The
PENGUIN
INTERNATIONAL
DICTIONARY

of

CONTEMPORARY
BIOGRAPHY

from 1900 to the Present

The
PENGUIN INTERNATIONAL DICTIONARY
of
CONTEMPORARY BIOGRAPHY

from 1900 to the Present

EDWARD VERNOFF
AND RIMA SHORE

PENGUIN REFERENCE

VIKING
Published by the Penguin Group
Penguin Putnam Inc., 375 Hudson Street,
New York, New York 10014, U.S.A.
Penguin Books Ltd, 27 Wrights Lane,
London W8 5TZ, England
Penguin Books Australia Ltd, Ringwood,
Victoria, Australia
Penguin Books
Penguin Books Canada Ltd, 10 Alcorn Avenue,
Toronto, Ontario, Canada M4V 3B2
Penguin Books (N.Z.) Ltd, 182–190 Wairau Road,
Auckland 10, New Zealand

Penguin Books Ltd, Registered Offices:
Harmondsworth, Middlesex, England

This revised and updated edition first published in 2001 by
Viking Penguin, a member of Penguin Putnam Inc.

1 3 5 7 9 10 8 6 4 2

Original edition published by New American Library under the title
The International Dictionary of 20th Century Biography

LIBRARY OF CONGRESS CATALOGING IN PUBLICATION DATA

Vernoff, Edward.
The Penguin international dictionary of contemporary biography from 1900 to the present /
Edward Vernoff and Rima Shore.
p.   cm.
Rev. ed. of: The international dictionary of 20th-century biography. © 1987.
Includes index.
ISBN 0-670-89470-2
1. Biography—20th century—Dictionaries.   I. Shore, Rima.   II. Vernoff, Edward.
International dictionary of 20th-century biography.   III. Title.

CT103.V39 2001
920'.003—dc21   00-040676

This book is printed on acid-free paper. ∞

Printed in the United States of America
Set in Sabon
Designed by Joseph Rutt

For Helene,
Notable Contemporary Friend and Wife—
whose love, patience, and generosity made this book possible
—E.V.

As always, for Daniel
And for Alex, Emily, Jake, Melissa, Rebecca, Reuben, Rob, and Tressa
each of whom will help to shape the new century
— R.S.

ACKNOWLEDGMENTS

First and foremost we wish to thank Carol Dunlap for her major contributions to this project. Her dedicated work, over several years, helped to make the dictionary a reality. We also wish to acknowledge the contributions of Tom Butler, Jan Clausen, Marlene Ellin, Edie Ellis, Ellen Garvey, Kathe Geist, Susan Goldberg, Diane Gruenberg, A. Tom Grunfeld, Erica Bonime, Genevieve Libin, Hope Ludlow, Martha McMaster, Rakhmiel Peltz, Mark Sher, Barbara Shore, Kenneth Shore, Judy Slawson, Anita Phillips Strauss, Doug Strauss, Helen Wilbur, and Don Young. We are indebted to Robert Rosenbaum and Joel Shapiro for their advice and support at the initial stages of the project, and to Wesley Strombeck and Marty Karlow who shared the task of copyediting the enormous manuscript. We also want to thank Edward Puccia who did the proofreading and Sylvia Dunkelblau who typed portions of the manuscript. Special thanks are extended to the reference librarians at New York University's Bobst Library for their assistance over the years. In addition, we want to thank Mel Schweitzer for his generosity and his wise counsel. Finally we owe a special debt of thanks to Hugh Rawson at New American Library, copy editor Susan Johnson, and proofreader Mary Flower for the skill, patience, and tolerance they displayed while ushering the manuscript through its various stages of production.

INTRODUCTION TO THE FIRST EDITION

The International Dictionary of 20th Century Biography is a reference work consisting of 5,650 concise biographies of notable modern men and women. The most comprehensive work of its kind, it includes figures, both living and dead, who have made their mark in almost every field of human endeavor.

Unlike most traditional reference works that emphasize Western European and North American politics, science, and "high culture," the present volume includes figures from around the world in such frequently underrepresented categories as social science, business, industry, labor, feminism, political dissent, journalism, photography, design, and all areas of popular culture and sports. In all, more than fifty categories are represented in the book.

Choosing the subjects proved to be a long, arduous, and extremely frustrating task. With no objective criteria available, we included both those individuals who we thought made significant contributions during the century, even if they are relatively unknown, and those whose contributions to civilization were less than monumental but whose fame is widespread. We also attempted to include individuals who have been omitted from previous works because of ethnic, racial, gender, national, or political bias.

Given these broad guidelines, we faced the unexpected problem of having to choose "only" 5,650 names. In the end, we sometimes found ourselves in the difficult if not absurd position of having to choose between a hockey star and a nuclear physicist or between a ballerina and a member of Congress. The final list represents a series of personal choices and compromises, but remains broadly based and representative of the major movements and trends of the twentieth century.

We have established no cut-off date for inclusion in the book, so while most subjects are either deceased or retired, many are still active.

In addition to basic biographical facts, we have incorporated information of a critical nature to help place each subject in a historical context or to clarify each individual's contribution to modern society. Each entry contains a brief bibliography listing any autobiographies and all significant book-length biographies.

Where the subject's original name differs from the name he or she is known by, the original name is given in parentheses following the popularly known name. In cases where the subject is known by two names, or where there is a variation in spelling, a cross-reference refers the reader to the article. Chinese names are transliterated according to the modern Pinyin system; cross-references are alphabetized according to the Wade-Giles system, which is rapidly becoming obsolete but was used in English-language books and periodicals published in the United States prior to the mid-1970s.

The index at the back of the book organizes the articles according to category, with the larger categories—including politics, literature and art—divided into national subgroupings.

Edward Vernoff
Rima Shore
1987

INTRODUCTION TO THE NEW EDITION
(REVISED BY EDWARD VERNOFF)

The Penguin International Dictionary of Contemporary Biography is a completely revised and updated edition of the *International Dictionary of 20th Century Biography,* which was published in 1987. All of the articles, where appropriate, were updated to reflect the recent activities of the biographees. The bibliographies following each biography were updated to list new biographies, autobiographies, or scholarly studies that have been published since the original edition appeared. In addition, 415 new articles were written, bringing the total number of biographies in the book to 6,065. Many of the new articles reflect the social changes

and trends that have developed over the past decade and a half. For example, we have included the biographies of pioneers in the field of computers and have added the category of computers to the index. We have also added biographies of several prominent musicians and singers from Europe, Africa, Asia, and Latin America to reflect the growing influence and popularity of folk and traditional music. We have also written biographies of all Nobel Prize winners, including winners of the 2000 awards.

2001

A

AALTO, (HUGO) ALVAR (1898–1976), Finnish architect. Aalto fought in Finland's war of independence (1917–19), then completed study (1921) at Helsinki Technical University and immediately established an architecture practice. His sanatorium at Paimio (1929–33), an austere structure eminently suited to purpose, earned him international acclaim. Aalto sought to relate architecture to nature; he often combined brick, copper, and timber to blend with Finland's landscape. His mature work, characterized by free-flowing lines and complex surface, followed the humanist or organic trend pioneered by Frank Lloyd Wright. In his interior designs, Aalto stressed lighting and acoustics. He also designed furniture. While teaching (1945–49) at the Massachusetts Institute of Technology, he designed a dramatic dormitory, Baker House (1947). ■ See study edited by Karl Fleig (Eng. trans. 1971); study by Richard Weston (1995); and Goran Schildt, ed., *Alvar Aalto in His Own Words* (1998).

AARON, HANK (Henry Louis Aaron; 1934–   ), U.S. baseball player. Aaron began his professional career with the Indianapolis Clowns of the Negro American League (1952) and broke into the majors with the National League's Milwaukee Braves (1954). A right-handed-batting outfielder, he led the league in batting (.328) in 1956 and was named Most Valuable Player (MVP) in 1957, leading the Braves to the World Series championship. In 23 seasons (1954–76) with the Braves (who moved to Atlanta after the 1965 season) and the Milwaukee Brewers, Aaron set major league career records for runs batted in (2,297), extra-base hits (1,477), times at bat (12,364), and games played (3,298). On April 8, 1974, he hit his 715th home run, breaking Babe Ruth's career record, which had stood for almost 40 years. He ended his career with 755 home runs. ■ See his *Home Run* (1999) and Stan Baldwin and Jerry Jenkins, *Bad Henry* (1974).

ABBAS, FERHAT (1899–1985), Algerian political leader. Abbas was a former student leader and pharmacist who during World War II abandoned the goal of assimilation to French culture and called for Algerian autonomy in a 1943 manifesto. When local French officials tried to repress the nationalist movement, he joined (1955) the revolutionary Algerian National Liberation Front (FLN) and he served as premier of the provisional government in exile in Tunisia (1958–61) and president of the national assembly of independent Algeria (1962–63). He was later defeated and detained (1964–65) in factional struggles that marked the end of middle-class domination of the nationalist movement.

ABBOT, CHARLES GREELEY (1872–1973), U.S. astrophysicist. As director (1907–44) of the Smithsonian Institution's Astrophysical Observatory, Abbot made major contributions to solar physics. With Samuel Langley he published a chart of the sun's infrared spectrum and studied solar radiation and its atmospheric absorption, deriving the solar constant. Author of over 300 scientific papers and numerous books, Abbot particularly researched the energy potential of solar radiation and its meteorological effects. He also designed numerous research instruments and received a patent for an apparatus to convert solar energy to power shortly before his 100th birthday.

ABBOTT, BERENICE (1898–1991), U.S. photographer. Abbott was a midwesterner who went to Paris (1921) to study sculpture but instead did an apprenticeship under photographer Man Ray and photographed the expatriate writers and artists of the day. She also discovered the photographs of Eugène Atget, about whom she published two books (1956; 1964). Returning to New York in 1929, she undertook a photographic documentation of the city (*Changing New York*, 1939; *Greenwich Village Today and Yesterday*, 1949). Late in her career Abbott specialized in portraits of physical phenomena. ■ See biography by Hank O'Neal (1982) and study by Bonnie Yochelson (1997).

ABBOTT, BUD (1895–1974), **and LOU COSTELLO** (1906–1959), U.S. comedians. The son of a circus bareback rider, Abbott filled in (1931) as a straight man for the burlesque comedian Lou Costello. They remained a team and became the kings of slapstick and buffoonery with comedy routines like the absurdist baseball discussion "Who's on First?" Abbott was the tall, thin, insulting straight man to Costello's dumpy, sympathetic bumbler. They built their reputation in vaudeville and on Broadway, on radio and television, and in an immensely popular and financially successful series of films in the 1940s including *Buck Privates* (1941) and *Who Done It?* (1942). They had a friendly parting (1957). Costello soon died, and Abbott eventually retired after losing most of his fortune to the government in back taxes. ■ See Bob Thomas, *Bud and Lou* (1977), and Chris Costello and Raymond Strait, *Lou's on First* (1981).

ABBOTT, GEORGE (1887–1995), U.S. theatrical director, producer, and playwright. Abbott's theatrical career began at Harvard College, where he wrote plays under the auspices of George Pierce Baker. After appearing on stage in a number of New York shows, he turned to directing. Together with Richard Rodgers and Lorenz Hart, he wrote and directed such smash hits as *On Your Toes* (1936), *The Boys from Syracuse* (1938), and *Pal Joey* (1944). Abbott's talents as an author-director continued to develop with *Where's Charley?* (1948), *A Tree Grows in Brooklyn* (1951), *The Pajama Game* (1954), and *Damn Yankees* (1955). He also directed a number of films and received a 1960 Pulitzer Prize for his production of *Fiorello!* He directed a revival of *On Your Toes* (1983) and assisted in a revival of *Damn Yankees* (1994) when he was more than 100 years old. ■ See his autobiography, *Mr. Abbott* (1963).

ABBOTT, GRACE (1878–1939), U.S. social reformer. Abbott was an associate at Jane Addams' pioneer Chicago settlement house, Hull House (1908–15), and director of the Immigrants' Protective League (1908–17). She directed the child-labor division of the U.S. Children's Bureau (1917–19), administering the first federal Child Labor Act. Abbott then headed the Children's Bureau (1921–34) and administered the Maternity and Infancy Act (1922–29). She was professor of public welfare at the University of Chicago (1934–39) and the author of *The Immigrant and the Community* (1917) and *The Child and the State* (2 vols., 1938). ■ See Lila B. Costin, *Two Sisters for Social Justice* (1983).

ABBOUD, (EL FERIK) IBRAHIM (1900–1983), Sudanese political leader. A military officer, Abboud rose through the ranks of the Sudanese branch of the Egyptian army and after Sudan gained independence (1956) became commander in chief. In 1958 he installed a military government, with himself as presiding officer. He charted a course of neutrality in foreign affairs, of agricultural diversification, and of industrialization. The failure of his economic program, however, coupled with his policy of "Islamization" of the black, non-Muslim south, created near civil war and led to his resignation (1964) and the restoration of civilian government.

ABD-EL-KRIM, MUHAMMAD BEN (1882–1963), Moroccan nationalist leader. Abd-el-Krim was a legendary figure in Moroccan history, a feared Berber chieftain who led an anticolonial rebellion in 1919. His Confederated Republic of Rif Tribes, created in 1921 and financed by German mining concessions, held out against Franco-Spanish forces until 1927. Abd-el-Krim, who spent the rest of his life in exile on Réunion Island (1927–47) and in Egypt (1947–63), was regarded as a hero by many Third World revolutionaries; his exploits inspired the operetta *The Desert Song* and the novel and films *Beau Geste*. ■ See biography by Rupert Furneaux (1967) and David S. Woolman, *Rebels in the Rif* (1968).

ABDUL HAMID II (1842–1918), sultan of the Ottoman Empire. Abdul Hamid (or Abd-al-Hamid II) was an autocratic ruler who instituted reforms that laid the foundation for modern Turkey. Amid the turbulence of the Balkan Wars

the sultan assumed absolute power (1877) and ruthlessly suppressed all opposition. He modernized the empire's educational, legal, military, financial, and railroad systems and emphasized his unifying role as caliph by actively pursuing pan-Islamic policies. In 1908 his autocratic rule was broken by the Young Turks, a revolutionary movement that forced him to restore the 1876 constitution and representative assembly. He was deposed in 1909. ■ See Joan Haslip, *The Sultan* (1958).

ABDUL-JABBAR, KAREEM (Lew Alcindor; 1947–   ), U.S. basketball player. A neighborhood basketball legend as a junior high school student—he was 6 feet, 8 inches tall by the time he was 13—Abdul-Jabbar led his high school team (Power Memorial Academy) to 71 straight wins and three consecutive New York City Catholic high school championships (1963–65). As the high-scoring 7-foot, 2-inch center for the University of California at Los Angeles (All-American 1967–69), he dominated college basketball in leading the Bruins to a record of 88 wins and 2 losses and three consecutive National Collegiate Athletic Association championships (1967–69). In the pros with the Milwaukee Bucks (1969–75) and the Los Angeles Lakers (1975–89), he was rookie of the year (1969) and led the National Basketball Association in scoring in 1971 (31.7 points per game) and 1972 (34.8 points per game). Outstanding on both offense and defense, he was the highest scorer in pro basketball history, breaking Wilt Chamberlain's record by scoring his 31,419th point on April 5, 1984, and was named most valuable player (MVP) a record six times (1971–72, 1974, 1976–77, 1980). He led his teams to NBA championships in 1971, 1980, 1982, 1985, 1987, and 1988 and was named MVP in the 1985 series. He retired holding 20 all-time career NBA records, including most games (1,560) and most regular season points (38,387). ■ See his autobiography, *Giant Steps* (1983; with Peter Knobler).

ABDULLAH IBN-HUSEIN (1882–1951), king of Jordan. Born into a politically powerful Arab family in Mecca, Abdullah participated in the Ottoman government before he became involved in the Arab nationalist movement. During World War I he participated in the Arab revolt against the Ottomans (1916) and helped the British drive the Turks out of Syria. He was installed by the British as head of the newly created (1921) emirate of Transjordan and became king when it gained its independence from Britain in 1946. The country was renamed the Hashemite Kingdom of Jordan in 1949. Abdullah earned the enmity of many Arabs during the war with Israel in 1948–49 by annexing central Palestine with his British-trained Arab legion. He was believed to favor an accommodation with Israel and was assassinated by a Palestinian nationalist in 1951. ■ See his *Memoirs* (Eng. trans. 1950) and *My Memoirs Completed* (Eng. trans. 1954).

ABDUL RAHMAN, TUNKU (1903–1990), Malaysian political leader. Abdul Rahman, a son of the sultan of Kedah, studied in Britain (1920–31) and, after his return, became a civil servant; later he again went to Britain to study law (1947–49). As president of the United Malay Nationalist Organization, the major political party (from 1951), he was elected chief minister (1955) and negotiated his country's independence from Britain. In 1957 he became independent Malaysia's first premier and he helped create the federation of Malaysia (1963), which he continued to lead until 1970. ■ See his books *Viewpoints* (1978) and *Lest We Forget* (1986) and autobiography, *Looking Back* (1977).

ABDUL RAZAK, TUN (1922–1976), Malaysian political leader. The son of a minor nobleman, Abdul Razak was educated in Malaya and London and served as a guerrilla fighter during World War II. A successful lawyer and a founder of the major political party, United Malay Nationalist Organization, he was first elected to parliament in 1955 and played a major role in gaining his country's independence from Britain (1957). He held several high posts, including that of deputy premier. In 1970 he became the second premier of Malaysia, succeeding Tunku Abdul Rahman. His administration moved Malaysia toward a neutralist international stance and carried out policies of economic development. He was unsuccessful, however, in solving the racial tensions that plagued his country. He died suddenly in 1976. ■ See biography by William Shan, *Tun Razak* (1976).

ABE, ISOO (1865–1949), Japanese political leader. A Christian minister, university professor (Waseda, 1903–26), and political organizer, Abe was one of the founders of the socialist movement in Japan. He helped form the Social Democratic party (1901) and the Fabian Society of Japan (1921) and was chairman of the new People's Socialist party (1926–32) and of the Social Mass party (1932–40). A pacifist and ardent supporter of women's rights and birth control, Abe served five terms in the Japanese Diet (1928–40).

ABE, KOBO (Kimifusa Abe; 1924–1993), Japanese writer. Although trained as a doctor, Abe decided, upon graduation from medical school (1948), to pursue a literary career. Influenced by existentialism, surrealism, and Marxism, he concerned himself with the themes of alienation, human freedom, and the loss of identity, and he was regarded as one of the most original avant-garde novelists of Japan. Although his themes were universal, his treatment of them, and his characters, were uniquely Japanese. His most important works included *The Sign at the End of the Road* (1947), *The Intruders* (1952), *Woman in the Dunes* (1962; Eng. trans. 1964), *The Face of Another* (1964; Eng. trans. 1966), *The Box Man* (1973; Eng. trans. 1974), *Secret Rendezvous* (1977; Eng. trans. 1979), and *Kangaroo Notebook* (1991; Eng. trans. 1996). ■ See Nancy K. Shields, *Fake Fish* (1996).

ABEL, RUDOLF IVANOVICH (1903–1971), Soviet spy. During the 1930s Abel entered the Soviet intelligence service

as a language instructor. After serving as an intelligence officer on the German front during World War II, he received intensive training in intelligence work (1945–47). Using a forged passport, he entered Canada (1947), then crossed the border to the United States, where he directed a network of Soviet spies from a studio apartment in Brooklyn. Using several aliases (including Emil R. Golfus) and living an unassuming life as an artist and photographer, he communicated with Moscow via shortwave radio. He was exposed (1957) only after an assistant defected. Although sentenced to 30 years' imprisonment, Abel was exchanged (1962) for U.S. pilot Francis Gary Powers, who had been forced down and captured in 1960 while making a U-2 reconnaissance flight over the Soviet Union for the CIA. The information that Abel passed to Soviet authorities was never revealed. ■ See James B. Donovan, *Strangers on a Bridge* (1964), and Louise Bernikow, *Abel* (1970).

ABELL, KJELD (1901–1961), Danish playwright. Abell rebelled against his conventional background and worked as a painter and stage designer in London and Paris (1927–32). His first play, *The Melody That Got Lost* (1933; Eng. trans. 1939), attacked middle-class conformism and broke with the prevailing naturalistic style. His witty plays were noted for their varied theatrical effects. A politically committed writer, he believed that the theater could be a means of pointing out major social and intellectual failures and problems in society. ■ See study by Frederick J. Marker (1976).

ABELSON, PHILIP HAUGE (1913–), U.S. physical chemist. Trained at the University of California at Berkeley (Ph.D. 1939), Abelson discovered (1939; with Edwin M. McMillan) radioactive element 93, later named neptunian. During World War II he was associated with the Manhattan Project, which developed the first atomic bomb, and he proposed (with John I. Hoover) the thermal-diffusion method of separating uranium isotopes that was a crucial development in the creation of the bomb. His report on the feasibility of nuclear-powered submarines was credited with initiating the development of the *Nautilus* and subsequent missile-carrying submarines. As director of the Carnegie Institution's geophysical laboratory in Washington, D.C. (1953–71), Abelson did important work in paleobiochemistry. He edited the influential journal *Science* (1962–85) and wrote *Energy for Tomorrow* (1975) and *Enough of Pessimism* (1985).

ABERHART, WILLIAM (1878–1943), Canadian educator and political leader. Born on a farm in Ontario, Aberhart was a schoolteacher and principal in Calgary, Alberta, 1915–35. Initially conservative and highly religious, he organized Bible classes and ran an evangelical radio program during the Depression. Moved by the plight of working people, Aberhart joined the social-democratic Social Credit party, leading it to victory in provincial elections in 1935. As premier of Alberta (1935–43) he was the first to put the social-credit theories of Clifford Hugh Douglas into practice—though not always successfully, since his attempts to take over banking and credit were declared unconstitutional. ■ See study by L.P.V. Johnson and Ola J. MacNutt (1970).

ABERNATHY, RALPH DAVID (1926–1990), U.S. civil-rights leader. The son of an Alabama farmer, Abernathy was a Baptist minister in Montgomery who worked with Martin Luther King, Jr., during the 1955 bus boycott by the black community. He helped found the Southern Christian Leadership Conference (SCLC; 1957) to carry out nonviolent resistance to segregation throughout the South. As King's successor as president of the SCLC (1968–77), Abernathy led the 1968 Poor People's march on Washington, where he declared: "You can kill the dreamer but you cannot kill the dream." Abernathy also led demonstrations against poverty, government repression, and the war in Vietnam. ■ See his autobiography, *And the Walls Came Tumbling Down* (1989).

ABRAHAM, KARL (1877–1925), German psychoanalyst. A collaborator of psychoanalyst Sigmund Freud, Abraham was an M.D. (University of Freiburg, 1901) who helped to establish the first branch of the International Psychoanalytic Institute in Berlin (1910). Abraham studied the stages of psychosexual development in infants, describing the characteristics associated with arrested development at each stage. He also explored the theory of myths, symbols, and dreams. ■ See his *Selected Papers* (Eng. trans. 1927, 1979); *Clinical Papers and Essays on Psycho-analysis* (Eng. trans. 1955); and *A Psychoanalytic Dialogue: The Letters of Sigmund Freud and Karl Abraham* (Eng. trans. 1966).

ABRAHAMS, PETER (1919–   ), South African-born writer. Abrahams, whose father was Ethiopian and mother was of mixed French and African ancestry, grew up in a Johannesburg slum. He attended mission schools and a teacher-training college before leaving South Africa (1939) and settling in Britain and later in Jamaica (1957). His early novels, *Song of the City* (1945), *Mine Boy* (1946), and *The Path of Thunder* (1948), were among the first to describe the effects of apartheid in their portrayal of the plight of South Africa's black and colored (mulatto) populations. These books, and his autobiography, *Tell Freedom* (1953), were widely translated; they established his reputation as a leading modern African author. Among his other works were *Wild Conquest* (1950), a novel about the conflict between the Boers and the Matebele in the 19th century, and *A Wreath for Udomo* (1956), a political novel set in a newly independent African nation. *This Island Now* (1967) was about a power struggle on a Caribbean island. He also wrote *The View from Coyaba* (1985). ■ See study by Michael Wade (1972) and Kolawole Ogungbesan, *The Writing of Peter Abrahams* (1979).

ABRAMOVITZ, MAX (1908–   ), U.S. architect. Abramovitz studied at the University of Illinois, Columbia University, and later the École des Beaux Arts in Paris. He established an architectural firm with Wallace K. Harrison (1940) and directed (1955) architectural design at Brandeis University, creating the acclaimed interfaith chapel group. The skyscrapers designed by Harrison and Abramovitz were distinguished by the innovative use of aluminum (the Alcoa Building in Pittsburgh, 1952), glass (the Corning Building in New York City, 1953), and stainless steel (the Four Gateway Center Building in Pittsburgh, 1955). They also designed the 48-story Time & Life Building in New York City (1960). Abramovitz was best known as the architect of New York City's Philharmonic Hall (now Avery Fisher Hall) at Lincoln Center, completed in 1962.

ABRAMS, CREIGHTON WILLIAMS, JR. (1914–1974), U.S. general. A graduate of West Point (1936), Abrams served as a tank battalion commander during World War II, went on to serve in Korea (1953–54), and was a division commander in Germany during the Berlin crisis (1960–62). As director of operations in the Pentagon he was sent to Mississippi (1962) and Alabama (1963) to command federal troops intervening in racial conflicts. Succeeding Gen. William C. Westmoreland as commander of U.S. forces in Vietnam (1968–72), he supervised the gradual withdrawal of U.S. troops and trained the South Vietnamese to assume greater responsibility for their own defense. His increased use of bombing missions and aggressive ground tactics raised controversy among antiwar forces. He later served as army Chief of Staff (1972–74). ■ See Lewis Sorley, *Thunderbolt* (1992).

ABRUZZO, BEN (1930–1985), **MAXIE ANDERSON** (1935–1983), and **LARRY NEWMAN** (1947–   ), U.S. balloonists. In 1978, they flew the *Double Eagle 2*—a silver-and-black nylon helium balloon—for six days and nights some 3,120 miles across the Atlantic Ocean. Landing in a barley field in Normandy, France, they became the first balloonists to complete the transatlantic crossing. For Abruzzo, a real-estate and resort developer, and Anderson, a mining-operation executive, it was a second attempt. Anderson, who made three aborted attempts to circle the earth in a balloon called the *Jules Verne*, set a ballooning mark with his son Kris by flying the *Kitty Hawk* across North America (1980). Abruzzo, Newman, and two partners made the first balloon crossing of the Pacific Ocean in the *Double Eagle 6* (1981). Anderson was killed in a balloon race; Abruzzo died when the twin-engine plane he was piloting crashed. ■ See Charles McCarry, *Double Eagle* (1979).

ABZUG, BELLA (Bella Savitsky; 1920–1998), U.S. feminist and political figure. Born in The Bronx, New York, Abzug began a law practice in New York City (1944). Her clients included individuals named by Sen. Joseph McCarthy as suspected communists. She also represented the American Civil Liberties Union. She was a founder of Women's Strike for Peace in the 1960s. Elected to Congress (1970) as a

Democrat to represent a Manhattan district, she became known as "Battling Bella"—a powerful speaker and aggressive legislator who pressed for welfare reform, mass-transit improvement, and women's rights. She also opposed U.S. military intervention in Vietnam. In 1976 she gave up her House seat to run for the U.S. Senate, but was unsuccessful. She remained politically active, supported the Equal Rights Amendment, founded the Women's Environment and Development Organization, and wrote *Gender Gap Nineteen Eighty-Four* (with Mim Kelber; 1984). ■ See *Bella!: Ms. Abzug Goes to Washington* (1972).

ACE, GOODMAN (1889–1982), and **JANE SHERWOOD ACE** (1905–1974), U.S. radio performers. "The Easy Aces" (1930–45), the popular radio program, originated in Kansas City when arts critic Goodman Ace teamed up with his wife, Jane Sherwood. At the end of a 1928 broadcast, the manager of the local station motioned to Goodman to stay on the air because the next act was delayed. When Ace's ad-libbing faltered, Jane barged in to help, and their airwave chitchat delighted audiences. The duo's witty interchanges became a permanent local feature, and from 1931 to 1945 the show was aired by the network. Goodman Ace wrote the quarter-hour shows, casting himself as a somewhat aggravated husband. Jane became famous for her malapropisms, such as "I'm really in a quarry!" or "Congress is still in season." Goodman called just one rehearsal for each show, eschewed the conventional studio audience, and refused to meet sponsors. He broke into television as a writer for Milton Berle (1952–55) and later wrote for Perry Como, Sid Caesar, and Bob Newhart.

ACHEBE, CHINUA (1930–), Nigerian novelist. A graduate of Ibadan University (1953), Achebe was one of Africa's most acclaimed and widely read novelists. Concerned with the regeneration of his people, he wrote of the disorientation and disorganization of society and of the individual brought about by Western customs and values. *Things Fall Apart* (1958), concerning a small Ibo village's exposure to the West, has been called "the archetypical African novel," and it is one of the best-known novels written by an African. Achebe's other novels include *No Longer at Ease* (1960), *Arrow of God* (1964), and *Man of the People* (1966). During the Nigerian civil war, Achebe served as a Biafran diplomat (1966–69). *Beware, Soul Brother* (1971) and *Christmas in Biafra* (1973) are volumes of war poetry, while *Morning Yet on Creation Day* (1975) is a collection of literary essays. His later works included the novel *Anthills of the Savannah* (1987) and *Girls at War and Other Stories* (1991). Achebe taught at the University of Nigeria, Nsukka (1976–81) and was president of the Association of Nigerian Authors (from 1981). After 1990 he lived in the United States and taught at several universities. ■ See his memoir, *Home and Exile* (2000); Robert M. Wren, *Achebe's World* (1980); and Bernth Lindfors, *Conversations with Chinua Achebe* (1997).

ACHESON, DEAN GOODERHAM (1893–1971), U.S. lawyer and public official. Son of the Episcopalian bishop of Connecticut, Acheson was educated in the patrician tradition at Groton, Yale (B.A. 1915) and Harvard Law School (LL.B 1918). He served as Supreme Court Justice Louis Brandeis' secretary for two years (1919–21) before joining a prominent Washington, D.C., law firm. Acheson worked as an undersecretary in the Treasury and State Departments before serving as Pres. Harry Truman's secretary of state (1949–53). As a developer of the Marshall Plan, the Truman Doctrine, and the North Atlantic Treaty Organization (NATO), he played a key role in U.S. efforts to contain Communism after World War II, but nevertheless was attacked by right-wing critics for cold-war defeats in China and Korea. ■ See his memoirs, *Morning and Noon* (1965) and *Present at the Creation: My Years in the State Department* (1969; Pulitzer Prize); and studies by Gaddis Smith (1972) and Douglas Brinkley (1992); and the biography by James Chace (1998).

ACHTERBERG, GERRIT (1905–1962), Dutch poet. Achterberg emerged after World War II as the foremost poet of his generation in the Netherlands. His idiosyncratic, incantatory poetry reinterpreted the Orpheus myth and focused on reunion after the death of the beloved. His metaphysical work gave expression to intense emotional stress and was influenced by Calvinist religious beliefs. English translations of his works are in *A Tourist Does Golgotha and Other Poems* (1972), *Hidden Weddings* (1987), and *Selected Poems* (1989).

ACUFF, ROY CLAXTON (1903–1992), U.S. country musician. Acuff grew up in a musical Baptist family in the foothills of eastern Tennessee. After high school he played semiprofessional basketball and baseball and was spotted by New York Yankees scouts, but he quit the ballpark after several bouts of sunstroke and an emotional breakdown. During a lengthy recuperation he began taking country music seriously, and he performed (1932) in a local medicine show. He made it big after 1939, when he formed the Smoky Mountain Boys. Acuff called himself "a seller, not a singer." His fiddling was ordinary, and his vigorous voice was never astonishing, but his earnest, emotional delivery of thousands of songs made him enormously popular throughout his long career. He wrote nearly 100 songs. ■ See study by Elizabeth Schlappi (1977).

ADAMOV, ARTHUR (1908–1970), French playwright. Born in Russia, Adamov lived in Paris (from 1924) and wrote in French. The major influences on his plays were the surrealists, the authors Angust Strindberg and Franz Kafka, and the terrible experience of his own nervous breakdown (1938). His early, metaphysical plays like *L'Invasion* (1950; Eng. trans. 1968) were nonrealistic antitheater, expressing human alienation and the futility and cruelty of life. His most acclaimed play, *Ping-Pong* (1955; Eng. trans. 1959), was an allegory of two men whose lives revolve around a pinball machine. His work influenced the theater of the absurd. Adamov moved toward communism and then wrote socially oriented plays, such as *Paolo Paoli* (1957; Eng. trans. 1959), in the style of Bertroit Brecht's epic theater. He committed suicide. ■ See study by John H. Reilly (1974).

ADAMS, ANSEL EASTON (1902–1984), U.S. photographer. Born in San Francisco, Adams trained as a concert pianist and first began taking photographs in mountains and parks. In 1930 he collaborated on *Taos Pueblo,* the first of several black-and-white photo essays on the natural splendor of the Southwest. One of the world's best-known photographers, Adams also wrote instructional books, stimulated the educational development of photography and its collection by museums, contributed to photographic technology, and pioneered in folio reproduction. In 1944 he departed from the celebration of nature to publish *Born Free and Equal,* a photo essay on the wartime internment of Japanese-Americans. ■ See his autobiography (1985; with Mary Street Alinder) and the biography by Jonathan Spaulding (1995). See also *The Eloquent Light: Ansel Adams* (1964), a study by Nancy Newhall, with whom Adams collaborated on several Sierra Club books, and the collection of photos in *Ansel Adams: Images 1923–1974* (1974).

ADAMS, BROOKS (1848–1927), U.S. historian. The younger brother of historian Henry Adams, Brooks Adams was a Harvard graduate (1870) who practiced law for a decade before turning to historical research. Under the influence of social Darwinism, he traced historical cycles of growth and decline and predicted a struggle for survival among nations. In *The Law of Civilization and Decay* (1895), *America's Economic Supremacy* (1900), and *New Empire* (1902), he predicted that the British Empire would dissolve, France would decline, and the United States would advance. However, in *The Theory of Social Revolutions* (1913) Adams foresaw the decline of America due to the accumulation of great wealth without social responsibility. ■ See biography by Arthur F. Beringause (1955).

ADAMS, FRANKLIN PIERCE (1881–1960), U.S. newspaper columnist and radio personality. Known as "FPA," Adams began his career as a columnist in Chicago in 1903. He moved to New York in 1913 and received wide acclaim for his witty, irreverent, and erudite column "The Conning Tower," which appeared in the *Tribune* (1914–22), *World* (1922–31), *Herald Tribune* (1931–37), and *Post* (1938–41). A social critic, punster, and master of humorous verse, Adams expressed his views on nearly everything, both in print and on the popular national radio show "Information Please" (1938–48). ■ See biography by Sally Ashley (1986).

ADAMS, HARRIET S. *See KEENE, CAROLYN.*

ADAMS, MAUDE (Maude Kiskadden; 1872–1953), U.S. actress. The daughter of a stock-company acting star, Adams first received critical attention at age 5 and went on to become a leading actress in Charles Frohman's acting company (from 1892). A dazzling beauty, she appeared in a wide variety of roles and became one of the country's most-beloved actresses. Her elfinlike quality perfectly suited her for the plays of James M. Barrie, including *The Little Minister* (1897), *Quality Street* (1902), *What Every Woman Knows* (1908–09), *A Kiss for Cinderella* (1916–18), and her greatest success, *Peter Pan* (1905–07; 1913; 1918), in which she appeared more than 1,500 times. She left the theater in 1918 but came out of retirement to appear in Shakespeare's *The Merchant of Venice* (1931) and *Twelfth Night* (1934). ■ See biography by Phyllis Robbins (1956).

ADAMS, WALTER SYDNEY (1876–1956), U.S. astronomer. Associated with Mt. Wilson Observatory in California from its inception in 1904 (director, 1923–46), Adams was known for his spectroscopic analyses. Through these, he ascertained the velocities and distances of thousands of stars, investigated sunspots and interstellar gases, studied the atmospheres of the planets, and contributed to the confirmation of Albert Einstein's general theory of relativity (1925). He helped design and develop the 200-inch telescope that was installed (1947–48) at California's Mt. Palomar Observatory.

ADDAMS, CHARLES SAMUEL (1923–1988), U.S. cartoonist. Addams began his career as a freelance cartoonist in 1935 when he sold a cartoon to the *New Yorker,* where his work continued to appear regularly. He was known for his macabre humor, which invoked supernatural characters and events. His endearing group of ghouls, vampires, and goblins inhabiting a dilapidated Victorian mansion later became the subject of a television series popular in the 1960s called "The Addams Family." Addams exhibited in several gallery shows, and his work was brought out in a number of albums, among them *Monster Rally* (1950), *Nightcrawlers* (1957), and *Creature Comforts* (1981).

ADDAMS, JANE (1860–1935), U.S. social reformer. Born into a wealthy family, Addams graduated from Rockford College, Illinois (1881), and traveled extensively in Europe. Inspired by a visit to Toynbee Hall, a settlement house in London, she established (with Ellen Gates Starr) Hull House in a working-class slum neighborhood in Chicago (1889). It provided numerous services, training courses, and cultural programs for the poor and became the most famous and influential settlement house in the United States. Addams became a leader of Prohibition, labor, and women's suffrage movements and fought for child-labor reform, housing and factory regulation, and workers' compensation. A pacifist, she sought a mediated end to World War I, headed the International Congress for Women (1915) and the Women's

International League for Peace and Freedom, and remained opposed to the conflict when the United States entered the war in 1917. She shared the 1931 Nobel Prize for Peace with Nicholas Murray Butler. She wrote several books including *Newer Ideals of Peace* (1907), *Twenty Years at Hull House* (1910), and *The Second Twenty Years at Hull House* (1930). ■ See Gioia Diliberto, *A Useful Woman* (1999).

ADDISON, CHRISTOPHER, 1st VISCOUNT ADDISON OF STALLINGBOROUGH (1869–1951), British physician and political leader. Addison was a professor of anatomy at Sheffield University who was so appalled by social conditions that he ran (successfully) for Parliament as a Liberal in 1910. As minister of reconstruction (1917) and health (1919–21), he helped establish the principle of state responsibility for working-class housing. He joined the Labour party (1922) and held a succession of cabinet positions (after 1929) before taking a seat in the House of Lords (1937; leader, 1945–51), where he was a rare liberal. ■ See his *Betrayal of the Slums* (1922); *Practical Socialism* (2 vols., 1926); biography by R. J. Minney (1958); and Kenneth and Jane Morgan, *Portrait of a Progressive* (1980).

ADE, GEORGE (1866–1944), U.S. humorist and dramatist. Born in Indiana, Ade graduated from Purdue University (1887). His clever sketches and colloquial dialogue, which grew out of his column in the *Chicago Record*, poked fun at midwesterners. He wrote many popular books, including *Fables in Slang* (1889), *People You Knew* (1903), *Handmade Fables* (1920), and *The Old Time Saloon* (1931). He was also the author of several successful Broadway shows such as *The County Chairman* (1903) and *The College Widow* (1904). Ade's selected writings are in *The America of George Ade* (1960). ■ See biography by Fred C. Kelly (1947) and study by Lee Coyle (1964).

ADENAUER, KONRAD (1876–1967), West German chancellor. A lawyer from Cologne, Adenauer became active in Catholic Center party politics and served as lord mayor of his hometown (1917–33). He was removed from office by the Nazis and lived in retirement during the Nazi era (1933–45). After World War II, as head of the centrist Christian Democratic Union (CDU), which dominated West Germany's first elections in 1949, he maneuvered skillfully to become chancellor. During his 14-year reign, West Germany regained its sovereignty, joined the Common Market, and recovered economic prosperity. A willful, sometimes autocratic leader, "Der Alte" was finally forced into retirement by his own party (1963). ■ See his *Memoirs: 1945–53* (Eng. trans. 1966) and biographies by Paul Weymar (Eng. trans. 1957), Charles Wighton (1964), and Terrence Prittie (1971).

ADLER, ALFRED (1870–1937), Austrian psychiatrist. Trained at the University of Vienna (M.D. 1895), Adler was associated with psychoanalyst Sigmund Freud early in his career, but disagreed with his emphasis on sex and broke away (1911) to form a comprehensive theory that stressed the uniqueness of the individual and the vital importance of society in shaping personality. Adler postulated an inherent striving for perfection that may take the form of a striving for superiority to compensate for feelings of inferiority. Adlerian methods of treatment, while including interpretation of early memories and dreams, are flexible and attempt to effect behavioral change by fostering social interaction and positive human relationships. He moved to the United States in 1932. His books included *Neurotic Constitution* (Eng. trans. 1917), *The Practice and Theory of Individual Psychology* (Eng. trans. 1923), *Understanding Human Nature* (Eng. trans. 1927), and *What Life Should Mean to You* (in English, 1931). ■ See studies by Phyllis Bottome (rev. ed. 1957); Manes Sperber (1974); Josef Rattner (Eng. trans. 1983); and Edward Hoffman, *The Drive for Self* (1994).

ADLER, CYRUS (1863–1940), U.S. educator. Adler earned the first U.S. doctorate in Semitics (Johns Hopkins University, 1887) and was for 20 years curator of the Smithsonian Institution's Eastern and religious collections (1889–1908). He was an important Jewish lay leader, a founder (1906) and later (1929) president of the American Jewish Committee, and an editor of numerous Jewish reference works. An anti-Zionist, he attended the 1919 Versailles Peace Conference as a spokesman for minority rights. He was president of Dropsie College for Hebrew and Cognate Learning (Philadelphia, 1908–40) and he headed the Jewish Theological Seminary (1916–40). ■ See his autobiography, *I Have Considered the Days* (1941), and the biography by Abraham Neuman (1942).

ADLER, JACOB (1855–1926), Russian-born Yiddish-language actor and theatrical manager. Adler left Russia after theatrical performances in Yiddish were banned (1883). He toured Eastern Europe and performed in London and Chicago before settling in New York City (1890), where he was an idol of Yiddish-speaking theater audiences for more than 30 years. A flamboyant personality and forceful actor, he helped inaugurate the "golden age" of Yiddish theater and was a cultural hero of New York's immigrant Jews. His great successes were in *Der Yidisher King Lear, The Great Socialist,* and *The Merchant of Venice.* His wife Sara (1858–1953) was one of the most prominent actresses in the Yiddish theater. His daughter Stella (1902–1992) was a founding member of New York's Group Theater and a noted acting teacher; his son Luther (1903–1983) was a well-known stage and screen actor. ■ See his memoir, *A Life on the Stage* (Eng. trans. 1999), and Lulla Rosenfeld, *Bright Star of Exile* (1977).

ADLER, LARRY (1914–   ), U.S. harmonica player. A self-taught virtuoso on the instrument he preferred to call the mouth organ, Adler broke into show business in New York

City at age 14 and appeared in nightclubs, vaudeville, and in films. His astonishing musicality inspired such composers as Darius Milhaud, Albert Roussel, and Ralph Vaughan Williams to write pieces for him, and he performed as a soloist with the world's leading symphony orchestras. During the 1940s he appeared in joint recitals with tap dancer Paul Draper. Accused of being procommunist during the late 1940s, he was blacklisted for many years and emigrated to Britain, where he pursued a musical and journalistic career. He composed the music for several films, including *Genevieve* (1954). ■ See his autobiographies, *It Ain't Necessarily So* (1984) and *Me and My Big Mouth* (1994).

ADLER, MORTIMER JEROME (1902–), U.S. philosopher and editor. Adler's specialty was to assemble massive reference works on the great ideas and issues of Western civilization. While teaching (1930–52) at the University of Chicago, he and Robert Maynard Hutchins coedited the 54-volume *Great Books of the Western World* (1952) series, and reorganized the curriculum to emphasize the classics. Adler also edited the 20-volume *Annals of America* (1969) and directed planning on the "micropedia," the innovative feature of the 15th edition of the *Encyclopedia Britannica*. His other books included *Dialectic* (1927), *How to Read a Book* (1940), *The Idea of Freedom* (2 vols.; 1958–61), *Six Great Ideas* (1981), *Reforming Education* (1988), and *Art, the Arts and the Great Ideas* (1994). ■ See his autobiography, *Philosopher at Large* (1977).

ADONIS (pen name of Ali Ahmad Sa'id; 1930–), Lebanese poet. Born in Syria, Adonis graduated from Damascus University (1954) with a degree in philosophy. After serving a jail sentence for his radical politics, he settled in Beirut (1956), where he began to develop a modernist Arabic poetry, cofounded two influential literary journals, *Shi'r* (Poetry; 1956–63) and *Mawaqif* (Attitudes: 1968–78), and taught Arabic literature at the Lebanese University. A controversial figure, he opposed conservative traditions in Arabic literature and culture. He transcended the formalism of traditional poetry by introducing free verse as well as new words, rhythms, and metaphors into his complex poetry. His socially committed works, which linked the personal and political, envisioned the revolutionary rebirth of Arab society from its contemporary humiliation and repression. Adonis also wrote important studies of intellectual history and literary theory, including *Introduction to Arab Poetics* (Eng. trans. 1990). He left Lebanon during the civil war (1975) and subsequently taught in France and Switzerland. English translations of his poems are in *Transformations of the Lover* (1983), *Victims of a Map* (1984), *Orbits of Desire* (1992), and *The Pages of Day and Night* (1994).

ADORNO, THEODOR WIESENGRUND (Theodor Adorno Wiesengrund; 1903-1969), German philosopher, sociologist, and musicologist. Adorno was a wealthy, cultured German Jew who studied 12-tone composition with

Alban Berg and received his Ph.D. in philosophy from the University of Frankfurt (1924). He was closely associated (from 1928) with the Frankfurt Institute for Social Research (popularly known as the Frankfurt School) that developed Marxist-influenced critical studies of modern culture and society. Dismissed from teaching by the Nazis (1933), he emigrated first to Britain (1934), and then to the United States (1938), where he wrote (with Max Horkheimer) *Dialectic of Enlightenment* (1947; Eng. trans. 1972), a study of how reason has been transformed into a weapon of totalitarian social control, and collaborated on *The Authoritarian Personality* (1950), a study of fascism. Adorno returned to Frankfurt (1949) and served as director of the institute (1958–69). His other books included *Prisms* (1955; Eng. trans. 1982), *Philosophy of Modern Music* (1949; Eng. trans. 1973), *Negative Dialectics* (1966; Eng. trans. 1973), and *Introduction to the Sociology of Music* (1962; Eng. trans. 1976). ■ See Susan Buck-Morss, *The Origin of Negative Dialectics* (1977); Rose Gillian, *The Melancholy Science* (1978); and studies by Martin Jay (1984) and Simon Jarvis (1998).

ADRIAN (Gilbert Adrian Greenburgh; 1903-1959), U.S. fashion designer. Composer Irving Berlin was struck by Adrian's prize-winning costume at a 1921 Beaux Arts ball for art students in Paris and hired the 18-year-old to design for his Music Box Revue. Adrian worked on Broadway in the 1920s, going to Hollywood (1928) under contract with Metro-Goldwyn-Mayer. The distinctive, personalized styles he created in the 1930s and 1940s for such film stars as Greta Garbo, Joan Crawford, Jean Harlow, and Katharine Hepburn helped give Hollywood its glamour image. Like Schiaparelli, he padded the shoulders of women's fashions; the Adrian suit, often done in seemingly unsuitable fabrics, became the rage. In the 1950s, Adrian designed a quality line of ready-to-wear apparel.

ADRIAN, EDGAR DOUGLAS, 1st BARON ADRIAN OF CAMBRIDGE (1889–1977), British neurophysiologist. A fellow at Trinity College, Cambridge, when he shared the 1932 Nobel Prize for Physiology or Medicine with Sir Charles Sherrington, Adrian was chiefly concerned with the study of nerve impulses. He devised a system for recording and amplifying the discharges of nerve fibers that enabled researchers to increase their understanding of the physical basis of sensation, perception, and neural activity. His later work included studies of the electrical activity of the brain that enhanced the use of electroencephalograms in the study of epilepsy and brain lesions. He served as professor (1937–51) and master (1951–65) at Trinity College and wrote several books, including *The Basis of Sensation* (1928) and *The Mechanism of Nervous Action* (1932).

ADY, ENDRE (1877–1919), Hungarian poet, critic, and journalist. Trained as a lawyer, Ady worked as a journalist from 1900 until his death, contributing numerous articles and poems to various revolutionary left-wing periodicals. His collection of modernist lyric poetry, *New Poems* (1906), created a literary sensation with its unconventional use of language and form and its provocative tone and political perspective. While Ady presented a broad view of Hungarian national life, he also wrote extremely intense personal poetry, filled with violent and tormented images, concerning erotic love, death, mysticism, and God. His works rejuvenated Hungarian poetry, and he was regarded as the greatest Hungarian lyric poet of the century. Translations of his work are in *Poems* (1969) and *The Explosive Country* (1977).

AFINOGENOV, ALEKSANDR NIKOLAYEVICH (1904–1941), Soviet playwright. The same year Afinogenov completed courses at the Moscow Institute of Journalism, he wrote his first play, *Robert Tim* (1924). During the 1920s he trained playwrights and actors, stressing political aspects of theatrical productions. His own plays were highly appreciated both by the Russian Association of Proletariat Writers (RAPP) and by the public. Afinogenov emphasized psychological rather than historical forces in such plays as *Fear* (1930; Eng. trans. 1934), which analyzed the motivations of Soviet officials, and *Far Taiga* (1936; Eng. trans. 1946). The comedy *Listen, Professor!* (1940; Eng. trans. 1944) idealized the uprightness of Soviet youth. Afinogenov was expelled from the Communist party in 1937 but reinstated the following year. Shortly after completing *On the Eve* (1941; Eng. trans. 1946), which expressed his outrage at the Nazi invasion of the Soviet Union, he was killed in an air attack on Moscow.

AFLAQ, MICHEL (1910–1989), Syrian political leader. A socialist political theorist and organizer, Aflaq was a leading Arab nationalist who founded the pan-Arab Ba'ath (Arab Renaissance) party with Salah al-Din Bitar during the early 1940s. The party's radicalism and well-formulated programs appealed to young intellectuals and military officers. During the 1950s it was influential in Syrian, Jordanian, Lebanese, and Iraqi politics and was the main force behind the short-lived union between Syria and Egypt (1958–61). During the 1960s the party split into several factions, and Aflaq and his followers were ousted from Syria after a coup in 1966 and expelled from the party. However, Aflaq maintained close ties with the rival Iraqi Ba'ath party, which came to power in a military coup in 1968. ■ See *Choice of Texts from the Ba'ath Party Founder's Thought* (1977).

AGEE, JAMES (1909–1955), U.S. novelist and film critic. Agree grew up in backwoods Tennessee and graduated from Harvard (1932). Critics agreed that he never fulfilled his promise as a novelist, but called him America's greatest film critic. His witty, discerning reviews for *The Nation, Time,* and other magazines were collected posthumously in *Agee on Film* (2 vols., 1958–60). His literary output consisted of one poetry collection (1934), the novella *The Morning Watch* (1951), and the Pulitzer Prize–winning semiautobio-

graphical novel *A Death in the Family* (1957). His report on Alabama sharecroppers during the Depression was published with photos by Walker Evans as *Let Us Now Praise Famous Men* (1941). Agee also wrote the scripts for several films, including *The Quiet One* (1949) and *The African Queen* (1951). ■ See David Madden, ed., *Remembering James Agee* (1974); Genevieve Moreau, *The Restless Journey of James Agee* (Eng. trans. 1977); and biography by Laurence Bergreen (1984).

AGNELLI, GIOVANNI (1866–1945), Italian industrialist and philanthropist. Educated at a military academy, Agnelli was a cavalry officer during the 1880s. He was a founder (1899) and chairman of FIAT (Fabbrica Italiana Automobili Torino), the largest industrial enterprise and automobile manufacturer in Italy and the chief arms supplier to the Italian government during World Wars I and II. During the fascist period he organized opposition to the socialist and union movements, wielded great political influence, and was appointed to the senate by Benito Mussolini (1923).

AGNEW, SPIRO THEODORE (1918–1996), U.S. political leader. A night-law-school graduate, Agnew served as chief executive of Baltimore County (1962–66) and as Republican governor of Maryland (1967–69). Although elected governor with liberal support, he took a conservative stand on law and order, civil rights, and social services once in office. Tall and natty, a popular after-dinner speaker and Republican fund-raiser, he became U.S. vice president in 1969. Speaking for Pres. Richard Nixon's administration, he criticized the liberal establishment, dissenters, and the press, which he called "an effete corps of impudent snobs," and he was reelected with Nixon in 1972. After it was revealed that he had received payoffs from Baltimore contractors while governor, Agnew pleaded no contest to income-tax evasion and resigned in disgrace in 1973. He was disbarred in 1974. ■ See his *Go Quietly . . . Or Else* (1980).

AGNON, SHMUEL YOSEPH (Samuel Yosef Czaczkes; 1888–1970), Galician-born Israeli Hebrew-language novelist and short-story writer. Agnon wrote Hasidic folklore and legends and stories concerning the East European Jews and their traditions. During the 1930s his work reflected the disintegration of the Jewish life he knew and was preoccupied with the themes of personal alienation and the search for redemption. Agnon's post–World War II works were symbolic, enigmatic, and filled with mystical allusions. His most famous novels were *The Bridal Canopy* (1931; Eng. trans. 1937), *A Simple Story* (1935; Eng. trans. 1985), *In the Heart of the Seas* (1935; Eng. trans. 1948), *A Guest for the Night* (1938–39; Eng. trans. 1968), and *The Day Before Yesterday* (1945). English translations of his works are in *Two Tales* (1966) and *Twenty-one Stories* (1970). He shared the 1966 Nobel Prize for Literature with Nellie Sachs. ■ See study by Harold Fisch (1975) and biography by Gershon Shaked (1989).

AGUINALDO, EMILO (1869–1964), Filipino revolutionary. During the 1890s Aguinaldo was a local government official, at the same time heading a revolutionary society against the Spanish colonialists. During the Spanish-American War (1898) he declared the Philippines independent and then led a three-year guerrilla war against the United States, which occupied the country and refused to allow an independent Philippine state. After his capture (1901), Aguinaldo signed a pledge to end the rebellion and work with the Americans. He unsuccessfully ran for president in 1935 and during World War II he collaborated with the Japanese. ■ See his autobiography, *A Second Look at America* (1957), and Carlos Quirino, *The Young Aguinaldo* (1969).

AHAD HA'AM (Asher Ginsberg; 1856–1927), Jewish philosopher and essayist. Born into a wealthy Hasidic family in the Ukraine, he received a traditional religious education but was deeply influenced by secular Western thought and rationalist philosophy. He adopted the name Ahad Ha'am ("one of the people") while writing articles attacking the early political Zionists for their neglect of the spiritual aspects of Judaism. Stressing the religion's moral and ethical aspects, he called for a "spiritual Zionism," a revival of Jewish national consciousness and Hebrew language and culture. He conceptualized Palestine as the spiritual center of Judaism and a model for Jewish life in the Diaspora, but not as a political homeland for world Jewry. His influential writings appeared in the Hebrew-language monthly *Hashiloach,* which was published in Odessa, Berlin, and Jerusalem (1896–1926). He was its editor (1896–1903). His clear and precise prose style influenced the development of modern Hebrew literature. He lived in London (1904–20), where he was an adviser to Zionist leader Chaim Weizmann, and spent his last years in Palestine. ■ See his *Selected Essays* (Eng. trans. 1970); the biography of Leon Simon (1960); and Steven J. Zipperstein, *Elusive Prophet* (1993).

AHIDJO, AHMADOU (1924–1989), Cameroonian political leader. Born of a Muslim family in the north, Ahidjo was elected to the trust territory's representative assembly (1947). He succeeded to the premiership (1958) during a period of widespread disorder, crushed terrorists, and initiated negotiations with the United Nations that led to complete independence (1960). As the first elected president (1960–82), he organized the southern territory into the eastern and western states of the Cameroon Republic. His great achievement was overcoming tribal and religious distrust to unify the state governments into the United Republic of Cameroon in 1972. The leader of a one-party state (after 1966), Ahidjo carried out successful economic policies that made his country self-sufficient in food and energy. After a 1983 power struggle he went into exile and never returned to his homeland.

AI-CH'ING. *See AI QING.*

AIKEN, CONRAD (1889–1973), U.S. poet and novelist. Despite more than 50 books—poetry, novels, short stories—

Aiken was overshadowed by his close friend Ezra Pound and his Harvard roommate T. S. Eliot. He won a Pulitzer Prize (1930) for his *Selected Poems,* in which he adapted musical idioms to poetry. His fiction reveals a morbidity that may be traced to childhood tragedy: when Aiken was 11, his father murdered his mother and then committed suicide, an event that Aiken recalls in his third-person autobiography, *Ushant* (1952). An early follower of Freud, Aiken explored levels of consciousness and employed symbolism in his poetry. ■ See Clarissa M. Lorenz, *Lorelei Two: My Life with Conrad Aiken* (1983); the biography by Edward Butscher (1988); and Ted R. Spivey, *Time's Stop in Savannah* (1997).

AIKEN, HOWARD HATHAWAY (1900–1973), U.S. mathematician and inventor. After receiving a Ph.D. in physics from Harvard (1939), Aiken joined a group of engineers from the International Business Machines Corp. that sought to develop an automatic calculating machine able to carry out any sequence of five fundamental arithmetical operations—addition, subtraction, multiplication, division, and reference to previously computed results. By 1944 he and his colleagues (Clair D. Lake, B. M. Durfee, and F. E. Hamilton) had created Mark I, a 35-ton machine that was the world's first large-scale electromechanical computer and the forerunner of the contemporary digital computer. It contained 500 miles of wire and 3 million connections and was used by the navy during World War II. Mark II, an all-electric computer, was completed in 1947. Aiken taught at Harvard (1939–61) and the University of Miami (1961–73). ■ See biography by I. Bernard Cohen (1999).

AILEY, ALVIN, JR. (1931–1989), U.S. choreographer and director. Born in Texas, Ailey studied with modern dance pioneer Lester Horton in Los Angeles and joined his company. He began his choreographic work in 1953, when after Horton's death the company began accepting work from its own members. Moving to New York (1954), Ailey studied ballet and trained in modern dance under Martha Graham, Hanya Holm, Doris Humphrey, Charles Weidman, and Anna Sokolow. In 1958 he formed his own company, the Alvin Ailey American Dance Theater. Composed primarily of black dancers, it gained an international reputation and brought many young dancers, especially African and European blacks and Japanese artists, to the United States. The troupe made famous such Ailey works as *Revelations* (1960), an emotional ballet rooted in the religious music of American blacks. Other works by Ailey included *Creation of the World* (1961), *Cry* (1971), and *At the Edge of the Precipice* (1983). ■ See his autobiography, *Revelations* (1995; with A. Peter Bailey), and the biography by Jennifer Dunning (1996).

AI QING (old style: AI-CH'ING; 1910–1996), Chinese poet. Ai Qing was the pseudonym of Jiang Haizheng (Chiang Hai-ch'eng). Born into a wealthy landowning family and educated in France (1928–32), Ai achieved fame as a socially conscious poet with the publication of the volume *Big*

Dike River (1936). In this volume, and others, he was mainly concerned with the miserable lives of the Chinese peasants. After the Japanese invasion in the 1930s he worked as a literary propagandist in various parts of China and in 1941 joined the communists at Yanan (Yenan). Thenceforth he was active in implementing communist leader Mao Zedong's (Mao Tse-tung) literary directives but believed that literature did not exist merely to serve politics. After 1949 he held several official literary posts, but he was accused of being a rightist (1958), stripped of his positions, and forced to live on remote state farms until 1975. He resumed publishing in 1978. His *Selected Poems* (Eng. trans. 1981) contains a brief autobiography.

AKELEY, CARL ETHAN (1864–1926), U.S. naturalist and sculptor. While associated with Chicago's Field Museum of Natural History (1895–1909) and New York's American Museum of Natural History (1909–26), Akeley developed and perfected taxidermic methods whereby animal skins were applied to finely contoured models. This process permitted the museums to display large groups of animals in their natural settings with an unprecedented degree of realism. Akeley, who made five trips to Africa between 1896 and 1926, was best known for his displays and sculptures of elephants and lions as well as those of Nandi tribesmen. He also invented the Akeley cement gun, widely used in the creation of museum models, and the Akeley camera, designed for wildlife photography. He was instrumental in founding Albert National Park animal sanctuary in Zaire. He wrote *In Brightest Africa* (1923). ■ See Seymour G. Pond, *African Explorer* (1957); Felix Sutton, *Big Game Hunter* (1963); and the biography by Penelope Bodry-Sanders (1991).

AKHMADULINA, BELLA AKHATOVNA (1937–), Soviet poet. Born in Moscow, Akhmadulina graduated from the Gorky Literary Institute (1960). Associated with the independent, liberal movement of Soviet writers, she published her first book of poetry (1962) during a period of political "thaw" in the Soviet Union. Her frank and introspective lyric poetry utilized startling imagery to depict aspects of contemporary urban life. English translations of her works are in *Fever and Other New Poems* (1969) and *The Garden* (1990). ■ See study by Sonia Ketchian, *The Poetic Craft of Bella Akhmadulina* (1993).

AKHMATOVA, ANNA (Anna Andreyevna Gorenko; 1889–1966), Russian poet. With poets Nikolai Gumilev and Osip Mandelstam, Akhmatova developed acmeism, the movement devoted to a return to precise and direct expression of poetic feeling. Before the Russian Revolution (1917) she won acclaim for the personal, reflective lyrics collected in *Evening* (1912) and *Rosary* (1914). After *Anno Domini MCMXXI* (1922) she was virtually unpublished for two decades but her poetry nevertheless remained popular. After World War II she was vilified by the government for her bourgeois "individualism" and expelled from the official writers' union (1946); Stalinist literary arbiter Andrei Zhdanov called her "half nun, half harlot." She reemerged at the 1954 Writers' Congress after the death of dictator Joseph Stalin. Written over two decades, her masterpiece *Poem Without a Hero* (1940–62; Eng. trans. 1971) was a retrospective on the revolution and a meditation on Russia's destiny. *Requiem* (1963; Eng. trans. 1964), essentially completed in 1940 and long unpublished, commemorated the suffering of Stalin's victims. In her last years Akhmatova continued to write and translate poetry, traveled in Western Europe, and was honored at home and abroad. English translations of her work are in *Selected Poems* (1969, 1974, 1976). ■ See studies by Sam N. Driver (1972); Amanda Haight (1976); and Lydia Chukovskaya, *The Akhmatova Journals* (Eng. trans. 1994).

AKSELROD, PAVEL BORISOVICH (1850–1928), Russian political leader. A revolutionary populist (Narodnik) during the 1870s, Akselrod (also known as Paul Axelrod) fled from Russia to Western Europe to avoid arrest and was a co-founder, in Switzerland, of the first Russian Social Democratic party (1883). He was a prominent Marxist theorist, helped found the influential revolutionary newspaper *Iskra* ("The Spark"; 1900), and was one of the founders of the Menshevik movement (1903). An opponent of bolshevism, he concentrated party work on trade-union organizing and parliamentary activities. After the March 1917 revolution he joined the organizing committee of the Social Democratic party, but he left Russia after the November revolution (1917) declaring that bolshevism represented a dictatorship *over* the proletariat rather than a dictatorship *of* the proletariat. He spent his last years in Berlin. ■ See biography by Abraham Ascher (1972).

AKSYONOV, VASILY PAVLOVICH (1932–), Soviet-born writer. Aksyonov was the son of Evgenia Ginsburg (1906?–77), who chronicled her 10 years in Stalinist labor camps in the remarkable memoirs *Journey into the Whirlwind* (Eng. trans. 1975) and *Within the Whirlwind* (Eng. trans. 1981). Trained at the Leningrad Medical Institute, Aksyonov practiced medicine (1956–60), then turned his full attention to writing. His first novella, *Colleagues* (1960; Eng. trans. 1962), pleased conservative critics; a second, *Starry Ticket* (1961; Eng. trans. 1962), used colloquial language to portray restless Muscovite youths and stirred controversy. Although widely known, he published little in the Soviet Union after 1968. After resigning from the official writers' union to protest the expulsion of two younger members for their part in publishing the anthology *Metropol*, Aksyonov emigrated to the United States (1980) and was stripped of Soviet citizenship. The work he published in emigration established Aksyonov as a leading writer of his generation. These included *The Island of Crimea* (1981; Eng. trans. 1983), a political fantasy about an independent Crimea; *The Burn* (1980; Eng. trans. 1984), a surrealistic vision of Soviet intellectuals linked by their prison camp experiences; and *Surplussed Barrelware* (Eng. trans. 1985), a collection of short fiction written between 1967 and 1980. *Say Cheese!* (Eng. trans. 1989) was a fictionalized version of the *Metropol* affair. *Generations of Winter* (Eng. trans. 1994) and *The Winter's Hero* (Eng. trans. 1996) comprised a monumental family saga covering the years 1925 to 1953. He also wrote *In Search of Melancholy Baby* (Eng. trans. 1987) and *The New Sweet Style* (Eng. trans. 1999). Aksyonov taught at Goucher College in Maryland and George Mason University in Virginia.

AKUTAGAWA, RYUNOSUKE (1892–1927), Japanese short-story writer and poet. He also used the pseudonyms Chokodo Shujin and Gaki. A hypersensitive intellectual, Akutagawa was a literary perfectionist who revolted against naturalism and upheld an art-for-art's sake philosophy. His pessimistic and often macabre tales, numbering more than 140, were often based on obscure classical tales but were replete with modern psychological insights and were highly original in style. Among his most famous works were *Rashomon* (1915; Eng. trans. 1952) and *In a Grove* (1921; Eng. trans. 1952)—upon which the movie *Rashomon* was based—*The Nose* (1916; Eng. trans. 1930), *Hell Screen* (1918; Eng. trans. 1948), and *Kappa* (1926–27; Eng. trans. 1970). He was regarded as the most brilliant writer of his time, and his suicide at the age of 35 shocked the Japanese literary world. ▪ See study by Beongcheon Yu (1972).

ALAIN (Émile Auguste Chartier; 1868–1951), French philosopher. Alain was a philosopher who wrote a daily newspaper column and an ideologist who stubbornly remained a secondary-school teacher most of his life. At the elite Lycée Henri IV in Paris he introduced a whole generation of French leaders to the doctrinaire democracy of the French radical party: "to represent the ordinary undistinguished citizen against the eternal conspiracy of the strong, the rich, and the powerful." Alain helped form an "antifascist vigilance committee" in 1934, but in 1940 he advocated peace with Germany as a lesser evil than war. His many books included *Mars or The Truth About War* (Eng. trans. 1930), *Alain on Happiness* (Eng. trans. 1973), and *The Gods* (Eng. trans. 1974).

ALAIN-FOURNIER (Henri-Alban Fournier; 1886–1914), French writer. Alain-Fournier was briefly a literary columnist before he was killed in action in World War I. *Le Grand Meaulnes* (1913; Eng. trans. *The Wanderer,* 1928, and *The Lost Domain,* 1959), a poetic work of love and adventure, was his only completed novel. Set in the countryside where he grew up, it was a dreamlike and magical evocation of the lost delight of his youth. It was very popular and highly influential. His early poems and poetic stories were published as *Miracles* (1924). ▪ See biography by David Arkell (1986).

ALANBROOKE, ALAN FRANCIS BROOKE, 1st VISCOUNT (1883–1963), British military leader. Brooke grad-

uated from the Royal Military Academy (Woolwich), served in France during World War I, and became an expert in mechanized warfare. During World War II he distinguished himself during the 1940 evacuation from Dunkirk and commanded the British home forces (1940–41). A "military intellectual," he was highly influential as British chief of staff (1941–46), working with U.S. Gen. George C. Marshall to devise Allied strategy. His wartime diaries, the basis of *The Turn of the Tide* (1957) and *Triumph in the West* (1959), provided an intimate portrait of Prime Minister Winston Churchill and presented a critical view of Allied commander Dwight Eisenhower. ▪ See biography by David Fraser (1982).

ALBEE, EDWARD (1928–   ), U.S. playwright. Albee was adopted as an infant by the son of Edward F. Albee, the millionaire cofounder of the Keith-Albee vaudeville empire. While living in New York City's Greenwich Village in the 1950s, he despaired of becoming a poet or novelist, but still determined to be a writer, typed out *The Zoo Story* (1959), a stark one-act drama in the absurdist tradition of Eugène Ionesco. By the mid-1960s, Albee was America's most frequently performed native playwright, having added to his credits *The American Dream* (1961), *Who's Afraid of Virginia Woolf?* (1962; first full-length play), and *Tiny Alice* (1964). He won a Pulitzer Prize for *A Delicate Balance* (1966). Albee's modern morality plays often treated alienation in modern society by combining comedy with terror in a domestic setting. His later plays, which sometimes adapted stream-of-consciousness technique to the stage, included *All Over* (1971), *Seascape* (1975; Pulitzer Prize), *The Lady from Dubuque* (1980), and the autobiographical *Three Tall Women* (1991; Pulitzer Prize). ▪ See F. Hirsch, *Who's Afraid of Edward Albee?* (1978); the collection of critical essays edited by C.W.E. Bigsby (1975); and the biography by Mel Gussow (1999).

ALBEE, EDWARD FRANKLIN. *See KEITH, BENJAMIN FRANKLIN.*

ALBERS, JOSEF (1888–1976), German-born U.S. artist. Albers, who taught at the Bauhaus School of Design (1923–33), used colored shards in his early glass pictures. Emigrating to the United States, he taught at Black Mountain College in North Carolina (1934–50) and directed Yale University's department of art (1950–58). Utilizing geometrical abstraction, he rejected expressionism, spontaneity, and emotionalism in art and was known for his exploration of the color properties of superimposed squares (see his *Homage to the Square* series, begun in 1949). He also wrote *Interaction of Color* (1963).

ALBERT I (1875–1934), king of the Belgians. Albert I ascended to the Belgian throne at the death of his uncle, Leopold II (1909). His predecessors had been reconciled to the concept of parliamentary monarchy, but not until Albert's reign was the government accountable to parliament. During World War I, Albert denied German troops free access to Belgian territory and, successfully retreating onto French territory, headed the government-in-exile. He commanded (1918) the Allied offensive that recaptured the Belgian coast. Faced with social and economic upheaval during the postwar years, Albert I concentrated on social welfare and the promotion of trade and industry. He was killed in a mountain-climbing accident and was succeeded by his son, Leopold III. ■ See his *War Diaries* (Eng. trans. 1954) and biography by Émile Cammaerts (1935).

ALBERTI, RAFAEL (1902–1999), Spanish poet. Alberti began as a cubist painter, directing his energies to literature after 1923. He became interested in folk poetry and mariners' songs; encouraged by the poet Juan Ramón Jiménez, he wrote surrealistic poetry with subtle irony. His best volume in this genre was *Concerning the Angels* (1929; Eng. trans. 1967). His work became increasingly political, and during the Spanish civil war (1936–39), Alberti emerged as the poet of the workers and the revolution. He was the first major Spanish poet to join the Communist party. After the war he lived in Argentina and Italy, continuing to publish such works as *Returns of Distant Life* (1952) and *Marine Seaboard* (1953). He was also a noted playwright. He returned to Spain (1977) and ran successfully for a seat in the Cortes, but resigned after three months. ■ See *Selected Poems* (Eng. trans. 1966); *The Owl's Insomnia* (Eng. trans. 1973); *The Other Shore: 100 Poems* (Eng. trans. 1981); the autobiographical *The Lost Grove* (2 vols., 1942–59; Eng. trans. 1976); and Robert Manteiga, *The Poetry of Rafael Alberti* (1975).

ALBIZU CAMPOS, PEDRO (1891–1965), Puerto Rican political leader. A Harvard-educated lawyer, the son of a wealthy Basque father and a black mother, Albizu was a fiery and militant leader of the Puerto Rican independence movement. He was a bitter opponent of U.S. domination of his homeland and a hero in much of Latin America. A powerful orator who headed the Nationalist party, Albizu was arrested in 1936 (and imprisoned until 1943) for conspiring to overthrow the government, jailed again (1950–53) after his followers attempted to assassinate Pres. Harry Truman, and yet again (1954–64) when his followers invaded the U.S. House of Representatives and shot five congressmen. ■ See study by F. Ribes Tovar (Eng. trans. 1971).

ALBRIGHT, MADELEINE (Madeleine Korbel; 1937–), U.S. cabinet officer. Albright, the daughter of a Czechoslovakian diplomat, was born in Prague and emigrated to the United States after the Communists came to power in Czechoslovakia (1948). She studied at Wellesley College (B.A. 1959) and Columbia University (M.A. 1968; Ph.D. 1976), served on the staff of the National Security Council (1978–81), and taught international relations at the Georgetown University School of Foreign Service. As U.S. ambassa-

dor to the United Nations (1993–97), she advocated an active U.S. role in international affairs. Appointed by President Bill Clinton to be secretary of state (1997–2001), Albright became the first woman to hold that office. She played a major role in negotiations leading to the expansion of NATO and called for strong actions against Serbia in the growing Balkan crisis. Shortly after taking office she learned that her parents, who had raised her as a Roman Catholic, were born Jewish and that her grandparents were murdered in Nazi death camps during World War II. ■ See Ann Blackman, *Seasons of Her Life* (1998), and the biography by Michael Dobbs (1999).

ALBRIGHT, WILLIAM FOXWELL (1891–1971), U.S. archaeologist and biblical scholar. The son of missionaries, Albright earned his Ph.D. in archaeology and linguistics at Johns Hopkins University (1916), where he taught for many years (1929–58). He also directed the American School of Oriental Research in Jerusalem (1920; 1921–29; 1933–36) and conducted many expeditions to the Middle East, identifying biblical towns and reconstructing the past via artifacts and scrolls. He played a major role in dating the famous Dead Sea scrolls, discovered in 1947. His books included *From the Stone Age to Christianity* (1940), *Archaeology and the Religion of Israel* (1942), and *Yahweh and the Gods of Canaan* (1968). ■ See biography by Leona G. Running and David N. Freedman (1975).

ALCALÁ ZAMORA, NICETO (1877–1949), Spanish political leader. A liberal lawyer, Alcalá Zamora was elected to parliament in 1905 and served as minister in several governments. He declared himself a republican (1930), and when King Alfonso XIII abdicated (April 1931) he became premier of the provisional government. Although he strongly disagreed with some of the anticlerical provisions of the new constitution, he was elected the first president of the new republic (December 1931). A middle-of-the-roader, he attempted to reconcile the policies of the right-wing and left-wing parties and was attacked by both groups. After the popular-front victory of February 1936 he was deposed as president; he went into exile in France and later Argentina (1942).

ALCOCK, SIR JOHN WILLIAM (1891–1919), British aviator. After serving in the Royal Air Force in World War I, Alcock, with his navigator Arthur Whitten Brown, made the first nonstop transatlantic flight (1919) from St. John's, Newfoundland, to Clifden, Ireland. The 1,960-mile flight set a record of 16 hours, 27 minutes, of which almost 16 hours were spent over water. Both aviators were knighted after their flight. One week later, Alcock died in an airplane accident in France. ■ See Alcock and Brown's *Our Transatlantic Flight* (1969).

ALDER, KURT (1902–1958), German organic chemist. Alder completed graduate training under Otto Diels at the

University of Kiel (1926). Two years later, he and his mentor devised the Diels-Alder reaction and synthesized diene, an organic compound. Their method facilitated the economical laboratory manufacture of thousands of organic compounds, including camphor, drugs, dyes, insecticides, and vitamin K substitutes. Because it led to the synthesis of very large molecules, the Diels-Alder reaction also proved invaluable to the plastics industry. Alder taught at the University of Cologne (from 1940) and shared, with Diels, the 1950 Nobel Prize for Chemistry.

ALDISS, BRIAN WILSON (1925–), British writer. A prolific and successful science-fiction writer, Aldiss worked as a bookseller in Oxford (1948–56) before publishing his first collection of short stories, *Space, Time and Nathaniel* (1957), and his first sci-fi novel, *Non-Stop* (1958). His ingenious works were praised for their convincing settings and atmosphere and for their wit and humor. His other novels included *Hothouse* (1962), *Report on Probability* (1968), *Barefoot in the Head* (1969), *The Malacia Tapestry* (1976), and the epic trilogy *Helliconia Spring* (1982), *Helliconia Summer* (1984), and *Helliconia Winter* (1985). He also wrote an acclaimed history of science fiction, *Billion Year Spree* (1973), and three autobiographical novels, *The Hand-Reared Boy* (1970), *A Solder Erect* (1971), and *Rude Awakening* (1978). He served as editor of the journal *SF Horizons* (from 1964). His later works included the non-science-fiction novel *Remembrance Day* (1993) and *The Detached Retina: Aspects of SF and Fantasy* (1995). ■ See his autobiographies, *Bury My Heart at W. H. Smith's* (1990) and *The Twinkling of an Eye* (1998).

ALDRICH, NELSON WILMARTH (1841–1915), U.S. political leader. A prominent Rhode Island financier, Aldrich served as a Republican U.S. senator for 30 years (1881–1911), during which he represented corporate interests and managed to thwart or at least modify much of the progressive legislation of his time. Believing that what was good for big business was good for America, he supported the gold standard and protective tariffs and opposed social legislation and the regulation of business. Aldrich's recommendations influenced the organization of the Federal Reserve System (1913). His daughter Abby married John D. Rockefeller, Jr. ■ See biography by Nathaniel W. Stephenson (1930).

ALEGRÍA, CIRO (1909–1967), Peruvian novelist. Absorbing the Indian customs of his native region, Alegría determined to improve the lot of the Indian and was associated with the *indianismo* movement. Jailed (1932) for his revolutionary poetry and activities, he was exiled to Chile (1934) and later lived in the United States, taught at the University of Puerto Rico, and lived in Cuba before returning to Peru (1959). He wrote in the genre known as the *indigenista* novel, producing such prize-winning works as *The Golden Serpent* (1935; Eng. trans. 1943) and *Broad and Alien Is the World* (1941; Eng. trans. 1941), which depicted the suffering and exploitation of the Indians and presented a sensitive account of traditional village life and customs.

ALEICHEM, SHOLEM. *See SHOLEM ALEICHEM.*

ALEIXANDRE, VICENTE (1898–1984), Spanish poet. Precarious health marked the life and work of Aleixandre. He figured among the "brilliant pleiade" of poets who began to publish in the 1920s; he did not emigrate after the Spanish civil war (1936–39) because of illness. Aleixandre's difficult poetry, whose strange imagery bears the surrealist imprint, sought a fusion of human love and nature. He also wrote on the theme of death, and many of his works were influenced by the ideas of Sigmund Freud. His collected poems (1960), many written in free verse, were followed by several subsequent volumes. Although his work was suppressed in Spain until 1944 due to his Loyalist sympathies, he exerted considerable influence on the younger Spanish poets. He won the 1977 Nobel Prize for Literature. Translations of his poetry are in *A Longing for the Light* (1979), *A Bird of Paper* (1981), and *World Alone* (1982). ■ See study by Kessel Schwartz (1970).

ALEKHINE, ALEXANDER (Aleksandr Aleksandrovich Alyokhin; 1892–1946), Russian-born French chess player. A chess master at age 16, Alekhine was one of the greatest chess players of the century. He was three-time champion in blindfold chess (1924; 1935; 1933) and won the world championship from José Raúl Capablanca in 1927. Though he lost it eight years later to Max Euwe, he regained the championship in 1937 and held it until his death. Alekhine won more first-class master tournaments than any other player and was renowned as a theorist and innovator. ■ See study by A. A. Kotov (Eng. trans. 1975).

ALEKSANDROV, ALEKSANDR VASSILIEVICH (1883–1946), Soviet composer. A professor at the Moscow State Conservatory (from 1918), Aleksandrov founded (1928) and directed the famed Soviet Army Song and Dance Ensemble—popularly known as the Red Army Chorus—which performed Russian folk and martial music throughout the world. Aleksandrov also composed operas, orchestral works, and more than 100 popular songs and choruses, including the "Hymn to the Bolshevik Party," which, with a new set of words, became the Soviet national anthem in 1944.

ALEMÁN VALDÉS, MIGUEL (1903–1983), Mexican political leader. A labor lawyer, Alemán served as governor of the state of Veracruz (1936–40) and as minister of the interior (1940–45) before being elected president (1946). He was a representative of the new generation of middle-class banking, industrial, and commercial interests that dominated post–World War II Mexican politics. His term (1946–52) was marked by increased industrial development and foreign investments but also by a diminishing concern with agrarian reform. Alemán oversaw the construction of major national highways and began the construction of University City, the site of the National University of Mexico. From the early 1960s he served as president of the National Tourist Council.

ALESSANDRI PALMA, ARTURO (1868–1950), Chilean political leader. Alessandri, whose political career spanned 53 years (1897–1950), was one of Chile's most controversial political figures. A grass-roots social reformer during his years in congress, the senate, and the cabinet (1897–1920), Alessandri was elected president (1920) as leader of the Liberal Alliance. Conservative forces blocked most of his reform measures and the military forced him to step down (1924). He served again as president during the Depression (1932–38) and helped restore economic stability, but he headed a repressive, right-wing government that alienated his former labor and liberal supporters. He served in the senate from 1944 to 1950.

ALESSANDRI RODRÍGUEZ, JORGE (1896–1986), Chilean political leader. The son of Pres. Arturo Alessandri, Jorge Alessandri was a successful businessman who served as minister of finance (1948–50) and senator from Santiago (1956–58). Austere, aloof, and conservative, Alessandri appealed to the middle and upper classes to narrowly defeat the left-wing candidate Salvador Allende for the presidency (1958). He utilized orthodox financial policies to curb Chile's runaway inflation, but he was unable to solve problems of land reform and unemployment, and his conservative coalition was defeated in the 1964 elections by Christian Democrat Eduardo Frei. In 1970 Alessandri was persuaded to come out of retirement to run for president again, but he was defeated by Allende.

ALEXANDER I (1888–1934), king of Yugoslavia. Alexander commanded the Serbian armies during the First Balkan War (1912) and World War I and served as regent (from 1914) before being named king of the Serbs, Croats, and Slovenes (1921). He struggled to keep his multiethnic state together within a parliamentary political framework, but after the assassination of Croatian leader Stjepan Radić (1928) he abrogated the constitution and set up a royal dictatorship (1929). In an effort at unity, he changed the name of the kingdom to Yugoslavia, outlawed all regional and ethnic political parties, and standardized the legal system and school curriculum. However, Alexander's policies alienated several separatist minority groups, and he was assassinated by a member of a Croatian terrorist organization while he was on an official visit to France. ■ See biography by Stephen Graham (1939).

ALEXANDER, FRANZ GABRIEL (1891–1964), Hungarian-born U.S. psychoanalyst. The first student at the Berlin Psychoanalytic Institute (1919), Alexander elaborated the theory of the superego and was a pioneer in applying psychoanalytic insights to the study of criminal behavior. He was invited (1930) to Chicago, where he founded and directed (1932–56) the Chicago Institute for Psychoanalysis. Looking to human relations and cultural settings rather than sexuality as the source of neuroses, he identified emotional factors causing psychosomatic illness. Alexander's many books included *Roots of Crime* (1935), *Fundamentals of Psychoanalysis* (1948), *Western Mind in Transition* (1960), which is partly autobiographical, and *Psychosomatic Medicine* (1965).

ALEXANDER, GROVER CLEVELAND (1887–1950), U.S. baseball player. One of the greatest pitchers in baseball history, Alexander won a record 373 National League games (shared with Christy Mathewson) during his career (1911–30) with the Philadelphia Phillies, Chicago Cubs, and St. Louis Cardinals. His best years were with Philadelphia (1911–17), where he won 190 games and led the league in victories and strikeouts five times. His earned-run average of 1.22 in 1915 was a record that stood for 54 years. Despite suffering from alcoholism and epilepsy late in his career, he led the Cardinals to victory in the 1926 World Series. Alexander was elected to the National Baseball Hall of Fame in 1938.

ALEXANDER, HAROLD RUPERT, 1st EARL ALEXANDER OF TUNIS (1891–1969), British field marshal. The third son of the 4th earl of Caledon, Alexander was a distinguished, supremely confident Sandhurst graduate whose troops forced Germany's retreat in North Africa during World War II and whose victory in Sicily (1943) brought down Italian dictator Benito Mussolini's government. He was promoted to supreme Allied commander in the Mediterranean, served as postwar governor-general of Canada (1946–52), and as British minister of defense (1952–54). ■ See *The Alexander Memoirs: 1940–45* (1962) and Nigel Nicolson, *Alex* (1973).

ALEXANDER, SAMUEL (1859–1938), Australian-born British philosopher. Alexander was educated at Oxford, where he was the first Jew to be named a fellow at a university in Britain (1882–93), and where he wrote his prize-winning essay *Moral Order and Progress* (1889). He later taught at the University of Manchester (1893–1924). His series of lectures given at the University of Glasgow (1916–18) and published as *Space, Time and Deity* (1920) posited a metaphysical system consisting of a hierarchy of several levels of reality: matter, life, and mind. Each level seeks to develop into the next higher one, eventually reaching a state of "deity." His other work was concerned with traditional philosophical problems of ethics, the universal, and the mind-body relationship. In *Beauty and Other Forms of Value* (1933), he developed an aesthetic theory. ■ See Milton R. Konvitz, *On the Nature of Value* (1946); John W. McCarthy, *The Naturalism of Samuel Alexander* (1948);

Bertram D. Brettschneider, *The Philosophy of Samuel Alexander* (1964); and Michael A. Weinstein, *Unity and Variety in the Philosophy of Samuel Alexander* (1984).

ALEXANDERSON, ERNST FREDERIK WERNER (1878–1975), Swedish-born U.S. electrical engineer. Alexanderson emigrated to the United States (1901) to work with Charles Steinmetz at the General Electric Co. He spent most of the next five decades at GE, making notable contributions in the field of electronics; he was granted more than 320 patents. He was best known for developing a powerful high-frequency alternator (1906) that greatly advanced the state of radio communications. He also invented a selective tuning system for radio (1916), an amplidyne automatic-control system, and an electronic amplification system. He also pioneered in the field of television, building a home receiver in 1927, a complete system in 1930, and a color receiver in 1955. ■ See biography by James E. Brittain (1992).

ALFEROV, ZHORES I. (1930–), Russian physicist. After graduating from the Department of Electronics at the Lenin Electrotechnical Institute in Leningrad (now St. Petersburg), Alferov joined (1953) the A. F. Ioffe Physico-Technical Institute in Leningrad. He spent his entire career there and became its director in 1987. A pioneer in semiconductor technology, he developed fast opto- and microelectronic components, called heterostructures, that became the basis for the development of personal computers, compact-disc players, bar-code readers, cell phones, and radio linked satellites. Herbert Kroemer, working independently in the United States, developed similar heterostructures and the two researchers shared the 2000 Nobel Prize in Physics with Jack Kilby. Alferov was elected to the Soviet Congress of People's Deputies (1990) and to the Duma (1995) and advocated government spending on basic scientific research.

ALFONSÍN, RAÚL (1927–), Argentine political leader. Alfonsín graduated from a military academy but disliked the idea of pursuing an army career and acquired a law degree (1950). He became active in the Radical Civic Union, a middle-class movement that opposed authoritarian rule. He rose in influence through provincial and national legislatures, but his decisive defeat in a bid for party control in 1972 appeared to ruin his political career. In 1983, when the military stepped down after eight disastrous years in control, Alfonsín won both his party's nomination and the presidential election. He quickly saw to it that top military figures, including three former presidents, were brought to trial for human rights abuses—some 9,000 persons had disappeared during their rule. Yielding to pressure from the International Monetary Fund, Alfonsín imposed economic austerity measures in order to gain more credits to help pay for an enormous international debt. By the end of his six-year term, the economy was crippled by hyperinflation, a $60 billion foreign debt, and rampant capital flight. His

party lost the 1989 elections to Peronist candidate Carlos Menem.

ALFONSO XIII (1886–1941), king of Spain. Born six months after the death of his father, Alfonso XII, Alfonso formally ascended the throne at age 16 (1902). On the day of his marriage (1906) to Princess Victoria Eugénie (granddaughter of Queen Victoria), an assassination attempt was made on his life, in which 20 people were killed. From then on, there was much political unrest in Spain. Alfonso maintained Spanish neutrality during World War I, but he was severely criticized for a disastrous military campaign in Morocco (1921) and for supporting the dictatorship of Gen. Miguel Primo de Rivera (1923–30). The dictatorship proved unpopular and after the republicans won the municipal elections (1931), Alfonso left Spain and lived in exile in Rome. He abdicated in favor of his son, Don Juan, shortly before his death. ■ See study by Sir Charles Petrie (1963).

ALFVÉN, HANNES OLOF GÖSTA (1908–1995), Swedish physicist. A pioneer of magnetohydrodynamics (MHD) and its subfield of plasma physics, Alfvén shared (with Louis Néel) the 1970 Nobel Prize for Physics. Although his work was considered critical to the potential control of thermonuclear fusion, he was a critic of nuclear-reactor development and nuclear weapons. A professor at the Royal Institute of Technology, Stockholm (1940–67), and the University of California at San Diego (1967–89), Alfvén wrote *Cosmical Electrodynamics* (1950) and several works on the origin of the solar system.

ALGREN, NELSON (Nelson Algren Abraham; 1909–1981), U.S. novelist and short-story writer. Algren recorded characters and language from his youth in Chicago slums in his brutal, fast-paced fiction. His novels included *Somebody in Boots* (1935), *Never Come Morning* (1942), *The Man with the Golden Arm* (1949), and *A Walk on the Wild Side* (1956); his short stories were collected in *The Neon Wilderness* (1947). He also wrote *Notes from a Sea Diary* (1965), essays and a commentary on Hemingway, and *Who Lost an American?* (1963), observations on life in Chicago and New York. The French writer Simone de Beauvoir described her relationship with Algren in her autobiography and in the novel *Les Mandarins* (1954), which she dedicated to him. ■ See H.E.F. Donohue, *Conversations with Nelson Algren* (1964) and the biography by Bettina Drew (1989).

ALI, MUHAMMAD (Cassius Marcellus Clay; 1942–), U.S. boxer. Clay, who started to box at age 12, won a gold medal at the 1960 Rome Olympics and gained the professional heavyweight championship by knocking out Sonny Liston (1964). After joining the Black Muslims (1964) and changing his name to Muhammad Ali, he criticized U.S. involvement in Vietnam and refused induction in the army on religious grounds. He was sentenced to five years in prison and stripped of his title (1967), but returned to boxing (1970) after the U.S. Supreme Court reversed his conviction. A quick, graceful, and powerful fighter—and an unparalleled showman and promoter—he regained his crown by defeating George Foreman (1974). After losing to Leon Spinks in 1978, he defeated him in a rematch later that year to become the first heavyweight boxer to regain a title twice. He "retired" as champion in 1979 but lost several fights in a comeback bid (1980–81). In a career spanning two decades he compiled a record of 56 victories (37 knockouts) against 5 defeats, and was regarded as one of the greatest boxers in history. He fought throughout the world, including title matches in Zaire and the Philippines, and became a popular international celebrity. In 1984 he was diagnosed as suffering from Parkinson's syndrome, a form of brain damage caused by repeated blows to the head. ■ See his autobiography *The Greatest* (1975; with R. Durham); José Torres, *Sting Like a Bee* (1971); and David Remnick, *King of the World* (1998).

ALIGER, MARGARITA IOSIFOVNA (1915–   ), Soviet poet. A graduate of Moscow's Gorky Literary Institute, Aliger began writing lyrics of the confessional genre, often about unhappy love. She later won popularity with verse narratives, including *Zoya* (1942), the story of a young Komsomol (communist youth organization) girl who works in the Russian underground during World War II and is martyred at the hands of the Germans. She also wrote essays and translations. *Lyrics and Poems* (1970) appeared in two volumes.

ALINSKY, SAUL DAVID (1909–1972), U.S. social reformer and author. Born in the slums of Chicago to Russian-Jewish parents, Alinsky became active in a coal miners' rebellion while still an undergraduate at the University of Chicago (Ph.B. 1930). His work with juvenile and adult offenders spawned a lifelong concern with the economic roots of social problems. After helping organize Chicago's "Back of the Yards" slum into a self-help participatory community, Alinsky founded the Industrial Areas Foundation in 1939 to train community organizers. During the 1950s he worked with anticommunist unions in Italy under the sponsorship of the bishop of Milan, later Pope Paul VI, and during the 1960s turned to black American ghettos. Irreverent and unsentimental, Alinsky rejected federal antipoverty programs as "pork-barrel politics" and advocated radical democracy and indigenous leadership. ■ See his *Reveille for Radicals* (1947) and *Rules for Radicals* (1971); Robert Bailey, Jr., *Radicals in Urban Politics* (1974); P. David Finks, *The Radical Vision of Saul Alinsky* (1984); and the biography by Sanford D. Horwitt, *Let Them Call Me Rebel* (1989).

ALLAIS, MAURICE (1911–   ), French economist. Allais worked in the French state-owned mine administration (1937–44) before serving as a professor at his alma mater, the National Superior School of Mines in Paris (1944–88). He directed the National Scientific Research Center in Paris (1954–79) and several other economic research institutions. His research works, published in the 1940s, developed the theoretical foundation for determining prices by state-run monopolies in the absence of a competitive market. His works advocated market principles, as opposed to direct government regulation, in the running of state monopolies and were particularly influential in the Western European economies in the post–World War II era. He was made an officer of the Legion of Honor (1977) and was awarded the 1988 Nobel Memorial Prize in Economics.

ALLAL AL-FASSI, MUHAMMAD (1910–1974), Moroccan nationalist leader. Allal al-Fassi came from a scholarly family tracing its ancestry back to a companion of the prophet Muhammad. Called the father of Moroccan nationalism, he was a powerful writer and speaker on behalf of independence, for which he suffered long periods of imprisonment and exile (1937–47). In 1943 he became head of the Istiqlal (Independence) party, the first mass nationalist group, which he led through the struggle for independence from France (granted in 1956). Thereafter he became a focus of opposition to the Moroccan monarchy. ■ See his *Independence Movements in Arab North Africa* (Eng. trans. 1954).

ALLEN, FORREST C. (1885–1974), U.S. basketball coach. "Phog" Allen, who was coached by basketball's inventor, Dr. James Naismith, was one of the sport's most prominent personalities. In a coaching career lasting almost half a century, including 39 years at the University of Kansas, Allen won 771 games and 30 conference championships. He was instrumental in having basketball added to the Olympic games (1936), and he helped organize the first National Collegiate Athletic Association (NCAA) tournament (1939). Allen was also a practicing osteopath.

ALLEN, GRACIE (1906–1964), U.S. comedienne. The daughter of a song-and-dance man, Gracie Allen was in front of footlights by age 3; she teamed up with her three sisters in a dance number in her teens but quit when she wasn't given top billing. While attending secretarial school in New York City she met vaudevillian George Burns, with whom she teamed up (1922) and whom she later married (1926). When they first worked together, Burns delivered the funny lines and Allen played the "straight man," but when she got more laughs, they exchanged roles. Allen played dumb with great shrewdness. Her search for her long-lost brother was a famous gag in the 1930s, when she interrupted "The Eddie Cantor Show," "The Jack Benny Show," and other broadcasts all over the radio dial to look for him. Her birdbrained schemes, brilliantly illogical explanations, and unmatchable advice were mainstays of Burns and Allen humor on the stage, in radio (1932–50), and on television (1950–58).

They also appeared in films. ■ See George Burns, *I Love Her, That's Why!* (1955) and *Gracie: A Love Story* (1988).

ALLEN, HERVEY (William Hervey Allen, Jr.; 1889–1949), U.S. novelist. Allen left the U.S. Naval Academy after sustaining an athletic injury and finished college at the University of Pittsburgh (B.S. 1915). He published the collection *Wampum and Old Gold* (1921) as part of the prestigious Yale Younger Poets series, establishing a reputation as a poet that faded by the end of the 1920s. He taught at Columbia University (1925–26) and Vassar College (1926–27), then, while living in Bermuda, started work on *Anthony Adverse* (1933), the huge, picaresque novel of the Napoleonic era that was one of the bestselling historical novels of all time and set a literary trend. The 1,224-page book, which was bold for its day in its treatment of sexuality, sold 395,000 copies in its first year (during the Depression) and was translated into many languages. His later novels included *Action at Aquila* (1938), a Civil War story, and *It Was Like This* (1940), war stories set in 1918. In the 1940s he completed three books of *The Disinherited*, a cycle of novels set in colonial America. He also wrote *Israfel* (2 vols., 1926), an important biography of Edgar Allan Poe, and *Toward the Flame* (1926; rev. ed. 1934), a diary of Allen's experiences as a first lieutenant in World War I. ■ See biography by Stuart E. Knee (1988).

ALLEN, STEVE (1921–2000), U.S. television performer, composer, and author. Steve "Steverino" Allen hosted (1954–57) NBC's original "Tonight Show," a nightly 90-minute variety program that showcased the multiple talents of comedian, pianist, composer, and writer Steve Allen. He also introduced to home viewers the new faces and voices of his supporting players, including singers Andy Williams, Steve Lawrence, and Eydie Gorme and comedians Don Knotts, Bill Dana, and Louis Nye. Later Allen appeared (1956–60), often with his wife Jayne Meadows, on the weekly "Steve Allen Show." He appeared on specials and on game shows and did "Meeting of Minds" (1977) for the Public Broadcasting Service. Allen also made a name as a composer with such tunes as "This Could Be the Start of Something Big" and was the author of more than 30 witty books. ■ See his autobiographies, *Mark It and Strike It* (1961) and *Hi-Ho, Steverino* (1992).

ALLEN, WILLIAM MCPHERSON (1900–1985), U.S. business executive. A Harvard Law School graduate (1925), Allen worked for the Seattle law firm that was counsel to the Boeing Airplane Co. He provided the legal work for the establishment of United Airlines, an outgrowth of the Boeing Air Transport division, and was appointed a director of Boeing in 1931. Named president of Boeing as World War II military contracts were being canceled (1945), he emphasized commercial transport and produced the first jet airliners. During his years as Boeing's leader (president, 1945–68; chief executive officer, 1968–72), he introduced the Stra-

tocruiser and the 707, 727, and 747 jets, and Boeing became the world's leading manufacturer of civilian passenger aircraft. For the military, Boeing built the first swept-wing jet bomber, the B-47, as well as the B-50 and B-52 bombers and the Minuteman missile. It also built the Saturn-Apollo moon rocket and the lunar orbiter spacecraft.

ALLEN, WOODY (Allen Stewart Konigsberg; 1935–), U.S. writer, film director, and actor. As a high school student in Brooklyn, Allen began writing gags for press agents. He wrote for TV comedians Sid Caesar, Art Carney, and Buddy Hackett, and in 1961 began performing his own material at New York nightclubs. An extraordinarily inventive and productive filmmaker, Allen debuted in *What's New, Pussycat?* (1965), for which he wrote the screenplay; over the next 20 years, he made some 15 films, many of which became cult classics. Most of them featured Allen himself, playing a hesitant, self-deprecating, relentlessly psychoanalyzed New Yorker. He often parodied classics of film and fiction. The actress Mia Farrow, who starred in many of his movies, was his companion for over a decade, but Allen subsequently married her adopted daughter in 1997. Allen's films included *Bananas* (1971), *Play It Again, Sam* (1972), *Take the Money and Run* (1969), *Sleeper* (1973), *Love and Death* (1975), *Annie Hall* (1977; Academy Award), *Manhattan* (1979), *Stardust Memories* (1980), *Zelig* (1983), *Hannah and Her Sisters* (1985), *Crimes and Misdemeanors* (1989), *Bullets Over Broadway* (1994), *Everyone Says I Love You* (1996), *Deconstructing Harry* (1997), and *Sweet and Lowdown* (1999). He wrote *Getting Even* (1971) and *Without Feathers* (1975). ■ See biographies by Lee Guthrie (1978); Eric Lax (1991); John Baxter (1998); and Marion Meade, *The Unruly Life of Woody Allen* (2000).

ALLENBY, EDMUND HENRY HYNMAN ALLENBY, 1st VISCOUNT (1861–1936), British field marshal. Allenby was educated at Sandhurst and served in Africa early in his career. As commander of the Egyptian expeditionary force (1917–18), he liberated Syria and Palestine from Turkish rule in World War I and thus paved the way for British control of the Middle East. Later Allenby served (1919–25) as British high commissioner for Egypt, where he was instrumental in the granting of Egyptian independence (1922). He was considered the last of the great cavalry men. ■ See biography by Archibald Wavell (2 vols., 1940–43) and study by Brian Gardner (1966).

ALLENDE, ISABEL (1942–), Chilean writer. The niece of Chilean president Salvador Allende, Isabel Allende was born into a diplomatic family and lived in Europe and the Middle East before returning to Chile at age 15. She worked as a journalist in Santiago before going into exile, first in Venezuela (1975) and then in the U.S. (1988), after her uncle's socialist government was overthrown in a military coup (1973). Her internationally acclaimed first novel, *The House of the Spirits* (1982; Eng. trans. 1985), written in the style of magical realism, told the story of three generations of a prominent family, based on her family's experiences, from a feminist perspective. Her next novel, *Of Love and Shadows* (1984; Eng. trans. 1987), described the terror unleashed by the Pinochet dictatorship after the 1973 coup. Her other works of fiction included *The Stories of Eva Luna* (1987; Eng. trans. 1988), *The Infinite Plan* (1991; Eng. trans. 1993), and *Daughter of Fortune* (1999; Eng. trans. 1999). Her nonfiction work, *Paula* (1994; Eng. trans. 1995) written as a letter to her terminally ill daughter, recounted a long legacy of female endurance in her family. She also wrote *Aphrodite: A Memoir of the Senses* (1997; Eng. trans. 1998).

ALLENDE GOSSENS, SALVADOR (1908–1973), Chilean political leader. A Marxist activist while a student at the University of Chile (M.D. 1932), Allende helped found the Chilean Socialist party (1933). He served in congress (1937–39), as minister of health (1939–42), and in the senate (1945–69) before being elected president of Chile (1970) on his fourth try. As the head of Popular Unity, a Socialist-Communist-Radical coalition, Allende attempted to implement a program of socialism within a constitutional and democratic framework. He nationalized mineral resources and major industries and banks, raised industrial wages, and initiated large-scale land reform. However, he was plagued by rampant inflation, opposition by the middle class, harassment by far-right and far-left elements, and the hostility and interference of the U.S. government and U.S. corporations. Overthrown by a military coup, he died during the attack on the presidential palace (Sept. 11, 1973). ■ See his *Chile's Road to Socialism* (Eng. trans. 1973); Robert Alexander, *The Tragedy of Chile* (1978); study by James Whelan (1981); and Nathaniel Davis, *The Last Two Years of Salvador Allende* (1985).

ALLPORT, GORDON WILLARD (1897–1967), U.S. psychologist. A professor at Harvard from 1924 until his death, Allport developed a theory of personality that largely rejected Freudian theory as well as behaviorism. He advanced a concept of personality that, while rooted in infantile drives, because independent of them. His theory of "functional autonomy," in which the individual is seen as unique, emphasized treating problems as they manifested themselves in the present rather than focusing on possible childhood traumas. His books included *Personality: A Psychological Interpretation* (1937), *The Individual and His Religion* (1950), and *The Nature of Prejudice* (1954). ■ See study by Richard I. Evans (1971).

ALMOND, GABRIEL ABRAHAM (1911–), U.S. political scientist. A specialist in comparative political systems, Almond earned his Ph.D. from the University of Chicago (1938) and taught at Yale (1947–51; 1959–63), Princeton (1951–59), and Stanford (from 1963). He was among the first to incorporate a functional approach to studies in political science. His main works were *The American People and Foreign Policy* (1950), *The Politics of the Developing Areas* (1960; with James Coleman), *The Civic Culture* (1963; with Sidney Verba), *Political Development* (1970), *The Civic Culture Revisited* (1980), *A Discipline Divided: Schools and Sects in Political Science* (1990), and *Plutocracy and Politics in New York City* (1998).

ALONI, SHULAMIT (Schulamit Adler; 1931–), Israeli feminist and writer. She was born in Tel Aviv to Russian-Jewish parents and was educated at a progressive school. In 1948, she fought with Haganah units in the Jewish quarter of Jerusalem. She graduated from Teacher's Training College (1948), earned a law degree at Jerusalem's Hebrew University (1956), and got involved in consumer issues. She aired listeners' problems and dispensed advice on the radio show "After Office Hours" and in the mid-1960s headed the Israeli Council for Consumers' Rights. Aloni served in the Knesset as a Labor party member (1965–69), and later as a member of the Citizens Rights party (from 1974), which she founded in 1973. A member of the Knesset Committee for Constitutional Law and Legislation, she wrote weekly political columns for Israeli publications, and wrote widely on the status of women in Israel, particularly on laws concerning marriage and the family. She served as minister of education (1991) and of communications, science, and technology (1993–96).

ALONSO, ALICIA (Alicia de la Caridad del Cobre Martínez Hoyo; 1921–), Cuban ballerina and ballet director. Alicia Alonso was identified for over four decades with the title role in *Giselle*, the ballet in which she made a brilliant debut in 1943 with the Ballet Theatre of New York. She danced in the United States for 23 years, often with partner Igor Youskevitch. Alonso founded (1948) her own troupe in Havana, and after Fidel Castro's accession to power in 1959, she became director and prima ballerina of the National Ballet of Cuba. She continued to dance into the 1970s, despite near blindness; her sight was restored by an operation in 1975. Alonso, who continued to direct the company through the 1990s, was a preeminent public figure in Cuba, where postage stamps bearing her image were issued. ■ See biography by Beatrice Siegel (1979).

ALSOP, JOSEPH WRIGHT, JR. (1910–1989), U.S. journalist. A member of "the eastern establishment" by birth, education, and affinity, Alsop turned to journalism after graduation from Groton and Harvard (B.A. 1932). As an aide to Gen. Claire Chennault in China during World War II and as a globe-trotting syndicated columnist (*New York Herald Tribune*, 1945–58; *Washington Post*, 1958–74), he was conservative regarding world politics but defended some of the victims of the extreme anticommunism of the Sen. Joseph McCarthy era. Alsop was also a bon vivant who took an annual rest cure in Baden Baden and an erudite amateur archaeologist who published a journalistic report on the Greek Bronze age, *From the Silent Earth* (1964). He also wrote an affectionate popular biography of his cousin, Franklin D. Roosevelt, *FDR, 1882–1945: A Centenary Remembrance* (1982). ■ See his memoirs *I've Seen the Best of It* (1992); studies by Leann Almquist (1993) and Edwin Yoder (1995); and Robert Merry, *Taking on the World* (1996).

ALTAMIRA Y CREVEA, RAFAÉL (1866–1951), Spanish historian and jurist. A proponent of "scientific" historical writing, Altamira y Crevea worked as a university professor (Oveido, 1897–1910; Madrid, 1914–36) to promote secondary and continuing education. Author of *A History of Spain* (1934; rev. ed. 1946; Eng. trans. 1949) and *A History of Spanish Law* (1903–04), he served on the Permanent Court of International Justice at The Hague (1921–45), where he was active in behalf of world peace. An opponent of the regime of Spanish dictator Francisco Franco, he emigrated to Mexico in 1945.

ALTERMAN, NATAN (1910–1970), Polish-born Israeli Hebrew-language poet. The most popular and influential Hebrew poet since C. N. Bialik (1873–1934), Alterman produced poems characterized by musical effects, fantastic imagery, and unique use of language and humor. He arrived in Palestine in 1925, where, in addition to poetry, he wrote plays, children's books, show lyrics, and translations from Yiddish, French, and English. Alterman's topical ballads, which appeared weekly in a newspaper under the heading "The Seventh Column" (1943–65), reflected the Zionist struggle against British policies and influenced public opinion. After Israeli independence (1948) he continued to write on political and social themes. The volumes *Stars Outside* (1938), *The Joy of the Poor* (1941), *The Ten Plagues of Egypt* (1945), and *Summer Festival* (1965) contained his lyric poetry. English translations are in *Selected Poems* (1978).

ALTHUSSER, LOUIS (1918–1990), Algerian-born French philosopher. Althusser served in the French army (1939–40), then was captured by the Germans and spent the duration of World War II in a prisoner-of-war camp. After the war he studied philosophy in Paris at the École Normale Supérieure, the institution with which he was affiliated throughout his career. He became the controversial leading figure of the influential school of Marxist-structuralists, which sought to reinterpret Marxism as a structural analysis of society. He attempted to reestablish Marxism as a materialist science and repudiated humanist and historicist interpretations of Marx's writings. Afflicted with manic-depression, he strangled his wife (1980) and was institutionalized in a psychiatric hospital (1981–84). His most important works were *For Marx* (1965; Eng. trans. 1969), *Reading Capital* (1965; Eng. trans. 1970), and *Politics and History* (1959; Eng. trans. 1978). ■ See Alex Callinicos, *Athusser's Marxism* (1976); Simon Clarke, et al., *One Dimension Marxism* (1980); Ted Benton, *The Rise and Fall of Structural Marxism* (1984); E. A. Kaplan and M. Sprinker, eds., *The Al-*

thusserian Legacy (1993); and Althusser's memoir, *The Future Lasts Forever* (Eng. trans. 1993).

ALTIZER, THOMAS (1927–), U.S. theologian. Altizer studied the history of religions at the University of Chicago (Ph.D. 1955) and taught religion and later English literature at Emory University (1956–68) and the State University of New York at Stony Brook (from 1968). He published his radical ideas on the place of Christianity in modern life but was little known outside academic circles until the media popularized his controversial views under the rubric "God Is Dead" (1965). Altizer's ideas derived in part from those of the German philosopher Friedrich Nietzche and also were influenced by Paul Tillich and Mircea Eliade. His books included *Mircea Eliade and the Dialectic of the Sacred* (1963), *The Gospel of Christian Atheism* (1966), *The New Apocalypse* (1967), *The Descent into Hell* (1970), and *Total Presence* (1980). His essays are collected in *Radical Theology and the Death of God* (1966; with William Hamilton).

ALTMAN, ROBERT (1925–), U.S. film director, producer, and writer. Altman attended the University of Missouri, served in the military (1943–47), and went to work directing industrial films. He made two feature films (1957), then moved into television, directing more than 300 hours of programming, including episodes of "Bonanza" and "Alfred Hitchcock Presents." Returning to feature films in 1968, Altman won recognition with the antiwar comedy *M*A*S*H* (1970). A series of antigenre films followed: *McCabe and Mrs. Miller* (1972), a western; *The Long Goodbye* (1973), a Raymond Chandler detective thriller; and *Thieves Like Us* (1974), a gangster film. Altman became known for fast-paced social satire conveyed by overlapping dialogue on a multitrack sound system. *Nashville* (1975) was a documentary-style drama depicting several days in the lives of 24 characters connected to the country-western music industry. After a setback in 1976, when the box-office disaster *Buffalo Bill and the Indians* led to the cancellation of major projects, Altman recovered with such films as *Three Women* (1977), *Popeye* (1980), *Fool for Love* (1985), *Vincent and Theo* (1990), *The Player* (1992), *Cookie's Fortune* (1998), and *Dr. T and the Women* (2000). ■ See Altman's *Buffalo Bill and the Indians, or Sitting Bull's History Lesson* (1976; with Alan Rudolf); Neil Feineman, *Persistence of Vision* (1977); studies by Judith M. Kass (1978), Alan Karp (1981), and Daniel O'Brien (1995); and the biography by Patrick McGilligan (1989).

ALTMAN, SIDNEY (1939–), Canadian-U.S. biologist. Altman earned a doctorate in biophysics from the University of Colorada (1967) and taught molecular biology at Yale (1971–). In experiments during the late 1970s and early 1980s he demonstrated that ribonucleic acid (RNA) was not merely a passive carrier of genetic information but also functions as an enzyme, which initiates vital biochemical reactions. (Previously it was believed that all enzymes were proteins.) Independent research by Thomas Cech also showed that RNA can be a catalyst of chemical reactions within living cells. Together their findings led to new theories of cell function, promised new biotechnological tools for genetic engineering, and provided a new explanation for how life arose on earth—with RNA serving as both a storehouse of genetic information and a catalyst of chemical reactions. Altman and Cech shared the 1989 Nobel Prize in Chemistry for their research.

ALVAREZ, LUIS WALTER (1911–1988), U.S. physicist. Alverez took a leave of absence (1940–43) from his teaching position (University of California at Berkeley) to work at the Massachusetts Institute of Technology, where he invented microwave beacons and worked on the development of radar. He devised a ground-controlled approach system for all-weather landing and developed a method for blind bombing using radar. Later (1944–45) he worked on the development of the first atomic bombs at the Los Alamos Laboratory in New Mexico. After World War II Alvarez returned to Berkeley and worked on the development of linear accelerators, bubble chambers for detecting subatomic particles, and stereo photography for recording their activity. His research led to the discovery of dozens of previously undetected particles and earned for him the 1968 Nobel Prize for Physics. ■ See his autobiography (1987).

AMADO, JORGE (1912–), Brazilian novelist. Born on a cacao plantation in turbulent northeast Brazil, Amado was drawn to radical politics while in law school and achieved fame for a series of popular proletarian novels published during the 1930s and 1940s, including *The Violent Land* (1943; Eng. trans. 1945). Frequently exiled and imprisoned, he served as a communist member of the Brazilian parliament (1946–48) until the party was outlawed. His later works, though comical and less overtly political, continued to depict sympathetically the life and struggles of the lower classes in his native northeast and were translated into more than 40 languages. Brazil's most widely read novelist, he was best known internationally for *Gabriela, Clove and Cinnamon* (1958; Eng. trans. 1962), *Home Is the Sailor* (1960; Eng. trans. 1964), *Doña Flor and Her Two Husbands* (1966; Eng. trans 1969), *Tent of Miracles* (1969; Eng. trans. 1971), *The Golden Harvest* (1981; Eng. trans. 1992), and *War of the Saints* (1988; Eng. trans. 1993). ■ See study by Bobby J. Chamberlain (1990).

AMAYA, CARMEN (1913–1963), Spanish Gypsy dancer. Amaya started her dancing career as a child and appeared with a professional troupe in Paris at age 10. She was the most celebrated flamenco dancer of her time, achieving phenomenal success throughout the world. A theater was named for her in Buenos Aires (where she lived from 1929 to 1940), and she made several highly acclaimed appearances in the United States (New York debut, 1941). She appeared in the movie *Los Tarantos* (1964), a Gypsy version of *Romeo and Juliet,* shortly before her death.

AMBARTSUMIAN, VIKTOR AMAZASPOVICH (1908– 1996), Soviet-Armenian astronomer. The leading theoretical astrophysicist in the Soviet Union, Ambartsumian lectured at Leningrad University (1931–43) and founded (1946) and directed the Byurakan Astronomical Observatory (near Yerevan), one of the country's most important observatories. In 1947 he discovered the existence of stellar associations, fields of comparatively recently formed stars in our galaxy, which demonstrated that star formation is still continuing. His studies of "radio galaxies," which led him to conclude that they represent exploding rather than colliding galaxies, greatly influenced the study of the origin and evolution of stars and stellar systems. His textbook, *Theoretical Astrophysics* (1939; Eng. trans. 1958), was translated into many languages.

AMBEDKAR, BHIMRAO RAMJI (1891–1956), Indian social reformer. Born into an untouchable Mahar family, Ambedkar was educated at Columbia University (Ph.D. 1926), where he came under the influence of the philosopher John Dewey. Committed to empowering the untouchable (pariah) castes, he organized political campaigns and gained clout by founding newspapers. He fought for reserved legislative seats and jobs for his people and came into conflict with national leader Mahatma Gandhi, who wanted to integrate the untouchables into the mainstream of Hindu society. As law minister of newly independent India (1947–51), he played a major role in writing the Indian constitution, which outlawed discrimination against untouchables. However, he subsequently became convinced that Hindu society would never grant equality to untouchables and he converted to Buddhism (1956) with several hundred thousand followers. ■ See his *What Congress and Gandhi Have Done to the Untouchables* (1945); biography by Dhananjay Keer (1962); and Gail Omvedt, *Dalits and the Democratic Revolution* (1994).

AMBLER, ERIC (1909–1998), British novelist. A former advertising copywriter and a military-film director in World War II, Ambler won fame with a series of witty spy thrillers and he was credited with redefining the genre and raising it to the level of literature. Written with tension and economy, his novels were set in exotic locales. Most concerned ordinary people caught in a web of intrigue and violence; their unlikely heroes are sympathetically roguish characters. His early work included *Epitaph for a Spy* (1938), *A Coffin for Dimitrios* (1939), and *Journey into Fear* (1940). Later novels, like *Dirty Story* (1967), *The Levanter* (1972), and *The Care of Time* (1981) used as backgrounds contemporary events in Africa and the Middle East. ■ See his autobiographies, *Here Lies* (1986) and *The Story So Far* (1993), and Peter Wolfe, *Alarms and Epitaphs* (1993).

AMENDOLA, GIOVANNI (1882–1926), Italian journalist and political leader. A journalist in Rome before World War I, Amendola was elected to parliament as a democratic liberal in 1919. He was appointed minister for the colonies in 1922 and became leader of the antifascist opposition. Fascist leader Benito Mussolini was "a pathological case not foreseen in the constitution," he wrote in *Il Mondo,* his newspaper, and he led the 1924 secession of opposition deputies from parliament. But Mussolini remained firmly in power, and Amendola died of wounds inflicted by a fascist gang.

AMERINGER, OSCAR (1870–1943), German-born U.S. writer, publisher, and political leader. Ameringer left Bavaria in 1885, lived with his brother in Ohio (1885–90) and became an American citizen. He returned to Germany and did not permanently move to the United States until 1895. At first he supported himself as an artist and musician. However, he was influenced by the writings of Henry George, Edward Bellamy, and the muckraking journalists and he became a union organizer, labor editor, and public speaker for the socialist movement. In the decade before U.S. entry into World War I he was a leader of the powerful Oklahoma Socialist Party and editor of its newspaper. His satirical history of the U.S., *Life and Deeds of Uncle Sam* (1912; new ed. 1985), was a best-seller and Ameringer became known as the "Mark Twain of American Socialism." He became a pacifist after World War I but remained an active and influential socialist. He edited the *Illinois Miner* (1922–31) and published the *American Guardian* (1931–42), an Oklahoma City weekly that was a vehicle for his satirical essays attacking the capitalist system. ■ See his autobiography, *If You Don't Weaken* (1940; new ed. 1983).

AMICHAI, YEHUDA (1924–2000), German-born Israeli Hebrew-language poet. A teacher of Hebrew literature and the Bible in a secondary school, Amichai published his first collection of poems in 1955 and pioneered in the use of the contemporary Hebrew vernacular as a poetic language. He was primarily a love poet whose poems, reflecting a sense of loss and a keen awareness of time, were filled with juxtapositions of biblical and contemporary allusions. He also wrote plays, the short stories in *The World Is a Room and Other Stories* (Eng. trans. 1984), and the novel *Not of This Time, Not of This Place* (1963; Eng. trans. 1968). Among his poetry collections in English were *Poems* (1969), *Songs of Jerusalem* (1973), *Amen* (1977), *Love Poems* (1981), *Great Tranquillity* (1983), *Selected Poems* (1986), *Yehuda Amichai: A Life of Poetry, 1948–1994* (1994), and *Selected Poetry* (1996). ■ See Glenda Abramson, *The Writing of Yehuda Amichai* (1989).

AMIN, IDI (Idi Amin Dada Oumee; 1925?–   ), Ugandan political leader. Born into a Muslim Kakwa family, Amin received little formal education. He joined the King's African Rifles (1946) and participated in the suppression of the Mau Mau uprising in Kenya (1952–56). He was also the Ugandan heavyweight boxing champion (1951–60). A supporter of Pres. Milton Obote, he rose through the ranks, becoming head of the army and air force (1966–70) before ousting Obote in a military coup (1971). Called a buffoon by some and a shrewd politician by others, Amin ruled as a dictator and instituted a reign of terror. He tortured and murdered thousands of Obote supporters, expelled most members of the Asian minority community, and weakened ties linking the East African Community (of Uganda, Kenya, and Tanzania). He chaired the Organization of African Unity (1975–76) and declared himself Uganda's president for life (1976). Following the outbreak of a rebellion in the late 1970s, Uganda was invaded by the Tanzanian army and Amin was overthrown (1979). He fled to Libya and later lived in Saudi Arabia. ■ See David Martin, *General Amin* (1974); Henry Kyemba, *A State of Blood* (1977); and biography by David Gwyn (1977).

AMIS, SIR KINGSLEY (1922–1995), British novelist and poet. A graduate of Oxford and a teacher of literature (1949–63), Amis was originally a poet, but his reputation rested on his novels. *Lucky Jim* (1954), a comic study of academia and social classes, caused Amis to be classified as one of Britain's "angry young men." His later novels, including *One Fat Englishman* (1963), *Girl, 20* (1971), *Jake's Thing* (1978), and *Stanley and the Women* (1985), satirized sexual mores in modern life. As a critic and essayist, Amis argued for "militant philistinism" and wrote studies of science fiction and the James Bond novels of Ian Fleming. He also edited *The New Oxford Book of English Light Verse* (1978). His later works included *The Old Devils* (1986) and *The Russian Girl* (1994). ■ See his *Collected Poems, 1944–1979* (1980); his *Memoirs* (1991); Paul Fussell, *The Anti-Egotist* (1994); and the biography by Eric Jacobs (1995).

AMMANN, OTHMAR HERMANN (1879–1965), Swiss-born U.S. bridge designer and engineer. Long associated with projects in New York City, Ammann served as chief engineer (1930–1937) and director of engineering (1937–39) of the Port of New York Authority. He designed the George Washington Bridge (1931), linking New York and New Jersey, and Verrazano Narrows Bridge (1965), linking Brooklyn and Staten Island. Each was the longest suspension bridge in the world at the time of its completion. Ammann also directed the planning and construction of the Triborough Bridge, the Bronx-Whitestone Bridge, and the Lincoln Tunnel in New York City and was on the board of engineers responsible for San Francisco's Golden Gate Bridge (1937). In private practice (from 1939), he designed the Throgs Neck Bridge (New York City) and Dulles Airport (near Washington, D.C.).

AMOS 'N' ANDY. *See GOSDEN, FREEMAN F., and CHARLES J. CORRELL.*

AMRAM, DAVID WERNER (1930–   ), U.S. composer. Amram played horn in the National Symphony while studying at George Washington University (B.A. 1953), and appeared with the 7th Army Symphony while doing military service. He was music director of the New York Shakespeare Festival (1956–67) and a guest conductor with many orchestras. He composed scores for television, plays, and for such films as *Splendor in the Grass* and *The Manchurian Candidate*. At one time he led his own Latin jazz folklore ensemble, and in his compositions combined folk elements and traditional instruments with symphonic music. His works included *En Memoria de Chano Pozo* (1977), *Zohar* (1978), a violin concerto (1980), *American Dance Suite for Orchestra* (1986), and *Conversations for Chamber Ensemble* (1988). ■ See his autobiography, *Vibrations* (1968).

AMUNDSEN, ROALD (1872–1928), Norwegian explorer. Amundsen studied medicine for two years and served in the Norwegian navy. He was a member of the Belgian Antarctic Expedition (1897), the first to winter in the Antarctic, and made the first voyage through the Northwest Passage from east to west (1903–6: aboard the 47-ton sloop *Gjöa*). He was the first explorer to reach the South Pole (Dec. 14, 1911) and, with American explorer Lincoln Ellsworth and Italian aviator Umberto Nobile, was the first to fly over the North Pole (May 1926: aboard the dirigible *Norge*). Amundsen's airplane disappeared (1928) in the Arctic while he was searching for Nobile, whose dirigible *Italia* had crashed after he had successfully flown over the Pole. Amundsen's books included *The South Pole* (Eng. trans. 1913), *The First Crossing of the Polar Sea* (with Ellsworth; 1927), and his autobiography, *My Life as an Explorer* (Eng. trans. 1927). ■ See Cateau DeLeeuw, *A World Explorer* (1965), and Roland Huntford, *Scott and Amundsen* (1980).

ANAND, MULK RAJ (1905–   ), Indian novelist and art critic. One of the most widely read Indian novelists of the century, Anand chose his heroes from among the exploited masses of Indians and wrote realistic, angry novels depicting suffering that he ascribed to traditional Hinduism, British imperialism, and modern capitalism. After studying in India, he was educated in Britain (University of London, 1926–29; Cambridge, 1929–30), where he lived for many years prior to 1945. He wrote all of his novels in English. His best-known early works were *Untouchable* (1935), *Coolie* (1936), *Two Leaves and a Bud* (1937), and the famous trilogy *The Village* (1939), *Across the Black Waters* (1940), and *The Sword and the Sickle* (1942). His celebrated later works included *Private Life of an Indian Prince* (1953), *Morning Free* (1968), and *Selected Short Stories* (1977). He taught at several Indian universities, founded (1946) and edited the art magazine *Marg* (Bombay), wrote books on Indian art, and headed the fine-arts section of the Indian National Academy of Art (1965–70). ■ See his reminiscences, *Conversations in Bloomsbury* (1961); his childhood autobiography (1985); and the studies by Krishna Sinha (1972) and M. K. Naik (1973).

ANDERS, WLADYSLAW (1892–1970), Polish general. The son of a Polish official in the Russian government, Anders was a cavalry officer in the Russian army during World War I, after which he joined the Polish campaign (1919–20) against Russia. In 1939 he was captured by the Russians, who kept him in solitary confinement for 20 months, finally releasing him to assume command of Polish war prisoners in the Soviet Union. Anders' Free Polish forces fought in the Middle East and North Africa, and in the 1944 Italian campaign they captured Monte Cassino. After the war the anti-Soviet general chose exile in England. ■ See his *An Army in Exile* (1949) and *Hitler's Defeat in Russia* (1953).

ANDERSEN, LALE (Liselotte Helen Beul; 1913–1972), German singer, A little-known Berlin cabaret singer with a soft and sexy voice, Andersen became famous for her recording of "Lili Marlene" (1939), which was the theme song of the German army's radio show emanating from Belgrade during World War II. The song was a favorite of both the British and German soldiers stationed in North Africa. They took the song home with them, and it was soon familiar throughout Europe and the rest of the world. Andersen received an estimated 1 million fan letters from German soldiers during the war.

ANDERSON, CARL DAVID (1905–1991), U.S. physicist. A student of Nobel laureate R. A. Millikan at the California Institute of Technology (Ph.D. 1930), Anderson discovered (1932) the positron in the course of research on the nature of cosmic rays. Subsequently (1933) he was able to produce positrons by gamma-ray bombardment. The positron was the first known particle of antimatter and the first known positively charged nuclear particle other than the proton, and its discovery revolutionized the field of particle physics. Anderson shared the 1936 Nobel Prize for Physics with Victor F. Hess for his discoveries. In 1936, aided by Seth Neddermeyer, he confirmed the existence of intermediate-mass particles in cosmic rays. He called them mesotrons, but they were later named mesons and are now called muons.

ANDERSON, JACK (1922–   ), U.S. columnist. At age 12 Anderson was writing the Boy Scout page of the *Deseret (Utah) News*; by age 22 he had advanced to war correspondent in China; and by 25 was chief investigative reporter for "Washington Merry-Go-Round" columnist Drew Pearson. After Pearson died in 1969 Anderson came into his own, exposing political scandal and corruption with a missionary zeal. He earned a Pulitzer Prize in 1972 for the story of U.S. policy in the India-Pakistan crisis. His books included *Washington Exposé* (1967), *The Case Against Congress* (1968), *Fiasco* (1988), and *Inside the NRA* (1996). ■ See his *Confessions of a Muckraker* (1979; with James Boyd) and his memoirs, *Peace, War and Politics* (1999; with Daryl Gibson).

ANDERSON, DAME JUDITH (Frances Margaret Anderson; 1898–1992), Australian-born British actress. Three years after her 1915 debut in Sydney, Australia, Anderson made her first American appearance in bit parts at New York's old Fourteenth Street Theater. A stage actress of unusual power, she preferred strong character roles and achieved stardom for her performances in *Mourning Becomes Electra* (1931), *Come of Age* (1934), *The Old Maid* (1935), and *Hamlet* (1936). She made her London debut as Lady Macbeth in 1937. She is perhaps best known for her portrayals of the title role in Robinson Jeffers' adaptation of *Medea* (1947) and of the housekeeper in Alfred Hitchcock's film *Rebecca* (1940). At age 86 she appeared in the film *Star Trek III* and the television soap opera *Santa Barbara*.

ANDERSON, MARIAN (1897–1993), U.S. concert and opera singer. Anderson started singing as a child in church choirs in her native Philadelphia and began formal training at age 19. Although recognized early for the richness and purity of her voice and her tremendous range, she was denied concert opportunities in the United States because of prejudice against blacks. Between 1925 and 1935 she made several tours of Europe, became the first African-American concert singer to receive international acclaim, and was considered by many to be the world's greatest contralto. After 1935 her career flourished in the United States, and when the Daughters of the American Revolution banned her (1939) from singing in Washington's Constitution Hall (which they owned), Eleanor Roosevelt resigned from the organization and sponsored an Easter-morning concert at the Lincoln Memorial featuring Anderson that drew 75,000 people. Her broad repertoire ranged from spirituals to German lieder and to Italian operatic arias, and in 1955 she became the first African American to perform at New York's Metropolitan Opera (in Verdi's *A Masked Ball*). ■ See her autobiography, *My Lord, What a Morning* (1956); study by Janet Stevenson (1963); and biography by Allan Keiler (2000).

ANDERSON, MARY (1872–1964), Swedish-born U.S. labor leader. Anderson emigrated to the United States in 1889 and was a shoe stitcher in Chicago for 18 years before becoming a Women's Trade Union League (WTUL) official. In 1920 she was named to head the Woman's Bureau of the U.S. Department of Labor and became the best-known woman in government service during the 1920s. In office until 1944, she advocated improved safety standards and equal pay and opportunity for women workers. ■ See her autobiography, *Woman at Work* (1951).

ANDERSON, MAXIE. *See ABRUZZO, BEN.*

ANDERSON, MAXWELL (1888–1959), U.S. playwright. Anderson abandoned his New York journalism career when his antiwar play *What Price Glory?* (1924; with Laurence Stallings) became a hit. Many of his dramas featured romance frustrated by political, social, or moral obstacles, and served as vehicles for strident social commentary. *Both Your*

Houses (1933; Pulitzer Prize), was a satirical attack on the U.S. Congress. Anderson often wrote in blank verse, notably the historical romances *Elizabeth the Queen* (1930) and *Mary of Scotland* (1933), and *Winterset* (1935), a tragedy inspired by the Sacco and Vanzetti case. His other plays included *High Tor* (1937), *Key Largo* (1939), and two musicals written with Kurt Weill, *Knickerbocker Holiday* (1938) and *Lost in the Stars* (1949). ■ See his collection of essays, *Off Broadway* (1947), and studies by Mabel D. Bailey (1957) and Alfred S. Shivers (1983).

ANDERSON, PERRY (1938–), British editor and historian. Anderson served as editor (1962–82) and editorial committee member (1982–) of London's *New Left Review*, one of the world's most influential left-wing journals. His first two books, *Passages from Antiquity to Feudalism* (1974) and *Lineages of the Absolutist State* (1974), a massive synthesis of European history that concentrated on the development of the state, were considered landmarks of Marxist historiography. His books on modern Marxism included *Considerations on Western Marxism* (1976), *Arguments within English Marxism* (1980), and *In the Tracks of Historical Materialism* (1983). He also wrote *The Origins of Postmodernity* (1998). His essays appeared in *English Questions* (1992) and *A Zone of Engagement* (1992). ■ See study by Gregory Elliott (1997).

ANDERSON, PHILIP WARREN (1923–), U.S. physicist. Anderson did antenna engineering at the Naval Research Laboratory during World War II, then completed graduate training at Harvard University (Ph.D. 1949), where he worked under mathematical physicist John H. Van Vleck. Thereafter he worked at the Bell Telephone Laboratories and taught at Cambridge (1967–75) and Princeton (1975–96) Universities. He made basic findings in the field of solid-state physics; his approach to the spectroscopy of gases permitted the solution of numerous problems involving molecular interactions. For his work on magnetism, spectroscopy, and superconductivity, he shared the 1977 Nobel Prize for Physics with Van Vleck and with Nevill F. Mott. Their research provided the foundation for such diverse electronic devices as the laser, high-speed computers, tape recorders, and copying machines.

ANDERSON, POUL (1926–), U.S. science-fiction writer. Anderson began selling science-fiction stories while majoring in physics at the University of Minnesota (B.S. 1948), *Brain Wave* (1954), about a quantum leap in human intelligence, and *High Crusade* (1960), in which a spaceship sets down in medieval England, put him on the map as a major science-fiction writer. Later books included *Tau Zero* (1970), *The Byworlder* (1971), *Conan the Rebel* (1980), *Orion Will Rise* (1983), *Past Times* (1984), *The Boat of a Million Years* (1989), *All One Universe* (1996), and *War of the Gods* (1997). Anderson also wrote adventure and historical fiction, mysteries, nonfiction, poetry, and criticism.

His stories were collected in *The Worlds of Poul Anderson* (1978).

ANDERSON, SHERWOOD (1876–1941), U.S. novelist and short-story writer. Unhappy with his life as a paint factory owner in small-town Ohio, Anderson moved to Chicago (1913) to pursue a literary career and befriended Carl Sandburg, Theodore Dreiser, and others of their circle. Although he published his first novel, *Windy McPherson's Son*, in 1916, Anderson first attracted critical attention with *Winesburg, Ohio* (1919), in which he focused on crucial moments in small-town existence. He developed his own brand of naturalism, writing candidly about sex as a humanizing force in the machine age. Anderson's forthright conversational style, influenced by the writings of Gertrude Stein, lent itself best to short stories such as those in *The Triumph of the Egg* (1921). His works, in turn, influenced such writers as Ernest Hemingway and William Faulkner. After producing several lesser novels and a volume of poetry, he edited two newspapers in Virginia. ■ See his *A Story Teller's Story* (1924), *Memoirs* (1942), and *Letters to Bab* (1985); biography by Kim Townsend (1987); and studies by Irving Howe (1951), James Schevill (1951), and David D. Anderson (1967).

ANDERSSON, JOHAN GUNNAR (1874–1960), Swedish geologist and archaeologist. Trained as a geologist and geographer, Andersson participated in several Arctic and Antarctic expeditions and headed the Geological Survey of Sweden (1906–16). Though he originally went to China (1914) to advise the government on the mining of mineral resources, he soon began to make studies of Chinese flora and fauna and eventually spent years making extensive archaeological investigations all along the Yellow River Valley of Northern China. He discovered (1921) the first Neolithic artifacts ever found in China—painted pottery of a primitive farming community later named Yang-shao culture—and thus threw light on the earliest Chinese settlements. His books included *Children of the Yellow Earth* (Eng. trans. 1934) and *Researches into the Prehistory of China* (1943).

ANDRADE, MÁRIO (RAÚL) DE (MORAIS) (1892–1945), Brazilian writer and critic. The century's most influential Brazilian author, Andrade was a pioneer of the modernist movement, which attempted to develop a modern and authentically Brazilian language and cultural perspective. He was best known for his poetry, including *Hallucinated City* (1922; Eng. trans. 1968), a hymn to his native São Paulo, and the novels *Fräulein* (1927; Eng. trans. 1977) and *Macunaíma* (1928; Eng. trans. 1984). He also wrote numerous collections of short stories and essays on Brazilian music and literature. A multifaceted genius, he organized and directed (1934–37) the São Paulo department of culture, founded the Brazilian Society of Ethnography and Folklore (1937), and did extensive research into Brazilian folklore and art history.

ANDRE, CARL (1935–), U.S. sculptor. Born in Massachusetts, Andre moved to New York City in the late 1950s, began painting, then shifted to sculpture, making tall wood structures influenced by the work of Constantin Brancusi. After working as a brakeman for the Pennsylvania Railroad (1960–64), he began creating the simpler, more horizontal work for which he won fame. Rejecting consumerism, Andre used really available materials to create "minimalist" sculptural environments, applying his formula, "form equals structure equals space." One of his works, *Equivalent VIII* (1978), a two-level arrangement of ordinary bricks, was purchased by the Tate Gallery for $12,000. The city of Hartford, Connecticut, acquired a row of boulders from Andre for $87,000. His arrest late in 1985 stirred controversy in the art world. Andre was charged with pushing his wife, sculptor Ana Mendieta, to her death from the window of their New York City apartment but was subsequently acquitted. ■ See Robert Katz, *Naked by the Window* (1990).

ANDRES, STEFAN (1906–1970), German novelist. Andres studied from age 11 to become a priest, and although at age 22 he decided against pursuing a monastic life, his early novels, notably *Brother Lucifer* (1932), reflected the conflict of Christian versus worldly values. Because of his disgust with the Nazis and his love for southern Italy, Andres emigrated to Positano (1937), where he wrote his best-known work, *We Are Utopia* (1943; Eng. trans. 1955). This powerful novella, set during the Spanish civil war, probes the question of individual responsibility in war. His best-known post–World War II works were *The Flood* (3 vols., 1949–59), a somber political fantasy that symbolically depicted the rise and fall of Nazi Germany, and *The Dumb Girl* (1969), a penetrating social critique of both East and West Germany ■ See study by John Klapper (1995).

ANDREWS, CHARLES MCLEAN (1863–1943), U.S. historian. Born in Connecticut of Pilgrim ancestry, Andrews was a student of American history from the British or "imperial" viewpoint. After earning his Ph.D. from Johns Hopkins (1889), he did research in England for his books on U.S. colonial history. A member of the Yale faculty (1910–31), Andrews won a Pulitzer Prize (1935) for volume one of *The Colonial Period of American History* (4 vols., 1934–38). His other works included *Colonial Self-Government, 1652–1689* (1904) and *The Colonial Period* (1912). ■ See study by Abraham S. Eisenstadt (1956).

ANDREWS, FRANK MAXWELL (1884–1943), U.S. Air Force officer. A graduate of West Point (1906), Andrews served in the new air service during World War I. An advocate of strategic air power, he commanded (1935–39) the general-headquarters air force, the first independent air unit (and forerunner of the army air corps) and played a major role in the development of the B-17 bomber. During World War II he commanded U.S. forces in the Caribbean and later the Middle East before replacing Gen. Dwight D. Eisenhower as commander of U.S. forces in Europe (February 1943). He helped initiate successful daylight bombing raids on Germany but was killed in a plane crash on May 3, 1943.

ANDREWS, ROY CHAPMAN (1884–1960), U.S. explorer and naturalist. Andrews was associated with the American Museum of Natural History (New York City) from 1906 and served as its director (1935–42). His expeditions to various corners of the earth yielded new facts about plant, animal, and prehistoric human life. He collected both live specimens and fossil remains in explorations of the Alaska coast, the Malayan seas, and central and east Asia. His popular books on natural history included *Ends of the Earth* (1929), *Meet Your Ancestors* (1945), and *In the Days of the Dinosaur* (1959). ▪ See his autobiographies, *Under a Lucky Star* (1943) and *An Explorer Comes Home* (1947); Jules Archer, *Science Explorer* (1968); and the biography by Alonzo W. Pond (1972).

ANDREWS SISTERS (Patty, 1920– ; LaVerne, 1915–1967; Maxene, 1918–1995), U.S. vocal group. The Andrews Sisters appeared in vaudeville, on network radio shows, and in numerous popular movies from 1937 to the 1950s and sold more than 50 million records. Their popularity peaked during World War II. Among their most famous songs were "Bei Mir Bist Du Schoen," "In Apple Blossom Time," "Beer Barrel Polka," and "Rum and Coca-Cola." ▪ See Maxene Andrews, *Over Here, Over There* (1993).

ANDREYEV, LEONID NIKOLAYEVICH (1871–1919), Russian writer. After receiving a law degree from the University of Moscow (1897), Andreyev gained a reputation as a journalist and later (after 1902) as a short-story writer and novelist. His works dealt primarily with themes of despair, isolation, and death. He was best known for the stories "The Abyss" (1902; Eng. trans. 1924) and "The Seven That Were Hanged" (1908; Eng. trans. 1909) and the novel *The Red Laugh* (1904; Eng. trans. 1905). He also wrote a series of notable allegorical and pessimistic plays, including *Life of a Man* (1906; Eng. trans. 1915), *King Hunger* (1907; Eng. trans. 1911), and *He Who Gets Slapped* (1916; Eng. trans. 1921). An opponent of the 1917 bolshevik revolution, Andreyev spent the last years of his life in exile in Finland. ▪ See studies by James B. Woodward (1969) and Josephine M. Newcombe (1973).

ANDRIĆ, IVO (1892–1975), Yugoslav novelist and short-story writer. Andrić was Yugoslavia's most illustrious literary figure. Although from a poor Bosnian family, he studied in Zagreb, Vienna, Cracow, and Graz (Ph.D. 1923) and then served as a diplomat. His three great epic novels, *Bosnian Chronicle* (Eng. trans. 1958, 1963, and as *The Days of the Consuls*, 1992), a story of the Napoleonic era; *The Woman from Sarajevo* (Eng. trans. 1966), which dealt with the World War I period; and his masterpiece, *The Bridge on the*

Drina (Eng. trans. 1959), which presented a tableau of Bosnian history from 1516 to World War I, were all written during World War II while he was living under voluntary house arrest in Belgrade and were published in 1945. Using Bosnian society as a microcosm. Andrić compassionately dealt with the universal themes of human suffering and the struggle to preserve one's dignity. Characterized by their concise, graphic language, psychological penetration, and lyrical quality, his novels earned him the Nobel Prize for Literature (1961). He also wrote *The Pasha's Concubine and Other Tales* (Eng. trans. 1968). ▪ See study by Celia Hawkesworth (1984) and the volume edited by Wayne Vucinich (1995).

ANDROPOV, YURI VLADIMIROVICH (1914–1984), Soviet political leader. The son of a railroad worker, Andropov graduated from a technical school and worked as a telegraph operator and Volga boatman before rising through the ranks of the Young Communist League (from 1936). He was a political commissar on the Finnish front during World War II and joined the Central Committee staff in Moscow (1951). As Soviet ambassador to Hungary (1954–57) he helped suppress the 1956 Hungarian revolution and later served as Communist party secretary in charge of relations with parties within the Communist bloc (1962–67). He headed the Soviet secret police (KGB; 1967–82) and played a major role in suppressing the dissident movement within the Soviet Union. Andropov became general secretary of the Communist party after the death of Leonid Brezhnev (1982). His campaigns to end corruption and increase economic efficiency were cut short by his death soon after he achieved power. ▪ See studies by Martin Ebon (1983), Zhores A. Medvedev (1983), and Jonathan Steele and Eric Abraham (1984).

ANDRZEJEWSKI, JERZY (1909–1983), Polish novelist and short-story writer. Although he achieved fame before World War II as a writer concerned with Catholic themes, Andrzejewski was best known for his postwar novels analyzing the moral conflicts facing the Polish people during and immediately after the war. His masterpiece, *Ashes and Diamonds* (1948; Eng. trans. 1962), was the most acclaimed postwar Polish novel. He joined the Communist party (1949) and served in parliament (1952–57) but later (1957) renounced socialist realism and artistic regimentation. *The Inquisitors* (1957; Eng. trans. 1960) attacked political fanaticism. He also wrote *The Gates of Paradise* (1960; Eng. trans. 1962), *A Sitter for a Satyr* (1963; Eng. trans. 1965), and *The Appeal* (1968; Eng. trans. 1971). He was a founder of the Workers Defense Committee (KOR; 1976), a dissident group of intellectuals that helped to organize the Solidarity labor union (1980).

ANFINSEN, CHRISTIAN BOEHMER (1916–1995), U.S. biochemist. Anfinsen earned a Harvard Ph.D. (1943) and directed laboratories at the National Heart and Lung Institute

(1950–62) and the National Institute of Arthritis and Metabolic Diseases (1963–82). For research done in the early 1950s on the enzyme ribonucleic acid (RNA), which determined the primary structure of proteins and the relationship between their molecular structure and genetic function, Anfinsen shared the 1972 Nobel Prize for Chemistry with Stanford Moore and William H. Stein. He wrote *The Molecular Basis of Evolution* (1959).

ANGELL, JAMES ROWLAND (1869–1949), U.S. psychologist and educator. The son of a university president, Angell was attracted to psychology by philosopher and teacher John Dewey. He became professor and first head (1905) of the University of Chicago's psychology department, where he helped found the functionalist school of psychology. Appointed (1921) president of Yale University, he presided for 16 years during a period when the university established new divisions and schools and substantially elevated its intellectual standards. He wrote a basic textbook, *Psychology* (1904), *Chapters from Modern Psychology* (1912), and *American Education* (1937).

ANGELL, SIR NORMAN (Ralph Norman Angell Lane; 1872–1967), British economist and peace activist. Angell wrote one of the most influential antiwar books of the first half of the century, *The Great Illusion* (1910: rev. ed. 1933). In this book he explained that the belief that victory in war would lead to increased economic strength was the "great illusion" because military conquest would only destroy the fabric of credit and trade relations upon which wealth in the modern world was based. He worked for international cooperation after World War I, served as a Labour member of the House of Commons (1929–31), and received the 1933 Nobel Peace Prize. ■ See his autobiography, *After All* (1952); biography by Albert Marrin (1979); and study by J.D.B. Miller (1986).

ANGELOU, MAYA (Marguerite Johnson; 1928–), U.S. writer. In her best-selling autobiography, *I Know Why the Caged Bird Sings* (1970), Angelou depicted her experience as an African American growing up in the 1930s and early 1940s in rural Arkansas as well as in St. Louis and San Francisco. It was followed by several further volumes of autobiography, including *Gather Together in My Name* (1974), which begins when Angelou is age 16, and *Singin' and Swingin' and Gettin' Merry Like Christmas* (1976). The fourth volume, *The Heart of a Woman* (1981), recounted her reactions to the civil-rights movement of the late 1950s and early 1960s, and the fifth, *All God's Children Need Traveling Shoes* (1986), told of her experience in a group of African-American expatriates in Ghana. Critics praised her lyrical prose and powerful descriptions. Angelou also wrote several volumes of poetry, including *Just Give Me a Cool Drink of Water 'Fore I Die* (1971), *Oh Pray My Wings Are Gonna Fit Me Well* (1975), *And I Still Rise* (1978), *Shaker, Why Don't You Sing?* (1981), and *The Complete Poems*

(1994). She wrote screenplays, directed several plays and films, and taught at Wake Forest University (1981–). Her essays are in *Lessons in Life* (1993) and *Wouldn't Take Nothing for My Journey Now* (1993). ■ See Dolly A. McPherson, *Order Out of Chaos* (1991), and Lyman B. Hagen, *Heart of a Woman* (1997).

ANIELEWICZ, MORDECAI (1919–1943), Polish-Jewish resistance leader. Born into a Jewish working-class family, Anielewicz became a leading member of Ha-Shomer ha-Za'ir, a Socialist-Zionist youth movement in Warsaw. After the German invasion of Poland in 1939, he advocated Jewish armed resistance and was named commander of the ZOB (Jewish Fighting Organization) when it was formed in the Warsaw ghetto (1942). He organized the heroic armed civilian uprising against the Nazis in April 1943 and died in battle.

ANKA, PAUL (1941–), Canadian-born U.S. singer and composer. The son of an Ottawa restaurant owner, Anka achieved rock-and-roll immortality at age 15 with the recording of his own song "Diana" (1957). He subsequently became an international teenage idol with 15 original gold-record hits including, "You Are My Destiny," "Lonely Boy," "Put Your Head on My Shoulder," and "Crazy Love." He also composed songs for many of the most popular recording stars of the 1960s and 1970s, including Frank Sinatra ("My Way") and Tom Jones ("She's a Lady") and appeared frequently on television and in nightclubs.

ANNAN, KOFI (1938–), Ghanaian diplomat. Descended from tribal chiefs on both sides of his family, Annan attended college in Ghana and subsequently studied economics at Macalester College, St. Paul, Minnesota (B.A. 1961), and management at the Massachusetts Institute of Technology (M.S. 1972). He joined the U.N. staff in 1962 as an administrative officer at the World Health Organization (WHO) and rose through the ranks in various planning, budgetary, and personnel positions. A soft-spoken, skillful negotiator, he was highly praised for his work as under-secretary-general for peacekeeping (1993–95) and as the U.N.'s special representative to the former Yugoslavia (1995–96). As the U.N.'s seventh secretary-general (1997–), he became a popular international celebrity. In his attempts to rejuvenate and reform the organization Annan severely reduced its budget and its administrative costs. He advocated (1999) the controversial doctrine of "humanitarian intervention" whereby the international community would be able to intervene in conflicts within national borders when human rights were violated.

ANNENBERG, WALTER HUBERT (1908–), U.S. publisher. Annenberg inherited from his father a Philadelphia-based publishing empire that included the *Inquirer* newspaper and the *Racing Form*. He founded *Seventeen* magazine (1944) and *TV Guide* (1953) and bought the

Philadelphia Daily News (1957). A philanthropist with conservative Republican beliefs, Annenberg founded schools of communications at the University of Pennsylvania and the University of Southern California and made substantial contributions to the election of Pres. Richard Nixon, who subsequently appointed him ambassador to Great Britain (1969–75). He was also an adviser to Pres. Ronald Reagan. ■ See John E. Cooney, *The Annenbergs* (1982), and Christopher Ogden, *Legacy* (1999).

ANOUILH, JEAN (1910–1987), French playwright. Born in poverty, Anouilh worked in advertising as a young man. His plays were well crafted and written with comic style and verve. His early plays were naturalistic; later works were more stylized and symbolic as Anouilh mixed illusion and reality. Continuing themes were the conflicts between personal moral values and purity and the hypocritical demands of a corrupt society. Among his best-known plays were *Antigone* (1942; Eng. trans. 1946), whose main character prefers death to compromise; *The Lark* (1953; Eng. trans. 1955), *The Waltz of the Toreadors* (1951; Eng. trans. 1956), and *Becket* (1959; Eng. trans. 1962). ■ See Leonard Pronko, *The World of Jean Anouilh* (1961); study by Alba della Fazia Amoia (1969); and H. G. McIntyre, *The Theater of Jean Anouilh* (1981).

ANSERMET, ERNEST (1883–1969), Swiss conductor. Ansermet studied at Lausanne University and taught mathematics there (1906–10) before turning to music. After studying counterpoint and composition, he made his conducting debut in 1912. Three years later Ansermet was hired by Sergei Diaghilev's Ballet Russe, where he conducted first performances of works by composer Igor Stravinsky. In 1918 Ansermet founded the Orchestre de la Suisse Romande, which he conducted until 1967. Under his baton it became widely known through its tours and recordings of modern French and Russian composers, notably Debussy, Ravel, and Prokofiev.

AN-SKI, S. (Solomon Zainwil Rapaport; 1863–1920), Russian-born Yiddish-language author and folklorist. His name is also spelled Ansky. Although he received a traditional Hasidic education, An-Ski was soon attracted to the secular trends of his time. He studied Russian, joined the Narodniks, a Russian populist movement, and in 1905 became a member of the Social Revolutionary party. His writings consisted mostly of folk legends, Hasidic tales, plays, and stories of Jewish poverty. As head of an ethnographic expedition through Jewish villages in the Ukrainian regions of Volhynia and Podolia (1911–14), An-Ski collected folk materials for his internationally famed play, *The Dybbuk* (1920; Eng. trans. 1926). ■ See *The Dybbuk and Other Writings* (Eng. trans. 1992).

ANTONESCU, ION (1882–1946), Rumanian dictator. Born into an aristocratic family, Antonescu received a military education, served in the Rumanian army in World War I, and was a military attaché in Rome and London. A fascist sympathizer, he was named premier in September 1940 and set up a military dictatorship in January 1941. Under Antonescu, Rumania became a German puppet state, and he joined German dictator Adolf Hitler in invading the Soviet Union in June 1941. As a result of military setbacks his support eroded; he was overthrown in August 1944. He was arrested, convicted of war crimes by a Rumanian military tribunal, and executed.

ANTONINI, LUIGI (1883–1968), Italian-born U.S. labor leader. Antonini emigrated to the United States in 1908 and found work as a dress presser. In 1919 he started the Italian Dressmakers Local 89, which became the largest local in the International Ladies' Garment Workers' Union (ILGWU). He later served as vice-president (1934–68) of the ILGWU and was the longtime president of the Italian-American Labor Council. An avowed antifascist and anticommunist, he left the American Labor party, which he considered to be communist-dominated, and was a founder of New York's Liberal party (1944).

ANTONIONI, MICHELANGELO (1912–), Italian film director. A political-economy graduate of the University of Bologna, Antonioni wrote film criticism and worked with director Roberto Rossellini before directing documentaries during the 1940s. He won international acclaim in 1960 with *L'Avventura*, a film exploring the modern burden of alienation, guilt, and betrayal. In *La Notte* (1961), *The Eclipse* (1962), and *Red Desert* (1964), all set in visually stark landscapes, Antonioni pursued his search for meaning and permanence in an alienating and hostile world. That quest took him to London for *Blowup* (1966), a mod-era mystery, and to California for the less successful *Zabriskie Point* (1970). He also made the philosophical thriller *The Passenger* (1975). ■ See his books, *That Bowling Alley on the Tiber: Tales of a Director* (Eng. trans. 1985) and *Architecture of Vision: Writings and Interviews on Cinema* (1996); and the studies by Seymour Chatman (1985), Sam Rohdie (1990), and William Arrowsmith (1995).

ANZILOTTI, DIONISIO (1867–1950), Italian legal scholar and statesman. A professor of law at Florence, Palermo, Bologna, and Rome, Anzilotti was a founder of the positive school of international law and cofounder of the *International Law Review* (1906). He began his public career as a member of the Italian delegation to the Paris Peace Conference (1919) and was later vice secretary-general of the League of Nations (1992) and president of the Permanent Court of International Justice (1928–1930).

APOLLINAIRE, GUILLAUME (Guillaume Apollinaris de Kostrowitzky; 1880–1918), French poet and critic. An illegitimate child born in Italy, Apollinaire became a patriotic French citizen and was wounded in World War I. He was a legendary figure in Parisian intellectual circles, with a forceful and exuberant personality, and he strongly influenced the modernist and avant-garde movements as a publicist and critic. He advocated and explained the new cubist art, coined the word "surrealism," and wrote one of the first surrealist plays. In his own poetry, collected in *Alcools* (1913; Eng. trans. 1964) and *Calligrammes* (1918; Eng. trans. 1980), he experimented with word pictures, typography, and disquieting juxtapositions of language and images. ■ See his poems in *Bestiary* (1911; Eng. trans. 1980), criticism in *Apollinaire on Art* (Eng. trans. 1972), his *Selected Writings* (Eng. trans. 1950); and biographies by Francis Steegmuller (1963) and Margaret Davies (1964).

APPLETON, SIR EDWARD VICTOR (1892–1965), British physicist. While serving as an army officer during World War I, Appleton, trained in physics at Cambridge, became acquainted with the phenomenon of fading radio signals and pursued the problem while teaching at the University of London (1924–36). He hypothesized that the phenomenon might be caused by the reflection of radio waves from layers of the upper atmosphere and devised (1924) an experiment that enabled him to calculate the height of such reflection. This investigation led Appleton to his most important achievement, the discovery of the existence and properties of the ionosphere, for which he received the 1947 Nobel Prize for Physics. ■ See biography by Ronald Clark (1971).

AQQAD, ABBAS MAHMUD AL- (1889–1964), Egyptian essayist, poet, literary critic, and biographer. Though largely self-educated, Aqqad became a prolific and influential innovator in Arabic letters. He was coauthor of *al-Diwan* (1921), an iconoclastic work of literary criticism that attacked the contemporary literary establishment, and he produced a body of poetry that represented a transition from traditional classicism to romanticism. He is also known for his 30 volumes of biography, with subjects ranging from Jesus and Muhammad to writers J. W. von Goethe and G. B. Shaw, and numerous works dealing with politics, literature, philosophy, and religion.

AQUINO, CORAZON (Corazon Cojuangco; 1933–), Filipino political leader. Born into one of the wealthiest landowning families in the Philippines, Cory Aquino studied at exclusive girls' schools in Manila, Philadelphia, and New York City, and graduated from Mt. St. Vincent College in New York (B.A. 1953). Returning home, she abandoned law studies to marry a young politician, Benigno S. Aquino, Jr. She remained in the background as her husband became a governor and senator and the most prominent opponent of Pres. Ferdinand Marcos. After Marcos declared martial law, Benigno Aquino was imprisoned (1972–80), but allowed to leave for the United States to have heart surgery. Upon his return to Manila (August 1983), he was assassinated at the airport, an event widely believed to have been planned by the Marcos government. Cory Aquino became a symbol of

opposition to Marcos and ran for president in the special election called for February 1986. The election, marked by widespread fraud and intimidation of Aquino supporters, was "officially" won by Marcos, but he faced growing domestic and international pressures to resign. After he and Aquino held rival inaugurations (Feb. 25, 1986), Marcos fled the country for exile in the United States and Aquino established a new government. As president (1986–92) she survived seven military coup attempts and a communist insurgency while helping to restore democracy and constitutional government. ■ See study by Robert H. Reid (1995).

ARAFAT, YASIR (1929–), Palestinian political leader. Born in Jerusalem, Arafat studied civil engineering at the University of Cairo, headed the League of Palestinian Students (1952–56), and served briefly in the Egyptian army (1956). After working as an engineer in Kuwait (1957–65) he headed Al Fatah, a Palestinian guerrilla movement that subsequently became the largest military component of the coalition Palestine Liberation Organization (PLO). In 1969 he was appointed chairman of the PLO. Arafat won Arab recognition for the PLO as the "sole legitimate" representative of the Palestinian people and gained diplomatic recognition from the United Nations (1974) and from more than 100 countries. Though he was subsequently regarded as a moderate for his apparent willingness to negotiate an end to the Israeli-Palestinian conflict, he never renounced armed struggle and the PLO never officially repudiated its goal of eliminating Zionism in Palestine. Arafat's political authority was challenged by radical elements within the PLO after he was forced to leave his base in Beirut during the 1982 Israeli invasion of Lebanon. However, from his new base in Tunisia he remained the leader of the majority of the PLO and in 1988 persuaded the PLO to accept Israel's right to exist alongside of an independent Palestinian state. In 1993 he negotiated a peace agreement with Israeli Prime Minister Yitzhak Rabin and Foreign Minister Shimon Peres that established mutual recognition and provided for Israeli withdrawal from the Gaza Strip and parts of the West Bank, as well as a Palestinian authority to govern those areas. Arafat, Rabin, and Peres shared the 1994 Nobel Peace Prize for their efforts. In 1996 Arafat was elected president of the Palestinian National Authority, and he continued to negotiate a comprehensive peace plan with Israeli leaders. ■ See studies by Thomas Kiernan (1976), Alan Hart (1984; rev. ed. 1994), and Andrew Gowers and Tony Walker (1994).

ARAGON, LOUIS (1897–1982), French novelist and poet. Aragon was a founder of the surrealist movement and in his early career wrote iconoclastic poetry. Profoundly moved by a visit (1931) to the Soviet Union, he joined the Communist party and became a major figure in left-wing French literature. He broke with the surrealists and wrote numerous well-constructed novels embodying the Soviet principles of socialist realism, including *The Bells of Basel* (1934; Eng. trans. 1936) and *Residential Quarter* (1936; Eng. trans.

1938). They described aspects of the class struggle and "the real world." At the same time he was writing more personal novels, including *Aurélien* (1944; Eng. trans. 1947), and working as a critic and editor. He was a leader of the Resistance during World War II. Much of his later, lyrical poetry was inspired by his great love for his wife, the novelist Elsa Triolet. His other works included the novels *Holy Week* (1958; Eng. trans. 1961) and *Henri Matisse* (1971; Eng. trans. 1972). ■ See study by Lucille F. Becker (1971).

ARAKI, SADAO (1877–1966), Japanese general. An ultranationalist, Araki was a leader of the Imperial Way (Kodoha) faction of the army and served as minister of war (1931–33). As minister of education (1938–39) he promoted military education throughout the country. He served the government throughout World War II and was convicted as a war criminal by the International Military Tribunal (1946). He was sentenced to life imprisonment but released because of illness in 1955.

ARAMBURU, PEDRO EUGENIO (1903–1970), Argentinian army officer and political leader. A career military officer, Aramburu was a leader of the coup that ousted Pres. Juan Perón (1955). Serving as provisional president (1955–58), he attempted to stabilize Argentinian society and ousted Peronists from positions in business, government, the armed forces, and the press. He returned the country to democratic rule (1958) and ran unsuccessfully for president (1963). He was kidnapped and assassinated (June 1970) by a Peronist guerrilla group.

ARANHA, OSVALDO (1894–1960), Brazilian political leader. Politically active in his home state of Rio Grande do Sul during the 1920s, Aranha was a leader in the coup that brought his close friend Getúlio Vargas to power (1930), and he served as minister of justice (1930–31), of finance (1931–34), and as ambassador to the United States (1934–38). As foreign minister (1938–44) he worked for Pan-American unity and was instrumental in securing Brazil's participation as one of the Allies during World War II. A well-known international figure, he served as president of the United Nation's General Assembly during the 1947–48 session.

ARBENZ GUZMÁN, JACOBO (1913–1971), Guatemalan political leader. A graduate of the National Military Academy, Arbenz participated in a coup (1944) that led to the establishment of Guatemala's first democratic government, in which he served as defense minister (1945–50). An independent radical, he had the support of both the army and left-wing political parties when elected president (1950), but his agrarian land reform and expropriation of some United Fruit Co. holdings provoked a revolt by right-wing forces— aided by the U.S. government—and he was overthrown in June 1954 and forced into exile. His ouster resulted in much anti-United States feeling throughout Latin America. ■ See

Stephen C. Schlesinger and Stephen Kinzer, *Bitter Fruit: The Untold Story of the American Coup in Guatemala* (1982).

ARBER, WERNER (1929–   ), Swiss molecular biologist. During the early 1960s, Arber, a professor at the University of Geneva (1962–70), postulated and demonstrated the existence of restriction enzymes (endonucleases) capable of cutting through deoxyribonucleic acid (DNA), the basic genetic material of life, and thus segregating and modifying pieces of genetic material. Further independent work by Hamilton Smith and Daniel Nathans, who isolated the enzymes and utilized them to manipulate gene structure, produced a revolution in genetic research. Arber, who subsequently did research at Basel University (1971–96), shared the 1978 Nobel Prize for Physiology or Medicine with Smith and Nathans.

ARBUS, DIANE (Diane Nemerov; 1923–1971), U.S. photographer. Arbus and her husband were fashion photographers for her father's New York department store for 20 years. During the last decade of her life she turned to the opposite extreme, photographing all manner of physically and psychologically distinctive people. Her disturbing images gained a cult following her death by suicide and were exhibited throughout the United States and Europe. She was the sister of poet Howard Nemerov. ■ See the collection of her photographs published by the Museum of Modern Art concurrently with its 1972 exhibition and the biography by Patricia Bosworth (1984).

ARCARO, EDDIE (George Edward Arcaro; 1916–1997), U.S. jockey. One of the most successful jockeys in racing history, Eddie Arcaro won 4,779 races in his 30-year career (1931–61). He was the only jockey to win the Kentucky Derby five times and the Triple Crown (Kentucky Derby, Preakness, and Belmont Stakes) twice (aboard Whirlaway, 1941, and Citation, 1948). Riding such famous mounts as Native Dancer, Nashua, Bold Ruler, and Kelso, Arcaro won 17 Triple Crown races and won more than $30 million in purses.

ARCHIPENKO, ALEXANDER (1887–1964), Russian-born U.S. sculptor, painter, and teacher. Born in Kiev, Archipenko worked primarily in Paris after 1908, then emigrated (1923) to the United States. He took part in the cubist movement and shared with Picasso and Braque an enthusiasm for primitive art. His use of concave and convex cavities to suggest movement in such works as *Walking Woman* (1912) decisively influenced modern sculpture, and his use of such diverse materials as wood, wire, glass, and color in the *Medranos* (1912) defied tradition and introduced "sculpto-painting." After 1946 he experimented with "light sculpture"—plexiglass structures lit from within. ■ See volume edited by Donald Karshan (1969) and K. J. Michaelson and N. Guralnik, *Alexander Achipenko: A Centennial Tribute* (1986).

ARDEN, ELIZABETH (Florence Nightingale Graham; 1878?–1966), Canadian-born U.S. businesswoman. After studying nursing, Arden opened a beauty salon on New York City's Fifth Avenue (1909) and eventually became one of the world's foremost producers of beauty aids. A pioneer in the advertising of cosmetics, she stressed youthfulness and the "ladylike" qualities of her products and was soon marketing up to 300 different beauty aids in pharmacies and department stores throughout the world. By the time of her death, her beauty empire included 100 salons and two luxury beauty resorts. ■ See biography by Alfred A. Lewis and Constance Woodworth (1972).

ARDEN, JOHN (1930–   ), British playwright. Arden originally trained and practiced as an architect. His plays *Live Like Pigs* (1958) and *The Workhouse Donkey* (1963), set in the north of England, were highly theatrical and employed the Brechtian device of mixing verse, prose, and ballads. While the plays concerned major issues, such as pacifism in *Serjeant Musgrave's Dance* (1959), Arden would not take sides on the moral issues he presented; he believed that the audience should make its own judgments on the characters and conflicts in the play. The plays he wrote with his wife Margaretta D'Arcy after 1972 reflected an explicit socialist revolutionary viewpoint. Many were produced in Ireland and advocated British military withdrawal from Ulster. Arden also wrote *To Present the Pretence: Essays on the Theater and Its Public* (1978) and the novels *Vox Pop* (1982), *Books of Bale* (1988), and *Jack Juggler and the Emperor's Whore* (1995). ■ See study by Malcolm Page (1984) and Jared Malick, *Toward a Theater of the Oppressed* (1995).

ARENDT, HANNAH (1906–1975), German-born U.S. political philosopher. Arendt earned her Ph.D. in philosophy under Karl Jaspers at Heidelberg University (1928). She fled the Nazis to Paris (1933) and later to the United States (1941), where she was initially active in Jewish cultural and relief organizations. After the publication of her books *The Origins of Totalitarianism* (1951) and *The Human Condition* (1958) she became a major figure in American intellectual life and taught at several universities. In her writings she was primarily concerned with the loss of freedom and thought in contemporary times and the growth of alienation and atomization which makes society prone to totalitarian political regimes. Her other works included *On Revolution* (1963), *On Violence* (1970), and *Crises of the Republic* (1972). Her book on the trial of Nazi leader Adolf Eichmann (*Eichmann in Jerusalem*, 1963), which she called a report on the "banality of evil," aroused controversy within the American Jewish community. ■ See biography by Elisabeth Young-Bruehl (1982).

ARÉVALO, JUAN JOSÉ (1904–1990), Guatemalan political leader. While serving as a university professor in Argentina, Arévalo was recalled to Guatemala by the revolutionaries who had overthrown the government (1944),

and he was overwhelmingly elected president. He described himself as a "spiritual socialist," and during his term (1945–51) he inaugurated a social-security system and instituted labor, health, and educational reforms. After the overthrow (1954) of his successor, Jacobo Arbenz, by U.S.-backed forces, Arévalo went into exile (until the mid-1970s) and wrote books highly critical of U.S. policy in Latin America, including *Anti-Kommunism in Latin America* (1959; Eng. trans. 1963) and *The Shark and the Sardines* (1961; Eng. trans. 1961).

ARGENTINA, LA (Antonia Mercé; 1888–1936), Argentine-born Spanish dancer. La Argentina left her position of prima ballerina at the Madrid Opera at age 14 to study and refine the native dances of Spain. She achieved fame in Paris after World War I and later made six successful transcontinental tours of North America (1928–36). La Argentina single-handedly established the Spanish dance as a theatrical art and was considered by many to be the greatest Spanish dancer of all time. She revolutionized the playing of the castanets and created ballets and dances to the music of Isaac Albéniz, Enrique Granados, Joaquín Turina, Ernesto Halffter, and Joaquín Nin. She was best known for her interpretation of de Falla's *El Amor Brujo*.

ARGHEZI, TUDOR (Ion N. Theodorescu; 1880–1967), Rumanian writer. The most prominent Rumanian poet of the century, Arghezi wrote lyrical poems filled with striking and unexpected imagery and introduced the language of the peasantry and the underworld to Rumanian verse. His major themes were the search for meaning and relationship to God in modern life, the opposition of the ideal and the real, and the joys of childhood. In addition to his poetry, he wrote several celebrated autobiographical novels. A pacifist, he was imprisoned for a year during World War I. He published several journals and pamphlets between the wars, in which he attacked the corruption of Bucharest society and the pro-fascist government, and he was imprisoned again during World War II. Officially honored after the war, he won several state poetry prizes and was regarded as the poet laureate of Rumania. ■ See his *Selected Poems* (Eng. trans. 1976) and study by Dumitru Micu (Eng. trans. 1965).

ARGUEDAS, JOSÉ MARIA (1911–1969), Peruvian writer. Arguedas, whose mother was a Quechuan Indian and whose father was of European origin, grew up in Indian communities, spoke and wrote both Spanish and Quechua, and was immersed in both cultures. Trained as an anthropologist, he was a university professor, government administrator, and director of the National Museum of History (1964–69). His novels, among the first written from an Indian perspective, utilized Quechua words and songs in sympathetically depicting traditional culture and in forcefully describing the oppression and discrimination faced by the Indians in contemporary Peruvian society. His works included the short-story collections *Water* (1935) and *The Singing Moun-*

taineers (1940; rev. ed. 1958; Eng. trans. 1971) as well as the novels *Yawar Fiesta* (1941; Eng. trans. 1985), *The Sixth One* (1961), and *All the Races* (1964). The autobiographical *Deep Rivers* (1958; Eng. trans. 1978) is considered to be his masterpiece. He committed suicide while writing *The Fox from Above and the Fox from Below* (1971?), a novel about a man disillusioned by life. ■ See Claudette Columbus, *Mythological Consciousness and the Future* (1986), and study edited by C. A. Sandoval and S. M. Boschetto-Sandoval (1998).

ARIAS SANCHEZ, OSCAR (1941–), Costa Rican political leader. Born into one of his country's wealthiest families, Arias studied at the London School of Economics and the University of Essex (Ph.D. 1972) in England. After stints as a professor, bank director, minister of national planning and secretary-general of the ruling National Liberation Party (PLN), he served as Costa Rica's youngest president (1986–90). A centrist, he proclaimed neutrality in the civil wars in neighboring Nicaragua and El Salvador and drafted a regional peace plan that was signed by Guatemala, Honduras, Nicaragua, El Salvador, and Costa Rica (1987). Although the conflicts remained unresolved, Arias was awarded the 1987 Nobel Peace Prize for his attempts at restoring regional stability. After his presidential term ended he established the Arias Foundation for Peace and Human Progress.

ARISTIDE, JEAN-BERTRAND (1953–), Haitian political leader. Born into a poor, devout Roman Catholic family, Aristide was educated by the Salesian order of the Roman Catholic Church in Port-au-Prince, earned a degree in psychology from the State University of Haiti (1979), and was ordained a priest in 1982. In his weekly sermons he advocated radical political change and justice for the poor and was exiled (1982–85) by the dictator Jean-Claude Duvalier. Upon returning to Haiti, he became the most influential of a group of progressive priests inspired by the Latin American liberation theology movement and played a major role in the popular movement that forced Duvalier into exile (1986). He continued to work closely with the poor and spoke out against the corrupt military elite and the conservative Roman Catholic hierarchy. He was elected to a six-year term as president in December 1990, with nearly 70 percent of the vote, but he was overthrown by the military in September 1991. In October 1994, after intense international pressure and the threat of a U.S. invasion, the military junta stepped down and Aristide returned to finish his term, which ended in January 1996. Barred from seeking immediate reelection, he was reelected in 2000. ■ See his autobiography (1993) and Amy Wilentz, *The Rainy Season* (1989).

ARLEDGE, ROONE PINCKNEY, JR. (1931–), U.S. television producer. A wrestler while at Columbia College (B.A. 1952), Arledge broke into television sports production with ABC Sports (1960) and became its president in 1968. One of the most successful and innovative producers in television

history, he introduced such popular shows as "Wide World of Sports," "Monday Night Football," and "The American Sportsman," and was lauded for his coverage of the Olympic games (from 1968). He revolutionized sports coverage with the introduction of the instant replay, slow motion, the split screen, stop action, and the isolated camera. He later served as president of ABC News (1977–98) and initiated such programs as "20/20," "Prime Time Live," and "Nightline." ■ See Marc Gunther, *The House That Roone Built* (1994).

ARLEN, HAROLD (Hyman Arluck, 1905–1986), U.S. composer. The son of a cantor, Arlen started out as a singer and pianist with the Buffalodians Band and graduated to writing music for Cotton Club reviews in Harlem, Broadway musicals, and Hollywood films, notably *The Wizard of Oz* (1939). His lyricists included Ted Koehler, E. Y. Harburg, and Ira Gershwin, and his many popular song classics included "Let's Fall in Love," "Get Happy," "It's Only a Paper Moon," "Stormy Weather," "That Old Black Magic," "Over the Rainbow," and "Ac-cent-tchu-ate the Positive." ■ See the *Harold Arlen Songbook* (1967) and biography by Edward Jablonski (1961; rev. ed. 1996).

ARMAH, AYI KWEI (1939–), Ghanaian writer. Educated at Harvard and the University of Ghana, Armah was known for his powerful novels depicting the greed and corruption of modern African political leaders and the cynicism, alienation, and disillusionment engendered by them. His best-known works were·*The Beautyful Ones Are Not Yet Born* (1968), *Fragments* (1970), *Are We So Blest* (1971), *Two Thousand Seasons* (1973), *The Healers* (1979), and *Osiris Rising* (1995). He taught at the University of Tanzania, Dar es Salaam (1972–). ■ See study by Robert Fraser (1980) and Derek Wright, ed., *Critical Perspectives on Ayi Kwei Armah* (1992).

ARMSTRONG, EDWIN HOWARD (1890–1954), U.S. engineer and inventor. Trained at Columbia University (B.E.E. 1913), where he later served as professor of electrical engineering (1934–54), Major Armstrong, as he was known, developed (1912) the regenerative or feedback circuit, which amplified current, and invented (1918) the superheterodyne circuit that served as the basic design for amplitude modulation (AM) radios. He later invented (1933) the radio-transmission technique of frequency modulation (FM). His technique reduced static interference and provided high-fidelity reception by using a wider band than AM. He spent his later years entangled in patent disputes. In 1954 Armstrong committed suicide. ■ See Lawrence Lessing, *Man of High Fidelity* (1956); Don V. Erickson, *Armstrong's Fight for FM Broadcasting* (1973); and Tom Lewis, *Empire of the Air* (1991).

ARMSTRONG, HAMILTON FISH (1893–1973), U.S. journalist and editor. An authority on international politics,

Armstrong was a cofounder (1922), managing editor (1922–28), and editor (1928–72) of *Foreign Affairs*, the establishment journal published by the Council on Foreign Relations. Armstrong knew and solicited articles from most of the important political leaders of the century, and under his leadership *Foreign Affairs* became the most influential U.S. magazine in the field of international relations. He also served as an adviser to the State Department and wrote numerous books on international politics. ■ See his memoirs, *Peace and Counterpeace* (1971).

ARMSTRONG, HENRY JACKSON, JR. (1912–1988), U.S. boxer. The 11th of 13 children, Armstrong was orphaned at age 5 and was raised by an aunt in East Saint Louis, where he learned to fight in gang wars. The only boxer to hold three world titles simultaneously (1938), he won his first in the featherweight division (1937). In 1938 he captured the welterweight title by defeating Barney Ross, and 10 weeks later he added the lightweight crown. Nicknamed "perpetual motion" and "Hurricane Henry" for his aggressive style, he lost the featherweight and lightweight titles in 1939 but successfully defended his welterweight title a record 20 times. With a slugging offense and very little defense, he took a great deal of punishment in the ring; outside the ring, he fell victim to bad business deals. After 261 bouts in a 15-year career, he retired, broke. He later became a Baptist minister (1951) and preached before large audiences. ■ See his autobiography, *Gloves, Glory and God* (1956).

ARMSTRONG, LOUIS DANIEL (1900–1971), U.S. jazz musician. The world's most famous jazz trumpeter, "Satchmo," as he was popularly known, learned to play the bugle and cornet in the Colored Waifs Home for Boys in his native city of New Orleans. While in his teens he became the protégé of Joe "King" Oliver, the finest cornetist in the city, and in 1918 joined Kid Ory's band. He joined Oliver's band in Chicago (1922) and Fletcher Henderson's Orchestra in New York (1924), then formed his own band, the Hot Five (1925). His recordings in the mid-1920s established his reputation as a virtuoso improvisational soloist and his playing transformed jazz from an ensemble-oriented form to one that featured a soloist and a small group. Armstrong also introduced "scat" singing, in which the voice imitated instrumental improvisations through nonsense syllables. From the 1930s on Armstrong toured the world as an "ambassador of goodwill"—and as an ambassador of New Orleans jazz—and was instrumental in making jazz known and loved throughout the globe. ■ See his autobiography, *Satchmo* (1954); biographies by Robert Hoskins (1979), James L. Collier (1983), and Laurence Bergreen (1997); Gary Giddens, *Satchmo* (1988); and Thomas Brothers, ed., *Louis Armstrong in His Own Words* (1999).

ARMSTRONG, NEIL ALDEN (1930–   ), U.S. astronaut. Trained as an aeronautical engineer, Armstrong was an experienced test pilot before being selected as America's first civilian astronaut in 1962. He first ventured into space as the command pilot of the 1966 *Gemini 8* mission, which achieved the first manual space-docking maneuver. His piloting skill and cool approach resulted in his selection as commander of *Apollo 11*, the first lunar-landing mission. On July 16, 1969, Armstrong, with veteran astronauts Edwin E. Aldrin, Jr., and Michael Collins, lifted off from Cape Kennedy, Florida, and on July 20, 1969, the *Eagle* craft touched down on the moon near the Sea of Tranquility. As Armstrong stepped out onto the moon's surface, he remarked: "That's one small step for man, one giant leap for mankind." The astronauts set up instruments on the moon's surface to convey scientific data back to Earth, and they returned to Earth (July 24, 1969) with samples of moon rock and soil. Armstrong later taught aerospace engineering at the University of Cincinnati (1971–79) and pursued business interests. He was vice chair of the presidential commission that looked into the explosion of the *Challenger* shuttle (1986). ■ See his *First on the Moon* (1970; with Gene Farmer and Dora Hamblin).

ARNO, PETER (Curtis Arnoux Peters; 1904–1968), U.S. cartoonist. The son of a judge, Arno left Yale (1924) to pursue a career as an illustrator and designer. His sophisticated cartoons, which satirized the world of New York City's high society, began appearing in the newly established *New Yorker* in 1925 and helped set the tone of the magazine. A noted wit and socialite, Arno contributed regularly to the *New Yorker* and other magazines until his death. He also wrote musical revues and was coauthor of the Broadway musical *Here Comes the Bride* (1931). Collections of his cartoons appeared in several volumes, including *Hullabaloo* (1930), *Peter Arno's Circus* (1931), *Man in the Shower* (1941), and *Hell of a Way to Run a Railroad* (1957).

ARNOLD, EDDY (1918–   ), U.S. country-and-western singer. Eddy Arnold grew up among sharecroppers and later was known as the "Tennessee Plowboy." He first sang at the Grand Ole Opry with the Golden West Cowboys, a group that mixed the cowboy image with electric guitars. His smooth, polished variations on western sounds and themes, including such hits as "It's a Sin" and "That's How Much I Love You," won him a wide and varied audience in the late 1940s and early 1950s, when he often had several records in the top ten. He remained popular in later decades with such top-ten hits as "Kentucky Waltz" (1951), "Make the World Go Away" (1965), "What in Her World Did I Do?" (1979), and "If I Ever Had to Say Goodbye to You" (1980). ■ See his autobiography, *It's a Long Way From Chester County* (1969), and the biography by Michael Streissguth (1997).

ARNOLD, HENRY HARLEY (1886–1950), U.S. Air Force general. A student of Orville and Wilbur Wright, Arnold was the commander of the U.S. Army Air Corps during World War II and a principal military strategist in the Allied effort. He was promoted (1944) to five-star general of the army, a title later changed (1949) to general of the air force. An ardent believer in air power as the decisive war weapon, Arnold maintained that the air force should be an independent service like the army and navy. Largely due to his efforts, the U.S. Air Force attained (1947) independent status. ▪ See biography by Flint O. DuPre (1972) and Thomas M. Coffey, *Hap* (1982).

ARNOLD, THURMAN WESLEY (1891–1969), U.S. jurist. The son of a Wyoming rancher and lawyer, Arnold was educated at Princeton and Harvard Law School, taught law at Yale (1930–38), and published *The Symbols of Government* (1935) and *The Folklore of Capitalism* (1937), realistic appraisals of U.S. political and industrial development. During five years as Pres. Franklin D. Roosevelt's assistant attorney general in charge of the Antitrust Division (1938–43), he became known as a "trustbuster," resigning when World War II brought a rapprochement between government and business. After serving briefly as an appellate judge (1943–45), he helped form the prestigious Washington, D.C., law firm of Arnold, Fortas and Porter, which gained a reputation for defending civil liberties during the era of Sen. Joseph McCarthy's anticommunist crusade. ▪ See his autobiography, *Fair Fights and Foul: A Dissenting Lawyer's Life* (1965).

ARON, RAYMOND CLAUDE (1905–1983), French sociologist and political commentator. Aron, who earned his doctorate with a thesis on the philosophy of history (1930), joined Gen. Charles de Gaulle in London as editor of *La France Libre*, the organ of the World War II Resistance. After the war he was chief news analyst of *Le Figaro* (1947–77), and later *Express*, and was a critic of both the Gaullists and the left-wing intellectual elite (see *Opium of the Intellectuals*, 1955; Eng. trans. 1957). He was a professor of political science and sociology at the Sorbonne (1955–68) and professor at the Collège de France (from 1970). A liberal in politics, an antideterminist in historical analysis, and a traditionalist in international affairs, Aron wrote several influential interdisciplinary analyses of contemporary ideologies, industrial society, international relations, and French politics, including *Peace and War* (1962; Eng. trans. 1966), *The Industrial Society* (1965; Eng. trans. 1967), *Main Currents in Sociological Thought* (1967; Eng. trans., 2 vols., 1965–68), *In Defense of Decadent Europe* (1977; Eng. trans. 1979), and *Thinking Politically* (1983; Eng. trans. 1997). ▪ See his *Memoirs* (Eng. trans. 1990) and study by Brian C. Anderson (1998).

ARONSON, BORIS (1899–1980), Russian-born U.S. stage designer. Son of the chief rabbi of Kiev, Aronson discovered a talent for drawing early in life and subsequently studied art in Moscow, Kiev, and Paris. In 1923, he went to New York to design sets and costumes for the Yiddish theater. He became involved with the leftist Group Theater and gradually moved on to Broadway, where he designed *South Pacific* (1943), *The Crucible* (1953), *The Diary of Anne Frank*

(1955), *J.B.* (1958), *Fiddler on the Roof* (1964), *A Little Night Music* (1973), and many other productions. He won six Tony Awards—for *The Rose Tattoo* (1951), *Cabaret* (1966), *Zorba* (1968), *Company* (1970), *Follies* (1971), and *Pacific Overtures* (1976). He also designed for ballet and opera and was continually praised for his original, evocative work. ▪ See Frank Rich, *The Theater Art of Boris Aronson* (1987).

ARP, JEAN (**Hans Arp; 1887–1966**), French sculptor. Arp was born in Strasbourg, and though a German national, he considered himself a Frenchman. He was associated with many artistic movements (the Blue Rider group, the cubists) and was a founder of the dada and surrealist movements (1916–30), but his work defied classification. It retained, throughout his career, a characteristic childlike quality that influenced other artists. He painted wooden reliefs, presented a series of "crumpled papers," and sculpted curved, abstractly biomorphic forms with highly polished surfaces that were freestanding and inventive. ▪ See his *On My Way: Poetry and Essays, 1912–47* (1948) and Herbert Read, *The Art of Jean Arp* (1968).

ARRABAL, FERNANDO (1932–), French playwright and novelist. Born in Spanish Morocco, Arrabal spent his youth in Spain during the dictatorship of Francisco Franco. His father, an army officer with Republican sympathies, was arrested (1936), confined to a psychiatric ward, and disappeared without a trace after escaping from prison (1942). Arrabal moved to France (1955) and wrote plays in French that reflected his hatred of Spanish repression, terror, and betrayal. He believed in an intense, surrealistic "panic theater," where the audience is involved in or shaken by the action. His plays mixed humor and horror, vulgarity and sophistication, and reality and fantasy amid brutal and violent scenes. Among his many plays are *Picnic on the Battlefield* (1952; Eng. trans. 1967), *The Car Cemetery* (1957; Eng. trans. 1962), and *And They Put Handcuffs on the Flowers* (1969; Eng. trans. 1974). ▪ See study by Peter L. Podol (1978).

ARRAU, CLAUDIO (1903–1991), Chilean pianist. A child prodigy who first performed in Santiago at age 5, Arrau studied at the Stern Conservatory in Berlin (1912–18) on a special Chilean government scholarship. Based in Berlin (until 1940) he toured extensively during the 1920s (U.S. debut, 1924) and gained an international reputation as an interpreter of the works of Beethoven, Brahms, Schumann, Liszt, and Chopin. An unostentatious virtuoso, he was known for the rich tones, deliberate tempos, and intellectual depth of his playing. In 1935 (in Berlin) he performed the entire keyboard works of Bach in 12 successive concerts and performed works of Mozart and Beethoven in similar concert series. After moving to the United States (1941) he recorded dozens of albums, including a 14-disk set of the complete Beethoven sonatas. He continued to perform in public into his eighties. ■ See Joseph Horowitz, *Conversations with Arrau* (1982).

ARREOLA, JUAN JOSÉ (1918–   ), Mexican short-story writer. Arreola studied acting in Mexico City and later in France, but he won recognition as a writer of short fiction, beginning with the clever story "He Did Good While He Lived" (1943). His ironic and fanciful stories about the ills of contemporary society were collected in *Confabulario and Other Inventions* (1962; Eng. trans. 1964). He also wrote the collection *Bestiary* (1959; Eng. trans. 1964; the play *Everyone's Hour* (1954); and the satirical novel *The Fair* (1963; Eng. trans. 1977), a collage of life in a town in the state of Jalisco. ■ See study by Yulan M. Washburn (1983).

ARROW, KENNETH JOSEPH (1921–   ), U.S. economist. Arrow studied at Columbia University (Ph.D. 1951) and taught at Stanford (1948–63; 1979–91) and Harvard (1968–79). In 1962 he served on the Council of Economic Advisers in the administration of Pres. John F. Kennedy. A leading theoretician in the field of general economic equilibrium, Arrow contributed to the theory of social choice, sparking controversy by asserting the impossibility of arriving at consensus by the voting mechanism. In *Social Choices and Individual Values* (1951), Arrow demonstrated how economic strategies apply to different political settings. In the 1960s and early 1970s, he wrote on the economics of uncertainty, risk-bearing, and insurance. *The Future and the Present in Economic Life* (1978) showed why and when market prices may be useful guides to social action. *Production and Capital* (1985) was a collection of essays. Arrow shared the 1972 Nobel Prize for Economics with Sir John R. Hicks. ■ See A. K. Sen, *Collective Choice and Economic Welfare* (1970).

ARTAUD, ANTONIN (1896–1948), French theorist of drama. Artaud was an actor, avant-garde producer, and unsuccessful playwright. He is best known for his writings on the theater in *The Theater and Its Double* (1938; Eng. trans. 1958) and his manifestos on the "theater of cruelty." He proposed an "antitheater" that does not rely on text and that surrounds the audience with action and forces viewers to become part of the drama. Using devices like meaningless sounds, pantomime, and lights, he sought to "cruelly" terrify the audience in order to release unconscious feelings. Always unstable, Artaud spent the last years of his life in a mental institution. His revolutionary views influenced post–World War II directors Peter Brook and Jean-Louis Barrault and such playwrights as Samuel Beckett, Jean Genet, and Eugène Ionesco. ■ See Artaud's *Selected Writings* (Eng. trans. 1976) and studies by Martin Esslin (1977), Julia F. Costich (1978), and Bettina Knapp (1980).

ARTIN, EMIL (1898–1962), Austrian-born U.S. mathematician. Artin taught at the University of Hamburg (1923–37) before emigrating to the United States, where he taught at Notre Dame (1937–38), the University of Indiana (1938–46), and Princeton (1946–58). He formulated the general law of reciprocity and did major work in abstract algebra and hypercomplex numbers and in the study of nodes in three-dimensional space. His books included *Geometric Algebra* (1957) and *Class Field Theory* (1961; with John T. Tate). ■ See Serge Lang and John T. Tate, eds., *The Collected Papers of Emil Artin* (1965).

ASCH, SHOLEM (1880–1957), Polish-born U.S. Yiddish-language novelist and dramatist. One of the most widely known modern writers in Yiddish, Asch was the first writer to bring the Yiddish world into the mainstream of European and American culture. He moved to New York City in 1914 and was naturalized in 1920. Among his great successes were the play *God of Vengeance* (1907; Eng. trans. 1918) and the novels *Three Cities* (3 vols., 1929–31; Eng. trans. 1933) and *The Mother* (1925; Eng. trans. 1930). A master storyteller, he stressed his characters' moral and religious strivings and dilemmas as well as their cultural environment. His attempt to relate Christianity to Judaism, which he viewed as "one culture and one civilization," is evident in his controversial trilogy on the life of Christ, *The Nazarene* (1943; Eng. trans. 1939), *The Apostle* (Eng. trans. 1943), and *Mary* (Eng. trans. 1949), and his New York novel, *East River* (1946; Eng. trans. 1946). Translations of his short stories are in *Children of Abraham* (1942) and *Tales of My People* (1948).

ASHBERY, JOHN LAWRENCE (1927–   ), U.S. poet. Educated at Harvard (B.A. 1949) and Columbia University (M.A. 1951), Ashbery was a prominent member of the "New York School" of poetry, whose works were influenced by surrealism, abstract painting, and serial music. Although many of his poems had a dreamlike quality and were difficult to interpret, he was praised as one of the most inventive poets of his generation, and his collection *Self-Portrait in a Convex Mirror* (1975) won the 1976 Pulitzer Prize. His other books of poetry included *Some Trees* (1956), *The Tennis Court Oath* (1962), *Rivers and Mountains* (1966), *Three Poems* (1972), *As We Know* (1979), *Shadow Train* (1981), *A Wave* (1984), *Selected Poems* (1985), *And the Stars Were Shining* (1994), *Can Your Hear, Bird* (1995), and *Girls on the Run* (1999). Ashbery was also coauthor of the comic novel *A Nest of Ninnies* (1969; with James Schuyler), wrote art criticism, was an editor of *Art News* (1966–72) and *Partisan Review* (1976–80), and a professor at Brooklyn College (1974–90) and Bard College (1990–   ). He was corecipient (with Fred Chappell) of the prestigious Bollingen Prize in Poetry (1985). ■ See study by David Shapiro (1979).

ASHE, ARTHUR, JR. (1943–1993), U.S. tennis player. As a student at the University of California at Los Angeles (UCLA; B.S. 1966), Ashe won the NCAA singles title and led the team to the national collegiate tennis championship. A graceful athlete with a powerful serve and backhand,

Ashe became the first African-American male to win the U.S. Open (1968), Australian Open (1970), and Wimbledon (1975) championships, and the first to serve on a U.S. Davis Cup team (1963–70, 1975–76, 1978). After his retirement from competitive tennis he served as the nonplaying captain of the Davis Cup team (1981–85) that won championships in 1981 and 1982. He was active in the movement opposed to apartheid in South Africa and helped to inaugurate tennis programs for inner-city black youth. After publicly announcing (1992) that he was suffering from AIDS, probably contracted as a result of a blood transfusion following a 1983 heart bypass operation, Ashe became active in the movement to educate the public about AIDS. He wrote *A Hard Road to Glory: A History of the African-American Athlete* (3 vols., 1988) and an autobiography, *Off the Court* (with Neil Amdur; 1981).

ASHKENAZY, VLADIMIR (1937–   ), Soviet-born pianist. A member of a musical family, Ashkenazy studied at the Moscow State Conservatory and achieved international prominence when he won the Queen Elizabeth Competition in Brussels (1956) and shared the first prize (with John Ogdon) in the Tchaikovsky Competition in Moscow (1962). Renowned for his elegant and restrained style, he was best known for his interpretations of the music of Rachmaninoff, Beethoven, Brahms, Scriabin, Prokofiev, and Chopin. After leaving the Soviet Union (1963), he lived in England and Iceland (from 1968) and performed as a concert recitalist and soloist with orchestras throughout the world. He was music director of the Royal Philharmonic Orchestra (1987–94), the Deutsches Symphonie Orchester, Berlin (1989–   ), and the Czech Philharmonic (1998–   ). ∎ See his autobiography, *Beyond Frontiers* (1985; with Jasper Parrott).

ASHTON, SIR FREDERICK (1904–1988), British ballet dancer and choreographer. Ashton was a member of the Ballet Club and Camargo Society before joining (1935) the Vic-Wells (later Royal) Ballet, which he served as associate director (from 1952) and director (1963–70). Classically oriented, he infused his works with a lyricism and precision that were particularly evident in his romantic pas de deux. His many world-famous ballets included *Les Patineurs, La Fille Mal Gardée, Symphonic Variations, Enigma Variations*, and *Monotones*. He provided Margot Fonteyn with some of her greatest roles. ∎ See study by David Vaughan (1977) and the biography by Julie Kavanagh, *Secret Muses* (1997).

ASIMOV, ISAAC (1920–1992), Russian-born U.S. writer. The recipient of a Ph.D. in biochemistry (Columbia University, 1947), Asimov quit teaching at age 38 to write full-time. As prolific as he was popular, Asimov published more than 300 books on an astounding variety of topics. His work included first-rate science-fiction novels and stories, among them the celebrated short story "Nightfall" (1941) and the landmark trilogy *Foundation* (1951–53), as well as

factual books on science for the layperson, such as *The Human Brain* (1964) and *The Collapsing Universe* (1977). He also wrote on humanistic topics such as literature, religion, and history—for example, *Asimov's Guide to the Bible* (1968). Asimov published *Opus 100* (1969), *Opus 200* (1979), and *Opus 300* (1984), guides to his work that contain excerpts. ∎ See his autobiographies, *In Memory Yet Green* (1979) and *In Joy Still Felt* (1980), and his memoir (1994). See also studies by James Gunn (1982) and Jean Fiedler and Jim Mele (1982).

ASQUITH, HERBERT HENRY, 1st EARL OF OXFORD AND ASQUITH (1852–1928), British political leader. H. H. Asquith was classics scholar at Oxford, a politically ambitious lawyer, and a Liberal member of Parliament (1886–1918; 1920–24) who became prime minister in 1908. During eight years in office he curbed the power (1911) of the House of Lords and enacted moderate socioeconomic reforms. He proved unequal, however, to the demands of leadership during World War I and resigned in 1916. He remained leader of the Liberal party until 1926. ∎ See his *Memories and Reflections* (1928) and biography by Roy Jenkins (1964).

ASSAD, HAFEZ AL- (1928–2000), Syrian president. Assad, a member of the poor, minority Alawite sect, joined the Ba'ath party, which advocated socialism and Arab nationalism, in 1946. He graduated from the Syrian military academy (1955) and received pilot training in the Soviet Union. After the Ba'ath coup in 1963, Assad became a general and commander of the air force. While he served as minister of defense (1966–70) Syria suffered a humiliating defeat in the Arab-Israeli War (1967) and lost control of the Golan Heights. Assad staged a bloodless coup in 1970 that secured him the presidency. He was elected president in 1971 and re-elected to his fifth seven-year term in 1999. While maintaining uneasy control at home, he pursued close relations with the Soviet Union while avoiding an outright break with the United States. He demanded that Israel withdraw from captured territories, forcefully opposed the U.S.-sponsored Camp David peace accords between Egypt and Israel (1980), repeatedly skirmished with Israel over control of Lebanon, and sought to dominate the Palestine Liberation Organization. In early 1991 his forces participated in the Gulf War as part of the anti-Iraq coalition. ∎ See biographies by Patrick Seale (1988) and Moshe Ma'oz (1988), and Lisa Wedeen, *Ambiguities of Domination* (1999).

ASTAIRE, FRED (Frederick Austerlitz; 1899–1987), U.S. dancer, actor, and choreographer. Astaire made his vaudeville debut with his sister Adele at age 5. The debonair partners from Omaha danced their way to Broadway in 1916 and to London during the 1920s. After Adele's marriage (1932), Astaire's search for new partners led him to Hollywood, where he teamed up with Ginger Rogers in 10 classic song-and-dance films including *Top Hat* (1935) and *Shall*

We Dance? (1937). Cool, sophisticated, and rakishly elegant, Astaire gave the illusion of ease to the most technically exacting dance routines. One of his best partners was Cyd Charisse in *The Band Wagon* (1953). After *Funny Face* and *Silk Stockings* (both 1957), Astaire appeared in Emmy Award–winning musical television shows and several dramatic films. ■ See his autobiography, *Steps in Time* (1959); biographies by Michael Freedland (1976) and Bob Thomas (1984); and John Mueller, *Astaire Dancing* (1985).

ASTON, FRANCIS WILLIAM (1877–1945), British chemist. While working under J. J. Thomson at Cambridge (from 1910), Aston realized that atoms of the same element can have different masses and that the weighted average of these masses yields the element's atomic weight. With his invention, the mass spectograph (1919), he confirmed Frederick Soddy's concept of isotopes and elaborated on it by relating the mass differentials to the energy that binds subatomic particles together. He understood that this energy, if harnessed, could produce devastating effects. When he accepted the 1922 Nobel Prize for Chemistry, Aston warned of the potential dangers of atomic energy. He died three months after the first atomic bombs were dropped on Japan.

ASTOR, NANCY WITCHER LANGHORNE ASTOR, VISCOUNTESS (1879–1964), British political leader. The U.S.-born wife of British politician and publisher Waldorf Astor, Lady Astor was the first woman to sit in the British House of Commons (1919–45). A Conservative, she championed women's rights, temperance, and education and was also the hostess of the "Cliveden set" (named after the Astors' country estate), which included many advocates of Britain's appeasement policy toward Nazi Germany during the 1930s. ■ See her autobiography, *My Two Countries* (1920); biographies by Maurice Collis (1960) and Anthony Masters (1981); and Christopher Sykes, *Nancy* (1972).

ASTOR, WALDORF ASTOR, 2nd VISCOUNT (1879–1952), U.S.-born British public official and publisher. A great-great-grandson of U.S. fur magnate John Jacob Astor, Waldorf Astor was a Conservative member of Parliament (1910–19) before being forced to step down when he inherited his father's viscountcy. (He was succeeded by his wife, Lady Nancy Astor, the first woman ever to serve in Parliament.) Astor published the *London Observer* (1915–45), was a noted authority on health and agricultural problems, and sponsored many socially progressive causes. He and his wife were leaders of the "Cliveden set" (named for their country house), a politically and socially prominent group who supported the British "appeasement" policy toward Nazi Germany during the 1930s.

ASTOR OF HEVER, JOHN JACOB ASTOR, 1st BARON (1886–1971), U.S.-born British publisher and philanthropist. A great-great-grandson of U.S. fur magnate John Jacob Astor, Lord Astor of Hever was educated at Eton and Ox-

ford and served as a Conservative member of Parliament from 1922 to 1945. He was chairman and chief proprietor of the *Times* of London (1922–59), the leading newspaper in England, and served as adviser to the British Broadcasting Corp. (1937–39) and chairman of the British Press Council (1953–55). Although a leading philanthropist and pillar of the British establishment, he left Britain to live in France (1962) in order to escape the large inheritance taxes on the family trust fund.

ASTURIAS, MIGUEL ÁNGEL (1899–1974), Guatemalan novelist. Asturias earned a law degree (1923) at the National University and began writing lyric poetry and prose while studying anthropology and Mayan civilization in Paris in the 1920s. He wrote the study *Guatemalan Sociology* (1923; Eng. trans. 1977). His first major work, which many critics regard as his finest, was *El Señor Presidente* (1946; Eng. trans. 1963), a novel based on the dictatorship of Manuel Estrada Cabrera (which ended in 1920). *Men of Maize* (1949; Eng. trans. 1975) and *Mulata* (1963; Eng. trans. 1967) drew on Mayan history, myths, and language. His so-called *Banana Trilogy* deplored U.S. exploitation of Guatemalan banana production. It encompassed the novels *Strong Wind* (1949; Eng. trans. 1968), *The Green Pope* (1954; Eng. trans. 1971), and *The Eyes of the Interred* (1960; Eng. trans. 1972). The Soviet Union awarded Asturias the Lenin Peace Prize for the trilogy in 1966. The following year, Asturias won the Nobel Prize for Literature. Asturias, who lived in exile in Argentina (1954–1961) and then settled in France, was Guatemala's ambassador to France (1966–70) until strongman Carlos Arana Osorio gained power. ■ See studies by R. Callan (1972) and C. Meneses (1975).

ATANASOFF, JOHN VINCENT (1903–1995), U.S. computer scientist. The son of an electrical engineer, Atanasoff studied physics at the University of Wisconsin (Ph.D. 1930) and taught at Iowa State University at Ames (1930–42). With graduate student Clifford Berry (1918–63), he developed (1939) the prototype of the first modern electronic serial, digital computer, later called the ABC (Atanasoff Berry Computer). The computer used a binary number system, and made use of logic circuitry and regenerative memory. (Although J. Presper Eckert and John W. Mauchly, the inventors of the ENIAC in the 1940s, were credited with being the creators of the first electronic computer, a 1973 patent lawsuit established that their invention was derived from Atanasoff and declared the ENIAC patent invalid.) Atanasoff subsequently worked with the U.S. Naval Ordinance Laboratory (1942–52) and later founded two engineering firms. ■ See Alice R. Burks and Arthur W. Burks, *The First Electronic Computer* (1988) and Clark R. Mollenhoff, *Atanasoff* (1988).

ATATÜRK, KEMAL (1881–1938), Turkish political leader. Mustafa Kemal (his original name) was a successful World

War I general, leader of the postwar nationalist movement, and the first president (1923–38) of the new Turkish republic. He was a Western-oriented reformer who abolished the sultanate, modernized and secularized his country's educational, economic, and legal systems, banned polygamy, and enhanced the status of women, but he ignored his own political institutions and ruled as a benevolent dictator. Atatürk, meaning "father of the Turks," remained in office until his death. ■ See Harold Armstrong, *Gray Wolf* (1961) and biography by Lord Kinross (1965).

ATGET, EUGÈNE (1857–1927), French photographer. Atget worked as a sailor and stage actor before finding his vocation at age 42 as a photographer. During 30 years of commercial photography he compiled an extensive record of the living history of the buildings, parks, and street scenes of Paris during the first quarter of the century. Examples of his more than 10,000 photos are in *The Work of Atget* (3 vols., 1981–83), edited by John Szarkowski and Maria M. Hambourg. Berenice Abbott, who was instrumental in publishing his simple, classical photos, also wrote a biography, *The World of Atget* (1964). ■ See study by James Borcoman (1984) and Molly Nesbit, *Atget's Seven Albums* (1993).

ATKINS, CHET (Chester Burton Atkins; 1924–), U.S. country musician and promoter. Tennessee-born Atkins came from a line of country fiddlers. After a difficult childhood, he became a semiprofessional musician as a teenager, playing guitar and fiddle. His early career was not remarkable; he achieved success only in the late 1940s and he joined the Grand Ole Opry in Nashville in 1950. He worked for RCA after 1947, and when he helped to sign Elvis Presley in 1955, his move up the executive ladder was assured. Atkins' sophisticated finger-style guitar technique was unique and influential, and he recorded dozens of albums, but he was even more important in his corporate role, imposing his tastes on country music as an industry. ■ See his autobiography, *Country Gentleman* (1974; with Bill Neely).

ATKINSON, (JUSTIN) BROOKS (1894–1984), U.S. theater critic. Known as "the autocrat of the aisle," the Harvard-educated Atkinson was the most influential critic of his time. As the reviewer of Broadway shows for the *New York Times* (1925–42; 1946–60), he reputedly had the power to make or break a show with a favorable or unfavorable review. From 1942 to 1946 he served as a foreign correspondent in China and the Soviet Union and was awarded a 1947 Pulitzer Prize in journalism.

ATLAS, CHARLES (Angelo Siciliano; 1894–1972), Italian-born U.S. body builder. A "97-pound weakling" as a youth, Atlas devised a system of muscle building, called "dynamic tension," with which he built up his body. He became a successful sculptor's model and in 1922 won the title of "World's Most Perfectly Developed Man." Subsequently, he

created a program of mail-order body-building lessons that he sold throughout the world. At the time of his death he was selling 70,000 courses a year. ■ See study by Charles Gaines (1982).

ATTLEE, CLEMENT RICHARD ATTLEE, 1st EARL (1883–1967), British political leader. Attlee was born to wealth, but the harsh poverty he witnessed as a social worker in London's East End turned him toward socialism and the Labour Party. He led the party for 20 years (1935–55) and served as deputy prime minister in Winston Churchill's coalition government during World War II (1942–45). He led the Labour party to victory in the 1945 elections, serving as prime minister from 1945 to 1951. His government was noted for its social legislation, particularly the establishment of the national health and insurance programs, the nationalization of major industries, and the granting of independence to India. ■ See his memoirs, *As It Happened* (1954) and *Twilight of Empire* (1962); and the biography by Kenneth Harris (1983).

ATWOOD, MARGARET ELEANOR (1939–), Canadian author. Atwood studied at the University of Toronto, Radcliffe College, and Harvard and taught English literature at several Canadian universities. Her controversial and widely read study of Canadian literature, *Survival* (1972), was viewed as a literary manifestation of a resurgent Canadian nationalism. A feminist, she was best known for her novels, including *The Edible Woman* (1969), *Surfacing* (1972), *Lady Oracle* (1976), *Life Before Man* (1979), and *Bodily Harm* (1982), which dealt primarily with women's search for identity and the deceptiveness of human relationships. *The Handmaid's Tale* (1986) described a future theocratic dictatorship written from the viewpoint of a female slave whose only function is to bear children. Her other novels included *Cat's Eye* (1988), *The Robber Bride* (1993), *Alias Grace* (1996), and *The Blind Assassin* (2000). Her poems were collected in several volumes, including *Double Persephone* (1961), *The Circle Game* (1966), *You Are Happy* (1974), *True Stories* (1982), and *Eating Fire* (1998). Her reviews, essays, and speeches are in *Second Words* (1982). ■ See Arnold and Cathy Davidson, eds., *The Art of Margaret Atwood* (1981); and studies by Jerome H. Rosenberg (1984) and C. A. Howells (1996).

AUCHINLECK, SIR CLAUDE JOHN (1884–1981), British military leader. Auchinleck was the outstanding British officer in the Indian army during the 1930s. During World War II he served as commander in chief in the Middle East (1941–42), where he defeated the German forces of Gen. Erwin Rommel in North Africa, but was subsequently forced to retreat. He was credited by the official war history with turning defeat (at Tobruk) into counterattack. He later returned (1943) to India to defend it against Japanese invasion. ■ See biography by John H. Robertson (1959).

AUDEN, WYSTAN HUGH (1907–1973), British-born U.S. poet. Born and raised in Britain, W. H. Auden was educated at Oxford. Influenced by both Freud and Marx, his poetry of the 1930s reflected his social concerns and left-wing attitudes. He was then often linked with his friends Stephen Spender, Louis MacNeice, and Christopher Isherwood, with whom he wrote some plays. Auden was always an intellectual and social poet, concerned more with the moral problems of civilization than private feelings and emotions. After he emigrated to the United States (1939) and became a citizen (1946), his poetry became more openly Christian and meditative. His work of this period included *The Age of Anxiety* (1948; Pulitzer Prize) and *The Shield of Achilles* (1955). *Selected Poems* appeared in 1979. Auden also collaborated on the libretto for Igor Stravinsky's opera *The Rake's Progress* (1951). Combining contradictory elements of lyricism and satire, faith and humor, all his writing reflected his erudite, urbane concerns and desire to instruct. After the death of T. S. Eliot (1965), Auden was considered the greatest living poet in English. ■ See biographies by Charles Osborne (1979), Humphrey Carpenter (1981), Edward Mendelson (2 vols, 1981, 1999), and R.P.T. Davenport-Hines (1995). See also Charles H. Miller, *An American Friendship* (1983), and Dorothy J. Farnan, *Auden in Love* (1984).

AUER, LEOPOLD (1845–1930), Hungarian-born violinist. Auer studied violin in Budapest, Vienna, and Hanover (Germany). While working as a concertmaster in Düsseldorf (1863–65) and Hamburg (1866–67), he developed a new bow technique that advanced the art of the violin. In 1868 Auer went to St. Petersburg, where he became a professor at the Imperial Conservatory, teaching Efram Zimbalist, Mischa Elman, Nathan Milstein, and Jascha Heifetz, and he was soloist to the last three czars. He left Russia in 1917 and after a U.S. tour took up residence and became a U.S. citizen (1926). Auer remained active as a teacher and wrote *Violin Playing as I Teach It* (1921) and a memoir, *My Long Life in Music* (1923).

AUERBACH, ARNOLD JACOB (1917–), U.S. basketball coach. "Red" Auerbach took over the last-place Boston Celtics in 1950 and rebuilt the club into the most dominating team in the history of professional sport. Led by Bill Sharman, Bob Cousy, and Bill Russell, the Celtics won nine championships in 10 years (1957; 1959–66). The volatile and controversial Auerbach (he was fined over $17,000 during his career) retired in 1966 after winning 1,037 professional games. He remained with the Celtics as the team's general manager (1964–84) and president (1970–97). ■ See his autobiography (1977) and *On and off the Court* (1985; with Joe Fitzgerald); and Dan Shaughnessy, *Seeing Red* (1994).

AUGSTEIN, RUDOLF KARL (1923–), West German publisher. After serving as a lieutenant in World War II, Aug-

stein worked briefly as a journalist, and in 1947 borrowed $5,000 to found the controversial *Der Spiegel* ("The Mirror"), a weekly newsmagazine on the American model that specialized in sensational exposés of German politics and business. In 1962 the police raided the magazine and Augstein was charged with treason and jailed (Oct. 1962–Feb. 1963) for allegedly publishing military secrets. The "Spiegel affair" led to a cabinet crisis and the forced resignation of Defense Minister Franz Josef Strauss because of the public outcry against him for his role in the raid. Increasingly influential at home and abroad, *Der Spiegel* claimed a circulation of 700,000. Augstein was elected to the Bundestag (Nov. 1972), but resigned in Jan. 1973.

AULARD, FRANÇOIS ALPHONSE (1849–1928), French historian. "In order to understand the revolution," declared Aulard, an anticlerical leftist professor at the Sorbonne (1887–1922) and the foremost historian of the French Revolution, "it is necessary to love it." During his long academic career Aulard founded a society to study the revolution and established and edited (1887–1927) its journal, *La Révolution Française*. He wrote many books on the political aspects of the revolutionary period including *The French Revolution: A Political History* (1901; Eng. trans. 4 vols., 1910) and *Christianity and the French Revolution* (Eng. trans. 1927, 1966).

AUNG SAN (1915–1947), Burmese political leader. Aung came from an affluent family and was politically active as a student. Frequently detained by the British for his nationalist activities, he went underground in 1940 and fled to Japan. Although he was always critical of the Japanese, Aung organized a Burmese army to fight with the Japanese against the Allies and joined the World War II puppet government; later (1945) he became an arch antifascist and led a rebellion against the Japanese. Aung negotiated (1947) Burmese independence from Britain. He was assassinated after his selection as the first premier-designate. ■ See study edited by U Maung Maung (1962).

AUNG SAN SUU KYI (1945–), Burmese political leader. Aung San Suu Kyi was the daughter of Aung San, the leader of the Burmese independence movement in the 1940s who is regarded as founder of modern Burma. She lived in India with her mother, who was Burma's ambassador (1960–64), studied at Oxford University (B.A. 1967), and worked at the United Nations Secretariat in New York. After marrying Oxford scholar of Asian civilizations Michael Aris, she spent time in several Asian countries and wrote scholarly books on Burma's modern history and culture. Returning to Burma (1988), which had been ruled by a military dictatorship since 1962, she condemned the repressive policies of the government and became the leader of the National League for Democracy (NDL). Although she was placed under house arrest (1989–95) and forbidden to run for office, the

NDL won 80 percent of the seats in the National Assembly in the election of May 1990. The government refused to surrender power and Aung San Suu Kyi remained a leader of the democratic forces of her country in spite of continued harassment by the government. She received numerous awards for her advocacy of democracy and human rights, including the 1991 Nobel Peace prize. ■ See her books, *Freedom From Fear* (1991) and *The Voice of Hope* (1998; with Alan Clements); the study by Bertil Lintner (1990); and Barbara Victor, *The Lady* (1998).

AURIC, GEORGES (1899–1983), French composer. Auric, who began composing as a child, was the youngest member of the antiromantic group of French composers called "The Six." He wrote ballets for Sergei Diaghilev (*Les Facheux*, 1923; *Les Matelots*, 1924) and film scores (*A Nous la Liberté*, 1931; *Beauty and the Beast*, 1946; *Moulin Rouge*, 1952), was a music critic for *Les Nouvelles Littéraires*, and served as general administrator of the Paris Opera and the Opéra Comique (1962–68).

AURIOL, VINCENT (1884–1966), French public official. A leader of the French Socialist party in the interwar period, Auriol opposed the Vichy government and became a leader of the Resistance during World War II. He was an architect of the Fourth Republic and served as its first president (1947–54). Auriol's tenure in office was marked by continuing economic and political crises, and his conciliatory policies were attacked by both the right and the left. In 1958 he helped Charles de Gaulle return to power but broke with him in 1960.

AUROBINDO, SRI. *See GHOSE, AUROBINDO.*

AUSTEN, ELIZABETH ALICE (1866–1952), U.S. photographer. Although not "discovered" until shortly before her death, Alice Austen was one of America's pioneering women photographers. From the time of her childhood until the end of World War I, she took approximately 5,000 photos, mostly depicting family, friends, and everyday upper-class life in her native Staten Island, New York. Few of her works were published or exhibited, and her collection was largely unknown until accidentally discovered by researchers in 1951, when the destitute and crippled Austen was living in a Staten Island poorhouse. ■ See Ann Novotny, *Alice's World* (1976).

AUSTIN, HERBERT AUSTIN, 1st BARON (1866–1941), British industrialist. An automative designer and racer during the 1890s, Austin established the Austin Motor Co. (1905) and by 1914 was producing 1,000 cars a year. In 1922 he produced the first "Baby Austin," the Austin Seven, a seven-horsepower vehicle that was only slightly larger than a motorcycle with sidecar and cost just over $200. The enormous success of the car—100,000 were manufactured by 1927—led to its being imitated both at home and on the Continent. Austin Motors became one of Britain's largest automobile manufacturers; in 1952 it merged with Morris Motors to form the British Motor Corp. Austin served in Parliament as a Conservative from 1919 to 1924. ■ See biography by Roy A. Church (1979).

AUSTIN, JOHN LANGSHAW (1911–1960), British philosopher. Austin led the linguistic-analysis approach to philosophy, which, under the influence of Ludwig Wittgenstein, attempted to resolve problems in philosophy by analyzing and clarifying the meaning of words. Austin's writings were collected in *Philosophical Papers* (1961), *How to Do Things with Words* (1962), and *Sense and Sensibilia* (1962). They were published posthumously, since Austin's career as a teacher at Oxford (from 1933) was cut short by his early death. ■ See study by Mats Furberg (1971); Isaiah Berlin, et al., eds., *Essays on J. L. Austin* (1973); and the study by Keith Graham (1978).

AUSTIN, MARY HUNTER (Mary Hunter; 1868–1934), U.S. author. Called the most intelligent woman in America by the British writer H. G. Wells, Austin was a prolific essayist and novelist (32 books and more than 200 articles) whose works reflected her beliefs in mysticism, socialism, and feminism. She was best known for her classic accounts of American Indian culture and desert life, *The Land of Little Rain* (1903), *The Basket Woman* (1904), *The Flock* (1906), *The American Rhythm* (1923), and *Children Sing in the Far West* (1928). She also wrote *A Woman of Genius* (1912). ■ See her autobiography, *Earth Horizon* (1932); biography by Augusta Fink, *I—Mary* (1983); and biography by E. L. Stineman (1989).

AUTRY, GENE (1907–1998), U.S. country singer and film star. While sending a wire from an Oklahoma depot, the humorist Will Rogers heard the relief telegrapher sing and encouraged him to go professional. The telegrapher—Gene Autry—took his advice but had only modest success until an American Record Corp. executive signed him in 1931, hoping to capitalize on Autry's studied imitation of Jimmie Rodgers' yodeling. The "Singing Cowboy" was catapulted to fame, particularly after his appearance in the Ken Maynard film *In Old Santa Fe* (1934). Recordings, stage shows, films, radio broadcasts, and television films steadily increased his popularity and his bank account. He wrote or collaborated on much of his own material, including his theme song "Back in the Saddle Again." His recording of "Rudolph the Red-Nosed Reindeer" (1949) became one of the best-selling singles in history. In the early 1950s, Autry and his horse Champion starred in 91 self-produced TV films. His popularity lagged in the late 1950s, and the millionaire cowboy appeared infrequently after 1961. Country-music buffs tend to minimize Autry's musical contribution, but he must be credited for popularizing the guitar and for making "country and western" a viable profession. Autry was also an active businessman who owned TV and radio stations, a hotel chain, and, from 1962, the California Angels baseball team. ■ See his autobiography, *Back in the Saddle Again* (1978).

AVEDON, RICHARD (1923–), U.S. photographer. Born in New York City, Avedon learned photography in the merchant marine and began doing fashion photography after World War II. During his years on the staff of *Harper's Bazaar* (1945–65) and later with *Vogue* (1966–90), he took his mannequins out of the studio to shoot fashion scenes at the zoo, on the beach, and even before the pyramids of the Nile. At the same time, the world's highest-paid fashion photographer was taking perceptive celebrity portraits published in *Observations* (1959), *Portraits* (1976), and *Avedon: Photographs, 1947–1977* (1978). In 1985 he published the collection *In the American West: 1979–1984*. Avedon's life inspired the 1957 movie, *Funny Face*. He was staff photographer of the *New Yorker* (1992–). ■ See his autobiography (1993).

AVERY, MILTON (1885–1965), U.S. painter. Born into a working-class family, Avery studied art while working at a variety of blue-collar jobs in Hartford, Connecticut, and moved to New York City in 1925. A colorist who was influenced by French painter Henri Matisse, he was neither a realist nor an abstract painter and was never in the mainstream of contemporary American art. His gently humorous canvases depicted commonplace landscapes, figures, and domestic interiors. However, through his use of vivid color zones and simple flattened forms that seemed to float on the surface of the painting, he influenced the development of abstract expressionism and color-field painting and established a reputation by the mid-1950s as one of the great masters and pioneers of modernist painting in the United States. ■ See the study and catalog by Barbara Haskell (1982).

AVERY, OSWALD THEODORE (1877–1955), Canadian-born U.S. bacteriologist. Avery graduated from Colgate (1900) and went on to Columbia University's College of Physicians and Surgeons (M.D. 1904). Preferring research to the practice of medicine, he worked at the Rockefeller Institute Hospital in New York (1913–47) to conduct long-term experiments with pneumococci. Examining the transformation of the pneumonia bacteria in the body, he was able to demonstrate that inheritable changes are caused by deoxyribonucleic acid, or DNA. His works provided the basis for subsequent research in immunochemistry and molecular biology. ■ See René Dubos, *The Professor, The Institute and DNA* (1976).

AVERY, SEWELL LEE (1874–1960), U.S. businessman. Avery served as president of the U.S. Gypsum Co. (1905–1937), which he developed into the nation's largest plaster company. From 1931 to 1956 he was chairman of Montgomery Ward and Co., the nation's second-largest mail-order and retail-merchandising house. An arch conservative and "rugged individualist," he was a bitter foe of the New Deal. A 1944 photo of soldiers carrying him out of his Chicago office after he refused to comply with a War Labor Board order regarding a union contract became identified with his defiance of what he called "un-American" interference with business.

ÁVILA CAMACHO, MANUEL (1897–1955), Mexican general and political leader. A career military officer, Ávila Camacho served as minister of defense (1938–39) before being elected president (1940). A moderate, he attempted to consolidate and institutionalize the reforms made during the presidency of Lázaro Cárdenas (1934–40). He slowed down agrarian reform but sponsored social-security legislation and literacy programs. He was credited with dramatically improving ties with the United States. He settled the long-standing dispute with the U.S. government over seized oil properties and entered World War II on the side of the Allies (1942).

AVON, 1st EARL OF. *See EDEN, SIR ANTHONY, 1st EARL OF AVON.*

AWOLOWO, OBAFEMI (1909–1987), Nigerian political leader. An important Yoruba chief, Awolowo studied law in London and founded the Action Group (1950) to demand self-government for a federal Nigeria. After serving as premier of the western region (1954–59), he became leader of the opposition in the federal house of representatives in 1960, but he was later imprisoned (1962–66) for plotting to overthrow the government. Following his release, he headed the federal ministry of finance (1967–71) and later maintained a private legal practice until the lifting of the ban on politics (1978). He unsuccessfully ran for president as the candidate of the Unity Party of Nigeria (UPN) in 1979 and 1983. ■ See his autobiography, *Awo* (1960).

AWOONOR, KOFI (1935–), Ghanaian poet, novelist, and playwright. After studying comparative literature at the State University of New York at Stony Brook (Ph.D. 1972), Awoonor taught there (1968–75). He utilized the forms of his native Ewe songs and poems to write of the nefarious influence of Western education and culture in luring young Africans away from their cultural roots. His books of poetry included *Rediscovery and Other Poems* (1964), *Night of My Blood* (1971), and *House by the Sea* (1978). A novel, *This Earth, My Brother* (1971), treated corruption in modern African life. He also wrote *Breast of the Earth: A Study of African Culture and Literature* (1975). After returning to Ghana (1975), he was arrested for suspected subversion but was pardoned (1976) and subsequently served as dean of the faculty of arts at the University of Cape Coast, secretary-general of the Action Congress party, ambassador to Brazil (1984–90) and the United Nations (1990–94). His later works included *Comes the Voyager at Last: A Tale of Return to Africa* (1992) and *Africa: The Marginalized Continent* (1994).

AXELROD, JULIUS (1912–), U.S. pharmacologist. Hampered by poverty and Jewish quotas, Axelrod was refused admission to medical school. He earned a master's degree (1941) in chemical pharmacology instead and eventually became chief of the pharmacology section of the National Institute of Mental Health (1955–84). For his discovery of the substance that inhibits neural impulses, Axelrod shared the 1970 Nobel Prize for Physiology or Medicine with Ulf von Euler and Sir Bernard Katz. His work helped lay the foundation for important research in neurophysiology and neuropharmacology, notably in the search for remedies for hypertension and schizophrenia.

AXELROD, PAUL. *See AKSELROD, PAVEL BORISO-VICH.*

AYER, SIR ALFRED JULES (1910–1989), British philosopher. A. J. Ayer was prominent in the movement of logical positivism in the 1930s. In his classic, *Language, Truth, and Logic* (1936), he argued for the positivistic position that only verifiable statements are possibly true or false. Other statements, like those of religion and art, were either trivially true or expressions of emotion. Ayer taught at Oxford University (1933–46; 1959–78) and at the University of London (1946–59), where his ideas greatly influenced younger philosophers. His other works included *The Problem of Knowledge* (1956), *Philosophy and Language* (1960), *The Central Questions of Philosophy* (1973), and *Voltaire* (1986). ■ See his memoirs, *Part of My Life* (1978); study by John Foster (1985); and biography by Ben Rogers (1999).

AYMÉ, MARCEL (1902–1967), French writer. Entirely self-educated, Aymé worked as a journalist before the great success of his novel *The Green Mare* (1933; Eng. trans. 1955). His varied, richly comic work included novels, plays, and short stories. Mixing wild fantasy and reality with Rabelaisian gusto and skillful insight, his work satirized the absurdities and corruption of contemporary life. Some of his best work was found in his short stories and popular fables like *The Wonderful Farm* (1934; Eng. trans. 1951) and *Across Paris* (1947; Eng. trans. 1958). ■ See Dorothy R. Brodin, *The Comic World of Marcel Aymé* (1964).

AYUB KHAN, MOHAMMAD (1907–1974), Pakistani military and political leader. A Muslim of Pathan stock, Ayub Khan was the son of a soldier and was educated at Sandhurst. Commissioned in the British Indian army in 1927, he saw action in Burma during World War II. By 1951 Ayub Khan was the Pakistani commander in chief and had built a formidable army with extensive U.S. aid. As president

(1958–1969), he improved relations with China and the Soviet Union and promulgated a new constituion, but he forbade opposition and jailed critics. Charges of corruption and the unsuccessful war with India (1965–66) lost him support; subsequent widespread violence forced Ayub Khan to resign. ■ See his autobiography, *Friends Not Masters* (1967), and Lawrence Ziring, *The Ayub Khan Era* (1971).

AZAÑA, MANUEL (1880–1940), Spanish political leader. Azaña studied law at the University of Madrid and later in Paris, where he acquired many of the literary and political traits that were to influence the Spanish "Generation of 1898" movement. When the republicans came to power, Azaña was named minister of war (1931), and he later was premier (1931–33) under President Niceto Alcalá Zamora. During that time, he pressed for military and educational reform, but his harsh treatment of political dissenters lessened his popularity. With the victory of the popular front in 1936, Azaña was reinstated as premier and later that year he became the president of the republic. When the civil war broke out (1936), Azaña left Madrid and was of little help to the Loyalist government. He left Spain (1939) after the fall of Barcelona and died in France. ■ See Frank Sedwick, *The Tragedy of Manuel Azaña and the Fate of the Spanish Republic* (1964).

AZHARI, (SAYYID) ISMAIL AL- (1900–1969), Sudanese political leader. Born into a prominent family, al-Azhari became president of the Sudan's first political organization, the Graduates General Congress in 1940, and of the National Unionist Party (NUP) in 1952. His opposition to British rule and support of unification with Egypt brought him national attention. As prime minister (1954–56), however, he led the Sudan to complete and separate independence in January 1956. Factionalism within his ruling party cost him his leadership role, and he was the opposition leader from 1956 to 1958. Following a six-year period of military rule, he was appointed president (1965) but was overthrown in a military coup (May 1969).

AZIKIWE, NNAMDI (1904–1996), Nigerian journalist and political leader. Popularly known as "Zik," Azikiwe received his college education and training as a reporter in the United States. After returning to Africa (1934), he became editor in chief of nationalist newspapers in Accra and Lagos. A founder of the independence movement, he lent the name "Zikism" to the nationalist effort. As one of the three delegates to the 1953 London Conference, Azikiwe helped pave the way for complete independence in 1960. Elected the country's first president (1963), he tried to overcome the problems of underdevelopment and tribal animosity. After he was overthrown by a military coup in 1966, he worked with the Biafran secession movement (1967–69) but subsequently supported the central government. He served as chancellor of the University of Lagos (1972–76) and ran unsuccessfully for president as the candidate of the Nigerian

People's party (1979 and 1983). ■ See his autobiography, *My Odyssey* (1970); the biography by K.A.B. Jones-Quartey (1965); and P.C. Uwazurike, *The Man Called Zik of Africa* (1996).

AZORÍN (José Martínez Ruiz; 1873–1967), Spanish novelist, dramatist, and critic. Although he moved from extreme left to right in his political stance, Azorín remained a revolutionary stylist who enlarged the Spanish vocabulary. His staccato prose reacted against the flowery declamatory tradition of Spanish letters. His critical views were representative of the "Generation of 1898," which sought to revitalize Spanish culture and rejected the traditional novel as too artificial. He dwelled on details and communicated a static view of life in more than 100 volumes. His fiction included *Don Juan* (1922; Eng. trans. 1923) and *The Sirens and Other Stories* (1929; Eng. trans. 1931). He was intent on keeping European currents flowing through Spain, and edited (1923–36) the journal *Revista de Occidente* ("Magazine of the West"). ■ See study by Kathleen M. Glenn (1981).

AZUELA, MARIANO (1873–1952), Mexican novelist. Azuela began writing while a medical student (M.D. 1899), becoming both a novelist and a doctor. He participated in the Mexican revolution and wrote several novels and novellas treating issues raised by it. In *The Underdogs* (1916; Eng. trans. 1929), *The Bosses* (1917; Eng. trans. 1956), *The Flies* (1918; Eng. trans. 1956), *Trials of a Respectable Family* (1918; Eng. trans. 1963), and other novels, he showed how individuals change when they become part of a mass movement. Azuela used a terse style and photographic observation to portray social upheaval. He also wrote plays and a volume of criticism. ■ See studies by Luis Leal (1971) and Stanley L. Robe (1979).

B

BAADE, WALTER (1893–1960), German-born U.S. astronomer. After studying at Göttingen (Ph.D. 1919) and teaching at the Hamburg Observatory (1919–31), Baade worked at the Mt. Wilson and later Mt. Palomar observatories (California; 1931–58), where he made his most significant discoveries. His detailed study of the galaxies in Andromeda during the 1940s led to his discovery of two discrete populations of stars, older ones in the central regions and newer ones in the arms of the spiral galaxies. As further studies necessitated the recalibration of the luminosity variables used in measuring distances between galaxies, he determined (1952) that the galaxies were twice as far and therefore twice as old as previously calculated. He also discovered the asteroids Icarus and Hidalgo and identified distant galaxies as the sources of radio emissions. ■ See his posthumously published *Evolution of Stars and Galaxies* (1963).

BAADER, (BERND) ANDREAS (1943–1977), and **ULRIKE MEINHOF** (1934–1976), West German terrorists. Baader was arrested in 1968 for setting fires in department stores to protest West Germany's smug affluence and its "imperialistic" government. He was interviewed by Meinhof, a respected left-wing journalist who made the leap from theory to practice by helping Baader to escape in 1970. The "Baader-Meinhof gang" (or Red Army Faction, as they named themselves) then underwent guerrilla warfare training from Palestinians in Jordan, returning home to rob banks and detonate bombs in protest against bourgeois society and American war policies in Vietnam. They were captured in 1972 and kept in solitary confinement. In the midst of a lengthy trial, Meinhof was found dead by hanging (1976). Baader was subsequently sentenced to life imprisonment (1977). Later that year, having spawned a new generation of terrorist hijackers and kidnappers, as well as repressive governmental reaction, he and the rest of the gang were also found dead in their cells. ■ See Julian Becker, *Hitler's Children* (1977) and volume of photographs, *Baader-Meinhof* (1998), edited by Astrid Proll.

BABBITT, IRVING (1865–1933), U.S. educator. A Harvard teacher of French and comparative literature (1894–1933), Babbit espoused a return to classical values. The neohumanist movement that he initiated advocated education based on ethical principles. It put forth a conservative social ideology and rejected the emotionalism and dilettantism of the romantic era, as well as realism and naturalism. Babbitt's books included *Literature and the American College* (1908) and *Rousseau and Romanticism* (1919). ■ See the memoirs edited by Frederick Manchester and Odell Shepherd (1941); J. David Hoeveler, *The New Humanism* (1977); and studies by Thomas R. Nevin (1984) and Milton Hindus (1994).

BABBITT, MILTON (1916–   ), U.S. composer. Among the most influential and cerebral composers of electronic music, Babbitt was influenced by composer Roger Sessions while studying at Princeton University (M.F.A. 1942). While teaching there (from 1938), he was the first to apply—in *Three Compositions* for piano (1946–47) and *Composition for Four Instruments* (1947)—the principles of the 12-tone system to durations, timbres, and dynamics as well as pitch to create total serialization. His pioneering work on the RCA Electronic Sound Synthesizer led, in 1959, to the establishment of the Electronic Music Center of Columbia and Princeton Universities, which he codirected. Among Babbitt's best-known compositions are *All Set* (1957), *Composition for Synthesizer* (1961), *Vision and Prayer* (1961), *Relata I and II* (1965–68), and *Consortini for Chamber Ensemble* (1989). ■ See study by Andrew Mead (1994).

BABEL, ISAAK EMMANUILOVICH (1894–1940), Soviet short-story writer and playwright. The son of a Jewish merchant, Babel left (1915) his native Odessa for Petrograd (now Leningrad), where the writer and editor Maxim Gorky accepted two witty and erotic early stories for the journal *Chronicle*. Babel was charged with pornography by the czarist court, but was saved by the 1917 Russian Revolution. He served the bolsheviks and was assigned (1920) as a political officer in the cavalry during the civil war. Babel wrote *Tales of Odessa* (1923–24; Eng. trans. 1955) in the Russian-Jewish idiom and the stunning short-story cycle *Red Cavalry* (1926; Eng. trans. 1929); his subtle, ornamental prose established him as a master of the genre. His best-known play was *Sunset* (1928; Eng. trans. 1960). Babel wrote little else, and he was denounced after he stated at the 1934 Writers' Congress that he was working in a new genre, "silence." He was arrested (1939), tortured, and forced to incriminate other Soviet authors before being executed in January 1940. He was formally cleared of charges posthumously in 1954. Translations of his work appear in *Collected Stories* (1957) and *You Must Know Everything* (1984). ■ See Nathalie Babel, ed., *Isaac Babel: The Lonely Years, 1925–1939* (1964); studies by Patricia Carden (1972) and James Falen (1974); and the memoir by his widow, A. N. Pirozhkova, *At His Side: The Last Years of Isaac Babel* (1989; Eng. trans. 1996).

BABITS, MIHÁLY (1883–1941), Hungarian poet, novelist, essayist, and translator. Born into an intellectual, middle-class family, Babits was for many years associated with the influential journal *Nyugat* ("West"; editor from 1929) and was a major figure in Hungarian literary life for more than 30 years. A Catholic humanist and pacifist, he was a professor of classical, European, and Hungarian literature and was renowned for his immense learning. He mastered many literary forms and produced literary criticism, lyric poetry, novels (*The Nightmare*, 1916, Eng. trans. 1966; *The Son of Virgil Timár*, 1922; *The Children of Death*, 1927), scholarly works (*History of European Literature*, 1934), and translations of Dante, Goethe, Shakespeare, and Sophocles.

BABSON, ROGER WARD (1875–1967), U.S. statistician. Combining folksy slogans ("buy wisely, buy now") with astute business analyses, Babson guided stock-market investors for 50 years—through the Babson Statistical Organization (incorporated 1904), a weekly column entitled "Be Right with Babson," and a newspaper syndicate service, the Publishers Financial Bureau (organized 1923). In 1919 he founded a business school for men, the Babson Institute, near Boston. Babson established Webber College, its counterpart for women, in 1927 in Florida. ■ See his autobiography, *Actions and Reactions* (1935), and Earl L. Smith, *Yankee Genius* (1954).

BABST, EARL (1870–1967), U.S. industrialist. As a lawyer representing the National Biscuit Co. (1902–15), Babst was instrumental in winning the right for companies to market products in packages identified by national trademarks and to advertise nationally. He was president (1915–25) and chairman (1925–51) of the American Sugar Refining Co. and played a leading role in the development and promotion of trademark packaging in the sugar industry.

BACALL, LAUREN (Betty Joan Perske; 1924–), U.S. actress. A New York dance student and model, Bacall appeared in two Broadway flops before her 1944 film debut in *To Have and Have Not*. Only 19, a sophisticated high-fashion blonde with a baby face, a deep sexy voice, and a smart comeback, she proved such a good match for her costar Humphrey Bogart that they later married (1945) and teamed up again in *The Big Sleep* (1946), *Dark Passage* (1947), and *Key Largo* (1948). Bacall's subsequent film career was not outstanding, but she made a successful return to Broadway in *Cactus Flower* (1965) and *Applause* (1970; Tony Award). She also won a Tony Award for *Woman of the Year* (1981). Her later movies included *The Shootist* (1976), *Health* (1980), *Misery* (1990), and *The Mirror Has Two Faces* (1996). ■ See her autobiographies, *By Myself* (1979) and *Now* (1994).

BACHARACH, BURT (1929–), U.S. composer. The son of a newspaper columnist, Bacharach broke into show business as a nightclub pianist, studied classical music with Henry Cowell and Darius Milhaud, and returned to pop music as an accompanist, conductor, and arranger for Vic Damone, the Ames Brothers, and Marlene Dietrich (1958–61). Combining unorthodox meter and harmonics with lush orchestrations, he became a popular songwriter ("Walk on By," "Raindrops Keep Fallin' on My Head," "What the World Needs Now," "Do You Know the Way to San José?," "I'll Never Fall in Love Again," "That's What Friends Are For"). He also composed scores for such films as *Casino Royale* (1967) and *Butch Cassidy and the Sundance Kid* (1969), and for the Broadway show *Promises, Promises* (1968).

BACHMANN, INGEBORG (1926–1973), Austrian poet. Bachmann wrote a doctoral thesis on the philosophers Martin Heidegger and Ludwig Wittgenstein. In the 1950s she earned critical attention for two volumes of somber and intensely personal poetry. She also wrote radio plays; the short fiction in the volume *The Thirtieth Year* (1961; Eng. trans. 1964); a novel, *Malina* (1971; Eng. trans. 1990); and *The Book of Franza and Requiem for Fanny Goldman* (Eng. trans. 1999).

BACKUS, JOHN (1924–), U.S. computer scientist. After studying mathematics at Columbia University (B.S. 1949; M.A. 1950), Backus joined IBM, where he remained for his entire career (1950–91). In 1954 he invented FORTRAN (FORmula TRANslator), the first general-purpose, high-level computer language. When it became commercially available in 1957, it opened up computer use to nonspecialists and ushered in the computer software revolution. It remained the most widely used scientific programming language for decades and was the forerunner of such popular programs as COBOL, BASIC, and ALGOL (versions of which Backus also helped to design). Backus also invented (1959) the metalanguage BNF (Backus Normal Form; later modified by Peter Naur and called the Backus-Naur Form), which became the standard method for describing programming language syntax.

BACON, FRANCIS (1909?–1992), Irish-born British painter. A self-taught painter who began his career by designing interior decor, Bacon developed in the immediate post–World War II period a unique style, compared by critics to the works of Henry Fuseli and Goya, which used a fluid technique to communicate horror and anguish. He frequently depicted a single figure in an eerily lit setting, conveying the isolation and terror of the human condition. Bacon often incorporated images of photographs, films, newspaper clippings, and old-master paintings in his work. In the 1960s his settings became simplified; the horror was concentrated in the distortion of features and the nude body. His later works included *Three Studies for a Crucifixion* (1962) and *Portrait of a Man Walking Down Steps* (1972).

■ See study by John Russell (rev. ed. 1979) and biography by Michael Peppiatt (1997).

BACON, HENRY (1866–1924), U.S. architect. One of the most celebrated architects of the first quarter of the century. Bacon was an adherent of the classical Greek revival style in vogue at the time. Although he designed many buildings, he was a specialist in public monuments and memorials, and was best known for designing the Lincoln Memorial in Washington, D.C. (1922). He collaborated frequently with the sculptors Daniel Chester French and Augustus Saint-Gaudens.

BADILLO, HERMAN (1929–), U.S. political leader. Born in Puerto Rico and raised in New York City's East Harlem, Badillo worked as an accountant to put himself through Brooklyn Law School (1954) at night. He became active in local Democratic party politics and was elected borough president of the Bronx in 1965. He served in Congress (1971–78) and was the most prominent Puerto Rican politician in the United States. He later served as a deputy mayor of New York City (1978–79). He opposed the open admissions policy of the City University of New York and as CUNY board member (1990–) and chairman (1999–) opposed remedial instruction for CUNY students in four-year colleges. He joined the Republican Party in 1998.

BADOGLIO, PIETRO (1871–1956), Italian general and political leader. The century's most prominent Italian military figure, Badoglio served in Ethiopia (1896) and Libya (1912) and was a war hero during World War I. Named commander in chief in 1918, he conducted the postwar armistice talks. Although a royalist rather than a fascist soldier, he served fascist leader Benito Mussolini as chief of the general staff (1925–28; 1933–40) and personally commanded the army to victory in Ethiopia (1936). Following Italy's military setbacks in Greece (1940) during World War II, Badoglio resigned and remained inactive until he was appointed by King Victor Emmanuel III to succeed Mussolini as premier (1943). He negotiated the armistice with the Allies (1943) but, bitterly opposed by many Italians, he resigned in 1944. Accused of being a fascist by Italian democrats and a capitulator by the fascists, he spent his last years in obscurity. ■ See his *War in Abyssinia* (Eng. trans. 1937) and *Italy in the Second World War* (Eng. trans. 1948).

BAECK, LEO (1873–1956), German-born Jewish religious leader and theologian. Baeck earned a Ph.D. (1895) in philosophy at the University of Berlin, was ordained two years later, and served as rabbi in Oppeln (1897–1907), Düsseldorf (1907–12), and Berlin (1912–42). Baeck's book *The Essence of Judaism* (1905; Eng. trans. 1936), which viewed Judaism as an expression of morality, made him a leading figure of Jewish liberal thought. In the 1920s he wrote "Romantic Religion," an essay contrasting Christianity's basis in feeling with Judaism's basis in reason. After 1933, Baeck,

with Otto Hirsch, headed the National Agency of Jews in Germany, becoming responsible for the welfare of Jews under Nazi rule; the Nazis detained him numerous times. During this period Baeck wrote *The Gospel as a Document of Jewish Religious History* (1938). He was finally interned (1943) in the Theresienstadt (Terezin) concentration camp, where he wrote his last book, *This People Israel: The Meaning of Jewish Existence* (1955; Eng. trans. 1965). The day before he was to be executed, Baeck was liberated by Russian troops. He later became a British subject. ■ See biography by A. H. Friedlander (1968) and Leonard Baker, *Days of Sorrow and Pain* (1978).

BAEKELAND, LEO HENDRIK (1863–1944), Belgian-born U.S. chemist. Baekeland earned his doctorate *maxima cum laude* at age 21 from the University of Ghent (1884). When his interest in technological research found little support in Belgium or England, he emigrated to the United States (1889), where his enthusiasm for photography soon earned him his first million dollars: he sold Kodak his Velox photographic printing paper, which could be developed under artificial light. He also developed (1909) Bakelite, the first "thermo-setting" or heat-resistant plastic, and served (1910–39) as president of the Bakelite Corp. ■ See Carl B. Kaufmann, *Grand Duke, Wizard and Bohemian* (1968).

BAEZ, JOAN (1941–), U.S. folksinger. Her father was a Mexican-American scientist, her mother a teacher of English literature. Baez was a student at Boston University when she began strumming the guitar and singing in Cambridge coffeehouses. Performing ballads in a pure, silvery soprano, she achieved stardom with folk-festival appearances and college tours before she was 20. The successful albums *Joan Baez in Concert* (vol. I, 1962; vol. II, 1964) included her famous recording of "We Shall Overcome." An early member of the anti–Vietnam War movement, Baez withheld part of her income taxes in 1964, founded an institute for the study of nonviolence in California (1965), and was twice arrested for protests at army-induction centers. She was president of Humanitas (1979–92). Her later albums included *Play Me Backwards* (1992) and *Gone From Danger* (1997). ■ See her autobiography, *Daybreak* (1968) and her memoir, *And a Voice to Sing With* (1988).

BAHAR, MOHAMMAD TAQI (1885–1951), Iranian poet and scholar. The son of an official court poet, Bahar was granted the title "king of poets," but he broke with the monarchy and joined the revolutionary movement (1905–12). He served in parliament, taught Persian literature at Teheran University (from 1928), and was the most renowned poet of his generation. His poems, though written in classical form, introduced modern social and political themes and simplified language into modern Persian poetry. Many of his best ones criticized the government and reactionary religious and political forces in the country.

BAILEY, FRANCIS LEE (1933–   ), U.S. lawyer. A celebrated specialist in the defense of controversial criminal cases, F. Lee Bailey won a scholarship to Harvard Law School but dropped out to join the military, serving as a pilot and legal officer. Back in law school he founded a detective agency to conduct the extensive case research for which he later became known. His first major case was the murder retrial of Dr. Sam Sheppard, for whom he won acquittal in 1966. Later clients were the accused Boston Strangler, the $1.5 million Plymouth Mail Robbers, kidnapped heiress Patty Hearst, and My Lai massacre defendant Capt. Ernest Medina. Despite his penchant for publicity, frowned on by a conservative profession, Bailey was considered a methodical and effective trial attorney. ■ See his *The Defense Never Rests* (1971), *For the Defense* (1975), *To Be a Trial Lawyer* (1983), and biography by Les Whitten (1971).

BAILEY, LIBERTY HYDE (1858–1954), U.S. botanist and educator. Bailey created the nation's first horticulture department (1885) at Michigan State University, his alma mater, developing an applied science out of pure biology. He greatly expanded the field of horticulture as a professor (1888–1903) and dean of the college of agriculture (1903–13) at Cornell University. He was also active in the field of secondary education, wrote poetry, and pursued an interest in rural sociology. The Bailey Hortorium, which he established in 1920 and directed until 1951, was the first institution for botanical identification and classification. In 1935 it became part of Cornell University. ■ See biographies by Andrew Rodgers III (1949) and Philip Dorf (1956).

BAILEY, MILDRED (Mildred Rinker; 1907–1951), U.S. jazz singer. One of the first successful female vocalists with a jazz group, Bailey sang with the Paul Whiteman Band (1929–33) and was known as the "Rockin' Chair Lady" for her broadcast renditions of Hoagy Carmichael's song, "Rockin' Chair." Known for her unique, light, and warm soprano sound and special sense of phrasing, she was regarded as one of the great jazz stylists of her time. She formed a band with her husband, jazz xylophonist Red Norvo (1936–1939), and they were known as "Mr. and Mrs. Swing." After 1940 she performed mostly as a soloist.

BAIRD, BIL (William Britton Baird; 1904–1987), U.S. puppeteer. Baird first staged puppet productions at age seven. In his lifetime he created more than 2,000 puppets, including many for film and television, and he collaborated with producers Orson Welles and Florenz Ziegfeld in the late 1930s and early 1940s. Baird performed with his wife Cora (1912–1967), who created voices for many puppet characters. He created puppet shows for world fairs (1939; 1965), for New York's Radio City Music Hall, and he toured India, the Soviet Union, and Afghanistan for the U.S. State Department. Baird opened (1967) a puppet theater in New York's Greenwich Village. He wrote *The Art of the Puppet* (1965).

BAIRD, JOHN LOGIE (1888–1946), Scottish inventor. When poor health forced Baird to abandon his boot-polish and jam-manufacturing business, he turned to the study of television. His research led to the invention and demonstration (1926) of the first practical television and to the first transatlantic television transmission (1928). His system was used by the British Broadcasting Corporation (BBC) from 1929 to 1937. Baird also demonstrated (1939) color television by using a cathode-ray tube and conducted research in stereoscopic television. ■ See Ronald Tiltman, *Baird of Television* (1933), and John Rowland, *The Television Man* (1967).

BA JIN (old style: PA CHIN; 1904–   ), Chinese novelist. Ba Jin was the pseudonym of Li Feigan (old style: Li Fei-kan). Born into a wealthy family, he was given a traditional as well as a Western education and was attracted to the radical writing of the time. He was greatly influenced by the Russian anarchists Mikhail Bakunin and P. A. Kropotkin. His novels of the 1930s and 1940s, notably *Family* (1931; Eng. trans. 1958, 1972) and *Cold Nights* (1947; Eng. trans. 1978), were extremely popular with Chinese youth; they attacked the stifling traditional Chinese family structure, presented socially conscious heroes and heroines, and expressed resentment over foreign domination of China. Although never a member of the Communist party, he held important literary posts after the communists took control in 1949. He renounced his anarchist ideals but was nevertheless denounced during the Cultural Revolution (1966) and forced to do manual labor. He reemerged in 1977 and, as chairman of the Writers Association, called for artistic freedom (1984). ■ See his *Random Thoughts* (1979; Eng. trans. 1984) and studies by Olga Lang (1967) and Nathan K. Mao (1978).

BAKDASH, KHALED (1912–   ), Syrian political leader. Born into a prominent Kurdish family, Bakdash studied law at the University of Damascus and joined the underground Syrian Communist party in 1930. As secretary-general of the party from 1936, he loyally followed the Moscow line and was frequently referred to as "communist number one of the Arab world." He was the first communist elected to any Arab parliament (1954), but opposed the Syrian-Egyptian union (1958) and went into exile in Eastern Europe. He returned to Syria after the 1966 coup and collaborated with the Ba'ath government.

BAKER, ELLA (1903–1986), U.S. civil-rights leader. The granddaughter of a slave who became a minister, Baker graduated from Shaw University (Raleigh, North Carolina; 1927) and moved to New York City, where she was active in the consumer-rights movement during the 1930s. In 1938 she joined the National Association for the Advancement of Colored People (NAACP), and as its national director of branches (1943–46), she traveled around the country helping to build up its membership. She was president of the New York City branch (1954). She worked with Martin Luther King, Jr., as executive secretary of the Southern Christian Leadership Conference (SCLC; 1958–60) and was the major catalyst in the formation of the Student Non-Violent Coordinating Committee (SNCC; 1960), which spearheaded voter registration drives among blacks throughout the south. To the left of the mainstream of the civil-rights movement, she had a large following among youthful activists and participated in education, human-rights, and liberation groups through the 1970s. ■ See Ellen Cantarow, *Moving the Mountain* (1980) and biography by Joanne Grant (1998).

BAKER, JAMES A. (1930–   ), U.S. political leader. The son of a wealthy Houston lawyer, Baker graduated from Princeton University (B.A. 1952) and the University of Texas (J.D., 1957). He practiced law in Houston and was active in national Republican politics, managing the presidential campaign of Gerald R. Ford (1976) and George Bush (1979–80, 1988) and serving as Ronald Reagan's White House chief of staff (1981–85) and secretary of the treasury (1985–88). As George Bush's secretary of state (1989–92), he shaped East-West relations at the end of the cold war, helped to negotiate nuclear arms reduction agreements, was instrumental in creating the coalition that defeated Iraq during the Gulf War, and organized the first face-to-face negotiations between the Israelis and Palestinians. ■ See his memoir, *The Politics of Diplomacy* (1995, with Thomas M. Franck).

BAKER, JOSEPHINE (1906–1975), U.S. entertainer. The daughter of an African-American St. Louis washerwoman, Baker danced (1925) with *La Revue Nègre* in Paris at age 18 and achieved success with her stylized, exotic dancing as well as with her distinctive delivery of lyrics. She was known as much for her daring costumes and astonishing entrances (she was sometimes carried onstage upside down, sometimes lowered before the audience) as for her eccentric habits; she often appeared in public walking a pet cheetah or leading swans on a leash. She won a devoted following in European capitals, never matched at home despite appearances in Ziegfeld's *Follies* in the mid-1930s. She became a French citizen in 1937 and was a member of the anti-German resistance movement during World War II. In the 1950s Baker was barred from segregated night clubs and hotels during an American tour; in 1963 she marched in Washington with civil-rights leader Martin Luther King. ■ See her autobiography, *Josephine* (Eng. trans. 1977; with Jo Bouillon); Lynn Haney, *Naked at the Feast* (1980); and Phyllis Rose, *Jazz Cleopatra* (1989).

BAKER, NEWTON DIEHL (1871–1937), U.S. cabinet officer and lawyer. A student of Woodrow Wilson at Johns Hopkins University, Baker served a reform mayor of Cleveland (1912–16) and played a key role in securing Wilson's presidential nomination in 1912. Wilson appointed him sec-

retary of war (1916) although he was a pacifist, and Baker was criticized severely during the early months of World War I. He served out his full term, however, and returned to private law practice after the war. In 1928 he was appointed to the Permanent Court of Arbitration at The Hague. ■ See biography by Clarence Cramer (1961).

BAKER, RAY STANNARD (1870–1946), U.S. journalist and author. A leading liberal, muckraking reporter and editor (*Chicago Record*, 1892–97; *McClure's Magazine*, 1897–1905; *American Magazine*, 1906–15), Baker wrote regularly on social and economic problems and exposed corruption in business and government. His book *Following the Color Line* (1908) was a pioneering study of American blacks. Under the pseudonym David Grayson he published several widely read volumes of philosophical essays dealing with problems of human nature. Baker became a close friend of Pres. Woodrow Wilson and wrote or edited 18 books about him, including a monumental eight-volume biography, *Woodrow Wilson: Life and Letters* (1927–39), which won a Pulitzer Prize (1940). ■ See his two-part autobiography, *Native American* (1941) and *American Chronicle* (1945), and studies by Robert C. Bannister, Jr. (1966) and John E. Semonche (1969).

BAKER, RUSSELL WAYNE (1925–   ), U.S. journalist. Born in a backwoods Virginia town, Baker grew up in Newark, New Jersey, and Baltimore, Maryland; after serving in the navy during World War II, he graduated from Johns Hopkins University (B.A. 1947). He was a reporter for the *Baltimore Sun* (1947–52) before joining the Washington bureau of the *New York Times* (1954). In his thrice-weekly "Observer" column (1962–98) Baker produced literate, witty, and irreverent political and social commentary, for which he won a 1979 Pulitzer Prize. He won a second Pulitzer Prize (in biography; 1983) for *Growing Up*, an account of his first 25 years. His other books include *An American in Washington* (1961); several collections of his columns, such as *So This Is Depravity* (1980); and a second autobiographical volume, *The Good Times* (1989).

BAKHTIN, MIKHAIL MIKHAILOVICH (1895–1975), Soviet literary critic. In the years following the Russian Revolution, Bakhtin studied philology in Odessa and then in St. Petersburg, where he worked under renowned classicist F. F. Zelinsky. Beginning his career in the heyday of formalism, he was active in Leningrad's literary circles in the 1920s, publishing books under the names of associates on such topics as Freudian thought, Marxism, and formalism. He published *Problems of Dostoevsky's Poetics* (1929, rev. ed. 1963; Eng. trans. 1984) under his own name. Just as it was published, he was arrested and spent six years in exile in Kazakhstan. Bakhtin defended a controversial dissertation at Moscow University in 1946; it is available in English as *Rabelais and His World* (1984). However, he remained apart from the academic mainstream until the republication of his study of Dostoevsky in 1963. His international reputation grew, and the appearance of previously unpublished works in the decade after his death made Bakhtin something of a cult figure among students of literary theory. Essentially a philosopher of language, Bakhtin sought a poetics rooted in the study of history, and made important contributions to the theory of the novel. A scholar of unusual breadth, he wrote on literature, linguistics, folklore, psychology, anthropology, and social history. His works included *The Formal Method in Literary Scholarship* (1928; Eng. trans. 1985; with P. N. Medvedev), and *The Dialogic Imagination* (1981), a collection of essays in English translation. ■ See biography by Katerina Clark and Michael Holquist (1984) and studies by Tzvetan Todorov (1984) and Ken Hirschkop (1999).

BAKST, LÉON (Lev Rosenberg; 1866–1924), Russian painter and theatrical designer. Bakst emerged from a poor Jewish family to establish himself as one of the world's most renowned artists. He began a career in theatrical design in 1900 at the Hermitage Court Theater and the Imperial Theater in St. Petersburg, where he was also involved in publishing the *World of Art* (1898–1904), and mounted an important exhibit of historical portraits (1905). In 1906, he exhibited in Paris, where he later settled. Despite his early contempt for ballet, Bakst became associated with Sergei Diaghilev's Ballet Russe (1909). The sumptuous decors and costumes he designed for such ballets as *Cleopatra* and *Scheherazade* revolutionized the decorative arts and influenced Art Deco. He also painted portraits of Diaghilev and others. ■ See biography by Charles Spencer (1973).

BALABANOFF, ANGELICA (1878–1965), Russian-born socialist leader. At the age of 19 Balabanoff renounced her upper-class existence and became a revolutionary in Western Europe. A confidante of the future Italian dictator Benito Mussolini (during his pre–World War I socialist days) and of the Russian revolutionary V. I. Lenin (see her *Impressions of Lenin*, 1964), Balabanoff was named first secretary of the Third International (1919). She traveled widely as a propagandist for the Soviet government before becoming disillusioned with the increasingly dictatorial methods of the bolsheviks. She left the Soviet Union (1923) and broke with the communists but remained an active international socialist leader for decades. ■ See her autobiography, *My Life as a Rebel* (1938) and Ronald Florence, *Marx's Daughters* (1975).

BALAGUER, JOAQUÍN (1907–   ), Dominican Republic political leader. Balaguer was a lawyer and law professor at the University of Santo Domingo (from 1938) who served as his country's ambassador to Colombia and Mexico during the 1940s. He advanced under the dictatorship of Rafael Trujillo to become a figurehead president (1960). After Trujillo's assissination (1961), Balaguer attempted to institute reforms but was forced to resign amid political turmoil (1962). He lived in exile in New York, founded the Reform party, and returned to Santo Domingo during the coup that provoked U.S. military intervention. He was elected president in 1966 with the support of business and the army, and was reelected in 1970 and 1974. He carried out effective reforms during his first term, but his last years in office were marked by high inflation rates and increasing political violence. He lost the election of 1978 but was returned to office in 1986 and served as president until 1996.

BALANCHINE, GEORGE (Georgi Balanchivadze; 1904–1983), Russian-born U.S. choreographer. The son of a prominent Georgian composer, Balanchine studied ballet and piano in St. Petersburg. After founding the Soviet State Dancers, he defected (1924) during a European tour. Impresario Sergei Diaghilev discovered him the following year; by age 21 Balanchine was ballet master and principal choreographer (1924–29) for the celebrated Ballet Russe, creating ten new ballets. In 1933 he was invited by Lincoln Kirstein to direct the new School of American Ballet in New York City. In this capacity, and later as founder (1948) of the New York City Ballet, Balanchine molded the classical style of contemporary American ballet. He stressed pure dance rather than storytelling in more than 90 choreographic works, which included *Serenade, Seven Deadly Sins, Don Quixote, The Nutcracker,* and *Agon.* ■ See study by George Taper (rev. ed. 1985) and Merrill Ashley, *Dancing for Balanchine* (1985).

BALCH, EMILY GREENE (1867–1961), U.S. pacifist leader. A graduate of Bryn Mawr College (1889), Balch helped found the Denison House settlement in Boston, the Women's Trade Union League, and taught politics and economics at Wellesley College (1897–1918). She actively promoted child-welfare and industrial reforms in Massachusetts and wrote a sympathetic study of immigration, *Our Slavic Fellow Citizens* (1910). During World War I she helped to organize the Women's International League for Peace and Freedom and served as its secretary (1919–22; 1934–35). Balch shared the 1946 Nobel Peace Prize with John R. Mott. ■ See Mercedes M. Randall, *Improper Bostonian* (1964).

BALCHEN, BERNT (1899–1973), Norwegian-born U.S. aviator and explorer. Initiated into polar aviation when he headed the successful Arctic air search (1925) for explorers Roald Amundsen and Lincoln Ellsworth, Balchen was brought to America by explorer Richard Byrd the following year. As copilot of Byrd's 1927 transatlantic flight, he successfully landed the fogbound and nearly fuelless craft within a short distance of the shore. He was later chief pilot for Byrd's first Antarctic expedition (1928–30), and was at the controls for the first flight over the South Pole (1929). Balchen became a U.S. citizen in 1931 and served in the U.S. Air Force. ■ See the autobiography, *Come North with Me* (1958) and Clayton Knight and Robert C. Durham, *Hitch Your Wagon* (1950).

BALCON, SIR MICHAEL ELIAS (1896–1977), British movie producer. A pioneer and legendary figure in the British film industry, Balcon made his first film in 1922. During the 1920s he "discovered" the director Alfred Hitchcock and produced some of his best films. Balcon was subsequently responsible for many of the most renowned English movies, including *Rome Express* (1932), *Man of Aran* (1934), *The 39 Steps* (1935), *Goodbye Mr. Chips* (1938), and *Tom Jones* (1963). He was best known for a series of post–World War II comedies that starred Alec Guinness and were produced at the Ealing Studios, which Balcon headed from 1938 to 1959. Known as the "Ealing comedies," they included *Kind Hearts and Coronets* (1949), *The Lavender Hill Mob* (1951), and *The Man in the White Suit* (1951). ■ See his autobiography, *Michael Balcon Presents . . . A Lifetime of Films* (1969).

BALDWIN, FAITH (1893–1978), U.S. writer. Baldwin shared the privileged world of her early life in upper-crust New York with millions of readers. Between 1921 and 1977 she published more than 85 books, including 60 novels that portrayed glamorous upright characters as they sorted out questions of love and affection. Her light fiction, which often reached the public through serializations or film adaptations, never reflected social reality and were most popular during the Depression years of the 1930s. Her books included *The Office Wife* (1930), *White Collar Girl* (1933), *Honor Bound* (1934), and *Private Duty* (1936).

BALDWIN, JAMES ARTHUR (1924–1987), U.S. writer. Born in Harlem, New York City's black ghetto, Baldwin was an ordained revivalist preacher at age 14 and a published essayist by age 21. Encouraged to pursue a literary career by novelist Richard Wright, he won two major literary fellowships and emigrated to Paris (1948), where he wrote the novels *Go Tell It on the Mountain* (1953) and *Giovanni's Room* (1956) and a collection of essays, *Notes of a Native Son* (1955), that probed the dehumanizing effects of racism and presented a frank treatment of homosexuality. Baldwin returned to the United States in 1957 and became a civil-rights activist. With the subsequent publication of his novels *Another Country* (1962) and *Tell Me How Long the Train's Been Gone* (1968), the plays *Blues for Mr. Charlie* (1964) and *The Amen Corner* (1965), and the essay collections *Nobody Knows My Name* (1961) and *The Fire Next Time* (1963), he was regarded as the most articulate literary spokesman of African Americans. His later works included *If Beale Street Could Talk* (1974) and *Just Above My Head* (1979). *The Price of the Ticket* (1985) was a collection of nonfiction. ■ See studies by Stanley Macebuh (1973), Louis H. Pratt (1978), and Carolyn W. Sylvander (1980); and the biography by James Campbell (1991).

BALDWIN, ROGER NASH (1884–1981), U.S. lawyer and reformer. Born into an aristocratic Boston family, Baldwin graduated from Harvard (B.A. 1904, M.A. 1905), and taught sociology at Washington University in St. Louis. He served as secretary of the reformist Civic League of St. Louis (1910–17) and was director of the American Union Against Militarism (1917). After spending nine months in prison as a conscientious objector during World War I (1918), he founded (1920) and directed (to 1950) the New York–based American Civil Liberties Union (ACLU), an organization dedicated to the protection of individual freedoms. He was also a member the International League for the Rights of Man and numerous civil rights and social welfare organizations. Although an active supporter of the left during the 1920s and 1930s, Baldwin joined no political parties and was primarily responsible for removing communists from the ACLU national board (1940). Over the years the ACLU defended such diverse clients as John T. Scopes in the "Monkey Trial" (1925), Sacco and Vanzetti, Henry Ford, the Jehovah's Witnesses, and the Ku Klux Klan. ■ See study by Peggy Lamson (1976).

BALDWIN, STANLEY, 1st EARL BALDWIN OF BEWDLEY (1867–1947), British political leader. Baldwin was a Conservative politician who cultivated the image of a simple country gentleman, campaigned under the slogan "safety first," and during three terms as prime minister (1923–24; 1924–29; 1935–37) tried to attain national "normalcy." Instead he was confronted with the 1926 general strike and the constitutional crisis arising from King Edward VIII's determination to marry a twice-divorced American woman, Wallis Simpson (1936). In the latter situation he intervened forcefully to secure the king's abdication. He was severely criticized for his lack of response to the growth of fascism in Europe. ■ See biographies by G. M. Young (1952), Keith Middlemas and John Barnes (1970), H. Montgomery Hyde (1973), and Kenneth Young (1976).

BALENCIAGA, CRISTÓBAL (1895–1972), Spanish fashion designer. A marquesa initially set up the 20-year-old Balenciaga—the son of a seamstress—in his own dressmaking firm. He established *couture* houses in San Sebastián, Madrid, and Barcelona, but was driven (1937) to Paris by the Spanish civil war. Backed by other refugees, he opened a new shop; winning fame for his first line, he was the most influential fashion innovator over the next three decades. Balenciaga gave women's dresses a new silhouette, doing away with the constructed, fitted tunic, and later the straight chemise, the famous "sack," and the shift, dressmakers around the world followed suit. Known as a "designers' designer," Balenciaga trained such prominent stylists as Hubert de Givenchy and André Courrèges. The rather solitary designer retired in the late 1960s, dispirited by declining taste in the fashion world. In 1973, he was the first couturier to be the subject of a solo exhibition at New York's Metropolitan Museum of Art. ■ See study by Marie-Andree Jouve (1989).

BALEWA, SIR ABUBAKAR TAFAWA (1912–1966), Nigerian political leader. The son of a slave, Balewa attended the school of education of the University of London (1945) and advanced to a senior position in the Nigerian civil service. A founder of the Northern People's Congress party, established to secure northern dominence in national politics, he was elected to the federal house of representatives in 1951 and in 1957 was appointed first chief minister (later called prime minister) of Nigeria. When Nigeria achieved independence from Britain (1960), he continued in that post. Although he was a popular, moderate reformer, he was confronted with constant unrest, which culminated in the 1966 coup in which he was killed. ■ See biography by Trevor Clark, *A Right Honourable Gentleman* (1989).

BALFOUR, ARTHUR JAMES BALFOUR, 1st EARL OF (1848–1930), British political leader. Balfour was a cultured intellectual who pursued an avocation in metaphysics during 50 years in politics. As Conservative prime minister (1902–05), he was responsible for educational reform, Irish land reform, and the 1904 entente with France. Later, as foreign secretary (1916–19), he gave his name to a 1917 declaration favoring a Jewish "national home" in Palestine. Balfour's writings included *Theism and Humanism* (1915) and *Chapters of Autobiography* (1930). ■ See biographies by Blanche Dugdale (2 vols., 1936), Kenneth Young (1963), Sidney H. Zebel (1973), and Ruddock F. Mackay (1985).

BALL, LUCILLE DESIREE (1911–1989), U.S. actress and producer. Ball began acting in high school theatricals, enrolled for a brief stint at New York City's John Murray Anderson–Robert Milton Dramatic School, and broke into show business using the stage name Diane Belmont. She had little success until appearances as the Chesterfield cigarette girl made her expressive features and flaming red hair familiar to the American public. Ball made more than 30 films in the 1930s and 1940s, and when it became increasingly clear that comedy was her forte, she moved into radio with a role in "My Favorite Husband" (1947). Her television show "I Love Lucy," with husband Desi Arnaz, premiered in 1951. Filmed before a live audience, the series showcased her zany slapstick talents and remained enormously popular, winning five Emmy Awards and extending to 179 episodes. Ball went on to make almost an equal number of episodes on "The Lucy Show" (1962–68) and "Here's Lucy" (1968–74). She also starred in the Broadway hit *Wildcat* (1960) and later in the film *Mame* (1974). She presided over Desilu Productions (1962–67) and founded (1968) Lucille Ball Productions. ■ See biography by James Gregory (1974); Bart Andrews and Thomas J. Watson, *Loving Lucy* (1980); Charles Higham, *Lucy* (1986); and Kathleen Brady, *Lucille* (1994).

BALLA, GIACOMO (1871–1958), Italian painter. Influenced by French impressionism during a visit to Paris, Balla returned to Italy with new interest in color and light problems in painting. He was a leader of the pre–World War I futurist movement, which utilized cubist techniques to translate to painting the physical aggression and speed of the modern machine world. His best-known painting was *Dynamism of a Dog on a Leash* (1912), which depicted in slow-motion style the aspects of a woman's and a dog's legs as they walk. He was particularly concerned with abstract arrangements of color, light, and rhythm. Balla designed futurist rooms for the International Exhibition of Decorative Arts (Paris, 1925) and continued experimenting with the expression of motion and light on canvas long after futurism declined. ■ See studies by Virginia Dorazio (1969) and Susan B. Robinson (1981).

BALLANTYNE, DAVID (1924–1986), New Zealand novelist. Ballantyne was a journalist in Auckland and London (1955–65). He recorded provincial scenes in realistic novels such as *The Cunninghams* (1948) and *The Last Pioneer* (1963), dreary glimpses of New Zealand during the Depression. He satirized the values of a business tycoon in *A Friend of the Family* (1966) and turned to parody in *Sydney Bridge Upside Down* (1968). His later novels included *The Talkback Man* (1978) and *The Penfriend* (1980). He also wrote short stories and numerous television scripts.

BALMAIN, PIERRE ALEXANDRE (1914–1982), French fashion designer. Balmain's architecture studies were cut short when financial difficulties forced him to go to work. He found employment in Paris' fashion industry, working for such renowned couturiers as Edward Molyneux (1934–39) and Lucien Lelong (1940–45). After he abandoned early plans to open a *couture* house with young colleague Christian Dior, he established his own house (1945), designing subdued fashions for an exclusive clientele that at one time included author Gertrude Stein, as well as the queen of Belgium and many movie stars of the 1950s. ■ See his memoirs, *My Years and Seasons* (Eng. trans. 1965).

BALTHUS (Balthasar Klossowski de Rola; 1908–2001), French-born artist. Balthus' Jewish mother and Polish aristocrat father were both artists and he spent his early years amidst artists and intellectuals in Paris, Berne, Geneva, and Berlin. A precocious talent, he was encouraged to paint by his parents' friends, including Rainer Maria Rilke, Pierre Bonnard, and André Derain, but avoided academies and was mainly self-taught. His style reflected the realism of the old masters but his subjects were influenced by his fascinations with surrealism and the unconscious. Balthus' large, mysterious, dreamlike canvases included pensive adolescent girls in disturbing poses (*The Guitar Lesson,* 1934; *The Room,* 1954), views of urban street life (*The Street,* 1933; *Passage du Commerce—St. André,* 1954), rustic landscapes (*The Mountain,* 1937), and striking portraits (*André Derain,* 1936). He also created notable stage designs for Antonin Artaud. He served as director of the French Academy in Rome (1961–77). ■ See biography by Nicholas Fox Weber (1999).

BALTIMORE, DAVID (1938–   ), U.S. microbiologist. Baltimore worked at the Salk Institute with Renato Dulbecco's virology group (1965–68) before joining the Massachusetts Institute of Technology's Center for Cancer Research in 1968. In researching the links between viruses and cancer he discovered the "reverse transcriptase" enzyme, which demonstrated how genetic information could be transferred from RNA (ribonucleic acid) to DNA (deoxyribonucleic acid) and thus helped scientists to understand how viruses could cause a normal cell to become malignant. He shared the 1975 Nobel Prize for Physiology or Medicine with Dulbecco and Howard Temin. He was named president of Rockefeller University (1990) but was forced to leave the post one year later after being enmeshed in a science-fraud scandal involving a scientist with whom he had coauthored a paper. All charges were eventually (1996) dismissed. Baltimore subsequently headed an AIDS-vaccine research committee set up by the National Institutes of Health (1996) and served as president of the California Institute of Technology (Caltech; 1997–   ). ■ See Daniel J. Kevles, *The Baltimore Case* (1998).

BA MAW (1893–1977), Burmese political leader. Ba Maw, the son of a former royal court official, received a Western education (Rangoon College, Calcutta University, Cambridge, and Bordeaux University) and converted to Christianity. He became a lawyer in Burma (1924) and gained wide recognition for his legal defense of fellow nationalist Saya Sen in the 1930s. He allied himself with the most radical nationalist factions and served as prime minister (1937–39). He later served the Japanese World War II puppet government (1942–45) as head of state, only to be jailed in 1945 by the Allies. Although never again a major actor in Burmese politics, he was a critic of Premier Ne Win's government and was jailed (1966–68). ■ See his memoirs, *Breakthrough in Burma* (1968).

BANACH, STEFAN (1892–1945), Polish mathematician. A student and later faculty member at the Institute of Technology in Lvov, USSR (1919–41; 1944–45), Banach introduced the concept of normed linear spaces (subsequently called Banach spaces) and made important contributions to the theory of measure and integration, orthogonal series, set theory, and general topology. He was best known, however, as the founder of modern functional analysis.

BANCROFT, ANNE (Anne-Marie Italiano; 1931–   ), U.S. actress. When Bancroft first acted professionally on such television shows as "Studio One" and "The Goldbergs," she was listed in the credits as Anne Marno. After her roles won her a screen test, she was given a contract and a new name. Bancroft made several films in the early 1950s, but she gained prominence with her performance (1958) opposite Henry Fonda in the stage play *Two for the Seesaw,* for which she won a Tony Award. She went on to play Anne Sullivan in *The Miracle Worker* (1959; Tony Award), perhaps her best-known role; she worked intensively with blind children to prepare for this role of Helen Keller's teacher. Her performance in the film adaptation won a 1962 Academy Award. Bancroft appeared onstage in such plays as *Mother Courage* (1963), *The Devils* (1965), and *Golda* (1977) and in numerous films, including *The Pumpkin Eater* (1964), *The Graduate* (1967), *The Turning Point* (1977), *To Be or Not to Be* (1983), *Agnes of God* (1985), *84 Charing Cross Road* (1987), and *Torch Song Trilogy* (1988). She was married to director Mel Brooks (from 1964). ■ See Will Holtzman, *Seesaw* (1979).

BANDA, HASTINGS KAMUZU (1902?–1997), president of Malawi. Born to a very poor family in Nyasaland, Banda worked his way to the United States, where he earned a medical degree (1937). He settled in Britain (1939–53) and in the Gold Coast (later Ghana; 1954–58) before he returned home in 1958 to lead the nationalist campaign against the white-dominated Central African Federation, which linked Nyasaland with the Rhodesias. Successfully dismantling the federation, Banda led the territory to independence (1964), proclaiming the republic of Malawi with himself as chief executive (1966). A pragmatist rather than idealist, he was the first black African leader to visit South Africa (1970) and establish commercial ties with it. A paternalistic ruler of a one-party state. Banda barred all public criticism of his government and was named president for life in 1971. Forced by international pressure to hold free presidential elections, he was defeated at the polls in 1994 and lost power. ■ See biography by Philip Short (1974) and T. David Williams, *Malawi, the Politics of Despair* (1978).

BANDARANAIKE, SIRIMAVO (Sirimavo Ratwatte; 1916–2000), Sri Lankan political leader. Bandaranaike was from a wealthy landowning family and received a Catholic convent education before she married (1940) Solomon Bandaranaike. In 1960, following the assassination (1959) of her husband, the prime minister, she became the world's first woman prime minister. As head of socialist coalition governments (1960–65; 1970–77) Bandaranaike nationalized schools, insurance companies, and foreign-owned tea and rubber plantations. In 1971 she barely survived a radical leftist revolt against her, and she imprisoned thousands of suspected opponents without charges or trial for five years. In 1972 a new constitution was proclaimed and the name of Ceylon was changed to the Republic of Sri Lanka. In 1980 she was accused of misuse of power, stripped of her civil rights, and expelled from parliament. She returned to parliament in 1987 and subsequently served as prime minister (1994–2000), a largely ceremonial position.

BANDARANAIKE, SOLOMON WEST RIDGEWAY DIAS (1899–1959), Ceylonese political leader. Bandaranaike was a wealthy, Oxford-educated, nationalist lawyer who gave up his Western ways and converted to Buddhism in 1931. He held many government posts until Ceylon (now called Sri

Lanka) achieved independence (1948) and then served in the House of Representatives; he was elected prime minister (1956) as head of a nationalist-socialist coalition. His government pursued a neutralist foreign policy, removed British military bases from Ceylon, and established Sinhalese as the official national language. He was assassinated by a fanatical Buddhist monk. ■ See James Manor, *The Expedient Utopian* (1989).

BANDEIRA, MANUEL (1886–1968), Brazilian writer. Bandeira's early poems were influenced by symbolism, but after 1922 he became a leader of the modernist movement and wrote simple, often despondent, poetry, using colloquial language to describe ordinary lives and situations. His *Collected Works* (2 cols.) appeared in 1958. English translations of his poems are in *This Earth, That Sky* (1989). A professor of literature in Rio de Janeiro (1938–56), he was also known for his essays, criticism, and biographies and for his *Brief History of Brazilian Literature* (1940; Eng. trans. 1958).

BANERJEA, SIR SURENDRANATH (1848–1925), Indian nationalist. A Bengali Brahmin who was educated in India and Britain, Banerjea was only the second Indian to pass the colonial civil-service examinations (1869). In 1874 he became a nationalist and the following year began a 37-year career as a professor in Calcutta. He also published the liberal, nationalist newspaper *Bengalee* (from 1878). A founder of the Indian National Congress party (1885) and later its president (1895, 1902), Banerjea was a moderate, committed to constitutional reforms and methods, who opposed the tactics of both Mahatma Gandhi and the extremists. Late in life he served as minister of local self-government in Bengal (1921–24) and he was isolated from the nationalist movement. ■ See his autobiography, *A Nation in the Making* (1925), and Daniel Argov, *Moderates and Extremists in the Indian National Movement* (1967).

BANERJI, BIBHUTI BHUSAN (1894–1950), Indian writer. One of the most popular and prolific modern Bengali writers, Banerji wrote compassionate novels reflecting his faith in essential human goodness and his love of nature. The novel *Pather Panchali* (1929; Eng. trans. as *Pather Panchali: Song of the Road*, 1968), a series of episodes in the life of a poor Bengali Brahmin family, was regarded as his masterpiece. Together with its sequel, *Aparajito* (1932), it was made into a celebrated film trilogy by director Satyajit Ray (*Pather Panchali*, 1955; *Aparajito*, 1956; *The World of Apu*, 1959). *Ashani Samket* (1959), a novel dealing with the Bengal famine of 1943, was filmed by Ray as *Distant Thunder* (1973).

BANKS, DENNIS (1931?–), U.S. Indian leader. Banks was a cofounder in the late 1960s of the militant American Indian Movement (AIM) and became a nationally known activist for Indian rights. Arrested (1973) and convicted (1975) of riot and assault during a protest demonstration in Custer, South Dakota, Banks jumped bail before sentencing and fled to California. He was granted sanctuary by Gov. Edmund G. Brown, Jr., and became a teacher and administrator of the Deganawidah-Quetzacoatl (D-Q) University (1979–83), a two-year community college near Davis, California. When Brown's term was up, Banks fled to an Indian reservation in New York State (1982), but he returned to South Dakota to serve his sentence (1984). He was paroled in 1985. He headed the organization Sacred Run and appeared in several films, including *The Last of the Mohicans* (1992). ■ See K.S. Stern, *Loud Hawk: The U.S. versus the American Indian Movement* (1994) and J. W. Sayer, *Ghost Dancing the Law: The Wounded Knee Trials* (1997).

BANNA, HASSAN AL- (1906–1949), Egyptian political leader. An Islamic fundamentalist, al-Banna was a schoolteacher who feared that Westernization was a threat to Islam. In 1929 he organized the Muslim Brotherhood, which sought to reform the political, economic, and social life of Muslim nations strictly according to the teachings of the Koran. A powerful orator and skilled organizer, he attracted thousands of followers in Egypt and throughout the Arab world in opposition to existing governments. Although never a parliamentary force, the brotherhood maintained a paramilitary youth wing, held numerous street demonstrations, and was involved in political assassinations. After the brotherhood was banned by Premier Nukrashi (December 1948), Nukrashi was assassinated by members of the brotherhood. In retaliation, al-Banna was assassinated two months later. ■ See *Five Tracts of Hasan al-Banna* (1978) and Richard P. Mitchell, *The Society of the Muslim Brothers* (1969).

BANNISTER, SIR ROGER GILBERT (1929–), British mile runner. In a track meet at Oxford on May 6, 1954, Bannister ran a mile in 3 minutes 59.4 seconds. He thus became the first man to run that distance in less than 4 minutes, a feat many had thought impossible. A graduate of St. Mary's Hospital Medical School (1954), Bannister subsequently wrote several articles on the physiology of exercise and became a succcessful London neurologist. ■ See his autobiographical *The Four Minute Mile* (1955).

BANTING, SIR FREDERICK GRANT (1891–1941), Canadian medical scientist. Banting's search for the internal secretion of the pancreas, conducted at the University of Toronto with assistant Charles Best, resulted in the successful extraction of the hormone insulin (1921). Insulin proved crucial for treating diabetes in humans; its injection allows diabetics to lead relatively normal lives. Banting shared the 1923 Nobel Prize for Physiology or Medicine with J. J. R. Macleod. The Banting Research Foundation was established in 1924, and six years later the Banting Institute was founded in Toronto. Banting was also a pioneer in aviation medicine and cancer research. He was killed in a plane crash while on a war mission. ■ See biography by Lloyd Stevenson (1946), John Rowland, *The Insulin Man* (1966) and Michael Bliss, *The Discovery of Insulin* (1982).

BAO DAI (Nguyen Vinh Thuy; 1913–1997), Vietnamese emperor. Bao Dai, the son of Annamese Emperor Khai Din, was brought up to believe that he would rule under the French colonial administration. Except for a brief stay in 1926 to attend formal ceremonies that made him the 13th emperor of Annam, he lived in France from 1922 to 1932. He then ruled powerlessly under the French and the Japanese (1932–45). In 1945, at the end of World War II, he was forced to abdicate in favor of Ho Chi Minh's leftist Vietnamese government, and he went into exile in 1946. In 1949 he returned to set up an anticommunist Vietnamese government subservient to the French. After the Geneva Settlement (1954), he was forced by France and the United States to accept Ngo Dinh Diem as premier, while he served as a figurehead monarch. In 1955 a referendum made South Vietnam a republic, and Bao Dai returned to France and remained there for the rest of his life.

BARA, THEDA (Theodosia Goodman; 1890?–1955), U.S. film actress. The daughter of a Jewish tailor, Theda Bara had a quiet and unexotic Cincinnati, Ohio, upbringing, but Fox Studio publicists successfully created the enticing myth that she was born in the Sahara and that her name was an anagram for "Arab Death." From 1915 to 1919, during which she starred in more than 40 films, she was the undisputed queen of the movies. The prototypical "vamp," she appeared as the sultry but heartless seductress in such films as *A Fool There Was, Sin, The Vampire, Salome, Carmen, Cleopatra, The She Devil,* and *Siren's Song* and was an international sensation. ■ See biography by Ronald Genini (1996) and Eve Golden, *Vamp* (1996).

BARAKA, IMAMU AMIRI (LeRoi Jones; 1934–), U.S. poet and playwright. A controversial and prolific African-American cultural figure, Jones grew up in Newark, New Jersey, studied at Howard University (B.A. 1954), and served (1954–57) in the air force. After several years as a Greenwich Village poet, he moved to Harlem, wrote a series of violently antiwhite plays, including *Dutchman* (1964), *The Slave* (1964), *The Baptism* (1966), and *The Toilet* (1966), and founded the Black Arts Repertory Theater. Returning to Newark (1966) to head Spirit House, a cultural center, he converted to Islam and adopted an African name. He became a leader of the black cultural nationalist movement and was active in local politics. In the 1970s he turned to Marxism and wrote *The Motion of History and Other Plays* (1978), in which he sought to unify blacks and whites in order to overcome the capitalist system, which he considered their common enemy. His other works included the novel *The System of Dante's Hell* (1965), *Tales* (1967), *Crit-*

ical Essays (1978), *Selected Plays and Prose* (1979), *The Music: Reflections on Jazz and Blues* (1987), and *Eulogies* (1996). His poetry appeared in *Selected Poetry* (1979), *Transbluesency* (1995), and *Funk Lore* (1996). Baraka taught at the State University of New York at Stony Brook (1983–). ■ See *The Autobiography of LeRoi Jones* (1984) and studies by Kimberly W. Benston (1976), Werner Sollors (1978), Lloyd W. Brown (1980), and William J. Harris (1986).

BARAN, PAUL (1910–1964), U.S. economist. A specialist in the study of underdeveloped countries, Baran was a professor at Stanford University (1949–64). His influential book, *The Political Economy of Growth* (1956), which dealt with underdevelopment, was considered a classic of Marxist analysis. He also wrote *Monopoly Capital* (1966; with Paul Sweezy) and *The Longer View* (1970). ■ See study edited by Paul Sweezy and Leo Huberman (1965).

BÁRÁNY, ROBERT (1876–1936), Austro-Swedish otologist. A Viennese-born-and-trained physician, Bárány was best known for his pioneering studies of the balancing apparatus of the inner ear and its relationship to the cerebellum. He devised tests to diagnose inner-ear diseases and was the first to treat otosclerosis, an important cause of deafness. While a prisoner of war of the Russians in Siberia (1915), Bárány learned that he had been awarded the 1914 Nobel Prize for Physiology or Medicine. From 1917 to 1936 he taught otology and headed the ear, nose, and throat clinic at Uppsala University in Sweden.

BARBER, SAMUEL (1910–1981), U.S. composer. A neoromantic in an age of dissonance, Barber established his reputation with *Adagio for Strings* (1936) and *Essay No. 1 for Orchestra* (1937). His music is traditional in form and noted for its lyricism, refinement, and logic of design. *Vanessa,* Barber's Pulitzer Prize–winning opera (1958), with text by his friend the composer and librettist Gian Carlo Menotti, is considered one of the most significant American operas of the century, but the composer was widely admired for many other works, including *Hermit Songs* (1952–53), *Concerto for Piano and Orchestra* (1962; Pulitzer Prize), and the opera *Antony and Cleopatra* (1966). ■ See biography by Nathan Broder (1954) and study by Barbara B. Heyman (1992).

BARBERA, JOSEPH. *SEE HANNA, WILLIAM.*

BARBIROLLI, SIR JOHN (Giovanni Battista Barbirolli; 1899–1970), British conductor. Son of an Italian father and French mother, Barbirolli was born over a London bakery shop and began to study music as a child. He attended the Royal Academy of Music and played cello for the Queen's Hall Orchestra before World War I. In 1924 he founded his own chamber orchestra and in 1927 began conducting opera at Convent Garden. Appointed to succeed Arturo

Toscanini as conductor of the New York Philharmonic (1937), he suffered by comparison to the old maestro but remained in New York for seven controversial years. He then returned to wartime England to restore the Hallé Orchestra of Manchester to European prominence (1943–68). A small, intense man renowned for his romantic repertory, Barbirolli made many guest appearances in Europe and the United States and between 1961 and 1967 divided his time between Hallé and the Houston (Texas) Symphony Orchestra. ■ See biographies by Charles Reid (1971) and Michael Kennedy (1972).

BARBOSA, RUY (1849–1923), Brazilian political leader, scholar, diplomat, and journalist. An ardent civil libertarian and political reformer, Barbosa, a lawyer, was a leader of the antislavery movement in the 1870s and 1880s. After the 1889 revolution he served as minister of finance and of justice and was chief architect of Brazil's new constitution (1891). An internationalist, he won acclaim for his eloquent pleas in favor of the legal equality of all nations (at the Second Hague Conference, 1907), and he was elected to the Permanent Court of Arbitration (1908) and the Permanent Court of International Justice (1921). Barbosa served for many years in the Brazilian senate and twice ran unsuccessfully for the presidency (1910; 1919). He also wrote prolifically on sociology, jurisprudence, and politics and was considered one of the foremost prose stylists in the Portuguese language. ■ See biography by Charles W. Turner (1945).

BARBUSSE, HENRI (1873–1935), French novelist. Barbusse was a journalist before he was wounded in World War I. He gained fame with his pacifist account of the horrors of trench warfare, *Under Fire* (1916; Eng. trans. 1917), which denounced the war and the exploitation of the soldiers. He became a militant communist (1923) and was a leader of the antifascist movements of the 1930s. His later works included biographies of *Jesus* (1927; Eng. trans. 1927) and *Zola* (1932; Eng. trans. 1932) and a Marxist epic, *Chains* (1925; Eng. trans. 1925). ■ See his memoirs *I Saw It Myself* (1928; Eng. trans. 1928).

BARDEEN, JOHN (1908–1991), U.S. physicist. Working at the Bell Telephone Laboratories (1945–51), Bardeen collaborated with William Shockley and Walter Brattain to develop (1947) the transistor, a solid-state device that proved more efficient than the bulky vacuum tube. Bardeen and his co-workers shared the 1956 Nobel Prize for Physics for their invention. He continued his research into semiconductors while a professor at the University of Illinois (1951–75) and helped to develop the "BCS" theory of superconductivity, demonstrating that the electrical resistance of some metals is eliminated at extremely low temperatures. When this work earned Bardeen and co-workers Leon Cooper and John Schrieffer the 1972 Nobel Prize for Physics, he became the first person to win two Nobel prizes in the same field.

BARDOT, BRIGITTE (1934–   ), French film actress. Daughter of a French industrialist, Bardot began as a model and became an international sex symbol with the release of *And God Created Woman* in 1956. After a series of sex comedies in which she occasionally appeared nude, the pouting, blond woman-child played a caricature of herself in *Contempt* (1963). She also starred in *The Truth* (1960) and *Viva Maria* (1965). After she retired (1973) she was active in the animal rights movement. ■ See study by Peter Evans (1973) and biographies by Will Frischauer (1978), Glenys Roberts (1985), and Jeffrey Robinson (1994).

BAREA, ARTURO (1897–1957), Spanish novelist. Barea is best known for his autobiographical trilogy *The Forging of a Rebel* (*The Forge* [Eng. trans. 1941], *The Track* [Eng. trans. 1943], *The Clash* [Eng. trans. 1946]), which first appeared in notable English translations by his Austrian wife Ilsa Barea. Through his personal experience, he recounts the anguish of the Spanish civil war (1936–39), and particularly the siege of Madrid, communicating spiritual as well as political resistance. *The Broken Root* (Eng. trans. 1952) fantasizes the secret return of an exile to Spain. See also his literary study, *Lorca: The Poet and His People* (Eng. trans. 1949).

BARKLA, CHARLES GLOVER (1877–1944), British physicist. In his third year at Cambridge, Barkla began research on X rays, a topic that occupied him for the rest of his life. From 1913 on he taught at the University of Edinburgh. His study of secondary radiation occurring when a gas is exposed to X rays resulted in the discovery that the emission of characteristic radiation is an atomic property. This research indicated a correlation between the number of electrons in an atom and the positioning of the element in the periodic table; it also supported the hypothesis that X rays are light rays of shortwave length. Barkla received the Nobel Prize for Physics in 1916 "for his discovery of the characteristic X radiation of the elements."

BARLACH, ERNST (1870–1938), German sculptor and graphic artist. Barlach's art studies in Hamburg, Dresden, and Paris enabled him to develop a distinct style based on German medieval sculpture. His medievalism sparked renewed interest in wood carvings; his sculptural style was heavily cubist with Gothic aspects of expression. Barlach's graphic art depicted human suffering. Named to the Berlin Academy of Fine Arts (1920), he achieved fame for German war memorials and religious sculptures created in the 1920s, but his work was later condemned as "degenerate" by the Nazi government and over 300 pieces were confiscated and destroyed. Barlach also wrote expressionist drama. ■ See studies by Alfred Werner (1966), Carl D. Carls (rev. ed. 1969), and Kent W. Hooper (1987).

BARNARD, CHESTER IRVING (1886–1961), U.S. businessman, public administrator and management theorist.

Barnard was an employee of the American Telephone and Telegraph Co. (from 1909) and president of its subsidiary, New Jersey Bell Telephone Co. (1927–48). His influential book, *Functions of the Executive* (1938), based on his organizational experiences, was regarded as a classic of business theory. He served as president of the United Service Organizations (USO) during World War II (1941–45) and helped write the state department's report on the international control of atomic energy (1946), which became the basis for postwar American nuclear policy. He later served as president of the Rockefeller Foundation (1948–52) and chairman of the National Science Foundation (1952–54). ■ See William B. Wolf, *The Basic Barnard* (1974).

BARNARD, CHRISTIAAN NEETHLING (1922–), South African surgeon. While a student at the University of Minnesota (1956–58), Barnard trained under the famed heart surgeon C. Walton Lillehei. Upon returning to Cape Town, he introduced open-heart surgery, designed artificial heart valves, and performed heart-transplant operations on dogs. On Dec. 3, 1967, Barnard performed the first human-heart transplant. Although the patient, Louis Washkansky, died 18 days later of pneumonia, the transplant itself was successful, and his second patient lived for 594 days with a new heart. ■ See his autobiography (1970; with Curtis Bill Pepper) and the biography by L. E. Leipold (1971).

BARNARD, EDWARD EMERSON (1857–1923), U.S. astronomer. Known chiefly for his work in celestial photography, Barnard was a professor at the University of Chicago (1895–1923) and astronomer at the Yerkes Observatory, Williams Bay, Wisconsin. He discovered 16 comets in his lifetime and was the first to observe (1892) Jupiter's fifth satellite, adding to those sighted by Galileo in 1610. Barnard's photographic study of the Milky Way elucidated the structural details of the galaxy and indicated that its darker regions were dark clouds of gases. In 1916 he discovered Barnard's star, a faint star with the largest-known proper motion (apparent shift in position relative to other stars). ■ See William Sheehan, *The Immortal Fire Within* (1995).

BARNES, ALBERT COOMBS (1872–1951), U.S. physician, scientist, and art collector. After medical and scientific training in America and Europe, Barnes developed an antiseptic, noncaustic silver nitrate compound called Argyrol (1902), which was a tremendous commercial success and made him a millionaire. He held informal seminars on philosophy and art for the employees of his Argyrol factory, and he decorated the workrooms with his first art purchases. In 1922, he established the Barnes Foundation, intended to foster impartial study of artistic expression of all periods; in 1925 he housed his collection in a 26-room gallery near Philadelphia. Recognized as the owner of the best and largest collection of 19th- and 20th-century French art— particularly works by Renoir and Cézanne—Barnes was in-

fluential in promoting such painters as Paul Guillaume, Pablo Picasso, and Henri Matisse. An art critic as well as collector, he wrote *The Art in Painting* (1926), which he dedicated to his friend and associate, the educator John Dewey, and collaborated with Violette de Mazia on many books of artists works. ■ See William Schack, *Art and Argyrol* (1960) and Howard Greenfeld, *The Devil and Dr. Barnes* (1987).

BARNES, DJUNA (1892–1982), U.S. novelist, playwright, and artist. Barnes, a well-known avant-garde figure of the 1920s and 1930s, began her career as a journalist. She herself illustrated her first book, *The Book of Repulsive Women* (1915); *A Book* (1923, republished as *A Night Among the Horses,* 1929), offered stories, poems, and illustrations. The satirical novel *Ryder* (1928) experimented with stream of consciousness, a technique used in Barnes' masterpiece, *Nightwood* (1937), which was characterized by the poet T. S. Eliot as having "a quality of doom and horror very nearly related to that of Elizabethan tragedy." Several of her plays were produced by the Provincetown Players. *Spillway* (1962) reprinted Barnes' short fiction of 1929. ■ See her *Selected Works* (1962); biographies by Andrew Field (1983) and Phillip F. Herring (1995); and Louis F. Kannenstine, *The Art of Djuna Barnes* (1977).

BARNES, HARRY ELMER (1889–1968), U.S. historian and sociologist. A wide-ranging and prolific scholar and polemicist, Barnes aroused great controversy by blaming the Allies for starting World War I (*Genesis of the World War,* 1926), by debunking orthodox religion (*The Twilight of Christianity,* 1929), by proposing revolutionary changes in the penal and judiciary systems, and by opposing U.S. entry into World War II. He was an advocate of the New History, which called for the integration of the social sciences into the discipline, and made important contributions in the areas of historiography and cultural history. He taught at several colleges and was a social commentator for the Scripps-Howard newspapers (1929–40). Among his best-known books were *The New History and the Social Studies* (1925), *History of Historical Writing* (1937), and *An Intellectual and Cultural History of the Western World* (1937). ■ See Arthur Goddard, ed., *The Learned Crusader* (1968).

BARNET, RICHARD J. (1929–), U.S. political analyst. A graduate of Harvard University (B.A. 1952, LL.B. 1954), Barnet worked for the U.S. Arms Control and Disarmament Agency and as a state department consultant during the administration of Pres. John F. Kennedy, but became disillusioned with U.S. foreign and domestic policies. In 1963 he cofounded (with Marcus Raskin) the Institute for Policy Studies, a Washington, D.C.–based left-liberal think tank that issued widely read scholarly critiques of U.S. national security policies, domestic economic programs, and international economic relations. Barnet, a prominent critic of U.S. involvement in Vietnam and other areas of the Third World, codirected the Institute until 1978. In his writings he urged a détente with the Soviet Union, a nuclear weapons freeze, and the conservation of oil and other vital natural resources. His books included *Intervention and Revolution: The United States in the Third World* (1968), *The Economy of Death* (1969), *Roots of War* (1972), *Global Reach: The Power of the Multinational Corporations* (1974; with Ronald E. Müller), *The Lean Years: Politics in the Age of Scarcity* (1980), and *Real Security* (1981).

BAROJA Y NESSI, PÍO (1872–1956), Spanish novelist. Baroja, of Basque descent, gave up his medical practice to run a Madrid bakery. When the shop failed, he devoted himself to literature at the age of 30. He produced over 100 novels with various settings, stressing action rather than plot or character. As part of the "Generation of 1898," he criticized Spanish decadence and political hypocrisy. He bypassed religion or art in his search for truth, trusting only philosophical speculation and science, and wrote brusque, direct accounts of rebels and outcasts. His best-known novels included the trilogy *La Lucha por la Vida* (1904; Eng. trans. *The Quest*, 1922; *Weeds*, 1923; *Red Dawn*, 1924), *Caesar or Nothing* (1910; Eng. trans. 1919), and *The Tree of Knowledge* (1911; Eng. trans. 1928). *Youth and Egolatry* (1917; Eng. trans. 1920) was autobiographical. ■ See study by Beatrice P. Patt (1971).

BARON, SALO WITTMAYER (1895–1989), Austrian-born U.S. historian and sociologist. Baron earned three doctorates from the University of Vienna—in philosophy (1917), political science (1922), and law (1923)—and was also ordained by Vienna's Jewish Theological Seminary (1920). He taught at Columbia University in New York (1930–63), directed its Center of Israel and Jewish Studies (1950–68), and occupied the first American chair in Jewish history. A prolific writer in many languages, Baron wrote a comprehensive *Social and Religious History of the Jews* (18 vols., 1952–83) as well as a history of the Jewish community in the American revolution (3 vols., 1942). ■ See biography by Robert Liberles (1995).

BARR, ALFRED HAMILTON, JR. (1902–1981), U.S. art historian and museum director. Barr studied art history at Princeton. In 1929, at age 27, he became the first director of New York's Museum of Modern Art (MOMA) and was instrumental in making it the world's leading institution for 20th-century art. His brilliant, daring acquisitions brought to MOMA an unmatched collection of modern paintings, sculpture, and artifacts that by the time of his retirement 38 years later included 2,622 items. The landmark exhibitions he mounted shaped American taste, and his innovative multidepartmental plan for organizing the museum helped to establish architecture, film, photography, and industrial and theater design as major art forms. Demoted in 1943 by trustees who questioned his administrative skill and deplored his more unconventional shows, Barr returned to ac-

ademia, earning a Harvard Ph.D. at age 44 (1946). Thereafter he was MOMA's director of museum collections (1946–67). Barr wrote *Cubism and Abstract Art* (1936), *What Is Modern Painting?* (1946), *Picasso: Fifty Years of His Art* (1946), and *Matisse: His Art and His Public* (1951). After his retirement he completed the catalog *Paintings and Sculpture in the Museum of Modern Art 1929–1967* (1977). ■ See Russell Lynes, *Good Old Modern* (1973), and biography by Alice G. Marquis (1989).

BARR, ROSEANNE. *See ROSEANNE.*

BARRACLOUGH, GEOFFREY (1908–   ), British historian. In *The Origins of Modern Germany* (1946), Barraclough, then professor of medieval history at the University of Liverpool (1945–56), sought the origins of contemporary problems in medieval history. In the vein of Arnold Toynbee, whom he succeeded at the University of London (1956–62), he conceived of history as a succession of cycles, not an unbroken continuum, and predicted the decline of the West in favor of "more efficient forms of mass democracy." Barraclough, who also favored the use of science and statistics to make history more than just "high-class entertainment," later taught modern history at the University of California, Brandeis, and Oxford. His other books included *An Introduction to Contemporary History* (1964) and *Main Trends in History* (1979).

BARRAULT, JEAN-LOUIS (1910–1994), French actor, director, and producer. Barrault worked (1931–35) under Charles Dullin at the Théâtre de l'Atelier and studied mime with Étienne Decroux. Forming an independent studio with other actors, he worked with such men as surrealist author André Breton and theorist Antonin Artaud. During World War II and the Nazi occupation of Paris, he acted under Jacques Copeau's direction at the Comédie Française. After the war, Barrault and actress wife Madeleine Renaud together formed their own company, which staged (1947–56) productions at the Théâtre Marigny. Barrault later directed (from 1959) the national Théâtre de France, staging many revivals; he was dismissed after the theater was occupied by student protesters in the 1968 uprising. Barrault stressed exaggerated gesture and pantomime techniques and was particularly skillful at farce and comedy. His own mime performance was featured in Marcel Carné's film *Children of Paradise* (1944). He wrote *Reflections on the Theater* (1949; Eng. trans. 1951), *The Theater of Jean-Louis Barrault* (1959; Eng. trans. 1961) and his memoirs, *Memories for Tomorrow* (1972; Eng. trans. 1974).

BARRE, MOHAMMED SIAD. *See SIAD BARRE, MOHAMMED.*

BARRELL, JOSEPH (1869–1919), U.S. geologist. A professor at Yale (1903–1919), Barrell was a pioneer dryland geologist who made fundamental contributions to the study of the earth's crust, the process of sedimentation, the origin of igneous rocks on the earth's surface, and the study of geological time. In his classic study, *Geology of the Marysville Mining District, Montana* (1907), he developed a theory of magmatic stoping. He challenged the then-accepted belief that most sedimentary strata were of marine origin and reported that at least one-fifth of the land was covered by sediment produced by the activity of rivers, wind, and ice. Barrell also explained (1914–15) geological phenomena by the dynamic interaction of two distinct layers of the earth's crust.

BARRIE, SIR JAMES MATTHEW (1860–1937), Scottish dramatist, novelist, and essayist. Educated at Edinburgh University (M.A. 1882) Barrie moved to England and worked as a journalist in Nottingham and London. His early novels, *Auld Licht Idylls* (1888) and *A Window in Thrums* (1889), placed him in the tradition of the Kailyard school, which depicted Scottish country society with humor and nostalgia but omitted the harsh realities of Scottish life. After 1900 he turned to the theater and, with *Quality Street* (1901), *The Admirable Crichton* (1903), and *What Every Woman Knows* (1908), became one of the most popular playwrights of his time. His classic fantasy, *Peter Pan* (1904), the story of a young boy who does not want to grow up, was a favorite of children. The sentimentality and sweetness of much of his work, however, has not endeared him as much to later generations of adults. ■ See biography by Denis MacKail (1941) and studies by Harry Geduld (1971) and Andrew Birkin (1979).

BARRIOS, EDUARDO (1884–1963), Chilean novelist and dramatist. Leaving home when he dropped out of military school (1902), Barrios took up odd jobs, including rubberworking, bookkeeping, and weightlifting with a circus troupe. Later he became minister of education and director of the National Library (1927–31). He was a psychological novelist, writing such works as *The Boy Who Went Mad for Love* (1915), written in diary form. *A Failure* (1917), recounting an intellectual's troubled adaptation to society, presents a cross section of Chile's social life. Barrios researched *Brother Ass* (1926; Eng. trans. 1969), a novel about monastery life, by living among the Franciscans. *The Men in the Man* (1950) treated the various sides of a single personality. He also wrote plays. ■ See study by Ned Davison (1970).

BARRON, CLARENCE WALKER (1855–1928), U.S. editor and publisher. Convinced of the importance of up-to-date and reliable financial news for businessmen, Barron established the Boston News Bureau (1887) and the Philadelphia News Bureau (1897). In 1901 he acquired Dow, Jones and Co. (which he built into the nation's leading financial news agency) and its daily, the *Wall Street Journal,* the most important financial newspaper in the United States. Barron further extended his readership by founding *Barron's National Business and Financial Weekly* (1921).

BARRY, PHILIP (1896–1949), U.S. playwright. Barry emerged from the Ivy League (he graduated from Yale in 1919 and worked under George Pierce Baker at Harvard) to become a leading dramatist of the 1930s. His reputation was founded on his satirical comedies of manners, including *Holiday* (1928) and *The Animal Kingdom* (1932). *The Philadelphia Story* (1939) became a movie classic. He also wrote serious, symbolic dramas, including *Hotel Universe* (1930) and *Here Come the Clowns* (1938), and was one of the first U.S. dramatists to incorporate Freudian psychology in his plays. ■ See study by Joseph P. Roppolo (1965).

BARRYMORES, THE, U.S. family of actors. The third generation of a distinguished theatrical family, Lionel (1878–1954), Ethel (1879–1957), and John Barrymore (1882–1942) were born in Philadelphia. All three originally sought other careers—Ethel as a pianist, Lionel and John as artists—before entering the theater. Ethel, with her grand voice and style, was most clearly identified with the theater, from her Broadway successes in *Captain Jinks of the Horse Marines* (1901) to *The Constant Wife* (1920) and *The Corn Is Green* (1942). She made one film with her brothers, *Rasputin and the Empress* (1933), and won an Academy Award for *None But the Lonely Heart* (1944). Lionel made his first film in 1909 and later gave up the stage altogether to play crusty film characters in *Treasure Island* (1934) and *David Copperfield* (1935) in addition to an annual radio performance as Scrooge in *A Christmas Carol.* Confined to a wheelchair by arthritis, he played Dr. Gillespie in the Dr. Kildare series and wrote *We Barrymores* (1951). John, widely touted as the greatest Hamlet of his day and as Hollywood's greatest lover, led a losing battle to justify his publicity. After a distinguished Broadway stage career (debut 1903), he went to Hollywood to make *Dr. Jekyll and Mr. Hyde* (1920), *Don Juan* (1926), *Svengali* (1931), *Grand Hotel* (1932), and *Dinner at Eight* (1933). Troubled by alcoholism and marital and financial difficulties, he also appeared as an unwitting parody of himself in *The Great Profile* (1940). His granddaughter Drew (1975–) was a noted Hollywood actress. ■ See Ethel's *Memories* (1955); John's *Confessions of an Actor* (1926); Hollis Alpert, *The Barrymores* (1964); John Kobler, *Damned in Paradise: The Life of John Barrymore* (1977); James Kotsilibas-Davis, *The Barrymores* (1981); and Margot Peters, *The House of Barrymore* (1991).

BARTH, JOHN SIMMONS (1930–), U.S. novelist. Barth was a professional drummer before making his mark as a writer. He taught English at several universities, including his alma mater, Johns Hopkins (1973-91). His ingenious novels used literary artifice to expose social artifice, pointing out the arbitrary nature of conventional mores and dealing with such themes as innocence and existential freedom. They included *The Floating Opera* (1956), *End of the Road* (1958), and *The Sot-Weed Factor* (1960). In his most acclaimed work, *Giles Goat Boy* (1966), Barth played on the myth of the errant folk hero. He called his fiction an effort to "imitate the form of the Novel, by an author who imitates the role of Author." *Lost in the Funhouse* (1968) is a collection of short experimental fiction. His later works included *Chimera* (1972), a collection of recycled ancient myths; *Letters* (1979), a novel composed of letters exchanged by characters from his previous novels; and *Sabbatical* (1982), an uncharacteristically straightforward story of a sailing trip taken by a former spy and his wife. His subsequent works included the novels *Tidewater Tales* (1987) and *Once Upon a Time: The Floating Opera* (1994); the short-story collection, *On with the Story* (1996); and *Further Fridays: Essays, Lectures, and Other Nonfiction* (1995). ▪ See studies by Gerhard Joseph (1970), Jac Tharpe (1974), David Morrell (1976), and Patricia Tobin (1992); and Charles B. Harris, *Passionate Virtuosity* (1983).

BARTH, KARL (1886–1968), Swiss theologian. One of the century's leading Protestant theologians, Barth studied in Berlin and Marburg, was appointed assistant pastor in Geneva (1909), and through the 1920s and early 1930s taught at various German universities. Opposing Nazism, he played a leading role in drafting the Barmen Declaration (1934) that discredited the regime's religious claims. The following year he refused to swear loyalty to Hitler and was removed from his post and deported to Switzerland. Barth's thinking was embodied in *Church Dogmatics* (Eng. trans., 4 vols., 1936–69), his unfinished life's work that occupied more than 9,000 pages. His confident stance stressed the individual's confrontation with God. Elaborating his "theology of the word," he argued that modern Christian religious thought has departed from the central concern of theology—the word of God and revelation of God to Jesus Christ. ▪ See his letters (Eng. trans. 1980), his correspondence with Rudolf Bultmann (Eng. trans. 1981) and with Carl Zuckmayer (Eng. trans. 1983); George Casalis, *Portrait of Karl Barth* (Eng. trans. 1963); and Eberhard Busch, *Karl Barth: His Life from Letters and Autobiographical Texts* (Eng. trans. 1976).

BARTHÉ, RICHMOND (1901–1989), U.S. sculptor. Barthé was born in Mississippi of mixed creole, black, and Indian ancestry. He studied at Chicago's Art Institute (1924–28) and began sculpting representational figures and busts in 1928. His works include *The Blackberry Woman,* in New York's Whitney Museum, a statue of Toussaint L'Ouverture in Haiti, a marble bust of Booker T. Washington in New York University's Hall of Fame, a bust and small figure of Paul Robeson for Actor's Equity, and a frieze called *Green Pastures* in a Harlem housing project. Barthé lived in New York City (1929–47); Jamaica (1947–late 60s); and Pasadena, California (1969–89).

BARTHELME, DONALD (1931–1989), U.S. author. Raised in Houston, Texas, the son of a professor of archi-

tecture, Barthelme worked as a journalist and magazine editor before his short stories began to appear in the *New Yorker* in the early 1960s. Influenced by surrealism, he expressed his despair at a mad, disordered, and wicked world in his comic experimental stories which were devoid of plot or traditional character development. Called a postmodernist by literary critics, Barthelme used literary allusions, mythological references, and neologisms to depict surrealistic and wildly incongruous situations, events, and characters. His best-known stories appeared in the collections *Come Back, Dr. Caligari* (1964), *Unspeakable Practices, Unnatural Acts* (1968), *City Life* (1970), *Great Days* (1979), and *Sixty Stories* (1981). Barthelme also wrote the novels *Snow White* (1967) and *The Dead Father* (1975) and won the National Book Award for his first children's book, *The Slightly Irregular Fire Engine or the Hithering Thithering Djinn* (1972). He served as vice president of the PEN (Poets, Playwrights, Essayists, Editors, and Novelists) American Center. ▪ See study by Lois Gordon (1981).

BARTHES, ROLAND (1915–1980), French semiotician and literary and cultural critic. After qualifying in French literature and classics at the University of Paris (1939), Barthes taught in Bucharest and Alexandria, and then in Paris (1960–80). A leader of France's *nouveaux critiques,* Barthes drew on the insights of Karl Marx, Sigmund Freud, and Ferdinand de Saussure to expand the science of semiology, the study of signs and symbols underlying all aspects of human culture. His iconoclastic analyses of literature (*Writing Degree Zero,* 1953; Eng. trans. 1967), popular culture (*Mythologies,* 1957; Eng. trans. 1972), fashion (*The Fashion System,* 1967; Eng. trans. 1983), and photography (*Camera Lucida,* 1980; Eng. trans. 1981) had an enormous impact on modern cultural criticism. His textural analyses included *The Pleasure of the Text* (1973; Eng. trans. 1975) and *A Lover's Discourse* (1977; Eng. trans. 1978). Selections of his works are in *A Barthes Reader* (1982), edited by Susan Sontag, and *The Rustle of Language* (1986). ▪ See the autobiographical *Roland Barthes by Roland Barthes* (1975; Eng. trans. 1977) and studies by Annette Lavers (1982) and Steven Ungar (1984).

BARTLETT, SIR FREDERIC CHARLES (1886–1969), British psychologist. While Bartlett's interest in psychology was inspired by issues of war as a result of the outbreak of World War I, he was best known for his work in applied experimental psychology. He taught at Cambridge from 1922 to 1952. Through a long series of experiments utilizing materials encountered in daily life, he investigated the processes of memory and thinking, which he described in *Remembering* (1932) and *Thinking* (1958). During World War II he focused his efforts on such wartime problems as equipment design, fatigue, and personnel selection. He also studied the relationship between psychology and anthropology and wrote *Psychology and Primitive Culture* (1923).

BARTÓK, BÉLA (1881–1945), Hungarian composer. A noted scholar of East European folk songs as well as a brilliant concert pianist, Bartók adapted Hungarian peasant tunes into the themes of his concert compositions. Some of his most important works, in which he experimented with new harmonic and rhythmic techniques, were the opera *Bluebeard's Castle* (1911), the ballet *Miraculous Mandarin* (1916), *Music for Strings, Percussion and Celesta* (1936), and *Concerto for Orchestra* (1943). He also wrote celebrated piano concertos (1927, 1930, 1945) and six string quartets (1909–39). He taught piano at the Academy of Music in Budapest (1907–34) and emigrated to the United States in 1940. ■ See Benjamin Suchoff, ed., *Bela Bartok Essays* (1977); biography by Halsey Stevens (rev. ed. 1964); and study by Paul Griffiths (1984).

BARTON, BRUCE (1886–1967), U.S. advertising executive. A journalist and magazine editor, Barton and two partners founded an advertising firm (1919) that, as Batten, Barton, Durstine and Osborne (from 1928), became one of the world's largest agencies. Barton's belief in individualism, self-improvement, and material progress was reflected in his copy as well as in his numerous articles and books. He created Betty Crocker (for General Mills), helped improve the image of the U.S. Steel Corp., promoted electrical appliances (for General Electric), and supplied the Salvation Army with its slogan, "a man may be down, but he's never out." His best-selling biography, *The Man Nobody Knows* (1925), described Jesus as "the greatest advertiser of his own day." A longtime publicist for the Republican party, he served in the House of Representatives (1937–41) from New York.

BARTON, SIR DEREK HAROLD RICHARD (1918–1998), British chemist. On the faculty of Imperial College, London (1945–49; 1957–78), Barton did pioneering work in conformational analysis that elucidated the three-dimensional geometric structure of molecules. His research, which revolutionized the study of organic chemistry, led to the development of new drugs and was essential to the discovery of the double helix of DNA (deoxyribonucleic acid), the carrier of the genetic code. Barton shared the 1969 Nobel Prize in Chemistry (with Odd Hassel) for his research. He subsequently taught at Texas A & M University (1986–98). ■ See his *Some Recollections of Gap Jumping* (1991).

BARTON, SIR EDMUND (1849–1920), Australian jurist and political leader. Barton became a lawyer in 1871 and in 1879 was elected to the New South Wales legislature, where he served for the next 15 years. After 1894 he devoted his time to bringing about the federation of the Australian colonies and headed the committee that drafted the commonwealth constitution bill (1897–98); he served as Australia's first prime minister (1901–03). Highly conservative, Barton coined the phrase "white Australian policy" in referring to his restrictive immigration act. He was knighted (1902) and served as a high court justice (1903–20). ■ See biography by John Reynolds (1948).

BARUCH, BERNARD MANNES (1870–1965), U.S. financier. Through shrewd investments, Baruch was a millionaire at age 30 when he founded his own industrial development firm. An active Democrat, he earned the sobriquet "park bench statesman" for his role as unofficial adviser to presidents, from Woodrow Wilson to John F. Kennedy. Baruch contributed significantly to the economic sections of the Versailles Treaty (1919). After World War II he helped shape U.S. policy on international control of atomic energy. Numerous educational institutions benefited from his philanthropies. ■ See his autobiographies (1957; 1960); Margaret L. Coit, *Mr. Baruch* (1957); Jordan Schwarz, *Speculator* (1981); and study by James Grant (1983).

BARYSHNIKOV, MIKHAIL NIKOLAYEVICH (1948–), Soviet-born U.S. ballet dancer. Baryshnikov started to study ballet at age 12, became a soloist with Leningrad's Kirov Ballet at 18, and was one of its principal dancers at 20. Renowned for his flawless technique and extremely popular with Soviet audiences, Baryshnikov was the most highly acclaimed male dancer of his generation. Seeking greater artistic freedom, however, he defected from the Soviet Union (1974) and became a ballet superstar in the United States. He danced with the American Ballet Theatre and the New York City Ballet and performed modern dance as well as classical ballets. He was director of the American Ballet Theatre (1980–90). He became a U.S. citizen in 1986. His movies included *The Turning Point* (1976) and *White Nights* (1985). He was the founder of the White Oaks Dance Project (1990), a modern-dance touring company. ■ See his *Baryshnikov at Work* (1976); study by Gennady Smakov (1980); and Nina Alovert, *Baryshnikov in Russia* (Eng. trans. 1984).

BARZANI, MUSTAFA AL- (1902?–1979), Kurdish nationalist leader. For more than four decades Barzani attempted to form an independent state of Kurdistan consisting of the 12 million Kurds living in Iraq, Iran, Turkey, and the Soviet Union. The leader of the nationalist forces in Iraq from the late 1930s, Barzani was president of the short-lived Soviet-backed Kurdish Mahabad Republic set up in northwestern Iran (1946) and headed the socialist Kurdish Democratic party. In exile in the Soviet Union after 1946, he returned to Iraq after the 1958 revolution, but he rejected the government's autonomy plan (1960) and led a 10-year guerrilla struggle against the Iraqi government. Fighting resumed in 1974 but ended the following year after the Iranian government withdrew its support of the Kurds.

BARZUN, JACQUES (1907–), French-born U.S. historian, educator, and author. On the faculty of Columbia University for nearly half a century (1927–75; dean of faculties and provost, 1958–67), Barzun championed a broad-based liberal arts education and opposed highly specialized and vocational undergraduate study. His controversial works, critical of American higher education, included *The Teacher in America* (1945), *The House of Intellect* (1959), and *The American University* (1968). His stylishly written scholarly cultural studies included *Darwin, Marx and Wagner* (1941), *Berlioz and the Romantic Century* (2 vols., 1950), *The Energies of Art* (1956), *Classic, Romantic and Modern* (1961), *Clio and the Doctors* (1974), and *A Stroll with William James* (1983). His later works included *A Word or Two Before You Go* (1986), *The Culture We Deserve* (1989), and *From Dawn to Decadence: 500 Years of Western Cultural Life, 1500 to the Present* (2000).

BASIE, COUNT (William Basie; 1904–1984), U.S. jazz bandleader, pianist, and composer. Basie began as a drummer, studied organ with Fats Waller in Harlem, worked as a vaudeville accompanist, then played with several bands (Walter Page, Benny Moten) before establishing his own internationally famous ensemble (1935) that quickly grew from 9 to 13 pieces. He was dubbed "Count" by a Kansas City radio announcer. His band's spirited rhythmic patterns and use of fine instrumentalists and vocalists (including singer Billie Holiday and saxophonist Lester Young) helped to maintain its dominant position among big bands in the jazz world for more than four decades. Among its best-known numbers were "One O'Clock Jump" and "One, Two, Three O'Lairy." The Basie band played at Pres. John F. Kennedy's inaugural ball (1961) and toured (1981) with Frank Sinatra. ▪ See his memoirs, *Good Morning Blues* (with Albert Murray; 1985); Stanley Dance, *The World of Count Basie* (1980); and studies by Raymond Horricks (1957; repr. 1971) and Alun Morgan (1984).

BASKIN, LEONARD (1922–2000), U.S. sculptor. The son of a New Jersey rabbi, Baskin received an extensive Talmudic education before studying at Yale's School of Fine Arts (1941–43). He worked in bronze, stone, wood, and relief, sculpting large representational figures preoccupied with death and spiritual decay (such as *Blake,* 1955, and *Barlach,* 1959). Many of his works were based on themes from the Bible and classical mythology. Baskin, who joined the faculty of Smith College in 1953, was also a printmaker and book illustrator, turning out limited editions of rare books at his own small Gehenna Press in Northampton, Massachusetts. His essays appeared in *Iconologia* (1988). ▪ See Irma B. Jaffee, *The Sculpture of Leonard Baskin* (1980).

BASOV, NIKOLAI GENNADIYEVICH (1922–), Soviet physicist. Basov began working at Moscow's Lebedev Institute in 1948 as a laboratory assistant and subsequently was its deputy director (1958–73) and director (1973–89). His work in quantum electronics—more specifically, on the interaction between incident electromagnetic waves and mat-

ter—provided a theoretical basis for Charles H. Townes' invention of the maser (a device for microwave amplification) and later for the development of the laser (a device for amplification of visible radiation). For this work Basov shared the 1964 Nobel Prize for Physics with Soviet co-worker Aleksandr M. Prochorov and American physicist Townes.

BASSANI, GIORGIO (1916–2000), Italian novelist. The son of a Jewish physician from Ferrara, Bassani served in the antifascist resistance after 1943. In the post–World War II years, he was a screenwriter and literary and magazine editor. When he won a prize for a novella (1956), he emerged as a fiction writer of considerable stature, known for compelling characterizations. His tales of fascist persecution of Jews in Ferrara were collected in *Five Stories of Ferrara* (1956; Eng. trans. 1971) and *A Prospect of Ferrara* (1960; Eng. trans. 1962). He also wrote *The Gold-Rimmed Spectacles* (1958; Eng. trans. 1960), a sensitive portrait of a Jewish homosexual. *The Garden of the Finzi-Continis* (1962; Eng. trans. 1965), which used the garden of a prominent Jewish family as a metaphor for a losing battle to retain human values in Mussolini's Italy, was filmed by Vittorio De Sica. *Behind the Door* (1964; Eng. trans. 1972) concerned the search for identity of a Jewish Italian youth during the 1930s, and *The Heron* (1968; Eng. trans. 1970) was a character study of an alienated landowner. Bassani served as a vice president of RAI, the state radio and television network (1964–66), and taught at the Rome Academy of Dramatic Art (1957–68). English translations of his poetry are in *Rolls Royce and other Poems* (1982).

BASSETT, JOHN SPENCER (1867–1928), U.S. historian. A professor at Trinity College (now Duke University; 1893–1906) and Smith College (1906–28), Bassett was one of the major historians of the American south. A liberal opponent of racism and provincialism, he founded the influential journal *South Atlantic Quarterly* (1902), wrote *The Federalist System, 1789–1801* (1906), *The Life of Andrew Jackson* (2 vols., 1911), and *The Middle Group of American Historians* (1917), and edited *The Correspondence of Andrew Jackson* (6 vols., 1926–35).

BATES, DAISY GATSON (1922?–1999), U.S. civil-rights leader. Bates was one of the African-American leaders who worked to demand compliance with the U.S. Supreme Court's 1954 ruling that segregated schools were unconstitutional. As head of the Arkansas chapter of the National Association for the Advancement of Colored People (1953–61) and publisher, with her husband, of the *Arkansas State Press* (established 1941), she mobilized the black community of Little Rock in support of the first integration confrontation in 1957. Bates, whose newspaper was forced out of business in 1959 by segregationist pressure, wrote a memoir, *The Long Shadow of Little Rock* (1962). She subsequently worked with antipoverty programs, served on the national board of the NAACP, and briefly resumed the publication of her newspaper (1984–88).

BATES, DAISY MAE (Daisy O'Dwyer Hunt; 1861–1951), Australian social worker. Born in Ireland, Bates first went to Australia in 1884 for health reasons. She worked in Britain as a journalist (1894–99) and returned to western Australia for the *London Times* to report on alleged cruelty to the aborigines. For the next 46 years Bates studied, nursed, taught, and negotiated disputes for the aborigines, who in return called her *kabbarli*—"Grandmother." A strong supporter of aborigine cultural and religious practices, she severely criticized missionaries and government administrators who tried to Westernize the aborigines. Her extensive ethnological research included participation in secret rituals from which even aboriginal women were excluded. ■ See her autobiography, *The Passing of the Aborigines* (1938; 2nd ed. 1966) and the study by Elizabeth Salter (1972).

BATESON, GREGORY (1904–1980), British-born U.S. anthropologist. The son of geneticist William Bateson, Gregory Bateson studied physical anthropology at Cambridge, but he became increasingly interested in questions of culture and personality. His fieldwork in New Guinea produced *Naven* (1936; rev. 1958), a study of ritualized cross-dressing. He also studied Balinese culture and art, collaborating with his wife Margaret Mead on *Balinese Character* (1942). Bateson analyzed the process of abstracting from raw data, using cybernetic concepts and terminology, in *Communication* (1950; with J. Ruesch). He later wrote *Steps to an Ecology of Mind* (1972) and *Mind and Nature* (1979). He also investigated schizophrenia, a disorder that he likened to a communications breakdown, and developed the "double bind" hypothesis. ■ See study by David Lipset (1980).

BATESON, WILLIAM (1861–1926), British geneticist. Called by many "the father of genetics," Bateson coined the name "genetics" and helped spread and popularize the Austrian monk Gregor Mendel's laws of heredity and variation. Bateson's experiments (with Reginald Punnett) demonstrated that certain combinations of characteristics are inherited together, a phenomenon subsequently called linkage, and that some genes influence the action of other genes. However, he rejected the chromosome theory of inheritance as too materialistic and offered instead a vibratory theory of inheritance (based on force and motion) that was rejected by most of his contemporaries. He was the first British professor of genetics (Cambridge University, 1908–10) and directed the John Innes Horticultural Institution at Merton, England (1910–26). With Punnett he founded (1911) and edited (1911–26) the *Journal of Genetics*. His books included *Mendel's Principles of Heredity: A Defence* (1902) and *Problems of Genetics* (1913).

BATISTA Y ZALDÍVAR, FULGENCIO (1901–1973), Cuban political leader. The son of a laborer and orphaned at age 13, Batista enlisted in the army at age 20. As the fastest stenographer in the military he was assigned to record the trials of enemies of the dictatorial regime that, as a sergeant, he helped to overthrow in 1933. The de facto head of government and army chief of staff after the revolution, he served as a reformist president of Cuba during World War II (1940–44) and returned to the presidency via coup d'état in 1952. Batista's second reign was marked by gangsterism, gambling, corruption, and terror. Faced with a mounting guerrilla war led by Fidel Castro, the right-wing dictator fled into exile on New Year's Day, 1959. ■ See his *Cuba Betrayed* (1962) and Edmund A. Chester, *A Sergeant Named Batista* (1954).

BATLLE Y ORDÓÑEZ, JOSÉ (1856–1929), Uruguayan political leader. The son of a former president of Uruguay, Batlle founded the newspaper *El Día* (1886) and became active in the Colorado party. As a reform-minded president of the republic (1903–07; 1911–15), he worked to create democratic socialist institutions and to promote the public welfare, advocating government ownership of basic enterprises, labor reforms, and universal suffrage. To forestall the emergence of a dictator, Batlle sought to amend the constitution to create a collegial executive. His plan aroused controversy, and in its place a new constitution (1918) established a bifurcated executive consisting of a president and a nine-member national council. Batlle presided over the council in 1920 and 1926. ■ See study by Milton I. Vanger (1963).

BAUDOUIN I (1930–1993), king of the Belgians. When Leopold III surrendered to the Nazis during World War II, Prince Baudouin was interned (1940–44) with his father and went into exile with him in Switzerland after the war. Leopold returned (1950) to the throne following a general referendum, but he appointed Baudouin regent in the midst of unrest. Baudouin ascended to the throne (1951) when his father abdicated, helping to rehabilitate the Belgian monarchy. During his reign the Belgian Congo (later the Republic of Zaïre) was granted independence (1960). His impartiality helped make progress toward a political rapprochement between the Walloons and the Flemish community.

BAUER, OTTO (1882–1938), Austrian political leader. The leading theoretician of the Austrian Social Democratic party, Bauer was a major voice of the noncommunist left after World War I. He founded Die Zukunft ("The Future"), a socialist education movement, and served briefly as Austria's foreign minister (1918–19). His best-known works were *The Nationalities Question and Social Democracy* (1907) and *The Austrian Revolution* (1923; Eng. trans. 1925, 1970). He was exiled from Austria after an abortive workers' revolt in 1934 and died in Paris. ■ See Anson Rabinbach. *The Crisis of Austrian Socialism* (1983).

BAUGH, SAMUEL ADRIAN (1914–), U.S. football player. Twice named to the All-America squad while at

Texas Christian University (1935–36), Baugh went on to become one of the greatest quarterbacks in the history of professional football. In 16 seasons (1937—52) as the star of the Washington Redskins, "Slingin' Sammy" developed the modern aerial game and established career records for most passes completed, most touchdown passes, and highest career completion percentage (56.6 percent). He also held records for the highest completion percentage in one season (70.3 percent; 1945) and for the most yards gained passing in one game (446; 1948) and in one season (2,938; 1947).

BAUMEISTER, WILLI (1889–1955), German painter. Baumeister was influenced by the work of Cézanne until 1920, when, after serving in World War I, he began to develop his own personal style, using sand, putty, and plaster to create sculpturesque murals. His work showed constructivist aspects (reliefs using modern industrial materials) until 1930, when he developed calligraphic figures on sand grounds, the most famous of which was *Ideograms* (1937). Dismissed (1933) from his Frankfurt teaching position by the Nazis and barred from exhibiting his work, Baumeister studied historic art, illustrated Bible stories and the *Epic of Gilgamesh* (1942–53), and described his method of drawing pictorial signs from the unconscious in *The Unknown in Art* (written 1943; published 1947). His most important works, *Montaru* (1953–55), *Monturi* (1953–54), and the *Safer* series, used geometric forms in brighter colors than in his earlier works. ■ See biography by Will Grohmann (Eng. trans. 1966).

BAUSCH, PINA (1940–   ), German ballet dancer and choreographer. Trained by Kurt Jooss in Essen and Anthony Tudor in New York City, Bausch headed the Dance Theater in Wuppertal (1973–   ), where she created controversial and influential choreographed theater pieces that combined dance, speech, pantomime, music, gadgets, and pictures. Her pioneering neoexpressionist works, frequently depicting alienation, angst, and the inability of individuals to achieve intimacy with one another, challenged spectators with disturbing and frequently violent images and repetitive gestures. Her creations influenced both modern dance and theater, and Wuppertal became a major center of the European avant-garde. Her best-known works included *Rite of Spring* (1975), *Seven Deadly Sins* (1976), *Kontakthof* (1978), *Bluebeard* (1984), and *Nur Du (Only You)* (1996).

BAUZA, MARIO (1911–1993), Cuban-born U.S. jazz musician and bandleader. Bauza graduated from the Havana Municipal Conservatory of Music and played in the Havana Symphony Orchestra before migrating to New York City (1930), where he had first been introduced to jazz during a 1926 visit. He played the trumpet in some of the best bands of the swing era, including those led by Chick Webb, Fletcher Henderson, and Cab Calloway, and cofounded with his brother-in-law Machito, the Afro-Cubans, a jazz-oriented Latin orchestra. Often called the man who invented

Latin jazz, Bauza almost single-handedly introduced Afro-Cuban music to the United States. His innovative rhythms and musical arrangements, developed during his 35 years with the Afro-Cubans, had an indelible effect on American music, influencing popular music and rock and roll as well as jazz and salsa. Bauza also helped introduce and popularize the rhumba, mambo, and cha-cha dance crazes of the 1940s and 1950s. He also helped foster the careers of Ella Fitzgerald and Dizzy Gillespie. He formed his own band, the Afro-Cuban Jazz Orchestra, in 1976, and continued to perform and record regularly until his death.

BAX, SIR ARNOLD EDWARD TREVOR (1883–1953), British composer. Bax studied piano (1900–05) at the Royal Academy of Music. He achieved recognition in 1917 for his symphonic poems, *The Garden of Fand* and *Tintagel,* conceived in a romantic style and richly orchestrated. During the interwar period he wrote seven symphonies, each dedicated to a favorite composer. Bax also spent many years in Ireland; he wrote short stories and poems on Celtic themes under the name Dermot O'Bryne. He was appointed master of the king's music, with musical duties on ceremonial occasions, in 1941. ■ See his autobiography, *Farewell My Youth* (1943).

BAXTER, JAMES KEIR (1926–1972), New Zealand poet and playwright. Baxter, a socially committed bohemian, was acclaimed for his first book of poetry, *Beyond the Palisade* (1944), when he was 18. His collections *The Fallen House* (1953) and *In Fires No Return* (1958) contained melancholy poems dealing with isolation, while his later works, including *Pig Island Letters* (1966), *Jerusalem Sonnets* (1970), *Jerusalem Daybook* (1971), and *Autumn Testament* (1972) were spiritual and optimistic and reflected his vision of a humanistic socialism. He set up a refuge for drug addicts and dropouts in a remote Maori village, Jerusalem (1969). ■ See study by Charles Doyle (1976).

BAYAR, (MAHMUD) CELÂL (1884–1986), Turkish political leader. A Young Turk who was President Kemal Ataturk's economics minister (1932–37) and premier (1937–39), Bayar presided over a predominantly state-owned and operated economy. In 1946 he cofounded the Democratic party, which championed private enterprise and called for limited government intervention in the economy. Bayar served as president of Turkey throughout the 1950s. He fell from power in a coup (1960) and was sentenced by his successors to life imprisonment for violating the constitution; he was pardoned, however, in 1966.

BAYES, NORA (Dora Goldberg; 1880–1928), U.S. singer and actress. One of the most popular musical-comedy and vaudeville entertainers during the first quarter of the century, Bayes appeared in the first Ziegfeld's *Follies* (1907) and in numerous musical productions in New York and London. She was closely associated with such songs as "Shine On,

Harvest Moon," which she wrote with her husband (1908), "Take Me Out to the Ball Game," and George M. Cohan's famous World War I song, "Over There."

BAYLIS, LILIAN (1874–1937), British theater promoter. Baylis spent the 1890s in South Africa, performing in a music hall and teaching voice. Just before the turn of the century she returned to Britain, working with her aunt to manage the Royal Victoria Coffee Music Hall, which offered amusement while preaching temperance. Baylis wanted the music hall to popularize opera and drama; under her management the enterprise became known as "Old Vic," and after 1914 it specialized in performances of Shakespeare's works. When drama overshadowed opera at the Old Vic, she reopened (1931) the Sadler's Wells Theatre, where her companies grew into the Royal Ballet and the English National Opera. ■ See biography by Richard Findlater (1975).

BAYLISS, SIR WILLIAM MADDOCK (1860–1924), British physiologist. Working at University College, Oxford, Bayliss conducted research into the digestive, vascular, and nervous systems. His collaboration at the turn of the century with Ernest Henry Starling resulted in the discovery of the hormone—a substance that is secreted by one internal organ, carried in the bloodstream, and stimulates a specific effect on another organ. Working alone, Bayliss investigated the nature of vasomotor reflexes and the physicochemical aspects of physiology. Bayliss introduced the use of saline injections to treat surgical shock—a technique that was widely used in World War I. His book, *Principles of General Physiology* (1915), was a standard reference work. ■ See Charles Evans, *Reminiscences of Bayliss and Starling* (1964).

BAYLOR, ELGIN (1934–   ), U.S. basketball player. A two-time All-American at Seattle (1957; 1958) and star of the Minneapolis (later Los Angeles) Lakers (1958–71), the 6-foot, 5-inch-tall Baylor was one of the greatest all-around players in the history of basketball. He dazzled crowds and stymied opponents with his graceful, acrobatic movements on the court. Despite frequent injuries he was on the All-Pro team 10 times and was one of the most prolific scorers in National Basketball Association history (23,149 career points).

BAZIN, ANDRÉ (1918–1958), French film critic. Bazin founded a film society during the World War II German occupation of Paris, providing a forum for intellectual exchange. In the postwar years, he fostered serious discussion of cinematic theory and practice, promoting film societies and publishing critical articles. He cofounded (1951) the influential journal *Cahiers du Cinéma* and was the leading theoretician of New Wave cinema. Bazin's theory, based on analysis of existing films, was systematic, opposing the Russian director Sergei Eisenstein's concept of montage. The French directors François Truffaut and Jean-Luc Godard were among Bazin's followers, *What is Cinema?* (2 vols., 1967–71) contains English translations of his writings. ■ See biography by Dudley Andrew (1978).

BAZIN, HERVÉ (Jean-Pierre-Marie Hervé-Bazin; 1911–1996), French writer. Bazin revolted against his ultraconservative Catholic monarchist background, supporting himself as a waiter while he earned a literature degree from the Sorbonne and taking revenge in a series of grim portraits of bourgeois family life. His *Viper in the Fist* (1948; Eng. trans. 1951), a novel about the intense hatred between a mother and her child, enjoyed success because it scandalized. Subsequent novels by Bazin included *Head Against the Wall* (1949; Eng. trans. 1952), *Tribe of Women* (1956; Eng. trans. 1958), *In the Name of the Son* (1960; Eng. trans. 1962), *Tristan* (1970; Eng. trans. 1971), and *Madame Ex* (1975; Eng. trans. 1978). He was a member (from 1958) and president (from 1973) of the Académie Goncourt.

BAZIOTES, WILLIAM (1912–1963), U.S. painter. A leading member of New York's post–World War II abstract-expressionist group, Baziotes was concerned with the universal basis of primitive forms. He was a subtle colorist who was influenced by cubism and surrealism and frequently painted amoebalike shapes that seemed to float on the surface of his paintings. Baziotes cofounded the "Subject of the Artist" group with Robert Motherwell, Barnett Newman, and Mark Rothko.

BAZNA, ELYEZA. *See CICERO.*

BEACH, AMY MARCY CHENEY (Mrs. H.H.A. Beach; 1867–1944), U.S. composer. Beach was a professional pianist who turned to composition after her marriage in 1885 but resumed her concert career after her husband's death in 1910. Her *Gaelic Symphony* (1896), written in a traditional, romantic style, was considered to be the first symphony composed by an American woman. She also wrote a piano concerto (1900) and numerous piano pieces, which she performed herself on extensive European tours. In all, she wrote over 150 works, including a string quartet (1929); a one-act opera, *Cabildo* (1932); and numerous songs. ■ See biography by Adrienne F. Block (1998).

BEACH, SYLVIA WOODBRIDGE (1887–1962), U.S. bookshop owner and publisher. Beach, whose father, a minister, headed the American Church in Paris (1902–05), opened Shakespeare & Co. (1919), a bookstore and lending library on the Left Bank in Paris. It was the center of expatriate literary life frequented by such writers as Ernest Hemingway, F. Scott Fitzgerald, Katherine Anne Porter, T. S. Eliot, and Ezra Pound. She also published James Joyce's *Ulysses* (1922), which was initially banned as obscene in the United States and Britain. The bookstore at 12 Rue de l'Odéon was closed (1942–43) during the Nazi occupation, while Beach was interned, and was not reopened after the war. ■ See her autobiography, *Shakespeare and Company* (1959), and study by Noel R. Fitch (1983).

BEACH BOYS, THE (Brian Wilson, 1942– ; Dennis Wilson, 1944–1983; Carl Wilson, 1946–1998; Mike Love, 1941– ; and Al Jardine, 1942–), U.S. singing group. A group of all-American clean-cut boys in Pendleton plaid shirts, the three Wilson brothers, their cousin, and their neighbor built successful singing careers on the beach party themes of long-haired girls, fast cars, and endless summer. They billed themselves as Carl and the Passions and Kenny and the Cadets, finding their identity as the Beach Boys when Brian Wilson wrote their first hit, "Surfin'" (1961). Harmonizing to create their smooth West Coast sound, the Beach Boys made a series of tremendous hits, including "Surfin' USA," "Surfer Girl," "Help Me Rhonda," "California Girls," and "Good Vibrations." After a period of eclipse in the late 1960s, when they took up transcendental meditation, the Beach Boys made a successful European tour in 1970 and a U.S. comeback the following year. They continued performing into the 1980s. Dennis Wilson drowned in 1983 and Carl Wilson died of cancer in 1998. Brian Wilson recorded several albums independently of the group, including *Pet Sounds* and *Imagination*. ■ See studies by Byron Preiss (1978) and Steven Gaines (1986); and Timothy White, *The Nearest Faraway Place* (1994).

BEADLE, GEORGE WELLS (1903–1989), U.S. geneticist and educator. A pioneer in the field of biochemical genetics, Beadle determined that genes affect heredity by controlling individual steps of the chemical synthesis in a cell. His most important work, done in collaboration with E. L. Tatum at Stanford University (1937–46), demonstrated that each gene was responsible for the structure of a specific enzyme, which allowed a single chemical reaction to take place. For their bringing to fruition the "one-gene, one-enzyme" concept, they were awarded the Nobel Prize for Physiology or Medicine (1958; shared with Joshua Lederberg). Beadle was a professor at the California Institute of Technology (1946–61) and served as chancellor and president of the University of Chicago (1961–68). He wrote *The Language of Life* (1966; with Muriel Beadle).

BEAMON, BOB (1946–), U.S. long jumper. While competing in the 1968 Mexico City Olympics, Beamon established a world and Olympic record by jumping 29 feet, 2¼ inches. The perfect leap, which bettered Ralph Boston's old world mark by nearly 2 feet, was considered by many to be the greatest track record of all time. Beamon retired prior to the 1972 Olympics. Beamon's record was broken by Mike Powell at the World Track and Field Championships in Tokyo (1991) with a leap of 29 feet, 4¼ inches. ■ See his autobiography (1999).

BEARD, CHARLES AUSTIN (1874–1948), U.S. historian. Beard earned his Ph.D. from Columbia (1904) and taught

there until 1917, when he resigned in protest against the dismissal of two colleagues who opposed U.S. entry into World War I. He helped found the New School for Social Research (1919) and became a leader of the progressive movement. Beard's best-known work was a vaguely deterministic *Economic Interpretation of the Constitution* (1913). With his wife Mary Ritter Beard (1876–1958), he wrote *The Rise of American Civilization* (4 vols., 1927–39), which viewed the Civil War in economic terms. An isolationist, he accused the U.S. government of leading the country into World War II in *American Foreign Policy in the Making, 1932–40* (1946) and *President Roosevelt and the Coming of War, 1941* (1948). ■ See Mary Beard, *The Making of Charles A. Beard* (1955), and biography by Ellen Nore (1983).

BEARD, JAMES ANDREW (1903–1985), U.S. cooking expert. Beard's interest in culinary arts was nurtured by his mother, a fine cook. He first gave private lessons in 1932, ran a catering business (1938–40), published his first cookbook in 1940, and hosted the first commercially televised food show, "Elsie Presents" (1946–47). He subsequently ran his own cooking school in New York City (from 1955), published more than 30 cookbooks, and was regarded as the foremost food authority and arbiter of taste in food in the United States. A food historian and champion of outdoor cooking and American cuisine, he was best known for *The James Beard Cookbook* (1959), *James Beard's American Cookery* (1972), *Beard on Bread* (1973), *James Beard's Theory and Practice of Good Cooking* (1977), and *The New James Beard* (1981). ■ See the autobiographical *Delights and Prejudices* (1964); Evan Jones, *Epicurean Delight* (1990); and biography by Robert Clark (1993).

BEARDEN, ROMARE HOWARD (1914–1988), U.S. artist. Bearden was a student of George Grosz at New York's Art Students League (1936–37). His early works were influenced by Mexican muralism and reflected the social and political plight of African Americans. During World War II he served in the all-black 372nd Infantry Regiment. His works after the war were more abstract, but in the 1960s he produced the series of powerful photomontages for which he was best known. These controversial and innovative works, which he called projections, were constructed from newspaper and magazine photos and starkly depicted the condition of black life in contemporary America. His work appeared in a retrospective at New York's Museum of Modern Art (1971). He wrote *The Painter's Mind: A Study of the Relations of Structure and Space in Painting* (1969; with Carl Holty). ■ See M. Bunch Washington, *The Art of Romare Bearden* (1974), and study by Myron Schwartzman (1990).

BEATLES, THE (John Lennon, 1940–1980; [James] Paul McCartney 1942– ; George Harrison, 1943– ; and Ringo Starr [Richard Starkey], 1940–), British singing group. In 1956, two working-class composers from Liverpool, Lennon and McCartney, formed the Quarrymen; in 1960 they were joined by George Harrison and Ringo Starr, changed their name to the Beatles, and were discovered by manager Brian Epstein, who got their act together to make musical history. Rock music's most popular and influential group, the Beatles introduced a new sophistication, a literary bent, and a broader range of themes into popular music. Beatles' albums, of which they sold 250 million in the 1960s, were musical milestones of the decade; they included *A Hard Day's Night* (1964), *Help* (1965), *Sergeant Pepper's Lonely Hearts Club Band* (1967), and *Let It Be* (1970). Lennon and McCartney wrote most of the Beatles' songs: Lennon contributed a complexity and social consciousness to their music; McCartney invented the appealing melodies that made him, according to the *Guinness Book of World Records,* the most successful composer of all time. The group popularized Eastern music and made long hair a token of disaffection. They made two films. The Beatles parted ways in 1971 in personal and financial disarray, with each member going on to a solo career. John Lennon was murdered in New York City in December 1980. McCartney subsequently wrote several classical pieces, including *Liverpool Oratorio* (1991) and *Standing Stone* (1997), and was knighted in 1997. ■ See Wilfrid Mellers, *Twilight of the Gods* (1977); Philip Norman, *Shout!* (1981); Terence J. O'Grady, *The Beatles: A Musical Revolution* (1983); Jon Wiener, *Come Together* (1984); *The Beatles Anthology* (2000); and the study of Paul McCartney by Barry Miles (1997).

BEATON, SIR CECIL WALTER HARDY (1904–1980), British designer and photographer. An influential cultural force in British life, the elegant Sir Cecil Beaton was known as much for his high-society adventures as for his designs and photographs. He was romantically linked with Greta Garbo in the 1940s. He designed stunning costumes and sets for operas, ballets, and Broadway shows, and won Academy Awards for his designs in the films *Gigi* (1959) and *My Fair Lady* (1965). Beaton was also known for his portraits of Britain's royal family and of the leading culturati of his day. He was knighted (1972) by his famous photographic subject, Queen Elizabeth II. A noted conversationalist, Beaton published numerous books, including *I Take Great Pleasure* (1957) and five volumes of diaries (1961, 1965, 1973, 1976, 1978) that were anthologized in *Self Portrait with Friends: Selected Diaries, 1926–1974* (1979). ■ See also James Danziger, ed., *Beaton* (1980); the biography by Hugo Vickers (1986); and the study edited by Philippe Garner and David A. Mellor (1994).

BEATTY, CLYDE RAYMOND (1903–1965), U.S. wild-animal trainer. Beatty joined the circus at age 15 and became the leading trainer and handler of lions and tigers in the United States. Carrying a chair, whip, and blank pistol, he performed with as many as 40 animals at once and perfected a daring "fighting act." He starred with the Ringling Broth-

ers circus before touring the country for more than 20 years with his own troupe (from 1935). He appeared in vaudeville and in the movies (including *The Big Cage,* 1933, and *Ring of Fear,* 1954) and wrote *The Big Cage* (1933), *Jungle Performers* (1941), and *Facing the Big Cats* (1965).

BEATTY, DAVID, 1st EARL BEATTY OF THE NORTH SEA AND OF BROOKSBY (1871–1936), British admiral. Commander of the battle cruiser squadron in the early years of World War I, Beatty fought many important naval battles, including the Battle of Jutland (1916), the major naval encounter (and an indecisive one) between the British and German fleets of World War I. Beatty was subsequently commander in chief of the Grand Fleet (1916–19) and first sea lord of the Admiralty (1919–27). ■ See Charles Beatty, *Our Admiral* (1980), and biography by Stephen Roskill (1981).

BEAUVOIR, SIMONE DE (1908–1986), French philosopher, novelist, and essayist. Reacting strongly against her conventional bourgeois background, Beauvoir insisted on the creation of individual values. Her novels explored the existentialist theme of the responsibility inherent in human freedom. Her search for the meaning of female identity culminated in *The Second Sex* (1949–50; Eng. trans. 1953), a critical examination of woman's fate now regarded as a pioneering effort in the new wave of feminism. Her novel *The Mandarins* (1954; Eng. trans. 1956) received the Prix Goncourt. Her autobiographical writings, including *Memoirs of a Dutiful Daughter* (1954; Eng. trans. 1959), *The Prime of Life* (1960; Eng. trans. 1962), *The Force of Circumstance* (1963; Eng. trans. 1964), and *All Said and Done* (1972; Eng. trans. 1974), reflect on the individual's quest for an "authentic" self while documenting the world of the French antiestablishment intelligentsia from 1929 to 1970. She also published *Adieux: A Farewell to Sartre* (Eng. trans. 1984) about the writer with whom she was closely allied. ■ See her *After the Second Sex: Conversations with Simone de Beauvoir* (1984; with Alice Schwarzer); biographies by Carol Asher (1981), Deirdre Bair (1990), Margaret Crosland (1992), and Toril Moi (1994); and the studies by Edward and Kate Fullbrook (1998) and Margaret A. Simons (1999).

BEAVERBROOK, WILLIAM MAXWELL AITKEN, 1st BARON (1879–1964), Canadian-born British financier, publisher, and political leader. After making a fortune as an investment banker in Canada, Aitken moved to Britain (1910) and was elected to Parliament as a Conservative (1910). A deft political manipulator, he played key roles in advancing the careers of Bonar Law and David Lloyd George, was raised to the peerage (1917), and served as minister of information during World War I (1918). Best known as a newspaper tycoon, he purchased the *London Daily Express* (1916), which he built into the daily with the world's largest circulation. He also founded the *Sunday Express*

(1921) and purchased the *Evening Standard* (1929). He used his newspapers to spread his conservative and imperialist views. A friend and supporter of Winston Churchill during the interwar years, he served as minister of aircraft production (1940–41) and minister of supply (1941–42) in Churchill's World War II Cabinet and was lord privy seal from 1943 to 1945. His books included *Politicians and War* (1928) and *Men and Power, 1917–1918* (1956). ▪ See biographies by Tom Driberg (1956), A.J.P. Taylor (1972), and Anne Chisholm (1992); and Gregory P. Marchildon, *Profits and Politics* (1996).

BECHET, SIDNEY (1897–1959), U.S. jazz musician. Among the first of the few jazz musicians to specialize in playing the soprano saxophone, Bechet was one of the early masters of New Orleans jazz. Known for his highly individualistic and intense style and technique, he appeared frequently with jazz bands in Chicago and New York in the 1920s and 1930s. Bechet was especially popular in Europe, where he was the first black jazz artist to be granted serious recognition by classical musicians. He settled in Paris in 1949. ▪ See his autobiography, *Treat It Gentle* (1960), and the biography by John Chilton (1987).

BECHTEL, STEPHEN DAVISON (1900–1989), U.S. businessman. The son of the founder of the W. A. Bechtel Co., one of the largest construction firms in the west, Stephen Bechtel served as the firm's president from 1936 to 1960 (senior director, 1960–89) and built it into what was believed to be the world's largest engineering and construction company. The firm helped build Hoover Dam, constructed hundreds of ships during World War II, and built many nuclear power plants in the United States and dozens of oil refineries, pipelines, power plants, mining projects, and factories throughout the world. Under the leadership of Stephen D. Bechtel, Jr., (president 1960–73; chairman 1973–90), the Bechtel Corp. built the trans-Alaska pipeline, the Washington, D.C., subway system, and greatly expanded operations overseas, especially in the Middle East, where it contracted to build multibillion-dollar projects in Saudi Arabia. Prominent U.S. government officials who worked for the company were Secretary of State George P. Shultz (president; 1974–82), Secretary of Defense Caspar Weinberger (general counsel and vice president; 1975–81), and CIA Directors John A. McCone and Richard Helms.

BECK, JÓSEF (1894–1944), Polish political leader. Beck was born into the Warsaw bourgeoisie and fought in Joseph Pilsudski's Polish Legions during World War I. After Pilsudski's 1926 coup, Beck became a trusted aide and confidant of the dictator. As minister of foreign affairs (1932–39) Beck negotiated alliances with France, Britain, and Rumania; he tried to maintain friendly relations with Germany and the Soviet Union as well, but his balancing act ended in 1939 when Germany invaded Poland. He was interned in Rumania, where he died. ▪ See his *Final Report* (Eng. trans. 1957).

BECK, JULIAN (1925–1985), and **JUDITH MALINA** (1926–), U.S. actors, directors, and producers. Beck grew up in a wealthy industrial family; Malina's parents were a rabbi and an actress. Both trained at Piscator's Theater Workshop in New York City. They introduced their "Living Theater" in the late 1940s by staging plays by Brecht, Lorca, Gertrude Stein, and Paul Goodman in their Manhattan apartment; they created (1951) avant-garde productions at the Cherry Lane Theater in Greenwich Village and later at other studios. They staged such new works as Jack Gelber's play about drug addiction, *The Connection* (1959), and K. H. Brown's play about the military, *The Brig* (1963). Their Living Theater concept was committed to joining together people who would share lives and work, breaking down distinctions between personal and professional, real and dramatic. They used radical styles of movement and self-expression in "street theater" that set forth their radical ideology and often encountered resistance because of the use of profanity and nudity in their theatrical exercises. ▪ See Malina's *The Enormous Despair* (1972) and her *Diaries: 1947–57* (1984) and Beck's *The Life of the Theater* (1972) and *Theaudric* (1992), his last notebooks.

BECK, LUDWIG (1880–1944), German general. A well-educated career officer, Beck served as head of the German army (1935–38). He played a major role in Germany's rearmament but disapproved of dictator Adolf Hitler's aggressive foreign policy and resigned in protest over plans to conquer Czechoslovakia. Henceforth Beck served as a focus of resistance and committed suicide after the failure of the July 20, 1944, plot against Hitler's life. ▪ See Nicholas Reynolds, *Treason Was No Crime* (1976), and Klaus-Jürgen Müller, *The Army, Politics and Society in Germany, 1933–1945* (Eng. trans. 1987).

BECK, MARTIN (1867–1940), Hungarian-born U.S. theatrical producer. One of the leading vaudeville impresarios, Beck managed the Orpheum Circuit (estab. 1903), which included 60 theaters and was the major vaudeville organization west of Chicago. He moved to New York City (1907), "discovered" many of the great entertainers of the day (including Harry Houdini), and built the legendary Palace Theater (1913), America's most celebrated vaudeville house. After serving as president of the Orpheum Circuit (1920–23), he built his own legitimate Broadway theater, the Martin Beck (1924).

BECKER, CARL LOTUS (1873–1945), U.S. historian. Becker studied at the University of Wisconsin (Ph.D. 1907) under Frederick Jackson Turner and taught at Cornell from 1917 until his retirement. An historian of ideas, he specialized in 18th-century philosophy and the American Revolution. Becker challenged the current historical vogue of "scientific" methodology, arguing that the historian works within a socially defined reality. His best-known works were *The Beginnings of the American People* (1915), *The Decla-*

ration of Independence (1922; rev. ed. 1942), and *The Heavenly City of the Eighteenth-Century Philosophers* (1932). ■ See biography by B. T. Wilkins (1961).

BECKER, GARY S. (1930–), U.S. economist. Becker was a pioneer in the application of economic analysis to such areas of human behavior as marriage, divorce, childbearing, education, racial discrimination, and crime, which had previously been considered the domain of sociologists, ethnologists, or demographers. He was a professor at the University of Chicago (1954–57; 1970–) and Columbia University (1954–57). His University of Chicago Ph.D. dissertation on the economics of racial discrimination (1955), in which he argued that discrimination was costly both to perpetrators as well as victims, was considered revolutionary at the time it was written. His book *Human Capital* (1964) analyzed education as an economic decision. In subsequent studies he analyzed the family as a productive unit and crime as a rational decision. For extending the bounds of economic theory he was awarded the 1992 Nobel Memorial Prize in Economics.

BECKETT, SAMUEL (1906–1989), Irish novelist and playwright. Born into a middle-class Protestant family in Dublin, Beckett taught in Paris (1928–30) after graduating from Trinity College and became a protégé of fellow Irish writer James Joyce, who was living in Paris at the time. He settled in Paris permanently in 1937 and wrote most of his major works in French. His difficult, unsettling, and strangely comic creations, including the internationally acclaimed play *Waiting for Godot* (1952; Eng. trans. 1954), were concerned with the ultimate absurdity, futility, and insignificance of human existence. His other well-known plays included *Endgame* (1957; Eng. trans. 1964), *Krapp's Last Tape* (1958), and *Happy Days* (1961). He also wrote the novels *Murphy* (1938); *Watt* (1953); and the trilogy *Molloy* (1951; Eng. trans. 1955), *Malone Dies* (1951; Eng. trans. 1956), and *The Unnamable* (1953; Eng. trans. 1958). He won the 1969 Nobel Prize for Literature. ■ See his *Collected Poems* (1977), *Collected Shorter Plays* (1984), *Complete Short Prose* (1996); biographies by Deirdre Bair (1978) and Anthony Cronin (1997); and James Knowlson, *Damned to Fame* (1996).

BECKMANN, MAX (1884–1950), German painter and graphic artist. One of the leading figures of expressionist art, Beckmann began painting at the turn of the century and exhibited (1913) in Berlin such epic canvases as the *Sinking of the Titanic* (1912). Influenced by medieval painting and impressionism, he was most affected by his disorienting, depressing experience as a medical corpsman in World War I (1914–15). His subsequent paintings often depicted nightmarish scenes of brutality and sadism, as in *The Night* (1919). After Beckmann's work was repudiated by Nazi authorities as "degenerate," he fled to the Netherlands. Despite hardships suffered during the German occupation, the

Amsterdam years (1936–47) resulted in several important canvases, including *Odysseus and Calypso* (1943). Beckmann emigrated (1947) to the United States, where he executed the triptych *The Argonauts* (1950). ■ See his *Self-Portrait in Words: Collected Writings and Statements, 1903–50* (1997) and studies by Friedhelm Fischer (Eng. trans. 1973), Stephan Lackner (1991), and Peter Selz (1996).

BEDNORZ, J. GEORG (1950–), German physicist. After graduating from the Swiss Federal Institute of Technology (Ph.D. 1982), Bednorz was invited to join a research team headed by K. Alex Müller at the IBM Zurich Research Laboratory. Searching for superconducting material, in which there is no electrical resistance, Bednorz and Müller discovered (1986) that a ceramic oxide of copper, lanthanum, and barium retained its superconductivity up to a room temperature of 12°C higher than that of any previously observed superconductor. Their work stunned the scientific community and inspired a torrent of new research. Many scientists predicted a new era of electricity, and prospects were raised for the production of ultraefficient power generators and transmitters, tiny superconductors, and levitating high-speed trains. Bednorz and Müller shared the 1987 Nobel Prize in Physics for their discovery.

BEEBE, LUCIUS MORRIS (1902–1966), U.S. journalist, socialite, and author. Born into a prominent Boston family, Beebe was a dandy, bon vivant, and irrepressible practical joker who, in elegant but archaic prose, chronicled the comings and goings of café society for the *New York Herald Tribune* (1933–50) and the *San Francisco Chronicle* (1960–66). An incurable romantic, he wrote several books on the history of the American west and on railroading. He was an authority on steam engines, regarding them as symbols of a vanishing past.

BEEBE, (CHARLES) WILLIAM (1877–1962), U.S. naturalist, explorer, and author. As curator of ornithology at New York's Bronx Zoo (1899–1919) and director of tropical research at the New York Zoological Society (1919–52), Beebe led numerous expeditions throughout the world and wrote of his experiences in a series of books that were praised for their literacy as well as scientific merit. Among his best-known works were *Jungle Peace* (1918), *Galápagos* (1924), *Jungle Days* (1925), *High Jungle* (1949), *Unseen Life of New York* (1953), and *Adventuring with Beebe* (1955). He made (1934) a record deep-sea dive in a bathysphere (3,028 feet) and wrote about it in *Half Mile Down* (1934). ■ See biography by Robert H. Welker, *Natural Man* (1975).

BEECHAM, SIR THOMAS (1879–1961), British conductor. Son of a wealthy pill manufacturer, Beecham attended Oxford but had little formal musical education. At age 20 he founded his first orchestra and six years later made his debut as a conductor with the Queen's Hall Orchestra. Beecham conducted his first opera at Convent Garden in 1910, after which he helped bring Russian opera and ballet to London and did much to revitalize operatic life. In 1932 he founded the London Philharmonic Orchestra, served as artistic director of Covent Garden (1933–40), and founded the Royal Philharmonic Orchestra (1947). Known for his wit and fiery temperament and for his preference for 18th-century and contemporary composers (notably Delius, Sibelius and Strauss), Beecham frequently performed in Europe and the United States. He wrote an autobiography, *A Mingled Chime* (1943), as well as a biography of the English composer Frederick Delius (1960). ■ See biography by Charles Reid (1961) and study by Alan Jefferson (1979).

BEE GEES, THE (Barry Gibb, 1946– ; Robin Gibb, 1949– ; Maurice Gibb, 1949–), pop-music group. Born in England, the sons of a bandleader, the Gibb brothers first achieved popularity as a rock group in Australia in the early 1960s. In Europe and the United States they were touted as "the second Beatles" and their recordings of soft ballads, marked by lush three-part harmonies, were best-sellers during the 1960s. After several years of decline, they switched to a modified disco-style-inspired rhythm-and-blues and dance music and launched a second career that included the sound-track album to the movie *Saturday Night Fever* (1977). It sold more than 23 million copies and spurred the "discomania" that swept America. Their big hit singles included "Nights on Broadway" and "Too Much Heaven."

BEERBOHM, SIR MAX (Henry Maximilian Beerbohm; 1872–1956), British writer, critic, and caricaturist. An Oxford-educated wit and literary personality. Beerbohm titled his first slim book *The Works of Max Beerbohm* (1896). He followed this with various collections of subtle caricatures of literary figures, prose parodies like *A Christmas Garland* (1912), comic novels like *Zuleika Dobson, or an Oxford Love Story* (1911), and collections of essays and critical pieces. George Bernard Shaw, whom Beerbohm succeeded as drama critic (1898–1910) of the *Saturday Review,* referred to the multitalented but modest Beerbohm as "the incomparable Max." Beerbohm spent much of his life after 1910 in Italy, but returned to Britain during World War II. ■ See S. N. Behrman, *Portrait of Max* (1960); Lord David Cecil, *Max* (1964); biography by Robert Viscusi (1985); and study by Lawrence Danson (1989).

BEERS, CLIFFORD WHITTINGHAM (1876–1943), U.S. social reformer. After recovering from a severe case of mental illness, during which he was confined (1900–03) in numerous institutions, Beers, a New York City businessman, led a crusade to reform the care and treatment of the mentally ill. His autobiography, *A Mind That Found Itself* (1908), heightened public understanding of mental illness and rallied many throughout the world to support his cause. He founded the National Commission for Mental Hygiene (1909), served as secretary of the American Foundation for

Mental Hygiene (1928–39), and organized the first International Congress for Mental Hygiene (1930). ■ See study by Norman Dain (1980).

BEGIN, MENACHEM (1913–1992), Polish-born Israeli political leader. A militant follower of Zionist Revisionist leader Vladimir Jabotinsky, Begin studied law at Warsaw University and graduated in 1935. He escaped to Lithuania after the German invasion (1939) but was imprisoned by the Soviets after they annexed Lithuania (1940) and was deported to Siberia. Released in 1941, he was allowed to join the Polish army in exile and was sent to Palestine (1942). There he headed the extremist underground military organization Irgun Zvai Leumi (1943–48), which played a major role in the struggle for Israeli independence. He founded the hawkish right-wing Herut party (1948) and served in the Knesset as a leader of the opposition (1948–67). Although viewed by many as a fanatic as he urged the establishment of Jewish rule on both sides of the Jordan River, he served in a national unity government (1967–70) and became prime minister as head of the right-wing coalition Likud party (1977). He entered into negotiations with Egyptian President Anwar Sadat and U.S. President Jimmy Carter which resulted in the 1979 Egypt-Israeli peace treaty and his receipt (with Sadat) of the 1978 Nobel Peace Prize. He also dramatically increased the number of Israeli settlements on the West Bank. Begin's invasion of Lebanon (1982), which led to the withdrawal of thousands of Palestinian guerrillas from Beirut, resulted in hundreds of Israeli military casualties and indirectly led to the massacre of hundreds of Palestinians in refugee camps. It provoked unprecedented antigovernment demonstrations, and influenced his decision to resign (1983). ■ See his memoirs, *The Revolt* (1950; Eng. trans. 1951) and *White Nights* (1953; Eng. trans. 1957); and biographies by Frank Gervasi (1979), Eric Silver (1984), and Amos Perlmutter (1987).

BEGLE, EDWARD GRIFFITH (1914–1978), U.S. mathematician. A professor at Yale (1942–61) and Stanford (1961–78), Begle was the person most responsible for devising the "new math" curriculum that was introduced to U.S. primary and secondary schools during the 1950s and 1960s. Emphasizing basic principles of mathematics and problem solving rather than rote learning of tables of numbers, the controversial "new math" revolutionized classroom instruction in the United States.

BEHAN, BRENDAN (1923–1964), Irish playwright. Behan drew on his experiences with the Irish Republican Army and his years in British jails and reformatories to create three celebrated plays: *The Quare Fellow* (1956), *The Hostage* (1958), and *Borstal Boy* (1958). Characterized by earthiness, gallow's humor, and unresolved endings, Behan's works were compared to those of Samuel Beckett and Jean Genet. He helped liberate the contemporary theatrical scene by introducing previously suppressed language and themes.

Known for his drinking, talking, and generally excessive public behavior, Behan was a New York City celebrity during the last four years of his life. His memoirs were *Brendan Behan's New York* (1964) and *Confessions of an Irish Rebel* (1965). ■ See Ulick O'Connor, *Brendan* (1971); E. H. Mikhail, *Brendan Behan: Interviews and Recollections* (1981); and biography by Michael O'Sullivan (1997).

BEHN, SOSTHENES (1882–1957), U.S. businessman. Born in the Virgin Islands to a French mother and a Danish father, Behn became a U.S. citizen in his youth. In partnership with his brother, he took over a Puerto Rican sugar brokerage concern (1904), purchased the Puerto Rican (1914) and the Cuban Telephone Co. (1916), and in 1920 founded the International Telephone and Telegraph Co. Under Behn's leadership—he was president (1920–48) and chairman of the board (1948–56)—IT&T grew into one of the world's largest communication companies with properties scattered worldwide.

BEHRENS, PETER (1868–1940), German architect, painter, and designer. One of the most influential architects of the first half of the 20th century, Behrens pioneered in the field of industrial design; his works were a point of departure for much of the architecture of this century. An artistic adviser to Emil Rathenau, director of the massive public-utilities company AEG, he designed everything from company brochures to factory complexes. His design for a turbine factory in Berlin (1909) is considered the first modern building using glass and steel. He also designed low-cost utilitarian workers' apartment houses in Vienna (1924–25) and Stuttgart (1927). The architects Le Corbusier, Walter Gropius, and Ludwig Mies van der Rohe worked for Behrens early in their careers. ■ See study by Alan Windsor (1981) and Tilmann Buddensieg, *Industriekultur* (Eng. trans. 1984).

BEHRMAN, SAMUEL NATHANIEL (1893–1973), U.S. playwright. After studying with George P. Baker at Harvard and Brander Matthews at Columbia, S. N. Behrman confronted the difficult social issues of the 1920s and 1930s in sophisticated drawing-room comedies such as *Biography* (1932), *Rain from Heaven* (1934), *End of Summer* (1936), and *No Time for Comedy* (1939). His casts of leisure-class characters generally featured an elegant, independent woman who provided the moral center of the plays. These roles attracted such actresses as Ina Claire, Katharine Cornell, and Lynn Fontanne. Later in his career he wrote reminiscences and a memoir of Max Beerbohm, *Portrait of Max* (1960). ■ See his memoirs, *The Worcester Account* (1954) and *People in a Diary* (1972), and study by Kenneth T. Reed (1975).

BEIDERBECKE, BIX (Leon Bismarck Beiderbecke; 1903–1931), U.S. jazz musician and composer. A legendary figure in jazz history, Beiderbecke was a self-taught cornetist, pianist, and composer who was the first acknowledged white innovator of jazz music. During a short career interrupted by illness and heavy drinking, he played with King Oliver, Louis Armstrong, and Paul Whiteman and was recognized as a master stylist on the cornet. Although relatively unknown during his lifetime, he achieved posthumous fame with the publication of Dorothy Baker's novel, *Young Man with a Horn* (1938), which was loosely based on his life. ■ See Richard M. Sudhalter and Philip R. Evans, *Bix: Man and Legend* (1974).

BÉJART, MAURICE (Maurice Jean Berger; 1927–), French ballet dancer and choreographer. Béjart's parents enrolled him in ballet school at age 14 to fortify his weak constitution. When he completed (1945) secondary school, he studied ballet in Paris and later in London. Appearing with the Royal Swedish Ballet, Béjart attempted his first choreography. He formed (1953) his own ballet company in Paris with Jean Laurent, experimenting with electronic *musique concrète*. He founded, and directed, in Brussels (1959–87) the controversial company with which he was identified— the Ballet of the Twentieth Century. He subsequently directed the Béjart Ballet Lausanne (1987–92). His popular experimental, theatrical, sometimes surrealistic creations were considered electrifying and daring by some critics, obscure and self-indulgent by others. Many of his ballets reflected his left-wing political beliefs and his interest in Eastern mysticism. ■ See Colette Masson, *Béjart by Béjart* (Eng. trans. 1980).

BÉKÉSY, GEORG VON (1899–1972), Hungarian-born U.S. physiologist. After receiving a Ph.D. in physics from the University of Budapest (1923), Békésy worked at the Hungarian telephone system research laboratory (1924–46). His extensive anatomical and physiological studies of the inner ear enabled him to demonstrate how membranes in the spiral canal called the cochlea analyze sounds and transmit them to the brain. For this discovery and his general contribution toward the understanding of "physical mechanics of acoustic stimulation," Békésy was awarded the 1961 Nobel Prize for Medicine or Physiology. After emigrating to the United States, he taught at Harvard University (1947–66) and wrote *Experiments in Hearing* (1960) and *Sensory Inhibition* (1967).

BEKHTEREV, VLADIMIR MIKHAILOVICH (1857–1927), Russian neuropathologist. Bekhterev studied in St. Petersburg (M.D. 1881), Leipzig, and Paris and taught psychiatry at Kazan University (1885–93), where he organized the first laboratory specializing in research on the anatomy and physiology of the nervous system. He later taught at the Military Medical Academy at St. Petersburg (1893–1913), founded and directed the Institute of Psychoneurology (1908) and the Institute for the Study of the Brain (1917), and founded the first Russian journals on nervous and psychic diseases. He did pioneering research on brain structure and functions, described and diagnosed several nervous diseases, and stressed the importance of conditioned reflexes in human behavior. His books included *General Principles of Human Reflexology* (4th ed. 1928; Eng. trans. 1932).

BELAFONTE, HARRY GEORGE (1927–), U.S. singer. Born in New York, Belafonte spent part of his childhood in Jamaica, where he absorbed an island culture that he would later turn to musical gold. After World War II he enrolled in the American Negro Theater on the GI bill, but it wasn't until the mid-1950s that he achieved stardom as a calypso singer with such songs as "Day-O," "Brown Skin Girl," and "Jamaica Farewell." Belafonte, who also made films and TV specials, was active in the civil-rights movement and produced the first black TV special. Belafonte remained politically active and was a moving force behind the U.S.A. for Africa recording and video, "We Are the World" (1985), in which top U.S. recording artists performed together, donating proceeds to famine relief.

BELASCO, DAVID (1853–1931), U.S. theatrical producer and playwright. A phenomenally successful Broadway producer (from 1890), Belasco claimed to have produced or written 374 plays. He launched the careers of many actors and playwrights while producing extremely popular romantic, escapist plays that appealed to what he termed "healthy" middle-class taste. His popularity waned after World War I when his audience became interested in socially significant drama. He is best remembered for his innovative lighting, lavish stage settings, and spectacular technical scenic effects that resulted in a sense of detail and realism unmatched in the theater of his day. Among his famous productions were *Madame Butterfly* (1900), *The Girl of the Golden West* (1905), and *The Return of Peter Grimm* (1911). ■ See the autobiographical *The Theater Through Its Stage Door* (1919); Craig Timberlake, *The Bishop of Broadway* (1954); and study by Lise-Lone Marker (1974).

BELAÚNDE TERRY, FERNANDO (1912–), Peruvian political leader. The son of a prime minister, Belaúnde was a prominent architect before entering politics and serving in the Chamber of Deputies (1945–48). He organized the reformist Popular Action party (1956) and twice ran unsuccessfully for the presidency (1956, 1962) before being elected in June 1963. He launched a program of economic and social reforms and attempted to maintain close relations with the United States. He was overthrown (1968), however, by the military after disagreement over the amount of freedom a U.S. oil company should have in exploiting Peruvian oil. He lived in exile until 1976 and was reelected to the presidency when political democracy was restored in 1980. His final term (1980–85) was marked by rising unemployment, the lowering of living standards, and the growth of the Maoist guerrilla movement, Shining Path. He wrote

Peru's Own Conquest (1959; Eng. trans. 1965). ■ See P. Kuczynski, *Peruvian Democracy Under Economic Stress* (1977).

BELIVEAU, JEAN (1931–), Canadian ice-hockey player. Beliveau was so highly prized as an "amateur" player that the Montreal Canadiens bought an entire hockey league in order to secure his services. The investment paid off, as Beliveau became the highest-scoring center in National Hockey League history with 1,219 points. He led the Canadiens to ten Stanley Cup championships in his 18 years of play (1953–71). He was named to the All-Star team 10 times and twice won the Hart Trophy as the league's Most Valuable Player (1956, 1964).

BELL, CLIVE (1881–1964), British critic. Bell married Vanessa Stephen, sister of Virginia Woolf, and figured in the Bloomsbury group (though he denied its existence and insisted that the label was imposed by antagonistic outsiders on a group of family and friends). Bell's astute articles in the *New Statesman* and the *Nation* dealt with the emotional impact of visual art; they also commented on literary and political matters. In *Art* (1914), he proposed that "significant form," rather than content or moral message, is the essential quality of a work of art. He also wrote *Peace at Once* (1915), *Poems* (1921), *Since Cézanne* (1922), *On British Freedom* (1923), *Landmarks in Nineteenth-Century Painting* (1927), *Civilisation* (1928), *Proust* (1928), *An Account of French Painting* (1931), and *Old Friends* (1956). ■ See William G. Bywater, Jr., *Clive Bell's Eye* (1975).

BELL, DANIEL (1919–), U.S. sociologist. A product of New York City's Lower East Side, Bell became a radical journalist during the late 1930s and studied sociology at Columbia and the University of Chicago. His politics changed from socialist to moderate liberal, and he spent a decade as labor editor of *Fortune* magazine (1948–58) and wrote *The End of Ideology* (1960), an influential collection of his articles on the declining appeal of the world's "isms." He cofounded (with Irving Kristol) and coedited (1965–73) the quarterly *Public Interest,* joined the Harvard faculty (1969–90), and ventured into social forecasting with *The Coming of Post-Industrial Society* (1973). He also wrote *The Cultural Contradictions of Capitalism* (1976), *The Winding Passage: Essays and Sociological Journeys, 1960–1980* (1981), and *Communitarianism and Its Critics* (1993). ■ See studies by Nathan Liebowitz (1985), Howard Brick (1986), and Malcolm Waters (1995).

BELL, LAWRENCE DALE (1894–1956), U.S. aircraft designer and manufacturer. Bell began (1912) his career as an airplane mechanic and went on to establish (1935) the Bell Aircraft Corp., the company that designed the first American jet planes. Bell Aircraft also designed World War II fighter planes as well as the first airplane to exceed the speed of sound in level flight (1947). An innovator in assembly-line production of airplanes, Bell was one of the few aviation pioneers to remain active well into the supersonic jet era. ▪ See biography by Donald J. Norton (1981).

BELL, VANESSA (1879–1961), British painter. Vanessa Bell was the older sister of Virgina Woolf; she, her sister, and brothers Thoby and Adrian Stephen formed the nucleus of the Bloomsbury group, a circle of artists, writers, and intellectuals who were widely influential in Britain before and after World War I. Bell's style during the period from 1910 to 20 was inspired by the fauvists and was characterized by the free use of flat, often unmodulated color areas. Her later work tended to be less decorative and more representational, though still very much governed by formal relationships. Bell's many portraits of the Bloomsbury circle reflected her movement from the early naturalistic style through a more abstract period to her intimate, psychologically revealing later works. ▪ See Richard Shone, *Bloomsbury Portraits* (1976), and biography by Frances Spalding (1983).

BELL BURNELL, JOCELYN (1943–), British astronomer. Born and raised on a family estate in rural Northern Ireland, Bell Burnell became interested in astronomy during her childhood and was the only woman in her class at the University of Glasgow to earn a degree in physics (B.Sc. 1965). As a graduate student of Anthony Hewish at Cambridge (Ph.D. 1968) she helped design and construct a large radio telescope. While meticulously analyzing the massive amount of data-filled paper emanating from the telescope's recorders, she discovered (1967) a new class of celestial object, the pulsar (pulsating radio star), a rapidly spinning superdense object composed almost entirely of neutrons. The discovery had a revolutionary effect on the field of astronomy and earned for Hewish (but not Bell Burnell) a share of the 1974 Nobel Prize in Physics. Bell Burnell subsequently made contributions in the areas of X-ray and gamma-ray astronomy and analyzed data from orbiting satellites and space observatories. She did research at the Mullard Space Science Laboratory at the University of London (1974–82) and The Royal Observatory, Edinburgh (1982–91) and was a professor of physics at the Open University (1991–).

BELLI, MELVIN MOURON (1907–1996), U.S. attorney. A San Francisco socialite from a gold-rush family, Belli graduated from the University of California Law School (1933) and went on to specialize in large personal injury and malpractice cases. The "king of torts," he was known for his theatrical presentation of evidence in the form of stomach-churning pictures and witnesses arriving by stretcher. Belli also wrote a number of litigation textbooks, as well as *Dallas Justice* (1964), the story of his defense of Jack Ruby, in the aftermath of Pres. John F. Kennedy's assassination. ▪ See his autobiography (1976).

BELLO, ALHAJI SIR AHMADU (1909–1966), Nigerian political leader. The descendant of a 19th-century Islamic leader, Ahmadu Bello was a powerful figure in Nigerian politics. He helped to found the Northern People's Congress (NPC) and served as a member of the federal house of representatives (1952–59) and as prime minister (1954–66) of the northern region. He espoused federalism, but after independence (1960) worked to achieve northern domination of the federal state. He was assassinated in the military coup that ended northern domination of the country. ▪ See his autobiography, *My Life* (1962).

BELLOC, (JOSEPH PIERRE) HILAIRE (1870–1953), French-born British essayist, poet, and historian. Belloc wrote widely in many genres and on many subjects but always from a distinctly European and Roman Catholic viewpoint. His poetry, including his first book *Verses and Sonnets* (1895) and *The Bad Child's Book of Beasts* (1896), won many readers. In a long career he wrote many volumes of essays and reflections on nature, life, and Christianity, such as *The Path to Rome* (1902) and *Essays of a Catholic Layman in England* (1931), satirical novels, and historical studies and biographies. *The Servile State* (1912) described his anticapitalist and antisocialist philosophy of distribution, which he shared with his close friend, the author G. K. Chesterton. ▪ See biographies by Robert Speaight (1957) and A. N. Wilson (1984), and study by Michael H. Markel (1982).

BELLOW, SAUL (1915–), Canadian-born U.S. novelist. Reared as an Orthodox Jew, Bellow identified closely with the traditions of his Eastern European immigrant family. He abandoned graduate study in anthropology when his thesis kept "turn[ing] out to be a story." Bellow's comic novels attempted to fathom the modern world by examining the obsessions of American city dwellers. *Dangling Man* (1944) was followed by well-received novels that portrayed self-deluding, anxiety-ridden characters, including *The Adventures of Augie March* (1953), *Seize the Day* (1956), *Henderson the Rain King* (1959), and *Mr. Sammler's Planet* (1970). His best-known novel, *Herzog* (1966), focused on a tormented middle-aged intellectual seeking peace of mind. He also wrote *Humboldt's Gift* (1975). When he won the Nobel Prize for Literature (1976), Bellow noted that that honor had seemingly silenced other American recipients, including Ernest Hemingway and John Steinbeck; Bellow reserved his preeminent place in American letters, however, publishing *The Dean's December* (1981), *A Theft* (1989), *The Actual* (1997), *Ravelstein* (2000), *Something to Remember Me By: Three Tales* (1991), and *Him with His Foot in His Mouth and Other Stories* (1984). ▪ See studies by Mark Harris (1980), Robert R. Dutton (rev. ed. 1982), Daniel Fuchs (1983), and L. H. Goldman (1983); and biographies by Ruth Miller (1991) and James Atlas (2000).

BELLOWS, GEORGE WESLEY (1882–1925), U.S. painter. One of the most popular American realist painters of his time, Bellows vividly depicted scenes of city life (*Forty-two Kids,* 1907), and sporting events (*Stag at Sharkey's,* 1907; *Dempsey Through the Ropes,* 1924). His exuberant, vital works were scorned by conservative critics, but he was nevertheless the youngest man, at age 27, to be elected to the National Academy of Design. Bellows was an organizer of the famous New York Armory Show (1913) that introduced modern European art to the United States. He produced a series of powerful paintings depicting World War I. In 1916 he turned to lithography and inspired a revival of interest in that medium, which was seldom used by serious artists of the time. ▪ See biography by Charles H. Morgan (1965) and study by Marianne Doezema (1992).

BELLUSCHI, PIETRO (1899–1994), Italian-born U.S. architect. A practicing architect in Portland, Oregon, from 1925 to 1950, Belluschi was best known for structures carefully designed to fit the physical and social environment of the Pacific Northwest. From 1950 to 1965 he served as dean of the school of architecture and planning at the Massachusetts Institute of Technology. His later buildings included the Bank of America World Headquarters (San Francisco, 1969) and the Juilliard School of Music at Lincoln Center (New York City, 1969). ▪ See study by Meredith L. Clausen (1994).

BELMONDO, JEAN-PAUL (1933–   ), French film actor. Son of a sculptor, Belmondo studied at the Paris Conservatory before his role in *Breathless* (1959) launched him as the Humphrey Bogart of French film. The young actor with the battered face of a prizefighter abandoned his cynical style briefly in *Two Women* (1961) but resumed the stance of a highly stylized hero in *That Man from Rio* (1963) and *Pierrot le Fou* (1965). He was France's most popular male film star in the 1960s and directed his own production company, Cerito Films. He won the Cesar Award for best actor in 1988.

BELMONTE Y GARCÍA, JUAN (1892–1962), Spanish bullfighter. The most revolutionary matador of the century, Belmonte fought closer to the bulls than any matador had previously dared and was regarded as the creator of modern bullfighting. He introduced the technique of standing motionless and erect and using the cape to divert the bulls rather than using footwork to escape being gored by the charging animals. Called the "King of Matadors," he was considered the greatest bullfighter of his time; he killed 1,650 bulls during his career (1910–35). By appearing in 109 *corridas* in 1919, he set a record that was not broken until 1965 (by El Cordobés). ▪ See his autobiography (Eng. trans. 1937).

BELO, CARLOS FILIPE XIMENES (1948–   ), Timorese religious leader. Belo was educated in Madrid and lived in Portugal for over a decade before becoming Roman Catholic bishop of his native East Timor (1983). The overwhelmingly Catholic former Portuguese colony had been invaded (1975) and annexed (1976) by Indonesia after a few months of independence. Belo immediately began to denounce the brutality and repression of Indonesian rule and called for international assistance in ending human rights abuses. Although the target of several assassination attempts, he continued to speak out on behalf of his people and helped keep the East Timor issue alive in international forums and in the press. He called for the Indonesians to reduce their military presence, end repressive policies, and allow the East Timorese to hold a referendum on self-determination. He shared the 1996 Nobel Peace Prize with José Ramos-Horta for working to bring about a nonviolent solution to the conflict. ▪ See Arnold S. Kohen, *From the Place of the Dead* (1999).

BELTRÁN, LOLA (**Maria Lucila Beltrán Ruiz; c. 1934–1996**), Mexican singer. While working as a secretary at a Mexico City radio station during the early 1950s, Beltrán persuaded a popular mariachi group singing in a rehearsal studio to allow her to perform with them. She was an immediate hit, and was soon given her own show. Her emotional interpretations of melancholy mariachi ballads, which focus on loneliness, suffering, abandonment, poverty, and loss, endeared her to millions of fans around the world. Known as "The Queen" and "Lola the Great," she recorded more than 100 albums and appeared in more than 50 movies during a career that spanned five decades. Among her most famous songs were *Cucurucucu Paloma, Three Days, Bed of Stone, To the Four Winds,* and *If You Should Return.*

BELY, ANDREI (**Boris Nikolaevich Bugaev; 1890–1934**), Russian poet, novelist, and critic. Bely studied science and mathematics before devoting himself to the symbolist literary movement, which tended to view the bolshevik revolution as an event of mystical significance. He wrote theoretical works, rejecting logic in favor of intuitive association as a literary principle. The rhythmic prose of Bely's masterpiece, *Petersburg* (1913–16; Eng. trans. 1978), decisively influenced the prose of Boris Pilnyak and Marina Tsvetaeva and was instrumental in the evolution of formalist criticism. He also wrote the four-volume poetry collection *Symphonies* (1901–08), the novels *The Silver Dove* (1910; Eng. trans. 1974) and *The Baptized Chinaman* (1927), studies of the writers Pushkin and Gogol, and four books of memoirs. Bely professed support of the Soviet regime but his writings were suppressed altogether after 1965. His *Complete Short Stories* appeared in English in 1979; translations of *Selected Essays* appeared in 1985. ▪ See studies by J. D. Ellsworth (1972), Konstantin Mochulsky (Eng. trans. 1977), and Vladimir Alexandrov (1985).

BEMELMANS, LUDWIG (1898–1962), Austrian-born U.S. writer and artist. A rambunctious son of a ne'er-do-well and mostly absent Belgian artist father and a Bavarian mother, Bemelmans was given the choice (at age 16) of reform school or emigration to the United States. He chose the latter and became one of America's best-loved and most widely read authors. His joie de vivre was expressed in numerous magazine pieces and in more than 30 wryly humorous books, ranging from *My War with the United States* (1937), based on his World War I army experiences, to *Dirty Eddie* (1947), a satire about Hollywood, to *On Board Noah's Ark* (1962), a travel book. He was best known for *Madeline* (1939), a story written in verse about a young girl living in Paris. ■ See his selected writings in *Tell Them It Was Wonderful* (1985); the study by Jackie F. Eastman (1996); and biography by John Bemelmans Marciano (1999).

BEMIS, SAMUEL FLAGG (1891–1973), U.S. historian. A Harvard-educated (Ph.D. 1916) expert on U.S. diplomatic history, Bemis taught at Yale for 25 years (1935–60). He won Pulitzer Prizes for *Pinckney's Treaty* (1926) and *John Quincy Adams and the Foundations of American Foreign Policy* (1949), and also wrote *John Quincy Adams and the Union* (1956) and the frequently revised text, *A Diplomatic History of the United States* (1936). Bemis was an ardent patriot and favored an active American role abroad.

BENACERRAF, BARUJ (1920–   ), Venezuelan-born U.S. immunologist. Benacerraf directed research at the National Center for Scientific Research in Paris (1950–56) and taught at New York University (1957–68) and Harvard Medical School (1970–91). His discovery of specific immune-response (Ir) genes that control responses to thymus-dependent antigens contributed greatly to the understanding of human diseases and made it possible to determine why some individuals are more likely than others to suffer from specific infections and diseases. He shared the 1980 Nobel Prize for Physiology or Medicine with George Snell and Jean Dausset.

BENAVENTE Y MARTÍNEZ, JACINTO (1866–1954), Spanish playwright. A dandy in his youth, Benavente became the most popular Spanish playwright of his day with his well-made comedies of manners. He wrote and staged 172 plays using deliberate frivolity and avoiding social commentary. After such plays as *Bonds of Interest* (1907; Eng. trans. 1915), *Señora Ama* (1908), and *La Malquerida* (1913; Eng. trans. 1917) earned him the 1922 Nobel Prize for Literature, his work declined. Despite the rather formulaic nature of his work, he helped establish modern theater in Spain by importing the techniques of such European playwrights as Pirandello, Giraudoux, Shaw, Cocteau, and Synge. ■ See studies by Marcelino C. Peñulas (Eng. trans. 1968) and José A. Diaz (1972).

BEN BELLA, AHMED (1918–   ), Algerian political leader. A veteran of the French army, Ben Bella assembled an extremist group of Algerian nationalists seeking an end to French colonialism (1947) and was an organizer of the armed rebellion that began in November 1954. He was a gunrunner and high-level diplomat with the National Liberation Front until he was arrested by French colonial authorities in 1956. Imprisoned for the next six years, he developed an ideology of Islamic traditionalism combined with Third World-style socialism. After his release he was elected president of independent Algeria in 1963 but was ousted by the army in 1965 and kept under house arrest until 1979. He subsequently lived in exile until returning to Algeria in 1990. ■ See biography by Robert Merle (1967).

BENCHLEY, ROBERT CHARLES (1889–1945), U.S. humorist, drama critic, and movie actor. A theater critic for *Life* (1920–29), Benchley later wrote the acerbic Guy Fawkes column in the *New Yorker* (1929–40), created 46 cinema "shorts" (including *How to Sleep,* 1935), and appeared in minor roles in 50 movies. His 15 books of humorous essays included *Of All Things* (1921), *My Ten Years in a Quandary and How They Grew* (1936), and *Benchley Beside Himself* (1943). A master of the nonsequitur and an after-dinner speaker par excellence, he was part of the Round Table, the literary circle that frequented New York's Algonquin Hotel. *Benchley Roundup* (1954), a posthumous collection, was edited by his son, the writer Nathaniel Benchley. *Benchley at the Theatre* (1985) includes drama criticism from the 1920s and 1930s. ■ See biographies by Nathaniel Benchley (1955) and Babette Rosmond (1970); and Billy Altman, *Laughter's Gentle Soul* (1997).

BENDA, JULIEN (1867–1956), French novelist and philosopher. Benda graduated (1894) from the University of Paris and first won critical attention for his novel *The Yoke of Pity* (1912; Eng. trans. 1913). At the same time he published a series of attacks on the intuitive metaphysics of Henri Bergson, establishing himself as leader among French rationalists. He was best known for the popular but often misrepresented work, *The Treason of the Intellectuals* (1927; Eng. trans. 1928), which decried the transformation of ideas into political and racial ideologies. Benda wrote the intellectual autobiographies *The Youth of an Intellectual* (1937) and *A Regulator in His Century* (1938). ■ See the study by Robert J. Niess (1956).

BENEDICT XV (Giacomo della Chiesa; 1854–1922), Italian-born pope of the Roman Catholic Church. Della Chiesa aspired to the priesthood but at his father's urging instead earned (1875) a doctorate in civil law. He was later ordained (1878) and earned further degrees in theology and canon law. Della Chiesa served in the papal diplomatic service, spent four years in Spain, and became papal under secretary of state and archbishop of Bologna (1907). Three months after Pope Pius X named him cardinal (1914), della Chiesa became Pope Benedict XV; the outbreak of World War I a month earlier underscored the need at the time for a pope skilled in diplomacy and jurisprudence. Benedict XV remained impartial, concentrating on humanitarian efforts. He offered a seven-point peace note to both sides, but it was rejected. His ultimate ineffectiveness resulted in lost prestige for the Vatican; Benedict was later excluded from peace negotiations. ▪ See biography by Walter H. Peters (1959).

BENEDICT, RUTH (Ruth Fulton; 1887–1948), U.S. anthropologist. A student of English literature at Vassar, Benedict studied anthropology under Franz Boas at Columbia University, where she received her Ph.D. (1923) and taught (1924–48). Her theories, especially in the area of culture and personality, attached great humanistic importance to the intellectual, aesthetic, and religious aspects of culture. Her most influential work, *Patterns of Culture* (1934) emphasized the role of human behavior and personality and the way these are shaped by societal patterns. Her investigation into the folklore and religion of American Indian peoples resulted in *Zuñi Mythology* (2 vols., 1935). She supported the concept of cultural relativism and wrote against racism (*Race: Science and Politics,* 1940) and ethnocentrism. ▪ See studies by Margaret Mead (1974) and Judith Modell (1983); and biography by Margaret M. Caffrey (1989).

BENEŠ, EDUARD (1884–1948), Czech political leader. The youngest of 10 children of a farmer, Beneš studied under the philosopher Tomáš Masaryk at the University of Prague before completing his education in France. He was a prominent member of the Czech national liberation movement and served as his country's first foreign minister (1918–35). He oriented his foreign policy toward France, strongly supported the League of Nations, and sought to establish a balance of power in Eastern Europe. He succeeded Masaryk as president (1935) but resigned and went into exile after the Munich Pact (1938) dismembered his country. Beneš was president of the World War II Czech provisional government in London, a position he retained after he returned to Prague (1945). He attempted to make Czechoslovakia a "bridge" between East and West Europe, but he resigned after the communist coup in 1948. ▪ See his *Memoirs* (Eng. trans. 1954) and study by Edward Taborsky (1981).

BENÉT, STEPHEN VINCENT (1898–1943), U.S. poet, novelist, and short-story writer. An "army brat," Benét developed an early interest in military history and writing and pursued a literary career after graduating from Yale (1919). He wrote the widely read narrative poem about the Civil War, *John Brown's Body* (1928; Pulitzer Prize), and many other patriotic works based on American folklore and history. His later work included *Western Star* (1943; Pulitzer Prize), a narrative of early American settlement, and a folk-opera libretto based on his short story "The Devil and Daniel Webster" (1937). His brother William Rose Benét (1886–1950) was a poetry critic for the *Saturday Review of Literature* and author of many verse collections, including *The Dust Which Is God* (1941; Pulitzer Prize). ▪ See studies by Charles Fenton (1958) and Parry E. Stroud (1963).

BEN-GURION, DAVID (David Gruen; 1886–1973), Israeli political leader. A Polish-born Zionist who went to Palestine as a farm laborer in 1906. Ben-Gurion fought in World War I with the British against the Turks for the liberation of Palestine. He was one of the founders of the Histadrut, the Jewish labor federation, and served as chairman of the Zionist Executive and of the Jewish Agency (from 1935). He headed the provisional government during Israel's war of independence (1948). After the war his Mapai (Zionist-Socialist) party gained dominance and Ben-Gurion served as Israel's prime minister (1948–53; 1955–63). By the time he retired from political life in 1970, he had come to symbolize the tenacity and determination of the young Jewish state. His books included *Rebirth and Destiny of Israel* (1954), *The Jews in Their Land* (1966), and *Israel: A Personal History* (1970). ▪ See his *Memoirs* (1970); biographies by Maurice Edelman (1964), Michael Bar-Zohar (Eng. trans. 1967), and Dan Kurzman (1983); and study by Shabtai Teveth (1985).

BENJAMIN, WALTER (1892–1940), German philosopher and critic. A brilliant but little-known radical writer and translator during his lifetime, Benjamin emigrated to Paris when the Nazis came to power (1933) and was associated with the Frankfurt Institute for Social Research (in exile) from 1935 until 1940. When his escape (to the United States) from German-occupied France seemed thwarted, he committed suicide. Influenced by Jewish mysticism as well as Hegelian and Marxist thought, Benjamin was primarily concerned with the symbolic nature, social functions, and political bases of art, as well as with the faulty consciousness of intellectuals and the ways in which perception is dependent upon technology and mass culture. With the posthumous publication and translations of his essays in book form, he came to be regarded as one of the most important social critics of the century. His major works included *The Origin of German Tragic Drama* (1928; Eng. trans. 1977), *Charles Baudelaire* (1969; Eng. trans. 1973), *Understanding Brecht* (1966; Eng. trans. 1973), the essays in *Illuminations* (1968), *Reflections* (1978), and *One-Way Street and Other Writings* (1979), and *The Arcades Project* (Eng. trans. 1999), a monumental study of 19th-century Paris. ▪ See his *Selected Writings* (2 vols., 1996, 1999); studies by Terry Eagleton (1981), Gershom Scholem (1975; Eng. trans. 1982), Richard Wolin (1982), and Julian Roberts (1983); and biography by Momme Brodersen (1990; Eng. trans. 1996).

BENN, GOTTFRIED (1886–1956), German poet and critic. Benn was a skin surgeon who served as a medical officer during World War I. He adapted the clinical language of medical literature to create a body of pessimistic expressionist poetry that used images of physical agony, degeneracy, and decay to depict the moral and spiritual condition of mankind. His works were influential in Germany after both world wars. Benn's important collections were *Morgue* (1912), *Flesh* (1917), and *Statistical Poems* (1948). English translations of his works are in J. M. Ritchie, *Gottfried Benn: The Unreconstructed Expressionist* (1972); E. B. Ashton, ed., *Primal Vision: Selected Writings* (1960); and Volkmar Sander, ed., *Prose, Essays, and Poems* (1987). ▪ See his autobiography *Double Life* (1950) and study by Mark W. Roche (1991).

BENN, TONY (Anthony Neil Wedgwood Benn; 1925–), British political leader. The president of the Oxford Union (M.A. 1949), Benn served as a Labour member of the House of Commons (1950–60) before being forced to step down when he inherited a peerage from his father. After lengthy legal battles, he disclaimed the title (1963), was reelected (1963), and served as minister of technology (1966–70) and secretary of state for energy (1975–79). A spokesman of Labour's left wing during the 1970s, Benn was instrumental in the adoption of new party rules that gave increased power to activists and trade unionists at the expense of parliamentary representatives. His book *Arguments for Socialism* (1979) called for public ownership of industry and self-management in the workplace, and he was the unofficial leader of the radical left of the Labour party during the early 1980s. He lost his seat in the landslide 1983 Conservative party election victory, but was reelected to the House of Commons in 1984. He was opposed to the Labour party's shift to the right in the 1990s and criticized many of Labour Prime Minister Tony Blair's policies (1997–). His six published volumes of diaries were excerpted in *The Benn Diaries, 1940–1990* (1995). ▪ See biographies by Robert Jenkins (1981) and Jad Adams (1992).

BENNETT, (ENOCH) ARNOLD (1867–1931), British novelist, dramatist, and critic. A prolific and popular writer, Bennett was considered one of the leading novelists of his day until his reputation slipped toward the end of his career. Influenced by the naturalism of French writers Émile Zola and Gustave Flaubert, he wrote about the difficult lives of the ordinary shopkeepers and potters of the "Five Towns" of northern Britain in *The Old Wives' Tale* (1908), considered his finest novel, and the trilogy *Clayhanger* (1910), *Hilda Lessways* (1911), and *These Twain* (1916). Bennett wrote many less serious popular novels and potboilers for money to support his lavish lifestyle. Several of his plays were successful, and he was also a prominent literary critic. ▪ See his *Journals* (3 vols., 1932–33); biographies by Reginald Pound (1952) and Margaret Drabble (1974); and studies by Olga Broomfield (1984) and Robert Squillace (1997).

BENNETT, FLOYD (1890–1928), U.S. aviator. A naval aviator during World War I, Bennett accompanied explorer Richard E. Byrd on the MacMillan expedition to Greenland (1925). He served as pilot for Byrd on his flight to the North Pole (1926), after which both men returned home as heroes and were awarded the Congressional Medal of Honor. Bennett was planning an expedition with Byrd to the South Pole when he was stricken with pneumonia and died.

BENNETT, HUGH HAMMOND (1881–1960), U.S. soil scientist. A pioneer in the field of soil conservation, Bennett joined the department of agriculture in 1903 and supervised large-scale soil surveys in the United States and Latin America before heading the department's Soil Erosion Bureau (1928–33). As director of the interior department's Soil Erosion Service (1933–35), he directed programs to stem the growing "dust bowl" and established control projects in 30 states. He was the first director of the agriculture department's Soil Conservation Service (1935–52). His books included *Soils of the U.S.* (1913), *Soil Erosion: A National Menace* (1928), and *Soil Conservation* (1939). ▪ See Wellington Brink, *Big Hugh* (1951).

BENNETT, MICHAEL (Michael Bennett DeFiglia, 1943–1987), U.S. choreographer, producer, and director. Bennett started dance lessons at the age of 3 and left high school at 16 to dance in the chorus of a touring company of *West Side Story*. He danced in the chorus of several Broadway musicals and assisted in choreographing several others before becoming sole choreographer for *A Joyful Noise* (1966). Thus began an amazingly productive Broadway career in which Bennett won eight Tony Awards and garnered Tony nominations for every musical he was associated with. Hailed as an innovative genius, Bennett used lighting, costumes, sets, and moving bodies to dramatic effect, and his dances evolved directly from the action and character development of the plays. He was best known as the choreographer of *Promises, Promises* (1968) and *Coco* (1969), choreographer and codirector (with Harold Prince) of *Follies* (1971), and director and choreographer of *Dream Girls* (1981). *A Chorus Line* (1975; Pulitzer Prize 1976), which Bennett choreographed and directed, became the longest-running show in Broadway history (1983) until being eclipsed by *Cats* (1997). Bennett died of AIDS-related cancer.

BENNETT, RICHARD BEDFORD BENNETT, 1st VISCOUNT (1870–1947), Canadian political leader. Born in New Brunswick, Bennett practiced law there and in Calgary before entering local politics in 1898. Elected to the Canadian House of Commons (1911), he served in two federal cabinets (1920–21; 1926) and was elected to head the Conservative party in 1927. In 1930 he led the party to victory, contributing $600,000 of his own money. The aloof Bennett was a highly unpopular prime minister; many of his protectionist policies aimed at ending the Depression failed. Badly beaten at the polls by the Liberals in 1935, he remained in opposition until 1938 and retired to Britain in 1939. ▪ See study by Ernest Watkins (1963); J.R.H. Wilbur, *The Bennett New Deal* (1968); and Larry A. Glassford, *Reaction and Reform* (1992).

BENNETT, TONY (Anthony Dominick Benedetto; 1926–), U.S. pop singer. A native of New York City, Bennett sang with various military bands while serving in the army during World War II and appeared on several television shows before signing a contract with Columbia records (1950). A polished ballad singer, Bennett projected warmth, relaxation, and sincerity with such hits as "Because of You," "Cold, Cold Heart," "Rags to Riches," "Stranger in Paradise," and "I Left My Heart in San Francisco," and was one of the most popular vocalists of his generation. Five albums that he recorded during the 1990s, including *Perfectly Frank* (1992), *MTV Unplugged* (1994), and *Tony Bennett on Holiday* (1996) won Grammy Awards. ■ See his memoir, *The Good Life* (1998; with Will Friedwald).

BENNY, JACK (Benjamin Kubelsky; 1894–1974), U.S. radio and television performer and comedian. After working the borscht circuit of Catskill resorts, Benny debuted (1931) in radio on "The Ed Sullivan Show" and soon launched (1932) his own series. He continued on radio until 1955 and then successfully transplanted his show—retaining its basic format—to the TV screen. The show featured Benny as an affected tightwad who celebrated yearly his 39th birthday and who squeaked out "Love in Bloom" on his violin. Known for his matchless timing and delivery rather than for joke-telling, Benny was himself the butt of his mordant humor. Part of his successful formula was the resident cast who filled out his sketches: his wife Mary Livingstone, announcer Don Wilson, and comedians Eddie (Rochester) Anderson and Mel Blanc. ■ See his *Sunday Nights at Seven* (1990) and biographies by Irving A. Fein (1976) and Mary Livingstone Benny and Hilliard Marks (1978).

BENSON, OSCAR HERMAN (1875–1951), U.S. educator. A former county superintendent of schools in Iowa, O. H. Benson founded the 4-H (hand, heart, head, health) movement in 1910 to encourage profit-making crafts and skills among rural youth. He was also involved with the Junior Achievement movement (1919–24), an effort to promote entrepreneurial ability among urban adolescents. He served as president of the Home Canners Association of America (1921–25) and was director of rural scouting services for the Boy Scouts of America (1926–40).

BENTLEY, ARTHUR FISHER (1870–1957), U.S. political scientist, sociologist, and philosopher. After earning his Ph.D. (1895) from Johns Hopkins, Bentley devoted his life to writing. Working as a reporter in Chicago until 1910, he made a firsthand study of interest groups the subject of his classic book, *The Process of Government: A Study of Social Pressures* (1908). He also wrote *Behavior, Knowledge, Fact* (1935), which developed from his desire to provide political science with a behavioral methodology. His other profound and iconoclastic books, including *Relativity in Man and Society* (1926), *Linguistic Analysis of Mathematics* (1932), and *Knowing and the Known* (1949; with John Dewey), influenced scholars in many fields. ■ See Paul Kress, *Social Science and the Idea of Progress: The Ambiguous Legacy of Arthur F. Bentley* (1970) and James F. Ward, *Language, Form and Inquiry* (1984).

BENTLEY, ELIZABETH TERRILL (1908–1963), U.S. spy. Claiming that she was troubled by her "good old New England conscience," Bentley revealed to the FBI (1945) the espionage activities she carried out during World War II on behalf of the Soviet Union. A 1930 Vassar graduate, she had been recruited by a master spy with whom she had a love affair. Her disclosures to congressional committees led to the conviction (1949) of 11 Communist party leaders for conspiracy to advocate the overthrow of the U.S. government. She made elaborate accusations against 37 government employees, but none was ever indicted for spying. Bentley testified as a government witness against Julius and Ethel Rosenberg, who were executed for treason in 1953. ■ See her *Out of Bondage* (1951).

BENTON, THOMAS HART (1889–1975), U.S. painter. Named after his great-uncle, the Missouri senator, Benton studied in Paris for several years before abandoning modernism and settling into a naturalistic, regional painting style (c. 1920). His works, extremely popular during the 1930s, glorified rural and small-town life, and he inveighed against both urban civilization and abstract art. In an effort to "democratize" art he painted murals in preference to canvases—huge creations full of "down-home" energy. There are examples in New York's Whitney Museum, the Jefferson City, Missouri, Statehouse, and the Post Office Department and Department of Justice buildings in Washington, D.C. ■ See his autobiography, *An Artist in America* (rev. ed. 1983), and Wilma Yeo and Helen K. Cook, *Maverick with a Paintbrush* (1977).

BENTON, WILLIAM (1900–1973), U.S. businessman, educator, and politician. A clergyman's son, Benton worked his way through Yale (B.A. 1921) as a high-stakes bridge player. He then founded an advertising agency with his friend Chester Bowles, pioneering in the field by using consumer-research surveys and airing singing commercials on radio. As he had planned, he quit advertising when he made his first million dollars at age 35. He was later vice-president of the University of Chicago (1937–45) and assistant secretary of state (1945–47). Benton was an appointed Democratic U.S. senator from Connecticut (1949) who was elected (1950) to serve two years of an unexpired term. His opposition to the "witchhunting" tactics of Sen. Joseph R. McCarthy helped bring about Benton's defeat. He published the *Encyclopedia Britannica* (1943–73) and used his clever, hard-selling techniques to make it a success. ■ See Sidney Hyman, *The Lives of William Benton* (1969).

BERCHTOLD, COUNT LEOPOLD VON (1863–1942), Austro-Hungarian statesman. One of the richest men in Austria-Hungary, Berchtold was foreign minister during the crucial years 1912 to 1915. His indecisive policies aggravated tensions between Austria-Hungary and Serbia, and the ultimatum he sent to Serbia following the assassination of Archduke Francis Ferdinand (1914) led to the outbreak of World War I. He resigned his post (1915) over disputes regarding Italian participation in the war and retired from public life.

BERDYAEV, NIKOLAI ALEKSANDROVICH (1874–1948), Russian religious philosopher. A Marxist during his early years, Berdyaev was exiled by the czarist government at the turn of the century. After the bolsheviks took power, he returned to accept a professorship in Moscow (1920). Berdyaev became identified with a group of intellectuals passionately interested in Russian Orthodoxy. Again at odds with official dogma, he was exiled in 1922. He founded an academy of religious philosophy in Berlin, then moved it to Paris, where he lived until his death. His extremely influential writings challenged numerous tenets of traditional Orthodox thought. He argued that human fulfillment lies in the free, creative act and that God is the source of human freedom. He saw technology as a dehumanizing force. His important works included *The Meaning of History* (1923; Eng. trans. 1936) and *The Destiny of Man* (1931; Eng. trans. 1937). ■ See his *Dream and Reality: An Essay in Autobiography* (Eng. trans. 1950); Donald A. Lowrie, *Rebellious Prophet* (1960); and Michael A. Vallon, *An Apostle of Freedom* (1960).

BERENSON, BERNARD (1865–1959), Lithuanian-born U.S. art critic and historian. Berenson was one of the most influential and respected art critics and scholars of the century and was also considered one of the greatest wits and conversationalists of his time. His special area of expertise was Italian Renaissance art, and he authenticated and helped build up many of America's most important art collections. From 1900 he lived in an 18th-century villa, I Tatti, outside of Florence, Italy, which became a major intellectual center housing his art collection and library. He bequeathed the villa to Harvard University, his alma mater, which turned it into the Center for Italian Renaissance Culture. In addition to his numerous works on art history and aesthetics, he wrote four volumes of autobiography: *Sketch for a Self Portrait* (1949), *Rumor and Reflection* (1952), *The Passionate Sightseer* (1960), and *Sunset and Twilight* (1963). ■ See biography by Ernest Samuels (2 vols., 1979, 1987); Meryle Secrest, *Being Bernard Berenson* (1979); and study by Mary Ann Calo (1994).

BERG, ALBAN (1885–1935), Austrian composer. Berg studied with Arnold Schoenberg (1904–08) and combined Schoenberg's radical doctrines in harmony and tonality with an original capacity of expression that made him one of the outstanding composers of the 20th century. He gained acceptance of his complex style by adapting the 12-tone method to more familiar classical forms of music. His expressionistic opera *Wozzeck* was written in this style, partly atonal but utilizing classical forms. It created a sensation at its premiere at the Berlin State Opera in 1925. His other opera, *Lulu* (first performed in 1937), was composed en-

tirely in the 12-tone method. Berg's other works included a chamber concerto (1925) and violin concerto (1935). ■ See biographies by Willi Reich (Eng. trans. 1965), Mosco Carner (rev. ed. 1983), and Karen Monson (1979).

BERG, GERTRUDE (Gertrude Edelstein; 1899–1966), U.S. radio and television actress, writer, and producer. Born in New York City, Berg gave up magazine writing to try her hand at radio scripts in the late 1920s. "The Goldbergs," which she created and starred in for $75 a week, premiered in 1929, and her Molly Goldberg became one of the great characters on the air. Called a Jewish "One Man's Family," the show was unique on radio, lowkeyed and nonsensational, portraying with warmth and feeling the lives of the poor Jews of New York City, and somehow managed to universalize their particular experience. Berg ran the show completely, later producing and directing as well as writing and starring in it. "The Goldbergs" was discontinued (1945), but it inspired the Broadway hit *Molly and Me* (1948) and a movie, *Molly* (1951). It reappeared (1949) on television, becoming one of that medium's early hits. ■ See her autobiography, *Molly and Me* (1961).

BERG, MOE (Morris Berg; 1902–1972), U.S. baseball player and intelligence agent. After graduating from Princeton with honors, Berg joined the Brooklyn Dodgers (1923) and played baseball, mostly as a catcher, for the next 16 years. On his retirement (1939) he had hit only six home runs and six triples and had a lifetime batting average of .243. But he became the "intellectual of baseball," for during the off-seasons he studied at the Sorbonne, learned ten languages, and received a law degree from Columbia University. In World War II he served as a U.S. agent in Nazi-occupied Europe, using his language facility to pose as a businessman and gather information on Nazi nuclear-weapon development, the strength of the anti-Nazi underground, and the location of German atomic scientists. ■ See biography by Louis Kaufman, Barbara Fitzgerald, and Tom Sewell (1974).

BERG, PAUL (1926–), U.S. biochemist. A professor at Stanford University (from 1959), Berg did pioneering research in the biochemistry of nucleic acids (DNA and RNA). His development of recombinant DNA technology (or "gene splicing") revolutionized the field of genetics by making it possible for scientists to dissect, reconstruct, and map small chromosomes and to manipulate, alter, and reproduce genetic material of cells from any species. Recognizing the potential danger of genetic manipulation, Berg was in the forefront of those seeking to establish safety guidelines in the field. He shared the 1980 Nobel Prize for Chemistry with Frederick Sanger and Walter Gilbert.

BERGELSON, DOVID (1884–1952), Russian Yiddish-language writer. The son of a wealthy merchant, Bergelson received a traditional Jewish education and began to write fiction in Yiddish in 1906. With the publication of the short novels *By the Depot* (1909), *Joseph Schur* (1913; Eng. trans. 1977), and *When All Is Said and Done* (1913; Eng. trans. 1971), which dealt with the decay of traditional East European Jewish society, he was recognized as a major prose stylist. Although sympathetic to the 1917 revolution, he lived abroad (in Berlin, 1921–33), before returning to the Soviet Union to become a leading proletarian novelist. His works of this period, which contained positive portraits of the new Jewish life under communism, included the semiautobiographical *Along the Dneiper* (2 vols., 1932–40). He was active in the Jewish antifascist committee during World War II and wrote numerous patriotic works on Jewish themes. After the war he was accused of Jewish nationalism and cosmopolitanism, arrested (1949), and executed, along with other prominent Yiddish writers, by the Soviet secret police. ■ See English translations of his work in Irving Howe and Eliezer Greenberg, eds., *Ashes Out of Hope* (1977), and *The Stories of David Bergelson* (1996).

BERGEN, EDGAR (1903–1978), U.S. performer and ventriloquist. Bergen's routines with his dummy and partner Charlie McCarthy were first featured in a popular radio show, "The Chase and Sanborn Hour," in the 1930s and 1940s. They later appeared in tandem in movies and on TV variety programs. They hosted the daytime quiz program "Do You Trust Your Wife?" in the 1950s. The well-appointed, monocled Charlie often accused Bergen of moving his lips during a performance. While Charlie was Bergen's principal dummy, the ventriloquist also appeared with dullard Mortimer Snerd and the husband-hunting Effie Klinker. Bergen's daughter Candice (1946–   ) made her movie debut in *The Group* (1965) and went on to become a prominent actress. Charlie McCarthy was acquired by the Smithsonian Institution.

BERGER, HANS (1873–1941), German psychiatrist. Berger received a medical degree at Jena (1897), where he practiced and taught psychiatry (1900–38) and investigated the physical basis of mental functioning. In 1929, he published his first paper on human electroencephalography (EEG), the procedure he devised to record human brain waves. He attached electrodes to the skull and connected them to an oscillograph, which gave a visual picture of the rhythmic electric potentials that are constantly shifting within the brain. The EEG became a standard diagnostic tool in neurology and psychiatry. Depressed after his retirement, Berger committed suicide.

BERGER, JOHN PETER (1926–   ), British art critic and author. Educated at the Central and Chelsea Schools of Art in London, Berger worked as a painter and teacher of drawing before pursuing a career as a critic and writer and earning a reputation as one of the foremost Marxist art critics of his time. His best-known critical works included *Toward Reality: Essays in Seeing* (1962), *The Moment of Cubism*

(1968), *Art and Revolution: Ernst Neizvestny and the Role of the Artist in the USSR* (1968), *Ways of Seeing* (1972), and *The Look of Things: Essays* (1972). His other works included the novels *A Painter of Our Time* (1958); *G* (1972), a study of migrant workers in Europe; *A Seventh Man* (1975) and *To The Wedding* (1995); the essay collections *The Sense of Sight* (1985) and *Keeping a Rendezvous* (1991); and the screenplays for Alain Tanner's films, *La Salamandre* (1971), *The Middle of the World* (1974), and *Jonah Who Will Be 25 in the Year 2000* (1976). *Into Their Labours: A Trilogy* (1991), which included the novels *Pig Earth, Once In Europa,* and *Lilac and Flag* was an evocation of French peasant life and its degradation by the intrusions of modernity.

BERGER, VICTOR LOUIS (1860–1929), Austrian-born U.S. political leader. After studying at universities in Vienna and Budapest, Berger emigrated to the United States (1878) and worked as a teacher and journalist in Milwaukee. A political activist, he helped form—with Eugene Debs and others—the Social Democratic party (1898) and the Socialist party of America (1901). In 1910 the party won control of the city administration, and Berger became the first socialist ever elected to the U.S. Congress. Although considered a right-winger within the party for his advocacy of gradual reforms, he was nevertheless barred from Congress (1918; 1919) and sentenced to 20 years imprisonment (1918) for sedition for advocating opposition to World War I. In 1921 the Supreme Court overturned his conviction, and Berger served in Congress again from 1923 to 1929. ■ See study by Sally M. Miller (1973).

BERGIUS, FRIEDRICH (1884–1949), German organic chemist. Like his mentor Fritz Haber, Bergius became interested in reactions that occur under pressure. He produced (1912) gasoline by hydrogenating coal under high pressure, and in another dozen years he adapted this method for industrial use. He also produced edible products by breaking down complex wood molecules. For his research in high-pressure processes. Bergius shared the 1931 Nobel Prize for Chemistry with Carl Bosch. Germany made great use of his findings in World War II. After the war, Bergius left Germany and lived in Austria, Spain, and finally Argentina, where he worked as a technical adviser for a year before his death.

BERGMAN, INGMAR (1918–   ), Swedish director. Son of a Lutheran minister, Bergman became involved with theater at the University of Stockholm and directed his first film *Crisis* in 1945. After several years as a theatrical and film director, he received international critical acclaim for two 1957 films, *The Seventh Seal* and *Wild Strawberries*. Writing his own scripts and working with his own company of actors (including Liv Ullmann and Max Von Sydow) and technicians, Bergman made many outstanding contributions to art-house cinema. His first trilogy (*Through a Glass Darkly,*

1961; *Winter Light,* 1963; and *The Silence,* 1963) explored the loneliness and vulnerability of faithless, loveless individuals. In a second trilogy *(Persona,* 1966; *Hour of the Wolf,* 1968; and *Shame,* 1968), he probed the role of the artist in society. His later films included *Cries and Whispers* (1972), *Autumn Sonata* (1978), *Fanny and Alexander* (1983), and the television series *Scenes from a Marriage* (1973). He also wrote the novels *The Best Intentions* (1991; Eng. trans. 1993), *Sunday's Child* (1993; Eng. trans. 1994), and *Private Confessions* (1996; Eng. trans. 1997) and wrote screenplays for all three. ■ See his autobiographical volumes *The Magic Lantern* (1987; Eng. trans. 1988) and *Images: My Life in Film* (1990; Eng. trans. 1994); the study by Lise-Lone and Frederick J. Marker (1982); and biography by Peter Cowie (1983).

BERGMAN, INGRID (1915–1982), Swedish actress. Bergman went to Hollywood in the late 1930s as a successor to Garbo but soon established her own persona as the innocent sufferer in *Casablanca* (1943) and *Gaslight* (Academy Award, 1944) and as *Joan of Arc* on Broadway and in the 1948 film. In private life, however, Berman was cast as a "scarlet woman" because of her affair with the Italian director Roberto Rossellini and the birth of their son three months before their marriage in 1949. After their divorce she made a comeback with *Anastasia* (Academy Award, 1956). Bergman later launched a second career, playing more mature roles in *Cactus Flower* (1969), *Murder on the Orient Express* (Academy Award, 1974), and *Autumn Sonata* (1978). She won an Emmy Award (1982) for her performance as Golda Meir in the television show *Golda,* completed shortly before her death. ■ See her autobiography (1980); the biography by Joseph H. Steele (1960); Laurence Leamer, *As Time Goes By* (1986); and Donald Spoto, *Notorious* (1997).

BERGSON, HENRI (1859–1941), French philosopher. One of the most influential thinkers of his time, Bergson taught at the Collège de France (1900–21) and espoused a philosophy that directly opposed the positivist movement prevalent in the century's early decades. Finding the logical model of the scientist insufficient to understand reality, Bergson argued that intuition is vital to attain absolute knowledge of such concepts as change, creation, and human liberty. Whereas philosophers from the time of Plato had ignored duration by regarding time as an illusion, Bergson proposed in *Time and Free Will* (1889; Eng. trans. 1910) that values of duration and change replace a nontemporal, static approach to philosophy. In his most famous work, *Creative Evolution* (1907; Eng. trans. 1911), Bergson maintained that the traditional approach to evolution was too mechanistic and ignored the factor of duration. He was awarded the 1927 Nobel Prize for Literature. A secular Jew, Bergson refused the Vichy government's offer to protect him from anti-Semitic policies during World War II. ■ See biography by

Jacques Chevalier (Eng. trans. 1928); studies by Ian W. Alexander (1957), A.R. Lacey (1989), and M.C.T. Moore (1996); and P.A.Y. Gunter, ed., *Bergson and the Evolution of Physics* (1969).

BERGSTRÖM, SUNE KARL (1916–), Swedish chemist. After receiving doctorates in both medicine and biochemistry (Karolinska Institute, Stockholm; 1943). Bergström taught at the University of Lund (1947–58) and the Karolinska Institute (1958–81). A pioneer (from 1947) of the chemical study of prostaglandins—the remarkably versatile hormonelike structures that play important roles in protecting the body from disease, pain, injury, and stress—Bergström was the first to purify prostaglandins, to determine their chemical structure, and to demonstrate that they are manufactured from unsaturated fatty acids. He shared the 1982 Nobel Prize for Physiology or Medicine with Bengt I. Samuelsson (his former student) and John R. Vane. He also chaired the Nobel Foundation in Stockholm (1975–87) and the World Health Organization's advisory committee on medical research (1977–82).

BERIA, LAVRENTI PAVLOVICH (1899–1953), Soviet political leader. Beria was studying in Baku at the outbreak of the 1917 revolution; he joined the bolsheviks there. He directed (1922–31) the Cheka (secret police) in Georgia and the Transcaucuses and became first secretary of the Georgian (1931) and Transcaucasian (1932) Communist party. Soviet dictator Joseph Stalin appointed (1938) Beria to head the NKVD, the Soviet security service. Serving for 15 years, he oversaw the liquidation, imprisonment, or deportation of millions of Soviet citizens and was elevated (1946) to membership in the Politburo. At Stalin's death in March 1953, Beria shared power with G. M. Malenkov and Nikita Khrushchev, but he was arrested later that year. He was allegedly tried and executed, but he was likely summarily killed by his associates by June. His dismissal from office was announced in July 1953. Apologists for Stalin continued to blame the dictator's excesses on acts carried out by Beria unknown to Stalin. ■ See Thaddeus Wittlin, *Commissar* (1972) and biography by Amy Knight (1993).

BERIO, LUCIANO (1925–), Italian composer. Born into a musical family, Berio dropped out of law school to study at the Milan Conservatory (1946–51). He joined the staff of RAI, the Italian State Radio, and founded the Studio di Fonologia Musicale (Milan; 1954), one of Europe's leading electronic music studios, and the journal of progressive music, *Incontri Musicali* ("Musical Encounters"). An influential avant-garde theorist, teacher, and composer, Berio wrote experimental music for traditional instruments as well as for voice, chorus, electronic devices, and tape. His works include *Différences* (1959), *Visage* (1960), *Passaggio* (1963), *Sinfonia* (1968), *Concerto for Two Pianos and Orchestra* (1973), and the stage works *Allez-Hop!* (1959), *Diario Im-*

maginario (1975), and *La Vera Stória* (1982). He was the artistic director of the Accademia Filarmonica Romana (from 1976). ■ See David Osmond-Smith, *Luciano Berio: Two Interviews* (1985), and Osmond-Smith's study (1991).

BERKELEY, BUSBY (William Berkeley Enos; 1895–1976), U.S. choreographer. Berkeley grew up in the theater, got his start on Broadway, and moved to Hollywood in 1930 to revolutionize the musical-production number. After choreographing *42nd Street* (1933) and *Gold Diggers of 1933* (1933), he directed *Stage Struck* (1936), *Babes on Broadway* (1941), and *For Me and My Gal* (1942)—all featuring lavish sets and kaleidoscopic views of revolving platforms filled with hordes of costumed dancing girls. He later designed aqua ballets starring Esther Williams *(Million Dollar Mermaid,* 1952). ■ See Tony Thomas and Jim Terry, *The Busby Berkeley Book* (1973), and Martin Rubin, *Show Stoppers* (1993).

BERKNER, LLOYD VIEL (1905–1967), U.S. physicist and engineer. Berkner's pioneering studies and measurements of the ionosphere led to the complete explanation of high-frequency radio-wave propagation. He proposed (1950) and organized (1957–59) the International Geophysical Year (IGY), the most comprehensive cooperative study of the earth ever undertaken. Berkner also worked on the development of radar, the Distant Early Warning System, and early spacecraft research, and developed (with L. C. Marshall) a theory of the origin and development of planetary atmospheres. His books included *Rockets and Satellites* (1958). *Science in Space* (1961), and *The Scientific Age* (1964).

BERLAGE, HENDRIK PETRUS (1856–1934), Dutch architect and town planner. One of the pioneers of functionalism, H. P. Berlage was primarily noted for his design of the Amsterdam Stock Exchange (1897–1903). Departing from his earlier use of Renaissance and Romanesque styles, he used steel and stone in innovative ways, creating wall surfaces undecorated except for the alternation of brick and pale stone. His buildings were known for their simplicity, directness, and geometric order. He also designed furniture and wallpaper, and worked on city-planning projects in Amsterdam, Rotterdam, and The Hague. ■ See study by Pieter Singelenberg (1972).

BERLE, ADOLF AUGUSTUS, JR. (1895–1971), U.S. lawyer, scholar, and economist. The son of a progressive Congregationalist minister, Berle received three degrees from Harvard (LL.B. 1916), taught at Columbia Law School (1927–64), and wrote a pioneering study of the power of corporation managers, *The Modern Corporation and Private Property* (1932; with Gardner C. Means). He first gained national prominence as a member of Pres. Franklin D. Roosevelt's brain trust (1932), a group of advisers, predominantly from the academic world, who devised many important New Deal programs. He served as assistant secretary of state for Latin American affairs (1938–44) and as ambassador to Brazil (1945–46). Berle maintained a partnership in the New York law firm of Berle and Berle from 1919 until his death and was founder and chairman (1952–55) of the Liberal party in New York State.

BERLE, MILTON (Milton Berlinger; 1908–   ), U.S. television performer. The man who became known as "Mr. Television" attended New York's Professional Children's School and appeared in vaudeville and on the New York stage (including Ziegfeld's *Follies* of 1936). His radio shows (1939–48) were unsuccessful, but television made the most of Berle's mugging and fanciful use of costume. His Tuesday night "Texaco Star Theater" (1948–54) was a fixture in many viewers' week. Berle's later shows also featured his brand of extravagant comedy routines, which had broad appeal and helped spread the sale of television sets to lower-income households. "Uncle Miltie's" popularity was such that NBC made a contract with him through 1981, which was honored although Berle did not appear regularly after the 1950s; an attempt to revive his show in the 1960s failed. Milton Berle also appeared in a dozen films and on various TV specials. ■ See his autobiography (1974) and *B.S. I Love You: My Life as a Friar* (1988).

BERLIN, IRVING (Israel Baline; 1888–1989), Russian-born U.S. songwriter. Berlin was a street singer as a child in New York City's Lower East Side and later worked as a singing waiter. Although he had no formal musical training, he began to write songs at an early age, and his first great hits, "Alexander's Ragtime Band" (1911) and "Everybody's Doin' It" (1911) popularized ragtime music and established his reputation. He became one of America's most prolific and consistently successful songwriters with such hits as "Always," "Easter Parade," "Blue Skies," "There's No Business Like Show Business," "All Alone," "Cheek to Cheek," "A Pretty Girl Is Like a Melody," and "God Bless America." For the Broadway stage he wrote songs for numerous revues during the 1920s and 1930s and for such later hits as *Annie Get Your Gun* (1946) and *Call Me Madam* (1950). He also wrote the scores for some of the best musical films of the 1930s and 1940s, including *Top Hat* (1935), *Carefree* (1938), and *Holiday Inn* (1942), which featured "White Christmas," one of the best-selling songs of all time. ■ See biography by Michael Freedland (1974) and Laurence Bergreen, *As Thousands Cheer* (1990).

BERLIN, SIR ISAIAH (1909–1997), British philosopher and historian. Born in Latvia, Berlin emigrated to England as a child and was a brilliant scholarship student at Oxford (B.A. 1931; M.A. 1935). His first book, a biography of Karl Marx, was published in 1939. During World War II he wrote distinguished dispatches from Washington, D.C., for Britain's foreign office. An erudite scholar and conversationalist in several languages, Berlin taught at Oxford (1932–67) and was president of Wolfson College, Oxford (1966–75). His best-known works were *The Hedgehog and the Fox: An Essay on Tolstoy's View of History* (1953); *Historical Inevitability* (1955), an attack on determinism: and *Two Concepts of Liberty* (1958). He also wrote six volumes of collected essays and articles, *Russian Thinkers* (1978), *Concepts and Categories* (1978), *Against the Current* (1979), *Personal Impressions* (1980), *A Sense of Reality* (1997), and *The Proper Study of Mankind* (1997). ■ See studies by Claude Galipeau (1994) and John Gray (1996); and the biography by Michael Ignatieff (1998).

BERLINGUER, ENRICO (1922–1984), Italian political leader. Born into a wealthy, landowning but politically radical Sardinian family, Berlinguer joined the Communist party (1943) and held many party positions prior to his election as secretary-general (1972). As leader of the largest and best-organized Communist party in Europe, Berlinguer advocated a moderate, nonrevolutionary brand of communism. He called for a "historic compromise" between the communist and noncommunist parties so that the two groups could govern Italy in a coalition. Berlinguer also spoke out for a pluralistic and democratic communist world system, free of Soviet constraints, and criticized the Soviet Union for its lack of democracy and political debate. During his years as leader (1972–84) the party garnered 34 percent of the vote in the 1976 parliamentary elections and controlled the municipal governments of Rome, Milan, Florence, Bologna, and Venice.

BERNADOTTE, COUNT FOLKE (1895–1948), Swedish army officer. Count Bernadotte was an official of the Swedish Red Cross during World War II who helped obtain the release of prisoners from German concentration camps. The United Nations Security Council appointed him to mediate between the Jews and the Arabs in Palestine after the outbreak of war in 1948. Both sides rejected his proposal for settlement. The Israelis felt that he was partial to the Arabs, and he was assassinated in Jerusalem by Jewish extremists in September 1948. Count Bernadotte's role of UN mediator was then filled by the U.S. diplomat Ralph Bunche. ■ See Sune Persson, *Mediation and Assassination* (1979); study by Amitzar Ilan (1989); and Ted Schwarz, *Walking with the Damned* (1992).

BERNAL, JOHN DESMOND (1901–1971), Irish-born British physicist. A researcher at Cambridge (1927–37) and professor of physics (1937–63) and the first professor of crystallography (1963–68) at London University, J. D. Bernal was a pioneer in the field of X-ray crystallography and helped lay the foundations of molecular biology. The possessor of encyclopedic scientific knowledge, he conducted research on sex hormones, the tobacco mosaic virus, the structure and property of water, the structure and composition of the earth's crust, and the chemical processes in-

volved in the origin of matter. Though an avowed Marxist and a member of many left-wing organizations during the 1930s, he was an important scientific adviser to the military during World War II. His books *The Social Function of Science* (1939), *The Freedom of Necessity* (1949), and *Science in History* (1954) reflected his analysis of science as a social phenomenon. He also wrote *The Origin of Life* (1967) and *The Extension of Man* (1972). ■ See biography by Maurice Goldsmith, *Sage* (1980), and study edited by Brenda Swann and Francis Abrahamian (1999).

BERNANOS, GEORGES (1888–1948), French novelist and essayist. A deeply religious Catholic, Bernanos was concerned in his novels with the struggle between good and evil for the human soul and the central problem of faith. His works *Star of Satan* (1926; Eng. trans. 1940) and *Diary of a Country Priest* (1936; Eng. trans. 1937) have priests as central characters. An ultraconservative politically, Bernanos nevertheless in many skillful diatribes and polemics attacked bourgeois materialism, the Spanish church hierarchy for its support of fascist atrocities, and the policy of appeasement toward Nazi Germany. He spent the World War II years in self-imposed exile in South America. His last works included the play *The Fearless Heart* (1947; Eng. trans. 1952), regarded as his spiritual testament, and *Tradition of Freedom* (1949; Eng. trans. 1950). ■ See study by William Bush (1969) and biography by Robert Speaight (1974).

BERNAYS, EDWARD L. (1891–1995), Austrian-born U.S. public-relations executive. A nephew of Sigmund Freud, Bernays utilized his own knowledge of psychology to create the profession of public relations. A pioneer and master of scientific public manipulation, Bernays (and his wife, Doris) set up the first public-relations firm (New York City, 1919) and wrote the first book and taught the first courses (New York University, 1923) on the subject. Over the years, he persuaded the public to watch Nijinsky dance and Caruso sing and to buy Ivory Soap, hair nets, and war bonds. His clients included the nation's largest corporations, the U.S. government, and several presidents. ■ See his memoirs, *Biography of an Idea* (1965) and *The Later Years* (1986), and Larry Tye, *The Father of Spin* (1998).

BERNBACH, WILLIAM (1911–1982), U.S. advertising executive, Bernbach instigated a creative revolution on Madison Avenue (1949) when his new agency, Doyle, Dane, Bernbach, stared producing intelligent, subtle, and above all, entertaining copy. Responsible for such slogans as "Think small" (for Volkswagen), "We try harder because we're only number 2" (for Avis Car Rental), and "You don't have to be Jewish to love Levy's real Jewish Rye Bread," and the creator of the Dreyfuss Fund Lion and Colombian Coffee's Juan Valdez, Bernbach's agency rapidly became a leader of the industry. Bernbach viewed advertising as the art of persuasion and not as the science that many of his competitors believed it to be.

BERNERS-LEE, TIM (1955–   ), British computer scientist. Berners-Lee studies physics at Oxford (B.A. 1976), was an engineer with Plessey Communications, in Poole, England (1976–78), and was a founding director of Image Computer Systems, Ltd. (1981–84). As a software engineer at CERN, the European Particle Physics Laboratory in Geneva, Switzerland (1984–94), he worked on systems for the acquisition of scientific data. In 1989 he proposed an Internet-based "hypertext system" whereby physicists in different geographical locations could easily and efficiently share information. The system, which became known as the World Wide Web, was first used within CERN in December 1990 and made generally available on the Internet in the summer of 1991. Berners-Lee continued to work on refining the Web, and it soon became the centerpiece of global Internet activity and an international cultural phenomenon, linking millions of computer users throughout the world. He subsequently directed the World Wide Web Consortium at the Laboratory for Computer Science at the Massachusetts Institute of Technology (1994–   ) with the goals of making the Web more interactive and keeping it inexpensive, easy to use, and out of the control of a single large corporation. ■ See his *Weaving the Web* (1999; with Frank Fischetti).

BERNSTEIN, CARL (1944–   ), U.S. journalist. Bernstein, whose parents were both labor leaders, attended the University of Maryland part-time while working his way up from copyboy at the *Washington Star* to reporter, in 1963, on the rival *Post*. Assigned to work with Bob Woodward on the story of the 1972 burglary of the Democratic headquarters at the Watergate apartment complex, he obtained possession of critical telephone and credit-card records to break the story of top-level White House involvement. The exposé won a 1973 Pulitzer Prize and led to the resignation of Pres. Richard Nixon. Bernstein injected a subjective "new journalism" style into the two Woodward-Bernstein books, *All the President's Men* (1974) and *The Final Days* (1976). He worked for ABC News (1979–84) and he subsequently wrote *Loyalties: A Son's Memoir* (1989) and *His Holiness: John Paul II and the Hidden History of Our Time* (1996; with Marco Politi). ■ See Adrian Havill's gossipy study, *Deep Truth* (1993).

BERNSTEIN, EDUARD (1850–1932), German political leader. Exiled from Germany (1878–1901) because of his active participation in the German Social Democratic party (SPD), Bernstein edited party newspapers in Zurich and London. Known as the "father of revisionism," he was one of the first socialists to revise some of Karl Marx's basic doctrines. He noted that capitalism was not on the verge of collapse and therefore advocated an evolutionary, reformist, and parliamentary path to socialism rather than a violent revolutionary one. His ideas, expressed in the book *Evolutionary Socialism* (1899; Eng. trans. 1909), were extremely controversial within the German socialist movement, but eventually became the accepted ideology of the SPD. Bernstein served in the Reichstag (1902–06; 1912–18; 1920–28) and briefly as secretary of state (1919), and was a dominant figure in the SPD during the Weimar Republic. ■ See his reminiscences, *My Years of Exile* (1917; Eng. trans. 1921); Peter Gay's *The Dilemma of Democratic Socialism* (1952); and Manfred B. Steger, *The Quest for Evolutionary Socialism* (1997).

BERNSTEIN, LEONARD (1918–1990), U.S. conductor and composer. Bernstein studied with Walter Piston (at Harvard) and Fritz Reiner (at the Curtis Institute) before becoming a protégé of Serge Koussevitsky, the conductor of the Boston Symphony. He made a spectacular conducting debut with the New York Philharmonic in 1943 as a last-minute substitute for Bruno Walter. In 1944 his composing career was launched with the *Jeremiah Symphony,* the ballet *Fancy Free,* and the hit Broadway musical *On the Town.* During the 1950s his television lectures attracted millions of viewers, and his 1957 musical *West Side Story* (film adaptation, 1958) was a great success. He also wrote the musical *Candide* (1956; rev. 1973). From 1958 to 1969 he conducted the New York Philharmonic in spirited style, and his recordings helped spark the Mahler revival of the 1960s. His other compositions, infused with modern jazz rhythms, included the opera *Trouble in Tahiti* (1952), the film score for *On the Waterfront* (1954), and the controversial *Mass* (1971). His writings included *The Joy of Music* (1959), *The Unanswered Question* (1976), and *Findings* (1982). ■ See John Gruen, *The Private World of Leonard Bernstein* (1968), and biographies by Joan Peyser (1987) and Meryle Secrest (1994).

BERRI, NABIH (1938–   ), Lebanese (Shiite) political leader. The son of an expatriate Lebanese merchant, Berri was born in Freetown, Sierra Leone, and raised in south Lebanon. After graduating from the University of Beirut Law School (1963) he practiced law in Beirut and lived for a short period in the United States. He was a member of the Shiite Muslim sect. Lebanon's numerically largest but most economically, politically, educationally, and socially depressed faction. In the mid-1970s, as Lebanon was plunged into civil war, Berri joined the Movement of the Dispossessed, a group dedicated to achieving Shiite equality, and he headed its military wing, Amal ("Hope"; from 1980). The Shiites were opposed to the Christian–Sunni Muslim domination of Lebanese politics and to the Palestinian presence in the country. Amal grew in strength after the Israelis drove the Palestinian forces out of south Lebanon (1982), becoming the largest private army in Lebanon and successfully attacking the Israeli occupation forces. After Amal drove the troops loyal to Pres. Amin Gemayel out of West Beirut (February 1984), Berri joined the "national unity" cabinet. A moderate secularist who was opposed to the radical Shiite religious fundamentalists, Berri worked for changes in the Lebanese constitution that would give Shiites political power reflective of their numbers. He was a member of the

National Assembly (1991–) and served as its president (1992–).

BERRIGAN, DANIEL (1921–), and PHILIP FRANCIS BERRIGAN (1923–), U.S. radical priests. The two youngest of six sons of a militant socialist labor organizer, Daniel Berrigan underwent rigorous Jesuit training to be ordained in 1952; his brother Philip, who had served in the infantry during World War II, was ordained into the Society of St. Joseph (the Josephite Fathers) in 1955. The ascetic, poetry-writing Daniel was first radicalized during a year spent with France's worker priests, and together the Berrigans founded a Catholic Peace Fellowship (1964). Daniel was a founder of the Clergy and Laity Concerned About Vietnam. Philip, who worked for many years with black ghetto youth, was the first to go beyond pacifism. In protest against the Vietnam War, he participated in the destruction of Baltimore draft records (1967), after which he persuaded his brother to join in a similar action in Catonsville, Maryland. After their trial, which Daniel reproduced as an Off-Broadway play (*The Trial of the Catonsville Nine, 1971*), the brothers went underground, but were eventually captured and served sentences in federal prison (Philip, 35 months; Daniel, 18 months). They were both arrested and convicted for damaging three nuclear warheads under construction at a General Electric plant in King of Prussia, Pennsylvania (1980), and continued to demonstrate against nuclear weapons with their peace group, Plowshares, after their release. Philip, who was excommunicated (1973) after his marriage to ex-nun and political activist Elizabeth McAlister, was subsequently imprisoned for damaging weapons in 1988, 1993, and 1997. Philip's books included *A Punishment for Peace* (1969), *Prison Journals of a Priest Revolutionary* (1970), *Of Beasts and Beastly Images: Essays Under the Bomb* (1978), and his autobiography, *Fighting the Lamb's War* (1996). Daniel's poetry appeared in *Selected and New Poems* (1973) and *Prison Poems* (1979). He also wrote *The Dark Night of Resistance* (1971), *Lights On in the House of the Dead: A Prison Diary* (1974), *Ten Commandments for the Long Haul* (1981), *Steadfastness of the Saints* (1985), *Isaiah* (1997), and his autobiography, *To Dwell in Peace* (1987). ■ See Richard Curtis, *The Berrigan Brothers* (1974) and M. Polner and J. O'Grady, *Disarmed and Dangerous* (1997).

BERRY, CHUCK (Charles Edward Berry; 1926–), U.S. singer. Some sources give his date of birth as 1931. Berry spent three years in reform school (1944–47) for attempted robbery, worked on an auto assembly line, and studied hairdressing and cosmetology before emerging as one of the first great rock stars with his 1955 hit, "Maybelline." A popular African-American performer who affected a bent-kneed "duck walk," he had two other big hits in "Johnny B. Goode" and "Sweet Little Sixteen." The most influential performer in the early years of rock music, he made his mark on the Beatles, the Rolling Stones, and others. In 1959 he was charged with "immoral purposes" by an underage hatcheck girl in his St. Louis club and eventually served two years in prison. Released in 1964, Berry resumed his recording career and made a Las Vegas debut (1972). In 1979, shortly before performing at the White House for Pres. Jimmy Carter, Berry served 100 days in jail for tax evasion. He continued releasing albums in the 1970s and 1980s, including *Chuck Berry—75* (1975) and *The Great Twenty-Eight* (1982). ■ See his autobiography (1987) and study by Howard A. DeWitt (1985).

BERRYMAN, JOHN (1914–1972), U.S. poet. Berryman began publishing poetry in the 1940s but remained unknown until "Homage to Mistress Bradstreet" (1956) appeared; its complex interior monologue provided poetry with a new idiom. Inspired by William Butler Yeats and W. H. Auden, Berryman experimented within traditional poetic forms. He achieved prominence in the 1960s with the publication of *77 Dream Songs* (1964; Pulitzer Prize) and *His Toy, His Dream, His Rest* (1968). In his later years he suffered from alcoholism; Berryman jumped to his death from a bridge over the Mississippi. A volume of poetry, *Delusions, etc.* (1972), and a novel, *Recovery* (1973), were published posthumously. ■ See biography by John Haffenden (1982) and Paul Mariani, *Dream Song* (1990).

BERTALANFFY, LUDWIG VON (1901–1972), Austrian-born Canadian biologist and social scientist. A brilliant and wide-ranging experimental and theoretical scientist, Bertalanffy taught at the University of Vienna (Ph.D. 1926) until 1948 and thereafter at many schools in North America, including the University of Ottawa (1948–54) and the University of Alberta, Edmonton (1961–69). In the field of biology he developed a quantitative determination of metabolism and a technique for the early diagnosis of cancer. He was best known, however, as a pioneer during the 1920s of the "organismic conception" of biology, one of the earliest presentations of a "holistic" theory of life and nature. This, in turn, was the basis of his general systems theory, an all-encompassing humanistic theory of human nature and behavior that rejected mechanistic concepts and emphasized human spontaneity and the ability to use symbols. He explained the theory, developed over a 30-year period, in detail in *General System Theory* (1969). ■ See Mark Davidson, *Uncommon Sense* (1983).

BERTOIA, HARRY (1915–1978), Italian-born U.S. sculptor. Bertoia, who emigrated to the United States as a teenager, designed furniture for Charles Eames and developed the revolutionary diamond-mesh chair (1951–52) constructed of welded steel rods, before making a name with his own "screen sculptures." These were large, abstract, gilded or metallic screens used as interior decor at the Massachusetts Institute of Technology Chapel and Dulles Airport (Virginia) and in commercial establishments and affluent residences. Bertoia also experimented with musical or "sound sculptures," activated manually or by air to produce sound. ■ See study by June K. Nelson (1970).

BERTOLUCCI, BERNARDO, (1940–), Italian film director. The son of a poet and film critic, Bertolucci won a literary award for his poetry before establishing himself as a filmmaker at a very young age. His controversial second film, *Before the Revolution,* won an award at the 1964 Cannes Film Festival. After working in the TV documentary field, joining the Italian Communist party, and entering psychoanalysis, Bertolucci won international acclaim with *The Conformist* (1970), a psychological drama of the fascist era that he wrote as well as directed. His *Last Tango in Paris* (1972) with its frank scenes of sex and sadism was internationally notorious. He also directed the epic *1900* (1976), *La Luna* (1979), *The Last Emperor* (1986; Academy Award), *Little Buddha* (1993), and *Besieged* (1999). ■ See biography by Robert P. Kolker (1985).

BESANT, ANNIE (Annie Wood; 1847–1933), British social reformer and theosophist. Besant ended a seven-year marriage to an Anglican vicar (1873) and became active in the atheist, birth-control, and Fabian socialist movements. In 1899, though, she joined the mystical Theosophical Society, and later became its president (1907–33). Besant lived at the society's headquarters in India, where she learned Sanskrit, championed Indian home rule, and served as president of the Indian National Congress party (1917). In 1919, however, she supported British suppression in the Punjab and lost many of her followers to nationalist leader Mahatma Gandhi. Her best-known works included *The Ancient Wisdom* (1897), *Evolution of Life and Form* (1899). and *The Spiritual Life* (1912). ■ See biographies by Arthur H. Nethercot, *The First Five Lives of Annie Besant* (1960) and *The Last Four Lives of Annie Besant* (1964), and the biography by Anne Taylor (1992).

BEST, CHARLES HERBERT (1899–1978), U.S.-born Canadian physiologist and medical researcher. Working in collaboration with Frederick G. Banting, Best discovered insulin while experimenting in a laboratory at the University of Toronto only weeks after receiving his B.A. degree (1921). The discovery saved the lives of millions of diabetics throughout the world. The recipient of an M.D. degree (1925, Toronto) and a Ph.D. (1928, London), Best taught at the University of Toronto and made many advances in the study of diabetes. He also introduced the first coagulant for the treatment of thrombosis and discovered histaminase, the enzyme that breaks down histamine, and choline, a vitamin that prevents liver damage. ■ See Michael Bliss, *The Discovery of Insulin* (1982).

BETANCOURT, RÓMULO (1908–1981), Venezuelan political leader. Exiled for leading student protests against the Juan Vicente Gómez dictatorship, Betancourt was one of the founders of the left-wing but anticommunist Acción Democrática movement (1941). Taking power in 1945 by coup d'état, he launched a program of democratic and economic reforms before he was forced into exile again in 1948. Betancourt served as his country's elected president (1959–64), resuming his reform and industrialization program. He wrote *Venezuela: Oil and Politics* (1979). ■ See study by Robert J. Alexander (1982).

BETHE, HANS ALBRECHT (1906–), German-born U.S. physicist. The son of a university professor, Bethe studied at the universities of Frankfurt and Munich (Ph.D. 1928) and taught physics at Munich and Tübingen (1930–33). After the Nazis came to power (1933), he left Germany for England and later the United States (1935). He taught at Cornell University (1935–75) and became a U.S. citizen in 1941. In the late 1930s he determined the precise mechanism of solar and stellar energy production, and he was subsequently awarded the 1967 Nobel Prize in Physics for this work. During World War II he worked on the Manhattan Project and headed the theoretical physics division of the Los Alamos (New Mexico) Laboratory (1943–46) that developed the atomic bomb. After the war he opposed the use of nuclear weapons and helped negotiate the 1963 test ban treaty with the Soviet Union. Bethe also made fundamental contributions to the field of quantum mechanics and other areas of nuclear physics. He continued to be active into his 90s, doing research on supernovas and urging (1997) President Clinton to forgo further development of new weapons of mass destruction. ■ See study by Jeremy Bernstein (1980).

BETHELL, MARY URSULA (1874–1945), British-born New Zealand poet. Under the pseudonym Evelyn Hayes, Bethell wrote of her own experiences as a British settler in New Zealand in *From a Garden in the Antipodes* (1929), a volume of sophisticated poetry influenced by D. H. Lawrence. Under her own name Bethell published *Time and Place* (1936) and *Day and Night : Poems 1924–34* (1939), more ambitious collections of explicitly Christian poetry. Her *Collected Poems* appeared posthumously (1950).

BETHUNE, MARY MCLEOD (Mary McLeod; 1875– 1955), U.S. educator. One of the most influential African-American leaders of the century, Bethune was the daughter of former slaves. She graduated (1895) from the Moody Bible Institute, Chicago, and taught in several Southern Presbyterian mission schools for the next eight years. In 1904 she founded the Daytona Literary and Industrial School for Training Negro Girls, which merged with Cookman Institute (1923) to form Bethune-Cookman College, of which she was president until 1942. Bethune was also the founder of the National Council of Negro Women (1935) and director of Negro Affairs of the National Youth Administration (1936–44: the first African-American woman to head a federal office). She was a special assistant to the secretary of war during World War II, special adviser to Pres. Franklin Roosevelt (1935–44), and consultant on interracial relations at the U.N. organizing conference at San Francisco (1945). ■ See biographies by Emma Sterne (1957) and Rackham Holt (1964).

BETHUNE, NORMAN (1899–1939), Canadian surgeon. Born in Ontario, Bethune interrupted his studies in 1914 to serve in World War I. He returned, wounded, to complete his medical education and reenlist as a surgeon lieutenant in the navy. Suffering from tuberculosis, he nevertheless fought (1936–37) with the Loyalists in the Spanish civil war. In 1937 Bethune went to China and spent two years as a front-line surgeon with the communist forces, operating in primitive conditions, training others, and setting up hospitals. Lacking medication, he died from a cut suffered during surgery. The Chinese revere Bethune as an example of a foreigner who selflessly gave his life for their cause. ■ See Ted Allen and Sydney Gordon, *The Scalpel, the Sword* (1952), and study by Roderick Stewart (1973).

BETI, MONGO (Alexandre Biyidi; 1932–   ), Cameroonian writer. A Sorbonne-educated Marxist, originally named Alexandre Biyidi, Beti was, along with Camara Laye, the most highly acclaimed novelist of Francophone Africa. His satiric novels depicted the dilemmas of alienated semi-Westernized Africans. They rejected European values, education, and Christianity and affirmed the positive values of African culture. His best-known works were *Cruel City* (1954), *The Poor Christ of Bomba* (1956; Eng. trans. 1971), *Mission to Kala* (1957; Eng. trans. 1958), and *King Lazarus* (1958; Eng. trans. 1961). After 1961 he lived in France and was a high school teacher, but he attacked neocolonialism, corruption, and authoritarianism in independent Africa in his later novels, including *Perpetua* (1974; Eng. trans. 1978) and *Remember Ruben* (1973; Eng. trans. 1980), which were both banned in Cameroon. ■ See Stephen H. Arnold, ed., *Critical Perspectives on Mongo Beti* (1998).

BETJEMAN, SIR JOHN (1906–1984), British poet. An architectural editor, guidebook writer, and lecturer, Betjeman treated the world of British suburbs, nature, love, and the ironies of life in his gently satirical verses. He expressed nostalgia for the artifacts of a disappearing Victorian world, especially its architecture, in lyrical poetry written in traditional forms but in vivid, contemporary language. His work, particularly his *Collected Poems* (1958; 4th ed. 1979), was very popular with the British public. Other collections included *A Few Late Chrysanthemums* (1954), *The Best of Betjeman* (1976), *Church Poems* (1981), and *Uncollected Poems* (1982). He served as poet laureate from 1972 until his death. ■ See his autobiography in verse, *Summoned Bells* (1960), and biography by Patrick Taylor-Martin (1983).

BETTELHEIM, BRUNO (1903–1990), Austrian-born U.S. psychologist. Originally trained as a psychoanalyst, Bettelheim first gained worldwide recognition with "Individual and Mass Behavior in Extreme Situations" (1943), a study of the psychological effects of tyranny based on his observations while incarcerated (1938–39) in two Nazi concentration camps. As director (1944–73) of the University of Chicago's Sonia Shankman Orthogenic School, a residential treatment institution for severely disturbed children, Bettelheim achieved success with children unresponsive to many other therapeutic techniques by using a method of unconditionally accepting all the children's behavior. He was also recognized as an authority on the problems of child care. His books include *Love Is Not Enough: The Treatment of Emotionally Disturbed Children* (1950); *The Children of the Dream* (1969), a study of children in the Israeli kibbutz setting; *The Uses of Enchantment: The Meaning and Importance of Fairy Tales* (1976); *On Learning to Read: The Child's First Fascination with Meaning* (1981); and *Freud and Man's Soul* (1982). After his suicide, several commentators charged that he was manipulative, abusive, and dishonest with his staff and his patients and that he misrepresented his research conclusions. These issues are discussed in the biography by Nina Sutton (1995; Eng. trans. 1996) and in the hostile account by Richard Pollak, *The Creation of Dr. B* (1997).

BETTI, UGO (1892–1953), Italian writer. A magistrate and later a judge in Rome (1930–43), Betti wrote poetry, essays and short stories, but he was best known for his plays, of which 24 were produced in his lifetime. Concerned with themes of justice, guilt, responsibility, and expiation, many of his dramas take the form of legal investigations and can be seen as allegories of the human condition. Among his best-known plays were *Landslide* (1935; Eng. trans. 1964), *Corruption in the Palace of Justice* (1944; Eng. trans. 1962), *Crime on Goat Island* (1950; Eng. trans. 1961), *The Gambler* (1951; Eng. trans. 1966), and *The Burnt Flower-Bed* (1952; Eng. trans. 1956). ■ See study by Emanuele Licastro (1985).

BEUVE-MÉRY, HUBERT (1902–1989), French journalist. Beuve-Méry began his newspaper career as a correspondent in Czechoslovakia, where he was director of the French Institute in Prague (1928–39). Back in France during World War II, he wrote columns under the pseudonym "Sirius," and after liberation he founded *Le Monde,* an austere, nonpartisan left-wing newspaper celebrated for lucid analysis. During the 25 years of Beuve-Méry's direction (1944–69), *Le Monde* opposed the wars in Algeria and Vietnam and was France's most influential newspaper. Its circulation rose to 500,000 and its readers included many world leaders.

BEUYS, JOSEPH (1921–1986), German sculptor. Conscious since his childhood in Kleve, Germany, of a sense of mission, Beuys was shot down during World War II in the

Crimea, where he was saved by Tartars who wrapped him in fat and felt. He studied art in Düsseldorf after the war, creating sculpture from found materials in the tradition of Kurt Schwitters. Fat and felt appeared regularly in his creations as symbols of healing and regeneration. His art, generally environments or "happenings," was iconoclastic and was always committed to the transformation of society. He was a professor of sculpture at the Academy of Arts in Düsseldorf. In 1979 he was honored by a retrospective at the Guggenheim Museum in New York. ■ See studies by Adriani Götz (1979) and Caroline Tisdall (1979).

BEVAN, ANEURIN (1897–1960), British political leader. The son of a Welsh miner, "Nye" Bevan became active in the trade-union movement and was elected to Parliament in 1929 as a left-wing Labour member. He originated the expression "commanding heights of the economy," which he believed the state ought to control; he designed the National Health Service as minister of health (1945–51) and was leader of the radical wing of the party in the early 1950s. His political, social, and economic views were set forth in *In Place of Fear* (1952). ■ See biographies by Mark Krug (1961) and Michael Foot (1962, 1973), and study by John Campbell (1987).

BEVERIDGE, ALBERT JEREMIAH (1862–1927), U.S. senator and historian. Beveridge was a progressive Republican senator from Indiana (1899–1911), the chief contemporary spokesman for U.S. imperialism, and a supporter of Pres. Theodore Roosevelt. After the failure of Roosevelt's Progressive party (1912), Beveridge turned to the writing of historical biography, winning a Pulitzer Prize for his *Life of John Marshall* (4 vols., 1916–19) and completing two volumes on Abraham Lincoln (1928). ■ See biography by John Braeman (1971).

BEVERIDGE OF TUGGAL, WILLIAM HENRY BEVERIDGE, 1st BARON (1879–1963), British economist. Born in India and educated at Oxford, Beveridge played a major role in bringing social and economic reform to Britain. As director of the labor exchange and head of the employment department of the Board of Trade prior to World War I, he analyzed unemployment and helped to create a system of unemployment insurance. Under his direction (1919–37) the London School of Economics became one of Britain's most prestigious universities. In 1942 the committee he chaired produced the immensely influential *Social Insurance and Allied Services,* popularly known as the Beveridge Report, which served as the basis for the comprehensive welfare-state legislation adopted after World War II. His book *Full Employment in a Free Society* (1944) elaborated on his views and reflected the influence of economist John Maynard Keynes. ■ See Beveridge's autobiography *Power and Influence* (1953); biography by Jose Harris (1977); and Philip B. Mair, *Shared Enthusiasm* (1982).

BEVIN, ERNEST (1881–1951), British labor leader and government official. The most influential trade unionist of his generation, Bevin organized the Transport and General Workers Union (1921), a conglomeration of 32 separate organizations that became the world's largest trade union. He served as its general secretary (1921–40) and was also a member (1925–40) and chairman (1937) of the general council of the Trade Union Congress (TUC). In 1940 he joined Prime Minister Winston Churchill's coalition government as minister of labour, mobilizing manpower for World War II. As foreign ministering Clement Attlee's Labour government (1945–51), Bevin strengthened Western European and British ties to the United States with his advocacy of the Atlantic alliance (1949) and support of the Marshall Plan. ■ See biographies by Alan Bullock (3 vols., 1960–83) and Peter Weiler (1993).

BHARATI, SUBRAMANIA (C. Subramania Iyer; 1882–1921), Indian writer. Bharati was a court poet of the raja of Ettayapuram in south India before moving to Madras and becoming deeply involved in the revolutionary nationalist movement. Forced into exile in neighboring, French-controlled Pondicherry (1910–20), he wrote hundreds of revolutionary essays and poems and gained recognition throughout the Tamil-speaking areas of south India. His lyrical poems on themes of patriotism, social reform, and spiritual devotion transformed the written Tamil language, and Bharati is considered the father of modern Tamil poetry. His best-known works were the three long poems *The Krishna Songs* (1917; Eng. trans. 1977), *Panchali's Vow* (1912–24; Eng. trans. 1977), and *Kuyil's Song* (1912; Eng. trans. 1977). Other works in English included *Agni and Other Poems and Translations* (1937), *Essays and Other Prose Fragments* (1937), and *Poems* (1977). ■ See studies by P. Nandakumar (1968) and S. V. Bharati (1972).

BHAVE, VINOBA (Vinayak Bhave; 1895–1982), Indian nationalist leader and social reformer. A Brahmin from Maharashtra, Bhave left school at age 20 to become an ascetic and joined nationalist leader Mahatma Gandhi's movement. He became Gandhi's chief aide, spent several years in jail for leading civil disobedience campaigns against British policies, and later inherited Gandhi's spiritual mantle. After Indian independence Bhave created the Bhoodan (land-gift) movement (1951) during which he walked thousands of miles, crisscrossing India, urging landlords and wealthy peasants to give land voluntarily to poor landless peasants. He also led a nationwide campaign in favor of cow protection laws. ■ See biography by Shriram Narayan (1970).

BHUMIBOL, ADULYADEJ (also Phumiphol Adulyadet; 1927–), king of Thailand. The grandson of King Chulalongkorn (Rama V), who was popularized in the novel *Anna and the King of Siam* and the show and movie *The King and I,* Bhumibol was born in the United States while his father was a student at Harvard Medical School. Educated in Switzerland, he spent very little time in his country until his coronation in 1950, although he had already succeeded to the throne (1946) after the mysterious death of his brother. As King Rama IX, he symbolized the unity of the Thai people but exerted little political power. He participated in many ceremonial events, including the bicentennial of his (Chakri) dynasty (1982).

BHUTTO, BENAZIR (1953–), Pakistani political leader. The daughter of Prime Minister Zulfikar Ali Bhutto, Benazir Bhutto was educated at Harvard (B.A. 1973) and Oxford (B.A. 1976). After her father's execution (1979), she lived under house arrest (1984–86) before returning to Pakistan to lead the opposition to the military government of General Mohammed Zia ul-Haq. After Zia's mysterious death in a plane crash (1988), Bhutto led her Pakistan People's Party (PPP) to an electoral victory (1988), and she became the first woman prime minister of a modern Muslim country. She was dismissed from office in August 1990 on grounds of corruption and misrule, and her party lost the subsequent elections (1990). However, she returned to power after a narrow election victory (October 1993) but was again dismissed from power (November 1996) for incompetence, corruption, and defiance of the constitution. The PPP decisively lost the February 1997 elections. Although she denied all charges, in 1998 she and her husband, Asif Zardari, were officially charged with corruption amid reports that the couple had amassed an illegal fortune of more than $100 million hidden in foreign bank accounts. They were convicted (1999) and she was sentenced in absentia, to five years in prison and fined $8.6 million. She lived in exile in London. ■ See her autobiography, *Daughter of Destiny* (1989).

BHUTTO, ZULFIKAR ALI (1928–1979), Pakistani political leader. Bhutto was born into a rich and influential family and educated at the University of California and at Oxford. A successful Karachi lawyer during the 1950s, he held several cabinet posts and frequently represented Pakistan at international forums. As foreign minister (1963–66), he shifted left politically, established close relations with China, and in 1967 formed the "Islamic socialist" Pakistan People's party (PPP). Although second in the 1970 elections, Bhutto rejected the results and civil war broke out between West and East Pakistan. East Pakistan, aided by Indian troops, emerged from the conflict as the independent nation of Bangladesh. Bhutto served as president of what was left of Pakistan (from 1971) and became prime minister in 1973. He initiated political and economic reforms and nationalized key industries, but critics charged him with corruption and dictatorial practices, and with "vote rigging" after the March 1977 elections, in which he won a landslide victory. Overthrown in a bloodless coup (July 1977), he was arrested, tried, and convicted of conspiring to commit a political assassination in 1974 and hanged (April 1979). ■ See

S. J. Burki, *Pakistan under Bhutto* (1980), and biographies by Stanley Wolpert (1993) and Rafi Raza (1997).

BIALIK, CHAIM NACHMAN (1873–1934). Russian-born Hebrew-language writer. Considered the foremost modern Hebrew poet, Bialik worked for many years as a Hebrew teacher, translator, and editor in Odessa before moving to Berlin (1921) and finally to Tel Aviv (1924). His passionate, lyrical poems reflected the disintegration of the traditional Eastern European Jewish world, the sorrow and suffering of exile, and the hope of a new homeland in Palestine. They played a major role in the revival and modernization of the Hebrew language. He also translated European and Yiddish language classics into Hebrew and wrote several volumes of Hebrew and Yiddish legends. English translations are in *Law and Legend* (1923), *And It Came to Pass* (1938), *Complete Poetic Works* (vol. I, 1948), *Selected Poems* (1965), *Bialik Speaks* (1969), and *Poems* (1972).

BIDAULT, GEORGES (1899–1983), French public official. A history teacher at a Paris lycée, Bidault founded during the 1930s a small Catholic daily paper in which he opposed his government's policy of appeasement of Nazi Germany. During World War II he worked to create the National Council of the Resistance of which he became president in 1943. After the liberation Biault served as foreign minister in Gen. Charles de Gaulle's provisional government and became premier in 1946 and again in 1949. A leading opponent of independence for Algeria, he went underground in 1961 and fled to Brazil in 1963 to avoid conspiracy charges but returned home to resume his political career after the 1968 amnesty. ■ See his political autobiography, *Resistance* (1965; Eng. trans. 1967).

BIELY, ANDREI. *See BELY, ANDREI.*

BIERMANN, WOLF (1936–), German poet, cabaret performer, and playwright. Biermann's father was a Jewish communist member of the anti-Nazi resistance movement who was killed at Auschwitz concentration camp. Raised as an idealistic socialist in Hamburg, Biermann emigrated to East Germany (1953), attended Humboldt University in East Berlin, and worked with the Berliner Ensemble theater group. Influenced by the works of Bertolt Brecht, he emerged in the late 1950s as an extremely popular poet and balladeer who protested against alienation, bureaucracy, and social conditions in both East and West Germany. Severely criticized by the government, he was forbidden to sing in public or publish in East Germany after 1965. He was given permission to give a concert in West Germany (1976) but not permitted to return to East Berlin. Though he settled in West Germany, he maintained his independent Marxist views and continued to write and perform. After German unification (1990) he continued to write on controversial social and political issues. He was awarded the Georg Büchner literary prize (1991). His best-known works are *The Wire Harp* (1965; Eng. trans. 1968) and *Poems and Ballads* (Eng. trans. 1977).

BIERUT, BOLESLAW (Boleslaw Krasnodebski; 1892–1956), Polish political leader. Bierut joined the Polish Communist party in 1918, served as a Comintern agent in various European cities, and was imprisoned several times for his activities during the interwar period. In 1938 he went to the Soviet Union, returning to Poland in 1943 with the backing of the Soviets, who installed him as provisional president of Poland (1944). A loyal follower of Moscow's line, he was elected president (1947), replaced Wladyslaw Gomulka as party secretary (1948), and served as premier (1952–54).

BIFFEN, SIR ROWLAND HARRY (1874–1949), British geneticist and plant breeder. A Cambridge professor, Biffen was the first to apply Mendelian genetic principles to the study of plant breeding and was responsible for the development of agricultural botany as a distinct field of study. His experiments, which led to the creation of improved cereal varieties and to the discovery (1905) that disease resistance in plants is inheritable, reduced crop losses throughout the world. He headed the Cambridge Plant Breeding Institute from 1912 to 1936.

BIGGERS, EARL DERR (1884–1933), U.S. novelist and playwright. The Harvard-educated (B.A. 1907) Biggers wrote a humorous column, drama criticism, and a play before achieving sudden success with his first mystery novel, *Seven Keys to Baldpate* (1913). He wrote other mysteries and romances, but he is known for creating the world-famous Charlie Chan—the humble Honolulu detective who spoke stylized English, often quoting apt aphorisms, and always got his man. Biggers wrote six Chan novels, beginning with *The House Without a Key* (1925); they generated countless comic strips, radio shows, films, and a Broadway play.

BIGGS, E. POWER (Edward George Power-Biggs; 1906–1977), British-born U.S. organist. Undoubtedly the most famous organist of the century, Biggs first received acclaim (1937) for his concerts on the newly built classic organ at the Germanic Museum at Harvard, which was modeled after the great 18th-century European instruments. For 16 years, starting in 1942, Biggs played weekly Sunday-morning recitals on the Harvard organ that were broadcast nationwide over the Columbia Broadcasting System. Through his broadcasts, frequent concert appearances, and more than 50 recordings he reached millions of listeners and was responsible for bringing serious organ music out of the churches. Not merely interested in the classical repertoire, he commissioned pieces from such modern masters as Benjamin Britten, Walter Piston, Roy Harris, Howard Hanson, and Alec Templeton. ■ See biography by Barbara Owen (1987).

BIKILA, ABEBE (1927–1973), Ethiopian marathon runner. A member of Emperor Haile Selassie's imperial guard, Bikila electrified the sports world and became a national hero by winning the 1960 Olympic 26-mile marathon race running barefoot through the streets of Rome. He repeated as marathon champion in the 1964 Tokyo Olympics, thus becoming the first man ever to win two Olympic marathons.

BIKO, STEVE (1946–1977), South African political leader. Biko, a medical student at the University of Natal (1966–72), was influenced by the writings of Tanzanian leader Julius Nyerere, psychiatrist Frantz Fanon, and U.S. black-power advocates. Rejecting artificial and symbolic racial integration and the leadership of white liberals, Biko advocated militant self-reliance for blacks and led the "black consciousness" movement. He was the founding president of the all-black South African Students Organization (1969) and a cofounder of the nonstudent Black People's Convention (1972). An uncompromising activist, he was arrested in August 1977 for subversion and died shortly afterward while in police custody. His funeral, held amid contradictory government accounts of his death, which was officially called an accident, was attended by diplomatic representatives from 13 nations and prompted a boycott by 200,000 students. In September 1997, in testimony before the Truth Commission, former police officers described how Biko was beaten to death during interrogation. ■ See *Steve Biko: Black Consciousness in South Africa* (1978), the record of his testimony at a trial describing the aims of organizations that he founded; the selections of his writings in *I Write What I Like* (1979); and study by Donald Woods (1978; rev. ed. 1987).

BILBO, THEODORE GILMORE (1877–1947), U.S. senator. A legendary racist and demagogue, Bilbo was Democratic governor of Mississippi (1916–20; 1928–32) and U.S. senator (1935–47). Preaching to the Senate the same venom and invective he used on the stump in manipulating the fears and prejudices of poor white farmers, he advocated white supremacy (he was a member of the Ku Klux Klan), proposed the deportation of millions of blacks to Africa, and filibustered passionately against antilynching and antipoll-tax bills. Barred from taking his Senate seat (January 1947) while being investigated for intimidating black voters and taking gifts from war contractors, he underwent surgery for mouth cancer and died shortly thereafter. ■ See A. Wigfall Green, *The Man Bilbo* (1963), and Chester M. Morgan, *Redneck Liberal* (1985).

BILL, MAX (1908–1994), Swiss artist. Bill apprenticed as a silversmith and studied at the Bauhaus, Germany's celebrated school of design. Known primarily for his sophisticated advertising designs, his geometric paintings, and his curvilinear stone and metal sculptures, he also designed chairs and buildings. Bill wrote on the mathematical underpinnings of abstract art. He was rector and teacher as well as campus architect at the College of Design in Ulm, Germany (1951–56), and later served as a delegate to the Swiss parliament (1967–71). ■ See study by Eduard Hüttinger (Eng. trans. 1978).

BILLINGS, WARREN KNOX. *See MOONEY, TOM.*

BINET, ALFRED (1857–1911), French psychologist. The founder of experimental psychology in France, Binet directed (1895–1911) the first French psychological laboratory (at the Sorbonne, Paris) and founded the journal *L'Année Psychologique* (1895). Primarily concerned with the study of human intelligence, he devised a series of tests to determine the intellectual development of his daughters. He later expanded the tests (with Théodore Simon, 1905) when the minister of public information requested an instrument for measuring whether retarded children would benefit from schooling. The tests were revised in 1908 and 1911 to measure the "mental level" of normal children. Binet's scale of measurement was adopted by American psychologist Lewis Terman (1916), who used it in his revised Stanford-Binet Intelligence Scale test, which became the best-known IQ test in the United States. Binet's translated works included *The Development of Intelligence in Children* (1916). Several of his papers are in Robert H. Pollack and Margaret Brenner, eds., *The Experimental Psychology of Alfred Binet* (1969). ■ See biography by Theta H. Wolf (1973).

BING, SIR RUDOLF (1902–1997), Austrian-born opera impresario. Raised in a musical Viennese family, Bing studied at the University of Vienna and worked in the administration of the Darmstadt (Germany) State Theater (1928–30) and the Charlottenburg (Berlin) Municipal Opera (1930–33). When the Nazis came to power, Bing left for England, where he was general manager of the Glyndebourne Opera Festival (1935–49) and helped organize the Edinburgh Festival in 1947. He became a British subject in 1946. He was general manager of the Metropolitan Opera in New York from 1950 to 1972, during which time he improved production standards, introduced black singers, extended the season, and supervised the company's move to Lincoln Center. ■ See his autobiographies, *5000 Nights at the Opera* (1972) and *A Knight at the Opera* (1981).

BINH, NGUYEN THI (1927–), Vietnamese political leader. Madame Binh, as she was known in the West, was born in Saigon into a family of revolutionaries. She joined a militant group in 1950 after participating in the anticolonial movement as a schoolgirl. Jailed for three years (1951–54), she was forced to go underground in 1956. In 1961 she joined the communist-led National Liberation Front (NLF) and fought against the South Vietnamese government of Ngo Dinh Diem. A member of its Central Committee from 1962, she traveled extensively as a roving ambassador and

headed the NLF delegation at the Paris Peace talks (1968–73). In 1969 she was named foreign minister of the NLF's Provisional Revolutionary Government of South Vietnam and served as foreign minister of the transitional Revolutionary Government (1975–76). After the official reunification of North and South Vietnam (1976), she served as minister of education (1976–87) and member of the council of state (from 1981) and vice president (from 1993) of the Socialist Republic of Vietnam.

BINNIG, GERD (1974–), German physicist. After graduating from the Goethe University in Frankfurt (Ph.D. 1978), Binnig joined the staff of the IBM Research Laboratory in Zurich. Collaborating with Swiss physicist Heinrich Rohrer, he developed the scanning tunneling microscope (STM), a device that can map surfaces in such detail that individual atoms are visible. The device has been widely used in the study of semiconductor physics and low-temperature physics as well as in the development of computers. He shared the 1986 Nobel Prize in Physics with Rohrer and Ernst Ruska, who was credited with designing the first electron microscope.

BINYON, (ROBERT) LAURENCE (1869–1943), British poet, art critic, and dramatist. Binyon's poetry was outstanding for its style rather than feeling and for the most part was not popular. One poem, "For the Fallen," was engraved on war memorials after World War I. In another of his best-known poems, "The Burning of the Leaves," his subject was World War II. He was associated with the department of prints and drawings of the British Museum (1893–1933) and his works on Asian art, notably *Painting in the Far East* (1908), introduced the subject to the English-speaking public. He also translated Dante's *Divine Comedy* (1933–43) in triple rhyme and wrote the verse dramas *Attila* (1907) and *The Young King* (1924). ■ See his *Collected Poems* (1931) and biography by John Hatcher (1995).

BIRCH, JOHN MORRISON (1918–1945), U.S. missionary and soldier. Birch was born in India to missionary parents and graduated from a Baptist university in Georgia, where he advocated vigilance against professorial heresies. He went to China as a missionary in 1940. During World War II he joined U.S. Gen. Claire Chennault's air unit, later transferred to the Office of Strategic Services, and was killed by Chinese communist guerrillas after the war ended. In 1954 retired candy manufacturer Robert Welch wrote a biography of Birch, whom he cast as the first hero of the cold war and the rallying symbol of the archconservative society he founded bearing Birch's name.

BIRD, LARRY (1956–), U.S. basketball player. A native of French Lick, Indiana, Bird was the star of the Indiana State University basketball team (1975–79) and was voted Player of the Year in 1979. Drafted as a forward by the Boston Celtics of the National Basketball Association

(NBA), the 6-foot, 9-inch, 220-pound Bird revitalized the team and was named NBA Rookie of the Year in 1980. One of the greatest all-around players in basketball history, he excelled in shooting, rebounding, and passing, and was named the league's Most Valuable Player in 1984, 1985, and 1986. He led the Celtics to NBA championships in 1981, 1984, and 1986. After he retired as a player (1992) he coached the Indiana Pacers (1997–   ).

BIRDSEYE, CLARENCE (1886–1956), U.S. business executive and inventor. Adapting to quantity production the food-freezing techniques he had observed while fur trading among Eskimos, Birdseye parleyed a $7 investment in a Massachusetts fish business into a billion-dollar industry that revolutionized America's eating habits. In 1929, he sold for $22 million his General Seafoods Corp. and 168 quick-freeze patents to the Postum Co. and the Goldman-Sachs Trading Corporation, which renamed the company the General Foods Corp. Subsequently he was president of the Birdseye Electric Co. (1935–38). His later inventions included a kickless harpoon gun and an anhydrous method for dehydrating foods.

BIRENDRA BIR BIKRAM SHAH DEVA (1945–   ), king of Nepal. Birendra was educated at Darjeeling (India), Eton, the University of Tokyo, and Harvard. In 1972 he became king, the tenth of his line, although his coronation was delayed until 1975 on the advice of royal astrologers. He maintained the nonparty panchayat system of government established by his father, King Mahendra, in 1962, and resisted pressures for political democratization. He concentrated on economic development and built roads, sanitation facilities, schools, and hospitals in order to modernize his country. He maintained friendly relations with both of his giant neighbors, India and China.

BIRKHOFF, GEORGE DAVID (1884–1944), U.S. mathematician. Birkhoff made his reputation for his proof of a geometric theorem postulated by the French mathematician Henry Poincaré and for his ergodic theorem on the kinetic theory of gases. A professor at Harvard (1912–44), he also developed his own theory of gravitation as well as a mathematical theory of aesthetics. His writings included *Relativity and Modern Physics* (1923) and *Aesthetic Measure* (1933).

BIRNEY, (ALFRED) EARLE (1904–1995), Canadian author. Raised in a pioneering family in a remote area of Alberta, Birney moved to British Columbia after World War I and graduated from the University of British Columbia (B.A. 1927). While a graduate student in London (1934–35) he was a left-wing political organizer and journalist. Returning to Canada, he received his doctorate at the University of Toronto (1936), taught English literature there (1936–42), and edited the *Canadian Forum* (1936–40). He later taught at the University of British Columbia (1946–65). His early poetry featured colloquial speech and was in-

fluenced by his radical politics and his readings of Middle English literature. He later experimented with concrete and sound poetry. His best-known works are in *Selected Poems: 1940–1966* (1966) and *Collected Poems* (2 vols., 1975). His social satires included the novel *Turvey: A Military Picaresque* (1949), a story of a naive Canadian soldier's adventures with the military bureaucracy during World War II. *Down the Long Table* (1955) was a semiautobiographical novel describing political activism and social turmoil during the Depression of the 1930s. ■ See his *Spreading Time: Remarks on Canadian Writing and Writers* (1980) and study by Peter Aichinger (1979).

BISHOP, ELIZABETH (1911–1979), U.S. poet. When her father died and her mother was committed to a mental institution, Bishop was raised by her grandparents, who sent her to boarding school and then to Vassar. She lived in Brazil from 1952 to 1969. Despite her 1956 Pulitzer Prize for the lyric poetry in *North and South–A Cold Spring* (1955), public recognition came slowly. Bishop wrote formal, structured verse that was concerned with proportion and physical detail; often it contrasted her experiences in South America with her New England origins. She avoided social criticism in her poems, of which the most acclaimed were "The Fish," "Roosters," and "The Monument." Her *Complete Poems* (1969) was followed by *Geography III* (1976). *The Collected Prose* (1984) included autobiographical writings. ■ See study by Anne Stevenson (1966); Lloyd Schwarz and Sybil P. Estess, eds., *Elizabeth Bishop and Her Art* (1983); Gary Fountain and Peter Brazeau, *Remembering Elizabeth Bishop* (1994); and the biography by Brett C. Miller (1993).

BISHOP, J. MICHAEL (1936–   ), U.S. virologist. Bishop, the son of a Lutheran minister, graduated from the Harvard Medical School (M.D. 1962) and taught microbiology at the University of California Medical School in San Francisco (1968–   ). During the early 1970s, with colleague Harold Varmus and postdoctoral fellows Dominique Stehelin and Deborah Spector, Bishop did pioneering genetic research that disproved the theory that dormant rival oncogenes within healthy cells cause cancer. Their finding that normal cellular genes, when disrupted by mutations or chemicals (carcinogens), can cause "uncontrolled cellular growth characteristic of cancer" ushered in a new era in cancer research. Bishop and Varmus shared the 1989 Nobel Prize for Physiology or Medicine for their research.

BISHOP, WILLIAM AVERY (1894–1956), Canadian military aviator. Known for his daring air exploits, Billy Bishop shot down 72 German airplanes during World War I—more than any other Allied pilot. He won (1917) England's highest military honor, the Victoria Cross, after single-handedly downing 7 German planes. After the war he lectured and wrote on air warfare. Bishop was director of training for the Royal Canadian Air Force during World War II. ■ See William Arthur Bishop. *The Courage of the Early Morning* (1966).

BITAR, SALAH AL-DIN (1912–1980), Syrian political leader. Bitar cofounded (with Michel Aflaq) the pan-Arab Ba'ath (Arab Renaissance) party during the early 1940s. Socialist and nationalist in orientation, the party spread throughout the Middle East and was instrumental in the short-lived union between Syria and Egypt (1958–61). After the Ba'ath coup in Syria (1963), Bitar headed five governments before being ousted in the coup of 1966. Bitar (with Aflaq) was expelled from the party and lived in exile in Lebanon. In Paris (from 1970), he edited an Arabic-language theoretical journal in which he criticized the Ba'ath parties of both Syria and Iraq. He was assassinated by an unidentified gunman in Paris on July 21, 1980.

BITZER, BILLY (George William Bitzer; 1872–1944), U.S. motion-picture cameraman. Bitzer joined the pioneer motion-picture firm American Mutoscope and Biograph Co. (1896) and became its principal studio cameraman (1900–13). A technical wizard, he teamed up with director D. W. Griffith (1908–24) to produce hundreds of silent films, including such classics as *Judith of Bethulia* (1913), *The Birth of a Nation* (1915), *Intolerance* (1916), and *Broken Blossoms* (1919). Bitzer was the first cameraman to film completely under artificial lights, to utilize soft-focus photography, and to use the iris shot, a technique of shading out portions of the frame to fade in or out of a scene. He also developed close-ups and long shots to heighten the dramatic tension of a scene. He founded a photographer's union in 1926 and was blacklisted in Hollywood when a local opened there in 1929. ■ See his memoirs, *Billy Bitzer, the Story* (1973).

BJERKNES, JACOB AALL BONNEVIE (1897–1975), Norwegian-born U.S. meteorologist. The son of meteorologist Vilhelm Bjerknes, Jacob Bjerknes headed the weather-forecasting service at Bergen, Norway (1920–31), and was a professor at the Bergen Geophysical Institute (1931–40) before joining the faculty at the University of California at Los Angeles as its first professor of meteorology (1940). His pioneering research on the structure and development of cyclones became the basis of weather forecasting in all middle- and high-latitude locations. He was also a pioneer in the use of photographs taken by high-altitude rockets for weather analysis.

BJERKNES, VILHELM FRIMAN KOREN (1862–1951), Norwegian meteorologist and physicist. A pioneer of the science of weather forecasting, Bjerknes was a professor at Stockholm (1895–1907), Oslo (1907–12); (1926–32), Leipzig (1912–17), and Bergen (1917–26). His development of circulation theorems of hydrodynamics and theories of thermodynamics led to theories of atmospheric movement that were essential to the accurate prediction of future weather conditions. He founded and directed (1917–26) the Bergen Geophysical Institute. His classic work, *On the Dynamics of the Circular Vortex with Applications to the At-mosphere and Atmospheric Vortex and Wave Motion* (1921), summarizes his research.

BJOERLING, JUSSI (Johan Jonaton Bjoerling; 1911–1960), Swedish opera singer. Born into a prominent musical family—his father had sung in New York's Metropolitan Opera—Bjoerling started singing professionally as a boy with his father and two brothers in the Bjoerling Male Voice Quartet. He made his operatic debut in Stockholm in 1930 and sang at the Met, with the exception of the war years, from 1938 until his death. Frequently compared to Enrico Caruso, Bjoerling had one of the most beautiful tenor voices of the century. Known for his incomparable grace, elegance, and musicianship, he sang more than 50 leading roles in Italian and French operas and was best known for his performances in *Don Giovanni, Tosca, Don Carlos, A Masked Ball, Manon, Faust,* and *Romeo et Juliette.* ■ See Anna-Lisa Björling and Andrew Farkas, *Jussi* (1996).

BJÖRNSSON, SVEINN (1881–1952), Icelandic political leader. Björnsson served in parliament (1914–16; 1920) and was a special envoy to the United States and Britain during World War I. He served as minister to Denmark (1920–24; 1926–41) and was regent of Iceland during World War II (1941–44). His government invited U.S. troops to Iceland (July 1941). Upon the inauguration of the republic (1944), Björnsson was elected president and reelected to four-year terms in 1945 and 1949.

BLACK, CONRAD (1944–), Canadian publisher. Black was the son of the director of Argus Corp., a prominent investment holding company. He studied political science at Carleton University, Ottawa (B.A. 1965), law at Laval University, Quebec (L.L.L. 1970), and history at McGill University, Montreal (M.A. 1973). He purchased his first newspaper in 1967 and when he assumed control of Argus, in 1978, he divested it of its industrial and retail holdings in order to concentrate on newspaper acquisition. By the late 1990s he was one of the world's most powerful press barons, controlling more than half of Canada's 105 daily newspapers (with 40 percent of the nationwide circulation) and more than 100 dailies in the United States, including the *Chicago Sun-Times.* He founded the Canadian national daily, *National Post,* in Toronto in 1998. Internationally he controlled the *Daily Telegraph* of London, the *Jerusalem Post,* and the *Sydney Morning Herald* in Australia, among others. He was controversial because of his power, his staff cuts, and his strongly conservative political and economic views. ■ See his autobiography, *A Life in Progress* (1993), and Richard Siklos, *Shades of Black* (1995).

BLACK, DAVIDSON (1884–1934), Canadian physician and anthropologist. Black received an M.D. (1906) from the University of Toronto, and traveled to China in 1918 to teach at Peking Union Medical College. In 1927, having been shown a single fossilized hominid tooth found in a cave near Peking, he inferred the existence of *Sinanthropus pekinensis* or "Peking man," a genus and species similar to *Pithecanthropus erectus* or "Java man." Through later excavation at the cave site, where Black was joined by Pierre Teilhard de Chardin, Franz Weidenreich, and other paleontologists, the tooth was dated as 450,000 years old. ■ See biography by Dora Hood (1964) and Harry L. Shapiro, *Peking Man* (1975).

BLACK, EUGENE ROBERT (1898–1992), U.S. banker. The son of a Georgia banker who was a governor of the Federal Reserve Board, Black was a vice president of the Chase National Bank in New York (1933–49) before heading the International Bank for Reconstruction and Development, commonly known as the World Bank (1949–62). He initiated the creation of the International Development Association and the International Finance Corporation within the bank and was largely responsible for reorienting it toward investment in the Third World from its original purpose of rebuilding post–World War II Europe. During Black's tenure the bank's membership increased from 48 to 80 members, its capital increased from $8.3 to $20.5 billion, and it lent over $6 billion of its own funds, mainly for economic development. After retiring from the bank he was a special financial consultant to the United Nations, was an adviser to U.S. President Lyndon Johnson, helped set up the Asian Development Bank, served as chairman of the Brookings Institution, and was on the board of directors of many large corporations. He wrote *The Diplomacy of Economic Development* (1963).

BLACK, HAROLD STEPHEN (1898–1983), U.S. electrical engineer. Associated with the Bell Telephone system research organization (1921–63). Black invented (1927) the negative-feedback amplifier, which revolutionized communications by providing steady amplification free of distortion. The invention was essential for the development of telephone communications, radar and radar-controlled bombs and missiles, and industrial control mechanisms. The principle of negative feedback has also been used by psychologists and physiologists in studies of the operation and mechanisms of the brain. Black wrote *Modulation Theory* (1953).

BLACK, HUGO LAFAYETTE (1886–1971), U.S. jurist. Alabama born and bred, Black won his reputation as a successful labor attorney for the United Mine Workers and other unions. Elected as a Democrat to the U.S. Senate in 1926 and 1932, he was instrumental in the enactment of the Tennessee Valley Authority and other public-utility legislation. In 1937 Black became Pres. Franklin Roosevelt's first appointment to the Supreme Court, where he was a defender of constitutional liberties. Although formerly a nominal member of the Ku Klux Klan (1923–25), he advocated judicial enforcement of desegregation and was a leader of the court's liberal wing. Black's "one-man, one-vote" opinion in 1964 was a judicial landmark in legislative reapportionment. ■ See study by Gerald T. Dunne (1977); James J. Magee, *Mr. Justice Black* (1980); and biographies by Roger K. Newman (1994) and Howard Ball (1996).

BLACK, SIR JAMES (1924–), British pharmacologist. Black studied at the University of St. Andrews in Scotland (M.D. 1946) and taught in Singapore and Glasgow before doing research at Imperial Chemical Industries (1958–64) and at Smith, Kline and French (1964–73). He later taught pharmacology at the University of London (1973–77; 1984–), and directed therapeutic research at the Wellcome Research Laboratories (1978–84) and served as chancellor of Dundee University (1992–). His 1950s research on heart disease led him to the study of cell receptor sites in the heart (which he called beta receptors) and the chemicals in the blood that stimulate them and trigger various physiological responses, such as heart rate. In 1964 he developed the beta-blocking drug propranolol, which prevented beta receptors from stimulating heart contractions and thus eased the pain of angina pectoris. The drug was later used to treat high blood pressure in the 1970s. Black utilized a similar approach for the treatment of stomach ulcers, and he developed the drug cimetidine (marketed as Tagamet), which blocked the secretion of gastric acid and became the leading treatment for stomach and duodenal ulcers. Black was knighted in 1981 and shared the 1988 Nobel Prize in Physiology or Medicine with Gertrude Elion and George M. Hitchings.

BLACKETT, PATRICK MAYNARD STUART BLACK-ETT, BARON (1897–1974), British physicist. After serving as a naval officer, P.M.S. Blackett studied physics at Cambridge and worked there (1921–33) at the Cavendish Laboratory under Lord Rutherford. In the 1920s he developed a cloud-chamber method of tracing the tracks of atomic particles, and he began his important lifelong researches on cosmic rays. He confirmed the existence of the positron (1933); he won the Nobel Prize for Physics (1948) for his work. He also taught at the University of Manchester (1937–53) and Imperial College, London (1953–65). During World War II he did crucial scientific research and analysis for the British government and during the cold war was a sharp critic of American nuclear-weapons policy. He was president of the Royal Society from 1965 to 1970. His books included *Fear, War and the Bomb* (1949) and *Studies of War* (1962).

BLACKMUR, RICHARD PALMER (1904–1965), U.S. critic and poet. R. P. Blackmur's formal education ended when he was expelled from school at age 15 (1918). He worked at menial jobs, writing stories and poetry in his free time. While running a bookstore in his hometown of Cambridge, Massachusetts, Blackmur made literary friends and began issuing the little magazine *Hound and Horn* (publisher, 1928–34; editor, 1928–30), gaining a reputation for brilliant critical essays on contemporary writers. Blackmur was an originator of the method of literary analysis that stressed close textual analysis and became known as the New Criticism; the essays collected in *The Double Agent* (1935) exemplified this approach. A freelance critic until his mid-30s, Blackmur gained a post at Princeton University in 1940 and remained there for the rest of his life. *Language as Gesture: Essays in Poetry* (1952; repr. 1977) collected his more important critical writings. His works were gathered in the posthumous volumes *Poems of R. P. Blackmur* (1977) and *Selected Essays of R. P. Blackmur* (1986). ■ See Russell Fraser, *A Mingled Yarn* (1981), and study by Robert Boyers (1980).

BLACKSTONE, HARRY (Harry Bouton; 1885–1965), U.S. magician and illusionist. Called the last of the great magicians, Blackstone dazzled audiences with his tricks from 1904 to 1959. He sawed women in half and made rabbits appear, donkeys disappear, and handkerchiefs dance. He was also famous for a Hindu rope trick in which a boy climbed a rope suspended in the air and disappeared. Blackstone traveled throughout the United States, earned more than $200,000 annually, and estimated that he gave away 80,000 rabbits during his career. His son Harry Blackstone, Jr. (1934–1997) was also a famous magician.

BLAIR, TONY (Anthony Charles Lynton Blair; 1953–), British political leader. The son of a middle-class lawyer, who was a Conservative party activist, Blair studied law (1972–75) at Oxford (where he also played guitar in a university rock group) and joined the Labour party in 1975. He worked as a lawyer in London for several years before being elected to the House of Commons (1983) at age 30. Eager to reform the Labour party and broaden its base, he rose rapidly through party ranks and was chosen leader after the sudden death of John Smith (1994). He campaigned successfully to have the party repeal (1995) its constitutional commitment to socialism ("the common ownership of the means of production, distribution and exchange") and openly courted the business community and the middle class. His "New Labour party" grew rapidly and he became prime minister (1997) in a landslide electoral victory in which Labour won 418 seats and the biggest majority (178 seats) in Labour party history. In office he established a minimum wage and created a jobs program for unemployed youth, cut welfare benefits, established regional legislatures in Scotland and Wales, helped to negotiate a peace settlement in Northern Ireland, granted the Bank of England the power to set interest rates, and improved relations with Europe while maintaining close ties to the United States. He was attacked by Labour's left wing for moving the party to the right, but he maintained extraordinary popularity with the public during his first years in power.

BLAIS, MARIE-CLAIRE (1939–), French-Canadian novelist and poet. Blais, who was born and educated in Quebec,

dropped out of a convent school and worked in a factory and an office. Her poetic, psychological novels are populated by tortured, violent personalities; her verse employs symbols and elisions to express emotions that have no verbal equivalents. Her first novel, *Mad Shadows* (1959; trans 1960), and *A Season in the Life of Emmanuel* (1965; Eng. trans. 1966), her masterpiece, dealt with adolescence and presented a powerful attack on the social ills of French-Canadian society. *The Manuscripts of Pauline Archange* (1968; Eng. trans. 1970) and *Dürer's Angel* (1970; Eng. trans. 1976) concerned the plight of the artist and were semiautobiographical. Her later works included *Nights in the Underground* (1978; Eng. trans. 1979), a novel of homosexual life in Montreal; *Deaf to the City* (1980; Eng. trans. 1981); *Anna's World* (1982; Eng. trans. 1985); and *The Angel of Solitude* (1989; Eng. trans. 1993). ■ See study by Mary Green (1995).

BLAKE, EUBIE (James Hubert Blake; 1883–1983), U.S. ragtime pianist and composer. A legendary figure in the history of show business, Blake, the son of former slaves, started his career at age 15 as a pianist in a bordello. He subsequently achieved fame as a singer, pianist, and Broadway show composer *(Shuffle Along,* 1921). He was best known for his songs, "I'm Just Wild About Harry" (with Noble Sissle), "Memories of You," and "Love Will Find a Way." Blake was closely associated with the revival of ragtime music in the late 1960s and 1970s and, well past age 90, performed frequently before enthusiastic audiences. ■ See biography by Al Rose (1979).

BLAKE, EUGENE CARSON (1906–1985), U.S. Protestant clergyman. A tough-minded and controversial liberal who advocated the unification of Protestant churches in the United States, Blake was president of the National Council of Churches (1954–57) and chief executive of the Presbyterian Church during the 1950s and 1960s. He was a leader of the ecumenical movement and general secretary of the World Council of Churches (1966–72), which represented over 200 Protestant, Anglican, Orthodox, and Old Catholic churches in more than 80 countries. ■ See study by R. Douglas Brackenridge (1978).

BLALOCK, ALFRED (1899–1964), U.S. surgeon and physiologist. A professor of surgery at Johns Hopkins Medical School (1941–63), Blalock performed, with Helen Taussig (1944), the first "blue baby operation," which relieved congenital circulatory disease. His pioneering work on the physiology of shock demonstrated that loss of blood was responsible for shock and that plasma or whole-blood transfusions could compensate for the loss.

BLANC, MEL (1908–1989), U.S. voice specialist. As a child in Portland, Oregon, Blanc started his collection of dialects and voice characterizations with the study of a Yiddish-speaking grocer. Master of "57 varieties" of dialect, character, and sound effect, he was known first to radio listeners as Pancho on "The Cisco Kid," as the sound of a Maxwell automobile on "The Jack Benny Show," and as Pedro on "The Judy Canova Show," famous for the line: "Pardon me for talking in your face, señorita!" As the voices of Bugs Bunny, Porky Pig, Daffy Duck, Woody Woodpecker, Tweety Pie, Sylvester, and other members of the Warner Brothers roster, he was heard by children across the country. Later, on television, he supplied the voices for the Flintstones and the Munsters. He also gave voice to the classic characters in the live-animation film *Who Framed Roger Rabbit* (1988). ■ See his autobiography, *That's Not All Folks* (1988; with Philip Bashe).

BLANCHOT, MAURICE (1907–), French novelist and critic. Blanchot is best known for his contribution to the "new critical" movement in France. *Aminadab* (1942) and other novels are set in imaginary worlds reminiscent of those of the novelist Franz Kafka. Strongly influenced by German writers, Blanchot was close to the existentialists. *Faux Pas* (1943), *The Work of Fire* (1948; Eng. trans. 1995), and *The Space of Literature* (1955; Eng. trans. 1982) are his major critical works; in the latter he investigates the psychology of the artist. His later works included *The Madness of the Day* (1973; Eng. trans. 1981), *The Infinite Conversation* (1969; Eng. trans. 1993), *The Step Not Beyond* (1973; Eng. trans. 1992), and *The Unavowable Community* (1983; Eng. trans. 1988). In keeping with his emphasis on the preeminence of art, Blanchot took pains to preserve his solitude; little is known of his personal life. English translations of his essays are in *The Siren's Song* (1982) and *The Gaze of Orpheus* (1981). ■ See study by Gerald Bruns (1997).

BLANDING, SARAH GIBSON (1898–1985), U.S. educator. Blanding taught physical education and political science before moving full-time into educational administration. Appointed acting dean at the University of Kentucky at age 24, she was the youngest person in the country to hold such a position. She was dean of the New York State College of Home Economics at Cornell University (1941–46), then became the sixth president of Vassar College (1946–64). Vassar's first woman president, she altered the school's curriculum, stressing independent study, and increased the institution's investment portfolio. She was known for her research on the psychological changes that students undergo during the college years. In 1961, eight years before Vassar admitted male students, Blanding predicted the eventual demise of women's colleges.

BLANKERS-KOEN, FANNY (Francina Elsje Kohn; 1918–), Dutch track athlete. At age 18, she won a place on the Dutch Olympic team and had respectable showings at the 1936 Berlin Olympics, but did not garner top honors. When the Olympic games resumed 12 years later, many considered her well past her prime at age 30, and unfit, as the mother of two, to compete. However, she dominated competition at the 1948 London games, winning gold medals in four of the nine track-and-field events open to women (100 meters; 200 meters; 80-meter hurdles; and the 400-meter relay). She was named "Woman Athlete of the Century (1999) by the International Amateur Athletic Federation (IAAF).

BLANSHARD, BRAND (1892–1987), U.S. philosopher. A teacher of philosophy all his life, Blanshard was a professor at Swarthmore (1925–45) and chaired the Yale philosophy department (1945–50; 1959–61). In his work, he attacked the trend toward linguistic technicality in philosophy. He was well known for his "coherence" theory of truth, which held that truth is apprehended not in parts but as a whole or gestalt. His important works were *The Nature of Thought* (1939), *Reason and Goodness* (1961), *Reason and Analysis* (1962), and *Reason and Belief* (1974). ■ See Paul Arthur Schilpp, ed., *The Philosophy of Brand Blanshard* (1980), which includes an intellectual autobiography.

BLASCO IBÁÑEZ, VICENTE (1867–1928), Spanish novelist and political leader. The best-known Spanish writer of his time, Blasco Ibáñez wrote naturalist novels whose themes reflected his concern for the poor and socially disadvantaged. An antimonarchist, he advocated a republican Spain while serving seven terms in the Spanish parliament (1898–1923). He was also an active propagandist for the Allies during World War I. In addition to the international best-selling World War I novel *The Four Horsemen of the Apocalypse* (1916; Eng. trans. 1918), he wrote many other popular novels, including *The Cabin* (1898; Eng. trans. 1917), *Reeds and Mud* (1902; Eng. trans. 1928), *The Mob* (1905; Eng. trans. 1927), *Blood and Sand* (1908; Eng. trans. 1919), and *Mare Nostrum* (1918; Eng. trans. 1919). ■ See study by A. Grove Day and Edgar C. Knowlton, Jr. (1972).

BLEGEN, CARL WILLIAM (1887–1971), U.S. archaeologist. A professor of classical archaeology at the University of Cincinnati (1927–57), Blegen led many expeditions to Greece. His findings helped reconstruct the history of ancient Greece, and his excavations substantiated the epic poet Homer's account of the sacking of Troy in the *Iliad*. He discovered (1939) the palace of Nestor, king of Pylos, also described by Homer. Blegen also unearthed hundreds of inscribed tablets containing Linear B, or Mycenaean script, previously found in Crete. In addition to six scholarly volumes describing the excavations at Troy and Pylos, he wrote *Troy and the Trojans* (1963) for a general readership.

BLÉRIOT, LOUIS (1872–1936), French aviator. Blériot was a successful manufacturer of automobile lights before turning to aviation. His 37-minute flight (1909) across the English Channel marked the first overseas flight in a heavier-than-air craft and focused attention on the crucial role of military air power. The 600-pound, 22-horsepower monoplane of his own design traveled at 35 to 40 miles per hour. During World War I, he developed airplanes for the French government and later helped design commercial aircraft including the autogiro. Blériot was on hand to meet U.S. aviator Charles Lindbergh on his arrival in Paris (1927).

BLEULER, EUGEN (1857–1939), Swiss psychiatrist. Bleuler, a professor at the University of Zurich (1898–1927), was a dissenter from the Freudian school of psychoanalysis. In *Dementia Praecox or the Group of Schizophrenias* (1911; Eng. trans. 1950) he advanced the notion that "dementia praecox" (early insanity), previously conceived of as a single disorder, was instead a group of disorders. He coined the word "schizophrenia," meaning splitting of the mind, to describe symptoms common to these disorders, most notably an absence of contact with reality, and he refused to accept the popularly held belief that schizophrenics were incurable. He also studied the tendency of some psychotic persons to retreat entirely from reality, which he termed "autism." The 1951 translation of his *Textbook of Psychiatry* (1916) contains biographical information.

BLITZSTEIN, MARC (1905–1964), U.S. composer. Blitzstein studied at the University of Pennsylvania and the Curtis Institute of Music in Philadelphia, and with Nadia Boulanger in Paris and Arnold Schoenberg in Berlin. Influenced by the "song plays" of Bertolt Brecht and Kurt Weill, he wrote a series of provocative anticapitalist musical dramas that included traditional arias and recitatives as well as jazz and pop elements. *The Cradle Will Rock* (1937) was his most famous work. He also wrote a symphony, *The Airborne* (1944), and the operas *Regina* (1949) and *Juno* (1959). His adaptation of the Brecht-Weill musical *The Threepenny Opera* (1954) ran Off-Broadway for nearly seven years. He was murdered while vacationing in Martinique. ■ See Eric A. Gordon, *Mark the Music* (1989).

BLIXEN, KAREN. *See DINESEN, ISAK.*

BLOBEL, GÜNTER (1936–), German-born U.S. biologist. Blobel studied at the University of Tübingen (M.D. 1960) and the University of Wisconsin (Ph.D. 1967) before joining the faculty of Rockefeller University in New York City (1967–). In a series of experiments over a period of three decades, Blobel discovered how proteins find their proper locations within the cell and how they travel to precise destinations in different parts of the body. He demonstrated that the molecular mechanisms were the same in animals and plants, and his findings had a revolutionary impact on the field of molecular biology. His research spurred the development of the biotechnology industry by helping to make possible the manufacture of drugs inside of living cells and enabled scientists to treat diseases caused by defects in the body's protein-signaling systems. For his pioneering research he received the 1999 Nobel Prize in Physiology or Medicine.

BLOCH, ERNEST (1880–1959), Swiss-born composer. Bloch became a conductor and lecturer on aesthetics in Geneva, where his father had a clock business. His best-known compositions, including the tone poem *Schelomo* (1916), the *Baal Shem Suite* (1923), and the *Sacred Service* (1933), were inspired by Jewish themes. In 1916 Bloch moved to the United States where he directed the Cleveland Institute of Music (1925–30). His other works included the rhapsody *America* (1926) and the Second String Quartet (1945). ■ See biography by Robert Strassburg (1977).

BLOCH, ERNST (1885–1977), German philosopher. A leading Marxist intellectual after World War I, Bloch published numerous articles on political, philosophical, and aesthetic subjects. His Marxism was tempered by a utopianism that led to his development of a "philosophy of hope" in his major work, *The Principle of Hope* (3 vols., 1954–59; Eng. trans. 1986), which he wrote while living in exile in the United States during World War II. Selections were translated in *On Karl Marx* (1971). Bloch returned to East Germany (1949) and taught at the University of Leipzig. His unorthodox Marxism, however, provoked the government to condemn his works (1957) and he was declared a revisionist. He defected to West Germany (1961) and taught at Tübingen University. English translations of his work included *Man on His Own* (1970) and *A Philosophy of the Future* (1970). ■ See Wayne Hudson, *The Marxist Philosophy of Ernst Bloch* (1982), and study by Vincent Geoghegan (1996).

BLOCH, FELIX (1905–1983), Swiss-born U.S. physicist. Educated in Leipzig (Ph.D. 1928), where he subsequently held a teaching post, Bloch left Germany for the United States upon Nazi leader Adolf Hitler's rise to power (1933). Applying the results of his work on radar during World War II, he devised (1945) a method for using a radio transmitter to measure the magnetic moments of atomic nuclei. Working independently, Edward Purcell developed a similar method employing electromagnets. These techniques made possible high-precision measurements of atomic magnetism and provided valuable information about the chemical structure of many substances. For this work Bloch shared with Purcell the 1952 Nobel Prize in Physics. He taught at Stanford University (1934–71) and was the first director general of the European Commission for Nuclear Research (CERN) in Geneva (1954–55).

BLOCH, KONRAD EMIL (1912–2000), German-born U.S. biochemist. A Jewish émigré from Nazi Germany, Bloch arrived in the United States in 1936 and received a Ph.D. in biochemistry at Columbia University two years later. His most significant work was the discovery of the steps in the natural formation of cholesterol, a vital body chemical. For his research concerning cholesterol and fatty-acid metabolism, he shared the Nobel Prize in Physiology or Medicine with Feodor Lynen (1964). He taught at Columbia, Chicago, and Harvard universities.

BLOCH, MARC (1886–1944), French historian. The son of a professor of ancient history, Bloch became an authority on the Middle Ages, paying particular attention to economic organization and belief systems. He fought in the infantry during World War I and was admitted to the Legion of Honor and given a Croix de Guerre. He taught at the University of Strasbourg (1919–36) and was a cofounder (with Lucien Febvre; 1929) of the journal *Annales,* which adopted techniques from sociology, geography, and other disciplines to the study of history. Bloch later taught at the Sorbonne (1936–39) until being recalled by the army during World War II; he was subsequently barred from teaching there by Nazi anti-Semitic laws. Active in underground activities with the French Resistance, he was captured and executed by the Germans. His major works included *French Rural History* (1931; Eng. trans. 1966), *Feudal Society* (1939; Eng. trans. 1961), and *The Historian's Craft* (1949; Eng. trans. 1953). ■ See also his *Memoirs of War, 1914–15* (Eng. trans. 1980) and *Strange Defeat* (1946; Eng. trans. 1949), a personal memoir of World War II, and the biography by Carole Fink (1989).

BLOCK, HERBERT LAWRENCE (1909–   ), U.S. political cartoonist. Block adopted the name "Herblock" when he began drawing editorial cartoons for the *Chicago Daily News* (1929). He subsequently worked for the Newspaper Enterprise Association (1933–43), the army's Information and Education Division (1943–46), and the *Washington Post* (from 1946). A liberal defender of civil liberties, he brilliantly satirized McCarthyism, political demagoguery, governmental bureaucracy, the atomic arms race, and American involvement in the war in Vietnam, and he was syndicated in more than 200 newspapers. He won three Pulitzer Prizes (1942; 1954; 1979) and published several cartoon collections, including *The Herblock Book* (1952), *Herblock's Here and Now* (1955), *Straight Herblock* (1964), *Herblock's State of the Union* (1972), and *Herblock at Large* (1987). ■ See his autobiography, *Herblock* (1993).

BLOEMBERGEN, NICOLAAS (1920–   ), Dutch-born U.S. physicist. Bloembergen taught himself quantum mechanics during the German occupation of Holland in World War II, when his university was closed, and then went to the United States (1946) to do research for his doctoral thesis at Harvard. He joined the Harvard faculty (1949) and pioneered in theoretical work that led to the development of the maser. He helped develop laser spectroscopy, established many of the laws of nonlinear optics, and shared the 1981 Nobel Prize in Physics with Kai Siegbahn and Arthur Schawlow. Among his books were *Nonlinear Optics* (1965) and *Encounters in Magnetic Resonances* (1996).

BLOK, ALEKSANDR ALEKSANDROVICH (1880–1921), Russian poet. The leading figure of the Russian symbolist movement, Blok gained recognition with his idealistic and mystical love poetry, *Verses About the Beautiful Lady* (1904). His poetry mirrored the spiritual and emotional turmoil of his life, and many of his later works betrayed a disillusionment with life, while others reflected a heightened social awareness and powerful nationalistic feelings. His support of the 1917 revolution was reflected in his poems *The Twelve* (1918; Eng. trans. 1920), a controversial, mystical representation of the bolshevik movement, and *The Scythians* (1918; Eng. trans. 1955), a depiction of postrevolutionary Russia as the leader of humankind. Blok held important cultural posts after the revolution, but toward the end of his life he grew disillusioned with political interference in the realm of art. English translations of his works are in *Selected Poems* (1968, 1972), and *Alexander Blok: An Anthology of Essays and Memoirs* (1982). ■ See biographies by Cecil Kischd (1960), Avril Pyman (2 vols., 1979–80), Kornei Chukovsky (Eng. trans. 1982), and Nina Berberova (Eng. trans. 1996); and study by Konstantin Mochulsky (Eng. trans. 1983).

BLOOMFIELD, LEONARD (1887–1949), U.S. linguist. Bloomfield first studied Indo-European comparative linguistics as a graduate student, but after studying in Germany (1913–14), he became interested in the scientific aspects of language. He conducted extensive field work and taught Germanic philology at the University of Chicago (1927–40) and linguistics at Yale (1940–49). His classic *Language* (1933) profoundly influenced American linguistic science. It stressed that the study of language must emphasize the spoken tongue rather than the written language and that language could be studied when isolated from nonlinguistic factors like climate, migrations, and intermarriages among different peoples. This doctrine was widely accepted until the mid-1950s. ■ See Charles F. Hockett, ed., *A Leonard Bloomfield Anthology* (1970) and Robert A. Hall, *A Life for Language* (1990).

BLOOR, MOTHER (Ella Reeve Bloor; 1862–1951), U.S. radical activist. Born into a wealthy old Republican New York family, "Mother Bloor" became involved at an early age in the women's suffrage and temperance movements and was a Socialist party organizer (1902–19). A left-wing militant, she left the party and became a founder of the U.S. Communist party (1919). Called the "matron saint" of the party, she was an activist for decades, a member of the party's national committee (1932–48), and the head of its women's division. ■ See her autobiography, *We Are Many* (1940).

BLUFORD, GUION S., JR. (1942–   ), U.S. astronaut. Fascinated by aviation from an early age, Bluford decided to study aerospace engineering while in high school. He graduated from Pennsylvania State University (B.A. 1964) as a distinguished member of the air force ROTC program. Bluford was trained for F-4C combat duty and was sent to Vietnam, where he flew 144 combat missions (1966–67). In 1978 he received his Ph.D. in aerospace engineering with a specialty in laser physics. That same year, Bluford was among the 35 candidates chosen by NASA to participate in the space program. As a member of the eighth mission of the space shuttle *Challenger* (August 1983), Guion Bluford became the first African American to fly in space. He retired from the air force (1993) and became a corporate executive.

BLUM, LÉON (1872–1950), French political leader. The son of a prosperous merchant, Blum studied philosophy and law at the best Paris schools before entering government service (1896) as an attorney for the council of state. An intellectual who wrote essays and poetry as well as journalism, Blum joined the Socialist party (1904) and became its leader after the assassination of Jean Jaurès (1914). He remained in government service until his election to the Chamber of Deputies in 1919. He was the first socialist and first Jewish premier of France, heading the popular-front government (1936–37; 1938), which inaugurated the 40-hour week and paid vacations and nationalized the Bank of France. In 1940 the former premier was arrested by the Vichy regime and later deported to the Buchenwald and Dachau concentration camps, but he lived through the Allied liberation and served briefly as interim premier (December 1946). ■ See biographies by Louise Dalby (1963), Joel Colton (1966), and Jean Lacouture (Eng. trans. 1982).

BLUMBERG, BARUCH SAMUEL (1925–), U.S. medical scientist. Blumberg received an M.D. degree from Columbia University (1951) and a Ph.D. in biochemistry from Oxford (1957). He taught medical anthropology at the University of Pennsylvania in addition to working at the university's Institute for Cancer Research (1964–86). He shared the 1976 Nobel Prize in Physiology or Medicine (with D. Carleton Gajdusek) for his discovery of the Australia antigen, a breakthrough in study of viral hepatitis that led to the development of a vaccine against hepatitis B.

BLUNT, ANTHONY (1907–1983), British art historian and Soviet spy. Blunt, the son of an Anglican clergyman, was a brilliant student at Cambridge and was a fellow of Trinity College (1932–37). While there, he befriended undergraduates Guy Burgess, Donald Maclean, and Kim Philby, who shared his antifascist and anticapitalist views. Together they joined a secret communist cell and decided to spy for the Soviet Union. They all worked for the foreign office or British military intelligence during World War II and supplied high-level secrets to Soviet contacts. (Burgess and Maclean defected in 1951 and Philby in 1963). After leaving government service (1945) Blunt resumed his academic career and became an internationally recognized authority on Nicholas Poussin, William Blake, Pablo Picasso, Baroque architecture, and French Renaissance art. He served as curator of the royal art collection (1945–72), director of the famed Courtauld Institute of Art in London (1947–74), and was knighted (1956). After his role as a spy was made public

(1979), it was revealed that he had secretly confessed to espionage (1964) and had been granted immunity in exchange for cooperating with British intelligence. His knighthood was annulled, he was expelled from the British Academy, and he withdrew from public life. ■ See Andrew Boyle, *The Fourth Man* (1979); Douglas Sutherland, *The Great Betrayal* (1981); Andrew Sinclair, *The Red and the Blue* (1986); and John Costello, *Mask of Treachery* (1988).

BLY, ROBERT (1926–), U.S. poet, editor, and translator. Born and raised in rural Madison, Minnesota, Bly studied poetry at Harvard (B.A. 1950) and taught at the University of Iowa (1954–55) before returning to his home town (1957). There he founded (1958) the literary magazine *The Fifties* (later *The Sixties, The Seventies,* etc.), and began publishing collections of his poems, including *The Light Around the Body* (1967), which won the 1968 National Book Award. During the 1960s he founded the organization American Writers Against the Vietnam War and supported antidraft organizations. Many of his best poems appeared in *Selected Poems* (1986). His best-selling nonfiction book, *Iron John: A Book about Men* (1990), urged men to nurture each other and become mentors to young men. It heralded "the men's movement," which inspired all-male retreats and led to the publication of numerous books about men's psyches and masculine consciousness. In *The Sibling Society* (1996), a critique of contemporary American culture, Bly argued that lack of authority figures had created a society dominated by adolescent values and activities. He advocated the emotional integration of the sexes in *The Maiden King: The Reunion of Masculine and Feminine* (1998), written with Jungian psychologist Marion Woodman.

BLYTON, ENID (1897–1968), British writer. Blyton wrote for magazines before publishing *Real Fairies* (1922), a volume of verse that was followed by some 400 books for children. After Agatha Christie and William Shakespeare, she was Britain's most translated author. Her didactic fantasies often irritated parents and teachers but enthralled generations of children—particularly girls aged 7 to 12—who followed the adventures of the Famous Five, the Secret Seven, Mr. Meddle, and Noddy. Blyton also wrote primers and books on nature and religion. ■ See her autobiography, *Story of My Life* (1952); biography by Barbara Stoney (1974); and Sheila G. Ray, *The Blyton Phenomenon* (1982).

BOAS, FRANZ (1858–1942), German-born U.S. anthropologist. Starting out as a geographer (Ph.D. 1881), Boas turned to anthropology at a time when it was barely established as a discipline and specialized in the culture and languages of the Indians of the Pacific Northwest. He formulated a central principle of cultural anthropology—that socialization, rather than instinct or heredity, conditions human institutions and behavior—and played a major role in attacking the racist ideologies of his era. He applied anthropology to education, political issues, and race relations, and as a professor at Columbia University (1896–1936) he shaped generations of American anthropologists. Boas wrote more than 30 books, including *The Mind of Primitive Man* (1911) and *Anthropology and Modern Life* (1928). Many of his major papers were collected in *Race, Language, and Culture* (1940). ■ See George W. Stocking, Jr., *A Franz Boas Reader* (1982), and studies by Melville Jean Herskovits (1953) and Marshall Hyatt (1990).

BOCCIONI, UMBERTO (1882–1916), Italian painter and sculptor. A founder and chief theoretician of the pre–World War I futurist movement in Italy, Boccioni was concerned with depicting movement and speed through "lines of force," representations of the energy in every physical object. Considerably ahead of his time in painting and sculpting techniques, he anticipated the dadaist and constructivist use of nontraditional substances such as glass in combination with other materials. He also suggested kinetic sculpture powered by electric motors and envisioned environmental sculpture; his own sculpture, however, was more conventional than his theoretical constructs. His best-known works included the paintings *The City Rises* (1910) and *Forces of a Street* (1911) and the sculpture *Unique Forms in Continuity and Space* (1913). Boccioni enlisted in the army during World War I and was killed when he fell off a horse. ■ See Joshua C. Taylor, *The Graphic Work of Umberto Boccioni* (1961).

BOCK, JERRY (1928–), **and SHELDON HARNICK** (1924–), U.S. musical-comedy writing team. Composer Bock, who collaborated on the score for the Broadway show *Mr. Wonderful* (1956), and lyricist Harnick, who wrote songs for several Off-Broadway revues, began their partnership in 1957. Their shows, known for brilliantly evoking the local color and historical era of their subjects, included *Fiorello* (1959; Pulitzer Prize and Tony Award), *Tenderloin* (1960), *She Loves Me* (1963), *The Rothschilds* (1970), and their greatest success, *Fiddler on the Roof* 1964; Tony Award), one of the biggest hits in Broadway history.

BOCUSE, PAUL, (1926–), French chef. The son of a bistro owner, Bocuse opened his own restaurant north of Lyons (1962) and became world famous as the creator of *nouvelle cuisine,* a simplified and nonfattening form of French cooking that featured fresh, natural dishes and light sauces. He established his own Beaujolais wine label, prepared meals for Air France, opened a restaurant in Tokyo and at Disneyworld (Orlando, Florida), and was awarded the Legion of Honor. He wrote *Paul Bocuse's French Cooking* (1977), *Paul Bocuse in Your Kitchen* (1982), and *Bocuse's Regional French Cooking* (1997).

BOEING, WILLIAM EDWARD (1881–1956), U.S. airplane manufacturer. A lumberman and a Sunday pilot, Boe-ing turned his hobby into a successful manufacturing concern, the Pacific Aero Products Co. (1916), which was later renamed Boeing Aircraft. He realized very early the potential of airplanes for transporting both passengers and cargo, and by 1934 his company was the recognized leader in the development of cargo planes. Boeing personally piloted the first international airmail run in a plane designed by his firm. The Boeing company produced military aircraft, including the B-17 (1939), B-29 (1942), B-47 (1947), and B-52 (1952) bombers, and built the first jet transport, the 707 (1957), and the first jumbo jet, the 747 (1970).

BOFF, LEONARDO (1938–), Brazilian Roman Catholic priest and theologian. Ordained a Franciscan priest, Boff studied at Wurzburg, Louvain, and Oxford, received his doctorate in theology from the University of Munich (1972), and taught theology at the Petrópolis (Brazil) Institute for Philosophy and Theology (1971–92) and at the University of Rio de Janeiro (1992–). He was a leading advocate of Liberation Theology, which blended elements of Marxist analysis and Christian doctrine in its commitment to end poverty and social injustice in Latin America. Boff emphasized the utopian, critical, and social aspects of Christianity in his widely read books, including *Jesus Christ Liberator* (Eng. trans. 1978), *St. Francis: A Model for Human Liberation* (Eng. trans. 1982), and *Salvation and Liberation* (with Clodovis Boff: Eng. trans. 1984). In *Church, Charism, and Power: Liberation Theology and the Institutional Church* (Eng. trans. 1985), he declared that the church must be liberated before the world can be, and advocated a decentralization of the church hierarchy and the formation of egalitarian base communities within the church. For these views he was condemned by the Vatican (1985) and ordered to keep one year of public silence. His later works included *The Maternal Face of God* (Eng. trans. 1987), *New Evangelization: Good News to the Poor* (Eng. trans. 1991), and *Cry of the Earth, Cry of the Poor* (Eng. trans. 1997). He resigned from the priesthood in 1992. ■ See Harvey Cox, *The Silencing of Leonardo Boff* (1989).

BOGAN, LOUISE (1897–1970), U.S. poet. Although she was poetry editor of the *New Yorker* for 38 years, Louise Bogan did not use that prestigious position to promote her own poetry, which was appreciated by other poets but long neglected by critics. Her most important collections were *Body of This Death* (1923), *Dark Summer* (1929), and *The Sleeping Fury* (1937). Encasing passionate feeling in rigid structures, she wrote modernist poetry that often dealt with the perplexities of love, but in ways that obscured the facts of her life. *The Blue Estuaries* (1968) assembled her complete poems. Her work received renewed attention in the years after her death, with the publication of her selected critical writings in *A Poet's Alphabet* (1970), her letters in *What the Woman Lived* (1973), and autobiographical fragments and poems in *Journey Around My Room* (1980), all edited by Ruth Limmer. ■ See biographies by Jacqueline Ridgway (1984) and Elizabeth Frank (1985), and Marie Collins, ed., *Critical Essays on Louise Bogan* (1984).

BOGARDE, SIR DIRK (Derek Van den Bogaerde; 1920–1999), British film actor. A promising artist whose father was art editor of the *London Times,* Bogarde decided to pursue an acting career after World War II service in army intelligence. His lead role in *Power Without Glory* (1947) on the London stage led to a movie contract with the J. Arthur Rank organization. During the next 14 years the tactful, urbane actor appeared in 30 films, including several war dramas, the popular "Doctor" films (*Doctor in the House,* 1954), and the romantic *Song Without End* (1960). But Bogarde was better known abroad for the "arty" films made after his Rank contract expired; *The Servant* (1963), *Darling* (1965), *Accident* (1967), *Death in Venice* (1971), *The Night Porter* (1974), *Providence* (1977), *Despair* (1978), and *Daddy Nostalgia* (1990). ■ See his memoirs, *A Postillion Struck by Lightning* (1977), *Snakes and Ladders* (1979), *An Orderly Man* (1983), *Backcloth* (1986), *A Particular Friendship* (1989), *A Short Walk from Harrods* (1993), and *Cleared for Take-Off* (1995) and biography by Sheridan Morley (1996).

BOGART, HUMPHREY (1899–1957), U.S. film actor. With his sardonic smile and cynical integrity, "Bogie" became a cult hero of American film. After World War I service in the navy, he appeared in several undistinguished Broadway plays. He made his mark as a psychotic gangster in the play *The Petrified Forest* (1935), and re-created the role in the celebrated 1936 film. Bogart was typecast as a gangster in *Dead End* (1937), *Kid Galahad* (1937), and *High Sierra* (1941) before coming into his own as a detective in *The Maltese Falcon* (1941). The bittersweet *Casablanca* (1943) was his most popular film, but critics consider *The Treasure of the Sierra Madre* (1948) his best dramatic effort. After winning an Academy Award as the grizzled, alcoholic skipper of *The African Queen* (1951), Bogart played the psychotic Captain Queeg in *The Caine Mutiny* (1954). He was married to actress Lauren Bacall (from 1945). ■ See Joe Hyams, *Bogie* (1966), and the biographies by Nathaniel Benchley (1975), A.M. Sperber and Eric Lax (1997), and Jeffrey Meyers (1997).

BOHLEN, CHARLES EUSTIS (1904–1974), U.S. diplomat. A graduate of Harvard, Charles (Chip) Bohlen joined the foreign service (1928) and specialized in Soviet affairs. He was appointed to the staff of the newly opened U.S. embassy in Moscow (1934–35; 1937–40) and served Presidents Franklin Roosevelt and Harry Truman as a translator and adviser at the Teheran, Yalta, and Potsdam conferences during World War II. He advised every postwar secretary of state on Russian affairs and served as ambassador to the Soviet Union (1953–57). Despite his advocacy of U.S. military strength, his strong disagreement with Soviet policies, and

his skepticism over détente, he nevertheless sought limited agreements with the Soviets and thereby earned the enmity of U.S. right-wing forces. At the end of his career he served as ambassador to France (1962–68) and undersecretary of state (1969). ■ See his autobiography, *Witness to History* (1973).

BOHR, AAGE (1922–), Danish physicist. Aage Bohr was born the year that his father, Niels Bohr, won a Nobel Prize for Physics. A half century later Aage Bohr shared the 1975 Nobel Prize in Physics with Ben Mottelson and James Rainwater. The distinction awarded his research on the structure and behavior of the atomic nucleus; with his corecipients, he established the relationship between collective motion and particle motion in the nucleus. Bohr, a professor at the University of Copenhagen (from 1956), succeeded his father as director of the Niels Bohr Institute of Theoretical Physics (1963–70) and directed the Nordic Institute for Theoretical Atomic Physics (1975–81). With Ben Mottelson he wrote *Collective and Individual Particle Aspects of Nuclear Structure* (1953) and *Nuclear Structure* (3 vols., 1969–80).

BOHR, HARALD AUGUST (1887–1951), Danish mathematician. The younger brother of physicist Niels Bohr, Harald Bohr taught at the Copenhagen College of Technology (1915–30) and at the University of Copenhagen (1910–15; 1930–51). One of the foremost analysts of his generation, Bohr did important work in the theory of numbers and the theory of analytic functions. He contributed to the theory of Dirichlet series and collaborated on the Bohr-Landau theorem (1914); his main achievement was the formulation of the theory of almost-periodic functions. An autobiographical lecture appears in his *Collected Mathematical Works* (3 vols., 1952).

BOHR, NIELS HENRIK DAVID (1885–1962), Danish physicist. After receiving his doctorate from the University of Copenhagen (1911), Bohr went to Manchester, England, to work with Ernest Rutherford exploring the ramifications of Rutherford's nuclear model of the atom. According to classic electrodynamic theory, the orbiting electrons posited by Rutherford should lose energy and fall into the nucleus; Bohr suggested that energy loss occurred only when an electron moved from one "quantum orbit" to another. He remained a major figure in the development of quantum physics for decades. Bohr became (1918) director of the Institute for Theoretical Physics, University of Copenhagen. He was awarded the Nobel Prize for Physics in 1922. During the 1930s he studied the mechanics of uranium fission. After escaping from German-occupied Denmark (1943), Bohr worked on the development of the atomic bomb in the United States, despite grave misgivings about the bomb's social consequences. He was president of the Royal Danish Academy of Sciences from 1939 until his death. The first six volumes of his *Collected Works* appeared between 1973 and 1984. Aage Niels Bohr, a Nobel laureate in physics (1975), was his son. ■ See biography by Ruth E. Moore (1966); the volume edited by S. Rozental (Eng. trans. 1967); and the study by Abraham Pais (1991).

BÖLL, HEINRICH (1917–1985), German writer. Infantryman Böll was wounded in World War II; in the postwar years he emerged as a major fiction writer with the stories collected in *Traveller, If You Come to Spa* (1950; Eng. trans. 1956) and the novels *The Train Was on Time* (1949; Eng. trans. 1956) and *Adam, Where Art Thou?* (1951; Eng. trans. 1955), about the uselessness of war and the disintegration of the Third Reich. His novels of the 1950s, realistic treatments of life in postwar Germany, diagnosed the disease implicit in economic "recovery." In later works Böll exploited intricate narrative structures, built of such modernist devices as flashback and stream of consciousness. These works included *Billiards at Half-Past Nine* (1959; Eng. trans. 1961) and *The Clown* (1963; Eng. trans. 1965). He also wrote *Group Portrait with Lady* (1971; Eng. trans. 1973), *The Lost Honor of Katharina Blum* (1974; Eng. trans. 1975), and *Safety Net* (1979; Eng. trans. 1983). His *Collected Stories* appeared in English translation in 1986. Böll, whose works were widely read in both East and West Europe, won the 1972 Nobel Prize for Literature. He spoke out in defense of persecuted authors, remained a frequent critic of West German society and the nuclear-arms race, and published the democratic socialist journal *L 76* (from 1976). ■ See studies by James H. Reid (1973), Robert C. Conard (1981), and J. H. Reid (1988).

BOLT, ROBERT (1924–1995), British dramatist. Bolt taught school and wrote radio plays for the British Broadcasting Corporation before achieving popular and critical success on the London stage with *Flowering Cherry* (1957). He won acclaim on Broadway as well as in London with his play *A Man for All Seasons* (1960), a drama of conviction and restraint based on the story of Sir Thomas More. His work for film included the screenplays of *Lawrence of Arabia* (1962), *Doctor Zhivago* (1965), *Ryan's Daughter* (1970), and *The Mission* (1986). *Vivat! Vivat Regina!* (1970) was a well-received drama about Mary Queen of Scots and Elizabeth I.

BOLTON, GUY REGINALD (1894–1979), British-born librettist. Bolton gave up a promising career as an architect in New York (1911) to write for the theater. He was the author or coauthor of dozens of romantic musical comedies, many of them written with or put to music by Jerome Kern, P. G. Wodehouse, George Gershwin, and Cole Porter. Among his best-known works, which played a major role in shaping the modern musical theater, were *Very Good Eddie* (1915), *Sally* (1920), *Sitting Pretty* (1924), *Lady Be Good* (1924), *Rio Rita* (1927), *Girl Crazy* (1930), *Anything Goes* (1934), and *Follow the Girls* (1944). He also adapted the play *Anastasia* from a French novel (1954). ■ See study by Lee Davis (1993).

BOMBECK, ERMA (1927–1996), U.S. writer. A newspaper reporter who gave up her career to raise a family (1953), Bombeck started to sell short humorous columns describing the foibles of a typical middle-class suburban housewife to her local Dayton, Ohio, newspaper in 1965. Within a few weeks her column, satirizing such topics as housework, car pooling, and child rearing, was syndicated and eventually appeared thrice-weekly in more than 800 newspapers throughout the United States. She wrote such best-selling books as *The Grass Is Always Greener over the Septic Tank* (1976), *If Life Is a Bowl of Cherries—What Am I Doing in the Pits?* (1978), and *Motherhood: The Second Oldest Profession* (1983), and became one of America's most widely read authors. ■ See *Forever Erma: Best-Loved Writing from America's Favorite Humorist* (1996).

BOND, CARRIE JACOBS (Carrie Jacobs; 1862–1946), U.S. composer. A cousin of John Howard Payne (composer of "Home Sweet Home"), Bond grew up in a musical Wisconsin family. Widowed in her early thirties, she found herself destitute, crippled by rheumatism, and without marketable skills. She scraped together a living by sewing and painting designs on china, but she devoted spare time to music. The self-taught composer eventually created music and lyrics for about 175 songs—many self-published—and performed them in a "talky" manner. Sentimental ballads such as "I Love You Truly" (1901), "Just A-Wearyin' for You" (1901), and "The End of a Perfect Day" (1910) became standards, making her rich and famous. Many of her songs were popular during World War I, and Bond often performed them for the troops. ■ See her autobiography, *The Roads of Melody* (1927).

BOND, JULIAN (1940–), U.S. political leader. Bond, whose father was president of a black college in Pennsylvania, attended a Quaker preparatory school and Morehouse College (B.A. 1971). He was one of the founders of the Student Nonviolent Coordinating Committee (SNCC; 1960) and its communications director (1961–66). In 1965 Bond was elected to the Georgia House of Representatives but was refused a seat because of his outspoken stand against the Vietnam War; the U.S. Supreme Court then intervened (1966) to rule Bond's exclusion unconstitutional. In 1968 Bond led an insurgent black delegation from Georgia to the Democratic national convention, and he was the first African American in history to receive a vice-presidential nomination. He remained in the House until 1975 and subsequently served in the Georgia Senate (1975–87). He taught history at American University and the University of Virginia and served as president of the NAACP (1998–). ■ See his *A Time to Speak: A Time to Act* (1972) and biography by John Neary (1971).

BONDARCHUK, SERGEI (1920–1994), Soviet actor and director. After making his acting debut in frontline army productions during World War II, Bondarchuk enrolled at the State Institute of Cinematography. He made his film debut in *The Young Guard* (1948), which was directed by one of his acting teachers. He starred in *Taras Shevchenko* (1951) and *Othello* (1956). In 1960 he appeared in an Italian film, thus becoming the first Soviet actor to work in the West. Bondarchuk made his directorial debut in 1959 and later was chosen to direct the four-part epic *War and Peace* (1966–77), in which he also acted the role of Pierre Bezhukov. He directed a Soviet-Italian coproduction of *Waterloo* (1970) as well as *Uncle Vanya* (1974) and *Father Sergius* (1979). He also directed and acted in *Boris Gudonov* (1987).

BONDFIELD, MARGARET GRACE (1873–1953), British labor and political leader. A union organizer, Bondfield was a national officer of the National Union of General and Municipal Workers (1898–1938) and was the first woman to chair the Trade Union Congress (1923). She served as a Labour member in the House of Commons (1923–24; 1926–31) and, as minister of labour (1929–31), was the first woman to hold cabinet rank in a British government. ■ See her reminiscences, *A Life's Work* (1948).

BONDI, SIR HERMANN (1919–   ), Austrian-born British mathematician and cosmologist. While teaching mathematics at Cambridge University (1945–54), Bondi became known for his research into the origins of the universe. He collaborated with Fred Hoyle and Thomas Gold in advancing the "steady-state" theory (1948). Astronomer Edwin Hubble had shown that the universe is expanding. The steady-state theory held that matter (in the form of hydrogen atoms) is constantly being created to fill the space resulting from that expansion. According to this model, this continuous, spontaneous process occurs at a rate too slow to be observed directly. An alternative to the "big-bang" theory, the model gained credibility in the 1950s. In recent years, however, evidence from radio astronomy and the detection of cosmic background radiation have cast doubt on the steady-state theory. Bondi later taught at the University of London (1954–84) and at Oxford (1984–90). He wrote *Cosmology* (1952; rev. ed. 1960), *The Universe at Large* (1960), and *Relativity and Common Sense* (1964). ■ See his autobiography, *Science, Churchill and Me* (1990).

BONHOEFFER, DIETRICH (1906–1945), German Protestant theologian. Bonhoeffer received his doctoral degree from the University of Berlin at age 21. After living in Barcelona, Spain, and in the United States, he returned to the University of Berlin (1931) as a lecturer in theology. Bonhoeffer centered his beliefs on the New Testament, advocating a total rejection of self and a commitment to others. He discarded the "inward" approach to religion and urged personal social involvement. He helped organize the Pastors' Emergency League against the Nazi regime and was a leading spokesman of the Confessing Church. He actively participated in the German resistance movement and he was

arrested (1943) and hanged for treason after he was implicated in the 1944 assassination attempt on dictator Adolf Hitler. He was formally exonerated by a German court in 1996. Some of his important works were *The Cost of Discipleship* (1937; Eng. trans. 1948) *Ethics* (1949; Eng. trans. 1955), and *Letters and Papers from Prison* (1951; Eng. trans. 1955). ■ See biographies by Eberhard Bethge (Eng. trans. 1970) and Mary Bosanquet (1969), and studies by André Dumas (Eng. trans. 1971) and Charles Marsh (1994).

BONNARD, PIERRE (1867–1947), French painter. While studying at the École des Beaux Arts (Paris, Bonnard became involved in the Nabi ("prophet") movement of Maurice Denis, Édouard Vuillard, and Paul Sérusier (1889). His flat, linear, "Japanized" work of this period gave way to a more impressionistic style that used bright colors to convey a sense of space and light. With Vuillard, he was known as an "intimist" due to his gracious depictions of domestic themes. His travels (1912–20) led him to produce landscapes and sumptuous room interiors. *Luncheon* (1927) and *The Breakfast Room* (1930–31) are among his best-known works. ■ See studies by Antoine Terrasse (Eng. trans. 1964), John Rewald (1948), and Nicholas Watkins (1994).

BONNET, GEORGES ÉTIENNE (1889–1973), French public official. The son of a magistrate, Bonnet earned a law degree from the University of Paris and a diploma in political science. He served in parliament as a radical-socialist deputy from Dordogne (1924–29; 1929–40) and participated in numerous Third Republic governments, also representing France at the League of Nations and as ambassador to the United States. An advocate of appeasement of Nazi Germany, he served as foreign minister (1938–39) and supported the Munich Pact. Later he opposed France's declaration of war against Germany and supported the Vichy regime, for which he was expelled from the Radical party in 1944. He moved to Switzerland after the war to avoid prosecution as a collaborator. Bonnet later returned to serve as a member of the Chamber of Deputies (1956–68). ■ See his memoir, *Quai d'Orsay* (1961; Eng. trans. 1965).

BONOMI, IVANOE (1873–1951), Italian political leader. A democratic socialist, Bonomi served in several ministerial posts (1916–21) before becoming premier (1921–22). Opposed to fascism, he retired from public life during dictator Benito Mussolini's rule, but joined the antifascist underground in 1940 and became its leader in 1942. He again served as premier from June 1944 to June 1945 and helped lay the groundwork for Italy's economic, administrative, and military reconstruction.

BONTECOU, LEE (1931–   ), U.S. sculptor. Bontecou studied at the Art Students' League (1952–55), then worked in Rome as a Fulbright fellow (1957–58). At the time of her first solo exhibition in New York City (1959), Bontecou was creating large-scale naturalistic bronze forms, suggesting animals and flowers. She was best known for the large canvas constructions that she began creating in the 1960s. These sculptures worked industrial materials (such as wire and welded steel) and found objects into organic forms. Bontecou's exhibitions, including a retrospective at Chicago's Museum of Contemporary Art (1972), have included drawings that use natural materials to depict phenomena of nature.

BONTEMPS, ARNA WENDELL (1902–1973), U.S. poet and novelist. A leader of the Harlem renaissance of the 1920s, Bontemps used a broad spectrum of literary forms to depict the lives and struggles of African Americans. His novel *God Sends Sunday* (1931) was considered the final work of the Harlem renaissance; he collaborated with Countee Cullen to adapt it into the 1946 musical *St. Louis Woman*. *Black Thunder* (1936) and *Drums at Dusk* (1939) were novels about slave revolts. The collection *Personals* (1963) included the well-known poem "Nocturne at Bethesda," which expressed identification with Africa. He was perhaps best known for his numerous anthologies of black writing, including *The Poetry of the Negro* (1949; with Langston Hughes) and *Great Slave Narratives* (1969). He directed Fisk University's library (1943–65) and taught at the University of Chicago (1966–69). ▪ See the *Arna Bontemps–Langston Hughes Letters, 1925–1967* (1980), and Kirkland C. Jones, *Renaissance Man from Louisiana* (1992).

BOONE, PAT (Charles Eugene Boone; 1934–), U.S. popular singer. Boone's clean-cut image, short hair, and white buck shoes set him apart in an era of rock and roll. He gained stardom as a romantic balladeer during the mid-1950s with such hits as "Love Letters in the Sand," "April Love," and "Goldmine in the Sky." He also had a network television show (1957–60) and made several films. A devout fundamentalist Christian, he wrote several inspirational books including *The Real Christmas* (1961), *My Faith* (1976), and *Pray to Win* (1980). Boone was a graduate of Columbia University (B.S. 1958) and served on the Board of Regents of Oral Roberts University. To the astonishment of his fans, he recorded an album of heavy metal songs (1997) in an attempt to revive his pop-singing career.

BOORSTIN, DANIEL JOSEPH (1914–), U.S. historian. Born in Atlanta of Russian-Jewish parentage, Boorstin edited the Harvard *Crimson* and won a Rhodes scholarship to Oxford, where he gained first-class honors degrees in jurisprudence (1936) and in civil laws (1937). He was admitted to the English bar in 1937. After lecturing on legal history at Harvard, he joined an interdisciplinary social-sciences program at the University of Chicago (1944–69), with time out for frequent lecture tours abroad. In *The Americans* (3 vols., 1958–73). Boorstin assembled a wealth of facts in support of his environmental interpretation of U.S. history as a pragmatic response to opportunity and circumstances. He emphasized the consensus, continuity, and homogenization he discerned in the American past. He also wrote *Democracy and Its Discontents: Reflections on Everyday America* (1974) and *The Discoverers* (1983), a wide-ranging intellectual history of western innovations. His later books included *The Creators* (1992), *Cleopatra's Nose* (1994), and *The Seekers* (1998). He served as director of history and technology at the Smithsonian Institution (1969–73) and Librarian of Congress (1975–87).

BORAH, WILLIAM EDGAR (1865–1940), U.S. senator. A powerful orator, Borah was a maverick Republican who served as a senator from Idaho for 33 years (1907–40). Known primarily for his isolationist and moralistic views on foreign affairs, he was a leading Senate opponent of U.S. membership in the League of Nations and the World Court, and he strongly opposed aiding France and Britain as World War II approached. Although he was the influential chairman of the Senate Foreign Relations Committee (1924–40), he never traveled abroad, believing that "one might become merely confused by firsthand information." ▪ See biography by Marian C. McKenna (1961) and study by Robert J. Maddox (1970).

BORCHERT, WOLFGANG (1921–1947), German writer. Borchert had a short career as an actor before being drafted into the German army and sent to the Russian front (1941) during World War II. He became ill; further service and a subsequent prison term for criticizing the government destroyed his health beyond repair. Heavily influenced by the expressionists, Borchert wrote furiously after the war and is best remembered for his immensely popular radio play *The Man Outside,* first broadcast in 1947. The play's bitter disillusionment with war and life echoed the mood of postwar Germany. A nihilist, Borchert still found hope in human contact in his story "Rats Do Sleep at Night." His collected works have been translated into English as *The Man Outside* (1971), *Selected Short Stories* (1964), and *The Sad Geraniums* (1974). ▪ See study by James L. Stark (1997) and Erwin T. Warkentin, *Unpublishable Works* (1997).

BORDEN, SIR ROBERT LAIRD (1854–1937), Canadian political leader. Born in Nova Scotia, Borden practiced law in Halifax from 1878. He was elected to Parliament in 1896, becoming the leader of the Conservative opposition in 1901. In 1911 Borden was elected prime minister, remaining in office through World War I and until 1920. In 1917 he led a campaign against French-Canadian opposition to conscription and polarized the country ethnically. After the war, Borden was successful in having Canada recognized as an entity separate from Britain at the Paris Peace Conference (1919) and the League of Nations. ▪ See his *Memoirs* (2 vols., 1938) and studies by Robert C. Brown (1975) and John English (1977).

BORDET, JULES JEAN BAPTISTE VINCENT (1870–1961), Belgian bacteriologist and immunologist. Bordet's most important work was done at the Pasteur Institute in Paris (1894–1901) and Brussels (1901–40), where he discovered the immunity factors of blood serum. His discovery permitted the diagnosis and treatment of such diseases as cholera, typhoid fever, tuberculosis, and syphilis. Bordet also discovered (with Octave Gengou, 1906) the bacillus that caused whooping cough. He was professor of bacteriology at the University of Brussels (1907–35) and received the 1919 Nobel Prize in Physiology or Medicine.

BOREL, (FELIX ÉDOUARD JUSTIN) ÉMILE (1871–1956), French mathematician. A professor at the Sorbonne (1909–40), Borel did pioneering work in set and measure theory and complex-function theory and was the inventor (1921–27) of game theory. In addition to his mathematical research, Borel served in the Chamber of Deputies (1924–36) and was minister of the navy (1925). His books in English translation included *Space and Time* (1926), *Probability and Certainty* (1963), and *Elements of the Theory of Probability* (1965).

BORG, BJORN (1956–   ), Swedish tennis player. Golden-haired Borg left school at age 14 to concentrate on tennis, turned pro at 16 (1972), and was the dominant male player of the 1970s. A strong, quiet, and graceful presence on the court, he was a peerless baseline player, known for his extraordinary concentration and his deadly topspin forehand. He won five straight Wimbledon singles titles (1976–80) and a record 41 consecutive matches at that tournament before losing the final of the 1981 championships. Considered by many to be the finest clay-court player in history, he won six French Open titles (1974–75; 1978–81). When he retired (January 1983), he had won more than $3.5 million as a pro. ■ See his autobiography, *My Life and Games* (1980).

BORGES, JORGE LUIS (1899–1986), Argentine writer. Borges was born in Buenos Aires to a prominent Spanish-English family; English was his first language. After studying in Switzerland, he returned home in 1921. Borges won recognition for his early, often nostalgic poems, included in *Selected Poems 1923–1967* (1967; Eng. trans. 1972), but he secured an international reputation with the unsentimental philosophical fiction published in *Fictions* (1944, rev. ed. 1961; Eng. trans. 1962) and *The Aleph* (1949, rev. ed. 1957; Eng. trans. 1970), *Labyrinths* (Eng. trans. 1972) contained English translations of selected fiction. His work was known for its concision of style, intricate architecture, and fantastic themes. He often used images of mirror and maze. An inveterate self-parodist, Borges also wrote clever detective tales, creating a homegrown Argentine private eye in *Six Problems for Don Isidro Parodí* (1982; Eng. trans. 1981; with Adolfo Bioy-Casares). He anthologized Argentine literature, wrote important literary criticism, and directed Argentina's National Library. In the last decades of his life his eyesight deteriorated and he dictated such later works as the stories in *The Book of Sand* (1975; Eng. trans. 1977). Borges' nonpo-

litical stance in his writings set him apart from most other leading Latin American writers; his apparent right-wing sympathies made him a controversial figure. He was a perennial Nobel Prize nominee. A selection of his writings is in *Borges: A Reader* (1981) and *Collected Fictions* (1998). ■ See his *Borges at Eighty: Conversations* (1982); biographies by Emir Rodriquez Monegal (1978) and George McMurray (1980); and James Woodall, *The Man in the Mirror of the Book* (1996).

BORGLUM, (JOHN) GUTZON (DE LA MOTHE) (1867–1941), U.S. sculptor. The son of Danish immigrants who settled in the Idaho Territory, Borglum sculpted on a scale as large as all outdoors. After a series of major commissions—12 apostles for the Cathedral of St. John the Divine in New York City, a six-ton bust of Abraham Lincoln for the Capitol rotunda in Washington, D.C.—Borglum began (1927) blasting and carving the heads of four U.S. presidents (Washington, Jefferson, Lincoln, and Theodore Roosevelt) out of the Black Hills of South Dakota. He died just before finishing the Mt. Rushmore National Memorial, which was completed by his son Lincoln. ■ See Robert J. Casey and Mary Borglum, *Give the Man Room* (1952); Rex Alan Smith, *The Carving of Mount Rushmore* (1985); and Howard and Audrey Shaff, *Six Wars at a Time* (1985).

BORING, EDWIN GARRIGUES (1886–1968), U.S. psychologist. Influenced by Edward Titchener, Boring was a noted and widely published experimental psychologist who championed his viewpoint over those of such rival schools as behaviorism and psychoanalysis. A professor at Harvard (1922–1957), he played a major role in the growth of the American Psychological Association, coedited the *American Journal of Psychology* (1925–46), and cofounded (1955) the journal *Contemporary Psychology*. His books included *History of Experimental Psychology* (1929; rev. ed. 1950) and an autobiography, *Psychologist at Large* (1961).

BORIS III (1894–1943), king of Bulgaria. Boris III succeeded his father, Ferdinand I, who abdicated in 1918. Until 1934 he ruled as a constitutional monarch, but in 1935 he established a royal dictatorship. Under strong pressure he joined the Axis powers (March 1941) and declared war on the United States and Britain (December 1941). However, aware of the Bulgarian population's sentimental attachment to Russia, he resisted German dictator Adolf Hitler's demand that he fight against the Soviet Union. Boris died unexpectedly and under mysterious circumstances after a stormy meeting with Hitler. ■ See Stephane Groueff, *Crown of Thorns* (1987).

BORLAUG, NORMAN ERNEST (1914–   ), U.S. agricultural scientist. Borlaug studied plant biology and forestry at the University of Minnesota (Ph.D. 1941). He joined the Rockefeller Foundation's International Maize and Wheat Improvement Center near Mexico City in 1944 and later served as its director (1964–79). There he developed new strains of grains that, although highly dependent on irrigation and large amounts of expensive herbicides, pesticides, and fertilizer, dramatically increased cereal yields in Mexico, India, Pakistan, and many other Third World countries. For this technological breakthrough, which helped create the "green revolution" of the 1960s and 1970s, Bourlaug was awarded the 1970 Nobel Peace Prize. ■ See Lennard Bickel, *Facing Starvation (1974).*

BORMANN, MARTIN (1900–1945?), German Nazi leader. Bormann joined a group of paramilitary terrorists after World War I, served a year in prison for complicity in a murder, and on his release in 1925 joined the Nazi party. He was chief of staff (1933–41) and successor to Rudolf Hess as party chancellor after Hess flew to Scotland in 1941, with control over the entire party organization. In 1942 he became Adolf Hitler's personal secretary and an intimate member of the inner circle. A ruthless master of intrigue, Bormann remained the most obscure of the top Nazis. He disappeared after witnessing Hitler's marriage and cremation in 1945 and was tried in absentia at the Nuremberg War Crimes Tribunal (1946) and sentenced to death. He was frequently reported to be living in South America. In 1973, after studying a skeleton, the West German government declared him officially dead, a suicide in 1945. ■ See biography by James McGovern (1968); Ladislas Farago, *Aftermath* (1974); Jochen von Lang, *The Secretary* (Eng. trans. 1979); and Louise Kilzer, *Hitler's Traitor* (2000).

BORN, MAX (1882–1970), German physicist. Born worked with Erwin Schrödinger and Werner Heisenberg on the mathematical aspects of the quantum theory during the 1920s. His statistical studies of Schrödinger's wave equations led to the development of quantum mechanics, which describes the behavior of atomic and subatomic particles, and he shared, with Walther Bothe, the 1954 Nobel Prize in Physics. A Jew, he had sought refuge in Britain (1933) from the Nazis and taught at the University of Edinburgh (1936–53). He also did research in other aspects of atomic structure and solid-state physics. His autobiography, *My Life* (Eng. trans. 1978), expressed his strong opinions on the political responsibilities of scientists.

BORODIN, MICHAEL (**Mikhail Markovich Gruzenberg;** 1884–1951?) Russian revolutionary. Borodin joined the Jewish Socialist Bund in 1903 but shortly thereafter became a bolshevik. After serving a jail sentence, he emigrated to he United States (1906), attended Valparaiso (Indiana) University, and was active in socialist politics. He returned to Russia (1918) after the Bolshevik revolution and represented the Comintern on missions to Scandinavia, Spain, Turkey, Britain, Mexico, and the United States. As special envoy both to the Chinese Communist party and to the revolutionary leader Sun Yatsen (1923–27), he attempted to bring about a "bourgeois" revolution that was seen as a prerequi-

site for a proletarian one. He played a major role in the alliance between the communists and the Guomindang (Kuomintang) party and helped develop the Guomindang into a centralized and highly organized political organization. After Nationalist leader Chiang Kai-shek massacred his communist allies (1927), Borodin was recalled to Moscow. He held several minor posts until his arrest in February 1949. He died in a Siberian labor camp. ■ See study by Dan N. Jacobs (1981).

BOROKHOV, BER (1881–1917), Russian-born Zionist theoretician and Yiddish philologist. Cofounder and predominant leader of the Poaley-Tsiyon party, Borokhov is best known for harmonizing Marxist materialist theory of the class struggle with socialist Zionism. His most popular political writing is found in *Nationalism and the Class Struggle* (1905; Eng. trans. 1937, 1972). Borokhov's multifaceted contributions spanned philosophy, economic history, and literary criticism. His Yiddish philological publications in the *Pinkes* (Vilna, 1913) set the scientific standards for this field.

BOSCH, CARL (1874–1940), German chemical engineer. A corecipient (with Friedrich Bergius) of the 1931 Nobel Prize in Chemistry, Bosch improved on the catalysts used by Fritz Haber to synthesize ammonia under high pressure and he adapted the Haber process for large-scale manufacture. Bosch's work boosted food production by supplementing nature's limited supply of nitrogenous fertilizers. It also revolutionized the explosives industry; his supervision of the construction of an ammonia plant that was nearing completion at the outbreak of World War I aided Germany's military effort. Bosch was chairman of the giant chemical corporation I. G. Farbenindustrie (from 1925) and, although opposed to the Nazi regime, served as president of the Kaiser Wilhelm Institute, the most prestigious position in the German scientific world.

BOSCH, JUAN (1909–   ), president of the Dominican Republic. A writer and social democrat, Bosch achieved fame while living in exile (1937–61) during the dictatorial rule of Rafael Trujillo. He cofounded the anti-Trujillo political party, Partido Revolucionario Dominicano (1939), and returned to his country after Trujillo's assassination (1961). He ran successfully for president (1963), but he was overthrown by the army after seven months for alleged incompetence and procommunist leanings. A countercoup by his followers (April 24, 1965) was suppressed by the intervention of 30,000 U.S. troops. Bosch was defeated in the 1966 elections and subsequently moved further to the Left in his political philosophy. He ran unsuccessfully for president in 1978, 1982, 1986, 1990, and 1994. His works included *Pentagonism, a Substitute for Imperialism* (1961; Eng. trans. 1968) and *The Unfinished Experiment: Democracy in the Dominican Republic* (1964; Eng. trans. 1965). He also wrote fiction and several biographies.

BOSE, SUBHAS CHANDRA ("NETAJI") (1897–1945), Indian nationalist. A wealthy, high-caste Bengali, Bose studied at Calcutta and Cambridge universities and joined the nationalist movement in 1920. A militant activist who advocated violence against the British to achieve Indian independence, he spent much of the 1920s and 1930s in jail or in exile. Although frequently at odds with nationalist leader Mahatma Gandhi, Bose served as president of the Indian National Congress party (1938–39). Arrested for civil disobedience (1940), he escaped to Germany and spent the years of World War II collaborating with the Nazis and Japanese. He organized propaganda broadcasts, headed the Japanese-sponsored Indian national army (INA) and government-in-exile, and fought against the Allies in Burma and Northeast India. He was reportedly killed in a plane crash in Taiwan on his way to the Soviet Union after the defeat of Japan. ■ See his *Essential Writings* (1997) and *An Indian Pilgrim: An Unfinished Autobiography* (1997); Hugh Toye, *The Springing Tiger* (1959); biography by Harihara Dasa (1983); and Leonard A. Gordon, *Brothers Against the Raj* (1990).

BOSMAN, HERMAN CHARLES (1905–1951), South African novelist and poet. An Afrikaner who received an English education in Johannesburg, Bosman taught for a year in a remote frontierlike town in western Transvaal. There he gathered the reminiscences and local lore that formed the basis of the wry and ironic stories published in *Mafeking Road* (1947), *Unto Dust* (1963), and *The Best of Bosman* (1967). He was often compared to his literary heroes, Mark Twain and O. Henry. He served a four-year sentence (1926–30) for shooting his stepbrother during a quarrel and wrote a sardonic account of his years in prison, *Cold Stone Jug* (1949). Bosman, whose other works included the novels *Jacaranda in the Night* (1946) and *Willemsdorp* (1977), also served as literary editor of the journal *South African Opinion*. ■ See his *Collected Works* (2 vols., 1981) and the study by Valerie Rosenberg, *Sunflower to the Sun* (1976).

BOTERO, FERNANDO (1932–), Colombian-born artist. Botero, who won a national prize for painting (1952), studied art in Madrid and Florence and was influenced both by Italian Renaissance masters and contemporary Mexican muralists. A figurative painter, he specialized in depicting plump, cartoonlike personages in a seemingly primitive style, and before he was 30 had a painting (*Mona Lisa, Age 12*; 1959) in New York's Museum of Modern Art. His subjects fall into four groups; Latin American cultural stereotypes (chubby tropical generals and puffed-up politicians like those in *The President's Family,* 1967, and *Military Junta,* 1973); religious figures, such as saints, bishops, or a Christ with dimpled knees; family groups, in which pets usually resemble their owners; and historical figures, like King Louis XIV of France. Botero lived in New York during the 1960s and in Paris after 1973. From the late 1970s he concentrated on sculpture. In 1992, 31 of his monumental bronzes, depicting men, women, children, and animals, were exhibited outdoors along the Champs-Élysées in Paris. ■ See studies by Kalus Gallwitz (Eng. trans. 1976), Cynthia J. McCabe (1980), and Werner Spies (1997), which includes six short stories by Botero.

BOTHA, LOUIS (1862–1919), South African political leader. When faced with defeat, Botha, a distinguished Afrikaner general in the Boer War (1899–1902), accepted peaceful reconciliation with the British. He helped found the Het Volk ("the people") party in 1905 and then served as the first prime minister (1910–19) of the Union of South Africa. He advocated racial segregation and supported the British effort in World War I. ■ See biography by Johannes Meintjes (1970).

BOTHA, PIETER WILLEM (1916–), South African political leader. P. W. Botha spent his entire career with the racist Afrikaner National party. He became a party organizer when he was 20, and from 1948, when the party gained control of the government, he represented it in parliament. He rose in power to the position of defense minister (1966) and later served as prime minister (1978–84) while heading the National Party (1978–89). He was determined to maintain white control in South Africa and the system of apartheid, or racial separation, despite growing domestic violence and increasing international pressures. He sponsored a new constitution that granted limited access to the political system to Asians and people of mixed race, but not to the black majority (1984). Under the new system Botha served as the country's first executive president (1984–89). He supported the establishment of so-called homelands, where most blacks would be required to live. His police and armed forces brutally suppressed antiapartheid demonstrations. After the fall of the Nationalist government, the Truth and Reconciliation Commission was established in 1995 to document apartheid-era abuses. It noted in its final report (1998) that Botha's government had committed gross human rights violations, including abductions, torture, and assassinations. Botha was found guilty of contempt (1997) for failing to appear before the commission, but his conviction was reversed on a technicality (1999).

BOTHE, WALTHER (1891–1957), German physicist. Bothe was educated at the University of Berlin (Ph.D. 1914), where he studied under Max Planck. He devised (1929) his method of "coincidence counting" while investigating the wave-particle duality of light. Using two Geiger counters that he bombarded with a stream of X rays, he was able to confirm the validity of the law of conservation of energy on the atomic level. The coincidence method quickly found application in the study of cosmic rays, which he proved were not exclusively composed of gamma rays, and nuclear reactions. For devising it, and for the research results he obtained, Bothe shared with Max Born the 1954 Nobel Prize for Physics. He also supervised the construction of Germany's first cyclotron (1943) and directed the Max Planck Institute for Medical Research at Heidelberg (1934–57).

BOTVINNIK, MIKHAIL MOISEYEVICH (1911–1995), Soviet chess player. Botvinnik gained the world chess championship (1948) by defeating the world's strongest players at a tournament held after the death of reigning champion Alexander Alekhine. A master of all aspects of the game, he held the championship until 1963, with the exception of 1957–58 and 1960–61. Botvinnik was also a prominent electrical engineer and received a doctorate in 1952. ■ See his *Achieving the Aim* (Eng. trans. 1981).

BOUDIN, LEONARD (1912–1989), U.S. attorney. A nephew of prominent socialist legal scholar and activist Louis Boudin, Leonard Boudin graduated from the City College of New York and the St. John's Law School (1936). Associated with the Emergency Civil Liberties Union and the National Lawyers Guild, he successfully represented numerous victims of the witch-hunting campaign of Sen. Joseph R. McCarthy during the 1950s and became one of the most prominent legal defenders of left-wing and dissident causes in the United States. His arguments in the "passport cases" of artist Rockwell Kent and singer Paul Robeson established that passports cannot be withheld by the government for political reasons. He also represented Judith Coplon at her conspiracy and espionage trial, and defended numerous opponents of the Vietnam War, including Julian Bond and Daniel Ellsberg. Boudin lectured at the Harvard, Yale, and Stanford law schools.

BOUDIN, LOUIS (1874–1952), Russian-born U.S. attorney, Boudin was a leading theoretician of the American socialist movement before 1919. His book *The Theoretical System of Karl Marx in the Light of Recent Criticism* (1907), which stressed Marxist orthodoxy, was translated into many languages and was highly influential among socialists. He branded the bolsheviks "unorthodox Marxists," claimed that the Russian Revolution was a tragedy, and left active involvement in politics (1919) to devote himself to the practice of law. He became one of America's most prominent labor lawyers and won several important Supreme Court cases that helped strengthen the labor movement.

BOULANGER, NADIA JULIETTE (1887–1979), French music teacher, composer, and conductor. Born into a prominent musical family, Boulanger studied at the Paris Conservatory (1897–1904) and taught composition there (from 1909) and at the École Normale de Musique (1920–39) and at the American Conservatory at Fontainebleau (from 1921). Called a "one-woman graduate school" by her former student Virgil Thompson, she taught such other prominent composers as Aaron Copland, Elliot Carter, Roy Harris, Darius Milhaud, Walter Piston, Roger Sessions, and Marc Blitzstein, and was regarded as the greatest and most influential music teacher of the century. She was also the first woman to conduct the Royal Philharmonic, London (1937), and the Boston Symphony (1938), New York Philharmonic (1938), and Philadelphia Orchestra (1938). ■ See Alan Kendall, *The Tender Tyrant* (1976); biography by Léonie Rosenstiel (1982); Bruno Mansangeon, *Mademoiselle: Conversations with Nadia Boulanger* (Eng. trans. 1985); and study by Jérôme Spycket (Eng. trans. 1992).

BOULEZ, PIERRE (1925–), French composer-conductor. Boulez, whose father was a steel manufacturer, was an uncompromising activist on behalf of contemporary music. His own compositions *(Les Marteau sans maître, 1955)* were written in a 12-tone style with echoes of Claude Debussy. As a conductor, he revived the modern German repertory in France, staging Alban Berg's *Wozzeck* at the Paris Opera in 1963. During his tenure as director of the New York Philharmonic (1971–77), he was known as the "20th-Century Limited" for his refusal to cater to traditional matinee preferences. He later returned to Paris to head IRCAM (1975–91), an electronic music research institute and reworked some early piano pieces into a composition called *Notations* (1979). His later compositions included *Répons* (1981), *Anthèmes* (1997), and *Sur Incises* (1998). He founded the Ensemble Intercontemporain orchestra (1977) and taught at the Collège de France (1976–95). His collected writings were published in *Orientations* (1981; Eng. trans. 1986). ■ See his *Boulez on Music Today* (Eng. trans. 1971), *Conversations with Célestin Deliège* (Eng. trans. 1976), studies by Joan Peyser (1976) and Georgina Born (1995); and the biography by Dominique Jameux (1984; Eng. trans. 1991).

BOULLE, PIERRE FRANÇOIS (1912–1994), French writer. Boulle drew on his experiences as a rubber planter in British Malaya and as a Japanese prisoner of war during World War II to write psychological novels of colonial intrigue and espionage. His popular novel *The Bridge on the River Kwai* (1952; Eng. trans. 1954) was made into a successful 1958 film. (Although Boulle's name went on the Academy Award–winning screenplay, it was actually written by two blacklisted writers, Carl Foreman and Michael Wilson.) Changing pace, Boulle invented the science fiction *Planet of the Apes* (1963; Eng. trans. 1963), which also became a film (1968). He later wrote several novels, including *The Whale of the Victoria Cross* (1983; Eng. trans. 1983), a book of short stories, *The Marvelous Palace* (1976; Eng. trans. 1978); and a memoir, *My Own River Kwai* (1966; Eng. trans. 1967). ■ See study by Lucille F. Becker (1996).

BOUMEDIENNE, HOUARI (nom de guerre of Mohammed Ben Brahim Boukharrouba; 1927?–1978). Algerian political leader. Boumedienne joined the anti-French Algerian nationalist movement as a guerrilla leader in 1955, rose to chief of staff of the liberation forces in 1960, and served as defense minister of newly independent Algeria (1962–65). He deposed Pres. Ahmed Ben Bella in a military coup (June

1965) and ruled Algeria as president until he died of a rare blood disease in 1978. A reserved, puritanical revolutionary from a poor peasant background, he developed heavy industry, established collective farms, expanded the Algerian education system, and was internationally recognized as a leading militant spokesman of the Third World.

BOURASSA, HENRI (1868–1952). French-Canadian political leader and editor. An inveterate pamphleteer and outstanding orator, Bourassa devoted his life to French-Canadian rights within a united Canada. Born in Montreal, he was elected in Parliament in 1896 as a Liberal, only to resign in 1898 over Canadian participation in the Boer War. Reelected as the leader of the Nationalists shortly thereafter, he resigned in 1907 and served in the Quebec legislature (1908–12). He again served in Parliament, as an independent, from 1925 to 1935. Bourassa founded (1910) and edited (1910–32) the French-language newspaper *Le Devoir*, which championed the cause of French-Canadians. ■ See his essays in *Henri Bourassa on Imperialism and Biculturalism* (1970) and studies by Casey Murrow (1968) and Joseph Levitt (1969).

BOURGEOIS, LÉON VICTOR AUGUSTE (1851–1925), French political leader and diplomat. A legal scholar, Bourgeois was elected to the national assembly, (1888) and was premier of a reform government (1895–96). He later served in the senate (from 1905; president, 1920–23). A delegate to the Hague peace conferences of 1899 and 1907, he was a member of the Permanent Court of Arbitration and was an early advocate of an international peace organization. After World War I he helped draft the Covenant of the League of Nations and became the French delegate to the League. He was awarded the 1920 Nobel Peace Prize.

BOURGEOIS, LOUISE (1911–   ), French-born U.S. sculptor. Bourgeois was exposed to art at an early age by her parents, who owned a workshop in Paris for restoring and selling tapestries. She studied mathematics at the Sorbonne before beginning formal art studies. She moved to New York after marrying American art historian and critic Robert Goldwater (1938) and studied painting at the Art Students League. She turned to sculpture in the late 1940s with a series of totemlike wooden images. She later used latex, plaster, bronze, and marble to produce a body of symbolic objects, some explicitly sexual, expressing loneliness, anxiety, and vulnerability. She claimed that her inspiration came from her childhood in a dysfunctional family. Her works appeared often in New York's Whitney Biennial. Her bronze sculpture *Welcoming Hands* (1996) is situated in a New York City park across the river from the Statue of Liberty. ■ See her *Destruction of the Father, Reconstruction of the Father: Writings and Interviews, 1923–1997* (1998).

BOURGUIBA, HABIB (1903–2000), Tunisian political leader. From the mid-1930s to the mid-1950s. Bourguiba,

the cofounder and secretary-general of the Neo-Destour party, spoke, wrote, negotiated, and suffered imprisonment on behalf of Tunisian independence from France. An astute, tenacious Paris-trained lawyer, he pressed for independence until France felt compelled to accede, after a damaging terrorist campaign, in 1956. As Tunisia's first premier and then, from 1957, president, Bourguiba, a moderate socialist, launched a Western-style modernization program. A secular civil code was adopted, women won the right to vote, and polygamy was outlawed. In the tumultuous Arab world, Tunisia became a bastion of individual liberty and literacy. Proclaimed president-for-life (1975), Bourguiba, though enfeebled, continued to lead the country while in his 80s, though an increasingly unresponsive political structure, declining agricultural output, and a disastrously high unemployment rate threatened the country's stability during the 1980s. Amid reports of his deteriorating mental capacity, he was overthrown in a bloodless coup (1987). ■ See biography by Norma Salem (1984) and study by Derek Hopwood (1992).

BOURKE-WHITE, MARGARET (Margaret White; 1904–1971), U.S. photojournalist. A native of New York, Bourke-White specialized in industrial photography as a staff member of *Fortune* magazine. On the staff of *Life* magazine (1936–1969), she covered wars, floods, and riots. In collaboration with writer Erskine Caldwell, her future husband, she published *You Have Seen Their Faces* (1937), a study of rural southern sharecroppers. During World War II, the aggressive and determined Bourke-White was the first woman photographer attached to the U.S. armed forces and the only U.S. photographer to cover the siege of Moscow (1941); she subsequently covered battles in North Africa, Italy, and Germany and the release of prisoners from Buchenwald concentration camp. ■ See her autobiography, *Portrait of Myself* (1963); *The Photographs of Margaret Bourke-White* (1972); and biography by Vicki Goldberg (1986).

BOURNE, RANDOLPH SILLIMAN (1886–1918), U.S. social critic. Bourne was a literary spokesman for the young radicals of his generation. After receiving his master's degree from Columbia University (1913), he published a book of essays, *Youth and Life* (1913), which called for a social renaissance. A prolific writer during the last five years of his life, he wrote two studies on progressive education and numerous antiwar articles, some of which were published posthumously in *Untimely Papers* (1919) and *The History of a Literary Radical* (1920). ■ See the anthology *The World of Randolph Bourne* (1965); his *Letters* (1984); biographies by John A. Moreau (1966), Louis Filler (1966), and James R. Vitelli (1981); and Bruce Clayton, *Forgotten Prophet* (1984).

BOUTROS-GHALI, BOUTROS (1922–   ), Egyptian diplomat. Born into a prominent Coptic-Christian family—his grandfather was a prime minister and his father a finance minister—Boutros-Ghali received a law degree from Cairo University (1946) and a doctorate in international law from the Sorbonne (Paris, 1949). He was a professor of international relations for many years at Cairo University and head of a Cairo think tank devoted to strategic studies before launching a diplomatic career. As acting foreign minister (1977), he accompanied President Anwar el-Sadat on his historic trip to Jerusalem, and as deputy foreign minister (1978–91), helped negotiate the Camp David accords (1979), which ended the 31-year state of war between Egypt and Israel. After a short stint as foreign minister (1991–92), he served as secretary-general of the United Nations (1992–96). His tenure at the U.N. was marked by a severe financial crisis and policy disputes with major powers over costly peacekeeping operations in Somalia, Rwanda, and Bosnia. Several U.S. officials accused him of waste and mismanagement, and the United States vetoed his bid for a second term. ■ See his memoirs, *Egypt's Road to Jerusalem* (1997) and *Unvanquished: A U.S.-U.N. Saga* (1999).

BOVET, DANIEL (1907–1992), Swiss-born Italian pharmacologist. The son of a professor of pedagogy, Bovet studied at the University of Geneva before becoming a researcher at the Pasteur Institute in Paris (1929–47), where he did his most famous work. For his development of the first antihistamine drug, which relieved the symptoms of millions of allergy sufferers, and for his work in synthesizing compounds that caused muscle relaxation and could be used in conjunction with anesthesia during surgery, Bovet received the Nobel Prize in Physiology or Medicine (1957). He emigrated to Italy (1947) and taught in Sassari and Rome. His later studies of the South American poison curare led to the development of pain-killing and muscle-relaxing drugs.

BOW, CLARA (1905–1965), U.S. film actress. As a 17-year-old from Brooklyn, Bow won a screen test as a prize in a beauty contest. With her role as Betty Lou, the shop girl who wows her boss in *It* (1927)—"it" being the suggestion of sex—she became Hollywood's first sex symbol. Her other hits included *Wings* (1927), *The Fleet's In* (1928), *Ladies of the Mob* (1928), and *The Wild Party* (1929). For three years Bow played the quintessential flapper with fluttering eyes and teasing looks, but the coming of sound apparently dampened her appeal. Her disorderly personal life also aroused a bourgeois backlash, and she retired to obscurity in 1933. ■ See Joe Morella and Edward Z. Epstein, *The "It" Girl* (1976), and biography by David Stenn (1988).

BOWEN, ELIZABETH (1899–1973), Irish-born British novelist. Bowen's Anglo-Irish family, described in *Bowen's Court* (1942), were landowners in County Cork, but she was educated in Britain and lived in Oxford and London for most of her life. Believing that the novel's task was the "nonpoetic statement of a poetic truth," she was concerned with personal relationships and feelings. She often focused on women's disillusionment and loss of innocence. Among her works are *The Last September* (1929), *The Death of the Heart* (1938), and *The Heat of the Day (1949)*. Her later novels, such as *A World of Love* (1955) and *Eva Trout* (1968), contained elements of myth and fantasy. ■ See her *Collected Stories* (1981); biography by Victoria Glendinning (1978); and studies by Allan E. Austin (1971) and Patricia Craig (1986).

BOWEN, NORMAN LEVI (1887–1956), Canadian-born geologist. A pioneer in the field of experimental petrology, Bowen made fundamental contributions to the study of rock origins (petrogenesis). His book, *The Evolution of the Igneous Rocks* (1928), exerted a profound influence on the field: he also did major studies of silicates and limestone, granite, and alkaline rocks. Long associated with the Carnegie Institution in Washington, D.C. (1912–19; 1920–37; 1947–52), Bowen was also a professor of petrology at the University of Chicago (1937–47).

BOWERS, CLAUDE GERNADE (1878–1958), U.S. journalist, historian, and diplomat. A journalist from Indiana who wrote *The Party Battles of the Jackson Period* (1922), Bowers wrote for the *New York World* (1923–31) and continued his historical studies on the Jeffersonian period. *Jefferson and Hamilton* (1925) was a best-seller. He was also active in contemporary Democratic politics, and his support for Franklin D. Roosevelt's successful quest for the presidency resulted in his appointments as ambassador to Spain (1933–39) and to Chile (1939–53). ■ See his diplomatic memoirs, *My Mission to Spain* (1954) and *Chile Through Embassy Windows* (1958), and an autobiography, *My Life* (1962).

BOWLBY, JOHN (Edward John Mostyn Bowlby; 1907–1990), British psychiatrist. Bowlby, the son of a surgeon, was educated at Cambridge University (B.A. 1928; M.A. 1932) and at London's University College Medical School (M.D. 1933) and served as an army psychiatrist during World War II. After the war he worked at the Tavistock Clinic in London (1946–90), where he directed its Department for Children and Parents (1946–68) and did pioneering work in the field of family therapy. He was best known for his studies of the emotional life of children and for developing "attachment theory," which stressed the importance of a warm and continuous relationship between mother and child and the negative effects on the child of maternal deprivation. His widely read and influential books included *Child Care and the Growth of Love* (1953), *Attachment and Loss* (3 vols., 1969–80), and *A Secure Base* (1988). ■ See study by Jeremy Holmes (1993).

BOWLES, CHESTER BLISS (1901–1986), U.S. advertising executive, politician, and diplomat. Born to a prominent New England family, Bowles graduated from Yale (1924) and cofounded the advertising firm of Benton and Bowles (1929). After leaving the highly successful company (1941), he entered government, serving as federal price administrator, and as a member of the War Production Board during World War II, and was governor of Connecticut (1949–51). A liberal Democrat and internationalist who believed strongly in foreign aid to developing countries, Bowles served as ambassador to India (1951–53; 1963–69), undersecretary of state (1961), and special adviser to Pres. John F. Kennedy (1961–63). His books included *Tomorrow Without Fear* (1946), *The Conscience of a Liberal* (1962), and *Promises to Keep: My Years in Public Life* (1971). ■ See study by Howard B. Schaffer (1993).

BOWMAN, ISAIAH (1878–1950), U.S. geographer. While teaching geography at Yale (1905–15), Bowman made three expeditions to South American and became a recognized expert in his field. He headed the American Geographical Society (1915–35) and developed it into a world-renowned institution. Under his leadership the society mapped the continent of South America, made important studies of polar geography, and undertook a worldwide study of land settlement. As an expert on political geography, Bowman served on the U.S. delegation to the Paris Peace Conference (1918–19), was an adviser to Pres. Franklin D. Roosevelt, and served on numerous commissions concerned with scientific and international questions. As president of Johns Hopkins University (1935–48) he established the departments of geography, oceanography, and aeronautics. Among his many books were *The New World: Problems of Political Geography* (1921) and *International Relations* (1930). ■ See Geoffrey J. Martin, *Life and Thought of Isaiah Bowman* (1980).

BOWMAN, SCOTTY (1933–   ), Canadian hockey coach. Bowman, the son of a blacksmith, was a promising junior hockey player until a head injury ended his playing career. He turned to coaching, first with a junior team and then with the National Hockey League (1967–   ) and became the most successful coach in hockey history. Known for his rigid discipline and fiery temper, Bowman won eight league championships and was the first coach to win the Stanley Cup with three different teams (Montreal Canadiens, 1973, 1976–79; Pittsburgh Penguins, 1992; Detroit Red Wings, 1997–98). He set a career record for most games coached (1,607) in 1995, and in 1997 he became the first coach in N.H.L. history to win 1,000 games. ■ See biography by Douglas Hunter (1998).

BOYD, LOUISE ARNER (1887–1972), U.S. explorer. The socially prominent daughter of a wealthy California businessman, Boyd began organizing, financing, and leading polar expeditions during the 1920s. She participated in the search for missing explorer Roald Amundsen in 1928 and during the 1930s explored eastern Arctic Canada and Greenland. A technical adviser to the U.S. government during World War II, Boyd was the first woman to fly over the North Pole (1955). She wrote *The Fjord Region of East Greenland* (1935) and *The Coast of Northeast Greenland* (1948).

BOYD, MARTIN À BECKETT (1893–1972), Australian novelist. The son of noted watercolorists, Boyd was born in Switzerland and spent much of his life in Britain. He served in World War I, joined a religious order, exhibited his paintings, and finally turned to full-time writing. In style and theme he was compared to the American novelist Henry James; Boyd wrote about the Australian's "geographical schizophrenia." Under the pseudonym Martin Mills, he published *The Montforts* (1928), a humorous and vivid saga of a British family's emigration to Australia. Among his later novels, *Lucinda Brayford* (1947), about Australians in Britain, had an aristocratic setting that set it apart from the working-class tradition of Australian literature. Boyd also wrote the verse collection *Retrospect* (1920), the family saga *Cardboard Crown* (1952), and the autobiographies *A Single Flame* (1939) and *Day of My Delight* (1965). ■ See biography by Brenda Niall (1988).

BOYD, WILLIAM (1898–1972), U.S. film actor. A romantic leading man in the silent films of the 1920s, Boyd starred in such films as *The Volga Boatman* (1926), *King of Kings* (1927), and *Two Arabian Knights* (1927). During the Depression, Boyd donned a black outfit and mounted a white horse to create the role of Hopalong Cassidy (1935), a virtuous cowboy who was a hero to two generations of American children. Boyd starred in 66 action-filled Hopalong western films (1935–48) and 106 television episodes (1948–53).

BOYD-ORR, JOHN BOYD ORR, 1st BARON (1880–1971), British medical scientist. A pioneer in the fields of animal and human nutrition, Boyd-Orr founded and directed (1922–45) the Rowett Institute in Aberdeen, Scotland. Through his journal, *Nutrition Abstracts and Views* (editor, 1930–45), he drew attention to the universal problem of malnutrition, demonstrated the correlation between poor food, poor health, and poverty, and worked to reconcile the interests of agriculture and public health and to increase food production. His studies inspired the creation of the League of Nations Committee on Nutrition (1935). He believed that an abundant food supply was essential for international peace and worked to eliminate worldwide food shortages as the founding director of the United Nations Food and Agricultural Organization (1945–48). An advocate of world federalism, Boyd-Orr was awarded the 1949 Nobel Peace Prize for his humanitarian work. His writings included *Food, Health and Income* (1936), *Food: Foundation of World Unity* (1948), *Feast and Famine* (1957), and *As I Recall* (1966). ■ See biography by Eva de Vries (1948).

BOYE, KARIN (1900–1941), Swedish poet and novelist. Boye studied at the Universities of Uppsala and Stockholm

(M.A. 1928) and became a leader of the idealistic left-wing Clarté movement. She was a major figure in modern Swedish poetry through her work as a founding editor (1931) of *Spektrum,* a journal espousing new poetic techniques; her translations of the poetry of T. S. Eliot; and her own writing. Intellectually she moved from a religious outlook to one embracing psychoanalysis and socialism. Her idealistic and humanistic poetry was noted for its rhythm, imagery drawn from nature, and emphasis on the problems of growth and change. It dealt with psychological conflicts, the outer and inner self, and the split personality, and reflected her own anguish over the conflict between a desire for rationality and purity, and the unconscious and instinctual forces of sensuality. *Kallocain* (1940; Eng. trans. 1996), written at the onset of World War II, was a powerful antiauthoritarian protest novel set in a future totalitarian state. Emotionally troubled, and in despair over political developments in Europe, she committed suicide.

BOYER, CHARLES (1899–1978), French-born U.S. actor. Boyer, who studied philosophy at the Sorbonne and drama at the Paris Conservatory, became a star of French stage and screen in the 1920s. Publicized as the greatest screen lover since Valentino, he made his Hollywood debut in 1931. He subsequently moved to Hollywood (1934) and became a U.S. citizen. With his seductive accent and continental charm, he played romantic leads in *Private Worlds* (1935), *The Garden of Allah* (1936), *Tovarich* (1937), *Algiers* (1938), and *Gaslight* (1944), appearing opposite such stars as Hedy Lamarr, Marlene Dietrich, Greta Garbo, and Ingrid Bergman. He later appeared in the French films *Madame de . . . (1953),* Nana (1955), and *Stavisky* (1974), and the U.S. films *Fanny* (1961), *Casino Royale* (1967), and *Barefoot in the Park* (1968). He died after taking an overdose of sleeping pills, two days after the death of his wife of 44 years. ■ See biography by Larry Swindell (1983).

BOYER, PAUL D. (1918–), U.S. biochemist. Boyer studied biochemistry at the University of Wisconsin, Madison (Ph.D. 1943), and taught at the University of Minnesota (1945–63) and the University of California at Los Angeles (1963–90). Starting in the 1950s, Boyer studied adenosine triphosphate (ATP), a tiny molecule that is the basic source of energy for all living things. He discovered how an enzyme, ATP synthase, played a role in the formation of ATP, which fuels such processes as muscle contraction, nerve impulse transmission, and protein building. He also described the complicated structure of the enzyme and its unusual molecular mechanism. For his pioneering research, Boyer shared the 1997 Nobel Prize in Chemistry with John E. Walker and Jens C. Skou.

BOYINGTON, GREGORY (1912–1988), U.S. marine officer. Colorful World War II hero "Pappy" Boyington served with the "Flying Tigers" in China (1941–42) and shot down six Japanese fighters. In 1943 he formed his own squadron of misfits, the "Black Sheep," which shot down nearly 100 Japanese planes in the South Pacific and became one of the most famous U.S. units in the war. Boyington personally shot down 28 enemy aircraft, more than any other marine pilot, before being shot down (Jan. 3, 1944) and captured by the Japanese. He returned home to a hero's welcome in September 1945 and was awarded the Congressional Medal of Honor. His autobiographical *Baa Baa Black Sheep* (1958) was made into a movie.

BOYLE, KAY (1902–1992), U.S. writer. Boyle studied music and architecture and spent the years 1923–41 in France, Britain, and Austria. She returned to Europe after World War II and was a correspondent for the *New Yorker* magazine (1946–53). She wrote about culture shock and American-European relations in the partially autobiographical novels *Plagued by the Nightingale* (1931) and *Generation Without Farewell* (1960). Her works reflected her concern for social justice. She won O. Henry Memorial Prizes for the best short story of 1935 ("The White Horses of Vienna") and 1941 ("Defeat") and published several important collections, including *The Smoking Mountain* (1951) and *Fifty Stories* (1980). Boyle wrote or translated more than 40 books, including poetry, juvenile literature, essays, and reminiscences, and taught at San Francisco State College (1963–79). She supported human rights causes and was active in the anti-Vietnam War movement. ■ See study by Sandra Whipple Spanier (1986).

BRACHER, KARL DIETRICH (1922–), German historian. Germany's foremost modern historian, Bracher wrote the first comprehensive history of the Nazi period with his *Dissolution of the Weimar Republic* (1955) and *The German Dictatorship* (1969; Eng. trans. 1970). *The German Dilemma* (1971; Eng. trans. 1974) extends his analysis to the post–World War II era. Bracher taught at the Free University in Berlin (1955–58) before his appointment (1959) as professor at the University of Bonn. His later works included *Age of Ideologies* (Eng. trans. 1984) and *Turning Points in Modern Times* (Eng. trans. 1995).

BRADBURY, RAY (1920–), U.S. science-fiction writer. Bradbury published (1939) a science-fiction fan magazine before selling his first story (1942). His writing—for the most part short fiction—bears the imprint of Edgar Allan Poe. Each story strives for a single effect, often deriving from the relationship between science and technology on the one hand and imagination and fantasy on the other. Bradbury is best known for the anti-utopian novel *Fahrenheit 451* (1953; film, 1966) and for the work collected in *The Martian Chronicles* (1950), *The Illustrated Man* (1951), *The Golden Apples of the Sun* (1953), *The Small Assassin* (1973), *A Memory of Murder* (1984), and *Quicker Than the Eye* (1996). Bradbury also wrote plays, screenplays, verse, and essays. His work is collected in *The Stories of Ray Bradbury* (1980) and *The Complete Poems* (1982). *Death Is a Lonely Business* (1985), a novel, was semiautobiographical. His later works included *Green Shadows, White Whale* (1992), and *Yestermorrow: Obvious Answers to Impossible Futures* (1991). ■ See studies by Wayne L. Johnson (1980) and David Mogen (1986).

BRADDOCK, JAMES JOSEPH (1905–1974), U.S. boxer. Born in New York City, Braddock began fighting professionally in 1926 and went undefeated until 1929, when he lost to Tommy Loughran in a light-heavyweight title bout. He suffered so many defeats in the next years that his prize-fighting future was dubious. In 1933, disheartened after breaking both hands in a match with Abe Feldman, he retired from the ring. Broke and on relief, he labored on the docks for a year, then decided to try a comeback. A steady fighter with a respectable left jab and a punishing right-hand punch, he fought his way back to the top against strong odds until finally, in 1935, he stunned the boxing world by outpointing champion Max Baer—the universal favorite—in a heavyweight title bout. Braddock's dramatic comeback earned him the nickname "Cinderella Man." In 1937 he lost the crown to newcomer Joe Louis.

BRADLEY, OMAR NELSON (1893–1981), U.S. general. A 1915 graduate of West Point, Bradley commanded armies during World War II in North Africa and Sicily before being appointed by Gen. Dwight D. Eisenhower to lead U.S. forces in the invasion of France at Normandy (1944). He later commanded the 12th army group, the largest field command in U.S. army history, which helped ensure the Allied victory over Germany. He was appointed to the rank of general of the army (1950), making him the fourth five-star general in U.S. history, and he served as the first permanent chairman of the U.S. Joint Chiefs of Staff (1949–53). ■ See his World War II memoirs, *A Soldier's Story* (1951); his autobiography, *General's Life* (1983; with Clay Blair); and study by Charles Whiting (1971).

BRADLEY, THOMAS (1917–1998), U.S. political leader. Bradley was born on a Texas cotton plantation, won an athletic scholarship to the University of California, Los Angeles, and during 21 years on the Los Angeles police force (1940–61) worked his way through night law school. He then turned to local Democratic politics in Los Angeles, establishing an image as a deliberate, self-contained exponent of the work ethic and winning election in 1973 as the first African-American mayor of a predominantly white U.S. city. He was reelected in 1977 and 1981 but lost a close gubernatorial race in 1982. He won a fourth term as mayor in 1985 but lost the 1986 gubernatorial race. He was reelected to a fifth term in 1989. During his 20 years in office the population of Los Angeles grew rapidly and the economy expanded. ■ See study by J. Gregory Payne and Scott Ratzan (1986).

BRADMAN, SIR DONALD GEORGE (1908–2001), Australian cricket player. The holder of numerous batting records. Bradman was statistically the most successful batsman in cricket history. He was an active player from 1927 through 1949 and was the first Australian cricket player to be knighted (1949). ■ See his *Farewell to Cricket* (1950), *The Bradman Albums* (1988), and the biography by Charles Williams (1996).

BRADY, WILLIAM ALOYSIUS (1863–1950), U.S. theatrical manager and producer. Brady ran his own touring company and managed professional boxers James J. Corbett and James J. Jeffries before going to Broadway. In a New York career that spanned four decades, Brady produced more than 250 shows, including such hits as *Way Down East* (1898), *Major Barbara* (1915), *What Every Woman Knows* (1926), and *Street Scene* (1929). He built the Playhouse (1910) and the Forty-eighth Street Theater (1912) and was instrumental in launching the careers of David Warfield, Douglas Fairbanks, Helen Hayes, Katharine Cornell, and Grace George, his wife. Also a pioneer movie producer, he was president of the National Assembly of the Motion Picture Industry (1915–20).

BRAGG, SIR (WILLIAM) LAWRENCE (1890–1971), Australian-born British physicist, Bragg, son of the eminent physicist Sir William Henry Bragg, was educated at the University of Adelaide and Cambridge University. He began (1912) an investigation of crystalline structure based on Max von Laue's discovery that X rays are diffracted by crystals and formulated a fundamental law of X-ray diffraction known as Bragg's law. His father became involved in the research, which created the science of modern crystallography, and the two were awarded the 1915 Nobel Prize in Physics. Bragg served as professor of physics at Manchester University (1919–37) and Cambridge University (1938–53). He continued to perform detailed studies of various minerals, especially silicates, and directed research teams investigating the structure of various metallic alloys and protein crystals. He directed the Royal Institution of Great Britain (1954–1966).

BRAGG, SIR WILLIAM HENRY (1862–1942), British physicist. Bragg studied at Trinity College, Cambridge, and was appointed (1885) to a professorship at the University of Adelaide, Australia. His research on alpha, beta, and gamma radiation (1904–08) made his reputation and he returned (1908) to an academic post in Leeds, England. His son, William Lawrence, became interested in Max Von Laue's discovery (1912) of the diffraction of X rays by crystals, and he involved his father in related research. The elder Bragg developed the X-ray spectrometer, which made possible many discoveries about atomic and crystalline structure. For this work, which laid the foundation for the science of solid-state physics, father and son shared the Nobel Prize in Physics in 1915. Bragg directed the Royal Institution in London (1923–42) and served as president of the Royal Society (1935–40). ■ See biography by G. M. Caroe (1978).

BRAIN, DENNIS (1921–1957), British French horn player. Brain was the third generation of his family to master the French horn, a notoriously difficult instrument. He played first horn with the Royal Philharmonic and Philharmonia Orchestra and gave solo performances as well, expanding the repertory with new compositions written for him by Malcolm Arnold, Benjamin Britten, and Paul Hindemith. He was killed in an auto accident at the peak of his career. ■ See biography by Stephen Pettitt (1976).

BRAIN, JOHN GERARD (1922–1986), British writer, Braine was a librarian convalescing from tuberculosis when he began his first novel, *Room at the Top* (1957), a classic about the angry working-class antihero who aspires to possess the proverbial fast cars, horses, and rich women. Its sequel, *Life at the Top* (1962), describes the moral corruption of the establishment. His later works included a religious novel, *The Jealous God* (1964); a study of marital discord, *Stay with Me till Morning* (1970); two spy novels, *The Pious Agent* (1975) and *Finger of Fire* (1977); and a novel about a middle-aged writer, *One and Last Love* (1981). ■ See his account of literary craftsmanship, *Writing a Novel* (1974), and study by James Ward Lee (1968).

BRANCUSI, CONSTANTIN (1876–1957), Rumanian-born sculptor. A shepherd and apprentice carver from the Carpathians, Brancusi moved to Paris (1904), where he continued to live like a peasant while developing his inimitable style. Working in stone, wood, and brass, eliminating all but the essential, he created highly polished abstract geometric forms such as *Bird in Space* (1919) and *Fish* (1930). A 1927 lawsuit brought by Brancusi against U.S. Customs resulted in duty-free importation of abstract art. He returned briefly to Rumania (1937) to design the 98-foot-high *Endless Column* for a park in Tirgu Jiu. His works expressed his spirituality and belief in the mystical unity of all life forms. ■ See studies by Sidney Geist (1968), Carola Giedion-Welcker (Eng. trans. 1959), Ionel Jianu (1963), and Anna C. Chave (1993).

BRAND, MAX. *See FAUST, FREDERICK.*

BRANDEIS, LOUIS DEMBITZ (1856–1941), U.S. jurist. Born in Kentucky to Bohemian-Jewish immigrants, Brandeis entered Harvard Law School at age 18 and graduated two years later at the head of his class. In private practice in Boston he delved into the socioeconomic issues of the turn of the century, including monopolistic practices and unfair labor standards, developing the "Brandeis brief," which cited the social sciences and expert opinions in support of law. Despite opposition from the legal profession, which considered him a radical, Brandeis became (1916) the first Jew to sit on the Supreme Court, where he later supported

New Deal legislation but is best remembered for his dissenting liberal opinions. After retiring from the court (1939), Brandeis devoted his last years to the Zionist movement. ■ See biographies by Alpheus T. Mason (1946) and Philippa Strum (1984), and Melvin Urofsky, *A Mind of One Piece* (1971).

BRANDO, MARLON (1924–), U.S. actor. A midwesterner with a military-academy education, Brando carried the Stanislavsky-inspired "method" of realism in representing human behavior to its greatest Broadway and Hollywood success. After an acclaimed two-year Broadway run (1947–48) as the mumbling, uncouth Stanley Kowalski in the Tennessee Williams play *A Streetcar Named Desire* (a role repeated in the 1951 film), Brando scored another success in the film *On the Waterfront* (Academy Award, 1954). In the 1960s Brando's fortunes declined as he made several critically and commercially unsuccessful films, but he recovered his authority and won an Academy Award for *The Godfather* (1972). He refused to accept the award, however, in order to protest the treatment of American Indians. He also starred in the controversial *Burn* (1969), *Last Tango in Paris* (1973), and *Apocalypse Now* (1979). His later films included *A Dry White Season* (1989) and *The Freshman* (1990). ■ See his autobiography (1994; with Robert Lindsey) and the biographies by Richard Schickel (1991) and Peter Manso (1994).

BRANDT, BILL (1905–1983), British photographer. Early in his career, Brandt assisted in Man Ray's Paris studio (1929–30), and many of his subsequent documentary photographs contained elements of surrealism. Brandt's collections *The English at Home* (1936) and *A Night in London* (1938) showed social class disparity in England during the Depression years. During World War II he documented Londoners' experiences and photographed eerie cityscapes of London during blackouts. His distorted renderings of nudes appeared in the influential collection *Perspective of Nudes* (1961). ■ See his photos in *Literary Britain* (1951), *Shadow of Light* (rev. ed. 1977), *Bill Brandt: Nudes, 1945–1980* (1980), and the volume edited by Bill Jay and Nigel Warburton (1999).

BRANDT, WILLY (Herbert Frahm; 1913–1992), West German political leader. The child of an unmarried working-class mother, Brandt was active in socialist youth activities and fled Nazi Germany (1933) to escape arrest. In Norway, and during World War II in Sweden, he worked as a journalist and supported the anti-Nazi underground movements. Returning to Berlin (1945), he served in the Bundestag (1949–57) and gained worldwide fame as the mayor of West Berlin (1957–66). He was chairman of the Social Democratic party (SPD, 1964–87) and he served as West German foreign minister (1966–69). As chancellor (1969–74), he advocated improved economic and political relations with East Germany and the Warsaw Pact countries, signed treaties with the Soviet Union and Poland, supported the nuclear nonproliferation treaty, and supported the expansion of the European Economic Community. He won the 1971 Nobel Peace Prize for efforts to ease East-West tension. After resigning (1974) over a spy scandal in his administration, he served as president of the Socialist International (1976–92), a member of the European parliament (1979–83), and as head of the Independent Commission on International Development Issues, which issued urgent reports (1979, 1983) advocating an immediate increase in aid to developing countries in order to avert a worldwide economic collapse. ▪ See his *In Exile: Essays, Reflections and Letters, 1933–47* (Eng. trans. 1971) and his political memoirs, *People and Politics: the Years 1960–75* (Eng. trans. 1978); his autobiography, *My Life in Politics* (1989; Eng. trans. 1992); and the political biography by Barbara Marshall (1997).

BRANNER, HANS CHRISTIAN (1903–1966), Danish novelist and playwright. Branner, who was once an actor, worked for Copenhagen publisher (1923–33) before embarking on a full-time literary career. A humanist who was influenced by Freudian psychoanalysis and by existentialism, he wrote psychological novels that dealt with the dangers and stress created by fear, power, and solitude. He was also noted as an interpreter of children's psyches. Among his best work are the short-story collection *Two Minutes of Silence* (1944; Eng. trans. 1966), the novels *The Riding Master* (1949; Eng. trans. 1951) and *No Man Knows the Night* (1955; Eng. trans. 1958), and the play *The Judge* (1952; Eng. trans. 1958). ▪ See study by T. L. Markey (1973).

BRANTING, (KARL) HJALMAR (1860–1925), Swedish political leader. The editor of the daily *Socialdemokraten.* Branting was a founder (1889) and chairman (1907–25) of the Social Democratic party. he was a member of parliament (1896–1925) and served for two years as finance minister (1917–19). He also served as premier (1920; 1921–23; 1924–25), sponsoring social-reform programs. For his effective handling of the 1920 controversy with Finland over the Åaland Islands, Branting shared the 1921 Nobel Peace Prize with Norwegian historian Christian Louis Lange.

BRAQUE, GEORGES (1882–1963), French painter, sculptor, and graphic artist. In his early work (1906–07), Braque was influenced by fauvism (noted for use of bright colors and sensual approach) and later by Paul Cézanne's technique of looking for geometric forms in nature. With Pablo Picasso, Barque evolved cubism, which sought to depict on flat canvas various surfaces of the subject (using muted colors) so that it could be seen from many viewpoints. His work constituted a sequence of experiments in cubist technique, especially in depicting still lifes and human figures. He developed the *papier collé* (collage of paper and painted forms) and was one of the first cubists to modify the movement's austere technique with brighter colors and more fluid lines. ▪ See studies by Jean Leymarie (Eng. trans. 1961) and

Francis Ponge, et al. (Eng. trans. 1971), and biography by Bernard Zurcher (Eng. trans. 1988).

BRASILLACH, ROBERT (1909–1945), French journalist. As a young man Brasillach contributed to the royalist newspaper *L'Action Française* and advanced in 1937 to the editorship of *Je Suis Partout,* a fascist newspaper inclined to violently nationalistic polemics. Brasillach was mobilized in 1939, captured by the Germans, and released through the offices of Adm. François Darlan to resume leadership of *Je Suis Partout.* After liberation, in one of the most controversial trials, the "literary traitor" was convicted and shot as a collaborator. ▪ See biography by William R. Tucker, *The Fascist Ego* (1975), and Alice Kaplan, *The Collaborator* (2000).

BRASSAÏ (Gyula Halász; 1899–1984), Transylvanian-born French photographer, sculptor, and poet. Brassaï trained as an artist in Budapest and Berlin, then spent six years as a journalist in Paris (1924–30). With a borrowed camera, he began (1930) to document his accounts of late-night Parisian life. The photos of lovers, streetwalkers, opium addicts, barflies, and petty criminals that Brassaï published in *Paris de Nuit* (1933; rev. ed. as *The Secret Paris of the Thirties,* 1976) created a sensation and established his international reputation. During the German occupation of World War II, when photography was forbidden on Paris streets, he returned to drawing (see *Trente Dessins,* 1946) and sculpture and wrote surrealistic poetry. He was a lifelong friend of many of the leading artists and sculptors of Paris. His photos and descriptions of them are in *Picasso and Company* (Eng. trans. 1966) and *The Artists of My Life* (Eng. trans. 1982). ▪ See study by Marja Warehime (1996).

BRATTAIN, WALTER HOUSER (1902–1987), U.S. physicist. The descendant of pioneers, Brattain was born in China and raised on his parents' cattle ranch in Washington. After receiving his Ph.D. from the University of Minnesota (1929), he did research at the Bell Telephone Laboratories (1929–67). There he and his colleague John Bardeen investigated the properties of semiconductors and developed the first transistor (1947). Tiny transistors eventually replaced the bulkier vacuum tube and revolutionized electronic technology. Brattain shared with Bardeen and William Shockley the 1956 Nobel Prize in Physics.

BRAUDEL, FERNAND (1902–1985), French historian. Born in rural northeastern France, Braudel was educated in Paris, where he was a student of Lucien Febvre, a cofounder of the Annales school of historiography. He taught in Algeria (1923–32) and Brazil (1935–38) before spending World War II in a German prisoner-of-war camp in Lübeck, where he wrote, from memory, the draft of his monumental work, published as *The Mediterranean and the Mediterranean World in the Age of Philip II* (1949; Eng. trans., 2 vols., 1972–73). This, and his other massive work, *Civilization* and *Capitalism, 15th–18th Century* (3 vols., 1979; Eng. trans. 1982–84; vol. I published separately as *Capitalism and Material Life*, Eng. trans. 1973), were regarded as classics of the "new history" of the Annales school, applying comparative and analytic methods from the social sciences to study the underlying economic and social structures of society. After World War II he was a professor at the Collège de France in Paris (1949–72), editor of the journal *Annales,* and founder of the Maison des Sciences de l'Homme.

BREAM, JULIAN (1933–   ) British guitarist. Inspired by the example of Andrés Segovia, who reestablished the guitar as a concert instrument. Bream became a virtuoso performer on the guitar and lute as well as a skilled musicologist. He transcribed classical piano compositions for the guitar, unearthed original compositions from the Elizabethan era, and, like Segovia, expanded the guitar repertory by commissioning new works. He had a lute constructed after a museum model to achieve greater authenticity in performance. ■ See biography by Tony Palmer (1982).

BREASTED, JAMES HENRY (1865–1935), U.S. archaeologist and historian. As a seminary student Breasted became so interested in Semitic languages that he transferred to the study of Oriental languages and Egyptology at Yale (M.A. 1892) and Berlin (Ph.D. 1894) universities. He collaborated on the *Berlin Egyptian Dictionary* for Berlin's Royal Academy and published a five-volume record of every known hieroglyph, *Ancient Records of Egypt* (1906). Breasted, who coined the term "fertile crescent," taught at the University of Chicago (from 1896) and established its Oriental Institute (1919) with a grant from John D. Rockefeller, Jr. His books included *Religion and Thought in Ancient Egypt* (1912), *Ancient Times* (1916), and *The Conquest of Civilization* (1926). ■ See Charles Breasted, *Pioneer to the Past* (1943).

BRECHT, BERTOLT (1898–1956), German playwright and poet. Perhaps the most controversial playwright of the century. Brecht created a revolutionary new form of drama, "epic theater," which aimed at educating his audience and inspiring it to change society. His medium was a frank and austere untraditional drama in which actors step out of character to comment on the action, reminding the audience that they are merely playing roles and that they matter less than the ideas they represent. His message was revolutionary Marxism. The most famous of Brecht's 46 plays were *The Threepenny Opera* (1928; Eng. trans. 1955; with Kurt Weill), *Mother Courage and Her Children* (1939; Eng. trans. 1941), *Galileo* (1947; in English), *The Good Woman of Setzuan* (1943; Eng. trans. 1961), and *The Caucasian Chalk Circle* (1945; Eng. trans. 1948). He worked in Hollywood during World War II and returned to (East) Germany in 1948 after a 15-year exile from his homeland. In 1949 he founded the Berliner Ensemble, which soon became one of Europe's most prominent theatrical companies. ■ See biographies by Frederic Ewen (1967), Martin Esslin (rev. ed.

1971), and Klaus Volker (Eng. trans. 1978) and studies by Claude Hill (1975) and Jan Needle and Peter Thomson (1981).

BRENNAN, CHRISTOPHER JOHN (1870–1932), Australian poet. Brennan studied at the University of Berlin and taught languages and literature at the University of Sydney (1908–25). Born to Irish parents, he broke with Catholic tradition, only to return to the faith in his last year. In the intervening years, he expressed his spiritual quest in highly personal poetry, the best of which appeared in *Poems 1913* (1914). He was also a theorist of symbolism and an eminent classicist whose university career ended (1925) when a divorce suit brought his drinking to public attention. He left much work in manuscript form: *Twenty-Three Poems* (1938) was published posthumously. His works were collected in *The Verse* (1960), *The Prose* (1962), and *Selected Poems* (1973). ■ See biography by Axel Clark (1980).

BRENNAN, WILLIAM JOSEPH JR. (1906–1997), U.S. jurist. The son of Irish-immigrant parents, Brennan graduated from Harvard Law School (1931) and practiced law in Newark, New Jersey, before becoming a New Jersey Superior Court (1949), appellate division (1951), and Supreme Court (1952) judge. Although he was a Democrat, Republican Pres. Dwight Eisenhower appointed him to the U.S. Supreme Court (1956), where he generally voted with the court liberals and became known for his strong defense of the Bill of Rights. His majority opinion in *Baker v. Carr* (1962) paved the way for nationwide legislative reapportionment under federal court scrutiny, and his opinion in *New York Times Co. v. Sullivan* (1966) imposed the first limitation on state libel laws by holding that malice was required for conviction. His other opinions sustained the constitutionality of affirmative action and reflected his (minority) view that the death penalty was unconstitutional. He retired in 1990. ■ See Kim Eisler, *A Justice for All* (1993) and study by Roger L. Goldman (1994).

BRENT OF BIN BIN. *See FRANLIN, MILES.*

BRESSON, ROBERT (1901–1999), French film director. Bresson studied philosophy and painting before becoming a screenwriter during the 1930s. After 18 months as a German prisoner during World War II, he directed his first film, *Angels of the Streets* (1943), which enjoyed some popular success despite its moral seriousness. Continuing in the same vein, using nonprofessional actors and spare dialogue in order to concentrate on visual expression and emotional undertone, Bresson directed *Diary of a Country Priest* (1951), *Pickpocket* (1959), *Au Hasard, Balthasar* (1966), *Une Femme Douce* (1969), and *Four Nights of a Dreamer* (1971), austere films with their own group of devotees. *L'Argent* (1983) won the grand prize at the Cannes Film Festival. ■ See his *Notes on Cinematography* (Eng. trans. 1977) and Lindley Hanlon, *Fragments* (1986).

BRETON, ANDRÉ (1896–1966), French poet and critic, Breton's literary views were influenced by the poets Paul Valéry and Guillaume Apollinaire and the writings of the psychoanalyst Sigmund Freud. One of the founders of surrealism, he remained its uncompromising spokesman and theoretician throughout his life. In manifestos (1924, 1930, 1942; Eng. trans. 1969) he defended surrealism's spontaneity of expression and claimed it could help bring self-knowledge and a true understanding of the unconscious, especially through "automatic writing." His most admired fictional work was his dreamlike novel *Nadja* (1928; Eng. trans. 1960). He also wrote *Surrealism and Painting* (1928; Eng. trans. 1972). ■ See his *Poems* (Eng. trans. 1982); *What Is Surrealism?: Selected Writings* (1978); biography by Anna Balakian (1971); and Mark Polizzotti, *Revolution of the Mind* (1995):

BREUER, MARCEL LAJOS (1902–1981), Hungarian-born U.S. architect. In 1924, Breuer enrolled at Germany's Bauhaus, where he later taught and designed his distinctive tubular furniture. When Adolf Hitler came to power, he fled to the United States where he joined a Cambridge, Massachusetts, architectural firm. He also taught at Harvard where, with Bauhaus associate Walter Gropius, he trained many prominent U.S. architects. After World War II, Breuer executed such important architectural commissions as the United Nations Education, Scientific, and Cultural (UNESCO) headquarters in Paris (1958), the Whitney Museum of American Art in New York City (1966), and the controversial Pan American Building adjacent to Grand Central Station, also in New York. The sculptural quality of Breuer's massive concrete buildings helped to change the face of modern architecture. ■ See studies by Peter Blake (1949) and Cranston Jones (1962) and David Masello, *Architecture Without Rules* (1993).

BREUIL, HENRI ÉDOUARD PROSPER (1877–1961), French archaeologist. An ordained priest, Abbé Breuil developed an interest in Paleolithic art by visiting Bronze Age sites in France. He was a skilled draftsman and he copied the remains of prehistoric cave paintings in southern France, northern Spain, and Africa. He developed methods for relating their style and color to specific periods of prehistoric culture and devised a technical vocabulary for analyzing the paintings. He taught at the Institute of Human Paleontology, Paris (1910–29) and at the Collège de France (1929–47) and wrote numerous books, including *Four Hundred Centuries of Cave Art* (1952; Eng. trans. 1952) and *The Men of the Old Stone Age* (with Raymond Lantier, 1959; Eng. trans. 1965). ■ See Alan H. Brodrick, *Father of Prehistory* (1963).

BREZHNEV, LEONID ILYICH (1906–1982). Soviet political leader. Brezhnev studied engineering in his native Ukraine and joined the Communist party in 1931. He became a party official (1938) and during World War II served (1941–45) as a military political commissar and was given the rank of major general. He rose to prominence during dictator Joseph Stalin's last years, when he became an alternate member of the party presidium. His career blossomed with that of fellow Ukrainian Nikita Khrushchev, and he became a member of the Politburo (1957). He served as nominal head of state as president of the presidium of the Supreme Soviet (1960–64) and succeeded Khrushchev as first secretary of the Communist party (1964–82). Although he shared collective leadership with Premier Alexei Kosygin, he emerged as principal leader. After the 1977 revision of the Soviet constitution, Brezhnev was also able to resume the presidency of the presidium, thus becoming the first soviet leader to head the party and the state simultaneously. Brezhnev's tenure marked the strengthening of Soviet military power as well as the development of détente with the West and the negotiation of strategic-arms-limitation accords. He was largely responsible as well for Soviet intervention in Czechoslovakia (1968) and the Soviet incursion into Afghanistan (1979–80). ■ See his autobiography (Eng. trans. rev. ed. 1982) and Harry Gelman. *The Brezhnev Politburo and the Decline of Détente* (1984).

BRIAND, ARISTIDE (1862–1932), French political leader. A lawyer from Nantes, an eloquent speaker and skillful debater, Briand was elected to parliament as a socialist in 1902. He also helped found (1904) *L'Humanité*, the socialist newspaper. As minister of education and religion in 1906 he helped implement the policy of separation of church and state. From 1909 through the mid-1920s he served 11 times as premier. After World War I Briand was foreign minister in several different governments (1925–32) and promoted Franco-German rapprochement. He shared the 1926 Nobel Peace Prize with Germany's Gustav Stresemann, a cosigner of the 1925 Locarno Pact guaranteeing certain European boundaries, and was a coauthor of the 1929 Kellogg-Briand agreement to outlaw war.

BRICE, FANNY (**Fannie Borach**; 1891–1951), U.S. singer and comedienne. A product of the Jewish ghetto that was New York City's Lower East Side, Brice was "discovered" by Florenz Ziegfeld (1910) and became the star of almost every edition of his annual *Follies*. Known for her roguish eyes and half-moon mouth, she delighted audiences with her renditions of ballet dancers, fan dancers, and vamps. Her renditions of the songs "My Man" and "Rose of Washington Square" were her trademarks. Brice also created the character of Baby Snooks and played the role of the incorrigible brat on radio from 1938 until her death. *Funny Girl* (staged 1964; filmed 1968) was based on her life. ■ See Norman Katkov, *The Fabulous Fanny* (1953); Barbara Grossman, *Funny Woman* (1991); and biography by Herbert G. Goldman (1992).

BRIDGES, HARRY (**Alfred Bryant Renton Bridges**; 1901–1990), Australian-born U.S. labor leader. A merchant seaman, Bridges arrived in the United States in 1920 and became a longshoreman and militant labor organizer in San Francisco. After two unsuccessful efforts, he formed an International Longshoremen's Association (ILA) local (1933) and initiated a strike (1934) that led to a three-day general strike in San Francisco. In 1937 he set up the International Longshoremen's and Warehousemen's Union (ILWU), was elected its president, and merged it with the newly formed Congress of Industrial Organizations (CIO). A political radical and iconoclast who supported the Soviet Union, Bridges was accused of being a communist and hounded by the U.S. government—which sought his deportation for 17 years (1938–1955)—and was made an outcast from the mainstream of organized labor (the ILWU was expelled from the CIO in 1950). In 1961 he negotiated a pattern-setting contract that led to waterfront automation. ■ See biography by Charles P. Larrowe (1972).

BRIDGMAN, PERCY WILLIAMS (1882–1961), U.S. physicist. Bridgman began his experiments in the field of high-pressure physics while working on his doctoral dissertation at Harvard (Ph.D. 1908), where he taught from 1908 to 1954. Limited by available equipment, previous investigators had never obtained pressures of more than 3,000 atmospheres: Bridgman invented a new type of seal that eventually enabled him to produce pressures of up to 425,000 atmospheres under limited circumstances. He measured the effects of high pressure on many substances. Also known as a philosopher of science, Bridgman wrote *The Logic of Modern Physics* (1927), *The Nature of Physical Theory* (1936), and *The Intelligent Individual and Society,* (1938). He received the 1946 Nobel Prize in Physics for designing equipment and techniques basic to the continued investigation of high-pressure physics. ■ See his *Reflections of a Physicist* (1950; 2d ed. 1955) and *Collected Experimental Papers* (7 vols., 1964) and Maila L. Walter, *Science and Cultural Crisis* (1990).

BRIERLY, JAMES LESLIE (1881–1955), British international law expert, J. L. Brierly was a distinguished scholar and teacher (1922–47) at Oxford who was also active in the movement to establish collective security. He was a member of the League of Nations committee on the codification of international law (1924–27), was Ethiopian Emperor Haile Selassie's legal adviser after the Italian invasion of Ethiopa (1935), and served on the United Nations international law commission (1949–51). Brierly's clear, concise study of *The Law of Nations* (1928) reflected his liberal values and went into several editions.

BRIGHTMAN, EDGAR SHEFFIELD (1884–1953), U.S. philosopher. An ordained Methodist minister, Brightman taught at Boston University (1919–53). He was an influential teacher and scholar, publishing prolifically. The most articulate American advocate of the values of "personalism," first enunciated by B. P. Bowne, Brightman gave Bowne's

theism and idealism a more experiential grounding. He argued that the concept of the "person"—as a self-conscious, moral entity—should replace the scholastic concept of the "soul." Brightman wrote *Introduction to Philosophy* (1925), *The Problem of God* (1930), *Personality and Religion* (1934), *Philosophy of Religion* (1940), *Nature and Values* (1945), and *Person and Reality* (1958).

BRINKLEY, DAVID. *See HUNTLEY, CHET.*

BRISBANE, ARTHUR (1864–1936), U.S. newspaper editor. The son of social-reformer Albert Brisbane, Arthur began his newspaper career at age 19 and became the most widely read and highly paid newspaper editor of his time. A master of "yellow journalism," he edited William Randolph Hearst's *New York Journal* and devised inflammatory atrocity stories (1897–98) that helped promote the Spanish-American War. His anecdotal and simplistic editorial column, "Today" (1917–36), featured pictures, cartoons, and boldface type to attract a mass readership and was syndicated in more than 1,400 newspapers. Among the targets of his columns, which critics called "brisbanalties," were trade unions, the New Deal, the League of Nations, and the World Court. ■ See biography by Oliver Carlson (1937).

BRITTEN, (EDWARD) BENJAMIN BRITTEN, BARON (1913–1976), British composer and conductor. One of the century's most prolific composers, Britten was influenced by the music of the Elizabethan and Tudor periods. His forte was vocal music, composed in a conservative idiom and cast in classical forms. His works included the operas *Peter Grimes* (1945), *Billy Budd* (1951), and *The Turn of the Screw* (1954)—all, as critics have noted, on the theme of injured innocence—the choral works *Ceremony of Carols* (1942) and *War Requiem* (1962); and the church pageant *Noye's Fludde* (1958). He was also a noted pianist and conductor and founded (1947) the Aldeburgh Festival. ■ See Alan Blyth, *Remembering Britten* (1981); studies by Christopher Headington (1981), Michael Kennedy (1981), and Eric W. White (rev. ed. 1983); and biographies by Humphrey Carpenter (1992) and Michael Oliver (1996).

BROAD, CHARLIE DUNBAR (1887–1971), British philosopher. On the faculty of Cambridge University (from 1923), Broad contributed to all of the major fields of philosophy. He was generally regarded as a realist and was best known for his work in the philosophy of science, the theory of knowledge, perception, and ethics. He joined the Society for Psychical Research (1920) and served as its president (1935; 1958). His works included *Scientific Thought* (1923), *The Mind and Its Place in Nature* (1925), *Ethics and the History of Philosophy* (1952), and *Religion, Philosophy and Psychical Research* (1953).

BROCH, HERMANN (1886–1951), Austrian-born novelist and poet. At the age of 41, Broch left the family textile business and turned to academic studies and then to writing. The novels that he termed "polyhistoric" included *The Sleepwalkers* (3 vols., 1930–32; Eng. trans. 1932) and *The Guiltless* (1950; Eng. trans. 1974). Broch employed complex, innovative narrative devices to convey the spiritual and cultural disintegration of modern German society. He also wrote the novels *The Unknown Quantity* (1933; Eng. trans. 1935) and *The Death of Vergil* (1945; Eng. trans. 1945) as well as drama, short fiction, criticism, and abstract poetry. He was detained (1938) by the Nazis but was allowed to emigrate to the United States after prominent foreigners interceded on his behalf. ■ See study by Ernestine Schlant (1978) and biography by Paul M. Lützeler (Eng. trans. 1987).

BROCKHOUSE, BERTRAM N. (1918–), Canadian physicist. After receiving a doctorate in physics from the University of Toronto (1950), Brockhouse did research at the Chalk River Nuclear Laboratories, operated by Atomic Energy of Canada Limited (1950–59). Working with an early nuclear research reactor, he developed the technique of neutron spectroscopy that enabled researchers to measure atomic vibrational energy of crystals and, subsequently, of different materials. Knowledge of this sort is important in determining how efficiently materials conduct heat or electricity and the technique played an important role in the development of semiconductors, superconducting materials, and catalytic converters. Brockhouse later was a professor at McMaster University in Ontario (1962–84) and shared the 1994 Nobel Prize in Physics with Clifford G. Shull.

BRODSKY, JOSEPH (1940–1996), Soviet-born poet. Born into a Jewish family in Leningrad, Brodsky dropped out of high school at age 15, studied languages and literature at home, and started to publish poems in underground magazines when he was 18. As his poems began to reach a wide audience, he was branded a dissident and social parasite by the government: he was exiled (March 1964) to a remote region but was permitted to return to Leningrad late the next year after his sentence sparked international protest. Forced to emigrate (1972), he became a U.S. citizen (1977) and taught at several universities. His powerful and innovative lyric poetry, influenced both by Russian- and English-language poets (notably Marina Tsvetaeva and W. H. Auden), dealt with existential themes of human suffering, loss, isolation, and death. He was virtually unpublished in the Soviet Union, but his name was a household word among its intelligentsia. English translations of his poems are in *Elegy to John Donne and Other Poems* (1967), *Selected Poems* (1973), and *A Part of Speech* (1979). *Less Than One* (1986) is a collection of critical prose. He was awarded the 1987 Nobel Prize in Literature and served as poet laureate of the United States (1991–92). His later works included the poetry collections *To Urania* (1988) and *Collected Poems in English* (2000) and the prose volume *Watermark* (1992). ■

See studies by Valentina Polukhina (1989) and David M. Bethea (1994).

BROGLIE, LOUIS VICTOR DE (1892–1987), French physicist. Born into a noted family, Broglie almost became a historian instead of a physicist. He received his doctorate at the University of Paris (1924) and taught there until his retirement (1962). Broglie was best known for his research in the 1920s on quantum theory. He proposed that matter and radiation have both wave and particle properties and discovered the wave character of the electron, thus laying the foundation of wave mechanics. He was awarded the 1929 Nobel Prize for Physics. His books in English translation included *Physics and Microphysics* (1955).

BRONK, DETLEV WULF (1897–1975), U.S. biophysicist and educator. Trained in physics and physiology, Bronk researched the nature of sensation, the chemical excitation of nerves, body-movement control, and related subjects. But his most important contributions were made as an administrator. He served as president (1949–53) of Johns Hopkins University and of the Rockefeller Institute for Medical Research (1953–68), which he transformed into Rockefeller University while influencing its development into a preeminent graduate-training institution. Bronk also chaired (1946–50) the National Research Council and presided (1950–62) over the National Research Council of the National Academy of Sciences.

BRONOWSKI, JACOB (1908–1974), Polish-born scholar. A recipient of a Ph.D. in mathematics (Cambridge, 1933), Bronowski was a poet, inventor, and playwright with a life-long interest in the philosophical bases of science. He studied the economic effects of World War II bombing, headed research for Britain's National Coal Board (1950–59), and was a fellow (1964–74) at the Salk Institute for Biological Sciences in California. His crowning achievement was "The Ascent of Man," a BBC-TV series on Western intellectual history that also became a best-selling book (1973). His other books included *The Common Sense of Science* (1953), *Science and Human Values* (rev. ed. 1965), and *William Blake and the Age of Revolution* (rev. ed. 1965).

BROOK, PETER (1925–), British theatrical and film director. Brook's earliest productions, such as *Dr. Faustus* (1942), *The Infernal Machine* (1945), *The Respectable Prostitute* (1946), *The Lark* (1955), and *The Visit* (1960), established him as an important theatrical director and provided the foundation for the more innovative productions that followed. His concepts of environmental staging were evolved from many sources, including Antonin Artaud's "theater of cruelty," Bertolt Brecht's "theater of alienation," the circus, and the *commedia dell 'arte*. His most influential productions were *Marat/Sade* (1964; film, 1967) and *A Midsummer Night's Dream* (1970). Brook directed a number of

Shakespearean productions at Stratford-upon-Avon and was appointed (1962) codirector of the Royal Shakespeare Company. To promote theatrical experimentation, he founded (1970) the International Center of Theatrical Research in Paris. He also staged his own version of Bizet's *Carmen, La Tragédie de Carmen* (1983). He was also acclaimed for his nine-hour production of *The Mahabharata* (1987), based on ancient Hindu texts, and his production of Mozart's *Don Giovanni* (1998). He recounted his theories of drama in *The Empty Space* (1968). ■ See his *The Shifting Point: 1946–1987* (1987) and *Threads of Time: Recollections* (1998); Edward T. Jones, *Following Directions* (1985); and the biography by John C. Trewin (1971).

BROOKE, ALAN FRANCIS. *See ALANBROOKE, ALAN FRANCIS BROOKE, 1st VISCOUNT.*

BROOKE, EDWARD WILLIAM (1919–), U.S. political leader. The son of a government attorney, Brooke graduated from Boston University Law School in 1948. As attorney general of Massachusetts (1963–66) he gained a reputation as a crime buster, handing down indictments against a former governor and two speakers of the state legislature and bringing in a clairvoyant to help identify the Boston Strangler. In 1967 Brooke, a Republican, an Episcopalian, and the chairman of the Boston Opera, became the first African-American U.S. senator since Reconstruction. He was defeated for reelection in 1978, after a divorce and a Senate investigation of his financial affairs, and he later practiced law and headed the National Low-Income Housing Coalition. ■ See his *Challenge of Change* (1966).

BROOKE, RUPERT (1887–1915), British poet. Educated at Rugby and Cambridge, Brooke achieved early fame through his *Poems* (1911), in which he concentrated on the details of everyday life. He showed greater maturity in his writings on World War I in the idealistic collection *1914* (1915), which included his famous poem "The Soldier." Just as his fame was increasing, he died of blood poisoning contracted as a soldier. Brooke was universally regarded as handsome, witty, and charming, and his tragic early death made him a symbol to the British of the idealism and nobility of their youth. ■ See biography by Christopher V. Hassall (1964); John Lehmann, *Strange Destiny of Rupert Brooke* (1980); and Mike Read, *Forever England* (1997).

BROOKINGS, ROBERT SOMERS (1850–1932), U.S. businessman and philanthropist. A multimillionaire merchant, builder, and manufacturer with an elementary-school education. Brookings launched a career at age 47 as an educational philanthropist. He began by upgrading the physical plant and the academic standards of Washington University in St. Louis, and went on to endow (1927) the Brookings Institution in Washington, D.C., as a center of independent research and graduate training in government and economics.

He was also one of the original trustees of the Carnegie Endowment for International Peace (1910) and a member of the War Industries Board during World War I. ■ See biography by Hermann Hagedorn (1936).

BROOKS, CLEANTH (1906–1994), U.S. literary critic. A leading advocate of the New Criticism, which stressed attention to imagery and structural analysis rather than the historical or social analysis of literary works, Brooks taught at Louisiana State University (1932–47) and Yale (1947–75). He edited, with Robert Penn Warren, *The Southern Review* (1935–42) and wrote several important works that helped popularize the New Criticism, including *Modern Poetry and the Tradition* (1939), *The Well-Wrought Urn* (1947), and *Literary Criticism: A Short History* (1957; with W. K. Wimsatt, Jr.). He was coauthor of the college textbooks *Understanding Poetry* (1938) and *Understanding Fiction* (1943) with Warren. His essays were collected in *Community, Religion and Literature* (1995). ■ See Lewis P. Simpson, ed., *The Possibilities of Order* (1976), and study by Mark R. Winchell (1996).

BROOKS, GARTH (1962–), U.S. country singer. Brooks, whose mother recorded for Capitol Records in the late 1950s, started singing while he was a student at Oklahoma State University. After moving to Nashville he signed a contract with Capitol and his first album, *Garth Brooks* (1989), was a sensational hit, selling more than 1 million copies in its first year of release. An easygoing and likable performer, Brooks became the youngest member of Nashville's Grand Ole Opry (1990) and appealed to both mainstream country music audiences as well as to rock and pop fans. His *Ropin' the Wind* (1991) was the first country album to debut as a number one on *Billboard* magazine's pop chart. He subsequently became the best-selling solo artist in U.S. musical history with sales of his albums allegedly topping 100 million through 2000. His other albums included *The Chase, No Fences,* and *Double Live,* which sold more than 1 million copies during its first week of sales (1998).

BROOKS, GWENDOLYN (1917–2000), U.S. poet. Brooks grew up in a black ghetto in Chicago. At age 13 her poem "Eventide" was published by *American Childhood.* After graduation (1936) from Wilson Junior College, she frequently contributed poetry to the black newspaper *Defender.* When she published *A Streetcar in Bronzeville* (1945), Brooks was selected by *Mademoiselle* as one of the year's 10 exceptional women. With *Annie Allen* (1949), poems about an African-American girl's Chicago youth, she became the first African-American woman to win a Pulitzer Prize. She also published *The Bean Eaters* (1960), *Selected Poems* (1963), *In the Mecca* (1964), *The Riot,* (1970), *Family Pictures* (1970), *Aloneness* (1971), *Black Love* (1982), and *Children Coming Home* (1991), and the autobiographies, *Report from Part One* (1972) and *Report From Part*

Two (1996). She was the poetry consultant to the Library of Congress (1985–86). ■ See study by Harry B. Shaw (1980) and biography by George Keat (1990).

BROOKS, MEL (Melvin Kaminsky; 1927?–   ), U.S. filmmaker and comedy writer. Brooks grew up in Brooklyn's Jewish Williamsburg section. While working as a drummer in the Borscht Belt of the Catskills, he launched a career in comedy and became social director at Grossinger's resort hotel, where he met Sid Caesar. Brooks later wrote gags for Caesar's popular television program "Your Show of Shows." In the 1960s he came into his own with the album *The 2,000-Year-Old-Man* (with Carl Reiner), developed the hit TV series "Get Smart" with Buck Henry, and began directing his own outrageous, irreverent film scripts, including *The Producers* (1968), *Blazing Saddles* (1974), *Young Frankenstein* (1975), *Silent Movie* (1976), *High Anxiety* (1978), *History of the World, Part I* (1981), *Spaceballs* (1987), and *Robin Hood: Men in Tights* (1993). He costarred with his wife, Anne Bancroft, in a remake of *To Be or Not to Be* (1983). His album *The 2,000-Year-Old Man in the Year 2000* (with Carl Reiner) won a 1998 Grammy Award. ■ See the biography by Bill Adler and Jeffrey Feinman (1976); Will Holtzman, *Seesaw* (1979); and Maurice Yacowar, *Method in Madness* (1981).

BROOKS, ROMAINE (Beatrice Romaine Goddard; 1874–1970), U.S. artist. Brooks was best known for her portraits in the symbolist style, executed in tones of black, white, and gray. Her subjects were frequently portrayed as remote, introspective, and isolated. She favored a slender, nearly emaciated female ideal, and some of her portraits had an androgynous quality, particularly evident in *The Crossing* (1911). Brooks frequently included symbolic animal images in her portraits and allusions to personal qualities of her subjects. Brooks was the model for Olympia Leigh in Compton McKenzie's novel *Extraordinary Women* (1928) about lesbian life, and she was also the model for a character in *The Well of Loneliness* (1928) by Radclyffe Hall. Brooks' line drawings, done largely in the 1930s, have been described as appearing to be "by Thurber out of Beardsley." ■ See Meryle Secrest, *Between Me and Life* (1974).

BROOKS, VAN WYCK (1886–1963), U.S. literary critic and historian. After graduating from Harvard (1907), Brooks wrote *The Wine of the Puritans* (1908) and *America's Coming of Age* (1915), which presented the radical thesis that America's cultural shortcomings and divided character were attributable to the Puritans' separation of spiritual and material matters. During the last 30 years of his life, though, he changed his views, idealized the American past, and rejected all modernist criticism. His masterpiece, *Makers and Finders: A History of the Writer in America, 1800–1915* (5 vols., 1936–52), presented a positive and sentimental treatment of U.S. culture and literary tradition. ■ See his *Autobiography* (1965); studies by James R.

Vitelli (1969), James Hoopes (1977); and William Wasserstrom, *The Legacy of Van Wyck Brooks* (1971).

BROPHY, BRIGID (1929–1995), British writer. The precocious daughter of an Irish novelist, Brophy began writing as a child, was sent down after one year at Oxford (1948), and published her first novel, *Hackenfeller's Ape,* a fantasy about a laboratory ape that acquires human inhibitions, in 1953. She was an outspoken Freudian and opponent of hypocrisy, censorship, philistinism, and vivisection. She was active in campaigns for women's rights and prisoners' rights. Her witty and iconoclastic novels, concerning the instinctual-rational conflict in human nature, included *The King of a Rainy Country* (1956), *Flesh* (1962), and *In Transit* (1969). Other novels included *The Snow Ball* (1964) and *Palace Without Chairs* (1978). Brophy also published a psychoanalytic study, *Mozart the Dramatist* (1964); a collection of journalistic writings, *Don't Never Forget* (1966); and studies of writer Ronald Firbank (*Prancing Novelist,* 1973) and artist Aubrey Beardsley (1976). In the essays in *Baroque 'n' Roll* (1987) she described the debilitating effects of multiple sclerosis, which was diagnosed in 1979 and eventually caused her death.

BROPHY, JOHN (1883–1963), British-born union leader. A coal miner from age 12, Brophy joined the United Mine Workers of America (1899) and served as president of its central Pennsylvania district (1916–26). He was a leading exponent of nationalizing the coal mines and a frequent critic of union president John L. Lewis. Brophy was a founder (1935) of the Congress of Industrial Organizations (CIO) and its national director (1935–39); he remained a high union official until 1961. ■ See his autobiography, *A Miner's Life* (1964).

BROSSOLETTE, PIERRE (1902–1944), French resistance leader. An influential socialist journalist, Brossolette served as chief editor of the government radio (1936–39). After the German invasion (1940) during World War II, he helped organize the resistance movement, became an adviser to Gen. Charles de Gaulle in London (1942), and returned to France to help found the National Council of the Resistance (March 1943), an organization set up to coordinate the activities of all anti-Nazi groups in France. Captured by the Germans in 1944, he committed suicide by jumping out of the window of the Gestapo headquarters in Paris, thus ensuring that he would not talk under torture.

BROTHERS, JOYCE (Joyce Bauer; 1927–   ), U.S. psychologist and media personality. Clinical psychologist Dr. Joyce Brothers trained at Columbia University and occupied (1948–52) teaching posts at Columbia and at Hunter College in New York City. She was introduced to television viewers when she won (1957) top prizes on the quiz shows "The $64,000 Question" and "The $64,000 Challenge" by answering questions in her chosen category—boxing. NBC hired her as cohost for "Sports Showcase," but she built her reputation in the late 1950s and early 1960s on TV and radio shows in which she advised members of the home audience—who would write or phone her—on personal problems. Her programs popularized psychological concepts and helped dispel the stigma attached to seeking professional counseling. In the 1970s and 1980s she appeared in other TV roles: as dramatic actress, variety-show host, and game-show panelist. She played herself on the soap opera "One Life to Live" and on the children's show "Captain Kangaroo." She wrote a syndicated column (after 1961) and numerous books, including *The Successful Woman* (1989) and *Positive Plus: The Practical Plan to Liking Yourself Better* (1994).

BROUN, HEYWOOD CAMPBELL (1888–1939), U.S. newspaper columnist and critic. One of the most widely read and controversial columnists of his time (*New York World,* 1921–28; *New York World Telegram,* 1928–39; *New Republic,* 1935–39; *New York Post,* 1939), Broun championed the underdog and crusaded against social injustice. He vigorously defended Sacco and Vanzetti (anarchists convicted of murder in 1921), baked the newly formed labor unions, unsuccessfully ran for Congress as a socialist (1930), and organized a campaign to find work for the unemployed during the Depression of the 1930s. Broun was also a novelist, lecturer, drama critic, playwright, biographer, and the founder and first president of the American Newspaper Guild (1933–39). ■ See biographies by Dale Kramer (1949) and Richard O'Connor (1975).

BROUWER, LUITZEN EGBERTUS JAN (1881–1966), Dutch mathematician. A professor at the University of Amsterdam (1912–51), L.E.J. Brouwer rejected the idea that formal logic was the foundation of mathematics and that every mathematical statement is either true or false. He developed instead the doctrine of intuitionism, which sees mathematics as a free activity of the mind based on self-evident primitive ideas, or intuition. He was a pioneer in the study of topology and made major contributions to the theory of aggregates, the theory of functions, and the field of differential equations. ■ See his *Cambridge Lectures on Intuitionism* (1981), *Collected Works* (Eng. trans., 2 vols., 1974–76); Walter P. Van Stigt, *Brouwer's Intuitionism* (1990), and Dirk van Dalen, *Mystic, Geometer and Intuitionist* (1999).

BROWDER, EARL RUSSELL (1891–1973), U.S. political leader. At age 15, following in his father's footsteps, Browder joined the Socialist party, but he left it (1912) to join the more radical Syndicalist League of North America. After serving prison terms for opposing the draft in World War I (1917–18; 1919–20), he joined the newly formed American Communist party and attended several conferences in Moscow during the 1920s. In 1930 he became secretary-general of the party and led it (until 1945) during the time of its greatest growth and influence and during a period marked by precipitous shifts in its policies dictated by Moscow. Browder himself became a victim of such a shift when he was denounced (1945) as a deviationist for advocating postwar cooperation and coexistence with liberal capitalism (the party's position during World War II) and was expelled from the party (1946). Although probably the best-known communist in American history (he ran for president in 1936 and 1940), he lived the last 27 years of his life in obscurity. ■ See study by James G. Ryan (1997).

BROWER, DAVID ROSS (1912–2000), U.S. environmentalist. An avid hiker and rock climber in his youth, Brower joined the Sierra Club in 1933 and served as a trainer and combat-intelligence officer with the U.S. Army's 10th Mountain Division during World War II (1942–45). As executive director of the Sierra Club (1952–69), he transformed the small, conservative, regional organization into a powerful, national, 70,000-member force that militantly championed environmental protection. Under Brower's leadership the club successfully opposed the construction of dams in the Grand Canyon and Dinosaur National Monument, and played a leading role in the creation of national parks (North Cascades, Washington, and Canyonlands, Utah) and national seashores (Cape Cod, Massachusetts, and Point Reyes, California) and in the protection of primeval forests and wilderness areas. Brower helped plan and edit the Sierra Club's series of best-selling books on scenic America featuring the works of Ansel Adams, Eliot Porter, and other leading photographers. Brower subsequently founded Friends of the Earth (1969; president 1969–79), a politically active environmental group; the John Muir Institute (1969), a nonprofit organization devoted to research and education; and Earth Island Institute (1969), an international organization established to facilitate ties between environmental and peace groups. ■ See his 2-volume autobiography, *For Earth's Sake* (1990) and *Work in Progress* (1991).

BROWN, SIR ARTHUR WHITTEN (1886–1948), British aviator. Trained as an engineer, Brown navigated (1919) the first nonstop crossing of the Atlantic. The record flight, with John Alcock at the controls of a twin-engine plane, averaged 120 miles per hour and took 16 hours, 27 minutes. Brown and Alcock were knighted and shared a £10,000 prize given by the *London Daily Mail.* ■ See Alcock and Brown's *Our Transatlantic Flight* (1969).

BROWN, DEE ALEXANDER (1908–), U.S. writer. Brown earned a library-science degree (1937) and worked for the U.S. government (1934–48) and the University of Illinois (1948–72) while researching his books on the American frontier. His first novel was about Davy Crockett (1942): *They Went Thataway* (1960) was made into a movie. But Brown's best-remembered work was *Bury My Heart at Wounded Knee* (1971), an account of "manifest destiny" from the Indian perspective. Later works included the novels *Creek Mary's Blood* (1980), an epic tale told from an old Indian storyteller's viewpoint, and *Killdeer Mountain* (1983), a mystery-and-adventure story. He also wrote *The American West* (1994) and *The Way to Bright Star* (1998). ■ See his *Growing Up Western: Recollections* (1990).

BROWN, EDMUND GERALD, JR. (1938–   ), U.S. political leader. The son of a California governor, Jerry Brown studied for the priesthood and worked briefly as a lawyer before going into Democratic party politics. Elected California secretary of state in 1970, he filed suit against oil companies and candidates over illegal campaign contributions. From 1975 to 1983 Brown served as a nonconformist governor, preaching a revolution of lowered expectations, following a Spartan lifestyle, and affecting disdain for conventional politics. He unsuccessfully sought the Democratic party's presidential nomination in 1980 and 1992. He subsequently ran a grassroots community organization, We the People, in Oakland, California, and served as Oakland's mayor (1999–   ). ■ See biographies by Orville Schell (1978) and Robert Pack (1978).

BROWN, ERNEST WILLIAM (1866–1938), British mathematician and astronomer. After distinguishing himself at Cambridge University, Brown spent his professional life in the United States and was a professor at Yale (1907–32). He completed the study of the motion of the moon initiated by G. W. Hill. In 1908, Brown published his theory and, in 1919, the tables that have been used to make accurate determinations of the moon's positions. His research suggests that the earth rotates at a variable rate.

BROWN, FREDERIC (1906–1972), U.S. novelist and science-fiction and mystery writer. Brown began his career as a journalist. He wrote several polished detective novels, beginning with *The Fabulous Clipjoint* (1947), before publishing *What Mad Universe* (1949), the first of the clever, satirical novels that established him in the science-fiction world as well. Psychological motivation was often the subject of his fiction. His other works included the thriller *Night of the Jabberwock* (1950) and the comic novel of an invasion of Earth, *Martians, Go Home* (1955). The novel *The Office* (1958) was partly autobiographical. ■ See Jack Seabrook, *Martians and Misplaced Clues* (1993).

BROWN, GEORGE HAROLD (1908–   ), U.S. electrical engineer. A researcher and executive with the Radio Corp. of America (1933–72), Brown was responsible for major improvements in the transmission of radio and television signals. He developed directional broadcast antennas (1934–36), invented the turnstile antenna used for television and FM radio broadcasting (1936), and devised the vestigial sideband filter (1938), which doubled the resolution of television pictures. After World War II he worked on the development of ultrahigh frequency (UHF) and color television. ■ See his autobiography, *And Part of Which I Was* (1982).

BROWN, H. RAP (Hubert Geroid Brown; 1943–   ), U.S. political activist. A charismatic young black-power leader from Baton Rouge, Louisiana, Brown became president of the Student Nonviolent Coordinating Committee (SNCC) in 1967. He bitterly denounced American society and advocated revolutionary violence. After being indicted in Maryland for riot and arson and convicted for violating federal firearms laws, Brown went underground (1970). "Violence is as American as cherry pie," he once declared; in 1971 he was caught in a New York City robbery shootout and sentenced (1973) to 5 to 15 years. In prison he converted to Islam and adopted the name Jamil Abdullah al-Amin. In October 1976, federal firearms charges were dropped and he was paroled. He later opened a grocery store in Atlanta, Georgia, and became leader of the Community Mosque. He was arrested (2000) and charged with shooting to death a deputy sheriff in Atlanta. ■ See his *Die Nigger Die* (1969) and *Revolution by the Book: The Rap Is Live* (1993).

BROWN, HERBERT (1912–   ), British-born U.S. organic chemist. Trained at the University of Chicago (Ph.D. 1938), Brown taught at Purdue University (1947–78). He shared the 1979 Nobel Prize in Chemistry with West German Georg Wittig for research that facilitated low-cost synthesis of chemical substances. Working independently of Wittig, Brown developed a method of joining large molecules by establishing temporary chemical links composed of boron and hydrogen, called boranes, which serve temporarily until permanent links are in place. This technique revolutionized the manufacture of many pharmaceutical and industrial chemicals. Brown wrote several books, including *Hydroboration* (1962), *Boranes in Organic Chemistry* (1972), and *The Nonclassical Ion Problem* (1977).

BROWN, JAMES (1933?–   ), U.S. singer. Backed by his group the "Famous Flames," Brown became famous in the mid-1950s for his "cry" ballads. "Please, Please, Please, (Pleeze)" he would cry with nearly trancelike repetition. Brown's popularity increased in the 1960s as rhythm and blues picked up a new mass market. He became known as "Soul Brother No. 1" and the "godfather of soul." His popularity waned with the advent of disco in the late 1970s, then revived in the mid-1980s. His recordings influenced funk jazz and the black urban street music of such rap performers as Grandmaster Flash and Kool DJ Herc, and hip-hop artist Afrika Bambaataa. Brown and Bambaataa together recorded "Unity" (1984). He won a Grammy Award (1987) for "Living in America." ■ See his autobiography (1986) and Cynthia Rose, *Living in America* (1990).

BROWN, JERRY. *See* BROWN, EDMUND GERALD, JR.

BROWN, JIM (1936–), U.S. football player. A superb all-around athlete, Brown was an All-America halfback at Syracuse University (1956). Drafted by the Cleveland Browns of the National Football League (NFL), he became the game's greatest ball carrier and led the league in rushing in eight of his nine seasons (1957–66). The 6-foot, 2-inch, 228-pound fullback established the NFL's single-season rushing record, the career rushing record (12.312 yards), the career touchdown record (126; broken by Jerry Rice), and the career yards per carry (5.2) and yards per game (104.3) records. Upon his retirement he became a movie actor. ■ See study by J. P. Terzian and J. Benagh (1964) and J. Toback, *Jim* (1971).

BROWN, LEW. *See DE SYLVA, BUDDY.*

BROWN, MICHAEL STUART (1941–), U.S. molecular geneticist. A graduate of the University of Pennsylvania Medical School (M.D. 1966). Brown did research on the chemistry and the abnormalities of the digestive system at the National Institutes of Health (1968–71). While a professor at the Southwestern Medical School of the University of Texas in Dallas (from 1971), Brown collaborated with Joseph Goldstein on cholesterol research. Their discovery (1973) of low-density lipoprotein (LDL) receptors, molecules that extract cholesterol from the blood and transport it inside the cell, revolutionized the study of cholesterol metabolism. It led to the development of new treatments for heart attacks, strokes, hardening of the arteries, and other diseases caused by clogging of the arteries by the accumulation of fatty cholesterol. For their research, Brown and Goldstein shared the 1985 Nobel Prize in Physiology or Medicine.

BROWN, NORMAN OLIVER (1913–), U.S. historian and social critic. Brown was educated at Oxford (1936) and the University of Wisconsin (Ph.D. 1942), served as a research analyst for the Office of Strategic Services during World War II, then taught classics at various universities. He wrote a pioneering Marxist analysis of an ancient myth, *Hermes the Thief* (1947), but he was best known for the popular and controversial book *Life Against Death: The Psychoanalytic Meaning of History* (1959), which applied to large patterns of history such related Freudian notions as the unconscious, repression, psychic determinism, and the death wish. Defining the human being as "the animal which represses himself," he suggested that humankind inevitably moves toward self-destruction and critiqued the "perversion of human drives from life and art to money and death." Various critics judged the book to be far-reaching or farfetched. Brown also wrote *Love's Body* (1966), which influenced the human potential movement, *Closing Time* (1973), and *Apocalypse and/or Metamorphosis* (1991).

BROWN, PAUL (1908–1991), U.S. football coach. Brown had a successful career in the college ranks before becoming a professional coach with the Cleveland Browns of the All-American Conference (1946). His team so overpowered its opponents (losing only 4 of its 54 games) that fans lost interest and the league broke up. In 1950 the Browns (named after him) joined the National Football League and stunned the gridiron world by quickly dominating the league. His teams captured a league or division title in each of its first 10 years, winning the overall championship in 1950, 1954, and 1955. In 1962, after Cleveland lost momentum, Brown was fired, but 5 years later he returned to the spot as head coach (1968–76) and general manager (1976–91) of the Cincinnati Bengals. Brown made the Bengals, an expansion club, a division winner in just 2 years. ■ See his autobiography, *PB* (1979; with Jack Clary).

BROWN, STERLING (1901–1989), U.S. poet and critic. Brown was educated at Williams College and Harvard University and later taught at Howard University. He figured in the Harlem renaissance (a term that struck him as too narrow); unlike its more urban-oriented writers, he focused on the rural south in his poetry collection *Southern Road* (1932), reproducing folk idioms, work songs, blues, and jazz rhythms. He rejected the use of stereotypic black dialect. During the Depression he worked in the Federal Writers' Project (1936–39) and later, under a Guggenheim Fellowship, wrote *The Negro in American Fiction* (1938) and *Negro Poetry and Drama* (1938). He anthologized African-American writing in *The Negro Caravan* (1941). ■ See his *Collected Poems* (1980) and study by Joanne V. Gabbin (1985).

BROWNING, JOHN MOSES (1855–1926), U.S. inventor. The son of a Mormon gunsmith, Browning designed his first gun from scrap metal at age 13. He went on to design small arms as well as automatic weapons, including a single-shot rifle, a repeating shotgun and rifle, and an automatic pistol. His automatic machine gun and Browning automatic rifle (BAR) were among the weapons purchased by the U.S. Army, and his inventions were used extensively during both world wars. ■ See biography by John Browning and Curt Gentry (1964).

BRUBECK, DAVE (1920–), U.S. pianist, composer, and quartet leader. A cellist and pianist in childhood, Brubeck studied composition under Arnold Schoenberg and Darius Milhaud, who encouraged his interest in jazz. He formed his modern jazz quartet in 1951, and although he was never fully accepted by the jazz world, he received great popular acclaim. Brubeck was the first well-known jazz musician to become famous without first working with other groups. His quartet made frequent international tours and many recordings. ■ See study by Ilse Storb (Eng. trans. 1994) and Fred Hall, *It's About Time* (1996).

BRUCE, DAVID KIRKPATRICK ESTE (1898–1977), U.S. diplomat. Born into an old and distinguished Maryland family, Bruce served briefly in the foreign service (1925–27) but resigned to enter the business world and to become a gentleman farmer after his marriage to industrialist Andrew Mellon's daughter Ailsa. During World War II he commanded the Office of Strategic Services (the precursor of the Central Intelligence Agency) in Europe. By all accounts a man of grace, wit, reason, and culture, Bruce served as ambassador to France (1949–52), West Germany (1957–59), and Britain (1961–69), where he worked for European unification. He came out of his 1969 retirement to head the Vietnam peace negotiations in Paris (1970) and later served as the first head of the U.S. liaison office in Beijing (Peking) (1973) and the chief U.S. delegate to the North Atlantic Treaty Organization (1974–76). ■ See Nelson D. Lankford, *The Last American Aristocrat* (1996).

BRUCE, LENNY (Leonard Alfred Schneider; 1927–1966), U.S. comedian. Bruce finished (1946) a stint in the navy and held down various jobs before gaining notoriety as a nightclub comedian whose "sick" jokes and irreverent humor sparked controversy wherever he performed. In his largely improvised act he touched on whatever subjects struck him as important, especially religion, sex, and politics, as he sought to provoke rather than entertain his audience. A hero of the mid-1960s counterculture, Bruce was continually harassed by authorities; he was imprisoned (1961) for obscenity, refused entry to Britain (1963), where he had a nightclub engagement, and banned (1963) in Austrialia. Bruce was convicted (1963) of illegal drug possession in Los Angeles. In 1966 he was found dead in Hollywood of an accidental drug overdose. ■ See his autobiography, *How to Talk Dirty and Influence People* (1965); Albert Goldman, *Ladies and Gentlemen—Lenny Bruce!* (1974); and study by William K. Thomas (1989).

BRUCE OF MELBOURNE, STANLEY MELBOURNE BRUCE, 1st VISCOUNT (1883–1967), Australian statesman and diplomat. An Anglo-Australian, Bruce devoted his life to nurturing ties between the two countries. Born in Melbourne, educated at Cambridge, he practiced law in London (1906–14) and served with the British in World War I, during which he was wounded and decorated. First elected to the Australian parliament as a Nationalist in 1918, he served as prime minister (1923–29). He also had a distinguished diplomatic career including posts as Australian representative to the League of Nations and as high commissioner in London (1933–45). He represented Australia in the British war cabinet (1942–45) and later headed the World Food Council (1947–51). ■ See biography by Cecil Edwards (1965).

BRUHN, ERIK (1928–1986), Danish ballet dance. Bruhn studied for 10 years before graduating (1947) into the Royal Danish Ballet. He accepted an invitation (1949) to dance with the American Ballet Theatre, becoming a permanent member of that troupe (1953–58). Bruhn won acclaim in America, appearing (1955) with Alicia Markova in *Giselle;* he also was known for his roles in *La Sylphide* and *Swan Lake.* He became ballet's leading *danseur noble,* impressing audiences and critics with his fastidious technique and his skill at pantomime, an art emphasized by the Royal Danish Ballet. He directed the Swedish Opera Ballet (1967–73), and he was a resident producer with the National Ballet of Canada (1973–81) and its artistic director (1983–86). ■ See biography by John Gruen (1979).

BRUMEL, VALERI (1942–), Soviet high jumper. An unknown when he placed second in the 1960 Olympics, Brumel was the first to jump 7 feet, 4 inches (1961) and 7 feet, 5 inches (1962). Employing the straddle technique, he relied on exceptional speed on his approach to the bar. His best jump was 7 feet 5¾ inches (1963), and he later won the 1964 Olympic gold medal by besting his arch rival John Thomas of the United States. He retired after a motorcycle accident (1965) but held the world record until 1971.

BRUNDTLAND, GRO HARLEM (Gro Harlem; 1939–), Norwegian political leader and environmentalist. The daughter of a medical doctor who was also a government minister, Brundtland earned a degree in medicine from Oslo University (1963) and a master's degree in public health from Harvard University (1965). While serving as a public health service medical officer she joined the Norwegian Labor Party (DNA), served as minister of the environment (1974–79), and was elected to parliament (1977). As Norway's first woman prime minister (1981; 1986–89; 1990–96) she promoted equal rights for women and appointed many women to her cabinet and other key government positions. She was best known as a forceful advocate of environmental issues. She chaired the United Nation's World Commission on Environment and Development (1983–92), whose report *Our Common Future* (1987), commonly known as the Brundtland Report, warned of worldwide environmental disasters and the depletion of nonrenewable resources, and called for sustainable development and global solutions to problems of the environment. She later served as director general of the World Health Organization (1998–).

BRUNER, JEROME SEYMOUR (1915–), U.S. psychologist. After serving under Gen. Dwight D. Eisenhower during World War II as a specialist in psychological warfare, Bruner joined the faculty at Harvard (1945), where he distinguished himself as a cognitive psychologist. The founder and director (1961–72) of Harvard's Center for Cognitive Studies, he studied children as young as one year to understand such processes as learning, perception, memory, language acquisition, and problem solving. Bruner also investigated factors conducive to learning in an educational setting. He later taught at Oxford, the New School for Social Research, and New York University. His books included *The Process of Education* (1960), *On Knowing* (1962), *Processes of Cognitive Growth* (1968), *The Relevance of*

Education (1971), *Actual Minds, Possible Worlds* (1986), and *The Culture of Education* (1996). ▪ See his *In Search of Mind: Essays in Autobiography* (1983).

BRÜNING, HEINRICH (1885–1970), German political leader. Brüning, a conservative politician with a reputation for financial expertise, entered parliament as a member of the Catholic Center party (1924). He formed a government in the Depression year 1930 and became known as "the hunger chancellor" for his policies of tax increases, salary and welfare cuts, and high tariffs. Lacking the votes to implement fiscal measures, he governed by emergency decree until 1932, when he was forced to resign. His policies failed to solve Germany's economic problems and helped to discredit the parliamentary system. Brüning emigrated to the United States after the Nazis assumed power and taught political science at Harvard (1937–52). ▪ See study by William L. Patch, (1998).

BRUNNER, (HEINRICH) EMIL (1889–1966), Swiss Protestant theologian. A professor of theology in Zurich (1924–53), Brunner was a foremost thinker of the "theology of crisis" or "dialectical theology" school and shaper (with Karl Barth) of the revolution in Protestant theology after World War II. He opposed liberal theologies and sought to reaffirm the major themes of the Protestant Reformation through a theology of revelation that was relevant to the modern world. His many books, which were read throughout the world, included *The Mediator* (1928; Eng. trans. 1934), *The Divine Imperative* (1932; Eng. trans. 1937), *Man in Revolt* (1937; Eng. trans. 1939), *Christianity and Civilisation* (2 vols., 1948–49), and *Dogmatics* (3 vols., 1946–60; Eng. trans. 1950-61). ▪ See study by J. Edward Humphrey (1976).

BRYAN, WILLIAM JENNINGS (1860–1925), U.S. political leader. Bryan was elected to Congress as a Democrat from Nebraska (1890; 1892) as a proponent of free coinage of silver. "You shall not crucify mankind on a cross of gold," he declared in a speech that won him the 1896 Democratic nomination for the presidency at age 36. He lost that and subsequent presidential elections in 1900 and 1908 but remained in the public eye through magazine articles and stirring speeches on social reform and economic evils in which he emerged as a spokesman for western and southern farmers. Appointed secretary of state by Pres. Woodrow Wilson, Bryan resigned rather than compromise his commitment to neutrality as the United States prepared to enter World War I. A flamboyant fundamentalist, he became a millionaire promoting real estate during the Florida boom and died shortly after participating in the successful prosecution of John T. Scopes for teaching evolution to Tennessee schoolchildren. ▪ See his memoirs (1925); biographies by Paolo E. Coletta (3 vols., 1964–69) and Louis W. Koenig (1971); study by Kendrick A. Clements (1983); and Robert W. Cherny, *A Righteous Cause* (1985).

BRYANT, BEAR (Paul William Bryant; 1913–1983), U.S. football coach. Born into a poor Arkansas family, 6-foot, 4-inch Bryant played right end on the University of Alabama football team that won the 1935 Rose Bowl game. During a 38-year coaching career (1945–82) at Maryland, Kentucky, Texas A&M, and Alabama (1958–82), he developed such stars as John David Crow, Joe Namath, George Blanda, Ken Stabler, and Richard Todd, and more than 40 of his players became college coaches. Six of his teams at Alabama (1961; 1964–65; 1973; 1978–79) were rated number one in the nation in various press polls. During the 1981 season he surpassed Amos Alonso Stagg's 315 victories and retired after the 1982 season as the most successful coach in college football history with a record of 323 wins, 85 losses, and 17 ties. His record was surpassed when Grambling coach Eddie Robinson won his 324th game during the 1985 season. ▪ See his autobiography, *Bear* (1975; with John Underwood).

BUBER, MARTIN (1878–1965), Austrian-born Israeli theologian and scholar. Buber studied philosophy and the history of art at the universities of Vienna and Berlin (Ph.D. 1904). He became involved with the Zionist movement in 1898, pursuing its cultural and political goals. He edited (1901) the Zionist publication *Die Welt* and later founded and edited (1916) *Der Jude*, an influential journal of German-speaking Jews. Buber's interest in the Hasidic movement, which sought the divine in the realm of the everyday human community, influenced his "philosophy of dialogue." Buber translated original Hasidic literature and wrote *The Legend of the Baal-shem* (1908; Eng. trans. 1955) and *Tales of the Hasidim* (1927; Eng. trans., 2 vols., 1947–48). In *I and Thou* (1923; Eng. trans. 1937), Buber posited two approaches to reality: the "I-it" relationship focused on a functional and manipulative treatment of other persons and things; the more profound "I-thou" provides for greater interpersonal knowledge and responsibility. This work strongly affected psychology and education as well as ethics and theology, and particularly influenced Christian theologians. Buber left his chair at the University of Frankfurt (1933), emigrated to Palestine (1938), and taught at the Hebrew University in Jerusalem (1938–51). He urged mutual respect and understanding between Arabs and Jews and advocated the establishment of a binational state in Palestine. He also wrote *Paths in Utopia* (1946; Eng. trans. 1940), a study of Utopian socialist thought. ▪ See his *A Believing Humanism: My Testament, 1902–1965* (Eng. trans. 1967); Maurice Friedman, *Martin Buber's Life and Work: The Early Years, 1878–1923* (1982), *The Middle Years, 1923–1945* (1983), and *The Later Years, 1945–1965* (1984); and studies by Werner Manheim (1974), Aubrey Hodes (rev. ed. 1972), Donald J. Moore (1996), and Dan Avnon (1998).

BUBKA, SERGEI (1963–   ), Ukrainian pole vaulter. Bubka started vaulting as a preteen and was advised to give up the sport after twice breaking bones in his left foot when he was 17 and 18. However, he persevered, graduated from the Institute of Physical Culture in Kiev, and became the first to vault over six meters (1985) and the first over 20 feet (1991). He won the gold medal (competing for the Soviet Union) in the 1988 Olympics in Seoul, South Korea, and won an unprecedented six consecutive world championships (1983, 1987, 1991, 1993, 1995, 1997). Bubka set more world records, both indoor and outdoor, than any other vaulter (35 through 1999), and by the late 1990s was earning more than $1 million a year in fees, endorsements, and prize money.

BUCHAN, SIR JOHN, 1st BARON TWEEDSMUIR (1875–1940), Scottish novelist, historian, and statesman. A clergyman's son, Buchan was educated at Glasgow and Oxford. He adroitly combined careers in business, writing, and public service—he served in Parliament (1927–35) and eventually became governor-general of Canada and a peer (1935). Though he wrote many historical and biographical studies, he is best remembered for his novels of international intrigue and adventure. These thrillers, such as *Prester John* (1910), *The Thirty-Nine Steps* (1915), and *The Three Hostages* (1924), were briskly written stories with a vivid sense of place and excitement, but imbued with his conservative beliefs in imperialism and in the superiority of his class and race. ■ See his memoirs, *Pilgrim's Way* (1940), and biographies by Janet A. Smith (1966) and Andrew Lownie (1995).

BUCHANAN, JAMES MCGILL (1919–), U.S. economist. The grandson of a governor of Tennessee, Buchanan studied at the University of Chicago (Ph.D. 1948), where he was imbued with conservative free-market principles. A founder of "public choice theory," he applied economic principles, notably the logic of self-interest, to the analysis of political decision making and advocated limited government and a constitutional amendment that would require a balanced federal budget. He taught at several universities and established the Center for the Study of Public Choice (1969). His numerous books and articles influenced many social scientists and political leaders during the 1980s and 1990s and he was awarded the 1986 Nobel Prize in Economics. His books included *The Calculus of Consent* (with Gordon Tullock; 1962), *The Limits of Liberty* (1975), *Democracy in Deficit* (with W. R. Wagner; 1977), and *Ethics and Economic Progress* (1994).

BUCHMAN, FRANK NATHAN DANIEL (1878–1961), U.S. evangelist. Raised in a devout Lutheran household in Pennsylvania, Buchman was ordained as a Lutheran minister (1902) and later headed a home for orphaned boys. A revelation in a village parish in Britain resulted in his establishment of the First Century Christian Fellowship, a controversial revivalist movement also known as the "Oxford Group" and later named Moral Re-Armament (MRA) when he published a book by that name (1938). Buchman proposed a Christian revolution to establish "the dictatorship of God" and advocated absolute moral standards. Buchman supported appeasement policies during the 1930s and he praised Nazi dictator Adolf Hitler as the man who "built a front line of defense against the anti-Christ of Communism." With the onset of World War II his movement lost much of its influence. Buchman wrote many books, including *Remaking the World* (1949) and *The World Rebuilt* (1951). ■ See A. W. Eister, *Drawing Room Conversion* 1950); Theophil Spoerri, *Dynamic out of Silence* (Eng. trans. 1976); and biography by Garth Lean (1988).

BUCHWALD, ART (1925–), U.S. humorist Buchwald joined the marines at age 17 and after World War II used his GI bonus to go to Paris, where he became a stringer for *Variety* and a restaurant reviewer for the *New York Herald Tribune*. By 1949 he was writing three humorous columns weekly on the lighter side of Europe. After 14 years as an expatriate, Buchwald moved to Washington, D.C., and began satirizing U.S. politics in his widely syndicated column and on the celebrity lecture circuit. He wrote one novel and published several collections of his columns, such as *Son of the Great Society* (1966), *Getting High in Government Circles* (1971), *I Am Not a Crook* (1974), *The Buchwald Stops Here* (1978), *While Reagan Slept* (1983) and *You Can Fool All of the People All of the Time* (1985) commented on the Reagan era. He won a 1982 Pulitzer Prize for commentary. ■ See his memoirs *Leaving Home* (1993) and *I'll Always Have Paris* (1996).

BUCK, FRANK (1884–1950), U.S. wild-animal hunter and explorer. Probably the world's most famous animal collector, Buck led numerous expeditions (from 1911) to the jungles of South America, Malaya, India, Borneo, New Guinea, and Africa to capture wild animals for zoos and circuses. He described his experiences in lectures and magazine articles and wrote several books, including *Bring 'Em Back Alive* (1930), *Wild Cargo* (1931), and *Fang and Claw* (1935), which were made into popular motion pictures starring Buck. ■ See his autobiography, *All in a Lifetime* (1941).

BUCK, PEARL S. (Pearl Comfort Syndenstricker; 1892–1973), U.S. novelist. The daughter of missionary parents, Pearl Buck called herself a "mental bifocal": she spent most of her first 40 years in China and spoke Chinese before English. Author of more than 80 books, the first published at age 38, she believed that critics disdained her for her prolific output and commercial success. When she won the 1938 Nobel Prize in Literature, the choice was widely assailed. *The Good Earth* (1931; Pulitzer Prize) blended regional and universal elements of Chinese life; written in eight weeks, it remained on the best-seller list for 21 months. Her other novels of China included *Sons* (1932). *A House Divided* (1935), *Dragon Seed* (1942), and *Imperial Woman* (1956). She was the mother of a retarded daughter and nine adopted children. ■ See her autobiography, *My Several Worlds* (1954), biographies by Theodore F. Harris (2 vols., 1969–

71), Irvin Block (1973), Nora Stirling (1983), and Peter Conn (1996).

BUCKLER, ERNEST (1908–1984), Canadian novelist and short-story writer. Buckler attended a one-room schoolhouse in Nova Scotia, the province where, except for a five-year stint as actuary for a Toronto life-insurance firm, he spent his life farming and writing. In the novel *The Mountain and the Valley* (1952), his poetic prose gleaned universal elements from local Nova Scotian situations, using psychological symbolism to express the complexity and frustration of rural existence. The novel *The Cruelest Month* (1962) was followed by *Ox Bells and Fireflies* (1968), "a fictive memoir" and folksy account of his native village at the turn of the century. He also wrote *The Rebellion of Young David and Other Stories* (1975) and *Whirligig: Selected Prose and Verse* (1977). ▪ See Robert Chambers, *Sinclair Ross and Ernest Buckler* (1975), and study by Charles Bissell (1989).

BUCKLEY, WILLIAM FRANK, JR. (1925–), U.S. editor and author. The son of a wealthy oilman, Buckley attended schools in the United States, France, Britain, and Mexico before going to Yale (B.A. 1950). The leading campus conservative ideologue, he was a talented debater, orator, and polemicist: he edited the *Yale Daily News.* His early controversial books, *God and Man at Yale* (1951) and *McCarthy and His Enemies* (1954), attacked liberal education and defended Sen. Joseph McCarthy's anticommunist crusade, while *Up from Liberalism* (1959) was an indictment of American liberal ideology. He founded and edited the weekly conservative journal *National Review* (1955–90), wrote a syndicated newspaper column (from 1962), hosted the weekly television show "Firing Line (1966–99), and was regarded as the most articulate conservative intellectual in the United States. *Right Reason* (1985) and *Happy Days Were Here Again* (1993) were collections of Buckley's newspaper columns. He also wrote several spy novels, several books on sailing, a study of anti-Semitism (1992), and *The Redhunter* (1999), a novel based on the life of Sen. Joseph McCarthy. ▪ See his *Overdrive: A Personal Documentary* (1983) and *Nearer My God: An Autobiography of Faith* (1997), and the biography by John Judis (1988).

BUDENNY, SEMYON MIKHAILOVICH (1883–1973), Soviet marshal. Budenny was a Don cossack and a sergeant in the czar's army before joining (1919) the Communist party. He shaped the Red army that Leon Trotsky, as minister of war, had created, and he became a hero of the civil war (1918–20). Budenny was promoted (1935) to marshal and given a command (1940) on the Finnish front in World War II. After a stunning defeat near Kiev (1941) at the hands of Nazi troops, Budenny was removed from command. ▪ See his memoirs, *The Path of Valour* (Eng. trans. 1972).

BUDENZ, LOUIS FRANCIS (1891–1972), U.S. journalist. Budenz received a law degree from Indianapolis Law School (1912) and began work as a journalist for labor publications (1921–31). Through his activities as a union organizer (1927–34), he became a member of the U.S. Communist party, serving on its Central Committee and editing its newspaper, the *Daily Worker* (labor editor, 1935–37; managing editor, 1940–45). Inspired by Bishop Fulton J. Sheen, in 1945 he returned to his Catholic faith and abruptly broke with the party. Budenz became a key anticommunist witness, testifying in some 60 proceedings before congressional committees, courts, and loyalty review boards, and naming many persons—including prominent personalities—as communists or communist sympathizers. In almost every case, the accusation was denied and was not substantiated. Budenz was the star witness in Sen. Joseph McCarthy's 1950 congressional hearings. He taught economics at Notre Dame (1945) and Fordham (1945–56) universities and wrote several books, including *This Is My Story* (1947) and *The Techniques of Communism* (1954).

BUDGE, DON (John Donald Budge; 1915–2000), U.S. tennis player. Combining a powerful serve with a dangerous backhand, Budge dominated men's tennis in the late 1930s. He won the U.S. amateur singles title and all three championships at Wimbledon (singles, doubles, and mixed doubles) in 1937 and 1938. In 1937 he was the mainstay of the American Davis Cup team that won the trophy that year. In 1938, he became the first man to win the grand slam of tennis (Australian, French, British, and U.S. singles titles). In 1939 he turned professional and was U.S. professional singles and doubles champion several times. He wrote *Budge on Tennis* (1939) and his memoirs (1969).

BUERO VALLEJO, ANTONIO (1916–2000), Spanish playwright. A Loyalist during the Spanish civil war (1936–39) and a political prisoner in the 1940s, Buero Vallejo focused on problems of communication in plays of social protest. His first naturalistic play, *Story of a Staircase* (1949), which he later repudiated, was written in the spirit of the U.S. dramatist Eugene O'Neill. His best works included *In the Burning Darkness* (1950; Eng. trans. 1985), *The Dream Weaver* (1952; Eng. trans. 1967), *Madrugada* (1953), *Today Is a Holiday* (1956), and a historical drama series including *A Dreamer for the People* (1958; Eng. trans. 1944), and *The Concert at Saint Ovide* (1963; Eng. trans. 1967). Writing in Spain, he often escaped censorship by using mythological or historical themes. He formulated a theory of tragedy that argues that the function of Aristotelian catharsis is improvement rather than purgation of the audience. Several of the plays, including *The Sleep of Reason* (1970; Eng. trans. 1989) and *The Shot* (1979; Eng. trans. 1989) concerned the role of the intellectual in a repressive society. ▪ See study by Martha T. Halsey (1973).

BUISSON, FERDINAND ÉDOUARD (1841–1932), French educator and political leader. A political exile in Switzerland (1866–70), Buisson taught philosophy at

Neuchâtel and advocated a United States of Europe during the first Geneva Peace Conference (1867). He returned to France after Napoleon III was deposed. As director of elementary education (1879–96), he helped draft bills providing for a free, compulsory, and secular school system in France. In 1898 he helped found the League for the Rights of Man (president, 1913–26) and served as a Radical-Socialist member of the Chamber of Deputies (1902–14; 1919–24). An ardent advocate of peace and supporter of the League of Nations, he attempted to promote Franco-German reconciliation after World War I and shared the 1927 Nobel Peace Prize with Ludwig Quidde.

BUKHARIN, NIKOLAI IVANOVICH (1888–1938), Soviet political leader. Bukharin joined the Moscow bolshevik committee in 1908. He encountered (1912) Lenin in exile in Cracow and remained his close associate, establishing a reputation through the revolutionary period as a shrewd theoretician. A participant in the November revolution (1917), he was a member of the Communist party's Central Committee (1917–34) and the Politburo (1924–29), and he edited (1934–37) the newspaper *Izvestia.* At Lenin's death, Bukharin backed Joseph Stalin against his political adversary Leon Trotsky. He directed (1926–29) the Third International until he opposed Stalin's collectivization policy. He articulated his dissent in the party's Central Committee but failed to depose Stalin. Finally, Bukharin was convicted (1938) of treason in the last great Moscow show trial and executed. He was posthumously rehabilitated by the government of Mikhail Gorbachev (1988) and an autobiographical novel, *How It All Began,* written while Bukharin was in prison, was published in Moscow in 1994 (Eng. trans. 1998). ■ See biography by Stephen F. Cohen (1973); studies by Roy A. Medvedev (Eng. trans. 1980) and Michael Haynes (1985); the memoirs of his widow, Anna Larina, *This I Cannot Forget* (Eng. trans. 1993); and Donny Glukstein, *The Tragedy of Bukharin* (1994).

BULATOVIC, MIODRAG (1930–1991), Yugoslav novelist and short-story writer. Bulatovic's works reflected the destruction, chaos, and anarchy he lived through during World War II in his native Montenegro. He was the first Yugoslav writer to take a skeptical attitude toward the partisan resistance movement and the first to introduce the character type of the antihero. His powerful, grotesque, and pessimistic works, which included intense portrayals of Montenegrin life, concerned alienation and the futile human quest for happiness. Bulatovic's novels *The Red Cock Flies to Heaven* (1959; Eng. trans. 1962), *Hero on a Donkey* (1964; Eng. trans. 1966), and *The War Was Better* (1968–69; Eng. trans. 1972) and his play *Godot Has Come* (1965) earned him an international reputation.

BULGAKOV, MIKHAIL AFANASYEVICH (1891–1940), Soviet writer. Bulgakov gave up the practice of medicine after World War I and devoted himself to writing. His novel

The White Guard (1925; Eng. trans. 1971) and its dramatic version, *The Days of the Turbins* (1926; Eng. trans. 1934, 1972), presented sympathetic accounts of the antibolshevik White Guards and were both highly successful. His satiric and allegorical short stories of the 1920s were critical of the government and of the new Soviet society, and many of his plays were banned (and not published until the 1960s), although he continued to work with the Moscow Art Theater (to 1936) and the Bolshoi Opera (1936–38). After the posthumous publication of the novels *Black Snow* (1965; Eng. trans. 1967) and his finest work, *The Master and Margarita* (1966; Eng. trans. 1967), bulgakov was internationally recognized as one of the finest Russian prose masters of the century. English translations are in *Diaboliad and Other Stories* (1972) and *Early Plays* (1972). ■ See biography by Leslie Milne (1990); Lyubov Beloverskaya-Bulgakova, *My Life with Mikhail Bulgakov* (1983); studies by A. Colin Wright (1978), Ellendea Proffer (1980; 1984), and Nadine Natov (1985); and J.A.E. Curtis, *Manuscripts Don't Burn* (1991).

BULGANIN, NIKOLAI ALEKSANDROVICH (1895–1975), Soviet political leader. Bulganin served during World War I and joined the communists during the bolshevik revolution (1917). He was a secret police operative (1918–22) and later worked in industrial administration. As mayor (1931–37) of Moscow, Bulganin implemented large-scale city-planning projects. During World War II he helped organize the 1941 defense of Moscow, was given high military rank, and served in the wartime cabinet (1944–45). Later he became minister of defense (1947–49) and full member of the Politburo (1948). With party secretary Nikita Khrushchev's support, he replaced G. M. Malenkov as premier, serving from 1955 to 1958; in his position he accompanied Khrushchev on visits to many world capitals. Bulganin was ejected from office in 1958 for having joined an "antiparty faction" against Khrushchev.

BULLOCK, WYNN (Percy Wingfield Bullock; 1902–1975), U.S. photographer. Bullock left a singing career to undertake (1938) serious photography. Influenced by László Moholy-Nagy, he devised technical methods for undercutting the reality of his subject. He reversed himself in the late 1940s when he fell under the influence of Edward Weston, who stressed realism in photographic art. Bullock became committed to creating a natural surface in his photographs but also to communicating the psychological or emotional reality beneath that surface. He was best known for his enigmatic photos of trees, seascapes, and nudes in nature. Two of his photographs were included in the *Family of Man* collection (1955). ■ See *Wynn Bullock Photography* (1973).

BÜLOW, BERNHARD HEINRICH VON (1849–1929), German political leader. The son of an imperial secretary of state, Bülow entered Germany's foreign service in 1874 and served in all the major capitals of Europe. He became foreign minister in 1897 and then chancellor (1900–09). In pursuit of Germany's "place in the sun," Bülow expanded the fleet, acquired a few colonies, and promoted the Berlin-to-Baghdad railroad. He sought to avoid entangling alliances, such as the entente suggested by the British. His policies antagonized the British, French, and Russians and resulted in Germany's isolation on the eve of World War I. ■ See his *Memoirs* (Eng. trans., 4 vols., 1931–32).

BULTMANN, RUDOLF KARL (1884–1976), German Protestant theologian. The son of an Evangelical Lutheran pastor, Bultmann studied theology at the University of Tübingen and later taught at Marburg (1921–51). His biblical interpretations were heavily influenced by Martin Heidegger, whose philosophies Bultmann adapted to clarify such religious concepts as the life of faith, sin and guilt, and death and resurrection. Bultmann also did extensive work in the reinterpretation of the New Testament scriptures, demythologizing 1st-century beliefs and providing a more modern understanding of recorded events. During World War II, he was a prominent member of the Confessing Church, refusing to support Nazi dictator Adolf Hitler's Aryan policies. His books included *Theology of the New Testament* (2 vols.; Eng. trans. 1951–55) and *Jesus and the Word* (1926; Eng. trans. 1934). ■ See Walter Schmithals, *An Introduction to the Theology of Rudolf Bultmann* (Eng. trans. 1968); Norman Perrin, *The Promise of Bultmann* (1969); and study by Gareth Jones (1991).

BUNAU-VARILLA, PHILIPPE JEAN (1859–1940), French engineer. Chief engineer of the Panama Canal Co. when the French firm went bankrupt, Bunau-Varilla formed a new company (1894) and through complex diplomacy and intrigue finally convinced the U.S. government to build the canal (1902). When Colombia, of which Panama was then a part, refused to ratify the project, he fomented a revolution in Panama that resulted in Panamanian independence (1903). Bunau-Varilla was named Panamanian ambassador to the United States—which immediately recognized the new country—and he negotiated the Hay-Bunau-Varilla Treaty (1903) that gave the United States the right to construct and control the Panama Canal. ■ See biography by Gustave Anguizola (1980).

BUNCHE, RALPH JOHNSON (1904–1971), U.S. diplomat. The grandson of a slave, Bunche earned a Ph.D. from Harvard (1934) and taught political science at Howard University. He collaborated with Gunnar Myrdal (1938–40) on the pioneering study of race relations, *An American Dilemma* (1944), before going into diplomatic service. He became director of the trusteeship department of the United Nations in 1947 and served as an international troubleshooter, winning the Nobel Peace Prize in 1950 for mediating the Arab-Israeli armistice in 1948. As U.N. undersecretary for special political affairs (1955–67) and undersecretary-general (1967–71), Bunche also directed peacekeeping efforts in the Suez,

the (Belgian) Congo, and Cyprus. ■ See study by Peggy Mann (1975) and biography by Brian Urquhart (1993).

BUNDY, MCGEORGE (1919–1996), U.S. educator and public official. An army intelligence officer during World War II and Harvard government professor (1949–53) and dean—the youngest ever—(1953–61), Bundy was one of the "best and brightest" recruited by Pres. John F. Kennedy. As special assistant for national security affairs to Kennedy and to Pres. Lyndon Johnson (1961–66), he directed the National Security Council and played a major role in foreign-policy formation. He supported and helped develop strategy for the Bay of Pigs invasion (1961), the Cuban missile crisis (1962), the invasion of the Dominican Republic (1965), and the escalation of the Vietnam War. Upon his resignation from government he headed the Ford Foundation (1966–79) where he emphasized race relations and civil rights. He later taught history at New York University (1979–89). During the 1980s he opposed the nuclear-arms policies of Pres. Ronald Reagan. He wrote *Danger and Survival: Choices About the Bomb in the First Fifty Years* (1988). ■ See Kai Bird, *The Color of Truth* (1998).

BUNIN, IVAN ALEKSEYEVICH (1870–1953), Russian writer. Born into a poor gentry family, Bunin began publishing poetry in 1887 and by 1909 he had gained prominence as a short-story writer and translator. He appealed to a wide readership by adhering to the 19th-century Russian tradition of direct but expressive narration of life among peasants and landowners. He briefly turned to remote lands in such works as the title story in *The Gentleman from San Francisco* (1916; Eng. trans. 1922), but after emigrating (1919) to France, he wrote only about Russia. He became preoccupied with death in such works as *Mitya's Love* (1925; Eng. trans. 1926), the autobiographical *The Well of Days* (1927; Eng. trans. 1933), and *Lika* (1939). His selected lyrical poetry (1929) was viewed by some critics as the verse of a prose writer. Bunin's selection as the first Russian recipient of a Nobel Prize for Literature (1933) was widely assailed as a political maneuver: Bunin was a vocal adversary of the Soviet regime. He was an aloof observer who skillfully verbalized the images stored in his retentive visual memory. Some of his best love stories were collected in *Dark Avenues* (1943; Eng. trans. 1949), *Memories and Portraits* (1950; Eng. trans. 1951) contains reminiscences of Russian writers Chekhov, Gorky, Tolstoy, and others. ■ See studies by James B. Woodward (1980) and Julian W. Connolly (1982).

BUNSHAFT, GORDON (1909–1990), U.S. architect. A graduate of the Massachusetts Institute of Technology, Bunshaft joined the firm of Skidmore, Owings and Merrill as chief designer (1937) and became a partner in 1946. He was best known for the Lever House (New York City, 1952), a slender curtain-walled, glass-covered skyscraper that greatly influenced American architecture in the 1950s and 1960s.

Bunshaft's other well-known buildings included the Connecticut General Life Insurance Co. (Bloomfield), Yale University's Beinecke Rare Book and Manuscript Library (New Haven), and the Joseph H. Hirshhorn Museum and Sculpture Garden (Washington, D.C.). He won the prestigious Pritzker Prize (1988). ■ See study by Carol H. Krinsky (1988).

BUÑUEL, LUIS (1900–1983), Spanish film director. The son of a Spanish landowning family, Buñuel was a Madrid University student when he met artist Salvador Dalí. Later in Paris they collaborated on the surrealist films *Un chein Andalou* (1928) and *L'age d'or* (1930), after which Buñuel worked in obscurity in France, the United States, and Mexico for 20 years. In 1950 he directed *Los Olvidados,* a bitter story about children of poverty that restored him to international celebrity. Buñuel returned to Spain to direct *Viridiana* (1961), an iconoclastic treatment of Catholic social and sexual mores that was banned by Spanish dictator Francisco Franco's government. In France, he directed *Belle de Jour* (1966), a film about the double sex life of a young wife, and *The Discreet Charm of the Bourgeoisie* (1972), a gentle surrealist satire on bourgeois pretensions. He continued his social criticism in *Le Fantôme de la Liberté* (1974) and *That Obscure Object of Desire* (1977). ■ See his selected writings in *An Unspeakable Betrayal* (Eng. trans. 2000); memoirs, *My Last Sigh* (Eng. trans. 1983); biographies by Raymond Durgnat (Eng. trans. 1968), Francisco Aranda (Eng. trans. 1976), and John Baxter (1998); and study by Virginia Higginbotham (1979).

BURBIDGE, (ELEANOR) MARGARET (1922?–   ), British astronomer. Burbidge specialized in the study of quasars, radio galaxies, and stellar formations. Her work led to the first accurate estimates of galactic masses. She was the first woman to serve as director of the Royal Greenwich Observatory (1972–73; 1984–90) and directed the Center for Astrophysics and Space Sciences at the University of California in San Diego (1979–88). She also was president of the American Astronomical Society (1976–78) and president of the American Association for the Advancement of Science (1981). She wrote *Quasi-Stellar Objects* (1967) with her husband, Geoffrey Burbidge, the director of the Kitt Peak National Observatory in Arizona (1978–84), with whom she collaborated on many astronomical observations.

BURCHFIELD, CHARLES EPHRAIM (1893–1967), U.S. artist. Burchfield was born in Ohio and graduated from the Cleveland School of Art (1916). His early works were depressive fantasies with surrealistic elements, but during the 1920s and 1930s he documented small-town America and painted realistic watercolors of weathered buildings and lonely cityscapes. In the 1940s he began to invent his own imaginary landscapes and depicted the mystery of nature. ■ See studies by Matthew Baigell (1976) and John Bauer (1981).

BURGER, WARREN EARL (1907–1995), U.S. jurist. Born in Minnesota, Burger graduated from the University of Minnesota and the St. Paul College of Law. He practiced law in St. Paul and became active in Republican politics, throwing key Minnesota delegation votes to Dwight Eisenhower for president at the end of the first ballot at the 1952 national convention. He served as an assistant attorney general (1953–55) in the Eisenhower administration and was named to the U.S. Court of Appeals for the District of Columbia in 1955. For 14 years on that court he was an outspoken opponent of what he believed to be excessive judicial concern over the protection of the rights of defendants in criminal cases. In 1969, Pres. Richard Nixon named him the 15th chief justice of the United States. On the Supreme Court he fulfilled expectations that he would end the era of liberal activism on the court and would instead apply the conservative principle of strict construction of the Constitution. In 1972 he voted against the majority that found the death penalty unconstitutional as then administered. But in 1973, in *Roe v. Wade,* he supported a woman's right to an abortion in the first three months of pregnancy. In public addresses, Burger offered many criticisms of the judicial system and complained about the lack of competence of many lawyers. He retired in 1986. ■ See Herman Schwartz, *The Burger Years* (1987) and *The Ascent of Pragmatism* (1990).

BURGESS, ANTHONY (John Anthony Burgess Wilson; 1917–1993), British novelist. A teacher, Burgess was working in Malaya and Borneo (1954–59) when he was told he had only a year to live. In order to leave his family an estate, he started to write seriously. *The Long Day Wanes* (3 vols., 1956–59) reflected his Malayan experiences. Although the diagnosis proved to be wrong, Burgess continued to write seriocomic novels, essays, and literary studies. He also wrote television scripts and musical compositions. He was noted for his verbal brilliance and wordplay and for his versatility. He wrote comic novels like *Honey for the Bears* (1963) and *Enderby* (1968), spy thrillers like *Tremor of Intent* (1966), the anti-utopian fable *A Clockwork Orange* (1962; film, 1971), and the historical novel *Napoleon Symphony* (1974). His later works included *Earthly Powers* (1980); *The End of the World News* (1983); *The Kingdom of the Wicked* (1985); *Any Old Iron* (1989); *A Dead Man in Deptford* (1993); and *Byrne* (1997), a novel written in verse. ■ See his autobiographies, *Little Wilson and Big God* (1986) and *You've Had Your Time* (1991), and studies by A. A. DeVitis (1972), Geoffrey Aggeler (1979), and John J. Stinson (1991).

BURGESS, GUY (1911–1963), British intelligence officer and Soviet spy. The son of a Royal Navy officer, Burgess attended Cambridge (1930–35), where he met Kim Philby. Donald Maclean, and Anthony Blunt. Sharing anticapitalist and antifascist views, the four secretly joined a communist cell and became undercover agents for the Soviet Union. While working as a journalist for the British Broadcasting

Corporation (BBC; 1935–39; 1941–44), military intelligence (1939–41), and the foreign office (1944–51), he passed secret information to the Soviets. As second secretary of the British embassy in Washington, D.C. (1950–51), he worked and lived with Kim Philby, who was the embassy's first secretary. Maclean, also a diplomat with the foreign office, had served in the Washington embassy (1944–48) and headed the U.S. desk in the foreign office in London (1951). Learning that British agents had suspicions of their activities, Burgess and Maclean escaped to Moscow (1951), though they did not surface until 1956. Philby remained with British intelligence until 1963, when he defected to the Soviet Union. Blunt, who also passed secrets to the Soviets during World War II and had subsequently become a world-famous and knighted art historian, was publicly revealed as the "fourth man" in 1979. ■ See Andrew Boyle, *The Fourth Man* (1979); Douglas Sutherland, *The Great Betrayal* (1981); and Andrew Sinclair, *The Red and the Blue* (1986).

BURGESS, THORNTON WALDO (1874–1965), U.S. writer of children's books. While working as an associate editor of *Good Housekeeping* magazine (1904–11), Burgess wrote his first children's book, *Old Mother West Wind*, for his son. The book grew into an 8-volume series published between 1910 and 1918; at the same time, he worked on a 20-volume series called *Bedtime Story* (1913–19). Burgess is remembered for whimsical, orally edifying animal stories, many featuring his famous character, Peter Rabbit. He insisted upon scientific accuracy in all his nature and animal tales and encouraged children to protect nature and wildlife. In 1925 he founded the Radio Nature League, an organization that eventually signed up 300,000 young conservationists. His books sold more than 7 million copies and were translated into many languages. A syndicated newspaper columnist (1912–60), Burgess wrote the autobiographical *Now I Remember* (1961) and *The Animal World of Thornton Burgess* (1961).

BURKE, BILLIE (**Mary William Burke; 1886–1970**), U.S. actress. The toast of Broadway during the early years of the century, Burke appeared in dozens of comedies and revues. She was married to Florenz Ziegfeld from 1914 until his death in 1932 and starred in several of his productions. She was a star of the silent screen and in her later years appeared in dozens of Hollywood sound movies, often portraying a charming but scatterbrained matron. He best-known roles were in *The Wizard of Oz* (1939), *The Man Who Came to Dinner* (1942), *Father of the Bride* (1950), and the Topper series (1937–41). ■ See her autobiography, *With a Feather on My Nose* (1949; with Cameron Shipp).

BURKE, KENNETH (1897–1993), U.S. literary critic. Originally a poet and music critic, Burke turned to literature, which he considered "symbolic action," and integrated anthropological, sociological, and psychological insights into his complex analyses. Among his influential works were *Counter-Statement* (1931), *Attitudes Toward History* (2 vols., 1937), *The Philosophy of Literary Form* (1941), *A Grammar of Motives* (1945), and *Language as Symbolic Action* (1966). *The White Oxen* (1924) is a book of stories; his poetry appeared in *Book of Moments* (1955) and *Collected Poems* (1968). ■ See studies by William H. Rueckert (1963), Armin Frank (1969), Stephen Bygrave (1993), Robert Wess (1966); and Herbert Simms and Trevor Melia, *The Legacy of Kenneth Burke* (1989).

BURLEIGH, HARRY T. (**Henry Thacker Burleigh; 1866–1949**), U.S. singer, composer, and arranger. The grandson of a slave, Burleigh studied music at the National Conservatory of Music, New York City (1892–96), and was a soloist with several choirs in the city. During a long and successful concert career, he introduced Negro spirituals to the concert halls of the United States and Europe. He composed more than 250 art songs and choral and violin pieces, but he was best known for making concert arrangements, and thus preserving and introducing to the general public more than 100 spirituals, including "Deep River" (1916), "Swing Low, Sweet Chariot" (1917), "Nobody Knows de Trouble I've Seen" (1917), "Sometimes I Feel Like Motherless Child" (1918), "My Lord What a Morning" (1918), and "Joshua Fit de Battle of Jericho" (1935). Among his protégés were Roland Hayes, Paul Robeson, and Marian Anderson. ■ See Anne K. Simpson, *Hard Trials* (1990).

BURNET, SIR FRANK MACFARLANE (1899–1985), Australian virologist and immunologist. A staff member for four decades at Melbourne's Walter and Eliza Hall Institute for Medical Research, Burnet was responsible for many advances in medical science. He perfected the technique of cultivating viruses in living chick embryos, initiated the study of the multiplication of bacteriophages, discovered the existence of multiple strains of the poliomyelitis virus, and isolated the rickettsial organism that causes Q fever. His most important work dealt with the body's immunological tolerance. Burnet's theory (1949) that an embryo, treated with foreign cells, would not form antibodies against them but would become tolerant of them was proven experimentally by Peter Medawar (1953). This discovery of acquired immunological tolerance profoundly affected research involving organ transplantation, cancer, allergies, and radiation damage and earned for Burnet and Medawar the 1960 Nobel Prize in Physiology or Medicine. ■ See his autobiographies *Changing Patterns* (1968) and *Credo and Comment* (1979), and Christopher Sexton, *The Seeds of Time* (1991).

BURNETT, CAROL (1936–   ), U.S. actress and television performer. Burnett studied at the University of California at Los Angeles. Early in her career she introduced (1957) the song "I Made a Fool of Myself over John Foster Dulles" and starred (1959) in the New York stage production *Once upon a Mattress*. She appeared (1959–62) on "The Garry Moore TV Show" before taking off with "The Carol Burnett Show" (1967–78), the comedy-variety hour that held huge audiences in an era when "family entertainment" was a precarious undertaking. With her troupe of players—Harvey Korman, Vicki Lawrence, and Lyle Waggoner—she created a vaudeville-type format, mixing musical sequences with zany sketches. Her show, which also featured a question-and-answer session with the studio audience, won five Emmy Awards and numerous others prizes. Burnett also acted in serious roles in films and TV dramas. On Broadway she acted in *Plaza Suite* (1970), *I Do I Do* (1973), and *Moon Over Buffalo* (1995). In 1981, she won a libel suit against the tabloid *National Enquirer*. ■ See her memoir, *One More Time* (1986) and biography by George Carpozi, Jr. (1975).

BURNHAM, DANIEL HUDSON (1846–1912), U.S. architect and city planner. Burnham designed the earliest skyscrapers in the United States, in Chicago, while in partnership with John W. Root (1873–91). The classical revival buildings he helped design and coordinate as chief of construction of the World's Columbian Exposition (Chicago, 1893) influenced American architecture for more than 30 years. Subsequently he designed the Flatiron Building (New York, 1901), Union Station (Washington, D.C., 1909), and Selfridge's (London, 1909) and Filene's (Boston, 1912) department stores. His plan for the redevelopment of Washington, D.C. (1902), heralded the beginning of the American city-planning movement, and his innovative and visionary long-range plans for Chicago (1907–09), which provided for the development of lakefront parks, boulevards, industrial areas, and residential and public buildings, were utilized in the modernization of the city. ■ See study by Thomas S. Hines (1974).

BURNHAM, (LINDEN) FORBES (SAMPSON) (1923–1985), Guyanese political leader. Burnham earned a law degree at the University of London (1947) and was a cofounder (with Marxist Cheddi Jagan) of the People's Progressive party (1949). After breaking with Jagan (1955), Burnham was a founder of the more moderate People's National Congress (1957), and he came to power (1964) with the help of the British government and U.S. Central Intelligence Agency (CIA; 1964). He led Guyana to independence (1966), and then shifted to the Left (1970), declaring Guyana a "Cooperative Socialist Republic." The government nationalized most industries and foreign-owned mines and plantations and carried out a modest social reform program. He was accused by critics of election rigging (1968 and 1973) and of suppressing opposition. He was widely believed to have been responsible for the assassination of radical scholar and political leader Walter Rodney (1980). After a constitutional change in 1980, Burnham served as president (1980–85).

BURNS, ARTHUR FRANK (1904–1987), Austrian-born U.S. economist. Burns emigrated to the United States with his parents (1914), graduated from Columbia University (Ph.D. 1934), and taught economics at Rutgers (1927–44) and Columbia (1944–53; 1957–69) Universities. He was director of research (1945–53) and president (1957–67) of the National Bureau of Economic Research and wrote important historical and statistical studies of economic fluctuations, especially business cycles. He was chairman of the Council of Economic Advisers during Pres. Dwight Eisenhower's administration (1953–56), chairman of the Federal Reserve Board (1970–78), and U.S. ambassador to West Germany (1981–85). ■ See his *Reflections of an Economic Policy Maker* (1978) and Wyatt C. Wells, *Economist in an Uncertain World* (1994).

BURNS, GEORGE (Nathan Birnbaum; 1896–1996), U.S. comedian. Burns first performed as a singer—in the Peewee Quartet. As an adult he continued singing, now in saloons, and broke into vaudeville in the comedy team of Burns and Billy Lorraine. But only after pairing up with Gracie Allen, whom he married in 1926, did his long apprenticeship pay off. Together they played vaudeville in the 1920s, became fixtures on radio in the 1930s and 1940s, and moved into television in the 1950s. At first Burns made the jokes, but it soon became clear that his talents lay elsewhere: he played the straight man with faultless timing and a wry edge to his voice, ending every show with the prompting, "Say good night, Gracie." After Allen's death (1964) he retired; but in the late 1970s, nearly 80 years old, he launched a film career, winning (1976) an Academy Award for his performance as a retired vaudevillian in *The Sunshine Boys*. His subsequent films included *Oh, God!* (1977) and *Eighteen Again* (1988). ■ See his books, *I Love Her, That's Why!* (1955), *Living It Up* (1976), *The Third Time Around* (1980), and *How to Live to Be 100—or More* (1983); Cherly Blythe, *Say Goodnight, Gracie* (1986); and study by Martin Gottfried (1996).

BURROUGHS, EDGAR RICE (1875–1950), U.S. novelist. Burroughs became a multimillionaire when *Tarzan of the Apes* (1914) and its 22 sequels sold more than 30 million copies in 58 languages and dialects. His chest-thumping character, Tarzan—an English infant raised by apes in the African jungle—was also the hero of dozens of movies and a comic strip that was syndicated in 400 newspapers. Burroughs, who wrote other jungle and space thrillers as well, died on his ranch near Tarzana, the town in California named for his hero. ■ See biographies by Irwin Porges (1975) and John Taliaferro (1999).

BURROUGHS, WILLIAM SEWARD (1914–1997), U.S. novelist. A Harvard graduate (1936), Burroughs worked as a private detective, exterminator, and reporter before turning to fiction writing. With Allen Ginsberg and Jack Kerouac in New York City in the 1940s, he formed the nucleus of what was later termed the Beat Generation. He attacked social and aesthetic convention by recording the hallucinatory, nightmarish impressions he experienced as a heroin addict (1944–57) in *Junky: Confessions of an Unredeemed*

Drug Addict (1953; published under the pseudonym William Lee) and *Naked Lunch* (1959), *Queer*, a companion piece to *Junky* written in 1952, was published in 1985. His other controversial works, which dealt with homosexuality, incorporated elements of science fiction, and offered glimpses of underworld life, included *The Soft Machine* (1961), *Nova Express* (1964), and *Wild Boys* (1971), *Cities of the Red Night* (1981), *The Place of Dead Roads* (1983), and *The Westernlands* (1987) constituted a trilogy about the end of the world. ▪ See his *Letters to Allen Ginsberg, 1953–1957* (1982); Victor Bokris, *With William Burroughs: A Report from the Bunker* (1981); study by Jennie Skerl (1985); Ted Morgan, *Literary Outlaw* (1988); and Graham Caveney, *Gentleman Junkie* (1998).

BURROWS, ABE (Abram Borowitz; 1910–1985), U.S. librettist and director. Burrows was a successful radio gag writer, party entertainer, and nightclub performer in Hollywood (from 1939), and he collaborated with composer Frank Loesser on two comedy record albums. He wrote scripts for Paramount Pictures and had his own radio show (1947) before adapting (with Jo Swerling) several Damon Runyon stories into the hit Broadway show *Guys and Dolls* (1950). He subsequently wrote the books for Cole Porter's *Can-Can* (1953) and *Silk Stockings* (1955) and wrote and directed Frank Loesser's *How to Succeed in Business Without Really Trying* (Pulitzer Prize, 1962). His other shows included the nonmusicals *Cactus Flower* (1965) and *Forty Carats* (1968). ▪ See his autobiography *Honest, Abe: Is There Really No Business Like Show Business?* (1980).

BURT, SIR CYRIL LODOWIC (1883–1971), British psychologist. A pioneer of applied psychology, Burt developed mental and scholastic tests for schoolchildren, and ran the first child guidance clinic in Britain while he was chief psychologist for the London Country Council (1913–32). He was a professor of education (1924–31) and psychology (1931–50) at the University of London and wrote several important studies of youth and intelligence, including *The Young Delinquent* (1925), *Measurement of Mental Capacities* (1927), *The Backward Child* (1937), and *Factors of the Mind* (1940). He helped found (1947) and edited (1947–63) the *British Journal of Statistical Psychology*. A disciple of Francis Galton, he stressed the importance of individual differences in intelligence and character and emphasized the role of heredity in determining these differences. After his death it was proven (1976) that he had published false data and invented facts in attempting to demonstrate that intelligence is largely inherited, and his scientific credibility was thus undermined. ▪ See biography by L. S. Hearnshaw (1979); Robert B. Joynson, *The Burt Affair* (1989); and Ronald Fletcher, *Science, Ideology and the Media* (1991).

BURTON, RICHARD (Richard Jenkins; 1925–1984), British actor. One of 13 children of a Welsh coal miner, Burton won a scholarship to Oxford, dropped out to join the Royal Air Force, and eventually became an actor in the grand romantic style. An intense, lusty baritone, he moved from Shakespearean roles at the Old Vic to play the archetypal "angry young man" in the film *Look Back in Anger* (1959), and on to the Broadway lead in *Camelot* (1960). During his frenetically publicized years of marriage to American actress Elizabeth Taylor, whom he wooed while filming *Cleopatra* (1963), Burton costarred with his wife in several films, the most successful of which was *Who's Afraid of Virginia Woolf?* (1966). His other films included *Becket* (1964), *Anne of the Thousand Days* (1969), and *Equus* (1977). ▪ See biography by Hollis Alpert (1986) and Melvin Bragg (1989) and studies by John Cottrell and Fergus Cashin (1971) and Paul Ferris (1981).

BURTON, WILLIAM MERRIAM (1865–1954), U.S. chemist. Burton joined Standard Oil of Indiana in 1890, a year after receiving his Ph.D. from Johns Hopkins University. Known as the father of modern petroleum refining, he developed a thermal-cracking process for refining gasoline from crude oil (patented 1913) that utilized chemical rather than physical methods and doubled the yield of the gasoline. Burton served as president of Standard Oil of Indiana (1918–27).

BURY, JOHN BAGNELL (1861–1927), Irish historian. Bury, a professor at Trinity College, Dublin (1893–1902), and at Cambridge (1902–27), was a leading scholar of ancient Greek, Roman, and Byzantine civilizations and wrote several important political and intellectual histories, including *A History of the Later Roman Empire* (1889) and *A History of the Eastern Roman Empire* (1912). Bury expressed his concept of history as a rational struggle toward progress in *The History of Freedom of Thought* (1914) and *The Idea of Progress* (1920). ▪ See the memoir and bibliography by Norman H. Baynes (1929).

BUSH, GEORGE HERBERT WALKER (1924–), U.S. political leader. Bush grew up in Connecticut (his father, Prescott Bush, became a U.S. senator from that state), served in the navy in World War II, and graduated from Yale (1948). Moving to Texas, he made a fortune in the oil business and sought to establish a political base. Though he lost two races for the U.S. Senate, he served two terms (1967–71) in the U.S. House of Representatives. During the 1970s he was ambassador to the United Nations, chairman of the Republican National Committee, head of the U.S. liaison office in China, and director of the Central Intelligence Agency. Seeking the GOP presidential nomination in 1980, Bush was beaten by Ronald Reagan, but accepted Reagan's invitation to be his vice presidential candidate. They were elected, and were reelected in 1984. Bush, though not generally seen as the strong ideological conservative that Reagan was, became the president's most stalwart public defender. Behind the scenes, he was one of Reagan's most trusted advisers and undertook many diplomatic assignments for the president. As president (1989–93) he was praised for his restrained response to the fall of the Communist governments in Eastern Europe and the dissolution of the Soviet Union (1989–1991). He gained popularity for organizing the international military response that successfully drove Iraqi forces out of Kuwait during the Persian Gulf crisis (1990–91). However, he was criticized by the Republican right wing for raising taxes and for compromising with Democrats. His popularity waned during the 1991–92 economic decline and he was defeated for reelection by Bill Clinton (1992). He wrote *A World Transformed* (1998; with Brent Scowcroft). His son George W. Bush became president in 2000. ▪ See his letters and other writings in *All the Best, George Bush* (1999) and the biography by Herbert S. Parmet (1997).

BUSH, GEORGE WALKER (1946–), U.S. political leader. The son of U.S. president George Bush, George W. Bush was raised in the oil boomtown of Midland, Texas. After graduating from Yale (B.A. 1968) he served in the Texas Air National Guard (1968–73), received an M.B.A. from Harvard University (1975), and set up an independent oil and gas exploration company in Midland. A politically conservative Republican, he ran unsuccessfully for Congress in 1978. In 1986 he sold his struggling company to a larger firm and Bush then worked for his father's successful presidential campaign (1987–88). He subsequently became part-owner of the Texas Rangers baseball team (1989). Elected governor of Texas (1994; reelected 1998) he initiated stricter welfare rules, curbs on large jury awards in civil cases, tougher treatment for juvenile offenders, and increased local control over public schools. He became president (2000) by defeating Al Gore in one of the closest presidential elections in U.S. history. ▪ See Bill Montuglio, *First Son* (1999); Elizabeth Mitchell, *W: Revenge of the Bush Dynasty* (2000); and Molly Ivins, *Shrub* (2000).

BUSH, VANNEVAR (1890–1974), U.S. engineer and inventor. With doctoral degrees (1916) in engineering from both Harvard and the Massachusetts Institute of Technology (MIT), Bush conducted research in submarine detection during World War I. Joining the MIT faculty, he made important contributions to the first generation of computers; he collaborated on the invention of the differential analyzer, a forerunner of the modern analog computer. He also contributed to the development of the vacuum tube and the typewriter. During World War II, Bush headed the Office of Scientific Research and Development, mobilizing U.S. scientists behind the war effort. His proposal for a parallel peacetime agency led to the formation of the National Science Foundation. He held numerous posts in government agencies and scientific organizations, including the presidency of the Carnegie Institution (1938–55). Bush wrote several books, including *Science: The Endless Frontier* 1945), *Endless Horizons* (1946), and *Modern Arms and Free Men* (1948). ▪ See G. Pascal Zachary, *Endless Frontier* (1997).

BUSIA, KOFI ABREFA (1913–1978), Ghanian political leader. Member of a royal clan, Busia received undergraduate and advanced degrees from Oxford University, taught African studies at the University of the Gold Coast (1949–59), and served in the preindependence legislature (1951–57). He opposed Prime Minister Kwame Nkrumah's regime and organized an effective opposition party, the United party (1957). Fearing arrest, he sought voluntary exile in the Netherlands and Britain (1959–66) and wrote *Africa in Search of Democracy* (1967). After the overthrow of Nkrumah (1966), he returned to Ghana, organized the liberal democratic Progress party, and became prime minister (1969). Unable to solve the country's severe economic problems, he was toppled by the military in 1972 and spent his last years at Oxford.

BUSONI, FERRUCCIO BENVENUTO (1866–1924), Italian-born composer and pianist. Pupil of his (Italian) clarinettist father and (German) pianist mother, Busoni made his debut in Vienna at age 8 and from then on went frequently on concert tours of Europe. His compositions were influenced by Bach and Liszt and he was best known for his *Piano Concerto* (104), *Fantasia Contrapputistica* for piano (1910–12), *Indian Fantasy* (1913) for orchestra and piano, and various operas, including *Doktor Faust* (unfinished). He made notable transcriptions of Bach organ works and Liszt piano pieces, worked extensively as a conductor and teacher in Helsinki, Moscow, Boston, and Berlin, and wrote the prophetic *Sketch of a New Esthetic of Music* (1907; Eng. trans. 1911). ▪ See study by H. H. Stuckenschmidt (Eng. trans. 1970) and biography by Edward J. Dent (1974).

BUSSOTTI, SYLVANO (1931–), Italian composer. Bussotti moved in avant-garde artistic circles and became interested in applying the principles of abstract expressionism to music. He believed that the performer should be given a good deal of flexibility in determining the final outcome of the musical composition. He abandoned traditional notation, using instead a series of doodles, blots, or line drawings that the performer was required to duplicate in sound. His compositions, such as *Five Pieces for David Tudor* (1959) and *Frammento* (1959), also required the use of such unconventional techniques as hitting the piano strings with tennis balls. Bussotti's absurdist opera, *Passion According to Sade* (1969), employed multimedia techniques and relied heavily on spontaneity. His other works included the cantata *Memoria* (1962) and the *Rara Requiem* (1970) and the operas *Lorenzaccio* (1972), *Fedra* (1988), and *L'ispirazione* (1988). In addition, he directed and designed several of his own stage works *(Bussottioperaballet)* and was the artistic director of the Teatro la Fenice, Venice (from 1975).

BUTENANDT, ADOLF FRIEDRICH JOHANN (1903–1995), German biochemist. After studying with Adolf Windaus at the University of Göttingen (Ph.D. 1927), Butenandt isolated various sex hormones and ascertained their molecular structure. He researched the female hormones estrone (1929) and progesterone (1934) and the male sex hormone androsterone (1931). Because these substances occur naturally in minute quantities, Butenandt's work depended on the microanalytical methods devised by Fritz Pregl. Butenandt shared (with Leopold Ružička) the 1939 Nobel Prize in Chemistry. He also did notable genetic and pheromone research. He directed the Kaiser Wilhelm (later Max Planck) Institute of Biochemisty (1936–72) and was president of the Max Plack Society 1960–72).

BUTLER, NICHOLAS MURRAY (1862–1947), U.S. educator. During Butler's 44 years as president of Columbia University (1901–45), it became one of the world's greatest centers of learning and research. Prominent both nationally and internationally, Butler was an influential Republican who advised U.S. presidents as well as foreign governments. He helped found the Carnegie Endowment for International Peace, served as its president (1925–45), and shared the 1931 Nobel Peace Prize (with Jane Addams). ▪ See his autobiography, *Across the Busy Years* (2 vols., 1939–40).

BUTLER, RICHARD AUSTEN, BARON BUTLER OF SAFFRON WALDEN (1902–1982), British political leader. Many times a cabinet minister during 36 years in the House of Commons, "Rab" Butler never achieved his ambition of becoming prime minister of Britain. He was a Conservative who defended the 1938 Munich agreement with Nazi dictator Adolf Hitler and favored nonintervention in Spain's civil war, but he was also considered a liberal reformer for his support of Indian home rule and his sponsorship of the progressive 1944 education act. He retired from politics in 1965 with a life peerage and served as master of Trinity College, Cambridge (1965–78). ▪ See his memoirs, *The Art of the Possible* (1971); study by Francis Boyd (1956); Gerald Sparrow, *"R.A.B."* (1965); and Anthony Howard, *R.A.B.* (1987).

BUTLER, SMEDLEY DARLINGTON (1881–1940), U.S. military leader. Born into a distinguished Quaker family, Butler joined the marine corps during the Spanish-American War (1898) by lying about his age. Over the next three decades he became a legendary and heroic warrior, seeing action in the Philippines, China, Nicaragua, Mexico, and Haiti, winning two Congressional Medals of Honor (1914; 1915), and advancing through the ranks. However, his bluntness and indiscretion antagonized senior military and political officials and he retired (1931) after being passed over for the post of marine corps commandant, despite his position as senior major general. In retirement he became a vocal critic of American imperialism, claiming that, "I spent 33 years and 4 months in active service . . . most of my time being a high-class muscle man for Big Business, for Wall Street and the bankers. In short, I was a racketeer for capitalism." In 1934 he exposed a plot by Wall Street financiers to organize a fascist march on Washington and place him

in power. (Much of Butler's account was confirmed in a Congressional investigation.) He subsequently wrote a best-selling book, *War Is a Racket* (1935), and became a leader of the peace movement. ▪ See Hans Schmidt, *Maverick Marine* (1987), and Jules Archer, *The Plot To Seize the White House* (1973).

BUTOR, MICHEL (1926–), French novelist and critic. Butor was a philosopher and teacher who initially wrote poetry. He was associated with the development of the "new novel"—a narrative form that challenged social and cultural values by discarding such traditional elements of fiction as plot, character, point of view, and linear development. Critics regarded his novels *Passing Time* (1956; Eng. trans. 1960) and *A Change of Heart* (1957; Eng. trans. 1959) as among the more successful "new novels." After 1960, Butor ceased to call his works novels and diminished the convention of the narrator to the vanishing point. His narrative experiments challenged traditional notions about the role of both writer and reader. Often collaborating with artists in various disciplines, he wrote texts whose physical appearance was an integral part of the work, or which were meant to be performed. *Niagara* (1965; Eng. trans. 1969) was designed for radio broadcast. His wide-ranging literary criticism was collected in the four-volume work *Repertoire* (1960–64); *Inventory* (1968) assembled selected criticism in English. Butor, who taught at the University of Geneva (1975–91), also wrote *Portrait of the Artist as a Young Ape: A Caprice* (1967; Eng. trans. 1995) and *Letters From the Antipodes* (1978; Eng. trans. 1981) ▪ See study by Michael Spencer (1974) and D. McWilliams, *The Narratives of Michel Butor* (1968).

BUTTERFIELD, SIR HERBERT (1900–1979), British historian. In a long career at Cambridge (1933–68), Butterfield specialized in modern history and made important studies of ideas in history. In *The Whig Interpretation of History* (1931), he examined political bias in historiography. Other works included *The Statecraft of Machiavelli* (1940), *Origins of Modern Science* (1949; originally a BBC lecture series), *History and Human Relations* (1951), *Man on His Past* (1955), and *International Conflict in the Twentieth Century* (1960). ▪ See Alberto R. Coll, *The Wisdom of Statecraft* (1985).

BUTTON, DICK (Richard Totten Button; 1929–), U.S. figure skater. America's foremost figure skater, Button held the U.S. senior men's championship for seven consecutive years (1946–52) and the world's championship five consecutive years (1948–52). While a student at Harvard, he achieved the unprecedented feat of holding the Olympic, World, European, North American, and U.S. championships simultaneously (1948). He repeated as the Olympic gold medalist in 1952. A spectacular skater—he introduced into competition the jump with three midair revolutions—Button turned professional in 1952 and toured with the *Ice Ca-*

pades. ■ See his autobiography, *Dick Button on Skates* (1956).

BUTTS, ALFRED MOSHER (1899–), U.S. game inventor. Born into a game-loving family, Butts graduated from the University of Pennsylvania (B. Arch., 1924) and worked as a draftsman for a New York City architectural firm. Temporarily unemployed during the Depression, he began working on a crossword puzzle–style word game (1931) based on anagrams, which he first called Lexiko and then Criss-Cross Words. A revised version, with a board and wooden lettered tiles, was completed in 1938, but was rejected by all of the major game companies. Finally, in 1948, the game—now called Scrabble—was produced privately by Butts and his friend James Brunot. As sales gradually increased, the rights to Scrabble were sold to the Selchow and Righter game company and it became a national fad in the 1950s and remained a perennial best-seller.

BUZZATI, DINO (1906–1972), Italian novelist and artist. Buzzati's reputation rested both on his independent journalism and on his fiction, which utilized allegory and surrealism to depict the absurd nature of the human condition. Due to fascist censorship, he employed abstract settings and ambiguous symbolism in such novels as *The Tartar Steppe* (1940; Eng. trans. 1952), the story of a frontier garrison awaiting the chance to be heroic; the censorship indirectly contributed to the books' ironic power. The realistic novel *A Love Affair* (1963; Eng. trans. 1964) was Buzzati's response to critics who called on him to give up his symbolism, *Larger than Life* (1960; Eng. trans. 1962) is a science-fiction novel. Several of his best short stories appeared in *Catastrophe* (1958; Engl. trans. 1966) and *Restless Nights* (Eng. trans. 1983).

BYRD, HARRY FLOOD (1887–1966), U.S. political leader. Born to a prominent and politically active Virginia family, Byrd served as Virginia's Democratic governor (1926–30) and senator (1933–65). A staunch conservative—some called him a reactionary—he opposed the New Deal, Fair Deal, the growth of federal power, school desegregation, and social welfare legislation, and built a solid rural power base that made him one of America's most influential politicians. Known for frugality when it came to government spending, he was called the "watchdog of the Senate" during his tenure as chairman of the powerful Finance Committee (1955–65). ■ See biography by Ronald L. Heinemann (1996).

BYRD, RICHARD EVELYN (1888–1957), U.S. aviator and explorer. A trip around the world, alone at age 12, spurred Byrd's interest in exploration. He graduated from the U.S.

Naval Academy (1912) and entered the navy's aviation service. He piloted the first flights over the North (1926) and South (1929) Poles and gained international acclaim as well as promotion to the rank of commander. Byrd subsequently explored Antarctica, discovering new mountain ranges and mineral deposits, mapping miles of coastline, and obtaining vital scientific data. One five-month unescorted mission (1934) nearly proved fatal, as he recounted in *Alone* (1938). He was selected (1939, 1947, 1955) by the U.S. government to command the Antarctic exploration program. Byrd also made major contributions to transatlantic flying and aviation safety. ■ See his books *Little America* (1930) and *Discovery* (1935); his diary and notebooks (1925–27) in *To the Pole* (1998); Eugene Rodgers, *Beyond the Barrier* (1990); and Edwin P. Hoyt, *The Last Explorer* (1968).

BYRNE, JANE (Jane Margaret Burke; 1934–), U.S. political leader. The daughter of a Chicago steel company executive, Byrne attended Catholic schools through college (Barat College of the Sacred Heart; B.A. 1955) and gained her first experience in politics as an organizer for John F. Kennedy during the 1960 presidential campaign. She subsequently was a protégé of Chicago's Mayor Richard J. Daley and served as his commissioner of consumer sales, weights, and measures (1968–77), and as cochair of the Cook County Democratic Committee (1975–76) and was regarded as a reformer within the powerful Democratic machine. After Daley's death (December 1976), she feuded with his handpicked successor, Michael Bilandic, and defeated him in the February 1979 primary. She was elected in a landslide and served as Chicago's first woman mayor (1979–83). ■ See Bill and Lori Granger, *Fighting Jane* (1980).

BYRNES, JAMES FRANCIS (1879–1972), U.S. public official. A South Carolina Democrat, Byrnes served in the U.S. House of Representatives (1911–25) and the U.S. Senate (1931–41) before being rewarded for his support for New Deal legislation and loyalty to Pres. Franklin D. Roosevelt with an appointment to the Supreme Court (1941). He resigned (1942) at Roosevelt's request to become director of the Office of Economic Stabilization and the Office of War Mobilization (1943–45), where he wielded great power over the economy and was known as "the assistant president for domestic affairs." During the early years of the cold war (1945–47) he served as Pres. Harry Truman's secretary of state and pursued tough anti-Soviet policies. After resigning from the cabinet, he denounced Truman's Fair Deal as socialistic, served as governor of South Carolina (1951–55), and supported racial segregation in the schools. ■ See his autobiography, *All in One Lifetime* (1958), and David Robertson, *Sly and Able* (1994).

C

CABELL, JAMES BRANCH (1879–1958), U.S. novelist and essayist. Born into a distinguished Virginia family, Cabell was influenced in his youth by the myths connected with the old Confederacy. He worked as a genealogist before publishing his first novel (1904). His novel *Jurgen* (1919), part of an 18-volume series (*Biography of the Life of Manuel;* 1917–29), reflected his skeptical views and attacked American pieties. Filled with sexual allusions, the book was banned in New York (1920) for being obscene, and Cabell was hailed by the youth of the day as a spokesman for the new morality. He produced more than 50 volumes, including novels, essays, and poetry, but his popularity plummeted in the 1930s. Cabell was closely associated with H. L. Mencken and the "smart set" and was an editor of *American Spectator* (1932–35). He published his recollections in *These Restless Heads* (1932), *Quiet Please* (1952), and *As I Remember It* (1955). ▪ See studies by Frances Joan Brewer (2 vols., 1957), Joe L. Davis (1962), and Desmond Tarrant (1967); and the biography by Edgar MacDonald (1993).

CABOT, RICHARD CLARKE (1868–1939), U.S. physician and educator. Cabot's discovery early in his medical career that certain illnesses increase the white-blood-cell count established an important diagnostic aid. Later, as professor at the Harvard Medical School (1899–1933) and chief of staff at Massachusetts General Hospital (1912–21), he introduced the case-history approach to medical education, which developed into the clinical pathological conference, a standard teaching method. He also wrote a landmark article on heart disease (1914). Cabot is best known, however, as the innovator of medical social work, as he was the first to organize a team of social workers to observe outpatients at home. His many books include *Social Service and the Art of Healing* (1909) and *What Men Live By* (1914). ▪ See Ida M. Cannon, *On the Social Frontier of Medicine* (1952).

CABRAL, AMILCAR (1926–1973), Portuguese Guinean nationalist. Born in the Cape Verde Islands, Cabral studied agronomy at Lisbon University and returned to Portuguese Guinea in 1952 a colonial civil servant. Becoming increasingly anticolonial, he resigned in 1954 and moved to Angola, where, in 1956, he helped found the Popular Movement for the Liberation of Angola (MPLA), the first important nationalist organization in that colony. After returning to Portuguese Guinea, Cabral formed a similar independence group, the African Party for the Independence of Guinea and Cape Verde (PAIGC), which, in 1963, began guerrilla operations within the colony. A scholarly Marxist and author of several books and articles, he stressed the importance of mass political education and participation in the revolution. He was assassinated in Conakry, Guinea, 20 months before Portuguese Guinea became the independent republic of Guinea-Bissau. His writings, in English translation, included *Revolution in Guinea* (1970), *Return to the Source* (1974), and *Unity and Struggle* (1979). ▪ See study by Patrick Chabal (1983); Jock McCulloch, *In the Twilight of Revolution* (1983); and Mustapha Dhada, *Warriors at Work* (1993).

CABRERA INFANTE, GUILLERMO (1929–), Cuban novelist. Cabrera Infante, whose parents were founders of the Cuban Communist party, wrote about Cuba under the rule of Fulgencio Batista (1952–58). *Writes of Passage* (1960; Eng. trans. 1993), a short-story cycle linked by vivid sketches of repressive measures taken against Batista's opponents, influenced younger writers. After working for the revolutionary Castro government, he became disillusioned with its policies and left Cuba (1965) to live in Britain. He wrote the linguistically inventive erotic novel *Three Trapped Tigers* (1967; Eng. trans. 1971) about Havana's prerevolutionary night life; *View of Dawn in the Tropics* (1974; Eng. trans. 1978), a series of vignettes relating to Cuban history and culture; *Infante's Inferno* (1979; Eng. trans. 1984), a witty fictional autobiography that describes the narrator's youthful sexual adventures in Havana during the 1940s; and *Holy Smoke* (Eng. trans. 1985), a whimsical history of the cigar. *Mea Cuba* (1992; Eng. trans. 1994) is a collection of writings on Cuba. ▪ See Study by Raymond D. Souza (1996).

CAESAR, SID (1922–), U.S. comedian. Sid Caesar studied the saxophone and played in small bands before World War II. After scoring a Broadway success and launching a promising film career, he began creating the sophisticated, zany sketches and pantomimes featured on "Your Show of Shows" (1949–54), the 90-minute television revue broadcast Saturday nights live from New York. Appearing solo, in tandem with Imogene Coca, and with supporting players Carl Reiner and Howard Morris, Caesar mocked pretension and parodied pop culture—especially movies. They created their own versions of *A Streetcar Named Desire, High Noon,* and other films; in his retake of foreign films he hilariously mimicked languages of which he knew not a word. Caesar's popularity waned when the Caesar-Coca team split up and when television audiences—broader in the mid-1950s—turned to the less sophisticated humor of Milton Berle and others. The movie *Ten from Your Show of Shows*

(1973) highlighted his most inspired sketches. ■ See his autobiography, *Where Have I Been* (1982).

CAGE, JOHN (1912–1992), U.S. composer. Cage studied under the Austrian composer Arnold Schoenberg. Abandoning 12-tone composition in the 1940s, he established rhythm and percussive textures as his prime concerns and experimented with the unpredictable, accidental sounds of music. His neodadaist compositions, which often incorporated bizarre visual effects, featured the sounds of radios, animals, static, shuffled cards, moving bicycles, or cascading water. *Speech* (1955) was written for newsreader and five radios played simultaneously. The first major figure of modern, experimental music, Cage emphasized the elaboration of an idea or way of thinking rather than the actual production of sounds by musicians. He pioneered in the musical genre of silence, believing that anything that transpires during a fixed time period can be called music. His controversial compositions included *Sonatas and Interludes* (1946–48), a series of *Imaginary Landscapes* (1942–51), *Water Music* (1952), *Variations V* (1965), *Études Australes* (1974–75) and *Europeras 1–4* (1987–89). Cage often collaborated with choreographer Merce Cunningham. His writings are collected in *Silence* (1961), *A Year from Monday* (1967), *M* (1973), and *Empty Words* (1979). ■ See study edited by Richard Kostelanetz (1970); interviews in Cage's *For the Birds* (1981); and David Revill, *The Roaring Silence* (1992).

CAGNEY, JAMES (1899–1986), U.S. film actor. After an early career as a vaudeville dancer, Cagney made his first film in 1930. He became one of the great Hollywood stars, since the lively combination of charm, cockiness, and suppressed anger and violence that he projected touched a responsive chord in the American public. In his classic gangster pictures like *The Public Enemy* (1931) and *The Roaring Twenties* (1939), he made crime, if not respectable, at least interesting and understandable as a way to success in Depression-era America. Until his retirement in 1961 he played both heroes and villains with a punchy intensity; he won critical praise as a strangely stiff-backed, loose-limbed dancer and singer in the musical biography of George M. Cohan, *Yankee Doodle Dandy* (Academy Award, 1942). He reemerged (1981) in a memorable supporting role in *Ragtime*. ■ See his autobiography, *Cagney by Cagney* (1976), and the biography by John McCabe (1997).

CAHAN, ABRAHAM (1860–1951), Russian-born U.S. newspaper editor and author. Cahan cofounded (1897) the *Jewish Daily Forward*, the most important Yiddish-language newspaper in the United States, and edited it for nearly 50 years. Infused with Cahan's socialist ideals, the paper was the major political, educational, and cultural medium and the foremost socializing agent for hundreds of thousands of newly arrived Jewish immigrants in New York City. Cahan also wrote several novels, including *The Rise of David Levinsky* (1917), a classic account of the Jewish immigrant experience. ■ See *The Education of Abraham Cahan* (Eng. trans. 1969), composed of excerpts from his five-volume Yiddish-language autobiography published between 1916 and 1936; Moses Rischin, ed., *Grandma Never Lived in America: The New Journalism of Abraham Cahan* (1985); and the study by Sanford E. Marovitz (1996).

CAHN, SAMMY (**Samuel Cohen;** 1913–1993), U.S. lyricist. Cahn grew up on New York City's Lower East Side, played the violin in variety shows, and became one of Hollywood's most facile songwriters. Collaborating with several different composers, including Jule Styne and Jimmy Van Heusen, he wrote the lyrics for the song hits "High Hopes," "I'll Walk Alone," "Love and Marriage," "It's Been a Long, Long Time," "All the Way," "Call Me Irresponsible," "Only the Lonely," and "Let It Snow." Many of his songs were recorded by Frank Sinatra. His best-known Broadway musical was *High Button Shoes* (1947). ■ See his autobiography, *I Should Care* (1974).

CAILLAUX, JOSEPH MARIE AUGUSTE (1863–1944), French political leader. A pacifist and fiscal expert, Caillaux was a controversial figure in French politics for more than 40 years and served five times as finance minister. Named premier in 1911, he was forced to resign the following year after concessions made to Germany in central Africa during the Agadir crisis provoked the hostility of the right. A "European" rather than a nationalist at heart, he opposed expenditures for war preparations (1912–13). After the outbreak of World War I, his continued opposition to it, his advocacy of a negotiated peace, and his friendship with German agents led to his imprisonment (1918–20) for "damage to . . . the state" by "communication's with the enemy." As chairman of the senate finance committee (1925–40) he was instrumental in the downfall of Léon Blum's popular-front government (1937). ■ See Rudolph Binion, *Defeated Leaders* (1960).

CAI YUANPEI (old style: TS'AI YUAN-P'EI; 1867–1940), Chinese educator. Born into a wealthy merchant family, Cai was a brilliant student who in 1890 became one of the youngest degree holders in the history of the imperial civil service. Believing that education was the key to strengthening and modernizing China, Cai devoted his life to educational improvement. He served as minister of education (1912–13) and chancellor of Beijing (Peking) University (1916–26) and was the founder and first president of the Academia Sinica (1928–35), China's most important research institute. A political liberal and independent scholar who synthesized Chinese and Western ideas, Cai was the foremost educator of republican China. ■ See study by William J. Duiker (1977).

CALDER, ALEXANDER (1898–1976), U.S. sculptor. In Philadelphia, the three generations of Calders who contributed civic statuary were known as the father, the son, and the unholy ghost. A mechanical engineer, Calder began achieving fame in the 1920s and 1930s for his wire and wood sculptures and the brightly colored wind-propelled discs that came to be called "mobiles." (Stationary versions were called "stabiles.") His reputation was sufficiently established by 1943 to justify a retrospective exhibition at New York City's Museum of Modern Art. Calder's mobiles and stabiles, including huge versions designed to adorn New York's Lincoln Center, the United Nations Educational, Scientific, and Cultural Organization Building in Paris, and Expo 67 in Montreal, became the preeminent art form of the urban industrial world. ■ See his autobiography (1966), the biography by H. H. Arnason (1966), and Margaret Calder Hayes, *Three Alexander Calders* (1978).

CALDICOTT, HELEN (Helen Broinowski; 1938–), Australian-born pediatrician, writer, and political activist. Caldicott first became concerned about the dangers of nuclear holocaust when she read Nevil Shute's 1957 novel *On the Beach.* In the 1960s, she completed her studies at the University of Adelaide Medical School, established a general medical practice, and worked under a fellowship at Harvard Medical School (1966–69). From 1972, she specialized in pediatrics, focusing on cystic fibrosis. Convinced that radioactive contaminants promote disease, Caldicott spearheaded a successful campaign in the early 1970s to ban French atmospheric nuclear testing in the South Pacific and to end Australia's exportation of uranium. She emigrated to the United States in 1977 to work at Harvard Medical School and Boston Children's Hospital Medical Center, and the following year revived Physicians for Social Responsibility (est. 1962). From 1980 she devoted her full-time efforts to antinuclear work, calling it essential preventive medicine. Caldicott opposed nuclear power as well as nuclear weaponry, a controversial stance that caused her resignation as president of Physicians for Social Responsibility in 1983. She also founded Women's Action for Nuclear Disarmament, a Washington-based lobbying group, and wrote *Nuclear Madness: What You Can Do* (1978) and *Missile Envy* (1984). ■ See her autobiography, *A Desperate Passion* (1996).

CALDWELL, ERSKINE (1903–1987), U.S. novelist and short-story writer. Having lived in every southern state, Caldwell reproduced country dialect faithfully in his realistic and earthy novels, which gained an enormous following all over the world. *Tobacco Road* (1932) was adapted for the stage and ran over seven years on Broadway; its title became synonymous with the poverty and degradation of the South's poor whites. His other books included *God's Little Acre* (1933), *Georgia Boy* (1943), and *Close to Home* (1962). His *Complete Short Stories* appeared in 1953. He collaborated with photographer Margaret Bourke-White, his future wife, on *You Have Seen Their Faces* (1937), a volume documenting the poverty of southern sharecroppers. ■ See his memoirs, *Call It Experience* (1951) and *Deep South*

(1968), and autobiography *With All My Might* (1987), and biographies by Harvey L. Klevar (1993) and Dan B. Miller (1995).

CALDWELL, SARAH (1924–), U.S. opera director and conductor. Caldwell's first operatic production, Vaughan Williams' *Riders to the Sea,* was staged in 1948 at the Berkshire Music Center, Tanglewood, whose faculty she joined shortly thereafter. In 1952 she was appointed head of Boston University's Opera Workshop. Five years later (1957) she founded the Opera Company of Boston and within a decade gained an international reputation for her highly dramatic, innovative productions of little-known or seldom-performed works—Offenbach's *Voyage to the Moon,* Berlioz's *Les Troyens,* Schoenberg's *Mathis der Maler*—and for her unusually perceptive character interpretation's. Caldwell conducted opera and symphony orchestras throughout the United States and became, in 1976, the first woman to conduct at the Metropolitan Opera in New York, directing eight performances of *La Traviata.*

CALDWELL, TAYLOR (Janet Taylor Caldwell; 1900–1985), British-born U.S. writer. Caldwell began writing as a child, winning a medal for an essay on Charles Dickens at age 6. Her family emigrated to the U.S., settling in Buffalo, New York; she graduated from the University of Buffalo (1931). Her first published novel, *Dynasty of Death* (1938), was a best-seller, and she continued to turn out, in rapid succession, long and suspenseful romantic melodramas, some under the pen names Max Reiner and Marcus Holland. She often treated New Testament and historical themes, as in the immensely popular *This Side of Innocence* (1946) and *Dear and Glorious Physician* (1959). Her *Captains and the Kings* (1972) became a television miniseries. At age 80, she published *Answer as a Man* (1981), her 35th novel and another best-seller. Many of her novels reflected her ultraconservative political beliefs. A bird-watcher, Caldwell was also interested in extrasensory perception: once, in a trance, she recalled 37 former lives.

CĂLINESCU, GEORGE (1899–1965), Rumanian novelist, poet, and literary historian. One of Rumania's most prominent literary personalities, Călinescu started his career by writing literary and cultural reviews. His sophisticated and ironic novels, studies of the private and social relations of exceptional individuals, included *The Wedding Book* (1933), *Otilia's Enigma* (1938), *Poor Ioanide* (1954), and *The Black Chest* (1960). Călinescu also wrote biographies of the writers Mihai Eminescu (1932) and Ion Creangă (1938), a highly acclaimed history of Rumanian literature (1941), and *Studies in Poetics* (Eng. trans. 1972).

CALKINS, RICHARD. *See NOWLAN, PHILIP.*

CALLAGHAN, MORLEY (1903–1990), Canadian novelist and short-story writer. A fellow *Toronto Star* reporter, the

American writer Ernest Hemingway encouraged Callaghan to publish his fiction. In 1928, the year he was admitted to the bar, he published the novel *Strange Fugitive*. He developed an economical, deliberately casual style for his short-story collection *A Native Argosy* (1929). Callaghan went to France (1929), as he later recalled in *That Summer In Paris: Memories of Tangled Friendships with Hemingway, Fitzgerald and Some Others* (1963). He invested his fiction with the conviction that Christian love will right social inequities, and he advocated a liberalized form of Christianity in novels including *Such Is My Beloved* (1934), *They Shall Inherit the Earth* (1935), *A Passion in Rome* (1961), and *The Many Colored Coat* (1963). His later novels included *Close to the Sun Again* (1977), *A Time for Judas* (1984), and *Our Lady of the Snows* (1986). *Morley Callaghan's Stories* appeared in 1959. ■ See studies by Brandon Conron (1966) and Victor Hoar (1969).

CALLAGHAN OF CARDIFF, (LEONARD) JAMES CALLAGHAN, BARON (1912–   ), British political leader. Too poor to attend college, Callaghan served as a government tax officer (1929–36) before taking a full-time trade-union post. A member of the Labour party (from 1931), he rose through the ranks of the Trade Union Congress and was elected to Parliament in 1945. He gained a reputation as a right-winger within the party and served as chancellor of the Exchequer (1964–67), home secretary (1967–70), and foreign secretary (1974–76). When Prime Minister Harold Wilson retired (1976), Callaghan replaced him, serving as prime minister until he was brought down by a vote of no confidence (1979). He retired as leader of the Labour party in 1980. ■ See his autobiography, *Time and Chance* (1987), and the biography by Kenneth O. Morgan (1997).

CALLAS, MARIA (Maria Anna Sophia Cecilia Kalogeropoulos; 1923–1977), U.S. opera singer. The most exciting operatic personality of the post–World War II era. Callas was regarded as one of the greatest dramatic sopranos ever. From her debut in 1947 until her retirement in the mid-1960s, she won acclaim throughout the world for her intense portrayals of dozens of roles in both the dramatic and lyric repertory and for single-handedly reviving the bel canto operas of Bellini, Donizetti, and Rossini, which were largely forgotten for decades and were considered too difficult to sing. A controversial prima donna both on and off stage, Callas was frequently involved in artistic and legal feuds with major opera companies that merely heightened her appeal to an adoring public. She was also acclaimed for her acting in the title role of Pier Paolo Pasolini's film *Medea* (1970). ■ See biographies by Arianna Stassinapoulos (1981), John Ardoin (rev. ed. 1982), Michael Scott (1992), and G. B. Meneghini, *My Wife Maria Callas* (1982).

CALLES, PLUTARCO ELÍAS (1877–1945), Mexican political leader. A radical in his early years, Calles joined the rev-

olution in 1910, modernized the revolutionary armies, and served as governor of Sonora (1915–19) and secretary of the interior (1920–24). His presidency (1924–28) was marked by radical agrarian reforms, educational expansion, anticlericalism, and disputes with the United States. After 1928, however, he became a landowner and financier and grew increasingly conservative. He organized the National Revolutionary party (1929) and molded it into Mexico's dominant political force. As the leader of a clique of financiers and industrialists who controlled Mexico's economy and politics, he systematically dismantled the revolutionary programs he had previously sponsored. He was forced into exile (1936–41) by his former radical protégé, President Lázaro Cárdenas.

CALLEY, WILLIAM LAWS, JR., (1943–   ), U.S. war criminal. Calley was an officer candidate from Florida who was commissioned a lieutenant during the manpower shortage of the Vietnam War. In 1971, a military jury convicted him of the premeditated murder of 22 unarmed Vietnamese civilians in the 1968 My Lai massacre, despite Calley's testimony that he had acted under orders from Capt. Ernest Medina. (Medina was acquitted in later proceedings.) Calley's life sentence was reduced on appeal to 20 years' imprisonment. Pres. Richard Nixon ordered that he be moved from the stockade at Fort Benning, Georgia, and placed under house arrest. He was released after 40 months. In the 1980s, he was sales manager in his father-in-law's jewelry store. ■ See *Lieutenant Calley: His Own Story* (1971; with John Sack).

CALLOWAY, CAB (1907–1994), U.S. singer and bandleader. Calloway arrived in Chicago in the early 1920s and began to make his way into the jazz world, first as a drummer, then as a bandleader and vocalist of the "Alabamians." He moved to New York's Savoy Ballroom (1929) and then, with his own band, to the Cotton Club. Known as the "King of Hi De Ho," Calloway was famous for his style of singing (he helped to develop the scat style) and for his spirited delivery. His best-known songs were "Minnie the Moocher" and "St. James Infirmary Blues." He appeared in several films, including *The Singing Kid* (1936); *Stormy Weather* (1943), for which he received an award from the Negro Actors' Guild; *Porgy and Bess* (1959); and *The Blues Brothers* (1980). He starred in an all-black Broadway production of *Hello Dolly* (1967). Calloway compiled the *Hepster's Dictionary* (1938), called the "official jive-language reference book," and coined the term "jitterbug." ■ See his autobiography *Of Minnie the Moocher and Me* (1976).

CALMETTE, ALBERT LEON CHARLES (1863–1933), French bacteriologist. A disciple of Louis Pasteur, Calmette founded the Pasteur Institute in Saigon (1891) and the Pasteur Institute in Lille (1894), which he headed from 1896 to 1919. He is famous for his discovery (with Camille Guérin) of the tuberculosis vaccine Bacillus Calmette-Guérin, known as BCG. Although used widely throughout the world after 1921, it was not adopted in the United States until 1940 or in Britain until 1956, long after Calmette's death.

CALVIN, MELVIN (1911–1997), U.S. chemist. The son of Russian immigrants, Calvin studied at the University of Minnesota (Ph.D. 1935) and taught at the University of California at Berkeley (1937–80), where he headed the Lawrence Radiation Laboratory (1963–80). He was best known for his analysis of the most fundamental of all biochemical reactions—photosynthesis. Using the radioactive isotope carbon 14 as a tracer, he determined how plants use the sun's energy to produce sugars and starches from water and carbon dioxide. Calvin wrote several books on isotopic carbon and photosynthesis and won the 1961 Nobel Prize for Chemistry. His theories on the chemical evolution of life are described in *Chemical Evolution* (1969). ▪ See his *Following the Trail of Light: A Scientific Odyssey* (1992).

CALVINO, ITALO (1923–1985), Italian writer. Born in Cuba to Italian parents, Calvino grew up in San Remo on the Italian Riveria. He was a resistance fighter during World War II, and his first novel, *The Path to the Nest of Spiders* (1947; Eng. trans. 1957) was an account of the resistance from a child's viewpoint that allied him with the Italian neorealitsts. Breaking out of that tradition, he established an international reputation as one of Europe's most inventive modernists and as Italy's most readable contemporary novelist. He wrote popular versions of *Italian Folktales* (1956; Eng. trans. 1980) and published light, allegorical tales in the tradition of the French *conte* and the Italian fable in *Our Ancestors* (1960; Eng. trans. 1980; also trans. as *The Nonexistent Knight* and *The Cloven Viscount,* 1962), *The Castle of Crossed Destinies* (1969; Eng. trans. 1977), and *Cosmicomics* (1965; Eng. trans. 1968). *If on a winter's night a traveler* (1979; Eng. trans. 1981), a novel about reading fiction, consisted of ten beginnings of novels and won many readers abroad. *Marcovaldo or The Seasons in the City* (1970; Eng. trans. 1983) offered 20 short stories about the same character, a naive laborer in a drab industrial city in northern Italy. *Difficult Loves* (1984) assembled English translations of stories written in the 1940s and 1950s. *Mr. Palomar* (1983; Eng. trans. 1985) was a novel about anxiety and consciousness. ▪ See studies by J. R. Woodhouse (1968), Sara Maria Adler (1979), and JoAnn Cannon (1981), and I. T. Olken, *With Pleated Eye and Garnet Wing* (1984).

CĂMARA, HELDER PESSOA (1909–1999), Brazilian theologian and archbishop. One of 13 children, Dom Helder Cămara entered a Catholic seminary in 1923 and was ordained eight years later. As a young priest he was briefly attracted to fascism; later, as the auxiliary bishop of Rio de Janeiro (1952–64) and archbishop of Olinda and Recife (1964–84), he became a champion of the poor and called for peaceful but radical social transformation and an end to "in-

ternal colonialism." He helped found the Brazilian Conference of Bishops and the Latin American Conference of Bishops and played a major role in the radicalization of the Latin American clergy. He was also an outspoken critic of the Brazilian military governments (1964–85). His translated works included *Race Against Time* (1971), *Revolution Through Peace* (1971), *The Conversions of a Bishop* (1979), and *Hoping Against All Hope* (1984). ▪ See study by José de Broucker (1970) and B. Moosbrugger and G. Weigner, *A Voice of the Third World* (1972).

CAMPBELL, DONALD MALCOLM (1921–1967), British auto and speedboat racer. The engineer son of the famed speed racer Sir Malcolm Campbell, Donald Campbell set world speed records on water (276.33 mph, 1964) and on land (403.1 mph, 1964). He was killed while attempting to break his own water speed record when his hydro plane crashed as it exceeded 300 mph. ▪ See biography by Arthur Knowles and Dorothy, Lady Campbell (1970).

CAMPBELL, JOHN W., JR. (1910–1971), U.S. science-fiction writer and editor. While a physics student at the Massachusetts Institute of Technology (B.S. 1932), Campbell published "When the Atoms Failed" (1930), which introduced one of science fiction's first computers. During the Depression he turned out numerous novels and stories; his popularity was rivaled by that of science-fiction writer Don A. Stuart—a Campbell pseudonym. After he became (1937) editor of the magazine *Astounding Science-Fiction* (later called *Analog*), he wrote little of his own fiction, but he enormously influenced a generation of science-fiction writers. He discovered budding writers Isaac Asimov, Robert Heinlein, and others. In 1944 Campbell was investigated by FBI agents; the atomic bomb fuse device mentioned in a story he edited was dangerously close to that being secretly developed at Los Alamos by government scientists. ▪ See his stories in *The Best of John W. Campbell* (1973) and John Bangsund, ed., *John W. Campbell: An Australian Tribute* (1974).

CAMPBELL, JOSEPH (1904–1987), U.S. writer and educator. Campbell, a professor of literature at Sarah Lawrence College, Bronxville, N.Y. (1934–72), was an authority on world mythology. Raised as a Roman Catholic, he became fascinated with American Indian folklore as a child and began studying Eastern religions after meeting with Jiddu Krishnamurti during the 1920s. His Jungian interpretations of dreams, fairy tales, and folklore sought to show that stories from diverse cultures have universal archetypes, themes, and functions. The best known of his widely read books are *The Hero With a Thousand Faces* (1949), *The Masks of God* (4 vols.; 1959–67), and *Myths to Live By* (1972). His views were further disseminated in a popular six-part public television series, *Joseph Campbell and the Power of Myth,* and a companion book (1988). ▪ See Phil Cousineau, ed.,

The Hero's Journey (1990); Michael Toms, *An Open Life* (1988); and Stephen and Robin Larsen, *A Fire in the Mind* (1991).

CAMPBELL, SIR MALCOLM (1885–1949), British auto and speedboat racer. The holder of the world speed record on land and on water at various times in his racing career, Campbell was the first person to attain an officially clocked land speed of 300 mph (301.1292 mph at Bonneville Salt Flats, Utah, 1935). Each of his racing cars and hydroplanes was named *Bluebird*, the symbol of the unattainable in Maurice Maeterlinck's play *The Bluebird*. The spitfire engines used by the Royal Air Force in World War II were developed from his racing engines. ■ See Leo Villa and Tony Gray, *The Record Breakers* (1969).

CAMPBELL, MRS. PATRICK (Beatrice Stella Tanner; 1865–1940), British actress. Tempestuous, witty, and beautiful, Campbell was a leading actress on the London stage for decades. She specialized in portraying passionate and intelligent characters and was best known for her roles in plays by Pinero, Ibsen, Maeterlinck, and George Bernard Shaw, who wrote the role of Eliza Doolittle in *Pygmalion* (1914) for her. She had a celebrated friendship with Shaw and published a series of their letters in *My Life and Some Letters* 1922. ■ See biography by Alan Dent (1961), his edition of *Bernard Shaw and Mrs. Patrick Campbell: Their Correspondence* (1952), and Margot Peters, *Mrs. Pat* (1984).

CAMPBELL, ROY (1901–1957), South African poet. Born into a wealthy Durban family and educated at Oxford (1919), Campbell was a perpetual outsider who was estranged from both the provincialism of South Africa and the left-wing literary circles in London. A colorful individualist and man of action, he lived most of his adult life in southern France, Spain, and Portugal and fought with Francisco Franco's fascist forces during the Spanish civil war. Although he was acclaimed for the powerful poem *The Flaming Terrapin* (1924), which dealt with the theme of regeneration; and the lyrical collections of short poems, *Adamastor* (1930); and *Flowering Reeds* (1933); he was best known for his scornful satirical attacks on the South African intellectual establishment (*Wayzgoose*, 1928), the Bloomsbury literary group in Britain (*The Georgiad*, 1931), and on left-wing ideas (*The Flowering Rifle*, 1939). In spite of his ultraconservative views, he fought with the British during World War II; he spent his last years in Portugal. ■ See his reminiscences, *Broken Record* (1934); his autobiography, *Light on a Dark Horse* (1952); and biography by Peter Alexander (1982).

CAMPBELL, WILLIAM WALLACE (1862–1938), U.S. astronomer. Campbell applied spectrographic analysis to a wide range of celestial subjects. As director of the Lick Observatory, Mt. Hamilton, California (1901–30), he accurately determined the radial velocities of thousands of stars by using a 36-inch telescope and a three-prism spectrograph. His statistical analysis led to his elucidation of the sun's motion in our galaxy, which he published in *Stellar Motions* (1913) and *Stellar Radial Velocities* (with J. H. Moore; 1928). He gathered a wealth of data on his seven solar-eclipse expeditions. He was among the first to conclude, on the basis of spectroscopic studies, that Mars's atmosphere contained little oxygen or water vapor. Campbell served as president of the University of California from 1923 to 1930.

CAMUS, ALBERT (1913–1960), French novelist, dramatist, philosophical essayist, and journalist. Born in Algiers, Camus worked his way through the University of Algiers, then became involved in a theatrical group and pursued numerous literary activities. During World War II he wrote for the clandestine newspaper *Combat,* earning a reputation that secured his position in postwar French intellectual life. Alienation and the meaning of human suffering are recurrent themes in his work. The protagonist in his first novel, *The Stranger* (1942; Eng. trans. 1946), displays an unnerving detachment from the values of his society. *The Myth of Sisyphus* (1942; Eng. trans. 1955) treats similar themes in essay form. *The Plague* (1947; Eng. trans. 1948), a parable of medieval disaster in a modern city, explores moral problems posed by the war. Though Camus' philosophy of the absurdity of the human condition brought him close to the existentialism of Jean Paul Sartre, Sartre sharply criticized Camus for his rejection of Marxism and Stalinism in *The Rebel* (1951; Eng. trans. 1954). Camus was awarded the Nobel Prize in Literature in 1957. Three years later he died in an automobile accident. ■ See his *Notebooks: 1935–1951* (2 vols.; Eng. trans. 1963) and biographies by Herbert R. Lottman (1979), Patrick McCarthy (1982), and Olivier Todd (1997).

CANARIS, WILHELM (1887–1945), German admiral. Born in Westphalia into a patriotic industrialist family, Canaris served during World War I in naval intelligence. Later he headed (1934–44) the Abwehr, the Third Reich's military intelligence agency. Convinced that dictator Adolf Hitler and Nazism were a threat to Germany, Canaris took part in the resistance from 1938. His role was ambiguous, however, since he continued to perform successful intelligence work against the Allies. The Abwehr—eventually a center of anti-Hitler sentiment—was disbanded in February 1944. Canaris was arrested after the June 20, 1944, attempt to assassinate Hitler, although he was not directly involved in the plot. He was imprisoned in Flossenburg fortress, charged with treason, and then executed (April 1945). He was formally exonerated by a German court in 1996. ■ See Roger Manvell and Heinrich Fraenkel, *The Canaris Conspiracy* (1969), and biographies by André Brissaud (Eng. trans. 1974) and Heinz Hohne (Eng. trans. 1979).

CANBY, HENRY SEIDEL (1878–1961), U.S. editor and literary critic. A major arbiter of literary taste in America,

Canby was the editor of the *Saturday Review of Literature* (1924–36) and chairman of the board of judges of the Book-of-the-Month Club (1926–58). A Yale-trained (Ph.D. 1905) upholder of 19th-century liberal values, he succeeded in bringing culture to the middle classes, but it was a culture devoid of modernism, avant-garde trends, and experimentation. He wrote many books, including *The Short Story in English* (1909), *Better Writing* (1926), studies of Thoreau (1939) and Walt Whitman (1943), *A Literary History of America* (coeditor, 1948), several volumes of essays, and his autobiography, *American Memoir* (1947).

CANDELA (OUTERIÑO), FÉLIX (1910–   ), Spanish-born Mexican architect. A Republican refugee from the Spanish civil war, Candela settled in Mexico (1939) to become the world's leading authority on reinforced concrete-shell architecture. Working as construction foreman and builder as well as engineer and designer, he created factories, schools, warehouses, and churches in a new idiom ideally suited to the climate and economy. Among Candela's best-known creations were the Cosmic Ray Laboratory at Mexico's University City (1952), shaped like a covered wagon with the thinnest concrete roof ever constructed; Church of the Miraculous Virgin, Mexico City (1953); and the Sports Palace for the Olympic games in Mexico City (1968). He taught at the National University in Mexico City (1953–70) and emigrated to the United States in 1971, where he taught at the University of Illinois, Chicago (1971–78), and at Cornell (1969–74). ■ See study by Colin Faber (1963).

CANETTI, ELIAS (1905–1994), Bulgarian-born German-language writer. Born into a prosperous Sephardic-Jewish family, Canetti learned Ladino, Bulgarian, English, and German in his youth and studied in Zurich, Frankfurt, and Vienna (Ph.D. in chemistry, 1929). He emigrated to Britain in 1938. His celebrated novel, *Auto-da-Fé* (1935; Eng. trans. 1946), reflected his preoccupation with the growth of totalitarianism and the disintegration of European culture. *Crowds and Power* (1960; Eng. trans. 1962) was a profound multidisciplinary study of the origins, structure, symbolism, and social psychology of fascism and other mass movements. He also wrote plays, several volumes of aphorisms, essays and notes, a study of the writer Franz Kafka (*Kafka's Other Trial*, 1969; Eng. trans. 1982), and three volumes of autobiography—*The Tongue Set Free* (1977; Eng. trans. 1979), *The Torch in My Ear* (1980; Eng. trans. 1982), and *The Play of the Eyes* (1985; Eng. trans. 1986). He was awarded the 1981 Nobel Prize in Literature. ■ See study by Thomas H. Falk (1993).

CANIFF, MILTON (1907–1988), U.S. cartoonist. A graduate of Ohio State University (1930), Caniff introduced the dashing adventurer who was to become his stock hero in the daily strip *Dickie Dare* (1932). In 1934 he caught the eye of *New York News* publisher Joseph Patterson, who was in the market for a suspenseful realistic action strip. Caniff re-

sponded with the inspired *Terry and the Pirates,* set in China, which grew quickly into a Sunday page. During World War II, Caniff created *Male Call* for servicemen. After contractual disputes forced him to abandon *Terry,* Caniff conceived *Steve Canyon* (1947), whom he described as "a sort of modern Kit Carson," a retired air-force captain who reenlisted for the Korean War, took on cold-war assignments, and later fought in Vietnam.

CANNON, ANNIE JUMP (1863–1941), U.S. astronomer. While on the staff of the Harvard College Observatory (1896–1940), Cannon studied the observatory's collection of astronomical photographs with the aim of classifying and cataloging the spectra of stars. The result was the *Henry Draper Catalogue,* a nine-volume work supplying spectral listings of over 225,000 stars. Published in sections between 1918 and 1924, the work demonstrated that almost all stars could be categorized into a few spectral types based on color and greatly influenced the evolution of astronomy. Cannon also discovered numerous stars and five novas.

CANNON, CLARENCE (1879–1964), U.S. political leader. A conservative Democrat from Missouri, Cannon went to Washington as a secretary to House of Representatives Speaker Champ Clark (1911). He was elected to the House in 1922 and served until his death. One of the most influential men in government, he chaired the powerful House Appropriations Committee (1941–47; 1949–53; 1955–64) and fought for economy in government. A master of parliamentary procedure, he wrote *Cannon's Procedure* (1928) and *Cannon's Precedents* (1936; 1949), which became standard reference works.

CANNON, JAMES PATRICK (1890–1974), U.S. political leader. A founder of the U.S. Communist party (1919), Cannon became a follower of the Russian bolshevik leader Leon Trotsky and was known as his American heir. He was expelled from the party (1928) for his support of the now-ousted Trotsky and helped found the Socialist Workers party (1938), later serving as its national chairman. Cannon was one of 18 members of the party sentenced to prison (1941) for violating the Smith Act, which outlawed advocating the overthrow of the U.S. government by force and violence. His books included *The History of American Trotskyism* (1944), *The First Ten Years of the Communist Party* (1962), *The Struggle for a Proletarian Party* (1943), and *Speeches for Socialism* (1971).

CANNON, JOSEPH GURNEY (1836–1926), U.S. congressman. An ardent defender of the status quo, Cannon, an Illinois Republican, served in Congress for 46 of the 50 years between 1873 and 1923 and dominated it through his control of the House Committee on Rules and his position as Speaker of the House (1903–11). He was an earthy and coarse small-town politician who opposed progressive legislation and government interference in private enterprise and supported high tariffs and government austerity. Cannon's arbitrary leadership, favoritism in appointments, and support of special interests gave rise to the term "Cannonism." His power was broken (1910), however, when a coalition of Democrats and insurgent Republicans voted to exclude the speaker from the Rules Committee and provide for election to that committee by the House. ■ See William R. Gwinn, *Uncle Joe Cannon* (1957).

CANNON, WALTER BRADFORD (1871–1945), U.S. physiologist. A professor at the Harvard Medical School (1899–1942), Cannon introduced the use of X rays in physiological studies. His work enabled doctors to view internal organs for the first time and supplied modern medicine with a vital diagnostic tool. He also formulated theory of "homeostasis," which described the body's ability to maintain a stable internal environment through various physiological processes, despite wide variations in the outside environment. Cannon was also known for the development (1931) of sympathin, an a adrenalinelike compound, and for his research on the sympathetic nervous system and hemorrhagic and traumatic shock. ■ See his autobiography, *The Way of an Investigator* (1945), and biography by S. Benison, A. C. Barger, and E. L. Wolfe (1987).

CANTINFLAS (Mario Moreno Reyes; 1911–1993), Mexican actor. Originally an acrobat, clown, and song-and-dance man, Cantinflas made his first film in 1936. Enormously popular at home and throughout the Spanish speaking world, he broke box-office records with *Neither Blood nor Sand* (1941). A Chaplinesque comedian, he specialized in bumbling antics. He appeared in two U.S. films, *Around the World in 80 Days* (1956) and *Pepe* (1960).

CANTOR, EDDIE (Edward Israel Iskowitz; 1892–1964), U.S. entertainer. A product of New York's Lower East Side, Cantor was a star of stage, screen, radio, and television who delighted audiences for more than half a century. With seemingly boundless energy and enthusiasm, he became famous by clapping his hands, goggling his "banjo" eyes, and dancing around the stage while clowning and singing simple, gay tunes. He appeared in Ziegfeld's *Follies* (1917–19) and starred in numerous Broadway productions of the 1920s and 1930s, including *Kid Boots* (1923) and *Whoopee* (1928). He also hosted a popular weekly radio show (1931–39) and a monthly television program (1950–53). ■ See his autobiography, *Take My Life* (1957); biography by Gregory Korselak (1995); and Herbert G. Goldman, *Banjo Eyes* (1997).

CAO YU (old style: TS'AO YU; 1910–1996), Chinese playwright. Cao Yu was the pseudonym of Wan Qiabao (Wan Ch'ia-pao). The most significant modern Chinese playwright, Cao masterfully utilized Western stage methods to convey Chinese themes. A realist who was inspired by the Norwegian Hendrik Ibsen and the Englishman John Galsworthy, he emphasized human tragedy and degradation and attacked the corruption of traditional society. *Thunderstorm* (1934; Eng. trans. 1964) and *Peking Man* (1940; Eng. trans. 1986), two of his most popular works, depicted the decadence and disintegration of wealthy middle-class families. His other plays included *Sunrise* (1936; Eng. trans. 1960), *The Wilderness* (1937; Eng. trans. 1980) and *The Consort of Peace* (1979; Eng. trans. 1980). After the communist takeover in 1949 he held numerous official cultural posts and joined the Communist party (1957). During the Cultural Revolution he was sent to the countryside for political reeducation but was rehabilitated in 1976. ■ See study by John Y. H. Hu (1972).

CAPA, CORNELL (Cornel Friedmann; 1918–), Hungarian-born U.S. photographer. Capa became a photographer like his older brother Robert, worked for *Life* magazine after World War II (1946–54), and in 1954 joined the photography cooperative, Magnum. With a New York exhibition in 1967 followed by two books, he developed the theme and movement of "the concerned photographer" as a documentarian of the human condition. He was also a founder and executive director of the International Center of Photography in New York City (1974–94). His work as photographer, editor, and administrator helped to establish photojournalism as a serious art form. His volumes of photos included *Margin of Life* (1974), *Children of War, Children of Peace* (1991), and *Cornel Capa: Photographs* (1992).

CAPA, ROBERT (Andre Friedmann; 1913–1954), Hungarian-born U.S. photographer. Capa left home for Paris at age 18 and adopted a pseudonym in order to get higher prices for his photos. He covered the civil war in Spain, where he took (1936) his most famous photograph. "The Death of a Loyalist Soldier." During the next 18 years he covered one conflict after another, compiling a shattering visual record later published as *Images of War* (1964). In 1947 Capa helped found the photo agency Magnum. He was killed by a land mine while covering the war in Indochina. His younger brother was photographer Cornell Capa. ■ See *Robert Capa* (1969; text by John Hersey, et al.); biography by Richard Whelan (1985); and Cornell Capa and Whelan, eds., *Robert Capa Photographs* (1985).

CAPABLANCA, JOSÉ RAÚL (1888–1942), Cuban chess player. The Cuban champion at the age of 12, Capablanca was a chess perfectionist who rarely lost a match and was known as the "chess machine." A deceptively simple stylist and master of the end game, he defeated Emanuel Lasker for the world championship (1921). Later, however, he lost the title to Alexander Alekhine in a great upset (1927). Capablanca served in the Cuban diplomatic corps from 1913 until his death.

ČAPEK, KAREL (1890–1938), Czech novelist and playwright. A student of philosophy in Prague, Berlin, and Paris, Čapek became internationally famous for his satiric and utopian plays. His works reflected a concern for the future of humanity in an age dominated by technology and materialism. His best-known works. including *R.U.R.* (1920; Eng. trans. 1923), which introduced the term "robot," *The Insect Play* (1921; Eng. trans. 1923), written with his brother Josef; and (the novel) *War with the Newts* (1936; Eng. trans. 1937), depicted forces of disintegration within European society and prophesied the rise of totalitarianism. A liberal, democrat, and humanitarian, Čapek was influenced by his friend, the political leader Thomas Masaryk, whose government he supported and whose popular biography he wrote (3 vols., 1928–35; Eng. trans., 2 vols., 1934–38). Čapek was a major Czech literary personality between the two world wars, and he wrote philosophical novels, detective stories, and whimsical travel essays in addition to his well known theatrical pieces. ■ See studies by William Harkins (1962), Alexander Matuška (Eng. trans. 1964), and B. R. Bradbrook (1998).

CAPONE, AL (Alphonse Capone; 1899–1947), Italian-born U.S. gangster. The son of an impoverished barber, Capone worked his way up from petty criminal in South Brooklyn to head of the organized-crime syndicate in Chicago (1925–31). Based on his control of vice, gambling, and bootleg liquor, he built a nationwide underworld empire, reaped annual profits estimated at $100 million, wielded immense political influence, and became the symbol of American lawlessness ("Public Enemy No. 1") during the Prohibition era. Although said to have been ultimately responsible for more than 300 murders (including the St. Valentine's Day Massacre of 1929), he was never tried for any of them. He was convicted of income tax evasion (1931), however, and spent eight years in prison. He led a reclusive life in Florida after his release in 1939. Rumors of hidden loot that circulated long after his death interested the Internal Revenue Service, which in 1985 refiled a lien against his estate in hopes of recovering outstanding taxes of $800,000. ■ See John Kobler, *Capone* (1971), and biography by Laurence Bergreen (1994).

CAPOTE, TRUMAN (1924–1984), U.S. novelist, journalist and celebrity. A high school dropout, one-time apprentice fortune-teller, and *New Yorker* writer, Capote attracted critical attention at age 23 for his first novel, *Other Voices, Other Rooms* (1948). Short stories, novellas, and reportage followed in such volumes as *The Grass Harp* (1951) and *Breakfast at Tiffany's* (1958). Capote cultivated famous friends and his own eccentric image. The celebrity he pursued came when he used his capacity for total recall to record verbatim accounts of the murder of an appointee in the administration of Pres. Dwight D. Eisenhower in *In Cold Blood* (1965). *Esquire* magazine called 1966 "the year of Capote" when the chilling nonfiction novel—the result of six years' research and writing—earned a 17-page spread in *Life* magazine and $2 million in advances on royalties. Capote also wrote drama, TV plays, documentaries, and screenplays. *Music for Chameleons* (1980), a collection of short writings, included a "self-interview," and *One Christmas* (1983) was autobiographical. ■ See also biography by Gerald Clarke (1985); studies by Helen S. Garson (1980) and George Plimpton (1997); and Lawrence Grobel, *Conversations with Capote* (1985).

CAPP, AL (Alfred Gerald Caplin; 1909–1979), U.S., cartoonist. Capp began his career working for other cartoonists and ghost-drew the *Joe Palooka* strip for several years before creating his own *Li'l Abner* hillbilly characters (1934). Set in mythical Dogpatch, Kentucky, the strip followed the adventures of huge and wholesome Abner Yokum, his buxom wife Daisy Mae, and other characters; some were clever caricatures of well-known public figures, through which Capp interjected political and social satire. In 1940 Capp wrote a screenplay based on the immensely popular strip, and in 1956 the Dogpatch characters appeared in a Broadway musical that was itself made into a movie in 1959. A popular personality, Capp was widely in demand as a public speaker, although his popularity dimmed somewhat in the 1960s as his formerly liberal politics turned conservative. ■ See his memoirs, *My Well-balanced Life on a Wooden Leg* (1991).

CAPRA, FRANK (1897–1991), U.S. film director. Capra arrived from Sicily as a child in steerage, grew up in Los Angeles, and bluffed his way with a California Institute of Technology engineering degree (1918) and a lot of moxie into Hollywood. His first big hit was a screwball comedy, *It Happened One Night* (1934), which he made in four weeks. More typical of the Capra style were *Mr. Deeds Goes to Town* (1936) and *You Can't Take It with You* (1938), Depression-era favorites about lone heroes winning out over cynicism, corruption, and big business. Capra won Academy Awards for all three movies. During World War II he directed the army's award-winning documentary series, "Why We Fight." The sentimental fantasy, *It's a Wonderful Life* (1946), became a perennial Christmas TV favorite. ■ See his autobiography, *The Name Above the Title* (1971); study by Charles J. Maland (1980); and biography by Joseph McBride (1992).

CARAMANLIS, CONSTANTINE. See *KARAMANLIS, CONSTANTINE.*

CARATHÉODORY, CONSTANTIN (1873–1950), German-born Greek mathematician. The most prominent Greek mathematician of modern times, Carathéodory received his Ph.D. from Göttingen University (1904) and taught at several German universities, including the University of Munich (from 1924). He made fundamental contributions to the calculus of variations, the theory of functions, the theory of real functions, and the theory of the measure of set points. His books in English translation included *Algebraic Theory of Measure and Integration* (1963) and *Theory of Functions of a Complex Variable* (1954).

CÁRDENAS, LÁZARO (1895–1970), Mexican political leader. Born into a mestizo peasant family, Cárdenas joined the revolutionary army in 1913, achieved the rank of general by 1923, and served as governor of his home state of Michoacán (1928–32). A protégé of political boss Plutarco Calles, Cárdenas was elected president in 1934, but he broke with the Callistas and implemented a series of radical policies during his term of office (1934–40). He expropriated 45 million acres of land and distributed them to the peasants, nationalized many industries and the railroads, sponsored educational reform and expansion, nationalized the foreign-owned oil industry, and became a hero of the peasant masses. He granted asylum to thousands of antifascist Spaniards during and after the Spanish civil war and allowed the Russian revolutionary Leon Trotsky to live in Mexico. After World War II he remained a leader of the Mexican left, and though never a communist, opposed U.S. expansionism, accepted the Stalin Peace Prize (1955), and supported Cuba's Fidel Castro. ■ See biography by William C. Townsend (1952) and Adrian A. Bantjes, *As If Jesus Walked on Earth* (1998).

CARDIN, PIERRE (1922–   ), French fashion designer. After studying architecture, Cardin began designing clothes. He worked for Paquin, Castillo, and Christian Dior before establishing his own firm (1949). Cardin's line introduced modernistic, abstract designs and synthetic fabrics to haute couture. His house was the first to offer both ready-made and custom-made fashions, as well as both men's and women's styles. His innovations influenced the unisex and space-age looks in fashion. He also created (1970) L'Espace Pierre Cardin, an avant-garde Paris arts complex, and acted in a film with Jeanne Moreau. In 1979 he made a trade agreement with the People's Republic of China. He also served as chairman of Maxim's Restaurant (1982–   ) in Paris.

CARDOSO, FERNANDO ENRIQUE (1931–   ), Brazilian political leader. A Marxist academic sociologist, trained at the University of São Paulo and the University of Paris, Cardoso lived in exile during most of the period that Brazil was ruled by a military dictatorship (1964–85). He taught at universities in Chile, France, England, and the United States and wrote many books, including *Dependency and Development in Latin America* (with Enzo Faletto, 1969; Eng. trans. 1979), a seminal contribution to dependency theory. He served in the Brazilian Senate (1983–92), helped draft the new democratic constitution (1988), and cofounded the center-left Brazilian Social Democratic party (1988). After serving as foreign minister (1992–93), he became finance minister (1993) and devised the tight-money Real Plan, a series of measures that brought Brazil's staggering inflation under control. As president (1993–   ) he carried out conservative free-market economic reforms that opened Brazil's market to foreign countries, privatized state-run concerns, cut government spending, and led to moderate economic growth, but had little effect in reducing the rate of poverty or the enormous gap between rich and poor. After his reelection amidst a growing budget deficit (1998), he announced an austerity plan of spending reductions and tax increases.

CARDOZO, BENJAMIN NATHAN (1870–1938), U.S. jurist. A Sephardic Jew from New York, Cardozo had a successful law practice for 20 years before his election (1913) to the state supreme court. He was appointed the following year to the New York Court of Appeals, winning election to a 14-year term in 1917. A devoted student of the evolution of the law, Cardozo was highly esteemed as an appellate judge for his learning and his gracious style of jurisprudence. Appointed to the U.S. Supreme Court (1932) by Pres. Herbert Hoover, he voted frequently with the "liberals" on the court in order to reconcile the law with social change. He wrote many works on law, including *The Nature of the Judicial Process* (1921) and *The Paradoxes of Legal Science* (1928). ■ See Joseph P. Pollard, *Mr. Justice Cardozo* (1935); biographies by George Hellman (1940) and Andrew L. Kaufman (1998); and study by Beryl H. Levy (rev. ed. 1969).

CAREY, JAMES BARRON (1911–1973), U.S. labor leader. Fiery and dynamic, Carey headed the Radio and Allied Trades National Labor Council at age 22 and was chosen president of the newly formed United Electrical, Radio, and Machine Workers of America (UE) at 24 (1936). He was elected national secretary of the Congress of Industrial Organizations (CIO) in 1938 and served as its second-ranking official (secretary-treasurer, 1942–55). An uncompromising anticommunist, he was defeated for reelection of the UE by a left-wing coalition (1941), but after it was expelled by the CIO for alleged communist domination (1949), Carey helped organize the rival International Union of Electrical, Radio, and Machine Workers (IUE). Carey was also a vice president of the AFL-CIO (from 1955) and labor representative of the United Nations Association (1965–72).

CARLSON, CHESTER FLOYD (1906–1968), U.S. inventor. A graduate (1930) of the California Institute of Technology, Carlson noted the constant need for multiple copies of documents while working as a patent lawyer in an electronics firm. He began experimenting with copying processes using photoconductivity and by 1938 he had refined the basic steps of electronics firm. He began experimenting with copying processes using photoconductivity and by 1938 he had refined the basic steps of what is now known as xerography, from the Greek word for "dry." His technique, patented in 1940, involved charging a sheet of insulating material with high-electric voltage to sensitize it to small amounts of light. His copier was publicly demonstrated in 1948 and commercially produced in 1959. Carlson became a multimillionaire by collecting royalties from the Xerox Corp., which bought rights to develop his process.

CARLSSON, ARVID (1923–), Swedish pharmacologist. Carlsson studied at the University of Lund (M.D. 1951) and taught at the University of Göteborg (1951–89). During the 1950s he discovered that dopamine is a chemical transmitter in the area of the brain that controls movement. His research led to the development of the drug L-dopa for the treatment of Parkinson's disease. His subsequent research into the effect of antischizophrenia drugs on neurons that pick up the dopamine signal led to the development of new drug treatments for the disease. For his pioneering research, Carlsson shared the 2000 Nobel Prize in Physiology or Medicine with Eric R. Kandel and Paul Greengard.

CARLTON, STEPHEN NORMAN (1944–), U.S. baseball player. A hard-throwing 6-foot, 5-inch pitcher who spent most of his career with the St. Louis Cardinals (1965–72) and Philadelphia Phillies (1972–86), Steve Carlton perfected a fluid motion that resulted in a seemingly effortless delivery. Batters exerted great effort, usually in vain, in trying to hit his pitches. The first lefthander to surpass 3,000 strikeouts in a career, he ended his career (1988) with 4,136 strikeouts which placed him second on the all-time major league list. He was the first pitcher to win four Cy Young Awards (1972, 27–10; 1977, 23–10; 1980, 24–9; 1982, 23–11), and he amassed a record of 329 wins and 244 losses.

CARMICHAEL, HOAGY (Hoagland Howard Carmichael; 1899–1981), U.S. jazz pianist and composer. Carmichael was an Indiana lawyer and jazz fan who sat down at the piano and composed such sentimental favorites as "Stardust," "Georgia on My Mind," "Lazy Bones," "Old Buttermilk Sky," and "In the Cool, Cool, Cool of the Evening." He also played in a few films (*To Have and Have Not*, 1944), had a popular radio program during the 1940s, and appeared in a TV western in the 1950s. ■ See his memoirs *Stardust Road* (1946) and *Sometimes I Wonder* (1965).

CARMICHAEL, STOKELY (1941–1998), Trinidad-born political activist. Carmichael graduated from the Bronx (New York) High School of Science (1960) and Howard University (B.A. 1964). As a college student he joined the Freedom Rides sponsored by the Congress of Racial Equality. In 1964 he was a field organizer for the Student Nonviolent Coordinating Committee (SNCC) in Mississippi and

later chaired (1966–67) that rural, South-oriented civil-rights organization. He gained nationwide publicity in 1966 when he raised the cry of "Black Power," a concept he explained in the book *Black Power: The Politics of Liberation in America* (1967; with Charles Hamilton). In 1967 Carmichael called for armed revolution in the United States and aligned himself with the urban-oriented Black Panthers party, but he resigned in 1969 in protest against its dogmatism and alliances with whites. He moved to Guinea (1969), changed his name to Kwame Touré, and worked for the pan-African movement. He was married for several years to singer Miriam Makeba.

CARNAP, RUDOLF (1891–1970), German-born U.S. philosopher. Carnap studied physics and mathematics, served in World War I, then earned a doctoral degree (1921). He occupied an important place in a group of philosophers, mathematicians, and semanticists in the period between World Wars I and II known as the Vienna Circle. A professor at Vienna University (1926–31) and at the German University of Prague (1931–35), he emigrated to the United States and joined the faculties of the University of Chicago (1936–52) and the University of California at Los Angeles (1954–62). Turning away from philosophy's traditional emphasis on ethics and metaphysics, Carnap was a founder of logical positivism. He held that philosophy's only legitimate function should be to characterize. clarify, and critique science and language, and that all knowledge should be derived through empirical observation and inductive logic. He made major contributions to the fields of logic, semantics, and probability theory. His writings included *The Logical Structure of the World* (1928; rev. ed. 1961; Eng. trans. 1967), *The Logical Syntax of Language* (1934; Eng. trans. 1937), *Meaning and Necessity* (1947; 2nd ed. 1956), and *Logical Foundations of Probability* (1950). ■ See Paul A. Schilpp, ed., *The Philosophy of Rudolf Carnap* (1963).

CARNÉ, MARCEL (1909?–1996), French film director. The son of a Parisian cabinetmaker, Carné was highly regarded during the 1930s and 1940s for the gloomy, melancholy films that he made in collaboration with poet Jacques Prévert, including *Port of Shadows* 11938) and *Daybreak* (1939). The best of these was *Children of Paradise* (1943), a nostalgic 19th-century theatrical romance shot during World War II and the German occupation of France. His last popular film was *The Cheaters* (1958). ■ See Edward B. Turk, *Child of Paradise* (1989).

CARNEGIE, DALE (1888–1955), U.S. author and lecturer. Born into a poor Missouri farming family, Carnegie graduated from Warrensburg State Teachers College (1908) and began his career as a teacher of public speaking in New York City (1912). His first book, *Public Speaking: A Practical Course for Businessmen* (1926), was a success, and he subsequently wrote a syndicated newspaper column, had his own radio show, and expanded the scope of his writing and lecturing to include all aspects of successful living. His most famous book, *How to Win Friends and Influence People* (1936), advised readers to smile, to be friendly, and not to argue or find fault with others; it became the best-selling nonfiction work of modern times, second only to the Bible. It sold 4,844,938 copies up to the time of Carnegie's death and was translated into 29 languages. His optimistic precepts ("Believe that you will succeed, and you will") also accounted for the popularity of his course (run by the Carnegie Institute for Effective Speaking and Human Relations), which, by 1955, had been taken by more 450,000 people in 750 U.S. cities and 15 foreign countries. ■ See biography by Giles Kemp and Edward Claflin (1989).

CARNEGIE, HATTIE (Henrietta Kanengeiser; 1886–1956), Austrian-born U.S. fashion designer. Carnegie was brought to the United States by her parents as a child and she grew up in New York City's Lower East Side. She adopted the *nom de mode* Carnegie because it stood for influence and fortune, and she opened her first business in 1909. She established a national reputation when she began (1928) manufacturing ready-to-wear copies of her own designs. Creating variations on Paris styles, she put the "little Carnegie suit" and the simple black dress into the closets of style-conscious women of the 1930s and 1940s. A number of well-known designers, including Claire McCardell and Norman Norell, trained under Carnegie.

CARNEY, DON (Howard Rice; 1897–1954), U.S. radio personality. A character actor and vaudeville performer—he was the first to play the piano while standing on his head—Carney joined New York radio station WOR as host of a children's show (1928) and as "Uncle Don" became one of the most popular personalities in radio history. For 20 years he told stories and jokes, read the comics, played tunes on the piano, advised against misbehaving, and was hailed as a "saint, oracle, and pal" to millions of children throughout the United States. Carney spent years denying an apocryphal—but classic—story in which, after signing off the broadcast one evening, and thinking he was off the air, he allegedly said, "There! I guess that'll hold the little bastards for another night."

CARO, SIR ANTHONY (1924–   ), British sculptor. Caro studied engineering at Cambridge and art at the Royal Academy schools in London and served as an assistant to sculptor Henry Moore (1951–53). In the early 1960s he created a new sculptural aesthetic with his large, abstract and brightly painted welded creations constructed out of steel rods and plates, I-beams, and aluminum tubes. He sought to convey mood and involve the viewer directly in the space occupied by the sculptures, which were set on the ground and not on traditional pedestals. Caro's later works utilized rusted and weathered steel. His works of the 1980s were increasingly representational and figurative and many referred to artworks of the past. ■ See studies by Richard Whelan (1974), Diane Waldman (1982), and John Riddy (1991).

CAROL I (1839–1914), king of Rumania. A German Hohenzollern prince, Carol was elected prince of Rumania in 1866 and became Rumania's first king in 1881. His years on the throne were marked by constitutional and monetary reform and the expansion of the industrial and military sectors. Rumania's oil industry began during his reign. He ignored rural problems, however, and brutally crushed the massive peasant rebellion of 1907.

CAROL II (1893–1953), king of Rumania. The flamboyant King Carol II led a scandal-ridden domestic life that forced him (as crown prince) to renounce his rights to the throne and go into exile with his mistress Magda Lupescu (1925). However, he returned to Rumania as king (1930) and, during a chaotic period, ruled in an increasingly authoritarian manner. In 1938, to counter the pro-Nazi Iron Guard movement, he declared a royal dictatorship and banned all political parties. He was forced to abdicate in favor of his son Michael and go into exile, (1940) due to German pressure, after being compelled to cede northern Transylvania to Hungary.

CAROSSA, HANS (1878–1956), German novelist and poet. A physician who lived his entire life in Bavaria, Carossa infused all of his works with his love of humanity and his desire to enlighten and regenerate mankind. He is best known for his autobiographical novels, *A Childhood* (1922; Eng. trans. 1930), *Boyhood and Youth* (1928; Eng. trans. 1930), *Guidance and Companionship* (1933), and *The Year of Sweet Illusions* (1941; Eng. trans. 1951), which, in addition to presenting memorable descriptions of the folklore and natural beauty of Bavaria, revealed Carossa's quest for a harmonious and essential life, free of inner turmoil. Called the closest to Goethe of all modern writers, he always emphasized the nobler aspects of humanity.

CAROTHERS, WALLACE HUME (1896–1937), U.S. chemist. Carothers abandoned a teaching career at Harvard (1928) to head the Du Pont Co.'s newly built research laboratory in organic chemistry. His initial triumph was the development of neoprene (1931), the first successful synthetic rubber. His later research in polymerization and polycondensation resulted in the creation (1935) of long and extremely strong fibers that have the characteristics of wool and silk. After several more years of experimentation, Du Pont announced (1938) the discovery of the versatile, durable substance that it named nylon and began commercial production the following year. Subject to deep depressions, Carothers committed suicide at age 41 and did not live to realize that his discovery would usher in a new era of synthetic fibers that would revolutionize the textile, automotive, and other industries. ■ See his *Collected Papers* (1940) and Matthew E. Hermes, *Enough for One Lifetime* (1996).

CARPENTIER, ALEJO (1904–1980), Cuban novelist. Carpentier was a musicologist and radio scriptwriter whose fiction incorporated aspects of the Afro-Cuban tradition as well as elements of surrealism that he assimilated during his many years in Paris. His major novel, *The Lost Steps* (1953; Eng. trans. 1956), concerned a musician's search for primitive wisdom and his eventual decision to return to civilization. *Explosion in a Cathedral* (1962; Eng. trans. 1963) was a more clearly ideological work set after the French Revolution. A later novel was *Reasons of State* (1974; Eng. trans. 1976), an attack on Latin American dictatorship. His powerful short fiction included *The War of Time* (1958; Eng. trans. 1970). After the Cuban revolution (1959), Carpentier represented the Castro government on diplomatic missions, served in the national assembly, and was the cultural attaché in Paris (1970–80). His last novel, *The Harp and the Shadow* (1979; Eng. trans. 1990), was an inquiry into the myths about Christopher Columbus. ■ See studies by Donald Shaw (1985) and Robert González-Echeverria (1990).

CARR, EDWARD HALLETT (1892–1982), British political scientist. After studying classics at Cambridge, E. H. Carr joined the British foreign service and was sent to the Paris Peace Conference (1919), to Latvia, and to the League of Nations. He later taught international politics, served as an editor of the *London Times* during World War II (1941–46), and was a fellow at Cambridge (1955–82). He wrote many books including *The Twenty Years' Crisis, 1919 39* (1939) and *What Is History?* (1961), a controversial volume discussing the social conditioning of historians and the impossibility of objective history. He was best known for the monumental *History of Soviet Russia, 1917–29* (14 vols., 1950–78), a detailed account of the bolshevik consolidation of power. The work, disparaged by some historians for its uncritical tone, was considered to be a landmark of modern scholarship. His *Twilight of the Comintern, 1930–35* (1983) was a related study.

CARR, EMILY (1871–1945), Canadian artist. Having studied in San Francisco, London, and Paris, Carr applied the intense colors of the fauves to landscapes and Indian motifs of her native British Columbia. When her health no longer permitted sketching trips into the wilderness, she began writing autobiographical sketches full of local lore: *Klee Wyck* (1941), *The House of All Sorts* (1944), *Growing Pains* (1946). ■ See biographies by Edythe Hembroff-Schleicher (1978), Maria Tippett (1979), Paula Blanchard (1987), and Doris Shadbolt (1990); and study by Marion Endicott (1981).

CARRÀ, CARLO (1881–1966), Italian painter. Primarily a self-taught painter, Carrà became interested in futurism, a dynamic new movement exalting technology and speed, in 1909. *The Funeral of the Anarchist Galli* (1911) is characteristic of this period. In 1917 he met fellow Italian painter Giorgio de Chirico, and the style they evolved became known as metaphysical painting. In 1918 Carrà published *Pittura Metafisica,* which explained the new aesthetic, a plastic reshaping of visual reality that produced an alien, arid atmosphere filled with sculptural figures and objects, as in *The Drunken Gentleman* (1917). Having broken with Chirico in 1918, however, he rejected his own earlier theories in 1920, returned to a classicist tradition, and exerted a major influence on the Italian art world between World War I and World War II.

CARRANZA, VENUSTIANO (1859–1920), Mexican political leader. A senator from Coahuila, Carranza supported Francisco Madero in the revolution against Porfirio Diaz (1910) and was a leader of the forces opposed to Victoriano Huerta, who had overthrown Madero (1913). He was named head of the provisional government (1914) and after a civil war against the forces of Pancho Villa and Emiliano Zapata, he was named the first president of the new Mexican republic (1917). However, he failed to implement the reforms called for in the 1917 constitution and was overthrown by radical generals, led by Álvaro Obregón (1920), and murdered. ■ See study by Douglas W. Richmond (1983).

CARREL, ALEXIS (1873–1944), French-U.S. surgeon. A graduate of the University of Lyon (M.D. 1900), Carrel did his most important work at the Rockefeller Institute for Medical Research (now Rockefeller University) in New York City. Primarily interested in organ transplants, he developed a method for suturing blood vessels end to end, enabling surgeons to connect them to transplanted organs. Carrel won the Nobel Prize in Physiology or Medicine (1912) for this work. During World War I he helped develop, with Henry Dakin, a sodium-hypochlorite solution for the sterilization of deep wounds. He also designed, in collaboration with famed aviator Charles A. Lindbergh, a mechanical "heart," a germ-proof perfusion pump that kept whole organs alive outside the body by supplying them constantly with blood. ■ See biographies by Robert Soupault (1952) and W. Sterling Edwards and Peter D. Edwards (1974).

CARRERA ANDRADE, JORGE (1903–1978), Ecuadorian poet. A diplomat and at times a political exile, Carrera Andrade traveled the world and lived for many years in Europe. He frequently wrote of the plight of the Ecuadorian Indian, and many of his poems reflected his commitment to social revolution. His poetry, replete with French, Spanish, and Japanese influences, fused simplicity of vocabulary with brilliant and original metaphorical images. Some of his best poems are included in *Secret Country* (1940; Eng. trans. 1946) and *Selected Poems* (Eng. trans. 1972). He also wrote essays, an autobiography, and several works on history and culture, including *Reflections on Spanish-American Poetry* (Eng. trans. 1973). ■ See study by P. R. Beardsell, *Winds of Exile* (1977).

CARRERAS, JOSÉ (1946–), Spanish opera singer. Carreras was inspired to become a singer at the age of 7 after seeing Mario Lanza in the film *The Great Caruso*. A lyric tenor with romantic good looks, he studied at the Barcelona Conservatory, and made his debut in Barcelona in Donizetti's *Lucrezia Borgia* (1972) and his Metropolitan Opera debut in Puccini's *Tosca* (1974). He was acclaimed for his interpretations of Verdi and Puccini roles and sang in opera houses around the world. In 1987 he was diagnosed with leukemia but miraculously returned to the stage a year later after chemotherapy and bone marrow treatment. During the 1990s he toured the world with Plácido Domingo and Luciano Pavarotti as a member of the "Three Tenors" concert series, the most lucrative event in classical music history. It was estimated that more than 2 billion viewers saw the concerts on television and the audio and video tapes of the events became the best-selling classical recordings of all time.

CARRIER, WILLIS HAVILAND (1876-1950), U.S. mechanical engineer and industrialist. The pioneer of modern air-conditioning, Carrier designed his first machine to control humidity for a Brooklyn, New York, lithographer (1902). By 1907, when the term "air-conditioning" was first used, Carrier's systems were installed in several factories, and in 1914 he published a theoretical paper, "Rational Psychometric Formulae," which became the standard work on air-conditioning design. He was a founder of the Carrier Corp. (1915), a leading manufacturer of air-conditioning equipment, and held more than 80 patents in the field. ■ See study by Margaret Ingels (1952).

CARRILLO, SANTIAGO (1915–), Spanish political leader. The son of a Socialist party leader, Carrillo became secretary-general of the Socialist Youth Federation in 1934 and joined the Communist party in 1936. During the Spanish civil war (1936–39) he took part in the Loyalist defense of Madrid and left Spain for France (1939) after Francisco Franco had established his dictatorship. Active in the Communist party, Carrillo shared power with Dolores Ibarruri from 1956 to 1960 and served as secretary-general of the party from 1960 to 1982. A pioneer Eurocommunist and proponent of a democratic form of socialism, he severely criticized the Soviet invasion of Czechoslovakia (1968) and advocated the independence of national communist parties from Soviet control. After Franco's death Carrillo returned to Spain (1976), successfully fought for the legalization of the Communist party (1977), and was elected to parliament (1977). He was expelled from the party's Central Committee (1985) after disagreeing with the political strategy of the new leadership, and he subsequently formed (1985) the

short-lived Spanish Worker's party–Communist Unity (PTE-U.C.). His books include *Problems of Socialism Today* (1967; Eng. trans. 1970) and *Eurocommunism and the State* (1977; Eng. trans. 1978).

CARRINGTON, ELAINE STERNE (1892–1958), U.S. writer. Known as the "Queen of the Soapers," Carrington wrote the first radio soap opera, "Red Adams." The show, concerned with the daily life of a middle-American family, was aired three times a week over the National Broadcasting Company in 1932 and was an enormous success with housewives. Carrington continued to write scripts for the show, whose name was changed to "Pepper Young's Family" (1936), until her death. She wrote more than 12,000 daily installments during her career and in the mid-1940s was writing three separate 15-minute shows.

CARROLL, VINNETTE (1922–), U.S. director and actress. Trained as a psychologist at New York University (M.A. 1946) and Columbia University, Carroll left the field to study acting with Erwin Piscator, Lee Strasberg, and Stella Adler. She made her Broadway debut in 1957. She appeared in Errol John's *Moon on a Rainbow Shawl* (1961, Obie Award), directed Langston Hughes' *Black Nativity* (1961) and *Prodigal Son* (1965), adapted and directed James Weldon Johnson's religious poems as *Trumpets of the Lord* (1963), and won a TV Emmy Award for *Beyond the Blues* (1964), a dramatization of selections by black poets. She was the founder (1967) and artistic director of the Urban Arts Corps, an experimental repertory theater group established to provide opportunities for minority playwrights, actors, and directors. Carroll's major Broadway stage-directing credits include the musicals *Don't Bother Me I Can't Cope* (1971) and *Your Arms Too Short to Box with God* (1975). She formed her own repertory company in 1986.

CARR-SAUNDERS, SIR ALEXANDER MORRIS (1886–1966), British demographer, sociologist, and academic administrator. Trained in zoology at Magdalen College, Oxford, Carr-Saunders became interested in biometrics and wrote *The Population Problem* (1922), a pioneering study of the relationship of population size to a country's social structure. He was one of the first to discuss birth control as a means of improving physical and social environment, urging the collection and analysis of demographic data as the basis for such a policy. He was a professor of social science at Liverpool University (1923–37) and director of the London School of Economics (1937–56). He also wrote a pioneering sociological study, *The Professions* (1933; with the P. A. Wilson), and chaired commissions on higher education (1943–55) that established universities in Malaya, Sudan, Nigeria, East Africa, and the West Indies.

CARSON, EDWARD. *See CARSON OF DUNCAIRN, EDWARD HENRY CARSON, BARON.*

CARSON, JOHNNY (1925–   ), U.S. television personality. America's best-paid television talent began his performing career with magic shows in Lincoln, Nebraska. He worked in radio in the 1940s, wrote comedy routines for Red Skelton in the 1950s, and hosted afternoon quiz shows like "Who Do You Trust" and "Earn Your Vacation." His monologues on the daytime "Johnny Carson Show" convinced NBC executives to give him (1962) Jack Paar's spot on "The Tonight Show." Carson's sharp quips, wry monologues, and "naughty boy" image appealed to late-night audiences, and his "desk and sofa" interview show was so popular that Carson, in typical fashion, termed himself America's most effective birth-control device. High ratings earned him multimillion-dollar contracts that allowed him extensive vacations. He retired in 1992. ■ See biographies by Douglas Lorence (1975) and Paul Corkery (1987).

CARSON, RACHEL LOUISE (1907–1964), U.S. biologist and science writer. A biologist with the U.S. Fish and Wildlife Service, Carson was the author of the highly acclaimed natural history of the sea, *The Sea Around Us* (1951). Her most influential work, the prophetic *Silent Spring* (1962), warned of the dangers of the indiscriminate use of insecticides and led to an increased awareness of environmental pollution. Few scientific works have had such an impact on the public. Her essays were published in *Lost Woods* (1998). ■ See Philip Sterling, *Sea and Earth* (1970); study by Carol B. Gartner (1983); and biography by Linda Lear (1997).

CARSON OF DUNCAIRN, EDWARD HENRY CARSON, BARON (1854–1935), Irish political leader. Born into a Protestant family in Dublin, Carson attended Trinity College and, in London, emerged as a brilliant lawyer. Elected (1892) to Parliament (as representative from Dublin), he proved to be a staunch unionist, opposing home rule in Ireland because of his sympathies with Protestant Ulster. Despite his conservative leanings, however, he favored such liberal notions as women's suffrage and the abolishment of capital punishment. His support for Northern Ireland led him to organize (1913) military rest resistance in Ulster, which eventually resulted in its exclusion from home rule. He was created a Baron in 1921. ■ See biographies by H. Montgomery Hyde (1953), A.T.Q. Stewart (1997), and John Hostettler (1997).

CARTAN, ÉLIE JOSEPH (1869–1951), French mathematician. A professor at the Sorbonne (1912–40), Cartan developed methods of analysis of the structure of continuous groups (Lie groups), differential systems, and differential geometry. His work played a crucial role in the development of quantum mechanics and general relativity and profoundly affected the shape of modern mathematics. He was elected to the French Academy of Sciences in 1931. ■ See *Élie Cartan–Albert Einstein: Letters on Absolute Parallelism, 1929–32* (Eng. trans. 1979) and biography by M. A. Akivis and B. A. Rosenfeld (Eng. trans. 1993).

CARTER FAMILY (Alvin Pleasant Carter, 1891–1960; Sara Dougherty Carter 1899–1979; Maybelle Addington Carter, 1990–1978), U.S. country singers. After the Victor Talking Machine invited local talent to audition in Bristol, Tennessee, the trio of A. P. Carter, his wife Sara, and his sister-in-law Maybelle began cutting recordings of country and sacred music that became immensely successful. A.P.'s songs (many of which he collected and "claimed" rather than composed), Sara's voice, and Maybelle's "thumb-brush" guitar style proved a matchless combination. The Carter Family's reputation was made largely through recordings, which sold well through the Depression. After 1938, younger Carters—including Anita, Janette, June, and Helen—joined the group, and the Carter Family began singing on the radio. The group disbanded (1943). Maybelle went on to produce many Nashville hits, forming the group Mother Maybelle and the Carter Sisters; she remained active in country music into the 1970s as part of Johnny Cash's road show. A.P., Sara, Joe, and Janette Carter appeared in the 1950s as the A. P. Carter Family. Country music—particularly bluegrass—was greatly influenced by the repertoire and style of the original Carter Family. ■ See Michael Orgill, *Anchored in Love* (1975), and study by Robert Krishof and Stacy Harris (1978).

CARTER, DON (1926–   ), U.S. bowler. Considered by many to be the greatest bowler in the history of the sport, Carter won six Professional Bowlers Association (PBA) championships, five World Invitational Singles championships, and four Bowling Proprietors' Association (BPA) All-Star championships. He was named Bowler of the Year six times (1953–54; 1957–58; 1960; 1962) and was selected as an All-American for eight consecutive years (1956–63). Utilizing an unorthodox bent-arm delivery, Carter rolled 11 perfect 300 games and was the star of the championship Budweiser team of St. Louis.

CARTER, ELLIOT COOK, JR. (1908–   ), U.S. composer. After earning a master's degree in music from Harvard (1932), Carter studied in Paris with the influential French musician Nadia Boulanger. One of the most important post–World War II U.S. composers, he was honored with Pulitzer Prizes for String Quartet No 2 (1960) and String Quartet No. 3 (1973). Carter's cerebral and difficult compositions, including *Sonata for Cello and Piano* (1948), String Quartet No. 1 (1951), *Double Concerto* (1961), *Concerto for Orchestra* (1969), and *A Symphony of Three Orchestras* (1977), were noted for their complex and innovative tempos, rhythms, and textures. His later works included Quartet No. 4 (1986), Quartet No. 5 (1995) for strings, and *Partita for Orchestra* (1994). ■ See *The Writings of Elliot Carter* (1977) and David Schiff, *The Music of Elliot Carter* (1983; rev. ed. 1998).

CARTER, HODDING, JR. (1907–1972), U.S. publisher and editor. A crusading liberal from the deep south who devoted his life to attacking racism and intolerance, Carter published the *Hammond* (Louisiana) *Daily Courier* (1932–36) and the *Greenville* (Mississippi) *Delta Democrat-Times* (1936–72). Known as "the spokesman for the new South," he won a 1945 Pulitzer Prize for his series of articles on racial, religious, and economic discrimination. His son, Hodding Carter 3rd (1935–), succeeded him at the *Delta Democrat-Times* and served as assistant secretary of state for public affairs (1977–80). ▪ See the autobiographical *Where Main Street Meets the River* (1953) and *First Person Rural* (1963).

CARTER, JIMMY (James Earl Carter, Jr.; 1924–), U.S. president. Born in rural Plains, Georgia (population 550), the son of a peanut farmer, Carter graduated from the U.S. Naval Academy (1947) and served in the navy as a nuclear engineering specialist. Returning to private life (1953), he built up the family farming business, participated in local affairs, and served in the state senate (1963–67) and as governor of Georgia (1971–75). A progressive Democrat, he reorganized the state bureaucracy, opened up the government to African-Americans and women, and inaugurated environmental and social programs. Campaigning as a trustworthy and truthful Washington outsider, he defeated incumbent Gerald R. Ford (1976) to become the 39th president of the United States. During his term he proposed a national energy policy, sponsored environmental legislation, signed the Panama Canal Treaty, was the major catalyst for the (Israeli-Egyptian) Camp David Treaty, and introduced a human rights component into U.S. foreign policy. He was viewed by many, however, as vacillating and lacking vision. His popularity waned as inflation increased and as the Iranian hostage crisis deepened in 1980, and he was badly beaten in his bid for reelection by Ronald Reagan (1980). After his presidency he was a board member of the organization Habitat for Humanity, and he led observer teams in monitoring elections in many countries around the world. He also played a major role in negotiations restoring peace in Ethiopia (1989) and in solving the crisis in Haiti (1994). ▪ See his autobiography, *Why Not the Best?* (1975); his memoirs, *Keeping Faith* (1982); his book on Middle East diplomacy, *The Blood of Abraham* (1985); his spiritual biography, *Living Faith* (1996); and biography by Betty Glad (1980). His post presidential activities are described in the study by Rod Troester (1996) and in Douglas Brinkley, *The Unfinished Presidency* (1998).

CARTIER-BRESSON, HENRI (1908–), French photographer. Cartier-Bresson was a student of painting who raised photography to an art. An unobtrusive character with an inconspicuous Leica camera, he traveled over Europe and Africa during the 1930s, taking pictures that he sold to newspapers and magazines and later exhibited at New York's Museum of Modern Art (1946) and the Louvre. In *The Decisive Moment* (1952) Cartier-Bresson explained his philosophy of "the accidental realism of the moment" in fa-

vor of which he rejected setups, retouching, and editing as well as color photography. He also published photo essays on Russia (1955), China (1956), Asia (1972), and composites of his work, *The World of Henri Cartier-Bresson* (1968), *Henri Cartier-Bresson, Photographer* (1979), *Henri Cartier-Bresson: Europeans* (1998), and *Tete à Tete* (1998). ▪ See study by Jean-Pierre Montier (1995; Eng. trans. 1996).

CARTLAND, BARBARA (1901–2000), British writer. Born into an aristocratic family, Cartland contributed articles to the *London Daily Express* before writing her first novel, *Jigsaw* (1925). Eventually known as the "queen of the romantic novel," she produced works of fiction at an astonishing pace for over 50 years, and by 1981 had written 304 books that sold more than 150 million copies. A champion of virginity and romantic love, her books featured (sexless) love affairs between young women and older noblemen who invariably married at the end of the story. She attributed the amazing popularity of her books with women in the 1960s and 1970s to a reaction against pornography. Cartland also wrote biographies, autobiographies (including *I Reach for the Stars,* 1994), and books on health, charm, etiquette, and cookery. She also published a romance magazine and comic strip and promoted "romantic tours" for British Airways. By the late 1990s, approximately one billion copies of her more than 700 books were in print, and the Guinness Book of World Records named her as the world's best-selling author. ▪ See biography by Henry Cloud (1980).

CARUSO, ENRICO (1873–1921), Italian opera singer. Caruso was born into an impoverished Neapolitan family, the 18th of 21 children and the first to survive past infancy. After brief schooling, he began singing in churches, street festivals, and to crowds lined up outside public baths. He was not a prodigy, but the voice that developed slowly into a rich, sonorous tenor became the best-known operatic voice of all time, almost legendary for its range, power, and emotional coloring. He sang at Milan's La Scala and London's Covent Garden, but was chiefly associated with the Metropolitan Opera in New York after his 1903 debut in *Rigoletto.* During his career, he sang more than 50 operatic roles, notably those in *La Bohème, I Pagliacci,* and *Tosca.* Numerous recordings preserved his renditions of arias as well as Neapolitan folk songs; his popularity continued to increase even after his death at age 48. ▪ See biographies by Dorothy Caruso (1945), Stanley Jackson (1972), Howard Greenfeld (1983), and Michael Scott (1988).

CARVER, GEORGE WASHINGTON (1861?–1943), U.S. chemist, botanist, and educator. Born a slave on a farm in Missouri, Carver supported himself as a laborer in a variety of occupations before graduating from high school in his middle twenties. He studied art and piano at Simpson College in Iowa, but was persuaded to study science, and transferred to Iowa State Agricultural College in Ames, where he received degrees in agricultural science (B.S. 1894; M.S.

1896). Hoping to improve the life of poor southern blacks, he accepted Booker T. Washington's invitation to head the newly organized department of agriculture at Tuskegee Institute in Alabama (1896), and he remained there for the rest of his life. His pioneering research indicated that peanuts and sweet potatoes could thrive in the depleted soil of the South, and he developed over 300 by-products from them, including dyes, food substitutes, oils, medicine, cosmetics, cereals, soaps, and plastics. He also developed numerous hybrids and fertilizers and taught poor farmers elements of crop diversity and soil enrichment. His efforts transformed southern agriculture, and he gained an international reputation as a leading scientist and humanitarian. ■ See biographies by Rackham Holt (1963), Linda O. McMurry (1981), and Gary R. Kremer (1987).

CARY, (ARTHUR) JOYCE (1888–1957), British novelist. Cary's first seven novels, notably *Aissa Saved* (1932) and *Mr. Johnson* (1939), reflected his own experiences in Africa as a colonial officer. Aspects of his own childhood are recaptured in *A House of Children* (1941). His later novels, set in Britain, demonstrated his belief in the creative potential of the individual. His best-regarded works are two humorous, ironic trilogies with strong, feisty characters as their protagonists: the first, concerned with art, is *Herself Surprised* (1941), *To Be a Pilgrim* (1942), and his most famous novel, *The Horse's Mouth* (1944); the second, about politics, is composed of *Prisoner of Grace* (1952), *Except the Lord* (1953), and *Not Honour More* (1955). ■ See biography by Malcolm Foster (1968) and Alan Bishop, *Gentleman Rider* (1988).

CASALS, PABLO (1876–1973), Spanish cellist. Born into a poor but musical family, Casals was a child prodigy but did not start playing the cello until age 11. His first solo recital (1899) was followed by a 75-year career as a cellist, composer, and conductor (in 1919 he founded his own orchestra in Barcelona). Regarded as the century's greatest cellist, Casals revolutionized cello-playing technique by his freer bowing and newer fingerings, which allowed him to obtain subtleties of tone and intonation. Trained in the romantic tradition, he emphasized the melodic and rhythmic contours of the music; his playing restored Bach's unaccompanied partitas to the recital repertoire. An ardent humanitarian and democrat, Casals protested the regime of dictator Francisco Franco in Spain by living in self-imposed exile after 1939. After years in France, he moved to Puerto Rico (1956), where he launched the Casals Festival (1957). He became a well-known figure in the United States. ■ See his memoirs, *Joys and Sorrows* (1970), and biographies by H. L. Kirk (1974) and Robert Baldock (1993).

CASELLA, ALFREDO (1883–1947), Italian pianist and composer. One of the most influential figures in contemporary Italian music, Casella pursued a successful solo, conducting, and teaching career while organizing concerts,

festivals, and periodicals aimed at promoting modern music. He founded the Italian Society for Modern Music (1917) and helped introduce the music of Ravel, Debussy, and Stravinsky. An extremely versatile composer, he wrote in all mediums in styles ranging from neoromantic to dissonant and polytonal. He is best known for the rhapsody *Italia* (1910), the ballet *La Giara* (1924), the *Partita for Piano and Orchestra* (1925), and the divertimenti *Scarlattiana* (1926) and *Paganiniana* (1942–43). ■ See his memoirs, *Music in My Time* (1941; Eng. trans. 1955).

CASEMENT, SIR ROGER DAVID (1864–1916), Irish revolutionist. Casement served in the British consular service (1895–1912) and was knighted for exposing colonial exploitation in the Belgian Congo (1904) and in South America. Becoming a fervent Irish nationalist, he sought aid for the nationalists during World War I first from the United States and later from Germany, but he was unable to obtain the help needed for the 1916 Easter Rebellion. On returning to Ireland, he was spotted disembarking from a German submarine by a farmer and was subsequently arrested, sent to London, tried, and hanged for treason. ■ See biographies by Brian Inglis (1974) and Roger Sawyer (1984) and B. L. Reid, *The Lives of Roger Casement* (1976).

CASH, JOHNNY (1932–), U.S. country-music singer and composer. The son of Arkansas sharecroppers, Cash recorded his first hit single in 1955 and began appearing regularly on the Grand Ole Opry radio show in Nashville. Within a few years he was one of the most popular country-music performers, although his problems with stimulants and tranquilizers nearly ended his career in the 1960s. The possessor of a distinctively deep and flat baritone voice, he recorded many songs dealing with prisoners, outlaws, and other luckless and trapped people. His biggest hits included "Folsom Prison Blues," "I Walk the Line," "A Boy Named Sue," and "Don't Take Your Guns to Town." Cash also appeared on his own television show (1969–71), acted in several movies, and frequently performed in prisons and at benefits for American Indians. ■ See Christopher S. Wren, *Winners Got Scars Too* (1971), and the autobiographies *Man in Black* (1975) and *Cash* (1997; with Patrick Carr).

CASONA, ALEJANDRO (Alejandro Rodriguez Alvarez; 1903–1965), Spanish playwright. In the witty tradition of the older Benavente, Casona wrote plays that derived from the Spanish brand of surrealism, which blurs distinctions between reality and illusion. A onetime school inspector, he examined other social institutions in plays that had a sharp satirical edge. After *The Stranded Mermaid* (1934) established his reputation, his plays of the 1930s, including *No Suicide Allowed in Spring* (1937; Eng. trans. 1950), anticipated the theater of the absurd. Casona was best known for *Trees Die Upright* (1949), Other works included *Lady of the Dawn* (1944; Eng. trans. 1972) and *The Boat Without a Fisherman* (1945; Eng. trans. 1970). He emigrated to Argentina during the Spanish civil war (1936–39), returning (1963) to Spain only shortly before his death. ■ See study by Harold K. Moon (1985).

CASSANDRE (Adolphe Mouron; 1901–1968), Russian born French poster artist. Cassandre studied at the Académie Julian in Paris and published his first poster in 1922; by the next year he was famous for *Le Bûcheron* "the woodcutter," stylized poster produced for a cabinetmaker. His concept of poster art's communicative function and his innovative use of color, design, and type powerfully affected advertising techniques and graphic arts in general and fostered acceptance of avant-garde art. His forceful depictions of tennis matches, wines, steamships, and horse races were seen on Parisian billboards throughout the 1920s and 1930s. Cassandre also designed stage sets and developed new typefaces. ■ See study by Henri Mouron (Eng. trans. 1985).

CASSIN, RENÉ (1887–1976), French statesman. Cassin was a professor of International law in Paris (1929–60) and served on the French delegation to the League of Nations (1924–38). During World War II he served under Gen. Charles de Gaulle as a prominent member of the French government-in-exile and held high legal and administrative positions in postwar France. In 1946 he became a member of the United Nations Human Rights Commission (president, 1955–57) and was a founder of UNESCO. Considered France's foremost expert on international law, he was the principal author (1948) of the U.N. Declaration of the Rights of Man and was president of the European Court of Human Rights (1965–68). He also headed several Jewish organizations in France. He was awarded the 1968 Nobel Peace Prize.

CASSIRER, ERNST (1874–1945), German philosopher. Cassirer, a prominent neo-Kantian, was a professor of philosophy at the University of Hamburg (1919–33). A Jew, he left Germany when the Nazis came to power and taught at Oxford (1933–35); Göteborg, Sweden (1935–41); and Yale University (1941–44). He wrote several books on the history of science, the problem of knowledge, and the theory of myth. He believed that human beings are primarily creators of symbols, including language, myth, art, history, and science, and that culture is the unity of these diverse symbolic forms. Cassirer's major works included *The Philosophy of Symbolic Forms* (3 vols., 1923–29; Eng. trans. 1953–57), *Language and Myth* (1925; Eng. trans. 1946), *An Essay on Man: An introduction to a Philosophy of Human Culture* (1944), and *The Myth of the State* (1946). ■ See P. A. Schilpp, *The Philosophy of Ernst Cassirer* (1949), and studies by Seymour W. Itzkoff (1977) and David R. Lipton (1978).

CASSOLA, CARLO (1917–1987), Italian novelist. Cassola participated in the antifascist resistance during World War II

in Tuscany, the setting of his fictional works. Originally committed to a literary aesthetic that valued narrative objectivity and the depiction of timelessness, a world devoid of action and development, his works eventually became broader in scope and treated social and political problems. He often wrote of the brief joys and subsequent disillusionment in the lives of his characters and of their acceptance of their destiny. His works, most of which have strong working-class women as protagonists, included *The Cutting of the Woods* (1950; Eng. trans. 1961), *Fausto and Anna* (1952; Eng. trans. 1960), *Bebo's Girl* (1960; Eng. trans. 1962), and *An Arid Heart* (1961; Eng. trans. 1964). His writings of the 1970s were concerned with the threat of nuclear war.

CASTANEDA, CARLOS ARANA (1931?–1998), Brazilian-born (?) U.S. anthropologist. Castaneda was a graduate student in anthropology at the University of California, Los Angeles, when he went to Arizona in 1960 to study the Indian use of medicinal plants; he remained to become the local sorcerer's apprentice. His master's thesis, *The Teachings of Don Juan: A Yaqui Way of Knowledge*, became a bestseller after its publication by the university press in 1968. An elusive cult figure, Castaneda then wrote four best-selling sequels (including his Ph.D. thesis, *Journey to Ixtlan*, 1972), which were considered anthropological classics by some and great works of fiction by others. His later books included *The Fire From Within* (1984), *The Power of Silence* (1987), and *The Wheel of Time* (1998), a reflection on his work. ■ See Richard DeMille, *Castaneda's Journey* (1976).

CASTELO BRANCO, HUMBERTO DE ALENCAR (1900–1967), Brazilian military officer and political leader. A career officer who worked his way up to being army chief of staff, Castelo Branco was a leader of the coup that overthrew the left-wing government of João Goulart (1964). Serving as president (1964–67), he dissolved political parties and disbanded civil liberties, concentrated political power in the hands of the executive, and instituted an economic austerity program that lowered inflation but also lowered the standard of living of Brazilian workers. He died in a plane crash shortly after retiring. ■ See studies by John W. F. Dulles (1978, 1980).

CASTLE, VERNON (1887–1918), **and IRENE CASTLE** (1893–1969), U.S. dancers. British-born engineer Vernon Castle Blythe traveled to the United States in 1906 and, dropping his surname, began a theatrical career in *The Girl Behind the Counter* (1907) before he married Irene Foote in 1911. The couple first won acclaim while dancing in a Paris café (1912) and later were widely sought after to perform in American cafés and theaters. Innovators in ballroom dancing, they introduced the one-step, the turkey trot, and the Castle-walk, and they popularized existing dances such as the hesitation waltz and the tango. The Castles' dancing popularity was cut short by Vernon's death in a crash while training fighter pilots In Texas (1918). Irene Castle, credited with starting the bobbed-hair fashion, was later known for her animal-welfare work. ■ See her *Castles in the Air* (1958).

CASTRO, JOSÉ MARIA FERREIRA DE. *See FERREIRA DE CASTRO, JOSÉ MARIA.*

CASTRO RUZ, FIDEL (1926–), Cuban political leader. The son of a moderately wealthy sugar plantation owner, Castro was a revolutionary student activist at the University of Havana (J.D. 1950). He practiced law among the poor in Havana and led an unsuccessful insurrection against the regime of dictator Fulgencio Batista (July 26, 1953). Amnestied from prison (May 1955), he went into exile in Mexico until December 1956, when he returned to Cuba with a small group of revolutionaries and established a guerrilla movement in the Sierra Maestra mountains. When Batista fled Cuba (Jan. 1, 1959), Castro assumed power and set up a government that nationalized industry, instituted radical agrarian and social reforms, and confiscated more than $1 billion of U.S.-owned property. After the abortive U.S.-backed Bay of Pigs invasion (1961), Castro declared himself a Marxist-Leninist. Cuba increasingly depended on the Soviet Union for economic and military aid, and the Cuban Communist party—which Castro headed—became the only legal political organization. A fiery orator and charismatic leader, Castro symbolized revolution and anti-capitalism for radicals throughout Latin America and the Third World. Economically isolated after the collapse of the Soviet Union in the early 1990s, Castro initiated a series of limited market reforms, decentralized state-owned enterprises, introduced agricultural cooperatives, encouraged foreign investment, and attempted to reinstate Cuba into the international capitalist economy while trying to maintain socialist principles and benefits. ■ See *Fidel Castro Speaks* (1970); biographies by Herbert L. Matthews (1969) and Robert E. Quirk (1993); Lee Lockwood, *Castro's Cuba, Cuba's Fidel* (1969); Edward Gonzalez, *Cuba Under Castro* (1974); Tad Szulc, *Fidel* (1986); and studies by Sheldon B. Liss (1994) and Thomas M. Leonard (1999).

CASTRO RUZ, RAÚL HÉCTOR (1931–), Cuban political leader. A member of his brother Fidel's guerrilla movement in Cuba, Raúl Castro was captured after the failure of the attack on the Moncada barracks (1953) and fled to Mexico after being amnestied in 1955. He returned the following year on board the yacht *Granma* to launch the final assault against the regime of Fulgencio Batista. In 1959 Castro became head of the armed forces and was later designated vice premier and successor to his brother. In these posts he negotiated in 1962 for Soviet missiles to be installed in Cuba, provided training and support to African independence movements a decade later, and delivered ardent anti-imperialist tirades against the United States.

CATHER, WILLA (1873–1947), U.S. novelist and short-story writer. A meticulous stylist, Cather mined the experiences of her Nebraska youth to depict midwestern frontier life of the late 19th century. A lesbian who wrote primarily about women's experience, Cather did not explore her characters' inner lives, but populated her novels with vigorous, substantial working women who defy the stereotype of feminine fragility. Moving to New York (1904), Cather was managing editor of *McClure's* magazine (1905–12), then devoted herself to writing novels and published *Alexander's Bridge* (1912) and *O Pioneers!* (1913). *My Antonia* (1918), her most admired work, is still read despite a general decline in Cather's popularity. Important later works included *One of Ours* (1922; Pulitzer Prize), *The Professor's House* (1925), *Death Comes for the Archbishop* (1927), and the best-selling *Shadows on the Rock* (1931). After viewing Hollywood's adaptation of the novel that brought her fame, *A Lost Lady* (1923), she stipulated in her will that no more of her fiction be made into movies. ■ See biographies by Phyllis Robinson (1983) and James Woodress (1970), and studies by Dorothy Van Ghent (1964), P. L. Gerber (1975), Sharon O'Brien (1987), Hermione Lee (1989), and Joan Acocella (2000).

CATROUX, GEORGES (1877–1969), French general. The son of a general, Catroux graduated from St. Cyr Military Academy in 1899 and served in the foreign legion in Indochina and North Africa. He was captured during World War I but decorated for valorous service; he later served as governor of Damascus and governor-general of Indochina. The only important general who refused to accept France's capitulation to Germany in 1940, Catroux joined in exile Gen. Charles de Gaulle, who appointed him commander in chief of the Free French in the Levant, where he proclaimed the independence of Syria and Lebanon (1941). He also served as governor-general in Algeria (1943–44) and as ambassador to the Soviet Union (1944–48).

CATT, CARRIE CHAPMAN (Carrie Lane; 1859–1947), U.S. suffragist and pacifist. Catt graduated from Iowa State College (1880) and served as school superintendent in Mason City, Iowa (1883–85). An Iowa delegate to the National American Woman Suffrage Association's first convention, she was an organizer (1890–1900) for that association succeeding Susan B. Anthony as its president (1900–04; from 1915). With Jane Addams, Catt established (1915) the Women's Peace party, and during World War I she worked toward pacifist goals while remaining a key figure in the suffragist movement. Her political strategy of working on both state and national levels resulted in the ratification (1920) of the 19th Amendment, which gave women the vote. She was also involved in organizing the League of Women Voters (1919) and served as president of the International Woman Suffrage Alliance (1904–23). She devoted the last decades of her life to the pacifist cause. Catt was coauthor with Nettie Shuler, of *Woman Suffrage and Politics* (1923). ■ See biographies by Mary G. Peck (1944), Robert B. Fowler (1986), and Jacqueline van Vorris (1987).

CAUDWELL, CHRISTOPHER (Christopher St. John Sprigg; 1907-1937), British writer. Caudwell wrote several books on aviation, seven mystery thrillers, and a few science-fiction short stories before becoming deeply involved with the study of Marxism (1934). He joined the Communist party (1935) and fought with the international brigade in Spain, where he was killed during the battle of Jarama River. His works of Marxist literary criticism, including *Illusion and Reality* (1937), which represented the first Marxist theory of poetry, were published posthumously. His other works included *Studies in Dying Culture* (1938), *Further Studies in a Dying Culture* (1949), and *Romance and Realism* (1970).

CAVAFY, CONSTANTINE (Konstantinos P. Kabaphes; 1863-1933), Egyptian-born Greek poet. Acclaimed during his lifetime as the greatest figure of modern Greek poetry, Cavafy never published his works and rarely left his native city of Alexandria, where he was a prominent member of international society and where he worked for the ministry of irrigation. Standing apart from contemporary Greek literary life, the pessimistic Cavafy evoked, with unique insight, the glory and decline of Pan-Hellenistic civilization. He was a master of free iambic verse who utilized a simple style and somewhat archaic but graceful language. Among his most-famous poems were "Waiting for the Barbarians," "The Town," "Ithaca," "In a Large Greek Colony," and "Myris: Alexandria A.D. 340." English translations appeared in *The Complete Poems of Cavafy* (1976) and *Collected Poems* (1975). ∎ See study by Robert Liddell (1976).

CAVELL, EDITH LOUISA (1865-1915), English nurse. Cavell first attracted notice as matron of the Berkendael Medical Institute (Brussels), where she helped (from 1907) to modernize the nursing profession in Belgium. In August 1915, during World War I, she was arrested by the German occupation authorities and accused of harboring Allied soldiers at her hospital and helping them to reach neutral Netherlands. She confessed to these charges and was executed (Oct. 12, 1915). Cavell was never accused of espionage and her execution was considered an outrage. Widely publicized by the Allies, it damaged Germany's reputation. ∎ See Adolph A. Hoehling, *Whisper of Eternity* (1958), and biography by Rowland Ryder (1975).

CAVETT, DICK (1936–), U.S. television personality. As a teenager Cavett played *The Winslow Boy* to a hometown Nebraska audience before going on to Yale and summer-stock acting. His career flourished, however, not onstage but before TV cameras; after writing comedy routines for Jack Paar, Johnny Carson, and others, he hosted the nightly program "The Dick Cavett Show," winning loyal audiences in the early 1970s with his dry wit, willingness to address controversial issues, and provocative interviews with usually uninterviewable guests, including Katharine Hepburn and Marlon Brando. Cavett's show was canceled when ratings dropped. He subsequently appeared regularly on the Public Broadcasting Service, hosting an interview show (1977–82) and offering backstage commentaries on "live" ballet and opera performances. ∎ See his autobiographies; *Cavett* (1974; with Christopher Porterfield) and *Eye on Cavett* (1983; with Porterfield).

CAYCE, EDGAR (1877–1945), U.S. psychic healer. The son of a Kentucky farmer, Cayce had visions as a child and (in a trance) began to prescribe cures for illnesses at age 16, although he had no knowledge of medicine. He treated more than 30,000 patients during his 43 years of healing and was said to have cured people that doctors claimed were incurable. He founded the Association for Research and Enlightenment, in Virginia (1931), to keep records of his work. He was reputed to be a clairvoyant and to be able to perceive human auras and to predict the future. ∎ See Thomas Sugrue, *There Is a River* (1942); the study by Joseph Millard (1956); biography by Jess Stearn (1967); and Edgar E. Cayce and Hugh L. Cayce, *The Outer Limits of Edgar Cayce's Power* (1971).

CEAUŞESCU, NICOLAE (1918–1989), Rumanian political leader. A youthful activist in the then-illegal Communist party. Ceauşescu was imprisoned for eight years before and during World War II. A protégé of party leader Gheorghe Gheorghiu-Dej, he served as minister of agriculture (1948–50), deputy armed-forces minister (1950–54), and Politburo member (from 1955) before being named party secretary-general (1965) and president of Rumania (1967). An orthodox Marxist-Leninist, he enforced rigid domestic controls while concentrating on Rumanian economic development. He advocated ideological and political independence from the Soviet Union, however, and pursued an independent foreign policy that included friendly relations with China, Israel, and most capitalist countries. The imposition of severe austerity policies and the razing of peasant villages in the pursuit of economic development in the 1980s led to growing unrest, and he was overthrown in a bloody revolution (December 1989). After a summary trial both he and his wife, Elena, his first deputy prime minister, were executed by firing squad. ∎ See studies by John Sweeney (1991) and Mark Almond (1992).

CECH, THOMAS R. (1947–), U.S. chemist. Cech earned a doctorate in chemistry from the University of California Berkeley (1975) and taught at the University of Colorado (1978–99). In a series of experiments during the late 1970s and 1980s Cech showed, contrary to prevailing scientific belief, that ribonucleic acid (RNA) was not only a carrier of genetic information, but was also able to act as an enzyme and initiate chemical reactions within the cell. (Previously it was thought that all enzymes were proteins.) Independent research by Sidney Altman also demonstrated that RNA can function as a catalyst. The findings of Cech and Altman gave rise to new theories of cellular functioning, promised new tools for genetic engineering, and provided a new explanation for how life on Earth began—with RNA serving as both carrier of genetic information and catalyst for chemical reaction. Cech and Altman shared the 1989 Nobel Prize in Chemistry for their research. Cech served as president of the Howard Hughes Medical Institute, Bethesda, Maryland (2000–   ).

CECIL, EDGAR ALGERNON ROBERT, 1st VISCOUNT CECIL OF CHELWOOD (called Lord Robert Cecil to 1923; 1864–1958), British political leader. The son of Lord Salisbury, who was three times British prime minister, Cecil studied law and served in Parliament as a Conservative from 1906 to 1923. He helped write (1919) the Covenant of the League of Nations, served as a delegate to the league and to the Geneva Disarmament Conference, and won the 1937 Nobel Peace Prize for his efforts on behalf of collective security. ■ See his autobiographies, *A Great Experiment* (1941) and *All the Way* (1949).

CELA, CAMILO JOSÉ (1916–   ), Spanish novelist and short-story writer. Cela established his reputation with *Pascual Duarte's Family* (1942; Eng. trans. 1946). Reflecting the chaos in post–civil war Spain, the novel introduced the technique known as *tremendisimo,* which uses grim humor, grandiose language, and alienated characters to communicate violence and absurdity. *The Hive* (1950; Eng. trans. 1953), a naturalistic novel with more than 200 characters, portrays Madrid society at its most sordid. Cela also wrote travel accounts, such as *Journey to the Alcarria* (1948; Eng. trans. 1964), and short fiction collected in *The Windmill* (1956). His stylistic innovations made him a leading writer of the post–civil war period. Despite his conservative political leanings, Cela's works were suppressed by dictator Francisco Franco's regime. He founded and edited (1956–79) the prominent literary review *Papeles de Son Armadans.* His civil-war novel, *Mazurka for Two Dead Men* (1983; Eng. trans. 1992), was acclaimed as his masterpiece. His other works included *San Camilo, 1936* (1969; Eng. trans. 1991). He won the 1989 Nobel Prize in Literature. ■ See Study by D. W. McPheeters (1969).

CELAN, PAUL (Paul Antschel; 1920–1970), Rumanian-born poet and translator. A survivor of the Holocaust whose parents died in concentration camps, Celan settled in Paris (after 1948) and was regarded as one of the most distinguished post–World War II German-language poets. His early poems, influenced by surrealism, the Jewish mystical tradition, and the genocide of the Jews during World War II, were filled with images of terror and death, while his later more abstract and fragmented works primarily concerned the nature of words and poetry. He explained his conception of poetry in the essay "The Meridian" (1961; Eng. trans.

1978). He committed suicide at age 49. English translations of his works are in *Speech-Grille* (1971), *Selected Poems* (1972), and *Poems* (1980). ■ See study by Jerry Glenn (1973).

CÉLINE, LOUIS FERDINAND (Louis Ferdinand Destouches; 1894–1961), French novelist. Céline was a medical doctor who ministered to the poor. His first novel, *Journey to the End of the Night* (1932; Eng. trans. 1934, 1983), was an immediate success, causing a furor with its hallucinatory style, harsh obscene language, and pessimistic viewpoint. He showed a contemporary world without values. Both that book, and his second, *Death on the Installment Plan* (1936; Eng. trans. 1938), with their use of slang and their nightmare visions, profoundly influenced other writers. A rabid anti-Semite, Céline collaborated with the Nazis during World War II and fled to Germany (1944). *Castle to Castle* (1957; Eng. trans. 1968) and *North* (1960; Eng. trans. 1972) describe the calamity of the war as seen from within Germany. After his eventual return to France (1951), he resumed his medical career. ■ See studies by Patrick McCarthy (1975), David O'Connell (1976), and Merlin Thomas (1980).

CELLER, EMMANUEL (1888–1981), U.S. congressman. Celler became head of his family at age 18 when his parents died, yet managed to finish Columbia College (1910) and Columbia Law School (1912) and establish a successful law practice. As a Democratic congressman from Brooklyn for 50 years (1923–73), he made a reputation by defending civil and constitutional liberties. A New Deal supporter who became head of the House Judiciary Committee in 1949, a position he held for 22 years, Celler was instrumental in the passage of the 1957, 1960, and 1964 civil-rights acts. ■ See his autobiography, *You Never Leave Brooklyn* (1953).

CENDRARS, BLAISE (Frederic-Louis Sauser; 1887–1961), Swiss-born French poet, essayist, and novelist. A world traveler and an adventurer who tried a number of occupations, Cendrars wrote poetry that was spontaneous, breathless, evocative, and very influential, notably, *Complete Postcards from the Americas* (1919; Eng. trans. 1976). Much of his writing, including *Lice* (1946; Eng. trans. 1973) and *Planus* (1948; Eng. trans. 1972), was semiautobiographical and extolled a life of danger and the importance of inner resilience in the face of adversity. He was a gifted storyteller. His novels include *Sutter's Gold* (1925; Eng. trans. 1926; as *Gold,* 1984). ■ See his *Sky: Memoirs* (Eng. trans. 1992), *Selected Writings* (Eng. trans. 1966); biography by Jay Bochner (1978); and study by Monique Chefdor (1980).

CERF, BENNETT ALFRED (1898–1971), U.S. publisher. A former editor of the Columbia College humor magazine, Cerf, and partner Donald S. Klopfer, bought Modern Library in 1925 and two years later launched their own firm to publish books at "random." Random House grew large and successful, counting James Joyce, Marcel Proust, William Faulkner, Sinclair Lewis, and Eugene O'Neill among its authors. Cerf became a celebrity himself with his syndicated joke column ("Cerfboard"), his anthologies of puns and anecdotes, and his weekly TV appearances on "What's My Line?" (1952–66). ■ See his reminiscences, *At Random* (1977).

CERNUDA, LUIS (1902–1963), Spanish poet. Cernuda wrote in exile after fighting for the republic in the Spanish civil war (1936–39). An uncompromising artist, he wrote technically superb verse, the best of which is collected in *Reality and Desire* (1936, 1940, 1958, 1964). He adhered to the tenet that one should "cultivate what others censure in you, for that is your true self." His poems constitute a search of lost innocence. Cernuda's last volume, *Desolation of the Chimera* (1958), contains some bitter attacks on his contemporaries. He also wrote prose poems, three stories, and a notable translation of Shakespeare's *Troilus and Cressida*. Translations of his works are in *The Poetry of Luis Cernuda* (1971) and *Selected Poems* (1977). ■ See study by Salvador Jiménez-Fajardo (1978).

CÉSAIRE, AIMÉ FERNAND (1913–   ), Martinican poet, playwright, and political leader. A master of the French language who was regarded as the most prominent poet of the Caribbean world, Césaire was a cofounder (with Léopold Senghor and Léon Damas) of the influential Négritude movement, which sought to restore the cultural identity and dignity of blacks. He was a militant anticolonialist whose writings inspired the leaders of the independence movements in West Africa. His best-known works, influenced both by Marxism and surrealism, were the fiery poem, *Return to My Native Land* (1939; Eng. trans. 1968), the plays *Tragedy of King Christophe* (1963; Eng. trans. 1970) and *A Season in the Congo* (1966; Eng. trans. 1969), and two historical works, *Discourse on Colonialism* (1950; Eng. trans. 1972) and *Toussaint L'Ouverture* (1961), a biography of the Haitian revolutionary hero. Césaire served in the French national assembly (1946–93) and was president of the Parti Progressiste Martiniquais and mayor of Fort-de-France, the capital of Martinique (from 1945). ■ See *Aimé Césaire, the Collected Poetry, 1939–1976* (Eng. trans. 1983), *Lyric and Dramatic Poetry, 1946–1982* (Eng. trans. 1990); and A. James Arnold, *Modernism and Negritude* (1981).

CHADWICK, FLORENCE MAY (1918–1995), U.S. distance swimmer. A stenographer from California who was a child prodigy at swimming (she swam the San Diego Bay Channel at age 10), Chadwick broke Gertrude Ederle's record by swimming the English Channel in 13 hours, 20 minutes (1950). In 1951 she swam the channel from England to France, thus becoming the first woman to swim it in both directions. She also broke the speed record while swimming from Catalina Island to the California mainland (1952). In 1953 she swam the Strait of Gibraltar, the Dard-

anelles, the Bosporus, and the English Channel (for the third time)—all within a matter of weeks. After she retired from swimming, she became a stockbroker.

CHADWICK, SIR JAMES (1891–1974), British physicist. Chadwick studied under and then for years collaborated with Ernest Rutherford as a lecturer and assistant director of radioactive research at the Cavendish Laboratory in Cambridge. There Chadwick proved the existence of the neutron (1932) by bombarding beryllium with alpha particles. He was awarded the 1935 Nobel Prize for Physics for this work. He also discovered that the collision of the neutron with atomic nuclei resulted in the release of protons. During World War II he was actively engaged in the United States in experiments that led to the development of the atomic bomb. He wrote *Radiation from Radioactive Substances* (1930; with Rutherford and C. D. Ellis).

CHAFEE, ZECHARIAH, JR. (1885–1957), U.S. lawyer and legal scholar. A professor at the Harvard Law School (1916–56), Chafee was one of the nation's leading civil libertarians. Although he was born to wealth and held conservative political beliefs, he was concerned with protecting freedom of speech during and after World War I and defended radicals whose views he abhorred. His book *Freedom of Speech* (1920; expanded as *Free Speech in the United States, 1941*) established his reputation, and he was actively involved in civil-rights cases for decades. His other books included *The Inquiring Mind* (1928) and *Blessings of Liberty* (1956). ■ See study by Donald L. Smith (1986).

CHAFFEE, ADNA ROMANZA, JR. (1884–1941), U.S. military leader. The son of a general who served as army chief of staff, Chaffee graduated from West Point (1906) and became one of the army's finest horsemen. After a distinguished battle record in World War I, he promoted the development of a mechanized army based on tanks and other mobile armor and was known as "the father of the armored force." In 1934 he organized and was given command of the army's first mechanized brigade.

CHAGALL, MARC (1887–1985), Russian-born French artist. Born into a devout Hasidic Jewish family in the provincial town of Vitebsk, Chagall was granted special permission to study art in St. Petersburg (1907–09). There he met a patron who enabled him to move to Paris (1910), where he befriended the cubist painters and surrealist poets who were transforming French cultural life. In Paris Chagall began to produce the colorful and whimsical canvases, filled with visions of Jewish folklore and elements of fantasy and the unconscious, that evoked his childhood memories. He returned to Russia (1915) and served briefly as cultural commissar for Vitebsk (1917–19) after the Russian Revolution. However, he met with official disapproval and left his homeland for Berlin (1922) and Paris (1923), where he settled and won international fame. During World War II he lived in

New York City (1941–47), but he returned to France after the war. In addition to hundreds of paintings and book illustrations, he designed stained-glass windows for the synagogue of the Hebrew University Medical Center near Jerusalem (1962), the ceiling for the Paris Opera (1964), and two large murals for the Metropolitan Opera in New York (1966). ■ See his autobiography (1931; Eng. trans. 1957), *My Life, My Dream: Berlin and Paris, 1922–40* (Eng. trans. 1990); the biographies by Franz Meyer (Eng. trans. 1964), Jean Cassou (1965), Jean Paul Crespelle (Eng. trans. 1970), and Sidney Alexander (1977); and studies by Monika Bohm-Duchen (1998) and Daniel Marchesseau (1998).

CHAIN, SIR ERNST BORIS (1906–1979), German-born British biochemist. The recipient of a degree in chemistry from the Friedrich-Wilhelm University in Berlin (1930), Chain, a Jew, emigrated to England at the outset of the Nazi era (1933). His most significant work, the extraction and purification of penicillin, was done in collaboration with Sir Howard W. Florey at Oxford. They shared the Nobel Prize in Physiology or Medicine (1945) with Sir Alexander Fleming, the discoverer of penicillin. Their work ushered in the modern era of antibiotics. Chain was professor of biochemistry at Imperial College of the University of London (1961–73).

CHALIAPIN, FEODOR IVANOVICH (1873–1938), Russian opera singer. Born into a poor family, Chaliapin was a rare outstanding boy soprano who survived the voice change to become a world-class opera star. He specialized in complex, tormented characters such as Boris Godunov or Mephistopheles, portraying them with great theatricality. Although sympathetic to the revolutionary government, which honored him as a People's Artist, Chaliapin spent the years after 1921 in the cultural capitals of the West. ■ See his memoirs, *Pages From My Life* (Eng. trans. 1927) and *Man and Mask* (Eng. trans. 1932), and his autobiography as told to Maxim Gorky (Eng. trans. 1967).

CHALIDZE, VALERY NIKOLAEVICH (1938–), Soviet-born human-rights activist and publisher. Chalidze, a physicist living in Moscow, edited and published the typescript journal *Social Problems* (1969–71), which included signed articles on questions of law, ethics, and other social issues. He was also a founding member of the Moscow Human Rights Committee, which sought to compel Soviet authorities to act in conformity with Soviet and international law. A self-taught legal expert, Chalidze dispensed counsel in Thursday night "at-homes" in his Moscow apartment. While he was lecturing in the United States in 1972, Soviet authorities revoked his citizenship—the first instance of a ploy later used to exile other Soviet dissidents. He remained in the United States, where he founded Khronika Press (1973; later Chalidze Publications) and wrote on legal, social, and political issues, venturing as well into psycholinguistics. In 1985 he won a prestigious MacArthur Fellowship. He wrote *To Defend These Rights* (Eng. trans. 1975) and *Criminal Russia* (Eng. trans 1977).

CHAMBERLAIN, SIR (JOSEPH) AUSTEN (1863–1937), British political leader. Chamberlain, whose father Joseph was an important politician and whose half brother Neville became prime minister, was elected a Conservative member of Parliament in 1892. He served as chancellor of the Exchequer (1903–05; 1919–21), secretary of state of India (1915–17), and head of the Conservative party (1921–22). He advanced to the foreign secretaryship (1924–29), sharing the 1925 Nobel Peace Prize (with Charles G. Dawes) for the Locarno Pact and mutual defense and arbitration treaties that he negotiated. ■ See his memoirs, *Down the Years* (1935), *Politics from Inside* (1936), and *Seen in Passing* (1937), and biography by Charles Petrie (2 vols., 1939–40).

CHAMBERLAIN, (ARTHUR) NEVILLE (1869–1940), British political leader. Neville Chamberlain, the son of Joseph Chamberlain and half brother of Austen Chamberlain, entered Parliament as a Conservative, at age 50, and held several posts including those of minister of health (1923; 1924–29; 1931) and chancellor of the Exchequer (1923–24; 1931–37) before serving as prime minister (1937–40). He is best remembered for his policy of appeasement toward Italy and Germany, which culminated in the Munich Pact (1938). After the signing he declared that there would be "peace in our time." When appeasement failed and World War II began, he was replaced as prime minister by his foremost critic, Winston Churchill (May 1940), but he served in the war cabinet until ill health forced him to resign from public life (September 1940). ■ See biographies by Iain MacLeod (1961), H. Montgomery Hyde (1976), and David Dilks (Vol. I. 1985).

CHAMBERLAIN, OWEN (1920–), U.S. physicist. Chamberlain worked on the Manhattan atomic bomb project (1942–46) and received his Ph.D. (1949) in physics at the University of Chicago, where he worked under Enrico Fermi. His main achievement was a laboratory demonstration of the existence of the antiproton—a particle predicted in 1930 by Paul Dirac, who theorized that electrons, protons, and neutrons have nuclear "twins" with identical mass but opposite charge. Many physicists were skeptical until Chamberlain used the Bevatron particle accelerator at the Lawrence Radiation Laboratory at Berkeley (1955) to bombard neutrons with high-energy protons, producing a particle with the mass of a proton but with a negative charge. Chamberlain solved the difficult problem of isolating and identifying these antiprotons. For this work, he shared the 1959 Nobel Prize in Physics with Emilio Segrè. Chamberlain taught at the University of California at Berkeley (1948–89).

CHAMBERLAIN, WILT (Wilton Norman Chamberlain; 1936–1999), U.S. basketball player. Nicknamed "Wilt the

Stilt," the 7-foot, 1-inch-tall Chamberlain was the most over-powering player up to his time. A two-time all-American at the University of Kansas (1957–58), he spent one season with the Harlem Globetrotters before playing with the Philadelphia (later San Francisco) Warriors (1959–68) and the Los Angeles Lakers (1968–73) of the National Basketball Association. He was the all-time NBA scorer and rebounder, the first player to score 30,000 career points and the first to score 100 points in one game (March 2, 1962); he was the league's Most Valuable Player four times and led his teams to two world championships (1967, 1972). ■ See his autobiographies, *Wilt* (1973; with David Shaw) and *A View from Above* (1992), and Bill Libby, *Goliath* (1977).

CHAMBERLIN, THOMAS CHROWDER (1843–1928), U.S. geologist. While associated with the Wisconsin Geological Survey (1873–82), Chamberlin gained recognition as the nation's outstanding glacial geographer. He headed the glacier division of the U.S. Geological Survey (1881–87) and then chaired the geology department at the University of Chicago (1892–1918). He also founded (1893) and edited (1893–1922) the *Journal of Geology.* His studies of past geological times led him to develop (with astronomer Forest R. Moulton) the planetesimal hypothesis, which held that a star passing near the sun caused the expulsion of material that later solidified into minute "planetesimals" and eventually into larger masses that formed the planets. His books included *The Origins of the Earth* (1961) and *The Two Solar Families* (1928). ■ See study by George L. Collie and Hiram D. Densmore (1932).

CHAMBERS, WHITTAKER (Jay Vivian Chambers; 1901–1961), U.S. journalist and spy. According to his own confession, Chambers, a writer, editor, and translator, joined the Communist party in 1925 and participated in a Washington, D.C., Soviet espionage ring. In 1938 he quit the party and went to work as an editor for *Time* magazine and in 1948 testified before the House Un-American Activities Committee, naming former state-department official Alger Hiss as an accomplice in spying. Hiss denied the charge. Chambers produced his "pumpkin papers," a collection of innocuous state-department microfilms and documents allegedly provided by Hiss, which eventually resulted in the latter's conviction (1950) for perjury. Subsequently Chambers was a senior editor for the conservative National Review (1957–59) and wrote an autobiography, *Witness* (1952). He was posthumously awarded a Medal of Freedom by Pres. Ronald Reagan (1984). ■ See Meyer A. Zeligs, *Friendship and Fratricide* (1967); Allen Weinstein, *Perjury* (1978); and biography by Sam Tanenhaus (1997).

CHAMOUN, CAMILLE (1900–1987), Lebanese president. A Maronite Christian, the pro-Western Chamoun was elected to parliament in 1934 and later held several government posts. He became president in 1952 after helping bring

down his elected predecessor. In 1958 an armed insurrection by Muslim groups forced Chamoun to ask for American help, which was provided as U.S. marines landed in Lebanon. The national crisis continued after Chamoun's term expired later in 1958. His National Liberal party played a pivotal role in the political balance of power, participating in coalition governments and entering the 1975 civil war on the Christian side. He still exercised influence within the Maronite community as Lebanon virtually disintegrated in the early 1980s. At the time of his death he was serving as minister of finance.

CHANDLER, NORMAN (1899–1973), U.S. publisher. The third-generation publisher of the *Los Angeles Times,* Chandler is said to have begun his apprenticeship as a paperboy driving a model-T Ford. He graduated from Stanford (1922), became assistant general manager of the *Times* (1934), and succeeded his father as publisher (1945). The *Times* under Chandler championed Republican causes and militant anticommunism. Chandler built up advertising linage, circulation, and profits before retiring in favor of his son in 1960. As chairman of the parent Times Mirror Co. (1961–68), he expanded into encyclopedias, books, and other publications.

CHANDLER, RAYMOND (1888–1959), U.S. novelist. Raised in Britain, Chandler moved to California after World War I and became a successful oil-company executive. When he lost his job during the Depression, he started to write stories. Inspired by the tough, realistic fiction of Dashiell Hammett, Chandler used the detective novel to explore dynamic and tawdry aspects of southern California society. His polished prose and vivid characterizations strongly influenced the contemporary American detective genre. The experiences of his battered, truth-seeking private eye Philip Marlowe were described in *The Big Sleep* (1939), *Farewell, My Lovely* (1940), *The Long Goodbye* (1953), *Playback* (1958), and three other novels. He also wrote screenplays. ■ See his *Selected Letters* (1981); biographies by Frank MacShane (1976) and Tom Hiney (1997); and study by Jerry Spier (1981).

CHANDRASEKHAR, SUBRAHMANYAN (1910–1995), Indian-born U.S. astronomer. Born in Lahore, now in Pakistan. Chandrasekhar studied at Cambridge (Ph.D. 1933), taught at the University of Chicago (from 1938), and was best known for his pioneering studies of the evolution of stars. Reacting to the theory, accepted in 1930 when he began his work, that all stars burn out and collapse into relatively small dense objects known as white dwarf stars, Chandrasekhar theorized that stars having a mass of more than 1.4 times that of the sun (now called the Chandrasekhar limit) would not compress in this manner but would explode as a supernova. He claimed that remaining matter would keep on shrinking and become so dense that no light would be able to radiate from it. Although initially dismissed by astrophysicists, Chandrasekhar's theories were confirmed by subsequent research, and the extremely dense residue of supernovas are now called neutron stars and black holes. He shared the 1983 Nobel Prize in Physics with William A. Fowler. He also did important research on the theory of radiation transfer in stellar atmospheres. His books included *An Introduction to the Study of Stellar Structure* (1939) and *Radiative Transfer* (1950).

CHANEL, COCO (Gabrielle Bonheur-Chanel; 1883–1971), French fashion designer. Chanel's fashion career began in 1911 when she set up a millinery shop in Paris. By the mid-1920s she dominated haute couture with adaptations of working-class wear: her unaffected line used soft, clingy fabrics to reinterpret trench coats and sailors' and schoolgirls' uniforms. Her other innovations included bobbed hair, costume jewelry, and tweed suits. She helped democratize the industry, never discouraging others from copying her designs. Her Chanel No. 5, introduced in 1922, became the world's most familiar perfume. She was a celebrity for six decades and one of the most influential couturiers of the century. Katharine Hepburn starred in *Coco* (1969), a musical adaptation of her life. ■ See Pierre Galante, *Mademoiselle Chanel* (Eng. trans. 1973), and biographies by Edmonde Charles-Roux (Eng. trans. 1981) and Axel Madsen (1990).

CHANEY, LON (1883–1930), U.S. film actor. The son of deaf mute parents, Chaney developed the ability to express himself in mime, an asset in his silent-film career, which began in 1913. Known as "the Man of a Thousand Faces," he was a skilled make up artist who played a wide variety of villainous and macabre characters in more than 150 films. He was celebrated for his sympathetic portrayal of grotesques, such as the deformed Quasimodo in *The Hunchback of Notre Dame* (1923) and the scarred musician in *The Phantom of the Opera* (1925). ■ See Forrest J. Anderson, *Lon of 1,000 Faces* (1983), and study by Don G. Smith (1996).

CHANG, MIN-CHUEH (1908–1991), Chinese-born U.S. biologist. M. C. Chang studied at Tsinghua University in Peking and Cambridge University in England (Ph.D. 1941) before emigrating to the United States (1945), where he did research at the Worcester Foundation for Experimental Biology (1945–82) and taught at Boston University (1951–74). Working in the 1950s with Worcester colleague Gregory Pincus and John Rock, head of the Rock Reproduction Clinic in Brookline, Massachusetts, Chang developed the oral contraceptive pill containing progesterone and estrogen that was approved by the U.S. Food and Drug Administration in 1960 and marketed as Enovid. The "pill" helped to foster the sexual revolution that began in the 1960s and revolutionized family planning through birth control. Chang also did research with rabbits in the 1950s that eventually led to in vitro fertilization, in which a human egg is fertilized outside the body and "test tube" babies are created.

CHANG HSUEH-LIANG. *See ZHANG XUELIANG.*

CHANG KUO-T'AO. *See ZHANG GUOTAO.*

CHANG TSO-LIN. *See ZHANG ZUOLIN.*

CHANNING, EDWARD (1856–1931), U.S. historian. Channing spent his entire career at Harvard, where he was a student (Ph.D. 1880), a rather unpopular professor (1883–1929), and a prodigious researcher. An exponent of nationalism and social Darwinism, he wrote a monumental *History of the United States* (6 vols., 1905–25), which stressed the forces of union and urbanization over those of regionalism and challenged the frontier thesis of Frederick Jackson Turner. The work was considered the most authoritative of the time and the final volume, *The War for Southern Independence* (1925), won a Pulitzer Prize.

CHAO TZU-YANG. *See ZHAO ZIYANG.*

CHAPLIN, CHARLIE (Sir Charles Spencer Chaplin; 1889–1977), British comedian and director. After a Dickensian childhood in London's slums, Chaplin became a popular music-hall comedian. He created (1915), in Hollywood, the world's most popular movie underdog, the tragicomic Little Tramp, who was melancholy but resilient, gallant though unkempt, and whose appeal transcended class, nation, and even cultural barriers. Chaplin's films—shorts such as *Easy Street* (1917) and *The Pawnshop* (1916), followed by *The Kid* (1920), *The Gold Rush* (1925), *City Lights* (1931), and *Modern Times* (1936)—were beloved all over the world. After his caricature of Adolf Hitler in *The Great Dictator* (1940), his popularity began to wane. In 1952 while he was abroad publicizing *Limelight*, an affectionate remembrance of his music-hall days, Chaplin received notice that his reentry to the United States would be challenged on grounds of moral turpitude and political unreliability—he was an advocate of leftist causes and had been involved in several paternity and divorce suits. For the next 20 years he remained in Europe, producing two relatively unsuccessful films and publishing his autobiography (1964). In 1972 Chaplin returned to Hollywood for an emotional tribute, and in 1975 he was knighted. ■ See studies by Theodore Huff (1951), Raoul Sobel and David Francis (1977), David Robinson (1984), Julian Smith (1984), and biography by Kenneth S. Lynn (1997).

CHAPLIN, RALPH (1888–1961), U.S. labor leader. Born in a Chicago slum, Chaplin was attracted to radical politics at an early age and joined the militant Industrial Workers of the World (IWW) in 1913. He edited its publication, *Solidarity*, wrote the words of its song, "Solidarity Forever"

(1915), and was jailed (1918–23) with other IWW leaders for violating the wartime Espionage Act by allegedly proposing a general strike if the United States entered World War I. Chaplin continued his labor activities during the 1920s and 1930s and was known in his later years for his violently anticommunist views. ■ See his autobiography, *Wobbly* (1945).

CHAPMAN, SYDNEY (1888–1970), British mathematician and geophysicist. A professor at Manchester (1919–24), Imperial College, London (1924–46), and at Oxford (1946–53), Chapman made major contributions to the kinetic theory of gases and to the study of geomagnetism. He discovered gaseous thermal diffusion and developed theories of atmospheric tides, magnetic storms, ionospheric layers, auroras, and the sun's corona. He also headed the committee that organized the International Geophysical Year (IGY; 1957–58), the most extensive international scientific undertaking carried out up to that time. His books included *Geomagnetism* (2 vols., 1940; with Julius Bartels) and *IGY: Year of Discovery* (1959).

CHAR, RENÉ (1907–1988), French poet. Char's early work reflected his attachment to surrealism. During World War II he was a resistance leader and a friend of the writer Albert Camus, whose philosophy he shared. His war journal, *Leaves of Hypnos* (1946; Eng. trans. 1973), was infused with his humanism. An admirer of the Greek philosopher Heraclitus, Char too wrote in a trenchant, aphoristic style, seeking to reveal in his abstract poetry some of the external truths and fleeting mysteries of nature. Among his admired collections were *Fureur et Mystère* ("madness and mystery"; 1948) and *Commune Présence* ("common presence"; 1964). English translations of his work are in *Hypnos Walking* (1956), *Poems* (1976), and *No Siege Is Absolute* (1983). ■ See studies by Mary Ann Caws (1977) and James R. Lawler (1978).

CHARLES (Charles Philip Arthur George Windsor; 1948–), prince of Wales (from 1969). The son of Queen Elizabeth of Britain and Prince Philip, Duke of Edinburgh, Prince Charles was the first heir to the British throne to receive a university bachelor's degree (Cambridge, 1970) and the first modern heir to command a Royal Navy warship (1976). Extremely popular with the British public, he ended years as "the world's most eligible bachelor" by marrying his seventh cousin once removed, Lady Diana Spencer (July 29, 1981). The spectacular royal wedding ceremony, held in London's St. Paul's Cathedral, was broadcast on television and witnessed by an estimated 500 million people throughout the world. Their first son, Prince William, was born in June 1982; a second, Prince Henry, was born in September 1984. Charles and Diana divorced in 1996. Charles spoke out on such issues as the environment, inner city poverty, and unemployment and established two charitable trusts. ■ See biography by Anthony Holden (1979) and Holden's *Charles at Fifty* (1998).

CHARLES, RAY (1932–), U.S. singer. Blind since the age of 6 and orphaned in his teens, Charles began memorizing music at Florida's St. Augustine School for the Blind. In the late 1940s he formed a rhythm-and-blues trio, and in 1956 he recorded "I Got a Woman," the first of many hit songs. His recording of "Georgia on My Mind" (1959) broke sales records. A gifted pianist with an eclectic repertoire of gospel, soul, country, and standard songs. Charles appeared with his musical entourage at New York's Carnegie Hall and London's Palladium, the Apollo in Harlem, and the Peacock Club in Atlanta. Other hits included the standards "Ruby" and "Yesterday." ■ See his autobiography, *Brother Ray* (1978) and biography by Michael Lydon (1998).

CHARPAK, GEORGES (1924–), Polish-born French physicist. Charpak served in the French army during World War II and survived a year-long imprisonment in the Dachau concentration camp. After the war he studied physics, received a Ph.D. from the Collège de France in Paris (1954), and did research at the National Center of Scientific Research in Paris (1947–59) and at the European organization for Nuclear Research (CERN; 1959–). Charpak invented the multiwire proportional chamber, an electronic particle detector that enabled scientists to trace the path of subatomic particles produced in particle accelerators. His device, which increased the speed of collecting data by a factor of a thousand, enabled scientists to discover the J/psi and W and Z particles and win Nobel Prizes in 1976 and 1984. Charpak's research revolutionized high-energy physics and he was awarded the 1992 Nobel Prize in Physics.

CHARTERIS, LESLIE (Leslie Charles Bowyer Yin; 1907–1993), U.S. mystery writer. Born in Singapore, Charteris had a British mother and a Chinese father; he spoke Chinese and Malay before learning English. A crime buff, he enrolled at Cambridge University (1926) but dropped out the first year after writing his first mystery. He called himself the twin brother of his character Simon Templar, the dashing Robin Hood type who first appeared in *Meet the Tiger* (1928) and became known to an immense British and American following as "the Saint." In 1932 Charteris moved to the United States to better his financial prospects; after 1933 he was a Hollywood screenwriter. Simon Templar did his good works on radio and television, in movies, in comics, and in mystery magazines named for him in the 1950s and 1960s. ■ See W.O.G. Lofts and Derek Adley, *The Saint and Leslie Charteris* (1972).

CHARTIER, ÉMILE AUGUSTE. *See ALAIN.*

CHASE, LUCIA (1897–1986), U.S. dancer and ballet company administrator. Born into a wealthy and socially prominent family, Chase studied at the Theater Guild School in New York City. After the death of her husband, Thomas Ewing. Jr. (1933), from whom she inherited a fortune, she pursued a career as a professional dancer and performed with the Mordkin Ballet (1938–40). She was a founder (1940), in New York City of the Ballet Theater (renamed the American Ballet Theater in 1957), which presented both classical and contemporary works. As its chief financial backer, codirector (with Oliver Smith, 1945–80), and one of its principal dancers, she built the company into one of the world's leading ensembles. The company introduced the works of Antony Tudor to U.S. audiences in the 1940s, produced ballets by such choreographers as Jerome Robbins, Agnes de Mille, Michel Fokine, and Léonide Massine, and gained a reputation for its dramatic orientation. Chase was best known for her roles in *La Fille Mal Gardée, Les Sylphides, Pas de Quatre, Pillar of Fire, Tally-Ho,* and *Fall River Legend* and danced character roles into her seventies.

CHASE, MARY ELLEN (1887–1973), U.S. author and educator. A professor at Smith College (1926–55), Chase wrote scholarly books on writing, literary criticism, and the Bible as well as several children's stories. She was best known, however, for her novels set in her native state of Maine. Among her most popular works, which were noted for their penetrating character portrayals, were *Uplands* (1927), *Mary Peters* (1934), *Silas Crockett* (1935), and *Windswept* (1941). *A Goodly Heritage* (1932), *A Goodly Fellowship* (1939), and *The White Gate* (1954) were autobiographical. ■ See study by Perry D. Westbrook (1965) and Evelyn H. Chase, *Feminist Convert* (1988).

CHATTERJI, SARATCHANDRA (1876–1938), Indian writer. Born into a poor Bengali Brahman family, Chatterji dropped out of college and wandered about India for several years. He then worked in Burma for more than a decade. His varied experiences are reflected in the episodes of his ambitious novel, *Srikanta* (4 vols., 1917–33; Eng. trans. vol. I, 1922), which established his reputation as a pioneer realist and a master of character delineation. Most of his works described traditional Hindu social values and family structures undergoing rapid change. In such novels as *Charitrabeen* (1917; Eng. trans. 1962) and *The Fire* (1920; Eng. trans. 1964), he condemned the oppression of women in traditional society. He played an active role in the independence movement and was a member of the Congress party for many years. His other works included *Queen's Gambit* (1916; Eng. trans. 1969), *The Deliverance* (1917; Eng. trans. 1944), and *The Elder Sister and Other Stories* (Eng. trans. 1950). ■ See study by V. S. Naravane (1976) and M. Mukopadhyay and S. Roy, eds., *The Golden Book of Saratchandra* (1977).

CHÁVEZ, CARLOS (1899–1978), Mexican composer and conductor. The most eminent Mexican musical personality of the century, Chávez organized the Mexican Symphony Orchestra, which he directed from 1928 to 1948. His music, which was performed throughout the world, mixed European styles with strong Mexican folkloric rhythms and tonalities. Among his best-known works were *Sinfortía de*

Antígona (1933), Concerto No. 1 for Piano and Orchestra (1940), Toccata for Percussion Instruments (1942), and *Sinfonía Romántica* (1953). He wrote *Toward a New Music* (Eng. trans. 1937). *Musical Thought* (1961) contains his lectures given at Harvard University. ■ See study by Robert L. Parker (1983).

CHAVEZ, CESAR ESTRADA (1927–1993), U.S. labor leader. After their farm in Arizona failed during the Depression, Chavez and his family moved to California to become migrant farm workers. He joined (1952) the newly formed grass-roots self-help political movement Community Service Organization (CSO) and served as its general director (1958–62) until he left it to organize the National Farm Workers Association, a union of migrant farm workers. Utilizing marches, picketing, strikes, fasts, and other nonviolent techniques developed during the civil-rights campaigns, Chavez won several important contracts, and in 1966 he helped form the United Farm Workers Organizing Committee of the AFL-CIO. Under Chavez's leadership, the union carried out national boycotts of California table grapes and lettuce and organized migrants in Florida and other states. In 1973 he organized the United Farm Workers of America. ■ See study by Jacques E. Levy (1975) and biography by Richard Griswold del Castillo and Richard A. Garcia (1995).

CHAYEVSKY, PADDY (Sidney Chayefsky; 1923–1981), U.S. playwright and screenwriter. Born in New York and educated at the City College of New York (B.S. 1943), Chayefsky wrote low-key dramas about simple people for television during the 1950s. Originally a TV play, *Marty* (1953), the poignant story of a butcher and a schoolteacher who fall in love, was an award-winning film in 1955. Writing directly for the screen and moving away from everyday life to a concern with large social institutions, Chayefsky wrote highly acclaimed original scripts for the films *Hospital* (1971) and *Network* (1975). His Broadway shows included *The Tenth Man* (1959) and *Gideon* (1961). ■ See study by John M. Clum (1976) and Shaun Considine, *Mad as Hell* (1994).

CHAZOV, YEVGENY (1929–   ), Soviet physician and peace activist. A prominent cardiologist and personal physician to Soviet political leaders, Chazov served as deputy minister of public health (1967–87), member of the Supreme Soviet (1974–84), director of the Moscow Cardiological Center (1975–82), and member of the Central Committee of the Communist party (1982–90). He cofounded, with U.S. cardiologist Bernard Lown (1980), International Physicians for the Prevention of Nuclear War, a group that publicized the dangers to human health caused by nuclear war and sought to prevent it by advocating an end to all nuclear testing, a verifiable freeze on development and deployment of nuclear weapons, and a declaration of no-first-use by all nuclear powers. The organization, which had a membership of about 135,000 in 41 countries, including about 60,000 in the Soviet Union and 28,000 in the United States, was awarded the 1985 Nobel Peace Prize. The award aroused controversy in the West when it was learned that Chazov had signed a published letter (1973) that denounced dissident Soviet physicist Andrei Sakharov, a winner of the 1975 Nobel Peace Prize.

CHEEVER, JOHN (1912–1982), U.S. novelist and short story writer. A compulsive diarist in his youth, Cheever at age 17 recounted his expulsion from Thayer Academy in the *New Republic.* For two years he wrote television scripts for "Life with Father." Cheever was closely identified with the New Yorker school of story writing. A sophisticated moralist, he wittily worked the affairs of middle-class America into myths and parables, finding spiritual resonance in humdrum doings. Loose plot and archetypal characters were typical of his more than 100 short stories and of the novels *The Wapshot Chronicle* (1957), *The Wapshot Scandal* (1964), *Bullet Park* (1969), and *Falconer* (1977). *Cheever's Collected Stories* (1979) was a best-seller and won a Pulitzer Prize. ■ See Susan Cheever, *Home Before Dark* (1984), and studies by Lynne Waldeland (1979) and Scott Donaldson (1988).

CHELMSFORD, FREDERIC JOHN NAPIER THESIGER, 3rd BARON and 1st VISCOUNT (1868–1933), British colonial official. Chelmsford was educated at Oxford University and served in local government before he became governor of Queensland (1905–09) and of New South Wales (1909–13) in Australia. He went to India in 1914 and served as viceroy from 1916 to 1921, a difficult time for him because the independence movement was gaining momentum. In 1918 Chelmsford was coauthor (with Edwin S. Montagu) of a report that pledged eventual Indian self-rule and led to electoral reforms. These reforms were rejected by nationalist leader Mahatma Gandhi, and Chelmsford used force to suppress Gandhi's nonviolent protest movement. After leaving India, Chelmsford was first lord of the Admiralty in the Labour government of 1924.

CHEN, EUGENE (Ch'en Yu-jen; 1878–1944), Chinese publicist and politician. Born in Trinidad, Chen worked as a lawyer there and in London where he met revolutionary leader Sun Yat-sen (1911) and became his protégé. He went to China and edited the Peking *Gazette* and the Shanghai *Gazette* and traveled abroad extensively (1918–20) seeking support for Sun; later he served as Sun's foreign affairs adviser (1922–25) and as foreign minister after Sun's death (1926–27). Chen joined the strongly anti-imperialist leftist Guomindang (Kuomintang) government in Wuhan (1927) and when the Guomindang party split and the right was victorious in the political struggles, he fled with the leftists to the Soviet Union. He returned later (1931), alternating between support and opposition to the surviving Guomindang government. In all, Chen was China's foreign minister four times under various governments until he retired from active politics in 1934.

CHEN BODA (old style: CH'EN PO-TA; 1905–1989), Chinese communist intellectual and propagandist. Little is known of Chen's early life. He began working underground for the communists in the 1920s and from 1926 to 1930 studied in Moscow. Emerging in the 1940s as the communists' leading ideologue, he was elected to the Central Committee in 1945. For many years Chen was party leader Mao Zedong's (Mao Tse-tung) political secretary and the chief interpreter of Mao's writings. Holding many high posts in the Communist party's propaganda bureau, Chen also edited the party journal *Red Flag* (from 1958) and contributed editorials to its paper, *People's Daily.* One of the leaders of the Cultural Revolution, he was named to the ruling Politburo (1969). However, in 1971 Chen disappeared from public view after being criticized for encouraging excesses during the Cultural Revolution and he was expelled from the party in 1973. He was sentenced to 18 years imprisonment in September 1981 but was released later that year. His books included *Notes on Ten Years of Civil War, 1927–36* (Eng. trans. 1954) and *A Study of Land Rent in PreLiberation China* (Eng. trans. 1958). ■ See Raymond Wylie, *The Emergence of Maoism* (1980).

CHEN DUXIU (old style: CH'EN TU-HSIU; 1879–1942), Chen Duxiu was the pseudonym of Chen Qiansheng (Ch'en Ch'ien-sheng). An editor of *New Youth,* the journal of the intellectual avant-garde, and a dean at Peking University, Chen was one of the leaders of the 1919 May Fourth movement, which called for a Chinese cultural revolution. In 1919 he became a Marxist and cofounded the Chinese Communist party in 1921. Chen led the party for six years, though he accepted Comintern discipline and agreed to the alliance with the Guomindang (Kuomintang) party reluctantly. When the Comintern policies failed, Chen was denounced as a deviationist, stripped of his leadership post (1927), and expelled from the party two years later. He spent the rest of his life in relative political obscurity, including five years in a nationalist prison. ■ See biography by Lee Feigon (1983).

CHEN KAIGE (1952–), Chinese film director. The son of a prominent Beijing filmmaker, Chen came into contact with impoverished peasants when he was sent to work on a rubber plantation in rural Yunnan province during the Cultural Revolution (1967). He subsequently spent five years in the army and worked in a film processing lab before studying at the Beijing Film Academy (1978–82). He was recognized as a leader of the "fifth generation" of Chinese filmmakers with the success of his early realistic films depicting developments in recent Chinese history, including *Yellow Earth* (1984), *The Big Parade* (1985), and *King of the Children* (1987). His epic film, *Farewell My Concubine* (1993), which followed the lives of two members of the Beijing Opera from the 1920s through the 1970s, shared first prize at the 1993 Cannes International Film Festival. *Temptress Moon* (1996) was a lush melodrama set in decadent Shanghai during the

1920s. He also directed the historical epic *The Emperor and the Assassin* (1998).

CH'EN PO-TA. *See CHEN BODA.*

CH'EN TU-HSIU. *See CHEN DUXIU.*

CHEN YI (1901–1972), Chinese communist political and military leader. A group of scholars sent Chen to study in France (1919–21), where he held various blue-collar jobs and was active in socialist movements. He joined the communists when he returned to China, and from 1927 to 1949 he held important military positions in the wars against the Japanese and the nationalists. He was elected to the Central Committee of the Chinese Communist party in 1945. His troops captured Shanghai, and he stayed there as an official until 1954, when he was named a vice premier. Chen became foreign minister in 1958, traveled extensively, and was known for his wit, candor, and skill as a negotiator. A target of Red Guard militants during the Cultural Revolution, he ceased to function actively as minister at the end of 1968 and was dropped from the ruling Politburo in 1969.

CHERENKOV, PAVEL ALEKSEYEVICH (1904–1990), Soviet physicist. While a graduate student of Sergei Vavilov at Moscow's Lebedev Physical Institute, Cherenkov began investigating the faint blue light emitted from liquids exposed to a source of fast gamma radiation. In 1934, Cherenkov attributed the luminescence, known later as the Cherenkov effect, to a new kind of radiation, caused by a particle traveling near the speed of light (in vacuo); when such a particle passes through a transparent medium that causes light to travel at a rate slower than that of the particle, the Cherenkov effect results. The Cherenkov counter was developed as a result of these findings; a critical lab instrument for detecting elementary particles, it facilitated the discovery of the antiproton. Cherenkov shared the 1958 Nobel Prize in Physics with compatriots Ilya Frank and Igor Tamm. In later years he did research in high-energy particle physics and worked on the development of electron accelerators.

CHERKASOV, NIKOLAI (1903–1966), Soviet actor. A Leningrad stage actor, Cherkasov played the lead in Sergei Eisenstein's two historical film epics, *Alexander Nevsky* (1938) and *Ivan the Terrible* (Part 1, 1944; Part 2, 1946). Tall, with an expressive face and deep voice, he also appeared in the Russian films *Battle of Stalingrad* (1950), *Rimsky-Korsakov* (1952), and *Don Quixote* (1956). A prominent public figure, Cherkasov became a member of the Supreme Soviet in 1938. ■ See his memoirs, *Notes of a Soviet Actor* (1953; Eng. trans. 1957).

CHERNENKO, KONSTANTIN USTINOVICH (1911–1985), Soviet political leader. Born into a peasant family in Siberia, Chernenko worked as a farm laborer at age 12 and joined the Young Communist League at age 15. A member of the Communist party from 1931, he attended party schools and worked his way up the party hierarchy in various organizational and propaganda posts. After World War II, while serving as propaganda chief in Moldavia, he met Leonid Brezhnev, then the party secretary in the region, became his protégé, and rose with him through the ranks. He was Brezhnev's chief aide (from 1960), and following Brezhnev's elevation to the post of party general secretary, he was named head of the party Central Committee's general department (1965), giving him control over party personnel. Named a Central Committee (1971) and Politburo (1974) member and head of the party ideological department (1982), Chernenko was chosen general secretary of the Communist party upon the death of Yuri Andropov (1984). In poor health when he took power, Chernenko made no major changes in Soviet domestic or foreign policy, but did resume arms negotiations with the United States. He died after 13 months in office.

CHERNOV, VIKTOR MIKILAILOVICH (1873–1952), Russian political leader. A peasant-oriented revolutionary theorist and propagandist, Chernov was a founder of the Russian Socialist Revolutionary party (1901–02) and believed that a socialist revolution would follow a democratic one. He advocated the socialization of agricultural land and after the February revolution (1917) attempted unsuccessfully to carry out this policy while serving as minister of agriculture in the government of Aleksandr Kerensky. He was elected president of the constituent assembly (January 1918), which lasted one day before being dispersed by the bolsheviks. Chernov briefly associated himself with an anti-bolshevik government in Samara during the Russian civil war (1918–20) but fled the country (1920) and spent the rest of his life in Prague, Paris, and New York. He wrote *The Great Russian Revolution* (Eng. trans. 1936). ■ See the memoirs of his stepdaughter, Olga C. Andreyev, *Cold Spring in Russia* (Eng. trans. 1978).

CHERWELL, FREDERICK ALEXANDER LINDEMANN, VISCOUNT (1886–1957), British physicist. Lindemann studied with Walther Nernst in Berlin (Ph.D. 1910) and developed the Nernst-Lindemann theory of specific heat and the Lindemann melting-point formula. He was a professor at Oxford (1914–56) and built the Clarendon Laboratory into a major research center. During World War II he was Prime Minister Winston Churchill's personal assistant and scientific adviser. He advised Churchill again during 1951–53 and played a major role in the development of atomic energy in Britain. He was crested a baron in 1941 and a viscount in 1956. ■ See Roy F. Harrod, *The Prof* (1959); Lord Birkenhead, *The Prof in Two Worlds* (1961); and Thomas Wilson, *Churchill and the Prof* (1995).

CHESSMAN, CARYL WHITTIER (1912–1960), U.S. convict. Two months after Chessman was released from prison for robbery, he was arrested and eventually convicted of kidnapping and raping two women (1948). Proclaiming his innocence, he began a 12-year campaign of appeals to reverse the verdict, financed by three books and a novel he wrote in prison. The autobiographical *Cell 2455, Death Row* (1954) became a best-seller. His case rallied opponents of capital punishment throughout the world. After eight stays of execution, Chessman died in the gas chamber at San Quentin (California) on May 2, 1960. ■ See William M. Kunstler, *Beyond a Reasonable Doubt?* (1961).

CHESTERTON, GILBERT KEITH (1874–1936), British essayist, poet, and novelist. G. K. Chesterton was one of the most prolific and popular writers of his age. He brought to his writing a strong social commitment to distributism (to restore land to the landless) and to the betterment of the poor and powerless. He held strong religious beliefs as an ardent Roman Catholic convert (1922). The essays collected in such volumes as *Tremendous Trifles* (1909) and *Come to Think of It* (1930) were famous for their wit and bright, light style. His poetry, collected in 1927, was popular, as were his novels, especially *The Napoleon of Notting Hill* (1904) and *The Man Who Was Thursday* (1908). Among his many other works is a five-volume series of detective novels featuring a priest, Father Brown (1911–35), and various literary and religious studies. ■ See his *Autobiography* (1936); biographies by Maisie Ward (1943), Garry Wills (1961), and Dudley Barker (1973); and Alzina S. Dale, *Outline of Sanity* (1982).

CHEVALIER, MAURICE (1888–1972), French entertainer. Chevalier began as a Parisian café singer. His break came in 1909 when he was hired by the Folies Bergère to perform with the music-hall star Mistinguett. Known for his straw hat and cane, his roguish smile and impersonation of the gay Parisian, Chevalier sang, danced, and talked in one-man shows and musical films throughout his long life and immortalized such songs as "Mimi" and "Valentine." He made a series of films with Jeanette MacDonald in the 1930s, among them *The Love Parade* (1929) and *The Merry Widow* (1934), and was particularly remembered for his role in *Gigi* (1958). During the World War II German occupation he stirred controversy for collaborating with the Nazis by performing for German-held French prisoners of war. ■ See his memoirs, *With Love* (1960) and *I Remember It Well* (Eng. trans. 1972); studies by Gene Ringgold (1973), Michael Freeland (1981), and James Harding (1982); and Edward Behr, *The Good Frenchman* (1993).

CHEVROLET, LOUIS (1879–1941), Swiss-born U.S. automobile racer and designer. Chevrolet emigrated to the United States in 1900 and soon was the world's leading racing-car driver. In 1905 he sped over a measured mile in the astonishing time of 52.8 seconds. He designed and built (1911; in collaboration with William Crapo Durrant) the first "Chevrolet," a light six-cylinder auto that was produced to compete with the Ford. Chevrolet, however, lost confidence

in the car and sold his interest to Durant, who incorporated the Chevrolet Motor Co. into his General Motors organization. Chevrolet thus benefited little from the incredibly successful car that bore his name. He subsequently designed racing cars—his racers won the 1920 and 1921 Indianapolis 500-mile race—and airplanes.

CHI PAI-SHIH. *See QI-BAISHI.*

CHIANG CH'ING. *See JIANG QING.*

CHIANG CHING-KUO (1909?–1988), Chinese Nationalist political leader. The son of Guomindang (Kuomintang) leader Chiang Kai-shek, Chiang was radicalized during his student days in Shanghai and went to the Soviet Union to study (1925). After his father broke with the communists (1927), Chiang denounced the move and remained in the Soviet Union. He was reconciled with his father (1937) following the establishment of the anti-Japanese United Front, and he held several important administrative positions in the Chinese government. He failed to curb the runaway inflation in Shanghai (1948) and fled with his father to Taiwan (1949) after the communist armies defeated the Nationalist forces. On Taiwan he headed the military intelligence and secret police and served as defense minister (1965–72) and premier (1972–78). He became head of the Guomindang after his father's death (1975) and served as president of the Republic of China (Taiwan) from 1978 until his death. During Chiang's years in power he tightly controlled the government and suppressed political opposition while presiding over a rapidly growing economy. In the last year of his rule he ended 38 years of martial law and allowed opposition parties to be formed. ■ See Jay Taylor, *The Generalissimo's Son* (2000).

CHIANG KAI-SHEK (old style: JIANG JIESHI; 1887–1975), Chinese military and political leader. The son of a village merchant, Chiang received military training in China and in Japan. He joined Sun Yat-sen's revolutionary movement (1911) and organized the Nationalist army; after Sun's death (1925) he led the Northern Expedition to unite China under one government (1926). His marriage to Song Mei-ling (Soong Mei-ling) in 1927 established his ties to the wealthy and influential Song (Soong) family. After massacring his Communist allies (1927), he set up a national government in Nanking (1928) and spent the next 21 years as head of a politically divided and war-torn China. Forced into an alliance with the Communists to fight the Japanese invaders (1937), he nevertheless concentrated his military efforts on attempting to destroy the Communist movement. Though he gained international prestige as an ally of the United States during World War II (1941–45), his corrupt and inefficient government could not solve China's economic and social problems and his forces were defeated by the Communist armies in the civil war (1945–49). He fled with his government to the island of Taiwan, where he continued to claim control over all of China. Remaining in power with large amounts of U.S. aid, he built up Taiwan (the Republic of China) into a significant regional military and economic power. His books included *China's Destiny* (1943; Eng. trans. 1947) and his autobiography, *Soviet Russia in China: A Summing Up at Seventy* (1957). ■ See biography by Robert Payne (1969) and Brian Crozier, *The Man Who Lost China* (1976).

CHIANG KAI-SHEK, MADAME. *See SONG MEILING.*

CH'IAO KUAN-HUA. *See QIAO GUANHUA.*

CHICAGO, JUDY (Judy Cohen; 1939–), U.S. artist. Judy Chicago founded the first women's art program in the United States (Fresno State College, California, 1970) and was instrumental in establishing the Feminist Studio Workshop in Los Angeles (1974). Her best-known work, *The Dinner Party* (1974–78), was a room-size sculpture executed by Chicago with a group of artists and craftswomen. It consisted of 39 place settings whose elaborate ornamentation represented women's contributions to Western civilization. *The Birth Project* (1980–85), created by Chicago and executed by 118 volunteer needleworkers (whose names appear with Chicago's on their work), explores woman's role as birthgiver in the traditional media of embroidery, quilting, needlepoint, appliqué, crochet, smocking, macramé, weaving, and beadwork. Chicago wrote that she sought "to use the physical process of giving birth as a metaphor for the birth of the universe and of life itself." In the mid-1980s she explored her Jewish roots and her book *Holocaust Project: From Darkness Into Light* (1993) was published in connection with a traveling exhibition of paintings, photos, tapestries, and texts. ■ See *The Complete Dinner Party* (2 vols., 1981), *The Birth Project* (1985), the autobiographical *Through the Flower* (1975; rev. ed. 1982), and *Beyond the Flower* (1996).

CHICHERIN, GEORGI VASILYEVICH (1872–1936), Soviet diplomat. A member of a noble family, Chicherin served in the foreign office in czarist Russia but resigned (1904) and joined (1905) the Social Democratic party in Berlin. Active in the socialist movements in France and Britain, he returned (1918) to Russia, where he succeeded Leon Trotsky as foreign commissar (May 1918); in that post he facilitated the de jure recognition of Soviet power by the major European powers, established good relation with Turkey, Persia, Afghanista, and China and was instrumental in concluding the Treaty of Rapallo (1922) with Germany. He lost influence in 1927 and was succeeded (1930) by his deputy, Maxim Litvinov. ■ See Timothy Edward O'Connor, *Diplomacy and Revolution* (1988).

CHICHESTER, SIR FRANCIS (1901–1972), British aviator and yachtsman. The son of a country minister, Chichester dropped out of Marlborough College at age 17, emigrated to New Zealand, and made a fortune in real estate. After returning to England (1929), he obtained a pilot's license and flew solo from England to Australia. His later solo crossing of the Tasman Sea from New Zealand to Australia (1930) was the first long-distance flight by seaplane. In the 1950s he took up sailing and made three solo transatlantic crossings (1960; 1962; 1964). After completing a record-breaking nine-month solo voyage around the world at age 65 (1967), he was knighted by Queen Elizabeth II with the same sword that Elizabeth I had used in knighting Sir Francis Drake. His books included *Seaplane Solo* (1933), *Alone Across the Tasman Sea* (1945), *Alone Across the Atlantic* (1961), *"Gipsy Moth" Circles the World* (1967), and the autobiography, *The Lonely Sea and the Sky* (1964).

CHIEFTAINS (est. 1963), Irish folk ensemble. Formed by four traditional instrumentalists who were members of a Dublin folk orchestra, the Chieftains became the most influential and renowned Irish folk group. Known for their virtuosity, exuberance and playfulness, they helped to launch the revival of traditional Irish music and were cultural ambassadors for decades. Although there were some personnel changes over the years, the core group consisted of **Paddy Maloney (1938–), Martin Fay (1936–), Derek Bell (1935–), Sean Keane (1946–), Kevin Conneff (1945–), and Matt Molloy (1947–)**. They experimented with Celtic music from France and Spain as well as with musical traditions from as far afield as Texas and China. Their soundtrack to *Barry Lyndon* won an Academy Award (1976) and their albums *An Irish Evening* (1991), *Another Country* (1992), *The Celtic Harp* (1993), and *Santiago* (1997) won Grammy Awards. Their numerous albums included notable collaborations with James Galway (1987) and Van Morrison (1988) as well as with traditional Chinese musicians (1985). ■ See John Glatt, *The Chieftains* (1997).

CHIFLEY, JOSEPH BENEDICT (1885–1951), Australian political leader. Chifley, who receive limited schooling, joined the New South Wales Railways at age 18 and became a railway union leader. From 1928 to 1931 he served in Parliament and was minister of defense in the Labour government (1931). After nine years in local politics, Chifley was reelected to the national Parliament (1940) and served as treasurer and minister of postwar reconstruction during World War II. As prime minister (1945–49), he restructured the banking system and expanded welfare state policies. After Labour lost the 1949 elections, he spent the last two years of his life as leader of the opposition. ■ See biography by L. F. Crisp, *Ben Chifley* (1961).

CHILD, JULIA (Julia McWilliams; 1912–), U.S. cooking expert. Child served with the Office of Strategic Services (OSS) in Ceylon and China during World War II. She lived with her diplomat husband in Paris (1948–54), where she attended the Cordon Bleu cooking school, became an avid chef, and established her own cooking school. Her book

Mastering the Art of French Cooking (1961; written in collaboration with Simone Beck and Louisette Bertholle; vol. II. 1970) was a best-seller and hailed as a classic. As hostess of the award-winning nationwide television series, "The French Chef" (1963–73), she built up a huge audience while candidly and humorously demystifying French cuisine. She subsequently hosted "Julia Child and Company" (1978–79), a cooking show that dealt primarily with native American cuisine, and wrote *From Julia Child's Kitchen* (1975), *Julia Child and Company* (1978), and *In Julia's Kitchen with Master Chefs* (1995). ■ See Noël R. Fitch, *Appetite for Life* (1997).

CHILDE, VERE GORDON (1892–1957), Australian archaeologist. V. Gordon Childe studied at Oxford (B. Litt., 1916) and taught at the University of Edinburgh (1927–46) and the University of London (1946–57). An independent Marxist, he revolutionized the field of archaeology and prehistory by using the social and physical sciences to describe a complex sequence of economic, technological, and cultural developments in *The Dawn of European Civilization* (1925) and *The Most Ancient East* (1928). He also wrote *Man Makes Himself* (1936) and *What Happened in History* (1942), popular introductions to the field.

CHILDERS, (ROBERT) ERSKINE (1870–1922), Anglo-Irish political leader and writer. Childers wrote a popular spy novel about a German invasion of Britain, *The Riddle of the Sands* (1903), which influenced defense policy and remained topical for 40 years. A Protestant, he gave up his position as a clerk in the House of Commons (1910) to work for Irish home rule, although he fought for the British in World War I. Elected to the Irish assembly (1921), he served as minister of propaganda and demanded republican status for all of Ireland. He opposed the 1921 treaty with Britain and fought with the Irish Republican Army (IRA) in the ensuing civil war. Captured by Free State forces, he was court-martialed and shot as a traitor. His son, Erskine Hamilton Childers, was president of Ireland (1973–74). ■ See Tom Cox, *Damned Englishman* (1975); Andrew Boyle, *The Riddle of Childers* (1977); and the study by Jim Ring (1996).

CHILUBA, FREDERICK (1943–), Zambian political leader. The son of a miner, Chiluba dropped out of high school because of family financial problems. While an office worker in a Swedish mining equipment company, he joined the National Union of Building, Engineering and General Workers (1967) and later chaired the organization (1971–87). After 1972 he became disillusioned with President Kenneth Kaunda's one-party rule, and as head of the Zambian Congress of Trade Unions (1974–88) led the movement protesting Kaunda's socialist economic policies and political repression. When popular pressure forced Kaunda to end his monopoly on power, Chiluba helped organize (1990) the Movement for Multiparty Democracy (MMD) and overwhelmingly won the 1991 presidential elections. He was re-

elected in 1996. As president Chiluba pursued free-market economic policies, privatized banks and the copper industry, and cut food subsidies and public spending. ■ See his book *Democracy: The Challenge of Change* (1995), and Julius O. Ohonvbere, *Economic Crisis, Civil Society, and Democratization* (1996).

CHIRAC, JACQUES RENÉ (1932–), French political leader. The son of a banker, Chirac served as an army officer in Algeria (1956–57), graduated from the École Nationale d'Administration (1959), entered the civil service, and was elected to the National Assembly (1967). He was a conservative who admired the policies of former President Charles de Gaulle and served as prime minister under President Valéry Giscard d'Estaing (1974–76). He organized the neo-Gaullist political party, Rally for the Republic (1976), was mayor of Paris (1977–95), and served again as prime minister in a power-sharing arrangement ("cohabitation") with Socialist President François Mitterrand (1986–88). Chirac advocated economic austerity, privatization, and a strengthening of France's nuclear arsenal. After twice being defeated for the presidency (1981, 1988), Chirac narrowly defeated socialist Lionel Jospin and served as president of France (1995–).

CHIRICO, GIORGIO DE (1888–1978), Greek-born Italian painter. Chirico spent his youth in Athens, Munich, Florence, and Turin: cities whose arcaded squares and massive, sculpturesque architecture figured in his disturbing cityscapes. From 1910 to 1919 Chirico created metaphysical pictures that decidedly influenced early surrealist painters. Canvases like *Melancholy and Mystery of a Street* (1914) and *The Great Metaphysician* (1917) depicted sinister, lifeless cities filled with faceless people. A mysterious revelation moved Chirico to renounce (1919) his modernist work. He called on the art world to "liberate the world from the melancholy dictatorship of so-called modern painting" and spent the next half century producing paintings in the neoclassic mode of the academy. ■ See his *Memoirs* (Eng. trans. 1971) and study by J. T. Soby (1955).

CHISHOLM, SHIRLEY (Shirley St. Hill; 1924–), U.S. political leader. A feisty, outspoken education specialist from Brooklyn, Chisholm served in the New York State Assembly (1964–68) before winning election in 1968 as the first African-American U.S. congresswoman. She served for seven terms (1969–83), supporting women's rights, job training, abortion reform, day care, environmental protection, and an end to the Vietnam War. In 1972 Chisholm ran unsuccessfully for the Democratic presidential nomination. ■ See her memoirs, *Unbossed and Unbought* (1970) and *The Good Fight* (1973).

CHOIBALSAN, HORLOOQIYAN (1895–1952), Mongolian political leader. Choibalsan (also spelled Choybalsan) studied in Moscow (1914–17) and founded in Urga (now

Ulan Bator) in 1919 one of the two Mongolian revolutionary groups that merged to form the Mongolian People's party (1920). He organized units of the Mongolian people's army during the 1921 revolution; with the help of Russian Red army forces it defeated an army of White Russians and a Chinese army and established a revolutionary government. Choibalsan served in the government, was elected to the party's Central Committee and Politburo (1924), commanded the army (1924–28), and served as deputy premier (1935–39). As premier (1939–52), he was called "the Mongolian Stalin" as he helped to transform traditional Mongolia into a modern communist state along Soviet lines.

CHOMSKY, NOAM (1928–   ), U.S. linguist. The son of a noted Hebrew language scholar, Chomsky studied at the University of Pennsylvania (Ph.D. 1955) and taught at the Massachusetts Institute of Technology (1955–   ). He revolutionized linguistic studies with the publication of a small book, *Syntactic Structures* (1957), which extended the thrust of his doctoral dissertation, *Transformational Analysis* (1955). His theory was further elaborated in *Aspects of a Theory of Syntax* (1965). Chomsky's approach broke with the earlier tradition of American structural linguistics by assuming that linguistic expressions have beneath their surface structure an underlying deep structure which is innate. He understood this deep structure to be basic grammatical forms from which a great diversity of surface structures, the various languages, could be generated. He presented a revised version of his theoretical framework, the Minimalist Program, in the early 1990s. A libertarian socialist, Chomsky was also a prominent political activist. He was an outspoken opponent of U.S. military involvement in Vietnam and elsewhere in the Third World, and of U.S. support of dictatorships around the world. His political books included *American Power and the New Mandarins* (1969), *At War with Asia* (1970), *The Political Economy of Human Rights* (1979; with Edward S. Herman; 2 vols.), *Towards a New Cold War* (1982), *The Fateful Triangle* (1983), *Manufacturing Consent* (1988; with Edward S. Herman), *Necessary Illusions: Thought Control in a Democratic Society* (1989), and *Power and Prospects: Reflections on Human Nature and the Social Order* (1996). ■ See biography by Robert F. Barskey (1997). For his linguistic theories, see *Chomsky: Selected Readings* (1971), *Language and Responsibility: Based on Conversations with Mitsou Ronat* (1979), and studies by Justin Leiber (1975) and John Lyons (rev. ed. 1978).

CHOU EN-LAI. *See ZHOU ENLAI.*

CHOU TSO-JEN. *See ZHOU ZUOREN.*

CHRÉTIEN, JEAN (1934–   ), Canadian political leader. Born into a French-Canadian family in Quebec, Chrétien attended Liberal party meetings and rallies with his father and headed the campus Liberal Club at Laval University, where he received a law degree (1958). As a member of parliament (1963–86), he served in nine cabinet posts, including finance minister (1977–79), and earned a reputation as an excellent administrator. As minister of justice (1980–82) he played a major role in the defeat of a referendum calling for the separation of Quebec from Canada. He was also instrumental in the repatriation of Canada's constitution from Great Britain, and in the creation of a national charter of rights. After four years in private life, he returned to politics (1990) as leader of the Liberal party and led it to victory in elections in 1993, 1997, and 2000. As prime minister (1993–   ) he maintained strong support for a united Canada, championed the North American Free Trade Agreement (NAFTA), and followed a policy of fiscal austerity that cut many social programs but ultimately ended a huge deficit and resulted in low inflation and a balanced budget in 1998. ■ See his autobiography, *Straight from the Heart* (1985).

CHRISTIAN X (1870–1947), king of Denmark. Christian X succeeded his father Frederick VIII in 1912 and in 1915 granted a new constitution that provided for two houses of parliament and extended the vote to women. He was also king of Iceland during the period that Iceland was an independent kingdom united with Denmark (1918–44). During the German World War II occupation (1940–45), Christian X defied Nazi pressure, refused to promulgate anti-Jewish laws, and frequently rode his horse through Copenhagen to assert his claim to authority. A national hero and symbol of Danish resistance, he was held under house arrest from 1943 to 1945.

CHRISTIE, DAME AGATHA (Agatha Miller; 1890–1976), British novelist. Agatha Christie turned from a singing career to writing. In a durable career that began in 1920, Christie published nearly 100 titles (novels, short-story collections, and plays) that sold more than 500 million copies in numerous languages. Fame came with her sixth novel, *The Murder of Roger Ackroyd* (1926); others included *Death on the Nile (1937), And Then There Were None* (1940), *Witness for the Prosecution* (1953), *Nemesis* (1971), and *Curtain* (1975). Models of the classic English detective novel, they relied on the formula of murder in middle- or upper-class settings, intricate plots laced with clues and red herrings, and eccentric sleuths like Hercule Poirot and Miss Jane Marple, who solved crimes by deduction. Her play *The Mousetrap* (1952) set a London record for its continuous run of some three decades. She also wrote romance novels under the pen name Mary Westmacott. ■ See her autobiography (1977); biographies by Gwen Robyns and Janet Morgan (1985), Gillian Gill (1990), and Charles Osborne (1999); and studies by Dennis Sanders and Len Lovallo (1984) and Dawn B. Sova (1996).

CHRISTOFF, BORIS (1918–1993), Bulgarian opera singer. Christoff graduated from law school in Sofia before being sponsored by King Boris to study singing in Rome and Salzburg in the early 1940s. He emerged after World War II as one of the greatest singer-actors of his era, hailed by many as the successor to the great Russian bass Feordor Chaliapin. A flamboyant and temperamental artist, Christoff sang in all of the world's great opera houses and was best known for his portrayals of Boris Godunov and of King Philip II in Verdi's *Don Carlo*.

CHRISTY, HOWARD CHANDLER (1873–1952), U.S. illustrator. Christy covered the Spanish-American War with the Rough Riders, drawing battle-scarred heroes for American magazines, and produced several popular World War I posters. He was best known, however, for creating the saucy but sweet "Christy girl," who appeared in the most popular magazines and epitomized beauty during the first two decades of the century. In the 1920s Christy moved into fashionable portraiture (Will Rogers, Amelia Earhart) and also painted murals (New York City's Café des Artistes) featuring the Christy-girl nude. His large oil painting, *Signing the Constitution* (1940), hangs in the U.S. Capitol.

CHRYSLER, WALTER PERCY (1875–1940), U.S. industrialist. Starting his career as a railroad machinist, Chrysler worked his way up to the position of works manager (American Locomotive Co.) before switching industries to become plant manager for the Buick Motor Co. (1912), the principal unit of General Motors. He became vice president of GM (1916) but resigned over policy differences (1920). Chrysler then took over the Maxwell Motor Corp. (1924) and brought out the first Chrysler car, which featured a high-compression engine, four-wheel hydraulic brakes, and other automotive innovations. The car was a great success, and the company—renamed the Chrysler Corp. (1925)—eventually became the country's second-largest auto producer. He also built the 1,046-foot-high Chrysler Building in New York City (1930). ▪ See his autobiography, *Life of an American Workman* (1937), and biography by Vincent Curcio (2000).

CHU, STEVEN (1948–), U.S. physicist. Chu studied at the University of California, Berkeley (Ph.D. 1976), and did research at Bell Laboratories in Holmdel, New Jersey (1978–87). He later was a professor of physics at Stanford University (1987–). With colleagues at Bell (1985), he devised a way of utilizing six concentrated laser beams to cool gases in order to dramatically slow down their atoms. This procedure, which lowered the temperature to 240 millionths of a degree above absolute zero, enabled scientists to capture individual atoms and study them in great detail. The technique was refined by William D. Phillips and Claude Cohen-Tannoudji and raised the possibility of creating supersensitive atomic clocks that would increase the accuracy of space and global navigation and would allow for precise measurements of gravitational forces. For their work, Chu, Phillips, and Cohen-Tannoudji shared the 1997 Nobel Prize in Physics.

CHUBAIS, ANATOLY BORISOVICH (1955–), Russian government official. Chubais was a research economist who studied (Ph.D. 1983) and taught (1977–90) at the Leningrad Institute of Economics and Engineering. During the 1980s, as a member of the Communist party, he was a leader of the democratic movement in Leningrad and supported the reform policies of Mikhail Gorbachev. He served on the Leningrad City Executive Committee (1990–91) and left the Communist party after the 1991 hard-line coup attempt. As head of the State Committee for the Administration of State Property of the Russian Federation (1991–96), Chubais aggressively advocated free-market reforms and designed and supervised the swift privatization of Russia's industries. The controversial reforms stabilized the currency and slashed state spending but resulted in the creation of a criminalized form of capitalism that was controlled by a handful of tycoons and worsened industrial stagnation. He organized President Boris Yeltsin's successful reelection campaign (1996) and, although accused of corruption by his political enemies, served Yeltsin as his chief of staff (1996–97) and as deputy prime minister (1997–98). He subsequently ran Russia's electrical monopoly, United Energy Systems and was the government's chief negotiator in securing a $17.1 billion loan from the International Monetary Fund and other international lenders (1998).

CH'U CH'IU-PAI. *See QU QIUBAI.*

CHUKOVSKY, KORNEI IVANOVICH (Nikolai Vasilyevich Korneychuk; 1882–1969), Soviet writer, translator, and critic. During the early decades of the century, Chukovsky mixed with avant-garde literary circles and took part in various publishing ventures. The lively children, animals, and insects created by "Uncle" Kornei Chukovsky have been loved by generations of young Russian readers, and by their parents. He wrote dozens of children's books, including *The Crocodile* (1916; Eng. trans. 1931, 1964). In *From Two to Five* (1933; Eng. trans. 1963) he recorded conversations with children. Chukovsky was also an intelligent and prolific translator of American and English literature, known particularly for his Russian rendering of Walt Whitman. *The Art of Translation* (1919; rev. 1941; Eng. trans. 1984) discussed his craft. Chukovsky's critical writings included books on the poets Alexander Blok (1924; Eng. trans. 1982) and Nikolai Nekrasov (1952; Eng. trans. 1977). His daughter, the scholar writer, and human-rights activist Lydia Chukovskaya (1907–1996), wrote the semiautobiographical novels *The Deserted House* (Eng. trans. 1977) and *Going Under* (Eng. trans. 1972).

CHUN DOO HWAN (1931–), South Korean political leader. Chun graduated from the Korean Military Academy (1955) and subsequently served in many high-ranking posts in the army. He was made a brigadier general in 1973 and named commander of the army intelligence unit in 1979. After the assassination of President Park Chung Hee (1979), Chun staged a coup within the military and seized control of the armed forces. He established a military government in May 1980, abolished civil rights, arrested prodemocracy leader Kim Dae Jung, and violently suppressed a protest movement in the city of Kwangju, during which at least 200 students and other civilians were killed. Elected to a seven-year term as president of South Korea by a newly created electoral college (1981), Chun led a brutally repressive regime that nevertheless presided over a period of dramatic economic growth. He was succeeded as president by Roh Tae Woo (1988), his former military academy classmate, who won the freely contested 1987 presidential election. Chun and Roh were both arrested in 1995 and convicted in 1996 of plotting the 1979 coup, of carrying out the Kwangju massacres, and of accepting hundreds of millions of dollars in bribes from businessmen. Chun's death penalty was reduced by an appeals court to life imprisonment. Both Chun and Roh were pardoned and released from prison at the urging of President-elect Kim Dae Jung in December 1997.

CHURCHILL, SIR WINSTON LEONARD SPENCER (1874–1965), British political leader. A descendant of the first duke of Marlborough, Churchill was the son of a Tory politician and a wealthy American woman. He graduated from the military academy at Sandhurst (1894), served in India and the Sudan, and covered the Boer War as a correspondent. He was elected to the House of Commons as a Conservative (1900) but switched to the Liberal party out of an interest in social welfare and served as president of the board of trade (1908–10) and home secretary (1910–11). As first lord of the Admiralty (1911–15), he helped prepare Britain for World War I, but the failure of the Dardanelles expedition led to his resignation. After the war he was colonial secretary (1921–22) and, rejoining the Conservatives, served as chancellor of the Exchequer (1924–29). He was politically isolated during much of the 1930s speaking out against Nazism and German rearmament, until being recalled to the admiralty at the outbreak of World War II (1939–40). As wartime prime minister (1940–45), he inspired the nation with his oratory, courage, optimism, and tenacity, and helped plan the strategy, with U.S. President Franklin D. Roosevelt and Soviet leader Joseph Stalin, that defeated the Axis powers. In retirement after his government's defeat by the Labour party (1945), he warned against Soviet expansionism in his famous "iron curtain" speech in Fulton, Missouri (1946) and wrote a history of *The Second World War* (6 vols., 1948–53). He served a second term as prime minister (1951–55). Churchill's other books included *The World Crisis* (6 vols., 1923–31), *Marlborough* (4 vols., 1933–38), and *A History of the English Speaking Peoples* (4 vols., 1956–58), and he was awarded the 1953 Nobel Prize in Literature. ■ See biographies by Reginald Thompson (1963), Randolph Churchill and Martin Gilbert (8 vols., 1967–88), and Henry Pelling (1974).

CHU TEH. *See ZHU DE.*

CIANO, GALEAZZO (1903–1944), Italian public official. A multimillionaire, the son of the count of Cortellazzo. Ciano participated in the fascist March on Rome (1922), received a law degree from the University of Rome (1925), married the daughter of fascist leader Benito Mussolini (1930), and quickly worked his way up to the highest ranks of the fascist ruling hierarchy. He was appointed foreign minister (1936), helped create the Italian-German alliance (1939), and was viewed as Mussolini's successor. After several military setbacks in 1942, however, Ciano advocated a separate peace with the Allies and was a leader of the coup that overthrew Mussolini (July 25, 1943). He was subsequently captured by the Germans and tried and executed for treason by the fascist puppet government in German-occupied Verona. ■ See Edda Mussolini Ciano, *My Truth* (Eng. trans. 1977).

CIARDI, JOHN ANTHONY (1916–1986), U.S. poet. The son of Italian immigrants who settled in Boston, Ciardi attended Tufts College (B.A. 1938) and the University of Michigan (M.A. 1939). Beginning with *Homeward to America* (1940), he published some 25 volumes of light and humorous poetry as well as noted verse translations of the Italian poet Dante Alighieri and an introduction to poetry, *How Does a Poem Mean?* (1959). His *Selected Poems* appeared in 1984. A member of the faculty at Harvard University (1946–53) and Rutgers (1953–61), Ciardi was also actively associated with the Bread Loaf Writers Conference (1947–73) and served as poetry editor of the *Saturday Review* (1956–72). Ciardi also wrote *A Browser's Dictionary* (1980) and its sequel, *A Second Browsers Dictionary, and Native's Guide to the Unknown American Language* (1983). ■ See autobiography (1987; with Vince Clemente) and studies by Edward Krickel (1980) and Edward M. Cifelli (1997).

CICERO (Elyeza Bazna; 1904–1970), spy for Germany during World War II. Bazna was born into an Albanian family and grew up in Ankara (later the capital of Turkey). Codenamed Cicero because his information spoke so eloquently, he was the valet of the British ambassador in Ankara (1943–44). He photographed and sold to the Germans top-secret information, including the minutes of the 1943 Tehran Conference of Allied leaders and details of the Normandy invasion planned for 1944. But the Nazi high command, believing Cicero to be a plant, disregarded his information. Cicero fled when the British detected the leak but was later apprehended passing counterfeit British notes that the Nazis had given him in large quantities in payment for his services. He spent his final years as a night watchman in Munich. ■ See his *I Was Cicero* (with Hans Nogly; Eng. trans 1962); Fitzroy Maclean, *Take Nine Spies* (1978); and Richard Wires, *The Cicero Spy Affair* (1999).

CIERVA, JUAN DE LA (1896–1936), Spanish aviator. Determined to make aviation a safer and more practical activity, Cierva designed the first autogiro (1919), the precursor of the helicopter, and made the first successful autogiro flight (1923). Cierva continued to refine his design, invoking many principles expounded by Leonardo da Vinci, until the autogiro was ready for commercial production (1925). Cierva's machine dominated the rotorcraft field for the next 12 years. He was working on the design for a modern helicopter when he died (1936) in an airplane crash.

CILLER, TANSU (1946–   ), Turkish political leader. The daughter of an affluent local official, Ciller studied economics at Bosporus University (B.A. 1967) and in the United States at the universities of New Hampshire and Connecticut (Ph.D. 1972). She became a professor of economics, joined the conservative True Path party (1990), and was elected to parliament in 1991. After serving as economics minister (1991–93), the youthful Ciller was elected leader of the True Path party (1993), and served as Turkey's first woman prime minister (1993–95). She maintained her office in coalition with the Islamist Welfare Party (1995–96) and subsequently served as foreign minister (1996–97). In office she advocated privatization and pursued controversial austerity policies in order to curb inflation and growing government debt. She was also faced with serious challenges from the Islamic fundamentalist movement and Kurdish separatists. At the end of her term in office she was investigated for financial impropriety and accused of condoning government-sponsored death squads aimed at supporters of the Kurdish separatist guerrilla army. However, the investigations were curtailed, she was not indicted, and she remained a major power broker in Turkish politics.

CITROËN, ANDRÉ GUSTAVE (1878–1935), French engineer and industrialist. Citroën achieved prominence during World War I when he applied mass-production techniques to increase dramatically the output of the French munitions industry. In May 1919 he built his first Citroën automobile and became known as the "French Henry Ford" for introducing Ford's methods of production and marketing to the French automotive industry. One of Europe's leading car manufacturers, he sponsored automobile crossings of the Sahara (1922–23), Asia (1931–32), and North America (to Alaska, 1934), and organized the traffic-light system in Paris. He introduced the first popular front-wheel-drive car (1934) shortly before his company went bankrupt and he lost control of it. ■ See biography by John Reynolds (1996).

CIXOUS, HÉLÈNE (1937–   ), French feminist and critic. Cixous was born to a Jewish family in Algeria, where her mother worked as a midwife. After finishing secondary school (1954), she went to France, took graduate degrees in English (1957; 1958), writing a dissertation on James Joyce, and taught. Cixous was active in the May 1968 student upheaval in Paris. In its aftermath. she organized experimental literature courses at Vincennes. where she became a professor, and cofounded the review *Poétique* (1969). An influential voice in French intellectual circles, Cixous explored the intersections between psychoanalysis and language, particularly as they relate to women, and the relationship between writer and reader in literary works. Her many books included *The Exile of James Joyce* (1968; Eng. trans. 1972), *Angst* (1977; Eng. trans. 1985), *First Days of the Year* (1990; Eng. trans. 1997), and a volume of lectures, *Three Steps on the Ladder of Writing* (Eng. trans. 1993). ■ See study by Lynn Penrod (1996).

CLAIR, RENÉ (René Chomette; 1898–1981), French film director. Clair began his career as a writer and continued to write his own scripts, as well as several novels, after he began directing. His first film, *Paris qui dort* (*The Crazy Ray,* 1923), was a surrealist venture in which tourists entered a Paris paralyzed by a magic ray. It was followed by *Entr'acte* (1924), a dadaist comedy whose cast included the artist Marcel Duchamp. Comedy and fantasy continued to predominate in Clair's work. *The Italian Straw Hat* (1927) was his most successful silent feature. With the advent of sound, Clair led the way in exploring fully the artistic possibilities of the new medium. He pioneered the musical-comedy film in *Under the Roofs of Paris* (1930), *Le Million* (1931), and *A Nous la Liberté!* (1931) and developed the principle of asynchronous sound, in which sound is used to counterpoint an image. He continued to make fanciful comedies in England (*The Ghost Goes West,* 1935) and in the United States (*I Married a Witch,* 1942), returning to France after World War II. ■ See his *Reflections on the Cinema* (Eng. trans. 1953) and study by Celia McGerr (1980).

CLAPHAM, SIR JOHN HAROLD (1873–1946), British economic historian. A Cambridge honors graduate (1895), dean, provost, and holder of the university's chair in economic history established for him (1928–38), Clapham rejected economic theory in favor of the systematic compilation of economic data. His major works were *The Economic Development of France and Germany* (1921), *Economic History of Modern Britain* (3 vols., 1926–38), and *The Bank of England* (3 vols., 1944–58). He was also active on the Board of Trade (1916–18), as president of the British Academy (1940–45), and as editor of the first volume of *The Cambridge Economic History of Europe* (1941).

CLAPTON, ERIC (1945–   ), British guitarist, singer, and composer. Influenced by the playing of Muddy Waters and other African-American blues musicians, Clapton was a member of several influential rock bands including the Yardbirds (1963–65), John Mayall's Bluesbreakers (1965–66), and Cream (1966–68). By the late 1960s he had achieved cult status as rock's greatest guitarist and was given the nickname "God." After near-fatal bouts of heroin and then alcohol addiction in the 1970s, he reemerged as a vocalist/songwriter in the 1980s and attracted a new generation of fans. His best-selling albums included *461 Ocean Boulevard* (1974), *Slowhand* (1977), *Journeyman* (1989), and *Unplugged* (1992). Among his most famous songs were "Sunshine of Your Love" (1967), "After Midnight" (1970), "Layla" (1970), "Lay Down Sally" (1971), "Cocaine" (1977), and "Pilgrim" (1998). "Tears in Heaven" (1991), inspired by the accidental death of his young son, was a worldwide hit. ■ See Marc Roberty, *Slowhand* (1993), and Michael Schumacher, *Crossroads* (1995).

CLARK, CHAMP (James Beauchamp Clark; 1850–1921), U.S. politician. An independent Democratic progressive from Missouri, Clark served in the U.S. House of Representatives for 13 terms (1893–95; 1897–1921). He led the revolt that unseated the dictatorial Speaker of the House Joseph G. Cannon (1910), and he himself served as speaker from 1911 to 1919. He narrowly lost the 1912 Democratic presidential nomination to Woodrow Wilson. ■ See his reminiscences, *My Quarter Century in American Politics* (1920).

CLARK, DICK (1929–), U.S. television personality. After graduating from Syracuse University (B.S. 1951), Clark worked as a radio newscaster and announcer before becoming host of the teenage pop-music television program "American Bandstand," on WFIL in Philadelphia (1956). A tremendous success, the show joined the ABC network in 1957, and the clean-cut and youthful-looking Clark became a national celebrity, an idol of American teenagers, and a major force in the growth of rock-and-roll music for more than 25 years. During the 1960s, 1970s, and 1980s he also hosted several game and comedy shows and produced movies and television musical specials. ■ See his *Rock, Roll and Remember* (1976) and John A. Jackson, *American Bandstand* (1997).

CLARK, JAMES (1936–1968), Scottish auto racer. The youngest driver to gain the world auto-driving championship (1963), Jim Clark was the first driver to win both the Indianapolis 500 and the world's championship (his second) in the same year (1965). Known as the "Flying Scot," he won a record 25 Grand Prix races. He was killed when his rear-engined Lotus-Ford crashed during the German championship race. ■ See study by Graham Gauld (1968).

CLARK, JOHN BATES (1847–1938), U.S. economist. Clark was educated at Brown University, Amherst College, and Heidelberg and Zurich universities. Influenced by the German historical school and by Christian socialism, he was an economic reformer early in his career, but his famous marginal productivity theory of wages justified the distribution of income under capitalism. He taught at Columbia University (1895–1923) and edited the Political Science Quarterly (1895–1911). His writings against monopoly influenced the formation of the antitrust legislation of 1914 and the establishment of the Federal Trade Commission.

Clark also directed economic and historical studies for the Carnegie Endowment for World Peace (1911–23), planned its multivolume study of World War I, and advocated a strong League of Nations to prevent war. His books included *The Distribution of Wealth* (1899), *The Problem of Monopoly* (1904), and *Social Justice Without Socialism* (1914). His son, John Maurice Clark (1884–1963), was also a noted economist.

CLARK, JOHN PEPPER (1935–), Nigerian poet and playwright. After graduating from University College, Ibadan (1960), J. P. Clark worked as a government information officer, journalist, editor, and college professor. He is best known for three frequently performed plays, *Song of a Goat* (1961), *The Masquerade* (1964), and *The Raft* (1964), which offer a tragic view of human experience. A fourth play, *Ozidi* (1966), a modern stage version of a traditional Ijaw drama, depicts corruption in a contemporary African state. Clark's poetry (*Poems,* 1962; *A Reed in the Tide,* 1965) is filled with traditional myths and allusions to local Nigerian customs and manners. *Casualties: Poems of 1966–68* (1970) is concerned with the Nigerian civil war. His notable critical essays appeared in *The Example of Shakespeare* (1970), and he spent 15 years translating and editing the Ijaw epic, *The Ozidi Saga* (Eng. trans. 1977). Clark was affiliated with the University of Lagos (1963–80) and directed Nigeria's only English-language repertory theater (in Lagos). His later works included *The Bikaroa Plays: The Bat, The Return Home and Full Circle* (1985) and *Collected Plays and Poems, 1958–1988* (1991). ■ See study by Robert M. Wren (1984).

CLARK, KENNETH BANCROFT (1914–), U.S. psychologist. Reared in New York City's Harlem, Clark studied at Columbia University (Ph.D. 1940), taught at the City College of New York (CCNY; 1942–75), and won renown for his work with emotionally disturbed ghetto children. His report (1950) on the psychological impact of racial segregation was an influential factor in the U.S. Supreme Court decision (1954) banning segregation in the public schools. Clark cofounded (1962) Harlem Youth Opportunities Unlimited to help school dropouts and unemployed youth and served on the New York State Board of Regents (1966–86). His writings included *Prejudice and Your Child* (1955), *Dark Ghetto: Dilemmas of Social Power* (1965), *The Negro American* (1966), *Pathos of Power* (1975), and *King, Malcolm, Baldwin: Three Interviews* (1984). With John H. Franklin he wrote *The Nineteen Eighties: Prologue and Prospect* (1981).

CLARK, KENNETH MACKENZIE CLARK, BARON (1903–1983), British art historian. Born to wealth, Clark studied at Oxford, worked with American art connoisseur Bernard Berenson in Florence, Italy, and served as fine-art curator at Oxford's Ashmolean Museum (1931–34). A major figure in Britain's cultural life for decades, Clark directed the National Gallery in London (1934–45), taught at Oxford (1946–50; 1961–62), chaired the Arts Council (1953–60), and presided over the introduction of commercial television in Britain. As a scholar Clark specialized in the Italian Renaissance and his works on art history included two studies on Leonardo da Vinci (1935, 1939), a book on Piero della Francesca (1951), and two surveys, *Landscape into Art* (1949) and *The Nude* (1955). *Civilisation* (1970) stemmed from his popular televised lecture series (1969) reviewing achievements in the fine arts, architecture, and music. He was made a life peer in 1969. ■ See his autobiographies, *Another Part of the Wood* (1975) and *The Other Half* (1977), and biography by Meryle Secrest (1984).

CLARK, MARK WAYNE (1896–1984), U.S. general. A 1917 graduate of West Point, Clark served in France during World War I. During World War II, as Gen. Dwight D. Eisenhower's deputy in the invasion of North Africa (1942), Clark was instrumental in securing the cooperation of Free French forces. He commanded Allied troops in Italy (1944), became a full general (1945), and commanded American occupation forces in Austria after the war. He held various army posts until his appointment as commander in chief of the United Nations forces in Korea (1952–53). He was also known as a prominent anticommunist propagandist. ■ See his war memoirs, *Calculated Risk* (1950) and *From the Danube to the Yalu* (1954), and the study by Martin Blumenson (1984).

CLARK, TOM CAMPBELL (1899–1977), U.S. jurist. After graduating from the University of Texas (B.A. 1921; LL.B. 1922), Clark worked for his father's law firm, then served as district attorney of Dallas (1927–32), where he was reputed never to have lost a case. In 1937 Clark joined the U.S. Department of Justice and rose to head the Antitrust and Criminal Divisions before Pres. Harry Truman appointed him U.S. attorney general in 1945 and associate justice of the Supreme Court four years later. His judicial opinions tended to support the government's position, especially in cases involving subversion and national security. He wrote the majority opinions in landmark decisions barring illegally obtained evidence in state trials (1961), banning prayers and Bible reading in public schools (1963), and upholding the public-accommodations provisions of the Civil Rights Act (1964). Clark resigned in 1967 to avoid conflict of interest when his son Ramsey became U.S. attorney general.

CLARKE, SIR ARTHUR C. (1917–   ), British science fiction writer. Clarke was trained in physics and mathematics and was a radar instructor and a flight lieutenant during World War II. He was credited with originating the idea of a satellite communication system in a 1945 article. Clarke's best-known early works were *Childhood's End* (1953) and *The City and the Stars* (1956). His science fiction viewed exploration of the universe through the eyes of a romantic humanism, while supplying convincing technological detail to make the journey credible. His works often held religious and philosophical implications. After writing *2001: A Space Odyssey* (1968), he collaborated on the film adaptation with Stanley Kubrick. He wrote the sequels *2010: Odyssey Two* (1982), which was also adapted for the screen, *2061: Odyssey Three* (1988), and *3001: The Final Odyssey* (1997). In 1984 he published *1984, Spring: A Choice of Futures*, a collection of addresses. essays, and lectures; *Profiles of the Future; and Ascent to Orbit: A Scientific Autobiography*. His later novels included *The Songs of Distant Earth* (1986). He emigrated to Sri Lanka in the mid-1950s and served as chancellor of Moratuwa University (from 1979). His nonfiction included *The Snows of Olympus: A Garden on Mars* (1995) in which he predicted human colonization of the planet. ■ See his autobiography (1990) and biography by Neil McAleer (1992).

CLAUDE, ALBERT (1898–1983), Belgian-born U.S. cell biologist. After receiving a medical degree from the University of Liege (1929), Claude joined the Rockefeller Institute for Medical Research in New York (now Rockefeller University), where he was the first to use the electron microscope for biological research. He published the first detailed anatomy of a cell (1945) and discovered mitochondria and the endoplasmic reticulum. Claude was also a pioneer in the use of the centrifuge to separate cells into their component parts. From 1948 to 1972 he directed the Jules Bordet Institute in Brussels. He shared the 1974 Nobel Prize in Physiology or Medicine with George S. Palade and Christian de Duve.

CLAUDE, GEORGES (1870–1960), French engineer. Claude developed a method for safely transporting acetylene gas (1896) and invented (1902) a process for making liquid air that he used as a cooling agent to separate hydrogen from illuminating gas. He then used the hydrogen to synthesize ammonia. He made his fortune by establishing that light can be produced by sending an electric current through a tube of inert gas, a discovery that led to neon lighting. Convicted (1945) of collaborating with the Germans during World War II, Claude was released from prison in 1949.

CLAUDEL, PAUL (1868–1955), French poet and playwright. As a French diplomat, Claudel traveled widely and served as ambassador to Tokyo, Washington, and Brussels. A deeply religious Catholic, he infused his writings with his spiritual beliefs; his poetry, notably *Five Great Odes* (1910; Eng. trans. 1967), expressed his faith in God and his joy in life. Eschewing traditional French rhyme and meter, he developed his own free form. Most of his plays were written between 1890 and 1924, though they were not produced until years later. They were symbolic and poetic metaphysical excursions on human love and God's redemption. Particularly noteworthy are *Tidings Brought to Mary* (1910; Eng.

trans. 1916) and the lengthy *Satin Slipper* (1929; Eng. trans. 1931). ■ See studies by Harold A. Waters (1970), Bettina L. Knapp (1982), and Joy Humes, *Two Against Time* (1978).

CLAY, LUCIUS DUBIGNON (1897–1978), U.S. general. The son of a U.S. senator from Georgia and a descendant of Henry Clay, Lucius Clay graduated from West Point (1918) and held a series of army engineering posts prior to World War II. From 1942 to 1944 he headed the army's procurement program and later served as deputy military governor of Germany (1945–47) in charge of civilian affairs. As commander of U.S. forces in Europe (1947–49) Clay, by then a full general, successfully organized the airlift during the 327-day Soviet blockade of Berlin. After his retirement from the army (1949) he served as chief executive of the Continental Can Co. (1949–62) and senior partner of the Lehman Brothers banking firm (1963–73). ■ See biography by Jean E. Smith (1990).

CLEAVER, ELDRIDGE (1935–1998), U.S. political activist and author. Born in Arkansas and raised in the black slums of Los Angeles, Cleaver was a street criminal as a teenager and spent most of the next two decades in prison. Self-taught while behind bars, he became a political radical and his angry prison book, *Soul on Ice* (1968), was an international best-seller. On parole, he was a leader of the Black Panther party in Oakland, a spokesman for radical causes, and presidential candidate for the Peace and Freedom party (1968). He was involved in a shootout between the Panthers and the Oakland police and left the United States (1968) rather than face charges of attempted murder. He lived in exile for seven years in Havana, Algiers, and Paris. After becoming a "born-again" Christian while in France, Cleaver returned home in 1975, abandoned his political militancy, and espoused conservative Republican views. He toured the country as a religious crusader and wrote an updated autobiography, *Soul on Fire* (1978). Attempted murder charges were dropped in 1979. During the 1990s he was treated for addiction to crack cocaine. ■ See biography by Kathleen Rout (1991).

CLEMENCEAU, GEORGES (1841–1929), French political leader. A public figure of great energy and determination, Clemenceau was called the "Tiger" for his anticlerical and anti-imperialist campaigns that challenged more than one government of the Third Republic. A journalist and editor of the newspaper *L'Aurore* (1893–1903), he spearheaded the campaign to exonerate the convicted Jewish army officer Alfred Dreyfus. Clemenceau served as premier (1906–09) and again during the World War I years (1917–20), when he proved a pillar of national strength. He helped draft the postwar Treaty of Versailles but felt that French security was compromised by the Allies and retired to write several volumes of memoirs and philosophy, including *In the Evening of My Thought* (Eng. trans. 1929). ■ See Wythe Williams,

The Tiger of France (1949); Edgar Holt, *The Tiger* (1976); Gregor Dallas, *At the Heart of a Tiger* (1993); and biography by David S. Newhall (1991).

CLEMENTE, ROBERTO (1934–1972), Puerto Rican–born U.S. baseball player. One of the greatest outfielders in baseball history, Clemente played for the Pittsburgh Pirates (1955–72), compiling a .317 lifetime batting average, 3,000 hits, and 240 home runs. Voted the National League's Most Valuable Player in 1966, he led the league in batting on five different occasions and spurred his team toward world series titles in 1960 and 1971. Clemente died in a plane crash while carrying food and supplies to the victims of the Managua, Nicaragua, earthquake. In the spring of 1973, the Baseball Writer's Association waived the five-year waiting period and voted him into the National Baseball Hall of Fame. ■ See biographies by Kai Wagenheim (1973) and Phil Musick, *Who Was Roberto?* (1974).

CLIBURN, VAN (Harvey Lavan Cliburn, Jr.; 1934–), U.S. pianist. Cliburn made his professional debut at age 13 in a concert with the Houston Symphony. He established himself as a major keyboard artist in 1958 by winning the Moscow International Tchaikovsky Piano Competition, a triumph that made him a national hero and led to extensive concert tours and recordings. He was best known for his interpretations of the romantic repertory, notably the works of Tchaikovsky and Rachmaninoff. He established a piano competition in his name in Forth Worth, Texas (1962). ■ See studies by Abram Chasins (1959) and Howard Reich (1993).

CLIFFORD, CLARK MCADAMS (1906–1998), U.S. lawyer and public official. Clifford was a special adviser and speechwriter for fellow midwesterner Harry Truman (1946–50), helping to devise the president's campaign strategy and foreign policy. Then, as later, he supported liberal domestic policies while shaping a tough anticommunist foreign policy. He served as foreign-policy adviser to Pres. John F. Kennedy; as Pres. Lyndon Johnson's secretary of defense (1968–69), he converted from hawk to dove when he decided the Vietnam War was unwinnable. Subsequently Clifford maintained his Washington contacts and became a wealthy lawyer, serving the nation's largest corporations. During his last years he was indicted for fraud, conspiracy, and bribe taking in the scandal involving the collapse of the Bank of Credit and Commerce International (B.C.C.I.). He insisted on his innocence but reached a $5 million settlement with the Federal Reserve in 1998. ■ See his memoir, *Counsel to the President* (1991).

CLINTON, BILL (William Jefferson Clinton; 1946–), U.S. political leader. Clinton was raised in Hope and later in Hot Springs, Arkansas, and developed a passion for politics while in high school. He graduated from Georgetown University (B.S. 1968), was a Rhodes Scholar at Oxford University (1968–70), studied law at Yale (J.D. 1973), and served as governor of Arkansas (1978–80; 1982–92). A pragmatic, nonidelogical, "new style" Democrat who believed that only by moving to the right could the Democratic party regain the White House after years of conservative Republican rule, he was elected president in 1992 and was reelected in 1996. Domestically he promoted market-driven economic policies, signed balanced budget and welfare reduction legislation proposed by the Republicans, and presided over the longest period of continuous economic growth in U.S. history. In foreign policy matters he successfully argued for passage of the North American Free Trade Agreement (NAFTA), sent troops to Haiti to ensure the return to power of ousted President Jean-Bertrand Aristide, bombed Iraq for its failure to comply with post–Gulf War military restrictions (1996) and for its defiance of U.N. arms inspectors (1998), arranged for a cease-fire in the Bosnian civil war (1995), and bombed Yugoslavia as part of NATO's attempt to halt attacks on ethnic Albanians in the Serbian province of Kosovo (1999). He was plagued by numerous allegations of financial and sexual misconduct and was impeached by the Republican-dominated House of Representatives (December 1998) for perjury and obstruction of justice relating to the cover-up of a sexual liaison (1995–97) he had with a White House intern. The Senate, however, acquitted Clinton of the charges (February 1999). His wife, Hillary Rodham Clinton (1947–   ), a lawyer, was a key presidential adviser and was elected to the U.S. Senate from New York State (2000). ■ See David Maraniss, *First in His Class* (1995), Jeffrey Toobin, *A Vast Conspiracy* (2000), and Joe Conason, *The Hunting of the President* (2000).

CLURMAN, HAROLD EDGAR (1901–1980), U.S. theatrical director and critic. A major force In the American theater for five decades, Clurman cofounded (1931) New York's Group Theater, which presented notable realistic dramas during the 1930s. It presented plays by Clifford Odets, William Saroyan, and Irwin Shaw, developed the careers of such actors as John Garfield, Luther Adler, Stella Adler, and Lee J. Cobb, and introduced the Stanislavsky method of acting to Broadway. Clurman directed such hit plays as *Awake and Sing!* (1935), *Member of the Wedding* (1950), and *Tiger at the Gates* (1955) and wrote criticism for the *New Republic* and the *Nation*. His books included *On Directing* (1972), *The Divine Pastime* (1974), *Ibsen* (1977), and *The Fervent Years* (1945), a history of the Group Theater. ■ See his memoirs, *All People Are Famous* (1974).

COASE, RONALD H. (1910–   ), British-born economist. Coase taught at the London School of Economics (1935–51), his alma mater, before moving to the United States (1951), where he was a professor at several universities. He served as a professor of law at the University of Chicago (1964–81), where he edited the *Journal of Law and Economics*. His reputation rests primarily on two papers that were practically devoid of mathematical analysis. The first, "The Nature of the Firm" (1937), analyzed why companies exist. The second, "The Problem of Social Cost" (1960), which became one of the most frequently cited works in modern economics, argued that social conflicts can most efficiently be solved through market mechanisms rather than through government intervention or costly litigation. His pioneering works on the institutional structure of the economy influenced legal studies, economic history, and organization theory, and he was awarded the 1991 Nobel Memorial Prize in Economics. His books included *The Firm, the Market and the Law* (1988) and *Essays on Economics and Economists* (1994).

COBB, IRVIN SHREWSBURY (1876–1944), U.S. writer. A newspaperman in his native Kentucky, Cobb moved to New York, where he edited the humor sections of the *Evening Sun* (1904) and the *Evening World* (1905–11) before giving up journalism to concentrate on writing fiction. A prolific writer of humorous books, short stories, essays, and plays, he contributed regularly to the *Saturday Evening Post* (1911–22) and *Cosmopolitan* (1922–32). The character of Judge Priest, featured in nearly 100 of his stories, was called by one critic "the best representative southerner ever presented in literature." *Speaking of Operations* (1916), a humorous account of an appendectomy, sold nearly 800,000 copies. Cobb's wit and unaffected humor made him a popular lecturer, after-dinner speaker, and radio (1930–36) and motion picture (1934–42) personality. ■ See his autobiography, *Exit Laughing* (1941); Elisabeth Cobb, *My Wayward Parent* (1945); and study by Anita Lawson (1984).

COBB, TY (**Tyrus Raymond Cobb; 1886–1961**), U.S. baseball player. Cobb was regarded by many as the greatest as well as the meanest player in major league history. Some attribute his nastiness to the fact that his beloved father was fatally shot by his mother, who had mistaken the elder Cobb for an intruder. In spite of his megalomania, cruelty, and violent outbursts, he created or equaled more individual records than any other player and was the first man elected to the Baseball Hall of Fame (1936). In a 24-year career in the American League, with the Detroit Tigers (1905–26) and Philadelphia Athletics (1927–28), Cobb, a left-handed hitting outfielder, established records for lifetime batting average (.367) and batting championships won (12) that still stand. Called the "Georgia Peach," he hit over .400 three times and over .300, 23 times, feats never equaled. His record of 892 career stolen bases was not broken until 1977 (by Lou Brock) and his lifetime tally of 4,191 hits was not surpassed until 1985 (by Pete Rose). ■ See his autobiography, *My Life in Baseball* (1961), and the biography by Al Stump (1994).

COBURN, ALVIN LANGDON (1882–1966), U.S. photographer. Coburn opened his first studio in New York City

(1902) and joined the newly formed Photo-Secession group, which sought recognition for photography as an art form. Working in London in the early years of the century, he compiled two volumes of portraits of *Men of Mark* (1913; 1922), including writer George Bernard Shaw posing as Auguste Rodin's statue *The Thinker*. His work became increasingly abstract, from his 1913 exhibit of aerial perspectives of New York City to his "vortographs" in 1917, the first nonobjective photographs. ■ See his autobiography (1966) and his photographs in *Alvin Langdon Coburn* (1998).

COCA, IMOGENE (1909–), U.S. comedienne. Coca made her "show biz" debut as a vaudeville tap dancer at age 11. She later performed in an adult camp in the Poconos, under Max Liebman's direction. Coca wanted to work with her first husband Robert Burton, but Liebman paired her up with Sid Caesar and produced "Your Show of Shows" (1949–54), the live Saturday night variety revue that showcased their witty sketches and pantomimes. Coca preferred satirizing movies like *A Place in the Sun;* her takeoff on the ballet *Afternoon of a Faun,* using Nijinsky's choreography, was famous. Neither Caesar nor Coca enjoyed particular success after the team split up (1954). Coca appeared onstage in *The Four Poster* (1973) and *Prisoner of Second Avenue* (1973), and in films.

COCHRAN, SIR CHARLES BLAKE (1872–1951), British impresario and theatrical producer. The greatest showman of his time, C. B. Cochran produced everything from rodeos and boxing matches to Max Reinhardt's spectacular show *The Miracle* (1911) and Sergei Diaghilev's ballets. He presented the illusionist Harry Houdini, introduced roller skating (1909), and promoted such stars as Beatrice Lillie, Noel Coward, and Eleonora Duse. Of the 128 productions he personally supervised (1914–50), he was best known for the elaborate and tasteful musical revues he produced during the 1920s and 1930s, including *Wake Up and Dream* (1929), and his collaborations with Noel Coward, *The Year of Grace* (1928), *Private Lives* (1930), and *Cavalcade* (1931). He wrote four books of reminiscences, *I Had Almost Forgotten* (1932), *Cock-a-doodle-do* (1941), *A Showman Looks On* (1945), and *Secrets of a Showman* (1951).

COCHRAN, JACQUELINE (1910?–1980), U.S. aviator. Cochran, who learned to fly at age 22, set more than 200 flying records during her career. The U.S. Air Force lent her a Seversky fighter plane in which she placed first in the Bendix Cup Air Race (1938). In World War II she headed Women's Auxiliary Service Pilots (WASP), a group of noncombatant flyers. She later became (1953) the first woman to break the sound barrier. The U.S. National Aeronautics Association recognized (1962) 49 new records set by her in a single jet flight from New Orleans to Germany. Two years later she became the fastest woman pilot on record, flying at 1,429 miles per hour. ■ See her informal autobiography, *The Stars at Noon* (1954).

COCKCROFT, SIR JOHN DOUGLAS (1897–1967), British physicist. Cockcroft studied engineering and then mathematics at Cambridge. There he joined (1922) Ernest Rutherford at the Cavendish Laboratory. He and E.T.S. Walton built the world's first atom-smashing machine, a linear accelerator, and split the nuclei of lithium and boron with a bombardment of protons (1932). For this major work in particle physics, they shared the 1951 Nobel Prize in Physics. Cockcroft played a leading role in the development of radar; after World War II he was the first director of Britain's atomic-research establishment at Harwell (1946–58). ■ See study by Ronald Clark (1960).

COCTEAU, JEAN (1889–1963), French poet, novelist, dramatist, and critic. Energy, dedication, and incredible versatility marked Cocteau's career. In addition to his prodigious literary output, he did graphic illustrations, worked in ceramics, created ballet scenarios, decorated buildings, composed music, made movies and acted. His name is associated with a number of aesthetic movements during the period between World War I and II. Like much of his work in other media, his poetry and novels are marked by fantasy and fascination with surfaces. The novel *Les Enfants Terribles* (1929; Eng. trans. 1930) and the play *The Infernal Machine* (1934; Eng. trans. 1936) are considered to be his masterpieces. He has been criticized for self-consciousness and lack of emotional depth. Cocteau's widely admired films included *The Blood of a Poet* (1932), *Beauty and the Beast* (1945), and *Orpheus* (1950). In 1955 he was elected to the Académie Française. ■ See Robert Phelps' collection of Cocteau's writings, *Professional Secrets: An Autobiography* (1970), and biography by Francis Steegmuller (1970). His diaries were published as *Past Tense* (2 vols. 1983; Eng. trans. 1987–88).

CODONA, ALFREDO (1893–1937), Mexican-born circus performer. When Codona first performed on the flying trapeze (1913), his father was his catcher. Later he performed with his brother, Lalo, and sister, Victoria, who eventually retired, and was replaced by Vera Bruce. Subsequently he toured for six seasons as a soloist with the Barnum and Bailey circus in the United States. He made circus history by performing the daring (some said suicidal) triple aerial somersault. He worked on the triple for three years, and after 1930 incorporated it into his act, with a 90 percent success record. He married famed aerial gymnast Lillian Leitzel in 1928. After her accidental death while performing (1931), Codona married Vera Bruce. When she sued him for divorce (1937), Codona shot her and committed suicide.

CODREANU, CORNELIU ZELEA (1899–1938), Rumanian political leader. An anti-Semitic and anticommunist agitator while a student at the University of Iasi (1919–21), Codreanu founded the Legion of the Archangel Michael (1927). Renamed the Iron Guard (1930), the paramilitary organization became Rumania's most prominent fascist movement. As the All for the Fatherland party, the movement received 16 percent of the votes in the 1937 elections to become Rumania's third-largest political party. Fearing its growing influence, King Carol II dissolved the party (1938) and arrested Codreanu, who was shot along with 13 of his followers, allegedly while attempting to escape from detention. ■ See Nicholas M. Nagy-Talavera, *The Green Shirts and the Others* (1970).

COFFIN, WILLIAM SLOANE, JR. (1924–   ), U.S. Presbyterian clergyman. An intelligence officer during World War II and Central Intelligence Agency operative (1950–53), Coffin graduated from the Yale Divinity school and served as Yale University chaplain (1958–76). He received nationwide recognition as a civil rights activist and as a leader of the anti–Vietnam War movement. His highly publicized 1968 conviction for conspiracy to violate federal draft laws was overturned two years later, and the charges were dropped. As senior minister of New York City's progressive inter-denominational Riverside Church (1977–87), he advocated a shift toward increased spiritualism but continued to speak out on major social issues through the 1980s. He headed the SANE/Freeze nuclear disarmament movement (1988–   ). ■ See his memoir, *Once to Every Man* (1977).

COHAN, GEORGE MICHAEL (1878–1942), U.S. actor, director, songwriter, playwright, and producer. Born into a family of vaudevillians, Cohan first appeared on the stage when he was an infant. He started writing songs as a teenager; he wrote his first musical comedy, *The Governor's Son,* in 1901. A boisterous and animated performer, he dominated and transformed the American musical theater during the next two decades, writing and starring in dozens of productions including *Little Johnny Jones, Forty-Five Minutes from Broadway,* and *George Washington, Jr.* Known for patriotic and sentimental songs, he was awarded the Congressional Medal of Honor (1940) for "Over There" and "You're a Grand Old Flag." His other popular hits included "The Yankee Doodle Boy," "Mary's a Grand Old Name," and "Give My Regards to Broadway." Late in his career he was acclaimed for his performances in Eugene O'Neill's *Ah, Wilderness!* (1933) and the Rodgers and Hart musical *I'd Rather Be Right* (1937). Cohan's life was the subject a of an Academy Award-winning film *Yankee Doodle Dandy* (1942) and a Broadway musical *George M.* (1968). ■ See his autobiography, *Twenty Years on Broadway* (1925), and biography by John McCabe (1973).

COHEN, LEONARD NORMAN (1934–   ), Canadian songwriter, poet, and novelist. The son of a prosperous Jewish merchant in Montreal, Cohen played electric guitar for the Buckskin Boys, a country band, as a teenager. Soon after

graduating from McGill University (1955), he published his first volume of poetry. He published the novel *Beautiful Losers* (1966), then turned to songwriting, recording *The Songs of Leonard Cohen* in 1967. He became famous for haunting, poetic songs such as "Suzanne," "Sisters of Mercy," "Bird on a Wire." and "Famous Blue Raincoat," which were performed by Cohen and others, notably Judy Collins. In the late 1970s, his popularity waned in the United States, but European fans remained loyal, and on a 1985 tour he found himself a hero of the Polish Solidarity movement. Later albums included *Recent Songs* (1979), *Various Positions* (1985), *I'm Your Man* (1988), and *The Future* (1992). He gave up touring, and making albums in 1993 and became a Buddhist monk in southern California. ■ See his *Stranger Music: Selected Poems and Songs* (1994) and study by Ira Nadel (1994).

COHEN, MORRIS RAPHAEL (1880–1947), Russian-born U.S. philosopher. Cohen arrived in the United States at age 12 and studied at New York's City College and later under Josiah Royce and William James at Harvard (Ph.D. 1906). He taught philosophy at City College (1912–38), where he was one of the most brilliant, popular, and influential members of the faculty. He was also a founder and president (1933–41) of the Conference on Jewish Relations. He applied his naturalistic mode of philosophic inquiry to such fields as the philosophy of science, metaphysics, and logic. Cohen advocated the inclusion of legal philosophy in university and law school curricula. He wrote *Reason and Nature* (1931), *Law and the Social Order* (1933), *Preface to Logic* (1944), *Faith of a Liberal* (1945), and other works. ■ See his autobiography, *A Dreamer's Journey* (1949); Leonora Rosenfield, *Portrait of a Philosopher* (1962); and study by David A. Hollinger (1975).

COHEN, STANLEY (1922–   ), U.S. biochemist. Cohen studied at the University of Michigan (Ph.D. 1948), did research on cell growth with Rita Levi-Montalcini at Washington University in St. Louis (1952–59), and taught at Vanderbilt University in Nashville, Tennessee (1959–   ). After Levi-Montalcini discovered nerve growth factor (NGF), a natural substance that stimulates the growth of nerve cells, Cohen purified it and demonstrated that it is a protein. He subsequently discovered and determined the molecular structure of epidermal growth factor (EGF), a natural substance that regulates the growth of several types of tissue within the body. Cohen and Levi-Montalcini's research influenced many areas of medical research, including the study of cancer, birth defects, senile dementia, and delayed wound healing, and they shared the 1986 Nobel Prize in Physiology or Medicine.

COHEN-TANNOUDJI, CLAUDE (1933–   ), French physicist. Born in Algeria, Cohen-Tannoudji studied in Paris and was a professor at the University of Paris (1964–73) and at the Collège de France (1973–   ). Between 1988 and 1995 he and his colleagues extended the pioneering work of Steven Chu and William D. Phillips, who developed methods to cool and capture atoms with laser beams and magnetic traps. These methods enabled scientists to study individual atoms in great detail. Cohen-Tannoudji and his team cooled gases to .2 millionth of a degree above absolute zero, revising the theoretical basis for the cooling of atoms and raising the possibility of the creation of atomic clocks that could accurately measure gravitational forces and allow for precise navigational measurements. For their pioneering work, Cohen-Tannoudji, Chu, and Phillips shared the 1997 Nobel Prize in Physics. Cohen-Taunoudji's books included *Atom-Photon Interactions* (1992; with J. Dupont-Roc and G. Grynberg) and *Atoms in Electromagnetic Fields* (1994).

COHN, EDWIN JOSEPH (1892–1953), U.S. biochemist. After studies at the University of Chicago (Ph.D. 1917), Cohn joined the faculty of the Harvard Medical School (1920), where he eventually headed the department of physical chemistry (1935) and the division of medical sciences (1936). He spent most of his career studying proteins and their components—amino acids and peptides; he was best known for separating, or fractionating, blood plasma into its various protein components—albumin, gamma globulin, thrombin, and fibrin. Developed at the start of World War II, these "Cohn fractions" were used to treat shock, stop hemorrhages, and prevent infection: they proved invaluable in the treatment of wartime casualties. Serum gamma globulin was later used as the basis for mass inoculations against polio and measles.

COHN, HARRY (1891–1958), U.S. film producer. The archetype of the autocratic Hollywood mogul, Cohn cofounded (1920) the company that became Columbia Pictures in 1924 and built it into a force beyond its size by hiring director Frank Capra, borrowing actors from other studios, and discovering new stars. (He personally groomed Rita Hayworth and Kim Novak for top parts.) Notable films made under Cohn's aegis were the Academy Award winners *It Happened One Night* (1934), *You Can't Take It with You* (1938), *All the King's Men* (1949), *From Here to Eternity* (1953), *On the Waterfront* (1954), and *The Bridge on the River Kwai* (1957). ■ See Bob Thomas, *King Cohn* (1967), and Bernard F. Dick, *The Merchant of Poverty Row* (1993).

COHN-BENDIT, DANIEL (1945–   ), Franco-German political activist. Cohn-Bendit was born in France to German-Jewish refugee parents. He returned to West Germany with his family (1958) and took German citizenship. Influenced by both anarchism and socialism, he espoused spontaneous political activity and was a member of the radical SDS student organization. While enrolled as a sociology student at the Nanterre campus of the University of Paris, he led the March 1968 student protest movement that inspired worker revolts and nearly brought down the French government. The charismatic Cohn-Bendit was subsequently expelled from France. With his brother Gabriel he wrote *Obsolete Communism: the Left-Wing Alterative* (Eng. trans. 1968). Back in Germany he worked in a day-care center, edited a political magazine, and became a leader of the Green party. As a member of the Frankfurt City Council (1989–97) he headed the municipal department of multicultural affairs. He also served in the European Parliament (1994–99; 1999–   ).

COLBERT, EDWIN HARRIS (1905–   ), U.S. paleontologist. An authority on the distribution, migration, and evolution of prehistoric animals, Colbert was curator of fossil reptiles and amphibians at the American Museum of Natural History in New York City (1945–70) and professor of vertebrate paleontology at Columbia University (1945–69). Called by *Time* magazine "the Dick Tracy of the Mesozoic Age," Colbert unearthed thousands of prehistoric fossil remains throughout the world and discovered 50 new species. His works included *The Dinosaur Book* (1945), *Evolution of the Vertebrates* (1955), *Men and Dinosaurs* (1968), and *Wandering Lands and Animals* (1973). ■ See his autobiographies, *A Fossil-Hunters Notebook: My Life with Dinosaurs and Other Friends* (1980) and *Digging into the Past* (1989).

COLE, GEORGE DOUGLAS HOWARD (1889–1959), British economist. As a student at Oxford, G. D. H. Cole edited the *Reformer,* became active in Fabian socialist politics, and earned a first-class degree. A romantic socialist who believed in individualism and pluralism, he helped found the National Guilds League (1915), which advocated public ownership of heavy Industry. Teaching economics and political theory at Oxford (1925–57), Cole wrote prolifically, occasionally collaborating with his wife, Margaret Postgate Cole, on academic works as well as detective novels. His books included *Principles of Economic Planning* (1935), *Case for Industrial Partnership* (1957), and the classic *History of Socialism* (5 vols., 1953–60). ■ See biography by his wife (1971), and A. W. Wright, *G. D. H. Cole and Socialist Democracy* (1979).

COLE, NAT "KING" (**Nathaniel Adams Coles;** 1919–1965), U.S. popular singer and jazz pianist. Cole sang and played the organ in his father's church. Although he made his professional debut as a jazz pianist, his soft, mellow vocal tones brought him international fame as a romantic singer. A star of vaudeville and night clubs, he formed the King Cole Trio (also known as the Fiddlers Three) in the late 1930s and was the first African American to have both his own radio (1948–49) and television (1956–57) series. His recorded ballads included "Too Young," "Mona Lisa," and "Nature Boy." His daughter Natalie (1949–   ) was also a popular singer. ■ See biographies by Maria Cole (1971), Leslie Gourse (1991), and David M. Epstein (1999).

COLEMAN, JAMES SAMUEL (1926–1995), U.S. sociologist and educator. A professor at Johns Hopkins University

(1959–73) and the University of Chicago (from 1973), Coleman wrote the controversial U.S. government report *Equality of Educational Opportunity* (1966). Known as the Coleman Report, it influenced the government to increase federal aid to schools and to implement desegregation programs during the 1970s. He also wrote *The Adolescent Society* (1961), *Adolescents and the Schools* (1965), and *Foundations of Social Theory* (1990), and was coauthor of *Youth: Transition to Adulthood* (1974) and *High School Achievement* (1982).

COLEMAN, MICHAEL (**1891–1945**), Irish musician. One of the most influential figures in Irish traditional music, Coleman was born in south Sligo, an area famous for its musical heritage. He emigrated to New York in 1914 and was recognized among Irish Americans as a master fiddler. He appeared in vaudeville and performed solo concerts throughout the United States during the 1920s. His flowing style was captured on dozens of popular 78-rpm records (1921–44), which helped to resuscitate what was then a dying musical form back in Ireland. His playing set a standard for the performance of traditional fiddle music and resulted in the Sligo style and Sligo melodies coming to predominate over much of Irish and Irish-American fiddling. Coleman's performances inspired generations of fiddlers and influenced the development of all aspects of traditional music in Ireland through the 20th century.

COLEMAN, ORNETTE (**1930–**), U.S. saxophonist and composer. Coleman bought an alto saxophone at age 14 and a tenor sax two years later. Unable to pay for lessons, he learned from an instruction book, a method that led to unorthodox fingering. As another money-saving measure, Coleman bought a white plastic (rather than brass) saxophone that later became his trademark. Through the 1950s he played in New Orleans, where jazz buffs rejected his idiosyncratic style; in Los Angeles, where he formed his first quartet; and in New York, where reviews were mixed. He remained obscure until the appearance of his first album, *Something Else* (1958); it found a following with its atonal sound and unusual phrasing. His other notable albums included *Change of the Century* (1959), *Free Jazz* (1960), and *The Skies of America* (1972). In 1976, after extended absences from the stage, Coleman again stirred controversy by assembling a new band, "Prime Time," which included two electric guitars, electric bass, and drums. His fusion of jazz and rock was well received by rock fans.

COLES, ROBERT (**1929–**), U.S. psychiatrist and writer. Coles received an M.D. from Columbia University (1954) and was affiliated with Harvard University throughout his career. He was an activist who wrote extensively about people caught up in the turmoil of social crisis. Equipped with a tape recorder and a sense of compassion, he lived and worked with the first black children to integrate southern schools and with migrant families and others. His five-volume *Children of Crisis* (1967–77) won a Pulitzer Prize. After completing a two-volume study of *Women of Crisis* (1978–80), he traveled to Ireland and South Africa to work with children involved in political crisis. *The Moral Life of Children* (1985) and *The Political Life of Children* (1985) were based on talks with children around the world. He also wrote on literary subjects in *Irony in the Mind's Life* (1974) and *Flannery O'Connor's South* (1980). His later works included *The Spiritual Life of Children* (1990), *The Call to Service: A Witness to Idealism* (1993), and *The Secular Mind* (1999). ■ See study by Susan Hilligoss (1997).

COLETTE (**Sidonie Gabrielle Colette; 1873–1954**), French novelist. Colette first started writing in collaboration with Willy, the first of her three husbands. After their divorce (1906), she continued to write while working as a music-hall dancer and mime. She recounted these experiences in the semiautobiographical *Vagrant* (1910; Eng. trans. 1912) and other writings. She was famed for her portrayals of the sadness of love, the yearnings of young girls and older women, and her vivid descriptions of animals and nature. She secured her reputation with such novels as *Chéri* (1920; Eng. trans. 1929) and *Gigi* (1945; Eng. trans. 1952) and her nostalgic memoirs and books celebrating turn-of-the-century French society. Her *Collected Stories* appeared in English translation in 1983. ■ See *Earthly Paradise,* an autobiography drawn from her writings by Robert Phelps (1966); biographies by Yvonne Mitchell (1975), Michele Sarde (Eng. trans. 1980), Joanna Richardson (1983) and Judith Thurman (1999); and Claude Francis and Fernaude Gontier, *Creating Colette* (2 vols., 1998, 1999).

COLLINGWOOD, ROBIN GEORGE (**1889–1943**), British historian. R. G. Collingwood was educated in the arts by his father, a painter and biographer of the critic John Ruskin. He studied at Oxford and later joined its faculty (1912–41). Specializing in the archaeology of Roman Britain, he wrote the *Roman Britain and the English Settlements* volume (1936) of the *Oxford History of England*. A scholar of great breadth, Collingwood sought to reconcile history and philosophy in *Essay on Philosophical Method* (1933) and *Essay on Metaphysics* (1940), asserting that cultural values are rooted in history and can be judged as such. A composer and painter in leisure hours, Collingwood studied the interplay between art and politics in *New Leviathan* (1942). His last book, *The Idea of History* (1946), which argued that the study of history involves reliving the past in the mind, influenced the teaching of history. ■ See his *Autobiography* (1939); Alan Donagan, *The Later Philosophy of R. G. Collingwood (1962);* and L. Rubinoff, *Collingwood and the Reform of Metaphysics* (1970).

COLLINS, EDDIE (**Edward Trowbridge Collins; 1887–1951**), U.S. baseball player. A star second baseman for the Philadelphia Athletics and the Chicago White Sox. Eddie Collins maintained an average of .333 over a 25-year playing career (1906–30). He amassed 3,311 hits, stole 743 bases, accounted for 7,629 assists, and was one of the original members of the National Baseball Hall of Fame.

COLLINS, JUDY (1939–), U.S. singer. The daughter of a radio entertainer, Collins studied classical piano for many years but gave it up to become a guitar-playing folksinger. Starting with her 1961 album *Maid of Constant Sorrow,* she repeatedly turned out carefully crafted albums, nearly one a year for 20 years, weathering shifts of popular-music taste. After two albums of traditional folk songs, she broadened her repertory to include the urban folk music of Bob Dylan, Leonard Cohen, and others, and eventually to encompass a discriminating inventory of modern pop standards by such composers as Jacques Brel, Kurt Weill, Joni Mitchell, and Stephen Sondheim. Her albums included *In My Life* (1966); *Wildflowers* (1967), which first included her own compositions; *Judith* (1975); *Hard Times for Lovers* (1979); *Amazing Grace* (1985); and *Shameless* (1995). Collins was active in the civil-rights and antiwar movements. ■ See her autobiographies *Trust Your Heart* (1987) and *Singing Lessons* (1998) and study by Vivian Claire (1977).

COLLINS, MICHAEL (1890–1922), Irish revolutionist. Collins spent his early manhood in Britain, where he was a postal clerk and joined the Fenian movement. Returning to Ireland (1916), he devoted himself entirely to the republican revolutionary cause. He led the guerrilla forces in the war against the British, organized an effective intelligence service for the Irish Republican Army (IRA), and served as finance minister in the republican government. Despite his revolutionary leanings, he supported the treaty of 1921 establishing the Irish Free State as a British dominion and was appointed president of the provisional government upon the death of Arthur Griffith. Ten days later he was gunned down by a republican extremist. ■ See Frank O'Connor, *The Big Fellow* (1937; rev. ed. 1965); and biographies by Rex Taylor (1958), Margery Forester (1971), T. Ryle Dwyer (1990), and James A. MacKay (1996).

COLMAN, RONALD (1891–1958), British-born actor. Active on the London and Broadway stages before appearing opposite Lillian Gish in the movie *The White Sister* (1923), Colman was one of the few screen stars to achieve popular success in both silent and sound films. A dignified and aristocratic romantic hero, he starred in such Hollywood films as *Dark Angel* (1924), *Beau Geste* (1926), *Arrowsmith* (1931), *A Tale of Two Cities* (1935), *Lost Horizon* (1937), *The Prisoner of Zenda* (1937), and *Random Harvest* (1942). He won an Academy Award for his role in *A Double Life* (1947). ■ See the biography by his daughter Juliet Benita Colman (1975).

COLTRANE, JOHN WILLIAM (1926–1967), U.S. jazz saxophonist and composer. The grandson of a minister and son of an amateur musician, Coltrane grew up in an at-mosphere filled with the religious melodies of the southern black church. During the early 1950s he toured with such widely divergent jazz stylists as Earl Bostic and Dizzy Gillespie, but when working with Miles Davis (1955–57) he began to develop his own sound—the piercing, keening dissonance and "sheets of sound" style that he perfected in his 1957 gigs in New York with Thelonius Monk. This style was controversial: some found it intentionally offensive, others an expression of modern soul. In the 1960s his sound changed again, to the mellower, pensive style of his famous and characteristic "My Favorite Things" (1960). "A Love Supreme" (1964) was a successful and powerful synthesis of his many styles and influences. ■ See J. C. Thomas, *Chasin' the Trane* (1975); Eric Nisenson, *Ascension* (1993); John Fraim, *Spirit Catcher* (1996); and biographies by Cuthbert O. Simpkins (1975), Bill Cole (1976), and Lewis Porter (1998).

COMANECI, NADIA (1962–), Rumanian gymnast. The most spectacular and acclaimed athlete of the 1976 Montreal Olympics, Comaneci won three gold medals for her near-perfect and seemingly effortless performances. Her exercises on the uneven bars and the balance beam (the sport's most difficult apparatus) were given the perfect score of 10, making her the first Olympic gymnast to accomplish such a feat. She also won two gold medals at the 1980 Moscow Olympics. She was coached by Bela Karolyi, who later was a coach of the U.S. gymnastic Olympic teams (1984–2000). ■ See Marion Connock, *Nadia of Romania* (1977).

COMDEN, BETTY (1919–) **and ADOLPH GREEN** (1915–), U.S. lyricists and librettists. Comden and Green were classmates at New York University and founding members of the satirical Greenwich Village nightclub troupe, the Revuers (1939). In 1944 they wrote the book and lyrics for the Broadway hit *On the Town,* with music by Leonard Bernstein, and they subsequently collaborated on a series of upbeat musicals set in New York City, including *Wonderful Town* (1953; Tony Award), *Bells Are Ringing* (1956), and *Subways Are for Sleeping* (1961). They also wrote the musical films *Singing in the Rain* (1952), *The Band Wagon* (1953), and *It's Always Fair Weather* (1955), and the Broadway musicals *Hallelujah, Baby!* (1968; Tony Award), *Applause* (1970; Tony Award), and *The Will Rogers Follies* (1991; Tony Award). ■ See Comden's autobiography *Off Stage* (1995).

COMMAGER, HENRY STEELE (1902–1998), U.S. historian. Commager earned a Ph.D. from the University of Chicago (1928). A Jeffersonian liberal, he explored the concept of social justice in the sweep of U.S. history. He collaborated with S. E. Morison on *The Growth of the American Republic* (1930), a textbook that went into several editions, and with Allan Nevins on two other big histories of the United States (1939; 1942). Commager taught at New York University, Columbia, and Amherst, edited *Documents of*

American History (1934), and wrote many other books, including *The American Mind* (1950), *Freedom, Loyalty, Dissent* (1954), *The American Character* (1970), *The Empire of Reason* (1978), and *Commager on Tocqueville* (1993). ■ See study by Neil Jumonville (1999).

COMMONER, BARRY (1917–), U.S. biologist and ecologist. Commoner was born in Brooklyn, the son of Russian immigrant parents. He earned a Ph.D. in cellular physiology from Harvard University (1940) and joined the faculty of Washington University (St. Louis) in 1947, serving as head of its Center for the Biology of Natural Systems (1965–80). In his books *Science and Survival* (1966), *The Closing Circle* (1971), *The Poverty of Power* (1976), and *The Politics of Energy* (1979) and *Making Peace with the Planet* (1990), he warned against technological threats to the environment, opposed nuclear power, advocated the widespread use of solar energy, and established a reputation as America's most influential environmentalist. He was the candidate of the Citizens' party, a coalition of environmentalists and democratic socialists, for the U.S. presidency in 1980.

COMMONS, JOHN ROGERS (1862–1945), U.S. economic historian. Commons taught at the University of Wisconsin (1904–32), where he was identified with the "Wisconsin school" of labor analysis or applied economics and helped draft progressive state legislation on unemployment insurance and workmen's compensation. With his students he wrote a *Documentary History of American Industrial Society* (10 vols., 1910–11) and a *History of Labor in the United States* (4 vols., 1918–35), tracing the evolution of the labor movement in terms of changes in the marketplace. He was also noted for *Legal Foundations of Capitalism* (1924) and *Institutional Economics* (1934). ■ See his autobiography, *Myself* (1934).

COMPTON, ARTHUR HOLLY (1892–1962), U.S. physicist. Compton studied at Princeton (Ph.D. 1916) and did postgraduate work in England with Ernest Rutherford and J. J. Thompson (1919–20). In 1923 he discovered the so-called Compton effect, noting that the scattering of X rays results in increased wavelength. His finding proved that radiation could behave both as a wave and as a particle and corroborated the quantum theory. For this research, he shared the 1927 Nobel Prize in Physics with C.T.R. Wilson. During the 1930s he investigated the nature of cosmic rays. Compton also dealt with the relationship between science and religion, insisting that there is no fundamental conflict between the two. During World War II, he played a major role on the Manhattan Project that developed the atom bomb. He described his role in that project in *Atomic Quest* (1956). ■ See his *Scientific Papers* (1973); see also Marjorie Johnston, ed., *The Cosmos of Arthur Holly Compton* (1967), and Roger H. Stuewer, *The Compton Effect* (1975).

COMPTON-BURNETT, DAME IVY (1892–1969), British novelist. Compton-Burnett's novels were all set in Victorian or Edwardian England, since she felt "no real or organic knowledge of life later than about 1910." Her novels had no objective descriptions of characters or surroundings and were written entirely in her special blend of stylized dialogue. The plots often concerned crimes in upper-middle-class society and revealed a bleak world of hypocrisy and hidden tensions, but they were written with sophistication and sardonic wit and irony. Her first novel was *Dolores* (1911), and among the many novels that followed were *Pastors and Masters* (1925), *Brothers and Sisters* (1929), *Parents and Children* (1941), *Manservant and Maidservant* (1947), and *A God and His Gifts* (1963). ■ See biography by Elizabeth Sprigge (1973) and Hilary Spurling, *Ivy* (1984).

CONANT, JAMES BRYANT (1893–1978), U.S. educator, scientist, diplomat, and author. Trained in chemistry at Harvard (B.A. 1913; Ph.D. 1916), Conant worked in the war gas production unit of the Chemical Warfare Service during World War I. Returning to Harvard, he taught chemistry (1919–33) and was president of the university (1933–53). During World War II, he headed the National Defense Research Committee, advised the government on the atomic bomb project, and was instrumental in selecting a target for the first bomb, dropped over Hiroshima (Aug. 6, 1945). He also advised the government on postwar atomic policy and was an early advocate of international control of nuclear weapons. After serving as U.S. high commissioner in Germany (1953–55) and then ambassador to West Germany (1955–57), Conant returned home and, in the midst of the post-*Sputnik* examination of American education, undertook a comprehensive study of public high schools. His report, *The American High School Today* (1959), influenced local efforts to raise educational standards. In *Slums and Suburbs* (1961), Conant warned that inadequate educational and vocational opportunities for underprivileged youth amounted to "social dynamite." In later works on U.S. education, he called teacher training " scandalous" and questioned the ways that public education is financed. ■ See his autobiography, *My Several Lives* (1970), and biography by James Hershberg (1993).

CONDON, EDDIE (Albert Edwin Condon; 1904–1973), U.S. jazz guitarist. The son of an Indiana Irish saloon keeper, Condon taught himself to play banjo and ukulele and made his debut at age 17 with Homer Peavey's Jazz Bandits. He was a leading figure in the "hot jazz" of the 1920s in Chicago, later moving to New York where he promoted jam sessions, concerts, and opened a Greenwich Village club (1946). The club moved uptown (1958) and remained a fixture of New York City nightlife until it closed (1985). In his autobiography, *We Called It Music* (1947; with Thomas Sugrue), Condon defined jazz as unscored music played by a small ensemble. He never played solo but was a celebrated solo conversationalist. ■ See *The Eddie Condon Scrapbook of Jazz* (1973; with Hank O'Neal).

CONDON, EDWARD UHLER (1902–1974), U.S. physicist. A pioneer in the field of quantum mechanics, Condon did important research on molecular structure and atomic radiation while a professor at Princeton (1930–37). He was associate director of research at Westinghouse (1937–45) and during World War II played a key role in the development of radar and was a leader of the Manhattan Project, which developed the first atomic bombs. Opposed to perpetuating wartime secrecy and military control of atomic research, he advocated international control of atomic weapons and helped draft legislation that placed atomic energy under civilian control. He was attacked as a security risk by the House Un-American Activities Committee (HUAC) at the height of the cold war (1948), and though strongly defended by Pres. Harry Truman, whom he served as director of the National Bureau of Standards (1945–51), he lost his security clearance (1954). He was a professor at Washington University, St. Louis (1956–63), and the University of Colorado (1963–70), and directed the air force study of unidentified flying objects during the 1950s.

CONNALLY, TOM (Thomas Terry Connally; 1877–1963), U.S. political leader. Elected to the U.S. Senate in 1928 from his native Texas, Connally, a Democrat, served with that body for 24 years and was known for his sharptongued debating style. He chaired the Foreign Relations Committee (1941–47; 1949–53) and was instrumental in securing Senate support of U.S. membership in the United Nations, whose charter he helped to draw in 1945. ■ See his autobiography. *My Name Is Tom Connally* (1954).

CONNELLY, MARCUS COOK (1890–1980), U.S. playwright. Marc Connelly, whose parents were both in vaudeville, became a reporter at age 17. In 1921 he began collaborating with George S. Kaufman on a succession of hit plays: *Dulcy* (1921), *To the Ladies* (1922), *Merton of the Movies* (1922), and *Beggar on Horseback* (1924). A gregarious member of the celebrated Round Table, a literary circle that met at New York's Algonquin Hotel, he also contributed articles to the *New Yorker,* wrote screenplays, and directed plays and films. He won a Pulitzer Prize for *Green Pastures* (1930), his play adapted from a black folk version of the Bible. ■ See his memoirs, *Voices Offstage* (1968), and study by Paul T. Nolan (1969).

CONNOLLY, CYRIL (1903–1974), British critic. After writing one satirical novel, *The Rock Pool* (1936), Connolly concentrated on literary criticism and essays. His work was published in various collections like *The Unquiet Grave* (1944), *Ideas and Places* (1953), and *Previous Convictions* (1964). He cofounded and edited the influential British literary monthly *Horizon* (1939–50) and subsequently wrote for various newspapers and magazines. An eclectic and entertaining critic, Connolly was not very sympathetic to newer fiction. Although he was a popular writer with the British public, other critics did not take him seriously, partly because he candidly admitted his own weaknesses and disarmingly disparaged the craft of criticism. ■ See the autobiographical *Enemies of Promise* (1938); *Selected Essays* (1984); David Pryce-Jones, ed., *Cyril Connolly: Journal and Memoir* (1984); and the biography by Jeremy Lewis (1998).

CONNOLLY, MAUREEN (1934–1969), U.S. tennis player. Known as "Little Mo," Connolly was one of the youngest players (at age 16) to win the U.S. tennis championship. A hard-hitting, vigorous player who was compared with Helen Wills for the power of her drives, she won three consecutive U.S. titles (1951–53) and British titles (1952–54). In 1953 she became the first woman to win the grand slam of tennis by sweeping the British, U.S., Australian, and French singles championships in one year. From 1951 to 1954, Connolly won every Wightman Cup match she played. At age 21, a horseback-riding accident cut short her tournament career.

CONNORS, JIMMY (James Scott Connors; 1952–), U.S. tennis player. Taught tennis by his mother, Connors developed into a powerful player as a teenager and won the National Intercollegiate Singles title while he was a student at the University of California at Los Angeles (1971). He was controversial as a professional for his frequently discourteous on-court behavior, but was also a dynamic shot maker and strong baseline player. He had a powerful two-handed backhand and devastating return of service. One of the most explosive competitors and top money winners of his time, he won five U.S. Open championships (1974, 1976, 1978, 1982, 1983), two Wimbledon Jones, titles (1974, 1982), an Australian championship (1974), and the World Professional championship (1977). Ranked number one in the world for five years (1974–78), Connors ended his career with 109 tournament wins and a record singles-match-winning percentage of .824.

CONQUEST, (GEORGE) ROBERT (1917–), British writer. An Oxford graduate (1939) with ten years service in the foreign office (1946–56), Conquest published a collection of his own poetry in 1955, followed by anthologies of British "movement" poetry (1956), science fiction, and "thaw" poetry from Eastern Europe (1958). He was also a respected Kremlinologist who wrote closely documented studies of *Power and Policy in the USSR* (1961), *The Great Terror: Stalin's Purges of the Thirties* (1968; rev. ed. 1990), *Kolyma: The Arctic Death Camps* (1978), and *The Harvest of Sorrow* (1986). His later works included *Stalin: Breaker of Nations* (1991) and *Reflections on a Ravaged Century* (1999).

CONRAD, FRANK (1874–1941), U.S. radio pioneer. As a young laborer with Westinghouse, Conrad began experimenting with electrical equipment and eventually built a crude wireless receiving set (1912). He started to broadcast records from his homemade station in his garage (1919) and, when he ran out of records to play, was able to borrow some from a local store, provided that he announced where he got them. Thus was born the first "sponsored broadcast." Conrad and Westinghouse vice president Harry P. Davis were convinced that regular broadcasting was commercially viable, and Westinghouse applied for a license from federal authorities to set up station KDKA at its plant in Pittsburgh, where the nation's first broadcasting station was born (1920). Conrad, by then Westinghouse's assistant chief engineer. was later known as "the father of radio broadcasting."

CONRAD, JOSEPH (Jósef Teodor Konrad Korzeniowski; 1857–1924), Polish-born British novelist. Born and raised in Poland, Conrad spent 20 years at sea and did not learn English until age 23. He retired in 1894 as a British subject and master mariner. Among his best-regarded works are his first novel, written when he was almost 40, *Aylmayer's Folly* (1895), *The Nigger of the Narcissus* (1897), *Lord Jim* (1900), *The Secret Agent* (1907), *Chance* (1913), *Victory* (1915), and the short story "Heart of Darkness" (1902). Written in a complex style, his works reflect his sailing experiences and exotic travels. They are not mere adventure stories, however, but pessimistic explorations of human psychology and of the tragic effects of isolation, guilt, and the inevitable responsibility that an individual bears for his actions. ■ See biographies by Jocelyn Baines (1960), Frederick R. Karl (1979), and Zdzislaw Najder (1983).

CONSIDINE, ROBERT BERNARD (1906–1975), U.S. journalist. Associated for nearly 40 years with conservative Hearst publications (*New York Mirror, New York Journal-American,* International News Service), Bob Considine covered some of the most important foreign and domestic stories of the century. He reported from Europe, Asia, and Africa during World War II, obtained an exclusive interview with Soviet leader Nikita Khrushchev in Moscow (1957), and accompanied Presidents Eisenhower, Kennedy, Johnson, and Nixon on worldwide tours. In addition to writing a widely distributed syndicated column, "On the Line," Considine was also the author or coauthor of 25 books, wrote several movie scripts, and appeared frequently as a TV and radio commentator.

COOKE, ALISTAIR (1908–), British-born U.S. journalist and broadcaster. Educated at Cambridge and interested in the theater, Cooke was deeply affected by travel in the U.S. He settled there permanently working as a correspondent for various British publications and broadcasting (from 1946) his weekly "Letter from America" for the BBC. He became a cultural intermediary, interpreting American affairs for Britons and British affairs for Americans. In the United States he was known for his many television appearances as narrator and host on such shows as the Emmy

Award–winning "Omnibus" (1952–61), NET's "Masterpiece Theater" (1971–93), and his own award-winning series, "America: A Personal History of the United States" (1972–73; 13 episodes). His books included *Douglas Fairbanks: The Making of a Screen Character* (1940), *Generation on Trial: USA versus Alger Hiss* (1950), *Alistair Cooke's America* (1973), *The Americans: Fifty Talks on Our Life and Times* (1979), *America Observed: From the 1940s to the 1980s* (1988), and *Memories of the Great and Good* (1999).

COOLEY, CHARLES HORTON (1864–1929), U.S. sociologist. The son of a jurist, Cooley studied economics at the University of Michigan, where he became a member of the faculty in 1892 and taught the new subject of sociology (1904–29). A pioneer of the sociopsychological approach, he introduced, in *Human Nature and the Social Order* (1902), the concept of "the looking glass self," which is determined by interaction with others. He described the role of primary groups in *Social Organization* (1909) and the process of social competition in *Social Process* (1918). ■ See biography by Edward Jandy (1942).

COOLEY, DENTON ARTHUR (1920–), U.S. surgeon. A graduate of Johns Hopkins Medical School (1944) and a professor at Baylor University (1954–69), Cooley was known as one of the world's fastest and most skillful heart surgeons—he frequently performed 8 to 12 operations a day. He had participated in more than 5,000 cardiac operations by 1969, when he became the first man to implant an artificial heart in a human being. The device functioned for 65 hours until a human heart was inserted to replace it. However, the patient died 38 hours after the second operation. The case aroused much controversy, sparked debate over the ethics of the procedure, and caused a rift between Cooley and his colleague Dr. Michael DeBakey. He was the founder (1962) and chief surgeon of the Texas Heart Institute in Houston. ■ See biography by Harry Minetree (1973).

COOLIDGE, (JOHN) CALVIN (1872–1933), U.S. president. A dour New England lawyer who was active in Republican politics, Coolidge was elected governor of Massachusetts in 1918 and gained national attention during a Boston police strike (1919) by denouncing the right to strike against the public safety and denying reinstatement to the strikers. Elected U.S. vice president on the ticket headed by Warren G. Harding (1920), he succeeded to the presidency (1923) on the death of Harding and won the 1924 election with the slogan "Keep Cool with Coolidge." He generally pursued a laissez-faire policy regarding big business and foreign affairs. Governing during a time of growing prosperity, he lowered the income tax and the national debt and raised tariffs. His policies created a surplus of capital and encouraged the speculation in stocks that preceded the stock market crash of 1929. Coolidge did not run for reelection in 1928. ■ See his autobiography (1929); William Allen White,

A Puritan in Babylon (1938); and biographies by Donald R. McCoy (1967) and Robert Sobel (1998).

COOLIDGE, WILLIAM DAVID (1873–1975), U.S. physical chemist. Coolidge graduated from the Massachusetts Institute of Technology (1896) and spent his career at the General Electric Research Laboratory (1905–44; director, 1932–44). He developed (1908) ductile tungsten filaments for the incandescent lamp. By making the tungsten pliable, he resolved the problem of the easy breakage of earlier tungsten filaments. Tungsten replaced the impractical carbon filaments used by Thomas A. Edison; it is still used today. In 1913 Coolidge used a hot tungsten cathode to create a high-vacuum X-ray tube. Called the Coolidge tube, it was less dangerous than previously designed tubes and proved a major breakthrough in radiology. ■ See John A. Miller, *Yankee Scientist* (1963), and study by Herman A. Liebhafsky (1974).

COON, CARLETON STEVENS (1904–1981), U.S. anthropologist. Coon, who studied at Harvard (Ph.D. 1928), made important contributions in various branches of anthropology. His investigations of contemporary tribal societies in the Middle East, South America, and India resulted in important ethnographies, including a definitive monograph on the Rif tribes of Morocco (1931). The archaeological excavations he undertook while doing fieldwork in those regions illuminated the transition of early human communities from hunting and gathering to cultivating. During World War II, he worked for the Office of Strategic Services (OSS) in Africa and the Middle East. After the War, he taught at the University of Pennsylvania (1948–63) and was curator of ethnology at Philadelphia's University Museum. He became well known for the books *The Story of Man* (1954; rev. ed. 1962) and *The Seven Caves* (1957). The theory elaborated in *Origin of Races* (1962), now disregarded by scholars, was sometimes exploited by racists to support their views, although Coon repudiated their beliefs. ■ See *A North Africa Story* (1980), which recounts his wartime experiences, and the autobiography *Adventures and Discoveries* (1981).

COOPER, GARY (Frank James Cooper; 1901–1961), U.S. film actor. Brought up on a Montana ranch, Cooper drifted in 1924 to Hollywood, where he began as a cowboy extra before winning lead roles in *Wings* (1927) and *The Virginian* (1929). Tall, lean, and laconic, he was a romantic lead in two Hemingway classics, *A Farewell to Arms* (1932) and *For Whom the Bell Tolls* (1943), but his greatest roles featured a simple man up against great trials of character. Cooper won an Academy Award for his portrayal of *Sergeant York* (1941), the religious young farm boy who became the outstanding U.S. World War I hero, and another as the steadfast ex-sheriff who stands alone in *High Noon* (1952). One of Hollywood's most popular actors, he won a special Academy Award (1960) for his career achievements.

■ See biographies by Hector Arce (1979) and Jeffrey Meyers (1998); Stuart M. Kaminsky, *Coop* (1980); and Larry Swindell, *Last Hero* (1980).

COOPER, LEON (1930–), U.S. physicist. A postdoctoral researcher in the laboratory of Nobel laureate John Bardeen at the University of Illinois during the mid-1950s, Cooper, along with doctoral student John R. Schrieffer, studied the phenomenon of superconductivity in metals. Their explanation (1957) of how many metals lose all resistance to electrical currents at temperatures near absolute zero (called the BCS theory after the three scientists) was a major breakthrough and earned for them the 1972 Nobel Prize in Physics. Cooper lectured extensively at many American and European universities and was on the faculty of Brown University from 1958. He wrote *An Introduction to the Meaning and Structure of Physics* (1968).

COPEAU, JACQUES (1879–1949), French actor and director. Copeau wrote theater criticism before establishing and editing (1909–11) *La Nouvelle Revue Française* with author André Gide and others. After his stage version of Dostoevsky's *The Brothers Karamazov* won (1911) critical notice, Copeau founded (1913) the influential Théâtre du Vieux-Colombier; after World War I he attached a drama school to the theater. Failing health and morale prompted an early retirement to Burgundy (1924–29), where with several followers Copeau staged classical farces at local fairs in the *commedia dell'arte* tradition. The group became known as "Les Copiaux." He later returned to Paris and was associated with the Comédie Française (from 1936). Copeau eschewed both artificiality and naturalism in his efforts to create "pure" theater. He stressed script rather than set, actor rather than star. His productions of plays by Claudel, Musset, Maeterlinck, Molière, Chekhov, Goldoni, and others markedly influenced modern French theater and American and European stage technique as well. ■ See study by John Rudlin (1986) and biography by Maurice Kurtz (1999).

ĆOPIĆ, BRANKO (1915–), Yugoslav novelist, poet, and short-story writer. A prolific writer who became a communist while a student at the University of Belgrade, Ćopić first achieved popularity among his fellow partisans as a writer of wartime poetry. His humorous World War II writings of the reactions of primitive peasant villagers in his native Bosnia to the war, the partisans, and the revolution brought him lasting fame. The comic peasant presented in Ćopić's *Adventures of Nikoletina Bursać* (1956) became a national folk hero.

COPLAND, AARON (1900–1990), U.S. composer. Brooklyn-born of Lithuanian-Jewish ancestry, Copland was Nadia Boulanger's first American student (1921–24) and the first American composer to make a living from music. He melded diverse ethnic styles—jazz, folk, Mexican—into an accessible American "sound." Copland's most popular compositions were *El Salón México* (1936), *Billy the Kid* (1938), *Fanfare for the Common Man* (1942), *A Lincoln Portrait* (1942), and *Appalchian Spring* (1944). He also composed film music, winning an Oscar for *The Heiress* (1949), conducted, taught, and wrote *What to Listen for in Music* (1939), *Music and Imagination* (1952), and *The New Music* (rev. ed. 1968). ▪ See his autobiography (1984; with Vivian Perlis); studies by Julia F. Smith (1955) and Arnold Dobrin (1967); and biography by Howard Pollack (1999).

CORDOBÉS, EL (nickname of Manuel Benítez Pérez; 1936?–   ), Spanish bullfighter. An idol throughout Spain and Latin America during the 1960s, El Cordobés was the highest-paid matador in history. Endowed with incredible reflexes and seemingly defiant of death, he worked closer to the horns than any matador of his time and fought in a record 111 corridas in 1965. His yearly earnings were estimated to be $2 million, and during August 1965, when he killed a record 64 bulls, it was said that he earned close to $600,000. He retired in 1972 but returned to the bullring in 1979.

COREY, ELIAS JAMES (1928–   ), U.S. chemist. Corey studied at the Massachusetts Institute of Technology (Ph.D. 1950) and taught at Harvard (from 1959). He was awarded the 1990 Nobel Prize in Chemistry for developing a technique known as retrosynthetic analysis, which enabled chemists to synthesize complex compounds, including pharmaceuticals, from simple component molecules. The technique, easily adapted to computer programs, made the synthesis of compounds faster, less costly, and more efficient than ever before and became standard practice in laboratories around the world. Among the drugs synthesized by Corey were prostaglandins, used to induce labor and treat infertility, and an extract from the ginkgo tree that was used to treat asthma and blood circulation problems.

COREY, LEWIS (Luigi Carlo Fraina; 1892–1953), Italian-born U.S. political theorist. Corey was a leader of the left wing of the Socialist party before World War I and helped found the U.S. Communist party (1919). Using the name Louis C. Fraina, he edited several revolutionary journals and translated and published the first postrevolutionary essays of V. I. Lenin and Joseph Stalin. During the early 1920s he left the communist movement and emerged as an independent socialist. He wrote several economic studies, including *The House of Morgan* (1931), *The Decline of American Capitalism* (1934), *The Crisis of the Middle Class* (1935), and was professor of economics at Antioch College (1942–51). ▪ See Paul Buhle, *A Dreamer's Paradise Lost* (1995).

CORI, CARL FERDINAND (1896–1984) and GERTY THERESA CORI (1896–1957), Czech-born U.S. biochemists. A husband-and-wife research team, the Coris both received M.D. degrees from the German University in Prague (1920), emigrated to the United States (1922), and were both professors at the Washington University (St. Louis) Medical School (from 1931). Their most important work demonstrated how glycogen, the carbohydrate stored in the liver and muscle, was changed into a form of glucose that could be used by the body. They also showed how some hormones, such as adrenaline and insulin, could affect the metabolism of carbohydrates. The Coris won the 1947 Nobel Prize for Physiology or Medicine (with Bernardo Houssay) for their research.

CORMACK, ALLAN MACLEOD (1924–1988), South African–born U.S. medical physicist. Cormack studied physics and engineering at the University of Cape Town (B.A. 1944; M.A. 1945) and did graduate work at Cambridge. While working as a medical physicist at Groote Shuur Hospital (1956) in Cape Town, he became interested in the deficiencies of X-ray technology. Later, as a physics professor at Tufts University (1957–94), he made mathematical analyses of the absorption of X rays by various tissues of the body. His calculations were essential for the development (1973) of the computerized axial tomography (CAT) scanner, which revolutionized radiology by enabling doctors to produce detailed X-ray pictures of specific "slices" of the human body in more detail than any nonsurgical technique. For his work, Cormack shared the 1979 Nobel Prize in Physiology or Medicine with Godfrey Hounsfield.

CORNELL, KATHARINE (1893–1974), U.S. stage actress. Cornell's father and grandfather were amateur actors, and she began her life in the theater as a playwright for school productions. She joined the Washington Square Players (New York City) in 1916 and achieved stardom in 1921 in *A Bill of Divorcement*. That same year she married Guthrie McClintic, who directed almost all of her subsequent performances. A star for 40 years, she was frequently called the "first lady of the American theater." Best known for her exacting performances of plays by G. B. Shaw and for her role in *The Barretts of Wimpole Street,* she appeared in New York and on extended tours in works by Chekhov and Shakespeare as well as in contemporary plays. She wrote the autobiographical *I Wanted to Be an Actress* (1939) and *Curtain Going Up* (1943). ▪ See Guthrie McClintic, *Me and Kit* (1955), and Tad Mosel and Gertrude Macy, *Leading Lady* (1978).

CORNFORTH, SIR JOHN WARCUP (1917–   ), Australian-born British organic chemist. Deaf since his teens, Cornforth communicated by means of sign language, labored speech, and writing. He nevertheless graduated from Oxford (Ph.D. 1941), worked on the staff of the National Institute of Medical Research (1946–62), and directed the Shell Research Laboratory (1962–75). His research gave the world an understanding of stereochemistry—the study of how the structure of molecules affects the properties of a chemical compound. Cornforth's collaboration with Robert

Robinson resulted in the determination of the structure of penicillin's central molecule. He also investigated the structure of sterols, including cholesterol. He shared, with Vladimir Prelog, the 1975 Nobel Prize in Chemistry. He taught at the University of Sussex from 1975 to 1982.

CORRELL, CHARLES J. *See GOSDEN, FREEMAN F.*

CORRIGAN, MAIREAD (1944–   ), **and BETTY WILLIAMS** (1943–   ), Northern Ireland peace activists. Appalled by the growing sectarian violence in Northern Ireland, Corrigan, a secretary, and Williams, a housewife, independently organized (in Belfast) petitions for peace and neighborhood peace marches. They joined forces to form the Northern Ireland Peace Movement (later renamed the Community of the Peace People), which spontaneously became a mass movement of Catholic and Protestant women seeking to end the bloodshed between the two religious groups. Although opposed by militants in both camps, the movement was successful in reducing the level of violence. For their efforts in sponsoring the peace campaign throughout Northern Ireland, Corrigan and Williams shared the 1976 Nobel Peace Prize. ■ See Richard Deutsch, *Mairead Corrigan—Betty Williams* (1977).

CORSO, GREGORY (Nunzio Gregory Corso; 1930–2001), U.S. poet. Corso grew up in foster homes in New York and in juvenile institutions and served time in prison (1947–50) before meeting and being influenced by poet Allen Ginsberg. He began to write spontaneous, streetsmart poetry, publishing *The Vestal Lady on Brattle* (1955) after a visit with friends at Harvard University. Corso traveled extensively, joining Ginsberg in San Francisco in 1956 as a major counterculture figure of the "beat" generation. His later works included *Gasoline* (1958), *Selected Poems* (1962), *Elegiac Feelings American* (1970), and *Minefield: New and Selected Poems* (1989). ■ See Gregory Stephenson, *Exiled Angel* (1989). The poems in *Herald of the Autochthonic Spirit* (1981) reflected on his literary career.

CORTÁZAR, JULIO (1914–1984), Argentine novelist. Opposed to the government of Juan Domingo Perón, Cotázar settled in France (1951), where 30 years later he accepted French citizenship, but did not renounce Argentine citizenship. His fiction was influenced by the "new novel"—a French literary movement that discarded such traditional elements of fiction as plot, character, and linear development. Cortázar sought to engage his audience directly with tricks and games that delighted some readers and frustrated others. His novels included *The Winners* (1960; Eng. trans. 1965), in which lottery winners embark on a voyage governed by complex rules; *Hopscotch* (1963; Eng. trans. 1966), whose parts can be read in any order, and which concerns an intellectual's futile quest for experience free of Western cultural values; and *Sixty-two: A Model Kit* (1968; Eng. trans. 1972), which challenges readers to assemble the

fiction. The novel *A Manual for Manuel* (1973; Eng. trans. 1978) presented documentary material to describe the torture of political prisoners in Latin America. Cortázar's short-story collections included *Blow-Up* (1959; Eng. trans. 1968), whose title story inspired Michelangelo Antonioni's 1966 film, and *We Loved Glenda So Much* (1981; Eng. trans. 1983). *The End of the Game* (1967) and *A Change of Light* (1980) presented English translations of stories from several collections. Cortázar was a leading figure in the renaissance of Latin American literature that began in the 1960s. ■ See studies by Evelyn Picon Garfield (1975) and Terry Peavler (1990); and J. Alazraki and I. Ivask, eds., *The Final Island* (1978).

CORTOT, ALFRED DENIS (1877–1962), French pianist and conductor. Cortot's keyboard artistry first gained recognition through a series of performances of Beethoven piano concertos in Paris, where the young Swissborn musician had come to study with one of Chopin's last disciples. At age 24, Cortot also established himself as a conductor and an interpreter of Wagner, directing the first Paris production of *Götterdammerung* (1902). Cortot was founder of the École Normale de Musique in Paris (1918), editor of a four-volume edition of Chopin's works, and member of a celebrated trio that also included violinist Jacques Thibaud and cellist Pablo Casals.

CORWIN, NORMAN (1910–   ), U.S. radio writer, producer, and director. Corwin was a journalist and local broadcaster in Boston and New York City before being hired by CBS radio (1938). For ten years, as creator of such network series as *Words Without Music, Pursuit of Happiness, Twenty-six by Corwin,* and *Columbia Presents Corwin,* he presented original, poetic, innovative dramas, fantasies, musicals, and documentaries that established his reputation as one of radio's few creative geniuses. His eloquent and emotional "We Hold These Truths" (1941), prepared to commemorate the 150th anniversary of the Bill of Rights, was aired as the United States entered World War II and was heard by an estimated 60 million listeners. His wartime productions celebrated the "common man" and his victories over injustice, and relentlessly attacked the evils of fascism. Among his best-known single programs were "The Plot to Overthrow Christmas," "The Undecided Molecule," and "On a Note of Triumph," a celebration of the end of World War II. For United Nations radio, he wrote "Document A/777," a powerful play advocating an international Bill of Human Rights. He subsequently wrote the screenplay for *Lust for Life* (1956) and several books, including *Greater Than the Bomb* (1981) and *Trivializing America* (1983). ■ See his *Years of the Electric Ear* (1994) and the study by R. LeRoy Bannerman (1986).

COSBY, BILL (1937–   ), U.S. comedian and actor. Cosby studied at Temple University in his hometown of Philadelphia. When he appeared (1965–68) in "I Spy," Cosby became the first African-American actor to star in a dramatic TV series. He was known mainly as a comedian, starring in the situation comedy "The Bill Cosby Show" (1969–71) as a high school gym teacher, and then on "The New Bill Cosby Show" (1972–73). He was especially skillful at entertaining children; he had regular spots on the Public Broadcasting Service's "The Electric Company" and on the Saturday-morning show "Fat Albert and the Cosby Kids." Yet another "Cosby Show" (1984–92), a top-rated situation comedy, was followed by "Cosby" (1996–). He made numerous recordings and films, won numerous Emmy and Grammy awards, and wrote several books, including *Fatherhood* (1986), *Time Flies* (1988), *Love and Marriage* (1989), and *Childhood* (1991).

COSELL, HOWARD (Howard William Cohen; 1920–1995), U.S. sportscaster. A frustrated actor who practiced law for 10 years, Cosell began moonlighting during the 1950s as an unpaid radio commentator of Little League baseball games. He graduated to his own ABC interview program (1956), to heavyweight boxing commentary (1959), the Olympics (1968), and "Monday Night Football" (1970–84, the most successful prime-time sports series in television history), gaining celebrity for his blunt, adversary style of interviewing and his controversial commentary. A nonathlete, Cosell also worked the lecture circuit and wrote the best-sellers *Cosell* (1973), *Like It Is* (1974), and *I Never Played the Game* (with Peter Bonventre, 1985).

COSGRAVE, WILLIAM THOMAS (1880–1965), Irish political leader. Cosgrave started out in the grocery trade but became interested in politics and joined (1913) the Sinn Fein nationalist movement. He fought (1916) under Patrick Pearse in the Easter Rebellion, for which he was sentenced to life imprisonment. Released under an amnesty the following year, he became (1917) a member of the British Parliament and later joined (1919) the Dáil Éireann (revolutionary parliament), serving as minister of local government for both the revolutionary government and the provisional government (after the treaty of 1921). Upon the sudden deaths of Pres. Arthur Griffith and his successor, Michael Collins, Cosgrave became (1922) president of the republic. An unambitious and peaceloving executive, he believed in a division of power and did much to bring order to a revolution-torn nation. He served in office until his party, Fine Gael, lost the 1932 elections, and he relinquished his position as party head in 1944. His son, Liam Cosgrave (1920–), served as prime minister (1973–77).

COSTA-GAVRAS (Konstantinos Gavras; 1933–), Greek-born film director. Born in Athens of Russo-Greek parentage, Costa-Gavras studied at the Sorbonne in Paris (1952–55), where he began his film career as an assistant to director René Clement. His first directing credit was an American-style thriller, *The Sleeping-Car Murder* (1965), which was

produced with the aid of actor Yves Montand. He subsequently turned to fast-paced political dramas that reflected his independent Marxist views. He directed *Z* (1969), a film about the right-wing assassination of a liberal Greek politician; *The Confession* (1970), an indictment of Stalinism in Eastern Europe; *State of Siege* (1972), about a U.S. Central Intelligence Agency operative kidnapped by leftist Latin American guerrillas; and *Missing* (1982), about alleged U.S. complicity in the overthrow of the government of Salvador Allende in Chile (1973). His later films included *Hannah K.* (1983), *Betrayal* (1988), and *Music Box* (1989). ■ See study by John J. Michalczyk (1984).

COSTAIN, THOMAS BERTRAM (1885–1965), Canadian born U.S. novelist. Costain moved to the United States (1920) and was a fiction editor for the *Saturday Evening Post* (1920–34). At age 57 he published the first of his popular historical romances, *For My Great Folly* (1942). His exciting plots focus on historical figures and are grounded in meticulous research on customs, speech, costumes, and events. *The Black Rose* (1945) is set in medieval England, and *The Silver Chalice* (1952) fictionalizes the plight of Christians in Rome. *High Towers* (1949) and *Son of a Hundred Kings* (1950) re-create moments in Canadian history. His nonfiction included *The Pageant of England* (4 vols., 1949–62), a history of the Plantagenets.

COSTELLO, FRANK (Francesco Castiglia; 1891–1973), Italian-born U.S. racketeer. Costello was an East Harlem street-gang member in his youth, a rumrunner during Prohibition, and a politically astute Mafia-syndicate power in middle age. A key member of Lucky Luciano's crime family, Costello looked after the Cosa Nostra's gambling interests and smuggled gems. He maintained the appearance of well-tailored respectability and stayed out of the limelight until his interrogation by the Senate crime-investigating committee (1954). Costello was subsequently convicted of contempt and tax evasion. He survived a 1957 assassination attempt and died of natural causes. ■ See Leonard Katz, *Uncle Frank* (1973), and biography by George Wolf and Joseph DiMona (1974).

COSTELLO, LOU. See *ABBOTT, BUD.*

COUDENHOVE-KALERGI, COUNT RICHARD NICOLAUS (1894–1972), political theorist and internationalist. An "internationalist" by birth—the Coudenhoves were Flemish nobles, the Kalergis were Greek, and his mother was Japanese—Coudenhove-Kalergi dedicated his life to the cause of European political and economic unification. Terrified by the growth of nationalism leading up to World War I, he wrote *Pan-Europe* (1923; Eng., trans. 1926), which advocated a United States of Europe, and organized the Pan-European Union (1923). An intimate of most of the European statesmen of the postwar period, he strove mightily to prevent another European war. In 1948 the European Parliamentary Union was founded, and Coudenhove-Kalergi, thrice nominated for the Nobel Peace Prize, served as its first secretary-general. In later years he campaigned to transform the Common Market into a political organization. Among his many books were *Europe Must Unite* (1940) and his autobiographies, *Crusade for Pan Europe* (1943) and *An Idea Conquers the World* (1954).

COUGHLIN, CHARLES EDWARD (1891–1979), Canadian-born U.S. Roman Catholic priest. Ordained (1916) in Toronto, Father Coughlin was transferred (1926) to the Detroit diocese, where he served as pastor of the Shrine of the Little Flower Church in the suburb of Royal Oak for 40 years. He began (1926) making religious broadcasts and became a celebrity and a major cultural and political force in the 1930s with his Sunday broadcasts touching on political and economic as well as religious questions. After 1935 he vociferously opposed Pres. Franklin D. Roosevelt and the policies of the New Deal. He established the National Union for Social Justice to bring about radical economic change and allied himself with anti-Semitic and pro-fascist forces. Coughlin's magazine, *Social Justice*, ceased publication (1942) when, under the Espionage Act, it was banned from the U.S. postal service. After Coughlin's church superiors silenced him (1942), his influence diminished, and he vanished from public view. ■ See biographies by Sheldon Marcus (1973) and Ronald H. Carpenter (1998), and Donald I. Warren, *Radio Priest* (1996).

COURANT, RICHARD (1888–1972), German-born U.S. mathematician. Courant studied under David Hilbert at Göttingen, completing a doctoral thesis on the calculus of variations in 1910. His work was disrupted by long years of military service before and during World War I; he returned (1920) to Göttingen to help establish the Mathematics Institute. When the Nazi government exerted pressure on the liberal Göttingen community, Courant emigrated to the United States, where he taught at New York University (1934–58). During World War II he was active in war-related technological research. His investigation of such problems as conformal mapping, aspects of partial differentiation equations, group theory, and the nature of vibration always placed mathematics in the context of general scientific knowledge. His classic work, *Methods of Mathematical Physics* (1924, with David Hilbert; Eng. trans. 1953), influenced the study of quantum mechanics and partial differential equations. Courant was a leader in the organization of research and teaching in the field of mathematics. ■ See study by Constance Reid (1976).

COURNAND, ANDRÉ FRÉDÉRIC (1895–1988), French-born U.S. physician and physiologist. Working in collaboration with Dickinson W. Richards at Columbia University's

College of Physicians and Surgeons (1935–64), Courand developed a body of knowledge basic to the study of heart and lung diseases. They were best known for the perfection of cardiac catheterization, first devised by Werner Forssmann (1929), which enabled physicians to study precisely the functioning of both normal and diseased human hearts and to diagnose heart disease more accurately. Cournand shared the 1956 Nobel Prize in Physiology or Medicine with Richards and Forssmann. ■ See his autobiography, *From Roots to Late Budding* (1986).

COURRÈGES, ANDRÉ (1923–), French fashion designer. Courrèges trained in civil engineering before entering the fashion world, demonstrating with his unique designs that the fields were not entirely unrelated. After working under Cristóbal Balenciaga for almost a decade (1952–60), Courrèges developed his own line (1961). His modernistic designs did not immediately catch on, but when he introduced (1964) the miniskirt and the "little girl look," he accomplished a style revolution. Disgusted with mass-produced copies of his designs, he abruptly closed his doors (1966), reopening a year later with both custom-made and ready-made offerings. He eventually opened boutiques in 10 countries around the world.

COURT, MARGARET SMITH (Margaret Smith; 1942–), Australian tennis player. Known for her endurance, power, and remarkably long reach, Court won 66 Big Four (Australian, U.S., Wimbledon, and French singles, doubles, and mixed doubles) titles (1960–75), setting a tennis record. She was the second woman to win the grand slam—all 4 major singles championships in one year (1970); she also won the grand slam in mixed doubles (1963; with Ken Fletcher). Among her singles victories were 11 Australian (1960–66; 1969–71; 1973), 7 U.S. (Amateur: 1962, 1965, 1968, 1969; Open: 1970, 1973), and 3 Wimbledon (1963, 1965, 1970) championships. ■ See her autobiography, *Court on Court* (1975).

COUSINS, NORMAN (1912–1990), U.S. editor. After studying at Columbia University's Teachers College (1933), Cousins became education editor of the *New York Post* and managing editor of *Current History* before moving to the *Saturay Review* in 1940. In 36 years as its editor (1940–71; 1973–77) he expanded the cultural review's field of intellectual inquiry, espoused such causes as world government and a nuclear-testing ban, and boosted circulation from 20,000 to 660,000. Cousins lectured widely on world affairs, served on the board of the Encyclopedia Britannica, and was active in the field of educational TV. His numerous books included *Modern Man Is Obsolete* (1945) and the autobiographical *Present Tense* (1968). His experiences as a cancer and heart patient prompted him to write *Anatomy of an Illness* (1980) and *The Healing Heart* (1983), in which he asserted that one's attitude can help combat an illness. His last book,

Head First: The Biology of Hope (1989), was about the effects of emotions on the body's resistance to disease.

COUSTEAU, JACQUES YVES (1910–1997), French marine explorer. An officer in the French navy (1939–57), Cousteau served in the underground during World War II. He Invented the Aqua-Lung (1943; with Emil Galgnon) and founded the French navy's undersea research group (1956). He also pioneered in underwater color photography and television; helped develop the one-man jet propelled submarine, the bathyscaphe, and devices for spending extended periods underwater; and directed the Museum of Oceanography at Monaco (from 1957). He led dozens of expeditions throughout the world and produced numerous award-winning television documentaries and movies, including the Academy Award–winning *The Silent World* (1956), *The Golden Fish* (1960), and *World Without Sun* (1964). He was also active in the movement to reduce marine pollution. His books include *Silent World* (1953), *The Living Sea* (1963), *World Without Sun* (1965), *The Ocean World* (1979), *The Cousteau Almanac of the Environment (1981),* and *Jacques Cousteau's Amazon Journey* (1984; with M. Richards).

COUSY, BOB (Robert Joseph Cousy; 1928–), U.S. basketball player. A ball-handling and pasting wizard, Cousy was one of the most exciting players in basketball history. Although only 6-feet, 1-inch tall, he sparked the Boston Celtics to six National Basketball Association championships (1957; 1959–63) while being named to the All-Star team in each of his 13 seasons (1950–63). Known as "Mr. Basketball," Cousy—the greatest playmaker of his time—scored over 16,000 points and made 6,949 assists during his career, while averaging 18.5 points per game. He later coached at Boston College and with the Cincinnati Royals and the Kansas City Kings of the N.B.A. ■ See his *Basketball Is My Life* (rev. ed. 1963) and biography by Bob Devaney (1965).

COUVE DE MURVILLE, MAURICE JACQUES (1907–), French diplomat. Born in Reims, the son of a judge, Couve de Murville studied literature, history, and law before entering government service in 1930. Dismissed by the Vichy government, he joined Gen. Charles de Gaulle's government in North Africa as a diplomat in 1943. In 1950 he was appointed French ambassador to Egypt and in 1954 representative to the North Atlantic Treaty Organization; he subsequently served as ambassador to West Germany and representative on the U.N. Security Council. A loyal Gaullist technocrat, Couve de Murville was foreign minister (1958–68), and he succeeded Georges Pompidou as premier (1968–69). He subsequently served as a deputy in the national assembly and as a senator.

COWARD, SIR NOEL PIERCE (1899–1973), British dramatist, actor, and composer. Born into a musical family, Coward entered the theatrical world as a child actor and emerged during the 1920s as a master of sophisticated and naughty comedies and musicals. A phenomenon on both sides of the Atlantic, he was best known for the comedies *Hay Fever* (1925), *Private Lives* (1930), *Design for Living* (1932), and *Blithe Spirit* (1941) and the musicals *Bitter-Sweet* (1929) and *Cavalcade* (1931). His songs included "I'll See You Again," "Mad Dogs and Englishmen," and "Marvelous Party." He wrote, acted in, and codirected the patriotic World War II naval film *In Which We Serve* (1942) and wrote the screenplay for the sentimental love story *Brief Encounter* (1945). After the war he became a noted nightclub and cabaret performer and witnessed numerous revivals of his works in the 1960s and 1970s. ■ See his two autobiographies, *Present Indicative* (1937) and *Future Indefinite* (1954); his *Diaries* (1982); Sheridan Morley, *A Talent to Amuse* (1969); Cole Lesley, *Remembered Laughter* (1976); Cole Lesley, Graham Payn, and Sheridan Morley; *Noel Coward and His Friends* (1979); and biography by Philip Hoare (1996).

COWELL, HENRY DIXON (1897–1965), U.S. composer. A former child musical prodigy from California, Cowell remained in the vanguard of musical innovation all his life. He introduced the tone cluster, a group of notes struck simultaneously, and invented the rhythmicon, an electronic keyboard percussion instrument. He incorporated rural American hymns, Irish reels, and Oriental and Middle Eastern melodies into his compositions and favored an "elastic form," leaving much discretion to the performer. Cowell also promoted the works of other composers through his quarterly *New Music,* established in 1927, and as the editor of *American Composers on American Music* (1933). His own compositions included *Hymns and Fuguing Tunes* (1941–45), *Gaelic Symphony* (1942), *Persian Set* (1957), and *Concerto for Koto and Orchestra* (1964). He wrote *New Musical Resources* (1919) and *The Nature of Melody* (1938).

COWEN, JOSHUA LIONEL (1880–1965), U.S. miniature electric-train inventor and manufacturer. Cowen set up his first miniature train in 1901 and sold the cars to novelty shops that used them in window displays. As they increased in popularity, he set up a company bearing his middle name to produce them, and soon "Lionel" toy electric trains were running on thousands of miles of miniature tracks in homes throughout the world. By 1960 his company had laid more miles of track than any real railroad line. ■ See Ron Hollander, *All Aboard!* (1981).

COWLES, GARDNER (1903–1985), U.S. magazine publisher. Born into a journalistic family, Cowles received a B.A. from Harvard University (1925), where he edited the *Crimson* before becoming city editor of his father's *Des Moines* (Iowa) *Register and Tribune*. A founder of *Look* magazine (1937), he developed the *Look* pictorial-feature news approach at the *Register.* Cowles was instrumental in launching the career of the pollster George Gallup by using Gallup's services to ascertain public preference in news packaging. He created Cowles Communications, Inc., which controlled radio and television stations and published numerous local newspapers as well as *Family Circle* and *Venture* magazines, and served as its board chairman (1937–71).

COWLES, HENRY CHANDLER (1869–1939), U. S. botanist and ecologist. On the faculty of the University of Chicago (1898–1934), Cowles pioneered in the development of the science of ecology. His seminal studies of sand dunes and plant societies stressed the relationship between vegetation and geology and led to his development of the concept of plant succession. He was a founder of the Ecological Society of America (1915), coauthor of the widely used *Textbook of Botany* (2 vols., 1910–11), and editor of the *Botanical Gazette.*

COWLEY, MALCOLM (1898–1989), U.S. literary critic. The literary editor of the *New Republic* (1929–44), Cowley was a leading intellectual figure in the United States. His poetry collection *Blue Juniata* (1929) and social and literary history *Exile's Return* (1934; rev. ed. 1951) established his reputation as the foremost chronicler and critic of the "lost generation" of the 1920s. His reputation was enhanced with the publication of *A Second Flowering: Works and Days of the Lost Generation* (1973) and *The Dream of the Golden Mountains: Remembering the 1930s* (1980). He also edited important popular editions of selected works of Hemingway (1944), Faulkner (1945), Hawthorne (1948), Whitman (1948), and F. Scott Fitzgerald (1951) and published several volumes of essays including *After the Genteel Tradition* (1937), *The Literary Situation* (1954), *Think Back on Us* (1967), *A Many-Windowed House* (1971), and *The Flower and the Leaf* (1985). ■ See his memoirs, —*And I Worked at the Writers' Trade* (1978), and *The View from 80* (1980), his account of aging, and study by Hans Bak (1993).

COX, ARCHIBALD (1912–), U.S. attorney and public official. As Pres. John F. Kennedy's solicitor general, Cox, a Harvard Law School professor (1946–61), gained a reputation for unflappable expertise while arguing the government's cases before the Supreme Court. Having returned to Harvard in 1965, he was recalled temporarily to Washington in May 1973 to assume the position of special Watergate prosecutor with authority to investigate everything from burglary to political espionage and illegal campaign contributions. After issuing a subpoena for the tape recordings of Pres. Richard Nixon in October 1973, Cox was abruptly dismissed in the "Saturday-night massacre." He later served as president of Common Cause (1980–93), a citizens' lobby. His books included *The Role of the Supreme Court in American Government* (1976) and *The Court and the Constitution* (1987). ■ See study by Ken Gormley (1997).

COZZENS, JAMES GOULD (1903–1978), U.S. novelist. Cozzens published in the *Atlantic Monthly* while enrolled in a Connecticut preparatory school and wrote his first novel as a Harvard sophomore (1924). He first attracted critical attention with the novella *S.S. San Pedro* (1931). His traditionally constructed novels analyzed institutions and professions rather than individual psyches. *The Last Adam* (1933) portrayed a doctor; *Men and Brethren* (1936) portrayed a clergyman; *Guard of Honor* (1948; Pulitzer Prize), a World War II story, drew on his experience as an air force major; *By Love Possessed* (1957), the book that established him as a popular author, examined the legal profession. Called the "champion of the status quo," Cozzens wrote from the detached viewpoint of white, Republican, Protestant America. His rise from relative obscurity in the 1950s sparked a critical controversy as to whether his conservative views accounted for his newfound popularity. ■ See *Just Representations* (1978), a collection of his writings; biography by Matthew J. Bruccoli (1983); and study by Frederick G. Bracher (1959; repr. 1972).

CRAIG, EDWARD GORDON (1872–1966), British actor, scene designer, and dramatic theorist. The son of famed actress Ellen Terry, Gordon Craig made his acting debut at age 17 but eventually turned to scenic design. He emphasized simplicity and suggestiveness and developed the concept of the "moving scene," in which all of the sets move accompanied by constantly changing lighting. Although many of his "visions" were technologically impossible to create, he devised notable productions for the Abbey Theatre in Dublin (1911), the Moscow Art Theater (1912), and the Royal Theater in Copenhagen, (1926). Many of his ideas subsequently became commonplace in the theatre. He was also noted for his etchings and engravings of theatrical scenes. He founded and edited the first theater journal, the *Mask* (1908–29), and wrote *The Art of the Theatre* (1905), *Towards a New Theatre* (1913), *The Theatre Advancing* (1919), and his memoirs of the years 1872 to 1907, *Index to the Story of My Days* (1957). ■ See biographies by Edward Craig (1968), Dennis Bablet (Eng. trans. 1966), Christopher Innes (1983); and Irène Eynat-Confino, *Beyond the Mask* (1987).

CRAM, DONALD (1919–), U.S. chemist. Cram studied at Harvard (Ph.D. 1947) and taught at the University of California, Los Angeles (1947–90). A pioneer in what he termed host-guest chemistry, a field based on the idea that the 3-D shape of a molecule is crucial to its functions, he synthesized three-dimensional molecules that could "recognize" and link up to their complementary structures within a cell. This allowed for the creation of artificial molecules that could mimic chemical and biological reactions that are vital to all living systems. Specifically, Cram produced molecules that mimic enzymes, which raised the possibility of creating artificial enzymes, more stable than their natural counterparts, for medical and industrial use. Cram shared the 1987 Nobel Prize in Chemistry with Charles Pedersen and Jean-Marie Lehn. He wrote *From Design to Discovery* (1990).

CRAM, RALPH ADAMS (1863–1942), U.S. architect. Inspired by medieval art and life and convinced that "religion is the essence of human life," Cram was internationally known as an advocate of the Gothic revival. Acclaimed for his church architecture based on French and English medieval models, the prolific Cram designed churches and cathedrals throughout the United States, including New York's Cathedral of St. John the Divine, part of the original design of which he altered from Romanesque to Gothic. ■ See studies by Harold F. Sheets (1978) and Douglas Shand-Tucci (1995).

CRANE, (HAROLD) HART (1899–1932), U.S. poet. After little formal education, Crane left his native Ohio for New York (1923); he worked out his mental adjustment to urban life in *White Buildings* (1926). In *The Bridge* (1930), the only other volume published in his lifetime, the Brooklyn Bridge served as Crane's mystical unifying image for a series of long poems that represented a spiritual affirmation of the American experience. He cultivated verbal ingenuity in his allusive, inventive poetry. Among his best works were "Praise for an Urn" and "Voyages." In 1932 Crane jumped from the SS *Orizaba* into the Caribbean, taking his own life. His collected poems (1933; 1966) and letters (1952) were published posthumously. ■ See biography by John Unterecker, *Voyager* (1969), and Paul L. Mariani, *The Brooklyn Tower* (1999).

CRANKO, JOHN (1927–1973), South African choreographer and ballet director. Cranko worked with a puppeteer troupe in his teens, then turned to dance. He went to London (1946) to study dancing with the Sadler's Wells Ballet, but he showed a greater gift for choreography. He won plaudits for *Beauty and the Beast* (1949), *Pineapple Poll* (1951), *Bonne-Bouchea* (1952), and later for the full-length ballet *The Prince of the Pagodas* (1959). Cranko wrote the London musical revue *Cranks* (1955). After 1961 he directed the Stuttgart Ballet, which, under his direction, developed a more eclectic repertoire and became a troupe of international stature. ■ See John Percival, *Theatre in My Blood* (1983).

CRAWFORD, CHERYL (1902–1986), U.S. theatrical producer. A major force in the repertory-theater movement in the United States, Crawford was a board member of the Theater Guild (1926–30) and a cofounder of the Group Theater (1930), American Repertory Theater (1946), and the Actors Studio (1947). She was also general director of the American National Theater and Academy (ANTA) play series (from 1950). Her best-known productions were *One Touch of Venus* (1943), *Brigadoon* (1957), *Sweet Bird of Youth* (1959), and the revivals of *Porgy and Bess* (1941), *Shadow of a Gunman* (1958), and *Mother Courage* (1963). She won a Tony Award for her production of *The Rose Tat-*

too (1951). ■ See her autobiography, *One Naked Individual* (1977).

CRAWFORD, JOAN (Lucille LeSueur; 1908–1977), U.S. film actress. In life as well as art, Crawford was a self-made woman, tenacious and tough-minded. She worked as a salesgirl in Missouri to pay for dancing lessons, a sacrifice that paid off when she was "discovered" in a Broadway chorus line (1924). After several dancing roles in movies, including *Dancing Lady* (1933), Fred Astaire's first film, Crawford was cast as a suffering woman striving for love and security in *Today We Live* (1933), *The Women* (1939), and *Mildred Pierce* (Academy Award, 1945). Low-voiced and broad-shouldered, with dark brows and bright red lipstick, Crawford involved herself in the business world after the death (1959) of her fourth husband, whom she replaced as a director of the Pepsi-Cola Co. ■ See her memoirs, *A Portrait of Joan* (1962) and *My Way of Life* (1971); the biography by Bob Thomas (1978); and the best-selling exposé by her daughter, Christina Crawford, *Mommie Dearest* (1978).

CRAXI, BETTINO (Benedetto Craxi; 1934–2000), Italian political leader. Craxi was born in Milan, where his father, a socialist lawyer and politician, had emigrated from Sicily. The younger Craxi joined the Socialist party at age 18 and left the University of Milan to concentrate on party work. An advocate of moderate social democratic domestic policies at home and pro-United States "Atlanticist" policies abroad, he was elected to the Milan City Council (1960) and the Italian Chamber of Deputies (1968). As Socialist party leader (1976–93), he purged its left wing, broadened its popular appeal, and served as the first socialist premier in Italian history (1983–87). As head of a five-party coalition, he pursued gradualist policies, rejecting the nationalization of industry and centralized economic planning. He authorized austerity budgets to cut inflation, initiated tough policies against organized crime, and signed the Concordat with the Vatican (1984) in which Roman Catholicism lost its status as the official state religion. Craxi publicly defended the right of the Palestine Liberation Organization (PLO) to struggle militarily against the state of Israel, and his coalition temporarily collapsed over his government's handling of the Palestinian hijacking of the cruise ship *Achille Lauro* (1985). Accused of corruption (1993), he fled to his villa in Tunisia. He was sentenced (in absentia) to 8½ years in prison for fraud (1994), 18 years for corruption (1996), and 4 years for illegally channeling funds to his party (1998).

CRAY, SEYMOUR (1925–1996), U.S. engineer. The son of a civil engineer, Cray studied electrical engineering and mathematics at the University of Minnesota before working as a designer on the Univac 1103 computer in the mid-1950s. Later, at the Control Data Corp. (1957–72), he designed the first transistor-based computer and the first supercomputer, an ultrafast device initially used in weapons design and military planning and then in weather forecasting, oil exploration, and complex scientific research. At Cray Research Inc. (1972–89), he designed the Cray 1 (1976) and the Cray 2 (1985), then the world's fastest computers. He continued his design of ever-faster computers at his Cray Computer Corp. (1989–95), but increasing competition and fewer government orders forced his company into bankruptcy. ■ See Charles J. Murray, *Supermen* (1997).

CREASEY, JOHN (1908–1973), British novelist. Creasey left school at age 14, lost numerous jobs, and received countless publishers' rejections before his first detective novel, *Seven Times Seven* (1932), was published. In the following years he wrote over 500 mystery novels, using numerous pseudonyms, among them J. J. Marric. The detectives he created included Inspector Roger West, Baron Mainwaring, and Gideon of Scotland Yard. Though his writing was undistinguished, his novels were enjoyed for their ingenious plots and good characterizations and sold more than 60 million copies in 23 languages. *Gideon's Fire* (1961) won an award from the Mystery Writers of America.

CREEL, GEORGE EDWARD (1876–1953), U.S. journalist and propagandist. A progressive and crusading journalist and editor (*Kansas City Independent*, 1899–1908; *Denver Post*, 1909–10; *Rocky Mountain News*, 1911–13). Creel was appointed by Pres. Woodrow Wilson as civilian head of the Committee on Public Information (1917–19). In his capacity as "propaganda minister" during World War I, he depicted the United States as a champion of freedom and democracy fighting to save European civilization from the German menace. He effectively mobilized public opinion in support of the war effort and Liberty Loan bond drive through the use of films, posters, speeches, and press releases. After the war he wrote several popular histories. During the 1930s he wrote a column for *Collier's* magazine and held several public positions. ■ See autobiography, *Rebel at Large* (1947), and James R. Mock and Cedric Larson, *Words That Won the War* (1939).

CRERAR, HENRY DUNCAN GRAHAM (1888–1965), Canadian military leader. Born in Hamilton, and educated at the Royal Military College, Crerar nonetheless opted for a civilian career in engineering. With the outbreak of World War I he became a professional soldier, rising to lieutenant colonel and receiving the Distinguished Service Order (1917). A student of military history and tactics, he served as director of military operations and intelligence (1935–38) and, after the outbreak of World War II, as chief of the general staff (1940). As commander of Canadian forces (1944–45) he led his troops, eventually numbering more than 500,000, during the D-Day invasion of Normandy, the liberation of the Netherlands, and in battles in northern Germany. He retired in 1946.

CRERAR, THOMAS ALEXANDER (1876–1975), Canadian political leader. Although born in Ontario. Crerar grew up in Manitoba where he became a teacher and a successful farmer. As president of the cooperative United Grain Growers Ltd. (1907–29), he opposed the railroad monopolies. During World War I Crerar, a Liberal, was Canadian minister of agriculture (1917–19), but he resigned over his opposition to high tariffs and conscription and returned to leading western farmers against the political and economic domination of big eastern financial interests as head of the new Progressive party (1920–21). He later served as minister of railways and canals (1929–30), minister of mines and resources (1936–45), and member of the Senate (1945–66).

CRICK, FRANCIS HARRY COMPTON (1916–), British molecular biologist. Working in collaboration with James D. Watson at Cambridge University (1953), Crick developed a double-helix model of a molecule of deoxyribonucieic acid (DNA), the basic substance controlling heredity. The model explained the baffling problem of how hereditary material duplicates itself and has been called the most important biological discovery of the century. He and Watson shared the 1962 Nobel Prize in Physiology or Medicine (with Maurice H. Wilkins) for their work. Crick retired from Cambridge (1976) and later wrote *Life Itself: Its Origins and Nature* (1981) and *The Astonishing Hypothesis* (1994). ■ See his autobiography, *What Mad Pursuit* (1988), and James D. Watson, *The Double Helix* (1968).

CRIPPS, SIR (RICHARD) STAFFORD (1889–1952), British political leader. A successful Oxford-educated lawyer, Cripps entered Parliament in 1931 as a left-wing Labourite, antiwar and pro-Soviet. He served as ambassador to Moscow (1940–42) and later served in Winston Churchill's wartime cabinet and was leader of the House of Commons. As chancellor of the Exchequer (1947–50), he presided over the postwar austerity program. ■ See biography by Colin Cooke (1957) and study by Christopher Bryant (1997).

CROCE, BENEDETTO (1866–1952), Italian philosopher and historian. Croce was trained as a historian, and he wrote widely on history and the philosophy of history. A master of clear Italian prose, he was a scholar of almost universal erudition. Starting in the 1890s, he influenced Italian intellectual life for 50 years through his voluminous writings and *La Critica* (1903–44), the journal he edited. A humanist, Croce was best known for his systematic study, *Philosophy of the Spirit* (4 vols., 1902–17; Eng. trans. 1909–21), which included volumes on aesthetics, logic, economics and ethics, and history, and for his study of *History as the Story of Liberty* (1938; Eng. trans. 1941). Appointed a lifetime senator (1910), he also served as minister of education (1920–21). Croce was a consistent opponent of fascism, but because of his enormous reputation and his value as a living "proof" that freedom of speech existed in dictator Benito Mussolini's Italy, he was never harmed or silenced. *Philosophy, Poetry, and History* (1951; Eng. trans. 1966) is his own anthology of essays. ■ See his *Autobiography* (Eng. trans. 1927) and studies by Cecil J. S. Sprigge (1952) and Gian N. G. Orsini (1961).

CROLY, HERBERT (1869–1930), U.S. journalist and political commentator. A graduate of Harvard, Croly was one of the most respected journalists in the United States in the first quarter of this century. His book *The Promise of American Life* (1909) influenced both Theodore Roosevelt and Woodrow Wilson. Croly criticized Americans for having an idealized Jeffersonian view of democracy, called for a revitalized nationalism, and advocated strong leadership to carry out domestic reforms and an effective foreign policy. In 1914 he founded the liberal weekly *New Republic,* which actively supported U.S. participation in World War I and helped mold intellectual thought during the 1920s. ■ See biography by David W. Levy (1985) and study by Edward A. Stettner (1993).

CRONIN, ARCHIBALD JOSEPH (1896–1981), Scottish-born British novelist. With the success of his first novel, *Hatter's Castle* (1931), A. J. Cronin abandoned his successful medical career to became a professional writer. Many of his novels, realistic works with elements of social criticism. were best-sellers and were made into popular movies. Cronin's most famous works were *The Stars Look Down* (1935), set in a Welsh coal-mining area; *The Citadel* (1937), which traces how economic pressures affect a doctor's career; and *The Keys of the Kingdom* (1942), which concerns a missionary priest in China. *Adventures in Two Worlds* (1952) and *Song of Sixpence* (1964) were autobiographical.

CRONIN, JAMES WATSON (1931–), U.S. physicist. A professor at Princeton (1958–71) and the University of Chicago (from 1971), Cronin conducted experiments with Val L. Fitch (1964) that disproved the seemingly inviolable law of symmetry governing the behavior of subatomic particles. Their demonstration of asymmetry during the decay of neutral K mesons was later used to support the "big bang" theory of the origin of the universe. It was theorized that similar asymmetries could have taken place at the birth of the universe and thus have permitted matter to survive. Previously it was thought that matter and antimatter, formed in a symmetrical "big bang," would have annihilated each other almost immediately. For their research Cronin and Fitch shared the 1980 Nobel Prize for Physics.

CRONIN, JOE (Joseph Edward Cronin; 1906–1984), U.S. baseball player, manager, and executive. A bank clerk turned shortstop, Joe Cronin became known during two decades in the major leagues as one of the outstanding clutch hitters of his day. He played for the Pittsburgh Pirates (1926–27), the Washington Senators (1928–34) and the Boston Red Sox (1935–45), and compiled a .302 lifetime average, with 2,285 hits, 1,233 runs, and 1,423 runs batted in. In 1930 he won the Most Valuable Player award. As a Boston Red Sox

he was a player-manager, manager, and then vice president. Elected to the National Baseball Hall of Fame in 1956, Cronin was president of the American League (1959–74).

CRONKITE, WALTER LELAND, JR. (1916–), U.S. broadcast journalist. Inspired by an *American Boy* short story to become a journalist, Cronkite dropped out of the University of Texas (1935) to go to work for the *Houston Post.* He covered World War II and the Nuremberg trials as a UPI correspondent before moving in 1950 to the Columbia Broadcasting System, where he participated in the first televised presidential nominating conventions (1952) and the "You Are There" documentary series. Cronkite was anchorman (1962–81) of his own nightly newscast, winning public confidence with his middle-of-the-road impartiality and his low-key reports. ■ See his memoirs *A Reporter's Life* (1996).

CRONYN, HUME (1911–), Canadian-born actor and director. Cronyn, who was nominated for the Canadian Olympic boxing team, considered studying law but opted for a stage career, training at New York's American Academy of Dramatic Arts. A versatile character actor, he played both goody-goodies and villains in plays and motion pictures. He accumulated a long list of credits over a half century on the stage, among them roles in *Three Men on a Horse* (1935), *Boy Meets Girl* (1936), *Big Fish, Little Fish* (1961), *The Caine Mutiny Court Martial* (1972), and *Krapp's Last Tape* (1973). He won a Tony Award (1964) for his performance in *Hamlet.* He often costarred with his wife Jessica Tandy, as in *The Fourposter* (1957) and *The Gin Game* (1977). Cronyn was also an award-winning director who wrote screenplays and produced films. He made frequent TV appearances and produced a dramatic radio and TV series. "The Marriage," in which he and Tandy costarred. He won an Emmy Award for *Broadway Bound* (1992). ■ See his autobiography *A Terrible Liar* (1991).

CROSBY, BING (Harry Lillis Crosby; 1904–1977), U.S. singer and actor. Crosby briefly studied law in his home state, Washington, but he was more dedicated to singing with a local band. In the mid-1920s he recorded with the Rhythm Boys. The development of electronic amplification systems brought his quiet, intimate baritone to live audiences and made feasible the crooning style that became Crosby's trademark. When CBS president William S. Paley heard a Crosby recording, he aired him on network radio (1931). Crosby was an instant success. His low-key optimism increased his popularity in the Depression years and reassured the GIs he entertained during World War II. In a career spanning five decades, Crosby sold more than 300 million records and made 50 movies, including the "Road" comedies with Bob Hope and Dorothy Lamour. ■ See his autobiography, *Call Me Lucky* (1953); C. Thompson, *Bing* (1976); B. Thomas, *The One and Only Bing* (1977); and G. Giddins, *Bing Crosby: A Pocketful of Dreams.*

CROSBY, CARESSE (Mary Phelps Jacob; 1892–1970), U.S.-born publisher and inventor. Born into a socially prominent New York family, Crosby was a member of the literary and avant-garde circles in Paris during the 1920s and 1930s. With her husband, Harry Crosby, she founded and edited Black Sun Press, which published such writers as D. H. Lawrence, Hart Crane, and James Joyce. She also established Crosby Continental Editions, which published paperback editions of works by Ernest Hemingway, William Faulkner, Dorothy Parker, Kay Boyle, and others. Prior to her life with the bohemians of Paris, she was granted a U.S. patent for her invention of the backless brassiere (1914). ■ See her autobiography, *The Passionate Years* (1953), and study by Anne Carson (1989).

CROSLEY, POWEL, JR. (1886–1961), U.S. industrialist. Describing himself as "a man of 50 jobs," Crosley achieved his greatest success as the founder of the Crosley Radio Corp., the world's largest radio manufacturer in the early 1920s, and the Crosley Broadcasting Corp., which set up (1921) and ran station WLW in Cincinnati. Crosley also manufactured the Shelvador refrigerator, the first with shelves built into the door; the Crosley automobile, one of the first of the American-built minicars; and owned the Cincinnati Reds baseball club (from 1936).

CROTHERS, RACHEL (1878–1958), U.S. playwright, producer, and actress. Crothers addressed feminist issues—the double standards of social mores, the conflicts common in women's experiences—in such plays as *A Man's World* (1909). *He and She* (1911), *As Husbands Go* (1931), and other works that were staged on Broadway at a rate of one per year for three decades (1906–37). She also acted in and produced plays and sponsored such actresses as Katharine Cornell and Gertrude Lawrence. Crothers established Stage Women's War Relief in World War I, promoted aid to theater professionals during the Depression years, and was instrumental in founding the Stage Door Canteens during World War II. ■ See study by Lois C. Gottlieb (1979).

CROUSE, RUSSEL M. *See LINDSAY, HOWARD.*

CRUMP, EDWARD HULL (1874–1954), U.S. political leader. One of the last of the old-time, big-city political bosses, Crump, a Democrat, controlled the politics of Memphis, Tennessee, for more than four decades. He served, as mayor (1909–16; 1939–41) and congressman (1931–35) and was a dominant force in state politics until his candidates were defeated in 1948. He opposed the Ku Klux Klan and strongly supported the New Deal and the Tennessee Valley Authority. ■ See William D. Miller *Mr. Crump of Memphis* (1964).

CRUTZEN, PAUL (1933–), Dutch atmospheric scientist. Trained as a meteorologist at the University of Stockholm (Ph.D. 1973), Crutzen taught himself chemistry and served

as a professor at the Max Planck Institute for Chemistry in Mainz, Germany (1980–). In a controversial paper (1970) he proposed that nitrogen oxides, released naturally on the earth's surface by soil bacteria, can destroy the ozone layer in the stratosphere that protects life on earth from harmful ultraviolet radiation. His paper inspired numerous research projects in the area of atmospheric chemistry, including one by F. Sherwood Rowland and Mario Molina showing that industrially produced chlorofluorocarbons (CFCs) widely used as refrigerants, plastic foams, and aerosol-spray propellants could also destroy the ozone layer. Although initially attacked by many industrialists and their conservative political allies, the research was eventually accepted by industry and government and led to international agreements (1987; 1992) by the industrial nations to end the production of CFCs. For their pioneering research, Crutzen, Rowland, and Molina shared the 1995 Nobel Prize for Chemistry.

CUGAT, XAVIER (1900–1990), Spanish-born U.S. bandleader. A prodigy on the violin, Cugat grew up in Cuba and played in the Grand Opera Company of Havana. He organized a dance orchestra in Hollywood (1928) and achieved nationwide popularity for his lively renditions of popular Latin American ballroom dances. Known as the "rhumba king" during the 1930s and 1940s, he broadcast nightly from New York's Waldorf-Astoria, appeared in several Hollywood movies, and was frequently on television during the early 1950s. His best-known musical numbers were "Babalu," "The Peanut Vendor," and "Mama Inez." ■ See his autobiography, *Rhumba Is My Life* (1949).

CUKOR, GEORGE (1899–1983), U.S. film director. After working in New York as a stage director, Cukor went to Hollywood in 1929, with the coming of sound movies. His favorite vehicles were polished social comedies, and his special talent lay in directing women. His great discovery was Katharine Hepburn, whom he directed in *Little Women* (1933), *Holiday* (1938), *The Philadelphia Story* (1940), *Adam's Rib* (1949), and *Pat and Mike* (1952), the latter two with Spencer Tracy. Cukor directed Greta Garbo in *Camille* (1937), Ingrid Bergman in *Gaslight* (1944), Judy Holliday in *Born Yesterday* (1950), Judy Garland in *A Star Is Born* (1954), and Audrey Hepburn in his Academy Award–winning *My Fair Lady* (1964). Cukor was the original director for *Gone With the Wind* (1939) but was replaced when actor Clark Gable allegedly objected to him as an "actress's director." ■ See Gavin Lambert, *On Cukor* (1972); study by Gene D. Phillips (1982); and biography by Patrick McGilligan (1992).

CULBERTSON, ELY (1891–1955), Rumanian-born U.S. bridge expert. Inventor of the first successful bidding system in contract bridge, Culbertson was the world's leading authority on the game and helped establish it as the most popular card game in the United States. He won many tournaments, founded and edited *The Bridge World*, and was captain of the American team in 1933, 1934, and 1937. After 1940 he wrote and lectured widely on world peace, advocating arms limitation and an international police force. ■ See his autobiography, *The Strange Lives of One Man* (1940).

CULLEN, COUNTEE (1903–1946), U.S. poet. The adopted son of a minister in New York City's Harlem, Cullen won citywide poetry contests as a schoolboy and earned a B.A. (1925) at New York University and an M.A. (1926) at Harvard. He took a job teaching French at a Harlem junior high school, remaining in the public-school system until his death. Cullen knew and worked with other leading African-American writers in the Harlem Renaissance but rejected their avant-garde viewpoint. For inspiration he looked instead to the great British lyric poets, especially John Keats, and adhered to traditional poetic forms. When at age 22 he published *Color* (1925), he won immediate recognition. Later collections included *Copper Sun* (1927), *Ballad of the Brown Girl* (1927), *The Black Christ and Other Poems* (1935), and the posthumous volume of selected poems, *On These I Stand* (1947). He also wrote the satirical novel *One Way to Heaven* (1932) about life in Harlem. ■ See studies by Blanche E. Ferguson (1966) and Alan Shucard (1984).

CULLEN, MAURICE GALBRAITH (1866–1934), Canadian artist. Cullen studied at the École des Beaux Arts in Paris (1889–92) and earned a European reputation for his paintings in the style of the French impressionists. Back in Canada (after 1895), he worked outdoors in his native New Foundland and along the St. Lawrence River to capture shadows over the landscape, but his cityscapes of Montreal and Quebec are seen through European mists. He was a pioneer of the Canadian national school of landscape painting.

CUMMINGS, EDWARD ESTLIN (1894–1962), U.S. poet. The son of a nonconformist Unitarian minister, e e cummings, as he spelled his name, recorded his brief experience in a World War I detention camp in France in *The Enormous Room* (1922). In the 1920s he remained on the periphery of the American expatriate colony in Paris, writing and painting. He was influenced by the poet Ezra Pound and the imagists who fractured traditional syntax, punctuation, and usage. Cummings resisted cold intellect and said, "Not for philosophy does this rose give a damn." His indefatigable sense of wonder throughout 11 volumes of verse won him great popularity, but critics tended to consider him a verbal comic. He also published two verse plays, an experimental prose book, and *i: six nonlectures* (1953) from his discussions on poetry at Harvard, his alma mater. ■ See biography by Charles Norman (1964), and Richard S. Kennedy, *Dreams in the Mirror* (1979).

CUNNINGHAM, GLENN (1909–1988), U.S. distance runner. Known as the "Kansas Ironman" and "Kansas Flyer," Cunningham overcame severe burns on his legs to become a world-class miler. A member of the 1932 and 1936 U.S. Olympic teams, he won a silver medal in the 1,500-meter

run in the 1936 games. In addition, the barrel-chested Cunningham set a world mark in the mile (4:067), and dominated that event throughout the 1930s, holding the Amateur Athletic Union title in 1933 and from 1935 to 1938.

CUNNINGHAM, IMOGEN (1883–1976), U.S. photographer. Cunningham worked for eight years in the photographic studio of Edward S. Curtis while he was compiling his famous portfolio of photographs of American Indians. She established her own studio (1910) after studying photographic chemistry for a year in Germany. Soon she was nationally famous for her portraits and her sensitive and unembellished photos of plants and flowers. She was a member of the "f/64" group of West Coast photographers—who favored sharply focused photos over the sentimental, soft-focus style—and was known throughout her career (which spanned eight decades) for the wit and freshness she brought to her subjects. ■ See the study by Judy Dater (1979) and biography by Richard Lorenz (1993).

CUNNINGHAM, MERCE (1919–), U.S. dancer and choreographer. Cunningham began dancing at age 8. He performed with Martha Graham's dance company (1939–45), at times in roles that he had choreographed, including *Mysterious Adventure* (1945), a dance that incorporated a technique associated with Cunningham—absence of motion. He began working independently, establishing a company (1953) and pursuing his experimentation with abstract form. His works did not adhere to narratives and stressed space rather than time; movement sometimes bore no formal relationship to music. Cunningham collaborated with innovators in other fields, including composer John Cage and artist Robert Rauschenberg, and was regarded as a seminal figure in modern dance. Among his creations were *Sixteen Dances for Soloist and Company* (1951), *Summerspace* (1958), *Winterbranch* (1965), *Sounddance* (1974–75), *Tango* (1978), *Torse* (1984), *Scenario* (1997), *Biped* (1999), and *Interscape 2000* (2000). ■ See his *The Dancer and the Dance: Merce Cunningham in Conversation with Jacqueline Lesschaeve* (1985) and *Chances: Notes on Choreography* (1968); studies by James Klosty (1975) and David Vaughan (1997); and his essays (1994–92) in Richard Kostalanetz, ed., *Merce Cunningham: Dancing in Space and Time* (1992).

CURIE, MARIE (Maria Sklodowska, 1867–1934), French physicist. Born in Warsaw, Poland, then a part of the Russian Empire, she moved to Paris (1891), studied mathematics and physics at the Sorbonne, and married physicist Pierre Curie in 1895. Mme. Curie did pioneering studies on the source of radioactivity and played a major role in the development of nuclear physics. Together with her husband she discovered new elements (radium and polonium) and they shared the 1903 Nobel Prize in Physics (with Henri Becquerel) for their research. She subsequently won the 1911 Nobel Prize in Chemistry for the isolation of pure radium. She was the founding director of the Radium Institute at the

University of Paris (1914–34) and spent her later years studying the medical applications of radioactive substances. Her daughter was physicist Irène Joliot-Curie (1897–1956).

CURL, ROBERT F., JR. (1933–   ), U.S. chemist. Curl graduated from the University of California, Berkeley (Ph.D. 1957), and taught at Rice University, Houston, Texas (1958–   ). Working on the formation of carbon chains with Sir Harold Kroto and Richard E. Smalley at the Rice University Laboratories (1985), he and his colleagues discovered a new form of carbon in which carbon atoms are linked in the form of a soccer ball. The scientists dubbed the new molecules "fullerenes" or "buckyballs" because they resembled the geodesic domes created by architect R. Buckminster Fuller. The discovery created a new branch of chemistry (fullerene chemistry) and promised to yield applications in such fields as ultrastrong fibers, lubricants, and superconductors. For their contributions to science, Curl, Kroto, and Smalley shared the 1996 Nobel Prize in Chemistry.

CURLEY, JAMES MICHAEL (1874–1958), U. S. political leader. A legendary political boss, Curley was a power in Boston for more than half a century. Irish, Catholic, and Democratic, he was the self-proclaimed champion of Boston's poor immigrant groups and they elected him to municipal offices (1900–11), the U.S. House of Representatives (1911–14; 1943–46), the mayoralty of Boston (1914–18; 1922–26; 1930–34; 1946–50), and the governorship of Massachusetts (1935–37). While mayor in 1947, he was convicted of mail fraud and served five months in prison. A colorful and shrewd political leader, he was said to be the model for the main character in Edwin O'Connor's novel, *The Last Hurrah*. ■ See his autobiography, *I'd Do It Again* (1957), and Jack Beatty, *The Rascal King* (1992).

CURRAN, JOSEPH EDWARD (1906–1981), U.S. labor leader. A seventh-grade school dropout who went to sea at age 16, Curran was the founding president (1937–73) of the National Maritime Union (NMU). He was a vice president of the Congress of Industrial Organizations (CIO) from 1940, and of the merged AFL-CIO (1955–73). His union membership reached 100,000 during World War II, and he won numerous wage hikes and benefits for the seamen. Although he supported left-wing causes during the 1930s, he launched a purge of communists from the union leadership in 1946. He retired in 1973 to Florida with a reported $1 million in severance and pension benefits.

CURRIE, SIR ARTHUR WILLIAM (1875–1933), Canadian general and educator. Born in Ontario, Currie was a teacher and businessman in British Columbia before joining the Canadian garrison artillery (1897). He went off to World War I as a lieutenant colonel and by 1917 was the commander of the Canadian corps, leading his troops at Passchendaele, Arras, and Amiens. He was promoted to general, Canada's first, on his return in 1919. In 1920 he retired from the army,

spending the next 13 years as principal and vice-chancellor of McGill University. ■ See biography by H. M. Urquhart (1950) and John Swettenham, *To Seize the Victory* (1965).

CURTIN, JOHN JOSEPH (1885–1945), Australian political leader. Curtin went to work at age 13 and was active in labor unions and the anticonscription movement in Melbourne during World War I. In 1916 he settled in Perth and edited (1917–28) the *Westralian Worker*. He was a Labour member of Parliament (1928–31; 1934–45), and head of the party from 1934 to 1945. As prime minister during World War II (1941–45), he led an all-out national mobilization, broadened conscription, initiated close ties with the United States, and introduced progressive welfare state legislation. He died in office. ■ See biographies by Alan Chester (1943) and Lloyd Maxwell Ross (1977).

CURTIS, CYRUS HERMANN KOTZSCHMAR (1850–1933), U.S. publisher and philanthropist. Creator of one of the world's richest publishing empires, Curtis founded the *Ladies' Home Journal* (1883), which transformed women's periodicals and became the leading magazine of its kind (circulation 2.5 million in 1933), *The Saturday Evening Post*, which he purchased in 1897, eventually embodied the virtues of American middle-class life and was one of the nation's most popular magazines (circulation 2.7 million in 1933). Among the newspapers Curtis controlled were the *Philadelphia Press*, the *New York Evening Post*, and the *Philadelphia Inquirer*. At his death he left millions of dollars to musical institutions, schools, and hospitals. ■ See Edward W. Bok, *Man from Maine* (1923).

CURTIS, EDWARD SHERIFF (1868–1952), U.S. photographer and historian. Curtis became fascinated with photography as a boy and after moving with his family to Seattle began making a photographic record of the North American Indian. The Indian way of life, which Curtis described as "near to nature," had already vanished east of the Mississippi, but Curtis traveled from Arizona to Alaska to find western remnants of Indian arts and crafts, society, and economy. His romanticized photos were published as *The North American Indian* (20 vols., 1907–30) under the patronage of the financier J. P. Morgan, who stipulated that the collection be "the handsomest ever published." ■ See biography by Barbara A. Davis (1985).

CURTISS, GLENN HAMMOND (1878–1930), U.S. aviator. Like the Wright brothers, Curtiss began his career as a bicycle mechanic. He designed (1904) the motor for the first dirigible balloon adopted by the U.S. Army. Turning to heavier-than-air craft, he won acclaim (1908) for the first one-kilometer public flight in the United States, averaging almost 40 miles per hour in his plane, the *June Bug*. He also invented the aileron (1911), a device used to maintain vertical stability, and developed the first viable seaplane (1911). Curtiss's factories produced military planes during World

War I, and his NC-4 flying boat, built for the U.S. Navy, made the first transatlantic flight (1919). ■ See biography by C. R. Roseberry (1972) and Clara Studer, *Sky Storming Yankee* (1937).

CURTIZ, MICHAEL (Mihaly Kertész; 1888–1962), Hungarian-born U.S. film director. Curtiz directed films in Hungary, Austria, Germany, France, and Scandinavia before being brought to Hollywood (by Harry Warner; 1926), where he was a fixture at Warner Brothers for a quarter of a century. He was best known for his films of the 1930s and 1940s, including *20,000 years in Sing Sing* (1933), *Black Fury* (1935), *Captain Blood* (1935), *Angels with Dirty Faces* (1938), *The Sea Hawk* (1940), *Yankee Doodle Dandy* (1942), *Mildred Pierce* (1945), and *Life with Father* (1947). He won (1943) an Academy Award for *Casablanca.* ■ See James C. Robertson, *The Casablanca Man* (1993).

CURZON OF KEDLESTON, GEORGE NATHANIEL CURZON, 1st MARQUESS (1859–1925). An arrogant aristocrat, educated at Eton and Oxford, Curzon traveled extensively as a young man, writing learned reports from remote corners of the globe. He was a protégé of the prime minister Lord Salisbury and was elected to Parliament in 1886. During his tenure as viceroy of India (1898–1905) he established the Northwest Frontier province, authorized an invasion of Tibet (1904) to counter a fear of Russian expansion, and partitioned Bengal for administrative efficiency. He was active in politics as a Conservative, serving as foreign secretary (1919–24)—a line that eventually became the Polish-Soviet border was known as the Curzon line—but was frustrated in his ambition to become prime minister. ■ See Leonard Mosley, *The Glorious Fault* (1960); Kenneth Rose, *Superior Person* (1970); and biography by Nayana Goradia (1993).

CUSHING, HARVEY WILLIAMS (1869–1939), U.S. neurosurgeon. Born into a medical family, Cushing graduated from the Harvard Medical School (1895) and achieved fame for his studies of, and pioneering survey on, the pituitary gland (1912). A professor of surgery at Harvard (1912–31), he introduced numerous technique for surgery of the brain and spinal cord. He was also the first to describe the pituitary disorder now known as Cushing's disease, wrote several important works on brain tumors, and contributed to the study of blood pressure in surgery. In addition to his numerous technical works, Cushing wrote a Pulitzer Prize–winning medical biography, *The Life of Sir William Osler* (1925). ■ See biography by Elizabeth H. Thomson (1950).

CUSHING, RICHARD JAMES (1895–1970), U.S. Roman Catholic cardinal. Cushing grew up in Boston and after ordination (1921) rose to become archbishop of his native city (1944). He was elevated to cardinal in 1958 and was a major figure in the second Vatican Council (1962–65). In the 1960s he spoke out for social justice and equality of opportunity and was a champion of ecumensism. He was close to the family of Pres. John F. Kennedy and was the first Roman Catholic clergyman to offer official prayers at a U.S. presidential inauguration ceremony. ■ See biography by John H. Cutler (1970).

CYRANKIEWICZ, JÓZEF (1911–1989), Polish political leader. The son of a well-to-do manufacturer, Cyrankiewicz studied law in Cracow before World War II and joined the Polish Socialist party. Active in the underground during the war, he was arrested in 1941 and spent four years in German concentration camps. Cyrankiewicz presided over the 1948 unification of the Polish Socialist and Communist parties and served as premier (1947–52 and 1954–70) through both Stalinist and anti-Stalinist eras.

D

DĄBROWSKA, MARIA (Maria Szumska; 1889–1965), Polish writer. A writer whose work reflected her humanitarian faith and hope in the everyday heroism of the Polish masses. Dąbrowska came from an impoverished landowning family and had firsthand knowledge of the Polish countryside and dialect. While the stories in *Folks from over Yonder* (1925) realistically portrayed the life of the rural proletariat during the early years of the 20th century, her masterpiece was the vivid epic *Nights and Days* (4 vols., 1932–34), a saga of several generations of a poor Polish family covering the period from the 1860s to World War I. *A Village Wedding* (1955; Eng. trans. 1957) contains stories that described peasant life in the 1950s. ▪ See study by Zbigniew Folejewski (1967).

DACHÉ, LILLY (1897?–1989), French-born U.S. milliner. Daché was apprenticed at age 12 to her milliner aunt and then to well-known Paris hat designer Caroline Reboux. After sailing to New York (1924), she sold hats off the shelf at Macy's, but by the decade's end was designing "made-on-the-head" creations that made the name Daché synonymous with hat. At the peak of her 50-year career, the House of Daché designed some 9,000 hats per year. Daché ran a prestigious shop on 56th Street and expanded her enterprise to encompass dresses, accessories, jewelry, and hair products. ▪ See her autobiography, *Talking Through My Hats* (1946).

DAGERMAN, STIG (1923–1954), Swedish novelist, short-story writer, and playwright. Dagerman at first wrote topical, propagandistic verse that was syndicated in newspapers; he then became the prodigy of the "Forties group." His first novel, *The Snake* (1945; Eng. trans. 1995), explored the perpetual struggle against fear and anxiety. His best works probed his characters' mental processes, as in the fictionalized autobiography *A Burnt Child* (1948; Eng. trans. 1950). He also wrote plays, including *The Condemned* (1947; Eng. trans. 1951) and *The Climber* (1949), and short stories, including those in the collection *The Games of Night* (1947; Eng. trans. 1961). He also wrote *Island of the Doomed* (1946; Eng. trans. 1992) and *German Autumn* (1947; Eng. trans. 1988). His suicide at age 31, when he was at the height of his popularity, traumatized the Swedish intelligentsia. ▪ See study by Laurie Thompson (1983).

DAHL, ROBERT ALAN (1915–   ), U.S. political scientist. A graduate of Yale (Ph.D. 1940) and professor there after 1946, Dahl specialized in the study of elites and groups, decision making, and liberal democratic theory. His works in-cluded *Congress and Foreign Policy* (1950); *Who Governs* (1961), a study of local government in New Haven, Connecticut; *Pluralist Democracy in the U.S.* (1967); and *Dilemmas of Pluralist Democracy* (1982). In such works as *Political Oppositions in Western Democracies* (1966), *After the Revolution* (1971), and *Polyarchy* (1971), he discussed the transformation of political systems and the preconditions of democracy. His later works included *A Preface to Economic Democracy* (1985), *Democracy and Its Critics* (1989), and *On Democracy* (1998).

DAHRENDORF, RALF DAHRENDORF, BARON (1929–   ), German sociologist. Born in Hamburg, the son of a Social Democratic politician, Dahrendorf was sent to a concentration camp in 1944 for anti-Nazi activities. He earned doctorates from the universities of Hamburg (1952) and London (1956) and wrote two important sociological studies, *Class and Class Conflict in Industrial Society* (1957; Eng. trans. 1959) and *Society and Democracy in Germany* (1965; Eng. trans. 1966). Elected to the West German Bundestag as a Free Democratic deputy, Dahrendorf was parliamentary secretary of state in the West German foreign office (1969–70) and a member of the European Economic Community Commission (1970–74). While serving as director of the London School of Economics (1974–84), he wrote *Life Chances* (1979), a study of social theory, and *On Britain* (1982). He taught at Oxford (1987–97) and also served as a director (1974–84) and governor (1986–   ) of the European Economic Commission. He became a British citizen (1988) and was created a life peer (1993). His later books included *The Modern Social Conflict* (1988) and *After 1989: Morals, Revolution and Civil Society* (1997).

DAIRO, I. K. (Isaiah Kehinde Dairo; 1930–1996), Nigerian musician. A self-taught drummer and drum maker, Dairo was a part-time musician before starting his own 10-piece Morning Star Orchestra (1957; renamed the Blue Spots in 1959) in Lagos. Called "the father of Juju Music," he transformed and modernized the popular Yoruba musical genre in the 1960s by introducing the accordion and talking drum and by blending call-and-response vocals, Latin American rhythms, traditional African songs, and Christian hymns. He recorded dozens of albums, toured the world, became one of the first African musicians to become an international star, and was the first African musician to be made a member of the British Empire (M.B.E.; 1963). Dairo was also a devout Christian and a leader of the Cherubim and Seraphim movement. ▪ See Chris Waterman, *Juju* (1990).

DALADIER, ÉDOUARD (1884–1970), French statesman. Son and grandson of rural bakers in the south of France, Daladier was a history teacher who became active in politics when elected mayor of his hometown. Elected to parliament as a radical socialist in 1919, he served briefly as premier in 1933, 1934, and also during the critical period of 1938–40, when he supported the policy of appeasing Nazi Germany and signed the Munich agreement (1938) that led to the partition of Czechoslovakia. Daladier was later arrested by the Vichy government, deported to Germany in 1943, and liberated by the Allies in 1945. He served again in parliament from 1946 to 1958. ■ See his speeches in *In Defense of France* (Eng. trans. 1939) and Stanton B. Leeds, *These Rule France* (1940).

DALAI LAMA, 14th (1935–   ). Tibetan religious leader. Considered by Tibetan Buddhists to be the 14th incarnation of Avalokitesvara, the Lord of Compassion, the Dalai Lama was born in China into a peasant family, identified by Buddhist monks when he was 2 years old, and installed on the throne in Lhasa on Feb. 22, 1940. He was named king at the age of 15 (Nov. 17, 1950) when the Chinese reasserted their control over Tibet. Accepting the reality of overwhelming Chinese power, he cooperated with them but attempted to resist encroachments on traditional Tibetan society. After the Chinese crushed a nationalist revolt against them (1959), the Dalai Lama fled to India and headed a large exile community in Dharamsala, a Himalayan town near the Pakistan border. He traveled the world to publicize the plight of the Tibetan people and, from the late 1970s, negotiated with the Chinese government over the terms of his possible return to Tibet. In 1988 he switched his position from advocating an independent Tibet to accepting a self-governing Tibet in association with China. Although the Chinese government rejected his plan, he was awarded the 1989 Nobel Peace Prize. He wrote several books, including *The Buddhism of Tibet and the Key to the Middle Way* (Eng. trans. 1975), *The Meaning of Life* (1990), *The Art of Happiness* (1998; with Howard C. Cutler), and *Ethics for the New Millennium* (1999). ■ See his autobiographies, *My Land and My People* (Eng. trans. 1962) and *Freedom in Exile* (Eng. trans. 1990), and John F. Avedon, *In Exile from the Land of Snows* (1984).

DALE, CHARLES. *See SMITH, JOE, and CHARLES DALE.*

DALE, SIR HENRY HALLETT (1875–1968), British biochemist. A graduate of Cambridge (M.D. 1909), Dale began to study the parasitic fungus ergot, a substance known to stimulate muscle contraction, in 1904. His later research with histamine led him to isolate a new substance named acetylcholine. Dale showed that this chemical substance was connected with nerve action as it carried nerve impulses from one nerve cell to another. For this discovery, he shared the 1936 Nobel Prize in Physiology or Medicine with Otto Loewi. He directed the National Institute for Medical Research (1928–42) and reprinted his major scientific papers in *Adventure in Physiology* (1953).

DALEY, ARTHUR JOHN (1904–1974), U.S. sportswriter. On the staff of the *New York Times* for nearly 50 years, Daley was the paper's chief sports columnist from 1942 to 1974. A longtime devotee of baseball, he was one of the sports world's most respected journalists and only the second sportswriter to win a Pulitzer Prize (1956).

DALEY, RICHARD JOSEPH (1902–1976), U.S. political leader. The last of the big-city political bosses, Mayor Daley of Chicago became a precinct captain at age 21 and rose in 1953 to Cook County Democratic chairman, a position he maintained firmly through six successful mayoral elections. An Irish-American resident of the same blue-collar neighborhood all his life, he had worked in the stockyards to put himself through law school (LL.B. 1933). As mayor (1955–76), Daley sponsored public works programs, expanded municipal services, and weathered recurring civic scandals to play a pivotal role in national politics through his leadership of the important Illinois Democratic delegation. A staunch advocate of law and order, he issued "shoot-to-kill" orders during the 1968 riots after civil-rights leader Martin Luther King's assassination and later the same year cracked down on demonstrators at the Democratic National Convention in Chicago. ■ See Mike Royko, *Boss* (1971); Eugene Kennedy, *Himself!* (1978); study by Roger Biles (1995); and Adam Cohen and Elizabeth Taylor, *American Pharaoh* (2000).

DALHART, VERNON (Marion Try Slaughter; 1883–1948), U.S. country singer. Dalhart moved from Texas to the Bronx at the urging of his voice coach and concocted a stage name from the two Texas towns between which he had worked as a cowpuncher—Vernon and Dalhart. He set his sights on grand opera and operetta and sang tenor roles in works by Puccini and Gilbert and Sullivan. But his great success came when he realized the commercial potential of the country music so close to his roots. His first two recordings, "The Wreck of the Old '97" and "The Prisoner's Song" (both 1924), effectively launched the county-music industry with their phenomenal sales. By the time of his death, "The Prisoner's Song" had sold some 25 million copies.

DALÍ, SALVADOR (1904–1989), Spanish artist. When told as an art student to copy a Gothic virgin, Dalí drew a pair of scales. His precise rendering of subconscious imagery, often phantasmagorical and fetishistic, made him a major figure in the surrealist and dada movements of the period between World Wars I and II. He collaborated with Spanish director Luis Buñuel on the surrealistic films *Un Chien Andalou* (1928) and *L'Age d'Or* (1930). During the 1940s, Dalí moved into a more serene classicism, painting "dream pictures" with photographic realism; in 1950 he turned to religious themes. A flamboyant, mustachioed celebrity, he wrote *The Secret Life of Salvador Dali* (Eng. trans. 1942) and *Diary of a Genius* (Eng. trans. 1965). ■ See studies by J. T. Soby (rev. ed. 1946), Conroy Maddox (1979), Dawn Ades (1978), and Meryle Secrest (1986); and Ian Gibson, *The Shameful Life of Salvador Dali* (1998).

DALLAPICCOLA, LUIGI (1904–1975), Italian composer. Trained as a pianist at the conservatory in Florence, where he later taught, Dallapiccola then turned to composition. Influenced by the work of Anton Webern and Alban Berg, he adopted their 12-tone technique and assimilated it to the traditions of Italian vocal lyricism, which resulted in serial music noted for its lyricism and melodic and expressive line. Also a teacher in various American universities and music schools, he influenced American composition. Among his chamber orchestral, choral, and operatic music are *Variazioni per Orchestra* (1954), *Il Prigioniero* ("the prisoner"; 1944–48), an operatic requiem, and *Canti di Liberazione* ("songs of liberation," 1952–55) a choral work.

DALY, HERMAN (1938–   ), U.S. economist. Daly was a professor of economics at Louisiana State University (1964–88), staff member at the World Bank (1988–94), and senior researcher of the School of Public Health at the University of Maryland (1994–   ). He is best known for linking economics with ecology by applying the insights of steady-state systems, developed by physicists studying thermodynamics, to the analysis of economic problems. In *Steady-State Economics* (1977), he argued that society must recognize the limitations of the physical world and adopt policies of sustainable development if humanity is to survive. In his writings he proposed economic incentives to maintain zero population growth and marketable quotas to regulate the production of goods at a level that does not exceed environmental limits. He also advocated limits on income and wealth. His books, including *Economics, Ecology, Ethics* (1980), *Energy, Economics and the Enviroment* (1981), *For the Common Good* (with John Cobb; 1989), *Valuing the Earth* (1993), and *Beyond Growth* (1996), influenced the international environmental movement.

DALY, MARY (1928–   ), American feminist and Roman Catholic theologian. Daly received doctorates from St. Mary's College, Indiana (1954). and from Switzerland's University of Fribourg (1965) and taught at Boston College (1966–99). Primarily concerned with women's liberation, she postulated a new theology, writing that in Western religion "The roles and structures of patriarchy have been developed and sustained in accordance with an artificial polarization of human qualities into the traditional sexual stereotypes." She analyzed the sexist ethos of the Roman Catholic Church and opposed what she termed "phallic morality." Daly wrote *The Church and the Second Sex* (1968; rev. ed. 1975), *Beyond God the Father* (1973), *Gyn/Ecology: The Metaethics of Radical Feminism* (1978), *Pure Lust: Elemental Feminist Philosophy* (1984), and

Quintessence—Realizing the Archaic Future (1998). From the early 1970s she barred men from her classes and she was forced to retire (1999) after losing a case in a Massachusetts Superior Court because of this practice. ■ See her autobiography, *Outercourse* (1992).

DALY, REGINALD ALDWORTH (1871–1957), Canadian-born U.S. geologist. A professor of geology at Harvard (1912–42), Daly developed theories explaining the origin of igneous formations and the formation of coral atolls, reefs, and submarine valleys. The most prominent American geologist of his time, Daly wrote seven books, including *Igneous Rocks and the Depths of the Earth* (1933), *The Changing World of the Ice Age* (1934), *The Strength and Structure of the Earth* (1940), and *The Floor of the Ocean* (1942).

DAM, (CARL PETER) HENRIK (1895–1976), Danish biochemist. While studying the cholesterol metabolism in chicks as a professor at the University of Copenhagen (1923–40), Dam discovered that some of the experimental animals developed internal hemorrhages and delayed blood coagulation. He attributed this to the lack of a fat-soluble substance in the diet that he named vitamin K (for the German word *koagulation*). Dam demonstrated that vitamin K, found naturally primarily in green leaves and tomatoes, could be useful in reducing bleeding during surgery and in preventing hemorrhaging in infants, especially those born prematurely. He shared the 1943 Nobel Prize for Physiology or Medicine with Edward Doisy.

DAMAS, LÉON GONTRAN (1912–1978), French Guianese author and political leader. Educated in Paris, Damas founded the literary magazine *L'Étudiant Noir* (The Black Student; 1934) with Léopold Senghor and Aimé Césaire and thus launched the cultural movement known as Négritude. His poetry, replete with African motifs and rhythms, violently attacked colonialism while championing the cultural values of Africa. He was best known for the poetry collections *Pigments* (1937), *African Songs of Love, War, Grief and Abuse* (1947; Eng. trans. 1961), *Graffiti* (1952), *Black-Label* (1956), and the autobiographical *Return from Guyana* (1938). A lifelong socialist, he participated in the Resistance during World War II, served in the French national assemble (1945–51), and traveled widely researching African culture. He lived in Washington. D.C. (from 1970), and taught at Georgetown and Howard Universities. ■ See study edited by Daniel L. Racine (1979).

DAMROSCH, WALTER JOHANNES (1862–1950), German-born U.S. conductor. A major force in American musical life for over 50 years, Damrosch conducted at New York's Metropolitan Opera (1885–91; 1900–02) and ran his own Damrosch Opera Company (1894–1900) before directing the New York Symphony Orchestra (1903–27). He introduced works by Wagner, Brahms, Tchaikoysky, Saint-Saëns, and Berlioz to the American public and his pioneering radio show, "Musical Appreciation" (National Broadcasting Company; 1928–42), was heard by millions of schoolchildren each week. He also composed several operas and wrote incidental music for the theater. ▪ See his autobiography, *My Musical Life* (1923), and George Martin, *Damrosch Dunasty* (1983).

DAN, BARON TAKUMA (1858–1932), Japanese business leader. Trained as a mining engineer at the Massachusetts Institute of Technology, Takuma directed the Mitsui Mining Co. (1894) and was board chairman of the Mitsui *zaibatsu* (1914–32), one of the largest family-owned industrial-financial empires in Japan. He wielded enormous power until he was assassinated by a member of a right-wing nationalist organization.

DANILOVA, ALEXANDRA (1904–1997), Russian-born ballet dancer and teacher. A soloist with the Maryinsky (now Kirov) Ballet in Leningrad (1922–24), Danilova toured Western Europe (1924) with a small ballet troupe (including George Balanchine) and decided against returning to the Soviet Union. She was a leading member of Sergei Diaghilev's Ballet Russe in Paris (1924–29) and was prima ballerina of the Ballet Russe de Monte Carlo (1938–52). Acclaimed throughout the world, she was noted for her wideranging and exterisive repertoire, which included *Le Beau Danube, Swan Lake, Les Sylphides, Gaieté Parisienne,* and *Coppélia.* After her retirement she choreographed at the Metropolitan Opera, La Scala (Milan), and the Washington, D.C., Ballet and taught at Balanchine's School of American Ballet in New York City. ▪ See her memoirs, *Choura* (1986).

DANNAY, FREDERIC. See QUEEN, ELLERY.

D'ANNUNZIO, GABRIELE (1863–1938), Italian writer. One of the most flamboyant and controversial European figures of his time, D'Annunzio was a prolific author of poetry, novels, and plays noted for their dazzling use of language and unrestrained sensuality. His best-known works include the novel *The Triumph of Death* (1894; Eng. trans. 1896), the drama *The Daughter of Jorio* (1904; Eng. trans. 1907), and the poetry collection *Alcyone* (1903). One of the most publicized lovers of his day, he wrote the erotic novel *The Flame of Life* (1900; Eng. trans. 1900), an account of his affair with the celebrated actress Eleonora Duse. D'Annunzio was a superpatriot who adhered to the myth of the "superman" championed by Friedrich Nietzsche and Richard Wagner. He urged Italian entry into World War I and was known for his daring military exploits during the conflict and for the capture, with 300 followers, of the disputed Dalmatian port of Fiume (1919), which he ruled as a dictator for two years. He retired from public life in 1921 as a living legend and later ardently supported the fascist regime of Benito Mussolini. ▪ See biographies by Anthony Rhodes (1960) and Philippe Jullian (Eng. trans. 1973).

DANQUAH, JOSEPH B. (1895–1965), Gold Coast nationalist and Ghanaian political leader. A scholar of history and law who proposed the name "Ghana" for a Gold Coast eventually independent from Britain, Danquah began a legal, journalistic, and political career in the 1920s. Although he founded the moderate nationalist party United Gold Coast Convention (1947), he was unable to compete with the more militant nationalist Kwame Nkrumah, who established his own party in 1949 and led the country to independence in 1957. Danquah lost the 1960 presidential election to Nkrumah and subsequently attacked Nkrumah's increasingly authoritarian rule. Despite international protest he was imprisoned in 1961–62 and again in 1964–65, during which time he suffered a fatal heart attack. His books included *Gold Coast* (1928) and *The Akan Doctrine of God* (1944).

DANTZIG, GEORGE BERNARD (1914–   ), U.S. mathematician. Dantzig's discovery in the late 1940s of linear programming and his invention of the simplex method of solving mathematical programs took place at the same time that computers were being introduced. These simultaneous developments, which enabled managers and researchers to assess large numbers of interdependent variables to allocate scarce resources, fostered a revolution in industrial and governmental evaluation and planning and gave rise to the new discipline of decision making called operations research (or management science). Dantzig was a mathematician with the U.S. Army Air Corps (1941–52) and a professor at the University of California, Berkeley (1960–66), and at Stanford University (from 1966). He wrote the standard reference, *Linear Programming and Extensions* (1963), and *Compact City: A Plan for a Liveable Urban Enrironment* (1973; with T. L. Saaty).

DARÍO, RUBÉN (Felix Rubén García Sarmiento; 1867–1916), Nicaraguan poet, journalist, critic, and diplomat. A child prodigy, Dario published his first poem at age 13 and revolutionized the world of Spanish letters with the publication of *Azul* ("Blue"; 1888), a collection of short stories and poems. He was the founder and leader of *modernismo*, the literary movement that had a profound effect on literature in Spain and throughout Latin America. His innovative poems, influenced by contemporary French writers, sought perfection of form and used objective language and exotic themes, while his prose used simple sentence structure and direct language. His poetry as well as his bohemian lifestyle influenced generations of Latin American youth. Among his important works were *Prosas Profanas* ("profane hymns"; 1896), *Cantos de Vida y Esperanza* ("songs of life and hope"; 1905), and *Poema del Otoño* ("autumn's poem"; 1910). ▪ See his *Selected Poems* (Eng. trans. 1965) and Charles D. Watland's biography, *Poet-Errant* (1965).

DARLAN, JEAN LOUIS FRANÇOIS (1881–1942), French admiral. Born into a seafaring family, Darlan graduated from the French Naval Academy (1902) and at age 48 became the youngest admiral in Europe. A supporter of appeasement who was also thought to be a royalist, during World War II he served the collaborationist Vichy regime as foreign minister. In 1942 the ambitious admiral became commander in chief of all French forces and was appointed Vichy high commissioner to French North Africa, where he was assassinated soon after he concluded an armistice with the Allies. ■ See Peter Tompkins, *The Murder of Admiral Darlan* (1965).

DARLING, JAY NORWOOD (1876–1962), U.S. cartoonist. "Ding" Darling's award-winning editorial cartoons (Pulitzer Prize, 1923 and 1943) appeared in the *Des Moines Register* (1906–11; 1913–49) and the *New York Tribune* (later *Herald Tribune;* 1917–49) and its syndicate. He was also an active conservationist and served as chief of the U.S. Biological Survey (1934–35) and president of the National Wildlife Federation (1936). A collection of his cartoons appeared in *Ding's Half Century* (1962), edited by John M. Henry. ■ See David L. Lendt, *Ding* (1979).

DARROW, CLARENCE SEWARD (1857–1938), U.S. attorney. The attorney for the defense in several historic trials, Darrow began his career as a small-town Ohio lawyer. By age 30 he was established as a Chicago railroad attorney, a position he abandoned to 1894 to defend railroad-union officials. Darrow devoted the next 15 years to union causes, until a 1911 bombing case in Los Angeles in which he was himself accused of bribing jurors. Acquitted, he salvaged his reputation by defending criminal cases. His defense of "thrill" murderers Nathan Leopold and Richard Loeb (1924) was an eloquent denunciation of capital punishment, and he saved his clients from the death sentence. In 1925 he squared off against fundamentalist lawyer William Jennings Bryan in the Tennessee trial of John Scopes for teaching evolution. A much-sought-after speaker and debater, Darrow wrote several books, including the novel *An Eye for an Eye* (1905) and *The Story of My Life* (1932). ■ See biographies by Kevin Tierney (1975) and James Charles Livingstone (1988), and Arthur and Lila Weinberg, *A Sentimental Rebel* (1980).

DART, RAYMOND ARTHUR (1893–1988), Australian-born South African physical anthropologist. Dart studied medicine at Sydney University, served with the Australian army medical corps in World War I, and taught anatomy. In 1923 he settled in South Africa and began teaching medicine at the University of the Witwatersrand in Johannesburg. His discovery of fossil remains of *Australopithecus africanus,* an early human ancestor, at Taung, South Africa, lent support to the view that human life originated in Africa, not Asia. He later found similar fossil remains at Makapansgat and Sterkfontein. Dart formulated a theoretical model of australopithecine culture based on the probable use of tools made of bone, tooth, and horn. ■ See his *Adventures with the Missing Link* (with Dennis Craig; 1959) and study by Frances Wheelhouse (1983).

DARWISH, MAHMUD (1942–   ), Palestinian poet. Darwish was born in an Arab village near Acre and fled to Lebanon with his family during the 1948 war. His village destroyed, he secretly reentered Israel a year later and was raised as a "refugee" in a border village in Galilee. He eventually settled in Haifa, worked as a journalist and literary editor, wrote poetry expressing resistance to Zionist rule, and became a prominent member of Rakah, a faction of the Israeli Communist party. Jailed and placed under house arrest several times, Darwish left Israel for Beirut (1971) and later moved to Paris (1982), where he edited the magazine *Karmal*. He served on the Palestine Liberation Organization (PLO) executive (1987–93) before resigning in protest over the Israel-PLO accord. He moved to the Palestinian city of Ramallah in 1996. His poems, which reflected his attachment to the Palestinian people and love for the land of Palestine, appeared in English translation in *Selected Poems* (1973), *Splinters of Bone* (1974), *The Music of Human Flesh* (1980), *Victims of a Map* (1984), and *Psalms: Poems* (1994).

DAS, CHITTA RANJAN (1870–1925), Indian nationalist. Born into a progressive Bengali family, Das was a successful lawyer in Britain and Calcutta before he became actively involved in the nationalist cause in 1917. A poet, author, and brilliant orator, Das held many posts in the Indian National Congress party (including the presidency, 1922). He cofounded the Swaraj or "Self-Rule" party (1923) in order to obstruct the British-sponsored legislative councils from within, and he was the first elected mayor of Calcutta (1924). He was particularly concerned with communal harmony and sponsored the Bengal Pact (1923) between the Hindus and Muslims of Bengal. ■ See biography by Hemendra Nath Das Gupta (1960).

DASSAULT, MARCEL (Marcel Bloch; 1892–1986), French industrialist and legislator. He graduated from the École Nationale Superieure de L'Aeronautique (1913) and during World War I worked on military aircraft for France. In the years between the world wars, he was responsible for the prototypes of numerous civil and military aircraft. When the Nazis occupied France during World War II, he resisted pressure to work for the Germans and was sent to the concentration camp at Buchenwald. After the war he took the name Dassault (his brothers code name in the Resistance) and converted from Judaism to Roman Catholicism. Dassault made a huge fortune by manufaturing the Mirage and Mystère fighterjets (introduced in the 1950s) and the executive's Falcon fan-jet. Smaller and less expensive than their U.S. or Soviet counterparts, Dassault's warplanes appealed to smaller nations. The Mirage was used successfully by the

Israelis in the 1967 war. From 1968, Dassault directed Dassault-Breguet Aircraft, which sold warplanes to such customers as Spain, India, and Greece during the 1970s and 1980s. His financial empire also encompassed electronics manufacturing, real estate, banking, and publishing; he published and edited the popular weekly *Jours de France*. One of France's most powerful investors, Dassault figured in a quartet of financiers that in the 1980s took control of some businesses that were not completely nationalized by the government of Pres. Francois Mitterand. Active in politics as a staunch supporter of Pres. Charles de Gaulle, Dassault was a legislator in the national assembly (1951–55).

DAUD KHAN, SARDAR MOHAMMAD (1909–1978), Afghan military and political leader. Daud Khan was born in Kabul and educated in Afghanistan and France. A brother-in-law and cousin of the king, he became commander in chief of the armed forces (1939) and served as defense minister (1946–53). As premier (1953–63) he outlawed the use of the veil by women and had the Soviet Union equip and train the army. A three-year famine (1970–73) created much discontent, and in 1973 Daud Khan overthrew the monarchy, declared a republic, and became president and premier. He was murdered during a left-wing military coup that overthrew his government.

DAUDET, LÉON (1867–1942), French writer. Son of author Alphonse Daudet, Léon Daudet was a right-wing polemicist who coedited and contributed satirical articles to *L'Action Française* (from 1908), the organ of the French royalist movement. Daudet was unsuccessful in promoting restoration, but he did a masterful job of sowing anti-Semitism and contempt for democratic institutions and the struggling Third Republic. He served in the Chamber of Deputies (1919–24) and was a member of the Goncourt Academy. He also wrote novels and works on psychology, history, literature, and politics. ■ See his *Memoirs* (Eng. trans. 1925).

DAUSSET, JEAN (1916–   ), French biologist. After studies at the University of Paris (M.D. 1945), Dausset begin immunological research that eventually enabled him to demonstrate the existence of histocompatibility antigens in humans. This discovery of the genetically determined cell structures that regulate immunological reactions paved the way for human organ transplants and enabled scientists to explain why some individuals are more disposed than others to certain diseases and infections. Dausset was a professor of medicine at the University of Paris (1968–77) and professor of experimental medicine at the College of France (1977–87). He shared the 1980 Nobel Prize in Physiology or Medicine with George Snell and Baruj Benacerraf. Among his books (in English) were *Human Transplantation* (1968; with Felix Rapaport) and *Histocompatability* (1976; with Snell and Stanley Nathanson).

DAVIČO, OSKAR (1909–   ), Yugoslav novelist and poet. A communist activist and surrealist poet before World War II, Davičo, a Jew, became one of socialist Yugoslavia's leading literary figures. Known for his modernist and nonconformist prose and poetry, he was an editor of *Delo,* one of Yugoslavia's most influential postwar literary magazines, and was granted his country's highest literary prize. Davičo's most famous works were his novels *The Poem* (1952; Eng. trans. 1959) and *Concrete and Fireflies* (1956) and his poetry, *The Cherry Tree Behind the Wall* (1950), *Hana* (1951), and *Man's Man* (1953).

DAVIDSON, BRUCE (1933–   ), U.S. photographer. A freelance photographer for *Life, Look, Réalités, and Queen* and a member of the Magnum photo collective (from 1958), Davidson was known for his sympathetic portraits of the poor and disenfranchised. He reversed the course of modern photography when he took a cumbersome studio camera into Spanish Harlem in New York City. Earning the occasionally shy, sometimes belligerent, but always honest participation of his subjects, he achieved a remarkable portrait of *East 100th Street* (1970) as "home." See also *Subsistence U.S.A.* (1973; with Carol Hill), *Bruce Davidson: Photographs* (1979), *Subway* (1986), *Central Park* (1995), *Brooklyn Gang* (1998), and *Bruce Davidson: Portraits* (1999).

DAVIDSON, JO (1883–1952), U.S. sculptor. Davidson, who was born on New York City's Lower East Side, left medical school to pursue his interest in art. He devoted his career as a sculptor to making "heroes out of mud," as one of his subjects put it. Obsessed by the mysteries of personality and character, he sculpted some 300 portraits of contemporary celebrities, from Einstein to Chaplin, using clay, marble, and bronze in a naturalistic style. His better-known works included portraits of Gertrude Stein (1920) and Will Rogers (1939). ■ See his autobiography, *Between Sittings* (1951), and Lois H. Kuhn, *The World of Jo Davidson* (1958).

DAVIES, JOSEPH EDWARD (1876–1958), U.S. diplomat. After chairing the Bureau of Corporations (1913–15) and the Federal Trade Commission (1915–16) and serving as economic adviser to Pres. Woodrow Wilson at the Paris Peace Conference (1919), Davies maintained a lucrative corporate law practice in Washington, D.C (to 1936). As ambassador to Moscow (1937–38) he traveled widely in the Soviet Union and was favorable impressed by the Russian people and their leaders. His best-selling account, *Mission to Moscow* (1941), was criticized by some for its naiveté (he wrote that "the Soviet leaders are moved, basically, by altruistic concepts" and concluded that the defendants at the purge trials, which he attended daily, were guilty), but it played an important role in gaining Arnerican sympathy for the Soviet Union during World War II. ■ See studies by Keith D. Eagles (1985) and Elizabeth K. MacLean (1992).

DAVIES, (WILLIAM) ROBERTSON (1913–1995), Canadian novelist and playwright. After earning an Oxford degree (1938), Davies remained in Britain to stage-manage, act, and direct for the Old Vic Repertory Company. Returning to Canada (1940), he wrote a wry column for the *Peterborough* (Ontario) *Examiner,* "The Diary of Samuel Marchbanks (collected 1947, 1949), which set the tone for his plays, including *Eros at Breakfast and Other Plays* (1949) and *Love and Libel* (1960). He also satirized Canadian provincialism in a trilogy *Tempest Tost* (1951), *Leaven of Malice* (1954), and *A Mixture of Frailties* (1958). Davies published essays in *A Voice from the Attic* (1960), the title a reference to the United States' upstairs neighbor; *One Half of Robertson Davies* (1978); *The Merry Heart* (1997); and *Happy Alchemy* (1998). The highly praised trilogy *Fifth Business* (1970), *The Manticore* (1972), and *World of Wonders* (1976) were concerned with illusion, Jungian psychology, and God and the devil. Davies also wrote an additional trilogy—*Rebel Angels* (1982), *High Spirits* (1983), and *What's Bred in the Bone* (1985). *The Cunning Man* (1995) was his last novel. He was a professor of English at the University of Toronto (1960–81). ■ See Patricia Monk, *The Smaller Infinity* (1982), and study by Judith S. Grant (1994).

DAVIS, ANGELA YVONNE (1944–), U.S. political activist. Born into a middle-class black family in Birmingham, Alabama, and recruited by Quakers to study at a progressive New York preparatory school, Davis won a scholarship to Brandeis University (1965), where she became the protégée of Marxist philosopher Herbert Marcuse. In 1969 she was hired to teach philosophy at the University of California, Los Angeles, but was dismissed (1970) for her radical views and her activity on behalf of the imprisoned Soledad brothers. Davis went underground after being linked to a courtroom shoot-out; subsequently acquitted of murder and conspiracy charges (1972), she returned to teaching and writing. She ran for vice president of the United States on the Communist party ticket (1980; 1984), continued to speak out against racism, and became a forceful advocate of penal reform. She wrote *Women, Race and Class* (1983), *Women, Culture and Politics* (1989), and *Blues Legacies and Black Feminism* (1998). ■ See her autobiography (1974) and *The Angela Davis Reader* (1998).

DAVIS, ARTHUR VINING (1867–1962), U.S. businessman. One of the most prominent and wealthy industrialists of the century, Davis was president (1910–28) and chairman (1928–57) of the Aluminum Co. of America (Alcoa) and a director of numerous other corporations and banks. In the course of popularizing aluminum pots and pans, household utensils, wire, ships, and airplane engines, he amassed a fortune of $400 million. After 1948 he purchased thousands of acres of land in southern Florida and played an important role in that area's economic development.

DAVIS, BENJAMIN OLIVER, SR. (1877–1970), U.S. general. Davis dropped out of Howard University during the Spanish-American War (1898) to enlist in the army, rising to sergeant during the Philippine insurrection and going on to teach military science at black colleges. During his 50-year army career he served as military attaché in Liberia and as commander of a national guard unit in Harlem. In 1940 Davis became the first African American to achieve the rank of brigadier general. His son, Benjamin O. Davis, Jr. (1912–), became the first African-American general in the air force (in 1954). ■ See Marvin Fletcher, *America's First Black General* (1989).

DAVIS, BETTE (Ruth Elizabeth Davis; 1908–1989), U.S. film actress. After a brief stage career, Davis started making films in Hollywood in 1931 and became an enduring movie star with her role in *Of Human Bondage* (1934). Not a classic Hollywood beauty, she specialized in playing intense, strong, often neurotic women in many melodramas in the 1930s and 1940s. She was famous (and often imitated) for her unique mannerisms and vocal quality. Among her more than 75 movies were *Dangerous* (Academy Award, 1935), *Jezebel* (Academy Award, 1938), *Dark Victory* (1939), *The Little Foxes* (1941), and *All About Eve* (1950). In later years she played more eccentric roles in less interesting movies. ■ See her autobiographies, *The Lonely Life* (1962) and *This N' That* (1987); Whitney Stine, *Mother Goddam* (1974); Charles Higham, *Bette* (1981); and Lawrence J. Quirk, *Fasten Your Seatbelts* (1990).

DAVIS, ELMER HOLMES (1890–1958), U.S. writer and broadcaster. A Rhodes scholar (1910–12) at Oxford, *New York Times* political commentator (1914–24), and novelist (1924–39), Davis joined CBS as a radio newscaster (1939) and became one of America's most prominent radio personalities. Known for his dry humor, calm and thoughtful comments, and unmistakable Hoosier drawl, Davis achieved fame for his analyses of the early years of World War II. When he headed the Office of War Information (1942–45), which coordinated the government's information and propaganda services, his liberal views on military censorship sparked controversy. Davis resumed his radio career (1945) with ABC. His best-selling *But We Were Born Free* (1954) attacked Sen. Joseph McCarthy and other political witchhunters. ■ See Roger Burlingame, *Don't Let Them Scare You* (1961).

DAVIS, HALLIE FLANAGAN. *See FLANIGAN, HALLIE.*

DAVIS, JOHN WILLIAM (1873–1955), U.S. lawyer and public official. A second-generation attorney from West Virginia, Davis was elected to Congress as a Democrat in 1910 but resigned in 1913 to become U.S. solicitor general and then ambassador to Great Britain (1918–21). He was a founding partner of a blue-chip Manhattan law firm, president of the American Bar Association (1922–24), and an unsuccessful Democratic compromise candidate for the U.S. presidency (1924). An opponent of the welfare state and a champion of conservative principles and states' rights, Davis held the record for the most cases argued before the Supreme Court (141), including his successful plea against Pres. Harry Truman's seizure of U.S. Steel and his unsuccessful defense of school segregation, both in 1952. ■ See William H. Harbaugh, *Lawyer's Lawyer* (1973).

DAVIS, MEYER (1895?–1976), U.S. bandleader and entrepreneur. Davis studied violin as a child; when he was barred from his school orchestra, he assembled his own five-piece band. He studied business and later law but dropped his studies when he found that his band could make money. He catered to the tastes of high society and formed a corporation that, at its height, booked as many as 1,000 musicians in 80 bands at one time. Davis himself conducted bands for the galas of uppercrust families and led bands at the inaugural balls of seven U.S. presidents. Among musicians emerging from Davis bands were Benny Goodman and the Dorsey Brothers.

DAVIS, MILES DEWEY, III (1926–1991), U.S. jazz trumpeter. Davis' father was a dental surgeon, his mother a music teacher. Both parents urged a medical career, but from age 12 Davis was determined to make the trumpet his life. After a brief, unhappy enrollment at the Juilliard School of Music, Davis worked in nightclubs in New York City with saxophonists Charlie Parker and Coleman Hawkins and later toured with the Billy Ekstine band. In the 1940s, he pioneered the movement called "cool jazz," characterized by less dominant horn techniques, which marked the transition from the "bebop" era. Over the next four decades he led many small groups, blending contemporary musical trends with jazz. In 1981, after a five-year hiatus, he resumed his performing career with appearances at the Kool Jazz Festival in New York City. ■ See biography by Bill Cole (1974); Eric Nisenson, *Round About Midnight* (1982); Jack Chambers, *Milestones: The Music and Times of Miles Davis* (2 vols., 1985); and his autobiography *Miles* (1989; with Quincy Troupe).

DAVIS, OSSIE (1917–), U.S. actor, director, and plawright. After attending Howard University (1938–41) and serving in the U.S. Army (1942–45), Davis pursued an acting career in New York and was associated with the American Negro Theater. He appeared in several Broadway shows during the 1950s, including *Raisin in the Sun* and *The Green Pastures*. Davis wrote and starred to *Purlie Victorious* (1961) and the movie based on it, *Gone Are the Days* (1963), and was also coauthor of the musical version, *Purlie* (1970). He directed the film *Cotton Comes to Harlem* (1970); acted in many films including *Do the Right Thing* (1989) and *I'm Not Rappaport* (1996); and appeared frequently on television and in movies with his wife, actress Ruby Dee (married 1948). They also were actively involved in the civil-rights movement. ■ See their joint autobiography, *With Ossie and Ruby* (1993).

DAVIS, SAMMY, JR. (1925–1990), U.S. entertainer. Born into a vaudeville family, Davis began his show-business career at the age of four as a singer and dancer with his father and adopted uncle, Will Mastin, in the Will Mastin Trio. The group played in the top nightclubs during the late 1940s and early 1950s and made numerous television appearances. An exuberant performer, Davis launched a solo career in the 1950s and starred in the popular Broadway musicals *Mr. Wonderful* (1956) and *Golden Boy* (1964) and in such Hollywood movies as *Anna Lucasta* (1959), *Ocean's 11* (1960), *Porgy and Bess* (1962), *A Man Called Adam* (1965), *One More Time* (1970), and *Tap* (1989). ■ See his autobiographies, *Yes I Can!* (1965), *Hollywood in a Suitcase* (1980), and *Why Me?* (1989).

DAVIS, STUART (1894–1964), U.S. painter. Davis began as a painter in the realist school that dominated American art at the turn of the century, but his style evolved and he became a leader of the American abstractionist movement. He was influenced by the work of the French modernists exhibited at the revolutionary Armory Show in New York City (1913). Throughout his career, cubist elements, the colors and themes of city life, and the rhythms of jazz were important aspects of his paintings. Among his best-known works were the *Eggbeater* series (1927–28), *Visa* (1951), and *Colonial Cubism* (1954). ■ See his autobiography (1945) and studies by Eugene C. Goosen (1959), John R. Lane (1978), and Patricia Hills (1996).

DAVIS, WILLIAM MORRIS (1850-1934), U.S, geologist and geographer. On the Harvard faculty from 1876 to 1912, Davis was responsible for systematizing the study and teaching of geography. He founded the science of geomorphology (the study of land forms) and wrote many authoritative books, including *Elementary Meteorology* (1894), *Geographical Essays* (1909), *The Coral Reef Problem* (1928), and *Origin of Limestone Caverns* (1930–31). Davis also founded the Association of American Geographers (1904).

DAVISSON, CLINTON JOSEPH (1881–1958), U.S. physicist. Davisson received a Ph.D. from Princeton (1911) and did research at the Bell Telephone Laboratories (1917–46). For his most important work, verifying Louis de Broglie's theory (1924) that particles of matter, particularly electrons, could behave like waves, Davisson shared the 1937 Nobel Prize in Physics with George P. Thomson. In addition to his pioneering experiments on electron diffraction, Davisson did important work in thermionic emission of metals and helped to develop the electron microscope.

DAWES, CHARLES GATES (1865–1951), U.S. banker and public official. A politically active (Republican) lawyer and banker, Davis served as U.S. comptroller of the currency (1897–1902), as the chief purchasing agent for U.S. forces in Europe during world War I, and as the first director of the U.S. budget (1921). For his proposal (1924; prepared with Owen D. Young), known as the Dawes Plan, which helped to stabilize post-war German finances, he shared the 1925 Nobel Peace Prize (with Sir Austen Chamberlain). Subsequently he was vice president of the United States (under Pres. Calvin Coolidge; 1925–29) and served Pres. Herbert Hoover as U.S. ambassador to Britain (1929-32), delegate to the London Naval Conference (1930), and president of the Reconstruction Finance Corp. (1932). His books included *A Journal of the Great War* (1921), *Notes as Vice President* (1935), and *Journal as Ambassador to Great Britain* (1939). ■ See biography by Bascom N. Timmons, *Portrait of an American* (1953).

DAWIDOWICZ, LUCY S. (1915–1990), U.S. historian. Dawidowicz studied at Hunter College (B.A. 1936), was a fellow at the YIVO Institute of Jewish Research in Vilna, Poland (1938–39), and during World War II worked at the YIVO in New York City (1940–46). After the war she was an education officer in displaced persons camps in Germany (1946–47). She conducted research on modern Jewish history under the aegis of the American Jewish Committee (1948–69), and received an M.A. from Columbia University (1961). A prominent scholar of the Holocaust, Dawidowicz taught at Yeshiva University in New York City (1969–78). Her major work, *The War Against the Jews, 1933–1945* (1975), asserted that extermination of the Jews was the centerpiece of Nazi leader Adolf Hitler's policies, not a byproduct of those policies. Her other books included *The Jewish Presence: Essays on Identity and History* (1977), *The Holocaust and the Historians* (1981), *On Equal Terms: Jews in America, 1881–1981* (1982), and *What is the Use of Jewish History?* (1992). ■ See her memoir of Vilna, *From That Place and Time* (1989).

DAWSON, WILLIAM LEVI (1899–1990), U.S. composer. One of the major African-American composers of the century, Dawson graduated from the Tuskegee Institute (1921) and headed the institute's School of Music (from 1931). He was best known for his choral arrangements and for the imaginative Negro Folk Symphony (1934), which utilized melodies and rhythms from Negro spirituals. He also headed the Tuskegee choir for 25 years and led the group on highly acclaimed world tours.

DAY, CLARENCE SHEPARD (1874–1935), U.S. essayist. Son of a Wall Street broker, Day graduated from Yale (1896) and pursued a business career until crippling arthritis forced him to retire (1903). He was an invalid for the rest of his life. Day turned to writing humorous essays and light verse and was a frequent contributor to the *New Yorker*. His three volumes of warm and witty family reminiscences, *God and My Father* (1932), *Life with Father* (1935), and *Life with*

Mother (1937), were extremely popular and were adapted for the stage by Howard Lindsay and Russel Crouse. Their play, *Life with Father* (1939), had one of the longest runs in Broadway history.

DAY, DORIS (Doris Kappelhoff; 1924–), U.S. singer and movie star. Doris Day was an aspiring dancer when at age 13 she was injured in a car crash. She later made a name as a band singer, working with Les Brown and others; radio familiarized millions of Americans with her lilting voice in such hits as "Que Sera Sera." Doris Day then became a box-office draw to the movies; she earned as much as a million dollars for movie roles that typically cast her as an innocent "girl next door." She appeared with Rock Hudson in *Pillow Talk* (1959) and with James Cagney in *Love Me or Leave Me* (1955), her finest role. She stopped making movies after *With Six You Get Eggroll* (1968). ■ See *Doris Day: Her Own Story* (1976; with A. E. Hotchner) and study by Eric Braun (1991).

DAY, DOROTHY (1897–1980), U.S. writer, publisher, and social activist. Day was a longtime socialist, a journalist on the *Call* and *The Masses*, a suffragist, and a supporter of the Industrial Workers of the World (the Wobblies). After long introspection led her to adopt Roman Catholicism, she founded (1933) the *Catholic Worker* with Peter Maurin (1877–1949). The monthly newspaper responded to Depression conditions by calling for social reconstruction. It urged establishment of hospitality houses for impoverished city dwellers; New York City's St. Joseph's House, located on the Lower East Side, was the prototype for this concept. By 1936 the *Catholic Worker* had achieved a circulation of 150,000 and the urban-shelter concept had spread to major U.S. cities. The newspaper advocated radical social views, supporting conscientious objectors during World War II, decrying the development and testing of nuclear arms in the postwar period, and opposing the Vietnam War. At its penny price, the paper promoted the Catholic Worker movement for five decades, and Dorothy Day continued to publish a regular column on its pages. ■ See her autobiography, *The Long Loneliness* (1954); Mel Piehl, *Breaking Bread* (1982); and James H. Forrest, *Love is the Measure* (1986).

DAY-LEWIS, CECIL (1904-1972), British poet and writer. Educated at Oxford, C. Day-Lewis was linked with his contemporaries W. H. Auden, Stephen Spender, and Louis MacNeice as a left-wing antifascist poet during the mid-1930s. After 1938, however, he became less political and wrote lyrical, traditional poetry, often in the form of heroic narrative. He was influenced at various times by the work of other poets, including Auden, John Donne, and W. B. Yeats. Among his works are *Collected Poems* (1935, 1954), *An Italian Visit* (1953), and *Poems* (1977). He also wrote literary criticism, well-known translations of Virgil from the Latin, and detective stories under the pseudonym Nicholas Blake. He succeeded John Masefield as poet laureate of England in

1968. ■ See his autobiography, *The Buried Day* (1960); biography by his son Sean Day-Lewis (1980); and study by Joseph N. Riddel (1971).

DAYAN, MOSHE (1915–1981), Israeli military and political leader. Born on a kibbutz, Dayan served with the Jewish militia in the 1930s and with the British army (in Syria) during World War II. He was an underground Haganah commando leader in the war for Israeli independence (1948), directing the final battles for Jerusalem. As chief of staff (1953–58) he commanded the 1956 Sinai campaign, and as minister of defense (1967–74) he planned the successful strategy during the 1967 Six-Day War. However, he was blamed for Israel's unpreparedness during the 1973 Arab-Israeli War and was dropped from the cabinet in 1974. Returning to government as Menachem Begin's foreign minister (1977–79), he was the chief architect of the 1979 Israeli-Eyptian peace treaty. He resigned over disagreements regarding the government's hard-line policy toward the Arabs on the West Bank. ■ See his books *Diary of the Sinai Campaign* (1966), *The Story of My Life* (1976), and *Breakthrough: A Personal Account of the Egypt-Israel Peace Negotiations* (1981); study by his daughter Yael Dayan, *My Father, His Daughter* (Eng. trans. 1985); biography by Shabtai Teveth (Eng. trans. 1972); and Robert Slater, *Warrior Statesman* (1991).

DAZAI, OSAMU (Tsushima Shuji; 1909–1948), Japanese novelist. The son of a wealthy landowner and politician, Dazai led a dark and dissipated life that was mirrored in his gloomy and despairing novels. He was an idol of post–World War II Japanese youth who, in the wake of Japan's defeat, nihilistically rejected traditional values. His best-known works were *Tsugaru* (1944), *The Setting Sun* (1947; Eng. trans. 1956), *Villon's Wife* (1947; Eng. trans. 1956), and *No Longer Human* (1948; Eng. trans. 1956). After several unsuccessful attempts, he finally succeeded in committing suicide in 1948. ■ See study by James A. O'Brien (1975).

DEACON, SIR GEORGE EDWARD RAVEN (1906–1984), British oceanographer. Deacon prepared comprehensive accounts of the water masses of the South Atlantic Ocean (1933) and the Southern Ocean (1937) for the British government's Antarctic Discovery Investigations project. During World War II he worked on underwater acoustics, and his research team was the first to make a spectrum analysis of sea waves and to demonstrate the value of such an analysis. He directed the National Institute of Oceanography in Britain (1949–71), which was responsible for many advances in oceanographic research including the development of methods of measuring deep currents.

DEAKIN, ALFRED (1856–1919), Australian political leader. A lawyer and journalist, Deakin served as a Liberal member of the Victoria legislature (1880–1900). During this period he was a strong proponent of the use of irrigation and wrote extensively on the subject. A leader of the federation movement, he drafted the constitution bill that created the Australian commonwealth and helped guide it through the British Parliament (1900). Deakin was Australia's first attorney-general (1901–03) and was prime minister three times (1903–04; 1905–08; 1909–10). Although he was responsible for instituting a protective tariff (1907), he sponsored such progressive legislation as child-labor laws, pensions for the aged, minimum-wage laws, and an easing of immigration curbs. ■ See his *The Federal Story* (1944); biography by J. A. La Nauze (1965); and Al Gabay, *The Mystic Life of Alfred Deakin* (1992).

DEAKIN, ARTHUR (1890–1955), British labor leader. A worker from age 13, Deakin became a full-time union official in 1919 and was appointed national secretary of the General Workers' Group (London) of the Transport and General Workers' Union, Britain's largest, in 1932. He worked closely with its general secretary, Ernest Bevin, whom he succeeded when Bevin joined the war cabinet (1940). The dominant voice of the British labor movement after World War II, he opposed wildcat strikes and advocated wage restraints and increased production. A tough anticommunist, he denounced the World Federation of Trade Unions as an instrument of Soviet policy (1948) and helped set up the rival International Confederation of Free Trade Unions. ■ See Victor L. Allen, *Trade Union Leadership* (1957).

DEAN, JAMES BYRON (1931–1955), U.S. actor. Catapulted to stardom with roles in three films, *East of Eden* (1954), *Rebel Without a Cause* (1955), and *Giant* (1956), Dean personified the confused, frustrated, and restless American youth of the mid-1950s. He became a cult hero, and his fame reached legendary proportions after his violent death in an automobile crash at age 24. ■ See biography by Venable Herndon (1974); David Dalton, and Ron Cayen, *James Dean: American Icon* (1984); Paul Alexander, *Boulevard of Broken Dreams* (1994); and Donald Spoto, *Rebel* (1996).

DEAN, JOHN WESLEY, III (1938–), U.S. attorney. An ambitious graduate of Georgetown Law School (1965), Dean became chief legal counsel to Pres. Richard Nixon at age 31. Assigned to conduct an in-house investigation when the Watergate crisis first broke, the president's counsel decided to "tell all" to the Senate investigating committee in 1973, implicating Nixon and other top administration figures in the Watergate cover-up; they eventually left office in disgrace. Dean was disbarred, served a brief prison sentence for conspiring to obstruct justice, and launched a lucrative new career on the lecture and publishing circuit, receiving a $350,000 advance on his book *Blind Ambition* (1976). He also wrote a sequel, *Lost Honor* (1983).

DEAN, MAN MOUNTAIN (Frank Simmons Leavitt; 1891-1953), U.S. wrestler. Leavitt began wrestling in New York City in 1906 and won the armed-forces championship during World War I. He changed his name (1931?), and as the awesome-looking Man Mountain—he weighed more than 300 pounds and sported a full beard—he was one of the first showman wrestlers of the Depression era. Before his retirement in 1937, he participated in close to 7,000 professional matches and was an internationally known celebrity. He also appeared in more than 30 Hollywood motion pictures.

DEBAKEY, MICHAEL ELLIS (1908–   ), U.S. surgeon. DeBakey received his medical training at Tulane, Strasbourg, and Heidelberg universities and became a pioneer in the field of heart surgery. He developed a pump that later became a component of the heart-lung machine (1932), originated surgical procedures to correct blockages of the aorta, developed a technique to replace diseased blood vessels with dacron tubing, and successfully implanted a mechanical device to aid a malfunctioning heart (1967). He was a professor of surgery (from 1948), president (1969–79), and chancellor (1979–96) of the Baylor University College of Medicine. He wrote several books, including *A Surgeon's Visit to China* (1974), *The Living Heart* (1977; with A. M. Grotto), and *The New Living Heart* (1997; with A. M. Grotto). He continued to perform operations into his nineties.

DEBREU, GERARD (1921–   ), French-born U.S. economist. Debreu received a doctorate in economics from the University of Paris (1946), was a researcher with the Cowles Foundation at the University of Chicago (1950–55) and Yale (1955-62), and was a professor of mathematics and economics at the University of California at Berkeley (from 1962). Influenced by the theories of John von Neumann, Debreu did theoretical research and developed mathematical models to analyze conditions that affect general market equilibrium. His work, which was influential among economic researchers and forecasters, attempted to demonstrate how prices operate to balance supply and demand in complex economies. His theories appeared in his book *Theory of Value: An Axiomatic Analysis of Economic Equilibrium* (1959), and in his papers collected in *Mathematical Economics* (1983). He was awarded the 1983 Nobel Prize for Economic Science.

DEBS, EUGENE VICTOR (1855–1926), U.S. political and labor leader. Debs, who went to work on the railroad at age 15, was a founder and president of the American Railway Union (1893). After spending six months in jail for leading the 1894 Pullman strike, he became a socialist and was a founder of the Socialist party of America. He was a charismatic public speaker and one of the most popular and respected socialist leaders in American history. Debs was a

candidate for the U.S. presidency five times (1900–12; 1920), but he never received more than 6 percent of the popular vote. A vocal opponent of World War I, he was imprisoned in 1918 for sedition. While in jail he polled nearly 1 million votes as the socialist candidate for president (1920). He was released in 1921. ■ See Ray Ginger, *The Bending Cross* (1949); study by Nick Salvatore (1982); and Marguerite Young, *Harp Song for a Radical* (1999).

DEBUSSY, (ACHILLE) CLAUDE (1862–1918), French composer. The "century's first musician," as composer Igor Stravinsky called him, Debussy created a new harmonic vocabulary in which timbre and rhythm functioned as melody had previously. After studying at the Paris Conservatory (1873–84), he achieved fame in 1894 with *Prélude à l'après-midi d'un faune,* controversy in 1902 with the dreamlike opera *Pelléas et Mélisande,* and sensuous beauty in 1905 with the tone poem *La Mer.* Moving away from impressionism, he wrote *Jeux* (1912) for the Ballet Russe and *Etudes* (1915), which explored fresh pianistic harmonies and colors. ■ See biography by Edward Lockspeiser (2 vols., 1962–65) and studies by Maurice Dumesnil (1979), Robert Orledge (1983), and Roger Nichols (1998).

DEBYE, PETER JOSEPH WILHELM (1884–1966), Dutch-born physical chemist. Trained in Munich (Ph.D. 1910), Debye taught at the universities of Zurich, Utrecht, Göttingen, and Leipzig before moving to Berlin as professor of theoretical physics and head of the new Kaiser Wilhelm Institute for Physics (1934-40), which he named the Max Planck Institute. He won the 1936 Nobel Prize in Chemistry for his work on X-ray diffraction and his investigations of dipole movements—the measurement of positive and negative electric charges within molecules. Refusing to assume German citizenship after the outbreak of World War II, Debye emigrated to the United States, where he taught chemistry at Cornell Universty (1940-50).

DE DUVE, CHRISTIAN RENÉ (1917–   ), British-born Belgian biologist. A pioneer in the field of cell biology, de Duve headed research laboratories at the University of Louvain, the Nobel Institute (Stockholm), Washington University (St. Louis), and the Rockefeller University (New York; 1962–88). He utilized the electron microscope in his research and discovered lysosomes, the cell components that, he said, act like "stomachs of the cell" by breaking down food particles for cellular digestion. He shared the 1974 Nobel Prize in Physiology or Medicine with Albert Claude and George Palade. In 1975 he was named president of the International Institute of Cellular and Molecular Pathology in Brussels.

DEE, RUBY (Ruby Ann Wallace; 1924–   ), U.S. actress. An African American raised in New York City's Harlem. Ruby Dee studied French and Spanish at Hunter College, then during World War II trained with other "apprentices," including Harry Belafonte and Sidney Poitier, at the American Negro Theater. She received favorable reviews for her first Broadway role in *Jeb* (1946), which also featured Ossie Davis (the play closed after a week). Dee won recognition in Davis' *Purlie Victorious* (1961), establishing herself as one of the few African-American character actresses performing on the American stage. Her 1970 performance with James Earl Jones in *Boesman and Lena*—a commentary on apartheid in South Africa—stunned critics. Dee also performed in television, winning a 1968 Emmy Award for the documentary *Now Is the Time,* and in motion pictures. She and husband Ossie Davis (married in 1948) were active in civil-rights and other political movements. ■ See their joint autobiography, *With Ossie and Ruby* (1988), and Dee's selected writings in *My One Good Nerve* (1998).

DE FOREST, LEE (1873–1961), U.S. inventor. A Yale graduate (Ph.D 1899), De Forest was a solitary and individualistic inventor who held more than 300 patents and made and lost four fortunes. He developed (1906) the triode electron tube, the precursor of the modern radio tube and one of the most influential inventions of the century. The audion, as he called the device, spurred growth in the fields of electronics and communications because of its potential for generating, detecting, and amplifying radio waves. Selling his rights to the audion, he later designed a movie-sound system and contributed to the development of the phonograph, telephone, television, radar, and diathermy. ■ See his autobiography, *Father of Radio* (1950); Israel E. Levine, *Electronics Pioneer* (1964); and study by James A. Hijiya (1992).

DE GASPERI, ALCIDE (1881–1954), Italian political leader. A leader of the Italian irredentist movement in his native Trentino, then part of Austria, de Gasperi served in the Austrian parliament (1911–16) and later in the Italian parliament (1921–24) after Trentino was united with Italy. A founder of the Italian Popular party, a Roman Catholic political organization, he was arrested by the fascists (1926) and served 16 months in prison. After his release he served as Vatican librarian, and during World War II he was a leader of the underground resistance and helped organize the center-right Christian Democratic party, which became the dominant party in postwar Italy. Serving as premier (1945–53), de Gasperi instituted land reforms and promoted economic growth. He ousted the communists and left-socialists from the central government, sought close ties with the United States, led Italy into the North Atlantic Treaty Organization, and championed European integration.

DE GAULLE, CHARLES ANDRÉ JOSEPH MARIE (1890–1970), French military and political leader. De Gaulle's father, a Lille schoolteacher who raised his sons to work for the restoration of French glory, sent Charles to the national military academy of St. Cyr; he graduated in 1912. He served in the infantry during World War I and was captured by the Germans during the Battle of Verdun. A lecturer at the Staff College during the interwar period, he lobbied for a mobile defense strategy based on the tank and became unpopular with the military establishment for his criticism of France's existing reliance on static fortifications. Promoted to brigadier general and undersecretary of war just before the fall of France (1940), he refused to capitulate to the Germans and fled to London. There, he announced the loss of a battle, not the war, and constituted himself leader of the Free French Resistance. In 1944 he was chosen to head the provisional government of liberated France, but he resigned in 1946 out of autocratic disdain for parliamentary politics. The 1958 coup d'état in Algeria and the threat of civil war brought the general out of retirement to create a Fifth French Republic with himself as a strong president. During the next 11 years Pres. de Gaulle supported independence for Algeria and other French African colonies, pulled the French military out of the North Atlantic Treaty Organization command, developed a French nuclear strike capacity, and opposed British entry into the Common Market. Although economic conditions generally improved, education and social welfare programs were neglected and widespread student and worker protests took place in 1968. De Gaulle resigned in 1969 over the failure of a referendum on constitutional reform. ■ See his *War Memoirs* (5 vols., Eng. trans. 1955–60) and *Memoirs of Hope* (Eng. trans. 1971), and biographies by Brian Crozier (1973), Bernard Ledwidge (1982), Don Cook (1983), and Jean Lacouture (3 vols., 1984–86; Eng. trans. 2 vols., 1990–92).

DE GENNES, PIERRE-GILLES (1932–), French physicist. Called by some of his colleagues "the Isaac Newton of our time," de Gennes taught at the University of Paris (1961–71) and Collège de France, Paris (from 1971) and earned an international reputation for devising rules and mathematical formulas to describe complex physical phenomena. He was best known for describing the structure and behavior of superconducting liquid crystals and polymers and was awarded the 1991 Nobel Prize for Physics for his research. His books included *The Physics of Liquid Crystals* (1974; 2nd ed. 1993), *Scaling Concepts in Polymer Physics* (1979), *Simple Views on Condensed Matter* (1992; rev. ed. 1998), and *Fragile Objects* (1996).

DE HAVILLAND, SIR GEOFFREY (1882–1965), British aircraft designer and manufacturer. Although the first plane De Havilland designed crashed on takeoff (1908), he flew his second plane successfully (1910) and designed fighter planes during World War I. Later designs by De Havilland Aircraft (estab. 1920) included the *Moth* sport biplane, the famous World War II fighter-bomber *Mosquito,* the first British plane to break the sound barrier (1941), and the world's first jet airliner (1948). By the early 1950s, his jets were in use worldwide. Knighted in 1944, De Havilland was the only civilian in aviation to receive (1962) the prestigious

Order of Merit. Two of his three sons were killed while testing his planes.

DEHMELT, HANS G. (1922–   ), German-born U.S. physicist. Dehmelt studied physics while serving in the German army during World War II, but became an American prisoner of war in 1945. He subsequently continued his studies at the University of Göttingen (Ph.D. 1950) and Duke University (1952–55), taught at the University of Washington (1961–   ), and became a U.S. citizen (1961). In 1955 he developed a device, using both electric and magnetic fields, to isolate and capture electrons and ions (electrically charged atoms) so that they could be accurately studied. In 1973 he was able to isolate a single electron, and in 1975 he devised a method for measuring atomic frequencies and quantum jumps with unprecedented accuracy. Dehmelt shared the 1989 Nobel Prize in Physics with Wolfgang Paul and Norman F. Ramsey.

DEISENHOFER, JOHANN (1943–   ), German biochemist. Deisenhofer studied at the Max Planck Institute for Biochemistry at Martinsried (Ph.D. 1974) and did research there until moving (1988) to the Howard Hughes Medical Institute and University of Texas in Dallas. An expert in X-ray crystallography, Deisenhofer worked (1982–85) with colleagues Hartmut Michel and Robert Huber in studying photosynthesis. The trio mapped the three-dimensional structure of the four-protein complex, consisting of more than 10,000 atoms, found in cell membranes. The cluster of proteins, called the photosynthetic reaction center, is essential to the process of photosynthesis. Deisenhofer, Michel, and Huber shared the 1988 Nobel Prize in Chemistry for their pioneering research.

DE KLERK, FREDERIK WILLEM (1936–   ), South African political leader. Born into a family active in National party politics—both his father and uncle were government ministers—de Klerk practiced law and entered Parliament in 1972. A staunch supporter of apartheid, he served in the cabinet (1978–89) and as Transvaal National party leader (1982–89) before becoming national leader (1989) of the party. After being elected president of South Africa (1989) he underwent an ideological conversion and sponsored a series of fundamental reforms that dismantled the system of racial segregation. He released Nelson Mandela after 26 years of imprisonment (1990), recognized the African National Congress, and played a major role in getting the minority white population to accept the peaceful transition to a nonracial democracy. After the election of 1994, the first open to all races, Nelson Mandela was elected president and de Klerk served as executive deputy president in a unity government. He left office in 1996 and led the Nationalists as an opposition party. He retired from politics in 1997. De Klerk and Mandela shared the 1993 Nobel Peace Prize. ■ See his autobiography, *The Last Trek: A New Beginning* (1999).

DE KOONING, WILLEM (1904–1997), Dutch-born U.S. painter. A leader in the abstract-expressionist movement that dominated American painting in the 1950s, de Kooning utilized violent brush strokes and brilliant colors to emphasize energy and spontaneity in his works. Although his paintings demonstrated the principles of the movement—the absence of visible reality and an emphasis on gesture—he retained an interest in the human figure, a theme that alternated with abstraction in his work and that was seen in his famous "Women" series (1950–52). During the 1970s he produced expressionistic sculptures. ■ See Thomas B. Hess, *Willem de Kooning* (1959, 1968); Paul Cummings, *Willem de Kooning* (1983); and study by Harry F. Gaugh (1983).

DE LA MARE, WALTER (1873–1956), British writer. After a career as an office worker (1890–1908), De la Mare devoted himself to writing. Belonging to no literary school or group, he wrote 50 volumes of essays, stories, novels, and poetry, much of it for children. He was uniquely able to evoke the grotesque and whimsical. His imaginative writing often revolved around spirits and dreams. Among his best-known works are the novel *Memoirs of a Midget* (1921), the anthology *Come Hither* (1923), and the poem "The Listeners." ■ See studies by John A. Atkins (1947) and Doris McCrosson (1966) and Theresa Whistler, *Imagination of the Heart* (1993).

DE LA ROCHE, MAZO (1879–1961), Canadian novelist. De la Roche studied art and attended the University of Toronto before writing short stories and one-act plays during the early 1920s. She made her mark when she won a coveted *Atlantic Monthly* prize for *Jalna* (1927), the gripping saga of the Whiteoak family, which she perpetuated in 15 additional books (1929–60). The Jalna cycle—more popular in the United States and Europe than in Canada—was acclaimed for its evocation of the rural Ontario setting and its individualized characters. De la Roche's other writings included *Portrait of a Dog* (1930), *Beside a Norman Tower* (1934), and the autobiographical *Ringing the Changes* (1957). ■ See studies by Ronald Hambleton (1966), George Hendrick (1970), and Joan Givner (1989).

DELAUNAY, ROBERT (1885–1941), French painter. Delaunay studied theater design (1902) and worked with a decorator before he completed the series of *Cathedrals* and *Cities* (1909–10) that reflected cubist influence. These paintings, especially *Tour Eiffel* (1910), indicated Delaunay's interest in the lyric-rhythmical qualities of color that later led him away from the cubists. His work eventually became completely abstract arrangements of colored discs that seemed to flash and spin on the canvas. Delaunay's style was dubbed "orphism" by the poet Guillaume Apollinaire in 1912, and Delaunay was credited with contributing to cubism an emphasis on color and abstraction. He was married to the artist Sonia Delaunay (from 1910). ■ See study by Michel Hood (Eng. trans. 1977).

DELAUNAY, SONIA (Sonia Stern; 1885–1979), Russian-born French artist. Sonia Delaunay exerted a major influence on 20th-century modernism. Her achievements ranged from painting to large-scale tapestries and fashion design. Her early work was influenced by folk art and by the artists Paul Gauguin, Vincent van Gogh, and particularly Henri Matisse. Her marriage to the artist Robert Delaunay (1910) was stimulating to both their creative efforts, and she encouraged Robert Delaunay's renewed concern with the creative possibilities of color after a period of monochrome cubism. She designed stage costumes and turned increasingly to fashion and textile design in the 1920s. After her husband's death (1941), she consolidated his work and theoretical contributions. Her later work included book illustrations, gouaches, drawings, oil paintings, and tapestries woven at Aubusson. ▪ See study by Arthur A. Cohen (1975) and biographies by Axel Madsen (1989) and Stanley Baron (1995).

DELBRÜCK, MAX (1906–1981), German-born U.S. biologist. A recipient of a Ph.D. in physics from the University of Göttingen (1930), Delbrück fled Nazi rule and emigrated to the United States in 1937. He did his most important work at Vanderbilt University (1940–47) and the California Institute of Technology (1947–77). Switching his research interests to biology and genetics, he developed the plaque technique that led to the purification of a virus. In collaboration with Salvador Luria (1943) he studied the interaction between viruses and the bacteria they infect and demonstrated that both could mutate, thus changing their resistance and infectious characteristics. This work proved essential to the development of vaccines against viral diseases. The informal collaboration of Delbrück, Luria, and Alfred Hershey, the pioneers of molecular biology, resulted in their joint award of the 1969 Nobel Prize in Physiology or Medicine. ▪ See Ernst P. Fischer, *Thinking About Science* (1988).

DELCASSÉ, THÉOPHILE (1852–1923), French public official. After graduating from the University of Toulouse (1874), Delcassé became a journalist in Paris. In 1889 he was elected to parliament and in 1893 became under secretary for colonies. As minister of foreign affairs (1898–1905). Delcassé reshaped the European balance of power by skillfully negotiating the Entente Cordiale (1904) with the British and mediating with the Russians. His policies led eventually to the creation of the Triple Entente (1907). He served as ambassador to Russia (1913–14) and returned to head the ministry of foreign affairs during World War I (1914–15). ▪ See study by Christopher Andrew (1968).

DELDERFIELD, RONALD FREDERICK (1912–1972), British novelist. Originally a journalist, R. F. Delderfield became a fiction writer after World War II, producing novels, successful plays, and popular historical works. His comic play about life in the Royal Air Force (R.A.F.) during World War II, *Worm's Eye View* (1945), played for more than five years on the London stage. He wrote massive, panoramic family sagas through which he hoped "to project the English way of life in the tradition of Hardy and Galsworthy." These novels, more popular in the United States than in Britian, sold in the millions in paperback, despite critics' complaints that they were long, tedious, and poorly written. Among them is the multivolume chronicle of the Swann family, *God is an Englishman* (1970), *Theirs Was the Kingdom* (1971), and *Give Us This Day* (1973). *For My Own Amusement* (1972) was autobiographical. ▪ See study by Sanford V. Sternlicht (1988).

DELEDDA, GRAZIA (1871–1936), Italian novelist. Deledda spent much of her adult life to Rome, but she evoked the rugged Sardinian setting of her youth in such novels as *Ashes* (1904; Eng. trans. 1908) and *The Mother* (1920; Eng. trans. 1923). Her narratives focused on the inner struggles of often inarticulate characters. Although some critics feel that her work has been overrated, she won the 1926 Nobel Prize in Literature. The autobiographical work *Cosima* (1937; Eng. trans. 1988) was published posthumously.

DE LEON, DANIEL (1852–1914), Curaçao-born U.S. political leader and theoretician. Greatly admired by V. I. Lenin, the founder of bolshevism, and considered by some to have been America's greatest socialist thinker, De Leon was leader of New York's tiny Socialist Labor party (1890–1914) and a founder of the Industrial Workers of the World (1905). He advocated socialist unions based on industries rather than crafts and criticized most contemporary union leaders and political socialists. Although his political following remained small, his vivid and erudite writings and speeches, concerned with the problems facing the revolutionary movement of the time, influenced the thinking of many American radicals. ▪ See biographies by Carl Reeve (1972) and Stephen Coleman (1990).

DELIBES, MIGUEL (1920–   ), Spanish novelist. A journalist and law professor, Delibes at first wrote realisitic novels that portrayed ordinary people in commonplace settings. His most popular work, written from the viewpoint of boyhood, was *The Path* (1950; Eng. trans. 1961). He was also noted for *Smoke on the Ground* (1962; Eng. trans. 1972), an account of the relationship of the individual and society to nature, and *Five Hours with Mario* (1966; Eng. trans. 1988), a long interior monologue consisting of the thoughts of a conservative, middle-class widow "conversing" with the corpse of her liberal husband shortly before the funeral. His later novels were increasingly experimental and concerned the threat to human dignity posed by technological society. *The Hedge* (1969; Eng. trans. 1983), influenced by the work of Franz Kafka, presented a nightmarish vision of dehumanization in which the protagonist turns into a sheep.

He also wrote *The Stuff of Heroes* (1987; Eng. trans. 1990) and *The War of Our Ancestors* (1990; Eng. trans. 1992). ■ See study by Janet Diaz (1971).

DELIUS, FREDERICK (1862–1934), British composer. After operating an orange grove in Florida (1884–85), Delius studied music in Leipzig, where he became a friend of the Norwegian composer Edvard Grieg. In 1888 he retired to Grez-sur-Loing, near Paris, with his wife, the painter Jelka Rosen, and he remained there for the rest of his life. In his last years he was blind and paralyzed, but he worked through an amanuensis, Eric Fenby. The conductor Sir Thomas Beecham promoted his work in Britain. Nostalgic, somewhat impressionistic, and rich and sweet in its harmonies, his music is best exemplified by works such as *On Hearing the First Cuckoo in Spring* (1912), *Summer Night on the River* (1912) for orchestra, and *Sea-Drift* (1903) for baritone, chorus, and orchestra. ■ See Eric Fenby, *Delius as I Knew Him* (rev. ed. 1981), and studies by Sir Thomas Beecham (1959) and Alan Jefferson (1972).

DELL, FLOYD (1887–1969), U.S. writer. A member of the avant-garde literary movement in Chicago before coming to New York (1913), Dell was a major figure in the bohemian world of Greenwich Village through the late 1920s. He treated love, marriage, and family life candidly and realistically in his novels, plays, and numerous articles; his best-known works include *Moon-Calf* (1920), *Janet March* (1923), and *Love in the Machine Age* (1930). A utopian radical, he served as editor of the prominent left-wing magazines *The Masses*, the *Liberator*, and *The New Masses*. ■ See his autobiography, *Homecoming* (1933); the study by John E. Hart (1971); and biography by Douglas Clayton (1994).

DELLER, ALFRED (1912–1979), British concert singer. A countertenor, Deller was born with such a rare voice that he was unable to find a teacher and instead became a consummate musician through his own efforts. He began singing in the chorus at his parish church and in 1940 was appointed lay clerk at Canterbury Cathedral. Deller gave his first London concert in 1944; in 1947 he joined the choir at London's St. Paul's Cathedral. In 1948 he formed the Deller Consort for the purpose of performing and recording authentic Renaissance and Baroque music, particularly Purcell and Handel, and he was credited with single-handedly reviving the countertenor repertory that had been ignored for almost 200 years. ■ See biography by Michael and Mollie Hardwick (1969).

DELLINGER, DAVID (1915–), U.S. political activist, writer, and editor. A Phi Beta Kappa graduate of Yale (1936), Dellinger studied English at Oxford (1936–37), then attended the Yale Divinity School (1937–39) and Union Theological Seminary (1939–40). Although best known as one of the "Chicago 7," Dellinger was a leader in social protest movements for nearly half a century. Despite his eligibility as a minister for an automatic draft exemption, he served two prison terms during World War II for refusing draft induction. During the 1950s he was active on behalf of Ethel and Julius Rosenberg, leftists who were convicted of espionage. While working as a printer (1946–67), Dellinger edited the magazine *Liberation* (1956–75); he later edited *Seven Days* Magazine (1975–80). He drew national attention as a leader of the peace movement during the Vietnam War. He chaired the National Mobilization Commission to End the War in Vietnam (1967–71). In 1969, Dellinger (then in his mid-50s) was one of the protestors indicted for conspiracy to incite a riot at the 1968 Democratic convention in Chicago. A much publicized trial followed, and the seven defendants were acquitted of conspiracy. He remained an active pacifist, practicing civil disobedience in antinuclear protests and opposing draft registration requirements. His writings included a volume of essays, *Revolutionary Nonviolence* (1970), *More Power Than We Know* (1975), and *Vietnam Memoirs* (1986). He edited *Beyond Survival: New Directions for the Disarmament Movement* (1983; with Michael Albert). ■ See his autobiography, *From Yale to Jail* (1993).

DEL MONACO, MARIO (1905–1982), Italian tenor. A handsome and dramatic tenor, Del Monaco made his Milan debut in 1941 as Pinkerton in *Madama Butterfly* and sang at New York's Metropolitan Opera from 1951 to 1959. He sang (and recorded) most of the great Verdi and Puccini roles and was particularly acclaimed for his portrayal of Otello. Del Monaco appeared in memorable performances with Maria Callas and Renata Tebaldi and was voted the world's best tenor by an international jury in 1957. He retired in 1973.

DELORIA, VINE VICTOR, JR. (1933–), U.S. writer and attorney. Rejecting the aid of missionaries, anthropologists, and other do-gooders, Deloria, a Sioux from South Dakota, became a spokesperson for his people as executive director of the National Congress of American Indians (1964–67) and as the author of *Custer Died for Your Sins, An Indian Manifesto* (1969). He then earned a law degree (1970) in order to help tribes secure their rights. His other works included *We Talk, You Listen* (1970), *Behind the Trail of Broken Treaties* (1974), *The Metaphysics of Modern Existence* (1979), *American Indians, American Justice* (1983; with Clifford M. Lytle), and *Red Earth, White Lies* (1995). He taught at the University of Arizona (1978–90) and the University of Colorado (1990–). ■ See Robert A. Warrior, *Tribal Secrets* (1995).

DELVAUX, PAUL (1897–1994), Belgian artist. Influenced by the surrealists Salvador Dalí and René Magritte, Delvaux began to paint improbable subjects in classic perspective and meticulous detail during the late 1930s. His canvases of nude women strolling somnambulistically with fully clothed men have been called "a commentary on sexual schizophrenia." Other dreamlike works depicted skeletons, empty railway stations, and deserted landscapes. He taught painting in Brussels (1950-62). ■ See study by Marc Rombaut (Eng. trans. 1990).

DE MILLE, AGNES GEORGE (1909–1993), U.S. dancer and choreographer. The daughter of playwright William de Mille, granddaughter of economist Henry George, and niece of movie director Cecil B. DeMille, Agnes de Mille toured Europe and the United States as a dancer (1929–40) after she joined the Ballet (now American Ballet) Theatre as a choreographer. Her best-known ballets included *Rodeo* (1942) and *Full River Legend* (1948). However, it was as a choreographer of such Broadway musicals as *Oklahoma!* (1943), *Carousel* (1945), *Brigadoon* (1947), and *Paint Your Wagon* (1951) that she received national acclaim. For the first time in the history of musical comedy, dance was used to advance the plot and enhance the drama of the show. Her innovative choreography exposed a mass audience to serious dance for the first time. Her later works included the ballets *The Informer* (1988) and *The Other* (1992). She wrote *To a Young Dancer* (1962), *Book of the Dance* (1963), and a study of Martha Graham (1991). ■ See her autobiographies, *Dance to the Piper* (1952), *And Promenade Home* (1958), *Speak to Me, Dance with Me* (1973), *Where the Wings Grow* (1978), and *Reprieve* (1981); and Carol Easton, *No Intermissions* (1996).

DEMILLE, CECIL B. (1881–1959), U.S. film producer and director. DeMille founded a studio with Jesse L. Lasky and Samuel Goldwyn (1913) that grew into Paramount Pictures. His production of the feature-length movie *The Squaw Man* (1914) put Hollywood on the map as a major film center. During the 1920s he directed a series of sociosexual comedies of contemporary manners (*Why Change Your Wife?*, 1920) that significantly influenced public taste. But DeMille was most closely identified with the mammoth epic. The Bible was his favorite source, and *The Ten Commandments* (1923; remake, 1956) and *King of Kings* (1927) were popular successes. Even his westerns (*The Plainsman*, 1937) were historical spectacles. *The Greatest Show on Earth* (Academy Award, 1952) was the only contemporary story produced by the master showman in the last decade of his career. ■ See his *Autobiography* (1959) and biography by Charles Higham (1973).

DEMIREL, SÜLEYMAN (1924–), Turkish political leader. Demirel, a graduate of the engineering school of Istanbul Technical University (1949), oversaw the construction of a series of hydroelectric dams while serving as head of the State Irrigation Administration (1955–60). He entered politics in the early 1960s and became leader of the conservative Justice party (1964). His first three terms as prime minister (1965–71) were marred by domestic violence

and he was forced to resign by the military (1971). He subsequently headed three additional coalition governments (1975–77; 1977–78; 1979–80), but ethnic clashes, parliamentary inaction, and increasing domestic violence led to his ouster by a military coup (1980). After democratic policies were restored in the late 1980s, Demirel headed the True Path party and served as prime minister of a right/left coalition government (1991–93). He was elected president of Turkey following the sudden death of President Turgut Ozal (1993) and served in office until 2000.

DEMPSEY, JACK (William Harris Dempsey; 1895–1983), U.S. boxer. Dempsey left grade school to work in the copper mines of his native Colorado. An aggressive, colorful fighter famous for his dangerous left hook and his bobbing-and-weaving style, Dempsey made his debut in the ring as Kid Blackie (1914) and five years later, at age 24, defeated 35-year-old Jess Willard for the heavyweight title (1919). In 1926 he was upset by Gene Tunney in a 10-round decision. A rematch bout with Tunney the next year, known as the "Battle of the Long Count," set a record for gate receipts and was one of the most controversial in boxing history. After Dempsey knocked Tunney to the floor in the seventh round, the referee stopped the count for four seconds until Dempsey retreated to a neutral corner; Tunney recovered and went on to win the bout on a decision. Dempsey never regained his crown and retired in 1940 to become a successful New York restaurateur. ■ See his autobiography (1977); studies by Nat Fleischer (1972) and Randy Roberts (1979); and Roger Kahn; *A Flame of Pure Fire* (1999).

DEMUTH, CHARLES (1883–1935), U.S. painter. Demuth studied at the Pennsylvania Academy of Fine Arts (1905–13) and traveled in Europe during the same period. He was best known for his watercolors of flowers and fruits and his paintings of theatrical figures. The influence of French cubism on his work was most apparent in his paintings of factories and industrial sites. Among his characteristic later paintings was *I Saw the Figure 5 in Gold* (1928). ■ See biography by Emily Farnham (1971).

DENEUVE, CATHERINE (Catherine Dorléac; 1943–), French film actress. An actor's daughter, Deneuve became a film star in her teens and subsequently acted in over 70 films. She appeared in two French musicals, *The Umbrellas of Cherbourg* (1964) and *The Young Girls of Rochefort* (1966), interrupted by her role as a mentally disturbed girl in *Repulsion* (1965). Director Luis Buñuel cast the cool blond beauty in *Belle de Jour* (1966) and *Tristana* (1970). She also starred in François Truffaut's *The Last Metro* (1980), and in *Scene of the Crime* (1986), *Indochine* (1992; Best Actress Award in France), *Place Vendôme* (1998), and *Dancer in the Dark* (2000).

DENG XIAOPING (old style: TENG HSIAO-PING; 1904–1997), Chinese political leader. Born into a wealthy landowning family in Sichuan (Szechwan) province, Deng participated in a work-study program in France (1920–25) and became friendly with fellow student Zhou Enlai (Chou En-lai). He joined the French Communist party, and studied Marxism in Moscow for six months (1925–26) before returning to China as a party activist. A supporter of Mao Zedong (Mao Tse-tung), Deng participated in the Long March (1934–35) and played a major role in the World War II struggle against the Japanese and in the civil war against the Nationalist armies (1945–49). After the establishment of the People's Republic of China (1949), he was the chief administrator of Southwest China, and was named a vice-premier (1952), member of the politburo (1955), and party general secretary (1956). After the failure of the Great Leap Forward (1958), he advocated pragmatic reforms, as a result of which he was branded a "revisionist" and "counterrevolutionary" during the Cultural Revolution (1966–69) and dismissed from his high posts. He reemerged as vice premier in 1973, but was purged once again by the radical Gang of Four (April 1976). However, after Mao's death (September 1976) the radicals were arrested and Deng returned to power as the dominant political figure in China (1977). Over the next two decades he transformed the Chinese economy by introducing elements of the free-market system in both the agricultural and the industrial sectors, and by emphasizing technical skills over ideological purity. He pursued close ties with the Western powers and increased trade and cultural and scientific exchanges with them. He negotiated (1984) the terms of the 1997 handover of Hong Kong to China and ordered the crackdown on demostrators in Beijing's Tiananmen Square in June 1989. Although he officially retired in late 1989, he wielded power behind the scenes during the 1990s. ■ See political biography by Benjamin Yang (1998).

DENIKIN, ANTON IVANOVICH (1872–1947), Russian general. At age 15 Deniken entered the czar's army; he rose through the ranks in World War I, becoming (February 1917) deputy chief of staff. Denikin commanded the western front for the provisional government in March 1917, moving to the southwest. After the October revolution he led the White army in the south that fought (1918–20) to wrest power from the bolsheviks and establish a "United Russia." His forces won control of the south, but despite British support they were defeated by the Red army at Orel (1919) and failed to seize Moscow. He resigned (1920) his command to Gen. Pyotr Wrangel and escaped to Constantinople. He later lived in France and the United States. ■ See his memoirs, *The Career of a Tsarist Officer* (Eng. trans. 1975), and Dimitry V. Lehovich, *White Against Red* (1974).

DE NIRO, ROBERT (1943–   ), U.S. actor. Robert De Niro was trained for the stage by Stella Adler and Lee Strasberg. After appearing in workshop and Off-Broadway productions, De Niro performed in a series of low-budget films by director Brian De Palma. Despite favorable reviews, De Niro

failed to attract the attention of major producers until his performances in *Bang the Drum Slowly* and *Mean Streets* (both 1973). He went on to memorable roles in *The Godfather Part II* (1974), *Taxi Driver* (1976), *New York, New York* (1977), *The Deer Hunter* (1979), *Raging Bull* (1981, Academy Award), *Falling in Love* (1984), *Goodfellas* (1990), *Awakenings* (1990), *Heat* (1995), *Wag the Dog* (1997), and *Analyze This* (1999). ■ See studies by John Parker (1995) and Andy Dugan (1996).

DENIS, MAURICE (1870–1943), French painter and decorator. During studies at the École des Beaux Arts (Paris), Denis was attracted by the French symbolist movement, but he later joined the Nabis ("prophets") who sought to emphasize and develop the theory that painting is the two-dimensional representation of a three-dimensional world. His most famous painting, *Homage to Cézanne* (1900), was a grouping of his friends around a still life. His interest in decorative patterning led Denis to create huge murals and panels for the Théâtre des Champs-Élysées (begun 1912) and the Petit Palace (1924–25). With Georges Desvallières, Denis founded Ateliers d'Art Sacré (1919), a studio-school of religious art.

DENISON, FLORA MACDONALD (Flora Merrill; 1867–1921), Canadian suffragist. Denison was a schoolteacher and seamstress who experienced firsthand the low wages and poor working conditions of women. Later she wrote an influential labor column in the Toronto newspaper *Sunday World* and agitated for women's rights. She headed the Canadian Suffrage Association (1911–14) and was a leader in the movement that secured the right to vote for women in the majority of Canada's provinces in 1918.

DENNIS, EUGENE (Francis Eugene Waldron; 1904–1961), U.S. political leader. A member of the militant Industrial Workers of the World (IWW), Dennis participated in the general strike in Seattle (1919) and joined the U.S. Communist party in 1926. He was elected general secretary of the party in 1945. In 1949 he was convicted, with 10 other communist leaders, of conspiracy to teach and advocate the overthrow of the government by force and imprisoned (1951–55). An advocate of greater party autonomy from Soviet control, he was replaced as a party leader in 1959.

DENNIS, LAWRENCE (1893–1977), U.S. journalist and writer. Called the "brains of American fascism," Dennis graduated from Harvard (1920), worked for the foreign service (1920–27), and was a Wall Street banker and consultant during the 1930s. An isolationist and elitist who opposed liberalism and parliamentary democracy, he achieved notoriety with such books as *Is Capitalism Doomed?* (1932), *The Coming of American Fascism* (1936), and *Dynamics of War and Revolution* (1940). He lectured widely and published *Weekly Foreign Letter* (1939–43) and later the newsletter *Appeal to Reason*. He was tried during World

War II (1944) with 28 others on charges of sedition, but charges were dropped after the judge died and a mistrial was declared.

DENVER, JOHN (1943–1997), U.S. singer and songwriter. Inspired by Elvis Presley, Denver took up the guitar in the 1950s. He dropped out of high school to play on the West Coast (where he changed his name from Henry John Deutschendorf, Jr., to John Denver) and later went (1965) to New York. His career blossomed in the 1960s with a series of campus tours that billed him as composer of "Leaving on a Jet Plane." Denver wrote and performed scores of songs, including "Rocky Mountain High," "Annie's Song," "Sunshine on My Shoulders," and "Take Me Home, Country Roads." Despite some criticism that his music was banal or sentimental, he developed a large following. Denver also appeared in the movie *Oh God* (1977). He was active in the environmental movement. ■ See his autobiography, *Take Me Home* (1994), and biography by Leonore Fleischer (1976).

DERAIN, ANDRÉ (1880–1954), French artist. Derain studied art (1895–98) at the Académie Camillo, where he met Henri Matisse, and later was influenced by a 1901 exhibition of paintings by Vincent van Gogh. He served in World War I before mounting his first one-man exhibition (1916). Derain combined the influences of fauvism and cubism, African primitive art, and classical masters to arrive at an avant-garde style (c. 1920) in the classical tradition of representation. In addition to his paintings, he also did sculptures, woodcuts, book illustrations, and designs for the Ballet Russe. ■ See the studies by Denys Sutton (1959) and Gaston Diehl (Eng. trans. 1964).

DEREN, MAYA (Eleanora Derenkowsky; 1908–1961), U.S. avant-garde filmmaker. Born in Russia, Deren emigrated to the United States in 1927. Trained as a dancer, she became interested in experimental film, making her first, *Meshes of the Afternoon,* in which a girl dreams her own suicide, in 1943. Known as "the mother of the underground film," she hired a theater in which to show her films when they were not accepted elsewhere, leading the way to commercial independence for underground films. She also founded the Creative Film Foundation (1955), which gave cash awards to help finance experimental cinema. Many of her films were based on choreographed dance, including her last, *The Very Eye of Night* (1959). She wrote *An Anagram of Ideas on Art, Form and Film* (1946) and *Divine Horsemen: The Living Gods of Haiti* (1953). ■ See Vèvè A. Clark, et al., *The Legend of Maya Deren* (1984).

DERRIDA, JACQUES (1930–   ), French philosopher and critic. Born in Algiers to Sephardic Jewish parents, Derrida went to France at age 19 and emerged as a leading voice in modern philosophy in the 1960s as one of a group writing for the influential journal *Tel Quel*. He taught at the prestigious École Normale Superieure in Paris (1965–84) and di-

rected the École des Hautes Études en Sciences Sociales in Paris (1984–   ). His early books were translations and analyses of the work of Edmund Husserl; he was also influenced by the writings of Hegel, Nietzsche, Freud, and Heidegger. Derrida brought their insights to bear on the meaning of writing (as inscription and as creative process) to Western tradition. Opposed to metaphysical formulations, he developed a strategy of "deconstructing" literary and philosophical texts in order to identify metaphysical assumptions by analyzing the language of the texts. The wide-ranging work *Of Grammatology* (1967; Eng. trans. 1976) was followed by several volumes including *Writing and Difference* (1967; Eng. trans. 1978), *Positions* (1972; Eng. trans. 1981), *Dissemination* (1972; Eng. trans. 1981), *Margins of Philosophy* (1972; Eng. trans. 1982), *The Post Card* (1980; Eng. trans. 1987), and *Specters of Marx* (1993; Eng. trans. 1994). ■ See Geoffrey H. Hartman, *Saving the Text* (1981); Joseph H. Smith, ed., *Derrida, Psychoanalysis and Literature* (1984); and the volume of conversations edited by John D. Caputo, *Jacques Derrida: Deconstruction in a Nutshell* (1997).

DÉRY, TIBOR (1894–1977), Hungarian novelist, short-story writer, and playwright. Although born into a wealthy family, Déry was a radical activist during the rebellion of 1918–19, and he joined the Communist party in 1919. He spent many years traveling through Europe as an exile activist and writer, but his works were concerned with the transformations occurring in contemporary Hungarian society. Most were not published until the end of World War II. Déry is best known for his novels *The Unfinished Sentence* (3 vols; written 1934–38, published 1947), *Response* (2 vols., 1950–52), and *Niki, the Story of a Dog* (1956; Eng. trans. 1958). Always a rebel and a non-conformist, he was arrested for his participation in the 1956 revolt. However, he was released three years later and resumed his literary career. English translations of his stories are in *The Giant, Behind the Brick Wall, Love* (1964), and *The Portuguese Princess and Other Stories* (1966).

DESAI, MORARJI (1896–1995), Indian political leader. Born into a Brahmin family in the state of Gujurat, Desai studied at the University of Bombay (B.S. 1917) and joined the civil service in Bombay State (1918). He resigned to participate in the independence movement (1930) and was arrested several times during the 1930s and 1940s for his nationalist activities. After Indian independence (1947) he served as chief minister of Bombay State (now Maharashtra; 1952–56) and in cabinet posts under Prime Ministers Jawaharlal Nehru and Indira Gandhi. After his dismissal as finance minister by Mrs. Gandhi (1964), he led the opposition to her government and he was imprisoned (1975–77) after she declared a state of emergency. Upon his release, he helped organize the Janata (People's) party, a coalition movement opposed to Mrs. Gandhi's authoritarian rule. Janata won the 1977 elections and Desai became India's first non-Congress Party prime minister. He restored democratic rights and institutions and improved relations with Pakistan, China, and the United States, but he was unable to resolve intraparty disputes and his coalition collapsed in 1979. ■ See his autobiography, *The Story of My Life* (3 vols., 1974–79), and the biography by S. R. Bakshi (1992).

DE SICA, VITTORIO (1902–1974), Italian actor and director. A popular stage and film actor during the interwar period, De Sica became dissatisfied with the direction of one of his films and decided to try his own hand. An early success was *The Children Are Watching Us* (1943), a film about the breakdown of a marriage as seen by the children. His postwar films *Shoeshine* (1946), *The Bicycle Thief* (1948), and *Umberto D* (1952) are considered classics of neorealism. His wartime drama, *Two Women* (1960), provided Sophia Loren with her greatest role. The popular comedies *Yesterday, Today and Tomorrow* (1963) and *Marriage Italian Style* (1964) were followed by *The Garden of the Finzi-Continis* (1971), about the plight of a Jewish family in fascist Italy, and *A Brief Vacation* (1973), about a working-class Italian woman.

DESNOS, ROBERT (1900–1945), French poet. A member of the surrealist group, Desnos experimented with his ability to relate dreams and to write while in a trance. His poetic works, characterized by free association and gentle irony, included *Liberty or Love* (1927; Eng. trans. 1993). During the 1930s he wrote movie and radio scripts. Active during World War II in the anti-Nazi Resistance, Desnos was deported to Theresienstadt concentration camp, where he died of typhus just after the liberation. Translations of his works are in *The Voice: Selected Poems* (1972), *Selected Poems* (1991), and *The Automatic Muse: Surrealist Novels* (1994). ■ See Mary Ann Caws, *The Surrealist Voice of Robert Desnos* (1977).

DE SYLVA, BUDDY (George Gard de Sylva; 1895–1950), **LEW BROWN** (Louis Brownstein; 1893–1958), **and RAY HENDERSON** (1896–1970), U.S. songwriters. Before teaming up in 1935, composer Henderson and lyricists De Sylva and Brown had individually written such song hits as "California Here I Come," "Somebody Loves Me," "April Showers," "I Used to Love You," "That Old Gang of Mine," "Alabamy Bound," and "Five Foot Two, Eyes of Blue." As the team of De Sylva, Brown, and Henderson they wrote some of the most popular musicals of the 1920s, including George White's *Scandals* of 1925, 1926, and 1928, *Good News* (1927), *Hold Everything* (1928), and *Flying High* (1930). Their most famous songs included "Sonny Boy," "The Birth of the Blues," "Black Bottom," "The Best Things in Life Are Free," "Button Up Your Overcoat," and "There's a Rainbow Round My Shoulder."

DETERDING, SIR HENRI WILHELM AUGUST (1866–1939), Dutch-born oil magnate. Bored with his Amsterdam banking job, Deterding sought his fortune in the East Indies and joined the Royal Dutch Oil Co. (1896), then a small concern, and became its managing director in 1900. He arranged a merger (1903) between Royal Dutch, the Rothschilds' Russian oil fields, and British Shell and exploited oil fields in Rumania, Egypt, Venezuela, Argentina, Mexico, and the United States in building Royal Dutch-Shell into one of the world's largest oil combines. When he retired in 1937, after having amassed a fortune reputed to be $200 million, Deterding was directing a group of 200 companies with 40,000 employees. ■ See his autobiography, *An International Oilman* (1934), and Glyn Roberts, *The Most Powerful Man in the World* (1981).

DEUTSCH, BABETTE (1895–1982), U.S. poet. A native of New York, Deutsch graduated from Barnard College (1917) and was secretary to economist Thorstein Veblen before beginning a long teaching career at Columbia University (1944–71). Her poetry, gathered in two volumes of *Collected Poems* (1963–1969), reflected the influence of the imagist poets who were important in the years when Deutsch began publishing. She also wrote astute criticism and literary history, including *This Modern Poetry* (1935) and *Poetry in Our Time* (1952; rev. ed. 1963), and four novels, including *Mask of Silenus* (1933) and *Rogue's Legacy* (1942), and collaborated with her husband, Avrahm Yarmolinsky, on translations from Russian and German.

DEUTSCHER, ISAAC (1907–1967), British writer. Born in Poland and educated in Jewish religious schools and at Cracow University, Deutscher edited communist periodicals and pamphlets (1926–32) until he was expelled from the Polish party as an anti-Stalinist. Emigrating to England (1939), he became a columnist and correspondent for the *Economist* (1942–49) and the *Observer* (1942–47), an occasional lecturer, and the author of radio-TV scripts and documentaries. An unrepentant independent Marxist with a gift for dramatic narrative, he wrote vivid political biographies of Stalin (1949) and Trotsky (3 vols. 1954-63) and *The Unfinished Revolution: Russia 1917–1967* (1967). He was active in the anti–Vietnam War movement in the United States and Europe. ■ See study by David Horowitz (1971).

DE VALERA, EAMON (1882–1975), U.S.-born Irish political leader. Born in New York City, De Valera was sent (1885) to Ireland after the death of his father. As one of the commanders of the anti-British Easter Rebellion (1916), De Valera received a sentence of life imprisonment, which was later commuted to one year. (He escaped execution because of his American citizenship.) After his release, he was elected (1917) to Parliament and later became president of the nationalist movement Sinn Fein (1917) and of the revolutionary assembly, the Dáil Éireann (1919). Imprisoned (1918) once again, he made a daring escape (1919), and journeyed to the United States, where he collected more than $5 million for the revolutionary movement. Opposing the treaty of

1921 because it excluded Northern Ireland from the Free State settlement, he resigned (1922) from the Dáil Éireann. His own political party, Fianna Fáil, did not gain control of the government until 1932, at which point De Valera became head of the government, abolishing the oath of allegiance to England and introducing (1937) a new constitution declaring Ireland an autonomous state. Defeated in 1948, he later returned as prime minister (1951–54; 1957–59). From 1959 to 1973, De Valera served as president of the republic. ■ See biographies by the Earl of Longford and Thomas P. O'Neill (1971), T. Ryle Dwyer (1988), and Tim Pat Coogan (1993).

DE VALOIS, DAME NINETTE (Edris Stannus; 1898–2001), Irish-born British ballet director. De Valois performed in revue and opera productions and was a soloist with Diaghilev's Ballet Russe (1923–25). She organized the Academy of Choreographic Art in London (1926) and was choreographic director of the Abbey (Dublin) and the Old Vic theatres (1926–30). With Lilian Baylis she undertook (1931) the training of the Sadler-Wells theatre's corps de ballet; as director (1931–63) and choreographer she developed the company, first known as Vic-Wells, then Sadler's Wells, and finally (after 1956) the Royal Ballet, and greatly enhanced the state of dance in Britain with her eye for talent and her sense of a unique "English" style. She choreographed many works, including *Job, Rake's Progress,* and *Checkmate.* ■ See her memoirs, *Invitation to the Ballet* (1937), *Come Dance with Me* (1957), and *Step by Step* (1977).

DEVLIN MCALISKEY, (JOSEPHINE) BERNADETTE (1947–), Northern Ireland political leader. Born into a working-class Roman Catholic family, Devlin was involved with the Civil Rights Association while a psychology student at Queen's University, Belfast (1966–69). A militant independent socialist who opposed the British presence in Northern Ireland, she called for Catholic and Protestant workers to unite and served as the youngest member in the British House of Commons (1969–74). She was arrested during the Londonderry riot of August 1969, the disturbance that sparked the wave of violence in Ulster of the 1970s and 1980s, and served four months in prison (1970). She remained politically active after leaving Parliament and was a founding member of the Irish Republican Socialist party (1975). ■ See her autobiography, *The Price of My Soul* (1969).

DE VOTO, BERNARD AUGUSTINE (1897–1955), U.S. writer. Born in Utah and educated at Harvard (B.A. 1920), De Voto was a versatile and controversial writer of novels, history, and literary criticism. Under the pseudonym John August he wrote potboilers to support his serious work on economic utopias, crank religions, and the exploration and settlement of the American West. He also wrote a widely read column for *Harper's* magazine (1935–52) and pro-

duced notable essays on conservation and civil rights. His most important books were *Mark Twain's America* (1932) and *Across the Wide Missouri* (1947). ■ See Wallace Stegner, *The Uneasy Chair* (1974), and study by Orlan Sawey (1969).

DE VRIES, HUGO (1848–1935), Dutch botanist and geneticist. The son of a Dutch prime minister, Hugo de Vries studied at the universities of Leiden, Heidelberg, and Würzburg, and was a professor of botany at the University of Amsterdam for 30 years. His research in plant physiology led him to studies of heredity and variation that revolutionized Mendelian genetics and evolutionary theory. De Vries observed that new plant forms appear unexpectedly among ordinary forms of the same species. He used these plants in breeding experiments and eventually concluded that the new plant forms resulted from gene mutation. His theory of mutation challenged Darwin's notion that variations within a species result from environmental factors. At the same time, his findings supported Darwin's evolutionary theory ("survival of the fittest") by showing how new forms, better fitted for survival, come about.

DE VRIES, PETER (1910–1993), U.S. novelist. A taffy-apple peddler and radio actor during the Depression of the 1930s, De Vries worked for *Poetry* magazine (1938–44) before joining the staff of the *New Yorker* (1944). His novels *Tunnel of Love* (1954), *Comfort Me with Apples* (1956), *The Tents of Wickedness* (1959), and *Reuben, Reuben* (1964) were irreverent commentaries on American life set in suburban Connecticut. Later comic novels included *Consenting Adults, or, the Duchess Will Be Furious* (1980), *Sauce for the Goose* (1981), and *The Prick of Noon* (1985). *No But I Saw the Movie* (1952) is a short-story collection. His writing parodied William Faulkner, Ernest Hemingway, and other literary masters. De Vries was an incomparable punster. ■ See studies by James H. Bowden (1983) and Dan Campion (1995).

DEWEY, GEORGE (1837–1917), U.S. naval officer. A career navy man, Dewey became a national hero when the Asiatic squadron under his command destroyed the Spanish fleet in Manila Harbor (May 1, 1898) during the Spanish-American War. As a result of his victory, which established the United States as a major Pacific power and paved the way for the conquest of the Philippines, Dewey was named admiral of the navy, the highest rank ever held by an American naval officer. Dewey served (1900–1917) as president of the General Board of the Navy, which was America's most important strategic militaty-planning agency. ■ See his autobiography (1913); Laurin Hall Healy and Luis Kutner, *The Admiral* (1944); and Ronald Spector, *Admiral of the New Empire* (1974).

DEWEY, JOHN (1859–1952), U.S. philosopher, psychologist, and educator. After receiving a Ph.D. from Johns Hopkins University (1884), Dewey taught at several universities before settling in at Columbia (1904-30), where he was the leading contributor to the *Journal of Philosophy*. One of the most influential—if controversial—U.S. thinkers of the century, Dewey maintained that the value of philosophy rests in its capacity to solve human problems. Dewey applied his pragmatist philosophy ("instrumentalism") to psychology, law, political science, and, most importantly, education. A reformer who rejected the authoritartian teaching methods prevalent at the turn of the century, Dewey emphasized active problem-solving and learning through experiece, and urged educators to relate curriculum to students' interests. In the 1930s, he was visible in public affairs as a defender of civil rights and advocate of progressive causes. His numerous books included *The School and Society* (1899; rev. ed. 1915), *The Quest for Certainty* (1929), *Art as Experience* (1934), *Freedom and Culture* (1939), and *Problems of Man* (1946). ■ See biographies by Sidney Hook (1939), Richard J. Bernstein (1966), and George Dykhuizen (1973); and Charles F. Howlett, *Troubled Philosopher* (1977).

DEWEY, THOMAS EDMUND (1902–1971), U.S. lawyer and political leader. Born in Michigan and graduated from Columbia Law School (1925), Dewey made his reputation as an assistant U.S. attorney prosecuting members of New York's organized-crime syndicate (1935). He was elected district attorney of New York County (Manhattan) in 1937 and in 1942 was the successful Republican candidate for governor. During three terms as governor (1943–55), Dewey sponsored labor-mediation procedures, prohibited racial and religious discrimination in employment, and extended the state's highway network, gaining a popular reputation for efficiency. He unsuccessfully challenged Franklin D. Roosevelt for the presidency in 1944 and narrowly lost to Harry Truman in 1948. ■ See the biography by Richard Norton Smith (1982).

DEWHURST, COLLEEN (1924–1991), Canadian-born U.S. actress. Dewhurst resolved to be a pilot, and later a journalist, before she took up acting. She dropped out of college after a year and worked at odd jobs in New York City while training for the stage. Her first Broadway role came in 1952 in Eugene O'Neill's *Desire Under the Elms,* for which she won an Obie Award; she subsequently performed in several O'Neill dramas, including a revival (1973) of *A Moon for the Misbegotten,* which was the first Broadway hit of her long career and, according to some critics, Dewhurst's finest hour. She won a Tony Award for her performance. Known for her subtle, multidimensional characterizations, she also won a Tony for her performance in *All the Way Home* (1961). She played numerous classical roles as well, particularly in Shakespearean tragedies, and in plays by Jean-Paul Sartre, Arthur Miller, Edward Albee, Athol Fugard, and others. Dewhurst also acted in films and on television, notably in the situation comedy *Murphy Brown.* ■ See her autobiography (1997; with Tom Viola).

D'HARNONCOURT, RENÉ (1901–1968), Austrian-born U.S. museum director. Born into an aristocratic family, d'Harnoncourt studied philosophy and chemistry in Vienna before traveling to Mexico in search of work when his family's fortune declined. An avid art collector and amateur artist, he failed to get a job as a chemist, but he amassed a large collection of Mexican contemporary and folk art and organized an exhibition for the Mexican ministry of education that toured the United States (1930–32). His reputation in the art world now established, he became active in the art community of New York City and in 1944 joined the staff of the Museum of Modern Art. He served as the museums director from 1949 to 1968.

DIAGHILEV, SERGEI PAVLOVICH (1872–1929), Russian ballet impresario and art critic. Diaghilev received early training in music. In his twenties he began arranging concerts and art exhibitions in Russia and abroad and established (1898) the influential journal the *World of Art*. In 1909 he organized his Ballet Russe; his troupe of Russian dancers brought modern ballet to the West. Collaborating with choreographer Michel Fokine, he staged ballets characterized by perpetual motion that integrated music and set design. Until his death, he toured Europe and the Americas with his company, which featured such celebrated dancers as Vaslav Nijinsky, Anna Pavlova, and Mikhail Mordkin. Diaghilev collaborated with the great choreographers, composers, and painters of his day. His productions of *Firebird* (1910), *Petrouchka* (1911), and particularly *The Rite of Spring* (1913), all based on music by Igor Stravinsky, revolutionized modern ballet. ■ See biographies by Arnold Haskell and Walter Nouvel (1935), Serge Lifar (Eng. trans. 1940), and Richard Buckle (1979); and John Drummond, *Speaking of Diaghilev* (1999).

DIAGNE, BLAISE (1872–1934), Senegalese political leader. A member of Senegal's educated, well-to-do native elite, Diagne served in the French customs service before his election (1914) as the first black African in the French parliament, where he served 20 years. During World War I, he recruited over 180,000 Senegalese to fight for France. Although originally a radical, he gradually assimilated French cultural and political values, defended the colonial system, and served as under secretary of state for colonies (1931–32).

DIANA (Diana Frances Spencer; 1961–1997), Princess of Wales (1981–1997). Born into an aristocratic family, Diana married (1981) Charles, Prince of Wales, the heir to the British throne, in a storybook wedding ceremony that was viewed on television by hundreds of millions of people around the world. A glamorous young woman with the common touch, she became the most popular member of the royal family and was the mother of two sons, Prince William (1982–) and Prince Henry (1984–). She became an international fashion trendsetter, was one of the most photographed women in the world, and was closely associated with numerous causes and charities, especially aid to children, the movement to help AIDS victims, and the campaign to ban land mines. Amidst charges and countercharges of adultery and revelations that the royal couple had few common interests and that the princess was suffering from severe eating disorders, Diana and Charles separated (1992) and were divorced (1996). Diana's death in an automobile crash in Paris was followed by an extraordinary week of public mourning in Britain and around the world. ■ See Andrew Morton, *Diana: Her True Story* (1992), and Sally Bedell Smith, *Diana in Search of Herself* (1999).

DICK, GEORGE FREDERICK (1881–1967) and GLADYS HENRY DICK (1881–1963), U.S. physicians. Working as a husband-and-wife team, the Dicks demonstrated that scarlet fever was caused by streptococcal organisms (1923), developed a toxin (Dick toxin) and antitoxin that prevented and cured the disease, and developed a skin test (the Dick test) that measured one's susceptibility to the disease (1924). George chaired the department of medicine at the University of Chicago (1933–45).

DICKEY, JAMES (1923–1997), U.S. poet, novelist, and critic. Dickey's poetry often appeared in the *New Yorker* as well as in little magazines; his published volumes included *Into the Stone* (1960), *Buckdancer's Choice* (1965), *Poems, 1957–1967* (1967), and *The Central Motion: Poems, 1968–1979* (1983). But Dickey gained fame for his best-selling novel *Deliverance* (1970), an allegory about men braving the elements on a white-water canoe venture. The novel, which pleased the reading public more than the critics, was adapted for the screen. *Night Hurdling* (1983) assembled "poems, essays, conversateons, commencements, and afterwords." He served as consultant in poetry at the Library of Congress (1966–68) and taught at the University of South Carolina (from 1969). ■ See his *Self-interviews* (1984); study by Richard J. Calhoun and Robert W. Hill (1984); Bruce Weigl and T. R. Hummer, eds., *The Imagination as Glory* (1984); memoir by his son Christopher Dickey, *Summer of Deliverance* (1998); and biography by Henry Hart (2000).

DIDION, JOAN (1934–), U.S. writer. Didion grew up in California's Sacramento Valley and won a *Vogue* magazine writing contest while an undergraduate at the University of California at Berkeley (1956). She subsequently worked for *Vogue* and contributed articles to several other popular periodicals. Her celebrated essays and columns, published as *Slouching Towards Bethlehem* (1968) and *The White Album* (1979), depicted her views on the spiritual desolation, nihilism, and malaise of California of the 1960s and 1970s. Some of these themes were also reflected in her novels *Run, River* (1963), *Play It as It Lays* (1970), *A Book of Common Prayer* (1977), and *Democracy* (1984), which featured women protagonists. She recounted her journey to Central America in *Salvador* (1983). Didion dissociated herself in

print from vocal feminists, many of whom she alienated with her portraits of women who seemed to accept victimization. She also collaborated on several screenplays with her husband, John Gregory Dunne. Her later works included nonfiction (*Miami*, 1987), a volume of essays (*After Henry*, 1992), and the novel *The Last Thing He Wanted* (1996). ■ See studies by Mark R. Winchell (1980) and Katherine U. Henderson (1981).

DIDRIKSON, BABE. *See ZAHARIAS, BABE DIDRIKSON.*

DIEFENBAKER, JOHN GEORGE (1895–1979), Canadian political leader. Born in Ontario, Diefenbaker moved to Saskatchewan in 1903, studied at the University of Saskatchewan Law School, and became a successful lawyer. Entering politics, he was defeated five times before being elected in 1940 to the Parliament as a Progressive Conservative. Diefenbaker worked his way up to the Conservative leadership in 1956 and was elected prime minister in a surprising victory the following year. His six years in office (1957–63) were marked by indecision, rising unemployment, and difficulties with the United States and with French-Canadian nationalists. He is best known for his policies of opening up Canada's vast Arctic lands for economic development. In 1967 Diefenbaker was ousted from party leadership but he retained his seat in Parliament until his death. ■ See his memoirs, *One Canada* (3 vols., 1975–77); Thomas Van Dusen, *The Chief* (1968); and study by Peter Stursberg (1976).

DIELS, OTTO PAUL HERMANN (1876–1954), German organic chemist. The son of a noted classical scholar, Diels studied at the University of Berlin (Ph.D. 1899) and taught at the University of Kiel (1916–48). The advances he made in steroid chemistry led to the elucidation of the carbon skeleton of steroids. With his student Kurt Alder, he identified the Diels-Alder reaction (1928) and devised a method for synthesizing a large variety of organic compounds. His research expanded knowledge of biologically important compounds such as cholesterol and also proved useful to the production of plastics and petrochemicals. Alder and Diels shared the 1950 Nobel Prize in Chemistry.

DIEM, NGO DINH (1901–1963), Vietnamese political leader. Born into an aristocratic Catholic family, Diem was an important official in Emperor Bao Dai's government (1933) but resigned his post in protest of French colonial rule. He lived to seclusion for a decade and refused offers to serve in Ho Chi Minh's government after World War II. An uncompromising anticommunist nationalist, he built a strong lobby in the United States and in 1954 became the American-sponsored president of South Vietnam. With U.S. support, he refused to allow the agreed-upon elections in 1956 and began a corruption-ridden, dictatorial rule in which opposition was brutally suppressed and communist-led insurgency grew. In May 1963, Diem allowed his troops to fire on Buddhist monks protesting his rule, thus setting off a chain of events culminating in the U.S. withdrawal of its support of him and tacit approval of a military coup in which Diem was killed. ∎ See Dennis Warner, *The Last Confucian* (1964).

DIES, MARTIN, JR. (1901–1972), U.S. political leader. A second-generation politician from Texas, Dies served in Congress as a Democrat (from 1931) and proposed as his first bill, which was unsuccessful, the expulsion of communist aliens. In 1938 he was appointed chairman of a "temporary" committee to investigate subversion, the first House Un-American Activities Committee (HUAC), which he used to launch a communist witch-hunt. Dies publicly attacked the Congress of Industrial Organizations (CIO) and the New Deal as communist-infiltrated, instigated the trial of Communist party secretary Earl Browder for passport fraud, and pioneered the technique of guilt by association. He retired in 1945 to practice law in Texas, then returned to Congress (1953–59), but he was unable to resume his old seat on HUAC. He wrote *The Martin Dies Story* (1963). ∎ See study by William Gellerman (1944).

DIETRICH, MARLENE (Maria Magdalene Dietrich; 1901–1992), German-U.S. actress and singer. Daughter of a Prussian policeman, Dietrich studied violin and drama and was a popular stage and screen actress by the late 1920s. Her role as the disdainful Lola in *The Blue Angel* (1930), Germany's first sound film, launched her international career. Director Joseph Von Sternberg took his seductive star to Hollywood that year and cast her in the classics *Morocco* (1931), *Blonde Venus* (1932), and *The Devil Is a Woman* (1935). She became an American citizen in 1937. During World War II she entertained Allied troops, made anti-Nazi radio broadcasts, and later toured as a cabaret star. Her subsequent films—*Rancho Notorious* (1952), *Touch of Evil* (1958), *Judgment at Nuremberg* (1961)—were not as successful as the vehicles Von Sternberg created for her. ∎ See Charles Higham, *Marlene* (1977); study by her daughter Maria Riva (1993); and biography by Stephen Bach (1992).

DIETZ, ROBERT SINCLAIR (1914–1995), U.S. geophysicist and oceanographer. Educated at the University of Illinois (Ph.D. 1941), Dietz served in the U.S. Army Air Corps during World War II and was a civilian scientist for the U.S. Navy and other governmental agencies for much of his career. He was in charge of oceanographic research on Admiral Richard E. Byrd's last Antarctic expedition (1946–47) and collaborated with Swiss engineer Jacques Piccard on the development of the bathyscaphe *Trieste*, which descended a record 35,800 feet (1960) in the western Pacific while exploring the world's deepest trench. He also did pioneering studies of the physical features of the moon and of the phenomenon of asteroid and meteor impacts on the surfaces of the earth and moon. Dietz was best known, however, for developing the theory of sea-floor spreading (1961) that he later incorporated into the theory of plate tectonics, which describes the Earth's surface as a mosaic of constantly moving crustal plates. His book *Seven Miles Down* (with Jacques Piccard; 1961) described the expedition of the *Trieste*.

DILLINGER, JOHN HERBERT (1903–1934), U.S. criminal. Released from prison in 1933 after serving a nine-year sentence for robbery and assault, Dillinger resumed his crime career and during the next 13 months became America's most daring and notorious bank robber. Like "Baby Face" Nelson, Bonnie Parker and Clyde Barrow—other midwestern Depression-era criminals—he captured the public imagination by holding up banks, institutions seen as exploiting the poor, and by eluding the police or making dramatic escapes from prison. He was gunned down by FBI agents in Chicago after being betrayed by his girlfriend's landlady. ∎ See biographies by Robert Cromie and Joseph Pinkston (1962) and G. Russell Girardin (1994); John Toland, *The Dillinger Days* (1963); and Lew Louderback, *He Only Robbed Banks* (1974).

DILLON, CLARENCE DOUGLAS (1909–), U.S. financier and public official. C. Douglas Dillon received a patrician education at Groton School and Harvard (B.A. 1931), after which he joined the family investment firm, Dillon, Read and Co., and served as its board chairman (1946–53). Active in Republican politics, he served as U.S. ambassador to France (1953–57) and undersecretary of state (1958–61) during the Eisenhower administration, and was the secretary of the treasury (1961–65) under Presidents Kennedy and Johnson. He was an innovator in foreign trade policy and played a role in the creation of the Inter-American Development Bank (IADB), the Organization for Economic Cooperation and Development (OECD), and the Alliance for Progress. He subsequently headed the Metropolitan Museum of Art in New York City (president, 1970–78; chairman, 1978–83), and served as chairman of the Brookings Institution (1970–76) and Rockefeller Foundation (1972–75) and returned to Dillon, Read as chairman of the executive committee (1971–81). ∎ See study by Robert C. Perez and Edward F. Willett (1995).

DIMAGGIO, JOE (Joseph Paul DiMaggio; 1914–1999), U.S. baseball player. The graceful and powerful DiMaggio, nicknamed "Joltin' Joe" and "the Yankee Clipper," was one of the greatest center fielders of all time. He succeeded Babe Ruth as a New York Yankee idol and superstar. In 13 seasons he compiled a .325 batting average, hit 361 home runs, led the American League twice in batting (1939, 1940), and was the league's Most Valuable Player three times (1939; 1941; 1947). His most notable achievement was hitting safely in 56 consecutive games during the 1941 season. For several generations of Americans he was a symbol of dignity, integrity, pride, and courtliness. His stormy and highly publicized marriage to actress Marilyn Monroe lasted for nine months in 1954. ■ See Maury Allen, *Where Have You Gone, Joe DiMaggio?* (1975), and biographies by George De Gregorio (1981) and Richard Ben Cramer (2000).

DIMITROV, GEORGI MIKHAILOVICH (1882–1949), Bulgarian communist leader. A printer by trade, Dimitrov was a founding member of the Bulgarian Communist party (1919) and was forced to flee the country after an unsuccessful uprising in 1923. He became a Comintern agent and was arrested in Germany (1933) for setting the Reichstag fire in Berlin. However, he successfully defended himself in a highly publicized trial that embarrassed the Nazi government. A hero of the communist movement, he headed the Comintern from 1934 until 1943, returning to Bulgaria at the end of World War II (1945). There, he directed the communist consolidation of power and served as Bulgaria's prime minister (1946–49). ■ See biography by Charles A. Moser (1979).

DINE, JIM (1935–), U.S artist. A graduate of Ohio University (1957) with training at the Boston Museum of Fine Arts School, Dine made a career out of exploring the imagery of objects. He started with old objects in an autobiographical context, as in *Shoes Walking on My Brain* (1960), with the shoes literally attached to the canvas, progressing to "found" or scavenged objects, store-bought objects, aluminum casts of objects, and a controversial 1966 series treating sex organs as objects. A prominent member of the pop-art movement, he was also a pioneer (1959–60) of "happenings" and, in the late 1960s and early 1970s, of performance art. Dine later painted more traditional, representational works. His sculptures of the 1990s included *Venus* (1990–91) and the *Ape and Cat* series (1992–93). ■ See studies by David Shapiro (1981) and Mario Livingstone (1998).

DINESEN, ISAK (Baroness Karen Blixen-Finecke; 1885–1962), Danish novelist and short-story writer. Dinesen was educated in Copenhagen, married her cousin (1914), and moved to Kenya, where the couple ran a coffee plantation. Though their marriage ended in 1921, she stayed on to run the plantation until 1931. She had been writing since 1905, but her first major work was *Seven Gothic Tales* (1934), first published in the United States. In such subsequent books as *Winter's Tales* (1942; Eng. trans. 1942) and the semiautobiographical *Shadows on the Grass* (1960; Eng. trans. 1960), she continued her series of unique gothic tales, which blended her aristocratic wit and storytelling with exotic intimations of mystery and the supernatural. *Out of Africa* (1937; Eng. trans. 1938) is a nonfiction account of the Africa she knew. She also wrote *Daguerreotypes and Other Essays* (Eng. trans. 1979) and *Carnival: Entertainments and Posthumous Tales* (Eng. trans. 1977). ■ See biographies by Judith Thurman (1982) and Olga Pelensky (1991); Parme-

nia Migel, *Titania* (1967); and Linda Donelson, *Out of Isak Dinesen in Africa* (1995).

DING LING (old style: TING LING; 1904?–1986), Chinese writer. Ding Ling was the pseudonym of Jiang Bingzhi (Chiang Ping-chih). Ding was born into a prosperous family, but her mother was a radical feminist who sent her to schools associated with the communist movement. Her extremely popular early stories, written during the 1920s, were concerned with the problems and conflicts of young women rebelling against patriarchal Chinese society. After 1930 her works, notably *Flood* (1931; Eng. trans. 1937), began to reflect a more proletarian outlook, and she joined the Communist party in 1933. Her best and most famous novel, *The Sun Shines over the Sangkan River* (1948; Eng. trans. 1954), which described the complex land-reform movement of the late 1940s, received the Stalin Prize for Literature in 1951. Continuously involved to intraparty literary disputes, she was dubbed a rightist and purged from the party and her important positions in the literary establishment (1957) in spite of her continuing popularity and fame as China's leading woman writer. After spending 20 years in remote work farms, she was released in 1978 and exonerated in 1979. English translations of her works appeared in *Miss Sophie's Diary and Other Stories* (1985). ■ See study by Yi-tsi Mei Feuerwerker (1982).

DINKELOO, JOHN GERARD (1918–1981), U.S. architect. Dinkeloo left his position as chief of production with Skidmore, Owings and Merrill to join Eero Saarinen and Associates (1950). After Saarinen's death (1961), he and Kevin Roche took over the firm and completed such structures as the Dulles International Airport Building near Washington, D.C.), the CBS Building (New York), the TWA terminal at Kennedy Airport (New York), and the Jefferson Memorial Arch (St. Louis). The firm also planned the Oakland (California) Museum and the Ford Foundation Building, One UN Plaza, and the new wings of the Metropolitan Museum of Art in New York City. Dinkeloo's innovations included the use of metalized, mirrorlike glass for exterior walls.

DIOP, BIRAGO (1906–1989), Senegalese short-story writer, poet, and diplomat. Born into a middle-class Muslim Wulof family in Dakar, Diop studied in Paris and collaborated with the poet and political leader Léopold Senghor on the pioneering literary journal, *The Black Student* (1934). He trained as a veterinarian and practiced throughout the French empire. Diop achieved fame with the publication of *Tales of Amadou Koumba* (1947; Eng. trans. 1966), tales told by his family *griot*—the traditional village storyteller and keeper of the oral tradition. The stories subtly evoked the humor, wisdom, and daily life of the African peasant and had a universal appeal. Diop also published a collection of poetry, *Lures and Gleams* (1960), and several additional volumes of tales.

DIOP, CHEIKH ANTA (1923–1986), Senegalese historian. While studying at the Sorbonne in Paris during the early 1950s, Diop was an important voice in the African intellectual community and helped shape the ideolgy of the Negritude movement. After Senegalese independence, he returned home (1961) and founded two opposition political parties. A third, formed in 1973, was not legally recognized until 1981, but both were outlawed by the government. He subsequently directed the research department of the Institut Fondamental d'Afrique Noire in Dakar, where he set up the first carbon-14 dating laboratory in Africa. A radical pan-Africanist, he was best known as the author of several controversial works, including *Cultural Unity of Black Africa* (1959; Eng. trans. 1980), *Black Africa: Economic and Cultural Basis for a Federated State* (1960; Eng. trans. 1978), and *The African Origin of Civilization* (1967; Eng. trans. 1974), which asserted that civilization arose below the Sahara and stressed the black origins of Egyptian culture and science. His view that the origins of Western and Near Eastern civilizations were predominantly African influenced the Afrocentric movement in the United States.

DIOR, CHRISTIAN (1905–1957), French fashion designer. Dior studied diplomacy before winning design jobs with Robert Piguet and Lucien Lelong. He opened (1947) his own couture salon, startling the industry and upstaging Schiaparelli with his initial "Corolle" line; featuring the tight bodice and full skirt suggested by classical ballet, it was called the New Look. Dior dominated fashion of the post-World War II era with consistently innovative new lines (including the A-line and the trapeze look), distinctive Dior accessories, and a flair for dramatic presentation of his elegent collections. He spotted and trained several younger designers, including Yves Saint-Laurent. He published *Talking About Fashion* (1951; Eng. trans. 1954). ■ See his autobiography, *Christian Dior and I* (Eng. trans. 1957), and the biography by Marie-France Pochna (Eng. trans. 1996).

DIRAC, PAUL ADRIEN MAURICE (1902–1984), British physicist. While a graduate student to the 1920s, Dirac began to build upon Werner Heisenberg's theory of quantum mechanics to reconcile conflicting versions of the quantum theory of matter. He formulated an elegant general mathematical concept of the atom based on Albert Einstein's theory of relativity. He shared the Nobel Prize in Physics with Erwin Schrödinger for his relativist theory of the electron (1933). With this theory he predicted (1931) the positron, the first known form of antimatter. He taught mathematics at Cambridge University (1932–69) and wrote several books including *Principles of Quantum Mechanics* (1930) and *The Development of Quantum Theory* (1971). ■ See study edited by Peter Goddard (1998).

DISNEY, WALT (Walter Elias Disney; 1901–1966), U.S. film producer. Disney was a high school dropout from the midwest who studied art by correspondence. In Hollywood after World War I, he pioneered in the production of animated cartoons starring such anthropomorphic animals as Mickey Mouse, Donald Duck, and the Three Little Pigs. The first Disney animated feature was *Snow White and the Seven Dwarfs* (1937), followed by *Fantasia* (1940) and *Bambi* (1942). After World War II Disney moved into the production of wholesome live-action films (*Treasure Island,* 1950), mature documentaries, and into television (1954), which financed his dream of an amusement park. Disneyland opened in California in 1955 to become one of the world's most successful tourist attractions, with a Florida branch opening in 1971. ■ See biographies by Bob Thomas (1958) and Marc Elliot (1993); Richard Schickel, *The Disney Version* (1968); Leonard Mosely, *Disney's World* (1985); and Steven Watts, *The Magic Kingdom* (1997).

DI SUVERO, MARK. *See SUVERO, MARK DI.*

DIVINE, FATHER (George Baker; 1880?–1965), U.S. religious leader. Baker was born into a poor, black, sharecropping family in Georgia. In his thirties he moved north, preaching as Major M. J. Divine and later as Father Divine. He founded the Peace Mission Movement (1919), a nonsectarian, interracial organization that established missions and sponsored "heavens" for reborn "angels." The movement reached its peak in the 1930s and 1940s and had its headquarters in Harlem (1933–42). Most members were in New York City and Philadelphia, but the movement spread to other cities in the United States and abroad. Many of Father Divine's followers declared him to be a messiah. ■ See study by Sara Harris (rev. ed 1971).

DIX, OTTO (1891–1969), German painter. A veteran of World War I, Dix expressed his horror at trench warfare in paintings that became increasingly abstract. He studied at the Dresden Academy (1919–21) and aligned himself with the antimilitaristic, antiaesthetic dadaists, creating montages of beads, paper, and poetical phrases. His political disenchantment led him to verism (the grotesque distortion of images presented with photographic clarity), in which he created violent paintings of cripples, war scenes, and power-corrupted men. He was also known for religious painting, and landscapes executed in a similarly violent manner. Dix was dismissed (1933) from his teaching post by the Nazis. He later fought in World War II and was a prisoner (1945–46) in France. ■ See biography by Linda F. McGreevy (1981) and study by Fritz Löffler (Eng. trans. 1982).

DIXON, THOMAS (1864–1946), U.S. author. Trained as a lawyer, Dixon spent a year in the North Carolina state legislature before becoming a Baptist minister (1886). After 1900 he concentrated on writing melodramatic plays and novels that were set in the South and reflected his white-supremacist views. His most famous novel, *The Clansman* (1905), which defended the Ku Klux Klan, served as the basis for D. W. Griffith's epic film *The Birth of a Nation* (1915) and helped promote the revival of the Klan. ■ See study by Raymond A. Cook (1974).

DJILAS, MILOVAN (1911–1995), Yugoslav political leader and writer. Djilas, a native of Montenegro, received a law degree from the University of Belgrade (1933). A member of the Yugoslav Communist party from 1932, he became a friend and colleague of Josip Broz Tito during the World War II partisan movement and was a prominent member of Marshal Tito's postwar government. In 1954 he was branded a heretic, ousted from his posts, and later imprisoned (1956–61) for his criticism of the new communist oligarchy, which he described in *The New Class* (published in New York in 1957) as poisoned by the "majestic and demonic pleasure of power." He was reincarcerated (1962–66) after the publication in the West of his autobiographical volume, *Conversations with Stalin* (1962), for which he was accused of revealing state secrets. His other writings included *The Unperfect Society* (Eng. trans. 1970), *Wartime* (Eng. trans. 1977), a biography of Tito (Eng. trans. 1980), and three additional volumes of autobiography, *Land Without Justice* (Eng. trans. 1958), *Memoir of a Revolutionary* (Eng. trans. 1973), and *Rise and Fall* (Eng. trans. 1985). After the collapse of communism in Yugoslavia (1990) Djilas criticized the emergence of Serbian nationalism and the Yugoslav war against Croatia. ■ See study by Stephen Clissold (1983) and C. L. Sulzberger, *Paradise Regained* (1989).

DMOWSKI, ROMAN (1864–1939), Polish political leader. Cofounder of Poland's National Democratic party (1897) and the leading Polish delegate in the Russian Duma, Dmowski identifed Germany as the foremost enemy of his partitioned nation. In 1917 he set up a national committee that won recognition by the Allied powers as the official representative of Poland. Dmowski was a delegate to the 1919 Paris Peace Conference and signed the treaty that established the new Polish republic. He retired from politics in 1924, but his National Democratic philosophy, which was anti-Semitic and antisocialist, and fearful of the "Teutonic menace" and "Masonic conspiracy," exercised a strong influence over national life. ■ See study by Alvin M. Fountain (1980).

DOBB, MAURICE HERBERT (1900–1976), British economist. Dobb studied economics at Cambridge and the London School of Economics (Ph.D. 1924) and taught at Cambridge (1924–67). A political activist as well as a scholar, he was a member of the British Communist party (from 1922) and was regarded as one of the foremost Marxist economists of the century. He was primarily concerned with the analysis of capitalism and its historical development, the theory of value, the history of economic thought, and the problems of socialist planning. His frequently revised *Russian Economic Development Since the Revolution* (1928) was a pioneering attempt to explain Soviet society. He collaborated with Piero Sraffa in editing and annotating

the *Works and Correspondence of David Ricardo* (11 vols.; 1951–73). His other books included *Studies in the Development of Capitalism* (1946), *An Essay on Economic Growth and Planning* (1960), *Socialist Planning* (1970), and *Theories of Value and Distribution Since Adam Smith* (1973).

DOBELL, SIR WILLIAM (1899–1970), Australian artist. Dobell studied and worked in London during the 1930s. He became the leader of Australia's modern-art movement in 1944 when a group of painters unsuccessfully challenged his right to an award for a portrait painted in a slightly distorted style. Dobell's style was actually eclectic, a mixture of Hogarth, Renoir, and Soutine. He specialized in local landscapes and insightful portraits, including a few *Time* magazine covers. ■ See Brian Adams, *Portrait of an Artist* (1983), and study by James Gleeson (rev. ed. 1981).

DÖBLIN, ALFRED (1878–1957), German writer. A physician, Döblin practiced psychiatry in the workers' district near the Alexanderplatz in Berlin, which provided him with the characters and setting for his most famous novel, *Berlin Alexanderplatz* (1929; Eng. trans. 1931, 1961), which was filmed in 1931 and again for television in 1980. Considered the most talented narrative writer of the German expressionists, Döblin dwelled on the emptiness of a self-destructive universe yet never lost faith in the human spirit. His successful novel, *The Three Leaps of Wang-Lun* (1915), tells of the victory of the nonviolent spirit over brute force. His other novels included *Men Without Mercy* (1935; Eng. trans. 1937) and the four-volume narrative of post–World War I Germany, consisting of *Citizens and Soldiers* (1939) and the *November 1918* trilogy, *A People Betrayed* (1948; Eng. trans. abridged 1983), *Return of the Frontline Troops* (1949; Eng. trans. abridged 1983), and *Karl and Rosa* (1950; Eng. trans. 1983). From 1933 to 1945 Döblin, a Jew, lived in exile in France and the United States. His last novel, *Tales of a Long Night* (1956; Eng. trans. 1984), expressed hope for a new Europe. ■ See his memoirs, *Destiny's Journey* (1949; Eng. trans. 1992), and study by Wolfgang Kort (1974).

DOBZHANSKY, THEODOSIUS (1900–1975), Ukrainian-born U.S. geneticist. A pioneer in the field of evolutionary genetics, which combined the theories of Darwin and Mendel, Dobzhansky is best known for studies that revealed great genetic diversity within species. Overturning views commonly held in the 1930s, he demonstrated that it was this diversity that gave the species a greater chance to adapt to a changing environment and be naturally selected in the evolutionary process. He taught at the California Institute of Technoloy (1929–40), Columbia University (1940–62), and Rockefeller University in New York (1962–71). Dobzhansky's best-known works were *Genetics and the Origin of Species* (1937) and *Mankind Evolving* (1962), an influential volume in the field of human evolution.

DOCTOROW, EDGAR LAURENCE (1931–), U.S. writer. E. L. Doctorow wrote two novels, *Welcome to Hard Times* (1960) and *Big as Life* (1966), before leaving a successful career as a literary editor to write full-time (1969). He was best known for *The Book of Daniel* (1971; filmed as *Daniel,* 1983), a powerful novel based on the story of Julius and Ethel Rosenberg, who were executed as spies; *Ragtime* (1975; film, 1981), a highly original novel set in pre–World War I America that interspersed fictional and historical characters; *Loon Lake* (1980), a picaresque novel set in the 1930s; and *World's Fair* (1985), a novel based on his 1930s boyhood in the Bronx, New York. His later novels, *Billy Bathgate* (1985; film, 1991), *The Waterworks* (1994), and *City of God* (2000) were also set in New York City. *Lives of the Poets* (1984) was a collection of short fiction. ■ See studies by Carol C. Herter and James R. Thompson (1990) and John G. Parks (1991), and Christopher D. Morris, ed., *Conversations with E. L. Doctorow* (1999).

DODERER, HEIMITO VON (1896–1966), Austrian writer. Incarcerated (1916-20) in Siberia during World War I, Doderer subsequently returned to Vienna and studied medieval history and psychology. His novels were concerned with his characters "becoming human" by going through a process blocked by false perceptions, obsessions, and mistaken judgements. He was best known for the novel *The Demons* (1956; Eng. trans. 1961), a monumental work that reflects the influence of the French novelist Marcel Proust and the Austrian Robert Musil. His fiction treated Austria's social history, at times idealizing pre–World War I Austrian society. His other novels included *Every Man a Murderer* (1938; Eng. trans. 1964) and *The Waterfalls of Slunj* (1963; Eng. trans. 1966). ■ See study by Michael Bachem (1981).

DOENITZ, KARL (1891–1980), German admiral. A submarine officer during World War I, Doenitz helped the Nazis build a submarine fleet during the 1930s in contravention of the Versailles treaty. Appointed commander of this fleet in 1936, he devised the "wolf pack" technique of concentrated attack against surface shipping. In 1943, during World War II, Doenitz became commander in chief of the German navy, and in 1945 briefly succeeded Adolf Hitler as chancellor before presiding over Germany's unconditional surrender to the Allies. At the Nuremberg trials (1946) he was sentenced to 10 years imprisonment for war crimes. During this period he wrote his *Memoirs* (Eng. trans. 1959). ■ See biography by Peter Padfield (1984).

DOESBURG, THEO VAN (Christian Emil Marie Kupper; 1883–1931), Dutch painter, decorator, poet, and art theorist. Van Doesburg was a naturalist painter until 1917, when the artist Piet Mondrian introduced him to the principles of geometric abstractionism. Together they published the avant-garde magazine *De Stijl* ("The Style"; 1917–31), which promoted the idea that modern art can best convey spiritual values through the use of such basic forms as cubes, verticals, and horizontal lines. De Stijl was also the name of the aesthetic creed that joined a group of artists in the aftermath of World War I. Briefly involved with dadaism (1922), Van Doesburg formulated a more dynamic version of De Stijl, based on the use of inclined planes, which he called elementarism. In the 1920s he became increasingly involved with architectural projects. ■ See study by Joost Baljeu (1974).

DOHERTY, HENRY LATHAM (1870–1939), U.S. businessman. An executive in several public-utilities companies (1890–1905) and founder of his own financial- and engineering-consultation firm (1905), Doherty formed Cities Service Corp. (1910), a gigantic utilities holding company. Over the years the company expanded into natural-gas, electricity, and petroleum production, and by the 1930s it controlled more than 200 light, gas, and power companies and had assets of more than $1.25 billion. Doherty's financial manipulations were in large measure responsible for the passage of the Securities Act (1933) and the Public Utilities Holding Company Act (1935).

DOHERTY, PETER C. (1940–), Australian immunologist. Doherty received a degree in veterinary medicine from the University of Queensland (1966) and a doctorate from the University of Edinburgh, Scotland (1970). He taught at the John Curtin School of Medical Research in Canberra (1972–88) and at the St. Jude Children's Research Hospital in Memphis, Tennessee (1988–). At Canberra, he collaborated with Rolf M. Zinkernagel on immune system studies using laboratory mice (1973–75). The two researchers discovered how white blood cells (cytotoxic T cells, or killer T cells) responsible for destroying cells in the body infected with viruses recognize infected cells and leave normal body cells alone. They discovered that the white cells simultaneously recognize two separate chemical signals form the target cell—one indicating that it is from the same individual and not from a foreign source, and the other indicating that the cell is infected with a virus. These findings revealed how the immune system works and led to new approaches to the treatment of cancer, AIDS, diabetes, and multiple sclerosis. For their pioneering research, Doherty and Zinkernagel shared the 1996 Nobel Prize in Physiology or Medicine.

DOISY, EDWARD ADELBERT (1893–1986), U.S. biochemist. Working in collaboration with Edgar Allen, Doisy, a Harvard-trained professor at the St. Louis University School of Medicine (1923–65), achieved prominence by isolating the female sex hormones estrone (1929), estriol (1930), and estradiol (1935). His most important work, though, was the isolation (1939) of two compounds of vitamin K—K_1 and K_2. Subsequently he elucidated the chemical structure of both compounds and synthesized vitamin K_1. Doisy shared the 1943 Nobel Prize in Physiology or Medicine with Henrik Dam.

DOLCI, DANILO BRUNO PIETRO (1924–1997), Italian writer and social reformer. A native of northern Italy, Dolci gave up his architectural studies in Milan (1950), moved to Sicily (1952), and devoted himself to improving the working and living conditions of the poverty-stricken peasants of the island through nonviolent means. Called the "Gandhi of Sicily" and a 20th-century saint, Dolci organized peasant and artisan cooperatives and led sit-ins, fasts, and "strikes-in-reverse"—actions in which the unemployed undertake needed public-works protects without pay or government authorization—to publicize the plight of the workers and to attempt to overcome their resignation and fatalism. His books, which included the peasants' own descriptions of their experiences, included *Report from Palermo* (1956; Eng. trans. 1959), *Waste* (1960; Eng. trans. 1963), *The Man Who Plays Alone* (1966; Eng. trans. 1969), and *Sicilian Lives* (Eng. trans. 1982). His poetry is in *Creature of Creatures* (Eng. trans. 1980). ■ See James McNeish, *Fire Under the Ashes* (1966)

DOLE, JAMES DRUMMOND (1877–1958), U.S. businessman. Born into a New England trading and missionary family, Dole moved to Hawaii (1899), then a one-crop (sugar cane) territory, and started to plant pineapples. Convinced of the fruit's commercial viability, he formed the Hawaiian Pineapple Co., opened a cannery (1903), started shipping pineapples to the mainland, and eventually controlled 84 percent of the total U.S. market and 72 percent of the world's supply. Known as the "pineapple king," Dole was personally responsible for the development of the Hawaiian pineapple industry.

DOLLFUSS, ENGELBERT (1892–1934), Austrian political leader. Active in the conservative, peasant-based Christian Socialist party, Dollfuss served as minister of agriculture (1931) before being elected chancellor (1932). He dismissed parliament (1933) and set up a dictatorial regime based on Italian fascist and conservative Catholic principles. Dollfuss used the fascist militia to crush the Social Democrats (1934), but he was assassinated during an abortive Nazi putsch (July 1934). ■ See biography by Gordon Brook-Shepherd (1961).

DOLMETSCH, ARNOLD (1858–1940), French-born British musicologist and instrument maker. The son of a piano maker and grandson of an organ builder, Dolmetsch began making instruments and playing the clavichord in his earliest childhood. After his formal musical studies, he devoted himself to the reconstruction, restoration, and revival of the harpsichord, viol, lute, recorder, and other obsolete instruments. He trained his family in the use and manufacture of the instruments, established a music center and workshop at Haslemere (1920), and sponsored annual festivals of antiquarian music. He also wrote the pioneering book, *The Interpretation of the Music of the Seventeenth and Eighteenth Centuries* (1915). ■ See biography by Margaret Campbell (1975)

DOMAGK, GERHARD JOHANNES PAUL (1895–1964), German bacteriologist and pathologist. Domagk trained at the University of Kiel (M.D. 1921) and taught at Greifswald and Münster universities before becoming director of the I. G. Farbenindustrie Laboratory for Experimental Pathology and Bacteriology (1927). While there, he discovered (1932) that the dye prontosil (sulfonamide-crysoidin) cured streptococcal infections in mice. Proved effective in humans (Domagk's daughter and Franklin D. Roosevelt. Jr., among others), the drug was the first of the so-called sulfa drugs, the "wonder drugs" that were widely used in treating the debilitating and often fatal streptococcic diseases including bacteremia, pneumonia, meningitis, and gonorrhea. Domagk was awarded the 1939 Nobel Prize for Physiology or Medicine.

DOMINGO, PLÁCIDO (1941-), Spanish-born opera singer. The son of celebrated zarzuela singers who moved to Mexico when he was 6, Domingo appeared in children's roles in his parents' company and later studied at the National Conservatory of Music in Mexico City. He made his debut in Monterrey, Mexico (1961), and gained valuable experience as the leading tenor of the Hebrew National Opera (Tel Aviv, Israel; 1962–65). Handsome and athletic, Domingo first sang with the New York City Opera in 1965 and at the Metropolitan in 1968, and he emerged in the 1970s as one of the international superstars of opera. Renowned for his musicianship and acting abiliy as well as for his warm, yet powerful, voice, he mastered more than 80 roles and was best known for his peformances in *Otello, Tales of Hoffmann, Carmen, La Bohème, Tosca,* and *La Traviata.* During the 1990s he toured with Luciano Pavarotti and José Carreras as part of the "Three Tenors" concert series, the most lucrative production in classical music history. An estimated audience of over 2 billion viewers saw the concerts on television, and the audio and video tapes of the events were the best-selling classical recordings of all time. Domingo also served as artistic director of the Washington Opera (1996–) and the Los Angeles Opera (2000–). ■ See his *My First Forty Years* (1983) and biography by Cornelius Schnauber (1997).

DOMINGUÍN, LUIS MIGUEL (Luis Miguel González Lucas; 1926–1996), Spanish matador. Trained by his father, a well-known matador, Dominguín began to fight bulls when he was a child and made his professional debut at age 11. He achieved prominence to the mid-1940s with his flashy and brash style and was the major rival of the great Manolete, whom he succeeded as number one after Manolete was fatally gored in 1947. In addition to being the highest-paid bullfighter in the world and a member of international society, he became friends with Ernest Hemingway and Pablo Picasso and was involved in a series of highly publicized love affairs. He retired (1961) after a fierce competition with his brother-in-law Antonio Ordóñez, but returned triumphantly to the ring in 1971. His last fight was in 1973. His duels with Ordóñez were chronicled by Hemingway in *The Dangerous Summer* (1960).

DONAHUE, PHIL (1935–), U.S. television personality. A veteran journalist and broadcaster, Phil Donahue hosted one of television's most popular talk shows. "The Phil Donahue Show" aired in Dayton, Ohio (1967), and as a result of syndication and increased popularity, the show was renamed "Donahue" and moved to Chicago (1974) and then to New York (1985). Best known for tackling controversial subjects and for a discussion format that encouraged audience and viewer participation. Donahue attributed much of his popularity to his largely female audience. Appealing to housewives and career women alike, he described himself as a feminist, a former male chauvinist, and a lapsed Catholic. He wrote *The Human Animal* (1985) and the autobiography *Donahue* (1979).

DONG, PHAM VAN (1906–2000), Vietnamese political leader. Dong came from a well-to-do family and began his career as a revolutionary while he was a student at the University of Hanoi in 1925. A colleague of communist leader Ho Chi Minh (from 1930), he spent several years in prison for inciting peasant revolts (1931–36). In China (1940–41) he was a founder of the Vietminh independence movement (1941), which engaged in guerrilla activities against the French and the Japanese. After the proclamation of Vietnamese independence in Hanoi (1945), Dong served as minister of finance (1945–47) and minister for foreign affairs (1954–61), and was the chief Vietminh delegate at the 1954 Geneva Conference on Indochina that divided Vietnam. As premier of the Democratic (later Socialist) Republic of Vietnam, commonly known as North Vietnam (1955–76), he was his country's chief spokesman during the Vietnam War. After the fall of the South Vietnamese government, Vietnam was officially reunified and Dong served as premier (1976–81; chairman of the council of ministers, 1981–86) of the Socialist Republic of Vietnam. During his years in power in reunited Vietnam, the country became a close ally of the Soviet Union, forced thousands of ethnic Chinese to flee, and invaded neighboring Kampuchea (Cambodia) to overthrow the barbarous Pol Pot government.

DONGEN, KEES VAN (**Cornelius Theodorus Marie van Dongen;** 1877–1968), Dutch-born French painter. Van Dongen studied in Rotterdam, then settled in Paris (1897). He came under the influence of fauvism, with its bright colors and sensual approach. He developed a characteristic portrait type of a slender woman, slightly clothed or nude, adorned with sparkling jewels—a curious cross between prostitute and princess. Known for cynical portraits that did not hide moral or physical flaws, van Dongen became in the 1920s the portraitist of fashonable French society. He is remembered mainly for his earlier work.

DONLEAVY, J. P. (**James Patrick Donleavy;** 1926–), U.S.-born Irish novelist, playwight, and short-story writer. After a less than distinguished high school career, he served in the U.S. Navy in World War II and later studied math and bac-teriology. At Trinity College in Dublin he steeped himself in literary studies, then left before graduation and produced the novel *The Ginger Man* (1955). Its hero, Sebastian Dangerfield, a comically depraved American expatriate in Dublin, scared off publishers and shocked some readers, but he ultimately took his place as a major fictional creation. Donleavy also wrote short stories, plays based on his fiction, and numerous other novels, including *A Singular Man* (1963), *The Saddest Summer of Samuel S* (1966), *The Destinies of Darcy Dancer, Gentleman* (1977), *Schultz* (1979), *Leila: Further in the Destinies of Darcy Dancer, Gentleman* (1983), *Are You Listening Rabbi Loew* (1987), *That Darcy, That Dancer, That Gentleman* (1990), and *The Lady Who Liked Clean Restrooms* (1997). Donleavy became an Irish citizen in 1967. ■ See study by Charles G. Masinton (1975).

DONOSO, JOSÉ (1924–1996), Chilean writer. A graduate of Princeton University (B.A. 1951), Donoso worked for a time as a shepherd, longshoreman, journalist, and university professor. He established his reputation as a novelist and short-story writer during the 1950s and was subsequently hailed as the finest Chilean novelist of his generation. His works, filled with grotesque characters and nightmarish visions, dealt with the themes of alienation, dehumanization, and the decadence of contemporary Chilean society. Among his best-known works were *Coronation* (1956; Eng. trans. 1965), *This Sunday* (1966; Eng. trans. 1967), *The Obscene Bird of Night* (1970; Eng. trans. 1973), *Sacred Families* (1973; Eng. trans. 1977), *Charleston and Other Stories* (Eng. trans. 1977), *A House in the Country* (1978; Eng. trans. 1984), *Curfew* (1986; Eng. trans. 1988), and *The Garden Next Door* (1981; Eng. trans. 1992). He also wrote *The Boom in Spanish American Literature: A Personal History* (1972; Eng. trans. 1977). ■ See study by George R. McMurray (1979).

DONOVAN, WILLIAM JOSEPH (1883–1959), U.S. soldier, attorney, and intelligence officer. "Wild Bill" Donovan came into public view when, as a colonel with the "fighting 69th," he won the Congressional Medal of Honor for valor during the Meuse-Argonne battle of World War I. He served as assistant U.S. attorney general (1924–25) in the Coolidge administration and later made an unsuccessful bid for governor of New York as a Republican. After undertaking a fact-finding mission (1940) in Europe for Pres. Franklin D. Roosevelt, Donovan forged and directed—often from the field—a new U.S. intelligence service that became known as the Office of Strategic Services (OSS; 1942–45). The most effective U.S. secret agency of the war, the OSS had agents behind the lines to facilitate crucial Allied operations. The OSS was the precursor of the Central Intelligence Agency (CIA), established in 1947; Pres. Harry Truman passed over Donovan and appointed Adm. Roscoe Hillenkoetter as its first director. Pres. Dwight Eisenhower, who called Donovan America's "last hero," appointed him ambassador to Thailand (1953–54). ■ See Corey Ford, *Donovan of OSS* (1970);

Anthony Cave Brown, *The Last Hero* (1983); and study by Thomas F. Troy (1996).

DOOLITTLE, HILDA (H. D.; 1886–1961), U.S. poet. Doolittle expatriated (1911) to live among London's Bloomsbury circle. A leader of imagism, a minimalist school of poets that thrived in the years before World War I, she discarded formal poetic prescriptions and arranged "words that make images" in collections such as *Sea Garden* (1916), *Collected Poems* (1925), and *Red Roses from Bronze* (1931), signing her poetry "H.D. Imagiste" and later simply "H.D." *Bid Me to Live: A Madrigal* (1960) is an autobiographical roman à clef dedicated to the novelist D. H. Lawrence. *Hermetic Statement* (1972), a philosophical reflection on her life, and *HERmione* (1981), an autobiographical novel about a woman torn between her love for a man and for a woman, appeared posthumously. H.D. also wrote a *Tribute* (1956; rev. ed. 1974) to her psychoanalyst, Sigmund Freud. ▪ See biography by Barbara Guest (1983).

DOOLITTLE, JAMES HAROLD (1896–1993), U.S. aviator. An army air corps officer (1920–30), Doolittle established speed records for land planes and was an expert in the fields of military navigation and strategic and tactical bombing. He was awarded the Congressional Medal of honor for his World War II raid on Tokyo with 16 B-25 bombers (1942). This spectacular daylight raid boosted U.S. morale. He later commanded U.S. air forces in North Africa and Europe, resigning from the army (1945) to become vice president and director of Shell Oil (1945–59). ▪ See Quentin Reynolds, *Amazing Mr. Doolittle* (1953), biography by Lowell Thomas and Edward Jablonski (1976), and study by Carroll V. Glines (1980).

DORIOT, GEORGES FREDERIC (1899–1987), French-born U.S. businessman and educator. Doriot studied at the University of Paris and then attended Harvard Business School, remaining in the United States. He served as a teacher and administrator at Harvard Business School (1926–66) and during his tenure decisively influenced American education in business administration. After directing military planning for the quartermaster corps during World War II, Doriot left the army as a brigadier general to direct the newly formed American Research and Development Corp. (ARD), the "grandparent" of venture-capital businesses, for its first 28 years.

DORNBERGER, WALTER ROBERT (1895–1980), German-born U.S. rocket scientist. Dornberger was an engineer and career officer in the German army. During the 1930s he worked with Wernher von Braun and others to develop rockets and guided missiles and he helped establish the test facility at Peenemünde on the Baltic coast. His pioneering work culminated in the development of the potent V-2 rocket, launched by Germany against England in World War II (1944–45). After spending three years (1945–47) as a pris-

oner of war in England, Dornberger accepted an invitation to work in the United States as an air force consultant. His rocket, which attained speeds of 3,500 miles per hour, served as the basis for American and Soviet space-rocket programs. After leaving the air force (1950), Dornberger was a vice president of Bell Aircraft. His book *V-2* (1952; Eng. trans. 1954) described his work in the field of jet propulsion.

DORRANCE, JOHN THOMPSON (1873–1930), U.S. industrialist. Trained as a chemist, Dorrance received a doctorate from Göttingen University (1897) and advanced culinary instruction from several famous Parisian chefs before producing the first lot of canned condensed soup (1899) for his uncle's firm, the Joseph Campbell Preserve Co. Dorrance thus originated the canned-soup industry and served as president (1914–30) of the renamed Campbell Soup Co.

DORSEY, JIMMY (1904–1957), and **TOMMY DORSEY** (1905–1956), U.S. bandleaders and instrumentalists. Trained by their bandleader father, Jimmy (a cornetist, saxophonist, and clarinetist) and Tommy (a trombonist) played in the nation's most famous dance bands during the 1920s before forming the Dorsey Brothers Orchestra (1933). Although highly successful, they had musical and personality differences that led to a separation (1935), and each formed bands that became legendary ensembles during the age of the big bands of the 1930s and 1940s. Jimmy's biggest hits were "Maria Elena," "Amapola," and "A New Shade of Blue," while Tommy's greatest triumphs were "I'm Getting Sentimental over You," "Marie," "I'll Never Smile Again," and "Boogie-Woogie." The brothers teamed up again (1953) to form a new band, the Fabulous Dorseys. ▪ See Herb Sanford, *Tommy and Jimmy* (1972).

DORSEY, THOMAS ANDREW (1899–1993), U.S. composer and pianist. Dorsey, whose mother was a church organist and whose father was an itinerant preacher, studied at the Chicago Music College and toured and recorded with several prominent blues and jazz artists during the 1920s. He accompanied Ma Rainey with his five-piece jazz band (1923–27) and composed songs for her shows. In the late 1920s he turned to sacred music, modernized traditional spirituals with elements of the blues, and became known as the father of gospel music. He coined the term "gospel song," organized the first gospel chorus (1931), and composed more than 1,000 gospel songs, many of which were sung in black churches throughout the United States. Among his best-known compositions were "If You See My Savior," "Precious Lord, Take My Hand," "When I've Done My Best," and "Peace in the Valley." Dorsey also founded the first gospel publishing house (1932), cofounded the annual National Convention of Gospel Choirs and Choruses (Chicago, 1932), and was musical director of the Pilgrim Baptist Church in Chicago (1932–83). ▪ See Michael W. Harris, *The Rise of Gospel Blues* (1992).

DORTICÓS TORRADO, OSVALDO (1919–1983), Cuban political leader. A successful lawyer who joined Fidel Castro's clandestine movement during the 1950s. Dorticós became minister of laws in Castro's revolutionary government (1959) and subsequently served as Cuba's president (1959–76). He helped revise the island's constitution and draft new laws on agrarian reform and nationalization of foreign enterprises. As minister of the economy (1964–76) he was the country's chief economic planner. He committed suicide in 1983.

DOS PASSOS, JOHN RODERIGO (1896–1970), U.S. novelist. An adamant leftist in the 1920s, Dos Passos wrote for the *New Masses*. His trilogy *U.S.A.* (1930–36) was an angry appraisal of industrial America of 1898–1929. A tireless traveler and observer, Dos Passos characterized America as a country with boundless energy but no direction. He used experimental techniques: "The Camera Eye"—impressionistic personal observations; "The Newsreel"—a pastiche of headlines, advertisements, song lyrics, and news clips; and verbal snapshots—thumbnail sketches of actual celebrities juxtaposed with fictional men-on-the-street. His disappointing later novels coincided with the sharp veer to the right that followed his disenchantment with communist politics during the early 1930s. They attacked mass organization, trade unionism, and the New Deal. In his later years he wrote for the conservative periodical the *National Review*. ■ See his memoirs, *The Best Times* (1966), and biographies by Townsend Ludington (1980) and Virginia S. Carr (1984).

DOUGLAS, AARON (1899–1979), U.S. painter. Douglas grew up in Kansas and later studied art in New York and Paris. He founded and for three decades directed Fisk University's art department. A leading figure of the Harlem Renaissance of the 1920s, Douglas incorporated the motifs of primitive African sculpture into his work. His murals at Fisk, at Bennett College (Greensboro, North Carolina), and at the 135th Street branch of the New York Public Library sparked public interest in the black cultural heritage. He illustrated books by Countee Cullen, James Weldon Johnson, and others and created a series of canvases entitled *Idyll of the Negro Past*. ■ See study by Amy Helene Kirschke (1995).

DOUGLAS, DONALD WILLS (1892–1981), U.S. aircraft designer and manufacturer. An aviation enthusiast, Douglas received an engineering degree (1914) from the Massachusetts Institute of Technology and established (1920) his own company, remaining president until 1957 and board chairman until 1967. Douglas Aircraft developed two twin-engine planes, the all-metal DC-1 (1933) and the more famous DC-3 (1936), which, by 1938, was transporting 95 percent of the nation's civilian air passengers. Douglas's planes dominated the commercial airline industry until the end of the piston era. His company, which later merged (1967) with McDonnell Aircraft, produced more than one-sixth of the U.S. planes manufactured during World War II

and later developed the DC-7 and DC-8 airliners and manufactured guided missiles. ■ See Frank Cunningham, *Skymaster* (1943).

DOUGLAS, (GEORGE) NORMAN (1868–1952), Scottish novelist and essayist. As a young man Douglas traveled to Italy, was enchanted by it, and after a short career in the foreign service (1893–96) lived there as an expatriate most of his life. His colorful travel books, including *Siren Land* (1911), *Old Calabria* (1915), and *Together* (1923), were erudite, cosmopolitan, and cheerfully pagan. They helped set a pattern for the genre by mixing history, philosophy, and personal experience in graceful and stylish prose. His popular *South Wind* (1917) was a satirical tale of hedonism on Capri. *Looking Back* (1933) and *Late Harvest* (1946) are autobiographical. ■ See biography by Mark Holloway (1976).

DOUGLAS, THOMAS CLEMENT (1904–1986), Canadian clergyman and political leader. "Tommy" Douglas moved to Canada in 1910 from Scotland. Ordained a Baptist minister in 1930, he was appalled by the economic conditions of the Great Depression and entered politics. In 1935 he was elected to Parliament as a member of the Cooperative Commonwealth Federation (CCF), a socialist party. After a decade Douglas resigned and was elected premier of Saskatchewan (1944). For the next 17 years his administration worked for such progressive social policies as expanded health care, laws favoring trade unions and small farmers, and public ownership of transportation and insurance. From 1961 to 1971 Douglas was the national leader of the CCF's successor, the New Democratic party (NDP), and again served in Parliament (1962–68; 1969–79). ■ See his memoirs, *Making of a Socialist* (1982).

DOUGLAS, WILLIAM ORVILLE (1898–1980), U.S. jurist. Douglas survived poverty and polio in his childhood in the state of Washington to graduate from college (1920) and then from Columbia Law School (1925). A specialist in business law, he taught at Columbia and at Yale. As chairman of the Securities and Exchange Commission (1937–39), he was instrumental in achieving stock-exchange reform. In 1939 Pres. Franklin D. Roosevelt appointed him to the U.S. Supreme Court; at age 41 he became the youngest justice in court history. He was always a controversial jurist who in his concern for the general welfare and for civil liberties sided with dissidents and the disadvantaged. He retired in 1975 after having served on the court longer than any other justice in history. Douglas was also known as an outdoorsman and conservationist. He wrote many books, including the memoirs *Go East, Young Man* (1974) and *The Court Years, 1939–1975* (1980) ■ See biography by James F. Simon, *Independent Journey* (1980).

DOUGLASS, ANDREW ELLICOTT (1867–1962), U.S. astronomer. Douglass did research at the Harvard and Lowell

(Flagstaff, Arizona) observatories before becoming professor of physics and astronomy at the University of Arizona (1906). While doing research on sunspot activity, he investigated the relationship between sunspots, weather, and tree growth. Examining and measuring tree rings, he found that variations in their width corresponded to patterns of distinct climatic cycles that he determined for a period of nearly 2,000 years. Utilizing his system of dendrochronology, scientists were able to date prehistoric ruins and accurately study the growth of forests.

DOUHET, GIULIO (1869–1930), Italian military strategist. The commander of Italy's first military aviation unit (1912–15), Douhet was the first to write about strategic air power. In *The Command of the Air* (1921; Eng. trans. 1942) and *The War of 19–* (1931), he predicted that future wars would be won by bombing attacks on population and industrial centers and that surface forces would play a purely defensive role. Although he overemphasized the role of bombing and did not consider the possibility of an effective antiaircraft defense, he enunciated many ideas that were adopted by strategists of the major military powers in the interwar period and during World War II. ■ See study by Louis A. Sigaud (1941).

DOVE, ARTHUR GARFIELD (1880–1946), U.S. painter. Dove worked as an illustrator before studying art in Paris (1907–09). He developed an abstract style based on forms in nature and first exhibited his work at the gallery of photographer Alfred Stieglitz in New York City (1912). Dove's paintings became increasingly abstract (*Rise of the Full Moon,* 1937), and he was generally regarded as a forerunner of the abstract expressionists. ■ See study by Frederick S. Wight (1958).

DOVE, RITA FRANCES (1952–   ), U.S. poet. Dove studied at the University of Iowa, Iowa City (M.F.A. 1977), and taught there (1975–87) and at the University of Virginia, Charlottesville (1989–   ). She won numerous awards for her concise, evocative poems, which were based on personal history as well as on the history of African Americans. Among her best-known collections were *Thomas and Beulah* (1986; Pulitzer Prize, 1987), *Grace Notes* (1984), *Selected Poems* (1993), *Mother Love* (1995), and *On the Bus with Rosa Parks* (1999). She was the youngest person and the first African-American poet to serve as poet laureate (1993–95) of the United States. Dove also published a volume of short stories, *Fifth Sunday* (1985); a novel, *Through the Ivory Gate* (1992); a verse drama, *The Darker Face of the Earth* (1994); and a collection of essays, *The Poet's World* (1995).

DOVZHENKO, ALEKSANDR (1894–1956), Russian film director. The son of illiterate peasants, Dovzhenko was a diplomat, painter, and cartoonist before turning to film at age 32. The most provincial of the great Soviet directors, he examined a peasant theme in *Zvenigora* (1928); his masterpiece, *Earth* (1930), was a stirring lyrical tribute to the Ukrainian peasantry. His talking films included the patriotic *Frontier* (1935) and *Shors* (1939). After *Michurin* (1948), a film about the life of the famous horticulturist, Dovzhenko again returned to the subject of his Ukrainian homeland for a trilogy that was completed by his widow after his death. Translations of his writings are in *The Poet as Filmmaker* (1973). ■ See Vance Kepley, *In the Service of the State* (1986).

DOWDING, HUGH CASWALL TREMENHEERE DOWDING, 1st BARON (1882–1970), British military leader. As a member of the Air Council (1930–36), Dowding was instrumental in the development of the all-metal monoplane fighter and radar. He served as commander in chief of the Fighter Command (1936–40) and organized the air defense that defeated the German air force during the Battle of Britain (1940). Involved in controversy, he was relieved of his post in November 1940. Many believe that he was shabbily treated at the time; he retired in 1942. Thereafter he became interested in spiritualism, and his *Many Mansions* (1943) deals with communications received from men killed in World War II. ■ See Basil Collier, *Leader of the Few* (1957).

DOWNES, (EDWIN) OLIN (1886–1955), U.S. music critic. Downes was the critic of the *Boston Post* (1906–24) before moving to the *New York Times* (1924–55), where he was regarded as the "dean" of U.S musical criticism during the 1940s and 1950s. He championed the music of romantic and nationalistic composers (notably Sibelius) while dismissing neoclassical and atonal works. In his attempts to bring classical music to the masses, he lectured widely, chaired the Metropolitan Opera's Saturday matinee radio quiz, and wrote several popular books, including *The Lure of Music* (1918) and *Symphonic Masterpieces* (1935). Selected reviews are to *Olin Downes on Music* (1957).

DOXIADES, CONSTANTINOS APOSTOLOS (1914–1975), Bulgarian-born Greek architect and city planner. Trained in architecture and engineering in Athens and Berlin, Doxiades was chief town planner of Athens (1937–39), regional planner (1939–44), and head of Greek reconstruction after World War II. A visionary concerned with human-centered rather than machine-dominated cities, he developed "ekistics," a multidisciplinary (architecture, sociology, town planning, geography, psychology) science of human settlement, and established a consulting firm to put his ideas into practice. He worked on projects in over 30 countries and was best known for rural and urban projects in Iraq, an urban-renewal project in Philadelphia, and the planning of the new Pakistani capital of Islamabad. Among his books were *Ekistic Analysis* (1946), *Architecture in Transition* (1963), and *Ekistics: An Introduction* (1968).

DOYLE, SIR ARTHUR CONAN (1859–1930), British writer. To supplement his physician's income, Doyle wrote his first story, "A Study in Scarlet" (1887), featuring his creation, the detective Sherlock Holmes. Doyle himself regarded his now-forgotten historical novels more highly than the Holmes tales, but Holmes became immensely popular and is still today the object of a cult of readers. Most of the Holmes stories were written in 1891–93 and 1901–02 and evoke late Victorian life. The last Holmes book was *The Casebook of Sherlock Holmes* (1927). Aided by his friend and narrator of the tales, the befuddled Dr. Watson, Holmes was a cerebral detective who solved crimes by the use of science and the deductive method; he influenced the development of the European detective novel. Doyle was knighted (1902) for services to the crown during the Boer War and spent his last years involved in spiritualism. ■ See his autobiography, *Memories and Adventures* (1924); Charles Higham, *The Adventures of Conan Doyle* (1976); biography by Ronald Pearsall (1977); and Daniel Stashower, *Teller of Tales* (1999).

DRABBLE, MARGARET (1939–), British writer. After graduating from Cambridge (1960), Drabble, newly married, wrote her first three novels during her three pregnancies. Her novels dealt not only with women in search of their place in the world, but also with the powerful claims of motherhood. Among her best works are *The Millstone* (1965; filmed as *A Touch of Love*, 1969, for which Drabble wrote the screenplay), *The Needle's Eye* (1972), *The Realms of Gold* (1975), and *The Ice Age* (1977). *The Middle Ground* (1980) examined a middle-aged journalist and feminist whose children are nearly grown. Her trilogy—*The Radiant Way* (1987), *A Natural Curiosity* (1989), and *The Gates of Ivory* (1991)—traced the lives of three women who first met as students at Cambridge during the 1950s. She later wrote the novel *The Witch of Exmoor* (1996) and a biography of Angus Wilson (1996). Drabble also edited the *Oxford Companion to English Literature* (1985). ■ See studies by Valerie G. Myer (1974) and Lynn V. Sadler (1986); and Ellen C. Rose, *The Novels of Margaret Drabble* (1980).

DRAGO, LUIS MARÍA (1859–1921), Argentine official and jurist. As Argentina's minister of foreign relations in 1902, Drago, a former newspaper editor, lawyer, and judge, proposed that foreign countries should not use force to compel Latin American repayment of indebtedness. The Drago Doctrine, which was adopted by a Pan-American conference (1906), fortified Latin America against foreign intervention. Drago served on the International Court of Justice (1906) and was subsequently called upon to arbitrate international disputes.

DRAKE, FRANK DONALD (1930–), U.S. astronomer. Drake was among the first Americans to receive a doctoral degree (Harvard, 1958) in the new field of radio astronomy, the science that explores astronomical phenomena through the radio waves emitted by celestial objects. Drake discov-

ered that Jupiter, like the earth, is girded by a radiation belt, and that Venus, with a temperature of approximately 585°F, is too hot to support life as it is known on Earth. Radio astronomy allowed Drake to penetrate the cosmic dust obscuring our galaxy—the Milky Way—and to make (1959) a high-resolution map of the galaxy. He also participated in the first major attempt to intercept radio signals from intelligent beings on other planets. He taught at Cornell University (1964–85) and the University of California, Santa Cruz (1984–), and directed the National Astronomy and Ionosphere Center (1971–81). His books included *Murmers of Earth* (1979) and *Is Anyone Out There?* (1992).

DRAPEAU, JEAN (1916–1999), French-Canadian political leader. Drapeau graduated from the University of Montreal (B.A. 1938; LL.B. 1941) and was involved with extremist French-Canadian political groups during World War II. A crusading lawyer and journalist, he was elected mayor of Montreal as the candidate of the reformist Civic Action League (1954). Although defeated for reelection three years later, he organized the Montreal Civic party (1960) and was returned to power in 1960, reelected in subsequent elections, and served until 1986. During his years in office, Drapeau helped build up the city as an international metropolis. He was largely responsible for bringing the 1967 World's Fair (Expo 67), the 1976 Olympic games, and the major-league baseball team, the Expos, to Montreal, and for building the subway system, new airports, and a new highway network. ■ See study by Brian McKenna and Susan Purcell (1980).

DRAPER, PAUL (1909–1996), U.S. dancer. Draper made his debut as a tap dancer in a London vaudeville theater in 1932. He later studied ballet (in New York), incorporated that discipline's techniques, elegance, and precision into his tap routines, and developed "ballet-tap," a unique combination of classical and modern dance. He created his own choreography, arranged numbers to the music of Bach, Handel, Dubussy, Couperin, and other classical composers, and gave highly acclaimed solo recitals throughout the world. From 1940 to 1949 he toured with harmonica virtuoso Larry Adler. Subsequently blacklisted as a communist sympathizer, Draper left the country (1951) and settled in Switzerland. He returned to the United States in 1954 and resumed his career as a dancer and choreographer.

DREES, WILLEM (1886–1988), Dutch political leader. A Social Democrat, Drees served as alderman of The Hague (1913) and member of parliament (1933–40). During World War II he was a member of the Dutch resistance and helped set up the first postwar government. He participated in forming a new non-Marxist Socialist party (1946) and served as premier in four successive governments (1948–58). During his years in power he intiated a comprehensive welfare system, presided over the transfer of sovereignty to Indonesia (1949), and led the Dutch into the North Atlantic

Treaty Organization and the European Economic Community.

DREISER, THEODORE (1871–1945), U.S. novelist. Distraught when his first novel, the classic *Sister Carrie* (1900), sold fewer than 500 copies, Dreiser didn't publish his next, *Jennie Gerhardt,* until 1911. Both were attacked for their unvarnished realism, but the second novel was sufficiently successful to allow Dreiser to abandon his journalism career and devote himself to fiction. Working in the naturalist mode, he portrayed the individual's struggle for survival in the face of injustice and his own ambition. Work on a trilogy about a driven, power-hungry business magnate—*The Financier* (1912), *The Titan* (1914), and *The Stoic* (1947)—spanned four decades. *An American Tragedy* (1925), Dreiser's most acclaimed novel, was based on a notorious murder case. It was adapted for the Broadway stage and the motion-picture screen and made Dreiser famous. Dreiser's interest in socialism led to two works of nonfiction: *Dreiser Looks at Russia* (1928) and *Tragic America* (1931). In his later years he devoted himself increasingly to political activism and joined the American Communist party. He wrote three autobiographies: *A Book About Myself* (1922), *A Traveler at Forty* (1931), and *Dawn* (1931). ■ See his *American Diaries, 1902–1926* (1982); and biographies by W. A. Swanberg (1965), Richard Lehan (1969), Robert H. Elias (1970), and Richard Lingeman (2 vols., 1986–90).

DRESSLER, MARIE (Leila Koerber; 1869–1934), Canadian-born U.S. actress. Dressler left home at age 14, toured with a light-opera company, and appeared in vaudeville, making a name for herself as a comedienne during the 1890s. In her fist movie, *Tillie's Punctured Romance* (1914), she acted with Charlie Chaplin and won audiences with her comic expressions. Her career waned until the late 1920s, when she renewed her dramatic repertoire with charming, comic portrayals of large, eccentric, and strong-willed older women. After playing the alcoholic Marthy in *Anna Christie* (1930), Dressler was typecast in this kind of role in such films as *Politics* (1931), *Dinner at Eight* (1933), and *Tugboat Annie* (1933). Her performance in *Min and Bill* (1931) earned her an Academy Award. ■ See her autobiography, *My Own Story* (1934), and biographies by Betty Lee (1997) and Matthew Kennedy (1999).

DREW, CHARLES RICHARD (1904–1950), U.S. surgeon and medical researcher. A graduate of Amherst (B.A. 1926) and McGill (M.D. 1933), Drew achieved prominence for his blood research done at Columbia University. His work, described in his 1940 thesis, *Banked Blood,* established that blood plasma could replace whole blood in transfusions. In that year he headed the British Blood Bank, which collected blood in New York, converted it to plasma, and shipped it to war-torn Britain. In 1941 he directed the American Red Cross blood-bank program; he resigned in protest when, a few weeks later, the Red Cross complied with an armed-forces directive to segregate blood donations. Drew, an African American, also chaired (from 1941) the department of surgery at the Howard University Medical School. He died after a car crash; the segregated hospital where he was treated lacked the blood plasma that might have saved his life. ■ See studies by Richard Hardwick (1967) and Charles E. Wynes (1988); Robert Lichello, *Pioneer in Blood Plasma* (1968); and Spencie Love, *One Blood* (1996).

DREYER, CARL THEODOR (1889–1968), Danish film director. An orphan who was raised in a strict Lutheran family in Copenhagen, Dreyer was a journalist, scriptwriter, and editor before directing his first film (1919). He subsequently directed 14 films during a long career in Scandinavia, Germany, and France. Dreyer's best-known films concerned the power of evil, human suffering, and spiritual conflicts. He used a slow pace, lingering close-ups, and stark lighting to heighten the dramatic effects of his works. *The Passion of Joan of Arc* (1928) examined the emotional trial of the martyr, and *Vampyr* (1932) explored the intensity of the feeling of horror. *Day of Wrath* (1943), made during the German occupation of Denmark, depicted 17th-century religious persecution, while *Ordet* (1955) was a study of faith, love, and resurrection. Dreyer's last film, *Gertrude* (1964), concerned a woman seeking perfect love. His writings on film are in *Dreyer in Double Reflection* (Eng. trans. 1973). ■ See Tom Milne, *The Cinema of Carl Dreyer* (1971) and David Bordwell, *The Films of Carl-Theodor Dreyer* (1980).

DREYFUSS, HENRY (1904–1972), U.S. industrial designer. A pioneer in his field, Dreyfuss gave up a successful career in stage design to become a designer of industrial and consumer products. From 1929, when he opened his first office, he helped modernize, simplify, and beautify American life with designs of such diverse items as telephones, refrigerators, plumbing fixtures, farm machinery, vacuum cleaners, typewriters, prosthetic devices, and airline, train, and ship interiors. He believed that form followed function, favored clean-cut lines in his designs, and opposed planned stylistic obsolescence. His books include *Designing for People* (1955), *The Measure of Man* (1960), and *Symbols Sourcebook* (1972). ■ See study by Russell Flinchum (1997).

DRIEU LA ROCHELLE, PIERRE (1893–1945), French novelist and essayist. A prominent political and literary intellectual during the period between World War I and II, Drieu La Rochelle wrote influential political tracts as well as notable autobiographical fiction, including *The Comedy of Charleroi* (1934; Eng trans. 1973), a series of short stories based on his World War I combat experiences; *The Fire Within* (1931; Eng. trans. 1965), the story of a young Parisian drug addict; and *Gilles* (1939), a rich fresco of the interwar period. Convinced of the decadence of modern France, he drifted politically from surrealism through socialist internationalism to fascism (from 1934) and advocated collaboration with Germany after the defeat of France in

1940. He served as editor (1940–43) of the prestigious *Nouvelle Revue Française* during the German occupation of Paris and committed suicide after the liberation of France. ■ See his *Secret Journal and Other Writings* (1961; Eng. trans. 1973), Robert Soucy, *Fascist Intellectual* (1979), and study by Robert B. Leal (1982).

DRUMMOND, JAMES ERIC. *See PERTH, JAMES ERIC DRUMMOND, 16th EARL OF.*

DRUMMOND DE ANDRADE, CARLOS (1902–), Brazilian poet. A leader of the modernist movement in his native state of Minas Gerais, and later (after 1934) in Rio de Janeiro, Drummond de Andrade was regarded as the greatest Brazilian poet of his generation. His simple, straightforward poems, at times humorous and ironic, reflected the sense of internal conflict and wistful nostalgia with which he viewed the human condition. He demanded intellectual honesty and integrity in his socially conscious poetry that frequently dealt with themes of injustice, reform, and human solidarity. For English translations of his poems, see *In the Middle of the Road* (1965), *An Anthology of Twentieth Century Brazilian Poetry* (1972), *The Minus Sign* (1980), and *Traveling in the Family* (1987).

DRYDEN, HUGH LATIMER (1898–1965), U.S. physicist and aeronautical engineer. Dryden studied at Johns Hopkins University (Ph.D. 1919) and worked at the National Bureau of Standards (1918–47). He did pioneering work on air turbulence that led to improvements in airplane design and headed the research team that developed (1944) the first U.S. guided missile, the *Bat*. He directed aeronautical research for the National Advisory Committee for Aeronautics (NACA; 1947–58) and was instrumental to the establishment (1958) of the National Aeronautics and Space Administration (NASA), which he served as deputy administrator (1958-65).

DRYSDALE, SIR (GEORGE) RUSSELL (1912–1981), Australian artist. Born in Britain and raised in the Australian outback, Drysdale was the first artist to paint the Australian heartland realistically, depicting the desolation, hardship, melancholy, and monotony of the area that had been ignored by previous artists. He recorded the effects of the severe drought in 1944 and depicted the plight of the aborigines. Other subjects included *The Drover's Wife* (1945) and *The Cricketers* (1948). ■ See study by Geoffrey Dutton (rev. ed. 1981) and biography by Lou Klepac (1996).

DUARTE, JOSÉ NAPOLÉON (1926–1990), Salvadoran political leader. Duarte graduated from the University of Notre Dame in South Bend, Indiana (1948), and became a prominent civil engineer in San Salvador. He helped found the reformist, anticommunist, Christian Democratic party (1960) and was elected mayor of San Salvador (1964) and reelected twice (1966, 1968). Having gained a reputation as

a populist, he was apparently elected president in 1972, but the military intervened and he was exiled to Venezuela. After the coup of October 1979, Duarte returned to El Salvador, joined the civilian-military junta, and served as its head (1980–82). The government inaugurated a land distribution program (never fully implemented) and was strongly supported by U.S. economic and military aid, but the Salvadoran army was unable to stem the growing leftist-led guerrilla insurgency and it was accused of committing widespread attocities against civilians. Although the civil war continued through the mid-1980s, Duarte was elected president for a five-year term in 1984 in a controversial election that was boycotted by the left. His administration was widely criticized as being corrupt and ineffective in solving El Salvador's social and economic problems. ■ See study by Stephen Webre (1979), Raymond Bonner, *Weakness and Deceit* (1984), and Duarte's autobiography (1986).

DUBČEK, ALEXANDER (1921–1992), Czechoslovak political leader. A patternmaker by trade, Dubček was active to the World War II underground in Slovakia and became a Communist party functionary after the war. As head of the Slovak Communist party (from 1963), he led the opposition against Czech leader Antonín Novotný, whom he succeeded as national party chief in January 1968. Dubček sought to humanize socialism, instituting political and economic liberalization during the "Prague Spring," but was forced by Soviet military intervention in August 1968 to renege on key reforms. He was replaced as party leader by Gustav Husak (April 1969) and ideological and political restrictions were reintroduced. After serving as ambassador to Turkey (1969–70), he faded from official life. He returned to public life to support the reform movement during the 1989 nationwide demonstrations that eventually swept the Communist party from power. After dissident playwright Vaclav Havel was elected president (1989) Dubček was unanimously elected speaker of the Parliament and subsequently served as a leader of the Social Democratic party of Slovakia and was a deputy in the Slovak National Assembly (1992). ■ See his autobiography, *Hope Dies Last* (Eng. trans. 1993); biography by William Shawcross (1970); Pavel Tigrid, *Why Dubček Fell* (Eng. trans. 1971); and *Dubček Speaks* (1990; with A. Sugár).

DUBE, JOHN LANGALIBALELE (1871–1946), South African writer and political leader. Dube studied in the United States (Oberlin College; B.A. 1893), became a Methodist minister, and returned home to found the first Zulu-language newspaper (1906) and the Zulu Christian Industrial School. He was the first president (1912–17) of the South African Native National Congress, the forerunner of the African National Congress, a political organization established to defend black interests, but he encountered factionalism and financial difficulty. He later served as a delegate from Natal to the Native Representative Council (1937–46). Dube wrote some of the first books in Zulu, including the historical novel *Jeqe, the Bodyservant of King Tshaka* (1930; Eng. trans. 1951), and was the first black African to be awarded a Ph.D. from the University of South Africa (1936).

DUBINSKY, DAVID (David Dobnievski; 1892–1982), U.S. labor leader. Arrested several times for labor activiy in his native Poland, Dubinsky emigrated to the United States in 1911, became active in the labor movement, and by 1932 was president of the International Ladies Garment Workers Union (ILGWU), retaining that position until his retirement (1966). He built up the union membership to 450,000 and was nationally known for securing benefits and shorter hours for his workers, for successfully combating racketeering, and for introducing educational and cultural programs. He served as vice president of the American Federation of Labor (AFL; later the AFL-CIO) from 1945 to 1966 and was a founder of the American Labor party (1936), the Liberal party (1944), and the Americans for Democratic Action (ADA; 1947). ■ See his autobiography (1977; with A. H. Raskin) and Max Danish, *The World of David Dubinsky* (1957).

DUBNOW, SIMON (1860–1941), Jewish historian. Born in Russia, Dubnow was a self-educated scholar of the Diaspora who taught Jewish history in St. Petersburg from 1906. He wrote a *History of the Jews in Russia and Poland* (3 vols; Eng trans. 1916–20). In 1922 he fled the bolshevik revolution to Germany, where he completed a *History of the Jews* (10 vols., 1925–29; Eng. trans. 5 vols. 1967–73). Dubnow was an anti-Zionist who also rejected assimilation, believing that the Jews could survive as "cultural nationalists." In 1933 he had to flee again, this time from the Nazis. He was killed during the Nazi occupation of Riga. ■ See his essays in *Nationalism and History* (Eng. trans. 1958); study edited by Aaron Steinberg (1963); biography by Sofia Dubnova-Erlikh (Eng. trans. 1991); and David H. Weinberg, *Between Tradition and Modernity* (1996).

DUBOIS, WILLIAM EDWARD BURGHARDT (1868–1963), U.S. scholar and political activist. W.E.B. DuBois was born and raised in Massachusetts and earned a Ph.D. from Harvard (1895) with a dissertation on the slave trade. An African-American intellectual who was one of the century's most influential interpreters of the black experience in America, he taught economics and sociology at Atlanta University (1897–1910; 1934–44), was a patron of the Harlem Renaissance after World War I, and wrote many important books, including *The Philadelphia Negro* (1899), *The Souls of Black Folk* (1903), *The Negro* (1915), *Black Reconstruction in America* (1935), *Color and Democracy: Colonies and Peace* (1945), and *The World and Africa* (1917). He helped form the Niagara protest movement (1905) and the National Association for the Advancement of Colored People (NAACP; 1909) and edited its journal *Crisis* (1910–34).

He headed a series of Pan-African conferences between 1900 and 1945 and was a leader of the anticolonial movement. A lifelong socialist, DuBois joined the U.S. Communist party in 1961 and later that year became a citizen of Ghana, where he died. ■ See his posthumously published autobiography (1968); biographies by Francis L. Broderick (1959), Elliot M. Rudwick (2d ed. 1968), and Daniel L. Lewis (2 vols., 1993, 2000); and Arnold Rampersad, *The Art and Imagination of W.E.B. DuBois* (1976).

DUBOS, RENÉ JULES (1901–1982), French-born U.S. microbiologist. A pioneer antibacterial researcher. Dubos spent practically his entire career at Rockefeller University in New York City, which he joined in 1927. He discovered tyrothricin (1939); the first commercially produced antibiotic, it was effective in treating several bacterial diseases. The discovery influenced S. A. Waksman and helped pave the way for his eventual discovery of streptomycin. In his later years Dubos wrote many books on scientific subjects for a general audience; *So Human an Animal* (1968) won the Pulitzer Prize (1968). He was particularly concerned with the social implications of science and advocated studying the effect of the total environment on human inhabitants.

DUBUFFET, JEAN (1901–1985), French artist. Dubuffet, who came from a family of bourgeois wine merchants, rejected prevailing aesthetic conventions to seek inspiration for an "art brut" (raw or naive art) from psychotics, criminals, and children. During the 1940s and 1950s he painted a series of flattened humanoids in varying textures and sculpted a succession of giant jigsaw-puzzle constructions. His deliberately antiaesthetic works foreshadowed pop art and other radical movements of the 1960s. ■ See study by Peter Selz (1962) and biography by Andreas Franzke (Eng. trans. 1982).

DUCHAMP, MARCEL (1887–1968), French artist. The brother of painter Jacques Villon and sculptor (Raymond) Duchamp-Villon, Marcel Duchamp was one of the most important figures of 20th-century avant-garde art. In his early works, which anticipated the dada and surrealist movements and inspired op art and pop art, he attempted to destroy the mystique of taste and aesthetic beauty. His cubist-influenced *Nude Descending a Staircase* (1912) created a sensation at the 1913 Armory Show in New York City. With his large wire and glass construction, *The Bride Stripped Bare by Her Bachelors, Even* (commonly called *Large Glass* 1913–23), he completely dispensed with traditional art forms. His well-known "readymades," including *Bicycle Wheel* (1913); a urinal entitled *Fountain* (1927); and *L.H.O.O.Q.* (1919), a photograph of the Mona Lisa with mustache and goatee, questioned traditional views of the role of the artist and the value of art and introduced the "mobile" and the "found object." Duchamp virtually abandoned his artistic work in 1923. He divided his time between Paris and New York, where he helped mount several important surrealist exhibitions. ■ See his *Salt Seller: The Writings of Marcel Duchamp* (Eng. trans. 1973). See also Arturo Schwarz, *The Complete Works* (1969), Calvin Tomkins, *The World of Marcel Duchamp* (1972), and Gianfranco Baruchello and Henry Martin, *Why Duchamp?* (1985).

DUCHAMP-VILLON, RAYMOND (1876–1918), French sculptor. Self-taught sculptor Duchamp-Villon, the brother of artists Jacques Villon and Marcel Duchamp, studied medicine before turning to art in 1898. His early work showed the influence of August Rodin, but his head of Baudelaire (1911) indicated a trend toward abstract principles that led him to cubism. His most daring and original sculpture, the bronze abstract *Horse* (1914), combined the fluid form of a leaping horse and the rigid parts of a machine to create a dynamic and powerful figure. It was considered the prototype of cubist sculpture.

DUCLOS, JACQUES (1896–1975), French political leader. A member of the French Communist party from its formation (1920), Duclos served in the national assembly (1926–32; vice president 1936–40) and was a member of the Central Committee of the Communist party (from 1926) and party secretary (1931-64). A loyal Stalinist, he adhered closely to the Moscow line and played a major role in the formation of the popular front (1936). He led the party (with Benoît Frachon) during World War II and thus played an important role in the Resistance. After the war he served in the consultative assembly (1944–45), constituent assembly (1945–46), and the national assembly (1946–58, heading the communist bloc), and the senate (1959–75). In 1969 he ran for the presidency of France against Georges Pompidou and received 21.3 percent of the vote.

DUFY, RAOUL (1877–1953), French painter. While studying at the École des Beaux Arts (Paris), Dufy found the museum masterpieces oppressive and turned to contemporary art galleries for stimulation and inspiration. He was attracted to the fauvists' bold use of color and the cubists' geometric structures, but he temporarily abandoned painting to make woodcuts and illustrate the first edition of poet Guillaume Apollinare's *Bestiary* (1911). His woodcuts were used by dress designers to paint silks. After World War I, Dufy began to paint again, creating bathers, sailboats, and racing scenes in vibrant colors and light brush strokes. Famous for his pottery and tapestries of the 1920s, Dufy also created watercolors, book illustrations, stage sets, and ornamental panels. ■ See studies by Raymond Cogniat (Eng. trans. 1962) and Dora Perez-Tibi (1989).

DUHAMEL, GEORGES (Denis Thévenin; 1884–1966), French novelist. Duhamel was a founder of a utopian group (1906-08) and espoused its doctrine of unanimism, which emphasized the fraternity of all social groups. A compassionate physician, he expressed his humanism, tolerance, and humor in his writing, which warned against the dehumanizing effects of industrial civilization. *Civilization: 1914–1917* (1918; Eng. trans. 1919) related his experiences as a surgeon during World War I and *America: The Menace* (1930; Eng. trans. 1931) deplored the unchecked industrialization in the United States. His major works were the novel cycles *Salavin* (5 vols., 1920–32; Eng. trans. 1936), and *The Pasquier Chronicles* (10 vols., 1933–45; Eng. trans. 1937–46), a sympathetic study of a bourgeois family over the course of 40 years. He was elected to the Académie Française (1935). ■ See his memoirs, *Light on My Days* (2 vols.; Eng. trans. 1948), and L. Clark Keating, *Critic of Civilization* (1965).

DUHEM, PIERRE MAURICE (1861–1916), French physicist and historian of science. While investigating the history of science, Duhem discovered ancient and medieval precursors of modern theories, which he described in his *Studies on Leonardo da Vinci* (3 vols., 1906–13) and *The System of the World* (10 vols., 1913–59). Duhem, who taught at the universities of Lille (1887–93) and Bordeaux (1894–1916), also made important contributions to the study of thermodynamics. His major philosophical work was *The Aim and Structure of Physical Theory* (1906; Eng. trans. 1954). He also wrote *Thermodynamics and Chemistry* (1902; Eng. trans. 1903) and *To Save the Phenomena* (1908; Eng. trans. 1969). ■ See Armand Lowinger, *The Methodology of Pierre Duhem* (1941), and Stanley L. Jaki, *Uneasy Genius* (1984).

DUKAS, PAUL ABRAHAM (1865–1935), French composer. Influenced by Dubussy while remaining an heir of the classical tradition of César Franck and Vincent d'Indy, Dukas was best known for his dazzling tone poem *The Sorcerer's Apprentice* (1897). His works—including the finely constructed *C Major Symphony* (1897), *Sonata* (1901) for piano, the opera *Ariane et Barbe Bleue* (1907), and the ballet *La Peri*, (1912)—are admired for their clarity, sensitivity, and fine orchestration. He was also a music critic, an editor of 18th-century music, and a noted teacher whose students included Olivier Messaien and Walter Piston.

DUKE, JAMES BUCHANAN (1856–1925), U.S. industrialist. The son of a North Carolina tobacco grower and processor, Duke joined his father's business, perfected an automatic cigarette-rolling machine, and through intensive advertising and reduced prices developed the firm into America's largest producer. In 1890 Duke, convincing his four leading competitors to merge with him, formed the American Tobacco Co., which controlled the industry until ordered to dissolve by the U.S. Supreme Court (1911). In his later years Duke formed the Southern Power System (later the Duke Power Co.) and heavily endowed Trinity College (Durham, North Carolina), which changed its name (1924) to Duke University. ■ See study by John W. Jenkins (1927) and John K. Winkler, *Tobacco Tycoon* (1942).

DULBECCO, RENATO (1914–   ), Italian-born U.S. biologist. Dulbecco received an M.D. degree from the University of Turin (1936) and worked with old friend and future Nobel laureate Salvador Luria at the University of Indiana (1947–49). At the California Institute of Technology and the Salk Institute, during the 1950s and 1960s, he developed laboratory techniques to study the molecular biology of animal viruses and to determine which viral gene is responsible for cancerous changes in a living cell. With his former students, David Baltimore and Howard Temin, he shared the 1975 Nobel Prize in Physiology or Medicine. He later worked at the Imperial Cancer Research Laboratory in London (1972–77) and did research at the Salk Institute (1977–   ; president, 1989–92) and the University of California at San Diego (1977–81).

DULLES, ALLEN WELSH (1893–1969), U.S. diplomat and intelligence expert. The younger brother of statesman John Foster Dulles, Allen Dulles served in various diplomatic posts during and after World War I. While a member of a Wall Street law firm, he continued to advise the government at several important international conferences during the 1920s and 1930s. From 1942 to 1945 he headed the Bern, Switzerland, headquarters of the U.S. Office of Strategic Services (OSS), the wartime intelligence service, and played a key role in the German surrender in northern Italy. During the cold-war era he served as deputy director (1951–53) and director (1953–61) of the Central Intelligence Agency (CIA), the newly established U.S. espionage establishment. He was responsible for such operations as U.S. involvement in right-wing coups in Iran (1953) and Guatemala (1953); the U-2 spy plane flights over the Soviet Union (1956-60), including the mission of Francis Gary Powers, who was forced down and captured by the Soviets in 1960; and the abortive Bay of Pigs landing in Cuba, which sought to overthrow Fidel Castro (1961). The Bay of Pigs operation prompted Dulles' resignation from the CIA. He wrote *The Craft of Intelligence* (1963) and *The Secret Surrender* (1966). ■ See Leonard Mosley, *Dulles* (1978), an account of the Dulles family, and Peter Grose, *Gentleman Spy* (1994).

DULLES, JOHN FOSTER (1888–1959), U.S. secretary of state. Dulles was a Wall Street international lawyer who attended the 1919 Paris Peace Conference, the 1945 conference on the United Nations in San Francisco, and helped negotiate the peace treaty with Japan (1951) and a Korean cease-fire (1951). As Pres. Dwight Eisenhower's secretary of state (1953–59), he replaced the cold-war policy of containment of communism with active intervention and "brinksmanship." His threats of "massive retaliation" against the Soviet Union inspired the slogan "better dead than red." Under Dulles' guidance, the United States intervened to

overthrow a leftist government in Guatemala (1954) and to restore "order" in Lebanon (1958); the United States sponsored the creation of the Southeast Asia Treaty Organization (1954) and supported Premier Ngo Dinh Diem as a bulwark against communism in South Vietnam. ■ See Townshend Hoopes, *The Devil and John Foster Dulles* (1973), and biography by Ronald W. Pruessen (1982).

DU MAURIER, DAME DAPHNE (1907–1989), British novelist and short-story writer. Du Maurier was the daughter of the actor Sir Gerald Du Maurier, whose life she recounted in *Gerald: A Portrait* (1934). She was a popular and successful author of romantic mystery and suspense stories in which she often employed supernatural and melodramatic elements. Her best-known work was *Rebecca* (1938), an atmospheric gothic novel set in Cornwall. Among her other novels were *Jamaica Inn* (1938), *The King's General* (1946), *My Cousin Rachel* (1951), *The House in the Strand* (1969), and *Rule Britannia* (1972). ■ See her autobiographies, *Myself When Young* (1977) and *The Rebecca Notebook* (1980); biography by Margaret Forster (1993); and study by Nina Auerbach (2000).

DU MONT, ALLEN BALCOM (1901–1965), U.S. engineer and inventor. Founder and president (1931–56) of the Du Mont Laboratories, Du Mont was the pioneer in television technology, who developed the first commercially practical cathode-ray tube. Du Mont's company manufactured the first commercial television receivers (1938) and marketed the first home television receivers after World War II. He also established experimental television stations and set up the Du Mont Television Network (1946).

DUNBAR, PAUL LAURENCE (1872–1906), U.S. writer. Son of former slaves, Dunbar worked as an elevator operator and wrote in his spare time until 1895, when he began to attempt to live from his writing. His poetry, much of it written in dialect, was published in several volumes. The second, *Majors and Minors* (1895), was well received by critic William Dean Howells; his introduction to Dunbar's *Lyrics of Lowly Life* (1895) launched a vogue for his poems. He also published four collections of short stories and four novels of which *The Sport of the Gods* (1902) is considered his best, and was one of the first African-American writers to attain national prominence. His *Complete Poems* (1913) was published posthumously. ■ See biography by Benjamin Brawley (1936); Addison Gayle, *Oak and Ivy* (1971); and study by Peter Revell (1979).

DUNCAN, DAVID DOUGLAS (1916–   ), U.S. photographer. In 1938 Duncan began roaming the world with his camera, covering World War II as a photographer with the marines and the Palestine conflict and Korean War for *Life* magazine (1946–56). *This Is War!* (1951), a collection of his Korean pictures, revealed the horror as well as the heroics of combat. Duncan then turned to art, photographing the treasures of the Kremlin (1960), completing several books on Picasso, *Sunflowers for Van Gogh* (1986), and *The World of Allah* (1982). ■ See also *Self-Portrait: U.S.A.* (1969), a photographic report of the 1968 political campaign; *War Without Heroes* (1970), photos of the war in Vietnam; and his pictorial autobiography, *Yankee Nomad* (1966).

DUNCAN, ISADORA (1878–1927), U.S. dancer. Duncan began her professional dance career at age 17. She rejected the constraints of formal ballet, insisting on her own lyrical free-form style. Her dances, based on classical Greek theme and costume, shocked American audiences, but were warmly received in Europe. She opened (1921) a dance school in the Soviet Union, where she married (1922–23) poet Sergei Yesenin. Isadora Duncan danced her last concert in 1927. She died later that year when, during a drive in an open car, the end of her long scarf caught in the rear-wheel spokes. ■ See her autobiography, *The Art of Dance* (1927); Allan R. MacDougall, *Isadora* (1960); Victor Seroff, *The Real Isadora* (1971); Fredrika Blair, *Isadora* (1985); and Lillian Loewenthal, *The Search for Isadora* (1993).

DUNHAM, KATHERINE (1910–), U.S. dancer and choreographer. Durham spent a year and a half in the West Indies studying the native dances and received an M.A. in anthropoloy from the University of Chicago. She combined the movements she learned with modern-dance technique and exerted a major influence on the anthropological dance movement. Her company performed colorful theatricalized versions of African and Caribbean dance rituals on Broadway, in films, and on concert stages throughout the world (1940–67). Her best-known works included *L'Ag'Ya, Choros, Shango,* and *Bal Negre.* She also choreographed the movies *Emperor Jones* (1939) and *Cabin in the Sky* (1940) and *Aida* at New York's Metropolitan Opera (1963), where she was the first African-American choreographer to work with the company. After her retirement in the mid-1960s she founded dance schools for poor children in Haiti and East St. Louis, Illinois. ■ See her autobiography, *A Touch of Innocence* (1959); Terry Harnan, *African Rhythm—American Dance* (1974); and biography by Ruth Beckford (1979).

DUNNE, FINLEY PETER (1867–1936), U.S. journalist and humorist. Dunne worked (from 1884) for various Chicago newspapers, specializing in political reporting. He started to write Irish-dialect sketches for the Chicago *Evening Post* (1892) in which a fictional Irish bartender, the witty and philosophical Mr. Dooley, delivered political and social commentary on the events of the day. Through Mr. Dooley, Dunne attacked governmental corruption, capitalism, and American imperialism, and like the muckrakers, he championed reform. His columns, which became nationally syndicated and appeared in eight collections, were extremely popular during the pre–World War I era. ■ See Elmer Ellis, *Mr. Dooley's America* (1941).

DUNNING, WILLIAM ARCHIBALD (1857–1922), U.S. historian. Dunning spent his academic career at Columbia Universiy, beginning as a student (Ph.D. 1885) and graduating to the teaching and writing of history. His works on the post–Civil War Reconstruction period, notably *Essays on the Civil War and Reconstruction* (1897; rev. ed. 1904) and *Reconstruction* (1907), were the first to claim dispassionate objectivity. He and his students examined the North as well as the South to conclude that the predominant motivation was political rather than economic. The "Dunning School" defended southern planters, criticized the abolitionists, and blamed the radical Republicans for transforming the South into a colony of the North. Dunning also wrote a *History of Political Theories* (3 vols., 1902–20) and *The British Empire and the United States* (1914).

DUNNINGER, JOSEPH (1896–1975), U.S. mentalist. Dunninger was astonishing audiences with magic shows at age 7. He began to concentrate on what he termed "thought reading," and just out of his teens was already calling himself "Dunninger—the Master Mind of Mental Mystery." Dunninger was asked to the White House by six presidents and guessed what was on their minds; Teddy Roosevelt was concentrating on a poker hand, Herbert Hoover on his mother. He demonstrated his telepathic powers on radio and TV shows and wrote the book *What's on Your Mind?* (1944). He dismissed the suggestion that his gift was supernatural; Dunninger asserted that telepathy is a latent ability in a tenth of any population.

DUPLESSIS, MAURICE LE NOBLET (1890–1959), French-Canadian political leader. Born in Quebec, Duplessis became a lawer in 1913 and was elected to the Quebec legislature as a Conservative in 1927. He rose to the leadership of the provincial party in 1933. An advocate of provincial autonomy, he founded the Union Nationale party (1936) and was premier of Quebec (1936–39; 1944–59). He built a formidable political machine, and promoted industrial development. His administration was marked by political patronage, favoritism to U.S. business interests, opposition to organized labor, close relations with the Catholic Church hierarchy, concessions to agricultural interests, and accusations of wide-spread corruption. ■ See Leslie Roberts, *The Chief* (1963), and biography by Conrad Black (1978).

DU PONT, PIERRE SAMUEL (1870–1954), U.S. industrialist. A graduate of the Massachusetts Institute of Technology (1890), Du Pont joined the family gunpowder and chemical firm and helped develop smokeless gunpowder. In 1902 he purchased the company (with two of his cousins) and as president (1915–20) and chairman of the board, modernized and rationalized its operations and built E. I. du

Pont de Nemours and Co. into the largest corporation of its kind in the United States. Over the years it introduced nylon, rayon, Lucite, synthetic rubber, and cellophane and manufactured more than 1,000 different substances. Pierre Du Pont also served as president of General Motors (1920–23) and remodeled it into one of the world's largest and most profitable industrial enterprises. Du Pont was probably America's greatest corporation builder. ■ See biographies by Alfred D. Chandler, Jr., and Stephen Salsbury (1970).

DUPRÉ, MARCEL (1886–1971), French organist. The foremost organist of his time, Dupré dazzled audiences throughout the world with his virtuosity and improvisational ability. He was chief organist at St. Sulpice Church—which housed the largest organ in Paris—and Notre Dame Cathedral, before being named professor at the Paris Conservatory (1926; director 1954–56). In a 10-recital series in 1920 he performed, from memory, the complete organ works of J. S. Bach. He was unrivaled in his improvisational ability, and two of his compositions, *Symphonie-Passion* (1924) and *Le Chemin de la Croix* (1932), were originally played as improvisations. Dupré also wrote works on organ technique, counter-point, and improvisation. ■ See study by Michael Murray (1985).

DURANT, WILL (William James Durant; 1885–1981), and ARIEL DURANT (Ida Kaufman; 1898–1981), U.S. historians and writers. Will Durant worked as a reporter, entered a seminary, but turned to the study of social history and philosophy. When he fell ill during travels in Syria (1912), he conceived the idea of a history of civilization. He set to work 15 years later with his wife Ariel, his former student whom he had married when he was 28 and she was 15. Royalties from Will Durant's first book, *The Story of Philosophy* (1926), which sold 2 million copies in the first three years, gave the Durants the economic freedom to support their joint venture. Over the next five decades, they labored on 11 volumes of *The Story of Civilization* (though Ariel was listed as coauthor only beginning with Volume 7). Their method, which they termed "synthetic history," stressed cultural and scientific achievement; their best-selling work was praised more for its erudition and readability than for its historical judgments. They won a Pulitzer Prize for Volume 10, *Rousseau and Revolution* (1968). Married for 68 years, the Durants died within two weeks of each other. ■ See their *Dual Autobiography* (1977); Will Durant's *Transition* (1978); and the biography of Will by Raymond Frey (1991).

DURANT, WILLIAM CRAPO (1861–1947), U.S. industrialist. Durant organized (1886) the Durant-Dort Carriage Co. in Flint, Michigan, and built it into the world's largest buggy manufacturer. An enthusiastic speculator, promoter, and visionary, he recognized the revolutionary potential of the automobile. He organized the Buick Motor Co. (1905) and consolidated it with a number of smaller firms to establish the General Motors Co. (1910), but he soon lost control of it. He regained control with the backing of the Du Pont family and formed the General Motors Corp. (1916). But as he was an erratic manager, easily diverted to grandiose schemes, he was forced out of GM (again) in 1920; under new management it became one of the world's largest corporations. Durant left the auto business for good in 1926 and lost his fortune in the 1929 Wall Street crash. ■ See Lawrence R. Gustin, *Billy Durant* (1973), and Bernard A. Weisberger, *The Dream Maker* (1979).

DURANTE, JIMMY (James Francis Durante; 1893–1980), U.S. comedian. Durante spent his boyhood in New York City's Lower East Side, soaping customer's physiognomies in his father's barber shop. When he entered "show biz," his own physiognomy became famous across America. Durante started out playing piano in Coney Island spots, sometimes accompanying singing waiter Eddie Cantor. He worked his way into the nightclub circuit and by 1923 was featured with the trio Clayton, Jackson, and Durante. He also appeared in film and on stage in the 1920s; only in the 1940s when he teamed up with youngster Garry Moore were his naturally gruff voice and low-brow comedy aired regularly on radio. Durante became famous for his legendary "schnozz," for his theme song "Inka Dinka Doo," and for his ad-libbed digressions that mangled the lexicon in a way that gave the illusion of logic. He began appearing (1950) on television, at times singing duets with the likes of Ethel Barrymore and Margaret Truman. He always ended broadcasts with the line "Good night, Mrs. Calabash, wherever you are!" ■ See Gene Fowler, *Schnozzola* (1951); William Cahn, *Good Night, Mrs. Calabash* (1963); and study by David Bakish (1995).

DURANTY, WALTER (1884–1957), British-born journalist. A first-class honors graduate of Cambridge University (1906), Duranty spent seven years wandering through Britain, France, and America, living a bohemian existence, before joining the *New York Times* Paris bureau (1913). As a foreign correspondent with the paper for 28 years, he was internationally regarded as an expert on the Soviet Union, which he covered from 1921 to 1934. His reports from Moscow won a 1932 Pulitzer Prize. Duranty's books on the Soviet Union included *The Curious Lottery and Other Tales of Russian Justice* (1929), *U.S.S.R.* (1944), and *Stalin and Co.* (1949). ■ See his memoirs, *I Write As I Please* (1935), and S. J. Taylor, *Stalin's Apologist* (1990).

DURAS, MARGUERITE (Marguerite Donnadieu; 1914–1996), French novelist and filmmaker. Duras was born in Indochina, which provided the background for some of her work. She was associated with several schools of writing; while her early work was realistic, her later fiction, with its lack of plot, obscure speech, and silences, was linked with the "new novel" in France. Her basic themes, the aspects of love and the importance of time and its effect on people, are seen in such novels as *The Sea Wall* (1950; Eng. trans.

1952), *Moderato Cantabile* (1958; Eng. trans. 1960), and *The Lover* (1984; Eng. trans. 1985), all of which were filmed. Duras also wrote the screenplay for Alain Resnais' *Hiroshima Mon Amour* (1960) and directed several films, including *Nathalie Granger* (1972) and *India Song* (1973). Her memoir, *The War* (1985; Eng. trans. 1986), described her life in Paris during World War II. She worked for the occupation government for a year before joining the Resistance in mid-1943. After the war she joined the Communist party and despite her subsequent expulsion, she remained committed to leftist causes. Her essays appeared in *Writing* (Eng. trans. 1998). ■ See study by Marilyn R. Schuster (1993) and biography by Laure Adler (1998; Eng. trans. 2000).

DURKHEIM, ÉMILE (1858–1917), French sociologist. Born into a Jewish rabbinical family in Alsace, Durkheim graduated from the École Normale Supérieure in Paris and taught law and philosophy. A founder of modern sociology, he taught the first sociology course in France (1887) and a decade later established France's first professorship in sociology at the University of Bordeaux (1896). Durkheim turned the methods of science to the study of society, stressing the importance of social cohesion and stability and studying the phenomena that result when that stability is disrupted. In his classic study *Suicide* (1897; Eng. trans. 1957), Durkheim classified the types of societies in which suicide rates tend to be high, and argued that individual acts of suicide reflect the dissolution of social ties. In *The Elementary Forms of Religious Life* (1915; Eng. trans. 1954), he examined the belief system as a social bond whose absence leads to social instability. ■ See biographies by Anthony Giddens (1979), Steven Lukes (1972), and Kenneth Thompson (1982); and studies by Steve Fenton (1984) and William W. Miller (1996).

DURRELL, LAWRENCE (1912–1990), British poet and novelist. Born and raised in India, Durrell spent most of his life outside Britain working as a journalist and British press attaché. He wrote sensual poetry, fiction, and notable travel books about the islands of Rhodes (*Reflections on a Marine Venus,* 1953), Cyprus (*Bitter Lemons,* 1957), and Corfu (*Prospero's Cell,* 1960). He was most famous for the bestselling novels forming *The Alexandria Quartet* (4 vols., 1957–60). The novels were set in the cosmopolitan society of Alexandria, Egypt, before and during World War II. In an elaborate, lush style, Durrell described, from different viewpoints, varieties of love and isolation. He subsequently wrote an Avignon Quintet, consisting of the novels *Monsieur* (1975), *Livia* (1979), *Constance* (1982), *Sebastian* (1984), and *Quinx* (1985). ■ See his *Collected Poems* (1980); studies by John A. Weigel (1966) and George S. Fraser (1968); and biography by Ian S. MacNiven (1998).

DÜRRENMATT, FRIEDRICH (1921-1990), Swiss (German-language) playwright and novelist. A student of philosophy and theology who originally planned to be a painter, Dür-

renmatt turned to writing after World War II and became one of the most popular European dramatists. His plays, characterized by grotesque plots and black humor, exposed hypocrisy and corruption in modern society. While he showed life as impersonal and cruel, his message was that individuals must assert themselves and never surrender to life's pressures. Dürrenmatt's most notable plays were *The Marriage of Mr. Mississippi* (1952; Eng. trans. 1964), *The Visit* (1956; Eng. trans. 1958), and *The Physicists* (1962; Eng. trans. 1963). Later plays were out of step with the highly politicized German theater of the late 1960s and 1970s. He also wrote detective novels, *The Judge and his Hangman* and *The Quarry* (Eng. trans. in one vol., 1983), the essays in *Writings on Theater and Drama* (1966; Eng. trans. 1976), and the novel, *The Execution of Justice* (1985; Eng. trans. 1989). ■ See study by Murray B. Peppard (1969).

DURRUTI, BUENAVENTURA (1896–1936), Spanish anarchist leader. An idealistic and militant miner and railway worker, Durruti was a cofounder of the Solidarios (1919), an anarcho-bolshevik group that assassinated several public figures as part of its campaign (1919–23) to bring about a Spanish social revolution. After several years in Latin America, France—including a period in prison—and Belgium, he returned to Spain (1931) and was imprisoned (1933–35) for participating in violent labor demonstrations. In 1936 he endorsed the popular front and participated in the leadership of the Federación Anarquista Ibérica (FAI), the most important anarchist movement in Europe, which sought to establish workers' councils and agricultural communes as the basis of a libertarian communist society. At the outbreak of the civil war (1936) the charismatic Durruti helped unite various forces on the left, headed the militia of the new Catalan government, and played a major role in the defense of Barcelona. His forces, however, failed to take Saragossa, and he was killed by a sniper during the defense of Madrid. His murder, which the anarchists blamed on the communists, led to bitter sectarian struggles. In death he became a legendary cult figure. ■ See study by Abel Paz (Eng. trans. 1978) and Robert Kern, *Red Years—Black Years* (1978).

DURYCH, JAROSLAV (1886–1962), Czech poet and novelist. A physician turned literary man, Durych was best known for his series of historical novels that re-created the Bohemia of the 17th century. His most famous work is *The Descent of the Idol* (3 vols., 1929; Eng. trans. 1935), which concentrated on the period of the Thirty Years' War and the figure of General von Wallenstein. All of Durych's works reflected a Roman Catholic—and at times mystical—outlook. He championed the poor, opposed modern civilization, and wrote of the human desire for divine grace.

DUTT, RAJANI PALME (1896–1974), British political leader. Born to a Bengali father and Swedish mother, R. Palme Dutt graduated from Oxford (1918) and was a founder of the British Communist party (1920) and a member of its Central Committee (1922–65). The party's leading theoretician and intellectual, he consistently followed and defended Soviet dictator Joseph Stalin's policies. He founded and edited the *Labour Monthly* (1921–74) and wrote many books, including *Fascism and Social Revolution* (1934), *World Politics, 1918–1936* (1936), *India Today* (1940), and *The Crisis of Britain and the British Empire* (1953). Dutt also affected the growth of communism in India by influencing three generations of Indian students in England.

DUVALIER, FRANÇOIS ("Papa Doc"; 1907–1971), Haitian political leader. A doctor who headed the national health service (1946–48) and the ministry of public health (1948–50), Duvalier was a member of the "Groupe des Griots," a group of writers that sought Haitian cultural roots in black nationalism and voodoo. As "president for life" (1957–71), he ruled dictatorially by a mixture of terrorism, corruption, and voodoo, bringing economic and political stagnation to the poverty-stricken and predominantly illiterate citizens of Haiti. He was succeeded as dictator by his son, Jean Claude, who fled the country in February 1986 following three months of protest demonstrations against the government. ▪ See biography by Al Burt and Bernard Diederich (1969) and James Ferguson, *Papa Doc, Baby Doc* (1987).

DUVEEN, JOSEPH, 1st BARON DUVEEN OF MILLBANK (1869–1939), British art dealer. The son of the founder of Duveen Brothers, art dealers, Joseph Duveen spectacularly expanded the firm until he practically monopolized the pre–World War I market of old masters in Europe and the United States. An expert in appraising the value and authenticity of a work of art, he helped form the vast Frick, Rockefeller, Mellon, Hearst, Widener, and Huntington collections, which eventually were housed in public museums. Duveen thus greatly influenced art tastes in America and indirectly made it possible for Americans to see the greatest European artworks without traveling abroad. He also patronized many young artists, donated a new wing and large collection to the Tate Gallery (London), and contributed an addition to the British Museum that houses the Elgin Marbles from the Parthenon. ▪ See S. N. Behrman, *Duveen* (1952; rev. ed. 1972), and Colin Simpson, *Artful Partners* (1986).

DU VIGNEAUD, VINCENT (1901–1978), U.S. biochemist. Du Vigneaud studied at the universities of Rochester (Ph.D 1927), Berlin, Edinburgh, and London and taught at Cornell University Medical College in New York City (1938–67). For the "historic feat" of isolating and synthesizing the pituitary hormones oxytocin, which controls uterine contractions, and vasopressin, which helps regulate blood pressure, he was awarded the 1955 Nobel Prize for Chemistry. Du Vigneaud also established the structure of the vitamin biotin (1942) and contributed to the synthesis of

penicillin G (1946). He wrote *A Trail of Research in Sulfur Chemistry and Metabolism and Related Fields* (1952).

DYER-BENNET, RICHARD (1913–1991), British-born U.S. musician. Dyer-Bennet emigrated to the United States as a boy and became a U.S. citizen in 1935. A singer, guitarist, lutist, and composer, he single-handedly revived the art of minstrelsy. He assembled a repertoire of Elizabethan, classic, and folk songs that he began presenting in churches and union halls. Dyer-Bennet made a New York concert debut in 1944, and thereafter his Town Hall (New York) recital became an annual event. He also sang in nightclubs. Known primarily for his renditions of English and American ballads, Dyer-Bennet also distinguished himself with performances of Schubert song cycles. He taught at the State University of New York, Stony Brook (1970–83).

DYLAN, BOB (Robert Allen Zimmerman; 1941–), U.S. singer and songwriter. Dylan dropped out of the University of Minnesota, renamed himself after the poet Dylan Thomas, and drifted to New York in the early 1960s to become a musical legend. Dylan enthralled young audiences with his sometimes raspy and whining but always compelling renditions of his own poetic lyrics and music. His career spanned several shifts of musical taste as he moved from urban folk and protest to country and rock, achieving success in each. Dylan's greatest hits included "It Ain't Me Babe," "The Times They Are A-Changin'," "Blowin' in the Wind," "Just Like a Woman," and "Lay Lady Lay." Many were recorded as well by other performers. The album *Biograph* (1985) and the book *Lyrics 1962–1985* (1985) reflected his work over three decades. His later albums included *Good As I Been To You* (1992) and the Grammy Award–winning *Time Out of Mind* (1997), a compilation of dark songs about aging and mortality. Dylan also wrote a stream-of-consciousness novel, *Tarantula* (1970), and produced and starred in a film, *Renaldo and Clara* (1978). ▪ See biographies by Anthony Scaduto (rev. ed. 1979), Jonathan Cott (1985), Bob Spitz (1989), and Clinton Heylin (2000).

DZERZHINSKY, FELIKS EDMUNDOVICH (1877–1926), Soviet political leader. Born into the Polish aristocracy, Dzerzhinsky joined the Social Democratic party in 1895, became a follower of bolshevik leader V. I. Lenin, and played a major role in the bolshevik seizure of power in October 1917. He served as first chief of the secret police, the Cheka (1917–22), and its successors the GPU and OGPU (1922–26). In 1919 he took charge of the commissariat of internal affairs (NKVD) as well, assuming responsibility for all police and security matters, and oversaw the series of repressions known as the "Red Terror." He later served as chairman of the Supreme Economic Council (1924–26) and was a strong supporter of the New Economic Policy (NEP). ▪ See Lennard D. Gerson, *The Secret Police in Lenin's Russia* (1976).

E

EAMES, CHARLES (1907–1978), U.S. furniture designer. Trained as an architect, Eames created the famous Eames chair, a molded plywood lounge chair structured by a metal underframe, which was exhibited (1946) at New York's Museum of Modern Art in its first one-person furniture show. Eames' innovative, prize-winning designs combined technical and aesthetic considerations with a view toward maximizing comfort. Much of his work was done in collaboration with his wife, Ray Kaiser Eames (1916–1988). Manufacturers of office and home furnishings copied and adapted many of Eames' designs. He was design consultant for several U.S. corporations, including the International Business Machines Corp. (IBM). ■ See Donald Alhrecht, et al., *The Work of Charles and Ray Eames* (1997).

EANES, ANTÓNIO RAMALHO (1935–   ), Portuguese political leader. The son of a building contractor, Eanes joined the army after he graduated from the national military academy (1956) and served in Portuguese India (1958–60), Macao (1962), and Mozambique (1964: 1966–68). While leading antiguerrilla forces in Portuguese Guinea (1969–73) and Angola (1973–74), he became disillusioned with his government's colonial policy and joined the Armed Forces movement, a group of dissident young officers. In April 1974 they overthrew the dictatorial regime of Marcello Caetano (successor of longtime fascist dictator Antonio de Oliveira Salazar) and Eanes served as director of the Portuguese television system in the transitional military government. For his role in suppressing a leftist military coup (November 1975) he was named a four-star general and was appointed army chief of staff. A believer in democratic socialism, he served as the first freely elected president of Portugal in half a century (1976–86) and helped reestablish parliamentary democracy.

EARHART, AMELIA (1898–1937), U.S. aviator. Defying the wishes of her family, Earhart abandoned her social-work career and turned to aviation. She was the first woman to fly across the Atlantic (1928), although only a passenger on that flight. Four years later she made the first solo transatlantic flight by a woman and received the Distinguished Flying Cross from the U.S. government. She also completed the first solo flights from Hawaii to California (1935) and from Mexico City to New York City's airport in Newark, New Jersey (1935). Earhart's career ended tragically in the first attempt to circumnavigate the earth near the equator. After safely negotiating two-thirds of the flight, her plane vanished in the South Pacific. A 16-day naval search produced no trace of Earhart or her navigator, Frederick Noonan. ■

See her memoirs, *The Fun of It* (1932), *Letters* (1983); and Paul L. Briand, Jr., *Daughter of the Sky* (1960); Fred Goerner, *The Search for Amelia Earhart* (1966); Richard O'Connor, *Winged Legend* (1970); and the biography by Doris L. Rich (1989).

EAST, EDWARD MURRAY (1879–1938), U.S. botanist and plant geneticist. East received a Ph.D. from the University of Illinois (1907) and worked at its experimental agriculture facility. From 1909 he taught experimental plant morphology and genetics at Harvard University. His studies of maize and tobacco provided important information on genetics and breeding and generated new methods of seed production. His work, together with that of George H. Shull, led to the development of hybrid corn, which revolutionized corn growing throughout the world. In *Mankind at the Crossroads* (1923) and *Heredity and Human Affairs* (1927), he warned against the continued rapid growth of human population. ■ See Alexander R. Crabb, *Hybrid-Corn Makers* (1947).

EASTMAN, GEORGE (1854–1932), U.S. inventor and manufacturer. While working as a bank clerk, Eastman designed (1879) a process for making dry photographic plates. Within a year he was working full time to develop and market photographic products. His paper-backed flexible film (1884) and single box camera called the Kodak (1888) made photography available to millions, and by 1927 the Eastman Kodak Co. virtually monopolized the American photographic industry. It also introduced pioneering employee profit-sharing and stock-option plans. Eastman contributed over $75 million, more than half his fortune, to philanthropies. Plagued by ill health, he committed suicide. ■ See biographies by Carl W. Ackerman (1930) and Elizabeth Brayer (1996).

EASTMAN, MAX FORRESTER (1883–1969), U.S. writer and editor. Eastman, both of whose parents were Congregational ministers, inclined to moralistic preaching in his literary endeavors. He started out on the left as a pacifist and editor of *The Masses* (1913–17) and the *Liberator* (1918–23), and was a leader of Bohemian society in New York's Greenwich Village. After a visit to the Soviet Union (1923–24), however, he became a leading anti-Stalinist. Eastman's first book, *The Enjoyment of Poetry* (1913), was his most successful. He also wrote poetry, translations from the Russian, several books attacking developments in the Soviet Union, and two memoirs, *Enjoyment of Living* (1948) and *Love and Revolution* (1965). ■ See William O'Neill, *The Last Romantic* (1978).

EASTWOOD, CLINT (1930–), U.S. movie actor and director. Eastwood grew up in California during the Depression, relocating repeatedly as his father searched for work. He finally settled down in Oakland, graduated from high school, worked as a logger, firefighter, and steelworker, and served in the army (1951–53). He appeared in the western television series "Rawhide"(1959–66) and achieved international fame as a laconic, violent loner (the "man with no name") in three "spaghetti westerns"—Italian director Sergio Leone's *A Fistful of Dollars* (1964), *For a Few Dollars More* (1965), and *The Good, the Bad and the Ugly* (1966). He maintained his antihero persona as rogue cop Harry Callahan in a series of films, including *Dirty Harry* (1971) and *Sudden Impact* (1983), in which he issued the notorious taunt, "Make my day." Although he was one of the world's top box-office attractions, and was considered an icon of American masculinity and individualism in the conservative 1980s and 1990s, he did not receive widespread critical acclaim until *Bird* (1988), a film he directed about jazz great Charlie Parker, and *The Unforgiven* (1992), a western he produced, directed, and starred in that won Academy Awards for best film and best direction. His later movies included *The Bridges of Madison County* (1995), *True Crime* (1999), and *Space Cowboys* (2000). Eastwood also served as mayor of Carmel, California (1986–88). ▪ See biography by Richard Schickel (1996).

EATON, CYRUS STEPHEN (1883–1979), Canadian-born U.S. financier and industrialist. A founder of the Republic Steel Corp. (1930) and director of many of the nation's largest utility, steel, coal, and railroad companies, Eaton was one of America's most successful capitalists. In his later years, however, he became increasingly critical of U.S. business practices, advocated nuclear disarmament, and called for improved U.S.-Soviet relations. He inaugurated (1957) the annual "Pugwash Conferences," at which scientists and scholars from around the world met and discussed contemporary world problems. The Soviet government awarded him the Lenin Peace Prize (1970). ▪ See Marcus Gleisser, *The World of Cyrus Eaton* (1965).

EBAN, ABBA (Aubrey Solomon; 1915–1997), Israeli diplomat. Eban was born in South Africa, educated in Britain, and served as a British officer in the Middle East during World War II. A major figure in the negotiations leading to the establishment of the state of Israel (1948), he served as Israel's representative to the United Nations (1948–59) and ambassador to the United States (1950–59), where he was an eloquent spokesman for his nation. He was foreign minister from 1966 to 1974. Eban's speeches were collected as *Voice of Israel* (1957). A political moderate, he served as a Labor member of the Knesset (parliament; 1959–88). His books on the history of the Jews included *My People* (1968), *My Country* (1972), and *Heritage: Civilization and the Jews* (1984), based on his acclaimed television series. His *Diplo-macy for the Next Century* (1998) was a concise introduction to realism in foreign affairs. ▪ See biography by Robert St. John (1972), his autobiography (1977), and his memoir *Personal Witness* (1992).

EBERHART, MIGNON G. (Mignon Good; 1899–1996), U.S. mystery writer. Mignon G. Eberhart abandoned a short-lived journalism career and wrote more than 50 mysteries. Her detectives attracted a large following and inspired many films. Eberhart's first five novels, including *While the Patient Slept* (1930), featured the inquisitive, trouble-prone Nurse Sarah Keate, who sometimes teamed up with Detective Lance O'Leary. Other Eberhart cases were taken on by Susan Dare, a young mystery writer (see *The Cases of Susan Dare*, 1934), and by Mr. Wickwire, an aging New York banker. Her best works, set in exotic locales, combined the elements of the gothic romance, adventure fantasy, and classic murder mystery novels. Her last novel was *Three Days for Emeralds* (1988).

EBERHART, RICHARD (1904–), U.S. poet. Eberhart spent time at Cambridge during a period when William Empson and other influential British writers were there. He later held many jobs, working as a tutor to Siam's royal family, schoolteacher, businessman, naval officer, and professor. A rhetorical poet, Eberhart imitated the Englishman William Blake in his early work. He wrote best about lost innocence and the acceptance of death, as in his famous poem "The Groundhog." His later works employed a simple direct style and language. ▪ See his *Collected Verse Plays* (1962), *Collected Poems* (1976), *Ways of Light: Poems, 1972–1980* (1980), *The Long Reach: New and Uncollected Poems, 1948–1984* (1984), *Collected Poems, 1930–86* (1988), and *New and Selected Poems* (1990). See also his critical essays in *Of Poetry and Poets* (1979).

ÉBOUÉ, (ADOLPHE) FÉLIX (1884–1944), French colonial administrator. Born in French Guiana and educated in France, Éboué joined the colonial civil service (1908) and was posted to the French Congo. Rising in the service, he served in Martinique and the Sudan and in 1936 was appointed governor of Guadalupe—becoming France's first black colonial governor—and in 1938 governor of Chad. Éboué declared for the Free French of General Charles de Gaulle in 1940, during World War II, and was named governor of French Equatorial Africa, where he spurred the war effort and introduced numerous reforms. Identifying more with France than with African nationalism, he nonetheless raised African national consciousness by his political success. ▪ See biography by Brian Weinstein (1972).

ECCLES, SIR JOHN CAREW (1903–1997), Australian neurophysiologist. A student of Charles S. Sherrington (at Oxford) and a colleague of Bernard Katz (at Sydney), Eccles taught at the Australian National University at Canberra (1952–66) and spent most of his scientific career examining how nerve cells communicate with each other. He demonstrated that synaptic transmission did not operate electrically, but chemically—one chemical substance acting to excite neurons, another acting to inhibit them. His work profoundly affected the study of nervous disorders, brain function, and kidney and heart disease, and he shared the 1963 Nobel Prize in Physiology or Medicine with Alan Hodgkin and Andrew Huxley. After 1966 he directed research institutes in Chicago and at the State University of New York, Buffalo. His books included *Physiology of Nerve Cells* (1957), *Physiology of Synapses* (1964), and *The Understanding of the Brain* (1973). ■ See *Nobel Prize Conversations* (1985).

ECCLES, MARRINER STODDARD (1890–1977), U.S. businessman and public official. The son of a Mormon polygamist, Eccles inherited and expanded a banking and industrial empire in Utah. Believing that only massive governmental expenditures could help the nation recover from the Depression of the 1930s, he helped shape and implement Pres. Franklin D. Roosevelt's New Deal programs as assistant secretary of the treasury (1934) and later as chairman of the Federal Reserve Board (1936–48). He cooperated with the Treasury Department to help finance the industrial production of the United States and the Allied powers during World War II and restored the board's independence after the war. ■ See his memoirs, *Beckoning Frontiers* (1951) and the biography by Sidney Hyman (1977).

ECKENER, HUGO (1868–1954), German dirigible pioneer. Eckener was trained as an economist but worked with the firm of Ferdinand Graf von Zeppelin and helped develop the dirigible in the early 1900s. He piloted more than 100 flights, including the first successful crossing of the Atlantic (1924) and the Graf Zeppelin flight around the world in 288 hours and 14 minutes (1929). He popularized airship travel and received numerous international awards.

ECKERT, JOHN PRESPER (1919–1995), U.S. engineer. After vastly improving the differential analyzer that proved valuable during World War II, Eckert was awarded a contract (with John Mauchly) to design an all-purpose digital machine. They produced (1946) what was for many years considered to be the first all-electronic computer, ENIAC, the model for most other modern computers. (However, a decision in a patent lawsuit in 1973 established that Eckert and Mauchly's invention was derived from a prototype built by John Atanasoff and declared the ENIAC patent invalid.) Joining Mauchly to form (1947) the Eckert-Mauchly Computer Corp., Eckert helped design a second computer, BINAC (1949), which used magnetic tape to store information. A third model, UNIVAC I (1951), contained many innovations and greatly advanced the field of electronic data processing. Eckert was granted more than 85 patents for his electronic inventions.

ECO, UMBERTO (1932–), Italian writer and semiotician. Eco lived through World War II as a boy in German-occupied Italy. He later studied philosophy at the University of Turin (Ph.D. 1954). While working for Italian television (1954–59), he also taught aesthetics at his alma mater (1956–64): he later taught communications theory at other universities. He was a key figure in Gruppo 63, an avant-garde literary group that emerged in Italy in the late 1950s and 1960s. From the late 1960s, he focused on semiotics, the study of signs in all realms of culture, and developed a theory of sign production. From 1971 he was a professor of semiotics at the University of Bologna. His books in English included *A Theory of Semiotics* (1976), *The Role of the Reader* (1979), *Semiotics and the Philosophy of Language* (1984), and *Travels in Hyperreality* (1986). Eco's novel *The Name of the Rose* (1980; Eng. trans. 1983), a challenging, suspenseful work set in the late middle ages, was a bestseller in Europe and the United States. His later works included the novels *Foucault's Pendulum* (1988; Eng. trans. 1989) and *The Island of the Day Before* (1994; Eng. trans. 1995), and the essay collections *The Limits of Interpretation* (Eng. trans. 1990), *Apocalypse Postponed* (Eng. trans. 1994), and *Serendipities* (Eng. trans. 1998).

EDDINGTON, SIR ARTHUR STANLEY (1882–1944), British astrophysicist. Eddington, long associated with Cambridge University, elucidated the process by which a star's energy is transmitted from its interior to its surface. He concluded that the energy emitted from the star's surface travels through the star by radiation and not by convection as had been previously thought. He determined that the luminosity of stars, most of which he found to be entirely gaseous, is related to their mass. Eddington also conducted tests that confirmed aspects of Albert Einstein's general theory of relativity, and he researched problems of stellar motion. His published works included *The Mathematical Theory of Relativity* (1923) and *The Expanding Universe* (1933). ■ See biography by Allie V. Douglas (1956) and study of C. W. Kilmister (1966).

EDDY, NELSON (1901–1967), U.S. singer and movie star. Nelson Eddy sang with the Savoy Opera Company and Philadelphia Civic Opera and made his New York debut in *Wozzeck* (1931). But his clear baritone resounded most often in movie theaters across America that, in the 1930s and 1940s, often featured the romantic duets of Jeanette MacDonald and Nelson Eddy. The suave blond singer and red-haired leading lady teamed up for eight musicals, popularizing such tunes as "Indian Love Call" and "Will You Remember." Eddy died while performing in a Miami Beach nightclub. ■ See Philip Castanza, *The Films of Jeanette MacDonald and Nelson Eddy* (1978).

EDELMAN, GERALD MAURICE (1929–), U.S. biochemist. Upon receiving his doctorate in biochemistry from Rockefeller University (1960), Edelman taught there (1960–

92) and specialized in the study of antibodies. He conducted grueling research into the chemical and molecular structure of the gamma-globulin blood molecule. Working along the same lines as Rodney Porter in England, Edelman succeeded in fragmenting the molecule and making a complete model of the complex Y-shaped biochemical unit. This work represented a breakthrough in immunological science and earned him a share of the 1972 Nobel Prize for Physiology or Medicine with Porter. During the 1980s, Edelman directed a research institute devoted to studying higher functions of the brain. He subsequently taught at the Scripps Research Institute, La Jolla, California (1992–   ). His books included *The Remembered Present* (1989) and *Bright Air, Brilliant Fire* (1992).

EDEN, SIR (ROBERT) ANTHONY, 1st EARL OF AVON (1897–1977), British political leader. Eden served as a Conservative member of Parliament (1923–57) and held several cabinet posts before becoming foreign secretary (1935–38). An opponent of fascism, he resigned over Prime Minister Neville Chamberlain's appeasement policy, but he returned as dominions secretary (1939). Under Winston Churchill, he served as foreign secretary (1940–45; 1951–55) and deputy prime minister (1951–55), gaining a reputation as a superb negotiator and persuader. As prime minister (1955–57), he joined with France and Israel in an invasion of Egypt after Egypt had nationalized the Suez Canal Co. (1956). The invasion, condemned by the United Nations, the United States, and many members of his own party, was a political disaster for Eden and led to his resignation in January 1957. ■ See his memoirs, *Full Circle* (1960), *Facing the Dictators* (1962), and *The Reckoning* (1965); and biographies by David Carlton (1981) and Robert Rhodes James (1987).

EDERLE, GERTRUDE CAROLINE (1906–   ), U.S. swimmer. In the early 1920s Trudy Ederle held 29 national and world swimming records and in 1924 won an Olympic gold medal as a member of the 400-meter freestyle relay team. One of the most famous athletes of the 1920s, she was the first woman to swim the English Channel (1926). Her time for the 35-mile swim was 14 hours and 31 minutes, 1 hour and 59 minutes faster than the existing men's record. She subsequently toured as a professional swimmer. After recovery from a serious injury, she appeared in the Aquacade at the 1939 New York World's Fair.

EDGERTON, HAROLD EUGENE (1903–1990), U.S. electrical engineer. Edgerton taught at the Massachusetts Institute of Technology (from 1928) and developed the modern stroboscope (1931), a sophisticated electronic device that made stop-action and high-speed photography possible by throwing a very intense light on the subject in extremely brief flashes. The strobe light greatly advanced motion-picture photography by increasing the number of possible frames per second from 250 to 6,000. Applying this concept to sound, Edgerton designed an instrument to determine ocean depths. He also invented ultrasonar "photography" for seismic probes beneath the ocean floor. The stroboscope concept proved important in numerous other fields, from medicine to aerial photography to nuclear-test measurement. ■ See his *Moments of Vision* (1979; with James R. Killian, Jr.) and *Sonar Images* (1986).

EDINBURGH, PHILIP MOUNTBATTEN, DUKE OF (1921–   ), British consort. The son of Prince Andrew of Greece and Princess Alice of Battenberg, whose father traded German for British citizenship during World War I, Philip was a great-great-grandson of Britain's Queen Victoria. He was educated in Britain and served in the Mediterranean with the Royal Navy during World War II. In 1947 he became a British subject and married his third cousin, who in 1952 succeeded to the throne as Elizabeth II. As prince consort, Philip was a top polo player and popular, informal, and occasionally outspoken public figure. His selected speeches and essays are in *Men, Machines and Sacred Cows* (1984). ■ See biographies by Basil Boothroyd (1971) and Denis Judd (1981).

EDISON, THOMAS ALVA (1847–1931), U.S. inventor. With only three months of formal education, Edison became a leading figure in the technological revolution. An extraordinarily prolific inventor, he received (1869) the first of more than a thousand patents—for the design of an electric vote recorder. Edison is best known as the inventor of the phonograph (1877) and the carbon-filament incandescent lamp (1879). Perhaps even more significant was his development of a central system for generating and distributing electricity and the accompanying improvements in motors and dynamos. In 1876 Edison moved to Menlo Park, New Jersey (and later to West Orange, New Jersey), where he established the first industrial research laboratory. Among his other inventions or research projects were the two-message "diplex" telegraph, the stock ticker, the carbon telephone transmitter, the dictating machine, the phonograph record, the fluoroscope (a movie-camera and peep-show device), the storage battery, the magnetic separation of iron ore, and the manufacture of cement. Also a manufacturer and businessman, Edison is regarded as a pioneer of organized research. ■ See Robert Conot, *A Streak of Luck* (1979); Wyn Wachhorst, *Thomas Alva Edison: An American Myth* (1981); and studies by A. J. Millard (1990), Neil Baldwin (1995), and Paul Israel (1998).

EDWARD VII (Albert Edward; 1841–1910), king of Great Britain and Ireland (1901–10). The eldest son of Queen Victoria, Edward served a 60-year apprenticeship as Prince of Wales during his mother's long reign. Penalized for a youthful indiscretion, he was denied meaningful responsibility most of that time, devoting himself instead to a sporting lifestyle in European café society. Succeeding to the throne in 1901, he restored vitality and pageantry to the monarchy after the long years of Victoria's widowhood and was a popular figure at home and abroad. ■ See biographies by Philip Magnus (1964) and George Plumptoe (1995).

EDWARD VIII (later Duke of Windsor; 1894–1972), king of Great Britain and Ireland (1936). Edward was a popular prince of Wales (1911–36) who saw World War I service as a naval officer and made lengthy state trips around the world. He succeeded to the throne in 1936 on the death of his father, George V, but was never crowned. Later that year he abdicated dramatically to marry Wallis Warfield Simpson (1896–1986), a twice-divorced American woman. He served as governor of the Bahamas during World War II. The Windsors lived the rest of their lives in exile, mainly in France. ■ See the duke's memoir, *A King's Story* (1951), and the biographies by Frances Donaldson (1975) and Philip Ziegler (1991).

EGAS MONIZ, ANTONIO CAETANO DE ABREU FREIRE (1874–1955), Portuguese neurologist and diplomat. Although trained in medicine, Egas Moniz first distinguished himself in the field of politics, serving in the Portuguese chamber of deputies (1903–17), becoming foreign minister (1917), and leading the Portuguese delegation to the Paris Peace Conference (1918–19). While a professor of neurology at the University of Lisbon (1911–44), he developed a nonsurgical procedure for examining blood vessels of the brain by injecting into them substances opaque to X rays. In addition, he conducted pioneer work on the treatment of certain mental disorders by the operation of prefrontal lobotomy. For this work he shared, with Walter Hess, the 1949 Nobel Prize for Physiology or Medicine.

EGLEVSKY, ANDRÉ (1917–1977), Russian-born U.S. dancer. Eglevsky learned the traditions and techniques of the classical Russian ballet from émigré artists in Paris, where his family had fled during the Russian Revolution. Acclaimed for his technical virtuosity, particularly for his spectacular pirouettes, he achieved international recognition during the 1930s and 1940s while dancing with such companies as the Ballet Russe de Monte Carlo and the Ballet (now American Ballet) Theatre. He emigrated to the United States in 1937. Considered by many to be the greatest male dancer of his generation, he was the principal male dancer at the New York City Ballet (1951–58), where George Balanchine created several new parts for him. His best-known roles were in *Giselle, Swan Lake, Helen of Troy, Apollo, Scotch Symphony, Mad Tristan*, and *Les Sylphides*. After he retired, he formed his own ballet company (1961) and taught at the School of American Ballet in New York.

EHRENBURG, ILYA GRIGORYEVICH (1891–1967), Soviet novelist and journalist. Jailed briefly for bolshevik activities at age 16, Ehrenburg emigrated (1908) and lived in Paris (1909–17), where he met French symbolists and exiled Russian revolutionaries. He returned an antibolshevik (1917), moved to Paris (1921), and with some waffling, ac-

commodated increasingly to the Soviet regime. In 1921 he published his most admired work, the satiric novel *The Extraordinary Adventures of Julio Jurenito and His Disciples* (1921; Eng. trans. 1930, 1976). Working as European correspondent for the government newspaper *Izvestia*, he lived mainly abroad until 1941, bridging Soviet and Western intellectual worlds. His vehemently anti-German World War II reports won official and public esteem, and despite his precarious position as a Jewish intellectual, he survived dictator Joseph Stalin's purges. In the 1950s Ehrenburg emerged as a liberal, speaking out against the drab state of Soviet literature in *The Thaw* (1954; Eng. trans. 1955), the controversial novel that gave a name to the de-Stalinization period. *In One Newspaper* (1984; with Konstantin Simonov), collected translations of articles published in *Red Star*, and Ehrenburg's six volumes of memoirs, *People, Years, Life* (1961–66; Eng. trans. 1962–67), illuminated the dilemma of the Russian intelligentsia in Soviet times; they restored the reputations of several writers, called for artistic flexibility, and condemned the crimes of his onetime admirer, Stalin. ■ See biography by Anatol Goldberg (1984).

EHRLICHMAN, JOHN DANIEL (1925–1999), U.S. presidential assistant. A graduate of Stanford Law School (1951) and a specialist in land use and zoning ordinances, Ehrlichman took leaves of absence from his law practice to work on Richard Nixon's 1960, 1962, and 1968 campaigns. The neat, efficient attorney was rewarded in 1969 with the position of assistant to the president for domestic affairs. In 1974 he was indicted for conspiracy to obstruct justice in the Watergate affair and also for the burglary of dissenter Daniel Ellsberg's psychiatrist's office. Ehrlichman moved to New Mexico and wrote a novel, *The Company* (1976), before entering an Arizona prison camp in October 1976, where he served 18 months of an eight-year sentence. He subsequently wrote the political novels *The Whole Truth* (1979) and *The China Card* (1986). ■ See his memoirs, *Witness to Power* (1982).

EICH, GÜNTER (1907–1972), German poet, fiction writer, and radio playwright. Eich established a reputation in Germany after World War II as a cofounder of the influential literary organization Gruppe 47 (1947) and as the author of several poetry collections published between 1948 and 1966. His lyrical and humanistic but unsentimental verse influenced younger German poets, but it was not well known abroad. Eich also furthered the development of radio plays as a recognized literary genre; two such plays were published in English as *Journeys* (1968). He also wrote short fiction. English translations of his work are in *Selected Poems* (1975), *Valuable Nail* (1981), and *Pigeons and Moles* (1991). ■ See study by Egbert Krispyn (1971).

EICHMANN, ADOLF OTTO (1906–1962), German Nazi officer. Eichmann was a traveling salesman selling vacuums when he joined the Nazi party in 1932. A fanatical anti-

Semite, he worked his way up through the ranks of the SS, the elite guard, and was especially concerned with the emigration and, later, the extermination of the Jews in Europe. Promoted to lieutenant colonel in November 1941, he was placed in charge of the deportation of Central European Jews to the extermination camps in Eastern Europe and was thus largely responsible for the death of millions of Jews. He escaped from Germany at the end of the war but was tracked down and abducted by Israeli agents in Argentina (1960) and tried in an Israeli court (1961). After a lengthy and highly publicized trial, Eichmann was found guilty of "crimes against the Jewish people . . . crimes against humanity . . . war crimes and membership in an 'enemy organization,'" and hanged. ■ See Hannah Arendt, *Eichmann in Jerusalem* (1963), and Jochen von Lang and Claus Sibyll, eds., *Eichmann Interrogated* (1983).

EIGEN, MANFRED (1927–   ), West German physical chemist. After receiving a Ph.D. from the University of Gottingen (1951), Eigen developed techniques for inducing and studying rapid chemical reactions; in the 1960s he applied these methods to problems of molecular biology. His technique involved destabilizing a chemical system and observing how it "relaxes" or seeks a new equilibrium state. For his research, Eigen shared the 1967 Nobel Prize for Chemistry with Ronald G. W. Norrish and George Porter. After 1953 he was associated with the Max Planck Institute for Physical Chemistry in Gottingen, West Germany (director, from 1964).

EIJKMAN, CHRISTIAAN (1858–1930), Dutch physician and pathologist. An army medical officer, Eijkman did research in Indonesia (1886–97) on beriberi. He found (1890) that chickens afflicted with the disease had been fed a diet of polished rice and that giving them the discarded rice hulls would cure it. Although Eijkman did not himself link beriberi with vitamin deficiency, he laid the groundwork for the eventual discovery of vitamin B and, thus, to the concept of nutritional deficiency as a cause of diseases. He taught at the University of Utrecht (1898–1928) and shared the 1929 Nobel Prize for Physiology or Medicine with Frederick Hopkins.

EINAUDI, LUIGI (1874–1961), Italian economist and statesman. A professor of economics at the University of Turin (1900–43), Einaudi, a liberal, won fame as a frequent contributor of economic and political analyses to the influential newspapers *La Stampa, Il Corriere della Sera,* and *La Riforma Sociale.* An outspoken opponent of fascism, he fled to Switzerland in 1943; returning after World War II, he served as governor of the Bank of Italy (1945–48). As vice premier and minister of the budget (1947), he coordinated financial policy and helped to stabilize the currency and curb postwar inflation. He was president of Italy from 1948 to 1955. His son, Giulio Einaudi (1912–1999), founded (1933) the Einaudi publishing house and was a prominent cultural figure in Italy.

EINSTEIN, ALBERT (1879–1955), German-born U.S. physicist. Denied a teaching post because he was a Jew, Albert Einstein accepted a position at the patent office in Bern, Switzerland (1901). He received a doctorate degree from the University of Bern in 1905, the year he published three landmark papers on the photoelectric effect, Brownian motion, and the special theory of relativity. The latter theory arose out of an attempt to explain certain paradoxes involved in measuring the speed of light, and incorporated the famous formula that relates energy to mass, $E = mc^2$. After 1905, Einstein held various academic posts. Settling in Berlin (1913) as a member of the Royal Prussian Academy of Sciences, Einstein published his fundamental paper on the general theory of relativity (1915), explaining certain gravitational phenomena incomprehensible in traditional Newtonian terms. The Nobel Prize for Physics awarded to Einstein (1922) recognized his important work on the photoelectric effect. Scientists were slower to acclaim the more radical theories of relativity that ultimately transformed their understanding of time and space. When Nazi leader Adolf Hitler came to power in Germany, Einstein accepted a position at Princeton University (1933), where he remained for the rest of his life. Known for his concern with the social impact of scientific discovery as well as for his monumental intellectual achievements, Einstein received popular recognition almost unprecedented for a scientist. He is generally regarded as the most influential theoretical physicist of the modern era. ■ See his autobiographical notes (Eng. trans. 1979) and Helen Dukas and Banesh Hoffmann, eds., *Albert Einstein, The Human Side: New Glimpses from His Archives* (1979). See also Abraham Pais, *"Subtle is the Lord"* (1982); study edited by Peter C. Aichelburg and Roman U. Sexi (1979); Jamie Sayen, *Einstein in America* (1985); and Roger Highfield and Paul Carter, *The Private Lives of Albert Einstein* (1994).

EINSTEIN, ISIDORE (1880–1938) and **MOE SMITH** (1887?–1960), U.S. civil servants. "Izzy and Moe," the legendary team of federal revenue agents during the Prohibition era, were said to have made more than 4,900 arrests and confiscated more than five million bottles of illegal liquor. Their comical antics and fantastic disguises made them great public favorites. They were most active putting the "Einstein theory of rum-snooping" into practice from 1922 to 1925. ■ See Einstein's memoirs, *Prohibition Agent No. 1* (1932).

EINTHOVEN, WILLEM (1860–1927), Dutch physiologist. The son of a physician, Einthoven received his medical degree from the University of Utrecht (1885) and served as professor of physiology at the University of Leiden (1885–1927). In 1903 he devised the first string galvanometer that was sensitive enough to measure the tiny electrical current caused by heart-muscle contraction. This allowed him to develop the first electrocardiograph, which recorded the current graphically. Over the next 18 years he perfected the process and demonstrated that different types of heart disease show different peaks and troughs on the graphs. Electrocardiograms eventually were used universally in the diagnosis of heart disease. Einthoven won the 1924 Nobel Prize for Physiology or Medicine. ■ See study by H. A. Snellen (1995).

EISENHOWER, DWIGHT DAVID (1890–1969), U.S. military and political leader. Born in Texas and raised in Kansas, Eisenhower, known popularly as Ike, graduated from West Point (1915) and rose steadily through the army ranks over the next 25 years. During World War II he was commander of U.S. forces in Europe (1942–43) and planned and directed the invasion of North Africa, Sicily, and Italy. As supreme commander of all allied forces in Europe (1944–45) he directed the D-Day invasion (June 6, 1944) and the subsequent campaigns leading to the German surrender. After the war he served as army chief of staff (1945–48), president of Columbia University (1948–50), and commander of NATO forces in Europe (1950–52), and wrote his best-selling war memoir, *Crusade in Europe* (1948). A genial and popular figure, he was persuaded to run for president by Republican party leaders and served for two terms (1953–61). He negotiated a truce to end the Korean War (1953) and kept the United States out of a major war for eight years. His foreign policy was pointedly anticommunist and he encouraged the "rollback" of Soviet power in Eastern Europe and authorized covert Central Intelligence Agency (CIA) operations to overthrow elected leftist governments in Guatemala and Iran. Domestically the economy prospered, with balanced budgets and minimal inflation. Eisenhower never publicly opposed Sen. Joseph R. McCarthy, whose anticommunist smear campaign flourished during his first administration, and he refused to endorse the 1954 Supreme Court school integration decision. At the end of his presidency he warned of the power and growth of the "military-industrial complex." Eisenhower's other books included *Mandate for Change* (1963), *Waging Peace* (1965), and *At Ease: Stories I Tell to Friends* (1967). ■ See biographies by Stephen E. Ambrose (2 vols., 1983–84) and Geoffrey Perret (1999); and Piers Brandon, *Ike* (1986).

EISENSTAEDT, ALFRED (1898–1995), German-U.S. photojournalist. Born in Germany, where he became a well-known photojournalist, Eisenstaedt emigrated to the United States (1935) and was a member of the staff of the picture magazine *Life* (1936–72). A master of the candid shot and telling expression, he shot photo essays on West Point plebes and dust-bowl farmers, kings and dictators, and movie stars and nobodies, some of whom are included in his books *Witness to Our Time* (1966; rev. ed. 1980), *The Eye of Eisenstaedt* (1969), *People* (1973), and *Eisenstaedt's Album*

(1976). *Eisenstaedt: Germany* (1981) documented a return visit to his native land. His best-known photo was of a sailor kissing a nurse in New York City's Times Square on V-J Day, August 14, 1945.

EISENSTEIN, SERGEI MIKHAILOVICH (1898–1948), Russian film director. After serving in the Red army during the civil war (1918–20), Eisenstein got involved with the Proletkult Theater and was selected by the government to make films commemorating the 1905 and 1917 revolutions. The results were *Potemkin* (1925), a powerful montage—a "collision of images," Eisenstein called it—on the 1905 battleship mutiny, and the visually striking *Ten Days that Shook the World* (1928). During three years in the West (1929–32), the Russian filmmaker was involved in several abortive film projects and shot some footage in Mexico that was later edited and released by others. After a period of political difficulties back in the Soviet Union, during which Eisenstein helped develop the art of film through writing and teaching, he was appointed to direct *Alexander Nevsky* (1938), a dramatic patriotic epic. He began work on *Ivan the Terrible* (1944–47) during World War II, completing two parts in a trilogy before his death. English translations of his influential theoretical writings on film are in *The Film Sense* (1943), *Film Form* (1949), *Notes of a Film Director* (1959), and *Film Essays* (1968). ■ See his autobiography, *Immoral Memories* (Eng. trans. 1983); the studies by Yon Barna (Eng. trans. 1973) and Marie Seton (rev. ed. 1978); and the biography by Richard Bergan (1999).

EISNER, MICHAEL (1942–), U.S. businessman. Born into a wealthy family in New York, Eisner graduated from Denison University, Ohio (B.A. 1964) and started his career in the entertainment industry as an executive at CBS and then at ABC (1966–76). After successfully heading Paramont Pictures (1976–84) he became chairman and CEO of the Walt Disney Company (1984–), an animation and theme-park business that had foundered after the death of Walt Disney in 1966. Eisner achieved phenomenal financial success by diversifying the company into television and film production, software, publishing, hotels, and professional hockey (the Mighty Ducks) and baseball (Anaheim Angels) franchises. The company also produced such popular feature-length animated films as *The Little Mermaid* (1989) and *The Lion King* (1994; transformed into a Tony Award–winning Broadway musical, 1997). In 1995 Eisner negotiated the $19 billion acquisition of Capital Cities/ABC, Inc., the giant communications company that owned the ABC Television Network. It also owned television and radio stations, newspapers, and magazines, an 80 percent interest in the ESPN cable television networks, and a 37.5 percent interest in the A&E television networks. As a result of the purchase, Disney's revenues reached $22.5 billion in 1997 and Eisner became one of the most powerful figures in the entertainment industry. His salary, bonus, and long-term compensation in

1998 was estimated to be $575,592,000. ■ See his memoir, *Work in Progress* (1998; with Tony Schwartz), and Ron Grover, *The Disney Touch* (1997).

EKELÖF, GUNNAR (1907–1968), Swedish poet. Ekelöf called his first book of poetry, *Late Arrival on Earth* (1932; Eng. trans. 1967), a "suicide book." Surrealistic and despairing, it had a major influence on Swedish poetry. His work showed great variety and intellectual depth, and his style mixed allusiveness with direct verse. Such later works as *The Ferry Song* (1941) and *In Autumn* (1951) were more analytical and lyrical and written in an experimental musical structure. *A Mölna Elegy* (1960; Eng. trans. 1979) was concerned with the nature of time, while *Selected Poems* (1966; Eng. trans. 1971) and *Guide to the Underworld* (1967; Eng. trans. 1980) explored mysticism and myth. Regarded as Sweden's greatest poet, he was elected to the Swedish Academy (1958). English translations of his works are in Robert Bly, ed., *Friends, You Drank Some Darkness* (1975), and in *Songs of Something Else* (1982) and *Modus Vivendi: Selected Prose* (1996).

EKMAN, VAGN WALFRID (1874–1954), Swedish oceanographer. A pioneer in the field of oceanography, Ekman made important studies of the dynamics of ocean currents. A 1905 paper established the importance to oceanic circulation of what was subsequently called the "Ekman layer" and the "Ekman spiral," and a 1923 study presented a complete mathematical theory for wind-driven oceanic circulation. He also invented the widely used Ekman current meter, which measured the speed and direction of ocean currents. He was a member of the International Laboratory for Oceanographic Research at Oslo (1902–09) and professor at the University of Lund, Sweden (1910–39).

EKWENSI, CYPRIAN (1921–   ), Nigerian writer. Ekwensi began his literary career in the 1940s with a series of short melodramatic pulp novels that were especially popular with students and middle-class readers. He subsequently established an international reputation with his novels *People of the City* (1954), *Jagua Nana* (1961), and *Beautiful Feathers* (1963), which brilliantly described the vibrant life of Lagos and the conflicts and frustrations of the newly urbanized generation of West Africans. *Burning Grass* (1962) concerned a nomadic Fulani family of northern Nigeria and *Survive the Peace* (1976) and *Divided We Stand* (1980) dealt with the Nigerian civil war. Trained as a pharmacist, Ekwensi worked for many years as a teacher, journalist, government information official, and manager of a publishing house. His later works included the novels *Jagua Nana's Daughter* (1986) and *For a Roll of Parchment* (1987) and several volumes of stories for children. ■ See study by Ernest Emenyonu (1974).

ELDRIDGE, (DAVID) ROY (1911–1989), U.S. jazz musician. Known as "Little Jazz," Eldridge played drums at age

6, then bugle and trumpet. In the 1920s and 1930s, he made a reputation as an instrumentalist as well as a vocalist and a composer. In the late 1950s, Eldridge toured with his own band, playing at Harlem's Apollo Theater and elsewhere. He worked with Gene Krupa, Benny Goodman, Artie Shaw, Ella Fitzgerald, Count Basie, and Coleman Hawkins. Noted for his power and originality, he displayed a virtuosity on the trumpet in many jazz styles and remained active for over six decades.

ELGAR, SIR EDWARD (1857–1934), British composer, violinist and organist. As part of his early training, Elgar was bandmaster (1879–84) at the county asylum in Worcester, England, with the attendants as musicians. His reputation was established with his *Enigma Variations* for orchestra (1899) and *Dream of Gerontius oratorio* (1900). His many compositions included the military march *Pomp and Circumstance No. I* (1901), a much-played Violin Concerto in B minor (1910), and the *Falstaff* overture (1913). His works were noted for their brilliant orchestration and emotional intensity, and Elgar was considered the outstanding figure of early 20th-century music in England. ■ See studies by Diana McVeagh (1956) and Simon Mundy (1980); Michael Kennedy, *Portrait of Elgar* (rev. ed. 1982); and biographies by Jerrold N. Moore (1984) and Robert Anderson (1993).

ELIADE, MIRCEA (1907–1986), Rumanian-born historian of religion. Eliade studied Indian philosophy and Sanskrit at the University of Calcutta (1928–31), wrote his doctoral dissertation on yoga (Ph.D. 1933; University of Bucharest) and taught at Bucharest (1933–39). A cultural attaché in Lisbon and London during World War II, he later taught at the Sorbonne (Paris, 1946–48) and at the University of Chicago (from 1956) and founded the journal *History of Religions* (1961). His controversial works on the history of religion and the meanings of religious symbols included *Patterns in Comparative Religion* (1949; Eng. trans. 1958), *The Myth of the Eternal Return* (1949; Eng. trans. 1954), and *The Sacred and the Profane* (1959). He also wrote the novel *Forbidden Forest* (1955); Eng. trans. 1978) and the journal *No Souvenirs: 1957–1969* (1973); Eng. trans. 1977). ■ See his autobiography (Vol. I, 1981) and Guilford Dudley, *Religion on Trial* (1977).

ELIJAH MUHAMMAD. *See MUHAMMAD, ELIJAH.*

ELION, GERTRUDE B. (1905–1999), U.S. biochemist. The daughter of immigrants, Elion graduated at age 19 from the tuition-free Hunter College in New York City (B.A. 1933) and worked as a substitute high school science teacher to help pay for tuition for her graduate studies in chemistry at New York University (M.S. 1941). In a long career as a researcher at the Burroughs Wellcome pharmaceutical company (1944–83), she collaborated with George H. Hitchings in designing drugs to specifically destroy pathogens, disease-causing microorganism, while leaving healthy cells undamaged. Their innovative approach enabled them to develop effective drugs for treating leukemia (thioguanine and 6-mercaptopurine), malaria (pyrimethamine), gout (allopurinol), urinary and respiratory infections (trimethoprim), and viral herpes (acyclovir). Azathioprine, a derivative of G-mercaptopurine, was used to treat rheumatoid arthritis and other autoimmune disorders, as well as to prevent the body's rejection of transplanted human kidneys. The anti-AIDS drug AZT was based on their research. Elion shared the 1988 Nobel Prize for Physiology or Medicine with Hitchings and Sir James Black and was the first woman elected to the Inventors Hall of Fame (1991).

ELIOT, THOMAS STEARNS (1888–1965), U.S.-born British poet and critic. T. S. Eliot was born in St. Louis and studied at Harvard, where he developed a keen interest in the French symbolists, Sanskrit, and Eastern religions, and took boxing lessons. The publication of his undergraduate poem "The Love Song of J. Alfred Prufrock" (1915) helped revolutionize post-Victorian poetic idioms, stressing imagery over ideas. Eliot went to Britain (1914), where he mixed with the Bloomsbury group, embraced Anglo-Catholicism, and became a British subject (1927). He worked full-time at Lloyd's Bank while writing and teaching. His erudite masterpiece *The Waste Land* (1922)—which poet Ezra Pound edited heavily—articulated the anguish of his post–World War I generation, but also reflected Eliot's own physical and emotional exhaustion. Poems of the next decade, including "Ash Wednesday" (1930) and *Four Quartets* (1935–43), laden with his characteristic religious symbolism and literary allusion, were more hopeful expressions of the quest for innocence and salvation. *Murder in the Cathedral* (1935) and *The Cocktail Party* (1950) revived verse drama. The most influential poet-critic of his day, Eliot readjusted the century's poetic sensibilities. He won the 1948 Nobel Prize for Literature. ■ See biographies by Peter Ackroyd (1984), Lyndall Gordon (1977), and Tony Sharpe (1991); and studies by Bernard Bergonzi (1972) and Stephen Spender (1976).

ELISOFON, ELIOT (1911–1973), U.S. photographer. Born in New York City, Elisofon took an early interest in painting, but was encouraged by his parents to pursue more practical goals. While working as a clerk and studying nights at Fordham University (B.S. 1935), he tried his hand at photography. In 1939, the Museum of Modern Art hired him as a staff photographer. He was a *Life* magazine staff photographer for three decades (1942–72), traveling some 2 million miles in a career that encompassed war reporting, social photojournalism, and food and glamour photography. Elisofon was best known for photographs of art and architecture, artifacts of ancient cultures, and exotic scenery. He traveled extensively through Africa, making the four-hour television documentary *Africa* (1967). He experimented with color (from 1949), using filters to achieve special effects, and was hired as a color consultant on such films as

Moulin Rouge (1953). Elisofon never abandoned his love of painting and mounted two well-received exhibits of watercolors (1958, 1960). His books included *Color Photography* (1961), *The Nile* (1964), *Java Diary* (1969), and *Hollywood Style* (1969).

ELIZABETH II (1926–), queen of the United Kingdom of Great Britain and Northern Ireland. The eldest daughter of the duke of York, who became King George VI when his brother, King Edward VIII, abdicated (1936). Elizabeth received a private education and served as a truck driver and mechanic with the auxiliary territorial service during World War II. She married her third cousin, Philip Mountbatten (1947), and had four children, Prince Charles (b. 1948), Princess Anne (b. 1950), Prince Andrew (b. 1960), and Prince Edward (b. 1964). Her father died in 1952, and she was crowned queen on June 2, 1953. Although she wielded no real power, she was an extremely popular figure; her reign was noted for its successful blend of traditional pomp and modern leadership. ■ See Robert Lacey, *Majesty* (1977), and biographies by Judith Campbell (1980) and Ben Pimlott (1997).

ELLINGTON, "DUKE" (Edward Kennedy Ellington; 1899–1974), U.S. jazz composer and conductor. The foremost figure in the history of jazz, Ellington conducted his original compositions everywhere from Harlem's Cotton Club to Carnegie Hall, Westminster Abbey, and the White House. He was a constant innovator, beginning with short pieces ("Black and Tan Fantasy," "Creole Love Call," "Mood Indigo") and moving into extended composition with "Black, Brown and Beige," "The Deep South Suite," and "Togo Brava." Ellington, whose bands maintained a high standard of orchestral jazz and improvisation for more than 50 years, also composed film scores (*Anatomy of a Murder* 1959) and, at the end of his long career, sacred music. ■ See his autobiography, *Music Is My Mistress* (1974); studies by Derek Jewell (1977) and Mercer Ellington and Stanley Dance (1978); and biography by James Lincoln Collier (1987).

ELLIS, (HENRY) HAVELOCK (1859–1939), British psychologist. The son of a sea captain, Ellis became a physician but preferred writing to the practice of medicine. The first volume of his pioneering scientific survey of sexuality, *Studies in the Psychology of Sex* (7 vols. 1897–1928), was banned by a British judge as a "filthy publication"; succeeding volumes were published in the United States and for many years available only to physicians. Ellis was an advocate of sex education, birth control, and women's suffrage. He wrote several other books, including a memoir, *My Life* (1940), largely about his own unconventional marriage. ■ See Arthur Calder-Marshall, *The Sage of Sex* (1960), and biographies by Vincent Brome (1979) and Phyllis Grosskurth (1980).

ELLISON, HARLAN JAY (1934–), U.S. science-fiction writer. A contributor to pulp magazines (in New York) during the 1950s and a successful television scriptwriter (in California) during the 1960s, Ellison developed into one of the world's most controversial and honored masters of science fiction. He was best known for short stories that portrayed the struggle of the human spirit with the forces of regimentation, hypocrisy, and derangement. His writings included the collections *I Have No Mouth and I Must Scream* (1967), *The Beast That Shouted Love at the Heart of the World* (1969), and *Deathbird Stories* (1975), which presented his bleak view of the world. He also edited the influential "new wave" science-fiction stories in *Dangerous Visions* (1967); *Again, Dangerous Visions* (1972); and *The Last Dangerous Visions* (1976). His essays were collected in *Sleepless Nights in the Procrustean Bed* (1984). *Stalking the Nightmare* (1982) contains autobiographical memoirs. His later collections of stories included *Angry Candy* (1988) and *Slippage* (1997).

ELLISON, RALPH WALDO (1914–1994), U.S. novelist. Born in Oklahoma. Ellison studied music for three years at Tuskegee Institute (1933–36) before traveling to New York. He was interested initially in sculpture, but when he met the novelist Richard Wright he directed his energies toward left-wing politics and writing. Five years' work resulted in *Invisible Man* (1952), a semiautobiographical novel of the black experience in America that anticipated the civil rights struggle. Its audacity, its convincing individual episodes, and its fusion of literary and political concerns established Ellison as a major writer. After its publication, Ellison lectured on black American culture and creative writing and was Albert Schweitzer professor at New York University (1970–79). He also wrote the short stories collected in *Flying Home and Other Stories* (1996) and two books of essays, *Shadow and Act* (1964) and *Going to the Territory* (1986). A long-awaited but unfinished novel, written over a period of 40 years, was assembled and arranged from typescripts and printouts by Ellison's literary executor, John F. Callahan, and published as *Juneteenth* (1999). ■ See Robert G. O'Meally, *The Craft of Ralph Ellison* (1980), and M. Graham and A. Singh, *Conversations with Ralph Ellison* (1995).

ELLSBERG, DANIEL (1931–   ), U.S. government official and political activist. Ellsberg studied economics and graduated third in his class at Harvard (B.A. 1952; M.A. 1953). He served as a marine (1954–57), then returned to Harvard to complete a doctoral thesis on game theory (Ph.D. 1962). While working for the Rand think tank (1959–64; 1967–70), he advised the U.S. Defense and State Departments on international security matters, including options in the Vietnam conflict and strategic nuclear war planning. In the late 1960s, after working at the U.S. embassy in Saigon (1965–67), Ellsberg took a stand against the Vietnam War. He came into public view in 1971 when he leaked to the *New York Times* a Pentagon study in which he had participated—*The History of U.S. Decision-making in Vietnam* (47 vols.,

1945–68). (He had provided these papers to the Senate Foreign Relations Committee in 1969.) The Pentagon Papers, as they became known, stirred controversy and led to criminal charges against Ellsberg that were later dropped. He appeared again in headlines during the Watergate probe of the early 1970s when it was revealed that government functionaries had authorized a burglary in the office of Ellsberg's psychiatrist, in the hopes of unearthing incriminating information. Ellsberg remained politically active in the 1980s and 1990s, practicing civil disobedience to protest nuclear weapons research, supporting the Greenpeace environmentalist group, and speaking out in defense of political dissidents at home and abroad. ■ See his book *Papers on the War* (1972).

ELLSWORTH, LINCOLN (1880–1951), U.S. explorer. The son of a millionaire mine operator and financier, Ellsworth used his inheritance to finance several polar expeditions and was the first person to fly over both the North (with Umberto Nobile and Roald Amundsen, 1926) and South (with Herbert Hollick-Kenyon, 1935) Poles. In Antarctica (1935 and 1939) he discovered new mountain ranges, photographed thousands of square miles from the air, and claimed nearly 400,000 square miles of territory for the United States. Ellsworth also led expeditions to the Andes(1924), Labrador (1931), and Peru (1941) and financed (1931) Sir Hubert Wilkins' early attempts at submarine exploration of the North polar basin. He wrote *Our Polar Flight* (1925; with Amundsen), *First Crossing of the Polar Sea* (1927; with Amundsen), *Search* (1932), and his autobiography, *Beyond Horizons* (1938).

ELMAN, MISCHA (1891–1967), Russian-born U.S. violinist. Son of a Jewish schoolmaster, Elman was a child prodigy who won a scholarship to the Royal Music School of Odessa at age 6. In 1903 he went to the St. Petersburg Conservatory, where he studied with Leopold Auer. At age 13 Elman made an enormously successful tour of Germany, followed by debuts in London (1905) and New York (1908). He settled in the United States in 1911. Noted for the sensuousness of his tone and the vibrancy of his playing, Elman performed all the great violin solos and concertos and was a highly sought-after performer all his life.

ELSASSER, WALTER MAURICE (1904–1991), German-born U.S. geophysicist, Elsasser received his Ph.D. from Göttingen University (1927) and subsequently taught in Berlin, Frankfurt, and Paris before going to the United States (1936).He made many fundamental contributions to geophysics, including the formulation of the "dynamo" theory of the earth's permanent magnetic field. He taught at several U.S. universities, including Pennsylvania, Utah, California at La Jolla, Princeton, and Maryland, and wrote *The Physical Foundation of Biology* (1958) and *Atom and Organism* (1966). ■ See his *Memoirs of a Physicist* (1978).

ELTON, CHARLES (1900–1991), British ecologist. A pioneer in the field of animal ecology, Elton did extensive research on several Arctic expeditions during the 1920s. He established and directed the British Bureau of Animal Population at Oxford (1932–67), which became a world-renowned research center, and taught at Oxford University (1936–67). His influential studies of animals and their natural environments included *Animal Ecology* (1927), *Animal Ecology and Evolution* (1930), and *The Pattern of Animal Communities* (1966). ■ See Peter Crowcroft, *Elton's Ecologists* (1991).

ÉLUARD, PAUL (1895–1952), French poet. Long associated with surrealism, Éluard wrote poetry that reflected that movement's attempts to explore dreams, the unconscious, and free expression. His popular poetry commented on love with sensual and lyric rhythms and evocative imagery. During World War II Éluard joined (1942) the Communist party. He wrote war poetry and was a leading poet of the Resistance. His translated verse is in *Uninterrupted Poetry: Selected Writings* (Eng. trans. 1951; 1975), *Capital of Pain* (1926; Eng. trans. 1973), and *Last Love Poems* (1962; Eng. trans. 1980). ■ See study by Robert Nugent (1974).

ELY, RICHARD THEODORE (1854–1943), U.S. economist and educator. The first professor of political economy at Johns Hopkins University (1881–92) and a professor at the University of Wisconsin (1892–1925) and Northwestern (1925–33). Ely was one of the most controversial economists of his time. A Christian socialist who worked for the Progressive movement before World War I, Ely challenged classical laissez-faire economics and advocated government control of natural resources and public utilities, the prohibition of child labor, and the growth of labor unions. He was a founder of the American Economics Association (1885; president, 1899–1901), president of the American Association for Labor Legislation (1907–08), and a founder of the Institute for Economic Research (1920) and was instrumental in popularizing the study of economics. His books included *Outlines of Economics* (1893), a standard text for decades, *Monopolies and Trusts* (1900), *Property and Contract in Their Relations to the Distribution of Wealth* (1914), and *Elements of Land Economics* (1924). ■ See his autobiography, *Ground Under Our Feet* (1938).

ELYTIS, ODYSSEUS (Odysseus Alepoudhelis; 1911–1996), Greek poet. Born into a prosperous Cretan industrial family, Elytis gave up his legal studies in the mid-1930s to concentrate on poetry. Influenced by French surrealism, his humorous and lyrical avant-garde poems formed a personal mythology that celebrated the Greek landscape, climate, history, and tradition, and he was known as "the poet of the Aegean." He fought in the antifascist resistance during World War II, and his poem "Heroic and Elegiac Song for the Lost Second Lieutenant of the Albanian Campaign" served as an inspiration for wartime Greek youth. His postwar works, more complex and philosophical than his earlier verse, included his masterpiece *The Axion Esti* (1959; Eng. trans. 1974), which the Swedish Academy called one of the century's "most concentrated and ritually faceted poems" when it awarded Elytis the 1979 Nobel Prize in Literature. English translations of his works are in *Orientations* (1974), *The Sovereign Sun* (1974), *Selected Poems* (1981), and *Analogies of Light* (1981).

EMERSON, ROY (1936–), Australian tennis player. Emerson grew up on an 800-acre farm in Queensland and began playing tennis on a court on his family's property. An excellent athlete, he quit school at age 16 to pursue a career in tennis and joined the junior squad of the powerful Australian Davis Cup team in 1954. Although never a flashy competitor, he was extremely fast and smooth, rarely made errors on the court, and excelled as both a singles and doubles player. He led Australia to 8 Davis Cup victories (1959–62; 1964–67) and won a record 12 Grand Slam titles, 6 Australian Championships (1961; 1963–67), 2 U.S. National Championships (1961, 1964), 2 French Championships (1963, 1967), and 2 Wimbeldon titles (1964, 1965). His record was broken by Pete Sampras in 2000.

EMPSON, SIR WILLIAM (1906–1984), British critic and poet. Empson studied mathematics at Cambridge before switching, in his last undergraduate year, to the English faculty. He was exposed to the techniques of the New Criticism through his teacher, I. A. Richards. Unlike the New Critics, however, Empson developed a critical approach that took into account the historical and sociological conditions that surround a literary work. In *Seven Types of Ambiguity* (1930), he tied the value of a literary work to its multiplicity of meanings; this idea linked him to Freudian critics, who held that the productions of the unconscious mind are overdetermined, i.e., have many meanings. *Some Versions of Pastoral* (1935) laid greater weight on structural considerations and offered some Marxist interpretations of literary works. *The Structure of Complex Words* (1951) reflected both the New Critics' interest in semantics and Empson's particular interest in the relationship between literature and psychology. Empson, who taught at the University of Tokyo (1931–34), Peking National University (1937–39; 1947–52), and the University of Sheffield (1953–71), published several books of poetry, including *Poems* (1935), *The Gathering Storm* (1940), and *Collected Poems* (1949; rev. ed. 1961). His volume of essays, *Using Biography* (1985), was published posthumously. ■ See study by Christopher Norris (1978).

ENDERS, JOHN FRANKLIN (1897–1985), U.S. virologist. A literature student at Harvard (M.A. 1922), Enders became interested in bacteriology and in 1930 received his Ph.D. in that field from Harvard. As a member of the Harvard faculty (1930–67), he developed techniques for detecting antibodies to the mumps virus that resulted in a skin test for mumps and the development of an attenuated live-virus vaccine. Enders also contributed to the development of a poliovirus vaccine by demonstrating (1949) that the virus could be grown in a culture of human nonnervous tissue cells. For this work he shared the 1954 Nobel Prize in Physiology or Medicine with Frederick C. Robbins and Thomas H. Weller. His application of the culture method to measles led to the development of an effective measles vaccine (1962).

ENRIGHT, DENNIS JOSEPH (1920–), British writer. After graduation from Cambridge (B.A. 1944), D. J. Enright became a peripatetic professor, teaching in Egypt (1947–50), Japan (1956–57), Thailand (1957–59), and Singapore (1960–70). He wrote satirical novels set in Asia (*Heaven Knows Where,* 1957), as well as literary criticism and travel articles and coedited the magazine *Encounter* (1970–72). He was best known, however, for his poems, which cut through cultural pretensions and hypocrisy to describe the human misery of the ex-colonial Third World. Enright also edited the *Oxford Book of Death* (1983) and the *Oxford Book of the Supernatural* (1994). His later works included the novel *The Way of the Cat* (1992), *Collected Poems, 1948–98* (1998), literary essays in *A Mania for Sentences* (1983), and the autobiographical poems in *Instant Chronicles* (1985). ■ See his *Memoirs of a Mendicant Professor* (1969) and study by William Walsh (1974).

ENSOR, JAMES (1860–1949), Belgian painter. Inheritor of Flemish tradition in painting and influenced by the French impressionists, Ensor combined an impressionist technique with fanciful and often grotesque subject matter. When his work was rejected by the Brussels salon in 1883, he helped form an avant-garde group called the Twenty. But even they rejected him for his bitterly irreverent *Entry of Christ into Brussels* (1888), which was not publicly exhibited until 1929. Ensor was fascinated by masks as symbols of evil and degeneracy, and they appear in many of his paintings. His painting changed little after 1900; nevertheless many critics consider him the most significant pioneer of fantastic art in the 20th century, forerunner to the expressionists and surrealists. ■ See studies by Paul Haesaerts (Eng. trans. 1959), Roger Van Gundertael (Eng. trans. 1975), and Diane Lesko (1985).

ENVER PASHA (1881–1922), Turkish soldier and dictator. A leader of the Young Turk revolution of 1908, Enver seized power in a coup d'état (1913). As a member of a ruling triumvirate, he was instrumental in bringing Turkey into World War I on the side of the Germans. He was minister of war (1914–18) and led Turkish forces to a disastrous defeat in the Caucasus (1914–15). After the armistice in Europe (1918), Enver took refuge in Germany. He was killed in action near Bukhara fighting with central Asian Turks against the bolsheviks, whom he had first approached as an ally and

then betrayed. ■ See Ernest Ramsaur, *The Young Turks* (1957).

ENZENSBERGER, HANS MAGNUS (1929–), German poet and critic. After studying languages, literature, and philosophy in Paris and at several German universities (Ph.D. Erlangen, 1955), Enzensberger emerged in the late 1950s as the "angry young man" of German letters. His brilliantly innovative poems utilized a montage of puns, slang, advertising slogans, political and scientific jargon, and biblical and mythological language to attack and parody the emergent post–World War II bourgeoisie and the corruption of contemporary Western society. His biting essays analyzed and debunked the media (*Consciousness Industry,* 1962; Eng. trans. 1974) and drew parallels between gangsters, businessmen, and politicians (*Politics and Crime,* 1964; Eng. trans. 1974). A nonideological left-wing revolutionary, he was a member of the influential literary movement Group 47 and founded and edited (1965–75) the critical journal *Kursbuch.* English translations of his poems are in *Poems* (1966), *Poems for People Who Don't Read Poems* (1968), *Selected Poems* (1968), and *Mausoleum* (1976). His later works included *Europe, Europe* (1987; Eng. trans. 1989); *The Number Devil* (1997; Eng. trans. 1997), a popular account of mathematical history and theory; and an essay collection, *Zig Zag: The Politics of Culture and Vice Versa* (1997; Eng. trans. 1997).

EPSTEIN, SIR JACOB (1880–1959), U.S.-born British sculptor. Born in New York City, Epstein trained in Paris (1902–05) and subsequently lived and worked primarily in Britain. He created controversial massive sculptures in stone and bronze. The 18 sizable nude figures that he created for the British Medical Association Building in London (1907–08) were deemed unsafe and unaesthetic and were destroyed (1937). Epstein also created the Oscar Wilde Memorial, a bronze Christ, a statue of the *Green Mansions* heroine Rima for the W. H. Hudson Memorial, and a *Madonna and Child.* He was best known for compelling and penetrating naturalistic portraits in bronze: he executed busts of Albert Einstein, Joseph Conrad, Jawaharlal Nehru, and others. ■ See his autobiography (rev. ed. 1955) and biographies by Richard Buckle (1963) and Stephen Gardiner (1992).

EPSTEIN, JASON (1928–), U.S. editor and writer. After graduation from Columbia (B.S. 1949; M.A. 1950), Epstein joined Doubleday and Co., the publishers, where he launched the paperback revolution with a series of softcover reissues of the classics. As editorial director for Random House (1958–97) and a founder of (1963) and contributor to the *New York Review of Books* (which was coedited by his wife Barbara), he exercised a major influence on U.S. intellectual life. Epstein wrote *The Great Conspiracy Trial* (1970), an account of the federal trial of the "Chicago Eight," a group of antiwar leaders charged with conspiracy to incite a riot during the 1968 Democratic Convention in Chicago. ■ See Philip Nobile, *Intellectual Skywriting* (1974).

EPSTEIN, JULIUS J. (1909–2000) and **PHILIP G.** (1909–1952), U.S. screenwriters. Julius and his twin brother Philip, whose father ran a livery stable on New York City's Lower East Side, both studied playwriting at Penn State. They wrote a social comedy for Broadway but gained fame after moving to Hollywood and forming a screenwriting team for Warner Bros. in 1938. They coauthored 29 films, including the classics *Yankee Doodle Dandy* (1942), *The Man Who Came to Dinner* (1942), *Casablanca* (1943; Academy Award), *Mr. Skeffington* (1944), and *Arsenic and Old Lace* (1944). After Philip's death, Julius wrote such movies as *Fanny* (1961), *Any Wednesday* (1966), *Pete 'n' Tillie* (1972), *House Calls* (1978), and *Reuben, Reuben* (1983).

ERDOS, PAUL (1913–1996), Hungarian-born mathematician. The son of mathematics teachers, the legendary Erdos was a math prodigy who received his doctorate in mathematics from the University of Budapest at age 21. He left Hungary for England shortly before World War II, thus escaping the fate of his Jewish family, nearly all of whom died in the Holocaust. Erdos never settled down, owned a home, married, or held a job, and he devoted his entire life to mathematics. He constantly traveled around the globe from conference to conference, and university to university, surviving on lecture fees, grants, prizes, and the generosity of colleagues. All the while, for up to 19 hours a day, seven days a week, he posed and solved problems in such fields as number theory, topology, combinatorics, and graph theory. He also discovered the field of discrete mathematics, which is the foundation of computer science. Erdos was one of the most prolific mathematicians in history, publishing more than 1,500 papers with more than 450 collaborators. ■ See Paul Hoffman, *The Man Who Loved Only Numbers* (1998).

ERHARD, LUDWIG (1897–1977), West German political leader. Erhard, a former director of the Nuremberg Institute for Economic Studies (1930–42), was elected as a Christian Democrat to parliament in the first post–World War II elections (1949). As minister of economics (1949–63) in Chancellor Konrad Adenauer's cabinet, he combined currency reforms and free-market policies to create the basis of West Germany's "Wirtschaftswunder," or economic miracle. A strong supporter of U.S. policies and the Atlantic partnership, he succeeded Adenauer as chancellor in 1963, but his government fell over economic difficulties in 1966. ■ See his books, *Germany's Comeback in the World Market* (1953; Eng. trans. 1954) and *Prosperity Through Competition* (1957; Eng. trans. 1958). His speeches and articles are in *The Economics of Success* (Eng. trans. 1963).

ERICKSON, MILTON HYLAND (1901–1980), U.S. psychiatrist. Nearly totally paralyzed by polio at age 17, Erick-son devoted himself to honing his powers of observation and rebuilding strength in his muscles; eventually, he walked with a cane. He studied at the University of Wisconsin under learning theorist Clark Hull, who interested him in hypnotism, and earned an M.D. there (1928). Based in Phoenix, Arizona (1948–80), Erickson sought to make hypnosis an effective tool in his clinical work. He often induced trances to make patients more receptive to his "teaching tales." These stories, which sometimes had no obvious tie to the patient's symptoms, were frequently paradoxical; Erickson did not hesitate to advise that a patient intensify a troubling symptom or substitute an even less comfortable one if he thought the suggestion would ultimately disrupt a destructive pattern. His work, which departed from Freudian techniques, influenced many psychotherapists, particularly those in the family therapy movement. A collection of teaching tales appear in Sidney Rosen, ed., *My Voice Will Go with You* (1982). ■ See *The Collected Papers of Milton Erickson on Hypnosis* (4 vols.; 1980); Ronald A. Havens, ed., *The Wisdom of Milton H. Erickson* (1982); and Jeffrey K. Zeig, *Experiencing Erickson* (1985).

ERIKSON, ERIK HOMBURGER (1902–1994), German-born U.S. psychoanalyst. Erikson studied art and traveled through Europe before moving (1927) to Vienna to enter analysis with Anna Freud and to teach in a private day school. He undertook psychoanalytic training (1929–33), working with child patients, then emigrated (1933) to the U.S., where he gained recognition as a specialist in child psychoanalysis. In *Childhood and Society* (1950), Erikson expanded the Freudian theory of child development by proposing eight stages of life, from infancy to old age, each characterized by a central crisis a person must resolve to be free of neuroses. His theory, which he developed with his wife and lifelong collaborator, Joan (1903–1997), emphasized the importance of cultural, social, and historical factors in the development of an individual identity. Erikson's anthropological investigations among Sioux and Yurok Indian children led him to conclude that each culture has its own unique way of progressing through the stages. Using his analytic theory, Erikson wrote psychohistorical studies of Martin Luther (*Young Man Luther*, 1958) and Mahatma Gandhi (*Gandhi's Truth*, 1969). Other writings included *Insight and Responsibility* (1964) and *Toys and Reasons: Stages in the Ritualization of Experience* (1977). His teaching career was linked chiefly with the University of California at Berkeley (which he left in 1950 after refusing to sign the required loyalty oath) and Harvard University (1960–70). ■ See study by Paul Roazen (1976) and Lawrence J. Friedman, *Identity's Architect* (1999).

ERLANDER, TAGE (1901–1985), Swedish political leader. Erlander began his political career in Lund, where he attended the university and later served on the city council (1930–36). A member of the Social Democratic party, he was elected to parliament (1932) and upon the death of party leader Per Albin Hansson, he was named (1946) premier, a position that he held until 1969. In power during a period of unprecedented industrial expansion, he sponsored social welfare legislation and education reforms and maintained a position of neutrality in foreign affairs. ■ See study by Olof Ruin (1990).

ERLANGER, JOSEPH (1874–1965), U.S. physiologist. A graduate of Johns Hopkins (M.D. 1899), Erlanger taught at the University of Wisconsin (1906–10) and Washington University, St. Louis (1910–46). He shared with Herbert S. Gasser, his former student, the 1944 Nobel Prize in Physiology or Medicine for the discovery of the "highly differentiated functions of single nerve fibers." Using a cathode-ray oscilloscope that they had developed, they discovered that nerve fibers conduct impulses at speeds that vary with the thickness of the fiber. The oscilloscope made possible the specialized field of neurophysiology. Erlanger and Gasser wrote *Electrical Signs of Nervous Activity* (1937).

ERNST, MAX (1891–1976), German-born French painter and sculptor. Educated in philosophy and abnormal psychology, Ernst became fascinated by the art of psychotics. Although influenced by Jean Arp, he was largely self-taught as an artist. After serving in World War I, Ernst became a leader of the antimilitarist, antiaesthetic dadaists in Cologne (1919–22), producing collages of magazine illustrations arranged in arresting images. His work became more illusionary, and he aligned himself with the Paris surrealists in 1924 with his *"frottage"* technique (patterns produced by random placement of tiles, fabric, or grained wood under paper or canvas that was rubbed with crayon or pencil). He was briefly interned during the Nazi occupation of France, then lived (1941–48) in the United States, where his painting became more crystalline. He spent his last years in France. ■ See biography by John Russell (1967); study by Uwe M. Schneede, (1973); and David Hopkins, *Marcel Duchamp and Max Ernst* (1998).

ERNST, RICHARD R. (1933–   ), Swiss chemist. After receiving a Ph.D. in physical chemistry from the Swiss Federal Institute of Technology in Zurich (1962), Ernst worked as a research scientist at Varian Associates in Palo Alto, California (1963–68). With a colleague (Dr. Weston A. Anderson) he developed refinements to nuclear magnetic resonance (NMR) spectroscopy, which increased its sensitivity as a chemical measuring technique by as much as a hundredfold. Back in Switzerland as a professor at his alma mater (from 1968), he made further advances to NMR spectroscopy that allowed for three-dimensional analysis of molecules and compounds and for the development of magnetic resonance imaging (MRI), a medical diagnostic tool that generates images of the interior of the human body in a noninvasive manner. Ernst was awarded the 1991 Nobel Prize in Chemistry.

ERSKINE, JOHN (1879–1951), U.S. educator. As professor of English at Columbia University (1909–37), Erskine emphasized the study of literary and philosophical classics, an approach later extended by his students Mortimer Adler and Carl Van Doren. He was also a lifelong student of music, a concert pianist until a 1935 injury, and president of the Julliard School of Music in New York (1928–37). Erskine wrote poetry, literary criticism, and several humorous novels that placed historical characters in contemporary settings (*The Private Life of Helen of Troy*, 1925; *Galahad*, 1926; *Adam and Eve*, 1927). ■ See his volumes of reminiscences, *The Memory of Certain Persons* (1947), *My Life as a Teacher* (1948), *My Life in Music* (1950), and *My Life as a Writer* (1951).

ERTÉ (Romain de Tirtoff; 1892–1990), Russian-born French fashion designer and illustrator. Erté, whose *nom de mode* derived from the French pronunciation of his initials, was born into St. Petersburg nobility. After seeing Poiret's collection as a child, he left (1912) his portfolio of designs at the couturier's Paris door and was hired as a sketcher. He was soon creating original designs for such clients as the dancer and spy Mata Hari. During World War I, he returned to illustration, drawing his exotic, extravagant fashions in fanciful settings. His art deco illustrations appeared (1915–36) in *Harper's Bazaar*. He designed for the Folies Bergère (1919–30) and for music-hall and theatrical productions in London and New York. Many of Erté's fashion ideas were ahead of their time, including metal hardware on clothes, cutout dresses, one-shoulder dresses, and loose caftans. ■ See his *Erté Fashions* (1972) and the autobiographies, *Things I Remember* (Eng. trans. 1975) and *My Life, My Art* (1989).

ERTEGUN, AHMET MUNIR (1923–   ), Turkish-born U.S. music producer. Born in Istanbul and raised in Paris, London, and Washington, D.C., where his father was the Turkish ambassador, Ertegun was a fan of jazz and blues as a teenager. After studying at St. Johns College in Maryland (B.A. 1944) and Georgetown University (1944–46), he founded Atlantic Records (1947). Ertegun signed the Bee Gees and the Rolling Stones; pioneering in the recording of black music for mass consumption, he also signed such major stars as Ray Charles and Aretha Franklin. He also wrote several award-winning songs. In 1967, Atlantic merged with Warner Bros., and Ertegun became a vice president of the Warner Communications conglomerate. He was a cofounder and president (1971–83) of New York City's Cosmos Soccer Club. ■ See Justine Picardie, *Music Man* (1990).

ERVIN, SAMUEL JAMES, JR. (1896–1985), U.S. political leader. The folksy, Bible-quoting head of the 1973 Senate Watergate investigation that led to the resignation of Pres. Richard Nixon in 1974, Ervin was educated at the University of North Carolina (B.A. 1917) and Harvard Law School (1922). He was a state legislator, judge, and justice of the

North Carolina supreme court (1948–54) before serving as a Democratic U.S. senator (1954–74). As a constitutional expert he was a defender of individual liberties against the state, opposing government surveillance and "no-knock" law enforcement yet also opposing civil-rights legislation and supporting the Vietnam War. He became a celebrity during the televised Watergate hearings for rejecting Pres. Nixon's pleas of executive privilege. ■ See Paul R. Clancy, *Just a Country Lawyer* (1974), and Dick Dabney, *A Good Man* (1976).

ERVING, JULIUS WINFIELD (1950–   ), U.S. basketball player. Erving dropped out of the University of Massachusetts after his junior year to join the Virginia Squires of the American Basketball Association and was named rookie of the year (1972). Known as "Dr. J.," the 6-foot, 7-inch forward was one of the most sensational offensive players in basketball history, capable of flashy dribbling and ball handling, unpredictable midair fakes and maneuvers, and dramatic slam dunks. He led the league three times in scoring (1973, 1974, 1976) and was Most Valuable Player (MVP) in 1974 and 1975. He played with the New York Nets from 1973 to 1976 and, after the merger with the National Basketball Association, with the Philadelphia 76ers (1976–87). He was voted MVP again in 1981. He scored 30,026 points during his career. He later was executive vice president of the Orlando Magic (1997–   ). ■ See Marty Bell, *The Legend of Dr. J.* (1975).

ERZBERGER, MATTHIAS (1875–1921), German political leader. Erzberger trained as a schoolteacher but in 1896 became active in the Catholic Center party. In 1903 he was elected to the Reichstag, where he specialized in fiscal legislation and Catholic rights. An imperialist at the outbreak of World War I, he sponsored a 1917 peace resolution and negotiated the 1918 armistice agreement when the military resisted. This, along with Erzberger's efforts at tax reform, earned him the hatred of ultra-nationalists, who were responsible for his assassination. ■ See study by Klaus Epstein (1959).

ESAKI, LEO (1925–   ), Japanese physicist. Esaki headed a research group at the Sony Corp. while studying for his doctorate in physics (Tokyo University, 1959). At Sony he created the Esaki diode, a tunnel diode that was a significant development in semiconductor electronics and earned him a share of the 1973 Nobel Prize in Physics with Ivar Giaever and Brian D. Josephson. He worked for International Business Machines Corp. (IBM) in the United States (1959–92) and was president of the University of Tsukuba, Ibaraki, Japan (1992–   ).

ESAU, KATHERINE (1898–1997), Russian-born U.S. botanist. Esau grew up in Russia, emigrating with her parents to Germany (1919), where she received a university ed-

ucation, and then to the United States (1922). She trained at the University of California at Berkeley (Ph.D. 1931) and spent her entire career in the University of California system (1931–65). Esau's research on plant development, particularly on the structure and ontogeny of the phloem (the complex tissue that conducts food materials in higher plants), led to significant contributions on the effects of viruses on plants. She elaborated the relationship between the plant virus and the plant host, devising a means of determining whether a virus selectively afflicts a specific tissue. Her books included the classic study *Plant Anatomy* (1953).

ESCHER, MAURITS CORNELIS (1898–1972), Dutch graphic artist. M. C. Escher studied at the School for Architecture and Decorative Arts in Haarlem (1919–22), where he specialized in drawing and printmaking. His realistically detailed lithographs and woodcuts, mostly in black and white, utilized conflicting perspectives, repetitive interlocking figures, and spatial puzzles to depict impossible architecture and such illusions as continuous waterfalls and endless staircases. Although outside the artistic mainstream, his dazzling and bizarre creations were among the most widely reproduced works of art of the century. Because of their perceptual and geometrical complexity they were of particular interest to psychologists and mathematicians. His best known works included *Encounter* (1944), *Relativity* (1953), *Waterfall* (1961), and *Metamorphosis III* (1968). ■ See his writings in *Escher on Escher: Exploring the Infinite* (Eng. trans. 1989); the biography (with complete graphics) by F. H. Bool (Eng. trans. 1982); and Douglas R. Hofstadter, *Gödel, Escher, Bach* (1979).

ESCOBEDO, DANNY (1937?–   ), U.S. convict. A Chicago laborer, Escobedo confessed to the murder of his brother-in-law (January 1960) after a lengthy interrogation by the police, who refused to let him see his lawyer. Sentenced to a 20-year term, he served 4 years before the U.S. Supreme Court, under Chief Justice Earl Warren, ruled five-to-four that his confession had been illegally obtained since he had been denied the effective assistance of counsel guaranteed by the Sixth Amendment. *Escobedo* v. *Illinois* (1964) was a landmark case and Escobedo's name became a byword for the revolution in criminal procedure and police practice carried out by the Warren Court. Escobedo, who was arrested several times in later years on various charges, claimed that police persisted in harassing him.

ESCOFFIER, GEORGES AUGUSTE (1846–1935), French chef. The son of a blacksmith, Escoffier started to cook at age 13 and apprenticed with a famous Parisian chef at 19. Regarded by many as the greatest chef of all time, he simplified and refined the French cuisine of his day, organized teams of cooks to prepare meals efficiently, and invented scores of new dishes, including peach Melba and Melba toast. Long associated with such luxurious hotels as the

Grand in Monte Carlo and the Savoy and Ritz-Carlton in London, he prepared meals for Napoleon III, Edward VII, Victoria, Kaiser Wilhelm, and George V and was known as the "king of cooks, who cooked for kings." (His wife cooked all of his meals at home.) He wrote several widely used cookbooks and a standard work for instructing chefs and was the first chef to be awarded the Legion of Honor (1920).

ESCUDERO, VICENTE (1889–1980), Spanish dancer. Escudero was a teenage runaway who learned authentic flamenco dancing from the Gypsies in Granada. Performing at first in small Spanish cafés, he developed a pure and refined style and graduated to the Olympia Theater in Paris (1920) and a tour of the United States in 1932. He also appeared in a memorable production of *El Amor Brujo* with La Argentina (1934). But Escudero refused to make commercial compromises, and his subsequent career was marked by periods of inactivity and business failure.

ESENIN, SERGEI ALEKSANDROVICH. *See YESENIN, SERGEI ALEKSANDROVICH.*

ESPOSITO, PHIL (1942–), Canadian ice-hockey player. Phil Esposito's scoring ability did not surface until he was traded from Chicago to the Boston Bruins (1967). In his seven years with Boston he won five scoring championships, was the first player to exceed 100 points in a single season, and scored an all-time record of 152 points and 76 goals in 1970–71. In 1970 and again in 1972, Esposito led the Bruins to the Stanley Cup championship, and he was named to the All-Star team for seven straight years. In 1969 and 1974 he was the Most Valuable Player of the National Hockey League (NHL). He played for the New York Rangers from 1975 to 1981, when he retired, having scored a total of 1,590 regular-season points. He later served as general manager of the Rangers (1986–89) and as the first general manager of the Tampa Bay Lightning.

ESTRADA CABRERA, MANUEL (1857–1924), Guatemalan dictator. A former lawyer, judge, and cabinet minister, Estrada Cabrera became in 1898 the first civilian head of the Guatemalan state in 50 years. He changed the constitution and manipulated elections to rule for the next 22 years. Although he improved public health, expanded the school system, and completed a railroad from the capital to the Atlantic coast, his time in office was primarily a period of repression, corruption, and growing United States economic influence. Estrada Cabrera was declared insane by the national assembly in 1920, tried, and imprisoned briefly.

ESTRADA PALMA, TOMÁS (1835–1908), Cuban politician. Estrada served as provisional president of the rebel republic during Cuba's ten-year war against Spain (1868–78), but was captured and exiled. After a period in Honduras, where he met and married the president's daughter, he settled in New York and was principal of a Quaker boys'

school. He headed the Cuban junta in exile (from 1895) and rallied support for the Cuban independence movement in the United States. In 1901 Estrada became the first president of independent Cuba, a paternalistic, nonpartisan figure who negotiated the 1903 treaty giving the United States a base at Guantánamo. He formed an alliance with Conservatives and was reelected in 1905 but withdrew from office after a revolt in 1906.

EULER, ULF SVANTE VON (1905–1983), Swedish physiologist. The son of Hans Euler-Chelpin (co-winner of the 1929 Nobel Prize in Chemistry), Ulf von Euler received his M.D. degree from Stockholm's Karolinska Institute in 1930 and taught there until 1971. He discovered (1935) prostaglandins, fatty acids that are involved in the contraction of smooth muscles and the regulation of pulse rate, blood pressure, and the central nervous system. For his identification (1946–48) of noradrenaline, the key impulse carrier of the sympathetic nervous system, he shared the 1970 Nobel Prize in Physiology or Medicine with Julius Axelrod and Sir Bernard Katz. He wrote *Noradrenaline* (1956) and *Postaglandins* (1967; with Rune Eliasson) and served as president of the Nobel Foundation (1965–75).

EULER-CHELPIN, HANS KARL AUGUST SIMON VON (1873–1964), German-born Swedish biochemist. A man who abandoned painting for science, Euler-Chelpin studied at the universities of Berlin and Göttingen and at the Pasteur Institute (Paris). On the faculty of the University of Stockholm (1900–41), he worked on enzymes, coenzymes, and vitamins. For his work, which described the role of enzymes in the fermentation of sugar, Euler-Chelpin shared the 1929 Nobel Prize in Chemistry with Sir Arthur Harden. His son, Ulf Svante von Euler, shared the 1970 Nobel Prize in Medicine or Physiology.

EUWE, MAX (Machgielis Euwe; 1901–1981), Dutch chess player. A mathematics professor who was an expert on chess-opening theory, Max Euwe was the Dutch chess champion from 1921 through 1957. In 1935 he defeated Alexander Alekhine for the world championship, but lost the title in a return match two years later. Known for his classic style of play, Euwe wrote numerous books and articles on chess and served as president of the International Chess Federation (1970–78).

EVANS, SIR ARTHUR JOHN (1851–1941), British archaeologist. The son of a prominent archaeologist, Evans studied at Oxford, where he became curator of the Ashmolean Museum (1884–1908). He first went to Crete in 1894 to study ancient script and worked there until 1935 uncovering the ancient city of Knossos and the ruins of a Bronze Age civilization that he called Minoan, one of the major finds in European prehistory. Evans described his work in *Scripta Minoa* (2 vols., 1909 and 1952) and in *Palace of Minos* (4 vols., 1921–36). ■ See Joan Evans, *Time and Chance* (1943).

EVANS, DAME EDITH (1888–1976), British actress. In a stage career stretching over six decades, Evans used her characteristic "swooping" voice to express a broad range of emotions in scores of stage and screen roles. She performed with rare intelligence and directness in comedy and drama, both classical and modern, and in Restoration drama. She is best remembered as Millamant in William Congreve's *The Way of the World* (1924), as the nurse in Katharine Cornell's production of *Romeo and Juliet* (1934), and as Lady Bracknell in Oscar Wilde's *The Importance of Being Earnest* (1939). Evans also made motion pictures, winning numerous awards for *The Whisperers* (1967). She made many recordings of Shakespearean roles and sonnets. ■ See biography by Bryan Forbes (1977).

EVANS, MAURICE (1901–1989), British-born U.S. actor. Evans' earliest roles were in his father's adaptations of Thomas Hardy's fiction. His professional career began in the mid-1920s. He played numerous parts before establishing himself (1934) in the Old Vic–Sadler Wells Company, where he became known for his interpretations of roles in the plays of Shakespeare and Shaw. He emigrated (1935) to the United States, toured with Katharine Cornell in *Romeo and Juliet,* and later appeared as Richard II, Hamlet, Malvolio, and Macbeth. Evans became (1941) a U.S. citizen; during World War II he headed (1942–45) the army entertainment section in the central Pacific, staging a "GI version" of *Hamlet.* Evans later appeared in such hit shows as *Man and Superman* (1949), *Dial M for Murder* (1952–54), and *Tenderloin* (1960) and in such films as *Macbeth* (1959), *Planet of the Apes* (1968), and *Rosemary's Baby* (1968). He also produced television shows and Broadway plays. ■ See his memoirs, *All This—and Evans Too* (1987).

EVANS, WALKER (1903–1975), U.S. photographer. Evans' early architectural photography of historic New England generated (1934) the first one-person exhibition of photography mounted at New York's Museum of Modern Art. The following year, as a staff photographer for the Farm Security Administration, he began documenting the impact of the Depression on rural Americans, particularly in the South. His direct, unpretentious photos of people, their artifacts, and their homes greatly influenced the development of American photography. His Depression scenes were collected in *American Photographs* (1938). Evans collaborated with James Agee on *Let Us Now Praise Famous Men* (1941), an account in words and images of southern sharecroppers. After World War II, he worked as an editor of *Fortune* magazine (1945–65). ■ See *Walker Evans* (1971) and *Walker Evans at Work* (1982) and biography by James R. Mellow (1999).

EVANS-PRITCHARD, SIR EDWARD EVAN (1902–1973), British social anthropologist. E. E. Evans-Pritchard, a professor at Oxford (1946–70), investigated almost every aspect of social anthropology, integrating ethnographic detail with illuminating theory. His fieldwork among the Azande of the southern Sudan and the Congo generated *Witchcraft: Oracles and Magic among the Azande* (1937), which suggested the internal logic of a preliterate culture, and also *The Azande* (1971). Another work, *The Nuer* (1940), analyzed the political organization of a society without government. Evans-Pritchard converted to Roman Catholicism during World War II, and his later work strove to reconcile the social sciences with religious faith. ■ See study by Mary T. Douglas (1980).

EVATT, HERBERT VERE (1895–1965), Australian statesman and jurist. Evatt excelled scholastically at Sydney University and was so successful as a lawyer that he became the youngest justice on the high court of Australia (1930). He resigned in 1940 and was elected a Labour member of Parliament, and he served as attorney general and minister for external affairs (1941–49). In the latter position Evatt solidified ties with the United States and New Zealand during World War II, extended Australia's participation in world affairs, and strongly supported the rights of small countries. An internationalist, he helped write the United Nations charter (1945) and was president of the General Assembly (1948). He later served as the leader of Labour opposition in Parliament (1951–60) and chief justice of New South Wales (1960–62). ■ See biographies by Allan Dalziel (1967) and Kylie Tennant (1970) and K. D. Buckley, *Doc Evatt* (1994).

EVERGOOD, PHILIP (Philip Blashki; 1901–1973), U.S. painter. Evergood was educated in Britain (Eton and Cambridge) and studied art in New York and Paris. Associated with the social realism that characterized American painting in the 1930s, he was best known for the murals he executed while working with the Federal Works of Art Project beginning in 1933, notably *American Tragedy* (1937). An example of his later work, which emphasized biblical and mythological symbolism, was *The New Lazarus* (1954). ■ See study by John Baur (1975).

EVERS, (JAMES) CHARLES (1922–), and MEDGAR WILEY EVERS (1925–1963), African-American U.S. civil-rights leaders. As field director for the National Association for the Advancement of Colored People in Mississippi, Medgar Evers was challenging white supremacy with a voter registration drive when he was assassinated. He was succeeded by his older brother Charles, who subsequently signed up enough black votes to become a political power in the state's Black Belt. "The only way to change the system is to become the system," according to Charles Evers, who served four non-continuous terms as the first African-American mayor since Reconstruction of a racially mixed town in the South (Fayette, Mississippi; 1969–89). ■ See Charles Evers' autobiography (1971) and his *Have No Fear* (1997); Jason Berry, *Amazing Grace* (1973); and John R. Salter, Jr., *Jackson, Mississippi* (1979).

EVERT, CHRIS (Christine Marie Evert; 1954–   ), U.S. tennis player. The daughter of a tennis teaching pro. Evert learned to play as a child and was the youngest player ever to participate on the U.S. Wightman Cup team (1971). Known for her powerful two-handed backhand and her intense concentration on the court, she turned professional in 1972 and was one of the dominant women players of the 1970s and 1980s. Among her victories were 6 U.S. Open championships (1975–78, 1980, 1982), 3 Wimbledon titles (1974, 1976, 1981), 7 French Open championships (1974–75, 1979, 1980, 1983, 1985, 1986), and 2 Australian Open championships (1982, 1984). She retired (1989) with 157 titles. ■ See her autobiography, *Chrissie* (1982; with Neil Amdur).

EWING, (WILLIAM) MAURICE (1906–1974), U.S. geophysicist. Raised on a Texas farm, Ewing became a noted geophysicist specializing in seismology and oceanography. He invented the SOFAR communications system during World War II; it used explosions to transmit long-distance underwater signals. Ewing founded and directed (1949–72) Columbia University's Lamont Geological Observatory, where he and his staff pioneered new methods and theories of modern geophysics. He helped develop seismic, or shock, wave exploration and mapping of the ocean's floor, which offered evidence to support the theory of continental drift. He advocated a controversial theory to explain ice ages and invented many geophysical instruments and a lunar seismograph.

EYSKENS, GASTON (1905–1988), Belgian premier and economist. Eyskens was a professor of economics when he entered Belgium's parliament, representing (1939–73) the Social Christian party. He was three times minister of finance and three times premier (1949–50; 1958–61; 1968–72). He resigned his first tenure during the dispute over King Leopold III's return to Belgium. During his second term, Eyskens negotiated (1958) the resolution of a controversy over government support of public and parochial schools. After he urged parliament to declare the Belgian Congo (later the republic of Zaire) independent (1960), the Congolese civil war that ensued and Belgium's internal strife toppled his coalition government. During his third term, he attempted unsuccessfully to reconcile Belgium's French-speaking and Flemish-speaking communities.

F

FADEYEV, ALEKSANDR ALEKSANDROVICH (1901–1956), Soviet novelist. The son of a village doctor, Fadeyev grew up in Siberia, joined the Communist party at age 17, and became a leader of the Russian Association for Proletarian Writers (1923–32). His first novel, *The Nineteen* (1927; Eng. trans. 1929; 1956 as *The Rout*), met with a warm official reception, and he later won a Stalin Prize for *The Young Guard* (1945; Eng. trans. 1958), which he revised (1951) to give the Communist party greater prominence. Fadeyev was more influential as a literary ideologue than as a writer and served as secretary of the official writers' union (1936–44; 1946–54). He urged imitation of the classics, which he equated with the works of Leo Tolstoy, and championed realism as the literary vehicle of Marxist-Leninist philosophy. He attacked romanticism, formalism, and modern Western literary trends. After the death of dictator Joseph Stalin (1953), he lost power and he committed suicide during the de-Stalinization campaign.

FADIMAN, CLIFTON PAUL (1904–1999), U.S. critic. Fadiman studied at Columbia (A.B. 1925) and worked as an editor at the publishing firm of Simon & Schuster (1929–35). As book editor for the *New Yorker* (1933–43), he gained a reputation as the "lord high executioner" of aspiring authors. As a member of the Book-of-the-Month Club's selecting committee (from 1944), Fadiman influenced the literary taste of generations of Americans. He hosted radio and television programs, assembled more than two dozen anthologies, and wrote many books, including *Party of One* (1955), *The Lifetime Reading Plan* (1959; rev. ed. 1977), *Enter Conversing* (1962), and *Empty Pages: A Search for Writing Competence in School and Society* (1979; with James Howard). ■ See his memoir, *Fifty Years* (1965).

FAHD IBN ABD AL-AZIZ AL SA'UD (1921–   ), king of Saudi Arabia. The eleventh son of King Ibn Saud, Fahd received a traditional court education. He served as minister of education (1953–62), minister of the interior (1962–75), and first deputy prime minister (1975–82) before ascending to the throne after the death of his half brother, King Khalid, in 1982. A pro-Western and pro-American modernizer, he sought to use his country's oil wealth to support rapid economic development, a position opposed by many traditionalists in the kingdom. Dwindling oil revenues in the 1980s forced him to carry out unpopular austerity measures. His 1981 Middle East peace plan, which called for Israel to withdraw from all Arab territories it occupied in 1967 in exchange for peaceful coexistence, was accepted by most Arab states. Fahd strongly supported the U.S. position against Iraq in the Persian Gulf War (1990) and allowed foreign troops to enter Saudi territory in preparation for the liberation of Kuwait. Accused of corruption and repression by his opponents, he nevertheless weakened his family's power by establishing a 60-member consultative council and 13 regional advisory councils (1993). ■ See study by N. I. Rashid and E. I. Shaheen (1987).

FAIRBANK, JOHN KING (1907–1991), U.S. historian. A Harvard graduate (B.A. 1929) who won a Rhodes scholarship to Oxford, Fairbank taught himself Chinese when he heard the Chinese government was going to publish its 19th-century archives, then spent a year reading them. He returned to teach at Harvard in 1936 and worked for the U.S. government in China (1942–43; 1945–46). He later published *The United States and China* (1948) and *China's Responses to the West* (1954). As a leader of American Asian scholars, he was accused during the witch-hunting era of Sen. Joseph McCarthy of being a communist—a charge he denied. In 1970 he led a group of scholars in protest against the Vietnam War. His other works included *China Perceived* (1974), *The Great Chinese Revolution, 1800–1985* (1986), and *China: A New History* (1992). ■ See his memoirs, *Chinabound* (1982), and study by Paul M. Evans (1988).

FAIRBANKS, DOUGLAS, SR. (Douglas Ulman, 1883–1939), U.S. film actor. Hollywood's first adventure hero, Fairbanks was the swashbuckling star of silent costume romances, including *The Three Musketeers* (1921), *Robin Hood* (1922), and *The Thief of Baghdad* (1924). He was a founder of United Artists (1919), first president of the Academy of Motion Picture Arts and Sciences, and with his wife Mary Pickford reigned over Hollywood society during the 1920s. A physical-fitness buff, he did all his own stunts and popularized the suntan as a sign of vitality. His son, Douglas Fairbanks, Jr. (1909–2000), was also a popular movie star. ■ See biography by Ralph Hancock and Letitia Fairbanks (1953) and Richard Schickel, *His Picture in the Papers* (1974).

FAIRCHILD, DAVID GRANDISON (1869–1954), U.S. botanist and agricultural explorer. Fairchild traveled the world for 50 years searching for new and useful plants. He served with the U.S. Department of Agriculture's division of foreign seed and plant introduction (explorer, 1898–1903; director, 1903–28; collaborator, 1928–54) and was responsible for the introduction of thousands of new plant species into the United States. His collection is at the Fairchild Tropical Garden near Coconut Grove, Florida. His popular books included *Exploring for Plants* (1930) and *The World Grows Round My Door* (1947). ■ See his autobiography, *The World Was My Garden* (1938).

FAIRCLOUGH, ELLEN (Ellen Louks; 1905–   ), Canadian political leader. Forced to leave school at age 16 when her father's farm failed, Fairclough held various jobs. In 1935 she set up an accounting firm in Hamilton, Ontario, and became an income-tax expert. From 1946 to 1951 she participated in municipal politics, being elected to Parliament (the only woman) as a Progressive Conservative in 1950. In 1957 Fairclough became the first woman cabinet minister in Canadian history on her appointment as secretary of state, and she later served as minister for citizenship and immigration (1958–62) and postmaster general (1962–63). After her defeat in the 1963 elections she was a prominent member of Hamilton's business community. ■ See her memoirs, *Saturday's Child* (1995).

FAISAL (Ibn-Abd-al-Aziz al-Saud; 1906?–1975), Saudi Arabian king. A son of King Ibn Saud, Faisal helped his father conquer Hejaz (1924–25) and served as his foreign minister (from 1930). Named crown prince in 1953, Faisal succeeded to the throne in 1964 after his brother, King Saud, was deposed. A devout Islamic traditionalist, he favored close ties to the West and was a bitter opponent of Zionism, Soviet influence, and indigenous radical movements. As his country's wealth from oil grew astronomically, he initiated programs of economic, agricultural, and educational development. He was a leader of the Organization of Petroleum Exporting Countries (OPEC) and cautiously used the "oil weapon"—a limited embargo—after the 1973 Arab-Israeli War. He was assassinated by his nephew. ■ See biography by Vincent Sheean (1975) and Willard Beling, ed., *King Faisal and the Modernization of Saudi Arabia* (1979).

FAISAL I (1883–1933), king of Iraq. Faisal was the third son of the Arab nationalist Husein ibn-Ali, a member of one of Mecca's leading families. In 1891 Faisal moved with his father to Constantinople, where he was raised and educated. After Husein proclaimed the Arab Revolt in Mecca (1916), Faisal and his older brother Abdullah led Arab troops against the Ottomans and assisted the British in their invasion of Palestine from Egypt. They occupied Syria in 1918, and Faisal was proclaimed king of Syria by an Arab national congress (1920). France ousted Faisal from Syria four months later and in 1921 his British friends secured for Faisal the newly created kingdom of Iraq, which he ruled until his death. He helped guide the country to complete independence in 1932. ■ See James Morris, *The Hashemite Kings* (1959).

FALKENHAYN, ERICH VON (1861–1922), German general. A Prussian career soldier, Falkenhayn served in the Far East as an instructor to the Chinese army and as governor of Tientsin before his appointments as a minister of war (1913) and as chief of the general staff (1914). His failure, during World War I, to take Verdun in 1916 and his neglect of the eastern front led to demotion. He later commanded forces in Rumania, Palestine, and Lithuania.

FALL, ALBERT BACON (1861–1944), U.S. cabinet officer. Fall was a rancher, miner, and lawyer before winning election as the first U.S. senator, a Republican, from the new state of New Mexico (1912). He was appointed secretary of the interior by Pres. Warren Harding in 1921 and resigned in 1923. It was later revealed (1924) that Fall was involved in the Teapot Dome oil scandal and had received $300,000 from oilmen who obtained leases on naval property without competitive bidding. Convicted of bribe taking (1929), he served nine months of a one-year sentence in prison (1931–32). He was the first cabinet officer convicted of a felony while in office. ■ See his *Memoirs* (1966); J. Leonard Bates, *The Origins of Teapot Dome* (1963); and David H. Stratton, *Tempest over Teapot Dome* (1998).

FALLA, MANUEL DE (1876–1946), Spanish composer. Falla frequently used the folk music of Andalusia and flamenco dance rhythms to give a passionate feeling to his characteristically Spanish compositions. His most famous works included the opera *La Vida Breve* (1905), the ballets *El Amor Brujo* (which included the "Ritual Fire Dance"; 1919), and *The Three-Cornered Hat* (1919). Unwilling to live under the dictatorship of Francisco Franco, he left his native Spain (1939) to live in exile in Argentina. ■ See studies by Jaime Pahissa (Eng. trans. 1954), Suzanne Demarquez (Eng. trans. 1968), and James Burnett (1979).

FALLACI, ORIANA (1930–   ), Italian journalist. Fallaci became a reporter at 16 and made her name with interviews of show-business personalities for *L'Europeo*, a popular news and feature magazine (1955–75). She recorded her experiences covering the Vietnam War (1967–68) in her book *Nothing, and So Be It* (Eng. trans. 1972). A journalist with strong leftist sympathies, Fallaci developed the art of the political interview. In conversations with her, U.S. Secretary of State Henry Kissinger described himself as the Lone Ranger, and Palestinian leader Yasir Arafat unveiled his terrorist ambitions. She wrote *Interview with History* (Eng. trans. 1976), the fictionalized account of her relationship with Greek poet and resistance hero Alexander Panagoulis; *A Man* (Eng. trans. 1980); and *Inshallah* (Eng. trans. 1992), a fictional account of Italian troops in Lebanon in 1983. ■ See biography by Santo L. Arico (1998).

FALLADA, HANS (Rudolf Ditzen; 1893–1947), German novelist. The son of a judge, Fallada was a journalist before writing the popular novels concerned with the problems confronting German society following World Wars I and II. The compassionate social realism of the novel *Little Man, What Now?* (1933; Eng. trans. 1933) won international attention and was twice filmed; *Wolf Among Wolves* (1937;

Eng. trans. 1938) was written in the same spirit. He also wrote *The World Outside* (1934; Eng. trans. 1934), *An Old Heart Goes A-Journeying* (1936; Eng. trans. 1936), *Sparrow Farm* (1938; Eng. trans. 1938), and *The Drinker* (1950; Eng. trans. 1952). His autobiographical writing recalls his experiences as a disaffected noncollaborator in Nazi Germany and exposes his alcoholism and drug abuse. ■ See study by Heinz Schueler (1970) and Jenny Williams, *More Lives Than One* (1998).

FALWELL, JERRY (1933–), U.S. clergyman and political activist. A promising youthful athlete and preengineering student, Falwell became a "born-again" Christian while studying at Lynchburg (Virginia) College (1952) and transferred to a Bible college. He founded an independent Baptist church in Lynchburg (1956) and became a popular evangelist. He inaugurated the televised "Old-Time Gospel Hour," which by 1971 was broadcast nationwide, and founded Liberty Baptist College. By the late 1970s he turned toward political activism to spread his traditional moral values and antiabortion, anti–Equal Rights Amendment, and antihomosexual views and founded Moral Majority, Inc. (1979). The organization endorsed and supported conservative candidates and played a leading role in the election of Pres. Ronald Reagan in 1980. Falwell wrote several books, including *Listen, America!* (1980). ■ See his autobiography, *Strength for the Journey* (1987), and biographies by Gerald Strober and Ruth Tomczak (1979) and Dinesh D'Souza (1984).

FANFANI, AMINTORE (1908–1999), Italian public official. Known as "the little professor," Fanfani was a distinguished economic historian and a prolific author before being elected to parliament (1946). As leader of the Christian Democrats, Fanfani was premier five times (1954; 1958–59; 1960–63; 1982–83). The government he formed in 1962 reflected the "opening to the left" as the Christian Democrats entered a parliamentary alliance with the socialists for the first time. Fanfani also served as foreign minister (1965; 1966–68) and was elected president of the U.N. General Assembly (1965–66) and president of the Italian senate (1968–73; 1976–82; 1985).

FANGIO, JUAN MANUEL (1911–1995), Argentine auto racer. Considered by many to be the greatest driver in auto-racing history, Fangio dominated the sport during the 1950s. A safe, smooth, and seemingly effortless driver for Alfa Romeo, Mercedes-Benz, Ferrari, and Maserati, he won 16 Grand Prix races and was the world driving champion in 1951 and from 1954 through 1957. After his retirement he was president of Mercedes-Benz, Argentina.

FANON, FRANTZ OMAR (1925–1961), Martinican-born psychiatrist and political theorist. A black victimized by both racism and colonialism, Fanon examined the psychology of racism in his first book, *Black Skin, White Masks*

(1952; Eng. trans. 1967). While directing the psychiatric department of an Algerian hospital (1953–56) he became sympathetic to the Algerian liberation movement, quit the hospital to work for the National Liberation Front (FLN) in Tunis, and became a leading ideologist of the revolution. In his most important work, *The Wretched of the Earth* (1961; Eng. trans. 1963), Fanon utilized Marxist, psychoanalytic, and sociological analysis in arguing that only a violent socialist revolution, led by the oppressed peasantry of Third World countries, could break the psychological and economic shackles of colonialism and bring true justice to the colonized. He also wrote *Studies in a Dying Colonialism* (1959; Eng. trans. 1965) and *Toward the African Revolution* (1964; Eng. trans. 1967). ■ See biographies by Peter Geismar (1971) and Irene Gendzier (1973).

FARINACCI, ROBERTO (1892–1945), Italian politician. A former railroad worker and socialist, Farinacci became the fascist party boss of Cremona, which he ruled like a medieval feudal baron. He was appointed secretary-general of the Fascist party in 1925 but, considered more extremist than fascist dictator Benito Mussolini, resigned a year later in disfavor. Recalled to power in 1935, he was the key fascist liaison with the Nazis and urged Mussolini to enter World War II in alliance with Germany. He was tried and executed by partisans at the end of World War II. ■ See Harry Fornari, *Mussolini's Gadfly* (1971).

FARLEY, JAMES ALOYSIUS (1888–1976), U.S. political leader. Farley began his career as a bookkeeper and in 1912 was elected town clerk of Stony Point, New York. His talent for Democratic party politics won him appointments to such sinecures as the New York State Boxing Commission. A hearty handshaker with a phenomenal memory for names and faces, Farley was appointed Democratic national chairman (1932) and U.S. postmaster general (1933) for valuable campaign services in Franklin D. Roosevelt's rise from governor of New York to the White House. He also successfully managed Roosevelt's 1936 reelection campaign. Farley broke with Roosevelt in 1940 and served as chairman of Coca-Cola (1940–73). ■ See his memoirs, *Behind the Ballots* (1938) and *Jim Farley's Story* (1948).

FARNSWORTH, PHILO TAYLOR (1906–1971), U.S. engineer and inventor. While still a teenager Farnsworth worked out the principles of electronically transmitting moving pictures and drew a schematic diagram of the first television system. After studying at Brigham Young University, Utah (1923–25), he found financial support for his project. He produced a working model of the electronic "image dissector" camera in 1928 and was granted numerous patents covering different aspects of television design. The Philco Corporation, which had supported his work for several years in the 1930s, withdrew its backing in 1938, and Farnsworth suspended work on the project during World War II. By the end of the war, a rival television system devised by Vladimir K. Zworykin was pushed into production by the giant Radio Corporation of America (RCA) and it soon became the industry standard. In 1949 Farnsworth's company became an electronic research division of the International Telephone and Telegraph Company (ITT), and Farnsworth subsequently worked on the peaceful uses of nuclear fission and fusion. ▪ See E. G. Farnsworth, *Distant Vision* (1990).

FAROUK I (1920–1965), king of Egypt. The only son of King Fuad I. Farouk ascended the Egyptian throne in 1936 as a teenager. Hemmed in on one side by the British, who during World War II curbed his profascist inclinations, and on the other by the popular nationalistic Wafd party, he turned increasingly to gambling, nightclubbing, and other pleasurable pursuits. Many in the army blamed him for Egypt's defeat in the war with Israel (1948), and he was overthrown by a military coup led by Gamal Abdel Nasser (1952). Farouk died in exile in Rome. ▪ See biography by Barrie McBride (1967).

FARRAKHAN, LOUIS ABDUL (Louis Eugene Walcott; 1933–), U.S. religious leader. The son of immigrants from the Caribbean, Farrakhan was born in New York City and raised in Boston. He was an honor student and outstanding violinist in high school and appeared on Ted Mack's "Original Amateur Hour," a popular television show. After studying at a teacher's college (1952–53), he pursued a career as a calypso singer. During this period he was recruited by Malcolm X into the black separatist Nation of Islam and became minister of its Boston mosque in 1956. When Malcolm X split with The Nation (1963–64), Farrakhan succeeded him as head of the Harlem mosque and as national spokesman of the movement. When, after the death of The Nation's leader Elijah Muhammad (1975), his son and successor, W. Dean Muhammad, gradually moved the group toward orthodox Islam and allowed members of all races to join, Farrakhan formed (1977) a new Nation of Islam, based on racial exclusivity and strict codes of behavior. An eloquent orator, he was known both for his advocacy of economic self-reliance for blacks as well as for his frequent antiwhite and anti-Semitic statements. In 1995 he organized a "Million-Man March" in Washington as a holy day of atonement and reconciliation for African-American men. ▪ See Arthur J. Magida, *Prophet of Rage* (1996); Robert Singh, *The Farrakhan Phenomenon* (1997); and Florence Levinsohn, *Looking for Farrakhan* (1997).

FARRAR, GERALDINE (1882–1967), U.S. opera singer. The daughter of a professional baseball player, Farrar started to sing publicly at age 14 and made her debut with the Berlin Royal Opera in 1901. Celebrated for her beauty, personal magnetism, and dramatic abilities, she was a leading lyric soprano at New York's Metropolitan Opera (1906–22), where she appeared frequently with Enrico Caruso. Her most famous roles were in *Madama Butterfly, Carmen, Manon, Tosca, Faust,* and *La Bohème.* ▪ See her autobiography, *Such Sweet Compulsion* (1938), and Elizabeth Nash, *Always First Class* (1981).

FARRELL, JAMES T. (1904–1979), U.S. novelist. Born and educated in Chicago, Farrell worked as a clerk, salesman, and undertaker. His trilogy, *Studs Lonigan,* narrated the protagonist's adventures on Chicago's South Side with blunt realism and a graphic treatment of sexuality that shocked some readers. The trilogy encompassed *Young Lonigan* (1932), *The Young Manhood of Studs Lonigan* (1934), and *Judgment Day* (1935). Studs Lonigan became a popular culture hero of the Depression years, and Farrell won praise as a leading writer of realistic fiction; critic H. L. Mencken called him "the best living American novelist." Undaunted by the sharp decline in his reputation in later years, Farrell published more than 50 novels. A prominent figure in the non-Stalinist left, he was, at the time of his death, at work on a novel depicting literary and political circles of the 1930s. He also wrote poetry, stories, and nonfiction, including *A Note on Literary Criticism* (1936) and *Reflections at Fifty* (1954). ▪ See study by Alan M. Wald (1978).

FARRELL, SUZANNE (Roberta Sue Ficker; 1945–), U.S. dancer. Farrell took her first ballet lessons at the age of 8. She won a scholarship to study at the School of American Ballet (1960), the training school of the New York City Ballet, joined the company in 1961 and became a principal dancer in 1965. An artist with flawless technique and an ethereal stage persona, she quickly became the muse of company director George Balanchine and was, to many, the personification of the modern ballerina. She danced in over a hundred ballets, more than 20 created for her by Balanchine, including *Meditation, Don Quixote, Variations, The Jewels, Slaughter on Tenth Avenue,* and *Mozartiana.* After a dispute with Balanchine (1970) she left the company and danced with Maurice Béjart's Ballet of the 20th Century in Brussels. However, she returned to the New York City Ballet in 1975 and danced with the company until her retirement in 1989. ▪ See her autobiography, *Holding on to the Air* (1990).

FASSBINDER, RAINER WERNER (1946–1982), German filmmaker. Trained as an actor, Fassbinder started an avant-garde theater group called Anti-Theater in 1968. The group produced its first film in 1969. In a career lasting 13 years, Fassbinder directed over 41 films, writing most of them, acting in many, and continuing to rely heavily on his repertory company. Severe in style, most of his films are bitingly political and satiric, and there is almost no group that they did not offend. A leftist and an open homosexual, he often portrayed the disrupted lives of people on the fringes of bourgeois society. *The Bitter Tears of Petra von Kant* (1972), depicting a lesbian relationship, won Fassbinder an international reputation. *Ali—Fear Eats the Soul* (1973) concerned an elderly cleaning woman who marries a young immigrant worker from North Africa. *Effi Briest* (1974), a period piece based on Theodor Fontane's novel, described the rigidity of 19th-century Prussian society. His other notable films included a trilogy about post–World War II West German society (*The Marriage of Maria Braun*, 1979; *Lola*, 1981; *Veronika Voss*, 1982) and the 15½-hour epic originally made for television, *Berlin Alexanderplatz* (1979). ■ See studies by Peter Iden (Eng. trans. 1981) and Ronald Hayman (1984), and Robert Katz, *Love Is Colder Than Death* (1987).

FAST, HOWARD (1914–), U.S. writer. Born into a poverty-stricken Jewish family in New York City, Fast worked as a garment worker and as a page in the New York Public Library after leaving high school. He began writing at an early age, publishing his first magazine story at age 17 and his first novel at age 18. In a literary career spanning over 60 years, he wrote more than 70 books and was one of the most widely read novelists of the 20th century. His historical fiction included works dealing with the American Revolution (*The Unvanquished*, 1942; *Citizen Tom Paine*, 1943; *April Morning*, 1961), the struggle of southern African-Americans during the Reconstruction era (*Freedom Road*, 1944; film 1980), and the attempt of the Cheyenne Indians to regain their homeland (*The Last Frontier*, 1941). He also wrote *Spartacus* (1952; film 1960) and the six-volume Lavette family saga (1977–97), which included the novels *The Immigrants* (1977) and *The Establishment* (1979). A politically active member of the U.S. Communist party (1944–56), Fast was jailed briefly (1950) for refusing to name fellow party members before a congressional committee and was blacklisted during the 1950s. His books *The Naked God* (1957) and *Being Red* (1990) describe his break with the party. ■ See study by Andrew Macdonald (1996).

FAULKNER, WILLIAM (**William Cuthbert Falkner; 1897–1962**), U.S. novelist. After serving in the Royal Canadian flying corps in World War I, Faulkner wandered between New York and New Orleans. After a jaunt to Europe, he settled in the South to write, in over a dozen novels, the epic and fragmented saga of Yoknapatawpha County, Mississippi, a mythical patch of land modeled on Faulkner's native Jefferson County in Mississippi. Faulkner's extraordinary experiments with interior monologue, sentence structure, and chronology in such works as *The Sound and the Fury* (1929), *Light in August* (1932), *Absalom, Absalom!* (1936), and *Go Down, Moses* (1942) baffled critics, and his passionate concern with moral responsibility in the new South aroused both praise and indignation. Faulkner's popularity declined in the 1930s and 1940s, but *A Fable* (1954) and *The Reivers* (1963) both won Pulitzer Prizes. His 1950 Nobel Prize acceptance speech struck the theme of his major novels: "I believe that man will not merely endure: he will prevail." ■ See biographies by Hyatt H. Waggoner (1959),

Joseph Blotner (2 vols., 1974), A. I. Bezzerides (1979), David Minter (1980), and Richard Gray (1994).

FAURE, EDGAR JEAN (1908–1988), French political leader. A brilliant lawyer from Béziers, Faure was a World War II Resistance leader who became director of legislative services to Gen. Charles de Gaulle's government in North Africa. In 1945 he was a French delegate to the International Military Tribunal in Nuremberg and in 1946 won election to the national assembly as a radical socialist. A skilled debater with an impressive command of facts and figures, Faure was premier twice (1952; 1955–56). He was a supporter of Pres. Charles de Gaulle (after 1958), served as minister of agriculture (1966–68) and education (1968–69), and was president of the national assembly (1973–78). He also wrote detective stories under the pseudonym Edgar Sanday.

FAURÉ, GABRIEL URBAIN (1845–1924), French composer. Fauré studied in Paris at the École Niedermeyer (1855–65) and worked as an organist and teacher of composition. He joined the faculty of the Paris Conservatory (1896–1920; director from 1905), where his students included composers Maurice Ravel and Georges Enesco. Best known for his melodies and piano accompaniments, Fauré composed chamber music, religious choruses, piano pieces, and many songs. His best-known work was *Requiem* (1888). His compositions made subtle changes to the traditional tonal system. ■ See studies by Norman Suckling (1946) and Robert Orledge (1979); Marguerite Long, *At the Piano with Fauré* (Eng. trans. 1981); and biography by Jean Michel Nectoux (Eng. trans. 1991).

FAUST, FREDERICK SCHILLER (**Max Brand; 1892–1944**), U.S. author. Faust was orphaned at age 13 and later attended the University of California. Able to write at an amazing pace, he began selling action stories to pulp magazines in 1917 under the pseudonym Max Brand. He wrote about 100 novels under that name, but used at least 18 other names as well. Known as "the king of the pulp writers," Faust is thought to have published 30 million words or the equivalent of a book every two weeks. His westerns were the most popular; among them *Destry Rides Again* (1930) is best known and was filmed three times. Faust also wrote for Hollywood, in particular the *Dr. Kildare* movie serials and features. In 1926 he purchased a villa in Florence, Italy, and lived there until 1938. A war correspondent during World War II, he was killed in action in Santa Maria Infante, Italy. ■ See Robert Easton, *Max Brand* (1970).

FAWZI, MAHMOUD (1900–1981), Egyptian political leader. A career diplomat with a Ph.D. from the University of Rome (1923) and a command of eight languages, Fawzi served as Gamal Abdel Nasser's foreign minister (1952–64), deputy prime minister (1964–67), and vice president (1967–

68). After Nassar's death in 1970 he was President Anwar el-Sadat's prime minister (1970–72) and vice president (1972–74).

FAY, SIDNEY BRADSHAW (1876–1967), U.S. historian. The first historian to challenge the assumption of sole German responsibility for the outbreak of World War I, Fay did exhaustive archival research to establish collective European complicity in *The Origins of the World War* (2 vols., 1928). He taught at Dartmouth, Smith, Harvard, and Yale before his retirement in 1946. Also an authority on Prussia, he wrote *The Rise of Brandenburg-Prussia to 1786* (1937).

FEBVRE, LUCIEN (1878–1956), French historian. One of the most influential European historians of the century, Febvre rejected the concept of history as a chronicle of narrowly defined political events; he utilized data from the social sciences and analyzed political, religious, geographic, economic, and cultural phenomena in writing the "total" history of society. He taught at Strasbourg (from 1919) and the Collège de France, Paris (1933–50), and cofounded the influential journal *Annales* (1929). He wrote *A Geographical Introduction to History* (1922; Eng. trans. 1924) before turning to the religious mentality of the Reformation with his *Martin Luther: A Destiny* (1928; Eng. trans. 1929) and *The Problem of Unbelief in the Sixteenth Century* (1942; Eng. trans. 1982). He also wrote *Life in Renaissance France* (1962; Eng. trans. 1977) and *The Coming of the Book* (1958, with H. J. Martin; Eng. trans. 1976). ▪ See translations of his writings in Peter Burke, ed., *A New Kind of History* (1973).

FEDIN, KONSTANTIN ALEKSANDROVICH (1892–1977), Soviet writer. Fedin was discovered by the writer Maxim Gorky (1920) and joined his Petrograd literary group. His early novels experimented with time and reflected his experience as a civilian interned in Germany during World War I. Fedin described Germany and Russia during war and revolution and expressed his preoccupation with the problems of an intellectual adjusting to revolution in *Cities and Years* (1924; Eng. trans. 1962) and *Brothers* (1928). He skillfully evoked atmosphere, particularly in his late trilogy of Soviet life from 1910 to World War II: *Early Joys* (1945; Eng. trans. 1948), *No Ordinary Summer* (1948; Eng. trans. 1950), and *The Conflagration* (1962; Eng. trans. 1968). He headed the official writers' union (1959–72) and served on the editorial board of the influential journal *Novy mir* (New World). Fedin's work was seen as a link between Soviet realism and the Russian narrative tradition of the 19th century. His *Gorky Among Us* (1943–44) recalls Russian literary life in the 1920s. ▪ See study by Julius Blum (1967).

FEIFFER, JULES (1929–), U.S. cartoonist. Known for his sparse drawing style and satiric wit, Feiffer won widespread recognition for a *Village Voice* comic strip called *Feiffer*, which began publication in 1956. Later syndicated (1959), the cartoon usually consisted of one or two characters in a series of poses or attitudes whose accompanying monologues exposed their insecurities and acted as social or political commentary. The cartoons were collected in several volumes, among them *Sick, Sick, Sick* (1958), *The Unexpurgated Memoirs of Bernard Mergendeiler* (1965), and *Feiffer* (1982). Feiffer also wrote the plays *Little Murders* (1967), *The White House Murder Case* (1970), *Grownups* (1981), and *Elliot Loves* (1990), the screenplay for *Carnal Knowledge* (1971), and created *Munro* (Academy Award, 1961), an animated cartoon about a 4-year-old drafted into the army. A vocal opponent of the Vietnam War, Feiffer was also a critic of conservative domestic policies and the nuclear arms race. He won the 1986 Pulitzer Prize for editorial cartooning. He also wrote the children's books *Man in the Ceiling* (1993) and *A Barrel of Laughs, A Vale of Tears* (1995).

FEININGER, ANDREAS (1906–1999), U.S. photographer. Born in Paris, son of the expatriate American painter Lyonel Feininger, Feininger was educated in Germany. While studying at the Bauhaus school of architecture (1925), he began taking the photographs of buildings and cities for which he is best known. During the 1930s Feininger wrote German textbooks on photography and worked as an architectural photographer in Stockholm (1933–39). After going to the United States (1939), he was a staff photographer for *Life* magazine (1943–62). He produced more than 30 books, including *The Creative Photographer* (1955), *Basic Color Photography* (1972), and the photo collections *The World Through My Eyes* (1963), *Forms of Nature and Life* (1966), and *Industrial America, 1940–1960* (1981). ▪ See his illustrated autobiography (1986).

FEININGER, LYONEL (1871–1956), U.S. painter. Feininger studied music in New York and Germany before he turned to art, training (1887–93) in Hamburg, Berlin, and Paris. Remaining in Europe, he worked as a cartoonist and graphic artist. After turning to oil painting (1907), he was influenced by Richard Delaunay and the cubists (1911). His prismlike style and use of planes and light brought him into association (1913) with the Blue Rider group, which was noted for pure abstraction and romantic imagery. He taught at the Bauhaus from 1919 to 1933. Feininger's subjects ranged from seascapes and sailboats to the urban skyscrapers he saw on his return to America (1937). His son was the noted photographer Andreas Feininger (1906–1999). ▪ See studies by Hans Hess (1961) and Ernst Scheyer (1964).

FELA (Olufela Ransome-Kuti; 1938–1997), Nigerian singer, composer, and musician. Born into a prominent Yoruban family—his father was a well-known Anglican priest and educator and his mother was a leader of the nationalist movement—Fela studied classical music in London (1959–63). However, after being exposed to American jazz, he began playing trumpet and keyboards in jazz bands and formed his own high-life jazz band, the Koola Lobitos, when he returned to Nigeria (1963). During a 10-month stay in the United States (1969), he was influenced by the writings of Malcolm X, the Black Panther party, and the Black Power movement. Upon returning home (1970), he formed a new band (Africa 70; later Egypt 80) and began playing a new kind of music, "Afro beat," a blend of jazz and pop elements with intricate traditional African rhythms. His scathing, satirical lyrics, delivered in pidgin English, the lingua-franca of the West African coast, attacked authoritarianism, injustice, and corruption, and he soon became Nigeria's most prominent political dissident and Africa's most famous and controversial musician. (In the 1970s he de-Anglicized his name, dropping Ransome in favor of the Yoruba Anikulapo.) Although his compound was burned down by the military (1977) and he was arrested more than a dozen times, he continued to tour and give flamboyant stage performances at his nightclub, the Shrine, through the 1990s. He died of complications due to AIDS. ▪ See Carlos Moore, *Fela, Fela* (1982), and studies by Frank T. Fairfax (1993) and Michael Veal (2000).

FELDMAN, MORTON (1926–1987), U.S. composer. Feldman studied with Wallingford Riegger and Stefan Wolpe and worked with David Tudor and John Cage in the 1950s. Primarily concerned with new types of sound relationships, he became known for his work in indeterminacy and for a kind of graphic notation that allowed a performer to select his own pitches against a predetermined rhythm. Most of Feldman's minimalist avant-garde works were scored for conventional forces, but were distinguished both by their low sound levels and the composer's individual conception of "pure" tones. His works included the *Projection* series (1950–51), *Atlantis* (1958), *Durations* series (1960–62), *In Search of an Orchestration* (1969), *The Rothko Chapel* (1971–72), *Neither* (an opera, 1977), *Three Voices* (1982), *Piano and String Quartet* (1985), and *Coptic Light for Orchestra* (1986).

FELLER, BOB (Robert William Andrew Feller; 1918–   ), U.S. baseball player. A hard-throwing pitcher for the Cleveland Indians (1936–42; 1944–56), Feller struck out 15 batters in his first major league appearance. Called "Rapid Robert," he used his blistering fastball to strike out 18 batters in a nine-inning game (1938). He led the American League in strikeouts seven times and set a record with 348 strikeouts in 1946. Wildness sometimes hampered his game; he set another record by issuing 208 walks in the 1938 season. Overall, Feller pitched in 570 games, winning 266 and losing 162, while pitching 3 no-hitters and 12 one-hit games. He was elected to the National Baseball Hall of Fame in 1962. ▪ See his autobiography, *Now Pitching, Bob Feller* (1990; with Bill Gilbert), and biography by Gene Schoor (1962).

FELLINI, FEDERICO (1920–1993), Italian film director. Fellini was a journalist, gagman, and scriptwriter on several films including Roberto Rossellini's *Open City* (1945) before evolving his own highly personal style of filmmaking. *La Strada* (1954) grew out of the director's lifelong fascination with the circus, introducing grotesques and caricatures who recur in later films. *La Dolce Vita* (1960) was hailed as a brilliant satire on European high society, while *8½* (1963) was an autobiographical trip into the director's stream of consciousness. Even richer in fantasy was Fellini's *Amarcord* (1974), an affectionate remembrance of his childhood. His other films included *Juliet of the Spirits* (1965), *Fellini Satyricon* (1969), *Casanova* (1976), *City of Women* (1981), and *Ginger and Fred* (1986). ▪ See his *Fellini on Film* (Eng. trans. 1976); study edited by Gilbert Salachas (Eng. trans. 1969); study by Frank Burke (1996); and biography by Hollis Albert (1986).

FENG YOULAN (old style: Fung Yu-lan; 1895–1990), Chinese philosopher. Considered to be the 20th century's foremost Chinese philosopher and historian of Chinese philosophy, Feng was trained at Beijing University and at Columbia University, New York City (Ph.D. 1923), where he studied under John Dewey. He taught at Yenching (Qinghua) University in Beijing (1933–52) and during the 1930s and 1940s created an original neo-Confucianist philosophical system that combined traditional Confucian thought with Western logical analysis. He remained in China after the 1949 Communist revolution, but was frequently criticized during the 1950s and 1960s for what were considered idealist, abstract, and ahistorical concepts and he repudiated many of his previously published ideas. English translations of his works are in his *Spirit of Chinese Philosophy* (1970) and *Selected Philosophical Writings* (Beijing, 1991). In the West he was best known for *A History of Chinese Philosophy* (2 vols., 1933; Eng. trans. 1937; rev. ed. 1962). ▪ See study by Michel C. Masson, *Philosophy and Tradition* (1985).

FENG, YÜ-HSIANG. See FENG YUXIANG.

FENG YUXIANG (old style: Feng Yü-hsiang; 1882–1948), Chinese warlord. Feng was born into a very poor family and taught himself to read. After joining the army in 1896, he rose rapidly; in 1911 he organized his own army, the Guominjun (Kuominchün). In 1914 he became a Methodist and was subsequently known as the "Christian general." One of the most progressive warlords in China, Feng wore ordinary soldier's clothing, and his troops were disciplined, well fed, well dressed, and taught to be moral; a unique situation for Chinese armies of the period. In 1927 he joined nationalist leader Chiang Kaishek and helped him to eliminate leftist factions in the Guomindang (Kuomintang) movement and achieve supremacy in China. Soon after his army occupied Beijing (Peking; 1928) he declared his independence from Chiang, but his forces were defeated and he left China. He supported the anti-Japanese movement during the 1930s but criticized the nationalist government after World War II. ■ See James E. Sheridan, *Chinese Warlord* (1966).

FENWICK, CHARLES GHEQUIERE (1880–1973), U.S. political scientist. Fenwick, whose specialty was international law, studied at Johns Hopkins University (Ph.D. 1912) and taught at Bryn Mawr (1915–45). A delegate to many international conferences, he campaigned for U.S. membership in the League of Nations (1919–20) and World Court and advocated collective security as a means of preventing war. He directed the department of international law and organization of the Pan American Union (later the Organization of American States; 1948–62). His writings included a standard text on *International Law* (1924), *American Neutrality, Trial and Failure* (1940), and *The Organization of American States* (1963).

FERBER, EDNA (1887–1968), U.S. novelist and playwright. Ferber's early years as a reporter in the Midwest furnished material for many of her panoramic best-selling novels. She portrayed the American roving spirit in the Pulitzer Prize–winning *So Big* (1924), as well as in *Cimarron* (1930), *Saratoga Trunk* (1941), *Giant* (1952), and *Ice Palace* (1958). Her novel *Show Boat* (1926) was made into a popular operetta by Jerome Kern and Oscar Hammerstein II (1927). She also collaborated with George S. Kaufman on several plays, including *The Royal Family* (1927), *Dinner at Eight* (1932), and *Stage Door* (1936). ■ See her autobiographies, *A Peculiar Treasure* (1939) and *A Kind of Magic* (1963), and biography by Julie G. Gilbert (1978).

FERDINAND (1865–1927), king of Rumania. Although a Hohenzollern, Ferdinand declared war on Germany and Austria-Hungary during World War I in order to gain Hapsburg-ruled lands inhabited by Rumanians. Although his armies were defeated (1917), the victorious Allies granted (1918) to Rumania Transylvania, Bukovina, Bessarabia, and part of the Banat, thus doubling the size of the country and completing the territorial claims of "Greater Rumania." Ferdinand's reign (1914–27) was also marked by moderate land reform (1921) and an army reorganization.

FERENCZI, SÁNDOR (1873–1933), Hungarian psychoanalyst. A longtime friend and collaborator of psychoanalyst Sigmund Freud, Ferenczi founded the Hungarian Psychoanalytic Society (1913) and conducted a private practice in Budapest. He wrote an important paper (1913) on the individual's development of the sense of reality; a theory of genitality, *Thalassa* (1924; Eng. trans. 1949); and *The Development of Psychoanalysis* (with Otto Rank, 1924; Eng.

trans. 1925). Departing from Freud's therapeutic methods, Ferenczi, in later years, favored a more permissive, relaxed, indulgent atmosphere of treatment. ■ See his *Selected Papers* (3 vols., Eng. trans. 1950–55), *Contributions to Psychoanalysis* (Eng. trans. 1916), and *Further Contributions* (Eng. trans. 1926).

FERGUSON, HARRY GEORGE (1884–1960), British engineer and inventor. An early auto enthusiast, Ferguson designed and built an airplane (1909) in which he made the first recorded flight over Ireland. He became interested in farm mechanization when he was assigned, during World War I, to the "Grow More Food" campaign. The prototype of his revolutionary Ferguson tractor, with its hydraulically controlled implements, was built in 1935 and mass-produced in 1939 in partnership with the Ford Motor Co. Ferguson later won a record out-of-court patent settlement from Ford, which had repudiated the original agreement. ■ See biography by Colin Fraser (1973).

FERGUSON, MA (Miriam Amanda Wallace Ferguson; 1875–1961), U.S. governor. The wife of James Ferguson, the governor of Texas who was impeached (1917) for misuse of state funds and prohibited from running again, Ma Ferguson ran for governor in his place (1924). With the support of the poor and tenant farmers she was elected by a large majority and thus became the first woman state governor—a distinction she shared with Nellie Ross, elected governor of Wyoming in 1924. While in office she broke the political power of the Texas Ku Klux Klan and obtained an amnesty for her husband. Responding to criticism that he wielded the real power in the government, she ran for reelection (1926) with the slogan "two Fergusons for the price of one." Although she lost that election, she won a second term at the height of the Depression in 1932. ■ See the account by her daughter, Ouida F. Nalle, *The Fergusons of Texas* (1946).

FERLINGHETTI, LAWRENCE (1919–   ), U.S. poet and publisher. Ferlinghetti was a naval commanding officer during the 1944 Normandy invasion and later earned a Sorbonne doctoral degree. Returning from Paris, he founded (1953) America's first paperback bookstore. A poet, painter, book designer, and graphic artist, he edited City Lights Books, a feature of the San Francisco poetry revival of the 1950s. Ferlinghetti was arrested (1956) for publishing Allen Ginsberg's *Howl* but was cleared of obscenity charges. His own audacious poetry, collected in such popular volumes as *A Coney Island of the Mind* (1958), was criticized by some fellow "beats" for its preoccupation with politics. He also wrote *Her* (1960), a baffling free-associative novel; later he turned to filmmaking. Other books included *Endless Life: The Selected Poems* (1981), *Seven Days in Nicaragua* (1984), *Love in the Days of Rage* (1988), *These Are My Rivers: New and Selected Poems* (1993), *Pictures of the Gone World* (2nd ed. 1993), and *A Far Rockaway of the*

Heart (1997). He was named San Francisco's first poet laureate (1998). ■ See biography by Barry Sileski (1990).

FERMI, ENRICO (1901–1954), Italian-born U.S. physicist. Educated in Italy and Germany, Fermi taught at the University of Rome (1926–38). He experimented with the bombardment of atoms and produced artificial radioactivity. Other scientists realized (1938–39) that his work was the beginning of nuclear fission. Fearing for the safety of his Jewish wife and their children under the fascist regime, he emigrated with them directly to the United States from Stockholm after accepting the 1938 Nobel Prize in Physics. For the U.S. government Fermi helped design and construct a nuclear reactor on a squash court at the University of Chicago; here the world's first self-sustaining nuclear reaction was achieved (1942). This led the way for the production of the atomic bomb (1945) and nuclear energy. ■ See Laura Fermi, *Atoms in the Family* (1954) and study by Emilio Segrè.

FERNANDEL (Fernand Contandin; 1903–1971), French actor. Fernandel made his music-hall debut at age 5, toured the vaudeville circuit in France and North Africa during the 1920s, and made his first film in 1930. He gained fame in serious roles in *Le Rosier de Madame Husson* (1932) and *Angèle* (1934) but was best known for more than 100 comic portrayals and was France's most beloved comedy star. Fernandel, whose long, sad horse face was transformed by a toothy grin, played the role of Don Camillo, an eccentric priest, in several films (from 1951).

FERRARO, GERALDINE (1935–   ), U.S. political leader. Ferraro taught grade school while attending Fordham University Law School at night. After passing the bar exam (1960), she spent 14 years working part-time as a civil lawyer while raising three children. In 1974, she took a full-time prosecutor's position in Queens, New York, heading a special bureau for victims of violent crime. Ferraro won election (1978) as the first female representative from the conservative 9th Congressional District in New York and was reelected in 1980 and 1982. A liberal Democrat and Roman Catholic, she took a pro-choice position on abortion rights and supported the Equal Rights Amendment. Known as a shrewd politician, she was a team player whose diligence and party loyalty contributed to a close alliance with House Speaker Thomas P. (Tip) O'Neill, and she won appointments to key congressional and party committees. As Walter Mondale's running mate in his unsuccessful 1984 presidential bid, Geraldine Ferraro was the first woman to be nominated by a major party for the vice presidency. The financial dealings of Ferraro and her husband, real-estate developer John Zaccaro, sparked controversy during the campaign. She appeared on the TV show "Crossfire" (1996–98) and ran unsuccessfully for the Democratic nomination for U.S. senator from New York (1998). ■ See her autobiography (1985); her family memoir, *Framing a Life* (1998); and Rosemary Breslin and J. Hammer, *Gerry!* (1984).

FERREIRA DE CASTRO, JOSÉ MARIA (1898–1974), Portuguese novelist. While living in Brazil (1910–19), Ferreira de Castro worked for nearly four years on an Amazon rubber plantation and wrote of his experiences among the exploited workers in the novels *Emigrants* (1928; Eng. trans. 1962) and *The Jungle* (1930; Eng. trans. 1934). His works, the first great social novels written in Portuguese, won international acclaim. These and subsequent novels, set in Portugal, demonstrated his deep concern for the oppressed and his opposition to the capitalist system. His later works, including *The Mission* (1954; Eng. trans. 1963), dealt with agonizing struggles of conscience in the face of conflicting political and social pressures. Internationally, he was the century's best-known Portuguese novelist.

FERRER, JOSÉ (1912–1992), U.S. actor, director, and producer. Ferrer was born in Puerto Rico and came to the U.S. at age 6. After graduating (1933) from Princeton University, Ferrer made his Broadway debut in *A Slight Case of Murder* (1935). He went on to great acclaim as an actor in such productions as *Charley's Aunt* (1940), *Cyrano de Bergerac* (1946), *Twentieth Century* (1950), *Man of La Mancha* (1966), and *A Life in the Theatre* (1978). He played Iago in the long-running production of Shakespeare's *Othello* starring Paul Robeson (1943). In addition to directing a number of Broadway productions (including *Stalag 17, The Fourposter,* and *O Captain*), Ferrer worked in films, receiving an Academy Award (1950) for his lead role in *Cyrano de Bergerac*. His other films included *Joan of Arc* (1948), *Moulin Rouge* (1952), and *The Caine Mutiny* (1954).

FERRERO, GUGLIELMO (1871–1942), Italian historian. Ferrero studied law but turned to history and political commentary through his involvement with the socialist movement. His six-volume history of *The Greatness and Decline of Rome* (1902–07; Eng. trans. 1907–09), a socioeconomic analysis of imperial politics, was a popular success all over Europe. Exiled in 1930 as an antifascist critic of dictator Benito Mussolini, Ferrero accepted a professorship in Geneva and continued to write historical studies, novels, and political essays. His other translated works included *Militarism* (1902), *Ancient Rome and Modern America* (1914), *The Unity of the World* (1930), and *Peace and War* (1933).

FEUCHTWANGER, LION (1884–1958), German-born author. Born into an orthodox Jewish family in Munich, Feuchtwanger gained fame through two early historical novels, *The Ugly Duchess* (1923; Eng. trans. 1928) and *Jew Süss* (1925; Eng. trans. 1926). Ironically, the latter was made into a wildly anti-Semitic propaganda film by the Nazis in 1940. *The Waiting Room* trilogy—*Success* (1930; Eng. trans.

1930), *The Oppermanns* (1933; Eng. trans. 1934), and *Paris Gazette* (1939; Eng. trans. 1940)—described the effects of the rise of Nazism on the Jews. Exiled from Nazi Germany in 1933, Feuchtwanger moved to France and then to the United States in 1941. Interested in the forces of religion, culture, and politics more than in the personalities of his historical subjects, Feuchtwanger raised the historical novel to new heights. Among his most famous works are his Josephus trilogy—*Josephus* (1932; Eng. trans. 1932), *The Jew of Rome* (1935; Eng. trans. 1936), and *Josephus and the Emperor* (1936; Eng. trans. 1942)—and *Rachel, the Jewess* (1954; Eng. trans. 1956) and *Jephta and His Daughter* (1957; Eng. trans. 1958). ■ See biography by Lothar Kahn, *Insight and Action* (1976).

FEYDEAU, GEORGES (1862–1921), French playwright. The son of a writer, and himself an actor and director, Feydeau wrote numerous farces poking fun at pre–World War I French society. His plays tended toward low comedy and depended upon swift action, ingeniously improbable plots and situations, the clever use of props, and witty dialogue. They included *Hotel Paradiso* (1894; Eng. trans. 1957) and *A Flea in Her Ear* (1907; Eng. trans. 1968). ■ See translations of his plays in *Feydeau, First to Last* (1982) and *Four Farces* (1970) and study by Manuel A. Esteban (1983).

FEYNMAN, RICHARD PHILLIPS (1918–1988), U.S. physicist. Feynman worked at Los Alamos, New Mexico, on the atomic bomb during World War II and returned to teaching in 1945, first at Cornell (1945–50) and later at the California Institute of Technology (from 1950). He made theoretical advances in quantum electrodynamics—a field developed in the 1920s by physicists who applied quantum mechanics to classical electrodynamic theory. This procedure created problems of measurement and computation; Feynman's hypothesis eliminated impediments to the study of interaction among electrons, positrons, and radiation by deriving new values for electron mass and charge, allowing more precise computation of the electron's behavior. For his work in this field, Feynman shared the 1965 Nobel Prize in Physics with Julian S. Schwinger and Shinichiro Tomonaga, who had developed similar theories by taking independent mathematical approaches. He also hypothesized (with Murray Gell-Mann) the existence of the "quark" as the fundamental building block of all matter. As a member of the presidential commission investigating the 1986 explosion of the space shuttle *Challenger,* he publicly demonstrated the vulnerability of the rubber O-rings that were designed to prevent the escape of hot gas from the rocket booster, and he severely criticized the National Aeronautics and Space Administration (NASA) for exaggerating the reliability of the shuttle. His books included *Quantum Electrodynamics* (1961), *Statistical Mechanics* (1972), and his memoirs, *Surely You're Joking, Mr. Feynman!* (1985), and *What Do You Care What Other People Think?* (1988). His lectures in *The Meaning of It All* (1998) were published posthumously.

■ See James Gleick, *Genius* (1992), and biography by John R. Gribbon (1997).

FIBIGER, JOHANNES ANDREAS GRIB (1867–1928), Danish pathologist. A student of famed bacteriologists Robert Koch and Emil von Behring in Berlin, Fibiger was a professor at the University of Copenhagen (from 1900). He was the first scientist to induce cancer in laboratory animals and was awarded the Nobel Prize in Physiology or Medicine (1926) for his experiments. Although his theory—that tumors that appeared in his laboratory rats were caused by tissue irritation—was superseded, his work represented an important step in modern cancer research.

FIEDLER, ARTHUR (1894–1979), U.S. conductor. Trained at the Royal Academy of Music in Berlin, Fiedler progressed from violinist with the Boston Symphony in 1914 to conductor in 1930 of the Boston "Pops" Orchestra. Adopting a businesslike attitude toward music, he emphasized the lighter classics and presented contemporary music, including jazz, folk, and rock, in symphonic arrangement. During five decades as the "Potentate of Pop," Fiedler sold more than 50 million records. ■ See study by Robin Moore (1968); Harry Ellis Dickson, *Arthur Fiedler and the Boston Pops: An Irreverent Memoir* (1981); and the volume by his daughter, Johanna Fiedler (1994).

FIELD, MARSHALL, III (1893–1956), U.S. publisher and philanthropist. The grandson of the noted 19th-century merchant and philanthropist, Field inherited a $160 million fortune from his father. He abandoned his banking and business career in the mid-1930s to concentrate on social and political problems. He established the Field Foundation, Inc. (1940), which was concerned with child welfare and interracial relations. The same year he established the experimental liberal New York daily newspaper *PM,* and in 1941 he launched the *Chicago Daily Sun* (later the *Sun-Times*) to oppose Robert McCormick's reactionary *Tribune.* By 1944 his publishing empire (Field Enterprises) included Simon & Schuster, Pocket Books, the *World Book Encyclopedia,* and *Parade* magazine. ■ See his *Freeedom Is More Than a Word* (1945) and biography by Stephen D. Becker (1964).

FIELDS, DOROTHY (1905–1974), U.S. songwriter. The daughter of vaudeville comedian Lew M. Fields, Dorothy Fields teamed up with many of the nation's most famous composers, including Jerome Kern, Harold Arlen, Arthur Schwartz, Sigmund Romberg, Cole Porter, and Cy Coleman to produce more than 400 songs and 19 Broadway musicals. With composer Jimmy McHugh she wrote "I Can't Give You Anything But Love, Baby"(1928), "Diga Diga Doo" (1928), "On the Sunny Side of the Street" (1930), and "I'm in the Mood for Love" (1935). For Jerome Kern's movie *Roberta* (1934) she wrote "Lovely to Look At" and for his *Swingtime* (1936) she did "A Fine Romance" and "The Way You Look Tonight." With her brother, Herbert Fields, she wrote the libretto for *Mexican Hayride* (1944), *Annie Get Your Gun* (1946), and *Redhead* (1959). She was the first woman elected to the Songwriters Hall of Fame. ■ See Deborah Winer, *On the Sunny Side of the Street* (1997).

FIELDS, W. C. (William Claude Dukenfield; 1879–1946), U.S. comedian. Son of an immigrant peddler, Fields became a runaway at age 11, a vaudeville master juggler in his teens, and a Ziegfeld's *Follies* star at 36. His first silent films in the 1920s were not well received, but he returned to conquer Hollywood in 1932. A pudgy misanthrope with a sad, mottled face, Fields was best known for his films *My Little Chickadee* (1940), *The Bank Dick* (1940), and *Never Give a Sucker an Even Break* (1941), malevolent visions of humankind that he wrote under the pseudonyms Otis Criblecoblis and Mahatma Kane Jeeves. ■ See the autobiographical *W. C. Fields by Himself* (1973); the study by Robert Lewis Taylor (1949); and Simon Louvish, *Man on the Flying Trapeze* (1997).

FIGL, LEOPOLD (1902–1965), Austrian political leader. A leader of the Agrarian Union party who opposed German-Austrian unification, Figl was arrested by the Nazis (1938) and spent most of the World War II period in German concentration camps. In 1945 he helped organize the Austrian People's party and served as chancellor (1945–53). He then served as foreign minister (1953–59) and was primarily responsible for obtaining neutrality for Austria and an end to the postwar Allied military occupation (1955).

FIGUERES FERRER, JOSÉ (1906–1990), Costa Rican political leader. A progressive young planter who studied at the Massachusetts Institute of Technology, Figueres led a volunteer army in 1948 to defeat the enemies of a legitimately elected president of Costa Rica. As a three-time president (1948–49; 1953–58; 1970–74), he instituted important economic and social reforms. He also dissolved the country's army as a precaution against possible antidemocratic military rule. Figueres championed "just prices" for the raw materials of underdeveloped nations and negotiated an agreement with the United Fruit Co. giving Costa Rica a greater share of the company's profits. He served as president of the social democratic National Liberation party (from 1951). ■ See biography by Charles Ameringer, *Don Pepe* (1978).

FILENE, EDWARD ALBERT (1860–1937), U.S. businessman and reformer. As president (from 1891) of William Filene's Sons department store—a Boston establishment founded by his father—Filene developed many new ingenious retailing techniques, including the "automatic bargain basement" designed to sell slow-moving items at low prices. A progressive civic and social reformer, Filene advocated high wages and unemployment and medical insurance for workers and was a pioneer in the credit-union and consumer cooperative movements. He founded (1919) the Coopera-

tive League (later called the Twentieth Century Fund) and organized the Boston, U.S., and International Chamber of Commerce, although he broke with them (1936) over their conservative views. He tried to turn over the management of his store to workers but, after much litigation, was overruled (1928). ■ See G. W. Johnson, *Liberal's Progress* (1948).

FIRBANK, (ARTHUR ANNESLEY) RONALD (1886–1926), British writer. An exotic aesthete, Firbank inherited the wealth to indulge his eccentricities and to write the short, highly stylized works of fiction for which he was celebrated. He published his first short novel at age 19, before enrolling at Cambridge, converting to Catholicism, and flirting with the idea of a Vatican post. *Prancing Nigger* (1924), perhaps Firbank's best-known novel, was inspired by a visit to Haiti. Other works included *Valmouth* (1919), and *Flowers Beneath the Foot* (1923). His brilliant dialogue, unconventional form, and perverse humor influenced such writers as Evelyn Waugh, Ivy Compton-Burnett, Graham Greene, Samuel Beckett, and Aldous Huxley. ■ See biography by Miriam J. Benkovitz (1969), and Brigid Brophy, *Prancing Novelist* (1973).

FIRESTONE, HARVEY SAMUEL (1868–1938), U.S. industrialist. A buggy salesman (1892–96), Firestone was convinced that rubber tires were soon to be standard equipment on vehicles of all kinds, and he established the Firestone Tire and Rubber Co. in Akron, Ohio (1900). The company became the principal supplier of tires to Henry Ford (1906), introduced the "dismountable rim" for quick tire replacement, and soon was one of the nation's largest corporations. Over the years it introduced low-pressure balloon tires and nonskid treads. It kept prices low by resisting unionization and securing its own rubber supply by leasing a one-million-acre plantation in Liberia (1926). Firestone actively promoted freight hauling by truck and vast highway construction projects. ■ See biography by Alfred Lief (1951).

FIRTH, JOHN RUPERT (1890–1960), British linguist. A teacher in India (1913–28) and lecturer at Oxford (1930–38), Firth was a professor of general linguistics at London University (1944–56), where he created what became known as the "London school of linguistics." His work, influenced by anthropologist Bronislaw Malinowski and the members of the Prague school of linguistics, emphasized the importance of the social (or situational) context in analyzing the sound as well as the grammatical structure of language. He wrote *Tongues of Men and Speech* (1964). ■ See his *Papers in Linguistics, 1934–51* (1957) and *Selected Papers, 1952–59* (1968) and D. Terence Langendoen, *The London School of Linguistics* (1968).

FIRTH, SIR RAYMOND WILLIAM (1901–), New Zealand-born British social anthropologist. A student of cultural anthropologist Bronislaw Malinowski at the London School of Economics (Ph.D. 1927), Firth gathered (1928–29) data on the people of the Solomon Islands, particularly on the Tikopia, which informed such works as *We the Tikopia* (1936) and *Social Change in Tikopia* (1959). He applied a functionalist approach to his analysis of the social organization and economic systems of Pacific and West African societies and, as a professor at the University of London (1944–68), helped to shape modern social anthropology. His other books included *Elements of Social Organization* (1951), *Economics of the New Zealand Maori* (1959), *Symbols: Public and Private* (1973), and *Religion: A Humanist Interpretation* (1996).

FISCHER, ABRAM LOUIS (1908–1975), South African lawyer and political leader. Born into a prominent Afrikaner family, Abram Fischer received a law degree in South Africa before studying at Oxford as a Rhodes Scholar in the early 1930s. An advocate of political rights for nonwhites, he joined the Communist party while in England and became head of the party in South Africa when it was banned in 1950. He was defense counsel for black nationalist leaders Nelson Mandela and Walter Sisulu, who were imprisoned for life after their sabotage trial in 1964. Fischer was arrested shortly thereafter and charged with conspiracy to commit sabotage and overthrow the government and with furthering the aims of the Communist party. He was convicted and sentenced to life imprisonment (1966).

FISCHER, BOBBY (Robert James Fischer; 1943–   ), U.S. chess player. Fischer learned to play chess at age 6 and at 13 became the youngest national junior champion in history and at 15, the youngest international grand master. An innovative strategist known for his brilliant end game, he left high school to devote himself to chess (1959) and was a seven-time winner of the U.S. championship. By 1972, when he defeated Boris Spassky of the Soviet Union to become the first U.S. player to win the world championship, he was the most widely known player in the world and considered by many to be the greatest player in history. Extremely temperamental, however, and frequently involved in disputes with chess officials, he periodically retreated from tournament play. He forfeited his world title in 1975 after a dispute with the International Chess Federation and lived thereafter in virtual seclusion. In a rare public appearance he defeated Boris Spassky in a 1992 exhibition match in Yugoslavia. ■ See Frank Brady, *Profile of a Prodigy* (rev. ed. 1973) and study by Max Euwe (1979).

FISCHER, EDMOND H. (1920–   ), U.S. biochemist. Born in Shanghai to Swiss parents, Fischer studied chemistry at the University of Geneva (Ph.D. 1947). He came to the United States in 1953 and taught biochemistry at the University of Washington in Seattle (1953–90), where he collaborated for many years with Edwin G. Krebs. During the 1950s, while studying glycogen metabolism in muscles, the two researchers discovered the process by which enzymes regulate the activity of cell proteins. They isolated and purified a protein kinase and a phosphatase, enzymes responsible for the regulation of muscle contraction and relaxation. Subsequent research demonstrated that other such enzymes govern almost all life processes and indicated that an imbalance of the enzymes can cause disease. For their research Fischer and Krebs shared the 1992 Nobel Prize in Physiology or Medicine.

FISCHER, ERNST (1899–1972), Austrian philosopher, journalist, and writer. Fischer joined the Communist party in 1934 and became a leading defender of the Stalinist position on cultural matters. After spending the World War II years in Moscow as a journalist and radio commentator, he returned to Austria and was elected to the national assembly and served as minister of culture and education. He eventually repudiated his Stalinist convictions in favor of a Marxist-humanist world view and frequently criticized the Soviet Union. *The Necessity of Art* (1959; Eng. trans. 1963) was regarded as a major work on Marxist aesthetics, as was *Art Against Ideology* (1966; Eng. trans. 1969). He was ousted from the party (1969) for demanding the immediate withdrawal of Soviet troops from Czechoslovakia. ■ See his autobiography, *An Opposing Man* (Eng. trans. 1974).

FISCHER, ERNST OTTO (1918–   ), German chemist. The son of a physics professor, Fischer received his doctorate (1952) from Munich's Technical University and taught there from 1954. For his work in explaining how metals and organic substances can merge in previously unknown ways to form sandwichlike organometallilc molecules, Fischer shared the 1973 Nobel Prize in Chemistry with Geoffrey Wilkinson. Their theoretical work held out promise for the development of gasoline additives that would be less toxic than lead and thereby diminish air pollution.

FISCHER, FRITZ (1908–1999), German historian. Fischer was born in imperial Germany, graduated from the University of Berlin during the Nazi era, and was taken prisoner during World War II. A history professor in Hamburg (1948–73), he aroused bitter feelings with the publication in 1961 of *Germany's Aims in the First World War* (Eng. trans. 1967), which blamed the conflict on his country's imperialistic ambitions. He also wrote *World Power or Decline* (1965; Eng. trans. 1974), *War of Illusions: German Policies, 1911–1914* (1969; Eng. trans. 1975), and *From Kaiserreich to Third Reich* (1979; Eng. trans. 1986).

FISCHER, HANS (1881–1945), German biochemist. Fischer studied at the universities of Marburg (Ph.D. 1904) and Munich (M.D. 1908). His research clarified the nature of complex animal and plant pigments. He climaxed a decade of work by synthesizing hemin (1929), the pigment that combines with a protein to form hemoglobin, the oxygen vehicle in blood, and earning the 1930 Nobel Prize in Chemistry. In the 1930s he investigated chlorophyll, analyzing and synthesizing this green-plant pigment, and he published the synthesis of bilirubin in 1944. Fischer committed suicide a month before his country's defeat in World War II, after an aerial bombardment of Munich obliterated his laboratory.

FISCHER, LOUIS (1896–1970), U.S. journalist and historian. A journalistic soldier of fortune from Philadelphia, Fischer served 15 months in Palestine with the British-sponsored Jewish Legion after World War I and fought in the Spanish Civil War (1936–39) as the first American member of the international brigade. In between he served as European correspondent for the *New York World* and *Evening Post* and *The Nation*. Fischer spent much of the period between World War I and World War II in the Soviet Union and wrote a sympathetic study of the *Soviets in World Affairs* (2 vols., 1930). He also published biographical works on Soviet leaders Joseph Stalin (1952) and V. I. Lenin (1964) and the Indian leader M. K. Gandhi (1950) as well as *Russia's Road from Peace to War: Soviet Foreign Relations, 1917–41* (1969). ■ See his autobiography, *Men and Politics* (1941).

FISCHER-DIESKAU, DIETRICH (1925–), German opera and lieder singer. One of the leading baritones of his generation, Fischer-Dieskau sang roles in the German and Italian repertory at the leading opera houses and music festivals throughout the world. Acclaimed for his resonant and flexible voice, flawless technique, and keen intelligence, he was primarily known as an interpreter of German lieder, especially the songs of Schubert and Schumann. His repertory of more than 1,000 songs was larger than that of any other modern singer, and he recorded more vocal compositions than any other artist. He compiled the *Fischer-Dieskau Book of Lieder* (1976) and wrote *Schubert's Songs: A Biographical Study* (1971; Eng. trans. 1977) and *Wagner and Nietzsche* (1974; Eng. trans. 1976). ■ See study by Kenneth S. Whitton (1981) and biography by Hans Neunzig (1995; Eng. trans. 1998).

FISHER, ANDREW (1862–1928), Australian labor and political leader. Fisher was born in Scotland and after he emigrated to Australia (1885) he worked as a coalminer and emerged as a labor leader. A socialist, he served as a Labour member of the Queensland legislature (1893–96; 1899), was elected to the first federal Parliament (1901), and was prime minister three times (1908–09; 1910–13; 1914–15). His administration enacted more than 100 measures, including a federal land tax, the creation of a commonwealth bank, and the initiation of a transcontinental railroad. Social services were expanded and included the granting of maternity allowances. Fisher was a strong advocate of Australian participation in World War I and of conscription. From 1916 to 1921 he was Australian high commissioner in London.

FISHER, BUD (Harry Conway Fisher; 1885–1954), U.S. cartoonist. Fisher created (1907) the comic strip *A. Mutt*, named for its only character, a chronic horseplayer, while working for the *San Francisco Chronicle* as a sports cartoonist. The first comic strip to be featured six days a week, it sold so many papers that the rival Hearst daily wooed Fisher away. Soon other characters, including Jeff, appeared and the famous *Mutt 'n' Jeff* strip was born. During the 1920s, when Fisher took over the distribution and syndication, he was America's highest-paid and most famous cartoonist, having proven that readers would buy a newspaper just for an outstanding comic strip.

FISHER, FREDERIC JOHN (1878–1941), U.S. industrialist. Fred Fisher learned the carriage-making trade from his father and worked for a Detroit carriage manufacturer before organizing the Fisher Body Co. (1908). The first company to design bodies specifically for automobiles, Fisher was responsible for numerous improvements in auto design and construction, and with the help of large orders from General Motors, became the largest firm of its kind in America. The trademark, "Body by Fisher" was familiar to millions of drivers. General Motors purchased the company for $208 million (1923), retaining Fisher and five of his brothers in executive positions. Fisher served as vice president and general manager of GM (1924–34).

FISHER, HAMMOND EDWARD (1901?–1955), U.S. cartoonist. Ham Fisher was a journalist and advertising salesman who created *Joe Palooka* a decade before the comic strip was finally accepted by the McNaught Syndicate (1930). Called "the most sentimental strip in America," it related the adventures of a naive boxer who personified traditional American ideals and virtues. In the 1930s Fisher hired such cartoonists as Al Capp and Moe Leff to draw the strip but he continued to create the story and dialogue. Over the years the strip appeared in more than 1,000 newspapers and was followed by tens of millions of readers. After a long public feud with Capp, Fisher charged him with public obscenity for including pornographic material in his *Lil Abner* comic strip. Capp claimed that Fisher had altered Capp's original drawings. Fisher was subsequently suspended from the National Cartoonists Society (1955) and committed suicide several months later.

FISHER, HERBERT ALBERT LAURENS (1865–1940), British historian and educational reformer. On the faculty of New College, Oxford (1888–1912; 1925–40), H.A.L. Fisher, a member of the Liberal party, served as minister of education (1916–22) and sponsored the act (1918) that set up a national public education system and provided for compulsory education to age 14. An advocate of historical liberalism, he wrote many works, including *The Republican Tradition in Europe* (1911), *The Commonweal* (1924), and *The History of Europe* (3 vols., 1935). ■ See biography by David Ogg (1947).

FISHER, IRVING (1867–1947), U.S. political economist. A student of mathematics at Yale University (Ph.D. 1891),

Fisher applied mathematical methods to solve fundamental economic problems. His main contribution was his investigation of the relationship between the supply of money and prices. To ensure stability he advocated the adoption of a "compensated" or "commodity dollar" of constant purchasing power; its worth would be fixed by its given value as determined by an index number of commodity prices of a given amount of goods. He taught economics at Yale (1895–1935), was active in many reform organizations, and wrote several books, including *The Purchasing Power of Money* (1911), *The Making of Index Numbers* (1922), and *The Theory of Interest* (1930). ■ See biography by Robert L. Allen (1993).

FISHER, JOHN ARBUTHNOT FISHER, 1st BARON (1841–1920), British admiral. As a midshipman Fisher served in the Crimean War and in China and later played a major role in the modernization of the navy during the 1890s. He worked for British naval supremacy as first sea lord (1904–10), introducing efficiency, organization, and the big-gun "dreadnought" battleships. Recalled to the Admiralty at the start of World War I (1914), he resigned over his opposition to the 1915 Dardanelles expedition, moving to the Board of Invention (1915–18). ■ See his *Memories and Records* (2 vols., 1919–20); his correspondence, *Fear God and Dread Nought* (3 vols., 1952–59); and Richard Hough, *Admiral of the Fleet* (1970).

FISHER, SIR RONALD AYLMER (1890–1962), British statistician and geneticist. Fisher, who studied math and physics at Cambridge (1909–15), gravitated to statistics and biology when he was appointed head of the statistics department at the Rothhamstead Experimental Station (1919). There he revolutionized the field of statistics by introducing the concept of randomization and the technique of analysis of variance. His pioneering work is described in his books *Statistical Methods for Research Workers* (1925) and *Design of Experiments* (1934). Applying his new methods to the field of genetics, he arrived at neo-Darwinian reconciliation of Darwin's evolutionary theories and Mendel's genetic theories, which he described in *The Genetical Theory of Natural Selection* (1930). Fisher taught eugenics at the University of London (1933–43) and genetics at Cambridge (1943–57). ■ See biography by Joan Fisher Box (1978).

FISKE, MINNIE MADDERN (Marie Augusta Davey; 1865–1932), U.S. actress. A professional performer from the age of 3, Fiske was one of the most popular and talented actresses of her time. She was a pioneer in theatrical realism and was best known for her portrayals of Ibsen and Shakespeare heroines. With her husband, playwright and manager Harrison Grey Fiske, she ran New York's Manhattan Theater (1901–07) and starred there in such productions as *Hedda Gabler, Rosmersholm,* and *Becky Sharp.* She encouraged young actors and playwrights and toured extensively until shortly before her death. ■ See Archie Binns, *Mrs. Fiske and the American Theater* (1955).

FITCH, VAL LOGSDON (1923–), U.S. physicist. After working on the Manhattan Project (1945), which created the first atomic bomb, Fitch received a Ph.D. in physics from Columbia University (1954). While a member of the faculty of Princeton University (from 1954), Fitch conducted experiments with James W. Cronin (1964) that demonstrated, contrary to the accepted laws of physics, that asymmetry governs the behavior of subatomic particles during the decay of neutral K mesons. Their findings were later incorporated into cosmological theory to explain that similar asymmetries could have taken place at the birth of the universe and thus have permitted matter to survive. Previously it was thought that matter and antimatter, formed in a symmetrical "big bang" at the birth of the universe, would have annihilated each other almost immediately. For their research, Fitch and Cronin shared the 1980 Nobel Prize in Physics.

FITZGERALD, ELLA (1917–1996), U.S. singer. Fitzgerald was discovered at a Harlem amateur night at age 16 and made her first record, "Love and Kisses," the following year. In the late 1930s she worked with bandleader William "Chick" Webb, winning fame and taking over his band at his death. Known for her technical virtuosity—a remarkably clear tone and flexible range—she endowed even trite music with style, as in her 1938 novelty hit, "A-tisket, A-tasket." Managed in the 1950s by jazz impresario Norman Granz, she gained new stature in the musical world with popular recordings of the smoothly sophisticated songs of Cole Porter, George Gershwin, and others. One of the most respected vocalists of her day, she performed at the Copacabana, the Hollywood Bowl, and Carnegie Hall and won 13 Grammy Awards. ■ See biography by Stuart Nicholson (1993).

FITZGERALD, F. SCOTT (Francis Scott Key Fitzgerald; 1896–1940), U.S. novelist and short-story writer. Fitzgerald left Princeton to enlist during World War I. In the first year of the decade so closely identified with his work he published the best-selling *This Side of Paradise* (1920), based on his Princeton experience. *The Great Gatsby* (1925), his masterpiece, concerned a bootlegger obsessed with making his fortune. Some of Fitzgerald's most brilliant writing went into short-story collections, notably *Tales of the Jazz Age* (1922) and *All the Sad Young Men* (1926). He captured poignant, lyrical moments of the 1920s, but these proved as elusive in his own life as in his fiction; after *Tender Is the Night* (1934), which reflected increasing strain on his psyche and marriage, Fitzgerald suffered the acute depression of a self-proclaimed has-been, titling his next book *Taps at Reveille* (1935). He was at work on the Hollywood novel *The Last Tycoon* (1941) when he died at age 44. Fitzgerald was married to the writer Zelda Sayre (1900–47), the inspiration for his heroines. She suffered mental breakdowns in 1930 and 1932 and spent the rest of her life in and out of sanitariums. She died in a fire in a mental institution. ■ See Arthur Mizener, *The Far Side of Paradise* (rev. ed. 1965); biographies by Andrew Turnbull (1962), André Le Vot (Eng. trans. 1983), and Jeffrey Meyers (1994); and Matthew J. Bruccoli, *Some Sort of Epic Grandeur* (1981).

FITZGERALD, GARRET (1926–   ), Irish political leader. FitzGerald's Roman Catholic father and Presbyterian mother both participated in the 1916 Dublin uprising against the British, and his father subsequently served as a cabinet minister in the Free State government (1922–32). After studying political economy at University College, Dublin (B.A. 1946; Ph.D. 1969) and earning a law degree (King's Inn, 1947), he worked for Irish Air Lines (Aer Lingus; 1947–58) and as an economic correspondent (1954–   ) and lecturer in political economy (1959–73). A member of the business-oriented Fine Gael party, he served in the Dáil Éireann (House of Representatives; 1969–92) and served as foreign minister (1973–77). As prime minister of coalition governments with the Labour party (June 1981–March 1982; December 1982–87), he raised taxes and cut government spending in order to alleviate the economic crisis, advocated the secularization of the Irish Republic, and worked to bring an end to the Catholic-Protestant conflict in Northern Ireland. In November 1985 he signed an accord with the British government giving the Irish Republic a formal consultative role in the governing of Northern Ireland. FitzGerald's books included *Planning in Ireland* (1968) and *Towards a New Ireland* (1972). ■ See his autobiography *All in a Life* (1991).

FITZGERALD, ROBERT DAVID (1901–   ), Australian poet. Like his father and grandfather, R. D. Fitzgerald was a surveyor (1926–65). He first achieved recognition with the long poem "Essay of Memory" (1937), a meditation on Australia's national destiny. Primarily a philosophical poet, he wrote on such themes as human transience, the role of history in shaping the present and future, and the need for personal commitment. His other well-known works include "The Hidden Bole" (1934), an elegy on the death of dancer Anna Pavlova, and the metaphysical narratives, *Between Two Tides* (1952) and *The Wind at My Door* (1959). His collections included *Southmost Twelve* (1962), *Forty Years' Poems* (1965), and *Robert D. Fitzgerald* (1987). *Of Places and Poetry* (1976) is a collection of reminiscences and literary essays. ■ See study by A. Grove Day (1974).

FITZPATRICK, JOHN (1870–1946), Irish-born U.S. labor leader. A journeyman horseshoer, Fitzpatrick became a union activist in the 1890s and served as president of the Chicago Federation of Labor (1899–1901; 1905–46). He was a progressive and honest leader who was among the

first to bring mass-production workers into the American Federation of Labor and among the first to help organize the clothing, packinghouse, and steel workers during the first quarter of the century. He was a leader of the historic 1919 steel strike and attempted, unsuccessfully, to form an independent left-wing Labor party after World War I. During the 1920s and 1930s he was a strong foe of racketeering and of communist infiltration in the labor movement.

FLAGG, JAMES MONTGOMERY (1877–1960), U.S. illustrator. Widely known for his portraits and magazine illustrations of beautiful, buxom young women. Flagg achieved his greatest fame with his World War I U.S. army recruiting poster ("I Want You") depicting a stern-faced Uncle Sam pointing directly at the viewer. More than 4 million copies were distributed at the time, and it was revived during World War II. A self-proclaimed bohemian and iconoclast, he wrote several satirical books, including *Yankee Girls Abroad* (1900) and *If—A Guide to Bad Manners* (1905). ■ See his autobiography, *Roses and Buckshot* (1946).

FLAGSTAD, KIRSTEN (1895–1962), Norwegian opera singer. A forceful soprano with an impressive vocal range. Flagstad was unknown outside of Scandinavia until she won recognition in Germany at the Bayreuth Wagner Festival (1934). She made her Metropolitan Opera (New York) debut in 1935 and reigned for the next 20 years as the world's most celebrated Wagnerian soprano. She served as director of Norway's new state opera (1958–60). ■ See her autobiography, *The Flagstad Manuscript* (narrated to L. Biancolli; 1952); the memoirs of Edwin McArthur (1965); and the biography by Howard Vogt (1987).

FLAHERTY, ROBERT (1884–1951), U.S. documentary filmmaker. As a child, Flaherty accompanied his miner father on expeditions to the Canadian northwest, where he later worked as a mapmaker and explorer. With the sponsorship of a fur company and the collaboration of his wife, he spent two years filming *Nanook of the North* (1922), a documentary about an Eskimo family that became a critical and commercial success. After *Moana* (1926), a South Seas documentary, Flaherty returned to his theme of man versus nature in *Man of Aran* (1934), filmed on the Aran Islands off the Irish coast. Next he traveled to India to shoot *Elephant Boy* (1936). Flaherty's last film was a prestige documentary sponsored by Standard Oil, *Louisiana Story* (1948). ■ See Richard Griffith, *The World of Robert Flaherty* (1953); Arthur Calder-Marshall, *The Innocent Eye* (1966); and biography by Paul Rotha (1983).

FLANAGAN, EDWARD JOSEPH (1886–1948), Irish-born U.S. educator. A Roman Catholic priest who believed that "there is no such thing as a bad boy," Father Flanagan opened a shelter for homeless boys in Omaha, Nebraska

(1917). The institution grew quickly and moved (1918) to a location 10 miles outside of town and was called Boys Town. It was incorporated as a village in 1936. The community, which was self-governing and which provided for the religious, social, and vocational education of the youths, was a great success. It gained international renown and established for Flanagan a reputation as an authority on the training and rehabilitation of underprivileged and delinquent youth. ■ See biography by Fulton Oursler (1949).

FLANAGAN, HALLIE (Hallie Ferguson; 1890–1969), U.S. educator and theatrical producer. A major force in the theatrical world for decades, Flanagan directed the Federal Theater Project (1935–39), which employed more than 15,000 theater workers and staged more than 1,000 productions in more than 40 cities during the Depression of the 1930s. She was a professor of drama and leader in the experimental stage at Vassar College (1925–42) and Smith College (1942–55). She also wrote, produced, and directed experimental plays for New York City's Off-Broadway theater. ■ See her *Shifting Scenes of the Modern European Theater* (1929) and *Arena* (1940), a history of the Federal Theater, and the biography by Joanne Bentley (1988).

FLATT, LESTER (1914–1979), and EARL SCRUGGS (1924–), U.S. country musicians. Both Flatt and Scruggs were born into large, musical families in the Appalachian foothills. Lead singer and guitarist Flatt met banjo-picking Scruggs while playing in Bill Monroe's Blue Grass Boys. They both left that group in 1948 and within a month teamed up to seek radio work. By the early 1950s, their act was drawing immense audiences. They formed their own band, the Foggy Mountain Boys, which performed on TV and radio, in concert, and at the Grand Ole Opry. In the late 1950s their bluegrass instrumentals survived rivalry with the rock-and-roll craze. They made the transition from bluegrass to folk in the 1960s. Many fans were unhappy with the innovations in their music, but Flatt and Scruggs were second only to Johnny Cash in country-music sales when they split up in 1969. Their careers continued independently during the subsequent country-music revival.

FLEMING, SIR ALEXANDER (1881–1955), Scottish bacteriologist. Fleming studied (1901–08) at St. Mary's Hospital Medical School, later a part of the University of London, and spent his entire career there. Concerned with antibacterial research from his student days, Fleming isolated and described lysozyme (1921), an antibacterial enzyme found in tears and mucous secretions; however, it failed to inhibit bacteria that were harmful to humans. While searching for such a substance, Fleming accidentally discovered penicillin (1928), the byproduct of a *Penicillium notatum* mold that dissolved the staphylococcus bacteria culture with which he was working. The substance was nontoxic and extremely powerful. Its discovery laid the groundwork for antibiotic therapy for infectious diseases, a great contribution to medical science. Fleming shared the 1945 Nobel Prize in Physiology or Medicine with Howard W. Florey and Ernst B. Chain, the two men who isolated, purified, and successfully tested penicillin. ■ See biographies by Laurence Ludovici (1955), André Maurois (Eng. trans. 1959), and Gwyn Macfarlane (1984), and Galdys L. Hobby, *Penicillin* (1985).

FLEMING, DENNA FRANK (1893–1980), U.S. historian. The dean of revisionist American historians of the cold war, D. F. Fleming earned a Ph.D. at the University of Illinois (1928), then served on the faculty of Vanderbilt University (1928–61). In *The Cold War and Its Origins* (2 vols., 1961), he described post–World War II Soviet-U.S. relations as a "balance of terror," with the United States pursuing a deliberate policy of intimidation and the Soviets intent upon security. He extended his analysis in *The Origins and Legacies of World War I* (1968) and *America's Role in Vietnam and Asia* (1969).

FLEMING, IAN (1908–1964), British novelist. His varied career as a banker, high-ranking naval intelligence officer, and journalist gave Fleming background material for his dozen novels featuring the suave British secret agent 007, James Bond. These well-written, imaginative thrillers, set in exotic locales, sold over 18 million copies and were turned into extremely popular movies. In such books as *From Russia with Love* (1957), *Dr. No* (1958), *Goldfinger* (1959), and *The Man with the Golden Gun* (1965), Bond emerged as a prototypical playboy-hero. The novels' popularity was increased by their sometimes snobbish and arcane details of gambling, gourmet food, lethal gadgets, and sex. ■ See biography by Andrew Lycett (1995); study by Richard Gant (1966); and Donald McCormick, *17F* (1993).

FLEMING, SIR JOHN AMBROSE (1849–1945), British electrical engineer and inventor. A professor of engineering at the University of London (1885–1926), Fleming invented (1904) the thermionic or "Fleming" valve, the precursor of the modern diode tube. He devised this wireless signal detector by making direct use of the Edison effect, a rule of unidirectional flow of electrical current between a heated filament and a cold electrode. Fleming made pioneering contributions to electrical lighting and heating and helped introduce the telephone and wireless into Britain. He was also a prolific writer. ■ See his *Fifty Years of Electricity* (1921) and *Memories of a Scientific Life* (1934).

FLESCH, CARL (1873–1944), Hungarian-born violinist. Flesch studied music in Vienna and Paris before his 1895 debut in Vienna. In addition to his career as an international soloist and chamber musician, renowned for his purity of tone, he was also an important teacher of the violin. Flesch taught in Bucharest (1897–1902), Amsterdam (1903–08), Philadelphia (1924–28), and Berlin (1928–34). In 1934 he settled in Britain, where violinists from many countries traveled to attend his master classes. His last teaching post was at the newly founded Lucerne Conservatory in Switzerland (1943–44). Flesch also wrote technical and educational studies on violin playing and new editions of violin music as well as his *Memoirs* (Eng. trans. 1957).

FLETCHER, HARVEY (1884–1981), U.S. physicist. Fletcher was associated with the Bell Telephone Laboratories from 1916 to 1949 (director of physical research from 1933), and he headed the research team that first developed and demonstrated (New York, 1934) stereophonic sound. He later established the department of acoustical engineering at Columbia University (1949) and held several research and administrative posts at Brigham Young University in Salt Lake City, Utah (from 1952). He wrote *Speech and Hearing* (1929; rev. ed. 1953).

FLETCHER, JOSEPH FRANCIS (1905–1991), U.S. philosopher. A lifelong social activist who advocated democratic socialism, Fletcher was an ordained (1928) Episcopal priest, dean of a cathedral (in Cincinnati), union organizer, labor educator, and college professor. He taught Christian social ethics at the Episcopal Theological School at Harvard University (1944–70) and was dubbed "the red professor" by Senator Joseph R. McCarthy during the 1950s. His book, *Morals and Medicine* (1954), is considered the pioneering work in the discipline of biomedical ethics. In his controversial best-seller, *Situation Ethics* (1966), he argued moral decision making in given situations should be guided by appraisals of consequences based on loving concern (agape) rather than by adherence to general and abstract moral laws or principles. In 1967 he gave up his faith in Christianity. He subsequently served as professor of medical ethics at the University of Virginia (1970–77). ■ See Harvey Cox, ed., *The Situation Ethics Debate* (1968).

FLEXNER, ABRAHAM (1866–1959), U.S. educator. The son of a Jewish immigrant from Bohemia, Flexner was the founding director of a successful college preparatory school in Louisville, Ky. (1890–1924). He advocated progressive education and criticized American higher education. He was most famous for his 1910 report, *Medical Education in the United States and Canada,* which led to dramatic reforms in American medical schools. As an executive with the General Education Board of the Rockefeller Foundation (1913–28), he helped raise and channel more than $500 million in private funds for the improvement of medical-school and university education. In 1930 Flexner founded the Institute for Advanced Study at Princeton, New Jersey, and during his tenure as director (1930–39) established it as a major world center of higher learning. ■ See his autobiography, *I Remember* (1940; rev. ed., 1960).

FLEXNER, SIMON (1863–1946), U.S. pathologist. Flexner taught at Johns Hopkins and the University of Pennsylvania before joining the newly founded Rockefeller Institute for Medical Research in New York (1903). During his tenure as director of the laboratories (1903–35) and head of the institute (1920–35), Flexner molded it into the world's foremost center for viral-disease research. An internationally renowned authority on infectious diseases, Flexner discovered the bacillus responsible for dysentery (1900), developed a serum for cerebrospinal meningitis (1907), and led the research team that determined the cause and method of transmission of poliomyelitis. He edited the *Journal of Experimental Medicine* (1905–46) and with his son wrote a biography of his friend and teacher, *William Henry Welch and the Heroic Age of American Medicine* (1941). ■ See James T. Flexner, *An American Saga* (1983).

FLICK, FRIEDRICH (1883–1972), German industrialist. A farmer's son, Flick graduated from Cologne College (1907), worked as head clerk in a coal mine, and within eight years was a member of its board of directors before World War II and was one of Nazi leader Adolf Hitler's biggest industrial backers; he was reputed to be the wealthiest person in Germany when the Nazi regime fell. Convicted by the U.S. military tribunal at Nuremberg of war crimes, including exploiting Russian slave labor and looting Nazi-occupied countries, he served three years in prison (1947–50). East Germany confiscated three-quarters of his holdings; U.S. and British authorities compelled him to break up his remaining holdings in West Germany. Nevertheless, he built a huge new coal and steel empire, expanding into the automobile industry with a 40 percent interest in Daimler-Benz. At the time of his death, he was thought to be West Germany's richest individual.

FLOREY, HOWARD WALTER, BARON FLOREY OF ADELAIDE (1898–1968), Australian pathologist. A medical student at Adelaide University, Rhodes scholar at Oxford, and graduate student at Cambridge, Florey later headed the Sir William Dunn School of Pathology at Oxford (1935–62). In 1938, he and Ernst B. Chain, whom he had invited to head the biochemistry department, began their research on penicillin, an antibacterial substance discovered 10 years earlier by Alexander Fleming. By 1941 they had isolated, purified, successfully tested, and directed the widespread production of penicillin, which became a tremendously important antibiotic drug. Florey shared the 1945 Nobel Prize in Physiology or Medicine with Chain and Fleming. ■ See Lennard Bickel, *Rise up to Life* (1973), and study by Gwyn Macfarlane (1979).

FLORY, PAUL JOHN (1910–1985), U.S. organic chemist. Flory's research in polymer chemistry began at Delaware's DuPont Experimental Station, where he worked under Wallace A. Carothers on the development of nylon and synthetic rubber. Working both in industry (Standard Oil, 1940–43; Goodyear, 1943–48) and in academia (Cornell, 1948–57; Stanford, 1961–75), Flory innovated analytic techniques used to establish the structure and properties of long-chain molecules. His research increased understanding, and ultimately production, of numerous synthetic polymers, including plastics. He wrote *Principles of Polymer Chemistry* (1953) and *Statistical Mechanics of Chain Molecules* (1969). A 1974 Nobel Prize in Chemistry recognized Flory's contributions. He was also active in the international movement for human rights.

FLYNN, ELIZABETH GURLEY (1890–1964), U.S. radical. A descendant of Irish revolutionaries, Flynn became a labor organizer for the Industrial Workers of the World (IWW) at age 16 and participated in the historic strikes at Lawrence, Massachusetts (1912), and Paterson, New Jersey (1913). Joe Hill's song "The Rebel Girl" was inspired by Flynn's early activism. A powerful orator, she also fought for freedom of speech and assembly and was a founding member of the American Civil Liberties Union (1920). Flynn joined the U.S. Communist party in 1937; arrested with 12 other communist leaders in 1951, she was convicted of advocating the government's overthrow (1953) and served two years in prison (1955–57). She chaired the Communist party's national committee (1961–64). Flynn died while visiting the Soviet Union. ■ See her autobiography, *I Speak My Own Piece* (1955; rev. ed. 1973), and Helen C. Camp, *Iron in Her Soul* (1995).

FLYNN, ERROL (1909–1959), U.S. film actor. Born in Australia, Flynn wandered the Orient as guide and adventurer before turning to acting. His 1935 film debut as *Captain Blood,* followed by *The Charge of the Light Brigade* (1936) and *The Adventures of Robin Hood* (1938), brought him worldwide popularity as a swashbuckling romantic hero. In addition to costume dramas, he appeared in *The Sun Also Rises* (1957) and portrayed his spiritual ancestor John Barrymore in *Too Much Too Soon* (1958). Flynn described his colorful private life in his autobiography, *My Wicked, Wicked Ways* (1960). ■ See Lionel Godfrey, *The Life and Crimes of Errol Flynn* (1977); Michael Freedland, *The Two Lives of Errol Flynn* (1979); and biography by Charles Higham (1980).

FO, DARIO (1926–), Italian playwright and actor. The son of a northern Italian railway stationmaster and part-time actor, Fo was immersed in working-class culture during his youth and developed a political and cultural radicalism that he maintained throughout his life. After dropping out of the Milan Academy of Fine Arts, he performed with several improvisational theatrical groups and, by the early 1950s, began writing satirical and irreverent reviews and plays that combined Marxist politics with the iconoclastic traditions of commedia dell'arte and the jesters of the Middle Ages. His targets included political, business, and church leaders, and the Vatican called his play *Mistero Buffo* (*The Comic Mystery,* 1969) the "most blasphemous show in the history of television" when it was broadcast in 1977. Among the best known of his more than 70 plays were *Accidental Death of an Anarchist* (1970), *We Can't Pay? We*

Won't Pay (1974), and *About Face* (1981). He wrote several plays with his wife, the actress Franca Rarme, including *Orgasmo Adulto Escapes from the Zoo* (1978), and formed the theater cooperatives *Nuova Scena* (1968) and *La Comune* (1970) with her. Fo was awarded the 1997 Nobel Prize in Literature. ■ See study by Tony Mitchell (1984).

FOCH, FERDINAND (1851–1929), French marshal. Born in the Pyrenees and educated by Jesuits, Foch enlisted in the Franco-Prussian War and was promoted to captain at age 26. As professor of strategy and tactics and later director of the French War College (1908–11), he developed a theory of massive attack that was published in two volumes. Foch was appointed chief of staff in 1917, during World War I, and the following year commander in chief of the Allied armies. After turning back the German offensive he counterattacked to force the Germans to the armistice of November 1918. ■ See his *Principles of War* (1903; Eng. trans. 1918), *Memoirs* (1931; Eng. trans. 1931), and studies by B. H. Liddell Hart (1932), Jere C. King (1960), and Sir James Marshall Cornwall (1972).

FOGEL, ROBERT W. (1926–), U.S. economic historian. Fogel studied at Johns Hopkins University (Ph.D. 1963) and taught economics at several schools, including Harvard (1975–78) and the University of Chicago (from 1981). He was a founder of "cliometrics," a school of historical analysis named after Clio, the muse of history in Greek mythology, which utilized quantitative methods and rigorous statistical analysis in studying history. Fogel wrote several controversial studies, including *The Union Pacific Railroad* (1960) and *Railroads and American Economic Growth* (1964), which argued that railroads contributed very little to the growth of the U.S. economy. In *Time on the Cross: The Economics of American Negro Slavery* (with Stanley Engerman, 1974) he argued that slavery was an economically efficient system and that it collapsed for political, not economic reasons. The furor that the book caused was so bitter that Fogel published a four-volume defense of his scholarship, *Without Consent or Contract: The Rise and Fall of American Slavery* (1989–92). His later works included a study of the cycles of reform in U.S. history, *The Fourth Great Awakening & the Future of Egalitarianism* (2000). He shared the 1993 Nobel Prize in Economics with Douglass C. North for his work in economic history.

FOKINE, MICHEL (Mikhail Mikhaylovich Fokine; 1880–1942), Russian-born choreographer and ballet dancer. Trained (1889–98) at St. Petersburg's Imperial Ballet School, Fokine introduced innovations into ballet choreography; he revitalized an art that had become static by employing all the possibilities of stagecraft. He worked with such celebrated dancers as Vaslav Nijinsky and choreographed *The Dying Swan* (1905) for Anna Pavlova. With Sergei Diaghilev, he left for Paris, creating (1909–14) new works for the Ballet Russe. Fokine emigrated (1919) to the United

States, where he formed several ballet troupes and a school. Among his approximately 70 ballets were *Les Sylphides* (1909), *The Firebird* (1910), and *Petrouchka* (1911), and the later works *Bluebeard* (1941) and *The Russian Soldier* (1942). ■ See his *Memoirs of a Ballet Master* (1961) and studies by Dawn L. Horowitz (1985) and Cyril W. Beaumont (1996).

FOKKER, ANTHONY HERMAN GERARD (1890–1939), Dutch aircraft designer and manufacturer. Born in Java, Fokker taught himself to fly at age 20 in a self-designed plane; two years later he opened his first aircraft plant near Berlin, Germany (1912). During World War I his factories manufactured thousands of pursuit planes for the German air force. Fokker also developed a mechanism that permitted machine guns to fire through propeller blades without damaging the blades. After the war he founded Fokker Aircraft Works in Holland, which became one of Europe's leading aeronautical firms. Fokker emigrated (1922) to the United States, where he designed the plane that made the first nonstop flight across the country (1923), as well as the plane flown by explorers Richard Byrd and Floyd Bennett over the North Pole (1926). Fokker's designs greatly expanded commercial air travel. ■ See his autobiography, *The Flying Dutchman* (1931, with Bruce Gold, Eng. trans. 1931), and studies by Henri Hegener (1961) and A. R. Weyl (1968).

FOLKS, HOMER (1867–1963), U.S. social reformer. The executive secretary of the New York State Charities Aid Association (1893–1902; 1904–47), Folks was one of America's foremost advocates of public health and child welfare for more than 50 years. A pioneer in linking dependency, delinquency, and the breakdown of the family with poverty and disease, he organized a children's home, founded the nation's first municipal tuberculosis hospital, sponsored innovative public-health legislation, and helped establish the New York Juvenile Court system and the nation's first state probation commission. He was instrumental in the founding of the U.S. Children's Bureau and was one of the founders and chairman (1935–44) of the National Child Labor Committee. His work in New York inspired many of Pres. Franklin D. Roosevelt's New Deal reforms. ■ See the collection of his papers, *Public Health and Welfare* (1958), edited by Savel Zimland, and biography by Walter I. Trattner (1968).

FONDA, HENRY (1905–1982), U.S. actor. Fonda made his stage debut in Omaha in 1925, and his Hollywood film debut ten years later in *The Farmer Takes a Wife*. Tall, blue-eyed, and boyish—once described as a "prairie Galahad"—he starred in *Young Mr. Lincoln* (1939), *The Grapes of Wrath* (1940), and *The Ox-Bow Incident* (1943), three American film classics. Frequently portraying idealistic heroes, he was a great success as *Mr. Roberts* both on Broadway and in the 1955 film, and in the films *12 Angry Men* (1957) and *The Best Man* (1964). He won a 1982 Academy Award for his performance opposite Katharine Hepburn in *On Golden Pond*. His other Broadway stage successes included *The Caine Mutiny Court-Martial* (1953); *Clarence Darrow* (1974), a one-man show; and *First Monday in October* (1978). He was the father of film stars Jane and Peter Fonda. ■ He collaborated with Howard Teichmann on *Fonda: My Life* (1981). See also biography by Allen Roberts (1984).

FONDA, JANE (1937–   ), U.S. actress. After two years at Vassar, Fonda enrolled at the Actors Studio in New York City and decided to follow her father Henry's footsteps into an acting career. In 1960 the kittenish blonde made her Broadway debut in *There Was a Little Girl* and appeared in her first film, *Tall Story*. While working in France, she was cast as a sexpot in *Barbarella* (1968). Shortly thereafter she returned to the United States, participated in the anti-Vietnam War movement, and toured U.S. military bases with an antiwar show. She was married to political activist Tom Hayden (1973–89) and was involved in the antinuclear movement. She won Academy Awards for her roles as the self-destructive but gutsy prostitute in *Klute* (1971) and as the wife of a soldier fighting in Vietnam in *Coming Home* (1978). Her other films included *Julia* (1977), *The China Syndrome* (1979), *Agnes of God* (1985), and *The Old Gringo* (1989). In the 1980s she wrote popular fitness and health books and made best-selling videos in which she demonstrated her exercise programs. She married media magnate Ted Turner in 1991. ■ See biographies by Fred L. Guiles (1982) and Christopher P. Anderson (1990) and study by Sean French (1997).

FONTANNE, LYNN. *See* LUNT, ALFRED.

FONTEYN, DAME MARGOT (Margaret Hookham; 1919–1991), British ballet dancer. A woman of legendary stamina, Fonteyn began dancing at age 5 and continued for decades. She made her debut (1934) as a snowflake in *The Nutcracker* in London's Vic-Wells (later the Royal) Ballet. A supple and disciplined dancer, she quickly advanced to prima ballerina, creating many important new roles. Fonteyn appeared regularly with the Royal Ballet for almost 30 years; notable performances included those in *The Sleeping Beauty, Swan Lake, Ondine,* and *Giselle*. When she danced with Rudolf Nureyev in the 1960s, the partners caused a sensation. After 1970 she continued to make guest appearances. ■ See her autobiography (1976) and biography by Keith Money (1974).

FOOT, MICHAEL MACKINTOSH (1913–   ), British political leader. A son of Isaac Foot, the noted bibliophile and Liberal member of Parliament, Michael Foot was active in student politics at Oxford and was president of the Oxford Union (1933). Influenced by the human suffering caused by the Depression, he joined the Labour party (1935) and became a friend and protégé of its left-wing leader, Aneurin Bevan. After World War II he wrote several widely read political pamphlets and edited the radical political weekly *Tribune* (1948–52; 1955–60). A brilliant and witty orator, he served in Parliament (1945–55; 1960–92) and was secretary of state for employment (1974–76) and leader of the House of Commons (1976–79). He was spokesman for his party's left wing and advocated nuclear disarmament and a "wide-ranging socialist program." In November 1980 he narrowly defeated Denis Healey for leadership of the Labour party but resigned after leading the party to a disastrous defeat in the 1983 elections. Among his many books were a biography of Bevan (2 vols., 1962–73), *The Politics of Paradise: A Vindication of Byron* (1988), and a collection of personal and literary essays, *Debts of Honour* (1980). ▪ See biography by Mervyn Jones (1994).

FORD, FORD MADOX (Ford Madox Hueffer; 1873–1939), British novelist and editor. Born into a prominent musical and artistic family, Ford maintained close contacts with the most important writers of his era. Among his early works are three novels written with Joseph Conrad, who greatly influenced his style. Ford founded and edited the literary journal *English Review* (1908–11), which published works by Henry James, H. G. Wells, John Galsworthy, and W. B. Yeats. Real fame, however, came with his novel *The Good Soldier* (1915) and the tetralogy (1924–28) that was published complete in 1950 as *Parade's End*. In these studies he subtly explored the corruption and decline of politics and society in pre–World War I Britain through a close study of the lives of a small group of people. After 1922 he lived in France, where he published James Joyce and Ernest Hemingway as the editor of the *Transatlantic Review* (1924), and in the United States, where he taught college. ▪ See his autobiographical writings in *Your Mirror to My Times* (1971); Arthur Mizener, *The Saddest Story* (1971); biographies by Frank MacShane (1965) and Alan Judd (1990); and study by Ann B. Snitow (1984).

FORD, GERALD RUDOLPH (1913–), U.S. political leader. Born in Nebraska, he was first named Leslie King, Jr., but he later took the name of his stepfather, Gerald R. Ford. He grew up in Grand Rapids, Michigan, and starred in football at the University of Michigan (B.A. 1935). He received a law degree from Yale in 1941. After navy service in World War II, Ford practiced law and was elected as a Republican to the U.S. House (1948). An effective legislator and a Republican party faithful, Ford rose to the position of minority leader (1965–73). He opposed most "big government" policies advanced by Democrats and advocated more forceful prosecution of the Vietnam War. After Spiro Agnew resigned (1973), Pres. Richard Nixon chose Ford to be vice president. When Nixon also stepped down, Ford became president of a nation stunned by the Watergate scandal. Calling for a period of healing, Ford sought to reassure the country with calm, stable leadership. His pardon of Nixon was a political setback. To constrain federal spending, Ford vetoed more

than 50 bills. He sought to improve relations with the Soviet Union and China but could do nothing to prevent the collapse of the anticommunist regime in South Vietnam. Ford edged out Ronald Reagan for the 1976 Republican presidential nomination, but he narrowly lost the November election to Democrat Jimmy Carter. ▪ See his autobiography, *A Time to Heal* (1979); Richard Reeves, *A Ford, Not a Lincoln* (1974); Robert T. Hartmann, *Palace Politics* (1980); and the political biographies by Edward L. Schapsmeier (1980) and James M. Cannon (1994).

FORD, HENRY (1863–1947), U.S. automobile manufacturer. At age 15, Ford was apprenticed to a Detroit machinist. Less an inventor than a coordinator of ideas, Ford applied the principle of internal combustion to the gasoline engine and created the Model T (1908). Produced on his pioneering assembly line, Ford was the first automobile that masses of the public could afford. His company, though highly paternalistic, was the first to pay a $5-a-day minimum wage and to establish the five-day week to its factories. When he retired in 1945, the Ford Motor Co., founded with $28,000, was valued at more than $1 billion. Ford was politically active, opposing U.S. intervention in both World Wars I and II and promoting his own anti-Semitic views. He ran unsuccessfully for the U.S. Senate (1918). ▪ See his *My Life and Work* (1922; with Samuel Crowther; repr. 1973) and *Today and Tomorrow* (1926; with Crowther). See also William C. Richards, *The Last Billionaire* (1948), and biographies by Allan Nevins and F. E. Hill (3 vols., 1954–63), Booton Herndon (1969), and Carol Gelderman (1981).

FORD, HENRY, II (1917–1987), U.S. automotive manufacturer. In 1945 the Ford Motor Co. was losing $10 million monthly under the management of old Henry Ford, the founder, when his 28-year-old grandson seized control. Henry Ford II, as president, drafted a team of "whiz kids," including Robert McNamara and several experts from rival General Motors, to rebuild the firm's fortunes. After his initial success in business, Ford gained notoriety for his jet-set lifestyle, spending extravagantly on his daughters' coming-out parties, collecting art, and yachting and skiing. He served as chief executive officer of Ford from 1960 to 1979. ▪ See biographies by Booton Herndon (1969) and Walter Hayes (1990), and Victor Lasky, *Never Complain, Never Explain* (1981).

FORD, JOHN (Sean O'Feeney; 1895–1973), U.S. film director. Youngest of 13 children of Irish-immigrant parents, Ford followed an older brother to Hollywood in 1914. He directed more than 20 short films before his first critical success, *The Iron Horse* (1924). Although *The Informer* (1935) was set in Ireland and *How Green Was My Valley* (1941) in Wales, most of his celebrated films were epic Americana: *Stagecoach* (1939), *The Grapes of Wrath* (1940), and *My Darling Clementine* (1946). He worked with the same group of technicians for many years, directing them with an imperious hand to achieve color, suspense, and original characterization in his films. After World War II Ford directed a trilogy about the U.S. cavalry. Among his later films were *The Quiet Man* (1952), *Mister Roberts* (1955), *The Last Hurrah* (1958), and *The Man Who Shot Liberty Valance* (1962). ■ See biographies by Andrew Sinclair (1979) and Ronald L. Davis (1995); Dan Ford, *Pappy* (1979); and Scott Eyman, *Print the Legend* (1999).

FORMAN, MILOS (1932–), Czech-born film director. Orphaned by the Nazis, Forman attended the Prague film school where he wrote one script and served as an assistant director. After directing at the Lanterna Magica Theater, he made his first film, *Talent Competition* (1963), out of documentary material edited into a fictional framework. He made his reputation abroad with his ironic comedies *Loves of a Blonde* (1965) and *The Fireman's Ball* (1967), which gently explored the daily lives of ordinary people. He left Czechoslovakia before the 1968 Soviet intervention and did not return. His American films included *Taking Off* (1971), *One Flew over the Cuckoo's Nest* (Academy Award, 1975), *Hair* (1979), *Ragtime* (1980), *Amadeus* (Academy Award, 1985), *Valmont* (1989), and *The People vs. Larry Flynt* (1996). ■ See his memoirs, *Turnaround* (1993; with Jan Novak).

FORRESTAL, JAMES VINCENT (1892–1949), U.S. public official. A partner (1923) and later president (1938) of the Wall Street investment firm of Dillon, Read and Co., Forrestal became friendly with Pres. Franklin D. Roosevelt and his adviser, Harry Hopkins, after testifying before Congress in favor of government regulation of the securities market. He was appointed presidential administrative assistant (1940); as undersecretary of the navy (1940–44), he was responsible for procurement and production during World War II. He became secretary of the navy (1944) and was named the nation's first secretary of defense (1947) after the unification of the armed forces. A virulent anticommunist and cold warrior, he advocated a buildup of the military establishment and a tough anti-Soviet foreign policy. Suffering from exhaustion and depression, he committed suicide two months after resigning from the cabinet. ■ See biography by Arnold A. Rogow (1963).

FORRESTER, JAY WRIGHT (1918–), U.S. electrical engineer and management expert. While doing military research at the Digital Computer Laboratory at the Massachusetts Institute of Technology (MIT), which he founded and directed (1945–52), Forrester invented (1949) the random-access magnetic core memory, the information-storage device used in nearly all digital computers. He later developed "system dynamics," utilizing computer simulations, to analyze behavior of social systems and design policy for industrial organizations. He was professor of management at MIT (1956–89). His books included *Industrial Dynamics* (1961), *Principles of Systems* (1968), and *World Dynamics* (1971).

FORSSMANN, WERNER (1904–1979), German physician. One year after he graduated from the University of Berlin (M.D. 1928), Forssmann proved that cardiac catheterization was possible by inserting a catheter tube into a vein in his own elbow and pushing it gently into his heart. He also injected contrast medium directly into his heart in order to X-ray it. Although the daring experiment proved painless and caused no damage, it was generally regarded as a stunt with no value to patients. Twelve years later, however, André Cournand and Dickinson W. Richards proved the practicality of the procedure, and it eventually was universally used to diagnose heart and pulmonary disease and to assess results of cardiac surgery. For his pioneering work in opening up a new era in heart research, Forssmann shared the 1956 Nobel Prize in Physiology or Medicine with Cournand and Richards. ■ See his autobiography, *Experiments on Myself* (Eng. trans. 1975).

FORSTER, EDWARD MORGAN (1879–1970), British novelist and essayist. E. M. Forster graduated from Cambridge (B.A. 1901; M.A. 1910) and was closely associated with the Bloomsbury group in London. His major novels, acclaimed for their style and sensibility, were *Where Angels Fear to Tread* (1905), *The Longest Journey* (1907), *A Room with a View* (1908), *Howard's End* (1910), and his most profound and ambitious work, *A Passage to India* (1924). Forster's basic themes were the hypocrisy and conventionality of the middle class and the relationship between society and civilized values and between different cultures and moral beliefs. Among his few later works were literary criticism in *Aspects of the Novel* (1927) and *Abinger Harvest* (1936), and essays permeated with his liberal beliefs. *Two Cheers for Democracy* (1951), *Maurice,* a semiautobiographical novel of a homosexual love affair, written in 1913–14, was published posthumously (1971). ■ See his *Commonplace Book* (1976, repr. 1985) and *Selected Letters* (2 vols., 1984); biographies by P. N. Furbank (1978), Nicola Beauman (1994), and Mary Lago (1995); and study by Frederick McDowell (rev. ed. 1982).

FORTAS, ABE (1910–1982), U.S. lawyer. An accomplished violinist, Fortas played his way through Southwestern College (1930) and went on to graduate first in his class from Yale Law School (1933). After nine years of government service in the Interior Department and the Securities and Exchange Commission, he helped form (1946) the corporate law firm of Arnold, Fortas and Porter. A noted civil libertarian, Fortas personally represented such precedent-making clients as Monte Durham, whose case gave rise to a new definition of criminal insanity, and Clarence Gideon, an indigent prisoner who promoted legal rights for the poor. He also represented his friend Lyndon Johnson, who as president appointed Fortas to the Supreme Court in 1965. Three years later Johnson nominated him to replace Chief Justice Earl Warren, but conservative forces in the Senate held up the nomination and Fortas withdrew his name. In a 1969 controversy over his acceptance of a fee from a foundation under investigation, Fortas became the first justice to resign in disgrace, returning to private practice. ■ See Robert Shogan, *A Question of Judgment* (1972), and biography by Laura Kalman (1990).

FOSDICK, HARRY EMERSON (1878–1969), U.S. Protestant clergyman. Fosdick graduated from Colgate University (1900) and Union Theological Seminary (1904) and was a professor of theology at Union (1915–46). While minister of the First Presbyterian Church, New York, he became widely known for his liberal position in the fundamentalist-modernist controversy of the 1920s as he sought to relate Christianity to modern scientific thought. His 1922 sermon "Shall the Fundamentalists Win?" drew sharp criticism from conservatives, especially William Jennings Bryan. In 1925, Fosdick resigned his pastorate and, with John D. Rockefeller, Jr., founded Riverside Church in New York City (1931), providing a forum for nonsectarian, interracial, and international ideals. One of the first to adapt Christian teachings to growing urban needs, he spoke on contemporary issues including support of Alcoholics Anonymous and the birth-control movement. ■ See his autobiography, *The Living of These Days* (1956), and biographies by Robert M. Miller (1985) and Halford R. Ryan (1989).

FOSS, LUKAS (Lukas Fuchs; 1922–   ), German-born U.S. composer, pianist, and conductor. A precocious child who published a piano piece at 15, Foss emigrated to the United States in 1937 and studied with Serge Koussevitzky and Paul Hindemith. His early neoclassical works included the Piano Concerto No. 2 (1951), *Song of Songs* (1957), and the *Symphony of Chorales* (1958). In the early 1960s he developed a method of simultaneous group improvisation and began to experiment with prerecorded tape, electronic effects, and aleatory or chance composition, often improvising on a borrowed theme, as in *Echoi* (1961–63) and *Cello Concerto* (1966). As conductor of the Buffalo Philharmonic Orchestra (1964–70), Brooklyn Philharmonic (1971–90), and Milwaukee Symphony Orchestra (1981–86), Foss championed the contemporary repertory. His later works included *Quartet for Saxophones* (1985).

FOSSE, ROBERT LOUIS (1927–1987), U.S. choreographer, dancer, and stage and film director. Son of a vaudeville entertainer, Bob Fosse performed as a professional dancer from age 13 and made his New York City debut in 1950. He staged innovative and jazzy dance sequences for such popular musicals as *Pajama Game* (1954) and *Damn Yankees* (1955). He directed and choreographed *Redhead* (1959), *How to Succeed in Business Without Really Trying* (1961), *Sweet Charity* (1966), *Chicago* (1975), and *Dancin'* (1978) and was one of Broadway's most prominent and honored personalities. He also choreographed and directed the films *Sweet Charity* (1966), *Cabaret* (1972), and the autobio-

graphical fantasy, *All That Jazz* (1979). ■ See Kevin B. Grubb, *Razzle Dazzle* (1989), and Martin Gottfried, *All His Jazz* (1990).

FOSTER, WILLIAM ZEBULON (1881–1961), U.S. political leader. A militant labor-union activist from his teenage years, Foster was affiliated with the Socialist party, the Industrial Workers of the World, and the American Federation of Labor before joining the Communist party (1921). He was the party's candidate for U.S. president in 1924, 1928, and 1932 and during the 1930s and 1940s criticized party chairman Earl Browder's policy of cooperation with liberals. Foster replaced Browder in 1945, toed the line established by Moscow, and was indicted (but not tried due to poor health) under the Smith Act for advocating the overthrow of the U.S. government (1948). He remained party chairman until 1956. A prolific author of pamphlets, essays, and books, he wrote two autobiographical works, *From Bryan to Stalin* (1937) and *Pages from a Worker's Life* (1939). ■ See Arthur Zipser, *Workingclass Giant* (1981) and biography by James R. Barrett (2000).

FOUCAULT, MICHEL (1926–1984), French philosopher, cultural historian, and social critic. A student of Marxist scholar Louis Althusser, Foucault taught at Clermont Ferrand and Paris before serving as a professor at the College de France (1970–84). He published important studies of social deviants and the growth of state institutions to control such individuals. *Madness and Civilization* (1961; Eng. trans. 1965) considered Western attitudes toward insanity from the 16th to the 18th centuries, while *Discipline and Punish* (1975; Eng. trans. 1977) discussed the development of prisons. Society's changing views of illness, science, and sex were traced in *The Birth of the Clinic* (1963; Eng. trans. 1973), *The Order of Things: An Archaeology of the Human Sciences* (1966; Eng. trans. 1971), and *The History of Sexuality* (3 vols. 1976–84; Eng. trans. 1978–85). *The Archaeology of Knowledge* (1969; Eng. trans. 1972) contains an analysis of his methodology and his study of the manipulation of language. A translated selection of his works is in *The Foucault Reader* (1984). ■ See his *Power-Knowledge: Selected Interviews and Other Writings* (1981); studies by Alan Sheridan (1980), Hubert L. Drefus (1982), Pamela Major-Poetzel (1983), and Mark Cousins and Athar Hussain (1984); and James Miller, *The Passion of Michel Foucault* (1993).

FOUJITA, TSUGUHARU or LÉONARD (1886–1968), Japanese-born French painter. After training at Tokyo's Imperial School of Fine Arts (1906–10) and traveling to China and Korea (1911) and London (1912), Foujita settled in Paris (1913), where he remained except for the years of World War II, which he spent in Japan. He associated with the leaders of the artistic avant-garde—especially Pablo Picasso and Henri Matisse—and his early style synthesized

Japanese tradition with Western consciousness. Particularly interested in painting female nudes, cats, and solemn little girls, Foujita employed precise line, harmony of color, and lacquerlike surfaces. In 1959, he changed his given name to Léonard to honor Leonardo da Vinci. In the same year he converted to Catholicism and concentrated on painting religious scenes and portraits of the Virgin. He also executed many landscapes and self-portraits and illustrated books.

FOWLER, HENRY WATSON (1858–1933), British lexicographer. Fowler was a retired schoolmaster who wrote literary essays and then collaborated with his brother, Francis George Fowler, on a four-volume translation of the Greek satirist Lucian (1870–1918). They then wrote *The King's English* (1906) and *The Concise Oxford Dictionary of Current English* (1911). During World War I, Fowler, who was approaching age 60, concealed his age and served as a private. After his brother's death (1918), H. W. Fowler completed the landmark *Dictionary of Modern English Usage* (1926), which influenced English usage by arbitrating points of grammar, style, punctuation, and pronunciation in favor of clarity and simplicity. He also worked on the *Shorter Oxford English Dictionary* (1933). ■ See his memoirs, *If Wishes Were Horses* (1929).

FOWLER, WILLIAM ALFRED (1911–1995), U.S. physicist. After graduating from the California Institute of Technology (Ph.D. 1936), Fowler joined its faculty and taught there until 1982. He worked on proximity fuses, rocket and torpedo ordinance, and the atomic bomb during World War II. He collaborated with E. Margaret Burbidge, Geoffrey R. Burbidge, and Fred Hoyle on a landmark paper (1957) that described the synthesis of all naturally occurring elements by means of stellar nuclear reactions. He also did important research on nucleosynthesis in places other than stars. His work is described in *Nucleosynthesis in Massive Stars and Supernovae* (1955; with Fred Hoyle) and *Nuclear Astrophysics* (1967). He shared the 1983 Nobel Prize in Physics with Subrahmanyan Chandrasekhar.

FOWLES, JOHN (1926–   ), British novelist. Fowles studied French at Oxford (B.A. 1950) and taught in France, Greece, and Britain before devoting himself exclusively to writing (1963). A brilliant storyteller, he peopled his complex philosophical novels with nonconforming existential heroes and heroines, and treated such themes as personal identity, religious and moral awareness, sexual love, the change of consciousness over time, and the role of the novelist in modern fiction. He was best known for *The Collector* (1963; film, 1963), *The Magus* (1966; rev. ed. 1978; film, 1968), *The French Lieutenant's Woman* (1969; film, 1981), *Mantissa* (1982), and *A Maggot* (1985). He also wrote *Wormholes: Essays and Occasional Writings* (1998). ■ See studies by Barry N. Olshen (1978), Peter Wolfe (1979), Robert Huffaker (1980), and James Acheson (1998).

FOX, FONTAINE TALBOT, JR. (1884–1964), U.S. cartoonist. Fox dropped out of Indiana University (1906) to pursue his career as a newspaper cartoonist. Hometown personalities from his boyhood on the outskirts of Louisville, Kentucky, became the unforgettable "Toonerville Folks" in the comic strip that appeared for over four decades (1915–55). The Terrible-Tempered Mr. Bang was based on Fox's father. Even better known than the comic strip's outlandish inhabitants was the Toonerville Trolly, along with the Skipper who engineered it along miles of rural and suburban track. The Trolley was in part inspired by Louisville's notoriously unreliable Brook Street trolley line. ■ See the collection in *Toonerville Folks* (1973).

FOX, WILLIAM (1879–1952), Hungarian-born U.S. film producer. One of the pioneers of the movie industry, Fox bought his first nickelodeon in 1904 and by 1913 was one of the major independent film exhibitors and distributors. In 1915 he founded the Fox Film Corp. (merged to form 20th Century-Fox in 1935) and began to produce films in Fort Lee, New Jersey. He helped develop the "star" system—launching the careers of Theda Bara and Janet Gaynor, among others—introduced organ accompaniment, ornate interiors, and comfortable seats to the theaters, developed *Movietone News* (1927), and eventually controlled more than 450 theaters. Although his empire was worth approximately $300 million in 1930, Fox seriously overextended himself, and the Depression witnessed the collapse of his empire and bankruptcy (1936). Involved in court proceedings for years, he was sentenced to a year's imprisonment for obstruction of justice and fraud (1941).

FOXX, REDD (John Elroy Sanford; 1922–1991), U.S. comedian and television actor. Foxx left home in his teens and played with a washboard band in Harlem. He worked the "chitlin circuit," making a name as a comedian; he delivered his gag lines on numerous record albums. Due to the limited demand for black performers, however, he was often out of work. When he played in the movie *Cotton Comes to Harlem* (1970), TV producers Norman Lear and Bud Yorkin spotted him as the ideal lead for their remake of the BBC series, "Steptoe and Son." They used Foxx's real name and packaged "Sanford & Son," a hit TV situation comedy (1972–77) that capitalized on Foxx's comic mannerisms and exquisite timing.

FOY, EDDIE (Edwin Fitzgerald; 1856–1928), U.S. entertainer. A street singer as a boy, Foy toured the mining and cattle towns of the West during the 1870s. He starred in several lavish revues in Chicago during the 1880s and 1890s, where he became known for his eccentric mannerisms, quizzical expressions, and clownlike makeup. He was a popular musical-comedy star on Broadway (1904–13), appearing in such shows as *The Earl and the Girl* (1905), *Up and Down Broadway* (1910), and *Over the River* (1911–13). With his children, "the Seven Little Foys," he entered vaudeville (1913); the act remained a top-billed favorite until his retirement (1923). He died while on a farewell vaudeville tour. ■ See his autobiography, *Clowning Through Life* (1928; with Alvin F. Harlow).

FOYT, ANTHONY JOSEPH, JR. (1935–), U.S. auto-racing driver. The only racer in history to capture seven national championships, A. J. Foyt was a four-time winner of the Indianapolis 500-mile race (1961; 1964; 1967; 1977). He was also a champion stock-car racer (1968; 1978; 1979) and won the Le Mans 24-hour race (1967; with Dan Gurney, the Daytona 500-mile race (1972), and the Daytona 24-hour race (1983; 1985). He retired (1993) with a record 67 Indy car victories. ■ See Lyle K. Engel, *The Incredible A. J. Foyt* (rev. ed. 1977).

FRACHON, BENOÎT (1893–1975), French labor and political leader. A miner from age 13, Frachon was a founding member of the French Communist party (1920) and was secretary-general of the Confédération Générale du Travail (CGT), France's largest national trade union (1936–39; 1945–67). He was one of the architects of the United Front with the socialists during the 1930s. A leader (with Jacques Duclos) of the Communist party during World War II, he played an important role in the Resistance movement. Although at one time able to command the allegiance of millions of French workers, Frachon was repudiated by militant autoworkers during the May 1968 upheavals and went into semiretirement.

FRAINA, LOUIS C. *See COREY, LEWIS.*

FRAME, JANET (1924–), New Zealand novelist. Frame wrote about the plight of the individual in a provincial, conformist society. The novels *Owls Do Cry* (1957) and *Faces in the Water* (1961) contain semiautobiographical accounts of her periods of confinement in a psychiatric hospital due to several nervous breakdowns. Her characters hover on the brink of madness and death in such works as *The Edge of the Alphabet* (1962), *Scented Gardens for the Blind* (1964), and *Yellow Flowers in the Antipodean Room* (1969). *Intensive Care* (1970), an antiutopian novel, describes a society dominated by computers in which all misfits are destroyed. Frame also wrote short stories, a volume of verse, and a children's book. Her later works included the novels *Living in the Maniototo* (1979) and *Daughter Buffalo* (1992); three volumes of autobiography, *To the is-land* (1982), *An Angel at My Table* (1984), and *The Envoy from Mirror City* (1985). ■ See study by Patrick Evans (1977) and Michael King, *Wrestling with the Angel* (2000).

FRANCIS FERDINAND (1863–1914), Austrian archduke. The heir of Emperor Francis Joseph (after 1889), Francis Ferdinand sought in vain for a solution to the nationality problem within the Hapsburg Empire and succeeded in winning the enmity of both the Pan-Serbians and the Pan-Germans. While visiting Sarajevo (Bosnia) in his role as in-

spector general of the army (June 1914), he was shot by a Serbian nationalist, Gavrilo Princip. The assassination was the immediate cause of World War I. ■ See Hertha Pauli, *The Secret of Sarajevo* (1965).

FRANCIS JOSEPH (Ger.: **Franz Josef**; 1830–1916), emperor of Austria. Francis Joseph succeeded his uncle Ferdinand as ruler of the Hapsburg Empire in 1848, governing as a benevolent despot during nearly 70 years of increasingly turbulent nationalism. After crushing the popular revolutions of 1848, he initiated several reforms and granted new rights to Jews and Protestants in the empire. He moved to create a new political structure by compromising with Hungary and creating the dual Austro-Hungarian Monarchy (1867). After losing land to Italy and Germany, he concentrated on the Balkans (after 1870), where his policies, particularly regarding Bulgaria and Serbia, antagonized Russia. After 1879 he maintained a secret defensive alliance with Germany. He exercised a restraining influence during the Balkan crises (1908–14), but after the assassination of his heir, Archduke Francis Ferdinand (1914), he was persuaded to issue the ultimatum to Serbia that resulted in the outbreak of World War I. The emperor died just before the final dissolution of his empire. ■ See biographies by Josef Redlich (1929) and Anatol Murad (1968).

FRANCK, JAMES (1882–1964), German-born U.S. physicist. Franck studied at the University of Berlin (Ph.D. 1906) and became professor of physics at the University of Göttingen (1920). With Gustav Hertz, he was awarded the Nobel Prize in Physics in 1925 for discovery of the laws governing the transfer of energy between molecules. By bombarding atoms of mercury vapor with electrons (1914), Franck and Hertz obtained results that confirmed Niels Bohr's quantum theory. Franck resigned his post in protest against Nazi leader Adolf Hitler's anti-Semitic policies, emigrated to the United States (1935), and taught at the University of Chicago (1938–49). He participated in the World War II development of the atomic bomb, but he chaired a committee of concerned scientists that wrote the "Franck Report" (June 11, 1945), which urged that the bomb not be used against Japanese cities and advocated the international control of atomic weapons. After the war Franck did research on photosynthesis.

FRANCO, FRANCISCO (1892–1975), Spanish political leader. Educated at the Toledo Infantry Academy, Franco entered the army in 1910. He served in Morocco during the 1920s and achieved the rank of general. As chief of the general staff (1935–36) he was one of the leaders of the military revolt against the Republican government (1936) that precipitated the Spanish Civil War (1936–39). Proclaimed head of state (1936) and leader of the Falange (Fascist) party (1937), he led the Nationalist forces to victory in the war and emerged as Spain's undisputed leader. Although he received military aid from Nazi Germany and fascist Italy, he remained neutral during World War II. Named head of state for life in 1947, he ruled Spain for almost 40 years as a traditional military dictator, controlling the army while keeping the domestic peace by suppressing dissident political and social movements. His successor, Prince Juan Carlos, grandson of (former) King Alfonso XIII, subsequently restored democracy to Spain. ■ See biographies by Brian Crozier (1967), Alan Lloyd (1969), Juan Pablo Fusi Aizparáa (Eng. trans. 1987), and Paul Preston (1994); and John W. D. Trythall, *El Caudillo* (1970).

FRANK, ANNE (1929–1945), German-born Dutch Jewish diarist. After fleeing the Nazi regime in Germany, Anne Frank and her family sought refuge in Amsterdam but were forced to go into hiding in a warehouse office (1942–44) after German forces occupied the Netherlands during World War II. On Aug. 4, 1944, the Gestapo discovered the family, and Anne was deported to the Bergen-Belsen concentration camp, where she died. After the war, her father, a survivor of the Auschwitz concentration camp, discovered a diary that Anne had written in their Amsterdam hiding place and had an edited version of it published in 1947. Movingly written with great insight, humor, and hope, it traced her emotional growth during her tragic confinement and came to be regarded as a monument to the human spirit. Translated into English (as *The Diary of a Young Girl*, 1953) and more than 30 other languages, it was an international best-seller and was made into a prize-winning play (1956) and film (1959). A more complete version of the diary was published in 1995. ■ See biography by Melissa Müller (Eng. trans. 1998); Lawrence Graver, *An Obsession with Anne Frank* (1995); and Ralph Melnick, *The Stolen Legacy of Anne Frank* (1997).

FRANK, GLENN (1887–1940), U.S. educator and editor. Frank, who worked as a Chautauqua lecturer during vacations from Northwestern University (B.A. 1912), edited *Century* magazine (1921–25), and became known as a liberal reformer. As the "boy president" of the University of Wisconsin (1925–37), he won a reputation for educational progressivism before his dismissal for anti–New Deal political activity. He was involved in state and national Republican politics and was killed in an auto accident while campaigning for the U.S. Senate. ■ See Lawrence H. Larsen, *The President Wore Spats* (1965).

FRANK, HANS (1900–1946), German Nazi official. An educated, cultivated young lawyer, Frank joined the Nazi party in 1927 and became commissioner of justice during the 1930s and later governor of the conquered eastern territories, which he ruled despotically. "The Poles shall be the slaves of the German Reich," he announced, proceeding to liquidate the Polish intelligentsia, conscript labor for work in Germany, and send hundreds of thousands of Jews to the Auschwitz and Treblinka extermination camps. Convicted at Nuremberg of war crimes, Frank was hanged, leaving behind a 42-volume memoir of his life and works. ■ See Niklas Frank, *In the Shadow of the Reich* (Eng. trans. 1991).

FRANK, ILYA MIKHAILOVICH (1908–1990), Soviet physicist. Frank earned a degree in physics from Moscow State University (1930). He was associated (from 1934) with Moscow's Lebedev Physical Institute, becoming (1941) director of its Atomic Nucleus Laboratory, and was a professor at Moscow State University (from 1944). Collaborating with Igor Tamm, Frank worked out the theoretical basis of the Cherenkov effect (1937)—the pale blue light emitted by a transparent medium when gamma radiation is passed through it at a speed greater than the speed of light in the medium. As a result of their research, new methods for detecting elementary particles were developed. Frank, Tamm, and Pavel Cherenkov shared the 1958 Nobel Prize in Physics.

FRANK, WALDO DAVID (1889–1967), U.S. writer. A noted radical critic of American society—*Our America* (1919), *The Rediscovery of America* (1929)—Frank was actively involved in left-wing causes from the 1930s to the 1960s. Among his best-known books were *Virgin Spain* (1926) and *South American Journey* (1943), sensitive and perceptive accounts of Hispanic culture. Known as a "literary ambassador" to Latin America, Frank was widely respected throughout the region. ■ See his *Memoirs* (1973) and study by Michael A. Ogorzaly (1994).

FRANKENTHALER, HELEN (1928–   ), U.S. painter. Frankenthaler studied with Mexican painter Rufino Tamayo and cubist Paul Feeley and was influenced by the abstract-expressionist painting of Jackson Pollock. Her technique of soaking raw canvas in diluted paint resulted in such characteristic paintings as *Mountains and Sea* (1952) and *Blue Territory* (1955), which were described as lyrical and sensuous in their use of color, shape, and space. Some of her techniques were incorporated by Morris Louis and Kenneth Noland, and her work was considered transitional between abstract expressionism and color-field painting. She had numerous one-woman shows around the world and was the first woman elected a fellow of Calhoun College, Yale University (1968). She also produced notable works in welded sculpture and designed sets and costumes for London's Royal Ballet (1985). ■ See study by Barbara Rose (1971).

FRANKFURTER, FELIX (1882–1965), U.S. jurist. Born in Vienna, Frankfurter emigrated with his family to New York City (1894), where he graduated from the City College of New York (1902). *Law Review* editor and honors graduate of Harvard Law School (1906), he returned to Harvard as a professor between periods of government service. Frankfurter attended the 1919 Paris Peace Conference as a representative of American Zionists seeking a Palestinian homeland and was one of the founders of the American Civil Liberties Union (1920). He was a leading adviser to Pres. Franklin D.

Roosevelt and helped frame Neal Deal legislation before his appointment to the Supreme Court in 1939. In spite of his liberal views he took an increasingly strict constructionist view of the Constitution and was reluctant to have the court overrule legislative acts. He retired in 1962. ■ See Joseph P. Lash, ed., *From the Diaries of Felix Frankfurter* (1975), and biographies by Livia Baker (1969) and Michael Parrish (1982).

FRANKL, VIKTOR E. (1905–1997), Austrian psychiatrist. Born into a religious middle-class Jewish family in Vienna, Frankl graduated from the University of Vienna Medical School (1930) and worked at several psychiatric clinics and hospitals during the 1930s. At that time he developed what subsequently became known as logotherapy, an approach to psychotherapy based on the insight that human behavior is driven by a search for meaning and purpose in life and that neurotic behavior is caused by an inability to find that meaning. Frankl and his family were arrested by the Nazis in 1942, and his experiences as a prisoner in four concentration camps (including Auschwitz) over the next three years, during which his entire family perished, dramatically reinforced his views of human behavior. After the war, Frankl headed the neurology department at the Vienna Policlinic Hospital, and logotherapy came to be regarded by some as the "Third Viennese School of Psychotherapy," succeeding those of Sigmund Freud and Alfred Adler. It had a great influence on the development of humanistic psychotherapy and existential psychiatry. Frankl's book *Man's Search for Meaning* (1946; Eng. trans. 1959; rev. ed. 1984), which described his experiences and his theory of logotherapy, was translated into 24 languages and had sold more than 10 million copies at the time of his death. He also wrote more than 30 other books, including *The Doctor and the Soul* (1947; Eng. trans. 1955; rev. ed. 1965), *The Will to Meaning* (1969; rev. ed. 1976), and *The Unheard Cry for Meaning* (1978). ■ See his autobiography, *Reflections* (1995; Eng. trans. 1997).

FRANKLIN, ARETHA (1942–), U.S. singer. The daughter of an African-American Baptist minister, Franklin grew up singing gospel during revival meetings in Detroit. At 18 she tried to break into the pop-music market. She made her first recording in 1954 but didn't find her level until 1967, when she recorded the hit album and single, *I Never Loved a Man (the Way I Love You),* followed by *Lady Soul* (1968). Both albums sold more than a million copies, as did a series of hits released in the late 1960s: "Respect," "Baby I Love You," and "I Say a Little Prayer." Trading her beauty-parlor hair and prom gown for a more natural "Afro" look in the 1970s, Franklin made a successful return to the concert circuit and to the top 10 with her album *Amazing Grace.* Her later recordings included *Queen of Soul* (1993) and *A Rose Is Still a Rose* (1998). She was the first woman elected to the Rock and Roll Hall of Fame. ■ See her autobiography, *Aretha* (1999; with David Ritz), and biography by Mark Bego (1989).

FRANKLIN, JOHN HOPE (1915–), U.S. historian. The son of a prominent attorney in Oklahoma, Franklin studied at Harvard (M.A. 1936; Ph.D. 1941) and taught history at several universities, including Howard (1947–56), Brooklyn College (1956–64), Chicago (1964–82), and Duke (1982–92). He did research on the legal, social, and economic status of African Americans for his books on abolition, emancipation, and reconstruction, including *From Slavery to Freedom* (1947), *The Militant South* (1956), *Reconstruction After the Civil War* (1961), *The Emancipation Proclamation* (1963), and *Racial Equality in America* (1976). He was the first African-American president of the American Historical Association (1978–79), and he headed Pres. Clinton's advisory panel on race relations (1997–98).

FRANKLIN, MILES (Stella Maraia Sara Miles Franklin; 1879–1954), Australian novelist. Franklin was born and raised on a farm in the Australian bush country. Her first novel, *My Brilliant Career* (1901; film, 1979), written when she was 16 but published several years later, combined fiction and autobiography. It realistically described the atmosphere of pioneer life and was hailed as the first truly Australian novel. A feminist and socialist, Franklin worked as a social worker and political and union organizer in the United States and Europe (1902–33) before writing her best-known novel, *All That Swagger* (1936), a saga detailing the emptiness of life in the bush. She also wrote several other novels of bush pioneering using the pen name "Brent of Bin Bin." These included *Up the Country* (1928), *Back to Bool Bool* (1931), and *Cockatoos* (1954). ■ See studies by Marjorie Barnard (1967) and Colin Roderick (1998).

FRANKLIN, ROSALIND (1920–1958), British X-ray crystallographer. After studying chemistry at Cambridge, Franklin worked on the crystallography of coal and granite in a Paris laboratory (1947–50), where she helped lay the foundation for carbon-fiber technology. Her experiments at Kings College, London (1951–53), notably her photograph of a hydrated (B form) deoxyribonucleic acid (DNA) molecule, played a major role in the elucidation of the structure of DNA, for which James Watson, Francis Crick, and Maurice Wilkins won the 1962 Nobel Prize in Physiology or Medicine. ■ See biography by Anne Sayre (1975).

FRASER, DOUGLAS ANDREW (1916–), Scottish-born U.S. labor leader. Fraser emigrated to the United States with his family at age 6 and became a United Auto Workers union organizer while working on a DeSoto assembly line in Detroit during the Depression. He participated in the struggles to gain union recognition by the auto industry and served as union president Walter Reuther's chief aide (1951–59) and UAW vice president (1970–77). A skilled negotiator who won numerous benefits for the union, Fraser was popular with the rank and file and was elected president of the 1.4-million-member UAW (1977). In the wake of the severe economic reverses suffered by the auto industry, Fraser was appointed to the board of directors of the Chrysler Corp. (1980). He was succeeded as UAW president by Owen Bieber (1983).

FRASER, (JOHN) MALCOLM (1930–   ), Australian political leader. Born in New South Wales to a wealthy family, Fraser studied at Oxford (M.A. 1952) and prospered as a sheep rancher after his return home. In 1955 he became the youngest person ever elected to Parliament. Fraser held several cabinet posts before he attained leadership of the conservative Liberal party in March 1975. In November 1975 he was appointed prime minister after the governor-general dissolved the previous administration, and the following month he won a landslide victory at the polls. In his eight years in power he pursued a pro-U.S., anti-Soviet foreign policy and increased aid to the noncommunist countries of Southeast Asia. Domestically he was unable to curb the high unemployment or inflation rates, and he was defeated in the 1983 elections. ■ See John Edwards, *Life Wasn't Meant to Be Easy* (1977).

FRASER, PETER (1884–1950), New Zealand political leader. Born in Scotland, the son of a shoemaker, Fraser emigrated to New Zealand (1911), where he worked as a longshoreman and became prominent in trade unionism and the Socialist party. A founder of the Labour party (1916) he was jailed for one year for his opposition to New Zealand's involvement in World War I (1916–17). First elected to Parliament in 1918, Fraser headed several ministries from 1935 to 1940 and sponsored innovative programs in health, education, social security, and Maori affairs. As prime minister (1940–49), Fraser moderated many of his radical socialist views. He led his country through World War II and was one of the architects of the United Nations. ■ See biography by James Thorn (1952).

FRAZER, SIR JAMES GEORGE (1854–1941), British classicist and anthropologist. Frazer devoted most of his life to library research at Cambridge University. His monumental work, *The Golden Bough: A Study in Magic and Religion*, originally appeared (1980) in two volumes but was ultimately expanded to 12 (1907–15). A study in comparative folklore and religion, it influenced thought in various disciplines, including literature and psychology. Frazer distinguished between religion (the propitiation of supernatural powers) and magic (pseudoscientific attempt to manipulate natural law). His work placed Christianity in cultural perspective and explained primitive customs to European readers. His later works included *Totemism and Exogamy* (1910) and its sequel *Totemica* (1937), and *Folklore in the Old Testament* (1919). ■ See study by Robert Angus Downie (1970); John B. Vickery, *The Literary Impact of the Golden Bough* (1973); and biography by Robert Ackerman (1987).

FRAZIER, EDWARD FRANKLIN (1894–1962), U.S. sociologist. A graduate of the University of Chicago (Ph.D.

1931), he was professor at Howard University (1934–59), where he headed the sociology department. E. Franklin Frazier specialized in systematic studies of the American black community, concentrating on the effects of racial prejudice. He wrote *The Negro Family in the United States* (1939) and *Black Bourgeoisie* (1957), concluding that the latter had achieved "status without significance." He was the first African-American scholar to head the American Sociological Association (1948). ■ See study by Anthony M. Platt (1991).

FRÉCHET, MAURICE RENÉ (1878–1973), French mathematician. A professor at the University of Strasbourg (1920–27) and the University of Paris (1927–49), Fréchet was the first to define and propose the theory of abstract spaces. He also made notable contributions to the fields of topology, mathematical statistics, differential and integral calculus, and the calculus of probability. His books included *Initiation to Combinatorial Topology* (Eng. trans. 1967; with Ky Fan).

FREED, ALAN (1922–1965), U.S. disc jockey. Freed was a radio announcer for a classical-music program and a songwriter before becoming known in the 1950s for his rock-and-roll shows. He was credited with coining the term "rock and roll," applying it to the rhythm-and-blues music that became popular after World War II. Freed announced live rock-and-roll stage shows, drawing thousands of teenagers, and his radio programs were taped and broadcast to audiences around the world. His radio career ended when he was accused of accepting bribes to publicize a recording company's releases. A composer as well as an announcer, Freed wrote "Sincerely" (1954) and appeared in several films including *Rock Around the Clock* (1956). ■ See John A. Jackson, *Big Beat Heat* (1991).

FREED, ARTHUR (Arthur Grossman; 1894–1973), U.S. film producer and lyricist. Freed began his career as a songwriter for MGM in 1929. In 1939 he was put in charge of what became known as the Freed Unit at MGM, which between 1939 and 1960 produced a new kind of musical film in which songs were submerged in an engrossing story. This series of films included *Meet Me in St. Louis* (1944), *On the Town* (1949), *An American in Paris* (Academy Award, 1951), *Singin' in the Rain* (1952), and *Gigi* (Academy Award, 1958). Freed promoted the talents of performers Judy Garland, Cyd Charisse, and Gene Kelly; directors Vincente Minelli and Stanley Donen; orchestrator André Previn; and choreographer Michael Kidd. ■ See Hugh Fordin, *MGM's Greatest Musicals* (1996).

FREEMAN, DOUGLAS SOUTHALL (1886–1953), U.S. journalist and historian. Born in Virginia, the son of a Confederate soldier, Freeman earned a Ph.D. in history from Johns Hopkins University (1908). During 34 years as editor of the *Richmond News Leader* (1915–49) he was also a historian and biographer of the Confederacy. A conservative southerner but a meticulous researcher, Freeman won a Pulitzer Prize (1935) for his biography of Robert E. Lee (4 vols., 1934) and shared another for his multivolume study of George Washington (1948–57), completed by others after his death. In his editorials during World War II he often drew learned analogies with the Civil War.

FREI MONTALVA, EDUARDO (1911–1982), Chilean political leader. Influenced by the social philosophy of the French thinker Jacques Maritain, Frei organized (1938) Argentina's National Falange, an antifascist, Catholic party opposed to both capitalism and communism. He served in several cabinets during the 1940s and was elected to the senate in 1949. The Falange merged with the Social Christian Conservatives (1957) to form the Christian Democratic party, and Frei served as the first Christian Democratic president in the Western hemisphere (1964–70). Under the watchword "revolution in liberty," he enacted land and tax reforms, improved health, education, and welfare, and brought Chile's copper industry under government control. He was succeeded by Salvador Allende, Chile's first Marxist president. After the 1973 military coup of Gen. Pinochet, Frei was a leading opposition figure and called for the restoration of democracy. His son Eduardo Frei Ruíz-Tagle (1942–   ) also served as Chile's president (1994–2000). ■ See his *Latin America, the Hopeful Option* (1967; Eng. trans. 1978) and Leonard Gross, *The Last, Best Hope* (1967).

FREIRE, PAULO (1921–1997), Brazilian educator. A radical educational theorist and expert on literacy and on the role of school in society, Freire spent years working in adult education programs with Brazilian and Chilean peasants. He taught at the University of Recife and at Harvard and worked on the 1980 literacy campaign in Nicaragua. He believed that education, practiced as dialogue, had a humanizing effect on people and led to critical consciousness (conscientization), self-dignity, and self-awareness, which were necessary elements in the struggle for the liberation of the oppressed masses. He was a member of the Socialist Workers party and was education secretary of the city of Sâo Paolo (1989–91). His translated books included *Pedagogy of the Oppressed* (1970), *Education for Critical Consciousness* (1973), *Pedagogy in Process* (1978), *The Politics of Education* (1985), *Literacy* (1987), *Pedagogy of the Heart* (1997), and *Teachers as Cultural Workers* (1998). ■ See his *Letters to Christina: Reflections on My Life and Work* (Eng. trans. 1996) and study by Denis E. Collins (1977).

FRELICH, PHYLLIS (1944–   ), U.S. actress. The oldest of nine deaf children born to deaf parents, Frelich became interested in theater while studying at Gallaudet College, a liberal-arts college for the deaf (B.S. 1967). A founding member and acting coach (1977–79) for the National Theater of the Deaf, Frelich appeared in many of its productions. She was acclaimed for her performance in the

Broadway production of Mark Medoff's *Children of a Lesser God* (1980, Tony Award), one of the first plays written for a deaf actor. She also appeared in *Poets from the Inside* (1980) at New York City's Public Theater, directed the New York Deaf Theater Production of *The Gin Game* (1980), and starred in the TV movie *Love Is Never Silent* (1985).

FRENCH, DANIEL CHESTER (1850–1931), U.S. sculptor. French grew up in Concord, Massachusetts, where Abigail May Alcott gave him his first lessons in sculpture. At age 23 he was commissioned to produce for Concord a statue of the Minute Man (1874), which was subsequently reproduced as a patriotic symbol on stamps and posters. Influenced by his exposure in Paris to the École des Beaux-Arts style, French sculpted large civic statuary, including the seated figure of Lincoln in the Washington, D.C., memorial (1922). ■ See the memoir by his wife (1928) and Margaret Cresson, *Journey into Fame* (1947).

FRENCH, JOHN DENTON PINKSTONE, 1st EARL OF YPRES (1852–1925), British field marshal. French was a cavalry leader in the Boer War (1899–1902), for which he was knighted. Promoted to field marshal (1913), he commanded British forces in France and Belgium during World War I. He resigned in December 1915 under pressure compounded by the enormous casualties suffered during the first and second battles of Ypres and the Battle of Loos, poor staff relations, and strain with the Allies. ■ See his war memoir, *1914* (1919); biography by his son Gerald French (1931); and George H. Cassar, *The Tragedy of Sir John French* (1985).

FREUD, ANNA (1895–1982), Austrian-born British psychoanalyst. The youngest daughter of Sigmund Freud, the founder of psychoanalysis, Anna Freud picked up where her father left off by elaborating the defensive capacities of the ego in her most famous book, *The Ego and the Mechanisms of Defense* (1936; Eng. trans. 1937), thus laying the groundwork for the ego-psychology movement. A staunch defender of psychoanalytic orthodoxy who was noted for her pioneering work with children, she broadened the scope of psychoanalytic theory to include normal psychological functioning. She left Vienna with her father after the Germans took over Austria (1938) and settled in Britain, where she founded (1947) and directed the Hampstead Child Therapy Clinic, London. ■ See *The Writings of Anna Freud* (8 vols., 1966–81) and biographies by Raymond Dyer, *Her Father's Daughter* (1983); Uwe H. Peter (1984); and Elizabeth Young-Bruehl (1988).

FREUD, LUCIAN (1922–   ), British artist. Born in Berlin, the grandson of Sigmund Freud, Lucian Freud moved to England with his family (1932), and became a naturalized British subject (1939). He was educated at several progressive boarding schools but only briefly attended art school.

Although he was attracted to surrealism and neoromanticism in the 1940s, he adapted an expressive figurative style in the 1950s and maintained it throughout his career. His meticulous, intense, and detailed renderings gained international attention during the 1970s and he was considered one of the greatest realist painters of his era. His typical subjects were posed images of alienated nude figures, often seen from unusual and unsettling angles, and depictions of squalid interiors and somber cityscapes. Freud's best-known works included *Girl with a White Dog* (1951), *Pregnant Girl* (1960–61), *Large Interior, W11 (After Watteau; 1981–83)*, *Reflection (Self-Portrait)* (1985), and *Naked Man, Back View* (1991–92).

FREUD, SIGMUND (1856–1939), Austrian psychoanalyst. Freud, a neurologist by training, was best known as the founder of psychoanalysis, a revolutionary, comprehensive theory of human behavior that emphasizes unconscious mental processes and the enduring influence of infantile sexuality. His collaboration (1882) with Joseph Breuer on treatment of a hysterical patient using cathartic methods that the patient called "the talking cure," and consultation with French neurologist Jean Charcot, led Freud to develop (1892–95) the technique of "free association" and to elaborate psychoanalysis as a method of treatment. Freud's self-analysis and his work with patients resulted in other treatment modes: the interpretation of dreams, the analysis of resistance to therapy, and the analysis of a patient's transference of emotions to the therapist. He laid out his theories in such seminal works as *The Interpretation of Dreams* (1990; Eng trans. 1913), *The Psychopathology of Everyday Life* (1904; Eng. trans. 1914), *Three Essays on the Theory of Sexuality* (1905; Eng. trans. 1910), *A General Introduction to Psychoanalysis* (1916; Eng. trans. 1920), and *The Ego and the Id* (1923; Eng. trans. 1927). *The Standard Edition of the Complete Psychological Works of Sigmund Freud* (24 vols., 1953–74) contains English translations of Freud's writings. Although psychoanalysis encountered intense opposition in the early years, it eventually became a dominant psychological theory and method of treatment as well as a major research technique. Freud's theories have influenced virtually every sphere of contemporary Western culture, but not one has escaped challenge or qualification. A Jew, Freud was forced to leave his home in Vienna when the Nazis seized Austria (1938) and he died in London. His daughter, Anna Freud (1895–1982), was a prominent psychoanalyst. ■ See biographies by Ernest Jones (3 vols., 1953–57), Peter Gay (1988), Paul Ferris (1998), and Louis Breger (2000); and study by Paul Roazen (1985).

FREYRE, GILBERTO DE MELLO (1900–1987), Brazilian social historian and novelist. A native of Recife in the racially mixed northeast of Brazil, Freyre studied cultural anthropology with Franz Boas at Columbia University (M.A. 1922) and applied his insights to analyze the culture and history of his homeland. His widely read masterpiece, *The Masters and the Slaves* (1933; Eng. trans. 1946), stressed the contributions of Indian and African culture to Brazilian civilization and offered Brazilians a special sense of identity. Related works, *The Mansions and the Shanties* (1936; Eng trans. 1963) and *Order and Progress* (1959; Eng. trans. 1970), traced the rise of 19th-century urban society and the emergence of modern Brazil. Freyre taught at several Brazilian, U.S., and European universities, organized the first Afro-Brazilian conference (1934), served in parliament (1946–50), and headed the Northeast Brazil Social and Educational Research Center (from 1957). Among his other books are *New World in the Tropics* (written in English; 1959), the novel *Mother and Son* (1964; Eng. trans. 1967), and *The Gilberto Freyre Reader* (Eng. trans. 1974).

FREY-WYSSLING, ALBERT FRIEDRICH (1900–1988), Swiss botanist. A faculty member of the Swiss Federal Institute of Technology (1932–70), Frey-Wyssling did pioneering research in the field of submicroscopic morphology in an effort to unite two disciplines of biology: histomorphology and biochemistry. His studies, corroborated by the electron microscope after 1940, laid the groundwork for the new field known as molecular biology. His books included *Submicroscopic Morphology of Protoplasm* (Eng. trans. 1948; rev. ed. 1953), *Ultrastructural Plant Cytology* (with K. Muhlethaler; Eng. trans. 1965), *Macromolecules in Cell Structure* (1957), and *Comparative Organellography of the Cytoplasm* (Eng. trans. 1973).

FRIEDAN, BETTY (Betty Goldstein; 1921–   ), U.S. feminist. Friedan was born in Illinois, attended Smith College, and moved (1942) to New York City. A onetime suburban housewife, she wrote the landmark best-seller *The Feminine Mystique* (1963), which analyzed the role of women in American society. Friedan founded (1966) the National Organization for Women (NOW), serving (1966–70) as its first president, and headed (1970) the national Women's Strike for Equality. She wrote *It Changed My Life* (1977), *The Second Stage* (1981; rev. ed. 1986), *The Fountain of Age* (1993), and *Beyond Gender* (1997). ■ See her memoir *Life So Far* (2000); study by Daniel Horowitz (1998); and biography by Judith Hennessee (1999).

FRIEDMAN, JEROME (1930–   ), U.S. physicist. The son of Russian-Jewish immigrants, Friedman turned down an art scholarship in order to pursue studies in physics at the University of Chicago (B.A. 1950; M.A. 1953; Ph.D. 1956), where Enrico Fermi was his mentor. He did research at Stanford (1957–60) and then taught at the Massachusetts Institute of Technology (1960–   ). Collaborating with Henry W. Kendall and Richard E. Taylor at the two-mile-long-high-energy particle accelerator at the Stanford Linear Accelerator Center (1967–73), Friedman performed electron-scattering experiments that confirmed the existence of quarks, subatomic particles that are the fundamental building blocks of protons and neutrons. The three scientists also identified electrically neutral particles called gluons, which bind quarks together. Friedman, Kendall, and Taylor shared the 1990 Nobel Prize in Physics for their experiments.

FRIEDMAN, MILTON (1912–   ), U.S. economist. A leading monetarist at the University of Chicago (1946–83), Friedman believed that only the amount of money in existence, and not the manipulation of it by government through taxes and expenditures, affects the level of production in an economy. Rejecting most of the widely accepted theories of British economist John Maynard Keynes, Friedman was a conservative who believed in a free laissez-faire capitalist economy with minimal governmental interference and was therefore opposed to tariffs, social welfare programs, corporate taxes, and wage and price controls. His prescription for halting inflation was to curb the money supply. He was an adviser to Sen. Barry Goldwater and presidents Richard Nixon and Ronald Reagan and was awarded the 1976 Nobel Prize in Economics. His books included *Essays in Positive Economics* (1953), *A Theory of the Consumption Function* (1957), *A Monetary History of the United States, 1867–1960* (1963; with Anna J. Schwartz), *The Optimum Quantity of Money and Other Essays* (1969), *Monetarist Ecnomics* (1991), and *Money Mischief* (1992). With his wife, Rose, he wrote *Capitalism and Freedom* (1962) and *Free to Choose* (1980; TV series 1980) and the memoir *Two Lucky People* (1998). ■ See study by Eamonn Butler (1985).

FRIML, (CHARLES) RUDOLF (1879–1972), Austrian-born composer and pianist. Rudolf Friml studied music at the Prague Conservatory with Antonin Dvořák. After settling in the United States (1906), he composed 33 light-hearted romantic operettas, including such popular favorites as *The Firefly* (1912), *Rose Marie* (1924), *The Vagabond King* (1925), and *The Three Musketeers* (1928). Among his best-known songs were "Indian Love Call" (1925), "Only a Rose" (1925), "Some Day" (1925), and "Donkey Serenade" (1937).

FRISCH, KARL VON (1886–1982), Austrian zoologist. A graduate of the University of Munich (Ph.D. 1910), Frisch set up a new zoological institute there (1932) and spent his entire career studying animal behavior. His numerous experiments over a period of five decades proved that fish hear and distinguish colors, that insects perceive polarized light, and that bees communicate with each other by means of circling and wiggling "dance" motions in order to convey information regarding food sources. This means of communication proved the most complex ever discovered in invertebrates. His books included *The Dancing Bees* (1927; Eng. trans. 1954) and *Animal Architecture* (1974; Eng. trans. 1974). Frisch shared the 1973 Nobel Prize in Physiology or Medicine with Konrad Lorenz and Nikolaas Tinbergen. ■ See his autobiography, *A Biologist Remembers* (1957; Eng. trans. 1967).

FRISCH, MAX (1911–1991), Swiss (German-language) novelist and playwright. When critics acclaimed his second novel, *I'm Not Stiller* (1954; abridged Eng. trans. 1958; 1994), Frisch abandoned a successful architecture career to write full-time. He wrote about alienation and collective war guilt, deploring anti-Semitism and the moral cowardice of the bourgeoisie. Frisch wrote several important novels, including *Homo Faber* (1957; Eng. trans. 1959), *A Wilderness of Mirrors* (1964; Eng. trans. 1965), *Montauk* (1975; Eng. trans. 1976), and *Man in the Holocene* (1979; Eng. trans. 1980), but established an international reputation primarily with his plays, which were influenced by the work of his friend Bertolt Brecht. They included *When the War Was Over* (1949; Eng. trans. 1967), *The Fire Raisers* (1953 for radio; 1958 for stage; Eng. trans. 1962), *Andorra* (1961; Eng. trans. 1962), *Biography: A Game* (1967; Eng. trans. 1969), and *Triptych* (1978; Eng. trans. 1981). ■ See the diaries published as *Sketchbook, 1946–1949* (Eng. trans. 1977) and *Sketchbook, 1966–1971* (Eng. trans. 1974), and studies by Ulrich Weisstein (1967), Carol Peterssen (Eng. trans. 1972), and M. Butler (1976).

FRISCH, RAGNAR (1895–1973), Norwegian economist. A graduate of Oslo University (Ph.D. 1926), Frisch was a professor of social economy and statistics there from 1931 to 1965. He was a developer of econometrics, the use of mathematical models and statistics to analyze economic data. Frisch used econometric techniques to solve problems of national economic planning and income accounting. He also studied trade cycles, index numbers, and demand theory. For his contributions to the development of econometrics he shared the first Nobel Prize in Economics (1969) with Jan Tinbergen.

FROBENIUS, LEO VIKTOR (1873–1938), German explorer, archaeologist, and ethnologist. Frobenius led 12 expeditions to Africa (1904–35) and wrote numerous works on the nature of culture. He originated the cultural-historical approach to ethnology, supported the idea of cultural diffusion, and regarded cultures as living organisms with unique souls that, independently of human will, grow and decay with age. A leading authority on prehistoric art, he founded the Institute for Cultural Morphology at Frankfurt am Main (1922) and established a collection of more than 3,500 facsimiles of prehistoric rock paintings and engravings. From 1932 he taught cultural anthropology at the University of Frankfurt. His numerous works included *The Voice of Africa* (2 vols., 1912–13; Eng. trans. 1913) and *African Genesis* (1921–24, 1931; Eng. trans. 1937). ■ See also Eike Haberland, ed., *Leo Frobenius: An Anthology* (1973).

FROHMAN, CHARLES (1860–1915), U.S. theatrical manager. Known as "the Napoleon of the drama," Frohman was the dominant theatrical personality of his time. He was responsible for organizing the modern theatrical booking system and for creating the "star" system. His Theatrical Syndicate, which emerged from his booking office in New York City, controlled theatrical touring in the United States during the early years of the century, and his Empire Theater Stock Company developed such stars as Maude Adams, Ethel Barrymore, Billie Burke, and William Gillette. He had a long association with playwright Sir James Barrie and promoted the plays of many young American playwrights, including David Belasco, Clyde Fitch, and Augustus Thomas. Frohman also controlled theaters in London and promoted the system of exchange of shows between London and New York. He died at sea in the sinking of the *Lusitania* (May 7, 1915). ■ See biography by Isaac F. Marcosson and Daniel Frohman (1916).

FROMM, ERICH (1900–1980), German-born U.S. psychoanalyst. Educated at the University of Munich (Ph.D. 1922) and the Psychoanalytic Institute in Berlin, Fromm approached the practice of psychoanalysis from the standpoint of philosophy rather than medicine. He treated patients from 1925 and began a distinguished teaching career in 1929. A lifelong pacifist, he emigrated to the U.S. (1934) soon after the Nazis assumed power in Germany. Inspired by fellow neo-Freudians, by the writings of Karl Marx, and by the humanistic tradition, Fromm lent a cultural and social perspective to psychoanalysis by contending that neurosis can result from culturally inspired needs rather than from frustration of biological drives. A profound critic of materialistic values, he argued for a society that fosters productive and meaningful relations with others and that responds to what he saw as a person's basic need to avoid loneliness. In the 1950s he warned against the dangers of a society dominated by technology and in 1957 helped to found the National Committee for a Sane Nuclear Policy (SANE), which took its name from his book *The Sane Society* (1955). Fromm's 20 books—many of them considered classics—included *Escape from Freedom* (1941), *Man for Himself* (1947), *The Art of Loving* (1956), *Marx's Concept of Man* (1961), and *The Anatomy of Human Destructiveness* (1973). ■ See Richard I. Evans, *Dialogue with Erich Fromm* (1966), and study by Don Hausdorff (1972).

FROST, LESLIE MISCAMPBELL (1895–1973), Canadian lawyer and politician. Born in Ontario, Frost served in the infantry in World War I and returned to become a lawyer in 1921. In 1937 he was elected to the Ontario legislature and held several ministerial posts. From 1949 to 1961 Frost was the leader of the provincial Progressive Conservative party and premier of Ontario. Frost's progressive administration enacted laws admitting women to jury duty and requiring equal pay for equal work, and passed a fair-employment-practices act. He vigorously supported the St. Lawrence Seaway project. He later served as the first chancellor of Trent University in Peterborough (from 1963). ■ See Roger Graham, *Old Man Ontario* (1990).

FROST, ROBERT LEE (1874–1963), U.S. poet. Born in San Francisco, Frost was taken at age 10 to his family's farm in New England. He studied briefly at Harvard, then went to Britain (1912–15), where he published his first poetry collection, *A Boy's Will* (1913). Immersed in the tradition of Emerson and Thoreau, Frost focused his simple-seeming verse on familiar pastoral landscapes. Some critics suggested that his cheerfulness belied a harrowing consciousness of tragedy. Frost resisted literary fashion and adhered to formal meter; he once compared writing free verse to "playing tennis with the net down." His infusion of everyday language into austere Yankee verse endeared Frost to the American public, which regarded him as the nation's unofficial poet laureate. Among his best-known poems were "A Servant to Servants," "Bond and Free," "Stopping by Woods on a Snowy Evening," "Mending Wall," "The Death of the Hired Man," "The Road Not Taken," and "Birches." Four books of poetry, *New Hampshire* (1923), *Collected Poems* (1930), *A Further Range* (1936), and *A Witness Tree* (1942), won Pulitzer Prizes. The most comprehensive collection is *The Poems of Robert Frost* (1969). ■ See biographies by Lawrence Thompson and R. H. Winnick (3 vols., 1966–76; abridged 1981), William H. Pritchard (1984), Jeffrey Meyers (1996), and Jay Parini (1999).

FRUNZE, MIKHAIL VASILYEVICH (1885–1925), Russian general. After being expelled from college for revolutionary activity, Frunze joined the bolsheviks (1904) and participated in the 1905 revolution. While in prison (1907–15) he studied military doctrines and after his escape became an agitator among the Russian troops. After the 1917 Bolshevik revolution he became a general in the Red army, and during the civil war (1918–20) he defeated the armies of Adm. A. V. Kolchak and Gen. P. N. Wrangel and secured Soviet control over Turkestan. As Leon Trotsky's replacement (1925) as people's commissar for the army and navy, he reorganized the Red army and devised a war strategy that was to prove instrumental in the army's victories in World War II. ■ See biography by Walter D. Jacobs (1969).

FRY, CHRISTOPHER (1907–   ), British playwright. Once a schoolteacher, Fry was also an actor and director. Frequently compared to T. S. Eliot, he was an exponent of poetic drama, written in blank verse and often based on ancient myths and history. His plays espoused the healing and positive powers of nature and religion. They included *A Phoenix Too Frequent* (1946); *The Lady's Not for Burning* (1948), his most famous play, a comedy of a medieval woman accused of being a witch; *A Sleep of Prisoners* (1951); and *The Dark Is Light Enough* (1954). Other comedies included *Venus Observed* (1950) and *A Yard of Sun* (1970). He also wrote the screenplays for the biblical epics *Ben Hur* (1959), *Barabbas* (1962), and *The Bible* (1966). ■ See his family history, *Can You Find Me* (1978), and studies by Emil Roy (1968) and Glenda Leeming (1990).

FRY, ROGER ELIOT (1866–1934), British art critic and artist. A champion of modern art, Fry introduced Cézanne and the postimpressionists to Britain (1910). He wrote extensively on the aesthetics of "pure form" and color in art and regarded content as incidental. Fry was closely associated with the London Bloomsbury group and founded (1913) the Omega Workshops, which produced avant-garde furniture, fabrics, and pottery. His best-known works were *Vision and Design* (1920), *Transformations* (1927), and *Cézanne* (1927). ■ See biographies by Virginia Woolf (1940) and Frances Spalding (1980).

FRYE, (HERMAN) NORTHROP (1912–1991), Canadian literary critic. Frye studied theology before concentrating on English at Oxford University (M.A. 1940). On the faculty of the University of Toronto (from 1939), he examined the role of symbolism and myth in literature in *Fearful Symmetry: A Study of William Blake* (1947) and gained international recognition for *Anatomy of Criticism* (1957), a systematic study of literary criticism. Regarded as a modern classic, it presented the theory that myth provides the underlying principle of all literature. His other works, including *Fables of Identity* (1963), *The Well-Tempered Critic* (1963), *Fools of Time* (1967), *The Great Code: The Bible and Literature* (1981), and *Words with Power* (1990), applied his theory to classics of the Western literary tradition. ■ See study by Robert Denham (1978).

FUAD I (Ahmed Fuad Pasha; 1868–1936), Egyptian king. Son of the khedive of Egypt, Ismail Pasha, Fuad was educated in Europe and became sultan in 1917. After the 1922 treaty with Britain that resulted in nominal Egyptian independence, he became the first king of modern Egypt. He ruled autocratically as a constitutional monarch under British protection and struggled to limit the influence of the popular, nationalistic Wafd party. Fuad was forced by nationalist pressure in 1935 to restore the constitution that he had abrogated in 1930. He was succeeded by his son Farouk.

FUCHS, KLAUS EMIL JULIUS (1911–1988), German-born physicist and spy. Fuchs studied physics at the University of Leipzig, where he became involved with the Communist party. Fleeing from Germany when Nazi leader Adolf Hitler rose to power (1933), he went to Britain. During World War II Fuchs worked in secret atomic research and in 1943 became a British subject. The same year, apparently convinced that the Soviets' tremendous losses in the Allied effort entitled them to a full share in military intelligence, he became an active Soviet agent. He joined (1943) the U.S. Los Alamos project and stayed with U.S. atomic research until the bombing of Hiroshima (1945). During this time, he supplied the Soviets with the design for the uranium and plutonium bombs. Returning to Britain (1945) to continue research, he became disillusioned with the Soviets and ended his spying activities. In 1950 an investigation into leaks from Los Alamos led to Fuchs' confession. His testimony sparked an investigation that ultimately resulted in the arrest of Julius and Ethel Rosenberg. Sentenced to a 14-year term, Fuchs was released (1959) and made his home in East Germany. ■ See Oliver Pilat, *The Atom Spies* (1952); H. Montgomery Hyde, *The Atom Bomb Spies* (1980); and studies by Norman Moss (1987) and Robert C. Williams (1987).

FUENTES, CARLOS (1928–   ), Mexican novelist. Fuentes held several government posts in the 1950s before devoting himself exclusively to writing. A prominent left-wing intellectual and leader of the modern generation of Mexican novelists, he established himself with his ambitious first novel, *Where the Air Is Clear* (1958; Eng. trans. 1960), a panorama of life in Mexico City. *The Good Conscience* (1959; Eng. trans. 1968) described the gradual corruption of an angry young man. Fuentes won critical acclaim in the mid-1960s for *The Death of Artemio Cruz* (1962; Eng. trans. 1964), the deathbed reminiscences of a revolutionary turned newspaper tycoon, and *A Change of Skin* (1967; Eng. trans. 1968), about the inner life of a failed writer. Later works included *Terra Nostra* (1975; Eng. trans. 1976), an imaginative treatment of Spanish and Mexican history; *The Hydra Head* (1978; Eng. trans. 1979), a heavy-handed thriller about Middle East interests; *Distant Relations* (1980; Eng. trans. 1982), about an archaeologist's search for his own roots; and *The Old Gringo* (1984; Eng. trans. 1985), a novel that draws on history and myth to link the destinies of Mexico and the United States. Fuentes also wrote literary criticism, short stories, and several volumes of essays. His later works in English translation included *Buried Mirror: Reflections on Spain in the New World* (1992); *Diana, The Goddess Who Hunts Alone* (1995), a semiautobiographical novel; *The Crystal Frontier* (1997), a novel about U.S.-Mexican relations; and *The Years with Laura Díaz* (2000). Widely read in the United States, he was regarded as a cultural mediator between North and South America. ■ See studies by Daniel de Guzmán (1972) and Wendy B. Faris (1983), and Robert Brady and Charles Rossman, eds., *Carlos Fuentes, A Critical View* (1982).

FUGARD, ATHOL (1932–   ), South African playwright and director. Born into a mixed English-Afrikaner family, Fugard dropped out of the University of Cape Town just before graduating and worked for two years as the only white crew member of a tramp steamer and then as a clerk in a Johannesburg court. He wrote his first play dealing with the brutalization of nonwhites in South Africa in 1958 and helped to form several theater groups. His powerful plays, which strongly condemned apartheid while examining the universal themes of boredom, despair, alienation, and the problem of identity, were presented throughout the world. He was best known for *The Blood Knot* (1961; pub. 1963), *Boesman and Lena* (1969), *Sizwe Bansi Is Dead* (1972; pub. 1974), *The Island* (1973; pub. 1974), *A Lesson from Aloes*

(1978), "Master Harold" and the Boys (1982), and The Road to Mecca (1988). His novel Tsotsi, written in 1961, was published in 1980. His plays of the postapartheid era included Valley Song (1996) and the autobiographical The Captain's Tiger (1998). ■ See his Cousins: A Memoir (1994), Notebooks, 1960–1977 (1983); study by Dennis Walder (1985); and Russell Vandenbroucke, Truths the Hand Can Touch (1985).

FUJIMORI, ALBERTO KENYO (1938–   ), Peruvian political leader. The son of Japanese immigrants, Fujimori received an agricultural science degree from the National Agrarian University (1961) and a master's degree in mathematics from the University of Wisconsin (1969). He taught mathematics and served as rector of the Agrarian University before he formed the Cambio 90 (Change 90) and won the presidency in a stunning electoral upset victory (1990). Opposed by a hostile legislature, he suspended the constitution and dissolved Congress (1992). He won a majority in subsequent congressional elections (1992), promulgated a new constitution with increased presidential powers (1993), and successfully eliminated hyperinflation (which peaked at 7,649 percent), and reduced guerrilla violence by defeating the Shining Path insurgency. Fujimori was overwhelmingly reelected in 1995. During his presidency (1990–2000), the autocratic Fujimori restructured the Peruvian economy through privatization and deregulation, but although the economy grew, by the late 1990s more than half of the Peruvian people lived in poverty and approximately 85 percent of workers did not have full-time jobs. He won a third term (May 2000) in a disputed election that was boycotted by the opposition. Following a sensational corruption scandal (September 2000) involving his intelligence chief, Fujimori resigned (Nov. 2000) and moved to Japan.

FUKUI, KENICHI (1918–1998), Japanese chemist. A professor of physical chemistry at Kyoto University, Fukui applied the theories of quantum mechanics to chemical reactions and developed, during the 1950s, a theory of "frontier orbitals." Although he demonstrated that the orbits of the outermost electrons play a decisive role in the reactivity of molecules, his work was largely ignored until similar conclusions were reached independently, in the United States, by Roald Hoffmann and Robert B. Woodward. Their theoretical work enabled scientists to predict and understand previously inexplicable laboratory reactions and had important practical applications in medicine and industry. Fukui and Hoffmann shared the 1981 Nobel Prize in Chemistry.

FULBRIGHT, JAMES WILLIAM (1905–1995), U.S. senator. A Rhodes scholar from Missouri, J. William Fulbright returned to his undergraduate alma mater, the University of Arkansas (B.A. 1925) to teach law and serve as its president (1939–41). In 1942 he was elected to Congress as a Democratic representative from Arkansas and two years later went to the U.S. Senate, where he sponsored the 1946 Fulbright Act for cultural exchange of students, scholars, and teachers. Fulbright was a traditional southerner in matters of civil rights but as chairman of the Senate Foreign Relations Committee (1959–74) took an increasingly liberal stance in world affairs. One of the leading critics of U.S. intervention in Vietnam, he was defeated in a primary election in his bid for a sixth term (1974). His books included Old Myths and New Realities (1964), The Arrogance of Power (1967), and The Crippled Giant (1972). ■ See studies by Tristram Coffin (1966), Haynes Johnson and Bernard M. Gwertzman (1968), Eugene Brown (1985), and Randall Bennett Woods (1995).

FULLER, ALFRED CARL (1885–1973), Canadian-born U.S. businessman. Fuller left his Nova Scotia farm home at age 18 to seek his fortune in Boston. He became a salesman for a brush company and was so impressed with the potential market that he invested $375 of his savings and went into business for himself (1906), manufacturing brushes in a basement workshop at night and selling them, mainly to housewives, door-to-door by day. He started recruiting salesmen, who were independent dealers, and soon the "Fuller brush man" became an American institution. The company was the first successful U.S. direct-sales enterprise. Yearly sales eventually reached $130 million. Fuller was president of his company until 1943 and chairman of the board until 1968. ■ See his autobiography, A Foot in the Door (1960), and study by Edward Allen (1964).

FULLER, (RICHARD) BUCKMINSTER (1895–1983), U.S. engineer and futurist. Born into an eminently traditional New England family, Fuller was a nonconformist who was twice expelled from Harvard University. Describing himself as an "explorer in comprehensive anticipation design," he used technology, a belief in basic geometric principles, and rational planning to devise futuristic solutions to contemporary social problems. He held more than 2,000 patents. Fuller's "Dymaxion" (for "dynamic plus maximum efficiency") house was conceived in 1927 as a functional solution to the housing shortage, but was not built until 1944. His Dymaxion auto (1932), an airplane-shaped, three-wheeled vehicle with the capacity to go 120 miles per hour, also remained on the drawing board. Although Fuller lacked an architect's formal training or credentials, he won acclaim for his geodesic dome, a tetrahedron enclosing the maximum space with the minimum materials. It was used for factories in the 1950s, houses in the 1960s, and for the translucent U.S. Pavilion at the Montreal Expo (1967). He wrote several books, including Ideas and Integrities: A Spontaneous Autobiographical Disclosure (1963). ■ See his Inventions: The Patented Works of R. Buckminster Fuller (1983); Hugh Kenner, Bucky (1973); and studies by Alden Hatch (1974) and Robert Snyder (1979).

FUNG YU-LAN. See FENG YOULAN.

FUNK, CASIMIR (1884–1967), Polish-born U.S. biochemist. A prominent scientist who headed research institutes in Poland (1923–27), France (1928–39), and the United States (1948–67), Funk is best known as the discoverer of vitamins. He demonstrated that diseases such as beriberi, scurvy, rickets, and pellagra were caused by the lack of a specific chemical substance in the diet, which he called "vitamines" (for vital amines). The "e" was later dropped when it was found that only B_I was an amine. Funk's theories on the importance of vitamins in the diet stimulated research in the field of nutrition and laid the foundation of modern dietetics. ▪ See biography by Benjamin Harrow (1955).

FURCHGOTT, ROBERT F. (1916–   ), U.S. pharmacologist. Furchgott studied biochemistry at Northwestern University (Ph.D. 1940) and taught at the State University of New York Health Science Center at Brooklyn (1956–   ). In a 1980 experiment on endothelial cells, which form the inner lining of blood vessels, he concluded that blood vessels widen and allow for increased blood flow because of the release of a signal molecule he called endothelium-derived relaxing factor (EDRF). Independent research by Louis J. Ignarro and Ferid Murad showed that the relaxing factor was the short-lived gas nitric oxide (NO). Subsequent research demonstrated that nitric oxide plays a major role in immunity, blood pressure control, and tumor suppression and led to the use of Viagra as an anti-impotence drug. For their research, Furchgott, Ignarro, and Murad shared the 1998 Nobel Prize for Physiology or Medicine.

FURTSEVA, EKATERINA ALEKSEYEVNA (1910–1974), Soviet political leader. A member of the Communist party from age 20, Furtseva was trained as a chemical engineer before being employed by the Moscow party organization (1942). A protégée of party leader Nikita Khrushchev, she headed the Moscow party (1954–57), served on the Supreme Soviet (from 1954) and the Central Committee of the Communist party (from 1956), and was minister of culture (from 1960). She was the only woman ever to serve on the Politburo (1957–61), the party's ruling body, and was the Soviet Union's only woman minister.

FURTWÄNGLER, WILHELM (1886–1954), German conductor. Son of an archaeologist and art critic, Furtwängler began to study music at age 8 and made his conducting debut in Lübeck in 1911. In 1922 he became a leader in the music world with his appointment to direct the Berlin Philharmonic, a post at which he remained for most of his life. At various times during his career he also directed the Berlin State Opera, the Vienna Philharmonic, and the Bayreuth and Salzburg festivals. Because he enjoyed a privileged position in the Third Reich, he was later accused of Nazi sympathies, even though he was officially cleared of pro-Nazi activities in 1946. Restrained in his personal manner, Furtwängler was best known for his profound interpretations of the works of Wagner and Beethoven and was regarded by many as the greatest conductor of the century. ▪ See his *Concerning Music* (Eng. trans. 1953); biography by Curt Riess (Eng. trans. 1955); study by Peter J. Pirie (1980); and Sam H. Shirakawa, *The Devil's Music Master* (1992).

FURUSETH, ANDREW (Anders Andreassen; 1854–1938), Norwegian-born U.S. labor leader and reformer. A seaman for 18 years, Furuseth dedicated his life to improving the wages, legal status, and living and working conditions of merchant seamen. He served as a Washington lobbyist for Seamen's unions (1894–1908) and was president of the International Seaman's Union (1908–38). Furuseth was primarily responsible for the La Follette Seamen's Act (1915), which abolished imprisonment for desertion and was the most important reform bill of its kind. He was also the major force behind the Norris-LaGuardia Act (1932), which restricted the use of injunctions against labor and helped establish the right of workers to strike. ▪ See biography by Hyman Weintraub (1959).

G

GABIN, JEAN (Jean Alexis Moncorgé; 1904–1976), French actor. Offspring of a theatrical family, onetime song-and-dance man Gabin was the most popular French film star of the 1930s. In *The Lower Depths* (1936), *Pépé le Moko* (1937), and *Grand Illusion* (1937), he played working-class loners who seemed the embodiment of the national ideal: brave, loyal, and kind. Other famous roles were in *Port of Shadows* (1938) and *The Human Beast* (1938). After a brief unsuccessful period in Hollywood, he joined the Free French navy during World War II. Continuing his career in France after the war, he appeared in dozens of movies, including *French Can-Can* (1955) and *Les Miserables* (1957).

GABLE, CLARK (1901–1960), U.S. film actor. The "king" of Hollywood, Gable was a tough, unsentimental "man's man" with a rakish appeal to women. He dropped out of school in Ohio to become a factory hand, oil-field roughneck, and lumberjack before trying to break into acting. During the 1920s he toured with stock companies and played bit film parts. His big break came with *It Happened One Night* (1934), followed by *Mutiny on the Bounty* (1935) and *Gone With the Wind* (1939). He also played leads opposite Greta Garbo, Jean Harlow, and Carole Lombard, the screwball comedienne who became his third wife in 1939. A top movie idol for three decades, Gable simply played himself in most of his post–World War II films. He died of a heart attack after finishing *The Misfits* (1960). ■ See Charles Samuels, *The King* (1962), and Lyn Tornabene, *Long Live the King* (1976).

GABO, NAUM (Naum Neemia Pevsner; 1890–1977), Russian-born sculptor. Naum Gabo studied medicine, natural science, and engineering before studying art in Munich (1911–12) and coming under the influence of Wassily Kandinsky's Blue Rider group. In Norway during World War I, he took the surname Gabo to distinguish himself from his brother, Antoine Pevsner. Together the brothers began experimenting with spatial concepts, constructing bold, abstract sculptures. They returned to Russia (1917), where they issued their important *Realistic Manifesto* (1920), a constructivist tract that reacted against the political use of art. Using nonconventional media, Gabo sought to express contemporary values and to join art with scientific technology. He created his first kinetic, motor-driven pieces while still in Russia. He emigrated to Berlin (1922) and later to Paris (1932), introducing constructivist sculpture to other European artists. After 1946 he lived in the United States. Gabo created sculptures for Rockefeller Center in New York City (1956) and the Bijenkorf Building in Rotterdam (1957). ■ See the biographical sketch by Aleksei Pevsner (1964).

GABOR, DENNIS (1900–1979), Hungarian-born British electrical engineer and inventor. Gabor was educated in Berlin (D.D.E. 1927) and worked there until the Nazis came to power in 1933. He emigrated to Britain, where, despite the Depression, he was hired as a research engineer based on his early invention of the plasma lamp; he later taught at the University of London (1949–67). He was best known, however, as the inventor of the technique of holography (1947), a system of three-dimensional photography that revolutionized the field of optical science. Using a laser as a light source, the hologram proved widely applicable in medicine, communications, and industry during the 1960s, and Gabor was awarded the 1971 Nobel Prize in Physics. His books on the social implications of technology included *Inventing the Future* (1963), *The Mature Society* (1972), and *Beyond the Age of Waste* (1980; with U. Colombo).

GADAMER, HANS-GEORG (1900–), German philosopher. Gadamer, the son of a prominent chemistry professor, studied humanities at several German universities. After earning a doctorate at the University of Freiburg (1922), he served as the assistant to renowned philosopher Martin Heidegger at the University of Marburg (1923–28) and subsequently taught philosophy at five universities, including Heidelberg (1949–68). He developed a system of philosophical hermeneutics that opposed a strict emphasis on methodology and proposed instead that understanding be sought through a reflective process that took into account one's own preconceptions, prejudices, history, and tradition. Gadamer's major work, *Truth and Method* (1960; Eng. trans. 1975), influenced philosophical studies throughout the world and particularly inspired growing interest in the field of hermeneutics in the United States. His other major works included *Plato's Dialectical Ethics* (1931; Eng. trans. 1991), *Hegel's Dialectic* (1971; Eng. trans. 1976), and *Reason in the Age of Science* (1976; Eng. trans. 1981). ■ See study by Georgia Warnke (1987) and Lewis E. Hahn, ed., *The Philosophy of Hans-Georg Gadamer* (1997).

GADDA, CARLO EMILIO (1893–1973), Italian novelist and short-story writer. Gadda was a prisoner of war in World War I. He abandoned his career as an electrical engineer (1935) to write fiction. He exploited every resource of the Italian language—and at times added to it—to create intricate and sophisticated parodies. His expressionistic works represent his response to a world in chaos and contain indictments of violence, hypocrisy, and fascism. The highly acclaimed but forbiddingly obscure detective novel *That Awful Mess on Via Merulano* (1957; Eng. trans. 1965) was written in standard Italian and three other dialects. He also wrote *Acquainted with Grief* (1963; Eng. trans. 1969) and several collections of short fiction. ▪ See study by Albert Sbragia (1996).

GAGARIN, YURI ALEKSEYEVICH (1934–1968), Soviet cosmonaut. Born on a collective farm, Gagarin was trained at the Orenburg Air Force School (1955–57) and entered the cosmonaut program in 1959. On April 12, 1961, he made the first manned space flight in history, orbiting the earth in the *Vostok I* spacecraft in one hour, 48 minutes at a maximum speed of nearly 18,000 miles per hour. He demonstrated during the flight that useful tasks may be performed in a state of weightlessness. He earned his country's highest honor, "Hero of the Soviet Union," and gained worldwide fame. He died near Moscow on a routine training flight and was buried in the Kremlin Wall. ▪ See Khwaja Abbas, *Till We Reach the Stars* (1962), and I. K. Golovanov, *Our Gagarin* (Eng. trans. 1978).

GAINES, WILLIAM MAXWELL (1922–1992), U.S. publisher. Gaines, the son of pioneering comic book publisher Max Gaines, inherited EC comics after his father died in 1947. He successfully published several lurid, horror comic-book series, including *Tales from the Crypt*, but toned down the illustrations after the Senate held hearings probing the influence of comics on teenage violence (1954). In 1952 he launched *Mad* comic book (expanded into the monthly *Mad* magazine, 1954), the brainchild of artist Harvey Kurtzman (1924–1993), who served as editor until 1955. Featuring the grinning, gap-toothed cover boy Alfred E. Neuman, whose motto was "What, me worry?," *Mad* lampooned every aspect of modern mainstream culture and had an immediate appeal to teenagers and college students. *Mad* exerted a powerful influence on U.S. popular culture for decades and reached a circulation high of more than 2.3 million copies in 1973. Gaines remained publisher of the magazine until shortly before his death. ▪ See Frank Jacobs, *The Mad World of William M. Gaines* (1973), and Maria Reidelbach, *Completely Mad* (1992).

GAITÁN, JORGE ELIÉCER (1898–1948), Colombian political leader. A leader of the left wing of the Liberal party, Gaitán was a champion of the Colombian masses who served as mayor of Bogotá (1936), minister of education, and minister of labor. He was famed as an orator and was a professor of criminal law. Although he ran unsuccessfully for president (1946), he gained control of the Liberal party (1947) and was expected to be elected Colombia's next president. He was assassinated in 1948, however, and his death led to widespread rioting in Bogotá. He was subsequently revered as a Liberal martyr.

GAITSKELL, HUGH TODD NAYLOR (1906–1963), British political leader. Gaitskell taught political economy at the University of London, served in the ministry of economic warfare during World War II, and entered Parliament as a Labourite in 1945. He rose rapidly and served as chancellor of the Exchequer (1950–51). He was elected Labour party treasurer (1951–55) and succeeded Clement Attlee as party leader (1955–63). When the 1960 party conference supported unilateral nuclear disarmament, he opposed it, and in 1961 the party reversed its decision. In 1962, he spoke against Britain's entry into the Common Market. He was undisputed leader of his party at the time of his sudden death. ▪ See Geoffrey McDermott, *Leader Lost* (1971).

GAJDUSEK, DANIEL CARLETON (1923–   ), U.S. medical scientist. The versatile D. Carleton Gajdusek was a virologist, pediatrician, anthropologist, linguist, and the adoptive father of 16 boys from the Pacific Islands. In 1957 he spent 10 months with a primitive tribe in New Guinea to study *kuru*, a fatal disease of the nervous system; he determined that it was caused by a virus transmitted by cannibalism. For his research on the origin and dissemination of infectious diseases, Gajdusek, who worked at the National Institutes of Health (1958–97) shared the 1976 Nobel Prize in Physiology or Medicine with Baruch Blumberg. ▪ See Richard Rhodes, *Deadly Feasts* (1997).

GALARZA, ERNESTO (1905–1984), Mexican-born U.S. labor leader and scholar. Brought to the United States by his family at age 6, Galarza was an agricultural worker in his youth. He graduated from Stanford University (M.A. 1929) and Columbia (Ph.D. 1946) and was chief of labor and social information of the Pan-American Union (1940–47). Thereafter he focused on the problems of farm workers in the United States and was an organizer, director of research and education, and eventually vice president of the National Farm Labor Union (1947–55) and secretary of the National Agriculture Workers Union (1955–60). He was also counsel to the U.S. House of Representatives Committee on Education and Labor and served on the U.S. Civil Rights Commission. Many of his writings, including *Strangers in Our Fields* (1956) and *Merchants of Labor* (1964), exposed abuses of the bracero system, under which Mexican farm workers were permitted to enter the United States. In the 1960s and 1970s he taught at several universities, was active in the bilingual education movement, and was honored as a pioneer in Mexican-American studies. His other books included *Spiders in the House and Workers in the Field* (1970), *Farm Workers and Agri-business in California, 1947–60* (1977), and the autobiographical *Barrio Boy* (1971).

GALBRAITH, JOHN KENNETH (1908–   ), Canadian-born U.S. economist and writer, Galbraith emigrated to the United States in 1931 and studied at the University of California, Berkeley (Ph.D. 1934). He was an administrator with the Office of Price Administration (OPA) during World War II

(1941–43), an editor of *Fortune* magazine (1943–48), and a professor of economics at Harvard (1949–75). He also served as U.S. ambassador to India (1961–63). In his numerous popular books, which reflected his humanistic and liberal outlook as well as his sardonic wit, he challenged traditional economic orthodoxies and the myth of the classic market economy. He emphasized the power of large corporations and their ability to transcend market forces, and noted the convergent paths of capitalist and socialist societies as a result of high levels of production and the growth of technology. His books included *The Affluent Society* (1958), *The New Industrial State* (1967), *Economics and the Public Purpose* (1973), *Money* (1975), *The Age of Uncertainty* (1977), *The Galbraith Reader* (1979), *The Anatomy of Power* (1983), *The Culture of Contentment* (1992), *The Good Society* (1996), and *Name-Dropping* (1999). ■ See his memoirs, *A Life in Our Times* (1981); C. Lynn Munro, *The Galbraithian Vision* (1979); and study by David A. Reisman (1980).

GALLAND, ADOLF (1912–1996), German military leader. A former commercial pilot, Galland flew 300 missions for Germany's Condor Legion during the Spanish Civil War and was credited with 103 air kills during World War II. He became head of the Fighter Arm (1941) and at the age of 30 he became the youngest major general in the German military. He was relieved of command (Jan. 1945) after disputes with his superiors. Shot down in 1945 and held prisoner for two years, Galland went to Argentina in 1948 as an adviser to the aeronautics ministry. He returned to West Germany in 1955 as a candidate for commander of the newly rearmed air force but instead became an aeronautics consultant. He wrote the autobiographical *The First and the Last* (Eng. trans. 1954) and *The Luftwaffe at War: 1939–45* (with K. Ries and R. Ahnert; Eng. trans. 1973). ■ See Raymond F. Toliver, *Fighter General* (1990) and the biography by David Baker (1996).

GALLEGOS, ROMULO (1884–1969), Venezuelan political leader and novelist. A high school and college teacher, Gallegos wrote several realistic social-protest novels that attacked economic exploitation and superstition and defended Indians and blacks. He was best known for *Doña Bárbara* (1929; Eng. trans. 1931), which explored the clash between intuitive, primitive existence and cultivated civilization. After the death of dictator Juan Vicente Gómez (1935), Gallegos served briefly as minister of education (1936), founded the Democratic Action party (1941), and served as the first popularly elected president of Venezuela (1948). His reformist government, however, was overthrown by the military after nine months in office, and he lived in exile in Mexico for 10 years before returning home. ■ See study by Lowell Dunham (1974).

GALLI-CURCI, AMELITA (Amelita Galli; 1882–1963), Italian opera singer. Completely self-taught, Galli-Curci made her debut in Rome (1909) and for the next two decades reigned as the world's unsurpassed coloratura soprano. Her brilliant golden voice and the effortlessness of her singing caused a sensation at her American debut (Chicago, 1916) and she had triumphant careers at both the Chicago Opera (1916–24) and New York's Metropolitan Opera (1921–30). She concertized throughout the world and made more than 144 recordings, notably "Caro nome" from *Rigoletto* and "The Bell Song" from *Lakmé*. After her retirement, due to a throat ailment, she settled in California and became a devotee of Hindu mysticism. ■ See C. E. Le Massena, *Galli-Curci's Life of Song* (1945).

GALLIÉNI, JOSEPH SIMON (1849–1916), French general. After graduating from St. Cyr military academy in 1870, Galliéni spent most of his military career in France's colonies, furthering his belief in conquest as a means of spreading French civilization. He conquered western Sudan (1886), served in Indochina (1892–96), and in 1896 became governor-general of the new colony of Madagascar, where he put down a rebellion in 1905. Galliéni retired in 1914 but was recalled the first year of World War I to defend Paris against German attack. He served as minister of war (1915–16) and was posthumously promoted marshal of France.

GALLIMARD, GASTON (1881–1975), French publisher. A dilettante scion of a wealthy Parisian family, Gallimard entered the publishing world as the cofounder, with André Gide and Jean Schlumberger, of the literary review *La Nouvelle Revue Française* (1908), which established itself as one of France's most influential intellectual journals. In 1911 they founded a firm, called Librairie Gallimard after 1919, which published such writers as Gide, Albert Camus, Paul Claudel, Guillaume Apollinaire, Paul Valéry, Antoine de Sant-Exupéry, André Malraux, Jean Paul Sartre, Marcel Proust, Roger Martin du Gard, Louis Aragon, and Simone de Beauvoir and was regarded as France's most important publishing house. By the time of Gallimard's death, the company was publishing 250 volumes a year, and its authors had won 25 Goncourt Prizes. ■ See biography by Pierre Assouline (1984; Eng. trans. 1988).

GALLUP, GEORGE HORACE (1901–1984), U.S. public-opinion analyst. A professor of journalism at Drake (1929–31) and Northwestern (1931–32) universities, Gallup developed techniques for measuring reader response to media. He worked for the advertising firm of Young and Rubicam in New York (1932–47) and in 1935 launched his American Institute of Public Opinion, which quickly gained stature by correctly predicting the outcome of the 1936 U.S. presidential election. Gallup continued to refine his survey methods and expanded into 30 countries with grass-roots polls on everything from new products to social and economic issues. ■ See his *Pulse of Democracy* (1940), *The Gallup Poll: Public Opinion, 1935–1971* (3 vols., 1972), and *The Sophisticated Poll Watcher's Guide* (rev. ed. 1976).

GALSWORTHY, JOHN (1867–1933), British novelist and dramatist. Galsworthy practiced law before turning to writing. His fame rests on his novels about the Forsyte family, which represented to Galsworthy some of the worst and most typical attributes of late Victorian and Edwardian England: a hypocritical business-oriented upper-middle class ruled by desire for money, acquisition, and property rights. The career of this fictional family was traced in three trilogies: *The Forsyte Saga* (1906–21), *A Modern Comedy* (1924–28), and *End of the Chapter* (1931–33). By the end of the series, however, Galsworthy had softened his original satirical intent. He also wrote many plays focusing on social inequalities. He was awarded the Nobel Prize in Literature in 1932. ▪ See Dudley Barker, *The Man of Principle* (1963), and studies by Catherine Dupré (1976) and James J. Gindin (1987).

GALTUNG, JOHAN (1930–), Norwegian peace researcher. Galtung, the son of a doctor, was born into an aristocratic Norwegian family. His lifelong commitment to peace and social justice was influenced by his experience of living under German occupation during World War II, the progressive traditions of his native society, and the writings on nonviolence of Indian leader Mahatma Gandhi. He was a student of philosophy, sociology, and mathematics, and served six months in prison for his opposition (1951) to compulsory military training. Galtung subsequently wrote prolifically on peace issues and was a pioneer in the academic field of peace studies. He was the founding director of the International Peace Research Institute, Oslo (1959–69), and the founding editor of the *Journal of Peace Research* (1964–74). He was a professor of conflict and peace research at the University of Oslo (1969–77) and taught at more than a dozen universities around the world. He also set up (with Robert Jungk) the first International Conference on Futurism (1967). He wrote or edited more than 50 books, including *Essays in Peace Research* (5 vols., 1974–80), *The Two Worlds* (1980), *There Are Alternatives* (1984), and *Peace by Peaceful Means* (1996). ▪ See Peter Lawler, *A Question of Values* (1995).

GÁLVEZ, MANUEL (1882–1962), Argentine novelist, Gálvez studied law, was an inspector of secondary schools in Argentina (1906–31), cofounded the literary journal *Ideas* (1903), and established (1917) a large publishing concern. His documented, realistic novels attracted a wide readership with their down-to-earth style. His best-known works included *The Schoolmistress* (1914), *Metaphysical Anguish* (1916), *Holy Wednesday* (1930; Eng. trans. 1934), and *Nacha Regules* (1919; Eng. trans. 1922). He also wrote histories and biographies. ▪ See study by Myron I. Lichtblau (1972).

GALWAY, JAMES (1939–), Irish flute virtuoso. Born into a working-class Belfast family, Galway was given his first flute at the age of 8 and studied informally with his father and paternal grandfather. He was a scholarship student at the Royal College of Music in London (1956–59) and the Paris Conservatory (1960–61). He spent the next 15 years as an instrumentalist with leading orchestras, including the Royal Philharmonic Orchestra (1967–69) and the Berlin Philharmonic (1969–75), before launching a spectacular career as a soloist in 1975. Known for his enormous range, unusually sweet and pure tone, remarkable agility, and eclectic repertory, he gained a huge cult following appearing with orchestras throughout the world and recording dozens of albums and CDs. He wrote *Flute* (1982) and an autobiography (1978).

GAMBINO, CARLO (1902–1976), Italian-born U.S. racketeer. Gambino sailed (1921) from Sicily to the United States as a stowaway. He soon joined the Mafia organization of Joseph (Joe the Boss) Masseria; he rose in the organization and became (1957) boss of a powerful crime family when Albert Anastasia was murdered, reputedly on orders by Gambino. As head of the country's largest, richest Mafia family, he was the central figure in American organized crime, overseeing a thousand men and extensive operations ranging from narcotics and gambling to labor racketeering. In a half century of criminal activities, he served less than two years in prison when he was convicted (1937) for operating a million-gallon still. In his last years, a heart condition prevented prosecution or deportation. He died of natural causes.

GAMELIN, MAURICE GUSTAVE (1872–1958), French general. Member of a distinguished French military family, Gamelin graduated first in his class from St. Cyr military academy (1893). As chief of staff to Marshal Joseph Joffre during World War I, he was credited with planning the successful defense of Paris and turning the tide at the Battle of the Marne (1914). Named chief of staff of the national defense (1938), he was commander of the French and British forces during the first nine months of World War II. A cautious and pessimistic military planner and an authority on Napoleonic battles, Gamelin was blamed for France's tragic reliance on the Maginot Line and the army's rapid collapse in 1940. He was arrested by the Vichy government that year and later interned by the Germans.

GAMOW, GEORGE (1904–1968), Russian-born U.S. physicist. Gamow did research in nuclear physics at the universities of Leningrad, Göttingen, Copenhagen, and Cambridge before emigrating to the United States, where he taught at George Washington University (1934–56) and the University of Colorado (1956–68). A renowned cosmologist, he was one of the leading exponents of the "big bang" theory of the origin of the universe. He also developed the quantum theory of radioactivity and proposed the existence of a genetic code determined by units of deoxyribonucleic acid (DNA). He was best known to the public as the author of numerous books that explained abstract concepts of modern science to the layperson, including *Mr. Tompkins Explores the Atom* (1944), *One, Two, Three . . . Infinity* (1947), *The Creation of the Universe* (1952), *A Star Called the Sun* (1964), and *Thirty Years That Shook Physics: The Story of Quantum Theory* (1966). ■ See his autobiography, *My World Line* (1970).

GANCE, ABEL (1889–1981), French film director. An actor, screenwriter, and playwright, Gance directed his first film in 1911 and achieved critical and commercial success with *Mater Dolorosa* ("Mother of Sorrow"; 1917) and *La Dixième Symphonie* ("Tenth Symphony"; 1918). A technical innovator, he was influenced by U.S. pioneer D. W. Griffith and was best known for three highly acclaimed epics: *J'accuse* ("I Accuse"; 1918), a sensational antiwar film; *La Roue* ("The Wheel"; 1922), a five-hour movie about the mechanization of modern life; and his best-known film, *Napoléon* (1926), which featured extensive use of the handheld camera, wide-angle photography, and triple-screen projection. His later films included *Austerlitz* (1960) and *Cyrano et d'Artagnan* (1963). ■ See biography by Steven Kramer and James Welsh (1978).

GANDHI, INDIRA (Indira Nehru; 1917–1984), Indian political leader. The only child of nationalist leader Jawaharlal Nehru, Gandhi was educated at Oxford and became an activist in the nationalist Indian Congress party (1938). In 1942 she married a Parsi lawyer, Feroze Gandhi (1913–60), no relation to Mahatma Gandhi. During her father's years as independent India's first prime minister (1947–64), she served as his official political hostess and confidante and was elected president of the Congress party (1959). Chosen by party leaders to be prime minister after the sudden death of Lal Bahadur Shastri (1966), Gandhi surprised the old-line political professionals who thought that they could control her, and she emerged as a powerful, decisive, independent, and popular ruler. However, as economic conditions worsened and a high court ruled that she had misappropriated funds, Gandhi declared a state of emergency (June 1975), arrested political opponents, and ruled by decree. Her popularity plummeted and she was decisively defeated by the coalition Janata party in the 1977 elections. However, the party was unable to rule effectively and Gandhi was swept back into power in the 1980 elections. Violent political agitation for an autonomous Sikh state in the Punjab resulted in her ordering the army to storm the Golden Temple in Amritsar, the Sikhs' holiest shrine (June 1984). Hundreds died in the attack. In retaliation she was assassinated by Sikh members of her bodyguard unit in her New Delhi compound. She was succeeded as prime minister by her son Rajiv Gandhi (1944–1991). ■ See study by Mary C. Carras (1979) and Pranay Gupte, *Vengeance* (1985).

GANDHI, MOHANDAS KARAMCHAND (1869–1948), Indian political and spiritual leader. Gandhi came from a wealthy Gujarati family and practiced law in Britain, India,

and South Africa. In South Africa (1893–1914) he became celibate, lived in voluntary poverty, and resolved to dedicate his life to the betterment of his people. Returning to India (1915) he joined the freedom movement and became a guiding force in the Indian National Congress party (president, 1924–34), transforming it into a mass organization. During major campaigns (1920–22; 1930–34; 1940–42) he initiated fasts, protest marches, strikes, boycotts, and other means of nonviolent civil disobedience and noncooperation toward the British in order to gain complete independence. He was repeatedly arrested for his activities. Opposed to industrialization and urbanization, he idealized the self-sufficient village and promoted cottage industries and agrarian reform. Known as the Mahatma ("Great Soul"), he attempted to foster Hindu-Muslim cooperation and improve the status of untouchables, and he became a worldwide symbol of pacifism, tolerance, and spirituality. Shortly after Indian independence (1947), which he helped negotiate, he was assassinated by a Hindu extremist. ■ See biographies by Louis Fischer (1950) and Robert Payne (1969); Joan V. Bondurant, *Conquest of Violence* (1965); and Erik H. Erikson, *Gandhi's Truth* (1969).

GANDHI, RAJIV (1944–1991), Indian political leader. The grandson of Jawaharlal Nehru and son of Indira Gandhi, both of whom served as prime ministers of India, Rajiv Gandhi eschewed a political career, studied mechanical engineering in London and Cambridge, and worked as a pilot for Indian Airlines (1972–81). However, after the accidental death of his politically active younger brother Sanjay (1980), he gave up his career and became an aide to his mother, the head of the government. He was elected to the lower house of Parliament (1981), became the leader of the Congress party (1983), and gained a reputation as a moderate reformer and technocrat. After his mother's assassination (October 1984) he was named prime minister by the cabinet and subsequently led his party to a landslide election victory (December 1984). As prime minister (1984–89) Gandhi was pragmatic and flexible and attempted to liberalize the Indian economy and reach accords and various regional and religious factions. However, his last years in office were marred by renewed political and ethnic factionalism, bribery and corruption scandals, and negative reaction to his (1987) decision to send Indian troops to intervene in the civil war in Sri Lanka. Gandhi led his party to defeat in the 1989 general elections, and he was assassinated while campaigning to regain power during the election campaign of 1991. ■ See biography by Nicholas Nugent (1990).

GANNETT, FRANK ERNEST (1876–1957), U.S. newspaper editor and publisher. A graduate of Cornell University (B.A. 1898), Gannett began a newspaper career as city editor of the *Ithaca Daily News*. In 1906, he became editor and part-owner of the *Elmira Star-Gazette*, launching a communications chain that ultimately controlled four radio stations, three television stations, and 22 newspapers (including the

Brooklyn Eagle and the *Rochester Times-Union,* his base. A candidate for the Republican presidential nomination in 1940 (which he lost to Wendell Willkie), Gannett was a conservative who opposed the New Deal and U.S. involvement abroad. ■ See biography by Samuel T. Williamson (1940).

GAO XINGJIAN (1940–), Chinese-born writer. A native of Jiangxi province, Gao received a degree in French from the Institute of Foreign Languages in Beijing (1962) and he was forced to spend six years in the countryside during the Cultural Revolution. Beginning in 1979 he published numerous essays and short stories reflecting both his skepticism and his linguistic ingenuity. His experimental plays, which championed the individual's struggle against the masses, were influenced by the modernism and absurdism of Western writers as well as by the traditions of Chinese theater and opera. His play *Bus Stop* (1983) was denounced by Communist party officials and Gao was placed under surveillance. After his play *The Other Shore* (1986; Eng. trans. 1999) was banned he left China (1987) and settled in France. His other works were banned after the publication of the play *Fugitives* (Eng. trans. 1993) whose backdrop was the bloody suppression of the 1989 Tiananmen Square demonstrations. Gao's most significant work was *Soul Mountain* (1990; Eng. trans. 1999), a massive, impressionistic novel based on his 10-month walk along the Yangtze River. In the novel Gao utilized a variety of styles, techniques, and viewpoints to describe an individual's search for inner harmony and freedom. He was awarded the 2000 Nobel Prize in Literature.

GARAUDY, ROGER (1913–), French philosopher. The leading intellectual and theoretician of the French Communist party during the 1950s and 1960s, Garaudy served as a parliamentary deputy (1946–51; 56–58) and senator (1959–62) and was a professor of philosophy at Clermont-Ferrand (1962–65) and Poitiers (1965–73). A member of the Politburo of the party (1956–70), he modified his once dogmatically orthodox party-line views during the late 1950s and by the late 1960s was criticizing Soviet bureaucratic centralism and intervention in Czechoslovakia. He also advocated a Christian-Marxist dialogue and argued for an opening of the party to technical and scientific workers and students. Branded a revisionist, he was expelled from the party in 1970. Late in life he converted to Islam, and many of his books of the 1980s and 1990s involved Islamic and Arabic issues. His numerous books included *Marxism in the Twentieth Century* (1966; Eng. trans. 1970), *A Christian-Communist Dialogue* (with Quentin Lauer, 1968), *The Crisis in Communism: The Turning Point of Socialism* (1969; Eng. trans. 1970), *The Alternative Future: A Vision of Christian Marxism* (1972; Eng. trans. 1974), and *The Mythical Foundations of Israeli Policy* (1996; Eng. trans. 1997).

GARBO, GRETA (Greta Gustafsson; 1905–1990), Swedish-born U.S. film actress. A shopgirl at age 14 and bathing beauty at 16, Garbo won a scholarship to Stockholm's Royal Dramatic Theater School. After two European films she moved (1925) to Hollywood, where she remained until her retirement in 1941. With her sculptured face, brooding eyes, and seductive voice, Garbo has been called the essence of a "star": magical but remote and unattainable. Most of her films were about ill-fated love affairs: *Mata Hari* (1931), *Queen Christina* (1933), *Anna Karenina* (1935), and *Camille* (1937). *Ninotchka* (1939), on the other hand, was a successful comedy. Despite repeated efforts to lure her out of retirement to play such roles as Sarah Bernhardt and George Sand, Garbo remained a legendary recluse. ■ See biographies by John Bainbridge (1971), Alexander Walker (1980), Antoni Gronowicz (1990), Barry Paris (1995), and Karen Swenson (1997); and Frederick Sands and Sven Broman, *Divine Garbo* (1979).

GARCÍA, CARLOS P. (1896–1971), Filipino political leader. A lawyer and governor of Bohol province (1933–41), García spent the years during World War II as an underground guerilla leader fighting the Japanese. After 1945 he rose quickly in government; by 1953 he was vice president, becoming president four years later upon the death of Ramón Magsaysay. García's foreign policy as president (1957–61) was staunchly anticommunist and pro-American. Domestically, he advocated Philippine economic independence from foreign (especially American) influence.

GARCÍA LORCA, FEDERICO (1898–1936), Spanish poet and dramatist. García Lorca gained an international reputation with his daring *Gypsy Ballads* (1928; Eng. trans. 1953), combining ballad and popular forms with avant-garde technique. He visited New York in the midst of an emotional crisis; his *Poet in New York* (1940; Eng. trans. 1955) was published posthumously, due to its homosexual themes. He returned (1930) to Spain, directing the experimental La Barraca theater troupe and writing such dramas as *Yerma* (1934, Eng. trans. 1945), *The House of Bernarda Alba* (1936; Eng. trans. 1947), and *Blood Wedding* (1938; Eng. trans. 1939). He continued to write poetry, including the long *Lament for the Death of a Bullfighter* (1935; Eng. trans. 1937). At the outbreak of the Spanish Civil War (1936), he returned to his native Granada and was taken into custody by nationalist forces, apparently because of his personal ties and sympathy with the loyalist cause. He was shot on Aug. 19, 1936, by a Falangist firing squad. His personal charm and dramatic death inflated his popularity; he is the most translated Spanish poet. ■ See his *Selected Letters* (1984); the study by Carl W. Cobb (1967); biographies by Mildred Adams (1977) and Leslie Stainton (1999); Ian Gibson, *The Assassination of Federico García Lorca* (1979); and Francisco García Lorca, *In the Green Morning: Memories of Federico* (Eng. trans. 1986).

GARCÍA MÁRQUEZ, GABRIEL (1928–), Colombian writer. A leading figure of the renaissance of Latin American literature that began in the 1960s, García Márquez was born and raised by grandparents in northern Colombia, studied law, and became a foreign correspondent. A political leftist (and friend of Cuban leader Fidel Castro), he lived mainly in Mexico after 1961. He created the fictional backwater town of Macondo in intricate fiction that mixed elements of the fantastic with social realism. The stories in *Leaf Storm* (1955; Eng. trans. 1972) and *No One Writes to the Colonel* (1961; Eng. trans. 1968) were preludes to his landmark novel, *One Hundred Years of Solitude* (1967; Eng. trans. 1970), which chronicles Macondo's history. It sold in the millions of copies and made readers throughout the world more receptive to Latin American writers. *The Autumn of the Patriarch* (1975; Eng. trans. 1976), a strange, haunting novel, portrays a tyrant who sells out to imperialist interests. The novella *Chronicle of a Death Foretold* (1981; Eng. trans. 1983), a murder tale that critics called a classic of that genre, investigates why two young men carry out a murder they did not want to commit. García Márquez wrote a column that was syndicated in many Spanish-language newspapers. He won the 1982 Nobel Prize in Literature. His later works included the novels *Love in the Time of Cholera* (1985; Eng. trans. 1988) and *The General in His Labyrinth* (1989; Eng. trans. 1990) and the nonfiction account *News of a Kidnapping* (1996; Eng. trans. 1997). In 1999 he bought the Bogotá newsweekly *Cambio* and joined its reporting staff. ■ See studies by Raymond L. Williams (1984) and G. H. McMurray (1977).

GARCÍA ROBLES, ALFONSO (1911–1991), Mexican diplomat. García Robles studied law in Mexico City, Paris, and the Hague before joining the Mexican foreign service (1939). He was a member of the Mexican delegation at the San Francisco Conference that founded the United Nations (1945) and worked in the U.N. Secretariat (1946–57). Alarmed by the Cuban missile crisis (1962), he began a personal international crusade for nuclear disarmament, and as Mexican undersecretary for foreign affairs (1964–71), he sponsored the Treaty of Tlatelolco (1967), which was intended to create a nuclear-free zone in Latin America. He also coauthored the 1968 Nuclear Nonproliferation Treaty, served as Mexico's foreign minister (1975–76), and represented Mexico at the U.N. (1971–75) and at the U.N. Disarmament Commission in Geneva (from 1977). He shared the 1982 Nobel Peace Prize with Alva Myrdal.

GARDEL, CARLOS (1890–1935), French-born Argentinian singer. The world's most famous singer of tangos, Gardel first achieved fame in Buenos Aires in the 1910s and was at the peak of his popularity during the 1920s and early 1930s. Through concert appearances, 900 recordings, and roles in numerous motion pictures, he became a sensation throughout South America and Western Europe. Called "the tango made flesh," he was still remembered more than six decades after his death in a plane crash in Colombia. ■ See biography by Simon Collier (1986).

GARDEN, MARY (Mary Davidson; 1877–1967), Scottish opera singer. One of the leading sopranos of the early part of the century, Garden achieved fame for her portrayals, at the Paris Opéra Comique, of *Louise* (1900) and Mélisande in *Pelléas et Mélisande* (1902), a role that Debussy created for her. She made her U.S. debut in *Thaïs* (1907) and became known for her temperament as well as her acting and singing abilities. Among her most noted characterizations were the title roles in *Tosca* and *Salome*. Garden was closely associated with opera in Chicago (1910–31) and directed the Chicago Opera Association (1921–22). ■ See her autobiography (1951) and biography by Michael Turnbull (1997).

GARDNER, ERLE STANLEY (1889–1970), U.S. novelist. As a very successful trial lawyer, Gardner was a defender of the poor. Long a contributor to pulp magazines, he devoted himself to full-time writing after the success of his first mystery featuring his hero, lawyer Perry Mason, in *The Case of the Velvet Claws* (1933). Though stylistically and artistically undistinguished, his intricately plotted mysteries sold more than 170 million copies in the United States alone. So prolific that he had to use several pseudonyms and was called the "fiction factory," Gardner wrote more than 140 mysteries, including 80 in the Perry Mason series. He was also the script supervisor for the popular *Perry Mason* television series (1957–66). ■ See biography by Dorothy B. Hughes (1978).

GARDNER, HOWARD (1943–), U.S. psychologist. Gardner, the son of German-Jewish immigrants from Nazi Germany, studied developmental psychology at Harvard (B.A. 1965; Ph.D. 1971) and specialized in the study of the evolution of human creativity. His work with brain-damaged adults at Boston's Veterans Administration Hospital (1972–) and with children as codirector of Harvard's Project Zero (1973–), led to the publication of *Artful Scribbles: The Significance of Children's Drawings* (1980) and *The Shattered Mind: The Person After Brain Damage* (1975). Convinced that human intelligence is complex and not a single faculty that can be measured by an IQ test, he proposed that humans have seven types of intelligence (verbal, mathematical, spatial, musical, physical, social, and self-knowledge), and that all must be addressed in schools. (He subsequently added spiritual, or "existential," intelligence to his list.) His controversial theory of multiple intelligences, presented in *Frames of Mind* (1984) and elaborated upon in *The Unschooled Mind* (1991), *Multiple Intelligences* (1993), and *The Disciplined Mind* (1999), influenced educational theory and planning in the United States. Gardner was a professor at Boston University School of Medicine (1979–87) and a professor of education at Harvard (1987–). His book *To Open Minds* (1989) contains autobiographical information.

GARDNER, JOHN WILLIAM (1912–), U.S. educator and public official. Having earned a Ph.D. in psychology from Stanford (1938), Gardner served with the Office of

Strategic Services during World War II, after which he joined the Carnegie Corp. As president of Carnegie (1955–65) he funded educational projects. Gardner was appointed U.S. secretary of health, education, and welfare by Pres. Lyndon B. Johnson in 1965, resigning in 1968 to head the National Urban Coalition, a private antipoverty organization. In 1970 he founded Common Cause (chairman 1970–77), a nonpartisan citizens' lobby group that opposed the Vietnam War and the B-1 bomber and supported full disclosure of campaign contributions and reform of the seniority system of the House of Representatives. He later taught at Stanford University (1989–96). His books included *Excellence* (1961; rev. ed. 1984), *The Recovery of Confidence* (1970), *In Common Cause* (1972), *Morale* (1978), and *On Leadership* (1990).

GARFUNKEL, ART. *See SIMON AND GARFUNKEL.*

GARLAND, (HANNIBAL) HAMLIN (1860–1940), U.S. writer. Garland first achieved recognition for his realistic novels, short stories, and sketches depicting the harshness and oppression of farm life, including *Main-Travelled Roads* (1891), *Prairie Folks* (1893), and *Wayside Courtships* (1897). His volume of criticism, *Crumbling Idols* (1894), advocated literary realism, or "veritism." He is best remembered, however, for his popular autobiographical and nostalgic accounts of his midwestern upbringing, *A Son of the Middle Border* (1917) and *A Daughter of the Middle Border* (1921; Pulitzer Prize). *The Book of the American Indians* (1923), a collection of magazine articles, was one of the earliest accurate and sympathetic accounts of Indian life. ■ See biography by Jean Holloway (rev. ed. 1971) and study by Joseph B. McCullough (1978).

GARLAND, JUDY (Frances Gumm; 1922–1969), U.S. singer and actress. As a toddler she appeared onstage with her vaudevillian parents; she later toured as one of the three Gumm Sisters. Garland was a film star by age 16, costarring with Mickey Rooney in the popular Andy Hardy films. She won a special Academy Award for her affecting performance in *The Wizard of Oz* (1939); its Arlen-Harburg song "Over the Rainbow" became her theme song. In the 1940s she made such box-office hits as *For Me and My Gal, Meet Me in St. Louis,* and *Easter Parade.* Her best dramatic performance was in *A Star Is Born* (1954). She was often directed by her husband, Vincente Minnelli; their daughter Liza Minnelli (1946–) became an Academy Award–winning actress and singer. In the 1950s and 1960s Garland's career was intermittently disturbed by periods of severe depression and marital problems. She appeared in a weekly TV show that featured her dramatic delivery of pop tunes and torch songs (1963) but it was a commercial failure. She continued to appear in concerts but grew increasingly dependent on drugs and was frequently ill. Her death was attributed to an accidental overdose of sleeping pills. ■ See biography by Anne Edwards (1975); Christopher Finch, *Rainbow* (1975);

James Spada, *Judy and Liza* (1983); and Gerald Clarke, *Get Happy* (2000).

GARNEAU, (HECTOR DE) SAINT-DENYS (1912–1943), French-Canadian poet. Heart disease made Garneau an invalid in his twenties. After helping to establish the French-Canadian literary journal *Le Relève* (1934), he became increasingly reclusive, living with his parents after 1941. Only one volume of his introspective, musical poetry appeared in his lifetime; his collected poetry was published posthumously in 1949. His morbidity and manipulation of symbols set him apart from the regionalist writers of the time. ■ See his intimate *Journal (1935–39)* (Eng. trans. 1962) and *Complete Poems* (Eng. trans. 1975).

GARNER, HUGH (1913–1979), Canadian novelist and short-story writer. Garner served in the international brigade during the Spanish Civil War (1936–39). He first published his direct, painstaking fiction in 1936–37, but his writing did not appear again until after his World War II service. *Storm Below* (1949) was a realistic novel about the navy. His identification with the working class permeated *Cabbagetown* (1950; unabridged, 1968), *Present Reckoning* (1951), *A Nice Place to Visit* (1970), and *The Intruders* (1976). Short stories in which he immediately pinpointed character and rendered a sense of speech and place contained his best writing and were collected in *Hugh Garner's Best Stories* (1963), *Men and Women* (1966), and *Violation of the Virgins* (1971). *Author, Author!* (1964), is a collection of humorous essays. ■ See his autobiography, *One Damn Thing After Another* (1973), and study by Doug Fetherling (1972).

GARNER, JOHN NANCE (1868–1967), U.S. vice president. A master of manipulation, persuasion, and parliamentary procedure, "Cactus Jack" Garner represented West Texas as a Democrat in the U.S. House of Representatives for 30 years before serving as vice president for Pres. Franklin D. Roosevelt (1933–41). Although more conservative than Roosevelt, he helped push through much New Deal legislation, but he opposed Roosevelt's bid for a third term. After leaving the vice presidency, the controversial, plain-talking, poker-playing Garner retired from politics to live on his Texas ranch. ■ See biography by Bascom N. Timmons (1948).

GARROWAY, DAVE (1913–1982), U.S. television performer. During the late 1940s, Garroway hosted several radio shows each day, as well as a Sunday night variety show. His broad interests, knowledge of jazz, and his relaxed, intimate style attracted a loyal following. In his early "distracted-prose" style, he addressed listeners affectionately as "old delicate" or "my so unfrowsy." Moving to television in its early years ("Garroway at Large"; 1949–52), he was identified with the "Chicago school" of television, noted for its imaginative use of the medium on a low budget. His horn-rimmed glasses and bow tie became familiar to early morning audiences when he created and hosted the "Today Show" (1952–61), on which he shared the spotlight with chimpanzee J. Fred Muggs. He later hosted NBC's "Wide, Wide World" (1955–58), NET's "Exploring the Universe" (1962–63), and the "Dave Garroway Show" (1969–71). Depressed over a debilitating heart condition, he committed suicide.

GARST, ROSWELL (1898–1977), U.S. businessman and agriculturist. Garst headed a multimillion-dollar seed business and cattle farm in Coon Rapids, Iowa, and devoted his considerable energies to breaking farmers' resistance to agricultural innovation. He distributed and endorsed a hybrid form of corn developed by his friend Henry A. Wallace, spoke to rural gatherings about chemical fertilizers, insecticides, and synthetic protein, and proposed use of ground corncobs to feed cattle. When Nikita Khrushchev toured the United States (1959), he made a highly publicized visit to Garst's farm, and Garst subsequently advised Soviet and East European agriculturalists and advocated the sale of U.S. seed and equipment to their governments. ■ See biography by Harold Lee (1984).

GARSTANG, JOHN (1876–1956), British archaeologist. A professor of archaeology at the University of Liverpool (1907–41), Garstang was an authority on the ancient civilizations of Asia Minor, Palestine, and the Sudan. He excavated many biblical sites, including Jericho (1930–36), as well as the ancient trading city of Mersin (1937) in Turkey. His books included *The Land of the Hittites* (1910), *Meroë: The City of the Ethiopians* (1911), *The Foundations of Bible History: Joshua, Judges* (1931), and *Prehistoric Mersin* (1953).

GARTH, DAVID (1930–), U.S. political consultant. Garth's interest in politics grew out of a sickly childhood spent listening to the radio commentaries of H. V. Kaltenborn and Edward R. Murrow. In the late 1950s, he bluffed his way into a New York television station and offered a plan to televise local football games. Soon after, Garth was also producing public affairs programs for the station. His reputation as a media specialist dated from the New York mayoral campaign of John V. Lindsay (1965), when Garth filmed the candidate walking the city streets with rolled shirtsleeves, loosened tie, and coat slung over his shoulder. This type of "cinéma vérité" commercial was quickly adopted by other candidates, setting a standard for political advertising. Considered a shrewd and aggressive public relations expert, Garth took part in the campaigns of such Democrats as presidential candidate Walter Mondale, Sen. H. John Heinz 3rd, Governors Hugh Carey and Brendan Byrne, and Mayors Edward Koch and Tom Bradley. Garth's New York firm also handled public relations for large corporate clients.

GARVEY, MARCUS MOSIAH (1887–1940), Jamaican-born black nationalist. Garvey traveled widely before World War I and returned home to Jamaica in 1914 to found the black nationalist Universal Negro Improvement Association (UNIA). Two years later he traveled to New York, where he established UNIA branches, and a newspaper, *Negro World,* in which he argued for a return to Africa or, failing that, black economic independence. With Harlem as its center, Garvey's movement grew to claim a following of millions. During a 1920 UNIA convention, the charismatic spokesman for black unity, pride, and power was elected president of the Republic of Africa, a kind of government in exile. In 1923 Garvey was convicted of mail fraud in connection with his Black Star Shipping Line and deported to Jamaica (1927) after serving two years in prison. His movement dwindled during the Depression and he moved to London (1935), where he died in obscurity. ■ See his *Philosophy and Opinions* (2 vols.; repr. 1968–69) and *More Philosophy and Opinions* (1977); Edmund David Cronon, *Black Moses* (1935); studies by Garvey's wife Amy (1963), Elton C. Fax (1972), and Rupert Lewis (1988); and Judith Stein, *The World of Marcus Garvey* (1985). His papers were edited by Robert A. Hill (1983–).

GARY, ROMAIN (Romain Kacewgari; 1914–1980), Lithuanian-born French writer and diplomat. Gary was raised by his Jewish mother, a milliner and onetime actress who had used the stage name Gary. She took him to France when he was 14 years old. During World War II, Gary was a war hero, flying with Britain's Royal Air Force and later with the Free French forces. After the war he won critical recognition for *A European Education* (1945; Eng. trans. 1960), sketches about a Polish partisan group. He wrote numerous books on a wide range of topics (some under pseudonyms) and wrote and directed films. His novels, which championed humanistic values, included *Roots of Heaven* (1956; Eng. trans. 1958), set in a Nazi concentration camp, and *Momo* (1975; written under the pseudonym Emile Ajar), both of which won the prestigious Prix Goncourt. A member of the French diplomatic corps (1945–55), Gary was consul general in Los Angeles (1956–60). There he met U.S. actress Jean Seberg, whom he married and divorced. Gary killed himself at age 66, 15 months after Seberg's death. He had claimed that Seberg committed suicide after the FBI spread damaging rumors about her to discredit her support of the Black Panther party. Gary's essay, "The Life and Death of Emile Ajar" was published posthumously with the translation of his novel *King Solomon* (1979; Eng. trans. 1983).

GASSER, HERBERT SPENCER (1888–1963), U.S. physiologist. Gasser studied at the University of Wisconsin (B.A. 1910) and Johns Hopkins University (M.D. 1915). Collaborating with Joseph Erlanger at Washington University in St. Louis (1916–31) in the study of the electrical impulses carried by nerve fibers, he demonstrated, with the aid of an oscillograph, that nerve impulses are transmitted at different velocities depending on the thickness of the fibers along which they travel and showed that there are essential differences between sensory and motor nerves. They shared the 1944 Nobel Prize in Physiology or Medicine. From 1935 to 1953 Gasser headed the Rockefeller Institute (now Rockefeller University) in New York City.

GATES, BILL (William Henry Gates, III; 1955–), U.S. business executive. Born into a wealthy Seattle, Washington, family, Gates became fascinated with computers as a school boy and began writing computer programs while in high school. He dropped out of Harvard after his sophomore year and (with his friend and fellow computer enthusiast Paul Allen) founded Microsoft (1975) in order to commercially produce computer programs. Gates and Allen adapted the computer language BASIC to microcomputers and developed the Microsoft Disk Operating System (MC-DOS) for IBM personal computers. Microsoft subsequently developed the Windows operating system. By the late 1980s Microsoft was the world's leading software company, and Gates became a billionaire at age 31. In 1999 his net worth was estimated to be $100 billion, making him the world's richest person and the first to amass a 12-figure fortune. In the 1990s he established a philanthropic foundation and in 1999 announced a $1 billion scholarship program for minority college students. The U.S. government sued Microsoft for antitrust law violations (1998). A federal judge ruled (2000) that Microsoft had violated antitrust laws through monopolistic, anticompetitive, and predatory behavior and ordered that the company be split into two separate and competing organizations. Microsoft appealed the ruling. Gates wrote *The Road Ahead* (1995) and *Business @ the Speed of Thought* (1999). ■ See Gary Rivlin, *The Plot to Get Bill Gates* (1999).

GATTI-CASAZZA, GIULIO (1869–1940), Italian opera manager. Born into a musical family, Gatti-Casazza gave up an engineering career (1893) for a life in the theater. As general manager of La Scala in Milan (1898–1908), he introduced many non-Italian operatic classics, provided a stage for such contemporary Italian composers as Leoncavallo, Mascagni, and Puccini, and transformed La Scala into one of the great operatic theaters of the world. Called to New York (with conductor Arturo Toscanini) to preside over the Metropolitan Opera (1908–35), he greatly improved the quality of performance and introduced such stars as Maria Jeritza, Lawrence Tibbett, Rosa Ponselle, Lily Pons, and Kirsten Flagstad. He presented dozens of world premieres, produced the Met's first American operas, and arranged its first radio broadcasts. His successful policies, which enabled the Met to build up a large reserve fund during the 1920s, contributed greatly to the house's survival during the Depression years. ■ See his *Memories of the Opera* (1941).

GAUDÍ I CORNET, ANTONI (1852–1926), Spanish architect. Gaudí apprenticed with a blacksmith before studying architecture. Unknown outside his native Catalonia during his lifetime, Gaudí designed some of Barcelona's most striking buildings. Working in several styles over many decades, he created a body of highly original work that defies neat classification. Its consistent features were his emphasis on form, his fluidity of design, and his technical ingenuity. He was best known for the achievements of his late career, when he introduced startling concepts in the use of form, material, and color. He added a curvilinear facade to a conventional structure, creating the Casa Battló (1905–07); at the same time, he designed the Casa Milá (1905–19) in the Art Nouveau style. Gaudí took over plans for his most significant work, the church of the Sagrada Familia, from another architect, then spent much of his life working on it (particularly after 1910). Proceeding skyward from a fairly traditional lower part, he created an increasingly elaborate and expressive structure. It remained unfinished. ■ See biography by G. R. Collins (1960) and studies by J. J. Sweeny and J. L. Sert (1960) and Joan Bergós (1947; Eng. trans. 1999).

GAVILAN, KID (Gerardo González; 1926–), Cuban-born U.S. boxer. One of the most talented welterweight fighters of the post–World War II period, Gavilan began boxing in 1943 and was undefeated in his first 26 fights. In 1949 he lost a world welterweight title match to Sugar Ray Robinson, but in 1951 he won the crown and successfully defended it until 1953. A contender for the middleweight title in 1954, he lost to Bobo Olson. The same year he lost his welterweight crown to Johnny Saxton; he retired shortly thereafter.

GAYNOR, JANET (Laura Gainor; 1906–1984), U.S. film actress. Gaynor won the first Academy Award for best actress for her roles in three silent classics, *Seventh Heaven* (1927), *Sunrise* (1927), and *Street Angel* (1928). She was generally typecast as a demure, saucer-eyed waif in light, sentimental films, and was one of Hollywood's greatest box-office draws in the early 1930s. She managed at least one creditable dramatic role (in *A Star Is Born,* 1937) before her retirement in 1938.

GEDDES, NORMAN BEL (Norman Geddes; 1893–1958), U.S. theatrical and industrial designer. Geddes designed his first set for New York's Metropolitan Opera Company in 1918 and over the next three decades designed or produced over 100 operas, dramas, musical comedies, and films. His most representative set designs (such as *The Miracle,* 1923) departed from the naturalist tradition by featuring innovative lighting that intensified the mood of the production. He established an industrial design firm (1932) and his numerous functional designs of trains, automobiles, ocean vessels, appliances, and office and airplane interiors pioneered the "streamline" style. Also an architect, Geddes designed the Ukrainian State Opera House (Kharkov, USSR), the Roxy Theatre (New York City), and the General Motors Futurama Exhibit at the 1939–40 New York World's fair. ■ See his autobiographies *Horizons* (1932) and *Miracle in the Evening* (1960).

GEDDES, SIR PATRICK (1854–1932), Scottish sociologist, biologist, and town planner. Geddes was a botanist at Edinburgh and Dundee universities who brought the concepts of life science, particularly the relationship of human communities to the environment, to bear on town and regional planning. He coined the concepts of "megalopolis" and "kakatopia" in his classic *Cities in Evolution* (1915), and he was also engaged in the practical work of urban renovation in Scotland, Cyprus, India, and Palestine. Geddes also taught sociology and civics at the University of Bombay (1919–24). ■ See Philip Mairet, *Pioneer of Sociology* (1957); Paddy Kitchen, *A Most Unsettling Person* (1975); Philip Boardman, *The Worlds of Patrick Geddes* (1978); and biography by Helen E. Meller (1990).

GEERTZ, CLIFFORD JAMES (1926–), U.S. anthropologist. Educated at Antioch College (A.B. 1950) and Harvard (Ph.D. 1956), Geertz taught anthropology at the University of California (1958–60), the University of Chicago (1960–70), and Princeton's Institute for Advanced Study (from 1970). He did fieldwork in Java (1952–54), Bali (1957–58), and Morocco (1965–66). A scholar of great breadth in the social sciences and humanities, he stressed the diversity of mental experience, resisted structuralism as "a sort of high-tech rationalism," and took an interpretive approach to human behavior, viewing society as a text that one can explore as a literary critic might delve into a novel. Noting a revolution in "the way we think about the way we think," he played an important role in the debate about the nature and role of anthropology that began in the 1960s. Known for his elegant prose, Geertz wrote *The Religion of Java* (1960), *Person, Time and Conduct in Bali* (1966), *Islam Observed* (1968), and *Local Knowledge* (1983). *The Interpretation of Cultures* (1973) was an influential collection of essays. He also edited *Old Societies and New States* (1964). His later works included *Works and Lives: The Anthropologist as Author* (1988) and *After the Fact: Two Countries, Four Decades, One Anthropologist* (1995).

GEHLEN, REINHARD (1902–1979), German intelligence director. Gehlen served in World War I, then opted for a military career. Rising quickly, he joined the staff of the Nazi high command (1940), and from 1942 directed Adolf Hitler's military espionage against the Soviet Union. Anticipating Germany's eventual defeat, Gehlen began to amass and hide, in 50 steel chests, his most important files. Surrendering himself to the Americans at the war's end, he transferred to the Allies his exhaustive documentation of Soviet affairs and the vast spy network he had in place in Soviet-occupied areas. For nearly a decade he supplied the CIA with information that apparently overestimated the strength and belligerent intent of Soviet military forces in Europe and influenced U.S. Cold War policies. As chief of West German intelligence (1955–68), he functioned completely incognito, known only as "Number 30," "the doctor," and "the man without a face." His agents were very successful in infiltrating East German intelligence circles and dug a tunnel into East Berlin to tap communication lines to Moscow. He forecast the 1968 Soviet-led invasion of Czechoslovakia. His memoirs, *The Service* (1971; Eng. trans. 1972), sparked controversy by claiming that Nazi official Martin Bormann, one of Hitler's most trusted aides, had been a Soviet agent. ■ See Heinz Höhne and Hermann Zolling, *The General Was a Spy* (1971; Eng. trans. 1972); biography by E. H. Cookridge (1972); and study by Mary Ellen Reese (1990).

GEHRIG, LOU (Henry Louis Gehrig; 1903–1941), U.S. baseball player. Gehrig studied at Columbia University (1921–23) before becoming a professional athlete. Known as the "Iron Horse" for his remarkable stamina (he played in 2,130 consecutive major league games), he was one of baseball's greatest players and one of its legendary figures. As first baseman for the New York Yankees (1923–39)—and one of the team's fabled "Murderers' Row"—he compiled a .340 lifetime average, with 493 home runs, 1,990 runs batted in, 1,888 runs, and 2,721 hits. He was voted the American League's Most Valuable Player four times (1927, 1931, 1934, 1936) and set a league record for runs batted in with 184 (1931). A retiring, self-effacing man, he was overshadowed by his gregarious teammate Babe Ruth. Gehrig had his career cut short by a terminal form of sclerosis which has come to be known as "Lou Gehrig's disease." He was elected to the National Baseball Hall of Fame in 1939. ■ See Eleanor Gehrig, *My Luke and I* (1976; with Joseph Durso).

GEHRY, FRANK (Frank Goldberg; 1929–), Canadian-born U.S. architect. Gehry and his family moved from Toronto to Los Angeles (1947), where he studied architecture at the University of Southern California (B.A. 1954) and founded his own firm (1962). He emerged as a major force in American architecture in the late 1970s with his playful, freewheeling, human-scale building designs, which were praised for their creative use of color, space, and irregular geometrical forms. Gehry's celebrated buildings, which he saw as sculptural objects, included his own house (a refurbished Dutch colonial revival bungalow; 1977–78), the Los Angeles Children's Museum (1980), the Loyola Marymount University Law School (1981–84), the American Center in Paris (1994), an asymmetrical twin-towered office building in Prague (which he nicknamed "Fred and Ginger"; 1996), and the shimmering titanium-paneled Guggenheim Museum in Bilbao, Spain (1997). Gehry also designed furniture (made of corrugated cardboard) and numerous museum exhibitions in Los Angeles. He won the prestigious Pritzker Architecture Prize (1989). ■ See Mildred Friedman, ed., *Gehry Talks* (1999).

GEIGER, HANS WILHELM (1882–1945), German physicist. While researching radioactivity with Ernest Rutherford in Britain, Geiger devised (1908–13) the prototype of the Geiger counter, an instrument that measured the number of alpha particles emanating from radioactive materials. Redesigned (1928) by Geiger and W. Müller, the counter contained an ionization chamber in which the radioactive particles generated electrical impulses. These impulses were then amplified and registered either on an electroscope or as clicks. This instrument had wide application in such fields as medicine, geology, and industry. Geiger's experiments on the scattering of atomic particles facilitated Ernest Rutherford's elaboration of atomic structure. Geiger taught at several German universities and participated in Germany's abortive effort to develop an atomic bomb during World War II.

GEISEL, THEODOR SEUSS. *See SEUSS, DR.*

GELFAND, IZRAIL MOISEEVICH (1913–), Soviet mathematician. Gelfand worked (1932–91) at the center of a group of Moscow State University mathematicians whose research dealt mainly with functional analysis; he investigated aspects of ring theory and set theory. Gelfand also worked in the area of computational mathematics. In the course of his work, he became increasingly interested in problems of biology and physiology, particularly the principles governing the organization of neurophysiological systems. His books included *Lectures on Linear Algebra* (Eng. trans. 1964), *Neoplastic and Normal Cells in Culture* (Eng. trans. 1981; with J. M. Vasilieu), and *Discriminants, Resultants, and Multidimensional Determinants* (Eng. trans. 1994); and he edited *Structural-Functional Organization in Biological Systems* (Eng. trans. 1971).

GELFOND, ALEKSANDR OSIPOVICH (1906–1968), Soviet mathematician. A professor at Moscow State University (from 1931), Gelfond made fundamental contributions to the study of transcendental numbers. He also influenced the development of the theory of interpolation and approximation of functions of complex variables and advanced the study of the history of mathematics. His works included *Transcendental and Algebraic Numbers* (1952; Eng. trans. 1960).

GELL-MANN, MURRAY (1929–), U.S. physicist. A precocious genius, Gell-Mann entered Yale at age 15 and received his Ph.D. from the Massachusetts Institute of Technology at 21. While on the faculty of the University of Chicago (1952–54), he introduced (1953) the concept of "strangeness" to describe the decay patterns of newly discovered elementary particles. In a further effort to bring order to the world of subatomic physics, he developed (1961) a scheme of classifying elementary particles that he called "the Eightfold Way." Likened to the classification of the periodic table of the elements, Gell-Mann's grouping of particles was confirmed by the discovery of the Omega-minus particle (1965), and he won the 1969 Nobel Prize in Physics. Gell-Mann also hypothesized (with Richard P. Feynman) the existence of the "quark" as the fundamental building block of all matter. He was a professor at the California Institute of Technology (1954–93) and wrote *The Eightfold Way* (1964; with Yuval Ne'eman) and *The Quark and the Jaguar* (1994). During the 1980s he was a pioneer in the multidisciplinary study of simplicity and complexity, and he cofounded the Santa Fe (New Mexico) Institute (1993–). ■ See George Johnson, *Strange Beauty* (1999).

GEMAYEL, AMIN (1942–), Lebanese (Maronite Christian) political leader. Gemayel was the oldest son of Pierre Gemayel, the founder of the right-wing Phalange party, the political movement of the Maronite Christian community. A lawyer and newspaper publisher, he was elected to parliament in 1970. Considered a moderate within the Maronite leadership, he was elected president (by parliament) following the assassination of his brother Bashir Gemayel, the president-elect (1982). In spite of his reputation as a conciliator during the civil war, he was unable to reassert central government control over the warring factions of Lebanon, and real power remained in the hands of the private Shiite, Druze, and Christian militias. Gemayel sought to uphold the constitution, which established the political domination of the Maronites and the Sunni Muslims, and was bitterly opposed by Shiite and Druze leaders, and—in the mid-1980s—by dissident members of the Maronite militia leadership. After his term ended in 1988 he moved to France and was a leader of the Lebanese opposition in exile.

GEMAYEL, PIERRE (1905–1984), Lebanese (Maronite Christian) political leader. Trained as a pharmacist in Beirut and Paris, Gemayel founded the Phalange (1936), a right-wing political party and paramilitary organization, in order to protect the interests of the Maronite Christian community in Lebanon. A shrewd and influential power broker for five decades, he opposed the expansion of Muslim political power and the growth of Syrian influence in Lebanon, and was a foe of Arab nationalism. During the 1958 crisis he led the resistance to pro-Nasser forces and served in the caretaker government at the end of the crisis. Gemayel was a member of parliament (1960–84) and held several cabinet posts during the 1960s. He was opposed to the Palestinian "state within a state" in Lebanon during the 1970s and early 1980s and led the Phalange militia forces during the civil war (1975–76). After his youngest son Bashir, the president-elect, was assassinated (1982), his oldest son, Amin, was elected president by the parliament (1982). Pierre Gemayel served in the national unity government in 1984.

GENEEN, HAROLD SYDNEY (1910–1997), U.S. business executive. When Geneen—an accountant with a photographic memory and a genius for organization—accepted the presidency of International Telephone and Telegraph Corp. (1959) at age 49, he had already established his business acumen by leading the Raytheon Manufacturing Co. out of serious financial difficulties (1956–59). Over the next 17 years, Geneen reorganized the loosely knit holding company, imposing strict divisional accountability and effecting his fabled accounting efficiencies in its increasingly diversified operations. By 1977, ITT was one of the largest multinational conglomerates, controlling more than 350 companies (including manufacturing companies, publishing houses, Avis Rent-A-Car, Sheraton hotels, the Hartford Fire Insurance Co., and Twinkies) in 80 countries with sales topping $16.7 billion. In 1975 a Senate committee reported that ITT gave $350,000 to opponents of Salvador Allende during the 1970 Chilean election campaign after Allende promised to nationalize ITT's Chilean Telephone Co. if his left-wing Popular Unity party came to power. ■ See his book, *Managing* (1984; with Alvin Moscow); Anthony Sampson, *The Sovereign State of ITT* (1980); and the biography by Robert J. Schoenberg (1985).

GENET, JEAN (1910–1986), French novelist and dramatist. Genet, who was abandoned soon after birth, spent much of his adolescent and adult life in prison, where he began to write. His novels, notably *Miracle of the Rose* (1946; Eng. trans. 1965) and *Thief's Journal* (1949; Eng. trans. 1964), superimpose rich, poetic language and fantastic imagery upon the brutal realities of homosexual prison life. Turning conventional morality upside down, he exalts the deeds of criminals and social outcasts. His first novel, *Our Lady of the Flowers* (1944; Eng. trans. 1963), features an obsessive quest for identity. This theme recurs in his plays *The Maids* (1948; Eng. trans. 1954), *The Balcony* (1956; Eng. trans. 1957), and *The Blacks* (1958; Eng. trans. 1960). Genet was hailed for his unflinching examination of the meaning of human values. ■ See Jean Paul Sartre, *Saint Genet* (1952; Eng. trans. 1963); Joseph H. McMahon, *The Imagination of Jean Genet* (1963); Richard N. Coe, *The Vision of Jean Genet* (1968); and studies by Bettina Knapp (1968) and Edmund White (1993).

GENOVESE, EUGENE DOMINICK (1930–), U.S. historian. The son of a Brooklyn dockworker, Genovese received a Ph.D. from Columbia University (1955) and studied the slavocracy of the American South from the standpoint of Marxist humanism. Using plantation records and slave memoirs, he examined the mutual interaction of master and slave in *Roll, Jordan, Roll* (1974). A frequent contributor to literary and scholarly journals, Genovese was a professor at the University of Rochester (New York; from 1969). His other books included *The Political Economy of Slavery* (1965); *The World the Slaveholders Made* (1969); *From Rebellion to Revolution* (1979); *Fruits of Merchant Capital: Slavery and Bourgeois Property in the Rise and Expansion of Capitalism* (1983; with Elizabeth Fox-Genovese); *The Slaveholder's Dilemma* (1992); and essays on the historiography of slavery, *The Southern Front* (1995).

GENSCHER, HANS-DIETRICH (1927–), German political leader. Born in eastern Germany, Genscher served in the army during World War II, and remained in the East after the war and studied law at Leipzig University. He fled to West Germany in 1952 and soon became a leader of the small but influential centrist political party, the Free Democrats. He was elected to parliament in 1965 and served as interior minister (1969–74) under Chancellor Willy Brandt. Later he was foreign secretary and deputy chancellor (1974–92) under Chancellors Helmut Schmidt and Helmut Kohl. He was best known for advocating European integration and closer German ties to the Soviet Union and Eastern Europe, and for playing a key role in the reunification of Germany (1990). ■ See his memoir, *Rebuilding a House Divided* (1995; Eng. trans. 1997).

GENTILE, GIOVANNI (1875–1944), Italian philosopher. Gentile taught philosophy at several universities and published extensively in *Critica*, the journal edited by Benedetto Croce. He formulated a neo-Hegelian philosophy known as actual idealism in *The Theory of Mind as Pure Act* (1916; Eng. trans. 1922), established (1920) the *Critical Journal of Italian Philosophy*, and oversaw work on a new *Italian Encyclopedia* (1925–43). He was also a public figure who became (1922) a senator; as minister of public instruction (1922–24), he restructured the educational system. Gentile, who early identified himself with fascist political doctrine, was considered its principal philosopher. He was shot by antifascist partisans. His other writings included *The Reform of Education* (Eng. trans. 1922) and *The Philosophy of Art* (Eng. trans. 1972). ■ See Roger W. Holmes, *The Idealism of Giovanni Gentile* (1937), and Henry S. Harris, *The Social Philosophy of Giovanni Gentile* (1960).

GEOFFRION, BERNIE (1931–), Canadian ice-hockey player. An outstanding forward on the Montreal Canadiens' Stanley Cup championship teams of the 1950s and early 1960s, Geoffrion never played minor-league hockey but jumped from the junior ranks directly to the National Hockey League (NHL) in 1951. His searing slap shot earned him the nickname "Boom Boom" and contributed to his record as one of the NHL's most prolific scorers. He twice led the league in scoring and was named the NHL Most Valuable Player in 1961. He later coached the New York Rangers (1971–72) and the Atlanta Flames (1972–73).

GEORGE V (1865–1936), king of Great Britain and Ireland. George, the son of Edward, prince of Wales (later Edward VII), ascended to the throne in 1910 and gained a reputation as a modest, frugal, and conscientious ruler. Sensitive to his role as a constitutional monarch, he mediated debate over the 1911 Parliament Act and the Irish Home Rule Act of 1914 and exercised discretion in the formation of new cabinets in 1923 and 1931. His actions enhanced the popularity of the monarchy. He was succeeded by his eldest son, Edward VIII. ■ See biographies by John Gore (1941), Harold Nicolson (1952), Denis Judd (1973), and Kennet Rose (1983); and Dennis Friedman, *Darling Georgie* (1998).

GEORGE VI (1895–1952), king of Great Britain and Ireland. As Prince Albert, the second son of the duke of York (later George V), he pursued the traditional naval career but succeeded to the throne in 1936 after the abdication of his brother, Edward VIII. George was a dignified, compassionate, and popular monarch who ruled during the devastation of World War II, the decline of empire, and the transition to the welfare state. He was succeeded by his eldest daughter, Elizabeth II. ■ See biographies by J. W. Wheeler-Bennett (1958), Patrick Howarth (1987), and Sarah Bradford (1989).

GEORGE, STEFAN (1868–1933), German poet and critic. George was the leader of an elite band of aesthete poets and critics who were united in their belief in art for art's sake and their idealization of Greek antiquity as well as their opposition to naturalism, materialism, and bourgeois values. Influenced by the French symbolists and by the philosopher Friedrich Nietzsche, George and his group attempted to revitalize and purify German poetry and to create a new, esoteric, humanistic religion, which would be led by the poet-priest. George was a prolific, refined, sophisticated, and difficult writer, and his collected works, which included the finest homosexual love poems in the German language, numbered 18 volumes (1927–34). Among his best-known works were *Year of the Soul* (1897), *The Seventh Ring* (1907–11), and *The New Reich* (1928). He also cofounded and edited the journal *Periodical for Art* (1892–1919). Although he was antidemocratic and a German nationalist, he hated the Nazis and left Germany (1933) for Switzerland, where he died. English translations of his work are in *Poems* (1943) and *Works* (1949; rev. ed. 1974). ■ See study by Michael and Erika Metzger (1972).

GERHARDSEN, EINAR HENRY (1897–1987), Norwegian political leader. Secretary of the Norwegian Labor party (1934–45) and mayor of Oslo (1940), Gerhardsen was a member of the resistance to German occupation during World War II before being arrested (1941) and sent to a concentration camp. After the war he served as chairman of the Labor party (1945–65) and was premier three times (1945–51; 1955–63; 1963–65). He led Norway's postwar rebuilding programs, brought Norway into NATO (1949), and initiated numerous social-welfare programs.

GERNREICH, RUDI (Rudolph Gernreich; 1922–1985), Austrian-born U.S. fashion designer. A refugee from Nazi-dominated Europe, Gernreich settled in Los Angeles (1938), studied art, and danced with the Lester Horton Modern Dance Troupe (1942–48). He started designing his youthful, colorful, and loose-fitting women's clothing in the late 1940s and set up his own firm in 1960. Among his best-known innovations were the topless swimming suit, the miniskirt, vinyl clothing, the see-through blouse, colored hosiery, and swimming suits without inner foundations. He retired from full-time fashion design in 1968.

GERNSBACK, HUGO (1884–1967), Luxembourg-born U.S. inventor, writer, and publisher. Gernsback received a technical education in Europe and became an active inventor. He went to the United States (1904) to sell his improved dry battery and stayed to open the first radio-supply house. He pioneered American science-fiction writing when, as publisher of the first radio magazine *Modern Electrics,* he introduced (1911) science romances as fillers. In 1926 he launched *Amazing Stories,* the first science-fiction magazine in English. Other publications followed, and his contribution to the genre was recognized by the establishment of the Hugo Award, an annual prize for science-fiction writing. In addition to holding more than 80 patents, Gernsback wrote stories that anticipated many inventions, such as radar and microfilm.

GERSHWIN, GEORGE (1898–1937), U.S. composer. A former rehearsal pianist in Tin Pan Alley and composer of the hit song "Swanee" (1919), Gershwin began writing musicals (*Lady, Be Good,* 1924, and *Funny Face,* 1927) as well as film music, often to lyrics by his brother Ira. Their show, *Of Thee I Sing* (1931), was the first musical comedy to win a Pulitzer Prize, and their hit songs included "The Man I Love," "'S Wonderful," "But Not for Me," and "I Got Rhythm." He also wrote serious compositions, including *Rhapsody in Blue* (1924) and *An American in Paris* (1928); his folk opera *Porgy and Bess* (1935) combined jazz and classical elements and enjoyed great popularity. ■ See biographies by Isaac Goldberg (1958), David Ewen (1970), Charles Schwartz (1973), Edward Jablonski (1987), and Rodney Greenberg (1998); and Joan Peyser, *The Memory of All That!* (1993).

GERSHWIN, IRA (1896–1983), U.S. lyricist. Gershwin worked in his father's Turkish bath before collaborating with his younger brother George on a 1924 stage hit, *Lady, Be Good.* Together they wrote the words and music to *Funny Face* (1927), *Girl Crazy* (1930), *Of Thee I Sing* (1931; Pulitzer Prize), and a folk opera adaptation of *Porgy and Bess* (1935). Their hit songs included "The Man I Love," "I Got Rhythm," "Embraceable You," "'S Wonderful," "Somebody Loves Me," and "They Can't Take That Away from Me." After George's death (1937), Ira Gershwin collaborated with Kurt Weill on the show *Lady in the Dark* (1941) and with Harold Arlen on the film *A Star Is Born* (1954). ■ See Robert Kimball and Alfred Simon, *The Gershwins* (1973), and study by Philip Furia (1996).

GESELL, ARNOLD LUCIUS (1880–1961), U.S. psychologist. A pioneer in the scientific study of child behavior, Gesell founded and directed the Clinic of Child Development, Yale University (1911–48), the most influential U.S. center of child study. In his widely read books he described the norms of behavior for children at various stages of development. Although a generation of Americans during the 1930s and 1940s raised their children in accordance with his guidelines, he was later criticized for being too rigid in his development schedule, for not accounting for individual variation among children, for not considering cultural influences on the children, and for basing his conclusions on a small, homogeneous, white middle-class group that was unrepresentative of the entire population. His books included *Infant and Child in the Culture of Today* (1943) and *The Child from Five to Ten* (1946), both written with F. L. Ilg. ▪ See study by Louise B. Ames (1989).

GETTY, JEAN PAUL (1892–1976), U.S. businessman and tycoon. The son of a wealthy oilman, J. Paul Getty made his first million dollars by age 21 buying and selling oil leases. He made even more money during the Depression and gained control of Tidewater Oil Co. in the 1940s. His fortune was later concentrated in Getty Oil and many other companies. He made so much money in oil all over the world, especially in his dealings with Saudi Arabia, that by the 1960s he was worth over a billion dollars and regarded as the world's wealthiest man. He was famed, however, for his miserliness: he installed a pay telephone for his guests in his 72-room English mansion. ▪ See his autobiographies, *My Life and Fortunes* (1963) and *As I See It* (1976); Richard Lenzner, *The Great Getty* (1986); and Russell Miller, *The House of Getty* (1986).

GHELDERODE, MICHEL DE (Adhemar Martens; 1898–1962). Belgian playwright. Born in Brussels into a Flemish family, Ghelderode was brought up speaking French and wrote all of his plays in that language. A visionary eccentric, strongly influenced by Flemish folklore, the Belgian puppet theater, and the paintings of Pieter Brueghel, Hieronymus Bosch, and James Ensor, Ghelderode created a violent, grotesque, and macabre theatrical world that served as a battleground for the conflict between God and the devil. His distorted morality plays were "total theater," featuring frenzied action, rhetorical language, pantomime, dance, and acrobatics. Although little known outside of Belgium until 1949, he was regarded by the time of his death as a master of the avant-garde theater and a forerunner of the theater of the absurd. Many of his best-known plays, including *Pantagleize* (written 1929; produced 1934), *Barabbas* (1928/1932), *Christopher Columbus* (1927/1929), *Chronicles of Hell* (1929/1943), and *Hop, Signor* (1935/1938) appeared in English in *Seven Plays* (2 vols., 1960–64).

GHEORGHIU-DEJ, GHEORGHE (1901–1965), Rumanian political leader. Born into a working-class family, Gheorghiu-Dej joined the outlawed Rumanian Communist party and was active as an agitator and railroad-worker organizer until he was jailed for 11 years (1933–44). After his escape from prison he became secretary-general of the party (1945) and emerged the victor in an intraparty struggle (1949–52). He served as premier (1954–61) and later president of the council of ministers (1961–65). During the late 1950s and early 1960s he skillfully led Rumania away from a position of total economic and political dependence on the Soviet Union, developed Rumania's industrial economy, and seized on the Sino-Soviet rift to create an independent foreign policy.

GHOSE, AUROBINDO (1872–1950), Indian nationalist and religious leader. Born into a high-caste, Westernized, atheistic Bengali family, Ghose was educated at Cambridge and was a professor in Baroda and Calcutta after returning to India (1892). A revolutionary nationalist, he was a radical critic of the Indian National Congress party. After his arrest (1908) he abandoned politics, devoted himself to religious pursuits, and established an ashram (1910) in Pondicherry that attracted followers from all over the world. Known as Sri Aurobindo, he sought to spiritualize human activity and to transform the world through the creation of a disciplined, religious elite. His books in English included *The Life Divine* (1940) and *The Synthesis of Yoga* (1948). ▪ See Robert A. McDermott, ed., *The Essential Aurobindo* (1973); A. B. Purani, *The Life of Sri Aurobindo* (1964); Satprem, *Sri Aurobindo* (Eng. trans. 1974); June O'Connor, *The Quest for Political and Spiritual Liberation* (1976); and Georges van Vrekhem, *Beyond Man* (1997).

GIACOMETTI, ALBERTO (1901–1966), Swiss sculptor and artist. Giacometti, whose father was also an artist, spent most of his adult life in Paris, where he was influenced by surrealism and existentialism. Working from inner visions for a time, later using models, he painted and sculpted, during the 1950s, elongated skeletal figures that were enigmatic but highly suggestive of despair. He was praised by such writers as Jean Paul Sartre, Albert Camus, and Jean Genet, and was regarded as the most important post–World War II European sculptor. ▪ See biography by James Lord (1985) and study by Reinhold Hohl (Eng. trans. 1972).

GIAEVER, IVAR (1929–   ), Norwegian-born U.S. physicist. Giaever received an electrical-engineering degree in Trondheim (1952) and emigrated to Canada (1954) to work for the General Electric Co. He later did research at GE's Research and Development Center in Schenectady, New York (1956–88), and earned a Ph.D. in physics at Rensselaer Polytechnic Institute (R.P.I.; 1964). A specialist in solid-state physics, he developed techniques of superconductivity that helped expand the field of miniature electronics and earned him a share of the 1973 Nobel Prize in Physics with Leo Esaki and Brian D. Josephson. After 1988 he taught at R.P.I. and the University of Oslo.

GIANNINI, AMADEO PETER (1870–1949), U.S. banker. A school dropout from San Francisco, Giannini founded the institution that became the largest bank in the United States. His Bank of Italy (established in 1904; later renamed the Bank of America) survived the 1906 earthquake solvent enough to loan San Francisco funds for reconstruction. Contrary to conventional banking practices, Giannini went out and solicited customers, offering liberal terms for loans to small farmers and gradually expanding throughout California. He retired in 1930 after organizing his holdings into the Transamerica Corp. (1928). ▪ See Paul Rink, *Building the Bank of America* (1963).

GIAP, VO NGUYEN (1912–), Vietnamese military leader. Giap came from a poor peasant family and was a student anticolonial leader in Hue, where he earned a law degree. He was active in the Indochinese Communist party during the 1930s and joined communist leader Ho Chi Minh in China in 1939 as a military aide. After he had led a successful World War II campaign against the Japanese, he served as defense minister of the newly proclaimed Democratic Republic of Vietnam (1945) and he masterminded the victory over the French at Dien Bien Phu (1954). As North Vietnamese vice premier, defense minister, and army chief, Giap formulated strategy that led to the withdrawal of U.S. forces (1973) and the defeat of South Vietnamese forces and subsequent reunification of Vietnam (1975). Giap served the new government as minister of defense (1976–80) and was a member of the politburo of the Communist party of Vietnam (1976–82). His book on guerrilla warfare, *People's War, People's Army* (Eng. trans. 1961), became a primer for revolutionaries around the world. ▪ See also his *Military Art of People's War* (Eng. trans. 1970), *Unforgettable Months and Years* (Eng. trans. 1975), and study by Robert J. O'Neill (1969).

GIAUQUE, WILLIAM FRANCIS (1895–1982), Canadian-born U.S. chemist. Giauque became interested in cryogenics, the study of the behavior of substances at low temperatures, as an undergraduate at the University of California at Berkeley, where he later earned a Ph.D. (1922) and spent his entire academic career. By examining the effect of magnetic fields on thermodynamic properties, he developed a technique for reaching temperatures approaching absolute zero and for studying substances at these temperatures. This work earned him the 1949 Nobel Prize in Chemistry. Giauque's earlier discovery (1929) that oxygen is a mixture of three isotopes sparked a controversy over the atomic weight of oxygen and allowed use of the isotope oxygen 18 as a tracer in experiments on photosynthesis and respiration.

GIBBON, JOHN HEYSHAM, JR. (1903–1973), U.S. surgeon. Gibbon graduated from Philadelphia's Jefferson Medical College (M.D. 1927), where his father was a professor, and became the institution's chief surgeon (1947–67). He spent 19 years developing a heart-lung machine that, when introduced in 1953, made possible open-heart surgery and paved the way to heart transplants. Gibbon also edited *Surgery of the Chest* (1962), a basic textbook that went through several editions. ▪ See study by Ada Romaine-Davis (1991).

GIBBS, WILLIAM FRANCIS (1886–1967), U.S. naval architect. The son of a wealthy Philadelphia financier, Gibbs

briefly practiced law but was more interested in studying naval history and British battleship plans. In 1922 he went into business with his brother to design yachts, luxury liners, and, when the U.S. Navy began expanding in 1933, naval vessels. Gibbs increased the number of watertight compartments in his ships' holds to help prevent sinking and standardized and simplified designs to save time and labor. His most famous designs were the *Liberty Ship* (1940), used to carry cargo during World War II, and the passenger liner *United States* (1952).

GIBRAN, KHALIL (Jubran Khalil Jubran; 1883–1931), Lebanese-U.S. Arabic novelist, essayist, poet, and painter. Gibran studied art with the sculptor Auguste Rodin in Paris and Arabic literature in Beirut before settling in New York City (1912). A romantic mystic and visionary, he preached love, beauty, freedom, and redemption in his works. *The Prophet* (1923), a mystical composition of prose poems, was a perennial best-seller and was translated into more than 20 languages. ▪ See Martin L. Wolf, ed., *A Treasury of Khalil Gibran* (1951); study by Joseph Ghougassian (1973); biographies by Mikhail Naimy (1985) and Suheil Bushrui and Joe Jenkins (1998); and Robin Waterfield, *Prophet* (1998).

GIBSON, ALTHEA (1927–), U.S. tennis player. Gibson played paddle tennis while growing up in Harlem. After winning American Tennis Association competition (for black players) for ten straight years (1947–56), Gibson became the first African-American player to win not only one championship but also all the world's single titles for women. A strong, aggressive competitor, Gibson dominated women's tennis in the late 1950s, when she was in her early thirties, and was the top-ranked woman player in the United States in 1957. She won consecutive British and U.S. titles (1957–58) and British doubles titles (1956–58). She was also the first African-American woman to compete for the Wightman Cup (1957, 1958). She turned professional in 1959 and won the women's professional singles crown in 1960. After 1963 she enjoyed some success in professional golf. ▪ See her *I Always Wanted to Be Somebody* (1958) and *So Much to Live For* (1968) and study by Sue Davidson (1997).

GIBSON, JOSH (1911–1947), U.S. baseball player. Excluded from the major leagues because he was African American, Gibson was a star catcher for the (Pittsburgh) Homestead Grays (1930–33; 1937–47) and Pittsburgh Crawfords (1933–37) of the Negro League. A powerful right-hand batter, he was the greatest power hitter in baseball history. Although no official records were kept, it was estimated that he hit more than 950 home runs during his career, including more than 70 in 1931 and 1933. He hit over .400 13 times and had a lifetime batting average of .423. He developed a brain tumor (1943) and died of a brain hemorrhage. In 1972 he was elected to the Baseball Hall of Fame. ▪ See Robert W. Peterson, *Only the Ball Was White*

(1970); John Holway, *Voices from the Great Black Baseball Leagues* (1975); and Mark Ribowsky, *The Power and the Darkness* (1996).

GIBSON, WILLIAM (FORD) (1948–   ), U.S.-born writer. Gibson was raised in a small town in Appalachia, where he became fascinated with science fiction and the novels of William Burroughs and Thomas Pynchon. He dropped out of high school, moved to Toronto, Canada, to escape the draft, and eventually settled in Vancouver, B.C., where he studied English (University of British Columbia, B.A. 1977) and began writing fiction. His award-winning science-fiction novel, *Neuromancer* (1984), presented the dark image of a future dominated by computers and multinational capitalism that threatened the existence of human autonomy. One of the first works in the new genre called "cyberpunk," the novel introduced the term "cyberspace" and gained a cult following. *Count Zero* (1986) and *Mona Lisa Overdrive* (1988) formed the remainder (with *Neuromancer*) of the *Sprawl* trilogy. Subsequent novels included *The Difference Engine* (with Bruce Sterling, 1991), a speculative work about the impact modern computers would have had in the 19th century, and a trilogy set in the 21st century—*Virtual Light* (1993), *Idoru* (1996), and *All Tomorrow's Parties* (1999). ■ See study by Lance Olsen (1992).

GIDDINGS, FRANKLIN HENRY (1855–1931), U.S. sociologist. Giddings was a journalist and political commentator from Connecticut who was appointed lecturer at Bryn Mawr in 1888. In 1894 he accepted Columbia University's new chair in sociology, a field that he helped transform over the next 35 years from a vague philosophy into a quantitative science. He explained social cohesiveness on the basis of a "consciousness of kind," shared feelings of similarity and belonging. Giddings was influenced by social Darwinism and espoused U.S. imperialism. His works included *Principles of Sociology* (1896), *Studies in the Theory of Human Society* (1922), and *The Scientific Study of Human Society* (1924).

GIDE, ANDRÉ PAUL GUILLAUME (1869–1951), French novelist, essayist, and playwright. In the 1890s, the decade when Gide began publishing his work, he discovered his identity as a homosexual, traveled in Africa, met Oscar Wilde, and married his cousin (1895). Throughout his long career, Gide sought a morality that would allow for the uniqueness and self-realization of each individual. Paradox was at the center of his life and work: he was torn between a strong puritanical streak and an equally strong attraction to physical pleasures; he was drawn to traditional Christian moral values but continually defied convention. He wrote about these struggles in such works as *The Immoralist* (1902; Eng. trans. 1930), a novel about illicit sensuality that reflected the dilemma of his own marriage; *Strait Is the Gate* (1909; Eng. trans. 1924), a book that urged restraint and self-denial; *Corydon* (1924; Eng. trans. 1950), a defense of

homosexuality; and *La Symphonie Pastorale* (1919; Eng. trans. in *Two Symphonies,* 1931), which deals with the impact of Calvinist morality. In *The Counterfeiters* (1926; Eng. trans. 1927), his most famous novel, Gide explored the problems of fiction writing while trying to reproduce on paper the untidiness of real life. He came close to joining the Communist party in 1934, then denounced it in *Return from the USSR* (1936; Eng. trans. 1937). Gide, who was also a distinguished playwright and translator, was awarded the Nobel Prize in Literature in 1947. ■ See his autobiography, *If It Die . . .* (1926; Eng. trans. 1935); his *Journals, 1889–1949* (Eng. trans., 4 vols., 1947–51); *Self-Portraits* (Eng. trans. 1966), which contains his correspondence with Paul Valéry; study by Thomas Cordle (1975); and J. Delay, *The Youth of André Gide* (Eng. trans. 1963).

GIDEON, CLARENCE EARL (1910–1972), U.S. plaintiff. A drifter of Missouri with a long record of petty crime, Gideon was jailed in 1961 for robbing a Florida poolroom, despite his protestations of innocence. Gideon sent a handwritten note to the U.S. Supreme Court, arguing that his conviction was unconstitutional since he could not afford a lawyer and the court had refused to appoint one for him. The Supreme Court, under Chief Justice Earl Warren, agreed to hear his case against the director of Florida's division of corrections and assigned lawyer Abe Fortas to represent him. In 1963, the court handed down a landmark decision in *Gideon* v. *Wainwright,* ruling that all poor people charged with serious crimes have the right to free defense counsel. Gideon was released along with 500 other prisoners whom the state of Florida believed it could not successfully reprosecute. A marker placed on Gideon's grave by the American Civil Liberties Union (1984) commemorated his historical challenge to the U.S. legal system. ■ See Anthony Lewis, *Gideon's Trumpet* (1964).

GIELGUD, SIR JOHN (1904–2000), British actor and director. The grandnephew of actress Ellen Terry, Gielgud made his acting debut at the Old Vic (1921) and had his first popular success in *Richard of Bordeaux* (1932). A versatile actor with a wonderfully controlled speaking voice, he was regarded as one the greatest Shakespearean actors of his generation and was particularly acclaimed for his interpretations of Hamlet and Richard II. He toured the world during the 1950s with *Ages of Man,* a one-man recital of passages from Shakespeare's plays. He also was admired for his roles in *The Importance of Being Earnest, The School for Scandal,* and *The Seagull,* and in such modern plays as *The Lady's Not for Burning, The Potting Shed, Tiny Alice, Home,* and *No Man's Land.* He also appeared frequently on television and in many films, including *Julius Caesar* (1953; 1970), *Becket* (1964), *Arthur* (1981; Academy Award), and *Prospero's Books* (1991). He wrote *Stage Directions* (1963) and four volumes of memoirs: *Early Stages* (1939), *Distinguished Company* (1972), *An Actor and His Time* (1979), and *Backward Glances* (1989). ■ See Ronald Harwood, ed.,

The Ages of Gielgud (1984), and study by Gyles Brandreth (1984; rev. ed. 1994).

GIEREK, EDWARD (1913–   ), Polish political leader. A miner like his father (who was killed in a Silesian mine disaster), Gierek was raised in France and joined the French Communist party in 1931. Deported to Poland (1934), he eventually turned up in Belgium, where he was active in the communist underground during World War II. Gierek returned to Poland in 1948 and worked his way up through the party bureaucracy in Silesia as a technocrat with a constituency in the mines. In 1970, after worker protests against rising food prices, he was chosen to replace Wladyslaw Gomulka as party secretary. As leader of Poland for a decade, he increased ties with the West and developed heavy industry. But economic conditions worsened in the late 1970s and after nearly 600,000 workers went on strike for the right to form independent unions (1980), Gierek fell from power. He was expelled from the Communist party (1981) and interned (1981–82).

GIESEKING, WALTER (1895–1956), German pianist. A master of subtlety whose refined touch was uniquely suited to the works of Debussy and Ravel, Gieseking was also celebrated for his interpretations of Beethoven, Schumann, Brahms, and Mozart. Strenuous tours between 1926 and 1953 took Gieseking throughout the Western world (although, considered a Nazi sympathizer in World War II, he was for a time unwelcome on the U.S. concert stage). Teaching at the State Conservatory in Saarbrücken, he promulgated an approach to the piano that demanded complete memorization of a piece—including fingering and pedaling—before actual keyboard practice.

GIFFORD, WALTER SHERMAN (1885–1966), U.S. industrialist. A Harvard graduate (1905), Gifford joined the American Telephone and Telegraph Co. (1908) as a statistician. He gained a reputation as an efficiency expert, worked his way up the corporate ladder and served as AT&T's president and chairman (1925–50). He was largely responsible for making the firm the world's largest corporation, raising its assets from $3 billion to $10 billion. Gifford also served as U.S. ambassador to Britain (1950–53).

GIGLI, BENIAMINO (1890–1957), Italian opera singer. One of the century's greatest singers, Gigli was the leading tenor of New York's Metropolitan Opera (1920–32) and was considered the successor to Enrico Caruso. Although not a great actor, he was known for the power, purity, and natural smoothness of his voice and was idolized throughout the world. After leaving the Metropolitan over a salary dispute, he performed mainly in European opera houses and gave frequent concerts that included arias as well as popular Neapolitan songs. He was cleared after World War II of alleged collaboration with the fascists that had alienated many of his American followers. ▪ See his memoirs (Eng. trans. 1957).

GILBERT, CASS (1859–1934), U.S. architect. A leader of the classical revival, Gilbert designed some of America's most famous public buildings, including the U.S. Customs House (New York City, 1907) and the Supreme Court Building in Washington, D.C. (completed 1935). He was best known for his design of the extravagantly ornate 66-story Woolworth Building (New York City, 1913). Adorned with pinnacles and gargoyles in the French Gothic style, the building was for many years the world's tallest and long served as a model for commercial skyscrapers. ▪ See his memoirs (1935).

GILBERT, JOHN (John Pringle; 1897–1936), U.S. film actor. Beginning as a scriptwriter, Gilbert became a popular romantic lead in *The Merry Widow* (1925) and *La Bohème* (1926). His appearances opposite Greta Garbo in *Flesh and the Devil* (1927) and *Love* (1927) solidified his position as Hollywood's greatest screen lover. However, with the advent of sound movies and the decline in popularity of the passionate dramas for which he was known, Gilbert's career waned. Garbo, rumored to be Gilbert's mistress, obtained for him his role in *Queen Christina* (1933). ▪ See biography by Leatrice G. Fountain, *Dark Star* (1985; with John Maxim).

GILBERT, WALTER (1932–   ), U.S. molecular biologist. After studies at Cambridge (Ph.D. 1957), Gilbert joined the Harvard faculty (1959). He developed methods for determining the chemical structure of deoxyribonucleic acid (DNA), which enabled scientists to learn the details of the structure of genes and to manufacture genetic material in the laboratory. For his research, he shared the 1980 Nobel Prize in Chemistry with Frederick Sanger and Paul Berg. Gilbert was also a founder (1978) of Biogen, a Swiss company specializing in "gene splicing" or recombinant DNA technology. During the 1980s and 1990s he supported the undertaking of a human genome project, whose purpose was to map all human genes, and he did research on the origin of genes and how the first ones were formed.

GILBRETH, FRANK BUNKER (1868–1924), U.S. industrial engineer. A pioneer in the field of industrial management, Gilbreth invented and developed time-and-motion studies aimed at simplifying industrial operations, increasing efficiency, and reducing fatigue of both laborers and executives. A follower of the "father of scientific management," Frederick W. Taylor, Gilbreth founded the Society for the Promotion of the Science of Management (later called the Taylor Society), and wrote, in collaboration with his wife Lillian, numerous books, pamphlets, and articles on scientific management. Two of their 12 children collaborated to write the popular *Cheaper by the Dozen* (1949; film, 1950) and *Belles on Their Toes* (1950; film, 1952), which described how the Gilbreths applied their efficiency methods at home.

GILELS, EMIL GRIGORYEVICH (1916–1985), Soviet pianist. At age 16, Gilels won first prize in the National Soviet Piano Competition and later won second prize (Vienna, 1936) and first prize (Brussels, 1938) in international competitions. He began to teach at the Moscow Conservatory (1938), played for Soviet forces during World War II, and was awarded the Stalin Prize (1946). Gilels was the forerunner of the dazzling postwar generation of Soviet pianists, and his tour of the United States in 1955 was an event of international magnitude. He had a prodigious technique, but he also possessed a magnificent musical intelligence that was capable of dealing idiomatically with music ranging from Bach to the Russian moderns.

GILL (ARTHUR) ERIC (ROWTON) (1882–1940), British sculptor, engraver, and writer. A convert to Roman Catholicism (1913), Gill executed several important works on religious and biblical themes, notably *The Stations of the Cross* (Westminster Cathedral, 1914–18) and the bas-reliefs *The Creation of Adam* (Palace of Nations, Geneva; 1935–38). He also sculpted the famous stone torso *Mankind* (1928) and *Prospero and Ariel* (1931). He was best known, though, for his design of elegantly styled lettering and typefaces and book engravings done for the Golden Cockerel Press (from 1924). Gill also wrote several books including *An Essay on Typography* (1931), *The Necessity of Belief* (1936), and *Work and Prosperity* (1937). ■ See his autobiography (1941) and studies by Robert Speaight (1966), Malcolme Yorke (1982), and Fiona MacCarthy (1989).

GILLESPIE, "DIZZY" (John Birks Gillespie; 1917–1993), U.S. jazz trumpeter and composer. One of the creators of modern jazz, Gillespie started playing the trumpet while he was a student at the Laurinburg Institute, a black industrial school in South Carolina. He modeled himself on Roy Eldridge, whose work he admired. His appearances with the Billy Eckstine band starting in 1944 brought him recognition for his originality. With saxophonist Charlie Parker, he pioneered the style known as "bebop" and in 1945 put together his first orchestra, which toured Europe under government subsidy, the first jazz orchestra to be so honored. He continued to make Grammy Award–winning recordings and to play in jazz festivals, clubs, and concert halls through the early 1990s. ■ See his memoirs, *To Be or Not . . . To Bop* (1979; with Al Fraser); biography by Barry MacRae (1988); and Alyn Shipton, *Groovin' High* (1999).

GILLETTE, KING CAMP (1855–1932), U.S. inventor, businessman, and social reformer. Gillette worked as a traveling salesman for many years before inventing the safety razor and disposable blade, which he started marketing in 1903. Although initial sales amounted to only 51 razors and 168 blades, they increased rapidly, and as Gillette established plants around the world, beards began to disappear. He was also a utopian socialist who believed that the competitive system fostered waste, greed, and strife. Seeking to create a giant trust that would run a planned and rational economy, he set up the "World Corporation" (1910) in Ari-

zona to promote his ideas. He elaborated his social theories in *World Corporation* (1910) and *The People's Corporation* (1924). ■ See biography by Russell B. Adams, Jr. (1978).

GILMAN, ALFRED G. (1941–), U.S. pharmacologist. The son of a prominent pharmacologist, Gilman studied at Case Western Reserve University in Cleveland, Ohio (M.D. and Ph.D. 1969), and taught at the University of Virginia (1971–81) and the University of Texas Southwestern Medical Center in Dallas (from 1981). In the 1970s Gilman discovered the chemical nature of G-proteins (guanosine triphosphate or GTP), natural substances that help cells convert signals from the environment (such as light and sound) and from chemicals within the body (such as hormones and neurotransmitters) to produce cellular chain reactions that give rise to fundamental life processes such as metabolism, vision, and smell. In 1980 Gilman and his research team purified the G-protein. Subsequent research determined that G-protein activity is linked to many health disorders, including cancer, diabetes, cholera, and alcoholism. For his research Gilman shared the 1994 Nobel Prize in Physiology or Medicine with Martin Rodbell, who discovered the G-protein. Gilman also served as coeditor of *Goodman and Gilman's The Pharmacological Basis of Therapeutics,* a widely used textbook that was coauthored by his father in 1941 (9th edition 1996).

GILRUTH, ROBERT ROWE (1913–2000), U.S. aeronautical and space engineer. Gilruth made pioneering engineering studies of military aircraft specifications and performed experiments that led to the design of the X-1 research airplane, the first to break the sound barrier. He founded and directed (1945–52) the Wallops Island, Virginia, missile research center and gathered a team of scientists who formed the core of the National Aeronautics and Space Administration (NASA) when it was founded in 1958. Gilruth led NASA's Project Mercury, which successfully launched the first American astronauts. He then built and directed (1961–72) the Manned Spacecraft Center (Houston, Texas), which developed Project Gemini to study the problems of long space flights, and Project Apollo, which resulted in the first lunar landing by a manned spacecraft (July 1969).

GILSON, ÉTIENNE HENRI (1884–1978), French philosopher and historian. Gilson earned a doctorate at the Sorbonne (1906). After serving in World War I, he taught at the University of Strasbourg (1919–20), the Sorbonne (1921–32), and the Collège de France (1932–51). Gilson helped establish the Pontifical Institute of Medieval Studies in Toronto, which became the center of his work after 1950. He was a leading scholar on the history of philosophy, a preeminent exponent of Thomism, the scholastic philosophical method developed by Thomas Aquinas, and a major figure in the neo-Thomist movement of Roman Catholicism. He was elected to the French Academy in 1946. Gilson's books included *The Philosophy of St. Thomas Aquinas* (1919; Eng.

trans. 1924), *The Christian Philosophy of Saint Augustine* (1929; Eng. trans. 1960), *The Spirit of Medieval Philosophy* (2 vols., 1932; Eng. trans. 1936), and *The Philosopher and Theology* (1960; Eng. trans. 1962). The *Gilson Reader* (1957) contains selections of his writings in English. ■ See study by Laurence K. Shook (1984) and J. M. Quinn, *The Thomism of Étienne Gilson* (1971).

GINASTERA, ALBERTO EVARISTO (1916–1983), Argentinian composer. In his early compositions, such as the ballets *Panambí* (1937) and *Estancia* (1941), Ginastera used folk-music themes and rhythmic patterns. Later he adopted 12-tone techniques, aleatory passages, and electronic effects and utilized modern and traditional forms in his celebrated operas, *Don Rodrigo* (1964), *Bomarzo* (1967), and *Beatrix Cenci* (1971). Active as a teacher in Argentina, he was founding director of the Latin American Center for Advanced Musical Studies, Buenos Aires (1963–70) and influenced many young Latin American composers.

GINGRICH, NEWT (1943–   ), U.S. political leader. Gingrich studied at Emory University (B.A. 1965) and Tulane University (M.A. 1968; Ph.D. 1971, in European history) and taught at West Georgia College (1970–78). Elected as a Republican U.S. congressman from suburban Atlanta (1978), he quickly emerged as a petulant and confrontational leader of conservative House Republicans. He sparked the investigation that led to the resignation of Democratic Speaker of the House of Representatives Jim Wright (1989). As minority whip (1989–94) he promoted a conservative agenda of cutting taxes and liberal social programs, balancing the federal budget, and restoring traditional values. He led the Republicans to a landslide congressional victory in 1994, their first House win in 40 years, and he was elected Speaker of the House. However, the "Republican revolution" was weakened as Gingrich's polarizing tactics were blamed for a government shutdown in late 1995, and the Republicans lost seats to the Democrats in the 1996 elections. Gingrich was further hobbled by ethical problems (he was fined $300,000 for using tax-exempt money to advocate Republican policies) and by dissatisfaction with his leadership. After his party again lost House seats in the 1998 elections, he resigned both the speakership and his congressional seat. ■ See his *To Renew America* (1995) and *Lessons Learned the Hard Way* (1998); the study by John K. Wilson (1996); and David Maraniss and Michael Weisskopf, *"Tell Newt to Shut Up"* (1996).

GINSBERG, ALLEN (1926–1997), U.S. poet. A major poet of the "beat" generation of the 1950s whose influence carried over to the "hippie" movement of the 1960s, Ginsberg was born in New Jersey and earned a scholarship to Columbia College (B.A. 1949). His best-known works were *Howl!* (1956), a long, rambling poetic indictment of American materialism, and *Kaddish for Naomi Ginsberg* (1961), a memorial to his mother. Ginsberg visited India (1962–63),

returning as a guru of the counterculture. An exponent of meditation and "flower power," he organized the first "be-in" in San Francisco in 1967. His *Selected Poems (1947–1995)* appeared in 1996. He was a prominent figure in the anti–Vietnam War movement and spoke out against homophobia, censorship, and the military-industrial complex throughout his career. ■ See his *Journals* (1977); studies by Jane Kramer (1969) and Paul Portuges (1978); Dick McBride, *Cometh with Clouds* (1982); and biography by Barry Miles (1989).

GINZBERG, LOUIS (1873–1953), Lithuanian-born U.S. Jewish scholar. One of the century's foremost scholars of Jewish law and biblical lore, Ginzberg was a professor of Talmud at the Jewish Theological Seminary of America (New York, 1902–53), and he exerted a great influence on the course of Conservative Judaism in the United States. He was best known for his *Legends of the Jews* (7 vols., 1909–38) and *Commentary on the Palestinian Talmud* (3 vols., 1941). He was also a founder (1919) and first president of the American Academy of Jewish Research. ■ See Eli Ginzberg, *Keeper of the Law* (1966).

GIOLITTI, GIOVANNI (1842–1928), Italian political leader. A government bureaucrat for more than 20 years, Giolitti entered parliament in 1882 and served as premier five times between 1892 and 1921. Although he was a progressive liberal, responsible for such measures as national insurance (1911), universal male suffrage (1912), and public-health and labor reforms, he was also associated with a special brand of political corruption and intimidation dubbed *giolittismo*. He kept power through shifting alliances based on personal rather than party loyalty and accepted the support of any group, including the fascists. ■ See his *Memoirs* (Eng. trans. 1923).

GIONO, JEAN (1895–1970), French novelist. Giono left school at 16 and worked in a bank until 1929. His novels, set mostly among simple peasants of his native Provence, illustrated his belief in the nobility and happiness of the individual working in harmony with nature. They included *Hill of Destiny* (1928; Eng. trans. 1929), *Harvest* (1930; Eng. trans. 1939), and *Song of the World* (1934; Eng. trans. 1938, 1981). He was jailed (1939) for his pacifist views and again briefly (1945) for suspicions (unfounded) of sympathizing with the Vichy government during World War II. His postwar novels, including *Horseman on the Roof* (1951; Eng. trans. 1952, 1982), were inspired by history and picaresque chronicles and were characterized by their liveliness and concise style. Among his last works was *Ennemonde* (1968; Eng. trans. 1970). ■ See the autobiographical *Blue Boy* (1932; Eng. trans. 1949, 1981) and W. D. Redfern, *The Private World of Jean Giono* (1967).

GIOVANNI, NIKKI (Yolande Cornelia Giovanni, Jr.; 1943–   ), U.S. poet. After her first poetry collections, *Black*

Feeling, Black Talk, and *Black Judgement,* appeared in 1968, Nikki Giovanni emerged as a spokeswoman for black concerns and the women's movement. These were followed by *Re: Creation* (1970) and *My House* (1972) and the essay collection *Gemini* (1971). She anthologized the poetry of black women in *Night Comes Softly* (1970). Later collections included *The Women and the Men* (1979), *Those Who Ride the Night Winds* (1983), *Sacred Cows and Other Edibles* (1988), *Love Poems* (1997), and the volume of essays, *Racism 101* (1994). She also wrote poems for children. ■ See her autobiographical statement, *Gemini* (1971); *A Poetic Equation: Conversations Between Nikki Giovanni and Margaret Walker* (1983); and Virginia C. Fowler, ed., *Conversations with Nikki Giovanni* (1992).

GIOVANNITTI, ARTURO (1884–1959), Italian-born U.S. labor leader and poet. Arriving in the United States in 1900, Giovannitti joined the Italian Socialist Federation (1908) and the Industrial Workers of the World (1912). He was an active and well-known labor leader for more than 40 years and a major figure among Italian immigrant workers. He was a Socialist party leader and a founder of the Antifascist Alliance of America (1923). Giovannitti was known as "the workers' poet," and his most famous poem, "The Walker" (1912), about a pacing prisoner, was written while he was serving time in jail for his activities during the Lawrence, Massachusetts, textile strike. ■ See his *Collected Poems* (1962).

GIRAUD, HENRI HONORÉ (1879–1949), French general. Giraud graduated from St. Cyr military academy (1900) and served in French colonies before and after World War I. He helped to direct the campaign against the rebellious Moroccan Rifs (1925–26). In 1936 he was appointed military governor of Metz and in 1938 commander of an army guarding a section of the Maginot line. A right-winger who scorned the Third Republic, Giraud achieved popular fame for his escapes from German prisons during World Wars I and II and from Vichy to North Africa in 1942. Following the World War II Anglo-American landings in North Africa, Giraud was named commander of the pro-Allied French forces in Tunisia (December 1942). In 1943 he became coleader with Gen. Charles de Gaulle of the French Committee of National Liberation but retired amid controversy the following year. ■ See study by G. Ward Price (1944).

GIRAUDOUX, JEAN (1882–1944), French novelist and playwright. A high-ranking French diplomat (1910–40), Giraudoux also wrote episodic, impressionistic novels, including *Suzanne and the Pacific* (1921; Eng. trans. 1923). He had an optimistic view of life and infused his work with his love of purity and human tenderness. Later he wrote plays; especially notable are *Amphitryon 38* (1929; Eng. trans. 1937), *Tiger at the Gates* (1935; Eng. trans. 1955), and *The Madwoman of Chaillot* (1945; Eng. trans. 1949). Written in a complex, stylized, poetic language, his plays are metaphor-ical studies of universal human concerns. ■ See biography by Laurent LeSage (1959) and studies by John H. Reilly (1978) and Jacques Body (Eng. trans. 1991).

GIRONELLA, JOSÉ MARÍA (1917–), Spanish novelist. Trained for the priesthood, Gironella fought for the victorious Francisco Franco during the Spanish Civil War (1936–39) but then lived among Spanish refugees in France; he experienced the war trauma from both sides. His ambitious, intelligent tetralogy on the civil war appeared in Spain after apparent negotiations with censors. The first volume, *The Cypresses Believe in God* (1952; Eng. trans. 1955), was least problematic since it treated the prewar era. *One Million Dead* (1961; Eng. trans. 1963) and *Peace After War* (1966; Eng. trans. 1969) strove for political balance; the ambivalent protagonist fights on both sides. The final volume was *Condemned to Live* (1971). ■ See study by Ronald Schwartz (1972).

GIROUD, FRANÇOISE (Françoise Gourdji; 1916–), Swiss-born French journalist and political leader. The facts of Giroud's life are inspirational magazine fare in France: school dropout and script girl for director Jean Renoir, World War II prisoner during the German occupation, and mother of an illegitimate son, she became editor of a top women's magazine in 1945 and was a cofounder and editor of the newsweekly *L'Express* (1953–71). She continued to break social taboos as secretary of state for the condition of women (1974–76) and secretary of state for culture (1976–77). She wrote many books, including *Women and Men: A Philosophical Conversation* (1993; Eng. trans. 1995) and was a columnist and literary critic during the 1980s and 1990s. ■ See her autobiography, *I Give You My Word* (1972; Eng. trans. 1974).

GISCARD D'ESTAING, VALÉRY (1926–), French political leader. Giscard was born in Koblenz, Germany, where his father was an economist with the French occupation forces in the Ruhr. After serving in the army during World War II, he graduated from the elite École Polytechnique and École Nationale d'Administration (in Paris) and entered the ministry of finance (1952). A political conservative from a patrician background, he was elected to the national assembly (1956) and became a supporter of Charles de Gaulle. He subsequently served as secretary of state for finance (1959–62) and minister of finance (1962–66) under de Gaulle and finance minister under Georges Pompidou (1969–74), balancing the budget and enacting an austerity program that laid the foundation for economic growth. However, his years as president (1974–81) were marked by a deepening world economic crisis and rising French unemployment and inflation rates. He was defeated for reelection by socialist François Mitterand in 1981, but subsequently served in the national assembly (1984–89; 1993–) and was a deputy in the European Parliament (1989–93). He wrote *French Democracy* (1976; Eng. trans. 1977).

GISH, LILLIAN (1896–1993), U.S. actress. A traveling child actress, Gish appeared with her younger sister Dorothy in such D. W. Griffith silent-film classics as *Birth of a Nation* (1915), *Way Down East* (1920), and *Orphans of the Storm* (1922). After leaving Griffith, she gave some of her finest performances in *The White Sister* (1923) and *The Scarlet Letter* (1926), but her virginal purity was out of key with the roaring 1920s. Returning to the stage, Gish appeared in *Uncle Vanya, Camille, Hamlet,* and *Life with Father.* In later years she played character roles in *Portrait of Jennie* (1949), *The Night of the Hunter* (1955), and other films. Her last film was *Whales of August* (1987). ■ See her autobiography, *The Movies, Mr. Griffith and Me* (1969).

GIVENCHY, HUBERT DE (1927–   ), French fashion designer. Givenchy put aside plans for a career in law and took his portfolio of fashion sketches to Paris at age 17. After designing for Jacques Fath, Robert Piguet, and Elsa Schiaparelli, he was encouraged by Cristóbal Balenciaga to establish his own house (1952). Givenchy's fashions epitomized classic aristocratic elegance.

GJELLERUP, KARL ADOLPH (1857–1919), Danish writer. The son of a parson, Gjellerup studied theology but, influenced by critic Georg Brandes and the writings of Charles Darwin and Herbert Spencer, he broke with Christianity. In several novels he attempted to combine his idealism with his belief in scientific truth, but after 1900 he was preoccupied with Eastern religions and metaphysics and eventually returned to Christianity. His best-known novels were the melancholy love story, *Minna* (1889; Eng. trans. 1913), the study of a crime of passion, *The Mill* (1896), and the tale of reincarnation, *The Pilgrim Kamanita* (1906; Eng. trans. 1911). He shared the 1917 Nobel Prize in Literature with Henrik Pontoppidan.

GLACKENS, WILLIAM JAMES (1870–1938), U.S. painter. Glackens was a magazine and newspaper illustrator before becoming associated with a group of painters called The Eight (also derisively called the Ashcan School), who introduced social realism into American painting around the turn of the century. Glackens painted middle-class people in streets and parks in a style reminiscent of the European masters Manet and Renoir. *Chez Mouquin* (1905) and *Nude with Apple* (1910) were characteristic of his work. ■ See studies by Ira Glackens (1957) and William H. Gerots (1996).

GLADKOV, FYODOR VASILYEVICH (1883–1958), Soviet novelist. A schoolteacher and editor, Gladkov joined a Moscow literary group (1923) and furnished the prototype for what became known as "Soviet five-year plan literature." His novel *Cement* (1925; Eng. trans. 1929), describing the reconstruction of a cement plant, was favored by dictator Joseph Stalin, and it was a best-seller at home and abroad. *Cement* underwent numerous revisions to reflect the Kremlin's ideological shifts. Its style is in keeping with its ti-

tle, but *Cement* nevertheless had an emotional appeal for Soviet readers. A later Gladkov work, *Energy* (1932–38), was weighed down by engineering specifications on the construction of the Dneprostroy Dam. Gladkov's autobiographical trilogy (1949–54) and the unfinished *Restless Youth* (1958; Eng. trans. 1959) contain his best writing and reflect the literary influence of Maxim Gorky.

GLASER, DONALD (1926–   ), U.S. physicist. Glaser received his Ph.D. from the California Institute of Technology (1950) and taught at the University of Michigan (1949–59) and the University of California at Berkeley (from 1959). He won the 1960 Nobel Prize in Physics for his invention (1952) of the "bubble chamber"—an apparatus that traces the paths of high-energy atomic particles. His invention generated a host of new data concerning these particles (including their mass, lifetimes, and decay modes) and high-energy reactions. It led to the detection of several new elementary particles. After the 1960s, Glaser did work in the field of molecular biology.

GLASGOW, ELLEN ANDERSON GHOLSON (1873–1945), U.S. writer. Born into a wealthy and socially prominent Richmond, Virginia, family, Glasgow produced a series of 19 novels that sought to portray realistically the social and political history of Virginia since 1850. She first attracted critical attention at age 52 for *Barren Ground* (1925). Other well-known works included *Vein of Iron* (1935), *In This Our Life* (Pulitzer Prize, 1941), and the comic trilogy of life in (thinly disguised) Richmond, *The Romantic Comedians* (1926), *They Stooped to Folly* (1929), and *The Sheltered Life* (1932). ■ See her autobiography, *The Woman Within* (1954), her *Letters* (1958), and biographies by E. Stanly Godbold, Jr. (1972) and Susan Goodman (1998).

GLASHOW, SHELDON LEE (1933–   ), U.S. physicist. Glashow studied at Harvard (Ph.D. 1958) and taught at the University of California, Berkeley (1962–66) and at Harvard (from 1966). He won the 1979 Nobel Prize for Physics for experiments in the early 1960s that contributed significantly to, and extended, the Weinberg-Salam Theory of Weak Interactions, advanced independently by corecipients Abdus Salam and Glashow's high school classmate, Steven Weinberg. Glashow resolved an obstacle to the concept that two essential natural forces, electromagnetism and the nuclear force known as "weak interaction," are aspects of the same phenomenon. His work decisively influenced research on quarks and leptons, leading to the discovery, in the mid-1970s, of a previously unknown type of quark, called the "charmed quark," and to the prediction of other quarks. His books included *The Charm of Physics* (1990) and *From Alchemy to Quarks* (1994). ■ See his memoirs, *Interactions* (1988; with Ben Bova).

GLASS, CARTER (1858–1946), U.S. senator. A newspaper publisher and local Democratic political leader in his native

Lynchburg, Virginia, Glass served in the U.S. House of Representatives (1902–18), where he was acknowledged as a financial expert and coauthored the Federal Reserve Act. After briefly serving as secretary of the treasury (1918–20), he entered the Senate (1920) and remained there for the rest of his life. Although he was coauthor of the bill that created the Federal Deposit Insurance Corp. (1933), he bitterly opposed most New Deal legislation (Pres. Franklin D. Roosevelt called him an "unreconstructed rebel") and led the southern conservative bloc in the Senate that resisted big government and advocated strict construction of the Constitution, racial segregation, and states' rights. ■ See the uncritical biography by Rixey Smith and Norman Beasley (1939).

GLASS, PHILIP (1937–), U.S. composer. Glass graduated from Juilliard (1962) and studied with the influential French musician Nadia Boulanger (1964–66) and the famed Indian performers Ravi Shankar and Alla Rakha. One of the leading minimalist composers of the late 1960s and early 1970s, Glass was influenced by Asian and African rhythms, and his music was noted for its modular form and rhythmic repetition. His later highly amplified works reflected his interest in contemporary rock and progressive jazz. He frequently performed them (from 1968) as a member of the Philip Glass Ensemble, a chamber group for winds, voice, and electronic keyboards. His best-known works were the avant-garde operatic epics *Einstein on the Beach* (1975; with playwright, director, and designer Robert Wilson) and *Satyagraha (M. K. Gandhi in South Africa, 1893–1914)* (1980), and music for the films *Koyanisqatsi* (1983), *Powaqqatsi* (1988), *The Thin Blue Line* (1988), and *Kundun* (1997). He also wrote several symphonies.

GLASSCO, JOHN (1909–1981), Canadian novelist and poet. Born in Montreal and educated at McGill University, Glassco joined the Parisian colony of American expatriates in the 1920s and described his experiences in the highly acclaimed autobiography *Memoirs of Montparnasse* (1970). "I look on myself mainly as a pornographic novelist, and have sought to create serious and artistic works in this genre," wrote this former mayor (1952–54) of Foster, Quebec. His pseudonymously written novels, including *The English Governess* (1960; by "Miles Underwood") and *Fetish Girl* (1972; by "Sylvia Beyer"), were calculated to outrage middle-class sensibilities. Glassco edited *The Poetry of French Canada in Translation* (1970) and published several volumes of his own verse, including *The Deficit Made Flesh* (1958) and *Selected Poems* (1971). ■ See study by Philip Kokotailo (1988).

GLATSTEIN, JACOB (1896–1971), Polish-born U.S. Yiddish-language poet and literary critic. Glatstein emigrated to New York, studied law, and worked for years as a newspaper columnist. A cofounder of the introspective school of Yiddish poetry, *inzikhism,* he was a master of linguistic and technical innovation as well as of surrealistic style. His poem "Good Night, World" (1938) shockingly forecast the destruction of European Jewry, and he wrote moving elegies after World War II. Glatstein's most notable poetic collections included *Jacob Glatstein* (1921), *The Joy of the Yiddish Word* (1961), and *A Jew of Lublin* (1966). English translations are in *Poems* (1970), *The Selected Poems* (1972; 1987), and *I Keep Recalling: The Holocaust Poems* (1993). He also wrote the autobiographical *Homeward Bound* (1938; Eng. trans. 1969) and *Homecoming at Twilight* (1940; Eng. trans. 1962). ■ See Janet R. Hadda, *Yankev Glatshteyn* (1979).

GLAZER, NATHAN (1923–), U.S. sociologist. The son of a New York City tailor, Glazer was active in both Zionist and socialist groups in his youth. After graduating from New York's City College (1944) he worked as an assistant editor at *Commentary* magazine (1944–53) and collaborated on two classics of American sociology: *The Lonely Crowd* (1950), with David Riesman and Reuel Denny, and *Beyond the Melting Pot* (1963) with Daniel Moynihan. While a professor at the University of California at Berkeley (1963–69) and at Harvard (from 1969), his political views shifted to the right and he became associated with the neoconservative movement. He was coeditor of the journal *The Public Interest* (from 1973) and wrote *Affirmative Discrimination* (1976), a controversial attack on government-enforced quotas in education and employment. Glazer's other books included *American Judaism* (1957), *The Social Basis of American Communism* (1961), *Ethnic Dilemmas* (1983), *The Limits of Social Policy* (1988), and *We Are All Multiculturalists Now* (1997).

GLEASON, JACKIE (1916–1987), U.S. comedian. After a career in nightclubs, radio, and the Broadway stage, the man who called himself "the Great One" played an average Joe in "Life of Riley" when the popular radio show came to television (1949). He then moved to "Cavalcade of Stars" and starred in "The Jackie Gleason Show" (1952–55); his show generated a feature sketch, "The Honeymooners," into a series (1955–56) that was hugely popular in its own right and suggested such later television comedies as "The Flintstones" and "All in the Family." While his variety shows were lavish productions, "The Honeymooners" was set in Ralph and Alice (Audrey Meadows) Kramden's bare Brooklyn kitchen at 328 Chauncey Street, an address shared with the Mullinses, the Manicottis, and notably Ed (Art Carney) and Trixie (Joyce Randolph) Norton. Gleason made numerous films over four decades, recorded dozens of record albums, and won (1959) a best-Broadway-actor award for *Take Me Along*. ■ See James A. Bishop, *The Golden Ham* (1956), and James Bacon, *How Sweet It Is* (1985).

GLENN, JOHN HERSCHEL, JR. (1921–), U.S. astronaut and political leader. A highly decorated marine-corps fighter pilot during World War II and the Korean War, Glenn was a test pilot during the 1950s and made the first nonstop transcontinental supersonic flight (1957). He was chosen to be one of the seven original U.S. astronauts (1959) and became a national hero after he made the first orbital flight aboard the space capsule *Friendship 7* (Feb. 20, 1962). After retiring from the space program (1964), Glenn pursued a business career and served as a Democratic U.S. senator from Ohio (1975–99). He made an unsuccessful bid to become the Democratic presidential candidate in 1984. In October 1998 the 77-year-old Glenn returned to space as a crew member on the space shuttle *Discovery,* acting as a test subject for the study of the physiological effects of weightlessness. ■ See his memoirs (1999; with Nick Taylor) and Richard F. Fenno, *The Presidential Odyssey of John Glenn* (1990).

GLIÈRE, REINHOLD MORITSEVICH (1875–1956), Soviet composer. Basically conservative in style, Glière combined elements of German romanticism and Russian nationalism in Symphony No. 3 (*Ilya Muromets,* 1912). His works frequently reflected his interest in folk music—e.g., the operas *Gyul'sara* (1936), written with the Uzbek composer Talib Sadïkov, and the Azerbaidzhan opera *Shakh Senem* (1923)—and he collected folk songs in Russia and the Ukraine. Other works, such as the ballet *The Red Poppy* (1927, revised 1949), have political overtones; he was active in the Union of Soviet Composers. He taught in the Kiev (1913–20) and Moscow (from 1920) conservatories; his students included Sergei Prokofiev, Nicolai Miaskovsky, and Aram Khachaturian.

GLUBB, SIR JOHN BAGOT (1897–1986), British military leader and commander of the Arab Legion. Glubb served on the western front in World War I and was wounded three times. In 1920 he was sent to Iraq as a lieutenant in the royal engineers; there he gained a reputation as a friend of the Arabs. In 1926 he resigned his British commission and became an administrative inspector for the Iraqi government. Five years later he transferred to the British mandate of Transjordan (later Jordan), where he commanded the desert patrol of the Arab Legion. Glubb later (1939–56) served as commander of the Arab Legion, in which post he combined respect for Arab tradition with the introduction of European techniques. The Arab Legion was acclaimed for brilliant military maneuvers, and Glubb Pasha, as he was called, achieved legendary status. His army was the only Arab force to defeat Israeli units during the 1948 Palestine war. ■ See his *Story of the Arab Legion* (1948), the autobiographical *A Soldier with the Arabs* (1957), *The Changing Scenes of Life* (1983), and the biography by James D. Lunt (1984).

GOBETTI, PIERO (1901–1926), Italian political writer. At age 22 Gobetti, a literary critic and advocate of democratic social reform, founded the weekly *Rivoluzione Liberale,* which became the most forceful organ of opposition to the fascist regime of Benito Mussolini. But the paper was suppressed in 1926, and its editor, who had been arrested and assaulted by the fascists the previous year, fled to Paris, where he died.

GODARD, JEAN-LUC (1930–), French film director. A student of ethnology at the Sorbonne, Godard began writing film criticism in 1950 and made his first film, about a Swiss dam, in 1954. With *Breathless* (1959), he became internationally celebrated for his idiosyncratic New Wave style of filmmaking. He utilized unorthodox filming methods while mixing interview techniques and gangster plots with literary allusions and in-group jokes. After directing a rapid succession of films during the 1960s—*Alphaville and Pierrot le Fou* (1965), *La Chinoise* (1967), *Weekend* (1968)—Godard became involved with Maoist political groups. He rejected narrative commercial filmmaking altogether and made 16mm and 8mm movies for politically committed leftist audiences, exploring the relationship between politics and aesthetics. In 1979, however, with *Every Man for Himself*—which he called his "second first film"—he resumed his innovative commercial work of the 1960s. *Hail Mary* (1985), his updated version of the story of the Virgin Mary and Joseph, was condemned by the Vatican. ■ See his collection of critical writings, *Godard on Godard* (Eng. trans. 1972); study by John F. Kreidl (1980); Wheeler W. Dixon, *The Films of Jean-Luc Godard* (1997); and David Sterritt, *Jean-Luc Godard: Interviews* (1998).

GODDARD, ROBERT HUTCHINGS (1882–1945), U.S. rocket scientist. Goddard, a professor of physics at Clark University (1914–43), did pioneering work that earned him the title "father of American rocketry." His now-classic report *A Method of Reaching Extreme Altitudes* (1919) elaborated his basic theories of rocket flight and generated financial support for further research. His interest turned from solid to liquid fuels, and in 1926 he launched the world's first liquid-propelled rocket. He later illustrated that rockets were more effective in a vacuum than in atmosphere and advanced the crucial theory that planetary rockets must consist of multiple stages. ■ See Milton Lehman, *The High Man* (1963).

GÖDEL, KURT (1906–1978), Austrian-born U.S. mathematician and logician. Gödel studied at the University of Vienna (Ph.D. 1930) and taught there from 1933 to 1938. Investigating the ramifications of non-Euclidian geometrics, he published "On Formally Undecidable Propositions of Principia Mathematica and Related Symptoms" (1931; Eng. trans. 1962), a paper that, by translating symbolic logic into numerical terms, demonstrated that no system of axioms within a mathematical system can be proved or disproved on the basis of the axioms within that system. "Gödel's proof" furthered the work of such mathematicians as Bertrand Russell and Alfred North Whitehead and demonstrated that certainty in mathematics is never absolute. Gödel emigrated to the United States, where he was associated with the Institute for Advanced Study in Princeton,

New Jersey (1938–76). He also wrote *The Consistency of the Axiom of Choice and of the Generalized Continuum-Hypothesis with the Axioms of Set Theory* (1940). ■ See Douglas R. Hofstadter, *Gödel, Escher, Bach* (1979), John W. Dawson, Jr., *Logical Dilemmas* (1997), and biography by John Casti and Werner DePauli (2000).

GODFREY, ARTHUR (1903–1983), U.S. radio and television performer. Godfrey first hit the airwaves as an amateur banjo and ukelele player on a Baltimore radio station. He later worked as a freelancer and local announcer for CBS. Following his dramatic coverage of Pres. Franklin D. Roosevelt's funeral, during which he wept into the microphone, he was moved (1945) into the regular morning lineup and went on to create an inexplicably popular early-morning show, heard by 40 million people a week. He snacked between records, discarded scripts, talked about products not belonging to his sponsors, and consistently debunked the commercial copy handed to him by his sponsors, preferring to ad-lib. Amazingly, sales of sponsors' products increased. Godfrey kept a group of young people around him on his "Arthur Godfrey's Talent Scouts" (on radio, 1946, and later, 1948–58, on television) and on "Arthur Godfrey and His Friends" (1949–56), and only began to lose popularity when he fired one of them, Julius LaRosa, on the air for "lack of humility." He continued his show until 1972 and later became involved with the causes of ecology and conservation.

GODOWSKY, LEOPOLD (1870–1938), Lithuanian-born pianist and composer. The son of a physician, Godowsky made his debut as a pianist in Wilno (Vilnius) in 1879, followed by a tour of Poland and Germany. A rich benefactor enabled him to enter the Berlin High School for Music at age 14, and he made his first U.S. tour the following year and became a U.S. citizen in 1891. Godowsky directed the piano department at the Chicago Conservatory of Music (1895–1900) and was a professor at Vienna's Master School of Piano Playing (1909–14), where he developed new theories of piano technique. He lived in New York after 1914. A stroke (1930) ended his career as a soloist. He also edited educational works, composed 53 studies on Chopin's *Etudes,* and wrote original concert studies for piano, violin, and symphony orchestra. ■ See biography by Jeremy Nicholas (1989).

GOEBBELS, PAUL JOSEPH (1897–1945), German Nazi political leader. Goebbels studied art and literature (Ph.D. from Heidelberg University, 1921) and dreamed of becoming a writer. Instead, he joined the Nazi party in 1924 and used his skill at demagoguery to help the Nazis gain control of Germany. As minister of propaganda (1933–45) with control over Germany's press, theater, art, and music, he stage-managed the mass meetings and orchestrated the official anti-Semitism of the Third Reich. The only one of the original top Nazis to remain faithful to the end, Goebbels

killed himself, his wife, and six children shortly after Adolf Hitler's suicide. ■ See his diaries (Eng. trans. 1948, 1962, 1965, 1978) as well as biographies by Roger Manvell and Heinrich Fraenkel (1960), Ernest Bramsted (1965), Viktor Reimann (Eng. trans. 1976), and Ralf G. Reuth (1990; Eng. trans. 1993).

GOEPPERT MAYER, MARIA. *See MAYER, MARIA GOEPPERT.*

GOERDELER, KARL FRIEDRICH (1884–1945), German political leader. A nationalist right-wing, anti-Nazi municipal administrator, Goerdeler resigned as mayor of Leipzig (1937) to organize a resistance movement against Nazi dictator Adolf Hitler. With the onset of World War II he hoped to win Allied support for his plans to overthrow the Nazi government and become the new chancellor. However, after the attempted assassination of Hitler failed (July 20, 1944), Goerdeler went into hiding. Captured in Poland, he was executed. ■ See Gerhard Ritter, *The German Resistance* (Eng. trans. 1958).

GOERING, HERMANN WILHELM (1893–1946), German Nazi political and military leader. A World War I flying ace, Goering joined forces with Adolf Hitler, who made him commander of the storm troopers in 1922. When Hitler was named chancellor (1933), Goering became minister of interior in Prussia and created the Gestapo, the Nazi secret police. He achieved more prominence as aviation minister (1933) by developing and expanding the air force. By 1936, Goering had accumulated vast economic influence, which he used to plunder German Jews and to bolster his personal finances. Although his reputation suffered from the defeat of the German air force in the Battle of Britain (1940) and from his frequent military miscalculations as World War II proceeded, Goering remained an influential promoter of Hitler's policies. His futile attempt (1945) to succeed Hitler resulted in his expulsion from the Nazi party. Sentenced to death by the Nuremberg tribunal, Goering committed suicide on the eve of his scheduled execution. ■ See biography by Roger Manvell and Heinrich Fraenkel (1962) and Leonard Mosley, *The Reich Marshal* (1974).

GOFFMAN, ERVING (1922–1982), Canadian-born U.S. sociologist. The recipient of a Ph.D. from the University of Chicago (1953), Goffman studied the effects of the total institution on the individual and wrote several books about the meaning of the seemingly innocuous social transactions of everyday life. He spent a year at St. Elizabeth's Hospital in Washington, D.C., preparatory to writing *Asylums* (1961), a detailed description of a mental hospital from the patient's viewpoint. Goffman also wrote *Stigma* (1963), *Behavior in Public Places* (1963), *Relations in Public* (1972), and *Forms of Talk* (1981). He taught at the University of California (1958–68) and the University of Pennsylvania (from 1968). ■ See study by Tom Burns (1992).

GOGARTY, OLIVER ST. JOHN (1878–1957), Irish novelist, poet, surgeon, and politician. An ebullient personality whose witticisms were legendary in Dublin, Gogarty was educated at Trinity College (Dublin) and Oxford and became a distinguished physician. His many literary friends included W. B. Yeats, George Moore, and George Russell, the leaders of the Irish literary renaissance. He was a classmate of James Joyce, who modeled Buck Mulligan in *Ulysses* after him. Gogarty was elected (1922) to the senate of the Irish Free State. His best-known works were *As I Was Going Down Sackville Street* (1937), a vivid collection of scenes depicting everyday life in Dublin; *Tumbling in the Hay* (1939), an autobiographical novel of his student days; and *Collected Poems* (1952). ■ See his autobiography, *It Isn't This Time of Year at All!* (1954); Ulick O'Connor, *The Times I've Seen* (1964); and biography by J. B. Lyons (1980).

GOKHALE, GOPAL KRISHNA (1866–1915), Indian political leader. Gokhale, who was named the secretary of the Indian National Congress party in 1895, was an illustrious college teacher, local politician, social reformer, and nationalist. A political moderate, he served in the Bombay and Imperial legislative councils (1899–1915), founded the Servants of India Society (1905), and was president of the Congress party (1905). He visited Britain (1905, 1908) to urge civil rights for Indian citizens. The great nationalist leader Mahatma Gandhi, who met Gokhale in South Africa, considered him a political mentor. ■ See biography by D. B. Mathur (1966) and study by Bal Ram Nanda (1977).

GOLD, MICHAEL (Irving Granich; 1893–1967), U.S. novelist, playwright, and journalist. A product of New York City's Lower East Side Jewish ghetto, Gold became one of America's best-known proletarian writers. His columns, plays, and novels all dealt with social protest and the need for revolutionary, socialist change through class struggle. He wrote a column, "Change the World," for the communist *Daily Worker* for more than three decades, wrote plays for the Provincetown Players during the 1920s, contributed to the radical literary magazine, *The Masses,* and edited the *Liberator* and *The New Masses* (1928–32). However, he was best known for his novel *Jews Without Money* (1930), a classic account of life in New York's slums prior to World War I. ■ See John Pyros, *Mike Gold: Dean of American Proletarian Writers* (1979).

GOLD, THOMAS (1920–   ), Austrian-born U.S. astronomer. Educated at Cambridge University (M.A. 1945), Gold formulated (with mathematician Hermann Bondi and cosmologist Fred Hoyle) the steady-state theory of the universe. The theory, which stated that matter is being created at a rate enabling the ever-expanding universe to maintain a constant mean density, was widely abandoned in favor of the "big bang" theory by the 1960s and 1970s. Gold directed the Center for Radiophysics and Space Research at Cornell University (1959–81) and made important contributions to the study of pulsars, quasars, planetary motion, the lunar surface, and solar flares and storms. In the late 1950s he developed the controversial "deep-earth gas" theory of the origin of oil and natural gas, which refuted the traditional organic theories relating to the formation of hydrocarbons. He believed that hydrocarbons were created when the earth was formed and were trapped deep inside and still remain there. He wrote *Power from the Earth: Deep Earth Gas-energy for the Future* (1987).

GOLDBERG, ARTHUR JOSEPH (1908–1990), U.S. public official and jurist. The son of Jewish immigrants from Russia, Goldberg received a law degree from Northwestern University (1929) and practiced law in Chicago. Closely associated with the organized labor movement, he represented several major unions during the late 1930s and early 1940s and was appointed general counsel for the Congress of Industrial Organizations (CIO) and the United Steelworkers Union in 1948. He gained a national reputation as a negotiator and mediator and was the chief architect of the merger of the American Federation of Labor (AFL) with the CIO in 1955. An influential supporter of Democratic presidential candidate John F. Kennedy in 1960, Goldberg served as his secretary of labor (1961–62) and was appointed to the Supreme Court (1962), where he created a liberal majority. He left the court (1965) to serve as ambassador to the United Nations (1965–68) and ran unsuccessfully for the governorship of New York (1970). He wrote *AFL-CIO: Labor United* (1956) and *Equal Justice* (1971). ■ See his public papers, *The Defenses of Freedom* (1966), and biography by David L. Stebenne (1996).

GOLDBERG, BERTRAND (1913–1997), U.S. architect. Goldberg studied at Harvard (1930–32) and worked under Ludwig Mies van der Rohe at the Bauhaus in Germany (1932–33). He returned home to Chicago to experiment with prefabricated projects and public housing on the city's South Side. Attracted by the possibilities of curvilinear shapes, he designed Mike Todd's Chicago Cinestage (1957) and Marina City (1963), soaring columns of apartments with petaled balconies. (He also designed, in 1987, River City, a pair of undulating 17-story apartment towers on the Chicago River.) From the 1960s he specialized in designing hospitals and health centers, including Saint Joseph Hospital (Tacoma, Washington) and the Health Science Center at the State University of New York, Stony Brook.

GOLDBERG, RUBE (Reuben Lucius Goldberg; 1883–1970), U.S. cartoonist. Trained in engineering, Goldberg turned from planning sewers to drawing sports cartoons for San Francisco newspapers (1904–07). He later worked for the *New York Mail* (1907–21) until his cartoons became syndicated. Goldberg championed the daily comic strip and poked fun at America's love affair with technology. His long-running strip *Boob McNutt,* as well as the series *Foolish Questions,* typically featured absurdly complex contraptions carrying out simple tasks, including a device for people who cannot tolerate the noise of celery chewing. After 1938 he turned to editorial cartooning and won a 1948 Pulitzer Prize for *Peace Today,* a cartoon about the dangers of nuclear weapons. Goldberg also wrote *How to Remove the Cotton from a Bottle of Aspirin* (1959). ∎ See biography by Peter C. Marzio (1973).

GOLDBERGER, JOSEPH (1874–1929), Austrian-born U.S. physician and medical researcher. A graduate of the City College of New York and the Bellevue Hospital Medical College (1895), Goldberger investigated yellow fever and typhus for the U.S. Public Health Service in Mexico and Cuba. From 1913 to 1925 he studied pellagra in the southern United States and proved that the disease was not infectious and was caused by a dietary deficiency. Goldberger cured the disease with a diet of milk, meat, and yeast, which was rich in what he called the "p-p" (pellagra-prevention) factor. This was later identified as niacin or nicotinic acid (a member of the vitamin-B-complex group). From 1904 to 1929 he worked at the Hygienic Laboratory in Washington, D.C.

GOLDEN, HARRY (Herschel Goldhirsch; 1902–1981), U.S. writer. Golden's family emigrated when he was a child from Austria-Hungary to the United States, where his father worked for the *Jewish Daily Forward.* After serving three years in prison (1929–32) for a fraudulent stock scheme, Golden worked as a reporter in New York City. He moved to Charlotte, North Carolina (1939) and published the *Carolina Israelite* (1941–68), a monthly newspaper, as a personal forum for his humorous reminiscences, social commentary, and attacks on bigotry and racism. Pointing out that whites were apparently willing to stand, if not sit, next to blacks, he proposed to end segregation with a "Golden Vertical Negro Plan," by which seats in public places would be abolished. In addition to *Only in America* (1958) and *For 2¢ Plain* (1959), two best-selling collections of his writings, Golden published works on American Jewish history and a study of Carl Sandburg (1961). ∎ See his autobiography, *The Right Time* (1969), and Clarence W. Thomas, *The Serious Humor of Harry Golden* (1997).

GOLDIN, HORACE (Hyman Goldstein; 1873–1939), Russian-born magician and illusionist. One of the highest-paid entertainers on the British and American stage, Goldin was known as the man who invented the trick of sawing a woman in half with a circular saw. He also was known for making people disappear, boring a hole through a man, shooting a canary into a burning light bulb, and stopping a bullet between his teeth. ∎ See his *It's Fun to Be Fooled* (1937).

GOLDING, SIR WILLIAM (1911–1993), British novelist. Educated at Oxford (B.A. 1935), Golding took from World War II naval service a lasting conviction of humanity's potential for irrational and barbaric acts. He later taught school. He wrote imaginative, dramatic novels which held, beneath realistic exteriors, symbolic moral fables. His most acclaimed work, *Lord of the Flies* (1954), concerned a group of proper English schoolboys who, isolated on a desert island, revert to savagery. Later novels included *The Inheritors* (1955), *Pincher Martin* (1956), *The Spire* (1964), *The Pyramid* (1967), *Darkness Visible* (1979), *Rites of Passage* (1980), *The Paper Men* (1984), *Close Quarters* (1987), and *Fire Down Below* (1989). He also wrote short stories, plays, and a book of criticism, *A Moving Target* (1982). *An Egyptian Journal* (1985) recounted a boat trip up the Nile River. Awarding Golding the 1983 Nobel Prize in Literature—a decision that sparked some controversy—the Swedish Academy cited his novels that "illuminate the human condition in the world today." ∎ See studies by Virginia Tiger (1974) and Lawrence J. Friedman (1983) and Arnold Johnson, *Of Earth and Darkness* (1980).

GOLDMAN, EMMA (1869–1940), Russian-born U.S. anarchist. At age 16 Goldman emigrated to the United States and found work in the garment industry. Goldman became involved in the anarchist movement in New York City (1889), winning attention with her stirring speeches on anarchism, women's emancipation, the institution of marriage, and other social issues. Goldman was sentenced (1893) to a year's imprisonment for inciting a riot when she urged unemployed workers to steal bread if they had no money to feed their families. With Alexander Berkman, Goldman published the anarchist monthly *Mother Earth* (1906–17); in 1908 her U.S. citizenship was revoked. She was imprisoned briefly in 1916 for publicly endorsing contraception and again the next year for opposing the draft. After serving a two-year sentence, Goldman was deported. She lived in the Soviet Union (1919–21), but broke with the bolsheviks and left for Sweden, thereafter living in Germany, France, England, and Canada. She actively supported the Loyalist forces in the Spanish Civil War. Goldman's writings included *Anarchism and Other Essays* (1911), *Social Significance of the Modern Drama* (1914), *My Disillusionment in Russia* (1923), and the autobiography *Living My Life* (1931). ∎ See Richard Drinnon, *Rebel in Paradise* (1961); Alix Kates Shulman, *To the Barricades* (1971); Candace Falk, *Love, Anarchy and Emma Goldman* (1984); and biographies by Alice Wexler (1984), Martha Solomon (1987), and John Chalberg (1991).

GOLDMAN, MAYER CLARENCE (1874–1939), U.S. lawyer. A pioneer in the legal-aid movement in the United States, Goldman spoke throughout the country and wrote some 800 articles in support of public defenders for poor people accused of a crime. His book *The Public Defender* (1917) was extremely influential. Although opposed by many lawyers, his plan was gradually adopted in San Francisco, Chicago, Hartford, New Haven, Bridgeport, St. Louis, Tulsa, and Miami, and during the 1930s it had the support of the U.S. Department of Justice and the American Bar Association.

GOLDMANN, LUCIEN (1913–1970), Rumanian-born French literary critic and philosopher. Goldmann studied at the University of Zurich (Ph.D. 1944) and taught at the University of Brussels (1946–58) and the École Pratiques des hautes études in Paris (1958–70). His writings, grounded in Marxist thought and structuralist concepts, are related both to the work of the Hungarian critic Gyorgy Lukács and to formalist criticism. *The Hidden God* (1956; Eng. trans. 1964), a Marxist/structuralist analysis of the classic French writers Pascal and Racine, elicited a response from the semiotician Roland Barthes in *On Racine* (1963; Eng. trans. 1964). *Towards a Sociology of the Novel* (1964; Eng. trans. 1975) included an extended study of André Malraux's fiction and also three essays that elaborated Goldmann's method of "genetic structuralism." His other works included *The Human Sciences and Philosophy* (1952; Eng. trans. 1969), *Cultural Creation in Modern Society* (1971; Eng. trans. 1976), *The Philosophy of the Enlightenment* (1968; Eng. trans. 1973), and *Essays on Method in the Sociology of Literature* (Eng. trans. 1980).

GOLDMARK, PETER CARL (1906–1977), Hungarian-born U.S. engineer and inventor. Born in Budapest, Goldmark emigrated to the United States in 1933 (U.S. citizen 1937). His work at the Columbia Broadcasting System (CBS) laboratories revolutionized television broadcasting and the recorded music and video industries. He made the first color-television broadcast (1940). A music lover, he hated listening to lengthy works on short-playing, 78-rpm records and invented the long-playing (LP) microgroove phonograph record (1948). He also pioneered in electronic videocassette recording. Goldmark was influential in the field of educational television. He died in a car crash at age 71. ■ See his memoirs, *Maverick Inventor* (with Lee Edson; 1973).

GOLDSCHMIDT, VICTOR MORITZ (1888–1947), Swiss-born Norwegian mineralogist and chemist. One of the pioneers of geochemistry, Goldschmidt taught at the University of Kristiania (now Oslo; 1914–29) and Göttingen, Germany (1929–35). Utilizing newly developed X-ray techniques, Goldschmidt and his colleagues made extensive crystallographic studies of 75 elements and related the hardness of crystals to their structures, the distance between adjacent charged atoms, and their ionic charges. Goldschmidt also devised geological maps of the earth and analyzed meteorites. Forced to leave Göttingen by rising anti-Semitism, he returned to Oslo, where he worked until the German World War II occupation of Norway (1940). He was interned in a concentration camp, but he escaped to Sweden (1942) and spent the remaining war years in Britain, where he did research in soil science. He returned to Oslo after the war. His book *Geochemistry* (1954), edited by Alex Muir, was published posthumously.

GOLDSTEIN, JOSEPH LEONARD (1940–   ), U.S. molecular geneticist. Goldstein graduated from the Southwestern Medical School of the University of Texas in Dallas (M.D. 1966) and did research in biomedical genetics at the National Heart Institute (1968–70) and the University of Washington in Seattle (1970–72). As a professor at the University of Texas Health Science Center in Dallas (from 1972), he collaborated with Michael Brown on cholesterol research. Their discovery (1973) of low-density lipoprotein (LDL) receptors, molecules that extract cholesterol from the blood and transport it inside the cell, revolutionized the study of cholesterol metabolism. It paved the way for new dietary and drug therapies for the prevention and treatment of strokes, hardening of the arteries, heart attacks, and other diseases caused by the clogging of the arteries by the accumulation of fatty cholesterol. For their research, Goldstein and Brown shared the 1985 Nobel Prize in Physiology or Medicine. Goldstein was the coauthor of *The Metabolic Basis of Inherited Disease* (5th ed. 1983).

GOLDWATER, BARRY MORRIS (1909–1998), U.S. political leader. Educated at a military academy, Goldwater dropped out of college when his father died (1929), joined the family's department store (Goldwater's, Inc., in Phoenix, Arizona), and later served as its president (1937–53). A Republican conservative, he was elected to the Phoenix City Council (1949) and later to the U.S. Senate (1952; 1958). One of the leading conservative politicians of the 1950s and 1960s, he espoused rugged individualism and the free-enterprise system and spoke out against big government, the welfare state, and international communism. Nominated for president (1964) and declaring, "Extremism in the defense of liberty is no vice! . . . Moderation in the pursuit of justice is no virtue!" he carried only six states and was overwhelmingly defeated by Democratic incumbent Lyndon Johnson. He was reelected, however, to the Senate (1968; 1974; 1980) and remained a spokesperson of the conservative movement. He wrote *Conscience of a Conservative* (1960), *Why Not Victory* (1962), and his memoirs, *With No Apologies* (1979). ■ See biography by Peter Iverson (1997).

GOLDWYN, SAMUEL (Samuel Goldfish; 1882–1974), Polish-born U.S. film producer. A former glove salesman, Goldwyn wheeled and dealed his way to power in Hollywood. He produced his first film in 1913 with his brother-in-law Jesse Lasky; he emerged from later partnerships with Adolph Zukor and the Selwyn Brothers with his new name and a company that he sold to MGM in 1924. Subsequently an independent producer, he concentrated on quality rather than quantity, turning out such classics as *Wuthering Heights* (1939), *The Little Foxes* (1941), *The Best Years of Our Lives* (1946), and *Guys and Dolls* (1955). His non sequiturs ("Include me out," "In two words—impossible") were celebrated as Goldwynisms. He wrote *Behind the Screen* (1923). ■ See Carol Easton, *The Search for Sam Goldwyn* (1976); studies by Arthur Marx (1976) and Lawrence J. Epstein (1981); and biography by A. Scott Berg (1989).

GOLITSYN, BORIS BORISOVICH (1862–1916), Russian physicist and seismologist. A member of an old, noble family, Golitsyn studied at the University of Strasbourg and taught at Moscow University (1891–93) and the naval academy in St. Petersburg (1894–1914). He was a pioneer in scientific seismometry, and he invented the first electromagnetic seismograph (1906), which was able to record seismic vibrations precisely. Used for the study of earthquakes and for mineral prospecting, the apparatus was a prototype of modern seismographs and gained international recognition for Russian seismometry.

GOLLANCZ, SIR VICTOR (1893–1967), British publisher, author, and humanitarian. Born into a rabbinic family, Gollancz rejected its orthodoxy and middle-class conservatism and committed himself to socialism and later to pacifism. In 1928 he founded Victor Gollancz, Ltd., one of Britain's most successful and controversial publishing houses, and in 1936 founded the influential Left Book Club, which sought to expose Nazism and stop German dictator Adolf Hitler without war. Gollancz also founded committees to aid victims of Nazism (1941), to set up food relief in postwar Germany (1945), and to aid Arab refugees. He headed the National Campaign for the Abolition of Capital Punishment (1960–64). He wrote several widely read books on religion, politics, music, and literary criticism as well as three autobiographical volumes, *My Dear Timothy* (1952), *More for Timothy* (1953), and *Reminiscences of Affection* (1968). ■ See study by Ruth D. Edwards (1987) and the story of the publishing house by Sheila Hodges (1978).

GÖMBÖS, GYULA (1886–1936), Hungarian military and political leader. Active in right-wing and anti-Semitic politics from 1919, Gömbös served as minister of war (1929–32) and premier (1932–36). A man of totalitarian inclinations, he fostered the growth of fascism in Hungary and hoped to set up a dictatorial state allied with Italy and Germany. He met with strong domestic opposition, however, and he died before any of his plans could be carried out.

GOMBRICH, SIR ERNST HANS JOSEF (1909–), Austrian-born British art historian. Gombrich's father was a prominent Viennese lawyer and his mother was a pianist and member of composer Gustav Mahler's circle. He received his Ph.D. from the University of Vienna (1935) and emigrated to London, where he began his long association with the Warburg Institute at the University of London (from 1936; director, 1959–76). A man of immense erudition and wit, he was one of the most respected and widely read art historians of his generation. His major works, praised for their clarity and insight, included the bestselling history, *The Story of Art* (1950; 16th ed. rev. 1995), *Art and Illusion: A Study in the Psychology of Pictorial Representation* (1960), *Meditations on a Hobby Horse* (essays; 1963), *Aby Warburg: An Intellectual Biography* (1970), *A Sense of Order: A Study in the Psychology of Decorative Art* (1979),

The Image and the Eye (1982), *New Light on Old Masters* (1986), and *Topics of Our Time* (1991).

GOMBROWICZ, WITOLD (1904–1969), Polish novelist. A member of a wealthy family, Gombrowicz abandoned his law career for a literary one. His most famous novel, *Ferdydurke* (1938; Eng. trans. 1961, 2000), about the transformation of an adult into a child, was an international success. In all of his satiric, ironic, and absurdist works he sought to expose the phoniness of social relations and explain that human life cannot be lived as an individual but only in interdependence with others. He called this the "interhuman church." Among his other important works were *Ivona, Princess of Burgundia* (1938; Eng. trans. 1970), *Transatlantic* (1953; Eng. trans. 1994), *Pornografia* (1960; Eng. trans. 1966), *Cosmos* (1965; Eng. trans. 1967), and *Possessed* (1939; Eng. trans. 1981). Stranded in Buenos Aires at the start of World War II, he lived there until his return to Europe in the 1960s. ■ See his *Diary* (3 vols., 1957–69; Eng. trans. 1988–93), the autobiographical *A Kind of Testament* (1969; Eng. trans. 1973), and study by Ewa M. Thompson (1979).

GÓMEZ, JUAN VICENTE (1857–1935), Venezuelan dictator. An untutored cowboy of mixed Indian and European parentage, Gómez led his own private army into politics in 1899 in support of Cipriano Castro, from whom he seized power in 1908. As dictator for 27 years (1908–35), he was known as the "tyrant of the Andes" for the reign of terror maintained by his secret police. After the discovery of oil in 1918 he shrewdly negotiated foreign concessions, using the proceeds to further Venezuelan industrialization, militarization, and his own personal wealth. ■ See biography by Thomas Rourke (1936) and John Lavin, *A Halo for Gómez* (1954).

GÓMEZ CASTRO, LAUREANO ELEUTERIO (1889–1965), Colombian political leader. An ultraright-wing admirer of the dictators Hitler and Franco, Gómez led the Conservative party from 1932 until his death. He personified authoritarianism and clericalism, and during his presidency (1950–53) he presided over a repressive neofascist government. Ousted by the military (1953) and exiled in Spain, he collaborated with the Liberals to overthrow the new Colombian government (1957) and agreed to a power-sharing plan by which the Liberals and Conservatives would alternately hold presidential power (1958–74).

GOMPERS, SAMUEL (1850–1924), U.S. labor leader. Gompers was born in London of Dutch-Jewish parentage and emigrated to the United States at age 13. He became a cigar maker like his father but worked his way up through the local union to found (1886) the American Federation of Labor (AFL), a group of autonomous craft unions. A skilled debater and respected leader, Gompers favored collective bargaining and strikes for bread-and-butter issues. Rejecting radicalism and political and ideological entanglements during nearly 40 years of leadership, Gompers built the AFL into the largest labor organization in the United States. ■ See his autobiography, *Seventy Years of Life and Labor* (2 vols., 1925), and studies by Bernard Mandel (1963) and Will Chasan (1971).

GOMULKA, WLADYSLAW (1905–1982), Polish political leader. Gomulka joined the Communist party (1926) and was imprisoned repeatedly during the interwar period for his activity in the workers' movement, but he escaped during World War II to join the underground. He became deputy premier of Poland (1945) and was also secretary of the Polish Workers' party until he was purged (1949) for nationalistic sympathies. Gomulka remained under virtual arrest until 1956, when he returned to power as first secretary of the party on a wave of economic unrest, to seek a "Polish way" to socialism. In 1970 a similar outbreak of unrest led to Gomulka's replacement by Edward Gierek. ■ See study by Nicholas Bethell (rev. ed. 1972).

GONCHAROVA, NATALIA SERGEEVNA (1881–1962), Russian artist and illustrator. A great-granddaughter of the poet Aleksandr Pushkin, Goncharova studied science at Moscow University, then trained in art in Moscow and Western Europe. In the years before the 1917 Bolshevik revolution, she was associated with such avant-garde art groups as the "Jack of Diamonds" and "Donkey's Tail" in Russia, and the Blue Rider group in Germany. Using folk-art motifs and drawing on the idioms of futurism, Goncharova figured prominently in the revolution in graphic design that took place in Russia early in the century. Her constructivist graphics combined the printed word with bold, visual images in book illustrations and posters. She worked closely with her husband, artist Mikhail Larionov. Goncharova emigrated to Paris (1915), where she created stage and costume designs for impresario Sergei Diaghilev. ■ See Mary Chamot, *Goncharova: Stage Designs and Paintings* (1979).

GONZALES, PANCHO (Richard Alonzo Gonzales; 1928–1995), U.S. tennis player. Born into a poor California Mexican-American family, Gonzales had little formal training when he began entering tournaments. His sensational career spanned an astonishing three decades. He won the U.S. amateur championship (1948) after only four years of tournament competition and successfully defended his title the next year, after helping the U.S. Davis Cup team to a victory over Australia. Gonzales turned professional (1949) at age 21 in an era when only amateurs qualified for major tennis tournaments and professionals played relatively unpublicized one-night stands. He dominated the men's pro tour in the 1950s with an aggressive, well-rounded game; throughout the 1960s and early 1970s he continued to play in the major tournaments, challenging younger rivals. His list of titles does not fully reflect his standing in the tennis world. ■ See his autobiography, *Man with a Racket* (1959).

GONZÁLEZ, JULIO (1876–1942), Spanish painter and sculptor. Born into a family of metalworkers, González was almost exclusively a painter until 1927, when at age 50 he began experimenting with metal sculpture, using his grounding in cubist painting as a point of departure. Working with wrought and welded iron, he developed new techniques and strongly influenced later metal sculptors, including the American David Smith. His best-known works included the *Monserrat* series (begun in 1932) and *Cactus People* (1939–40).

GONZÁLEZ MÁRQUEZ, FELIPE (1942–   ), Spanish political leader. Born into a farming family, González joined the clandestine Socialist Youth movement in 1962 and the outlawed Spanish Socialist Workers party (PSOE) in 1964. After graduating from the Seville University Law School (1966) he worked as a labor lawyer and joined the PSOE executive committee (1970). A moderate who worked to broaden the base of the party, he was elected PSOE leader in 1974. He maintained close ties with other European socialists and served as vice president of the Socialist International (1976–   ). In 1977, the year that the PSOE was legalized, it won the first free elections in Spain in more than 40 years (capturing 28.5 percent of the popular vote) and became the largest single party in the country. González, a fiery orator, led the party to a landslide victory in the 1982 elections. As prime minister (1982–96) he carried out social reforms, decentralized the government, extended welfare benefits, and led Spain into the European Common Market (January 1986).

GONZÁLEZ MARTÍNEZ, ENRIQUE (1871–1952), Mexican poet. After practicing medicine for nearly two decades, González Martínez devoted himself to poetry. His serious, careful verse reacted against the coldness of modernist poetry. Exploring inner experience and describing serene landscapes, he influenced postmodernist poets of the late 1920s and 1930s who attempted to utilize universal symbols and images to express Mexican themes. He served as Mexican ambassador to Spain. Argentina, and Chile and helped found the National College (1943). ■ See study by John H. Brushwood (1969).

GOOCH, GEORGE PEABODY (1873–1968), British historian. G. P. Gooch was a Liberal member of Parliament (1906–10) and editor of the *Contemporary Review* (1911–60). An authority on diplomatic history, he coedited *The Cambridge History of British Foreign Policy* (3 vols., 1922–23) and the British documents on the origins of World War I (13 vols., 1926–38). He was an early opponent of fascism, and presided over the antifascist National Peace Council (1933–36). He also wrote important works on modern German history and a notable study of historiography, *History and Historians in the Nineteenth Century* (1913). ■ See his autobiography, *Under Six Reigns* (1958), and study by Frank Eyck (1982).

GOOD, ROBERT ALAN (1922–   ), U.S. immunologist. Born in Minnesota, Good graduated from the state university medical school (1947), where he became head of the pathology department and professor of pediatrics. A specialist in pediatric immunological disorders, he discovered that the thymus gland regulates part of the immunity system and pioneered the technique of bone-marrow transplants. He headed New York City's Sloan-Kettering Institute for Cancer Research (1973–80). He later taught at the University of Oklahoma (1982–85) and the University of South Florida (1985–   ).

GOODALL, JANE (1934–   ), British ethologist. Goodall's childhood dream, while growing up in London and Bournemouth, was to study animals in Africa. Although she had no training in animal behavior, her dream became a reality when famed paleontologist Louis Leakey, for whom she worked as an assistant secretary (1957), arranged for her to study chimpanzees in the wild at the Gombe Stream Game Reserve (now Gombe National Park) on Lake Tanganyika in northern Tanzania. Her research, which began in 1960, continued through the 1990s and became the longest continuous field study of animals in their natural habitat. Developing her own methodology she was able, over time, to gain the trust of a group of animals and to observe their daily activities at close quarters. Her findings, for example, that chimpanzees are meat eaters, that they make tools, that they display affection and tenderness as well as warlike behavior, and that they communicate by means of nonverbal "body language," demonstrated that the behavior of chimpanzees was remarkably similar to that of human beings and revolutionized the field of primatology. She described her ongoing research, for which she earned a Ph.D. in ethology at Cambridge University (1965), in *My Friends the Wild Chimpanzees* (1967), *In the Shadow of Man* (1971), *The Chimpanzees of Gombe: Patterns of Behavior* (1986), and *Through a Window* (1990). In 1990 she cofounded the Committee for the Conservation and Care of Chimpanzees to protect threatened populations of chimpanzees around the world. ■ See her *Reason for Hope: A Spiritual Journey* (1999; with Phillip Berman).

GOODMAN, BENNY (Benjamin David Goodman; 1909–1986), U.S. musician. A virtuoso clarinetist who spent a decade playing with various dance and jazz bands, Goodman formed his own band (1934) and developed (with arranger Fletcher Henderson) a new kind of jazz called "swing." Characterized by driving, insistent rhythms interspersed with brilliant improvisational solos, "swing" introduced jazz to a mass white audience. Goodman's music swept the country, and he was hailed as "the king of swing." His band, featuring such soloists as Lionel Hampton, Teddy Wilson, Harry James, and Gene Krupa, was the first racially mixed jazz ensemble and one of the nation's most popular bands for a decade. Among his most famous recordings were "Let's Dance," "Avalon," "Tiger Rag," and "Sing, Sing,

Sing." In a spectacularly successful concert in 1938, Goodman introduced jazz to New York's Carnegie Hall. He organized a new band in 1955, played the music for the film *The Benny Goodman Story* (1956), and continued playing his old standards in the United States and on numerous world tours through the 1980s. He was also noted as a classical clarinetist and performed and recorded with many leading orchestras. ■ See his autobiography, *The King of Swing* (1939); biography by Stanley Baron (1979); and Ross Firestone, *Swing, Swing, Swing* (1993).

GOODMAN, PAUL (1911–1972), U.S. writer. Calling himself a humanist, Paul Goodman disregarded critics who, while conceding his brilliance, complained that he spread himself too thin. A scholar, Reichian lay therapist, city planner, radical social critic, and writer of drama, short stories, novels, and poetry, he grew up in New York City's Greenwich Village and attended the City College of New York. Goodman informed all of his work with the conviction that organized structures stifle individual creativity, and he inspired political thinkers of the New Left. The best-selling *Growing Up Absurd* (1960) attacked American materialism and advocated dropping out. *Compulsory Mis-Education* (1964) was a critique of standardized schooling, and *People or Personnel* (1965) and *Like a Conquered Province* (1967) were attacks on centralism and militarism. Goodman considered himself first and foremost a poet and was a superb technician in both fixed and free forms. ■ See his *Collected Poems* (1974) and *Collected Stories* (4 vols., 1978–80); his memoirs, *Five Years: Thoughts in a Useless Time* (1966); and study by Kingsley Widmer (1980).

GOODPASTURE, ERNEST WILLIAM (1886–1960), U.S. pathologist. A graduate of Vanderbilt University (1907) and Johns Hopkins (M.D. 1912), Goodpasture taught at Harvard Medical School (1915–22) and at Vanderbilt Medical School (1924–55). Working first with fowl-pox virus and later with rickettsia and herpes simplex, he succeeded in cultivating the organisms in fertile chicken eggs. Goodpasture's success with chicken eggs as a cheap and sterile medium led to the large-scale production of vaccines for smallpox, typhus, yellow fever, mumps, influenza, and other diseases.

GOODSON, MARK (1915–1992), **and WILLIAM SELDEN TODMAN** (1916–1979), U.S. television producers. Goodson, a radio announcer, and Todman, a radio writer and producer, teamed up in 1946 to produce the popular radio quiz shows "Winner Take All" (1946), "Stop the Music" (1947), and "Hit the Jackpot" (1947). They soon switched to television and devised and produced the most popular and successful quiz shows in TV history, including "The Price Is Right," "I've Got a Secret," "To Tell the Truth," "Password," "Beat the Clock," "Stop the Music," and "What's My Line?" (1950–67), the second-longest running show in the history of television. The shows were most popular in the 1950s and 1960s, but many were revived in the 1970s. Goodson and Todman also produced dramatic shows and owned several newspapers and radio stations.

GOODSPEED, EDGAR JOHNSON (1871–1962), U.S. biblical scholar and educator. Goodspeed was a University of Chicago professor of Greek and religion (1902–37) who translated the New Testament (1923) and the Apocrypha (1938) into the American vernacular. He also collaborated on the translation of *The Complete Bible* (1939), participated in the preparation of the 1946 Revised Standard Version of the New Testament, and wrote extensively on biblical subjects, including *An Introduction to the New Testament* (1937) and *A Life of Jesus* (1950). ▪ See his autobiography, *As I Remember* (1953).

GORBACHEV, MIKHAIL SERGEYEVICH (1931–), Soviet political leader. Born into a peasant family, Gorbachev was active in the Komsomol and joined the Communist party in 1952. He earned a law degree (Moscow State University, 1955) and a diploma in agronomy (1967), and worked as a party official in the Stavropol area. A protégé of party officials Mikhail Suslov and Yuri Andropov, Gorbachev was appointed to the Supreme Soviet (1970) and the Central Committee of the party (1971), served as agriculture secretary (1978–85), and was named to the Politburo (1980), becoming its youngest member. Elected party general secretary after the death of Konstantin U. Chernenko (March 1985), he continued the broad program of economic and social reforms first enunciated by Andropov, the party leader from 1982 to 1984. At a Geneva summit meeting with U.S. Pres. Ronald Reagan (November 1985) he expressed his opposition to Reagan's Strategic Defense Initiative ("Star Wars") and subsequently offered a plan (1986) to eliminate all nuclear weapons by the year 2000. Presiding at the 27th Party Congress (1986), he proposed the introduction of economic incentives, price flexibility, and limited aspects of private enterprise to spur economic growth and modernization. His book *A Time for Peace* (Eng. trans. 1985) was aimed at readers in the West. He signed a treaty with Reagan abolishing intermediate-range nuclear weapons (1987). By the late 1980s his reform policies of *glasnost* (openness) and *perestroika* (restructuring) transformed Soviet society. As president of the Soviet Union (1988–91) he withdrew Soviet troops from Eastern Europe, paving the way for the fall of the Communist regimes there. He improved relations with the West, and was awarded the 1990 Nobel Peace Prize. However, his policies led to inflation and food shortages and to the growth of independence movements by nationalities within the Soviet Union. He was severely criticized by both Communists and radical reformers and after an abortive coup by Communist hardliners (August 1991), his political rival Boris Yeltsin emerged as a national hero and wielded effective power. In the wake of the failed coup, Gorbachev resigned as leader of the Communist party, the party was suspended by Parliament, and most of the constituent republics of the Soviet Union declared their independence. Unwilling to accept the breakup of his country, Gorbachev resigned the presidency (December 25, 1991). Running for president in 1996 he received 0.5 percent of the vote. ▪ See his *Memoirs* (1995; Eng. trans. 1996) and *On My Country and the World* (1998; Eng. trans. 1999); biographies by Zhores Medvedev (1986) and Christian Schmidt-Häuer (Eng. trans. 1986); and study by Martin McCauley (1998).

GORDIMER, NADINE (1923–), South African writer. Born in the suburbs of Johannesburg into a Jewish middle-class family, Gordimer rejected the fears and prejudices of her social milieu and created a body of literature (in English) that described the destructive and alienating effects of the authoritarian and racially segregated society of South Africa. Although she was a passionate foe of apartheid, her writings were devoid of polemicism and sentimentality and were praised for their subtlety and precision. She was best known for the short-story collections *Soft Voice of the Serpent* (1952), *Friday's Footprint* (1960), *A Soldier's Embrace* (1980), *Something Out There* (1984), and *Jump* (1991) and the novels *The Lying Days* (1953), *The World of Strangers* (1958), *A Guest of Honour* (1970), *The Conservationist* (1974), *Burger's Daughter* (1979), *July's People* (1981), and *My Son's Story* (1990). She was awarded the 1991 Nobel Prize in Literature. Her novels concerning post-apartheid society included *None to Accompany Me* (1994) and *The House Gun* (1998). ▪ See studies by Robert F. Haugh (1974) and Michael Wade (1978) and Nancy T. Bazin and Marilyn D. Seymour, *Conversations with Nadine Gordimer* (1990).

GORDON, AARON DAVID (1856–1922), spiritual leader of the Palestinian Jewish labor movement. Gordon was born and raised in czarist Russia. In 1904 he emigrated to Palestine and moved from place to place doing agricultural work. Gordon formulated a doctrine of "religion of labor" that formed the basis of his labor Zionism and became a cornerstone of the non-Marxist Israeli labor movement. He believed that the return of the Jewish people to nature and to manual labor would be a source of renewal and he spent the last ten years of his life at Degania, the first kibbutz. Gordon typified the idealism of the first generation of Jewish pioneers in Palestine, whose ideological roots were in Russian socialism as well as in Zionism. ▪ See his *Selected Essays* (Eng. trans. 1938) and Herbert H. Rose, *The Life and Thought of A. D. Gordon* (1964).

GORDY, BERRY, JR. (1929–), U.S. record producer. Born in Detroit's black ghetto, Gordy wrote some moderately successful songs, including "Lonely Teardrops," before turning to production. In the late 1950s, when black rhythm and blues was attracting a larger audience, he founded Motown Records (1959), later becoming chairman of the board of Motown Industries. Gordy carefully groomed his stars— the Temptations, Diana Ross and the Supremes, Stevie Wonder, the Jackson Five, Marvin Gaye, Lionel Richie, and others—to produce a slick, chromed "Motown" sound that greatly affected popular music in the 1960s and beyond. The recording empire he established was a major breakthrough for African-American entrepreneurs in the entertainment industry. ∎ See his autobiography, *To Be Loved* (1994), and Nelson George, *Where Did Our Love Go?* (1986).

GORE, AL (Albert Gore, Jr.; 1948–), U.S. political leader. The son of a liberal Democratic congressman and senator from Tennessee, Gore grew up in Washington, D.C., and graduated from Harvard (B.A. 1969). He worked as a reporter before serving as a Democratic congressman (1977–85) and senator (1985–92) from Tennessee. Associated with the Democratic Leadership Council, he believed that only by moving to the right could the Democrats regain the White House. He ran unsuccessfully for president in the 1988 primaries. As U.S. vice president under President Bill Clinton (1993–97; 1997–2001), he gained a reputation as an advocate of streamlining federal agencies and of protecting the environment, and was a close and trusted adviser to the president. He wrote the best-selling *Earth in the Balance: Ecology and the Human Spirit* (1992). He was defeated for president (2000) by George W. Bush in one of the closest presidential elections in U.S. history. ∎ See biography by Bob Zelnick (1999) and Bill Turque, *Inventing Al Gore* (2000).

GÓRECKI, HENRYK (1933–), Polish composer. Górecki trained at the Katowice Conservatory (1955–60) and later studied in Paris with Olivier Messiaen. While still a student, he emerged as a leader of the Polish avant-garde by composing a series of atonal experimental pieces, including *Scontri* (1960). He changed his style, however, with *Three Pieces in the Olden Style* (1963), and most of his subsequent orchestral and choral works were influenced by Polish folk melodies, medieval Polish laments, and Roman Catholic devotional music. His compositions, referred to by some critics as "holy" or "mystical" minimalism, utilized simple, repetitive motives and slow tempi and were based on themes of human suffering. They included *Beatus Vir* (1979), *Misererre* (1981), and *Totus Tuus* (1987). He achieved international superstar status with the 1992 recording of his *Symphony No. 3: Symphony of Sorrowful Songs* (1976), a hauntingly beautiful and hypnotic 55-minute work for soprano and orchestra that became a best-selling album in the United States and Britain and sold hundreds of thousands of copies throughout the world. ∎ See study by Adrian Thomas (1997).

GOREN, CHARLES HENRY (1901–1991), U.S. expert on bridge. Goren gave up a legal practice in Philadelphia (1936) to concentrate on bridge, becoming one of the world's most famous players and winning the U.S. national championship over 30 times. His books, notably *Winning Bridge Made Easy* (1936) and *Contract Bridge Complete* (1951; rev. ed. 1957), which popularized and expanded the point-count bidding system, sold over four million copies and were translated into many languages. His bridge column was syndicated to more than 200 newspapers.

GOREY, EDWARD (1925–2000), U.S. writer and illustrator. Gorey served in the army (1944–46), finished undergraduate work at Harvard (1950), and later worked in Adlai Stevenson's presidential campaign (1952). At the same time he tried to sell his drawings and wrote *The Beastly Baby*, which he self-published (1962) under the Fantod Press imprint. Gorey created dozens of small books that won a large cult following. His fanciful and gory illustrations, executed in the style of steel and wood engravings, accompanied wittily grim texts about bizarre and often sadistic characters who commit awful acts in Gothic settings. His books included *The Hapless Child* (1961), *The Epiplectic Bicycle* (1968), *Dancing Cats and Neglected Murderesses* (1980), *The Eclectic Abecedarium* (1983), and the popular anthologies *Amphigorey* (1972) and *Amphigorey, too* (1975). He won a Tony Award (1978) for costume design for the Broadway show *Dracula*. ∎ See Clifford Ross, *The World of Edward Gorey* (1996).

GORGAS, WILLIAM CRAWFORD (1854–1920), U.S. sanitarian. An army doctor, Gorgas undertook a mosquito control and sanitary program in Panama (1904–14) that effectively cut the incidence of yellow fever and malaria and thus ensured the construction of the Panama Canal. As surgeon general of the army (1914–18), he was responsible for the organization of medical personnel in World War I. ∎ See the biography by Marie D. Gorgas and Burton J. Hendrick (1924) and John M. Gibson, *Physician to the World* (1950).

GORGEOUS GEORGE (George Raymond Wagner; 1915–1963), U.S. wrestler. A showman first and a wrestler second, George Wagner changed his name to "Gorgeous George," bleached blond and waved his long hair, donned flashy robes, and hired a bodyguard and valet to accompany him into the ring. He became the most popular wrestler in America and one of the most popular of the early television stars (1947–52).

GORKY, ARSHILE (Vosdanig Manoog Adoian; 1904–1948), Turkish-born U.S. painter. When he was a child, Gorky's family fled their homeland to escape the Turkish persecution of Armenians, and he emigrated to the United States in 1920. He taught at the Grand Central School of Art in New York (1926–32) and painted murals for the Federal Art Project (1935–38). Originally imitative of Picasso, Cézanne, and Miró, his style evolved into a more personal idiom under the influence of the surrealism of the Chilean painter Matta and the abstract expressionism of Kandinsky. By 1943 he was established as a major figure in American art and regarded as an important link between cubism, surrealism, and American abstract expressionism. Among the paintings that demonstrated these influences were *Water of the Flowery Hill* (1944) and *Agony* (1947). He committed suicide in 1948. ∎ See studies by Harold Rosenberg (1962) and Melvin P. Lader (1985) and Matthew Spender, *From a High Place* (1999).

GORKY, MAXIM (Aleksey Maximovich Pyeshkov; 1868–1936), Soviet writer. Gorky left home at age 12, living as a vagabond. He supplied the details of his youth in the autobiographical masterpieces *My Childhood* (1913; Eng. trans. 1915), *Apprenticeship* (1916; Eng. trans. 1917), and *My Universities* (1922; Eng. trans. 1949). Revolutionary zeal and literary renown both came early: when he was arrested by czarist police (1905), public pressure facilitated his release. Gorky won fame with dramas such as *The Lower Depths* (1902; Eng. trans. 1912). With colloquial, individualized dialogue, he authentically rendered the hardships of peasant life. Gorky's international reputation, his prominent position in the publishing world, and his friendship with bolshevik leader V. I. Lenin gave him influence that he used to protect writers and their work from the brutal confusion of cultural life in the years surrounding the 1917 Russian Revolution. Disillusionment led to a decade of voluntary exile in the West; when he repatriated (1931), his apparent endorsement of Joseph Stalin's regime assured him a place of honor. Soviet critics have called his novel *Mother* (1907; Eng. trans. 1907)—which he wrote during a visit to the United States—the first work of socialist realism, although it was not until 1932 that Gorky, as first president of the Union of Soviet Writers, articulated that literary doctrine. The circumstances of his death remain clouded. Gorky's *Reminiscences* (1924–31; Eng. trans. 1946) included portraits of his friends, the writers Leo Tolstoy and Anton Chekhov. ■ See studies by D. Levin (1965), Irwin Weil (1966), and Barry P. Scherr (1988).

GOSCINNY, RENÉ (1926–1977), and ALBERT UDERZO (1927–   ), French cartoonists. Goscinny, a cofounder of the adult comic weekly *Pilote* (1959), teamed up with Uderzo to create a French answer to the American comic strips that were inundating Europe. The result was *Astérix,* a strip about the adventures of a feisty and quick-witted Gallic warrior (in 50 B.C.) and his fellow Breton villagers (including the giant Obélix, the druid Panoramix, and the dog Idéfix) who manage to defend themselves against occupying Roman soldiers. The strip, with text by Goscinny and drawings by Uderzo, featured puns, innuendo, exaggerated facial expressions, and zany stereotypical characters representing different ethnic groups. Astérix quickly became a French national hero and between 1961 and 1996, 30 adventures were published in book form, selling more than 90 million copies. After Goscinny's death, Uderzo both wrote and illustrated the strip, and he eventually became the best-selling author in French history. By the late 1990s his books were translated into 78 languages, and worldwide sales exceeded 280 million copies. Astérix also appeared in seven movies and was the focus of a theme park near Paris.

GOSDEN, FREEMAN F. (1899–1982), and CHARLES J. CORRELL (1890–1972), U.S. radio performers. Born in Richmond, Virginia, and Peoria, Illinois, respectively, white vaudevillians Gosden and Correll met in the early 1920s in Durham, North Carolina, where they were members of the same road company. Together they originated (1929) the "Amos 'n' Andy" show, the first of the great radio comedy shows, which nightly occupied a 15-minute prime-time spot until 1943, when it began to appear weekly, continuing until 1954. In the early years Gosden and Correll wrote and acted their black-dialect show entirely themselves, making "Kingfish," Lightnin'," "the Fresh Air Taxicab Co. of America," and "I's regusted" household words. So popular was the show during the 1930s that movie theaters interrupted their films at 7 P.M. to pipe in "Amos 'n' Andy." But the responsiveness of a Depression audience in the plight of these jobless, futureless characters began to wane in the 1940s; in the 1950s, when the show took to television with African-American actors, it was criticized for its stereotypic portrayal of blacks. The show was last aired in 1966.

GOTTLIEB, ADOLPH (1903–1974), U.S. artist. Gottlieb studied art in New York and Paris and was a noted expressionist during the 1930s. He subsequently developed a style based on "pictographs," abstract universal symbols placed in a grid arrangement. In the 1950s he moved to abstract-expressionist landscapes, large canvases dominated by "bursts" of color, which were a commercial success and were widely exhibited. ■ See study by Robert Doty and Diane Waldman (1968).

GOTTWALD, KLEMENT (1896–1953), Czech political leader. A founder of the Czech Communist party (1921), Gottwald served as the party's secretary-general (from 1927) and was a member of the executive committee of the Comintern (1928–43) and of the Czech parliament (1928–38). He spent World War II in Moscow organizing Czech exiles, then returned to Czechoslovakia and served as deputy premier (1945–46) and premier (1946–48). An organizer of the communist coup (February 1948), he succeeded Edward Beneš as president (1948–53). He brought Czechoslovakia firmly into the Soviet orbit, rigidly dominated the government and party, and created a Stalinist state in Czechoslovakia. He suppressed both communists and noncommunists and conducted the infamous prude trials (1952) that sentenced 11 prominent communist leaders to death. ■ See his *Selected Speeches and Articles, 1929–53* (Eng. trans. 1954).

GOUDSMIT, SAMUEL ABRAHAM (1902–1978), Dutch-born U.S. physicist. While a graduate student (1925) at the University of Leiden, Goudsmit (and fellow student George Uhlenbeck) formulated the theory of electron spin, which profoundly influenced subsequent atomic theory and research. He emigrated to the United States (1927), taught at the University of Michigan (1927–46), was senior scientist at the Brookhaven National Laboratory (1948–70), and edited the influential journal, *Physics Review* (1951–62). During World War II he did radar research at the Massachusetts Institute of Technology and headed Alsos, a secret mission set up (1944) to determine if German scientists were developing an atomic bomb. He wrote *The Structure of Line Spectra* (1930; with Linus Pauling), *Atomic Energy States* (1932; with Robert F. Bacher), and *Alsos* (1947).

GOULART, JOÃO (1918–1976), Brazilian political leader. A practicing lawyer before entering politics as a member of the Brazilian Labor party (PTB), Goulart was a protégé of Getúlio Vargas, Brazil's most powerful political figure, and served as Vargas' minister of labor (1953–54). He became head of the PTB after Vargas' suicide (1954) and was elected vice president of Brazil in 1955 and 1960 and succeeded to the presidency when Pres. Jânio Quadros resigned (1961). He attempted to reform the economy fundamentally and to pursue a program of agrarian reform and economic development, but he was unable to control spiraling inflation or get many of his programs through the conservative and hostile congress. As he moved further to the left, military and conservative forces conspired against him, and he was overthrown by a military uprising (April 1, 1964) and fled into exile.

GOULD, CHESTER (1900–1985), U.S. cartoonist. Outraged by the mob violence of the time, Gould, a Chicago newspaper cartoonist, created the comic strip *Dick Tracy* for the *Chicago Tribune* and the *New York Daily News* (1931). Featuring the clean-cut, square-jawed detective Dick Tracy battling such bizarre characters as Mole, Pruneface, Flattop, and B-B Eyes, the strip introduced violence and crime-fighting realism into the cartoon world and was an immediate success. Aided by his friends Tess Trueheart and Sam Catchem and his famous two-way wrist radio and closed-circuit television, Tracy inevitably foiled the criminals, proving that "crime doesn't pay." The strip remained enormously popular for half a century and eventually appeared in six hundred newspapers in the United States and abroad with an estimated readership of one hundred million.

GOULD, GLENN HERBERT (1932–1982), Canadian pianist. A child prodigy who began playing the piano at age 3, Gould enrolled at Toronto's Royal Conservatory at age 10 and made his debut with the Toronto Symphony at 14. Assuming an unorthodox posture—seated on a 14-inch chair, with head bent close to the keyboard—he launched a successful concert career in 1955. Critics admired the translucent quality of his compelling performances, but sometimes questioned his personal, provocative interpretations of classics. He gained a reputation as an eccentric by humming along with the music, canceling concert dates, or appearing in an overcoat in warm weather. Preferring recording studio to concert hall, the reclusive Gould retired from the stage altogether in 1964 and worked exclusively for the microphone, viewing the recording of music as a distinct art form. He made an important series of some 80 records, including landmark recordings of the music of Bach and Beethoven. Gould also composed music in a conventional tonal idiom. The memo-

rial volume edited by John McGreevy, *Glenn Gould Variations* (1983), contains essays by and about Gould. ■ See also John Cott, *Conversations with Glenn Gould* (1984); Tim Page, ed., *The Glenn Gould Reader* (1984); the biography by Otto Friedrich (1989); and the psychological study by Peter F. Ostwald (1997).

GOULD, MORTON (1913–1996), U.S. composer. A piano prodigy, Gould received a scholarship to study at the new York Institute of Musical Art (later the Juilliard School) at age 8 and gave improvised-jazz piano recitals as a teenager. He ran the weekly radio program *Music for Today* (for the Mutual Network's New York radio station WOR; 1934–42) and other network musical programs during the 1940s. As a composer he was noted for introducing American jazz, folk, pop, and marching themes into symphonies, concerti, and other music for the concert stage. His best known pieces included *Boogie Woogie Etude, Lincoln Legend, Tap Dance Concerto, Cowboy Rhapsody,* and *Latin American Symphonette. Stringmusic* won the 1995 Pulitzer Prize. Gould also wrote ballets (*Fall River Legend,* 1947), Broadway musicals (*Billion Dollar Baby,* 1945; *Arms and the Girl,* 1950), and music for television ("Holocaust," 1978). He also made over 100 recordings as a conductor, including an album of Charles Ives's *First Symphony* (Grammy Award, 1966). He served as president of the American Society of Composers, Authors and Publishers (ASCAP) from 1986 to 1994.

GOULD, STEPHEN JAY (1941–), U.S. paleontologist. A graduate of Antioch College (B.A. 1963) and Columbia University (Ph.D. 1967), Gould was a professor at Harvard (from 1967) and a contributor of scientific essays to *Natural History* magazine (from 1974). He gained attention with two articles on "Punctuated Equilibria" (written with Niles Eldredge; 1972, 1977) that modified Darwinian evolutionary theory by proposing that new species could arise relatively rapidly (over a few hundred thousand years) rather than evolving gradually and steadily by means of natural selection over millions of years. In his other writings he attacked creationism and biological determinism and discussed the social context of scientific theories. His books include *Ontogeny and Phylogeny* (1977), *The Mismeasure of Man* (1981, rev. ed. 1996), *Wonderful Life* (1989), and *Fall Mouse* (1996) and the essay collections *Ever Since Darwin* (1977), *The Panda's Thumb* (1980), *Hen's Teeth and Horse's Toes* (1983), *The Flamingo's Smile* (1985), *Dinosaur in a Haystack* (1996), *Leonardo's Mountain of Clams and the Diet of Worms* (1998), and *The Lying Stones of Marrakech* (2000).

GOULDNER, ALVIN WARD (1920–1981), U.S. sociologist. An independent, neo-Marxist scholar, Gouldner believed that sociologists should be concerned with contemporary issues in order to help overcome social injustice. He attacked "value-free" sociology as helping to maintain societal inequalities and enabling scholars to avoid moral obligations.

Gouldner taught at Washington University in St. Louis (1959–64; 1967–81), was the founding editor of the journals *Trans-Action* (1963) and *Theory and Society* (1974), and wrote several books, including *Enter Plato* (1965), *The Coming Crisis of Western Sociology* (1970), *For Sociology* (1970), and the trilogy *The Dialectic of Ideology and Technology* (1977), *The Future of Intellectuals and the Rise of the New Class* (1979), and *The Two Marxisms* (1979).

GOUZENKO, IGOR (1919–1982), Soviet spy and defector. An art and architecture student in Moscow (1937–38), Gouzenko was recruited into the NKVD—the Soviet intelligence service—in 1939. After serving as an intelligence officer during World War II, he was assigned (1945) to the Soviet embassy in Ottawa, Canada, as a cipher clerk and became a member of the Soviet espionage network in Canada. He prepared to seek asylum for himself and his family by copying more than 100 classified Soviet documents. In September 1945, he walked out of the embassy with documents concealed under his shirt. In each of his several attempts, at newspaper and government agencies, to get the documents to the authorities, Gouzenko was dismissed as a lunatic. Fearing for his life, he finally turned to his neighbor, a Royal Canadian Air Force sergeant who secured the help of local police, and eventually Gouzenko won his asylum. The information he supplied disclosed the identities and techniques of a huge network of Soviet spies operating in North America, including British atomic scientist Alan Nunn May. Relocated with a new identity, Gouzenko turned to writing. ▪ See his *The Iron Curtain* (1948).

GOWON, YAKUBU (1934–), Nigerian military and political leader. A Christian from the largely Muslim north, Gowon was a career military officer with training at Sandhurst and experience with the 1961–62 U.N. Congo peacekeeping mission. After the 1966 Nigerian coup d'état, he emerged as Africa's youngest head of state and presided over the tragic civil war (1967–70). Known as the "gentle general," he led Nigeria through the subsequent period of national reconciliation and was chairman of the Organization of African Unity (1973–74). He was ousted by a coup while out of the country in 1975 and remained in exile. He earned a Ph.D. from Warwick University (1984), was pardoned by the government (1991), and returned to Nigeria, where he chaired the Nigerian National Oil and Chemical Marketing Co. (formerly Shell Nigeria Ltd., 1996–).

GRABLE, BETTY (Elizabeth Grable; 1916–1973), U.S. film actress. A teenage chorine from St. Louis, Grable played ingenue film roles during the 1930s, until *Million Dollar Legs* (1939) and a series of musical films propelled her to stardom. During World War II she was the favorite "pinup girl" of U.S. soldiers. Postwar fashions changed, but Grable kept to form in *My Blue Heaven* (1950) and *Call Me Mister* (1951). She was upstaged by another blond pinup, Marilyn Monroe, in *How to Marry a Millionaire* (1953). In addition to later TV and nightclub appearances, she starred on Broadway in *Hello Dolly* in 1967. ▪ See biography by Doug Warren (1981) and Spero Pastos, *Pin-Up* (1986).

GRACE OF MONACO, PRINCESS. See KELLY, GRACE.

GRADE, CHAIM (1910–1982), Lithuanian-born Yiddish-language poet and novelist. Grade was educated in traditional religious schools, but became a leading secular poet in the "Young Vilna" group during the 1930s. He escaped to the Soviet Union after the German invasion (1941) and lived in New York after 1948. In addition to his nature poetry, poems about his mother, and famed portraits of traditional Jewish life, he wrote emotional and prophetic poems on the Holocaust and Jewish refugees. Critical acclaim followed the English translations of Grade's prose works, many of which described the inner spiritual struggles of East European Jews. They included *The Well* (1958; Eng. trans. 1967), *The Seven Little Lanes* (1949; Eng. trans. 1972), *The Agunah* (1961; Eng. trans. 1974), *My Mother's Sabbath Days: A Memoir* (1959; Eng. trans. 1986), *The Yeshiva* (2 vols., 1967–68; Eng. trans. 1976–77), and *Rabbis and Wives* (Eng. trans. 1982).

GRADE OF ELSTREE, LEW GRADE, BARON (Louis or Lewis Winogradsky; 1906–1998), British television and film producer. The eldest son of a Jewish tailor, Lew Grade emigrated to Britain with his family as a boy (1912). He started out as a vaudeville dancer, and during World War II organized tours to entertain the troops. After the war, he created Lew and Leslie Grade, Ltd., building it into Europe's largest theatrical agency. He sold the agency in 1967, moving full-time into television. His Associated Television Corp., Ltd. (later Associated Communications Corp., Ltd.), was the largest supplier of commercial television offerings in Great Britain, responsible for a quarter of all programming. In addition, the firm syndicated reruns all over the world, including multimillion-dollar sales of such serials as "The Saint," "The Avengers," and "The Muppet Show" to the United States. He also produced movies, including *The Return of the Pink Panther* (1975), *The Boys from Brazil* (1978), *Capricorn One* (1978), *Movie Movie* (1978), *Autumn Sonata* (1978), *Blood Feud* (1980), *On Golden Pond* (1981), and *Sophie's Choice* (1982). ▪ See his autobiography *Still Dancing* (1987).

GRAF, STEFFI (Stephanie Maria Graf; 1969–), German tennis player. Graf was introduced to tennis at age 4 by her father, who ran a small tennis school. She turned professional at 13 (1982) and developed into one of the world's top players by 1985. Ranked number one for eight years (1987–90; 1993–96), the 5-foot, 10-inch Graf became (1988) only the third woman to win the grand slam (British, U.S., Australian, and French singles titles). In addition she won four more U.S. Opens (1989, 1993, 1995–96), three more Australian Opens (1989–90, 1994), five more French Opens (1987, 1993, 1995–96, 1999) and six more Wimbledon Championships (1989, 1991–93, 1995–96). She also won the 1988 Olympic gold medal. She retired (August 1999) after having won 107 titles and earning $21.8 million in prize money, more than any other woman in sports history.

GRAHAM, BILL (Wolfgang Wolodia Grojonca; 1931–1991), U.S. music producer. Born in Berlin to parents who had immigrated from Eastern Europe, Graham was evacuated from a French orphanage during World War II and sent to New York City (1941), where he grew up in a Jewish foster home. He served in the U.S. Army during the Korean War (1951–53), became a U.S. citizen (1953), and earned a B.A. in business administration (1955). Moving to California, Graham gained prominence as a concert promoter and manager, signing such rock stars as the Jefferson Airplane, Santana, Van Morrison, and Ronnie Montrose. He opened the famous Fillmore West (1965) and Fillmore East (1968) auditoriums, which housed psychedelic light shows and concerts by all the top groups of the 1960s and 1970s. Graham also produced the outdoor concert at Watkins Glen, New York (1973), that attracted 600,000 people and produced nationwide tours, including the landmark tour of Bob Dylan and the Band (1974). Known for his aggressive style, the flamboyant Graham often clashed with the stars he promoted. During the 1980s he produced concerts to raise money for Amnesty International, Live Aid, and other social and political causes. ▪ See his memoirs, *Bill Graham Presents* (1992; with R. Greenfield).

GRAHAM, BILLY (William Franklin Graham; 1918–), U.S. evangelist. Steeped in Protestant fundamentalism during his North Carolina boyhood, Billy Graham served as a lay preacher (1936–40) during student days at Bob Jones University and the Florida Bible Seminary. After ordination as a Southern Baptist minister, he became a preacher for American Youth for Christ (1944), then launched an evangelical campaign that brought him into public view (1949). Graham's dramatic, persuasive preaching appealed to radio and television audiences and made him an enormously visible and forceful presence in American life. He promoted a clean-cut, optimistic Christianity, took publicized political positions (supporting, for example, U.S. intervention in Vietnam and other anticommunist policies), and befriended powerful people, including every president from Eisenhower to Clinton. He traveled widely, including tours of Korea (1973) and the Soviet Union (1982, 1984). Graham wrote numerous books, including *Revival in Our Times* (1950), *Peace with God* (1953), *The Seven Deadly Sins* (1955), *My Answer* (1960), *How to Be Born Again* (1977), and *Answers to Life's Problems* (1988). ▪ See his autobiography *Just As I Am* (1997) and biographies by John Pollock (1977) and Marshall Frady (1979).

GRAHAM, KATHARINE (Katharine Meyer; 1917–), U.S. publisher. The daughter of banker Eugene Meyer, who bought the *Washington Post* in 1933, Graham worked there summers while earning her B.A. at the University of Chicago (1938) and then during World War II. She married Philip Graham (1940), a *Harvard Law Review* editor and clerk to Supreme Court Justice Felix Frankfurter. Philip Graham became publisher of the *Post* in 1946, but after his suicide in 1963 his wife took over the company, which now included *Newsweek* magazine and TV holdings. Many admired her courage in printing the Pentagon Papers (concerning U.S. involvement in Southeast Asia) in 1971 and for pursuing the Watergate story—the scandals (1972–74) involving Pres. Richard Nixon's administration. After 10 years as publisher of the *Post* (1969–79), she was succeeded by her son, Donald E. Graham. However, she remained the company's CEO until 1991 and chair until 1998. ▪ See her autobiography, *Personal History* (1997; Pulitzer Prize); biography by Deborah Davis (1979); and Howard Bray, *Pillars of the Post* (1980).

GRAHAM, MARTHA (1894–1991), U.S. dancer, choreographer, and teacher. Graham studied modern dance at the Denishawn School, making her professional debut in 1920 in Ted Shawn's *Xochitl*. She was solo dancer (1923–24) in the Greenwich Village Follies and began (1924) the career in choreography that produced more than 180 dances, dramatizing diverse aspects of human experience—historical, psychological, and mythological. Among her best-known works were *Primitive Mysteries* (1931), *Appalachian Spring* (1944), and *Clytemnestra* (1958). She developed "percussive movements," based on natural body structure, and influenced generations of modern-dance teachers, performers, and choreographers throughout the world. Graham was the first choreographer to employ a racially integrated troupe. Her notebooks were published in 1973. ▪ See her memoirs, *Blood Memory* (1991); biographies by Don McDonagh (1973) and Agnes de Mille (1991); and Ernestine Stodelle, *Deep Song* (1984).

GRAHAM, OTTO (1921–), U.S. football player. An All-American at Northwestern University (1943), Graham developed into one of the greatest "T-formation" quarterbacks of the National Football League (NFL) and led the Cleveland Browns to world championships in 1950, 1954, and 1955. He completed 1,464 passes for 23,584 yards and 174 touchdowns during his NFL career and was elected to the National Professional Football Hall of Fame (1965).

GRAHAM, SHEILAH (Lily Shiel; 1908?–1988), British-born U.S. gossip columnist. A great rival of Louella Parsons and Hedda Hopper, Graham was one of Hollywood's most influential columnists. Starting in 1935, she reported film gossip for the North American Newspaper Alliance and was eventually syndicated in more than 175 newspapers. Her celebrated love affair with the novelist F. Scott Fitzgerald, during the last three years of his life, is recounted in her book *Beloved Infidel* (1958). ■ See also the autobiographical *The Rest of the Story* (1964) and *Confessions of a Hollywood Columnist* (1969).

GRAINGER, (GEORGE) PERCY ALDRIDGE (1882–1961), Australian-born U.S. composer, pianist, and conductor. A child prodigy, Grainger studied piano in Germany and began an international concert career in 1900. He settled in the United States (1914) and became one of America's best-loved pianists, although he was regarded as an eccentric because of his bizarre public statements and behavior. Influenced by his friend, Norwegian composer Edvard Grieg, whose piano concerto he performed frequently, Grainger collected folk music from around the world and created memorable arrangements for numerous traditional English, Scottish, and Irish folk songs, including "Irish Tune from County Derry" (better known as "Danny Boy"), "Brigg Fair," and "Shallow Brown." He was best known for the piano pieces *Country Gardens* and *Shepherd's Hey* and the ensemble works, *Molly on the Shore, Mock Morris,* and *Lincolnshire Posy.* In addition to these pleasantly melodic pieces, he spent years developing an experimental and complex dissonant "beatless music" that was ignored during his lifetime. ■ See biographies by Thomas C. Slattery (1974), John Bird (1977), and Wilfrid H. Mellers (1992).

GRAMSCI, ANTONIO (1891–1937), Italian political theorist and activist. Gramsci was active in the factory workers' council movement in Turin and a cofounder of the movement's journal, *L'Ordine Nuovo* (1919). He left the Socialist party to help found the Italian Communist party (1921) and served in the Comintern secretariat (1922–24). He became the party chief (1924), founded its newspaper, *Unità,* and was elected to parliament before the party was outlawed by fascist leader Benito Mussolini and he was imprisoned (1926–37). Gramsci's prison writings, published posthumously, included *Letters from Prison* (1947; Eng. trans. 1975), *The Modern Prince* (1949; Eng. trans. 1957), and *Prison Notebooks* (Eng. trans. 1971). In them he developed the theory of hegemony, which explained how a dominant class controlled society through ideological as well as economic means. Gramsci emphasized the importance of political and ideological struggle to create a new world view in order to combat bourgeois hegemony and establish true human freedom. He was one of the most influential Western Marxist thinkers of the century. ■ See studies by John Cammett (1967), Martin Clark (1977), Paolo Spriano (Eng. trans. 1979), Christine Buci-Glucksmann (Eng. trans. 1980); Walter L. Adamson, *Hegemony and Revolution* (1980); James Martin, *Gramsci's Political Analysis* (1998); and Terry Robson, *The State and Community Action* (2000).

GRANADOS, ENRIQUE (1867–1916), Spanish pianist and composer. An internationally acclaimed piano virtuoso, Granados was a leading member of the nationalist school of Spanish composers. He based much of his music on Spanish folk songs and folk dances and was best known for two series of love songs for voice and piano, *Twelve Spanish Dances* for piano (1892) and *Goyescas* (1911–13), a piano suite inspired by Goya's paintings and tapestries. He adapted the melodies of *Goyescas* into an opera of the same name (1916) and died while returning home from its premiere in New York City when his ship was torpedoed by a German submarine.

GRANGE, RED (Harold Edward Grange; 1903–1991), U.S. football player. The best-known gridiron star of the 1920s, Grange was one of the greatest runners in football history. An All-American at halfback (1923–24) and quarterback (1925) at the University of Illinois, he scored 31 touchdowns and gained 3,637 yards in 20 varsity games. Called the "Galloping Ghost" because of his dazzling runs and elusive maneuvers, Grange left college early to play professionally with the Chicago Bears (1925; 1929–35) and did more than any other player to stimulate public interest in the fledgling National Football League (NFL). ■ See his autobiography (1953).

GRANIT, RAGNAR ARTHUR (1900–1991), Finnish-born Swedish physiologist. Granit received an M.D. degree from Helsinki University (1927) and worked under Charles Sherrington as a research fellow at Oxford (1928; 1931–32). He later served as a professor of neurophysiology at the Karolinska Institute in Stockholm (1940–67) and director of the Nobel Institute for Neurophysiology (1945–67). Primarily known for his research on the physiology of vision, he was a pioneer in the use of microelectrodes and was the first to demonstrate that different nerves in the retina react to different wavelengths of light. For his work in explaining the mechanisms of visual perception, he shared the 1967 Nobel Prize in Physiology or Medicine with George Wald and Haldan K. Hartline.

GRANT, CARY (Archibald Leach; 1904–1986), British-born U.S. film actor. A teenage runaway who spent five years with an English acrobatic troup, Grant matured into one of Hollywood's most polished performers. Mae West invited the tall, dark, handsome young actor to "come up and see me sometime" in *She Done Him Wrong* (1933), and he was an inspired match for Katharine Hepburn in *Bringing Up Baby* (1938) and *The Philadelphia Story* (1940). But his most interesting roles were as a charming innocent in four classics of director Alfred Hitchcock, *Suspicion* (1941), *Notorious* (1946), *To Catch a Thief* (1955), and *North by Northwest* (1959). A master of studied nonchalance and sophisticated comedy, Grant received a 1970 Academy Award for general excellence. ■ See biographies by Albert Govoni (1972), Lee Guthrie (1977), Lionel Godfrey (1981), and Graham McCann (1997), and Geoffrey Wansell, *Haunted Idol* (1984).

GRANT, LEE (Lyova Haskell Rosenthal; 1931–), U.S. actress and director. Born in New York City, Grant acted on the stage, screen, and in television over three decades. Her early films were *Detective Story* (1951) and *Storm Fear* (1955). Blacklisting made her unemployable in the entertainment industry for years during the anti-communist fervor of the 1950s; she made a strong comeback in the 1960s, winning Emmy Awards for TV performances in *Peyton Place* (1966) and *The Neon Ceiling* (1971) and an Academy Award for her supporting role in *Shampoo* (1975). She turned to filmmaking in the mid-1970s, directing a feature movie of Tillie Olsen's *Tell Me a Riddle* (1981); a docudrama (1984) on the Wilmar Eight, a group of eight women employees who undertook a two-year strike against a Minnesota bank; and the television movies *Nobody's Child* (1986) and *No Place Like Home* (1989). Grant won an Academy Award for her documentary *Down and Out in America* (1985). She debuted as a theatrical director in 1983 at New York City's Public Theater.

GRANT, MADISON (1865–1937), U.S. lawyer and publicist of nativism. A lawyer with independent means, Grant was a founder of the New York Zoological Society in 1895 and later its president (1925–37). A hunter, explorer, and conservationist, he had an Alaskan caribou named after him as well as a redwood grove in California. He was best known to the public as an advocate of "Nordic" racial superiority and an activist in the eugenics movement. A powerful force in the movement to limit immigration after World War I, he helped frame the Johnson Act (1924), which codified the quota system. He wrote *The Passing of the Great Race* (1916) and coedited *The Alien in Our Midst; or "Selling Our Birthright for a Mess of Pottage"* (1930), two tracts that presented his racist views.

GRANT, WILLIAM T. (1876–1972), U.S. businessman. When high school dropout W. T. Grant opened (1906) his first retail department store in Lynn, Massachusetts, no item cost more than 25 cents, the "magic price" that he had determined optimal for rapid sales. Operating with a formula that included quick merchandise turnover, strict economy, and good customer relations, Grant built his W. T. Grant Co. store into a retail chain-store empire that by his death included 1,176 stores in over 40 states, employed 60,000 people, and registered sales of $1.2 billion. Grant served as chairman of the board of his company until he was 90.

GRANVILLE-BARKER, HARLEY GRANVILLE (1877–1946), British actor, dramatist, director, and critic. A major influence in the modern British theater, Granville-Barker managed (with J. E. Vedrenne) the Court Theatre (London; 1904–07) and organized there the most celebrated repertory company in Britain. He championed naturalism and introduced plays by George Bernard Shaw, John Galsworthy, John Masefield, Henrik Ibsen, and Maurice Maeterlinck.

His own plays included *The Voysey Inheritance* (1905) and *The Madras House* (1910). His revolutionary productions of Shakespeare's plays at the Savoy Theatre (London; 1912–14) influenced generations of actors and directors. He settled in Paris after World War I and retired from active participation in theatrical productions, but his written works, including *The Exemplary Theatre* (1922) and the mulitvolume *Prefaces to Shakespeare* (1927–47), remained important contributions to theatrical criticism. ■ See biographies by Charles B. Purdom (1955) and Eric Salmon (1984) and study by Dennis Kennedy (1985).

GRASS, GÜNTER (1927–), German writer. The literary spokesman for his generation, Grass was best known for the novels of the Danzig trilogy: *The Tin Drum* (1959; Eng. trans. 1962), *Cat and Mouse* (1961; Eng. trans. 1963), and *Dog Years* (1963; Eng. trans. 1965). Brilliantly inventive and graphic, they presented a panorama of German society during the Nazi era and post–World War II period and represented a scathing attack on the refusal of Germans to accept responsibility for Nazi crimes. An active member of the Social Democratic party, he produced works, including the novel *Local Anaesthetic* (1969; Eng. trans. 1969) and the play *The Plebians Rehearse the Uprising* (1966; Eng. trans. 1969), that reflected his nonrevolutionary socialist views. His other well-known works included the novels *The Flounder* (1977; Eng. trans. 1978) and *The Call of the Toad* (1992; Eng. trans. 1992), *The Meeting of Telgte* (1979; Eng. trans. 1981). His novel *Too Far Afield* (1995; Eng. trans. 2000) criticized the 1990 reunification of Germany. He won the 1999 Nobel Prize in Literature. ■ See also his *Headbirths; or the Germans Are Dying Out* (1980; Eng. trans. 1983); *On Writing and Politics: 1967–1983* (Eng. trans. 1985), a collection of essays and speeches; *My Century* (1999; Eng. trans. 1999); and studies by W. Gordon Cunliffe (1969), Kurt Lothar Tank (1965; Eng. trans. 1969), Keith Miles (1975), and Michael Hollington (1980).

THE GRATEFUL DEAD (Jerry Garcia, 1942–1995; "Pig Pen" McKernan, 1945–1973; Phil Lesh, 1940– ; and Keith Godchaux, 1948–1980), U.S. rock group. In 1964 they called themselves Mother McCree's Uptown Jug Band; in 1965 they were the Warlocks; and in 1966 they came up with the name Grateful Dead, which was also the title of their first album (1967). Under lead guitarist Jerry Garcia, the Dead became a San Francisco institution and, for many fans, personified the Haight-Ashbury hippie culture of the 1960s. They made innovative use of electronic amplification, and their music, a deafening synthesis of country, blues, and acid rock, was more successful in live performances than on recordings. The band's popularity grew in the 1980s and 1990s and their loyal fans, known as Deadheads, became a cultural phenomenon. The group's albums included *Workingman's Dead* (1970), *American Beauty* (1970), and *In the Dark* (1987). ■ See Blair Jackson's biography of

Jerry Garcia (1999) and Carol Brightman, *Sweet Chaos* (1999).

GRAU SAN MARTÍN, RAMÓN (1887–1969), Cuban doctor and political leader. A graduate of the University of Havana's medical school, Grau was teaching physiology there when he became involved in student protests against the dictatorship of Gerardo Machado. After the 1933 coup led by Fulgencio Batista, the professor presided over a reformist alliance of students and the military. However, the new regime was too radical for the U.S. government, which refused to recognize it, and Grau was forced to resign (January 1934) after four months. In a political comeback, he was elected president in 1944 for a four-year term, a period of peace, prosperity, and corruption. He remained active as an opponent of Batista during the 1950s and chose to remain in Cuba after Batista fled (1959).

GRAVES, ROBERT RANKE (1895–1985), British poet and novelist. Educated at Oxford, an officer in World War I and a teacher in Cairo (1926), Graves pungently recounted his early career and the passage of an era in *Good-bye to All That* (1929). He was a full-time resident of Majorca from the 1930s and wrote prolifically in many fields, producing some 140 books in a 60-year career. A brilliant classical scholar, he published several highly acclaimed historical novels, including *I Claudius* (1934), and a controversial interpretive study, *The Greek Myths* (1955). His poetry, collected in various yearly volumes, carried on the formal conventions of British verse and included intense, graceful love poems. *Collected Poems* appeared in 1965. Graves also wrote literary criticism. ■ See biographies by Martin Seymour-Smith (1983), Miranda Seymour (1995), and Richard P. Graves (2 vols., 1986–90), and study by Robert H. Canary (1980).

GRAY, HAROLD LINCOLN (1894–1968), U.S. cartoonist. Gray worked for the *Chicago Tribune* and was an assistant draftsman for *The Gumps* cartoon strip before creating his own strip, *Little Orphan Annie* (1924). Featuring Annie, the round-eyed, frizzy-haired 12-year-old (whom Gray described as "tougher than Hell, with a heart of gold, but a fast left"); her faithful dog Sandy; and her guardian, the bald and ultraconservative billionaire Daddy Warbucks, the strip became one of the most popular cartoon series of all time. More serious than comic, the often violent and controversial strip depicted Annie defending the American way of life from the onslaught of criminals, liberals, communists, and other "subversives." At the time of Gray's death it was carried in more than 400 newspapers in the United States and abroad.

GRAZIANI, RODOLFO (1882–1955), Italian general. One of fascist leader Benito Mussolini's most trusted colleagues, Graziani established a reputation as a brilliant but barbarous military commander and colonial administrator in Libya (1921–34), Somaliland (1935), and Ethiopia (1936–39). As governor-general and commander of Italian troops in Libya, Graziani was decisively defeated by the British (1940–41), and he resigned his posts. He reappeared as defense minister in Mussolini's puppet fascist republic in northern Italy (1943) but failed to raise an army and was captured (1945). Although found guilty of collaboration with the Nazis and sentenced by an Italian tribunal to 19 years' imprisonment (1950), he was released under an amnesty the same year and became an active leader in the neofascist movement.

GRECHKO, ANDREI ANTONOVICH (1903–1963), Soviet marshal and defense minister. At age 16, Grechko joined Gen. S. M. Budenny's legendary Red cavalry as it was defeating the White forces in the civil war (1918–20). He rose through the ranks and, in the wake of dictator Joseph Stalin's prewar army purges, was given a command at the outbreak of World War II. He distinguished himself in the defense of the Caucasus (1942–43) and led (1944) the First Guards army across the Carpathians from Poland into Czechoslovakia. He later commanded Soviet forces in East Germany (1953–57), where he was involved in quashing the 1953 uprising, and commanded the Warsaw Pact forces (1960–67). As minister of defense (1967–76), he modernized the Soviet military. His appointment to the Politburo (1973) signaled the increased influence of the military in Soviet political deliberations. He wrote *Through the Carpathians* (1970), *Battle for the Caucasus* (1969; Eng. trans. 1971), and *The Armed Forces of the Soviet State* (1974; Eng. trans. 1975).

GRECO, JOSÉ (1918–2000), Spanish-U.S. dancer. Born to Spanish parents in Italy, Greco was taken to the United States as a boy and acquired (1928) U.S. citizenship. At age 19 he made his debut (1937) in *Carmen*, later appearing in nightclubs and on the resort circuit. He danced in films and in touring ballet troupes, then formed (1949) his own company, Ballets y Bailes de España. He was best known for his flamboyant *farruca*, the Gypsy dance that is related to the flamenco. The most famous Spanish dancer outside of Spain, he established a foundation for Hispanic dance in New York (1971) and retired in 1975. ■ See his autobiography, *The Gypsy in My Soul* (1977).

GREEN, ADOLPH. *See COMDEN, BETTY.*

GREEN, HENRY (Henry Vincent Yorke; 1905–1973), British novelist. After two years at Oxford, Green entered his family's manufacturing business and eventually became its managing director. A keen and detached observer of both upper- and lower-class society with a brilliant ear for colloquial speech, Green wrote a series of lyrical and sophisticated social comedies that concentrated on the emotional experience of his characters. His best-known works, noted for their poetic descriptive passages and their haunting symbolism, included *Living* (1929), a proletarian novel; *Party Going* (1939), about the idle rich; *Caught* (1943), *Loving*

(1945) and *Back* (1946), all dealing with aspects of World War II; and *Nothing* (1950) and *Doting* (1952), dealing with upper-class life in post–World War II London. ▪ See his autobiography, *Pack My Bag* (1940), and study by John Russell (1960).

GREEN, JULIEN (1900–1998), French novelist. Born to American parents who lived in France, Green was educated in part in the United States and was bilingual. His writing was influenced by American literature and his own conversion to Catholicism. His novels, set in provincial towns, concern anguished people who are "dead to life" and have a pervading gothic atmosphere and a sense of spiritual presence. Among his works are the novels *The Closed Garden* (1927; Eng. trans. 1928), *Moira* (1950; Eng. trans. 1951), and *The Other One* (1971; Eng. trans. 1973); the autobiographical *Memories of Happy Days* (1942, written in English) and *To Leave Before Dawn* (1963; Eng. trans. 1967); *Diary, 1928–57* (Eng. trans. 1964); and *Memories of Evil Days* (Eng. trans. 1976). His later works included two novels of the old South, *Distant Lands* (1987; Eng. trans. 1990) and *Stars of the South* (1996; Eng. trans. 1998). He was elected (1971) to the Académie Française. ▪ See biography by Glenn S. Burne (1972) and study by Michael O'Dwyer (1997).

GREEN, WILLIAM (1873–1952), U.S. labor leader. The son of a miner, Green became one at age 16 and soon involved himself in union activities. He worked his way up through the ranks of the United Mine Workers, becoming secretary-treasurer (1912–24) and a vice president of the American Federation of Labor (1913–24). With the support of his close associate John L. Lewis, Green was elected AFL president (1924) and steered a moderate course of peaceful coexistence with management and support of the New Deal. He opposed the militant dissidents, led by Lewis, who formed the Committee for Industrial Organization (1935), and expelled the CIO from the AFL (1938). After the split the AFL became more aggressive in its organizing activities, and Green helped transform the labor movement into a powerful nonradical political and economic force. An ardent foe of communism, he resisted communist influence in the unions at home and sent union experts overseas to counteract communism abroad. ▪ See pictorial biography by Max Danish (1952) and biography by Craig Phelan (1989).

GREENBERG, CLEMENT (1909–1994), U.S. art critic. Born in New York City, Greenberg studied at the Art Students League (1924–25) and Syracuse University (B.A. 1930). While working as a Customs Service clerk (1937–42) he began writing art criticism for the *Partisan Review* and later served as art critic for *The Nation* and as an associate editor of *Commentary*. A formalist who upheld aesthetic standards in art, he championed abstract expressionism during the 1940s, 1950s, and 1960s and he was a major cultural arbiter during the postwar era. Widely regarded as the most influential commentator on art in U.S. history, he promoted and helped to shape the careers of such artists and sculptors as Jackson Pollack, David Smith, Hans Hofmann, Helen Frankenthaler, Morris Louis, Jules Olitski, Anthony Caro, and Kenneth Noland. His books included *Joan Miró* (1948), *Matisse* (1953), and *Art and Culture* (1961). ▪ See his *Collected Essays and Criticism* (4 vols., 1986–93) and *Homemade Esthetics: Observations on Art and Taste* (1999); study by Donald Kuspit (1979); and biography by Florence Rubenfeld (1997).

GREENBERG, HANK (Henry Benjamin Greenberg; 1911–1986), U.S. baseball player. One of the finest first basemen ever to play the game, Hank Greenberg was a powerful hitter who threatened Babe Ruth's record one-season total of 60 home runs when he hit 58 in 1938. Playing for the Detroit Tigers (1933–42; 1944–46), he led the American League in runs batted in four times and was named Most Valuable Player twice (1935, 1940). He hit 331 home runs during his career. After his retirement (1947), Greenberg became a successful businessman and baseball executive; in 1956 he was elected to the National Baseball Hall of Fame.

GREENE, GRAHAM (1904–1991), British novelist. Greene was an Oxford-educated journalist, book reviewer, and film critic before devoting himself full-time to fiction writing. His many "entertainments"—literate spy thrillers like *Orient Express* (1933) and *Ministry of Fear* (1943)—raised the standards for popular fiction. A convert to Roman Catholicism (1926), Greene also wrote serious novels that made him one of the most esteemed writers of his generation. Expressing moral concerns about grace, alienation, and redemption, he depicted individuals trying to escape society, the police, God, or themselves. He adopted some stylistic techniques from movies. His novels were often set in exotic locales, reflecting his wide travels, and mirrored contemporary events. His works included *England Made Me* (1935), *The Power and the Glory* (1940), *The Quiet American* (1955), and *Our Man in Havana* (1958). Later books included *The Honorary Consul* (1973), *The Human Factor* (1978), *Dr. Fischer of Geneva, or The Bomb Party* (1980), and *Monsignor Quixote* (1982). *Getting to Know the General* (1984) is a nonfiction account of the Panamanian leader Gen. Omar Torrijos Herrara. ▪ See his autobiographies, *A Sort of Life* (1971) and *Ways of Escape* (1980); study by A. A. De Vitis (1964); and biography by Norman Sherry (Vol. 1, 1989).

GREENGARD, PAUL (1925–), U.S. neurobiologist. Greengard studied at Johns Hopkins University (Ph.D. 1953) and taught at the Albert Einstein School of Medicine, New York (1961–70), Yale Medical School (1968–83), and The Rockefeller University (1983–). He did pioneering work in the biochemistry of nerve cells and discovered how dopamine and other neurotransmitters act in the nervous system. His findings spurred research in the study of synaptic transmissions and he shared the 2000 Nobel Prize in

Physiology or Medicine with Eric R. Kandel and Arvid Carlsson.

GREENSPAN, ALAN (1926–), U.S. economist. A native New Yorker, Greenspan studied the clarinet at Juilliard and played professionally in a touring dance band before studying economics at New York University (B.A. 1948; M.A. 1950; Ph.D. 1977). He headed a firm providing economic forecasts to corporations (1953–87) before becoming an economic adviser to President Richard Nixon (1968–74). A free-market advocate and libertarian who was influenced by his friendship with Ayn Rand, Greenspan headed President Gerald Ford's Council of Economic Advisers (1974–77) and chaired the National Commission on Social Security Reform (1981–83). He was appointed chairman of the Federal Reserve Board by President Ronald Reagan (1987) and reappointed by President George Bush (1991) and President Bill Clinton (1996, 2000). As Fed chairman he pursued a tight money policy and was widely credited for helping the economy to grow while keeping inflation low. ■ See D. B. Sicilia and J. Cruikshank, *The Greenspan Effect* (1999), Bob Woodward, *Maestro* (2000), and biography by Justin Martin (2000).

GREER, GERMAINE (1939–), Australian feminist and writer. Born in Melbourne, Greer attended a convent school, studied at Melbourne University and the University of Sydney, and then moved to Britain (1964), where she acquired a doctorate at Cambridge (1967) and taught literature at Britain's University of Warwick (1967–73). Her book *The Female Eunuch* (1970) established her reputation internationally. This influential work analyzed Western attitudes toward womanhood, called for an end to sexual repression, and asserted her refusal "to be a female impersonator," that is, to conform to conventional, historical notions of the role of women. She later wrote a volume on women artists through history, *The Obstacle Race* (1979). In her controversial book *Sex and Destiny: The Politics of Human Fertility* (1984), she asserted that women have been harmed by sexual permissiveness and modern contraceptives. She called for sexual restraint and an enhanced status for motherhood, and condemned the West for proselytizing about birth control to the Third World. Greer directed the Tulsa Center for the Study of Women's Literature (1979–83) and taught at Cambridge University (1989–). Her later books included *The Change: Women, Aging and the Menopause* (1991), *Slip-Shod Sibyls: Recognition, Rejection and the Woman Poet* (1995), and *The Whole Woman* (1999). ■ See biography by Christine Wallace (1999).

GREGORY, DICK (1932–), U.S. comedian and political activist. Gregory ran the third-fastest half mile in the United States as a student at Southern Illinois University. He began performing in 1958 at Chicago's South Side black nightclubs as a stand-up comic, telling "healthy race jokes" and satirizing racial tensions. In 1961 he moved into more lucrative club bookings, TV talk shows, and recordings. By the late 1960s, Gregory was actively involved in the civil-rights and anti–Vietnam War movements, and his comedy was increasingly influenced by his radical social and political views. He ran for U.S. president on the Peace and Freedom party ticket (1968). He subsequently became a proselytizer for good nutrition and founded Dick Gregory Health Enterprises (1984). He also wrote *From the Back of the Bus* (1962), *Nigger: An Autobiography* (1965), *Write Me In* (1968), *Dick Gregory's Political Primer* (1972), *Up from Nigger* (1976), and *Murder in Memphis: The FBI and the Assassination of Martin Luther King* (1993; with Mark Lane).

GRETZKY, WAYNE (1961–), Canadian hockey player. The son of a former amateur hockey player, Gretzky entered organized hockey at age 6 and starred on every team for which he played. He joined professional hockey with the Edmonton Oilers of the short-lived World Hockey Association (1978), and when the club joined the National Hockey League (1979) Gretzky immediately electrified the league with his pinpoint passing and prolific scoring. Although relatively small (5 feet, 11 inches; 170 lbs.) and deceptively slow and casual on the ice, he became a perennial scoring leader (1981–87, 1990–91, 1994) and Most Valuable Player (1980–87, 1989), and set records for most assists (163; 1985–86) and most points (215; 1985–86) in a regular season. From October 1983 to January 1984 he scored one or more points in 51 consecutive games (61 goals; 92 assists). He led the Oilers to league championships in 1984, 1985, 1987, and 1988. He subsequently played for the Los Angeles Kings (1988–96), St. Louis Blues (1996), and the New York Rangers (1996–99). When he retired after 20 seasons (April 1999), he held 61 league scoring records, including career points (regular season, 2,857; play-offs, 382), career goals (regular season, 894; play-offs, 122), and assists (regular season, 1,963; play-offs, 260). ■ See biography by Barry Wilner (1982).

GREW, JOSEPH CLARK (1880–1965), U.S. diplomat. A Harvard graduate (B.A. 1902) from a Boston banking family, Grew joined the consular service in 1904, transferred to the foreign service in 1906, and served in Egypt, Mexico, Russia, Austria, and Germany. As undersecretary of state (1924–27) he oversaw the transformation of the service from patronage to professionalism. As ambassador to Japan (1932–41) he tried to ameliorate the growing tensions between the two countries; he gave advance warning of a possible attack on Pearl Harbor. He returned to the State Department during World War II and retired to private life in 1945. ■ See his autobiography, *Turbulent Era* (2 vols., 1952), and Waldo H. Heinrichs, Jr., *American Ambassador* (1966).

GREY, EDWARD, 1st VISCOUNT GREY OF FALLODON (1862–1933), British diplomat. Grey was elected to Parliament as a Liberal in 1885. As foreign secretary (1905–16), he negotiated alliances with France, Russia, and Italy. "The lamps are going out all over Europe" were his immortal words when the German invasion of Belgium prompted Britain's declaration of war in 1914. In 1919 he traveled to the United States to urge U.S. entry into the League of Nations. ■ See his memoirs, *Twenty-five Years, 1892–1916* (1926); as well as collections of his papers (1926) and speeches (1931); and biographies by G. M. Trevelyan (1937) and Keith Robbins (1971).

GREY, ZANE (1875–1939), U.S. novelist. Grey gave up his New York dental practice when his books, such as *The Spirit of the Border* (1905), a pioneer tale based on a relative's diary, became best-sellers. He romanticized the old West in 54 mediocre adventure novels that sold over 30 million copies. *Riders of the Purple Sage* (1912) was the most popular. ■ See biography by Frank Gruber (1978) and studies by Carlton Jackson (1973, rev. ed. 1989) and Stephen May (1997).

GRIERSON, JOHN (1898–1972), Scottish film director and producer. The most important figure in British documentary, Grierson spent three years in the United States on a Rockefeller Foundation fellowship studying communications and public opinion. On his return home in 1928 he joined the Empire Marketing Board, for which he directed *Drifters* (1929), a documentary about the daily life of British fishermen. From 1933 to 1937 Grierson headed the General Post Office (GPO) film unit, which attracted a group of progressive young filmmakers who made hundreds of films exploring social issues. With the outbreak of World War II, the GPO unit became the main British film and propaganda agency. Grierson then went to Canada, where he was instrumental in setting up the National Film Board and producing outstanding documentaries (1939–45). He worked for the United Nations Educational, Scientific, and Cultural Organization briefly before producing an anthology of international documentary (1957–65) for Scottish television. ■ See his writings in *Grierson on Documentary* (rev. ed. 1966) and *John Grierson* (1978) and the documentary biography by Forsyth Hardy (1979).

GRIFFITH, ARTHUR (1872–1922), Irish nationalist leader. A Dublin printer, Griffith founded several nationalist newspapers including *The United Irishman* (1899). He founded Sinn Féin ("ourselves alone"; 1905), a nationalist party advocating the organization of a separate Irish parliament. After the Easter Rebellion of 1916, in which he took no part, he was elected to Parliament but refused to sit at Westminster. Instead he helped form the separatist revolutionary assembly, the Dáil Éireann, in Dublin, and was elected its vice president. He led the Irish delegation that negotiated the Treaty of 1921, which established the Irish Free State. Griffith died shortly after he succeeded Eamon De

Valera as president of the Dáil. ■ See biography by Padraic Colum, *Ourselves Alone!* (1959).

GRIFFITH, DAVID WARK (1875–1948), U.S. film director. The descendant of an impoverished southern family, D. W. Griffith became an actor at age 18. He also wrote stories, some of which he sold to the Biograph Co. in 1908 to launch his film career. During the next five years Griffith directed over 400 short films, inventing as he went along many of the basic techniques of filmmaking—the close-up, long shot, fade out, and crosscutting—that liberated the art from a fixed theatrical point of view. In 1914 he directed *The Birth of a Nation,* an enormously successful film about the aftermath of the Civil War. A technical triumph, it carried a racist message and was censored in many cities. Griffith responded to his critics with his next film, the epic *Intolerance* (1915), his masterpiece. He was cofounder (1919) of United Artists, which released his *Broken Blossoms* (1919), a love story, and *Orphans of the Storm* (1922), a drama of the French Revolution. Then the director's films began to lose their popularity. Griffith made his last film, a failure, in 1931, and lived on alone and forgotten in Hollywood until his death. ■ See his autobiography, *The Man Who Invented Hollywood* (1972; edited by James Hart), and biographies by Robert M. Henderson (1972) and Richard Schickel (1984).

GRIN, ALEKSANDR (Aleksandr Stepanovich Grinevsky; 1880–1932), Soviet writer. Expelled from school and beaten at home, Grin at age 15 set out for Odessa, where he acquired his lifelong love of the sea. He took odd jobs, was jailed for socialist revolutionary activities, and after the 1917 Russian revolution, with the help of the writer Maxim Gorky, began to publish his fantastic tales. He set these stories in a mythical country whose oddly named cities convinced many readers that Grin was a foreigner whose works had been translated. *Scarlet Sails* (1923; Eng. trans. 1967), *On the Slope of the Hill* (1927), *Fire and Water* (1930), and other works won him increasing popularity. Grin remained apart from literary movements and relatively free of political pressures during his career, but in 1950 he was posthumously charged with "decadentism" and publication of his works was suspended. Reissued in 1956, his books found their way into the hands of millions of Soviet children and adults. *Selected Short Stories* (1984) contains English translations. ■ See study by N. Luker (1973).

GRIS, JUAN (José Victoriano González; 1887–1927), Spanish painter. After studying engineering and painting in Madrid, Gris emigrated to Paris (1906) and lived near Pablo Picasso and Georges Braque, whose cubist style influenced him. Discovering that their cubism was too analytic for his expression, he developed a style of synthetic cubism in which he built up and organized fragments of objects and geometric shapes to create, "architecturally," an artistic structure. He was best known for his collages, or *papiers* *collés,* in which he applied glued paper to the surface to be painted. *Breakfast* (1914) was a notable example of this style. His works became increasingly complex, featuring interplays of objects, shadows, colors, and textures. Through his artwork and his writings and lectures he disseminated cubist ideas to a wide public. ■ See biography by Daniel Henry Kahnweiler (Eng. trans. 1969) and study by Antonio Gaya Nuño (Eng. trans. 1975).

GRIVAS, GEORGE (Georgios Theodorus Grivas; 1898–1974), Greek Cypriot general. A lifelong soldier, Grivas fought in the Greek resistance against the Germans during World War II and subsequently against Greek communist partisans. A conservative, he ran unsuccessfully for a seat in the Greek parliament in 1946, 1950, and 1951. He came out of retirement in 1955 to lead the guerrilla war against the British that culminated in independence for Cyprus (1960). But Grivas wanted *enosis,* Cypriot union with Greece, and for this he resumed terrorist guerrilla operations against Pres. Makarios of Cyprus in 1971. He was a fugitive at the time of his death, at age 75, in his hideout in Limassol. ■ See study by Dudley Barker (1960).

GROCK (Charles Adrien Wettach; 1880–1959), Swiss-born circus clown. Grock was one of the best known and wealthiest clowns in circus history. A master of pantomime, he mixed pathos and comedy in delighting European audiences for more than 50 years. He elicited laughter thousands of times by removing a minuscule violin from a huge case and by moving a grand piano closer to a piano stool so that he could sit closer to the instrument. Grock spent his last years primarily in his 40-room lakeside mansion in Switzerland. ■ See his autobiography (Eng. trans. 1957).

GROENING, MATT (1954–), U.S. cartoonist. An inveterate doodler in high school, Groening published his first cartoons in his student newspaper at Evergreen State College in Olympia, Washington. After he graduated (1977) he moved to Los Angeles, where he conveyed his reaction to the city and to life in general in the gloomy comic strip *Life is Hell.* Featuring a victimized bug-eyed rabbit named Binky, the strip unsentimentally commented on modern life and was nationally syndicated by the late 1980s. Collections of the cartoon strip were published in book form as *Love is Hell, Work is Hell, School is Hell,* and *Childhood is Hell.* In 1990 Groening created the wildly successful satirical half-hour animated television series for the Fox network, "The Simpsons," which featured the misadventures and humiliations of a "typical" contemporary American family. It "starred" 10-year-old Bart Simpson, a complex underachieving, sarcastic brat who became a cultural icon of the 1990s. Groening subsequently created the animated series "Futurama," set in New York City in the year 3000.

GROFÉ, FERDE (Ferdinand Rudolph von Grofé; 1892–1972), U.S. composer, conductor, and arranger. Grofé was a

violist with the Los Angeles Symphony and a pianist with dance orchestras. His music bridged the gap separating popular, jazz, and classical music, and he achieved recognition for his arrangement of George Gershwin's *Rhapsody in Blue* (1924). His own compositions treated popular music symphonically. They included *Metropolis* (1927), *Grand Canyon Suite* (1931), and *Café Society* (1938), all of which were based on American influences.

GROMYKO, ANDREI ANDREYEVICH (1909–1989), Soviet diplomat and political leader. Gromyko, who was born into a peasant family, taught agricultural economics in Moscow (1936–39) before joining the foreign service in 1939. He succeeded Maxim Litvinov as wartime ambassador in Washington (1943–46), participated in the international conferences at Dumbarton Oaks, Yalta, Potsdam, and San Francisco, and headed the Soviet delegation to the United Nations (1946–48). He was deputy foreign minister (1946–52; 1953–57) and ambassador to Great Britain (1952–53) before serving as foreign minister (1957–58). A dour figure on the international scene, Gromyko was a champion of détente in the 1970s and an outspoken opponent of the Reagan administration's policies in the 1980s. He was a member of the ruling Politburo (1973–88), first deputy premier (1983–85), and president (chairman of the presidium of the Supreme Soviet; 1985–88). ■ See his *Memoirs* (Eng. trans. 1989).

GRONCHI, GIOVANNI (1887–1978), Italian political leader. Elected to parliament as a member of the Italian Popular party (1919), a Roman Catholic organization, Gronchi was forced to leave politics by the fascists (1924). A member of the underground during World War II, he helped found the Christian Democratic party and served as minister of commerce and industry (1944–46) and as speaker of the Chamber of Deputies (1948–55). He was president of Italy from 1955 to 1962.

GROPIUS, WALTER (1883–1969), German-born U.S. architect and industrial designer. A pioneer of modern "functional" architecture, Gropius directed (from 1915) the Weimar School of Art, which he reorganized (1919) as the Bauhaus and directed until 1928. Designing in a mode known as the International Style, he utilized glass, metal, and modern materials in such structures as the Fagus shoe factor at Alfeld (1911) and the Bauhaus buildings at Dessau (1924–26). He worked (1934–37) in London, and emigrated (1937) to the United States, where he directed Harvard's architecture school until 1952. He wrote *The New Architecture and the Bauhaus* (Eng. trans. 1935) and *Scope of Total Architecture* (1955). ■ See studies by Sigfried Giedion (1954), James M. Fitch (1960), and Reginald R. Isaacs (1991).

GROSS, MILTON (1895–1953), U.S. cartoonist. Milt Gross began cartooning in the sixth grade. His talent caught the attention of the New York *American* editors for whom he worked as a teenage copyboy. He created several short-lived features and strips, but first attracted attention with a satirical weekly column in the *New York World, Gross Exaggerations,* in which he introduced the Yiddish dialect of the Jewish immigrants among whom he had grown up in the Bronx. Many words and expressions featured prominently in his ludicrous comic strips *Nize Baby* and *Hiawatha* (published as books in 1926) were adopted into American slang. His other popular strips included *Count Screwloose of Toulouse* (1922), *He Done Her Wrong* (1930), *Dave's Delicatessen* (1931), *That's My Pop* (1935), and *Dear Dollink* (1945).

GROSVENOR, GILBERT HOVEY (1875–1966), U.S. editor, writer, and geographer. Born in Turkey to American parents, Grosvenor graduated from Amherst College (1897). Two years later, he joined the National Geographic Society. As editor in chief (1903–54) of *National Geographic Magazine,* he introduced color photography (1910), broadened the publication's scope by introducing nontechnical articles on travels to exotic regions, and greatly increased its circulation. During Grosvenor's tenure as president (1920–54), the National Geographic Society sponsored scientific expeditions throughout the world. He was also a leading figure in the areas of conservation and wildlife protection.

GROSZ, GEORGE (1893–1959), German-born U.S. artist. Profoundly affected by the horrors of World War I, Grosz drew such bitter satirical caricatures of German bourgeois society (especially in Berlin) that he was tried three times for blasphemy and defamation of public morality. Branded "cultural bolshevist no. 1" by the Nazis, he took refuge in the United States and began teaching at the Art Students League (1933). He became a U.S. citizen in 1938. Soon after returning to live in Berlin, Grosz suffered an accidental fall and died. *Ecce Homo* (1967) is a collection of his drawings. ■ See his autobiography, *A Little Yes and a Big No* (1946; rev. ed. 1983); study by Beth I. Lewis (1971) and study ed. by Uwe M. Schneede (Eng. trans. 1979); and Serge Sabarsy, *George Grosz: The Berlin Years* (1986).

GROTOWSKI, JERZY (1933–1999), Polish theater director. Trained at the National Theater Academy in Cracow (1951–59), Grotowski founded the Theater with 13 Rows (in Opole, 1959), which was renamed the Laboratory Theater when it moved to Wroclaw (1965). Seeking to eliminate the barriers between actors and spectators, Grotowski created a revolutionary minimalist theater. It consisted only of actor, audience, and basic settings and lighting in order to emotionally confront the audience with archetypal images in ritualist performances. Actors were specially trained with rigorous vocal and psychological exercises and communicated to the audience through disciplined body movements and vocalization. His innovative ideas, described in *To-wards a Poor Theater* (1968; Eng. trans. 1968), influenced theatrical productions around the world. He worked with the Royal Shakespeare Company in London and trained actors in Denmark, Sweden, and France. The Laboratory Theater was disbanded in 1976 and Grotowski left Poland during the period of martial law (1981–82). He subsequently taught at the University of California, Irvine, and at his Centro di Lavoro in Pontedera, Italy. ■ See Jennifer Kumiega, *The Theater of Grotowski* (1985), and L. Wolford and R. Schechner, eds., *The Grotowski Sourcebook* (1997).

GROVE, FREDERICK PHILIP (1871?–1948), Canadian novelist. The son of an Anglo-Swedish father and Scottish mother, Grove was born in Russia and grew up in Sweden but spent his youth absorbing a broad education in various European countries. In 1892 he extended his travels to North America and was stranded in Toronto when he learned that his father had died bankrupt in Sweden. He spent the next 20 years as a harvest laborer and then was a teacher in Manitoba (1912–24) and an editor in Ottawa. He failed to publish his work until *Over Prairie Trails* (1922), descriptive narrative essays that were well received. His best novels, including *Settlers of the Marsh* (1925), *Our Daily Bread* (1928), and *Fruits of the Earth* (1933), realistically depict in starched prose the hardships of pioneer life. A semiautobiographical novel, *A Search for America* (1927), enjoyed great popularity. ■ See his autobiography, *In Search of Myself* (1946), and study by Margaret R. Stobie (1973).

GROVE, LEFTY (Robert Moses Grove; 1900–1975), U.S. baseball player. One of the all-time great left-handed pitchers, Grove pitched for manager Connie Mack's Philadelphia Athletics (1925–33) and the Boston Red Sox (1934–41), winning a total of 300 games. Learning to control the baseball and his notorious temper, Grove developed one of the best fastballs in the history of the game. He led the American League in strikeouts for seven consecutive seasons (1925–31) and won 20 or more games in seven consecutive years (1927–33). His greatest year was 1931, when he compiled a 31–4 mark and was voted the league's Most Valuable Player. When elected to the National Baseball Hall of Fame in 1947, Grove had the best winning percentage of any pitcher (.682).

GROZA, PETRU (1884–1958), Rumanian politician. A highly educated and wealthy landowner, Groza practiced law before entering parliament (1919) and serving in several cabinet posts during the 1920s. He founded the left-wing Ploughman's Front (1933) and was imprisoned during World War II. In 1945, at the insistence of the Soviet Union, King Michael named Groza premier, and when the king was forced to abdicate (Dec. 30, 1947), Groza proclaimed Rumania a people's republic. He served as a premier until 1952, and was subsequently chairman of the presidium of the Grand National Assembly (the titular head of government) until his death.

GRUEN, VICTOR (Victor Gruenbaum; 1903–1980), Austrian-born U.S. architect and city planner. Trained in his native Vienna, Gruen practiced architecture there before emigrating to New York before World War II. He achieved fame in the 1950s for his pioneering designs of regional shopping centers (in the suburbs of Detroit, Minneapolis, Indianapolis, San Francisco, and Los Angeles) and for his renewal and redesign of the inner city (Fort Worth). Referred to as "the father of the downtown mall," Gruen advocated multifunctional urban centers to counter inner-city blight. He wrote *The Heart of Our Cities* (1964) and *Centers for the Urban Environment* (1973).

GRUENING, ERNEST HENRY (1887–1974), U.S. political leader. A graduate of the Harvard Medical School (1912), Gruening left medicine to pursue a career in journalism and served as an editor of the *Nation* and several newspapers in New York and Boston. He was a New Deal Democrat and Pres. Franklin D. Roosevelt appointed him head of the division of territories and island possessions in the Department of the Interior (1934); he subsequently served as the appointed governor of Alaska (1939–53). Gruening was an influential lobbyist for Alaskan statehood and served as a prestatehood (1956–58) and poststatehood (1959–68) senator from Alaska. An outspoken liberal, he was one of the first critics of U.S. involvement in Vietnam and was one of the two senators (with Wayne Morse) to vote against and strongly denounce the Tonkin Gulf resolution (Aug. 8, 1964), which escalated the war. ■ See his autobiography, *Many Battles* (1973), and study by Robert D. Johnson (1998).

GRUMMAN, LEROY RANDLE (1895–1982), U.S. engineer and aviation pioneer. A graduate of Cornell University (1916), Grumman was a navy flight instructor and test pilot during World War I. He established his own aircraft repair shop on Long Island (New York) in 1929 and began producing planes in 1932. During the 1930s he won numerous naval contracts by developing amphibious aircraft, retractable landing gear for military planes, and folding-wing systems for carrier-based fighters. Grumman produced thousands of fighters and torpedo-bombers during World War II, including the *Wildcat, Hellcat,* and *Avenger,* and his company remained one of the largest defense contractors after the war, employing more than 20,000 people. Blinded due to an allergic reaction to penicillin (1946), he relinquished the presidency of his company but remained a board chairman until 1966.

GUDERIAN, HEINZ (1888–1954), German general. The genius of the panzer (tank) corps, Guderian commanded Germany's first armored, motorized forces in 1935 and wrote *Achtung! Panzer!* (1937) to describe how he would employ them in lightning attacks on the enemy. His bold techniques were largely responsible for the German break-through to the west that drove France out of World War II (1940). Guderian also penetrated to the gates of Moscow before he was forced to retreat (1941). The great offenses over, he served as inspector general of armored troops (1943–44) and as acting chief of staff (1944–45). ■ See his *Panzer Leader* (Eng. trans. 1952) and biography by Kenneth Macksey (1976).

GUEST, EDGAR ALBERT (1881–1959), British-born U.S. writer. A reporter for the *Detroit Free Press* at the turn of the century, Guest contributed light homey verse to a weekly column that became so popular that he was given a column of his own. The popularity of his folksy, optimistic rhymes, dealing with the virtues of motherhood, home, friendship, humility, and hard work, grew to the extent that Guest was eventually syndicated in more than 300 newspapers across the country and his name became a household word. His first book of verse, *A Heap o' Livin'* (1916), sold millions of copies, and subsequent volumes, including *When Day Is Done* (1921), *Harbor Lights of Home* (1928), and *Today and Tomorrow* (1942), were also best-sellers. Although scorned by the critics and intellectuals, he remained popular for decades and was known as "the poet of the plain people." ■ See biography by Royce Howes (1953).

GUEVARA, CHE (Ernesto Guevara de la Serna; 1928–1967), Argentinian-born revolutionary. After receiving his medical degree from the University of Buenos Aires (1953), Guevara sought to put his revolutionary views into practice. He joined Fidel Castro's Cuban revolutionary movement in Mexico (1955) and was a leader in the guerrilla war against Cuban dictator Fulgencio Batista (1956–59). A trusted aide and confidant of Castro, Guevara was the chief theoretician of the revolution and held many important posts, including that of minister of industry (1961–65). He advocated moral versus material work incentives, emphasized the creation of a "new socialist man," called for armed struggle to bring about the revolution throughout Latin America, and became a legendary hero to socialist revolutionaries throughout the world. He left Cuba (1965) and established a guerrilla base in Bolivia (1966), but he failed to win the support of the peasantry and was captured and executed by a Bolivian army unit. His remains, which were hastily buried in a secret location, were exhumed in 1997 and interred in a mausoleum in Santa Clara, Cuba. His writings included *Guerrilla Warfare* (1960; Eng. trans. 1961) and *Man and Socialism in Cuba* (1965; Eng. trans. 1967). ■ See biographies by Andrew Sinclair (1970) and Jon Lee Anderson (1997).

GUÈVREMONT, GERMAINE (Germaine Grignon; 1893?–1968), French-Canadian novelist. A journalist in Sorel, Quebec (1928–35), and later in Montreal, Guèvremont was known for her portrayals of life in rural French Canada, which won acclaim for their natural dialogue and credible characterizations. Her two novels, translated into English as

The Outlander (1950), depicted peasant life with a mixture of realistic and poetic prose.

GUGGENHEIM, DANIEL (1856–1930), U.S. industrialist and financier. Oldest of the seven sons of mining magnate Meyer Guggenheim, Daniel Guggenheim became the acknowledged head of the House of Guggenheim, which from the time it took control of the American Smelting and Refining Co. (1901) dominated the U.S. mining industry. As head of the company (1901–19), he integrated the domestic mining, smelting, and refining operations and expanded the family interests abroad to include mines in Bolivia, Chile, Canada, the Belgian Congo, and Angola. He also established the Daniel and Florence Guggenheim Foundation (1924) and the Daniel Guggenheim Fund for the Promotion of Aeronautics (1926). ■ See studies of the Guggenheim family by Edwin P. Hoyt, Jr. (1967), and John H. Davis (1978).

GUGGENHEIM, PEGGY (Marguerite Guggenheim; 1898–1979), U.S. art collector. Guggenheim was the niece of Solomon R. Guggenheim (1861–1949), whose foundation promoted Americans' appreciation of nonobjective art. Peggy Guggenheim in her twenties went to Paris and then to London, where, with the help of artist Marcel Duchamp, she established Guggenheim Jeune, a gallery of contemporary art. She showed work by Jean Cocteau, Wassily Kandinsky, Picasso, Braque, Miró, and others, and made a practice of purchasing at least one work by each artist. She amassed and preserved an extraordinary collection. Returning to New York (1941) with Max Ernst, whom she married, Guggenheim opened Art of This Century, a gallery that exhibited established European artists as well as Mark Rothko, Jackson Pollock, and others. After 1951 she housed her collection at her palazzo, the Venier dei Leoni, in Venice. ■ See her autobiography, *Out of This Century* (1979), and Jacqueline B. Weld, *Peggy* (1986).

GUGGENHEIM, SIMON (1867–1941), U.S. industrialist. The sixth son of Meyer Guggenheim (founder of the Guggenheim mining empire), Simon managed the family's Colorado enterprises and served as senator from Colorado (1907–13). From 1919 until his death, he was president of the American Smelting and Refining Co., through which the family dominated the U.S. mining industry. In memory of his son, he established the John Simon Guggenheim Memorial Foundation (1925), which provided "Guggenheim fellowships" to scholars and artists doing advanced study abroad. ■ See studies of the Guggenheim family by Edwin P. Hoyt, Jr. (1967), and John H. Davis (1978).

GUGGENHEIM, SOLOMON ROBERT (1861–1949), U.S. industrialist and art collector. One of the seven Guggenheim brothers who operated the largest mining and smelting company in the United States, Solomon retired from the family business in 1919 and devoted much of his time to amassing one of the world's great art collections. A champion of modern—particularly nonobjective—art, he established (1937) the Solomon R. Guggenheim Foundation for the advancement of art, which set up (1939) the Museum of Non-Objective Painting in New York City. Later called the Solomon R. Guggenheim Museum, it contained one of the world's largest collections of abstract art and was housed in a unique concrete, inverted conelike structure designed by Frank Lloyd Wright and completed in 1959. ■ See studies of the Guggenheim family by Edwin P. Hoyt, Jr. (1967), and John H. Davis (1978).

GUHA, RANAJIT (1922–   ), Indian historian. Born into a landlord family in eastern Bengal, Guha studied history at Presidency College and Calcutta University (M.A. 1946). He joined the Communist party of India while in college and worked as a full-time party activist (1947–53) before leaving the party (1956) after the Soviet invasion of Hungary. He lived in England for 21 years (1959–80), teaching at the University of Manchester and at Sussex University. He later taught at the Australian National University, Canberra (1980–   ). Influenced by his interest in peasant insurgency and colonial Indian history, he organized a series of meetings with young historians in England (1979–80) that resulted in the conceptualization of subaltern studies, an approach to colonial Indian history concentrating on the lower classes and castes rather than on the elites. Guha edited the first six volumes of *Subaltern Studies: Writings on South Asian History and Society* (1982–89), and his approach influenced historians throughout the world. His best-known historical studies included *Elementary Aspects of Peasant Insurgency in Colonial India* (1983), *An Indian Historiography of India* (1988), and *Dominance Without Hegemony: History and Power in Colonial India* (1988).

GUILBERT, YVETTE (1867–1944), French entertainer. One of France's most popular singers during the early part of the century, Guilbert achieved fame for her innocently delivered renditions of risqué songs and ballads drawn from the Latin Quarter and lower-class Parisian life. Habitually appearing in a yellow dress and black gloves, she was the subject of several famous posters and caricatures by Henri Toulouse-Lautrec. She was also a recording star and appeared in several popular movies. ■ See her *Song of My Life: My Memories* (Eng. trans. 1929) and Bettina Knapp, *That Was Yvette* (1964).

GUILLAUME, CHARLES ÉDOUARD (1861–1938), Swiss physicist. Guillaume spent his entire career at the International Bureau of Weights and Measures at Sèvres, near Paris (director 1915–36). His work included research and improvements on thermometers (1889) and the redetermination of the volume of the liter. He discovered "invar," an inexpensive steel and nickel alloy that barely expanded under wide changes in temperature. This and related alloys are widely used in surveyor's tapes, clock pendulums, and other scientific instruments and make possible more precise measurements in physics. He was awarded the 1920 Nobel Prize in Physics.

GUILLEMIN, ROGER CHARLES LOUIS (1924–), French-born U.S. medical researcher. A resistance fighter during World War II, Guillemin received an M.D. degree (1949) and worked as a research professor at the University of Montreal, Baylor University, and at the Salk Institute (1970–94). He shared the 1977 Nobel Prize in Physiology or Medicine (with Andrew Schally and Rosalyn Yalow) for discovering and synthesizing hormones produced by the hypothalamus. These hormones govern the action of the pituitary gland, which governs the sex, adrenal, and thyroid glands. They, in turn, regulate such bodily functions as reproduction, adaption to heat and cold, appetite, the level of sugar in the blood, and emotional response. Guillemin's research revolutionized the study of brain control over body chemistry. ■ See Nicholas Wade, *The Nobel Duel* (1981).

GUILLÉN, JORGE (1893–1984), Spanish poet. An academic who taught at the Sorbonne and Oxford, Guillén sided with the Loyalists during the Spanish Civil War (1936–39), went into exile (1938), and was a professor at Wellesley College (1941–57). He spent most of his life developing a single volume of poetry. His original *Cántico* (1928) contained 75 poems. Three subsequent editions appeared; the last (1950; Eng. trans. 1965) included 334 poems. He produced a continuous, if uneven, flow of poetry and also translated the work of the French poet Paul Valéry. Influenced by the poet J. R. Jiménez, he captured simple moments in traditional forms, stressing surface reality in his highly visual poetry; "Look. Do you see? Enough," is a telling line from his verse. His later collections included *Clamor* (3 vols., 1957, 1960, 1963) and *Homage* (1967). A bilingual selection of his poetry is in J. Palley, ed., *Affirmation* (1968). ■ See also *Guillén on Guillén* (1979); Ivar Ivask and Juan Marichal, eds., *Luminous Reality* (1969); and study by C. Grant MacCurdy (1982).

GUILLÉN, NICOLÁS (1902–1989), Cuban poet. A mulatto of African and Spanish descent, Guillén led the school known as *Poesía negra*. He infused Afro-Cuban dialects, rhythms, and folklore into his early collections of verse and registered social protest most effectively in his bitter satires, such as *West Indies Ltd.* (1934). He fought with the Loyalists in the Spanish Civil War (1936–39). Guillén became a communist (1937), and his later poetry was increasingly political and didactic, using more traditional forms. He celebrated the triumph of the Cuban revolution in *Tengo* (1964; Eng. trans. 1974) and served as president of the Cuban Writers Union (from 1961). English translations of his works are in *Man-making Words* (1972), *Patria O Muerte! The Great Zoo and Other Poems* (1972), *The Daily Daily* (1989), and *New Love Poetry* (1994). ■ See Lorna V.

Williams, *Self and Society in the Poetry of Nicolás Guillén* (1983).

GUIMARÃES ROSA, JOÃO (1908–1967), Brazilian novelist and short-story writer. Guimarães Rosa was a physician who became a diplomat (1934–51) and later a fiction writer. His writing captured the language, myths, and customs of the *sertão*, Brazil's northern backlands. A linguistic and stylistic innovator, he was regarded by many critics as the leading Brazilian fiction writer of the century. His major work was *The Devil to Pay in the Backlands* (1956; Eng. trans. 1963), an epic multilayered monologue about a bandit who strikes a pact with Satan. His stories appeared in *Sagarana* (1946; Eng. trans. 1966) and *The Third Bank of the River* (1962; Eng. trans. 1968). ■ See study by Jon S. Vincent (1978).

GUINAN, TEXAS (Mary Louise Cecilia Guinan; 1884–1933), U.S. entertainer and nightclub owner. Born in Waco, Texas, Guinan was a vaudeville singer and silent-film star during the first two decades of the century. Subsequently known as the "queen of the nightclubs," she reigned on Broadway during the Prohibition era of the 1920s. She was a wisecracking and colorful hostess who greeted her patrons with the phrase "Hello Sucker" and thrived on brassily insulting them. She ran numerous nightclubs, most of which were eventually closed by federal agents for selling liquor. Guinan also appeared in several talking pictures and musical revues during the 1920s and 1930s. ■ See Glenn Shirley, *"Hello, Sucker!"* (1989), and biography by Louise Berliner (1993).

GUINNESS, SIR ALEC (1914–2000), British actor, Guinness established his reputation in the classical theater, acting with the Old Vic in 1936 and later with the John Gielgud Company. After World War II service in the Royal Navy, he made his film debut in *Great Expectations* (1946), followed by *Oliver Twist* (1948). A masterful character actor, Guinness developed a genius for eccentric comedy in the classic *Kind Hearts and Coronets* (1949) and *The Lavender Hill Mob* (1951). He received an Academy Award for his dramatic performance in *The Bridge on the River Kwai* (1957). Guinness assumed another eccentric role in *The Horse's Mouth* (1959) before appearing in the Hollywood extravaganzas *Lawrence of Arabia* (1962) and *Dr. Zhivago* (1965). He was also acclaimed for his portrayal in the televised adaptations of the spy novels *Tinker, Tailor, Soldier, Spy* (1979) and *Smiley's People* (1981–82). His later films included *Star Wars* (1977), *Little Dorrit* (1988), and *Kafka* (1991). ■ See his autobiography, *Blessings in Disguise* (1986); his journals *My Name Escapes Me* (1996) and *A Positively Final Appearance* (1999), and studies by John R. Taylor (1984) and Garry O'Connor (1994).

GÜIRALDES, RICARDO (1886–1927), Argentine novelist and poet. The rich and well-traveled Güiraldes used the technique of poetic prose learned from European avant-garde writers to treat Argentine history and culture. *Don Segundo Sombra: Shadows on the Pampas* (1926; Eng. trans. 1935), the most celebrated South American novel of the 1920s, developed the gaucho myth; the novel was significant as allegory as well as history as it described a free lifestyle that was fast disappearing. His colorful language and striking imagery made him the most brilliant stylist among the "gauchesque" writers. ■ See study by Giovanni Previtali (1963).

GUITRY, SACHA (1885–1957), French actor and playwright. The son of a famous actor, Guitry left school early to write for the theater. His first success, *Nono* (1905), was followed by more than 100 witty and ephemeral plays, farces, and comedies as well as 33 films. Occasionally all the leading roles were acted by his father, himself, and his current wife, since he coached all five of his wives in acting. A flamboyant theatrical personality and a fine comedian and improviser, Guitry often produced and directed his own plays for the stage and the screen. ■ See his autobiography, *If Memory Serves* (1935; Eng. trans. 1935), and biography by James Harding (1968).

GU JIEGANG (old style: KU CHIEH-KANG; 1893–1980), Chinese historian. Born into a scholarly family, Gu was early exposed to both the classical and folkloric traditions of China. He was trained at Beijing (Peking) University and subsequently taught Chinese history and edited historical journals throughout China. Gu's most notable work, *Discussions on Chinese Ancient History* (7 vols., 1926–41), reinterpreted ancient Chinese history by demonstrating that the classical texts describing the "earliest" traditions of the so-called "golden age" were those that had actually been invented last. This thesis undermined the orthodox Confucian view of history and legitimacy. ■ See Laurence A. Schneider, *Ku Chieh-kang and China's New History* (1971).

GULBENKIAN, CALOUSTE SARKIS (1869–1955), Turkish-born British financier, industrialist, and philanthropist. The son of an Armenian oil importer and exporter, Gulbenkian was educated in England (naturalized 1902) and was a major stockholder in the Royal Dutch–Shell Oil group. He pioneered in the development of the Middle Eastern oil industry: the Turkish Petroleum Co. (later called the Iraq Petroleum Co.), which he helped set up (1911), was the first company to exploit the Iraqi oil fields. One of the world's richest men, Gulbenkian held a 5 percent interest in the company and was frequently called "Mr. 5 percent." He also owned one of the world's greatest private art collections.

GULLSTRAND, ALLVAR (1862–1930), Swedish ophthalmologist. A professor at the University of Uppsala (1894–1927), Gullstrand made important contributions to knowledge of the light-refracting qualities of the eye. He also

helped to elucidate the structure and function of the cornea and to improve methods for estimating astigmatism and corneal abnormalities. Gullstrand's major inventions, the slit-lamp and the reflex-free ophthalmoscope, enabled doctors to make minute examinations of the anterior part of the eye, and they became indispensable to the practice of ophthalmology. He won the Nobel Prize in Physiology or Medicine in 1911.

GUNN, NEIL MILLER (1891–1973), Scottish writer. The son of a Highland (Caithness) fisherman, Gunn was educated in a village school and by private tutors. He passed the civil service examination (1907) and worked as a civil servant in England and Scotland until 1937, when he quit to devote himself entirely to writing. Considered to be the most significant novelist of northern Scotland, his best works illuminate Highland history and probe the Highland character. His novels include *Morning Tale* (1931), about a boy's experience in a changing Highland village; *Sun Circle* (1933), an account of the ninth-century conflict between the Picts and Vikings; *Butcher's Broom* (1934), a story of the Highland Clearances; and *Highland River* (1937), a celebration of a boy's growing awareness. *The Silver Darlings* (1941), a novel of the clearances and the development of the fishing industry, is considered to be Gunn's masterpiece. ■ See his autobiographical volume, *The Atom of Delight* (1952), and biography by F. R. Hart and J. B. Pick (1985).

GUNN, THOM (Thomson William Gunn; 1929–), British poet. Educated in London, Cambridge, and Stanford, Gunn first published while still an undergraduate. His poetry was noted for its powerful and adroit language and for syllabic experimentation. He valued toughness, energetic movement, and the power of the will in works like *The Sense of Movement* (1957), *Selected Poems* (1962), written with Ted Hughes, and *Touch* (1967). His images bordered on the violent, and his subjects included "rockers" and motorcyclists in America, where he spent much of his time (after 1954) and was, occasionally, a university instructor. His later collections included *To the Air* (1974), *Jack Straw's Castle* (1976), *The Passages of Joy* (1982), which candidly views homosexual life, *Selected Poems, 1950 to 1975* (1979), *Collected Poems* (1994), and *Boss Cupid* (2000). ■ See his *Occasions of Poetry: Essays in Criticism and Autobiography* (1982) and *Shelf Life: Essays, Memoirs and an Interview* (1993).

GUNTHER, JOHN (1901–1970), U.S. journalist and author. Gunther began his career in Europe in the early 1920s working first for United Press and then for the *Chicago Daily News* bureau in London. In 1936, he published the first of his "Inside" books, *Inside Europe*— a panoramic, informal sociopolitical report based on personal impressions and analyses, interviews with political leaders, and biographical studies. Subsequent "Inside" books focused on Asia (1939), Latin America (1941), the United States (1947),

Africa (1955), and Russia (1958), sold millions of copies, and were translated into dozens of languages. ■ See his *Death Be Not Proud* (1949), *A Fragment of Autobiography* (1962), and *Procession* (1965) and Ken Cuthbertson, *Inside* (1992).

GUO MORUO (old style: KUO MO-JO; 1892–1978), Chinese writer. Guo Moruo was the pseudonym of Guo Kaizhen (Kuo K'ai-chen). An intimate of communist leader Mao Zedong (Mao Tse-tung) and the leading literary personality in the People's Republic of China, Guo began writing (1917) while studying medicine in Japan. Influenced by various Western writers, he cofounded the Creation Society (1921), an organization dedicated to romanticism and art for art's sake. He embraced Marxism in 1924, however, and his subsequent works reflected his new social orientation. A prolific poet, essayist, playwright, historian, translator, and autobiographer, Guo broke with the rigid traditions of the past to help create a modern Chinese literature. His works translated into English included *Selected Poems from the Goddesses* (1958) and the historical play *Chu Yuan* (1955). After the communists took power in 1949 he held important political and cultural positions, including the presidency of the Chinese Academy of Sciences. Although he confessed at the height of the Cultural Revolution (1966) to ideological shortcomings and declared that his books should be burned, he was not purged and retained his positions. ■ See David Tod Roy, *Kuo Mo-jo: The Early Years* (1971).

GURDJIEFF, GEORGEI IVANOVITCH (1877?–1949), Russian-born mystic and occultist. Born near the Russian-Persian border, Gurdjieff learned the legends and epics of Central Asia from his father, a traditional bard, and modern science from the dean of the cathedral of Kars. He left home as a young man and traveled through Tibet, Central Asia, India, and the Middle East seeking out the sources of the ancient esoteric knowledge that formed the basis of his subsequent psychophysical insights and teaching methods. He founded (Moscow, 1912) an "Institute for the Harmonious Development of Man"—reestablished after the Russian Revolution in Tiflis, Constantinople, Berlin, and finally in Fontainebleau (1922–36) and Paris—where he taught the "Fourth Way." The system aimed at awakening a higher consciousness through a combination of learning, group movement, dance, manual labor, and a minimum of sleep. His prominent disciples included P. D. Ouspensky, Katherine Mansfield, A. R. Orage, Hart Crane, and Margaret Anderson. His best-known book was *Meetings with Remarkable Men* (Eng. trans. 1963). ■ See study by J. G. Bennett (1973); James Webb, *The Harmonious Circle* (1980); and biography by James Moore (1992).

GUREVICH, MIKHAIL I. *See MIKOYAN, ARTEM I.*

GUSTAV V (1858–1950), king of Sweden. The son of Oscar II, Gustav V ascended (1907) to the Swedish throne at age 59 and ruled until he was 92. He opposed the Liberal ministry with his policy of expanded defense prior to World War I; nevertheless, his conservative leanings created a stabilizing element in Sweden's domestic affairs. Under his rule, Sweden was able to remain neutral during both world wars. He was succeeded by his son Gustav VI.

GUSTAV VI ADOLF (1882–1973), king of Sweden. Gustav, who did not become king until late in his life, devoted much of his career to nonpolitical interests. As a student of archaeology, he assisted in numerous excavations, both in Sweden and abroad. His work in Greece and in Rome later led to the establishment of the Swedish Institute in Rome (1926). Gustav also possessed a large treasure of Chinese art, and his work in the field of botany was recognized by the British Royal Academy, which granted him membership (1958). He also served in the Swedish army and attained the rank of general in 1932. On the death of his father, Gustav V, Gustav VI ascended (1950) the Swedish throne, reigning for 23 years. On his death, he was succeeded by his grandson, Charles XVI Gustav.

GUSTON, PHILIP (1913–1980), Canadian-born U.S. painter. Initially a figurative painter of social themes, Guston painted murals for the Federal Works of Art Project (1935–42). Moving toward abstraction in the late 1940s, he developed a style frequently referred to as abstract impressionism, which was characterized by subdued colors on a white background. In the late 1960s he returned to representational painting with a controversial series of politically inspired canvases done in the style of pop art. ■ See Dore Ashton, *Yes, but . . . : A Critical Study of Philip Guston* (1976); study by Robert Storr (1986); and Musa Mayer, *Night Studio* (1988).

GUTENBERG, BENO (1889–1960), German-born U.S. geologist and seismologist. On the faculty of the University of Frankfurt-am-Main (from 1918), Gutenberg emigrated to the United States (1930) and was professor of geophysics (1930–58) and director of the Seismological Laboratory (1947–58) at the California Institute of Technology. He was an authority on earthquakes and worked with Charles F. Richter to develop the Richter scale (1935) for measuring the intensity of earthquakes. He also edited *Internal Constitution of the Earth* (1939) and wrote (with Richter) *The Seismicity of the Earth* (1941; rev. ed. 1954), both of which became standard works in their field.

GUTHRIE, EDWIN RAY, JR. (1886–1959), U.S. psychologist. Guthrie, a behaviorist, was a University of Washington psychologist (1914–56) who specialized in learning theory. He gained celebrity in a 1930 dispute with Russian physiologist Ivan Pavlov over the necessity of reward-reinforcement for motivation. Guthrie attributed learning to specific motor and glandular patterns, denying the necessity for reward and for repetition. He believed that there was only one type of learning, based on a single pairing of stimulus and response. He wrote *The Psychology of Learning* (1935), *The Psychology of Human Conflict* (1938), and *Educational Psychology* (1950; with F. F. Powers).

GUTHRIE, SIR (WILLIAM) TYRONE (1900–1971), British theatrical director. Guthrie graduated from Oxford (1923) and directed plays for the BBC, the Scottish National Theater, and the Festival Theater, Cambridge, during the 1920s. He gained an international reputation for his innovative interpretations of plays directed in London during the early 1930s and his Shakespearean productions at the Old Vic (1933–45). He was also acclaimed for his direction of the operas *Peter Grimes* (1946) and *Carmen* (1949; New York, 1952). He directed plays in Ireland, Finland, and Israel, helped launch the Stratford (Ontario) Shakespeare Festival (1953), and founded the Tyrone Guthrie (Repertory) Theater in Minneapolis, Minnesota (1963). Guthrie was appointed chancellor of Queen's University, Belfast, Ireland, in 1953. He wrote *A New Theater* (1964), *In Various Directions* (1965), and an autobiography, *A Life in the Theater* (1959). ■ See biographies by James Forsyth (1976) and Alfred Rossi (1980).

GUTHRIE, WOODY (Woodrow Wilson Guthrie; 1912–1967), U.S. folksinger and songwriter. Born in Oklahoma Indian territory, Guthrie left home as a teenager to make his way by odd jobs and singing. In California during the Depression he landed a job at a radio station, singing songs he had collected and others he had written, about crop failures and outlaws and hard times. He also performed for unions and migrant laborers. In the late 1930s he moved to New York, where he wrote for the *Daily Worker*, sang with Pete Seeger and others, and made 12 records of "Dust Bowl Ballads" for the Archive of American Folk Song. A prolific songwriter, Guthrie made an incalculable contribution to American folk music. His most beloved song was "This Land Is My Land"; others included "So Long—It's Been Good to Know You" and "Hard Traveling." Guthrie spent 13 years in state hospitals before his death at age 55 from the hereditary nervous disease Huntington's chorea. Folksinger Arlo Guthrie (1947–) was his son. ■ See his *Bound for Glory* (1943; illustrated by Guthrie), *Born to Win* (1965), *Woody Says* (1975), and biography by Joe Klein (1980).

GUTIÉRREZ, GUSTAVO (1928–), Peruvian Roman Catholic priest and theologian. Gutiérrez studied medicine for five years at the National University in Lima before preparing for the priesthood. He studied philosophy and psychology at the University of Louvain (Belgium; M.A. 1955), received a doctorate in theology at the University of Lyon (France; 1959), and was ordained a priest in 1959. He returned to Lima (1960) to teach theology at the Catholic University and work among slum dwellers to link Bible study and theological issues to the everyday concerns of the poor. Influenced by the growing poverty and violence in Latin America and by his belief in the poor as a social class and the bearer of God's word, Gutiérrez, a mestizo, broke with traditional church teachings during the 1960s and developed Liberation Theology. Blending elements of Marxist analysis and Christian doctrine, it was committed to ending poverty and injustice in Latin America and represented a challenge to entrenched political, economic, and religious institutions. Gutiérrez's best-known book was *A Theology of Liberation* (1971; Eng. trans. 1973). His other works included *Power of the Poor in History* (1979; Eng. trans. 1983), *We Drink from Our Own Wells* (1983; Eng. trans. 1984), *The God of Life* (1983; Eng. trans. 1991), *On Job* (1986; Eng. trans. 1987), *Las Casas: In Search of the Poor of Jesus Christ* (1992; Eng. trans. 1993), and *Essential Writings* (Eng. trans. 1996). ■ See study by Robert McAfee Brown (1980).

GUTTMACHER, ALAN (1898–1974), U.S. physician and birth-control advocate. The son of a rabbi, Guttmacher graduated from the Johns Hopkins Medical School (1923) and taught there and at Columbia before chairing the department of obstetrics and gynecology at Mount Sinai Hospital in New York (1952–62). Regarded in his later years as the elder statesman of the birth-control movement and the successor to Margaret Sanger, he advocated freedom of choice for women regarding childbirth for over four decades. He crusaded for unrestricted access to contraceptive information for all and fought for liberalized abortion laws. From 1962 until his death he was president of the Planned Parenthood Federation of America. ■ See his *Pregnancy, Birth and Family Planning* (1973).

GUY-BLACHÉ, ALICE (Alice Guy; 1873?–1968), French-born filmmaker. The daughter of a book publisher, she was educated in a convent. She was exposed to the early developments in motion pictures as secretary to camera and film manufacturer Léon Gaumont, who established a film studio in 1901. Directing all the Gaumont studio productions until 1905, Alice Guy-Blaché pioneered in silent filmmaking and was among the first to use the medium to tell a story; she also made films with sound, using a wax cylinder to record a soundtrack. Between 1896 and 1920, she made more than 150 films. Many showed singers in performance or tableaux accompanied by choral singing and ran no more than a minute or two; others were longer narratives. *The Life of Christ* (1905), an early film extravaganza, used 25 sets, some 300 extras, and a soundtrack. She worked in France and Spain (1896–1907), and in the United States after 1910.

H

HAAKON VII (1872–1957), King of Norway. A Danish prince, Haakon VII was elected the first king of Norway after its independence (from Sweden) was restored (1905). A champion of democracy who was extremely popular with the Norwegian people, he headed the Norwegian government-in-exile in London during World War II (1940–45) and symbolized Norwegian resistance to German occupation. ▪ See biographies by M. A. Michael (1958), and Tim Greve (Eng. trans. 1983).

HAAS, ERNST (1921–1986), Austrian-born U.S. photographer. A foremost exponent of color photography, Haas emigrated to the United States in 1949. He was a member of Magnum photo agency (1949–62) and produced innovative photo essays for *Life* magazine. In 1962 the Museum of Modern Art in New York chose his work for its first display of color photography. Continuing to experiment, Haas created "a tone poem based on Genesis" in *The Creation* (1971) and used multiple color exposures to create a cubist style in his portraits of *In America* (1975). ▪ See also his *In Germany* (1976) and *Himalayan Pilgrimage* (1978).

HAAS, WALTER ABRAHAM (1889–1979), U.S. businessman. When Haas returned from service in World War I, his father-in-law, Levi Strauss, took him into his dry-goods wholesale business. The company began manufacturing blue-denim pants whose riveted seams and pockets could hold rocks collected by prospectors. Haas became (1928) president of Levi Strauss & Co. and over the next 40 years built it into an international corporation whose annual sales were nearly $2 billion. Haas was known for his fair labor practices.

HAAVELMO, TRYGVE (1911–), Norwegian economist. Haavelmo graduated from the University of Oslo (1933) and subsequently worked as a researcher at the university's Institute of Economics under its founder, Ragnar Frisch (1933–38). Stranded in the United States at the outbreak of World War II, he studied at Harvard, where he presented his doctoral dissertation, "The Probability Approach in Economics" (1941). This work, which integrated statistical probability theory into economic analysis and was published in the journal *Econometrica* (1944), had an immediate influence on the field of econometrics and paved the way for modern economic forecasting and planning. For his pioneering econometric studies, he was awarded the 1989 Nobel Memorial Prize in Economics. He was a professor at the University of Oslo (1948–79) and wrote *A Study in the Theory of Economic Evolution* (1954) and *A Study in the Theory of Investment* (1960).

HABER, FRITZ (1868–1934), German chemist. A professor of physical chemistry at Karlsruhe, Haber invented (1907–09) a process of synthesizing ammonia, which helped to avert potential food shortages by guaranteeing increased supplies of nitrogen fertilizer. He was named director (1911) of the Kaiser Wilhelm Institute for Physical Chemistry (Berlin), which he built into the world's leading center for research in physical chemistry, and was awarded the 1918 Nobel Prize in Chemistry. He worked closely with German industry and headed Germany's chemical-warfare program during World War I. With the rise of the Nazis in 1933, Haber, a Jew, was forced to resign from the institute and flee Germany. ▪ See Morris Goran, *The Story of Fritz Haber* (1967).

HABERMAS, JÜRGEN (1929–), German philosopher. One of post–World War II Germany's most influential thinkers, Habermas developed ideas of Hegel, Marx, and Talcott Parsons to expand the scope of "critical theory" first propounded by Marxist philosophers and social scientists at the Frankfurt Institute for Social Research during the 1920s. He was especially noted for his work on epistemology, communication theory, the theory of capitalist crisis, and the legitimation function of science and technology. Habermas taught philosophy and sociology at the University of Frankfurt (1971–83) and later headed the Max Planck Institute. Among his most important works were *Theory and Practice* (1963; Eng. trans. 1973), *Towards a Rational Society* (1968; Eng. trans. 1970), *Knowledge and Human Interests* (1968; Eng. trans. 1971), *Legitimation Crises* (1973; Eng. trans. 1975), *The Theory of Communicative Action* (1981; Eng. trans. 1984), and *A Berlin Republic: Writings on Germany* (1995; Eng. trans. 1997). ▪ See Thomas A. McCarthy, *The Critical Theory of Jürgen Habermas* (1978); John B. Thompson, ed., *Habermas: Critical Debates* (1982); and study by Rick Roderick (1986).

HACKWORTH, GREEN HAYWOOD (1883–1973), U.S. international jurist and legal scholar. Hackworth began his 30-year legal career with the U.S. State Department in 1916. As legal adviser (1931–46) he played an important role in policy formation and helped to shape many important international treaties and agreements. He also served as a member of the Permanent Court of Arbitration (1937–46). In 1945 he helped prepare the statute for the International Court of Justice and the Charter of the United Nations. He served on the International Court from 1946 to 1961 (president, 1955–58). His authoritative eight-volume reference work, *Digest of International Law* (1940–44), covered the major legal issues from 1906 up to World War II.

HADAMARD, JACQUES SALOMON (1865–1963), French mathematician. A lecturer at the Sorbonne (1897–1909) and professor at the Collège de France (1909–37) and the École Polytechnique (1912–37), Hadamard made fundamental contributions to the fields of complex variables, prime numbers, differential geometry, and partial differential equations. His published works influenced the development of functional analysis—he introduced the term "functional"—and general topology, and also contributed to the fields of hydrodynamics, mechanics, and probability theory. In addition to numerous technical works, he wrote, in English, the *Essay on the Psychology of Invention in the Mathematical Field* (1945). ■ See biography by V. G. Maz'ia and T. O. Shaposhnikova (Eng. trans. 1998).

HADJIDAKIS, MANOS (1925–1994), Greek composer. A major figure in the post–World War II musical life of Greece, Hadjidakis financed competitions in Athens to promote young Greek composers and to introduce works of Greeks living abroad. His own song cycles and instrumental compositions incorporated folk melodies and instruments and led to a revival of the Greek popular-song movement. He wrote for the theater and cinema and was best known internationally for the "bauzouki" folk music for the films *Never on Sunday* (1960), *America, America* (1963), and *Topkapi* (1964). He was appointed deputy director general of the National State Opera (1974) and director general of the Athens State Orchestra (1976).

HAEGG, GUNDER. *See HÄGG, GUNDER.*

HAFIZ IBRAHIM, MUHAMMAD (1872?–1932), Egyptian poet. Known as the "poet of the Nile," Hafiz was one of the geniuses of 20th-century Arabic poetry. Like Ahmad Shawqi, his illustrious compatriot, he wrote on many contemporary themes. A lawyer, army officer, and director of literature in the National Library in Cairo (1911–31), he achieved fame mainly through his prolific output of nationalistic and antiimperialist poems. He was a provincial who knew only Arabic, and his style was dignified and conservative.

HAGEN, UTA (1919–   ), German-born U.S. actress. The daughter of an art-history professor, Hagen left college to begin a professional acting career. She made a celebrated Broadway debut in *The Seagull* (1939) and appeared in several notable dramatic productions with José Ferrer (to whom she was married from 1938 to 1948), including *Key Largo* (1939; with Paul Muni) and *Othello* (1943; with Paul Robeson). One of Broadway's most versatile stars, she won Tony Awards for her performances in *The Country Girl* (1950) and *Who's Afraid of Virginia Woolf?* (1962). She cofounded the Herbert Berghof [Acting] Studio (1947) with Berghof, whom she married in 1951. Her later starring roles were in *Mrs. Klein* (1995) and *Collected Stories* (1998). She wrote *Respect for Acting* (1973; with Haskel Frankel); *A Challenge for the Actor* (1991); and a memoir, *Sources* (1983).

HAGEN, WALTER CHARLES (1892–1969), U.S. golfer. A caddy in his teen years, Hagen won his first major championship in 1914 at age 22. In his remarkable career he won 11 major titles and 13 other important titles. A shrewd, confident player, he won the U.S. Open twice, the British Open four times, and played on the Ryder Cup team for five years. Hagen's showmanship helped to popularize the game and to raise the professional golfer's status in the 1920s. ■ See his autobiography (1956).

HÄGG, GUNDER (1918–   ), Swedish distance runner. A professional firefighter, Hägg broke 15 world records in distances ranging from one to three miles. During the summer of 1942 he established 10 world records. The next year he made a successful tour of the United States and won the Amateur Athletic Union (AAU) 5,000-meter title. He also set world marks in the 1,500-meter and the 2-mile run, and his time of 4:01.4 for the mile (July 1945) was the world record until Roger Bannister ran the first sub-4-minute mile (3:59.4) in May 1954. He was barred for life from amateur track competition (1946) for accepting money to appear at track events.

HAGIWARA, SAKUTARŌ (1886–1942), Japanese poet. The son of a wealthy doctor, Hagiwara was a lonely and introspective youth who failed to complete university studies and rejected a traditional career. He studied poetry and philosophy on his own, and was especially influenced by the works of Edgar Allan Poe, Charles Baudelaire, Friedrich Nietzsche, and Arthur Schopenhauer. His poems, first published in 1913, were the first in Japanese to express the modern themes of world-weariness, spiritual dislocation, and existential anxiety, and were the first to make poetic use of the Japanese vernacular. His late works were increasingly nihilistic. His best-known poems are in the collections *Howling at the Moon* (1917; Eng. trans. 1978), *Blue Cat* (1923; Eng. trans. 1978), and *Face at the Bottom of the World and Other Poems* (Eng. trans. 1969). Hagiwara also wrote collections of essays, aphorisms, treatises on poetry, and a novel (*The Cat Town*, 1935; Eng. trans. 1948), and taught at Meiji University in Tokyo (1934–42).

HAGUE, FRANK (1876–1956), U.S. political leader. One of the most powerful local political figures in American history, Hague was a symbol of big-city bossism from the 1920s through the 1940s. As mayor of Jersey City, New Jersey (1917–47), he controlled the local Democratic party organization and through it spread his influence into state politics. Elected a Democratic national committeeman (1922), Hague later supported Franklin D. Roosevelt (1932) and New Deal policies. After his retirement in 1947, he gradually began to lose his influence, and by 1950 the Hague era in New Jersey politics had ended after his nephew Frank Hague Eggers was defeated (1949) for reelection as mayor of Jersey City. ■ See Dayton McKean, *The Boss* (1940), and Richard J. Connors *A Cycle of Power* (1971).

HAHN, OTTO (1879–1968), German physical chemist. Hahn worked on problems of radioactivity with William Ramsay in London and Ernest Rutherford in Canada (1904–06). After returning to Germany, he discovered (1918), with Lise Meitner, the new element protactinium and developed the important concept of nuclear isomerism (1921). He later served as director of the Kaiser Wilhelm Institute of Chemistry (1928–45). Hahn's most significant breakthrough came on the verge of World War II after Meitner, a Jew, had fled to Stockholm. Working with Fritz Strassman, he bombarded enriched uranium with slow neutrons and suspected that the resulting atoms were actually a uranium atom split in half. When he described his research in a letter to Meitner, she explained the process, named it nuclear fission, and published the results of Hahn's experiment. The German government overlooked his results, and Hahn conducted only minor research throughout the war. But in the United States, Enrico Fermi seized on the theory, which proved crucial in the development of the atom bomb. Hahn won the 1944 Nobel Prize in Chemistry. After the war he was president of the Max Planck Society (1946–60) and campaigned for nuclear disarmament. ■ See his *A Scientific Autobiography* (1962; Eng. trans. 1966) and *My Life* (1968; Eng. trans. 1970).

HAIG, ALEXANDER MEIGS, JR. (1924–), U.S. military leader and public official. A career army officer, Haig served in Korea (1950–51) and Vietnam (1966–67) and did years of staff work in the Pentagon. After serving as assistant to presidential adviser Henry Kissinger (1969), he rose meteorically; he was promoted to four-star general (1972), served as Pres. Richard Nixon's White House chief of staff (1973–74), and was military commander of the North Atlantic Treaty Organization (NATO) from 1975 to 1979. As Pres. Ronald Reagan's secretary of state (1981–82), he helped develop a tough anti-Soviet foreign policy. ■ See his memoirs, *Caveat* (1984), and Roger Morris, *General's Progress* (1982).

HAIG, DOUGLAS HAIG, 1st EARL (1861–1928), British field marshal. A graduate of Oxford and Sandhurst who served in India and Africa, Haig assumed command of the British army in late 1915, during World War I. The controversial strategy of attrition by trench warfare on the western front, especially during the Somme (1916) and Passchendaele (1917) campaigns, took a heavy toll, but Haig was promoted to field marshal and led the counteroffenses of 1918, which eventually defeated the German armies. ■ See *Private Papers: 1914–19* (1952) and biographies by Duff Cooper (1936), E.K.G. Sixsmith (1976), and Phillip Warner (1991).

HAILE SELASSIE (Tafari Makonnen; 1892–1975), emperor of Ethiopia. A cousin of Emperor Menelik II, Tafari became a regent in 1916, established a strong central government, and was crowned emperor in 1930. After Ethiopia

was invaded by Italy, he pleaded in vain for aid from the League of Nations (1936) and remained in exile until 1941. Upon his return, he rebuilt his autocratic government, attempted to modernize the country, ended its traditional isolation, and gained immense international prestige as a spokesman for Africa. However, power in the country remained in the hands of a narrow, feudal, landed elite who dominated millions of poverty-stricken peasants. Accused of fostering a vast system of graft and corruption, he was overthrown by a military coup (1974) and kept in confinement until his death. ■ See biography by Leonard Mosley (1964), and Ryszard Kapuscinski, *The Emperor* (1978; Eng. trans. 1983).

HAKIM, TAWFIQ AL- (1902?–1987), Egyptian novelist, essayist, and playwright. A native of Alexandria, Hakim studied law in Cairo and Paris and worked as a public prosecutor in the provinces before becoming a full-time writer (1938). Called the creator of modern Arabic literary theater, he achieved fame for intellectual dramas that frequently treated contemporary social themes and for symbolist plays. His masterpiece, *The People of the Cave* (1933), was an adaptation of an Islamic legend. A prolific author who was widely translated into European languages, he was best known in the English-speaking world for his absurdist play *The Tree Climber* (Eng. trans 1966) and for his amusing novel of life in provincial Egypt, *The Maze of Justice* (Eng. trans. 1947). He also wrote a novel of the 1919 revolution, *Return of the Spirit* (1988; Eng. trans. 1990) and a short-story collection, *In the Tavern of Life* (Eng. trans. 1998). ■ See *Fate of a Cockroach: Four Plays of Freedom* (1973); *Plays, Prefaces and Postscripts* (2 vols., Eng. trans. 1981–84); and study by Richard Long (1979).

HALAS, FRANTIŠEK (1901–1949), Czech poet. A Communist party member who extolled collectivism in his poetry, Halas later became increasingly pessimistic in outlook and was preoccupied with death, decay, and pain. He was one of the foremost innovators in modern Czech poetry and was known for his innovative combinations of sound and imagery. Halas' most famous collections were *The Rooster Frightens Death* (1930), *The Face* (1931), *Old Women* (1935; Eng. trans. 1948), and *Wide Open* (1936). *Torso of Hope* (1938) described the suffering of the Czechs during the German occupation.

HALAS, GEORGE STANLEY (1895–1983), U.S. football player, coach, and owner. A cofounder of the National Football League (1920) and founder and coach of the Chicago Bears, "Papa Bear" Halas revolutionized football strategy in the 1930s by creating the modern "T-formation." Active in the sport for almost half a century and a coach for 40 years, his teams featured such stars as Red Grange, Bronko Nagurski, Sid Luckman, Johnny Lujack, and Gale Sayers. Halas won a record 321 regular-season games as he led the Bears to six league championships. He retired in 1968. ■ See his autobiography (1979).

HALBERSTAM, DAVID (1934–), U.S. journalist. The son of an army surgeon, Halberstam graduated from Harvard (1955), having been managing editor of the *Crimson,* and worked as a journalist in the South. While on the staff of the *New York Times* (1960–67), he covered the postindependence upheaval in the Congo in 1961 and the Vietnam War, for which he won a Pulitzer Prize in 1964. He wrote *The Best and the Brightest* (1972), a study of the decision-making processes that got the United States involved in the Vietnam War, and *The Powers That Be* (1979), about media in the United States. His later books included *The Reckoning* (1986), a study of the auto industry; *The Fifties* (1993); *The Children* (1998), a study of the early civil rights movement; and *Playing for Keeps: Michael Jordan and the World He Made* (1999).

HALDANE, JOHN BURDON SANDERSON (1892–1964), British biometrician and geneticist. The son of a noted physiologist, J.B.S. Haldane was introduced to science at an early age and was educated at Eton and Oxford. He was best known for his work in theoretical genetics, and he helped formulate the mathematical theory of natural selection that related Mendelian genetics to evolution. Haldane also mathematically analyzed mutation rates and rates of evolutionary change, studied statistically the occurrence of hemophilia and color blindness, and did experiments in enzyme kinetics and human physiology. A professor at London University (1933–57), he was a lifelong Marxist who quit the Communist party as a result of the T. D. Lysenko genetics controversy with the Soviet Union (1950). He left England in 1957 in protest over the government's policy in Egypt and settled in India. ■ See Ronald William Clark's biography, *JBS* (1968), and biography by Jean G. Hall (1996).

HALDANE, RICHARD BURDON, VISCOUNT HALDANE OF CLOAN (1856–1928), British political leader. Haldane was a lawyer, a neo-Hegelian philosopher, and a cofounder of the London School of Economics (1895). He sat in the House of Commons (1885–1911) and later the House of Lords as a member of the Liberal party; as secretary of state for war (1905–12) he enacted wide-ranging military reforms. He also served as lord chancellor (1912–15; 1924). His writings included *The Philosophy of Humanism* (1922) and an autobiography (1929). ■ See biography by Dudley Sommer (1960).

HALDEMAN, BOB (Harry Robbins Haldeman; 1926–1993), U.S. presidential assistant. Born into a wealthy family in Beverly Hills, California, Haldeman graduated from the University of California at Los Angeles (U.C.L.A., 1948) and began a successful career in advertising with the J. Walter Thompson Company (1949). An admirer of Richard Nixon, he worked on his national political campaigns in 1956 and 1960 and served as his campaign manager during his successful run for the presidency in 1968. As Nixon's chief of staff (1969–73), he controlled access to the president and was one of the most influential people in Washington. Caught up in the Watergate scandal that eventually led to Nixon's downfall (1974), Haldeman resigned his post in April 1973. He was convicted of perjury, conspiracy, and obstruction of justice, and served 18 months in federal prison (1977–78). He subsequently became a successful businessman in California. ■ See his Watergate chronicle, *The Ends of Power* (1978).

HALDEMAN-JULIUS, EMANUEL (1889–1951), U.S. author and publisher. A free-thinking iconoclast and socialist and a journalist turned publisher, Haldeman-Julius was called "the Henry Ford of publishing," "Voltaire from Kansas," and "the Prince of Pamphleteers." Hoping to raise the cultural level of the ordinary American, he launched (1919) an inexpensive series of small paperback books, later called Little Blue Books, which he sold by mail from his printing plant in Girard, Kansas. As sales increased he lowered the price of each book to five cents and in more than 30 years of publishing he printed thousands of titles and sold more than 500 million books. He also wrote numerous polemical works, two novels, and the three autobiographical works, *The First Hundred Million* (1928), *My First 25 Years* (1949), and *My Second 25 Years* (1949).

HALE, GEORGE ELLERY (1868–1938), U.S. astronomer. After graduating from the Massachusetts Institute of Technology (1890), Hale invented the spectroheliograph, a device for photographing the sun in monochromatic light. He organized and directed (1892–1904) the Yerkes Observatory (Williams Bay, Wisconsin) and built its 40-inch refracting telescope. He then organized and directed the Mt. Wilson Observatory (near Pasadena, California; 1904–23), where he discovered magnetic fields in sunspots (1908) and built its 60-inch and 100-inch reflecting telescopes. Hale planned (from 1928) the 200-inch reflector at the Mt. Palomar Observatory (near Pasadena; completed 1948). He also founded the *Astrophysical Journal* (1895) and wrote *Beyond the Milky Way* (1920), *Depths of the Universe* (1924), and *Signals from the Stars* (1931). ■ See Helen Wright, *Explorer of the Universe* (1966), and Donald E. Osterbrock, *Pauper and Prince* (1993).

HALÉVY, ÉLIE (1870–1937), French historian. Son of the writer and librettist Ludovic Halévy, Halévy taught English political philosophy and the history of socialism for 40 years at the École Libre des Sciences Politiques in Paris (1892–1932). His interest in the British utilitarian philosophers and his study trips to England and extensive contacts there led to his major works, *The Growth of Philosophic Radicalism* (3 vols., 1901–04: Eng. trans. 1949) and A *History of the English People in the Nineteenth Century* (6 vols., 1912–30; Eng. trans. 1949–52). In *The Era of Tyrannies* (1938; Eng. trans. 1965) Halévy underscored the similarities between communism and fascism. ■ See biography by Myrna Chase (1980).

HALEY, ALEX PALMER (1921–1992), U.S. writer. Haley began writing while at sea during a coast guard tour in World War II. Later a magazine journalist, he conducted numerous interviews for *Playboy;* an interview with Malcolm X resulted in collaboration on the important document, *The Autobiography of Malcolm X* (1965), which Haley compiled from extensive interviews. He received little credit for this labor. But sudden fame came to him at age 55 with the publication of his best-selling, Pulitzer Prize–winning *Roots: The Saga of an American Family* (1976), in which Haley traced his maternal lineage through seven generations back to the African village of Juffure in what is now Gambia. Haley's account of the odyssey of his ancestor Kunta Kinte, a slave, and of his own search, sold millions of copies and was serialized (1977) for television, where it was seen by 130 million viewers.

HALEY, BILL (William John; 1927–1981), U.S. musician and bandleader. Haley was performing as a professional guitarist at 13; by the time he was 15 he had his own band, the Saddlemen (renamed the Comets in 1952), which played country songs with a new "rock" beat. Rolling and bobbing in plaid sports jackets, led by Haley with a blond spit curl falling in his face, the Comets sang some of the earliest, biggest hits of the rock-and-roll era: "Shake, Rattle and Roll" (1954); "Rock Around the Clock" (1955), an original Haley composition; and "See You Later Alligator" (1956). The group continued into the 1960s and 1970s with European tours and rock-and-roll revivals. His recordings decisively influenced the Beatles and other rock artists in the 1960s and 1970s.

HALEY, JAY (1923–   ), U.S. psychologist. Born in Wyoming, Haley studied communications at Stanford University (M.A. 1953). While taking part in anthropologist Gregory Bateson's research on communication theory, he became interested in issues of control within families. He worked under Salvador Minuchin at the Philadelphia Child Guidance Clinic (1967–74) and later founded the Family Therapy Institute in Chevy Chase, Maryland (1974). A leader in strategic family therapy, Haley sought to clarify and strengthen confused family hierarchies. He preferred short-term treatment during which the therapist observes how a family interacts, then intervenes in ways that disrupt destructive alliances. His books included *Techniques of Family Therapy* (1967; with Lynn Hoffman), *Uncommon Therapy* (1972), *Probem-Solving Therapy* (1976), *Leaving Home* (1980), *Reflections on Therapy* (1982), and *Learning and Teaching Therapy* (1996).

HALEY, SIR WILLIAM (1901–1987), British editor. Haley began his journalistic career with the *London Times* (1921). He was soon thereafter sent to Brussels to organize a news service, proving so successful that he was asked to join the staff of the *Manchester Evening News* (1922). As its managing editor (1930–39) and as board secretary of the Man-

chester Guardian and Evening News, Ltd. (1930–39), he gained a reputation as a brilliant editor and news manager. He was director of Reuters (1939–43) and editor in chief (1943–44) and then director general (1944–52) of the British Broadcasting Corp. before returning to the *Times* as editor in chief (1952–66).

HALIFAX, EDWARD FREDERICK LINDLEY WOOD, 1st EARL OF (1881–1959), British political leader and diplomat. Halifax served in the House of Commons as a Conservative from 1910 to 1925. As viceroy of India (1926–31), he befriended nationalist leader Mohandas K. Gandhi and pledged that dominion status was Britain's goal for India (1929). He later served as secretary of war (1935), Lord Privy Seal (1935–37), and foreign secretary (1938–40). Although he had strongly supported Prime Minister Neville Chamberlain's appeasement policy, he served in Winston Churchill's war cabinet (1940) and as ambassador in the United States (1941–46), a delicate diplomatic post at the time. ■ See autobiography, *Fullness of Days* (1957), and study by Andrew Roberts (1991).

HALL, GUS (Arvo Kusta Halberg; 1910–2000), U.S. political leader. The son of Finnish immigrants, Hall was a steelworker who joined the Communist party at age 17. He spent eight years (1949–57) in Leavenworth prison for "conspiring to teach or advocate overthrow of the U.S. government" and became secretary-general of the U.S. Communist party in 1959. He followed the Soviet line, with occasional attempts at American relevance, and ran for president in 1972, 1976, 1980, and 1984. His books included *Ecology: Can We Survive Capitalism?* (1972) and *Basics: For Peace, Democracy and Social Progress* (1980).

HALL, JOYCE CLYDE (1891–1982), U.S. businessman. Hall and his brother Rollie purchased a small engraving plant in Kansas City, Missouri (1916), and, as Hall Bros., Inc., began manufacturing attractive, high-quality greeting cards with a "Hallmark" label. The firm pioneered in developing independent card-display racks and creating special-occasion cards and achieved a nationwide reputation by the 1920s. Under Joyce Hall's leadership, the firm held international competitions for artists, sponsored numerous radio and television shows (including the much-admired "Hallmark Hall of Fame on NBC television) and was the first to utilize the work of well-known artists, including Norman Rockwell, "Grandma" Moses, and Winston Churchill, on Christmas cards. By the time Hall retired from the presidency (1966), Hallmark was the largest greeting-card manufacturer in the world, employing more than 300 artists to devise approximately 14,000 designs a year.

HALL, SIR PETER (1930–   ), British director. Hall directed his first plays while a student at Cambridge University during the early 1950s. After several successful Shakespearean productions at Stratford-upon-Avon, he served as managing director of the Royal Shakespeare Company (1960–68), which he established as a permanent ensemble. He was highly acclaimed both for his emphasis on the contemporary political and social relevance of the plays as well as for his sparse, symbolic stagings. His best-known productions of this period included *The War of the Roses* cycle (1963–64), *Hamlet* (1965), and *Macbeth* (1967). He also directed many of Harold Pinter's plays, including *The Homecoming* (1965), *Old Times* (1971), *No Man's Land* (1975), and *Tantalus* (2000). As director of the National Theater (1972–1988) and later as an independent director, he was responsible for such notable productions as *Amadeus* (1979), *Betrayal* (1980), *The Oresteia* (1981), *The Tempest* (1988), *Orpheus Descending* (1988), and *An Ideal Husband* (1992). He formed his own company in 1988. He also directed operatic productions at Convent Garden and the Glyndebourne Festival and made several films. He was knighted in 1977. ■ See *Peter Hall's Diaries* (1983).

HALLIBURTON, RICHARD (1900–1939), U.S. adventurer and writer. A graduate of Princeton (B.A. 1921), Halliburton was a noted world traveler and explorer who retraced Ulysses' journey as recounted in the *Odyssey* (1925), Cortez's route in the conquest of Mexico (1928), Balboa's march across Darién in the discovery of the Pacific (1928), and Hannibal's journey (on an elephant) across the Alps (1934–35). He participated in expeditions in western Tibet, Peru, Brazil, Russia, Arabia, and Ethiopia; climbed the Matterhorn (1921), Fujiyama (1923), Olympus (1925), and Popocatepetl (1928); flew 50,000 miles around the world in his own plane (1931–32); and swam the Hellespont (1925) and the Panama Canal from the Atlantic to the Pacific (1928). He was lost at sea while trying to cross the Pacific on a Chinese junk. His popular books included *The Royal Road to Romance* (1925), *The Glorious Adventure* (1927), *New Worlds to Conquer* (1929), *The Flying Carpet* (1932), and *Seven League Boots* (1935). ■ See biography by Jonathan Root (1965).

HALLSTEIN, WALTER (1901–1982), West German government official. A law professor (1927–41) who served in the army during World War II, Hallstein finished his military career as a prisoner of war in Mississippi. As West Germany's state secretary for foreign affairs (1951–58) he proposed (1955) the doctrine, in effect from 1955 until the late 1960s, of breaking off diplomatic relations with any state, other than the Soviet Union, recognizing East Germany. He was a founder of the European Coal and Steel Community and the European Economic Community (EEC or Common Market) and promoted European integration as the first president of the EEC Commission (1958–67). His numerous books included *United Europe* (1962) and *Europe in the Making* (1969; Eng. trans. 1972).

HALPERN, MOISHE LEIB (1886–1932), Polish-born U.S. Yiddish-language poet. Although a member of the New York literary group "Di Yunge," which experimented in poetic form, Halpern wrote brash and often grotesque works and was a unique literary personality. In his volumes *In New York* (1919; Eng. trans. 1982) and *The Golden Peacock* (1924), he evolved an unconventional, fierce style, juxtaposing refined lines with jarring coarseness. His constant questioning of style and subject had an important modernizing influence on Yiddish poetry. English translations of his poems are in I. Howe and E. Greenberg, eds., *A Treasury of Yiddish Poetry* (1969). ■ See Ruth Wisse, *A Little Love in Big Manhattan* (1988).

HALSEY, WILLIAM FREDERICK, JR., (1882–1959), U.S. fleet admiral. Known as "Bull," Halsey was a vice admiral with the Pacific fleet at the time of the Japanese attack on Pearl Harbor (1941). During the early days of World War II, his carrier task force was the heart of the American fleet, launching several surprise attacks against the Japanese, including the Doolittle raid on Tokyo (1942). As commander of the U.S. 3rd Fleet (1944–45), Halsey led his carrier task force on raids on the Japanese home islands, and he won one of the greatest naval battles in history at Leyte Gulf (October 1944). Promoted to the largely ceremonial rank of fleet admiral in 1945, he retired two years later. ■ See his *Admiral Halsey's Story* (1947); biography by E. B. Potter (1985); and James M. Merrill, *A Sailor's Admiral* (1976).

HALSMAN, PHILIPPE (1906–1979), Latvian-born U.S. photographer. Halsman grew up in Riga, Latvia, and studied electrical engineering in Germany. He ran (1930–40) a photo studio in Paris, winning renown as a fashion photographer. Moving (1940) to the United States, he became the American Society of Magazine Photographers' first president (1944). Halsman took well over 100,000 photographs, including psychologically penetrating portraits of Winston Churchill, Albert Einstein, John Steinbeck, and Eleanor Roosevelt. He produced 101 covers for *Life* magazine, more than any other photographer. He sometimes created "stunt" portraits; his photograph of Salvador Dalí depicted the artist as a fetus in an egg. *Philippe Halsman's Jump Book* (1959) captured famous people, including Richard Nixon and Paul Tillich, in the pose that he believed best revealed character: at the peak of a jump. ■ See his essay, *Halsman on the Creation of Photographic Ideas* (1961), and his photos in *Portraits* (1983).

HAMER, FANNIE LOU (**Fannie Lou Townsend**; 1917–1977), U.S. civil-rights activist. The youngest of 20 children in a family of Mississippi sharecroppers, Hamer worked in the fields from age 6, attending school only in the off-season. She left sharecropping at age 45, joined the Student Nonviolent Coordinating Committee (SNCC; 1962), and began agitating for civil rights for blacks in the Mississippi Delta region. She worked for voter registration, urged agricultural workers to organize, and became one of the most influential and respected African-American leaders in the South. She was a cofounder of the Mississippi Freedom Democratic party, which was seated at the 1972 Democratic National Convention, and helped to unite the black and white factions of the Democratic party in 1976. ▪ See study by Susan Kling (1979) and Kay Mills, *This Little Light of Mine* (1993).

HAMILTON, ALICE (1869–1970), U.S. physician. A feminist, medical researcher, and social reformer, Hamilton was the first to study industrial diseases and industrial hygiene in the United States. Concerned with the plight of workers, she spent years identifying health hazards in mines and factories. Her work was instrumental in advances in industrial hygiene and in the passage of workers' compensation laws. She was the first woman to serve on the faculty of the Harvard Medical School (1919–35). ▪ See her autobiography, *Exploring the Dangerous Trades* (1943), and the biographies by Madeleine P. Grant (1967) and Barbara Sicherman (1984).

HAMILTON, EDITH (1867–1963), U.S. classicist. Born in Germany to American parents, Hamilton graduated from Bryn Mawr and became the first woman admitted to study at the University of Munich. She worked as headmistress of a Baltimore school for girls from 1896 to 1922, when she retired to interpret classical culture for a broad audience in readable works: *The Greek Way* (1930), *The Roman Way* (1932), and *Mythology* (1942). Hamilton also translated Greek plays, restoring a simplicity of spirit after the florid translations of the Victorian era. ▪ See study by Doris F. Reid (1967).

HAMMARSKJÖLD, DAG (1905–1961), Swedish diplomat. A career civil servant, Hammarskjöld held high administrative posts in the finance and foreign ministries before heading the Swedish United Nations delegation (1951–53). As the second U.N. secretary-general (1953–61), he expanded the scope of the office by initiating practical peace moves at times of international crises in the Third World. Acknowledged for his moral courage and personal integrity, he helped resolve the Suez Crisis (1956) by establishing the first U.N. Emergency Force (in Sinai and Gaza) and helped settle the Lebanon Crisis (1958). He helped create the U.N. force during the Congo Crisis (1960–61) and died in an air crash in Africa while seeking to negotiate an end to the conflict. Although severely criticized for his active and independent diplomacy by the British, French, and Soviet governments, he was praised for his efforts by most members of the international community and was posthumously awarded the 1961 Nobel Peace Prize. ▪ See *Markings* (Eng. trans. 1964), his journal of personal reflections and meditations, and studies by Brian Urquhart (1972), Joseph Lash (1961), and Robert S. Jordan, ed., *Dag Hammarskjöld Revisited* (1983).

HAMMER, ARMAND (1898–1990), U.S. business executive. The son of a New York City doctor and pharmaceutical wholesaler, Hammer reportedly built up his father's business and earned more than $1 million while he was a student at Columbia Medical School (M.D. 1921). Before beginning his internship, he traveled to the Soviet Union to help the government fight a series of epidemics sweeping the country, but he was persuaded by Soviet leader V. I. Lenin to use his business acumen to help the country. Abandoning medicine, Hammer obtained sales concessions for major U.S. corporations, developed an asbestos mine, and established a pencil factory. He returned to New York City (1930) with the good will of the Soviet government and with a vast collection of czarist treasures and paintings that he eventually sold in his New York art gallery. In the United States he made additional fortunes in whiskey, cattle, and broadcasting. In 1957 he purchased the tiny Occidental Petroleum Corporation in California, worth approximately $125,000, and after striking oil, built it into a multibillion-dollar operation. He played an important role in arranging East-West cultural exchanges and signed an $8 billion chemical fertilizer barter deal with the Soviet government (1973). During the 1980s he signed a contract to build the world's largest open-pit coal mine in China. ▪ See his autobiography (1987; with Neil Lyndon); Robert Considine, *The Remarkable Life of Dr. Armand Hammer* (1975); and John Bryson, *The World of Armand Hammer* (1985). Edward Jay Epstein's *Dossier: The Secret History of Armand Hammer* (1996) documents numerous instances of fraud, deception, and bribery perpetrated by Hammer over the years.

HAMMERSTEIN, OSCAR, II (1895–1960), U.S. lyricist. Hammerstein was the grandson of the operatic impresario Oscar Hammerstein I. He practiced law for a year before pursuing a theatrical career and collaborating with such composers as Rudolf Friml (*Rose Marie,* 1924), Sigmund Romberg (*Desert Song,* 1926), and Jerome Kern (*Show Boat,* 1927). He wrote many memorable musicals during a 16-year collaboration with Columbia College classmate Richard Rodgers: *Oklahoma!* (1943), *Carousel* (1945), *South Pacific* (1949), *The King and I* (1951), and *The Sound of Music* (1959), all imbued with sophisticated nostalgia. ▪ See Hugh Fordin, *Getting to Know Him* (1977).

HAMMETT, (SAMUEL) DASHIELL (1894–1961), U.S. novelist and short-story writer. After leaving school at age 13, Hammett held a variety of jobs; he was a soldier in World Wars I and II and also a Pinkerton detective for eight years. Hammett began writing stories for the pulp magazines in the 1920s, and his tough, hard-boiled detective novels set a new pattern for the genre and also influenced writers working in other genres. In economical language he realistically depicted crime and violence in such novels as *The Maltese Falcon* (1930; film, 1941), with its unsentimental detective Sam Spade, and *The Thin Man* (1932; film, 1934), with its pair of flip sleuths, Nick and Nora Charles. A political radical, Hammett served six months in jail (1951) for refusing to testify before a congressional committee investigating a left-wing organization of which he was a trustee. Hammett lived for many years with the writer Lillian Hellman and appears frequently in her memoirs. ■ See biographies by Diane Johnson (1983), William Marling (1983), and Julian Symons (1985); Peter Wolfe, *Beams Falling* (1979), and Richard Layman, *The Shadow Man* (1981).

HAMMOND, SIR JOHN (1889–1964), British animal scientist. Hammond was a pioneer in the study of animal growth and reproduction, and his work affected livestock production and feeding throughout the world. His introduction of artificial insemination of dairy cattle in Britain (1942) dramatically improved the country's beef and milk output. He spent most of his career as an agricultural physiologist at Cambridge University, where he created a school of animal science that attracted students of animal husbandry from around the globe.

HAMMOND, JOHN HAYS, JR. (1888–1965), U.S. inventor. The son of a prominent mining engineer, Hammond was the inventor of radio remote control. He founded the Hammond Radio Research Laboratory (1911) and was responsible for hundreds of devices used to direct ships, planes, torpedoes, and guided missiles. His other inventions contributed to the development of radio, television, and radar.

HAMMOND, JOHN HENRY, JR. (1910–1987), U.S. record producer and jazz promoter. A great-great-grandson of Commodore Cornelius Vanderbilt, Hammond grew up in a Manhattan mansion. Involved with music from his childhood, he developed a passionate interest in jazz as a teenager and regularly attended Harlem theaters and nightclubs. Over the years, from the early 1930s, he used his substantial inheritance and executive positions at several record companies (including Columbia; 1959–75) to promote the careers of dozens of jazz and popular singers and musicians and to sponsor numerous jazz concerts and recordings. Among the stars he discovered or made famous were Benny Goodman, Billie Holiday, Count Basie, Lionel Hampton, Teddy Wilson, Aretha Franklin, Bob Dylan, and Bruce Springsteen. He also wrote jazz columns for several newspapers. He was active in the civil-rights struggle for decades and was a member of the board of directors of the National Association for the Advancement of Colored People (NAACP) from 1934 to 1967. ■ See his autobiography, *John Hammond on Record* (1977).

HAMMOND, JOHN LAWRENCE LE BRETON (1872–1949), **and LUCY BARBARA HAMMOND** (1873–1961), British historians. The Hammonds both earned degrees at Oxford before their marriage in 1901. Lawrence became involved in Liberal journalism and published a number of biographies in addition to collaborating with his wife, who devoted her life to archival research. Together they wrote a series of histories on the degradation of the working class in the course of the industrial revolution: *The Village Laborer* (1911), *The Town Laborer* (1917), *The Skilled Laborer* (1919), and *The Rise of Modern Industry* (1925). ■ See Stewart A. Weaver, *The Hammonds* (1998).

HAMPDEN, WALTER (Walter Hampden Dougherty; 1879–1955), U.S. actor. Hampden graduated from Brooklyn Polytechnical Institute (1900) before joining a British Shakespearean company, learning more than 70 parts in three years. He won recognition as Hamlet (1905) and, after returning to the United States (1907), appeared on Broadway with Alla Nazimova. In subsequent years he appeared on the American stage in numerous Shakespearean roles as well as in works by Ibsen and other modern dramatists. He managed his own Broadway theater (1925–30) and toured widely during the 1930s. He played more than 150 roles in a career that spanned half a century, often turning down more commercially appealing roles for challenging parts. He was best known for his portrayal of Cyrano de Bergerac, a character he recreated in more than 1,000 performances. Hampden also appeared in several movies, including *The Hunchback of Notre Dame* (1939) and *All About Eve* (1950), and starred in radio and television roles as well.

HAMPTON, LIONEL LEO (1908–   ), U.S. jazz musician. The first jazz virtuoso on the vibraphone, Hampton began his career as a drummer in a newsboy jazz band sponsored by the black newspaper the *Chicago Defender*. He also played jazz piano with a two-finger "trigger style." During the 1930s he toured as a member of the Benny Goodman Quartet with Goodman, Teddy Wilson, and Gene Krupa and by the 1940s had his own successful big band. Hampton moved into rhythm and blues during the 1950s and gave performances during Republican political campaigns. He made several worldwide tours and performed at the White House for Presidents Carter and Reagan. ■ See his autobiography, *Hamp* (with James Haskins, 1989).

HAMSUN, KNUT (1859–1952), Norwegian novelist. Hamsun was born into a peasant family and worked at many different jobs before he published his first novel, *Hunger* (1890; Eng. trans. 1899; new trans. 1967), a vivid description of the mind of a starving writer, and *Mysteries* (1892; Eng. trans. 1927; new trans. 1971). He disliked the contemporary emphasis on the novel of social problems and instead proposed a literature that focused on the individual ego, "the unconscious life of the mind." This approach and his impressionistic, spontaneous style strongly influenced European writing. His later work, including the semiautobiographical *Growth of the Soil* (1917; Eng. trans. 1920), concerned modern society's pernicious influence on the individual. He further developed this theme in the "August trilogy," *Wayfarers* (1927; Eng. trans. 1931; new trans. 1980), *August* (1930; Eng. trans. 1931), and *The Road Leads On* (1933; Eng. trans. 1935). Though he was considered the greatest literary figure in Norway after Henrik Ibsen and was awarded the Nobel Prize in Literature (1920), Hamsun's reputation suffered after World War II because of his strong pro-Nazi views. ■ See his memoirs, *On Overgrown Paths* (1949; Eng. trans. 1967); study by Harald Naess (1984); and biography by Robert Ferguson, *Enigma* (1987).

HAND, (BILLINGS) LEARNED (1872–1961), U.S. jurist. Learned Hand was a graduate of Harvard (M.A. 1894, LL.B. 1896), where he studied philosophy and law. After a brief career as a corporation lawyer, he was appointed (1909) a federal district judge for the Southern District of New York. In 1924 he was elevated to the U.S. Circuit Court of Appeals for the 2nd Circuit (New York, Connecticut, and Vermont) and served there until his death, although he officially retired in 1951. Hand's decisions and opinions, which reflected his belief in judicial restraint, were considered among the most important outside the rulings of the Supreme Court. Particularly notable were his decisions that expounded the Sherman Act's provisions against monopolies. Their clarity, depth, and elegance often influenced the reasoning behind Supreme Court decisions on the same subject matter. ■ See his lectures and articles in *The Bill of Rights* (1958) and *The Spirit of Liberty* (rev. ed. 1960); his opinions in Hershel Shanks, ed., *The Art and Craft of Judging* (1968); and studies by Kathryn P. Griffith (1973) and Gerald Gunther (1994).

HANDKE, PETER (1942–   ), Austrian-born author. Handke was raised in rural Austria. He had published one novel (*The Hornets*, 1966) and some poetry when he leaped into the international spotlight after a speech to Gruppe 47, Germany's leading literary society. In the same year such antitheater pieces as *Offending the Audience* (1966; Eng. trans. 1970) made him a leader in avant-garde German theater. Obsessed with the limitations of language, Handke wrote his play *Kaspar* (1968; Eng. trans. 1971) about the systematic destruction of Kaspar Hauser through his acquisition of language. The novella *The Goalie's Anxiety at the Penalty Kick* (1969; Eng. trans. 1972) and the film script *Wrong Move* (1975) pushed this issue further. The latter was modeled on the traditional German journey novel, as was the semiautobiographical *Short Letter, Long Farewell* (1971; Eng. trans. 1974). In 1977 he directed the film version of his novella *The Left-Handed Woman* (1976; Eng. trans. 1978). His later works included *Repetition* (1986; Eng. trans. 1988), *Absence* (1987; Eng. trans 1990), *My Years in the No-Man's-Bay* (1994; Eng. trans. 1998), and *On a Dark Night I Left My Silent House* (Eng. trans. 2000). ■ See his volume of reflections and opinions, *The Weight of the World* (1978; Eng. trans. 1984); the heavily autobiographical *Slow Homecoming* (1979; Eng. trans. 1985); and study by Nicolas Hern (1971).

HANDLIN, OSCAR (1915–   ), U.S. historian. Handlin was born in Brooklyn, where his Russian immigrant parents ran a grocery, and studied at Harvard (Ph.D. 1940) and taught there from 1939 to 1986. A prolific writer of social history on every phase of the American republic, his work was a deeply felt marriage of literature and scholarship. He was particularly interested in the role of immigration in U.S. life, the subject of *Boston's Immigrants* (1941), the Pulitzer Prize-winning *Uprooted* (1951), and *The Americans* (1963).

His later works included *Truth in History* (1979), *The Distortion of America* (1981), and *Liberty in America* (4 vols., 1986–94).

HANDY, WILLIAM CHRISTOPHER (1873–1958), U.S. jazz musician and composer. Known as "the father of the blues," W. C. Handy was born in Alabama, the son of former slaves. Interested in music from his childhood, he drew on the music he had grown up with—work songs, spirituals, folk ballads, and the melancholy songs of itinerant singers—in developing, for the first time in written form, the music that came to be known as "blues." Handy's most famous compositions were *Memphis Blues* (1911), *St. Louis Blues* (1914), and *Beale Street Blues* (1917). He conducted his own orchestra (1903–21) and later published several anthologies of spirituals and blues. ■ See his autobiography, *Father of the Blues* (1941).

HANKS, TOM (1956–   ), U.S. actor. Hanks trained with Shakespearean companies in Cleveland, Ohio, and New York City before costarring in the television situation comedies "Bosom Buddies" (1980–82), "Happy Days" (1982), and "Family Ties" (1983–84). Roles in such films as *Splash* (1984) and *Big* (1988) established his reputation as a leading Hollywood comedy actor. Switching to dramatic roles in the 1990s, he became one of the most popular and honored stars in film history. He received Academy Awards for his portrayal of a gay lawyer with AIDS in *Philadelphia* (1993) and for his performance as the slow-witted hero of *Forrest Gump* (1994). He was also acclaimed for his portrayals of an astronaut in *Apollo 13* (1995) and a World War II soldier in *Saving Private Ryan* (1998).

HANNA, WILLIAM (1910–   ), and **JOSEPH BARBERA** (1911–   ), U.S. cartoonists. Hanna, a banker, and Barbera, a structural engineer, both gave up their professions during the 1930s to become cartoonists. They met while working at M-G-M Studios in Hollywood, teamed up (1938), and created Tom and Jerry, the cat-and-mouse duo that starred in more than 100 short films, including *Yankee Doodle Mouse* (1943), *Kitty Foiled* (1947), and *The Two Mouseketeers* (1951). They left M-G-M (1957), set up their own production company, Hanna-Barbera Productions (1957), and developed a simplified, computerized system of animation that enabled them to dominate the television animated market with such popular series as "Huckleberry Hound," "The Flintstones," "Yogi Bear," "The Jetsons," "The Smurfs," and "Scooby-Doo, Where Are You." ■ See Hanna's autobiography, *A Cast of Friends* (1996), and Barbera's autobiography, *My Life in 'Toons* (1994).

HANSBERRY, LORRAINE (1930–1965), U.S. playwright. The daughter of a wealthy Chicago real-estate broker and banker, Hansberry wrote *A Raisin in the Sun* (1959), the first play by an African-American woman to appear on Broadway and the first by an African-American to win the New

York Critics' Circle Award for best play of the year. Based on a true incident in her life, the play presented the frustrations and aspirations of an African-American family desirous of moving into a white neighborhood. It sensitively explored the themes of racism, cultural pride, honor, and self-respect and was translated into more than 30 languages, filmed (1961), and adapted into the musical *Raisin* (1973). Hansberry also wrote the play *The Sign in Sidney Brustein's Window* (1964). After her early death from cancer, excerpts from her journals, letters, speeches, and plays were compiled in *To Be Young, Gifted, and Black* and presented as dramatized readings (1969) and published in book form (1970). ▪ See *Lorraine Hansberry: Art of Thunder, Vision of Light* (1979; special issue of *Freedomways* and study by Anne Cheney, 1984).

HANSEN, ALVIN (1887–1975), U.S. economist. A professor at the University of Minnesota (1919–37) and at Harvard (1937–58), Hansen made major theoretical advances in Keynesian economics. Through his role as an economic adviser during the 1930s and 1940s he was influential in getting the government to accept spending, borrowing, and tax policies to stimulate economic growth and protect the economy against high rates of unemployment. He was instrumental in the creation of the social security system and the establishment of the Council of Economic Advisers. His books included *Economic Stabilization in an Unbalanced World* (1932), *Full Recovery or Stagnation?* (1938), *Fiscal Policy and Business Cycles* (1941), *Economic Policy and Full Employment* (1947), and *A Guide to Keynes* (1953).

HANSEN, MARCUS LEE (1892–1938), U.S. historian. A doctoral student of Frederick Jackson Turner at Harvard (Ph.D. 1924) and professor at the University of Illinois (1928–38), Hansen wrote the first comprehensive histories of European immigration to the United States. He spent years searching through previously unexamined archives in Europe and America to find the data upon which his studies were based. His best-known works, all published posthumously, were *The Atlantic Migration, 1607–1860* (1940), *The Mingling of the Canadian and American Peoples* (1940), and *The Immigrant in American History* (1940).

HANSON, HOWARD (1896–1981), U.S. composer and conductor. As director of the Eastman School of Music in Rochester, New York, for 40 years (1924–64), Hanson taught several generations of musicians and performed more than 1,200 compositions of young American composers at his music festivals. He also composed symphonies with romantic northern inflections, winning a Pulitzer Prize in 1944 for No. 4. (the *Requiem*). His other popular works included Symphony No. 1 (*Nordic;* 1923), Symphony No. 2 (*Romantic;* 1930), and the opera *Merry Mount* (1934). He wrote *Harmonic Materials of Modern Music* (1960).

HANSSON, PER ALBIN (1885–1946), Swedish political leader. Hansson edited Social Democratic party newspapers before being elected to parliament (1918). He served as minister of defense in the early 1920s and became head of the Social Democratic party in 1925. As four-time premier (1932–46) he implemented economic reforms that helped Sweden recover from the Depression and carried out a foreign policy that maintained neutrality throughout World War II. He initiated social-welfare programs for the aged, sick, and unemployed that laid the foundation of the postwar Swedish welfare state.

HAPGOOD, NORMAN (1868–1937), U.S. editor. Hapgood was educated at Harvard (B.A. 1890; LL.B. 1893), worked for several years as a reporter, and served as editor of *Collier's Weekly* (1903–12). He was responsible for exposing the Alaskan land-grab scandals of Pres. William H. Taft's administration, for leading a crusade for a pure food and drug act, and for campaigning against the dictatorial policies of Speaker of the U.S. House of Representatives Joseph G. Cannon. As editor of *Harper's Weekly* (1913–16), he supported the policies of Pres. Woodrow Wilson and as editor of *Hearst's International Magazine* (1923–25) he attacked the Ku Klux Klan and the anti-Semitism of Henry Ford. He was also a founder of the Foreign Policy Association (1918). ▪ See his reminiscences, *The Changing Years* (1930), and Michael D. Maraccio, *The Hapgoods* (1977).

HARA, TAKASHI (also called Hara Kei; 1856–1921), Japanese political leader. Hara received a missionary education and converted to Catholicism. He was a journalist and diplomat before he entered politics in 1900 as a cofounder and secretary-general of the Seiyukai party, the first modern political party in Japan. He served as home minister (1906–08; 1911–12; 1913–14) and rose to the premiership in 1918. Called the "commoner premier" because he refused a peerage, Hara tried to curb the power of the bureaucracy and the military and doubled the size of the electorate. His popularity waned as corruption marred his administration; he was assassinated by a young right-wing fanatic. ▪ See Tetsuo Najita, *Hara Kei in the Politics of Compromise* (1967).

HARBACH, OTTO (Otto Hauerbach; 1873–1963), U.S. lyricist and librettist. Harbach taught English in college and worked as a New York City newspaper reporter before entering show business. He collaborated with the greatest composers of his time and became one of the most prolific and distinguished figures in the musical theater in the United States. His shows included *The Fire Fly* (1912) and *Rose Marie* (1924) with Rudolf Friml; *Wildflower* (1923) and *No, No, Nanette* (1925) with Vincent Youmans; *Desert Song* (1926) with Sigmund Romberg; and *Sunny* (1925) and *Roberta* (1933) with Jerome Kern. Among his song hits were "Indian Love Call," "One Alone," "The Night Was Made for Love," and "Smoke Gets in Your Eyes."

HARBORD, JAMES GUTHRIE (1866–1947), U.S. general. Harbord joined the army in 1889 and rose through the ranks. In May 1917, his old friend Gen. John J. Pershing, the newly named commander of the American expeditionary forces in World War I, picked Harbord to be his chief of staff. Promoted to brigadier general (August 1917), Harbord led U.S. forces to victories in the Battle of Belleau Wood (May 1918) and the counteroffensive at Soissons (July 1918). After the war he served as army chief of staff (1921–22) and was president (1923–30) and chairman of the board (1930–47) of the Radio Corp. of America (RCA).

HARBURG, E. Y. "YIP" (Edgar Harburg; 1896–1981), U.S. lyricist. Born and raised in New York City's Lower East Side, Harburg discovered Gilbert and Sullivan in his youth and wrote verse with City College classmate Ira Gershwin for the school newspaper. After an early failure in the electrical business, he turned to lyrics and scored a Depression-era hit with the song "Brother, Can You Spare a Dime?" He wrote the more lyrical "April in Paris" for a 1932 revue; "It's Only a Paper Moon" for the show *The Great Magoo* (1933); "Over the Rainbow" for the film *The Wizard of Oz* (1939); and collaborated on the libretto of *Finian's Rainbow* (1947). Many of his lyrics reflected his antiestablishment political views, and he was blacklisted in Hollywood after World War II. ■ See his verse collections, *Rhymes for the Irreverent* (1965) and *At This Point in Rhyme* (1976), and Harold Meyerson, *Who Put the Rainbow in the Wizard of Oz?* (1993).

HARDEN, SIR ARTHUR (1865–1940), British biochemist. After teaching and writing textbooks for a decade, Harden was struck by Eduard Buchner's discovery that alcoholic fermentation is possible in the absence of living cells and commenced his studies of sugar fermentation at the Jenner (later Lister) Institute (1897), where he headed the biochemistry department from 1907 to 1930. Studying the yeast enzyme by means of dialysis, he discovered that the enzyme consisted of two molecules: the smaller molecule was not a protein but proved necessary for the enzyme to function. This was the first isolation of a coenzyme. It later turned out that vitamins are important because they function as parts of coenzymes. Harden also pioneered research on intermediary metabolism, looking for those compounds produced in the course of chemical reactions taking place in living tissue. His work led to the realization of the importance of phosphate groups in every biochemical reaction. Harden shared the 1929 Nobel Prize in Chemistry with Hans von Euler-Chelpin.

HARDIE (JAMES) KIER (1856–1915), British labor and political leader. An uneducated coal miner and union activist, Hardie founded the Scottish Labour party (1888) and served in the House of Commons (1892–95) as the first independent representative of British workers. His newspapers the *Miner* (1887–89) and *Labour Leader* (from 1889) propagated his Christian socialist and (from 1899) pacifist views. He was a founder of the Independent Labour party

(1893) and helped form the Labour Representation Committee (1900), the forerunner of the Labour party (founded 1906), which he chaired from 1906 to 1907. He represented a Welsh constituency in Parliament from 1900 until his death. Hardie broke with leaders of the Labour party when he was unable to prevent them from supporting British participation in World War I. ■ See biographies by Emrys Hughes (1956), K. O. Morgan (1967), and Ian McLean (1975).

HARDING, WARREN GAMALIEL (1865–1923), U.S. president. A newspaper editor in Marion, Ohio, Harding entered politics as a Republican and served as a state senator (1899–1902) and as lieutenant governor (1903–04). Although defeated for governor in 1910, he was elected to the U.S. Senate in 1914. Handsome, genial, and a party regular, the mediocre Harding was in the perfect position to become the compromise choice of GOP bosses for the presidential nomination in 1920. His call for a "return to normalcy" appealed to a war-weary nation, and Harding was elected in a landslide. Though generally conservative, Harding established the Bureau of the Budget and he appointed blacks to federal positions and spoke out for racial equality. Treaties negotiated following the Washington Naval Conference limited war-ship construction. Harding named a number of able men to high office, but he also chose badly. In the Teapot Dome scandal, Interior Secretary Albert Fall (who eventually went to prison) took money in return for secret oil leases. Several other officials were convicted in separate scandals, and Harding's crony Harry Daugherty, whom he had named attorney general, was tried (but not convicted) for conspiring to defraud the government. Harding, shattered by the revelations of betrayal, died in office. ■ See Francis Russell, *The Shadow of Blooming Grove* (1968).

HARDWICK, ELIZABETH (1916–), U.S. writer and critic. Born in Kentucky, Hardwick moved to New York in 1939 and by 1941 was writing full-time. Author of several novels, numerous short stories, and essays, Hardwick was an influential member of New York's intelligentsia and cofounded (1963) and edited the *New York Review of Books.* Among her short stories that have been anthologized are "The Golden Stallion" and "The Classics Society." Her novels included *The Ghostly Lover* (1945) and the semiautobiographical *Sleepless Nights* (1979). Many of her essays were collected in *A View of My Own* (1962), *Bartleby in Manhattan and Other Essays* (1983), and *Sight Readings* (1998). She wrote *Seduction and Betrayal: Women and Literature* (1974) and edited the series *Rediscovered Fiction by American Women: A Personal Selection* (1977).

HARDY, GODFREY HAROLD (1877–1947), British mathematician. The leading British pure mathematician of his time, G. H. Hardy taught at Cambridge (1906–19; 1931–42) and Oxford (1919–31) and made important contributions to almost every branch of mathematical analysis. One of his papers (1908) proved vital to the development of population genetics and the study of blood-group distribution. Much of Hardy's most important work was done in collaboration with mathematicians J. E. Littlewood and Srinivasa Ramanujan. He wrote numerous technical works as well as the influential text *A Course in Pure Mathematics* (1908) and the popular *A Mathematician's Apology* (1940). ■ See his *Collected Papers* (7 vols., 1966–79).

HARDY, OLIVER. *See LAUREL, STAN.*

HARKNESS, EDWARD STEPHEN (1874–1940), U.S. philanthropist. The son of Stephen Vanderberg Harkness (one of John D. Rockefeller's original partners and one of the six original stockholders of the Standard Oil Co.), Edward Harkness inherited one of America's largest fortunes and gave away more than $130 million. His gifts made possible the merger of Presbyterian Hospital and the Columbia University Medical School, and he donated the land in New York City on which the massive Columbia-Presbyterian Medical Center was built. He conceived the idea of a decentralized college campus and gave $12 million each to Harvard (1928) and Yale (1930) to set up their "house" plans. He gave more than $7 million to Phillips Exeter Academy to develop its tutorial teaching system and reorganize its curriculum.

HARLAN, JOHN MARSHALL (1899–1971), U.S. jurist. A fourth-generation lawyer whose grandfather (and namesake) was a Supreme Court justice, Harlan spent 25 years working for a Wall Street Corporate law firm after his graduation from New York Law School (1924). In 1954 he was named to the U.S. Court of Appeals and in 1955 to the Supreme Court, where he gained a reputation as a conservative dissenter. A Republican, a Presbyterian, and a strict adherent to legal precedent, Harlan believed that social and political change should come through the legislature, not the judiciary, and that federal courts should not interfere in state and local affairs. He resigned from the court (1971) several months before his death.

HARLOW, JEAN (Harlean Carpenter; 1911–1937), U.S. film actress. A brassy, wisecracking blonde from Kansas City, Harlow eloped and became a film extra at age 16. The marriage didn't last, but with her first big part in *Hell's Angels* (1930) she became the sex archetype of the next decade. In *Platinum Blond* (1932) Harlow displayed her voluptuous curves under clinging gowns; in *Red Dust* (1932) and *China Seas* (1935) she played a salty "man's woman" opposite Clark Gable. Her brief career was frequently interrupted by illness and she died at age 26 from cerebral edema. Two films were made about her life. ■ See biography by Irving Shulman (1964) and David Stenn, *Bombshell* (1993).

HARMON, THOMAS DUDLEY (1919–1990), U.S. football player. Tom Harmon was the outstanding college football player in the era immediately preceding World War II

and was the University of Michigan's greatest football hero. A two-time All-America selection (1939, 1940) as a running and passing back, he broke most of Red Grange's Big Ten records and scored 33 touchdowns, passed for 16 more, and ran for 2,338 yards—just under 6 yards per carry. He was a pilot during World War II, and after playing professional football with the Los Angeles Rams (1946–47), he became a radio and television sportscaster.

HARNICK, SHELDON. *See BOCK, JERRY, and SHELDON HARNICK.*

HARRIMAN, (WILLIAM) AVERELL (1891–1986), U.S. public official and diplomat. Son of financier and railroad magnate E. H. Harriman, Averell Harriman served as chairman of the board of the Merchant Shipping Corp. (1917–25) and the Union Pacific Railroad (1932–46). He entered government service in 1934 and was an administrator of the National Recovery Administration, chairman of the Business Advisory Council, and coordinator of lend-lease aid to Britain and the Soviet Union. As ambassador to the U.S.S.R. (1943–46) and Britain (1946) he helped shape U.S. foreign policy at the beginning of the cold war. Under Pres. Harry Truman he was secretary of commerce (1946–48), director of Marshall Plan aid to Europe (1948–50), and director of the Mutual Security Agency (1951–53). After four years as a liberal Democratic governor of New York (1955–58), he served in various high-level State Department and diplomatic posts and was chief negotiator of the 1963 Nuclear Test Ban Treaty and the 1968–69 Paris peace talks with North Vietnam. He wrote *America and Russia in a Changing World* (1971) and *Special Envoy to Churchill and Stalin, 1941–46* (1975; with Elie Abel). ■ See biography by Rudy Abramson, *Spanning the Century* (1992).

HARRINGTON, (EDWARD) MICHAEL (1928–1989), U.S. political leader and writer. Harrington, who came from a "lace-curtain Irish" family in St. Louis, was radicalized during a college summer spent in the South. He joined the Catholic Worker movement in 1951 and the Young Socialist League the following year. In *The Other America* (1962), Harrington described the fate of the "invisible poor" so effectively as to be credited with sparking the federal antipoverty program. He headed the U.S. Socialist party (from 1968) but resigned in 1972 over its lukewarm endorsement of George McGovern's presidential candidacy. He later chaired the Democratic Socialist Organizing Committee and its successor, Democratic Socialists of America (from 1973). His other books included *Twilight of Capitalism* (1976), *Decade of Decision* (1980), *The Politics at God's Funeral* (1984), *The Next Left* (1987), and *Socialism: Past and Future* (1989). ■ See the autobiographical *Fragments of a Century* (1973) and *Taking Sides: The Education of a Militant Mind* (1985); his autobiography, *The Long-Distance Runner* (1988); biography by Robert Gorman (1995); and Maurice Isserman, *The Other American* (2000).

HARRIS, FRANK (James Thomas Harris; 1856–1931), British-U.S. writer and editor. Harris is best known for his apocryphal, sexually explicit autobiography *My Life and Loves* (3 vols., 1923–27), which was banned in the United States and Britain. Born in Ireland, he came to the United States at age 15 and worked at odd jobs, one of which inspired *My Reminiscences as a Cowboy* (1930). He earned a law degree at the University of Kansas, then went to Britain, where he edited several important publications, including the *Saturday Review* (1894–98), and befriended such notables as Sir Max Beerbohm, George Bernard Shaw, and Oscar Wilde. He returned briefly to the United States to edit *Pearson's Magazine,* but became a German sympathizer in World War I and left again. Other writings included short stories, the novel *Great Days* (1913), several studies of Shakespeare, an impressionistic biography of Wilde (1920), and five volumes of provocative *Contemporary Portraits* (1915–23). ■ See biographies by Vincent Brome (1959), Hugh Kingsmill (1974), and Philippa Pullar (1975).

HARRIS, JULIE (1925–), U.S. actress. Harris was, from her youth, doggedly set on a stage career; she acted at summer drama camps and in school. She made her Broadway debut in 1945 while a student at the Yale School of Drama, later worked at New York's Actors Studio, and in the late 1940s performed in Old Vic productions of Shakespeare. After creating numerous roles on Broadway, 24-year-old Harris won lavish praise as the 12-year-old Frankie Adams in the stage production of Carson McCullers' *The Member of the Wedding* (1950; film, 1953). She subsequently appeared in more than 30 stage roles and won Tony Awards for her performances in *I Am a Camera* (1951), *The Lark* (1955), *Forty Carats* (1959), *The Last of Mrs. Lincoln* (1973), and *The Belle of Amherst* (1976), a play based on the life and work of the poet Emily Dickinson in which she appeared alone. The indefatigable Harris made numerous films and gave more than 50 television performances.

HARRIS, LOUIS (1921–), U.S. pollster. Louis Harris studied economics at the University of North Carolina. His first poll, taken at the end of World War II, revealed the attitudes of sailors awaiting demobilization. In 1947 Harris joined the Elmo Roper polling organization and in 1956 established Louis Harris and Associates. He used opinion polls to help John F. Kennedy develop strategy for his successful 1958 Senate and 1960 presidential bids. He introduced sophisticated polls that probed the sentiments underlying respondents' initial answers. By scrutinizing election returns at the precinct level, Harris gauged shifts in political attitudes by ethnic and religious groups. While continuing to conduct market research, Harris became best known as a political pollster, usually for Democrats or liberal Republicans. He replaced Roper as public opinion analyst for the CBS network (1962–68), then went to work for ABC (1971–72). Harris was a columnist for the *Washington Post* and

Newsweek in the 1960s and for the Daily News Syndicate (1969–88). He wrote several books, including *Inside America* (1987).

HARRIS, MARVIN (1927–), U.S. cultural anthropologist. Harris studied at Columbia University (Ph.D. 1953), where he taught (1952–81). He made important theoretical contributions to cultural ecology and economic anthropology, wrote extensively on the development of anthropological theory, and was a leading advocate of cultural materialism. His books included *The Nature of Cultural Things* (1964), *The Rise of Anthropological Theory* (1968), *Cows, Pigs, Wars, and Witches* (1974), *Cultural Materialism* (1979), *America Now* (1981), *Good to Eat: Riddles of Food and Culture* (1986), *Our Kind* (1989), and *Theories of Culture in Postmodern Times* (1999).

HARRIS, ROY (1890–1979), U.S. composer. One of the numerous prominent students of the influential French musician Nadia Boulanger, Harris was a leading composer of symphonies and choral works. His best-known pieces, traditional in form and influenced by folk music and hymns, reflected his attachment to America's landscape, history, and traditions. Of his 16 symphonies, No. 3 (1937) is one of the most frequently performed of all American symphonies. His other notable works included *When Johnny Comes Marching Home* (1935), Symphony No. 4 (*Folksong Symphony,* 1940), and Symphony No. 7 (1952). He taught at several universities and organized many music festivals. ■ See study by Dan Stehmann (1984).

HARRISON, SIR REX (Reginald Carey Harrison; 1908–1990), British actor. After a London stage career in the 1930s and World War II service in the Royal Air Force, Harrison appeared in *Blithe Spirit* (1945) and *Rake's Progress* (1945) before his successful Hollywood debut in *Anna and the King of Siam* (1946). Alternating between the stage and film, he was a popular Professor Higgins in *My Fair Lady* on Broadway (1956–57) and won an Academy Award for his performance in the film (1964). The tall, debonair actor with the high-pitched voice also starred in *Cleopatra* (1962) and *Dr. Dolittle* (1967). ■ See his autobiography, *Rex* (1975), and memoirs, *A Damned Serious Business* (1991).

HARRISON, ROSS GRANVILLE (1870–1959), U.S. biologist. Harrison received a Ph.D. (Johns Hopkins, 1894) and M.D. (University of Bonn, 1899) before serving on the faculty at Yale (1907–38). He developed a method of culturing animal tissue in a liquid medium that permitted, for the first time, the study of isolated living cells in a controlled environment. He also demonstrated that nerve fibers are outgrowths from cells of the central nervous system and formulated general laws regarding the asymmetry of all vertebrate forms. As chairman of the National Research Council (1938–46) he helped organize the scientific community during World War II.

HARRISON, WALLACE KIRKMAN (1895–1981), U.S. architect. A New Englander who studied in Paris after World War I, Harrison devoted his career as an architect to the construction of Rockefeller family projects, beginning with Rockefeller Center in New York City (1929–40). He was a partner in the firm of Harrison and Abramovitz (1945–79) and played a major role in the design of the 1939 World's Fair (New York) and the Empire State Plaza in Albany. Harrison supervised the design of the United Nations headquarters (1947–50) on a New York City site donated by the Rockefellers and was the overall design coordinator of New York's Lincoln Center for the Performing Arts (1962). ■ See biography by Victoria Newhouse (1989).

HARSANYI, JOHN C. (1920–2000), Hungarian-born U.S. economist. Harsanyi studied mathematics at the University of Budapest (Ph.D. 1947) before emigrating to Australia (1950) and then to the United States (1956). He earned a second doctorate from Stanford University (1959) and taught economics at the Haas School of Business at the University of California, Berkeley (1964–90). A pioneer in the field of game theory, Harsanyi extended the work of John F. Nash by introducing probability functions to the analysis of how rivals interact with each other in such situations as business competition, trade negotiation, and conflicts between nations. He collaborated with Reinhard Selten, a visiting professor at Berkeley (1967–68), on *A General Theory of Equilibrium Selection in Games* (1988). Harsanyi shared the 1994 Nobel Memorial Prize in Economics with Nash and Selten for their contributions to game theory.

HART, LORENZ (1895–1943), U.S. lyricist. A descendant of the poet Heinrich Heine, Hart was born in New York and studied at Columbia University, where he collaborated with composer Richard Rodgers on the varsity show in 1920. During the next 20 years they wrote 28 Broadway shows, including *On Your Toes* (1936), *Babes in Arms* (1938), and *Pal Joey* (1940), and hundreds of songs. Hart's literate, expressive, and bittersweet lyrics—"Blue Moon," "Where or When," "There's a Small Hotel," "My Funny Valentine," "The Lady Is a Tramp," "Bewitched, Bothered and Bewildered"—epitomized witty sophistication. ■ See Dorothy Hart, *Thou Swell, Thou Witty* (1976), and biography by Frederick Nolan (1994).

HART, MOSS (1904–1961), U.S. playwright and director. The son of a Jewish cigar maker, Hart worked at odd jobs in the theatrical world. Six summers of directing amateur productions on the Catskill Mountains resort-hotel "borscht circuit" in upstate New York prefaced his success as a comedy writer. He collaborated with George S. Kaufman on *Once in a Lifetime* (1930), *You Can't Take It with You* (1936; Pulitzer Prize), and *The Man Who Came to Dinner* (1939) and with Kurt Weill and Ira Gershwin on *Lady in the Dark* (1941). A would-be actor, Hart also wrote books for musi-

cals by Irving Berlin and Cole Porter, and directed *My Fair Lady* (1956) and *Camelot* (1960). Hart earned over $5 million and once confessed "I have none of the money left and I have no regrets." ■ See his autobiography, *Act One* (1959).

HART, WILLIAM S. (1870–1946), U.S. film actor and director. A cowboy in his youth, Hart had a successful career on the New York stage for 20 years (1890–1910) before becoming the first cowboy film star. An austere, middle-aged man with solemn manners, Hart created Rio Jim, "the good badman," in *The Disciple* (1915). Writer and director of many of his films, he re-created a West without glamour and artifice in *The Gun Fighter* (1917), *Square Deal Sanderson* (1919), *The Covered Wagon* (1923), and *Wild Bill Hickok* (1923). But popular taste inclined to more contrived westerns, and Hart retired after making *Tumbleweeds* (1925). ■ See his autobiography, *My Life East and West* (1929).

HARTACK, BILL (1932–   ), U.S. jockey. One of the most successful jockeys in history, Hartack won the Kentucky Derby five times (1957, 1960, 1962, 1964, 1969), the Preakness three times (1956, 1964, 1969), and the Belmont once (1960). The leading jockey in 1955, 1956, 1957, and 1960, he was the first to win $2 million (1956) and $3 million (1957) in one year. In 1972 he became the fifth jockey to win 4,000 races. He retired from U.S. racing with 4,272 winners and then raced for six years in Hong Kong.

HARTLEY, LESLIE POLES (1895–1972), British writer. L. P. Hartley was a gentleman writer in the style of Henry James, concerned with guilt, evil, and psychological nuance. He is best known for his trilogy about two children growing up: *The Shrimp and the Anemone* (1944), *The Sixth Heaven* (1946), and *Eustace and Hilda* (1947). Another novel of childhood was *The Go-Between* (1953; film 1971). ■ See his essays in *The Novelist's Responsibility* (1967), his *Collected Short Stories* (1968), and study by Peter Bien (1963).

HARTLEY, MARSDEN (1877–1943), U.S. painter. Hartley studied art in Cleveland and New York and exhibited his landscapes at the gallery of Alfred Stieglitz (1909). He traveled extensively in Europe throughout his life; his abstract paintings reflected the influence of French cubism and German expressionism. After 1920, Hartley turned from abstraction to more realistic depiction of natural scenes, and he was best known for his colorful paintings of the people and scenes of his native Maine. ■ See his autobiography, *Somehow a Past* (1997), and study by Elizabeth McCausland (1952).

HARTLINE, HALDAN KEFFER (1903–1983), U.S. neurophysiologist. Working with the eyes of horseshoe crabs and frogs, Hartline isolated individual nerve fibers and recorded their reactions to light. He discovered how receptor cells are interconnected to allow the eye to sharpen contrasts and differentiate between form and movement. Hartline taught at the University of Pennsylvania (1931–40; 1942–49), Johns Hopkins (1949–53), and the Rockefeller Institute (now Rockefeller University, 1953–74) and shared the 1967 Nobel Prize in Physiology or Medicine with George Wald and Ragnar Granit.

HARTMANN, CARL SADAKICHI (1867?–1944), Japanese-born U.S. writer and art critic. Born to a German father and a Japanese mother, Sadakichi Hartmann was one of the authentic bohemian figures of the century. Characterized by his friend John Barrymore, the actor, as "presumably sired by Mephistopheles out of Madame Butterfly," Hartmann was a protégé of poets Walt Whitman and Stéphane Mallarmé and was well known as "the king of Bohemia" in pre–World War I Greenwich Village (New York). Although never steadily employed, Hartmann wrote free-verse dramas, short stories, and poetry, but he survived by lecturing, panhandling, and writing critical books on art and the dance. Among his best-known works were *Japanese Art* (1904) and *A History of American Art* (1902; rev. ed. 1932). ■ See Gene Fowler, *Minutes of the Last Meeting* (1954).

HARTMANN, HEINZ (1894–1970), Austrian-born U.S. psychoanalyst. Hartmann came from a distinguished family of Viennese Jews; his father was at one time Austrian ambassador to Germany. He earned his M.D. from the University of Vienna (1920) and published the important pioneering paper *Ego Psychology and the Problem of Adaptation* (1939; Eng. trans. 1958). Emigrating to the United States in 1941, he joined the faculty of the New York Psychoanalytic Institute and became one of the leaders of the second generation of Freudian psychoanalysts. Expanding the basic theory of the ego, he wrote *Essays on Ego Psychology* (1964) and collaborated on *The Psychoanalytic Study of the Child,* an annual publication updating the basic works of psychoanalysis.

HARVEY, PAUL (Paul Harvey Aurandt; 1918–), U.S. news commentator. A descendant of five generations of preachers, Harvey started delivering his news commentary on ABC radio in 1944. Thirty years later the melodramatic Chicago-based broadcaster was appearing on more than 600 radio stations and could boast of having the largest audience of any network radio show, reaching more than 4 million listeners. A staunch conservative, impassioned enemy of communism, and favorite of middle America, Harvey also wrote a thrice-weekly opinion column that appeared in 300 newspapers, made daily television commentaries for approximately 100 stations, and constantly crisscrossed the country giving lectures at conventions, colleges, and civic associations.

HAŠEK, JAROSLAV (1883–1923), Czech novelist, journalist, and short-story writer. A schoolmaster's son who wrote poetry and short stories and edited anarchist journals prior to 1914, Hašek served in the Austrian army, Czech legion,

and the Red army during and after World War I. In a series of four loosely organized, anecdotal, coarse, and antimilitaristic novels, Hašek created the *Good Soldier Schweik* (1920–23; Eng. trans. 1974). The story of Schweik, an insignificant soldier whose wit and naiveté preserved him through the war and the trials of official bureaucracy, has been called one of the great satires of world literature. Some saw Schweik as a representative of one aspect of the Czech national character, while others stressed the universal message that craftiness and idiocy were the only defenses against authoritarianism and regimentation. Further adventures of Schweik, along with other stories, appeared in *The Red Commissar* (Eng. trans. 1981). ■ See Cecil Parrott, *The Bad Bohemian* (1978), and biography by Emanuel Frynta (Eng. trans. 1965).

HASKINS, CHARLES HOMER (1870–1937), U.S. historian. Haskins received his Ph.D. from Johns Hopkins (1890) at age 20, the first medievalist to be trained in the United States. As professor of history (1902–31) and dean (1908–24) of Harvard's graduate school, he trained a whole generation of U.S. scholars in his subject. Haskins wrote *The Normans in European History* (1915) and *Norman Institutions* (1918), the definitive work on the subject. He also studied the transmission of Greek and Arabic scholarship to Europe in *The Renaissance of the Twelfth Century* (1927).

HASS, ROBERT (1941–), U.S. poet. A native of San Francisco, Hass was educated at St. Mary's College, California (B.A. 1963), and Stanford University (M.A. 1965; Ph.D. 1971) and taught at St. Mary's College (1971–89) and the University of California, Berkeley (1989–). In his highly acclaimed poems he creatively combined apparently unrelated images and objects in writing about such topics as the natural environment and human relationships. He was best known for his poetry collections, *Field Guide* (1973), *Praise* (1979), *Human Wishes* (1989), and *Sun Under Wood* (1996), and his volume of essays, *Twentieth Century Pleasures: Prose on Poetry* (1985). Hass also served as U.S. poet laureate (1995–97), translated several volumes of poetry by Czeslaw Milosz, and edited *The Essential Haiku* (1994).

HASSAM, (FREDERICK) CHILDE (1859–1935), U.S. painter and etcher. Hassam studied in Paris, where he was influenced by impressionism. Settling in New York (1889), he became known for his vibrant landscapes, cityscapes, and interiors. His best canvases, which related impressionism to his American heritage, included *Church at Gloucester, Washington Arch, Spring, The New York Window, Broad and Wall Streets,* and *The Strawberry Tea-Set.* His works hang in major museums, including New York's Metropolitan Museum and the Chicago Art Institute. ■ See study by Donelson Hoopes (1979).

HASSAN II (Moulay Hassan; 1929–1999), king of Morocco. The son of King Muhammad V, Hassan II received a traditional Islamic as well as a French education (University of Bordeaux) and succeeded to the throne following the death of his father (Feb. 26, 1961). A nationalistic and autocratic leader, he built up the Moroccan armed forces, developed close ties with the West, and ruled through a subservient parliament. His forces occupied Spanish (later Western) Sahara in November 1975 but were bogged down in a long war with the Polisario Front (backed by Algeria), which sought independence for the region. His forces emerged victorious and controlled most of the land after a 1991 cease-fire. He met with Israeli Prime Minister Shimon Peres in 1986 and Yitzhak Rabin in 1993, and played the role of a mediator between Arabs and Israelis. During the 1990s he increased political freedoms, established an elected lower house of Parliament, and initiated market-oriented reforms, but he was unable to solve the problems of poverty, unemployment, and illiteracy. ■ See his memoirs, *The Challenge* (1976; Eng. trans. 1978).

HASSAN, MUHAMMAD ABDULLAH (1864-1920), Somali religious and political leader. The major event in the modern history of Somaliland (now Somalia) was the rebellion launched by Hassan in 1900. A poet, Islamic scholar, reformer, and teacher, he led a nomadic guerrilla force of dervishes in a messianic protonationalist crusade against the "corrupting colonial infidel," the Christian Europeans (primarily the British), and the Christian Ethiopians. The rebellion was finally suppressed by punitive British expeditions and aerial bombardment in 1920, soon after which Hassan died. He is regarded as the father of Somali nationalism and his poetry is still sung in Somalia. ■ See Douglas Jardine, *The Mad Mullah of Somaliland* (1923).

HASSEL, ODD (1897–1981), Norwegian chemist. Hassel made pioneering studies of the three-dimensional arrangement of molecules while he was on the faculty of the University of Oslo during the 1930s and 1940s. His work was advanced by Derek H. R. Barton in the 1950s and together they were awarded the 1969 Nobel Prize in Chemistry for their work in conformational analysis. Hassel's research revolutionized the study of molecular structure and led to the synthesis of new drugs and, indirectly, to the cracking of the genetic code. His books included *Crystal Chemistry* (1934; Eng. trans. 1935).

HASTIE, WILLIAM HENRY (1904–1976), U.S. jurist. A graduate of Harvard Law School (1930), Hastie served as dean of the Howard Law School (1939–46) and consultant on race relations to the secretary of war (1940–43), a post from which he resigned in protest over continued discrimination against blacks in the armed forces. A skillful lawyer, he successfully argued several civil-rights cases before the Supreme Court, including decisions that outlawed all-white primaries and prohibited segregation of passengers using interstate transportation. Hastie was the first African-American governor of the Virgin Islands (1946–49) and the first

African American to hold a judgeship on the U.S. Court of Appeals (3rd Circuit, Philadelphia; 1949–71). ■ See study by Gilbert Ware (1984).

HATEM, GEORGE (1910–1988), U.S.-born Chinese physician and public health official. Born into a family of Lebanese origin in Buffalo, New York, Hatem studied medicine at the American University in Beirut, Lebanon, and the University of Geneva, Switzerland, and began practicing medicine in Shanghai (1933). Fed up with working in a "gangster society," he went to the Communist base in Yenan, in northern Shaanxi Province (1936), and became the only American to join the Red army. As Ma Haide, he served as an army doctor until the Communists took control of the country in 1949. At that point he became the first foreigner to be naturalized by the new government and he served as an adviser to the Ministry of Public Health. He helped to organize the vast new public health program and became a legendary figure in China for his work in eradicating venereal disease by the 1960s. His work also helped to limit the incidence of leprosy. He was credited with saving millions of lives and being one of the most successful figures in medical history. ■ See Edgar A. Porter, *The People's Doctor* (1997).

HAUPTMAN, HERBERT AARON (1917–), U.S. chemist. Hauptman studied at City College of New York (B.S. 1937), Columbia, and the University of Maryland (Ph.D. 1955). Working at the Naval Research Laboratory in Washington, D.C., with CCNY classmate Jerome Karle during the 1950s and 1960s, he helped to develop a mathematical technique, known as the "direct method," to determine the three-dimensional structures of molecules. Analyzing the intensity of points visible as dots on X rays of substances in crystal form, they were able to determine the detailed structure of molecules in a few days, a task that previously took years. Although their technique was not generally accepted for more than 15 years, it was eventually used throughout the world and had extensive applications in medical and pharmaceutical research. Hauptman and Karle shared the 1985 Nobel Prize in Chemistry for their research. Hauptman taught at the University of Buffalo (from 1970) and was president of the Hauptman-Woodward Medical Research Institute (1988–).

HAUPTMANN, BRUNO RICHARD (1899–1936), German-born convicted criminal. After escaping from prison in Germany, Hauptmann stowed away on a transatlantic liner and entered New York illegally in 1923. Over the next 10 years he worked as a dishwasher and carpenter and was a partner in a fur business. In September 1933, he was arrested for the kidnap-murder (1932) of aviator Charles A. Lindbergh's two-year-old son. The crime was one of the most publicized of the century. Hauptmann was found guilty and executed. John V. Haring, *The Hand of Hauptmann* (1937), supports the guilty verdict, while Anthony Scaduto, *Scapegoat* (1976), and Ludovic Kennedy, *The Air-*

man and the Carpenter (1985) and *Crime of the Century* (1996), argue that Hauptmann was the innocent victim of a frame-up.

HAUPTMANN, GERHART (1862–1946), German playwright. Ranked with the great Scandinavian dramatists Henrik Ibsen and August Strindberg, Hauptmann was one of the pioneers of naturalistic drama. His powerfully written and compassionate plays were not mere entertainment but social commentary that dramatized the moral corruption and ugliness of modern materialistic life. His most famous plays were *Before Dawn* (1889; Eng. trans. 1909), *Lonely Lives* (1891; Eng. trans. 1898), *The Weavers* (1892; Eng. trans. 1899), and *Drayman Henshel* (1899; Eng. trans. 1913). Hauptmann won the Nobel Prize in Literature (1912). The epic poem *Till Eulenspiegel* (1928) told of the chaotic conditions of post–World War I Germany, while the Atrides tetralogy (1941–48) reflected the horrors and despair of World War II. *The Book of Passion* (1929) and *The Adventure of My Youth* (1937) were autobiographical.

HAUSER, ARNOLD (1892–1978), Hungarian-born art historian. Hauser studied at the University of Budapest and belonged to the "Sunday Circle," a group of left-liberal intellectuals (including Gyorgy Lukács) who did pioneering work on the sociology of art and literature. After participating in the Hungarian Soviet Republic (1918–19), he lived in exile in Italy (1919–21), Berlin (1922–24), and Vienna (1925–38) before settling in Britain (1938). A critical Marxist who rejected the dogmatism of many of his left-wing colleagues, he developed his own Marxist method of analysis, which was most prominently displayed in his magnum opus, *The Social History of Art* (Eng. trans. 1951). His other works included *The Philosophy of Art* (1958; Eng. trans. 1959), *Mannerism: The Crisis of the Renaissance and the Origin of Modern Art* (2 vols., 1964; Eng. trans. 1965), and *The Sociology of Art* (1967; Eng. trans. 1982).

HAUSER, GAYELORD (Helmut Eugene Benjamin Gellert Hauser; 1895–1984), German-born U.S. nutritionist. A health-food evangelist, Hauser believed that a diet of fruits, vegetables, and herb teas cured his tuberculosis of the hip after surgery proved futile. He learned about nutrition from specialists in Dresden and Vienna, then began dispensing advice on diets in Chicago (1923). Moving to California (1927), Hauser became internationally famous during the 1930s for vegetable diets that featured such "wonder foods" as brewers' yeast, yogurt, skim milk, wheat germ, and blackstrap molasses. He had a large following in the Hollywood film set and among many international celebrities. Although medical doctors regarded his theories with skepticism, Hauser published numerous best-selling books, including *Diet Does It* (1944), the *Gayelord Hauser Cookbook* (1946), *Look Younger, Live Longer* (1950), and *Be Happier, Be Healthier* (1952). He died at age 89.

HAUSHOFER, KARL ERNST (1869–1946), German geopolitician. A major general, Haushofer retired from the military to pursue a second vocation (1921) as professor of geography and director of the Institute of Geopolitics at the University of Munich. Under the influence of the English geopolitician Sir Halford Mackinder's theory of the ascendance of the heartland, he advocated a German-Soviet alliance and in his first major work, *Geopolitics of the Pacific Ocean* (1924), he predicted the rise of Japan. Haushofer was an influential adviser to Nazi dictator Adolf Hitler. In 1946, depressed by the murder of his son by the Gestapo and by his investigation for war crimes, Haushofer and his wife committed suicide. ■ See Andreas Dorpalen, *The World of General Haushofer* (1942), and Edmund A. Walsh, *Total Power* (1948).

HAVEL, VACLAV (1936–   ), Czech playwright. While working in a chemical factory, Havel completed high school at night and began writing poetry and drama while attending a technical college. Finding work at Prague's Theater on the Balustrade (1960), he went from stagehand to resident playwright in eight years. Widely regarded as the leading Czech playwright of his generation, he commented satirically on the struggles of contemporary Czech intellectuals and bureaucrats in such plays as *The Garden Party* (1964; Eng. tans. 1969), *The Memorandum* (1965; Eng. trans. 1965), and *The Increased Difficulty of Concentration* (1968; Eng. trans. 1972). After the Soviet invasion of Czechoslovakia (1968), Havel's works were banned from the Czech stage; however, such plays as *Interview* (1975), *A Private View* (1975), and *The Protest* (1978) were produced abroad. In 1977 Havel was one of three main spokespersons for the Charter 77 manifesto, which charged the Czech government with violations of the human rights provisions of the 1975 Helsinki agreement. Arrested several times, he was convicted of subversion (1979) and spent four and half years in prison. In November 1989 he was a founder and a leading spokesman and negotiator for Civic Forum, the political organization that played a major role in bringing down the Communist government and restoring democracy. He was elected president in December 1989, but resigned in June 1992, when he failed to receive the support of Slovak legislators in Parliament. After Czechoslovakia split into two countries, Havel was elected president of the Czech Republic in 1993 and reelected in 1998. His later translated works included *Open Letters: Selected Writings, 1964–1900* (1991) and *The Art of the Impossible: Politics as Morality in Practice—Speeches and Writings, 1900–1996* (1997). ■ See Michael Simmons, *The Reluctant President* (1991), and the biography by John Keane (2000).

HAWKE, BOB (Robert James Lee Hawke; 1929–   ), Australian political leader. Influenced by his father, a Congregationalist minister, and his mother, an activist in the temperance movement, Hawke joined the Australian Labour party (ALP) at age 17. He received degrees in economics and law from the University of Western Australia, and was a Rhodes scholar at Oxford (1953–55). Abandoning an academic career, he joined the Australian Council of Trade Unions (ACTU; 1958), an umbrella organization of the country's organized labor movement, as a researcher and advocate at wage-arbitration hearings. A successful negotiator, he served as ACTU president (1970–80) and revitalized and unified the movement. He also was ALP vice president (1971–73) and president (1973–78), and became one of Australia's most visible and popular public figures. He was elected to parliament (1980) and led the ALP to victory in the 1983 elections. As prime minister he was frequently criticized by the left wing of the party, but negotiated a historic wage and price accord (1983; extended 1985) and sponsored tax reforms and free-market policies that cut inflation, established industrial peace, and resulted in significant economic growth. His government was reelected in 1984, 1987, and 1990, but he lost support as the economy slumped in the early 1990s. He was ousted by Labour party leaders (December 1991) and replaced by Paul Keating. Hawke gave up his parliamentary seat in 1992 and retired from politics. ■ See *The Hawke Memoirs* (1994) and biography by Stan Auson (1992).

HAWKES, JOHN (John Clendennin Burne, Jr.; 1925–1998), U.S. novelist. Hawkes' academic career at Harvard was interrupted by service as an ambulance driver in World War II, which generated his first novel, *The Cannibal* (1949). He injected gallows humor into his suspenseful, macabre novels *The Beetle Leg* (1951), *The Goose on the Grave* and *The Owl* (1954), *The Lime Twig* (1961), *Second Skin* (1964), *The Passion Artist* (1979), and *Virginia: Her Two Lives* (1981). The novel *Adventures in the Alaskan Skin Trade* (1985) was based in part on his family's experiences in Alaska (1935–40). Hawkes created complex fantasies with great stylistic discipline, exploring the border between dream and reality. "I want to try to create a world, not represent it," he wrote. After 1958, he taught at Brown University. His later works included *Whistlejacket* (1988), *Sweet William: A Memoir of Old Horse* (1993), *The Frog* (1996), and *An Irish Eye* (1997). ■ See study by Patrick O'Donnell (1982).

HAWKING, STEPHEN WILLIAM (1942–   ), British theoretical physicist. Educated at Oxford and Cambridge, Hawking served on the Cambridge faculty from 1968 to 1979. He incorporated insights from the general theory of relativity and quantum mechanics to support the "big bang" theory of the origin of the universe, to attempt to develop a quantum theory of gravity, and to work out complex equations pertaining to the formation, size, and radiation emission ("Hawking radiation") of black holes in space. Hawking managed to do this theoretical work despite the fact that he suffered (from 1962) from amyotrophic lateral sclerosis, a crippling disease that confined him to a wheelchair and left him physically unable to speak clearly or to write. He was the author of *Large-scale Structure of Space-Time* (with G.F.R. Ellis, 1973) and a book of essays, *Black Holes and Baby Universes* (1993). His book about the origin of the universe, *A Brief History of Time* (1988; film 1992), was written for a popular audience and became a best-seller. ■ See study by Michael White (1992).

HAWKINS, COLEMAN (1904–1969), U.S. jazz saxophonist. One of the pioneers of jazz, Hawkins studied music as a child, joined his first band at age 17, and was a member of Fletcher Henderson's band from 1923 to 1934. His virtuosity, improvisational genius, and powerful tone transformed the saxophone from what was essentially a comic instrument into a major instrument of jazz performance. His 1939 recording of "Body and Soul" is considered a classic. Hawkins' style constantly evolved, and even in his later years he was in the vanguard of jazz development.

HAWKINS, ERICK (Frederick Hawkins; 1909–1994), U.S. dancer and choreographer. A native of the Southwest, Hawkins studied under George Balanchine and danced with the American Ballet (1935–37) and then with the Martha Graham Dance Company (1938–51). He won acclaim as the dance partner of Graham (who was his wife from 1948 to 1954) in such Graham works as *Appalachian Spring*. His early choreography, rooted in Americana, included *Trickster Coyote* (1941) and *God's Angry Man: A Passion Play of John Brown* (1945). In 1951 he formed his own company, choreographing and dancing ritualistic, free-form, metaphoric dances. His avant-garde, abstract, mystical style reflected his interest in Eastern philosophy. His later works included *Hurrah!* (1975) and *The Joshua Tree, Or Three Outlaws* (1984). At age 75, Hawkins celebrated a half century in dance by appearing in four of his own works.

HAWKS, HOWARD (1896–1977), U.S. film director. Born in Goshen, Indiana, Hawks worked as a studio propman in Hollywood during vacations from Cornell University. He was a professional automobile and airplane racer, then returned to Hollywood (1922). There he became a film editor and wrote scripts before directing his first feature (1926). During a long and highly respected career Hawks directed every conceivable type of film: *Scarface* (1932), a gangster story; *Bringing Up Baby* (1938), a sophisticated comedy; the western *Red River* (1948); and the musical *Gentlemen Prefer Blondes* (1953). His films are distinguished by their incisive dialogue, visual clarity, and the absence of "arty" effects. ■ See study by Robin Wood (1968); Joseph McBride, *Hawks on Hawks* (1981); and biography by Todd McCarthy (1997).

HAWORTH, SIR (WALTER) NORMAN (1883–1950), British organic chemist. Haworth taught at several universities, including St. Andrews, Scotland (1912–20), and Birmingham (1925–48). He elaborated on the research of Emil H. Fischer, who had isolated and analyzed structures of pure sugars. His conception of sugar molecules in terms of ring formations provided a more accurate representation of their structure and yielded the useful Haworth formulas—descriptions of chemical reactions involving sugars. He investigated and synthesized (1934) vitamin C, which allowed wider and cheaper production of the antiscurvy vitamin. With Paul Karrer, Haworth received the 1937 Nobel Prize in Chemistry. He wrote *The Constitution of Sugars* (1929).

HAY, HARRY (Henry Hay, Jr.; 1912–   ), U.S. writer and gay liberation pioneer. Hay was born in England but spent most of his life in southern California. Influenced by leftist activists during the 1930s, he saw parallels between exploited workers and the experience of homosexuals in the United States and he initiated the idea of gays as an "oppressed minority." He viewed homosexuals as basically altruistic, community-minded, and progressive people who are essentially different from conservative and tradition-bound heterosexuals. The Mattachine Society, which he founded in 1950 to promote his ideas, constituted a unique brotherhood organization for gay men, and ushered in the modern gay liberation movement. Hay believed that as marginal people gays had become artists and spiritual leaders who had historically provided mainstream society with critical insights and visions that had enabled it to survive. Consequently, he helped launch the Radical Faeries (1978), a gay spiritual movement based on the concepts of sharing and consensus. ■ See Hay's writings in *Radically Gay* (1996; edited by Will Roscoe) and Stuart Timmons, *The Trouble with Harry Hay* (1990).

HAYA DE LA TORRE, VICTOR RAÚL (1895–1979), Peruvian political leader. An eloquent and charismatic figure, Haya was one of the century's leading Latin American advocates of social and national revolution. He founded the APRA (Popular Revolutionary Alliance for America) movement in 1924 and spent the ensuing years either in exile, jail, or underground; he became an international symbol during five years of asylum (1949–54) in the Colombian embassy in Lima. After constitutional government was restored (1957), his movement attracted wide support, but he found his legitimate political aspirations perennially blocked by the ruling Peruvian oligarchy. ■ See Robert J. Alexander, ed., *Aprismo* (1973), and Steve Stein, *Populism in Peru* (1980).

HAYAKAWA, SAMUEL ICHIYE (1906–1992), Canadian-born U.S. linguist, university administrator, and senator. The son of a Japanese businessman, S. I. Hayakawa taught English and linguistics at several U.S. universities and, after publishing *Language in Action* (1941), was recognized as a popularizer of general semantics. His other books included *Symbol, Status and Personality* (1963), *Language in Thought and Action* (3rd ed. 1972), and *Through the Communica-*

tion Barrier (1979). He became president of San Francisco State College in 1968, in the wake of student unrest, and took a controversial law-and-order stance in dealing with student demonstrators. When his goal of "restoring order" was achieved, he resigned the college presidency (1972) and later represented California in the U.S. Senate (1977–83). Hayakawa, a conservative Republican, supported tax cuts, decentralization of government, and noninterference in business.

HAYASHI, FUMIKO (Fumiko Miyata; 1903–1951), Japanese novelist. Raised in a poverty-stricken lower-class urban environment and having worked as a laborer for many years, Hayashi understood the humiliations and hardships of the poor. She skillfully and unsentimentally depicted the life and loves of these people in a series of realistic and popular works, notably the novels *Journal of a Vagabond* (1928–30; Eng. trans. 1951) and *A Life of Poverty* (1931) and the short story "The Late Chrysanthemum" (1948; Eng. trans. 1970). Her popularity peaked with the publication of her works depicting the harsh realities of post–World War II life, *Downtown* (1948; Eng. trans. 1961) and *Floating Clouds* (1949; Eng. trans. 1965). At the time of her death she was Japan's most popular woman writer. ■ See Joan E. Ericson, *Be a Woman* (1997) and Susanna Fessler, *Wandering Heart* (1998).

HAYDEN, CARL TRUMBULL (1877–1972), U.S. senator. The son of a pioneer in the territory of Arizona, Hayden served as the state's first congressman (1912–27) and later as a U.S. senator for seven terms (1927–69). His congressional career was the second longest in American history. A taciturn, unassuming Democrat who rarely made a speech, Hayden was nevertheless one of the Senate's most powerful figures for decades. He was closely associated with highway, water, land-reclamation, and mining bills that aided the development of the West. From 1957 to 1969 he was chairman of the powerful Appropriations Committee. ■ See study by Ross R. Rice (1994).

HAYDEN, THOMAS EMMETT (1940–   ), U.S. social activist. Born in Detroit and educated at the University of Michigan (B.A. 1961), Tom Hayden joined the Student Nonviolent Coordinating Committee (SNCC) as a civil-rights worker in the South and served as theorist and first president of the radical Students for a Democratic Society (SDS; 1962–63). He also worked as a community organizer in Newark (1964–67) and as a leader of the protest movement against the Vietnam War, in the course of which he made two trips to North Vietnam. He stood trial as one of the "Chicago 7" for conspiracy to disrupt the 1968 Democratic National Convention, and was acquitted. He later was married (1973–89) to fellow activist Jane Fonda, the actress. He was a founder and chair (from 1977) of the California Campaign for Economic Democracy and served as a Democratic member of the California State Assembly (1982–

92) and California State Senate (1992–2000). His early writings included *Rebellion in Newark* (1967), *The Other Side* (1967; with Staughton Lynd), and *Trial* (1970). His critique of U.S. foreign and domestic policies and his alternative visions are in *The American Future* (1980), while his *Lost Gospel of the Earth: A Call for Renewing Nature, Spirit and Politics* (1996) is a plea for environmental awareness. ■ See his *Reunion: A Memoir* (1988).

HAYEK, FRIEDRICH AUGUST VON (1899-1992), Austrian-born U.S. economist. The son of a botany professor, Hayek earned doctoral degrees in law and political science from the University of Vienna (1921–23) and in economics from the London School of Economics (1944), where he also taught (1931–50). He later joined the faculties of the University of Chicago (1950–62) and West Germany's University of Freiburg (1962–69). A leading conservative voice in modern economics, Hayek opposed government intervention in the economy and criticized the welfare state. He did pioneering work on business cycles, price theory, and production, and was one of the few experts to anticipate the 1929 stock market crash. His book *The Road to Serfdom* (1944), a controversial attack on state planning, was a bestseller in 12 languages. For three decades, Hayek's views departed from mainstream Keynesian economic thought, but he reemerged in the 1970s and 1980s when British leader Margaret Thatcher and U.S. Pres. Ronald Reagan and other conservatives embraced his economic philosophy. Hayek shared the 1974 Nobel Memorial Prize in Economics with the Swede Gunnar Myrdal, whose views were antithetical to his own. ■ See his *Hayek on Hayek: An Autobiographical Dialogue* (1994; with S. Kresge and L. Wenar); Fritz Machlup, ed., *Essays on Hayek* (1976); and N. P. Barry, *Hayek's Economic and Social Philosophy* (1979).

HAYES, BOB (Robert Hayes; 1942–   ), U.S. track star and football player. Sportswriters called Hayes "Bullet Bob" and the "World's Fastest Human" when he ran the hundred-yard dash in 9.1 seconds. A member of the 1964 U.S. Olympic team, he won gold medals in two events (100 meters and 400-meter relay team). A star in both track and football at Florida A&M University, Hayes later played for the Dallas Cowboys football team (1964–74) and became an All-Pro wide receiver. He was sentenced in 1979 to five years in prison for selling cocaine but was paroled the following year.

HAYES, HELEN (Helen Hayes Brown; 1900–1993), U.S actress. Called "the first lady of the American theater," Hayes delighted theater, movie, radio, and television audiences for more than 75 years. She made her stage debut at age 5 and was acclaimed on Broadway for her comic roles in *Penrod* (1918), *Dear Brutus* (1918), *Caesar and Cleopatra* (1925), and *What Every Woman Knows* (1926). Her later stage successes, which demonstrated her range and versatility, included starring roles in *Victoria Regina* (1935), *Happy*

Birthday (1946; Tony Award), *A Touch of the Poet* (1957), *Time Remembered* (1958; Tony Award), and *Long Day's Journey into Night* (1971). She appeared in many films including *Arrowsmith* (1931), *The Sin of Madelon Claudet* (1931; Academy Award), *A Farewell to Arms* (1932), *Anastasia* (1956), and *Airport* (1970; Academy Award). ■ See her memoirs, *A Gift of Joy* (1965), *On Reflection* (1968), *Twice Over Lightly* (1972; with Anita Loos), and *My Life in Three Acts* (1990); and study by Kenneth Barrow (1985).

HAYES, IRA (1922–1955), U.S. marine. A Pima Indian from Arizona, Hayes was one of the six World War II soldiers who raised the United States flag on Iwo Jima after the defeat of the Japanese in 1945, a scene immortalized by an Associated Press photographer. Back home on the reservation after the war, he was frequently arrested for drunk and disorderly behavior. After his death from exposure and alcoholism, "the tragic Indian marine" was buried in Arlington National Cemetery near the recently dedicated statue of the Iwo Jima flag raising. ■ See study by Albert Hemingway (1988).

HAYES, PATRICK JOSEPH (1867–1938), U.S. Roman Catholic clergyman. Called "the Cardinal of Charity," Hayes first served as curate of St. Gabriel's parish (New York City) and then became secretary to Bishop (later archbishop and cardinal) John Farley. During World War I he served on the executive committee of the National Catholic War Council and was named the first bishop of the armed services (1917). As archbishop of New York (from 1919), he established more than 60 new parishes and diocesan schools and founded Catholic Charities (1920), which incorporated over 200 diocesan charitable agencies and served as a model for charity centralization across the United States. Elevated to cardinal in 1924, Hayes generally avoided public controversy but spoke out against prohibition and opposed the American Birth Control League. ■ See study by John B. Kelly (1940).

HAYES, ROLAND (1887–1976), U.S. concert singer. Son of a former slave, Hayes worked in a Chattanooga factory before his first voice lessons at age 16. A tenor, he studied voice at Fisk University and in 1911 traveled with the Fisk Jubilee Singers to Boston, where he remained to study and give a successful solo concert in 1917. However, unable to get backing by white promoters, he began giving recitals in Europe after World War I, singing classical songs as well as spirituals, which he interpreted and arranged. He appeared as soloist with many orchestras and gave command performances for the royal houses of Britain and Spain. He returned to the United States in triumph (1923) and thereafter sang throughout the country. He published *My Songs: Aframerican Religious Folk Songs* (1948). ■ See MacKinley Helm, *Angel Mo' and Her Son, Roland Hayes* (1942).

HAYFORD, JOSEPH EPHRAIM CASELY (1866–1930), pan-African leader. J. E. Casely Hayford was a journalist from the Gold Coast (later Ghana) who studied law in England and served on the Gold Coast legislative council (1916–25; 1927–30). An elder statesman of the pan-African movement, he founded the national congress of British West Africa (1920) to press for self-government for the British West African colonies. He wrote three books on the land question. arguing against alienation of African holdings, and was a pioneer in the Africanization of education. His writings included *Gold Coast Native Institutions* (1903), *Ethiopia Unbound* (1911), and *United West Africa* (1919).

HAYNES, GEORGE EDMUND (1880–1960), U.S. sociologist. The first African American to receive a Ph.D. from Columbia University (1912), Haynes pioneered the study of black urban life. He was a cofounder and first executive director (1910–18) of the National Urban League. A leader in the movement for improved interracial relations, he served as the first executive secretary of the department of race relations of the Federal (now National) Council of Churches of Christ (1922–46). He was a founder of the Association of Negro Colleges and Secondary Schools and taught at Fisk University (1910–18) and the College of the City of New York (1950–59).

HAYNES, MARQUES (1926–   ), U.S. basketball player. Known as the "World's Greatest Dribbler" (he was able to dribble a ball three times a second), Haynes was a star with the Harlem Globetrotters from 1947 to 1953. He and teammate Goose Tatum were the chief attractions during the team's first worldwide tour. After leaving the Globetrotters, he formed his own touring club, the Fabulous Magicians.

HAYS, ARTHUR GARFIELD (1881–1954), U.S. lawyer. A highly successful corporation lawyer, Hays was internationally known for his defense work in some of the century's most important civil-liberties cases. Associated for most of his professional career with the American Civil Liberties Union, Hays played major defense roles in the Scopes evolution trial (1925), the *American Mercury* censorship trial (1926), the Sacco-Vanzetti murder case (1921–27), and the Scottsboro rape case (1931). He defended Georgi Dimitrov (1933), the Bulgarian communist accused of setting fire to the Reichstag Building in Berlin, and conducted an investigation into alleged civil-liberties violations in Puerto Rico (1937). ▪ See his autobiography, *City Lawyer* (1942).

HAYS, WILL (William Harrison Hays; 1879–1954), U.S. public official and motion-picture executive. A lawyer active in Indiana politics, Hays served as Republican national chairman (1918–20) and engineered Warren G. Harding's successful presidential race (1920). He became postmaster general (1921) but resigned to serve as president of the Motion Picture Producers and Distributors of America (1922–43) and was known as the "czar" of the motion-picture industry. A strict Presbyterian churchman, he developed and enforced codes of morality and censorship (the "Hays Code") that controlled the content of almost all American movies until 1966. His work contributed to the public acceptance of Hollywood movies and forestalled threatened government censorship. ▪ See his *Memoirs* (1955).

HAYWARD, LELAND (1902–1971), U.S. theatrical producer. A flamboyant and legendary entrepreneur, Hayward was (from 1926) a Hollywood talent agent who helped break producers' control over actors' salaries and negotiated extraordinarily lucrative contracts for James Stewart, Clark Gable, Katharine Hepburn, Henry Fonda, and Fred Astaire. As a literary agent he represented Ernest Hemingway, Edna Ferber, and Dashiell Hammett. He merged his operations with the Music Corp. of America (1945) and served as one of the organization's vice presidents. He produced such Broadway hits as *A Bell for Adano* (1944), *State of the Union* (1945), *Mister Roberts* (1948), *South Pacific* (1949), *Gypsy* (1959), and *The Sound of Music* (1959), and such films as *Mister Roberts* (1955), *The Spirit of St. Louis* (1957), and *The Old Man and the Sea* (1958). ▪ See Brooke Hayward, *Haywire* (1977).

HAYWOOD, WILLIAM DUDLEY (1869–1928), U.S. labor leader. One of the most prominent and controversial U.S. social radicals, Bill Haywood began his career as an organizer for the Western Federation of Miners and served on its executive board (1899–1908). He was also an activist with the Socialist party (1901–13). A militant who advocated violence as a means of changing society, "Big Bill," as he was known to his followers, was a founder of the Industrial Workers of the World (1905) and helped make it the foremost American radical labor organization of its time. After being indicted and then acquitted (1907) of the murder of a former Idaho governor, he became a popular hero. He called for "one big union" of all workers and led famous strikes at Lawrence, Massachusetts (1912), and Paterson, New Jersey (1931). He was convicted (1918) of sedition during World War I and sentenced to 20 years. Out on bail (1921), Haywood fled to the Soviet Union, where he remained until his death. ▪ See his autobiography, *Bill Haywood's Book* (1929); Joseph R. Conlin, *Big Bill Haywood and the Radical Union Movement* (1969); and Peter Carlson, *Roughneck* (1983).

HAZELTINE, (LOUIS) ALAN (1886–1964), U.S engineer and inventor. Fascinated by algebra as a boy, Hazeltine was drawn to radio research because of its potential for mathematical investigation. His successful design of a radio receiver during World War I led to his invention of the neutrodyne receiver (1919), which eliminated most of the noise found in early radios. The most important of his many radio inventions, this receiver was the first commercial apparatus suitable for broadcast reception by the general public. Also known for his educational innovations, Hazeltine developed new methods of teaching physics and mathematics. He taught at Stevens Institute of Technology (1907–25; 1933–44) and founded the Hazeltine Electronics Corp. (1945). ■ See Harold A. Wheeler, *Hazeltine the Professor* (1978).

HEAD, EDITH (1907–1981), U.S. costume designer. Head was chief designer for Paramount Pictures (from 1938) and worked for Universal Studios (from 1967). She introduced many new Latin American and American Indian design concepts to Hollywood fashions and created costumes for such stars as Mae West, Marlene Dietrich, Ingrid Bergman, and Ginger Rogers. Hollywood's most prominent designer, she won Academy Awards for *The Heiress* (1949), *All About Eve* (1950), *Samson and Delilah* (1950), *A Place in the Sun* (1951), *Roman Holiday* (1953), *Sabrina* (1954), *The Facts of Life* (1960), and *The Sting* (1973). She wrote the autobiographical *Dress Doctor* (1959) and *How to Dress for Success* (1967).

HEALEY, DENIS WINSTON HEALEY, BARON (1917–), British political leader. A brilliant student at Oxford (B.A. 1938), Healey headed the international department of the Labour party secretariat (1945–52) before serving in the House of Commons (1952–92). He held the posts of defense minister (1964–70) and chancellor of the Exchequer (1974–79). A moderate, he was defeated for Labour leadership by leftist Michael Foot (1980) but served as deputy leader of the party (1980–83) until the landslide 1983 Conservative party election victory. He served as president of Birkbeck College, London (1993–). ■ See his autobiography, *The Time of My Life* (1989), and study by Bruce Reed and Geoffrey Williams (1971).

HEALY, WILLIAM (1869–1962), U.S. psychiatrist. Healy was a leader in the study of juvenile delinquency. After earning an M.D. from the University of Chicago (1900), he set up that city's first child-guidance clinic, the Juvenile Psychopathic Institute (1902). Working with his first wife, Grace Fernald, he devised performance tests to supplement IQ testing for adolescents. The Individual Delinquent (1915), considered a classic in the field, examined the psychological roots of adolescent antisocial behavior. Healy directed the Judge Baker Foundation in Boston (1917–46) and with his second wife, Augusta Bronner, wrote *New Light on Delinquency and Its Treatment* (1936).

HEANEY, SEAMUS JUSTIN (1939–), Irish poet. Heaney was born into a rural Roman Catholic family in Northern Ireland and educated at Queens College, Belfast (B.A. 1961), where he later taught (1966–72). In four volumes, subsequently republished as *Poems: 1965–75* (1980), he established a reputation as the most prominent Ulster poet of his generation. His honest and courageous poems of self-definition combined personal childhood experiences with Irish and British traditions and confronted the contemporary political violence of his native region. He left Northern Ireland (1972) and taught at Caryfort College, Dublin (1975–81), Harvard University (1982–88), and Oxford

(1989–94). His later works included the poetry collections *Field Work* (1979), *Station Island* (1985), *The Haw Lantern* (1987), *Seeing Things* (1991), *The Spirit Level* (1996), and *Open Ground: Selected Poems, 1966–1996* (1998), the prose anthology *Preoccupations* (1980), and a verse translation of *Beowulf* (2000). He won the 1995 Nobel Prize in Literature. ■ See study by Helen Vendler (1998).

HEARST, PATRICIA CAMPBELL (1954–), U.S. kidnap victim and convicted bank robber. Until she was kidnapped by a left-wing terrorist group in February 1974, Patty Hearst was an apolitical art student who, as daughter of newspaper magnate Randolph A. Hearst, enjoyed a life of privilege. After two months with the Symbionese Liberation Army (SLA), her captors, she emerged as "Tania," urban guerrilla and bank robber. The SLA demanded a ransom of $2 million in foodstuffs, which eventually were handed out to minority communities in California. Arrested after 16 months underground, she soon reverted to her previous persona. An expensive defense conducted by F. Lee Bailey in one of the country's most publicized trials claimed that Hearst had been brainwashed and tortured; nevertheless, she was convicted of armed robbery and sentenced to a seven-year term. She served 22 months before Pres. Jimmy Carter commuted her sentence (1979). ■ See Hearst's *Every Secret Thing* (1982; with Alvin Moscow) and Shana Alexander, *Anyone's Daughter* (1979).

HEARST, WILLIAM RANDOLF (1863–1951), U.S. publisher. In 1887, after expulsion from Harvard, Hearst took over the *San Francisco Examiner,* which his millionaire father had acquired for a bad debt. In 1895 he moved to New York, where he bought the *Morning Journal* and boosted its circulation tenfold with aggressive, sensational journalism. His jingoistic and falsified articles and editorials played a major role in instigating the war with Spain (1898). Hearst also entered politics, winning election to Congress in 1902 and 1904 as a Democrat but losing later races for mayor and governor of New York. He then turned to art, accumulating a $50 million collection that he displayed at his huge San Simeon, California, ranch and castle, where he lived a cheerfully hedonistic life with former showgirl Marion Davies. By 1920 Hearst owned 20 daily newspapers and 6 magazines—the world's biggest publishing empire; by 1937 he was nearly bankrupt, but his fortunes revived during World War II and his empire outlived him. The film masterpiece *Citizen Kane* (1939) was inspired by Hearst's life. ■ See W. A. Swanberg, *Citizen Hearst* (1961); biography by Frank Brady (1974); study by R. Everett Littlefield (1980); and David Nasaw, *The Chief* (2000).

HEARTFIELD, JOHN (Helmut Herzfelde; 1891–1968), German artist. A pioneer in the field of photomontage, Heartfield juxtaposed images in a dadaist style to create highly politicized works that were intended as weapons against autocracy. He anglicized his name in 1913 in protest against German Junkerism and founded (with his brother Wieland and artist George Grosz) the Malik Verlag publishing house (1916), a pacifist journal (1916), and a satirical magazine. He joined the Communist party (1918) and cofounded the Berlin Dada group (1919). He was best known for his powerful anti-Nazi posters and magazine covers, many of which were created for the widely distributed worker's paper *AIZ* (1930–38). He fled Nazi Germany on foot in 1933 and lived in Prague (1933–38) and in London (from 1938). After World War II he returned to East Germany to work as a teacher, stage designer, and propaganda adviser. ■ See his *Photomontages of the Nazi Period* (Eng. trans. 1977).

HEATH, SIR EDWARD RICHARD (1916–), British prime minister. Heath won a scholarship to Oxford and worked for a merchant bank before his election to Parliament in 1950 as a "new style" (middle-class) Conservative. He held several cabinet positions and was chosen party leader in 1965. He led the Conservative party to an upset victory in the 1970 elections and served as prime minister until 1974. It was a period of labor unrest and high inflation, which Heath was unable to control. His major accomplishment was negotiation of British entry (1973) into the Common Market. He wrote *Old World, New Horizons* (1970). ■ See his autobiography, *The Course of My Life* (1998), and study by John Campbell (1993).

HEATTER, GABRIEL (1890–1972), U.S. newscaster. One of the most popular American radio personalities, Heatter dramatically and optimistically reported the news in a career that lasted 34 years (1932–65). He started his nightly broadcasts with the reassuring phrase, "Ah—there's good news tonight!" and unfailingly found the brighter side of any event he reported. He was especially popular during World War II and confidently predicted the survival of Britain and the successful defense of Stalingrad, though he told an interviewer after the war that despite his public optimism he feared that Britain would fall and that the Nazis would invade the United States.

HÉBERT, ANNE (1916–2000), Canadian writer. Born into a prominent French-Canadian literary family, Hébert wrote for the theater, film, and television but was best known for austere and introspective poems dealing with love, sorrow, solitude, and death that appeared in the collections *The Tomb of the Kings* (1953; Eng. trans. 1967) and *Poems* (1960; Eng. trans. 1975). Her prose works, dealing with the familiar Quebec theme of the burden of the past, included the short-story collection *The Torrent* (1950; Eng. trans. 1972) and the novels *The Silent Rooms* (1958; Eng. trans. 1974), *Kamouraska* (1970; Eng. trans. 1973), *Children of the Black Sabbath* (1975; Eng. trans. 1977), and *In the Shadow of the Wind* (1982; Eng. trans. 1984). Her later works included *Selected Poems* (Eng. trans. 1987). ■ See study by Delbert W. Russell (1983).

HECHT, BEN (1894–1964), U.S. journalist and author. While in his teens, Hecht landed jobs on Chicago newspapers and became active in the city's literary circles. He founded and edited (1923–25) the irreverent *Chicago Literary Times*. Hecht's wide-ranging career encompassed fiction, nonfiction, drama, and scriptwriting. He was coauthor (with Charles MacArthur) of the classic newsroom drama *The Front Page* (1928), and of several notable films, including *Twentieth Century* (1934), *The Scoundrel* (1935), and *Wuthering Heights* (1939). He supported creation of an independent Jewish state in the 1940s; the pageant *A Flag Is Born* (1946) supported anti-British terrorism in Palestine. ■ See his autobiographies, *A Child of the Century* (1954) and *Gaily Gaily* (1963); Doug Fetherling, *The Five Lives of Ben Hecht* (1977); and biography by William MacAdams (1990).

HECKMAN, JAMES J. (1944–), U.S. economist. Heckman studied at Princeton University (Ph.D. 1971) and taught at the University of Chicago (1973–). He developed widely used methods for analyzing selective samples in studying the behavior of both individuals and households. They have been used in evaluating the impact of social programs on the economy, in the analysis of consumer preferences, and in the correction of selection bias in statistical studies. For his innovations, Heckman shared the 2000 Nobel Memorial Prize in Economics with Daniel L. McFadden. Heckman's books included *Evaluating Social Programs* (2000) and *Incentives in Government Bureaucracies* (2000).

HEDAYET, SADEQ (1903–1951), Iranian writer. Born into a wealthy and distinguished family, Hedayet studied in Europe during the 1920s. He was influenced by the works of Poe, Maupassant, Chekhov, Dostoyevsky, and Kafka, and translated their writing into Persian. His short stories and novellas, which sympathetically probed the psychological distress and anxiety of the poor, reflected his deep pessimism, sense of alienation and isolation, and obsession with the absurdity of the human condition. He committed suicide in Paris (1951). His best-known works included *The Blind Owl* (1937; Eng. trans. 1957, 1974) and *Haji Agha: Portrait of an Iranian Confidence Man* (1945; Eng. trans. 1979). Extremely influential among Iranian writers, he was considered the century's foremost Persian author. ■ See *Sadeq Hedayet: An Anthology* (1979), and Michael C. Hillmann, ed., *Hedayet's "The Blind Owl" Forty Years After* (1978).

HEDIN, SVEN ANDERS (1865–1952), Swedish explorer. Hedin spent nearly 40 years exploring uncharted regions of Central Asia, Tibet, and China. He was a tutor in Persia (1885) and was employed as an interpreter for a Swedish-Norwegian mission to the shah (1890). He made his first extensive travels in Central Asia in 1891, and from 1893 to 1898 he crossed the Urals, Pamirs, and the Tibetan plateau en route to Peking. During his 1905–1908 expedition he explored the sources of the Indus, Sutlej, and Brahmaputra

Rivers, prepared the first reliable maps of the trans-Himalayan mountains of Tibet, and collected valuable geological specimens. He organized and led the historic Sino-Swedish Scientific Expedition to the northwest provinces of China (1927–35), which investigated the geology, meteorology, botany, and ethnography of areas of Inner Mongolia, Sinkiang, and Western Kansu and unearthed hundreds of archaeological sites indicating an extensive Stone Age culture. His numerous works included *Through Asia* (1898; Eng. trans. 1898), *Southern Tibet* (9 vols., 1916–22), *The Silk Road* (1936; Eng. trans. 1938), and *History of the Expedition in Asia, 1927–35* (4 vols., Eng. trans. 1943). ■ See his autobiography, *My Life as an Explorer* (Eng. trans. 1925), and George Kish, *To the Heart of Asia* (1984).

HEEGER, ALAN J. (1936–), U.S. chemist. Heeger studied at the University of California, Berkeley (Ph.D. 1961) and taught at the University of Pennsylvania (1962–82) and the University of California, Santa Barbara (1982–). During the late 1970s, with University of Pennsylvania colleague Alan G. MacDiarmid and Tsukuba (Japan) University professor Hideki Shirakawa, Heeger helped to develop conductive ploymers, plastics that conduct electricity like metals. The discovery had a profound impact in both chemistry and physics and influenced the growth of molecular electronics. Conductive polymers were soon used in light-emitting diodes, photographic film, computer screens, mobile telephone displays, and solar cells. For their innovative research, Heeger, MacDiarmid, and Shirakawa shared the 2000 Nobel Prize in Chemistry.

HEEZEN, BRUCE CHARLES (1924–1977), U.S. geologist and oceanographer. Heezen, who was associated with Columbia University's Lamont-Doherty Geological Observatory (1956–77), made notable contributions to the study of the ocean floor. He explained the erosional effects of turbidity currents and was among the first to propose that the mid-Atlantic ridge was part of a globe-encircling system of ridges (or fracture zones) that were characterized by rift valleys along the center of the ridges. He was best known for the widely circulated physiographical and topological maps of the Atlantic, Pacific, and Indian ocean floors he prepared with his colleagues Marie Tharp and Maurice Ewing (1959–71). *The Face of the Deep* (1971; with C. Hollister), a volume with 600 photographs of the ocean floor, is a summation of his life's work.

HEFNER, HUGH MARSTON (1926–), U.S. publisher. Raised in the Midwest as a strict Methodist, Hefner graduated from the University of Illinois (1949), then joined the subscriptions department at *Esquire* magazine. In December 1953, having raised an investment of $10,000, he came out with the first issue of *Playboy* magazine. Addressed to the young, affluent, urban male, *Playboy* incorporated nude photography and prestige nonfiction, advice, and glossy ad-

vertising into an argument for sexual permissiveness. Hefner, who also operated a network of private clubs staffed by "Playboy bunnies," pursued the kind of hedonistic lifestyle extolled by his successful magazine. He remained head of *Playboy* until 1988. ■ See Russell Miller, *Bunny* (1984).

HEIDEGGER, MARTIN (1889–1976), German philosopher. Heidegger was raised as a Catholic and studied theology before turning to philosophy. He was a student of phenomenologist Edmund Husserl at the University of Freiburg (Ph.D. 1914), where he returned to teach (1928–51) with an introductory lecture on metaphysical "nothingness." Receptive to the Nazis' promise of a cultural renaissance, he won their appointment as rector (1933–34) of the university, but was soon disillusioned with Nazism. After World War II, forbidden to teach by occupation authorities, he isolated himself in the Black Forest to learn the secret of "being" from nature. Heidegger's major work was *Being and Time* (1927; Eng. trans. 1962). A difficult and often obscure writer, he described the three basic features of the structure of being as facticity, existentiality, and fallenness. He considered the basic characteristic of an authentic existence to be "angst," or anxiety, which he considered a creative force. Heidegger's theories influenced psychoanalysis and theology as well as philosophy. His other works included *An Introduction to Metaphysics* (1953; Eng. trans. 1959) and *What Is Philosophy?* (1956; Eng. trans. 1958). ■ See David F. Krell, ed., *Basic Writings* (1977); Magda King, *Heidegger's Philosophy* (1964); study by George Steiner (1979); and biography by Rüdiger Safranski (1994; Eng. trans. 1998).

HEIDEN, ERIC (1958–), U.S. speed skater. Heiden, whose mother and father were both athletes, started skating as a young child and trained as a speed skater at the country's only rink (prior to 1977) in West Allis, Wisconsin. After participating in the 1976 Olympics at Innsbruck, Austria, he raced in Europe and became the first American to win the world speed-skating championship (1977). He later won the world junior all-around title (1977) and the world sprint championship (1977) and repeated his victories during the next two years. At the 1980 Lake Placid Olympics he won the 500-meter, 1,000-meter, 1,500-meter, 5,000-meter, and 10,000-meter races to become the first athlete in Winter Olympic history to win five gold medals. From 1981 to 1986 he competed as a professional cyclist. ■ See biography by Suzanne L. Munshower (1980).

HEIFETZ, JASCHA (1901–1987), Russian-born U.S. violinist. Heifetz was a child prodigy who made his debut at age 6 and, after study in St. Petersburg, toured Europe at age 12. He matured into one of the century's greatest violinists. Heifetz settled in the United States (1917) and became a U.S. citizen (1925). His digital dexterity and the strength of his bow arm were legendary, and during 60 years on the international concert circuit he set the world standard for flawless execution. Heifetz extended the violin literature by transcribing classical compositions and commissioning new works by contemporary composers. He taught at the University of Southern California (from 1962). ■ See Herbert R. Axelrod, ed., *Heifetz* (1976).

HEIKAL, MUHAMMED HASSANEIN (1923–   ), Egyptian journalist. Heikal covered the 1948 Arab–Israeli War and the Korean War as a war correspondent before assuming editorship (1957–74) of the newspaper *Al Ahram*. He enjoyed daily access to Egyptian leader Gamal Abdel Nasser, accompanying him abroad, writing his speeches, and ghosting a book for him. Heikal, whose weekly column was considered as expressing the views of the government, built his newspaper into the most important political journal in the Arab world. After protesting President Anwar el-Sadat's negotiations with Israel, he was arrested (1981) but was released several months later after Sadat's assassination. His books (in English) included *The Cairo Documents* (1973), *Sphinx and Commissar* (1978), *Autumn of Fury: The Assassination of Sadat* (1979), *Cutting the Lion's Tail: Suez Through Egyptian Eyes* (1986), *Illusions of Triumph: An Arab View of the Gulf War* (1992), and *Secret Channels: The Inside Story of the Arab-Israeli Peace Negotiations* (1996). ■ See Munir K. Nasser, *Press, Politics and Power* (1979).

HEILBRONER, ROBERT LOUIS (1919–   ), U.S. economist. The son of a prosperous New York City businessman, Heilbroner graduated from Harvard in 1940. He was a bestselling popularizer of economics and a perceptive social critic. *Worldly Philosophers* (1953) brought economic theory to the lay reader, while *The Making of Economic Society* (1962) examined economies of the past. He earned his Ph.D. (1963) at the New School for Social Research and joined its faculty in 1972. His later writings, including *The Limits of American Capitalism* (1966), *An Inquiry into the Human Prospect* (1975), *Beyond Boom and Crash* (1978), and *Marxism: For and Against* (1980), were influenced by socialist theory but were pessimistic about the future of humanity. He also wrote *The Nature and Logic of Capitalism* (1985), *Visions of the Future* (1995), *The Crisis of Vision in Modern Economic Thought* (1995; with William Milberg), and *Teachings from the Worldly Philosophy* (1996).

HEIN, MEL (1909–1992), U.S. football player. One of the great centers in gridiron history, Hein played for Washington State and then with the New York Giants (1931–45). Playing in the era when the same personnel handled offense and defense, he was a center and a linebacker and never missed a game in 15 seasons. Hein was a moving force behind the Giants' seven Eastern division titles and two National Football League (NFL) championships. An All-Pro center for eight straight years, he became the NFL's highest-paid lineman. After his retirement he was a coach at the University of Southern California and a supervisor of officials for the American Football League and later for the NFL.

HEINKEL, ERNST HEINRICH (1888–1958), German aircraft designer and manufacturer. Heinkel's career as a pilot ended abruptly (1911) when he was severely injured in a crash in his homemade plane, but his career as an aircraft designer was just beginning. He designed military aircraft during World War I and built the HE-178 (1939), the first jet plane. Heinkel's work with rocket-propelled aircraft included the 550-mph HE-176 (1939). His bombers were widely used during World War II. ■ See his memoirs, *Stormy Life* (Eng. trans. 1956).

HEINLEIN, ROBERT ANSON (1907–1988), U.S. science-fiction writer. Heinlein studied engineering at the U.S. Naval Academy (1925–29). After physical disability cut short his navy career, he traveled and wrote pulp fiction and then juvenile novels before settling into science fiction in the 1950s. At a time when futurist fiction was bogged down in gadgetry, Heinlein's tales mused about how the evolution of human society would mold behavior and values. He wrote many stories and dozens of novels that combined compelling narration with unusual ingenuity. *Stranger in a Strange Land* (1961; uncut ed. 1990) sold more than three million copies and appealed to students as a "counterculture" phenomenon. *The Best of Robert Heinlein* (1939–1959) appeared in 1973. His 39th novel, *The Number of the Beast* (1980), followed four geniuses from a California party to a journey through alternate universes. *The Cat Who Walks Through Walls* (1985) is a social satire that begins in the year 2188. Although his social and political views stirred controversy, he was one of the most influential science-fiction writers of the century. ■ See essays edited by Joseph D. Olander and Martin H. Greenberg (1978) and study by H. Bruce Franklin (1980).

HEISENBERG, WERNER KARL (1901–1976), German physicist. A year after he finished his doctorate, Heisenberg went to Copenhagen to work under physicist Niels Bohr (1924–27). During this period, he made vital contributions to quantum mechanics. After 1913, quantum theory gained hold in the scientific community, but the absence of a coherent, rigorous mathematical basis for the theory undermined it. In 1925, Heisenberg used matrices to provide this mathematical foundation, introducing the principles of quantum mechanics. Max Born and others soon elaborated upon his work. Two years later, while working on atomic structure, Heisenberg stated the uncertainty principle, which is crucial to quantum mechanics: a subatomic particle's exact position and exact momentum cannot be determined simultaneously. For his role in developing quantum mechanics, Heisenberg received the Nobel Prize in Physics (1932). He was a professor at Leipzig (1927–41), worked in the German atomic research program during World War II, and after the war headed the Max Planck Institute. He later introduced the concept of the unified-field theory to explain the structure of elementary particles. *Physics and Beyond* (Eng. trans. 1971) is semi-autobiographical. ■ See Patrick A. Heelan, *Quantum*

Mechanics and Objectivity (1965); David C. Cassidy, *Uncertainty* (1992); and study by Paul L. Rose (1998).

HELBURN, THERESA (1887–1959), U.S. theatrical personality. Helburn studied theater at Bryn Mawr, the Sorbonne, and Yale and was a drama critic for the *Nation* (1918–19). She was a founding member of the Theater Guild in New York (1919), which revolutionized the theater in the United States by presenting serious new dramatic productions. As its codirector (with Lawrence Langner; 1919–58), Helburn was instrumental in getting it to produce plays of Robert Sherwood, Maxwell Anderson, William Saroyan, and Philip Barry. She also persuaded Richard Rodgers to write the musical *Oklahoma!* (1943), which was one of the most successful shows in theatrical history. ■ See her autobiography, *A Wayward Quest* (1961).

HELD, ANNA (1865?–1918), Polish-born musical-comedy star. A headline performer in Paris and London, Held was brought to the United Sates (1896) by Florenz Ziegfeld (whom she later married) to star in his musical production *A Parlor Match*, in which she won over her audience with the song "Won't You Come and Play Wiz Me?" Held subsequently appeared in numerous musicals (including the *Follies* of 1907, Ziegfeld's first), and became a favorite of Broadway audiences. The subject of nationwide publicity campaigns, she became a legendary figure and lent her name to cigars, corsets, and face powder, and reputedly took daily baths in gallons of milk. Separated from Ziegfeld in 1908, she was divorced from him in 1913 and made her last stage appearance in 1916. ■ See Liane Carrera, *Anna Held and Flo Ziegfeld* (Eng. trans. 1979), and biography by Eve Golden (2000).

HELD, JOHN, JR. (1889–1958), U.S. cartoonist and illustrator. The most prominent graphic interpreter of the 1920s, Held achieved national renown for his line drawings depicting the "flaming youth" of the "jazz age." His renditions of fashion-conscious "flappers," with their short skirts, bobbed hair, and cigarette holders, and of their young male escorts, with their patent-leather hair, raccoon coats, and hip flasks, appeared regularly in such magazines as the *New Yorker, Smart Set, Vanity Fair, Harper's Bazaar,* and *College Humor* as well as in numerous books. He also drew the comic strip *Margy* during the 1920s and wrote several books, including *Grim Youth* (1930), *Women Are Necessary* (1931), and *Crosstown* (1934). ■ See *The Most of John Held, Jr.* (1972) and study by Shelley Armitage (1987).

HELLER, JOSEPH (1923–1999), U.S. novelist. Heller flew 60 combat missions during World War II. His abhorrence of war, incubated during the complacent 1950s, generated the brilliant and popular comic novel *Catch-22* (1961; film 1970), a zany, pointed satire set on a bomber base. Later novels included *Something Happened* (1974), a pessimistic view of contemporary middle-class American life; *Good as Gold* (1979), a biting satire of the Washington establish-

ment; and *God Knows* (1984), a comic novel set in biblical times. Heller also wrote *We Bombed in New Haven* (1967), a play about the changing American attitudes toward war. *No Laughing Matter* (1986; with Speed Vogel) is an account of Heller's struggle with Guillain-Barré syndrome. *Closing Time* (1994) involved characters from *Catch-22* in the 1990s. His *Portrait of an Artist, As an Old Man* (2000) was published posthumously. ■ See his nostalgic autobiography, *Now and Then: From Coney Island to Here* (1998), and Adam Sorkin, ed., *Conversations with Joseph Heller* (1993).

HELLMAN, LILLIAN (1905–1984), U.S. writer. As a child Hellman was shuttled between her father's New Orleans family and her mother's monied New York connections. She worked in publishing before scoring her first success at 28 with *The Children's Hour* (1934), a play that examines truths and untruths about the bond between two women. Her plays, incisive social commentaries characterized by credible dialogue and tight construction, included *The Little Foxes* (1939), *Watch on the Rhine* (1941), and *Toys in the Attic* (1960). She also wrote screenplays. *An Unfinished Woman* (1969) and *Pentimento* (1973), two memoirs, portrayed the important people in her life, including the writers Dashiell Hammett (with whom she lived for many years), Dorothy Parker, and Ernest Hemingway. A political activist, Hellman was associated with many left-wing causes. *Scoundrel Time* (1976) recalled the early 1950s, when she refused (1952) to cooperate with the House Un-American Activities Committee and was blacklisted by the film industry. ■ See studies by Richard Moody (1972) and Katherine Lederer (1979) and biographies by William Wright (1986) and Carl Rollyson (1988).

HELMS, RICHARD MCGARRAH (1913–), U.S. public official. After attending preparatory school in Switzerland and graduating from Williams College (1935), Helms became a journalist, securing an exclusive interview with German dictator Adolf Hitler as a cub reporter for United Press. A veteran of the intelligence service during World War II, he helped create the Central Intelligence Agency (CIA) in 1947 and remained with it as a career officer, rising to the directorship in 1966. A cool professional, Helms left the CIA in 1973 to serve as ambassador to Iran (1973–76). ■ See Thomas Powers, *The Man Who Kept the Secrets* (1979).

HELPMANN, SIR ROBERT MURRAY (1909–1986), Australian dancer, choreographer, actor, and director. Helpmann joined the Vic-Wells (later the Royal) Ballet in 1933 and became known for the wide range of his roles. As principal male dancer (1933–50), he partnered Margot Fonteyn and helped establish the international reputation of the company. He choreographed *Comus* (1942), *Hamlet* (1942), and *Adam Zero* (1946), dance pieces noted for their drama and theatricality. Helpmann danced in the well-known ballet films *The Red Shoes* (1948) and *Tales of Hoffmann* (1950) and had dramatic roles in several other movies. On the stage he starred in Old Vic productions of *A Midsummer Night's Dream, The Merchant of Venice,* and *Hamlet.* He also directed operas, plays, and musicals in London and was a director and choreographer of the Australian Ballet (1965–76). ▪ See biographies by Katherine Sorley Walker (1958) and Elizabeth Salter (1978).

HEMINGWAY, ERNEST (1899–1961), U.S. novelist and short-story writer. Born in Illinois, Hemingway became a reporter right out of high school in 1917 but soon volunteered for World War I duty in Europe as an ambulance driver. Remaining in Paris during the 1920s as a foreign correspondent, he described his own "lost generation" of hard-drinking, thrill-seeking American expatriates in his first major novel, *The Sun Also Rises* (1926). His next two novels, written in the spare, laconic style for which he became famous, glorified the "grace under pressure" of man in war: *A Farewell to Arms* (1929), set during World War I, and *For Whom the Bell Tolls* (1940), about the Spanish Civil War. An aficionado of bullfighting, big-game hunting, and prizefighting, Hemingway settled in Cuba after World War II. His contemplative novella about a Cuban fisherman alone against the elements, *The Old Man and the Sea* (1952), won a Pulitzer Prize; Hemingway was awarded the Nobel Prize in Literature in 1954. Forced to leave his home in Cuba after the 1959 revolution, he became increasingly despondent and committed suicide. *Selected Letters* appeared in 1981. Several uncompleted manuscripts were published posthumously, including the fictional memoir set in Africa, *True at First Light* (1999). ▪ See biographies by Carlos Baker (1969) and Jeffrey Meyers (1985), and Peter Griffin, *Along with Youth* (1985).

HENCH, PHILIP SHOWALTER (1896–1965), U.S. physician. Hench studied at the University of Pittsburgh (M.D. 1920) and spent his career at the Mayo Clinic (1923–57). Discovering that the adrenal glands played a role in rheumatoid arthritis, he was the first to treat the disease with an adrenal hormone (later known as cortisone). Working with Edward C. Kendall, his longtime colleague at the clinic who isolated the hormone, he proved that the disease was reversible. They shared the 1950 Nobel Prize in Physiology or Medicine (with Tadeus Reichstein) for their discoveries.

HENDERSON, ARTHUR (1863–1935), British political leader. The major organizer of the Labour party, Henderson served as party secretary (1911–34) and with Sidney Webb wrote most of the Labour party constitution (1918), which established the party as a centralized, mass-based socialist entity. He served in the coalition cabinets of Prime Ministers Herbert Asquith and David Lloyd George (1915–17) and was home secretary (1924) and foreign secretary (1929–31), actively supporting the League of Nations. He resigned from government in 1931 and devoted his energies to disarmament. He was president of the World Disarmament Conference of 1932 and was awarded the Nobel Peace Prize

(1934). ▪ See biographies by Mary Agnes Hamilton (1938) and F. M. Leventhal (1989).

HENDERSON, (JAMES) FLETCHER (1898–1952), U.S. jazz musician. Henderson, who was born in Georgia and educated at the all-black Atlanta University (B.S. 1920), founded the first great jazz orchestra during the 1920s in New York City. Using written arrangements as well as improvisation, he brought rags, blues, and stomp as well as jazz to an expanding public at the Club Alabam and Roseland. Henderson also played piano accompaniment for singers Bessie Smith and Ethel Waters and wrote arrangements for the Dorsey Brothers and Benny Goodman. ▪ See Walter C. Allen, *Hendersonia* (1973).

HENDERSON, LAWRENCE JOSEPH (1878–1942), U.S. biochemist. A member of the Harvard Medical School faculty (1904–42), Henderson was the first to recognize the importance of the acid-base equilibrium in animal organisms and to discover how the balance is maintained in the body. Impressed with the order of natural systems, he wrote two books, *The Fitness of the Environment* (1913) and *The Order of Nature* (1917), which elaborated on his views of the harmonious unity of nature. His pioneering studies of the mutually interacting components of blood, published as *Blood: A Study in General Physiology* (1928), and his exposure to the writings of sociologist Vilfredo Pareto inspired him to apply his physical-science insights to the study of society. His seminars in sociology at Harvard (from 1932) stressed the regulatory and stabilizing forces in both nature and society and influenced such thinkers as George Homans, Talcott Parsons, and Crane Brinton. His sociological writings are in *On the Social System* (1970).

HENDERSON, RAY. *See* DE SYLVA, BUDDY.

HENDRIX, JIMI (James Marshall Hendrix; 1942–1970), U.S. singer. Hendrix was an accomplished guitarist from Seattle who worked as a sideman for the Isley Brothers and Little Richard before putting together his own distinctive group. With two English musicians, he formed the Jimi Hendrix Experience in 1966, making a successful debut at the Olympia in Paris and returning in triumph to the 1967 Monterey Rock Festival with a hit single, "Hey Joe." His memorable performance at the August 1969 Woodstock festival is recorded in the film *Woodstock.* Hendrix's style relied heavily on eroticism, a pulsating beat, and the innovative use of electronic feedback. He wrote much of his own music. *Rolling Stone* magazine called him the "first black performer to take on white rock'n'roll head on and win." Hendrix died of a drug overdose at age 27. ▪ See biographies by Curtis Knight (1974) and David Henderson (1978) and studies by John McDermott (1992) and Harry Shapiro (1992).

HENIE, SONJA (1912–1969), Norwegian-U.S. figure-skating champion and actress. Henie won her first figure-skating title in Norway at age 8. In 1927 she captured the first of her 10 straight world amateur championships in figure skating, and in 1928, 1932, and 1936 she won Olympic gold medals at the winter games. Henie won the grand slam of figure skating twice (1932, 1936) by winning the World, European, and Olympic titles in the same year. She turned professional in 1936, earning $47.5 million with appearances in ice revues and 10 motion pictures, including *One in a Million* (1936). An astute businesswoman, she was also a collector and patron of modern art. ■ See her *Wings on My Feet* (1940) and Raymond Strait, *Queen of Ice, Queen of Shadows* (1985).

HENLEIN, KONRAD (1898–1945), Czech Sudeten-German political leader. A leader of the Sudeten-German minority between World Wars I and II, Henlein agitated, in collusion with the Nazis, for German annexation of the Sudetenland and thus paved the way for the cession of the territory at the Munich Conference (1938). During World War II he was district leader of the Nazi party and Reich commissioner in the Sudetenland. He committed suicide (1945) while a prisoner of war of the Allies.

HENRI, ROBERT (1865–1929), U.S. artist and teacher. Henri was born in Ohio, spent a decade in Europe, and returned to teach at the Philadelphia School of Design and Art Students League of New York (1915–28). Rebelling against the prevailing academic standards of genteel conservatism, he taught his students to paint from real life with all its blemishes. Henri's "Ashcan" school, also known as "The Eight," introduced social realism into American art and held major exhibitions in 1908 and 1910. His book *The Art Spirit* (1923) influenced many younger artists. ■ See studies by Helen Evelyn Goodman (1975), William Innes Homer (1969; rev. ed. 1988), and Bernard B. Perlman (1991).

HENSON, JIM (James Maury Henson; 1936–1990), U.S. puppeteer. Henson signed up for a puppet club in his Maryland high school and landed a puppeteering job on a Washington, D.C., local TV program in the 1950s. When his show "Sam and His Friends" won an Emmy Award (1958), Henson began taking the trade more seriously. He won numerous awards for his famous and fanciful creations, the Muppets, a name Henson gave to his hybrid of puppets and marionettes. Designed for television, most of the foam-rubber Muppets were operated by a single puppeteer, often Henson himself. They were featured on various variety shows in the 1960s, then found a home on the National Educational Televison's "Sesame Street," the preschoolers' program whose resident Muppets (including Big Bird, Oscar the Grouch, Ernie, and the Cookie Monster) became household names. In 1976 Henson's creations began appearing on their own weekly TV broadcast, "The Muppet Show" (featuring Kermit the Frog and Miss Piggy), and subsequently "starred" in several movies. Henson also directed fantasy films and appeared on the TV series "The Jim Henson Hour" and "The Ghost of Faffner Hall."

HENZE, HANS WERNER (1926–   ), German composer. One of the most prominent German composers of the post–World War II era, the eclectic Henze incorporated many musical styles in his work. He abandoned the 12-tone technique in the mid-1950s and concentrated on more accessible "expressive" music. He lived in Italy after 1954. Although he composed several symphonies and other orchestral music, he was best known for his ballet music, including *Undine* (1958), and the operas *Boulevard Solitude* (1951), *The Stag King* (1955), *Elegy for Young Lovers* (1961), and *The Bassarids* (1966). His works of the late 1960s and 1970s, notably the operas *El Cimarrón* (1970) and *We Come to the River* (1974–76), reflected his revolutionary Marxist political views. His later works included Symphony No. 7 (1983–84), *Requiem* (1993), and the opera *Venus und Adonis* (1997). ■ See his *Music and Politics: Collected Writings, 1953–81* (Eng. trans. 1982) and his autobiography, *Bohemian Fifths* (1996; Eng. trans. 1998).

HEPBURN, KATHARINE (1907–   ), U.S. actress. After an upper-crust New England upbringing and graduation from Bryn Mawr (1928), Hepburn set out to conquer the theater. She made her stage debut in *The Czarina* in Baltimore later that year and her film debut in *A Bill of Divorcement* (1932). Despite her commanding accent and manner, Hepburn found her sharp edges melted away by Cary Grant in *Bringing Up Baby* (1938) and *The Philadelphia Story* (1940). She also formed a strong professional and private relationship with Spencer Tracy, with whom she bantered through *Adam's Rib* (1949), *Pat and Mike* (1952), and seven other films. Hepburn also played several "spinsters," most memorably the missionary who finds love and adventure with the improbable captain (Humphrey Bogart) of *The African Queen* (1951). She won Academy Awards for *Morning Glory* (1933), *Guess Who's Coming to Dinner* (1967), *The Lion in Winter* (1968), and *On Golden Pond* (1981), and was highly praised for her performance in *Long Day's Journey into Night* (1962). Late in her career she appeared on Broadway in the musical *Coco* (1970) and the play *The West Side Waltz* (1981). ■ See her autobiography, *Me* (1991); the biography by Gary Carey (rev. ed. 1983); Charles Higham, *Kate* (1975); and Anne Edwards, *A Remarkable Woman* (1985).

HEPBURN, MITCHELL FREDERICK (1896–1953), Canadian farmer and political leader. Born in Ontario, Hepburn worked as a bank clerk before serving in World War I and returned to become an onion farmer. He entered politics in 1926 when he was elected to Parliament; in 1930 he became the leader of Ontario's Liberal party. From 1934 to 1942 Hepburn was the premier of Ontario, heading a controversial administration, highlighted by a personal feud with Canadian Prime Minister Mackenzie King. He proposed progressive social legislation, similar to New Deal policies in the United States, but opposed the extension of federal authority in the provinces. After being defeated in the election of 1945, he retired from politics to return to his farm. ■ See study by N. McKenty (1967) and John T. Saywell, *Just Call Me Mitch* (1991).

HEPWORTH, DAME (JOCELYN) BARBARA (1903–1975), British sculptor. Hepworth studied at the Royal College of Art (1921–24) and later in Italy (1924–26). In the 1930s, influenced by her close association with sculptors Ben Nicholson (her husband) and Henry Moore, she produced increasingly abstract works; the three sculptors were at the heart of Britain's abstract movement. Her use of the hole in Pierced Form (1931) was imitated by Moore the following year and decisively influenced the course of modern sculpture. In subsequent years, Hepworth used the hole in more complex works. She also introduced color into her sculpture and moved in the 1950s from direct carving in wood and stone to creating pieces cast in bronze—some monumental in scale. She died in a fire in her studio-home at St. Ives, England. ■ See her *Pictorial Autobiography* (1970) and studies by J. P. Hodin (1961), Michael Shepherd (1963), A. M. Hammacher (1968), and Sally Festing (1995).

HERBERT, FRANK PATRICK (1920–1986), U.S. science-fiction writer. A West Coast photographer, news reporter, and lay analyst, Herbert published his first science-fiction story in 1952 and his first book, *The Dragon in the Sea*, in 1956. He achieved fame with the award-winning novel *Dune* (1965) and its sequels, *Dune Messiah* (1969), *Children of Dune* (1976), *God Emperor of Dune* (1981), *Heretics of Dune* (1984), and *Chapterhouse: Dune* (1985), a complex series dealing with political, religious, and military developments on a water-starved planet. His other books included *Soul Catcher* (1972) and *Hellstrom's Hive* (1973). Herbert was also an ecological consultant and active in the World Without War Council. ■ See study by Timothy O'Reilly (1981).

HERBERT, VICTOR (1859–1924), U.S. composer. Irish-born and German-trained, Herbert emigrated to the United States in 1886. A cello soloist, bandmaster, symphony conductor (Pittsburgh, 1898–1904), and opera composer (*Natoma* and *Madeleine*), Herbert was best known for his enormously popular romantic operettas, including *Babes in Toyland* (1903), *Naughty Marietta* (1910), and *Sweethearts* (1913). His songs included "Kiss Me Again," "Ah, Sweet Mystery of Life," "The Gypsy Love Song," and "Toyland." He composed the first original background film score, *The Fall of a Nation* (1916), initiated the legal suit that guaranteed copyright owners the receipt of royalties (1909), and helped found the American Society of Composers, Authors and Publishers (ASCAP, 1914). ■ See biography by Edward Waters (1955).

HERBERT, ZBIGNIEW (1924–1998), Polish poet and playwright. Herbert was active in the Polish underground during the World War II Nazi occupation. He studied law, philosophy, and art and emerged after the liberalization of 1956 as a major intellectual poet. Preoccupied with the events of contemporary history, his poems indicted totalitarianism, explored questions of conscience, and expressed his compassion for human suffering. He dispensed with traditional rhyme and meter and utilized biblical and mythological allusions as well as satire and irony in his pessimistic and reflective poetry. ■ See English translations in *Selected Works* (1968; 1977), *Barbarian in the Garden* (1985), *Report from the Besieged City* (1985), *Still Life with a Bridle: Essays and Apocryphas* (1993), *Mr. Cogito* (1993), *Elegy for the Departure and Other Poems* (1999), and *The King and the Ants: Mythological Essays* (1999).

HERBLOCK. *See BLOCK, HERBERT.*

HERCZEG, FERENC (1863–1954), Hungarian novelist, short-story writer, and dramatist. A politically active conservative who was born to wealth and power, Herczeg was Hungary's most popular and successful literary figure in the first part of the century. He was an elegant stylist who portrayed and supported the Hungarian gentry in a series of witty, urbane, and colorful novels that were devoid of social concern. Among his best-known works were the novels *Heathens* (1902), *The Golden Violin* (1916), and *The Gates of Life* (1919) and the plays *Seven Sisters* (1893; Eng. trans. 1937), *Byzantium* (1904), *The Colonel* (1914; Eng. trans. 1920), and *Blue Fox* (1917).

HERGÉ (Georges Rémi; 1907–1983), Belgian writer and cartoonist. Hergé began his career, at the age of 16, as the creator of a comic strip for a Boy Scout magazine in Brussels. In 1929 he created the comic strip *Tintin* for the weekly children's supplement of the Brussels newspaper *Le Vingtieme Siècle*. The strip featured the adventures of Tintin, an intrepid boy reporter; his dog Milou (Snowy); Captain Haddock, a retired, frequently tipsy sailor; Professor Tournesol (Calculus), an absentminded, nearly deaf scientist; and Dupont and Dupond (Tomson and Thompson), identical-twin bumbling detectives as they traveled the world solving mysteries and battling the forces of evil. *Tintin,* which was acclaimed for both its humor and its artistry, appealed to both children and adults. Appearing for more than 50 years, it was syndicated in newspapers throughout the world and was translated in 33 languages. Hergé also produced more than 20 books featuring Tintin and his friends. ■ See Benoit Peeters, *Tintin and the World of Hergé* (1992).

HERNÁNDEZ, MIGUEL (1910–1942), Spanish poet. Hernández had little formal education and worked as a goatherd and farmhand. His precocious early volume *Expert on Moons* (1933) and the more mature *The Lightning That Never Ceases* (1936) were recognized by the established poets J. R. Jimenez and Antonio Machado for their daring imagery within classical forms. Hernández fought for the republic in the Spanish Civil War (1936–39), and in his role as popular peasant-poet wrote such works as *Wind of the People* (1937) to hearten his fellow soldiers. He was imprisoned and deprived of nutritional and medical care, and succumbed to tuberculosis. Some of his finest poetry appeared in *Songbook of Absences* (1939; Eng. trans. 1972). ■ See *Selected Poems: Miguel Hernández and Blas de Otero* (Eng. trans. 1972) and study by Geraldine C. Nichols (1978).

HERRIMAN, GEORGE JOSEPH (1880–1944), U.S. cartoonist. While Herriman worked as a newspaper office boy, the *Los Angeles Herald* published his sketches (1897) and his first full-page cartoons (1901). His first comic strip, *Lariat Pete,* appeared in the *San Francisco Chronicle* (1903). After 1908 he worked for Hearst publications. His most memorable characters, first conceived for the farcical strip *The Dingbat Family* (1910), appeared in the classic strip *Krazy Kat,* which was introduced in 1911. Written in a unique style and language and filled with allegory and myth, the strip centered on the romantic triangle of Krazy Kat, Ignatz Mouse, and Offissa Bull Pupp set in a surrealistic desert. The strip had a mass as well as an avant-garde following and was the subject of a full-length jazz pantomime by John Alden Carpenter (1922). ■ See the *Krazy Kat Anthology* (1969) and *Krazy Kat: The Comic Art of George Herriman* (1986), which contains a short biography.

HERRIOT, ÉDOUARD (1872–1957), French political leader. The son and grandson of army officers, Herriot was a brilliant student who attended elite schools and wrote his Ph.D. thesis in music. In 1904 he was elected mayor of Lyons, a post he held continuously until his death, except during wartime internment by the Nazis. An eloquent, forceful politician in the radical-socialist tradition, Herriot was first elected to parliament in 1912. As premier (1924–25) he recognized the Soviet Union, accepted the Dawes plan to solve the German reparations problem, and evacuated the Ruhr. President of the Chamber of Deputies from 1936 to 1940, he refused to recognize the collaborationist Vichy regime and was imprisoned by the Germans (1942–45). After World War II he was president of the national assembly (1947–54). Herriot wrote a biography of Beethoven (1929; Eng. trans. 1935) and other works on history, philosophy, and travel. ■ See biography by Sabine Jessner (1974).

HERRMANN, BERNARD (1911–1975), U.S. film composer. The chief conductor of the Columbia Broadcast Symphony (1942–59), Herrmann wrote innovative, impressionistic scores for Orson Welles' two film classics, *Citizen Kane* (1941) and *The Magnificent Ambersons* (1942) and won an Academy Award for the score of *All That Money Can Buy* (1941). He also explored the instrumentation of suspense in several Alfred Hitchcock films, including *Vertigo* (1958), *North by Northwest* (1959), and *Psycho* (1959), but he considered himself primarily a serious composer, completing a symphony, a violin concerto, an opera, and a cantata.

HERSCHBACH, DUDLEY (1932–), U.S. chemist. Herschbach, a highly touted football player at Stanford, traded in his helmet for a microscope and received a Ph.D. in chemical physics from Harvard University (1958). A professor at the University of California, Berkeley (1956–63), and later at Harvard (1963–), he was one of the first scientists to use molecular beams for the study of chemical reactions. He devised the "crossed molecular beam technique" and (with Yuan T. Lee) developed the apparatus that enabled scientists, for the first time, to study changes that take place in chemical reactions molecule by molecule. For their development of reaction dynamics, a new field of chemical research, Herschbach and Lee shared the 1986 Nobel Prize in Chemistry with John C. Polanyi.

HERSEY, JOHN (1914–1993), U.S. novelist. Born to missionary parents, Hersey was raised in China, educated at Yale (B.A. 1936), and worked briefly as novelist Sinclair Lewis' secretary. His global travels as a World War II correspondent furnished material for the novel *A Bell for Adano* (1944, Pulitzer Prize) and *Hiroshima* (1946), a powerful nonfiction account of the atomic bombing. Later novels included *The Wall* (1950), on the Warsaw Ghetto; *The War Lover* (1959), on war's psychological devastation; and *The Child Buyer* (1960), on modern education. Hersey defined the novel of contemporary history as a "clarifying agent" that "makes truth plausible." A collection of nine "studies in human tenacity" was published as *Here to Stay* (1963). His other works included *The Algiers Motel Incident* (1968), a nonfiction account of the 1967 Detroit riots; *The Call* (1985), a novel about an American missionary in China; *Antonietta* (1991), a novel about a Stradivarius violin; and *Key West Tales* (1994), a short-story collection. ■ See study by David Sanders (1967).

HERSHEY, ALFRED DAY (1908–1997), U.S. biologist. A professor at the Washington University (St. Louis) School of Medicine (1934–50) and the Carnegie Institution's genetic-research unit at Cold Spring Harbor, New York (1950–74), Hershey worked informally with Salvador Luria and Max Delbrück for more than 25 years and made major discoveries regarding the replication mechanism and the genetic structure of viruses. He is best known for demonstrating, through the use of radioisotopes, that deoxyribonucleic acid (DNA) was responsible for the genetic continuity of the bacteria cells he was studying (1952). Hershey shared with Luria and Delbrück the 1969 Nobel Prize in Physiology or Medicine.

HERSHEY, LEWIS BLAINE (1893–1977), U.S. general. Hershey participated on the 1936 army-navy preparedness committee that set up the draft and served as director of the U.S. Selective Service for over a generation (1941–46; 1948–70). A target of antiwar sentiment during the Korean and Vietnam conflicts, he was accused of setting up a deferment system that discriminated against the poor and of punishing protestors by having them drafted. The draft was replaced by the lottery in 1969, but Hershey remained in service until 1973, the oldest man on active duty. ■ See study by George O. Flynn (1985).

HERSHEY, MILTON SNAVELY (1857–1945), U.S. businessman. Apprenticed as a young man to a Lancaster, Pennsylvania, confectioner, Hershey began to manufacture chocolate bars in 1903, a venture that became the Hershey Chocolate Co.—the world's largest manufacturer of chocolate products. Known also as a philanthropist, Hershey founded (1909) and later heavily endowed the Hershey Industrial School, a home and school for orphan boys. ■ See Joseph R. Snavely, *An Intimate Story of Milton S. Hershey* (1957), and Joël G. Brenner, *The Emperors of Chocolate* (1999).

HERSKOVITS, MELVILLE JEAN (1895–1963), U.S. anthropologist. A student of Franz Boas at Columbia University (Ph.D. 1923), Herskovits was associated after 1927 with Northwestern University, where he founded (1951) the first U.S. university program in African studies. He was a leading cultural relativist and a pioneer in applying principles of cultural anthropology to the study of black Americans. In *Myth of the Negro Past* (1941), he formulated the controversial principle that American black culture had absorbed and retained elements of African culture; he dispelled the myth that antebellum slave culture had wiped out all traces of the black American's roots. Herskovits wrote other works on cultural change, economic anthropology, and African culture, including *Man and His Works* (1948) and *The Human Factor in Changing Africa* (1962). ■ See study by George E. Simpson (1973).

HERTZ, GUSTAV (1887–1975), German physicist. Hertz and James Franck shared the Nobel Prize in Physics (1925) for their work on the impact of electrons on atoms, which proved the quantum-theory postulate that energy can be absorbed by the atom only in definite amounts. Among his other research were the separation of isotopes by diffusion cascade and work on separating U-235 from uranium. He resigned his teaching position (1934) in protest against Nazi policies and worked as an industrial physicist. After World War II he agreed to work for the Soviets (1945–54) and helped develop their atomic bomb. He returned to East Germany, where he taught until his retirement (1961).

HERTZOG, JAMES BARRY MUNNIK (1866–1942), South African political and military leader. A European-educated judge in the Orange Free State and a Boer general during the Boer War (1899–1902), Hertzog opposed reconciliation with the British. He formed the Nationalist party (1914) and became prime minister of the Union of South Africa (1924), working during the next 15 years to create a society based on Afrikaner superiority and African powerlessness. His government fell (September 1939) after losing a vote in parliament advocating neutrality during World War II. In 1941 he called for a National Socialist (Nazi) government in South Africa. ■ See study by C. M. van den Heever (1946).

HERTZSPRUNG, EJNAR (1873–1967), Danish astronomer. Trained as a chemical engineer, Hertzsprung became active in many phases of stellar astronomy. He did research at the Göttingen and Potsdam observatories in Germany before joining the Leiden Observatory (director 1935–45). In two papers (1905; 1907), he correlated the color of stars with their true brightness and also demonstrated the existence of giant and dwarf stars. He collaborated with American astronomer Henry Russell to classify stellar types, developing the Hertzsprung-Russell, or H-R, diagram. A fundamental analysis of stellar astronomy, the diagram plotted stellar magnitudes against stellar color.

HERUY WALDA SELLASE (1878–1938), Ethiopian writer. A protégé of regent Ras Tafari, the future Emperor Haile Selassie, Heruy became mayor of Addis Ababa and director of the government printing office in 1917. Considered the father of modern Amharic literature, he published his own works on religion, history, philosophy, and travel as well as novels with constructive social messages. He traveled widely with Ras Tafari during the 1920s and was appointed foreign minister when the regent acceded to the imperial throne (1930). In 1936 he followed the emperor into exile in Britain, where he died.

HERZBERG, GERHARD (1904–1999), German-born Canadian physicist. Trained at the Darmstadt Institute of Technology, Göttingen University, and Bristol University (England), Herzberg fled from the Nazi regime to Canada (1935) and taught at the University of Saskatchewan (1935–45). Associated with the National Research Council of Canada at Ottawa (1948–94), Herzberg did pioneering research in molecular microscopy that enabled him to determine the electron structure and geometry of molecules. His spectrographic studies were of fundamental importance to such wide-ranging fields as chemical physics, quantum mechanics, chemical kinetics, and cosmic chemistry and earned him the 1971 Nobel Prize in Chemistry. He wrote numerous scientific studies, including *Molecular Spectra and Molecular Structure* (3 vols., 1939–66).

HERZOG, MAURICE (1919–   ), French mountain climber and government official. Herzog led the nine-man French Alpine Club expedition that reached the summit of the 26,502-foot peak Annapurna on June 3, 1950. Located in the Nepalese Himalayas, it was the first mountain over 26,000 feet to be climbed. Subsequently Herzog served as high commissioner (1958–63) and secretary of state (1963–66) for youth and sport, was a deputy in the national asssembly (1962–63; 1967–78), held several other government positions, and was a member of the International Olympic Committee (from 1970). ■ See his *Annapurna* (Eng. trans. 1952) and David Roberts, *True Summit* (2000).

HESBURGH, THEODORE MARTIN (1917–), U.S. educator. Ordained as a Roman Catholic priest (1943), Hesburgh studied theology at Catholic University (Ph.D. 1945). He was affiliated with the University of Notre Dame from 1945, and as president of the university (1952–87), transformed it from an all-white Catholic school known primarily for football into a respected secular, multiracial academy. A social activist, he was most committed to combatting racism, which he considered the key problem in the United States. Hesburgh served for 15 years on the U.S. Commission on Civil Rights (1957–72; chair 1969–72). He left the commission after protesting the civil rights policy of Pres. Richard Nixon. He chaired the Overseas Development Council during the administration of Pres. Jimmy Carter. As chair of the Select Commission on Immigration and Refugee Policy, Hesburgh recommended (1981) amnesty for illegal aliens already in the United States and penalties for employers hiring illegal aliens in the future. He wrote numerous books. ■ See his autobiography, *God, Country, Notre Dame* (1991; with Jerry Reedy).

HESCHEL, ABRAHAM JOSHUA (1907–1972), Polish-born U.S. Jewish religious leader and philosopher. After earning (1933) a doctoral degree in Berlin, Heschel directed Frankfurt's Central Organization for Jewish Adult Education; he succeeded Martin Buber, the philosopher whose reformulation of Hasidic mysticism and whose concept of the direct dialogue between man and God influenced Heschel's own thinking. Heschel taught philosophy in Warsaw and London, then emigrated (1940) to the United States, where he taught at the Jewish Theological Seminary in New York City (1945–72). Many of his scholarly works dealt with revelation and inspiration, and he elaborated upon an existential philosophy of Judaism. Heschel set forth his influential philosophy in such works as *Man Is Not Alone: A Philosophy of Religion* (1951), *God in Search of Man: A Philosophy of Judaism* (1955), and *The Prophets* (1962). He was also active in the civil rights, peace, and ecumenical movements. ■ See Franklin Sherman, *The Promise of Heschel* (1970), and study by Edward K. Kaplan and Samuel H. Dressner (1998).

HESS, DAME MYRA (1890–1965), British pianist. Hess studied at the Royal Academy of Music (1902–07) and made her recital debut in 1907, playing the music of Bach, Mozart, and Scarlatti with classical precision and graceful execution. Her World War II lunchtime concerts in London's National Gallery boosted public morale, and she was made a dame of the British Empire in 1941. ■ See study edited by Denise Lassimonne (1967).

HESS, RUDOLF (1894–1987), German Nazi leader. Born in Egypt of German parents, Hess was a naive and reckless fanatic who became a friend and confidant of Adolf Hitler. While they were serving prison sentences for the 1923 Munich "beer-hall putsch," Hitler dictated the text of "Mein Kampf" to Hess, who became his secretary and deputy Nazi party leader. In 1941, during World War II, Hess created international astonishment with his unauthorized flight to Britain, evidently to negotiate peace. After the war he was convicted of war crimes at Nuremberg and sentenced to life imprisonment (1946). He remained incarcerated for the rest of his life, for years the only prisoner in Berlin's Spandau jail. He committed suicide. ■ See the biography by J. Bernard Hutton (1971); Eugene K. Bird, *Prisoner 7* (1974); W. Hugh Thomas, *The Murder of Rudolf Hess* (1979); and John Costello, *Ten Days to Destiny* (1991).

HESS, VICTOR FRANCIS (1883–1964), Austrian physicist. While teaching at the University of Vienna, Hess discovered via a series of balloon ascents (1911–13) that the high-energy radiation found in the earth's atmosphere comes neither from the earth nor the sun but originates in outer space. For his discovery of what was later named "cosmic rays" by R. A. Millikan (1925), Hess shared the 1936 Nobel Prize in Physics with Carl D. Anderson. Subsequent research in cosmic radiation led to the discovery of several new elementary particles. Hess emigrated to the United States (1938) and became a professor of physics at Fordham University in New York.

HESS, WALTER RUDOLF (1881–1973), Swiss neurophysiologist. Originally trained as an ophthalmologist, Hess switched to physiology and specialized in brain research. By planting electrodes in the brains of laboratory animals, he demonstrated that the diencephalon, or interbrain (the hypothalamus, subthalamus, and parts of the thalamus), was responsible for many autonomic activities (such as digestion, excretion) as well as moods and drives (fear, anger, lethargy). The director of the Physiological Institute at the University of Zurich (1917–51), Hess shared the 1949 Nobel Prize in Physiology or Medicine with António Egas Moniz. His books included *The Functional Organization of the Diencephalon* (Eng. trans. 1957) and *The Biology of Mind* (Eng. trans. 1964).

HESSE, HERMANN (1877–1962), German-born Swiss novelist, poet, and essayist. Hesse's grandfather and father were missionaries in India; he ran away from the seminary at a young age. His early novels, including *Peter Camenzind* (1904; Eng. trans. 1969), *The Prodigy* (1905; Eng. trans. 1957), *Gertrud* (1910; Eng. tran. 1969), and *Rosshalde* (1914; Eng. trans. 1970), described the artist's inner struggles. Following a journey (1911) to India, he wrote novels reflecting his fascination with Eastern religion and his experience in Jungian analysis; they treated the split between nature and spirit, body and mind. Novels of this period, *Demian* (1919; Eng. trans. 1965), *Steppenwolf* (1927; Eng. trans. 1963), and *Siddhartha* (1922; Eng. trans. 1951), aroused great interest among young intellectuals, particularly Americans, when they appeared in translation some 40 years later. *Magister Ludi* (1943; Eng. trans. 1970) is considered by many to be his masterpiece. Hesse won the 1946 Nobel Prize in Literature. ■ See his *Autobiographical Writings* (1972) and biographies by Joseph Mileck (1978) and Ralph Freedman (1997).

HEVESY, GEORG CHARLES DE (1885–1966), Hungarian-born chemist. Hevesy worked with Ernest Rutherford in Manchester (1911–13) and later with Niels Bohr at the University of Copenhagen (1920–26; 1934–43). After 1944 he taught at the University of Stockholm. He made two breakthroughs in 1923. He added to the periodic chart a new element that he called hafnium (the Latin name for Copenhagen). More significantly, he developed the concept of radioactive-isotope tracing, on the basis of data gathered from watering plants with a lead isotope. This research technique, which revolutionized research in physiology, pathology, botany, and even metallurgy, aroused little interest when it was proposed, and it was not until 1943 that Hevesy was awarded the Nobel Prize in Chemistry. His books included *Adventures in Radioisotope Research* (2 vols., 1962). ■ See study by Hilde Levi (1985).

HEWISH, ANTONY (1924–), British astrophysicist. Hewish studied at Cambridge University (Ph.D. 1952), where he conducted research under Sir Martin Ryle. He remained at Cambridge, ultimately serving as full professor (1971–89). He was best known for the 1967 discovery of pulsars, phenomena in space that emit radio waves at regular intervals. The initial detection of pulsars was made by Jocelyn S. Bell, a graduate student in Hewish's research team. At first the group believed that the phenomenon signaled intelligent life in space; they ultimately concluded that the energy emissions originated from relatively small, rapidly spinning celestial objects. (Most astronomers now believe that pulsars are neutron stars.) The discovery was made possible by Hewish's introduction of equipment that permitted shorter time exposures than had previously been recorded. Hewish shared the 1974 Nobel Prize in Physics with Ryle; they were the first astronomers to be honored by the Nobel committee.

HEWLETT, WILLIAM R. (1913–2001), and PACKARD, DAVID (1912–1996), U.S. engineers and industrialists. Hewlett and Packard met while they were both undergraduates at Stanford University in the early 1930s. After earning master's degrees in electrical engineering, the two men formed (1939) an electronics firm, the Hewlett-Packard Company, in a small garage in Palo Alto, California, with an initial investment of $538. The company, whose first product was an audio oscillator developed by Hewlett in graduate school, ultimately became a giant multinational concern and the nation's second largest computer company, with revenue of $31 billion in 1996. (The firm's first home became a California historical landmark and was labeled "the birthplace of Silicon Valley.") Hewlett-Packard was known for developing the first handheld calculator and the first ink-jet computer printer as well as for its egalitarian management approach and organizational environment that encouraged worker initiative and creativity. The company's philosophy was described in Packard's book, *The HP Way* (1995). Hewlett was president of Hewlett-Packard (1964–71) and chief executive officer (1969–78). Packard was president (1947–64) and chief executive officer (1964–68). Packard also served as U.S. deputy secretary of defense (1969–71) and was a member of the Trilateral Commission (1973–81).

HEYDRICH, REINHARD (1904–1942), German Nazi official. Heydrich was a teenage street fighter in the disorders that followed World War I, then joined the navy (1922). Sacked for misconduct (1931), he became a black-shirted SS leader and was promoted (1934) to deputy chief of the Gestapo (secret police) and (1939) to the head of security and intelligence. He played a major role in planning the mass extermination of European Jews. His brutality in suppressing anti-Nazi opposition both within and outside of Germany during World War II earned him the title of "hangman of Europe." He was assassinated by Czech patriots; in revenge the Nazis executed the male population of Lidice and demolished the town. ■ See biographies by G. S. Graber (1980), Günther Deschner (Eng. trans. 1981), and Edouard Calic (Eng. trans. 1985), and studies by Charles Wighton (1962) and Alan Wykes (1973).

HEYERDAHL, THOR (1914–), Norwegian ethnologist and explorer. While conducting zoological research in Polynesia (1936–38), Heyerdahl noted striking parallels there to aspects of pre-Inca South American civilization. He formulated the controversial theory that parallel cultural phenomena had resulted from actual contact and migration. Heyerdahl collected archaeological data in South America to support his hypothesis, but anthropologists dismissed the idea that primitive people could have navigated the transoceanic voyage. Finally, Heyerdahl himself crossed the Pacific (1947) on a raft made of balsa logs; the best-selling book *Kon-Tiki* (1948; Eng. tran. 1950) and a film (1951) documented his journey. Heyerdahl crossed the Atlantic (1969–70) in *Ra II,* a facsimile of an ancient boat, demonstrating the possibility of cultural links between Egypt and pre-Inca South American civilization. *The Ra Expeditions* (1971) recounted this crossing. He later tested the capability of a Sumerian-type reed boat, *Tigris,* to travel from Asia to Africa (recorded in *The Tigris Expedition,* 1979) and undertook archaeological digs on the Maldive Islands (documented in *The Maldive Mystery,* 1985), in Peru (1988), and on the Canary Islands (1990). His later books included *Easter Island—The Mystery Solved* (1989) and *Green Was the Earth on the Seventh Day* (1996), a description of environmental degradation. ■ See Arnold Jacoby, *Señor Kon-Tiki* (1966; Eng. trans. 1968), and Christopher Ralling, *The Kon-Tiki Man* (1990).

HEYM, STEFAN (1913–), German writer. Heym was born to Jewish parents in Chemnitz, which is now part of

East Germany. He attended the University of Berlin, left Germany at age 20 when the Nazis came to power (1933), spent two years in Prague, and then emigrated to the United States, where he attended the University of Chicago (M.A. 1935). In the 1940s he published *Hostages* (1942; reprinted as *The Glasenapp Case*, 1962) and *The Crusaders* (1948). Heym was decorated for U.S. Army service during World War II; a lifelong activist in the noncommunist left, he returned his Bronze Star to Pres. Dwight Eisenhower during the anticommunist fervor of the early 1950s and moved to East Germany, giving up his U.S. citizenship. He won East Germany's national prize in 1969, but his insistence on challenging official ideology antagonized the government; his later novels, which often treated events in Eastern Europe during and after World War II, were banned in East Germany but were well received in West Germany and elsewhere. These included *Five Days in June* (1974; Eng. trans. 1978), *Collin* (1979; Eng. trans. 1980), *The Wandering Jew* (1981; Eng. trans. 1984), and *Schwarzenberg* (1984). His short fiction appeared in *The Queen Against Defoe* (German trans. 1970; Eng. orig. 1974). Heym, who wrote in German and English, traveled outside of East Germany but chose to remain a dissident voice there rather than to emigrate. After German reunification he served as a Social Democratic party member of parliament (1994–96). ▪ See study by Peter Hutchinson (1992).

HEYMANS, CORNEILLE JEAN FRANÇOIS (1892–1968), Belgian physiologist and pharmacologist. Heymans collaborated with his father, the prominent researcher J. F. Heymans, on many of his early experiments on blood pressure and circulation, and succeeded him as professor of pharmacology at the University of Ghent (1930). His most important work demonstrated that the carotid sinus and aortic mechanisms play key roles in the regulation of respiration. Heymans was awarded the 1938 Nobel Prize in Physiology or Medicine for his research.

HEYROVSKÝ, JAROSLAV (1890–1967), Czech physical chemist. Heyrovský was educated in Prague and London and taught at Charles University in Prague (1920–54). He received little attention when he first developed (1922) polarographic analysis, a delicate electrochemical method of measuring and identifying the constituents of an unknown solution, but his technique proved applicable to fields as diverse as metallurgy and medicine and was eventually universally accepted. Heyrovský was appointed director (1950–63) of the Polarographic Institute of the Czechoslovak Academy of Sciences and was awarded the 1959 Nobel Prize in Chemistry.

HICKS, GRANVILLE (1901–1982), U.S. literary critic. A solid member of the Communist party until his resignation (1939), Hicks served as a literary editor and staff critic for the *New Masses*. He applied his Marxist orientation to literary criticism in his study of American literature, *The Great

Tradition* (1933). Hicks' political shift after 1939 was reflected in his cooperation with the House Committee on Un-American Activities during the 1950s. He edited an anthology of criticism, *The Living Novel* (1957), and in 1970 he published *Literary Horizons: A Quarter Century of American Fiction,* a collection of his critical writing on Saul Bellow, Bernard Malamud, Vladimir Nabokov, and others. Hicks also wrote several novels. ▪ See his autobiography, *Part of the Truth* (1965); Jack A. Robbins, ed., *Granville Hicks in the "New Masses"* (1974); and study by Leah Levenson (1993).

HICKS, SIR JOHN RICHARD (1904–1989), British economist. Educated at Balliol College, Oxford, Hicks taught at the London School of Economics (1926–35), the University of Manchester (1938–46), and at Oxford (1946–71). He made important contributions to economics in the 1930s; his *Value and Capital* (1939) was a classic work that resolved fundamental conflicts between business-cycle theory and equilibrium theory. Hicks maintained that economic forces do not simply reflect cyclical trends, but tend to balance each other. Rather than studying the dynamics of markets one by one, he emphasized the relationship among them, analyzing the impact of broader economic and social phenomena on the stability of multimarket systems. He made contributions to many branches of economics, including wages, money, and welfare economics. Such later works as *A Theory of Economic History* (1969) and *Causality in Economics* (1979) explored the relationship between theory and economic history. Hicks shared the 1972 Nobel Prize in Economics with Kenneth J. Arrow. ▪ See his *Collected Papers* (2 vols., 1981–82).

HIGGINS, MARGUERITE (1920–1966), U.S. journalist. A war correspondent during World War II and the Vietnam War, Higgins achieved her greatest glory—and a Pulitzer Prize—for her vivid frontline reporting during the Korean War (1951). She was the only woman correspondent at the front, and her book *War in Korea* (1951) became a bestseller. Higgins reported for the *New York Herald Tribune* (from 1942) and was a syndicated columnist for *Newsday* (from 1962). ▪ See biography by Antoinette May, *Witness to War* (1983).

HIKMET, NAZIM (1902–1963), Turkish writer. While a student of economics and sociology in Moscow (1922–24), Hikmet joined the Communist party and was influenced by poets Vladimir Mayakovsky, Sergey Yesenin, and other Russian futurists and constructivists. Returning home in 1924, he began to write avant-garde plays, novels, and poetry that had a revolutionary effect on Turkish literature during the 1920s and 1930s, and he became Turkey's best-known literary figure. He introduced free verse, new poetic forms, and Marxist-Leninist themes into Turkish poetry and was a hero of the Turkish left. A revolutionary political activist, he was imprisoned from 1938 to 1950 and lived (from 1951 until his death) in the Soviet Union, Poland, and Bulgaria. Among his best-known works was *The Epic of Sheikh Bedreddin* (1936; Eng. trans. 1977). English translations of his poems are in *Poems* (1954), *Selected Poems* (1967), *The Moscow Symphony* (1970), *The Day Before Tomorrow* (1972), *Things I Didn't Know I Loved* (1975), *Human Landscapes* (1983), and *Poems of Nazim Hikmet* (1994).

HILBERT, DAVID (1862–1943), German mathematician. A professor at the universities of Königsberg (1886–95) and Göttingen (1895–1943), Hilbert was a legendary figure in the world of mathematics. He formulated modern algebraic number theory, developed the basis of functional analysis, and advanced a formalistic, axiomatic approach to mathematics. His famous enunciation of 23 unsolved problems (1900) challenged scholars throughout the world and influenced the development of new theorems and branches of mathematics. His work on infinite-dimensional space (later called Hilbert space) contributed to the development of quantum mechanics. His books included *The Foundations of Geometry* (1899; Eng. trans. 1902), *Principles of Mathematical Logic* (1928; with W. Ackermann; Eng. trans. 1950), and *Methods of Mathematical Physics* (1931; with R. Courant; rev. ed. Eng. trans. 1953). ▪ See study by Constance Reid (1970).

HILFERDING, RUDOLF (1877–1941), Austrian-born German Marxist theoretician and government official. Born into a wealthy Jewish family, Hilferding joined the socialist movement while a medical student. He wrote the influential Marxist book *Finance Capital: A Study of the Latest Phase of Capitalist Development* (1910; Eng. trans. 1981), and he served as political editor of the journal *Vorwärts* (1907–15) and editor of *Die Freiheit* (1918–22). He joined the German Social Democratic party (1922) and became its leading theorist and financial expert. A Reichstag deputy (1924–33), he served as finance minister in two German Social Democratic governments (1923; 1928–1929) and published the journal *Die Gesellschaft* (1924–33). He escaped from Nazi Germany to Prague (1933) and later to Paris (1938), where he was arrested by the Gestapo (during the German occupation) and was found hanged in a prison cell. ▪ See studies by Peter F. Wagner (1996) and William Smaldone (1998).

HILL, ARCHIBALD VIVIAN (1886–1977), British physiologist. A graduate of Cambridge (1907), A. V. Hill began conducting experiments with heat measurements of muscles in 1911. He showed that oxygen is not needed for the contraction phase of muscular activity and discovered the series of biochemical reactions that results in muscle contraction. For this work, Hill shared the 1922 Nobel Prize in Physiology and Medicine with Otto Meyerhof. He was the Foulerton research professor of the Royal Society (1926–51), an Independent Conservative member of parliament (1940–45), member of the War Cabinet Scientific Advisory Committee (1940–46), and author of several books, including *Muscular Activity* (1926), *Muscular Movement in Man* (1927), and *Trails and Trials in Physiology* (1965).

HILL, (JOHN EDWARD) CHRISTOPHER (1912–), British historian. Christopher Hill concluded his long career at Oxford (B.A. 1934; M.A. 1938, faculty member 1938–65) as master of Balliol College (1965–78). A Marxist who specialized in 16th- and 17th-century history, Hill emphasized the economic and social causes of the English Revolution, paying particular attention to populist elements and radical intellectuals. His best-known works included *The Century of Revolution, 1603–1714* (1961), *Society and Puritanism in Pre-Revolutionary England* (1964), *The Making of Modern English Society* (1967), *The World Turned Upside Down* (1972), *Milton and the English Revolution* (1977), *The Experience of Defeat: Milton and Some Contemporaries* (1984), and *The English Bible and the Seventeenth-Century Revolution* (1993).

HILL, GEORGE WASHINGTON (1884–1946), U.S. businessman. Hill joined the American Tobacco Co. in 1904 and succeeded his father as president (1925). He introduced Lucky Strike, one of the first nationally marketed cigarettes, and relying heavily on advertising (much of it written by himself), he made the brand one of the world's most popular smokes. Through catchy slogans ("It's Toasted," "Reach for a Lucky instead of a sweet," "LS/MFT—Lucky Strikes Means Fine Tobacco"), sponsorship on the Walter Winchell, Jack Benny, and "Your Hit Parade" radio programs, and a special campaign to make smoking by women socially acceptable, Hill kept his company profitable throughout the Depression and was one of America's highest-paid executives.

HILL, JOE (Joel Emmanuel Hagglund; 1879–1915), Swedish-born U.S. labor organizer. Hill emigrated to the United States (1902) and drifted around the country working in factories, on farms and waterfronts, and on coastal schooners. Fed up with working conditions, he joined the San Pedro (California) branch of the radical labor organization, the Industrial Workers of the World (IWW) or "Wobblies" (1910), and spent five years traveling through the western states organizing farm, mine, and mill workers. During his wanderings he wrote a number of famous labor songs, including "The Preacher and the Slave," "Casey Jones—the Union Scab," and "The Rebel Girl." In January 1914, he was arrested in Utah on a murder charge and convicted on circumstantial evidence. Many thought he was framed; despite national and international protests, he was executed in November 1915. One of his last messages, "Don't waste time in mourning. Organize!" became a well-known labor movement slogan. ▪ See Philip Foner, *The Case of Joe Hill* (1965), and biography by Gibbs M. Smith (1969).

HILL, PHIL (1927–), U.S. auto-racing driver. Three-time winner of both the renowned Le Mans 24-hour race (with

Olivier Gendebien; 1958; 1961; 1962) and Sebring 12-hour race (1958 with Peter Collins; 1959 and 1961 with Gendebien), Hill was America's most successful endurance driver. He was the first American to win the World Driving Championship (1961). ■ See biography by William F. Nolan (1963).

HILLARY, SIR EDMUND PERCIVAL (1919–), New Zealand mountain climber and explorer. A beekeeper by profession, Hillary became interested in mountain climbing at an early age and on May 29, 1953, he and Nepalese Sherpa mountaineer Tenzing Norgay became the first people to reach the summit of Mt. Everest, the world's highest mountain (29,028 feet). Hillary was knighted later that year. He subsequently led several other Himalayan expeditions and helped to build schools, hospitals, and clinics for the Sherpa people. He led the New Zealand section of the Commonwealth Trans-Antarctic Expedition (1955–58) and participated in the first mechanized journey to the South Pole (1958). *From the Ocean to the Sky* (1979) describes his 1977 expedition on the Ganges River, from its mouth to the Himalayas. His books included *Ecology 2000: The Changing Face of Earth* (1984) and *Indigenous Peoples and Protected Areas* (1993). ■ See his autobiography, *Nothing Venture, Nothing Win* (1975).

HILLMAN, BESSIE (Bessie Abramowitz; 1889–1970), Russian-born U.S. labor leader. Hillman fled from her native town during anti-Jewish pogroms (1905) and settled in Chicago. A militant garment worker, she protested the low wages she received at the Hart, Schaffner and Marx men's clothing plant and led a walkout of 16 women that precipitated the landmark 1910 garment workers' strike. The strike led to the formation of the Amalgamated Clothing Workers of America (1914) and she married Sidney Hillman (1916), the union's first president. Moving to union headquarters in New York, she worked as an organizer and led the union's educational programs. She served on government commissions during World War II. After her husband's death, she served as vice president of the union (1946–70) and was active in the civil-rights, peace, and child-welfare-reform movements. She advocated equal rights for women and participated in United Nations–sponsored conferences on the status of women (1962–63).

HILLMAN, SIDNEY (1887–1946), U.S. labor leader. Born in Lithuania, Hillman was an organizer for the Jewish trade union movement, the Bund. He emigrated to the United States in 1907, became a garment worker, and led an important strike in Chicago (1910–11). As president of the Amalgamated Clothing Workers of America (1914–46), he expanded union functions to include banking, unemployment insurance, housing, and other social services for members, and he encouraged labor support for political candidates. He helped to found (1935) the Committee for (later Congress of) Industrial Organization (CIO) and served as its vice president (1935–40). Hillman held various posts

in Pres. Franklin D. Roosevelt's administrations, gaining influence in the Democratic party. After World War II he helped to create (1945) and was vice president of the World Federation of Trade Unions. ■ See biographies by Matthew Josephson (1952) and Jean Gould (1952) and Steve Fraser, *Labor Will Rule* (1991).

HILLQUIT, MORRIS (Morris Hillkowitz; 1869–1933), Russian-born U.S. lawyer, author, and political leader. After emigrating to New York City's Lower East Side (1886), Hillquit joined the Socialist Labor party, wrote for the first American-Yiddish newspaper, and earned a law degree (1893). He helped form (1897) the coalition Social Democratic party, led by Eugene V. Debs, and was a cofounder (1901) and chief spokesman of the Socialist party. He was well known as a debater, publicist, lawyer, and union organizer, and he attempted to adapt socialist theory to American reality. He condemned World War I and advocated the formation of an independent labor party after the war. Between 1906 and 1932 he ran unsuccessfully for Congress five times and for New York city mayor twice. His books included *History of Socialism in the U.S.* (1903) and *Socialism in Theory and Practice* (1909). ■ See his autobiography, *Loose Leaves from a Busy Life* (1934), and study by Norma F. Pratt (1979).

HILTON, CONRAD NICHOLSON (1887–1979), U.S. hotel executive. Hilton purchased his first hotel in Cisco, Texas (1919), and eventually built up the largest hotel organization in the world. Originally aimed at traveling salesmen and businessmen, his hotels offered efficiency, standardization, and a degree of luxury. Hilton controlled such famous hotels as the Waldorf-Astoria and Statler Hilton in New York, Palmer House and Conrad Hilton in Chicago, and the Beverly Hilton in Beverly Hills, California, as well as dozens of others scattered around the globe. The new hotels built by the Hilton International Co. (founded 1948) provided affluent travelers with American oases throughout Europe, Asia, and Latin America. ■ See his autobiography, *Be My Guest* (1957), and Whitney Bolton, *The Silver Spade* (1954).

HIMES, CHESTER (1909–1984), U.S. novelist. Himes was convicted of armed robbery at age 19 and began writing while serving a seven-year prison term at the Ohio State Penitentiary. He lived in France after 1953 and amassed a fortune with a series of mystery thrillers set in Harlem that adopted a detective team from a Langston Hughes story. When he later turned to social novels, Himes was a cutting satirist and skilled raconteur. *If He Hollers Let Him Go* (1945) and *Lonely Crusade* (1947) were based on his experience as a defense-plant worker during World War II. Himes also wrote *The Third Generation* (1954), *Cotton Comes to Harlem* (1965), *Pinktoes* (1965), *Blind Man with a Pistol* (1969), *Hot Day Hot Night* (1970), and *A Case of Rape* (1980). ■ See his autobiographies, *The Quality of Hurt* (1972) and *My Life of Absurdity* (1976); study by Stephen F. Milliken (1976); and Edward Margolies, *The Several Lives of Chester Himes* (1997).

HIMMLER, HEINRICH (1900–1945), German Nazi official. Himmler was the son of a Bavarian schoolmaster and a participant in Adolf Hitler's 1923 "beer-hall putsch." He became head of the elite Nazi SS corps (1929), head of the German police (1936) with authority over the Gestapo (secret police), and minister of the interior (1943) with extensive control over domestic politics. He established an extensive network of concentration camps and instituted a reign of terror throughout German-occupied Europe during World War II. Captured by the British after trying unsuccessfully to negotiate Germany's surrender, Himmler committed suicide by poison. ■ See biographies by Willi Frischauer (1953), Roger Manvell and Heinrich Fraenkel (1965), Bradley F. Smith (1971); and Richard Breitman, *The Architect of Genocide* (1992).

HINDEMITH, PAUL (1895–1963), German composer and theorist. Germany's leading composer during the 1920s, Hindemith was a radical in the European classical tradition. An exponent of *Gebrauchmusik* (functional music) and dissonant counterpoint, his masterpiece was the symphony (1934) drawn from his opera *Mathis der Maler* (1938). Branded a "cultural bolshevik" by the Nazis, he emigrated to Turkey (1935) and then to the United States, where he became an influential teacher (Yale, 1940–53) and wrote *The Craft of Musical Composition* (1941) and *Traditional Harmony* (1943). He spent his last decade in Switzerland teaching at the University of Zurich. ■ See his *A Composer's World* (1952) and biography by Geoffrey Skelton (1977).

HINDENBURG, PAUL VON (1847–1934), German field marshal and statesman. A veteran of the Franco-Prussian War, Hindenburg came out of retirement to command the German army on the eastern front during World War I and to stabilize the western front at what became known as the "Hindenburg line." He served as chief of the General Staff from 1916 to 1919. Acclaimed a hero despite Germany's defeat, the aged field marshal was elected president of the republic in 1925 and 1932. In 1933, in the midst of crisis, he appointed Adolf Hitler chancellor, remaining in office as a figurehead president until his death. ■ See his memoirs, *Out of My Life* (Eng. trans. 1920), and biographies by Margaret Goldsmith and Frederick Voight (1930), John Wheeler-Bennett (1936), and Andreas Dorpalen (1964).

HINE, LEWIS WICKES (1874–1940), U.S. photographer. A sociology student at the University of Chicago and New York University (Pd.M. 1905), Hine took up photography as a means of documenting social conditions. He went to Ellis Island (New York) to photograph the arrival of the immigrants (1904–08) and followed them into the tenements and factories of the promised land, taking pictures that were compassionate without being didactic. Hine's depiction of immigrant life, published in the reformist journal *Charities and the Commons* (1908), is considered the first "photo story." The pictures of child labor that he took as the official photographer of the National Child Labor Committee (1911–16) resulted in corrective legislation. His book *Men at Work* (1932; rev. ed. 1977) documented the construction of the Empire State Building in New York City. Selections of his photos are in *America and Lewis Hine* (1976). ■ See study by Judith Gutman (1967).

HINES, EARL "FATHA" (1905–1983), U.S. jazz pianist and bandleader. Born into a musical family in Pittsburgh, Hines started his professional career while still a teenager and achieved prominence during the 1920s for the amazing technical command he displayed while playing with several jazz ensembles. He developed a "trumpet style" of playing and was the first virtuoso piano soloist in jazz history. He made a series of legendary recordings with Louis Armstrong (1928) and led his own bands during the big-band era (1928–48). After World War II he toured with Louis Armstrong's All Stars (1948–51) and other small and more modern groups (during the 1960s and 1970s) and made several solo albums. ■ See Stanley Dance, *The World of Earl Hines* (1977).

HINSHELWOOD, SIR CYRIL NORMAN (1897–1967), British physical chemist. Hinshelwood's research at Oxford during the 1920s in chemical kinetics—the study of the rate at which chemical reactions occur—afforded insights into the mechanisms involved in these reactions. His analysis of the combination of hydrogen and oxygen to form water clarified the phenomena of chain reactions and chain branching. He shared the 1956 Nobel Prize in Chemistry with Soviet chemist Nikolai Semenov, who had independently reached similar conclusions. A practical application of their work was the elucidation of the hydrocarbon chain reaction, which allowed improvement of the octane rating of gasoline. Hinshelwood, who taught at Oxford from 1921 to 1964, also investigated chemical reactions in living organisms. His books included *Kinetics of Chemical Change* (1926; 4th ed. 1947) and *The Chemical Kinetics of the Bacterial Cell* (1946).

HIROHITO (1901–1989), Japanese emperor. Named heir apparent to the throne in 1912, Hirohito became the first crown prince to leave Japan when he toured Europe in 1921. In 1926 he succeeded his father, Emperor Taisho, as the 124th emperor of Japan and was formally crowned two years later. Though he was revered, he generally accepted policies developed by his ministers. His degree of support for militaristic policies leading to World War II has been the subject of historical debate. In 1945, Hirohito read the announcement of Japan's surrender, and in 1946 he declared that he was a mere mortal. The Japanese, though initially shocked, adjusted to democratic government, and Hirohito continued as a ceremonial ruler only. He traveled extensively abroad—the first sitting emperor to do so in more than 2,000 years. Hirohito was an authority on marine biology and wrote several books on the subject. ▪ See biographies by Leonard Mosley (1966), Edward Behr (1989), and Herbert Bix (2000).

HIRSCH, ELROY LEON (1923–   ), U.S. football player. Known as "Crazylegs" for his elusiveness in the open field, Hirsch made an inauspicious professional debut as back end for the Chicago Rockets of the All-America Conference, where he spent three injury-filled seasons. Joining the Los Angeles Rams (1949–57) of the National Football League (NFL), Crazylegs Hirsch became football's most reliable receiver of the early 1950s. As the league's leading pass receiver in 1951, Hirsch was central to the aerial game that helped his team gain 5,506 yards and capture the NFL championship. *Crazylegs* (1953) was a movie about his life. He was the Rams' general manager (1960–69) and director of athletics at the University of Wisconsin (1969–87).

HIRSCHBEIN, PERETZ (1880–1948), Polish-born Yiddish-language dramatist. A world traveler who visited farflung Jewish communities, Hirschbein wrote, in addition to drama, lyric poetry, music, short stories, novels, children's literature, travelogues, and memoirs. He was a master of natural dialogue; his depiction of characters had a positive influence on the literary quality of the Yiddish theater. His plays *The Haunted Inn* (1912; Eng. trans. 1921) and *A Wayside Nook* (1912) uniquely juxtaposed mysticism and realism. Hirschbein's most popular play, *Green Fields* (1916; Eng. trans. 1966), dealt with the struggle of values in an idyllic rural settlement. The novel *Red Fields* (1935) concerned Jews in the Soviet Union, and *Babylon* (1942) dealt with three generations of an American Jewish family. He lived in New York City (1911–21; 1929–40) and Los Angeles (1940–48).

HIRSCHFELD, MAGNUS (1868–1935), German physician and sex researcher. Born into a Jewish family in the Baltic town of Kolberg (now Kolobrzeg, Poland), Hirschfeld practiced medicine in Berlin and was a pioneer sexologist and world-renowned advocate for the decriminalization of homosexuality. He believed that homosexuals represented an intermediate sexual stage between masculinity and femininity, an innate third sex, and his publication *Yearbook for Sexual Intermediacy* (1899–1923) was the world's first scholarly journal devoted to the study of homosexual behavior. His book *Transvestites* (1910; Eng. trans. 1991) was a pioneering study in which he coined the term, and his monumental work, *Male and Female Homosexuality* (1914), based on historical research and data from questionnaires, remained a standard work in the field for decades. He founded the Institute for Sexual Science in Berlin (1919) and

presided over four conferences of the World League of Sexual Reform (1921–30). While Hirschfeld was abroad, the Nazis destroyed his institute and its unique archive and library (1933), and he died in exile in southern France. A summary of his works, in English, was published as *Sexual Anomalies* (1936; rev. ed. 1948). ▪ See biography by Charlotte Wolff (1987).

HIRSHHORN, JOSEPH HERMAN (1899–1981), Latvian-born U.S. financier, mining tycoon, and art collector. Brought to the United States by his widowed mother at age 6, Hirshhorn was raised in poverty in a Jewish neighborhood in Brooklyn, New York. He was a Wall Street office boy at age 14 and became a successful broker and analyst while still in his teens. He amassed a fortune during the 1920s and was one of the few large investors to sell his holdings just before the 1929 stock market crash. He made additional fortunes in Canadian gold mining during the 1930s and uranium mining during the 1940s and 1950s. All the while, he was amassing one of the world's largest private art collections, which was particularly strong in the areas of 19th- and 20th-century sculpture and in modern American painting. He donated the collection to the U.S. government, which built the Joseph H. Hirshhorn Museum and Sculpture Garden on the Mall in Washington, D.C. (1974), to house it. ▪ See study by Barry Hyams (1979).

HISS, ALGER (1904–1996), U.S. public official. Hiss was a member of the eastern establishment—a graduate of the Harvard Law School (1929) and protégé of Justice Oliver Wendell Holmes—who had a distinguished career in the State Department. He played a key role in the founding of the United Nations and had just been appointed president of the Carnegie Endowment for World Peace in 1948, at the height of the cold war, when he was accused by confessed spy Whittaker Chambers (at a session of the House Committee on Un-American Activities) of having been a communist from 1934 to 1938 and of having passed confidential documents to the Soviets. Hiss denied the charges, but the case against him was relentlessly pursued by the then unknown congressman from California, Richard M. Nixon. Hiss's trial and conviction for perjury (1950) aroused an ongoing debate and a voluminous literature. He was imprisoned from 1950 to 1954. In 1978, citing government documents newly available under the Freedom of Information Act, Hiss filed a petition to have his conviction overturned, but his plea was rejected by a federal judge in 1982. Some documents discovered in the 1990s seemed to indicate that Hiss was a spy, but a Russian general in charge of KGB and military-intelligence archives announced in 1992 that no evidence was found in the archives to indicate that Hiss was a Soviet agent. ▪ See his memoirs, *In the Court of Public Opinion* (1957) and *Recollections of a Life* (1988), and the informal biography by his son Tony Hiss, *Laughing Last* (1997). The study by John C. Smith (1976) supports Hiss's innocence while Allen Weinstein's *Perjury* (1978) claims that Hiss was guilty.

HITCHCOCK, SIR ALFRED JOSEPH (1899–1980), Anglo-American film director. A Jesuit-educated engineer, Hitchcock began writing silent-film titles in 1920 and directed his first film in 1925. By the 1930s he had developed the techniques of infusing everyday events with terror and of staging the predictable unpredictably that made him a master of the suspense thriller. Early Hitchcock suspense classics were *The Thirty-Nine Steps* (1935) and *The Lady Vanishes* (1938). In 1940 Hitchcock moved to Hollywood, where he directed *Rebecca* (1940) and *Rear Window* (1954), followed by two "chase" films, *To Catch a Thief* (1955) and *North by Northwest* (1959). From suspense Hitchcock progressed to outright terror with *Psycho* (1960). His later films included *The Birds* (1963), *Frenzy* (1972), and *Family Plot* (1976). He also produced, occasionally directed, and always introduced in a tantalizing manner his two American TV series, "Alfred Hitchcock Presents" (1955–62) and "The Alfred Hitchcock Hour" (1963–65). ■ See François Truffaut's book-length interview (rev. ed. 1985); John Russell Taylor, *Hitch* (1978); and Donald Spoto, *The Dark Side of Genius* (1983).

HITCHCOCK, THOMAS, JR. (1900–1944), U.S. polo player. Considered by many to be the greatest player in polo history, Hitchcock achieved a 10-goal rating, the highest handicap awarded, in all but one season from 1922 to 1940. He was on four U.S. National Open championship teams and led the U.S. team to five victories over Great Britain in Westchester Cup competition. A combat pilot, Hitchcock was a member of the Lafayette Escadrille during World War I and was killed in England during World War II while commanding a fighter group.

HITCHINGS, GEORGE H. (1905–1998), U.S. biochemist. Hitchings studied biochemistry at Harvard (Ph.D. 1933) and taught there and at Western Reserve University in Ohio before being hired by the Burroughs Wellcome pharmaceutical company (1942) to establish the firm's biochemistry department. He did research at the company until his retirement in 1975, but remained as an emeritus scientist until 1994. During a decades-long collaboration with Gertrude B. Elion, whom he hired in 1944, he designed drugs to destroy pathogens, disease-causing microorganisms, while leaving healthy cells unimpaired. Their pioneering methods, based on the chemical disruption of nucleic acid metabolism, enabled them to develop effective drugs for treating malaria (pyrimethamine), leukemia (thioguanine and 6-mercaptopurine), gout (allopurinol), urinary and respiratory infections (trimethoprim), viral herpes (acyclovir), and rheumatoid arthritis and other autoimmune disorders (azathioprine). The anti-AIDS drug AZT was based on their research. Hitchings shared the 1988 Nobel Prize in Physiology or Medicine with Elion and Sir James Black.

HITLER, ADOLF (1889–1945), German political leader. The son of an Austrian customs official, Hitler drifted to Vienna at age 18 to study art. After serving in the German army during World War I, he became the charismatic leader of the nationalistic, anti-Semitic, and anticommunist National Socialist (Nazi) party, spending nine months in prison for the abortive 1923 Munich "beer-hall putsch." In *Mein Kampf* (2 vols., 1925–26), which he wrote in prison, Hitler asserted the superiority of the "Aryan race," of which he considered the German people the leaders. He identified Germany's enemies as liberalism and Marxism, both, he claimed, directed by international Jewry, and asserted Germany's need for *Lebensraum*—territorial expansion. A mesmerizing orator, Hitler gained popularity as elements of German society sought scapegoats on which to blame their growing economic problems. Aided by leading industrialists, the Nazi party polled 6.5 million votes in 1930 and Hitler, its *führer* (leader), was appointed chancellor in 1933. He gradually eliminated all political opposition and assumed dictatorial powers. A vast building and rearmament program alleviated Germany's economic plight, and in 1938 Hitler began his search for empire, annexing Austria and the Czech Sudetenland. In 1939 he took the rest of Czechoslovakia and invaded Poland, precipitating World War II. Invasions of France (1940), the Low Countries (1940), and the Soviet Union (1941) enslaved whole nations and sent their Jewish populations—along with the Jews of Germany—to the "final solution" of the death camps. But the tide finally turned against Hitler, and in May 1945, with Allied armies at the gates of Berlin, he committed suicide. ■ See biographies by Alan Bullock (rev. ed. 1962), Joachim Fest (Eng. trans. 1974), John Toland (1976), and Ian Kershaw (2 vols., 1999, 2000); Eberhard Jäckel, *Hitler in History* (1985); Alvin H. Rosenfeld, *Imagining Hitler* (1985); and Ron Rosenbaum, *Explaining Hitler* (1998).

HJELMSLEV, LOUIS TROLLE (1899–1965), Danish linguist. A pioneer of structural linguistics, Hjelmslev founded the influential Linguistic Circle of Copenhagen (1931), cofounded the journal *Acta Linguistica* (1939), and taught at the University of Copenhagen (from 1937). Influenced by the work of Ferdinand de Saussure—the pioneer of semiotics—he developed the theory of glossematics, in which language was viewed as a symbolic system, and made major contributions to phonological and grammatical theory. His works included *Prolegomena to a Theory of Language* (1943; Eng. trans. rev. ed. 1961) and *Language: An Introduction* (Eng. trans. 1970).

HLINKA, ANDREJ (1864–1938), Slovak priest and political leader. A leader of the clerical Slovak People's party, Hlinka advocated Slovak autonomy during the 1920s and 1930s. He frequently attacked the Czech government for not granting Slovakia a separate parliament. The Germans used his party to help dismember Czechoslovakia (1938), and his deputy, Jozef Tiso, became the president of the German puppet state of Slovakia (1939). ■ See Yeshayahu Jelinek, *The Parish Republic* (1976).

HOARE, SAMUEL JOHN, 1st VISCOUNT TEMPLE-WOOD (1880–1959), British political leader. A history scholar from Oxford, Hoare was elected to the House of Commons in 1910 as a Conservative. During the interwar period he served as secretary of state for air (1922–29), secretary of state for India (1931–35), and foreign secretary (1935). He was forced to resign as foreign secretary after revelation of the secret Hoare-Laval Pact (1935) that would have surrendered Ethiopian territory to Italy, and he was subsequently known as an appeaser. He later went to Spain (1940–44) as a special ambassador and was instrumental in securing Spanish neutrality during World War II. Hoare wrote several memoirs, including *Ambassador on Special Mission* (1946) and *Nine Troubled Years* (1954).

HOBBS, JACK (Sir John Berry Hobbs; 1882–1963), British cricket player. The Surrey opening batsman (1905–35), Hobbs held the record for the most runs scored (61,237) in first-class matches, exceeded 2,000 runs in a season 17 times, and completed 197 centuries. As a professional (1905–37, excluding the war years), he played for the All-England team in 61 test matches—the world series of cricket. He had a long opening partnership with cricketer Herbert Sutcliffe (1894–1978). The greatest and most popular batsman in cricket history, Hobbs was the first cricket player to be knighted (1953). After he retired, he ran a sports shop.

HOBBY, OVETA CULP (1905–1995), U.S. public official. A graduate of the University of Texas Law School, Hobby served as the first woman parliamentarian of the Texas House of Representatives (1926–31). After her marriage to William Pettus Hobby (1931), former Texas governor and publisher of the *Houston Post*, she joined the newspaper and became its editor in 1938. During World War II she helped develop plans for a women's auxiliary army corps, later called the Women's Army Corps (WAC), and directed it from 1942 to 1945. Active in national Republican politics, she was named the first head of the Department of Health, Education, and Welfare by Pres. Dwight Eisenhower (1953), thus becoming the second woman to serve in a cabinet post. She resigned in 1955 to direct the *Post* as president and editor.

HOBHOUSE, LEONARD TRELAWNY (1864–1929), British sociologist. Rejecting the turn-of-the-century vogues of laissez-faire and social Darwinism, Hobhouse worked as a journalist, labor arbitrator, and professor of sociology at the University of London (1907–29) to reconcile the conflicting claims of individualism and collectivism. His *Morals in Evolution* (1906) was a wide survey of historical data indicating progress in the harmonious organization of social

life. In *Liberalism* (1911), Hobhouse advocated a form of "liberal socialism." He also wrote *Elements of Social Justice* (1923) and *Social Development* (1924). ■ See study by John E. Owen (1975).

HOBSBAWM, ERIC JOHN (1917–), British historian. Hobsbawm was born in Alexandria, Egypt, educated in Vienna, Berlin, London, and Cambridge, and taught at Cambridge and at the University of London (1970–82). A prominent Marxist scholar, he was an authority on the history of the working classes, archaic social movements, and modern European history. His books included a notable four-volume history of the modern world, *The Age of Revolution: Europe, 1789–1848* (1962), *The Age of Capital, 1848–1875* (1975), *The Age of Empire, 1875–1914* (1987), and *The Age of Extremes: A History of the World, 1914–1991* (1994). His other books included *Primitive Rebels* (1959), *Labouring Men* (1964), *Bandits* (1964), *Nations and Nationalism Since 1780* (1990), *The Invention of Tradition* (1992), and *Uncommon People: Resistence, Rebellion and Jazz* (1998).

HOBSON, JOHN ATKINSON (1858–1940), British economist. Hobson was a popular lecturer and prolific author who was concerned with the reform of capitalism, which he viewed as essential if the problems of unequal distribution of wealth and monopoly control were to be solved. In *Imperialism* (1902), a work that influenced Marxist thinkers, he attributed the rise of the new imperialism of the late 19th century to the economics of the capitalist system. His other works included *The Physiology of Industry* (1889), *The Evolution of Modern Capitalism* (1894; rev. ed. 1926), *The Economics of Unemployment* (1922), *Wealth and Life* (1930), *Poverty and Plenty* (1931), and the autobiographical *Confessions of an Economic Heretic* (1938). ■ See John Allett, *New Liberalism* (1981).

HOCHHUTH, ROLF (1931–), German dramatist. Born into a middle-class Protestant family, Hochhuth studied history and philosophy at Heidelberg and Munich (1952–55) and worked as an editor before the publication and simultaneous production (Berlin) of his play *The Deputy* (1963; Eng. trans. 1964). Accusing Pope Pius XII of refusing to speak out against the Nazi genocide of the Jews during World War II, the play aroused controversy throughout the world, inspired a debate on moral and historical responsibility, and initiated the trend of documentary theater in Europe. Hochhuth's subsequent works continued to probe controversial moral and political issues through a mixture of fact and fiction. Best known are the play *Soldiers* (1967; Eng. trans. 1968) and the novel *A German Love Story* (1978; Eng. trans. 1980). *Tell '38* (1979; Eng. trans. 1984) is a short biography of Maurice Bavaud, a Swiss divinity student who attempted to assassinate Nazi leader Adolf Hitler in 1938. ■ See study by Margaret E. Ward (1977).

HO CHI MINH (Nguyen That Thanh; 1890–1969), Vietnamese political leader. Ho was born into a family involved in the anti-French nationalist movement. He lived abroad after 1911, settling in France (1917), where he petitioned for Vietnamese independence at the Paris Peace Conference following World War I (1919) and helped establish the French Communist party (1920). After studying in Moscow (1923–24) he became a Comintern agent in China, organized the Vietnamese nationalist movement, and founded the Indochinese Communist party (1930). At the outbreak of World War II he organized the Vietminh independence movement, led raids against the Japanese, and proclaimed the Democratic Republic of Vietnam in Hanoi (1945). The French return to Vietnam to reclaim the colony led to an eight-year war (1946–54) that resulted in French withdrawal and the division of Vietnam, with Ho serving as president of communist-dominated North Vietnam (1954–69). After 1959 he supported the Viet Cong guerrilla movement against the U.S-backed government of South Vietnam. However, he did not live to see the realization of his dream, in 1975, of a united independent Vietnam under communist rule. In his later years he personified the Vietnamese struggle and became a symbol of the unification of Marxism and revolutionary nationalism. His translated works included *On Revolution: Selected Writings, 1920–1966* (1967) and *Selected Works* (4 vols., 1960–62). ■ See biographies by Jean Lacouture (1967; Eng. trans. 1968), David Halberstam (1971), and William J. Duiker (2000).

HOCKING, WILLIAM ERNEST (1873–1966), U.S. philosopher. Hocking was raised in the Midwest as a strict Methodist and studied at Harvard (Ph.D. 1904), where he was influenced by Josiah Royce and William James. He taught there from 1914 to 1943. His philosophical writings, classified by some as "objective realism," dealt primarily with questions of religion. However, he was also deeply concerned with contemporary problems and wrote several books on world politics, education, the cold war, and freedom of the press. His best-known works included *The Meaning of God in Human Experience* (1912), *Man and the State* (1926), *The Coming World Civilization* (1956), and *The Meaning of Immortality in Human Experience* (1957). ■ See John Howie and Leroy Rouner, eds., *The Wisdom of William Ernest Hocking* (1978); Leroy Rouner, *Within Human Experience* (1969); and Robert B. Thigpen, *Liberty and Community* (1973).

HOCKNEY, DAVID (1937–), British artist. Hockney held his first one-man show in 1963, soon after leaving the Royal College of Art. He traveled extensively in the United States, where he completed a number of etchings entitled *Rake's Progress* (1963), inspired by his adventures in New York. He also painted a series of swimming pool pictures in Southern California. He taught at the University of California (1966–67). Hockney's style evolved from "pop" to realism to a "new cubism" in the 1980s, and his works were accorded important exhibitions in Europe and the United States. He also designed sets for several operas, produced a book of photomontages, *Cameraworks* (1984), and created abstract computer graphics. ■ See his autobiography (1977) and his *That's the Way I See It* (1993) and studies by Marco Livingstone (1981) and Peter Clothier (1995).

HODGKIN, SIR ALAN LLOYD (1914–1998), British physiologist. Educated at Cambridge, Hodgkin taught there as assistant director of research (1945–52), Foulerton research professor of the Royal Society (1952–69) and professor of biophysics (1970–81). He began (1935) to investigate the mechanism of nerve conduction and in 1949 he proved, with Bernard Katz, that the action potential of nerves is generated by an increase in the permeability of the cell membrane to sodium ions, enabling an exchange of sodium and potassium ions between the nerve cell and its surrounding solution. This process was further analyzed by Hodgkin and his student, Andrew F. Huxley, who devised a system of measuring the transmission of nerve impulses. For this research, Hodgkin shared the 1963 Nobel Prize in Physiology or Medicine with Huxley and John C. Eccles. ■ See his *Conduction of the Nervous Impulse* (1964) and *Chance and Design: Reminiscences of Science in Peace and War* (1992).

HODGKIN, DOROTHY CROWFOOT (1910–1994), British chemist. Born in Cairo, Egypt, Hodgkin was educated at Oxford (1928–31) and Cambridge (1932–34) and taught at Oxford (1934–77). A noted crystallographer, she made the first X-ray diffraction photograph of a protein (pepsin; 1933) and studied the structure of sterols (1934), penicillin (1942–49), cholesterol iodide (1945), and insulin (1969). For her elucidation of the structure of vitamin B_{12}, the complex molecule that is essential for building red blood cells and treating pernicious anemia, she won the 1964 Nobel Prize in Chemistry. She later served as chancellor of Bristol University (1970–88). ■ See study by Georgina Ferry (1998).

HOFFA, JAMES RIDDLE (1913–1975?), U.S. labor leader. Jimmy Hoffa was a grocery warehouseman in 1931 when he joined the International Brotherhood of Teamsters union, then a series of disorganized locals. He organized, centralized, and—elected president in 1957—negotiated the union's first national contract in 1964. He was investigated for several years by U.S. Attorney General Robert F. Kennedy and he was convicted of jury tampering, fraud, and looting pension funds (1964), and he served four years in prison (1967–71) before Pres. Richard Nixon commuted his sentence. He resigned as union president in 1971. Hoffa was attempting to resume control of his 2-million-member union (in violation of his parole) when he disappeared, presumably murdered. ■ See his autobiographies, *The Trials of Jimmy Hoffa* (1970) and *Hoffa: The Real Story* (1975); Walter Sheridan, *The Rise and Fall of Jimmy Hoffa* (1972); Dan Moldea, *The Hoffa Wars* (1978); and study by Arthur A. Sloane (1991).

HOFFMAN, ABBIE (Abbott Hoffman; 1936–1989), U.S. radical activist. Hoffman studied psychology at Brandeis (B.A. 1959) and at the University of Calfornia, Berkeley (M.A. 1960) and participated in the civil-rights movement in the early 1960s. He was the merry prankster of the anti-Vietnam War movement, staging absurdist antics to dramatize the evil of the conflict. Widely recognized as a spokesperson for the counterculture during the 1960s, he organized "happenings" and "be ins" and founded the anarchist Youth International Party, or Yippies (1968). He was indicted, as one of the Chicago 7, for conspiracy to incite a riot at the 1968 Democratic National Convention in Chicago. His conviction was overturned on appeal, but in 1974 he went underground to avoid trial on cocaine possession charges. He surrendered to authorities in 1980 and revealed that he had undergone plastic surgery and had lived (from 1976) in conservative upstate New York. There, as "Barry Freed," he was a leader of an environmental and antinuclear crusade and had testified before a U.S. Senate committee, had been commended by the governor of New York, and had been appointed to a federal commission. After serving a sentence in a work-release program (1981–82), he resumed his political work and supported himself mainly through public speaking. His books included *Revolution for the Hell of It* (1968), *Steal This Book* (1971), *Square Dancing in the Ice Age: Underground Writings* (1982), and *Steal This Urine Test* (1987; with Jonathan Silvers). ■ See his memoirs, *Soon to Be a Major Motion Picture* (1980); Jack Hoffman, *Run, Run, Run* (1994); and Larry Sloman, *Steal This Dream* (1998).

HOFFMAN, DUSTIN (1937–), U.S. actor. Born in Los Angeles, where his father handled props at a film studio, Hoffman studied acting at the Pasadena Playhouse and with Lee Strasberg in New York. At age 30, he was spotted by Mike Nichols, who cast him in *The Graduate* (1967). His natural vulnerability impressed critics and the public, and numerous offers came his way. Choosing roles carefully, Hoffman appeared in such films as *Midnight Cowboy* (1969), *Little Big Man* (1971), *Lenny* (1974), and *All the President's Men* (1976). He won an Academy Award for his performance as a divorced father in *Kramer vs. Kramer* (1979), and rose to superstardom with his comic portrayal of a man and a woman in *Tootsie* (1982). Known more for versatility than glamour, Hoffman achieved star status with character acting. He won a second Academy Award for his performance in *Rainman* (1988). His later films included *Billy Bathgate* (1991) and *Wag the Dog* (1997). He appeared on Broadway in *Death of a Salesman* (1984), which was also produced for television (1985). ■ See Douglas Brode, *The Films of Dustin Hoffman* (1983) and study by Ronald Bergan (1991).

HOFFMAN, MALVINA CORNELL (1885–1966), U.S. sculptor. The daughter of a pianist with the New York Philharmonic, Hoffman was encouraged to pursue her artistic goals and studied with Gutzon Borglum and Auguste Rodin. She created fountains, statues, and architectural sculpture as well as finely detailed portrait sculpture of several celebrities, including dancer Anna Pavlova and pianist Ignace Paderewski. Her most ambitious creation was *Races of Mankind,* a series of 110 lifesize figures commissioned by the Field Museum of Natural History in Chicago (1930). Her other works included *The Sacrifice* (1922), a war memorial at Harvard University; the American War Memorial at Épinal, France (1948), and 13 bas-relief panels for the Joslin Clinic in Boston (1956). She wrote *Sculpture Inside and Out* (1939) and two autobiographical works, *Heads and Tales* (1936) and *Yesterday Is Tomorrow* (1965).

HOFFMAN, SAMUEL KURTZ (1902–1995), U.S. propulsion engineer. Associated with North American Aviation, which later became Rockwell International (1949–70), Hoffman developed a 75,000-pound-thrust rocket engine (1949) that boosted the Navaho intercontinental missile. The following year he developed the prototype of the rocket that launched the first U.S. satellite and the first crewed space flights. His rockets also powered the Atlas, Thor, and Jupiter missiles that were deployed throughout the country. He later served as president of his company's Rocketdyne Division (1960–70), and he headed the team that developed the cluster of eight rocket engines for the multistaged Saturn 5 vehicle, which ultimately carried American astronauts to the moon.

HOFFMANN, JOSEF (1870–1956), Austrian architect. As a founder-member of the Vienna Secession (1897) and Wiener Werkstätte (workshops devoted to crafts development, 1903), Hoffmann was instrumental in introducing and continuing art nouveau in Austria. His style employed contrasting black-and-white cubic volumes, and his architectural reputation was gained by his Pukersdorf Sanatorium (1903–04), noted for its simple white-stucco form. Called Hoffmann's masterpiece, the Stoclet House (Brussels, 1905–11) was an asymmetrical design in marble with a copper roof and bronze ridges. He was city architect of Vienna (from 1920) and designed the Austrian pavilion for the 1934 Venice Biennale. He devoted his later years to the design of inexpensive working-class housing. ■ See study by Eduard F. Sekler (1985).

HOFFMANN, ROALD (1937–), Polish-born U.S. chemist. A Holocaust survivor, Hoffmann emigrated to the United States in 1949. He received a Ph.D. in chemical physics from Harvard (1962) and taught at Cornell University (from 1965). In collaboration with Robert B. Woodward, he developed (1965) rules of orbital symmetry by applying principles of quantum theory to chemical behavior. His research, showing that wave and orbital motion of electrons have a primary effect on chemical reactions, enabled scientists to predict the feasibility and results of many laboratory experiments in the areas of medical and industrial research. Hoffmann shared the 1981 Nobel Prize in Chemistry with

Japanese chemist Kenichi Fukui, who independently developed an orbital theory in the 1950s.

HOFMANN, HANS (1880–1966), German-born U.S. painter. Hofmann was a successful and internationally known art teacher in Munich before emigrating to the United States (1930). In 1934 he established an art school in New York and through his effect on younger artists was influential in the growth of abstract expressionism as the dominant style of the late 1940s and 1950s. Hofmann was known particularly for his use of vibrant color. His influential writings were collected in *Search for the Real,* edited by Sara T. Weeks and Bartlett H. Hayes, Jr. (1948; rev. ed. 1967). ■ See studies by Clement Greenberg (1961) and Cynthia Goodman (1986).

HOFMANN, JOSEF (1876–1957), Polish-born U.S. pianist. Born in Cracow, Hofmann was a child prodigy who made his piano debut at age 6. At 11 he made a sensational debut at the Metropolitan Opera House in New York, followed by a grueling U.S. tour that was interrupted by the Society for Prevention of Cruelty to Children. Hofmann then retired for six years of study, including two years as Anton Rubinstein's only pupil. At age 18 he resumed his concert career by revisiting the scenes of his earlier triumphs. Hofmann was renowned for his free, romantic style, and was acclaimed for his performances of the works of Chopin and Liszt. He became a U.S. citizen (1926) and directed the Curtis Institute of Music in Philadelphia (1926–38). He published several books on piano playing and also wrote compositions for piano under the pseudonym Michel Dvorsky.

HOFMANNSTHAL, HUGO VON (1874–1929), Austrian writer. A precocious literary genius, Hofmannsthal published the first of his impressionistic lyrical poems and verse plays in Vienna at age 16. After renouncing purely lyrical forms in his famous essay *The Letter of Lord Chandos* (1902; Eng. trans. 1952), he turned to the theater and wrote such works as *The Play of Everyman* (1911; Eng. trans. 1917), *The Difficult Man* (1921; Eng. trans. 1963), *The Salzburg Great Theater of the World* (1922; Eng. trans. 1963), and *The Tower* (1924; rev. ed. 1927; Eng. trans. 1963). A representative of the humanistic tradition of European culture who dwelled on such themes as community, reconciliation, and ethical responsibility, he never fully adjusted to the demise of the aristocracy after World War I. His works were frequently performed at the Salzburg Festival, which he cofounded with theatrical director and producer Max Reinhardt (1920). He was best known for the librettos to the operas *Elektra* (1906), *Der Rosenkavalier* (1912), *Ariadne auf Naxos* (1912), *Die Frau ohne Schatten* (1919), *Die ägyptische Helena* (1928), and *Arabella* (1933), which were set to music by Richard Strauss. ■ See the English translations of his work in *Selected Prose* (1952), *Poems and Verse Plays* (1961), and *Selected Plays and Libretti* (1963) and study by Lowell A. Bangerter (1977).

HOFSTADTER, RICHARD (1916–1970), U.S. historian. Hofstadter earned his Ph.D. from Columbia (1942) with a thesis published as *Social Darwinism in American Thought* (1944) and served on the Columbia faculty (1946–70). He was a fluent writer on the intellectual, social, and political history of the United States, and his works—*The American Political Tradition* (1948) and the Pulitzer Prize-winning *Age of Reform* (1955) and *Anti-Intellectualism in American Life* (1963)—reflected his liberalism as well as his skeptical views of U.S. politics. They enjoyed popular as well as academic acclaim. ■ See Stanley Elkins and Eric McKitrick, *The Hofstadter Aegis* (1974), and Susan S. Baker, *Radical Beginnings* (1985).

HOFSTADTER, ROBERT (1915–1990), U.S. physicist. In 1950 Hofstadter joined the faculty of Stanford University, where a large linear accelerator was being built. He devised experiments using this instrument that would allow him to study the arrangement of protons and neutrons in nuclei. By analogy with earlier investigations of molecular and atomic structure, Hofstadter trained an intense beam of monoenergetic electrons at the nuclei, then studied the number of electrons scattered at various angles. He later (1954) applied this method to the study of the proton and neutron, which he discovered to be complex and not, as had been thought, pointlike or "elementary" structures. He evaluated their sizes and magnetic moment and determined their electromagnetic "form factors"—technical quantities that characterize how the particles interact with other particles and fields. For this work Hofstadter shared the 1961 Nobel Prize in Physics with Rudolph Mössbauer. He headed Stanford's High Energy Physics Laboratory (1967–74).

HOGAN, BEN (William Benjamin Hogan; 1912–1997), U.S. golfer. One of golf's greatest players, Hogan dominated the game throughout the late 1940s and early 1950s. He won the U.S. Open four times (1948, 1950, 1951, 1953), the U.S. Masters twice, the U.S. Professional Golfers' Association tourney twice, and the British Open. In 1949, at the peak of his career, Hogan was critically injured in a car accident; he returned to the fairways 11 months later and went on to win 11 major tournaments in 1951. A film about his life, *Follow the Sun,* was made in 1951. ■ See biography by Gene Gregston (1978).

HOKINSON, HELEN ELNA (1893–1949), U.S. cartoonist. Helen Hokinson's satiric drawings of middle-aged society matrons, matinee-goers, shoppers, and ladies' club members appeared in the *New Yorker* from the magazine's inception (1925). She supplied the illustration; captions were written by her collaborator James Reid Parker or by gag writer Richard McAllister. When Hokinson died in a plane crash, newspapers mourned the loss of her astringent vision of leisured Americans. Books featuring her drawings included *My Best Girls* (1941), *There Are Ladies Present* (1952), and

The Hokinson Festival (1956). *The Ladies, God Bless 'Em!* (1950) contains a memoir by Parker.

HOLAN, VLADIMIR (1905–1980), Czech poet and translator. Born in Prague, Holan was associated, in the early 1920s, with the poetist school of pure poetry that stressed fantasy and free association. The poetry collections he published in the decades between the world wars reflected metaphysical concerns; after World War II, he wrote in a more realistic vein, but he clashed with the Stalinist regime that came to power in 1948 and did not publish poetry for more than a decade, producing instead translations and books for children. He reemerged in the 1960s as a leading poet of his generation; his melancholic free verse, expressing his sense of alienation, won acclaim at home and abroad. *A Night with Hamlet* (1964; Eng. trans. 1980), a long, meditative poem written in the 1950s, is widely regarded as his finest work. *Selected Poems* (1971) is a selection of his work in English. ▪ See A. French, *The Poets of Prague* (1969).

HOLIDAY, BILLIE (Eleanora Fagan; 1915–1959), U.S. jazz singer. The daughter of an unwed African-American domestic, Holiday began singing professionally in Harlem nightclubs in 1930 and made her first record in 1933. In the mid-1930s she toured as a vocalist with the bands of Benny Goodman, Artie Shaw, and Count Basie and became recognized as a major jazz artist. Her records, notably "Strange Fruit," "Fine and Mellow," and "Them There Eyes," became international hits, and she began a highly successful solo career in 1940. Known as "Lady Day" and the "first lady of the blues," she possessed an incomparable voice and was known for her dramatic intensity and highly individual phrasing and intonation. The last few years of her life were marked by personal tragedies, including an addiction to heroin that ruined her career and led to her death. ▪ See her autobiography, *Lady Sings the Blues* (1956); John Chilton, *Billie's Blues* (1975); and biography by Stuart Nicholson (1995).

HOLLEY, ROBERT WILLIAM (1922-1993), U.S. biochemist. Trained at Cornell University (Ph.D. 1947), Holley worked there for two decades, then became a fellow of the Salk Institute in California (1966–93). After working on the team that synthesized penicillin during World War II, Holley focused his research on the basic biochemical mechanisms and substances that govern genetic inheritance. He elucidated the structure of the chainlike RNA (ribonucleic acid) molecule and demonstrated how transfer-RNA functions. For this work he shared with Har Gobind Khorana and Marshall W. Nirenberg the 1968 Nobel Prize in Physiology or Medicine.

HOLM, HANYA (Johanna Eckert; 1893–1992), German-born U.S. dancer and choreographer. One of the pioneers of modern dance, Holm performed with Mary Wigman's company in Germany during the 1920s and directed the Wigman School in New York (1931–36) before opening her own studio there in 1936. Among her students were Alwin Nikolais, Valerie Bettis, and Glen Tetley. Though basically abstract, many of her works, notably *Trend* (1937), *Metropolitan Daily* (1938), and *Tragic Exodus* (1939), alluded to contemporary events. She also choreographed the popular Broadway musicals *Kiss Me Kate* (1948), *My Fair Lady* (1956), and *Camelot* (1960) and staged the world premiere of the opera *Ballad of Baby Doe* (1956). ▪ See biography by Walter Sorell (1969).

HOLMAN, NAT (1896–1995), U.S. basketball player and coach. One of the greatest players of all time, Holman, known as "Mr. Basketball," was the star of the original Celtics, the professional team that was considered to be the finest in the early history of the sport. A playmaking artist, excellent dribbler and passer, and accurate shooter, he was one of the first to average in double figures and led the Celtics to a 720–75 record (1921–28). He won 421 games as a coach of the City College of New York (1920–52; 1955–56; 1959–60), and his 1950 squad won both the National Invitational Tournament and National Collegiate Athletic Association championships. In 1951, after several of his star players were arrested for point shaving in college basketball's biggest scandal, Holman was suspended, although he denied any knowledge of his players' wrongdoing. He was subsequently vindicated and was reinstated as coach.

HOLMES, ARTHUR (1890–1965), British geologist. A pioneer in geochronology, Holmes was the first to use radioactive measurements to determine the age of rocks; he eventually concluded that the earth was at least 4.5 billion years old. He refuted the theory that the earth was contracting and advocated a theory of alternating cycles of expansion and contraction to explain movements of the earth's crust. Holmes was one of the first scientists to support the continental-drift theory and the first to propose the existence of convection currents in the mantle of the earth. He taught at Durham (1924–43) and Edinburgh (1943–56) Universities. His textbook, *Principles of Physical Geology* (1944), is considered a classic in the field.

HOLMES, (ELIAS) BURTON (1870–1958), U.S. travel lecturer and filmmaker. World-traveler Burton Holmes delivered more than 8,000 travel lectures throughout the United States during a career that lasted more than 50 years. The father of the "travelogue," Holmes was the first person to illustrate his talks with motion pictures, and his travel films produced for Paramount Pictures (1915–21) were the longest-running shorts in movie history. He made six round-the-world trips before his 1950 retirement. Holmes was interested in photographing beautiful scenery and showing pleasant aspects of foreign countries. His most popular films were on the Panama Canal, Russia, Mexico, Paris, and Oberammergau. ▪ See his autobiography, *The World Is Mine* (1953), and the collection of pictures and writings *Burton Holmes* (1977).

HOLMES, JOHN HAYNES (1879–1964), U.S. clergyman. Holmes studied at Harvard Divinity School. Ordained as a Unitarian minister, he was assigned (1907) to the Community Church in New York, where he remained for 42 years. A compassionate and dynamic social reformer, he became a vice president of the National Association for the Advancement of Colored People (NAACP) in 1909 and was a moving spirit behind the formation of the American Civil Liberties Union (ACLU) in 1917. A pacifist, Holmes was investigated for sedition during World War I. He left the Unitarian fold (1919) and renamed his congregation the Community Church of New York to express the "unity of all men in the spirit." During World War II, his church was a center for conscientious objectors. He wrote several books, including a two-volume study, *My Gandhi* (1953). *A Summons unto Men* (1971) is an anthology of his writings. ■ See his autobiography, *I Speak for Myself* (1959), and Carl Hermann Voss, *Rabbi and Minister: The Friendship of Stephen S. Wise and Jon Haynes Holmes* (1980).

HOLMES, OLIVER WENDELL, JR. (1841–1935), U.S. jurist and legal scholar. Considered by many to be one of the greatest justices of the Supreme Court, Holmes played a major role in the development of U.S. constitutional law. A graduate of Harvard Law School (1866), he was a professor of law at Harvard (1873–82) and a justice of the Massachusetts Supreme Court (1882–1902) before being appointed to the U.S. Supreme Court by Pres. Theodore Roosevelt (1902). He retired in 1932. Called the "Great Dissenter," Holmes, unlike most of his colleagues on the court, believed that the law should not be narrowly interpreted as it should serve the contemporary human needs of a changing society. A humanist and libertarian, he advocated free expression and dissent and upheld laws that allowed the Congress to regulate economic activity. His writings are in *Speeches* (1891; rev. ed, 1934) and *Collected Legal Papers* (1920). ■ See Felix Frankfurter, *Mr. Justice Holmes and the Supreme Court* (1938); Catherine Bowen, *Yankee from Olympus* (1944); biography by Sheldon M. Novick, *Honorable Justice* (1989); and Albert W. Altschule, *Law Without Values* (2000).

HOLST, GUSTAV THEODORE (1874–1934), British composer. Holst, descended from professional musicians, played symphony trombone and enjoyed a long career as a teacher. His romantic music, influenced by the English folk-song revival as well as contemporary European innovations, was never quite in fashion, but he won respect for his *St. Paul's Suite* for strings (1913), the orchestral suite *The Planets* (1916), his opera *The Perfect Fool* (1921), and the *Choral Symphony* (1925). ■ See biography by Imogen Holst (2nd ed. 1969) and studies by Michael Short (1990) and Paul Holmes (1997).

HOLT, HAROLD EDWARD (1908–1967), Australian political leader. Holt was born in Sydney and practiced law until his election to Parliament (1935). A founder of the Liberal party (1944) and a political protégé of Robert Menzies, he held several cabinet posts in Prime Minister Menzies' administrations (minister of labor, 1940–41, 1949–58; minister of immigration, 1949–56; treasurer, 1958–66). As prime minister (1966–67), he supported U.S. foreign policy, sent Australian troops to Vietnam to combat communism, and eased, somewhat, barriers against immigration of Asians. He died in 1967 in a swimming accident. ■ See Dame Zara Holt, *My Life and Harry* (1968).

HOLT, LUTHER EMMETT (1855–1924), U.S. pediatrician and educator. A specialist in children's diseases, Holt directed the Babies Hospital of New York (1888–90), the first hospital of its kind in the United States, and was professor of diseases of children at New York Polyclinic (1890–1901). His book *The Care and Feeding of Children* (1894), written for the use of mothers in the home, was the most successful medical book published up to that time and was reprinted 75 times. Holt's *The Diseases of Infancy and Childhood* (1896) became the standard text in the field and remained so for decades. During his tenure as professor of pediatrics at Columbia University's College of Physicians and Surgeons (1901–21), he exerted a profound influence on the development of pediatrics as a specialized field of medicine and was a member of numerous organizations dedicated to the promotion of children's health. ■ See biography by R. L. Duffus and L. Emmett Holt, Jr. (1940).

HOLUB, MIROSLAV (1923–1998), Czech poet and immunologist. Holub studied at Charles University (M.D. 1953), then earned a Ph.D. (1958) in immunology at Prague's Institute of Microbiology, where he was a researcher (1954–65; 1968–71). After 1972 he worked at the Institute for Clinical and Experimental Medicine. He considered himself a scientist first, a poet second, and published more than 100 papers on cellular immunology. He was best known, however, for cerebral poetry characterized by the precise use of language and by metaphors drawn from the realm of science. Although his witty and ironic poems were never overtly political, they were banned for many years by the Communist government. Several collections of Holub's poetry are available in English translation, including *Selected Poems* (1967), *Although* (1971), *Notes of a Clay Pigeon* (1977), *Sagittal Section* (1980), *Interferon: or, On Theater* (1982), *Poems Before and After* (1990), and *Intensive Care* (1996). His essays appeared in *The Dimension of the Present Moment* (1990) and *Shedding Life: Disease, Politics and Other Human Conditions* (1997).

HOLYOAKE, SIR KEITH JACKA (1904–1983), New Zealand political leader. Holyoake was a farmer from 1917 to 1932, when he was elected, as the youngest member, to Parliament as a representative of the National party. Defeated in 1938, he returned to farming until his reelection in 1943. Holyoake rose quickly to be deputy prime minister and minister of agriculture in 1949; he served as prime minister for three months in 1957. He was subsequently leader of the opposition from 1957 to 1960 and prime minister and minister of foreign affairs from 1960 to 1972. Holyoake's administration was marked by his conservatism, anticommunism, and strong support of the Southeast Asia Treaty Organization (SEATO) and the U.S. war policies in Vietnam. He negotiated favorable trading terms for New Zealand when its markets were threatened after Britain joined the Common Market. He later served as governor-general (1977–80).

HOMMA, MASAHARU (1887?–1946), Japanese general. Homma, who had served in India and as a military attaché in London (1930), commanded Japanese forces in Tientsin, China (1939). He led the World War II Japanese invasion of the Philippines in December 1941, herding the surviving U.S. and Filipino prisoners in what became known as the Bataan death march. Of the 70,000 troops that surrendered to Homma (April 1942), 17,000 died during the nine-day, 75-mile march to a railroad line. After the war he was tried, convicted, and executed for war crimes.

HONDA, SOICHIRO (1906–1991), Japanese businessman. Starting out as a garage mechanic, Honda founded a company (1948) that used army surplus parts and ingenuity to become the world's largest manufacturer of motorcycles. During the 1960s he expanded into small economy cars, another successful undertaking. An unconventional tycoon who preferred the machine shop to the boardroom, Honda also acquired a fleet of ships in which to export his products. He was president of the company until 1973, and remained on its board of directors until 1983, when he became a "supreme adviser."

HONECKER, ERICH (1912–1994), East German political leader. Son of a communist coal miner in the Saar, Honecker was active in the communist youth movement. Convicted by the Nazis of treasonous activities, he spent ten years in Brandenburg prison (1935–45). After World War II he worked with East Germany's paramilitary youth groups (1946–55) and studied for two years in the Soviet Union. He returned home to become a member of the party secretariat (1958) and head of security. He was regarded as a protégé of party leader Walter Ulbricht, whom he succeeded (1971) as party secretary-general and head of national defense. He continued his predecessor's policies of close ties to the Soviet Union, hostility to the West, and severe domestic repression, while presiding over a strong government-controlled industrial economy. The policies of openness and economic restructuring in the Soviet Union during the late 1980s led to unrest and calls for reform in East Germany, and Honecker was forced out of office in 1989. After German reunification (1990) he was charged with ordering the killing of East Germans trying to escape over the Berlin Wall. However, he was too ill to stand trial and he died in exile in Chile. ■ See his memoirs, *From My Life* (Eng. trans. 1980), and biography by Heinz Lippmann (Eng. trans. 1972).

HONEGGER, ARTHUR (1892–1955), French-Swiss composer. Born in France of German-Swiss parentage, Honegger studied at the Paris Conservatory and became a member of the antiromantic group "The Six." The most accessible of the group, he strove to write comprehensibly without banality. In addition to his dramatic oratorios *King David* (1923) and *Joan of Arc at the Stake* (1938), he wrote five symphonies, chamber music, operas, and 40 film scores. ■ See his *I Am a Composer* (Eng. trans. 1966) and study by Harry Halbreich (Eng. trans. 1999).

HOOD, RAYMOND MATTHEWSON (1881–1934), U.S. architect. Hood studied at the Massachusetts Institute of Technology (1903) and at the École des Beaux Arts in Paris. In collaboration with J. M. Howells he submitted a neo-Gothic design that won the international competition for the Chicago Tribune Building in 1922. Best known for his New York City skyscrapers, he designed (with J. André Fouilhoux) the McGraw-Hill Building (1930–31) and the Daily News Building (1930). His last big assignment was as a consultant on the Rockefeller Center complex in New York City, which used his slab design. ■ See studies by Walter H. Kilham, Jr. (1974), and Raymond Hood (1982).

HOOK, SIDNEY (1902–1989), U.S. philosopher and social critic. A student and biographer (1939) of John Dewey and professor at New York University (1927–72), Hook was involved in public controversy for decades. He wrote *Towards the Understanding of Karl Marx* (1933) and was close to the Communist party during the early 1930s but became an intellectual leader of the anticommunist left later in the decade and was known as a passionate defender of freedom in his subsequent scholarly works and political and cultural activities. He advocated conservative defense and foreign-policy views during the 1960s and 1970s and vigorously opposed preferential hiring and affirmative-action quotas for minorities. His other well-known books were *The Hero in History* (1943), *Marx and the Marxists* (1955), *The Paradoxes of Freedom* (1962), *From Hegel to Marx* (1968), and *Pragmatism and the Tragic Sense of Life* (1974). ■ See his autobiography, *Out of Step* (1987); Christopher Phelps, *Young Sidney Hook* (1997); and studies edited by Paul Kurtz (1968; 1983).

HOOKER, EVELYN (Evelyn Gentry; 1907–1996), U.S. psychologist. Hooker studied at Johns Hopkins University (Ph.D. 1932) and taught psychology at the University of California at Los Angeles (1939–1970). Her pioneering study of male homosexuals, begun in the 1940s and published in 1957 as *The Adjustment of the Male Overt Homosexual*, demonstrated that there was no measurable psychological difference between heterosexual and homosexual men and challenged the prevailing beliefs that homosexuality was an abnormality or mental illness. Her controversial report encouraged the fledgling gay rights movement and helped to legitimize homosexuality as a field of study. It also led the

American Psychiatric Association to remove homosexuality from its list of mental disorders (1973). Hooker chaired the National Institute of Mental Health's Task Force on Homosexuality (1967), which recommended a repeal of sodomy laws and advocated better public education about homosexuality.

HOOTON, EARNEST ALBERT (1887–1954), U.S. anthropologist. On the Harvard faculty from 1913 to 1954, Hooton was a pioneer in the systematic presentation of physical anthropology in the United States, and he exerted a great influence on the field for decades. He was especially interested in human evolution and racial classification, and his major early works included studies of prehistoric populations of the Canary Islands (1925) and of pueblos near Pecos, New Mexico (1930). *The American Criminal* (1939) and *Crime and Man* (1939) were controversial studies linking body traits and racial factors to criminal behavior. His widely read popular books included *Up from the Ape* (1931), *Apes, Men and Morons* (1937), and *Why Men Behave Like Apes and Vice Versa* (1940).

HOOVER, HERBERT CLARK (1874–1964), U.S. president. Hoover obtained a degree in engineering from Stanford University (1895) and while still a young man made a fortune as a mining engineer. During and after World War I he directed relief efforts in Europe and served as U.S. food administrator. As secretary of commerce (1921–28) he reorganized and expanded the department, focusing on the problems of unemployment and foreign trade. He received the Republican nomination for president in 1928 and was elected in a landslide. The stock market crash of 1929 and the ensuing Great Depression dominated his administration. The high rates of the Smoot-Hawley tariff act, which Hoover reluctantly signed, made matters worse. Hoover believed that state and local governments should provide aid for the unemployed, though he did support creation of the Reconstruction Finance Corp. (1932), which lent money to stimulate the economy. In 1932, with unemployment approaching 14 million, Hoover was overwhelmingly defeated for reelection by the Democratic candidate, Franklin D. Roosevelt. After World War II he again helped with relief efforts, and he headed two commissions that made major recommendations for reorganizing the executive branch of the federal government. He wrote three volumes of memoirs (1951–52). ■ See also study by Harris Warren (1959) and biographies by Eugene Lyons (1964), Gary D. Best (1983), George H. Nash (1983), and Richard N. Smith (1984).

HOOVER, JOHN EDGAR (1895–1972), U.S. crime fighter and public official. Director of the U.S. Federal Bureau of Investigation (FBI) for almost half a century (1924–72), J. Edgar Hoover served under eight presidents beginning with Calvin Coolidge and ending with Richard Nixon. An innovator in the use of scientific criminal-investigation techniques, including the use of fingerprint files, he built the FBI into the most professional and respected U.S. law-enforcement organization. He was primarily concerned with capturing gangsters and kidnappers during the 1930s. Increasingly turning his attention to the problem of wartime domestic espionage, foreign intrigue, and alleged communist subversion during the 1940s and 1950s, Hoover and the FBI became deeply involved in U.S. politics. By the late 1960s he had become a very controversial figure as a result of his denunciation and harassment of antiwar activists and black and student radicals, and his alleged illegal wiretapping of political foes. ■ See Jay Robert Nash, *Citizen Hoover* (1972); Ovid Demaris, *The Director* (1975); Richard G. Powers, *Secrecy and Power* (1987); Athan Theoharis and John S. Cox, *The Boss* (1988); and biography by Curt Gentry (1991).

HOOVER, WILLIAM HENRY (1849–1932), U.S. businessman. A politically active Ohio manufacturer, Hoover developed the vacuum cleaner from the crude prototype brought to him by its inventor, a Cleveland janitor. He formed the Electric Suction Sweeper Co. (1908; later called the Hoover Co.) and began selling vacuum cleaners throughout the United States and, after World War I, throughout the world. Soon "hoovering" became synonymous with vacuum cleaning.

HOPE, ALEC DERWENT (1907–2000), Australian poet and critic. The son of a Presbyterian minister, A. D. Hope graduated from Sydney (B.A. 1928) and Oxford (B.A. 1930) universities and taught English at several Australian colleges, including the Australian National University (1951–68). A controversial foe of modernism, Hope produced a body of formally traditional poetry that reflected a tension between a classical concern for order and structure and a romantic view of human nature. In addition to his candid and satirical poems that indict contemporary mechanized mass society, modern literary criticism, and the erosion of rationalism and intellectual tradition, he wrote sumptuous love poetry. Among his best-known collections were *The Wandering Islands* (1955), *Poems* (1960), *Collected Poems: 1930–65* (1966), *New Poems* (1969), *A Late Picking: Poems 1965–74* (1975), and *Selected Poems* (1992). His critical works included *The Cave and the Spring* (1965), *A Midsummer Eve's Dream* (1970), *Native Companions* (1974), and *The New Cratylus* (1979). ■ See study by Robert Darling (1997).

HOPE, BOB (Leslie Townes Hope; 1903–), U.S. comedian. Born in England and raised in Ohio, Hope rose through vaudeville and Broadway appearances to make his radio debut as a comedian (1935) and his film debut in *The Big Broadcast of 1938*. Beginning with *Road to Singapore* (1940), the cheerfully incompetent gagster teamed with Bing Crosby and Dorothy Lamour for six popular "Road" films (1940–1953). Alone, he made *Monsieur Beaucaire* (1946), a costume spoof, and *Paleface* (1948), a burlesque of the classic western. Hope appeared on TV (from 1950) and gave many benefits and military entertainment tours. As a comedian, he was best known for his rapid-fire technique and encyclopedic memory of jokes prepared by an army of gag writers. He had numerous real-estate and business interests and was one of the wealthiest entertainers in the world. ■ See his memoirs, *Have Tux, Will Travel* (1954) and *The Road to Hollywood* (1977), and the biography by Lawrence J. Quirk (1998).

HOPE, JOHN (1868–1936), U.S. educator. The first African-American president of a college established for blacks after the Civil War (Morehouse College, Atlanta, Georgia; 1906), Hope advocated advanced liberal arts education for blacks. He opposed Booker T. Washington's program calling for blacks to concentrate on achieving technical skills while abandoning agitation for political and social rights, and he joined the militant Niagara Movement (1906) and was at the founding meeting of the National Association for the Advancement of Colored People (1909). Hope was also the prime force behind the consolidation of Atlanta University, the first black graduate school, and served as its president (1924–36). ■ See Frederic Ridgely Torrence, *The Story of John Hope* (1948), and Leroy Davis, *A Clashing of the Soul* (1998).

HOPKINS, SIR FREDERICK GOWLAND (1861–1947), British biochemist. A lecturer and professor at Cambridge University (1898–1943), Hopkins insisted that many biological problems could be solved by chemical means and was one of the pioneers of biochemistry in England. He was most famous for his work leading to the discovery of vitamins, for which he shared the 1929 Nobel Prize in Physiology or Medicine with Christiaan Eijkman. Hopkins is known for the isolation of the amino acid tryptophane, the discovery of the connection between muscular contractions and lactic acid, and for the isolation of the tripeptide glutathione, which plays a major role in biochemical oxidation.

HOPKINS, HARRY LLOYD (1890–1946), U.S. public official. An administrator of various health and welfare agencies in New York City during the 1920s, Hopkins served as Gov. Franklin D. Roosevelt's director of the Temporary Emergency Relief Administration (1931–33). After Roosevelt became president (1933), Hopkins played a major role in the formulation of New Deal policies. He headed the Emergency Relief Administration and the Works Progress (later Works Projects) Administration (WPA), which created public-works projects to aid the poor and unemployed. He also helped establish the social security system. After two years as secretary of commerce (1938–40) he became personal adviser to the president. In that capacity he was Roosevelt's closest confidant, and during World War II he served as his chief emissary to Britain and the Soviet Union. He also headed the lend-lease program and attended, with Roo-

sevelt, all of the major wartime Allied conferences. ■ See Robert E. Sherwood, *Roosevelt and Hopkins* (rev. ed. 1950), and biographies by Henry H. Adams (1977) and June Hopkins (1999).

HOPPE, WILLIAM FREDERICK (WILLIE) (1887–1959), U.S. billiards player. Regarded as the greatest carom billiards player of all time, Willie Hoppe won 51 world championships between 1906 and 1952. A player from his childhood days, he mastered all aspects of billiards and was the 18.1 balkline champion (1906–07; 1909–11; 1914–27), 18.2 balkline champion (1907; 1910–20; 1923–24; 1927), and the dominant figure of the three-cushion game, winning the world title in 1936, 1940–44, and 1947–52. ■ See his *Thirty Years of Billiards* (1925).

HOPPER, EDWARD (1882–1967), U.S. painter. Hopper studied (1900–6) with Robert Henri of the "Ashcan" school of realism; disassociating himself from that movement's stress on social content, he developed a style that remained constant over 60 years of painting. Hopper's canvases often depicted anonymous figures and scenes of urban life. His masterful use of light and shadow communicated a bleak, haunting solitude. *Early Sunday Morning* (1930), *Nighthawks* (1942), and *Second Story Sunlight* (1960) are characteristic of Hopper's work. The architecture of New England towns was often the subject of his watercolors. Hopper's work affected the pop artists of the 1960s and the new realist painters of the 1970s and 1980s. ■ See biography by Gail Levin (1995) and studies by Lloyd Goodrich (1971) and Gail Levin (1980).

HOPPER, GRACE (Grace Brewster Murray; 1906–1992), U.S. computer scientist. A computer pioneer, Hopper studied mathematics at Yale (Ph.D. 1934) and taught at Vassar College (1934–43) before joining the navy (1943). She worked at the Bureau of Ordnance's Computation Project at Harvard University (1944–46), where she was a programmer on Mark I, the first large-scale automatic calculating device, which was a precursor of electronic computers. After World War II she joined private industry but remained in the naval reserve until her retirement, as a rear admiral, in 1986. She helped develop UNIVAC I, the first commercial electronic computer, and helped invent COBOL, the programming language that was widely used in business. Hopper also developed an improved compiler, a program that translates instructions into codes that can be read by a computer, and helped standardize the navy's computer languages and programs. ■ See biography by Charlene Billings (1989).

HOPPER, HEDDA (Elda Furry; 1890–1966), U.S. newspaper columnist. One of Hollywood's most influential and flamboyant personalities, Hopper appeared in more than 100 films, ran a weekly network radio show (1936–51), and wrote a daily syndicated gossip column about movie stars from 1938 until her death. ■ See the autobiographical *From Under My Hat* (1952) and *The Whole Truth and Nothing But* (1963), and George Eells, *Hedda and Louella* (1972).

HORKHEIMER, MAX (1895–1973), German philosopher and sociologist. Horkheimer studied at the University of Frankfurt (Ph.D. 1922) and joined its Institute for Social Research (1923), popularly known as the Frankfurt School, which utilized a Marxist analysis in its critical studies of modern culture and society. He directed the institute from 1930 to 1958. After the Nazis came to power (1933), the institute and its staff moved first to Paris and then to New York City, taking up residence at Columbia University (1935–46). Horkheimer wrote *Eclipse of Reason* (1947) and collaborated with Theodor Adorno on *Dialectics of Enlightenment* (1947; Eng. trans. 1972), which described how reason was transformed into a weapon of totalitarian social control under capitalism. He returned to Germany after World War II, reestablished the institute at the University of Frankfurt, and lived to see the ideas of the Frankfurt School play a major role in the development of the New Left during the 1960s. His essays are in *Critical Theory* (1968; Eng. trans. 1972) and *Dawn and Decline: Notes 1926–1931 and 1950–1969* (Eng. trans. 1978). ■ See Zoltan Tar, *The Frankfurt School* (1977), and David Held, *Introduction to Critical Theory* (1980).

HORNE, LENA (1917–), U.S. singer and actress. Horne's mother was an actress who often took her on tour. She studied dance, appearing for a week in a ballet at the Harlem Opera House. During the Depression she left her Brooklyn high school and found work as a chorus girl in Harlem's Cotton Club. When she sang with Charlie Barnet's orchestra, Horne was the first African-American woman vocalist to be featured with a white band. She toured for the military during World War II but left a tour when German prisoners were given front-row seats and African-American soldiers were seated in the rear. Horne launched a movie career in the 1940s, appearing in the all-black cast of *Cabin in the Sky* (1943). After Horne returned to Broadway in *Jamaica* (1957), her popularity grew. At age 63, she scored a hit with her one-woman Broadway show, *The Lady and Her Music* (1981), a musical retrospective on her nearly 50 years in show business. Her hit songs included "Stormy Weather," "Deed I Do," and "As Long as I Live." ■ See her autobiography, *Lena* (1965).

HORNE, MARILYN (1934–), U.S. opera singer. The most acclaimed mezzo-soprano of her era, Horne was known for the purity and richness of her voice, which covered a range from low E to high C. She gained an international reputation in Europe (1956–59) before making her debut at the San Francisco Opera in *Wozzeck* (1960). Horne sang her first role at New York's Metropolitan Opera in a memorable performance of *Norma* (1970) with Joan Sutherland. Her other notable roles were in *The Barber of Seville, Carmen,*

The Siege of Corinth, L'Italiana in Algeri, and *Semiramide.* She established the Marilyn Horne Foundation (1993) to aid young recitalists. ■ See her autobiography (1983; with Jane Scovell).

HORNEY, KAREN (Karen Danielsen; 1885–1952), German-born U.S. psychoanalyst. Horney taught at the Psychoanalytic Institute in Berlin (1918–32), where she also had a private practice, before moving to the United States in 1932. She was a neo-Freudian who stressed the environmental and cultural rather than instinctual factors in the development of neuroses and considered sexual problems a result and not the cause of all neuroses. She also rejected Freudian antifeminism, specifically the concept of penis envy. After the publication of her critique of Freudianism, *New Ways in Psychoanalysis* (1939), she was expelled from the New York Psychoanalytic Institute (1941) and she founded the Association for the Advancement of Psychoanalysis. She also wrote *The Neurotic Personality of Our Time* (1937), *Self-Analysis* (1942), *Our Inner Conflicts* (1945), *Neurosis and Human Growth* (1950), and *Feminine Psychology* (1967). ■ See biography by Jack L. Rubins (1978).

HORNSBY, ROGERS (1896–1963), U.S. baseball player. Considered by many to be the greatest right-handed hitter in baseball history, Hornsby compiled a lifetime (23-season) batting average of .358, highest in National League history and second only to Ty Cobb's .367. A second baseman for the St. Louis Cardinals, he had his greatest years in the early 1920s when he led the league in batting for six consecutive seasons (1920–25) and averaged .401 for five years (1921–25). His .424 average in 1924 was the highest ever achieved in the 20th century. ■ See his autobiographies, *My Kind of Baseball* (1953) and *My War with Baseball* (1962), and biography by Charles Alexander (1995).

HOROWITZ, VLADIMIR (1904?–1989), Russian-born pianist. Horowitz enjoyed a comfortable musical upbringing, entered the Kiev Conservatory at age 12, and made his debut (1922) with a dazzling repertory amid the turmoil of postrevolutionary Russia. He never returned after a 1924 European tour, settling in New York and winning an international following with his great technique and brilliance at the keyboard. His long career was marked by extended sabbaticals. Returning after 12 years to Carnegie Hall in 1965, he gave a bravura performance that also became a best-selling recording. On his first visit to his homeland in over 60 years (1986) he gave a series of highly publicized concerts. He was best known for his interpretations of works by Rachmaninoff, Liszt, Schumann, Chopin, and Scriabin. ■ See biographies by Glenn Plaskin (1983) and Harold C. Schonberg (1992).

HORST, LOUIS (1884–1964), U.S. musician and modern-dance choreography teacher. Horst was the music director of the Denishawn Concert Group (1915–25) before joining forces with Martha Graham (1926–48). He was Graham's mentor, encouraging her to develop her own school of movement and composed music for many of her dances. He advocated the natural posture or gesture as the point of departure for modern dance. This was in contrast to the ballet principle of an upright back, from which the stylized movements of arms and legs emerge. Horst used the preclassic forms—pavane, galliard, minuet, gavotte—as a basis for teaching students to think choreographically. He demonstrated how to transform these movements into modern-dance styles. He taught at many schools, including New York's Neighborhood Playhouse (1928–64) and the Juilliard School (1958–63). ■ See his *Modern Dance Forms* (1960) and biography by Janet M. Soares (1992).

HORTHY DE NAGYBANYA, MIKLÓS (1868–1957), Hungarian admiral and regent. A former aide-de-camp to Emperor Francis Joseph and a commander in chief of the Austro-Hungarian navy during World War I, Horthy assumed leadership of the counterrevolutionary "white terror" in Hungary after the war. In 1920 he was elected regent pending restoration of the Hungarian monarchy, but as no king was chosen, he remained in office until 1944. Although not a Nazi, he hoped to regain territory lost in World War I and allied Hungary with Germany during World War II. His efforts to limit German influence in Hungary failed, and he was arrested by the Germans after publicly calling for an armistice with the Allies (October 1944). Captured by American troops (1945), he was released and went into exile in Portugal. ■ See his *Memoirs* (Eng. trans. 1957) and study by Mario D. Fenyo (1972).

HORTON, MYLES (1905–1990), U.S. educator. A socially conscious, statewide student secretary with the YMCA, Horton left his native Tennessee to study at the Union Theological Seminary in New York City (1929). There he came under the influence of radical theologian Reinhold Niebuhr, familiarized himself with socialist thought, and learned of the labor schools in Britain and the folk schools in Denmark. Determined to set up a school for adults that would address the problems of the Appalachian poor, Horton returned home and founded (1932) the Highlander Folk School (Monteagle, Tennessee—moved to Knoxville, 1960; and to New Market, 1971) and actively participated in its programs until his retirement (1973). Although frequently harassed by local, state, and federal authorities, the school provided a training ground for southern labor organizers and social activists during the 1930s and 1940s and for an entire generation of African-American and white civil-rights leaders (including Martin Luther King, Jr.) during the 1950s and 1960s. ■ See his autobiography, *The Long Haul* (1990), and Frank Adams, *Unearthing Seeds of Fire* (1975).

HOSTOVSKY, EGON (1908–1973), Czech novelist. Born into a family of writers, Hostovsky published the first of his 14 novels while a student at Prague University and won Czechoslovakia's highest literary award. He was an assimilated Jew, and many of his early works, including *The Closed Door* (1926), *The Ghetto Inside Them* (1928), and *The Case of Professor Körner* (1933), dealt with the problems of alienated Czech Jews. The best of his later psychological novels, including *Missing* (Eng. trans. 1952), *Midnight Patient* (Eng. trans. 1955), *The Charity Ball* (Eng. trans. 1958), and *Three Nights* (Eng. trans. 1964), were concerned with refugees who were fleeing from persecution, war, and tyranny. A refugee himself, Hostovsky left his homeland in 1938, returned after World War II, and fled again after the communist coup in 1949. He lived in the United States until his death.

HOUDINI, HARRY (Ehrich Weiss; 1874–1926), Hungarian-born U.S. illusionist and escape artist. The son of a rabbi, Houdini was brought to the United States by his family and lived in Wisconsin and later New York City. A trapeze artist and magician, he gained international fame in the early 1900s for his escape act in which he was able to extract himself from ropes, chains, handcuffs, and locked cabinets as well as from prison cells, submerged weighted locked boxes, and from a straitjacket while suspended 75 feet in the air. He toured Europe and the United States and starred in three film serials after World War I. He campaigned against fraudulent mind readers and mediums and wrote *Miracle Mongers and Their Methods* (1920) and *A Magician Among the Spirits* (1924) to discredit them. He also served as president of the Society of American Magicians and founded the Magicians' Club of London. ■ See study by Walter B. Gibson; Morris N. Young, *Houdini's Fabulous Magic* (1961); Raymund Fitzsimons, *Death and the Magician* (1980); and biography by Kenneth Silverman (1997).

HOUNSFIELD, SIR GODFREY NEWBOLD (1919–), British electrical engineer. A Royal Air Force radar lecturer during World War II, Hounsfield graduated from Faraday House Electrical Engineering College (London, 1951) and joined the research staff of EMI, Ltd., an international electronics and entertainment conglomerate. He headed the team that developed the first solid-state computer built in Britain and developed computers that could interpret X-ray signals to form a two-dimensional image of a complex object. He applied the new technology to medical diagnosis and built the first prototype of the computerized axial tomography (CAT) scanner, which revolutionized radiology by producing detailed X-ray pictures of specific "slices" of the human body in more detail than any nonsurgical technique. He shared the 1979 Nobel Prize in Physiology or Medicine with Allan Cormack.

HOUPHOUËT-BOIGNY, FÉLIX (1905–1993), president of the Ivory Coast. The son of a chief, Houphouët-Boigny became a wealthy planter and doctor. He helped organize the Ivory Coast Democratic party (1945) and served in the French national assembly (1946–59) and from 1956 to 1959 in successive French cabinets. Although he headed the interterritorial party Rassemblement Démocratique Africain (RDA), he opposed a federation after independence and worked with Pres. Charles de Gaulle to establish independence for individual colonies within the French community. First elected president of the newly independent Ivory Coast in 1960, he headed a one-party state for more than 30 years, maintaining close ties with France while presiding over one of the most prosperous economies in Africa until the early 1980s, when the economy collapsed. However, he spent more than $200 million at the time to build the world's largest Roman Catholic cathedral, the Basilica of Our Lady of Peace, in his home town of Yamoussoukro. ■ See Virginia Thompson, *West Africa's Council of the Entente* (1972), and Jon Woronoff, *West African Wager: Houphouët versus Nkrumah* (1974).

HOUSE, EDWARD MANDELL (1858–1938), U.S. diplomat and political adviser. An independently wealthy banker and plantation owner, Col. House was a political adviser to Democratic governors in his home state of Texas before assuming an active role in Woodrow Wilson's successful campaign (1912) for the presidency. Refusing a cabinet post in the new administration, he became Wilson's closest aide and personal confidant. Particularly effective as a promoter of Wilson's domestic legislative program in the Congress, he also served as the president's chief diplomatic agent abroad. His most significant work began in the closing days of World War I, when he was assigned the task of organizing the American program for the Paris Peace Conference, including the drafting of the original version of the famous "Fourteen Points." Always a realist, House attempted to reach a compromise with the Allied powers on the issue of punitive measures against Germany, which alienated the idealistic Wilson, and after the signing of the Treaty of Versailles (1919) the two men never met again. ■ See Charles Seymour, ed., *The Intimate Papers of Colonel House* (4 vols., 1926–28); biography by Arthur D. Howden Smith (1940); and Alexander and Juliette George, *Woodrow Wilson and Colonel House* (1956).

HOUSMAN, ALFRED EDWARD (1859–1936), British poet and scholar. A. E. Housman was an eminent classical scholar and translator and a professor of Latin at Cambridge (1911–36). He achieved general fame with his poetry collections *A Shropshire Lad* (1896) and *Last Poems* (1922). Among his most famous poems are "When I Was One-and-Twenty" and "To an Athlete Dying Young." Housman's poetry was extremely popular with both critics and the general public because of its simplicity, melodiousness, and taste. His poems pondered nature, the passing of youth, and the problems of friendship. ■ See biography by Richard P. Graves (1980); study by Tom Haber (1967); and Jeremy Bourne, *The Westerly Wanderer* (1996).

HOUSSAY, BERNARDO ALBERTO (1887–1971), Argentinian physiologist. Houssay was the son of French immigrants. Concerned with the pituitary gland from his medical-school years at the University of Buenos Aires (M.D. 1911), he was best known for proving that hormones from the frontal lobe of that gland play a major role in carbohydrate metabolism. His research showed that insulin works in treating diabetics by acting against pituitary secretions that block the burning of sugar. Although dismissed from his professorship at the University of Buenos Aires by strongman Juan Perón (1943), Houssay was awarded the 1947 Nobel Prize in Physiology or Medicine (with Carl and Gerty Cori). He founded the independent Institute of Biology and Experimental Medicine in Buenos Aires (1944) and was reinstated at the university after Perón's ouster in 1955.

HOVHANESS, ALAN (1911–2000), U.S. composer. Born into a family of Armenian-Scottish descent, Hovhaness received classical training at the New England Conservatory of Music (1932–34) and composed award-winning romantic orchestral and instrumental pieces during the 1930s. However, influenced by mysticism, meditation, Eastern religion, and traditional Indian, East Asian, and Armenian music, he developed a new, personal style in the early 1940s that blended oriental and occidental forms and techniques. He traveled frequently to India, Japan, and Korea and composed hundreds of meditative and mystical works, many utilizing Asian themes and instruments. His best-known works included *Prayer of St. Gregory* (1946), Symphony No. 2 (*Mysterious Mountain;* 1955), Symphony No. 6 (*Celestial Gate,* 1960), and *And God Created the Great Whales* (1970). He also composed the music for the Broadway show *The Flowering Peach* (1954) and for two Martha Graham ballets, *Ardent Song* (1955) and *Circe* (1964).

HOVING, THOMAS PEARSALL FIELD (1931–   ), U.S. art administrator. A native New Yorker who earned a Ph.D. (1959) in art history from Princeton University, Hoving left New York's Metropolitan Museum of Art in 1965 to become city parks commissioner. He was a dynamic bureaucrat, launching new recreational facilities and filling them with people, music, art, and "happenings." He returned to the Metropolitan as director (1967–77), again arousing controversy, interest, and growth with his acquisitions and exhibitions. ■ See his *Tutankhamun: The Untold Story* (1978), *King of the Confessors* (1981), *Masterpiece* (1986), *Making the Mummies Dance* (1993), and *False Impressions* (1996).

HOVLAND, CARL IVER (1912–1961), U.S. psychologist. Hovland earned his Ph.D. at Yale (1936) and remained there as a member of the faculty for the rest of his life. A pioneer in the field of social communications, he studied effects of prestige and of one-sided and two-sided presentations on attitude formation and modification. He also described a "sleeper effect," whereby information from a suspicious source gradually attains credibility, and he moved into computer simulation of human thought processes. He was co-author of *Experiments on Mass Communication* (1949) and *Communication and Persuasion* (1953).

HOWARD, JOHN (1939–), Australian political leader. Howard, a graduate of the University of Sydney (1961), was a lawyer before being elected to Parliament (1974) as a member of the conservative Liberal party. He served as federal treasurer (1977–83) and later as leader of the opposition (1987–89; 1995–96) and became known as an advocate of economic deregulation and reduced governmental spending. As prime minister, leading a Liberal-National party coalition (1996–98; 1998–), he maintained tariff protections to save jobs, reduced immigration quotas, and advocated a broad-based tax reform featuring a 10 percent tax on all goods and services.

HOWARD, LESLIE (Leslie Stainer; 1893–1943), British actor. Son of Hungarian immigrants, Howard made some early silent films and became popular on the London stage after World War I, appearing opposite Tallulah Bankhead in *Her Cardboard Lover* (1928). *Outward Bound,* in which the delicate, whey-faced actor had starred on stage, was his first Hollywood film (1930), followed by *The Scarlet Pimpernel* (1934), *The Petrified Forest* (1936), and *Gone With the Wind* (1939). After an emotional return to World War II England, Howard directed and acted in *Pimpernel Smith* (1941) and other films. His plane was shot down while returning from a secret wartime mission to Lisbon. ■ See Leslie Ruth Howard, *A Quite Remarkable Father* (1959), and Ronald Howard, *In Search of My Father* (1981).

HOWARD, ROY WILSON (1883–1964), U.S. journalist and newspaper publisher. One of the century's most influential publishers, Howard began as a reporter in Indianapolis and Cincinnati. In 1908 he became general manager of United Press (UP) wire service and served as its president (1912–21). In 1918 he gained notoriety for his premature reporting (four days early) of the World War I armistice. Three years later, however, he became board chairman of United Press and of the Scripps-McRae (later Scripps-Howard) chain. He served as the chain's president from 1936 to 1952. Howard controlled more than 30 major newspapers throughout the United States but focused particularly on the *New York World Telegram and Sun,* which he edited until 1960. His newspapers were generally liberal during the 1920s and 1930s, but opposed Franklin D. Roosevelt's reelection in 1940 and grew increasingly conservative thereafter.

HOWE, FREDERICK CLEMSON (1867–1940), U.S. public official. Howe was a well-known liberal activist and reformer. In a career spanning the period from the Progressive era to the New Deal, he was a leader in the civic-reform (in Cleveland, 1894–1910), labor-reform, consumer reform, and cooperative movements and wrote numerous books on taxation and urban affairs. He served as federal commis-

sioner of immigration in New York (1914–19) and helped establish the Conference for Progressive Political Action (1922), a forerunner of the Progressive party. ■ See his autobiography, *The Confessions of a Reformer* (1925).

HOWE, GEORGE (1886–1955), U.S. architect. During the late 1920s, Howe gave up a successful career designing country houses and estates in various historical styles and embraced the modern International Style that had recently been developed in Europe. In partnership (1929–34) with Swiss architect William Lescaze, he designed the landmark Philadelphia Savings Fund Society Building (1931), considered to be the first International Style skyscraper in the United States and one of the classics of 20th-century American architecture. Howe subsequently designed several other notable houses, projects, and office buildings and chaired the department of architecture at Yale University (1950–54). ■ See study by Robert A. M. Stern (1975) and the reminiscences by his daughter Helen Howe West (1973).

HOWE, GORDIE (1928–), Canadian ice-hockey player. Widely regarded as the greatest player in the history of the game, Gordie Howe was respected as much for his staying power in this grueling sport as for his brilliant playmaking and prolific scoring. In the midst of his career with the Detroit Red Wings (1946–71), he recovered from a severe brain injury (1950) and went on to set league marks for the most games played (1,687), most goals (801), most assists (1,023), and most points (1,809). (His scoring records were subsequently broken by Wayne Gretzky.) He was named to the National Hockey League's All-Star team 21 times, won the league's scoring title six times, and was a six-time winner of the Hart Trophy as the league's Most Valuable Player. In 1973, at age 45, he came out of retirement to join his two sons on the Houston Aeros of the World Hockey Association (which gave him a four-year $1 million contract), and led that team to a championship. He kept playing into his fifties with New England-Hartford (1977–80), retiring in 1980. ■ See biography by Stan Fischler (1967) and Don O'Reilly, *Mr. Hockey* (1975).

HOWE, IRVING (1920–1993), U.S. social and literary critic. A Trotskyist student leader at the College of the City of New York (CCNY; B.A. 1940), Howe emerged during the 1950s as a leading literary and social critic and a prominent spokesman of the anticommunist left. He taught at Brandeis University (1953–61) and Hunter College (New York City; 1963–86), edited the independent left-wing magazine *Dissent* (from 1953), and wrote several important books including *Politics and the Novel* (1957), *The Decline of the New* (1969), and *The Critical Point: On Literature and Culture* (1973). Best known for the book *World of Our Fathers* (1976), a social history of East European Jewish life in New York's Lower East Side, he also wrote *Socialism in America* (1985) and *The American Newness* (1986). Howe also edited several volumes of Yiddish stories and poetry. ■ See his autobiography, *A Margin of Hope* (1982), and biography by Edward Alexander (1998).

HOWE, JAMES WONG (Wong Tung Jim; 1899–1976), Chinese-born U.S. cinematographer. Howe got his first job in the movie industry (1917) as a cutting-room helper and later was a slate boy and assistant cameraman for Cecil B. DeMille. He became a director of photography in 1922 and developed a reputation for realistic effects and for filming actresses in a way that dramatically enhanced their beauty. In a career lasting 53 years, he was nominated for 16 Academy Awards, won Oscars for *The Rose Tatoo* (1955) and *Hud* (1966), and filmed such popular hits as *The Power and the Glory* (1933), *The Thin Man* (1934), *The Prisoner of Zenda* (1937), *King's Row* (1942), *Yankee Doodle Dandy* (1942), *Body and Soul* (1947), *Picnic* (1956), *The Old Man and the Sea* (1958), and *Funny Lady* (1975). ▪ See study by Todd Rainsberger (1981).

HOWE, LOUIS MCHENRY (1871–1936), U.S. journalist and political adviser. Howe was the *New York Telegram*'s correspondent in Albany in 1911 when he befriended state senator Franklin D. Roosevelt. He became his political mentor and (from 1913 until 1935, when he was critically ill) served as Roosevelt's personal secretary, strategist, and alter ego. He persuaded Roosevelt to remain in politics after being stricken with polio (1921) and successfully managed Roosevelt's gubernatorial and presidential campaigns. "There has never been a story of greater devotion to another man's success," Eleanor Roosevelt, the president's wife, once said. ▪ See Lela Stiles, *The Man Behind Roosevelt* (1954).

HOWEY, WALTER CRAWFORD (1882–1954), U.S. journalist. A legendary editor on four Chicago newspapers (1904–1922), Howey was the inspiration for the Ben Hecht and Charles MacArthur play *The Front Page* (1928). Exuberant and hard driving, he specialized in presenting sensationalized local news stories in a concise and visually compelling format. From 1917 he was associated with Hearst publications, editing Hearst newspapers in New York, Boston, and, again, Chicago. He served as special organizational assistant to William Randolph Hearst for many years. A strong advocate of news photography, Howey pioneered in the development of an automatic photoelectrical engraving system and in the transmission of photos by wire.

HOXHA, ENVER (1908–1985), Albanian political leader. A high school French teacher from a middle-class Muslim background, Hoxha was a founder of the Albanian Communist party (1941), party secretary-general (1943–48), and a leader of the anti-Italian resistance during World War II. As a loyal Stalinist premier of the new postwar government (1944–54) and as party first secretary (from 1954) he isolated his country from Western influences, collectivized agriculture, began the process of industrialization, and claimed

to have eliminated illiteracy and created the world's first atheist state. Hoxha managed to maintain Albanian independence by skillfully exploiting the rivalries between neighboring Yugoslavia and the Soviet Union (1940s and 1950s) and the Soviet Union and China (1960s and 1970s). He wrote numerous books, including *Imperialism and the Revolution* (Eng. trans. 1979), *The Khrushchevites: Memoirs* (Eng. trans. 1980), and his war memoirs, *The Anglo-American Threat to Albania* (Eng. trans. 1982).

HOYLE, SIR FRED (1915–), British astronomer. Hoyle gained prominence as the spokesman for the controversial theory of a steady-state universe, which rejects any claim that the universe had a beginning or can have an end. Developed (1948) by Hoyle with astronomers Hermann Bondi and Thomas Gold, the theory posits that a universe that is homogeneous in space must necessarily be homogeneous in time—that the physical state of the universe at the present is the same as that of the past or future. Hoyle maintained that the universe evolved through a process of continuous growth and that matter is continually being formed to fill the voids resulting from the universe's constant expansion. He taught at Cambridge (1945–72) and Cornell (1972–78) universities and wrote many technical books, science fiction novels, and popular accounts of astronomy, including *Frontiers of Astronomy* (1955), *Men and Galaxies* (1964), *Lifecloud* (1979; with C. Wickramasinghe), *The Intelligent Universe* (1984), *Our Place in the Cosmos* (1993), and *A Different Approach to Cosmology* (2000; with G. Burbidge and J. V. Narlikar). *Encounter with the Future* (1965) contains an autobiographical essay. ▪ See his autobiographical volumes, *The Small World of Fred Hoyle* (1986) and *Home Is Where the Wind Blows* (1994).

HRDLIČKA, ALEŠ (1869–1943), Czech-born U.S. anthropologist. Trained as a physician, Hrdlička turned to physical anthropology and helped establish the field in the United States. He organized the division of physical anthropology (1903) of the National Museum of the Smithsonian Institution in Washington, D.C., and as its curator (1910–42) amassed one of the world's largest collections of skeletal remains. He specialized in early human history in the Americas and, through his anthropometric studies, advanced the theory of the Asiatic origin of North American Indians. Hrdlička was founder (1918) and editor (1918–42) of the *American Journal of Physical Anthropology* and founder (1929) of the American Association of Physical Anthropologists. His numerous studies included *The Old Americans* (1925) and *The Skeletal Remains of Early Man* (1930).

HRUSHEVSKY, MIKHAILO (1866–1934), Ukrainian historian and nationalist leader. A professor at the University of Lvov (1894–1914), Hrushevsky launched a Ukrainian national awakening with his definitive ten-volume history of the Ukraine (1899–1937) and a five-volume history of its literature (1922–27). He became president of the Ukrainian republic created (1918) out of the chaos of World War I, but German occupiers soon forced him to flee. He returned home (1924) but was exiled from Kiev by the Soviets (1930), for whom Ukrainian nationalism was an inconvenience, and he died in the Caucasus. See his *A History of Ukraine* (Eng. trans. 1941).

HSU CHIH-MO. *See XU ZHIMO.*

HUA GUOFENG (old style: HUA KUO-FENG; 1920–), Chinese communist leader. Born in Shanxi (Shansi) province, Hua joined the Communist party (1935) and served as a Red army officer. He gained prominence in Hunan province, after 1949, as an expert in agriculture. A loyal supporter of party leader Mao Zedong (Mao Tsetung), Hua was named the head of the Communist party in Hunan in 1970, a member of the Politburo in 1973, and was unexpectedly chosen to be premier in 1976. On the death of party chairman Mao in 1976, Hua quickly purged numerous party radicals, including the powerful "gang of four," and climaxed his rapid rise by gaining the posts of chairman of the Chinese Communist party and of the military commission. He was the first person in the history of the People's Republic of China to simultaneously head the party, government, and army. However, Hua was soon overshadowed by vice-premier Deng Xiaoping (Teng Hsiao-p'ing) and his followers who advocated policies of modernization and reform. Criticized for "leftist" errors, he was ousted from his party (1980) and state (1981) leadership positions, but retained his membership on the party's Central Committee through the 1990s. ▪ See study by Wang Ting (Eng. trans. 1980).

HUA KUO-FENG. *See HUA GUOFENG.*

HUANG HSING. *See HUANG XI-JUNG.*

HUANG HUA (1913–), Chinese diplomat. Huang Hua was the pseudonym of Wang Rumei (old style: Wang Jumei). A student leader at Yanjing (Yenching) University during the 1930s, Huang was the interpreter for U.S. journalist Edgar Snow on his visit to the communist base at Yan'an (Yenan) while he was writing *Red Star Over China* (1936). During the 1940s he was the liaison between the communists and Western journalists. After joining the foreign ministry (1953), he served as chief negotiator during the Korean War (1953), as adviser to Premier Zhou En-lai (Chou En-lai) at international conferences (Geneva, 1954; Bandung, 1955), and as ambassador to Ghana (1960–66), Egypt (1966–70), Canada (1971), and the United Nations (1971–76). In these positions and as foreign minister (1976–82), he played a major role in expanding China's contacts with Africa and the West. He also served as a member of the Central Committee of the Chinese Communist party.

HUANG XING (old style: HUANG HSING; 1874–1916), Chinese political leader. The son of a schoolteacher, Huang received a traditional Confucian education and studied in Japan (1902–03). There he became involved in anti-Manchu activities and founded a revolutionary society upon his return to China. With revolutionary leader Sun Yat-sen he organized the Tongmeng Hui (T'ung-meng-hui; Chinese United League), a union of revolutionary movements (1905). He organized several abortive uprisings including the famous Canton revolt (1911), commanded forces in the Yangzi (Yangtze) region, and helped establish a provisional government in Shanghai headed by Sun (1912). After Yuan Shikai (Yuan Shih-k'ai) assumed leadership and moved the government to Beijing (Peking), Huang helped organize the Guomindang (Kuomintang; 1912) as a parliamentary political party. When Yuan banned the party, Huang and Sun organized a revolution against his rule. Huang went to the United States to raise funds (1914–16) and returned to China shortly after Yuan's death. ▪ See Hsüeh Chün-tu, *Huang Hsing and the Chinese Revolution* (1961).

HUBBARD, L. RON (Lafayette Ronald Hubbard; 1911–1986), U.S. scientologist. Hubbard wrote pulp-magazine science fiction, westerns, and screenplays during the 1930s. After World War II service in the navy, he published *Dianetics: The Modern Science of Mental Health* (1950) and *This Is Scientology* (1952) and founded the Church of Scientology (1952). Hubbard returned to science fiction writing after a 30-year hiatus, and his novels *Battlefield Earth* (1982) and *The Invaders Plan* (1985) were both best-sellers. ▪ See Jon Atack, *A Piece of Blue Sky* (1990), and Russell Miller, *Bare-Faced Messiah* (1987).

HUBBELL, CARL OWEN (1903–1988), U.S. baseball player. An outstanding left-handed pitcher for the New York Giants (1928–43), Hubbell was the master of the screwball pitch and won 253 games during his career. Though he won 24 consecutive games (1936–37) and won 20 or more games for five straight years (1933–37), Hubbell is best remembered for striking out Babe Ruth, Lou Gehrig, Jimmy Foxx, Al Simmons, and Joe Cronin in succession in the 1934 All-Star game. He directed the Giants minor-league system from 1943 to 1976.

HUBBLE, EDWIN POWELL (1889–1953), U.S. astronomer. While engaged in the telescopic study of nebulas—enormous masses of stars—at Mt. Wilson Observatory in California (1919–53), Hubble demonstrated that certain nebulas were in fact independent galaxies located vast distances from our own. By determining the distance of relatively nearby galaxies, Hubble and his colleagues were able to estimate the distances of those farther away. In 1929 he announced "Hubble's constant," which posited that the more distant a galaxy is, the faster it is receding from our own. The discovery that the universe is constantly expanding profoundly influenced the study of the cosmos. ■ See study by Gale E. Christianson (1995).

HUBEL, DAVID HUNTER (1926–), Canadian-born U.S. neurobiologist. A graduate of Montreal's McGill University (M.D. 1951), Hubel did research at Johns Hopkins Medical School (1954–59), where he began a long collaboration with Torsten Wiesel that continued when they both joined the faculty of Harvard Medical School (1959). To study the complex manner in which the brain processes information received through the eyes, they performed experiments on cats and monkeys and were able to determine specific functions of individual cells in the brain's visual cortex. For their pioneering work in showing how the nerve cells of the brain translate patterns of light and color into a coherent picture, they shared the 1981 Nobel Prize in Physiology or Medicine with Roger W. Sperry. His books include *Eye, Brain and Vision* (1988).

HUBER, ROBERT (1937–), German biochemist. Huber graduated from the Technical University of Munich (Ph.D. 1963) and did research at the Max Planck Institute for Biochemistry in Martinsried (1972–76; 1987–). An expert in the area of X-ray diffraction, Huber worked with colleagues Hartmut Michel and Johan Deisenhofer in the study of the process of photosynthesis. The trio mapped (1982–85), atom by atom, the three-dimensional structure of the protein complex found in cell membranes (called a photosynthetic reaction center), which is crucial to photosynthesis. For his research in explaining what has been called "the most important chemical reaction on earth," Huber shared the 1988 Nobel Prize in Chemistry with Michel and Deisenhofer. He subsequently edited the *Journal of Molecular Biology* (1996–).

HUBERMAN, LEO (1903–1968), U.S. editor and writer. A Marxist humanist, Huberman sought to teach the American public the basic principles of socialism and the irrationalities, inefficiencies, and injustices of capitalism, which he saw as a dying system. To that end he founded and edited (with Paul Sweezy) *Monthly Review,* an independent socialist magazine (1949) that soon became one of the world's leading Marxist journals, and established Monthly Review Press (1952). In addition to hundreds of magazine articles, he wrote *Man's Worldly Goods* (1936), which sold more than 500,000 copies in English and millions more in translations throughout the world. His other books included *We the People* (1932), *The Labor Spy Racket* (1937), and *The Truth About Unions* (1946).

HUCH, RICARDA (1864–1947), German novelist, poet, and cultural historian. Huch was the first woman student admitted to the University of Zurich; she received a Ph.D. in history in 1892. She became known with the publication of *Recollections of Ludolf Urslev the Younger* (1893; Eng. trans. 1913–15), a fictional account of the decline of an aris-

tocratic family. Although she produced several volumes of lyric poetry, she was best known for her historical novels and histories of Germany and Italy, including *Garibaldi and the New Italy* (2 vols., 1906–07; Eng. trans. 1928–29). Her psychological novel *The Deruga Trial* (1917; Eng. trans. 1927) is considered a classic of detective fiction. She was the first woman elected to the Prussian Academy of Arts, but she resigned in 1933 and refused any honors bestowed by the Nazis.

HUDSON, MANLEY OTTMER (1886–1960), U.S. legal scholar. A professor of international law at Harvard (1923–54), Hudson was legal adviser to the U.S. delegation to the post–World War I Paris Peace Conference (1919) and worked on the legal staff of the League of Nations Secretariat. A judge on the Permanent Court of Arbitration (1933–45) and the Permanent Court of International Justice (1936–45), he later chaired the International Law Commission of the United Nations (from 1949). He was editor of the *American Journal of International Law* (1923–59) and author of many books including *The Permanent Court of International Justice* (1934). He also edited four volumes of *World Court Reports* (1934–43) and compiled *International Legislation* (9 vols., 1931–50), which made the texts of hundreds of multilateral treaties available to lawyers and scholars.

HUDSON, ROCK (**Roy Scherer, Jr.;** 1925–1985), U.S. film actor. He grew up in Illinois and took the surname Fitzgerald when his mother remarried. During World War II he served in the navy (1944–46), then moved to Los Angeles. A truck driver, he was discovered by a talent scout for the Selznick Studio, who immediately changed his name (1947) and arranged for acting lessons. After playing numerous small roles, Hudson came into his own in *Magnificent Obsession* (1954), opposite Jane Wyman. His role in *Giant* (1956) secured his reputation and merited an Academy Award nomination. Paired with Doris Day in a string of romantic comedies, including *Pillow Talk* (1959), *Lover Come Back* (1962), and *Send Me No Flowers* (1964), he became a matinee idol and the personification of masculine good looks. He later starred in the TV series *McMillan & Wife* and *The Devlin Connection* and appeared on *Dynasty*. Hudson was the first major public figure to state publicly that he had acquired immune deficiency syndrome (AIDS), a devastating illness that in the United States afflicted many male homosexuals. His announcement turned worldwide attention on the disease, the plight of its victims, and the search for a cure. He succumbed to AIDS at age 59. ■ See his autobiography (with Sara Davidson; 1986); Jerry Oppenheimer and Jack Vitek, *Idol* (1986); and J.E.S. Parker, *The Trial of Rock Hudson* (1990).

HUERTA, DOLORES (**Dolores Clara Fernandez;** 1930–), U.S. labor leader. Born in New Mexico, Huerta moved as a child to Stockton, California, where she worked with the Community Service Organization (CSO), promoting voter registration and organizing within the Mexican-American community. Through the CSO she met Cesar Chavez, and worked with him to establish the Farm Workers of America in Delano, California. As the United Farm Workers' first woman organizer, she helped bring about the lettuce and grape boycotts that turned national attention to the union. In the process, she was arrested 20 times and concluded one of the first UFW contracts with Delano grape growers (1970). She lobbied state and federal legislators for unemployment insurance, disability insurance, and pensions for migrant workers. Huerta was elected UFW vice president (1970, 1973), directed its political department, and served as its secretary-treasurer.

HUERTA, VICTORIANO (1854–1916), Mexican general and political leader. A Huichol Indian, Huerta received military training and advanced to the rank of general during the reign of dictator Porfirio Díaz. After Díaz was forced into retirement (1911), Huerta fought to suppress the uprisings of Emiliano Zapata (1911) and Pascual Orozco (1912) and in February 1913 overthrew the regime of liberal Pres. Francisco Madero and named himself president. He suppressed all political opposition and dissolved congress, but the combined opposition to his counterrevolutionary regime from Zapata, Venustiano Carranza, Pancho Villa, and the U.S. government forced him into exile (July 1914). ■ See study by Michael C. Meyer (1972).

HU FENG (1903–1985), Chinese literary critic, poet, and essayist. An independent and influential Marxist who apparently never joined the Communist party, Hu was involved in major ideological disputes with orthodox communists throughout the 1930s and 1940s. He believed that ideology and politics were secondary to literary value, that literary personages should have universal characteristics and not be stereotypes, and that literature should portray all men and not merely certain classes. Although he held several literary posts after the communists took control in 1949, he never conformed to the orthodox line and was denounced as a counterrevolutionary in 1955 and arrested. He spent several years in prison and was not allowed to publish until 1981, when he was officially rehabilitated.

HUGENBERG, ALFRED (1865–1951), German financier and political leader. A former director of the Krupp industrial empire who became a powerful press and film magnate during the interwar period, Hugenberg used all his influence to undermine the post–World War I German republic. He cofounded the nationalist Pan-Germanic League, chaired the German Nationalist party (1928–33), promoted the 1929 plebiscite against the "enslavement" of reparations, and put together the 1931 Harzburg front, which funneled political and financial support to Nazi leader Adolf Hitler. Hugenberg received a cabinet post in Hitler's government in January 1933 but was forced out later that year. ■ See study by John A. Leopold (1977).

HUGGINS, CHARLES BRENTON (1901–1997), Canadian-born U.S. surgeon and cancer researcher. A Harvard-trained professor at the University of Chicago Medical School (1927–72), Huggins was a pioneer in cancer chemotherapy. The first to demonstrate that cancer could be controlled through the use of nontoxic and nonradioactive agents, he successfully administered female hormones to men with prostate cancer and male hormones to women with breast cancer. For his experiments, conducted in the 1930s, he shared the Nobel Prize in Physiology or Medicine with Peyton Rous (1966).

HUGHES, CHARLES EVANS (1862–1948), U.S. political leader and jurist. A lawyer, college teacher, and legislative investigator, Hughes began his political career as Republican governor of New York (1907–10). Appointed an associate justice of the Supreme Court by Pres. William H. Taft (1910), Hughes left the court in 1916 to run for president against Woodrow Wilson, but he narrowly lost. As Pres. Warren Harding's secretary of state (1921–25), he attempted to secure American entry into the League of Nations and successfully organized the Washington naval disarmament conference of 1921–22. A true internationalist, he served on the Permanent Court of Arbitration (1926–30) and as a judge on the World Court (1928–30). Appointed chief justice of the Supreme Court by Pres. Herbert Hoover in 1930, Hughes led the court through one of its most controversial periods (1930–41). While striking down some of Pres. Franklin D. Roosevelt's New Deal legislation as unconstitutional, the Hughes court upheld many other acts while expanding constitutional liberties. ■ See his *Autobiographical Notes* (1973), edited by David Danelski and Joseph Tulchin; biography by Merlo J. Pusey (2 vols., 1951); and study by Dexter Perkins (1956).

HUGHES, HOWARD ROBARD, JR. (1905–1976), U.S. tycoon. Hughes' father invented a rotary bit for oil-well drilling and left his 17-year-old son the prosperous Hughes Tool Co. Hughes was also a tinkerer, but his passion was aviation. He set several world flying records during the 1930s, survived a number of crashes, established Hughes Aircraft, and bought into three commercial airlines. He also considered himself a Hollywood mogul, producing *Hell's Angels* (1930), the most expensive film of its day, and *The Outlaw* (1946), the first sexy western. Obsessive about privacy and increasingly eccentric on the subject of germ contamination, Hughes began to withdraw from public view in the 1950s. In 1966, after selling his Trans World Airline holdings for $566 million, he took up penthouse seclusion in Las Vegas, where he invested $150 million in hotels, real estate, abandoned gold mines, and a TV station. He was the center of a scandal in 1971 when a manuscript represented as his "memoirs" sold for $1 million, then proved to be fraudulent. After Hughes died, his estate (valued at more than $1.5 billion) was the subject of a legal tangle over contested wills. ■ See biographies by John Keats (1966), Noah

Dietrich (1976), and Peter H. Brown (1996); and Michael Drosnin, *Citizen Hughes* (1985).

HUGHES, (JAMES MERCER) LANGSTON (1902–1967), U.S. novelist, poet, and playwright. While working as a busboy in a Washington, D.C., hotel, Hughes was discovered (1925) by the poet Vachel Lindsay. Within a year he won recognition with his first poetry collection, *Weary Blues* (1926), and went on to become a major figure of the Harlem Renaissance of the 1920s and to pioneer black realism in novels, stories, autobiographies, poetry, songs, blues, speeches, and children's books. He treated race issues with insight and sophistication, wit and anger. His best-known works included the novels *Not Without Laughter* (1930); the short-story collections *Laughing to Keep from Crying* and *The Ways of White Folks* (1930); the poetry collections *Shakespeare in Harlem* (1942), *One-Way Ticket* (1949), and *Selected Poems* (1959); and the play *Mulatto* (1935). *The Best of Simple* (1961) assembled newspaper columns in which Hughes spoke through his mouthpiece, the social commentator Jesse B. Simple. The posthumous collection *The Panther and the Lash* (1967) reflected the black militancy of the 1960s. Hughes wrote two autobiographical works, *The Big Sea* (1940) and *I Wonder as I Wander* (1956). ■ See study by James A. Emanuel (1967) and biographies by Milton Meltzer (1968), Faith Berry (1983), and Arnold Rampersad (2 vols., 1986–88).

HUGHES, TED (1930–1998), British poet. Cambridge-educated (B.A. 1954; M.A. 1959), Hughes was regarded as a leading poet of his generation. In contrast to the less dynamic verse of his contemporaries, his poetry was written in powerful, emphatic language. It took as its basic theme the struggle between life and death in the human and animal world. He was famed for brutal nature poems in which he viewed the violence and predatory cunning of animal life. Many of his poems were conceived with myth and ritual, and his later work employed more disjunctive syntax and experimental rhymes. Among his works were *The Hawk in the Rain* (1957), *Selected Poems* (1962, 1972), *Crow* (1970), *Gaudete* (1977), *New Selected Poems* (1982), *The River* (1984), *Tales from Ovid* (1997), and numerous children's stories and plays. He was married (1956–63) to the U.S. writer Sylvia Plath, who committed suicide shortly after their separation. Hughes refused to discuss their relationship for 35 years until he broke his silence with publication of *Birthday Letters* (1998), a collection of poems about Plath and their years together. In 1984 Hughes succeeded Sir John Betjeman as poet laureate. ■ See Margaret Dickie Uroff, *Sylvia Plath and Ted Hughes* (1979), and studies by Ekbert Faas (1980) and Terry Gifford and Neil Roberts (1981).

HUGHES, WILLIAM MORRIS (1864–1952), Australian political leader. Hughes emigrated to Australia from his native London (1884) and worked as an itinerant laborer and labor organizer. He served in the New South Wales legislature (1894–1901) as a Labourite and after federation was elected to the first federal Parliament (1901), holding his seat until his death. As prime minister (1915 to 1923) he supported conscription during World War I and helped form the Nationalist party (1917) when the Labour party failed to support him. At the Versailles Peace Conference (1919) he gained Australian control over most German colonies in the South Pacific. Hughes subsequently served in the cabinet (1934–41) and on the Advisory War Council (1941–44). ■ See his memoirs, *Crusts and Crusades* (1947) and *Policies and Potentates* (1950), and biography by L. F. Fitzhardinge (2 vols., 1964–79).

HUIDOBRO, VICENTE (1893–1948), Chilean poet. The controversial Huidobro, the first avant-garde poet in Latin America, formulated the radical poetic doctrine known as creationism in Paris during World War I. Inspired by the work of the French poet Guillaume Apollinaire, it asserted that a poem must be autonomous, and characterized the poet as a "little God." Among Huidobro's poems illustrative of creationism are those in *Tour Eiffel* (1917) and *Arctic Poems* (1918; Eng. trans. 1974). In Madrid (1921) he helped found the *ultraísmo* (ultraism) movement, an offshoot of creationism. He later fought for the Republicans in the Spanish Civil War during the 1930s and was a correspondent during World War II. He also wrote several literary manifestos and the novels *Mirror of a Mage* (1926; Eng. trans. 1931) and *Portrait of a Paladin* (1929; Eng. trans. 1931). English translations are in *The Selected Poetry* (1981). ■ See Cecil G. Wood, *The Creacionismo of Vicente Huidobro* (1978).

HUIZINGA, JOHAN (1872–1945), Dutch historian. A conservative professor at Leiden University (1915–42), Huizinga was a specialist in Indian literature who wrote several important works in European intellectual and cultural history, including *The Waning of the Middle Ages* (1919; Eng. trans. 1924), a study of 15th-century France and Holland; a biography of Erasmus (1924; Eng. trans. 1924); and a collection of essays, *Men and Ideas* (Eng. trans. 1959). *Homo Ludens* (1938; Eng. trans. 1949) was an examination of the role of play in culture. He was held as a hostage by the Nazis during World War II from 1942 until his death.

HULL, BOBBY (Robert Marvin Hull; 1939–), Canadian ice-hockey player. Known as the "Golden Jet," Hull was the first true "superstar" of hockey. He joined the Chicago Black Hawks in 1957 and in his 15-year career became one of the most prolific scorers in hockey history. He led the National Hockey League in scoring in 1960, 1962, and 1966. He also led in goals scored six times, going over the 50 mark on five occasions, and won the Hart Trophy for Most Valuable Player in 1965. In 1972 he became the first million-dollar hockey player when he jumped to the World Hockey Association, giving that new league immediate credibility. He scored 913 goals during his career in the two leagues.

His son was hockey star Brett Hull (1964–   ). ■ See study by Jim Hunt (1971).

HULL, CLARK LEONARD (1884–1952), U.S. psychologist. Hull was a neobehaviorist who defined basic human motivation as "drive." A recipient of a Ph.D. from the University of Wisconsin (1918), he taught at Wisconsin and Yale. He was best known for his experimental studies of learning, which formed the basis of his "mathematico-deductive" theory described in *Principles of Behavior* (1943). In his efforts to devise a rigorous system of behavior prediction he was influenced by Darwinian evolutionary theory, the physiological studies of Ivan Pavlov, and Freudian psychiatric concepts. A scholar of diverse interests, he coined the phrase "aptitude testing," the subject of his 1928 book of that name, and wrote the classic *Hypnosis and Susceptibility* (1933).

HULL, CORDELL (1871–1955), U.S. public official. Hull was a Tennessee state legislator, judge, Democratic congressman (1907–21; 1923–31), and U.S. senator (1931–33) before being appointed secretary of state by Pres. Franklin D. Roosevelt. As head of the State Department longer than anyone else in U.S. history (1933–44), Hull promoted the Good Neighbor policy with Latin America and advocated tariff reductions and expanded international trade. He pursued a cautious policy toward Japan and Germany during the 1930s, but drew closer to the Allies after the outbreak of World War II. During the war his role in foreign-policy formulation was less significant, but he played an important role in the establishment of the United Nations and won the 1945 Nobel Peace Prize for this work. ■ See his *Memoirs* (2 vols., 1948) and biographies by Harold B. Hinton (1942) and Julius W. Pratt (1964).

HULSE, RUSSELL A. (1950–   ), U.S. physicist. Hulse was a student of radio astronomer Joseph H. Taylor, Jr., at the University of Massachusetts, Amherst (Ph.D. 1975). While searching for pulsars with the radio telescope at Arecibo, Puerto Rico (1974), the two scientists discovered the first binary pulsar, two dense rapidly spinning neutron stars rotating around a common center of mass with one emitting pulsing radio waves. They found that the rotational speed of the pulsars was increasing as was their proximity to each other, and they theorized that the orbital decay was due to energy loss in the form of gravitational waves. Their study provided the first indirect experimental evidence for gravitational waves that were predicted by Albert Einstein in his theory of gravitation. Hulse and Taylor shared the 1993 Nobel Prize in Physics for their discovery. Hulse subsequently changed fields from astrophysics to plasma physics and did research at the Princeton University Plasma Physics Lab (1977–   ).

HUMBERT-DROZ, JULES (1891–1971), Swiss Comintern leader. A Protestant pastor, Humbert-Droz refused to serve in the army during World War I, joined the Socialist party, and embraced communism after the Bolshevik revolution in Russia (1917). He was a founder of the Swiss Communist party (1921) and a high official of the Comintern (1921–35) and directed its activities in Latin America and the Latin countries of Europe. After an intraparty conflict in 1943, he was expelled from the Swiss party. He joined the Swiss Social Democratic party and served as its secretary (1947–58).

HUME, JOHN (1937–   ), Northern Ireland political leader. A graduate of the National University of Ireland, Hume was founder of the Credit Union party, the forerunner of the Social Democratic and Labor Party (SDLP), and served in the Northern Ireland Parliament (1969–72) and Northern Ireland Assembly (1972–73; 1982–86). A leader of the moderate, nonviolent forces within the Roman Catholic community, he headed the SDLP, the largest Roman Catholic party in Northern Ireland (1979–   ), and served in both the European Parliament (1979–   ) and the British Parliament (1983–   ). He was a tireless advocate of peace and reconciliation between the Catholics and Protestants in Northern Ireland and played a key role in the negotiations leading to the Good Friday Agreement (April 1998), which provided for a respite in sectarian violence and the creation of a new Northern Ireland Assembly. He shared the 1998 Nobel Peace Prize with Northern Ireland Protestant political leader David Trimble.

HUMPHREY, DORIS (1895–1958), U.S. dancer, choreographer, and dance theorist. Humphrey worked in the Denishawn company (1917–28), then formed her own troupe and school with mime artist Charles Weidman (1928). For over fifteen years their company influenced modern dance, producing such accomplished dancers as José Limón. Humphrey originated (1935) the Juilliard Dance Theatre and was (1934–42) the moving force behind the Bennington College Summer School of Dance. Humphrey's dance creations included *Water Study* (1928) and the *Life of a Bee* (1929). She stopped performing in 1945 due to arthritis but continued to teach and choreograph. She wrote *The Art of Making Dances* (1959). ■ See her autobiography (1972) and Marcia B. Siegel, *Days on Earth* (1987).

HUMPHREY, HUBERT HORATIO (1911–1978), U.S. political leader. A former pharmacist and teacher, Humphrey became active in politics as a supporter of New Deal social ideals. He engineered a merger of Minnesota's Democratic and Farmer-Labor parties to win election as mayor of Minneapolis (1945–48) and U.S. senator (1949–65, 1971–78). He was defeated for the 1960 Democratic presidential nomination by John F. Kennedy. A leading supporter of civil-rights and social-welfare legislation, Humphrey was also known as a dedicated anticommunist. However, he continually called for contacts with communist nations and for disarmament agreements with the Soviet Union. He served as vice president (1965–69) under Pres. Lyndon B. Johnson, compromising his liberal reputation, many felt, by supporting the Vietnam War. He was defeated for the presidency in 1968 by Republican Richard Nixon. ■ See biographies by Robert Sherrill (1968) and Carl Solberg (1984) and study by Charles L. Garrettson (1993).

HUNSACKER, JEROME CLARKE (1886–1984), U.S. aeronautical engineer. A graduate of the U.S. Naval Academy (1908), Hunsacker studied engineering at the Massachusetts Institute of Technology and instituted (1914) the nation's first college course in aeronautics and design. In charge of aircraft design for the navy during World War I, he designed the NC-4 flying boat, which made the first transatlantic flight (1919), and the *Shenandoah* (1923), the first helium-filled airship. Hunsacker subsequently aided in the development of the torpedo plane, takeoff and landing devices for aircraft carriers, and lightweight carrier airplanes. He left the navy in 1926 and taught at Massachusetts Institute of Technology (1933–51).

HUN SEN (1951–), Cambodian political leader. The son of peasant farmers, Hun Sen joined the revolutionary Khmer Rouge movement as a teenager and was the commander of a guerrilla regiment when the movement seized power (April 1975). Two years later, however, disgusted by the murderous policies of the new government, he deserted the Khmer Rouge and in 1978 he helped organize a united front against it. He participated in the 1978 Vietnamese invasion of Cambodia that ousted the Khmer Rouge, and he served as foreign minister (1979–91) and prime minister (1985–91) in the new Vietnamese-dominated government. For years, however, civil war continued in the countryside, and various rebel factions vied for power. A 1991 U.N. peace accord resulted in a cease-fire and the formation of a provisional government led by then-Prince Norodom Sihanouk but which included Hun Sen. As a result of negotiations after a disputed 1993 election sponsored by the United Nations, Hun Sen became co-prime minister with royalist party leader Prince Norodon Ranariddh. Hun Sen consequently ousted Ranariddh in a bloody coup (1997) and formed a new government after winning the 1998 national elections.

HUNT, FRAZIER (1885–1967), U.S. journalist. The prototype of the foreign correspondent, Spike Hunt roamed the world for 30 years (from World War I through World War II) covering major news stories and interviewing nearly every important political figure of the era as a reporter for several news agencies. His most famous scoop was his acquisition of a copy of the Treaty of Versailles before its public release; he delivered it personally to the *Chicago Tribune,* which published it. His dramatic account of U.S. troop intervention in northern Russia (1918–19) during the civil war was instrumental in Pres. Woodrow Wilson's decision to withdraw the soldiers. Among his 14 books were two biographies of Gen. Douglas MacArthur, whose campaigns he covered during World War II. ■ See his autobiography, *One American and his Attempt at Education* (1938).

HUNT, HAROLDSON LAFAYETTE (1889–1974), U.S. oilman. The recipient of a fifth-grade education, H. L. Hunt left his father's farm at age 16 and worked as a ranch hand. He used a modest inheritance to speculate and trade in oil leases in Arkansas and struck oil on his first try. Extending his operations throughout the Southwest, he founded the Hunt Oil Co. (1937), which soon became the largest independent producer of oil and gas in the United States. His income was estimated at $1 million per week and his fortune was said to be worth $2 to $3 billion. Hunt's ultraconservative political views were broadcast on hundreds of radio and television stations throughout the country during the 1960s and his column was published in approximately 80 newspapers. Sons (Nelson) Bunker Hunt and W. Herbert Hunt caused a brief financial panic in 1980. Their efforts to control the price of silver were undermined when the margin requirements were raised by the government and the price of silver collapsed. They were forced to borrow $1.1 billion to save their financial and oil empire. In 1986, they and their brother Lamar filed a petition of bankruptcy for the Placid Oil Company, their key enterprise. ■ See biography by Stanley H. Brown (1976) and Harry Hurt, *Texas Rich* (1981).

HUNTINGTON, ANNA HYATT (Anna Hyatt; 1876–1973), U.S. sculptor. Huntington's interest in animals stemmed from her youth on a Maryland farm; she began sculpting as a child. At age 24 she exhibited 40 animal sculptures at a one-person exhibition, winning recognition for her anatomical precision. She later studied in France and Italy and became known for her heroic statuary. The French government awarded her a prize for a statue of Joan of Arc, cast in bronze and erected (1915) in New York City. Her other award-winning sculptures included *Diana of the Chase* (1922), *El Cid Compeador* (1927), *Bulls Fighting* (1928), and *Greyhounds Playing* (1937). With her husband, the philanthropist Archer M. Huntington, she was an active patron of the arts.

HUNTINGTON, ELLSWORTH (1876–1947), U.S. geographer. A Yale researcher and professor (1907–45), Huntington was best known for his influential, though ethnocentric, theories concerning the relationship of climate and environment to human civilization and progress. He did extensive fieldwork in the Middle East, Central Asia, Iran, India, China, Siberia, Central America, and the United States and wrote 28 books, including *The Pulse of Asia* (1907), *Civilization and Climate* (1915), *The Character of Races* (1924), and *Mainsprings of Civilization* (1945). He believed in the cultural superiority of the Nordic races, advocated restrictive immigration policies, and was a powerful force within the American Eugenics Society (president, 1934–38). ■ See biography by Geoffrey J. Martin (1973).

HUNTLEY, CHET (1911–1974), and **DAVID BRINKLEY** (1920–), U.S. broadcast journalists. Huntley and Brinkley reported the nightly news for NBC television from 1956 to

1970. Huntley, solemn and unflappable, and Brinkley, wry and witty, mixed humor, human interest, and authoritative national and international reporting in commanding an audience of 17 million viewers. They achieved the highest ratings in the news field and won every major news-broadcasting award. Brinkley remained with NBC until joining ABC News in 1981. He hosted the influential Sunday morning show "This Week with David Brinkley" (1981–96), which featured political news and commentary.

HUROK, SOLOMON (1888–1974), Russian-born impresario. Sol Hurok arrived in the United States in 1906 and worked briefly as a hardware salesman and streetcar conductor. As an impresario he discovered, promoted, and presented some of the world's great performing artists, including Efrem Zimbalist, Mischa Elman, Isadora Duncan, Anna Pavlova, Marian Anderson, Feodor Chaliapin, and Artur Rubinstein. Hurok took particular pride in creating an audience for ballet in the United States, beginning with his sponsorship of Diaghilev's Ballet Russe (1914) and continuing over the years with the Sadler's Wells, Royal, and Bolshoi ballets. He was a consummate showman with a lavish lifestyle and a genius for publicity. ■ See his memoirs, *Impresario* (1946) and *Sol Hurok Presents* (1953).

HURSTON, ZORA NEALE (1901–1960), U.S. novelist. Hurston was one of eight children born to the family of a Baptist preacher in Florida. After going north as a maid to an actress in a Gilbert and Sullivan company, Hurston studied literature and anthropology at Howard University (1921–24), Barnard College (B.A. 1928), and Columbia University, where she studied under anthropologist Franz Boas. Her study, *Mules and Men* (1935), and novels, *Jonah's Gourd Vine* (1934), *Their Eyes Were Watching God* (1937), *Moses, Man of the Mountain* (1938; repr. 1984), and *Seraph on the Suwanee* (1948), were set in the Deep South and the West Indies and reflected her fascination with folklore, magic, and dialect. Hurston was an important figure of the Harlem Renaissance of the 1920s and 1930s and appeared on the cover of the *Saturday Review* in 1942. In later years, however, she dropped out of the literary scene, worked as a domestic, and apparently grew increasingly conservative. Critics continue to debate her politics. Hurston died in poverty and obscurity in a Florida welfare home. Her work was neglected for two decades, until Alice Walker's essay "Looking for Zora" (1975) revived interest in her work. Selections of Hurston's writings were subsequently collected in *I Love Myself When I Am Laughing... & Then Again When I Am Looking Mean & Impressive* (1979) and *Spunk* (1985). ■ See her autobiography, *Dust Tracks on a Road* (1942; enlarged ed. 1984); biography by Robert E. Hemenway (1977); and study by Lillie Howard (1980).

HUSÁK, GUSTAV (1913–1991), Czechoslovak political leader. A Slovak Communist party activist (from 1933), Husák, a lawyer, was a leader of the anti-Nazi Slovak na-

tional uprising (1944). After World War II he was a party and state official but, as a victim of the Stalinist purges, was charged with treason and sabotage, expelled from the party, and imprisoned (1951–60). Rehabilitated (1963), he became deputy premier (1968) and helped formulate some of the liberal reforms of the Alexander Dubček regime. However, after the Soviet invasion (August 1968), Husák became increasingly pro-Soviet. He replaced Dubček as party secretary (1969), suppressed the liberals, and reinstated strict party control throughout Czech society. He was named president of Czechoslovakia in 1975. As the wave of reform, initiated by Mikhail Gorbachev in the Soviet Union, reached Czechoslovakia in the late 1980s, Husák gave up his party leadership post (1987), resigned as president (1989), and was again expelled from the Communist party (1990).

HUSAYN, TAHA (1889–1973), Egyptian writer and educator. Husayn was probably the century's greatest Arabic literary figure. Though blind from the age of 3, he studied at Al Azhar University in Cairo and received a Ph.D. from the Sorbonne and the first doctorate granted by the University of Cairo. The author of more than 40 volumes of fiction, essays, criticism, history, and philosophy, he was most famous for his autobiography, *Al-Ayyam* (3 vols., 1929–67), which was translated as *An Egyptian Childhood* (1932), *The Stream of Days* (1943), and *A Passage to France* (1976). A landmark in Arabic literature, it was the first modern literary work to be acclaimed in the West. As a professor in Egypt, Husayn was frequently involved in controversies with conservatives for his application of modern Western critical methods to Arabic and Islamic literature and religion. In *The Future of Culture in Egypt* (1938; Eng. trans. 1954), he advocated a mixture of Arab and Western cultures and saw Egypt as part of a Euro-Arabic Mediterranean civilization. Husayn was minister of education from 1950 to 1952. His other translated works included *The Dreams of Scheherazade* (1974), *The Call of the Curlew* (1980), *The Sufferers: Stories and Polemics* (1993), *A Man of Letters* (1994), and *The Tree of Misery* (1997). ■ See study by Pierre Cachia (1956).

HUSAYNI, HAJ AMIN AL-. *See HUSSEINI, HAJ AMIN AL-.*

HUSEIN IBN-ALI (1854?–1931), Arab national and political leader. Born into a prominent family that claimed descent from the Prophet Muhammad, Husein served as sharif of Mecca (1908–16). During World War I he and his sons supported the British against the Ottomans, and he proclaimed the Arab revolt in June 1916 and was named king of Hejaz. Following World War I, he felt betrayed by the British, who had made conflicting territorial promises to the Arabs, French, and Zionists. Though the British named Husein's sons Abdullah and Faisal as emir of Transjordan and king of Iraq, respectively, Husein rejected the mandate system and the peace treaties. His rivalry with Ibn-Saud of the

Nejd (now in central Saudi Arabia) intensified when Husein proclaimed himself caliph (1924). Saud captured Mecca and forced Husein to abdicate and flee (1924). ■ See James Morris, *The Hashemite Kings* (1959).

HU SHIH (1891–1962), Chinese scholar and reformer. A graduate of Cornell (B.A. 1914) and Columbia (Ph.D. 1917) universities, Hu became an influential leader of the May Fourth movement (1919), which sought to transform Chinese culture and politics. Opposed to a political revolution that would precede cultural changes, Hu successfully advocated the use of a new Chinese vernacular that would make literature and scholarship available to the masses. He utilized experimental methodology in his numerous scholarly endeavors and sought precedents in traditional thought for modern scientific ideas. A disciple of the U.S. pragmatist John Dewey, Hu was a politically independent opponent of Marxism and champion of liberalism, pragmatism, and gradualism. His influence waned after 1937, when he left his post as dean of the College of Arts at Beijing (Peking) University, and he spent only two of his last 25 years on the mainland. He served as China's ambassador to the United States (1938–42) and served the nationalist government as U.N. ambassador (1957). At his death, he was president of the Academia Sinica on Taiwan. His books in English translation included *The Development of the Logical Method in Ancient China* (1922; 2nd ed. 1963) and *The Chinese Renaissance* (1934; 2nd ed. 1963). ■ See studies by Jerome B. Grieder (1970) and Min-chih Chou (1984).

HUSSEIN, SADDAM (1937–   ), Iraqi political leader. Born into a landless peasant family, Hussein joined the Ba'ath Socialist party (1957) and was active in nationalist student groups. Wounded in an assassination attempt against head-of-state Gen. Abdel Karim Kassem (1959), he escaped to Syria and then to Egypt, where he was influenced by the ideology of Pres. Gamal Abdel Nasser. Returning to Iraq after Kassem's downfall (1963), Hussein was imprisoned (1964–66), but he escaped and reorganized the Ba'ath party. He played a major role in the bloodless coup that brought his party to power (July 1968), and served as deputy chairman of the Revolutionary Command Council (1969–79) and as president of Iraq (from 1979). He established a repressive, dictatorial regime, created a personality cult, and maintained close ties with the Soviet Union, which became his chief arms supplier. He used Iraq's oil revenues for industrial development, agricultural modernization, rural electrification, and numerous social, educational, and literacy programs. His invasion of Iran (September 1980) led to an inconclusive war that damaged Iraq's economy and caused an estimated one million casualties. Fighting continued until 1988. His invasion of neighboring oil-rich Kuwait (August 1990) led to the Persian Gulf War (January–February 1991) in which a U.N.-sponsored army composed of U.S., European, and Arab forces defeated the occupying Iraqi army. Hussein ruthlessly suppressed Shi'ite and Kurdish rebellions in Iraq in the wake of the war. His failure to fully comply with terms of the cease-fire agreement led to a U.N.-approved trade embargo that was maintained through the 1990s. ■ See studies by Effraim Karsh and Inari Rautsi (1991) and Said K. Abarish (2000), and Andrew and Patrick Cockburn, *Out of the Ashes* (1999).

HUSSEIN I (1935–1999), Jordanian king. Hussein succeeded to the throne in 1952, after his father was deposed because of mental illness. A Sandhurst alumnus, Hussein survived assassination attempts and political and economic crises to maintain his grip on the monarchy. With the help of U.S. financial aid, he modernized Jordan's military forces. Although a moderate, pro-Western Arab, he took his country into the 1967 war against Israel, was defeated decisively, and lost Jordan's territory on the West Bank of the River Jordan. In 1970, Hussein routed Palestinian commandos who were using Jordan as a base for attacks on Israel. Later, though declining to go as far as Egypt in developing relations with Israel, he worked with the Palestine Liberation Organization and with moderate Arab regimes to find a solution to the Middle East crisis. He subsequently relinquished Jordan's claim to the West Bank (1988) and signed a peace treaty with Israel (1994). He wrote an autobiography, *Uneasy Lies the Head* (1962), and *My War with Israel* (1968; Eng. trans. 1969). ■ See biography by Peter J. Snow (1972) and Robert B. Satloff, *From Abdullah to Hussein* (1994).

HUSSEINI (OR HUSAYNI), HAJ AMIN AL- (1893?–1974), Palestinian Arab political and religious leader. Born into a prominent family, Husseini was opposed to the Zionist movement and accused of instigating anti-Jewish riots (1920). Named mufti of Jerusalem (1921) and president of the Supreme Muslim Council (1922), he was the most important Palestinian politician and religious leader during the British mandate period. He formed the militant Arab High Committee (1936), a coalition of Arab groups, and attempted to force the British to end Jewish immigration. After the outbreak of an anti-British and anti-Jewish terror campaign, Husseini was removed from office by the British, his committee was banned, and he went into exile in Lebanon (1937) and then in Iraq. He spent most of World War II in Germany, where he worked as a propagandist and advised the Nazis on Middle East policies. After the war he headed the Palestine Arab Higher Committee in Egypt and fought against the Zionists in the 1948 war. After Israeli independence he sought to revive the committee in Lebanon, but his influence declined. He continued to publish anti-Israel propaganda. ■ See Joseph B. Schechtman, *The Mufti and the Fuehrer* (1965), and Philip Mattar, *The Mufti of Jerusalem* (1988).

HUSSERL, EDMUND (1859–1938), German philosopher. Husserl, who taught philosophy at Göttingen (1901–16) and Freiberg (1916–28), was the founder of phenomenology and one of the century's most influential philosophers. He sought to describe subjective experience by "bracketing" the data of consciousness, that is, by considering that data without reference to preconceived notions. He used this method to study the structure of experience. Influenced by his mentor, Franz Brentano, Husserl concluded that consciousness exists only in relation to the objects that it considers. His phenomenology influenced Martin Heidegger, Jean Paul Sartre, and scholars in many disciplines. His writings included *Logical Investigations* (1900–01; Eng. trans. 1970), *Ideas* (1913; Eng. trans. 1931), *Formal and Transcendental Logic* (1929; Eng. trans. 1969), and *The Phenomenology of Internal Time-Consciousness* (1928; Eng. trans. 1964). ■ See studies by Paul Ricoeur (Eng. trans. 1967) and Maurice Natanson (1973) and Dorian Cairns, *Conversations with Husserl and Fink* (1976).

HUSTON, JOHN (1906–1987), U.S. film director. Son of the character actor Walter Huston, John enjoyed an adventurous youth before turning to film. He made his directorial debut with *The Maltese Falcon* (1941), now a cult classic, spent the World War II years filming army documentaries, and later directed such memorable features as *Key Largo* (1948), *The Treasure of the Sierra Madre* (Academy Award, 1949), *The Asphalt Jungle* (1950), *The African Queen* (1952), and *The Misfits* (1961). Huston also produced and directed *The Man Who Would Be King* (1975) and *Annie* (1981), and directed *Prizzi's Honor* (1985). He was an original; he never established a consistent style, but his films have in common a love of adventure and fascination with honor. He also did some acting, specializing in his later years in roles of great patriarchal authority. His daughter was the actress Anjelica Huston (1951–   ). ■ See his autobiography, *An Open Book* (1980); biographies by Axel Madsen (1978) and Stuart Kaminsky (1978); and Lawrence Grobel, *The Hustons* (1989).

HUTCHINS, ROBERT MAYNARD (1899–1977), U.S. educator and social critic. For more than half a century Hutchins was an influential voice in American education and public affairs. Appointed to the presidency of the University of Chicago at age 30, he reorganized the curriculum (by stressing liberal arts), spoke out against the trends of specialization and vocationalism, and abolished football and fraternities (as unrelated to the aims of education). After leaving Chicago in 1951, he was president of the Fund for the Republic (1954–69) and founded the Center for the Study of Democratic Institutions (1959) in Santa Barbara (chairman, 1959–74), an internationally known "community of scholars" that ran seminars and conferences and issued publications dealing with major contemporary social and political issues. His books included *The Higher Learning in America* (1936) and *The University of Utopia* (1953). ■ See study by Mary Ann Dzuback (1991).

HUTSON, DONALD MONTGOMERY (1913–1997), U.S. football player. One of the greatest pass catchers in football history, Don Hutson was an All-American end at the University of Alabama (1934) and a star with the Green Bay Packers (1935–45). Speedy, graceful, and a master at faking, he was professional football's outstanding receiver and was named All-Pro in 9 of his 11 seasons. He led the National Football League in scoring five times, pass receptions eight times, touchdowns eight times, and retired with 20 league records—including most points, most pass receptions, most yards gained by receiving passes, and most touchdowns in a career and during one season.

HUXLEY, ALDOUS LEONARD (1894–1963), British novelist and essayist. The son of the biologist Thomas Henry Huxley, Aldous Huxley studied at Eton and Oxford (B.A. 1915). Though virtually blind as an adult, he worked for a time as a journalist and drama critic. His early novels and short stories, including *Crome Yellow* (1921) and *Antic Hay* (1923), were satirical studies of British society. His later novels were more serious and included *Point Counter Point* (1928), a depiction of the hollowness of modern life, and *Brave New World* (1932), a bitter, anti-utopian view of a sterile future. Living in California after 1937, Huxley continued to write novels, essays, and historical studies on such varied topics as witchcraft, mysticism, and the effects of hallucinatory drugs. ■ See biography by Sybille Bedford (1974); study by Harold H. Watts (1969); and George Woodcock, *Dawn and the Darkest Hour* (1972).

HUXLEY, SIR ANDREW FIELDING (1917–   ), British physiologist. A member of a distinguished family of scientists and literary figures, Huxley taught at Cambridge (1941–60) and at the University of London (1960–83). For his pioneering physicochemical analysis of nerve cells and of the mechanism of the transmission of nerve impulses he shared the 1963 Nobel Prize in Physiology or Medicine with Alan Hodgkin and Sir John Eccles. He later did important research in the area of muscle contraction. He served as president of the Royal Society (1980–85).

HUXLEY, SIR JULIAN SORELL (1887–1975), British biologist, humanist, and science writer. Born into an illustrious English family, Huxley was educated at Eton and Oxford and did important work in many fields of biology including ecology, ethology, and genetics. He was a professor of zoology at King's College, London (1925–35) and secretary of the London Zoological Society (1935–42). His most important book, *Evolution: The Modern Synthesis* (1942), concerned the fusion of Darwin's natural selection theory with Mendelian genetics. Huxley was a proponent of "evolutionary humanism," a philosophy that rejected a belief in God but proposed a system of ethics and psychosocial evolution that involved eugenics and that placed ultimate faith in the possibilities of humanity. Widely respected throughout the world, he served as the first director general (1946–48) of the United Nations Educational, Scientific, and Cultural Organization (UNESCO). ■ See his two-volume autobiography, *Memories* (1970–73); the studies by Ronald Clark (1961) and J. R. Baker (1978); and Krishna R. Dronamraju, *If I Am to Be Remembered* (1993).

HUXTABLE, ADA LOUISE (Ada Louise Landman; 1921?–), American architecture critic. Born in New York City, Huxtable studied at Hunter College, New York University's Institute of Fine Arts, and later in Italy. She was associated with New York's Museum of Modern Art (1946–50), and wrote on architecture for various magazines. In 1963, she became architecture critic for the *New York Times,* and a decade later joined the newspaper's editorial board. Huxtable brought social conscience and eclectic interests to her lively columns, exposing bland design and inept city planning while praising elegance and efficiency. She was largely responsible for the creation of the New York City Landmarks Preservation Commission. Huxtable wrote *Pier Luigi Nervi* (1960), *Classic New York* (1964), *Will They Ever Finish Bruckner Boulevard?* (1970), *Kicked a Building Lately?* (1976), *The Tall Building Artistically Reconsidered: The Search for a Skyscraper Style* (1985; rev. ed. 1992), *Architecture, Anyone* (1986), and *The Unreal America: Architecture and Illusion* (1997).

HU YAOBANG (old style: **HU YAO-PANG;** 1915–1989), Chinese political leader. Born into a poor peasant family in Hunan province, Hu left home to join the communist forces in the Jinggang Mountains when he was 14. He joined the Communist party in 1933. As a political commissar with the Red army during World War II, he met Deng Xiaoping (Teng Hsiao-p'ing) and became his protégé, serving with him in the army and later (after the establishment of the People's Republic) in Sichuan (Szechwan) province (1949–52) and in Beijing (Peking; from 1952). Hu held important party and government posts during the 1950s, including leader of the Communist Youth League (1952–67), but during the Cultural Revolution (1966–69) he was accused of being a "capitalist roader," purged from his positions, and sent to a reeducation camp. Rehabilitated in 1973, he worked to improve morale at the Academy of Sciences, but was purged again, by the radical Gang of Four (April 1976). After the death of Mao Zedong (Mao Tse-tung; September 1976) the radicals were arrested and Hu was restored to power once again. A pragmatist and modernizer, he advocated material incentives for workers and the introduction of aspects of the free-enterprise and free-market systems. Elevated to the Politburo (1978) and named party secretary-general (1979), he replaced Hua Guofeng (Hua Kuo-feng) as chairman of the Chinese Communist party (1981). He was forced to re-

sign as party secretary (1987) in the wake of large demonstrations by university students in several cities calling for greater democracy in China. He was accused of tolerating dissidents and of introducing market reforms too rapidly and he was replaced as acting general secretary by Zhao Ziyang. His death triggered widespread demonstrations by students that culminated in the government suppression of the movement in Tiananmen Square in Beijing. ■ See biography by Zhong Mei Yang (Eng. trans. 1988).

HYDE, CHARLES CHENEY (1873–1952), U.S. international jurist and educator. Hyde was educated at Yale and Harvard (LL.B. 1898). While teaching at the Northwestern University Law School (1899–1925) he wrote *International Law, Chiefly As Interpreted and Applied by the U.S.* (2 vols., 1922; rev. ed., 3 vols., 1945), which became a standard reference work cited by international tribunals. From 1923 to 1925 he served as a solicitor for the U.S. Department of State, and he subsequently taught international law and diplomacy at Columbia University (1925–45).

HYDE, DOUGLAS (1860–1949). Irish scholar and political leader. Hyde collected folktales and poetry and published verse translations from the Irish that influenced William Butler Yeats and other writers. An interest in reviving the Irish language prompted the Protestant Hyde to found the Gaelic League (1893). The organization thrived, with 550 branches by 1919, and was an important force in the movement for national revival. Hyde, the league's first president, was also known in Gaelic as *An Craoibhin Aoibhinn* ("the Delightful Little Branch"). Believing that the league should remain apolitical, he left when its goals became decidedly nationalist (1915). At the National University, he held the chair of modern Irish (1909–32). When the constitution of 1937 created the office of president of Ireland, Hyde was unanimously selected by all parties and served throughout World War II (1938–45). ■ See study by Janet E. Dunleavy (1991).

HYMAN, LIBBIE HENRIETTA (1888–1969), U.S. zoologist. Hyman trained at the University of Chicago (Ph.D. 1915), where she remained for two decades until becoming associated with New York's American Museum of Natural History (1937–69). Her research on such organisms as protozoa, sponges, jellyfish, and flatworms led to the classic reference work *The Invertebrates* (6 vols., 1931–68), which describes various aspects of animals without backbones ranging from the single-cell protozoa to the giant squid. Her research and prolific publications gained her many international prizes.

I

IACOCCA, LEE (Lido Anthony Iacocca; 1924–   ), U.S. businessman. The son of Italian immigrants, Iacocca studied engineering at Lehigh (B.S. 1945) and Princeton (M.E. 1946) and joined the Ford Motor Co. in 1946. Gaining a reputation as a marketing genius, he developed such successful models as the Ford Mustang, Maverick, Fiesta, Continental Mark III, and the Econoline truck, and worked his way up the corporate ladder, eventually serving as president of the company (1970–78). Forced out of his job because of personal disputes with Henry Ford II, Iacocca took over Ford's financially ailing competitor, the Chrysler Corp. (president, 1978–79; chairman, 1979–93). Through layoffs, production cutbacks, union wage concessions, and, most importantly, an unprecedented $1.2 billion loan guarantee and tax concessions granted by Congress, he was able to restore the company to financial health by 1983 and to gain $2.4 billion in profits in 1984. His autobiography, *Iacocca* (1984; with William Novak), which extolled the work ethic, patriotism, and family values, became one of the century's best-selling books, with more than 2.5 million hardcover copies in print by 1986. He also wrote *Talking Straight* (1988). ■ See Peter Wyden, *The Unknown Iacocca* (1987).

IAKOVOS (Demetrios A. Coucouzis; 1911–   ), Greek Orthodox archbishop. A storekeeper's son, Coucouzis was born on a Turkish island and entered theological school at age 16. He was ordained a deacon in 1934 and went to the United States (1939), where he taught at the Archdiocese Theological School in Connecticut. When he was ordained a priest (1940), he took the name Iakovos (James). While dean of Boston's Cathedral of the Annunciation (1942–54), Iakovos studied at Harvard Divinity School (S.T.M. 1945). In 1959, he was named archbishop of North and South America and served in that post until 1996. Iakovos, who became a U.S. citizen, was active in the ecumenical movement and served as a copresident of the World Council of Churches (1959–68). He sought a renewal of faith among his 2 million subjects and wrote books in Greek, French, and English.

IBÁÑEZ DEL CAMPO, CARLOS (1877–1960), Chilean general and political leader. Ibáñez was a career officer who participated in a 1925 coup to restore to power the legally elected president of Chile. He was himself elected president in 1927 but reigned as a dictator, suppressing opposition and strengthening ties with foreign reactionaries. Economic failures prompted Ibáñez to flee the country in 1931, but he returned to lead unsuccessful revolts in 1937 and 1939 that were supported by Chilean Nazis. Elected to the senate (1949), he appealed to depressed urban workers and won a plurality of the votes in the 1952 presidential election that returned him to power for six years. Although his policies led to industrial growth, he was unable to solve Chile's basic economic problems.

IBARRURI, DOLORES (La Pasionaria; 1895–1989), Spanish political leader. Born into an impoverished family of miners, Ibarruri was a founder of the Spanish Communist party (1920) and an activist among the Asturian miners during the 1920s and 1930s. She edited several communist newspapers and served in parliament (1936–39). A militant supporter of the Second Republic, she became an internationally known figure during the Spanish Civil War (1936–39) as she exhorted the Spanish people, on radio and in the streets, to fight against the fascist forces: "It is better to die on your feet than live on your knees! They shall not pass." A living legend, she left Spain after the Franco dictatorship was established (1939) and lived for most of the next 38 years in exile in the Soviet Union, where she served as general secretary of the Spanish Communist party (1942–60). She returned to Spain in 1977 and was again elected to parliament but withdrew because of infirmity and old age. She wrote several books, including the autobiography, *They Shall Not Pass* (Eng. trans. 1966).

IBERT, JACQUES (1890–1962), French composer. A student of Gabriel Fauré, Ibert directed the French Academy in Rome (1937–61) and the Paris Opera (1955–56). His music, known for its elegance and craftsmanship, is marked by coloristic orchestration, rich harmonies, and influences of impressionism and neoclassicism—and often by a streak of humor. His orchestral works include *Escales* ("Ports of Call"; 1919), *Divertissement* (1930), and the ballet *The Ballad of Reading Gaol* (1922). His well-known piano piece *Le Petit Ane Blanc* ("the little white donkey") is from the suite *Histoires* (1943).

IBN-SAUD (Abd al-Aziz ibn-Saud; 1880–1953), Saudi Arabian king. A desert sheik who extended his authority over most of the Arabian peninsula, Ibn-Saud consolidated this area into the kingdom of Saudi Arabia in 1932. In 1933 he granted the first oil concession to the American company that later was known as Aramco. Following World War II, oil production grew spectacularly, and government income, which was essentially the king's personal funds, jumped from less than $1 million in 1920 to $7 million in 1939 and to over $200 million at the time of his death in 1953. Ibn-Saud captured the world's imagination as the first of the fabulously wealthy Arab rulers of an oil-rich nation. ■ See David Howarth, *The Desert King* (1964), and study by Leslie J. McLoughlin (1993).

IBUKA, MASURU (1908–1997), **AKIO MORITA** (1921–1999), **and KAZUO IWAMA** (1919–1982), Japanese physicists and industrialists. Ibuka and Morita met while doing scientific research during World War II and cofounded, with an investment of $500, the Tokyo Telecommunications Engineering Corp. (1946). They were soon joined by Iwama, Morita's brother-in-law. The trio developed the world's first AM transistor radio (1955) and the first pocket-size radio (1957). Changing the name of their firm to the Sony Corp. (1958), they developed it into one of the world's largest producers of electronics equipment. Over the years, Sony introduced the all-transistor TV, the videotape recorder, the Trinitron color TV tube, the compact color videocassette recorder, and the digital audio system. Ibuka, president of the company until 1971, was succeeded by Morita (1971–76) and then by Iwama (1976–82). ■ See Nick Lyons, *The Sony Vision* (1976), and Akio Morita, *Made in Japan* (1986).

IBUSE, MASUJI (1898–1993), Japanese novelist and short-story writer. A native of Hiroshima, Ibuse was known for his humorous, lyrical, and compassionate depictions of ordinary people. Artistically he strove for a middle ground between the proletarian writers and those who sought only technical perfection. Although his satire *The Salamander* (1929; Eng. trans. 1971) and his historical novel *John Manjiro, the Castaway* (1937; Eng. trans. 1940) were widely read, Ibuse achieved his greatest renown after World War II with the publication of the novels *No Consultation Today* (1949; Eng. trans. 1964), a description of postwar city life; *The Far-Worshipping Commander* (1950; Eng. trans. 1966), an antimilitary satire; and his masterpiece, *Black Rain* (1965; Eng. trans. 1971), an account of the Hiroshima atom bombing and its aftermath. ■ See his *Lieutenant Lookeast and Other Stories* (1971), *Salamander and Other Stories* (1981), and *Waves: Two Short Novels* (1986).

ICAZA, JORGE (1906–1978), Ecuadoran novelist. An actor and director, Icaza wrote about the exploitation of Indians in *Huasipungo* (1934; Eng. trans. 1962; also trans. as *The Villagers,* 1964) and other novels of social protest. His realistic works influenced writers throughout Latin America and he was regarded as Ecuador's foremost novelist. He served as secretary-general of the Union of Writers and Artists (1944–60), director of the National Library (1960–73), and ambassador to the Soviet Union (from 1973).

ICE-T (**Tracy Morrow; c. 1958–**), U.S. rap artist and actor. Orphaned at age 12, Ice-T moved from his native Newark, New Jersey, to Los Angeles, California, where he was raised by an aunt in a middle-class neighborhood. He joined a street gang and after graduating from high school

and serving a four-year stint in the army, rejoined the gang. He engaged in criminal activity and served several short terms in jail before turning his life around and becoming involved in the world of rap. He worked as a deejay in several Los Angeles dance clubs, and appeared in the break-dance movie, *Breakin'* (1984). The profanity-laced raps on his albums *Rhyme Pays* (1987), *Power* (1988), *The Iceberg/Freedom of Speech . . . Just Watch What You Say* (1989), and *OG: Original Gangster* (1991) angrily described the street life, crime, and fantasies of urban black youth and inaugurated the style known as "gangsta rap." The lyrics to his song "Cop Killer" (1991) which he performed with his rock band Body Count, provoked a storm of protest, was denounced by President George Bush, and led to a national debate on free expression. Ice-T also starred in several movies, including *New Jack City* (1991) and *Trespass* (1992), and the television series "Players" (1997). He wrote *The Ice Opinion* (1994).

ICHIKAWA, FUSAYE (1893–1981), Japanese feminist and legislator. Rebelling against her father's view of women as inferior, Ichikawa moved to Tokyo in her twenties. There she became involved in trade unionism and met feminists Hiratsuka Raicho and Oku Mumeo. With them, she founded the New Women's Association (1920), which supported legislation entitling women to take part in political gatherings; the legislation was passed in 1922. Influenced by the U.S. suffrage movement and by Alice Paul's National Women's party during a stay in the United States (1921–24), she formed the Woman's Suffrage League in Japan (1924; dissolved by the military in 1940). In the 1920s she headed the Women's Committee of the International Labor Organization, and in the 1930s protested fascist trends. After World War II she led the New Japan Women's League, which became the League of Women Voters when Japanese women secured the vote (1945). She agitated against licensed prostitution and sought fair election practices. Fusaye Ichikawa served five terms in the Diet (1952–71), where she campaigned against government corruption; she was defeated in 1971 but regained her seat by wide margins in two subsequent elections (1975, 1980), waging her last successful campaign at age 86. She wrote widely on the feminist movement.

ICKES, HAROLD LECLAIRE (1874–1952), U.S. government official. Ickes, a liberal Republican Chicago lawyer, began his political career as an activist in municipal reform movements. A supporter of Theodore Roosevelt's Progressive party (1912), he later became a Democrat and supported Franklin D. Roosevelt (1932). As FDR's secretary of the interior (1933–46; the longest tenure in American history), he fought for the preservation of natural resources, spoke out against the large private oil and utility companies, and developed publicly owned power projects. He also headed the Public Works Administration (1933–39), which supervised New Deal programs aimed at recovery from the Depression. ■ See his *Autobiography of a Curmudgeon* (1943) and *Secret Diary* (3 vols., 1953–54); biographies by Linda J. Lear (1981) and Graham White and John Maze (1985); and T. H. Watkins, *Righteous Pilgrim* (1990).

IDRIS I (1890–1983), king of Libya. In 1917 Idris became leader of the Sanusi brotherhood, or Senussi Muslim sect, the austere religious reform order that challenged foreign sovereignty over Libya. After fleeing the Italian overlords of Libya and spending 20 years of exile in Egypt, he returned home in 1943 during World War II with Allied occupation troops. In 1951, with the support of the British authorities and conservative tribal leaders, Idris was proclaimed king of Libya. He ruled autocratically over a country transformed by the discovery of oil (1959) and maintained close political and economic ties with Great Britain and the United States. A 1969 coup led by Col. Muammar el-Qaddafi sent him back to exile in Egypt.

IGLESIAS, JULIO (1943–   ), Spanish popular singer. Son of a wealthy Madrid doctor, Iglesias wrote his first song (1968) while convalescing after a serious auto accident, and won a Spanish song-festival contest with it. After completing his law school studies, he gained attention at the Eurovision Festival in Holland (1970) and launched his spectacular singing career. The elegant, handsome, and perpetually suntanned Iglesias sang his melodramatic love songs and ballads to adoring fans throughout Europe, Latin America, and Japan before making his U.S. debut in 1983. He subsequently appeared on popular U.S. television shows and gave special performances at the White House. Called the world's most popular singer, and the best-selling musician in recording history, he sold (by 1984) more than 100 million albums. His first all-English language album, *1100 Bel Air Place* (1984), sold over a million copies within five days of its release.

IGNARRO, LOUIS J. (1941–   ), U.S. pharmacologist. Ignarro studied at the University of Minnesota (Ph.D. 1966) and taught at the Tulane University Medical School (1972–86) and the University of California at Los Angeles (1986–   ). As a result of analyses done during the 1980s, he concluded that the short-lived gas nitric oxide (NO) was the signaling mechanism produced by endothelium cells, the inner lining of blood vessels, which relax the vessels, allow them to widen, and allow for increased blood flow in the body. Subsequent research demonstrated that nitric oxide plays a major role in immunity, blood pressure control, and tumor suppression, and led to the use of Viagra as an anti-impotence drug. Ignarro's work complemented the independent research done by Robert F. Furchgott and Ferid Murad, and the three scientists shared the 1998 Nobel Prize in Physiology or Medicine.

IKEDA, HAYATO (1899–1965), Japanese political leader. Ikeda was a tax official in the ministry of finance (1925–45)

before being elected to Japan's House of Representatives (1949) as a member of the Liberal party. Throughout the 1950s he held key economic posts, including those of minister of finance and minister of international trade and industry, and played a major role in Japan's dramatic post–World War II economic expansion. He served as premier from 1960 to 1964, carrying out policies aimed at stimulating trade and economic growth.

ILF and PETROV (Iliya Arnoldovich Faynzilberg, 1897–1937, and Yevgeny Petrovich Katayev, 1903–1942), Soviet comic novelists. Together, the retiring Jew Ilf and the talkative Russian Petrov created the happy novel *The Twelve Chairs* (1928; Eng. trans. 1961) and gave the Soviet public a popular culture hero—the happy-go-lucky opportunist Ostap Bender. While parodying 19th-century Russian novels and making light of Soviet foibles, they communicated their country's mood on the verge of its first five-year plan. *The Little Golden Calf* (1931; Eng. trans. 1932; 1962), a more solemn satire, also featured the ingenious Bender, but because the rogue never clashes directly with officialdom, his creators were only briefly out of favor. *Little Golden America* (1936; Eng. trans. 1937) recorded witty impressions of a trip to the United States. After Ilf's death, Petrov wrote several screenplays and was a correspondent during World War II.

ILLICH, IVAN (1926–   ), Austrian-born educator and social critic. A polymath, Illich studied histology, crystallography, psychology, art history, theology, and philosophy in Vienna, Florence, and Rome before receiving his Ph.D. in history (University of Salzburg, 1951). He was ordained in the Roman Catholic Church (1951) and was a priest in New York City (1951–56) and vice rector of the Catholic University in Ponce, Puerto Rico (1956–60). He founded and directed (1961–76) the Intercultural Center of Documentation (Cuernavaca, Mexico), a think tank for those seeking radical social, economic, and political change in Latin America. Attacked by the church for his radical views, he resigned from the priesthood in 1969. A critic of highly centralized Western industrial society, he advocated the deinstitutionalization of education, religion, medicine, and transportation and a rearranging of social priorities to benefit the poor. His best-known books included *De-Schooling Society* (1971), *Tools for Conviviality* (1973), *Celebration of Awareness* (1970), *Toward a History of Needs* (1978), *Limits to Medicine* (1978), *Shadow Work* (1981), *Gender* (1982), and *ABC: The Alphabetization of the Popular Mind* (1988). *In the Mirror of the Past* (1991) contains lectures and addresses.

ILLYÉS, GYULA (1902–1983), Hungarian poet, essayist, and novelist. Hungary's unofficial poet laureate, Illyés was an important cultural figure for more than 40 years. As a youth he participated in the communists' seizure of power in 1919 and remained committed to radical social change throughout his life. The foremost populist writer of his time, he produced a largely autobiographical social portrait of the Hungarian peasantry, *People of the Puszta* (1936; Eng. trans. 1967) that is regarded as a classic. His colorful lyric poems, which also drew their inspiration from the peasantry, were noted for their bold images, strong rhythms, and exuberant language. English translations are in Thomas Kabdebo and Paul Tabori, eds., *A Tribute to Gyula Illyés* (1968), and *Selected Poems* (1971).

ILYUSHIN, SERGEI VLADIMIROVICH (1894–1977), Soviet aircraft designer. An engine mechanic, Ilyushin learned to fly in 1917 and graduated from the Zhukovski Military Aviation Academy in 1926. He designed more than 50 planes, including the famous IL-28 Shturmovik (1939), the Soviet World War II dive-bomber, and the Il-28 (1948), the first Soviet jet bomber. He was also responsible for the Il-4 World War II medium bomber, the Il-18 four-engine turbo-prop (1957), the Il-62 180-passenger jet airliner (1962), and the wide-body Il-86 350-passenger airbus introduced in the late 1970s.

INBER, VERA MIKHAYLOVNA (1890–1972), Soviet writer. A leading constructivist poet after the 1917 Russian Revolution, Inber became a supporter of the Bolshevik government and wrote stories and poems about Lenin, Moscow, and the revolution during the 1920s and 1930s. She joined the Communist party during World War II and gained fame for her patriotic writing. Her poem *Pulkovo Meridian* (1941; Stalin Prize, 1946) and her *Leningrad Diary* (1946; Eng. trans. 1971) described the hardships of life during the World War II siege of Leningrad.

INDIANA, ROBERT (Robert Clarke; 1928–   ), U.S. artist. Indiana, who borrowed his name from his birthplace, made his reputation in New York City as a painter of artistic signs and was a major figure in the pop art movement. His *American Dream* series (1961–   ) concentrated on verbs (hug, err) and numbers. He painted *EAT* on a pavilion at the New York World's Fair, and his *LOVE* emblem was a best-selling poster and appeared on 400 million U.S. postage stamps. Though he left New York (1978) for a small island off the coast of Maine, he continued to produce paintings, prints, and sculpture in the same style of his earlier works.

INDY, (PAUL MARIE THÉODORE) VINCENT D' (1851–1931), French composer. D'Indy was the leading musical heir of César Franck and a proponent of adapting to French music the musical nationalism of Richard Wagner. He helped found (1894) the Schola Cantorum in Paris, where he became an influential teacher (his pupils included Paul Dukas and Albert Roussel) and stimulated the revival of interest in Gregorian chant and French music of the 16th and 17th centuries. Many of his works incorporated Gregorian chant melodies and French folk songs, which he collected in great quantity. His music included *Symphony on a French Mountain Air* (1886), *Istar,* variations for orchestra (1896), and the *Suite for Flute, String Trio, and Harp* (1927). He wrote works on Franck, Beethoven, Wagner, and on the craft of composition. ■ See studies by Norman Demuth (1951) and Andrew Thomson (1996).

INGE, WILLIAM RALPH (1860–1954), British Anglican clergyman. Inge was educated at King's College, Cambridge, taught at Hertford College, Oxford, and Jesus College, Cambridge, and served as dean of St. Paul's Cathedral (1911–34). He was widely known as a writer and lecturer, and his approach to topics ranging from democracy to euthanasia was marked by pessimism and nonconformity, earning him the title "gloomy dean." His writings included *Christian Mysticism* (1897), *Outspoken Essays* (1919), *Christian Ethics and Modern Problems* (1930), and *Mysticism in Religion* (1948). ■ See his *Diary of a Dean* (1949); studies by Adam Fox (1960) and Robert Helm (1962); and biography by Ralph V. Foss (1989).

INÖNÜ, ÌSMET (1884–1973), Turkish political leader. Inönü ranks second only to Kemal Atatürk in modern Turkish history. As the first premier of the Turkish republic (1923–37), he administered Atatürk's modernization program and succeeded Atatürk as president (1938–50). After World War II he fostered the growth of a multiparty system, and his Republican People's party was defeated in the 1950 elections. Inönü returned to power (1961–65) as premier in a left-of-center coalition government, but the Republicans were badly defeated in the 1965 and 1969 elections and Inönü was replaced as party leader in 1972. ■ See study by Metin Heper (1998).

INUKAI, TSUYOSHI (1855–1932), Japanese political leader. Although Inukai came from a samurai family and received a Confucian education, he was very interested in Western learning. He started out as a journalist and was elected to the Diet (parliament) in 1890, remaining a member until his death. Inukai held many positions, including that of premier (1931–32), and spent his career in a struggle to defend parliamentary democracy, control the military, and widen the political decision-making process beyond a small elite. He was assassinated by ultranationalist military officers after he tried to halt Japanese military activity in Manchuria and negotiate with the Chinese government.

IONESCO, EUGÈNE (1912–1994), Rumanian-born French playwright. As a major figure in the development of the theater of the absurd, Ionesco disdained the traditional theater of social realism. He claimed his role was to be the "objective witness" of his own "subjectivity." In *The Lesson* (1951; Eng. trans. 1958) and other works, including *The Chairs* (1952; Eng. trans. 1958) and *The Bald Soprano* (1953; Eng. trans. 1958), Ionesco emphasized the alienation and isolation of contemporary individuals by his use of abstract characters, repetitive, disjointed, and meaningless dialogue, and fantastic and irrational plots. In *Rhinoceros* (1959; Eng. trans. 1960), an attack on conformity and obedience to authority, the characters were transformed into raging pachyderms. He also wrote the novel *The Hermit* (1972; Eng. trans. 1974). Ionesco was elected (1970) to the Académie Française. ■ See his *Fragments of a Journal* (1967; Eng. trans. 1968), his memoir *Present Past, Past Present* (1968; Eng. trans. 1971), and studies by Ronald Hayman (1976) and Deborah B. Gaensbauer (1996).

IORGA, NICOLAE (1871–1940), Rumanian historian and political leader. A history professor at the University of Bucharest from 1895, Iorga published the standard history of his country in a one-volume German edition in 1905 and in a 10-volume Rumanian edition in 1936–39. An English-language *History of Roumania* appeared in 1925. He also wrote a history of the Ottoman empire (5 vols. in German, 1908–13). Elected to the National Assembly (1907), he founded the National Democratic party (1910). Iorga served as premier (1931–32) during the reign of his former pupil, King Carol II. He was later assassinated by members of the fascist Iron Guard. ■ See biography by M. M. Alexandrescu-Dersca Bulgaru (Eng. trans. 1972) and William O. Oldson, *The Historical and Nationalist Thought of Nicolae Iorga* (1973).

IPATIEFF, VLADIMIR NIKOLAEVICH (1867–1952), Russian-born chemist. Trained at a military school, Ipatieff became an officer in the Russian army (1887) and taught chemistry at the Mikhail Artillery Academy (1898–1906). He was well known for the synthesis of isoprene, the basic unit of natural rubber (1897). He was most famous, however, for his discovery of high-pressure catalytic reactions of hydrocarbons that were used extensively in the petrochemical industry. During World War I he coordinated Russia's chemical-warfare program and directed the entire chemical industry under the Soviet government (until 1926). Not in sympathy with the bolsheviks, he left the Soviet Union (1930) and settled in the United States, where he worked for private industry and directed a laboratory at Northwestern University. There he developed a process for producing high-octane gasoline for automobiles and airplanes. ■ See his memoirs, *Life of a Chemist* (1946) and *My Life in the U.S.* (1959).

IQBAL, SIR MUHAMMAD (1877?–1938), Indian Muslim poet and political philosopher. Iqbal graduated from Government College in Lahore (1899) and taught there (1899–1905). He later earned a doctorate at Cambridge (1908) and practiced law upon his return to India. Iqbal was a Pan-Islamist reformer who wrote extensively, particularly Persian and Urdu poetry; he was knighted in 1922. Becoming president of the Muslim League in 1930, he gave up his Pan-Islamic views to promote a separate Muslim state. For this, many regard him as the "spiritual father" of Pakistan. ■ See his *Reconstruction of Religious Thought in Islam* (1934) and biographies by S. A. Vahid (1959) and Rafiq Zakaria (1993).

IRIGOYEN, HIPÓLITO (1852–1933), Argentine political leader. A rancher, lawyer, and teacher, Irigoyen succeeded his uncle (1896) as leader of the Radical party, a middle-class group protesting against political fraud and violence. After implementation of the secret ballot (1912), Irigoyen's party began participating in politics, and in 1916 he was elected president of Argentina for six years. An austere, authoritarian leader, he failed to enact the reforms he had advocated. He was reelected in 1928 but corruption and the effects of the worldwide Depression weakened the government, and he was deposed by the military in 1930.

IRONSIDE, WILLIAM EDMUND IRONSIDE, 1st BARON (1880–1959), British field marshal. Ironside had an adventurous military career as a secret agent during the Boer War (1899–1902) and as commander of the Archangel expedition (1918–20) that intervened in the Russian civil war. "Big Bill" (6 feet 4 inches) was considered the model of a British officer, and a light armored vehicle was named after him. He was chief of staff during the early period of World War II (1939–40) and served briefly as commander of the home forces. ■ See his *Time Unguarded: The Ironside Diaries, 1937–40* (1962).

ISAACS, ALICK (1921–1967), British virologist. Isaacs earned a medical degree at Glasgow (1944), carried out research on viruses in Melbourne, Australia, and joined the virology division of England's National Institute for Medical Research (1950–67; division head 1961–67). His early research on influenza viruses focused on the way that one virus could impede the growth of another. In 1957, collaborating with J. Lindenmann, he found that cells treated with a dead or damaged virus could release a protein that interfered with virus growth. He called this protein interferon. The discovery, a major breakthrough in immunology, contributed to scientists' understanding of viral infections and the body's response to them. It showed that antibody production is not the body's only fast, effective means of defense against viruses.

ISELIN, COLUMBUS O'DONNELL (1904–1971), U.S. oceanographer. Iselin taught physical oceanography at Harvard and the Massachusetts Institute of Technology and was the assistant curator of the Harvard University Museum of Comparative Zoology (1929–48). On the original staff of the Woods Hole Oceanographic Institute (founded 1930), he was named captain (1931) of the *Atlantis*, the first privately operated full-time oceanographic research vessel in the United States, and he made important studies of the Gulf Stream and the North Atlantic region. He directed the

Woods Hole Oceanographic Institution (1940–50; 1956–58) during the period of its greatest expansion.

ISHERWOOD, CHRISTOPHER (1904–1986), British-born U.S. novelist, short-story writer, and playwright. The Cambridge-educated Isherwood first achieved fame as the author of three plays written in collaboration with W. H. Auden during the 1930s. His most celebrated works, *Mr. Norris Changes Trains* (1935), *Sally Bowles* (1937), and *Goodbye to Berlin* (1939), were realistic accounts of the social and moral decay of contemporary Germany, where Isherwood lived and taught English (1930–33). The Broadway hit *I Am a Camera* (1951) and the musical and movie *Cabaret* were based on two of his Berlin stories. Isherwood's later works, written after he emigrated to the United States (1939), included *Down There on a Visit* (1962), *A Single Man* (1964), and *A Meeting by the River* (1967). In the autobiographical *Lions and Shadows* (1938), *Kathleen and Frank* (1971), *Christopher and His Kind* (1976), and *My Guru and His Disciple* (1980), he discussed his family life, his years at college, his homosexuality, and his belief in Hindu (Vedanta) philosophy. ■ See his *Diaries—Vol. 1: 1939–1960* (1979); biography by Brian Finney (1979); and study by Claude J. Summers (1980).

ISHII, VISCOUNT KIKUJIRO (1866–1945), Japanese diplomat. Ishii entered the diplomatic service after studying English law at Tokyo Imperial University (1890). He negotiated with the United States the "gentlemen's agreement" (1907–08), which limited Japanese emigration, and the Lansing-Ishii Agreement (1917), which acknowledged Japan's special interests in China while recognizing the U.S. open-door policy. He advocated Japanese cooperation with the West and was foreign minister (1914–16) and ambassador to the United States (1918–19) and to France (1912–15; 1920–27). He was president of the council and assembly of the League of Nations (1923, 1926) and represented Japan at numerous international conferences. He was killed in a U.S. bombing raid during World War II. ■ See his *Diplomatic Commentaries* (1931; Eng. trans. 1936).

ISHIKAWA, TAKUBOKU (Hajime Ishikawa; 1886–1912), Japanese poet. The poverty-stricken, chronically ill son of a Zen priest, Ishikawa was known as a master of the traditional Japanese tanka poetry. But he infused this classical form, long a vehicle for expressions of elegant sentiment, with startling imagery, vivid language, and an intellectual and often cynical content frequently relating to everyday experience. Many of the poems in his most famous collections, *A Handful of Sand* (1910; Eng. trans. 1934), *The Flute* (1912), and *Sad Toys* (1912; Eng. trans. 1977), reflect the socialist views he embraced shortly before his early death. His *Romaji Diary*, not published in full until 1954 (Eng. trans. 1956), further revealed the complexity and modernity of his thought. English translations of his works are in

Takuboku: Poems to Eat (1966). ■ See study by Yukihito Hijiya (1979).

ISHIZAKA, TAIZO (1886–1975), Japanese industrialist. A successful insurance executive before World War II, Ishizaka served as chairman of the giant Toshiba Electric Co. and the Nippon Atomic Industry Group in the postwar years. As president (1956–68) of the powerful Federation of Economic Organizations, Japan's most important business group, Ishizaka was virtual ruler of the nation's economy. He also served as president of Expo '70, the World's Fair held in Osaka.

ISLAM, KAZI NAZRUL (1899–1976), Bengali poet. One of the foremost 20th-century poets of the Indian subcontinent, Islam was a "people's poet" whose poetry and songs called for revolution against the British and glorified the Indian freedom movement. His more than 3,000 poems, which denounced injustice and championed egalitarianism, were read throughout Bengal. He was a leader of the Indian National Congress in Calcutta during the 1920s and 1930s. A serious brain disease, contracted in 1942, cut short his literary and political career. The study by Mizanur Rahman (1966) contains translations of his poems. ■ See biography by Rezaul K. Talukdar (1994).

IVANOV, VSEVOLOD VYACHESLAVOVICH (1895–1963), Soviet novelist and short-story writer. In his youth Ivanov worked as a sailor, a clown, a sword swallower, and at other odd jobs. He fought with the Whites, and later with the Reds, during the Russian civil war (1918–20). His four early works, set in his native Siberia, contained straightforward descriptions of the conflict. The most highly regarded of these is the novel *Armoured Train 14–69* (1922; Eng. trans. 1933). They all were praised by contemporary critics but later criticized for their pessimism and cynicism. Ivanov also wrote an enthusiastic socialist realist novel and a fictionalized account of his circus days, *The Adventures of a Fakir* (1934–35; Eng. trans. 1935). His short stories in English translation appeared in *Selected Stories* (1983) and *Fertility and Other Stories* (1998).

IVANOV, VYACHESLAV IVANOVICH (1866–1949), Russian poet. After studying classics in Moscow and Berlin, Ivanov settled into a St. Petersburg (now Leningrad) apartment called the "Tower," which from 1904 until 1913 was headquarters for symbolist poets. His first volume, *Pilot Stars* (1903), established him immediately as an important poet of that movement. Other collections of his ornate, esoteric verse included *Eros* (1907), *Cor Ardens* (1911), and *Winter Sonnets* (1920). He considered art to be a mystical form of communion, and he emphasized the mythic dimension of fiction in his critical study of Dostoyevsky, *Freedom and the Tragic Life* (Eng. trans. 1952). He also did numerous translations. Ivanov taught classical philology at the

University of Baku (1920–24) and then emigrated (1924) to Italy, where he converted to Roman Catholicism. *Correspondence Across a Room* (1921; Eng. trans. 1985) contains his exchange with literary historian Mikhail Gershenzon. ■ See James D. West, *Russian Symbolism* (1970).

IVENS, JORIS (1898–1989), Dutch-born documentary filmmaker. One of the most prolific and widely traveled filmmakers of the century, Ivens made dozens of films that supported his socialist and internationalist political views. He shot *Song of Heroes* (1932) in the Soviet Union and made several films in China, including *The Four Hundred Million* (1938) and a six-part documentary, *How Yukong Moved the Mountains* (1976). *The Spanish Earth* (1937) eloquently demonstrated his support for the Republican side during the Spanish Civil War. He produced *Power and the Land* (1940) and *Our Russian Front* (1941) in the United States. After World War II his films sympathetically portrayed anticolonialist and anti-imperialist struggles throughout the world. ■ See his autobiography, *The Camera and I* (1969).

IVES, CHARLES EDWARD (1874–1954), U.S. composer. Ives was long considered the great unsung American composer. He chose, on graduation from Yale University (1898), to become an insurance salesman—and proved very successful. He continued to compose music but remained isolated from the company of musicians and the rigor of performance and did not publish his music until later in life. His complex music featured polyrhythmic structures and polytonal harmonies interspersed with traditional New England dances, hymns, and marches. Among his most popular works were *Three Places in New England* (1903–14); *Concord Sonata* (1909–15), dedicated to the New England transcendentalists; and his third symphony, *The Camp Meeting,* for which he won a Pulitzer Prize in 1947. ■ See biographies by Henry and Sidney Cowell (1955), Stuart Feder (1992), and Jan Swafford (1996); David Wooldridge, *From the Steeples and Mountains* (1974); and Frank R. Rossiter, *Charles Ives and His America* (1975).

IVORY, JAMES. *See MERCHANT, ISMAIL.*

IWAMA, KAZUO. *See IBUKA, MASURU.*

IWASAKI, KOYATA (1879–1945), Japanese industrialist. The grandson of the founder of the Mitsubishi Co., Japan's largest industrial, commercial, and banking group, Iwasaki was trained at Tokyo Imperial and Cambridge universities. He ran the company from 1916 to 1945 and produced much of the industrial goods and armaments (including the Zero fighter planes) used by Japan during World War II. It was estimated that his company alone accounted for more than 10 percent of Japan's national income. After the war the U.S. occupation authorities disbanded the *zaibatsus,* Japan's giant monopolies, and Iwasaki, one of Japan's richest citizens and one of the "four great outlawed capitalists," was forced to retire.

J

JABOTINSKY, VLADIMIR EVGEN'EVICH (1880–1940), Zionist leader. Born and raised in Russia, Jabotinsky studied law and languages and was a popular journalist. Following the Kishinev pogrom (1903) he became an active Zionist, and during World War I he opposed the neutrality of the official Zionist leaders by insisting on active Jewish participation in the Allied conquest of Palestine. He helped form three Jewish battalions that participated in the British victory over the Turks in Palestine. He served on the Zionist Executive (1921–25) but resigned to form the World Union of Zionist Revisionists (1925) and the New Zionist Organization (1935), groups that called for militant opposition to the British mandate authority and that advocated the transformation of Palestine, by unlimited immigration, into a Jewish state. He also commanded the underground military organization, Irgun Tz'vai Le'umi. Israeli Prime Minister Menachem Begin was a disciple of Jabotinsky. ■ See his *The War and the Jew* (1942); biography by Joseph B. Schechtman (2 vols., 1956–61); and Shmuel Katz, *Lone Wolf* (1995).

JACKSON, GLENDA (1936–   ), British actress. A scholarship student at the Royal Academy of Dramatic Arts, Jackson first won celebrity as a mad woman in the 1966 Broadway production (and 1967 film) of *Marat/Sade*. She received an Academy Award (1970) for her role as the cold, inscrutable sister in *Women in Love* and was also acclaimed for her performance in *Sunday, Bloody Sunday* (1971) and for her portrayal of Queen Elizabeth in the 1972 BBC-TV series, "Elizabeth R." She displayed a flair for comedy in *A Touch of Class* (Academy Award, 1973), *House Calls* (1978), and *Hopscotch* (1980). She left films for politics and served as a Labour party MP in the House of Commons (1992–   ). ■ See study by Ian Woodward (1985).

JACKSON, JESSE (1941–   ), U.S. civil rights activist and political leader. The youngest of Dr. Martin Luther King, Jr.'s, aides, Jackson helped found the Chicago branch of Operation Breadbasket (1966), an arm of the Southern Christian Leadership Conference, and was ordained a Baptist minister in 1968. After King's death, he founded his own movement in Chicago, People United to Save Humanity (PUSH; 1971), a civil-rights and self-help organization for African Americans. An articulate advocate of political and economic reform, he became the first African American to make a serious bid for the U.S. presidency, winning over 3.2 million votes (approximately 17 percent) in the 1984 Democratic primaries. Although he lost the nomination to Walter Mondale, he was credited with dramatically increasing the number of African-American voters throughout the country.

After the election he headed the Rainbow Coalition, an independent political organization aimed at uniting racial minorities, the poor, peace activists, and environmentalists. He ran again, unsuccessfully, for the Democratic presidential nomination in 1988 but remained a public champion of liberal causes. ■ See studies by Barbara A. Reynolds (1975) and Thomas Landess and Richard Quinn (1985), and Marshall Frady, *Jesse* (1996).

JACKSON, MAHALIA (1911–1972), U.S. gospel singer. The granddaughter of a slave, Jackson began her career singing devotional songs in black churches and revival tents; she began to record in 1934. Her remarkably rich contralto voice became widely known outside of the black community during the mid-1940s with her recordings of "Move on up a Little Higher" and "Silent Night," and she subsequently sang frequently on radio and television and gave annual concerts at New York's Carnegie Hall (from 1950). She was deeply religious, and although her style was infused with jazz and blues rhythms, she sang only gospel songs and never appeared in nightclubs. During the 1960s she was closely associated with the civil-rights movement. Among the other recordings that helped establish her worldwide reputation were "He's Got the Whole World in His Hands," "I Can Put My Trust in Jesus," "Just over the Hill," and "When I Wake Up in Glory." ■ See her autobiography, *Movin' on Up* (1966; with Evan Wylie); Laurraine Goreau, *Just Mahalia, Baby* (1984); and Jules Schwerin, *Go Tell It* (1992).

JACKSON, MAYNARD HOLBROOK (1938–   ), U.S. political leader. Jackson was born into the black aristocracy and graduated from Morehouse College at age 18. He became a lawyer (1965), founded the first and largest black law firm in Atlanta, and served as the first African-American mayor of a major southern city—Atlanta—from 1974 to 1982 and again from 1990 to 1994.

JACKSON, MICHAEL JOSEPH (1958–   ), U.S. singer and songwriter. Jackson was born to a family of nine children in Gary, Indiana, where he began singing with his brothers. By age 11 he was a star of the Jackson 5, whose early Motown hits included "I Want You Back" (1969) and "I'll Be There" (1970). He made his first solo release, "Got to Be There," in 1971, but it was nearly a decade later that Michael Jackson emerged as a rock-and-roll phenomenon comparable to Elvis Presley or the Beatles. An androgynous figure bedecked in gaudy clothes with epaulets and a sequinned glove, his trademark, Jackson combined his childlike high-pitched voice, upbeat songs, and fancy dancing with high-tech showmanship. A pioneer of rock-music video, he issued his solo LP *Thriller* (1982), a best-selling album, with a blockbuster video. A separate 60-minute video documentary on the making of *Thriller* also had big sales. The album *Victory* (1984) marked the 1984 "Victory Tour," promoted as the last that Jackson would make with his brothers; it made lavish use of visual effects and was among rock music's most lucrative ventures. With Lionel Richie, Jackson wrote "We Are the World" (1985), the Grammy-winning song recorded by a large group of prominent performers to benefit USA for Africa. A reclusive performer whose air of mystery titillated fans, Jackson broke into music publishing by securing the rights to 251 songs by John Lennon and Paul McCartney (1985). He subsequently recorded the albums *Bad* (1987), *Dangerous* (1991), and *History* (1995) and the videos *Black or White* (1991) and *Leave Me Alone* (1993). ■ See his autobiography *Moonwalk* (1988) and biographies by Nelson George (1984) and Christoper P. Andersen (1995).

JACKSON, REGGIE (Reginald Martinez Jackson; 1946–), U.S. baseball player. An intense and controversial long-ball-hitting outfielder, Jackson played for the Athletics (in Kansas City, 1967, and Oakland, 1968–75; 1987), the Baltimore Orioles (1976), the New York Yankees (1977–81), and the California Angels (1982–86). He led the American League in home runs four times (1973, 32; 1975, 36 tie; 1980, 41 tie; 1982, 39), was the league's Most Valuable Player (1973), and hit 563 career home runs. He also held the record for most career strikeouts (2,597). Known as Mr. October for his stellar postseason performances, he batted .357 in five World Series and held several series records, including most home runs in one series (5; 1977) and most home runs in one game (3, on three consecutive pitches; Oct. 18, 1977). ■ See his autobiography, *Reggie* (1984; with Mike Lupica), and Maury Allen, *Mr. October* (1981).

JACKSON, ROBERT HOUGHWOUT (1892–1954), U.S. Supreme Court justice. A lawyer active in municipal government and Democratic politics in Jamestown, New York, Jackson served Pres. Franklin D. Roosevelt as general counsel of the Bureau of Internal Revenue (1934–36), assistant attorney general (1936–38), U.S. solicitor general (1938–40), and U.S. attorney general (1940–41). Appointed to the Supreme Court by Roosevelt (1941), Jackson went on leave from the bench (1945) to serve as U.S. chief prosecutor at the post–World War II Nuremberg war-crimes trials. Jackson was a devoted civil libertarian who defended freedom of religion with particular distinction, but he nevertheless believed that the court should exercise judicial restraint and not become a superlegislature. His books included *The Struggle for Judicial Supremacy* (1941) and *The Nürnberg Case* (1947). ■ See Eugene C. Gerhardt, *America's Advocate* (1958), and Glendon Schubert, ed., *Dispassionate Justice* (1969), a synthesis of Jackson's judicial opinions.

JACKSON, SHIRLEY (1919–1965), U.S. writer. Jackson was best known for the short story "The Lottery" (1948) and the novels *Hangsaman* (1951), *The Haunting of Hill House* (1959), and *We Have Always Lived in the Castle* (1962)—macabre tales that added cryptic Freudian symbolism to the classic ghost story. Although highly regarded for her depictions of loneliness and alienation, she also wrote rollicking accounts of her happy home life in *Life Among the Savages* (1953) and *Raising Demons* (1957). Her short-story collections, *The Magic of Shirley Jackson* (1966) and *Come Along with Me* (1968), were edited by her husband, literary critic Stanley Edgar Hyman. ■ See study by Lenemaja Friedman (1975) and Judy Oppenheimer, *Private Demons* (1988).

JACKSON, "SHOELESS JOE" (Joseph Jefferson Jackson; 1881–1951), U.S. baseball player. Called by star player Ty Cobb the finest natural hitter in the game, Jackson was an outfielder for Philadelphia (1908–09), Cleveland (1910–15), and the Chicago White Sox (1915–20) and had a career batting average of .356. Due to a heel injury he supposedly played a game in the minors without shoes and thus earned the nickname "Shoeless." After the 1919 World Series, which the White Sox lost, Jackson and seven other players were accused of taking bribes to "throw" the games and were barred from baseball for life. Upon hearing of the "Black Sox" scandal, a young fan supposedly tugged at Jackson's sleeve, begging him to "say it ain't so, Joe." Jackson always denied any wrongdoing. ■ See Donald Gropman, *Say It Ain't So, Joe!* (1979).

JACKSON OF LODSWORTH, BARBARA MARY JACKSON, BARONESS (née Barbara Ward; 1914–1981), British economist and journalist. Educated at Oxford (1932–35), Ward joined the staff of the *Economist* (1939) and became its foreign editor in 1940. She stressed Western unity, rapprochement between the noncommunist and communist blocs, and aid to Third World countries, and was one of the most influential political and economic commentators of the post–World War II era. She was a visiting scholar at Harvard (1957–68), a professor at Columbia (1968–73), and president of the International Institute for Environment and Development (1973–80). She was made a life peeress in 1976. Her books included *Faith and Freedom* (1954), *The Rich Nations and the Poor Nations* (1962), *Spaceship Earth* (1968), and *Progress for a Small Planet* (1979).

JACOB, FRANÇOIS (1920–), French biochemist. Jacob served in the Free French forces in World War II, then studied at the University of Paris (M.D. 1947) and at the Sorbonne (D.Sc. 1954). He was affiliated with the Pasteur Institute in Paris (1950–92) and the Collège de France (1964–92). Working with Jacques Monod, Jacob conducted research into cell physiology, in the decade following World War II, which contributed to the understanding of protein synthesis. Establishing that there are at least three types of genes (ordinary structural, regulator, and operator), they found that these genes control one another by holding each other in check. They concluded that protein synthesis is regulated by a process of negative controls. Their findings had important implications for cancer research. Jacob shared the 1965 Nobel Prize in Physiology or Medicine with Monod and André Lwoff. His books included *The Logic of Life: A History of Heredity* (1970; Eng. trans. 1993) and *Of Flies, Mice and Men* (1997; Eng. trans. 1998). ■ See his autobiography, *The Statue Within* (1987; Eng. trans. 1988).

JACOB, MAX (1876–1944), French poet. Jacob was a legendary personality in the Parisian avant-garde as a painter, writer, humorist, bohemian, and deeply religous convert (1915) to Catholicism from Judaism. He was a close friend of the painter Pablo Picasso and the poet Guillaume Apollinaire and a major figure in the cubist and surrealist movements. His poetry merged humor, fantasy, and mysticism with a variety of verbal tricks and puns. Tormented by the contradictions between his actions and his religious beliefs, after 1921 he lived as a recluse in a monastery. He died in a Nazi concentration camp. Translations of several of his works are in Michael Brownstein, ed., *The Dice Cup: Selected Prose Poems* (1980), and *Hesitant Fire: Selected Prose* (1991). ■ See Gerard Kamber, *Max Jacob and the Poetics of Cubism* (1971).

JACOBS, HELEN HULL (1908–1997), U.S. tennis player. The national junior tennis champion in 1924–25, Jacobs won fame as rival to the "queen of courts," Helen Wills Moody. She was the first player to win the national women's singles title at Forest Hills for four straight years (1932–35). She also won the unofficial 1936 world singles title at Wimbledon (where she was a finalist on six separate occasions), won several doubles and mixed doubles crowns, and played on the U.S. Wightman Cup team for 13 consecutive years (1927–39). During World War II she served as a commander of a U.S. Navy intelligence unit. She retired from tennis in 1947.

JACOBS, HIRSCH (1904–1970), U.S. racehorse trainer. Although he began his sports career by racing pigeons when he was 12, Jacobs switched to horses 10 years later and became the most successful trainer in racing history. He saddled 3,569 winners (including 177 in 1936), led trainers in winnings 11 times (1933–39; 1941–44), and won more than $12 million in purses. Few of Jacobs' winners were high-priced horses, and he was known as the "voodoo veterinarian" for his ability to rejuvenate rundown horses. Stymie, the horse he purchased for $1,500 in 1944, eventually won $918,485 and was the all-time money-winning horse at the time of its retirement in 1949.

JACOBS, JANE (1916–), U.S. writer and urban theorist. After graduating from high school in Scranton, Pennsylvania, Jacobs moved to New York City to become a freelance writer and subsequently an associate editor of *Architectural Forum* (1952–68). She was an advocate of community, diversity, and human-scale architecture in urban locales. In her most influential work, *The Death and Life of American Cities* (1961), she attacked the urban renewal projects of orthodox urban planners for destroying old buildings, small businesses, and settled neighborhoods and replacing them with highways and housing projects. She successfully led movements of urban conservation in both New York City and Toronto, Canada, where she moved (1968) with her architect husband. She also wrote *The Economy of Cities* (1969), *Cities and the Wealth of Nations* (1984), *Systems of Survival* (1993), and *The Nature of Economies* (2000). Always a supporter of decentralization and small-scale entities, she argued for the breakup of Canada in *The Question of Separatism: Quebec and the Struggle over Sovereignty* (1980).

JAGAN, CHEDDI (1918–1997), Guyanese political leader. Jagan was born on a sugar plantation into a poverty-stricken family that had migrated to what was then British Guiana, from India, as indentured laborers. In the United States (1936–43) he studied history and economics, earned a degree in dentistry from Northwestern University, and married Janet Rosenberg, a left-wing student activist who became his political partner and adviser. Back in Guiana, Jagan became a labor organizer, entered politics, and founded (1950), with his wife and Forbes Burnham, the People's Progressive party (PPP), a socialist movement seeking an end to British colonial rule. Jagan was elected head of the colonial government (1953), but was ousted by the British for his radical leanings after less than six months in office. When the PPP won the 1957 elections, Jagan headed the government (1957–61). He later served as prime minister at the height of the cold war (1961–64), during which the United States destabilized his government by supporting labor unrest, racial strife, and acts of sabotage. After Guyana gained independence (1966), Jagan led the opposition in the National Assembly. Elected president (1992), he advocated privatization and free-market reforms in order to solve Guyana's economic crisis. Following his death in office, his widow served as president (1997–99). His books included *The West on Trial* (1966) and *Forbidden Freedom* (1989).

JAIN, DEVAKI (**Mandyam Ananth Devaki**; 1933–), Indian feminist. Devaki Jain was one of seven children in the family of a civil servant. In the 1950s she studied economics, political science, and statistics at Oxford University in Britain, earned bachelor's and master's degrees, and took research jobs (including as an assistant to Swedish economist Gunnar Myrdal). Returning to India (1959), Jain lectured in economics at a women's college at Delhi University for a decade. As an associate of the Institute of Social Studies, she conducted research on the political, social, and economic status of Indian women, treating such issues as employment opportunities, prostitution, domestic violence, and the implications for women of the caste system. An influential voice in the international women's movement, Jain edited *Indian Women* (1976), published *Women's Quest for Power: Five Indian Case Studies* (1980; with Nalini Singh and Malini Chaud), and coedited *Tyranny of the Household* (1985) and *Speaking of Faith: Global Perspectives on Women, Religion and Social Change* (1987).

JAKOBSON, ROMAN OSIPOVICH (1896–1982), Russian-born linguist and literary critic. Jakobson was born in Moscow, where he became acquainted with the poet Vladimir Mayakovsky and other literati who were his contemporaries. After emigrating in the late 1920s, he was a cofounder of the movement known as the Prague school of linguistics. A pioneering structuralist, Jakobson believed that all languages and poetic forms, regardless of their superficial variations, have a similar fundamental structure. Forced to leave Czechoslovakia after the German invasion (1939), he taught at Columbia University (1943–49), Harvard (1949–67), and the Massachusetts Institute of Technology (1957–67), and elaborated his structuralist theories in numerous books and more than 600 scholarly papers. He spoke 6 languages, read 25, and was an authority on Slavic literatures. His best-known works included *Child Language, Aphasia,* and *Phonological Universals* (1941; Eng. trans. 1968), *Preliminaries to Speech Analysis* (1952; with G. Fant and M. Halle), and *Fundamentals of Language* (1956; rev. ed. 1971; with M. Halle). ■ See also his *Selected Writings* (8 vols., 1962–82), *Verbal Art, Verbal Sign, Verbal Time* (1985), and studies by Elmar Holenstein (Eng. trans. 1976) and Rodney B. Sangster (1982).

JAMALZADEH, SAYYED MOHAMMAD ALI (1896?–1997), Iranian writer. After studying in Lebanon, France, and Switzerland, Jamalzadeh joined a group of progressive Iranians in Berlin and helped edit an influential journal, *Kava.* His collection of satirical short stories, *Once upon a Time* (1921; Eng. trans. 1985) introduced social criticism into modern Persian prose literature with its depiction of the hypocrisy, corruption, and decay of contemporary Iranian society. The introduction to the collection, a manifesto on the importance of the modern short story as a literary genre, inspired a generation of Iranian writers. He later wrote numerous short stories, novels, and essays as well as historical and economic studies. He worked for the International Labor Organization in Geneva from 1931 to 1956. ■ See his autobiographical novel *Isfahan Is Half the World* (1956; Eng. trans. 1983).

JAMES, CYRIL LIONEL ROBERT (1901–1989), Trinidadian-born historian, political theorist, novelist, and journalist. A member of the West Indian intellectual avant-garde of the 1930s, C.L.R. James was the first to write short stories dealing with the manners and morals of the poor indigenous population of the islands. In Britain (1932–38), he worked as the cricket correspondent of the *Manchester Guardian*; published the novel *Minty Alley* (1936), which

concerned the paradoxical position of the black middle class; and collaborated with Jomo Kenyatta and George Padmore on the International African Service Bureau, an organization whose aim was the independence of African colonies. He was also a leader of the Pan-Africanist movement. His other books of this period included *The Case for West Indian Self-Government* (1933), and the highly acclaimed study of the Haitian revolution *Black Jacobins* (1938). James lived in the United States (1938–52) before returning to Trinidad, where he played an important role in the independence movement, and finally to London. A Marxist adherent of the political views of Leon Trotsky (from 1934), James wrote several works on contemporary politics and political theory, including *World Revolution: 1917–1936* (1937), *Marxism and the Intellectuals* (1962), and *Notes on Dialectics* (1981). *Beyond a Boundary* (1963) is an insightful study of cricket and anticolonialism. ■ See biography by Paul Buhle (1988).

JAMES, WILLIAM (1842–1910), U.S. psychologist and philosopher. Son of the theologian Henry James and brother of the novelist also named Henry, William James studied at Harvard (M.D. 1869) and taught anatomy, physiology, philosophy, and psychology there. He established the first psychology laboratory in the United States, and his comprehensive treatise *Principles of Psychology* (2 vols., 1890) was universally acclaimed. In *The Varieties of Religious Experience* (1902), he applied the insights of psychology to the study of religion. His philosophical views reflected his belief in a dynamic, pluralistic, and interconnected universe in which there were no eternal truths and in which human freedom and individuality were of primary importance. His views were elaborated in *Pragmatism* (1907) and *Essays in Radical Empiricism* (1912). James also helped organize the American Society for Psychical Research (1884). ■ See Ralph B. Perry, *The Thought and Character of William James* (2 vols., 1935); Howard M. Feinstein, *Becoming William James* (1984); and Linda Simon, *Genuine Reality* (1998).

JAMESON, SIR LEANDER STARR (1853–1917), British political leader. Jameson abandoned a career in medicine to seek adventure in the mines and politics of South Africa. He was a friend and business representative of Cecil B. Rhodes and led the abortive Jameson raid (1895) on the Transvaal, which sought to overthrow Boer rule. It was repudiated by the British government and Jameson was imprisoned for 15 months in England. An advocate of South African unity, Jameson later served as prime minister of the Cape Colony (1904–08) and led the Progressive party opposition in the first parliament of the Union of South Africa.

JAMISON, JUDITH (1944–), U.S. dancer. Jamison grew up in Philadelphia, where she studied piano and violin and sang at the Mother Bethel African Methodist Episcopalian Church. Since she was tall for her age at 6, her parents hoped dance lessons would make her less awkward. Jamison continued dance training and was noticed (1964) at the Philadelphia Dance Academy by choreographer Agnes de Mille, who cast her in *The Four Marys* at the American Ballet Theatre. The next year, the statuesque Jamison began her association with the Alvin Ailey American Dance Theater; by the late 1960s she had won acclaim for her dramatic, emotional performances, which fused classical technique with modern-dance movement in a strikingly original idiom. She was best known for her roles in *Cry* and *Revelations*. She also starred in the Broadway show *Sophisticated Ladies* (1981). Jamison later directed the Alvin Ailey company (1990–   ). ■ See her autobiography *Dancing Spirit* (1993).

JANÁČEK, LEOŠ (1854–1928), Czech composer. Janáček's music reflects a personal style of great integrity and vitality and draws heavily on the inflections of the Czech language and on the rhythmic, melodic, and harmonic traits of Czech folk music. After study abroad, he worked in relative isolation in Brno, collecting folk music and becoming an influential teacher as well as composer; the 1918 Vienna premiere of his opera *Jenufa* (1904; rev. 1916) made him an international figure. His monumental *Glagolitic Mass* (*Slavonic Mass*; 1926) and the powerful *Diary of One Who Vanished* (1919) are among the finest choral works of the century. His other works include the orchestral rhapsody *Taras Bulba* (1918) and the operas, *Katya Kabanova* (1921), *The Makropulos Affair* (1926), and *From the House of the Dead* (1930). ■ See studies by Hans Hollander (Eng. trans. 1963) and Jaroslav Vogel (Eng. trans. rev. ed. 1981).

JANIS, SIDNEY (1896–1989), U.S. art dealer. A shirt manufacturer with a good eye for modern art, Janis first exhibited his collection, then including six paintings by the Spaniard Pablo Picasso and three by the Swiss Paul Klee, in 1935. He retired from business in 1939, later (1948) opening a gallery on 57th Street in New York City where he exhibited and exclusively represented the work of Jackson Pollock, Mark Rothko, and other contemporary American artists. He played a major role in the growth of abstract expressionism and both pop and op art. He also wrote about art in *They Taught Themselves: American Primitive Painters of the 20th Century* (1942) and *Abstract and Surrealist Art in America* (1944). He donated his important personal collection to New York's Museum of Modern Art in 1967.

JANOV, ARTHUR (1924–   ), U.S. psychologist. A native of Los Angeles with a Ph.D in psychology from the Claremont Graduate School (1960), Janov practiced standard "insight" therapy until witnessing (1967) a formerly withdrawn patient emit what has been called a "primal scream" on reenacting a traumatic childhood experience. He then devised an intensive course of treatment using cribs and baby bottles as aids to reach the "pool of pain" buried in the childhood of every neurotic. "Primal therapy," as described by Janov in *The Primal Scream* (1970) and *Primal Man: The*

New Consciousness (1975), was claimed by him to be the only cure for neurosis. See also his *Prisoner of Pain* (1980), *Imprints: The Lifelong Effects of the Birth Experience* (1983) and *The New Primal Scream: Primal Therapy 20 Years On* (1991).

JANOWITZ, MORRIS (1919–1988), U.S. sociologist. After working as a morale analyst for the U.S. Army during World War II, Janowitz studied sociology at the University of Chicago (Ph.D. 1948) and joined its faculty. He became the leading U.S. sociologist of military institutions and of the social and political consequences of war. He gained prominence in the 1960s with such works as *The Professional Soldier: A Social and Political Portrait* (1960) and *The Military in the Political Development of New Nations* (1964). Later books included *The Last Half Century: Societal Change and Politics in America* (1978), *CivilMilitary Relations: Regional Perspectives* (1981), and *The Reconstruction of Patriotism: Education for Civic Consciousness* (1983).

JANSKY, KARL GUTHE (1905–1950), U.S. engineer. While working at the Bell Telephone Laboratories, Jansky studied (1931–32) the atmospheric static that interfered with transoceanic telephone calls. He concluded that the radio waves he detected emanated from a fixed source outside of the solar system, in the Milky Way galaxy. This discovery generated the development of radio astronomy, which enabled scientists to observe celestial bodies beyond the reach of ordinary telescopes.

JARA, VICTOR (1934?–1973), Chilean folk musician. Born into a poor peasant family, Jara was a scholarship student at the University of Chile in Santiago. As a theater director at the university (1960–70), he produced plays by Brecht and Gorky and toured Latin America. During the late 1960s and early 1970s he turned to music to spread his message of social justice, and began to write and sing politically charged folk songs. His compositions were inspired by the indigenous folk melodies he learned in rural villages and urban slums, and he became an internationally known representative of the "new song" movement. A socialist, he was a supporter of the left-wing government of Salvador Allende (1970–73) and was publicly tortured and murdered by Chilean soldiers after the military coup that overthrew Allende (Sept. 1973). ■ See biography by his widow, Joan Jara, *An Unfinished Song* (1984).

JARRELL, RANDALL (1914–1965), U.S. poet and critic. Jarrell began as a war poet with *Blood for a Stranger* (1942) and *Losses* (1948) and he never lost his sense of tragedy. His poetry, which was influenced by W. H. Auden, T. S. Eliot, and Rainer Maria Rilke, was published in *Selected Poems* (1955), *The Woman at the Washington Zoo* (1960), and *The Lost World* (1965). He railed at academic pretension in the satirical novel *Pictures from an Institution* (1954) and despaired of American culture in the essay collection *A Sad Heart at the Supermarket* (1962). He taught at the University of North Carolina (from 1947). *The Complete Poems* (1969), *The Third Book of Criticism* (1969), and the essays in *No Other Book* (1999) appeared posthumously. ■ See *Randall Jarrell's Letters: An Autobiographical and Literary Selection* (1985); studies by Bernetta Quinn (1981) and William H. Pritchard (1990); and Mary von Schrader Jarrell, *Remembering Randall* (1999).

JARUZELSKI, WOJCIECH (1923–   ), Polish military and political leader. Born into the landed gentry, Jaruzelski was deported to the Soviet Union after the partition of Poland (1939). He served in the Soviet-sponsored Polish army during World War II, joined the Communist party (1947), and attended officers' training school (1948–51). He worked his way up the ranks of the military and the party, serving as chief of the general staff (1965–68), defense minister (1968–83), and party Politburo member (1971–89). Amid continuing economic crises and the rise of the independent union Solidarity, which called for radical changes in Poland's economic and political structure, Jaruzelski was named prime minister and party leader (1981), with a mandate to blunt the effect of the reformers and maintain Communist party domination of Poland. Unable to reach a lasting compromise agreement with Solidarity leaders, he declared martial law (Dec. 1981), curtailed civil liberties, and arrested the union's leaders. Supported by the Soviet leadership, he maintained martial law until July 1983. However, he was unable to solve Poland's basic economic problems and maintained the ban on Solidarity. In 1985 he stepped down as prime minister and was elected president by the parliament. Solidarity was legalized in 1989 and that year won the free parliamentary elections that ended Communist rule. When Jaruzelski's presidential term ended in 1990, he apologized for the "harm, pain, and injustice" suffered by Poles during his years in power.

JASPERS, KARL THEODOR (1883–1969), German psychiatrist and philosopher. Jaspers first began observing the basic personality types he described in *General Psychopathology* (1913; Eng. trans. 1965) as a psychiatrist at Heidelberg's university hospital. From psychology he gravitated to philosophy, which he defined as the "never-ending search for the ultimate reality." Jaspers' philosophy, with its emphasis on individual existence and freedom, had an important influence on existentialism. He was forced into retirement by the Nazis and left Germany after World War II to teach in Switzerland (University of Basel; 1948–61), where he wrote works on such moral problems as German war guilt and world confederation. His best-known works included *Philosophy* (3 vols., 1932; Eng. trans. 1969), *Reason and Existence* (1935; Eng. trans. 1955), *Philosophy and Existence* (1938; Eng. trans. 1971), and *The Origin and Goal of History* (1949; Eng. trans. 1953). ■ See P. A. Schilpp, ed., *The Philosophy of Karl Jaspers* (rev. ed. 1981);

studies by Charles F. Wallraff (1970) and Leonard H. Ehrlich (1975); and Elisabeth Young-Bruehl, *Freedom and Karl Jaspers's Philosophy* (1981).

JAURÈS, JEAN (1859–1914), French political leader. A brilliant student, teacher, and orator, Jaurès served in parliament (1885–89; 1893–98; 1902–14), where he espoused an idealistic type of reform socialism. He completed his Ph.D. thesis on the philosophical roots of German socialism (1891), wrote an eight-volume *Socialist History of the French Revolution* (1901–07), and was a cofounder of the newspaper *L'Humanité* (1904). In 1905 Jaurès paved the way for the unification of the French socialist movement into a single party by agreeing not to participate in bourgeois governments; he remained in the opposition the rest of his life. An advocate of Franco-German reconciliation, he was assassinated on the eve of World War I by a right-wing fanatic. ■ See biography by Harvey Goldberg (1962).

JAWLENSKY, ALEKSEY VON (1864–1941), Russian-born artist. An officer in the Imperial Guard, Jawlensky gave up his career to study art and to paint. He moved to Munich (1896), where he met expressionist painter Wassily Kandinsky, whose artistic theories greatly influenced him. Jawlensky's work also showed the influence of Cézanne, Matisse, and Van Gogh as well as the fauves and cubists. His still lifes, landscapes, and portraits were characterized by vivid colors and simplified forms, and many had a folklike quality. The mystical abstract faces he painted after 1917 are reminiscent of Russian icons and are his best-known works. Before World War I he exhibited with members of the Blue Rider group, and during the 1920s he formed the Blue Four, a short-lived association with Paul Klee, Lyonel Feininger, and Kandinsky. ■ See study by Clemens Weiler (Eng. trans. 1971).

JEANS, SIR JAMES HOPWOOD (1877–1946), British mathematician and astrophysicist. Jeans applied mathematical principles to problems in physics and astronomy. He taught at Cambridge and Princeton universities before World War I and later did research at the Mt. Wilson Observatory in California. In the field of statistical mechanics, he worked out proofs for various laws of the kinetic theory of gases. Jeans developed new theories of astronomy, demonstrating the inaccuracy of the earlier French astronomer Laplace's theory of the origin of the solar system; he researched the origin of binary-star systems and star-cluster movement and theorized that matter is constantly being formed in the universe. He wrote numerous science texts and popularizations of science and philosophy. ■ See biography by Edward A. Milne (1952).

JEFFERS, ROBINSON (1887–1962), U.S. poet and playwright. A clergyman's son, Jeffers took up classical and modern languages in European and American schools and later studied medicine and forestry. Violent imagery characterized his striding, unrhymed poetry. Despising "civilization," he built a house on an isolated California bluff and wrote by the light of a kerosene lamp in a stone tower 100 feet over the Pacific. He glorified nature and often used Greek myth to express his radical pessimism. Heralded in the 1920s for such works as *Roan Stallion, Tamar, and Other Poems* (1925), *The Woman at Point Sur* (1927), *Cawdor and Other Poems* (1928) and *Dear Judas and Other Poems* (1929), he saw his reputation decline during the Depression of the 1930s when the public spurned his gloomy outlook. His adaptations of Greek tragedies, notably *Medea* (1946), brought him recognition in the 1940s and 1950s. *Selected Poems* (1965) and *Selected Letters* (1968) appeared posthumously. ■ See biography by Clark Powell (1983) and studies by Arthur B. Coffin (1971), Robert J. Brophy (1973), and William H. Nolte (1978).

JEFFREYS, SIR HAROLD (1891–1989), British geophysicist, astronomer, and mathematician. Associated with Cambridge University as a lecturer, reader, and professor from 1914 until his retirement in 1958, Jeffreys was one of the most wide-ranging and productive scientists of the century. He played a major role in systematizing and unifying the field of geophysics and calculated (1926) that the earth's core is liquid, devised tables (1930–40) giving the travel time of earthquake waves, and explained the causes of monsoons and sea breezes. In astronomy, he calculated that the surface temperatures of the outer planets (Jupiter, Saturn, Uranus, and Neptune) are more than 100° below zero centigrade, thus upsetting previously held views and leading to a complete revision of the study of the composition and the structure of the planets. He also contributed to probability theory, operational calculus, and other fields of mathematics. His books included *The Earth* (1924), *Earthquakes and Mountains* (1935), *Methods of Mathematical Physics* (1946; with Bertha Jeffreys), and *Collected Papers* (6 vols., 1971–77).

JEFFRIES, JAMES J. (1875–1953), U.S. boxer. Known as the "Boilermaker" because he had worked in a boiler factory, Jeffries was a strong, agile fighter who began his career as James J. Corbett's sparring partner. At age 24 he won the heavyweight crown by knocking out Bob Fitzsimmons in 11 rounds (1899). From then until his retirement in 1905, he successfully defended his title against such formidable challengers as Tom Sharky and Jim Corbett. In 1910 he was persuaded to try a comeback against the new champion, Jack Johnson—an African-American fighter whose domination of the sport outraged many in the boxing world. Johnson knocked him out in the 15th round.

JELLICOE, JOHN RUSHWORTH JELLICOE, 1st EARL (1859–1935), British admiral. Jellicoe, who joined the navy at age 13, led a relief force to Peking during the Boxer Rebellion (1898–1900). He became commander in chief of the British fleet in 1914 but was removed after heavy losses during the Battle of Jutland (1916), a strategic but indecisive victory over the German navy during World War I. He briefly served as first sea lord (1916–17) and later was governorgeneral of New Zealand (1920–24). ■ See biographies by Reginald H. Bacon (1936), A. Temple Patterson (1969), and John Winton (1981).

JENKINS OF HILLHEAD, ROY HARRIS JENKINS, BARON (1920–   ), British political leader. The son of a miner who was later elected to Parliament, Jenkins was a Labour member of the House of Commons (1948–76) and served as home secretary (1965–67; 1974–76) and chancellor of the Exchequer (1967–70). He was president of the Commission of the European Economic Community from 1977 until 1981, when he returned to British politics. He cofounded the centrist Social Democratic party (1981) and was reelected to Parliament, as a Social Democrat, in March 1982 and served until 1987. He later served as chancellor of Oxford University (1987–   ), president of the Royal Society of Literature (1988–   ), and as a member of the House of Lords (1988–   ). ■ See his autobiography, *A Life at the Centre* (1991), and biography by John Campbell (1983).

JENKS, CLARENCE WILFRED (1909–1973), British legal scholar. C. Wilfred Jenks studied at Cambridge University (B.A. 1931; M.A. 1936) and became a lawyer in 1936. In 1932 he joined the legal section of the International Labor Organization (ILO), where he spent his entire career (director, 1970–73). He quickly established himself as an expert on international labor standards and was a delegate to many international bodies. He wrote articles and books on many aspects of international law, including the award-winning volume *The Common Law of Mankind* (1959) and the pioneering study *Space Law* (1965). His major concerns are reflected in the titles of other books, including *The International Protection of Trade Union Freedom* (1957), *Human Rights and International Labour Standards* (1960), *Law, Freedom and Welfare* (1963), and *Social Justice in the Law of Nations* (1970). A principal architect of the concept of the international civil servant, Jenks was a delegate to the historic San Francisco Conference (1945), which established the United Nations.

JENSEN, JOHANNES HANS DANIEL (1907–1973), German physicist. The son of a gardener, J. Hans D. Jensen prepared for his work in nuclear physics by studying physics, mathematics, and philosophy at Hamburg University. He became interested in nuclear structure during visits to Niels Bohr's Institute in Copenhagen. He shared the 1963 Nobel Prize in Physics with Maria Goeppert Mayer and Eugene P. Wigner for the elaboration of nuclear shell structure, worked out in 1949 in collaboration with chemist H. E. Suess and physicist O. Haxel. Jensen's model posited a strong coupling of the spin and the orbital motion of each proton and neutron in the nucleus—an assertion that, although not consistent with theory of the day, elucidated a good deal of nuclear data and was corroborated in many experiments involving nucleon scattering. He was a professor at Heidelberg University (from 1949).

JENSEN, JOHANNES VILHELM (1873–1950), Danish writer. In his many "Himmerland Tales" (1898–1910) Jensen depicted the people and country of his native Jutland. An amateur anthropologist and Darwinist, he described humankind's ascent from baboon origins to the voyages of Columbus in his most important work, the epic novel *The Long Journey* (6 vols., 1908–22; Eng. trans. 1922–24). He was also known for his lyric poetry and his historical novel, *The Fall of the King* (1900–01; Eng. trans. 1933). His *Myths* (11 vols., 1907–44) are poetic collections of ruminative essays and tales. Selections in English were published in *The Waving Rye* (1958). Jensen was awarded the Nobel Prize in Literature in 1944.

JERITZA, MARIA (Maria Jedlicka; 1887–1982), Czech-born opera singer. A glamorous blond prima donna known for her brilliant voice and dramatic acting, Jeritza was a star of the Vienna Opera (1912–35) and the leading soprano at New York's Metropolitan Opera (1921–32). She appeared with all of the major opera houses of Europe and made numerous recordings (1908–30). Best known for her portrayals of Puccini, Strauss, and Wagner heroines, she performed in many of the traditional operas of the Italian and French repertory and sang in the world premiers of Strauss's *Ariadne auf Naxos* (1912) and *Die Frau ohne Schatten* (1919), and in the U.S. premiers of Janáček's *Jenufa* (1924), Puccini's *Turandot* (1926), and Strauss's *Die ägyptische Helena* (1928). ■ See her memoirs, *Sunlight and Song* (1924).

JERNE, NIELS KAJ (1911–1994), Danish-British immunologist. Born to Danish parents in London, Jerne worked for the Danish State Serum Institute (1943–55) and received his medical degree from the University of Copenhagen (1951). He was the chief medical officer of the World Health Organization (1956–62), taught at several universities in Europe and the United States, and was the founding director of the Basel (Switzerland) Institute of Immunology (1969–80). Recognized as a major theoretician in the field of immunology, he explained how the immune system supplies sufficient amounts of antibodies to destroy invading viruses and bacteria, described how the immune system develops and matures, and developed the "network theory" to explain the complex interaction processes by which the immune system protects the body against disease. He shared the 1984 Nobel Prize in Physiology or Medicine with César Milstein and Georges J. F. Köhler.

JESSUP, PHILIP CARYL (1897–1986), U.S. lawyer, educator, and judge. Jessup taught international law at Columbia University (1925–60), was a legal adviser to the State Department, and a prominent member of the Institute of Pacific Relations. After World War II, as a U.S. representative to the United Nations (1949–52) and U.S. ambassador-at-large (1949–52) and close adviser to Secretary of State Dean Acheson, he played a major role in the diplomatic negotiations ending the Soviet blockade of West Berlin, and coordinated the preparation of the famous State Department White Paper on *United States Relations with China* (1949), which charged the Nationalist government of Chiang Kai-shek with corruption and incompetence. He resigned from the government after being attacked as procommunist by Sen. Joseph R. McCarthy, the China Lobby, and other right-wing forces. He later served as a judge on the International Court of Justice (World Court; 1961–70). A pragmatist who believed in a functional approach to law, he developed the concept of "transnational law," which broadened the scope of international law to include areas that are both in the public and private spheres, and proposed the idea of an international "community interest." He wrote several important books, including *A Modern Law of Nations* (1948), *Transnational Law* (1956), *The Use of International Law* (1959), and *The Birth of Nations* (1974).

JHABVALA, RUTH PRAWER (Ruth Prawer; 1927–   ), German-born writer. Born into a Jewish family in Cologne, Jhabvala and her family escaped Nazi persecution by emigrating to England (1939). After graduating from the University of London (M.A. 1951), she married Indian architect Cyrus Jhabvala and moved with him to New Delhi. As a housewife, she began writing a series of satirical, nuanced novels of urban middle-class life in India and of the conflicts between Indians and westerners. These works included *Esmond in India* (1958), *The Householder* (1960), and *Heat and Dust* (1975). In 1963 she began a long collaboration with filmmakers Ismail Merchant and James Ivory, writing screenplays for many highly successful films, including *The Householder* (1963), *Bombay Talkie* (1970), *The Europeans* (1979), *Heat and Dust* (1983), *The Bostonians* (1984), *A Room with a View* (1986), *Howard's End* (1992), and *Jefferson in Paris* (1995). In 1976 she moved to New York City, the setting of her novels *In Search of Love and Beauty* (1983) and *Poet and Dancer* (1993). She also wrote *East into Upper East: Plain Tales from New York and New Delhi* (1998). ■ See study by Ralph Crane (1992).

JIANG JIESHI. *See CHIANG KAI-SHEK.*

JIANG QING (old style: CHIANG CH'ING; 1914?–1991), Chinese political leader. Jiang joined a theatrical troupe at age 13 and lived a bohemian life as a film actress in Shanghai during the 1930s. She established many connections on the left, joined the Communist movement in Yanan (Yenan) in 1937, and married party leader Mao Zedong (Mao Tsetung) in the early 1940s. After the establishment of the People's Republic of China (1949) she remained in political obscurity until 1964, when she sponsored a movement aimed at introducing proletarian themes at the Beijing (Peking) Opera. With Mao's blessing the movement grew and developed into the Cultural Revolution (1966), which had a revolutionary—and disruptive—effect on Chinese society for nearly a decade. Jiang, along with Zhang Chunqiao (Chang Ch'un-ch'iao), Wang Hongwen (Wang Hung-wen), and Yao Wenyuan (Yao Wenyuan), dominated the ultra-leftist "Cultural Revolution group" within the politburo during this period. Thousands of intellectuals, artists, and moderate government and party officials were purged and banished to the countryside, and many committed suicide or died in prison. In Oct. 1976, one month after Mao's death, Jiang and her three colleagues were arrested, expelled from the party, and accused (as the Gang of Four) of committing numerous crimes. Jiang defiantly maintained her innocence at a dramatic trial (1980–81) and was sentenced to death (1981), which was later commuted to life imprisonment. She reportedly committed suicide in 1991. ■ Roxane Witke's *Comrade Chiang Ch'ing* (1977) was based on a series of interviews with Jiang. See also Ross Terrill, *The White-Boned Demon* (1984).

JIANG ZEMIN (1926–), Chinese political leader. Born into an intellectual family in Jiangsu Province, Jiang learned English at an American missionary school and graduated from Shanghai's prestigious Jiaotong University (1947) with a degree in electrical engineering. He joined the Communist party in 1946. After training at a Moscow automobile factory (1955–60) he held a series of technical positions during the 1960s and 1970s. He was made a full member of Central Committee of the Communist party (1982) and served as mayor of Shanghai (1985–88) and member of the Politburo (1987–). A supporter of Deng Xiaoping's policies of economic liberalization while maintaining strict party political control, Jiang was named general secretary of the Communist party following the suppression of the Tiananmen demonstrations (June 1989). He subsequently served as president of China (1993–) and became the country's primary leader after the death of Deng Xiaoping (1997). His policies maintained China's market-oriented reform and high level of economic growth. ■ See Bruce Gilley, *Tiger on the Brink* (1998), and Hung-mao Tien and Yun-Han Chu, eds., *China Under Jiang Zemin* (2000).

JIMÉNEZ, JUAN RAMÓN (1881–1958), Spanish poet. One of the major Spanish poets of the century, Jiménez exerted enormous influence on modern poets with his symbolic lyric poetry. Always of precarious health and aesthetic temperament, he wrote about nature, music, and art and formulated (1916–17) *la poesía desnuda,* poetry stripped of its trappings. He experimented with free verse but also wrote in traditional forms, as in *Spiritual Sonnets* (1914–15; Eng. trans. 1996) and *Diary of a Newly Married Poet* (1917). His later work, gathered in *Total Season* (1946) was more precise. Jiménez emigrated after the Spanish Civil War (1936–39) and lived in the United States and Puerto Rico. He won the 1956 Nobel Prize in Literature. Translations of his work are in *Platero and I: An Andalusian Elegy, 1907–*

1916 (1917; Eng. trans. 1956), *Selected Writings* (1957), *Three Hundred Poems* (1962), *God Desired and Desiring* (1987), *Invisible Reality: 1917–20, 1924* (1987), *The Complete Perfectionist: A Poetics of Work* (1997), and *Time and Space: A Poetic Autobiography* (1988). ■ See study by Donald F. Fogelquist (1976).

JINNAH, MOHAMMAD ALI (1876–1948), Indian-Pakistani political leader. The secular and Westernized Jinnah studied law in Britain (1892–95) and was a successful criminal lawyer in Bombay. A nationalist, he joined the Indian National Congress party (1906) and the Muslim League (1913) and advocated Hindu-Muslim cooperation, but resigned from the Congress in opposition to Mahatma Gandhi's policy of mass demonstrations for independence (1920). Fearful of growing Hindu revival movements, Jinnah tried to convince the Congress leaders to grant Muslims separate electorates and other political protections, but his ideas were rejected. As president of the Muslim League (from 1934), he revitalized it into a mass movement and, after Hindu-Muslim relations deteriorated in the late 1930s, demanded (1940) the creation of a separate Muslim state. Although opposed by both the Congress party and the British government, separatists won almost every seat in predominantly Muslim areas in the 1946 elections. The rioting and killing that followed convinced the British and the Congress to accept Jinnah's plan, and when Pakistan was created as a Muslim state (1947), he was appointed its first governor-general and was regarded as the country's founder. ■ See biography by Hector Bolitho (1954) and study by Akbar S. Ahmed (1997).

JOBIM, ANTONIO CARLOS (1927–1994), Brazilian composer, musician, and songwriter. Trained in classical music and architecture, Jobim decided to pursue a career in popular music after hearing the big band jazz of Duke Ellington and other Americans in Rio during the 1940s. He wrote many songs in Brazil before becoming internationally known for composing (with Luis Bonfá) the pulsating samba-laden score for the film *Black Orpheus* (1958). His song "Chega de Saudade" ("No More Blues," 1958), recorded by Joao Gilberto, combined samba rhythms with cool jazz harmonies in a style that Jobim called "bossa nova." The style was popularized in the United States by jazz musicians Stan Getz and Charlie Byrd in the early 1960s and became an international craze. Subsequent bossa nova compositions by Jobim, such as *"Desafinado"* (1962), "The Girl from Ipanema" (1963), "How Insensitive" (1963), and "Wave" (1969), became jazz standards and were performed by artists such as Frank Sinatra, Ella Fitzgerald, and Sarah Vaughn. Jobim also wrote hundreds of other songs and instrumental works and recorded several solo albums.

JOBS, STEVEN PAUL (1955–), U.S. computer corporation executive. Jobs studied at Reed College and worked for the California-based computer firms Hewlett-Packard and Atari, Inc. With Stephen Wozniak, he developed the Apple I computer in 1976, and the two young men set up Apple Computer in a garage in 1976. The firm took off, with Jobs as chairman, becoming a major force in the high-tech world; as the industry's boy wonder, Jobs came to personify the Silicon Valley version of the American dream. In the 1980s he stirred controversy within the firm by stressing development of the Macintosh computer. After hiring John Sculley as Apple's chief executive (1983), Jobs increasingly lost clout in the firm, and at age 30 resigned as chairman late in 1985. He remained the firm's largest shareholder. He founded NeXT computer company (1985) and bought Pixar Animation Studio (1986) that produced the first entirely computer-generated full-length film, *Toy Story* (1995). Jobs sold NeXT to Apple for $400 million in Dec. 1995 and he rejoined Apple as interim president in 1997. ■ See Lee Butcher, *Accidental Millionaire* (1988); study by Jeffrey S. Young (1988); Owen W. Linzmayer, *Apple Confidential* (1999); and Alan Deutschman, *The Second Coming of Steve Jobs* (2000).

JODL, ALFRED (1890–1946), German general. As dictator Adolf Hitler's personal commander in chief during World War II, Jodl acted as liaison between the cabinet and the army and was active in planning the eastern campaign. Wounded during the 1944 attempt to assassinate Hitler, he became chief of the Joint Staff in 1945 and signed the German capitulation that year. At the Nuremberg trials Jodl testified that Hitler, nervous over Allied inactivity, repeatedly delayed his attack on the western front. He was convicted of war crimes and hanged.

JOFFRE, JOSEPH JACQUES CÉSAIRE (1852–1931), French marshal. Joffre served in the Franco-Prussian War and joined the engineering corps (1872), achieving promotion to captain at age 24. He served in France's colonies (1885–97), building a railroad in Senegal and a naval base in Madagascar and leading an attack against Timbuktu, about which he published a book in 1915. As chief of staff of the French army after 1911 he was responsible for lack of preparedness for World War I, but he endured as commander in chief on the western front to become known as the "victor of the Marne" for his successful counterattack against the German army (1914). He was replaced after the Germans nearly captured Verdun (1916). ■ See his *Personal Memoirs* (2 vols.; Eng. trans. 1932) and the biographies by Raymond Recouly (1931) and Arthur Conte (1991).

JOFFREY, ROBERT (Abdullah Jaffa Bey Khan; 1930–1988), U.S. choreographer, ballet-company director, and dancer. Ballet study was prescribed for Joffrey as a child to improve his asthmatic condition. He studied from age 12, appeared professionally after 1949, and began choreographing. Joffrey became known in New York as a dance teacher and founded (1953) the American Ballet Center. He established (1956) the eclectic Robert Joffrey Ballet (later the City Center Joffrey Ballet), which became one of the most important American dance troupes, known for its energetic performances of both classical ballet and modern dance. Its repertoire included works choreographed by George Balanchine, Anthony Tudor, Frederick Ashton, and Alvin Ailey as well as Joffrey's own *Astarte* (1967), *Remembrances* (1973), and *Beautiful Dreamer* (1975). Joffrey also choreographed many works for the New York City Opera. ■ See Sasha Anawalt, *The Joffrey Ballet* (1996).

JOHANSON, DONALD CARL (1943–), U.S. physical anthropologist. Johanson studied at the University of Chicago (Ph.D. 1974), working under F. Clark Howell and taking part in a major fossil-hunting expedition in the Omo valley of Ethiopia. He worked at the Cleveland Museum of Natural History (1972–81; curator, 1974–81). Johanson made a series of important fossil discoveries in eastern Africa, including a human knee joint that provided evidence of early upright posture and locomotion 3.3 million years ago (1973); the most nearly complete skeleton of a human ancestor, a female he called Lucy (1974); and bones from 13 individuals, apparently from one extended family, whom Johanson claimed represented a previously unknown, humanlike species (1975–76). Johanson's views were often at odds with those of Kenyan anthropologist Richard Leakey. Johanson claimed, on the basis of his findings, that the human species emerged from more primitive ancestors as recently as 2 million years ago; Leakey argued that the species appeared more than 4 million years ago. Johanson was later associated with the Institute for the Study of Human Origins in Berkeley, California (1981–) and taught at Stanford University (1983–89). He produced the films *The First Family* (1981) and *Lucy in Disguise* (1982) and coauthored (with M. A. Edey) *Lucy: The Beginnings of Human Kind* (1982).

JOHN, AUGUSTUS EDWIN (1878–1961), British painter. John studied at London's Slade School of Art (1894–98). A rebellious and legendary individualist during the first quarter of the century, he frequently lived with gypsy bands and featured gypsies, tramps, and beggars in many of his works. He was best known for his keen realization of character in portraits of political and literary figures, including Queen Elizabeth II, David Lloyd George, T. E. Lawrence, James Joyce, Sean O'Casey, George Bernard Shaw, and Dylan Thomas. Other canvases included *The Smiling Woman* and *Rachel,* which hang in the Tate Gallery (London). ■ See his autobiography, *Chiaroscuro* (1952), and biography by Michael Holroyd (1975; rev. ed. 1996).

JOHN, ELTON (Reginald Kenneth Dwight; 1947–), British rock composer and musician. John started taking piano lessons at the age of 4, studied at the Royal Academy of Music, and launched his first band in the early 1960s. In 1968, he began writing songs with lyricist Bernie Taupin, with whom he collaborated for most of his career. After the success of his 1970 albums *Elton John* and *Tumbleweed Connection,* he became one of the most popular rock singers in the world, performing in lavishly staged concerts wearing outlandish costumes and outrageous eyeglasses. He wrote such rock classics as "Rocket Man," "Your Song," "Daniel," "Don't Let the Sun Go Down on Me," "Someone Saved My Life Tonight," "Candle in the Wind," and "Can You Feel the Love Tonight?" and sold more than 200 million records. In spite of a turbulent personal life, including a long period as an alcoholic and drug addict, John remained popular through the late 1990s and broke Elvis Presley's record by having a top-40 single in *Billboard* magazine for 27 straight years. He sang "Candle in the Wind '97", a newly written version of his hit song, at Princess Diana's funeral (1997), and his recording of it became the world's biggest-selling single of all time. He shared a Tony Award for the score of the Broadway musical *Aida* (2000). He was knighted in 1998.

JOHN XXIII (Angelo Giuseppe Roncalli; 1881–1963), Italian-born pope of the Roman Catholic Church. Born of pious peasant stock, Roncalli entered the local seminary at age 12, was ordained in 1904, and became secretary to the progressive bishop of Bergamo. He was made an archbishop (1925), then served in the Vatican diplomatic corps for more than 30 years as envoy to Bulgaria (1925–34), Greece and Turkey (1935–44), and France (1945–52). Elevated to cardinal (1944), he was patriarch of Venice for five years before his election as pope (1958). Widely expected to act as a caretaker, John XXIII stunned churchmen by announcing, in the third month of his papacy, his intention to summon an ecumenical council to consider the role of the church in the modern world. Convened in 1962, the Second Vatican Council (Vatican II) introduced far-reaching reforms. John XXIII issued eight encyclicals, including *Pacem in Terris* (1963), which addressed all "men of good faith," enumerating human rights and obligations and urging a halt to the arms race. *Journey of a Soul* (1964; Eng. trans. 1965) included passages from his diaries. ■ See studies by Meriol Trevor (1967), Paul Johnson (1974), and Peter Hebblethwaite (1985); and G. Zizola, *The Utopia of Pope John XXIII* (Eng. trans. 1978).

JOHN PAUL I (Albino Luciani; 1912–1978), Italian-born pope of the Roman Catholic Church. John Paul I, who characterized himself as "only a poor man, accustomed to small things and silence," was the son of an artisan and a scullery maid who inhabited a mountain village. A frail child, he contracted tuberculosis in his youth. Long sure of his vocation, Luciani began preparing for the priesthood at age 11. After ordination (1934) and graduate study he combined parish work with teaching and compiled the popular book of aphoristic catechism lessons *Catechism Crumbs* (Eng. trans. 1949). He was named a bishop by Pope John XXIII and a cardinal and patriarch of Venice by Pope Paul VI. The sense of calm instilled on the Roman Catholic world by the election of this pastor pope, a moderate traditionalist, was suddenly disrupted when, a month after his election, John

Paul I succumbed to a heart attack, ending the shortest papal reign in nearly four centuries. ■ See Peter Hebblethwaite, *The Year of Three Popes* (1979), and Andrew Greeley, *The Making of the Popes, 1978* (1979).

JOHN PAUL II (Karol Jozef Wojtyla; 1920–), Polish-born pope of the Roman Catholic Church. After working as a laborer and performing with an avant-garde theater group in German-occupied Cracow during the early years of World War II, Wojtyla studied for the priesthood in an underground seminary (from 1942) and was ordained in 1946. He served as a parish priest after studying at the Angelicum in Rome (Ph.D. 1948) and taught social ethics at the Catholic University of Lublin (from 1954). He wrote scholarly articles and several books and also published poetry (under the pseudonym Adrzej Jawien). He served as auxiliary bishop (1958–64) and archbishop (from 1964) of Cracow and cardinal (from 1967) and was elected pope in 1978—the first non-Italian to hold the office in 455 years. A charismatic personality, he traveled to the United States, Latin America, Africa, and his native Poland during his years as pope, espousing universal human rights and strict doctrinal conservatism. He survived an assassination attempt in St. Peter's Square (May 1981). The longest-serving pope of the 20th century, he played a major role in the defeat of communism in Eastern Europe but also denounced the materialism and social injustices of capitalist societies. ■ See his *Collected Poems* (Eng. trans. 1982); biography by Lord Longford (1982); Gordon Thomas and Max Morgan-Witts, *Pontiff* (1983); Carl Bernstein and Mario Politi, *His Holiness* (1996); and George Weigel, *Witness to Hope* (1999).

JOHNS, JASPER (1930–), U.S. painter. Born in Georgia and raised in South Carolina, Johns went to New York City (1952) after an army stint and set up a studio in the same building as painter Robert Rauschenberg, who became a friend and mentor. Diverging from the abstract expressionism that dominated American art in the 1950s, Johns painted common objects (the U.S. flag, targets, beer cans, maps), modifying reality in a way that challenged viewers to rethink their usual way of seeing. His paintings of the late 1950s heralded the pop art movement in the United States. He also created such sculptures as his two *Painted Bronzes* (1960). After 1961, Johns began affixing actual objects to his canvases, as in the series called *Devices*. In 1980, Johns' *Three Flags* (1958) was sold to New York's Whitney Museum for $1 million, and he became the first living artist to command such a sum for a work. His later, more personal works, included *Perilous Night* (1982) and *The Seasons* (1985–86). ■ See studies by Michael Crichton (1977, 1994) and Jill Johnston (1996).

JOHNSON, ALVIN SAUNDERS (1874–1971), U.S. economist, educator, and editor. The son of an immigrant Danish farmer, Johnson was a professor of economics at several major universities and an editor of the influential liberal journal

New Republic (1917–23) before becoming the director of the innovative New School for Social Research in New York City (1923–45), the school for adults that he had cofounded in 1919. In 1933 he organized the "University in Exile," a refuge for European scholars threatened by the Nazis. The faculty, which included many of the world's foremost scholars, became the New School's graduate faculty of political and social science and profoundly affected American intellectual life. With the aid of the Rockefeller Foundation, Johnson arranged for more than 200 scholars to be brought to the United States. He was also associate editor of the *Encyclopedia of the Social Sciences* and the author of hundreds of scholarly articles. ■ See his autobiography, *Pioneer's Progress* (1952).

JOHNSON, AMY (1903–1941), British aviator. Johnson took an undergraduate degree in economics at Sheffield University (1925), then worked as a typist. In her free time she joined the London Aeroplane Club and was certified as a ground engineer and pilot (1929). In 1930 she found financial backing for a solo flight from Britain to Australia in her craft, *Jason*. She completed the itinerary but damage to her aircraft kept her from breaking the record. Nevertheless she won celebrity, as well as £10,000 from the *Daily Mail*. The next year, she made an 80-hour London-Moscow-Tokyo junket in a light airplane. In 1933, Johnson crossed the Atlantic in a de Havilland biplane in 39 hours with her husband, pilot James A. Mollison (1905–59). She set a London to Cape Town solo record in 1936. During World War II, Johnson joined the British Air Transport Auxiliary. She died in the line of duty when her plane disappeared over the Thames estuary.

JOHNSON, CHARLES SPURGEON (1893–1956), U.S. sociologist and educator. A pioneer in the systematic study of race relations, Johnson was an African-American sociologist (Ph.B., University of Chicago, 1917) who wrote *The Negro in Chicago* (1922), a landmark study of the causes of the 1919 race riots. Moving to New York, he joined the Urban League and was the founder and editor (1923–29) of *Opportunity*, a leading journal of black life and culture during the Harlem renaissance of the 1920s. While chair of the sociology department (from 1928) and later president of Fisk University (1947–56), Johnson wrote *The Negro in American Civilization* (1930), *Growing Up in the Black Belt* (1941), and *Patterns of Negro Segregation* (1943). ■ See Richard Robbins, *Sidelines Activist* (1996).

JOHNSON, EYVIND (1900–1976), Swedish novelist. Born into a working-class family and largely self-educated, Johnson was noted for narrative innovation and psychological insight. His masterpiece was published under the general title *The Novel About Olof* (4 vols., 1934–37; vol. 1, Eng. trans. as *1914*, 1970), based on his hard early life in northern Sweden. Always concerned with moral and political issues of freedom and democracy, he wrote a series of anti-Nazi novels during World War II; *The Days of His Grace* (1960; Eng. trans. 1968), an antitotalitarian novel; and *Dreams of Roses and Fire* (1949; Eng. trans. 1984), an account of persecution in 17th-century France. He is best known for *Return to Ithaca* (1946; Eng. trans. 1952), a modern version of the *Odyssey*. He shared the Nobel Prize in Literature in 1974 with his compatriot Harry Martinson. ■ See study by Gavin Orton (1972).

JOHNSON, HEWLETT (1874–1966), British clergyman. Johnson studied engineering and geology and worked in a factory before deciding to become a "missionary engineer." After four years of theology study at Oxford, he was assigned (1905) to a wealthy suburban parish. Johnson became interested in social planning and communism, which in his view did not conflict with Christian faith. Appointed dean of Canterbury by a Labour government, Johnson served for more than three decades (1931–63). Early in his tenure he visited the Soviet Union (1932) and Loyalist Spain (1937), and wrote a 1939 book describing the *Socialist Sixth of the World* as morally and economically superior. Known as the "red dean," Johnson won the Stalin Peace Prize in 1951. ■ See his autobiography, *Searching for Light* (1968), and Robert Hughes, *The Red Dean* (1987).

JOHNSON, HIRAM WARREN (1866–1945), U.S. political leader. A former reporter and lawyer, Johnson became widely known as a prosecuting attorney in San Francisco. Elected governor of California (1910), he sponsored many political and social reforms and ended the dominance of the Southern Pacific Railroad in state politics. He was the vice-presidential candidate on Theodore Roosevelt's unsuccessful Progressive party ticket (1912). Reelected governor (1914), he resigned in 1917 to enter the U.S. Senate, where he served until his death. Best known for his isolationist policies, Johnson opposed American entry into World Wars I and II and participation in the League of Nations and the United Nations. ■ See Spencer C. Olin, *California's Prodigal Sons* (1968); Richard C. Lower, *A Bloc of One* (1993); and study by Michael A. Weatherson (1995).

JOHNSON, HOWARD DEERING (1896–1972), U.S. businessman. An elementary-school dropout, Johnson sold the debt-ridden cigar-store business he had inherited from his father and purchased (1924) a run-down drugstore and soda fountain in Wollaston, Massachusetts. He purchased, for $300, the ice-cream recipe of an elderly German pushcart vendor, created 28 separate flavors, and saw his business boom. In 1929 he became a pioneer in franchising when he sold the use of his name and products to a restaurateur who opened the first "Howard Johnson's" in southern Massachusetts. Soon dozens of white clapboard restaurants trimmed with orange and blue began appearing on highways throughout the East Coast. Winning exclusive rights to build restaurants on many new turnpikes after World War II, Johnson's firm prospered (reaching $200 million a year);

at the time of his retirement (1964) his chain was the largest private U.S. food distributor.

JOHNSON, HUGH SAMUEL (1882–1942), U.S. military leader and public official. A 1903 graduate of West Point, Johnson served as judge advocate during Gen. John J. Pershing's Mexican campaign (1916), directed the conscription program during World War I, and served on the War Industries Board before resigning from the army as a brigadier general (1919). During the 1920s he served in private business and became an adviser to Bernard Baruch (1927). A tough-minded and energetic administrator, he served the New Deal as director (1933) of the National Recovery Administration (NRA), but he was not an effective leader and resigned when the agency was reorganized (1934). From 1935 until his death he wrote a nationally syndicated Scripps-Howard news column. He broke with Pres. Franklin D. Roosevelt over the attempt to enlarge the Supreme Court (1937) and was thereafter a bitter enemy of the New Deal. ■ See biography by John K. Ohl (1985).

JOHNSON, JACK (John Arthur Johnson; 1878–1946), U.S. boxer. The first African-American prizefighter to win the world heavyweight championship, the legendary Johnson was one of the most controversial figures in sports history. In 1908 he won the world title by defeating Tommy Burns in Sydney, Australia. Many in the boxing world were outraged that an African American stood at the pinnacle of their sport, and sought a white boxer (a "great white hope") who could depose the champion. For seven years Johnson defeated all challengers with a combination of assets that some ring experts say have never been matched: a formidable physical presence in the ring, flawless defense, the ability to hit hard with either hand, and superb balance. In 1915 he lost his crown to 6-foot 6-inch Jess Willard when he was "knocked out" in the 26th round in Havana, Cuba. Years later, Johnson admitted in writing that he had "thrown" the fight. His relationship with a white woman sparked controversy, and in 1913, Johnson was convicted under the Mann Act for transporting a white woman across state lines for immoral purposes. He spent many years in exile. A 1968 play about Johnson's life, *The Great White Hope*, was produced on Broadway. ■ See the autobiography, *Jack Johnson Is a Dandy* (1969); Finis Farr, *Black Champion* (1964); and Randy Roberts, *Papa Jack* (1983).

JOHNSON, JAMES P. (1894–1955), U.S. pianist and composer. A pioneer of the New York–stride style of jazz piano playing, Johnson was a teacher of Fats Waller and the inspiration of many young jazz musicians of the 1920s and 1930s, including Duke Ellington. He led his own band in New York, performed as a concert pianist, accompanied singers Bessie Smith and Ethel Waters, and composed the music for the review *Runnin' Wild* (1923), including his song "Charleston," which helped launch an international dance craze. His other popular songs included "Old Fashioned Love," "If I Could Be with You (One Hour Tonight)," and "Way Down Yonder in New Orleans." He also wrote several large-scale works that incorporated African-American folk themes, including *Yamekraw: A Negro Rhapsody* (1928), *Harlem Symphony* (1932), and *The Organizer* (c. 1939), an opera with a libretto by Langston Hughes. ■ See study by Scott E. Brown (1986).

JOHNSON, JAMES WELDON (1871–1938), U.S. writer and civil-rights leader. Trained at Atlanta and Columbia universities, Johnson became a high school principal and later was the first African American admitted to the Florida bar (1897). With his brother John Rosamond Johnson, a composer and singer, he wrote over 200 songs, including "Lift Ev'ry Voice and Sing." After serving in consular posts in Venezuela (1907–09) and Nicaragua (1909–13), he published (anonymously) his only novel, *Autobiography of an Ex-Colored Man* (1912; reissued in 1927 with his acknowledgment as author.). He also wrote *Fifty Years and Other Poems* (1917); the acclaimed *God's Trombones* (1927), dialect sermons in verse; and *Black Manhattan* (1930); and edited the pioneering anthology *American Negro Poetry* (1922). As field secretary (1916–20) and executive secretary (1920–30) of the National Association for the Advancement of Colored People, he was a highly successful organizer and outspoken champion of equal rights for blacks. ■ See his autobiography, *Along This Way* (1933), and the biography by Eugene Levy (1973).

JOHNSON, JOHN HAROLD (1918–), U.S. publisher. The most successful African-American publisher in the United States, Johnson, founded *Negro Digest* (1942), a news magazine modeled after *Reader's Digest,* and *Ebony* (1945), a slick picture and feature-story magazine modeled after *Life.* He also published *Jet* and *Tan* as well as *Black World,* an important literary journal. His magazines were the first black publications with substantial national advertising, and his Johnson Publishing Co. was second in earnings among black-owned businesses in the early 1970s. ■ See his autobiography, *Succeeding Against the Odds* (1989; with Lerone Beannett, Jr.).

JOHNSON, LYNDON BAINES (1908–1973), U.S. president. A Texas teachers' college graduate (1930) first elected to Congress as a New Deal supporter (1937), Johnson became a powerful Democratic political operator and was elected to the Senate in 1948. As majority leader (1955–61), he secured the passage of important and controversial pieces of legislation, including the civil-rights acts of 1957 and 1960. After losing the 1960 presidential nomination to John F. Kennedy, he agreed to be Kennedy's vice-presidential running mate, and they narrowly defeated the Republican ticket headed by Richard Nixon. Johnson succeeded to the presidency after the assassination of Kennedy (Nov. 22, 1963) and helped obtain congressional passage of tax and civil-rights legislation originally proposed by Kennedy. After a landslide victory over conservative Republican Barry Goldwater in the 1964 presidential election, he got Congress to pass his "Great Society" program of domestic reforms, including health care, civil rights, social welfare, education, urban development, and antipoverty legislation. However, his prestige and popularity waned as he dramatically increased the U.S. military presence in South Vietnam and initiated bombing of the North. As domestic opposition increased, he decided not to run for reelection in 1968 and he retired to his ranch in Texas. ■ See his memoirs, *The Vantage Point* (1971); biography by Merle Miller (1980); Ronnie Dugger, *The Politician* (1982); Kathleen J. Turner, *Lyndon Johnson's Dual War* (1985); Robert Dallek's *Lone Star Rising* (1991) and *Flawed Giant* (1998); Robert A. Caro, *The Path to Power* (1982) and *Means of Ascent* (1990); and Michael Beschloss, ed., *Taking Charge: The Johnson White House Tapes, 1963–1964* (1997).

JOHNSON, MAGIC (Earvin Johnson, Jr.; 1959–), U. S. basketball player. As an All-America sophomore at Michigan State University, the 6-foot, 9-inch Johnson led his team to the 1979 NCAA championship. He then began a remarkable 13-season career (1979–91; 1996) with the Los Angeles Lakers of the National Basketball Association. The tallest guard in league history, Johnson was an excellent shooter and phenomenal passer who won three Most Valuable Player awards (1987; 1989–90), played on five NBA championship teams (1980; 1982; 1985; 1987–88), scored 17,707 points and made 10,141 assists during his career. One of the most popular and highest paid athletes of his generation, he shocked the sports world in 1991 when he announced that he was infected with HIV, the virus that causes AIDS, and retired. Although he briefly returned to competition in 1996, he spent most of his time as an AIDS activist, preaching safe sex to teenagers and establishing a charitable foundation to fund HIV and AIDS organizations. He also founded a TV and movie production company and hosted a syndicated late-night television talk show, *The Magic Hour* (1998–).

JOHNSON, MARTIN (1884–1937), and OSA LEIGHTY JOHNSON (1894–1953), U.S. photographers and explorers. The Johnsons were happy wanderers in an era when the camera was still a novelty. An itinerant photographer who accompanied Jack London on the *Snark's* round-the-world voyage in 1906, Martin married Osa Leighty in 1910 and collaborated with her on film expeditions to the South Seas, the New Hebrides, Borneo, and Africa. They made documentaries for the American Museum of Natural History in New York, feature films including *Simba* (1928) and *Congorilla* (1932), and published several books, including *Lion* (1929) and *Over African Jungles* (1935). After her husband's death in a plane crash, Osa wrote a best-selling auto-biography, *I Married Adventure* (1940). ■ See Kenhelm W. Stott, Jr., *Exploring With Martin and Osa Johnson* (1978), and Pascal J. Imperato, *They Married Adventure* (1992).

JOHNSON, PHILIP CORTELYOU (1906–), U.S. architect. Johnson was a classics major at Harvard who became director of the (New York) Museum of Modern Art's architectural department in 1931. That year he mounted an exhibition and was coauthor of a monograph on *The International Style* (1931), which defined the terms of modern architecture. Johnson returned to Harvard in 1940 to study architecture; as his first project he designed his own home, a glass box in a parklike Connecticut setting. He collaborated with his mentor Ludwig Mies van der Rohe on the Seagram Building (New York City, 1958) before evolving his own personal, more monumental style with Lincoln Center's New York State Theater (1963). The controversial granite skyscraper he designed with his partner John Burgee for the American Telephone and Telegraph Co. in New York City (1983) represented the trend in architecture known as post-modernism. Johnson and Burgee also designed the "Crystal Cathedral" (1980) in Garden Grove, California; the 56-story Republic Bank Center (1984) in Houston, Texas; and the 64-story Transco Energy Co. Building (1985) in suburban Houston. Johnson was awarded the 1979 Pritzker Prize. ■ See his *Writings* (1978) and studies by John M. Jacobus (1962) and Franz Schulze (1994).

JOHNSON, RAFER LEWIS (1935–), U.S. decathlon champion. One of the greatest all-around athletes of the century, Johnson won the Pan American championship (1955) and the silver medal at the 1956 Melbourne Olympics. A one-man track team, he set a world record of 8,683 points in the 1960 Olympic trials and subsequently won the gold medal in Rome by defeating his archrivals C. K. Yang (Taiwan) and Vasily Kuznetsov (Soviet Union). After his retirement he became a sportscaster and film actor. ■ See his autobiography, *The Best That I Can Be* (1998).

JOHNSON, ROBERT (1911–1938), U.S. singer. Johnson, an itinerant African-American singer and guitar player from the Mississippi Delta, was the most influential blues singer of his time. His precise, rhythmic guitar playing; powerful, dignified voice; and emotional delivery of lyrics reflected the violence, lust, self-pity, and despair he experienced during his lifetime and are evident in the 29 songs he recorded (1936–37). His compositions included such blues standards as "Terraplane Blues," "Dust My Broom," "Love in Vain," "Crossroads," "Walkin' Blues," and "Home Sweet Chicago." His work not only influenced such pioneers of electric blues as Howlin' Wolf, Muddy Waters, and Elmore James, but also exerted a major influence on rock music through the recordings of his songs by The Rolling Stones, Cream, and Eric Clapton. Johnson was murdered by the jealous husband of a woman he was flirting with while playing at a house party. A two-CD compilation, *Robert Johnson: The Complete Recordings* (1990), won a Grammy Award and sold more than one million copies worldwide. ∎ See Peter Guralnick, *Searching for Robert Johnson* (1989).

JOHNSON, TOM LOFTIN (1854–1911), U.S. entrepreneur and political leader. A millionaire businessman who owned several street-railway lines in Cleveland, Detroit, and New York, Johnson disposed of his holdings to enter politics as a member of the Democratic party. Elected to Congress in 1890 and 1892, he advocated free trade, a single-tax system first proposed by Henry George, and public ownership of utilities and public transportation. As a four-term mayor of Cleveland (1901–09), he contributed greatly to the development of modern municipal government and was one of the best-known urban reformers in the United States. He fought the political bosses successfully, introduced scientific management techniques, and established bureaucratic administration on a nonpartisan basis. ∎ See his autobiography, *My Story* (1913), and Hoyt L. Warner, *Progressivism in Ohio* (1964).

JOHNSON, UWE (1934–1984), German novelist. Raised in Mecklenburg, East Germany, Johnson moved to West Berlin in 1959 and received immediate acclaim with the publication of *Speculations About Jacob* (1959; Eng. trans. 1963). Written in an unusual conjectural and detached style, featuring shifting narrative techniques and perspectives, minute detail, and experimental language and punctuation, it was the first major fictional work to confront the theme of a divided Germany. He returned to the same theme in his subsequent novels, *The Third Book about Achim* (1961; Eng. trans. 1967) and *Two Views* (1965; Eng. trans. 1966). *Anniversaries* (4 vols., 1970–83; Eng. trans. vols. I-II, 1975) develops the history of a Mecklenburg family over three generations. ∎ See study by Mark Boulby (1974) and Gary Lee Baker, *Understanding Uwe Johnson* (1999).

JOHNSON, VIRGINIA. *See MASTERS, WILLIAM.*

JOLIOT-CURIE, FRÉDÉRIC (1900–1958), French physicist. After joining the Radium Institute in Paris (1925), he married Irène Curie, the daughter of Marie Curie. They discovered artificial radioactivity, for which they were awarded the Nobel Prize in Chemistry (1935). During World War II he remained in France and pursued scientific work on biological aspects of isotopes and played an active part in the French Resistance movement. After the war, while holding the chair of nuclear chemistry at the College de France, he became high commissioner of France's atomic-energy program. Because of his political activities and his membership in the Communist party (from 1942), he was relieved of that post (1950). He was an active and outspoken advocate of world peace. ∎ See biographies by Pierre Biquard (Eng. trans. 1965) and Maurice Goldsmith (1976).

JOLIOT-CURIE, IRÈNE (Irène Curie; 1897–1956), French physicist. The daughter of Nobel laureates Pierre and Marie Curie, the joint discoverers of radium, she worked as her mother's assistant at the Radium Institute in Paris (from 1914). After graduating from the Sorbonne (Ph.D. 1925), she married (1926) physicist Frédéric Joliot (who took the name Joliot-Curie) and worked closely with him throughout her career. Together they won the Nobel Prize in Chemistry (1935) for their discovery (1934) of artificial radioactivity. Irène Joliot-Curie also made major contributions leading to the discoveries of the neutron and of nuclear fission. She was undersecretary of state for scientific research (1936), professor at the Sorbonne (from 1937), director of the Radium Institute (from 1946), and a member of the French atomic energy commission (1946–51). Like her mother, she died as a result of leukemia caused by prolonged exposure to radiation.

JOLSON, AL (Asa Yoelson; 1886–1950), U.S. singer and actor. The son of a rabbi, Jolson fled his native Russian Lithuania with his family and settled in Washington, D.C. (1894). He began singing in the streets as a child, and after an apprenticeship in the circus, vaudeville, burlesque, and minstrel shows, he became one of Broadway's top entertainers during the 1920s. Frequently appearing in blackface and singing on one knee with his arms extended to his audience, he immortalized such sentimental songs as "Swanee," "Mammy," "California, Here I Come," "Sonny Boy," and "April Showers." He starred in *The Jazz Singer* (1927), a sentimental treatment of his life story that was the first part-sound feature film. He made several other movies and frequently sang on popular radio programs. ∎ See Pearl Sieben, *The Immortal Jolson* (1962); and biographies by Michael Freedland (1972), Robert Oberfirst (1980), and Herbert Goldman (1988).

JONATHAN, CHIEF (JOSEPH) LEABUA (1914–1987), Lesothoan political leader. A descendant of the 19th-century leader who unified the Sotho people, Chief Jonathan helped found the Basutoland National Party (BNP) in 1959. He became prime minister of Basutoland in 1965, just before the enclave, completely surrounded by South Africa, achieved independence from Britain as Lesotho (1966). As prime minister (1966–86), he suspended the constitution and declared a state of emergency after the BNP was on the verge of losing the 1970 election, and he subsequently presided over an increasingly despotic government. Although the Lesothoan economy was almost totally dependent on South Africa, he became a vocal critic of apartheid in the early 1970s. He further antagonized the South Africans by allowing communist nations to establish embassies (1982) and by giving asylum to members of the African National Congress (ANC), a group seeking to overthrow the South African government. In the midst of a South African economic blockade (January 1986), Chief Jonathan was overthrown in a military coup.

JONES, BOB, SR. (Robert Reynolds Jones; 1883–1968), U.S. evangelist. Jones was conducting revivals at age 13, was licensed by the Methodists to preach at 15, and spread an old-time, fundamentalist religion by conducting revival meetings across the United States. To train missionaries and ministers, he established Bob Jones College in Florida in 1927, moving it to Tennessee (1933) and then to South Carolina (1947; renamed Bob Jones University). Jones left the Methodist Church (1939), which he regarded as too liberal, and had no formal church affiliation in his later years. He opposed dancing and drinking, racial integration, and the election of Catholics to public office. Jones wrote religious books that were published by the Bob Jones University Press, preached over the school's radio station WMUU ("World's Most Unusual University"), and claimed that he had made more converts in his lifetime than anybody except Billy Sunday. His son, Bob Jones, Jr. (1911–1997), succeeded him as president of Bob Jones University.

JONES, BOBBY (Robert Tyre Jones, Jr.; 1902–1971), U.S. golfer. Arguably the greatest golfer of all time, Bobby Jones won his first tournament at age 9. He captured 13 major championships in an eight-year span, including the U.S. Open four times (1923, 1926, 1929, 1930), the British Open three times (1926, 1927, 1930), and the U.S. Amateur championship five times. He played on the U.S. Ryder Cup team seven times and won all of his singles matches. Retaining his amateur status, Jones never played golf for money. His sweep (1930) of the American and British Open and amateur championships was a golf landmark. Retiring that year at age 28 to practice law, Jones nevertheless remained involved in the game and was responsible for initiating (1934) the Masters tournament in Augusta, Georgia. ■ See his autobiography, *Golf Is My Game* (1960); biography by O. B. Keeler and Grantland Rice (1953); and Dick Miller, *Triumphant Journey* (1980).

JONES, (ALFRED) ERNEST (1879–1958), British psychoanalyst. Jones was a young doctor studying neurology and psychiatry in Germany when he discovered the work of psychoanalyst Sigmund Freud. As a member of Freud's inner circle, he helped disseminate the new theory of psychoanalysis in Great Britain, Canada, and the United States; founded and edited the *International Journal of Psychoanalysis* (1920–39); and wrote a definitive three-volume biography, *The Life and Work of Sigmund Freud* (1953–57). Jones, who conceptualized the process of "rationalization," also applied the principles of psychoanalysis to literature and myth in *Hamlet and Oedipus* (1949). ■ See his *Papers on Psycho-analysis* (1913), *Essays in Applied Psycho-analysis* (2 vols., 1951), his autobiography, *Free Associations: Memoirs of a Psychoanalyst* (1959); and biography by Vincent Brome (1983).

JONES, SIR HAROLD SPENCER (1890–1960), British astronomer. As government astronomer (1923–33) at the Cape of Good Hope and astronomer royal (1933–55) at the Royal Observatory in Greenwich, Jones researched the motion of the earth's poles and determined the mass of the moon. His study of the solar parallax facilitated calculation (published in 1941) of the mean distance (c. 93 million miles) between Earth and the sun. This distance, called the astronomical unit, has been used to determine the distances of planets, as well as the distances and determinations of stars. Jones also conducted research in geophysics, particularly on the irregularity of earth rotation, and magnetism.

JONES, JAMES (1921–1977), U.S. writer. The son of an Illinois dentist, Jones joined the U.S. Army at age 18 and boxed as a welterweight in the service and in Golden Gloves tournaments. A sergeant in World War II, he earned a Purple Heart. His novel of army life in Hawaii just prior to Pearl Harbor, *From Here to Eternity* (1951), was a great popular and critical success. Continuing in the same tough, unsentimental vein, he wrote *The Thin Red Line* (1962) and *Whistle* (completed in 1978 by Willie Morris), the other panels of his World War II trilogy. He reported on the war in Vietnam in *Viet Journal* (1974) and wrote an illustrated memoir, *WWII* (1975). Jones moved to Paris in 1958, returning to the U.S. in 1975. ■ See Willie Morris, *James Jones: A Friendship* (1978); study by James R. Giles (1981); biography by George Garrett (1984); and Frank MacShane, *Into Eternity* (1985).

JONES, JAMES EARL (1931–   ), U.S. actor. Born in Mississippi and raised by his grandparents on a farm in Michigan, Jones overcame severe stammering in his youth and went on to major in drama at the University of Michigan. His first major role as a professional was Deodatus Village in Jean Genet's *The Blacks* (1961). Jones shot to stardom as black prizefighter Jack Jefferson in *The Great White Hope* (1968), a play based on the life of heavyweight champion Jack Johnson. He won a Tony Award for his performance and subsequently starred in the film version (1970). A veteran Shakespearean actor, Jones was acclaimed for his interpretations of Othello and King Lear as well as his roles in the plays of South African Athol Fugard, *The Blood Knot* (1964), *Boesman and Lena* (1970), and *A Lesson from Aloes* (1980), and for his role in August Wilson's *Fences* (1985–87; Tony Award). He also did the voice of Darth Vader in the film *Star Wars* (1977) and its sequels. His later films included *Field of Dreams* (1989) and *Cry the Beloved Country* (1995). ■ See his autobiography (1993; with Penelope Niven).

JONES, JESSE HOLMAN (1874–1956), U.S. public official. A conservative Democratic businessman from Texas, Jones was one of the ablest and most prominent New Deal administrators. He served as chairman of the Reconstruction Finance Corp. (1933–45), administrator of the Federal Loan Agency (1939–45), and secretary of commerce (1940–

45). Through his control of billions of federal dollars, he was perhaps the most powerful financial figure in America. During World War II he headed several public corporations and played a key role in industrial mobilization. ▪ See his memoir of the New Deal, *Fifty Billion Dollars* (1951), and biography by Bascom N. Timmons (1956).

JONES, LEROI. *See BARAKA, IMAMU AMIRI.*

JONES, ROBERT EDMOND (1887–1954), U.S. stage designer. After graduating from Harvard (1910), Jones worked with the Austrian producer Max Reinhardt in Berlin (1913) and developed ideas for the "new stagecraft," which was to revolutionize the American theater. Reacting against the dominant trend of realism, Jones designed sets and costumes that drew on abstract suggestion, color, and lighting to enhance the emotional impact of the play. His spare sets, emphasizing only the essentials, allowed for a fluidity of action comparable to that which existed on the Shakespearean stage. Jones' first triumphs were Anatole France's *The Man Who Married a Dumb Wife* (1915) and *The Devil's Garden* (1915). He subsequently designed dozens of New York shows, including Eugene O'Neill's *The Hairy Ape* (1921), *Desire Under the Elms* (1924), *Mourning Becomes Electra* (1931), and *The Iceman Cometh* (1946). Among his last works were *Lute Song* (1946) and *Green Pastures* (1951). He wrote *Continental Stagecraft* (1922; with Kenneth Mac-Gowan) and *The Dramatic Imagination* (1941).

JONES, RUFUS MATTHEW (1863–1948), U.S. Quaker leader. A member of a pious Quaker family from Maine, Jones was "recorded" a minister in 1890, became editor of a Quaker publication in Philadelphia (1893), and taught philosophy at Haverford College (1893–1934). He wrote more than 50 books, many of them on mysticism, his specialty, and collaborated on a six-volume study of Quakerism. A committed pacifist, Jones founded (1917) and led (1917–28; 1935–44) the American Friends Service Committee to aid war victims in Europe and the underprivileged in America. The organization shared the 1947 Nobel Peace Prize for its work during World War II. ▪ See his autobiographies, *Finding the Trail of Life* (1926), *The Trail of Life in College* (1929), *The Trail of Life in Middle Years* (1934), and *A Small Town Boy* (1941); see also biography by David Hinshaw (1951) and Elizabeth G. Vining, *Friend of Life* (1958).

JONG, ERICA (Erica Mann; 1942–   ), U.S. poet and novelist. Jong wrote the poetry collections *Fruits and Vegetables* (1971) and *Half-Lives* (1973) before soaring to fame with *Fear of Flying* (1973), a best-selling, trendy novel that introduced to readers the writer-heroine Isadora Wing and her search for fulfillment. After her novelistic success, a third volume of poetry, *Loveroot* (1975), became a Book-of-the-Month Club alternate; poetry by only two other Ameri-

cans—Robert Frost and Rod McKuen—had been selected for that distinction. *How to Save Your Own Life* (1977) and *Parachutes and Kisses* (1984), often humorous accounts of marital discord, followed Isadora Wing's further adventures. *Fanny* (1980) was a "mock-18th-century novel" about a lusty Englishwoman. Her other books included *Serenissima* (1987), *Any Woman's Blues* (1990), *Inventing Memory: A Novel of Mothers and Daughters* (1997), and *What Do Women Want?: Bread, Roses, Sex, Power* (1998). ▪ See her memoir, *Fear of Fifty* (1994), and Charlotte Templin, *Feminism and the Politics of Literary Reputation* (1995).

JOOSS, KURT (1901–1979), German ballet choreographer. Jooss, whose dance company performed in Essen (1927–33), was the first choreographer to combine modern dance with ballet. From classical ballet he incorporated fundamental steps and positions but eschewed virtuoso tricks such as pirouettes or dancing on toe. Jooss desired to create a theater with dance as the medium of expression; every movement for him had to further a plot. His dances communicated in allegorical and dramatic terms, including his masterpiece, *The Green Table* (1932), a powerful portrayal of the futility of war. Following Jooss's initiative, modern dance and ballet began to borrow movement ideas freely from each other. He left Germany when the Nazis came to power (1933) and moved to Britain where he continued to direct his company until his return to Germany in 1951. ▪ See A. V. Coton, *The New Ballet* (1946).

JOPLIN, JANIS (1943–1970), U.S. singer. Joplin left Port Arthur, Texas, at age 17 to hitchhike across the country. Drifting into the hippie subculture of San Francisco, in 1966 she became female vocalist with Big Brother and the Holding Company, with whom she gave an electric performance at the 1967 Monterey Rock Festival. An earthy woman with an extensive four-letter-word vocabulary and a raspy, bawdy voice, Joplin said she would "rather not sing than sing quiet." Her most successful album, *Pearl,* with the number-one-hit single "Me and Bobby McGee," was released posthumously, after Joplin's death from a heroin overdose. ▪ See David Dalton, *Janis* (1971); Myra Friedman, *Buried Alive* (1973); and Alice Echols, *Scars of Sweet Paradise* (1999).

JOPLIN, SCOTT (1868–1917), U.S. ragtime pianist and composer. The son of a former slave, Joplin studied music at the George R. Smith College for Negroes in Sedalia, Missouri. Known as "the king of ragtime composers," he was a serious musician whose pre–World War I compositions (including the "Maple Leaf Rag," "Gladiolus Rag," "Magnetic Rag," and "The Entertainer") were among the most popular jazz compositions of their time. Extremely lyrical and innovative, his pieces transformed ragtime music from the realm of honky-tonk to art. The failure of his opera *Treemonisha* to gain recognition, however, combined with the public's declining interest in ragtime, severely affected his personality, and he spent the last year of his life in a New York mental hospital. His music was successfully revived in the late 1960s and 1970s; it was featured in the film *The Sting* (1973). ■ See biography by James Haskins (1978); Edward A. Berlin, *King of Ragtime* (1994); and Susan Curtis, *Dancing to a Black Man's Tune* (1994).

JORDAN, DAVID STARR (1851–1931), U.S. scientist and educator. A prominent ichthyologist, Jordan was a professor at Butler and Indiana universities before being appointed the first president of Stanford University (1891–1913). He was also an anti-imperialist and peace advocate who opposed U.S. participation in World War I, promoted the cause of world federalism, and served as director of the World Peace Foundation (1910–14) and president of the World Peace Congress (1915). A prolific author, Jordan wrote more than 50 volumes on such diverse subjects as fish, education, and world peace. ■ See his autobiography, *The Days of a Man* (2 vols., 1922), and the biography by Edward M. Burns (1953).

JORDAN, MICHAEL (1963–), U.S. basketball player. Considered by many to be the greatest player in basketball history, the 6-foot, 6-inch Jordan was a star at the University of North Carolina (1982–84) and a superstar with the Chicago Bulls of the National Basketball Association (1984–93; 1994–98). (He interrupted his career in 1993 in an unsuccessful attempt to become a professional baseball player). A phenomenal leaper, dazzling playmaker, and accurate shooter, he was the NBA's Most Valuable Player five times (1988; 1991–92; 1996; 1998) and led the league in scoring 10 times. Through the 1997–98 season he scored 29,277 regular season points and achieved a record career-scoring average of 31.5 points per game. He led the Bulls to six NBA championships (1991–93; 1996–98), was named play-off MVP for each series, and set the career record of 5,987 play-off points. Jordan also led the U.S. team to victories in the 1984 and 1992 Olympic Games. He was the first basketball player to be pictured on a Wheaties cereal box (1988) and he costarred in the film *Space Jam* (1996) with Bugs Bunny and Daffy Duck. He was an extremely popular public figure, endorsed numerous products (notably Nike sneakers), and was estimated by *Fortune* magazine to have had a $10 billion impact on the world economy during his professional career (1998). ■ See his picture-book autobiography, *For the Love of the Game* (1998), and Michael Halberstam, *Playing for Keeps* (1998).

JOSELITO (nickname of José Gómez; 1895–1920), Spanish bullfighter. The youngest man to be given the title of matador (1912), Joselito was considered one of the greatest bullfighters of all time. He adopted the revolutionary style of his close friend and rival Juan Belmonte and remained motionless during the bull's charge, using the cape to manipulate the animal. The two matadors launched (1914) what has become known as "the golden age of bullfighting" and fought together until Joselito was gored to death on May 16, 1920.

JOSEPH, MICHAEL KENNEDY (1914–1981), British-born New Zealand novelist. An established scholar who taught at the University of Auckland (1945–79), M. K. Joseph was one of New Zealand's most sophisticated writers. With mild irony he contrasted his characters' theoretical free will with the reality of their ideological victimization. *I'll Soldier No More* (1958), based on his World War II experience in the British army, described the tedium of war and documented Germany in defeat. *A Pound of Saffron* (1962) was a campus novel about academic power play. *The Hole in the Zero* (1969) confronted a space crew with various planes of reality and nonreality. His later novels included *A Soldier's Tale* (1976) and *The Time of Achamoth* (1977).

JOSEPHSON, BRIAN DAVID (1940–). British physicist. While a 22-year-old graduate student at Cambridge (Ph.D. 1964), Josephson made theoretical predictions of the properties (later called Josephson effects) of the electron flow through a tunnel barrier. His work led to extremely accurate measurement of electronic currents, opened the field of superconductivity to rigorous exploration, and earned him a share of the 1973 Nobel Prize in Physics with Leo Esaki and Ivan Giaever. At Cambridge he was assistant director of research in physics (1967–72) and professor of physics (from 1974). ■ See *Nobel Prize Conversations* (1985).

JOSEPHSON, MATTHEW (1899–1978), U.S. biographer. On the fringe of the bohemian New York City literary world while a student at Columbia (B.A. 1920), Josephson spent the 1920s in Paris in the company of American expatriate writers and Parisian surrealists. His *Life Among the Surrealists* (1962) chronicled these times. Returning to the United States in the 1930s, he joined a circle of prominent and politically active left-wing intellectuals and wrote *The Robber Barons* (1934), the now-classic muckraking account of the careers of John D. Rockefeller, Andrew Carnegie, J. P. Morgan, and other notable 19th-century American capitalists. In addition to his other books on American history, *The Politicos* (1938) and *The President Makers* (1940), he wrote memorable biographies of Emile Zola (1928), Jean-Jacques Rousseau (1931), and Stendhal (1946), and a memoir of the 1930s, *Infidel in the Temple* (1967). ■ See biography by David E. Shi (1981).

JOSPIN, LIONEL ROBERT (1937–), French political leader. The son of a socialist schoolteacher, Jospin was raised in a suburb of Paris, graduated from the prestigious Institute of Political Studies and the National School of Administration, and served as a bureaucrat in the Ministry of

Foreign Affairs (1965–70). Inspired by the student demonstrations in Paris during the 1960s, he became politically active in the Socialist party and served as a professor of economics at the University Institute of Technology in Paris (1970–81). He worked his way up through the Socialist party ranks during the 1970s, became a protégé of François Mitterand, and won a seat in the National Assembly (1981–88). He served as a reformist Minister of Education, Youth and Sport (1988–92) and narrowly lost the 1995 presidential election to Jacques Chirac. After the left won the 1997 parliamentary election, Jospin became prime minister of a left-wing coalition government. His policies led to a dramatic lowering of unemployment and a thriving economy. Although accused by leftist critics of adopting free market policies, he remained extremely popular and sponsored legislation, which became law, to lower the work week to 35 hours.

JOUHAUX, LÉON (1879–1954), French labor leader. Jouhaux was the leader of the matchworkers' union (1906–1909) and rose to head the national General Confederation of Labor (CGT; 1909–40; 1945–47). A socialist, he tried, unsuccessfully, to form an antimilitaristic movement with German union leaders prior to World War I. After the war he was a founder of the International Labor Organization and was a French delegate to the League of Nations (1925–28). He was imprisoned in a German concentration camp during World War II (1943–45). Jouhaux split with the CGT after Communists took control of it (1947) and he helped to organize the independent Force Ouvrière (Workers' Force, 1948) and the International Confederation of Free Trade Unions (1949). He was awarded the 1951 Nobel Peace Prize.

JOUVET, LOUIS (1887–1951), French actor, producer, and director. The director of the Comedic des Champs-Elysées (1924–34) and the Théâtre de l'Athénée (1934–51) in Paris, Jouvet exerted a major influence on French theatrical life. One of the most popular actors of his time, he was also known for his innovations in lighting and stage design. In his celebrated productions of the plays of Jean Giraudoux, Jules Romains, and Moliere, he frequently served as actor, producer, and director. He appeared in numerous motion pictures, including *Carnival in Flanders* (1935), *The Lower Depths* (1936), and *Volpone* (1940). ■ See biography by Bettina Knapp (1957).

JOYCE, JAMES AUGUSTINE (1882–1941), Irish writer. Born and educated in Dublin (University College, B.A. 1902), Joyce left Ireland in 1904 and lived for the remainder of his life in self-imposed exile in Paris, Trieste, Rome, and Zurich. His early experiences in Dublin, however, informed all of his work, including the notable collection of short stories *Dubliners* (1914) and the autobiographical novel *A Portrait of the Artist as a Young Man* (1916). His masterpiece, *Ulysses* (1922), although originally banned in most countries because of its frank language, came to be accepted as a modern classic and one of the most influential books of the century. A description of one day (June 16, 1904) in the life of Dubliner Leopold Bloom, the novel featured unique mythic symbolism and extraordinarily detailed character portrayal and utilized the narrative techniques of interior monologue and stream of consciousness to an extent unparalleled in modern literature. His last and most difficult work, *Finnegans Wake* (1939), was remarkable for complex symbolism, puns, and double meaning and was filled with dozens of mythical and historical characters. ■ See biographies by Richard Ellmann (1959; rev. ed. 1982), Peter Costello (1992), and Edna O'Brien (1999).

JOYCE, WILLIAM (known as "Lord Haw-Haw"; 1906–1946), U.S.-born Nazi propagandist. Joyce was taken to London at an early age but never took British nationality. An honors graduate from the University of London, he was a believer in fascism from his teenage years and was a deputy leader of Sir Oswald Mosley's British Union of Fascists before founding his own British National Socialist League. Fleeing to Germany just before World War II, Joyce became the chief English-language propagandist for the Nazis. His regularly scheduled wartime broadcasts, aimed at inducing Britain to capitulate, made him one of Britain's most hated and ridiculed men. After the war he was found guilty of high treason by a British court and hanged. ■ See J. A. Cole, *Lord Haw-Haw and William Joyce* (1965).

JÓZSEF, ATTILA (1905–1937), Hungarian poet. Poverty-stricken throughout his life, József wrote of the suffering and oppression of the Hungarian proletariat in modern, cerebral verse. Influenced by surrealism, expressionism, and the Magyar folk song, he assimilated Marxist and Freudian concepts to create a unique body of poetry. A lifelong radical, József was expelled from Szeged University (1924) because of the controversy over the publication of his revolutionary poem, *With a Pure Heart,* and was expelled from the Communist party for his unorthodox views. (After World War II he was posthumously honored by the communist government as the greatest national poet.) Plagued by schizophrenia, he committed suicide in 1937. Translations of his poetry and a brief biography are in Anton N. Nyerges, *Poems of Attila József* (1973). See also *Poems* (1966), *Selected Poems and Texts* (1973), *Works* (1973), and *Winter Night* (1997).

JUAN CARLOS I (1938–), Spanish king. Juan Carlos was the great-great-grandson of Queen Victoria and the grandson of Alfonso XIII, the last king of Spain before the establishment of the republic in 1931. Designated by dictator Francisco Franco as his legal heir in July 1969, Juan Carlos assumed the throne after Franco's death in 1975 and engineered the reestablishment of political freedoms. A dynamic and popular leader, he emerged as a strong symbol of democracy and attempted to separate the throne from the world of politics. However, he played a major role in suppressing the attempted military coup of Feb. 23, 1981, and thus alienated many military leaders and right-wing politicians. Over the next two decades he retained his popularity with the Spanish people and restored the legitimacy of the Spanish monarchy. ■ See biography by Charles T. Powell (1996).

JUDD, CHARLES HUBBARD (1873–1946), U.S. educator. Judd was born in India, where his parents were Methodist missionaries; he earned his Ph.D. in psychology from the University of Leipzig (1896). As director of the school of education at the University of Chicago (1909–38), he promoted the application of scientific methods to educational problems. His educational surveys, research studies, and textbook on introductory psychology (1907) influenced teacher education. His well-known books included *Genetic Psychology for Teachers* (1903), *Psychology of Social Institutions* (1926), and *Education as Cultivation of the Higher Mental Processes* (1936).

JUDSON, ARTHUR LEON (1881–1975), U.S. concert manager. After abandoning a career as a conductor and concert violinist, Judson launched a new one as a "salesman" of classical music and became the most influential impresario in the United States. During the 1920s and 1930s he managed, simultaneously, the New York Philharmonic and the Philadelphia Orchestra and also managed most of the great conductors and many of the leading pianists and violinists of his time. He founded the Judson Radio Program Corp. (1926), which inaugurated classical concerts on radio, and organized a chain of radio stations (1927), which became the Columbia Broadcasting System (1928). His own management company, Columbia Concerts Corp. (1930), brought, for the first time, world-class musicians and orchestras to small towns and cities throughout America. Among the artists he managed or introduced to American audiences were Vladimir Horowitz, Jascha Heifetz, Rudolf Serkin, Joseph Szigeti, José Iturbi, and John Barbirolli.

JUHÁSZ, FERENC (1928–), Hungarian poet. Regarded by many as the finest Hungarian poet of his generation, Juhász achieved fame as a teenager with the publication of his social-realist poem, *The Winged Colt* (1947). He later rejected the literary principles imposed by the communist government, though he maintained his belief in a popular socialism akin to the populism of the 1930s. Juhász's *Ode to Flight* (1953) and *The Prodigal Country* (1954) championed personal freedom and denounced tyranny, while *The Boy Changed into a Stag* (1957; Eng. trans., with other selected poems, 1970) represented a private vision of a chaotic universe derived from nature, folktales, and technology. See his *Selected Poems* (Eng. trans. 1970).

JULIAN, PERCY LAVON (1899–1975), U.S. chemist. Born into a poor black family in Montgomery, Alabama, Julian

graduated as a Phi Beta Kappa from DePauw University (1920), did graduate work at Harvard (1922–26), and received his Ph.D. at the University of Vienna (1931). While on the faculty of DePauw (1932–35) he synthesized the drug physostigmine, which was used in the treatment of glaucoma. From 1936 until 1953 he headed the soya-products division of the Glidden Co. in Chicago and developed dozens of soya derivatives, including a soya protein used in paper production and in fire extinguishers, and steroids used in the treatment of arthritis and other diseases. He founded his own drug company (1954) and held more than 50 patents. Julian was also active in the civil-rights movement.

JULIANA (1909–), queen of the Netherlands. The only child of Queen Wilhelmina and Prince Henry of Mecklenburg-Schwerin, Juliana studied at the University of Leiden (1927–30) and helped form the National Crisis Committee (1931) to try to alleviate the distress caused by the Great Depression. She married German Prince Bernhard of Lippe-Biesterfeld in 1937. She was enthroned (1948) after the abdication of her mother and reigned for more than 31 years, during which Indonesia was granted its independence (1949) and the Netherlands recovered from the ravages of World War II and joined the European Common Market. Juliana abdicated (1980) in favor of her daughter Princess Beatrix (1938–). ■ See study by William Hoffman (1979).

JUMBLAT, KAMAL (1919–1977), Lebanese (Druze) political leader. Jumblat, head of a powerful Druze community and founder in 1949 of the Progressive Socialist party, played a crucial role in the bitter religious factionalism of Lebanese politics. After his election to parliament in 1947, he became a key power broker and held several major cabinet posts during the 1960s. Frequently at odds with the Maronite Christian leadership, he sided with the Muslims in the 1958 disorders that prompted U.S. intervention, and he headed the leftist-Muslim coalition in the 1975–76 civil war, after which he was assassinated. He was succeeded as community and party leader by his son Walid.

JUMBLAT, WALID (1947?–), Lebanese (Druze) political leader. Jumblat was the son of Kamal Jumblat, the leader of the Druze community in Lebanon and head of the left-wing Progressive Socialist party (PSP). After his father's assassination (1977) in the aftermath of the 1975–76 Lebanese civil war, Walid inherited the family business and real estate empire as well as his father's political leadership. Jumblat advocated the secularization of Lebanese politics; with Syrian help and in alliance with Shiite Muslims, Greek Orthodox Christians, and left-wing forces, he fought to change the Lebanese constitution, which established the political domination of Maronite Christians and Sunni Muslims. His militia controlled the Shuf mountains and remained a major force in the ongoing civil turmoil through the mid-1980s, seeking the ouster of Pres. Amin Gemayel. After Gemayel's term ended in 1988, Jumblat served in ministerial posts and in the Lebanese parliament (1991–   ), but his militia was disbanded and his power declined.

JUNG, CARL GUSTAV (1875–1961), Swiss psychiatrist. The recipient of an M.D. degree from the University of Zurich (1902), Jung was psychoanalyst Sigmund Freud's heir apparent and, briefly, the first president of the International Psychoanalytic Society. Breaking with Freud, the founding father of psychoanalysis, in 1914, over the primacy of early sex conflicts, he went on to establish his own school of "analytic psychology." Jung introduced the concepts of introversion and extroversion, further distinguishing between manifest and latent. A man of immense erudition, he traveled to Africa, India, and the U.S. southwest to pursue his cross-cultural studies of myth and symbol; these studies led him to posit the existence of archetypes of the collective unconscious, "expressions of man's basic psychic nature" that are common to diverse cultures. He wrote the autobiographical *Memories, Dreams, Reflections* (Eng. trans. 1963), and his *Collected Works* were published in English translation in 20 volumes. ■ See studies by Barbara Hannah (1976) and Paul J. Stern (1977).

JÜNGER, ERNST (1895–1998), German novelist and essayist. An ardent militarist and leader of a shock-troop unit in World War I, Jünger glorified the heroic deeds and sacrifice of the German soldiers in his most widely read novel, *Storm of Steel* (1920; Eng. trans. 1929). Although he espoused totalitarianism and military mobilization, he was repelled by dictator Adolf Hitler and Nazism. *On the Marble Cliffs* (1939; Eng. trans. 1947), an allegorical novel, was clearly anti-Nazi and reaffirmed the humanistic tradition. Jünger associated with anti-Hitler officers during World War II, and his pamphlet, *The Peace* (1943; Eng. trans. 1948), which represented their views, called for peace, renunciation of nationalism, affirmation of individual dignity, and a postwar federation of European nations. ■ See studies by Gerhard Loose (1974) and Thomas Nevin (1996).

JUSTO, AGUSTÍN PEDRO (1876–1943), Argentine general and political leader. The son of a politician, Justo studied at Argentina's military academy and remained there as a mathematics teacher (1904–15) and director (1915–22). He reorganized the army as minister of war (1922–28), participated in the Conservative coup of 1930, and in 1932 was elected to a six-year term as president of his country. He sponsored significant economic legislation that softened the impact of the Depression and was instrumental in ending the Chaco war between Peru and Bolivia. He retained influence in the army after 1938, and despite strong pro-Axis sentiment within Argentina, he was a strong supporter of the Allies during World War II.

K

KABALEVSKY, DMITRI BORISOVICH (1904–1987), Soviet composer. Kabalevsky studied piano and composition at the Moscow Conservatory, joining the faculty in 1932. Tonal and energetic, his music is nationalistic in idiom. His piano pieces for children, *Children's Songs from Pioneer Life* (1930; referring to the communist Young Pioneer movement), were followed by his Second Symphony (1934), the Piano Concerto in G Minor (1936), the orchestral suite *The Comedians* (1940), and the Cello Concerto in C Minor (1964). His operas, such as *Nikita Vershinin* (1954), often reflected the heroism of the worker.

KÁDÁR, JÁNOS (1912–1989), Hungarian political leader. A mechanic, Kádár joined the illegal Communist party in 1932. Though he sat on the party's Central Committee (1942) and the Politburo (1945), his differences with the Stalinist faction kept him out of the party leadership after World War II. He became minister of the interior after the Communists took control of Hungary (1948), only to be purged for pro Titoist views and imprisoned (1950–54). Rehabilitated in 1954, he served in Imre Nagy's insurrectionary government (Oct. 1956) but abandoned it before it was crushed by the Soviets. He set up a new government with Russian support, serving as premier until 1958, and again from 1961 to 1965, and initiated a program of gradual economic and social reforms that made Hungary the least repressive of East European nations. Kádár continued to wield power as party secretary until 1988. ■ See William Shawcross, *Crime and Compromise* (1974), and Andrew Felkay, *Hungary and the USSR, 1956–1988* (1989).

KADARE, ISMAIL (1936–   ), Albanian writer. The most prominent cultural figure in Albania during the 20th century, Kadare grew up during the World War II occupation of his country, earned a teaching diploma from the University of Tirana (1956), and studied languages and world literature in Moscow. He gained fame for his historical novels, which were nonideological and written in a subtle, oblique style. He supported the Communist government and its efforts to modernize Albania during the 1950s and 1960s and served in the People's Assembly (1970). However, after writing a poem critical of the party bureaucracy he was sent into internal exile and forbidden to publish (1975–78). He subsequently resumed his literary career, but sought political asylum in France (1990) and settled in Paris. His best-known novels included *The General of the Dead Army* (1963; Eng. trans. 1971), a portrait of Albania under Italian occupation during World War II; *Chronicle in Stone* (1971;

Eng. trans. 1987), a child's view of Albania during the war; *The Three-Arched Bridge* (1978; Eng. trans. 1997), a novel set in medieval times; and *The Concert* (1988; Eng. trans. 1994) and *The Palace of Dreams* (1980; Eng. trans. 1993), antiestablishment political novels that criticized Albania's totalitarian system. He also wrote several volumes of poetry and literary studies.

KADDAFI, MUAMMAR AL-. *See QADDAFI, MUAMMAR AL-.*

KAFKA, FRANZ (1883–1924), Austrian writer. A member of the German-speaking Jewish community in Prague, then part of the Austro-Hungarian empire, Kafka earned a doctorate in jurisprudence (1906) and worked for years at a government insurance office (1908–22). He was a sensitive, alienated intellectual whose brilliant short stories and novels—most unpublished during his lifetime—came to symbolize the anxieties of modern Western society. His enigmatic works, which portrayed a world in which individuals struggled unsuccessfully against ubiquitous and anonymous forces, had a major effect on the course of post–World War II European literature. He was best known for the novels *The Trial* (1925; Eng. trans. 1937), *The Castle* (1926; Eng. trans. 1930; rev. ed. 1969), and *Amerika* (1927; Eng. trans. 1938) and the short stories "The Judgment" (1916; Eng. trans. 1945), "Metamorphosis" (1915; Eng. trans. 1937), and "In the Penal Colony" (1919; Eng. trans. 1948). ■ See the autobiographical writings in *I Am a Memory Come Alive* (1974); biographies by Max Brod (1937; 2nd Eng. ed. 1960), Ronald Hayman (1982), and Frederick R. Karl (1991); Ernst Pawel, *The Nightmare of Reason* (1984); and Peter Mailloux, *A Hesitation Before Birth* (1989).

KAGAWA, TOYOHIKO (1888–1960), Japanese social reformer and evangelist. A convert to Christianity, Kagawa was educated at the Presbyterian College in Tokyo and Princeton Theological Seminary and then became an evangelist and social worker in the slums of Kobe. Influenced by the "social gospel" movement, he took part in the organization of the Japanese Federation of Labor, helped to establish agricultural cooperatives, and participated in the campaign for universal suffrage. A pacifist opposed to the imperialist policies of Japan during the 1930s and early 1940s, Kagawa was influential in the democratization of Japan after World War II. His autobiographical novel, *Before the Dawn* (1920; Eng. trans. 1924), was a best-seller. ■ See study by J. M. Trout (1959).

KAHANAMOKU, DUKE PAOA (1890–1968), Hawaiian swimmer. Called the "human fish," Kahanamoku was the greatest freestyle swimmer of his time. Among the first to use the flutter kick, he won two Olympic gold medals in the 100-meter freestyle (1912; 1920), set three world records in the 100-yard freestyle (between 1913 and 1917; best time, 53 seconds), and was U.S. champion in the event in 1916, 1917, and 1920. One of Hawaii's best-known citizens, he appeared in several motion pictures, was sheriff of Honolulu (1932–61), and served as official greeter of the state of Hawaii (from 1961).

KAHLO, FRIDA (1910–1954), Mexican painter. Kahlo's paintings explored her Mexican identity and reflected her experience with physical disability. A serious bus accident when she was 15 crushed her pelvis and led to a lifetime of pain. She was forced to abandon her plans for a medical career, but the paintings she did while convalescing attracted the notice of the muralist Diego Rivera, whom she married (1928). Kahlo's style was influenced by Mexican colonial and popular art, employing frontal figures, spare stagelike space, and bright colors. Although the French surrealist André Breton described her as a surrealist, Kahlo contended that she painted her own reality. After her death, Diego Rivera gave her house in Coyoacán to Mexico as the Frida Kahlo Museum. ▪ See her *Diary* (1995); biographies by Malka Drucker (1991) and Raquel Tibol (Eng. trans. 1993); Hayden Herrera, *Frida* (1983); and Margaret A. Lindauer, *Devouring Frida* (1999).

KAHN, ALBERT (1869–1942), German-born U.S. architect. While other top architects were vying for monuments and prestige commissions, Kahn, whose family settled in Detroit in 1881, was (from 1905) helping to make Detroit the mass-production capital of the country with his huge glass-walled, reinforced-concrete automobile factories. He designed more than 1,000 factories in 25 cities in the Soviet Union under its first five-year plan (1928–32). During World War II Kahn turned to the construction of U.S. military bases and defense plants, including Ford's giant Willow Run bomber plant (1941–43). ▪ See study by Federico Bucci (1993).

KAHN, GUSTAV GERSON (1886–1941), German-born U.S. songwriter. The son of a cattle dealer, Gus Kahn grew up in Chicago, where he first wrote songs for vaudevillians. Eventually a songwriter for both Broadway shows and Hollywood movies, he published more than 500 songs and was one of the most successful lyricists of his time. He put simple, direct, and colloquial words and phrases to the music of Walter Donaldson, Sigmund Romberg, and others to create many of America's best-known songs. Among his numerous hits were "My Blue Heaven," "Carolina in the Morning," "Mammy," "Memories," "Yes Sir, That's My Baby," "Makin' Whoopee," "Pretty Baby," "Toot, Toot, Tootsie," and "It Had to Be You."

KAHN, HERMAN (1922–1983), U.S. physicist and futurologist. As a member of the Rand Corp. think tank (1948–60), Kahn became a leading student of nuclear war strategies, which he discussed matter-of-factly in *On Thermonuclear War* (1960) and *Thinking About the Unthinkable* (1962). Long a controversial figure, he wrote that nuclear war was a probability, that it would not necessarily mean the end of civilization, and that the United States should defend itself with nuclear and nonnuclear forces. He was criticized for minimizing the dangers of nuclear war and thereby making it more likely, and was a prototype of Stanley Kubrick's cinematic Dr. Strangelove. In 1961 he founded his own think tank, the Hudson Institute, which consulted on national security and also branched out into social issues and nonmilitary futurology. Kahn also wrote *On Escalation* (1965) and *The Japanese Challenge* (1979), and coauthored two optimistic studies, *The Year 2000* (1967; with Anthony Wiener) and *The Next 200 Years* (1976; with William Brown and Leon Martel). In *The Coming Boom* (1982) he forecast a rosy economic future for the United States.

KAHN, LOUIS ISADORE (1901–1974), Russian-born U.S. architect. Born to a Jewish family in Russian Estonia, Kahn was taken to the United States at age 4. He studied at the University of Pennsylvania (B. Arch. 1924) and worked under Paul Cret (1929–30). He later taught at Yale University (1947–57) and at the University of Pennsylvania (1957–74). Philosopher and architect, his ideas provided a foundation for later developments in architectural thought. His expressive designs, which Kahn often characterized in terms of silence and light, were less abstract and more personal than those of the Bauhaus-influenced modernist movement and gave modern architecture greater ideological breadth. Kahn's major buildings included the Yale University Art Gallery (1954); the Richards Medical Research Building at the University of Pennsylvania (1962), which was accorded a "one-building show" at New York's Museum of Modern Art; and the Salk Institute in La Jolla, California (mid-1960s). ▪ See biography by Vincent Scully (1962); study by R. Giurgola and J. Mehta (1975); J. Lobell, *Between Silence and Light* (1979); Alexander Tyng, *Beginnings* (1984); and study by David B. Brownlee and David G. De Long (1992).

KAHN, OTTO HERMAN (1867–1934), German-born U.S. banker, philanthropist, and art patron. Born into a wealthy banking family, Kahn emigrated to New York (1893) and became a partner in the banking firm of Kuhn, Loeb and Co. (1897). He was closely associated with E. H. Harriman's reorganization and financing of the Union Pacific and other railroads. Perhaps the greatest patron of the arts in U.S. history, Kahn cofounded the Chicago Opera Co. and supported countless museums, theaters, orchestras, and cultural institutions throughout the country. He heavily supported and reorganized New York's Metropolitan Opera (1907–08), brought Arturo Toscanini and Giulio Gatti-Casazza to the company, and served as the opera's chairman and then president (1903–31). He was also a founder of the Federation of Jewish Philanthropies of New York. ■ See Mary Jane Matz, *The Many Lives of Otto Kahn* (1963), and John Kobler, *Otto the Magnificent* (1988).

KAHNWEILER, DANIEL HENRY (1884–1979), German-born French art dealer. The son of a banker, Kahnweiler began collecting art when he was a young stockbroker's clerk in Paris (1902–05). He discovered the Spanish painter Pablo Picasso in 1907 and represented his work for 65 years. His exhibit of Georges Braque's paintings in 1908 aroused the first mention of "cubes" in art. Kahnweiler ran the Simon Gallery in Paris from 1920 to 1941, when it was taken over by his sister-in-law and renamed the Galerie Louise Leiris while Kahnweiler, a Jew, went into hiding from the Nazis. He wrote many books on art, including *The Rise of Cubism* (1920; Eng. trans. 1949), *The Sculptures of Pablo Picasso* (1948; Eng. trans. 1949), *My Galleries and My Painters* (1961; Eng. trans. 1971), and *Esthetic Confessions* (1963). ■ See Pierre Assouline, *An Artful Life* (1988; Eng. trans. 1990).

KAISER, GEORG (1878–1945), German dramatist and novelist. The son of a wealthy merchant who left high school to enter business, Kaiser turned to the theater and became the most frequently performed post–World War I playwright in Germany until being suppressed by the Nazis (1933). An expressionist, he was interested in ideas, not in mere entertainment. He attacked the brutality of the machine age and celebrated the hero who sacrificed for the common good. His best-known works were *The Burghers of Calais* (1914; Eng. trans. 1971), *From Morn to Midnight* (1916; Eng. trans. 1922), and the trilogy *The Coral* (1917; Eng. trans. 1929), *Gas I* (1918; Eng. trans. 1929), and *Gas II* (1920; Eng. trans. 1929). ■ See study by Ernst Schürer (1971).

KAISER, HENRY JOHN (1882–1967), U.S. businessman. A high school dropout, Kaiser moved from New York to the West (1906) and founded a highway construction company (1914) that built roads throughout California and the Pacific Northwest. During the 1930s he organized and headed construction companies that built the Boulder (now Hoover) Dam, the Bonneville Dam, and the Grand Coulee Dam, and was involved in the construction of the San Francisco–Oakland Bay Bridge. He established shipyards on the West Coast and became the industrial hero of World War II by devising prefabrication and rapid assembly techniques that enabled him to build almost 1,500 cargo ships, nearly one-third of U.S. wartime production. He also built California's first integrated steel mill and produced aluminum and automobiles after the war. His pioneering nonprofit medical-care program (established 1942) served as a model for health care delivery systems throughout the country. At the time of his death, Kaiser Industries was producing approximately 300 different products at 180 plants located in 32 states and

40 countries. ■ See study by Mark S. Foster (1989) and Stephen B. Adams, *Mr. Kaiser Goes to Washington* (1997).

KALDOR OF NEWNHAM, NICHOLAS KALDOR, BARON (1908–1986), Hungarian-born British economist. Raised in Budapest, Kaldor moved to London during the 1920s and graduated from the London School of Economics (B.Sc. 1930). He taught there (1932–47) until he moved to Cambridge (1949–75), where he became a leader, with Joan Robinson and Piero Sraffa, of the post-Keynesian school of economic theory. He made important studies of trade cycles, economic growth, welfare economics, and income distribution. A liberal advocate of equitable taxes, he wrote a classic study, *An Expenditure Tax* (1955), in which he proposed to replace income taxes with taxes on expenditures. He was a tax adviser to many governments around the world, including Labour governments in Britain (1964–68; 1974–76), and was made a life peer in 1974. He criticized the British Conservative government's monetarist policies in *The Scourge of Monetarism* (1982) and *The Economic Consequences of Mrs. Thatcher* (1983). He also wrote *Economics Without Equilibrium* (1985). ■ See his *Collected Economic Essays* (8 vols., 1960–79) and studies by A. P. Thirlwall (1987) and Marjorie S. Turner (1993).

KALECKI, MICHAŁ (1899–1970), Polish economist. Kalecki studied engineering at polytechnics in Warsaw and Gdansk, but was self-taught in economics. During the 1930s, while working in a research institute, he independently published theories of savings, investment, and employment that anticipated the influential work of British economist John Maynard Keynes. An independent Marxist thinker, he was primarily concerned with macroeconomic dynamics, imperfect competition, and distribution of national income. He worked at the Oxford (England) Institute of Statistics (1940–45) and as a United Nations economist (1946–54) before returning to Poland as a teacher and researcher (1955). His books, in English, included *Essays in the Theory of Economic Fluctuations* (1939), *Studies in Economic Dynamics* (1943), *Introduction to a Theory of Growth in a Socialist Economy* (1969), and *Selected Essays on the Dynamics of the Capitalist Economy: 1933–70* (1971). ■ See George R. Feiwel, *The Intellectual Capital of Michal Kalecki* (1975).

KALININ, MIKHAIL IVANOVICH (1875–1946), Soviet political leader. Kalinin, an industrial worker, joined the Russian Social Democratic party (1898) and was an early follower of V. I. Lenin. After the creation of an independent Bolshevik party (1912), he helped found the party newspaper *Pravda* and served as mayor of Petrograd (later Leningrad) after the October revolution (1917). As chairman of the Presidium of the Supreme Soviet (1922–46), Kalinin was nominal president of the Soviet Union and was a member of the Politburo (from 1925). The city Tver on the Volga River was renamed Kalinin in his honor (1931).

KALLET, ARTHUR (1902–1972), U.S. author and consumer advocate. A graduate of the Massachusetts Institute of Technology (1924), Kallet entered the field of consumer protection as coauthor of *100,000,000 Guinea Pigs: Dangers in Everyday Foods, Drugs and Cosmetics* (1932), which was a best-seller for two years. He was a founder and director of Consumers Union (1936–57), which became the nation's preeminent product-testing organization; *Medical Letter* (1957), a publication that evaluated new drugs; and Buyers Laboratory (1961), which tested office-equipment machinery and maintenance supplies.

KALTENBORN, HANS VON (1878–1965), U.S. radio and news commentator. A pioneer in his field, H. V. Kaltenborn started broadcasting news analysis in 1922 while a reporter for the *Brooklyn Eagle*. As a full-time broadcaster for CBS (1929–40) and NBC (1940–55), he was known both for his knowledgeable, frank, and often controversial commentaries and for his rapid delivery, dignified diction, and famous Kaltenborn-clipped consonants. ■ See his autobiography, *Fifty Fabulous Years* (1950).

KAMARAJ, KUMARASWAMI (1903–1975), Indian political leader. Born into a low-caste Tamil family, Kamaraj received little education; in 1921 he joined the Indian National Congress party. A lifelong bachelor, Kamaraj devoted himself to the Congress party and drew his support from the poorer classes in his elections to the Madras legislative assembly and the Indian parliament. He served as chief minister of Madras (now Tamil Nadu) from 1954 to 1963. As president of the Congress party (1963–68), he was the party's chief power broker and played a major role in installing Lal Bahadur Shastri (1964) and Indira Gandhi (1966) as prime ministers. However, in 1969 Kamaraj and other older party leaders sought to oust Mrs. Gandhi from power. The Congress party split into two factions and Kamaraj and his group lost the power struggle and became relatively insignificant factors in Indian politics. ■ See biography by V. K. Narasimhan (1967).

KAMENEV, LEV BORISOVICH (L. B. Rosenfeld; 1883–1936), Soviet political leader. Kamenev joined (1903) the Bolshevik wing of the Russian Social Democratic party. Exiled (1915) to Siberia, he returned after the February revolution (1917), became a member of the first Politburo, and was a highly respected and effective administrator. When Lenin died (1924), Karnenev assumed, with G. E. Zinoviev and Joseph Stalin, collective rule. He was instrumental in denying power to his brother-in-law, Leon Trotsky. When Stalin's supporters defeated Kamenev and Zinoviev (1925), he allied with Trotsky (1926) and was expelled from the party the following year. He recanted and gained readmission but was arrested (1935) and sentenced to imprisonment in the aftermath of the murder of Stalin's associate S. M. Kirov. Stalin had Kamenev shot after the first of the celebrated show trials.

KAMMERER, PAUL (1880–1926), Austrian biologist. Kammerer was a musician and zoologist who worked by day at Vienna's Institute for Experimental Biology and by night as a composer of symphonies. Expert at catching and breeding toads and lizards, he conducted experiments with the midwife toad that seemed to prove the inheritance of acquired characteristics. He was a socialist and was preparing to depart to work in the Soviet Union when he committed suicide over allegations of fraud in his experiments. ■ See Arthur Koestler, *The Case of the Midwife Toad* (1971).

KANDEL, ERIC R. (1929–   ), Austrian-born U. S. neurobiologist. Kandel fled from Nazi-dominated Austria at the age of 9 and settled in the United States. He studied at New York University (M.D. 1956) and taught at New York University (1965–74) and at Columbia University (1974–   ). A pioneer in the study of the nervous system, he examined the nerve cells of a sea slug and determined the changes that take place in the brain when learning occurs and memories are formed. His findings applied to humans as well as to simpler animals and he shared the 2000 Nobel Prize in Physiology or Medicine with Paul Greengard and Arvid Carlsson for his innovative research.

KANDINSKY, WASSILY (1866–1944), Russian-born painter. Deeply affected by Russian folk art and French impressionism, Kandinsky abandoned a promising law career at age 30 and went to Munich to study art. He was a pioneer of abstract art and with Franz Marc developed the expressionist Blue Rider movement (1911). He returned to Russia in 1914, but soon after the revolution he fell out of official favor and emigrated to Germany (1921), where he taught at the Bauhaus School of Design. In 1933 he settled in France. Kandinsky wrote two important theoretical treatises: *On the Spiritual in Art* (1912; Eng. trans. 1947), which treated the idea of totally nonrepresentational art, and *Point and Line to Plane* (1926; Eng. trans. 1947), which explored the limits of creative freedom. He also produced woodcuts and designed costumes and sets for M. P. Mussorgsky's *Pictures at an Exhibition* (1928). ■ See Kenneth C. Lindsay and Peter Vergo, eds., *Kandinsky: Complete Writings on Art* (2 vols., 1982), and studies by Will Grohmann (Eng. trans. 1958), Paul Overy (1969), Rose-Carol Washton Long (1980), Peg Weiss (1995), and Thomas M. Messer (1997).

KANE, JOHN (1860–1934), Scottish-born U.S. painter. Kane emigrated to the United States in 1879 and worked as a steelworker in Pittsburgh and as a coal miner in Alabama. After losing his leg, he became a railway watchman and began painting landscapes on boxcars during his lunchtime, painting over them when he returned to work. His primitive paintings of the Pennsylvania countryside and the industrial sites of Pittsburgh became well known after 1927 when one of his paintings was accepted for the Carnegie Institute International Exhibition. His *Self-Portrait* (1929) is part of the collection of the Museum of Modern Art (New York City). ■ See his autobiography, *Sky Hooks* (1938).

KANE, ROBERT (1916–1998), **and BILL FINGER** (1917–1974), U.S. cartoonists. Commissioned by National Comics (1939) to create a counterpart to *Superman,* cartoonist Kane and writer Finger conceived *The Batman,* who, lacking supernatural powers, stalked Gotham City by night with companion Robin, avenging wrong. Finger suggested the bat ears and cowl that helped distinguish Batman from Superman. One of the most original comic books, *Batman* was an immense success. Other writers and artists worked on the books, but only Kane's by-line appeared until 1964 when the comic was revamped. The comic spawned two movie serials during the 1940s, a radio program, a television series (1966–67), and Hollywood films in 1989 and 1995.

KANTOROVICH, LEONID VITALIEVICH (1912–1986), Soviet economist and mathematician. A graduate of Leningrad University (1930) and a teacher there (1932–60), Kantorovich extended his mathematical studies in linear programming into economics with a 1939 paper on "Mathematical Methods of Organizing and Planning Production." He proposed the adoption of economic techniques that were widely used in the West but were resisted by orthodox Marxist economists. He shared the 1975 Nobel Prize in Economics with Tjalling C. Koopmans for his work on optimum allocation of resources. He directed the mathematical economics laboratory at the Institute of National Economic Management, Moscow (1971–76) and headed the laboratory at the Institute of System Studies at the Academy of Sciences, Moscow (from 1976). His books included *Management Science* (1939; Eng. trans. 1960) and *Functional Analysis* (1977; Eng. trans. 1981).

KAPITZA, PETER (Pyotr Leonidovich Kapitza; 1894–1984), Soviet physicist. Kapitza spent 13 years in Britain (1921–34) studying at Cambridge under Ernest Rutherford and conducting research on magnetic fields and low-temperature physics that was considered so important that a special laboratory was built for him (1933). The next year, during a visit to Moscow, authorities barred him from returning to Cambridge. The Soviets bought the entire contents of his laboratory, installing it at the Institute of Physical Problems, which was established for Kapitza. When he clashed with authorities—he apparently refused to contribute to atomic weapons development—he was removed from his post and placed under house arrest (1946). He was rehabilitated politically in 1955 and took part in research supporting the Soviet space effort. Kapitza advocated the free exchange of scientific thought and in the 1970s defended dissident physicist Andrei Sakharov from expulsion from the Soviet Academy of Sciences. In 1978 he shared the Nobel Prize in Physics with Arno A. Penzias and Robert W. Wilson for his work on the superconductivity of liquid helium at temperatures approaching absolute zero. His three

volumes of *Collected Papers* appeared in English (1964–67). ■ See his *Experiment, Theory, Practice* (Eng. trans. 1977) and Lawrence Badesh, *Kapitza, Rutherford, and the Kremlin* (1985).

KAPLAN, MORDECAI MENAHEM (1881–1983), U.S. Jewish philosopher and religious leader. Born in a Lithuanian *shtetl* (Jewish settlement), Kaplan was taken to the United States at age 8. He graduated from New York's City College (1900) and was ordained a rabbi by the Jewish Theological Seminary (1903). Kaplan viewed Judaism as the broad, dynamic religious civilization of the Jewish people, not as a religion alone. He founded the Society for the Advancement of Judaism (1922) and was appointed dean of the pedagogical division of the Jewish Theological Seminary (1931). Seeking to bridge the gap between traditional Jewish principles and modern thought, Kaplan founded the Reconstructionist movement, which took shape in the 1930s and 1940s; he founded the Jewish Reconstructionist Foundation in 1940. He profoundly influenced contemporary Judaism by recognizing equality for women in Jewish life (including the *bat mitzvah,* a celebration for girls at age 13), rejection of the "chosen people" doctrine, and the concept of the synagogue as a Jewish center. He wrote ten major books, including *Judaism as a Civilization* (1934; repr. 1981), *Judaism Without Supernaturalism* (1958), and *The Religion of Ethical Nationhood* (1970), and kept a daily journal for more than eight decades. ■ See Mel Scult, *Judaism Faces the Twentieth Century* (1993), and Jeffrey S. Gurock, *A Modern Heretic and a Traditional Community* (1997).

KAPP, WOLFGANG (1858–1922), German nationalist politician. Born in New York, where his father emigrated after the revolution of 1848, Kapp returned to Germany in 1870 to earn a law degree and join the bureaucracy. A nationalist and imperialist, he founded the German Fatherland party (1917) and was elected to the Reichstag (1918). Kapp staged a putsch in 1920 aimed at restoring the monarchy, but after four days was forced by a general strike to flee to Sweden. He returned in 1922 but died while awaiting trial.

KAPTEYN, JACOBUS CORNELIUS (1851–1922), Dutch astronomer. Although not the first to apply photography to celestial objects, Kapteyn, a professor at the University of Groningen (1877–1921), greatly expanded the field of photographic astronomy. Using the photographs of Sir David Gill, he plotted (1886–96) the positions of more than 400,000 stars in the Southern Hemisphere. He discerned the phenomenon of star streaming, in which stars move in opposite directions in space and not at random, and discovered the second-most-rapid star, now known as Kapteyn's star. His work allowed a more profound understanding of star arrangement and distances.

KARAJAN, HERBERT VON (1908–1989), Austrian conductor. Born into a highly cultured family, von Karajan was a child prodigy on the piano, studied in Salzburg and Vienna, and conducted at Ulm and Aachen before World War II. He was a member of the Nazi party (1933–42) and led orchestras and opera companies in Berlin during the war. His international career blossomed during the 1950s as he directed the Berlin Philharmonic (from 1955), the Vienna State Opera (1957–64; 1976–81), the Salzburg Festival (1956–60; board of directors from 1965), and was a principal conductor at La Scala, Milan, and with the London Philharmonia. One of the most influential and charismatic maestros of his generation, he specialized in the late romantics, notably Bruckner, Mahler, Strauss, and Wagner, and was noted for the tonal elegance, refinement, clarity, and precision of his performances. He recorded more than 280 major works. ■ See study by Paul Robinson (1976); biography by Roger Vaughan (1986); and Robert C. Bachmann, *Karajan: Notes on a Career* (1983; Eng. trans. 1990).

KARAMANLIS, CONSTANTINE (1907–1998), Greek political leader. A lawyer, Karamanlis was elected to parliament (1935), served in several cabinet posts, and was named premier in 1955. The founder and head of the National Radical Union, a conservative political party, he followed a pro-Western foreign and domestic policy and promoted independence for Cyprus. In 1963, after a disagreement with King Paul, he resigned his post and went into a self-imposed exile in France. When the military junta that took power in 1967 collapsed (1974), Karamanlis returned to Greece and as premier (1974–80), restored democracy and civil liberties. He later served as president (1980–85; 1990–95). ■ See study by C. M. Woodhouse (1982).

KARDELJ, EDVARD (1910–1979), Yugoslav political leader. A schoolteacher from Slovenia, Kardelj published a study of the Slovenian national question (1939) and was a prominent colleague of Josip Broz Tito in the pre–World War II communist underground and in the wartime partisan resistance movement. After the war he served as vice president in Marshal Tito's government and drew up the Yugoslav federal constitution. As minister of foreign affairs (1948–53) he provided the ideological underpinnings for Yugoslavia's split with the Soviet Union and helped develop the policy of nonalignment. He later played a major role in developing the concept of worker self-management, which represented a middle ground between Western capitalism and Soviet communism. He held high government positions until his death. His many books included *Socialism and War* (Eng. trans. 1960) and *Reminiscences* (Eng. trans. 1982).

KARLE, JEROME (1918–), U.S. chemist. Karle studied at City College of New York (B.S. 1937), Harvard, and the University of Michigan (Ph.D. 1943), and worked briefly on the Manhattan Project, which developed the atomic bomb in the 1940s. While working at the Naval Research Laboratory in Washington, D.C., with CCNY classmate Herbert

Hauptman during the 1950s and 1960s, he helped devise the "direct method," a mathematical technique used to determine the structures of molecules. Analyzing the intensity of points visible as dots on X rays of substances in crystal form, they were able to reduce drastically the time for determining detailed molecular structure. Although ignored for years, their technique was eventually utilized in laboratories throughout the world, particularly in medical and pharmaceutical research centers. Karle and Hauptman shared the 1985 Nobel Prize in Chemistry for their research. Karle spent his entire career at the Naval Research Lab, eventually directing its research on the structure of matter.

KARLFELDT, ERIK AXEL (1864–1931), Swedish poet. Born on a provincial farm, Karlfeldt worked as a Stockholm librarian. He was a popular lyric poet, and his work reflected his passionate love of nature and peasant culture. His nostalgic but unsentimental verse was gathered in several collections. Since he had been secretary of the Swedish Academy, he refused the Nobel Prize in Literature when it was offered to him (1918). He was awarded the prize posthumously (1931). English translations of his works are in *Arcadia Borealis* (1938).

KARLOFF, BORIS (William Henry Pratt; 1887–1969), British-U.S. actor. Instead of following the family footsteps into the British diplomatic service, Karloff worked as a laborer in Canada (1909) and later in Hollywood between acting stints until he made his name as *Frankenstein* (1931). Tall, gaunt, and heavily made up, Karloff gave a frightening yet sympathetic portrayal of the man-made monster. In addition to the sequels (*Bride of Frankenstein,* 1935; *Son of Frankenstein,* 1939) he appeared in several other Hollywood horror films, including *The Mummy* (1933) and *The Walking Dead* (1936). In 1941 Karloff made his New York stage debut in the successful *Arsenic and Old Lace,* which ran for 1,444 performances. In the film *Targets* (1967), he appeared as himself. ■ See biographies by Peter Underwood (1972) and Denis Gifford (1973).

KARMAL, BABRAK (1929–1996), Afghan political leader. The son of an army general, Karmal studied law and political science at Kabul University, joined the procommunist People's Democratic party (PDP), and served in the national assembly (1965–73). When the PDP split on ideological grounds (1973), Karmal headed the pro-Soviet Parcham wing while Nur Mohammad Taraki and Hafizullah Amin led the more radical Khalq group. When Pres. Daoud outlawed all political parties (1977) the PDP reunited. After a military coup overthrew Daoud and established the Democratic Republic of Afghanistan (April 1978), Taraki was named president and prime minister and Karmal and Amin were appointed vice presidents. When the PDP split reemerged, Karmal was "exiled" to Czechoslovakia as ambassador (July 1978) and stripped of his citizenship two months later. He sought asylum in Eastern Europe as the Taraki-Amin government began to carry out coercive policies of radical social change. In the midst of a civil war provoked by government policies, Amin overthrew Taraki in a coup (September 1979), but a countercoup led by several thousand airlifted Soviet combat troops (December 1979) ousted Amin—who was executed—and installed Karmal as president. Although Karmal espoused more moderate views than his predecessors, the Islamic, anticommunist insurgents extended their control over much of the country, and the government was able to survive only because of the continuing presence of thousands of Soviet troops. The stalemated war continued through the mid-1980s. Karmal resigned as Afghan leader in 1986 and subsequently lived quietly in the Soviet Union.

KÁRMÁN, THEODORE VON (1881–1963), Hungarian-born U.S. aeronautical engineer. Sometimes called the "father of the supersonic age," von Kármán directed the Aeronautical Institute at Aachen, Germany (1912–29), the Guggenheim Aeronautical Laboratories (1930–49), and the Jet Propulsion Laboratory (1942–45) at the California Institute of Technology, and chaired the aeronautical research group of the North Atlantic Treaty Organization (NATO; 1951–63). He developed the vortex trail theory (1935), the first theory of supersonic drag that accounted for the air resistance of bodies moving at supersonic speed. His innovations, including a supersonic wind tunnel for testing aircraft, proved crucial in the development of supersonic jets, guided missiles, and rockets. ■ See his autobiography, *The Wind and Beyond* (1967), and D. S. Halacy, Jr., *Father of Supersonic Flight* (1965).

KÁROLYI, COUNT MIHÁLY (1875–1955), Hungarian political leader. Károlyi was a conservative turned radical who became premier of Hungary in 1918 and president in Jan. 1919. After spending several months trying in vain to reconcile the right and left factions of parliament, he turned his administration over to the communists under Béla Kun (March 1919). With the fall of Kun's government (Aug. 1919), Károlyi fled the country. During World War II he headed the Free Hungary movement in London; he returned to Hungary in 1946. He served as ambassador to France (1947–49), then returned to exile after protesting the death sentence in the trial of László Rajk. ■ See his *Fighting the World* (1924) and his *Memoirs* (Eng. trans. 1956).

KARPOV, ANATOLY EVGENYEVICH (1951–), Soviet chess player. A child prodigy, Karpov learned chess from his father at age 4 and was a chess master at 15. He was the World Junior Champion in 1969, an international grand master by 1970, and was designated World Champion, when Bobby Fischer forfeited the title in a dispute with the International Chess Federation, in 1975. A brilliant and coldly mathematical strategist, he defeated Viktor Korchnoi

in highly publicized matches in 1978 and 1981 to retain the title. He lost the championship (1985) to 22-year-old Soviet challenger Gary Kasparov. He lost again to Kasparov in 1986, 1987, and 1990. A 1993 split in the chess world led to two championships, with Karpov winning the World Chess Federation title (1993, 1997, 1998) and Kasparov the Professional Chess Association crown (1993, 1995). Karpov studied economics at Leningrad University and was a member of the Central Committee of Komsomol, the Young Communist League before the collapse of the Soviet Union. ■ See his autobiography, *Chess Is My Life* (Eng. trans. 1980).

KARRER, PAUL (1889–1971), Swiss organic chemist. Born in Russia to Swiss parents, Karrer studied at the University of Zurich (Ph.D. 1911) and taught there from 1918 to 1959. A pioneer in vitamin research, he studied carotenoids, the coloring substances found in eggs and carrots as well as lobster shells and human skin, and found them to be structurally related to vitamin A (1930). Karrer deduced the molecular structure of vitamin A (1931) and, by synthesizing the molecule, confirmed his scheme. He later synthesized other vitamins including vitamin B_2 (1935) and vitamin E (1938), and he shared the 1937 Nobel Prize in Chemistry with Walter N. Haworth, who had synthesized vitamin C in 1934. Karrer also wrote the influential textbook *Organic Chemistry* (1928; 4th Eng. ed. 1950).

KARSH, YOUSUF (1908–), Armenian-born Canadian photographer. Karsh survived the Turkish massacres in Armenia to join a photographer uncle in Canada (1924) and open his own studio in Ottawa (1932). He became famous in 1941 for his *Life* magazine portrait of a belligerent Prime Minister Winston Churchill (whose cigar he had just snatched away) and was sent by the Canadian government to England to photograph its celebrities and statesmen. Karsh later completed a similar series of U.S. portraits for *Life*. He published several collections, including *Faces of Destiny* (1946), *Portraits of Greatness* (1959), *Karsh Portraits* (1976), *Karsh: American Legends* (1992), and *Karsh: A Sixty-Year Retrospective* (1996). ■ See his autobiography, *Search for Greatness* (1962).

KARUME, SHEIKH ABEID (1905–1972), labor organizer and political leader of Zanzibar/Tanzania. After 18 years as a merchant seaman, Karume entered Zanzibar politics in 1954 as a town councillor. He became president of the African Association and leader of the Afro-Shirazi party (1957), which opposed the political hegemony of the Arab clove plutocracy. Following Zanzibar's independence from Britain (1963), he briefly led the parliamentary opposition, but he became president of the Zanzibar People's Republic after a bloody anti-Arab revolution in 1964. Seeking a self-sufficient, egalitarian society, he nationalized land and entered into a union with Tanganyika, forming Tanzania, which he served as first vice president (1964–72). His growing monopolization of power within Zanzibar, however, embittered opponents and led to his assassination in 1972.

KASAVUBU, JOSEPH (1910–1969), Congolese political leader. Although trained for the priesthood, Kasavubu joined the administrative service of the Belgian Congo (1942). In 1955 he became leader of Abako, the nationalist movement of the Bakongo people; his goal was the restoration of the ancient Kongo kingdom. Consequently, when the Congo (later Zaire) gained independence (1960), he favored the formation of a loose federal state. As president of the Congo (1960–65) he was a bitter rival of Premier Patrice Lumumba, and during the bloody disturbances of 1960 he signed the warrant for Lumumba's arrest. Kasavubu, a shrewd politician, survived intervention and civil war only to be toppled by Gen. Mobutu Sese Seko in 1965. He then retired to his farm and never returned to politics.

KÄSEBIER, GERTRUDE (**Gertrude Stanton; 1852–1934**), U.S. photographer. Käsebier took up photography while studying art in Brooklyn, New York, during the 1890s, and by the turn of the century she was recognized as a leading portrait photographer. She was a founding member of the Photo-Secession group (1902), and her work appeared in many of the country's most popular magazines. Best known during the pre–World War I era, she was acclaimed for her photos of mothers and children, her studies of the French sculptor Auguste Rodin and his works, and her series of portraits of American Indians. She cofounded the Pictorial Photographers of America (1916) with Clarence H. White and A. L. Coburn. ■ See biography by B. L. Michaels (1992).

KASPAROV, GARRY (**Garry Veinshtein; 1963– **), Russian chess player. Born in Baku to a Jewish father and an Armenian mother, Kasparov was a chess prodigy who won the U.S.S.R. junior championship at the age of 12. Known for his bold, iconoclastic moves at the board, he became a grand master in 1980 and the youngest world chess champion by defeating Anatoly Karpov in 1985. He successfully defended his title against Karpov (1986, 1987, 1990) but broke with FIDE, the governing body of chess (1993), founded the Professional Chess Association (1993), and defended his title independently (1993, 1995). In 1997 he was defeated 3½ to 2½ by IBM computer Deep Blue (officially called RS/6000 SP), the first time a chess champion was beaten by a machine in a traditional match and the first time Kasparov lost a multi-game contest to an individual foe. He lost the championship to Vladimir Kramnik, a human, in November 2000. ■ See his autobiography, *Child of Change* (1987; with D. Trelford).

KASSÁK, LAJOS (1887–1967), Hungarian novelist and poet. A revolutionary in his politics and his art, Kassák was a leading Hungarian proletarian writer and the first to depict working-class life realistically. His best-known work

was his autobiography, *The Life of a Man* (8 vols., 1928–39). Kassák is also regarded as the pioneer of Hungarian avant-garde poetry, since he was the first to experiment with expressionist, futurist, and dadaist techniques.

KASSEM, ABDUL KARIM (1914–1963), Iraqi military and political leader. After lengthy plotting, Kassem, a general, overthrew the monarchy (July 1958) and became premier of the new republic of Iraq. His tenure was brief and chaotic as he attempted to steer a middle course between the communists and the pro-Nasser pan-Arabic forces. He survived an Egyptian-sponsored rebellion (1959), purged communists from the army and the police, and suspended political activity (1960). He was unable, however, to suppress a Kurdish revolt (1961) or carry out promised reforms, and he was overthrown by a military coup and murdered.

KASTLER, ALFRED (1902–1984), French physicist. A faculty member of the University of Paris (1941–68) and laboratory director at the École Normale Supérieure in Paris (1941–72), Kastler developed an "optical pumping" technique to raise momentarily the energy level of atoms in order to study their structures when the surplus radiation is released. His work led to new knowledge of atomic structure and a new method for measuring weak magnetic fields, and laid the groundwork for the subsequent development of lasers and masers. He won the 1966 Nobel Prize in Physics.

KÄSTNER, ERICH (1899–1974), German writer. Kästner became a freelance writer in 1927, producing poetry, novels, light verse, essays, plays for stage and later for television, and books for children. He was internationally known for his children's fable, *Emile and the Detectives* (1929; Eng. trans. 1930), which was both dramatized and filmed and also translated into 24 languages. His *Lisa and Lottie* (1949; Eng. trans. 1951) was the basis of the Walt Disney film *The Parent Trap* (1961). He combined the quintessential elements of the pre-Nazi era German intellectual in his sparse, satiric, and witty style. He remained in Germany during World War II, publishing abroad until the Nazis forbade him to continue. After the war his work contained more social criticism but remained entertaining. ■ See study by R. W. Last (1974).

KATAYAMA, SEN (**Sugataro Yabuki; 1860–1933**), Japanese socialist leader. Katayama was educated in Japan and in the United States (1884–1895), where he was influenced by Christian socialist ideas. He founded the first settlement house (1897) and the first labor journal, *Rodo Sekai* ("Labor World"), in Japan and helped form several socialist and pacifist groups. After another stint overseas (1903–07), Katayama returned to Japan to become a labor organizer; he was forced into exile in 1914. He returned to the United States and was a founding member of the U.S. Communist party (1921). He spent the last years of his life in Moscow, where he helped found the Communist party of Japan (1922) and served as a high official of the Communist International. ■ See Hyman Kublin, *Asian Revolutionary* (1964).

KATAYEV, VALENTIN PETROVICH (1897–1986), Soviet writer. Katayev was at his best as a humorist and satirist. His first novel, *The Embezzlers* (1926; Eng. trans. 1929), was a takeoff on Soviet bureaucrats in the satiric tradition of Nikolai Gogol. The play *Squaring the Circle* (1928; Eng. trans. 1934) made light of domestic strife and Moscow's housing shortage. Katayev also wrote outstanding novels of industrialization, including *Time, Forward!* (1932; Eng. trans. 1933), which adapted cinematic techniques to emphasize the fast pace of Soviet construction. Later he edited the journal *Yunost* ("Youth"; 1955–62) and wrote the experimental novels *The Holy Well* (1966; Eng. trans. 1967) and *The Grass of Oblivion* (1967; Eng. trans. 1969). ■ See his memoirs of childhood, *A Mosaic of Life* (1972; Eng. trans. 1976), and study by Robert Russell (1981).

KATO, TAKAAKI (also known as Komei Kato; 1860–1926), Japanese diplomat and political leader. Closely associated with the giant Mitsubishi Co., Kato served as foreign minister four times between 1900 and 1915. He drew up the controversial Twenty-One Demands (1915), an ultimatum that greatly increased Japan's influence in China. During his term as premier in a coalition government (1924–26), he established universal manhood suffrage, reduced the size and influence of the army, and introduced moderate social legislation. However, he also promulgated the Peace Preservation law, which provided for prison terms for political dissidents and expanded military education in the schools.

KATZ, SIR BERNARD (1911–), German-born British biophysicist. A Jewish refugee from Nazi Germany (1935), Katz settled in London and spent most of his teaching and research career at University College, where he was a professor and department head from 1952 to 1978. For his discovery of how the neural transmitter acetylcholine—which carries information between nerves and muscles—is released by neural impulses, he shared the 1970 Nobel Prize in Physiology or Medicine with Julius Axelrod and Ulf von Euler.

KAUFMAN, GEORGE S. (1889–1961), U.S. journalist, playwright, and director. When Kaufman's first sales job fell short of his expectations, he began to write for Franklin P. Adams' satirical newspaper column and soon had one of his own in the *Washington Times* (1912). Later, as *New York Times* drama writer and editor (1917–30), he earned national recognition with his critical acumen and searing wit. After the opening of a decidedly mediocre play, he wrote, "I was underwhelmed." Kaufman's own stage productions met with a better reception: he won Pulitzer Prizes for *Of Thee I Sing* (1931; with Morrie Ryskind and George and Ira Gershwin) and *You Can't Take It with You* (1936; with Moss Hart). *The Man Who Came to Dinner* (1939; with Moss Hart), *The Solid Gold Cadillac* (1952; with Howard Teichman), and *Silk Stockings* (1955; with Abe Burrows) were also popular. ■ See biographies by Howard Teichmann (1973) and Malcolm Goldstein (1979).

KAUFMANN, YEHEZKEL (1889–1963), Ukrainian-born Jewish historian and philosopher. Kaufmann studied in Odessa, St. Petersburg, and Bern (Ph.D. 1918) before emigrating to Palestine (1929). Known primarily for his biblical studies, he served as professor of Bible at Hebrew University (1949–63). He stressed the role of monotheism in Jewish history and rejected the notion that it developed gradually out of paganism during biblical times. His writings include the eight-volume *Religion of Israel from Its Beginnings to the Babylonian Exile* (1937–57; abridged Eng. trans. 1960), *The Biblical Account of the Conquest of Canaan* (1953; Eng. trans. 1985), and *Christianity and Judaism: Two Covenants* (1961; Eng. trans. 1988).

KAUNDA, KENNETH DAVID (1924–), president of Zambia. Born in what was then known as Northern Rhodesia, Kaunda began his career as a teacher. Subsequent experience as a welfare worker in the copper belt drew him to the nationalist movement. In 1958 he formed his own party to promote national independence. With self-government for the territory (1962), he became prime minister and negotiated complete independence (1964) for the country that was renamed Zambia. He became Zambia's first president (1964) and despite strong opposition he was reelected in 1968; in 1972 he formed a one-party state. An opponent of apartheid, he nonetheless maintained secret contacts with South Africa, upon which Zambia relied economically. He played a major role in the settlement of the (Southern) Rhodesian conflict during the 1970s and in the negotiations regarding the territory of Namibia during the 1980s. He was elected to a sixth term in 1988 but after being pressured to legalize the opposition, he was defeated in a multiparty election in 1991. Accused, in 1997, of plotting a coup against the new government, he was detained for nearly six months, after which charges were dropped and he was freed. ■ See his autobiography, *Zambia Shall Be Free* (1962); further autobiographical writings in *The Riddle of Violence* (1981); study by Fergus MacPherson (1974); and John Hatch, *Two African Statesmen* (1976).

KAUTSKY, KARL JOHANN (1854–1938), Austrian-born Marxist theoretician and political leader. Kautsky was born in Prague, then part of the Austro-Hungarian empire, and became interested in Marxism while studying at the University of Vienna. He founded and edited the German Marxist journal *Neue Zeit* (1883–1917), wrote the 1891 Erfurt program, which committed the German Social Democratic party (SPD) to an orthodox "evolutionary" approach, and was a leading figure in the Second International. A pacifist who opposed the Bolshevik revolution as undemocratic, Kautsky broke with the SPD during World War I. He was chosen to edit Germany's official documents on the outbreak of the war (1919). After 1924 he pursued literary activities in Vienna. His books included *The Economic Doctrines of Karl Marx* (1887; Eng. trans. 1925) and *The Social Revolution* (1902; Eng. trans. 1903). ■ See studies by Gary P. Steenson (1978) and Massimo Salvadori (Eng. trans. 1979).

KAWABATA, YASUNARI (1899–1972), Japanese novelist. An experimentalist during the 1920s, Kawabata reverted to the traditional Japanese style and produced some of the most sophisticated writing of modern Japan. In his most famous works, *The Izu Dancer* (1925; Eng. trans. 1974), *Snow Country* (1935–47; Eng. trans. 1956), *Thousand Cranes* (1949–51; Eng. trans. 1958), and *The Sound of the Mountain* (1949–54; Eng. trans. 1970), he explored the themes of loneliness, eroticism, death, and deprivation. He was primarily known as a master of female psychology. Kawabata encouraged many younger Japanese writers, including his protégé Yukio Mishima, and was the first Japanese to win the Nobel Prize in Literature (1968). He committed suicide in 1972. ■ See Gwenn Petersen, *The Moon in the Water* (1979).

KAWAKAMI, HAJIME (1879–1946), Japanese economist and political leader. One of Japan's first Marxist theoreticians, Kawakami was a journalist before serving on the economics faculty of the prestigious Kyoto Imperial University (1908–28). His influential magazine *Research in Social Problems* (1919–30) dealt with economic problems from a Marxist perspective. His books, including *Tale of Poverty* (1917), *Studies in Historical Materialism* (1921), *Fundamental Principles of Economics* (1928), and a translation and guide to *Das Kapital,* influenced a generation of students and intellectuals. He became actively involved in politics in the late 1920s, joined the Communist party (1932), and was imprisoned (1933–37) for his illegal political activities. ■ See Gail Bernstein, *Japanese Marxist* (1976).

KAWAWA, RASHIDI MFAUME (1929–), Tanzanian political leader. A social worker employed by the colonial government, Kawawa was president of the Civil Service Association (1954–55) and helped form (1955) the Tanganyikan Federation of Labour, an association of unions that supported nationalist goals. An ally of Julius Nyerere, he was elected to the legislative council (1958) and the vice presidency of the Tanganyika African National Union (1960). After independence he served briefly as prime minister (1962) and subsequently as Nyerere's vice president (1962–77) and prime minister (1972–77). He played an important role in the economic development of the countryside through his sponsorship of ujamaa villages and the National Service for Youth. He later served as secretary-general of the ruling Revolutionary party (1982–93).

KAYE, DANNY (David Daniel Kominski; 1913–1987), U.S. comedian and actor. After working for years as an all-around entertainer at resort hotels in New York's Catskill Mountains, Kaye achieved success on Broadway in Moss Hart's *Lady in the Dark* (1940) and Cole Porter's *Let's Face It* (1941) in roles written especially for him. He subsequently appeared in such popular movies as *The Secret Life of Walter Mitty* (1947), in which he played seven roles; *The Inspector General* (1949); *On the Riviera* (1950); *Hans Christian Andersen* (1954); *White Christmas* (1954); and *The Court Jester* (1955). He starred in his own television show (1963–67), frequently toured the world to entertain children on behalf of the United Nations Children's Emergency Fund (UNICEF), and appeared as guest "conductor" with major symphony orchestras.

KAYSONE, PHOMVIHANE (1920?–1992), Laotian political leader. Kaysone came from a middle-class mixed Lao-Vietnamese family and studied medicine at the University of Hanoi, where he became a dedicated nationalist. At the urging of Vietnamese communist leader Ho Chi Minh, he returned to Laos in 1945 and began his career as an underground communist organizer and military leader, eventually holding such important posts as commander in chief of the Pathet Lao forces (1954–57) and vice chairman of the Lao Patriotic Front (1959–). Although the Pathet Lao participated in coalition governments from 1962 to 1964, civil war condictions prevailed during most of the 1960s as the war in neighboring Vietnam intensified. After a 1973 cease-fire, a new government was formed with Pathet Lao membership (1974). In the spring of 1975, after the Communist takeover of Vietnam, many conservative Lao political leaders fled and the Pathet Lao (now called the Lao People's Liberation army) took control of the country. The Lao People's Democratic Republic was founded (Dec. 1975) with Kaysone, the secretary-general of the Lao People's Revolutionary party, serving as prime minister (1975–91) and then as president (1991–92). A pragmatic leader, his government maintained close ties with Vietnam during the 1980s and pursued policies of market reform and privatization. ■ See his book *Revolution in Laos* (Eng. trans. 1981).

KAZAN, ELIA (1909–), U.S. stage and film director. Kazan was born in Istanbul, Turkey, into a Greek family that emigrated to the United States in 1913. He grew up in New York City, graduated from Williams College (B.A. 1930), studied drama at Yale University (1930–32), and became associated with New York's left-wing Group Theater as an actor and director (1932–39). He was a celebrated Broadway director during the 1940s, with such productions as *The Skin of Our Teeth* (1942), *One Touch of Venus* (1943), *All My Sons* (1947), *A Streetcar Named Desire* (1947), and *Death of a Salesman* (1949), and was a cofounder of the Actors Studio (1947). Most of the films he directed were concerned with controversial contemporary social issues, including *Gentlemen's Agreement* (1947) and *On the Waterfront* (1954), for which he won Academy Awards as best director. His other films included *A Tree*

Grows in Brooklyn (1945), *Pinky* (1949), *A Streetcar Named Desire* (1952), *Viva Zapata!* (1952), *East of Eden* (1955), and *Splendor in the Grass* (1961). His appearance as a friendly witness before the House Un-American Activities Committee (1952), in which he admitted being a member of the Communist party (1934–36) and named fellow members, tarnished his reputation among many of his former colleagues and admirers. His written works included the novels *America, America* (1962), *The Arrangement* (1967), *The Anatolian* (1982), and *Beyond the Aegean* (1994), which tells the story of a Greek immigrant in America. ■ See his autobiography (1988); Michael Ciment's volume of taped interviews, *Kazan on Kazan* (1974); and the interviews in Jeff Young's *Kazan* (1999).

KAZANTZAKIS, NIKOS (1883–1957), Greek novelist and poet. Kazantzakis was born in Crete and educated in Athens and Paris. His works reflected, and attempted to synthesize, the conflicts between involvement and discipline, between the flesh and the spirit. To Kazantzakis, the greatest virtue was the passionate quest for freedom. His best-known works were *Zorba the Greek* (1946; Eng. trans. 1953), *The Greek Passion* (1948; Eng. trans. 1953), *The Last Temptation of Christ* (1955; Eng. trans. 1960), and the epic poem *The Odyssey: A Modern Sequel* (1938; Eng. trans. 1958). Kazantzakis was also a world traveler and wrote several highly praised travel books. ■ *Report to Greco* (1961; Eng. trans. 1965) was autobiographical. See biography by Helen Kazantzakis (1968).

KAZIN, ALFRED (1915–1998), U.S. critic. Born in Brooklyn, New York, Kazin graduated from City College and did graduate work at Columbia University (M.A. 1938). He taught at many universities and was best known for his incisive critical writings, including four comprehensive collections of essays that focused primarily on 20th-century U.S. literature: *On Native Grounds* (1942), *The Inmost Leaf* (1955), *Contemporaries* (1962), and *Bright Book of Life* (1973). *An American Procession* (1984) treated classic U.S. writers from the mid-19th to the mid-20th century. Kazin also wrote several autobiographical accounts: *A Walker in the City* (1951) recalled his early childhood in Brooklyn; *Starting Out in the Thirties* (1965) recounted his experiences as a young critic; *New York Jew* (1978) chronicled his life into the 1970s. *Writing was Everything* (1995) was a blend of autobiography, history, and criticism. He also wrote *God and the American Writer* (1997). ■ See his journals in *A Lifetime Burning in Every Moment* (1996).

KEATING, PAUL (1944–), Australian political leader. Keating, a native of Sydney, left school at age 14 to work for the municipal workers' union and joined the Australian Labor party (ALP) at age 15. He was elected to the federal House of Representatives (1969) and became treasurer (1983), and later deputy prime minister (1990) in the Labor government headed by Bob Hawke. He carried out defla-

tionary and deregulatory policies and replaced Hawke as party leader and prime minister (1991). He subsequently led the Labor party to victory in the 1993 elections. His attempts to generate economic growth through tax reductions and privatization of state-owned businesses alienated the left wing of the ALP. His government improved relations with Indonesia and other Asian countries and advocated severing political links with Great Britain and transforming Australia into a fully independent republic. After the ALP lost the 1996 election to a Liberal-National party coalition, Keating resigned from parliament.

KEATON, BUSTER (Joseph Francis Keaton; 1895–1966), U.S. comedian and film director. Beginning at age 3, Keaton worked with his parents in an acrobatic comedy act in vaudeville for 20 years. He made his film debut in 1917 in a series of shorts (with Roscoe "Fatty" Arbuckle) that established his style of deadpan impassivity in the face of extreme physical hazard. By 1923 Keaton graduated to features, the most outstanding of which were *Sherlock Junior* (1924), *The Navigator* (1924), and *The General* (1926). With his unique style and economy of humor, he rivaled Charlie Chaplin in popularity. But Keaton's film creativity came to an end in 1928 due to studio conflicts and personal problems. He subsequently made only budget shorts and guest appearances, as in Chaplin's *Limelight* (1952) and *A Funny Thing Happened on the Way to the Forum* (1966). ■ See his *My Wonderful World of Slapstick* (1960) and studies by Rudi Blech (1966), Tom Dardis (1979), and Marion Meade (1995).

KEENE, CAROLYN (Harriet Stratemeyer Adams; 1893–1982), U.S. mystery writer. Adams wrote under the names Laura Lee Hope and Franklin W. Dixon, but was best known as Carolyn Keene, author of the popular series of mysteries solved ingeniously by teenage sleuth Nancy Drew. Nancy Drew was originated by Adams' publisher-father Edward Stratemeyer, but was inherited by Adams at his death (1930). In the last 50 years of her life, she wrote 59 Nancy Drew mystery tales. With chums Bess and George and beau Ned Nickerson, Nancy pursued loathsome criminals in her sporty roadster. Her adventures have sold some 60 million copies.

KEFAUVER, (CAREY) ESTES (1903–1963), U.S. senator. A corporate lawyer from a socially prominent southern family, Kefauver adopted a coonskin cap and homespun manners as his political trademarks. After five terms as a Democratic congressman from Tennessee, he moved (1949) to the Senate, where he gained national exposure as chairman of the televised crime-investigation hearings, the subject of his *Crime in America* (1951). An unsuccessful seeker of his party's presidential nomination in 1952 and 1956, Kefauver ran unsuccessfully for vice president (1956) on the ticket headed by Adlai Stevenson. He also chaired Senate investigations into the pharmaceutical industry and professional sports. ■ See biographies by Joseph B. Gorman (1971) and Charles L. Fontenay (1980).

KEILLOR, GARRISON (1942–), U.S. radio personality, storyteller, and writer. Garrison Keillor grew up in small-town Minnesota, as millions of Americans found out from listening to "The Prairie Home Companion," the weekly radio show he hosted—purportedly from his fictional hometown, Lake Wobegon, Minnesota—for American Public Radio (1974–). A humorist in the tradition of James Thurber and Ring Lardner, Keillor gave to the mythic Midwest such heroes as Art, proprietor of Art's Bait & Night O'Rest Motel, and such landmarks as the Statue of the Unknown Norwegian. A frequent contributor to *The New Yorker,* Keillor wrote *Happy to Be Here* (1982), a collection of sketches and short stories, and the best-seller *Lake Wobegon Days* (1985), chronicling 150 years of that town's finest hours. He also wrote the short-story collections *Leaving Home* (1987), *We are Still Married* (1989), and *The Book of Guys* (1993), and the novels *WLT: A Radio Romance* (1991) and *Wobegon Boy* (1997). ■ See Michael Fedo, *The Man from Lake Wobegon* (1987).

KEITA, MODIBO (1915–1977), Malian political leader. After a brief teaching career in the French Sudan (later Mali), Keita became involved in politics and in 1946 helped form the Rassemblement Démocratique Africain (RDA), a pan-Africanist association of French-speaking colonies. As a left-wing anticolonialist, he was elected to the territorial assembly (1948) and subsequently was elected to the French assembly (1956) and became a cabinet member. He was president of the Mali Federation (1959) and was bitterly disappointed when the grouping of former French West African colonies (Sudan, Senegal, Upper Volta, and Dahomey) broke up (1960). He became increasingly radical as president of an independent Mali (1960–68) and attempted to develop a socialist economy along Soviet lines. He was overthrown in 1968 amid a growing economic and financial crisis and held in detention until his death.

KEITEL, WILHELM (1882–1946), German general. Keitel's appointment in 1938 as second to dictator Adolf Hitler in command of Germany's armed forces signaled Nazi ascendance over the military. Generally regarded as Hitler's "lackey," he dictated the French surrender in 1940, helped direct the war's major campaigns, and survived to ratify surrender in 1945. Convicted by the Nuremberg tribunal of war crimes, he was hanged. ■ See his memoirs, *In the Service of the Reich* (Eng. trans. 1979).

KEITH, BENJAMIN FRANKLIN (1846–1914), and ED-WARD FRANKLIN ALBEE (1857–1930), U.S. theater owners. Keith, a circus concessionaire and theater owner, and Albee, a circus ticket seller, joined forces in 1885 with the aim of improving the image and quality of vaudeville shows. They transformed Boston's Bijou Theater into Amer-

ica's first continuous variety theater, achieved great success, and began to set up a chain of modern, popular priced theaters throughout the country. By 1914 the Keith-Albee circuit controlled nearly 400 theaters and in conjunction with its United Booking Office virtually monopolized vaudeville entertainment in the United States. Shortly before retiring, Albee merged his interests with the Orpheum Circuit of the Pacific Coast (1927) and then with the Radio Corporation of America (1928), at which time the organization became known as RKO (Radio-Keith-Orpheum).

KEITH, MINOR COOPER (1848–1929), U.S. businessman. The nephew of Henry Meiggs (a builder of railroads in Peru), Keith started his career by building a railroad in Costa Rica. As a sideline he began to develop banana plantations; soon these were more valuable than his railroad. He expanded his holdings, acquired other plantations in Colombia and Panama, and in 1899 combined his interests with the West Indian–based Boston Fruit Co. to form the United Fruit Co., which became the most powerful economic influence in Central America. He delegated power in United Fruit, organized the International Railways of Central America, and, from 1912 to 1929, constructed 800 more miles of railroad. ■ See Watt Stewart, *Keith and Costa Rica* (1964).

KEKKONEN, URHO KALEVA (1900–1986), Finnish political leader. A leader of the Center party, Kekkonen served as premier (1950–56) and president (1956–81) of Finland. As chief executive, he authorized and administered Finland's policy of friendly but independent relations with the Soviet Union. ■ See his *Neutrality: The Finnish Position* (Eng. trans. 1970).

KELDYSH, MSTISLAV VSEVOLODOVICH (1911–1978), Soviet mathematician and physicist. After graduating from Moscow University (1931), Keldysh did pioneering studies in aerodynamics and oscillation theory. He directed the Institute of Applied Mathematics of the Soviet Academy of Sciences (from 1953) and helped initiate the Soviet space program. As president of the Academy of Sciences (1961–75), Keldysh was the chief spokesman, organizer, and administrator of Soviet science and played a major role in the rapid development of Soviet space, computer, and nuclear technology.

KELLER, HELEN ADAMS (1880–1968), U.S. educator and author. Keller overcame blindness and deafness caused by an early childhood disease to graduate cum laude from Radcliffe College (1904) and to become a lifelong crusader for the welfare of people who have disabilities. Through her numerous books and lectures she educated the public regarding the problems and potentialities of the blind and inspired blind people throughout the world. She joined the Socialist party in 1909. Keller's childhood experiences were recorded in the autobiographical *Story of My Life* (1902), which was eventually published in 50 languages, and in William Gibson's plays *The Miracle Worker* (1960) and *Monday After the Miracle* (1983). She also wrote *Midstream: My Later Life* (1929). ▪ See Richard Harrity and Ralph G. Martin, *The Three Lives of Helen Keller* (1962); Joseph P. Lash, *Helen and Teacher: The Story of Helen Keller and Anne Sullivan Macy* (1980); and biography by Dorothy Herrmann (1998).

KELLEY, FLORENCE (1859–1932), U.S. social reformer. Kelley graduated from Cornell (1882) but was barred from the University of Pennsylvania Law School, which accepted only male students. She subsequently studied in Europe at the University of Zurich, where she became a socialist. While living at Chicago's Hull House (1891–99), she wrote reports on slums and sweatshop conditions, worked as Illinois' first factory inspector (1892–97), and finally earned a law degree from Northwestern University (1894). In New York City, Kelley directed the National Consumers' League (1899–1932), which used consumer pressure to assure that goods were manufactured under proper working conditions. She continued her work for industrial reform, sought protective labor legislation, particularly for children and women, and lobbied for minimum wage, workmen's compensation, and other social legislation. She was also a founder of the National Association for the Advancement of Colored People (NAACP; 1909) and the Women's International League for Peace and Freedom (1919), and a vice president of the National Woman Suffrage Association. She wrote *Some Ethical Gains Through Legislation* (1905) and *Modern Industry* (1914). ▪ See Josephine Goldmark, *Impatient Crusader* (1953), and biographies by Dorothy Blumberg (1966) and Kathryn K. Sklar (1995).

KELLOGG, FRANK BILLINGS (1856–1937), U.S. senator and secretary of state. As special counsel for the U.S. government, Kellogg conducted several successful antitrust prosecutions against the Standard Oil Co. and the Union Pacific Railroad. He served in the U.S. Senate as a Republican (1917–23), and subsequently was ambassador to Britain (1923–25). As Pres. Calvin Coolidge's secretary of state (1925–29) he promoted the Kellogg-Briand Pact (1928), a multilateral agreement designed to outlaw war as an instrument of national policy. Although the pact proved completely ineffective, Kellogg received the 1929 Nobel Peace Prize and served as a member of the Permanent Court of International Justice (the World Court) at The Hague (1930–35). ▪ See biography by David Bryn-Jones (1937) and study by L. Ethan Ellis (1961).

KELLOGG, PAUL UNDERWOOD (1879–1958), U.S. editor and social reformer. An editor of the social-work magazine *Survey* (originally called *Charities*) from 1909 to 1952, Kellogg was a highly influential champion of social reform and a leader in the developing social-work profession. As director of the Pittsburgh Survey (1910–1914), he exposed the inhuman working conditions of steelworkers and was instrumental in ending the seven-day work week and in forming workers' compensation laws. He supported the New Deal and helped design the Social Security Act (1935). Kellogg was also a founder of the Foreign Policy Association (1918) and served as president of the National Conference of Social Work (1939).

KELLOGG, WILL KEITH (1860–1951), U.S. manufacturer. In collaboration with his brother, a physician who ran a sanitarium in Battle Creek, Michigan, Kellogg developed ways of rolling and toasting cooked wheat and corn into crisp flakes to be eaten as a nutritious breakfast cereal. Consumed at first exclusively by sanitarium patients, the new flakes were soon sold through the mail, and in 1906 the W. K. Kellogg Co. was founded and the cereal made nationally available. Heavily promoted through advertising, the new flakes created a revolution in American breakfast-eating habits and made Kellogg a millionaire. He served as president of the company until 1929 and in 1930 established the W. K. Kellogg Foundation, which became one of the nation's most important philanthropic institutions.

KELLY, EDWARD JOSEPH (1876–1950), U.S. political boss. As chief engineer of the Chicago Sanitary District (1920), Kelly supervised multimillion-dollar projects that were riddled with graft, nepotism, and mismanagement. He befriended Patrick A. Nash, an influential sewer contractor and prominent Democratic party leader, and together they built up a powerful political machine. After the death of Mayor Anton Cermak, Kelly was appointed mayor and was subsequently elected three times to serve for 14 years (1933–47). As the political boss of Chicago—he controlled 40,000 patronage jobs—he was one of America's most powerful politicians and was influential in three of Franklin D. Roosevelt's presidential campaigns (1936, 1940, 1944). Although Kelly's administration was marked by intermittent scandals, he restored the city financially, leaving it solvent, and sponsored major civic improvements. ▪ See Roger Biles, *Big City Boss* (1984).

KELLY, ELLSWORTH (1923–), U.S. painter and sculptor. Kelly studied in Boston at the Museum of Fine Arts School and at the Académie des Beaux Arts in Paris (1948–54). Absent from New York during the developmental years of the abstract-expressionist movement, he maintained an independent painting style based on geometric shapes and flat colors that was also carried out in his sculpture. He was commissioned to create sculpture for the New York State pavilion at the New York World's Fair (1964–65). His later steel sculptures emphasized shape and were devoid of color while his later large paintings were increasingly refined and abstract. ▪ See study by John Coplans (1973).

KELLY, EMMETT (1898–1979), U.S. clown. One of America's best-known circus performers, Kelly created the character of "Weary Willie," the mournful circus clown. Not the usual happy clown in white face and bright costume, "Willie" made people laugh, Kelly believed, because he maintained dignity as he chased elusive spotlights, cracked peanuts with a sledgehammer, and swept the circus ring with a frayed broom. Clowning with circuses in Britain and America, Kelly often appeared with The Ringling Brothers, Barnum and Bailey Circus (1942–57) and provided pregame entertainment for the Brooklyn Dodgers (1957) and the St. Louis Hawks (1958). ■ See his autobiography, *Clown* (1954).

KELLY, GENE (Eugene Curran Kelly; 1912–1996), U.S. dancer, actor, choreographer, and director. After working his way through college in Pennsylvania as a dancer and teacher, Kelly started out in a Broadway chorus line in 1938 and won the Broadway lead in *Pal Joey* two years later. He made his film debut in *For Me and My Gal* (1942) and choreographed his famous shadow routine in *Cover Girl* (1944). A spirited and athletic performer, he danced in and choreographed such successful films as *Anchors Aweigh* (1945), *On the Town* (1949), *An American in Paris* (1951), and *Singin' in the Rain* (1952). Kelly played straight dramatic roles in *Marjorie Morningstar* (1958) and *Inherit the Wind* (1960). Retired as a performer, he directed the 1969 film of *Hello, Dolly!* ■ See biographies by Clive Hirschhorn (1975), Sheridan Morley (1996), and Alvin Yudkoff (1999).

KELLY, GRACE (1928–1982), U.S. movie actress and princess of Monaco. Born into a wealthy Philadelphia family, Kelly studied acting in New York and starred in such popular movies as *Mogambo* (1953), *Dial M for Murder* (1954), *Rear Window* (1954), *To Catch a Thief* (1955), and *High Society* (1956). An elegant beauty, she generally played icily aloof heroines whose warmth and sensuality lay just beneath the surface. She stepped out of character, however, in *The Country Girl* (1954) and won an Academy Award. At the height of her popularity (1956) she married Prince Rainier III of the principality of Monaco and retired from the screen. She died in an automobile accident. ■ See Gwen Robyns, *Princess Grace* (1976), and Sarah Bradford, *Princess Grace* (1984).

KELLY, HOWARD ATWOOD (1858-1943), U.S. gynecologist and surgeon. A member of the original faculty of the Johns Hopkins Medical School (1889–1919), Kelly was one of the most skillful surgeons of his day. An influential teacher, researcher, and author of more than 500 articles and numerous books, Kelly devised several new surgical techniques and pioneered in the use of radium in the treatment of cancer. He also pioneered in the use of detailed drawings to illustrate medical texts by employing German artist Max Brödel to illustrate his books, thus inaugurating the field of medical art in the United States.

KELLY, PETRA (Petra Karin Lehmann; 1947–1992), German political leader. Kelly was brought to the United States

(1960) by her mother and her stepfather, U.S. Army Lt. Col. John E. Kelly, and was active in the student protest movements of the 1960s. She was a volunteer in the presidential campaign of Robert F. Kennedy (1968), worked in the office of Sen. Hubert Humphrey, and studied political science at American University, Washington, D.C. (B.A. 1970), and at the University of Amsterdam (M.A. 1971). She worked for the European Economic Community (EEC) in Brussels as a civil servant (1971–82) and was a member of the German Social Democratic party (SPD; 1972–78) before becoming disillusioned with its moderate policies. In 1979 she helped found the Green party, a loose alliance of environmentalists, antinuclear activists, feminists, and independent Marxists, and became its major spokesperson. Campaigning against the deployment of U.S. nuclear missiles on German soil, the Greens captured 5.6 percent of the vote in the 1983 national elections, and Kelly and 26 of her party colleagues were elected to parliament. They served until 1990, when the Greens received less than the required 5 percent of the vote needed for representation in parliament. In October 1992 she and her companion and fellow Green party leader Gert Bastian, a 69-year-old former major general in the West German army, were found dead in their home. The police theorized that Bastian shot Kelly and then committed suicide. ■ See her book, *Fighting for Hope* (1983; Eng. trans. 1984), and Sara Parkin, *The Life and Death of Petra Kelly* (1994).

KELLY, WALT (1913–1973), U.S. cartoonist. The son of a theatrical scene painter, Kelly worked as a newspaper reporter in his hometown, Bridgeport, Connecticut, then went to Hollywood (1935) to work as an animator at Walt Disney Studios. While illustrating children's books during World War II, he created his famous talking opossum, Pogo. The comic strip *Pogo* first appeared in the *New York Star* in 1948, and Kelly populated the Okefenokee bogs of his strip with more than 150 politically meaningful animals, whom he once characterized as "nature's screetures." Pogo came to national attention during the 1952 presidential campaign, when he won a considerable number of write-in votes. Kelly continued the strip for 25 years; by 1960 more than 450 newspapers carried it. His strip changed with the political scene: Joseph McCarthy, Nikita Khrushchev, J. Edgar Hoover, and Spiro Agnew visited the swamp as a wildcat, pig, bulldog, and hyena. In addition to his daily strip and Sunday page, Kelly published 14 *Pogo* cartoon books.

KELSEN, HANS (1881–1973), Austrian-born U.S. legal scholar. A native of Prague, Kelsen was a professor of law at the University of Vienna (1911–17; 1919–29), a drafter of the Austrian Constitution (1920), and a judge on the Austrian Constitutional Court (1920–29). He was forced out of teaching posts by the Nazis in Germany (1933) and Czechoslovakia (1938) and emigrated to the United States, where he taught at Harvard Law School (1940–43) and the University of California at Berkeley (1943–73). One of the century's most influential legal theorists, he attempted to develop a positivist "pure theory" of law, which would be applicable to all legal systems. He believed that law is a hierarchy of norms, ultimately rooted in an independent basic or fundamental norm—different in each society—and that the study of law should be concerned with the logical relationships between the "basic norm" and the laws within the system, and not deal with extraneous questions of morality, culture, ethics, history, or politics. His books included *General Theory of Law and the State* (1945), *The Law of the United Nations* (1950), *Principles of International Law* (1952), and *Pure Theory of Law* (1967). See also his essays in *What Is Justice?* (1957).

KEMAL, YASHAR (Yasar Kemal Gökçeli; 1922–), Turkish novelist. Hounded out of his native village in remote southern Turkey for his radical views, Kemal, a Kurd, moved to Istanbul (1951) and became a prominent journalist. His first novel, *Memed, My Hawk* (1955; Eng. trans. 1961), an action-filled saga of a folk hero who rebelled against exploiting landowners, became Turkey's all-time best-selling novel. Its sequel was *They Burn the Thistles* (1969; Eng. trans. 1977). His powerful "village novels," which described the plight of the impoverished peasants in his home region, included *The Wind from the Plain* (1960; Eng. trans. 1964), *Iron Earth, Copper Sky* (1963; Eng. trans. 1979), *The Undying Grass* (1968; Eng. trans. 1978), and *The Lords of Akchasaz: Murder in the Ironsmiths Market* (1974; Eng. trans. 1979). He also wrote modern versions of southern Turkish tales and legends (*The Legend of Ararat*, 1970; Eng. trans. 1975, and *The Legend of the Thousand Bulls*, 1971; Eng. trans. 1976) and notable short stories (*Anatolian Tales*; Eng. trans. 1968). *Seagull* (1976; Eng. trans. 1981) was set in a Black Sea fishing village, and *The Sea-Crossed Fisherman* (1979; Eng. trans. 1985), in Istanbul. His other novels included *To Crush the Serpent* (1976; Eng. trans. 1992), *The Birds Have Also Gone* (1978; Eng. trans. 1987), and *Salman the Solitary* (1980; Eng. trans. 1997). Arrested several times for his political views, he was a leader of the banned Turkish Workers' party and published the Marxist weekly *Ant* during the 1960s. He was placed on trial (1995) for accusing the Turkish government of oppressing the Kurdish minority.

KEMPTON, (JAMES) MURRAY (1917–1997), U.S. columnist. Kempton worked as a labor organizer and socialist pamphleteer before becoming a columnist for the *New York Post* (1949–69). Temperamentally inclined to support underdogs, he used his column to defend civil liberties during the "witch-hunt" era of Sen. Joseph R. McCarthy in the 1950s and civil rights during the later voter-registration and integration drives. Collections of Kempton's columns were published as *America Comes of Middle Age* (1963) and *Rebellions, Perversities and Main Events* (1994). In his own middle age Kempton attended the 1968 Democratic Convention as a delegate for Eugene McCarthy. He also wrote *The Briar Patch* (1973), a study of the prosecution of the Black Panthers. He was a columnist for *Newsday,* a Long Island, New York, newspaper (from 1981) and won the 1985 Pulitzer Prize for commentary.

KENDALL, EDWARD CALVIN (1886–1972), U.S. chemist. Shortly after joining the staff of the Mayo Clinic, where he worked from 1914 to 1951, Kendall isolated thyroxin, the hormone of the thyroid gland that was widely used to help patients with glandular deficiencies. He is most famous, however, for the isolation of adrenal hormones, which resulted in the eventual synthesis and widespread production of cortisone and hydrocortisone. These "miracle drugs" have been successfully used to treat rheumatoid arthritis, Addison's disease, and various diseases of the skin, eye, and intestines. Kendall shared the 1950 Nobel Prize in Physiology or Medicine with Philip S. Hench and Tadeus Reichstein.

KENDALL, HENRY W. (1926–1999), U.S. physicist. Kendall studied nuclear physics at the Massachusetts Institute of Technology (Ph.D. 1955) and taught there from 1961. In collaboration with Jerome Friedman and Richard E. Taylor, Kendall performed electron-scattering experiments at the two-mile-long high-energy particle accelerator at the Stanford Linear Accelerator Center(1967–73), which confirmed the existence of subatomic particles called quarks, the basic building blocks of protons and neutrons. The three scientists also identified electrically neutral particles called gluons, which bind quarks together. The trio shared the 1990 Nobel Prize in Physics for their experiments. Kendall was also an advocate of the control of nuclear weapons, and was a founder of the Union of Concerned Scientists (1969; chair, 1973–99) and a board member of the Arms Control Association (from 1979).

KENDREW, SIR JOHN COWDERY (1917–1997), British biochemist. A cofounder (with Max Perutz) and deputy director (1946–75) of the Medical Research Council Unit for Molecular Biology at Cambridge, Kendrew utilized X-ray diffraction techniques and high-speed electronic digital computers to produce a three-dimensional picture of the muscle protein myoglobin (1957) and became the first scientist to determine the detailed atomic structure of a complex protein molecule (1959). His work revolutionized the study of enzymes, and he shared the 1962 Nobel Prize in Chemistry with Perutz. Kendrew later wrote *The Thread of Life* (1966) and was director general of the European Molecular Biology Laboratory in Heidelberg, West Germany (1975–82). He was the founding editor of the *Journal of Molecular Biology* (1959–87).

KENEALLY, THOMAS (1935–), Australian novelist. An ex-seminarian, Keneally was regarded as one of the finest Australian novelists of the post–World War II era. Highly praised for his realistic characterizations and sensitivity to style, he was best known for the historical novels *The Chant* *of Jimmy Blacksmith* (1972), an account of the conflict of a mission-reared aborigine torn between white society and tribal traditions in the Australia of 1900; *Blood Red, Sister Rose* (1974), a retelling of the story of Joan of Arc; and *Schindler's List* (1982), an account, based on fact, of a German wheeler-dealer who saved the lives of Jews working in his prison-camp factory during World War II. *A Family Madness* (1986) is about a family of Byelorussian origin that had collaborated with the Nazis during World War II and emigrated to Australia after the war. He also wrote a novel about a doubting priest, *Three Cheers for the Paraclete* (1968); several powerful war novels, *Gossip from the Forest* (1975), *Season in Purgatory* (1976), and *Confederates* (1979); and *Passenger* (1979), a novel whose narrator is a fetus. His later works included the novels *To Asmara* (1989) and *Jacko: The Great Intruder* (1994) and the nonfiction account, *The Great Shame—And the Triumph of the Irish in the English-Speaking World* (1999). ■ See his memoir, *Homebush Boy* (1995), and study by Peter Quartermaine (1991).

KENNAN, GEORGE FROST (1904–   ), U.S. diplomat and historian. Kennan joined the foreign service after graduating from Princeton (1925) and served in a series of "listening posts" in northern and central Europe near the Soviet Union to become a "Kremlinologist," a student of Soviet political affairs. Following U.S. recognition of the Soviet Union (1933), he spent two years at the American embassy in Moscow and returned to that post during World War II (1944–46). As director of policy planning for the State Department in 1947, he helped replace the World War II spirit of compromise toward the Soviet Union with the containment policy he described in an anonymous article in *Foreign Affairs*. He served as ambassador to Moscow briefly (1952–53), was declared persona non grata (1953), and retired from government to join the Institute of Advanced Study, Princeton, New Jersey (1953–74). His books included *Realities of American Foreign Policy* (1954), the prize-winning *Russia Leaves the War* (1956), two volumes of *Memoirs* (1967, 1972), *Sketches from a Life* (1989), *Around the Cragged Hill: A Personal and Political Philosophy* (1993), and *At a Century's Ending: Reflections, 1982–1995* (1996). He returned to diplomacy as ambassador to Yugoslavia (1961–63). In his later years he was an outspoken opponent of the nuclear arms race and advocated a 50 percent reduction of all nuclear weapons in *The Nuclear Delusion* (1982). ■ See Barton Gellman, *Contending with Kennan* (1985).

KENNEDY, EDWARD MOORE (1932–   ), U.S. political leader. The youngest of nine children of businessman Joseph P. Kennedy, "Ted" Kennedy graduated from Harvard (1956) and the University of Virginia Law School (1959) and helped manage the political campaigns of his brothers John and Robert, including John's successful run for the presidency (1960). He was elected to the U.S. Senate as a Democrat from Massachusetts in 1962. After the death of his brother Robert (1968), he moved into leadership of liberal congressional forces, vigorously supporting social-welfare legislation and advocating a comprehensive national health insurance plan. However, his standing was damaged by his conduct in the 1969 drowning of a woman campaign worker at Chappaquiddick, Massachusetts. He unsuccessfully challenged incumbent Jimmy Carter for the Democratic presidential nomination in 1980. He was elected to his sixth Senate term in 1998. ■ See Joe McGuinness, *The Last Brother* (1993); B. Hersh, *The Shadow President* (1997); and biography by Adam Clymer (1999).

KENNEDY, JACQUELINE. *See ONASSIS, JACQUELINE KENNEDY.*

KENNEDY, JOHN FITZGERALD (1917–1963), U.S. political leader. The second son of millionaire businessman and Democratic party powerbroker Joseph P. Kennedy, John F. Kennedy graduated from Harvard (1940) and commanded a PT-boat during World War II. Groomed for high political office by his father, he served as a Democratic U.S. congressman from Massachusetts (1947–53) and U.S. senator (1953–61) before becoming the youngest man—and first Roman Catholic—to be elected president of the United States (1960). Vigorous, intelligent, charming, and handsome, Kennedy became a symbol of hope and renewal, both at home and abroad, as he called for a New Frontier of service and social justice. However, his domestic programs, including tax cuts, aid to education, medical care for the aged, and civil-rights legislation, were blocked by Congress. Internationally, he authorized the disastrous Bay of Pigs invasion of Cuba by Cuban exiles (1961) and faced down the Soviets during the Cuban missile crisis (1962), which brought the superpowers to the brink of nuclear war before the Soviets agreed to remove their missiles from Cuba. Subsequently Kennedy initiated a period of détente with the Soviet Union and signed the Nuclear Test Ban Treaty (1963). Kennedy also established the Peace Corps and increased U.S. military aid to South Vietnam. He was assassinated, allegedly by Lee Harvey Oswald, while on a visit to Dallas, Texas (Nov. 22, 1963). Kennedy's book, *Profiles in Courage* (1956), won a Pulitzer Prize for biography. ■ See Arthur M. Schlesinger, Jr., *A Thousand Days* (1965); study by Theodore Sorensen (1965); Nigel Hamilton, *JFK: Reckless Youth* (1992); and Seymour Hersh, *The Dark Side of Camelot* (1997).

KENNEDY, JOSEPH PATRICK (1888–1969), U.S. financier and diplomat. The patriarch of the family that included Pres. John F. Kennedy and Senators Robert and Edward Kennedy, Joseph Kennedy amassed a multimillion-dollar fortune in stock speculation, the motion-picture industry, and liquor importing in the 1920s and 1930s. He actively supported Pres. Franklin D. Roosevelt and served as first chairman of the Securities and Exchange Commission (1934–35) and as ambassador to Great Britain (1938–40), a post he resigned when his support of U.S. isolationism and appeasement of Nazi Germany conflicted with Roosevelt's policies. After World War II he bought Chicago's Merchandise Mart, the world's largest commercial building, made millions in real estate and oil ventures, and launched the political careers of his sons. ■ See Richard J. Whalen, *The Founding Father* (1964); biography by David E. Koskoff (1974); Ralph G. Martin, *Seeds of Destruction* (1995); and Ronald Kellser, *The Sins of the Father* (1996).

KENNEDY, ROBERT FRANCIS (1925–1968), U.S. political leader. A graduate of Harvard (1948) and the University of Virginia Law School (1951), "Bobby" Kennedy managed the successful senatorial and presidential campaigns of his older brother John F. Kennedy. Appointed U.S. attorney general in 1961, he was his brother's closest adviser. After the assassination of Pres. Kennedy in 1963, Robert Kennedy set out to become president himself. Elected to the U.S. Senate as a Democrat from New York (1964), he emerged as a leader of the liberal wing of the party and was a contender for the 1968 Democratic presidential nomination when he was assassinated by Sirhan Sirhan on the night of a primary victory in California. He wrote *The Enemy Within* (1960) and *Thirteen Days: A Memoir of the Cuban Missile Crisis* (1969). ■ See studies by Arthur M. Schlesinger, Jr. (1978), and Jack Newfield (1978); C. David Heymann, *RFK* (1998); Michael K. Beran, *The Last Patrician* (1998); Ronald Steel, *In Love with Night* (2000); and biography by Evan Thomas (2000).

KENNEDY, TED. *See KENNEDY, EDWARD MOORE.*

KENNY, ELIZABETH (1886–1952), Australian nurse. While practicing in the bush country of Australia, Sister Kenny devised (1910) a method of physical therapy to treat victims of poliomyelitis that opposed the orthodox treatment of immobilizing paralyzed limbs with casts and splints. She opened several clinics in Australia (1933–37) and Britain (1937) but was strenuously opposed by the medical establishment. A visit (1940) to the United States was highly successful, however, and she received the support of the American Medical Association. The Sister Kenny Foundation was established (1942) in Minneapolis, Minnesota, to train nurses and physiotherapists, and clinics were set up throughout the country. She wrote several books on her method of treatment as well as the autobiographical *And They Shall Walk* (1943) and *My Battle and Victory* (1955). ■ See biography by Victor Cohn (1975).

KENT, (ARTHUR) ATWATER (1873–1949), U.S. manufacturer. Kent was a pioneer in the automotive and radio industries and also a noted philanthropist. His Atwater Kent Manufacturing Works (established 1902) introduced the single-spark ignition system (1905) that soon became standard equipment on automobiles. In the 1920s he was a leading manufacturer of radio equipment, producing more than 6,000 receivers a day. "The Atwater Kent Hour" (1925) was the first network radio program to bring classical music to the public.

KENT, ROCKWELL (1882–1971), U.S. painter and illustrator. In a career that spanned six decades, Kent sought adventure in his life (he sailed alone around Cape Horn and traveled in Newfoundland, Alaska, and Greenland) and in his art. He painted vivid depictions of people and animals in dramatic natural settings. Influenced by Winslow Homer, his early works like *The Road Roller* (1909) were somber, raw landscapes and seascapes. His mature works, such as *Summer Night* (c. 1942), were symbolic rather than realistic treatments of nature, executed with a limited palette in a style characterized by the use of silhouette and parallelism. Kent's wood engravings were among his best-known works. He illustrated many volumes, including the classics and his own travel accounts. A supporter of leftist causes from the 1920s, Kent was awarded a Lenin Peace Prize (1967) by the Soviet Union. ■ See his autobiographical *This Is My Own* (1940) and *It's Me, O Lord* (1955); David Traxel, *An American Saga* (1980); and Fridolf Johnson, ed., *Rockwell Kent: An Anthology of His Works* (1982).

KENYATTA, JOMO (Johnstone Kamau Ngengi; 1891?–1978), president of Kenya. Kenyatta was a member of the Kikuyu tribe; as secretary of the nationalist Kikuyu Central Association (1928), he used issues of land shortage and restrictions on circumcision rites to politicize many Kikuyu. Living in London (1931–46), he studied anthropology with Bronislaw Malinowski, published his classic account of Kikuyu society, *Facing Mount Kenya* (1938), and avoided the bitter factional struggles of the 1930s. Upon returning to Kenya (1946) he became president of the Kenyan African Union, the most effective nationalist organization. Although imprisoned during and after the Mau-Mau Emergency of the 1950s (1952–61), he continued to be looked upon as the national leader. After his release, he led his party, the Kenya African National Union (KANU), to victory in the 1963 preindependence elections. He became prime minister in 1963, the first president of the new republic of Kenya in 1964, and led the country until his death in 1978. He established close ties with the West and maintained a capitalist economic system. His dedication and personal stature helped surmount tribal rivalry and create a sense of Kenyan nationalism. ■ See his *Suffering Without Bitterness: The Founding of the Kenya Nation* (1968) and biography by Jeremy Murray-Brown (2nd ed. 1979).

KENYON, DOROTHY (1888–1972), U.S. social reformer. The daughter of a lawyer, Kenyon earned a law degree (1917) at New York University and went into partnership during the 1930s with another woman attorney. She served as a New York City municipal court judge (1939–40), a member of the League of Nations and United Nations commissions on the status of women, and a longtime leader of the American Civil Liberties Union. She was also an early advocate of consumer cooperatives and a proponent of liberalized abortion laws and helped create free legal services for the poor.

KENYON, DAME KATHLEEN MARY (1906–1978), British archaeologist. Kenyon participated in major excavations in Southern Rhodesia, now Zimbabwe (1929); England (1930–35); and North Africa (1948–49; 1951) and was a lecturer in Palestinian archaeology at the University of London's Institute of Archaeology (1948–62). Her most important work was the excavation of the site of the ancient city of Jericho in Jordan (1952–58), which she was able to date back to 7000 B.C. She directed the British School of Archaeology in Jerusalem (1952–66) and wrote *Digging Up Jericho* (1957), *Archaeology in the Holy Land* (1960), *Excavations at Jericho* (2 vols., 1960–65), and *Digging Up Jerusalem* (1974).

KERENSKY, ALEKSANDR FEODOROVICH (1881–1970), Russian political leader. Like bolshevik leader V. I. Lenin, Kerensky was born in Simbirsk; his father was Lenin's schoolteacher. Kerensky trained in law at St. Petersburg University and was the defense attorney in several celebrated political trials. A moderate democratic socialist, he served in the Duma (1912–17) and became vice chairman of the Petrograd (St. Petersburg) Soviet at the outbreak of the 1917 revolution. His vigorous orations gained him great popularity and he became minister of justice and then minister of war in the provisional government. When he assumed the premiership in July 1917, he advocated continuing World War I against Germany instead of responding to the popular call for immediate peace and land reform. His position deteriorated quickly, and the bolsheviks overthrew his government in the October revolution. After several months of unsuccessful efforts to regain power, Kerensky left for France and emigrated to Australia in 1940. He spent the last 25 years of his life in the United States and taught at Stanford University (from 1956). His books in English include *The Prelude to Bolshevism* (1972) and *The Catastrophe: Kerensky's Own Story of the Russian Revolution* (1927). ■ See also his memoirs, *Russia and History's Turning Point* (1965), and biography by Richard Abraham (1987).

KERN, JEROME DAVID (1885–1945), U.S. composer. The son of a New York businessman, Kern studied music in New York and Heidelberg before working in Tin Pan Alley (1904). Between 1915 and 1918 he collaborated with P. G. Wodehouse on a series of intimate and integrated comedies, including *Oh Boy!* (1917) and *Oh, Lady! Lady!* (1918), that helped to reshape the Broadway musical theater. He subsequently wrote dozens of hit musicals including *Sally* (1920), *Sunny* (1925), *Show Boat* (1927), *Music in the Air* (1932), and *Roberta* (1933). His Hollywood movies included *Swing Time* (1936), *You Were Never Lovelier* (1942), and *Cover Girl* (1944). His songs, written with Otto Harbach, included "Make Believe," "Ol' Man River," "Smoke Gets in Your Eyes," "All the Things You Are," "The Way You Look Tonight," and "The Song Is You." He also collaborated with such lyricists as Dorothy Fields, Ira Gershwin, Oscar Hammerstein II, and Johnny Mercer. ■ See biography by Gerald Bordman (1980).

KERNER, OTTO (1908–1976), U.S. political leader. Often said to have been "born with a golden ballot in his mouth," Kerner, the son of a leader of Chicago's Czech community, was socially prominent, highly educated, and an apparently incorruptible politician. A member of Chicago's Cook County Democratic organization, noted for its frequently questionable political tactics, Kerner served as a U.S. attorney (1947–54), judge (1954–60), and governor of Illinois (1960–68). He was named chairman of Pres. Lyndon Johnson's National Advisory Committee on Civil Disorders; the committee's powerful "Kerner Report" declared that white racism was a major cause of the 1967 urban riots and warned that the United States was becoming a dual society based on race. After he was appointed to the U.S. Court of Appeals (1968), Kerner saw his world collapse when he was convicted (1973) of corruption, income-tax evasion, and lying to a grand jury regarding improprieties committed while he was governor. He was the first sitting judge on the nation's second highest court to be convicted of a serious crime.

KEROUAC, JACK (Jean Louis Lebris de Kerouac; 1922–1969), U.S. novelist. While studying at Columbia University in the 1940s, Kerouac met poet Allen Ginsberg and fiction writer William Burroughs; the three young men became known in the 1950s as voices of the "beat" generation. After serving in the U.S. Navy and the merchant marine, Kerouac published his first novel, *The Town and the City* (1950), an account of his family's decline. He chronicled his frenetic travels around the United States in *On the Road* (1957), which had enormous appeal for his generation and made Kerouac a cult hero. Its energetic prose, typed on long sheets of art paper, recounted experiences with sex, drinking, and drugs, chronicling and popularizing youthful rebellion against convention. *The Dharma Bums* (1958) and *Satori in Paris* (1966) sparked interest in Zen Buddhism. His other works included *Subterraneans* (1958), *Dr. Sax* (1959), *Mexico City Blues* (1959), *Book of Dreams* (1961), *Scattered Poems* (1971), and *Visions of Cody* (1973). ■ See Barry Gifford and Lawrence Lee, *Jack's Book* (1978); Dennis McNally, *Desolate Angel* (1979); Joyce Johnson, *Minor Characters* (1983); Gerald Nicosia, *Memory Babe* (1983); biographies by Ann Charters (1994) and Barry Miles (1998); and Ellis Amburn, *Subterranean Kerouac* (1998).

KERR, CLARK (1911–   ), U.S. educator. A leading labor economist and arbitrator, Kerr earned his Ph.D. from the University of California (1939), taught there (from 1945), and in 1958 became president of the expanding statewide California system, which he called "multiversity." Fired by Gov. Ronald Reagan in 1967 for tolerating free political activity on campus, he became director of the Carnegie Commission on Higher Education (1967–73) and the Carnegie Council on Policy in Higher Education (1974–79). Kerr wrote *The Uses of the University* (1963), *Education and National Development* (1979), and other works on education and economics including *The Great Transformation in Higher Education, 1960–1980* (1991).

KERST, DONALD WILLIAM (1911–1993), U.S. physicist. While a professor at the University of Illinois (1938–43), Kerst invented the betatron (1939), a machine that, when perfected, increased the speed of electrons to the point where they released mesons (subatomic particles) upon impact with atomic nuclei. In addition to playing an important role in the World War II atomic bomb project at Los Alamos, the betatron proved useful in the treatment of cancer. Kerst supervised the construction of a 300-million-volt betatron (1950), which enabled him to conduct fundamental nuclear research into the meson. After conducting research for the general atomic division of General Dynamics Corp. (1957–62), Kerst taught at the University of Wisconsin (1962–80).

KERTÉSZ, ANDRÉ (1894–1985), Hungarian-born U.S. photographer. Kertész began taking photographs on glass plates in 1912, moved to Paris in 1925, and soon adopted the new miniature camera. One of the greatest 35mm imagists, he specialized in old-world pictures of lovers, Gypsies, and peasants. His unpretentious, witty, and compassionate work was published throughout Europe and influenced many photographers, including Robert Capa, Brassaï, and Henri Cartier-Bresson. When Kertész moved to the United States in 1936, his style was considered too European for slick American magazine and advertising photography. He did conventional commercial photography during the 1940s and 1950s, but retrospective exhibitions held in New York, Paris, and Venice in 1963 once again earned him critical recognition. ■ See his photos in *Sixty Years of Photography* (1972), *J'aime Paris* (1974), and *André Kertész: The Manchester Collection* (1984). See also study by Sandra S. Phillips and David Travis (1985).

KESSELRING, ALBERT (1885–1960), German field marshal. An army veteran of the aerial dogfights of World War I, Kesselring transferred to the new Luftwaffe in 1933. Early in World War II he coordinated the air attacks on Poland and France, but his tactics failed in the Battle of Britain. Appointed supreme commander in Italy in 1943, he managed to forestall the Allies for a year but finally surrendered Germany's southern army in 1945. Kesselring was convicted of war crimes (1947) but released in 1952 because of ill health, which did not, however, prevent his activity in veterans' organizations. ■ See his memoirs, *A Soldier's Record* (Eng. trans. 1954), and study by Kenneth Macksey (1978).

KESSLER, COUNT HARRY (Harry Klemens Ulrich, Graf von Kessler; 1868–1937), German writer, diplomat, art patron, and publisher. Born in Paris, Kessler was the son of a German banker but was rumored to be the illegitimate son of Kaiser Wilhelm. He was a major figure in the artistic and intellectual life of Germany between the two world wars and was a prominent, but rare, aristocratic supporter of the Weimar Republic. He was an art patron, art museum director (Weimar), and founder (1913) of the Cranach Press, which produced high-quality limited editions of literary classics. He was Germany's first ambassador to Poland after World War I, a founder of the Democratic party, and president of the German Peace Society (1918–21). He wrote a well-known biography of his friend, the social theorist and statesman Walter Rathenau (1928; Eng. trans. 1930), and a contemporary analysis of international affairs, *Germany and Europe* (1923), as well as numerous other works on art and politics. He left Germany after Nazi leader Adolf Hitler came to power. His diaries, *In the Twenties* (1961; Eng. trans. 1971), present an unsurpassed insider's account of life in Germany during the Weimar period.

KETTERING, CHARLES FRANKLIN (1876–1958), U.S. engineer and inventor. Kettering graduated from Ohio State University with a degree in electrical engineering (1904) and worked for the National Cash Register Company (1904–09), where he developed the first electrically operated cash register. In 1909 he cofounded the Dayton Engineering Laboratories Company (Delco), where, before World War I, he invented the first battery-powered electric ignition system and the first electric starting and lighting systems for automobiles. In 1916 Delco was purchased by United Motors (later General Motors) and Kettering became a vice president of GM and member of its board of directors. As head of the GM Research Laboratories (1919–47) he helped develop high-octane, knock-free gasoline, quick-drying automobile paint, safety glass, the refrigerant Freon, and the efficient two-cycle diesel engine (for trains). After his official retirement, he developed (1951) the high-compression automobile engine. With GM President Alfred P. Sloan, Jr., he founded the Sloan-Kettering Institute for Cancer Research in New York City (1945). ■ See Thomas A. Boyd, *Professional Amateur* (1957; reprinted 1972), and Stuart W. Leslie, *Boss Kettering* (1983).

KEYNES, JOHN MAYNARD KEYNES, 1st BARON (1883–1946), British economist. The son of a Cambridge professor, Keynes studied there with Alfred Marshall and Arthur Pigou and was subsequently a fellow of King's College, his alma mater (1909–46). He was a treasury official (1915–19) and wrote two books, *The Economic Consequences of the Peace* (1919) and *A Revision of the Treaty* (1922), that attacked the harsh economic terms imposed on Germany in the Versailles treaty ending World War I. He was a noted patron of the arts and a member of the Bloomsbury group during the 1920s. His best known work, *The General Theory of Employment, Interest and Money* (1936), revolutionized the field of economics by showing that only an increase in aggregate demand, stimulated by government spending (via public works projects and organized investing), could solve the problems of stagnation and unemployment in capitalist economies. His ideas were widely accepted by both economic theorists and government leaders and the "Keynesian revolution" had a worldwide effect. As leader of the British delegation at the Bretton Woods Conference (1944) he played a major role in the creation of the post–World War II international monetary system. He was raised to the peerage in 1942. ■ See biographies by Roy Harrod (1952), D. E. Moggridge (1976 and 1992), Charles H. Hession (1984), Robert Skidelsky (1983), and David Felix (1999).

KEYSERLING, LEON (1908–   ), U.S. economist. A graduate of Columbia University and Harvard Law School (LL.B., 1931), Keyserling became a legislative assistant to Sen. Robert F. Wagner of New York (1933). As a consultant to numerous Senate committees, he was responsible for drafting important pieces of legislation during the New Deal era of Pres. Franklin D. Roosevelt (1933–45). During Pres. Harry Truman's administration (1949–53) he chaired the President's Council of Economic Advisers. He subsequently focused mainly on the fields of employment and production and was a primary author of the Humphrey-Hawkins Full Employment Act of 1978. His books included *The Federal Budget and the General Welfare* (1959) and *The Role of Wages in a Great Society* (1966).

KHACHATURIAN, ARAM ILICH (1903–1978), Soviet-Armenian composer. The son of an Armenian bookbinder in Tiflis, Khachaturian went to Moscow to study the cello at age 19 but became interested in composition. In 1934 he graduated from the Moscow Conservatory and gained international recognition with the publication of his Symphony No. 1, followed by a piano concerto (1936) and violin concerto (1940), both of which were popular abroad. For the 25th anniversary of the Russian Revolution in 1942, Khachaturian presented his ballet *Gayne,* which included the well-known "Sabre Dance," and his Symphony No. 2. His lively, brilliantly orchestrated music showed the influence of Armenian and other folk themes. Khachaturian also composed some film scores and a series of patriotic songs for the Red army.

KHAMA, SIR SERETSE (1921–1980), president of Botswana. Hereditary chief of the largest tribe in Bechuanaland (later Botswana), Khama studied law at Oxford, married an Englishwoman (1948), and was required by the British colonial rulers to renounce his hereditary rights before being allowed to return home in 1956. Instead of a tribal chieftain he became a nationalist leader and served as the first president of independent Botswana (1966–80). A moderate who believed in multiracialism and democracy, Khama was active in negotiations leading to the establishment of majority black rule in neighboring Zimbabwe.

KHAN, NUSRAT FATEH ALI (1948–1997), Pakistani singer. Born into a family who had sung quawwali, mystical Sufi devotional songs, for six centuries, Khan gave his first public singing performance at his father's funeral (1964). He became the leader of the family ensemble in 1971 and soon was recognized as the greatest quawwali virtuoso of his generation. Accompanied by a tabla, harmonium, and backing vocals, he enthralled audiences with his highly expressive voice and mesmerizing improvisations and became a superstar throughout the Islamic world. After appearing in a world music festival in England (1985), he became a popular performer in Europe and the United States, singing secular songs and modifying his style to appeal to young audiences. He collaborated with several rock singers and instrumentalists and appeared on MTV, allowed his music to be modified for dance clubs, and recorded the sound tracks for several Hollywood films, including *The Last Temptation of Christ* (1988) and *Dead Man Walking* (1996).

KHIEU SAMPHAN (1931–   ), Cambodian (Kampuchean) political leader. The son of a civil servant in the French colonial administration, Khieu studied economics at the University of Paris (Ph.D. 1959) and headed the communist-dominated Union of Cambodian Students. Elected to parliament in 1960, he served as a state secretary in the commerce ministry in Prince Sihanouk's government until he joined the communist Khmer Rouge insurgents (1967). After Sihanouk's overthrow by U.S.-backed Gen. Lan Nol, Sihanouk allied himself with the Communists, and Khieu served as deputy premier of the Communist government-in-exile (1970–75). After the Khmer Rouge forces seized power (1975), Khieu served as president of the newly proclaimed republic (1976–79). The new government attempted to transform society rapidly and established a reign of terror that allegedly resulted in the deaths of more than 2 million citizens. Following the 1979 Vietnamese invasion that overthrew his government, Khieu headed the Khmer Rouge forces fighting a guerrilla war against the Vietnamese and served as vice president of a coalition government-in-exile led by Prince Sihanouk (1982–91). He returned to Cambodia (1991) and continued to fight the government as head of the Cambodian National Unity party, but his forces dwindled and he surrendered to the government (Dec. 1998) after negotiating a deal for amnesty.

KHOMEINI, RUHOLLAH (Ruhollah Hendi; 1901?–1989), Iranian religious and political leader. A Shiite Islamic scholar, Khomeini was named "ayatollah" (religious leader) by public acclamation during the 1950s despite conflicts with religious and political authorities. Exiled (1964) for denouncing the reform policies of the shah, he became a focus of opposition during 16 years in Iraq (1964–78) and France (1978–79). He coordinated the antishah movement from his home in France and advocated the establishment of an Islamic republic. After a series of strikes and riots the shah fled (1979) and Khomeini returned in triumph to Teheran as his unofficial successor. A referendum (1979) created an Islamic republic and Khomeini was recognized as the supreme religious authority and ultimate source of power in the country. Fiercely autocratic, anticommunist, anti-Zionist, and puritanical, he set out to eradicate Western (particularly American) political and cultural influences as well as corruption. Thousands of opponents were executed, moderate and left-wing political parties were banned, and he supported Islamic fundamentalist movements throughout the Middle East. Domestic turmoil was compounded by an Iraqi invasion (1980) which provoked an inconclusive war that dragged on for more than eight years. ■ See Khomeini's speeches and writings in *Islam and Revolution* (Eng. trans. 1981); Shaul Bakhash, *The Reign of the Ayatollahs* (1984); Farhang Rajaee, *Islamic Values and World View* (1983); biographies by Mir Ali Asghar Montazam (1994) and Baqer Moin (1999); and Ervand Abrahamian, *Khomeinism* (1993).

KHORANA, HAR GOBIND (1922–   ), Indian-born U.S. biochemist. Khorana was educated at Punjab University and Liverpool University (Ph.D. 1948). As head of the organic chemistry section of the British Columbia Research Council in Vancouver, Canada (1952–60), he synthesized several nucleotide coenzymes, including coenzyme A. In the process, he confirmed Marshall Nirenberg's findings that four basic substances make up genetic material, and that a new cell's chemical composition and function hinge on the arrangement of these basic substances in large molecules of DNA (deoxyribonucleic acid). At the University of Wisconsin (1960–70), Khorana shed further light on the genetic code by synthesizing complex polynucleotides that had a known base sequence. Khorana shared the 1968 Nobel Prize in Physiology or Medicine with Nirenberg and Robert Holley. At MIT (1970–   ), Khorana focused on the complete synthesis of genes.

KHRUSHCHEV, NIKITA SERGEYEVICH (1894–1971), Soviet political leader. The son of a miner, Khrushchev grew up in the Ukraine. He joined the Communist party in 1918, served in the Red army during the civil war (1918–20), and then worked as a mining technician while finishing high school. After taking on full-time political responsibilities (1931), he rose rapidly to prominence, becoming head of the Moscow party apparatus (1935) and gaining full membership on the Politburo. He headed the Ukrainian party organization (1938–47) and organized post–World War II reconstruction of the region. Dictator Joseph Stalin named him to revitalize Soviet agriculture (1949) and within six months of Stalin's death (1953) Khrushchev emerged as the party's first secretary. His famous secret speech at the twentieth party congress (1956) denounced Stalin's abuses and cult of personality. He purged his rivals on the Politburo (1957) and was named premier in 1958. Khrushchev conducted a foreign policy of peaceful coexistence with the West and traveled extensively, but he alternated conciliatory

gestures with bald threats. His fall from power (1964) was laid to his mishandling of the 1962 Cuban missile crisis, his attempt at economic decentralization, and the deterioration of Sino-Soviet relations, as well as to disapproval of his sometimes crude style of self-expression. Publication in the West of his candid memoirs, *Khrushchev Remembers* (2 vols., 1970–74), stirred controversy; Western experts generally judged them authentic. ■ See biography by Edward Crankshaw (1966) and studies by Roy and Zhores Medvedev (Eng. trans. 1976); William J. Thompson (1995); and his son, Sergei Khrushchev, *Khrushchev on Khrushchev* (Eng. trans. 1990).

KIDDER, ALFRED VINCENT (1885–1963), U.S. archaeologist. The foremost American archaeologist of his time, Kidder developed the first pottery typology of the American Southwest in his Harvard Ph.D. thesis (1914). He directed excavations in Pecos, New Mexico, for the Phillips Academy in Andover, Massachusetts (1915–29), the first systematic stratigraphic field study in American archaeology. At the Carnegie Institution (1927–50) he organized an interdisciplinary program on the cultural history of the Maya. Kidder's *Introduction to the Study of Southwestern Archaeology* (1924), the pioneering and standard work in the field, traces the development from basketweaving to Pueblo culture. ■ See biography by Richard B. Woodbury (1973).

KIKUCHI, KAN (1888–1948), Japanese playwright, journalist, novelist, and publisher. He was also known as Hiroshi Kikuchi. A prolific and popular author, Kikuchi was one of Japan's leading literary figures of the 1920s. He was best known for his straightforward, realistic, and moralistic plays, such as *The Madman on the Roof* (1916; Eng. trans. 1956), *The Father Returns* (1917; Eng. trans. 1925), and *On the Conduct of Lord Tadanao* (1918; Eng. trans. 1961). Kikuchi was also known for encouraging many young writers (notably Yasunari Kawabata) and for publishing their works in the influential journal *Bungei Shunju* ("The Literary Review"), which he founded in 1923. He also established (1935) the Akutagawa Prize and the Naoki Prize, Japan's most prestigious literary awards.

KILBY, JACK (1923–   ), U.S. electrical engineer. The son of an electrical engineer, Kilby studied electrical engineering at the University of Illinois (B.S. 1947) and the University of Wisconsin (M.S. 1950). After working with transistors at the Centralab Division of Globe-Union, Inc. (1947–58), he switched to Texas Instruments, Inc., an innovative Dallas firm (1958–70). Within a short time, Kilby built the first monolithic integrated circuit, a transistor connected with resistors and capacitors on a single silicon semiconductor chip (1959). (Robert N. Noyce, working independently, is also recognized as an inventor of the integrated circuit.) He proved the practicality of his invention by developing a computing system and electronic pocket calculator. His pioneering work laid the groundwork for the development of microelectronics. After 1970 he worked as an independent inventor and was a professor at Texas A & M University (1977–85). He shared the 2000 Nobel Prize in Physics with Herbert Kroemer and Zhores I. Alferov. ■ See T. R. Reid, *The Chip* (1985).

KILGALLEN, DOROTHY MAE (1913–1965), U.S. journalist and radio and television personality. A journalist's daughter, Kilgallen started out as a cub reporter for the *New York Evening Journal.* In 1936, she and two other reporters raced around the world on commercial airliners. Kilgallen did not win, but her account of the race catapulted her into public view. In 1938 she launched her influential syndicated gossip column, "The Voice of Broadway," and she later was heard, with her husband Richard Kollmar, on the radio show, "Breakfast with Dorothy and Dick" (1945–63). Her appearances as a panelist on the TV show "What's My Line?" (1950–65) made her name a household word. After she covered the trial of Jack Ruby, who killed the alleged assassin of Pres. John F. Kennedy, Kilgallen sparked controversy by publishing Ruby's Warren Commission testimony a month before it was released to the public. Her death, which occurred shortly thereafter, was caused by a combination of barbiturates and alcohol and was called accidental. The biography by Lee Israel (1979) alleges that Kilgallen was murdered because she was unearthing information about Kennedy's assassination; this has not been substantiated. ■ See her selected newspaper pieces in *Girl Around the World* (1936) and *Murder One* (1967).

KILLY, JEAN CLAUDE (1943–), French skier. A national hero during the 1960s, Killy was one of the greatest skiers in the history of the sport. Winner of the French championship in all Alpine events (1965), the European championship (1966), the world championship (1967), and the first World Cup for Men (1967; by winning every downhill race he entered), Killy achieved his greatest glory at the 1968 Winter Olympic Games at Grenoble when he became only the second man in history to win gold medals in each of the Alpine events—downhill, slalom, and giant slalom. (Toni Sailer of Austria won the events in the 1956 Olympics.) He retired from amateur skiing in 1968. He became a business executive and was a member of the International Olympic Committee (1995–). ■ See his autobiography, *Comeback* (1974; with Al Greenberg).

KILPATRICK, WILLIAM HEARD (1871–1965), U.S. educator. After provoking controversy in his native Georgia for his unorthodox teaching methods, Kilpatrick studied at Columbia University (Ph.D. 1912) and became a disciple of philosopher John Dewey. He applied many of Dewey's theories to the classroom, developed the "project method" of teaching and the "purposeful activities program" for young students, and was often called "the father of progressive education" in the United States. He taught philosophy of education at Columbia Teachers College (1909–38) and wrote many books, including *Education and the Social Crisis* (1932) and *Philosophy of Education* (1951). ■ See biography by Samuel Tennenbaum (1951).

KIM DAE-JUNG (1925–), South Korean political leader. Born into a Roman Catholic farming family in the Cholla region of Korea, one of the poorest areas of the country, Kim headed a trading company and daily newspaper before entering politics. He was elected to the National Assembly, (1960), became widely known as a prodemocracy advocate and a supporter of the poor, and narrowly lost the 1971 presidential election (to Park Chung Hee), which many believed was rigged against his candidacy. During the years of martial law and military dictatorship (1972–87), Kim was branded by the military leaders as a radical and communist sympathizer, was kidnapped by the Korean CIA (1973), and served nearly six years in prison. A death sentence on charges of sedition (1980) was reduced to life imprisonment, but he was allowed to go into exile in the United States (1982–85). After returning to Korea, he lost the presidential elections of 1987 and 1992 but was elected president in 1997, becoming the first opposition candidate ever chosen as leader of South Korea. As president (1998–) he urged the Western powers to end economic sanctions against North Korea in order to reduce tensions and improve relations between the north and south. He travelled to North Korea (June 2000) to meet with North Korean leader Kim Jong Il. It was the first meeting between leaders of the two countries. He was awarded the 2000 Nobel Peace Prize. His books in English include *Mass-Participatory Economy* (1985; rev. ed. 1996), *Building Peace and Democracy* (1987), *Prison Writings* (1987), *A New Beginning* (1996), and *Kim Dae-Jung's "Three-Stage" Approach to Unification* (1997).

KIM IL SUNG (Sung Chu; 1912–1994), Korean political leader. A member of a middle-class, revolutionary family that fled to Manchuria (1925) to escape Japanese rule, Kim joined the Korean Communist party (1931) and fought the Japanese as a guerrilla leader along the Sino-Korean frontier. During World War II he received military and political training in the Soviet Union (1941), joined the Red army, and, with it, entered Pyongyang in 1945. Under Soviet occupation he established a communist provisional government (1946–48) and became premier when the Democratic People's Republic of Korea was established in the northern half of Korea (1948). After the Korean War (1950–53), he crushed his domestic opponents and became absolute ruler, buttressing his power with a personality cult rarely matched in history. Under Kim's rule, North Korean society became highly regimented and militarized. The economy was industrialized and the material standard of living rose sharply. Kim's policy of reunification of Korea by force was moderated in the 1970s, but he continued his hostility toward the

U.S. government. He was designated president and head of state in 1972, and his son, Kim Jong Il (1942–　), was officially confirmed as his political heir in 1984 and he became general secretary of the Communist party in 1997. ■ See biography by Baik Bong (3 vols., 1969–70).

KIMMEL, HUSBAND EDWARD (1882–1968), U.S. naval officer. A 1904 graduate of the U.S. Naval Academy, Kimmel became a rear admiral in 1937 and was appointed commander of the Pacific Fleet in Feb. 1941. He was at Pearl Harbor with the fleet when the Japanese attacked on Dec. 7, 1941, and was relieved of his command ten days later. A presidential board of inquiry (1942) charged him with "dereliction of duty," and he was retired. A 1946 congressional committee, however, after hearing that he had received no information regarding the possibility of such an attack, charged him only with "errors in judgment." ■ See Edward L. Beach, *Scapegoats* (1995).

KING, B. B. (Riley B. King; 1925–　), U.S. blues singer and guitarist. Born into a black sharecropping family in the Mississippi delta, King sang in a church choir in his youth. He began to sing professionally after World War II and worked as a disc jockey on WDIA in Memphis during the late 1940s. Known as the "Blues Boy from Beale Street," his nickname was soon shortened to "B.B." After making his first record (1950), he toured the country for almost two decades, performing in black bars and dance halls and remaining far out of the popular music mainstream. However, his style was widely copied by white rock guitarists, and his career changed dramatically when he was introduced by them to white rock audiences during the late 1960s. His performances gave the blues a respectability and visibility it had never had before, and he was hailed as the greatest blues musician of his time. He toured the world, recorded numerous best-selling albums, and remained popular through the 1990s. ■ See his autobiography, *Blues All Around Me* (1996; with David Ritz); Charles Sawyer, *The Arrival of B. B. King* (1980); and Sebastian Danchin, *Blues Boy* (1998).

KING, BILLIE JEAN (Billie Jean Moffitt; 1943–　), U.S. tennis player. Top ranked for more than 20 years, King won a record 20 Wimbledon championships (6 singles; 10 doubles; 4 mixed doubles) from 1961 to 1979 and was the major figure in the growth of women's professional tennis. King championed the cause of equal prize money for women players. She helped organize the Women's Tennis Association, the World Team Tennis League, and the first magazine dealing with women's sports. Shrewd and strong, she overpowered most of her female opponents and defeated former champion Bobby Riggs in a televised winner-take-all $100,000 "battle of the sexes" match before 30,000 fans in the Houston Astrodome (1973). Ranked number one in the United States seven times, she won four U.S. singles championships (1967; 1971–72; 1974), two Australian titles (1968,

1971), and a French championship (1972). ■ See her autobiography, *Billie Jean* (1982).

KING, ERNEST JOSEPH (1878–1956), U.S. admiral. A graduate of the U. S. Naval Academy (1901), King became knowledgeable in the new areas of naval aviation and submarine operations during World War I and the interwar period. As commander in chief of the U.S. fleet after the attack on Pearl Harbor, as well as chief of naval operations (1942–45), he shifted the emphasis of naval strategy from the battleship to the aircraft carrier. He was also Pres. Franklin D. Roosevelt's naval adviser at the Casablanca, Teheran, Cairo, and Yalta wartime Allied conferences. ■ See his memoirs, *Fleet Admiral King* (1952), and Thomas Buell, *Master of Sea Power* (1980).

KING, FRANK O. (1883–1969), U.S. cartoonist. Except for a year at the Chicago Academy of Fine Arts, King worked on newspapers from age 19; he attracted little attention until his *Bobby Make-Believe* appeared in the *Chicago Tribune* (1915). While continuing this popular strip, King introduced (1918) a new feature that drew an immense following for half a century: *Gasoline Alley*. Featuring Walt, his adopted son Skeezix, and their friends, the strip portrayed typical Americans living and growing day by day. Its appeal derived largely from its focus on the familiar. The circulation of *Gasoline Alley* increased steadily, and the prospering King spent more and more time pursuing his interests in sculpting, horticulture, and map collecting.

KING, MARTIN LUTHER, JR. (1929–1968), U.S. civil-rights leader. Ordained a Baptist minister in 1947, King studied theology at Crozer Theological Seminary in Chester, Pennsylvania (B.D. 1951), and Boston University (Ph.D. 1955). As a pastor of a black church in Montgomery, Alabama (1955), he led a successful year-long bus boycott protesting racial segregation on public transport and helped found the Southern Christian Leadership Conference (SCLC; 1957), which organized civil-rights activities throughout the South. An advocate of Mahatma Gandhi's philosophy of nonviolence, he led marches, demonstrations, and campaigns of civil disobedience in his quest for racial equality. He was frequently arrested, spied on, and harassed by the FBI. A brilliant orator, he electrified a crowd of 250,000 demonstrators during a march on Washington (1963) with his "I Have a Dream" speech. In 1964 he was awarded the Nobel Peace Prize. During the mid-1960s he campaigned against de facto segregation in the North and the continuation of poverty in America, and he became a critic of the Vietnam War. He was shot to death by James Earl Ray in Memphis, Tenn. After his death, his widow, Coretta Scott King (1927–　), carried on his work through the Martin Luther King, Jr., Center for Social Change in Atlanta. His books included *Stride Toward Freedom* (1958) and *Where Do We Go From Here* (1967). His shorter writings appeared in James M. Washington, ed., *A Testament of Hope* (1986). ■ See biography by David L. Lewis (2nd ed. 1978); Coretta Scott King's *My Life With Martin Luther King* (1969); Stephen B. Oates, *Let the Trumpet Sound* (1984); David J. Garrow, *The FBI and Martin Luther King, Jr.* (1981) and *Bearing the Cross* (1986); and Clayborne Carson, ed., *The Autobiography* (1998), a compilation of autobiographical writings, letters, and statements.

KING, STEPHEN (1947–), U.S. writer. A graduate of the University of Maine (B.Sc. 1970), King worked as a laborer and high school English teacher (1971–73) before becoming a full-time writer after the success of his horror novel *Carrie* (1974; film 1976). A prolific author, he produced dozens of best-selling novels, utilizing horror, fantasy, and science fiction to symbolically depict the fears and nightmares of late 20th-century America. He was one of the world's best-selling authors with sales of over 160 million copies through 1997. His best-known works included *The Shining* (1977; film 1980), *Firestarter* (1980; film 1984), *Misery* (1987; film 1990), *Insomnia* (1994), *Bag of Bones* (1998), and *Hearts in Atlantis* (1999). King also wrote numerous short stories and novellas, including those filmed as *The Shawshank Redemption* (1994) and *Apt Pupil* (1998). He was the first major author to self-publish a novel (*The Plant*) on the Internet (2000). His *On Writing* (2000) was autobiographical. ■ See studies by Jonathan P. Davis (1994) and Amy and Marjorie Keyishian (1995).

KING, WILLIAM LYON MACKENZIE (1874–1950), Canadian political leader. The grandson and namesake of a famous Canadian rebel, King was born in Ontario and educated at Harvard (Ph.D. 1909). A Liberal, he served as Canada's first minister of labor (1909–11) and was prime minister longer than anyone else (1921–26; 1926–30; 1935–1948). He stayed in power because of his determined methods and political astuteness. His greatest achievement was guiding Canada through World War II despite its being ethnically split on the issue of French opposition to and English approval of conscription. King strengthened ties with the United States while establishing Canadian sovereignty apart from Britain. ■ See Bruce Hutchinson, *The Incredible Canadian* (1952); Joy Esberey, *Knight of the Holy Spirit* (1980); and biography by R. M. Dawson and H. Blair Neatby (3 vols., 1958–77).

KINGSLEY, ELIZABETH (Hannah Elizabeth Seelman; 1871–1957), U.S. word-puzzle expert. Kingsley spent her early years working word puzzles in Brooklyn, New York, and contributed scrambled word games to *St. Nicholas* magazine. She attended Wellesley College (B.A. 1898) and New York University (M.A. 1905), and taught English at a Brooklyn high school (1900–14). Kingsley moved with her husband to Boston, returning to Brooklyn after his death (1926). There she took clerical jobs and concocted a new type of puzzle that combined crossword-type clues with quotations from monuments of U.S. and British literature. The Kingsley Double-Crostic was adopted by the *Saturday Review of Literature* in 1934 and has been a standard feature there, in the *New York Times* magazine, and in other periodicals ever since. She retired in 1951, turning over her puzzle-making duties to Doris Nash Wortman.

KINGSTON, MAXINE HONG (Maxine Hong; 1940–), U.S. writer. Born into an immigrant Chinese family in Stockton, California, Kingston grew up speaking a dialect of Cantonese and listening to "talk stories" concerning both Chinese legends and family history. She studied English literature at the University of California, Berkeley (B.A. 1962), and taught English at several high schools and colleges in California and Hawaii (1966–77). Her highly praised best-selling volumes, *Woman Warrior: Memoirs of a Girlhood among Ghosts* (1976; National Book Critics Circle Award) and *China Men* (1980; American Book Award), creatively blended autobiography and family history with myth and folklore. They told of struggles against prejudice and exploitation and they helped to introduce the experience of Chinese Americans into American literature and into mainstream American culture. Her best-selling novel, *Tripmaster Monkey: His Fake Book* (1989), recorded the adventures of a 1960s Chinese-American beatnik and his attempt to write a play celebrating the Chinese-American experience.

KINKAID, THOMAS CASSIN (1888–1972), U.S. admiral. The son of an admiral, Kinkaid served as a naval attaché during World War I and was promoted to rear admiral a month before the Japanese attacked Pearl Harbor on Dec. 7, 1941. Noted for his coolness under pressure, Kinkaid commanded the aircraft carrier *Enterprise* in the battles of Midway, the Coral Sea, Guadalcanal, and the Solomon Islands. Called by Gen. Douglas MacArthur "one of the great naval leaders of our day," he led the Seventh Fleet in plans for the invasion of the Philippines (1944) and accepted the Japanese surrender in Korea (1945).

KINNELL, GALWAY (1927–), U.S. poet. A graduate of Princeton (B.A. 1948), Kinnell taught at several universities in the United States, France, and Iran. His early free verse, lyric poems in *What a Kingdom It Was* (1960), influenced by Walt Whitman, represented a search for the sacred in the ordinary lives of poor people living in New York City. Many of his later poems in *Flower Herding on Mount Monadnock* (1964), *Body Rags* (1968), *The Book of Nightmares* (1971), *Mortal Acts, Mortal Words* (1980), and *The Long Approach* (1986) were haunted by suffering, alienation, and death, while others expressed gratitude for the pleasures in life. Kinnell was also a noted translator of French poetry and wrote the novel *Black Night* (1966). His collection, *Selected Poems* (1982), won the 1983 Pulitzer Prize in poetry. His later collections included *When One Has Lived a Long Time Alone* (1990) and *Imperfect Thirst* (1994). ■ See study by Richard J. Calhoun (1992).

KINOSHITA, JUNJI (1914–   ), Japanese dramatist. The leading figure in the post–World War II Japanese theater, Kinoshita was influential both as a playwright and as a commentator on the theory and technique of drama. His plays such as *Winds and Waves* (1947) represent his commitment to left-wing politics; other plays, such as *Twilight Crane* (1949; Eng. trans. 1956), reflect his interest in Japanese folklore. His plays after 1960, notably *Between God and Man: A Judgment on War Crimes* (1970; Eng. trans. 1979), deal with the individual's resistance to overwhelming historical forces. He was also known for his translations of Western plays.

KINSEY, ALFRED CHARLES (1894–1956), U.S. zoologist and sex researcher. A highly respected zoologist, Kinsey was a cofounder (1942) and director of the Institute for Sex Research at Indiana University (1942–56). His two controversial, pioneering studies, *Sexual Behavior in the Human Male* (1948), known as the "Kinsey Report," and *Sexual Behavior in the Human Female* (1953), were based on extensive interviews and indicated a wide variation in behavior. The best-selling books were defended and condemned on both moral and scientific grounds. ■ See biography by Cornelia V. Christenson (1971); Wardell B. Pomeroy, *Dr. Kinsey and the Institute for Sex Research* (1982); study by James H. Jones (1997); and Jonathan Gathorne-Hardy, *Sex the Measure of All Things* (2000).

KIPLINGER, WILLARD MONROE (1891–1967), U.S. journalist. A journalism-school graduate (1912) and financial writer (1916–19), Kiplinger started the *Kiplinger Letter* (1923), a newsletter, based in Washington, D.C., for businessmen. Featuring "inside" information from government and big-business sources and amazingly accurate predictions, it was written in a semiliterate staccatolike telegram style that executives were used to. The publication had a circulation of 5,000 by 1929 and reached more than 200,000 subscribers by the 1950s. Kiplinger also founded *Changing Times* magazine (1947) and the *Kiplinger Foreign Trade Letter* (1953).

KIRBY, ROLLIN (1875–1952), U.S. cartoonist and illustrator. Kirby studied painting in Paris under James McNeill Whistler and was a popular illustrator for many magazines before turning in his late thirties to political cartoons, which appeared in the liberal *New York World* (1914–31), *World-Telegram* (1931–39), and *New York Post* (1939–42). He was the first editorial cartoonist to win a Pulitzer Prize (1922) and won two more during his career (1924, 1928). Prohibition, personified by the sour "Mr. Dry," was a major target of his cartoons; he also attacked imperialism, fascism, financial manipulators, and corrupt politicians. He relentlessly satirized the Republicans of the 1920s, particularly after the exposure of corruption in Pres. Warren Harding's administration. Kirby's widely syndicated cartoons advocated civil liberties, progressive causes, and the election of

Franklin D. Roosevelt to the presidency. After 1942 they appeared in *Look* Magazine.

KIRCHNER, ERNST LUDWIG (1880–1938), German painter and graphic artist. With friends Kirchner founded (1905) Die Brücke, an art movement noted for intense and violent emotionalism, which sparked the expressionist movement and altered the course of modern painting. Influenced by Edvard Munch and Vincent Van Gogh, as well as by medieval woodcuts, Japanese prints, and primitive sculpture, he created early works marked by brilliant color and increasingly bold lines. When he moved to Berlin (1911), his colors became more subdued but the figures assumed a tense, brutalized stance and masklike expressions. After suffering a war-related nervous breakdown, Kirchner settled in Switzerland (1917–38), where he concentrated on producing peasant scenes and mountain landscapes, introducing a serenity not found in his earlier paintings. Soon after Nazi officialdom condemned his work as "degenerate," Kirchner committed suicide. ■ See studies by W. Grohmann (1961) and Donald E. Gordon (1968).

KIRKLAND, (JOSEPH) LANE (1922–1999), U.S. labor leader. Born into an old and wealthy South Carolina family, Kirkland studied at the Merchant Marine Academy, New York, and spent most of World War II as a deck officer. He graduated from Georgetown University's School of Foreign Service (1948) and took a research job with the American Federation of Labor. He worked his way up through the organization (which later merged with the Congress of Industrial Organizations) to become executive assistant to AFL-CIO president George Meany (1961) and secretary-treasurer of the organization (1969). A tough negotiator and skillful mediator, Kirkland succeeded Meany as head of the 14-million-member AFL-CIO (1979–95).

KIROV, SERGEI MIRONOVICH (S. M. Kostrikov; 1886–1934), Soviet political leader. Kirov joined the Russian Social Democratic party in 1904, sided with the Bolsheviks in intraparty disputes, and played a major role in establishing Soviet power in the Caucasus during the civil war (1918–20) and later in Georgia. He headed the Leningrad Communist party organization (from 1926), became a member of the Politburo (1930), and was numbered among dictator Joseph Stalin's closest associates. His assassination, reputedly inspired by Stalin, instigated a period of massive reprisals by which Stalin eliminated all of his potential rivals. Leon Trotsky, G. E. Zinoviev, L. B. Kamenev, A. I. Rykov, and others were accused of complicity in the murder and thousands of lesser officials were purged in the aftermath of the assassination. ■ See Amy W. Knight, *Who Killed Kirov?* (1999).

KIRSTEIN, LINCOLN (1907–1996), U.S. impresario and writer. A Harvard graduate (B.S. 1930), Kirstein was an art historian and writer and an ardent spectator of the dance. On a trip to Europe he convinced the Russian émigré George

Balanchine to come to the United States (1933). Determined to create a great American ballet company, Kirstein was the moving force behind the success of the New York City Ballet (est. 1948) and the School of American Ballet (est. 1933) until his retirement in 1989. A writer with a gift for explaining dance, literature, and the fine arts to the American public, he was a founding editor of *Dance Index Magazine* (1942–48) and published numerous books on the dance, including the classics *Dance* (1935), which was reprinted many times, and *Movement and Metaphor* (1970), which treated dance as a metaphoric system, not just as a storytelling mode. He also published volumes of poetry, including *Low Ceiling* (1935) and *Rhymes of a P.F.C.* (1964), essays in *Ballet: Bias and Belief* (1983), and the memoirs *Thirty Years with the New York City Ballet* (1978), *Quarry* (1986), and *Mosaic* (1994).

KISHI, NOBUSUKE (Nobusuke Sato; 1896–1987), Japanese political leader. Kishi received an elitist education in preparation for a bureaucratic career. He joined the government immediately after graduation from Tokyo University (1920), and during the 1930s he played a major role in converting peacetime industries to wartime production. He served as minister for commerce and industry during World War II (1941–44). He was jailed as a war criminal (1945–48) but resumed his career and was elected to the Diet as a member of the Liberal Democratic party in 1953. With wide business and political connections, Kishi rose to the premiership (1957–60). He advocated Japanese rearmament, pursued a strongly anticommunist foreign policy, and signed a controversial revised U.S.-Japan security treaty. Although unpopular because of his fascist background, Kishi remained a powerful, behind-the-scenes figure even after his retirement. ▪ See Dan Kurzman, *Kishi and Japan* (1960).

KISSINGER, HENRY ALFRED (1923–), German-born U.S. political scientist and secretary of state. After World War II service with the U.S. Army in Germany, Kissinger attended Harvard, earning a Ph.D. in 1954. He served on the Harvard faculty (1957–69), became director of a Rockefeller Brothers Fund project (1958) and an adviser to Republican presidential aspirant Nelson Rockefeller, and was a consultant on foreign policy to three presidents. As assistant for national security affairs (1969–73) to Pres. Richard Nixon and then as secretary of state (1973–77), Kissinger negotiated cease-fires in Vietnam (for which he shared the 1973 Nobel Peace Prize with Le Dui Tho) and the Middle East and negotiated a U.S. rapprochement with the People's Republic of China. However, he was criticized for his role in the bombing of Cambodia and the prolongation of the war in Vietnam, and for the role he played in the downfall of Chilean Pres. Salvador Allende, a socialist. His memoirs were published as *White House Years* (1979), *Years of Upheaval* (1982), and *Years of Renewal* (1999). ▪ See his *Observations: Selected Speeches and Essays, 1982–1984* (1985) and *Diplomacy* (1994); studies by David Landau (1974),

Marvin and Bernard Kalb (1974), and Walter Isaacson (1992); Seymour Hersh, *The Price of Power* (1983); and William Burr, ed., *The Kissinger Transcripts: The Top Secret Talks with Beijing and Moscow* (1999).

KITA, IKKI (1883–1937), Japanese political leader. An advocate of revolutionary changes in Japanese society and institutions, Kita was the leading theorist of the National Socialist movement of the 1920s and 1930s. In his best-known work, *An Outline for the Reorganization of Japan* (1923), he advocated the establishment of an authoritarian government and the expansion of Japanese influence throughout Asia. It was enormously influential among young army officers. Implicated in an abortive 1936 military coup, Kita was arrested and executed. ▪ See George M. Wilson, *Radical Nationalist in Japan* (1969).

KITCHENER, HORATIO HERBERT KITCHENER, 1st EARL (1850–1916), British field marshal. Kitchener came to epitomize the spirit of aggressive nationalism during colonial service in Africa and India. He conquered the Sudan (1896–98) and ruthlessly suppressed Boer guerrillas in South Africa (1899–1902), herding survivors into concentration camps. Appointed British secretary of war in 1914, he created a new mass army and enjoyed public adulation before the ship bearing him on a mission to Russia hit a German mine and sank. ▪ See biographies by George Arthur (1920) and Philip Magnus (1958); Trevor Royle, *The Kitchener Enigma* (1985); and A. J. Smithers, *The Fighting Nation* (1994).

KITTREDGE, GEORGE LYMAN (1860–1941), U.S. scholar and educator. "Kitty," as he was affectionately called by generations of students at Harvard (1888–1936), taught classics, medieval literature, and Shakespeare and was the best-known American literary scholar of his time. He produced the leading U.S. edition of the *Complete Works of Shakespeare* (1936) and was also an authority on Chaucer and Sir Thomas Malory. His books included *Words and Their Ways in English Speech* (1901; with J.B. Greenough), *Shakespeare* (1916), and *Witchcraft in Old and New England* (1929). ▪ See biography by Clyde Kenneth Hyder (1962).

KLEE, PAUL (1879–1940), Swiss artist. The son of two musicians, Klee studied in Germany, Italy, and France, absorbing various influences. He was a superb draftsman who began painting on glass. After serving in World War I, he won international fame when a Munich dealer mounted a large exhibition of his work (1919). A prolific artist, Klee invented a childlike but sophisticated pictorial language that decisively influenced artistic innovation throughout the century. He was also an important writer on aesthetics and a gifted violinist. Klee taught at the Bauhaus School and in Düsseldorf until he was dismissed (1933) by the Nazis, who labeled his work "degenerate." Disgusted by their policies,

Klee returned to Switzerland. ■ See his notebooks (Eng. trans., vol. 1, 1961; vol. 2, 1970); *Diaries* (Eng. trans. 1964); and studies by Will Grohmann (Eng. trans. 1967), Norbert Lynton (1975), Robert Short (1979), and Douglas Hall (rev. ed. 1992).

KLEIN, CALVIN (1942–), U.S. fashion designer. Klein's interest in fashion design dated from an adolescence spent sketching and sewing clothes. After graduating from New York City's Fashion Institute of Technology (1962), he worked as an apprentice designer in the garment district. Klein's first fashion success, a version of the trench coat, showed his ability to create fashions that fit the times without sacrificing classic lines. Klein emphasized elegant simplicity and high-quality natural fabrics in neutral shades. His designs expanded from chic women's sportswear to include eveningwear, activewear, menswear, underwear, cosmetics, and accessories. Provocative, sexy advertisements for his line, particularly designer jeans, set an industry trend and helped put him at the forefront of fashion in the 1970s, 1980s, and 1990s. ■ See Steven Gaines and Sharon Churcher, *Obsession* (1994).

KLEIN, LAWRENCE ROBERT (1920–), U.S. economist. Klein studied economics with Paul A. Samuelson at the Massachusetts Institute of Technology (Ph.D. 1944) and was a professor at the Wharton School of the University of Pennsylvania (1958–). Known as the "father of econometric model-making," he developed mathematical models, used by governments and private businesses throughout the world to forecast economic trends and business fluctuations. He led research teams at the Brookings Institution (1963–72) and the Wharton School (1969–), was an economic adviser to Pres. Jimmy Carter (1976–81), and won the 1980 Nobel Prize in Economics. His books included *The Keynesian Revolution* (1947), *An Introduction to Econometrics* (1962), and *Economic Theory and Econometrics* (1985).

KLEIN, MELANIE (Melanie Reizes; 1882–1960), Austrian-born psychoanalyst. Klein was a 30-year-old housewife and mother when she entered psychoanalysis in 1912. She applied the insights of her own analysis to disturbed children and she became the first major child psychoanalyst. Using play therapy to delve into the subconscious of her small subjects, she discovered unexpected funds of aggression and sadism in the "preoedipal" years up to age 2. Klein moved to England (1926) and developed a following of "Kleinians" in the British Psychoanalytical Society. She wrote *The Psychoanalysis of Children* (1932), *Envy and Gratitude* (1957), and *Narrative of a Child Analysis* (1961). ■ See study by Hanna Segal (1980) and biography by Phyllis Grosskurth (1986).

KLEM, BILL (William Joseph Klem; 1874–1951), U.S. baseball umpire. Baseball's foremost umpire, Bill Klem had a career in the National League that stretched to a record 37 years (1905–41). Known as the "Old Arbitrator," he was famous for his statement, "I never called one wrong." Klem sought better treatment and pay for umpires, stressing their vital role in the game. From 1942 until his death he was the league supervisor of umpires, and in 1953 he became the first umpire voted into the National Baseball Hall of Fame.

KLEMPERER, OTTO (1885–1973), German conductor. Klemperer was a severely exacting yet musically sensitive conductor, particularly noted for his interpretations of the classic German repertory. As director of opera companies throughout Germany, including the Berlin State Opera (1927–33), he championed the avant-garde music of contemporaries like Schoenberg, Stravinsky, Janáček, Hindemith, and Krenek. Forced into exile (1933) by the Nazis, he directed the Los Angeles Philharmonic Orchestra (1933–39). Despite partial paralysis from a brain operation in 1939 and a prolonged unsuccessful period in his career, Klemperer reestablished himself as world-renowned conductor of the New Philharmonia Orchestra in London (1959–72). ■ See his *Minor Recollections* (Eng. trans., 1964); biography by Peter Heyworth (1983); and Peter Heyworth, ed., *Conversations with Klemperer* (1973).

KLIMT, GUSTAVE (1862–1918), Austrian artist. A founder of the antiacademic Vienna Secession movement (1897), Klimt was a leading Art Nouveau painter who was best known for his highly decorative allegorical murals and his portraits of women. His controversial works, many of which included erotic symbolism, featured bold colors, abstract forms, and forceful linearity, and were regarded as forerunners of expressionism. His most famous works included the murals for the University of Vienna (1899–1907) and the Palais Stoclet, Brussels (1909–11), as well as the paintings *Frau Fritsa Riedler* (1906) and *The Kiss* (1908). ■ See studies by Fritz Novotny and Johannes Dobai (Eng. trans. 1968) and Frank Whitford (1990).

KLINE, FRANZ (1910–1962), U.S. painter. Kline studied in Philadelphia, Boston, and London (1937–38) and taught in New York City at the Pratt Institute (1953) and Cooper Union (1956). Initially a representational painter, he began around 1950 to evolve a style characterized by broad black strokes on a white background and became a leader of the abstract-expressionist movement. Among his best-known works were *Chief* (1950), *Ancient Grave* (1955), and "*Mahoning*" (1956). ■ See Fielding Dawson, *An Emotional Memoir of Franz Kline* (1967) and study by Harry F. Gaugh (1994).

KLINE, NATHAN SCHELLENBERG (1916–1983), U.S. psychologist. Trained at New York University (M.D. 1943) and Clark University (M.A. in psychology, 1951), Kline pioneered in the development of drugs used to treat mental disorders. He twice won the prestigious Lasker Award for developing tranquilizers (1957) and antidepressants (1964) which enabled many mental patients, previously considered untreatable, to lead useful lives. He was the founding director (1952–82) of the Rockland Research Institute, Orangeburg, New York (originally part of the Rockland State Hospital), and a professor at the Columbia College of Physicians and Surgeons (1948–50; 1952–80).

KLUCKHOHN, CLYDE (1905–1960), U.S. anthropologist. In his youth, Kluckhohn was sent to a New Mexico ranch to recuperate from rheumatic fever; he retained a fascination for the Southwest, which was to become the site of his anthropological fieldwork. He specialized in the culture of the Navaho Indians, but his interests included linguistics, the theory of culture, and the nature of values. He served on the faculty of Harvard University (1935–60), where he was involved in interdisciplinary collaboration; he was determined to apply scientific principles to the social sciences without sacrificing either the insights or the concerns of the humanities. Kluckhohn's books included *Navaho Witchcraft* (1944) and *Mirror for Man* (1949).

KLUG, SIR AARON (1926–   ), Lithuanian-born British molecular biologist. Brought by his parents to South Africa at the age of 3, Klug moved to Britain in 1949. He received his Ph.D. at Cambridge (1952) and did research at the Medical Research Council Laboratory of Molecular Biology, Cambridge (1962–   ; director 1986–96). He developed a technique of electron microscopy, called image reconstruction, by which researchers could study three-dimensional images of the structures of viruses and the subunits of chromosomes. He led the team that traced the complete details of the tobacco mosaic virus, determined the structure of the important segment of ribonucleic acid (RNA) known as transfer RNA, and made detailed studies of chromosome subunits known as nucleosome core particles, considered to be the smallest building blocks of chromosomes. He won the 1982 Nobel Prize in Chemistry and subsequently served as president of the Royal Society (1995–   ).

KNIGHT, DAMON (1922–   ), U.S. science-fiction writer. Knight began reading *Amazing Stories* magazine at age 11 and in his teens gave up hopes of becoming a cartoonist to write science fiction. He published his first story at 18, going on to write scores of stories as well as essays and novels. His first full-length novel, *Hell's Pavement* (1955), depicted the horrors of a "utopian" society. He was the foremost critic of science fiction; the essays collected in *In Search of Wonder* (1956) considered the fantastic from the viewpoint of psychology. Later books included *The Futurians* (1977), an informal history of a group of influential science-fiction writers active in New York (1938–45), *The Man in the Tree* (1984), and *Humpty-Dumpty: An Oval* (1996). *The Best of Damon Knight* appeared in 1976.

KNIGHT, FRANK HYNEMAN (1885–1972), U.S. economist. Knight was a neoclassical economist at the University of Chicago (1928–51) and leader of the laissez-faire-oriented "Chicago school" of economic thought. He and his students, notably Milton Friedman, exerted a great influence on applied economic theory. In *Risk, Uncertainty and Profit* (1921), Knight contributed to economic theory through his description of a model of perfect competition and his introduction of the problem of uncertainty into decision theory. His text, *The Economic Organization* (1933), presented an integrated approach to the economy as a social organization and influenced many introductory economics textbooks. His essays were published in *The Ethics of Competition* (1935), *Freedom and Reform* (1947), and *Economic Freedom and Social Responsibility* (1952).

KNIGHT, JOHN SHIVELY (1894–1981), U.S. newspaper publisher. Knight inherited the *Akron Beacon Journal* when his father died (1933), and he eventually assembled a 34-newspaper publishing empire, the Knight-Ridder Newspapers, Inc., which by 1981 had the largest weekly circulation in the United States. Located in 17 states, his dailies included the *Miami Herald*, the *Detroit Free Press*, the *Charlotte Observer*, and the *Philadelphia Inquirer* and had an aggregate weekly circulation of 25 million copies. His weekly column, "The Editor's Notebook," won a 1968 Pulitzer Prize for distinguished editorial writing. ■ See biography by Charles Whited (1988).

KNIPLING, EDWARD FRED (1909–2000), U.S. entomologist. The son of a cotton farmer, E. F. Knipling began his research on insect control when he joined the U.S. Department of Agriculture (1931). During World War II he headed the research laboratory that developed DDT and other insecticides that were used to protect military personnel from disease-carrying pests. He was best known for his development of pest control through nontoxic and environmentally sound sterilization techniques, whereby millions of sterilized males were airdropped over infested areas to mate with females that were capable of mating only once. Entire populations of insects were eradicated by this procedure. Knipling later headed the USDA entomology research division (1954–71). His books included *Principles of Insect Population Suppression* (1979) and *Principles of Insect Parasitism—Analysis from New Perspectives* (1992).

KNOPF, ALFRED ABRAHAM (1892–1984), U.S. publisher. After graduating from Columbia University (1912), Knopf forsook his intended law career for literature and publishing. He worked as a clerk and an editor of Doubleday, Page and Co. before he started his own firm, Alfred A. Knopf, Inc., with the publication of a collection of French plays (1915). Striving for quality in the manuscripts he selected and in book design, Knopf produced beautiful and distinctive volumes, including translations of major European writers. Known by its borzoi (Russian wolfhound) symbol, Knopf's company published many Nobel Prize–winning authors, among them Thomas Mann, Albert Camus, T. S. Eliot, Knut Hamsen, Jean Paul Sartre, and André Gide. (It was sold to Random House in 1960, but the Knopf imprint was retained.) With H. L. Mencken and George Jean Nathan, Knopf founded (1924) and published the magazine *American Mercury* to launch young American writers, and he was its editor from 1924 to 1934.

KNOX, PHILANDER CHASE (1853–1921), U.S. senator and cabinet officer. A prominent corporate lawyer during the 1880s and 1890s, Knox served as U.S. attorney general (1901–04) and directed the antitrust suits against the Northern Securities Co. (the railroad holding company) and the Beef Trust, drafted legislation that created the Departments of Commerce and Labor, and helped the U.S. government gain clear title to the land on which the Panama Canal was built. He served in the U.S. Senate as a Republican from Pennsylvania (1904–09) before becoming secretary of state (1909–13). The most powerful member of Pres. William H. Taft's cabinet, he reorganized the State Department and initiated a policy of "dollar diplomacy," which he hoped would ensure peace and stability by encouraging U.S. investments in China and Latin America. He served again in the Senate (1917–21), where he was a leading opponent of the League of Nations and the Versailles Peace Treaty.

KNUDSEN, WILLIAM S. (Signius Wilhelm Paul Knudsen; 1879–1948), Danish-born U.S. industrialist. The personification of the self-made man, Knudsen was an obscure immigrant (1899) who worked his way up to the pinnacle of American industrial power. A production and marketing genius, he was head of production at the Ford Motor Co. (1914–21), vice president and later president of the Chevrolet Division of General Motors (1922–33), and president of GM (1937–40), which he helped build into one of the world's largest multinational corporations. During World War II he was the War Department's director of armament production.

KOBAYASHI, TAKIJI (1903–1933), Japanese novelist. The most prominent Japanese proletarian writer, Kobayashi was best known for *The Factory Ship* (1929; Eng. trans. 1973) and *The Absentee Landlord* (1929; Eng. trans. 1973). These short novels described the miserable lives of exploited seamen and tenant farmers. *The Fifteenth of March, 1928* (1928; Eng. trans. 1933) described the suppression of the Japanese Communist party, which he joined in 1931. All of his works conveyed a sense of outrage and a conviction that eventually justice and the working class will triumph. In 1931 he became chief secretary of the powerful League of Proletarian Writers; he was forced to go underground in 1932. The following year he was arrested and died in custody, apparently murdered by the police.

KOCH, EDWARD IRVING (1924–), U.S. political leader. The son of Polish-Jewish immigrants, Koch served in the infantry during World War II and became politically active in

New York City after graduating from New York University Law School (1948). A reform Democrat, he served in the City Council (1967–69) and then in the U.S. House of Representatives (1969–77), where he opposed the war in Vietnam and was a leading proponent of liberal causes. Elected mayor of New York City (1977, 1981), he helped solve the financial crisis that he had inherited, but adopted increasingly conservative policies and alienated many in the black community. Despite the growing housing and transportation problems in the city, Koch remained extremely popular with the voters and was reelected to a third term (1985) with a record 78 percent of the vote. His administration was shaken in 1986 when several of his appointees and political allies were indicted on corruption charges. ■ See his autobiography, *Mayor* (1984), and *Politics* (1985), *Citizen Koch* (1992), and *Ed Koch on Everything* (1994). He appeared as a judge on the nationally syndicated daily TV show "The People's Court" (1997–).

KODÁLY, ZOLTAN (1882–1967), Hungarian composer. Kodály studied at the Budapest Conservatory and earned a Ph.D. in philology (1906) for his work on the structure of the Hungarian folk song. He and his colleague Béla Bartók took extensive field trips through Central Europe collecting ethnic music. Kodály, whose own best compositions were *Psalmus Hungaricus* (1923) and the folk opera *Háry János* (1926), was also a critic, essayist, pedagogue, and Hungarian national hero. ■ See his *Folk Music of Hungary* (Eng. trans. 1960) and biography by Percy Young (1964).

KODAMA, YOSHIO (1911–1984), Japanese businessman and political figure. An archnationalist from his youth, Kodama made a fortune in China during World War II buying goods looted by Japanese soldiers. After the war he was imprisoned in China as a war criminal (1945–48). Upon his return home, his extensive contacts with politicians, the right-wing underground, and businessmen and journalists enabled him to become Japan's most powerful behind-the-scenes figure. In 1955 he financed the establishment of the Liberal party (later Liberal-Democratic party), a conservative, generally pro-American coalition that controlled the government through the 1980s. Kodama had very close ties to Nobosuke Kishi and Kakuei Tanaka, who became premiers, and was connected with U.S. intelligence in the 1950s. He gained public notoriety (1976) when it was alleged that he had also been an agent for the Lockheed aircraft company (1958–75) and had received $7 million in bribes for persuading Japan's airlines to buy Lockheed manufactures. Although he was indicted for violating the foreign-exchange control law and had a lengthy trial, the verdict was suspended as he was too ill to attend court sessions.

KOERNER, THEODOR (1873–1957), Austrian military and political leader. A career military officer and World War I hero, Koerner resigned his post as inspector general of the Austrian army (1920) and served in parliament as a Social

Democrat (1925–34). He was arrested by Chancellor Engelbert Dollfuss' government (1934) and later by the Nazis, whom he refused to serve. After World War II he was lord mayor of Vienna (1945–51) and president of Austria (from 1951).

KOESTLER, ARTHUR (1905–1983), Hungarian-born British novelist and essayist. Raised in Vienna, Koestler studied science and at 17 joined a Zionist dueling fraternity. In more than 30 books, he drew on his firsthand experience on a succession of political and military fronts. After traveling in the Middle East, he went to Spain as a reporter during the Spanish Civil War. *Spanish Testament* (1937) followed four months of imprisonment by the fascists. A Communist (1932–38), he was one of the first influential intellectuals of the left to renounce Stalinism, but remained allied with leftist causes. His celebrated novel *Darkness at Noon* (1940) was set against the Moscow purge trials. The anthology edited by Richard Crossman, *The God That Failed* (1949), included Koestler's memoir of his years as a Communist. *Scum of the Earth* (1941) described his experiences in a concentration camp in France (1939–40) during World War II. After 1940 he lived in Britain and he served with the British army during the war. He later wrote on scientific ideas, spirituality, and parapsychology. In *Bricks to Babel* (1981), he assembled selections from a half century of his writings. After he became gravely ill, Koestler and his wife committed suicide. ■ See his two volumes of autobiography, *Arrow in the Blue* (1951) and *The Invisible Writing* (1954); biographies by Iain Hamilton (1982) and David Cesarani (1999); and study by Sidney A. Pearson (1978).

KOFFKA, KURT (1886–1941), German psychologist. Koffka, Max Wertheimer, and Wolfgang Köhler founded (1912) the Gestalt school of psychology, which taught that learning, thinking, and perception involved the appreciation of patterned and structured wholes and not merely isolated and individual elements. The Gestalt approach emphasized the integrative aspects of experience and had a profound effect on 20th-century social science and psychotherapy. Koffka, who taught at the University of Giessen (1911–24), was the most prolific of the three pioneers. He introduced Gestalt ideas to the United States (1922), where he settled permanently and taught at Smith College (1927–41). His book, *The Growth of the Mind* (1921; Eng. trans. 1924), applied Gestalt concepts to developmental psychology, and his classic work, *Principles of Gestalt Psychology* (1935), presented a complete theory of behavior. ■ See study by Molly Harrower (1983).

KOHL, HELMUT (1930–   ), German political leader. Born into a nationalistic and religious Roman Catholic family, Kohl joined the conservative Christian Democrat Union (CDU) at age 17 and studied at the universities of Frankfurt and Heidelberg (Ph.D. in political science, 1958). A centrist, he served in the Rhineland parliament (1959–69) and as minister-president of the Rhineland-Palatinate (1969–76) before becoming the leader of the opposition in the federal Bundestag (parliament; 1976–82). As chancellor (1982–98), he cut social welfare spending and public sector pay, pursued a tough law and order policy, and was strongly pro-American in international matters, approving U.S. intermediate range missiles on German soil (1983) and endorsing Pres. Ronald Reagan's Strategic Defense Initiative ("Star Wars") plan. He was Reagan's host at a controversial visit to Bitburg cemetery (1985), where Nazi SS troops were buried. His administration was weakened by the continuing high unemployment rate, which reached over 12 percent in 1997, and recurring financial scandals within his administration. He played a major role in the rapid reunification of Germany (1990), 11 months after the fall of the Berlin Wall, and was a powerful advocate of European integration. In 1996 he became the longest-serving chancellor since Otto von Bismarck in the 19th century, but his party was defeated in the 1998 elections and he was replaced by Social Democrat Gerhard Schröder. In December 1999 he admitted that he had illegally accepted more than $1 million in anonymous party donations during his years as chancellor. He refused to disclose the names of the donors and resigned as honorary chairman of the CDU (January 2000). ■ See biographies by Karl Pruys (1995; Eng. trans. 1996) and Henrik Bering (1999).

KÖHLER, GEORGES J. F. (1946–1995), West German immunologist. Köhler studied biology at the University of Freiburg (Ph.D. 1974) and spent two years (1974–76) as a postdoctoral fellow in the laboratory of César Milstein at the (British) Medical Research Council Laboratory of Molecular Biology at Cambridge University. Together, they developed (1975) a procedure for producing virtually unlimited amounts of pure, uniform, and easily reproducible antibodies. They created these "monoclonal antibodies" by fusing antibody-producing cells with tumor cells. Their procedure revolutionized biomedical research and became widely used in medical diagnosis and in the treatment of cancer, leukemia, and other diseases. After leaving Cambridge, Köhler did research at the Basel (Switzerland) Institute of Immunology (1976–84) and served as director of the Max Planck Institute of Immune Biology in Freiburg (from 1984). He and Milstein shared the 1984 Nobel Prize in Physiology or Medicine with Niels K. Jerne.

KOHLER, KAUFMANN (1843–1926), Bavarian-born U.S. Jewish scholar and religious leader. Kohler emigrated (1869) to the United States and served (1879–1903) as rabbi at New York City's Temple Beth-El. He was an important voice in the formulation of Reform Judaism in the United States and served as president of Hebrew Union College (1903–22), the major seminary of the Reform movement. He was an editor of *The Jewish Encyclopedia* and wrote *Backwards or Forwards: Lectures on Reform Judaism* (1885), *Jewish Theology Systematically and Historically*

Considered (1918), and *Heaven and Hell in Comparative Religion* (1923). *The Origins of the Synagogue and the Church* (1929) was published posthumously, as was *Studies, Addresses, and Personal Papers* (1931), which contained a brief autobiography.

KÖHLER, WOLFGANG (1887–1967), German psychologist. Together with Max Wertheimer and Kurt Koffka, Köhler founded (1912) the Gestalt school of psychology, which taught that learning, thinking, and perception involved the appreciation of patterned and structured wholes and not merely isolated and individual elements. The Gestalt approach emphasized the integrative aspects of experience and had a profound effect on 20th-century social science and psychotherapy. While director of the anthropoid research station of the Prussian Academy of Sciences in the Canary Islands (1913–20), Köhler conducted learning experiments with chimpanzees that were recorded in his classic study, *The Mentality of Apes* (1917; Eng. trans. 1924). He headed the Psychological Institute at the University of Berlin (from 1922). After the Nazis came to power, he emigrated to the United States and taught at Swarthmore College (1935–55). Among his books (in English) were *Gestalt Psychology* (1929), *Dynamics in Psychology* (1940), and *The Task of Gestalt Psychology* (1969). His selected papers were edited by Mary Henle (1971).

KOHN, HANS (1891–1971), U.S. historian. Kohn was born and reared in Prague in the turbulent last days of the Austro-Hungarian Empire and became a scholar of the phenomenon of nationalism. He earned a doctorate in jurisprudence, fought in World War I, and spent four years as a Russian prisoner of war (1915–19). After the war he migrated via Jerusalem to the United States and taught at Smith College (1934–49) and City College of New York (1949–62). Equally distrustful of totalitarianism on the right and on the left, Kohn equated communism with fascism. In addition to *The Idea of Nationalism,* his 1944 classic, he wrote several works in intellectual history and an autobiography, *Living in a World Revolution* (1964).

KOHN, WALTER (1923–), Austrian-born U.S. physicist. Kohn studied at Harvard (Ph.D. 1948) and taught at the University of California at San Diego (1960–79) and Santa Barbara (1979–). A pioneer in the field of quantum chemistry, Kohn discovered (1964) that the total energy of an atomic or molecular system can be calculated by determining the density of electrons in the system. Known as the Density-Functional Theory, Kohn's approach enabled scientists to map the geometrical structure of molecules and to predict their interactions. Kohn shared the 1998 Nobel Prize in Chemistry (with John A. Pople) for his research.

KOHOUT, PAVEL (1928–), Czech-born playwright, director, and novelist. Kohout wrote lyric poetry before devoting his energies to dramatic forms, including adaptations and radio plays. A Communist party member from the 1950s, he served as president of the party organization of the Council of Czechoslovak Writers. During the mid-1960s, the period of liberalization in the arts that culminated in the "Prague spring" of 1968, Kohout was a leader in the movement to bring greater political and social awareness to government-sponsored theaters. Related to the theater of the absurd, his work combined fantasy with political insight. When the Prague spring came to an end, he was expelled from the Communist party (1968) and was stripped of Czech citizenship (1979) during a stay in Austria. He remained there, becoming dramaturge-in-residence at Vienna's state theater, the Burgtheater. His works included the plays *Poor Murderer* (Eng. trans. 1977), *August August, August* (1968; Eng. trans. 1980), and the novels *The Hangwoman* (Eng. trans. 1981), *The Widow Killer* (Eng. trans. 1998), and *I Am Snowing* (Eng. trans. 1994).

KOHUT, HEINZ (1913–1981), Austrian-born U.S. psychoanalyst. Kohut, whose father was a Jew, fled the Nazis and emigrated to the United States (1940) soon after receiving a medical degree at the University of Vienna. He trained in neurology and psychiatry at the University of Chicago, where he spent his career. He received analytic training at the Chicago Institute for Psychoanalysis. He was president of the American Psychoanalytic Association (1964–65) and a vice president of the International Psychoanalytic Association (1965–73). Kohut devoted more than 20 years to clinical work on narcissism, departing from traditional Freudian thought by emphasizing the narcissistic struggle as central to human development and downplaying the importance of the Oedipal complex, intrapsychic conflict, libido, and other psychoanalytic concepts. His influential self-psychology, which he viewed as complementary to Freudian theory, held that the analyst should support a healthy self-love in patients. He considered the Freudian view of an infant as "a bundle of untamed drives" to be "nonsense," taking a more upbeat view of human nature. His major books were *The Analysis of the Self* (1971), *The Restoration of the Self* (1977), and *The Search for the Self* (1978).

KOKOSCHKA, OSKAR (1886–1980), Austrian-born painter and writer. After leaving (1908) the Vienna School of Decorative Arts, where his work was thought too exotic, Kokoschka wrote political dramas and painted a series of portraits (1909–14) remarkable for their psychological approach to the subjects' personalities. After being wounded in World War I, Kokoschka took a teaching position at Germany's Dresden Academy and executed a group of landscapes that have been termed "portraits of cities" (1919–31). His canvases were noted for their flowing lines and heavy colors, said to be drawn not painted with a brush, and for their unflinching concern for psychological truth. When the Nazis labeled his work "degenerate," Kokoschka painted *Self-Portrait of a Degenerate Artist* (1937) and fled to London (1938). He lived in Switzerland after 1953. ■ See his *My Life* (Eng. trans. 1974), study by J. P. Hodin (1966), and biography by Frank Whitford (1986).

KOLAKOWSKI, LESZEK (1927–), Polish philosopher. A graduate (Ph.D. 1953) and professor of philosophy at the University of Warsaw (1950–68), Kolakowski was a leading Marxist revisionist who served as a focal point for Poland's dissident students and intellectuals. He played an important role in the return to power of "nationalist" Wladyslaw Gomulka in 1956, only to be expelled from the Polish Communist party and dismissed from the university for political reasons when Gomulka's line hardened (1968). A collection of Kolakowski's writings was translated as *Toward a Marxist Humanism* (1968). After leaving Poland he became a severe critic of the communist governments of Eastern Europe, taught at Oxford University (1970–95), and wrote *Positive Philosophy* (Eng. trans. 1972), *Main Currents of Marxism* (3 vols.; Eng. trans. 1978), *Religion* (1982), *The Presence of Myth* (Eng. trans. 1989), *Modernity on Endless Trial* (1990), and *God Owes Us Nothing* (1995).

KOLBE, MAXIMILIAN MARIA, SAINT (Raymond Kolbe; 1894–1941), Polish priest. Kolbe joined the Franciscan Conventuals (1907), studied in Rome, and was ordained in 1918. A fervent adherent of the cult of the Virgin Mary, he edited a popular Polish Catholic monthly, *The Knight of Mary Immaculate*. In 1927 he founded a religious community outside Warsaw; Niepokalanów (the City of Mary Immaculate) became the world's largest friary and a powerful communications center. Kolbe did missionary work in Japan and India in the early 1930s, then returned to Poland due to poor health. The Catholic publishing organization he headed at Niepokalanów took an anti-Semitic stance in the years leading up to World War II. When the Germans invaded Poland in 1939, Kolbe was briefly imprisoned; he was arrested again in 1941 for anti-Nazi activities and was sent to the Nazi concentration camp at Auschwitz. There, Kolbe volunteered to take the place of a fellow inmate selected for execution. Pope Paul VI beatified Kolbe in 1971, and Pope John Paul II proclaimed him a saint in 1982, waiving the requirement of miracles. ■ See Diana Dewar, *Saint of Auschwitz* (1982), and Patricia Treece, *A Man for Others* (1982).

KOLCHAK, ALEKSANDR VASILIEVICH (1873–1920), Russian admiral and political leader. After distinguished service in the Russo-Japanese War (1905) and in the early stages of World War I, Kolchak won command of the Black Sea fleet (1916). After the October revolution (1917), he became war minister (1918) in an antibolshevik "all Russian government" in Siberia. Successful in controlling the central portion of the Trans-Siberian Railway, he pronounced himself Russia's "supreme ruler," but after his 1919 offensive failed, his support deteriorated, and he relinquished the leadership of the "White" forces to Gen. Anton Denikin. The Bolsheviks shot Kolchak at Irkutsk. ■ See Peter Fleming,

The Fate of Admiral Kolchak (1963), and John Smele, *Civil War in Siberia* (1996).

KOLEHMAINEN, HANNES (1889–1966), Finnish distance runner. The first of the durable Finnish competitors who dominated distance running in the early decades of the century, Kolehmainen set the first world record in the 1912 Stockholm Olympics when he captured the gold medal for the 5,000-meter event. In remarkable performances, he then won two more gold medals for the 10,000-meter race and for the cross-country competition. A record holder for the 20,000-meter (1913) and 25,000-meter (1920) distances, he won the marathon at the 1920 Antwerp Olympics.

KOLFF, WILLEM JOHAN (1911–), Dutch-born U.S. physician. A doctor's son, Kolff studied at the University of Leiden (M.D. 1938). During World War II, he took part in the Dutch resistance and developed the first crude kidney dialysis machine to remove urea and other retention products from a patient. After emigrating to the United States (1950), Kolff spent 17 years working on artificial organs at the Cleveland Clinic Foundation (1950–67). He refined the dialysis process, giving new hope to people suffering from kidney malfunction, and in the 1950s he designed a heart-lung machine that helped prepare the way for open-heart surgery. He directed the University of Utah's Institute for Biomedical Engineering (1967–86). In 1982, a quarter century after Kolff first implanted a mechanical heart in a dog, his team (including Robert Jarvik and William de Vries) replaced a dying patient's heart with an aluminum and plastic device. The patient, Dr. Barney Clark, survived 112 days. Kolffs books included *Artificial Organs* (1976).

KOLKO, GABRIEL (1932–), U.S. historian. A Harvard-educated (Ph.D. 1962) professor at York University, Canada (from 1970), Kolko adopted a revisionist, Marxist approach to U.S. history with particular attention to the progressive era of the early 20th century. Disputing the popular view of government as intervening to regulate business, he argued in *The Triumph of Conservatism* (1963) and *Railroads and Regulation, 1877–1916* (1965), that business had instead "captured" government. Kolko's other works included *Wealth and Power in America* (1962), *The Roots of American Foreign Policy* (1969; with Joyce Kolko), *The Politics of War: The World and U.S. Foreign Policy, 1943–45* (1969), *The Limits of Power: The World and U.S. Foreign Policy, 1945–54* (1972), *Main Currents in Modern American History* (1976), *Anatomy of a War: Vietnam, the United States, and the Modern Historical Experience* (1986), *Century of War: Politics, Conflicts and Society Since 1914* (1994), and *Vietnam: Anatomy of a Peace* (1997).

KOLLEK, THEODORE (1911–), Austrian-born Israeli political leader. Teddy Kollek emigrated to Palestine in 1934 and worked for the Jewish Agency Political Department during the 1940s. After Israeli independence he was director general of the prime minister's office (1952–65) and head of the government tourist office (1955–65). As mayor of Jerusalem for almost 30 years (1965–93) the energetic, gregarious politician encouraged normalization of relations with Arabs in the reunited city after the 1967 war, opposed the bill formally establishing Jerusalem as Israel's capital (1980), and proved an effective international fund-raiser for civic development. ■ See his autobiography, *For Jerusalem* (1978) and Naomi Shepherd, *The Mayor and the Citadel* (1987).

KOLLONTAI, ALEKSANDRA MIKHAILOVNA (Aleksandra M. Domontovich; 1872–1952), Russian political leader, diplomat, and writer. Though married to an officer of the czarist army, Kollontai joined the Russian Social Democratic party, took part in revolutionary activities, and was compelled to leave Russia (1908). An ardent pacifist during World War I, she campaigned against the war in Europe and the United States, then returned to Russia (1917) and participated in the Bolshevik revolution. She became people's commissar for social welfare (1920) and advocated free love, simplified divorce procedures, and legal rights for women. She was a leader of the "workers' opposition" (1920–21), which supported the independence of trade unions, a position opposed by Bolshevik leader V. I. Lenin. Appointed minister to Norway (1923), Kollontai later served in Sweden (1930–45), where she played a key role in negotiating the Soviet-Finnish armistice of 1944. ■ See her *Autobiography* (Eng. trans. 1971); *Selected Writings* (Eng. trans. 1977); Barbara E. Clements, *Bolshevik Feminist* (1979); and biographies by Cathy Porter (1980) and Beatrice Farnsworth (1980).

KOLLWITZ, KÄTHE (Kathe Schmidt; 1867–1945), German graphic artist and sculptor. After studying art in Berlin (1884–85) and Munich (1888–89), Kollwitz resided in a working-class neighborhood. With great emotional force she portrayed the grim existence of the urban poor. *The Weavers' Rebellion* (1894–98), a series of etchings and lithographs, was inspired by a Gerhart Hauptmann play; the theme of revolt by oppressed workers was reiterated in *Peasant War* (1902–08), an experimental series executed using several graphic techniques. After her youngest son was killed in World War I (1914), she repeatedly depicted a mother sheltering her children or grieving for a dead child; her sculpture *Monument to the Dead* (1932) was a modern version of medieval mourners. Throughout her life, Kollwitz committed her artistic energies to political causes, decrying war and fascism and supporting trade unions and communist organizations. She was denounced by the Nazis. Much of her life's work was destroyed during World War II when her residence and studio were bombed. Kollwitz was the first woman elected to the Berlin Academy of Art (1919). ■ See her diary and letters (Eng. trans. 1955) and studies by Otto Nagel (Eng. trans. 1971), Mina C. and H. A. Klein (1975), and Martha Kearns (1976).

KOLMOGOROV, ANDREY NIKOLAYEVICH (1903–1987), Soviet mathematician. The most influential Soviet mathematician of the century, A. N. Kolmogorov made fundamental contributions to many branches of mathematics, including probability theory, topology, and the theory of functions. A professor at Moscow State University (from 1931), Kolmogorov also contributed to the growth of cybernetics and information theory. In addition to training an entire generation of top Soviet mathematicians, he wrote introductory texts and pedagogical papers and helped devise mathematics curricula used in Soviet secondary schools. His books included *Foundations of the Theory of Probability* (1933; Eng. trans. 1950), *Elements of the Theory of Functions and Functional Analysis* (1954; Eng. trans., 2 vols., 1957–61: with S. V. Fomin), and *Introductory Real Analysis* (1968; Eng. trans. 1970, 1975).

KONOE, PRINCE FUMIMARO (1891–1945), Japanese political leader. Known as a "melancholy Marxist" in his early years, Prince Konoe entered the House of Peers in 1920 and rose to the presidency of that body in 1933. In 1937 he was named premier and quickly set out to conquer China, believing that Japan should be the master of east Asia. However, the war dragged on and he resigned in 1939. After returning to power (1940) he disbanded all political parties and signed a military alliance with Germany and Italy and a nonaggression pact with the Soviet Union. He attempted to prevent the spread of the Sino-Japanese War and avert American participation in the conflict, but he resigned in Oct. 1941 in a dispute with the prowar faction headed by war minister Hideki Tojo. After the war he was scheduled to be tried as a war criminal by the occupation authorities and he committed suicide.

KONRAD, GEORGE (1933–), Hungarian writer. Born into a Jewish family, Konrad escaped from his hometown in Nazi-occupied eastern Hungary (1944) one day before the Jewish community was deported to concentration camps. Trained as a social worker and sociologist, he was briefly arrested (1974) when police discovered the manuscript of *The Intellectuals on the Road to Class Power* (with Ivan Szelenyi; Eng. trans. 1979), a social and historical analysis of the intellectual class in Eastern Europe. His humanistic novels, which gained him international recognition, demonstrated his stylistic agility, ability to combine reality and fantasy, and linguistic originality. *The Case Worker* (1969; Eng. trans. 1974) described the cruel life of the Budapest poor. *The City Builder* (Eng. trans. 1979) consisted of the meditations of a disillusioned socialist state bureaucrat. *The Loser* (Eng. trans. 1982) detailed the experiences of a veteran communist government official currently incarcerated in a psychiatric hospital. The essays contained in *Antipolitics* (Eng. trans. 1984) advocated an end to cold-war confrontation between East and West, the neutralization and unification of Europe, and a reduction of state power. His later works included *A Feast in the Garden* (1989; Eng.

trans. 1992), *The Melancholy of Rebirth: Essays from Post-Communist Central Europe, 1989–1994* (Eng. trans. 1995), and *Stonedial* (Eng. trans. 2000).

KOO, VI KUIYUIN WELLINGTON (Ku Wei-chün; 1887–1985), Chinese Nationalist diplomat. V. K. Wellington Koo traveled to the United States (1904) and earned a Ph.D. (1912) at Columbia University, where he was active in Chinese student affairs. On his return to China (1912) he joined the ministry of foreign affairs. He was a member of the Chinese delegation to the Paris Peace Conference (1919) and helped strengthen China's international position during the 1920s. He was his country's foremost diplomat in the periods 1915–28 and 1931–49, representing China as ambassador in the United States, Britain, and France and at the League of Nations and the United Nations, as well as at countless international conferences. During the civil war he attempted to secure American aid for the nationalist cause and after the Communists gained control of China (1949), he continued to serve the nationalist government on Taiwan. He moved to the United States after he completed his term (1957–67) on the International Court of Justice. ■ See study by William L. Tung (1977).

KOOPMANS, TJALLING CHARLES (1910–1985), Dutch-born U.S. economist. Educated at the universities of Utrecht (M.A. 1933) and Leiden (Ph.D. 1936), Koopmans emigrated to the United States (1940) and taught at Princeton and at the University of Chicago (1948–55) before serving as professor of economics at Yale (1955–81). His principal contribution to economic theory was in the area of econometrics and activity analysis, and he developed mathematical formulations for determining the optimum allocation of resources. For this contribution to improved economic planning, Koopmans shared the 1975 Nobel Prize in Economics with Leonid V. Kantorovich. ■ See his *Three Essays on the State of Economic Science* (1957).

KORBUT, OLGA (1955–   ), Soviet gymnast. A diminutive 4-foot 11-inch, 84-pound athlete, Korbut was the first person to do a backward somersault on the uneven parallel bars in competition and one of the few to do a backward flip on the balance beam. She captivated the crowd at the 1972 Munich Olympics—and the hundreds of millions watching on television around the world—with her daring and graceful performances. She won gold medals for the balance beam and floor exercises, a silver medal for the parallel bars, and a third gold medal as a member of the winning Soviet team. She was named Female Athlete of the Year by the Associated Press (1973) and was world champion in 1974. She later moved to the United States (1991) and taught gymnastics in Atlanta, Georgia.

KORDA, SIR ALEXANDER (1893–1956), British film producer and director. A Hungarian Jew by birth, Korda had become his country's leading filmmaker before working in Vienna, Berlin, and Hollywood during the 1920s. He emigrated to Britain (1932), where he established London Film Productions. His historical extravaganzas—*The Private Life of Henry VIII* (1933), *Catherine the Great* (1934), and *Rembrandt* (1936)—won international recognition for the British film industry and a knighthood (1942) for Korda, the first ever awarded to a filmmaker. He later produced such films as *The Third Man* (1949), *The Man Between* (1953), and *Richard III* (1956). ■ See Michael Korda, *Charmed Lives: A Family Romance* (1979), and biography by Karol Kulik (1975).

KORN, RACHEL (1898–1982), Austrian-born Yiddish-language poet. Korn was born and educated in Galicia, a part of the Austrian Empire that was annexed to Poland after World War I. Regarded as an important literary figure after the publication (in Vilna) of her first book of poems (1928), she published numerous poems, essays, and stories in Yiddish journals throughout the world. She fled to the Soviet Union during World War II where she became part of the Yiddish writers' community in Moscow. After the war she returned to Poland and emigrated to Montreal, Canada (1949), where she lived until her death. She is known both for her lyric verse, depicting country life, as well as her poems concerning exile, suffering, and human endurance. Her short stories were noted for their psychological presentation and complex style. ■ See her volume of selected poems in English translation, *Generations* (1982).

KORNBERG, ARTHUR (1918–   ), U.S. biochemist. A graduate in medicine (1941) from the University of Rochester, Kornberg directed enzyme research at the National Institutes of Health (1947–52) and headed the department of microbiology at Washington University (St. Louis; 1953–59). Between 1955 and 1960, he discovered and then purified the DNA (deoxyribonucleic acid) enzyme polymerase. He found that the enzyme could, under appropriate conditions, initiate the synthesis of short DNA molecules. For this work, which advanced the understanding of the hereditary process, he shared the 1959 Nobel Prize in Physiology or Medicine with Severo Ochoa. While teaching at the Stanford University Medical School (1959–88), he and Mehran Goulian utilized DNA polymerase to become the first to synthesize viral DNA (1967). His books included *DNA Replication* (1980). ■ See his autobiography, *For the Love of Enzymes* (1989).

KORNBLUTH, CYRIL M. (1923–1958), U.S. science-fiction writer. Kornbluth earned a Bronze Star in the Battle of the Bulge during World War II; later he began writing detective fiction. He collaborated in the early 1950s with science-fiction writers Judith Merril and Frederik Pohl, coauthoring (with Pohl) *The Space Merchants* (1952), one of the best-known science-fiction novels. On his own, he published *Takeoff* (1952), in which scientists and bureaucrats clash. In *The Syndic* (1953) and *Not This August*

(1955), Kornbluth speculated not only about technological advance but also about future social structures. His politically sophisticated stories applied the techniques of conventional fiction to science fantasy. Kornbluth died of a heart attack at the age of 35. ■ See the collection *Best Science Fiction Stories of Cyril M. Kornbluth* (1968).

KORNILOV, LAVR GEORGIEVICH (1870–1918), Russian general. A division commander during World War I, Kornilov was captured (1915) by the Austrians but escaped (1916). After the February revolution (1917), he became commander in chief of Russian forces under the provisional government; he restored order among the troops and attracted conservatives to the cause of a reformulated provisional government. However, Premier A. F. Kerensky ordered Kornilov dismissed and later arrested, suspecting him of planning a military coup. After the October revolution Kornilov escaped and raised troops against the bolsheviks in the Don area. When the Don cossacks abandoned (1918) the "White" cause, Kornilov's forces diminshed; he was killed in combat and was succeeded by Gen. Anton Denikin.

KOROLEV, SERGEI PAVLOVICH (1906–1966), Soviet space scientist. Korolev studied aeronautical engineering in Moscow (1927–30) and formed (1931; with F. A. Tsander) the Moscow Group for the Study of Jet Propulsion, which launched the Soviet Union's first liquid fuel rocket (1933). He designed rockets and missiles during the 1930s and 1940s and was responsible for rocket systems that launched the Soviets' first intercontinential ballistic missiles and spacecraft during the 1950s and 1960s. As chief designer of Soviet space vehicles, he was responsible for many firsts in the history of space exploration, including the *Vostok* and *Voskhod* manned spacecraft, the unmanned probes of the moon, Venus, and Mars, and the Cosmos series of satellites. ■ See biography by James Harford (1997).

KOROVIN, YEVGENY ALEKSANDROVICH (1892–1964), Soviet jurist and historian. Korovin graduated from Moscow University (1915). An authority on international law, he frequently accompanied Soviet delegations to international conferences. After a period of disfavor, he emerged after dictator Joseph Stalin's death to serve as a member of the Permanent Court of Arbitration in The Hague (1957–64). During that period he chaired a Soviet commission on the legal problems of interplanetary space (1959–64) and won the 1958 Grotius Medal for development of the international law of space. Korovin taught at the Higher Diplomatic School attached to the foreign affairs ministry and wrote 13 books, including law textbooks and volumes on such subjects as the history of international law, disarmament, and world politics.

KORSCH, KARL (1886–1961), German philosopher. A prominent member of the German Communist party (from 1920), Korsch concerned himself with problems of the economic transformation of society and of the preconditions for revolution. He wrote numerous pamphlets and books, became one of the party's leading spokesmen, and edited its theoretical journal, *Die Internationale*. However, the party condemned his major work, *Marxism and Philosophy* (1923; Eng. trans. 1970), which emphasized Marx's relationship to Hegel and stressed the subjective or voluntaristic factors necessary for a successful revolution. Korsch subsequently criticized many aspects of Soviet domestic and international policies, and he was expelled from the party (1926). He left Germany (1933) and lived in the United States (from 1936), where he maintained his independent Marxist views. He also wrote *Karl Marx* (1938) and *Three Essays on Marxism* (1972). ■ See additional writings in *Karl Korsch: Revolutionary Theory* (1977) and biography by Patrick Goode (1979).

KORZYBSKI, ALFRED HABDANK SKARBEK (1879–1950), Polish-born U.S. linguist and philosopher. Educated as an engineer, Korzybski was an intelligence officer in the Russian army during World War I. Sent to North America on a military mission, he remained in the United States after the Bolsheviks seized power. Korzybski formulated general semantics, a linguistic theory stressing the importance of clear and precise communication. He believed that linguistic confusion was the cause of many social and psychological ills and proposed a sweeping language reform as a cure. He posited the human "time-binding capacity," that is, the possibility of increasing the capacity for transmitting ideas from one generation to the next through analysis of language usage. He wrote *Manhood of Humanity: The Science and Art of Human Engineering* (1921) and *Science and Sanity: An Introduction to Non-Aristotelian Systems and General Semantics* (1933), and founded (1938) the Institute of General Semantics in Chicago. ■ See Ross Evans Paulson, *Language, Science and Action* (1983).

KOSAMIBI, DAMODAR DHARMANAND (1907–1966), Indian mathematician and historian. A prize-winning Harvard-trained (B.S. 1929) mathematician, D. D. Kosambi taught at several Indian universities and worked at the Tata Institute of Fundamental Research (1947–62). He was best known, however, for his research in ancient Indian history and culture and for his contributions to Indian numismatics. An independent Marxist thinker, he wrote dozens of scholarly articles and essays and several influential books reflecting a creative, materialist interpretation of the Indian past. His best-known works included *An Introduction to the Study of Indian History* (1956), *Myth and Reality: Studies in the Formation of Indian Culture* (1962), and *Ancient India: A History of Its Culture and Civilization* (1965).

KOSINSKI, JERZY (1933–1991), Polish-born U.S. writer. Born into a Jewish family, Kosinski was separated from his parents during World War II and lived with Polish peasants.

He received master's degrees in history and political science from the University of Łódź and taught there (1955–57) before emigrating to the United States. His fiction, filled with violent and sexual images, presented a harrowing view of life, with many of his characters trapped in situations beyond their control. His first novel, *The Painted Bird* (1965), considered a classic of Holocaust literature, recounted the wanderings of a young boy in Nazi-occupied Eastern Europe. *Steps* (1968) won a National Book Award, and *Being There* (1971) was made into a popular movie in 1979. His later works included *Blind Date* (1977), *Passion Play* (1979), *Pinball* (1982), and *The Hermit of 69th Street* (1988). ▪ See study by Norman Lavers (1982) and biography by James P. Sloan (1996).

KOSTERLITZ, HANS WALTER (1903–1996), German-born pharmacologist. Kosterlitz studied at the University of Berlin (M.D. 1929) and worked there until 1933, when he fled to Scotland after the Nazis seized power. He joined the staff of the University of Aberdeen, earned Ph.D. (1936) and D.Sc. (1944) degrees there, and remained at the school for the rest of his career (1934–73). As a professor emeritus, collaborating with younger colleague John Hughes, he discovered (1975) the existence of naturally occurring opiates in the brain, known as endorphins. He isolated and determined the chemical structure of two almost-identical proteins, which were named enkephalins, and proved that they were potent painkillers. The discovery accelerated pharmacological research in the development of nonaddictive opiates. Because endorphins also act as chemical messengers in the brain and influence mood and hunger, Kosterlitz's work stimulated research in many areas of brain chemistry.

KOSYGIN, ALEXEI NIKOLAYEVICH (1904–1980), Soviet political leader. Kosygin joined the Red army (1919), participated in the Russian civil war (1918–20), and joined the Communist party in 1927. Trained as a textile engineer, he worked in Leningrad textile mills and became active in the city's political structure. He served as mayor (1938–39), then became a member of the Communist party's Central Committee and minister of the Soviet textile industry (1939–40). As deputy premier during World War II, he played a major role in relocating Soviet industry and in maintaining production. In the post–World War II years, Kosygin served as minister of finance and minister of light industry (1948–53), and as he rose in the economic structure he gained full membership in the Politburo (1948). Under Party Secretary Nikita Khrushchev he was a leading economic planner and served as chairman of the powerful state economic-planning commission (1959–60) and was named first deputy premier (1960). As Khrushchev's successor as premier (1964–80), Kosygin was regarded as a pragmatic economic reformer who emphasized the production of consumer goods. In foreign affairs he was considered a moderate and pursued a policy of peaceful coexistence with the West. In the 1970s his influence diminished as party secretary Leonid Brezhnev emerged as principal leader.

KOTT, JAN (1914–), Polish literary critic, scholar, and translator. Kott edited several clandestine journals during World War II while a member of the communist-led underground movement. After the war, however, as a professor of literature at Warsaw University, he was one of the most articulate opponents of socialist realism and he resigned from the Communist party in 1957. Primarily concerned with the theater, he was best known for *Shakespeare Our Contemporary* (1961; Eng. trans. 1964), which emphasized the political nature of the plays and showed how the tyranny, spying, political murder, and power struggles of the Elizabethans related to 20th-century social and political reality. *Theater Notebook: 1947–1967,* a collection of essays on modern drama, was published (in English) in 1968, two years after Kott settled in the United States, where he taught at the State University of New York, Stony Brook (1969–83). His later works included *The Eating of the Gods: An Interpretation of Greek Tragedy* (Eng. trans. 1973), *The Theater of Essence* (1984), *The Bottom Translation* (Eng. trans. 1987), and *The Memory of the Body: Essays on Theater and Death* (Eng. trans. 1992). ▪ See his *Still Alive: An Autobiographical Essay* (Eng. trans. 1994).

KOUFAX, SANDY (**Sanford Koufax; 1935–**), U.S. baseball player. The outstanding pitcher of the mid-1960s, Koufax was a hard-throwing left-hander who set several strikeout marks and led the Los Angeles Dodgers to four pennants (1959, 1963, 1965, 1966) and three world championships. He averaged better than one strikeout for each of the 2,324 innings he pitched, pitched four no-hit games, and set a record, subsequently broken, by striking out 382 batters in one season (1965). He pitched a perfect game on Sept. 9, 1965. His career was cut short by an arthritic elbow condition, and he retired at the height of his skills in 1966 (record that year: 27–9; ERA 1.75) to be a TV sports commentator. In 1971, Koufax became the youngest man (at age 36) ever elected to the National Baseball Hall of Fame. ▪ See biographies by Arnold Hano (1964), Jerry Mitchell (1966), and Edward Gruver (2000).

KOUSSEVITSKY, SERGE (1874–1951), Russian-born conductor. Koussevitsky was the world's leading soloist on the double bass, and he gave recitals throughout Europe. In 1910 he and his wife formed a symphony orchestra that toured Russia for seven years. After the 1917 revolution, he emigrated to France, where he organized the Concerts Koussevitsky in 1920. He was conductor of the Boston Symphony Orchestra (1924–49), which he raised to world standards, and he performed new works by such composers as Aaron Copland, Walter Piston, and Samuel Barber. He excelled at the brilliant epic music of Beethoven, Wagner, and Scriabin. As founding musical director of the Berkshire

Symphonic Festivals (1934) and later the Berkshire Music Center (1940) at Tanglewood, Massachusetts, he taught such younger conductors as Leonard Bernstein and Lukas Foss. ▪ See studies by Arthur Lourié (Eng. trans. 1931), Hugo Leichentritt (1946), and Moses Smith (1947).

KOVACS, ERNIE (1919–1962), U.S. television performer and comedian. Kovacs' black mustache, horn-rimmed glasses, and cigar became familiar in the 1950s to television audiences who either loved or hated his dry wit and madcap humor. His unorthodox slant on life was matched by innovative special visual effects and bizarre camera angles, which were completely new in TV's early days. He once sawed through the tripod of a camera while a show was running live. Kovacs starred in "It's Time for Ernie," "Ernie in Kovacsland," and "The Ernie Kovacs Show"; he also wrote, directed, and produced his own shows. A car crash in Hollywood ended his life just as his career was peaking. His gravestone was inscribed: "Nothing in Moderation"; this became the title of a biography by David G. Walley (1975).

KOZINTSEV, GRIGORI (1905–1973), Soviet director. Kozintsev studied at the Leningrad Academy of Fine Arts. At age 16, with Leonid Trauberg and Sergei Yutkevich, he founded (1921) the Factory of the Eccentric Actor (FEKS), which adapted circus and vaudeville motifs in shaping a new socialist theater. With Trauberg, Kozintsev made such innovative, stylized films as *The Overcoat* (1926), *Alone* (1931), and the *Maxim* trilogy (1935–39). He made patriotic war films during World War II; after the war he worked independently, directing *Don Quixote* (1957), then concentrating on his acclaimed film adaptations of Shakespeare's *Hamlet* (1964) and *King Lear* (1971). He wrote *Shakespeare: Time and Conscience* (Eng. trans. 1967), *The Deep Screen* (1971), and *King Lear, The Space of Tragedy* (Eng. trans. 1977). ▪ See study by Barbara Leaming (1980).

KRAFT, CHRISTOPHER COLUMBUS, JR. (1924–), U.S. aeronautical engineer. After studying at Virginia Polytechnical Institute (B.S. 1944), Kraft joined (1945) the research laboratory of the National Advisory Committee for Aeronautics (the predecessor of NASA, the National Aeronautics and Space Administration) and helped develop ground-control techniques for rocket planes. An original member of the U.S. space team assembled in 1958 after the launching of the Soviet space satellite *Sputnik,* Kraft was flight director of the Project Mercury (1959–63) and Project Gemini (1964–69) manned space flight programs and played a major role in the Project Apollo lunar missions. He directed the Johnson Space Center (1970–82) during the period that the winged rocket ship *Columbia* was developed.

KRAG, JENS OTTO (1914–1978), Danish political leader. A Social Democrat, Krag pursued the goal of European integration as Denmark's minister of commerce (1947), minister

of foreign economic affairs (1953–58), foreign minister (1958–62), and premier (1962–68; 1971–72). After leading a successful but bitterly fought campaign for Danish membership in the Common Market (1972), he unexpectedly resigned. He subsequently represented the Common Market in Washington, D.C. (1974).

KRAMER, JACK (**John Albert Kramer;** 1921–), U.S. tennis player and promoter. A remarkable tennis player and arguably the game's greatest promoter, Jack Kramer began winning tournaments at age 15. In 1946 and 1947 he won the U.S. and British singles crowns with aggressive, accurate play, and contributed to the U.S. Davis Cup championships. In 1948 he became the U.S. professional champion and in 1949 the world professional titleholder. After back injuries caused his retirement, he promoted pro tours that attracted the top international players. He was instrumental in opening up the major tennis tournaments to all players—amateur and professional (1968). ▪ See his memoirs, *The Game* (1979).

KRAMER, LARRY (1935–), U.S. writer and AIDS activist. After graduating from Yale (B.A. 1957), Kramer worked as a production assistant for Columbia Pictures and United Artists. His screenplay for the film *Women in Love* (1969), which he also produced, was nominated for an Academy Award. He then turned to gay themes and gained national attention with the semiautobiographical novel *Faggots* (1978), a controversial depiction of the promiscuous gay lifestyle in New York. Learning, in 1981, that a rare form of skin cancer was afflicting young male homosexuals, he cofounded the Gay Men's Health Crisis (GMHC) to gather and disseminate information on the disease that would later be known as AIDS. He vocally criticized political leaders, medical researchers, and the gay community for not doing enough to stop the disease and broke with the GMHC (1983) and eventually formed ACT UP (the AIDS Coalition to Unleash Power; 1987), a radical activist group that initiated demonstrations and confrontational meetings with government and medical leaders. Kramer, who was diagnosed as being HIV positive in 1988, wrote several powerful works related to the AIDS crisis, including the semiautobiographical plays *The Normal Heart* (1985) and *The Destiny of Me* (1992), and the collection of essays, speeches, and letters, *Reports from the Holocaust* (1989; rev. ed. 1994).

KRASNER, LEE (**Lenore Krasner;** 1908–1984), U.S. artist. Born in Brooklyn, Lee Krasner was one of the New York School of abstract-expressionist painters credited with moving the artistic avant-garde from Europe to America. Her early experimental work was influenced by Picasso, Mondrian, and Matisse. While she was studying with Hans Hoffman, she worked in a cubist style using nature as a model, but she later gave up external sources in favor of internalized images that she expressed in abstract form. Both Krasner and the painter Jackson Pollock, whom she married in 1945, were influenced by Jungian concepts and surrealist theories of unconscious creative sources. Krasner considered painting an act of self-revelation, preferring not to discuss the meaning of her images. ■ See studies by Barbara Rose (1983) and Robert Hobbs (1999).

KRAUS, KARL (1874–1936), Austrian writer. Born into a Jewish family in Bohemia, then part of the Austro-Hungarian empire, Kraus lived out his life in Vienna. After a brief career as a journalist, he founded and edited the journal *Die Fackel* ("The Torch"; 1899–1936), which exerted a major influence on Viennese cultural life. A brilliant satirist and social critic, Kraus exposed corruption in the realms of politics, law, literature, and art and stressed the importance of preserving the purity of language from distortions of politicians and journalists. In addition to essays, poems, and aphorisms, he wrote the powerful antiwar play *The Last Days of Mankind* (1922; Eng. trans. 1974) and gave numerous public readings of Shakespeare and the great German poets. English translations of his works are in *Poems* (1930), *In These Great Times* (1976), *Half Truths and One-and-One-Half Truths: Selected Aphorisms* (1976), and *No Compromise: Selected Writings* (1977). ■ See Erich Heller, *The Disinherited Mind* (1957); study by Harry Zohn (1971); and John Theobald, *The Paper Ghetto* (1996).

KREBS, EDWIN G. (1918–), U.S. biochemist. Krebs studied at Washington University in St. Louis (M.D. 1943), did research there in the laboratory of Carl and Gerty Cori (1946–48), and subsequently spent most of his career as a professor at the University of Washington in Seattle (1957–68; 1977–83), where he collaborated with Edmond H. Fischer. During the 1950s, while carrying out research on muscle contraction, the two scientists discovered the biochemical mechanism by which enzymes govern the activity of proteins within a cell. They isolated and purified the enzymes, a protein kinase and a phosphatase, that are responsible for the regulation of muscles. Subsequent research discovered that other such enzymes regulate almost all processes important to life, and indicated that an imbalance of the enzymes can cause disease. For their research, Krebs and Fischer shared the 1992 Nobel Prize in Physiology or Medicine.

KREBS, SIR HANS ADOLF (1900–1981), German-born British biochemist. The son of a Jewish physician, Krebs discovered the series of chemical reactions, called the urea cycle, which explain how urea is formed from amino acids and ammonia (1932). He was forced to leave Germany in 1933 and emigrated to Britain, where he continued his studies at Cambridge University (M.A. 1934) and later taught at Sheffield (1935–54) and Oxford (1954–81). In 1937 he documented a cycle of chemical reactions (now known as the Krebs cycle) that involved the conversion of sugars, fats, and proteins into carbon dioxide, water, and energy-rich com-

pounds in the presence of oxygen. This discovery, which relates to all metabolic reactions, was critical to basic understanding of cell metabolism and earned Krebs the 1953 Nobel Prize in Physiology or Medicine, which he shared with Fritz Lipmann. He wrote *Energy Transformation in Living Matter* (1957; with H. Kornberg). ■ See his *Reminiscences and Reflections* (1981; with Anne Martin).

KREHBIEL, HENRY EDWARD (1854–1923), U.S. music critic. Krehbiel was a scholar of music and the influential music critic of the *New York Herald Tribune* for over 40 years (1880–1923). He championed such contemporary romantic composers as Wagner, Tchaikovsky, and Brahms, but rejected neoclassicism and serial music. Krehbiel wrote extensively, including the program notes for the New York Philharmonic; *Afro-American Folk-Songs* (1914); and an adaptation of A. W. Thayer's *Life of Beethoven* (3 vols., 1921).

KREISKY, BRUNO (1911–1990), Austrian political leader. Kreisky came from a well-to-do Jewish family, joined the socialist youth movement at age 15, and was imprisoned (1935–36) for his political activities. He subsequently received a doctorate of law from the University of Vienna and spent World War II in exile in Sweden. Returning to Austria in 1946, Kreisky rose rapidly through the diplomatic service. He helped design the neutrality policy required by the 1955 treaty restoring Austrian independence and served as foreign minister (1959–66). He was chairman of the Socialist party (1967–83) and federal chancellor (1970–83), when Austria's welfare-state policies expanded and its international stature was enhanced. He was best known for his efforts to gain Western diplomatic recognition for the Palestine Liberation Organization (PLO), which he believed was essential for any Middle East peace settlement.

KREISLER, FRITZ (1875–1962), Austrian violinist and composer. A child prodigy at the Vienna Conservatory, Kreisler was an internationally known virtuoso by the early 1900s. In addition to his superlative skill as a violinist, he was a composer, linguist, artist, book collector, and, briefly, a World War I army officer (see his *Four Weeks in the Trenches; the War Story of a Violinist,* 1915). He also published violin "arrangements" that he attributed to the masters but later (1935) acknowledged as his own compositions. He lived in the United States after 1939. ■ See biographies by Louis P. Lochner (1950) and Amy Biancolli (1998).

KŘENEK, ERNST (1900–1991), Austrian-born U.S. composer. Křenek, who studied in Vienna and Berlin, worked as a conductor-director in several small German theaters before making his name with the jazz opera *Jonny spielt auf* (1926). He later experimented with 12-tone and electronic techniques, which he adapted to his own purposes in such works as *Sestina* (1957), *Spiritus Intelligentiae* (1958), and *Eleven Transparencies* for orchestra (1956). Křenek settled in the United States in 1938 and taught. ■ See his *Music Here and Now* (Eng. trans. 1939), *Exploring Music* (1966), and *Horizons Circled: Reflections on My Music* (1974); and study by John L. Stewart (1991).

KRETSCHMER, ERNST (1888–1964), German psychiatrist. Kretschmer, who enjoyed a long career as professor of psychiatry and neurology at the universities of Marburg (1926–46) and Tübingen (1946–59), subscribed to a "constitutional theory of personality" linking behavior to physical stature. Schizophrenia is more common among thin people, he believed, and manic-depression among the overweight, while athletes are least prone to mental illness. These ideas, developed in *Physique and Character* (1921; Eng. trans. 1925), were not widely accepted. He later wrote *Hysteria, Reflex and Instinct* (1923; Eng. trans. 1960), *The Pyschology of Men of Genius* (1929; Eng. trans. 1931), and did notable research in the fields of childhood psychopathology and compulsive criminality.

KREUGER, IVAR (1880–1932), Swedish industrialist, financier, and swindler. A successful engineer and construction-firm owner, Kreuger inherited his family match manufacturing business and reorganized it as the Swedish Match Co. (1913). He soon controlled the entire match industry in Sweden and attempted to gain a worldwide monopoly by granting foreign governments loans (for post–World War I reconstruction) in exchange for a monopoly over their match production. By 1928, Kreuger—known as the "Match King"—controlled approximately half the world's match production and was a trusted figure in European and American financial circles. However, after his suicide at the height of the Depression, it was discovered that his empire was based on fraud, forgery, and financial manipulations. ■ See study by Robert Shaplen (1960).

KRIS, ERNST (1900–1957), Austrian-born psychoanalyst. Kris was an art historian and assistant curator at the Vienna Kunsthistorisches Museum in 1922 when he was asked to advise psychoanalyst Sigmund Freud on his collection. Kris underwent analysis, became one of Freud's protégés, and followed Freud to Britain in 1938. During World War II he analyzed enemy broadcasts for the British Broadcasting Corp. In New York after the war he wrote several important studies of child behavior and development and he worked with Heinz Hartmann and Anna Freud on the annual publication *The Psychoanalytic Study of the Child,* clarifying and updating Freudian theories. ■ See his *Psychoanalytic Explorations in Art* (1952), *Legend, Myth and Magic in the Image of the Artist* (Eng. trans. 1979), and *Selected Papers* (1975).

KRISHNAMURTI, JIDDU (1895–1986), Indian spiritual philosopher. A Brahman child named after the Hindu divinity, Krishnamurti was adopted as a young man by the Theosophical Society, which welcomed him as a messiah and sent him to Britain for an education. He was introduced to the Western public by British social reformer and theosophist Annie Wood Besant, who toured with him in Britain and the United States (1926–27). In 1929 he broke away from the society and repudiated the role of cult leader, declaring, "My only concern is to set men absolutely, unconditionally free." He adopted an ascetic lifestyle, explained world crises in psychological terms, and published numerous books of verse, thoughts, and lectures, including *The Songs of Life* (1931) and *Commentaries on Living* (1956–60). Enjoying a second vogue among young people, he established headquarters in Ojai, California, in 1969. ■ See *Krishnamurti's Notebook* (1976) and biographies by Pupul Jayakar (1986) and Mary Lutyens (1990).

KRISTEVA, JULIA (1941–   ), Bulgarian-born French theorist and critic. A practicing psychoanalyst and member of the editorial board of the influential avant-garde journal *Tel Quel* (1970–   ), Kristeva was a leading voice among French intellectuals. Drawing on the ideas of Sigmund Freud and Jacques Lacan, she questioned Western premises about philosophy, linguistics, political theory, and literary criticism. In *Semeiotiké* (1969), she analyzed how meaning is produced. *Desire in Language* (1977; Eng. trans. 1980) applied the apparatus of semiotics to art and literature. *Powers of Horror* (1980; Eng. trans. 1982) discussed the notions of abjection and self-loathing. Regarded as the most systematic presentation of Kristeva's theories, *Revolution in Poetic Language* (1974; Eng. trans. 1984) focused on the writings of Comte de Lauréamont and Stephane Mallarmé and prepared the way for a sociology of literature based on attention to language. *About Chinese Women* (1975; Eng. trans. 1976) and *Polylogue* (1977; Eng. trans. 1980) involved Kristeva in feminist dialogue. Her other works included *Language—The Unknown* (1981; Eng. trans. 1989), *Black Sun: Depression and Melancholia* (1987; Eng. trans. 1989), and the novels *The Samurai* (1990; Eng. trans. 1992), *The Old Man and the Wolves* (1991; Eng. trans. 1994), and *Possessions* (1996; Eng. trans. 1998). Further translations of her works are in *The Kristeva Reader* (1986) and *The Portable Kristeva* (1997). ■ See Ross M. Guberman, ed., *Julia Kristeva Interviews* (1996).

KRISTOL, IRVING (1920–   ), U.S. social critic and editor. The son of a New York City garment worker, Kristol was a member of a left-wing student group at New York's City College (B.A. 1940). He soon abandoned his socialist views, and during the 1950s he was associated with a series of liberal anticommunist intellectual magazines, including *Commentary,* the *Reporter,* and *Encounter.* Moving further right politically during the 1960s, he cofounded the journal the *Public Interest* (1965), which attacked Great Society welfare programs, affirmative action, government regulation of industry, and the prevailing liberal attitudes of the day. His influence grew among former liberals who were repelled by the New Left, black militancy, student antiwar protesters, and the growth of the "counterculture." Subsequently known as "the godfather" of the neoconservative movement, Kristol spread his ideas through his positions as senior editor at Basic Books (1961–69), professor at New York University (1969–88), columnist for the *Wall Street Journal* (1972–   ), and board member of the American Enterprise Institute (1973–   ). His ideas were particularly influential during the years of the presidency of Ronald Reagan. In 1985 he founded *National Interest,* a quarterly focusing on foreign policy issues. His books include *On the Democratic Idea in America* (1972), *Two Cheers for Capitalism* (1978), *Reflections of a Neoconservative* (1983), and *Neoconservatism: The Autobiography of an Idea* (1995).

KRLEŽA, MIROSLAV (1893–1981), Yugoslav novelist, playwright, short-story writer, and poet. The most prominent Croatian writer of the century, Krleža published the first of his more than 50 volumes of prose and poetry immediately after World War I. He was a revolutionary socialist whose plays and novels, notably *The Glembays* (1936), *The Return of Philip Latinovicz* (1932; Eng. trans. 1959), *On the Edge of Reason* (1938; Eng. trans. 1976) and *Banquet in Blitvia* (1938–39), depicted the social injustice and decadence rife in Croatia under the Austrians. After World War II he was an outspoken advocate of artistic freedom and was president of the Yugoslav Writers Union. Additional works in English appeared in *The Cricket Beneath the Waterfall and Other Stories* (1972).

KROC, RAY ALBERT (1902–1984), U.S. restaurateur. A onetime paper-cup salesman, milk-shake-machine mechanic, and jazz musician, Kroc purchased a fast-food hamburger restaurant franchise (1955) from two brothers named McDonald—Richard (1909–1998) and Maurice (1922–71)—who were achieving high-volume sales using assembly-line techniques in their California restaurants. Kroc, who opened his McDonald's in Des Plaines, Illinois, bought the McDonald Corporation in 1961 for $2.7 million and dramatically expanded the company. Meticulously researching each outlet location, sending its owners for training at his Hamburger University in Elk Grove, Illinois, and enforcing high cleanliness standards, Kroc was a leader in the fast-food industry and amassed some $500 million. McDonald's eventually appeared in more than 100 countries and revolutionized food consumption around the world. Kroc was also the outspoken owner of the San Diego Padres baseball team (from 1974). ■ See his *Grinding It Out* (1978); Max Boas and Steve Chain, *Big Mac: The Unauthorized Story of McDonald's* (1976); and John F. Love, *McDonald's: Behind the Arches* (rev. ed. 1995).

KROCK, ARTHUR (1886–1974), U.S. journalist. Krock had a long and distinguished career as a political reporter, editor, and author. Beginning as a cub reporter for the *Louisville Herald* (1908), he worked 60 years and became the chief correspondent (1932–53) and bureau chief (1932–53) of the

New York Times Washington office. He covered every president from William Howard Taft to Richard Nixon and was the only reporter granted exclusive interviews with Franklin D. Roosevelt and Harry Truman. His pioneering editorial-page column "In the Nation" (1933–66) was a major outlet of conservative opinion. Krock was the only person ever to win four Pulitzer Prizes (1935, 1938, 1950, 1955). ■ See the collection of his columns, *In the Nation* (1966), and his *Memoirs* (1968).

KROEBER, ALFRED LOUIS (1876–1960), U.S. anthropologist. As a Columbia University undergraduate, A. L. Kroeber became interested in the languages, folklore, and art of North American Indians. After completing his doctoral work there under Franz Boas (1901), he established the anthropology department at the University of California at Berkeley and remained there until 1946. He wrote an influential introductory text, *Anthropology* (1923; rev. ed. 1948), and collaborated on *A Sourcebook in Anthropology* (1925). A major force in modern anthropology, Kroeber was remarkably eclectic; he synthesized knowledge and methodology from various disciplines in characterizing the interplay between individuals and groups in society. He investigated the ethnology of Southwest archaeology and, later, Mexican and Peruvian ruins. His later publications included *The Nature of Culture* (1952) and *Style and Civilization* (1957). ■ See studies by Theodora Kroeber (1970) and Julian H. Steward (1973).

KROEMER, HERBERT (1928–   ), German-born U.S. physicist. Kroemer studied theoretical physics at the University of Göttingen (Ph.D. 1952) and did research in several laboratories in Germany and the United States before becoming a professor at the University of Colorado, Boulder (1968–76) and the University of California, Santa Barbara (1976–   ). A pioneer in semiconductor technology, he proposed the concept of the double-heterostructure laser (1963) and helped to develop the fast opto- and microelectronic components (heterostructures) that became the basis for the development of compact-disc players, personal computers, bar-code readers, cell phones, and radio-linked satellites. Zhores Alferov, working independently in the Soviet Union, invented similar components and the two scientists shared the 2000 Nobel Prize in Physics with Jack Kilby.

KROGH, SHACK AUGUST STEENBERG (1874–1949), Danish physiologist. A pioneer of modern biology and physiology, Krogh studied zoology at the University of Copenhagen (Ph.D. 1903) and was professor of zoophysiology there from 1916 to 1945. His research on the anatomy and physiology of the blood capillaries showed how capillaries are regulated to supply muscle tissue with the required amount of blood. Krogh's findings had great influence because of their implications for metabolism, respiration, water balance, circulation, inflammation, and disease. He received the Nobel Prize in Physiology or Medicine (1920) for his experiments. A memoir is included in a 1959 edition of his *Anatomy and Physiology of the Capillaries*.

KROTO, SIR HAROLD W. (1939–   ), British chemist. Kroto studied at the University of Sheffield (Ph.D. 1964) and taught at the University of Sussex (1967–   ). While studying the formation of carbon chains in giant stars and gas clouds in outer space, Kroto utilized a specially designed laser apparatus at the Rice University Laboratories in Houston, Texas (1985). Working there with Robert F. Curl, Jr., and Richard E. Smalley, he and his colleagues discovered a previously unknown class of carbon molecule in which dozens of carbon atoms are linked together in the shape of a soccer ball. The researchers called the new molecules "fullerenes" or "buckyballs" because they resembled the geodesic domes designed by architect R. Buckminster Fuller. The discovery established a new branch of science, fullerene chemistry, and promised to lead to numerous practical applications in such fields as ultrastrong fibers, superconductors, and lubricants. Kroto, Curl, and Smalley shared the 1996 Nobel Prize in Chemistry for their pioneering work.

KRUPA, GENE (1909–1973), U.S. jazz musician. The most famous drummer in jazz history, the flamboyant Krupa was the first virtuoso jazz soloist on his instrument. As a main attraction with the Benny Goodman band (1935–38) and as an original member of the Goodman Trio (with Teddy Wilson), Krupa was a dominant personality of the swing era. He subsequently led his own bands (1938–42; 1944–51) and made numerous recordings. His life story was filmed as *The Gene Krupa Story* (1959). ■ See study by Bruce Crowther (1987).

KRUPP, GUSTAV (1870–1950) **and ALFRIED KRUPP** (1907–1967), German industrialists. The Krupps, who first began to make guns during the Thirty Years' War, developed Germany's first major steelworks (1811) and built the largest munitions factory in the world at Essen. Gustav von Bohlen und Halbach became a Krupp through marriage and named the 98-ton howitzer ("Big Bertha") of World War I after his wife. He and his son Alfried financed the Nazi party in the 1930s. Alfried was sentenced at the Nuremberg trials (1948) to 12 years' imprisonment for use of slave labor and misappropriation of property during World War II. Alfried was released in 1951 to resume ownership of the family firm, which underwent expansion thanks to the Common Market. In 1967, however, the firm, in debt, went public, and the family relinquished control in 1968. ■ See Peter Batty, *The House of Krupp* (1967), and William Manchester, *The Arms of Krupp* (1968).

KRUPSKAYA, NADEZHDA KONSTANTINOVNA (1869–1939), Soviet political figure. Krupskaya, a teacher and Marxist propagandist, met Vladimir Lenin in 1893 or 1894 in St. Petersburg. They both were sentenced to internal exile in Siberia and were married there in 1898. After her release she edited several Marxist journals and helped Lenin organize the Bolshevik party. After the 1917 revolution she served on the commissariat of education, helped establish the system of preschool education, and wrote extensively on education and women's issues. After Lenin's death (1924), she served on the Communist party's Central Committee and Control Commission and briefly opposed Joseph Stalin, but she played no role in the intraparty struggles among her husband's successors after 1926. ■ See her *Memories of Lenin* (Eng. trans. 1970); her articles and speeches in *On Education* (Eng. trans. 1957); and study by Robert H. McNeal, *Bride of the Revolution* (1972).

KRUTCH, JOSEPH WOOD (1893–1970), U.S. literary-critic and naturalist. After earning his Ph.D. from Columbia University (1923), Krutch worked for the *Nation* as a literary and dramatic critic (1924–52). He also taught at Columbia (1937–53) and wrote a study of Edgar Allan Poe (1926) and biographies of Samuel Johnson (1944) and Henry D. Thoreau (1948). A dedicated naturalist, he rejected science and technology as incompatible with humanism in *The Modern Temper* (1929). In 1950 Krutch moved to the Arizona desert, which served him as the subject of several books and TV specials. ■ See *The Best Nature Writing of Joseph Wood Krutch* (1970); *A Krutch Omnibus* (1970); his autobiography, *More Lives Than One* (1962); and the biography by John D. Margolis (1980).

KUBITSCHEK D'OLIVEIRA, JUSCELINO (1902–1976), Brazilian political leader. Kubitschek was a surgeon who became mayor of Belo Horizonte (1940) and governor of Minas Gerais (1950), acquiring a reputation as an efficient administrator. He was elected president of Brazil (1955) on a slogan of "power, transportation, and food." During his tenure (1956–61), his extensive public-works programs, including the construction of the new capital of Brasília, encouraged high levels of production and resulted in an inflated national debt.

KÜBLER-ROSS, ELISABETH (1926–   ), U.S.-Swiss psychiatrist and writer. Born in Switzerland, Kübler-Ross was one of triplets. She studied medicine at the University of Zurich (M.D. 1957), was a general practitioner in Switzerland, did an internship in the United States, worked at Manhattan State and Montefiore hospitals in New York City, and taught psychiatry at the University of Chicago. She held dual Swiss and U.S. citizenship. A pioneer in the care of dying patients, she sought to understand the experience of terminally ill patients and to help them and their families live without guilt or fear. She lectured extensively, treated individual patients, and chaired the board of Shanti-Nilaya, a nonprofit therapeutic and teaching center in California (1977–   ). Her books included *On Death and Dying*

(1969), *Questions and Answers on Death and Dying* (1974), *Death—the Final Stages of Growth* (1975), *To Live Until We Say Goodbye* (1978), *Working It Through* (1981), *Living with Death and Dying* (1981), *Remember the Secret* (1981), *On Children and Death* (1985), and *On Life After Death* (1991). She was a founder of the American Holistic Medicine Association. In her autobiography, *The Wheel of Life* (1997), she claims to have undergone out-of-body experiences and to have met spirit guides. ■ See Derek Gill, *Quest* (1980).

KUBRICK, STANLEY (1928–1999), U.S. film director. After four years as a photojournalist for *Look* magazine, Kubrick began producing documentaries in 1950 and completed his first feature in 1953. *Paths of Glory* (1957), a powerful view of military injustice, was his first critical success, followed by a number of outstanding and unique films: *Lolita* (1962), from the novel by Vladimir Nabokov; the black comedy *Dr. Strangelove, or How I Learned to Stop Worrying and Love the Bomb* (1963); and *2001* (1968), a science-fiction epic. Subsequently he adapted two English novels to film: *A Clockwork Orange* (1971), a violent view of contemporary life, and the 18th-century period piece *Barry Lyndon* (1975). He also directed *The Shining* (1979), *Full Metal Jacket* (1987), and *Eyes Wide Shut* (1999). ■ See studies by Alexander Walker (1972), Thomas Allen Nelson (1982), Michel Ciment (Eng. trans. 1983), and biography by John Baxter (1997).

KU CHIEH-KANG. *See GU JIEGANG.*

KUENEN, PHILIP HENRY (1902–1976), Dutch geologist. A professor at Gröningen (from 1946), Kuenen conducted oceanographic research that yielded significant data relating to the formation of coral atolls and the shape of oceanic basins. One of the very few experimental geologists, he used laboratory models to demonstrate that submarine canyons were formed during the Ice Age by the eroding action of turbidity currents. He also conducted laboratory studies of salt domes, volcanic cones, and other tectonic and sedimentary structures. His best-known book was *Marine Geology* (1950).

KUHN, MAGGIE (Margaret E. Kuhn; 1905–1995), U.S. political activist. Kuhn graduated from Case Western Reserve University and worked as an editor, a YWCA staff worker, and coordinator for the United Presbyterian Office of Church and Society. Her retirement at age 64 (1970) actually marked the intensification of her social activism: in that year she founded the Gray Panthers, a network supporting the rights of older Americans and, as Kuhn stressed, advocated social changes benefiting all people. The Gray Panthers opposed the depiction of older Americans in the media as senile and helpless, and influenced legislation by demanding better medical care, better nutrition, and changes in Social Security laws. Kuhn, who rejected the term "senior

citizen" and preferred to be called "an old woman," helped to found the Citizens Party with Barry Commoner and others (1980), supported the antinuclear movement, and protested Pres. Ronald Reagan's proposals to trim programs that benefit aging Americans. ■ See her autobiography *No Stone Unturned* (1991); her resource book, *Let's Get Out There and Do Something About Injustice* (1972); and Dieter Hessel, ed., *Maggie Kuhn on Aging* (1977).

KUHN, RICHARD (1900–1967), Austrian-born German organic chemist. Kuhn studied at the University of Munich (Ph.D. 1922) and was director of the Kaiser Wilhelm (later Max Planck) Institute for Medical Research and professor at the University of Heidelberg (from 1929). Working independently of Paul Karrer, Kuhn and his colleagues synthesized vitamins A and B_2 at about the same time as Karrer did. He also did research on carotinoids and prepared eight of them in pure form. Although he won the 1938 Nobel Prize in Chemistry, the Nazi government refused to allow Germans to accept the award and Kuhn did not receive the prize until after World War II.

KUHN, THOMAS SAMUEL (1922–1996), U.S. historian of science. Kuhn studied physics at Harvard (Ph.D. 1949), where, as an assistant to Harvard president James B. Conant in a science course for nonspecialists, he became interested in the sociology of knowledge and discovery. He analyzed the importance of accepted scientific "paradigms" in his influential book *The Structure of Scientific Revolutions* (1962), which sold hundreds of thousands of copies worldwide and influenced philosophers and social scientists as well as natural scientists. In it he argued that science did not advance through a steady, progressive growth of knowledge but rather by periodic "intellectually violent revolutions" in which one conceptual view, or paradigm, was replaced by a new one. He also wrote *The Copernican Revolution* (1957); *Black-Body Theory and the Quantum Discontinuity, 1894–1912* (1978); and a collection of articles, *The Essential Tension* (1977). He taught at the University of California, Berkeley (1958–64), Princeton (1964–79), and the Massachusetts Institute of Technology (1979–91). ■ See study by Steve Fuller (2000).

KUHN, WALT (1877–1949), U.S. painter and sculptor. Kuhn was born in Brooklyn and studied in New York and abroad. He was a professional bicycle racer in the 1890s and then a successful cartoonist, set designer, and director of revues before turning to painting. Kuhn played a key role in organizing the 1913 New York Armory show, introducing the work of impressionists and cubists—including Matisse, Van Gogh, Picasso, and others—to the American public. He often painted clowns and acrobats in a bold, simple style. In the 1940s he painted still lifes and landscapes. ■ See Paul Bird, *Fifty Paintings by Walt Kuhn* (1940), and study by Philip R. Adams (1978).

KUIPER, GERARD PETER (1905–1973), Dutch-born U.S. astronomer. Kuiper made several discoveries about the earth's solar system and influenced the direction of new investigations into this field of astronomy. He joined the staff of the University of Chicago's Yerkes Observatory in 1936 and later served as director of the Yerkes and McDonald observatories (1947–49; 1957–60). He discovered (1948) carbon dioxide in the atmosphere of Mars and later found that Titan, Saturn's largest moon, may be the only moon to have an atmosphere. He discovered (1948–49) previously unknown moons of Uranus and Neptune, and he revised astronomers' estimates as to the size of Pluto. He played a key role in the early U.S. space program and headed the Lunar and Planetary Laboratory at the University of Arizona (from 1960).

KUN, BÉLA (1886–1939), Hungarian political leader. As a World War I prisoner of war in Russia, Kun joined the bolsheviks, who trained him as a revolutionary. Pursuing the dream of a worldwide revolution, he returned to Hungary in 1918, founded the Hungarian Communist party, and set up a Hungarian Soviet Republic, which survived for 133 days (Mar. 21–Aug. 1, 1919). After its collapse, Kun worked as a leading Comintern official during the 1920s and 1930s until he was accused of Trotskyism (1937) during the Stalinist purges and arrested. He died in Soviet captivity but was rehabilitated, posthumously, in 1956. ■ See study by Rudolf L. Tökés (1967) and György Barsányi, *The Life of a Communist Revolutionary* (Eng. trans. 1993).

KUNDERA, MILAN (1929–), Czech-born writer. The son of a pianist, Kundera grew up in Prague, where his fiction is generally set. After being expelled from the Communist party (1948) he worked as a laborer and dance-band pianist. *The Joke* (1967; Eng. trans. 1982), his satirical novel about life under Stalinism, appeared in Czechoslovakia shortly before the liberal period known as the "Prague spring" came to an end. After 1968, his works were not published in his homeland and were unavailable in libraries or bookstores. He emigrated to France (1974), winning recognition in the West as one of the most original and important writers of his generation. After he published *The Book of Laughter and Forgetting* (1979; Eng. trans. 1980)—which characteristically combined history and fantasy with humor reminiscent of that of Franz Kafka—Czechoslovakia revoked his citizenship. He became a French citizen in 1980 and taught at the École des Hautes Études en Sciences Sociales, Paris (1980–). *The Unbearable Lightness of Being* (1982; Eng. trans. 1984), a seven-part narrative about the closely linked destinies of two pairs of lovers, reflected the rage and disillusionment of Czech intellectuals in the wake of the 1968 Soviet invasion. While he rejected the label "dissident writer," Kundera noted that his focus on psychological and sexual experience is subversive because it shows the inevitable ambiguity of social and moral issues. Kundera

also wrote plays and stories. His later works include the novels *Immortality* (1990; Eng. trans. 1991), *Slowness* (1996; Eng. trans. 1996), and *Identity* (1997; Eng. trans. 1998), and *Testaments Betrayed: An Essay in Nine Parts* (1993; Eng. trans. 1995).

KÜNG, HANS (1928–), Swiss theologian. After ordination as a Roman Catholic priest (1954), Kung made a reputation with *Justification: The Doctrine of Karl Barth and a Catholic Reflection* (1957; Eng. trans. 1964) and became a professor of theology at the University of Tübingen (1960). After publishing *The Council and Reunion* (1960; Eng. trans. 1961) on opportunities for ecumenical work at the Second Vatican Council, he was appointed by Pope John XXIII as an official theologian at that council (1962–65). A critic of papal authority, Küng was the first major Roman Catholic theologian to reject the doctrine of papal infallibility in his book *Infallible? An Inquiry* (1970; Eng. trans. 1971; rev. ed. 1994). He later challenged the views of Pope John Paul II. After publishing the best-selling *On Being a Christian* (1974; Eng. trans. 1976) and repeating in print his views on papal infallibility and the suppression of dissent within the church (1979), Küng was censured by the Vatican and forbidden to teach theology under Roman Catholic church auspices. Küng also wrote *Does God Exist?* (1978; Eng. trans. 1980), *Christianity and the World Religions* (1984; Eng. trans. 1986), *Judaism* (1991; Eng. trans. 1992), *Dying with Dignity* (1995, with Walter Jens; Eng. trans. 1995), and the essay collection *Theology for the Third Millennium* (Eng. trans. 1988). ■ See the National Catholic Bishops Conference (Washington, D.C.) publication *The Küng Dialogue* (1980) and a study of the debate by L. Scheffczyk (1982). See also the study edited by H. Haring and K.-J. Kuschel (1979). and Robert Nowell, *A Passion for Truth* (1981).

KUNITZ, STANLEY JASSPON (1905–), U.S. poet and editor. Kunitz studied at Harvard (A.B. 1926; M.A. 1927) and taught poetry at various institutions, including the New School for Social Research in New York City (1950–57) and Columbia University (1963–85). He wrote modern metaphysical verse, winning a Pulitzer Prize for *Selected Poems* (1958). His poetry was gathered in *The Poems of Stanley Kunitz, 1928–1978* (1979); *The Wellfleet Whale and Companion Poems* (1983), *Passing Through* (1995), and *The Collected Poems* (2000) followed. *A Kind of Order, A Kind of Folly* (1975) assembled critical essays and other prose written over four decades. *Next-to-Last Things* (1986) contained poems, essays, and aphorisms. Kunitz also wrote several reference books on writers (the first under the pseudonym Dilly Tante). They included *Twentieth Century Authors* (1942; with Howard Haycraft), *British Authors before 1800* (1952), and *European Authors 1000–1900* (1967). He served as U.S. poet laureate (2000–). ■ See studies by Marie Henault (1980) and Gregory Orr (1985).

KUNIYOSHI, YASUO (1893–1953), Japanese-born U.S. artist. Kuniyoshi studied weaving and dye technique in Japan; in his teens he moved (1906) to the United States, and he studied at the Art Students League of New York, where he later taught (1933–53). The Japanese artistic tradition influenced his work throughout his career: Kuniyoshi's fanciful early work gave way to more somber landscapes and sensual portrayals of the human figure. During and after World War II his work addressed political and social issues. He was also a leading figure in artists' associations.

KUNSTLER, WILLIAM MOSES (1919–1995), U.S. lawyer. An honors graduate of Yale (1941) and Columbia Law School (1948), Kunstler practiced conventional law until he began defending Freedom Riders during the civil-rights struggles of the early 1960s. He subsequently became identified as the foremost defender of New Left, antiwar, and counterculture leaders such as Lenny Bruce, Martin Luther King, Jr., the Chicago seven, the Catonsville nine, and the Black Panthers. A prolific writer and popular speaker, Kunstler likened himself to a "worker priest" in his emotional involvement and personal solidarity with his "movement" clients. ▪ See his account of his civil-rights cases, *Deep in My Heart* (1966); his autobiography, *My Life as a Radical Lawyer* (1994; with Sheila Iseuberg); and biography by David J. Laugum (1999).

KUO MO-JO. *See GUO MORUO.*

KUPKA, FRANK or FRANTIŠEK (1871–1957), Czech-born painter. Considered one of the earliest abstract painters to work with geometrical forms, Kupka studied at the School of Fine Arts in Prague and in Vienna before he settled permanently in Paris (1895). After establishing a reputation as a book illustrator, he produced his first entirely abstract paintings (1911–12) and developed a style consisting of varicolored shapes superimposed on each other that associated him with the orphists (whose geometric style used vivid colors). Titles like *Fugue for Two Colors* (1912), *Jazz-Hot No. 1* (1935), and *Music* (1936) expressed his conviction that color, like music, stirs strong feeling. His work was not fully recognized and his influence on modern art was not appreciated until after World War II. ▪ See study by Ludmila Vachtova (Eng. trans. 1968).

KURCHATOV, IGOR VASILYEVICH (1903–1960), Soviet physicist. A graduate of the Crimean University (1923), Kurchatov joined the Leningrad Physico-Technical Institute (1925) and began work in nuclear physics in 1933. Under his direction the first Soviet cyclotrons were developed and studies were published describing nuclear chain reactions (1939) and the spontaneous fission of uranium (1940). He founded (1943) and headed the Institute of Atomic Energy of the Academy of Sciences (Moscow), and he supervised the development of the first atomic reactor in Europe (1946), the first Soviet atomic bomb (1949) and thermonuclear (or hydrogen) bomb (1953), and the world's first industrial atomic-power plant (1954). He also directed research on controlled thermonuclear reactions.

KUROSAWA, AKIRA (1910–1998), Japanese film director. Kurosawa studied Western painting and worked as an illustrator before writing his first screenplays in the late 1930s. He made his directorial debut with *Sanshiro Sugata* (1943), an original screenplay about a judo champion. In 1951 he won the grand prize at the Venice Film Festival for direction of *Rashomon* (1950), the first Japanese film to attract Western attention. Other sword-fighting costume epics directed by Kurosawa included *The Seven Samurai* (1954) and *Yojimbo* (1961), both of which inspired foreign imitations. Kurosawa's films were noted for their visual elegance, precise composition, and the studied character analysis of his screenplays. The most Western of Japanese filmmakers, he made film adaptations of Dostoevsky's *The Idiot* (1951), Gorky's *The Lower Depths* (1957), and Shakespeare's *Macbeth* (*The Throne of Blood,* 1957). His later films included the epics *Dersu Uzala* (1975), *Kagemusha* (1980), *Ran* (1985), and *Akira Kurosawa's Dreams* (1990), a Samurai epic based on *King Lear.* ▪ See Kurosawa's *Something Like an Autobiography* (Eng. trans. 1982) and Donald Richie, *The Films of Akira Kurosawa* (rev. ed. 1984).

KURUSU, SABURO (1886–1954), Japanese diplomat. Kurusu entered the foreign ministry immediately upon graduation from college in 1909. He gained wide experience through his posts in China, the United States, Peru, Chile, Greece, Italy, and Belgium, as well as at the ministry in Japan. As ambassador to Germany, Kurusu signed the Berlin (Axis) Pact in 1940. Since he spoke English fluently and was married to an American, he was sent to Washington, D.C., as a special envoy in Nov. 1941 and was negotiating with Secretary of State Cordell Hull when the Japanese attacked Pearl Harbor (Dec. 7, 1941), the event that brought the United States into World War II. Kurusu insisted that he had no prior knowledge of the attack. After the war he was a professor at Tokyo University.

KUSCH, POLYKARP (1911–1993), German-born U.S. physicist. Brought to the United States as an infant, Kusch studied physics at the University of Illinois (Ph.D. 1936) and taught at Columbia University (1937–41; 1946–72) and at the University of Texas at Dallas (1972–82). At Columbia he worked with Isidor I. Rabi on the first radio-frequency atomic-beam experiments. For his further experiments, which resulted in the precise determination of the magnetic moment of the electron and revolutionized the study of quantum mechanics, Kusch shared the 1955 Nobel Prize in Physics with Willis E. Lamb, Jr.

KUWATLI, SHUKRI AL- (1891–1967), Syrian political leader. An activist in the nationalist movement from his youth, Kuwatli worked against the Turks—and then the

French—for the independence of Syria. During the 1930s he was a member of the "National Bloc," the major anticolonial movement; and when Syria was made an independent republic (1943), Kuwatli was elected president. He was elected to a second term in 1948 but was overthrown in a military coup in March 1949. After a five-year exile in Egypt, however, he returned home and served as president (1955–59). He and Egyptian leader Gamal Abdel Nasser formed the short-lived United Arab Republic (1958–61), a union of Syria and Egypt.

KUZMIN, MIKHAIL ALEKSEYEVICH (1875–1936), Russian poet. Kuzmin figured prominently among the St. Petersburg (now Leningrad) symbolists, but he did not embrace their mystical or philosophical stance. He advanced the principle of "beautiful clarity," later adopted by members of the acmeist school: Osip Mandelstam, Anna Akhmatova, and Nikolai Gumilev. Kuzmin adapted *Songs of Alexandria* (1908) from the French writer Pierre Louÿs's *Chansons de Bilitis* and composed music for his own pastoral, *Seasons of Love* (1907). His prose includes *Wings* (1906; Eng. trans. 1972), a defense of homosexuality, and *Travelers by Land and Sea* (1915; Eng. trans. 1983), an erotic account of St. Petersburg bohemian circles. Kuzmin has not been published in the Soviet Union. English translations of his work are in *Selected Prose and Poetry* (1980).

KUZNETS, SIMON SMITH (1901–1985), Russian-born U.S. economist. Emigrating from the Ukraine to the United States at age 21, Kuznets entered Columbia University as an undergraduate and received a Ph.D. four years later (1926). As a staff member of the National Bureau of Economics during the Great Depression, he began studying business cycles. His landmark work, *National Income and its Composition, 1919–1938* (2 vols., 1941), introduced a conceptual framework that allowed economists to measure national income with confidence. Kuznets was largely responsible for the statistical methods that governmental and private agencies use to gauge economic progress. He developed the concept of gross national product. He taught at the University of Pennsylvania (1930–54), taking leave during World War II to work as associate director of the Bureau of Planning and Statistics of the War Production Board. He later taught at Johns Hopkins (1954–1960) and Harvard (1960–71).

KY, NGUYEN CAO (1930–   ), Vietnamese military and political leader. Ky began his military training (1948) at a French colonial academy and traveled to France and North Africa (1952) for aviation training. After his return to South Vietnam (1954) the flamboyant Ky received U.S. training, gained a reputation as a militant anticommunist, and achieved high rank in the air force, eventually becoming its commander (1963). He served as premier (1965–67) and vice president (1967–71) during the period when the Vietnam War was expanding and U.S. military involvement was increasing. His authoritarian government failed to carry out social reforms and was charged with nepotism and corruption. As the South Vietnamese government was on the verge of collapse (1975), Ky fled to the United States and became a businessman. ■ See his autobiography, *Twenty Years and Twenty Days* (1976).

L

LABAN, RUDOLF VON (1879–1958), Slovakian-born dance theorist. A philosopher and teacher who established dance institutes throughout Europe, Laban was the pioneer theoretician of modern dance. His work inspired the "movement choirs" popular in Germany after World War I and he developed ideas about movement in space that influenced choreographers Mary Wigman and Kurt Jooss and subsequently led to expressionism in modern dance. He was best known for inventing a system for notating choreographic movement called Labanotation (1928). He directed the Allied State Theaters of Berlin (1930) before leaving Germany in the late 1930s for Britain, where he continued to teach and do research. In the 1940s, Laban applied his notation system to describe, in the booklet *Laban Lawrence Industrial Rhythm* (1945), how "choreographing" the movements of industrial workers could boost production and safety.

LACAN, JACQUES (1901–1981), French psychiatrist, philosopher, and literary critic. A Freudian, Lacan received a medical degree in Paris, then specialized in neuropsychiatry and psychoanalysis. He was associated with the École Pratique des Hautes Études in Paris, and he founded the École Freudienne de Paris (1963), but dissolved it amid controversy in 1980. His unorthodox methods included dispensing with the standard 50-minute therapy session and replacing it with one lasting from 5 to 10 minutes. His writings, which reflect the influence of structural linguists Ferdinand de Saussure and Roman Jakobson, were assembled in the collection *Écrits* (1966; Eng. trans. 1977). He pioneered structural studies in psychoanalysis, stressing the Freudian concept of repression (which itself had been repressed, according to Lacan), and posited that psychoanalysis had discovered, in the unconscious, the "whole structure of language." His controversial theories influenced contemporary studies of literature, philosophy, and ideology. English translations of his writings are in *The Four Fundamental Concepts of Psychoanalysis* (1978), *Speech and Language in Psychoanalysis* (1981), and *Feminine Sexuality* (1983). ▪ See studies by Anika Rifflet-Lemaire (Eng. trans. 1977), Stuart Schneiderman (1983), Elisabeth Roudinesco (Eng. trans 1997); and Catherine Clément, *The Lives and Legends of Jacques Lacan* (Eng. trans. 1983).

LACERDA, CARLOS (1914–1977), Brazilian political leader. A radical in his youth, Lacerda adopted conservative views in the 1940s and founded the newspaper *Tribuna da Imprensa* in 1949. He carried his opposition to Pres. Getúlio Vargas into active politics and represented Rio de Janeiro in congress (1954–60) and served as governor of the state of Guanabara (1960–65). It is said that largely due to his influence, three presidents fell from power in the period 1954–64, but he was unable to realize his ambition to replace them. Although he supported the 1964 military coup, he soon broke with the new regime. Deprived of his political rights in 1968, Lacerda undertook a successful career in business and investments.

LACHAISE, GASTON (1882–1935), French-born U.S. sculptor. The son of a Parisian cabinetmaker, Lachaise studied at the École des Beaux Arts before moving with his American bride to the United States (1906), where he became a pioneer of modern sculpture and produced notable portrait busts. He was best known for his large figures of nude women conceived as earth goddesses, with massive breasts and thighs and tapered waist and limbs, such as *Standing Woman* (1912–27) and *Floating Figure* (1935). ▪ See study by Gerald Nordland (1974).

LADYSMITH BLACK MAMBAZO. *See SHABALALA, JOSEPH.*

LAEMMLE, CARL (1867–1939), German-born U.S. motion-picture producer. Emigrating to the United States at age 17, Laemmle held a series of clerical jobs before buying his first nickelodeon (1906) in Chicago. An immediate success, he started his own movie-distribution company and started to produce his own films in 1909. In 1912 he merged several small firms to form Universal Pictures and in 1914 began construction of Universal City (north of Los Angeles), which was to become one of the world's largest and most successful studios. Laemmle was responsible for establishing the "star" system in Hollywood, for launching the careers of Lon Chaney, Erich von Stroheim, and Irving Thalberg, among others, and for such movie classics as *Traffic in Souls* (1912), *The Hunchback of Notre Dame* (1923), and *All Quiet on the Western Front* (1930). He held control of Universal from 1920 through 1936. ▪ See biography by John Drinkwater (1931) and Bernard F. Dick, *City of Dreams* (1997).

LA FOLLETTE, ROBERT MARION (1855–1925), U.S. politician. The leading progressive politician of his time, "Fighting Bob" La Follette served as Republican governor of Wisconsin (1901–06) and initiated the "Wisconsin Idea," a program that reorganized state politics by establishing direct primary elections, state regulation and equitable taxation of railroads and corporations, state civil service, and commissions of technical experts to help regulate and administer railroads, conservation programs, and tax assessments. His program influenced reformers throughout the country. As a U.S. senator (1906–25), La Follette continued to sponsor and support progressive legislation. Advocating the nationalization of railroads, collective bargaining for labor, the destruction of monopolies, and the establishment of public-works programs, La Follette ran for president on the Progressive party ticket (1924) and polled nearly five million votes but carried only Wisconsin. ■ See his autobiography (1913); biographies by Belle C. and Fola La Follette (2 vols., 1953) and David Paul Thelen (1976); and Nancy C. Unger, *Fighting Bob La Follette* (2000).

LA FONTAINE, HENRI MARIE (1854–1943), Belgian legal scholar. La Fontaine was a professor of international law in Brussels and a socialist member of the Belgian senate (1895–1936). As a member of the International Peace Bureau (president, 1907–43) he was influential in its efforts to bring about the Hague peace conferences of 1899 and 1907. He was active in many peace organizations and he received the 1913 Nobel Peace Prize. He also was a member of the Belgian delegation to the Paris Peace Conference (1919) and to the League of Nations Assembly (1920–21) and wrote numerous books on domestic and international law.

LAGERKVIST, PÄR (1891–1974), Swedish novelist, poet, and dramatist. Lagerkvist rebelled against his conservative, peasant background and was a youthful radical. Contact with fauvist and cubist painting on a visit (1913) to Paris influenced his work toward the same kind of expressionism. Books and plays like his poetry collections *Anguish* (1915) and *Evening Land* (1953; Eng. trans. 1975) revealed his despair over the tragedy of war and his pessimism about the future. Later he developed a greater faith in human goodness and the possibilities for hope. He regarded himself as a "believer without faith—a religious atheist." His metaphorical plays, poems, and novels, written in stark prose, reflected this belief. His major novels, *The Hangman* (1933; Eng. trans. 1936, 1954), *The Dwarf* (1944; Eng. trans. 1945), and his most important work, *Barabbas* (1950; Eng. trans. 1951), explored hypocrisy, evil, and the possibility of faith. English translations of his stories are in *The Marriage Feast* (1973) and translations of his plays, and an essay, are in *Modern Theater* (1966). He was awarded the Nobel Prize for Literature in 1951. ■ See study by Robert Spector (1973).

LAGERLÖF, SELMA (1858–1940), Swedish novelist. As a young woman, Lagerlöf qualified as a schoolteacher when her family suffered financial setbacks. Her hugely successful first book, *The Story of Gösta Berling* (1891; Eng. trans. 1898), depicted life in rural Värmland, the southeastern Swedish province where she grew up. She portrayed its patriarchal society in later works as well, including the autobiographical *Mårbacka* (1922; Eng. trans. 1923). Lagerlöf's

best works powerfully combined vivid description, recurrent symbols, and folk elements. The unfinished *The Ring of the Löwenskölds* (1925–28; Eng. trans. 1931) reflected the spiritualism of her later years. She won the 1909 Nobel Prize in Literature. ■ See *Memories of My Childhood* (1930; Eng. trans. 1934), *The Diary of Selma Lagerlöf* (1932; Eng. trans. 1936), and the study by Hanna Larsen (1936).

LA GUARDIA, FIORELLO HENRY (1882–1947), U.S. political leader. Known as "the Little Flower," La Guardia represented New York City in Congress (1917–19; 1923–33) and gained recognition as a leading liberal reformer. He cosponsored the Norris-La Guardia Act (1932), which restricted the use of injunctions against unions and thus helped establish labor's right to strike. Although a lifelong Republican, he was elected mayor of New York City on a Fusion party ticket (1933) and became a colorful national symbol of progressive urban government. Serving for 12 years, he initiated a vast series of political and social reforms and was regarded as the city's most effective and beloved mayor. ■ See his autobiography (1948); biographies by Arthur Mann (2 vols., 1959–65); Thomas Kessner (1989); and William Manners, *Patience and Fortitude* (1976); and Lawrence Elliott, *Little Flower* (1983).

LA GUMA, ALEX (Justin Alexander La Guma; 1925–1985), South African writer. The son of the president of the South African Coloured People's Congress, La Guma was imprisoned and placed under house arrest several times for his struggles against apartheid. His three short, naturalistic English language novels, *A Walk in the Night* (1962), *And a Threefold Cord* (1964), and *The Stone Country* (1967), vividly described the misery of the lower-class nonwhites in South Africa and established his reputation as one of his country's most militant and politically committed writers. Living in exile in England (1966–78), he wrote *In the Fog of the Season's End* (1972), *Time of the Butcherbird* (1979), and edited *Apartheid: A Collection of Writings on South African Racism by South Africans* (1971). He later served as the African National Congress (ANC) representative in Havana, Cuba (1978–85). ■ See study by Cecil Abrahams (1985).

LAHEY, FRANK HOWARD (1880–1953), U.S. surgeon. A graduate of the Harvard Medical School (M.D. 1904), Lahey was a pioneer in the surgical treatment of thoracic diseases, ulcers, and cancer. At the Lahey Clinic in Boston (founded 1922) he specialized in operations on the thyroid gland. He served as president of the American Medical Association (1941–42) and during World War II chaired the War Manpower Commission's medical procurement and assignment service.

LAHR, BERT (Irving Lahrheim; 1895–1967), U.S. entertainer. High school dropout Lahr toured America with a vaudeville troupe for three years before establishing his reputation with the Columbia burlesque circuit. Launching his career as a comedian in *Hold Everything* (1928), he appeared regularly in Broadway shows, including *The Show Is On* (1936; with Beatrice Lillie), *Du Barry Was a Lady* (1939; with Ethel Merman), and *Two on the Aisle* (1951–52; with Dolores Gray). Lahr also performed in plays by Shakespeare and Aristophanes, as well as in Samuel Beckett's *Waiting for Godot* (1956). His film credits included *The Wizard of Oz* (1939), in which he combined his mournful features and gentle humor to create the role of the Cowardly Lion. ▪ See John Lahr, *Notes on a Cowardly Lion* (1969).

LAING, RONALD DAVID (1927–1989), Scottish psychiatrist. A precocious child of working-class parentage, R. D. Laing studied at the University of Glasgow (M.D. 1951), then undertook research on schizophrenia. In *The Divided Self* (1960), he explained the disease as a defensive response to an insane world, a therapeutic "trip" possibly leading to transcendence. In *The Politics of Experience* (1967), he continued his argument that a sick society damages the individual. Laing favored the establishment of communes where the "mad" would live together with sympathetic companions. Other books included *Knots* (1970), *The Politics of the Family* (1976), *Sonnets* (1980), and *The Voice of Experience* (1982). ▪ See his *Wisdom, Madness and Folly: The Making of a Psychiatrist* (1985); study by Martin Howarth-Williams (1977); Richard Evans, *Dialogue with R. D. Laing* (1981); and Bob Mullan, *Mad to Be Normal: Conversations with R. D. Laing* (1995).

LAJPAT RAI, LALA (1865–1928), Indian nationalist. Lajpat Rai, a lawyer, was a leading nationalist in the Punjab. He believed in self-reliance and was a leader of the Hindu revivalist Arya Samaj Society (from 1882) and the Indian National Congress party (from 1888). A militant, he presided over the Congress party session (1920) that launched the nonviolent, noncooperation movement. He later joined the Swaraj party (1923) and served in the legislative assembly. He died after being beaten by the police during a mass demonstration. His books included *Young India* (1916), *England's Debt to India* (1917), and *Unhappy India* (1928; a refutation of Katherine Mayo's *Mother India*). ▪ See his *Autobiographical Writings* (1965) edited by Vijaya C. Joshi; Daniel Argov, *Moderates and Extremists in the Indian National Movement 1883–1920* (1967); and studies by P. Nagar (1978) and Shayamnandan Shahi (1986).

LAKE, SIMON (1866–1945), U.S. naval architect and engineer. Born into a family of inventors, Lake pioneered in ship construction and design and contributed to the development of the modern submarine. He invented the even-keel submarine torpedo boat and built the first experimental underwater boat (1894). In 1897 he constructed the gasoline-powered *Argonaut I,* the first submarine to be used successfully in open waters. Lake advised the British, Russians, and Ger-

mans on torpedo boats, although he was more interested in peaceful uses of his inventions. In the 1920s, his Lake Torpedo Boat Co. (est. 1900) went under. In debt in his last years, he used underwater apparatus he had designed (1932) to search for sunken treasure, unsuccessfully.

LAMB, WILLIS EUGENE, JR. (1913–), U.S. physicist. While on the faculty of Columbia University (1938–51), Lamb used an electron beam to measure precisely the energy levels in a hydrogen atom. For his pioneering research, which led to refinements in quantum theory and to a new understanding of the interaction of electrons and electromagnetic radiation, he shared the 1955 Nobel Prize in Physics with Polykarp Kusch. Lamb subsequently taught at Stanford, Harvard, Oxford, Yale, and the University of Arizona.

LAMMING, GEORGE (1927–), Barbadian novelist and poet. Lamming taught school in Trinidad before emigrating to London (1950). His novels focused on the social, psychological, and political conflicts that abounded in the West Indies as they emerged from colonial rule to independent status. His best-known works were the autobiographical *In the Castle of My Skin* (1953), which recounted scenes from his childhood, and *Of Age and Innocence* (1958), which presented the conflict of youth and age—of the colonized versus the untainted—in a newly independent Caribbean island. As in *Season of Adventure* (1960), he suggested that true personal and national fulfillment could be achieved only through the destruction of the old slave and colonial mentality. *The Emigrants* (1954) and *Water with Berries* (1972) dealt with the problems of West Indians living in Britain, and *Natives of My Person* (1972) was a novel about the slave trade in the 17th century. ▪ See Sandra P. Paquet, *The Novels of George Lamming* (1982).

LAMONT, THOMAS WILLIAM (1870–1948), U.S. banker. The son of a small-town Methodist minister, Lamont graduated from Harvard (1892) and entered the business world shortly thereafter. He was secretary and treasurer of the Bankers Trust Co. (1903) and vice president of the First National Bank (1909) before becoming a partner in the firm of J. P. Morgan and Co. (1911). From that time on, he concentrated on international finance and was one of the world's most powerful bankers. He was largely responsible for debt adjustment or multimillion-dollar loans to China (1920), Mexico (1922), Austria (1923), France (1924), Italy (1925), and Japan (1927); he worked on the Dawes Plan for German reparations (1924). His son was the noted humanist philosopher and civil libertarian Corliss Lamont (1902–1995). ▪ See Edward M. Lamont, *The Ambassador from Wall Street* (1994).

L'AMOUR, LOUIS DEARBORN (1908–1988), U.S. writer. A best-selling writer of westerns, L'Amour was born in

North Dakota and for two decades drifted around the world as a seaman and adventurer. He published a volume of poetry in 1939, turned to pulp-magazine fiction after World War II, and in 1951–52 wrote four books about Hopalong Cassidy under the pseudonym Tex Burns. Subsequent westerns, turned out by L'Amour at the rate of three a year, included *Hondo* (1953), *Shalako* (1962), *How the West Was Won* (1962), and *Catlow* (1963). The best-seller *Jubal Sackett* (1985) was the 18th book in a series chronicling settlement of the U.S. West. A scholar of old-West folklore, diaries, and genealogical records, he described the conflict between builders and exploiters and the meeting of cultures on the frontier. He was said to be one of the world's most widely read authors: nearly 200 million copies of his 101 books were in circulation in 1988, and 16 more books were published posthumously. His last best-seller was *Last of the Breed* (1986), a modern novel about an American-Indian pilot. He was awarded a Congressional gold medal in 1983. ■ See his autobiography, *Education of a Wandering Man* (1990).

LAMPRECHT, KARL (1856–1915), German historian. Instead of focusing narrowly on heroes and politics, Lamprecht argued in his monumental, 21-volume study of Germany (1891–1913) that history should deal with the whole of human experience. The Leipzig University professor (1891–1915), one of the first to introduce psychological factors to historical studies, devised a descriptive characterization of historical epochs as symbolic, individualistic, impressionistic, or nervous, and he founded an Institute for Cultural and Universal History to train followers. His work helped legitimize social and cultural history. ■ See his lectures in *What Is History?* (Eng. trans. 1905) and study by Roger Chickering (1993).

LANCEFIELD, REBECCA C. (Rebecca Craighill; 1895–1981), American bacteriologist. Working primarily at Rockefeller University (1918–80), Lancefield conducted crucial research on streptococci, a genus of bacteria, and on their relationship to rheumatic fever. The research procedures and the Lancefield classification system that she designed permitted advances in knowledge of the organism and of the disease. Lancefield was the first woman elected (1961) president of the American Association of Immunologists; she was later named (1970) to the U.S. National Academy of Sciences.

LAND, EDWIN HERBERT (1909–1991), U.S. inventor and businessman. Eager to pursue research on polarized light, Land dropped out of Harvard College to set up his own laboratory (1932). He had already invented the sheet polarizer. Previous light polarizers had been crystals, which were hard to use. Land lined up many of these microscopic crystals in the same direction and embedded them in a clear plastic sheet to retain their alignment. He used this inexpensive, useful material, which he called Polaroid, to manufacture camera filters and sunglasses. His "one-step" Polaroid Land camera (1947) featured one-minute film development inside the camera and earned more than $5 million in its first year on the market. Land presided over his own company until 1982. He also made theoretical contributions to the understanding of vision, including the "retinex" theory (1977) that altered scientists' understanding of the process of color perception. In 1980 he founded the Rowland Institute for Science in Cambridge, Massachusetts. ■ See Victor K. McElheny, *Insisting on the Impossible* (1998).

LANDAU, LEV DAVIDOVICH (1908–1968), Soviet physicist. Landau received his doctorate from Leningrad University when he was 19 and later studied with Niels Bohr in Copenhagen. In the 1930s he made an important mathematical explanation of atomic magnetism in substances like iron. This work had implications for the understanding of metals and ferromagnetism. An independent, outspoken scientist, he was briefly arrested (1938) by the Soviet secret police but was saved by the intervention of physicist Peter Kapitza. Landau was best known for continuing and expanding research begun by Kapitza on the properties of helium in its solid and liquid states, which Landau explained through quantum mechanics. He received the 1962 Nobel Prize in Physics; that same year he was injured in an automobile accident and was kept alive (he clinically died several times) through massive medical efforts. He never regained his former creative ability. ■ See Alexander Dorozynski, *The Man They Wouldn't Let Die* (1965), and study by Anna M. Livanova (Eng. trans. 1980).

LANDERS, ANN (Esther Pauline Friedman Lederer; 1918–), U.S. columnist. In 1955, at age 37, housewife Lederer applied for the "Ann Landers" slot at the *Chicago Sun-Times* and proceeded to fill her advice column with pithy, no-nonsense counsel. A bundle of energy, Landers didn't smoke or drink but was in many respects more "hip" than her identical twin and rival-columnist sister, Abigail Van Buren. She came out in favor of gun control, advised against the Vietnam War, and replied to one husband worried about his wife, "Many are cold, but few are frozen." By 1974 Landers claimed 60 million readers, received 1,000 letters daily, and had published several collections of her columns. ■ See her *Ann Landers Speaks Out* (1975); Margo Howard, *Eppie* (1982); Janice Pottker, *Dear Ann, Dear Abbey* (1997); and David Grossvogel, *Dear Ann Landers* (1997).

LANDIS, KENESAW MOUNTAIN (1866–1944), U.S. lawyer, judge, and baseball executive. Appointed U.S. district judge in Illinois (1905), Landis made headlines (1907) when he fined the Standard Oil Co. more than $29 million (the decision was reversed on appeal) for unlawful freight rebates. In the wake of the 1919 "Black Sox" baseball bribery scandal, he was appointed baseball's first commissioner, and although resented for his autocratic rule, he did much to restore the game's reputation through his honesty and integrity. In 1944 Landis was elected to the National Baseball Hall of Fame.

LANDON, ALFRED MOSSMAN (1887–1987), U.S. businessman and political leader. Born in a Pennsylvania parsonage and graduated from the University of Kansas (1908), Alf Landon began as a bookkeeper and invested his savings shrewdly in oil to become a millionaire by 1929. He was elected governor of Kansas in 1932, one of few successful Republican candidates during the Depression. A paragon of midwestern folksiness, he opposed government intervention in the economy and was nicknamed "Frugal Alf" for his balanced state budgets. The 1936 GOP nominee for president, Landon carried only two states in his landslide loss to Franklin D. Roosevelt. His daughter, Nancy Kassebaum (1932–   ), served as a Republican U.S. senator from Kansas (1979–96). ▪ See biography by David R. McCoy (1966).

LANDOWSKA, WANDA (1877–1959), Polish harpsichordist. A Warsaw-born musical prodigy, Landowska moved to Paris in 1900 to study and compose for piano. Near Paris, in 1925, she founded a school devoted to the interpretation of early music. She became an authority on 17th- and 18th-century music and was solely responsible for reviving popular interest in the harpsichord, which for 200 years had been relegated to museums. Her technical and artistic mastery of the instrument, displayed in countless recitals and recordings of works by Bach, Handel, Couperin, and Rameau, was legendary. Francis Poulenc (1928) and Manuel de Falla (1926) wrote concertos especially for her. Landowska lived in the United States from 1941 until her death. Her books included *Music of the Past* (1908; Eng. trans. 1924).

LANDRU, HENRI DÉSIRÉ (1869–1922), French murderer. Frequently referred to as "the modern Bluebeard," Landru was one of the century's most notorious criminals. The police accused him of murdering up to 300 lonely women. He operated by gaining control of the finances of his victims after first promising to marry them. Although the number of his victims was probably exaggerated, he was convicted of murdering 10 women and a boy (1921) and was executed. The case against him was based on circumstantial evidence and no bodies were ever found, though the prosecution claimed that Landru incinerated the bodies at his villa. ▪ See biography by René Masson (Eng. trans. 1965).

LANDRY, THOMAS WADE (1924–2000), U.S. football coach. Tom Landry played football at the University of Texas (B.S. 1949) and received a degree in mechanical engineering at the University of Houston (1952). A cornerback with the New York Giants (1950–55), he served as the

team's defensive coach (1956–59), introduced the 4–3 "flex" defense, and gained a reputation as a coaching genius. He was head coach of the Dallas Cowboys from the team's inception (1960–89) and methodically developed a dazzling multiformation offense and disciplined coordinated defense to lead the team to numerous division championships and two Super Bowl victories (1972, 1978). His regular-season record of 250–162–6 was one of the most successful in pro football history. A devout Christian, he participated in evangelist Billy Graham's crusades and directed the Fellowship of Christian Athletes. ▪ See his autobiography (1990).

LANDSTEINER, KARL (1860–1943), Austrian-born U.S. pathologist and immunologist. A research assistant at the Vienna Pathological Institute (1898–1908), Landsteiner found (1900–02) that there were at least four major types of human blood, A, B, O, and AB, which vary according to the antigens attached to the red blood cells. He discovered (1927) the additional blood types M and N, and the Rhesus (Rh) factor (1940; with A. S. Wiener). For this work, which made possible the safe transfusion of blood, he was awarded the 1930 Nobel Prize in Physiology or Medicine. He moved to the United States in 1922 and taught at the Rockefeller Institute for Medical Research (1922–39).

LANE, SIR ALLEN (1902–1970), British pubisher. With little formal education behind him, Lane joined his uncle's publishing firm, Bodley Head, at age 17 (1919), and succeeded his uncle as managing director six years later. In 1935, with Bodley Head failing, Lane, with two brothers, invested $500 to launch his own firm, Penguin Books. Wagering that good titles would have mass appeal, he bought rights to reprint quality fiction, scholarly books, and classics in inexpensive paperback editions. Works by Ernest Hemingway, André Maurois, and Compton Mackenzie were on his initial list. Penguin Books got off to a slow start, but when Woolworth's began stocking his books, Lane's concept proved successful. His approach revolutionized British publishing and influenced the reading habits of Britons and readers in other English-speaking countries. By 1945 he was selling more than 8 million books a year. His best-seller was D. H. Lawrence's *Lady Chatterley's Lover,* which sold millions of copies after a British court declared that it was not obscene (1960). ▪ See study by J. E. Morpurgo (1979).

LANE, BURTON (**Burton Levy; 1912–1997**), U.S. composer. Lane was a songwriter at 15 and a contributor to New York musical revues before he moved to Hollywood in 1933. For 20 years he composed songs and scores for such films as *Dancing Lady* (1933), *I Hear Music* (1941), and *Royal Wedding* (1951). His hit Broadway shows were *Finian's Rainbow* (1947), which included the songs "Old Devil Moon," "How Are Things in Glocca Morra," and "If This Isn't Love," and *On a Clear Day You Can See Forever* (1965). As president of the American Society of Composers,

Authors and Publishers (1957–67) he worked to improve copyright rules and royalties.

LANE, GERTRUDE BATTLES (1874–1941), U.S. magazine editor. The editor of *Woman's Home Companion* from 1912 until her death, Lane was the most prominent and highest-paid woman in the magazine-publishing industry of her era. She introduced many new features in the magazine (including a column with medical information for mothers), provided information on family psychological problems, encouraged the new field of home economics, and editorialized against Prohibition and child labor. She boosted the magazine's monthly circulation from 738,000 to 3,500,000, making it the most widely read women's magazine in the country. She was also a vice president and director of the Crowell-Collier Publishing Co. and adviser to the editors of *Collier's* and the *American Magazine.*

LANG, FRITZ (1890–1976), German-U.S. film director. Born and educated in Vienna, Lang traveled around the world before serving in the Austrian army in World War I. In Berlin after the war he directed *Metropolis* (1926), *M* (1931), and the "Dr. Mabuse" films (1922, 1933). These highly stylized dramas of criminals and psychopaths living in a world of acute socioeconomic tension became film classics. Fleeing from the Nazis (1933), he began a second career in Hollywood, where he directed *Fury* (1936), *You Only Live Once* (1937), *Scarlet Street* (1945), and *Rancho Notorious* (1952), skillful films but less highly regarded than his early work. In the 1950s Lang returned to Germany and directed a third film in the "Dr. Mabuse" series (1960). ■ See studies by Robert A. Armour (1978) and Frederick W. Ott (1979) and biography by Patrick McGilligan (1997).

LANG, JOHN THOMAS (1876–1975), Australian political leader. Lang was first elected to the New South Wales legislature, as a Labourite, in 1913. He twice served as provincial premier and treasurer (1925–27; 1930–32) and pursued policies hostile to business and favorable to labor. Lang was dismissed from office by the governor after defying a federal law ordering the banks to pay to the central government money held on state accounts. He remained party leader until 1939 and later served in the federal Parliament (1946–49). After his retirement (1949), he spent several years as the editor of a vehemently anticommunist weekly newspaper and remained a controversial figure. He wrote several books, including *I Remember* (1956), *The Great Bust* (1962), and *The Turbulent Years* (1970).

LANGE, CHRISTIAN L. (1869–1938), Norwegian historian and statesman. A graduate of the University of Oslo (1893), Lange taught history at the Nobel Institute (1890–1909) and served as secretary of the Nobel Committee in Oslo (1900–09). He was a delegate to the 1907 Hague Peace Conference and was secretary-general of the InterParliamen-

tary Union (1909–33), an international organization of parliamentarians established to promote world peace. For these activities he shared the 1921 Nobel Peace Prize with Karl Hjalmar Branting. As Norwegian delegate to the League of Nations (1920–37), he promoted the cause of disarmament.

LANGE, DAVID RUSSELL (1942–), New Zealand political leader. The son of a doctor, Lange studied law at the University of Auckland (LL.B. 1966; LL.M. 1970) and worked as a crusading lawyer among the poor in Auckland. A moderate socialist, he joined the Labour party and was elected to the House of Representatives (1977–89). Elected party leader in 1983, he led the Labourites to an overwhelming victory in the 1984 elections. As prime minister (1984–89; foreign minister, 1984–87), Lange devalued the dollar by 20 percent, cut the federal budget, and embraced free-market principles. He signed a pact with Australia and other nations of the region declaring the South Pacific a nuclear-free zone (1985), and instigated a major dispute with the United States, its Anzus treaty ally (along with Australia), by banning nuclear-armed or nuclear-powered ships from New Zealand ports (1985). This had the effect of blocking U.S. Navy ships from docking in the country. In retaliation the U.S. suspended the treaty. He wrote *Nuclear Free: The New Zealand Way* (1990) and *Broadsides* (1992).

LANGE, DOROTHEA (Dorothea Nutzhorn; 1895–1965), U.S. photographer. Disabled by polio as a child in New Jersey, Lange was a survivor with a lifelong sympathy for the disadvantaged. She operated a portrait studio in Oakland, California (1919–40), but went forth with her camera during the Depression to document social problems. She collaborated with her husband, economist Paul Taylor, on *An American Exodus: A Record of Human Erosion* (1939), a testimony to the extent of rural poverty, and traveled throughout the United States taking pictures for the Farm Security Administration (1935–42), some of which were later published in *Dorothea Lange Looks at the American Country Woman* (1967). Her photo "Migrant Mother" (1936) is one of the most widely recognized images of the Depression. ■ See biography by Milton Meltzer (1978) and study by Karin B. Ohrn (1980).

LANGE, OSKAR RICHARD (1904–1965), Polish-U.S. economist. Lange studied at the University of Cracow (LL.D. 1928) before arriving in the United States as a fellow of the Rockefeller Foundation in 1932. He taught economics at the University of Michigan (1936–43) and the University of Chicago (1943–45), but after World War II he renounced his U.S. citizenship and returned to Poland. He was appointed ambassador to the United States (1945–46) and Poland's delegate to the United Nations (1946–49). A specialist in socialist economic theory and in economic fluctuations, he headed the economic council of the Polish cabinet and was deputy chairman of the council of ministers (1957–65) and professor at the University of Warsaw (1955–65). He was an undogmatic socialist whose works, including *Political Economy* (1959; Eng. trans. 1963), incorporated modern economic techniques into Marxist analysis and influenced many East European economists.

LANGER, FRANTIŠEK (1888–1965), Czech novelist and playwright. Born into a Jewish family in Prague, Langer was an army doctor who eventually became head of the Czech army medical corps. He was a member of the Czech Legion and a close friend and follower of its founder, Thomas Masatyk. Langer's themes were wide-ranging and frequently dealt with the moral problems of ordinary people. His best-known plays were *The Camel Through the Needle's Eye* (1923; Eng. trans. 1929), a comedy about lower-class Prague society, and *The Outskirts* (1925; Eng. trans. n.d.), a psychological drama concerned with the anguish of a murderer who wants to be convicted of his crime.

LANGER, SUSANNE (Susanne Knauth; 1895–1985), U.S. philosopher and educator. A graduate of Radcliffe College (B.A. 1920; Ph.D. 1926), Langer studied with Alfred North Whitehead, whose influence is reflected in *The Practice of Philosophy* (1930) and *An Introduction to Symbolic Logic* (1937). Langer's major work, *Philosophy in a New Key* (1942), argues that all intellectual activity—in the arts as well as the sciences—takes place in the symbolic mode. She proposed a rigorous and systematic study of language, both the discursive symbols of scientific inquiry and the nondiscursive language of art and myth. She treated music as a symbolic form that can mediate between insight and feeling. Langer's later works included *Feeling and Form* (1953) and *Mind: An Essay on Human Feeling* (3 vols., 1967–82).

LANGER, WILLIAM LEONARD (1896–1977), U.S. historian. Born in Boston and educated at Harvard (Ph.D. 1923), Langer was a diplomatic historian who taught at Harvard from 1927 to 1964. His major works were *European Alliances and Alignments 1871–90* (1931) and *The Diplomacy of Imperialism 1890–1902* (1935). An intelligence expert during World War II, he remained associated with the Central Intelligence Agency after the war. Langer's book, *Our Vichy Gamble* (1947), based on classified government documents, was criticized as an apologia for U.S. policy. He also edited *An Encyclopedia of World History* (1940) and the *Rise of Modern Europe* series (from 1932). ■ See his autobiography, *In and Out of the Ivory Tower* (1977).

LANGMUIR, IRVING (1881–1957), U.S. chemist. One of the century's most versatile scientists, Langmuir earned (1906) a Ph.D. from the University of Göttingen, Germany, and became (1909) an industrial researcher at the General Electric Research Laboratory, which he directed from 1932 to 1950. His work at GE led to the development of the gas-filled incandescent lamp, the atomic-hydrogen welding

torch, the mercury-condensation vacuum pump, and the high-vacuum tube that was used in radio broadcasting. Langmuir also did pioneering studies of electron emissions, atomic structure, chemical bonding, and artificial rainmaking. His best-known research, which investigated oil films on water, created the new field of surface chemistry and won for him the 1932 Nobel Prize in Chemistry. ■ See Albert Rosenfeld, *The Quintessence of Irving Langmuir* (1966), and Virginia V. Westervelt, *Incredible Man of Science* (1968).

LANGNER, LAWRENCE (1890–1962), Welsh-born U.S. theatrical figure. Langner emigrated to the United States (1911) and became a successful patent attorney in New York. His first love, however, was the theater, and he helped establish the Washington Square Players (1914) and wrote several plays for the Provincetown Players. He was a founder (1919) and codirector (with Theresa Helburn; 1919–62) of the Theatre Guild, which transformed the American theater by presenting serious contemporary drama to a mass audience. Langner was responsible for securing plays of George Bernard Shaw and Eugene O'Neill for the guild, which also produced notable productions of plays by Robert Sherwood, Maxwell Anderson, Philip Barry, S. N. Behrman, and Elmer Rice. ■ See his autobiography, *The Magic Curtain* (1951).

LANSBURY, GEORGE (1859–1940), British political leader. A founder and editor of the socialist *Daily Herald* (1912), Lansbury was a popular left-wing Labourite whose devotion to pacifism and humanitarianism severely curtailed his career. He was a member of the House of Commons (1910–12; 1922–40) and leader of the Labour party (1931–35). After he was forced to relinquish party leadership, he personally visited (1937) fascist dictators Adolf Hitler and Benito Mussolini in an effort to forestall war. ■ See biographies by Raymond Postgate (1951) and Jonathan Schneer (1990).

LANSING, ROBERT (1864–1928), U.S. lawyer and public official. A prominent international lawyer, Lansing represented the U.S. government before various international tribunals (from 1892) prior to being named counselor of the State Department (1914) and secretary of state (1915) by Pres. Woodrow Wilson. Envisioning U.S. entry into World War I, he urged a policy of friendship toward Britain, sought peace with Mexico, helped negotiate the purchase of the Virgin Islands, and signed the Lansing-Ishii agreement (1917), which reaffirmed the open-door policy in China but acknowledged Japan's special interests. He also carried out a nonrecognition policy toward the bolshevik government in Soviet Russia. A conservative and a realist in foreign affairs, he broke with the more idealistic Wilson over aspects of the League of Nations and its covenant and was asked to resign (February 1920). His books included *The Peace Conference: A Personal Narrative* (1921), *The Big*

Four and Others of the Peace Conference (1921), and *War Memoirs* (1935).

LANSKY, MEYER (Maier Suchowljansky; 1902–1983), Russian-born U.S. organized-crime leader. A product of New York City's Lower East Side Jewish ghetto, Lansky befriended future crime bosses Charles (Lucky) Luciano and Benjamin (Bugsy) Siegel in his youth and got involved in gangland activities during the 1920s. He was a leader of organized-crime syndicates from the 1930s, a director of Murder Inc., and an alleged financial genius who reputedly amassed a personal fortune of $300 million from bootlegging, loan sharking, stock manipulation, the numbers racket, Cuban gambling casinos, Miami Beach real estate, Las Vegas hotels, and legitimate businesses backed by underworld money. Although frequently in court, he went to jail only once—for two months on a gambling conviction in Saratoga Springs, New York (1953). ■ See biographies by Hank Messick (1971) and Dennis Eisenberg, et al. (1979) and Robert Lacey, *Little Man* (1991).

LANTZ, WALTER (1900–1994), U.S. cartoonist and film animator. Lantz studied at the Art Students League in New York and got his start as an animator of Hearst newspaper cartoons. Moving to Hollywood in 1927, he set up his own cartoon unit at the Disney and Universal studios before becoming an independent in 1936. His most enduring cartoon character was a brash, noisy woodpecker named Woody (born 1940). ■ See study by Joe Adamson (1985).

LANVIN, JEANNE (1867–1946), French fashion designer. Lanvin was a milliner and designer of juvenile wear before introducing (1909) the line of women's formal attire that became the height of fashion in the years after World War I. Her designs were influenced by the costumes of her native Brittany. The name Lanvin was associated not only with the long-waisted *robe de style* of the 1920s but also with a famous line of perfumes, including My Sin and Arpège.

LAO SHE (pseudonym of Shu Qingqun; old style: SHU CH'ING-CH'UN; 1899–1966), Chinese novelist. Lao lived in London (1924–30), where he taught Chinese at the School of Oriental and African Studies and wrote *Zhao Ziyue* (Chao Tzu-yueh; 1929), which has been called the first serious comic novel in Chinese literature. His early works reflected his belief that individualism would save China, but after 1934 he concentrated his works on the social environment and the futility of individual struggle. His finest novel, *Camel Xiangzi* (Camel Hsiang-tzu; 1938), was a best-seller in the United States in an unauthorized and bowdlerized translation called *Rickshaw Boy* (1945). A 1979 English translation, *Rickshaw,* is faithful to the original. His other translated works included the satirical novel *Cat Country* (1970), *Crescent Moon and Other Stories* (1986), and the plays *Dragon Beard Ditch* (1956) and *Teahouse* (1980). During World War II Lao wrote many patriotic and propagandistic novels, plays, and short stories, and he continued his literary output after the communists came to power in 1949. He was denounced during the Cultural Revolution of the 1960s and his death was attributed to persecution by the Red Guards. ■ See Zbigniew Slupski, *The Evolution of a Modern Chinese Writer* (1966) and study by Ranbir Vohra (1974).

LARA, AGUSTÍN (1900–1970), Mexican composer. Often compared to Irving Berlin, Lara was the most prolific and successful composer of popular music in Mexican history. A self-taught musician, he began his career as a piano player in a bordello and later (1930) had his own Mexico City radio program. In a career spanning five decades, he composed more than 500 songs, and more than 30 film scores. An idol, whose many love affairs and wives made him a favorite of gossip columnists, he made frequent public appearances as a pianist, conductor, and singer and was honored by both the Mexican and Spanish governments. Among his most popular songs were "Granada," "Be Mine Tonight," "You Belong to My Heart," "The Nearness of You," and "Woman."

LARBAUD, VALÉRY (1881–1957), French writer. Larbaud's considerable fortune enabled him to devote his life to reading, writing, and travel. In *Fermina Marquez* (1911; Eng. trans. 1988), he sensitively captured the social atmosphere of an exclusive boys' boarding school. *A. O. Barnabooth, His Diary* (1913; Eng. trans. 1924), his most-discussed work, purports to be the journal of a wealthy young Peruvian vagabond in search of his identity. Larbaud also wrote *Childish Things* (1945; Eng. trans. 1990), stories, poems, travel notes, criticism, a *Journal: 1912–1935* (1955), and translated many world-famous authors into French, including Walt Whitman and James Joyce. ■ See biography by John L. Brown (1981).

LARDNER, RING (Ringgold Wilmer Lardner; 1885–1933), U.S. short-story writer. "This story is slightly immoral, but so, I guess, are all stories based on truth," Lardner wrote of one of his characteristic works, which exposed the mean spirits and petty concerns of "normal" people. Drawing on his experience as a baseball writer (1913–19) in Chicago and New York, Lardner published the mildly satiric *You Know Me Al: A Busher's Letters* (1916). After moving (1919) to New York City, he developed his sardonic view of American sports and business types in *How to Write Short Stories* (1924), *Round Up* (1929), and other collections. He wrote *June Moon* (1929), a satirical play about Tin Pan Alley, with George S. Kaufman. *Some Champions* (1976) appeared posthumously. ■ See his comic autobiography, *The Story of a Wonder Man* (1925; repr. 1975); Ring Lardner, Jr., *The Lardners* (1976); and biography by Jonathan Yardley (1977).

LARGO CABALLERO, FRANCISCO (1869–1946), Spanish political leader. A national trade-union leader and secretary of the Socialist party, Largo Caballero served as minister of labor (1931–33). Moving increasingly leftward, he advocated a socialist revolution, and his radical rhetoric and intransigent policies after the popular-front electoral victory (February 1936) helped bring about the split between moderate and revolutionary socialists and was considered an important factor in precipitating the military coup (July 1936) and subsequent civil war. He was named premier and defense minister of a coalition government (September 1936), but internal dissension led to the government's collapse (September 1937). He went into exile in France (1939) and was imprisoned in a German concentration camp during World War II.

LARIONOV, MIKHAIL (1881–1964), Russian-born painter and illustrator. Larionov studied art in Moscow. With his wife, painter Natalia Goncharova, he turned away from such European-oriented artists as Burlink and Kandinsky and founded (1912) the Donkey's Tail group, which considered itself an independent Russian school. His early works reflected strong interest in Russian folk painting and primitive art; after 1911 he worked in various abstract modes, introduced a short-lived movement called rayonism, and organized several landmark exhibitions. With Goncharova, Larionov left Russia (1914) to design for Sergei Diaghilev's Ballet Russe (1914–29). Larionov also made numerous drawings and illustrated poems by futurists. ■ See studies by Anthony Parton (1993) and E. F. Koutun (1998).

LARKIN, PHILIP (1922–1985), British poet. Larkin recounted his years as a scholarship student at Oxford (B.A. 1943; MA. 1947) in his novel *Jill* (1946); he later worked as a university librarian and jazz critic. Inspired by Thomas Hardy's poetry to write from his own experience, he reacted against recent British romantic and politically committed poetry. He wrote clearly and simply, in an amused, wry tone about ordinary people in provincial settings and was pointedly antimodernist. His books, including *The Less Deceived* (1955), *The Whitsun Weddings* (1964), and *High Windows* (1974), showed his resigned and understanding acceptance of life's defeats and joys. ■ See his *Required Writing: Miscellaneous Pieces: 1955–1982* (1984) and studies by David Timms (1973) and Andrew Motion (1993).

LARROCHA, ALICIA DE (1923–), Spanish pianist. A prodigy who made her debut at age 5, de Larrocha studied the classical German masters before moving on to the Spanish composers at age 15. After several years of recording and touring in Europe and the United States, she gained recognition as the finest contemporary Spanish pianist. In 1959 she opened a music school in Barcelona with her husband. Known for precision and delicacy, she was among the most frequently recorded artists of her day, and was a featured performer at the annual "Mostly Mozart" festival in New York City.

LARSON, GARY (1950–), U.S. cartoonist. As a child, Larson assembled a menagerie consisting of snakes, frogs, tarantulas, lizards, and pigeons and spent a great deal of time sketching his animals. After graduating from Washington State University (1972), he toured as part of a jazz duo and then worked for the Seattle Humane Society as an animal abuse investigator. He began producing a one-panel whimsical cartoon called *Nature's Way* for a local magazine and newspaper, and eventually for the San Francisco Chronicle Features syndicate (1979), which changed the name of the strip to *The Far Side*. Depicting bizarre, often macabre situations, the strip featured cunning and resourceful animals with human quirks and characteristics along with vulnerable human beings who acted in weirdly foolish ways. Although considered by some to be sick and offensive, the strip became extremely popular. It was syndicated in more than 900 newspapers by the late 1980s and became a staple of pop culture. *The Far Side* was avidly read by members of the scientific community and an exhibition of 400 of Larson's scientifically oriented cartoons toured natural history museums around the country. More than a dozen *Far Side* collections were published in book form, and cartoons appeared on greeting cards, mugs, calendars, and posters. Larson stopped producing new cartoons in the early 1990s.

LARTIGUE, JACQUES HENRI (1894–1986), French painter and photographer. At age 7 Lartigue began taking delightful photographs of his family and friends at play in an elegant world of privilege and sport. Later, he photographed his wife, child, and mistress with the same free and childlike pleasure. Lartigue was known primarily as a painter until his photos were first exhibited in 1962 and later published as *Diary of a Century* (1970).

LASCH, CHRISTOPHER (1932–1994), U.S. social historian. Born in Omaha and educated at Harvard (B.A. 1954) and Columbia (Ph.D. 1961), Lasch taught at the University of Rochester (from 1970). A democratic socialist, he wrote works of revisionist history including *American Liberals and the Russian Revolution* (1962) and *The Agony of the American Left* (1969). *Haven in a Heartless World* (1977) was an indictment of the effects of capitalism and consumerism in destroying the family as a realm of private relations. He also wrote *The Culture of Narcissism* (1979), a pessimistic critique of capitalism and the atomization of modern society, and its sequel, *The Minimal Self: Psychic Survival in Troubled Times* (1984). His last books were *The True and Only Heaven: Progress and Its Critics* (1991), *The Revolt of the Elites and the Betrayal of Democracy* (1995), and *Women and the Common Life: Love, Marriage and Feminism* (1997).

LASHLEY, KARL SPENCER (1890–1958), U.S. psychologist. A professor at the universities of Minnesota (1920–26), Chicago (1929–35), and Harvard (1935–55) and director of the Yerkes Laboratory of Primate Biology (1942–55), K. S.

Lashley did pioneering research into the relationship between brain mass and learning ability. Experimenting primarily with white rats, he discovered that the rate and accuracy of learning is proportionate to the total amount of cerebral cortex tissue available and that every psychological function does not have a specific localization in the cortex. His major findings appeared in *Brain Mechanisms and Intelligence* (1929). His research led to efforts by psychologists to teach chimpanzees and dolphins to communicate by language. Selected papers are in *The Neuropsychology of Lashley* (1960). See Nadine Weidman, *Constructing Scientific Psychology* (1999).

LASKER, ALBERT DAVIS (1880–1952), U.S. advertising executive and philanthropist. The dominant force in American advertising for four decades, Lasker invented the notion of "salesmanship in print" in transforming advertising from the mere dispensing of information about a product to the changing of public attitudes toward it. By supplying a "reason why" a consumer should buy a product, Lasker, who headed the Lord and Thomas agency (1908–42), made a fortune convincing people to buy (Sunkist) orange juice, Kleenex, and Kotex and to smoke when they wanted to lose weight–"Reach for a Lucky instead of a sweet." With his wife, he set up the Albert and Mary Lasker Foundation (1943), which funded many medical research and public-health projects and granted an annual award for outstanding medical research. ▪ See John Gunther, *Taken at the Flood* (1960).

LASKER, EMANUEL (1868–1941), German chess player. The grandson of a rabbi and son of a cantor, Lasker was considered by many to be the greatest chess player of all time. A master at analyzing the board as well as the psychological characteristics of his opponent, he held the world chess championship from 1894 until 1921, when he was defeated by José Raúl Capablanca.

LASKI, HAROLD JOSEPH (1893–1950), British political scientist. Laski was a popular and influential professor at the London School of Economics (1920–50), an authority on the United States, a friend of such international statesmen as U.S. Pres. Franklin D. Roosevelt and French Premier Léon Blum, and an active member of the Labour party executive (1936–49). His Marxism became more orthodox over the years along with his conviction of the inevitability of revolution at home and abroad. He wrote many books including *A Grammar of Politics* (1925), *Liberty in the Modern State* (1930), *Reflections on the Revolution of Our Times* (1943), and *American Democracy* (1948). ▪ See biography by Kingsley Martin (1953); Herbert A. Deane, *The Political Ideas of Harold J. Laski* (1955); and study by Granville Eastwood (1977).

LASKY, JESSE LOUIS (1880–1958), U.S. film producer. Lasky lost small fortunes as an Alaskan gold prospector and

a New York City cabaret producer before entering the motion-picture business in partnership with Samuel Goldwyn and Cecil B. DeMille (1913). They produced the first feature-length film made in Hollywood, *The Squaw Man* (1914), and merged their firm with several others to form Paramount Pictures, one of Hollywood's leading studios until it went bankrupt in 1932. Lasky produced more than 1,000 pictures in his career, including *Wings* (1927), *The Covered Wagon* (1923), and *Beau Geste* (1926), and developed the careers of actors Clara Bow, Gloria Swanson, Pola Negri, and Gary Cooper. In the 1940s and 1950s he made a series of film biographies, including *Sergeant York* (1941), *Rhapsody in Blue* (1945), and *The Great Caruso* (1951). ▪ See his autobiography, *I Blow My Own Horn* (1957).

LASSWELL, HAROLD DWIGHT (1902–1978), U.S. political scientist. Born in Illinois and educated at the University of Chicago (B.A. 1922; Ph.D. 1926), Lasswell was psychoanalyzed by one of Sigmund Freud's protégés while doing postgraduate work in Europe. Adapting the Freudian approach to politics, he wrote *Psychopathology and Politics* (1930), *World Politics and Personal Insecurity* (1935) and *Power and Personality* (1948), which emphasized the personal and sexual dimensions of political leadership. Lasswell, who taught at the University of Chicago (1924–38) and at Yale University (1945–75), also did pioneering work in the areas of communication, content analysis, policy sciences, systems theory, legal theory, and world trend studies.

LATTIMORE, OWEN (1900–1989), U.S. orientalist. Lattimore spent several years in China as a young man, involved in business, research, and writing. He became an expert in Chinese, Manchurian, and Mongolian history and culture and served as editor of the magazine *Pacific Affairs* (1934–41), published by the Institute of Pacific Relations. He later served as director of the Page School of International Relations at Johns Hopkins (1939–53) and served in several government posts during World War II. In 1950 his career was disrupted when he was accused by Sen. Joseph McCarthy of being a top Soviet spy. Although cleared by a Senate committee later that year, he was indicted for perjury (1952). All charges were dropped in 1955. Lattimore worked abroad after 1953 and was founding director (1963–70) of the Department of Chinese studies at the University of Leeds, England. He also wrote *Ordeal by Slander* (1950) as well as many works on Asian history, including *Asian Frontiers of China* (1940), *Solution in Asia* (1945), *Nationalism and Revolution in Mongolia* (1955), and *Nomads and Commissars* (1970). ▪ See study by Robert P. Newman (1992).

LATTRE DE TASSIGNY, JEAN DE (1889–1952), French general. A graduate of St. Cyr Military Academy, Jean de Lattre saw action during World War I and in the Rif War (Morocco, 1920s) before being named the youngest French general on the eve of World War II. Although arrested by the collaborationist Vichy government for resisting German entry into unoccupied France (1943), he escaped from prison, joined the Free French forces, and led the French army in the recapture of southern France and in the invasion of Germany (1944–45). He represented France at the signing of the German surrender, May 8, 1945. After the war he was inspector general of the French army (1945–48), commander in chief of the Western European ground forces (1948–50), and French high commissioner and military commander in chief in Indochina (1950–52). He was posthumously granted the rank of marshal. ■ See Guy Salisbury-Jones, *So Full a Glory* (1955).

LAUDER, SIR HARRY MACLENNAN (1870–1950), Scottish singer and comedian. A music-hall comedian known for his quaint Scottish songs, Lauder worked in a flax mill and coal mine before he became a professional singer. His first London appearance was at Gatti's Music Hall (1900), where his charm and gay humor won him rapid success. He was knighted in 1919 for entertaining servicemen during World War I, work he resumed during World War II. Lauder wrote many of his own songs, including "Roamin' in the Gloamin'" and "I Love a Lassie." He made several world tours and performed frequently in North America. ■ See his memoirs, *Between You and Me* (1919), *Wee Drappies* (1931), and *Ticklin' Talks* (1934).

LAUE, MAX THEODOR FELIX VON (1879–1960), German physicist. After graduating from the University of Berlin (Ph.D. 1903), Laue assisted (1905–09) Max Planck at the Institute of Theoretical Physics, Berlin. Laue's study of wave optics led to his experiment at the University of Zurich (1912) that proved that X rays are diffracted by a crystal, the diffraction effects obtained being proportional to the crystal's symmetry. This discovery provided strong evidence for the electromagnetic wave nature of X rays; it paved the way for a study of crystal structure, the beginning of solid-state physics, and made possible the measurement of X-ray wavelengths (X-ray spectroscopy). Laue was awarded the 1914 Nobel Prize in Physics for his discovery. From 1919 to 1943 he was professor of theoretical physics at the University of Berlin, and he played a major role in the rebuilding of German science after World War II.

LAUGHLIN, ROBERT B. (1950–), U.S. physicist. Laughlin studied at the Massachusetts Institute of Technology (Ph.D. 1979), worked at Bell laboratories, and subsequently taught at Stanford University (1985–). After Bell colleagues Daniel C. Tsui and Horst Störmer devised (1982) an experiment with electrons that led to the discovery of the phenomenon known as the fractional quantum Hall effect, Laughlin explained the effect. The three scientists demonstrated that at temperatures near absolute zero, electrons exposed to a powerful magnetic field act as if they were a fluid and form new "quasi particles," each having a fraction of the charge of an electron. The experiment yielded insights into the inner structure and dynamics of matter. Laughlin, Tsui, and Störmer shared the 1998 Nobel Prize in Physics.

LAUGHTON, CHARLES (1899–1962), British actor. Laughton worked in his family's hotel for seven years before enrolling at the Royal Academy of Dramatic Art (London) in 1925. His stage debut (1926) launched him as a major character actor with roles in *The Government Inspector, The Cherry Orchard,* and *Payment Deferred.* He joined the Old Vic in 1933 and appeared with the Comédie Française in 1936. A large man with bulging eyes and a leering smile, Laughton was usually cast as a tyrant or an ogre in his films: *The Private Life of Henry VIII* (Academy Award, 1933), *Mutiny on the Bounty* (1935), *The Hunchback of Notre Dame* (1939). In 1955 he directed a minor film classic, *The Night of the Hunter.* For 33 years he was married to actress Elsa Lanchester, who wrote *Charles Laughton and I* (1938). ■ See biographies by Charles Higham (1976) and Simon Callow (1988).

LAUREL, STAN (Arthur Stanley Jefferson; 1890–1965), **and OLIVER HARDY** (1892–1957), U.S. comedy team. Son of a British showman, Laurel was a music-hall comedian who made an unsuccessful solo film debut in *Nuts in May* (1917). Producer Hal Roach teamed (1926) the thin comic with fat Oliver Hardy, a former cinema owner from Georgia, in *Putting Pants on Philip* and *The Battle of the Century,* two 1927 shorts that launched their career as the most successful comedy duo in film history. Laurel conceived many of the gags and helped direct features such as *Babes in Toyland* (1934), *Way Out West* (1937), and *Swiss Miss* (1938). A pair of overgrown children playing cat and mouse, the silly, shuffling Laurel and the frustrated, tie-twiddling Hardy specialized in boisterous, knockabout comedy. In 1940 they formed their own production company to make *Great Guns* (1941), *The Big Noise* (1944), and *The Bullfighters* (1945). ■ See John McCabe, *Mr. Laurel and Mr. Hardy* (1961) and *The Comedy World of Stan Laurel* (1974); Fred L. Guiles, *Stan* (1980); and study by Bruce Crowther (1987).

LAURENCE, MARGARET, (Jean Margaret Wemys; 1926–1987), Canadian writer. Born and raised in Neepawa, a small prairie town in Manitoba, Laurence was educated in Winnipeg and lived in Somaliland (now Somalia; 1950–52) and Ghana (1952–57) with her engineer husband. Her first published works, including the novel *This Side Jordan* (1960), the travel journal *The Prophet's Camel Bell* (1963), and the short-story collection *The Tomorrow-Tamer* (1963), were all set in Africa. She is best known, however, for a series of four linked novels about the lives of courageous women striving for personal fulfillment. The novels, *The Stone Angel* (1964), *A Jest of God* (1966; filmed as *Rachel, Rachel,* 1968), *The Fire-Dwellers* (1969), and *The*

Diviners (1974), were set in Manawaka, a fictionalized version of Neepawa. Laurence also wrote children's stories, a volume of essays, (*Heart of a Stranger; 1976*), and the autobiographical *Dance on the Earth: A Memoir* (1989).

LAURENCE, WILLIAM L. (William L. Siew; 1888–1977), Lithuanian-born U.S. journalist. One of the nation's first full-time science reporters, the Harvard-educated Laurence wrote for the *New York Times* for 34 years (1930–64; Pulitzer Prize, 1937 and 1946). Nicknamed "Atomic Bill," he was the first journalist to write extensively about atomic-energy research and was the only journalist allowed to witness the first atomic bomb explosion at Alamogordo, New Mexico (July 16, 1945), and to witness the atomic bombing of Nagasaki, Japan (Aug. 9, 1945). Among his books were *Dawn Over Zero—the Story of the Atomic Bomb* (1946), *The Hell Bomb* (1951), and *Men and Atoms* (1959).

LAURIER, SIR WILFRID (1841–1919), Canadian statesman and politician. Born in what is now the province of Quebec, Laurier practiced law before turning to politics as a Liberal (1871). Elected to Parliament in 1874, he was soon recognized as a major spokesman for the province, and he served as leader of the federal Liberal party (1887–1919). In 1896 he became Canada's first French-Canadian prime minister, but in his 15 years in office (1896–1911) he found himself torn between the French and English political viewpoints. Under Laurier, however, Canada attained a large measure of autonomy from Britain: the last British troops left Canada, the great western prairies were settled, immigration was encouraged, and the economy boomed. An advocate of a reciprocity treaty with the United States, he was defeated in the 1911 elections by a coalition of militant French nationalists and conservative English manufacturers. His stand against conscription as leader of the opposition during World War I precipitated a split in the Liberal party, and it carried only Quebec in the 1917 national elections. ■ See biography by Joseph Schull (1965), and studies by Barbara Robertson (1971) and Richard Clippingdale (1979).

LAUTERPACHT, SIR HERSCH (1897–1960), British legal scholar and international jurist. Born in the Russian Ukraine, Lauterpacht studied at the University of Vienna (Ph.D. 1922), where he was a student of Hans Kelsen, and at the University of London (LL.D. 1925). He edited the *Annual Digest of Public International Law Cases* (1935–60), was a professor of international law at Cambridge (1938–55), and was a member of the British executive at the Nuremberg war crime trials (1945–46). After World War II, as an adviser to the U.N. Secretariat on the codification of international law (1948) and a member of the U.N. International Law Commission (1951–55) he helped develop international legal protection of human rights. He later served on the International Court of Justice (1955–60). His books *The*

Function of Law in the International Community (1933) and *International Law and Human Rights* (1950) became standard reference works.

LAVAL, PIERRE (1883–1945), French political leader. The son of a café owner in southern France, Laval was first elected to parliament (as a socialist) in 1914 from the "red" Paris suburb of Aubervilliers, which he also served as mayor (1923–44). A political opportunist who traveled the French ideological spectrum from left to right, he served as premier (1931–32; 1935–36) and foreign minister (1931–32; 1934–36). He was repudiated in 1936 on the revelation of his secret agreement with British foreign secretary Sir Samuel Hoare that would have allowed Italy to control much of Ethiopia. Laval returned to power during World War II, after the fall of France in June 1940, serving as vice premier in the collaborationist Vichy regime and in 1942 succeeding Marshal Henri Pétain as premier of France. He tried to defend French interests while acceding to German demands, for which he was convicted of treason and executed after the war. ■ See his *Diary* (Eng. trans. 1948); biographies by Hubert Cole (1963) and Fred Kupferman (1987); and study by Geoffrey Warner (1968).

LAVER, ROD (Rodney George Laver; 1938–   ), Australian tennis player. Widely considered to be the greatest male player in the post–World War II period, Laver competed in his first tournament at age 13. A wiry left-hander, he won the 1956 U.S. junior championship and the next year joined the Australian Davis Cup team. Throughout the late 1950s and early 1960s, he completely dominated men's amateur tennis with powerful ground strokes and quick thinking. He won the grand slam (Wimbledon, U.S., Australian, and French singles titles) in 1962 and contributed to the Australian Davis Cup team's world championship. In 1962 he turned professional and won the professional world singles title five times (1964–67; 1970) and the men's doubles twice (1965, 1967). After major tennis tournaments were opened to both amateur and professional players (1968), Laver set a tennis record by winning a second grand slam (1969). He also won the 1960 Australian singles title and the 1961 and 1968 Wimbledon titles.

LAVISSE, ERNEST (1842–1922), French historian. After the Franco-Prussian War (1870–71), Lavisse, a professor of history at the Sorbonne, undertook to reform French education by introducing the German seminar method, uniting the university's faculties, and revising history textbooks. He also wrote two studies of the Prussian ruler Frederick the Great, including *The Youth of Frederick the Great* (1891; Eng. trans. 1892), and edited several important multidisciplinary studies, notably *The History of France from the Beginnings to the Revolution* (9 vols., 1900–11), to which he contributed the two volumes on King Louis XIV, and *The History of Contemporary France* (10 vols., 1920–22).

LAW, (ANDREW) BONAR (1858–1923), British political leader. Bonar Law was born in New Brunswick, Canada, of Scottish Presbyterian parentage; he went to Scotland as a youth and made his fortune in the iron business. He was 42 when he entered Parliament in 1900 but 11 years later he had risen to leadership of the Conservative party. Cautious and reserved, morally and politically tough, he led the opposition to Irish home rule and favored tariff reform. During World War I he served as colonial secretary (1915), chancellor of the Exchequer (1916–18), and leader of the House of Commons (1916–21), and from 1922 to 1923 he served as "the unknown prime minister," as Robert Blake's 1955 biography is entitled.

LAWRENCE, DAVID (1888–1973), U.S. journalist. Lawrence reported on national affairs from Washington for more than 60 years. Conservative and Republican in outlook, he wrote a nationally syndicated column (from 1916) that appeared in some 300 newspapers. He was also a pioneer radio political commentator (1929–33). In 1947 he founded *U.S. News and World Report,* a popular weekly news magazine that featured his signed editorial in each issue.

LAWRENCE, DAVID HERBERT (1885–1930), British novelist, poet, and critic. The son of a coal miner and a teacher, D. H. Lawrence described the tensions of his early life in the semiautobiographical *Sons and Lovers* (1913). After his marriage to Frieda von Richthofen, Lawrence lived and traveled in various parts of the world, including Australia, Italy, and the United States, about which he wrote travel books and which provide the background for much of his fiction. His novels and short stories focused on the seemingly impossible necessity of human fulfillment in the context of an overly intellectualized culture and a decadent civilization. Lawrence emphasized sex as a means of developing inner freedom. He explored these themes in his novels *The Rainbow* (1915), *Women in Love* (1920), and *Lady Chatterley's Lover* (1928), which was banned for many years in Britain and the United States because of its sexual content. ■ See Harry T. Moore, *The Priest of Love* (1974); biographies by Keith Sagar (1980), Anthony Burgess (1985), and Jeffrey Meyers (1990); and study by Daniel J. Schneider (1984).

LAWRENCE, ERNEST ORLANDO (1901–1958), U.S. physicist. Lawrence was awarded the 1939 Nobel Prize in Physics for his development during the 1930s of the first successful cyclotron, a device that uses a circular magnetic field to accelerate atomic particles. The cyclotron is of importance in particle-physics research, in the formation of artificial radioactive elements, and is crucial for certain kinds of chemical, medical, and biological research. During World War II Lawrence helped isolate U-235 for use in the atomic bomb. A professor of physics at the University of California at Berkeley (1928–58), Lawrence founded and directed the Radiation Laboratory there, which set a new pattern for the organization of science. ■ See Herbert Childs, *An American Genius* (1968) and Noel Pharr Davis, *Lawrence and Oppenheimer* (1968).

LAWRENCE, JACOB (1917–2000), U.S. painter. Lawrence was born in Atlantic City, New Jersey, and trained in fine arts at the American Art School and the Harlem Art Workshop in New York. Working primarily in tempera, he produced cycles of canvases that treat social history and issues, particularly black American history; they include *Harlem, Migration of the Negro, War,* and *Tombstones.* A leading social realist, he was the first African-American painter to gain national recognition. He taught at the Pratt Institute in New York City (1955–70) and at the University of Washington in Seattle (1971–83).

LAWRENCE, THOMAS EDWARD (1888–1935), British soldier and writer. T. E. Lawrence, known as "Lawrence of Arabia," was an Oxford-trained archaeologist who served with British intelligence in World War I and organized Arab tribesmen to fight a successful guerrilla war against the Turks. *The Seven Pillars of Wisdom* (1926), his powerful, exciting account of his Arabian exploits, is generally considered a literary masterpiece. While his partisans hailed him as a hero, however, others accused him of self-glorification and of falsifying history. Bitterly dissatisfied and troubled with Britain's refusal to free Syria after World War I, Lawrence refused a knighthood and deliberately sought obscurity by joining the military under a pseudonym. He died in a motorcycle accident shortly after retiring from the Royal Air Force. *The Mint* (1955), a semifictional account of the dehumanization of military recruits, was, at his request, published posthumously. ■ See John E. Mack, *A Prince of Our Disorder* (1976); Lawrence James, *The Golden Warrior* (1990); and biographies by Jeremy Wilson (1990) and Michael Asher (1999).

LAWSON, HENRY (1867–1922), Australian writer. Lawson was the son of a Norwegian gold miner who settled in New South Wales. Deaf from age 9, he began working at 14, and when his parents separated (1883), he went with his mother to Sydney. There, he expressed socialist views in his poems and stories printed in the radical magazine, the *Bulletin* (from 1887). His experiences living in Australia's outback (1892–93) influenced the characterizations and language of his work. He blended humor, irony, and pathos in his realistic and sympathetic depictions of poor working people and exerted a strong influence on modern Australian writing. His works are in *The Stories of Henry Lawson* (3 vols., 1964), *Collected Prose* (2 vols., 1972), and *Collected Verse* (3 vols., 1967–69). ■ See studies by Denton Prout (1963), Judith Wright (1967), Arthur Phillips (1970), and Robyn Burrows (1996); and Colin Roderick, *Real Henry Lawson* (1982).

LAWSON, JOHN HOWARD (1895–1977), U.S. writer. Lawson was a successful New York playwright (from 1923), the head of the New York Workers Revolutionary Theater, and the author of a standard textbook on writing for the theater. He was active on behalf of the anarchists Sacco and Vanzetti, who were executed in Boston (1927), and the Scottsboro boys, accused of rape in Birmingham (1931). Moving to Hollywood (1928), he was one of the first to write for the "talkies." He became the first president of the Screen Writers Guild (1933) and polarized the film community by announcing his membership in the Communist party. Lawson's screenplays included *Blockade* (1938), *Algiers* (1938), *Action in the North Atlantic* (1943), and *Sahara* (1943). He was the leader of the "Hollywood Ten," who each served a year in jail for their refusal to testify before the House Un-American Activities Committee (HUAC) in 1947. Subsequently he was blacklisted and his career was destroyed. His books included *Film in the Battle of Ideas* (1953), *Film: The Creative Process* (1964), and *The Hidden Heritage* (rev. ed. 1968).

LAXNESS, HALLDÓR (Halldór Gudjónsson; 1902–1998), Icelandic writer. Born of peasant stock, Laxness was influenced early in his career by German expressionism, the Norwegian novelist Knut Hamsun, and French surrealism. His *The Great Weaver from Kashmir* (1927) was considered a milestone of Icelandic writing because of its individual, free style and its personal elements. Considered Iceland's greatest writer, he revolutionized the traditional literary language with his lyricism and colloquial style. Influenced in the 1920s by Roman Catholicism, he later became a communist and endowed his work with deep social significance. His multivolume realistic novels like *Salka Valka* (1931–32; Eng. trans. 1936), *Independent People* (1934–35; Eng. trans. 1946), and *World Light* (1937–41; Eng. trans. 1969) and his satirical novel, *The Atom Station* (1948; Eng. trans. 1982), examined the lives of poor people with compassion. From the late 1950s through the 1970s his works became more philosophical and conservative. He also wrote criticism, plays, and several historical novels. He was awarded the Nobel Prize in Literature (1955). ■ See study by Peter Hallberg (Eng. trans. 1971).

LAYDEN, ELMER (1903–1973), U.S. football player, coach, and executive. One of Notre Dame's "Four Horsemen"—the football team's legendary backfield—Layden was fullback and punter (1922–25) under Coach Knute Rockne, achieving All-America status in 1924. He was also star sprinter on the track team. After one season of professional football, he coached at Duquesne (1927–33) and then at Notre Dame (1933–41), compiling a career coaching record of 103–34–11. He served as commissioner of the National Football League (1941–46) during its years of conflict with the All-America Conference. ■ See his memoirs, *It Was a Different Game* (1969).

LAYE, CAMARA (1928–1980), Guinean writer in French. Educated in Muslim and French schools, Laye won a scholarship to study automotive engineering in Paris. While there, he wrote his fictionalized autobiography, *Dark Child* (1953; Eng. trans. 1954), an account of his childhood that was also a celebration of traditional village life and culture. *The Radiance of the King* (1954; Eng. trans. 1956), an ambitious multilayered allegorical novel, described the wanderings of a white man in Africa. Laye returned to Guinea (1955) and held several diplomatic and cultural posts before coming into conflict with the regime of Pres. Sékou Touré. He fled to Senegal (1965), where he taught at the University of Dakar. His third work, *A Dream of Africa* (1966; Eng. trans. 1968), a continuation of *Dark Child,* bitterly attacked the Touré government, which he accused of destroying local traditions and transforming his homeland into a neocolony. The last work published before his death was *The Guardian of the Word* (1978; Eng. trans. 1981), a modern version of an ancient legend. ■ See Adele King, *The Writings of Camara Laye* (1980), and study by Sonia Lee (1984).

LAYTON, IRVING PETER (1912–   ), Canadian poet. Layton's Jewish family emigrated to Canada from Rumania (1913). He earned a degree in agriculture and, upon his return from World War II service, he studied history at McGill University (M.A. 1946) and published his first volumes. Influenced by the writings of Karl Marx and Friedrich Nietzsche, he became known for his prolific outpouring of iconoclastic and sensuous verse in the 1950s and was a hero of the 1960s counterculture. Many of his poems of the 1970s were concerned with Jewish themes. He was a professor of English literature at York University, Toronto (1969–82). His numerous volumes of poetry included *The Cold Green Element* (1955), *A Red Carpet for the Sun* (1959), *Collected Poems* (1971), *The Unwavering Eye* (1975), *Selected Poems* (1977), *A Wild Peculiar Joy* (1982), *Dance with Desire* (1986; rev. ed. 1993), and *Fornalutx: Selected Poems, 1928–90* (1992). His social and political essays appeared in *Taking Sides* (1977). ■ See his memoir, *Waiting for the Messiah* (1985), and the critical volume edited by Seymour Mayne (1978).

LAZARSFELD, PAUL FELIX (1901–1976), Austrian-born U.S. sociologist. Lazarsfeld studied mathematics at the University of Vienna (Ph.D. 1924) but soon shifted into the field of social psychology. In the United States after 1933, he researched radio-listening patterns for the Rockefeller Foundation, collaborating with Frank Stanton (later head of CBS) on a device enabling listeners to register their response. One of the earliest investigators of popular culture, Lazarsfeld applied sophisticated mathematical analysis to compelling questions about the tastes and habits of Americans. Studying the influence of the media on voting, Lazarsfeld concluded in *The People's Choice* (1944) that mass media had little effect on the 1940 U.S. presidential election. Appointed to the Columbia University faculty in 1940, he taught there for more than three decades, and built up and directed its Bureau of Applied Social Research (1944–49).

LEACH, SIR EDMUND RONALD (1910–1989), British anthropologist. Leach served on the faculties of the London School of Economics (1947–53) and of Cambridge University (1953–89) and was considered the foremost advocate of structural analysis in the English-speaking world. His research on kinship and mythology, particularly in relation to South Asia, and his theoretical contributions are contained in such works as *Political Systems of Highland Burma* (1954), *Rethinking Anthropology* (1961), *Lévi-Strauss* (1970), *Genesis as Myth* (1970), *Culture and Communication* (1976), *Social Anthropology* (1982), and *Structuralist Interpretations of Biblical Myth* (1983; with D. A. Aycock).

LEACOCK, STEPHEN BUTLER (1869–1944), British-born Canadian humorist. Leacock emigrated to Canada with his parents (1876), studied at the University of Chicago (Ph.D. 1903), and headed the department of economics and political science at McGill University(1903–36). A highly regarded social scientist, he produced a score of books on history, economics, and political science. He was best known, however, for his hilarious commentaries on small-town Canadian life, notably in *Sunshine Sketches of a Little Town* (1912) and *Arcadian Adventures of the Idle Rich* (1914). His other humorous works included *Literary Lapses* (1910), *Nonsense Novels* (1911), and *Winnowed Wisdom* (1926). He also wrote *Humour: Its Theory and Technique* (1935) and analyses of his literary heroes, Mark Twain (1932) and Charles Dickens (1933). ■ See his autobiography *The Boy I Left Behind Me* (1946), and studies by Ralph L. Curry (1959) and David Legate (1970).

LEADBELLY (Huddie Ledbetter; 1888?–1949), U.S. folksinger and guitarist. Louisiana-born Leadbelly learned the country blues by traveling with Blind Lemon Jefferson, and mastered the "bad-man blues" in prison, where he served terms for murder (1918–25) and attempted homicide (1930–34). In 1932 he was discovered in the Louisiana penitentiary by folk-music expert John Lomax, who worked to get Leadbelly released, recorded his first performances, and helped launch his career. Leadbelly was a master of the 12-string guitar and revived interest in folk music with renditions of such classic folk songs as "On Top of Old Smoky," "The Midnight Special," "Rock Island Line," and "Goodnight Irene." In the 1940s he recorded many songs for the Library of Congress. He performed in nightclubs, on college campuses, and on the radio and was one of the first southern African-American folksingers to gain a national reputation. ■ See biography by Charles Wolfe (1994).

LEAKEY, LOUIS SEYMOUR BAZETT (1903–1972), British physical anthropologist. The son of British mission-aries, Leakey was born in Kenya and grew up among Kenya's Kikuyu—about whom he was later to write an exhaustive monograph—and actually underwent rites of passage into that tribe. Trained in anthropology at Cambridge, he returned to Africa, where the fossil discoveries made by him and by his wife Mary Leakey, an expert field collector, supported Charles Darwin's theory that human evolution centered not in Asia but in Africa. His expeditions established that human history was far older than had been suspected. Leakey also directed (1964) excavations in California that uncovered evidence that humans inhabited America more than 50,000 years ago. He wrote many volumes on Stone Age culture and on East Africa, as well as *White African: An Early Autobiography* (1937). Paleontologist Richard Leakey (1944–) was the second of the Leakeys' three sons. ■ See S. Cole, *Leakey's Luck* (1975); G. L. Isaac and E. R. McCown, *Human Origins* (1976); and Virginia Morell, *Ancestral Passions* (1995).

LEAKEY, MARY DOUGLAS (Mary Douglas Nicol; 1913–1996), British archaeologist. Working at Olduvai Gorge in Tanzania, Mary Leakey made some of the more significant discoveries that were widely credited to her husband, anthropologist Louis Leakey. Her 1959 discovery of a fossilized skull, some 1.8 million years old, modified theories of human evolution. The skull was attributed to *Proconsul Africanus*—also called "nutcracker man" due to powerful jaws and teeth—an ancestor who deviated from the main line of human evolution. The Leakeys separated after 30 years of marriage. After Louis Leakey's death (1972), Mary Leakey remained at Olduvai, studying prehistoric tools. In 1976 she discovered humanlike footprints made in volcanic ash some 3.5 million years ago. This discovery suggested that walking erect was an earlier development than toolmaking and challenged scientists' assumptions about those activities. Leakey's discoveries helped to transform paleontology from fossil hunting to a more sophisticated investigation of human origins. Paleontologist Richard Leakey (1944–) was the second of the Leakeys' three sons. Mary Leakey wrote *Africa's Vanishing Art: The Rock Paintings of Tanzania* (1983) and the autobiographies *Disclosing the Past* (1984) and *Lasting Impressions* (1984). ■ See Virginia Morell, *Ancestral Passions* (1995).

LEAKEY, RICHARD ERSKINE FRERE (1944–), British archaeologist. The second of three sons born to anthropologists Louis and Mary Leakey, Richard Leakey was raised and educated in Kenya. In his teens and twenties he worked as a tour guide and animal trapper and directed photographic safaris. After 1968 he was associated with the National Museums of Kenya (director from 1974). Working in northern Kenya, Leakey unearthed fossils that helped to trace humankind's lineage. In 1984, working with Alan Walker, he found a nearly complete skeleton of a 5-foot, 5-inch 12-year-old male who lived 1.6 million years ago. This unique specimen proved that humankind's early ancestors more closely resembled modern humans in appearance and height than most scientists had assumed. Leakey wrote *Origins* (1978; with Roger Lewin), *People of the Lake* (1978; with Lewin), *The Making of Mankind* (1981), *Human Origins* (1982), *Origins Reconsidered* (1992; with Lewin), and *The Sixth Extinction: Patterns of Life and the Future of Humankind* (1995; with Lewin). He subsequently entered Kenyan politics and served as a member of parliament (1995–99) and as head of the civil service (1999–   ) ▪ See his autobiography *One Life* (1984).

LEAN, SIR DAVID (1908–1991), British film director. Lean rose from performing studio odd jobs to editing *Movietone News* in 1930. After a dozen years of editing he got his chance to codirect a 1942 film with Noel Coward, after which he alone directed Coward's *Blithe Spirit* (1945) and *Brief Encounter* (1945). An admirer of Charles Dickens' novels, Lean directed successful productions of *Great Expectations* (1946) and *Oliver Twist* (1948). His later films were expensive international extravaganzas: *The Bridge on the River Kwai* (Academy Award, 1957), *Lawrence of Arabia* (Academy Award, 1962), and *Doctor Zhivago* (1965). Even *Ryan's Daughter* (1970), described as "a simple love story," cost $13 million under Lean's direction. He made a critically acclaimed adaptation of E. M. Forster's novel, *A Passage to India* (1984). ▪ See Gerald Pratley, *The Cinema of David Lean* (1974), and studies by Michael A. Anderegg (1984), S. M. Silverman (1992), and K. Brownlow (1996).

LEAR, NORMAN (1922–   ), U.S. television producer, director, and writer. In television's early days, Lear wrote comedy shows for Dean Martin and Jerry Lewis, George Gobel, and Martha Raye. With Bud Yorkin he created many TV specials in the 1960s; at the same time he began working in films. In the 1970s Lear came into his own, stunning the industry with "adult" situation comedies. Packaging hit after hit, he became American television's most daring and successful producer. Shows like "All in the Family," "Maude," "Good Times," "The Jeffersons," "Sanford and Son," and "Mary Hartman, Mary Hartman" revitalized old serial formulas by dealing with issues previously unheard of on television such as racial bias, homosexuality, and current political issues. His shows offered a comparatively realistic approach to modern life and moved network executives to reassess the range of subject matter and language appropriate for prime time. He was a founder of People for the American Way (1981), an organization opposed to the Moral Majority.

LEAR, WILLIAM POWELL (1902–1978), U.S. industrialist, engineer, and inventor. Lear quit school after the eighth grade and joined the navy at age 16. He studied radio electronics during World War I and flying after the war. An inventive genius, he designed the first practical car radio (1924), the first radio amplifier that could be used in any radio set (1934), and the first commercial radio compass for airplanes (1935); he held more than 150 patents in the fields of electronics, aviation, and automobile engineering. His company, Lear, Inc., filled more than $100 million worth of defense contracts during World War II. After the war he invented the automatic pilot for jet aircraft (1962) and developed, and became the world's largest manufacturer of, the small private jet airplane. He also invented (1966) and produced the eight-track stereo cartridge. ▪ See Victor Boesen, *They Said It Couldn't Be Done* (1971), and Richard Rashke, *Stormy Genius* (1985).

LEARY, TIMOTHY FRANCIS (1920–1996), U.S. psychologist. The creator of a widely used personality test, Leary taught (1959–63) at Harvard University but was dismissed after he began to experiment with consciousness-altering drugs. His name became a byword for the hippie "drug culture" in the mid-1960s when in public appearances he spoke glowingly of LSD (lysergic acid diethylamide) and advised the world to "turn on, tune in, drop out." Leary's Texas conviction for marijuana possession was overturned by the U.S. Supreme Court, but he went to prison in California for a similar offense. He escaped (1970) and went abroad but was extradited to California in 1973. Released from prison in 1976, he continued to lecture. His books included *Politics of Ecstasy* (1968), *Exo-Psychology: A Manual on the Use of the Nervous System According to the Instructions of the Manufacturers* (1977), *Changing My Mind Among Others: Lifetime Writings* (1982), *Design for Dying* (1997), and the autobiography *Flashbacks* (1983). In April 1997, 10 months after his death, his ashes, along with those of 23 others, were launched into space attached to a satellite expected to orbit the earth for up to 10 years.

LEAVIS, FRANK RAYMOND (1895–1978), British critic. As a teacher of English literature at Cambridge (1925–62) and the editor of the literary quarterly *Scrutiny* (1932–53), F. R. Leavis was one of the most influential literary critics of his day. He was not concerned with close textual criticism; instead, he believed that the task of the critic and of education was to see how a work of art relates to the world and life. He insisted upon viewing literature from a moral perspective. Among his many works were *New Bearings in English Poetry* (1932); *Revaluation* (1936); *The Great Tradition* (1948), a study of the English novel; *D. H. Lawrence, Novelist* (1955); and *Dickens the Novelist* (1970), written with his wife, the critic Q. D. Leavis. ▪ See studies by Ronald Hayman (1976) and William Walsh (1980).

LEAVITT, HENRIETTA SWAN (1868–1921), U.S. astronomer. A graduate of Radcliffe College (B.A. 1892), Leavitt joined the staff of the Harvard College Observatory (1902), and subsequently headed its photographic photometry department. She researched stellar luminosity, and by photographically measuring the brightness of stars, she established a celestial pattern. Her analysis of the luminosity of stars from two nearby galaxies led Leavitt to conclude (1908) that star brightness is directly proportional to the length of its period of variation. This period-luminosity relationship was later used by others to determine the distances of certain stars from Earth as well as to map out the size of the Milky Way. Leavitt also discovered four novas and 2,400 variable stars.

LEBESGUE, HENRI-LÉON (1875–1941), French mathematician. Lebesgue's theory, which he first developed in his doctoral dissertation (University of Paris, 1902), revolutionized the theory of integration and its applications. It was regarded as one of the most significant advances of modern real analysis. Lebesgue also developed the pavement theorem, a major contribution to research in topology, and worked on trigonometric series and potential theory. He taught at Rennes, Poitiers, and the Sorbonne before becoming a professor at the Collège de France (1921). ■ See Thomas Hawkins, *Lebesgue's Theory of Integration* (1970).

LEBRUN, ALBERT (1871–1950), French political leader. Lebrun was educated as a mining engineer. A leader of the moderate conservatives, he served in the Chamber of Deputies (1900–20) and the senate (1920–32). He held several cabinet posts, including minister of colonies and minister of war, before his elevation to president of the republic (1932). A modest, self-effacing man, he did not seek to influence policy. During the fall of France in 1940 he personally opposed armistice with Germany but quietly gave way to the collaborationist Vichy government.

LE CARRÉ, JOHN (David John Moore Cornwell; 1931–), British novelist. Oxford-educated (B.A. 1956) and briefly an Eton schoolmaster, Le Carré was a British diplomat in Germany (1961–64). His third novel, *The Spy Who Came in from the Cold* (1963), was an international best-seller that exposed the hypocrisy and betrayal within the intelligence services during the cold war. He was best known for the trilogy *Tinker, Tailor, Soldier, Spy* (1974), *The Honourable Schoolboy* (1977), and *Smiley's People* (1980), which related the story of retired spymaster George Smiley's attempt to uncover counterspies within British intelligence and to destroy his infamous Russian counterpart Karla. Other novels included *The Looking Glass War* (1965), *A Small Town in Germany* (1968), *The Little Drummer Girl* (1983), and *A Perfect Spy* (1986). His post–cold war novels included *The Tailor of Panama* (1996) and *Single & Single* (1999). ■ See study by Lynn Beene (1992).

LECLERC, JACQUES PHILIPPE (Philippe de Hauteclocque; 1902–1947), French general. Member of an old, aristocratic French family, Leclerc graduated from St. Cyr military academy (1924) and returned as an instructor after distinguished service in Morocco. Wounded and captured during the fall of France during World War II, he escaped to London to join Gen. Charles de Gaulle, who sent him to North Africa. Leclerc, who adopted a pseudonym to protect his family, led the desert army in daring raids against the Italians in Libya. He also participated in the 1944 Normandy landing and led the liberation of Paris, where he accepted the German surrender. As commander of French Far Eastern forces in 1945 he also accepted the Japanese surrender for France. He was killed in a plane crash while serving as inspector general in North Africa.

LE CORBUSIER (Charles Édouard Jeanneret-Gris; 1887–1965), Swiss-born French architect. Le Corbusier was an ideologue among architects, a widely traveled intellectual who was as important for his concepts as for his constructions, and he thought in terms of "modulor man," purist simplicity, and ideal cities; and he designed the new Punjabi capital of Chandigarh (begun 1951), a beautifully realized cubist chapel in Ronchamp (1950–55), and the "vertical city" of the Unité d'Habitation in Marseilles (1946–52). His writings included *Towards a New Architecture* (1923; Eng. trans. 1927), *The City of Tomorrow* (1925; Eng. trans. 1929), *When the Cathedrals Were White* (1937; Eng. trans. 1947), and *The Modulor* (1948; Eng. trans. 1954). ■ See studies by Peter Blake (1964), Stephen Gardiner (1975), and Geoffrey H. Baker (1996).

LECUONA, ERNESTO (1896–1963), Cuban composer and pianist. A musical prodigy, Lecuona gave his first public piano performance at age 5 and graduated from the National Conservatory of Music in Havana at the age of 15. A master of both pop and classical music, he toured Europe, the United States, and South America as leader of his own Cuban dance band (Lecuona Cuban Boys); gave piano recitals in Paris, Buenos Aires, and New York; and composed some 400 songs, 160 piano pieces, and 30 orchestral scores as well as film scores and numerous works for the theater. He is credited with introducing rumba and conga rhythms to the United States and is best known for songs that became standards, including "Siboney" (1929), "Jungle Drums" (1930), "Malagueña" (1927), "Say Si Si" (1933), "The Breeze and I" (1930), "It's No Secret I Love You" (1937), and "Always in My Heart" (1942). His concert works include the orchestral pieces *Andalucia* (1931), *Rapsodia Negra* (1943), and *Rapsodia Cubana* (1955) and the *Danzas Afro-Cubanas* (1937) for piano. Lecuona left Cuba after Fidel Castro came to power.

LEDERBERG, JOSHUA (1925–), U.S. biologist. A pioneer in the field of bacterial genetics, Lederberg demonstrated how genes are exchanged, recombined, and inherited in bacteria. He showed that bacteria combined in a sexual process and discovered the gene-transmission mechanism known as transduction, the process by which a bacterial virus carries hereditary material from one bacterial cell to another. Subsequently he was able to alter the heredity of bacterial cells. His work opened up the possibility of controlling genetic structure and profoundly affected cancer research. A professor at the University of Wisconsin (1947–59) and Stanford University (1959–78), Lederberg shared the 1958 Nobel Prize in Physiology or Medicine with George W. Beadle and Edward L. Tatum. He served as president of Rockefeller University, New York (1978–90).

LEDERMAN, LEON (1922–   ), U.S. physicist. The son of Russian immigrants, Lederman grew up in the Bronx, studied at the City College of New York and Columbia University (Ph.D. 1951), and taught physics at Columbia (1951–79). With colleagues Melvin Schwartz and Jack Steinberger, he performed (1960–62) a landmark experiment that generated the first laboratory-made beam of neutrinos, subatomic particles with no electrical charge and no detectable mass. The development gave scientists a powerful tool with which to study the "weak" nuclear force that influences radioactive nuclear decay. The experiment also revealed a previously unknown type of neutrino, the muon neutrino, whose existence subsequently led to the formation of the "standard model" theory describing the fundamental particles that are the components of all matter. For their research Lederman, Schwartz, and Steinberger shared the 1988 Nobel Prize in Physics. Lederman also discovered the upsilon particle (1972) and served as director of the Fermi National Accelerator Laboratory in Batavia, Illinois (1979–89). ■ See his *God Particle* (with Dick Teresi, 1994) and *From Quarks to Cosmos* (with David Schramm, 1995).

LE DUC THO (1911–1990), Vietnamese revolutionary leader. Le, whose original name was Phan Dinh Khai, was a cofounder of the Indochinese Communist party (ICP) in 1930. Jailed for 11 of the next 15 years, he rose to membership on the central committee of the ICP in 1945. In the 1950s he led Viet Minh insurgents in the south of Vietnam. After the French withdrew from Vietnam (1954), he returned to Hanoi and became a leader of the Workers' party. From 1968 to 1973 he represented North Vietnam in negotiations with the United States to end the war in Vietnam. An agreement was reached in 1973, although fighting did not end until 1975. In 1973 he was corecipient (with U.S. Secretary of State Henry Kissinger) of the Nobel Peace Prize; he rejected the prize on the grounds that there was still no peace in Vietnam. He was a member of the Politburo and Secretariat of the Communist party of Vietnam (1976–86).

LEDUC, VIOLETTE (1907–1972), French novelist and memoirist. Leduc was an illegitimate child; her painful, ambivalent relationship with her mother figured heavily in her autobiographical writings. Fascinated by writers, she found employment on the fringes of the Parisian literary world (1927–39). Writer Maurice Sachs encouraged her to write down her life story, and the author Albert Camus published *In the Prison of Her Skin* (1946; Eng. trans. 1970) in his

"Espoir" series. Encouraged by other important literary figures, she continued to write but did not receive widespread recognition until *La Bâtarde: An Autobiography* (1964; Eng. trans. 1965). Although the personality she reveals is not always pleasing, the details of her love affairs with women and men and her wartime black-market activities are always recounted with courage and imagination. She also wrote *Thérèse and Isabelle* (1966; Eng. trans. 1967) and *The Woman with the Little Fox* (three novellas; Eng. trans. 1966). ■ See study by Isabelle Courtivron (1985).

LEE, BRUCE (1941–1973), Chinese-U.S. actor. The son of a star of the Chinese opera, Lee was born in San Francisco and raised in Hong Kong, where he began studying the martial arts at age 13. Returning to the United States to study philosophy at the University of Washington, he founded three kung-fu academies on the West Coast and became a television actor. Back in Hong Kong, he created a kung-fu cult and world box-office sensation as the star of a series of low-budget films. Using an eclectic approach to the martial arts, he choreographed complicated tableaux of graceful violence in *Fists of Fury* (1972) and *The Chinese Connection* (1972). *Enter the Dragon* (1973), the last film he made before his sudden and mysterious death, earned over $100 million. ■ See Alex Ben Block, *The Legend of Bruce Lee* (1974).

LEE, DAVID M. (1931–   ), U.S. physicist. Lee graduated from Yale University (Ph.D. 1959) and taught at Cornell University (1959–   ). While performing experiments (1972) in low-temperature physics with fellow researcher Robert Richardson and graduate student Douglas Osheroff, Lee and his colleagues discovered superfluidity—the ability to flow without resistance—in helium-3, a rare form of liquid helium. The discovery enabled scientists to directly observe quantum effects that previously could only be indirectly detected through the study of molecules, atoms, or subatomic particles. The discovery also provided insight into the formation of the first physical structures microseconds after the "big bang" and the creation of the universe. Lee, Richardson, and Osheroff were awarded the 1996 Nobel Prize in Physics for their research.

LEE, GYPSY ROSE (Rose Louise Hovick; 1914–1970), U.S. entertainer. The "Queen of Burlesque," Gypsy Rose Lee was America's most famous striptease artist. Witty and sophisticated, she transformed stripping from lowbrow entertainment to a graceful and stylish art, which prodded critic H. L. Mencken to coin the word "ecdysiast" to describe, in respectable terms, what her act was all about. Intelligent as well as beautiful, she became the darling of a group of New York City's most prominent writers and intellectuals and frequently contributed articles to the *New Yorker, Harper's, American Mercury,* and *Collier's.* After her "retirement" from stripping in 1937, she appeared in several movies, wrote two best-selling mystery novels, *The G-String Mur-*

ders (1941) and *Mother Finds a Body* (1942), and wrote an autobiography, *Gypsy* (1957), which was the basis of the hit Broadway musical (1959) and movie (1962). ■ See Erik Lee Preminger, *Gypsy and Me* (1984).

LEE, IVY LEDBETTER (1877–1934), U.S. public-relations consultant. After graduating from Princeton (1898), Lee worked as a reporter before starting a career as a publicist (1903). Convinced that big business needed a more wholesome public image, Lee advised that openness and honesty could arouse public support. He helped clean up the image of the Pennsylvania Railroad, John D. Rockefeller, Bethlehem Steel, the Guggenheim and Chrysler interests, and the Nazi-controlled I. G. Farben Co. Dubbed by his enemies "Poison Ivy Lee" for his work for large corporations and millionaires, he was known to his supporters as the "physician to corporate bodies." A pioneer public-relations man, and not, he insisted, a glorified press agent, Lee wrote *Publicity: Some of the Things It Is and Is Not* (1925). ■ See Ray E. Herbert, *Courtier to the Crowd* (1966).

LEE, MANFRED B. *See QUEEN, ELLERY.*

LEE, PEGGY (**Norma Engstrom;** 1920–), U.S. jazz singer. Peggy Lee was appearing with a Chicago band when bandleader Benny Goodman spotted her (1941). She became vocalist for his group and recorded the hit song "Why Don't You Do Right?" Later she appeared with Bing Crosby in *Mr. Music* (1950) and starred in *The Jazz Singer* (1953). Also a lyric writer, she wrote and recorded "Mañana" (1951), which reflected her feeling for Latin rhythms. In a similar vein, she made a famous recording of Richard Rodger's song "Lover." Lee remained a popular nightclub attraction, known for her sultry delivery of "Fever," "Is That All There Is?," and other numbers. ■ See her autobiography *Miss Peggy Lee* (1989).

LEE, SPIKE (**Shelton Jackson Lee;** 1957–), U.S. film director, producer, and screenwriter. Lee grew up in Brooklyn, New York, graduated from Morehouse College in Atlanta (B.A. 1979), and studied filmmaking at New York University (M.A. 1983). His controversial films, starting with *She's Gotta Have It* (1986), depicted the lives of blacks in contemporary America, and he became the first African-American filmmaker to gain critical acclaim and commercial success in the United States. His best known movies were *School Daze* (1988), a musical spoof of color consciousness at a black college; *Do the Right Thing* (1989), a drama about relations between blacks and Italians in a Brooklyn neighborhood; *Mo' Better Blues* (1990), a story about New York jazz musicians; and *Jungle Fever* (1991), a provocative exploration of an interracial romance. His most ambitious work was *Malcolm X* (1992), a 3½-hour biography of the militant black Muslim leader. He also directed *Crooklyn* (1991), *Clockers* (1995), *Get on the Bus* (1996), *He Got Game* (1998), *Summer of Sam* (1999), *Bamboozled* (2000), and a

documentary on the Birmingham church bombing of 1962, *Four Little Girls* (1997). He founded his own production company, Forty Acres and a Mule Filmworks, in Brooklyn.

LEE, TSUNG-DAO (1926–), Chinese-born U.S. physicist. Together with Chen Ning Yang, Lee hypothesized that the law of parity conservation, which stated that subatomic particles behaved the same way as their mirror images, was invalid for weak interactions. Experiments performed by Chien-shiung Wu (1957) proved that they were correct, and Lee and Yang shared the 1957 Nobel Prize in Physics. Their work paved the way for revolutionary advances in particle physics. Lee was a member of the faculty of Columbia University (1953–60) before becoming a professor at the Institute for Advanced Study, Princeton (1960–63). He returned to Columbia as the first Enrico Fermi professor of physics in 1963.

LEE, YUAN T. (1936–), Taiwan-born U.S. chemist. Lee moved to the United States to study chemistry at the University of California, Berkeley (Ph.D. 1965). He worked in Dudley Herschbach's research lab at Harvard (1967–68), and the apparatus he designed there, utilizing Herschbach's "crossed molecular beam technique," enabled scientists to study changes that take place in chemical reactions at the level of individual molecules. He shared the 1986 Nobel Prize in Chemistry with Herschbach and John C. Polanyi for creating the new field of chemical-reaction dynamics. Lee taught at Berkeley (1974–) and became a U.S. citizen in 1974.

LEE KUAN YEW (1923–), Singaporean political leader. Born into a wealthy Chinese family, Lee was an outstanding law student at Cambridge who worked for militant labor unions before entering politics (1954). He founded the People's Action party and was elected to the legislative council (1955). In 1959 when Singapore became a self-governing state, Lee was elected the first prime minister and held power until 1990. He led Singapore into a short-lived merger with Malaysia (1963–65) and declared Singapore an independent republic (1965). Originally a socialist, Lee became progressively more conservative and ruled with virtual dictatorial powers, allowing no substantive opposition, while at the same time creating an economic boom for his city-state. An advocate of regional cooperation, he was a major spokesman of the anticommunist Association of Southeast Asian Nations (ASEAN). After he resigned the office of prime minister he maintained power as the cabinet's senior minister. ■ See his memoirs, *The Singapore Story* (1998), and *From Third World to First* (2000).

LEFEBVRE, GEORGES (1874–1959), French historian. Lefebvre was a provincial schoolteacher for 20 years while finishing his doctoral thesis on the peasantry and the French Revolution. He incorporated social psychology, statistical research, and Marxist humanism into his major, authoritative works on the French revolutionary period and taught at the Sorbonne from 1937 to 1945. His well-known works included *The Coming of the French Revolution* (1939; Eng. trans. 1947), *The French Revolution* (rev. ed. 1951; Eng. trans., 2 vols., 1962–64), and *Napoleon* (1935–36; Eng. trans., 2 vols., 1969).

LE GALLIENNE, EVA (1899–1991), British-born U.S. actress and director. Le Gallienne first achieved fame portraying Julie in Molnar's *Liliom* (New York City; 1921) and later became the outstanding interpreter of Ibsen and Chekhov, whose works she also translated and directed. She founded and directed the famed Civic Repertory Theater (1926–32), the first repertory group in New York, and the American Repertory Theater (New York City; 1946). She continued to appear on Broadway and in films through the 1980s. ■ See her autobiographies *At 33* (1934) and *With a Quiet Heart* (1953), and biography by Helen Sheehy (1996).

LÉGER, FERNAND (1881–1955), French painter. Trained as an architect, Léger was influenced by the cubists in Paris. His interest in modern machinery as artistic subject was spurred by his military service during World War I, after which his canvases often represented machines and people with mechanical parts. He collaborated on an early "art" movie, *Ballet Mécanique* (1923), which used simple mechanical objects. In a series of abstract murals (1924–26), he experimented with the use of color; later work explored the interplay between space and movement and was primarily figurative. Noted for artistic independence, Léger found his subjects in personal experience, not in literature, history, or other artists; he was particularly fond of painting acrobats, cyclists, and construction workers. ■ See study by Robert T. Buck, et al. (1982).

LEGUÍA, AUGUSTO BERNARDINO (1863–1932), Peruvian political leader. A wealthy insurance executive from an elite Peruvian family, Leguía served two terms as a modernizing but repressive president of his country (1908–12; 1919–30). He settled boundary disputes with Bolivia, Chile, and Brazil; enacted educational reforms; and borrowed from New York banks to begin Peru's industrialization. However, his policies resulted in huge foreign debts, high inflation, and food shortages, and he was overthrown by the army in 1930. He died in prison.

LE GUIN, URSULA K. (Ursula Kroeber; 1929–), U.S. author. The daughter of anthropologist Alfred L. Kroeber, Le Guin graduated from Radcliffe College (B.A. 1951) and Columbia University (M.A. 1952) and taught French at several universities. A writer from the age of 9, she produced five unpublished novels before the publication of her first science-fiction short story in 1962. In the 1960s her "Hainish cycle," a series of novels concerning future colonizers from the planet Hain, gained critical acclaim. She subsequently was recognized as a creator of "anthropological science fiction"

as she described alternative societies with great concern for physical and cultural detail. *The Left Hand of Darkness* (1969) described an androgynous society, while *The Dispossessed: An Ambiguous Utopia* (1974) concerned the differences between two planets, one dominated by anarchists and the other by materialistic bureaucrats. The complex fantasy novels comprising the "Earthsea Trilogy" (*Wizard of Earthsea*, 1968; *The Tombs of Atuan*, 1971; *The Farthest Shore*, 1972) were widely read. *The Word for World is Forest* (1976), a novel of interplanetary exploration, was a parable of U.S. involvement in Vietnam. *Always Coming Home* (1985) was an ethnography of the future in narratives, poems, and expositions. She returned to the Hainish universe in *The Telling* (2000). Her short-story collections included *Orsinian Tales* (1976) and *The Compass Rose* (1982). ■ See George Slusser, *The Farthest Shores of Ursula K. Le Guin* (1976), and study by Barbara Bucknall (1981).

LEHMAN, HERBERT HENRY (1878–1963), U.S. banker, philanthropist, and political leader. Lehman was a textile executive before joining his family investment banking house, Lehman Brothers (1908). He helped found the philanthropic American Jewish Joint Distribution Committee (1914). In 1926 Lehman managed the New York gubernatorial campaign of liberal Democrat Alfred E. Smith and subsequently served as lieutenant governor (1928–32) and four-time governor (1932–42) of New York. Closely associated with Pres. Franklin D. Roosevelt, whom he succeeded as governor, Lehman sponsored a "Little New Deal" that made New York one of the most progressive states in the Union. Lehman later was the first director of the United Nations Relief and Rehabilitation Agency (UNRRA; 1943–46), which aided more than 1 billion people in 25 war-ravaged countries. In the U.S. Senate (1949–57), he was a leading liberal and was one of the few to speak out against the witch-hunting tactics of Sen. Joseph R. McCarthy. ■ See biography by Allen Nevins (1963) and study by Robert P. Ingalls (1975).

LEHMANN, JOHN FREDERICK (1907–1987), British writer and publisher. After graduation from Cambridge, followed by a period of writing in Vienna, Lehmann was general manager of the Hogarth Press (1938–46), the publishing concern founded by Leonard and Virginia Woolf. In a series of volumes entitled *New Writing,* he introduced the work of such writers as George Orwell, Lawrence Durrell, and Edith Sitwell. He subsequently presided over his own publishing firm (1946–53) and then founded and edited *London Magazine* (1954–61). In addition to his poetry and several anthologies and studies of modern writers, Lehmann wrote three volumes of memoirs that were condensed into *In My Own Time* (1969).

LEHMANN, LOTTE (1888–1976), German-born U.S. opera singer. One of the most beloved and respected opera and lieder singers of her time, Lehmann was a leading soprano at the Vienna State Opera (1914–38) before emigrating to the United States. A member of New York's Metropolitan Opera from 1934 to 1945, Lehmann was most famous for her portrayals of Leonore in *Fidelio,* Sieglinde in *Die Walküre,* and the Marschallin in *Der Rosenkavalier.* She was an actress and singer of great intelligence, expressiveness, and emotional range and had an extraordinary rapport with her audiences during her 41-year singing career (1910–51). ■ See her autobiographies, *Midway in My Song* (1938) and *My Many Lives* (1948), and study by Beaumont Glass (1988).

LEHMBRUCK, WILHELM (1881–1919), German sculptor. Lehmbruck studied in Düsseldorf at the School of Decorative Arts (1895–99) and the Academy of Fine Arts (1901–07), experimenting in the sculptural styles of Auguste Rodin and Constantin Meunier. Working in bronze and artificial stone, he was influenced by medieval sculptural figures and the elongated human forms of Amadeo Modigliani. In his search for a modern expression of heroism, Lehmbruck gave his sculptures a grave and melancholic aspect, especially in *Kneeling Woman* (1911), which critics praised as the apex of German expressionism. But *Dying Warrior,* an unconventional memorial to soldiers slain in World War I, alienated critics when it was shown in Berlin (1916). Lehmbruck committed suicide in 1919. ■ See study by August Hoff (Eng. trans. 1969).

LEHN, JEAN MARIE (1939–   ), French chemist. Lehn studied at the University of Strasbourg (Ph.D. 1963) and taught at the Louis Pasteur University in Strasbourg (1970–79) and the Collège de France in Paris (1979–   ). He was a pioneer, in the 1960s, of what he called supramolecular chemistry, a field, also known as host-guest chemistry, that is based on the premise that the three-dimensional shape of a molecule is vital to its functions. Work in this area of research allowed for the creation of synthetic molecules that could mimic the behavior of the natural molecules that control all life processes. Specifically, Lehn produced a molecule that acts as a host for acetylcholine, a chemical neurotransmitter in the human brain and nervous system. His research raised the possibility of producing artificial enzymes for medical and industrial use. Lehn shared the 1987 Nobel Prize in Chemistry with Charles J. Pedersen and Donald Cram.

LEIBER, FRITZ (1910–1992), U.S. science-fiction writer. Leiber was a divinity student, editor, and drama coach. His first published story (1939) introduced science-fiction readers to Fafhrd the Barbarian and the Gray Mouser—two rogues whose adventures in mythical Nehwon were gathered in several volumes, notably the novel *The Swords of Lankhmar* (1968). Leiber's works did not always sell well; some were satiric to the point of acidity in their portrayal of American life, and others verged on the surreal. But as increasingly sophisticated science-fiction readers caught up

with him, he won recognition, including awards for *The Big Time* (1958), *The Wanderer* (1964), and several stories. Much of his earlier work was reissued in such collections as *The Best of Fritz Leiber* (1974) and *The Worlds of Fritz Leiber* (1976). Later works included the horror novel *Our Lady of Darkness* (1977), *The Ghost Light* (1983), and his final novel, *Gummitch and Friends* (1992).

LEINSDORF, ERICH (1912–1993), Austrian-born U.S. conductor. Leinsdorf studied at the University of Vienna and the Vienna State Academy of Music. He was assistant to Bruno Walter and Arturo Toscanini at the Salzburg festival (1934–37). He emigrated to the United States in 1937 and by 1940 had become a principal conductor at New York's Metropolitan Opera. A man with a strong-willed, exacting personality, he was music director of the Rochester (1947–56) and Boston (1962–69) Symphony orchestras and principal conductor of the Radio Symphony Orchestra of West Berlin (from 1977). He was best known for his interpretations of the works of German composers, notably Beethoven, Wagner, Brahms, and Richard Strauss. He wrote *The Composer's Advocate* (1981) and his memoirs, *Cadenza* (1976).

LEINSTER, MURRAY (**William F. Jenkins;** 1896–1975), U.S. science-fiction writer. In a career that began in 1918, Leinster published more than 1,000 stories in national magazines and wrote no fewer than a dozen screenplays. In the 1930s and 1940s he wrote mainly adventure and mystery tales, many under his original name, William Jenkins; beginning in the 1950s he produced the science-fiction thrillers for which he is best known. His books, which often depict time and space travel, have been translated into 15 languages; many were transcribed into braille. *A Murray Leinster Omnibus* (1968) contained three novels. His short-story collections included *Monsters and Such* (1959) and *The Best of Murray Leinster* (1976).

LEIRIS, MICHEL (1901–1990), French anthropologist, poet, and memoirist. Born in Paris, Leiris was a surrealist poet who, after a personal crisis in 1929, turned to a new career as an anthropologist with the Musée de l'Homme, Paris, and embarked on expeditions to Africa (1931–33; 1945), the Antilles (1948–52), and China (1955). His anthropological writings included *L'Afrique Fantôme* (Phantom Africa; 1934), *Race and Culture* (1951; Eng. trans. 1951), and *African Art* (1967; with J. Delange; Eng. trans. 1968). Leiris was best known for keenly intelligent but intensely self-deprecating memoirs, including *Manhood* (1939; Eng. trans. 1963) and the four-volume confession, *Rules of the Game* (1948–76; Eng. trans. 1991). ■ See Jeffrey Mehlman, *A Structural Study of Autobiography* (1974).

LEITZEL, LILLIAN (**Leopoldina Alitza Pelikan;** 1892–1931), German-born U.S. circus aerial gymnast. Her mother came from a Bohemian circus family and formed the aerial team "Leamy Ladies" with her two sisters. Trained in piano, dance, and foreign languages, Lillian Leitzel nevertheless joined her mother's daring act and came to the United States to appear In the Barnum & Bailey Circus (1908). "Mlle. Leitzel" was spotted by Ringling Brothers Circus, and after 1914 her "flying" was featured in the center ring of "The Greatest Show on Earth." She became America's most celebrated circus showwoman by accomplishing miraculously agile feats—including the "one-arm plunge"—on ropes and rings some 50 feet in the air (without a net). When a ring snapped during a trapeze performance in Copenhagen, Leitzel fell nearly 30 feet; she died two days later.

LEIVICK, H. (Leivick Halpern; 1888–1962), Russian-born U.S. Yiddish-language poet and playwright. Imprisoned (1906) for revolutionary activity, Leivick escaped to New York in 1913 and began to write poems based on his prison experiences. Turning to the suffering of East European Jews after World War I, he used historical symbolism to stress social criticism and messianic themes in the play *The Golem* (1921; Eng. trans. 1927), his most popular work. Leivick's anguished reactions to the Holocaust were expressed in poetry (*I Was Not in Treblinka*, 1945), and in drama (*Rabbi Mair of Rothenberg*, 1945; *A Wedding in Fernwald*, 1949; and *The Days of Job*, 1953) and he was regarded as the most prominent figure in Yiddish literature following World War II.

LELOIR, LUIS FEDERICO (1906–1987), French-born Argentinian biochemist. Leloir received an M.D. from the University of Buenos Aires (1932) before undertaking research in carbohydrate metabolism with leaders in the field at Cambridge, Buenos Aires, Washington, and Columbia universities. He founded the Institute for Biochemical Research in Buenos Aires (1946) and continued his research into ways that complex sugars are broken down into simpler carbohydrates. For his discovery of sugar nucleotides, substances that enable the body to synthesize carbohydrates, and his synthesis of the body sugar, glycogen, Leloir was awarded the 1970 Nobel Prize for Chemistry.

LEM, STANISLAW (1921–), Polish science-fiction writer. Lem received an M.D. degree (1946) and wrote several essays on scientific methodology before abandoning his scientific career for one as a writer. His novels, concerned with the impact of science and technology on modern society, were informed by his vast knowledge of the natural sciences, history, philosophy, and cybernetics. Utilizing paradox, wordplay, and a brilliantly comic style, he satirized some of the most serious contemporary social problems, including militarism and overpopulation, and he was translated into more than 30 languages. His best-known translated works included *The Star Diaries* (1976), *Solaris* (1970), *Memoirs Found in a Bathtub* (1973), *The Futurological Congress* (1974), *A Perfect Vacuum* (1979), *Memoirs of a Space Traveler* (1983), *Imaginary Magnitude* (1984), *Fiasco* (1987),

and *Eden* (1989). ■ See also his *Microworlds: Writings on Science Fiction and Fantasy* (1985) and *Highcastle* (1991; Eng. trans. 1995), a childhood autobiography.

LEMAÎTRE, GEORGES ÉDOUARD (1894–1966), Belgian astrophysicist. Ordained as a priest in 1923, Abbé Lemaître returned to his research on the theory of general relativity and its application to the concept of the expanding universe and served as a professor of astrophysics at the University of Louvain (from 1927). Inspired to investigate star dynamics by Sir Arthur Eddington, he developed (1925–31) what is now called the "big bang" theory of the origin and structure of the universe. This theory maintains that the universe began to expand billions of years ago with a nuclear explosion of a minute volume of high-density, high-temperature matter. He wrote *The Primeval Atom* (1946; Eng. trans. 1950).

LEMAY, CURTIS EMERSON (1906–1990), U.S. Air Force officer. As a bombardment division commander in World War II, LeMay developed new B-17 bomber formations and bombing techniques and directed raids on Japanese weapons factories. He supervised (1948–49) the airlift to West Berlin during the Soviet blockade, and during the 1950s he developed the newly formed Strategic Air Command into a strong deterrent force. He was air-force chief of staff from 1961 to 1965 and was an advocate of the use of nuclear weapons. An ultraconservative, LeMay ran (1968) unsuccessfully for vice president on the American Independent party ticket headed by George Wallace. ■ See his autobiography, *Mission With LeMay* (1965; with MacKinlay Kantor), and Thomas M. Coffey, *Iron Eagle* (1986).

LEMELIN, ROGER (1919–), French-Canadian novelist. Born into a poor working-class family in Quebec City, Lemelin started to work at age 14 and was self-educated. His novels, *The Town Below* (1944; Eng. trans. 1948), *The Plouffe Family* (1948; Eng. trans. 1950), and *In Quest of Splendour* (1952; Eng. trans. 1955), depicted the life of the lower classes in Quebec and were among the first works of social realism in French-Canadian fiction. His short story, "The Stations of the Cross" (1949: Eng. trans. 1960), a satire on the Quebec clergy, was frequently anthologized. He published the Montreal newspaper La Presse from 1972 to 1981.

LEMMON, JACK (1925–), U.S. actor. Educated at Andover and Harvard (BA. 1947), Lemmon worked in New York as a singing waiter before his first jobs on Broadway, radio, and television. One year after his movie debut he won an Academy Award for best supporting actor in *Mister Roberts* (1955). He established himself as a leading man in a series of light comedies and sex farces, which included *Some Like It Hot* (1959) and *The Great Race* (1965). As a comic hero he was known for his double takes and his projection of earnest frustration. He was also lauded for his serious roles as the alcoholic in *Days of Wines and Roses*

(1962) and the desperate businessman in *Save the Tiger* (Academy Award, 1973). He also gave memorable dramatic performances in *The China Syndrome* (1979), *Missing* (1981), *Dad* (1989), and *Glengarry Glen Ross* (1992). ▪ See the biography by Don Widener (1975).

LENGLEN, SUZANNE (1899–1938), French tennis player. An important influence in the early development of women's tennis, Lenglen won her first championship in 1914 at age 15. Between 1919 and 1926 she dominated the game, losing only one match and winning at Wimbledon six times. Lenglen intimidated opponents with blazing ground strokes and unnerving consistency. The first tennis player to turn professional (1926), she made a triumphant tour of the United States. She appeared in several motion pictures featuring tennis and wrote several books on the game. ▪ See Larry Englemann, *The Goddess and the American Girl* (1988).

LENIN, VLADIMIR ILYICH (V. I. Ulyanov; 1870–1924), Russian political leader. Lenin was drawn to Marxism when he was a student. He practiced law, was arrested for revolutionary activities (1895), and was exiled to Siberia (1897–1900). After leaving Russia (1900) he undertook political work in Brussels, Paris, London, and Geneva. A leader with great intellectual grasp and a basically pragmatic approach, he published such effective pamphlets as *What Is to Be Done?* (1902; Eng. trans. 1929), advocating a working-class struggle for socialism led by a small disciplined "vanguard" party of professional revolutionaries. His writings in the newspaper *Iskra* ("The Spark") circulated his theories, and he led the wing of the Russian Social Democratic Workers party known, after 1903, as bolsheviks. He returned to Russia during the 1905 revolution, but he was soon forced to resume exile. After the czar's forced abdication in the spring of 1917, he returned to Russia and led the bolsheviks in overthrowing the provisional government during the October revolution (1917). As head of the new government, he established communist rule, implemented land distribution, nationalized property and banks, and concluded an armistice with Germany (1918). After three years of devastating civil war, he instituted the New Economic Policy (NEP), partially restoring the capitalist market economy. He also founded the Third, or Communist, International (1919), aimed at fostering revolution throughout the world. He was incapacitated by a series of strokes (1922–23). His last writings reflect wariness of excessive bureaucratization and of the accumulation of power by party secretary Joseph Stalin. His major works included *The Development of Capitalism in Russia* (1899; Eng. trans. 1956), *Imperialism: The Highest Stage of Capitalism* (1916; Eng. trans. 1924), and *The State and Revolution* (1917; Eng. trans. 1919). ▪ See biographies by Louis Fischer (1964), David Shub (1966), Ronald W. Clark (1988), and Dmitri Volkogonov (Eng. trans. 1994), and studies by Moshe Lewin (1968) and Neil Harding (2 vols., 1978–81). Richard Pipes, ed., *The Un-*known *Lenin* (1996) contained 122 formerly secret documents from the Soviet archives.

LENYA, LOTTE (Karoline Blamauer; 1898–1981), Austrian-born singer and actress. Lenya won international acclaim for her performances in Berlin in plays by Bertolt Brecht with music by her husband Kurt Weill—particularly in *The Threepenny Opera* (1928; film, 1931) and *Mahagonny* (1930). Lenya and Weill fled Germany after the Nazis came to power (1933) and lived and worked in the United States (from 1935). She recorded Weill's theater songs, with which she was identified, and won a Tony Award for her performance in the 1955 Off-Broadway revival of *The Threepenny Opera*. On stage she also appeared in *The Eternal Road* (1937), *The Seven Deadly Sins* (1958), *Brecht on Brecht* (1962), and *Cabaret* (1966). Her film credits included *From Russia with Love* (1963) and *Semi-Tough* (1977). ▪ See biography by Donald Spoto (1989).

LEONOV, ALEKSEI ARKHIPOVICH (1934–), Soviet cosmonaut. An air-force instructor and pilot before joining the cosmonaut program (1959), Leonov was the first person to "walk" in space. On March 18, 1965, he emerged from an orbiting spacecraft and floated for 10 minutes in the vacuum of outer space. Connected to the spaceship only by a 16-foot cable, Leonov traveled at the same velocity as the craft, covering 3,000 miles at an altitude of 110 miles. The "walk" allowed Leonov to gather data that would have been inaccessible from within the space capsule. He later took part in the joint U.S.–U.S.S.R. Apollo-Soyuz space mission (1975). He served as deputy director of the Cosmonaut Training Center (1972–92).

LEONOV, LEONID MAKSIMOVICH (1899–1994), Soviet novelist and playwright. Leonov dropped out of Moscow University and served for three years in the Red army cavalry. He began writing in the 1920s, first poetry and then prose, and figured among the "fellow travelers"—the term coined by revolutionary Leon Trotsky for intellectuals who greeted the Russian Revolution, but with ambivalent feelings. Leonov's best novels, *The Badgers* (1924; Eng. trans. 1947), *The Thief* (1927; Eng. trans. 1931), *Road to the Ocean* (1935; Eng. trans. 1944), and *The Russian Forest* (1953: Eng. trans. 1966), reflect the influence of the great novelist Dostoyevsky in their complex, melodramatic plots and their emphasis on psychological motivation. Also a leading playwright, Leonov emphasized emotional rather than historical conflict in such plays as *The Orchards of Polovchansk* (1936: Eng. trans. 1946 in *Seven Soviet Plays*). His World War II plays included *Invasion* (1942; Eng. trans. 1944 in *Four Soviet Plays*). ▪ See study by George Harjan (1979).

LEONTIEF, WASSILY (1906–1999), Russian-born U.S. economist. A graduate of the University of Leningrad (MA. 1925) and the University of Berlin (Ph.D. 1928), Leontief taught at Harvard (1931–75) and New York University (1975–91). During World War II, when U.S. industries were expanding rapidly, Leontief's analysis of the interdependencies among basic industries, developed in the celebrated study *The Structure of the American Economy, 1919–29* (1941), was recognized as crucial for modern economic development. His input-output model, used in economic planning and in forecasting output and growth requirements, provided a practical application of the general equilibrium theory and was subsequently adopted by more than 50 countries as well as the United Nations. For this original technique of studying and predicting economic trends, Leontief was awarded the 1973 Nobel Memorial Prize for Economics. He proposed the creation of a federal government office of economic planning and wrote of the important role the government played in creating a prosperous economy after the 1930s. His other books included *Input-Output Economics* (1966) and *Essays in Economics* (1978). ▪ See Estelle Leontief, *Genia and Wassily* (1987).

LEOPOLD III (1901–1983), king of the Belgians. When his father Albert I died (1934) in a mountain-climbing accident, Leopold III inherited the throne and the responsibility for dealing with Belgium's social and economic upheaval. He called for a coalition government, making clear strides in domestic affairs. Leopold declined to ally with France or Britain against Nazi Germany, insisting on Belgium's neutrality. He led the Belgian forces' unsuccessful defense against the World War II German invasion of Belgium; refusing to set up a government-in-exile, he unconditionally surrendered Belgium to the Germans (1940). When Belgium was liberated (1944), parliament voted to end Leopold's reign, exiled him, and elected his brother, Prince Charles, as regent. After the Belgian electorate voted (1950) to approve Leopold's return to the throne, he resumed his reign, but his return sparked intense political dissension. He abdicated (1951) in favor of his son, Prince Baudouin (1930–1993). ▪ See Roger Keyes, *Outrageous Fortune* (1984).

LEOPOLD, ALDO (1886–1948), U.S. ecologist and conservationist. Leopold joined the U.S. Forest Service in 1909 and became a forceful advocate of wilderness protection. He succeeded in persuading the service to set aside (1924) 574,000 acres to establish Gila National Forest, New Mexico, the first of more than 14 million acres of forest land reserved for recreation and scientific research as well as for aesthetic appreciation. He served as professor of wildlife management at the University of Wisconsin (1933–48) and wrote a pioneering textbook, *Game Management* (1935), which was based on the new sciences of systems ecology and population dynamics. Leopold also helped organize the Wilderness Society (1935) and the Wildlife Society (1937). His concept of the "land ethic," whereby human beings would view nature as part of a shared living community, was fully developed in *A Sand County Almanac* (1949), regarded as a classic of environmental and ecological litera-

ture. His writings also appeared in *Aldo Leopold: For the Health of the Land* (1999) and *The Essential Aldo Leopold* (1999). ▪ See Susan L. Flader, *Thinking Like a Mountain* (1974), and study by Curt Meine (1988).

LEOPOLD, NATHAN, JR. (1904–1971) and **RICHARD LOEB** (1905–1931), convicted U.S. murderers. Both were sons of wealthy Chicago families. Loeb, one of the youngest graduates of the University of Michigan, and Leopold, a brilliant graduate in philosophy from the University of Chicago, kidnapped and murdered 14-year-old Bobby Franks in an effort to carry out the "perfect murder" (1924). Their guilty plea afforded Clarence Darrow, their lawyer, a forum for his case against capital punishment. The court sentenced both to life imprisonment plus 99 years. Loeb died in prison, slashed by a fellow inmate. Leopold volunteered to participate in malaria experiments, organized the prison library, and studied 37 languages during his 33-year-imprisonment. After his release (1958), Leopold worked as a medical technician in Puerto Rico. ▪ See Leopold's *Life Plus 99 Years* (1958) and Hal Higdon, *The Crime of the Century* (1975).

LERNER, ALAN JAY (1918–1986), U.S. lyricist and playwright. Active in student theatrical productions while at Harvard, Lerner became a radio scriptwriter before turning to Broadway and Hollywood. He met composer Frederick Loewe in 1942; together they wrote some of the most successful musical shows in Broadway history, including *Brigadoon* (1947), *Paint Your Wagon* (1951), *Camelot* (1960), and their greatest hit, *My Fair Lady* (1956). They also collaborated on the romantic film *Gigi* (Academy Award, 1958). Lerner independently wrote the screenplay for the movie *An American in Paris* (Academy Award, 1951). ▪ See biography by Edward Jablonski (1996).

LERNER, GERDA (Gerda Kronstein; 1920–   ), Austrian-born U.S. historian and writer. Born in Vienna, Lerner took part in the Austrian underground during World War II and was arrested and imprisoned by the Nazis before fleeing to the United States in 1939. The only member of her Jewish family to survive the Holocaust, she became a U.S. citizen in 1943. After raising a family, working as a writer and translator, and publishing the novel *No Farewell* (1955), Lerner earned a BA. (1963) and a Ph.D. (Columbia University, 1966) in her mid-40s. She taught at several colleges, including Sarah Lawrence (1968–80) and the University of Wisconsin (1980–   ), and gained a reputation as a leading scholar of women's history. Her books included *The Grimké Sisters from South Carolina: Rebels Against Slavery* (1967), *The Woman in American History* (1971), *The Majority Finds Its Past: Placing Women in History* (1979), *Teaching Women's History* (1981), *The Creation of Patriarchy* (1986), *The Creation of Feminist Consciousness* (1993), and *The Feminist Thought of Sarah Grimké* (1998). She also assembled primary documents in *Black Women in White America* (1971) and *The Female Experience* (1976). *A*

Death of One's Own (1978), Lerner's moving account of her husband's death from brain cancer, also delves into her own past. ■ See her reminiscences and a summation of her work in *Why History Matters* (1997).

LERNER, MAX (1902–1992), Russian-born U.S. writer. Lerner was taken to the United States at age 5 and earned a scholarship to Yale (BA. 1923). As a teacher (Williams College, 1938–43; Brandeis, 1949–73) and writer and editor (the *Nation*, 1936–38; *PM*, 1943–48), he confronted the political and social issues of the day from a left-wing point of view. Lerner wrote a column for the *New York Post*, (1949–92), broadening his beat to cover the world from an increasingly mainstream liberal perspective. His magnum opus was *America as a Civilization* (1957). ■ See biography by Sanford Lakoff (1998).

LESAGE, JEAN (1912–1980), French-Canadian political leader. Lesage was a practicing attorney in Quebec before he was elected a Liberal member of Parliament (1945). He held several cabinet posts in the next 13 years and was then named to head the Quebec provincial Liberal party (1958). As premier of Quebec (1960–66), he was the chief architect of the "quiet revolution," which resulted in enhanced powers for the provincial government. He exposed corruption in the previous administration, lessened the power of the Roman Catholic Church, nationalized the schools and the hydroelectric-power industry, instituted broad social, economic, and educational reforms, and fought U.S. cultural and economic dominance. After retiring as party leader (1970), he campaigned against the movement calling for an independent Quebec nation. ■ See study by Dale C. Thomson (1984).

LESCAZE, WILLIAM (1896–1969), Swiss-born U.S. architect. A master of the International style, Lescaze was best known for his design (with George Howe) of the 33-story Philadelphia Savings Fund Society Building (1932), one of the most significant examples of pre–World War II modern architecture. He designed many well-known commercial office towers, schools, residences, and public buildings in New York City and was responsible for the Williamsbridge Housing in Brooklyn, one of the early modern housing developments.

LEŚMIAN, BOLESLAW (Boleslaw Lesman; 1878–1937), Polish poet. Leśmian studied law in Kiev, lived for a period in Paris, and wrote some early verse in Russian. His four volumes of poetry (1912, 1920, 1936, 1938) contained what some consider to be the most consistently original and haunting poetry of modern Polish literature. Influenced by symbolism, he used mythic and folklore elements in traditional forms. He also wrote *Sinbad the Sailor* (1913; Eng. trans. 1980), a volume of Oriental fairy tales in poetic prose. His literary criticism is in *Mythematics and Extropy*

(Eng. trans. 1992). ■ See study by Rochelle Heller Stone (1976).

LEŚNIEWSKI, STANISLAW (1886–1939), Russian-born Polish logician and mathematician. Leśniewski was professor of the philosophy of mathematics at the University of Warsaw (1919–39) and cofounder of the Warsaw school of logic. His major work, which he began to publish in 1927, constituted an original and comprehensive system of logic and of the foundations of mathematics. His work and that of his colleagues helped make the University of Warsaw a world-famous center for research in mathematics and logic in the 1920s and 1930s. ■ See Eugene C. Luschei, *The Logical Systems of Leśniewski* (1962).

LESSING, DORIS (Doris May Tayler; 1919–), British writer. Lessing lived in Rhodesia (now Zimbabwe; 1924–49) before settling in England. She was a member of the Communist party (1944–56) and many of her early semiautobiographical novels, including *The Grass Is Singing* (1950) and *The Children of Violence* series (1952–69), reflected her opposition to colonialism and racism and described the experience of political activists. The influential feminist novel *The Golden Notebook* (1962), her best-known work, described the lives of strong independent women. Her involvement with R. D. Laing and the radical psychiatry movement was reflected in *Briefing for a Descent into Hell* (1971), while her subsequent study of Sufi mysticism influenced her visionary "space-fiction" series, *Canopus in Argos: Archives* (5 vols., 1979–83). She returned to the theme of political activism in *The Good Terrorist* (1985). Lessing published a collection of short novels, *Five* (1953), and several collections of short stories, including *A Man and Two Women* (1965) and *The Story of a Non-Marrying Man* (1972), *London Observed* (1992), and *The Real Thing* (1992). Her later novels included *Love Again* (1996) and *Mara and Dann: An Adventure* (1999). ■ See her two volumes of autobiography, *Under My Skin* (1994) and *Walking in the Shade* (1997); Betsy Draine, *Substance Under Pressure* (1983); study by Mona Knapp (1984); and biography by Carole Klein (2000).

LE SUEUR, MERIDEL (1900–1996), U.S. writer. Le Sueur was born in Iowa to a political family: her mother was an ardent feminist, her stepfather a lawyer and the first socialist mayor of Minot, North Dakota. Her work was rooted in the Midwest, where she spent most of her life, and in the radical left. During the 1930s she joined the Communist party and achieved a national reputation for the stories she placed in such publications as the *Daily Worker, Partisan Review, American Mercury, and New Masses. Salute to Spring* (1940) assembled short fiction that described the political struggles of the Depression years, particularly women's experiences. *North Star Country* (1945) was a history of the northern Midwest. During the years of anticommunist fervor in the 1950s, her publishing options were limited to radical publications, and Le Sueur turned to writing stories for children. Several works were published or reissued in the 1970s: *Rites of Ancient Ripening* (1975), poetry; *Women on the Breadlines* (1977), journalism from the 1930s; *Harvest* (1977), journalism and fiction, 1929–46; *Song for My Time* (1977), journalism and fiction, 1947–58; and *The Girl* (1978), a novel written in 1939. ■ See also *Ripening: Selected Work, 1927–1980* (1982). The journals she kept over several decades filled some 125 volumes.

LEVENE, PHOEBUS AARON THEODOR (Fishel Aaronovich Levin; 1869–1940), Russian-born U.S. chemist. After receiving an M.D. degree from the St. Petersburg Imperial Military Medical Academy (1892), Levene left Russia because of growing anti-Semitism. He practiced medicine in New York City (1892–96) but gave it up to pursue a career in biomedical research. Associated with the Rockefeller Institute for Medical Research (1905–39), Levene did pioneering work on the nucleic acids RNA and DNA, which subsequently were shown to play a key role in the transmission of hereditary information. A skilled and tireless researcher, he published more than 700 scientific papers.

LEVERHULME, WILLIAM HESKETH LEVER, 1st VISCOUNT (1851–1925), British manufacturer. Lever entered his father's grocery business but left it in 1884 to form a partnership with his brother to manufacture soap. Lever Brothers soap, made primarily of vegetable oils rather than tallow, was a huge success; the brothers soon amassed a soap empire through mergers and takeovers. They set up Port Sunlight, the site of their factory, as a model industrial town. The firm, renamed Unilever after Lever's death, developed more than 250 branches and associations throughout the world. Lever also invested heavily in palm oil production in West Africa; set up the United Africa Co., a large trading complex; and served in Parliament from (1906–09). He became Viscount Leverhulme in 1922.

LEVERTOV, DENISE (1923–1997), British-born U.S. poet. Levertov was born to a Welsh mother and a Russian Jewish father who converted to Christianity and became an Anglican clergyman. Educated at home, she was a nurse during World War II, then published *The Double Image* (1946), which was influenced by English romanticism. She emigrated (1947) to the United States and associated with the Black Mountain literary group. *Here and Now* (1957) reflected the influence of American poets such as William Carlos Williams and introduced to readers a transformed Levertov, whose verse was more vigorous, powerful, and political. *The Jacob's Ladder* (1961) exhibited a fascination with mysticism. *The Sorrow Dance* (1968) dealt with the Vietnam War, which she actively opposed. Levertov returned to her earlier lyricism in *Footprints* (1972). Two editions of collected poems spanned the years 1940–60 (1979) and 1960–67 (1983). *Oblique Prayers* appeared in 1984

and *Sands of the Well* in 1996. ■ See her *Tesserae: Memories and Suppositions* (1995); John K. Atchity, *Denise Levertov: An Interview* (1980); and study by Linda W. Wagner (1967).

LÉVESQUE, RENÉ (1922–1987), French-Canadian political leader. Born on Quebec's Gaspé Peninsula, Lévesque dropped out of law school to become a war correspondent in World War II. In the 1950s he was a popular radio and television personality, denouncing the Quebec provincial administration at that time. He was elected to the provincial legislature as a Liberal (1960) and held several cabinet posts in the reformist government of Jean Lesage. In 1967 Lévesque split with his party and in 1968 he helped found the Parti Québecois, which stood for democratic socialism and a sovereign status for Quebec. The Parti Québecois took power in Quebec in 1976 with Lévesque as premier. Although a referendum calling for Quebec's sovereignty was rejected by a three-to-two margin in 1980, Lévesque led his party to an overwhelming victory in the 1981 provincial elections. As public support for independence waned, however, the party voted (1985) to set aside the goal of separation for the foreseeable future, and Lévesque resigned as party leader and premier. ■ See his *My Québec* (Eng. trans. 1979) and Peter Desbarats, *René* (1976).

LEVI, CARLO (1902–1975), Italian writer and painter. A physician and a painter, Levi was exiled (1935) to a small town in a backward section of Italy for his antifascist activity. Moved by the difficult life of the peasants in this primitive village, he recounted their poverty, hopelessness, and faith in a sensitive documentary novel, *Christ Stopped at Eboli* (1945; Eng. trans. 1947). An international success, it greatly influenced the trend to social realism in post–World War II Italian literature. His later work included *Of Fear and Freedom* (1946; Eng. trans. 1950), *The Watch* (1950; Eng. trans. 1951), *The Linden Trees* (1959; Eng. trans. 1962), and numerous essays. He was active in left-wing politics, served in the Senate (1963–72), and also devoted much of his time to his painting.

LEVI, PRIMO (1919–1987), Italian writer. Born into an assimilated middle-class Jewish family in Turin, Levi was a descendant of Jews who had settled in northern Italy after being expelled from Spain in the late 15th century. He studied chemistry at the University of Turin (B.S. 1941) and worked at a pharmaceutical company until joining the anti-Fascist partisans (1943) during World War II. Captured by a fascist militia, he was deported to Auschwitz concentration camp, where he survived because his knowledge of chemistry enabled him to get a job in the synthetic-rubber factory attached to the camp. After the war he wrote a remarkable autobiographical trilogy, *Survival in Auschwitz* (1947; Eng. trans. 1959), *The Reawakening* (1963; Eng. trans. 1965), and *Moments of Reprieve* (1981; Eng. trans. 1986), which described the degradation and anguish of the concentration camp without hatred, bitterness, or self-pity. His works were seen by many as symbols of the triumph of reason over Nazi barbarism. He also wrote *The Periodic Table* (1975; Eng. trans. 1984), a volume of memoirs; the novels *The Monkey's Wrench* (1978; Eng. trans. 1986) and *If Not Now, When* (1982; Eng. trans. 1985); and *The Drowned and the Saved* (1986; Eng. trans. 1988), a book of meditations on the meaning of the Holocaust. He suffered from depression during the last months of his life and he reportedly committed suicide, although no note was found and there was no conclusive proof that he killed himself. ■ See Nicholas Patruno, *Understanding Primo Levi* (1995); study by Mirna Cicioni (1995); and biography by Myriam Anissimov (1996; Eng. trans. 1998).

LEVI-CIVITA, TULLIO (1873–1941), Italian mathematician. A professor at Padua (1897–1918) and Rome (1918–38), Levi-Civita was one of the most influential and versatile mathematicians of the century, contributing to the fields of analytic and celestial mechanics, hydrodynamics, elasticity, electromagnetism, and atomic physics. He helped developed differential calculus (tensor calculus) and applied it to differential geometry, mechanics, and relativity. His work proved essential for the formulation of Albert Einstein's general theory of relativity. He also introduced (1917) the concept of parallelism in curved spaces, the theory of "parallel displacement." A Jew, he was forced to give up his teaching post after the implementation of the fascist anti-Semitic laws. His books included *The Absolute Differential Calculus* (Eng. trans. 1926) and *The n-body Problem in General Relativity* (Eng. trans. 1964).

LEVI-MONTALCINI, RITA (1909–), Italian biochemist. Born into an ancient Jewish family in Turin, Levi-Montalcini studied at the University Turin (M.D. 1936) and did medical research there until forced out by anti-Semitic laws (1939). She continued her research in a laboratory in her home until the German occupation (1943) forced her to flee. She and her family lived in hiding in Florence until the end of the war (1945) and she then resumed her university career. As a researcher and later professor at Washington University in St. Louis (1947–77) she discovered nerve growth factor (NGF), the natural substance that stimulates the nerve cells and plays a crucial role in the development of the brain and nervous system. She pursued her research in collaboration with Stanley Cohen, and they shared the 1986 Nobel Prize for Physiology or Medicine. She also served as the director of the Institute of Cell Biology in Rome (1969–78). ■ See her autobiography, *In Praise of Imperfection* (1987; Eng. trans. 1988).

LEVINE, JACK (1915–), U.S. artist. Levine grew up in the slums of Boston and studied art at the Boston Museum of Fine Arts and at Harvard (1929–31). His expressionistic works commented on the corruption and dehumanization of modern capitalist society. With the Federal Arts Project during the 1930s, he painted plutocrats and politicians in a distorted, satiric style reminiscent of the older artists Chaim Soutine and George Grosz. Among his outstanding canvases are *Brain Trust* (1936), *The Feast of Pure Reason* (1937), and *Gangster Funeral* (1952–53). In the 1980s he produced several works on biblical themes, including *David and Saul* (1987–89).

LEVINE, JAMES (1943–), U.S. conductor. Born into a musical family, Levine made his professional piano debut at age 10, conducted orchestras as a teenager, and was an apprentice and later assistant to George Szell (1964–70), the conductor of the Cleveland Orchestra. His first love was opera, however, and he made his debut at New York's Metropolitan Opera in 1971 and served as its principal conductor (1972–) and musical director (1975–). Although he was de facto artistic director of the company from the late 1970s, he was not given the title until 1986. At the Met he dramatically improved the quality of the orchestra, conducted most of its televised broadcasts, and expanded the repertory to include many 20th-century works. In addition to his duties in New York, he continued to appear as guest conductor with orchestras throughout the world and served as artistic director of the Munich Philharmonic Orchestra (1999–). ■ See Robert C. Marsh, *Dialogues and Discoveries* (1998).

LEVITT, WILLIAM JAIRD (1907–), U.S. builder. Levitt founded the building firm of Levitt and Sons with his father and brother in 1929. He revolutionized the U.S. housing industry after World War II with the development of mass-produced, one-family suburban homes. Moderately priced and available to the lower middle class, his houses helped establish part of the Great American Dream of the 1950s, and by 1981 he had constructed more than 125,000 units. He was best known for creating the communities of Levittown on Long Island (New York), in Pennsylvania, and in New Jersey.

LÉVI-STRAUSS, CLAUDE GUSTAVE (1908–), French social anthropologist. Widely acclaimed as the founder of structural anthropology, Lévi-Strauss studied philosophy at the Sorbonne. While holding provincial teaching posts, he associated with the circle around Jean Paul Sartre. He did fieldwork among Brazilian Indian tribes while teaching sociology in Brazil (1935–39). Lévi-Strauss gained fame with *Tristes Tropiques* (1955; Eng. trans. 1961), an autobiographical, philosophical work based on his observations of four primitive South American tribes that reflected Marxist and psychoanalytic concepts, *Structural Anthropology* (1958; rev, ed. 1961; Eng. trans. 1963) established Lévi-Strauss as the leading voice of the structuralist school of thought, which worked a revolution not only in anthropology but also in philosophy, psychology, literary theory, and many other fields. *The Savage Mind* (1962; Eng. trans. 1966) sought to characterize "mind in its natural state" and elaborated his view of culture as a system of communication structured by the unconscious workings of the mind. The four-volume *Mythologiques* (1964–71), which received France's highest scientific honor, analyzed South and North American mythology to show "not how men think in myths, but how myths operate in men's minds without their being aware of it." This landmark work included *The Raw and the Cooked* (1964; Eng. trans. 1969), *From Honey to Ashes* (1967; Eng. trans. 1973), *The Origin of Table Manners* (1968; Eng. trans. 1981), and *The Naked Man* (1971; Eng. trans. 1979). The essays collected in *The View from Afar* (Eng. trans. 1984) discussed the genesis and methods of his work. ■ See studies by Edmund Leach (rev. ed. 1976) and David Pace (1983); Simon Clarke, *Foundations of Structuralism* (1981); and Didier Eribon, *Conversations with Claude Lévi-Strauss* (1988; Eng. trans. 1991).

LÉVY-BRUHL, LUCIEN (1857–1939), French anthropologist, philosopher, and sociologist. Lévy-Bruhl's earliest writings traced the history of French and German philosophy. The influence of positivist philosopher Auguste Comte marked *Ethics and Moral Science* (1903; Eng. trans. 1905), which asserted that cultural relativity obviates any absolute ethic. It called for scientific study of specific moral systems and paved the way for relativistic sociology. Lévy-Bruhl taught at the Sorbonne (1899–1927); he undertook no fieldwork himself but produced six books that generalized about primitive thought patterns and emphasized the distinctions between the primitive and civilized mentality. Among these were *How Natives Think* (1910; Eng. trans. 1926), *Primitive Mentality* (1922; Eng. trans. 1923), and *Primitives and the Supernatural* (1931; Eng. trans. 1935). ■ See his *Notebooks on Primitive Mentality* (1949; Eng. trans. 1975) and study by Jean Cazeneuve (Eng. trans. 1972).

LEWIN, KURT (1890–1947), German-born U.S. social psychologist. A Gestalt psychologist at the University of Berlin (1921–33), Lewin was a leader in the study of group dynamics, a major figure in the development of social psychology, and the originator of field theory. A refugee from Nazism, he taught child psychology at the University of Iowa (1935–44) and in 1945 founded the Research Center for Group Dynamics at the Massachusetts Institute of Technology. His studies of democratic and autocratic leadership indicated less resistance to change in democratically ruled groups, although their leaders enjoyed no less power than autocrats; ideological change, he concluded, was possible only by redistributing power. English translations of his papers are in *Resolving Social Conflicts* (1948) and *Field Theory in Social Science* (1963). ■ See Alfred J. Marrow, *The Practical Theorist* (1969), and Martin Gold, ed., *The Complete Social Scientist: A Kurt Lewin Reader* (1999).

LEWIS, SIR (WILLIAM) ARTHUR (1915–1991), West Indies-born British economist. An expert in the economic problems of developing nations, Lewis criticized the emphasis on industrialization in the Third World and advocated instead the development of a strong agricultural base. He served as vice-chancellor of the University of the West Indies (1959–63), was an economic adviser to the governments of Ghana, Nigeria, and Jamaica, and was a founder (1970) and president (1970–73) of the Caribbean Development Bank. He wrote many books and pamphlets, including the influential *Theory of Economic Growth* (1955), and served as a professor at Princeton University (1963–83). Lewis shared the 1979 Nobel Prize for Economics (with Theodore Schultz), thus becoming the first black to receive a Nobel award in a category other than Peace.

LEWIS, CARL (1961–), U.S. track-and-field athlete. Lewis' parents, both former star athletes at the Tuskegee Institute, founded the Willingboro (New Jersey) Track Club, where Carl began to run as a child. As a teenager he was the top-ranked high school track athlete in the United States and was a star of the University of Houston track team (1979–82). A champion sprinter and long jumper, he was designated the top amateur athlete in the country by virtue of winning the Sullivan Award (1981), and he won three gold medals in the 1983 world championships in Helsinki, Finland. In the 1984 Los Angeles Olympics he won gold medals in the 100-meter and 200-meter races, the long jump, and the 400-meter relay, duplicating Jesse Owens' remarkable feat at the 1936 Berlin Olympics. In the 1988 Seoul Olympics he won gold medals in the 100-meter race and the long jump and won two more gold medals in the 1992 Barcelona Olympics in the long jump and the 400-meter relay. At the age of 35, in the 1996 Atlanta Olympics, Lewis won the long jump for a fourth consecutive time, equaling the feats of Ray Ewry in the standing high jump and Al Oerter in the discus. It was Lewis' ninth Olympic track-and-field gold medal, tying a record held by Finnish runner Paavo Nurmi. He was named "Male Athlete of the Century" (1999) by the International Amateur Athletic Association (IAAF).

LEWIS, CLARENCE IRVING (1883–1964), U.S. philosopher. Lewis earned his Ph.D. from Harvard (1910) and returned there to teach for over 30 years (1920–53) while developing his ideas on epistemology and symbolic logic. Sensory impressions are subjective and must be verified empirically, he concluded. His writings included *A Survey of Symbolic Logic* (1918), *Mind and the World-Order* (1929), *An Analysis of Knowledge and Valuation* (1947), and *Our Social Inheritance* (1957). ■ See studies by Paul A. Schilpp, ed., *The Philosophy of C. I. Lewis* (1966), and J. Roger Saydah, *The Ethical Theory of C. I. Lewis* (1969).

LEWIS, C. S. (Clive Staples Lewis; 1898–1963), British scholar and writer. A teacher of medieval and renaissance studies at Oxford (1925–54) and Cambridge (1954–63) universities, Lewis wrote several important scholarly works, including *The Allegory of Love: A Study in Medieval*

Tradition (1936) and *English Literature in the 16th Century* (1954). However, he was best known to the public for his works on Christian themes, including *The Screwtape Letters* (1942; rev. ed. 1961) and an allegorical science-fiction trilogy, *Out of the Silent Planet* (1938), *Perelandra* (1943), and *That Hideous Strength* (1945). He also wrote an extremely popular series of allegorical children's stories, *The Chronicles of Narnia* (7 vols., 1950–56). ■ See the autobiographical *Surprised by Joy* (1955) and studies by W. Griffith (1986), D. Barratt (1987), J. R. Christopher (1987), A. N. Wilson (1990), and D. T. Myers (1994).

LEWIS, EDWARD B. (1918–   ), U.S. biologist. Lewis studied at the California Institute of Technology in Pasadena (Ph.D. 1942) and taught there from 1946 to 1988. In pioneering studies during the 1940s of genetic mutations in the fruit fly, Drosophila, he discovered a cluster of genes that control how specific regions of the body develop. The genes were arranged on the chromosome in the same order, head to tail, as the body segments they controlled. He demonstrated that mutations in such genes were responsible for dramatic abnormalities and malformations. His work represented a new approach to the study of developmental biology and led to the understanding that growth in most animals, including human beings, is regulated by a set of master genes that function early in the development of the embryo. Lewis shared the 1995 Nobel Prize in Physiology or Medicine with Eric Wieschaus and Christiane Nüsslein-Volhard.

LEWIS, JERRY (Joseph Levitch; 1926–   ), U.S. comedian. A show-business brat, Lewis made his borscht-circuit Catskill Mountains resort hotel debut at age 5 and dropped out of high school to develop a comedy act. From 1946 to 1956 he teamed with singer Dean Martin in one of the most successful partnerships in show-business history. As Martin and Lewis, they appeared in 16 popular movies (*My Friend Irma,* 1949: *That's My Boy,* 1951; *Pardners,* 1956) and starred in nightclubs and on TV. After the pair's breakup, the crew-cut comedian with the manic energy and raucous style made it on his own as actor-director-producer (*Rock-a-Bye Baby,* 1958; *The Bellboy,* 1960; *The Nutty Professor* 1963). His later films included *King of Comedy* (1983) and *Mr. Saturday Night* (1992). He was also an active fundraiser for charitable causes and the telethon host for the Muscular Dystrophy Association. ■ See his autobiography (1982; with Herb Gluck); Shawn Levy, *King of Comedy* (1996); and Frank Krutnik, *Inventing Jerry Lewis* (2000).

LEWIS, JOHN LLEWELLYN (1880–1969), U.S. labor leader. The son of a Welsh immigrant coal miner, Lewis headed the United Mine Workers of America (UMWA) from 1920 to 1960. One of the century's most powerful labor leaders, he was a principal founder and first president (1936–40) of the Congress of Industrial Organizations (CIO), the American Federation of Labor offshoot that unionized workers in mass-production industries. He supported Franklin D. Roosevelt for president (1932; 1936) but broke with the Democrats in 1940. Miners' strikes that he called during and after World War II secured new benefits for his workers but alienated elements of the public and were partly responsible for enabling conservatives to secure the passage of the antilabor Smith-Connally Act (1943) and Taft-Hartley Act (1947). He was instrumental in the passage of federal mine-safety legislation and cooperated with mine owners in permitting the mechanization and automation of many mining procedures. ■ See biographies by Saul Alinsky (1949) and Melvyn Dubofsky and Warren Van Tine (1977).

LEWIS, JOSEPH (1889–1968), U.S. atheist. Lewis was a lifelong crusader against religion and devoted considerable energy to get "God out of public institutions." He founded (1920) and was president of Freethinkers of America and served as president of the Thomas Paine Foundation. A self-styled "infidel," Lewis campaigned (unsuccessfully) for removing the phrase "under God" from the Pledge of Allegiance, for doing away with chaplains in the armed forces and the houses of Congress, and for having elections held and mail delivered on Sundays. Among his more than 20 books, reflecting his view that religion was superstition that caused strife between men, were *The Tyranny of God* (1921), *The Bible Unmasked* (1926), *In the Name of Humanity* (1949), and *An Atheist Manifesto* (1954).

LEWIS, MEADE "LUX" (1905–1964), U.S. jazz pianist. A nightclub performer during the 1920s, Lewis was rediscovered in 1935 and recognized as one of the greatest of the boogie-woogie stylists. At the peak of his popularity during the late 1930s and early 1940s, he displayed remarkable technical ability in creating the powerful crossrhythms that characterized his playing. He formed a shortlived trio (1939) with Albert Ammons and Pete Johnson, the other great pianists of the boogie-woogie era. Among his best-known recordings were *Honky Tonk Train Blues* (1929, 1935) and *Yancey Special* (1936).

LEWIS, OSCAR (1914–1970), U,S, anthropologist. Lewis studied history at Columbia University until he was drawn to anthropology by Prof. Ruth Benedict. He taught at the University of Illinois (from 1948) and wrote animated, immediate accounts of Mexican and Puerto Rican slum dwellers, often using tape-recorded monologues, in such books as *Five Families* (1959) and *The Children of Sanchez* (1961). The controversial *La Vida* (1966), which presented the first-person narrative of a Puerto Rican mother and former prostitute, won a National Book Award. Lewis put forth the controversial thesis that poverty may be treated as a culture in itself, transcending national boundaries. He also wrote three posthumously published oral histories of contemporary Cuba, *Four Men* (1977), *Four Women* (1977), and *Neighbors* (1978).

LEWIS, SINCLAIR (1885–1951), U.S. novelist and social critic. The son of a small-town Minnesota doctor, Lewis lashed out against both the spiritual bankruptcy of middle Americans and the snobbery of the educated elite. After early success as a fiery journalist, he won critical attention with *Main Street* (1920), an expose of pettiness and intolerance in the "everytown" called Gopher Prairie. His later works were hailed as vital, accurate portrayals of American middle-class values, but his style was often criticized as heavy-handed. *Arrowsmith* (1926), an attack on the medical establishment, brought Lewis a Pulitzer Prize, which he declined. In 1930, however, after dominating the American literary scene for a decade, Lewis became the first American writer to receive the Nobel Prize in Literature. His best-known works included *Babbitt* (1922), which depicted the ravages of conformity on the individual spirit, *Elmer Gantry* (1927), which satirized religious hypocrisy, and *Cass Timberlane* (1945), which explored the problems of a May-December marriage. He was married to journalist Dorothy Thompson from 1928 to 1942. ■ See biography by Mark Schorer (1961); studies by Richard O'Connor (1971) and Martin Light (1975); and James M. Hutchisson, *The Rise of Sinclair Lewis* (1996).

LEWIS, (PERCY) WYNDHAM (1884–1957), U.S.-born British artist, novelist, essayist, and poet. The iconoclastic Lewis founded vorticism, a pre–World War I avant-garde artistic movement, similar to cubism and futurism, which sought to relate art to the modern machine world. He also edited *Blast,* the movement's journal, with Ezra Pound (1914–15). Lewis is known for his satiric and complex novels, notably *Tarr* (1918), *The Childermass* (1928), and *The Apes of God* (1930). He wrote provocative books on political theory, art, philosophy, literature, and contemporary society. A frequent critic and satirist of the ways of democracy, he espoused profascist views between the wars, and his reputation suffered. *Blasting and Bombardiering* (1937) and *Rude Assignment* (1950) were autobiographical. ■ See *The Letters of Ezra Pound and Wyndham Lewis* (1985); study by Geoffrey Wagner (1957); Jeffrey Meyers, *Enemy* (1980); and Anne Quéma, *The Agon of Modernism* (1999).

LEYENDECKER, JOSEPH CHRISTIAN (1874–1951), German-born U.S. illustrator. A star pupil at the Chicago Art Institute and the Académie Julian in Paris (1897–98), Leyendecker opened a commercial-art studio with his younger brother Frank to produce magazine covers—up to 16 a year for *Collier's* and the *Saturday Evening Post*—and advertisements that made him wealthy. Most distinctive were his spare, boldly painted, posterlike Arrow collar, Chesterfield cigarette, and men's clothing ads featuring civilized, self-confident models with chiseled features. ■ See study by Michael Schau (1974).

LEZAMA LIMA, JOSÉ (1910–1976), Cuban writer. Called the "Proust of the Caribbean," Lezama Lima established his reputation with *Hostile Sounds* (1941), a collection of dense, hermetic baroque poems, and cofounded and edited (1944–57) the influential avant-garde journal *Origins*. His major work was the novel *Paradiso* (1966; Eng. trans. 1974), which exploited diverse modernist techniques and drew on religion, mythology, and musical imagery to portray the inner life of a poet. He was appointed by Fidel Castro's government to several key cultural positions, but after the publication of the distinctly apolitical *Paradiso,* which included frank discussions of homosexuality, he fell out of favor.

LHEVINNE, JOSEF (1874–1944), Russian-born U.S. pianist. Lhevinne studied at the Moscow Conservatory and graduated in 1891. He won the coveted Rubinstein Prize in 1895. In 1900 he became a piano teacher in Tiflis, returning to Moscow two years later as a professor at the Moscow Conservatory. Lhevinne made his U.S. debut in 1906 with a Russian symphony orchestra and returned for many subsequent tours to gain a reputation for his brilliant and poetic playing of romantic music, particularly Chopin and Tchaikovsky. Lhevinne lived in Berlin from 1907 until 1919, when he and his wife. Rosina Lhevinne, emigrated to the United States, where they opened a music studio and became members of the faculty of the Juilliard School of Music in New York ■ See Robert K. Wallace, *A Century of Music-making* (1976).

LHEVINNE, ROSINA (Rosina Bessie; 1880–1976), Russian-born U.S. pianist and teacher. Bessie was admitted to the Imperial Russian Conservatory at age 9 and graduated nine years later with a gold-medal award. Shortly after graduation she married pianist Josef Lhevinne and gave up a promising career as a solo pianist in favor of her husband. Together they played two-piano recitals until Josef's career as a soloist accelerated. The Lhevinnes were interned in Berlin during World War I, after which they went to the United States (1919) and joined the faculty of the Juilliard School of Music in New York. In 1939 they celebrated the 40th anniversary of their duo-piano debut with a concert at Carnegie Hall. After her husband's death in 1944, Lhevinne took over many of his pupils to become one of the century's great piano teachers. During 1945–56 she gave summer master classes in Los Angeles; subsequently she spent her summers at the Aspen Music Festival. Among Lhevinne's pupils were Van Cliburn, John Browning, and Mischa Dichter. ■ See Robert K. Wallace, *A Century of Music-making* (1976).

LIANG CH'I-CH'AO. *See LIANG QICHAO.*

LIANG QICHAO (old style: LIANG CH'I-CH'AO; 1873–1929), Chinese reformer. One of the foremost intellectual leaders of his time, Liang was a disciple of the scholar Kang Youwei (K'ang Yu-wei; from 1890) and aided him in initiating and carrying out the 100 Days of Reform (1898), an attempt at modernizing Confucian China. When the movement collapsed Liang fled to Japan and became a journalist. During the next 14 years his writings influenced scores of China's future leaders. After his return to China (1912) he formed the Progressive party (1913) and supported the government of Yuan Shikai (Yuan Shihk'ai), but resisted his attempts to overthrow the republic (1916). Liang began to lose favor among students because of his belief in gradualism (the slow evolution of reforms) and he spent the last nine years of his life in academic obscurity in Tianjin (Tientsin). His works in English included *Intellectual Trends in the Ch'ing Period, 1644–1912* (1959). ■ See Joseph R. Levenson, *Liang Ch'i-ch'ao and the Mind of Modern China* (1953; rev. ed. 1967) and Hao Chang, *Liang Ch'i-ch'ao and the Intellectual Transition in China, 1890–1907* (1971).

LIAQUAT ALI KHAN (1895–1951), Indian-Pakistani Muslim political leader. A wealthy Punjabi, Liaquat studied law at Oxford University, joined the Muslim League (1923), and participated in local politics (1926–40). He was named Pakistan's first prime minister (1947), and after the death of Pakistan's founder, Muhammad Ali Jinnah (1948), he was the most powerful man in Pakistan. He was bitterly criticized, however, by fanatics for signing a trade treaty with Prime Minister Jawaharlal Nehru of India and for not basing Pakistani law on the Koran, and he was assassinated. ■ See his speeches in *Pakistan, the Heart of Asia* (1950).

LIBBY, WILLARD FRANK (1908–1980), U.S. chemist. Willard Libby worked on the creation of the atomic bomb during World War II (1941–45) and taught at the University of Chicago (1945–54) and the University of California, Los Angeles (1959–80). He won the 1960 Nobel Prize in Chemistry for his introduction of radiocarbon dating, a technique used by geologists and archaeologists to determine the age of ancient organic materials. Libby's method was based on the presence of a small quantity of the isotope carbon 14 in every living cell. Unlike common carbon, carbon 14 undergoes gradual radioactive decay after a cell's death and is half depleted after 5,600 years. Libby suggested that by calculating the depletion of carbon 14, the age of dead organic matter could be determined. Using radiocarbon dating, archaeologists analyzed wood from Egyptian tombs to learn the chronology of ancient dynasties. By using other radioactive isotopes, scientists can date inorganic matter as well. ■ See his *Radiocarbon Dating* (2nd. ed. 1955).

LIBERACE (Wladziu Valentino Liberace; 1919–1987), U.S. pianist. Born in Wisconsin to parents of Italian and Polish heritage, Liberace received early musical training from his father, a french-horn player. He was encouraged by the celebrated Polish pianist Ignace Paderewski to study piano. Liberace played at local nightclubs under the name Walter Busterkeys, then moved to New York (1940). Assembling a repertoire of semiclassical arrangements, he appeared in elaborate costumes (often with sequins and furs) and was a novelty on the nightclub circuit. Inspired by a prop in a movie about the composer Chopin, Liberace placed a candelabrum on his piano, and it became the hallmark of his romantic style. He gained popularity with saccharine television performances. Liberace sold tens of millions of records, secured annual multimillion-dollar Las Vegas contracts, and was said to be the highest-paid pianist of all time. In 1984, he celebrated 40 years in show business with a sellout show at Radio City Music Hall (New York City). He published a cookbook (1970) and an autobiography (1973). ■ See biography by Bob Thomas (1987).

LIBERMAN, YEVSEI GRIGORIEVICH (1897–1983), Soviet economist. Liberman was initially denied admission to the University of Kiev because of the quota on Jewish entrants; he was admitted during World War I, but his education was interrupted by military service. He graduated in 1920 and later earned a graduate degree at the Kharkov Labor Institute (1940). He taught there (1933–40; 1947–63) and at Kharkov State University (after 1963). He became famous when "Plan, Profit, Bonus" (1962), an article he published in *Pravda,* proposed that a factory's efficiency be measured in terms of its ability to generate profit rather than in terms of output alone, and that managers and workers earn bonuses for surpassing their planned profit level. Liberman also recommended that factories be given greater autonomy. These views were published while Nikita Khrushchev was in power, presumably with his backing, but were put into effect only after Leonid I. Brezhnev assumed leadership in 1964. The progressive economic policies that resulted became known as "Libermanism." See his *Economic Methods and the Effectiveness of Production* (Eng. trans. 1972).

LICHTENSTEIN, ROY (1923–1997), U.S. painter. Lichtenstein experimented with several art styles, including abstract expressionism, before evolving the art based on popular culture for which he was known. Using characters from comic books, advertisements, and romance magazines, he employed commercial-art techniques to create brilliantly colored parodies of the originals. He also painted geometrical compositions and parodies of the works of Picasso, Mondrian, and Monet. His controversial work placed him in the vanguard of the pop-art movement of the early 1960s. His later works included the 68-foot-high *Mural With Blue Brushstroke* (1986) for the lobby of the Equitable Center in New York City. ■ See studies by Diane Waldman (1971) and Lawrence Alloway (1983).

LICKLIDER, JOSEPH C. R. (1915–1990), U.S. computer scientist. Though trained as a psychologist at the University of Rochester (Ph.D. 1942), Licklider achieved prominence as a computer pioneer and visionary. While a vice president of the engineering firm of Bolt Beranek and Newman in Cambridge, Massachusetts (1957–62), he wrote a seminal paper, "Man-Computer Symbiosis" (1960), which envisioned a "massive network" in which interactive home-based computer consoles would be linked. As a director of the Defense Department's Advanced Research Projects Agency (ARPA; 1962–64), he was instrumental in creating the computer network that became ARPANET, the forerunner of the Internet. Licklider, who taught at Harvard (1941–49) and the Massachusetts Institute of Technology (1949–57; 1964–85), also made contributions in areas of information storage and retrieval and developed a system for creating programs by drawing diagrams on a computer screen. He also helped establish large-scale experimental research projects in computer science at universities around the country. The first, which was called Project Mac, located at the Massachusetts Institute of Technology, later became the university's Laboratory for Computer Science.

LI DAZHAO (old style: LI TA-CHAO; 1889?–1927), Chinese revolutionary. As an editor of *New Youth* magazine and as chief librarian (1918) and later professor of history, economics, and political science (1920) at Beijing (Peking) University, Li profoundly influenced and radicalized many students during the upheaval of the May Fourth movement (1919). Among these students was the future communist leader Mao Zedong (Mao Tse-tung), whom he hired as a clerk in the library. Li led many antiimperialist and antiwarlord demonstrations, wrote numerous articles, organized Marxist study groups, and helped found the Chinese Communist party (1921). A theoretician, propagandist, and organizer, Li played a crucial role in the Communist–Guomindang (Kuomintang) alliance (1922–27) and was the key communist organizer in north China until his execution by the warlord Zhang Zuolin (Chang Tso-lin). ■ See study by Maurice Meisner (1967).

LIDDELL HART, SIR BASIL HENRY (1895–1970), British military strategist. A student of military history, Liddell Hart left Cambridge University to serve as an officer in the British army (1914–27). He was a leading advocate of mechanized warfare, surprise attack, mobility, and air power, and was a military correspondent for the *London Daily Telegraph* (1925–35), *Times* (1935–39), and *Daily Mail* (1941–45). He was a military adviser to the British government in the 1930s and many of his ideas were adopted by the Germans during World War II. He wrote some 30 books, including *The Tanks* (1959), *Strategy* (rev. ed. 1967), *A History of the Second World War* (1970), and his *Memoirs* (2 vols., 1965–66). ■ See Alex Danchev, *Alchemist of War* (1998).

LIDMAN, SARA (1923–   ), Swedish novelist, essayist, and dramatist. Sara Lidman grew up in a deeply religious home in remote northern Sweden. Using dialect and evocative narration, she revived the tradition of the regional novel with *Tjärdalen* (1953) while attacking injustice and championing the cause of the oppressed. These themes were repeated in *The Rain Bird* (1958; Eng. trans. 1963), her novels set in

South Africa (1960) and Kenya (1964), her reportage from North Vietnam (1966; 1972), and her writings about the lives of Swedish miners (1968). She also wrote *Naboth's Stone* (1981; Eng. trans. 1989).

LIE, TRYGVE HALVDAN (1896–1968), Norwegian diplomat. Lie was a leading member of the Norwegian Labor party and served as foreign minister of the Norwegian government-in-exile during World War II. Elected as the first secretary-general of the United Nations (1946), he dealt with such crises as the war in Palestine (1947) and the Kashmir conflict (1948). However, after U.N. forces were sent to aid South Korea during the Korean War (1950), Lie was attacked by the representatives of the Soviet Union and he resigned his office in 1953. He returned to Norway and served in several ministerial posts. ■ See his *In the Cause of Peace* (1954) and study by James Barros (1989).

LIEBERSON, GODDARD (1911–1978), British-born U.S. businessman. As chief promoter and salesman for the newly invented 33-rpm long-playing record (1948), Lieberson, a Columbia Records vice president (later president, 1956–66; 1973–75), created a revolution in the record industry and music world. Trained as a composer, he carefully selected the music that Columbia recorded and made it a leader in the new industry. He set up the Columbia Records Club (1955), which became the world's largest; recorded original-cast Broadway musicals, including *South Pacific, My Fair Lady, West Side Story,* and *The Sound of Music;* and pioneered in the recording of serious 20th-century music and complete classical and modern dramas. He also persuaded CBS to become the sole financial backer of the musical *My Fair Lady* (1956), which resulted in millions of dollars in profit for the company.

LIEBKNECHT, KARL (1871–1919), German socialist leader. Son of a revolutionary leader of 1848, Liebknecht, a lawyer, was convicted of high treason (1907) for antimilitaristic writings and jailed for 18 months. Elected to the Reichstag in 1912 as a left-wing member of the Social Democratic party (SPD), he was a leader of the opposition to the government during World War I and was expelled from the SPD for his radical views (1916). He and Rosa Luxemburg formed the Spartacus League, which advocated violent overthrow of the government, and helped found the German Communist party (KPD) in 1918. He was murdered by soldiers after the failure of a 1919 uprising. ■ See study by Karl W. Meyer (1957).

LIEBLING, ABBOTT JOSEPH (1904–1963), U.S. journalist. During his 28 years on the staff of the *New Yorker* (1935–63), A. J. Liebling wrote with affection about the affairs, large and small, of the patrons of the I & Y Cigar Store, the tenants of the Jollity Building, and other Broadway characters. He was also a devout Francophile and a student of cooking, boxing, and medieval history, but he is probably best remembered for his World War II reportage and his critical commentary on the American press. Liebling's books included *The Telephone Booth Indian* (1942), *The Wayward Pressman* (1947), *The Honest Rainmaker* (1953), and *The Press* (1961). ▪ See Raymond Sokolov, *Wayward Reporter* (1980).

LIFAR, SERGE (1905–1986), Russian-born French dancer, choreographer, and writer. Lifar studied dance in Kiev and joined Sergei Diaghilev's Ballet Russe in Paris in 1923. An athletic dancer with a magnetic stage presence, he was *premier danseur* with the company (1925–29) and created the title roles in George Balanchine's *The Prodigal Son* (1929) and *Apollo* (1929). As dancer, ballet master, and choreographer at the Paris Opera Ballet (1929–44; 1947–58), he completely revitalized the company by introducing dramatic modern ballets, enhancing the position of male dancers, and emphasizing dance, rather than music, as the dominant element in his productions. After 1958 he choreographed ballets for companies around the world. His writings included a biography of Diaghilev (1939; Eng. trans. 1940), *Lifar on Classical Ballet* (Eng. trans. 1951), *A History of the Russian Ballet* (1950; Eng. trans. 1954), *Ballet: Traditional to Modern* (Eng. trans. 1938), and an autobiography, *Ma Vie* (1965; Eng. trans. 1970).

LIFTON, ROBERT JAY (1926–   ), U.S. psychiatrist. A graduate of New York Medical College (M.D. 1948), Lifton served as an air force psychiatrist in the Far East, a region that provided the background of several major studies in which he linked psychiatry with ethics and history. In *Thought Reform and the Psychology of Totalism* (1961), he studied brainwashing by the Chinese during the Korean War; *Death in Life: Survivors of Hiroshima* (1968), Lifton's report on survivors of the atomic holocaust, won a National Book Award; *Home from the War: Vietnam Veterans* (1973) examined the psychomythology of warmaking. In *Indefensible Weapons: The Political and Moral Case Against Nuclear Arms* (1982; with Richard A. Falk), he argued that the very existence of nuclear weapons undermines mental health. Lifton taught at the Yale School of Medicine (1961–   ) and at the City University of New York (1985–   ). He also wrote *In a Dark Time* (1984), *The Nazi Doctors* (1986), *The Genocidal Mentality* (1990), *Hiroshima in America* (1995; with W. G. Mitchell), and *Who Owns Death* (2000).

LILIENTHAL, DAVID ELI (1899–1981), U.S. public official. A graduate of Harvard Law School (1923), Lilienthal practiced law in Chicago (1923–31) before serving on the Wisconsin Public Service Commission (1931–33). A political liberal and an expert in public-utility regulation, he was appointed as one of the three directors of the controversial Tennessee Valley Authority (1933) and served as its chairman (1941–46). His book, *TVA: Democracy on the March* (1944), described his work with the authority. As chairman of the Atomic Energy Commission (1946–50) he helped de-

velop national policy on nuclear research and atomic weapons. He was the founder (1955) and president (1955–79) of the Development and Resources Corp., which planned industrial, agricultural, and housing projects throughout the world. He also wrote *This I Do Believe* (1949), *Big Business in a New Era* (1953), *The Multinational Corporation* (1960), *Change, Hope and the Bomb* (1963), *Management: A Humanist Art* (1967), and six volumes of *Journals* (1964–76). ▪ See biography by Steven M. Neuse (1989).

LI LI-SAN (1899–1967), Chinese political leader. Born into a poor rural family, Li first met the future communist leader Mao Zedong (Mao Tse-tung) in 1917. He worked in a factory in France on a work-study program (1919) and later helped found, in that country, a branch of the Chinese Communist party (1921). Expelled from France in 1922, he returned to China and worked as a labor organizer and agitator. Li became de facto head of the party in 1928 and pursued a plan to have urban workers lead a national revolutionary uprising. The plan was opposed by Mao, who saw the peasantry as the leading force in the revolution. The policy failed, and Li was ousted in 1930 and exiled to Moscow until 1945. He was reelected to the party's Central Committee and held various posts in the People's Republic of China until 1956, when he was ousted from power once again. He confessed his "errors" of sectarianism and subjectivism and was reinstated in ceremonial positions in 1962. He reportedly committed suicide after being persecuted during the Cultural Revolution. He was officially rehabilitated in 1980.

LILLEHEI, CLARENCE WALTON (1918–1999), U. S. surgeon. The son of a dentist and the brother of two prominent physicians, C. Walton Lillehei was a pioneer in the field of open-heart surgery. He taught at the University of Minnesota Medical School (1949–67) and the Cornell Medical Center, New York (1967–74). He was the first to perform (1954) an intracardiac operation utilizing cross-circulation of the blood of the patient and of a donor. He was a coinventor (1955) of the heart-lung machine and was the first to replace damaged heart valves with prosthetic plastic devices (1957). His work paved the way for heart-transplant operations, which were first performed by his former students, Christiaan N. Barnard and Norman E. Shumway. Lillehei was also the first to report on the successful use of electronic heart pacemakers (1960). He was a medical director at St. Jude's Medical Inc. (1979–   ), a St. Paul Minnesota medical equipment manufacturer.

LILLIE, BEATRICE (1894–1989), Canadian-born British actress and comedienne. Bea Lillie studied singing and "gesture" as a schoolgirl. She clowned her way to celebrity on the American stage in revues and cabarets, beginning with an appearance in *Charlot's Revue of 1924*. She later starred in several Noel Coward shows. Her style of comedy was rollicking; she delighted audiences in London and New York with her distinctive mimicry, ad-libs, and gags. Lillie once left the stage on a pair of roller skates that were hidden under an elaborate formal gown. The pinnacle of her career was the one-woman show, *An Evening with Beatrice Lillie* (1952). ■ See her autobiography, *Every Other Inch a Lady* (1972), and biography by Bruce Laffey (1989).

LIMBAUGH, RUSH (1951–), U.S. radio personality. Limbaugh dropped out of Southeast Missouri State University to pursue a career in radio. After his controversial right-wing commentary got him fired from several stations, he became a successful talk show host in Sacramento, California (1983), and eventually hosted a nationally syndicated, three-hour program in New York City (1988–). Ridiculing liberals, feminists, the homeless, abortion advocates, and the Democratic party through the use of satire, mimicry, songs, and sound effects, he became one of the most influential and controversial political commentators of his era, heard on approximately 600 stations. Although many of the "truths" he broadcast were shown by his critics to be lies or distortions, his audience peaked at 21 million listeners per week (1996) and he was credited with helping to revitalize AM radio. He also hosted a nightly television program (1992–97) and wrote two best-selling books, *The Way Things Ought to Be* (1992) and *See, I Told You So* (1993). ■ See biography by Paul D. Colford (1993).

LIMÓN, JOSÉ (1908–1972), Mexican-born U.S. dancer and choreographer. Limón's parents emigrated (1915) to the United States, where Limón grew up. He studied fine arts until, overwhelmed by a performance by German modern dancer Harold Kreutzberg, he began to study at the Doris Humphrey–Charles Weidman Studio (1930). He later danced and choreographed in their company (1930–40). An artist of great dignity and intensity, he sought to develop a masculine style to portray both the tragic and noble aspects of humanity. After founding his own company (1946), he created powerful ballets drawing on themes from history, literature, legend. and religion, including *The Moor's Pavanne* (1949), *Malinche* (1949), *The Traitor* (1954), and *Missa Brevis* (1958). ■ See his *An Unfinished Memoir* (1999).

LIN BIAO (old style: **LIN PIAO**; 1907–1971), Chinese military and political leader. Trained at Whampoa Military Academy, Lin joined the Communist party (1927) and helped devise guerrilla strategy. A commander during the Long March (1934–35), he headed the Red Army Academy at Yanan (Yenan) and scored a major victory over the Japanese (1937). Wounded in battle, he recuperated in the Soviet Union (1939–42). After returning to China he was named to the Communist party's Central Committee (1945) and led communist armies to victory in the civil war (1945–49) following World War II. After the establishment of the People's Republic of China (1949), Lin held high government posts, including defense minister (from 1959). He sponsored political training for army members, emphasized the teachings of

party leader Mao Zedong (Mao Tse-tung), and was officially designated as Mao's heir during the Cultural Revolution (1969). At the height of his power, he was reported to have died in a plane crash in Mongolia. The official explanation was that he had attempted a coup d'état and failed, and was fleeing to the Soviet Union when his plane crashed. An account by pseudonymous author Yao Ming-le, *The Conspiracy and Death of Lin Biao* (Eng. trans. 1983), claimed that Mao had Lin murdered after learning of his plans for a coup. ■ See biography by Martin Ebon (1970); Thomas W. Robinson, *A Politico-Military Biography of Lin Piao—Part I* (1971); Michael Y. M. Kau, ed., *The Lin Piao Affair* (1975); study by Tien-wei Wu (1983); and Frederick C. Teiwes, *The Tragedy of Lin Biao* (1996; with Warren Sun).

LINDBERGH, CHARLES AUGUSTUS (1902–1974), U.S. aviator. Internationally acclaimed as the hero of the age, Lindbergh made the first nonstop solo transatlantic flight—from New York to Paris—in 1927. Called "Lucky Lindy" and "the Lone Eagle," he made the 33½-hour trip in the *Spirit of St. Louis,* a Ryan monoplane, and was given the Congressional Medal of Honor and numerous other international awards. The 1932 kidnap-murder of his infant son was the most sensational crime of the 1930s, and Lindbergh moved to England (1935 39) to escape the intense publicity surrounding it and the capture and execution of the murderer, Bruno Richard Hauptmann. He aroused great controversy in the United States by accepting an award from the German Nazi government (1938) and by speaking in favor of U.S. neutrality as a leading member of the isolationist America First movement (1940–41). During World War II he served as a civilian technician and flew 50 combat missions in the Pacific. After the war he advised the government and was appointed a brigadier general in the air force reserve (1954). He wrote *We* (1927), *Of Flight and Life* (1948), and the autobiography, *The Spirit of St. Louis* (1953; Pulitzer Prize). ■ See Walter S. Ross, *The Last Hero* (1968), and the biographies by Leonard Mosley (1976) and A. Scott Berg (1998).

LINDGREN, WALDEMAR (1860–1939), Swedish-born U.S. geologist. After graduating from the Royal Academy of Mines at Freiberg, Germany, Lindgren emigrated to the United States (1883) and worked for the U.S. Geological Survey (1884–1912). He made extensive studies of ore deposits in the western states, established the dominance of igneous processes in the formation of ores, developed a widely used system of classification of ore deposits, and pioneered in the use of the petrographic microscope. His book *Mineral Deposits* (1913) was a standard textbook in economic geography for decades. Lindgren was a professor at the Massachusetts Institute of Technology from 1912 to 1933.

LINDSAY, HOWARD (1889–1968), **and RUSSEL M. CROUSE** (1893–1966), U.S. playwrights. Lindsay, an actor and director, and Crouse, a reporter and press agent, teamed up in 1934 to write the libretto for Cole Porter's *Anything Goes.* They subsequently wrote *Life with Father* (1939), which starred Lindsay and ran on Broadway for nearly eight years (3,213 performances), *State of the Union* (1945), *Call Me Madam* (1950), *Mr. President* (1952), and *The Sound of Music* (1959). They also coproduced such hits as *Arsenic and Old Lace* (1941) and *Detective Story* (1949). ■ See Cornelia Otis Skinner, *Life with Lindsay and Crouse* (1976).

LINDSAY, JACK (1900–1990), Australian-born British writer, the son of illustrator-writer Norman Lindsay, Jack Lindsay studied classics at the University of Queensland (BA., 1921) and moved to Britain (1926), where he directed the Fanfrolico Press in London (1927–30). A prolific writer, he produced nearly 40 novels, notably *1699* (1938) and *Fires in Smithfield* (1950), 11 plays, 11 verse collections, numerous short stories, biographies, translations, and children's books. His many volumes of nonfiction included studies in history, classics, literary criticism, art history, and astrology. His historical novels and his novels of contemporary Britain are concerned with revolutionary struggle and reflected his Marxist views. *Meetings with Poets* (1968) recalled such writers as Dylan Thomas, Edith Sitwell, and Louis Aragon. His later works included *The Crisis of Marxism* (1981). ■ See his autobiographies, *Life Rarely Tells* (1958), *The Roaring Twenties* (1960), and *Fanfrolico and After* (1962), and study by John Hetherington (1973).

LINDSAY, NORMAN (1879–1969), Australian artist and novelist. Lindsay's reputation rested on his political cartoons for the *Sydney Bulletin,* his illustrations of erotic classics in the art nouveau style, and his own racy fiction. A bohemian, influenced by Nietzsche and Rabelais, he sought to scandalize middle-class morality, and he influenced many writers during the early years of the century. Lindsay's first novel, *Redheap* (1930), was banned in Australia for 28 years. His later works included *Saturdee* (1933), *Age of Consent* (1938), *The Cousin from Fiji* (1945), and *Rooms and Houses* (1968). He also wrote a children's classic, *The Magic Pudding* (1918). ■ See his autobiographies, *Bohemians of the Bulletin* (1965), *The Scribblings of an Idle Mind* (1966), and *My Mask* (1970), and biography by John Hetherington (1973).

LINDSAY, (ROBERT BLAKE) THEODORE (1925–), Canadian-U.S. ice-hockey player. In 1944, at age 19, Ted Lindsay signed with the Detroit Red Wings and played 13 seasons on the legendary "Production Line" (with Gordie Howe and Sid Able) that led the team to eight league titles and four Stanely Cup championships. He earned the nickname "Terrible Ted" for his aggressive, rugged playing style. After retiring in 1960, Lindsay made an amazing comeback in 1964–65 when he helped the Red Wings capture the league championship.

LINDSAY, (NICHOLAS) VACHEL (1879–1931), U.S. poet. Lindsay grew up in the Midwest. He left college to study art, supporting himself by lecturing for the YMCA and Anti-Saloon League. After several summers of chanting his rhythmic poems for bed and board and peddling such works as *Rhymes to be Traded for Bread* (1912), he published "General William Booth Enters into Heaven" in *Poetry* magazine (1913). Lindsay anticipated a later revival of oral poetry, infusing the intonations and emotional fervor of revival meetings into his recitations, which he called "higher vaudeville." *General William Booth Enters into Heaven and Other Poems* (1913) and *The Congo and Other Poems* (1914) were his finest collections. Afflicted by emotional turmoil in his later years, he committed suicide by drinking Lysol. ■ See Mark Harris, *City of Discontent* (1952); Eleanor Ruggles, *The Westgoing Heart* (1959); and study by Ann Massa (1970).

LINDSEY, BENJAMIN BARR (1869–1943), U.S. judge and reformer. A zealous legal, political, and social reformer who constantly sought public notice, Ben Lindsey achieved fame as the judge of the first juvenile court in the United States (Denver. 1900–27). Organized on the basis of his philosophy that juveniles should be protected as wards of the court and that treatment rather than punishment should be the goal, his court was a model for similar courts throughout the country. A controversial foe of puritanical values, he advocated "companionate marriage," in which couples would practice birth control until the marriage proved sound. If the couples proved incompatible and had no children, they would be able to divorce by mutual consent. Lindsey moved to California in 1931 and served as superior court judge (from 1934) and judge of the new Court of Conciliation (from 1939), which he helped establish. He wrote numerous books, including an autobiography, *The Dangerous Life* (1931). ■ See Charles Larsen, *The Good Fight* (1972).

LIN PIAO. *See LIN BIAO*

LINS DO REGO, JOSÉ (1901–1957), Brazilian novelist. Lins do Rego was born on his grandfather's plantation in northeast Brazil, and the focus of his first five novels was on Brazil's rapidly changing sugar industry. Three of them, (*Plantation Boy, Doidinho,* and *Banqüê*) in English translation, were published in the volume *Plantation Boy* (1966). The fiction of Lins do Rego is valued more for its social and psychological insights and evocative descriptions than for its stylistic qualities. *Dead Five* (1943), his masterpiece, also dealt with plantation life.

LIN SEN (1868–1943), Chinese revolutionary and president of China. After receiving Confucian and Western educations, Lin became involved in anti-Manchu activities prior to 1898. He joined revolutionary leader Sun Yat-sen's Tong meng hui (T'ung meng hui) party in 1905, and after the

1911 overthrow of the Manchus he was elected to the senate. After a brief period overseas (1913–16) soliciting funds for Sun's efforts, Lin returned to hold many government and Guomindang (Kuomintang) party leadership posts, culminating in that of the presidency of China (1931–43). Lin, however, was a titular head of state with few responsibilities and less power. He was, nevertheless, popular for his simple tastes, compatibility, and lack of personal ambition.

LINTON, RALPH (1893–1953), U.S. cultural anthropologist. The eclectic investigations of Ralph Linton, who taught at the University of Wisconsin, Columbia, and Yale, did much to unify cultural anthropology. Fieldwork in the Marquesas Islands drew his attention to ethnology, and after two years (1925–27) in Madagascar (later the Malagasy Republic) and East Africa he produced his major ethnological work, *The Tanala, a Hill Tribe of Madagascar* (1933). *The Study of Man* (1936), his major theoretical work, combined principles of anthropology and psychology with social theory. *The Cultural Background of Personality* (1945) put forward the concept of a basic personality type in a given culture. He speculated, in characteristically clear prose, about the origins and evolution of human life in *The Tree of Culture* (1955). ■ See study by Adelin Linton and Charles Wagley (1971).

LIPCHITZ, JACQUES (Chaim Jacob Lipchitz; 1891–1973), Lithuanian-born sculptor. Lipchitz, who was of Polish-Jewish descent, studied engineering in Vilna before moving to Paris in 1909 to study art. He befriended Pablo Picasso and other early cubists and became one of the first to apply cubist principles to sculpture. In the mid-1920s he began to produce abstract, spontaneous "transparent sculptures," inspired by African and Oceanic art. They were among the first sculptures to explore the contrasts and interactions of solid forms and empty space. During the late 1930s he began to produce emotional, monumental works based on mythological and biblical themes. He continued to work in this style after he emigrated to the United States (1941), a refugee from the German occupation of France. ■ See studies by Abraham Hammacher (1961) and Deborah A. Scott (1978).

LI PENG (1928–), Chinese political leader. After his father, a Communist party revolutionary, was executed by the Guomindang (Kuomintang; 1930) Li Peng was raised in the household of Zhou Enlai. He studied at the communist base at Yan'an as a teenager, joined the party in 1945, and studied electrical engineering in Moscow (1948–55). Upon his return to China he held important posts in the electric power bureaucracy and eventually served as minister of power (1981). He subsequently became a party central committee member (1982), minister of education, and member of the Politburo (1985). As premier (1987–98) he was seen as a conservative among the leaders as he advocated a slowing down of the rapid economic reforms sponsored by Deng Xiaoping and a continuation of central planning. He advocated the suppression of the student-led "democracy" movement in the spring of 1989 and declared martial law in Beijing (May 1989) during the massive demonstration in Tiananmen Square.

LIPMANN, FRITZ ALBERT (1899–1986), German-born U.S. biochemist. A graduate of the University of Berlin (M.D. 1922; Ph.D. in chemistry, 1927), Lipmann was an associate of the Carlsberg Institute in Copenhagen (1932–39) before emigrating to the United States in 1939. He did research at the Massachusetts General Hospital (1941–57) and taught at the Harvard Medical School (1949–57) and Rockefeller University (from 1957). While investigating the role of phosphates in animal tissue, Lipmann isolated (1947) and elucidated the molecular structure (1953) of coenzyme A, a compound involved in sugar, fat, and protein metabolism in the cell. For this work, Lipmann shared the 1953 Nobel Prize for Physiology or Medicine with Hans A. Krebs. ■ See his *Wanderings of a Biochemist* (1971).

LIPPMANN, WALTER (1889–1974), U.S. journalist. The only child of affluent German-Jewish parents, Lippmann might have remained at Harvard as a philosopher. Instead he became an editor of the *New Republic* (1914–17; 1919–21) and the *New York World* (1921–31). He helped draft Pres. Woodrow Wilson's Fourteen Points during World War I and in 1931 began covering the world as a syndicated columnist. His style was Olympian and judicious, and he was personally acquainted with heads of state. He expressed opinions (opposition to the New Deal, the Korean War, Sen. Joseph R. McCarthy's "witch-hunting" anticommunism, and the Vietnam War) on matters of highest national policy and was regarded as one of the nation's foremost social and political analysts. Lippmann's books included *Public Opinion* (1922), *U.S. Foreign Policy* (1943), *Isolation and Alliances* (1952), and *The Public Philosophy* (1954). ■ See his selected letters in *Public Philosopher* (1985); the studies by John Luskin (1972) and Barry D. Riccio (1994); and biography by Ronald Steel (1980).

LIPSCOMB, WILLIAM NUNN, JR. (1919–), U.S. chemist. During World War II, Lipscomb worked on scientific research and development projects; he then completed graduate training at the California Institute of Technology (Ph.D. 1946). He taught at the University of Minnesota (1946–59) and at Harvard (1959–90). Lipscomb devised low-temperature X-ray diffraction techniques to discover how molecules of borane, unstable compounds of boron and hydrogen, are held together. His demonstration of how a pair of electrons could be shared by three atoms had wide application, and he was awarded the 1976 Nobel Prize for Chemistry. ■ See his book, *Boron Hydrides* (1963).

LIPSET, SEYMOUR MARTIN (1922–), U.S. social scientist. Born and raised in New York City, Lipset studied at

Columbia University (Ph.D. 1949). He taught sociology and political science at Columbia, Berkeley, Harvard, Stanford and George Mason University. Lipset applied a dynamic equilibrium model to the study of political culture. He argued that a complex society is under constant pressure to adjust its institutions to its central value system, and that failure to do this results in political disturbance. He made contributions to the study of class structures, comparative politics, and systems of elites and political parties. Among his many books were *Agrarian Socialism* (1950), *Political Man* (1960), *The First New Nation* (1963), *Class, Status, and Power in Comparative Perspective* (1966), and *The Politics of Unreason* (1970). Later books included *Dialogues on American Politics* (1978), *The Confidence Gap* (1983), and *Failure of a Dream?: Essays in the History of American Socialism* (rev. ed. 1984), *Jews and the New American Scene* (1995; with Earl Raab), and *American Exceptionalism* (1996).

LISPECTOR, CLARICE (1925–1977), Russian-born Brazilian writer. Brought to Brazil as an infant by her family, Lispector spent her childhood in Recife and then moved to Rio de Janeiro. In 1943 she graduated from law school, wrote her first novel, and married a Brazilian diplomat. After living abroad for many years, she was divorced (1959) and returned to Rio, where she became a noted literary figure. Her psychological and symbolic novels and short stories were concerned with the universal existential themes of isolation, despair, and uncertainty, and played a major role in moving Brazilian literature away from regional and sociological concerns. She explored the inner world of her anguished characters, utilizing such experimental devices as stream of consciousness and interior monologue. Her best-known works included the short story collection *Family Ties* (1960; Eng. trans. 1972), the novels *The Apple in the Dark* (1961; Eng. trans. 1967), *Near to the Wild Heart* (1963; Eng. trans. 1990), *An Apprenticeship, or, The Book of Delights* (1969; Eng. trans. 1986), and *Discovering the World* (1984; Eng. trans. 1992) and the novella *The Hour of the Star* (1977; Eng. trans. 1986).

LISSITZKY, EL (Eliezer Markowich; 1890–1941), Soviet painter, sculptor, and graphic artist. Lissitzky launched (1915) an architecture career and simultaneously worked in painting and graphic arts. He was influenced by painters Marc Chagall, with whom he collaborated in illustrating Jewish books, and Kasimir Malevich. Lissitzky lived abroad in the early 1920s, establishing a reputation for graphic design and typography with such experimental works as the 10-page book, *The Story of Two Squares* (1922). Returning to the Soviet Union (1925), he directed a woodworking studio. Lissitzky powerfully influenced the fields of industrial design, typography, and graphic design in mass publications. He was also art director (1932–34) for the periodical *The USSR in Construction*. ▪ See study by Sophie Lissitzky-Kuppers (Eng. trans. 1980).

LISTON, SONNY (Charles Liston; 1932?–1971), U.S. boxer. Liston was the 24th in a family of 25 children. While serving time for robbery at Missouri State Penitentiary, he was encouraged to box by a prison chaplain. He launched a professional career in 1953, and over the next decade won some 40 bouts, most by knockouts. Liston was a controversial figure due to his two prison terms (the second served in 1957) and was barred from the ring in some states. Known for his dynamite punches and his staying power, Liston captured the world heavyweight crown in 1962 when he knocked out Floyd Patterson in the first round. He defended his title with a repeat performance, again knocking out Patterson in the first round, but in 1964 he lost the title to Cassius Clay (later known as Muhammad Ali). In a rematch bout with Clay he again lost; this time Liston was the victim of a first-round knockout. His death was caused by an apparent overdose of narcotics. ▪ See study by A. S. "Doc" Young (1963) and Nick Tosches, *The Devil and Sonny Liston* (2000).

LI TA-CHAO. *See LI DAZIIAO.*

LI TSUNG-JEN. *See LI ZONGREN.*

LITTLE RICHARD (Richard Wayne Penniman; 1932?–   ), U.S. singer. Born into religious black family in Macon, Georgia, Little Richard sang in a church choir and recorded his first blues numbers while still a teenager. He emerged, in the mid-1950s, as one of the most flamboyant, unrestrained, and influential of the early rock-and-roll singers, with such million-selling records as "Tutti Frutti" (1956), "Long Tall Sally" (1956), "Lucille" (1957), "Keep A-Knockin'" (1957), and "Good Golly Miss Molly" (1958). Screeching, shouting, pounding his piano, and leaping all over the stage during his live performances, Little Richard personified the raucousness and exuberance of rock and roll and exerted a lasting influence on such stars as James Brown, Otis Redding, Jerry Lee Lewis, Jimmy Hendrix, John Lennon, and Mick Jagger. After a religious experience in 1957, he suddenly quit pop music, became a minister, and denounced rock and roll. However, he returned to singing both gospel and rock in the 1960s and continued to appear in nostalgia revival shows through the 1990s. ▪ See Charles White, *The Life and Times of Little Richard* (1984; rev. ed. 1994).

LITVINOV, MAXIM MAXIMOVICH (Meyer Wallach; 1876–1951), Soviet diplomat. Litvinov engaged in revolutionary activities during the 1890s and after imprisonment fled to Europe (1902). He joined the bolsheviks (1903) and represented the movement, in various capacities, throughout Western Europe. In Britain he worked in publishing and married Ivy Low (1890?–1977), who later was known under her married name as a fiction writer. At the outbreak of the Russian Revolution (1917), he became the bolshevik representative in London until he was expelled (1918) from the country. As deputy cornmissar of foreign affairs during the 1920s, he was the chief spokesman for the policy of international disarmament and he became commissar in 1930. Litvinov sought closer ties with the West and vigorously supported the League of Nations and antifascist "collective security" policy. He was replaced (1939) by V. M. Molotov when dictator Joseph Stalin, anxious to conclude the NaziSoviet Pact, found his Jewish foreign minister an embarrassment. He later served (1941–43) as Soviet ambassador in Washington. His grandson, Pavel Litvinov, emerged in the 1960s as a champion of human rights in the Soviet Union and later emigrated to the United States. The diary attributed to Maxim Litvinov, *Notes for a Journal* (Eng. trans. 1955), is generally believed to be fabricated. ■ See the uncritical study by Arthur U. Pope (1943).

LIU SHAO-CH'I. *See LIU SHAOQI.*

LIU SHAOQI (old style: LIU SHAO-CH'I; 1898–1969), Chinese political leader. Born into a landowning family in Hunan province, Liu was a schoolmate of Mao Zedong (Mao Tse-tung) and studied in Moscow (1921–22), where he joined the Chinese Communist party. An effective labor organizer in Shanghai and Beijing (Peking), he was named to the party's politburo in 1934 and became an expert on party organization and a leading theoretician. His most famous work was *How to Be a Good Communist* (1939; rev. ed. 1962). When the People's Republic of China was established (1949), Liu was named the second-ranking vice chairman, and he replaced Mao as head of state (1959) following the failure of the Great Leap Forward. Attempting to restructure the Chinese economy, he pursued technological approaches to economic growth, and advocated free markets, monetary incentives, private plots for peasants, and independent management of state enterprises. He declared that the class struggle was over and foresaw a peaceful transition to socialism. Attacked during the Cultural Revolution (1966–69) as a "capitalist roader," "renegade," and "traitor," he was demoted (1966), denounced at mass meetings, and purged. He reportedly died of pneumonia while under detention. He was rehabilitated posthumously (1980). His writings in English included *Collected Works* (3 vols., 1968–69), *Quotations from President Liu Shao-ch'i* (1968), and *Selected Works* (1984). ■ See Li Tien-min, *Mao's First Heir Apparent* (1975), and the study by Lowell Dittmer (1974).

LIVERIGHT, HORACE BRISBIN (1886–1933), U.S. publisher and theatrical producer. A major figure in the publishing world of the 1920s, Liveright (and partner Charles Boni) published (1917–25) "The Modern Library," the most popular series of reprinted classics in the United States. He was influential in furthering the careers of Eugene O'Neill, Ernest Hemingway, Ben Hecht, Theodore Dreiser, and Robinson Jeffers, and he published such radicals as Max Eastman, Michael Gold, and John Reed as well as poets Ezra Pound and T. S. Eliot. His works were constantly attacked by the Society for the Suppression of Vice and he was

an active foe of state and city censorship. ■ See his autobiography, *The Turbulent Years* (1934); study by Walker Gilmer (1970); and Tom Dardis, *Firebrand* (1995).

LI ZONGREN (old style: LI TSUNG-JEN; 1890–1969), Chinese military and political leader. After receiving military training, Li joined a warlord army in 1916 and was subsequently involved in warlord intrigues until he emerged (1925) as sole ruler of Guangxi (Kwangsi) province. Li joined forces with Chiang Kai-shek's Guomindang (Kuomintang) party and helped reunite China. After helping Chiang liquidate the communist faction (1927), Li broke with Chiang and ruled Guangxi as an autonomous region. He was reconciled with Chiang in 1937 and became a hero in the war against Japan. He was vice president of China (1948–49) and acting president (1949), but broke relations with Chiang and called him a dictator when the government moved to Taiwan. He settled in the United States, but from 1965 until his death he lived in the People's Republic of China. ■ See his *Memoirs* (1978).

LLERAS CAMARGO, ALBERTO (1906–1990), Colombian political leader. A journalist and Liberal politician, Lleras was prominent in Pan-American diplomacy between his terms as president of Colombia (1945–46: 1958–62). He was one of the founders and first secretary-general of the Organization of American States (1948–54), after which he helped negotiate the end (1957) of the bloody dictatorship of Gustavo Rojas Pinilla In Colombia. According to a unique pact Lleras' Liberals worked out with the Conservatives, the two parties agreed to form a national front to share patronage and to alternate the 4-year presidency for 16 years. During his presidency Lleras maintained close ties with the United States and introduced a series of moderate economic, social, and agrarian reforms.

LLOYD, HAROLD (1893–1971), U.S. film comedian. A child actor who became one of the highest-paid male silent-film stars, Lloyd invented the stereotype of the wide-eyed, bumbling, bespectacled cliff-hanger. He dangled from a skyscraper in *Safety Last* (1923) as audiences laughed and screamed at his predicaments. His most successful silent-film features were *Grandma's Boy* (1922), *The Freshman* (1925), and *The Kid Brother* (1927). Lloyd made the transition to "talkies" with *Movie Crazy* (1932) and *Professor Beware* (1938), then retired to produce films. A shrewd businessman, he retained the rights to his films, which he reissued as *Harold Lloyd's World of Comedy* (1962) and his *Funny Side of Life* (1964). Living to a wealthy old age in California, he was active in Republican politics and civic clubs. ■ See biographies by Adam Reilly (1977) and Tom Dardis (1983).

LLOYD GEORGE, DAVID, 1st EARL LLOYD-GEORGE OF DWYFOR (1863–1945), British prime minister. The son of a schoolmaster, Lloyd George became the first of his class to achieve the pinnacle of British political power. Elected to

Parliament in 1890 as an aggressively partisan Liberal, highly ambitious and brilliantly eloquent, he began as a pacifist opponent of the Boer War, rose as a champion of the underprivileged, and peaked as a bold, aggressive World War I–era prime minister (1916–22). He is credited with mediating between American idealism and French vengeance at the Paris Peace Conference (1919) and with hastening the decline of his own party. ■ See biographies by Thomas Jones (1951), Chris Wigley (1992), and Ian Packer (1998) and Frank Owen, *Tempestuous Journey* (1954).

LLOYD WEBBER, ANDREW LLOYD WEBBER, BARON (1948–   ), British composer. Lloyd Webber, whose mother was a piano teacher and whose father was the director of the London College of Music, began writing music at age 9 and received classical training at the Royal College of Music. His spectacular career in the musical theater began when he teamed with lyricist Tim Rice to write the pop oratorio *Joseph and the Amazing Technicolor Dreamcoat* (1968). His other hits, which combined folk, pop, rock and roll, and British music hall elements, were *Jesus Christ Superstar* (London, 1970; Broadway, 1971; Tony Award, best musical) and *Evita* (London, 1978; Broadway, 1979), both written with Rice. *Cats* (London 1980; Broadway, 1982; Tony Award, best musical), based on poems by T. S. Eliot, surpassed *A Chorus Line* in 1997 as Broadway's longest-running show (with its 6,138th performance. It closed in September 2000 after its 7,485th performance. He also wrote *Song and Dance* (London, 1982; Broadway, 1985); *Starlight Express* (London, 1984), a musical whose entire cast is on roller skates; *Phantom of the Opera* (London 1986; Broadway 1987; Tony Award, best musical); *Sunset Boulevard* (London 1993; Broadway 1995; Tony Award, best musical); a *Requiem* (1985); and several film scores. ■ See biographies by Gerald McKnight (1985) and Michael Walsh (1997).

LOCKE, BESSIE (1865–1952), U.S. educator. Locke founded the National Kindergarten Association (1909), which was responsible for opening more than 3,200 kindergartens in the United States (most in public schools), which served more than 1.6 million children. She served as chief of the U.S. Bureau of Education (1913–19) and helped develop teacher-training courses. Locke also inaugurated a series of home-education articles for parents (1917) that reached close to 40 million readers in the United States and 43 other nations.

LODGE, HENRY CABOT (1850–1924), U.S. senator. A wealthy Boston Brahmin, Lodge was an editor and author of several historical biographies (Alexander Hamilton, 1882; Daniel Webster, 1883; and George Washington, 1889). As a Republican U.S. congressman (1887–93) and U.S. senator (1893–1924), he supported conservative economic legislation at home and expansionist policies abroad. A major critic of Pres. Woodrow Wilson, he led congressional opposition to Wilson's League of Nations' Covenant (1919),

which was rejected as a threat to U.S. sovereignty. He played a major role in securing the Republican presidential nomination for Warren G. Harding (1920). ■ See his *Early Memories* (1913), biography by John A. Garraty (1953), and study by William C. Widenor (1980).

LOEB, RICHARD. *See LEOPOLD, NATHAN, JR.*

LOESSER, FRANK HENRY (1910–1969), U.S. composer and lyricist. Loesser worked in a variety of odd jobs before achieving success as a Hollywood songwriter with such hits as "Two Sleepy People" (1938; music by Hoagy Carmichael), "On a Slow Boat to China" (1948), and "Baby, It's Cold Outside" (Academy Award, 1949). During World War II he wrote "Praise the Lord and Pass the Ammunition," one of the biggest song hits of the war. His Broadway shows, *Where's Charley?* (1948), *Guys and Dolls* (1950), *The Most Happy Fella* (1956), and *How to Succeed in Business Without Really Trying* (Pulitzer Prize, 1962), included such songs as "Once in Love with Amy." "I've Never Been in Love Before," "Luck Be a Lady," "I Believe in You," and "Standin' on the Corner." ■ See Susan Loesser, *A Most Remarkable Fella* (1995).

LOEW, MARCUS (1870–1927), U.S. theater owner and film producer. Loew, who left school at age 9, started in the entertainment industry by running profitable penny arcades in New York City. With the rising popularity of motion pictures, he developed a chain of theaters that featured vaudeville and film shows. By 1912 he controlled more than 400 movie houses throughout the country and was one of America's most prosperous theater owners. To guarantee a supply of films for his theaters, Loew purchased Metro Pictures Corp. (1920) and merged the Goldwyn Pictures Corp. and the Louis B. Mayer Co. (1924) to create Metro-Goldwyn-Mayer (MGM), which became the world's largest motion-picture company.

LOEWE, FREDERICK (1901–1988), Austrian-born U.S. composer and pianist. A child prodigy on the piano, Loewe was a soloist with the Berlin Symphony at age 13. After emigrating to the United States (1924), he played in several nightclubs but could not support himself with a musical career and was forced to take a series of odd jobs. He wrote several musicals during the 1930s but did not achieve success until he began to collaborate with Alan Jay Lerner (1942). Together they wrote some of the most successful musicals in Broadway history, including *Brigadoon* (1947), *Paint Your Wagon* (1951), *Camelot* (1960), and their greatest hit, *My Fair Lady* (1956). They also wrote the romantic film *Gigi* (Academy Award, 1958). ■ See Gene Lees, *Inventing Champagne* (1990).

LOEWI, OTTO (1873–1961), German physician and pharmacologist. A graduate of the University of Strasbourg (M.D. 1896), Loewi taught at the University of Graz (1909–

38). He conducted (1921–26) neurological research that demonstrated the chemical transmission of nerve impulses. For this discovery Loewi shared the 1936 Nobel Prize in Physiology or Medicine with Sir Henry H. Dale. Because he was a Jew, he was forced out of Austria by the Nazis (1938). He arrived in the United States in 1940 and was a professor at the New York University College of Medicine (1940–55). In addition to research on the nervous system, he studied diabetes and adrenaline and devised a test for detecting disease of the pancreas.

LOEWY, RAYMOND (1893–1986), French-born U.S. industrial designer. Lowey studied engineering, then emigrated (1919) to the United States. After working as a fashion illustrator, he embarked (1926) on a career in industrial design, opening his own firm (1929). Loewy's designs streamlined everyday artifacts, from the toothbrush and razor to furniture and department store layout. He was best known for his vehicle design—from the Studebaker auto to the railway car. Loewy's achievements were instrumental in legitimizing industrial design as a career. He wrote *The Locomotive (Its Esthetics)* (1937) and *Industrial Design.* (1979). ■ See biography by Paul Jodard (1992).

LOGAN, JOSHUA LOCKWOOD, JR. (1908–1988), U.S. director, producer, and playwright. While a student at Princeton (1927–30) Logan was president of the dramatic society and helped organize the University Players, a summer stock group that included such future luminaries as Henry Fonda, James Stewart, Margaret Sullavan, and Myron McCormick. He studied with Constantin Stanislavsky at the Moscow Art Theater (1931) and made his Broadway acting debut in 1932. He directed a series of Broadway hits during the late 1930s but had his greatest success after World War II directing *Annie Get Your Gun* (1946), *Mister Roberts* (1948: coauthor), *South Pacific* (1949; coauthor; film, 1958), *Picnic* (1953; film, 1956), *Fanny* (1954; coauthor; film, 1961), and *The World of Suzie Wong* (1958), among others. He also directed the movies *Bus Stop* (1956) and *Sayonara* (1957) and the screen versions of *Camelot* (1967) and *Paint Your Wagon* (1969). ■ See his memoirs, *Josh* (1976) and *Movie Stars, Real People and Me* (1978).

LOISY, ALFRED FIRMIN (1857–1940), French biblical scholar. Ordained as a Catholic priest in 1879, Loisy became a lecturer in scripture and Hebrew at the Catholic Institute in Paris but was dismissed in 1893 for radicalism. With *The Gospel and the Church* (1902; Eng. trans. 1903), an attack on traditional dogma, he became the father of Catholic modernism. Loisy was excommunicated in 1908 and his books banned, but he continued to teach the history of religions at the Collège de France (1909–26). He also wrote *The Birth of the Christian Religion* (1933; Eng. trans. 1948) and *The Origins of the New Testament* (1936; Eng. trans. 1950). ■ See his autobiography, *My Duel with the Vatican* (Eng. trans. 1924), and John Ratté, *Three Modernists* (1967).

LOMAX, ALAN (1915–   ), U.S. folk-music expert. The son of musicologist John Lomax, Alan Lomax went on the road with his father collecting folk songs during the Depression and worked as his father's assistant and successor at the Archive of American Folk Song of the Library of Congress. He was the first to record the music of Leadbelly, Woody Guthrie, and Muddy Waters. He also prepared folk-music programs for radio, lectured at universities, recorded traditional music around the world, and directed folk-music recordings for Decca and Columbia records, including a 1958 disc of *Texas Folk Songs* sung by Lomax himself. Lomax wrote *The Folk Songs of North America* (1960). Later works included *Cantometrics: A Method in Musical Anthropology* (1977), *World Dance and Movement Style* (1981; with Forrestine Paulay), and *Land Where the Blues Began* (1993). Music from his archive was released in a collection of over 100 hour-long CDs called *The Alan Lomax Collection* (1997–   ). He also created *Global Jukebox,* a multimedia database of folk music from more than 600 different cultures.

LOMAX, JOHN AVERY (1875–1948), U.S. folk-music expert. Lomax began collecting folk ballads as a teenager in Texas, and after earning a master's in English literature from Harvard (1907) he began systematically collecting and recording America's folk music. In 1910 he published *Cowboy Songs and Other Frontier Ballads,* and in 1932, after years as an English professor, university administrator, and a brief, unsuccessful career as a banker, he hit the road again to compile *American Ballads and Folk Songs* (1934). Lomax became curator of the Archive of American Folk Song of the Library of Congress. ■ See Nolan Porterfield, *Last Cavalier* (1996).

LOMBARD, CAROLE (Jane Alice Peters; 1908–1942), U.S. film actress. After her film debut (1921) in a tomboy role, Lombard made two-reelers for Mack Sennett and developed into one of Hollywood's greatest comediennes. Blond, beautiful, and an audaciously sexy screwball, she starred in the classics *Twentieth Century* (1934), *My Man Godfrey* (1936), *Nothing Sacred* (1937), and *To Be or Not to Be* (1942). Lombard was already a legend in her own right before her celebrated marriage to actor Clark Gable in 1939 and her death in a plane crash. ■ See Larry Swindell, *Screwball* (1975).

LOMBARDI, VINCENT THOMAS (1913–1970), U.S. football coach. Intending to enter the priesthood, Lombardi studied at Fordham University (B.S. 1937), where he was an outstanding football player. Changing his career plans, he became a winning high school football coach (1939–47) and assistant coach at the U.S. Military Academy at West Point (1949–54) before his successful stint as offensive coach with the New York Giants (1954–59). He gained national prominence as general manager and head coach of the Green Bay Packers (1959–69) as he molded a last-place squad of losers into the dominant power in the National Football League. An intense, dedicated, and authoritarian taskmaster, he compiled a record of 141 wins, 39 loses, and 4 ties in leading the Packers to five league championships and victories in Superbowls I and II (1967 and 1968). Believing that "winning isn't everything, it is the only thing," Lombardi symbolized conservative values and rigid moral codes at a time when authority was questioned throughout society. ■ See his *Run to Daylight!* (1963; with W. C. Heinz), *Vince Lombardi on Football* (2 vols., 1973), and David Maraniss, *When Pride Still Mattered* (1999).

LOMBARDO TOLEDANO, VICENTE (1894–1968), Mexican labor and political leader. A liberal lawyer and professor of law and philosophy at the National University (1918–33), Lombardo was active in governmental and union affairs during the 1920s and 1930s. After declaring himself "a radical Marxist, although not a communist" (1932), he founded (1936) and led (1936–41) the Confederation of Mexican Workers, which grew into Mexico's largest and most influential labor organization. He also founded and directed the Workers University (1936), the international Confederation of Latin American Workers (1936), and the Popular party (1948), which was renamed the Popular Socialist party (1960). He ran unsuccessfully for the presidency in 1952. ■ See biography by Robert Millon (1966).

LON NOL (1913–1985), Cambodian military and political leader. Born into a family of minor officials of Khmer-Chinese ancestry, Lon Nol entered the civil service immediately after concluding his education. He rose quickly, held the governorships of two provinces, and directed the administrative service (1949). Commissioned a lieutenant (1952), he commanded an infantry battalion, served as military chief of staff (1955), and was named a lieutenant general in 1961. He subsequently headed several government ministries and became a leader of the conservative forces in the country. During his second term as prime minister (1969–70) he overthrew neutralist Prince Norodom Sihanouk as head of state (1970), abolished the monarchy, and established a pro-American government. Lacking popular support, and thoroughly corrupt, Lon Nol's regime was unable to stop the communist Khmer Rouge guerrilla insurgency, despite the infusion of massive amounts of U.S. financial and military aid, including extensive B-52 bombing raids. As communist troops overwhelmed his forces (April 1975), he went into exile in the United States. ■ See William Shawcross, *Sideshow* (1979).

LONDON, GEORGE (George Burnstein; 1920–1985), Canadian-born U.S. opera singer. A leading singer of the post–World War II era, London sang with New York's Metropolitan Opera (1951–66). He was the first American to sing the title role of Mussorgsky's *Boris Godunov* (New York City, 1953) and the first to sing the role at the Bolshoi Opera (Moscow, 1960). Critically acclaimed as the greatest

dramatic bass since Chaliapin, London appeared regularly at the world's major opera houses until his career was cut short by a paralyzed vocal cord (1967). ■ See Nora London, *Aria for George* (1987).

LONDON, JACK (John Griffith London; 1876–1916), U.S. novelist and short-story writer. London sailed to Japan and the Bering Sea as a seaman at age 17, became an oyster pirate, panned for gold in the Klondike rush, reported on the Russo-Japanese War (1905), and filed reports from Mexico (1914). His vivid adventure tales, proletarian novels, and animal stories won enormous popularity, especially *The Call of the Wild* (1903), one of literature's great dog stories. In *The Iron Heel* (1907) he predicted that the capitalist system would give rise to a totalitarian government in the United States. He wrote three autobiographical novels, including *Martin Eden* (1909). London himself attached greater importance to the tracts that expressed his views—a curious mix of socialism and white supremacy—than to his fiction. At age 40, he intentionally took an overdose of morphine at his California ranch. *John Barleycorn: or, Alcoholic Memoirs* (1913) is autobiographical. ■ See Irving Stone, *A Sailor on Horseback* (1938), and biographies by Richard O'Connor (1964), Andrew Sinclair (1977), Joan D. Hedrick (1982), and Alex Kershaw (1998).

LONG, HUEY PIERCE (1893–1935), U.S. political leader. A one-time traveling salesman and lawyer from the backcountry, Long became Democratic governor of Louisiana in 1928 on a populist platform of "Every Man a King," the title of his autobiography (1933). He carried out a massive public-works program and taxed big business to pay for public services, cowing the legislature into submission to his demagogic will. Known as "the Kingfish," Long served in the U.S. Senate from 1932, but continued to run Louisiana affairs from Washington. He was mounting a third-party challenge to Pres. Franklin D. Roosevelt when he was assassinated in the marble corridors of his own capitol, to be succeeded by members of his family dynasty. ■ See the Pulitzer Prize–winning biography by T. Harry Williams (1969) and William Ivy Hair, *The Kingfish and His Realm* (1991).

LONGDEN, JOHN ERIC (1907–   ), British-born U.S. jockey. A jockey for 40 years (1927–66), Johnny Longden won 6,032 races, a world's record at the time of his retirement. Subsequently, Willie Shoemaker surpassed that mark (1970). Longden won the Triple Crown (Kentucky Derby. Preakness, and Belmont Stakes) aboard Count Fleet in 1943, led U.S. jockeys in wins for three seasons (1938; 1947–48), and won close to $25 million in purses during his career. ■ See B. K. Beckwith, *The Longden Legend* (1973).

LONGO, LUIGI (1900–1980), Italian political leader. One of the founders of the Italian Communist party (1921). Longo was active in the Comintern during the 1920s and 1930s and was inspector general of the pro-Loyalist international brigades during the Spanish civil war (1936–39). Arrested in France on the eve of World War II, Longo was extradited to Italy, where he was imprisoned until dictator Benito Mussolini's fall in 1943. After his release he led the partisan anti-Nazi military resistance in northern Italy, and one of his bands captured and executed Mussolini (April 1945). From 1945 to 1964 he was second in command of the Italian Communist party; he succeeded his chief, Palmiro Togliatti, as party secretary-general (1964–72). While he was party leader he supported the policy of an "Italian road to socialism," advocated diversity within the world communist movement, and witnessed the strengthening of party influence in Italian politics.

LONSDALE, DAME KATHLEEN (Kathleen Yardley; 1903–1971), British physical chemist. Lonsdale was the tenth and youngest child in a postmaster's family. After graduating (1922) in physics from the University of London, where she later served as a professor of chemistry (1949–68), she worked with William Bragg (1922–27;1937–42), whose research on the structure of the diamond formed the basis of her own contribution. Lonsdale demonstrated, by elaborating the crystal structure of hexamethylbenzene and hexachlorobenzene, the distinctive way in which carbon atoms are arranged in the benzene nucleus. She later demonstrated the existence of molecular orbitals, a notion that had been only theoretically advanced. Lonsdale also used X-ray techniques to study intramolecular phenomena and applied X-ray crystallography to various medical problems. A Quaker and a pacifist, she wrote several books on issues of war and peace in addition to *Crystals and X-rays* (1949) and other scientific works.

LOPEZ, NANCY (1957–), U.S. golfer. Born into a Mexican-American family in California, Lopez was raised in Roswell, New Mexico, where she received her first golf lessons from her father. She won her first tournament at age 9 and her first state women's tournament at age 12. An intercollegiate champion while a student at the University of Tulsa, she dropped out after her second year to turn pro and registered her first victory on the tour in 1978. Later that year she won a record five consecutive tournaments and was the leading money winner in 1978 and 1979. A long driver and excellent putter, she won many major tournaments including two Ladies Professional Golf Association (LPGA) championships (1978, 1985). In 1985 she won the Vare Trophy for the lowest stroke average on the tour (a record 70.73) and finished the year with a record $416,472 in official prize money. Still competing in her 40s, Lopez amassed 48 career victories and won more than $5 million through 1999. ■ See her autobiography, *The Education of a Woman Golfer* (with Peter Schwed, 1979).

LÓPEZ PORTILLO Y PACHECO, JOSÉ (1920–), Mexican political leader. The son of a prominent historian, López Portillo studied in Mexico and at the University of Chile and taught law, political science, and public administration at the National University of Mexico (1952–62). He entered government service in 1959, held several important posts, including that of minister of finance and public credit (1973–76), and was highly praised for his administrative abilities and management of fiscal policy. He served as president of Mexico from 1976 to 1982. During the first five years of his term, new oil reserves were exploited, and Mexico enjoyed an unprecedented economic boom. In 1982, however, the economy collapsed, inflation soared, the currency was devalued, and the foreign debt reached $80 billion; López Portillo dramatically announced the nationalization of private banks to help alleviate the economic crisis.

LORDE, AUDRE GERALDIN (1934–1992), U.S. poet. Born in Harlem (New York City), Lorde wrote poetry from childhood and published her first poem in *Seventeen* while a student at Hunter High School. She continued writing over the next two decades, but as she later wrote, her lesbianism made her persona non grata in black literary circles, and she began publishing collections of her powerful, political poetry only in the late 1960s. Lorde's work sought intellectual and moral clarity about everyday events. Her books included *The First Cities* (1968), *Cables to Rage* (1970), *From a Land Where Other People Live* (1973), *New York Head Shop and Museum* (1974), *Coal* (1976), *Between Our Selves* (1976), *The Black Unicorn* (1978), and *Chosen Poems—Old and New* (1982; rev. ed. as *Undersong*, 1992). A prose book, *The Cancer Journals* (1980), recounted her experiences with breast cancer and mastectomy. She worked as a librarian (1960–68), then taught in New York City at John Jay College (1970–81) and Hunter College (from 1981). An important figure in the women's movement in the 1970s and 1980s, Lorde was a cofounder of Kitchen Table–Women of Color Press. In 1991 she was named official state poet of New York. *Zami, A New Spelling of My Name* (1982) is autobiographical.

LOREN, SOPHIA (Sofia Scicolone; 1934–), Italian film actress. After a poverty-stricken childhood in Naples, Loren placed second in a beauty contest in 1949 and made her first American film as an extra in *Quo Vadis* (1951). The tall, statuesque brunette had made 20 Italian films before her U.S. film debut in *Boy on a Dolphin* (1957). Usually cast as a sex object, Loren proved her dramatic ability in *Two Women* (Academy Award, 1961) and demonstrated a flair for elegant comedy in *The Millionairess* (1960). She also starred in *Yesterday, Today and Tomorrow* (1963), *Marriage Italian Style* (1964) and *A Special Day* (1977). She costarred with Marcello Mastroianni in 12 movies. ■ See her autobiography, *Sophia* (1979; with A. E. Hotchner) and biography by Warren G. Harris (1998).

LORENTZ, PARE (1905–1992), U.S. filmmaker. Lorentz was a New York film critic who made beautifully realized and commercially successful documentary films for the government during the Depression. *The Plow That Broke the Plains* (1936) was a graphic depiction of the human and ecological disaster of the dust bowl, while *The River* (1937) was a lyric portrayal of conservation and flood control in the Mississippi basin. Lorentz's film unit, the United States Film Service, made *The Fight for Life* (1940), a powerful drama about childbirth in the slums, before it was disbanded by Congress in 1941. ■ See his memoris, *FDR's Moviemaker* (1992), and study by Robert Snyder (1968).

LORENZ, KONRAD (1903–1989), Austrian zoologist. A graduate of the University of Vienna (M.D. 1928; Ph.D. 1933), Lorenz conceded, late in life, that some of his early research reflected Nazi views. He was acknowledged as the founder of ethology, the study of animal behavior in natural environments. Primarily concerned with instinctive behavior in birds, he described the process of imprinting, by which visual or auditory stimuli elicit fixed behavior patterns in newborn birds that had not had any previous experience or learning. His later work dealt with the evolution of behavioral patterns that enable species to survive. In the controversial *On Aggression* (1963; Eng. trans. 1966). Lorenz argued that aggression is genetically programmed in humans but can be environmentally modified. After 1950 he did most of his work at the Max Planck Institute (West Germany) and in 1973 shared the Nobel Prize for Physiology or Medicine with Karl von Frisch and Nikolaas Tinbergen. ■ See study by Alec Nisbett (1976).

LORIMER, GEORGE HORACE (1867–1937), U.S. editor. Lorimer worked in the Chicago meat-packing industry, failing in an attempt to go into business for himself before taking over as editor in chief of the declining *Saturday Evening Post* (1899). An advocate of rugged individualism, he shrewdly steered the magazine into the "romance" of American business, with folksy illustrations and light literary entertainment by authors like Stephen Crane, Jack London, and Ring Lardner. The *Post* became an all-American success story with a weekly circulation of 3 million, while its editor became increasingly reactionary. Lorimer considered the New Deal un-American and in 1936, just before his retirement, came out in favor of child labor. ■ See biography by John Tebbel (1948) and Jan Cohn, *Creating America* (1989).

LORRE, PETER (Laszlo Lowenstein; 1904–1964), Hungarian-born actor. At age 15 Lorre ran away from home to work in theaters in Vienna and Zurich. A short, sadlooking man with protuberant eyes, he played the child murderer in *M* (1931), the German silent-film classic. After making two films in England for director Alfred Hitchcock, he starred in eight Hollywood films (1937–39) as Mr. Moto, novelist John Marquand's oriental detective. Lorre played small but studied roles in such film classics as *The Maltese Falcon* (1941), *Casablanca* (1943), and *Confidential Agent*

(1945). In 1949 Lorre returned to Europe, where he wrote, produced, and directed *The Lost One* (1951). ■ See Ted Sennett, *Masters of Menace* (1979).

LOSEY, JOSEPH (1909–1984), U.S. film director. Educated at Harvard (M.A. 1930), Losey was a stage manager and Broadway director (*Galileo Galilei,* 1947) before making the first of his feature films (1948) that dealt with controversial social issues. Accused of communist affiliations, he was blacklisted during the anticommunist witch-hunting era of Sen. Joseph McCarthy; he moved to England (1952) and resumed directing under a pseudonym. Losey returned to his own name with the thriller *Time Without Pity* in 1957. During the 1960s, working with a regular team of collaborators, including actor Dirk Bogarde and playwright Harold Pinter, he directed several "arty" British films about spiritual corruption and the social determinants of morality: *The Servant* (1963), *Accident* (1967), and *The Go-Between* (1971). His later films included *Mr. Klein* (1976) and *Don Giovanni* (1979). ■ See his *Losey on Losey* (1968; edited by Tom Milne) and the studies by Foster Hirsch (1980) and David Caute (1994).

LOTMAN, YURY (or **JÜRI**) (1922–), Soviet literary theorist and historian. Lotman was born in Leningrad, but his academic life was associated with the Estonian Republic, where after 1963 he taught at Tartu State University. His early work focused on Russian thought of the 18th and 19th centuries. He formed (1964) the Moscow Tartu semiotics group, which emphasized a comprehensive theory of culture described in terms of social function. His most influential works included *Lectures on Structural Poetics* (1964) and *The Structure of the Artistic Text* (1970; Eng. trans. 1977). Lotman's contributions significantly widened the scope of literary and linguistic inquiry in the Soviet Union and introduced an expanded language of criticism. His other works included *Analysis of the Poetic Text* (1972; Eng. trans. 1976), *Semiotics of Cinema* (1973; Eng. trans. 1976), and *Universe of the Mind: A Semiotic Theory of Culture* (Eng. trans. 1990). ■ See Ann Shukman, *Literature and Semiotics* (1977).

LOUBET, ÉMILE FRANÇOIS (1838–1929), French political leader. The son of a farmer, Loubet was educated as a lawyer and elected to the Chamber of Deputies (1876) and to the senate (1885). As president of the Third Republic (1899–1906), he was instrumental in the resolution of the Dreyfus affair (the scandal arising from the unjust conviction of Capt. Alfred Dreyfus for espionage) and of the anticlerical agitation that culminated in the 1905 separation of church and state.

LOUIS, JOE (Joseph Louis Barrow; 1914–1981), U.S. boxer. Joe Louis began boxing in amateur events at age 18; two years later he made his professional debut (1934). In

1936 the German champion Max Schmeling, a supporter of Nazi leader Adolf Hitler, became the first professional prizefighter to defeat Louis (by a 12th-round knockout), then exploited the victory to publicize his white-supremacist views. After deposing heavyweight champion James J. Braddock (1937), Louis again fought Schmeling, this time knocking him out in little more than two minutes. Known to fans as the "Brown Bomber," Louis combined superb conditioning, fast hands, and a devastating punch. A legendary champion, he put his title on the line more often (25 bouts, winning 21 by knockouts) and held it longer (11 years, 8 months) than any other heavyweight titleholder. Louis retired in 1947 at age 34. Staging a comeback, he lost the championship bout to Ezzard Charles (1950) and was knocked out by Rocky Marciano (1951). Boxing's second African-American heavyweight champion, Louis is credited by many with opening up boxing to black fighters. ■ See his autobiography (1978); Barney Nagler, *Brown Bomber* (1972): and Chris Mead, *Champion* (1985).

LOVE, IRIS CORNELIA (1933–), U.S. archaeologist. Born into a wealthy family of art collectors, Love grew up in New York City, where an English governess often took her to Central Park to hunt fossils. After graduating from Smith College (1955), Love did graduate work at New York University but did not complete her doctoral dissertation. Her controversial career in archaeology began in 1961, when she published a revised version of her undergraduate thesis, which claimed that three "Etruscan warrior" statues owned by New York's Metropolitan Museum of Art were forgeries. Forewarned of her claim, the museum publicized the forgeries before the book was in print. Love made annual expeditions to the ruins at Cnidus in western Turkey between 1967 and 1977. Her numerous significant discoveries there included the great circular temple of Aphrodite (1969). The next year, she claimed that a badly damaged sculptured head she found in the basement of London's British Museum was from Praxiteles' statue of Aphrodite, which had been missing from the temple. Her discovery of the remains of a Minoan settlement at Cnidus (1977) altered scholars' thinking about the scope of Minoan culture. Love wrote *Greece, Gods, and Art* (1968).

LOVECRAFT, HOWARD PHILLIPS (1890–1937), U.S. writer. A loner who was frequently in poor health and socially ill at ease, the idiosyncratic H. P. Lovecraft created bizarre supernatural horror tales set in New England and pioneered science-fiction stories. Most of his works originally appeared in the magazine *Weird Tales* and were anthologized posthumously. *The Dunwich Horrors and Others* (1985) assembled 16 major Lovecraft tales. His novellas included *The Case of Charles Dexter Ward* (1928), *At the Mountains of Madness* (1931), and *The Shadow over Innsmouth* (1936). His stories of the Cthulhu Mythos, concerning the dislocation of space and time, gained wide appeal

during the 1950s. ■ See studies by L. Sprague de Camp (1975), Barton L. Armand (1977), Donald R. Burleson (1983), and P. H. Cannon (1989).

LOVEJOY, ARTHUR ONCKEN (1873–1962), U.S. philosopher. Educated at Harvard, A. O. Lovejoy taught philosophy at Johns Hopkins University (1910–38). He concentrated on studying and tracing the evolution of basic philosophical concepts or "unit-ideas" and their influence upon each other. His chief works—*The Great Chain of Being* (1936) and *Essays in the History of Ideas* (1948)—traced the "unit-ideas" of Western thought through history. He also wrote *The Revolt Against Dualism* (1930) and was a founder of the *Journal of the History of Ideas* (1939). ■ See biography by Daniel J. Wilson (1980).

LOVELL, SIR (ALFRED CHARLES) BERNARD (1913–), British astronomer. Lovell became interested in radar during World War II and later pioneered the field of radio astronomy. He applied radio techniques to trace meteor showers, which allowed him to determine the orbits and radiants of meteors as well as to illustrate that meteors were part of the solar system. Lovell's investigation of radio emission from flare stars in the galaxy led to further exploration of stellar atmospheres. The founder and director of the Jodrell Bank Experimental Station, now Nuffield Radio Astronomy Laboratories (1951–81), he was instrumental in constructing the first large radio telescope, completed in 1957. His books included *Radio Astronomy* (1951), *Discovering the Universe* (1963), *Emerging Cosmology* (1980), *The Jodrell Bank Telescopes* (1984), *Astronomer by Chance* (1990), and *Echoes of War* (1991). ■ See biography by Dudley Saward (1984).

LOVELOCK, JAMES EPHRAIM (1919–), British scientist and inventor. Trained as a chemist at the University of Manchester (B.Sc. 1941), Lovelock subsequently earned degrees in medicine (1949) and biophysics (D.Sc. 1959) from the University of London and was a staff scientist at the National Institute for Medical Research in London (1941–61). He invented the electron-capture detector (1957), which identified and measured minute amounts of hazardous substances in the environment and provided data for Rachel Carson's pioneering book on environmental pollution, *Silent Spring* (1962). By attaching a gas chromatograph to the detector he was able to demonstrate, in the 1960s, that ozone-depleting chlorofluorocarbons were accumulating in the earth's atmosphere and that chemically polluted air was moving across national and continental boundaries. While working as a consultant for NASA in Houston, Texas, during the 1960s, he formulated the controversial Gaia hypothesis, which proposed that the earth is a self-regulating and self-sustaining system, with the air, rocks, biota, and oceans acting as a "single physiological system," akin to a superorganism. The theory, first presented in 1969, was ridiculed by many scientists as fanciful and metaphoric, but influenced environmental and ecological studies. Lovelock wrote *Gaia: A New Look at Life on Earth* (1979) and *The Ages of Gaia* (1988). ■ See L. E. Joseph, *Gaia* (1991).

LOVETT, ROBERT MORSS (1870–1956), U.S. scholar and political activist. A professor of English at the University of Chicago (1893–1939), Lovett was associated with the influential *Dial* and *Poetry* literary magazines and was coauthor of a standard college text, *History of English Literature* (1902). It was as an independent leftwing political activist and journalist, however, that he achieved wider prominence. He was an associate editor of the *New Republic* (1921–40), wrote numerous articles on social, economic, and political reform, and was a confidant of most of the radical leaders of his generation and a member of dozens of radical organizations.

LOW, SIR DAVID (1891–1963), New Zealand-born British cartoonist. After moving to Britain at age 28, Low created caricature emblems for British political and social institutions: a two-headed horse for Prime Minister David Lloyd George's coalition party, Colonel Blimp for the typical British archconservative. His brilliant liberal cartoons appeared in the *London Star* (1919–27), and in Lord Beaverbrook's right-wing *Evening Standard* (1927–50). Low's agitational World War II cartoons included a famous drawing of dictators Hitler and Stalin conversing across the corpse of Poland in 1939. His cartoons were collected in *A Cartoon History of Our Times* (1939), *Low on the War* (1941), and *Years of Wrath.* (1946). ■ See his *Autobiography* (1956).

LOW, JULIETTE GORDON (Juliette Gordon: 1860–1927), U.S. youth leader. Born in Savannah, Georgia, "Daisy" Low spent many years in Britain as an Edwardian socialite. After the death of her husband, she met Lord Baden-Powell, founder of the Boy Scouts, and she became interested in its counterpart, the Girl Guides. She brought the idea to the United States, organizing the first troop in Savannah (1912). In 1915, she founded a national organization renamed Girl Scouts of America and served as its president until 1920.

LOWELL, AMY (1874–1925), U.S. poet. A member of a prominent Boston family, Lowell began writing seriously at age 28, publishing her first poem at age 36. In 1913, the year after she published her first collection, she met the poet Ezra Pound and soon replaced him as leader of the imagists (whom Pound then called the "Amygists"), expanding on their innovative free-verse techniques with her own polyphonic prose. "Patterns" and "Lilacs," her most famous poems, are rich with sensuous imagery. Her best-known works were *A Critical Fable* (1922), humorous verse portraits of contemporary poets; a biography of *John Keats* (2 vols., 1925); and the collection *What's O'clock* (1925; Pulitzer

Prize). Her *Complete Poetical Works* appeared in 1955. Lowell's cigar smoking and blunt manners made her notorious in the literary world. ■ See biographies by Horace Gregory (1958) and Jean Gould (1975), and Glenn R. Ruthley, *The Thorn of a Rose* (1975).

LOWELL, PERCIVAL (1855–1916), U.S. astronomer. After a decade of travel in Asia, Lowell turned to astronomy. He established (1894) the Lowell Observatory in Arizona with the aim of studying Mars. Inspired by Giovanni Schiaparelli's observation of channels on Mars, he produced the first good photograph of the planet (1907) and concluded that intelligent inhabitants had constructed the channels for irrigation purposes. He believed that an advanced civilization existed on Mars and wrote several books on the subject. His 1905 prediction of the position of a planet beyond Neptune was borne out in 1930, when Pluto was first sighted. See William G. Hoyt, *Lowell and Mars* (1976).

LOWELL, ROBERT TRAIL SPENCE, JR. (1917–1977), U.S. poet. Born to one of Boston's patrician literary families, Lowell forged his own moral and aesthetic values. He left Harvard to study at Kenyon College (B.A. 1940) under John Crowe Ransom and Allen Tate, whose New Criticism school was moving American literary criticism away from the political concerns of the 1930s. Lowell converted to Catholicism (1940) and served time during World War II as a conscientious objector. His volume of personal, discordant poetry, *Lord Weary's Castle* (1946), won a Pulitzer Prize. Lowell's other writings included *Life Studies* (1959), *For the Union Dead* (1964), *The Dolphin* (1973, Pulitzer Prize), and a trilogy of plays, *The Old Glory* (1968). *Day by Day* (1977) was his last collection. Lowell's highly introspective poetry—which often described his manic-depression—sounded a new voice in American poetry, crossing the "natural speech" of William Carlos Williams with the formal diction of T. S. Eliot and Ransom. Lowell was active in the civil-rights and antiwar movements. ■ See biographies by Steven G. Aexlrod (1978) and Ian Hamilton (1982); study by Richard J. Fein (rev. ed. 1979); and Paul L. Mariani, *Lost Puritan* (1994).

LOWENTHAL, LEO (1900–1993), German-born U.S. sociologist. Lowenthal graduated from the University of Frankfurt (Ph.D. 1923) and was a member of its Institute of Social Research (1926–49), which developed a Marxist-influenced critique of modern capitalist society and culture. He followed the institute, popularly known as the Frankfurt School, to New York after the Nazis came to power and taught at Columbia University (1940–56). He also was director of research for the Voice of America (1949–55) and in 1956 became professor of sociology at the University of California, Berkeley. Lowenthal's works included *Prophets of Deceit: A Study in the Techniques of the American Agitator* (1949), *Literature and the Image of Man* (1957), *Literature, Popular Culture, and Society* (1961), *Communication in So-*

ciety (3 vols., 1984–86), *False Prophets: Studies on Authoritarianism* (1987), and *Critical Theory and Frankfurt Theorists* (1989). ■ See his memoirs, *An Unmastered Past* (1987).

LOWIE, ROBERT HARRY (1883–1957), Austrian-born U.S. anthropologist. Lowie was among the first to do extensive fieldwork on a single tribe of Native Americans. The investigations he undertook while associated with the American Museum of Natural History (1907–21) resulted in *The Crow Indians* (1935) and the popularized *Indians of the Plains* (1954). He later taught at the University of California, Berkeley (1921–50). Lowie's major theoretical contributions came in *Primitive Society* (1920) and *Social Organization* (1948). Influenced by the pioneering anthropologist Franz Boas, he related the concept of culture to race, psychology, and environment and applied anthropological concepts to the study of modern society. *Toward Understanding Germany* (1945) examined the impact of war on the personality. ■ See his autobiography (1959) and study by Robert F. Murphy (1972).

LOWN, BERNARD (1921?–), U.S. physician and peace activist. Born in Lithuania, Lown emigrated to the United States in 1935, graduated from the Johns Hopkins University Medical School (1945), and was a professor of cardiology at Harvard University, where he developed several machines and drugs to prevent sudden death caused by heart attacks. Concerned about the devastating medical effects of a possible nuclear war, he helped found Physicians for Social Responsibility (1961) and contributed to a major study on the subject published in the *New England Journal of Medicine* (1962). In 1980 he cofounded International Physicians for the Prevention of Nuclear War, with Yevgeny I. Chazov, a Soviet physician and high-ranking member of the Communist party. The group publicized the dangers to human health caused by nuclear war and sought to prevent it by advocating an end to all nuclear testing, a verifiable freeze on development and deployment of nuclear weapons, and a declaration of no-first-use by all nuclear powers. The organization, which had a membership of about 135,000 in 41 countries, including 60,000 in the Soviet Union and 28,000 in the United States, was awarded the 1985 Nobel Peace Prize. His books included *The Lost Art of Healing* (1996).

LOWRY, (CLARENCE) MALCOLM (1909–1957), British novelist. Lowry's first novel *Ultramarine* (1933), a semiautobiographical description of a youth's adventures at sea, was written while he was a student at Cambridge. It was constantly revised by him and republished in final form in 1962. The only other novel he published in his lifetime is considered a modern masterpiece; *Under the Volcano* (1947) recounts the last day in the disintegrating life of a failed, alcoholic British consul in Mexico. Lowry made his story a tragedy of faith and despair and called it "a drunken *Divine Comedy.*" Several less-successful novels, a collection of short stories, and his poems were published after his early

death. ■ See biography by Douglas Day (1973) and Gordon Bowker, *Pursued by Furies* (1993).

LUBAC, HENRI SONIER DE (1896–1991), French religious philosopher. The son of a banker, Lubac taught theology and history of religion at the University of Lyons (1929–61). He was the director of *Sources Chrétiennes,* editing and translating ancient Christian literature in inexpensive editions, and he wrote the standard study of medieval biblical scholarship, *Exégèse Médiévale* (4 vols., 1959–64). Although once ordered to silence for his liberal views, he was named a cardinal in 1983. His translated books included *The Un-Marxian Socialist: A Study of Proudhon* (1948), *The Drama of Atheist Humanism* (1949), *Aspects of Buddhism* (1953), *The Mystery of the Supernatural* (1967), *A Brief Catechesis on Nature and Grace* (1984), and five studies on Teilhard de Chardin (1962, 1964, 1966, 1971, 1977).

LUBITSCH, ERNST (1892–1947), German-born U.S. film director. Son of a Berlin storekeeper, Lubitsch made his name as an actor and director in Germany before going to the United States in 1924. His silent Hollywood satires on sex and money were great successes, but his gift for verbal subtleties remained unrealized until the advent of sound. Films such as *Monte Carlo* (1930), *Trouble in Paradise* (1932), *The Merry Widow* (1934), and *Ninotchka* (1939) were celebrated for their continental wit and sophistication and for the "Lubitsch touch." a combination of tragedy and comedy producing a moment of ironic truth. *To Be or Not to Be* (1942), his anti-Nazi comedy, stirred controversy. ■ See Herman G. Weinberg, *The Lubitsch Touch* (rev. ed. 1971), and biography by Scott Eyman (1993).

LUCAS, GEORGE (1944–), U.S. film director and producer. A prize-winning student filmmaker at the University of Southern California (B.A. 1966), Lucas was a protégé of director Francis Ford Coppola, at whose studios he made the science-fiction film *THX 1138* (1971) and the nostalgic evocation of adolescence in the early 1960s, *American Graffitti* (1973). *Star Wars* (1977), the science-fiction adventure saga, which he wrote and directed, was one of the most popular movies ever made. He also produced and wrote the story for *The Empire Strikes Back—Star Wars II* (1980), *Return of the Jedi—Star Wars III* (1983), and a prequel, *Star Wars: Episode I—The Phantom Menace* (1999). As executive producer, he played a major role in the creation of director Steven Spielberg's *Raiders of the Lost Ark* (1981), *Indiana Jones and the Temple of Doom* (coauthor, 1984), and *Indiana Jones and the Last Crusade* (coauthor, 1989), colorful re-creations of exotic 1930s adventure movies. ■ See Dale Pollock, *Skywalking* (1999).

LUCAS, ROBERT E., JR. (1937–), U.S. economist. Lucas studied with Milton Friedman at the University of Chicago (Ph.D. 1964) and later taught there (from 1974). A critic of Keynesian economics, he developed and applied the theory of "rational expectations" to show that workers and firms anticipate policies of government intervention in the economy (through monetary and fiscal policies) and react in ways that may counteract the intention of government planners. Lucas' work transformed macroeconomic analysis, influenced the economic tactics of government planners, and was responsible for his winning the 1995 Nobel Memorial Prize in Economics. His books include *Studies in Business-Cycle Theory* (1981) and *Rational Expectations and Econometric Practice* (1981; with T. J. Sargent).

LUCE, CLARE BOOTHE (Clare Boothe; 1903–1987), U.S. writer and diplomat. Born into genteel poverty in New York City, Boothe married a millionaire at age 20, became a top New York magazine editor before she was 30, and wrote a successful Broadway play, *The Women* (1936), satirizing her class. Her second husband was publisher Henry Luce, who was supportive of her career as a Republican congresswoman from Connecticut (1943–47) and joined her in Rome during her service as ambassador to Italy (1953–57). Nominated and confirmed as ambassador to Brazil in 1959, she resigned after making some impolitic remarks during Senate hearings. She supported conservative causes throughout her career. ■ See biography by Stephen Shadegg (1971); memoir by Wilfrid Sheed (1982); and Sylvia J. Morris, *Rage for Fame* (1997).

LUCE, HENRY ROBINSON (1898–1967), U.S. publisher. Born in China, the son of Presbyterian missionaries, Luce attended Yale and Oxford Universities before pursuing a career in journalism. In 1923 he and his close friend Briton Hadden (1898–1929) launched *Time,* the first modern weekly newsmagazine. Marked by its innovative departmentalized news coverage, slanted reportage, and distinctive writing style noted for its brevity, brashness, and syntactical eccentricities, *Time* became enormously successful and was frequently imitated. A vehicle for Luce's Americanism, Republicanism, internationalism, and anticommunism, it became the nation's most influential popular magazine. Through his sole control of Time Inc. (1929–64), which eventually included *Fortune* (1930), *Life* (1936), *Sports Illustrated* (1954), a book division, and several radio and television stations, Luce gained immense power and influence. A noted cold warrior, he was particularly hostile to the Chinese communists and the Americans who "lost" China. He was married to Clare Booth Luce (from 1935). ■ See biographies by John Kobler (1968) and R. E. Herzstein (1994) and W. A. Swanberg, *Luce and His Empire* (1972).

LUCIANO, CHARLES "LUCKY" (Salvatore Lucania; 1897–1962), Italian-born U.S. racketeer. Luciano was first arrested at age 10 for shoplifting. He dropped out of grade school at age 14, peddled drugs, and spent six months in jail. He had refused to name his contacts and was rewarded with acceptance into the Five Points Gang (1916). Eventually, Luciano became one of the most powerful figures of organized crime. Between 1919 and 1936 he was arrested 25 times on charges ranging from possessing drugs to assault, bootlegging, promoting prostitution, and homicide. He was convicted only once (in 1936, for running New York's vice ring) and did not serve out his sentence. While in jail during World War II, Luciano helped U.S. military intelligence by securing mob cooperation on the docks and Mafia cooperation in Sicily. In 1946, having served only 10 years of his 30-to-40 year sentence, he was freed on the condition that he leave the country. He returned to Naples, where he lived out his life in luxury with no visible means of support. ■ See Martin A. Gosch and Richard Hammer, *The Last Testament of Lucky Luciano* (1975).

LUCKMAN, SID (1916–1998), U.S. football player. An All-America selection at Columbia and star of the Chicago Bears (1939–50), Luckman was the best of the modern "T-formation" quarterbacks. A superb passer, scrambler, and field strategist, Luckman passed for 14,683 yards and 139 touchdowns in his National Football League career. He was the NFL's Most Valuable Player in 1943.

LUCKNER, COUNT FELIX VON (1881–1966), German naval officer. A Prussian aristocrat who ran away at age 13 to join the navy, Luckner captured the imagination of the world during World War I as captain of the raider *Seeadler.* Slipping through the British blockade in 1916, the raider, disguised as a full-rigged sailing vessel, sank 16 Allied ships, whose passengers and crew were rescued and delivered to neutral ports. Luckner earned the nickname "Sea Devil" for his exploits. The *Seeadler* made its way to the Pacific, where it was destroyed by a tidal wave, and Luckner was captured and interned in New Zealand. ■ See his memoir, *Out of an Old Sea Chest* (Eng. trans. 1958). and biography by Edwin P. Hoyt (1969).

LUDENDORFF, ERICH (1865–1937), German general. The son of a Prussian cavalry officer, Ludendorff played a key role in Germany's domestic and military affairs during World War I as chief of staff to Field Marshal Paul von Hindenburg. Subordinating the political decisionmaking process to military necessity, he insisted on unrestricted submarine warfare in 1917, thus prompting the United States to enter the war, and dictated harsh terms to the defeated Russians at Brest-Litovsk (1917). After Germany's defeat in 1918 Ludendorff fled to Sweden, nursing the legend of Germany's "stab in the back." He returned to participate in the abortive Kapp putsch (Berlin, 1920) and in the Nazi "beer-hall putsch" (Munich, 1923) and to serve as a Nazi deputy in the Reichstag (1924–28). He wrote *Ludendorff's Own Story* (Eng. trans. 1919). ■ See study by D. J. Goodspeed (1966) and Roger Parkinson, *Tormented Warrior* (1979).

LUDWIG, DANIEL KEITH (1897–1992), U.S. shipping magnate. In the 1930s D. K. Ludwig turned a small tanker company into the largest shipping fleet in the United States and the largest privately owned multinational company in the world (National Bulk Carriers, Inc.) A reclusive billionaire unknown to the general public, Ludwig was the "father" of the supertankers. He developed worldwide interests (employing more than 20,000 workers in more than 20 nations) in oil refining, coal mining, saltwater conversion, agriculture, real estate, hotels, and banking, in addition to shipping. He was best known for Jari, a billion-dollar development project in the Brazilian Amazon begun in 1967 but abandoned in 1982. ■ See Jerry Shields, *The Invisible Billionaire* (1986).

LUDWIG, EMIL (1881–1948), German-born writer. Trained in law, Ludwig began writing at age 25. He specialized in vividly written psychological biographies of major historical figures. Following a new trend, he emphasized the personalities of his subjects by blending real quotations with invented dialogue. His *Napoleon* (1925; Eng. trans. 1927), *Goethe* (1920: Eng. trans. 1928), *Lincoln* (1930; Eng. trans. 1930), and *Bolivar* (Eng. trans. 1942; 1939), among others, earned him an international reputation. He lived in Switzerland after 1907.

LUENING, OTTO (1900–1996), U.S. composer, conductor, and flutist. A widely traveled flutist and conductor of opera and symphony, Luening composed an opera (*Evangeline,* 1930; rev. 1948), chamber music, and other orchestral and choral works in which he juxtaposed many different styles. He also pioneered (from 1952) in the use of tape and electronic music, alone and in combination with live performance, such as *Gargoyles* (1961) for violin and synthesizer. Luening taught at Columbia University (1947–68), trained many prominent composers, and cofounded (1959) and directed the Columbia-Princeton Electronic Music Center. ■ See his autobiography, *The Odyssey of an American Composer* (1980).

LUGARD, FREDERICK JOHN LUGARD, 1st BARON (1858–1945), British colonial administrator. Born in India, where his parents were missionaries, and trained at Sandhurst, Lugard played an important role in securing British control over Uganda in the 1890s. He served as governor of northern Nigeria (1900–06), of Hong Kong (1907–12), and finally of all Nigeria (1912–19), where he forged a single unit out of two protectorates. He favored a humane, culturally tolerant imperialism, ruling indirectly through indigenous institutions. ■ See his *Dual Mandate in British Tropical Africa* (1922) and biography by Margery Perham (2 vols., 1956–60).

LUGONES, LEOPOLDO (1874–1938), Argentine writer. A versatile modernist in the pre–World War I era, Lugones influenced the course of Latin American poetry by importing European avant-garde techniques. He was prolific and energetic and often flamboyant. Lugones' best collection, *Sentimental Lunar Poems* (1909), reflected French symbolist

influence. His later literary career veered from romanticism to realism; his political career from socialism to extreme nationalism. He directed the Argentinian National Council of Education (1914–38).

LUGOSI, BELA (Bela Blasko; 1882–1956), Hungarian-born actor. Lugosi was a leading character actor with the Hungarian National Theater from 1901 until the fall of the 1919 Hungarian Soviet Republic, which he had supported. Fleeing to Germany and then to New York (1921), he won the part of Dracula in the 1927 Broadway play and the 1931 film, after which he was consistently typecast as a sinister, bloodcurdling horror-film heavy (*Murder in the Rue Morgue,* 1932; *Mark of the Vampire,* 1935; *The Wolf Man,* 1941). ■ See study by Robert Cremer (1976); Arthur Lennig, *The Count* (1974); and biography by Gary Rhodes (1997).

LU HSUN. See LU XUN.

LUJACK, JOHN (1925–), U.S. football player. A dazzling college quarterback and great all-around player, Lujack was a unanimous All-American at Notre Dame (1946, 1947) and a Heisman Trophy winner (1947). In 1949 he was named the outstanding quarterback of the previous quarter century by the *All America Review.* From 1948 to 1952 he played for the Chicago Bears of the National Football League and passed for 6,295 yards and 41 touchdowns.

LUKÁCS GYORGY (1885–1971), Hungarian philosopher and literary critic. Born into an aristocratic Jewish family, Lukács received a doctorate in sociology (Berlin, 1906) and joined the Hungarian Communist party in 1918. During the next 10 years he wrote numerous theoretical papers. His most famous book, *History and Class Consciousness* (1923: Eng. trans. 1971), which stressed the role of self-awareness in social struggle, was denounced by orthodox Marxist-Leninists. He lived in Moscow (1933–44), published numerous, more orthodox articles, and established his reputation as a foremost Marxist literary historian. His major works included *Studies in European Realism* (1946; Eng. trans. 1950) and *The Historical Novel* (1955; Eng. trans. 1962), as well as *Goethe* (1947; Eng. trans. 1969) and *The Young Hegel* (1948; Eng. trans. 1976). Lukács returned to Hungary in 1945, served in parliament, became a professor at the University of Budapest, and was an important force in Hungarian intellectual life. In the West, his work revived interest in Marxist criticism and the theory of alienation. ■ See studies by George Lichtheim (1970), George H. Parkinson (1977), and Mary Gluck (1985); Andrew Arato and Paul Breines, *The Young Lukács and the Origins of Western Marxism* (1979); and Lee Congdon, *Young Lukács* (1983).

LUKS, GEORGE BENJAMIN (1867–1933), U.S. painter. Luks studied art in Philadelphia, London, Düsseldorf, and Paris before becoming a newspaper illustrator (1894). He served as a correspondent artist in Cuba during the independence struggle (1895) and later worked as a cartoonist in New York. He was associated with The Eight, a group of early-20th-century social-realist painters, and was known for his scenes of New York City's Lower East Side. *The Spielers* (1905) and *The Wrestlers* (1905) were among his most famous works.

LUMUMBA, PATRICE (1925–1961), Congolese political leader. A veteran of the Belgian colonial administrative corps, Lumumba became a fiery pamphleteer and orator in Leopoldville (now Kinshasa). He was a founder of the Congolese National Movement (MNC) party (1958), and after the first elections in 1960 he became premier of independent Congo (later Zaïre). A supporter of a strong unitary state, he opposed tribal federalism, the position espoused by his rival, Pres. Joseph Kasavubu. In the summer of 1960, government authority disintegrated as military rebellion, Belgian intervention, and the succession of copper-rich Katanga (now Shaba) province occurred in rapid succession. Shortly after Lumumba appealed for aid from the Soviet Union he was dismissed from office (Sept. 5, 1960). Ten days later Gen. Mobutu Sese Seko assumed power in a coup. Lumumba fled but was captured and murdered by Katanga secessionists in February 1961. In death, he became a "national hero" and a martyr to the cause of militant African nationalism. ■ See his *Congo My Country* (1956; Eng. trans. 1962), *Lumumba Speaks* (1963; Eng. trans. 1972), and Thomas R. Kanza, *The Rise and Fall of Patrice Lumumba* (1978).

LUNACHARSKY, ANATOLI VASILYEVICH (1875–1933), Soviet political and cultural figure. A Marxist propagandist in his teens, Lunacharsky was deported from Russia (1898) and joined the bolsheviks in Switzerland (1904). He was a highly cultivated intellectual, and he broke with party leader V. I. Lenin after the 1905 revolution to form a leftist faction with Maxim Gorky and A. A. Bogdanov (1905). He lectured widely on politics and culture (1905–17). Rejoining the bolsheviks (1917), he returned to Russia with Lenin, and after the October revolution he served as the first Soviet commissar of enlightenment (1917–29). Believing that intellectual and cultural development was essential to the strengthening of the proletariat, he advocated moderation and tolerance in cultural affairs. As supervisor of cultural and educational life, he protected traditional works of art and literature and fostered new proletarian and experimental ones. He planned the expansion of free public schools and advocated the activity method of instruction, student self-government, and a well-rounded curriculum to include academic, political, and polytechnical studies. With the rise of rigid Stalinist orthodoxy, Lunacharsky was replaced. He died shortly after being named ambassador to Spain. He wrote hundreds of articles and numerous books on cultural subjects, as well as several plays. English translations of his work are in *On Literature and Art* (1965) and *On Education* (1981). ■ See Sheila Fitzpatrick, *Commissariat of En-*

lightenment (1970), and Timothy E. O'Connor, *The Politics of Soviet Culture* (1983).

LUNN, SIR ARNOLD HENRY MOORE (1888–1974), British skiing authority and author. A lifelong alpinist, Lunn founded the Alpine Ski Club (1908), organized the world's first downhill ski race (1911), and founded (1919) and edited *The British Ski Year Book*. He was best known for inventing the slalom ski race (1922). In addition to numerous books on skiing, the Alps, and politics, Lunn wrote several volumes on Roman Catholicism, his adopted religion. ■ See his autobiography, *Come What May* (1940), and his memoirs, *Unkilled for So Long* (1967).

LUNT, ALFRED (1893–1977), and **LYNN FONTANNE** (1887–1983), U.S. actors. Lunt and the British-born Fontanne were both Broadway stars when they married in 1922. They first appeared together in 1923 and became the most celebrated and best-loved couple in the history of theater in the United States, appearing in 27 productions together. Although they starred in such diverse dramas as *There Shall Be No Night* (1940) and *The Visit* (1960), they were best known for appearing in such sophisticated comedies as *The Guardsman* (1924), *Pygmalion* (1926), *Design for Living* (1933), *Idiot's Delight* (1936), *O Mistress Mine* (1946), and *The Great Sebastians* (1956). Broadway's Lunt-Fontanne Theater was named in their honor (1958). ■ See George Freedley, *The Lunts* (1957); Maurice Zolotow, *Stagestruck* (1965); and Jared Brown, *The Fabulous Lunts* (1986).

LURIA, ALEKSANDR ROMANOVICH (1902–1977), Soviet neuropsychologist. A physician's son who pioneered in psychosomatic medicine, Luria experimented with new laboratory techniques to measure human emotion while a 17-year-old student at the Moscow Medical Institute. He earned degrees in psychology, education, and medicine and headed the neuropsychology department at Moscow University. Among his many interests was the role of speech in mental development and retardation. During World War II, he made important advances in brain surgery and postsurgical restoration of brain function. Later research led to new findings on disturbances in intellectual functioning. His articles were widely translated and he lectured abroad. Luria's books included *Higher Cortical Functions in Man* (Eng. trans. 1966), *The Mind of a Mnemonist* (Eng. trans. 1968), *The Man with a Shattered World* (Eng. trans. 1972), *The Working Brain* (Eng. trans. 1973), and *Basic Problems of Neurolinguistics* (Eng. trans. 1976). ■ See his *The Making of Mind: A Personal Account of Soviet Psychology* (Eng. trans. 1979).

LURIA, SALVADOR EDWARD (1912–1991), Italian-born U.S. biologist. One of the pioneers of modern molecular biology, Luria emigrated to the United States (1940) after having studied at the Institute of Radium in Paris. Working formally and informally with Max Delbrück and Alfred Hershey, he demonstrated how phages (viruses that infect and destroy bacterial cells) multiply and undergo changes in their hereditary material. The three scientists shared the 1969 Nobel Prize for Physiology or Medicine. Luria was an activist in the anti-Vietnam War movement and was on a federal government blacklist the year he won the Nobel award. He wrote the pioneering study *General Virology* (1953) and *Life: The Unfinished Experiment* (1973) and taught at the Massachusetts Institute of Technology (1959–85). ■ See his autobiography, *A Slot Machine, a Broken Test Tube* (1984).

LURIE, RANAN RAYMOND (1932–), Israeli-U.S. political cartoonist. Raised and educated in Israel, Lurie worked for several Israeli newspaper and magazines and by the 1960s he was Israel's leading political cartoonist. After service as a reserve major in the Six-Day War (1967) he moved to New York to work as an editorial cartoonist for *Life* magazine (1968–73) and became a naturalized U.S. citizen in 1974. Subsequently he worked on the staffs of *The Honolulu Advertiser* (1979), *Die Welt* (Bonn; 1980–81), the *London Times* (1981–83), *Asahi Shimban* (Tokyo; 1983–84), *US. News and World Report* (1984–85), and *Time International* (1994–). By the mid-1990s he was the world's most widely syndicated cartoonist, appearing in 1,100 publications (in 104 countries) with a circulation of approximately 104 million. His cartoons appeared in several books, including *Nixon Rated Cartoons* (1973), *Lurie's Worlds* (1980), and *Lurie's Almanac* (1983). An international award for political cartooning was named in his honor by the United Nations Society of Writers (UNSW; 1995).

LUTHULI, ALBERT JOHN (1898?–1967), South African political leader. Luthuli was a mission teacher and minor Zulu chieftain when he joined the African National Congress (ANC) in 1946. He promoted nonviolent resistance to achieve a "colorless" Christian democracy, for which he was repeatedly arrested and harassed by the apartheid South African government. He was president of the ANC (1952–67) and was awarded the 1960 Nobel Peace Prize for his moderating moral force, but he was increasingly outflanked by more radical figures within his own movement. ■ See his autobiography, *Let My People Go* (1962), and biography by Mary Benson (1963).

LUTOSLAWSKI, WITOLD (1913–1994), Polish composer. Lutoslawski, active in reorganizing Poland's musical life after World War II, was the most prominent of a group of influential young avant-garde composers. He often wrote experimental music that called for improvisation on the part of individual members of the orchestra (*Venetian Games*, 1961) or chorus (*Three Poems by Henri Michaux*, 1963). His most famous works, influenced by Debussy, Bartók,

Stravinsky, and Varèse, were *Little Suite* (1951), *Concerto for Orchestra* (1954), *Funeral Music* (1958), *Cello Concerto* (1970), and *Chain 2* (1985). His Symphony No. 3 (1983) won the first Grawemeyer Award from the University of Louisville, a prize of $150,000. ■ See the study by Steven Stucky (1981).

LUTYENS, SIR EDWIN LANDSEER (1869–1944), British architect. A designer of English country houses during the Edwardian period, Lutyens was commissioned in 1912 to supervise the planning of the city of New Delhi, the new Indian capital. Outstanding among the buildings he designed was the Viceroy's Residence (1915–30), which combined classical motifs with Mogul domes and other Indian decoration. He was regarded as the most distinguished British architect of his era and served as president of the Royal Academy (from 1938). ■ See studies by Christopher Hussey (1950), Mary Lutyens (1980), Roderick Gradidge (1981), and Robert Irving, *Indian Summer* (1981).

LUXEMBURG, ROSA (1871–1919), Polish-born revolutionary. The daughter of a Jewish merchant, Luxemburg was born in Russian Poland, where she helped found the Polish Socialist party (1892). She fled the czarist police and earned a doctorate from the University of Zurich (1898). She then settled in Berlin, where she became a leader of the left wing of the German Social Democratic party (SPD) and of the international Marxist movement. She wrote and spoke forcefully against militarism and imperialism, founded (with Karl Liebknecht) the revolutionary antiwar Spartacus League during World War I, and was imprisoned from 1915 to 1918. Subsequently she cofounded the German Communist party (1918), which in 1919 attempted to transform the bourgeois revolution into the dictatorship of the proletariat. She was rearrested and then murdered by counterrevolutionary soldiers. Her books included *The Mass Strike* (1906; Eng. trans. 1971), *The Accumulation of Capital* (1913; Eng. trans. 1951), and *The Crisis in the German Social Democracy* (1916; Eng. trans. 1919). A film of her life was made in 1986. ■ See her *Selected Political Writings* (Eng. trans. 1971), *Letters* (Eng. trans. 1978), and biographies by Paul Frolich (Eng. trans. 1972), J. P. Nettl (2 vols., 1966), and Richard Abraham (1989).

LU XUN (old style: LU HSUN; 1881–1936), Chinese writer. Lu Xun is the pseudonym of Zhou Shuren (old style: Chou Shu-jen). He is also known as Lusin and Lu Hsin. Regarded by many as the greatest modern Chinese writer, Lu did not achieve literary success until 1918 with the publication of his short story "A Madman's Diary," the first modern short story written in vernacular Chinese. This, and subsequent tales, notably "The Story of Ah Q" (1921), and those in the volumes *Call to Arms* (1923) and *Hesitation* (1926), sardonically attacked the exploitative nature of traditional society and established Lu as a hero to an entire generation of Chinese. Although he never became a communist, he supported the party, regarding it as the major force of the Chinese revolution, and headed the League of Left-Wing Writers (1930). Lu was also known for his poetry, translations, essays, and the volume *A Brief History of Chinese Fiction* (1923; Eng. trans. 1977). English translations of his works are in *Selected Works* (4 vols., 1956–60) and *The Complete Stories* (1981). ■ See studies by Huang Sung-k'ang (1957) and William A. Lyll, Jr. (1976); Leo Ou-Fan Lee, ed., *Lu Xun and His Legacy* (1985); and *Voices from the Iron House* (1987).

LVOV, PRINCE GEORGI YEVGENYEVICH (1861-1925), Russian political figure. A lawyer, Prince Lvov left his civil service position (1893) to work in the *zemstvo* (local government) movement. A leader of the liberal Constitutional Democratic party, he served in the Duma (from 1906), headed the all-Russian union of *zemstvos,* and became leader of the provisional government following the February revolution (1917). He worked unsuccessfully to institute a constitutional government, while radical Social Democrats and Bolsheviks garnered power by organizing the workers' and peasants' soviets. He resigned in July 1917; he was succeeded by Aleksandr Kerensky, who formed a moderate socialist government. Lvov was imprisoned after the October revolution (1917), but he escaped and fled to Paris, where he lived until his death.

LWOFF, ANDRÉ (1902–1994), French biochemist. A member of the French Resistance during World War II, Lwoff was associated with the Pasteur Institute in Paris (1921–68) and the University of Paris (1959–68). His investigation of the genetics of bacterial virus, or bacteriophage, demonstrated the process known as lysogeny, in which the DNA (deoxyribonucleic acid) of a virus is incorporated into a bacterial chromosome and infects it, that is, causes its destruction. His further studies of the infected, or lysogenic, bacteria showed that after infection, the viral DNA passes on to succeeding generations of bacteria. For these discoveries, Lwoff shared the 1965 Nobel Prize for Physiology or Medicine with François Jacob and Jacques Monod. Lwoff's books, in English, included *Biological Order* (1962), *Of Microbes and Life* (1971), and *Origins of Molecular Biology* (1979).

LYAUTEY, LOUIS HUBERT GONZALVE (1854–1934), French marshal and colonial administrator. Lyautey was educated at St. Cyr military academy and served as an officer in Algeria, Indochina, and Madagascar. In 1912, when the French proclaimed their protectorate, Lyautey was named high commissioner to Morocco, which he developed into a model of pacification and colonial administration, preserving native institutions and improving public health, education, and welfare. Despite orders to withdraw, the general held Morocco through World War I; he was appointed a marshal of France in 1921 and left Morocco in 1925. ■ See

biography by André Maurois (Eng. trans. 1931)and Alan Scham, *Lyautey in Morocco* (1970).

LYND, ROBERT STAUGHTON (1892–1970), and HELEN MERRELL LYND (1896–1982), U.S. sociologists. Robert Lynd, a graduate of Princeton (1914), was a magazine editor from Indiana who earned a divinity degree from the Union Theological Seminary (1923) and became a research director of the Institute of Social and Religious Research. With his wife Helen, another midwesterner—and a graduate of Wellesley College (1919)—he brought the methods of cultural anthropology to bear on an average American community, *Middletown* (1929), describing its middle class as a tribe and discussing the town's class differences and materialistic ethos. The Lynds were accused of muckraking and of Marxist influences, but *Middletown* (later identified as Muncie, Indiana) became a classic of American sociology and gave rise to a follow-up study (*Middletown in Transition,* 1937) on the effects of the Depression. Robert Lynd. who received his Ph.D. at Columbia (1931) and taught there (1931–61), also wrote *Knowledge for What?* (1939), a book about the moral responsibility of social scientists. Helen Lynd received her Ph.D. from Columbia (1944), taught at Sarah Lawrence College (1928–64), and wrote several books, including *On Shame and the Search for Identity* (1958), and a collection of essays, *Towards Discovery* (1965). Their son was the historian and social activist Staughton Lynd (1929–).

LYND, STAUGHTON (1929–), U.S. historian. The son of the sociologists Robert and Helen Lynd, the authors of *Middletown* (1929), Lynd was a graduate of Columbia (Ph.D. 1962) who taught history at black colleges and freedom schools in the South. A conscientious objector, he became directly involved in the historical process with a 1965 trip to North Vietnam and became a leading spokesman for the antiwar movement. Although denied tenure at Yale (1968), Lynd wrote *Class Conflict, Slavery and the U.S. Constitution* (1968), and *Intellectual Origins of American Radicalism* (1968), and was considered a leading New Left historian of the revolutionary and confederation periods. He subsequently became a lawyer (1976) and worked for democratic socialism as a representative of steelworkers who opposed the shutdown of plants in Youngstown, Ohio. He wrote *Strategy and Program* (1973; with Gar Alperovitz), *Labor Law for the Rank and Filer* (rev. ed. 1982), *The Fight Against Shutdowns* (1982), and *Solidarity Unionism* (1992; rev. ed. 1994) and edited *Rank and File: Personal Histories by Working Class Organizers* (1981; with Alice Lynd) and *"We Are All Leaders": The Alternate Unionism of the Early 1930s* (1996). ■ See his *Living Inside Our Hope: A Steadfast Radical's Thoughts on Rebuilding the Movement* (1997).

LYNEN, FEODOR FELIX KONRAD (1911–1979), German biochemist. A graduate of the University of Munich (Ph.D. 1937), Lynen taught there (from 1942) and directed the Max Planck Institute for Cell Chemistry (1954–72) and Biochemistry (1972–79). He was the first to isolate "active acetate," which plays a vital role in the formation of both cholesterol and fatty acids. His research helped explain how fatty acids are synthesized and metabolized. For this work, which had important implications for the possible role of cholesterol in coronary and circulatory disease, Lynen shared the 1964 Nobel Prize for Physiology or Medicine with Konrad E. Bloch.

LYNN, LORETTA (Loretta Webb; 1935?–   ), U.S. singer and songwriter. Born in the depressed coal-mining hill country of eastern Kentucky, Lynn married at age 14 and had four children by the age of 18. Encouraged by her husband to sing professionally, she began (1961) to appear in dance halls and on local radio stations and by 1962 was a regular on radio's Grand Ole Opry in Nashville. She regularly toured the country, appeared frequently on nationwide television, and by the mid-1960s was one of the most popular country-music singers in the United States. Her songs were infused with the homespun philosophy of her native region, and she frequently sang of the problems of rural women. Her best-known hits included "Don't Come Home A-Drinkin' (with Lovin' on Your Mind)." "You Ain't Woman Enough (to Take My Man)," and "Coal Miner's Daughter," which was also the title of her autobiography (1976) and the movie based on it (1980). A three-time winner of the Country Music Association's Female Vocalist of the Year Award (1967, 1972, 1973), she was named entertainer of the decade by the Academy of Country Music (1980).

LYONS, JOSEPH ALOYSIUS (1879–1939), Australian political leader. Lyons began to work at age 12 and later taught school. He was elected as a Labour member to the Tasmanian legislature (1909) and held many cabinet posts until his tenure as premier (1923–28). In 1929 he switched to the federal arena and again held cabinet rank. He resigned from the Labour party (1931) to help found the United Australia party, and he served as Australia's prime minister from 1931 to 1939. His reorganization of Australian finances aided in the recovery from the Depression. He also sponsored an expansion of the navy and air force. ■ See biography by his widow Enid Lyons, *So We Take Comfort* (1965).

LYONS, LEONARD (Leonard Sucher; 1906–1976), U.S. journalist. The son of a sweatshop worker from New York City's Lower East Side Jewish ghetto, Lyons graduated from law school (1928) and became a Broadway columnist with the *New York Post* (1934). For the next 40 years his column, "The Lyons Den," chronicled the comings and goings of celebrities and theatrical people at the time when Broadway, "the Great White Way," was America's entertainment center. His columns, filled with anecdotes and trivia, were syndicated in more than 100 newspapers with a total circulation of 15 million.

LYOT, BERNARD FERDINAND (1897–1952), French astronomer. Lyot earned an engineering degree (1917), and after 1920 worked at the observatory at Meudon. In the 1920s, he measured the polarization of light from the moon and planets, using an instrument of his own invention, and made discoveries about the moon's surface and about the atmospheres of Mercury, Mars, and Venus. He then investigated the solar corona, the luminous phenomenon that envelops the sun and is visible to the naked eye only during a total eclipse. Devising a new kind of telescope called the coronagraph and carrying it on skis to a mountain peak in the Pyrenees, Lyot was the first to observe the solar corona in broad daylight (1931). In 1933 he developed a polarizing filter that he used to measure changes in the solar corona, making important photographic and motion-picture records of these events.

LYSENKO, TROFIM DENISOVICH (1898–1976), Soviet agronomist and geneticist. Influenced by the work of Russian horticulturalist I. V. Michurin, Lysenko attracted attention in 1929 when he identified "vernalization"—a process that he claimed could alter the genetic properties of plants by subjecting the seeds to environmental changes. When reputable Soviet geneticists assailed his theory, Lysenko retaliated with ferocity, using political clout to silence his opponents. The Communist party officially endorsed his views (1948), which meshed well with the Marxist-Leninist view that environment can shape character and society. Lysenko remained the Soviet Union's most visible authority on agriculture and genetics for nearly three decades (1934–63), suppressing the teaching of Mendelian genetics there until the early 1960s. His ideas and influence undercut the stature and progress of Soviet biological science for much of the century. He wrote *Heredity and Its Variability* (1943; Eng. trans. 1946) and *The Situation in Biological Science* (1948; Eng. trans. 1948). ■ See Zhores Medvedev, *The Rise and Fall of T. D. Lysenko* (Eng. trans. 1969), and Dominique Lecourt, *Proletarian Science?* (Eng. trans. 1977).

M

MA, YO-YO (1955–), French-born cellist. Born in Paris, Ma received his early musical education from his father, a composer and violinist who had emigrated to France from China during the 1930s. The family moved to New York City when Ma was 6 and he studied at Juilliard (under Leonard Rose) and then at Harvard. A virtuoso who distinguished himself with his combination of technical prowess and lyricism, he won recognition as the preeminent cellist of his generation. He appeared as a soloist with U.S. and European orchestras, and was known as well for performances of chamber music. He made notable recordings of the works of Bach, Haydn, and Mozart. ■ See Marina Ma, *My Son Yo-Yo* (1996).

MAAZEL, LORIN (1930–), U.S. conductor. A rare child prodigy in the field of conducting, Maazel led orchestras at the New York World's Fair and the Hollywood Bowl at age 9. In the 1940s he appeared with most of the major American orchestras. A Fulbright Fellowship (1952) enabled him to study in Europe, where he spent most of the following decade. In the 1960s he recorded regularly with the Vienna Philharmonic, directed the Berlin Opera and Berlin Radio Symphony, and was one of the most popular conductors on the Continent. He later conducted the Cleveland Symphony Orchestra (1972–82), served as director of the Vienna State Opera (1982–84), and conducted the Pittsburgh Symphony (1988–96) and the Bavarian Radio Symphony Orchestra (1993–). Maazel was best known for his meticulous and passionate performances of the late romantics.

MCADOO, WILLIAM GIBBS (1863–1941), U.S. senator and cabinet officer. An energetic administrator, McAdoo served in several important posts under Pres. Woodrow Wilson, including those of secretary of the treasury (1913–19) and chairman of the Federal Reserve Board. He was a strong contender for the 1924 Democratic party presidential nomination, but he was indirectly linked with the Teapot Dome scandal and other improprieties in the 1920s and was regarded by many as a political opportunist. He later practiced law in California and served in the U.S. Senate (1933–38). ■ See his autobiography, *Crowded Years* (1931), and study by John J. Broesamle (1973).

MCALISKEY, BERNADETTE DEVLIN. *See DEVLIN MCALISKEY, (JOSEPHINE) BERNADETTE.*

MACAPAGAL, DIOSDADO (1910–1997), Filipino political leader. Born into a poor, devout Catholic family, Macapagal worked his way through the University of the Philippines (LL.B. 1936) and pursued a successful legal career in Manila. After World War II he worked in the Department of Foreign Affairs and was elected to congress as a Liberal (1949). He represented his country at the United Nations and was elected vice president in 1957. As president (1961–65), he decentralized the economy, developed heavy industry, dismissed corrupt officials, and attempted land reforms, but corruption and poverty continued to flourish. In 1971 Macapagal presided over the constitutional convention that established a parliamentary form of government, and in 1976 he became a public critic of the martial-law dictatorship of Ferdinand Marcos. ■ See biography by Quentin J. Reynolds and Geoffrey Bocca (1965).

MACARTHUR, DOUGLAS (1880–1964), U.S. general. Descendant of a long line of military men, MacArthur graduated from West Point (1903). First assigned to the Philippines, he spent much of his life in military and civilian assignments in Asia and was army chief of staff from 1930 to 1935. In 1932, during the Depression, he led an infantry assault upon a shantytown in Washington, D.C., against the veterans who were petitioning Congress for early payment of their World War I bonuses. During World War II he led the American campaign in the Pacific, directing his main energy toward recapturing the Philippine Islands. After the war MacArthur was made supreme commander of Allied forces in Japan and was in charge of reviving Japanese economic life and introducing social reforms. He led U.N. troops when war broke out in Korea in 1950 but was removed from his command by Pres. Harry Truman for attempting to widen the war into China in 1951. An outspoken anticommunist, he was a hero of U.S. right-wingers during the cold war. ■ See his *Reminiscences* (1964); D. Clayton James, *The Years of MacArthur* (3 vols. 1970–85); William Manchester, *American Caesar* (1978); and Geoffrey Perrett, *Old Soldiers Never Die* (1996).

MACARTHUR, JOHN DONALD (1897–1978), U.S. insurance magnate. The son of a minister, MacArthur owned a small insurance company when he purchased the bankrupt Chicago-based Bankers Life and Casualty Co. for $2,500 in 1935. As larger companies with greater liabilities failed during the Depression, MacArthur gobbled them up, becoming one of the wealthiest men in the United States. Known as an eccentric and parsimonious billionaire, he owned Citizens Bank and Trust Co. (Illinois), Union Bankers Insurance Co. (Dallas, Texas), and several valuable properties in New York City and was the largest landowner in Florida, controlling more than 100,000 acres. In 1980 the directors of the huge

Catherine and John D. MacArthur Foundation initiated the MacArthur Prize and in 1981 named 21 "exceptionally talented" artists, scientists, educators, and scholars as the first recipients of five-year fellowships worth up to $60,000 annually.

MACAULAY, HERBERT (1864–1945), Nigerian political leader. The grandson of the first black Anglican bishop in West Africa, Macaulay joined the colonial civil service and after engineering studies in England became a crown surveyor in 1893. Resigning in protest over racial discrimination in 1898, he became an outspoken opponent of British rule and a politically active supporter of the *eleko,* traditional ruler of Lagos. When a limited franchise was granted in 1922, he organized, in Lagos, the Nigerian National Democratic party, the country's first modern political organization. As nationalism grew, his concern extended beyond Lagos to all of Nigeria and he cofounded, with Nnamdi Azikiwe, the National Council of Nigeria and Cameroons (NCNC), the first nationwide political party (1944). ■ See biography by Isaac B. Thomas (1946).

MACAULAY, DAME ROSE (1881–1958), British novelist. Oxford-educated Macaulay's first published novel was *The Valley Captives* (1911). She gained recognition with *Potterism* (1920), one of her many satires of middle-class life. With her deft comic touch, Macaulay was able to make serious points. Her other novels included *Told by an Idiot* (1923) and *The Towers of Trebizond* (1956). She was a member of the Bloomsbury group in the 1930s, and one of her critical works was a study of fellow member E. M. Forster (1938). She also wrote several travel books and was a popular literary journalist. ■ See study by Alice R. Benson (1969) and biography by Jane Emery (1992).

MCBRIDE, MARY MARGARET (1899–1976), U.S. radio commentator. As New York WOR-Radio's first Martha Deane, the helpful "grandmother" with household hints, McBride was one of the most effective salespeople on the airwaves. She was a *New York Evening Mail* reporter (1920–24), contributed to *Cosmopolitan, Saturday Evening Post,* and *Good Housekeeping* magazines, and collaborated on travel books (with Helen Josephy, 1929–32) before she turned to broadcasting in 1934. Listeners approved of her casual approach, and she eventually adlibbed her program as she talked about her travels and the people she met. McBride was a radio columnist continuously from 1937 to 1960 and also produced an Associated Press syndicated column (1953–56). A prolific writer, she wrote a cookbook, biographies, and her childhood memoirs, *How Dear to My Heart* (1940). ■ See her autobiography, *A Long Way from Missouri* (1959).

MACBRIDE, SEAN (1904–1988), Irish statesman. The son of Irish nationalist leader Major John MacBride and the actress and revolutionary Maud Gonne, MacBride was born and raised in Paris. He returned to Ireland after his father was executed by the British (1916) for his part in the Easter Rising of 1916, and he joined the underground Irish Republican Army (IRA), eventually becoming its chief of staff. He quit the IRA in 1937 and became a successful trial lawyer in Dublin, often defending accused IRA terrorists. He founded the Republican party (1946), served in parliament (1947–57) and was foreign minister (1948–51) in the coalition government that declared Ireland a republic (1949). He was a vice president of the newly formed Organization for European Economic Cooperation (1948–51) and president of the Council of Foreign Ministers of the Council of Europe (1950). He subsequently devoted himself to the causes of international human rights and disarmament. He was a founder (1961) and chairman (1961–75) of Amnesty International, secretary-general (1963–70) of the International Commission of Jurists, chairman of the International Peace Bureau (1972–85), assistant secretary-general of the United Nations, and U.N. commissioner for South-West Africa (Namibia; 1973–76). He won the Lenin Peace Prize (1976) and shared the 1974 Nobel Peace Prize with Eisaku Sato.

MCCARDELL, CLAIRE (1905–1958), U.S. fashion designer. McCardell, a graduate of the Parsons School of Design (1928), modeled fashions before designing for Hattie Carnegie and Townley Frocks, Inc. When Townley's principal stylist died (1932) before completing a new line, McCardell proved herself by finishing the collection. Concerned with popular-priced, ready-to-wear clothes, she created the first "separates," introduced the leotard or "body suit," and designed simple and comfortable dresses. Her distinctive use of line and color in such styles as the loose monastic dress, the hooded sweater, and the "popover" helped to define the "American look" during the 1940s, McCardell wrote *What Shall I Wear?* (1956). ■ See study by Yohannan Kohle and Nancy Nolf (1998).

MCCARTHY, EUGENE JOSEPH (1916–   ), U.S. senator. A college teacher, McCarthy entered politics in 1947 as an organizer for the Minnesota Democratic-Farmer-Labor party, winning a congressional election in 1948. He was known throughout his years in the House of Representatives (1949–59) and later in the Senate (1959–71) as a supporter of liberal legislation. He criticized Pres. Lyndon Johnson's intervention in the Dominican Republic in 1965 and later opposed U.S. involvement in Vietnam. McCarthy embarked on a campaign for the Democratic nomination for president in 1968, winning wide support in the primaries with a grassroots organization of students and suburban volunteers. Although he lost the nomination to Hubert Humphrey, he is credited with forcing Pres. Johnson's withdrawal from the race. He later ran as an independent for president in 1976. His books included *The Limits of Power* (1968), *The Hard Years* (1975), *The Ultimate Tyranny* (1980), and *A Colony of the World: The U.S. Today* (1992). *Complexities and Contraries* (1982) was a book of collected essays. ■ See his memoirs, *The Year of the People* (1968) and *Up 'Til Now* (1987); Arthur Herzog, *McCarthy for President* (1969); and George Rising, *Clean for Gene* (1997).

MCCARTHY, JOHN (1927–), U.S. mathematician. The son of Communist party organizers, McCarthy was influenced by his family's belief in the virtues of science and technology for the benefit of humanity. He studied mathematics at Princeton University (Ph.D. 1951) and did innovative work in computer science while teaching at Dartmouth College (1955–57), the Massachusetts Institute of Technology (1957–61), and Stanford University (1953–55; 1962–). A pioneer in the field of artificial intelligence, he coined the term (1955), organized a conference at Dartmouth (1956) that defined the new area of study, and established the first artificial intelligence laboratory (at M.I.T., 1957). He later invented the computer language LISP (1958), the vehicle for much of the research in artificial intelligence, and directed the Stanford Artificial Intelligence Laboratory (SAIL; 1965–80). ■ See Philip J. Hilts, *Scientific Temperaments* (1982).

MCCARTHY, JOSEPH RAYMOND (1908–1957), U.S. senator. As a Republican senator from Wisconsin (1947–57), McCarthy used a number of unprincipled tactics that made his name synonymous with political deception and dishonesty. In 1950, as his political career began to falter, he launched a campaign based on unfounded allegations that there were hundreds of communists in the State Department and the U.S. Army. His crusade helped to create the anticommunist hysteria of the early 1950s. The televised Army-McCarthy hearings (1954) were seen by millions and led to his censure by the U.S. Senate for misconduct and to the loss of his power and prestige. ■ See biographies by Richard H. Rovere (1959) and Thomas C. Reeves (1982) and David M. Oshinsky, *Conspiracy So Immense* (1983).

MCCARTHY, JOSEPH VINCENT (1887–1978), U.S. baseball manager. After 20 years as a minor-league player and manager, McCarthy was named manager of the Chicago Cubs (1926) and won his first pennant with them (1929). In 1931 he became manager of the New York Yankees, whose lineup featured Babe Ruth and Lou Gehrig, and in 15 seasons (1931–46) he won eight pennants and seven World Series. A quiet, conservative team leader, McCarthy had one of the most successful careers in baseball history and was the first manager to win pennants in both leagues and the first to win four straight World Series titles (1936–39). He was elected to the National Baseball Hall of Fame in 1957.

MCCARTHY, MARY (1912–1989), U.S. critic and novelist. Surviving her difficult Seattle childhood as the orphan ward of abusive foster parents, McCarthy fought her way to Vassar (BA. 1933) and stung New York with her acerbic literary and drama criticism. Sharp satire pervaded her fiction, including *The Company She Keeps* (1942), *The Groves of*

Academe (1952), and *The Group* (1963), her spicy bestseller about eight Vassar graduates. A vehement critic of U.S. involvement in Southeast Asia, McCarthy gathered firsthand evidence for *Vietnam* (1967) and *Hanoi* (1968). She wrote more than 20 books of fiction, essays, and reportage. Later works included *Ideas and the Novel* (1980) and *Occasional Prose* (1985). ■ See *Memoirs of a Catholic Girlhood* (1957), *How I Grew* (1987), and *Intellectual Memoirs–New York, 1935–1938* (1992); the biography by Carol Gelderman (1988); and Frances Kiernan, *Seeing Mary Plain* (2000).

MCCAY, WINSOR ZENIC (1886–1934), U.S. cartoonist and film animator. A newspaper cartoonist in New York (1902–34), McCay was the originator of the animated cartoon. His earliest film cartoons included *Little Nemo in Slumberland, Little Nemo and the Princess,* and *Gertie the Dinosaur* (1909), for which McCay produced 10,000 individual drawings. His *Sinking of the Lusitania* (1918) was the first feature-length animated film. ■ See biography by John Canemaker (1987).

MCCLINTIC, GUTHRIE (1893–1961), U.S. theatrical director and producer. A stagestruck youth, McClintic studied at the American Academy of Dramatic Arts and worked as a stage manager, casting director, and talent scout for Broadway producer Winthrop Ames (1913–22). He "discovered" actress Katharine Cornell, whom he married in 1921, and they worked together as director and leading lady in many notable Broadway productions, including *The Green Hat* (1925), *The Barretts of Wimpole Street* (1931), *Romeo and Juliet* (1934), *Saint Joan* (1936), *Candida* (1937), *The Three Sisters* (1942), *Antigone* (1946), and *The Constant Wife* (1957). Among his other productions were *Winterset* (1935), *Key Largo* (1939), and *Medea* (1949). He also introduced Maurice Evans, Brian Aherne, and Emlyn Williams to the American stage. ■ See his autobiography, *Me and Kit* (1955).

MCCLINTOCK, BARBARA (1902–1992), U.S. geneticist. Trained as a botanist at Cornell University (Ph.D. 1927), McClintock worked at the Carnegie Institution's laboratory in Cold Spring Harbor, New York (1941–92). Working with Indian corn at a time when chromosomes were thought to be stable arrangements of genes, she discovered (1951) that certain genetic material, "transposable elements" (later recognized as bits of deoxyribonucleic acid or DNA), shifted unpredictably from generation to generation and therefore provided the key for understanding the mechanism of cell differentiation. Although she was isolated and ignored for years, her work was reexamined after transposable elements were discovered in bacteria and other organisms and was recognized as a major contribution to recombinant-DNA technology. She was awarded the 1983 Nobel Prize in Physiology or Medicine. ■ See Evelyn F. Keller, *Feeling for the Organism* (1983).

MCCLOY, JOHN JAY (1895–1989), U.S. lawyer, diplomat, and banker. Born into a Philadelphia family of modest means, McCloy graduated from the Harvard Law School (1921) and worked for prestigious Wall Street law firms during the 1920s and 1930s. His successful handling of the Black Tom case (1930–39), which resulted in the German government's paying his client, Bethlehem Steel, $2 million, brought him to the attention of Secretary of War Henry Stimson, who appointed him assistant secretary of war (1941–45). During World War II, he helped plan major military campaigns, handled sensitive diplomatic missions, and oversaw the Allied occupation of conquered territories. He played a major role in postwar financial recovery and in the formation of the Western Alliance as president of the World Bank (1947–49) and as high commissioner in occupied West Germany (1949–52). Called "the most influential private citizen in America," he subsequently served as president of the Chase National Bank (1952–60, where he directed its merger with the Bank of Manhattan to form the Chase Manhattan Bank); chairman of the Council of Foreign Relations (1953–70) and the Ford Foundation (1953–65); and chief counsel to "the Seven Sisters," the major petroleum companies, during the 1960s and 1970s. ■ See Kai Bird, *The Chairman* (1992).

MCCLURE, SAMUEL SIDNEY (1857–1949), Irish-born U.S. editor and publisher. McClure was brought to the United States at age 9. While studying at Knox College in Illinois (B.A. 1882; M.A. 1887), he launched the McClure Syndicate (1884), the first newspaper organization that furnished written material for simultaneous release by all member publications. As the syndicate grew, McClure bought rights to novels by famous writers, including Rudyard Kipling, Robert Louis Stevenson, and Thomas Hardy, and serialized them in subscribers' newspapers. In 1893, he established *McClure's* magazine, which gained fame for its muckraking articles. Written by such writers as Lincoln Steffens, Ray Stannard Baker, and Ida M. Tarbell, its dramatic exposés shaped public opinion and often prompted legislation. The magazine won a broad readership and attracted advertisers who wanted to be identified with the magazine's reputation for integrity and high standards. McClure, however, alienated his staff, and several key writers left him to found their own journal (1906). *McClure's* declined and McClure lost control of it in 1912. During the 1930s he wrote several books on political philosophy and U.S. democracy. ■ See his autobiography (1914) and Peter Lyon, *Success Story* (1963).

MCCORMACK, JOHN (1884–1945), Irish tenor. McCormack, who began studying music seriously in his twenties, sang in opera houses throughout the world (from 1906) but soon switched to song recitals for which his relatively small but extraordinarily rich and controlled voice was better suited. He had great box-office appeal, and sales of his records of Irish folk songs, ballads, arias, and lieder were enormous. Among his best-loved recordings were "Mother Machree," "I Hear You Calling Me," and Mozart's "Il Mio Tesoro." He lived in the United States from 1914 to 1937 and became a U.S. citizen in 1919. ■ See his autobiography (1918; repr. 1973); biography by Raymond Foxall (1964); and Gordon T. Ledbetter, *The Great Irish Tenor* (1978).

MCCORMACK, JOHN WILLIAM (1891–1980), U.S. congressman. An Irish-Catholic lawyer from South Boston, McCormack served in the U.S. House of Representatives (1929–71). He was a loyal Democrat who supported party policy from the New Deal to U.S intervention in Vietnam. He also upheld the archaic rules of Congress and the rigid seniority system, under which he became speaker of the House in 1961, at age 70, and remained in that position until 1971.

MCCORMICK, ANNE O'HARE (Anne O'Hare; 1882–1954), U.S. journalist. McCormick was raised in Ohio, graduated from a Catholic college, and became editor of a weekly church publication. After her marriage (1910) to an Ohio businessman whom she frequently accompanied on trips abroad, she began (1920) contributing articles to the *New York Times,* including the first interview with Italian fascist leader Benito Mussolini. She became a regular *Times* correspondent in 1922. During the 1920s and 1930s McCormick interviewed many world leaders, became the first woman on the *Times* editorial board (1936), and won a 1937 Pulitzer Prize for foreign correspondence—the first awarded to a woman. She wrote a study of the Soviet Union, *The Hammer and the Scythe* (1928); two collections of her columns were published posthumously, *The World at Home* (1956), and *Vatican Journal, 1921–54* (1957).

MCCORMICK, ROBERT RUTHERFORD (1880–1955), U.S. newspaper editor and publisher. Outspoken nationalist and champion of right-wing Republicanism, McCormick published and edited the *Chicago Tribune* for over 40 years and was cofounder of the *New York Daily News* (1919). Popularly known as Colonel McCormick, he adopted the slogan "the world's greatest newspaper" (1911) for the *Tribune* and transformed it into the most widely read standard-sized U.S. newspaper. An upholder of individualism, free enterprise, and isolationism, he attacked the League of Nations, Presidents Franklin D. Roosevelt and Harry Truman, the United Nations, the welfare state, labor unions, socialism, and communism. His critics referred to him as "the greatest mind of the 14th century." ■ See study by Frank C. Waldrop (1966); Joseph Gies, *The Colonel of Chicago* (1979); and Richard N. Smith, *The Colonel* (1997).

MCCULLERS, CARSON (Carson Smith; 1917–1967), U.S. novelist. Although she spent her adult life in New York, McCullers set her five gothic novels in her native Georgia, exposing both poignant naiveté and terrifying brutality in her small-town characters. She wrote sensitively about loneliness, adolescence, and the plight of the eccentric. *The Heart is a Lonely Hunter* (1940), about a deaf mute's encounters with his fellow townspeople, won immediate recognition. Her other well-known works included *The Member of the Wedding* (1946; play, 1950) and the title story of the collection *The Ballad of the Sad Café* (1951). ■ See her unfinished autobiography, *Illumination and Night Glare* (1999); Oliver Evans, *The Ballad of Carson McCullers* (1965); Virginia S. Carr, *The Lonely Hunter* (1976); and study by Margaret B. McDowell (1980).

MCCULLOCH, WARREN STURGIS (1898–1969), U.S. neurophysiologist. A teacher and researcher at Yale (1934–52) and the Massachusetts Institute of Technology (MIT, 1952–69), McCulloch made significant contributions to psychiatry, experimental psychology, and the study of the brain. He was a pioneer in the field of cybernetics and information theory and wrote a paper (with Walter H. Pitts, 1943) that described the brain as a computer composed of an electrical network that manipulated information. *Embodiments of Mind* (1965) included his important papers.

MACDIARMID, ALAN G. (1927–   ), New Zealand–born U.S. chemist. MacDiarmid studied at the University of New Zealand, the University of Wisconsin, and Cambridge University and taught at the University of Pennsylvania (1955–   ). During the 1970s, in collaboration with University of Pennsylvania colleague Alan J. Heeger and Tsukuba (Japan) University professor Hideki Shirkawa, MacDiarmid helped to develop plastics that can conduct electricity like metals. These conductive polymers spurred research in both chemistry and physics that played a major role in the development of molecular electronics. They were soon put to practical use in computer screens, solar cells, photographic film, light-emitting diodes, and mobile telephone displays. For their contributions to science, MacDiarmid, Shirakawa, and Heeger shared the 2000 Nobel Prize in Chemistry.

MACDIARMID, HUGH (Christopher Murray Grieve; 1892–1978), Scottish poet. Educated to be a teacher, MacDiarmid became a journalist and writer. The major figure in the modern Scottish literary renaissance, he anthologized Scottish verse in the 1920s and published his own poetry, written in a combination of Scots dialect, English, and middle Scots. These works, including *Penny Wheep* (1926) and *A Drunk Man Looks at the Thistle* (1926), were praised for their imaginative use of dialects and folk ballads. A Marxist and, at times, a Communist party member, MacDiarmid championed Scottish nationalism and exposed the pretensions of modern society. His later poetry, written in more diluted Scots and then in English, included "poetry of pure fact," characterized by extravagant detail. ■ See his *Complete Poems: 1920–76* (2 vols., 1978) and *Selected Essays* (1969); his autobiographies, *Lucky Poet* (1943) and *The Company I've Kept* (1966); and study by Alan N. Bold (1984).

MACDONALD, DWIGHT (1906–1982), U.S. political, social, and film critic. A literary editor while a student at Yale (B.A. 1928), Macdonald became a follower of exiled Russian revolutionary Leon Trotsky while working as a staff writer for *Fortune* magazine (1929–36). He subsequently wrote penetrating political and social criticism for the influential socialist (but anti-Stalinist) journal *Partisan Review* (1938–43). An opponent of World War II, he published the antiwar journal *Politics* (1944–49), which printed the views of leading radical intellectuals from throughout the world. At this time his views veered toward anarchism, and he wrote several important essays criticizing mass culture as an antirevolutionary and antisocial force. Macdonald was a staff writer for the *New Yorker* (1951–71) and a perceptive film critic for *Esquire* (1960–66). He returned to the political battles during the 1960s as a vocal critic of the Vietnam War. His books included the essay collections *The Memoirs of a Revolutionist* (1957), *Against the American Grain* (1963), and *Discriminations: Essays and Afterthoughts: 1938–1974* (1974). ■ See Stephen J. Whitfield, *A Critical American* (1984), and Michael Wreszin, *A Rebel in Defense of Tradition* (1994).

MACDONALD, JEANETTE (1907–1965), U.S. singer and movie star. MacDonald made her debut (1920) in New York in the chorus of *The Demi-Tasse Revue* and sang in grand opera in *Romeo and Juliet* and *Faust*. But after 1925, she made films and is best remembered as the sweet soprano who sang romantic duets with Nelson Eddy in eight musical hits, including *Naughty Marietta* (1935), *Rose Marie* (1936), *The Girl of the Golden West* (1938), and *Sweethearts* (1938). ■ See biographies by James Parish (1976), Lee Edward Stern (1977), and Edward B. Turk (1998); and Philip Castanza, *The Films of Jeanette MacDonald and Nelson Eddy* (1978).

MACDONALD, (JAMES) RAMSAY (1866–1937), British prime minister. Born out of wedlock to a working-class woman, MacDonald acquired social status by marriage. First elected to Parliament in 1906, he attained power as head of the new Labour party (1911–14) that replaced the Liberals as Britain's second major party. He headed Britain's first two Labour governments (1924; 1929–31) and was denounced by many of his followers for remaining in office as head of the Depression-era National Coalition Cabinet (1931–35), when effective state power was wielded by Conservative Stanley Baldwin. His books included *Socialism and Society* (6th ed, 1908), *Parliament and Revolution* (1920), and *Socialism: Critical and Constructive* (1924). ■ See biographies by David Marquand (1977), Austen Morgan (1987), and Stephen R. Ward (1990).

MACDONALD, ROSS (Kenneth Millar; 1915–1983), U.S. novelist. Born in California to Canadian parents, Macdonald was raised in Ontario and graduated from the University of Western Ontario. A former college teacher and a wartime naval officer with a Ph.D. (1951), he lived (from the 1950s) in Southern California, a region whose crazy extremes he wrote about in his more than 20 popular and acclaimed detective novels. His hero was the middle-aged and sympathetic private detective Lew Archer. Macdonald used the mystery form to explore the effects of love, greed, and deeply buried hatreds. He developed these themes, often structured around the quest for the solution to a long-hidden murder or search for a missing child in such novels as *The Far Side of the Dollar* (1965), *The Goodbye Look* (1969), and *Sleeping Beauty* (1973). Other books included *The Underground Man* (1971) and his last novel, *The Blue Hammer* (1976). ▪ See studies by Matthew J. Bruccoli (1984) and Tom Nolan (1999).

MCDOUGALL, WILLIAM (1871–1938), British-born U.S. psychologist. McDougall received an M.D. (London, 1897) and was a specialist in physiology and neurology. He conducted some early Oxford experiments in psychology and wrote the influential *Introduction to Social Psychology* (1908). Critical of mechanistic behaviorism, he believed that humans are guided by instincts and cognition in seeking goals, a position known as purposive or "hormic" psychology. Moving to the United States in 1920, McDougall wrote a book on Nordic superiority (1921) while teaching at Harvard (1920–27). At Duke University after 1927 he conducted research into parapsychology, including clairvoyance and telepathy, and attempted to demonstrate that acquired behavior characteristics could be inherited. His other books included *Outline of Psychology* (1923), *Outline of Abnormal Psychology* (1926), and *Modern Materialism and Emergent Evolution* (1929).

MACFADDEN, BERNARR (Bernard Adolphus McFadden; 1868–1955), U.S. physical culturist and publisher. A messianic advocate of the natural approach to health and the cult of the body, MacFadden founded *Physical Culture* magazine (1899), which achieved great nationwide popularity by stressing the value of health foods, periodic fasting, vegetarianism, exercise, natural cures, and walking barefoot—while attacking traditional medical care and drugs. He wrote more than 100 short books and a five-volume encyclopedia on the subject of natural health, and he established physical culture sanitariums and health-food restaurants throughout the country. His *True Story* magazine, founded in 1919, featured true-to-life melodramatic stories and helped to bring the sexual revolution to the masses. His other widely read pulp magazines included *True Romances* (1923), *True Detective Mystery Magazine* (1925), and *Master Detective* (1929). The flamboyant MacFadden also published the lurid New York daily tabloid, *Evening Graphic* (1924–30), *Liberty* magazine (1931–42), and newspapers in several cities that reached an estimated annual circulation of 35 to 40 million. ▪ See Mary MacFadden and Emile Gauvreau, *Dumbbells and Carrot Strips* (1953); William R. Hunt, *Body Love* (1989); and Robert Ernst, *Weakness Is a Crime* (1991).

MCFADDEN, DANIEL L. (1937–), U.S. economist. McFadden studied at the University of Minnesota (Ph.D. 1962) and taught at the University of California, Berkeley (1963–79; 1990–) and the Massachusetts Institute of Technology (1978–90). His development of theory and methods for analyzing discrete choice transformed empirical research in microeconomics. For his innovations he shared the 2000 Nobel Memorial Prize in Economics with James J. Heckman.

MCGILL, RALPH EMERSON (1898–1969), U.S. journalist and publisher. A champion of civil rights who was called "the conscience of the south," McGill was the editor (from 1942) and publisher (from 1960) of the *Atlanta Constitution,* the paper he joined as sports editor in 1929. He supported school desegregation, attacked all forms of injustice in his daily columns, and won a 1959 Pulitzer Prize for his editorial condemning the bombing of a synagogue in Atlanta and a high school in Tennessee. His award-winning *The South and the Southerners* (1963) is semiautobiographical. ▪ See biographies by Harold H. Martin (1973) and Barbara Clowse (1998).

MCGOVERN, GEORGE STANLEY (1922–), U.S. senator. Torn between following an academic career or becoming a minister, McGovern, who was deeply involved with social issues during the post–World War II period, became first a political organizer and then a Democratic congressman (1957–61) from his native state of South Dakota. He was later elected (1962) to the U.S. Senate. He won the Democratic party's nomination for president in 1972 against several other contenders as a strong critic of U.S. involvement in Vietnam. He pledged that if elected he would remove all U.S. troops from Southeast Asia. He was, however, overwhelmingly defeated by Pres. Richard Nixon in that election. McGovern lost his Senate seat in the 1980 elections and he unsuccessfully sought the 1984 Democratic presidential nomination. ▪ See his autobiography, *Grassroots* (1977), and biography by Robert S. Anson (1972).

MCGWIRE, MARK DAVID (1963–), U.S. baseball player. The son of a dentist, McGwire grew up in the suburbs of Los Angeles and began playing Little League baseball at the age of 8. He was a power hitter at the University of Southern California (1982–84) before becoming a minor-league player in the Oakland Athletics system (1984). In his first full season with the As (1987) he hit 49 home runs, a record for a rookie, and was named Rookie of the Year. He led the As to three consecutive pennants (1988–90) and a 1989 World Series victory before suffering serious injuries in the early 1990s. He recovered, continued to hit towering home runs, and set a season record (1995) for hitting one home run per 8 at bats, breaking the mark of one per 8.5 set by Babe Ruth (in 1920). After hitting 52 homers in 1996, the 6-foot 5-inch, 250-pound slugger was traded in midseason in 1997 to the St. Louis Cardinals and finished the year with 58 homers. He set a torrid home-run hitting pace during the 1998 season and hit his 50th homer in August, becoming the first player to hit 50 in three consecutive seasons. Involved in a slugging contest with Sammy Sosa of the Chicago Cubs, in which both players broke Roger Maris's 37-year-old record of 61 homers in one season, McGwire set a new major-league record by hitting 70 home runs, narrowly beating out Sosa, who ended the 1998 season with 66 homers. McGwire led the majors again during the 1999 season with 65 homers.

MACHADO Y MORALES, GERARDO (1871–1939), Cuban dictator. The son of a cattle rancher and a hero of the Cuban war for independence (1895–98), Machado became wealthy and powerful during his dual career as a businessman and politician. Elected president of Cuba in 1924 on a platform of "water, roads, and schools," he brought the island into increasing dependence on the United States and achieved reelection in 1928 by repressing the opposition. He countered opposition violence with a virtual reign of terror (1931–33). After a 1933 general strike and the threat of an armed revolt, Machado went into exile in Miami Beach.

MACHADO Y RUIZ, ANTONIO (1875–1939), Spanish poet. The first edition of Machado's collected poems, *Poesías Completas* (1917), established him as one of Spain's greatest poets. He taught French literature and lived and studied in Paris; he figured among the Spanish "Generation of 1898." His spare, melancholy verse longs for lost innocence and romantic love. Rooted in early Spanish literature, his poems attempt to re-create medieval Spanish romances in a modern idiom. He wrote several plays with his brother Manuel Machado (1874–1947), known in literary history as "the bad Machado." Antonio Machado sided with the republic in the Spanish Civil War (1936–39) and fled on foot to France. He died under unknown circumstances three weeks later. Translations of his work are in *Juan de Mairena: Epigrams, Maxims, Memoranda, and Memoirs of an Apocryphal Professor* (1936; Eng. trans. 1963), *Eighty Poems of Antonio Machado* (1959), *Selected Poems* (1982), *The Dream Below the Sun* (1981), and *Times Alone* (1983). ■ See study by Carl W. Cobb (1971).

MACHEL, SAMORA MOISES (1933–1986), Mozambican political leader. A former male nurse, Machel joined the Mozambique Liberation Front (FRELIMO) in 1963, underwent guerrilla training in Algeria, and in 1964 commanded the troops that launched the war for national liberation from the Portuguese. Elected president of FRELIMO in 1970, he became the first president of the People's Republic of Mozambique, a Marxist, one-party state, when the Portuguese withdrew in 1975. Although he tried to rapidly transform the country along socialist lines, economic reversals and political and military pressure from South Africa forced him to moderate his policies. Collective farms were dismantled in 1983 and private enterprise and Western for-

eign investment were encouraged. In 1984 he signed a nonaggression treaty with South Africa, which in turn withdrew its support for guerrillas fighting against the Mozambican government. However, the pact was never fully implemented and the civil war continued through the mid-1980s. He died in a plane crash in South Africa. ■ See biography by Iain Christie (1989).

MACHLUP, FRITZ (1902–1983), Austrian-born U.S. economist. Machlup studied economics under Ludwig Von Mises at the University of Vienna, earned a Ph.D. at age 21, and launched a successful career in industry. He left Germany when Nazi leader Adolf Hitler came to power, emigrating to the United States (1933; U.S. citizen 1940). He taught at several universities, including Johns Hopkins (1947–60), Princeton (1960–71), and New York University (1971–83). The author of more than 25 books (and coauthor of 11 others), Machlup contributed to many branches of economics, notably international trade and the international monetary system. He criticized government intervention in a private-enterprise economy and was concerned with safeguarding individual liberties. Machlup pioneered in a field he called "the economics of knowledge," completing three volumes of a major work, *Knowledge: Its Creation, Distribution, and Economic Significance* (1980–84).

MACIVER, ROBERT MORRISON (1882–1970), Scottish-born U.S. sociologist and political theorist. MacIver was educated in the classics at Edinburgh and Oxford universities before he taught sociology at Columbia University (1929–50). A noted humanist who insisted on the importance of theory in the social sciences, he was particularly interested in the evolution from primitive community to modern state and in the relationship of the individual to society. He immersed himself in a broad range of social issues, including labor relations, juvenile delinquency, and academic freedom. He also served as president and chancellor of the New School for Social Research (1963–66). His books included *Community* (1917), *The Modern State* (1926), *The Web of Government* (1947), *Academic Freedom in Our Time* (1955), and *The Prevention and Control of Delinquency* (1966). ■ See his autobiography, *As a Tale That is Told* (1968).

MACK, CONNIE (Cornelius Alexander McGillicuddy; 1862–1956), U.S. baseball player and manager. Involved in organized baseball for seven decades, Mack managed the Philadelphia Athletics from 1901 through 1950 and was one of the pioneers of the American League. Under his guidance the Athletics won nine pennants and five World Series. During his career his teams won 3,776 games and lost 4,025, both major-league records. ■ See his autobiography, *My Sixty-six Years in the Big Leagues* (1950).

MACKAY, CLARENCE HUNGERFORD (1874–1938), U.S. businessman. The son of John William Mackay, a Nevada mining millionaire and founder of the Postal Telegraph and Cable Corp., Clarence Mackay supervised the completion of the laying of the first transpacific cable (1903) and also laid the first cables to Cuba (1907) and the Azores and Ireland (1923). He merged his interests (1928) with the International Telephone and Telegraph Corp. (IT&T) and thus became the first to combine cable, telegraph, and radio in one company. Mackay was a leader of New York society, a prominent sportsman and patron of the arts, and chairman of the New York Philharmonic Society and director of the Metropolitan Opera.

MCKAY, CLAUDE (1889–1948), U.S. poet and novelist. McKay's first published poems used the dialect of his native Jamaica. He left home for the United States, where he first studied agriculture (1912–14) and later worked as a laborer. He moved to New York City, where his poems were published in leading left-wing literary magazines. His powerful sonnet "If We Must Die" (1919), a protest against racial intolerance, and *Harlem Shadows* (1922), a militant poetry collection, set the tone for the Harlem renaissance. An inveterate traveler and radical political activist, he lived in the Soviet Union, Germany, Holland, France, Spain, and Morocco from 1922 to 1934. During this time he published his three popular novels, *Home to Harlem* (1928), *Banjo* (1929), and *Banana Bottom* (1933), which emphasized the vitality and "primitive" aspects of black lower-class life. After returning to the United States (1934) he became disillusioned with communism and criticized integrationist schemes but continued to champion civil rights and racial solidarity. He became a U.S. citizen (1940) and converted to Roman Catholicism (1944). ■ See *Selected Poems* (1953); his autobiography, *A Long Way From Home* (1937); Wayne Cooper, *The Passion of Claude McKay* (1973); and biography by Tyrone Tillery (1992).

MCKAY, DAVID OMAN (1873–1970), U.S. religious leader. An 1897 graduate of the University of Utah, McKay was the spiritual leader and president of the Church of Jesus Christ of Latter-day Saints (Mormons) from 1951 until his death. In 1934 he was named second counselor in the church's highest executive body; in his early 30s, he was appointed (1906) to the Council of Twelve Apostles, the governing body of the Mormon church. During his two decades as church president, Mormon relations with other Christian faiths improved substantially, and the church expanded into a worldwide organization.

MACKE, AUGUST (1887–1914), German painter. Macke was a founder-member of the expressionist Blue Rider movement (noted for pure abstraction and romantic imagery). He was first influenced by impressionism, then discovered cubism in 1911 and became interested in Robert Delaunay's bold treatment of color. Macke frequently painted strollers and window-shoppers, relaxed yet elegant in posture. Combining the warmth and sensuality of French painting with the cosmic sense of German art, Macke was

one of the few painters in his circle whose work did not take on the anguish and political overtones of pre–World War I Europe. Shortly before his death in the war, he traveled through Tunisia and completed a series of vivid watercolors that are believed to have influenced his traveling companion, Paul Klee. ■ See Klaus Lankheit, ed., *The "Blaue Reiter" Almanac* (Eng. trans. 1974).

MACKENZIE, SIR (EDWARD MONTAGUE) COMPTON (1883–1972), Scottish writer. The son and grandson of actors, MacKenzie wrote his first play shortly after earning a history degree from Oxford (1904). Best known for his atmospheric early novels, *Carnival* (1912) and *Sinister Street* (2 vols., 1913–14), and his comic later ones, *Whisky Galore* (1947) and *The Monarch of the Glen* (1941), he wrote more than 100 volumes, including poetry, plays, biographies, literary criticism, and political commentary. He was the founder and editor (1923–62) of *Gramophone* magazine. An exponent of Scottish nationalism and president of the Siamese Cat Club of Great Britain, MacKenzie became a familiar television personality. ■ See his 10-volume memoir, *My Life and Times* (1963–71), and biography by Andro Linklater (1987).

MCKIM, CHARLES FOLLEN (1847–1909), U.S. architect. The son of a prominent abolitionist, McKim studied at the École des Beaux Arts in Paris and became the senior partner of the leading U.S. architectural firm of his day, McKim, Mead and Bigelow (after 1879, McKim, Mead and White). His lucid geometry and severe classical styling moved architecture away from the romanticism that prevailed at the turn of the century. He designed New York's Pennsylvania Station (1902–10), worked on the Senate Park Commission's plans for redesigning Washington, D.C., and in 1907 helped draft guidelines for the preservation of Niagara Falls. ■ See studies by Alfred H. Granger (1913), Charles Moore (1929), F. P. Hill (1950), and Leland M. Roth (1983).

MACKINDER, SIR HALFORD JOHN (1861–1947), British political geographer. An exponent of what he called the "new geography," a discipline that bridged the gap between the natural sciences and the humanities, Mackinder taught at Oxford (1887–99, and was director of the School of Geography, 1899–1904) and the London School of Economics (director, 1904–08; reader in economic geography, 1908–23). He served in Parliament from 1910 to 1922. Mackinder was best known for his theory (1904) that the Eurasian "heartland" (Eastern Europe and interior Asia) had gained ascendance over the coastland or "maritime lands" and had become the "pivot" of history. His ideas were adapted by German geopoliticians before and during World War II. In *Democratic Ideals and Reality* (1919), he wrote that Britain and the United States should preserve a balance between those forces seeking control of the heartland. He later (1924) advocated the formation of an Atlantic community of North America and Western Europe to offset the power of the heartland. His other books included *Britain and the British Seas* (1902) and *The Nations of the Modern World* (1911). ■ See studies by William Henry Parker (1982) and Brian W. Blouet (1987).

MCKISSICK, FLOYD BIXLER (1922–1991), U.S. attorney and civil-rights activist. The first African-American student to graduate from the University of North Carolina Law School (Ll.B. 1951), McKissick went into practice in 1952 and successfully pleaded suits to get his children into all-white schools. As legal counsel for the Congress of Racial Equality (CORE; 1960–63) he defended Freedom Riders and worked on public-accommodation test cases. McKissick served as national chairman (1963–66) and director (1966–68) of CORE, espousing increasingly militant and black separatist positions. He subsequently became the developer of the town of Soul City, North Carolina, an unsuccessful attempt to create a community controlled by blacks. ■ See his *Three-Fifths of a Man* (1969).

MCKUEN, ROD (1933–   ), U.S. performer-poet and composer. McKuen launched his career as a California disc jockey, dispensing lyrical advice to "Rendezvous with Rod" listeners. After being drafted for the Korean War, he published the first of his fast-selling slim volumes, *And Autumn Came* (1954). He wrote and performed more than 1,000 songs and composed classical works and film and television scores. McKuen also had a brief, undistinguished Hollywood acting career. His volumes of poetry, including *Listening to the Warm* (1967) and *Lonesome Cities* (1968), sold more than 2 million hardcover copies. Later volumes included *Celebrations of the Heart* (1978), *Suspension Bridge* (1984), and *Intervals* (1986). His collected writings (1950–82) appeared in 1982.

MACLAINE, SHIRLEY (Shirley Beatty; 1934–   ), U.S. actress, dancer, and writer. MacLaine began studying ballet before her third birthday and made her Broadway debut in the chorus of the Rodgers and Hammerstein musical *Me and Juliet* (1953). Producer Hal B. Wallis spotted her and gave her a start in film. She made dozens of movies, including *Can-Can* (1959), *The Apartment* (1959), *The Children's Hour* (1961), *Irma La Douce* (1963), *Sweet Charity* (1968), *The Turning Point* (1977), *Being There* (1979), *Madame Sousatzka* (1988), *Steel Magnolias* (1989), and *Postcards from the Edge* (1990), and won an Academy Award for her performance in *Terms of Endearment* (1983). A political activist, MacLaine took part in the Vietnam War protest movement and campaigned for Democratic candidates Robert Kennedy (1968) and George McGovern (1972). The one-woman show she created at age 50, *Shirley MacLaine on Broadway* (1984), drew record audiences. Her books included *Out on a Limb* (1983), *Dancing in the Light* (1985), and *Many Happy Returns* (1986), accounts of her spiritual growth and discovery. Her brother is the actor and director Warren Beatty. ■ See her memoirs, *It's All in the Playing* (1987), *Dance While You Can* (1991), and *My Lucky Stars* (1995); and James Spada, *Shirley and Warren* (1985).

MCLAREN, NORMAN (1914–1987), Scottish-born Canadian animator. McLaren created his first animated film, *Camera Makes Whoopee*, at age 21. He was an innovator, experimenting with abstract designs, working directly on celluloid, ignoring frame boundaries, and experimenting with music. His films included *Neighbors* (Academy Award, 1952), *Blinkety Blank* (1954), *Rhythmetic* (1955), *Short and Suite* (1959), *Pas de Deux* (1968), and *Animated Motion* (1977–78). He became director of animated films for the National Film Board of Canada in 1943 and remained there for over four decades. He also worked in China and India on assignment for the United Nations Educational, Scientific, and Cultural Organization. ■ See study by Maynard Collins (1976).

MACLEAN, DONALD (1913–1983), British diplomat and Soviet spy. Son of a Liberal cabinet minister, Maclean studied at Cambridge (1931–35), where he met Guy Burgess, Kim Philby, and Anthony Blunt. The four, who shared anticapitalist and antifascist views, joined a secret communist cell and were recruited by Soviet intelligence. MacLean entered the foreign office (1935), served as first secretary of the British embassy in Washington, D.C. (1944–48), where he helped coordinate Allied atomic energy development, and directed the U.S. desk of the British foreign office in London (1951). His disappearance with Burgess (1951), a member of British intelligence who had also served at the embassy in Washington (1950–51), constituted a severe breach in British security. Their whereabouts were unknown until they surfaced in Moscow in 1956. Philby, who worked for British intelligence (from 1940) and was the first secretary of the Washington embassy (1949–51), defected to the Soviet Union in 1963. Blunt, who had supplied secrets to the Soviets while working for British intelligence during World War II and had subsequently become a prominent and knighted art historian, was publicly revealed as the "fourth man" in the spy ring in 1979. ■ See Andrew Boyle, *The Fourth Man* (1979) and Douglas Sutherland, *The Great Betrayal* (1981).

MACLEISH, ARCHIBALD (1892–1982), U.S. poet and public official. MacLeish practiced law (1920–23), then went to Paris to write. His early poetry, heavily influenced by Ezra Pound and T. S. Eliot, presented a bleak view of the individual's importance in the chaotic post–World War I era, Focusing on the American situation in the 1930s, he championed democracy in both his public addresses and in such works as *Conquistador* (1932, Pulitzer Prize). MacLeish urged intellectuals to aid the Loyalist cause in Spain (1937), and he stressed the artist's social responsibility in *A Time to Speak: Selected Prose* (1941), *A Time to Act: Selected Addresses* (1943), *Collected Poems, 1917–1952* (1952, Pulitzer

Prize), and *J. B.* (1958, Pulitzer Prize), a verse drama based on the book of Job. MacLeish served as librarian of Congress (1939–44), assistant secretary of state for cultural affairs (1944–45), and professor of rhetoric and oratory at Harvard (1949–62). *New and Collected Poems, 1917–1976* appeared in 1976. ■ See studies by Signi L. Falk (1965) and Scott Donaldson (1992).

MACLENNAN, HUGH (1907–1990), Canadian novelist. Trained at Oxford and Princeton, MacLennan was a noted classics scholar and professor at McGill University (1951–79). His novels examined Canadian national identity. *Barometer Rising* (1941), his most successful fusion of theme and narration, re-created the calamitous ship explosion in Halifax in 1917. *Two Solitudes* (1945) considered Anglo-French relations in Montreal, and *The Precipice* (1948) contrasted Canadians and Americans. He became increasingly didactic in *The Watch That Ends the Night* (1959) and *Return of the Sphinx* (1967). *Voices in Time* (1980) was set in 2030 A.D. after a global war had destroyed civilization. MacLennan used internal monologue and cinematic techniques in his fiction and focused on the special problems of the Canadian novelist who is at a loss for stereotypic characters. ■ See his selected essays in *The Other Side of Hugh MacLennan* (1978) and studies by Elspeth Cameron (1981) and T. D. MacLulich (1983).

MACLEOD, JOHN JAMES RICKARD (1876–1935), British physiologist. Educated at the universities of Aberdeen, Leipzig, and Cambridge, MacLeod was professor of physiology at Western Reserve University in Cleveland (1903–18) and at the University of Toronto (1918–28). His research on the nature of carbohydrate metabolism in animals laid the foundation for his later discovery of insulin (with Sir Fredrick Grant Banting and Charles H. Best). For this achievement he shared with Banting the 1923 Nobel Prize for Physiology or Medicine. His books included *Diabetes* (1913) and *Carbohydrate Metabolism and Insulin* (1926). ■ See Michael Bliss, *The Discovery of Insulin* (1982).

MCLUHAN, (HERBERT) MARSHALL (1911–1980), Canadian communications theorist. Trained in English literature at the University of Manitoba (M.A. 1934) and Cambridge University (Ph.D. 1942), McLuhan was a scholar of impressive erudition. He taught at St. Louis University (1937–44) and thereafter at the University of Toronto. Concerned with the impact of media on culture, he described the ascendance of movable type in *The Gutenberg Galaxy* (1962) and its replacement by television in *Understanding Media* (1964). He argued that while the print culture locked each individual into his own consciousness, the electronic media had the opposite effect of creating a "global village." To make ideas more accessible, he published a book of aphorisms, *The Medium is the Message* (1967; with Quentin

Fiore). McLuhan's life was, inevitably, the subject of a television documentary (written by Tom Wolfe; 1985). ■ See studies by Jonathan Miller (1971), Gordon W. Terrence (1997), and Phillip Marchand (1998).

MCMANUS, GEORGE (1884–1954), U.S. cartoonist. The familiar phrase "Let George Do It" comes from a comic strip drawn by McManus during his long stint with Joseph Pulitzer's *World,* where the first of his many family comic strips, *The Newlyweds,* appeared (1904). It was only after nearly a decade of experimentation and a move (1912) to the Hearst-owned *New York American,* however, that McManus created the comic strip that won him fame around the world: *Bringing Up Father* (1913). Suggested by William Gill's play *The Rising Generation* (1893), it characterized all corners of society in episodes starring the working-class Jiggs and Maggie, who have to cope with their newly acquired wealth. *Bringing Up Father* inspired books in many languages, film and radio adaptations, and plays; in the 1920s McManus personally played Jiggs in several productions of *Father.* He wrote *Fun for All* (1948).

MCMASTER, JOHN BACH (1852–1932), U.S. historian. Born in Brooklyn, the son of a former Mississippi planter. McMaster was deeply interested in the Civil War. He earned an engineering degree in 1873, published a book on masonry dams, and taught civil engineering at Princeton, all the while reading deeply in American history. His magnum opus was *A History of the People of the United States* (8 vols., 1883–1913), in which he was one of the first historians to emphasize socioeconomic factors, stress the role of the American west, and utilize newspapers as sources of information. After his retirement from the University of Pennsylvania, where he taught history from 1883 to 1920, he wrote *A History of the People of the United States During Lincoln's Administration* (1927). ■ See biography by Eric Goldman (1943).

MCMILLAN, EDWIN MATTISON (1907–1991), U.S. physicist. Associated with the Lawrence Radiation Laboratory at the University of California at Berkeley (1934–73; director, 1958–73), McMillan discovered (1939) and isolated, in collaboration with Philip H. Abelson, element 93—neptunium. This research led to the discovery (1940) of plutonium, element 94, by a team of physicists headed by Glenn Seaborg. Plutonium became a crucial ingredient of atomic weapons and nuclear-energy plants, and McMillan and Seaborg shared the 1951 Nobel Prize for Chemistry. During World War II McMillan worked on radar, sonar, and the development of the first atomic bombs. In 1945, independent of Soviet physicist Vladimir I. Veksler, he conceived the synchrotron, a high-energy accelerator that was an improvement over the cyclotron. It enabled physicists to discover antimatter and new particles and made possible revolutionary advances in the study of the structure of matter.

MACMILLAN, (MAURICE) HAROLD, EARL OF STOCKTON (1894–1986), British political leader. A grandson of the founder of the Macmillan publishing company, Macmillan graduated from Eton and Oxford and served in Parliament as an independent Conservative (1924–29; 1931–64). He advocated a neo-Keynesian approach to the Depression, opposed appeasement policies toward Nazi Germany during the 1930s, and joined Winston Churchill's coalition government in 1940. During World War II he was a special representative of the cabinet with Allied forces in the Mediterranean. He served in several important cabinet posts in the 1950s. During his tenure as prime minister (1957–63), he advocated granting independence to British colonies in Africa, helped negotiate the Nuclear Test Ban Treaty, and made Britain's first bid to join the Common Market. He resigned (because of ill health) in the wake of the scandal centering on John Profumo, secretary for war, who had associated with a call girl also involved with a Soviet official. He subsequently served as chairman (1963–74) and president (from 1974) of the Macmillan publishing house and was made an earl in 1984. He wrote six volumes of memoirs (1966–73) as well as *The Past Masters: Politics and Politicians, 1906–1939* (1975) and World War II *War Diaries* (1984). ■ See biographies by Anthony Sampson (1967), Nigel Fisher (1982), and Alistair Horne (2 vols., 1988–89).

MACMILLAN, SIR KENNETH (1929–1992), British choreographer. Born into a poor family, MacMillan was inspired to become a dancer by watching the films of Fred Astaire and Ginger Rogers. He studied at London's Sadler's Wells Ballet School (1945) and joined the newly founded Sadler's Wells (later Royal) Ballet in 1946. He choreographed his first work in 1955 and subsequently created more than 40 intense and expressive classical ballets that were performed by dance companies throughout the world. He directed Berlin's Deutsche Oper Ballet (1966–70) and London's Royal Ballet (1970–77; principal choreographer, 1977–92) and served as associate artistic director of New York's American Ballet Theater (1984–90). Among his best-known works were *Romeo and Juliet* (1965), *Song of the Earth* (1965), *Sleeping Beauty* (1967), *Manon* (1972), *La Fin du Jour* (1979), *Gloria* (1980), and *Winter Dreams* (1991).

MCNAMARA, ROBERT STRANGE (1916–), U.S. business and public official. After teaching at the Harvard Business School, where he developed management systems for the air force, McNamara went to the Ford Motor Co., where he rose from "whiz kid" (1946) to president (1960). In 1961 he became Pres. John F. Kennedy's secretary of defense, asserting civilian control and efficiency over the business of war. Retained in that post by Pres. Lyndon B. Johnson, McNamara increased the nation's tactical military forces and was a leading proponent of U.S. involvement in Vietnam. He later took on the problems of international underdevelopment and poverty as head of the World Bank (1968–81). In his book *In Retrospect: The Tragedy and Lessons of Vietnam* (1995), he stated that he and other U.S. officials had been "wrong, terribly wrong" about the war and that the U.S. should have withdrawn in the early 1960s. His other books included *The Essence of Security* (1968), *Blundering into Disaster* (1986), and *Out of the Cold* (1989). ■ See Paul Hendrickson, *The Living and the Dead* (1996).

MCNAMEE, GRAHAM (1888–1942), U.S. radio announcer. McNamee gave up a sagging concert-singing career to become a radio announcer (1923). Assigned to cover sports events, he delivered vivid rapid-fire narratives that won him immense popularity and made him the nation's premier sportscaster. As he branched out to cover major news stories, he established a reputation for accurate, fast-moving, dramatic accounts as he transformed extemporaneous radio reportage into an art form. Widely recognized as the dean of radio announcers, he was frequently imitated. ■ See his memoirs, *You're on the Air* (1926; with Robert Anderson).

MACNEICE, LOUIS (1907–1963), Anglo-Irish poet. MacNeice was educated in the classics at Oxford and worked as a university lecturer and as a scriptwriter for the British Broadcasting Corporation. In the 1930s he was associated with the group of poets led by W. H. Auden and Stephen Spender, but he was less politically or socially concerned in his poetry than they. He believed that "the poet is only an extension . . . of the ordinary man," and he infused his vivid, humanistic poetry with concern for the traditional problems of life. *Collected Poems, 1925–1948* (1949) and *Solstices* (1961) are personal, wry, and seemingly spontaneous, though written with great skill and control. ■ See his *The Strings Are False: An Unfinished Autobiography* (1966), study by Elton Smith (1970), and William T. McKinnon, *Apollo's Blended Dream* (1971).

MCNEILL, BRIAN (1950–), Scottish musician, folksinger, and songwriter. A native of Falkirk, McNeill was part of the Edinburgh folk scene during the 1970s and was cofounder (1972) and guiding spirit of the Battlefield Band, which became one of the most innovative and popular Scottish folk ensembles. A superb fiddler and masterful songwriter, he pursued a solo career after leaving the band (1990) and recorded several notable CDs that included songs relating to Scotland's heritage as well as to contemporary issues. Some of his best works are in the CDs *The Back o' the North Wind* (1991), which contains songs about Scottish émigrés, and *No Gods* (1995), whose title song powerfully debunks myths of Scottish history. McNeill also wrote the novels *The Busker* (1989) and *To Answer the Peacock* (1999).

MCNEILL, WILLIAM HARDY (1917–), U.S. historian. McNeill, the son of a church historian, was educated at the University of Chicago (B.A. 1938; M.A. 1939). After military service in the Caribbean and Greece during World War II, he studied at Cornell (Ph.D. 1947) and subsequently taught at the University of Chicago (1947–82). He is best known for *The Rise of the West* (1963), a one-volume world history in which he emphasized that contacts between civilizations, whether peaceful or warlike, are the driving force of historical change. This diffusionist view of history is also reflected in *Europe's Steppe Frontier* (1964), *A World History* (1967), and *The Pursuit of Power* (1982). His other important works included *Plagues and Peoples* (1976), a study of the impact of epidemics on civilizations; *The Human Condition: An Ecological and Historical View* (1980); and several books on modern Greek history, notably, *The Metamorphosis of Greece Since World War II* (1978). He also wrote a biography of one of his mentors, Arnold J. Toynbee (1989).

MACON, UNCLE DAVE (David Harrison Macon; 1870–1952), U.S. country musician and entertainer. Macon worked a small farm and founded the Macon Midway Mule and Wagon Transportation Co. before beginning a musical career at age 50. This banjo-playing, stomping Nashville man became the most popular performer during the first 15 years of the Grand Ole Opry. Beginning in the late 1920s, his radio broadcasts attracted large audiences, but his rapport with live audiences—his miming and trick playing—remained the key to his popularity. Macon made nearly 200 commercial recordings, including the humorous "Keep My Skillet Good and Greasy," "Chewing Gum," and "Hungry Hash House." His early song "Hill Billie Blues" was the source for the term that came to stand for early country music.

MCPHERSON, AIMEE SEMPLE (Aimee Elizabeth Kennedy; 1890–1944), U.S. evangelist. McPherson went to China as a missionary with her first husband and left her second husband to go on the road as an evangelist and faith healer. She founded the Four-Square Gospel movement in Los Angeles (1918), using costume, music, lighting, and other theatrical effects at her Angelus Temple (opened 1923) to attract the thousands of followers who knew her as Sister Aimee. At its peak, the empire she created encompassed $1.5 million in assets, a radio station (est. 1924), and 400 branch churches. After she disappeared for five weeks in 1926 (she claimed she had been kidnapped), she and her mother were indicted for fraud. The charges were eventually dropped for lack of evidence. McPherson died of an overdose of sleeping pills. Her son Rolf McPherson (1913–) carried on her work, and the movement claimed nearly 90,000 adherents in the 1980s. ■ See her *This Is That* (1919; repr. 1985) and *The Story of My Life* (1951); Robert V. P. Steele, *Storming Heaven* (1970); Robert Bahr, *Least of All Saints* (1979); Daniel Epstein, *Sister Aimee* (1993); and biography by Edith Blumhofer (1993).

MCREYNOLDS, JAMES CLARK (1862–1946), U.S. jurist. A professor of law at Vanderbilt University (1900–03),

McReynolds served as assistant U.S. attorney general (1903–07) and gained a reputation as a vigorous trustbuster. He continued to prosecute violators of the Sherman Antitrust Act as attorney general in Pres. Woodrow Wilson's cabinet (1913–14); he was appointed to the Supreme Court in 1914. A legal conservative, he believed in a strict and literal interpretation of the Constitution, upheld laissez-faire economics, supported states rights, and opposed the growth of governmental power. He was a bitter opponent of Pres. Franklin D. Roosevelt and his policies and opposed almost all of the New Deal legislation, including social-security measures and the Tennessee Valley Authority. Although he wrote very few opinions, he recorded a record number of 310 dissents during his 26-year career. He retired in 1941.

MCWILLIAMS, CAREY (1905–1980), U.S. editor. The son of a Colorado cattle rancher, McWilliams became a labor and civil-liberties lawyer, writing on the side about the issues he encountered in his California practice (1927–38). A crusader for civil rights and the rights of minorities, he wrote more than 20 books, including *Factories in the Field* (1939), a classic account of the plight of migratory labor during the Depression; *Prejudice* (1944), a study of discrimination against Japanese-Americans; and *Anti-Semitism in America* (1948). McWilliams served as California's commissioner of immigration and housing (1938–42). Associated with the liberal magazine the *Nation* for 35 years, he was its editor from 1955 to 1975. ■ See his autobiography, *The Education of Carey McWilliams* (1979).

MADARIAGA, SALVADOR DE (1886–1978), Spanish writer and diplomat. Salvador de Madariaga headed the disarmament section of the League of Nations (1922–27), taught Spanish studies at Oxford (1928–31), and served republican Spain as ambassador to Washington (1931) and Paris (1932–34). He was also Spain's delegate to the League of Nations (1931–36). When dictator Francisco Franco gained power, Madariaga went into exile in Britain (1936). Although he was not active in the Spanish Civil War, he became a leader of the anti-Franco opposition in exile in the 1950s and 1960s. While in exile, he wrote prolifically in Spanish, French, and English, publishing numerous volumes of fiction, drama, essays, poetry, psychology, and history. An authority on the Spanish empire, he wrote such books as *Christopher Columbus* (1939), *The Rise of the Spanish-American Empire* (1945; Eng. trans. 1947), and *The Fall of the Spanish-American Empire* (1945; Eng. trans. 1947). *Victors, Beware* (1946) set forth his liberal, humanist philosophy. Madariaga returned to Spain (1976) after Franco's death. ■ See his memoirs, *Morning Without Noon* (Eng. trans. 1974).

MADERO, FRANCISCO INDALECIO (1873–1913), Mexican revolutionary leader. The son of a wealthy landowner, Madero ran for president (1910) on a reformist, antireelection platform against longtime dictator Porfirio Diaz. Arrested on the eve of the election, he escaped and issued a call for armed revolt. The Diaz regime quickly collapsed, and Madero was elected president (1911). His administrative inexperience and the pent-up pressures of the Diaz years, however, made his presidency brief and chaotic. In February 1913, his army commander, Victoriano Huerta, overthrew him, and he was assassinated by his army escort on the way to prison. In death, as a martyr, Madero proved more useful to Mexican democracy than he had been as an indecisive leader while alive. ▪ See biography by Stanley R. Ross (1955).

MADONNA (Madonna Louise Veronica Ciccone; 1958–   ), U.S. singer, songwriter, and actress. Madonna abandoned her dance studies at the University of Michigan to move to New York City, where she danced briefly with the Alvin Ailey Dance Theater's third company, worked as an artist's and photographer's model, and sang with several disco bands. Her debut album, *Madonna* (1983), was a hit, and her recordings of "Like a Virgin" (1984) and "Material Girl" (1984), accompanied by provocative music videos, launched her into superstardom. Her subsequent hits, "Papa Don't Preach" (1986), "Justify My Love" (1990), and "Vogue" (1990); her elaborate live performances around the world; and her shrewd manipulation of glamour and sexuality made her one of the world's most widely known and influential performers. Her book *Sex* (1992), a collection of erotic photographs and musings, was released in conjunction with her album *Erotica*. She changed direction, however, with *Ray of Light* (1998), an album dealing with spiritual themes. Madonna appeared in the documentary *Truth or Dare* (1991) and starred in the films *Desperately Seeking Susan* (1986), *Dick Tracy* (1990), and *Evita* (1996).

MAETERLINCK, MAURICE (1862–1949), Belgian poet and dramatist. Born into a French-speaking upper-middle-class family in Ghent, Maeterlinck gave up a law practice, moved to Paris, and concentrated on writing the symbolist poems and plays that established his international reputation. His mysterious, dreamlike, and mystical works reflected the ennui and fatalism of the pre–World War I period. He is best known for the poetry collection *Hot Houses* (1889; Eng. trans. 1915) and the plays *Pelléas et Mélisande* (1892: Eng. trans. 1895; set to music by Debussy, 1902) and *The Blue Bird* (1908; Eng. trans. 1909). After winning the 1911 Nobel Prize for Literature, he wrote a patriotic anti-German wartime play, *The Burgomaster of Stilmonde* (1918; Eng. trans. 1918), and several volumes of speculative essays. ▪ See studies by W. D. Halls (1960), Una Taylor (1968), and Bettina L. Knapp (1975).

MAGNANI, ANNA (1908–1973), Egyptian-born Italian actress. Born into poverty and raised in a slum, Magnani was already an actress and vaudeville performer when she first received acclaim for her role in director Roberto Rossellini's neorealist film *Open City* (1945). Magnani usually played tempestuous, full-bodied characters, and because of her seething style she was considered "the last of the great shameless emotionalists." Her film and stage roles in the United States and Italy included an Academy Award-winning portrayal in *The Rose Tattoo* (1955).

MAGNES, JUDAH LEON (1877–1948), U.S. religious leader and educator. A rabbi and leader of the Jewish community in New York (1904–22), Magnes emigrated to Palestine (1922) and helped establish the Hebrew University, which he served as chancellor (1925–35) and president (1935–48). Although an early supporter of Zionism, Magnes split with the movement during World War I to advocate Arab-Jewish reconciliation within a binational state. He worked closely with the philosopher Martin Buber in Ihud (Unity), an organization Magnes founded to promote Arab-Jewish unity. ▪ See Norman Bentwich, *For Zion's Sake* (1954).

MAGRITTE, RENÉ (1898–1967), Belgian painter. Magritte's mother committed suicide when he was 15 years old. He enrolled at the Brussels Academy of Fine Arts (1916–18), then designed wallpaper patterns. He was attracted to surrealism by the works of Giorgio de Chirico. Magritte juxtaposed realistic images of incongruous but familiar objects in startling arrangements, extending surrealism with intellectual explorations of the unconscious. His early paintings depicted benign gentlemen in bowler hats in threatening situations: *The Threatened Murderer* (1926), *Threatening Weather* (1928), and *The Ladder of Fire* (1933). He painted surrealistic renderings of such celebrated paintings as Jacques Louis David's *Madame Récamier* and Édouard Manet's *The Balcony*, replacing figures with coffins. In his attempts to jar the viewer's consciousness, Magritte gave his paintings ambiguous titles. ▪ See studies by Suzi Gablik (1985), Harry Torczyner (1979), and David Sylvester (1993).

MAGSAYSAY, RAMÓN (1907–1957), Filipino political leader. Magsaysay studied engineering and commerce and worked as an auto mechanic and trucking-firm manager until he joined the army in World War II. He fought with U.S. troops and became a guerrilla leader in Luzon. In 1946 he was elected to the Philippine congress, and later served as secretary of national defense (1950–53). He reformed a corrupt army (with massive U.S. aid) and then used it to suppress a communist-led guerrilla army (the Hukbalahaps) as well as Muslim rebels. As president from 1953 until his death in a plane crash, the charismatic Magsaysay launched a series of agricultural reforms, opened the Philippine economy to widespread American investment, and pursued an anticommunist foreign policy. ▪ See biography by Carlos P. Romulo and Marvin M. Gray (1956).

MAHARAJ JI (Prem Pal Singh Rawat; 1957–   ), Indian spiritual leader. The youngest of five children born to the founder of the Divine Light Missions, Guru Maharaj Ji was a school dropout who was proclaimed "perfect Master" upon his father's death in 1966. He made his first international tour as a 13-year-old guru in 1971 and claimed a large international following and was supported by a chain of thrift shops and other enterprises. A controversial figure—called a phony by some, an enlightened soul by others—Maharaj Ji practiced the laying on of hands and addressed audiences in parables and clichés, such as, "Knowledge is the taste of an orange," and "Try it, you'll like it." In the 1980s he renamed his movement Elan Vital. ■ See study edited by Charles Cameron (1973).

MAHATHIR BIN MOHAMAD (1925–), Malaysian political leader. An ardent Malay nationalist, Mahathir joined the United Malays National Organization (UMNO) at its founding (1946) and became active in politics. He gave up a medical practice to serve in parliament (1964–69) and wrote an influential book, *The Malay Dilemma* (1970), which inspired the radical youth within the party. He was minister of education (1974–76) and deputy prime minister (1976–81) before serving as prime minister (1981–). Although a vituperative critic of the West, he encouraged foreign investment and his policies led to rapid economic growth and industrial development during the 1980s and 1990s. He blamed the 1997–98 financial crisis and economic downturn on foreign currency speculators and on Jews seeking to victimize his predominantly Muslim country. He subsequently banned the trading of Malaysia's currency and advocated controls on the international flow of capital in order to help small countries survive the excesses of capitalism.

MAHENDRA BIR BIKRAM SHAH DEVA (1920–1972), king of Nepal. Mahendra was educated by tutors and was a virtual prisoner in the palace until he was nearly 30. Crowned king in 1956, he promulgated a democratic constitution (1959) that resulted in the formation of Nepal's first popularly elected government. However, in December 1960 he dismissed the government, jailed its leaders, suspended the constitution, and banned all political parties. The new constitution, promulgated in 1962, set up a nonparty panchayat system of government, with the king maintaining executive authority. Mahendra opened Nepal to visitors for the first time, instituted land reforms, and settled Nepal's border issues with China.

MAHFOUZ, NAGUIB (1911–), Egyptian novelist and short-story writer. Mahfouz worked as a civil servant in several cultural institutions. One of the century's most important Arabic novelists, he started his literary career by writing historical novels but soon turned to naturalist realism. His most famous works, known as the Cairo Trilogy—*Palace Walk* (1956; Eng. trans. 1989), *Palace of Desire* (1957; Eng. trans. 1991), and *Sugar Street* (1957; Eng. trans. 1992)—follow a middle-class Egyptian family from 1917 to 1944. Praised for its realistic descriptions and dialogue, it portrays an entire era. His later works were more subjective, allegorical, and symbolic. English translations of his works included *Mirrors, a Novel* (1977), *Miramar* (1978), *Midaq Alley* (1981), *Children of Galselawi* (1981), *Adrift on the Nile* (1993), and *Arabian Nights and Days* (1995). He was awarded the 1988 Nobel Prize in Literature. After the publication of his novel *Children of the Alley* (1959; Eng. trans. 1996), which was banned in Egypt for 35 years as heretical, he was stabbed (1994) by an Islamic militant. ■ See his *Echoes of an Autobiography* (1995; Eng. trans. 1997) and Sasson Somekh, *The Changing Rhythm* (1973).

MAHLER, GUSTAV (1860–1911), Austrian composer and conductor. An alumnus of the Vienna Conservatory, Mahler found the time during a busy European career as a conductor to compose profusely romantic music in classical form. During 10 years as head of the Vienna Imperial Opera (1897–1907), he set new standards for operatic production and also composed 5 symphonies and numerous song cycles, including the *Kindertotenlieder* (1901–04) and *Das Lied von der Erde* (1907–10). Mahler wrote 10 symphonies in all (the last incomplete), sometimes incorporating his own song themes. In 1908 he traveled to New York to conduct for the Metropolitan Opera and the Philharmonic, but his high standards of musicianship made him unpopular among American performers. ■ See biographies by Bruno Walter (1936, Eng. trans. 1941), Kurt Blaukopf (Eng. trans. 1973), Henry L. de La Grange (Eng. trans. 1973), and Jonathan Carr (1998).

MAHLER, MARGARET S. (1897–1985), Hungarian-born U.S. child psychiatrist. Born in Sopron, Mahler studied medicine and psychiatry in Germany and Austria (M.D., University of Vienna, 1923), headed a well-baby clinic in Vienna in the late 1920s, then established and directed a psychoanalytic child-guidance clinic. After emigrating to the United States (1938), she taught at Columbia University's medical school (1941–55) and at the Albert Einstein College of Medicine (1955–74). Mahler considered the first three years of life the crucial period of character development; she stressed the difficult transition a child must make from the conviction, in infancy, of being one with the mother, to the sense of separate identity that comes in the third year. Her influential writings included *The Psychological Birth of the Human Infant* (1976). ■ See her memoirs (1988); Louise J. Kaplan, *Oneness and Separateness* (1978); and Lloyd H. Silverman, *The Search for Oneness* (1982).

MAILER, NORMAN (1923–), U.S. writer. Brooklyn-born and Harvard-educated (B.S. 1943), Mailer gained recognition with his best-selling realistic novel, *The Naked and the Dead* (1948), which was hailed as the greatest work of fiction to come out of World War II. *Advertisements for Myself* (1959), a collection of stories, essays, and interviews, established his reputation as a social critic and gadfly, and he was frequently involved in public controversies. His celebrated "nonfictional novels," *The Armies of the Night* (1968, Pulitzer Prize), an account of a massive anti–Vietnam

War demonstration in Washington, D.C.; *Miami and the Siege of Chicago* (1968), a treatment of the 1968 political conventions; and *Of a Fire on the Moon* (1970), a description of lunar exploration, combined brilliant reportage with incisive political and philosophical speculation. Among his other works were *The Executioner's Song* (1980, Pulitzer Prize), a huge documentary narrative of the last year of the life of convicted killer Gary Gilmore; *Pieces and Pontifications* (1982); and *Ancient Evenings* (1983), a massive novel set in ancient Egypt. His later works included *Harlot's Ghost* (1991), *Oswald's Tale* (1995), and *The Gospel According to the Son* (1997), an account of the life of Jesus. *The Time of Our Time* (1998) contained lengthy excerpts from his fiction and nonfiction published over the years. ■ See studies by Richard Poirier (1972) and Robert Merrill (1978) and biographies by Hilary Mills (1982), Peter Manso (1985), Carl Rollyson (1991), and Mary Dearhorn (1999).

MAILLART, ROBERT (1872–1940), Swiss engineer. Maillart revolutionized bridge design with his graceful and inexpensive reinforced-concrete structures constructed in the Swiss Alps. His designs, first applied on a bridge in Zuoz (1901), integrated the arch, stiffening wall, and roadway into a cohesive unit. His best known work was the spectacular curving Schwandbach Bridge at Schwarzenburg (1933). ■ See studies by Max Bill (3rd ed. 1969) and David P. Billington (1997).

MAILLOL, ARISTIDE JOSEPH BONAVENTURE (1861–1944), French sculptor and painter. Although his formal training was in painting, Maillol became interested in making tapestries and wood carvings and began (c. 1900) to work in clay, bronze, and marble sculpture. Influenced by Paul Gauguin, he was primarily concerned with sculpting the nude female form, mature yet innocent. Maillol's figures, serene and ordered, with a minimum of detail, contrasted with those of Auguste Rodin and exuded little sense of movement or facial expression. His style, which changed little throughout his lifetime, had a classical Greek quality, exemplified by *Chained Action* (1906), his monument to socialist revolutionary Louis Auguste Blanqui. ■ See biography by Dina Vierny (Eng. trans. 1965).

MAIMAN, THEODORE HAROLD (1927–   ), U.S. physicist. The son of an electrical engineer, Maiman studied engineering at the University of Colorado and at Stanford University before earning his Ph.D. in physics from Stanford (1955). At the Hughes Research Laboratories, Miami (1955–61), he studied stimulated emission of microwave energy, and he made important advances in the design of the solid-state maser and built the first practical laser (1960). He founded the Korad Corp. (1962), which manufactured high-powered lasers; cofounded the Laser Video Corporation (1972), which developed large-screen color video displays; and was vice president for advanced technology at TRW Electronics (1975–83).

MAINBOCHER (Main Rousseau Bocher; 1891–1976), U.S. fashion designer. After serving in World War I, Mainbocher stayed in Europe. He studied voice in Paris and supported himself by sketching fashions for *Vogue* and *Harper's Bazaar*. Establishing his own dressmaking house (1930), he designed dresses characterized by their understated elegance and he became the first American to score a major success in Parisian haute couture. After the outbreak of World War II, he moved his salon to New York City and during the war he created women's uniforms for the U.S. Navy and Marine Corps. He designed made-to-order clothes in New York until 1971, when he returned to Europe.

MAJOR, JOHN (1943–   ), British political leader. Born into a lower-middle class family—his father was a circus performer—Major was a banker until being elected to Parliament as a Conservative in 1979. A protege of Prime Minister Margaret Thatcher, Major served in her cabinet as chief secretary to the Treasury (1987–89), foreign secretary (1989), and chancellor of the Exchequer (1989–90). When Thatcher resigned (1990), the Conservatives picked Major to replace her and he led the Conservatives to victory in the 1992 elections. As prime minister (1990–97) he emerged as a centrist and he abolished the unpopular poll tax, strengthened relations with the European Community, and attempted to placate contending wings of his party. Although the British economy grew and unemployment fell during the 1990s, Major's popularity declined. He was attacked by party members opposed to his European policy and he was weakened by a series of political and sex scandals involving cabinet members and prominent Conservative politicians. As a result he led the Conservatives to a devastating defeat in the 1997 elections. ■ See biographies by Penny Junor (1996) and Anthony Seldon (1997).

MAJUMDAR, ROMESH CHANDRA (1888–1980), Indian historian. Majumdar studied at Calcutta University (Ph.D. 1918) and taught there (1914–21), at the University of Dacca (1921–42), and at several other universities. A specialist in the history of India and the influence of India on Southeast Asia, he was one of India's most prolific and influential historians. He also wrote several important works on the history of Bengal and was the general editor of *The History and Culture of the Indian People* (11 vols., 1951–1969) and of the *History of the Freedom Movement in India* (3 vols., 1961–62). His works on modern India, written late in his career, were controversial because he emphasized the tensions between Hindus and Muslims as an enduring aspect of Indian life and culture. His best-known works included *Corporate Life in Ancient India* (1919), *History of Bengal, Vol. 1: Hindu Period* (1943), and *The Sepoy Mutiny and the Revolt of 1857* (1957; rev. ed. 1963).

MAKARENKO, ANTON SEMENOVICH (1888–1939), Soviet educator. Makarenko came into prominence in the years after the 1917 bolshevik revolution, when the rampant delinquency of homeless children troubled Soviet society and strategies for educating them were a matter of public concern. He ran a colony for delinquents in the Ukraine (1920–27), where his methods for molding character evolved. His stress on rigid discipline and strenuous peer pressure was controversial in the early 1920s, when more progressive currents dominated education, but served the political ends of leader Joseph Stalin. After Stalin consolidated power, Makarenko was put in charge of an orphans commune in Kharkov (1927) and was regarded as an authority on child rearing. Over the next decade, he published and lectured widely on the molding of a "new Soviet man" and other educational issues. His books included *The Collective Family: A Handbook for Russian Parents* (1937; Eng. trans. 1967) and *The Road to Life: An Epic in Education* (3 vols., 1935–37; Eng. trans. 1951; repr. 1973). Several of his lectures and articles appeared in *Problems of Soviet School Education* (Eng. trans. 1965). ■ See study by W. L. Goodman (1949) and James Bowen, *Soviet Education* (1962).

MAKARIOS III (Mikhail Khristodolou Mouskos; 1913–1977), Cypriot religious and political leader. The son of a shepherd, Mouskos entered an Orthodox monastery at age 13 and was ordained as a deacon (1938). In 1950 he became Archbishop Makarios, primate of the Orthodox Church of Cyprus. He built the church into a major landowner and developer. During the British occupation that followed World War II, he assumed leadership of the island's Greek majority, advocating union (*énosis*) with Greece. Makarios discarded his policy of *énosis* in 1949 to become president of the independent republic of Cyprus, fusing the island's church and state in the Byzantine tradition. He weathered outbreaks of communal strife and intervention by both Greece and Turkey. Forced to flee after a 1974 coup d'état and Turkish invasion, he soon returned and spent his last years negotiating inconclusively with Turkish representatives. ■ See biography by Stanley Mayes (1981) and study by P. N. Vanezis (1972).

MAKAROVA, NATALIA (1940–), Soviet-born ballerina. Makarova grew up in Leningrad and studied under Natalia Dudinskaya at the Kirov Ballet School, where her long, slender figure earned her the nickname "Giraffe." A soloist with the Kirov (from 1959), she won critical acclaim for her lyrical, expressive interpretation of *Giselle*. She often performed in the West; in 1970 she defected and subsequently danced with the American Ballet Theatre in New York (1970–92). She also performed with Rudolf Nureyev in London and appeared with the Royal Ballet. Known for her aristocratic and intense style, she was acclaimed for her performances in *Les Sylphides, Swan Lake,* and *La Bayadère.* She formed her own company in 1980 and made her Broadway debut in *On Your Toes* (1983). ■ See *A Dance Autobiography* (1979) and the study by Richard Austin (1978).

MAKEBA, (ZENSI) MIRIAM (1932–), South African-born singer. A survivor of a Johannesburg slum, Makeba be-

gan singing professionally in 1954. She appeared in *Come Back Africa* (1958), an antiapartheid film documentary, and won a starring role in the Johannesburg folk opera *King Kong* (1959), which led to a U.S. tour with Harry Belafonte and a career of TV and radio appearances and recordings of an international folk repertoire, including the "click" songs of her native Xhosa tribe. Makeba spoke out against apartheid at the United Nations. Her albums included *Makeba* (1963), *Pata, Papa* (1972), and *Sangoma* (1989). She was married for several years to black radical Stokely Carmichael. ■ See her autobiography (1988).

MAKONNEN ENDALKACAW (1892–1963), Ethiopian writer and political leader. A member of a prominent court family, Makonnen befriended his contemporary, the future Emperor Haile Selassie, as a young man, and Selassie assured Makonnen's political rise. He filled a variety of executive and diplomatic posts, and after the departure of the Italian occupiers in 1941 became premier (1943–57) under the new constitution and president of the senate (1957–61). He was also an important literary figure whose many moralistic, religious, and patriotic novels contributed to a renaissance of vernacular Amharic literature.

MALAMUD, BERNARD (1914–1986), U.S. novelist and short-story writer. From his Brooklyn youth, Malamud internalized the values and mythology of the Russian-Jewish immigrant milieu. He defined the Jew as an individual who endures, and his characters learn that no one who suffers and loves is beyond redemption. In spare, lyrical language, with Yiddish rhythms and warm humor, he used the idioms of that folk culture to explore the human condition in such novels as *The Assistant* (1957), *A New Life* (1961), and *The Fixer* (1966, Pulitzer Prize). *Dubin's Lives* (1979) depicted the search for a new direction in life. The hero of Malamud's eighth novel, *God's Grace* (1982), is a rabbi's son and lonely survivor of a nuclear war. His first novel, *The Natural* (1952), was adapted for the screen in 1984. Malamud's short-story collections included *The Magic Barrel* (1958), *Idiots First* (1963), and *The Complete Stories* (1997). He taught at Oregon State University (1949–61) and at Bennington College in Vermont (from 1961). ■ See his *Talking Horse: Bernard Malamud on Life and Work* (1996; with Alan Cheuse and Nicholas Delbanco), and studies by Sidney Richman (1966) and Sheldon J. Hershinow (1980).

MALAN, DANIEL FRANÇOIS (1874–1959), South African political leader. Malan studied in Holland to become a minister in the Dutch Reformed Church (1905) but turned to politics at the time of World War I. A member of the Nationalist party, he was elected to the South African parliament (1918) and became minister of the interior (1924). In 1948 he led a "purified" party faction to electoral victory and served as prime minister (1948–54) of the nation's first exclusively Afrikaner government. A white supremacist, Malan introduced the laws establishing apartheid, or racial separation.

MALAPARTE, CURZIO (Kurt Suckert; 1898–1957), Italian political writer, filmmaker, and novelist. An intellectual gadfly, Malaparte joined Italy's Fascist party in the early 1920s but soon fell out of favor. His reports from the Russian front during World War II, collected in *The Volga Rises in Europe* (1943; Eng. trans. 1957), discomforted Nazi authorities; he was ordered to remain in Finland, where he wrote *Kaputt* (1945; Eng. trans. 1946), a bleak depiction of senseless destruction of Europe. *The Skin* (1949; Eng. trans. 1952) was a controversial surrealistic vision of postwar Italy. In the amusing and parodoxical *Those Cursed Tuscans* (1956; Eng. trans. 1964), he analyzed the Tuscan character.

MALATESTA, ERRICO (1853–1932), Italian anarchist leader. Born into a liberal middle-class family near Naples, Malatesta was inspired by the Paris Commune of 1871 and the anarchist writings of Michael Bakunin and Peter Kropotkin to devote his life to revolutionary anarchism. During a remarkable 60-year career as an activist—half of which was spent in exile and more than 10 years of which were spent in prison—he helped to organize and inspire revolutionary groups throughout Europe as well as in Egypt, Argentina, and the United States. In his writings he opposed determinism, dogmatism, and indiscriminate terrorism while emphasizing voluntarism, the organization of anarchists into a revolutionary vanguard, and the necessity of insurrection as a weapon against the existing order. He edited several newspapers and magazines before returning to Italy (1919), where he founded and edited the daily *Umanità Nova* (1920–22), which had a circulation of 50,000 copies at its peak, and *Pensiero e Voluntà* (1924–26). He helped to organize the Unione Sindicale Italiana (1919), a revolutionary syndicalist union that had a membership of more than 400,000, but the movement was suppressed by Benito Mussolini's fascist government, and Malatesta spent the last six years of his life (1926–32) under house arrest in Rome. A selection of his writings are in Vernon Richards, ed., *Errico Malatesta: His Life and Ideas* (1965).

MALCOLM X (Malcolm Little; 1925–1965), U.S. black-nationalist leader. Malcolm X, the son of a Baptist minister who was a follower of Marcus Garvey, was converted to Islam in 1952 while serving a prison term for burglary. Angry, militant, and articulate, he spent more than a decade speaking and organizing on behalf of the black separatist Nation of Islam and its leader Elijah Muhammad. He condemned white America and the integration movement, advocated violence in self-defense, and called for blacks to control their own communities. In 1963 Malcolm broke with the movement and, after a 1964 trip to Mecca, turned against black separatism and substituted elements of orthodox Islam, African socialism, anticolonialism, and racial solidarity. He was preaching from his New York City base at Harlem's Audubon Ballroom when he was assassinated. ■ See his speeches in George Breitman, ed., *Malcolm X Speaks* (1965), and *By Any Means Necessary* (1970); *The Autobi-*ography of Malcolm X* (1965); Peter Goldman, *The Death and Life of Malcolm X* (rev. ed. 1979); and E. Victor Wolfenstein, *The Victims of Democracy* (1981).

MALENKOV, GEORGI MAKSIMILIANOVICH (1902–1988), Soviet political leader. Malenkov joined the Communist party at age 18, helped dictator Joseph Stalin implement forced collectivization, and rose through the party secretariat. As a member (1942–44) of the state defense committee, Malenkov was considered Stalin's spokesman. He became deputy premier and a full member of the Politburo in 1946 and was regarded as Stalin's heir apparent. At Stalin's death in March 1953, Malenkov became first secretary of the party and premier; Nikita Khrushchev soon took over party leadership, but Malenkov remained premier (1953–55). His tenure was characterized by a shift of priorities from heavy industry to consumer goods, a moderate external policy, and restriction of the power of the secret police. Under attack for agricultural failures, he was replaced (1955) by Nikolai Bulganin. Two years later, Malenkov and V. M. Molotov were denounced as members of an "antiparty" group, expelled from all key posts, and stripped (1961) of party membership. He subsequently lived in obscurity.

MALEVICH, KASIMIR (1878–1935), Russian painter. A pioneer of abstract art, Malevich founded suprematism, a movement that repudiated representation in art. His series of abstract, geometrical paintings of plainly colored squares, triangles, and circles on a white background included his famous *Supermatist Composition: White on White* (1918). A professor of art at Moscow and Leningrad throughout the 1920s, Malevich described the principles of suprematism in *The Non-Objective World* (1927; Eng. trans. 1959). During the early 1930s Soviet officials denounced his style as contrary to the principles of socialist realism and he died in obscurity. ■ See studies by A. B. Novak (1976) and Larissa Zhadova (Eng. trans. 1982), and Charlotte Douglas, *Swans and Other Worlds* (1980).

MALINA, JUDITH. *See BECK, JULIAN.*

MALINOVSKY, RODION YAKOVLEVICH (1898–1967), Soviet marshal. Malinovsky was born in the Ukraine, joined the Communist party in 1926, and fought in the Spanish Civil War (1936–39). He distinguished himself in World War II, commanding Red army troops at Stalingrad and later in the Ukraine. Named a marshal of the Soviet Union (1944), he rose to membership (1956) in the party's central committee and succeeded Marshal Georgi Zhukov as minister of defense (1957–67).

MALINOWSKI, BRONISLAW (1884–1942), British anthropologist. After receiving a doctoral degree (1908) in physics and mathematics in his native Poland, Malinowski studied anthropology at the London School of Economics. He did fieldwork among the people of the Trobriand Islands

(1915–16; 1917–18) and among American Pueblo Indians (during the 1920s). Fluent in seven languages, he taught at the University of London (1924–38) and founded a functional school of social anthropology that stressed that the biological needs of society were fulfilled by cultural institutions like custom, religion, sexual taboos, ceremonies, and beliefs. His writings included *Crime and Custom in Savage Society* (1926) and the posthumous *Magic, Science and Religion* (1948). ■ See his *Diary* (Eng. trans. 1967) and Raymond Firth, ed., *Man and Culture* (1957).

MALIPIERO, GIAN FRANCESCO (1882–1973), Italian composer. Malipiero turned to the study of composition after failing examinations in violin, and with Alfredo Casella, he became a leader of the Italian school of modern classical music. His highly individual and intellectual works were influenced by Stravinsky, the French impressionists, and the works of 17th- and 18th-century Italian composers. Malipiero composed about 40 operas, as well as works in every other major musical genre: eight major symphonies, seven quartets, and five oratorios. He directed (1940–52) the Venice Conservatory and was known for his scholarly essays and books on music as well as for his editions of the complete works of Monteverdi and Vivaldi.

MALLE, LOUIS (1932–1995), French film director. Born into a wealthy industrial family, Malle studied political science at the Sorbonne and filmmaking at the Institute of Advanced Cinematographic Studies, Paris (1951–53). He served as codirector, with oceanographer Jacques-Yves Cousteau, on the Academy Award–winning documentary, *The Silent World* (1956), and worked as an assistant to director Robert Bresson (1956) before directing his first films, the psychological thriller *Frantic* (1957) and the sexually explicit *The Lovers* (1958). He subsequently became internationally known for his eclectic output of personal, reflective films that explored such themes as alcoholism (*The Fire Within,* 1963), incest (*Murmur of the Heart,* 1971), collaboration during World War II (*Lacombe, Lucien,* 1973), child prostitution (*Pretty Baby,* 1978), and the fate of French Jews during the Nazi occupation (*Au Revoir Les Enfants,* 1987). A six-month stay in India yielded the feature-length documentary *Calcutta* (1969) and the controversial seven-part, six-hour television documentary series, *Phantom India* (1972). He also collaborated with actor Wallace Shawn and stage director Andre Gregory on two highly unusual films, *My Dinner with Andre* (1981) and *Vanya on 42nd Street* (1994). ■ See Philip French, ed., *Malle on Malle* (1993).

MALLEA, EDUARDO (1903–1982), Argentine novelist. Mallea abandoned legal studies to pursue a literary career. His fiction represented a search for what he called the "invisible" Argentina of precapitalist spiritual and intellectual values beneath the surface of materialism, opportunism, and superficiality that he saw pervading contemporary society. He wrote about the dilemmas of modern civilization in terms of individual characters and their inner turmoil. He searched for the meaning of authentic existence in such books as the autobiographical *The Bay of Silence* (1940; Eng. trans. 1944), which was well received in the United States. The collection of novellas, *All Green Shall Perish* (1941; Eng. trans. 1966), whose title story was a grim account of a woman's isolation, also contained *Fiesta in November,* inspired by the murder of Spanish poet Federico García Lorca, and *Chaves,* a story of an emotionally withdrawn sawmill worker. His essay *History of an Argentine Passion* (1937; Eng. trans. 1983) treats many of the themes he developed in his fiction. ■ See study by H. Ernest Lewald (1977).

MALLON, MARY (1870?–1938), U.S. cook and typhoid carrier. Known as "Typhoid Mary," Mallon was the first carrier of typhoid bacilli identified in the United States. She was suspected as a carrier of the disease in 1904, when she was working as a cook at a home in Oyster Bay, New York. Although pursued by the authorities, she eluded them until 1907, when she was captured and committed to the isolated Riverside Hospital on New York City's North Brother Island; there it was confirmed that she was indeed the disease carrier. She was released in 1910 after she promised not to take a job involving food handling, but she was pursued four years later when typhoid broke out again at two hospitals where she had been employed as a cook. She was recaptured and sent back to Riverside Hospital, where she lived a cloistered existence for the rest of her life. Although she herself was immune to the disease, she was reportedly responsible for 51 cases of typhoid and three deaths.

MALONE, DUMAS (1892–1986), U.S. historian. Born and raised in Mississippi, Malone earned his Ph.D. at Yale (1923) and taught there, at the University of Virginia, and at Columbia (1945–59). He also worked as director of the Harvard University Press (1936–43) and as editor of the *Dictionary of American Biography* (1931–36). His extensive biography of Thomas Jefferson, *Jefferson and His Time* (6 vols., 1948–81), won a 1975 Pulitzer Prize in History.

MALOUF, DAVID (1934–), Australian writer. Malouf, whose paternal ancestors were Lebanese Christians and whose maternal ones were English Jews with Portuguese roots, grew up in Brisbane and studied there at the University of Queensland (B.A. 1954). His first collections of prize-winning poems were published while he was a lecturer in English at the University of Sydney (1968–77). He began his highly successful career as a novelist with *Johnno* (1975), a semiautobiographical account of growing up in Brisbane. In this and subsequent works, he examined issues of Australian identity through the presentation of pairs of characters, representing opposites, who live in exile or on the margins of society. He looked at situations from a multidirectional point of view, and frequently combined the past, present, and future in his narratives. His best-known novels were *An*

Imaginary Life (1978), *Fly Away Peter* (1982), *Harlands Half Acre* (1984), *The Great World* (1990), *Remembering Babylon* (1993), and *The Conversations at Curlow Creek* (1996). His stories were published in *Dream Stuff* (2000). ■ See the autobiographical *12 Edmundstone Street* (1985); the study by Ivor Indyk (1993); and Philip Neilsen, *Imagined Lives* (1996).

MALRAUX, ANDRÉ (1901–1976), French novelist, essayist, philosopher, and political figure. Malraux's preoccupation with "the human condition" extended beyond his famous novels of action. His spectacular career included revolutionary activism in China during the 1920s and outspoken antifascism and involvement with the republican cause in the Spanish Civil War during the 1930s. His novels *The Conquerors* (1928; Eng. trans. 1929) and *Man's Fate* (1933; Eng. trans. 1934) are set in China against a backdrop of revolutionary struggle. *Man's Hope* (1938; Eng. trans. 1938) deals with the early stages of the Spanish civil war. During World War II Malraux figured prominently in the French Resistance. His view of art as the human being's assertion of freedom over destiny is developed in *The Voices of Silence* (1951; Eng. trans. 1953). A supporter of Gen. Charles de Gaulle, Malraux served as de Gaulle's minister of cultural affairs (1959–69). ■ See his *Antimemoirs* (1967; Eng. trans. 1968); biographies by Jean Lacouture (Eng. trans. 1975) and Cate Curtis (1995); and Herman Lebovics, *Mona Lisa's Escort* (1999).

MAMET, DAVID (1947–   ), U.S. playwright. Mamet graduated from the experimental Goddard College in Vermont (1969) and studied acting in New York. After a brief period of employment in a Chicago real estate firm, he began to work in the Chicago theater, where many of his plays were first performed. He established his reputation with three 1975 Off-Broadway productions: *Sexual Perversity in Chicago,* a play about the fragility of contemporary relationships; *The Duck Variations,* a comedy featuring the ramblings of two elderly men on a park bench; and *American Buffalo,* a drama depicting the pervasive viciousness and betrayal in American business. His other plays included *The Water Engine* (1976), *The Woods* (1977), *Edmond* (1983), *Speed-the-Plow* (1988), and *The Old Neighborhood* (1997). *Glengarry Glen Ross,* a dark comedy portraying unscrupulous practices of a Chicago real estate company, won the 1984 Pulitzer Prize. All of Mamet's works were praised for their natural dialogue and precision of expression. Mamet also wrote the screenplays for *The Postman Always Rings Twice* (1981), *The Verdict* (1982), *Things Change* (1987), *The Spanish Prisoner* (1996), *Wag the Dog* (1997), and *The Winslow Boy* (1999), which he also directed. He also wrote the novels *The Village* (1994) and *The Old Religion* (1996) and a book on acting, *True and False* (1997). ■ See his *Make-Believe Town: Essays and Remembrances* (1996) and volume of reflections, *Jafsie and John Henry* (1999).

MAMONOVA, TATIANA (1943–   ), Soviet-born feminist. Mamonova trained for a pharmaceutical career in Leningrad (1962–64), then worked in a laboratory (1961–66), as a TV writer (1967–68), and as a magazine editor, reviewer, and translator (1969–72). Also a painter, she organized exhibitions with nonconformist artists, but became disillusioned when she encountered sexism in these groups. Collaborating with Tatiana Goricheva, Natalia Malakhovsksaya, and Julia Voznesenskaya, Mamonova edited the underground feminist journal *Woman and Russia* (1979), publishing articles on such topics as the patriarchal nature of Soviet ideology, conditions in maternity hospitals, abuse of women in Soviet prisons, the impact of male alcoholism on women, and birth control. Stripped of Soviet citizenship and forced to emigrate in 1980, she settled in Paris, then in Connecticut. She edited *Women and Russia* (Eng. trans. 1984) and wrote *Russian Women's Studies: Essays on Sexism in Soviet Culture* (Eng. trans. 1989) and *Women's Glasnost vs. Naglost* (Eng. trans. 1994).

MAMOULIAN, ROUBEN (1897–1987), U.S. theatrical and film director. Born in Tiflis (now Soviet Georgia), Mamouhan trained at the Moscow Art Theater and later directed plays in his native city and in London before emigrating to the United States (1923). After achieving prominence as a Broadway director, he was summoned to Hollywood, where he directed some of the best of the early sound movies, including *Applause* (1929), *City Streets* (1931), *Dr. Jekyll and Mr. Hyde* (1932), and *Queen Christina* (1933). He reintroduced camera mobility to the screen by utilizing a sound camera on wheels and skillfully blended motion, music, and lighting in his films. He directed the first Technicolor film, *Becky Sharp* (1935), and such innovative musicals as *Love Me Tonight* (1932), *Summer Holiday* (1948), and *Silk Stockings* (1957). He also directed the original stage productions of the musicals *Porgy and Bess* (1935), *Oklahoma!* (1943), and *Carousel* (1945). ■ See biography by Tom Milne (1969).

MAN, FELIX H. (Hans Felix Baumann; 1893–1985), German-born photographer. Man was an art student from Freiburg who became a pioneer of European photojournalism. Drafted in 1914, he recorded his war experiences with a pocket camera. During the interwar period he photographed the Italian dictator Mussolini, the composer Igor Stravinsky, and the Irish playwright George Bernard Shaw, as well as aspects of Africa and the Arctic, for German magazines. Man moved to London in 1934 and back to the Continent in 1958; he was still active in his eighties as a German correspondent in Rome. ■ See his *Man with Camera: Photographs from Seven Decades* (1984).

MANCINI, HENRY (1924–1994), U.S. composer. Mancini studied piano and flute as a child. His studies at Juilliard (1942) were interrupted by wartime service in the U.S. Air

Force. After the war, he continued to study composition and was a pianist and arranger for the Tex Beneke Orchestra (1945–47). During six years as staff composer for Universal Pictures (1952–58), Mancini wrote music for more than 100 films; he later scored television series and made recordings for the RCA Victor label (from 1959). Mancini composed scores for *The Glenn Miller Story* (1954), *The Benny Goodman Story* (1956), *Breakfast at Tiffany's* (1961; Academy Award), *The Return of the Pink Panther* (1975), and *Victor/Victoria* (1982; Academy Award). With collaborator Johnny Mercer, he won Academy Awards for the sophisticated, popular classics "Moon River" (1961) and "Days of Wine and Roses" (1962). He also won 20 Grammy Awards during his career. ■ See his *Sounds and Scores* (1962) and autobiography *Did They Mention the Music?* (1989).

MANDEL, GEORGES (Louis Georges Rothschild; 1885–1944), French political leader. Born into a wealthy Jewish family, Mandel served on the staff of Premier Georges Clemenceau (1906–09; 1917–20) and was a member of the national assembly (1919–24; 1928–40). Staunchly opposed to Nazi Germany and the profascists within France during the 1930s, Mandel, as minister of the interior, refused to sign an armistice with the Germans in June 1940 and supported Premier Paul Reynaud's resistance policy. He was arrested by the collaborationist Vichy government in Morocco, tried in France, and handed over to the Germans (November 1942). After incarceration at Oranienburg and Buchenwald concentration camps, he was returned to France (1944) and murdered by the French police. ■ See the study by John M. Sherwood (1970).

MANDELA, NELSON ROLIHLAHLA (1918–), South African political leader. Mandela renounced a hereditary Tembu chieftainship in order to become a lawyer, earning his degree from the University of South Africa (1942). He joined the African National Congress (ANC) in 1944, cofounded the Congress Youth League, and led a "defiance campaign" against discriminatory apartheid laws (1951–52). He was named deputy national president of the ANC (1952) and advocated nonviolent resistance and the establishment of a nonracial state. However, after the Sharpeville massacre (1960), in which 69 unarmed black protesters were killed by the police, Mandela headed a paramilitary group that carried out sabotage against targets symbolizing apartheid. Acquitted of treason in an epic mass trial (1961), he was subsequently convicted of sabotage (1964) and sentenced to life imprisonment. His speeches and articles were collected in *No Easy Road to Freedom* (1965; rev. ed. 1990). For decades he remained a symbol of resistance to apartheid and when he was released in 1990, after 27 years, he was elected president of the ANC (1991). He negotiated a peaceful transition to a multiracial democracy with South African President F. W. de Klerk and he shared the 1993 Nobel Peace Prize with him. In the first elections open to all South African citizens (April 1994), Mandela was elected president. In office until 1999, he attempted to improve the living conditions of the black majority but was unable to solve the severe problems of unemployment and crime. He was married to Winnie Mandela from 1958 until 1996, when he was granted a divorce. He married Graça Machel, the widow of Mozambican President Samora Machel, in 1998. ■ See his autobiography, *Long Walk to Freedom* (1994), and biographies by Martin Meredith (1997) and Anthony Sampson (1999).

MANDELA, WINNIE (Nkosikazi Nobandle Nomzamo Madikizela; 1936–), South African political activist. Winnie Mandela grew up in Transkei, the official "homeland" of the Xhosa people from whom she descended. She went to Johannesburg to study at the Jan Hofmeyr Social Centre (1953–55), and was said to be her country's first black medical social worker. In Johannesburg she met lawyer and political activist Nelson Mandela in 1956; the next year she joined the Women's League of the African National Congress. She married Mandela in 1958. After her husband was sentenced to life imprisonment on charges of sabotage and plotting a violent revolution (1964), Winnie Mandela emerged as a leading opponent of apartheid. She was banned (forbidden to meet in public with more than one person at a time) and was detained or imprisoned several times. In the aftermath of the 1976 Soweto riots, she helped to found the Black Parents' Association. After 1977 she lived in forced exile in a black township in the Orange Free State, where she ran a clinic and nursery school. After her home and clinic were burned (1985), Mandela broke her ban, appearing at political events and issuing strong public statements, and became involved in militant Soweto politics. In the late 1980s her bodyguards, members of the Mandela United Football Club, were accused of murder and assault and she was convicted of kidnapping (1991) but her sentence was commuted to a fine (1993). After her husband was released from prison (1990) she separated from him (1992), was divorced (1996), and thereafter used the name Madikizela-Mandela. She subsequently served as deputy minister in the first postapartheid government and was president of the ANC's Women's League (1997–). In 1998 the Truth and Reconciliation Commission found that she and members of her football club were responsible for "gross violations of human rights." ■ See the interviews in Anne Benjamin, ed., *Part of My Soul Went with Him* (1984), and biographies by Nancy Harrison (1986) and Emma Gilbey, *The Lady* (1993).

MANDELBROT, BENOIT (1924–), Polish-born French mathematician. Mandelbrot was born into an educated Jewish family in Warsaw. He moved to France (1936), where his uncle was a prominent analytical mathematician, and he spent several years (1942–44) during World War II moving around the country in order to avoid capture by the Nazis.

After the war he studied aeronautics at the California Institute of Technology (M.S. 1948), served in the French air force for one year, and received a doctorate in mathematics from the University of Paris (1952). In 1958 he moved to the United States, where he worked at IBM (researcher, 1958–74; fellow, 1974–93) and taught at Harvard (1962–64; 1984–87) and Yale (1987–   ). An interdisciplinary scholar, Mandelbrot was best known for developing fractal geometry, which enabled scientists to discover patterns and order in seemingly random and chaotic aspects of natural systems. His work had applications in such diverse fields as physiology, meteorology, physics, astronomy, and economics and was recognized as one of the most significant contributions to 20th-century mathematics. He described his work in *Fractals: Form, Change and Dimension* (1975; Eng. trans. 1977) and *The Fractal Geometry of Nature* (1982).

MANDELSTAM, NADEZHDA YAKOVLEVNA (Nadezhda Khazina; 1899–1980), Russian memoirist. Khazina grew up in Kiev, where she studied art, traveled with her family, and became sufficiently proficient in several Western European languages to undertake translation work. She met the poet Osip Mandelstam in 1919 and spent the next 20 years with him. In *Hope Against Hope* (1970; Eng. trans. 1970) and *Hope Abandoned* (1972: Eng. trans. 1974), she chronicled her husband's life and death and her own experiences, both with Mandelstam and during the three decades after his death that she wandered through Soviet Russia giving English lessons to earn money. Her memoirs provide an important account of 20th-century Russian literary life. She also wrote the literary study *Mozart and Salieri* (Eng. trans. 1973).

MANDELSTAM, OSIP EMILYEVICH (1892–1938), Russian poet. The brilliant son of a Jewish merchant, Mandelstam drew on his vast knowledge of literary culture to produce exact, exquisite poems that many consider the best ever written in Russian. Mandelstam's first volume, *Stone* (1913: Eng. trans. 1980), included short poems in classic meters; *Tristia* (1922) and *Poems* (1928) added to the body of his complex, philosophical verse. In an era of political upheaval and repression, he composed graceful, calm poetry, drawing strength from fellow poets Nikolai Gumilev and Anna Akhmatova, with whom he formed the acmeist movement. After reading one of his poems that derided the dictator Joseph Stalin to a few acquaintances, he was arrested (1934) and exiled for three years. Rearrested in 1938, he died in a Siberian transit camp. Much of his poetry was preserved by his widow, Nadezhda Mandelstam. Mandelstam was also a brilliant prose writer: *The Noise of Time* (1925; Eng. trans. 1965) and *The Egyptian Stamp* (1928; Eng. trans. 1965) were autobiographical. Translations of his works are in *Selected Poems* (1975, 1984), *The Complete Prose and Letters* (1979), and *Selected Essays* (1977). ■ See Nadezhda Mandelstam, *Hope Against Hope* (Eng. trans. 1970) and

Hope Abandoned (Eng. trans. 1974), and studies by Clarence Brown (1973) and Ryszard Przybylski (Eng. trans. 1986).

MANGER, ITZIK (1901–1969), Rumanian-born Yiddish-language poet, dramatist, and novelist. A tailor, Manger became one of the most widely read Yiddish poets before World War II. Favored by intellectuals as well as by the Jewish masses, he was known primarily for his poems in which biblical figures were portrayed as contemporary Jews who inhabited the villages of Eastern Europe. His poems, which combined sophisticated rhythms with the simplicity of folk songs, were translated into every major European language. He escaped to London during World War II and later lived in New York (from 1951). He died in Israel. Manger is most famous for his collections *Stars on the Roof* (1929), *Lantern in the Wind* (1933), *Pentateuch Songs* (1935), and *Scroll Song* (1936) and his novel, *The Book of Paradise* (1939; Eng. trans. 1965). Selected poems are in S. Z. Betsky, ed., *Onions and Cucumbers and Plums* (1958) and I. Howe and E. Greenberg, eds., *A Treasury of Yiddish Poetry* (1969).

MANIU, IULIU (1873–1953), Rumanian political leader. A native of Transylvania, a part of Hungary prior to 1920, Maniu took an active part in the Rumanian national movement in the province. After 1926 he headed the Rumanian National Peasants' party and served twice as premier (1928–30; 1932–33). A reformer, he was thwarted by the Depression and by King Carol's opposition to his policies. He opposed Ion Antonescu's dictatorship but initially supported the war against the Soviet Union (1941). As the war spread beyond Bessarabia, however, he opposed the government and was a principal organizer of the Aug. 23, 1944, coup that brought Rumania into the war against Germany. He tried, vainly, after the war, to prevent the communists from seizing power. In 1947 he was denounced as a reactionary by the communists, convicted of treason, and sentenced to life imprisonment.

MANKIEWICZ, JOSEPH LEO (1909–1993), U.S. screenwriter, producer, and director. Mankiewicz began his career in Berlin translating subtitles for UFA, Germany's leading film-production company. In 1929 he joined his writer-brother Herman (1897–1953) in Hollywood, where he became a leading writer for Paramount (*Million Dollar Legs*, 1932). His predilection was for witty and sophisticated comedies of manners. Promoted to producer, he first brought out Fritz Lang's *Fury* (1936). He also produced and wrote *The Bride Wore Red* (1937), *The Philadelphia Story* (1940), and *Woman of the Year* (1942). In 1945 he turned to directing, most memorably with *A Letter to Three Wives* (1949) and *All About Eve* (1950), which won him Academy Awards both for script and direction, *Guys and Dolls* (1955), and *Sleuth* (1972). He also directed *Cleopatra* (1962), a $40 million production that was one of the greatest box office failures in Hollywood history. ■ See Kenneth L. Geist, *Pictures Will Talk* (1978), and study by Bernard F. Dick (1983).

MANLEY, MICHAEL (1923–1997), Jamaican political leader. The son of Norman Manley, a prime minister and founder of the socialist People's National party (PNP), Michael Manley served in the Royal Canadian Air Force during World War II and studied at the London School of Economics (1945–49). A leader of the National Workers' Union during the 1950s, he served in the senate and the house of representatives during the 1960s and was elected president of the PNP (1969). As two-term prime minister (1972–80), he nationalized much of the economy, expanded social welfare and public-works programs, denounced capitalist imperialism, and emerged as an influential spokesperson for the Third World and a critic of the world economic order. However, by the late 1970s the economy was near collapse, the foreign debt had grown, and mounting street violence was keeping both investors and tourists away from the island. As a result, Manley was defeated in the 1980 elections by Edward Seaga of the Jamaica Labour party. He subsequently moderated his views and during a third term as prime minister (1989–92) he pursued free-market economic policies, removed price controls and subsidies, and encouraged foreign investment and the privatization of state-owned enterprises. Manley's books included *The Politics of Change* (1975), *The Search for Solutions: Selections From Speeches and Writings* (1976), *Jamaica: Struggle in the Periphery* (1982), *Up the Down Escalator* (1985), and *Poverty of the Nations* (1991). ■ See biography by Darrell E. Levy (1990).

MANN, HEINRICH (1871–1950), German novelist. Heinrich, the older brother of the novelist Thomas Mann, was a prolific author and social critic. A socialist from a wealthy and prominent family, he bitterly attacked the military and the bourgeoisie and perceptively criticized Wilhelmine, Weimar, and Nazi Germany. An early satire, *Professor Unrat* (1905; Eng. trans. as *Small Town Tyrant,* 1944), was the basis of the well-known movie *The Blue Angel.* His political novels *The Patrioteer* (1918; Eng. trans. 1921), *The Poor* (1917; Eng. trans. 1917), and *The Chief* (1925; Eng. trans. 1925) and his historical novels *Young Henry of Navarre* (1935; Eng. trans. 1937) and *Henry, King of France* (1937; Eng. trans. 1939) were his most admired works. He emigrated to France (1933) and spent the last decade of his life in the United States. ■ See study by Rolf Linn (1967) and biography by Nigel Hamilton, *The Brothers Mann* (1978).

MANN, THOMAS (1875–1955), German novelist. Born into a prosperous and influential family in Lübeck, Mann produced a distinguished body of fiction that, on one level, presented a spiritual history of modern Europe. His early successes, the novel *Buddenbrooks* (1900; Eng. trans. 1924) and novellas *Tonio Kröger* (1903; Eng. trans. 1928) and

Death in Venice (1913; Eng. trans. 1925) concerned the conflict between the artistic spirit and bourgeois values. In the novel *The Magic Mountain* (1924; Eng. trans. 1927), Mann presented a symbolic panorama of decaying pre–World War I European society in which his young hero opts for life and social responsibility. His novella *Mario and the Magician* (1930; Eng. trans. 1930) reflected his antifascist views; his outspoken opposition to the Nazis forced him to leave Germany in 1933 and settle in Switzerland (1933–38; 1952–55) and the United States (1938–52). His later works included the tetralogy, *Joseph and His Brothers* (1933–43; Eng. trans. 1934–44) and *Doctor Faustus* (1947; Eng. trans. 1948). Mann also wrote important political, literary, philosophical, and historical essays and was awarded the 1929 Nobel Prize for Literature. His son Golo Mann (1909–1994) was a prominent historian. ■ See studies by Hans Bürgin and Hans-Otto Mayer (1965; Eng. trans. 1969), T. J. Reed (1974), Anthony Heilbut (1996), and Nigel Hamilton, *The Brothers Mann* (1978).

MANN, TOM (1856–1941), British labor leader. A worker from age 9, Mann joined the labor movement in 1881 and the socialist movement in 1885. He was a fiery orator and achieved prominence as a leader of the great London dock strike (1889). For more than 50 years he was one of the most active and militant left-wing labor leaders in Britain, leading more than 150 strikes and participating in the founding of numerous unions and labor organizations. He joined the newly founded British Communist party (1920) and held several leadership positions in the Comintern during the 1920s. ■ See *Tom Mann's Memoirs* (1923; 1967) and biography by Joseph L. White (1991).

MANNERHEIM, BARON CARL GUSTAV EMIL (1867–1951), Finnish soldier and statesman. Mannerheim was an officer in the Imperial Russian army until 1917, when Finland declared its independence after the bolshevik revolution. He returned home to command anticommunist forces against the bolsheviks. Upon crushing the revolt, Mannerheim served as regent but was defeated in the 1919 presidential election. As head of the National Defense Council (1931–39), he reorganized the army and built fortifications along the Russian border (the Mannerheim Line). He commanded Finland's armed forces during the 1939–40 Winter War with the Soviet Union, and in 1941–44, during World War II, when Finland was allied with the Axis. He was president of Finland from 1944 to 1946. ■ See his *Memoirs* (Eng. trans. 1954).

MANNHEIM, KARL (1893–1947), Hungarian-born sociologist. A Jewish-Hungarian intellectual who was influenced by Marxist thought, Mannheim fled to Germany after the fall of the radical Béla Kun government (1919). After teaching sociology at Frankfurt (from 1926) he was forced to flee, again, after the Nazis came to power (1933), and served as a professor at the University of London (1933–47). His major work, *Ideology and Utopia* (1929; Eng. trans. 1936), a pioneering study in the sociology of knowledge, attempted to demonstrate that all thought has a social function and is related to specific social groups, and that the truth of any proposition could not be determined without considering the author's class position. According to Mannheim, only free-floating, socially unattached intellectuals could transcend class-based ideological thinking and achieve disinterested knowledge. His late works, including *Man and Society in an Age of Reconstruction* (1935; Eng. trans. 1940) and *Diagnosis of Our Time* (1943), were studies of contemporary social crises in which he advocated democratic social planning and sociologically oriented education. ■ See G. W. Remmling, *The Sociology of Karl Mannheim* (1975), and study by David Kettler (1984).

MANNING, WILLIAM THOMAS (1866–1949), British-born U.S. Protestant clergyman. Manning emigrated to the United States at age 16 and studied at the University of the South. He was rector of Trinity parish in New York (1908–21), the nation's wealthiest church corporation, and served as the Protestant Episcopal bishop of New York (1921–46). He was inclined to take uncompromising public stands on matters of morality. He opposed remarriage after divorce and spearheaded the 1940 drive to prevent British philosopher Bertrand Russell—in his view a "defender of adultery" who had an "immoral and salacious attitude toward sex"—from teaching at the City College of New York. Manning also raised funds for the construction of the nave of New York's enormous Cathedral of St. John the Divine. He supported the ecumenical movement and aided social and political reform movements. ■ See W.D.F. Hughes, *Prudently with Power* (1964).

MANNIX, DANIEL (1864–1963), Australian Roman Catholic religious leader and social reformer. Mannix was born in Ireland, where he was ordained a priest (1890) and became a professor of theology and philosophy (1891). Sent to Australia (1913), he served as archbishop of Melbourne from 1917 to 1963. Politically progressive, Mannix was a spokesman for the Irish nationalists (Sinn Fein) and led opposition to conscription during World War I, calling it a "trade war between rival capitalists." He was a promoter of Catholic Action (1937–54), a highly organized lay social movement, and he lectured extensively around the world. For years he was associated with the Labour party, but his militant anticommunism helped splinter the party during the 1950s. ■ See biographies by Niall Brennan (1964) and Frank Murphy (rev. ed. 1973) and study by Colm Kiernan (1984).

MANOLETE (nickname of Manuel Laureano Rodríguez y Sánchez; 1917–1947), Spanish bullfighter. The son and grandson of matadors, Manolete was the greatest bullfighter of his generation. A hero in Spain and Latin America, he was known for his coolness and restrained style. He died after being gored in a bullfight at Linares. ■ See Barnaby Conrad, *The Death of Manolete* (1958).

MANSFIELD, KATHERINE (Kathleen Mansfield Beauchamp; 1888–1923), New Zealand–born short-story writer. After attending schools in Wellington and London (Queen's College, 1903–06), Mansfield returned to Britain (1908) and began her literary career. She was closely associated with the editor and critic John Middleton Murry (from 1911); they were married in 1918. Many of her sensitive, impressionistic, and evocative stories were set in the New Zealand of her childhood and were influenced by the works of Anton Chekhov. Ill with tuberculosis for the last five years of her life, she died in France while under the supervision of the mystic Gurdjieff. Her best-known works appeared in *Bliss and Other Stories* (1920) and *The Garden Party* (1922). Murry edited her *Journal* (1927), *Letters* (2 vols., 1928), and *Scrapbook* (1939). ■ See *The Collected Short Stories* (1937); biographies by Jeffrey Meyers (1980), Antony Alpers (1980), and Claire Tomalin (1988); and Nora Crone, *A Portrait of Katherine Mansfield* (1985).

MANSHIP, PAUL HOWARD (1885–1966), U.S. sculptor. Trained in the United States and Rome (1909–12), Manship was influenced by classical sculpture but developed a distinctive style characterized by purity and simplicity of line. He produced stylized representations of animal and human forms, frequently drawing upon mythological and allegorical figures for his subjects. He executed numerous monumental sculptures, including his most famous work, the *Prometheus Fountain* (1934) in Rockefeller Center, New York City. ■ See study by Edwin Murtha (1957).

MANTLE, MICKEY (1931–1995), U.S. baseball player. Baseball's greatest switch-hitter, Mantle played centerfield for the New York Yankees from 1951 to 1968, during which the team won 12 pennants. Although plagued by injuries, he compiled a .298 lifetime batting average, with 536 home runs, 2,415 hits, 1,509 runs batted in, and 1,677 runs scored. He was voted the American League's Most Valuable Player in 1956, 1957, and 1962 and won the triple crown in 1956; in 1961 he hit a career high of 54 home runs. Mantle was voted into the National Baseball Hall of Fame in 1974. ■ See his memoirs, *The Mick* (1985; with Herb Gluck), and biographies by Milton Shapiro (1962) and Al Silverman (1963).

MANTOVANI (Annunzio Paolo Mantovani; 1905–1980), Italian-born British conductor. The son of a violinist, Mantovani conducted light classical and popular music at the Hotel Metropole (London) during the 1920s and toured and recorded with his own orchestra during the 1930s. He achieved international fame in the 1950s with his "shimmering strings" renditions of such melodies as "Charmaine," "Misty," and "Greensleeves," which epitomized the mood music and easy-listening sound heard in elevators, restaurants, and on radio stations throughout the United States. His pseudosymphonic style remained popular through the 1970s despite the disdain of classical critics and the popularity of rock and roll, and he made frequent concert tours and sold more than 100 million albums.

MANUILSKY, DMITRI ZAKHAROVICH (1883–1959), Russian revolutionary. The son of an orthodox priest in the Ukraine, Manuilsky joined the bolsheviks (1903) and became a political activist before being arrested and going into exile in Western Europe (1907–17). After returning to Russia in the spring of 1917, he played an active role in the Comintern and was elevated to the Central Committee of the Communist party (1923). He was elected to the Comintern's presidium (1924) and political secretariat (1926) and, as dictator Joseph Stalin's official Comintern spokesman, was leader of the organization from 1928 until its dissolution in 1943. From 1944 to 1952 he was foreign minister of the Ukrainian government and represented it at the United Nations.

MANZÙ, GIACOMO (Giacomo Manzoni; 1908–1991), Italian sculptor. Apprenticed as an engraver and stucco worker. Manzù briefly studied sculpture but was largely self-taught. His sculptural style, combing classicism and modernity, was influenced by Auguste Rodin and Aristide Maillol. Beginning in 1933, he established his reputation as a portraitist with a series of women's figures in wax, wood, and bronze. The sculptures of cardinals, for which he was well known, were begun in the late 1930s, but his *Self-Portrait with the Model* (1943–46) and *Portrait of a Woman* (1946) were considered the apex of his creations. He won commissions for the bronze doors of St. Peter's in Rome (1950) and Salzburg Cathedral in Austria (1955), and for the portrait bust *Pope John XXIII* (1963), which is in the Vatican collection. Manzù also created etchings and lithographs. ▪ See study by John Rewald (1967) and Curtis B. Pepper, *An Artist and the Pope* (1968).

MAO DUN (old style: MAO TUN; 1896–1981), Chinese novelist. Mao Dun was the pseudonym of Shen Yanbing (Shen Yen-ping). A left-wing intellectual who was a prominent literary figure in China from 1920, he helped found the Literary Research Society (1920) and the proletarian League of Left-Wing Writers (1930), two of China's most influential literary organizations. His trilogy, *The Eclipse* (1930), which related his experiences on the Northern Expedition (1926), and his novel *Midnight* (1933; Eng. trans. 1957), which realistically depicted the world of exploitative speculators in the decadent Shanghai of the 1930s, were extremely popular and regarded among the finest Chinese novels of the century. His other works in English included *Spring Silkworms and Other Stories* (1956). After the communists took power in 1949 Mao held many official literary and cultural posts and was minister of culture from 1949 to 1965. A victim of the Cultural Revolution, he was confined to his house in Beijing (Peking) from 1966 to 1978. He later served as president of the Chinese Writers Association.

MAO TSE-TUNG. *See MAO ZEDONG.*

MAO TUN. *See MAO DUN.*

MAO ZEDONG (old style: MAO TSE-TUNG; 1893–1976), Chinese political leader. Born into a peasant family in Hunan province, Mao was a politically active student in Beijing (Peking; 1919) and a cofounder of the Chinese communist party (1921). Alone among the communist leaders he recognized the revolutionary potential of the peasantry. He headed the Soviet Republic established in Jiangxi (Kiangsi) province (1931–34). Forced to abandon the region by attacks from the Nationalist armies, he and his guerrilla fighters embarked on the epic 6,000-mile Long March to northwest China (1934–35), at the end of which he gained control of the Communist party. At his remote headquarters at Yanan (Yenan) he developed theories of peasant guerrilla warfare that influenced revolutionary movements throughout the world. He led the communist forces against the Japanese during World War II (1937–45), and against the Nationalists during the civil war (1945–49). The victory over the Nationalists resulted in the establishment of the People's Republic of China in Beijing (1949). Mao's plan to rapidly increase industrial output within the framework of the "people's communes" (the Great Leap Forward, 1959) and his attempt to renew the revolution by radicalizing society and purging the party bureaucracy (the Great Proletarian Cultural Revolution, 1966–69) resulted in massive social dislocation. During the 1960s Mao's thoughts (*The Little Red Book*) became official doctrine and he was the object of a personality cult. After Deng Xiao-ping (Teng Hsiao-ping) consolidated power (1980), most of Mao's policies were abandoned and his official image was significantly deflated. ▪ See his *Selected Works* (4 vols., Eng. trans. 1965); Benjamin Schwartz, *Chinese Communism and the Rise of Mao* (1951); and biographies by Jerome Ch'en (1965), Stuart Schram (1966), and Ross Terrill (1980).

MARAN, RENÉ (1887–1960), French writer. Born in Martinique, the son of an official of the French colonial service, Maran was educated in France (1894–1909), and he served in the colonial service (in Equatorial Africa) from 1909 to 1923. His best-known novel, *Batouala* (1921; Eng. trans. 1973), vividly described traditional African life as well as the horrors of colonial rule. The book created a sensation, and Maran became the first black writer to be awarded the prestigious Prix Goncourt (1921). After he left the colonial service he settled in Paris and wrote other novels and animal tales set in Africa and also several volumes of poetry. ▪ See study by Keith C. Cameron (1985).

MARBLE, ALICE (1913–1990), U.S. tennis player. In 1932 Marble won the California women's title, and by 1933 she had become the third-ranked woman tennis player in the United States. She suffered from anemia and tuberculosis, and when she collapsed on a Paris court (1934), she was advised never to play competitive tennis. She went on to a brilliant career, however, dominating competition in the late 1930s by capturing four U.S. singles championships (1936; 1938–40) and winning the singles crown at Wimbledon (1939). In 1945 she served as a spy against the Germans for U.S. Army Intelligence in Switzerland. ■ See Sue Davidson, *Changing The Game* (1997).

MARC, FRANZ (1880–1916), German painter. The son of a landscape painter, Marc studied at the Munich Academy (1900–03) before traveling to Paris, where he was influenced by the impressionists and art nouveau. After studying and drawing animals (1903–07), he taught human anatomy (1907–10) but continued to treat animals, especially deer and horses, in symbolic paintings. *His Blue Horses* (1911) expressed the innocent, spiritual nature of animals. With Wassily Kandinsky in 1911, Marc founded the Blue Rider movement, noted for pure abstraction and romantic imagery. His later work became increasingly abstract until few objects could be distinguished among the clashing lines and colors. He was killed while fighting in World War I. ■ See Frederick S. Levine, *The Apocalyptic Vision* (1979).

MARCANTONIO, VITO (1902–1954), U.S. political leader. A protégé of New York City's Fiorello La Guardia, Marcantonio was a fiery radical who served as a congressman from East Harlem first as a Republican and Fusion member (1935–37), and later as an American Labor party representative (1939–51). He supported antilynching and civil rights legislation and spoke out against the defamation of the foreign born. He was a power in New York City politics, and although he denied that he was a communist, he consistently supported Communist party causes and was frequently red-baited. ■ See studies by Alan Schaffer (1966) and Salvatore J. Lagumina (1969) and biography by Gerald Meyer (1989).

MARCEAU, MARCEL (1923–   ), French mime. Marceau served in the French underground during World War II and later in the French army of occupation in Germany. After the war he studied mime in Paris, joined the theatrical company of Jean-Louis Barrault (1946), and created the character of Bip (1947), a sad, white-faced clown clad in sailor pants and striped jacket through whom he created a silent world of human activity and emotion. He presented both full-length "mimodramas" and short sketches on his world tours with his own company (from the 1940s) and revived the art of mime in Europe and the United States. ■ See study by Ben Martin (1978).

MARCEL, GABRIEL HONORÉ (1889–1973), French philosopher and playwright. Marcel studied philosophy at the Sorbonne (1910) and was a Red Cross worker during World War I. He taught intermittently while working as an editor, writer, and critic. A convert to Roman Catholicism (1929), he viewed humans as breaking free from social roles and constraints and gaining fulfillment through faith in a transcendent deity. He reluctantly accepted the label "Christian existentialist" as a stand against philosopher Jean Paul Sartre's "atheist existentialism." His writings included *Metaphysical Journal* (1927; Eng. trans. 1952), *The Mystery of Being* (2 vols.; Eng. trans. 1951), and *The Existentialist Background to Human Dignity* (Eng. trans. 1963). ■ See studies by Z. T. Ralston (1961), K. T. Gallagher (1962), and Seymour Cain (1963).

MARCH, FREDRIC (Frederick McIntyre Bickel; 1897–1975), U.S. actor. One of the century's most versatile and sensitive stage and screen actors, March starred in 69 films and numerous Broadway productions. He occasionally appeared with his wife, the actress Florence Eldridge, whom he married in 1927. Handsome, well trained, and endowed with a resonant voice, March broke into films (1929) shortly after the advent of sound and was an immediate hit. Active for more than four decades, he won Academy Awards for his performances in *Dr. Jekyll and Mr. Hyde* (1932) and *The Best Years of Our Lives* (1946) and starred in such hit films as *Anthony Adverse* (1936), *A Star Is Born* (1937), *The Adventures of Mark Twain* (1944), *Death of a Salesman* (1951), *Inherit the Wind* (1960), and *The Iceman Cometh* (1973). His Broadway hits included *The Skin of Our Teeth* (1942), *A Bell for Adano* (1944), and his greatest triumph, *Long Day's Journey into Night* (1956), for which he won a Tony Award. ■ See biography by Deborah C. Paterson (1996).

MARCHAIS, GEORGES (1920–1997), French political leader. The son of a miner, Marchais claimed he was drafted for forced labor in Germany during World War II, but escaped in 1943. According to German documents he volunteered and worked in Germany through 1945. He was a metalworkers' union leader after the war and joined the Communist party (1947). Rising through the party's ranks he joined its Central Committee (1959) and served as secretary-general (1972–94). He forged a coalition with the socialists in the early 1970s and served in the national assembly (1973–97). Marchais endorsed a Eurocommunist policy, asserting the party's independence from the Soviet Union, in 1976, but alienated many supporters when he readopted a tough pro-Moscow line in 1979. He lost in the first round of the 1981 presidential elections and supported the eventual winner, socialist François Mitterand, during the second round, for which the communists were given four posts in the new government. Although Marchais retained his assembly seat, Communist party strength fell from 86 to 44. In 1984 the communists withdrew from the government and received only 11.2 percent of the vote in the elections for the European parliament. By 1993 the Communist share of the popular vote fell to 9.2 percent.

MARCIANO, ROCKY (Rocco Francis Marchegiano; 1923–1969), U.S. boxer. Marciano was a powerfully built fighter whose devastating punch compensated for a short reach and sometimes awkard style. He began his career in 1947 and four years later impressed boxing fans by defeating former champion Joe Louis. The following year, at age 29, he won the heavyweight crown by knocking out Jersey Joe Walcott. In the next three years he successfully defended his title six times, retiring undefeated in 1956. Marciano won 43 of his 49 professional bouts by knockouts. He died in a plane crash. ■ See biographies by Bill Libby (1971) and Everett M. Skehan (1977).

MARCOS, FERDINAND EDRALIN (1917–1989), Filipino political leader. Marcos studied law at the University of the Philippines and served in the anti-Japanese resistance during World War II. He was a Liberal member of the House of Representatives (1949–59) and Senate (1963–65), but switched to the Nationalist party and defeated incumbent Liberal Diosdado Macapagal in the 1965 presidential election. His government was successful in increasing industrial output and agricultural productivity, and despite urban guerrilla activity and the growing Communist and Muslim insurgencies in rural areas, he was reelected (1969). He maintained close ties with the United States and supported U.S. policy in Vietnam. As violent protests mounted against his government, he suspended the constitution and imposed martial law (1972–81). A new constitution (1973) gave him semidictatorial powers; he served as both president and prime minister and amassed a huge fortune. Opposition to his rule increased during the 1980s due to widespread corruption and ruinous economic policies. The assassination of popular opposition leader Benigno S. Aquino, Jr. (1983) was widely believed to have been carried out by his government. As opposition grew, he called for a presidential election (February 1986) and was challenged by Aquino's widow, Corazon (Cory) Aquino, who galvanized the opposition. The election, which Marcos "officially" won, was marked by widespread fraud and intimidation of Aquino supporters, and Marcos was pressured by domestic and international forces to resign. After he and Aquino held rival inaugurations (Feb. 25, 1986), he fled the country for exile in the United States. The Aquino government subsequently claimed that Marcos (and his wife, Imelda, who reportedly left behind 1,060 pairs of shoes and slippers at the presidential palace) stole more than $5 billion during his years in office. Marcos wrote *The Democratic Revolution in the Philippines* (1974) and *The New Philippine Republic—A Third World Approach to Democracy* (1982). ■ See biography by Hartzell Spence (1969); David A. Rosenberg, ed., *Marcos and Martial Law in the Philippines* (1979); Raymond Bonner, *Waltzing with a Dictator* (1987); and Sterling Seagrave, *The Marcos Dynasty* (1988).

MARCUS, RUDOLPH A. (1923–), Canadian-born U.S. chemist. Marcus earned a Ph.D. in physical chemistry from McGill University, Montreal (1946), and moved to the United States to pursue a career in theoretical research (1949). As a professor at the Polytechnic Institute of Brooklyn, New York, (1951–64) and at the University of Illinois (1964–78) he developed a controversial mathematical theory regarding electron-transfer reactions in chemical systems. Although not verified until 1985, his theory helped scientists explain such complex phenomena as photosynthesis, chemiluminescence, corrosion, and electricity-conducting polymers, and he was awarded the 1992 Nobel Prize for chemistry. He was also a professor at the California Institute of Technology (Caltech) (from 1978).

MARCUSE, HERBERT (1898–1979), German-born U.S. Marxist philosopher. An active member of the renowned Frankfurt Institute for Social Research before emigrating to the United States (1934), Marcuse taught philosophy at Columbia, Harvard, Yale, Brandeis, and the University of California at San Diego. His work, influenced by Marx and Freud, described the repressive nature of contemporary society and the need for revolutionary change. He gained great popularity with the young radicals of the 1960s and was regarded as the major intellectual influence on the "New Left" movement. Among his best-known works were *Reason and Revolution* (1941), *Eros and Civilization* (1955), *Soviet Marxism* (1958), and *One-Dimensional Man* (1964). ■ See Harold Bleich, *The Philosophy of Herbert Marcuse* (1977); Morton Schoolman, *The Imaginary Witness* (1980); and biography by Barry Katz (1982).

MARGAI, SIR MILTON (1895–1964), Sierra Leonean political leader. A member of a wealthy commercial family, Margai was trained as a medical doctor and worked for the British colonial medical service (1928–50). In 1949 he began his active political career in the protectorate assembly, and he founded (1951) the conservative Sierra Leone People's party with the goal of self-government within the Commonwealth. As leader of the majority party, he was named chief minister in 1954, prime minister in 1960, and presided over the transition to independence in 1961. He was succeeded (1964) as prime minister by his brother, Sir Albert Margai. ■ See John Cartwright, *Political Leadership in Sierra Leone* (1978).

MARIÁTEGUI, JOSÉ CARLOS (1895–1930), Peruvian political theorist. One of the most influential South American Marxist thinkers of the century, Mariátegui was a largely self-taught reformist journalist whose radical views were solidified during four years of travel and study in Western Europe (1919–23). He joined the newly formed radical political party APRA (1924) and founded the journal *Amauta* (1926), which contained articles by the most prominent left-wing intellectuals of the Americas. His articles on contemporary Peruvian and world affairs were noted for their incisive analyses and his book, *Seven Interpretive Essays on Peruvian Reality* (1928; Eng. trans. 1971) contained the first Marxist interpretations of Peruvian history, culture, and economy. He left APRA and formed the Socialist party (1928), which split into orthodox communist and independent socialist organizations after Mariátegui's death. ■ See John M. Baines, *Revolution in Peru* (1972), and the study of Jesús Chavarría (1979).

MARIN, JOHN (1870–1953), U.S. painter. Marin traveled in Europe (1905–09), where he came under the influence of the painter James McNeill Whistler. Despite his participation in group exhibitions in Paris, he had little contact with new movements in art until returning to New York. He showed in the influential 1913 Armory Show along with Picasso, Matisse, and others. His work was affected by cubism, German expressionism, and particularly Cézanne's late watercolors. Mann had numerous exhibitions of forceful watercolors, many of them New England seascapes and views of Manhattan. Among his best-known works are *Lower Manhattan* (1920) and *Maine Islands* (1922). ■ See study edited by Cleve Gray (1970).

MARINETTI, FILIPPO TOMMASO (1876–1944), Italian writer. Born in Egypt, Marinetti studied in Paris and his first writings were in French. He is remembered less for his literary output than for his role in formulating (1909) Italian futurism, an iconoclastic avant-garde literary movement that in the early years of the century attracted a number of writers, composers, and artists. Futurists repudiated common usage in such spheres as language and literary convention; they gave modern technology a leading place in artistic creation and celebrated action, aggressiveness, nationalism, warfare, and the destruction of traditional culture. Many, including Marinetti, became fascists. Russian futurism, as formulated by the poet Vladimir Mayakovsky and others, was in part a reaction against the views of Marinetti, whom they regarded as politically retrograde. English translations of his works included R. W. Flint, ed., *Marinetti: Selected Writings* (1972), *Let's Murder the Moonshine: Selected Writings* (1991), *The Futurist Cookbook* (1989), and *Untameables* (1994), a collection of humorous stories.

MARING, H. *See SNEEVLIET, HENDRICUS.*

MARINI, MARINO (1901–1980), Italian sculptor and graphic artist. A portraitist and graphic artist who stood apart from the artistic movements of his day, Marini contributed significantly to a modern renaissance in Italian sculpture during the first half of the century. Influenced by German Gothic and ancient Etruscan and Roman sculpture, he was best known for his horse-and-rider series (begun in 1936); the equestrian figures are motionless but have a dynamic quality that suggests an inner energy. He sculpted strong female figures such as *Dancer* (1953) and executed such portraits as *Igor Stravinsky* (1951). In the 1950s he turned to more abstract work. ■ See his *Complete Works,* with text by Patrick Waldberg (1970), and studies by A. M. Hammacher (1970) and Alberto Busignani (1971).

MARINO, DAN (Daniel Constantine Marino, Jr.; 1961–   ), U.S. football player. Marino played for the University of Pittsburgh (1979–83) before becoming a star quarterback for the National Football League's Miami Dolphins (1983–2000). During the 1984–85 season he set league single-season passing records for most yards gained (5,084) and most touchdown passes (48) and won the league's Most Valuable Player award. Despite numerous injuries he was one of the most successful players in NFL history, setting regular-season career records for passes thrown (8,358), completed passes (4,967), yards gained through passes (61,361), and touchdown passes (420).

MARION, FRANCES (Marion Benson Owens; 1888–1973), U.S. screenwriter. Marion was a successful commercial artist and newspaper reporter in her native San Francisco before joining the movie industry as a $15-a-week studio assistant at the age of 26. She wrote her first original scenario in 1916 and soon became one of Hollywood's most prolific and highest-paid screenwriters. In a career lasting more than 20 years, spanning both the silent and the early talking-picture eras, she wrote the scenarios, original stories, or adaptations for some of the most popular movies in cinema history, including *Stella Dallas* (1925), *The Son of the Sheik* (1925), *The Scarlet Letter* (1926), *Anna Christie* (1930), *Min and Bill* (1930), *Dinner at Eight* (1933), and *Camille* (1937). She wrote many films starring her close friend Mary Pickford, including *Poor Little Rich Girl* (1917), *A Little Princess* (1917), and *Pollyanna* (1920). Marion won Academy Awards for *The Big House* (1930) and *The Champ* (1931). She also wrote *How to Write and Sell Film Stories* (1937) as well as six novels and numerous short stories. ■ See her autobiography, *Off with Their Heads* (1972), and Cari Beauchamp, *Without Lying Down* (1997).

MARIS, ROGER (1934–1985), U.S. baseball player. A better-than-average player who played the outfield for Cleveland (1957), Kansas City (1958–59), the New York Yankees (1960–66), and the St. Louis Cardinals (1967–68), Maris made baseball history in 1961 when he broke Babe Ruth's 1927 single-season home-run mark with 61 round-trippers. The record sparked sharp controversy since it was accomplished in a 162-game schedule and not, like Ruth's, in 154. Voted the Most Valuable Player for 1960 and 1961, Maris never again approached the home-run record, but as a St. Louis Cardinal he helped the team to National League pennants in 1967 and 1968. He hit 275 home runs during his career.

MARISOL (Marisol Escobar; 1930–   ), U.S. sculptor. Born in Paris to wealthy Venezuelan parents, Marisol was raised in France, South America, and southern California. Inspired by the painted figurines of South American folk art, she created life-size figures out of clay and wood, many of them caricatures of current celebrities, that were the sensation of the 1962 New York art season. Some of Marisol's humanoids bore her own face. Most of her work combined humor and social criticism, but her sculptures of the 1970s depicted a mythical underwater world of sharks and fishes. Her works of the 1980s included large-scale figural assemblages.

MARITAIN, JACQUES (1882–1973), French philosopher. Influenced by philosopher Henri Bergson, Protestant-born Maritain and his Russian-Jewish wife started a trend among French intellectuals by converting to Roman Catholicism in 1906. In the 1920s he hosted a salon for such culturati of the "Catholic revival" as the artist Georges Rouault and the philosopher Emmanuel Mounier. He was a teacher, editor, and writer on contemporary political and social issues, and became a leading modern interpreter of St. Thomas Aquinas. He was known as well for his own Thomist thought, which draws from other philosophies as well. After post–World War II service as France's ambassador to the Vatican (1945–48), Maritain taught at Princeton University for 12 years. He wrote many books, including *Art and Scholasticism* (1920; Eng. trans. 1930) and *The Degrees of Knowledge* (1932; Eng. trans. 1937), in which he argued that an abstract concept has greater reality than a physical object. ■ See memoirs by Raïssa Maritain (1942, 1945), studies by Bernard E. Doering (1983) and John M. Dunaway (1978), and biographies by G. Phelan (1937) and H. Bans (1959).

MARKANDAYA, KAMALA (Kamala Purnaiya; 1924–), Indian novelist. The daughter of a south Indian rail transport officer, Markandaya traveled extensively throughout India and Europe during her youth. After working as a journalist in Madras and Bombay, she emigrated to London (1948), where her novel *Nectar in a Sieve* was published (1954). This highly praised study of south Indian village life was followed by a series of novels noted for their variety of social settings and skillful character development. She was particularly praised for her portrayals of the problems of the educated middle class. Her other well-known works, all written in English, Included *A Silence of Desire* (1960), *Possession* (1963), *A Handful of Rice* (1966), *The Coffer Dams* (1969), *Two Virgins* (1973), and *Shalimar* (1983).

MARKIEVICZ, CONSTANCE GEORGINA, COUNTESS (Constance Gore-Booth; 1868–1927), Irish revolutionary. Born in London, Constance Gore-Booth married the Polish count Casimir Markievicz (1900). When her marriage failed, she became a follower of the independence movement Sinn Féin, although disagreeing with its pacifist stance. She organized the Fianna Éireann (1909), a national boy-scout organization, and personally instructed its members in the martial arts. Her scouts were later active in the Irish revolution. For her role in the Easter Rebellion of 1916, she was sentenced to death but freed a year later. Shortly after, she converted to Roman Catholicism. Following her release, she was the first woman elected to the British House of Com-

mons (1918) but refused to take the oath of allegiance and did not take her seat; later she served as minister of labor for the Dáil Éireann, the Irish parliament (1919–21), spending much of her tenure behind bars. She opposed the free state and supported the republicans during the civil war, for which she was jailed (1923–24). Countess Markievicz was also active in the suffrage movement. ■ See Anne Marreco, *The Rebel Countess* (1976); Diana Norman, *Terrible Beauty* (1987); and studies by Jacqueline Van Voris (1967) and Anne Haverty (1988).

MARKISH, PERETZ (1895–1952), Russian-born Yiddish-language poet, novelist, and playwright. The recipient of a traditional Jewish education, Markish became a secular Yiddish poet who acclaimed the new Soviet revolution. He left Soviet Russia for Poland and France (1921) but returned five years later and actively supported the government, writing of industrialization, collectivization, and the socialist reconstruction of the Jewish masses. During World War II Markish wrote many patriotic epic poems that were filled with praise for Soviet leader Joseph Stalin. However, he was arrested in 1948, accused of Jewish nationalism, and executed on Aug. 12, 1952, with several other prominent Jewish writers. ■ See the autobiography of his widow, Esther Markish, *The Long Return* (1974; Eng. trans. 1978).

MARKOVA, DAME ALICIA (Lilian Alicia Marks; 1910–), British ballerina. Markova joined (1925) Diaghilev's Ballet Russe, dancing for Diaghilev until his death (1929). She became (1932) prima ballerina of the Vic-Wells (later the Royal) Ballet and was the first British ballerina to dance the principal roles in *Giselle* and *Swan Lake* and to win international renown. Markova formed (1935) a company with Anton Dolin, and later appeared (1938–41) with the Ballet Russe de Monte Carlo. She retired (1962) but later directed (1963–69) the Metropolitan Opera (New York) Ballet. Markova wrote *Giselle and I* (1960). ■ See her memoirs, *Markova Remembers* (1986); biography by Maurice Leonard (1995); and study by Anton Dolin (1953).

MARKOWITZ, HARRY M. (1927–), U.S. economist. Markowitz received a Ph.D. in economics from the University Chicago (1955), worked at the Rand Corporation (1952–60; 1961–63) and at IBM (1974–83), and taught finance at Baruch College of the City University of New York (1982–93). In pioneering studies in the 1950s he developed portfolio theory, which provided quantitative methods for analyzing how wealth or savings can be optimally invested in corporate stocks and bonds. He showed how risks and rewards associated with different investments can be measured and demonstrated that a diversification of holdings yields the maximum returns. His research, along with the related studies of Merton H. Miller and William F. Sharpe, created the modern discipline of financial economics and provided the theoretical underpinnings of the mutual fund business. The three researchers shared the 1990 Nobel

Memorial Prize in Economics. Markowitz's books included *Portfolio Selection: Efficient Diversification of Investments* (1959).

MARKS, SIMON, 1st BARON (1888–1964), British retailer. His father was a Jewish immigrant from Poland who developed a chain of penny bazaars. Simon Marks joined the family business at age 19 and eventually built it into a network of 237 Marks & Spencer department stores that appealed to consumers with low-priced items. Working with his brother-in-law Israel Sieff, Marks stressed quality control and economies of scale, specification buying, and merchandising. In 1938, he helped to found Britain's Air Defence Cadet Corps (later the Air Training Corps). He was also known for his philanthropy and for his lifelong support of Zionism. ■ See study by Paul Bookbinder (1993).

MARLEY, BOB (1945–1981), Jamaican reggae singer and composer. Marley emerged from the slums of Kingston to worldwide fame as the most influential star of reggae, the popular Jamaican music infused with African, Caribbean, and black American soul rhythms. A charismatic stage personality who was closely associated with the Rastafarian religious movement, Marley reached millions of his followers around the world through his mesmerizing concert appearances and his numerous recordings with his group, the Wailers (from 1963). His militancy and revolutionary lyrics symbolized, for many, the black consciousness movement of the 1970s. He died of cancer. ■ See Timothy White, *Catch a Fire* (1983; rev. ed. 1989) and the biographies by Adrian Boot and Vivien Goldman (1982) and Stephen Davis (1985).

MARQUAND, JOHN PHILLIPS (1893–1960), U.S. novelist. Harvard-educated Marquand spent 15 years (1922–37) cranking out popular fiction for magazines, including the adventures of the inscrutable Japanese detective Mr. Moto. His series of satiric novels featuring upper-class Bostonians began with *The Late George Apley* (1937, Pulitzer Prize). Marquand studied New England social patterns and regional influences in *Wickford Point* (1939), *Point of No Return* (1949), *Sincerely, Willis Wayde* (1955), *Timothy Dexter Revisited* (1960)—an autobiographical work set in Newburyport, Massachusetts—and numerous other works. *Thirty Years* (1954) is a collection of stories and articles. ■ See Stephen Birmingham, *The Late John Marquand* (1972), and biography by Millicent Bell (1979).

MARQUÉS, RENÉ (1919–1979), Puerto Rican short-story writer and dramatist. An advocate of Puerto Rican independence, Marqués wrote about the cultural and economic domination of Puerto Rico by North America, couching his political concerns in psychological explorations. He wrote short stories, including the collection *Another One of Our Days* (1955), and plays such as *The Oxcart* (1951–52; Eng. trans. 1969) and *The House of the Setting Suns* (1958; Eng.

trans. 1965). He dealt with the anguish of emigration, both from rural Puerto Rico to cities and from Puerto Rico to the United States. ■ See his collected essays, *The Docile Puerto Rican* (Eng. trans. 1976), and study by Eleanor Martin (1979).

MARQUIS, DONALD ROBERT PERRY (1878–1937), U.S. writer. Don Marquis was an Illinois-born peripatetic journalist who wrote satirical columns for the *New York Sun* (1913–22) and *Herald Tribune* (from 1922) featuring such characters as "archy" the cockroach and "mehitabel" the alley cat. He expressed his cynical philosophy in *The Almost Perfect State* (1927), *The Old Soak's History of the World* (1937), and *Sons of the Puritans* (1939), an unfinished autobiographical novel. He also wrote plays, poetry, and short stories. ■ See Edward Anthony, *O Rare Don Marquis* (1962).

MARQUIS, FREDERICK JAMES. *See* WOOLTON, *FREDERICK JAMES MARQUIS, 1st EARL OF.*

MARR, NIKOLAI YAKOVLEVICH (1864–1934), Soviet linguist and archaeologist. Born in Georgia (his grandfather was a Scot who went to the Caucasus to cultivate tobacco), Mann researched Caucasian linguistics and history. His Marxist-inspired theory of language, which claimed that language was based on socioeconomic factors and that the vocabularies of all known languages derived from four primordial roots, retarded Soviet linguistics; his influence in his field has been compared to that of T. D. Lysenko in the realm of biology. His views were ultimately discredited when Soviet dictator Joseph Stalin published the essay "Marxism and Questions of Linguistics" (1950), which rehabilitated pre-Marrist linguistic principles. ■ See Lawrence L. Thomas, *The Linguistic Theories of N. Ja. Marr* (1957).

MARSALIS, WYNTON (1961–), U.S. trumpeter. Marsalis was born into a New Orleans family steeped in the black jazz idiom. His mother was a onetime jazz singer, his father an instructor of jazz improvisation and a pianist in the band of trumpeter Al Hirt. Hirt gave Marsalis his first trumpet. From age 12, he studied seriously, and began winning competitions at age 14. In 1979, Marsalis entered Juilliard in New York City, but found there a bias against jazz. The following year, he joined Art Blakey's jazz ensemble; at age 19, Marsalis became the band's musical director, and his virtuosity won national attention. In 1981 Marsalis formed his own band (with his brother, saxophonist Branford Marsalis) and signed a contract with Columbia Records to make both jazz and classical recordings. He impressed critics with his exceptional tone, phrasing, and interpretations in both realms. Marsalis was the first musician to win Grammy Awards for both classical and jazz albums in a single year (1984); the 1983 albums, *Think of One* and *Trumpet Concertos,* were released simultaneously and each sold 100,000 copies. He subsequently made the jazz album *Wynton*

Marsalis: Hot House Flowers (1984), and the television special *Wynton Marsalis: Catching a Snake* (1985). With his jazz oratorio, *Blood on the Fields* (1994), a three-hour meditation on slavery, he became the first jazz artist to win a Pulitzer Prize for Music (1997). He also created a four-hour series, *Marsalis on Music* (1995), for the Public Broadcasting System, and a symphonic piece, *All Rise* (1999), on the theme of the millennium. He was a cofounder and artistic director of Jazz at Lincoln Center (1987–) and leader of the Lincoln Center Jazz Orchestra. ▪ See his *Sweet Swing Blues on the Road* (1994; with Frank Stewart) and Leslie Gourse, *Skain's Domain* (1999).

MARSH, DAME (EDITH) NGAIO (1899–1982), New Zealand writer. Marsh's literary detective thrillers were set in New Zealand and Britain and drew on her early experiences as an art student and actress. Her many popular books included *A Man Lay Dead* (1934), *Artists in Crime* (1938), *Died in the Wool* (1945), *Night at the Vulcan* (1951), *False Scent* (1959), and *Black as He's Painted* (1974). They featured a cultured detective, Roderick Alleyn of Scotland Yard, and were noted for their ingenuity, style, and realistic characterizations. Marsh was also a theatrical producer. ▪ See her autobiography, *Black Beech and Honeydew* (1965) and the biography by Margaret Lewis (1991).

MARSH, REGINALD (1898–1954), U.S. painter. Born in Paris of American artist parents, Marsh studied at Yale and at the Art Students League of New York and was influenced both by the old masters, whom he studied, and contemporary social realists. He sketched vaudeville acts for the *New York Daily News* and was an original staff member of the *New Yorker* (1925). His humorous and realistic illustrations of New York City life set a standard for that magazine and established Marsh's reputation. He worked on the city streets, sketching people and places for such paintings as *In 14th Street* (1934) and *Twenty-Cent Movie* (1936). Many of his vigorous, baroque compositions depicted Coney Island and the Bowery. Several of his egg-tempera paintings are permanently installed at the Whitney Museum of American Art (New York), the Chicago Art Institute, and other major museums. ▪ See study by Lloyd Goodrich (1972).

MARSHALL, GEORGE CATLETT (1880–1959), U.S. general and cabinet officer. A career military officer, Marshall was army chief of staff during World War II (1939–45). He was a close adviser to Presidents Franklin D. Roosevelt and Harry Truman at the Allied wartime conferences. He failed in his mission to negotiate between the communists and the nationalists in ending the Chinese civil war (1945–47). As secretary of state (1947–49) he launched a plan (1947), subsequently known as the Marshall Plan, for the recovery of Europe; for that work he received the Nobel Peace Prize (1953). He played a central role in the formation of the North Atlantic Treaty Organization (NATO) and served as secretary of defense (1950–51) during the Korean War. ▪ See

biographies by Forest C. Pogue (2 vols., 1963–67) and Leonard Mosley (1982) and Ed Cray, *General of the Army* (1990).

MARSHALL, SIR JOHN HUBERT (1876–1958), British archaeologist and explorer. As director general of the Indian Archaeological Survey (1902–31), Marshall directed the excavation of the previously unknown ancient buried cities of Harappa and Mohenjo-Daro in the Indus River delta, which flourished from about 2500 to 1750 B.C. As described in *Mohenjo-Daro and the Indus Civilization* (3 vols., 1931), these cities paralleled the development of the Tigris-Euphrates river valley and may have been in communication with the Fertile Crescent. Marshall was also instrumental in preserving the Buddhist structures at Sanchi and Sarnath, and he wrote *The Monuments of Sanchi* (3 vols., 1939).

MARSHALL, LOUIS (1856–1929), U.S. lawyer and Jewish community leader. As a lawyer in Syracuse (1878–94) and New York City (from 1894), Marshall defended minorities in cases involving constitutional rights and appeared frequently before the U.S. Supreme Court. His mediation of the cloakmakers' strike (1910) became a model for subsequent arbitration. He was a founder (1906; president, 1912–29) of the American Jewish Committee, the Jewish Welfare Board, and the Joint Distribution Committee; chairman of the board of the Jewish Theological Seminary; and director of the Educational Alliance and the National Association for the Advancement of Colored People (NAACP). He was largely responsible for the abrogation of the 1832 Russian-American Treaty (1911), which he attacked for Russia's refusal to honor passports of U.S. Jews. He championed minority rights at the Paris Peace Conference (1919) and helped draft treaties that guaranteed civil, religious, and political rights in Poland, Rumania, and other nations of Eastern Europe. ▪ See his writings, edited by Charles Reznikoff (1957), and study by Morton Rosenstock (1965).

MARSHALL, THOMAS RILEY (1854–1925), U.S. vice president. Riley was a reform Democratic governor of Indiana (1909–13) before serving as Pres. Woodrow Wilson's vice president (1913–21). As chief officer of the Senate, he personally influenced the passage of much of Wilson's legislation, and he was a strong supporter of the League of Nations concept. A popular and whimsical politician, he once remarked during a tedious Senate debate on the nation's needs that "what this country needs is a really good five-cent cigar." ▪ See his memoirs (1925).

MARSHALL, THURGOOD (1908–1993), U.S. jurist. Marshall was born in Baltimore, worked his way through Lincoln University (B.A. 1930), and graduated from Howard University at the head of his law class (1933). Joining the National Association for the Advancement of Colored People as legal counsel (1936), he argued numerous cases before the Supreme Court, which resulted in landmark decisions ending segregation in voting, housing, jury selection, and interstate transportation. His work on school cases culminated in the Supreme Court's 1954 ruling that segregation in public education was unconstitutional. Marshall was appointed to the U.S. Court of Appeals (1961) and to the U.S. solicitor generalship (1966). He was the first African American to serve on the U.S. Supreme Court (from 1967) and was one of its most liberal members. ▪ See Randall W. Bland, *Private Pressure on Public Law* (1973); Carl T. Rowan, *Dream Makers, Dream Breakers* (1993); and biography by Juan Williams (1998).

MARTIN, ARCHER JOHN PORTER (1910–), British biochemist. Martin's nutrition studies in the 1930s led him to confront the problem of protein structure. The amino acids that constitute a protein are so similar that scientists had failed to separate them by ordinary chemical means. Collaborating with Richard Synge, Martin solved (1941) this problem by developing paper-partition chromatography, improving on the process introduced earlier by Mikhail Tsvett and Richard Willstätter. Martin and Synge took advantage of the capillary action of porous filter paper, realizing that various amino acids would creep up the paper at different rates depending on their solubility. This quick procedure of separating the components of complex mixtures generated data permitting calculation of the quantity and sequence of amino acids in a protein. The method was immediately seized upon by such chemists as Frederick Sanger, who isolated insulin, and Melvin Calvin, who investigated photosynthesis. Martin and Synge shared the 1952 Nobel Prize for Chemistry. The following year Martin, working with A. T. James, introduced gas chromatography. He worked at the Wool Industries Research Association (1938–46), the Medical Research Council (1948–59), Abbotsbury Laboratories Ltd. (1959–70), and taught at several universities.

MARTIN, DEAN (Dino Crocetti; 1917–1995), U.S. singer and entertainer. After stints as a boxer, steelworker, croupier, and dance-band singer, Martin teamed up with comedian Jerry Lewis (1946) to form one of the most successful partnerships in show-business history. For ten years, Martin and Lewis starred in nightclubs and on television and appeared in 16 popular films, including *My Friend Irma* (1949), *That's My Boy* (1951), and *Pardners* (1956). After the pair's breakup, the suave romantic crooner recorded several hit record albums and became a popular dramatic movie actor, television host, and solo nightclub performer. His best-known songs included "That's Amore," "Everybody Loves Somebody," and "Memories Are Made of This." ▪ See Nick Tosches, *Dino* (1992).

MARTIN, FRANK (1890–1974), Swiss composer. Martin's early works were influenced by French impressionism; he later adopted a modified 12-tone technique, but a highly individualistic neoclassical spirit characterized his works and he never fully abandoned tonality. His compositions include orchestral and chamber music, two operas, the oratorios *Le Vin Herbé* (1941) and *Golgotha* (1948), and a requiem (1972). He taught at the Jaques-Dalcroze Institute, Geneva, and the Cologne Conservatory.

MARTIN, GLENN LUTHER (1886–1955), U.S. aircraft designer and manufacturer. Martin began marketing aircraft at age 8, when he sold homemade kites. He built his first plane in 1909 and attracted public attention with flying exhibitions (1909–15) and with the first American aerial-bombing experiments. He set up his own company (1917) and developed the bombers that were used by Billy Mitchell in his bombing tests, proving that planes could sink battleships (1921). By the outset of World War II his airplane manufacturing firm was the largest in the United States, and it designed and constructed thousands of planes, including bombers and transports used extensively during the war. ▪ See Henry Still, *To Ride the Wind* (1964).

MARTIN, JOSEPH WILLIAM, JR. (1884–1968), U.S. congressman. A Massachusetts newspaper publisher, Martin was a state legislator (1912–17) before serving in the U.S. House of Representatives for 42 years (1925–67). Known for his conservative views and mastery of political strategy and organization, he was the House Republican leader over a 20-year period (1939–59) and was twice speaker of the House (1947–48: 1953–54). He also served as permanent chairman of five Republican national conventions (1940–56). He was defeated for reelection in the 1966 Republican primary. ▪ See his autobiography, *My First Fifty Years in Politics* (1960).

MARTIN, (BASIL) KINGSLEY (1897–1969), British journalist and editor. Martin taught political science at the London School of Economics (1923–27) before taking an editorial position with the *Manchester Guardian,* which he left for the *New Statesman,* a small left-wing weekly. Under his brilliant editorial leadership (1931–60), the magazine became one of the most influential radical journals in the world, perfectly reflecting the mood of Britain's independent left-wing intellectuals. Over the years, his weekly column strongly advocated friendship with the Soviet Union, a united front against Nazi Germany, and independence for Britain's colonies. He wrote several works of history and political analysis as well as two autobiographical volumes, *Father Figures* (1966) and *Editor* (1968).

MARTIN, MARY (1913–1990), U.S. singer and actress. After leaving the University of Texas, Mary Martin studied and taught dancing. She made her Broadway stage debut in Cole Porter's Broadway show *Leave It to Me* (1938), popularizing the tune "My Heart Belongs to Daddy," and made films in Hollywood but was never enthusiastic about movies. Martin acted before live audiences across America in musical-comedy roles, touring (1947–48) in *Annie Get*

Your Gun and creating Ensign Nellie Forbush in a two-year run (1949–51) in *South Pacific.* She won critical acclaim for *The Sound of Music* (1959–60), *I Do! I Do!* (1966), and for her TV performance in *Peter Pan* (1955). Her son is the actor Larry Hagman (1931–   ), best known for his role as J. R. Ewing, Jr., in the television series "Dallas." She wrote the autobiographical *Mary Martin's Needlepoint* (1969) and *My Heart Belongs* (1976).

MARTIN, WILLIAM MCCHESNEY (1906–1998), U.S. economist and government official. The son of a St. Louis banker, Martin graduated from Yale (B.A. 1928) and was the "boy wonder" president of the New York Stock Exchange (1938–41). He was an army economist during World War II and played a major role in supervising lend-lease aid to the Soviet Union. After the war he served as president of the Export-Import Bank (1946–48) and assistant secretary of the treasury (1949–51) before being appointed by Pres. Harry Truman to chair the Federal Reserve Board (1951). In the early 1950s he was the architect of the accord with the Treasury Department that enabled monetary policy to be linked to government planning. Reappointed as "Fed" chairman by presidents Eisenhower, Kennedy, and Johnson, Martin was the dominant figure in the financial world for two decades (1951–70). Although he basically favored anti-inflationary, tight-money policies, he moderated them to meet current needs.

MARTIN DU GARD, ROGER (1881–1958), French novelist. Trained as an archivist and paleographer, Martin du Gard served in World War I and then spent the rest of his life writing in quiet seclusion. His major works explored the intellectual conflicts of his generation. *Jean Barois* (1913; Eng. trans. 1949), with its striking dialogue, concerned the conflict between rationalism and science and religious faith. *The World of the Thibaults* (8 vols., 1922–40; Eng. trans., 2 vols., 1939–41) was a vast and detailed realistic chronicle of two families set amid the intellectual and social currents of Europe before and during World War I. He was awarded a Nobel Prize for Literature (1937). ■ See biography by David L. Schalk (1967).

MARTINELLI, GIOVANNI (1885–1969), Italian opera singer. One of the greatest Italian dramatic tenors of his time, Martinelli made his debut at La Scala (Milan) in 1910 and sang at New York's Metropolitan Opera from 1913 to 1946. A brilliant and powerful tenor, he had one of the longest careers and most diverse repertories (56 roles) in operatic history. He was best remembered for his singing in *Aïda, La Juive, Norma, Tosca,* and *Il Trovatore* and was regarded as the greatest Otello of his generation. Although he officially retired in 1946, he continued to perform in public and last appeared, in the role of the emperor in *Turandot,* in 1967.

MARTÍNEZ RUIZ, JOSÉ. *See* AZORÍN

MARTINS, PETER (1946–   ), Danish dancer, ballet master, and choreographer. Born in Copenhagen, Martins trained at the School of the Royal Danish Ballet and graduated into its company (1965). Acclaimed for performances in the Bournonville repertory, Martins was invited to join the New York City Ballet in 1969, after making an impressive fill-in appearance for an injured dancer in the title role of George Balanchine's *Apollo* while the troupe was on tour. He made a career with the City Ballet (principal dancer, 1970–83) and was often paired with Kay Mazzo and Suzanne Farrell in the 1970s. He danced roles in such Balanchine works as *Chaconne* (1976), *Union Jack* (1976), *Vienna Waltzes* (1980), and Schumann's *Davidsbundlertanze* (1980). Martins made his debut as a choreographer with *Calcium Light Night* (1977); he also choreographed *Five Easy Pieces* (1980) and collaborated with Andrew Lloyd Webber on the Broadway musical *Song and Dance* (1985). After Balanchine's death in 1983, Peter Martins and Jerome Robbins took over the New York City Ballet as co-ballet masters-in-chief, with Martins responsible for the troupe's day-to-day operation. He became sole master-in-chief in 1990 and choreographed numerous ballet pieces. ■ See his autobiography, *Far from Denmark* (1982; with Peter Cornfield).

MARTINSON, HARRY EDMUND (1904–1978), Swedish novelist and poet. Largely self-educated, Martinson wrote several travel books, including *Cape Farewell* (1933; Eng. trans. 1934), studies, and novels, all based on his own experiences as a poor orphan, sailor, and vagabond. His novel *The Road* (1948; Eng. trans. 1955) was a sympathetic study of tramps and outcasts in an age of growing industrialization. Martinson was best known, however, for such lyric poems as "Trade Winds" (1945), which revealed his verbal invention and great love of nature. His later work expressed profound pessimism about modern society. His most famous work was *Aniara* (1956; Eng. trans. 1963), a verse fantasy of a spaceship off course and journeying into the void. *Flowering Nettle* (1935; Eng. trans. 1936) was autobiographical. He shared the Nobel Prize for Literature in 1974 with his compatriot Eyvind Johnson. Translations of his poems appeared in Robert Bly, ed., *Friends, You Drank Some Darkness* (1975), and *Wild Bouquet* (1985).

MARTINŮ, BOHUSLAV (1890–1959), Czech composer. Expelled from the Prague Conservatory, he studied privately with the Czech nationalist composer Josef Suk and in Paris with Albert Roussel. Though he lived abroad after 1923 and became a U.S. citizen in 1952, elements of Czech folk music persist in his music, often integrated with international musical trends—for example, in the neoclassical *Concerto Grosso* (1941) for orchestra. His varied and prolific output included six symphonies, chamber music, choral pieces, operas, and the memorable orchestral works, *Double Concerto* (1938) and *Memorial to Lidice* (1943). ■ See study by Brian Large (1976).

MARTOV, L. or JULIUS (Iulii Osipovich Tsederbaum; 1873–1923), Russian political leader. An activist in the Jewish Socialist Bund in Vilna (Vilnius), Martov joined V. I. Lenin to found the St. Petersburg Union of Struggle for the Emancipation of the Working Class (1895) and the Marxist journal *Iskra* ("the spark"; Geneva, 1900). However, at the second congress of the Russian Social Democratic party (1903) he advocated a mass revolutionary workers' party rather than a narrow party of professional revolutionaries and broke with Lenin. Thereafter he was a leader of the anti-Leninist Mensheviks and after the 1917 revolution opposed the dictatorial methods of the Bolshevik government. He supported the bolsheviks in the Russian civil war (1918–20), but when the Menshevik party was outlawed (1920) he emigrated to Berlin, where he led the Mensheviks in exile. ■ See biography by Israel Getzler (1967).

MARTY, ANDRÉ PIERRE (1886–1956), French political leader. The son of a participant in the Paris Commune (1871), Marty joined the French navy (1908) and instigated the Black Sea Mutiny (1919) aboard two warships sent to fight the Bolsheviks during the civil war in the Soviet Union (1918–20). After serving four years in prison, he was amnestied; he joined the Communist party and served in parliament (1924–28; 1929–40; 1945–55). He also served on the Central Committee of the Communist party (from 1925) and was a member of the Executive Committee of the Comintern (1932–43). Marty was the organizer and commander in chief of the international brigades that fought against the forces of Francisco Franco during the Spanish civil war (1936–39). He lived in Moscow from 1939 to 1943 and returned to France at the end of World War II. He was expelled from the Communist party in a factional dispute in 1953.

MARX BROTHERS, U.S. comedy team. Sons of German immigrants, the five Marx brothers were pushed by their mother Minnie from vaudeville to Broadway and Hollywood. Chico (**Leonard, 1887–1961**), who spoke Italian gibberish, formed a duo with the silent, curly-haired Harpo (**Adolph, 1888–1964**), nicknamed after the instrument he played. Groucho (**Julius, 1890–1977**), with his arched eyebrows, greasepaint mustache, and cigar, specialized in puns and insults: "I could dance with you till the cows come home," he quipped in one film. "On second thought, I'd rather dance with the cows until you come home." Gummo (**Milton, 1894–1977**) worked with his brothers on stage but left show business before their films. And Zeppo (**Herbert, 1901–1979**) played straight man until he left the group in the 1930s. The Marx Brothers' spoof on the Florida land boom, *Coconuts* (1926), was a big success on the New York stage, as was *Animal Crackers* (1928); both were later filmed. Moving to Hollywood they made the memorable *Monkey Business* (1931), *Duck Soup* (1933), *A Night at the Opera* (1935), and *A Day at the Races* (1937). Groucho, who carried the weight of the absurd film plots, was the only

brother to establish a successful solo career. He hosted the television quiz show "You Bet Your Life" for 15 years (1947–62). ■ See the autobiographies *Groucho and Me* (1959) and *Harpo Speaks!* (1962); Joseph Adamson, *Groucho, Harpo, Chico and Sometimes Zeppo* (1973); Charlotte Chandler, *Hello, I Must Be Going* (1978); Stefan Kanfer, *Groucho* (2000); and Simon Louvish, *Monkey Business* (2000).

MASARYK, JAN (1886–1948), Czech diplomat. His father was Tomáš Masaryk, the first president of the Czech republic (1918–35). Jan Masaryk served as his country's chargé d'affaires in the United States (1919) and as minister to Great Britain (1925–38). As foreign minister of the World War II Czech government-in-exile in London, Masaryk favored cooperation with the Soviet Union. He retained his position in the postwar government until he died under questionable circumstances after the communist coup in 1948. ■ See study by Claire Sterling, *The Masaryk Case* (1969), and Zbyněk Zeman, *The Masaryks* (1976).

MASARYK, TOMÁŠ GARRIGUE (1850–1937), Czech statesman. The son of a coachman, Masaryk earned a Ph.D. from the University of Vienna (1876) and became a professor of philosophy at the Czech University of Prague (1882). A liberal democrat and champion of unpopular causes, he advocated progressive social reform and national autonomy within the Austro-Hungarian Empire as a member of the Austrian parliament (1891–93; 1907–14). After the outbreak of World War I he successfully lobbied West European governments in seeking the dismemberment of Austria-Hungary and the creation of a Czech state. Masaryk led the Czech national council, which was recognized by the Allies as a de facto government in 1918, and later that year he was elected his country's first president, a position he held until his retirement (1935). He took little part in international politics during the 1920s and 1930s. His books included *The Spirit of Russia* (Eng. trans. 1919) and *The Making of a State* (Eng. trans. 1927). ■ See Karel Čapek, *President Masaryk Tells His Story* (Eng. trans. 1934) and *Masaryk on Thought and Life* (Eng. trans. 1938); biography by E. W. P. Newman (1960); Roman Szporluk, *The Political Thought of Thomas G. Masaryk* (1981); and Hanus J. Hajek, *T. G. Masaryk Revisited* (1983).

MASEFIELD, JOHN (1878–1967), British poet and novelist. Masefield ran away to sea as a youngster and traveled widely. He worked in a factory in the United States and was a journalist after he returned to Britain in 1897. He wrote romantic adventure novels and much verse; the lyrical sea poems "Cargoes" and "Sea Fever" are especially well known. He was also noted for his long, realistic narrative poems, including *The Everlasting Mercy* (1911) and *Reynard the Fox* (1919), which shocked readers by their earthy, boisterous speech. He was poet laureate of Britain from 1930 until his death. ■ See his *Letters from the Front: 1915–*

1917 (1985); the autobiographical *In the Mill* (1941), *So Long to Learn* (1952), and *Grace Before Ploughing* (1966); and biography by Constance Babington-Smith (1978).

MASERATI, ERNESTO (1898–1975), Italian automobile manufacturer. Maserati built and drove the famous racing car that bears his name during the 1920s and 1930s. He sold his interest in the company just before World War II but remained as company director. Maseratis dominated the international Grand Prix circuit before and just after the war and won two Indianapolis 500-mile races.

MASLOW, ABRAHAM HAROLD (1908–1970), U.S. psychologist. Maslow studied psychology at the University of Wisconsin (Ph.D. 1934) and spent much of his career at Brandeis University (1951–69). A leading proponent of "third-force psychology," Maslow advocated a humanist approach to psychology as an alternative to behaviorism or psychoanalysis. His well-known books *Motivation and Personality* (1954) and *Toward a Psychology of Being* (1962) portrayed human nature as creative, idealistic, and striving for self-actualization. Maslow's hierarchy of human motives challenged psychologists' assumptions by placing physiological needs (such as hunger or thirst) at the bottom, with the need for safety, a sense of belonging and love, and esteem in the middle, and self-actualization at the top. He argued that lower needs dominate behavior unless fulfilled, and that an individual must defy society's pressure to conform in order to achieve self-actualization. Maslow's ideas influenced the encounter movement and humanistic psychotherapy. ■ See his *Journals* (2 vols., 1979; abridged, 1982); study by Richard Lowry (1973); Frank G. Goble, *The Third Force* (1970); and Edward Hoffman, *The Right to Be Human* (1988).

MASON, MAX (1877–1961), American inventor, mathematical physicist, and educator. In addition to inventing acoustical compensators and submarine-detection devices, Mason made theoretical contributions to mathematics and physics. He developed the relationship between the algebra of matrices and integral equations and did research in differential equations and the calculus of variations. In physics, his research focused on electromagnetic theory. Mason taught at the University of Wisconsin (1908–25), and served as president of the University of Chicago (1925–28) and of the Rockefeller Foundation (1929–36). He chaired the council that supervised construction of the Mt. Palomar Observatory (completed 1948).

MASSEY, VINCENT (1887–1967), Canadian statesman. Born into a wealthy Canadian-U.S. family, Massey was educated in Toronto and at Oxford. (His brother, Raymond, became a famous actor.) He was initially in government service (1915–21) before he served as president (1921–25) of the family business, one of the world's largest manufacturers of farm implements. He then launched a career as a diplomat, highlighted by his terms as minister to the United States (1926–36) and high commissioner to Britain (1935–46). He served as chancellor of the University of Toronto (1947–53) and as governor-general of Canada (1952–59), the first native-born Canadian to hold that post. A well-known and popular figure, Massey advocated the creation of a distinctive Canadian national culture, independent of influences from the United States. His books included *On Being Canadian* (1948), *Speaking of Canada* (1959), and his memoirs, *What's Past Is Prologue* (1964). ■ See Claude T. Bissell, *The Young Vincent Massey* (1981) and *The Imperial Canadian* (1986).

MASSEY, WILLIAM FERGUSON (1856–1925), New Zealand political leader. Massey emigrated to New Zealand (1870) from his native Ireland and became a farmer. He was first elected to Parliament as a Conservative in 1894 and spent the next 18 years with his party in opposition to Liberal governments. (The Conservatives were known as the Reform party after 1909.) Massey was prime minister (1912–25), leading New Zealand through World War I, in a coalition with the Liberals for a time. Throughout his career he was the spokesman for farming interests and an opponent of the labor and socialist movements.

MASSINE, LÉONIDE (Leonid Fedorovitch Myassin; 1895–1979), Russian-born choreographer and ballet dancer. Massine trained at St. Petersburg's Imperial Ballet School and at age 18 joined Diaghilev's Ballet Russe, attracting attention as the lead in Michel Fokine's *The Legend of Joseph*. He became a noted character dancer, but his greatest contribution to dance was his choreography, in the Diaghilev tradition. *Parade* (1917), on which he collaborated with Pablo Picasso, Jean Cocteau, and Erik Satie, was a landmark in modernist ballet. His other notable ballets included *La Boutique Fantasque* (1919), *Gaieté Parisienne* (1939), and *Jeux d'Enfants* (1943). He worked with the Ballet Russe (1914–21; 1925–28), the Ballet Russe de Monte Carlo (1932–42), and later founded his own troupe. His choreography for and performance in the movie *The Red Shoes* (1948) brought him great popularity. ■ See his autobiography, *My Life in Ballet* (1968), and *Massine on Choreography* (1976) and study by Vicente García-Márquez (1995).

MASSON, ANDRÉ (1896–1987), French painter. After study in Brussels and Paris, Masson was influenced by cubist Juan Gris, but his symbolic *Four Elements* (1923–24) brought him attention from surrealists, with whom he aligned himself until 1928. Franz Kafka's psychological literature and William Blake's dreamlike paintings influenced Masson as his works probed the inner self to determine human motivation. Cruelty was expressed in his series *Massacres* (1931–32). He lived in the United States (1940–45), where his method of spontaneous, nonrational, automatic painting influenced the early abstract expressionists Arshile

Gorky and Jackson Pollock. His later work lost its harshness, and he developed a landscape style that emphasized spiritual rapport with nature. ▪ See study by William Rubin and Carolyn Lanchner (1976).

MASTERS, EDGAR LEE (1869–1950), U.S. poet. Born and raised in the Midwest, Masters gave up his successful Chicago law practice after the publication of his highly regarded work, *Spoon River Anthology* (1915). A series of free-verse epitaphs in the form of monologues in which the inhabitants of a fictitious Illinois town speak from the grave of their unfulfilled lives, the book was hailed for its depiction of small-town America. His later works included the volume of poetry *Domesday Book* (1920) and biographies of Abraham Lincoln (1931), Vachel Lindsay (1935), Walt Whitman (1937), and Mark Twain (1938). ▪ See his autobiography, *Across Spoon River* (1936), and study by John H. and Margaret M. Wrenn (1983).

MASTERS, WILLIAM HOWELL (1915–2001), **and VIRGINIA ESHELMAN JOHNSON** (1925–), American sex researchers. A research team—he, a gynecologist: she, a psychologist—Masters and Johnson were known primarily for their book *Human Sexual Response* (1966), the first comprehensive study of the anatomy and physiology of human sexual activity. While Kinsey utilized only secondhand data in his studies, Masters and Johnson studied (from 1964) sexual activity with the aid of modern laboratory equipment at their Reproductive Biology Research Foundation in St. Louis, known after 1973 as the Masters and Johnson Institute. Although criticized by some for "dehumanizing" sex, their highly technical book was well received by the scientific community, became a best-seller, and was translated into more than 10 languages. The researchers were married from 1971 to 1993. They later wrote *On Sex and Human Loving* (1986; with Robert Kolodny).

MASTROIANNI, MARCELLO (1924–1996), Italian actor. The son of a carpenter, Mastroianni had a distinguished stage career playing roles in Shakespeare as well as in modern drama before achieving stardom as the melancholy, apathetic antihero of *La Dolce Vita* (1960) and *8½* (1963). He made several Italian sex comedies, as well as the more serious *The Tenth Victim* (1965) and *The Stranger* (1967). Later films included *A Special Day* (1977), *City of Women* (1979), *La Nuit de Varennes* (1982), and *Ginger and Fred* (1986). He costarred with Sophia Loren in 12 movies.

MATA HARI (Margaretha Geertruida Zelle; 1876–1917), Dutch dancer, courtesan, and convicted spy. A great beauty, Mata Hari gained fame during the first decade of the century as an exotic dancer. She performed on vaudeville stages throughout Europe but preferred to give private performances for exclusive gatherings. During World War I, she had numerous love affairs with highly placed military and government officials on both sides of the conflict. She was arrested by the French (Feb. 13, 1917) for transmitting to the Germans secrets confided to her by Allied officers, convicted by a military court, and shot by a firing squad. Her name has since become synonymous with the seductive female espionage agent. ▪ See studies by Thomas Coulson (1930), Sam Waagenaar (1964), and Russell Warren Howe (1986).

MATHER, STEPHEN TYNG (1867–1930), U.S. conservationist. A descendant of the famous Mather family of 17th-century Massachusetts, Mather gave up a successful business career in 1915 to become assistant secretary of the interior. In 1917 he organized and became first director of the National Park Service. Under his idealistic leadership (1917–29), high standards of excellence were established for the inclusion of parks into the new federal system, industry was excluded from park areas, and the Grand Canyon, Bryce Canyon, Grand Teton, Rocky Mountain, Mt. McKinley, Hawaii, Zion, and Great Smoky Mountains parks were added to the National Park System. ▪ See study by Robert Shankland (rev. ed. 1970).

MATHEWS, SHAILER (1863–1941), U.S. theologian. A leader of the "social gospel" movement, Mathews was a modernist who interpreted religion as part of the social process and sought to get the church involved with social issues and contemporary problems. He was a leader of the ecumenical and peace movements and was dean of the University of Chicago's Divinity School (1908–33). He de-emphasized revelation and metaphysics and utilized a sociohistorical method to interpret Christian doctrine and educate the public to critical understanding of religion. Among his important books were *The Social Teaching of Jesus* (1897), *The Faith of Modernism* (1924), and *The Atonement and the Social Process* (1930). ▪ See his autobiography, *New Faith for Old* (1936).

MATHEWSON, CHRISTY (Christopher Mathewson; 1880–1925), U.S. baseball player. One of the first college men to join the major leagues, Mathewson was a star right-handed pitcher for the New York Giants for 17 seasons (1900–16). He won 373 games (a National League record shared with Grover Alexander), struck out 2,499 batters, and won more than 20 games in each of 13 seasons. A master of the fadeaway, an early version of the screwball, he was known for his exceptional control. He pitched three shutouts in the 1905 World Series and during the 1913 season hurled 68 consecutive innings without a walk. Mathewson was one of the first five players named to the National Baseball Hall of Fame (1936). ▪ See his *Pitching in a Pinch* (1912) and biography by Gene Schoor (1953).

MATHIAS, BOB (Robert Bruce Mathias; 1930–), U.S. Olympic athlete and congressman. The youngest trackman (at age 17) to qualify for a U.S. Olympic team, Mathias made history by winning gold medals in the decathlon in two Olympic games (1948, 1952). An exceptionally versatile athlete, he won national decathlon titles four times and also played football as a fullback at Stanford University. From 1967 to 1975 Mathias was a Republican congressman from California's 18th district. ■ See biography by Jim Scott (rev. ed. 1963).

MATHIEZ, ALBERT (1874–1932), French historian. Mathiez, who taught at the University of Dijon (1919–26), interpreted the French Revolution as a class conflict in his history of the period, *The French Revolution* (3 vols., 1922–27; Eng. trans. 1928). He considered the moderate leader Danton a corrupt demagogue—taking issue with his teacher Alphonse Aulard, who admired Danton as a patriot—and viewed the fall of the radical Robespierre as the triumph of the bourgeoisie. Other books by Mathiez included *The Fall of Robespierre* (1925; Eng. trans. 1927) and *After Robespierre: The Thermidorian Reaction* (1929; Eng. trans. 1931).

MATISSE, HENRI (1869–1954), French painter and sculptor. Often considered the most influential modern French painter, Matisse studied in Paris at the Académie Julian and with Gustave Moreau at the École des Beaux Arts (1895). He was influenced by impressionist Claude Monet's use of color, but he strove to simplify and sharpen forms rather than blur and soften them. A leader of fauvism—the first 20th-century avant-garde movement—Matisse stressed color and line; in his work there were no gradual transitions of shades and lines but bold clashes of color and, eventually, an austerity that bordered on cubism. He experimented in artistic expression, creating, in addition to his paintings, a large body of lithographs and sculpture and the *papiers découpés* (imaginative paper cutouts) to which he devoted his last years. ■ See Jack D. Flam, ed., *Matisse on Art* (1973); studies by Alfred H. Barr (1951), Pierre Schneider (Eng. trans. 1984), and Nicholas Watkins (1985); and Hilary Spurling, *The Unknown Matisse* (1998).

MATSUOKA, YOSUKE (1880–1946), Japanese political leader and diplomat. After graduating from the University of Oregon Law School (1900), Matsuoka joined the diplomatic corps (1904) and later served in high executive positions with the South Manchuria Railway Co. (1921–26; 1927–29; president, 1935–39). He advocated Japanese expansion in China and became a national hero when he led the Japanese delegation out of the League of Nations (1933). He promoted close ties with the fascist powers, and as foreign minister (1940–41) he signed the Tripartite Pact (1940) that linked Japan with Italy and Germany. He also drew up plans for Japanese expansion into Southeast Asia. Although he successfully negotiated a neutrality pact with the Soviet Union (1941), he left the cabinet after the German invasion of Russia (June, 1941).

MATTEI, ENRICO (1906–1962), Italian industrialist. A war hero and leader of the largest noncommunist resistance movement during World War II, Mattei was a controversial figure in postwar Italy. He chaired (1945–53) the state-run Italian General Petroleum Industry, which, by discovering methane gas and oil, greatly aided Italy's industrial development. As head of the newly formed Italian National Hydrocarbon Authority (1953–62), which controlled the nation's oil and gas resources, Mattei exerted great influence on the national scene. An ardent foe of foreign oil investment in Italy, he arranged lucrative deals for Italian oil concessions in Egypt, Iran, and Morocco and concluded controversial trade pacts with China and the Soviet Union. His enemies claimed that he conducted a private foreign policy. He died in a plane crash.

MATTEOTTI, GIACOMO (1885–1924), Italian political leader. Matteotti was secretary-general of the Socialist party and a member of the Chamber of Deputies (from 1919). The most prominent opponent of the fascist government, he was abducted and murdered by fascist thugs in June 1924, shortly after denouncing fascist leader Mussolini in parliament. The murder produced a national outcry and precipitated a parliamentary crisis, but the antifascist forces were unable to act decisively and Mussolini used the crisis to consolidate his dictatorial rule by strengthening the secret police and destroying political opposition in Italy.

MATTHEW, SIR ROBERT HOAG (1906–1975), British architect. As London's principal municipal architect in the post–World War II years (1946–53), Matthew and his successor Sir Leslie Martin brought the functional design concepts of Walter Gropius to British architecture. During his tenure, teams of professionals from various disciplines designed school campuses, large housing projects (including Alton East at Rochampton), and London's Royal Festival Hall (1949–50), the first public building in Europe executed in the modern style. Matthew later taught architecture at Edinburgh University (1953–67) and managed a firm that stressed collectivity in the architectural process.

MATTHEWS, HERBERT LIONEL (1900–1977), U.S. journalist. After graduating from Columbia College (1922), Matthews went to work for the *New York Times* and remained with the newspaper as foreign correspondent and editorial writer for 45 years. His reporting was always controversial. Covering the Italian invasion of Ethiopia, he was inclined to favor the fascists; assigned to the Spanish civil war, he made clear his bias toward the republicans. A generation later, he climbed into Cuba's Sierra Maestra mountains to file sympathetic reports on guerrilla leader Fidel Castro (1957). ■ See his *Education of a Correspondent* (1946), *The Cuban Story* (1961), and *Revolution in Cuba* (1975).

MATTHEWS, SIR STANLEY (1915–2000), British soccer player. Matthews, whose father was a featherweight boxer, began playing semiprofessional soccer at age 14 and three years later made his first appearance as a professional for the Stoke City club. In his 33-year career, he played in 886 first-class matches that included 54 appearances for Britain in full international matches. A superb stylist who excelled at eluding the opposition, he was one of the finest dribbling wingers in soccer history.

MATUTE, ANA MARÍA (1926–), Spanish novelist. Matute's poetic novels focused with keen psychological powers on the discontent of alienated youth in modern Spain. Her first novel, *Los Abel* (1948), reflected the influence of the English writer Emily Brontë. Her other works included *Celebration in the Northwest* (1952; Eng. trans. 1997), *The Lost Children* (1958; Eng. trans. 1965), and the trilogy *The Merchants: Awakening* (1959; Eng. trans. 1963), *Soldiers Cry by Night* (1964; Eng. trans 1995), and *The Trap* (1969; Eng. trans. 1996), which presents a panorama of Spanish life from the beginning of the civil war (1936) through the 1960s. She also wrote *School of the Sun* (1960; Eng. trans. 1963, 1991) and *The Heliotrope Wall and Other Stories* (1968; Eng. trans. 1989). *Olvidado Rey Gudú* (1996) was an allegorical epic set in a mythical medieval kingdom. ■ See studies by Janet Diaz (1971) and Margaret E. W. Jones (1970).

MAUCHLY, JOHN WILLIAM (1907–1980), U.S. engineer. A professor of engineering at the University of Pennsylvania, Mauchly and graduate engineer J. Presper Eckert were given a contract by the War Department during World War II to develop a system of high-speed computation. By 1946 they had completed work on what was considered for years to be the world's first all-electronic computer, the Electrical Numerical Integrator and Computer (ENIAC). (However, a ruling in a 1973 patent lawsuit found that their invention was derived from a model built by John Atanasoff and declared the ENIAC patent invalid.) They formed their own company (1947) and developed the faster and more economical BINAC computer (1949) and the universal automatic computer, UNIVAC I (1951).

MAUGHAM, WILLIAM SOMERSET (1874–1965), British novelist, playwright, and short-story writer. An impeccable technician and stylist, W. Somerset Maugham is considered "the English Maupassant." His works are facile but entertaining in their sentimental and sometimes cynical attitude toward life. His most famous novels are *Of Human Bondage* (1915), a semiautobiographical account of his medical training; *The Moon and Sixpence* (1919), based on the painter Paul Gauguin's career; *Cakes and Ale* (1930); and *The Razor's Edge* (1944). His numerous plays and short stories were also great successes for over three decades, helping to make him one of the world's richest authors. ■ See *The Complete Short Stories* (2 vols., 1952), the autobiographical *The Summing Up* (1938), *A Writer's Notebook* (1949); biography by Ted Morgan (1979); and study by Forrest D. Burt (1985).

MAULDIN, WILLIAM HENRY (1921–), U.S. cartoonist. While a soldier assigned to the newspaper *Stars and Stripes* during World War II, Bill Mauldin created Willie and Joe, two cartoon soldiers whose disenchantment with army life and war made them extremely popular with the troops, though not with Gen. George Patton. The cartoons were also published in 100 stateside newspapers and were collected in several volumes, including *Up Front* (1945), and Mauldin was awarded a 1945 Pulitzer Prize. *Back Home* (1947) showed Willie and Joe adjusting to civilian life. Subsequent Mauldin cartoons satirized racism, jingoism, and empty liberalism, while *Bill Mauldin in Korea* (1952) described his visit to the Korean War zone. He was editorial cartoonist with the *St. Louis Post-Dispatch* (1958–62) and *Chicago Sun-Times* (from 1962), was syndicated in more than 200 newspapers, and won a second Pulitzer Prize in 1959. ■ See his memoirs, *The Brass Ring* (1971).

MAURER, ION GHEORGHE (1902–), Rumanian political leader. Maurer was a politically active lawyer during the 1930s when he defended such radicals as the communist Gheorghe Gheorghiu-Dej, whom he is said to have helped escape execution by the Nazis. Maurer became Gheorghiu-Dej's protégé in the post–World War II government but lost his job as minister of industry and trade in the 1948 purges and remained in obscurity until the 1956 "thaw." He served as Rumania's foreign minister in 1957–58 and in 1961 became chairman of the Council of Ministers, or premier, articulating the new Rumanian economic and foreign policy of independent roads to socialism. He resigned in 1974.

MAURIAC, FRANÇOIS (1885–1970), French novelist, playwright, and critic. Raised in a middle-class Catholic milieu, Mauriac confronted in his novels the dilemma of the misery of existence without God. He emphasized human helplessness in the face of evil and the problems and tragedy of love. Such novels as *Genitrix* (1922; Eng. trans. 1930), *The Desert of Love* (1925; Eng. trans. 1929), and *The Vipers' Tangle* (1932; Eng. trans. 1933) were thus very pessimistic. Later novels reexamined his beliefs and showed a greater optimism and faith in the healing powers of love. In the 1940s Mauriac became a noted political commentator and journalist for *Figaro*. Elected a member of the Académie Française (1933), he also received a Nobel Prize for Literature (1952). ■ See his intellectual and spiritual autobiography, *Mémoires Intérieurs* (Eng. trans. 1961); *Second Thoughts: Reflections on Literature and on Life* (Eng. trans. 1961); biography by Maxwell A. Smith (1970); and study by Malcolm Scott (1980).

MAUROIS, ANDRÉ (Émile Herzog; 1885–1967), French novelist and biographer. Born into a wealthy Jewish family, Maurois was influenced by his teacher, the humanist philosopher Alain. Long and sympathetic contact with the Anglo-Saxon world enabled Maurois to interpret British and American life to the French through historical studies and fiction such as his very sucessful *The Silence of Colonel Bramble* (1918; Eng. trans. 1920). He wrote many sensitive novels and essays but was best known for his "romanticized" biographies of Disraeli (1924; Eng. trans. 1928), Byron (1930; Eng. trans. 1930), George Sand (1952; Eng. trans. 1953), Balzac (1965; Eng. trans. 1965), and others. He was elected to the *Académie Française* (1938). ▪ See his autobiography, *I Remember, I Remember* (1942; Eng. trans. 1942), *Memoirs, 1885–1967* (1970; Eng. trans. 1970), and study by L. Clark Keating (1969).

MAURRAS, CHARLES MARIE PHOTIUS (1868–1952), French writer. The product of a royalist, Catholic upbringing, Maurras began his long literary career as a poet and scholarly critic in the classical tradition. He was a founder and the editor (1899–1944) of the right-wing, monarchist journal and later newspaper *L'Action Française,* which supported the doctrine of an austere, authoritarian, and nationalistic France. Maurras violently opposed Jews, Protestants, and foreign influences. In a stormy career he was condemned by the church (1926) and even by the pretenders to the throne but was elected to the Académie Française (1938) for his literary achievement. After World War II he was sentenced to life imprisonment for collaboration with the German wartime occupiers. ▪ See William C. Buthman, *The Rise of Integral Nationalism in France* (1939), and Michael Sutton, *Nationalism, Positivism and Catholicism* (1982).

MAUSS, MARCEL (1872–1950), French anthropologist. He taught (1900–39) Hindu and Buddhist philosophy and history at the University of Paris, where he helped to found the Institute of Ethnology (1925), and at the Collège de France (1930–39). A political activist, he helped establish (1904) the socialist newspaper *L'Humanité.* He studied and collaborated with his uncle and professor, the sociologist Émile Durkheim. In his writings, Mauss stressed the role of ethnographic research, rather than armchair theorizing. His *The Gift* (1925; Eng. trans. 1954) explained that cultural exchange was heavily dependent on economic and social factors. He also wrote extensively on the link between psychology and anthropology. His other books included *A General Theory of Magic* (Eng. trans. 1972) and *Sociology and Psychology* (Eng. trans. 1979).

MAX, PETER (1937–), German-born U.S. artist. Refugees from Nazi Germany, Max and his family lived in China, Israel, France, and Italy before settling in New York (1953), where he studied art and Eastern mysticism, practiced yoga, and founded a successful graphicarts business. He became a "hippie millionaire" at age 30 thanks to mass marketing of his psychedelic-styled household and personal products—everything from checkbook covers to upholstery fabrics. His designs—a kaleidoscope of op and pop, peace and love—also turned up on subway posters, telephone directories, and a 1974 U.S. postage stamp. ▪ See *The Peter Max Poster Book* (1970).

MAXIMILIAN OF BADEN, PRINCE (Maximilian Alexander Wilhelm; 1867–1929), German chancellor. Heir to the duchy of Baden, Prince Max gained a reputation as a liberal humanitarian with his World War I activities on behalf of German and Russian prisoners of war. Appointed imperial chancellor in October 1918 to bring the war to an end, he began negotiations with the Allies, announced the abdication of Emperor William II, and resigned in favor of the parliamentary socialist leadership five weeks later. ▪ See his *Memoirs* (1927; Eng. trans. 1928).

MAY, ALAN NUNN (1911–), British physicist and spy. Trained in research physics at Cambridge (Ph.D. 1936), May visited Leningrad (1936), where Soviet communism made a dramatic impression on him. During World War II he signed the Official Secrets Act and headed the Montreal Chalk River atomic project. Soviet intelligence recruited him and in 1944 received not only a full report on atomic development in the United States but also samples of uranium 233 and 235. May received only $700 and two bottles of whiskey for his espionage, apparently acting on the conviction that knowledge of atomic energy should not be confined to the West. He was exposed when Soviet cipher clerk Igor Gouzenko defected from the Soviet embassy in Ottawa, Canada. Arrested in London, May served 6 years of a 10-year sentence. He was released from prison (1952) and became (1962) a professor of physics at the University of Ghana. ▪ See H. Montgomery Hyde, *The Atom Bomb Spies* (1980).

MAY, ROLLO REESE (1909–1994), U.S. psychoanalyst. May studied under Paul Tillich at Union Theological Seminary and served as a Congregational minister for two years before returning to Columbia University, where he earned a Ph.D. (1949) in clinical psychology. As a leader in the "third force" or humanistic movement in psychology, he rejected sexual and environmental determinism to focus on higher human strivings. A member of the William Alanson White Institute in New York after 1948, he wrote two works of popular psychology, *The Meaning of Anxiety* (1950) and *Love and Will* (1969). Later books included *The Courage to Create* (1975), *Freedom and Destiny* (1981), and *The Discovery of Being: Writings in Existential Psychology* (1983), and *My Quest for Beauty* (1985). ▪ See study by Clement Reeves (1977).

MAYAKOVSKY, VLADIMIR VLADIMIROVICH (1893–1930), Soviet poet. Mayakovsky was a poet, revolutionary, painter, and stage and screen star. At age 20 he led the Russian futurist movement and won fame with imaginative, rhythmic poems, including "A Cloud in Trousers" (1914–15; Eng. trans. 1945). Although he sought public exposure and focused on himself in such works as "A Few Words About Myself" and "Vladimir Mayakovsky" (1913; Eng. trans. 1968), he remained inscrutable, masking his feelings behind drama and insolence. Mayakovsky was the only poet clearly identified with the bolshevik movement. His play

Mystery-Bouffe (1918; Eng. trans. 1933) and his poem "150,000,000" (1919–20) celebrated the Russian Revolution. His poem "Vladimir Ilich Lenin" (1924) eulogized the bolshevik leader as a historic force. Mayakovsky's enthusiasm for the Soviet regime seemed tempered in his two dramatic satires, *The Bedbug* (1928; Eng. trans. 1960) and *The Bath-House* (1930; Eng. trans. 1963). Under attack by the Russian Association of Proletarian Writers, entangled in painful love affairs, and apparently disillusioned with Soviet reality, he stunned the public by committing suicide. He left incomplete the poem that many consider his masterpiece, "At the Top of My Voice" (1930). In *How Are Verses Made?* (1926; Eng. trans. 1971) Mayakovsky recounted the process of writing a poem on the suicide of poet Sergei Yesenin. *The Bedbug and Selected Poetry* (1975) contains English translations of his works. ▪ See studies by Edward Brown (1973), Victor Terras (1983), and Juliet R. Stepanian (1986).

MAYER, ARNO JOSEPH (1926–), Luxembourg-born U.S. historian. Mayer earned his Ph.D. at Yale (1950) and taught modern European history at Princeton (from 1961). His specialty was diplomatic history, particularly of the World War I era. In *Political Origins of the New Diplomacy: 1917–1918* (1959), he discussed the conflicting views of Woodrow Wilson and Soviet leader V. I. Lenin, while in *Politics and Diplomacy of Peacemaking* (1967) he showed that the peril of bolshevism dominated the 1919 Paris Peace Conference. He also wrote *Dynamics of Counterrevolution in Europe, 1870–1956: An Analytic Framework* (1971); *The Persistence of the Old Regime* (1981), a Marxist analysis of the landed elite in Europe from the 18th century up to World War I, *Why Did the Heavens Not Darken?: The "Final Solution" in History* (1988), and *The Furies: Violence and Terror in the French and Russian Revolutions* (2000).

MAYER, CARL (1894–1944), German screenwriter. Forced to support his family at an early age, Mayer worked at odd jobs connected with the theater. With Hans Janowitz he conceived and wrote the script for *The Cabinet of Dr. Caligari* (1919), whose expressionist acting and decor marked the advent of the "golden age" of German cinema. Mayer was the most influential scriptwriter of this period, always working out his scripts cinematically. Many of his films dispensed with titles because they were so pictorially conceived. The originator of the *Kammerspielfilm*—intimate, psychologically probing dramas—Mayer influenced the direction and editing of many of these films, which included *Backstairs* (1921). He worked closely with director F. W. Murnau, scripting *The Last Laugh* (1924) and *Sunrise* (1927), which Murnau directed in Hollywood. Mayer refused offers to emigrate to Hollywood but settled in London after the Nazis came to power in Germany. He produced little, however, in the sound era.

MAYER, LOUIS BURT (1885?–1957), Russian-born U.S. film magnate. Mayer was a scrap-metal dealer who bought up a chain of New England theaters and made his fortune distributing *Birth of a Nation* (1914). He established (1917) his own production company, which in 1924 became part of Metro-Goldwyn-Mayer. As MGM general manager for 27 years, Mayer built the studio up by insisting on high-gloss wholesomeness and by astutely manipulating the star system. The highest-paid executive in the country for many years, he fell increasingly out of touch with popular tastes and was forced out in 1951. ▪ See Bosley Crowther, *Hollywood Rajah* (1960); Gary Carey, *All the Stars in Heaven: Louis B. Mayer's MGM* (1981); and Diana Altman, *Hollywood East* (1992).

MAYER, MARIA GOEPPERT (Maria Goeppert; 1906–1972), German-born U.S. physicist. Goeppert studied at Göttingen University (Ph.D. 1930) and moved to the United States (1931) after she married American physical chemist Joseph E. Mayer, with whom she later coauthored the book *Statistical Mechanics* (1940). While at Columbia University (1939–46) she worked on the atomic bomb project. Originally a physical chemist, she became interested in nuclear physics in 1945 while working with Enrico Fermi at the University of Chicago's Institute for Nuclear Studies. She later worked at the Argonne National Laboratory (1946–60) and taught at the University of San Diego (from 1960). She shared the 1963 Nobel Prize for Physics with J. Hans D. Jensen for her work on nuclear shell theory. Eugene P. Wigner also shared the award. Her proposal that the atomic nucleus consists of neutrons and protons arranged in concentric shells enabled physicists to explain why some nuclei are stable and others unstable. She wrote *Elementary Theory of Nuclear Shell Structure* (1955) with Jensen. ▪ See Joan Dash, *A Life of One's Own* (1973).

MAYO, (GEORGE) ELTON (1880–1949), Australian-born U.S. psychologist. Mayo taught psychology at the University of Adelaide before going to the United States (1922), where he was a professor in Harvard University's department of industrial research (1926–47). He launched (1927) the famous study of working conditions at the Hawthorne plant of the Western Electric Co. (Chicago), which spurred the development of organizational behavior research after its publication in 1939. He was criticized for subordinating individual and group interests in order to achieve organizational harmony that benefited the administrative elite and allowed it to retain power. In *The Human Problems of an Industrial Civilization* (1933), Mayo described the important role of informal groups in industrial organizations. He advocated personal counseling or psychotherapy for workers in industry. He also wrote *The Social Problems of an Industrial Society* (1945). ▪ See biography by L. F. Urwick (1960) and R.C.S. Trahair, *The Humanist Temper* (1984).

MAYO, WILLIAM JAMES (1861–1939), and CHARLES HORACE MAYO (1865–1939), U.S. surgeons. The Mayo brothers, recent medical school graduates, joined their father, William Worrall Mayo, to staff the newly opened St. Mary's hospital in Rochester, Minnesota (1889). They soon formed a group practice with several other specialists, the first such cooperative endeavor in the United States, and their clinic, known as the Mayo Clinic after 1905, became internationally renowned for the surgery performed there. Charles Mayo specialized in goiter, devising a treatment that significantly reduced the death rate, and made advances in the areas of orthopedic and cataract surgery and neurosurgery. William Mayo was a specialist in abdominal surgery. The clinic kept extensive records that influenced the future practice of surgery. ■ See Gunther W. Nagel, *The Mayo Legacy* (1966), and Helen B. Clapesattle, *The Doctors Mayo* (2nd ed. 1960).

MAYR, ERNST (1904–   ). German-born U.S. biologist. Mayr studied at the University of Berlin (Ph.D. 1926) and led three scientific expeditions to New Guinea and the Solomon Islands (1928–30), where he documented the importance of geographic variation in the process of evolution. He emigrated to the United States to serve as curator of birds at the American Museum of Natural History, New York (1932–53), and later served as professor of zoology at Harvard (1953–75). One of the most influential evolutionary biologists of the century and an architect of the modern neo-Darwinian evolutionary synthesis, Mayr made major contributions to the fields of genetics, avian taxonomy, and scientific methodology. His books included *Systematics and the Origin of Species* (1942); *Methods and Principles of Systematic Zoology* (with E. G. Linsley and R. L. Usinger; 1953); *Animal Species and Evolution* (1963); *Evolution and the Diversity of Life* (1976), *The Growth of Biological Thought* (1982), the first major history of ideas in biology; *Toward a New Philosophy of Biology* (1988); *One Long Argument* (1991); and *This Is Biology* (1997).

MAYS, WILLIE HOWARD, JR. (1931–   ), U.S. baseball player. Mays played in the Negro National League in Birmingham, Alabama (1948), while he was still in high school and developed into one of the greatest players in the history of the game. Called the "Say Hey Kid," he played the outfield for the New York–San Francisco Giants for over 20 years (1951–52; 1954–72), ending his career with the New York Mets (1973). A swift base runner, exceptional fielder, and powerful hitter, he compiled a career .302 batting average, with 660 home runs (third best in history), 3,283 hits, 2,062 runs, 1,903 runs batted in, and 338 stolen bases. The Most Valuable Player in the National League in 1954 and 1965, he was named the Baseball Player of the Decade (1960–69) by the *Sporting News* and was selected to the All-Star squad every season between 1954 and 1973. He was voted into the National Baseball Hall of Fame in 1979. ■ See his autobiography (1966) and Charles Einstein, *Willie's Time* (1979).

MBOYA, THOMAS JOSEPH (1930–1969), Kenyan labor and political leader. When Kenyan African political parties

were banned during the Mau-Mau emergency, Tom Mboya used the labor movement as a vehicle of anticolonial nationalism. As secretary-general of the Kenyan Federation of Labor (1953–63), he mediated the significant Mombasa dock strike of 1955 and won a popular settlement. Elected to the legislative council in 1957, he bolstered his reputation by his opposition to the British colonial administration. With the goal of self-government, he helped form (1960) the Kenya African National Union political party (KANU). After independence Mboya served in Jomo Kenyatta's government as minister for economic planning and development (1964–69). A Luo tribesman, Mboya was frequently blamed for the problems of the Kikuyu-dominated government; he was assassinated in Nairobi. ■ See the autobiographical *Freedom and After* (1963) and biography by David Goldsworthy (1982).

MEAD, GEORGE HERBERT (1863–1931), U.S. social psychologist. Mead taught a highly regarded course on social psychology for 30 years at the University of Chicago, the material for which was posthumously published as *Mind, Self and Society* (1934). He focused in particular on the role of language and the origin of the self in social interaction. His social behaviorism, which identified conduct as the unit of experience, was an important strand in the development of American pragmatism. His other books included *The Philosophy of the Present* (1932). ■ See study by David L. Miller (1973) and biography by Gary A. Cook (1993).

MEAD, MARGARET (1901–1978), U.S. anthropologist. Born in Philadelphia, Mead graduated from Barnard College (1923) and earned her Ph.D. at Columbia University (1929) under anthropologist Franz Boas. Beginning her fieldwork in Samoa (1925), she used a multidisciplinary approach strongly influenced by psychoanalytic themes to examine the cultural conditioning of sexual behavior in *Coming of Age in Samoa* (1928). Later she used new photographic techniques to compile an extensive documentary on *Balinese Character* (1942; with Gregory Bateson). Also concerned with the relevance of anthropology to contemporary life, she wrote *Male and Female* (1949) and frequently spoke out in favor of civil liberties, population control, women's liberation, and ecological sanity. Mead served as a member of the curatorial staff of the American Museum of Natural History in New York from 1926 until her death and as an adjunct professor of anthropology at Columbia University after 1954. Derek Freeman's controversial study, *Margaret Mead and Samoa: The Making and Unmaking of an Anthropological Myth* (1983) sparked debate about Mead's methods and conclusions. ■ See her *Blackberry Winter* (1972); biography by Jane Howard (1984); the memoir by her daughter, Mary Catherine Bateson, *With a Daughter's Eye* (1984); and Lowell Holmes, *Quest For the Real Samoa* (1987).

MEADE, JAMES EDWARD (1907–1995), British economist. Meade served with the League of Nations during the

1930s and was the British cabinet's chief economist during World War II. He later taught at Oxford, the London School of Economics, and Cambridge, also serving as a Labour party economic adviser and consultant on the General Agreement on Tariffs and Trade. A specialist in the relationship between domestic economic policy and foreign trade (*The Theory of International Economic Policy*, 2 vols., 1951–55), he shared the 1977 Nobel Memorial Prize in Economics with Bertil Ohlin. His other books included *Principles of Political Economy* (4 vols., 1965–76) and *The Intelligent Radical's Guide to Economic Policy* (1975).

MEANS, RUSSELL CHARLES (1939–), U.S. Indian leader. Born of Sioux ancestry on the Pine Ridge, South Dakota, reservation, Means was a college dropout and drifter who participated in a 1964 attempt to reclaim Alcatraz Island in San Francisco Bay for the Indians. Joining the American Indian Movement (AIM) in the late 1960s, he directed a Thanksgiving 1970 Indian demonstration in Plymouth, Massachusetts, and filed a $9 million damage suit against the Cleveland Indians baseball team for demeaning American Indians. In 1973, in a dispute with Pine Ridge tribal president Richard Wilson, Means and his armed followers took over the historic village of Wounded Knee, where the U.S. Cavalry massacred more than 350 Indians in 1890. Charges against Means were later dismissed by a federal judge after a lengthy trial (1974). In the early 1980s he founded a new tribal party, TREATY (True Revolution for the Elders, Ancestors, and Youth), which advocated the establishment of a sovereign Indian nation. After visiting Nicaragua (1985), he announced his support of the Miskito Indians in their rebellion against the Sandinista government. He left AIM in 1988 and founded the American Indian Anti-Defamation League (1988). He played a major role in the film *The Last of the Mohicans* (1992). ■ See Robert Burnette and John Koster, *The Road to Wounded Knee* (1974), and his autobiography, *Where White Men Fear to Tread* (1995; with Marvin J. Wolf).

MEANY, GEORGE (1894–1980), U.S. labor leader. A plumber of Irish-Catholic background from New York, Meany rose to the presidency of his state's Federation of Labor during the Depression. He became head of the American Federation of Labor (1952) and negotiated its merger with the Congress of Industrial Organizations (1955). Meany remained president of the AFL-CIO—which comprised 90 percent of U.S. union members—from its inception until 1979. The colorful, cigar-smoking labor leader, an ally of the Democratic party establishment, was a national figure, favoring moderate civil-rights and social-welfare legislation, expelling the Teamsters (1957) for corruption, and supporting cold-war foreign policy. But he was primarily concerned with bread-and-butter issues—wages and working conditions. Meany never walked a picket line or led a strike; he preferred to arbitrate and to lobby in order to build American labor into a significant mainstream political force. ■ See

biographies by Joseph C. Goulden (1972) and Archie Robinson (1982).

MEDAWAR, SIR PETER BRIAN (1915–1987), British biologist. Born in Brazil, Medawar studied zoology at Oxford. During World War II, the need to treat burn victims drew his attention to problems of immunology, since the body tends to reject skin grafted from one individual to another. Proceeding from Sir Macfarlane Burnet's ideas about acquired immunology, Medawar confirmed Burnet's theory that cells "learn" during embryonic life to differentiate between their own tissue and foreign cells or materials. He showed that if substances that would be antigenic to an adult were injected during embryonic life, they would inhibit the normal rejection response in the adult. For this discovery, which advanced organ-transplant and skin-graft techniques, Medawar shared the 1960 Nobel Prize for Physiology or Medicine with Burnet. He subsequently headed the National Institute of Medical Research (1962–71). Medawar won praise for his witty, elegant writings and lectures on science, philosophy, and culture. His books included *The Uniqueness of the Individual* (1957), *The Future of Man* (1959), *The Art of the Soluble* (1967), *The Hope of Progress* (1972), *Advice to a Young Scientist* (1979), and *Pluto's Republic* (1982). ■ See his autobiography, *Memoir of a Thinking Radish* (1986).

MÉDICI, EMÍLIO GARRASTAZÚ (1905–1985), Brazilian general and political leader. A career soldier with intelligence and staff experience, Médici was promoted to brigadier general in 1961. He was military attaché in Washington, D.C. (1964–66) and head of Brazil's civilian intelligence agency (1966–69). Chosen by the ruling military junta as the "least controversial" candidate for the presidency in 1969, he vowed to achieve full industrialization within a generation. To this end Médici gave carte blanche to foreign capital and right-wing vigilantes and instituted censorship, preventive detention, and torture of dissidents in a "war against subversion." He was succeeded by Gen. Ernesto Geisel in 1974.

MEDVEDEV, ROY ALEKSANDROVICH (1925–), Soviet historian. The son of a Russian civil-war hero who disappeared during the Stalinist purges of the 1930s. Medvedev was a dedicated Marxist who advocated democracy, human rights, and internal reforms within the Soviet Union. He taught high school history, edited textbooks, and did research at the Research Institute of Vocational Education (1962–71) before turning to history. His book *Let History Judge; The Origins and Consequences of Stalinism* (Eng. trans. 1971) was the first critique of Stalinism written by an insider, while *A Question of Madness* (written with his twin brother, scientist Zhores Medvedev; Eng. trans. 1971) recounted Zhores' temporary imprisonment in a psychiatric hospital for criticisms of the scientific establishment. Although he placed hope on liberals within the Communist party to reform Soviet society, he was expelled from the party for his dissident views. During the Gorbachev era he rejoined the party (1989–91), was a member of its Central Committee (1990–91), and served as a People's Deputy (1989–91). He later served as co-chair of the Socialist Party of Labor (1991–). Among his other books were *On Socialist Democracy* (1972; Eng. trans. 1975), *The October Revolution* (Eng. trans. 1979), *On Stalin and Stalinism* (Eng. trans. 1979), *Leninism and Western Socialism* (Eng. trans. 1981), *An End to Silence* (Eng. trans. 1982), *All Stalin's Men* (Eng. trans. 1983), *China and the Superpowers* (Eng. trans. 1986), *Time of Change* (Eng. trans. 1990), and *Post-Soviet Russia* (Eng. trans. 2000).

MEDVEDEV, ZHORES ALEKSANDROVICH (1925–), Soviet-born biologist and dissident writer. The son of a Russian civil war hero and member of the Communist party, Medvedev earned degrees in biology (M.A. 1950) and biochemistry (1954) and gained an international reputation for his scholarly works on genetics, gerontology, and biochemistry. His attacks on T. D. Lysenko's genetic theories drew rebuttals from the government, and he was imprisoned in a psychiatric hospital for his dissident views and released only after intellectuals in the Soviet Union and abroad protested. With his twin brother Roy, he wrote *A Question of Madness* (Eng. trans. 1971), which recounted his experiences. He also wrote *The Rise and Fall of T. D. Lysenko* (1966; Eng. trans. 1969) and *The Medvedev Papers* (1970; Eng. trans. 1971), in which he discussed the status and role of Soviet scientists. His Soviet citizenship was revoked while Medvedev was conducting research in London (1973). He remained there as a research scientist at the National Institute for Medical Research until 1992. His Soviet citizenship was restored in 1990. His later works included *Ten Years After* (1972; Eng. trans. 1973), a study of the persecution of Aleksandr Solzhenitsyn; *Soviet Science* (1978); *The Nuclear Disaster in the Urals* (1979); and *Gorbachev* (1986).

MEHTA, SIR PHEROZESHAH (1845–1915), Indian political leader. A middle-class Parsi, Mehta was one of the first Indians to receive a Western education. He practiced law (from 1868) and was prominent in Bombay politics for nearly 50 years. He was one of the founders of the Indian National Congress party (1885) and served as its president (1890–1909). Mehta was a board member of Bombay University, a founder of the Indian-controlled Central Bank of India, and the founder of the *Bombay Chronicle* (1913), an English-language newspaper. ■ See biographies by Hormasji P. Mody (1921) and V. S. Srinivasa Sastri (1945; rev. ed. 1975).

MEHTA, ZUBIN (1936–), Indian-born conductor. Mehta, a Parsi whose father founded the Bombay Symphony, studied at the Vienna Academy of Music (1954–60) and won a Liverpool competition that led to conducting positions with the Montreal Symphony (1961–67) and the Los Angeles Philharmonic (1962–78). A celebrity conductor with matinee-idol looks, who specialized in the music of the late romantics, he led the New York Philharmonic (1978–91) as well as the Israel Philharmonic (1969–), the Maggio Musicale, Florence (1986–), and the Bavarian State Opera (1998–). ■ See Martin Bookspan and Ross Yockey, *Zubin* (1978).

MEIER, RICHARD ALAN (1934–), U.S. architect. After earning an architecture degree at Cornell University (1957), Meier worked for several New York firms, spending free hours painting abstract canvases. In 1963 he launched his own practice, designing private houses that departed from the style set by Frank Lloyd Wright by contrasting with (rather than blending into) their environment. He won recognition for the Smith House (1967; Darien, Connecticut) and for his first large commission, the Westbeth Artists' Housing (1970) in New York's Greenwich Village. Known for elegant buildings that use white and silver surfaces and clean lines to create a "high-tech" appearance, he designed such buildings as The Atheneum (1979; New Harmony, Indiana), the Hartford (Connecticut) Seminary (1981), and Atlanta's High Museum of Art (1983). In 1984, Meier was awarded the prestigious Pritzker Prize. He subsequently designed the Getty Center for the Arts and Humanities, a six-building complex on a mountaintop in Los Angeles (1984–97), and the Museum of Contemporary Art, Barcelona (1987–95).

MEIGHEN, ARTHUR (1874–1960), Canadian political leader. Meighen practiced law in Manitoba before he was elected to Parliament as a Liberal Conservative in 1908. He was an excellent orator and parliamentary debater and held several cabinet appointments under Prime Minister Robert Borden (1917–20). Meighen was prime minister from 1920 to 1921; he was defeated because of strong French-Canadian opposition to conscription and farmer and worker opposition to his high tariff and antilabor policies. During the next four years he led the opposition; in 1926 he was again prime minister for a short time. He served in the Senate (1932–41) and again as leader of the conservatives (1941–42). ■ See his speeches in *Unrevised and Unrepented* (1949) and biography by Roger Graham (3 vols., 1960–65).

MEIKLEJOHN, ALEXANDER (1872–1964), British-born U.S. educator. Meiklejohn taught philosophy at Brown University (1897–1912), presided somewhat autocratically over Amherst College (1912–24), and headed an experimental college at the University of Wisconsin (1927–32). A reformer and advocate of the "Great Books" approach to higher education, he was best known as an outspoken champion of academic freedom and free speech. He lectured widely and published several works on education, including *The Liberal College* (1920) and *Education Between Two Worlds* (1942), *Alexander Meiklejohn: Teacher of Freedom* (1981), edited by Cynthia S. Brown and Ann F. Ginger, contains a collection of his writings and a biography.

MEI LAN-FANG (1894–1961), Chinese actor. The most prominent Chinese actor of the century, Mei Lan-fang mastered over 400 *tan* (female) roles and served as a link between the old acting tradition of imperial China and the contemporary theater. He preserved the essential heritage of the dramatic art while introducing dance, acrobatics, mime, and modern makeup and costume techniques. The first Chinese actor to appear on a foreign stage (Tokyo, 1915), he made a triumphal tour of the United States (1930) and toured the Soviet Union and Western Europe (1935). He held important cultural posts after the 1949 revolution.

MEINECKE, FRIEDRICH (1862–1954), German historian. The most distinguished historian in post–World War I Weimar Germany, Meinecke developed the history of political ideas as editor of the *Historische Zeitschrift* (1893–1935) and as professor at the University of Berlin (1914–1928). A liberal nationalist, he wrote many important works, including *Cosmopolitanism and the Nation State* (1908; Eng. trans. 1970), on the development of German nationalism; *Machiavellism* (1924; Eng. trans. 1957), a condemnation of power politics; and *Historism: The Rise of a New Historial Outlook* (1936; Eng. trans. 1972). He was removed from all teaching and editing posts by the Nazis (1935), and after World War II he wrote *The German Catastrophe* (1946; Eng. trans. 1950), which traced the roots of Nazism in German culture. After the post–World War II partition of Berlin, he became rector of the new Free University in the western zone. ▪ See study by Robert A. Pois (1972) and Richard W. Sterling, *Ethics in a World of Power* (1958).

MEINHOF, ULRIKE. *See BAADER, ANDREAS.*

MEINONG, ALEXIUS, RITTER VON HAND-SCHUCHSHEIM (1853–1920), Austrian psychologist and philosopher. Meinong studied under philosophical psychologist Franz Brentano in Vienna (1875–78) and later taught at the University of Gnaz (1889–1920). In 1894 he established the Institute of Experimental Psychology, the first of its kind in Austria. Associated with the Austrian school of values, he was concerned with the assumptions people make when they think that they know (or do not know) something to be true. He influenced phenomenology, a philosophical school that sought to take a fresh look at experience by analyzing the data of consciousness. His theory of objects expanded the term to include that which is intentional as well as that which exists physically. In *On the Foundations of the General Theory of Values* (1924), Meinong framed his theory in ethical as well as aesthetic terms, showing that values are a class of objects apprehended through feeling. His translated works included *On Emotional Presentation* (1972) and *On Assumptions* (1983). ▪ See study by Reinhardt Grossman (1974), David F. Lindenfeld, *The Transformation of Positivism* (1980), and Richard Routley, *Exploring Meinong's Jungle and Beyond* (1980).

MEIR, GOLDA (Golda Mabovitch; 1898–1978), Israeli political leader. Born in Russia, Meir was taken to the United States as a child (1906) and became a schoolteacher in Milwaukee, Wisconsin. She was active in the Labor Zionist panty, and in 1921 she emigrated to Palestine. She worked for Histadrut (the General Federation of Labor), and headed the Jewish agency's political department (1946–48). After Israeli independence she was appointed minister plenipotentiary to Moscow (1948). She returned to Israel to serve as minister of labor and social insurance (1949–56). From 1956 to 1966 Meir served as foreign minister, and in 1969 she assumed the post of prime minister, serving in that capacity during the difficult period of the Yom Kippur War in October 1973. She retired from public life in 1974 after her government was changed with being "unprepared" for the war. ▪ See her autobiography, *My Life* (1975), and biography by Ralph G. Martin (1988).

MEITNER, LISE (1878–1968), Austrian-born physicist. One of the first women to receive a doctorate in physics (1906) in her native Vienna, Meitner studied under Max Planck and then collaborated (1907–38) with the physicist Otto Hahn in Berlin. They discovered and named a new element, protactinium (1918), studied beta decay, and investigated the properties of uranium bombarded with neutrons (1934–38). A Jew, Meitner fled Nazi Germany (1938) to Sweden. There, with her nephew Otto Robert Frisch, in an extremely influential paper (1939) she coined the word "fission" to explain what happened to uranium under bombardment and elucidated the possibilities of a resulting chain reaction. For this work she shared the Enrico Fermi Award (1966). ▪ See biographies by Deborah Crawford (1969) and Ruth L. Sime (1996).

MELBA, DAME NELLIE (Helen Porter Mitchell; 1861–1931), Australian opera singer. Born in Australia of Scottish descent, Melba received a good musical education but due to her father's opposition to a musical career did not study voice until her marriage (1882). She went to Europe (1886) and after a year of study in Paris made her debut in Brussels. Taking the name Melba for Melbourne, she rapidly became an international opera star with regular appearances at London's Covent Garden (from 1888) and New York's Metropolitan Opera (from 1893) and on world tours. Melba also became a member of London society and was immortalized in peach Melba and Melba toast. A pure coloratura soprano with a flawless, seemingly effortless voice, she sang such roles as Gilda, Lucia, Desdemona, and Mimi, until her retirement to Australia in 1926. ▪ See her autobiography, *Melodies and Memories* (1925) and Joseph Wechsberg, *Red Plush and Black Velvet* (1961).

MELCHIOR, LAURITZ (1890–1973), Danish opera singer. The most prominent Wagnerian tenor of the century, Melchior sang the great heldentenor roles, including Tristan, Lohengrin, and Siegfried, at the Bayreuth (Germany) Festival (1924–31), New York's Metropolitan Opera (1926–50), and at opera houses throughout the world. A huge man with an unusually rich, dramatic, and powerful voice, he appeared in nearly 1,000 performances of the exhausting Wagnerian repertoire during his long career.

MÉLIÈS, GEORGES (1861–1938), French film director. Méliès worked in his father's shoe factory until 1888, when, with a passion for conjuring, he bought a theater to produce magic-lantern shows. Inspired by the Lumière brothers and their cinematography, Méliès bought an English camera and experimented with trick photography to create "magical" effects. Using six "tricks," including superimposition and stop-motion, he made his first film in 1896. He built the world's first true film studio (1897) and directed over a thousand short films, including *Bluebeard* (1901), *A Trip to the Moon* (1902), *20,000 Leagues Under the Sea* (1907), and *The Conquest of the Pole* (1912). But filmmaking was rapidly becoming more sophisticated, and Méliès failed to keep pace. He went bankrupt in 1923, and many of his films were melted down into a substance used in the making of shoes. ▪ See Paul Hammond, *Marvellous Méliès* (1975).

MELLON, ANDREW WILLIAM (1855–1937), U.S. financier and cabinet officer. Establishing his career as the manager of his family's banking firm, Mellon provided the financial backing for what became the Aluminum Co. of America. Investing in the oil industry (he organized Gulf Oil Corp. in 1901) and in a variety of industrial firms, he became one of the richest men in the United States. A major financial backer of the Republican party and influential behind the scenes, Mellon was appointed secretary of the treasury by Pres. Warren G. Harding and continued on under Calvin Coolidge and Herbert Hoover (1921–32). Politically conservative, Mellon drastically reduced taxation of the wealthy. He believed no special government intervention should be taken to counter the effects of the Depression. A prominent art collector, he gave his huge collection to the government and money to build the National Gallery of Art in Washington. D.C. (1937). ▪ See Harvey O'Connor, *Mellon's Millions* (1933).

MENCHÚ, RIGOBERTA (1959–), Guatemalan peace activist. Menchú, a Christian Quiché Indian, was born into a family of poverty-stricken subsistence farmers. Her family was victimized by local landowners and murderous Guatemalan military forces during the 1970s. Her father was a founder of the Committee of Peasant Unity (1977), known by its Spanish abbreviation CUG, which became the country's major peasant opposition group. She joined the CUG as an organizer in 1979 and learned Spanish and several Indian dialects. After her mother, father, and brother were killed in separate incidents by the Guatemalan military, she went into exile in Mexico (1981) and became an eloquent spokesperson for indigenous people and victims of government repression. Her book, *I, Rigoberta Menchú: An Indian Woman in Guatemala* (1983; Eng. trans 1983), written with the help of sociologist Elisabeth Burgos-Debray, was translated into more than a dozen languages and publicized the plight of indigenous Guatemalans. She helped found the National Committee for Reconciliation (1987), which advocated a negotiated settlement to the decades-long civil war, and was awarded the 1992 Nobel Peace Prize. *Crossing Borders* (1999; Eng. trans. 1999) was the second installment of her memoir. In his book, *Rigoberta Menchú and the Story of All Poor Guatemalans* (1999), U.S. anthropologist David Stoll claimed that Menchú fabricated many of the autobiographical details of her book, and she subsequently admitted that she blended her own personal experiences with those of other victims of the violent civil war.

MENCKEN, HENRY LEWIS (1880–1956), U.S. editor, writer, and critic. One of the most influential journalists of the century, H. L. Mencken was known for his hard-nosed attacks on the hypocrisies of the American middle class. He started his career on the staff of the *Baltimore Morning Herald*, later moving (1906) to the *Baltimore Sun*, where he remained for the rest of his life. He edited (1914–23) the *Smart Set*, a literary trendsetter, then with George Jean Nathan founded and edited (1924–33) *American Mercury*. Many of his articles were assembled in a six-volume collection, *Prejudices* (1919–27). Mencken also extensively studied the differences between British and American English in *The American Language* (1919; rev. ed. 1948), and furthered interest in the works of such U.S. writers as Theodore Dreiser, Sinclair Lewis, and Eugene O'Neill. ▪ See his autobiographical works *Happy Days: 1880–1892* (1940), *Newspaper Days: 1899–1906* (1941), and *Heathen Days: 1890–1936* (1943). A sampler of these works appeared as *A Choice of Days* (1980). See also biography by Charles Bode (1969) and studies by Charles Fecher (1978) and Edward A. Martin (1984).

MENDELSOHN, ERICH (1887–1953), German architect. Mendelsohn's first major commission was the Einstein Tower in Potsdam (1919–21), a sculptured concrete observatory distinctly expressionistic in inspiration. He later designed German factories and department stores, utilizing glass and poured concrete in increasing conformity to the International Style. Forced to flee the Nazis in 1933, he designed buildings in England and Palestine. He settled in the United States (1941), designing a number of synagogues in the Midwest as well as the Maimonides Hospital in San Francisco (1946). ▪ See studies by Arnold Whittick (2d ed. 1956) and Wolf von Eckardt (1960).

MENDES, CHICO (Francisco Alves Mendes Filho; 1944–1988), Brazilian labor leader and environmental activist. Born in Xapuri in the upper reaches of the Amazon River, the son of a rubber tapper, Mendes received no formal education and began working as a tapper in the rain forest at an early age. He did not learn to read or write until age 20.

Concerned both about the exploitation of his fellow rubber workers and the destruction of the Amazon rain forests by wealthy cattle ranchers, Mendes tried, unsuccessfully, to organize the workers (1968). He later joined the state-controlled Confederation of Rural Workers' Union (1974), became a branch secretary, and eventually became president of the local Xapuri Rural Workers' Union. He joined the Worker's Party (1979), ran unsuccessfully for elective office, established literacy programs, and helped organize the First National Rubber Tappers Congress in Brasília (1985), which focused national and international attention on the problem of the rain forest destruction. After Mendes and his colleagues persuaded the government to establish several forest reserves, many ranchers reacted violently against union leaders. Mendes was assassinated and a powerful rancher, Darli Alves da Silva, and his son, Darci Alves Pereira, were convicted of the murder. ■ See A. Revkin, *The Burning Season* (1991), and A. Dwyer, *Into the Amazon* (1990).

MENDÈS-FRANCE, PIERRE (1907–1982), French political leader. Born into a middle-class Jewish family whose ancestors had emigrated to France from Portugal in the 16th century, Mendès-France was a brilliant student of law and political science at the University of Paris and became the youngest lawyer in France (1928). A member of the Radical Socialist party, he served in the national assembly (1932–40) and with Gen. Charles de Gaulle's Free French forces, based in London, during World War II. He was briefly minister of national economy in the first postwar government (1944–45) and served again in the national assembly (1946–58), where he became a critic of French colonial policy. As premier from June 1954 to February 1955, he negotiated an end to the Indochina War and French withdrawal from the region. He subsequently became a symbol of opposition to Gaullist policies and a respected leader of the noncommunist left. He served in the assembly, once again, from 1967 to 1968 and campaigned, unsuccessfully, as Gaston Deferre's running mate in the 1969 presidential election. ■ See study by Alexander Werth (1958) and biography by Jean Lacouture (Eng. trans. 1984).

MENEM, CARLOS (1930–   ), Argentine political leader. Menem studied law at the Argentinian National University in Córdoba and was a founding member of the Peronista Youth Movement in his native province of La Rioja (1955). As a leader of the Justicialist (Peronist) party, he was elected provincial governor (1973), was imprisoned by the military junta (1976–81), and was reelected governor in 1983 and 1987. Elected president of Argentina during a period of economic crisis (1989), he pursued free-market policies, opened the economy to international investment, privatized state-owned businesses, curtailed government spending, and restructured the foreign debt. He improved relations with Great Britain and the United States, but aroused controversy by pardoning military officers accused of human rights abuses. After the constitution was amended (1994) to allow

an incumbent president to seek a second consecutive term, he was reelected (to a four-year term) in 1995.

MENGELBERG, JOSEF WILLEM (1871–1951), Dutch conductor. Director of Amsterdam's Concertgebouw Orchestra (1895–45), Mengelberg built it into one of the world's most prestigious ensembles. An exemplar of the romantic tradition, he was best known for his interpretations of Beethoven, Mahler, Tchaikovsky, and Richard Strauss. He conducted throughout the world and was associated with the New York Philharmonic (1921–30). His collaboration with the Nazis during World War II damaged his reputation, and barred from performing in Holland after 1945, he lived in exile in Switzerland until his death.

MENGELE, JOSEF (1911–1979), German war criminal. His family operated an agricultural-machinery company in Günzburg. In the 1920s, he studied philosophy in Munich and became a devoted adherent of Adolf Hitler's doctrine of Aryan superiority. He earned a medical degree at the University of Franfurt am Main. In 1939, he entered the Waffen-SS as a second lieutenant, served as a medical officer in France and Russia, and served as chief physician at Auschwitz concentration camp (1943–44). During his 19 months there, he sent some 400,000 victims, primarily Jews, to the gas chambers in mass selections that designated prisoners for death or work details, and conducted grotesque "medical" experiments on prisoners. The most elusive of the major Nazi war criminals, Mengele left Auschwitz with false papers in December 1944. In 1947 he was briefly in the custody of U.S. occupying forces but either escaped or was released; intense investigation in the mid-1980s raised questions about whether U.S. officials deliberately allowed him to escape. He spent most of the next decade in Argentina and Paraguay, obtaining Paraguayan citizenship in 1959; under intense international pressure, Paraguay officially revoked his citizenship in 1979. In June 1985, an international team of forensic scientists concluded that the body of a man buried six years earlier in Sao Paulo, Brazil, was that of Josef Mengele. He had allegedly drowned at a Brazilian beach resort at age 67. ■ See Gerald Astor, *The "Last" Nazi* (1985), and biography by Gerald Posner (1986).

MENGISTU HAILE MARIAM (1937–   ), Ethiopian military and political leader. A former army ordnance officer, Mengistu rose to leadership of the Marxist military junta that overthrew Emperor Haile Selassie in 1974 by purging and executing his opponents. With Soviet financial and military aid, he established a dictatorship, nationalized the economy, decreed a land reform, launched a personality cult complete with public photographs and quotations, and continued the long-standing military campaigns against Eritrean and Somali separatists. The Workers party, a communist political organization based on the Soviet model, was established in 1984 with Mengistu as secretary-general. It was the only legal party in Ethiopia. Mengistu's government was criticized for hindering international relief efforts during the disastrous 1984–85 famine. He was overthrown in 1991 and granted political asylum in Zimbabwe. In 1995 the Ethiopian government charged him with genocide and crimes against humanity.

MENNIN, PETER (Peter Mennini; 1923–1983), U.S. composer. One of the most widely performed American composers of the post–World War II era. Mennin was a member of the composition faculty of New York's Juilliard School of Music (1947–58) and president of Baltimore's Peabody Conservatory of Music (1958–62). As president of Juilliard (1962–83), he established its Theater Center, American Opera Center, and Contemporary Music Festival. Mennin's ambitious symphonies, concertos, and choral music, written in his distinctive idiom, are characterized by dissonant harmonies, lively rhythms, and restless energy and tension.

MENNINGER, KARL AUGUSTUS (1893–1990), U.S. psychiatrist. A graduate of the Harvard Medical School (1917), Menninger returned to his native Topeka, Kansas, to found, with his father, Dr. Charles Frederick Menninger (1862–1953), the Menninger Clinic, a center for psychiatric research and therapy. Karl's brother, Dr. William Claire Menninger (1899–1966), also a psychiatrist, joined the clinic in 1925; together they established the Menninger Foundation (1941), which helped promote the acceptance of mental health treatment in the United States and became one of the largest and most prestigious psychiatric centers in the world. Karl helped develop the Winter Veterans Administration Hospital in Topeka, a major psychiatric training institution (1946), and was professor of psychiatry at the University of Kansas (1946–62). His books included *The Human Mind* (1930), the first best-selling book on psychiatry, *Man Against Himself* (1938); *The Vital Balance* (1963); *The Crime of Punishment* (1968); and *Whatever Became of Sin?* (1973). ■ See his collected articles and letters in *Sparks* (1973); Walker Winslow, *The Menninger Story* (1956); and Lawrence J. Friedman, *The Family and the Clinic* (1990).

MENOCAL, MARIO GARCÍA (1866–1941), Cuban political leader. The son of a sugar planter, he earned an engineering degree from Cornell (1888) and fought in the 1895–98 war against Spain. After independence he went into politics as a Conservative, winning election as president of Cuba (1912). Menocal's two-term "businessman's government" (1913–21) promulgated administrative and financial reform but was accused of corruption. The economic and political influence of the United States in Cuba grew during this period. World War I led to a sugar boom called "the dance of the millions," followed by an economic collapse (1920). Menocal returned to business (1921) but lost bids for reelection in 1924 and 1936.

MENON, (VENGALIL KRISHNAN) KRISHNA (1897–1974), Indian diplomat and political leader. Menon was in-

fluenced by Marxism while he was a student at the London School of Economics and at the University of Glasgow during the 1920s. Remaining in Britain for almost 30 years, he worked tirelessly as a lobbyist for Indian independence and pursued careers as a lawyer, book editor, and London borough councilor (1934–47). A friend and confidant of Prime Minister Jawaharlal Nehru (from the 1930s), Menon served as high commissioner to London (1947–52) after independence was achieved. As Indian ambassador to the United Nations (1953–62), he was known for his anti-imperialist and anti-U.S. speeches and his defense of India's policy of neutrality. He also gained worldwide attention as a negotiator at the Korean armistice talks and at the Geneva Indochina Conference (1954). As minister of defense (1957–62) he developed India's arms industry, but he was held responsible for India's disastrous defeat in the war with China (1962) and was forced to resign. After leaving the Congress party in 1967, he served in parliament as an independent leftist (1969–74) but never regained his powerful role in Indian politics. ■ See biography by T.J.S. George (1964).

MENOTTI, GIAN CARLO (1911–), Italian-U.S. composer. Menotti went to the United States in 1928 (retaining Italian citizenship), where he studied (1928–33) and taught from 1941 at the Curtis Institute in Philadelphia. He composed chamber music, ballets, and songs. He was best known, however, for operas—the most popular composed in this century—that combined realistic contemporary plots with features of traditional Italian opera. His opera *The Consul* (1950) was staged on Broadway and won a Pulitzer Prize. Writing his own librettos, Menotti updated the Christmas story with *Amahl and the Night Visitors* (1951) and injected social commentary into *The Saint of Bleecker Street* (1954), for which he won his second Pulitzer Prize. His later works included the operas *Juana, la Loca* (1979) and *Goya* (1986) and the choral works *Landscapes and Remembrances* (1976), *Mass* (1978), *Llama de Amor Viva* (1991), and *Jacob's Prayer* (1997). Menotti also founded (1958) the successful Spoleto summer Festival of Two Worlds and (1977) the Spoleto Festival USA, Charleston, South Carolina. ■ See biography by John Gruen (1978).

MENUHIN, LORD YEHUDI SINAI (1916–1999), U.S. violinist. As a boy from San Francisco, Menuhin was a musical prodigy who enjoyed great international celebrity in the 1920s and 1930s. Taking a year off at age 19, he made a successful transition to musical and social maturity, emerging as a concert artist of great sensitivity and dedication. Béla Bartók composed a sonata for solo violin for him (1944). Critics noted problems of technique in his later career, but he remained one of the foremost violinists of his generation. For a half century, his accompanist was his sister, Hephzibah Menuhin (1920–81). Based in Britain as a peripatetic citizen of the musical world, he established a music school there (1963), an annual music festival (1969), and a health-food store. He became a British subject in 1985.

Menuhin was also an advocate of Eastern music and made a series of notable albums with Indian musicians Ravi Shankar and Ali Akbar Khan. He also conducted major orchestras throughout the world (from the 1950s) and made numerous recordings as both a violinist and conductor. His books included *The Compleat Violinist* (1986) and *The Music of Man* (1979; with C. W. Davis). ▪ See his memoirs, *Unfinished Journey* (1977) and *Unfinished Journey: Twenty Years Later* (1997); studies by Robert Magidoff (1955; repr. 1974) and Tony Palmer (1991); and Robin Daniels, *Conversations with Menuhin* (1979).

MENZIES, SIR ROBERT GORDON (1894–1978), Australian political leader. Menzies, a lawyer, served in the Victoria legislature (1929–34) before he entered the federal Parliament (1934) as a member of the United Australia party. As prime minister (1939–41), Menzies took Australia into World War II. He helped found the conservative Liberal party (1944) and was again prime minister (1949–66). During his long second term he spurred industrial growth, developed mineral and energy resources, increased immigration, and expanded the university system. An ardent foe of communism at home and abroad, he tied Australia closer to the United States and Britain and sent Australian troops to fight in Korea and Vietnam. ▪ See his memoirs, *Afternoon Light* (1967), and biographies by Kevin Perkins (1968) and A.W. Martin (1993).

MERCER, JOHNNY (1909–1976), U.S. songwriter. One of the most versatile and prolific songwriters of the century, Mercer teamed with many of America's best popular composers (including Jerome Kern, Hoagy Carmichael, Harold Arlen, Henry Mancini, and Gordon Jenkins) and wrote the lyrics of dozens of the most popular songs of the 1930s, 1940s, and 1950s. "On the Atchison, Topeka and Sante Fe," "In the Cool, Cool, Cool of the Evening," "Moon River," and "Days of Wine and Roses" won Academy Awards, and "That Old Black Magic," "Lazybones," and "Blues in the Night" are considered modern classics. Although he couldn't read music, he composed the melodies for "I'm an Old Cowhand" and "Something's Gotta Give" and the entire score for the musical *Top Banana* (1951).

MERCHANT, ISMAIL (1936–) **and JAMES IVORY** (1928–), U.S. filmmakers. Merchant began producing films shortly after emigrating to the United States from his native city of Bombay, India. Ivory studied cinema at the University of Southern California (M.A. 1957) and had directed two films before meeting Merchant and forming Merchant Ivory Productions in 1962. They teamed up with novelist Ruth Prawer Jhabvala, who became their screenwriter, to create a series of films set in India, including *The Householder* (1963), *Shakespeare Wallah* (1965), *Bombay Talkie* (1970), and *Heat and Dust* (1983). They were best known for their thoughtful, sensitive, and beautifully filmed adaptations of such serious literary works as *The Europeans*

(1979), *The Bostonians* (1984), *A Room with a View* (1986), *Maurice* (1987), and *Howard's End* (1992). They also created *Mr. and Mrs. Bridge* (1990), *The Remains of the Day* (1993), *Jefferson in Paris* (1995), and *Surviving Picasso* (1996). In 1996 they were recognized by the *Guinness Book of World Records* as the longest-running partnership in cinema history. See Robert E. Long, *The Films of Merchant Ivory* (1997).

MERCOURI, MELINA (Maria Amalia Mercouri; 1923–1994), Greek actress and government official. Born in Athens, Mercouri studied at the National Theater academy and won international fame for her portrayal of a prostitute in *Never on Sunday* (1960). Her other films included *He Who Must Die* (1957), *Phaedra* (1961), *Topkapi* (1964), and *Promise at Dawn* (1970). A vocal opponent of the right-wing military junta that seized power in Greece in 1967, Mercouri was stripped of her citizenship and spent most of the next seven years as an exile in Paris, combining a show business career with political activism. She returned to Athens days after the junta collapsed (1974). Mercouri won a landslide victory in her second bid to represent one of the capital's poorest districts in parliament (1977). When the Socialist party came to power (1981), she served as minister of culture (1981–89; 1993–94). Mercouri supported feminist causes, urged Greek independence in cultural spheres, and was a powerful public relations figure for her government. ▪ See her autobiography, *I Was Born Greek* (Eng. trans. 1973).

MEREDITH, JAMES HOWARD (1933–), U.S. civil-rights worker. The son of a Mississippi farmer, Meredith spent nine years in the U.S. Air Force before becoming the first African-American student at the University of Mississippi (1962). His application to the university provoked bitter opposition from the state government, but protected by federal court orders and federal marshals, Meredith survived harassment and ostracism to graduate from the formerly segregated university (B.A. 1963). After studying in Nigeria and at Columbia Law School in New York City, he set out from Memphis in 1966 with a handful of followers on a civil-rights march that was aborted when Meredith was shot. He recuperated; graduated from Columbia (J.D. 1968), and became a businessman in New York. Returning to Jackson, Mississippi, in 1971, Meredith went into business and ran unsuccessfully for Congress (1972). ▪ See his *Three Years in Mississippi* (1966).

MERLEAU-PONTY, MAURICE (1908–1961), French philosopher. Merleau-Ponty graduated from the elite École Normale Supérieure in Paris (1930) and returned to teach there in 1935. He was active in the anti-Nazi Resistance during World War II, after which he taught at the University of Lyons, the Sorbonne, and the Collége de France, and coedited with Jean Paul Sartre the journal *Les Temps Modernes* (1945–52). An opponent of psychological behaviorism,

Merleau-Ponty drew on Gestalt psychology and existentialism in his major works, *The Structure of Behavior* (1942; Eng. trans. 1963) and *Phenomenology of Perception* (1945; Eng. trans. 1962). He was also concerned with contemporary political, social, and cultural questions. He defended the Soviet Union in *Humanism and Terror* (1947; Eng. trans. 1969), but broke with communism during the Korean War and wrote *Adventures of the Dialectic* (1955; Eng. trans. 1973). His other works included *Sense and Non-Sense* (1948; Eng. trans. 1964) and *Signs* (1960; Eng. trans. 1964). ■ See John F. Bannan, *The Philosophy of Merleau-Ponty* (1967), and studies by Albert Rabil (1967), Samuel B. Mallin (1979), Barry Cooper (1979), and James Schmidt (1985).

MERMAN, ETHEL (Ethel Zimmerman; 1909–1984), U.S. singer and actress. Merman, a secretary and part-time nightclub singer in New York City, made her first stage appearances in vaudeville (1929) with the team Clayton, Jackson, and Durante before astonishing Broadway musical-comedy audiences with her vocal powers; theater lore had it that she could "hold a note as long as the Chase Manhattan Bank." The vivacious Merman bellowed catchy numbers in such memorable musicals as *Girl Crazy* (1930), *Anything Goes* (1934), *Annie Get Your Gun* (1946–49), *Call Me Madam* (1950), and *Gypsy* (1959). She also appeared in films and on television. ■ See her autobiographies, *Who Could Ask for Anthing More* (1955) and *Merman* (1978), and Bob Thomas, *I Got Rhythm!* (1985).

MERRIAM, CHARLES EDWARD, JR. (1874–1953), U.S. political scientist. A scholar-politican, Merriam taught political science at the University of Chicago (1900–40) and was an activist in Chicago politics. He was considered the father of behaviorism in political science; he advocated empirical research and democratic social planning. Merriam successfully utilized his positions as president of the American Political Science Association (1925), head of the Social Science Research Council (1923–27), vice chairman of the Research Committee on Recent Social Trends (1929–32), and head of the National Resources Planning Board (1933–43) to foster the expansion and influence of social science and social scientists in American life. Among his works were *American Political Ideas* (1920), *New Aspects of Politics* (1925), and *Political Power* (1934). ■ See biography by Barry D. Karl (1974).

MERRICK, DAVID (David Margulies; 1912–2000), U.S. theatrical producer. Merrick gave up a successful law practice (1949) to devote himself full-time to the theater, his first love. He produced dozens of Broadway hits and became known for his publicity stunts, masterly public relations, and feuds with critics. Known as "The Barnum of Broadway producers," Merrick produced *Fanny* (1954), *The Matchmaker* (1955), *The World of Suzie Wong* (1958), *Gypsy* (1958), *Irma La Douce* (1960), *Stop the World—I Want to* *Get Off* (1962), *Oliver!* (1962), *Oh What a Lovely War* (1964), and *42nd Street* (1980) as well as Tony Award winners *Becket* (1960), *Luther* (1963), *Hello, Dolly!* (1964), *Marat/Sade* (1965), and *Rosencrantz and Guildenstern Are Dead* (1967). ■ See biography by Howard Kissel (1995).

MERRIFIELD, ROBERT BRUCE (1921–), U.S. chemist. R. Bruce Merrifield studied at the University of California at Los Angeles (B.A. 1943; Ph.D. 1949) and worked at the Rockefeller Institute for Medical Research (now Rockefeller University) in New York City (1949–92). In 1959, he conceived of the idea of solid-phase peptide synthesis, a rapid, automated, "assembly-line" method for preparing chainlike molecules called peptides, the building blocks of proteins. First put to use in 1962, the research method greatly simplified and quickened the pace of protein synthesis and enabled Merrifield (working with Bernd Gutte; 1969) to synthesize the complex enzyme ribonuclease, which processes genetic information, in a few weeks. Merrifield's method was used by researchers throughout the world in the fields of protein and nucleic acid chemistry and had a practical application in the design and manufacture of drugs and in gene research technology. Merrifield was awarded the 1984 Nobel Prize in Chemistry.

MERRILL, CHARLES EDWARD (1885–1956), U.S. investment banker. Merrill founded (1914) the investment firm that eventually became (1941) Merrill, Lynch, Pierce, Fenner and Beane, the world's largest brokerage house. The man who brought Wall Street to Main Street, Merrill was one of the first to seek out small investors and furnish them with simple and conservative financial advice. Among his Wall Street innovations were the granting of salaries rather than commissions to salespeople, the elimination of service charges, a sales training program, an annual report of the firm's operations, and the establishment of informative advertising and investment studies aimed at the small investor. He also was a founder of Safeway Stores, Inc. (1926) and *Family Circle* magazine (1932), which was distributed by Safeway. His son was the noted poet James Merrill (1926–1995). ■ See Edwin J. Perkins, *From Wall Street to Main Street* (1999).

MERRILL, JAMES INGRAM (1926–1995), U.S. poet. Merrill, the son of a founder of the brokerage firm of Merrill, Lynch, Pierce, Fenner and Smith, grew up in Greenwich Village in New York City and graduated from Amherst College (B.A. 1947). He started to write poetry in high school and developed into one of the most celebrated poets of his generation, winning the Pulitzer Prize for *Divine Comedies* (1977) and National Book Awards for *Nights and Days* (1967) and *Mirabell: Books of Number* (1979). His graceful, witty, and urbane poems, many dealing with childhood memories and the theme of love, were concerned with the relationship between reality and appearance and revealed Merrill as a serious philosopher. He was highly praised for the complex and cosmic trilogy, "The Book of Ephraim" (1976), "Mirabell" (1978), and "Scripts for the Pageant" (1980), published in *The Changing Light at Sandover* (1982). He also wrote the collections *From the First Nine: Poems 1946–76* (1982), *Late Settings* (1985), and *A Scattering of Salts* (1995). ■ See Guy L. Rotella, ed., *Critical Essays on James Merrill* (1996).

MERRILL, ROBERT (Robert Miller; 1917–), U.S. opera singer. The son of immigrants—his father was a garment worker and his mother a singer on a local Brooklyn, New York, radio station—Merrill sang in synagogues, hotels, Yiddish theaters, and on the radio before winning the Metropolitan Opera Auditions of the Air (1945). A leading baritone at the Met for three decades (1945–73), Merrill was known for his powerful voice and technical command and sang more than 500 performances with the company. Renowned for his interpretation of the elder Germont in *La Traviata*, he sang most of the major roles in the Italian and French repertory. He was also the official singer of the New York Yankees (1969–). ■ See the autobiographical *Once More from the Beginning* (1965; with S. Dody) and *Between Acts* (1976; with R. Saffron).

MERTON, ROBERT C. (1944–), U.S. economist. The son of the renowned sociologist Robert K. Merton, Robert C. Merton studied economics at the Massachusetts Institute of Technology (Ph.D. 1970), where he was an assistant to Paul Samuelson. He taught at M.I.T. (1969–88) and at the Harvard University Business School (1988–). During the 1970s, with Myron S. Scholes and Fischer Black (1938–1995), he helped develop a mathematical formula for measuring the worth of stock options, and he subsequently applied the formula to a wide variety of financial instruments. His work helped revolutionize modern finance by facilitating the growth of options trading and spawning a huge worldwide market in derivatives, financial instruments whose value is linked to price fluctuations of other assets, such as stocks, bonds, and currencies. For their pioneering work, Merton and Scholes shared the 1997 Nobel Memorial Prize in Economics. In 1998, Long Term Capital Management, a hedge fund (specializing in speculative high-risk trades in securities around the world) that was cofounded by Merton and Scholes, nearly collapsed. The fund, and its superrich investors, were saved only after the Federal Reserve Bank of New York negotiated a controversial bailout by arranging for a payment of $3.6 billion in cash put up by a consortium of Wall Street banks and brokerage houses.

MERTON, ROBERT KING (Meyer R. Schkolnick; 1910–), U.S. sociologist. Merton was born into an immigrant Jewish family in the slums of Philadelphia and won scholarships to Temple University (B.A. 1931) and to Harvard (Ph.D. 1936). He taught at Columbia University (1941–84) and was the associate director (with Paul Lazarsfeld) of its Bureau of Applied Social Research (1942–71). A

leading structural-functionalist, he rejected all-inclusive theoretical models as well as totally empirical studies in favor of "middle-range theories," which apply to a limited range of social phenomena. His studies of social deviance and anomie, mass persuasion, bureaucracy, and sociological theory were highly influential during the 1940s and 1950s. He was also a pioneer in the field of the sociology of science. His major works included *Social Theory and Social Structure* (1949), *On Theoretical Sociology* (1967), *Science, Technology and Society in Seventeenth-Century England* (1938; 2nd ed. 1970), and *The Sociology of Science* (2 vols., 1973–79). His son was economist Robert C. Merton (1944–). ■ See study by Piotr Sztompka (1986).

MERTON, THOMAS (1915–1968), U.S. Trappist monk. Born in France of Anglo-American parentage, Merton was educated at Columbia University (B.A. 1938) and taught English there. In 1938, he converted to Roman Catholicism and in 1941 joined the Trappist order at the monastery of Our Lady of Gethsemane in Kentucky. There he was ordained a priest (1949) and lived in relative seclusion, though he participated in the civil-rights, peace, and ecumenical movements. His autobiography, *The Seven Storey Mountain* (1948), was a best-seller and his other books on spirituality included *Seeds of Contemplation* (1949), *No Man Is an Island* (1955), *Mystics and Zen Masters* (1967), and *Faith and Violence* (1968). *The Hidden Ground of Love* (1985) contained his letters. ■ See study by George Woodcock (1978); biography by Monica Furlong (1980); Michael Mott, *The Seven Mountains of Thomas Merton* (1984); and James H. Forest, *Living with Wisdom* (1991).

MERWIN, WILLIAM STANLEY (1927–), U.S. poet. Graduating from Princeton (1947), W. S. Merwin lived abroad, returning (1956) to write plays for the Poet's Theater in Cambridge, Massachusetts. His first book of poetry, *A Mask for Janus* (1952), and three subsequent volumes appeared as *The First Four Books of Poems* (1975). These were followed by *The Moving Target* (1963) and *The Lice* (1967). *The Carrier of Ladders* (1970) won the 1971 Pulitzer Prize. Later collections included *The Compass Flower* (1977); *Opening the Hand*, (1983); *The Second Four Books of Poems* (1993); *East Window: The Asian Poems* (1998); *The River Sound* (1998); and *The Folding Cliffs* (1998), a story in verse of 19th-century Hawaii. His prose works included *Lost Upland* (1992) and *Regions of Memory: Uncollected Prose, 1949–1982* (1987). Merwin's works, which often dealt with ecological issues and modern society's desecration of nature, were characterized by startling imagery. He also produced notable translations of French and Spanish poetry and drama and a translation of Dante's *Purgatorio* (2000). ■ See the autobiographical collection *Unframed Originals* (1982).

MESSERSCHMITT, WILLY (1898–1978), German engineer and aircraft designer. Messerschmitt graduated from the Munich Institute of Technology in 1923, the same year that he established his own aircraft factory. His single-engine monoplane Me-109 set a world speed record in 1939 and over 35,000 of these planes were produced for the Luftwaffe during World War II. Probably the most famous German plane ever produced, the Me-109 was the principal defender against Allied bombers during the war. Messerschmitt also designed the Me-110 bomber, the Me-163 rocket-driven interceptor, and the Me-262 fighter plane, the world's first production-model jet aircraft. In 1958 he resumed aircraft production, and during the 1970s his company (Messerschmitt-Bolkow-Blohm) produced satellites, missiles, and airplanes. ■ See biography by Frank Vann (1993).

MESSIAEN, OLIVIER (1908–1992), French composer. Messiaen, whose music focused on the themes of Catholicism, love, and nature, led the "Jeune France" protest during the 1930s against the dry technicality of the group called "The Six." Imprisoned by the Germans for two years during World War II, he wrote *Quartet for the End of Time* (1941), and after his release was an influential teacher at the Paris Conservatory (retired 1978). Other compositions included *Turangalila* (1949), *Modes of Duration and Loudness* (1950), *Catalog of Birds* (1959), *Seven Hai-Kai* (1962), *The Transfiguration* (1969), and *Reflections on the Hereafter* (1991). He also wrote *The Technique of My Musical Language* (2 vols., 1944; Eng. trans. 1956). ■ See study by Paul Griffiths (1985).

MESSICK, DALE (Dalia Messick; 1906–   ), U.S. cartoonist. After studying briefly at the Chicago Art Institute and designing greeting cards, Messick broke into the world of cartooning, changing her name to overcome the field's bias against women. She created the red-headed career woman who was inspired by movie star Rita Hayworth and became known to readers of comics as *Brenda Starr, Reporter*. The strip first appeared in Sunday editions in 1940, and became a daily feature in 1945. Brenda's farfetched romantic escapades culminated in wedded bliss with the dashing Basil St. John. She nevertheless pursued her journalistic calling and in her fifth decade was flourishing as a successful working mother.

MESTA, PERLE (Perle Skirvin; 1890–1975), U.S. political hostess and diplomat. Once a society hostess in Newport, Rhode Island, Mesta became active in the National Woman's party during the 1930s. She switched her locale to Washington. D.C., and her party affiliation from Republican to Democratic during the 1940s. She was a fund-raiser for her friend Pres. Harry Truman, who rewarded her with an appointment as U.S. envoy to Luxembourg (1949–53). Returning to Washington, Mesta continued her nonpartisan social activities through subsequent administrations. She was the prototype of "the hostess with the mostest" of the musical *Call Me Madam*. ■ See her autobiography, *Perle* (1960).

MEŠTROVIĆ, IVAN (1883–1962), Yugoslav-U.S. sculptor. Apprenticed to a stonecutter at age 13, Meštrović later studied at the Vienna Academy of Fine Arts (1900–04). He exhibited with the avant-garde Vienna Secession (1902, 1909). Employing massive, elongated human forms, Meštrović became known for his colossal civic sculpture, especially his *Monument to the Unknown Soldier* (1934), a mausoleum with four caryatids reminiscent of Yugoslav peasant women in traditional costume. Emigrating to the United States after World War II, he adopted textured surfaces and executed religious themes using his earlier monolithic technique. Meštrović was also known for portrait busts. ■ See study by Dusko Keckemet (1970).

METAXAS, IOANNIS (1871–1941), Greek general and political leader. A career military officer with strong monarchist leanings, Metaxas served during World War I as chief of the general staff (1915–17) and chief military adviser to King Constantine I, and sought unsuccessfully to maintain Greek neutrality during World War I. After Constantine's abdication, Metaxas followed him into exile (1917), returned to Greece after his restoration (1920), and fled once more into exile with the fall of the monarchy and the establishment of a republic (1923). Granted an amnesty, he returned to Greece, served briefly as a minister, won election to parliament, and led an ultraroyalist opposition party. After the restoration of the monarchy (1935), he became premier (April 1936) and, in a coup d'état (August 1936), he set up a fascist state and ruled as a dictator until his death. During World War II he successfully defended Greece against the Italian invasion (1940–41) and died before the German invasion and occupation of the country (April 1941). ■ See Jon V. Kofas, *Authoritarianism in Greece* (1983).

MEYER, ADOLF (1866–1950), Swiss-born psychiatrist. After studying at the University of Zurich (M.D. 1892), Meyer emigrated to the United States and taught at the Cornell (1904–09) and Johns Hopkins (1910–41) medical schools. He combined elements of psychology and physiology in his psychobiological approach to treatment, which emphasized social factors and called for the study of the whole personality in the entire life situation. He introduced the practice of compiling case histories and was a founder (1908) of the mental hygiene movement. His teaching reforms elevated professional standards in psychiatric training. See his selected papers in *Commonsense Psychiatry* (1948) and *Psychobiology* (1957).

MEYER, EUGENE (1875–1959), U.S. banker, government official, and newspaper publisher and editor. The son of a banker, Meyer established his own Wall Street investment-banking house (1901) and made a fortune before dissolving the firm and entering government service (1917). He held important positions under seven presidents (Wilson to Eisenhower), including those of director of the War Finance Corp. (1918–20), governor of the Federal Reserve Board

(1930–33), first chairman of the Reconstruction Finance Corp. (1932), and first president of the International Bank for Reconstruction and Development (1946). In 1933 he bought, at auction, the *Washington Post*, served as its publisher (1933–46), editor (1940–46), and chairman of the board (from 1947), and built it into one of the country's most widely read newspapers. His daughter was publisher Katharine Graham (1917–). ■ See biography by Merlo J. Pusey (1974).

MEYERHOF, OTTO (1884–1951), German biochemist. Meyerhof studied at the University of Heidelberg (M.D. 1909); under the influence of Otto Warburg he turned to physiology and physical chemistry. Focusing his attention on the chemical processes involved in muscular action, he discovered that glycogen was broken down into lactic acid without the consumption of oxygen, and that the lactic acid was reconverted into glycogen through oxidation when the muscle was at rest. For this contribution he shared the Nobel Prize for Physiology or Medicine with A. V. Hill in 1922. Because he was Jewish, the Nazis forced him out as head of the department of physiology at the Kaiser Wilhelm Institute for Medical Research in Heidelberg (1938). He worked in Paris (1938–40) and in 1940 he escaped to the United States, where he was research professor in physiological chemistry at the University of Pennsylvania (1941–51). His books included *The Chemical Dynamics of Life Phenomena* (1924).

MEYERHOLD, VSEVOLOD EMILIEVICH (Karl Theodore Kasimir Meyerhold; 1874–1940?), Russian theatrical director and producer. Asked to join the Moscow Art Theater when it was founded (1898), Meyerhold soon rejected (1902) its realistic approach. He developed an avant-garde theatrical style based on symbolism and stylization that diminished the individualism of the actors and relied on sparse constructivist settings. He was responsible for notable nonrealistic productions in Moscow and St. Petersburg; in 1918 he joined the Communist party and produced the first Soviet plays. One of the most powerful figures in the theatrical world of the 1920s, he lost favor during the 1930s for his opposition to socialist realism and was denounced for his "formalism" and decadence. A victim of the Stalinist purges, he was arrested in 1939 and disappeared. ■ See studies by Marjorie L. Hoover (1974) and Konstantin Rudnitskii (Eng. trans. 1981).

MIASKOVSKY, NIKOLAI YAKOVLEVICH (1881–1950), Russian composer. Miaskovsky abandoned his career as a military engineer (1907) to study music and became a professor at the Moscow Conservatory (1921). For the next 30 years he trained many of the younger Russian composers and was Russia's most prominent teacher of composition. Miaskovsky's works were characterized by the optimistic expression favored by the Soviet government. He composed 27 symphonies, more than any other modern composer. ■ See biography by Alexei Ikonnikov (1946).

MICHAEL (1921–), king of Rumania. Michael became Rumania's boy king in 1927, after his father Prince Carol had renounced the succession. His father returned in 1930, however, as King Carol II. Michael again assumed the throne in 1940, when his father abdicated. He asserted himself in 1944 to overthrow the military dictatorship of Gen. Ion Antonescu and make peace with the Allies, but in 1947 he was forced into exile by the communists.

MICHAËLIS, KARIN (Karin Marie Bech Brondum; 1872–1950), Danish novelist and short-story writer. Michaëlis spent considerable time in the United States. Much of her work appeared in translation. Early stories like "The Child: Andrea" (1940) were issued in more than a dozen languages. The novel *The Dangerous Age* (1910; Eng. trans. 1911, 1991) described a woman's midlife crisis. Her other novels included *Elsie Lindtner* (1912; Eng. trans. 1912), *The Governor* (1912; Eng. trans. 1913), *Venture's End* (1927; Eng. trans. 1927), and *The Green Island* (1935; Eng. trans. 1936). Her series of "Bibi" books found many adolescent readers. ■ See her autobiography, *Little Troll* (1946).

MICHEL, HARTMUT (1948–), German biochemist. After graduating from the University of Würzburg (Ph.D. 1977), Michel did research at the Max Planck Institute for Biochemistry in Martinsried (1979–87). He was the first scientist to isolate and crystallize (1982) a four-protein complex found in cell membranes called a photosynthetic reaction center, which is essential for the process of photosynthesis. He then joined (1982–85) with colleagues Robert Huber and Johann Deisenhofer, experts in X-ray crystallography, to map out, atom by atom, the three-dimensional structure of the macromolecule that consists of more than 10,000 atoms. For their work in explaining the mechanism of photosynthesis, the trio was awarded the 1988 Nobel Prize for Chemistry. In 1987 Michel became head of the Max Planck Institute for Biophysics in Frankfurt.

MICHELANGELI, ARTURO BENEDETTI (1920–1995), Italian pianist. Michelangeli studied in Brescia and Milan before winning first prize at the International Musical Competition in Geneva in 1939. During World War II he served in the Italian air force and later as a member of the antifascist resistance. After his London debut in 1946 he was considered one of the most musically brilliant of post–World War II pianists, with stunning technical powers and interpretation. Michelangeli taught piano in Italy between world concert tours. He was best known for his performances of Scarlatti, Ravel, and Beethoven.

MICHELS, ROBERT (1876–1936), German political sociologist. Michels came from a wealthy, cosmopolitan family and was active as a young man in the socialist movement, where he observed leaders employing techniques of authoritarianism and bureaucracy to maintain their power. Applying the insights of sociology to politics, he proposed his "iron law" of oligarchy: "who says organization says oligarchy." According to Michels, the more complex and bureaucratized an organization, the more likely it is to be controlled by an elite. Michels spent much of his adult life in Italy and Switzerland, teaching at the universities of Turin, Basel, and Perugia. He refused to support Germany's participation in World War I, but later he did not oppose fascism. ■ See his classic study *Political Parties* (1911; Eng. trans. 1949) and *First Lectures in Political Sociology* (1927; Eng. trans. 1949).

MICHENER, JAMES ALBERT (1907–1997), U.S. short-story writer and novelist. Abandoned as an infant and raised in Pennsylvania, Michener attended Swarthmore College and later served as a naval historian in the South Pacific (1944–46). Richard Rodgers and Oscar Hammerstein II adapted his *Tales of the South Pacific* (1947, Pulitzer Prize) into the hit Broadway musical *South Pacific* (1949). His best-selling, epic novels *Hawaii* (1959), *Caravans* (1963), *The Source* (1965), *Centennial* (1974), *Chesapeake* (1978), *The Covenant* (1980), *Space* (1982), *Poland* (1983), and *Texas* (1985) won him praise for exhaustive research and skill in blending fact and fiction. He published nonfictional accounts of the 1960 presidential campaign, the Vietnam War, and the student protest at Kent State University, and also wrote on art history. After he died it was revealed that he had given more than $117 million to various universities and charities, more than 90 percent of his lifetime earnings. ■ See his memoir, *The World is My Home* (1991), and study by A. Grove Day (rev. ed. 1977).

MICHURIN, IVAN VLADIMIROVICH (1855–1935), Russian horticulturist. Working in his private nursery in Kozlov (later named Michurinsk), Michurin developed many new varieties of fruits and berries. During the 1920s his nursery was transformed into a state-supported plant-breeding station. His theories of hybridization accepted the idea that acquired characteristics could be inherited; "Michurinism" was adopted as the official position on genetics in the Soviet Union from the mid-1930s to the mid-1960s, and Mendelian genetics was suppressed. T. D. Lysenko was the most influential exponent of Michurin's theories. Michurin's ideas, which were never accepted by scientists in the West, were eventually discredited in the Soviet Union. See his *Selected Works* (Eng. trans. 1949).

MIDGLEY, THOMAS, JR. (1889–1944), U.S. chemist. While working as an engineer for the Dayton (Ohio) Engineering Laboratories Co. (Delco), Midgley resolved to make gasoline a more efficient power source by minimizing knocking. He trained himself rigorously in chemistry and discovered (1921) that adding tetraethyl lead to fuel makes it burn more smoothly, increasing significantly its octane rating. "Ethyl" gasoline was made available to the public in 1923. His later search for a safe refrigerant led to the discovery of freon (1930), a gas now used in refrigerators,

freezers, and air conditioners. Midgley was paralyzed (1940) by polio, and he devised a harness with pulleys that allowed him to get out of bed. In 1944 he accidentally strangled himself with his invention.

MIELZINER, JO (1901–1976), U.S. scenic designer. Viewing the stage as an environment and not merely a setting, Mielziner revolutionized stage design in the United States, creating innovative sets and lighting for more than 300 productions, including *South Pacific, The King and I, Carousel, Gypsy, Pal Joey, Street Scene, A Streetcar Named Desire, Winterset, Guys and Dolls, Cat on a Hot Tin Roof, Death of a Salesman,* and *The Glass Menagerie.* He won five Tony Awards and five Donaldson Awards. He also did designs for the Metropolitan Opera and New York City Ballet (notably *Pillar of Fire,* 1942) and for motion pictures (Academy Award for *Picnic,* 1955). ■ See his *The Shapes of Our Theater* (1970; edited by C. Ray Smith) and his memoirs, *Designing for the Theater* (1965).

MIES VAN DER ROHE, LUDWIG (1886–1969), German-born U.S. architect. In Berlin during the 1920s and as director of the Bauhaus (1930–33), Mies designed early prototypes of his glass skyscrapers—reinforced-concrete structures without ornamentation ("skin-and-bones construction" was his term)—but his ideas remained largely on paper until he emigrated to the United States in the late 1930s. While serving as director of architecture at the Illinois Institute of Technology (1938–58), where he taught that "less is more," Mies designed two glass-sheathed apartment towers on Chicago's Lake Shore Drive (1951) and the Seagram Building (with Philip Johnson) in New York (1958). In the mid-1980s, his famous German Pavilion, a landmark of modern architecture that was dismantled after a brief existence at the 1929 International Exposition, was reconstructed in Barcelona, Spain. Mies also created furniture designs that are considered classics. ■ See biographies by Franz Schulze (1985) and Philip Johnson (1947; rev. ed. 1978) and studies by David Spaeth (1985) and Wolf Tegethoff (1985).

MIFUNE, TOSHIRO (1920–1997), Japanese actor. A photographer before World War II, Mifune won his first small acting part in a 1945 talent contest. Director Akira Kurosawa then chose him to play the lead in his Japanese film classics *Rashomon* (1950), *The Seven Samurai* (1954), *The Throne of Blood* (1957), and *Yojimbo* (1961). Mifune formed his own production company to direct *Legacy of the 500,000* (1963). He also appeared in the American productions of *Hell in the Pacific* (1960) and *Grand Prix* (1966) and was featured in the movie *Midway* (1976). He also starred in the television series "Shogun" (1980).

MIHAJLOVIĆ, DRAŽA OR DRAGOLJUB (1893–1946), Yugoslav military leader. A royalist and a Serbian nationalist, Mihajlović fought with the Chetniks (Serbian guerrilla forces) during the Balkan wars and World War I, and he organized underground Chetnik bands to oppose the Germans after the 1941 invasion. Although originally supported by the Allies, he clashed with Josip Broz Tito's communist partisans—viewing them as a greater threat than the Axis powers—and reportedly collaborated with the Nazis. In 1944 the Allies withdrew their support for Mihajlović's dwindling band, and he was captured by the Titoist forces and tried and executed in Belgrade. ■ See David Martin, *Ally Betrayed* (1946), and *Patriot or Traitor* (1978).

MIKAN, GEORGE LAWRENCE (1924–), U.S. basketball player. In a 1950 Associated Press poll, the 6-foot, 9-inch-tall Mikan was selected as the greatest player of the first half of the 20th century. He was the first of the outstanding professional centers in the post–World War II era, leading the Minneapolis Lakers to six championships from 1948 through 1954. In nine years as a pro, Mikan scored 11,764 points and averaged 22.6 points a game. After his retirement (1956) he was a successful lawyer and businessman and served as commissioner of the American Basketball Association (1967–69).

MIKHAILOVICH, DRAJA. *See MIHAJLOVIĆ, DRAŽA.*

MIKHOELS, SOLOMON MIKHAILOVICH (S. M. Vovsi; 1890–1948), Russian (Yiddish) director and actor. Mikhoels was the leading actor of the Yiddish-language Moscow State Jewish Theater founded in 1918, and its director after 1928. He mastered both tragic and comic roles, from King Lear to Sholem Aleichem's Tevye. He was chairman of the Jewish Antifascist Committee during World War II and was a spokesman for the Jewish community after the war. In 1948, a *Pravda* obituary reported Mikhoels' sudden death; rumor attributed his death to a drunken driver, but Svetlana Alliluyeva, daughter of dictator Joseph Stalin, later confirmed that Stalin had ordered his execution. The following year the State Jewish Theater was officially closed, and during the next few years most leading Jewish cultural figures were executed and Jewish cultural institutions were disbanded.

MIKI, TAKEO (1907–1988), Japanese political leader. Of middle-class origins, Miki studied at the University of California and received a law degree from Meiji University (1937). He was first elected to the diet (parliament) in 1937; because he had opposed war with the United States, he was permitted to continue in the diet after World War II. Miki joined the Liberal Democratic party (1955) and held many cabinet posts, including that of foreign minister (1966–68), before serving as premier (1974–76). His tenure in office was marred by the recession following the 1973 oil crisis and the disclosure of the Lockheed bribery scandal, which resulted in the arrest of former Liberal Democratic premier Tanaka Kakuei.

MIKOLAJCZYK, STANISLAW (1901–1966), Polish political leader. The founder and leader (1931–39) of Poland's Peasant party, Mikolajczyk served as premier (1943–44) of the Polish government-in-exile in London during World War II. Back in Poland after the war, he led the noncommunist opposition until the 1947 elections, which resulted in a communist takeover. Mikolajczyk fled first to England and then to the United States, where he was active in exile politics and wrote *The Rape of Poland* (1948).

MIKOYAN, ANASTAS IVANOVICH (1895–1978), Soviet political leader. Born into a middle-class Armenian family, Mikoyan studied at a theological seminary and joined the bolsheviks in 1915. He did political work in the Caucasus until 1926 and supported the wing of the Communist party headed by Joseph Stalin. A specialist in foreign and domestic trade, he held top posts in these areas for more than 30 years and was linked with efforts to increase the production and improve the distribution of consumer goods. A member of the ruling Politburo (1935–1966) and a deputy premier (1937–53), he was one of the few "old bolsheviks" to survive the Stalinist purges of the 1930s and 1940s. His 1956 speech at the 20th Party Congress helped launch the de-Stalinization campaign and he helped Nikita Khrushchev consolidate his power (1955–58). He played a major role in the formulation of foreign policy during the 1950s and served as chairman of the presidium of the Supreme Soviet (1964–65).

MIKOYAN, ARTEM IVANOVICH (1905–1970), **and MIKHAIL IOSIFOVICH GUREVICH** (1892–1976), Soviet aircraft designers. Mikoyan, an engineer in the Soviet air force, and Gurevich, a deputy chief of Aircraft Factory No. 1 in Moscow, established their own design bureau (1939) and developed the MiG series of fighter aircraft. The MiG-1 high-altitude interceptor (1940) and the refined MiG-3 were widely used against the Germans during World War II. Mikoyan and Gurevich also designed the MiG-9 (1946), one of the Soviet Union's first jet aircraft; the MiG-15 and -17, jet fighters used during the Korean War; and the MiG-19 (1955), a supersonic all-weather fighter. The MiG-25, a reconnaissance fighter that established a speed record of over 1,800 mph and an altitude record of over 118,000 feet, went into service in 1971.

MILCH, ERHARD (1892–1972), German general. A protégé of Nazi leader Hermann Goering, Milch used his position as chairman of Lufthansa, the new German national airline, as a cover to develop secretly the German air force (Luftwaffe) during the early 1930s. When the Luftwaffe was officially announced (1935), Milch was given the rank of lieutenant general and later promoted to field marshal (1940) and air force chief of staff. Convicted of war crimes at Nuremberg for his recruitment of slave labor and use of laborers for medical experiments, he served seven years in prison (1947–54). ■ See David Irving, *The Rise and Fall of the Luftwaffe* (1973).

MILGRAM, STANLEY (1933–1984), U.S. social psychologist. Milgram studied at Harvard (Ph.D. 1960), then taught at Yale (1960–63), where he conducted the controversial experiments that culminated, a decade later, in *Obedience to Authority: An Experimental View* (1974). His famous experiments demonstrated that people from all walks of life were willing to inflict a painful shock to a stranger they thought to be a helpless victim if encouraged to do so by an authority figure—a "scientist" dressed in a white lab coat. (The shocks were not real, and an actor played the role of the victim.) More than 60 percent of the volunteers who thought they were taking part in a study of learning and memory complied with the experimenter's request despite cries of pain from the actor who played the role of the victim. Milgram's findings stirred public discussion and inspired a play and a TV drama. The traumatic effects of the research on its subjects sparked controversy, and many institutions thereafter adopted more rigorous standards for safeguarding human subjects in social-science research. Milgram taught at the City University of New York (1967–84). He applied ingenious methods to investigations of such varied subjects as television violence, mental mapping, crowds, and urban living, and produced six scientific films. He succumbed to a heart attack at age 51.

MILHAUD, DARIUS (1892–1974), French composer. A cultivated member of The Six, Milhaud was a prolific composer in every genre whose works were influenced by jazz, Brazilian folk rhythms, Hebraic chants, and melodies of his native Provence. Many of his 441 works, which included 12 symphonies, 15 operas, and 19 ballets, were written in a polytonal style. He frequently collaborated with poet and librettist Paul Claudel. His best known works included the ballets *Le Boeuf sur le Toit* (1919) and *La Création du Monde* (1923), the opera *Christophe Columb* (1930), and the orchestral *Suite Provençale* (1937). A Jew, he fled France after the German invasion (1940) and taught at Mills College (California). After returning to France (1947) he alternately taught at the Paris Conservatory and at Mills. ■ See his autobiographies *Notes Without Music* (1949; Eng. trans. 1952) and *My Happy Life* (Eng. trans. 1995).

MILIUKOV (OR MILYUKOV), PAVEL NIKOLAYEVICH (1859–1943), Russian political leader and historian. A specialist in Russian history, Miliukov was a member of the Duma, a leading voice in the liberal Constitutional Democratic party, and an opponent of bolshevism. He was foreign minister in the first government of Prince Lvov after the February Revolution (1917), but when he favored meeting commitments to the Allies in World War I, his support eroded and he was forced to resign after three months in office. He emigrated to Paris, where he was active in émigré politics and wrote several works of history. His best-known work was *Outlines of Russian Culture* (3 vols., Eng. trans. 1942). ■ See his *Political Memoirs, 1905–1917*

(Eng. trans. 1967) and Thomas Riha, *A Russian European* (1969).

MILK, HARVEY (1931–1978), government official and gay rights activist. Milk worked as a financial analyst in New York City before moving (1969) to San Francisco. In his third bid for election to the San Francisco Board of Supervisors, he defeated 16 other candidates and became the city's first openly homosexual candidate to win election to high office (1977). A liberal Democrat, he advocated civil rights for minorities and for women. He helped to defeat Proposition 6 (1978), an initiative that would have allowed local school districts in California to discharge homosexual teachers. Milk and San Francisco Mayor George Moscone were assassinated (Nov. 1978) by former city supervisor Dan White, who was attempting to withdraw his resignation in order to remain in office. When White, who was charged with first-degree murder, was found guilty of voluntary manslaughter and sentenced to five-to-seven years' imprisonment, the verdict sparked protest. White was released in January 1984, and committed suicide in October 1985. *The Times of Harvey Milk* (1984) was an award-winning documentary film. ■ See Randy Shilts, *The Mayor of Castro Street* (1982).

MILLAY, EDNA ST. VINCENT (1892–1950), U.S. poet. The year she graduated from Vassar College (1917), she attracted critical attention with her first collection, *Renascence and Other Poems*. It was followed by *A Few Figs from Thistles* (1920) and *Second April* (1920). "The Harp Weaver" won a 1923 Pulitzer Prize and was the title poem of a 1923 collection. Millay's poetry was gathered in *Collected Sonnets* (1941), *Collected Lyrics* (1943), and *Collected Poems* (1956). She also wrote prose under the name Nancy Boyd and participated in the Provincetown Players, a troupe that produced several of her plays, including *Aria da Capo* (1920). She was among the most esteemed and widely read poets of her generation. Her letters appeared in 1952. ■ See biographies by Miriam Gurko (1962), Jean Gould (1969), and Anne Cheney (1975), and study by Norman A. Brittin (rev. ed. 1982).

MILLER, ARNOLD RAY (1923–1985), U.S. labor leader. A third-generation coal miner from West Virginia, Miller left the mines in 1970 partially disabled by black lung disease. In a 1972 election under U.S. Department of Labor supervision, he ousted the long-standing president of the United Mine Workers, W. A. Boyle, by promising to improve mine safety, increase pensions, and sell the union's limousines. During his term in office (1972–79) the union was beset by layoffs, wildcat strikes, and internal dissension. He resigned because of ill health. ■ See Paul F. Clark, *The Miners' Fight for Democracy* (1981).

MILLER, ARTHUR (1915–   ), U.S. playwright. Miller exposed family conflict and shallow American values in *All My*

Sons (1947) and in his masterpiece, *Death of a Salesman* (1949, Pulitzer Prize). After disparaging McCarthyism in *The Crucible* (1953), a play about Salem witch trials, Miller himself was convicted of contempt of Congress (1957) when he refused to divulge the names of writers present at a 1947 political gathering; the conviction was later reversed on appeal. *After the Fall* (1964) was based on his marriage (1956–61) to actress Marilyn Monroe, for whom he wrote the screenplay *The Misfits* (1961). Miller sought to bring to the stage the texture and complexity of the novel. Other plays included *A View from the Bridge* (1955, Pulitzer Prize), *Incident at Vichy* (1965), and *The Price* (1968). His later plays met less critical success. *The American Clock* (1980) and *Broken Glass* (1994) were more popular in London than in New York. *I Don't Need You Any More* (1968) is a short-story collection. ▪ See his autobiography, *Timebends* (1987), and studies by D.S.R. Welland (1979) and Leonard Moss (rev. ed. 1980).

MILLER, ARTHUR C. (1895–1970), U.S. cinematographer. A pioneer newsreel cameraman and recognized master of black-and-white cinematography, Miller filmed the famous serial *The Perils of Pauline* (1914) and films for George Fitzmaurice during the 1920s. At 20th Century-Fox (1932–50) he shot all of the Shirley Temple films, worked on several movies with John Ford, and won Academy Awards for *How Green Was My Valley* (1941), *The Song of Bernadette* (1943), and *Anna and the King of Siam* (1946). He wrote (with Fred Balshofer) an account of early moviemaking, *One Reel a Week* (1967).

MILLER, GLENN (1904–1944), U.S. bandleader. After years as a trombonist and arranger with the bands of Ben Pollack, Tommy and Jimmy Dorsey, and Ray Noble, among others, Miller formed his own ensemble in 1938. Featuring a distinctive "sweet" and smooth sound based on a disciplined combination of reeds and brasses, the Glenn Miller Orchestra soon became the nation's most popular "big band." It recorded such hit records as "Moonlight Serenade," "Chattanooga Choo Choo," "In the Mood," "Tuxedo Junction," and "Little Brown Jug," appeared in the films *Sun Valley Serenade* (1941) and *Orchestra Wives* (1942), and established an international reputation. Miller disbanded his orchestra in 1942 and became leader of the U.S. Army Air Force Band in Europe, which made World War II broadcasts to troops throughout the world. He disappeared while on a flight from England to Paris, and no wreckage of the plane was ever discovered. A film biography, *The Glenn Miller Story*, was released in 1953. ▪ See John Fowler, *Moonlight Serenade* (1972), and George T. Simon, *Glenn Miller and His Orchestra* (repr. 1980).

MILLER, HENRY (1891–1980), U.S. writer. Miller grew up in Brooklyn, worked for New York's Union Telegraph Co., and lived in Paris in the 1930s, where he began writing seri-

ously at age 40. His infamous books, including *Tropic of Cancer* (1934), *Black Spring* (1936), and *Tropic of Capricorn* (1939), were comic quasi-philosophical, autobiographical narratives that showed great powers of observation and an ear for natural conversation, but were better known for their explicit descriptions of sex. They were banned in the United States until the 1960s. Miller strongly influenced the anti-intellectual, unconventional tradition of modern American letters, although his prose style was actually quite conventional. His other writings included *The Cosmological Eye* (1939), *The Air-Conditioned Nightmare* (2 vols., 1945–47), *The Books in My Life* (1952), and *Big Sur and the Oranges of Hieronymus Bosch* (1957). ▪ See his autobiography, *My Life and Times* (1971); Jay Martin, *Always Merry and Bright* (1978); Mary V. Dearborn, *The Happiest Man Alive* (1991); and biography by Robert Ferguson (1991).

MILLER, JONATHAN (1934–), British physician. actor, director. and writer. While a student at Cambridge (1953–56) Miller appeared in several comic revues and, after receiving a medical degree from the University of London Medical School (1959), coauthored and costarred (with Peter Cook, Dudley Moore, and Alan Bennett) in *Beyond the Fringe* (1960), a hit satirical revue in London (1961–62) and New York (1962–63). He later directed provocative interpretations of Shakespearean plays at the National Theatre, the Old Vic, and for the BBC-TV's Shakespeare series and also directed at the English National Opera and at the world's leading opera houses, including the Metropolitan in New York and La Scala in Milan. He presented *The Body in Question* (1978), a thirteen-part television series on the history of medicine, and *States of Mind* (1983), a television series based on his book about the workings of the human mind. In 1986 he directed a Broadway production of Eugene O'Neill's *Long Day's Journey Into Night*. His books included *Marshall McLuhan* (1971), *Darwin for Beginners* (1982), *The Human Body* (1983), *The Facts of Life* (1984), *Subsequent Performances* (1986), and *On Reflection* (1988). ▪ See Michael Romain, *A Profile of Jonathan Miller* (1992).

MILLER, KELLY (1863–1939), U.S. sociologist and educator. A professor (1890–1934) and dean (1907–18) at Howard University, Miller did much to build up the university and was one of the most influential black academics of his time. He believed that the racial problem in the United States was part of the general problem of humanity, and he believed that reason and conscience would prevail and that blacks would eventually attain full equality in America. A civil-rights activist, he helped edit the journal *Crisis* with W. E. B. DuBois, but he took a middle position in the debate between "higher education" versus "industrial education" in which DuBois and Booker T. Washington were the main adversaries. His best-known works were *Race Adjustment* (1908), *Out of the House of Bondage* (1914), *An Appeal to Conscience* (1918), and *The Everlasting Stain* (1924).

MILLER, MERTON H. (1923–　), U.S. economist. Miller worked as a tax expert at the Treasury Department before getting a Ph.D. in economics from Johns Hopkins (1952) and teaching at the Carnegie Institute of Technology in Pittsburgh (1958–61) and the University Chicago (1961–96). A specialist in corporate finance, he collaborated (1958) with Franco Modigliani (who won the 1985 Nobel Memorial Prize in Economics) on an article that explained that the method of corporate financing does not determine the value of the firm, but rather it is determined by the skills of its managers and the productivity of the company. This Miller-Modigliani theorem, along with the research findings of Harry M. Markowitz and William F. Sharpe, created the modern discipline of financial economics and provided the theoretical underpinnings of the mutual fund business. Miller, Markowitz, and Sharpe shared the 1990 Nobel Memorial Prize for Economics.

MILLER, PERRY GILBERT (1905–1963), U.S. historian. A native of Chicago and graduate of the University of Chicago (Ph.D. 1931), Miller taught at Harvard from 1931 until his death. His field was early New England, and he used diaries and religious texts to re-create the historical reality of Puritanism. Miller, who was in nonacademic life an avid baseball fan, wrote *The New England Mind* (2 vols., 1939–53) and biographies of Jonathan Edwards (1948–49) and Roger Williams (1953). These influential works reawakened an interest in Puritan life in America. His later works included *Life of the Mind in America* (1965).

MILLER, STANLEY LLOYD (1930–　), U.S. biochemist. In 1953, while a graduate student of Harold Urey at the University of Chicago (Ph.D. 1954), Miller performed the first experiment replicating primitive conditions of the earth. His work demonstrated that amino acids, basic to life, could have been produced when lightning struck a primordial mixture of methane, ammonia, water vapor, and hydrogen. Miller was a professor at the University of California at San Diego (from 1960) and wrote *The Origins of Life* (1974; with L. E. Orgel).

MILLERAND, ALEXANDRE (1859–1943), French public official. A law graduate of the University of Paris and editor of the Socialist party newspaper, Millerand served in the Chamber of Deputies from 1885 to 1920. His appointment (1899) as minister of commerce was denounced as participation in a bourgeois government and caused a split in socialist ranks. The independent-minded Millerand eventually drifted to the nationalist right, serving as minister of war (1912–15), premier (1920), and president of France (1920–24). He served in the senate from 1925 to 1940. ■ See the study by Leslie Derfler (1977).

MILLETT, KATE (Katharine Murray Millett; 1934–　), U.S. feminist, writer, and artist. Millett attended Catholic schools, then studied English literature at the University of Minnesota, Oxford, and Columbia. Her doctoral thesis was published as *Sexual Politics* (1970), a study that explored the implications—in literature and in life—of the pattern of domination and subordination reflected in male-female relationships. Her book powerfully influenced the women's liberation movement as it gained momentum in the early 1970s. Millett treated sexual politics and relationships between women in the fictional works *Flying* (1974) and *Sita* (1975). Her later works included *The Loony-Bin Trip* (1990), *The Politics of Cruelty: An Essay on the Literature of Political Imprisonment* (1994), and *A.D., A Memoir* (1995), a book about growing up gay during the 1950s. She was also a graphic artist and sculptor.

MILLIKAN, ROBERT ANDREWS (1868–1953), U.S. physicist. Millikan studied at Columbia University (Ph.D. 1895) and did postgraduate work in Germany with Max Planck and Walther Nernst. While teaching at the University of Chicago (1896–1921), he conducted experiments that enabled him to determine the electric charge of the electron (1912) and to confirm Albert Einstein's formula describing the photoelectric effect (1916). For measuring these two basic constants in atomic physics, Milliken received the 1923 Nobel Prize for Physics. He later did important research on cosmic rays. As chairman of the California Institute of Technology (1921–45), he helped build that once-small school into one of the world's most important centers of scientific research and training. ■ See his *Autobiography* (1950).

MILLS BROTHERS (John Sr., 1889–1967; Herbert, 1912–1989; Harry, 1913–1982; Donald, 1915–1999), U.S. vocal group. John Mills, Sr., joined his sons' singing group, the Mills Brothers, in 1936 after the death of his eldest son, John Mills, Jr. Popular from the early 1930s, they starred on Broadway, in nightclubs, in movies, and on radio and television. The group originally specialized in instrumental imitations, but they were later known for their rhythmic and jazzy renditions of both old standards and new songs and were regarded as the founders of contemporary black-harmony singing. After the death of John Sr., his sons continued the act as a trio and remained popular into the 1980s. Among the group's hit recordings were "Tiger Rag," "Paper Doll," "Lazy River," "I'll Be Around," and "Glowworm."

MILLS, C. WRIGHT (1916–1962), U.S. sociologist. A professor at Columbia (1946–62) who was educated at the University of Wisconsin (Ph.D. 1941), Mills was a radical sociologist from Texas who rejected "abstracted empiricism" and value-free objectivity as supporting the status quo. In his quest for a concerned, socially responsible sociology, he wrote *White Collar* (1951), an analysis of America's new alienated and apathetic middle classes, and *The Power Elite* (1956), a study of the power of the leaders of the military-industrial complex. His other books included

The Sociological Imagination (1959), *Listen, Yankee: The Revolution in Cuba* (1960), and *The Marxists* (1962). All of his works, inspired by a radical humanist vision and influenced by Marxist thought, had a profound effect on the development of the New Left during the 1960s. ■ See *C. Wright Mills: Letters and Autobiographical Writings* (2000); the study by Howard Press (1978); and biographies by Irving Louis Horowitz (1983) and Rick Tilman (1984).

MILLS, FLORENCE (1895–1927), U.S. singer. At the age of 5 Mills was "Baby Florence," singing and dancing for Washington, D.C., society gatherings. When she was 8, her family moved to Harlem in New York City; she appeared in vaudeville acts, including the Mills Sisters, formed (1910) by Florence and her two sisters. She achieved stardom in the all-black Broadway musical revue *Shuffle Along* (1921), and subsequently her name illuminated New York marquees as she delighted audiences by singing and dancing in *Plantation Revue* (1922), *Dixie to Broadway* (1924–25), and *Blackbirds* (1926). She also appeared in nightclubs and starred in revues in Paris and London. She died following an operation on her appendix.

MILLS, WILBUR DAIGH (1909–1992), U.S. political leader. Mills graduated from Harvard Law School (1933) and served as an Arkansas county judge (1934–38). A Democratic member of the U.S. House of Representatives (1938–77), he showed a talent for tax law and committee politics. As chairman of the House Ways and Means Committee (1958–74) he became one of the nation's most powerful legislators. In 1974, a scandal involving his relationship with a stripper forced his resignation from the committee. ■ See Julian E. Zelizer, *Taxing America* (1998).

MILNE, ALAN ALEXANDER (1882–1956), British writer. An assistant editor of Punch (1906–14) and a successful playwright and detective novelist, A. A. Milne became world famous for his children's poems (*When We Were Very Young*, 1924; *Now We Are Six*, 1927) and stories (*Winnie-the-Pooh*, 1926; *The House at Pooh Corner*, 1928). The stories and poems related the adventures of Christopher Robin (a young boy named after Milne's son) and his toy animals that came to life, including Winnie-the-Pooh (his teddy bear), Piglet, Eeyore, Tigger, Kanga, and Roo, and were translated into many languages, including Latin. ■ See his autobiography, *It's Too Late Now* (1939), and biography by Ann Thwaite (1990).

MILNE, DAVID BRUCE (1882–1953), Canadian artist. A former country schoolteacher and commercial artist, Milne studied at the Art Students League in New York City (1904) and exhibited in the famous 1913 Armory Show. He spent many years in the backwoods of New England and Canada, painting watercolor flowers and landscapes with the dignity and fastidiousness of traditional Chinese painters, and was considered a pioneer of postimpressionism in Canadian art.

His later works included whimsical religious paintings. ■ See Rosemarie L. Tovell, *Reflections in a Quiet Pool: Prints of David Milne* (1981) and David P. Silcox, *Painting Place* (1996).

MILNE, EDWARD ARTHUR (1896–1950), British mathematician and astrophysicist. A professor at Oxford (from 1929), Milne did pioneering studies of stellar and planetary atmospheres, the ejection of fast particles from the sun, and the constitution and internal structure of stars. In order to explain the growth of the universe he developed the controversial theory of kinematic relativity, an alternative to Albert Einstein's general theory of relativity, which was based on atomic phenomena and the measurement of time. His books included *Relativity, Gravitation and World Structure* (1935) and *Kinematic Relativity* (1948).

MILNER, ALFRED MILNER, 1st VISCOUNT (1854–1925), British colonial administrator. Of British and German ancestry, Milner was an imperialist who believed implicitly in the British colonial destiny. As British high commissioner in South Africa (1897–1905), he was variously credited with keeping the colony within the empire and with precipitating the Boer War. He later served in Britain's World War I cabinet (1916–21). Milner's writings included *The Nation and the Empire* (1913) and *Questions of the Hour* (1923). ■ See *The Milner Papers* (2 vols., 1931–33), biography by John E. Wrench (1958), and study by Vladimir Halperin (1952).

MILOSEVIC, SLOBODAN (1941–), Yugoslavian political leader. Milosevic, the son of a Serbian Orthodox theology professor, graduated from the University of Belgrade with a law degree (1964) and held a series of economic posts, including president of the United Bank of Belgrade. As Serbian Communist party chief (1987–89) he emerged as a champion of the Serbian minority population in Kosovo, a Serbian province (autonomous since 1974) with an Albanian majority, although it was considered by Serbs to be the historic birthplace of the Serbian nation. After becoming Serbian president (1989), he appealed to "Greater Serbia" nationalist sentiments by abolishing autonomous rights in the provinces of Kosovo and Vojvodina. His policies of opposing political liberalization in the other Yugoslav republics, and of supporting Serb minorities in those areas, helped to precipitate the disintegration of the Yugoslav federal state (1991) and ultimately led to war between Serbia and Croatia. He was accused of aggression and "ethnic cleansing" after the Republic of Bosnia-Herzegovina declared independence (1992), and sanctions were imposed on Serbia by the United Nations. As president (1997–2000) of Yugoslavia (consisting of Serbia and Montenegro) he intimidated the Albanian community in Kosovo. His policies led to a war with the Kosovo Liberation Army (1999) and the forced expulsion of hundreds of thousands of Albanians from their homes in Kosovo. NATO intervention on behalf of the Albanians, in the form of a two-and-a-half-month air war against targets in Kosovo and Serbia (March–June 1999), led to the withdrawal of Serbian forces from Kosovo and a return of the refugees. Although Milosevic lost the September 2000 presidential election to Vojislav Kostunica, he called for a second round of elections claiming that his challenger failed to receive the required 50 percent of the vote. However, widespread demonstrations and strikes in support of Kostunica forced Milosevic to concede defeat and leave office. ■ See biography by Dusko Doder and Louise Branson (1999).

MILOSZ, CZESLAW (1911–), Lithuanian-born Polish poet, novelist, and critic. Milosz grew up in Vilna, a city where many intellectual currents crossed in the century's early decades. A law graduate, he went to Paris (1934) and later moved to Poland (1937). He spent most of World War II in occupied Warsaw, where he was active in the literary underground; many powerful poems came out of these years. A noncommunist intellectual with leftist leanings, Milosz joined the new government's diplomatic corps after the war, serving in Washington and then Paris, where he defected (1951). In 1960 he left France for the United States to teach at the University of California at Berkeley (1961–78). Milosz's poetry cast his humanist, introspective vision in traditional forms. Couching historical issues and ideas in the subjective form of the lyric, he expressed in some poems the impossibility of committing to paper the overwhelming experiences of his times. English translations of his poems appeared in *Selected Poems* (rev. ed. 1981); *Collected Poems, 1931–1987* (1988); *Provinces* (1991); and *Facing the River* (1995). His novels included *Issa Valley* (1955–57; Eng. trans. 1981), about his Lithuanian boyhood, and *The Seizure of Power* (1955; Eng. trans. 1982). Milosz also wrote nonfiction. *The Captive Mind* (1953; Eng. trans. 1953), which first brought him to readers' attention in the West, treated the effects of communist rule and ideology on some Polish intellectuals. *Visions from San Francisco Bay* (1969; Eng. trans. 1982) treated uprootedness as a pivotal fact of his life and of the American experience. He also published a *History of Polish Literature* (1969; rev. ed. 1983) and numerous translations. Milosz won the 1980 Nobel Prize for Literature. ■ See his *Native Realm: A Search for Self-Definition* (1968; repr. 1980); *The Separate Notebook* (Eng. trans. 1984); *Unattainable Earth* (Eng. trans. 1986); *A Roadside Dog* (Eng. trans. 1998); and his recollections, *Beginning with My Street* (Eng. trans. 1992).

MILSTEIN, CÉSAR (1927–), Argentine-British immunologist. Milstein was educated at the University of Buenos Aires and at Cambridge (Ph.D. 1960), where he did research at the Medical Research Council Laboratory of Molecular Biology (1963–95). Shifting from enzyme to antibody research, he developed (1975; with visiting postdoctoral fellow Georges J. F. Köhler) a procedure for producing virtually unlimited amounts of pure, uniform, and easily reproducible antibodies by fusing antibody-producing cells with tumor cells. The "monoclonal antibodies" they produced revolutionized biomedical research and became widely used in medical diagnosis and in the treatment of cancer, leukemia, and other diseases. Milstein and Köhler shared the 1984 Nobel Prize for Physiology or Medicine with Niels K. Jerne.

MILSTEIN, NATHAN (1904–1992), Russian-born U.S. violinist. As a child, Milstein began playing the violin in Odessa and studied at the St. Petersburg Conservatory under legendary violinist Leopold Auer. In the early 1920s he performed with Vladimir Horowitz in the Soviet Union. He went to Paris in 1925 and later settled in the United States. An intense musician with dazzling technique, a specialist in the classical and romantic repertory, he toured Europe annually and made numerous acclaimed recordings. He was also a collector of famous violins. ■ See his memoirs, *From Russia to the West* (1990; with Solomon Volkov).

MINDSZENTY, JÓZSEF (József Pehm; 1892–1975), Hungarian Roman Catholic prelate. Ordained in 1915, Mindszenty brought to his vocation a lifelong commitment to political activism. Shortly after he became bishop of Veszprém, he was arrested by the Hungarian fascists (1944). After the war (1945), he became prelate of Hungary. The following year, Pope Pius XII made him a cardinal. Arrested by the communists in 1948, he was tortured and forced to confess to a series of trumped-up charges and sentenced to life imprisonment. Temporarily released in the wake of the 1956 uprising, he sought refuge in the U.S. embassy, where he remained for the next 15 years. In 1971, Mindszenty was finally convinced to leave Hungary under safe conduct. After he criticized the Vatican's stance toward the Hungarian government, Pope Paul VI asked him to resign the primacy of Hungary. He was regarded in the West as a personification of Hungarian resistance to oppression. ■ See his *Memoirs* (Eng. trans. 1974) and George N. Shuster, *In Silence I Speak* (1956).

MINGUS, CHARLES (1922–1979), U.S. jazz musician and composer. Classically trained, Mingus performed as a professional musician from age 18 and helped introduce the bass as a solo instrument in jazz. He was known for his eclectic style, unusual technique, and improvisational genius, and he worked with Kid Ory. Louis Armstrong, and Lionel Hampton during the 1940s in Los Angeles and with Miles Davis, Charlie Parker, Duke Ellington, and Thelonius Monk during the 1950s in New York, where he established a jazz workshop. A fiery and temperamental personality, he was known as "the angry man of jazz" and was particularly outspoken against racial prejudice. His compositions included "The Black Saint and the Sinner Lady," "Revelations," "Tijuana Table Dance," and "Mingus Dances;" he recorded several popular albums. ■ See his autobiography, *Beneath the Underdog* (1971); biography by Brian Priestley (1982); and Gene Santoro, *Myself When I Am Real* (2000).

MINNAERT, MARCEL GILLES JOZEF (1893–1970), Belgian astrophysicist. Minnaert earned doctorate degrees in botany (1914) and a decade later in physics (1925). He was exiled from Belgium because of his support for the Flemish nationalist movement and worked in the Netherlands, at the Utrecht Observatory (from 1921; director, 1937–63). There he conducted studies of solar radiation that expanded knowledge of the Fraunhofer lines, the lines in the solar spectrum that are darker than the surrounding continuous spectrum but are nevertheless characterized by light. His measurement of the intensity distribution of these lines provided significant data on the sun's outer layers.

MINNELLI, LIZA (1946–), U.S. actress and singer. Minnelli was the daughter of movie star Judy Garland and director Vincente Minnelli. She early embarked on an entertainment career and won (1962) a Tony Award for her performance in the Broadway musical *Flora, the Red Menace*. But she leaped to superstardom when she won the 1972 Academy Award for Best Actress for her role in the movie *Cabaret*. She subsequently appeared in the films *Lucky Lady* (1975), *Silent Movie* (1976), *A Matter of Time* (1976), *New York, New York* (1977), *Arthur* (1981), and *Arthur 2: On the Rocks* (1988). She won a 1978 Tony Award for her performance in the Broadway musical *The Act,* and starred in several televised revues. ■ See James Robert Parish, *Liza!* (1975); Wendy Leigh, *Liza* (1993); and biography by Peter Carrick (1993).

MINNELLI, VINCENTE (1910–1986), U.S. film director. After a childhood spent touring with the Minnelli Brothers tent show, Minnelli became a stage manager and costume designer. He worked in New York City at Radio City Music Hall, in Ziegfeld's *Follies*, and on Broadway before moving (1937) to Hollywood, where he directed musicals: *Meet Me in St. Louis* (1944), *An American in Paris* (1951), *The Band Wagon* (1953), and *Gigi* (Academy Award, 1958). These stylish films were made in brilliant color, with the musical numbers integrated into the plot and characterization. Minnelli also directed psychological dramas (*Undercurrent,* 1946), comedies (*Father of the Bride,* 1950), and a powerful Hollywood melodrama, *The Bad and the Beautiful* (1952). He was married to Judy Garland (1945–51) and was the father of Liza Minnelli (1946–). ■ See his autobiography, *I Remember It Well* (1974), and study by Joseph Andrew Casper (1977).

MINOBE, TATSUKICHI (1873–1948), Japanese legal scholar. A law professor at Tokyo University (1902–34) and member of the Imperial Academy (from 1911), Minobe was Japan's leading authority on constitutional law. He advanced the theory that sovereign power rested with the

people and that the emperor was merely an "organ of the state" and not its divine embodiment. His views supported the democratic movement in Japan and weakened the theoretical basis for the growing autocratic rule of the 1930s. Attacked by the militarists, he was charged with lese majesty (1935) and forced to resign his seat in the upper house of the diet (parliament). His books were banned until the end of World War II. He helped draft Japan's postwar constitution. ■ See biography by Frank O. Miller (1965).

MINOR, ROBERT (1884–1952), U.S. cartoonist and political leader. The son of a Texas judge, Minor had little formal eduction and worked as a signmaker and reporter before being hired as a cartoonist for the *St. Louis Post Dispatch* (1904). After studying art in Paris (1912), he joined the *New York World* and the journal *The Masses* and drew effective antiwar cartoons, including "At Last a Perfect Soldier!" which depicted an army medical examiner looking at a giant muscular headless man (*The Masses,* July 1916). He subsequently covered World War I as a journalist for the socialist daily *New York Call,* visited the Soviet Union and met bolshevik leader V. I. Lenin (1918), and joined the newly formed American Communist movement (1920) and served on its Central Committee. Abandoning art he attended Communist International meetings during the 1920s and 1930s and faithfully supported the Moscow line, edited the *Liberator* and *Daily Worker,* and ran (unsuccessfully) for New York City mayor, New York state governor, and U.S. senator during the 1930s. He covered the Spanish Civil War for the *Daily Worker* (1936–37) and was acting general secretary of the Communist party (1941–42) during the imprisonment of Earl Browder. ■ See biography by Joseph North (1956).

MINUCHIN, SALVADOR (1921–), Argentine-born U.S. psychiatrist. After completing training in child psychiatry in Argentina, Minuchin, a lifelong Zionist, went to Israel to fight in the 1948 war of independence. He received analytic training in the United States, and directed the Philadelphia Child Guidance Clinic (1965–81). He taught at the University of Pennsylvania (1965–83) and at New York University (1983–). In the 1960s, Minuchin devised therapeutic techniques for work with inner-city families that could not afford, and often did not want, traditional therapy. He developed family structural therapy—short-term treatment in which, according to Minuchin, "the therapist joins the [family] system and uses himself to transform it." He did not delve into the past, but instead sought to disrupt or shift alliances within a family, and in this way to change family members' experiences of each other. Minuchin viewed psychosomatic illnesses such as anorexia nervosa as symptoms induced and supported by families. His books included *Families of the Slums* (1967), *Families and Family Therapy* (1974), *Family Therapy Techniques* (1981; with H. Charles Fishman), *Family Kaleidoscope* (1984), and *Family Healing* (1993; with Michael Nichols).

MIRANDA, CARMEN (Maria do Carmo da Cunha; 1913–1955), Portuguese-born Brazilian entertainer. One of Brazil's most celebrated entertainers, Miranda spent the last 14 years of her life in the United States, where she appeared on TV, in musical revues, and in more than a dozen movies, including *Down Argentine Way* (1940) and *That Night in Rio* (1941). Wearing colorful, elaborate tunics and turbans topped with extravagant fruit arrangements, "the Brazilian bombshell" executed the samba in exaggerated platform shoes, winning large audiences. Rio de Janeiro honored her by establishing the Carmen Miranda Museum, but some Brazilians criticized her extended absences from her homeland. ■ See Martha Gil-Montero *Brazilian Bombshell* (1989).

MIRANDA, ERNESTO (1940?–1976), U.S. convict. Miranda appealed his Arizona conviction for kidnapping and rape all the way to the U.S. Supreme Court. In 1966 the court, under Chief Justice Earl Warren, reversed the conviction, handing down the landmark "Miranda decision" that set guidelines on confessions and self-incrimination. It ruled that police must advise suspects of their rights at the time of arrest. Miranda was subsequently retried and convicted on the basis of new evidence. Released in 1972, he was later killed in a barroom brawl in Phoenix. His name became a byword for a revolution in criminal procedure and police practice carried out by the Warren Court.

MIRÓ, JOAN (1893–1983), Spanish painter. Miró absorbed the influences of fauvism, cubism, surrealism, and his native Catalonian folklore to create a distinctive pictorial language of signs, symbols, images, and metaphors, ranging from the playful to the nightmarish. In addition to his paintings, he did collages, murals, ceramic walls (for the United Nations Educational, Scientific, and Cultural Organization Building in Paris, 1957–59), and designed ballet decor and costumes. ■ See study by Ronald Penrose (1970).

MIRÓ FERRER, GABRIEL (1879–1930), Spanish writer. Miró studied law, held several minor governmental posts, worked as a journalist, and edited a Catholic encyclopedia. His impressionistic and sensuous early novels and short stories, set in his native Mediterranean region of Spain, established his reputation as an innovative prose stylist. His works reflected his love of nature and his religious and aesthetic preoccupations. Among his best known later works were *Figures of the Passion of Our Lord* (1916; Eng. trans. 1924), a series of vignettes of the life of Jesus; *The Book of Sigüenza* (1917), a series of vignettes describing the life of his alter ego, a meditative Franciscan monk; and *Our Father San Daniel* (1921); Eng. trans. 1930), a novel that reflected his early years at Jesuit schools. ■ See study by Ian R. Macdonald (1975) and the critical essays edited by Ricardo Landeira (1979).

MIRRLEES, JAMES A. (1936–), Scottish economist. Mirrlees studied at Cambridge University (Ph.D. 1963) and taught economics at Oxford (1968–95) and Cambridge (1995–). In a series of highly technical and mathematically refined microeconomic studies in the 1960s and 1970s he extended the work of William S. Vickery on the theory of incentives under asymmetric information, situations in which parties involved in economics transactions have different information from their counterparts. Related to game theory, the new means of analysis was applied by Mirrlees to such problems as determining levels of income taxation and commodity taxation that are both fair and efficient. The analysis was also applied in the theory of auctions, environmental policy, and the regulation of public utilities and public transport. Mirrlees and Vickery shared the 1996 Nobel Memorial Prize in Economics for their pioneering work.

MISES, LUDWIG EDLER VON (1881–1973), Austrian-born U.S. economist and social philosopher. Trained at the University of Vienna (Ph.D. 1906), where he later taught (1913–38), Ludwig Von Mises was a leader of the Austrian school of economics. Leaving Vienna on the eve of World War II, he emigrated to the United States (1940), where he taught at New York University (1954–69). A laissez-faire economist, he argued that socialist planning cannot result in a rational allocation of resources because it lacks a true price system. He broadened this view into a general critique of government intervention in private enterprise, asserting that the free market should determine the type and price of goods produced. He wrote on the theory of money and credit and developed an influential theory of business cycles that attributed booms to bank credit expansion. His students included Fritz Machlup, Oskar Morgenstern, Friedrich von Hayek, Rudolf Carnap, and Karl Popper. ■ See his *Notes and Recollections* (1978) and Margit Von Mises, *My Years with Ludwig Von Mises* (1976). See also study edited by L. S. Moss (1974).

MISES, RICHARD VON (1883–1953), Austrian-born mathematician. A professor of applied mathematics at the University of Strasbourg (1909–18), von Mises did pioneering work in aerodynamics and helped design Austrian military airplanes during World War I. He developed a new concept of probability, the relative-frequency (or limiting-frequency) theory (1919), that profoundly influenced modern statistics. Von Mises was a professor at the University of Berlin (1920–33) but left Germany when the Nazis came to power and taught at the University of Istanbul (1933–39) and Harvard (1939–53). He also published a major work in philosophy, *Positivism: A Study in Human Understanding* (1951). His other works included *Probability, Statistics and Truth* (1939) and *Theory of Flight* (1945).

MISHIMA, YUKIO (Hiraoka Kimitake; 1925–1970), Japanese writer. A brilliant and versatile stylist, Mishima wrote short stories and poetry as well as 40 novels and 18 plays. In real life, as in his fiction, he glorified the ancient Samurai warrior traditions and denounced the Westernization of contemporary Japan. Many of his novels depicted the frustrations of post–World War II youth and were filled with images of death, blood, and suicide. His best-known novels included the autobiographical *Confessions of a Mask* (1949; Eng. trans. 1958), *The Sound of Waves* (1954; Eng. trans. 1956), *The Temple of the Golden Pavilion* (1956; Eng. trans. 1959), and the *Sea of Fertility* tetralogy, *Spring Snow* (1966; Eng. trans. 1972), *Runaway Horses* (1968; Eng. trans. 1973), *The Temple of Dawn* (1969; Eng. trans. 1973), and *The Decay of the Angel* (1970; Eng. trans. 1974). Members of the Shield Society, a small private army of reactionary university students he founded (1968), were with him as he committed suicide by hara-kiri after raiding military headquarters in Tokyo and calling on the Self-Defense Forces to restore the prewar Japanese state. ■ See the biographies by John Nathan (1974) and Henry S. Stokes (1975).

MISTINGUETT (Jeanne Marie Bourgeois, 1875–1956), French entertainer. The greatest star in the history of the French music hall, Mistinguett appeared in spectacular revues at the Moulin Rouge, Folies-Bergère, and Casino de Paris. A talented low comedienne known for her magnetic stage personality and her beautiful legs, she was a frequent partner of Maurice Chevalier. Mistinguett also appeared in numerous stage productions and movies. ■ See David Bret, *The Mistinguett Legend* (1991).

MISTRAL, GABRIELA (Lucila Godoy Alcayaga; 1889–1957), Chilean poet. Mistral was a teacher and school administrator and later a diplomat. Her poetry mourned the suicides of a lover (1909) and of an adopted son (1944). A Roman Catholic, Mistral wrote traditional, unaffected poetry in a religious tone. She revised her four volumes of poetry throughout her life, producing many versions of the poems in *Desolation* (1922; rev. 1954), *Tenderness* (1924; rev. 1938), *Felling of Trees* (1938), and *Winepress* (1954). She was the first Latin American to win the Nobel Prize for Literature (1945). English translations of her works are in *Selected Poems* (1957, 1971) and *A Gabriela Mistral Reader* (1993). ■ See study by Margot Arce de Vasquez (Eng. trans. 1964).

MITCHELL, BILLY (William Mitchell; 1879–1936), U.S. aviator. The son of a U.S. senator, Billy Mitchell returned from World War I a military hero after fighting in 14 air campaigns. As assistant chief of the air service, he urged air-force independence but was overruled by his conservative superiors. In numerous articles and speeches he stated that the airplane had made the battleship obsolete, stressed the importance of air superiority and strategic bombing, and warned against the Japanese military threat. His criticism of the Departments of War and the Navy for "incompetency, criminal negligence, and almost treasonable administration of the national defense" led to his court-martial conviction (1925) for insubordination. He resigned (1926) from the

army to take up stock farming but continued to write on aeronautics. Many of Mitchell's prophecies were borne out in World War II, and in 1946 Congress awarded him a special Medal of Honor posthumously. ■ See the biography by Isaac Don Levine (rev. ed. 1958); Burke Davis, *The Billy Mitchell Affair* (1967); and the study by Alfred Hurley (1975).

MITCHELL, HARRY LELAND (1906–1989), U.S. labor leader. The son of a tenant farmer, H. L. Mitchell became a sharecropper in Tennessee (1924) and later operated a dry-cleaning business in Tyronza, Arkansas. There, in 1934, he founded (with 17 other men), the interracial Southern Tenant Farmers Union, which organized more than 30,000 agricultural workers by 1937. The union, which advocated higher wages and the eventual establishment of tenant-owned cooperative farms, met with opposition from plantation owners and many government officials, but won several strikes and publicized the plight of poor landless tenants. Mitchell served as the union's executive secretary (1934–39; 1941–44) and led it into the American Federation of Labor (AFL) under the name of National Farm Labor Union (1945). He served as its president (1945–55) and president of its successor, the National Agricultural Workers Union (1955–60). Subsequently he worked as a union organizer and agricultural specialist. ■ See his autobiography, *Mean Things Happening in This Land* (1979); David E. Conrad, *The Forgotten Farmers* (1965); and Donald H. Grubbs, *Cry from the Cotton* (1971).

MITCHELL, JOHN (1870–1919), U.S. labor leader. A coal miner at age 12, Mitchell joined the Knights of Labor in 1885 and the United Mine Workers (UMW) in 1890. As president of the UMW (1898–1908), he worked to secure better wages and hours for previously unorganized miners who had emigrated to the United States from eastern and southern Europe. An advocate of harmonious relations between capital and labor, he gave up the UMW presidency when his conservative position alienated elements of the union membership. He served as vice president of the AFL (1899–1914) and chaired the New York State Industrial Commission (1915–19). He wrote *Organized Labor* (1903) and *The Wage Earner* (1913). ■ See biography by Elsie Gluck (1929) and Craig Phelan, *Divided Loyalties* (1994).

MITCHELL, JOHN NEWTON (1913–1988), U.S. attorney. A graduate of Fordham (1938) and a former law partner of Republican leader Richard Nixon, Mitchell was a $200,000-a-year specialist in municipal bonds before his selection to run Nixon's successful 1968 presidential campaign. As attorney general in the new administration (1969–72) he favored wiretapping and preventive detention of criminal suspects and took a hard line against political dissent. Incidentally a resident of the Watergate apartment complex with his voluble wife Martha. Mitchell was convicted (1975) of conspiracy, obstruction of justice, and perjury in the aftermath of the scandal stemming from the break-in (1972) of the Democratic headquarters at the Watergate. He served 19 months in prison (1977–79).

MITCHELL, JONI (Roberta Joan Anderson; 1943–), Canadian singer and songwriter. Mitchell left the Alberta College of Art in Calgary after one year (1963) to pursue a folksinging career in Toronto and subsequently in New York City and Los Angeles. She first achieved fame as the writer of "Both Sides Now" (recorded by Judy Collins, 1968) and "Circle Game" (recorded by Tom Rush, 1968). She recorded the first of her numerous albums in 1968 and was immediately acclaimed for her expressive and wide-ranging soprano voice as well as for her poetic and intensely personal lyrics. The albums *Blue* (1971) and *Court and Spark* (1974) contained some of her best-known confessional-style songs. Always an innovator, she recorded albums influenced by jazz and rock as well as others containing topical songs critical of capitalism and consumerism. Her most famous songs included "Michael from Mountains," "Woodstock," "Chelsea Morning," "Big Yellow Taxi," and "Help Me." Her *Turbulent Indigo* (1994) won the Grammy Award for best pop album.

MITCHELL, MARGARET (1900–1949), U.S. novelist. Born in Atlanta, the daughter of the president of the Atlanta Historical Society, Mitchell was imbued with stories of the old confederacy from childhood. After working as a reporter for the *Atlanta Journal* (1922–26), she spent 10 years writing a panoramic historical novel concerned with presenting an account of the Civil War and Reconstruction from a southern perspective. Published as *Gone With the Wind* (1936; Pulitzer Prize), the novel sold a record 1,383,000 copies in its first year and eventually became the all-time best-selling novel in U.S. publishing history. The movie (1939; Academy Award), starring Clark Gable and Vivien Leigh, was the greatest moneymaker produced by the Metro-Goldwyn-Mayer (MGM) studios and one of the most popular films ever made. ■ See biography by Finis Farr (1965); Anne Edwards, *Road to Tara* (1983); and Darden A. Pyron, *Southern Daughter* (1991).

MITCHELL, PETER (1920–1992), British chemist. A Cambridge graduate (Ph.D. 1950), Mitchell taught there (1943–55) and then at Edinburgh (1955–63), where he investigated the manner in which plants and animals store and transfer the energy needed for the processes of life. In the early 1960s he explained that energy transfer, involving adenosinetriphosphate (ATP) was accomplished by an electrochemical process involving mitochondrial membranes. Although he was at first considered an eccentric, his experiments (with colleague Jennifer Moyle) were gradually recognized and accepted by the scientific community, and Mitchell won the 1978 Nobel Prize for Chemistry. From 1964 to 1986 he directed the Glynn Research Laboratories. His books included *Chemiosmotic Coupling and Energy Transduction* (1968).

MITCHELL, WESLEY CLAIR (1874–1948), U.S. economist. Mitchell studied under Thorstein Veblen and John Dewey at the University of Chicago (B.A. 1896; Ph.D. 1899). During World War I he was director of the price section of the War Industries Board, and in 1920 he helped organize the National Bureau of Economic Research, which he directed until 1945. He taught at Columbia University (1913–19; 1922–44) and chaired (1937–40) the Social Science Research Council. Mitchell was a pioneer in the study of money economies and an authority on business cycles. He played a major role in the development of quantitative studies of economic behavior and interdisciplinary social science research in the United States. ■ See volume edited by Arthur F. Burns (1952) and Lucy S. Mitchell, *Two Lives* (1953).

MITCHELL, WILLIAM ORMOND (1914–1998), Canadian writer. A salesman and highschool teacher. W. O. Mitchell earned a reputation as a homespun philosopher by writing with understated humor about the hardships of (Alberta) prairie life. The novel *Who Has Seen the Wind* (1947) was a sensitive, unpretentious view of small-town life through the eyes of a growing boy. *How I Spent My Summer Holidays* (1981) was its sequel. He adapted his classic radio and TV series "Jake and the Kid" into a short-story cycle (1962). *The Kite* (1962) featured a columnist's venture into the foothills to interview the weathered old-timer Daddy Sherry. Mitchell also wrote *The Vanishing Point* (1973), the story of a teacher on an Indian reservation. His other works included the play *Back to Beulah* (1974) and the novels *Roses Are Different Here* (1990) and *For Art's Sake* (1992).

MITTELHOLZER, EDGAR (1909–1965), British Guianan novelist. Of mixed European and black ancestry, Mittelholzer was the product of a strict middle-class colonial upbringing. He lived in Trinidad (1941–48) until emigrating to London (1948), where he wrote the novels *Morning in Trinidad* (1950) and *Shadows Move Among Them* (1951), which helped to create an authentically Caribbean literary consciousness. Although he subsequently wrote numerous mystery and political novels set in Guiana, the West Indies, and England, he is best known for his violent, macabre, and erotic stories. His most popular work was the melodramatic, historical trilogy set in Guiana, *Children of Kaywana* (1952), *Kaywana Stock* (1954), and *Kaywana Blood* (1958). Shortly after finishing *The Jilkington Drama* (1965), a novel dealing with the theme of suicide, Mittelholzer committed suicide. ■ See his autobiography, *A Swarthy Boy* (1963).

MITTERRAND, FRANÇOIS MAURICE (1916–1996), French political leader. The son of a railroad stationmaster in southwestern France, Mitterrand earned degrees in law, letters, and political science at the University of Paris before World War II, during which he was a leader of the Resistance. He was elected to the national assembly in 1946 and participated in several Fourth Republic cabinets, but became the leader of the left-wing opposition to Gen. Charles de Gaulle's Fifth Republic, which he called "a permanent coup d'état." Mitterrand lost the 1965 presidential election to de Gaulle, and, as first secretary of the Socialist party (1971–81), lost the 1974 presidential election to Valéry Giscard D'Estaing. However, Mitterrand dramatically built up the strength of the party and, in alliance with the communists, defeated Giscard for the presidency in 1981. Early in his term he nationalized the remaining private banks and several key industries, reduced the work week to 39 hours, lowered the retirement age to 60, and began to decentralize the government. However, as economic conditions worsened in the mid-1980s, he turned toward austerity, adopted free-market principles, and cut government spending and services. Reelected in 1988, he strongly supported the Maastricht Treaty on European Union (1991) and built or restored many public buildings in Paris. When he left office (1995) he had served longer than any other French president of the 20th century. ■ See his memoirs, *The Wheat and the Chaff* (Eng. trans. 1982) and Franz-Olivier Giesbert, *Dying Without God: François Mitterrand's Meditations on Living and Dying* (Eng. trans. 1998).

MIX, TOM (1880–1940), U.S. film actor and director. Mix reportedly fought in the Spanish-American War, the Boxer Rebellion, and the Mexican civil war before becoming a Wild West show cowboy (1906) and movie cowboy (1909). He wrote and directed many of his westerns, which featured spectacular photography and skilled horsemanship. Films such as *Desert Love* (1920) and *Riders of the Purple Sage* (1925) enjoyed tremendous popularity, and Mix was one of the leading box-office attractions of the 1920s. In 1928 he left Hollywood to join a circus, but he returned in 1932 to make *Destry Rides Again*. He died in a car crash. ■ See Olive Stokes Mix, *The Fabulous Tom Mix* (1957), and biography by Paul E. Mix (1972).

MIZNER, WILSON (1876–1933), U.S. playwright and raconteur. Born in California, Mizner accompanied his father, a minister, to Guatemala (1889) and studied there (1889–91) and at Santa Clara (California) College (1892–94). A veteran of the Klondike (Alaska) gold rush at the turn of the century, Mizner prospected in Nevada, then worked as a New York hotel manager and a Florida real-estate promoter. He collaborated on several plays, including *The Only Law* (1909; with G. Bronson Howard), *The Deep Purple* (1910; with Paul Armstrong), and *The Greyhound* (1912; with Armstrong), but his greatest talent was for the coolly underplayed quip. When informed that Pres. Calvin Coolidge was dead, he asked, "How do they know?" He achieved his finest hour as part-owner and resident wit of the Brown Derby Restaurant in Los Angeles. ■ See John Burke, *Rogue's Progress* (1975).

MIZOGUCHI, KENJI (1898–1956), Japanese film director. Trained as a painter, Mizoguchi got his first opportunity to direct in 1922 during a walkout at the studio where he was employed. The walkout was a protest against the studio's new policy of using women in women's roles. Of the 87 films he directed, many were devoted to exposing the degradation of Japanese women. *Sisters of Gion* (1936), *Women of the Night* (1948), and *Street of Shame* (1956) depicted the plight of prostitutes, while *The Life of Oharu* (1952) described the tribulations of a highborn woman fallen from favor. *The Story of the Last Chrysanthemums* (1939) depicted the sacrifices of an altruistic young woman helping a young man achieve success as an actor. *Sancho the Bailiff* (1954) was a general denunciation of the injustices of feudalism. *Utamaro and His Five Women* (1946) and *Ugetsu* (1953) treated the problems of the artist as well as those of the women in the films. Mizoguchi's style, with its carefully composed frames, atmospheric effects, and sensitivity to nature, reflected his background as a painter. ■ See study by Keiko McDonald (1984).

MOBERG, VILHELM (1898–1973), Swedish novelist and dramatist. Born into a peasant family and largely self-educated, Moberg set most of his fiction among the independent but terribly poor peasant communities of Sweden. His major works included the partly autobiographical *This Earth Is Ours* (3 vols., 1935–39; Eng. trans. 1940) and *When I Was a Child* (1944; Eng. trans. 1957). He was best known for his best-selling, earthy epic of Swedish emigration to America in the 1850s: *The Emigrants* (1949; Eng. trans. 1951), *Unto a Good Land* (1952; Eng. trans. 1954), *Nybyggarna* (1956), and *The Last Letter Home* (1959; Eng. trans. 1961). He also wrote an anti-Nazi novel, numerous problem plays, and an unfinished history of the Swedish peasantry, *A History of the Swedish People* (2 vols., 1970–71; Eng. trans. 1972–73). ■ See study by Philip Holmes (1980).

MOBUTU SESE SEKO (Joseph Désiré Mobutu; 1930–1997), president of Zaïre. A veteran of the Belgian army, Mobutu left the military in 1956 to edit a weekly Belgian Congolese newspaper. He joined Patrice Lumumba's Congolese National Movement (MNC) party in 1958. Appointed army chief of staff when the Congo gained independence (June 1960), he shortly thereafter overthrew Premier Lumumba. Despite a nominal civilian government, real control rested with the army, and following the bloody civil war (1963–65), Mobutu became president under a nationalist banner. In 1971, he changed the Congo's name to Zaïre. Often accused of pro-Americanism and corruption, he preserved Zaïre's independence and avoided civil war by ruthlessly suppressing all opposition. Twice when copper-rich Shaba (formerly Katanga) province rose in rebellion, he called in foreign troops to quell the disturbances. In the 1980s, the fall of the price of copper and the government's increasing corruption and stealing of national resources led to severe economic problems. Mobutu's government grew increasingly unpopular and he was overthrown (May 1997) after a seven-month rebellion led by Laurent Kabila and backed by several African countries, including Angola, Rwanda, and Uganda. (Kabila immediately renamed the country The Congo.) Mobutu fled to Morocco, where he died of cancer in September 1997. His wealth was estimated to be $5 billion. ■ See Crawford Young, *The Rise and Decline of the Zaïrian State* (1985), and Sean Kelly, *America's Tyrant* (1993).

MODIGLIANI, AMEDEO (1884–1920), Italian artist. Modigliani grew up in a once-wealthy Jewish family, which he left in 1906 to pursue a bohemian life in Paris. Painting in the classical Italian tradition, he created distinctively mannered and elongated portraits and nudes (*Reclining Nude*, 1919) before his premature death, in a charity ward, of tuberculosis. He also produced sculpture—carved works apparently influenced by his acquaintance Constantin Brancusi. ■ See biographies by Pierre Sichel (1967) and William Fifield (1976).

MODIGLIANI, FRANCO (1918–), Italian-born U.S. economist. Born into a Jewish family in Rome, Modigliana fled fascist Italy at the outbreak of World War II, shortly after he received a doctorate of law at the University of Rome (1939). He settled in New York City (1940), studied economics at the New School for Social Research (Ph.D. 1944), and taught economics at several major U.S. universities, including the Massachusetts Institute of Technology (1962–88). He was recognized as the first economist to integrate monetary considerations into Keynesian economics. He did pioneering work in the early 1950s (with Richard Brumberg) on household savings, and developed the life-cycle hypothesis that stated that people save for their own old age—not for their descendants. The theory explains why countries with younger populations have higher rates of savings than those with older populations and why a growing economy results in a redistribution of income favoring the young. His work in the late 1950s (with Merton Miller), which demonstrated that expectations of future earnings was the key factor in determining a company's market value, provided the basis for the field of corporate finance. For these contributions he was awarded the 1985 Nobel Memorial Prize for Economics. See his *Collected Papers* (3 vols., 1980).

MOFFETT, WILLIAM ADGER (1869–1933), U.S. naval officer. A highly decorated career naval officer and aviation enthusiast, Moffett was appointed chief of the new Bureau of Aeronautics (1921) with the rank of rear admiral. In 12 years at the post, Moffett, despite great hostility within the army and navy, waged a crusade for the development of naval air power and the aircraft carrier, and he was recognized as "the father of naval aviation." His successful campaign led to the formation of the carrier force, which played a crucial role in World War II and in subsequent military encounters. He was killed in the crash of the dirigible *Akron*.

■ See Edward Arpee, *From Frigates to Flat-tops* (1953); study by Paolo Coletta (1997); and biography by William F. Trimble (1994).

MOFOLO, THOMAS (1876–1948), Lesothoan novelist. Educated at Christian mission schools, Mofolo was encouraged to write while working as a clerk and proofreader at the mission book depot in Morija. His first novel, *The Traveller of the East* (1907; Eng. trans. 1934), described a young African chief's conversion to Christianity. It was the first novel in the Sesotho (Southern Sotho) language, and it launched one of the earliest literary movements in black Africa. His masterpiece, *Chaka, A Historical Romance* (1925; Eng. trans. 1931), a fictionalized account of the great 19th-century Zulu king, influenced writers throughout the continent and was considered to be the first major black African contribution to modern world literature.

MOHOLY-NAGY, LÁSZLÓ (1895–1946), Hungarian-born U.S. photographer and designer. After World War I Moholy-Nagy settled in Germany, where he was active in the Bauhaus movement. He emigrated to the United States in 1937 and founded the Chicago School of Design (1938) on the model of the Bauhaus. Moholy-Nagy created new forms of visual communication by exploring the fertile territory between art and photography. His pedagogical concepts and experimental works greatly influenced photography and commercial design in the United States. His books included *New Vision* (1928; Eng. trans. 1932), and *Vision in Motion* (1947). ■ See the memoir by his wife Sibyl (1950) and studies by Richard Kostalanctz (1970) and Krisztina Passuth (Eng. trans. 1985).

MOHOROVIČIĆ, ANDRIJA (1857–1936), Croatian geophysicist. A graduate of the University of Prague and the University of Zagreb (Ph.D. 1897), Mohorovičić was associated with the meteorological observatory in Zagreb (1900–21). After studying the seismic waves set up by the Kulpa Valley earthquake of 1909, he deduced that a boundary (subsequently called the Mohorovičić Discontinuity or Moho) exists between the earth's crust and mantle, at a depth varying from 10 to 40 miles below sea level. Project Mohole (1961–66), sponsored by the U.S. government, attempted to drill holes through the crust to study the nature of the discontinuity but was abandoned because of high cost.

MOI, DANIEL ARAP (Torotich arap Moi; 1924–), Kenyan political leader. A member of the Kalenjin tribal group, Moi was born into a poor farming family. He attended a teacher training college and became a teacher and school administrator. He was named to the Kenya legislative council (1955) and helped found the Kenya African Democratic Union (KADU) to challenge the Kenya African National Union (KANU), a political party dominated by the powerful Kikuyu and Luo peoples. He served as minister of education and minister for local government (1961–63), and after KADU was dissolved, he rejoined KANU (1964) and served as minister of home affairs. Moi was named vice president (1967) and became president when Jomo Kenyatta died (1978). He maintained a relatively stable leadership, promoting national unity, running a scandal-free administration, and expanding the base of KANU, the only legal political party. He survived an attempted coup in 1982. Over the years he was accused of corruption and mismanagement, but he kept domestic peace in a multiethnic society. He bowed to domestic and international pressure in 1992 and held multiparty elections, which he won with less than 40 percent of the vote. In 1998, with the opposition divided along ethnic lines, he won a fifth term with approximately 40 percent of the vote.

MOISEYEV, IGOR (1906–   ), Soviet dancer and choreographer. A soloist and choreographer with the Bolshoi Ballet (1924–39), Moiseyev was appointed the head of the dance department of Moscow's newly founded Theater of Folk Art (1936). He organized a national folk-dance festival, out of which developed the State Folk Dance Ensemble, which Moiseyev founded (1937) and directed for more than 60 years. His choreography, which combined authentic folk dances with theatrical effects, was acclaimed throughout the world as his troupe grew from a primarily amateur group of 35 dancers to one with 116 professionals with a repertory of over 300 dances.

MOLEY, RAYMOND CHARLES (1886–1975), U.S. political scientist, public official, and author. A professor at Columbia University (1923–54), Moley was a key adviser to Pres. Franklin D. Roosevelt during the early years of his administration and was an important member of the brain trust, Roosevelt's group of academic advisers. He helped shape much of the early New Deal economic policy and was one of the most powerful people in Washington. Basically a conservative, however, he broke with Roosevelt (1936) over what he considered the radical trend the New Deal was taking. He later was a columnist for *Newsweek* (1937–68), supported Republican candidates after 1940, and wrote *After Seven Years* (1939) and *The First New Deal* (1966).

MOLINA, MARIO (1943–   ), Mexican-born U.S. atmospheric scientist. Molina studied physical chemistry at the University of California, Berkeley (Ph.D. 1972), worked at the California Institute of Technology's Jet Propulsion Laboratory (1983–89), and was a professor at the Massachusetts Institute of Technology (1989–   ). As a postdoctoral fellow at the University of California, Irvine (1973–75), Molina did research into atmospheric pollution with lab director F. Sherwood Rowland, and together they showed that industrially produced chlorofluorocarbons (CFCs), widely used as refrigerants, plastic foams, and aerosol-spray propellants, were destroying the earth's protective ozone layer.

Their findings were attacked by big business and its conservative political supporters, but they eventually became widely accepted and led to international agreements (1987, 1992) by the industrial nations to end production of CFCs. For their influential environment research Molina and Rowland shared the 1995 Nobel Prize in Chemistry with Paul Crutzen, who first reported ozone-layer destruction.

MOLLET, GUY (1905–1975), French political leader. Born in Normandy and orphaned during World War I, Mollet became a teacher of English and Latin but was dismissed in 1932 for his Socialist party activities and turned to full-time party work. Active in the underground during World War II, he was elected to parliament in 1945 and to leadership of the French Socialist party the following year. A key player in Fourth Republic politics. Mollet served as premier in 1956–57, and was responsible for sending draftees to fight in Algeria and for French involvement in the Suez crisis. He was minister of state in 1958, a position he retained in Pres. Charles de Gaulle's first cabinet of the Fifth Republic, but he later worked to unify opposition to de Gaulle's domestic policies. He led the socialists until 1969.

MOLNÁR, FERENC (1878–1952), Hungarian novelist and playwright. The most widely known and successful Hungarian author of the century, Molnár was born into an upper-middle-class Jewish family in Budapest. His works were characterized by their sophistication, wit, cynicism, and sentimentality. Most dealt with city life and were popular throughout the world. He is best known for the novel *Paul Street Boys;* (1907; Eng. trans. 1927) and the plays *The Devil* (1907; Eng. trans. 1908), *Liliom* (1909; Eng. trans. 1921; the basis of *Carousel*), and *The Guardsman* (1910; Eng. trans. 1924; the basis of *The Chocolate Soldier*). Molnár left Hungary in 1940 and settled in New York City, where his suite at the Plaza Hotel became a mecca for his international literary following. ■ See the autobiographical *Companion in Exile* (Eng. trans. 1950) and the study by Clara Györgyey (1980).

MOLOTOV, VYACHESLAV MIKHAILOVICH (V. M. Skriabin; 1890–1986), Soviet political leader. Molotov studied in Kazan, became a bolshevik (1906), and took the name Molotov, meaning "hammer." In the years before the 1917 revolution he was an editor of the bolshevik newspaper *Pravda* (1912–17). Until Lenin's return to St. Petersburg, Molotov was that city's leading bolshevik and a member of the committee that helped organize the October revolution (1917). At age 31, he became the Politburo's youngest member (1921–57). For the next 32 years, Molotov was dictator Joseph Stalin's loyal ally, serving in key posts: secretary of the All-Russian Communist party (1921–30); chairman of the council of people's commissars, equivalent to premier (1930–41); and commissar (later minister) for foreign affairs (1939–49; 1953–56). He won recognition for his role in concluding the 1939 German-Soviet pact; he was apparently caught unaware by the 1941 Nazi invasion. He remained foreign minister, cautiously working during World War II with the Allied forces and later developing ties with East European countries and overseeing negotiations with the West during the onset of the cold war. An opponent of party leader Nikita Khrushchev, Molotov was demoted (1956) and removed from all party posts (1957) for "antiparty" activity. In the late 1950s he was ambassador to Mongolia and representative to the International Atomic Energy Commission in Vienna. He was expelled from the party in 1962 and lived as a pensioner in Moscow. In 1984, when Molotov was age 94, he was reinstated into the party; some observers interpreted this as a sign of the increased influence of neo-Stalinist elements in Soviet politics. ■ See study by Bernard Bromage (1956).

MOLTKE, HELMUTH JOHANNES VON (1848–1916), German general. Nephew and namesake of the victor of the Franco-Prussian War, Moltke "the Younger" exploited high-level patronage to achieve rank that he may not have deserved. As chief of the General Staff in 1914, during World War I, he critically weakened deployment on the western front, with the result that the Marne offensive dissipated into trench warfare. He was replaced in 1914. ■ See Otto Friedrich, *Blood and Iron* (1995).

MOLYNEUX, EDWARD HENRY (1894–1974), British fashion designer. After losing an eye as a British soldier in World War I, Molyneux established (1919) a house of couture in Paris that became famous overnight for simple, lithe, delicate dresses. He opened a branch in London (1933) and worked in it during World War II. He reopened (1946) the doors of his Paris firm, but faced with possible loss of his sight, he retired in 1950, returning to business only briefly in the 1960s. Molyneux was also known as a painter and art collector.

MOMADAY, NAVARRE SCOTT (1934–   ), U.S. writer. Born in Oklahoma of Kiowa Indian ancestry, N. Scott Momaday earned a Ph.D. (1963) from Stanford University and subsequently taught there (1973–82) and at the University of Arizona (1982–   ). His specialty was Indian folklore, which, in his view, made the Indian the most culturally secure of all Americans. Momaday won a Pulitzer Prize for *House Made of Dawn* (1968), his novel about growing up as an Indian. He also wrote *The Way to Rainy Mountain* (1969), a collection of Kiowa stories and legends, and *The Names: A Memoir* (1976). His poetry was collected in *Angle of Geese and Other Poems* (1974) and *The Gourd Dancer* (1976). His later works included the novel *The Ancient Child* (1989), *In the Presence of the Sun: Stories and Poems, 1961–1991* (1992), and *The Man Made of Words: Essays, Stories, Passages* (1997). ■ See Matthias Schubnell, *Conversations with N. Scott Momaday* (1997).

MONACO, MARIO DEL. *See DEL MONACO, MARIO.*

MONDADORI, ARNOLDO (1889–1971), Italian publisher. After finishing elementary school, Mondadori became an apprentice printer and opened his own shop (1907). He published numerous periodicals and children's books, expanded into serious literature, and developed Arnoldo Mondadori Editore into a vast literary empire. In addition to publishing such famous Italian authors as D'Annunzio, Pirandello, Quasimodo, and Silone, he introduced the work of foreign writers Steinbeck, Hemingway, Faulkner, Galsworthy, Gide, Mauriac, Thomas Mann, and Aldous Huxley to Italian readers. He also published the Mondadori Encyclopedia and the news magazine *Epoca* (from 1950), and introduced Mickey Mouse (known as Topolino) to Italian children.

MONDALE, WALTER FREDERICK "FRITZ" (1928–   ), U.S. political leader. The son of a Methodist minister, Mondale graduated from law school and became an activist in Minnesota's Democratic-Farmer-Labor party and a protégé of Sen. Hubert H. Humphrey. After serving as attorney general of Minnesota (1960–64), he moved to the U.S. Senate (appointed 1964; elected 1966, 1972), where he championed such issues as open housing, civil rights, education, child care, federal aid to cities, and increased controls over the FBI and CIA, becoming one of the most influential liberals in Congress. He served as Pres. Jimmy Carter's vice president (1977–81); they were defeated for reelection (1980) by Republican candidate Ronald Reagan. Running for president with Rep. Geraldine Ferraro as his vice-presidential running mate (1984), Mondale was decisively defeated as Pres. Reagan won a second term. He subsequently served as U.S. ambassador to Japan (1993–96). ■ See biography by Finlay Lewis (1980).

MONDLANE, EDUARDO (1920–1969), Mozambican political leader. The son of a Tsonga chief in Mozambique, then a Portuguese colony, Mondlane was educated in South Africa before being expelled from the country (1949) for political activities at Witwatersrand University. He continued his studies in the United States at Oberlin College and at Northwestern University (Ph.D. 1960). After serving with the United Nations Secretariat and teaching at Syracuse University, he moved to Tanzania (1962) and formed the Mozambique Liberation Front (FRELIMO), the united front of Mozambican nationalism. He worked tirelessly for the movement, training guerrilla fighters and raising funds for scholarships as well as weapons. Military operations were launched in 1964. Reelected president of FRELIMO in 1968, he was assassinated in 1969, six years before Mozambique gained independence. ■ See his book, *The Struggle for Mozambique* (1969).

MONDRIAN, PIET (Pieter Cornelis Mondriaan; 1872–1944), Dutch painter. As a teenager Mondrian began painting naturalistic landscapes. He went to Paris (1910), where exposure to cubism affected his compositions and his aesthetic stance. He was instrumental in founding (1917) the De Stijl group, and he published (1917–25) articles in the journal *De Stijl*. After 1919 Mondrian evolved a style that he termed neoplasticism: his canvases used vertical and horizontal lines to create a grid of rectangles; the rectangles were areas of primary colors. He elaborated on the possibilities created by this structure in *Neo-Plasticism* (1920); his collected essays appeared in English in *Piet Mondrian: Plastic Art and Pure Plastic Art* (1947). After 1940 he worked in New York. He influenced the Bauhaus movement and architects working in the International Style. ∎ See studies by L. J. F. Wijsenbeek (Eng. trans. 1968) and Frank Elgar (Eng. trans. 1968).

MONK, MEREDITH (1942–   ), U.S. dancer, choreographer, composer, singer. and filmmaker. After studying performing arts at Sarah Lawrence College (B.A. 1964), Monk joined the experimental Judson Dance Theater in New York City and became a pioneer of the multimedia theatrical revolution of the 1960s. She combined dialogue, music, dance, vocalization, film, and video to create theater pieces that explored space, movement, and sound. Her best-known larger thematic works included *Vessel* (1971), an "opera epic" based on the life of Joan of Arc; *Education of the Girlchild* (1973), a solo piece depicting the stages of a woman's life; *Quarry* (1976), a symbolic work portraying a child's perception of the rise of a dictatorship; and *The Games* (1983), a parable about a society following a nuclear war. Subsequent works included *American Archeology* (1994) and *The Politics of Quiet* (1996). Several of her musical compositions, which became the focus of her later works, were recorded as *Dolmen Music* (1981), *Turtle Dreams* (1983), *Book of Days* (1990), and *Volcano Song* (1997).

MONK, THELONIUS SPHERE (1917?—1982), U.S. jazz pianist and composer. An innovator of modern jazz, Monk was known for his wry and unconventional melodies and unusual harmonic progressions. He jammed during the early 1940s in Harlem with Charlie Parker, Dizzy Gillespie, and others who developed "bebop," and although he made several recordings in the late 1940s, he did not receive widespread recognition and popularity until the acceptance of cool jazz in the late 1950s. He led several small groups during his career, including a quartet that included saxophonist John Coltrane. His compositions included "Round Midnight," "Misterioso," "Blue Monk," "Epistrophy," "Straight No Chaser," and "Well, You Needn't."

MONNET, JEAN (1888–1979), French economist and diplomat. Born in Cognac, Monnet dropped out of school to join the family brandy business. During World War I he worked in Allied shipping and supply and served (1919–23) as a deputy secretary-general of the League of Nations, which he left to become an international financial adviser. In May 1943, Monnet joined the French Committee of National Liberation as commissioner of supply and reconstruction; subsequently he was responsible for France's postwar economic-planning program (1947–55). A leading figure behind the formation of the Common Market, he was primarily responsible for the Schuman Plan (1950), which led to the organization of the European Coal and Steel Community. Monnet was its first president (1952–55) and was founding president of the Action Committee for the United States of Europe (1956–75). ∎ See his *Memoirs* (Eng. trans. 1978) and study by Merry and Serge Bromberger (Eng. trans. 1969).

MONOD, JACQUES (1910–1976), French biochemist. Monod earned a Ph.D. in 1941, was decorated for valor in World War II, and was associated with the Pasteur Institute in Paris from 1945. He conducted vital research into cell physiology, demonstrating the regulatory activities that control protein synthesis. Collaborating with François Jacob in the decade following the war, he discovered new types of genes that regulate other genes. Their concept of "messenger RNA" (ribonucleic acid) and the operon (a cluster of genes that govern a particular sequence of reactions) contributed to the understanding of protein synthesis. Their discovery had many implications for cancer research. He shared the 1965 Nobel Prize for Physiology or Medicine with Jacob and André Lwoff. His book *Chance and Necessity* (1970; Eng. trans. 1971) discussed the role of chance in evolution.

MONROE, BILL (1911–1996), U.S. musician and singer. The popularizer of the bluegrass style of country music, Monroe began has professional career (1927) playing the mandolin and singing in a band led by his older brothers Birch and Charlie. He later formed a duet with Charlie, who played guitar, and they toured widely in the South and Midwest and recorded 60 of their songs (1936–37). Bill formed his own band, the Bluegrass Boys (1938), and they became featured performers on the Grand Ole Opry musical radio show in Nashville, Tennessee. The bluegrass sound, characterized by driving syncopated rhythms and complex harmonies, attained national popularity. Monroe continued to perform and record until shortly before his death. ∎ See James Rooney, *Bossmen: Bill Monroe and Muddy Waters* (1971) and Richard D. Smith, *Can't You Hear Me Callin'* (2000).

MONROE, HARRIET (1860–1936), U.S. editor and poet. Monroe founded and edited (1912–36) *Poetry: A Magazine of Verse*, which became the most important poetry journal in the English-speaking world. Published in Chicago, the magazine was initially identified with the Chicago renaissance and such poets as Carl Sandburg, Vachel Lindsay, and Edgar Lee Masters. Her poetic tastes were catholic, however, and she published poets from every school. Among her contributors, many of whom were introduced to poetry lovers through the magazine, were Ezra Pound (the magazine's London editor), T. S. Eliot, Rupert Brooke, Rabindranath Tagore, Wallace Stevens, Amy Lowell, William Carlos Williams, and Marianne Moore. With Alice Henderson she edited the influential *The New Poetry: An Anthology of Twentieth Century Verse in English* (1917; rev. eds. 1923, 1932). ■ See her autobiography, *A Poet's Life* (1938).

MONROE, MARILYN (Norma Jean Mortensen; 1926–1962), U.S. film actress. From a childhood in a Los Angeles orphanage and foster homes, Monroe matured into the archetypal Hollywood love goddess. A voluptuous calendar girl with wide eyes and a breathless voice, she achieved superstardom as the dumb blonde in *How to Marry a Millionaire* and *Gentlemen Prefer Blondes* (both 1953). In *The Seven Year Itch* (1955) and *Some Like It Hot* (1959) Monroe developed a flair for light comedy, while *Bus Stop* (1956) and *The Misfits* (1961), her final film, represented her claim to serious consideration as an actress. But her success was achieved at enormous personal cost, and her death, due to an overdose of barbiturates, was ruled a possible suicide. She was married to baseball star Joe DiMaggio (1954) and playwright Arthur Miller (1956–61). After her death journalists persisted in publishing rumors regarding alleged amorous links with both John and Robert Kennedy. ■ See her autobiography, *My Story* (1974); Fred Guiles, *Norma Jean* (1969); biographies by Norman Mailer (1973), Donald Spoto (1993), and Barbara Leaming (1998); and Anthony Summers, *Goddess* (1985).

MONTAGU, ASHLEY (Israel Ehrenberg; 1905–1999), British-born U.S. anthropologist and writer. After studying biology and physical anthropology at the University of London (1922–25), Montagu worked at the British Museum, then went to New York for graduate training at Columbia University (Ph.D. 1937). He taught anthropology and began writing books that popularized anthropological issues. His views on race and relations between the sexes earned him the reputation of a gadfly in academic circles; he wrote on other controversial topics, including creationism, sociobiology, and the nature of aggression. His many books included *Man's Most Dangerous Myth: The Fallacy of Race* (1942; 6th ed. 1997), *The Natural Superiority of Women* (1953; rev. ed. 1992), *The Elephant Man* (1971), and *The Dehumanization of Man* (1983; with F. Matson). He edited *Race and I.Q.* (1975; rev. ed. 1999) and *Science and Creationism* (1984). *His Growing Young* (1981) attacked "psychosclerosis," the hardening of the psyche. Montagu also wrote *Up the Ivy* under the pseudonym Academicus Mentor.

MONTALE, EUGENIO (1896–1981), Italian poet. Influenced by French symbolism and its use of language, Montale was grouped with Salvatore Quasimodo and Giuseppe Ungaretti as a leading "hermetic" poet. Montale's deliberately nonrhetorical poetry was considered difficult. It expressed meaning and pessimism about life in novel rhyme and word orders and in personal, sometimes obscure, symbolism. His

later work was more simple and direct. Due to his antifascism, he lost his job as a librarian (1938) and was forced to earn his living as a translator. After 1948 he worked as a literary and music critic for a Milanese newspaper. He was awarded the Nobel Prize for Literature (1975) for his poetry, which gave "an indelible feeling for the value of life and the dignity of mankind." English translations of his poetry are in *Poems* (1959), *Provisional Conclusions* (1970), *New Poems* (1976), *It Depends* (1980), *First and Last Poems* (1984), *The Storm and Other Things* (1985), and *Collected Poems, 1920–1954* (1997). ■ See his essays in *The Second Life of Art* (Eng. trans. 1982), his autobiographical prose pieces in *The Butterfly of Dinard* (Eng. trans. 1971), and studies by G. Singh (1973), Guido Almansi and Bruce Merry (1977), Rebecca J. West (1981), and Jared Becker (1986).

MONTANA, JOE (1956–), U.S. football player. After leading Notre Dame to a national collegiate championship (1977), Montana became a star quarterback for the San Francisco 49ers (1979–92) and Kansas City Chiefs (1993–94) of the National Football League. He led the 49ers to four Super Bowl victories (1982, 1985, 1989, 1990) and was named the game's Most Valuable Player (MVP) three times (1982, 1985, 1990). Known for his dramatic fourth-quarter comebacks, he completed 3,409 passes for 40,551 yards and 273 touchdowns during his career. In spite of numerous injuries, he established a career record for the highest percentage of completed passes in NFL history, nearly 64 percent. ■ See his memoirs, *Montana* (1999; with Dick Schaap).

MONTAND, YVES (Yves Livi; 1921–1991), Italian-born French actor and singer. Montand's Jewish family fled Benito Mussolini's fascist rule when Yves was two and settled in the rough Marseilles neighborhood where he grew up. He acted in school plays but left school at age 11. He later worked on the docks and performed in music halls; in the 1940s his singing career was promoted by Edith Piaf. He married actress Simone Signoret in 1951. Montand was a hit on the Broadway stage in a 1959 one-man show, and American movies cast him as a vacuous ladies' man, as in *On a Clear Day You Can See Forever* (1970). European films gave him more substantial roles, as in *Z* (1969), *The Confession* (1970), and *State of Siege* (1973). Later films included *Clair de Femme* (1979), *Garcon!* (1983), *Jean de Florette* (1986), and *Manon of the Spring* (1986). He often appeared on television and made numerous recordings of popular French songs, including the album *Yve Montand's Paris* (1974). Montand was also known as a supporter of left-wing political causes. ■ See his memoirs, *You See, I Haven't Forgotten* (Eng. trans. 1992).

MONTESSORI, MARIA (1870–1952), Italian educator, physician, and feminist. The first woman to receive a medical degree in Italy (University of Rome, 1894), Montessori became world famous for her theories of early childhood education. She emphasized the development of the child's freedom of expression and individual initiative and utilized special teaching materials and games to develop body coordination and sense perception. The teacher's role was one of adviser and guide rather than formal instructor. Her first "Children's House" in Rome (1907) served as the prototype for similar Montessori schools set up throughout the world. ■ See biographies by E. Mortimer Standing (1957) and Rita Kramer (1976).

MONTEUX, PIERRE (1875–1964), French-born U.S. conductor. Monteux studied violin and viola at the Paris Conservatory. As conductor of Sergei Diaghilev's Ballet Russe (1911–14) he led the world premieres of works by Stravinsky, Debussy, and Ravel. After military service in World War I, Monteux was invited to conduct French operas at New York's Metropolitan Opera. He also conducted the Boston Symphony (1919–24), organized and conducted the Paris Symphony Orchestra (1929–38), and conducted the San Francisco Symphony (1936–52) and the London Symphony (1960–64). Monteux, who became a U.S. citizen in 1942 and ran a New Hampshire summer school for conductors, was known for his restrained, objective interpretations of contemporary French and Russian composers. ■ See Fifi Monteux, *Everyone Is Someone* (1962).

MONTGOMERY, BERNARD LAW, 1st VISCOUNT MONTGOMERY OF ALAMEIN (1887–1976), British field marshal. The son of an Anglican bishop, Montgomery was educated at Sandhurst and served with distinction in World War I. During World War II, his victory at Alamein (1942) was considered the turning point of the North African campaign. He participated in the 1943 invasion of Sicily and commanded all ground forces in the 1944 Normandy landing. A dour figure in beret and pullover, Montgomery was popular with his troops but tactless in his dealings with the Allies and had serious conflicts with U.S. Gen. Dwight D. Eisenhower. After the war he was deputy supreme commander of Allied (NATO) troops in Europe (1951–58). ■ See his war *Memoirs* (1958); biography by Alan Moorehead (1967); Nigel Hamilton, *Monty* (3 vols., 1981–86); and Richard Lamb, *Montgomery in Europe, 1943–45* (1984).

MONTHERLANT, HENRY DE (1896–1972), French novelist, essayist, and playwright. Born into an aristocratic French family, Montherlant fought in World War I, traveled widely, and lived adventurously. He even tried bullfighting, an experience recounted in his novel *The Bullfighters* (1926; Eng. trans. 1927). Emphasizing masculine conceptions of honor, solitary pride, independence, and duty, he derided weakness, especially in the form of sentimental or romantic love. His novels included *The Bachelors* (1934; Eng. trans. 1960) and *The Girls* (4 vols., 1936–39; Eng. trans. 1937–40, 1968), while *The Queen After Death* (1942; Eng. trans. 1951) and *The Cardinal of Spain* (1960; Eng. trans. 1969)

are among his successful, traditional plays. He committed suicide when faced with the prospect of blindness. ■ See biography by Lucille Becker (1970).

MONTY PYTHON (Graham Chapman, 1941–1989; John Cleese, 1939– ; Terry Gilliam, 1940– ; Eric Idle, 1943– ; Terry Jones, 1942– ; and Michael Palin, 1943–), British–U.S. comedy team. British writers and performers Chapman, Cleese, Idle, and Jones, all Oxbridge graduates, joined forces with American animator Gilliam to create the free-form iconoclastic BBC television series "Monty Python's Flying Circus" (1969–74). The satirical show—which blended nonsense, sarcasm, and absurdism—mocked convention and authority and gained a cult following in Britain and the United States. Among the most popular sequences from the series were "The Ministry of Silly Walks" and "The Dead-Parrot Sketch." In addition to the 45 30-minute BBC episodes (and two shows for German television), the Python troupe created four movies (*And Now for Something Completely Different,* 1971; *Monty Python and the Holy Grail,* 1975; *Monty Python's Life of Brian,* 1979; and *Monty Python's Meaning of Life,* 1983) and several books and recordings. After the group split up, the individual members pursued solo careers as directors, writers, and actors. Cleese starred in *A Fish Called Wanda* (1988) and created the TV series "Fawlty Towers" (1975–76). Palin starred in *A Fish Called Wanda* and *Brazil,* and TV travel shows. Gilliam directed the movies *Time Bandits* (1981), *Brazil* (1985), and *Twelve Monkeys* (1995). Idle wrote the novel *The Road to Mars* (1999). ■ See David Morgan, *Monty Python Speaks* (1999), and Kim Howard Johnson, *The First 28 Years of Monty Python* (1999).

MOODY, HELEN WILLS. *See WILLS, HELEN NEWINGTON.*

MOOG, ROBERT (1934–), U.S. inventor. Moog studied physics at Queens College (B.S. 1957) and physics and engineering at Cornell University (Ph.D. 1965). While still an undergraduate, he formed the R. A. Moog Co. (1954) with the goal of creating an instrument (called the synthesizer) that would produce music electronically. Introduced at an audio convention a decade later, the keyboard instrument was soon in such demand by popular musicians that "Moog" became virtually synonymous with "synthesizer." Moog incorporated his business in 1968 and introduced the Polymoog, the first synthesizer with chord capabilities, in 1976. His inventions gave rise to a generation of Moog virtuosos, including Walter Carlos, who performed Bach's keyboard music on the synthesizer.

MOON, REVEREND SUN MYUNG (1920–), Korean evangelist. Moon was born in a rural town that is now part of North Korea; his family joined the Presbyterian Church when he was 10 years old. Claiming to be clairvoyant and to have had conversations with Jesus, Buddha, and Moses, he began preaching his doctrines (1946) as a self-ordained minister. He was arrested by the government and excommunicated by his church. After settling in South Korea (1950), he established what was to become the Unification Church (1954) and was known as a militant anticommunist. He built up a business empire that produced ginseng tea, paints, and pharmaceuticals as well as heavy machinery and armaments. He required his followers to give up all of their possessions, live communally with other church members, and work as recruiters and fund-raisers. He brought the church to the United States in 1973 and claimed to have 40,000 American followers (most of them young, clean-cut, and middle class) and close to 3 million worldwide by 1982. Extremely controversial, Moon was accused by many American parents of "brainwashing" their children. Alleged by U.S. congressional committees to have close ties to the Korean government and to have been involved in several bribery and illegal tax, immigration, and banking schemes, he was convicted of income-tax fraud in 1982. *Divine Principle* (2nd ed., 1973) contains his autobiography and theological views. ■ See George D. Chryssides, *The Advent of Sun Myung Moon* (1991), and Carlton Sherwood, *Inquisition* (1991).

MOONEY, THOMAS JOSEPH (1882–1942), and WARREN KNOX BILLINGS (1893–1972), U.S. labor organizers. Tom Mooney, a socialist antiwar labor organizer, and Billings, his assistant, were arrested for allegedly setting off a bomb at the San Francisco Preparedness Day Parade (July 22, 1916) that killed 10 people and wounded 40. In the tense atmosphere created by union-management conflicts and the imminent entry of the United States into World War I, Billings was sentenced to life imprisonment (1916) and Mooney sentenced to hang (1917), but it was soon discovered that they were convicted on false testimony. Mooney's case, called "the American Dreyfus case," became an international cause célèbre, and such prominent Americans as Roger Baldwin, Fremont Older, and Samuel Gompers aided in the legal battle that finally led to the commutation of Mooney's sentence to life imprisonment (November 1918). His legal battles for freedom lasted another 20 years, for while "Free Tom Mooney" became a well-known cry, he was not pardoned until Jan. 7, 1939. Billings was freed by commutation of sentence (October 1939) but not officially pardoned until 1961. ■ See Curt Gentry, *Frame-Up* (1967); Richard H. Frost, *The Mooney Case* (1968); and Estoly Ward, *Gentle Dynamiter* (1983).

MOORE, ARCHIE (Archibald Lee Wright; 1913–1998), U.S. boxer. Moore launched his career in 1936 but had no opportunity to fight for a title until 16 years later when he deposed light-heavyweight champion Joey Maxim (1952). A shrewd fighter with a powerful punch, Moore successfully defended his crown, then sought the heavyweight title but was knocked out by Rocky Marciano (1955). In 1956, he was again defeated for the heavyweight crown, this time by the agile 21-year-old, Floyd Patterson. From 1957 until

his retirement in 1962, he successfully defended his light-heavyweight title. In 220 recorded professional bouts, he registered 136 knockouts. The National Boxing Association stripped Moore of his title in 1962 for failing to fight challenger Harold Johnson, but other boxing associations recognized his crown. Moore also appeared in films, winning recognition for his portrayal of the slave Jim in *The Adventures of Huckleberry Finn* (1959). ■ See his autobiography, *Any Boy Can* (1971; with Leonard B. Pearl).

MOORE, BARRINGTON, JR. (1913–), U.S. political scientist. Moore graduated from Yale (Ph.D. 1941) and worked as a political analyst for the Office of Strategic Services (OSS) during World War II before serving on the faculty of the Russian Research Center at Harvard (1948–). A specialist in the fields of comparative politics and political ideology, he wrote *Soviet Politics* (1950), *Terror and Progress USSR* (1954), and *Social Origins of Democracy and Dictatorship* (1966), in which he made a strong case for revolution as a prerequisite to industrial democracy. His other works included *Reflections on the Causes of Human Misery* (1972), *Injustice: The Social Bases of Obedience and Revolt* (1978), *Privacy: Studies in Social and Cultural History* (1984), and *Moral Aspects of Economic Growth and Other Essays* (1996). ■ See study by Dennis Smith (1983).

MOORE, BRIAN (1921–1999), Irish-born Canadian novelist. Moore left Belfast after serving in World War II and lived in Montreal, California, and New York. The first of his realistic novels, *The Lonely Passion of Judith Hearne* (1956), brought him immediate recognition. *The Feast of Lupercal* (1957) and *The Luck of Ginger Coffey* (1960) described social misfits in an unpretentious, compassionate, often humorous manner. Many of his works dealt with guilt-ridden characters who have liberated themselves from traditional Irish-Catholic religious and family traditions. Two novels, *An Answer from Limbo* (1962) and *The Emperor of Ice Cream* (1962), drew on his own struggles as an expatriate writer. Later novels included *I Am Mary Dunne* (1968), *Fergus* (1970), *Catholics* (1972), *The Doctor's Wife* (1976), *The Mangan Inheritance* (1979), *Black Robe* (1985), *No Other Life* (1993), *The Statement* (1995), and *The Magician's Wife* (1998). ■ See studies by Hallyard Dahlie (1981) and Denis Sampson (1998).

MOORE, COLLEEN (Kathleen Morrison; 1900–1988), U.S. actress. Moore, the star-struck daughter of an irrigation engineer, attended a convent school and studied piano at the Detroit conservatory of Music. She got her start in Hollywood (1917) as repayment by director D. W. Griffith to her uncle, *Chicago Examiner* editor Walter Howey, for helping him get his epic movies, *The Birth of a Nation* and *Intolerance,* approved by the censors. She created a sensation as the wide-eyed, lighthearted, Jazz-Age flapper in *Flaming Youth* (1923) and such other silent films as *Flirting with Love* (1924), *The Perfect Flapper* (1924), *We Moderns* (1925),

Naughty But Nice (1927), and *Why Be Good?* (1929). With bobbed hair, slim figure, and short skirts, she personified the emancipated young woman of the 1920s, became one of Hollywood's richest stars, and remained a popular culture icon and fashion setter for years. She appeared in several talkies, including *The Power and the Glory* (1933) and *The Scarlet Letter* (1934) before her retirement in 1934. A successful investor, she wrote *How Women Can Make Money in the Stock Market* (1969). ▪ See her autobiography, *Silent Star* (1968).

MOORE, GEORGE EDWARD (1873–1958), British philosopher. Moore studied at Cambridge and taught there for most of his career (1911–39). He figured prominently in London's Bloomsbury group and edited the journal *Mind* (1921–47). Moving philosophy toward realism in two works of 1903—"The Refutation of Idealism" (reprinted in his *Philosophical Studies,* 1922) and *Principia Ethtca*—Moore discarded the idealist notion that we perceive only our own sensations and can know nothing with certainty about the material world. His ideas about the nature of philosophical inquiry powerfully influenced British thought in the century's early decades. He argued that if a philosophical notion defies common sense, it is probably wrong. Moore, who believed in stating philosophical ideas as simply as possible, held that philosophy should not attempt to undermine convictions that rest on common sense, but rather to clarify them through rigorous analysis. In the field of ethics, Moore's doctrine of ideal utilitarianism linked the notions of "good" and "right" to value and obligation. ▪ See the autobiographical statement in Paul A. Schilpp, ed., *The Philosophy of G. E. Moore* (2nd ed. 1968); biography by Paul Levy (1980); and Tony Gray, *A Peculiar Man* (1996).

MOORE, HENRY (1898–1986), British sculptor. The son of a coal miner, Moore achieved recognition as Britain's most important avant-garde sculptor in the 1930s. He absorbed a variety of influences, from pre-Columbian to cubist, into a distinctive, naturalistic treatment of the human figure, solitary and in intimate groupings. Moore's most effective themes are the mother with child and the reclining figure. His major commissions included massive reclining figures for the United Nations Educational, Scientific, and Cultural Organization Building in Paris (1958) and for Lincoln Center in New York (1965). In the post–World War II era he was regarded by many as the world's greatest living sculptor. ▪ See his autobiography (1968), biographies by William Packer (1985) and Roger Berthoud (1987), and studies by Donald Hall (1966) and Herbert Read (1966).

MOORE, HUGH (1887–1972), U.S. businessman and crusader. With his brother-in-law, Moore created the first commercial paper drinking cup, which they later called the Dixie cup, and he served as chairman of the Dixie Cup Co. He was also a crusader for world peace, supporting the League of Nations and the United Nations, and a leading advocate of population control. An officer of International Planned Parenthood, he coined the phrase "population bomb," the title of a pamphlet he wrote in 1955.

MOORE, JOHN BASSETT (1860–1947), U.S. jurist and diplomat. Moore was an assistant secretary in the Department of State (1886–91) and taught international law and diplomacy at Columbia University (1892–1924). A U.S. representative on many important international commissions and a foreign policy adviser during the early 1900s, he was a member of the Permanent Court of Arbitration (1912–38) and the first American judge on the World Court (Permanent Court of International Justice; 1921–28). A prolific writer on law and diplomacy, Moore wrote three monumental digests that became standard reference works: *A History and Digest of International Arbitration* (6 vols., 1898), *Digest of International Law* (8 vols., 1906), and *International Adjudications* (8 vols., 1937).

MOORE, MARIANNE (1887–1972), U.S. poet. After she graduated from Bryn Mawr (1909), Moore taught in a U.S. Indian school. She began to contribute to the *Egoist,* a British imagist magazine, and published *Poems* in 1921. *The Complete Poems* (1981), assembled from 11 books written over 60 years, contained a modest 125 works and was not in fact complete. It included poems from *Selected Poems* (1935) introduced by T. S. Eliot and *Collected Poems* (1951, Pulitzer Prize). Her works were praised for their wit and microscopic concentration and criticized for their obscure allusions. In *Predilections* (1955), a collection of essays, Moore expressed her desire for "impassioned exactitude" in poetry. She made her last public appearance in 1967, wearing the cape and tricorn hat that had become her trademark. Moore was also a lifelong baseball fan. ▪ See studies by Pamela Hadas (1977), Laurence Stapleton (1978), Bonnie Costello (1981), Elizabeth Phillips (1982), and Charles Molesworth (1990).

MOORE, MARY TYLER (1936–   ), U.S. actress. Brooklyn-born Mary Tyler Moore began her career as a dancer at age 17. Her first television role was as the private eye's secretary on "Richard Diamond," but the camera showed audiences only her legs, and she begged out of her contract after 16 weeks. Her face became familiar to viewers when she costarred on "The Dick Van Dyke Show" in the 1960s. After not altogether successful appearances in a half dozen films and on Broadway, she devoted herself to television, becoming star of "The Mary Tyler Moore Show," a mainstay of Saturday evening TV fare through most of the 1970s; she portrayed the all-American happy and unmarried career woman. With onetime husband Grant Tinker, Moore created MTM productions (1970), which offered the networks successful spinoffs and other shows. In 1980 Moore appeared on Broadway in *Whose Life Is It Anyway?* and in the film *Ordinary People.* In the mid-1980s she launched the new TV series, *Mary* (1985), and starred in the film *Just Be-*

tween *Friends* (1986). She won an Emmy Award for her role in the TV movie *Stolen Babies* (1993). ■ See her memoirs, *After All* (1995), and J. Feuer, P. Kerr, and T. Vahimagi, eds., *MTM: "Quality Television"* (1985).

MOORE, STANFORD (1913–1982), U.S. biochemist. After joining the faculty of the Rockefeller University (1939), Moore began collaborating with colleague William H. Stein in pioneering research on protein chemistry. They utilized the technique of chromatography to analyze the structure and activity of the enzyme ribonuclease (RNA) and were awarded the 1972 Nobel Prize for Chemistry (with Christian Anfinsen) for their work. Shortly before the announcement of the Nobel award, Moore and Stein published their analysis of the action of deoxyribonuclease (DNA), a much more complex enzyme. As RNA and DNA control the chemistry of life, the determination of their structures raised hopes for using chemical means to modify defective enzymes that can cause inherited diseases and mental retardation.

MORANDI, GIORGIO (1890–1964), Italian painter and engraver. Although briefly associated with the futurists and the metaphysical painting movement, Morandi was primarily an independent artist who created quiet, unheroic canvases even during the fascist period. After his early landscapes, he turned to the small, meditative still lifes for which he was best known. Their subject matter—mainly cups, bowls, and long-necked bottles painted in earth tone—reflects an attempt to strike a balance between form and color and creates an impression of spiritual purity and aesthetic conviction. Morandi spent virtually his entire life in his native Bologna but enjoyed an international following. ■ See study by Guido Giuffre (Eng. trans. 1971).

MORANTE, ELSA (1918–1985), Italian writer. A native of Rome, Morante was forced to leave the city (1943) with her husband at the time, novelist Alberto Moravia, during the World War II German occupation. She took refuge in southern Italy, where two of her best-known novels, the family saga *House of Liars* (1948; Eng. trans. 1951) and the poetic study of adolescent disillusionment *Arturo's Island* (1957; Eng. trans. 1959), were set. Her highly acclaimed and widely read *History: A Novel* (1974; Eng. trans. 1977), a tragic story of a woman and her son, set in wartime and postwar Rome, was written from a Christian-Marxist perspective. Her other works included *Aracoeli* (1983; Eng. trans. 1985), a novel about the relationship between a homosexual man and his mother.

MORAVIA, ALBERTO (Alberto Pincherl; 1907–1990), Italian novelist. Moravia's frail health in his youth prevented formal schooling, but it led to much reading and introspection. At age 22 he published *The Time of Indifference* (1929; Eng. trans. 1953; also translated as *The Indifferent Ones*, 1932), which flouted fascist literary dictates by treating corruption among Rome's middleclass bureaucrats. His

second novel, *Wheel of Fortune* (1935; Eng. trans. 1937), was officially censured, and the third, *The Fancy Dress Party* (1941; Eng. trans. 1952), was banned personally by dictator Benito Mussolini. *The Conformist* (1951; Eng. trans. 1952) portrayed the opportunistic behavior of the bourgeoisie during the fascist era, while *Agostino* (1944; Eng. trans. 1947) and *Two Woman* (1957; Eng. trans. 1958; film 1961) demonstrated his Marxist leanings and sympathy for the lower classes. His novels and short stories often treated human isolation and the ways in which people use sex to battle boredom and alienation, as in *The Woman of Rome* (1947; Eng. trans. 1949), *Conjugal Love* (1949; Eng. trans. 1951), and *The Empty Canvas* (1960; Eng. trans. 1962). Moravia's entire corpus was placed (1952) in the Index of the Roman Catholic Church. He also wrote notable accounts of his travels to the Soviet Union (1958), India (1962), China (1967), and Africa (1972) as well as a comic Freudian work, *Two: A Phallic Novel* (1971; Eng. trans. 1972), and *Erotic Tales* (1983; Eng. trans 1985). His later political novels included *Time of Desecration* (1978; Eng. trans. 1980) and *1934* (1982; Eng. trans. 1982). He was married to novelist Elsa Morante (1941–1963). ■ See study by Jane E. Cottrell (1974) and the interview autobiography, *Life of Moravia* (with Alain Elkann; 1990, Eng. trans. 2000).

MOREAU, JEANNE (1928–), French film actress and director. At age 20 Moreau became the youngest member of the Comédie Française and also made her film debut. But it was only as a mature woman that Moreau made her mark in such films as *La Notte* (1961), *Jules and Jim* (1961), *Eva* (1962), and *Diary of a Chambermaid* (1964), which demonstrated her wide range as well as her sophistication and sensuality. She also appeared in *Mr. Klein* (1976), *The Last Tycoon* (1976), *The Summer House* (1993), and *The Proprietor* (1996), and directed *La Lumière* (1975) and *L'Adolescente* (1979). ■ See Marianne Gray, *La Moreau* (1996).

MORENZ, HOWIE (Howarth William Morenz; 1902–1937), Canadian ice-hockey player. Morenz played center for the Montreal Canadiens (1922–34; 1936–37) and led the team to three Stanley Cup championships (1924, 1930, 1931). A dashing skater, ferocious bodychecker, and prolific scorer, he won the Hart Trophy for Most Valuable Player three times (1928, 1931, 1932). Morenz was the leading player of his era and was largely responsible for the expansion of the National Hockey League to the United States. After breaking his leg during a game in Montreal (January 28, 1937), he suffered a nervous breakdown and developed heart trouble while in the hospital, and died on March 7, 1937. ■ See biography by Dean Robinson (1983).

MORGAN, EDMUND SEARS (1916–), U.S. historian. Born in Minnesota and educated at Harvard (Ph.D. 1942), Morgan taught early American history at Brown (1946–55) and Yale (1955–86). His many works on the period included

The Puritan Family (1944; rev. ed. 1966), The Puritan Dilemma (1958), and a biography (1967) of Roger Williams, the founder of Rhode Island, described by Morgan as being more concerned with developing institutions than with theology. He also wrote The Birth of the Republic (1956; rev. ed. 1977), American Slavery, American Freedom: The Ordeal of Colonial Virginia (1975), and Inventing the People: The Rise of Popular Sovereignty in England and America (1988).

MORGAN, HELEN (1900–1941), U.S. singer. Morgan's greatest stage success was her triumph as Julie in the Broadway musical Show Boat (1927). She was best known, however, as a performer of "torch songs," a blues-influenced genre that conveyed the pain of unrequited love. Seated on a piano and twisting a chiffon handkerchief in her hands while singing such songs as "Why Was I Born?," "The Man I Love," and "Bill," she symbolized the newly "liberated" but lonely urban woman of the 1920s and 1930s and became one of the most famous entertainers in the United States. Her melancholy songs seemed to reflect her unhappy personal life and her death was attributable to alcoholism. ■ See biography by Gilbert Maxwell (1974).

MORGAN, JOHN PIERPONT (1837–1913), U.S. banker. The son of a merchant banker, J. P. Morgan was the foremost U.S. financier in the early years of the century. He built up the country's most important private banking house, powerful enough to bail out the U.S. Treasury during the depression of 1895 and to play a key role in stabilizing the economy after the financial crisis of 1907. J. P. Morgan & Co. was active in railroad development; it created U.S. Steel (1901) and International Harvester (1902) corporations. Morgan compiled the greatest private art collection of his day, leaving it to New York's Metropolitan Museum. John Pierpont Morgan, Jr. (1867–1943) inherited more than $50 million and took over his father's investment house. ■ See Lewis Corey, The House of Morgan (1930); biographies by Frederick Lewis Allen (1949) and Cass Canfield (1974); and Andrew Sinclair, Corsair (1981).

MORGAN, JULIA (1872–1957), U.S. architect. Trained in engineering at the University of California at Berkeley, Morgan was the first woman licensed as an architect in California. In 1896 she went to Paris, where she was the first woman to study architecture at the École des Beaux Arts. She returned home (1902) to work with Galen Howard on design of the university campus at Berkeley. Breaking out on her own, she designed the Mills College Library (1906). Her career thrived in the flurry of architectural activity following the San Francisco earthquake of 1906. Integrating various traditions, she won renown for sophisticated, finely crafted work, and designed more than 700 buildings in her 45-year career. She was best known for projects she undertook for newspaper magnate William Randolph Hearst. The residence she designed for him, San Simeon (1919–40), became

a state landmark. ■ See Carleton Winslow, The Enchanted Hill (1980), and biography by Sara Boutelle (1988).

MORGAN, THOMAS HUNT (1866–1945), U.S. biologist and geneticist. One of the founders of modern genetics, Morgan studied at Johns Hopkins (Ph.D. 1891) and taught at Columbia University as professor of experimental zoology (1904–28) and at the California Institute of Technology (1928–45). At Columbia (1907) he began his work in genetics and, while experimenting with the fruit fly (Drosophilia), developed the main outlines of the chromosome theory of heredity. It was the most important contribution to genetics since Gregor Mendel's basic discoveries. Morgan proved the existence of genes as discrete entities, mapped their positions along the chromosomes, and described linkage groups and the phenomenon of crossing over. For his major breakthrough in genetics he received the 1933 Nobel Prize for Physiology or Medicine. His books included Mechanism of Mendelian Heredity (1915; with A. H. Sturtevant, H. J. Muller, and C. B. Bridges), Theory of the Gene (1926), and Embryology and Genetics (1934). ■ See biographies by Ian Shine and Sylvia Wrobel (1976) and Garland E. Allen (1978).

MORGENSTERN, OSKAR (1902–1977), German-born U.S. economist. A graduate of the University of Vienna (1925), Morgenstern later taught there (1929–38) and served as director of the Austrian Insititute of Business Cycle Research (1931–38). After the German occupation of Austria, he emigrated to the United States and taught at Princeton University (1938–70). He was best known for work on game theory that sought to devise mathematically the most advantageous strategies for engaging in competitive or cooperative behavior. He wrote, with John von Neumann, Theory of Games and Economic Behavior (1944), and later applied game theory and other mathematical theories to such problems as unemployment, defense strategy, and stock-market prices.

MORGENTHAU, HANS JOACHIM (1904–1980), German-born U.S. political scientist. Morgenthau, who emigrated to the United States in 1937 and taught political science at the University of Chicago (1943–71) and the New School for Social Research (1974–80), considered himself a realist in world politics. In Politics Among Nations (1948), which became a popular college textbook, he defined power as the dominant goal of international relations and advocated the pursuit of national interest rather than world approval. A prominent foreign policy analyst during the 1960s and 1970s, he was a leading critic of U.S. participation in the Vietnam War. His other books included Politics in the Twentieth Century (3 vols., 1962) and A New Foreign Policy for the United States (1969).

MORGENTHAU, HENRY, JR. (1891–1967), U.S. cabinet officer. Born into a prosperous Jewish family, Morgenthau studied agriculture before starting his own farm in Dutchess County, New York. A neighbor and friend of Franklin D. Roosevelt and a Democrat active in state politics, Morgenthau supported Roosevelt for governor and then for president in 1932. During the New Deal, Roosevelt appointed him first as head of the Farm Credit Administration, which aided debt-ridden farmers, and then as secretary of the treasury. Although a fiscal conservative, he presided, during his long tenure as secretary (1934–45), over the most rapid expansion of federal expenditures in U.S. history. Morgenthau was an early advocate of collective action against Nazi expansion in Europe in the 1930s and was responsible for seeing that Britain and France received early assistance against German aggression. He resigned (1945) after his "Morgenthau Plan," which would have subdivided and deindustrialized Germany after World War II, was rejected by Pres. Harry Truman. ■ See John Morton Blum, *From the Morgenthau Diaries* (2 vols., 1959–65).

MORI, OGAI (Rintaro Mori; 1962–1922), Japanese novelist, poet, and translator. A prolific man of letters, Mori was a German-trained career army surgeon who headed the Army Medical College and served as Surgeon General. His novel *The Girl Who Danced* (1890; Eng. trans. 1964) helped initiate the romantic movement in Japanese literature, and he remained an antinaturalist throughout his career. Mori's most famous novel, *The Wild Geese* (1911–13; Eng. trans. 1973), is marked by a sense of detachment, melancholy, and resignation that is characteristic of much of his fiction. He was also known for his translations of Goethe, numerous critical and philosophical articles, and three pioneering scholarly biographies of 19th-century doctors of Chinese medicine. Other translated works include the novel *Vita Sexualis* (1909; Eng. trans. 1972) and the selections in *The Historical Literature of Mori Ogai* (1977), *The Historical Fiction of Mori Ogai* (1991), and *Youth and Other Stories* (1994). ■ See study by J. Thomas Rimer (1975).

MÓRICZ, ZSIGMOND (1879–1942), Hungarian novelist, short-story writer, and dramatist. The son of a peasant, Móricz studied law and theology and worked as a reporter and editor in Budapest. He achieved fame with the publication of his short story "Seven Pennies" in 1908, and he developed into one of the most important Hungarian novelists of the century. The first to portray realistically the brutality and poverty of peasant life and the decadence of the provincial gentry, Móricz produced a series of powerful novels, notably *Golden Mud* (1910), *Be Faithful unto Death* (1921; Eng. trans. 1962), *The Torch* (1917; Eng. trans. 1931), and *Transylvania* (3 vols., 1922–35), which placed him in the naturalistic tradition of the French novelist Émile Zola.

MORIN, PAUL (1889–1963), French-Canadian poet. Morin was born in Montreal, acquired degrees in the arts and law at Laval University, then continued his education at the University of Paris (Ph.D. 1912). He traveled widely and taught French literature at McGill, the University of Minnesota, and Smith College. His poetry, written in French and published in book form in 1911, 1922, and 1960, was remarkable for its sure craft, sensuous imagery, and exotic non-Canadian settings. Although attacked for the hedonism and amorality of his verse, Mono was generally regarded as the first Canadian master of French poetry.

MORÍNIGO, HIGINIO (1897–   ), Paraguayan political leader, Morínigo graduated from military college (1922), was promoted eventually to general and minister of war (1939), and became president of Paraguay in 1940. Stability and order were achieved at the price of censorship, suppression, and pro-Axis neutrality for most of World War II. Moríngo's attempts to establish a nationalist revolutionary state and replace the three traditional parties were unpopular, and civil war broke out in 1947 after an abortive attempt to democratize the regime. The following year Moríngo was overthrown and exiled. He lived in Argentina and Brazil before returning to Paraguay (1956) but subsequently resettled in Argentina.

MORISON, SAMUEL ELIOT (1887–1976), U.S. historian. A Boston Brahmin who taught at Harvard for 40 years (1915–55) and served as the university's official historian, Morison collaborated with Henry Steele Commager on *The Growth of the American Republic* (1930), a widely used textbook. But Morison's passion was maritime history, and in 1939 he retraced Columbus' route in sailing vessels and won a Pulitzer Prize for his biography of Columbus, *Admiral of the Ocean Sea* (1942). He was also the U.S. Navy's official historian, writing the 15-volume *History of U.S. Naval Operations in World War II* (1947–62). Morison wrote a biography of John Paul Jones (1959; Pulitzer Prize), an account of the northern voyages in *The European Discovery of America* (1971), and several other works of maritime history.

MORITA, AKIO. *See IBUKA, MASURU.*

MORLEY, JOHN, VISCOUNT MORLEY OF BLACKBURN (1838–1923), British political leader and author. Morley left Oxford University in 1859 and became a radical author, editor, and critic. As a Liberal member of Parliament (1883–96; 1896–1908) he served as secretary for Ireland (1886; 1892–95) and supported home rule. As secretary of state for India (1905–10), Morley was a reformer who advocated more local participation in government. He was a pacifist and resigned from the government in 1914, at the start of World War I. Morley was also noted for his biographies of, among others, Voltaire (1872), Rousseau (1873), and Gladstone (1903). ■ See his *Recollections* (1917); Francis W. Knickerbocker, *Free Minds: John Morley and His Friends* (1943); study by Stanley A. Wolpert (1967); and biography by David A. Hamer (1968).

MORO, ALDO (1916–1978), Italian political leader. A lawyer, law professor, and author of legal texts, Moro was first elected to parliament as a Christian Democrat in 1946. He served in several cabinet posts during the 1950s and was his party's secretary (1959–63). Known as a conciliator, he formed a center-left coalition with the Socialists, Social Democrats, and Republicans and served as premier (1963–68). He subsequently served as foreign minister (1969–72; 1973–74), effected a temporary accommodation with the Communist party, and headed two other governments during 1974–76. Moro continued to exercise political influence as party president (from 1976) until kidnapped by Red Brigade terrorists. They murdered him after two months of captivity when the government refused to release 13 captured members of the Red Brigades in exchange for his safe return. ▪ See Robert Katz, *Days of Wrath* (1980).

MOROZOV, PAVEL (1918–1932), Soviet paragon. The name Pavlik Morosov in the Soviet Union of the 1930s was a byword for loyalty to the state. At the time of collectivization, Morozov, a village boy of 14, denounced his father as a *kulak* sympathizer. His father was shot, and Pavel in turn was murdered by peasants instigated by his uncle. Dictator Joseph Stalin's propagandists seized on the event, honoring Pavel Morozov as a model of youth who put patriotic duty above all. Books and poems commemorated his deed, and his statue was erected in public places.

MORRICE, JAMES WILSON (1865–1924), Canadian artist. The son of a textile merchant, Morrice lived most of his adult life in Paris, with periodic painting trips home and abroad. His bright, intimate compositions, both landscapes and figure studies, were conceived in a "purist" postimpressionist style. His *Ferry, Quebec* (1909), is perhaps the best-known and most highly regarded Canadian painting of the century. Morrice was the model for Cranshaw in W. Somerset Maugham's *Of Human Bondage,* and the subject of a biography by Donald W. Buchanan (1936).

MORRISON, TONI (1931–), U.S novelist. Morrison was born in Lorain, Ohio, studied at Howard (B.A. 1953) and Cornell (M.A. 1955) Universities, and then taught English literature before working in publishing. She won acclaim for her novels, including *The Bluest Eye* (1970), *Sula* (1973), *Song of Solomon* (1977), which won a 1978 National Book Award, and *Tar Baby* (1981). Her fiction created stunning portraits from black American life, particularly exploring the inner lives and relationships of and among black women. Her later novels included *Beloved* (1987; Pulitzer Prize; film 1998), *Jazz* (1992), and *Paradise* (1998). She left publishing in 1985 and taught at several universities, including Princeton (1989–). Three of her speeches on racism in literature appeared in *Playing in the Dark: Whiteness and the Literary Imagination* (1992). She was awarded the 1993 Nobel Prize in Literature. ▪ See D. Taylor-Guthrie, ed., *Conversations with Toni Morrison* (1994).

MORSE, WAYNE LYMAN (1900–1974), U.S. senator. The son of a Wisconsin cattle farmer, Morse was a professor at the University of Oregon Law School (dean, 1931–44) who made his reputation as a labor arbitrator and specialist in criminal-law administration. During 24 years as a U.S. senator from Oregon (1945–69), he twice changed his party affiliation but always remained faithful to his liberal beliefs. Outspoken and long-winded, he once filibustered for a record 22½ hours against an offshore oil bill (1953). He cast one of only two votes against the Tonkin Gulf resolution (1964), which legitimized U.S. intervention in Vietnam, condemned the United States as "the greatest threat to world peace," and was defeated for reelection in 1968 over his opposition to the Vietnam War. ▪ See Arthur R. Smith, *The Tiger in the Senate* (1962).

MORTON, JELLY ROLL (Ferdinand Joseph LaMenthe Morton; 1885–1941), U.S. jazz musician, composer, and singer. Born into a Creole family in New Orleans, Morton was one of the pioneer ragtime piano players. He achieved national recognition in the late 1920s with a series of recordings he made with Morton's Red Hot Peppers. He was an innovator of orchestral jazz and composed such pieces as "King Porter Stomp," "London Rag," and "Jelly Roll Blues." Although regarded by many as a genius and the greatest New Orleans pianist, he enraged many contemporaries with his braggadocio, moodiness, and snobbery—he claimed to have "invented jazz in 1902"—and some critics considered him vastly overrated. ▪ See Alan Lomax, *Mister Jelly Roll* (1950).

MOSCA, GAETANO (1858–1941), Italian political scientist. Mosca taught constitutional law for many years, became a member of the Italian Chamber of Deputies in 1908, and served as under secretary of state for colonies (1914–16) before the rise of fascist leader Benito Mussolini put an end to his political career. Although Mosca was a political liberal, his concept that a ruling minority exists in all societies, published in his *Elements of Political Science* (1896) and translated as *The Ruling Class* (1939), was used by apologists to justify fascism. ▪ See James H. Meisel, *Myth of the Ruling Class* (1958).

MOSER-PROELL, ANNEMARIE (1953–), Austrian skier. The daughter of a mountain farmer, Moser-Proell learned to ski at age 4. Primarily self-taught, she developed an aggressive, natural technique and gained a reputation as a daredevil on the slopes. A downhill specialist, she joined the Austrian National Team at age 15 and won the World Cup Championship an unprecedented six times (1971–75, 1979), and registered 62 victories in individual races, more than any other woman in skiing history. She retired after she won a gold medal in the 1980 Lake Placid Olympics. ▪ See biography by Linda Jacobs (1975).

MOSES, GRANDMA (Anna Mary Robertson Moses; 1860–1961), U.S. painter. During a life of farming in Virginia and New York State, Moses embroidered country scenes in wool; when arthritis impeded that hobby, she took up painting at age 76. Her work was exhibited (1939) at a "contemporary unknown American painters" show at New York's Museum of Modern Art; over the next quarter century "Grandma Moses" became one of America's best-known artists. Entirely self-taught, she created more than 1,000 colorful canvases (at least 25 of them after her 100th year), depicting nostalgic rural scenes in a primitivist manner. Her paintings were installed in museums in America and Europe. *The Grandma Moses Storybook* (1961) sold 20,000 copies before publication. ■ See her autobiography, *My Life's History* (1952), and studies by Otto Kallir (1973) and Jane Kallir (1982).

MOSES, ROBERT (1888–1981), U.S. public official. Moses studied at Yale (B.A. 1909) and Oxford (MA. 1913) and earned a Ph.D. in political science from Columbia University (1914). Although never elected to public office, he exerted enormous power in New York City and New York State politics for over 40 years (1924–68) as chairman of the New York State Park Commission (1924–63), New York City Park Commission (1934–60), the Triborough Bridge and Tunnel Authority (1946–68), and the New York State Power Authority (1954–63). He was a planner, policy maker, and builder whose parks, highways, and urban renewal projects transformed the environment of New York City—for better and worse—and exerted a profound influence on cities throughout the country. He was the driving force behind such monumental public works as the St. Lawrence and Niagara power projects, the Henry Hudson Parkway, Jones Beach, the Triborough Bridge, and the 1964–65 New York World's Fair. At the height of his power (1960) he personally controlled 161 square miles of state and city land. ■ See Robert A. Caro, *The Power Broker* (1974).

MOSLEY, SIR OSWALD ERNALD (1896–1980), British political leader. In 1918 Mosley, then young and wealthy, was elected to Parliament as a Conservative with prospects. He soon went over to the Labour party (1924) and, under the impact of the Depression, became a Keynesian. But in 1932 he went beyond the pale to found the violently pro-German, anti-Semitic British Union of Fascists. Interned by the British government during World War II (1940–43), Mosley lived mainly in France and Ireland after the war. ■ See his autobiography, *My Life,* (1968); biography by Robert Skidelsky (1975); and Nicholas Mosley, *Rules of the Game* (1982).

MOSS, STIRLING CRAUFORD (1929–), British auto racing driver. Only mechanical mishaps and unsuccessful experiments prevented Moss from winning the world driving championship: he was runner-up five times (1955–58; 1961) and placed third twice (1959; 1960). Recognizing only Juan Manuel Fangio as his superior, Moss was regarded by many as the fastest, shrewdest, and most perfect driver of his time

and was probably the world's best-known racer. He retired after being critically injured in a crash in 1962. During his career he won 194 races and 16 Formula One events. ■ See his autobiography, *All But My Life* (2d ed. 1973).

MÖSSBAUER, RUDOLF LUDWIG (1929–), German physicist. "The Mössbauer effect" is the name given to the phenomenon discovered by the corecipient (with Robert Hofstadter) of the 1961 Nobel Prize for Physics. He found that certain atomic nuclei, bound in solid crystals, can emit and absorb gamma rays without losing energy through nuclear recoil. This observation proved an invaluable research tool for investigations in various fields, including general relativity theory and solid-state physics. Applied to chemistry, it elucidated the relationship between nuclear characteristics and valence properties of the atom. Mössbauer taught at the Technical University in Munich (1964–72; 1977–); and directed the Institute Max von Laue and the French-German-British High Flux Reactor in Grenoble (1972–77).

MOTHER TERESA (Agnes Gonxha Bojaxhiu; 1910–1997), Roman Catholic nun and poverty worker. Mother Teresa was born to Albanian parents in Skopje, now part of Macedonia. After receiving a religious education, she joined the Sisters of Loretto, an Irish order in India, and took her vows as a nun (1928). She taught in a convent school for upper-class Indian girls in Calcutta for two decades before founding a slum school (1948) and, subsequently, the Order of the Missionaries of Charity (1950), which was dedicated to serving the poor. Established to provide food and medical care and personal contact to the destitute, particularly to lepers and the dying, the order grew into a worldwide movement of more than 4,500 nuns in nearly 600 sites in over 100 countries. Mother Teresa was widely known and admired across India but was little known in the West until she was awarded the 1979 Nobel Peace Prize. She adhered strictly to the conservative social views of her church and was strongly opposed to contraception, abortion, and divorce. ■ See study by Desmond Doig (1976); Eileen Egan, *Such a Vision of the Street* (1985); the authorized biography by Kathryn Spink (1997); and the critical study by Christopher Mitchens, *The Missionary Position* (1995).

MOTHERWELL, ROBERT (1915–1991), U.S. painter. Motherwell studied aesthetics and psychoanalytic theory at Stanford and Harvard; at Columbia University (1940), Prof. Meyer Schapiro urged him to devote himself to painting. Contact with surrealists during World War II—particulary with artists in exile, including Max Ernst—confirmed his decision to paint. He began creating collages; with painters Jackson Pollock, Mark Rothko, and others, he pioneered abstract expressionism. Motherwell was one of the first American artists to experiment with automatism; using accidental, intuitive elements in his paintings, he sought to externalize unconscious motivation in his work. From 1949 until the mid-1990s, Motherwell worked on an extended series of stark black-and-white mural-sized canvases, *Elegy for the Spanish Republic*. In the 1960s he worked on a more massive scale in the emerging mode known as color-field painting. ■ See study by H. H. Arnason (rev. ed. 1982) and his *Collected Writings* (1993), edited by Stephanie Terenzio.

MOTLEY, CONSTANCE BAKER (1921–), U.S. jurist. Born in New Haven to West Indian parents, Motley graduated from Columbia University Law School (1946) and was associate counsel of the National Association for the Advancement of Colored People's Legal Defense Fund (1945–65). She worked primarily on school-segregation cases, winning 9 out of 10 suits before the U.S. Supreme Court, including James Meredith's successful plea to enter the University of Mississippi (1962). Motley served as a New York State senator (1964-65) and as Manhattan's borough president (1965-66). In 1966 she became the first African-American woman appointed to the federal judiciary (Southern District, New York). She later served as chief judge (1982–86) and senior judge (1986–). ■ See her autobiography, *Equal Justice Under Law* (1998).

MOTT, CHARLES STEWART (1875–1973), U.S. industrialist and philanthropist. A trained mechanical engineer, Mott moved his family-owned axle company from Utica, New York, to Flint, Michigan (1906), and sold it to General Motors (49 percent in 1908; 51 percent in 1913) for shares of stock. He eventually became the largest stockholder in GM, the world's largest industrial corporation. Amassing a fortune as a director (from 1913) and a vice president (1916–37) of GM, he established the Mott Foundation in 1926 (1969; assets, $300 million), which gave millions of dollars to educational, health, and recreational programs in Flint and throughout the country. His son, Stewart Rawlings Mott (1937–), was a business executive and philanthropist who was active in various peace, population control, and political reform organizations.

MOTT, JOHN RALEIGH (1865–1955), U.S., religious leader and social worker. A Methodist layman, Mott organized Christian youth and student organizations throughout the world and was a pioneer in the ecumenical movement. He presided over the World Missionary Conference (1910) and chaired its World Missionary Council (1921–42), which joined other groups to form the World Council of Churches in 1948. He chaired the executive committee of the Student Volunteer Movement for Foreign Missions (1888–1920), was general secretary of the Young Men's Christian Association (YMCA; 1915–31), and was president of the World Alliance of YMCAs (1926–37). He shared the 1946 Nobel Peace Prize with Emily Balch. ■ See biographies by Galen Fisher (1952) and Charles H. Hopkins (1979), and Robert C. Mackie, *Layman Extraordinary* (1965).

MOTT, SIR NEVILL FRANCIS (1905–1996), British physicist. Mott's parents were both physicists associated with the Cavendish Laboratory at Cambridge. He undertook research at the same institution in 1927, soon after the formulation of quantum mechanics by Werner Heisenberg and Erwin Schrödinger, and was a professor there from 1953 to 1971. His reputation was founded largely on his application of quantum mechanics to the elucidation of various physical phenomena, including the scattering of alpha particles by an atomic nucleus; he collaborated with H.S.W. Massey on *The Theory of Atomic Collisions* (1934). His later writings set forth *The Theory of the Properties of Metals and Alloys* (1936), a theory of semiconductors, the characteristics and application of wave mechanics, and the relationship between atomic structure and the strength of metals. Mott shared the 1977 Nobel Prize for Physics with John H. Van Vleck and Philip W. Anderson. The research of the three scientists provided a foundation for such developments in electronics as the laser, tape recorders, copying machines, and high-speed computers.

MOTTELSON, BEN ROY (1926–), U.S.-born Danish physicist. Mottelson obtained a Ph.D. in theoretical physics from Harvard University (1950), then worked in Copenhagen at the Bohr Institute and the Nordic Institute for Theoretical Atomic Physics (1957–94). He became a naturalized Danish citizen (1973). The articulate physicist worked closely with Aage Bohr in investigating the atom's internal structure; he advanced influential theories about distortion in atomic nuclei. With Bohr he wrote *Collective and Individual-Particle Aspects of Nuclear Structure* (1953) and *Nuclear Structure* (3 vols., 1969–80). Mottelson shared the 1975 Nobel Prize for Physics with Bohr and James Rainwater. He subsequently directed the European Center for Theoretical Studies in Nuclear Physics and Related Areas in Trento, Italy (1993–).

MOULIN, JEAN (1899–1943), French Resistance leader. A prefect in the French civil service, Moulin joined the World War II Resistance shortly after the German Invasion (1940) and fled to London to join General Charles de Gaulle. Parachuted back to France (1942) as "Max," he became a legendary figure who played the leading role in organizing and coordinating the French guerrillas who fought the Nazis. In May 1943 he was chosen the first president of the National Council of the Resistance, but shortly thereafter he was captured, tortured, and murdered by the Gestapo.

MOULTON, FOREST RAY (1872–1952), U.S. astronomer. While a professor at the University of Chicago (1896–1926), Moulton investigated the origin of the earth. Collaborating with geologist Thomas Chamberlin, he refuted the earlier French astronomer Laplace's nebular hypothesis, and by 1904 he had developed a new theory of the origin of the solar system called the planetesimal hypothesis. Moulton and Chamberlin postulated that the earth was created when the sun encountered a passing star, causing the ejection of molten material from the sun. The materials that remained within the sun's gravitational pull were drawn into orbit and became planets. Moulton also did important ballistics research during World War I, was a pioneer in educational broadcasting, and wrote extensively on scientific topics for both the specialist and layperson.

MOUNIER, EMMANUEL (1905–1950), French philosopher. The founder and director of the Catholic monthly review *Esprit* (1932), Mounier attracted a small but dedicated following to his "personalist" beliefs, a Christian philosophy related to existentialism. Traveling and lecturing widely on spiritual renewal and the evils of capitalism, he exhorted his followers to "change the heart of your heart." Mounier's movement was suppressed by the collaborationist Vichy regime during World War II, and he was arrested, but he survived to write *Existentialist Philosophies* (1946; Eng. trans. 1948), *The Character of Man* (1946; Eng. trans. 1958), and *Personalism* (1949; Eng. trans. 1970). ■ See study by Eileen Cantin (1973); Michael Kelly, *Pioneer of the Catholic Revival* (1979); and John Hellman, *Emmanuel Mounier and the New Catholic Left* (1981).

MOUNTBATTEN OF BURMA, LOUIS MOUNTBATTEN, 1st EARL (1900–1979), British admiral. Mountbatten, a greatgrandson of Queen Victoria and cousin of Queen Elizabeth II, became a naval cadet at age 13 and entered the Royal Navy in 1916. A vain, yet inspiring officer, he served during World War II as chief of combined operations (1942–43). As Allied commander in Southeast Asia (1943–46) he directed the recapture of Burma. While serving as the last viceroy of India (1947), he negotiated the transition from colony to independence, for which he was held by many to be a traitor to his class and party. He later served as first sea lord of the Admiralty (1955–59) and chief of the defense staff (1959–65). Mountbatten was killed by a bomb planted by Irish terrorists. ■ See biographies by John Terraine (1968), Richard Hough (1981), Philip Ziegler (1985), and Brian Hoey (1994), and Ian McGeoch, *The Princely Sailor* (1996).

MOUSKOURI, NANA (1934–), Greek singer. Mouskouri studied classical music at the Athens Conservatory of Music (1951–59) before pursuing a career as a popular singer. She achieved fame by winning the first Greek Song Festival contest and by performing songs written especially for her by composer Manos Hadjidakis. She moved to Paris (1962) and by the early 1960s her shimmering soprano voice was heard all over Europe singing both folk and pop songs. She remained a star for four decades, touring the world and recording more than 1,000 songs in 10 languages. By the late 1990s she had sold more than 800 million records, including more than 300 gold or platinum ones, making her the world's best-selling female artist of all time. Her biggest hits included "The White Rose of Athens" (1962), "Guantanamera" (1967), and "Only Love" (1986). She also served as a goodwill ambassador for UNICEF and

as an elected Greek deputy to the European Parliament (1944–99).

MOYNIHAN, DANIEL PATRICK (1927–), U.S. social scientist, diplomat, and political leader. An Irish-American who grew up in the slums of New York City, Moynihan worked as a longshoreman and bartender in his youth. He studied at Tufts University (B.A. 1948; Ph.D. 1961) with a year at the London School of Economics on a Fulbright fellowship (1950–51). Joining the U.S Department of Labor (1961), he helped draft antipoverty legislation and wrote a controversial report on the instability of the black family (*The Negro Family;* 1965). He was also coauthor of *Beyond the Melting Pot* (1963; with Nathan Glazer), a study of ethnicity in the United States. Moynihan directed the joint Harvard–Massachusetts Institute of Technology Center for Urban Studies before returning to Washington. D.C. (1968) as a presidential urban-affairs counselor. He later served as ambassador to India (1973–75) and ambassador to the United Nations, where he sharply criticized anti-American policies of Third World governments. As a four-term Democratic U.S. senator from New York (1977–2001) he initially supported neoconservative policies but emerged in the 1980s as a critic of Pres. Ronald Reagan's cuts in social programs, his nuclear weapons buildup, and his policies in Central America. His other books included *Maximum Feasible Misunderstanding* (1969) and *The Politics of a Guaranteed Income* (1973), two studies of government welfare policies; a volume of essays, *Counting Our Blessings* (1980); *Family and Nation* (1986); and *Secrecy: The American Experience* (1998). ■ See biography by Douglas Schoen (1979) and Godfrey Hodgson, *The Gentleman From New York* (2000).

MPHAHLELE, EZEKIEL or ES'KIA (1919–), South African writer. Mphahlele grew up in a large village and later in a squalid black slum area in Pretoria. He taught high school (1945–52) and contributed short stories to various magazines while continuing his higher education as an external student (M.A., University of South Africa, 1956), but he left South Africa (1957) as the pressures of apartheid became intolerable. In exile (1957–77) in Nigeria, France, Kenya, and the United States (Ph.D., University of Denver, 1968), he emerged as one of the most influential and versatile of modern African writers. His works included the celebrated autobiography *Down Second Avenue* (1959), the pioneering works of literary criticism *The African Image* (1962) and *Voices in the Whirlwind* (1972), the short-story collection *In Corner B and Other Stories* (1967), and the novels *The Wanderers* (1972) and *Chirundu* (1979). He returned to his homeland of Lebowa in South Africa (1977) and taught at Witwatersrand University (1979–88). His later works included *Afrika, My Music* (1984), *The Story of African Literature* (1986), and *Renewal Time* (1988). ■ See studies by Ursula A. Barnett (1976) and Ruth Obee (1998).

MQHAYI, SAMUEL EDWARD KRUNE (1875–1945), South African novelist, poet, and scholar. Born into a prominent Xhosa family, Mqhayi was imbued both with the Christianity of his teachers and the history and lore of his people. His novels, *The Case of Twins* (1914; Eng. trans. 1966) and *U-Don Jadu* (3 parts, 1929–35), were considered classics of the Xhosa language, and he spent years standardizing the Xhosa orthography and recording its grammar and syntax. Called "the father of Xhosa poetry," he was a master of the traditional praise poem, which he adapted to modern themes, and was considered the poet laureate of his people. He also wrote several important biographies and an autobiography. ■ See Patricia E. Scott, ed., *Mqhayi in Translation* (1976).

MUBARAK, (MOHAMED) HOSNI (1928–), Egyptian political leader. The son of an inspector of the Ministry of Justice, Mubarak graduated from the national Military Academy (1949) and trained as a pilot. He taught at the Air Force Academy (1952–59), received advanced training in the Soviet Union, and subsequently served as air force chief of staff (1969–72) and commander in chief (1972–75). His forces successfully attacked Israeli positions on the east bank of the Suez Canal during the 1973 Arab-Israeli War and Mubarak emerged as a war hero. As vice president (1975–81) he was a confidant of Pres. Anwar el-Sadat, and he became president after Sadat's assassination (1981). A moderate and pragmatist, he maintained close ties with the West and remained committed to the controversial 1979 peace treaty with Israel. The stability of his government was threatened in the 1980s and 1990s by the growing disparity between the rich and the poor, deteriorating economic conditions, and the growth of Islamic fundamentalism. He participated (1991) in the Persian Gulf War against Iraq and played a major role in arranging the 1993 accord between Israel and the Palestine Liberation Organization (PLO).

MUGABE, ROBERT GABRIEL (1924–), Zimbabwean political leader. The son of a laborer, Mugabe was a schoolteacher for eight years (in Southern Rhodesia, Northern Rhodesia, and Ghana) before joining the nationalist movement in 1960. A Marxist, he was a cofounder of the Zimbabwe African National Union (ZANU; 1963), but was arrested for "subversive speech" in 1964. During his 11 years in jail he earned university degrees in law, administration, and education. After his release he joined Joshua Nkomo as coleader of the Patriotic Front, which waged a long and successful guerrilla war against the white supremacist government of Ian Smith. Following a cease-fire, he won the British-supervised election (1980) by a wide margin to become the first prime minister of independent Zimbabwe. Mugabe's socialist policies resulted in improved economic conditions for the majority black population and he announced plans to establish a one-party socialist state gradually. In the 1985 election ZANU won 64 of the 80 seats reserved for blacks in the 100-seat national parliament. As

president (1987–) he presided over a weakening economy and in 1991 embraced capitalist policies. During the 1990s Mugabe's increasingly repressive government was weakened by corruption scandals and continuing economic hardships.

MUHAMMAD V (Sidi Muhammad Ben Youssef; 1911?–1961), king of Morocco (1957–61). Muhammad succeeded his father, Moulay Youssef, as sultan in 1927 and after World War II gave support to the Moroccan nationalist movement. Deposed and exiled (1953) by the French authorities, he returned (1955) to lead Morocco into independence in 1956 and the following year took the title of king. A reform-oriented, pro-Western monarch, he was succeeded by his son, Hassan II (1929–99).

MUHAMMAD ALI. *See ALI, MUHAMMAD.*

MUHAMMAD, ELIJAH (Robert Poole; 1897–1975), U.S. religious leader. The son of a Georgia sharecropper, Poole migrated north in 1923 to the auto assembly lines of Detroit. There he met (1930) an itinerant peddler, W. D. Fard, the founder of the Nation of Islam or Black Muslim movement, and became his disciple. Upon Fard's disappearance (1934) he changed his name to Muhammad and took over the movement, claiming to be Allah's divinely chosen messenger. Muhammad began advocating black nationalism, separatism, self-respect, and self-reliance. He was sentenced to prison for draft evasion during World War II (1942–46), but he never ceased preaching his stern, puritanical version of Islam for American blacks. By the 1970s his movement had a following of up to 250,000 with its own schools, businesses, mosques, and a weekly newspaper, *Muhammad Speaks*. ■ See Claude A. Clegg III, *An Original Man* (1997), and Karl Evanzz, *The Messenger* (1999).

MUHAMMAD REZA SHAH PAHLEVI. *See PAHLEVI, MUHAMMAD REZA SHAH.*

MUIR, EDWIN (1887–1959), Scottish writer. After a childhood in rural Scotland, Muir moved to Glasgow and then London (1919), where he was exposed to socialism, nihilism, and psychoanalysis. He and his wife lived on the Continent for many years, supporting themselves by translating from the German, including works of Franz Kafka, and contributing articles to the British press. Muir began writing philosophically oriented poetry at age 35 but did not achieve recognition until the publication of *The Voyage* (1946) and *Collected Poems* (1952). His poems depicted the evils and dislocations of modern society but affirmed a faith in the human spirit to endure and be regenerated. He also wrote an autobiography, *The Story and the Fable* (1940), as well as *Essays on Literature and Society* (1949). ■ See studies by P. H. Butter (1966), Allie C. Hixson (1977), and Elgin W. Mellown (1979).

MUJIBUR RAHMAN. *See RAHMAN, MUJIBUR.*

MULDOON, SIR ROBERT DAVID (1921–1992), New Zealand political leader. An infantryman in World War II, Muldoon joined an Auckland accounting firm in 1947. Elected to Parliament in 1960, on his third try, as a member of the conservative National party, he rose quickly to the posts of finance minister (1967–72) and deputy prime minister (1972), and gained a reputation as a fiscal conservative. In 1975 Muldoon ran a successful populist and chauvinist electoral campaign calling for the reduction of immigration, an end to "creeping socialism," and the passage of a drastic austerity budget. As prime minister and finance minister (1975–84), he emphasized New Zealand's close ties with the United States, proposed controversial internal security legislation, and pursued generally probusiness and antilabor policies that failed to solve the growing debt and unemployment crisis. ■ See his autobiography, *The Rise and Fall of a Young Turk* (1974), and Bob Jones, *Memories of Muldoon* (1997).

MULLER, HERMANN JOSEPH (1890–1967), U.S. biologist. A student of geneticist Thomas H. Morgan at Columbia University (Ph.D. 1916), Muller began genetics experiments in 1911 with fruit flies. He continued these experiments as professor at the University of Texas (1920–32) and in 1926 discovered that X rays cause genetic mutations. This discovery demonstrated that exposure to X rays could cause harmful mutations (i.e. cancer), enabled scientists to create mutations at will, and facilitated the mapping of chromosomes. Muller worked at the Institute of Genetics in Moscow (1933–37), taught at the University of Indiana (1945–64), and campaigned against atomic bomb tests. He was awarded the 1946 Nobel Prize for Physiology or Medicine. ■ See his selected papers in *Studies in Genetics* (1962) and biography by Elof Axel Carlson (1981).

MÜLLER, K. ALEX (1927–), Swiss physicist. Müller, a physics graduate of the Swiss Federal Institute of Technology (Ph.D. 1958), did research at the IBM Zurich Research Laboratory (from 1963), where he was a specialist in ceramic oxides. In a search for superconducting material, in which electrical resistance vanishes, Müller and IBM colleague J. Georg Bednorz discovered (1986) that an oxide of copper, lanthanum, and barium retained its superconductivity up to 35 Kelvins, or 12°C higher than the previous record. Their work, which stunned the scientific world and touched off a wave of new research, raised prospects for the production of ultraefficient power generators and transmitters, tiny supercomputers, and levitating high-speed trains. Müller and Bednorz shared the 1987 Nobel Prize in Physics for their achievement.

MÜLLER, PAUL HERMANN (1899–1965), Swiss chemist. Müller received a Ph.D. from the University of Basel (1925) and worked for the J. R. Geigy Co. (1925–65). In the 1930s, he undertook pesticide research for agriculture and began his search for a nonirritant, odorless, economical insecticide that would be lethal to insects on contact. He developed (1939) DDT (dichlorodiphenyltrichloroethane), which became widely used to prevent diseases carried by insects and to protect crops. During World War II, DDT was used by the Allies, for example, to stop a typhus epidemic in Naples. Müller won the 1948 Nobel Prize for Physiology or Medicine for his research. After more than 20 years of use it was determined that DDT is harmful to animal and human life, and its use was discontinued in the United States and several other countries.

MULLIKEN, ROBERT SANDERSON (1896–1986), U.S. physical chemist. Mulliken, who called himself a "middleman between experiment and theory," did most of his research at the University of Chicago, where he earned his Ph.D. (1921) and held appointments in the physics and chemistry departments (1928–61). During World War II he worked on the Plutonium Project, which was connected with the development of the atomic bomb. He won the 1966 Nobel Prize for Chemistry for his application of the principles of quantum mechanics, the branch of mathematical physics that describes the motion of subatomic particles, to chemical bonding. He worked on the structure of polyatomic molecules and conceptualized molecular orbitals as electrons of constituent atoms that bond chemically with other electrons and become associated with the molecule as a whole. He described the shape of these orbitals and applied group theory to describe the electronic states of molecules. ■ See his autobiography, *Life of a Scientist* (1989).

MULLIN, WILLARD (1902–1978), U.S. cartoonist. Mullin's sports cartoons appeared in the *New York World Telegram* six days a week from 1934 to 1966. He was best known for creating the "Brooklyn Bum," a bearded cigar-smoking tramp who became the symbol of the Brooklyn Dodgers baseball team. In 1971 he was named "the sports cartoonist of the century" by the National Cartoonist Society.

MULLIS, KARY B. (1944–), American biochemist. Mullis believed that the best science doesn't come from hard work but "from people on the fringes, being playful." While studying at the University of California at Berkeley (Ph.D. 1973) he became part of the counterculture and taught a course on the neurochemistry of hallucinogens. As a researcher at the Cetus Corporation in Emeryville, California (1979–86), Mullis invented (1983) the polymerase chain reaction (PCR), a simple technique for cheaply producing billions of copies of a discrete fragment of DNA in a few hours. The technique revolutionized research in molecular biology and was immediately adapted by scientists in such diverse fields as forensic medicine, paleontology, genetic screening, and AIDS research. For his invention, Mullis shared the 1993 Nobel Prize for Chemistry with Michael Smith. Cetus, which paid Mullis a $10,000 bonus for his invention, sold the rights to part of it for $300 million (1991). Mullis subsequently worked as a freelance consultant and interspersed periods of genetic research with surfing, skiing, and in-line skating. ■ See his autobiography, *Dancing Naked in the Mind Field* (1998).

MULRONEY, (MARTIN) BRIAN (1939–   ), Canadian political leader. The son of an electrician, Mulroney was born in Quebec province and became active in Progressive Conservative party politics while a student at St. Francis Xavier University in Nova Scotia. After receiving a law degree from Laval University in Quebec City, he became a corporate lawyer in Montreal (1962) and gradually began to build a political base. After losing an election for party leader (1976), he became president of the Iron Ore Co. of Canada (1977). A handsome and dynamic figure, he was elected party leader in 1983 and became prime minister after leading the party to the largest political majority in Canadian history in the 1984 elections. (The Progressive Conservatives won 211 of the 282 seats in the House of Commons, including 58 of the 75 seats from Quebec.) During Mulroney's tenure, the economy grew, but unemployment hovered at 10 percent, the debt reached unprecedented levels, and the Canadian dollar reached its lowest value ever. He signed a free-trade agreement with the United States (1988) and the North American Free Trade Agreement (NAFTA; 1992), which extended the pact to include Mexico. He lost popularity by sponsoring a controversial federal sales tax (1991), and he failed in his attempts to have the Canadian Constitution amended to recognize Quebec as a distinct society (1992). He resigned in 1993. ■ See biography by L. I. MacDonald (1984).

MUMFORD, LEWIS (1895–1990), U.S. social critic and teacher. Mumford was associated with Stanford (1942–44), the University of Pennsylvania (1951–59), the Massachusetts Institute of Technology (1957–60), and Wesleyan University (1963–64). Known particularly for his works on architecture and town planning, he was most concerned with the dehumanization of the individual in response to a deadening environment. His writings reflected his faith in the human capacity to renew the world. Mumford's essays focused on various aspects of social thought, including psychology, literature, and architecture. His more important works included a tetralogy. *Renewal of Life—Technics and Civilization* (1934), *The Culture of Cities* (1938), *The Condition of Man* (1944), and *The Conduct of Life* (1951). *The City in History* (1961) was a study reflecting the problems of urban development, and *The Myth of the Machine* (2 vols., 1967–70) was a warning against the dangers of technology and overmechanization. ■ See the autobiographical *My Works and Days* (1979) and *Sketches from Life* (1982) and biography by Donald L. Miller (1989).

MÜNCH, CHARLES (1891–1968), French-born conductor. The son of an Alsatian choral conductor, Münch studied violin in Paris and conducting in Leipzig with Wilhelm Furtwängler. He was celebrated in Paris during the 1930s for his dynamism, grace, charm, and the precise Germanic style in which he conducted modern French music. He later became conductor of the Boston Symphony Orchestra (1949–62). ■ See his autobiography, *I Am a Conductor* (1954; Eng. trans. 1955).

MUNCH, EDVARD (1863–1944), Norwegian painter and graphic artist. A sickly child confronted with the deaths of loved ones, Munch developed a sensitivity and anxiety that pervaded his art. Adapting impressionist technique to his own emotional expression, he created paintings and graphics in which the somber colors and distorted bodies and faces communicated a sense of isolation and longing. Munch selected his colors for their symbolic value—red for passion, green for jealousy—and his range of colors brightened after treatment for nervous depression in 1908. The paintings of peasants and working people he produced in his later years were calmer and less agonized than his earlier works. Munch experimented in graphic techniques, and he was an eloquent portraitist. His work influenced the development of German expressionism. ■ See studies by J. P. Hodin (1972), Ian Dunlop (1977), Ragna Stang (Eng. trans. 1979), Elizabeth Prelinger (1983), and Reinhold Heller (1984).

MUNDELEIN, GEORGE WILLIAM (1872–1939), U.S. Roman Catholic cardinal. A New Yorker who studied at the Urban College of the Propagation of the Faith in Rome, earning a divinity degree in 1895, Mundelein was a popular archbishop of Chicago (1915–39). He was elevated to cardinal in 1924. He raised funds to build churches, schools. and hospitals, organized such charitable activities as a Catholic "Big Brothers" group, and during the Depression of the 1930s supported New Deal programs, and supplemented them with church relief programs. The town of Mundelein, Illinois, where he hosted a 1921 Eucharistic Congress, was named after him. Mundelein wrote *Two Crowded Years* (1918) and *Letters of a Bishop to His Flock* (1927). ■ See Paul R. Martin, *The First Cardinal of the West* (1934).

MUNDELL, ROBERT (1932–   ), Canadian-born economist. Mundell studied at the University of British Columbia, the London School of Economics, and at the Massachusetts Institute of Technology (Ph.D. 1956). He did research at the International Monetary Fund (1961–63) and taught at the University of Chicago (1966–71) and Columbia University (1974–   ). His pioneering studies, begun in the early 1960s, analyzed the effects of floating exchange rates and high capital mobility on a government's monetary and fiscal policies. His research on the advantages of a regional common currency contributed to the creation of the euro as the common currency of Europe. His advocacy of large tax cuts to stimulate economic expansion influenced the growth of supply-side economics in the United States and the conservative economic policies of President Ronald Reagan. His books included *International Economics* (1968) and *Macropolicies* *in the World Economy and the New Capitalist Revolution* (1985). He was awarded the 1999 Nobel Memorial Prize in Economics.

MUNI, PAUL (Muni Weisenfreund; 1895–1967), U.S. actor. Muni's actor parents emigrated (1902) to the United States from Austria when he was 7. He acted at New York's Yiddish Art Theater as a boy and through his twenties, then debuted in an English-speaking role as Morris Levine in *We Americans* (1926). In the next three decades he created memorable characters on the New York stage in such dramas as *Counsellor-at-Law* (1931) and *Death of a Salesman* (1949); he played Clarence Darrow in *Inherit the Wind* (1955). Muni gave cerebral performances in motion pictures, particularly at the height of his film career in the 1930s when he convincingly portrayed markedly different character types, showing his great emotional range. He portrayed a gangster based on Al Capone in *Scarface* (1931) and won an Academy Award for his lead role in *The Story of Louis Pasteur* (1936). ■ See biography by Michael B. Druxman (1974) and Jerome Lawrence, *Actor* (1974).

MUNK, KAJ (1898–1944), Danish playwright. Munk studied theology and was a village parson. Influenced by Shakespeare and Ibsen, he wrote strong religious dramas, including *Ordet* (1932; Eng. trans. 1953), noted for their passionate poetic quality, and he was regarded as Denmark's leading dramatist. Among his plays were *Herod the King* (1928; Eng. trans. 1953), *The Word* (1932; Eng. trans. 1953), and *He Sits by the Melting-Pot* (1938; Eng. trans. 1953), which attacked the persecution of the Jews. Though he once briefly admired fascism, he became an outspoken foe of Nazi Germany and its terror both in his plays and sermons. For his defiant resistance, he was murdered by the Gestapo during World War II. English translations of his work are in *Five Plays by Kaj Munk* (1953).

MUNKACSI, MARTIN (1896–1963), Transylvanian-born fashion photographer. A self-taught photographer, Munkacsi worked for magazines in Budapest and Berlin (1921–34) before impressing *Harper's Bazaar*'s fashion editor Carmel Snow with his candid fashion shots. He moved to New York (1934) and worked for *Harper's Bazaar* (1934–40) and *Ladies Home Journal* (1940–46). He introduced realism into fashion photography and established it as an art form with his dramatic angles, spontaneous poses, and action photos. His work altered the look of fashion magazines and he was one of the highest-paid photographers in the world. ■ See his semiautobiographical novel, *Fool's Apprentice* (1945), and picture books, *How America Lives* (1941) and *Nudes* (1951). Photographs and background information are in Nancy White and John Esten, *Style in Motion* (1979).

MUÑOZ MARÍN, (JOSÉ) LUIS ALBERTO (1898–1980), Puerto Rican political leader. Son of publisher and patriot Lujs Muñoz Rivera, Muñoz Marín was a socialist who sup-

ported Puerto Rican independence during his years as a poet and journalist in New York City during the early 1920s. Returning to Puerto Rico (1926), he edited his father's newspaper, *La Democracia,* joined the Liberal party, won election to the senate, and became a popular political leader. He founded the Popular Democratic Party (1938), renounced his earlier views, and advocated social and economic progress under U.S. guidance. As Puerto Rico's first freely elected governor (1948–64), he advocated commonwealth status for the island (1952) and was an architect of Operation Bootstrap, and economic-development program whereby the government aided private enterprise. ■ See Thomas Aitken, *Poet in the Fortress* (1964).

MUÑOZ RIVERA, LUIS (1859–1916), Puerto Rican political leader. A leader of the struggle for Puerto Rican independence from Spain, Muñoz Rivera founded the newspaper *La Democracia* (1889), obtained a home-rule charter from Spain (1897), and headed the island's first home-rule cabinet (1898). He resigned after U.S. military rule was installed (1899) and soon thereafter left for the United States, where he staunchly advocated Puerto Rican self-government. He served as Puerto Rico's resident commissioner in Washington, D.C. (1910–16), and supported the Jones bill (1916), which granted Puerto Ricans a measure of self-government and U.S. citizenship. His son, Luis Muñoz Marín, served as governor of Puerto Rico (1948–64). ■ See Marianna Norris, *Father and Son for Freedom* (1968).

MUNRO, HECTOR HUGH (pseud.: Saki; 1870–1916), Scottish writer. H. H. Munro was born in Burma, where his father was a police inspector. He began his literary career with political sketches and short stories for the Westminster *Gazette,* completed a serious but unenthusiastically received study on Russian history, and served as foreign correspondent for the conservative *Morning Post* (1902–08). He is best remembered, however, for the inventive, satirical short stories about Edwardian life assembled in such collections as *Reginald* (1904), *The Chronicles of Clovis* (1912), and *Beasts and Super-Beasts* (1914). In his mid-forties, he enlisted for service in World War I and was killed in action. ■ The biography by A. J. Langguth (1981) includes stories not previously collected.

MUNSEY, FRANK ANDREW (1854–1925), U.S publisher. Munsey managed a Maine Western Union Telegraph office before becoming editor and publisher of a New York–based juvenile weekly magazine, *Golden Argosy* (1882). A pioneer in mass-production publishing techniques, he subsequently created numerous weekly pulp magazines, including *Argosy, All-Story,* and *Munsey's* magazine, which led the country in circulation. He also established an independent magazine distribution company, effectively breaking the American News Co.'s monopoly. Munsey believed that weak and unprofitable newspapers should be consolidated with viable ones, and between 1891 an 1924, he purchased and merged many floundering newspapers including New York's *Sun, Telegram, Daily News,* and *Herald,* as well as papers in Baltimore, Boston, and Philadelphia. ■ See George Britt, *Forty Years—Forty Millions* (1935).

MUNSHI, KANAIYALAL MANEKLAL (1887–1971), Indian writer and political leader. A graduate of Bombay University (B.A. 1906; LL.B. 1910). K. M. Munshi worked for Indian independence as a journalist, editor, and government official. He was a noted novelist and playwright in his native Gujarati, and he wrote several works in English, including *Gujarat and Its Literature* (1935), *I Follow the Mahatma* (1940), and *The End of an Era: Hyderabad Memories* (1957). He was also a founder (1938) and president of the Bharatiya Vidva Bhavan, the largest educational and cultural organization in India. He was a member of the committee that drafted the Indian constitution (1946–47), and after independence he served as the central government's food and agriculture minister (1950–52) and governor of the state of Uttar Pradesh (1953–58).

MÜNZENBERG, WILLI (1889–1940), German political leader. A socialist youth leader in Germany and Switzerland before and during World War I, Münzenberg was a founding member of the German Communist party (1918) and served as head of the Communist Youth International (1919–21). In 1921 he began his long career as an organizer and propagandist for Comintern front causes and organizations including the Workers' International Relief (1921), the League Against Imperialism (1927), the campaign in favor of Georgi Dimitrov, the Relief Committee for the Victims of Fascism, and, during the Spanish Civil War, the Committee for the Aid of the Spanish People. In Paris after 1933, he published numerous books and articles attacking German dictator Adolf Hitler and the Nazi party. He died in an internment camp in France in June 1940. ■ See biography by Babette Gross (Eng. trans. 1974) and Stephen Koch, *Double Lives* (1994).

MURAD, FERID (1936–), U.S. pharmacologist. Murad studied at Western Reserve University (Ph.D. 1965) and taught at the University of Virginia (1970–81), Stanford University (1981–89), and the University of Texas Medical School in Houston (1997–). He also was a vice president of Abbott Laboratories (1988–92) and president and CEO of Molecular Geriatrics Corp. (1993–95). After a series of studies in the late 1970s, Murad concluded that nitroglycerin and other related molecules caused blood vessels to dilate and relax by inducing the formation of nitric oxide (NO). Initially scientists doubted that a gas could act as a signal mechanism in the body to increase blood flow, but independent experiments by Robert F. Furchgott and Louis J. Ignarro during the 1980s proved that the short-lived NO was indeed the signaling agent. Subsequent research showed that nitric oxide plays a major role in immunity, blood pressure control, and tumor suppression, and led to the use of

Viagra as an anti-impotence drug. For their research, Murad, Furchgott, and Ignarro shared the 1998 Nobel Prize for Physiology or Medicine.

MURCHISON, CLINTON WILLIAMS (1895–1969), U.S. oilman and entrepreneur. The son of a bank president from Athens, Texas—a town of 5,000 that produced more than 50 millionaires—Murchison made a fortune during the 1920s exploiting Texas oil and natural gas. A wheeler-dealer with a Midas touch, he expanded his interests into railroads, life-insurance and investment companies, publishing, racetracks, real estate, candy manufacturing, sporting goods, bus companies, and cattle ranches and simultaneously controlled more than 115 companies with assets of approximately $600 million. He was a rightwing Democrat who opposed Presidents Franklin D. Roosevelt and Harry Truman. ■ See Jane Wolfe, *The Murchisons* (1989).

MURDOCH, (JEAN) IRIS (1919–1999), British novelist. Murdoch taught philosophy at Oxford (1948–63) and wrote a study of Jean Paul Sartre's existentialism (1953). A prolific writer, she produced nearly a novel a year for decades, as well as plays, poetry, and philosophical studies. Characterized by brilliant narration, intricate plots, and large casts of distinctive characters, her fiction explored the boundaries of human freedom and the relationship between art and morality. They often portrayed people struggling to see life as it really is, often in the context of complex configurations of love. Her novels included *Under the Net* (1953), *A Severed Head* (1961), *The Black Prince* (1973), *The Sacred and Profane Love Machine* (1978), *Nuns and Soldiers* (1980), *The Philosopher's Pupil* (1983), *The Good Apprentice* (1985), *The Message to the Planet* (1989), *The Green Knight* (1993), and *Jackson's Dilemma* (1995). Her struggle with Alzheimer's disease was described in *Elegy for Iris* (1998), a memoir by her husband, the novelist and critic John Bayley. ■ See studies by Elizabeth Dipple (1981), Angela Hague (1983), and Peter J. Conradi (1985).

MURDOCH, (KEITH) RUPERT (1931–), Australian-born newspaper publisher. The Oxford-educated Murdoch inherited a small newspaper in Adelaide from his father (1952) and used lurid, screaming headlines and sensationalistic sex and murder stories to boost circulation dramatically. He subsequently purchased newspapers in Perth and Sydney as well as several magazines and televison stations, and by 1968 his properties were worth an estimated $50 million. Seeking influence and riches overseas, he purchased London's *News of the World* and *Sun* in 1969 and the *Times* and *Sunday Times* in 1981. In the United States he bought the *New York Post, Chicago Sun-Times, Boston Herald,* and *New York* magazine. By the mid-1980s he had purchased 20th Century Fox film studios, 14 magazines from Ziff-Davis, and six television stations owned by Metromedia, thus controlling one of the world's largest communications empires. During the 1990s he founded the Fox television network and purchased satellite broadcasting companies in the United States, Asia, Europe, and Latin America. His holding company, The News Corporation, had revenues of $14 billion for the fiscal year ending in June 2000. His political views became more conservative over the years, and he pursued tough union-busting tactics in dealing with his employees. He became a U.S. citizen in 1985. ■ See studies by Simon Regan (1976) and William Shawcross (1997).

MURNAU, FRIEDRICH WILHELM (Friedrich Wilhelm Plumpe; 1888–1931), German film director. After completing studies in art history at Heidelberg, F. W. Murnau began directing propaganda films for the German government during World War I. His first important feature, the early vampire film *Nosferatu* (1922), won widespread critical attention, as did *The Last Laugh* (1924) and *Faust* (1926), for their sensitive and poetic interpretation of nature and human emotion. Murnau and his cameraman, Karl Freund, experimented with distorting lenses and, most importantly, with the moving camera. In 1927 he made *Sunrise* in Hollywood (scripted in Germany by Carl Mayer). His last film, *Tabu* (1931), was made in the South Seas with documentarist Robert Flaherty. Murnau died in an auto accident soon afterward in Hollywood. ■ See biography by Lotte H. Eisner (Eng. trans. rev. 1973).

MURPHY, AUDIE (1924–1971), U.S. soldier and movie actor. A sharecropper's son, Murphy lied about his age and joined the army in June 1942. He served in Europe and North Africa to become the most-decorated American soldier of World War II. He was awarded the Congressional Medal of Honor (for heroism displayed in battle against the Germans on Jan. 26, 1945) as well as 27 other medals, including the Distinguished Service Cross and the Croix de Guerre (with palm). After the war he appeared in about 40 movies, including the film version of his autobiography, *To Hell and Back* (1955). ■ See biography by Harold B. Simpson (1975) and Charles Whiting, *Hero* (1990).

MURPHY, CHARLES FRANCIS (1858–1924), U.S. political boss. A saloon operator and neighborhood notable in New York City's East Side tenement district, Murphy was the boss of Tammany Hall, the New York County Democratic party (1902–24). Wielding enormous political power in the city and state, his efficient machine secured the election of three mayors and three governors, and he helped guide the careers of Alfred E. Smith and Robert F. Wagner, Sr. In tune with the needs and desires of his constituents, he was called the ablest leader in the history of Tammany Hall. ■ See biography by Nancy J. Weiss (1968).

MURPHY, FRANK (1890–1949), U.S. public official and jurist. A lifelong defender of the oppressed, Murphy was a judge who was elected mayor of Detroit (1930) and won national attention for his relief programs. He was a strong supporter of the New Deal, and Pres. Franklin D. Roosevelt appointed him governor general (1933–35) and high commissioner (1935–36) of the Philippines. He was governor of Michigan (1936–38) and then served briefly as U.S. attorney general (1939–40), when he actively pursued antitrust and political-corruption cases and established the first civil-liberties unit in the Department of Justice. Murphy was named to the Supreme Court in 1940 and joined the liberal bloc in upholding civil liberties, supporting the rights of racial and religious minorities, and defending the rights of labor. He vigorously dissented (*Korematsu* v. *United States,* 1944) from the court's decision upholding the government's right to intern Japanese-Americans during World War II. ■ See J. Woodford Howard, Jr., *Mr. Justice Murphy* (1968), and study by Sidney Fine (1979).

MURPHY, ROBERT DANIEL (1894–1978), U.S. diplomat. The son of a railroad worker, Murphy graduated from George Washington University Law School (1920) and began a foreign-service career that was to last four decades (1921–59) and take him to the top levels of the state department. Best remembered for his part in planning the Allied invasion of North Africa during World War II, Murphy played key diplomatic roles as a negotiator of the Italian armistice (1943) and as political adviser to the U.S. military government in Germany (1944–49), and he served as ambassador to Belgium (1949–52) and Japan (1952–53). During Pres. Dwight Eisenhower's administration, Murphy, a conservative, was under secretary of state for political affairs (1953–59). A key government troubleshooter, he was an adviser to Secretary of State John Foster Dulles during the height of the cold war. ■ See his memoirs, *Diplomat Among Warriors* (1964).

MURPHY, WILLIAM PARRY (1892–1987), U.S. physician. A faculty member at the Harvard Medical School (1923–58), Murphy was noted for his success in treating pernicious anemia, a previously fatal disease, with a liver diet. The success of Murphy and his collaborator George R. Minot eventually led to vitamin B_{12} therapy, developed in 1948. Murphy and Minot shared the 1934 Nobel Prize for Physiology or Medicine with George H. Whipple.

MURRAY, ARTHUR (Arthur Murray Teichman; 1895–1991), U.S. dance instructor. Murray grew up in New York City's Lower East Side. Shy and awkward as a teenager, he was determined to go to school socials, but didn't know how to dance. After a friend gave him a few pointers, he began attending local weddings to practice, won many dance contests, and worked as an instructor. In the 1920s he made his mark by selling footprint diagrams by mail order; within a few years he had sold a half million home dance courses. After marrying (1925) Kathryn (1906–1999), well known as his dance partner, the couple opened a dance school. Their fame reached its peak in the late 1930s when they spread the "Big Apple" and the "Lambeth Walk"—relatively obscure dances—onto dance floors across the nation. Eventually the

Arthur Murray Dance Studio became the world's largest dance-school chain. ■ See Kathryn Murray, *My Husband Arthur Murray* (1960).

MURRAY, (GEORGE) GILBERT (1866–1957), Australian-born British scholar. Murray was an outstanding classical scholar, a brilliant Oxford graduate and professor (1908–36) who translated the Greek plays into rhymed heroic couplets and revived them on the modern stage. Applying Hellenic ideals to contemporary affairs, he was also a pacifist and a leading supporter of the League of Nations and the United Nations. His books included *The Rise of the Greek Epic* (1907), *Liberality and Civilization* (1938), *From the League to the United Nations* (1947), and *Hellenism and the Modern World* (1953). ■ See his autobiography (1960) and biography by Francis West (1984).

MURRAY, JOSEPH E. (1919–   ), U.S. surgeon. Trained at Harvard Medical School (M.D. 1943), Murray served as chief plastic surgeon at Boston's Peter Bent Brigham Hospital (1964–86) and Children's Hospital Medical Center (1972–85). He first became interested in transplants, and the problem of transplant rejection by the recipients' immune systems, while performing skin-graft operations on soldiers during World War II. In 1947, he turned his attention to kidney failure, a fatal disorder at the time. After successfully experimenting with animals, he performed the first human kidney transplant (1954) by using a kidney of his patient's genetically identical twin brother. In 1962, utilizing newly developed immunosuppressive drugs, he performed the first successful transplant using a kidney from a donor unrelated to the recipient. The operation had an immediate worldwide impact and paved the way for effective transplantation of the heart, liver, and lungs. By the time Murray shared the 1990 Nobel Prize in Physiology or Medicine (with E. Donnall Thomas) more than 200,000 kidney transplants had been performed.

MURRAY, PHILIP (1886–1952), Scottish-born U.S. labor leader. The son of a coal miner active in the union movement, Murray worked in the mines in Pennsylvania from age 16. He was active within the ranks of the United Mine Workers of America and served as its international vice president (1920–42). He was a founder (1935), with John L. Lewis, of the Congress of Industrial Organizations (CIO) and succeeded Lewis as its president(1940–52). Murray also set up the Steelworkers Organizing Committee (1936) and became president of its successor, the United Steelworkers of America (1942). During the height of the cold war (1949–50) he led a purge of communists from the CIO.

MURROW, EDWARD ROSCOE (1908–1965), U.S. broadcast journalist. The most influential radio and television news commentator of his time, Edward R. Murrow achieved fame for CBS broadcasts during World War II de-

scribing, in his somber and authoritative manner, the German occupation of Austria (1938), the Nazi bombings of London, the Allied bombing of Berlin, and the liberation of Buchenwald concentration camp. After the war he pioneered in-depth television news reporting with his award-winning weekly program "See It Now" (1951–58). Renowned for his integrity and forceful personality, he produced a series of memorable news documentaries, including a celebrated exposé of Sen. Joseph R. McCarthy (1954) and "Harvest of Shame" (1960), an account of migratory farm workers in the United States. Murrow's "Person to Person" interview program was extremely popular during the 1950s. From 1961 to 1963 he headed the U.S. Information Agency. ■ See Alexander Kendrick, *Prime Time* (1969), and the biographies by A. M. Sperber (1986) and Joseph E. Persico (1988).

MURRY, JOHN MIDDLETON (1889–1957), British literary critic, journalist, and editor. A graduate of Oxford (1912), Murry was a close friend of many of the leading literary intellectuals of his day, including D. H. Lawrence, T. S. Eliot, and Virginia Woolf. He was founding editor of the literary magazine, *Adelphi* (1923–48) and wrote widely on religion, economics, psychology, and current affairs. After the death (1923) of his wife, the author Katherine Mansfield, at age 33, a mystical world view informed much of his writing. He wrote *The Necessity of Pacifism* (1937) and edited *Peace News* during World War II, but renounced his pacifism after the war. Among his best-known works were *The Problem of Style* (1922); *Keats and Shakespeare* (1925); *The Necessity of Communism* (1932); and studies of Lawrence (1931), William Blake (1933), Jonathan Swift (1935), and Mansfield (1949). ■ See his autobiography, *Between Two Worlds* (1935), and the biographies by Frank A. Lea (1959) and Ernest G. Griffin (1968).

MUSEVENI, YOWERI (1944–   ), Ugandan political leader. The son of a landowner and cattle rancher, Museveni studied economics and political science at the University of Dar es Salaam in Tanzania (B.A. 1970) and was influenced by the socialist policies of Tanzanian President Julius K. Nyerere. He returned home to work for the government of President Milton Obote, but after Idi Amin seized power (1971), Museveni fled to Tanzania and helped to organize a guerrilla movement as part of a Tanzanian-led military offensive that eventually ousted Amin (1979). He served as a cabinet minister in transitional governments and ran for president in December 1980. Defeated by Obote, he claimed fraud, retreated to the bush and raised a guerrilla army that ultimately defeated the government forces and overthrew Obote (1986). After declaring himself president (1986), Museveni created a government transcending tribal differences, banned political parties, restored law and order, and rooted out corruption. Economically, he renounced his socialist past and implemented free-market principles and privatized state-owned enterprises in an attempt to encourage private enterprise and create a middle class. Museveni also became a regional power broker, supporting rebel movements that seized power in Rwanda (1994) and the Congo (1997). He won the nonparty presidential elections in 1996.

MUSHANOKOJI, SANEATSU (1885–1976), Japanese novelist and playwright. Influenced by Christianity and by the writings of the Russian Leo Tolstoy and the Belgian Maurice Maeterlinck, Mushanokoji, the son of a viscount, rejected the gloomy naturalism in vogue during his student days at Tokyo University. He helped found the influential journal *White Birch* (1910) and became a popular writer noted for his idealism and optimistic humanism. His best-known works were *The Good-Natured Soul* (1911), *Friendship* (1919; Eng. trans. 1958), *The Passion* (1926; Eng. trans. 1933), *Dr. Truth* (1949), and *Three Cheers for Man* (1963; Eng. trans. 1963). Putting his ideas into practice, he started two Tolstoyan agricultural communities on which he lived for eight years.

MUSIAL, STAN (Stanley Frank Musial; 1920–), U.S. baseball player. Known as "Stan the Man," Musial switched from pitcher to outfielder while still in the minor leagues and, adopting a distinctive left-handed stance, became one of the game's greatest sluggers. An outfielder and first baseman for the St. Louis Cardinals (1941–63), he set several National League records, including games played (3,026), at bats (10,972), runs scored (1,949), hits (3,630), extra base hits (1,377), doubles (725), total bases (6,134), and runs batted in (1,951). Voted the league's Most Valuable Player three times (1943, 1946, 1948), Musial won seven batting championships and compiled a .331 career batting average with 475 home runs. Selected to 24 consecutive All-Star squads, he was elected to the National Baseball Hall of Fame in 1969. ■ See his autobiography (1965) and the biographies by Ray Robinson (1963) and Bob Broeg (new ed. 1977).

MUSICA, PHILIP (1877?–1938), Italian-born U.S. swindler. Emigrating to the United States in 1883, Musica led his family into a series of fraudulent business deals, notably one involving the U.S. Hair Co. (1912–13), for which he served nearly three years in a New York City jail. Under the alias of F. Donald Coster, he bought (1926) McKesson and Robbins, a pharmaceutical firm, and made huge profits by fraudulent bookkeeping—buying and selling imaginary drugs. When the elaborate scheme was revealed and his identity uncovered, Musica shot himself. ■ See Charles Keats, *Magnificent Masquerade* (1964).

MUSIL, ROBERT (1880–1942), Austrian novelist. Musil dropped out of military school, trained in engineering, and later earned a doctorate in philosophy and psychology (1908). He published the novel *Young Törless* (1906; Eng. trans. 1955), which reflected the influence of the French novelist Marcel Proust, and a volume of short fiction *Unions*

(1911; Eng. trans. 1965). Following service in World War I, Musil devoted himself to writing. His masterpiece, *The Man Without Qualities* (3 vols., 1930–42; Eng. trans. 1953–60), chronicles the life of a Viennese intellectual in 1913–14; it encompasses Musil's reflections on the sense of cultural disintegration and spiritual crisis treated by other writers of his day. Musil faced financial ruin due to inflation in the 1930s; he fled Berlin and Nazi-occupied Vienna and died in penury in Switzerland. His work was little read until the early 1950s, when critics reestablished his important place in modern fiction. ■ See biography by David S. Luft (1980) and study by Hannah Hickman (1984).

MUSSADEGH, MUHAMMAD (1880–1967), Iranian political leader. A member of Iran's ruling elite, Mussadegh was governor of Fars province, foreign minister (1922), and member of parliament during the 1920s. A longtime political opponent of Reza Khan, he retired when Khan became shah, and did not reemerge politically until he became the parliamentary leader of the militant National Front party (1944–53), which opposed foreign influence in Iran. His bill to nationalize the British-dominated oil industry was passed by parliament in 1951 and Mussadegh was named premier. With the withdrawal of British experts and the inability of the government to find alternative markets, the economy was pushed into a deep crisis. Mussadegh, a mercurial and highly emotional leader, was granted dictatorial powers (1952) and he attempted to carry out a social revolution. However, he lost the support of key sectors of the Iranian army and aristocracy and he was overthrown by Reza Khan's son and heir, Muhammad Reza Shah Pahlevi, with the assistance of the U.S. Cetral Intelligence Agency (CIA; 1953). He was imprisoned from 1953 to 1956 and lived the rest of his life under house arrest.

MUSSOLINI, BENITO (1883–1945), Italian political leader. The son of a socialist blacksmith, Mussolini was a Socialist party journalist and propagandist until expelled from the party for supporting World War I. Switching his political views from left to right, he created an organization of black-shirted nationalistic and anticommunist terrorists, the *Fasci di Combattimento* ("fighting leagues"; 1919). A powerful demagogic orator, he was elected to parliament (1921) as leader of the National Fascist party (1921) and asked to form a government (1922), both in response to the prevailing anarchic conditions in much of Italy and to his threat to seize power by force. As *il Duce* (the leader) he quickly established a fascist dictatorship, outlawed other political parties, and set up a corporate state with the support of big business, the military, and the church. His rule was characterized by political repression and extensive public works projects at home, and imperialistic expansion abroad, with invasions of Ethiopia (1936) and Albania (1939). Allied with Nazi Germany (from 1936) he entered World War II in 1940, but Italy was unprepared and his armies were defeated on all fronts. He was dismissed by King Victor Emmanuel III after the Allied invasion of Sicily (July 1943) and imprisoned. Rescued by the Germans in September, Mussolini headed a Nazi-supported government in northern Italy until the German collapse, after which he was captured and shot by partisans. ■ See biographies by Laura Fermi (1961), Ivone Kirkpatrick (1964), Denis Mack Smith (1982), and Jasper Ridley (1997), and Richard Collier, *Duce!* (1971).

MUSTE, ABRAHAM JOHANNES (1885–1967), Dutch-born U.S. pacifist and labor leader. Known as "the American Gandhi," A. J. Muste, an ordained minister, was a lifelong pacifist who was national chairman (1926–29) and executive secretary (1940–53) of the Fellowship of Reconciliation. He was a leader of numerous peace groups for more than 50 years. Influenced by the writings of Karl Marx, V. I. Lenin, and Leon Trotsky, he became a radical labor organizer during the 1930s and was the educational director of the Brookwood Labor College (1921–33), a major training ground for militant labor leaders. In his later years he worked for nuclear disarmament and an end to the Vietnam War. His books included *Nonviolence in an Aggressive World* (1940) and *Not by Might* (1947). ■ See Nat Hentoff, *Peace Agitator* (1963), and JoAnn O. Robinson, *Abraham Went Out* (1981).

MUTESA II (1924–1969), king of Buganda. The last kabaka, or king, of Buganda (now in Uganda), he succeeded to the throne in 1939. An opponent of British colonial policy that would create a unitary Ugandan state in which Buganda's power would be diminished, he boycotted the 1960 elections, but in 1961 he allied himself and his party with Milton Obote's Uganda Peoples' party in return for a promise of Bugandan autonomy. After the political coalition won the 1962 elections and Uganda received its independence (1962), Mutesa II was appointed to the largely ceremonial position of president (1963). However, as prime minister (later president) Obote became more powerful; he reduced Bugandan freedom and in 1966 suspended the constitution, abolished the federal status of Buganda, and forced its king into exile, where Mutesa II wrote his autobiography, *Desecration of My Kingdom* (1967).

MUZOREWA, ABEL TENDEKAYI (1925–), Rhodesian-Zimbabwean political leader. Born at a Methodist mission station and educated in the United States (1958–63), Muzorewa was the first black African bishop of the United Methodist Church (1968–92). As head of the umbrella African national council (1971–85), he quickly became involved in nationalist Rhodesian politics, but split with more militant nationalists Robert Mugabe and Joshua Nkomo, who established the Patriotic Front (1976) to fight a guerrilla war against the white government of Ian Smith. In 1979 he became Rhodesia-Zimbabwe's first black prime minister at the head of a transitional cabinet under a constitution that guaranteed considerable power to the white minority. In a British-supervised election in February 1980, he was

overwhelmingly defeated by Robert Mugabe, who became prime minister of an independent Zimbabwe. He remained in parliament until 1985, when he retired from politics. However, he subsequently returned as president of the United Parties (1994–98). ■ See his autobiography, *Rise Up and Walk* (1978).

MYDANS, CARL (1907–), **and SHELLY SMITH MYDANS** (1915–), U.S photojournalists. Born in Boston, where he earned a journalism degree (1930), Carl Mydans worked for Roy Stryker at the Farm Security Administration (1935), for which he documented rural poverty during the Depression. He served on the staff of *Life* magazine (1936–72), covering major news events in the United States, Europe, and Asia. Shelly Smith, the daughter of a Stanford journalism professor, was a researcher for *Life* who collaborated with Mydans after their marriage (1938). They were assigned to Europe in 1939 and in 1940 to the Far East, where they were interned by the Japanese for 22 months, the subject of Shelly Mydans' novel, *The Open City* (1945). A later collaboration was *The Violent Peace* (1968), an account of continuing postwar conflicts. Shelly Mydans later wrote the historical novels *Thomas* (1965) and *Vermilion Bridge* (1980). ■ Carl Mydans' *More Than Meets the Eye* (1959) recounted his experiences as a *Life* photographer. See also his *Carl Mydans: Photo-Journalist* (1985).

MYRDAL, ALVA (Alva Reimer; 1902–1986), Swedish sociologist, diplomat, and writer. An advocate of women's rights and population control, Myrdal was a teacher and college director before heading the United Nations department of social welfare (1949–50) and directing the department of social sciences of the UN's Educational, Scientific, and Cultural Organization (UNESCO; 1950–56). She was Sweden's ambassador to India (1956–61) and served in the Swedish parliament (1962–70). As her country's delegate to the U.N. Disarmament Conference in Geneva (1962–73) and minister for disarmament and church affairs (1966–73), she emerged as a major voice in the international movement for nuclear disarmament; her angry book, *The Game of Disarmament: How the United States and Russia Run the Arms Race* (1977; rev. ed. 1982), denounced both superpowers and was widely read throughout the world. Myrdal shared the 1982 Nobel Peace Prize with Alfonso García Robles. She was married to Nobel Prize–winning economist Gunnar Myrdal. ■ See study by Sissela Bok (1991).

MYRDAL, (KARL) GUNNAR (1898–1987), Swedish social scientist. Myrdal earned both a law degree (1923) and a doctorate in economics (1927) before serving on the economics faculty of the University of Stockholm (1927–50; 1960–67). With his wife Alva, a sociologist, he wrote an analysis of Sweden's declining birthrate (1934) that had an important influence on Scandinavian social planning. After preparing his classic work on race relations in the United States, *An American Dilemma* (1944), for the Carnegie

Corp., Myrdal served as Sweden's minister of trade and commerce (1945–47) and was executive secretary of the U.N. Economic Commission for Europe (1947–57). Later works included *Beyond the Welfare State* (1960), *Challenge of Affluence* (1963), and *Asian Drama* (3 vols. 1968), a massive, interdisciplinary study of poverty and economic development. See also his *Against the Stream: Critical Essays on Economics* (1973). He shared the 1974 Nobel Memorial Prize in Economics (with Friedrich von Hayek). His wife subsequently shared the 1982 Nobel Peace Prize.

N

NABOKOV, VLADIMIR (Vladimir Sirin; 1899–1977), Russian-born U.S. writer, translator, and critic. Nabokov was trilingual from childhood and read English before Russian or French. His aristocratic St. Petersburg family fled to Britain (1919) after the bolsheviks took power in Russia. He earned a Cambridge degree (1922), then settled in Berlin (1922–37), where he wrote, taught tennis, and composed the first Russian crossword puzzles. He moved to Paris, then to the United States (1940), where he taught at Cornell and other universities and distinguished himself as a lepidopterist. Many critics extolled Nabokov's lexical, narrative, and parodic genius; others labeled his verbal trickery superficial. His novels written in Russian included *Laughter in the Dark* (1932; Eng. trans. 1938) and *The Gift* (1937; Eng. trans. 1963). His short stories, which some critics consider his finest work, are available in English translation in *Nabokov's Dozen* (1958), *Nabokov's Quartet* (1967), and *Nabokov's Congeries* (1968). After 1940 he wrote primarily in English, publishing such works as the controversial *Lolita* (1955), *Pnin* (1957), *Pale Fire* (1962), and *Ada or Ardor* (1969). He also wrote poetry, plays, literary monographs, a translation and analysis of Aleksandr Pushkin's *Eugene Onegin* (1963), and the autobiographies *Conclusive Evidence* (1951) and *Speak Memory* (1966), *Lectures on Literature* (1980) and *Lectures on Russian Literature* (1981) appeared posthumously. ■ See biographies by Andrew Field (1977) and Brian Boyd (2 vols., 1990–91).

NADELMAN, ELIE (1882–1946), Polish-born U.S. sculptor. Nadelman was born into the Warsaw bourgeoisie and studied in Munich and Paris, where he was influenced by art nouveau techniques and classical museum sculpture. In 1909 he held a successful one-man show in Paris of his abstract geometric figures (notably *Abstract Head*) and stylized, curvilinear manikins. A London exhibition two years later was entirely bought out by the cosmetician Helena Rubinstein, and in 1915 Nadelman's works were shown in New York, where the Museum of Modern Art purchased his humorous bronze caricature *Man in the Open Air*. He also produced popular portrait busts and doll-like figures of dancers and circus performers.

NADER, RALPH (1934–   ), U.S. reformer. A graduate of Princeton (1955) and Harvard Law School (1958), Nader gained fame for his best-selling exposé of the auto industry, *Unsafe at Any Speed* (1965), which contributed to the passage of the National Traffic and Motor Vehicle Safety Act (1966). Subsequently he became the most prominent consumer advocate in the United States, setting up such groups as the Center for the Study of Responsive Law, the Project on Corporate Responsibility, the Public Interest Research Group, and Public Citizen. With the help of students and volunteers, called "Nader's Raiders," these organizations investigated governmental agencies and industrial hazards and published reports and brought class-action suits that led to increased public awareness of many social problems and influenced legislation regulating slaughterhouses, gas pipelines, coal-mine safety, radiation dangers, and the use of DDT to control insects. During the 1990s he actively opposed several international free-trade agreements that he feared would send jobs overseas and weaken U.S. consumer and environmental laws, and he opposed legislation that would place caps on punitive damages awarded by juries in civil liability cases. He also criticized what he considered the monopolistic power of the Microsoft Corporation in the computer software industry. Nader was the Green Party's presidential candidate in 1996 and 2000. Nader collaborated on several books, including *The Consumer and Corporate Responsibility* (1973), *The Menace of Atomic Energy* (1977), *Who's Poisoning America* (1981), and *The Big Boys: Power and Position in American Business* (1986) and wrote *The Case Against Free Trade: GATT, NAFTA and the Globalization of Corporate Power* (1993) and *The Ralph Nader Reader* (2000). ■ See studies by Charles McCarry (1972) and Hays Gorey (1975).

NAGAI, KAFU (Sokichi Nagai; 1879–1959), Japanese novelist. A native of Tokyo, the locale of his fictional works, Nagai formally studied Chinese but was privately tutored in the traditional Japanese arts of the Edo period. After returning from five years in the United States and France (1903–08), Nagai became increasingly nostalgic for the fast-disappearing, premodern Tokyo culture—especially its demimonde—and produced a series of lyrical novels evoking the past and depicting the few remaining vestiges of traditional society in modern Tokyo. His best-known works were *The River Sumida* (1909; Eng. trans. 1965) and *A Strange Tale from East of the River* (1937; Eng. trans. 1965). His other translated works included the novellas *During the Rains & Flowers in the Shade* (1994). Nagai's works were also known for their insights into the psychology of Japanese women. He was an antimilitarist who opposed the military government both before and during World War II. ■ See Edward Seidensticker, *Kafu the Scribbler* (1965).

NAGANO, OSAMI (1880–1947), Japanese admiral. Nagano graduated from the naval academy (1900), studied law at Harvard (1913), and was a naval attaché in Washington

(1920–23). He participated in the Washington (1921–22) and London (1930; 1935–36) naval conferences and advocated the expansion of Japanese naval power. He subsequently served as navy minister (1936–41) and naval chief of staff (1941–44). Nagano planned and ordered the Japanese attack on Pearl Harbor (Dec. 7, 1941), which brought the United States into World War II. He died while on trial for committing war crimes.

NAGEL, ERNEST (1901–1985), Czech-born U.S. philosopher. Nagel, a Columbia University Ph.D. (1930) and member of the faculty (1931–70), collaborated with Morris R. Cohen on a basic textbook, *Introduction to Logic and Scientific Method* (1934). He also edited the *Journal of Philosophy* (1939–56) and *Journal of Symbolic Logic* (1940–46). In his frequent journal articles, many of which were later collected in book form, Nagel introduced European ideas in philosophy and tried to reconcile logical positivism with American pragmatic naturalism. His important works in the philosophy of science included *Logic Without Metaphysics* (1957), *The Structure of Science* (1961), and *Teleology Revisited and Other Essays* (1979).

NAGURSKI, BRONKO (1908–1990), Canadian-born U.S. football player. One of the greatest players in football history, Nagurski was an All-American at the University of Minnesota (1930), where he was a star end, guard, tackle, and fullback. He later was an outstanding runner and defenseman for the Chicago Bears (1930–37; 1943). A big, powerful man (6 feet, 2 inches, 230 pounds) in what was then a small man's game. Nagurski was a virtually unstoppable rusher who gained more than 4,000 yards in his career. He also was a professional wrestler (1933–43) and won more than 300 matches.

NAGY, IMRE (1896–1958), Hungarian political leader. Nagy was a World War I prisoner of war in Russia who joined the Red army (1918) and returned to live in Moscow after the failure of the Hungarian Soviet Republic (1919). Involved in left-wing politics in Hungary (1921–30), he later worked as an agricultural economist in the U.S.S.R. (1930–44). He served in several posts in the post–World War II Hungarian government; as premier (1953–55), he attempted to set a "new course" of economic reforms and political liberalization. Although forced out of office, he was called to head a coalition government during the October 1956 Hungarian revolution and he proclaimed Hungarian neutrality and pleaded for aid from the United Nations. After the Soviet intervention he was arrested, tried secretly, and executed. ■ See his *On Communism, In Defense of the New Course* (1957); Tibor Méray, *Thirteen Days That Shook the Kremlin* (1959); and Peter Unwin, *Voice in the Wilderness* (1991).

NAHAS PASHA, MUSTAFA (1876–1965), Egyptian political leader. A lawyer, Nahas was one of the founders of the Wafd, the most important nationalist party of Egypt. During the years that Nahas led the Wafd (1927–52), he served as premier five times (1928; 1929–30; 1936–37; 1942–44; 1950–52). He frequently fought with the monarchy over its attempts to curb parliamentary power. He negotiated the Anglo-Egyptian alliance of 1936 and was placed in power (1942) by the British, who believed that he would cooperate with them during World War II. During his final term, however, he formulated violently anti-British policies (1951). Unable to cope with the ensuing crisis and accused of corruption, his government was dismissed in January 1952.

NAIDU, SAROJINI (Sarojini Chattopadhyay; 1879–1949), Indian poet and political leader. The daughter of a prominent Bengali Brahman, Naidu was educated at Madras University, the University of London, and Cambridge. Known as "the nightingale of India," she published three volumes of lyric poetry in English (*The Golden Threshold,* 1905; *The Bird of Time,* 1912; and *The Broken Wing,* 1915; combined in *The Sceptered Flute,* 1928) that were widely read throughout Europe and India. She was an active feminist and social reformer and trusted follower of Mohandas K. Gandhi. The first Indian woman president of the Indian National Congress (1925), she was arrested several times for her anti-British political activity, and she participated in the negotiations leading to Indian independence (1947). As the first woman governor in India, she headed the United Provinces (now Uttar Pradesh) from 1947 until her death. ■ See biography by Padmini Sengupta (1966) and study by V. S. Naravane (1980).

NAIPAUL, VIDIADHAR SURAJPRASAD (1932–), Trinidadian-born novelist. The grandson of an émigré indentured laborer from India, V.S. Naipaul was recognized as the finest novelist of the English-speaking Caribbean. After moving to Britain (1950) he gained a reputation for his social and political satires of West Indian life, notably *Miguel Street* (1959), which dealt with lower-class Trinidadians, and *A House for Mr. Biswas* (1961), which portrayed the dissolution of Indian family life in the islands. His works, which viewed the human condition as inherently lonely and alienated, were noted for their irony, comic invention, linguistic flair, and rich characterization. Naipaul's nonfiction included *A Middle Passage* (1962), impressions of five Caribbean societies, and *An Area of Darkness* (1964), an account of his first trip to India. His later works, which depicted the decay, rootlessness, and pretensions of postcolonial Third World societies, included the novel *A Bend in the River* (1979) and the nonfiction accounts in *India: A Wounded Civilization* (1977), *The Return of Eva Peron* (1980), and *Among the Believers: An Islamic Journey* (1982) and *Beyond Belief: Islamic Excursions Among the Converted Peoples* (1998). *Finding the Center* (1984) contained an uncharacteristically sympathetic account of the Ivory Coast and a brief autobiographical study. He also wrote the autobiographical novels *The Enigma of Arrival*

(1987) and *A Way in the World* (1994) and the essay collection, *Reading and Writing: A Personal Account* (2000). ■ See R. K. Morris, *Paradoxes of Order* (1975), and studies by Landeg White (1975), Sudha Rai (1982), and Richard Michael Kelly (1989).

NAJIBULLAH (Najibullah Ahmadzi; 1947–1996), Afghan political leader. Born into a prominent Pathan family, Najibullah rejected his traditional Islamic beliefs while a student at Kabul University (M.D. 1975) and joined the Communist party (1965). After the pro-Soviet party took control of Afghanistan (1978), precipitating a brutal civil war and massive Soviet military intervention, he served as chief of the secret police (1979–86) and subsequently as president (1987–92), replacing Babrak Karmal. Despite the help of more than 100,000 Soviet troops, his government was unable to defeat the U.S.–backed Muslim guerrillas. After the withdrawal of Soviet troops (1989), he initiated constitutional reforms and economic liberalization but was unable to negotiate a peace settlement with the guerrilla movement. After his government fell to the Islamic militia (April 1992), he took refuge in a U.N. diplomatic compound in Kabul and remained there until he was executed (September 1996) by the fundamentalist Islamic Taliban force that captured the city and established a new government.

NAKASONE, YASUHIRO (1918–), Japanese political leader. Nakasone graduated from Tokyo Imperial University (1941) and served in the navy during World War II. A member of the generally pro-Western, conservative, and business-oriented Liberal Democratic party (LDP), he was first elected to parliament in 1947 and held several cabinet posts (from 1959) including minister of international trade and industry (1972–74). After directing the Administrative Management Agency (1980–82). he was elected president of the LDP and served as premier (1982–87). Fiscally conservative, promilitary, and nationalistic, he had much in common with his U.S. counterpart, Pres. Ronald Reagan. Presiding during a period of economic stability and relative political calm at home, he strengthened Japan's military and improved relations with China. South Korea, and Southeast Asia.

NAMATH, JOE (Joseph William Namath; 1943–), U.S. football player. A star quarterback under coach Paul "Bear" Bryant at the University of Alabama (1962–64), Namath signed an unprecedented $400,000 professional contract with the New York Jets of the American Football League (AFL; 1965) to become the highest-paid rookie in football history. After being named rookie of the year (1965), he led the AFL in pass completions and yards gained (1966–67) and passed for a record 4,007 yards during the 1967 season. His phenomenal passing boosted the league's prestige and was responsible for the Jets stunning upset win over the Baltimore Colts in the 1969 Superbowl. Although his career (with the Jets until 1976; with the Los Angeles Rams, 1977–78) was shortened due to repeated knee injuries. Namath set

seasonal and career records for most games passing for 300 or more yards, and he passed for a total of 27,663 yards and 173 touchdowns. Known as a high-living playboy off the field, "Broadway Joe" appeared in TV commercials, films, TV shows, and theatrical productions after he retired. ■ See his autobiography, *I Can't Wait Until Tomorrow* (1969; with Dick Schaap).

NAMIER, SIR LEWIS BERNSTEIN (Ludvik Bernstein; 1888–1960), British historian. Namier was born in Poland and educated in Britain. During World War I he worked for the British foreign office and attended the Paris Peace Conference (1919) as an expert on Eastern Europe. For nearly three decades after the war he played a leading role in the Zionist movement. Turning to scholarship, he wrote *Structure of Politics at the Accession of George III* (1929), in which he used political biographies to plot the family relationships and personal interests that preceded party politics. The work was a great critical success and spurred a reevaluation of 18th-century British history. Namier's later works included *1848: Revolution of the Intellectuals* (1946) and *Diplomatic Prelude, 1938–39* (1948). He taught modern history at Manchester University (1931–53). ■ See biographies by Julia Namier (1971) and Linda Colley (1989) and Norman Rose, *Lewis Namier and Zionism* (1980).

NANSEN, FRIDTJOF (1861–1930), Norwegian Arctic explorer, oceanographer, statesman, and humanitarian. Nansen studied animal life in the Arctic (1882), successfully crossed Greenland (1886), and led the famous "Fram" expedition that investigated the drift of polar sea ice (1895–96). On that expedition he nearly reached the North Pole on skis, but was forced to turn back due to treacherous ice conditions. Upon returning home, he switched his interest to oceanographic studies, was named director of the International Commission for the Study of the Sea (1901), and led several oceanographic expeditions. After Norway's independence from Sweden (1905), he was appointed minister to Britain (1906–08) and he headed the Norwegian delegation to the League of Nations (1920). He subsequently served as the league's high commissioner for refugees (1921–30) and was awarded the 1922 Nobel Peace Prize for his work in repatriating World War I prisoners, for directing the relief program to famine-stricken Russia, and for creating the "Nansen passport," an internationally recognized identification card for refugees. ■ See studies by Anna G. Hall (1940), F. E. Noel-Baker (1958), and Per Vogt (1962), and biography by Roland Huntford (1999).

NARAYAN, JAYA PRAKASH (1902–1979), Indian nationalist and social reformer. Born in a village in Bihar. J. P. Narayan quit school to join nationalist leader Mahatma Gandhi's movement. After studying in the United States (1922–29) he returned home a Marxist, helped found the Congress Socialist party (1934), and organized a violent resistance movement during World War II. He left the Congress party (1948) and formed the Indian Socialist party (1952), but quit organized politics (1954) and joined the land-gift movement of Vinoba Bhave. In 1974 students called him out of retirement to lead a movement against poverty and corruption; he quickly gained a following of millions that threatened Prime Minister Indira Gandhi's government. He was arrested in 1975 but was soon released because he suffered from diabetes. He united the opposition forces into the Janata party (1977), which defeated Mrs. Gandhi's government and ruled India from March 1977 to January 1980. Narayan retired from public life in 1978. ▪ See his selected writings in *Socialism, Sarvodaya and Democracy* (1964).

NARAYAN, RASIPURAM KRISHNASWAMI (1906–), Indian novelist. One of the foremost Indian authors writing in English, R. K. Narayan created the fictitious south Indian town of Malgudi, which, like the U.S. southern novelist William Faulkner's Yoknapatawpha, was a microcosm of his culture. His most famous novels, *The Bachelor of Arts* (1937), *The Financial Expert* (1952), *The Guide* (1958), and *The Vendor of Sweets* (1967), related the ironies of daily Malgudian existence in a humorous and simple style. The chaotic lives of many of his characters, attributed to their lack of self-knowledge, place Narayan firmly in the tradition of Hindu philosophy. His short stories are in *Malgudi Days* (1982), *Under the Banyan Tree* (1985), and *The Grandmother's Tale and Selected Stories* (1994). His other works included the novels *Talkative Man* (1986) and *The World of Nagaraj* (1990), and *A Writer's Nightmare: Selected Essays, 1958–1988* (1988). ▪ See his autobiography, *My Days* (1974), and study by William Walsh (1983).

NASH, JOHN F. (1928–), U.S. mathematician. Recognized as a genius during his undergraduate years, Nash received a doctorate in mathematics from Princeton University (1950). His Ph.D. thesis, *Non-cooperative Games,* laid out the formal mathematical principles of game theory and made it applicable to real-world situations, such as business competition, trade negotiation, and conflicts between nations. As a professor at the Massachusetts Institute of Technology (1951–59) he made important contributions in pure mathematics, but his brilliant career was halted when he was struck down by schizophrenia. After suffering from the disease for more than 15 years he recovered and returned to Princeton as a visiting scholar. For his work in game theory he shared the 1994 Nobel Memorial Prize in Economics with John C. Harasanyi and Reinhard Selten. He described his illness in a paper delivered at the World Conference of Psychiatry in Madrid, Spain (1996), and suggested that there might be a connection between mathematical genius and mental disorder. ▪ See Sylvia Nasar, *A Beautiful Mind* (1998).

NASH, (FREDERIC) OGDEN (1902–1971), U.S. poet and humorist. Nash spent a year at Harvard, then worked in advertising and publishing. The *New Yorker* first published

his verse (1930) and brought Nash onto its staff. Ending his lengthy and sardonic lines with preposterous rhymes ("boomerang" with "kangaroo meringue"), Nash affected doggerel for comic purposes and made the pun almost respectable. He became enormously popular by versifying familiar gripes in his prolific and highly quotable verse. He often read his work on radio and television. Nash also wrote children's books and collaborated on a musical, *One Touch of Venus* (1943), with Kurt Weill and S. J. Perelman. His 20 volumes of verse included *Hard Lines* (1931), *The Bad Parents' Garden of Verse* (1936), and *Collected Verses* (1961).

NASH, PAUL (1889–1946), British painter. Nash trained at the Slade School of Art in London (1910–12). He served in World War I, and, after suffering combat injuries, returned to the front as an official war artist. He later assumed that post in World War II, recording visual impressions of combat. He was also known for seascapes, landscapes, and wood engravings. During the 1930s his work featured symbolic and surrealistic elements and he cofounded (1933) the circle of avant-garde artists and architects known as Unit One. ▪ See his *Outline: An Autobiography* (1949); biography by Andrew Causey (1980); and James King, *Interior Landscapes* (1987).

NASSER, GAMAL ABDEL (1918–1970), Egyptian political leader. The son of a petty bureaucrat, Nasser was a graduate of the Royal Egyptian Military Academy (1938). He masterminded the 1952 overthrow of King Farouk, and as premier (1954–56) and later president (1956–70) of Egypt, he initiated such socioeconomic measures as land reform, industrialization, and the construction of the Aswan High Dam on the Nile River. A proud, charismatic advocate of Arab unity and an opponent of imperialism, Nasser succeeded in nationalizing the Suez Canal (1956) in spite of an invasion by Britain, France, and Israel, and he became a symbol of Arab nationalism throughout the world. But military glory escaped him in the 1967 war with Israel when he was crushingly defeated and lost the Sinai peninsula. Although a champion of nonalignment, he became increasingly dependent on the Soviet Union for arms, aid, and wheat. Shortly before his death he helped mediate an end to the civil war in Jordan between the army and the Palestinian guerrillas. ▪ See his *Philosophy of Revolution* (Eng. trans. 1959); biographies by Robert Stephens (1971), Jean Lacouture (1971; Eng. trans. 1973), and Anthony Nutting (1972); and Mohamed Heikal, *The Cairo Documents* (1973).

NAST, CONDÉ (1874–1942), U.S. publisher. Born in New York City. Nast was advertising manager of Collier publications (1900–07) after graduating from law school. In 1909 he bought *Vogue,* a modest pattern magazine, which he transformed into the elegant fashion journal that helped to establish fashion as an art form in the United States. His publishing empire later expanded to include *Vanity Fair, House and Garden,* and *Glamour.* Nast's elaborate penthouse parties attracted members of café society during the 1920s. With Irene Lewisohn, he began the fashion collection that was the foundation for the New York Metropolitan Museum of Art's Costume Institute. ■ See Caroline Seebohm, *The Man Who Was Vogue* (1982).

NATHAN, GEORGE JEAN (1882–1958), U.S. drama critic and editor. The foremost theatrical critic of his time, Nathan was a drama reviewer for numerous influential magazines and newspapers for more than 50 years. An associate of H. L. Mencken—they were coeditors of *Smart Set* magazine (1914–23) and cofounders of the *American Mercury* (1924)—he was the author of hundreds of lively, erudite, sophisticated, and audaciously outspoken reviews and essays that helped raise the cultural standards of the American public. Nathan championed the plays of O'Neill, Pirandello, O'Casey, Molnar, Saroyan, Giraudoux, and Arthur Miller and played a major role in their public acceptance. Selections of his work are in *The World of George Jean Nathan* (1952). ■ See also his Autobiography of an *Attitude* (1926); Constance Frick, *Dramatic Criticism of George Jean Nathan* (1943); and Thomas Q. Curtiss, *The Smart Set* (1998).

NATHANS, DANIEL (1928–1999), U.S. microbiologist. A professor at Johns Hopkins University (from 1962), Nathans was a pioneer in using restriction enzymes (endonucleases), discovered by his colleague Hamilton Smith, to study the structure and function of deoxyribonucleic acid (DNA) molecules. His experiments with tumor virus, in which he used the enzymes as a "scissors" to cut out cancer-causing DNA molecules, helped to produce a revolution in genetics by fostering recombinant DNA research (or gene splicing). He shared the 1978 Nobel Prize for Physiology or Medicine with Smith and Werner Arber.

NATSUME, SOSEKI (Kinosuke Natsume; 1867–1916), Japanese novelist. One of Japan's greatest and most-popular novelists, Natsume resigned his prestigious teaching position at Tokyo University (1907) to pursue a literary career. His early comic works, *I Am a Cat* (1905; Eng. trans. 1971) and *Botchan* (1906; Eng. trans. 1972) established his reputation, but he was best known for the brooding psychological novels that followed: *Mon* (1910; Eng. trans. 1972), *The Wayfarer* (1912–13; Eng. trans. 1967), *Kokoro* (1914; Eng. trans. 1957), and the unfinished *Light and Darkness* (1916; Eng. trans. 1971). Concerned with isolation and betrayal, he summed up his fatalistic philosophy with the phrase *sokuten kyoshi*, "conform to heaven and foresake the self." He was the first to write of the alienation of the modern Japanese intellectual, free from constraining tradition but a helpless and isolated prisoner of the strains of modernity. ■ See study by Beongcheon Yu (1969) and Angela Yiu, *Chaos and Order in the Works of Natsume Soseki* (1998).

NATTA, GIULO (1903–1979), Italian chemist. While investigating petrochemical problems as director of Milan's

Institute of Industrial Chemistry (1938–74), Natta learned of Karl Ziegler's use of metal-organic catalysts for the manufacture of strengthened plastics. He began working with propylene and quickly developed a polymer with a regular structure resulting in superior characteristics such as increased strength and a high melting point. This discovery of stereospecific polymerization (1954) earned him a share of the 1963 Nobel Prize for Chemistry with Karl Ziegler and led to the development of improved plastics, films, and synthetic fibers. ■ See Sergio Carrà, ed., *Giulio Natta, Present Significance of his Scientific Contribution* (1982).

NAVRATILOVA, MARTINA (1956–   ), Czech-born U.S. tennis player. Her grandmother was an excellent tennis player; her mother a fine skier. Coached by Geroge Parma from age 9, Navratilova rose to prominence in the Czech tennis federation. After holding the Czechoslovak national singles title for three years (1972–74), she defected to the United States in 1975. A left-handed player who excelled in the serve-and-volley game, Navratilova overcame problems with concentration and conditioning in the 1980s to become a powerful competitor, widely regarded as the best woman player of all time. She daunted opponents, including rival Chris Evert Lloyd, with a big serve, aggressive style, and quick reflexes, Navratilova captured titles at Wimbledon (1978, 1979, 1982–87, 1990), the U.S. Open (1983, 1984, 1986, 1987), the French Open (1982, 1984), and the Australian Open (1981, 1983, 1985). In 1983 she set a professional tennis record by winning more than $6 million in one year. Paired with Pam Shriver, Navratilova also dominated women's doubles competition. She retired (1994) with a record 167 titles, including 18 Grand Slam singles championships, and amassed a 1,443–211 won-lost singles record. ■ See her autobiography, *Martina* (1985; with George Vecsey).

NAZIMOVA, ALLA (Alla Leventon; 1878–1945), Russian-born U.S. actress. Nazimova pursued a career in music before undertaking drama training under Constantin Stanislavsky (1898). She played at the Moscow Art Theater prior to emigrating (1905) to the United States, where she performed in Russian on the New York stage. She made her first appearance in an English-language production only a year after emigrating when she starred (1906) in *Hedda Gabler;* she was admired for her powerful depiction of other Ibsen characters too. She began a film career in 1916, appeared in many exotic and passionate roles, and soon commanded a weekly salary of $13,000. Although she continued to make films, Nazimova was most at home on the stage and was highly acclaimed for her Broadway performances in *The Cherry Orchard* (1928) and *Mourning Becomes Electra* (1931).

NAZRUL ISLAM, KAZI. *See ISLAM, KAZI NAZRUL.*

N'DOUR, YOUSSOU (1959–   ), Senegalese singer. Born into a family of traditional singing griots (oral historians), N'Dour began singing at ceremonial parties as a child and was a featured performer in a pop band as a teenager. With his own dance band, Star of Dakar (renamed the Super Star during the early 1980s), N'Dour developed a new "Afropop" style of music based on traditional Senegalese rhythms, singing techniques, and chanting but mixed with elements of jazz and Cuban rhythms and played on combinations of traditional and Western instruments. Performing original Wolof-language songs with political and social commentary, N'Dour became one of Africa's most famous singers. He became known in Europe with his album *Immigrés* (1985). He collaborated with Peter Gabriel and Paul Simon and traveled the world as part of Amnesty International's "Human Rights Now!" tour (1988). His best-known albums included *Set* (1990), *Eyes Open* (1992), *The Guide* (1994), and *Joko* (The Link) (2000). N'Dour also served as a roving ambassador for UNICEF, composed an African opera for the Paris Opera (1993), and wrote the official anthem for the World Cup soccer competition (1997). ■ See Jenny Cathcart, *Hey You!* (1989).

NEAR, HOLLY (1949–　), U.S. singer and songwriter. Near grew up in a rural California farming community. Her parents were labor and peace activists. After high school, she studied acting, landed television and film roles, and won a part in the Broadway musical *Hair*. Her political and professional concerns merged when she joined the international anti–Vietnam War show *Free the Army* (1971). During the 1970s, Near continued her antiwar work and began writing and recording songs, drawing from folk, pop, and country music and jazz. She played a key role in the development of "women's music" that grew out of the feminist and gay rights movements. In the 1980s she was active in the antinuclear movement and opposed U.S. intervention in Central America. Near recorded numerous albums, including *Hang In There* (1973), *Imagine My Surprise* (1978), *Lifeline* (1983; with Ronnie Gilbert), and *Don't Hold Back* (1987). ■ See her autobiography *Fire in the Rain . . . Singer in the Storm* (1990).

NEARING, SCOTT (1883–1983), U.S. social scientist. A radical economist at the University of Pennsylvania (1906–15), Nearing gained national publicity when he was dismissed from his job because of his crusade against child labor. In 1917 he wrote an antiwar tract, *The Great Madness,* and was indicted for inspiring resistance to military recruitment. Although acquitted, he lost his teaching job at the University of Toledo, his books were withdrawn from school curricula, and popular magazines refused to publish his articles. An independent Marxist and pacifist for most of his career, he wrote more than 50 books and pamphlets dealing with U.S. social problems and world affairs, including *Dollar Diplomacy* (1925, 1969), *Must We Starve* (1932), *United World* (1944), *The Tragedy of of Empire* (1945), *Democracy Is Not Enough* (1945), and *Civilization and Beyond* (1975). He moved to rural Vermont in 1932, and *The Maple Sugar Book* (1950) and *Living the Good Life* (1954), written with his wife Helen, describe their successful experiment in homesteading and subsistence organic farming. The books established Nearing's reputation as the spiritual father of the back-to-nature movement of the 1960s and 1970s. ■ See his autobiography, *The Making of a Radical* (1972), and biography by John A. Saltmarsh (1991).

NEEDHAM, JOSEPH (1900–1995), British historian of science. Needham, who taught biochemistry at Cambridge (1928–66), was a specialist in embryology who was fascinated by the social implications of science. He became interested in Chinese science, learned the language, and during World War II traveled to China as head of a British scientific mission. A left-wing socialist, he became a supporter of the Chinese communist revolution. The outcome of Needham's interest was the monumental *Science and Civilization in China,* considered to be one of the major scholarly achievements of the century. Begun in 1949, 16 books were published during Needham's lifetime. He was also the first director of the natural science department of the United Nations Educational, Scientific, and Cultural Organization (UNESCO; 1946–48). His other works included *The Grand Titration* (1970) and *Celestial Lancets* (1980), a history of acupuncture.

NEEL, ALICE HARTLEY (1900–1984), U.S. painter. Called "the quintessential bohemian," Neel spent most of her creative life painting the human comedy in New York's Greenwich Village and Spanish Harlem. Her disturbing. expressionistic, psychological portraits of friends and neighbors, delineating their inner struggles and anxieties, were neglected for many years because they were out of the mainstream of American painting. Recognition came in the 1960s and she was honored with a one-person retrospective show at New York's Whitney Museum in 1974. ■ See study by Patricia Hills (1983) and volume edited by Ann Temkin (2000).

NÉEL, LOUIS EUGÈNE FÉLIX (1904–2000), French physicist. A professor at the universities of Strasbourg (1937–45) and Grenoble (1946–76), Néel did pioneering work in the field of magnetism (antiferromagnetism and ferrimagnetism) that led to significant developments in solid-state physics. Among the applications of his work were the development of "memories" in computers and tape recorders and the creation of new synthetic ferrite materials used in microwave communications. He shared the 1970 Nobel Prize for Physics with Hannes Alfvén.

NEGRÍN, JUAN (1891–1956), Spanish political leader. A professor of physiology at the University of Madrid (1923–31), Negrín was elected to the Cortes (parliament) as a socialist (1931) and served as minister of finance (1936–37) and premier (1937–39) during the civil war. Dependent on the Soviet Union for arms and on the support of the Spanish Communist party, he was severely limited politically and was viewed with suspicion by members of the anticommunist left. After fighting broke out in Madrid between communists and anticommunists, Negrín fled (1939) to France and later to Britain, and headed the republican government-in-exile until 1945.

NEHER, ERWIN (1944–), German biophysicist. Neher studied at the University of Wisconsin (M.S. 1967) and the Technical University of Munich (Ph.D. 1970), and did research at several universities and institutes in Germany and the United States, including the Max Planck Institute for Biophysical Chemistry in Gottingen, Germany (1972–75; 1976–). Working with colleague Bert Sakmann in the early 1970s, Neher confirmed the existence of ion channels, tunnellike structures in cells that regulate the cell's ability to function and communicate. They developed the patch-clamp technique, a laboratory method utilizing a tiny glass pipette fitted with a recording electrode, to detect the electrical current that passes through a single ion channel. The technique had a revolutionary effect in the field of cell biology, led to new insights into the causes of cystic fibrosis, diabetes, epilepsy, and several disorders of the nervous and muscle systems, and enabled scientists to tailor drugs to act directly on the ion channel involved in a specific disease. For the pioneering research, Neher and Sakmann shared the 1991 Nobel Prize for Physiology or Medicine.

NEHRU, JAWAHARLAL (1889–1964), Indian political leader. Nehru was born into a westernized, nationalistic high-caste Kashmiri Brahman family and was educated, in Britain, at Harrow and Cambridge. He practiced law (1912–19) before joining the Indian National Congress party (1919) and devoting his life to the cause of Indian independence. A chief lieutenant of Mahatma Gandhi and frequent president of the congress, he was incarcerated for nine years in British jails (between 1921 and 1945) before serving as independent India's first prime minister (1947–64). A reformist democratic socialist, he stressed secularism, unity, modernization, and large-scale industrial development during his years in power, although he failed to make major inroads against poverty. He forged an anticolonialist, nonaligned foreign policy, but failed to settle the Kashmir problem and waged a disastrous war with China (1962). His daughter Indira Gandhi also served as prime minister (1966–77; 1979–84). His books include *Glimpses of World History* (1942), *The Discovery of India* (1946), and his autobiography, *Toward Freedom* (1941). ■ See biographies by Michael Brecher (1959), Michael Edwardes (1971), Sarvepalli Gopal (3 vols., 1976–84), and Stanley Wolpert (1996).

NEHRU, MOTILAL (1861–1931), Indian political leader. A Kashmini Brahman from Allahabad, Nehru became a lawyer in 1886. He lived the life of an English gentleman and did not get involved in nationalist politics until 1907. Originally a moderate, he became a radical leader of the Indian National Congress party after World War I, joining Mahatma Gandhi's noncooperation movement and adopting a simpler lifestyle. After serving a six-month jail sentence

(1921–22), he cofounded the Swaraj party (1923) in order to obstruct the British-sponsored legislative councils from within, and he served in the central legislative assembly. He was arrested again after participating in the 1930 civil disobedience movement. He collaborated closely with his son, Jawaharlal, who became the first prime minister of independent India in 1947. ■ See the essays in S. P. Chablani, ed., *Motilal Nehru* (1961), and B. R. Nanda, *The Nehrus* (1974).

NEILL, ALEXANDER SUTHERLAND (1883–1973), Scottish educator and psychologist. The son of a village schoolmaster, A. S. Neill pioneered in the free-school movement. Convinced that traditional schools merely coerce children into the neurotic patterns of their elders, Neill sought to develop a school to "fit the child—instead of making the child fit the school." Thus he founded Summerhill School in Leiston, Suffolk (1924; originally an international school organized in Dresden, Germany, in 1921), which was self-governing and allowed the students maximum freedom and spontaneity. The controversial school discouraged antisocial behavior but allowed students the choice of attending classes, taking exams, or participating in extracurricular activities. He wrote *That Dreadful School* (1937), *Summerhill* (1962), and *Talking of Summerhill* (1967). ■ See his autobiography, *Neill! Neill! Orange Peel!* (1972) and biography by Jonathan Croall (1983).

NEILSON, NELLIE (1873–1947), U.S. historian. Born in Philadelphia and graduated from Bryn Mawr (B.A. 1893; Ph.D. 1899), Neilson headed the history department at Mount Holyoke College, where she taught from 1902 to 1939. In 1943 she became the first woman to head the American Historical Association. An authority on medieval England, Neilson was also the first woman contributor to the Oxford Studies in Social and Legal History and to the Harvard Law Review. Her works included *The Terrier of the Fleet* (1920), *The Cartulary of Bilsington* (1927), and *Medieval Agrarian Economy* (1936).

NEIZVESTNY, ERNST (1925–), Russian-born graphic artist and sculptor. In his teens Neizvestny was a volunteer paratrooper in World War II; wounded and left for dead, he nonetheless recovered and later studied art in Riga and Moscow and worked in a foundry. He won recognition in the early 1960s for energetic drawings and monumental sculpture, particularly portrait sculpture, that strove to communicate the anguish—and resilience—of the human spirit, and specifically of the Russian experience. His work was denounced (1962) by Soviet premier Nikita Khrushchev, but after the leader was deposed they exchanged cordial letters and Neizvestny carved the headstone for Khrushchev's grave. By the 1970s Neizvestny's work was known in the West, though he was unable to exhibit in the Soviet Union. He emigrated (1976) and resumed work in a duplex studio in New York City's SoHo district. ■ See John Berger, *Art and Revolution* (1969).

NELSON, (JOHN) BYRON, JR. (1912–), U.S. golfer. One of the game's outstanding shot makers, Nelson won every major U.S. championship and set several records. He won the U.S. Open (1939), the Masters (1937, 1942), and the Professional Golfers' Association championship (1940, 1945). In 1944, he won 13 of the 23 tournaments he entered and captured 11 consecutive open titles, a record that has never been approached. After retiring (1955), he became a coach and broadcaster.

NELSON, WILLIE (1933–), U.S. country-music singer and composer. After years of singing in rowdy honkytonk Texas bars, Nelson became a successful songwriter in Nashville and member of the Grand Ole Opry during the 1960s. Finding Nashville too conservative for his tastes, however, he returned to his native Texas (1972) and developed and performed his own blend of country, blues, gospel, and rock music, frequently called "outlaw country" or "redneck rock." The "king of country music" during the 1970s, Nelson sang plaintive songs of everyday dreams and disappointments and gained a huge and devoted nationwide following. He recorded numerous bestselling albums and was named Entertainer of the Year by the Country Music Association in 1979. His repertory broadened to include standard modern pop tunes, and Nelson's stature in the music world grew in the 1980s. In 1985, he organized "Farm Aid," a 12-hour concert to benefit U.S. farmers. ■ See his autobiography, *Willie* (1988; with Bud Shrake).

NEMEROV, HOWARD (1920–1991), U.S. writer. Nemerov graduated from Harvard (B.A. 1941) and served in the Royal Canadian Air Force during World War II. He subsequently taught in the English departments of several universities, including Washington University in St. Louis (from 1976). He was best known for his numerous volumes of witty and ironic verse that combined humor with poignancy. His *Collected Poems* (1977) won the 1978 Pulitzer Prize and National Book Award. He also wrote novels (*Federigo*, 1954; *The Homecoming Game*, 1957) and books of essays (*Journal of the Fictive Life*, 1965; *Figures of Thought*, 1978; *The Oak in the Acorn*, 1987). He served as poet laureate of the United States from 1988 to 1990. His sister was the photographer Diane Arbus. ■ See *A Howard Nemerov Reader* (1991) and studies by R. Labrie (1980) and D. L. Potts (1994).

NÉMETH, LÁSZLÓ (1901–1975), Hungarian novelist, playwright, and essayist. Trained as a physician, Németh achieved fame and a wide following as an independent and versatile writer and social critic who was devoted to social justice and reform. Through the vehicle of *Witness* (1932–36), a journal he founded and wrote, he produced numerous erudite articles on subjects ranging from cultural history to contemporary Hungarian affairs. In his fiction he was primarily concerned with crises forced on the individual by society. His best-known novels, *Guilt* (1936; Eng. trans.

1966), *Revulsion* (1947; Eng. trans. 1965), and *Egető Eszter* (1956), were psychological studies. Németh also wrote historical dramas and two important cultural histories.

NENNI, PIETRO (1891–1980), Italian journalist and political leader. The son of a peasant, Nenni succeeded Benito Mussolini as editor of the socialist newspaper *Avanti* (1922). After Mussolini changed his politics and established his fascist dictatorship, Nenni was forced into exile (1926). Settling first in Paris, he later fought as a volunteer (1936–38) on the Loyalist side during the Spanish Civil War. As the post–World War II leader of the Italian Socialist party (1949–69), Nenni pursued a policy of alliance with the communists in opposition to the government, but after the Soviet invasion of Hungary (1956), he broke with the communists and soon cemented an alliance with the Christian Democrats. He received several cabinet appointments and was a pivotal figure in the coalition governments of the 1960s.

NERNST, WALTHER HERMANN (1864–1941), German chemist. A professor at Göttingen (1891–1904) and Berlin (1905–33), Nernst was a pioneer physical chemist whose works extended the boundaries of physics and chemistry. He was best known for his formulation (1906) of the third law of thermodynamics, which stated that at a temperature of absolute zero, entropy (the energy of a substance due to the internal motion of its molecules, and therefore not available for mechanical work) is zero. The law, for which Nernst won the 1920 Nobel Prize for Chemistry, was first used to study chemical equilibria, but later it influenced the fields of statistical mechanics and quantum theory. ■ See study by Diana K. Barkan (1999).

NERUDA, PABLO (Ricardo Eliecer Neftali Reyes y Basoalto; 1904–1973), Chilean poet, diplomat, and political leader. After early volumes of rather conventional poetry, Neruda found a distinct voice in the enormously popular *Twenty Love Poems and a Song of Despair* (1924; Eng. trans. 1969), his verse account of a love affair. *Residence on Earth* (1933; Eng. trans. 1946) contained surrealistic impressions of his travels as a diplomat. Neruda was traumatized by the Spanish civil war (1936–39), which he witnessed as Chilean consul in Madrid. His later poetry became less symbolic and more vigorously political. A prolific poet who introduced innovative techniques and wrote in a variety of styles, Neruda produced more than 2,000 pages of poetry. Collections of his poetry in English translation included *The Early Poems* (1969), *Five Decades: Poems 1925–1970* (1974), and the posthumously published, autobiographical *Isla Negra: A Notebook* (Eng. trans. 1982). A communist and lifelong political activist, Neruda was elected (1944) to Chile's national senate. In 1970 he was the Communist party candidate for Chile's presidency, but withdrew to support Salvador Allende, whom he served as ambassador to France. Neruda died 12 days after the military coup that overthrew Allende; his last poem denounced that coup.

Neruda won the 1971 Nobel Prize in Literature. ■ See his *Memoirs* (Eng. trans. 1977); Manuel Durán and Margery Safir, *Earth Tones* (1981); and study by E. M. Santí (1982).

NERVI, PIER LUIGI (1891–1979), Italian civil engineer. Nervi acquired a degree in civil engineering (1913) and had no formal architectural training, but profoundly influenced the course of modern architecture. He applied his confidence in the possibilities of reinforced concrete to the design of numerous innovative structures in Italy and abroad. Nervi experimented with the possibilities of prefabrication. His designs, characterized by dramatic curves and arches, included the conference hall for the United Nations Educational, Scientific, and Cultural Organization in Paris (1953–57); a series of structures for the 1960 Olympic games in Rome (including the round Palazzetto dello Sport); and the George Washington Bridge Bus Station in New York City (1963). Nervi taught technology and construction at the University of Rome (1947–61). ■ See study by A. L. Huxtable (1960).

NESSLER, KARL (CHARLES) LUDWIG (**Charles Nestle**; 1872–1951), German-born U.S. hair curler. Nessler's lifelong interest in hair led him to seek employment at an exclusive Paris salon (1899), where he learned the most modern hair-curling procedures. While there, he developed a permanent-wave technique and, as Charles Nestle, set up his own salon in London (1900) and later New York (1915). Although at first unpopular, Nessler continually improved his equipment and advertised extensively; the permanent wave soon became internationally accepted and the basis of the modern beautyparlor industry. In 1927 he opened up the world's largest beauty salon in New York and the following year published his pseudoscientific study, *The Story of Hair*.

NETANYAHU, BENJAMIN (1949–), Israeli political leader. Netanyahu, the son of a prominent right-wing Zionist historian, spent his teenage years in the United States, where he learned to speak perfect, idiomatic English with an American accent. After serving in an elite commando unit of the Israeli army (1967–72), he studied at the Massachusetts Institute of Technology (B.S. 1974; M.S. 1976) and worked in private industry (1976–78, 1980–82). Following the death of his brother, Jonathan, while leading a raid on a hijacked plane in Entebbe, Uganda, Netanyahu organized a series of seminars on terrorism that attracted international attention. He subsequently served as deputy chief of mission at the Israeli embassy in Washington, D.C. (1982–84), Israeli permanent representative to the United Nations (1984–88), deputy minister of foreign affairs (1988–91), and deputy in the prime minister's office (1991–92). He was elected to the Knesset (parliament) as a member of the right-wing Likud party (1988) and became party leader in 1993. He waged an American-style campaign in winning the 1996 election, becoming the youngest prime minister in Israeli history. An opponent of relinquishing to the Arabs substantial

amounts of land captured in the 1967 war, he stymied negotiations with the Palestinians stemming from the Oslo peace agreements. He lost the 1999 election and was replaced as prime minister by Ehud Barak. He wrote *Fighting Terrorism* (1995). ■ See Neill Lochery, *The Difficult Road to Peace* (1999), and biography by Ben Kaspit (1998).

NETO, (ANTÓNIO) AUGUSTINHO (1922–1979), Angolan political leader. As a physician employed by the Portuguese colonial health service, Neto became embroiled in questions of health care and politics. A Marxist, nationalist poet, and political agitator, he was arrested and imprisoned several times during the 1950s; in 1957, he joined the Popular Movement for the Liberation of Angola (MPLA), a left-wing nationalist coalition. Arrested again in 1960 and removed to Portugal after the outbreak of guerrilla war in 1961, he escaped in 1962 and was elected president of the MPLA. After the departure of Portuguese troops (1975), Angola became independent under a nationalist-front government made up of the various factions—the MPLA, the National Front for the Liberation of Angola (FNLA), and the National Union for the Total Independence of Angola (UNITA)—that had fought for liberation from Portugal. Divided by ethnic and political differences, the coalition quickly collapsed, and the MPLA, supported by Cuban troops, formed a national government under Pres. Neto. He died in Moscow after a cancer operation while civil war continued to divide his country.

NEUMANN, FRANZ LEOPOLD (1900–1954), German-born U.S. political scientist. A teacher, labor lawyer, and adviser to the Social Democratic party in Berlin during the 1920s and early 1930s, Neumann was imprisoned by the Nazis (1933) but escaped to England. After receiving a Ph.D. in political science from the London School of Economics (1936), he emigrated to New York City and joined the Institute for Social Research at Columbia University (1936–42). While there he wrote his most famous book, *Behemoth: The Structure and Practice of National Socialism* (1942), a sophisticated Marxist analysis of Nazism. He worked for the Office of Strategic Services (1943–45), headed the German research section of the State Department (1945–47), and served as professor of government at Columbia University (from 1947). After Neumann's premature death in an automobile accident, Herbert Marcuse edited a collection of his essays published as *The Democratic and Authoritarian State* (1957).

NEUMANN, JOHN VON (1903–1957), Hungarian-born U.S. mathematician. Von Neumann was a polymath, a brilliant mathematician who also played a key role in the development of game theory, computers, and cybernetics. At age 20 he presented his theory of numbers as sets; at 30, his theory of rings of operators, known as von Neumann algebras. He emigrated to the United States (1930) and was long associated with the Institute for Advanced Study at Princeton

(1933–57). He was also a consultant to the U.S. government on the development of the atomic and hydrogen bombs. He wrote *Mathematical Foundations of Quantum Mechanics* (1926; Eng. trans. 1955), *The Theory of Games and Economic Behavior* (1944; with Oskar Morgenstern), and *Theory of Self-reproducing Automata* (1966). ▪ See study by Steve Heims (1981).

NEURATH, OTTO (1882–1945), Austrian sociologist and philosopher. An independent Marxist and one of the founders of logical empiricism, Neurath played a prominent role in the Vienna Circle of logical positivists during the 1920s. He was a polymath with broad interests who advocated a scientific behaviorist sociology through the use of a physicalist language. He developed isotypes, a pictographic language, which he hoped would overcome barriers separating scholars from workers and national and linguistic groups from each other. After leaving Vienna (1934), he headed the International Institute for Visual Education, in The Hague, and became a professor at Oxford University (1940). He planned and edited *The International Encyclopedia of Unified Science* (1938). Among his works were *International Picture Language* (1936), *Modern Man in the Making* (1939), *Foundations of the Social Sciences* (1944), and the collection *Empiricism and Sociology* (1973).

NEUTRA, RICHARD JOSEPH (1892–1970), Austrian-born U.S. architect. A student of Otto Wagner and apprentice of Erich Mendelsohn, Neutra emigrated to the United States (1923) and worked with Louis Sullivan and Frank Lloyd Wright before opening his own practice in Los Angeles (1925). He was instrumental in introducing the International Style to the United States and achieved fame for his Lovell House (Los Angeles, 1927–29), a pioneering structure noted for its use of glass and prefabricated components and its integration with the natural landscape. One of the most influential architects of the century, he designed offices, schools, private homes, and housing projects throughout the world. His books included *Mystery and Realities of the Site* (1951), *Survival Through Design* (1954), and *Building with Nature* (1971). ▪ See his autobiography, *Life and Shape* (1962), and studies by Esther McCoy (1960) and Thomas Hines (1982).

NEVELSON, LOUISE (Louise Berliawsky; 1900–1988), U.S. sculptor. Nevelson's Russian-Jewish family emigrated to the United States when she was 5 years old. She grew up in Maine, moved to New York City at age 20, studied drama, and enrolled at the Art Students League (1929–30). Nevelson studied in Germany (1931–32) and worked as muralist Diego Rivera's assistant in Mexico City. Extensive travel in Latin America influenced the terracotta and wood pieces she showed at her first one-person exhibition (1941). Critical recognition did not come until the mid-1950s, when New York City museums acquired *Black Majesty, Sky Cathedral,* and *First Personage.* She experimented with the size, shape, and positioning of a variety of parts, at first milk crates and later play-school blocks and plexiglass cubes. She was famous for sculptured walls—reliefs composed of compartments containing everyday objects, often painted black. In the 1960s and 1970s she used other materials (including lucite, Formica, and cor-ten steel) and more open forms appropriate to environmental sculptures. Work of this period included *Transparent Sculpture VI* (1968) and *Transparent Horizon* (1975). In later work she returned to work in wood. ▪ See her memoirs, *Dawns and Dusks* (1976), and studies by Mary Buxton (1970), Arnold B. Glimcher (1972), and Laurie Lisle (1990).

NEVINS, ALLAN (1890–1971), U.S. historian. After graduating from the University of Illinois (M.A. 1913), Nevins went to work in New York as a journalist, writing what he called "living history." As a member of the history faculty at Columbia University (1928–58), he wrote or edited more than 60 books covering every period of American history, including Pulitzer Prize–winning biographies of Grover Cleveland (1932) and Hamilton Fish (1936); notable studies of John D. Rockefeller, *A Study in Power* (2 vols. 1953), and *Henry Ford* (3 vols. 1954–63; with F. E. Hill), and a history from 1850 to the Civil War, *Ordeal of the Union* (8 vols., 1947–71). He also launched Columbia's Oral History Project (1948) and was a founder of American Heritage magazine.

NEWHOUSE, SAMUEL IRVING (1895–1979), U.S. newspaper publisher. Newhouse began acquiring newspapers in 1922 and by the late 1970s had amassed an empire of 31 dailies in 22 cities, including the *Newark Star Ledger,* the *Cleveland Plain Dealer,* the *Portland Oregonian,* and the *New Orleans Times-Picayune.* He also controlled numerous magazines, including *Parade, Vogue, Glamour, House and Garden,* and *Mademoiselle,* as well as five radio stations and several cable-television systems. Strictly a businessman, with a collector's fascination and an ability to revive financially ailing properties, he allowed local editors to control the editorial content and political slant of his publications. His son, S. I. Newhouse, Jr. (1928–) headed Condé Nast Publications in New York City. ▪ See Richard H. Meeker, *Newspaperman* (1983).

NE WIN, U (Maung Shu Maung; 1911–), Burmese political leader. Born into a family of minor officials, Ne Win abandoned his studies at Rangoon to become an activist in the anti-British nationalist movement. A member of the most radical group, the We Burmans Association, he was trained by the Japanese after their invasion of Burma during World War II and became chief of staff of the collaborationist army. However, in 1944 he began a guerrilla war against the Japanese and joined forces with the Allies. He was promoted to major general and second in command of the army when Burma gained its independence (1948). After serving as a "caretaker" premier (1958–60), he seized power in a military coup (1962). Ruling as head of the Burmese Socialist Program party (BSPP), he established a rigid single-party state, nationalized the economy, and pursued a nonaligned foreign policy. Under the 1974 constitution, he served as president (1974–81) and subsequently maintained an influential role in Burmese affairs as BSPP chairman until his resignation in 1988. During his years in power the economy deteriorated and his government was continually challenged militarily by communist and minority insurgent groups.

NEWMAN, ALFRED (1901–1970), U.S. film composer. Newman was a former piano prodigy and Broadway conductor who was music director at United Artists, Goldwyn Studios, and 20th Century Fox (1939–60) was a key figure in the development of film music. His own preference was for romantic, melodic, and emotional "mood music." He won nine Academy Awards for the scores of such movies as *Alexander's Ragtime Band* (1938), *The Song of Bernadette* (1943), and *Love Is a Many Splendored Thing* (1955).

NEWMAN, BARNETT (1905–1970), U.S. painter. A City College of New York graduate (1927) of Russian-Jewish origin. Newman was an abstract expressionist who defined space in terms of color in varying densities. A cofounder in 1948 of the "Subject of the Artist" groups, he was one of the most influential artists of the New York School and his large monochromatic canvases helped establish colorfield painting. His best-known works included *Vir Heroicus Sublimis* (1950–51) and *Stations of the Cross* (1966), a series of 14 color-field paintings. ■ See biography by Thomas B. Hess (1969) and study by Harold Rosenberg (1978).

NEWMAN, LARRY. *See ABRUZZO, BEN.*

NEWMAN, PAUL (1925–), U.S. actor. After managing his family's sporting-goods store for two years, Newman enrolled at the Yale School of Drama and the Actors Studio. He was a Broadway success in *Picnic* (1953) before his first film role in *The Silver Chalice* (1955). A cool, handsome, blue-eyed actor with a cocky smirk, he played a prizefighter in *Somebody Up There Likes Me* (1956), a pool shark in *The Hustler* (1961), and a gigolo in *Sweet Bird of Youth* (1962). Newman directed his wife Joanne Woodward in the sensitive *Rachel, Rachel* (1968); costarred with Robert Redford in two exceedingly popular films, *Butch Cassidy and the Sundance Kid* (1969) and *The Sting* (1973); and won acclaim for his roles in *The Verdict* (1982), *The Color of Money* (1986; Academy Award), *Mr. and Mrs. Bridge* (1989), and *Nobody's Fool* (1994). He was a spokesperson for liberal causes and a successful automobile racer and a food manufacturer (with all profits going to charity). ■ See biography by Lionel Godfrey (1979) and Joe Morella, *Paul and Joanne* (1988).

NEWTON, HUEY PERCY (1942–1989), U.S. political activist. Born in Louisiana and raised in Oakland, California,

Newton was a cofounder (1966) and minister of defense of the revolutionary Black Panther party, a paramilitary organization for black self-defense. The party set up breakfast programs and free clinics in ghettos and allied with white radicals in opposing racism and the Vietnam War. Dressed in a beret and black leather jacket, Newton led armed street patrols that brought him into constant conflict with local police. He spent two years in prison (1968–70) for shooting a policeman before his conviction was overturned by the California Court of Appeals. Indicted for another murder in 1974, he went underground for three years before returning from Cuba to face charges. The charges were dropped after two trials ended in hung juries (1979). He received a Ph.D. (1980) from the University of California, Santa Cruz. His thesis was entitled, *War Against the Panthers*. During the 1980s he suffered from drug and alcohol abuse, had numerous encounters with the law, and served time in jail for gun possession, misappropriation of public funds, and parole violations. He was shot to death on a street in Oakland, near where he began organizing for the Panthers. ■ See his *To Die for the People* (1972) and *Revolutionary Suicide* (1973) and study by Hugh Pearson (1994).

NEXØ, MARTIN ANDERSON (1869–1954), Danish novelist. Nexø spent a tough youth in Copenhagen slums and eventually worked as a laborer. He finally became a teacher and by 1901 a professional writer. He was a socialist, and his work reflects his concern about the plight of the poor. His international fame rests on his proletarian epics, *Pelle the Conqueror* (4 vols., 1906–10; Eng. trans. 1913–16), about a trade unionist and strike leader, and *Ditte* (5 vols., 1917–21; Eng. trans. 3 vols., 1920–23), about a poverty-stricken woman. After the Russian revolution (1917) Nexø became a communist. He moved to East Germany (1951), where he died. ■ *Under the Open Sky* (1932–35; Eng. trans. 1938) was autobiographical.

NEYMAN, JERZY (1894–1981), Russian-born U.S. mathematician and statistician. Neyman received a Ph.D. from the University of Warsaw (1923) and taught at the universities of Warsaw and Cracow (1923–34), London (1934–38), and California at Berkeley (from 1938). During the 1930s he developed a behavioristic statistics that was widely used to test hypotheses in the fields of medicine, genetics, astronomy, physics, meteorology, and agriculture. At Berkeley he established a world-renowned center for mathematical statistics. Neyman wrote *First Course in Probability and Statistics* (1950). ■ See study by Constance Reid (1982).

NEZVAL, VÍTĚZSLAV (1900–1958), Czech poet. One of Czechoslovakia's most prolific poets. Nezval abandoned the school of proletarian poets—although not his commitment to communism—in the mid-1920s to found his own movement of "poetism." He proclaimed a poetry of fantasy and free association and produced poems of vivid imagery and fantastic rhymes. Soon, though, his mood darkened, and visions of death, horror, and night infused his works, especially his volume *Poems of the Night* (1930). By 1934 he turned to surrealism and continued to display great verbal artistry and invention. After the pre–World War II German occupation, however, his poetry became patriotic, and, following the postwar communist coup. he produced propaganda pieces such as *Stalin* (1949) and *Song of Peace* (1950; Eng. trans. 1951). Toward the end of his life, though, he broke with the pro-Soviet regime. English translations of his work are in *Three Czech Poets* (1971),

NGATA, SIR APIRANA TURUPA (1874–1950), New Zealand Maori leader and scholar. One of 15 children, Ngata was the first Maori graduate of the University of New Zealand (1893). He became a lawyer and served as a Liberal member of Parliament (1905–43), championing his people, writing extensively about them, and struggling for better educational and health facilities and for the preservation of their culture. His greatest efforts were focused on Maori land development, and he served as minister of native affairs (1928–34). ■ See study by Eric Ramsden (1948).

NGO DINH DIEM. *See DIEM, NGO DINH.*

NGO DINH NHU. *See NHU, NGO DINH.*

NGUGI WA THIONG'O (formerly James T. Ngugi; 1938–), Kenyan writer. Ngugi, one of East Africa's most important English-language writers, was educated at Makerere College and Leeds University. Known for his "situation" or communal novels, most notably *Weep Not, Child* (1964), *The River Between* (1965), and *A Grain of Wheat* (1967), he explored the effects of British colonization and the subsequent Mau Mau rebellion on his native Kikuyu society. He was also a journalist and literary editor, and he taught at the University of Nairobi (1972–77) until he was dismissed from his post and imprisoned for nearly a year after his play *I Will Marry When I Want* (Eng. trans. 1982) was banned. His later novels include the revolutionary *Petals of Blood* (1977), an attack on neocolonialism, and the allegorical *Devil on the Cross* (1980, in Kikuyu; Eng. trans. 1982), which attempted to heighten the political consciousness of Kenya's peasants. His novel *Matigari* (1986; Eng. trans. 1989), a revolutionary political fantasy, was banned in Kenya. His works of nonfiction included *Decolonising the Mind: The Politics of Language in African Literature* (1986), *Moving to the Centre: The Struggle for Cultural Freedom* (1993), and *Penpoints, Gunpoints and Dreams: Towards a Critical Theory of the Arts and the State of Africa* (1998). He lived in exile in Britain (1982–88) and the U.S. (1989–). ■ See his *Detained: A Writer's Prison Diary* (1981); studies by D. Cook (1983), and F. Odun Balogun (1997); and G. D. Killam, *An Introduction to the Writings of Ngugi wa Thiong'o* (1980).

NGUYEN CAO KY. *See KY, NGUYEN CAO.*

NGUYEN THI BINH. *See BINH, NGUYEN THI.*

NGUYEN VAN THIEU. *See THIEU, NGUYEN VAN.*

NHU, NGO DINH (1910–1963), Vietnamese political leader. The brother of Ngo Dinh Diem, Nhu was French-educated and considered himself an intellectual and a political philosopher. From 1938 to 1945 he worked as chief archivist in the Indochina Library. After a period of exile, he returned to edit a newspaper that lobbied political support for his brother. After his brother achieved the presidency of South Vietnam (1954), Nhu founded the Can-Lao, or Revolutionary Personalist Labor party (1954), in order to consolidate economic and political control. He and his wife wielded enormous power and lived in the presidential palace. As head of the secret police, Nhu was the most feared man in South Vietnam until his death in the military coup that toppled his brother.

NIARCHOS, STAVROS SPYROS (1909–1996), Greek shipping magnate. Niarchos—the name means "master of ships"—established a shipping company in 1939. He bought his first ships at Depression prices and leased them to the Allies during World War II, while serving in the Greek navy. With the insurance from his wartime shipping casualties he built up a fleet of 80 ships, pioneering in supertankers. Niarchos amassed a personal fortune estimated at $4 billion and one of the world's great art collections. An intense, magnetic personality. Niarchos pursued an opulent lifestyle with a succession of wives (one of whom he was accused of murdering), his three-masted yacht, and his private island south of Athens.

NICHOLAS II (1868–1918), last czar of Russia. The son of Alexander III and Danish-born Maria Feodorovna, Nicholas married Princess Aix of Hesse-Darmstadt (later called Alexandra), a granddaughter of Queen Victoria. A believer in unlimited royal power, he declined to grant liberal concessions on assuming the throne and curtailed rights of national minorities. His reign (1894–1917) was marked by social unrest, agricultural reverses, military disaster, and finally political upheaval. When defeat by Japan led to the 1905 revolution. Nicholas convened an elected Duma (parliament) but continued to discourage political reform. He followed poor counsel, including that of his wife, who had fallen under the influence of the mystic Rasputin. During World War I, Nicholas assumed supreme command at the front (1915), though he was ill suited for that responsibility. Public discontent with the war and the monarchy grew and Nicholas was forced to abdicate in March 1917. During the civil war following the October 1917 bolshevik revolution, Nicholas and his family were murdered by a local bolshevik official who feared that they could be rescued by anticommunist forces. The remains of Nicholas, Alexandra, and three of their five children were located and exhumed (1991) after the collapse of the Communist government. They were reburied in a lavish funeral ceremony in SS. Peter and Paul Catheral in St. Petersburg (1998). The czar and his immediate family were canonized by the Russian Orthodox Church (2000). ■ See Richard Charques, *The Twilight of Imperial Russia* (1965); Robert K. Massie, *Nicholas and Alexandra* (1967); and S. S. Oldenberg, *Last Tsar* (4 vols., 1975–78).

NICHOLS, MIKE (Michael Igor Peschowsky; 1931–   ), German-born U.S. comedian and director. Nichols left the University of Chicago after two years in order to study acting in New York with Lee Strasberg, but returned to Chicago to join an improvisational nightclub troupe that included Alan Arkin, Barbara Harris, and Elaine May. He formed a comedy team with May (1957), and they gained a national reputation for their satire and wit through appearances in nightclubs, on television, and on Broadway (*An Evening with Mike Nichols and Elaine May,* 1960). Nichols established an independent career as a director during the early 1960s and was responsible for such critical and popular Broadway successes as *Barefoot in the Park* (Tony Award, 1963), *The Odd Couple* (Tony Award, 1965), *The Prisoner of Second Avenue* (Tony Award, 1971), *The Gin Game* (1977), and *The Real Thing* (Tony Award, 1984); he produced the one-woman show *Whoopi Goldberg* (1984). His best-known films were *Who's Afraid of Virginia Woolf* (1965), *The Graduate* (Academy Award, 1967), *Catch-22* (1969), *Carnal Knowledge* (1971), *Silkwood* (1983), *Working Girl* (1988), *The Bird Cage* (1995), and *Primary Colors* (1998). ■ See biography by H. Wayne Schuth (1978).

NICHOLSON, BEN (1894–1982), British painter. With only a few months of formal art training, Nicholson traveled frequently to Europe, developing a personal style characterized by freedom in scale and perspective. In the 1930s, under cubist and constructivist influence, he stressed spatial order and, impressed with the work of Piet Mondrian, he developed a series of white geometric shapes in slight relief. His association with the Paris Abstraction-Création group and with an English abstract-art group, Unit One, made him the principal connection between British and continental modern art. Nicholson worked in a less severe style after 1940, melding figurative and nonfigurative techniques in monumental still lifes and reliefs. He gained international recognition in the 1950s and was regarded as one of the foremost exponents of geometrical abstraction. ■ See study by John Russell (1969).

NICHOLSON, JACK (1937–   ), U.S. film actor. Nicholson appeared in low-budget horror and action films for ten years before achieving fame, and an Academy Award nomination, for his performance in *Easy Rider* (1969). He subsequently emerged as one of Hollywood's most versatile stars, frequently appearing as an outsider and antihero. He won Oscars for his roles in *One Flew Over the Cuckoo's Nest* (1975), *Terms of Endearment* (1983), and *As Good as It Gets* (1997), and starred in such other films as *The Last De-*

tail (1973), *Chinatown* (1974), *The Passenger* (1975), *The Shining* (1979), *Prizzi's Honor* (1985), *Ironweed* (1987), *Batman* (1989), and *Hoffa* (1992). ■ See study by David Downing (1984).

NICKLAUS, JACK (1940–   ), U.S. golfer. Nicklaus started to play golf at age 10 and developed into one of the hardest and most accurate (and unquestionably the most successful) hitters in golf history. The winner of two U.S. Amateur championships (1959, 1961) while he was a student at Ohio State University (1957–62). Nicklaus joined the professional tour in 1962 and posted more victories in major tournaments than any player in the history of golf. Called the "Golden Bear," he won six Masters (1963, 1965, 1966, 1972, 1975, 1986), five Professional Golfers' Association (1963, 1971, 1973, 1975, 1980), four U.S. Open (1962, 1967, 1972, 1980), and three British Open championships (1966, 1970, 1978) and became the first golfer to win more than $4 million as a pro (1983). He captured his 100th pro victory (including 70 on the regular tour) in 1996. ■ See his *My Story* (1997; with Ken Bowden).

NICOLLE, CHARLES JULES HENRI (1867–1936), French bacteriologist. Noted for his research on cholera, tuberculosis, measles, and diphtheria. Nicolle received the 1928 Nobel Prize for Medicine or Physiology for his 1909 research in connection with typhus. He discovered that the carrier of the disease was the louse, and as a result of this discovery all the armies in World War I introduced delousing as part of their operations. He also demonstrated that individuals could carry and transmit diseases without having any symptoms. He directed the Pasteur Institute in Tunis (1903–32) and developed it into a major center of research in bacteriology.

NIDETCH, JEAN (Jean Slutsky; 1923–   ), American businesswoman. Brooklyn-born Nidetch enlisted the help of friends to adhere to a weight-loss program. After losing 72 pounds, she founded Weight Watchers, Inc. (1963), which provided dieters with a food program and weekly instruction in behavior modification. Her organization developed into a multimillion-dollar business that used sophisticated advertising techniques to encourage membership and promote a line of foods, a magazine, cookbooks, and other products, including summer camps. ■ See her book, *The Story of Weight Watchers* (1970).

NIEBUHR, HELMUT RICHARD (1894–1962), U.S. Protestant theologian. The younger brother of theologian Reinhold Niebuhr, H. Richard Niebuhr followed his brother to Elmhurst (Illinois) College, Eden Theological Seminary, and Yale Divinity School (Ph.D. 1924), where he taught from 1931 until his death. Niebuhr wrote several studies on Protestantism in U.S. history, culture, and social science, including *The Kingdom of God in America* (1937), *Christ and Culture* (1957), and *Radical Monotheism and Western Cul-*

ture (1960). He also helped organize the United Church of Christ, a 1957 merger of the Congregational and Evangelical churches. ▪ See the symposium on his work edited by Paul Ramsey, *Faith and Ethics* (1957); John D. Godsey, *The Promise of H. Richard Niebuhr* (1970); and the study by Lonnie H. Kliever (1978).

NIEBUHR, REINHOLD (1892–1971), U.S. theologian. The son of a German Protestant minister who emigrated to Missouri, Niebuhr studied at Yale (B.D. 1914), was ordained an Evangelical minister in 1915, and preached for the next 13 years in working-class Detroit, where he embraced socialism and pacifism. He later modified his views and urged U.S. intervention in the war against German dictator Adolf Hitler. After World War II he recanted his socialism, embraced political "realism," anticommunism, and the expansion of U.S. power internationally, and exerted a great influence in intellectual and foreign policy-making circles. A member of the faculty of Union Theological Seminary in New York City (1928–60), Niebuhr attacked liberal Protestantism for its failure to deal with everyday moral predicaments. His major writings on the relation between religion, politics, and social problems included *Moral Man and Immoral Society* (1932), *The Nature and Destiny of Man* (2 vols., 1941–43), *The Irony of American History* (1952), and *The Structure of Nations and Empires* (1959). ▪ See biography by Richard Wightman Fox (1986); studies by Ronald H. Stone (1972) and Paul Merkley (1975); and June Bingham, *Courage to Change* (1993).

NIELSEN, CARL (1865–1931), Danish composer. Nielsen was a powerful symphonist in the tradition of Scandinavian romanticism. In his six symphonies (1894–1925) he experimented with "progressive tonality," beginning and concluding in different keys. His 1906 opera *Maskarade* became a Danish national epic. His other works included a violin concerto (1911), the *Luciferiske Suite* for piano (1919) and *Commotio* for organ (1931). In 1931 he was appointed director of the Royal Conservatory. ▪ See his *Living Music* (Eng. trans. 1953) and *My Childhood* (Eng. trans. 1953), and studies by Robert W. Simpson (1964) and Jack Lawson (1997).

NIEMEYER, OSCAR (1907–), Brazilian architect. A well-to-do graduate of the National School of Fine Arts in Rio de Janeiro (1934), Niemeyer joined the firm of Lúcio Costa, with whom he collaborated on the Ministry of Education and Health Building (1937–42) in Rio de Janeiro and the Brazilian Pavilion at the 1939 World's Fair in New York. He also helped plan the United Nations Building in New York (1947) and was the chief architect of the new capital of Brasília (1957–64). Having gained an international reputation for his sculptured, free-flowing concrete buildings, he designed a new city for Israel's Negev Desert (1964), Constantine University in Algeria (1969), the Mondadori Headquarters in Milan (1967–72), and numerous other buildings

around the world. A winner of the Lenin Peace Prize (1963), Niemeyer also designed the French Communist Party Headquarters in Paris (1967–72). He was also awarded the 1988 Pritzker Prize. ▪ See studies by Rupert Spade (1971) and David Underwood (1994).

NIEMÖLLER, MARTIN FRIEDRICH GUSTAV EMIL (1892–1984), German theologian. After commanding a U-boat in World War I. Niemöller became pastor of a Lutheran parish in Berlin-Dahlem in 1931. Although he initially supported national socialism, the policies of Nazi leader Adolf Hitler (after 1933) led him to form and direct the Pastors' Emergency League to Resist Hitlerism, which opposed anti-Semitic policy and government interference in affairs of the Evangelical church and of the Confessing church. He was the most prominent advocate of clerical resistance to Nazi policy. Suspended from the pastorate by the regime, he continued to preach against Nazism until his arrest and imprisonment in Sachsenhausen and Dachau concentration camps (1937–45). After World War II, Niemöller helped rebuild the Evangelical church and sparked controversy with his pacifist views and his contention that Germans bore collective guilt for the war. He served (1961–68) as one of the six presidents of the World Council of Churches. ▪ See his memoirs, *From U-Boat to Concentration Camp* (1934; rev. ed. Eng. trans. 1939); Clarissa S. Davidson, *God's Man* (1979); Dietmar Schmidt, *Pastor Niemöller* (Eng. trans. 1959); and biography by James Bentley (1984).

NIEUWLAND, JULIUS ARTHUR (1878–1936), Belgian-born U.S. organic chemist. A Roman Catholic priest (ordained 1903), Nieuwland taught botany (1904–18) and organic chemistry (1918–36) at Notre Dame University. His early experiments with acetylene, which he abandoned because of the poisonous properties of the compound (divinylchlorarsine) he had discovered, led to the development of lewisite, the deadly poison gas used during World War I. His discovery (1920) that acetylene molecules could be polymerized led to the development (by chemists of the E. I. Dupont de Nemours Co.) of neoprene (marketed in 1931), the first commercially successful synthetic rubber.

NIJINSKY, VASLAV FOMICH (1890–1950), Russian ballet dancer and choreographer. The son of Polish ballet dancers, Nijinsky enrolled at the Russian Imperial Theater at age 10, and at 17 entered the Imperial Ballet, dancing mainly as a partner for ballerinas. He met (1908) ballet master Sergei Diaghilev, who became his lover; Nijinsky created a sensation when he began (1909) touring with Diaghilev's Ballet Russe. He never returned to Russia. Nijinsky was the first to dance many ballets choreographed by Michel Fokine, including *Petrushka, Les Sylphides, Spectre de la Rose,* and *Schéhérazade.* He often gave the impression of being suspended in midair and was considered to be the greatest dancer of his time. Nijinsky also created his own dances, including *The Afternoon of a Faun* (1912), *The Rite of Spring*

(1913), and *Till Eulenspiegel* (1916). His tumultuous relationship with Diaghilev ended when Nijinsky married (1913); his illustrious career ended due to a mental breakdown (1919). He lived in Britain and Switzerland until his death. ■ See his *Diary* (1936), which was published in an unexpurgated version in 1999; biographies by his wife Romola Nijinsky (1933), Francoise Reiss (Eng. trans. 1960), and Richard Buckle (1971); and the memoirs of his sister Bronislava Nijinska (Eng. trans. 1981).

NIKOLAIS, ALWIN (1910–1993), U.S. choreographer. A puppeteer and pianist for silent films, Nikolais turned to dance after seeing a performance by German modern dancer Mary Wigman (1933). He studied with Hanya Holm and served as dance director at New York City's Henry Street Settlement Playhouse (1948–70), where he organized his own company in 1953. Believing that dance should be about motion, not emotion, he reacted to the psychological dance dramas that were popular during the 1940s and 1950s, and created an abstract, high-tech, multimedia dance theater that featured ingenious props and costumes, special lighting effects, and electronic music. Many of his works that featured the interplay of dancers with mobile props and changing lights suggested the interrelationship of human beings and their environment. His best known works included *Masks, Props and Mobiles* (1953), *Kaleidoscope* (1956), *Imago* (1963), and *Gallery* (1978). Choreographer Murray Louis was Nikolais's collaborator and companion for over 40 years.

NILSSON, BIRGIT (1922–   ), Swedish opera singer. The greatest Wagnerian soprano of her time, Nilsson made her debut with the Stockholm Royal Opera (1947). She achieved international fame in the mid-1950s for her portrayals of Isolde and Brünnhilde (in *Die Walküre*) and was hailed as the successor to Kirsten Flagstad. Possessor of one of the purest and most powerful voices in opera, Nilsson was also acclaimed for her performances in *Turandot, Salomé, Elektra, Aida,* and *Fidelio.* She made her debut at New York's Metropolitan Opera in 1959.

NIMEIRY, GAAFAR AL- (1930–   ), Sudanese political leader. Nimeiry studied in Islamic schools before graduating from the Military College at Khartoum (1952). He continued his training in Egypt (1955–56), where he became an enthusiastic admirer of Egyptian revolutionary leader Gamal Abdel Nasser. Considered the spokesman and leader of Sudan's younger officers, he led a successful coup against the government (May 1969), headed the revolutionary council, and was elected president in a plebiscite (1971). Initially pro-Soviet, he maintained close ties with Egypt and the West after the early 1970s. He ended the 17-year civil war by granting limited autonomy to the south (1972). By the 1980s his one-party rule had become increasingly authoritarian and unpopular; he imposed Islamic law throughout the country (including the non-Islamic south) in 1983 and instituted an austerity program, including increased food prices, to bolster a deteriorating economy in 1985. Following protest demonstrations and strikes, he was overthrown in a bloodless military coup (April 1985).

NIMITZ, CHESTER WILLIAM (1885–1966), U.S. naval officer. Nimitz served as chief of staff to the commander of the Atlantic submarine force during World War I. In 1926 he designed the prototype Naval Reserve Officers' Training Program (University of California). He served on various sea commands during the 1930s and was named rear admiral (1938) and chief of the Bureau of Navigation (1939). After the Japanese bombed Pearl Harbor (1941), Nimitz was named commander of the Pacific fleet. A brilliant strategist and innovator, he directed the series of sea battles and island landings (Guadalcanal, Midway, Solomon Islands, Gilbert Islands, Marshall Islands, the Marianas, the Philippines, Iwo Jima, and Okinawa) that crushed the Japanese. As the official representative of the United States, he signed the instrument of the Japanese surrender on his flagship, the U.S.S. Missouri, in Tokyo Harbor (Sept. 2, 1945). ■ See biographies by E. B. Potter (1976) and Frank Driskill and Dede Casad (1983).

NIN, ANAÏS (1903–1977), U.S. novelist. Born in France to parents of Spanish-Cuban descent, Nin was brought to the United States at age 11, left school at 15 to become a fashion and artist's model, then returned to Europe where, before the outbreak of World War II, she studied Spanish dance, underwent psychoanalysis with Otto Rank, and was a lay analyst. She returned to the United States in 1940. Intensely interested in unraveling women's inner lives, Nin wrote four volumes of essays and 12 books of fiction, including the short-story collections *This Hunger* (1945) and *Cities of the Interior* (1959), the novel *House of Incest* (1936), and two volumes of sophisticated erotica. She was best known, however, for her relentlessly introspective *Diaries* (11 vols., 1966–85) that span the years from 1914 (when she was age 11) to 1974. ■ See Noël Riley Fitch, *Anaïs* (1993) and the biography by Dierdre Bair (1995).

NIRENBERG, MARSHALL W. (1927–   ), U.S. biochemist. Nirenberg studied at the University of Michigan (Ph.D. 1957) and was associated with the National Institutes of Health (from 1957). Proceeding from the premise that cells carry hereditary messages through the DNA (deoxyribonucleic acid) molecule, Nirenberg showed that DNA works indirectly, using RNA (ribonucleic acid) as an intermediary. His work helped to crack the genetic code, and Nirenberg shared the 1968 Nobel Prize for Physiology or Medicine with Robert Holley and Har Gobind Khorana.

NITTI, FRANCESCO SAVERIO (1868–1953), Italian economist and political leader. Nitti left his teaching post at the University of Naples to enter parliament as a left-liberal deputy (1904) and subsequently became minister of agriculture, industry, and commerce (1911–14) and minister of finance (1917–19) before serving as premier (1919). Beset with a series of foreign and domestic crises, he resigned after one year in office but served again in parliament (1921–24). An opponent of the fascists, he refused to run in the elections of 1924 and went into exile in France. Returning to Italy (1945), he was again elected to parliament, helped form the Democratic Union party, and became a senator (1948).

NIVEN, (JAMES) DAVID (GRAHAM) (1910–1983), British actor. Born to wealth, Niven graduated from the Royal Military College at Sandhurst and served briefly in the British army before going to Hollywood in the early 1930s. There he joined the social set that included Errol Flynn, Tyrone Power, and Clark Gable, and gained fame for his film portrayals of charming and debonair English gentlemen. He appeared in such hits as *The Charge of the Light Brigade* (1936), *Prisoner of Zenda* (1937), *Dawn Patrol* (1938), and *Wuthering Heights* (1939) before returning to Britain to serve as an army officer during World War II (1939–45). He starred in dozens of films after the war, including *Stairway to Heaven* (1946), *Around the World in 80 Days* (1956), and *The Pink Panther* (1964), and won an Oscar for his performance in *Separate Tables* (1958). He wrote two best-selling memoirs, *The Moon's a Balloon* (1971) and *Bring on the Empty Horses* (1975). ▪ See Tom Hutchinson, *Niven's Hollywood* (1984), and Sheridan Morley, *The Other Side of the Moon* (1985).

NIXON, RICHARD MILHOUS (1913–1994), U.S. political leader. A lawyer and World War II naval veteran, Nixon was elected to Congress as a California Republican (1946) and gained publicity as an aggressive anticommunist crusader on the House Un-American Activities Committee, notably in the Alger Hiss case. He was elected to the U.S. Senate after a campaign marked by smear tactics (1950) and served as vice president in the administration of Pres. Dwight David Eisenhower (1953–61). After losing the 1960 presidential election to John F. Kennedy, his political career seemed to end, but he made a remarkable recovery and defeated Hubert H. Humphrey in the 1968 presidential race. Foreign affairs dominated the first years of his presidency as he gradually decreased direct U.S. military involvement in Vietnam, reestablished diplomatic ties with China (1972), and signed the SALT-I arms limitation treaty with the Soviet Union (1972). Following his landslide reelection victory over George McGovern (1972), he withdrew U.S. troops from Vietnam (1973), but soon became embroiled in the Watergate scandal. Nixon was accused of being involved in the coverup of an illegal break-in of Democratic campaign headquarters by men linked to his reelection campaign committee. Amid congressional calls for his impeachment, he became the first U.S. president to resign from office (Aug. 9, 1974). His books included his memoirs, *RN* (1978); *Six Crises* (1962); *The Real War* (1980); *Leaders* (1982); *No More Vietnams* (1985); *In the Arena: A Memoir of Victory, Defeat and Renewal* (1990); *Seize the Moment: America's*

Challenge in a One-Superpower World (1992); and *Beyond Peace* (1994). ▪ See study by Fawn M. Brodie (1981); biographies by Stephen E. Ambrose (3 vols. 1987–91) and Roger Morris (1989); Stanley I. Kutler, *Abuse of Power* (1997); and Anthony Summers, *The Arrogance of Power: The Secret World of Richard Nixon* (2000).

NIZER, LOUIS (1902–1994), U.S. attorney. Born in London and educated in New York, Nizer was admitted to the New York bar in 1924 and became known for his representation of celebrity clients in libel, proxy, and divorce actions. He argued the author Quentin Reynolds' successful suit against columnist Westbrook Pegler, prevented movie mogul Louis B. Mayer from regaining control of MGM, and earned a $288,200 fee in the divorce of a liquor magnate. Nizer was a popular speaker and author of magazine articles and other works on the law. A chapter from his best-selling *My Life in Court* (1961) was dramatized as the Broadway play *A Case of Libel* (1963). His other books included *The Jury Returns* (1966), *Catspaw* (1992), and his autobiography, *Reflections Without Mirrors* (1978).

NKOMO, JOSHUA (1917–), Zimbabwean political leader. The son of a teacher and Protestant lay preacher, Nkomo was educated in social work in South Africa and worked as a railway union official. He attended the 1953 London conference on federation and became a leader of successive nationalist parties, the African National Congress (ANC), the National Democratic party (NDP), and the Zimbabwe African Peoples Union (ZAPU), each replacing the prior banned party. With the election of the white minority Rhodesian Front government and the Unilateral Declaration of Independence (UDI), he was arrested and detained (1964–74). Although a moderate who was consulted by the British and Rhodesian governments about a possible political settlement, he led one of the major guerrilla factions in the liberation struggle and formed the Patriotic Front (1976) with Robert Mugabe, the leader of the Zimbabwe African National Union (ZANU). Nkomo was defeated by Mugabe in the British-supervised 1980 elections, winning only 20 seats in the 100-member parliament, but he nonetheless joined the Mugabe government. As tribal rivalries emerged (Mugabe was a leader of the Shona majority, while Nkomo was a leader of the Ndebele-speaking minority), Nkomo was dismissed from the cabinet (1982) and central government troops were accused of massacring civilians in Nkomo's native Matabeleland (1983). Increasingly isolated from national influence, Nkomo fled into exile (1983) and his party won only 15 seats in the 1985 elections. He returned home in 1987, reached an accord with Mugabe, and served as senior minister in the president's office (1988–90) and as vice president of Zimbabwe (1990–99) but wielded little influence. ▪ See his autobiography (1984).

NKRUMAH, KWAME (1909–1972), Ghanaian political leader. While studying in the United States (Lincoln University and the University of Pennsylvania) and Britain (Gray's Inn and the London School of Economics), Nkrumah became an active anticolonialist and pan-Africanist. Returning home to the Gold Coast, a British colony (now Ghana), he joined the moderate political party United Gold Coast Convention (UGCC), but broke with it to form his own more militant organization, the Convention People's party (CPP; 1949). He became prime minister after the 1951 national elections and led the colony to independence as Ghana (1957). He became president of the Republic of Ghana in 1960. As leader of the first black colony to achieve independence, Nkrumah became a revered figure throughout Africa, stimulated anticolonial movements throughout the Third World, and inspired the formation of the Organization of African Unity (1963). Responsible for domestic economic improvements, he nonetheless gradually eliminated political opposition. and his Marxist rhetoric and pan-African vision cloaked a growing dictatorship. He was overthrown by a military coup in 1966, after which he lived in exile in Guinea. His books included *Consciencism* (rev. ed. 1970), *Neo-Colonialism* (1966), and *Revolutionary Path* (1973). ■ See his autobiography (1957); Henry L. Bretton, *The Rise and Fall of Kwame Nkrumah* (1967); Basil Davidson, *Black Star* (1974); and biographies by David Rooney (1988) and David Birmingham (1998).

NOBILE, UMBERTO (1885–1978), Italian aeronautical engineer and explorer. With polar explorers Roald Amundsen and Lincoln Ellsworth among his passengers, Nobile, a general in the Italian air force, piloted (1926) the Norge, a 350-foot dirigible of his own design, over the North Pole only two days after Richard Byrd had reached it by plane. Two years later he set out to repeat the feat in the small and delicate airship Italia, but he crashed after crossing the North Pole. Nobile was rescued, but the accident resulted in 17 deaths; he was criticized by an official board of inquiry and resigned his commission. From 1932 to 1943 he worked and taught in the Soviet Union and the United States and was reinstated as a general in 1945. His account of his controversial career is in *My Polar Flights* (1959; Eng. trans. 1961). ■ See Alexander McKee, *Ice Crash* (1979).

NOEL-BAKER, PHILIP JOHN, BARON (Philip Baker; 1889–1982), British political leader and peace advocate. A Quaker and pacifist, Noel-Baker served in the ambulance corps during World War I. As a member of the British delegation to the Paris Peace Conference (1919), he helped establish the League of Nations and subsequently served on its secretariat (1920–22). During the 1920s he helped organize relief efforts to alleviate the Russian famine. He was a Labour member of the House of Commons (1929–31; 1936–70) and held several cabinet positions after World War II. He also helped draft the United Nations Charter (1945) and wrote numerous books on world peace and disarmament, including *The Private Manufacture of Armaments* (1936) and *The Arms Race* (1958). He was awarded the Nobel Peace Prize (1959) and made a life peer (1977). ■ See David J. Whittaker, *Fighter for Peace* (1989).

NOETHER, (AMALIE) EMMY (1882–1935), German mathematician, Noether was raised in a family of mathematicians, was tutored by eminent academicians, and received her Ph.D. at the University of Erlangen (1907). After 1915 she applied her knowledge of abstract algebra to research being conducted at Gottingen University, but because that university denied faculty positions to women, she lectured on a regular basis, "substituting" for her colleague, David Hilbert, whose name was announced. Ultimately (1922) she was named to the faculty, and by 1930 she was acknowledged internationally as a major mathematician. In 1933, when the Nazis came to power, Noether, a Jew, was dismissed from her post and emigrated to the United States, where she taught at Bryn Mawr and at the Institute for Advanced Study in Princeton. New Jersey ■ See study by Auguste Dick (Eng. trans. 1981) and the collection edited by J. W. Brewer and Martha K. Smith (1981).

NOGUCHI, HIDEYO (1876–1928), Japanese bacteriologist. A graduate of the Tokyo Medical College (1897). Noguchi arrived in the United States in 1899 and joined the Rockefeller Institute for Medical Research in New York (1904). He was best known for isolating the spirochete that causes syphilis and for developing the skin test for the disease. He also devised new techniques for producing cultures of numerous pathogenic organisms and demonstrated that two different diseases, Oroya fever and verruga peruana, were produced by the same bacterium. He died after contracting yellow fever while doing research on the disease in West Africa.

NOGUCHI, ISAMU (1904–1988), Japanese-U.S. sculptor. The son of two writers—one Japanese and one American—Noguchi spent most of his childhood in Japan, returning to the United States as an adolescent. He worked in Paris for two years as an apprentice to sculptor Constantin Brancusi, with whom he shared a love of stone artifacts. It was during the 1940s, after his brief World War II internment in an Arizona camp, that Noguchi began to produce his major work—powerful, abstract shapes in stone, wood, and bronze. Some later commissions included monumental granite sculptures for the Connecticut General Life Insurance Co., the *Red Cube* for New York's Marine Midland Building, and Detroit's Civic Center Plaza with its 120-foot steel pylon. In 1984 he erected in Philadelphia *A Bolt of Lightning—A Memorial to Benjamin Franklin,* an asymmetrical 102-foot-high piece conceived 50 years earlier. A tremendously versatile artist, he also created small-scale sculptures, furniture, gardens, and stage decor (collaborating with choreographer Martha Graham). Part of his Long Island City, New York, studio became the Noguchi Garden Museum (1985). ■ See Noguchi's memoir, *A Sculptor's World* (1967), and biography by Sam Hunter (1979).

NOLAN, SIR SIDNEY ROBERT (1917–1992), Australian painter. One of his country's foremost artists, Nolan painted landscapes and legends in a naive-sophisticated style, blending realism and fantasy, myth and history. He was best known for his series on bushranger Ned Kelly, a Robin Hood of colonial Australia. Nolan lived abroad after 1958, painting cosmopolitan themes such as *Leda and the Swan*, the subject of a 1958–60 series. He also designed operatic productions of *Samson and Dalila* (1981) and *Abduction from the Seraglio* (1987) at London's Covent Garden. ■ See study by Elwyn Lynn (1967).

NOLAND, KENNETH (1924–), U.S. painter. Noland was born in North Carolina and attended Black Mountain College; after serving in the air force in World War II, he studied (1948–49) at the Zadkine School of Sculpture in Paris. Working with Morris Louis in the 1950s, he innovated color-field painting, a technique that involved using thinned paints of brilliant color to stain a canvas in arresting geometrical patterns. His canvases used color and proportion to make emotional statements. ■ See studies by Kenworth Moffett (1977) and Diane Waldman (1977).

NOLDE, EMIL (**Emil Hansen; 1867–1956**), German painter and graphic artist. Emil Hansen taught drawing and painting (1892–99), then visited Paris (1900), where the work of Honoré Daumier and Édouard Manet deeply affected him. In 1904 he adopted the name of his birthplace, Nolde. Two years later he joined the expressionist Die Brücke group, but by 1908 he left the group, preferring to work in solitude. Nolde was an intensely religious man whose fervor was not without conflict. He painted distorted, primitive figures in bold, clashing colors symbolic of sinfulness. He was also a prolific graphic artist. Nolde was an early Nazi supporter, but in 1941 his works were condemned as "degenerate" and he was forbidden to paint. He secretly created small watercolors, which he called "unpainted pictures." ■ See study by Peter Selz (1963).

NONO, LUIGI (1924–1990), Italian composer. With the premieres of several of his works in 1950, Nono was recognized as a leading avant-garde composer. He rejected conventional theme development for his own system of intertonal relationships that constantly changed. Yet in his desire to reach the masses and not just the educated elite, he included such "concrete" sounds as street and factory noises in his music. A politically active communist, Nono based much of his vocal music, including his opera *Intolerance* (1960–61) and his setting of *The Communist Manifesto, A Spectre Rises over Europe* (1971), on radical political topics. His music after the late 1970s was less political and more meditative and intimate. His later works included the opera *Prometeo* (1984) and numerous pieces of electronic music.

NOONUCCAL, OODGEROO (**Kathleen Jean Mary Ruska; 1920–1993**), Australian Aboriginal writer and political activist. Noonuccal was known as Kath Walker for most of her life. She was born and raised on Stradbroke Island, Queensland, where many traditional Aboriginal customs were still practiced. She left school at 13 to work as a domestic, served in the Australian Women's Army Service during World War II, and joined the Communist party after the war and became an activist for Aboriginal rights. With the appearance of her books of poetry, *We Are Going* (1964) and *The Dawn is at Hand* (1966), she became the first Aboriginal woman to have her works published. Her best-known poems dealt with the dispossession of the Aboriginal people, asserted their rights, and idealized their traditional culture. Her other books included *Stradbroke Dreamtime* (1972), a collection of traditional stories, and *The Rainbow Serpent* (1988), a retelling of the Aboriginal creation myth. As state secretary of the Federal Council for the Advancement of Aboriginals and Torres Strait Islanders in the 1960s, she played a major role in the campaign to secure constitutional recognition for Aboriginals (1967). She was awarded the M.B.E. (Member of the Order of the British Empire) in 1970, but returned the honor in protest of government policies against Aboriginals (1988) and changed her name to Oodgeroo Noonuccal. ■ See Ulli Beier, *Quandamooka: The Art of Kath Walker* (1985).

NORDHOFF, HEINZ (1899–1968), German industrialist. Trained as an engineer, Nordhoff headed the Opel truck plant (1936), which he developed into Europe's biggest truck producer. In 1948 he became head of the Volkswagen Works, a bombed-out plant employing 7,000 workers. Despite criticism, he started mass-producing the "beetle," the people's car that dictator Adolf Hitler had promised but never delivered. His striking success was a major factor in the postwar German economic recovery. By 1967 Volkswagen was producing more than 2 million cars a year, employing almost 100,000 workers, and was the world's fourth-largest producer (behind General Motors, Ford, and Chrysler) and the world's largest exporter of cars.

NORELL, NORMAN (**Norman Levinson; 1900–1972**), U.S. fashion designer. At age 18, Norell went to New York from Indiana, where his family ran a men's clothing store. He studied fashion illustration at the Parson's School of Design, and worked in the 1920s and 1930s for Charles Armour and Hattie Carnegie. Norell both adapted French models and introduced original designs, but when he became associated with Anthony Traina (1941), his forte proved to be creating high-fashion styling in ready-made clothing. He headed his own firm (from 1960), won many fashion awards, and was called the "dean of American fashion designers."

NORIEGA, MANUEL (1934–), Panamanian military and political leader. Noriega escaped from poverty by gaining a scholarship to a military academy in Peru (1958). He subsequently became an intelligence officer in the Panamanian National Guard (1962), began a long relationship with the U.S. Central Intelligence Agency (CIA), and became chief of intelligence (1970). As national guard chief of staff (1982–89), he was the de facto ruler of the country and was supported by the U.S. government. However, in the late 1980s he defied U.S. policy in Central America and was accused of human rights abuses and indicted by two U.S. grand juries for drug trafficking, money laundering, and racketeering (1988). After Noriega voided the results of democratically held elections (1989), the United States invaded Panama and he surrendered to U.S. troops (1990). He was taken to Florida to stand trial, was convicted of eight counts of racketeering and drug trafficking, and sentenced to 40 years in prison. ■ See his memoirs, *America's Prisoner* (1997); Steve Albert, *The Case Against the General* (1993); and Frederick Kempe, *Divorcing the Dictator* (1990).

NORMAN, JESSYE (1945–), U.S. opera singer. Born into a middle-class black musical family in Georgia, Norman was inspired to become an opera singer after listening to radio broadcasts of the Metropolitan Opera while still a child. She studied music at Howard University (B.M. 1967) and the University of Michigan (M. Mus. 1968) and won the prestigious Munich International Music competition (1968). The prize led to a contract with the Deutsche Oper in Berlin (1969), where she made her sensational debut as Elisabeth in *Tannhäuser*. She sang her first performance at La Scala, Milan (1972), in *Aida* and at Covent Garden, London (1972), and at the Metropolitan Opera, New York (1983), in *Les Troyens*. The possessor of an enormously powerful and vibrant soprano voice, Norman was a magnetic stage personality and an imposing physical presence. She was also a highly acclaimed concert singer and recitalist, known for her refined interpretations of songs from the French, German, Italian, and Russian repertory. She recorded more than 50 albums, and won Grammy awards in 1980, 1982, and 1985. Widely regarded as the greatest female singer of her generation, she was invited to sing "La Marseillaise," the French national anthem, in Paris during the bicentennial of the French Revolution.

NORMAN, MARSHA (Marsha Williams; 1947–), U.S. playwright. Born in Louisville, Kentucky, to parents who were strict fundamentalists, Norman earned degrees from Agnes Scott College in Georgia (1969), where she majored in philosophy, and the University of Louisville (M.A. 1971). Her experience teaching disturbed teens at Kentucky Central State Hospital inspired the play *Getting Out* (1976). A tremendous success, the play received critical acclaim in a New York Off-Broadway production. It was followed by such plays as *Third and Oak* (1979), *The Shakers* (1983), *The Holdup* (1983), and *Traveler in the Dark* (1984). Norman won a Pulitzer Prize for *'night, Mother* (1983), an intense work about life-and-death issues in the relationship between a mother and daughter. She won a 1991 Tony Award for the musical play *The Secret Garden* (1989). She

also wrote the play *Traveler in the Dark* (1984) and the novel *The Fortune Teller* (1987).

NORMAN, MONTAGU COLLET, 1st BARON NORMAN OF ST. CLERE (1871–1950), British banker. A member of a British banking family, Norman was educated at Eton and Cambridge and elected a director of the Bank of England in 1907. Arrogant, taciturn, and financially orthodox, he served as the bank's governor for 24 years (1920–44), longer than any other person. No important financial move was made without him; he was especially influential in handling post–World War 1 economic reconstruction, German reparations, and the restoration (1925) and abandonment (1931) of the gold standard. He thus played a major role in the economic and social turmoil of the late 1920s, and his politics were said to have resulted in the fall of Prime Minister Ramsay MacDonald's Labour government in 1931.

NORRIS, GEORGE WILLIAM (1861–1944), U.S. political leader. A Nebraska judge before serving in the U.S. House of Representatives (1903–13), Norris was elected as a liberal Republican but quickly became known as an independent. His first great act of courage was leading the movement to dethrone the autocratic Speaker of the House, Joe Cannon (1910). In 1913 he began a 30-year career in the U.S. Senate, during which he opposed U.S. entry into World War I and the Versailles Treaty, wrote the 20th Amendment to the Constitution, which abolished the "lame duck" sessions of Congress, urged farm supports, and cosponsored (1932) the Norris-LaGuardia Act, which restricted the use of injunctions against unions. He supported Pres. Franklin D. Roosevelt's policies, and his sponsorship of the Tennessee Valley Authority (TVA) led to its first dam being named for him. An amiable but passionate man, Norris was the living link between the Progressive Era and the New Deal. ■ See his autobiography, *Fighting Liberal* (1945), and biography by Richard Lowitt (3 vols., 1963–78).

NORRISH, RONALD (1897–1978), British physical chemist. Norrish received a Ph.D. from Cambridge (1924) and taught there until his retirement in 1965. He shared the 1967 Nobel Prize for Chemistry with George Porter and Manfred Eigen for work in photochemistry, the study of very fast chemical reactions resulting from exposure of a system to light. This field emerged in the 1920s on the theoretical basis of work by Max Planck and Albert Einstein. With his collaborators, Norrish devised the techniques of flash photolysis and kinetic spectroscopy, which involved infusing "flashes" of power into a photochemically active system at precise intervals to permit observation and measurement of the system's dissociation into atoms or radicals.

NORTH, DOUGLASS C. (1920–), U.S. economic historian. North studied at the University of California at Berkeley (Ph.D. 1952) and taught at the University of Washington (1950–83) and Washington University in St. Louis (from

1983). He also directed the Institute for Economic Research (1960–66) and the National Bureau of Economic Research (1967–87). A founder of the school of historical analysis known as "cliometrics," named after Clio, the muse of history in Greek mythology, North applied economic theory and quantitative methods to the study of historical events. He published many studies as an editor of the *Journal of Economic History* (1960–66) and analyzed masses of quantitative data in his pioneering study of *The Economic Growth of the United States, 1790–1860* (1961). His later works, including *Structure and Change in Economic History* (1981) and *Institutions, Institutional Change and Economic Performance* (1990), emphasized the roles of social and political institutions in economic development. He shared the 1993 Nobel Memorial Prize in Economics with Robert W. Fogel for his work in economic history.

NORTHCLIFFE, ALFRED CHARLES WILLIAM HARMS-WORTH, VISCOUNT (1865–1922), British newspaper publisher. One of the century's most powerful newspapermen, Northcliffe was a pioneer of popular modern journalism. He began his career in 1888 by establishing a successful weekly called *Answers to Correspondents* and subsequently acquired the *London Evening News* (1894), founded the *Daily Mail* (1896) and the tabloid *Daily Mirror* (1903), and secured control of the *Times* (1908). He introduced short news stories, women's features, political gossip columns, and serials in building his papers' readership. From the 1890s he exercised a strong influence on British public life, especially during World War I, when he criticized the war office and its methods. In 1905 he was raised to the peerage as a baron, and in 1917 he was made viscount. ■ See biography by Reginald Pound and Geoffrey Harmsworth (1959).

NORTHROP, JOHN HOWARD (1891–1987), U.S. biochemist. After completing his education at Columbia University (Ph.D. 1916), Northrop did research at the Rockefeller Institute for Medical Research (1916–61) and became involved in the enzyme controversy sparked by Richard Willstätter's assertion that enzymes are not proteins. After James Sumner reversed Willstätter's theory, Northrop confirmed that enzymes *are* proteins when he crystallized pepsin (1930), trypsin (1932), and chymotrypsin (1935). He also isolated the first bacterial virus (1938) and confirmed that it too was a protein. He shared the 1946 Nobel Prize for Chemistry with Sumner and W. M. Stanley. His books included *Crystalline Enzymes* (2nd ed. 1948; with M. Kunitz and R. M. Herriot).

NORTHROP, JOHN KNUDSEN (1895–1981), U.S. aircraft designer and manufacturer. With only a high school degree, Northrop worked his way from garage mechanic to president of his own company, Northrop Aircraft, Inc., established in 1939. An engineer who patented numerous devices and designs, Northrop built the first Vega airplane (1927), which set numerous speed and endurance records.

He also helped develop (1939–40) the tailless "Flying Wing," which housed the pilot, cargo, and motor unit inside the wing and served as a "flying laboratory" for three years. He constructed several outstanding military planes during World War II and advanced the field of unmanned missiles and rockets before retiring in 1952. ■ See biography by Theodore Coleman (1988).

NOSSACK, HANS ERICH (1901–1977), German writer. Trained in philosophy and law, Nossack was a businessman before World War II. His work was banned by the Nazis because he was a Communist party member (1930–33), and his unpublished manuscripts were lost (1943) during air raids on Hamburg. His fiction, published after 1947, focused on existential crises of protagonists faced by external chaos or by evidence of their own failures. Influenced by the work of Franz Kafka, he questioned ideas and perceptions that are taken for granted and warned against the increasing bureaucratization and institutionalization of society. His novels included *Wait for November* (1955; Eng. trans. 1982), *The Impossible Proof* (1959; Eng. trans. 1968), *An Offering for the Dead* (1961; Eng. trans. 1992), *The D'Arthez Case* (1968; Eng. trans. 1971), and *To the Unknown Hero* (1969; Eng. trans. 1974).

NOVAËS, GUIOMAR (1896–1979), Brazilian pianist. Novaës, one of 19 children in her family, was a child prodigy who made her debut at age 8. She won a prestigious scholarship to the Paris Conservatory (1909) and made celebrated debuts in London (1912) and New York (1915). Renowned for her elegant and aristocratic style of playing, she was best known for her interpretations of the works of Chopin, Schumann, Bach, Mozart, and Debussy, which she performed in concert halls throughout the world.

NOVOTNÝ, ANTONÍN (1904–1975), Czech political leader. An efficient, humorless organization man, Novotný joined the Communist party in 1921. He was a leader of the anti-German underground during World War II until his arrest and incarceration in Mauthausen concentration camp (1941–45). Elected to the party Central Committee (1946), he played a leading role in the 1948 communist coup and became first secretary of the party—and virtual dictator of Czechoslovakia—in 1953. A dedicated Stalinist, he advanced oppressive economic and cultural policies that aroused resentment both within and outside of the party; he was ousted from the leadership during the liberalization period in January 1968 and replaced by Alexander Dubček.

NOWLAN, PHILIP (1888–1940), **and RICHARD CALKINS** (1895–1962), U.S. cartoonists. In 1928 Nowlan, a journalist, published a novel, *Armageddon 2419 A.D.*, about a contemporary American pilot, Anthony Rogers, who is overcome by gas and reawakens in the 25th century. John F. Dille persuaded Nowlan to turn the story into a comic strip and rename the hero Buck. The first American science-fiction strip, *Buck Rogers 2429 A.D.,* appeared on Jan. 7, 1929, illustrated by Richard Calkins, a newspaper cartoonist and illustrator. Calkins continued to draw the strip and took over the writing after Nowlan's death until a dispute with his employers caused him to quit in 1947. In the late 1940s and early 1950s he wrote stories for the *Red Ryder* comic books.

NOYCE, ROBERT N. (1927–1990), U.S. inventor. Noyce, the son of a Congregational minister, studied physical electronics at the Massachusetts Institute of Technology (Ph.D. 1953) and worked at the Shockley Semiconductor Laboratory, Palo Alto, California (1956–57). A research director (1957–59) of Fairchild Semiconductor Corp., Mountain View, California, which he cofounded in 1957, he invented (1959) the integrated circuit, a system of interconnected transistors on a single microchip made of silicon. (Jack Kilby of Texas Instruments, Inc., working independently, also developed a microchip in 1959.) The microchip revolutionized the electronics industry, became the basic component of the modern computer, and helped transform a Santa Clara Valley orchard area into "Silicon Valley," the center of high-tech industry. Noyce subsequently cofounded (1968), with Gordon E. Moore, the Intel Corporation, which developed the microprocessor and became one of the world's leading semiconductor companies. He also served as the first chief executive of Sematech (1988), a giant research consortium in Austin, Texas. ■ See T. R. Reid, *The Chip* (1985).

NOYES, ALFRED (1880–1958), British poet. Noyes was an Oxford-educated traditionalist whose prolific output of sentimental, straightforward, and rhythmic lyric verse made him the most popular poet of his generation. He was able to earn his living solely on the basis of his poetry. Noyes' epics, *The Flower of Old Japan* (1903) and *The Forest of Wild Thyme* (1905), have been called the finest fairy poetry since the Elizabethans. His lifelong interest in the sea was best reflected in his 12-volume masterpiece, *Drake* (1906–08), an epic of Elizabethan maritime power. Noyes is also known for *Tales of the Mermaid Tavern* (1913), *The Torchbearers* (1922–30), and his ballads "The Highwayman" and "The Barrel-Organ." ■ See his autobiography, *Two Worlds for Memory* (1953).

NOYES, FRANK BRETT (1863–1948), U.S. newspaper publisher. The son of Crosby Noyes, who edited the *Washington Star,* Noyes began working for the *Star* at age 13 and became its successful treasurer and business manager (1886–1901). As editor and publisher of the *Chicago Record Herald* (1902–10) and president of the *Washington Star* (1910–48), Noyes earned a reputation as a solid and effective—if dull—newspaperman. Noyes is best remembered for his role in the Associated Press (AP). As a director (1894–1947) and president (1900–38) of the nonprofit press agency, he helped to build it into the nation's most important wire service,

known for its impartial reporting. He helped set up AP's foreign news coverage and to form the AP Wirephoto service (1935).

NU, U (1907–1995), Burmese political leader. Nu graduated from Rangoon University (B.A. 1929) and became a teacher and journalist. A devout Buddhist and ardent nationalist, he was imprisoned by the British prior to World War II. He held cabinet posts in the Japanese puppet government during the war but later broke with it and served as an official of the Antifascist People's Freedom League. He negotiated Burmese independence with the British (1947) and became the first premier of independent Burma in 1948. During his years in power (1948–56; 1956–58; 1960–62) he attempted to revive Buddhism, build a welfare-state economy, and enhance the influence of the nonaligned movement. However, his government was thwarted by economic setbacks and communist and ethnic minority insurrections. Overthrown by a military coup led by Ne Win (1962), he was jailed (1962–66) and subsequently tried unsuccessfully to regain power as head of a Thailand-based resistance movement (1969–74). Allowed to return to Burma in 1980, he translated Buddhist scriptures into English. In 1988, during nationwide prodemocracy demonstrations, he became the leader of a new civilian political alliance and formed a provisional opposition government. However, the military reasserted its control and U Nu was placed under house arrest (1989–92). ■ See his autobiography (Eng. trans. 1975), and biography by Richard A. Butwell (1969).

NUFFIELD, WILLIAM RICHARD MORRIS, 1st VISCOUNT (1877–1963), British industrialist and philanthropist. A onetime bicycle mechanic, Nuffield mass-produced inexpensive, reliable, and economical motor cars. His Morris-Oxford (1913) and Morris-Cowley (1919) revolutionized the British automotive industry and were the basis of Morris Motors Ltd., which Nuffield founded in 1919 and headed until 1952. He produced the first "MG" in 1923. The merger of Morris with Austin (1952) established the British Motor Corp. as one of the world's largest motor companies. A leading philanthropist—his bequests totaled more than £30 million—Nuffield established the postgraduate Nuffield Institute for Medical Research (1937) and Nuffield College (1943), both at Oxford. He was created a viscount in 1938. ■ See biography by Martin Adeney (1993).

NUNN MAY, ALAN. *See MAY, ALAN NUNN.*

NUREYEV, RUDOLF (1938–1993), Soviet-born ballet dancer. A soloist with Leningrad's Kirov Ballet (from 1958), Nureyev defected while on tour in Paris (1961) and became the world's most famous and acclaimed male ballet dancer. Compared by many to Nijinsky, he had a magnetic stage presence and was able to perform dazzling leaps and turns. He joined London's Royal Ballet (1962) as guest artist and began a historic partnership with ballerina Margot Fonteyn. He performed with ballet companies throughout the world and frequently appeared in New York. Although best known for his interpretations in such classics as *Giselle, Swan Lake,* and *Les Sylphides* and modern ballets as *Petrushka, Apollo, The Prodigal Son,* and *La Fille Mal Gardée,* he also was acclaimed for performing modern-dance works of Paul Taylor, José Limón and Martha Graham. He also staged many productions, including the *Nutcracker, Don Quixote,* and *Raymonda.* He directed the Paris Opera Ballet (1983–1989). He died of AIDS. ■ See his autobiography (1962) and biographies by John Percival (1975), Clive Barnes (1982), and Diane Solway (1998).

NURI AL-SAID (1888–1958), Iraqi political leader. An officer in the Ottoman army (from 1909), Nuri joined the Arab Revolt (1916) and was closely associated with Emir Faisal, who was king of Iraq from 1921 to 1933. After serving as minister of defense and army chief of staff during the 1920s, he was named premier (1930–32). He ended Iraq's mandate status by negotiating its independence with the British. Over the next three decades he was Iraq's most important political figure, serving as premier 13 more times. Autocratic, pro-British, and anticommunist, Nuri attempted to assert Iraqi leadership in pan-Arab affairs and joined the U.S-sponsored Baghdad Pact (1955). However, he was out of touch with the political currents sweeping the Arab world and was murdered during the military coup that overthrew the Iraqi monarchy (July 14, 1958). ■ See Waldemar J. Gallman, *Iraq Under General Nuri* (1964).

NURMI, PAAVO JOHANNES (1897–1973), Finnish long-distance runner. Called the "Flying Finn," Nurmi was one of the century's great track stars and a Finnish national hero. The dominant runner of the 1920s, he won nine Olympic gold medals in three Olympics (1920; 1924; 1928), including six at Paris in 1924 (1.500 meter, 3,000 meter, 5,000 meter, and cross-country individual and team events). Known for his long, high strides, he ran at a swift, steady, and seemingly effortless pace and held 12 world records including the record for the mile run (4 minutes, 10.4 seconds; from 1923 to 1931).

NÜSSLEIN-VOLHARD, CHRISTIANE (1942–), German biologist. Nüsslein-Volhard studied at the University of Tübingen (Ph.D. 1973), and did research at the European Biology Laboratory in Heidelberg (1978–80) and at the Max Planck Institute for Developmental Biology in Tübingen (1981–). With her colleague at Heidelberg in the late 1970s, Eric Weischaus, she followed up on the pioneering genetic mutation studies of the fruit fly Drosophila done by Edward B. Lewis in the 1940s. Minutely studying the fly's 20,000 genes by breeding 40,000 fly families, they determined how the newly fertilized egg divided into segments

during the earliest stages of embryonic development. Their research opened up a new approach to the study of developmental biology, and they shared the 1995 Nobel Prize in Physiology or Medicine with Lewis.

NUVOLARI, TAZIO GIORGIO (1892–1953), Italian autoracing driver. A champion motorcycle racer before turning to automobiles, Nuvolari, known as "the Flying Mantuan" and "Il Maestro," was the most successful European Grand Prix racer of the 1930s. Many consider him to be the greatest racer of all time. Unorthodox in his animated driving style, daring in his devilishly skillful maneuvering (he rarely used brakes), and nonconforming in his choice of outrageous and colorful driving clothes, Nuvolari won 72 major races in his career, which lasted more than 30 years. He retired in 1947. ■ See biography by Count Giovanni Lurani (Eng. trans. 1960).

NYE, GERALD PRENTICE (1892–1971), U.S. senator. A progressive Republican, Nye served as a U.S. senator from North Dakota from 1925 to 1945. He was chairman of the committee that investigated the Teapot Dome scandal (1926) and the munitions industry (1934–36), and he won national recognition for his speeches blaming the "merchants of death" for U.S. entry into World War I. During the 1930s Nye was a leading Senate isolationist, a prominent member of the America First Committee, and a cosponsor of the Neutrality Act (1936). ■ See study by Wayne S. Cole (1962).

NYERERE, JULIUS KAMBARAGE (1922–1999), Tanzanian political leader. The son of a Zanaki chief, Nyerere studied at Makerere University College and at Edinburgh University, where he was influenced by Fabian socialism. He was the founding president of the Tanganyika African National Union (TANU; 1954), the nationalist political party, that led the country to independence (1961). As president (1962–85) he established a one-party state, based on principles of African socialism and self-reliance. Although the cooperative *Ujamaa* villages and nationalized industries were not economically successful, he arranged the union of Tanganyika with Zanzibar (1964), instilled a sense of national unity, promoted Swahili as the national language (and achieved a literacy rate of 83 percent), and dramatically improved health care for his people. Internationally he aided the independence movements in Mozambique and Zimbabwe and helped overthrow Ugandan dictator Idi Amin (1979). A universally respected elder statesman in Africa, he retired from government in 1985, but remained as party leader until 1990. His books included *Freedom and Socialism* (1968) and *Freedom and Development* (1973). ■ See William E. Smith, *We Must Run While They Walk* (1972); John Hatch, *Two African Statesmen* (1976); and William R. Duggan and John R. Civille, *Tanzania and Nyerere* (1976).

O

OAKLEY, ANNIE (Phoebe Anne Oakley Moses; 1860–1926), U.S. rodeo performer. Annie Oakley measured just under five feet tall and frequently did needlework between appearances in Buffalo Bill's Wild West Show (1885–1901). Her trick shooting—she could hit the edge of a playing card some hundred feet away and shoot cigarettes from her husband's lips—won her a worldwide reputation. Her sharpshooting days were fictionalized in a television series and in the musical comedy *Annie Get Your Gun* (1946), which starred Ethel Merman. ■ See biographies by Walter Havighurst (1954), Doris Garst (1958), and Glenda Riley (1994).

OATES, JOYCE CAROL (1938–), U.S. writer. Raised in a Catholic family in a small town near Buffalo, New York, Oates graduated from Syracuse University (B.A. 1960) and the University of Wisconsin (M.A. 1961) and taught English at the University of Windsor, Canada (from 1967). A prolific writer whom critics have compared to Melville, Dreiser, Zola, and Faulkner, she wrote of violence, sex, murder, and wasted lives in her numerous novels, short stories, and poems. Her best-known novels included *Them* (1969, National Book Award), *Unholy Loves* (1980), *Bellefleur* (1980), *A Bloodsmoor Romance* (1982), *Mysteries of Winterthurn* (1984), *Solstice* (1985), *Marya* (1986), *Because It Is Bitter, and Because It Is My Heart* (1990), *Man Crazy* (1997), *My Heart Laid Bare* (1998), *Broke Heart Blues* (1999), and *Blonde* (2000). She also published the short-story collections *By the North Gate* (1963), *Wheel of Love* (1970), *Marriages and Infidelities* (1972), *A Sentimental Education* (1981), and *Last Days* (1984), and several poetry collections, including *Anonymous Sins* (1969), *Angel Fire* (1973), *The Fabulous Beasts* (1975), and *Invisible Woman* (1982). Her literary criticism appeared in *The Edge of Impossibility* (1972), *New Heaven, New Earth* (1974), and *Contraries* (1981). ■ See studies by Joanne V. Creighton (1979) and Ellen G. Friedman (1980) and Greg Johnson, *Invisible Writer* (1998).

OBERTH, HERMANN JULIUS (1894–1989), Hungarian-born German astrophysicist. A pioneer of modern astronautics, Oberth had developed by 1922 his mathematical calculation demonstrating how a rocket might achieve a speed enabling it to escape the earth's gravitational force. His books, including *Big Rocket to Interplanetary Space* (1923) and *Way to Space Travel* (1929), anticipated later advances in rocketry and helped to finance his research. With his assistants, he demonstrated the possibility of rocket propulsion by liquid and, later, solid propellants. Oberth joined Wernher von Braun at the German rocket center at Peenemünde (1941–43) and later worked with him to develop space vehicles for the U.S. Army (1955–58). ■ See his *Man into Space* (Eng. trans. 1957) and the biography by Helen B. Walters (1962).

OBOTE, MILTON APOLLO (1924–), Ugandan political leader. A graduate of Makerere College, Kampala (1949), Obote served in the legislative council (from 1957), where he criticized British government policies, and founded the Uganda People's Party (1960). As prime minister of a coalition government, he led Uganda to independence from Britain (1962). In 1966 he abolished the constitution that granted semiautonomous status to Buganda and three other traditional kingdoms and became interim president. He continued in that office under the new constitution (1967) which gave broad powers to the central government and the presidency. Obote was overthrown by a military coup led by Idi Amin (1971) and remained in exile in Tanzania until Amin was overthrown (1980). Subsequently elected president once again (1980), Obote was unsuccessful in his attempts to quell intertribal warfare and antigovernment rebellions. His security forces were accused of torture and of massacring civilians and his government was deposed in a bloodless coup (1985). He subsequently lived in exile in Zambia. ■ See James H. Mittleman, *Ideology and Politics in Uganda* (1975).

OBREGÓN, ÁLVARO (1880–1928), Mexican political leader. A small landholder, Obregón entered politics in 1911 and raised a peasant army to defend the government of Pres. Francisco Madero. After Madero's murder (1913), he supported Venustiano Carranza (1913–17) and commanded the Constitutional Army to victories over the forces of Emiliano Zapata and Pancho Villa. He served as president of Mexico (1920–24) and was the first leader with a plan to carry out the program of the Mexican revolutionaries. He initiated significant agrarian, labor, and educational reforms and negotiated outstanding oil claims and land disputes with the U.S. government. He retired to pursue a business career but was reelected to the presidency in 1928. Before he could be sworn in, however, he was assassinated by a religious fanatic, apparently in revenge for his anticlerical policies. ■ See study by Linda B. Hull (1981).

O'BRIEN, FLANN (Brian O'Nolan; 1911–1966), Irish novelist and columnist. O'Brien studied Gaelic language and poetry at Dublin's University College and began (1940) writing humorous newspaper columns in Gaelic under the name

Myles na gCopaleen (or Gopaleen). He continued writing columns for a quarter of a century, for the most part in English. His grueling labors as journalist and civil servant diminished his output of fiction. O'Brien's early work is considered his finest. *At Swim-Two-Birds* (1939), the comic product of his imaginative linguistic trickery, was admired by James Joyce, the writer whose career overshadowed O'Brien's. He also wrote *The Hard Life: An Exegesis of Squalor* (1961) and *The Dalkey Archive* (1964). *The Third Policeman* (1967) and *Slattery's Sago Saga* (1973) appeared posthumously. *The Best of Myles* (1968) contained his newspaper columns. O'Brien wrote fiction in Gaelic as well. ■ See *A Flann O'Brien Reader* (1978); study by Anne Clissmann (1975); and Anthony Cronin, *No Laughing Matter* (1989).

O'CASEY, SEAN (1884–1964), Irish playwright. Born into a slum-dwelling Protestant family in Dublin. O'Casey did not learn to read until he was 14 and was largely self-educated. He worked as a laborer and organizer for the Irish revolutionary movement before becoming a full-time playwright. His most enduring works, *Shadow of a Gunman* (1923), *Juno and the Paycock* (1924), and the controversial *The Plough and the Stars* (1926), were naturalistic tragicomedies that depicted the life of the Dublin poor during the Easter rebellion (1916) and the civil war of the 1920s. A socialist who always championed the workers, O'Casey mocked patriotism, condemned war, and, after breaking with the middle-class leadership of the Irish revolutionary movement and settling in Britain (1926), became increasingly radical in his political views. Many of his later works were satirical fantasies of Irish life. His six volumes of autobiography (1939–54) were republished as *Mirror in My House* (1956). ■ See biographies by David Krause (enl. ed. 1975) and Garry O'Connor (1988).

OCHOA, SEVERO (1905–1993), Spanish-born U.S. physician and biochemist. Ochoa emigrated to the United States (1941) after having done research at Heidelberg (1936–38) and Oxford (1938–41). He served on the faculty of the New York University Medical School from 1942 to 1974. His major contributions were in the area of enzyme action, and he isolated (1955) the bacterial enzyme used for the synthesis of compounds resembling naturally occurring ribonucleic acid (RNA). For this discovery, which helped scientists understand how genes transfer hereditary information, he shared the 1959 Nobel Prize in Physiology or Medicine with Arthur Kornberg.

OCHS, ADOLPH SIMON (1858–1935), U.S. newspaper publisher. The son of Jewish immigrants from Bavaria, Ochs purchased the *Chattanooga* (Tennessee) *Times* (1878) and made it one of the south's leading papers. He bought the declining *New York Tmes* in 1896, chose the slogan "All the news that's fit to print," and transformed it into the newspaper of record for the United States. Unlike the sensational publishers of the day, Ochs insisted on quality journalism, stressed accuracy, nonpartisanship, and thoroughness, and helped raise the standard of journalism throughout the country. Among his innovations were the book-review supplement and *The New York Times Index,* which was the only complete U.S. newspaper index and served as an indispensable source for historians. ■ See Gerald W. Johnson, *An Honorable Titan* (1946).

OCHS, PHIL (1940–1976), U.S. singer. Ochs dropped out of Ohio State University, where he was studying journalism, and joined the burgeoning folk-protest movement in New York City's Greenwich Village (1962). His topical and satirical songs attacking U.S. imperialism and exposing injustice and political hypocrisy, became anthems of the New Left during the height of the civil-rights and anti–Vietnam War movements. Among his best-known songs were "I Ain't Marchin' Anymore," "Love Me, I'm a Liberal," "There but for Fortune," "The War Is Over," and "Outside of a Small Circle of Friends." He was, however, unable to successfully adapt his acoustic style to the electric folk-rock revolution of the late 1960s, and he was frustrated by the lack of change in American politics and society. During the mid-1970s he suffered from writer's block and severe depression and he committed suicide. ■ See biography by Marc Eliot (1990) and Michael Schumacher, *There but for Fortune* (1996).

O'CONNOR, (MARY) FLANNERY (1925–1964), U.S. writer. A religious Catholic, O'Connor was born in the South's Bible Belt. She inherited from her father disseminated lupus, a debilitating, incurable disease that gradually crippled and weakened her over the last 12 years of her life. She was, however, extremely productive during this period, working in short, intense bursts each day to produce the powerful, traditionally constructed novels and short stories that established her as a leading fiction writer of her generation. The novels *Wise Blood* (1952) and *The Violent Bear It Away* (1960) delved into religious fanaticism. The stories in *A Good Man Is Hard to Find* (1955) and *Everything That Rises Must Converge* (1965) depicted terrifying sequences of events that compel characters to seek redemption through an act of self-sacrifice. ■ See her *Complete Stories* (1971): her collection of letters, *The Habit of Being* (1979); studies by Kathleen Feeley (1972) and Dorothy T. McFarland (1976); and Josephine Hendin, *The World of Flannery O'Connor* (1970).

O'CONNOR, FRANK (Michael O'Donovan; 1903–1966), Irish short-story writer. Despite his poverty-stricken family background and his lack of a university education, O'Connor became one of Ireland's leading writers. His short stories, concerning everyday Irish life, were noted for their humor, realism, rich characterization, and their great sensitivity to Irish speech. Among O'Connor's best-known collections were *Guests of the Nation* (1931), *The Saint and Mary Kate* (1932), and *Crab Apple Jelly* (1944). He also translated several Gaelic literary classics, wrote studies of the Russian writer Ivan Turgenev and the Irish revolutionary Michael Collins, and was a director of Dublin's Abbey Theatre. *An Only Child* (1961) and *My Father's Son* (1968) were autobiographical. ■ See his *Collected Stories* (1981) and *Voices* (1983); biography by James Matthews; and studies by William M. Tomory (1980) and Jim McKeon (1998).

O'CONNOR, SANDRA DAY (Sandra Day; 1930–), U.S. jurist. O'Connor grew up on her family's 160,000-acre ranch on the Arizona–New Mexico border and graduated from Stanford Law School (1952), where she was a classmate of Supreme Court Chief Justice William Rehnquist. A conservative Republican Arizona state senator (1969–74), she was the first woman in the country to serve as a majority leader (1973–74). She subsequently was a Maricopa County Superior Court judge (1975–79) and an Arizona Court of Appeals judge (1979–81) before being appointed by Pres. Ronald Reagan (1981) to the Supreme Court. She was the first woman to serve on the nation's highest court. During her early years on the court, her votes and written decisions adhered closely to Reagan administration views in such areas as church and state, search and seizure, and social issues. Subsequently regarded as a centrist and an ideological moderate, she supported cases favoring women's equality but not those favoring affirmative action to combat racial discrimination. She also supported decisions favoring greater autonomy for the states. ■ See study by Nancy Maveety (1996) and Robert W. Van Sickel, *Not a Particularly Different Voice* (1998).

ODETS, CLIFFORD (1906–1963), U.S. playwright. The son of a prosperous Bronx, New York, printer, Odets dropped out of high school to act (1923–28) but had little success. He took up playwriting and was hailed by young socialists of the Depression era as the dramatist of social protest after well-received productions of *Waiting for Lefty* (1935) and *Awake and Sing!* (1935) by the influential Group Theatre in New York City. *Golden Boy* (1937; musical adaptation, 1964) was his last major success until *The Country Girl* (1950). Odets spent much of his later life in Hollywood doctoring scripts for large fees and writing and directing his own screenplays. *The Big Knife* (1949) expressed his disenchantment with the film industry. ■ See biographies by Gerald Weales (1971) and Margaret Brenman-Gibson (1981), and study by Edward Murray (1968).

ODETTA (Odetta Holmes; 1930–), U.S. folksinger. Born in Alabama, Odetta moved to California with her family at age 6 and studied music privately and at Los Angeles City College. When she was introduced to folk music (1949) she abandoned her plans for a classical career and soon began to appear in nightclubs in San Francisco. Her powerful dusky contralto voice and emotional delivery set her apart in the folk music world, and she gained national attention during the folk music revival of the late 1950s and early 1960s. Ac-companying herself on the guitar, she sang traditional folk songs as well as spirituals, work and prison songs, blues, gospel songs, and lullabies. She remained popular through the 1980s.

ODINGA, (AJUMA) OGINGA (1911–1994), Kenyan political leader. A Luo tribesman, Odinga received teacher training at Makerere College and was active in the tribal self-help movement. After meeting nationalist leader Jomo Kenyatta in 1948, he became a committed member of his movement. Not arrested during the Mau-Mau emergency of the 1950s, he continued the anticolonial struggle and was elected to the first legislative council (1957). In 1960 he was named vice president of the Kenya African National Union (KANU), and he subsequently served as vice president of an independent Kenya (1964–66). As a result of his split with KANU in 1966 and his forming a radical socialist opposition party, the Kenya People's Union (1966), he was arrested (1969–71) and the party was banned. He was not allowed to run for office in 1977 and 1981 and was under house arrest from November 1982 to October 1983. ■ See his autobiography, *Not yet Uhuru* (1967).

ODUM, HOWARD WASHINGTON (1884–1954), U.S. sociologist. A native of rural Georgia, Odum was an authority on black folk culture and an early advocate of equal opportunity. While on the faculty of the University of North Carolina (1920–54), he established a school of public welfare and a social science research institute, founded the *Journal of Social Forces,* and continued his inquiry into the transition from folk society to complex state civilization. Odum's *Rainbow Round My Shoulder: The Blue Trail of Black Ulysses* (1928) was a literary as well as sociological classic, and his *Southern Regions of the United States* (1936) a plea for responsible regionalism.

OE, KENZABURO (1935–), Japanese novelist. Oe was born into a wealthy family that lost its land following World War II. A graduate of Tokyo University (1959), he became one of the most significant Japanese novelists of the postwar years and a spokesperson for the younger generation of left-wing intellectuals. His short story "The Catch" (1958: Eng. trans. 1966) and his novels, notably *Screams* (1962) and *Perverts* (1963), reflected the frustration, rebellion, violence, and search for identity of the alienated postwar youth who were cut off from their past. *A Personal Matter* (1964; Eng. trans. 1968), about a young husband who seeks to escape from responsibility, and *The Silent Cry* (1967; Eng. trans. 1974), which contained his reflections on the course of modern Japanese history, both won major literary awards. His later novels and essays reflected his involvement in the anti-nuclear movement and his concern for problems of the Third World. Further English translations of his works are in *Teach Us to Outgrow Our Madness* (1972), *The Pinch Runner Memorandum* (1976; Eng. trans. 1994), *An Echo of Heaven* (1989; Eng. trans. 1996), *A Quiet Life* (1990; Eng.

trans. 1996), and *Hiroshima Notes* (1968; Eng. trans. 1995), a nonfiction account of the meaning and legacy of the atomic bombing. He was awarded the 1994 Nobel Prize for Literature. ■ See L. Cameron, *The Music of Light* (1998).

OERTER, AL (1936–), U.S. discus thrower. Oerter won four consecutive Olympic gold medals (1956–68), breaking the Olympic record, and his personal record, each time. Ray Ewry, a competitor in the discontinued standing-high-jump event, was up to that time, the only other man to accomplish the feat (1900, 1904, 1906, 1908). Subsequently Carl Lewis duplicated the feat and British rower Steve Redgrave won gold medals in five consecutive Olympics (1984–2000). Oerter was the first athlete to throw the discus 200 feet (200 feet, 5 inches, 1962) and was the national Amateur Athletic Union champion six times. His career best was in 1980 when at age 43 he threw the discus 227 feet, 11 inches.

O'FAOLÁIN, SEÁN (John Whelan; 1900–1991), Irish writer, A soldier in the Irish Republican Army (1918–1921), O'Faoláin wrote stories about the lower and middle classes that reflected the renewed interest in Irish culture after Irish independence. He taught in universities until his first works, *Midsummer Night Madness and Other Stories* (1932) and the novel *A Nest of Simple Folk* (1933), met with success. Controversial because of his anticlericalism, O'Faoláin edited *The Bell* (1940–45), which sought to stimulate Irish letters. Among his other well-known works are the biography of Daniel O'Connell (1938) and *An Irish Journey* (1940), a travel book, and *The Story of the Irish People* (rev. ed. 1982). He also wrote the novel *And Again?* (1979). ■ See also *Collected Stories* (1983); his autobiography, *Vive Moi!* (1964); and studies by Maurice Harmon (1967) and Paul A. Doyle (1969).

O'FLAHERTY, LIAM (1896–1984), Irish writer O'Flaherty fought in the Irish rebellion and later turned to writing. His realistic and intense psychological novels focus on common people during turbulent periods in Irish history. They include *Thy Neighbor's Wife* (1923); *The Informer* (1925), which John Ford turned into an Academy Award–winning film (1935); *Famine* (1937), considered his finest; and *Insurrection* (1950). Among his collections of lyrical and poetic short stories are *Spring Sowing* (1923), *Two Lovely Beasts and Other Stories* (1950), and *The Pedlar's Revenge* (1976). ■ See the autobiographical works *Two Years* (1930) and *Shame the Devil* (1934) and studies by James H. O'Brien (1973) and Angeline Kelly (1976).

OGBURN, WILLIAM FIELDING (1886–1959), U.S. sociologist. The son of a Georgia planter, Ogburn received a Ph.D. in sociology from Columbia University (1912) and taught there (1919–27) and at the University of Chicago (1927–51). In *Social Change* (1922) he identified the concept of "cultural lag," or societal disequilibrium brought about by differential rates of change. A pioneer in the application of statistical methods to the social sciences, Ogburn helped move the focus of sociology away from philosophy. His other books included *Recent Social Trends in the United States* (2 vols., 1933) and *Sociology* (1940). ■ See study by Otis Dudley Duncan (1964).

OGILVY, DAVID MACKENZIE (1911–1999), British-born U.S. businessman. Ogilvy worked as a Paris chef, a stove salesman, a market researcher, an intelligence agent, and a tobacco farmer before establishing the New York City advertising agency of Ogilvy & Mather (1948). His firm's breakthrough came with an ad for Hathaway shirts; Ogilvy, on an impulse, bought an eye patch for the model, who became the "Man in the Hathaway shirt." He also devised memorable ads for Rolls-Royce cars, Pepperidge Farm bread, and Schweppes beverages. Creating "long copy" ads that detailed a product's selling points, he advanced both the techniques of mass marketing and advertising—and the fortunes of his firm, which became one of the world's largest agencies. ■ See his *Confessions of an Advertising Man* (1964), *Blood, Brains and Beer* (1978), *Ogilvy on Advertising* (1983), and *The Unpublished David Ogilvy* (1986).

OHAIN, HANS PABST VON (1911–1998), German jet-propulsion pioneer. Ohain received his Ph.D. from Göttingen University and joined the firm of pioneer aircraft builder Ernst Heinkel in 1936. He built the first turbojet engine (1937) and designed the first fully operational jet aircraft, the HE-178 (first flight, Aug. 27, 1939). After World War II he emigrated to the United States where he helped to develop jet aircraft for the U.S. Air Force.

O'HAIR, MADALYN MURRAY (Madalyn Mays; 1919–1995?), U.S. atheist. Born into a wealthy churchgoing family, O'Hair studied religion and intellectual history in college and worked as a lawyer and social worker during the 1950s. She achieved notoriety as an atheist activist when she sued the Baltimore school board (1960) to eliminate prayers in the schools and became, in her own words, "the most hated woman in America" after the U.S. Supreme Court ruled in her favor and outlawed prayer in the public schools (1963). Believing that Christianity "held mankind back in politics, in economics, in industry, in science, in philosophy, [and] in culture," and that the church has "warped and brainwashed countless millions," O'Hair challenged the inclusion of the word "God" in the Pledge of Allegiance and sued to end tax exemptions for houses of worship and to prohibit Bible readings during space flights. She founded the American Atheist Center (1965); edited a monthly newsmagazine, *American Atheist;* and ran a weekly radio show, "Atheist Point of View," and a cable TV show, "American Atheist Forum." In September 1995, O'Hair, her son, and her adopted granddaughter, the three principals of her organization American Atheists Inc. based in Austin, Texas, disappeared without a trace. Among her books were *An Atheist Epic* (1970) and *What on Earth Is an Atheist* (1972).

O'HARA, JOHN (1905–1970), U.S. novelist and short-story writer. O'Hara worked on the *New York Herald Tribune*, became football editor for the *New Yorker*, and later wrote screenplays. His first and perhaps finest novel, *Appointment in Samarra* (1934), recreated his Pennsylvania hometown as a microcosm of America. His conviction that character can be defined in terms of perceivable behavior informed his cynical chronicles of the newly rich. O'Hara relied more on brisk dialogue and detail than on imagery in such novels as *Butterfield 8* (1935), *Ten North Frederick* (1955), and *From the Terrace* (1958). He also wrote the libretto for the Broadway hit *Pal Joey* (1940) and more than 300 short stories. His *Selected Letters* appeared in 1974. ■ See biography by Frank MacShane (1981) and Matthew Bruccoli, *The O'Hara Concern* (1975).

OHLIN, BERTIL (1899–1979), Swedish economist. Ohlin was a precocious scholar who earned a full professorship at the University of Copenhagen at age 25 and taught at the University of Stockholm (1931–65). He was also politically ambitious, but despite 23 years as leader of Sweden's Liberal party (1944–67), he failed to become prime minister. An expert on import-export behavior, he contended that as trade—and thus demand for products—increases, the special advantages that each nation initially has over its partners is diminished. His books included *Interregional and International Trade* (1933). He shared the 1977 Nobel Memorial Prize in Economics with James E. Meade.

OISTRAKH, DAVID (1908–1974), Soviet violinist. The son of poor Jewish parents, Oistrakh was raised in Odessa. He graduated from the Odessa Conservatory (1926) and in 1934 started teaching at the Moscow Conservatory, where he remained until his death. Worldwide fame came to him through international competitions in the 1930s and his early recordings. After his American debut in 1955 (one of the first cultural thaws in the cold war), he was recognized as one of the great violinists of his age. Oistrakh concentrated on the concertos of Brahms, Beethoven, and Tchaikovsky and the work of modern Soviet composers. His powerful virtuoso playing was characterized by its warmth and humanity, pure tone, and a sweeping melodic line. His son Igor (1931–) was also a brilliant violinist.

OJUKWU, CHUKWUEMEKA ODUMEGWU (1933–), Nigerian general. The son of a wealthy Ibo businessman, Ojukwu graduated from Oxford (1955) and joined the Nigerian army in 1957. He became military governor of the eastern region (1966) and headed the secessionist Biafran state (1967–70). After losing the war with Nigeria, he took refuge in the Ivory Coast. He returned to Nigeria (1982) and ran unsuccessfully for the senate as a candidate of the National Party of Nigeria (NPN) in 1983. He subsequently went into private business. His speeches and account of the civil war are in *Biafra* (1969).

OKAWA, SHUMEI (1886–1957), Japanese political theorist. An extremely popular and highly influential advocate of fascist policies and foreign expansion, Okawa was founder of the Yuzonsha (Society for the Preservation of the National Essence; 1919) and editor of magazines and pamphlets that advocated military government and inspired many right-wing extremist groups. He was involved in several abortive military coups and served five years in prison (1932–37). After his release he worked in governmental positions to propagate traditional values, ultranationalism, and expansionism among the Japanese people. Following World War II, war-crimes charges against him were dropped on the grounds of insanity.

O'KEEFFE, GEORGIA (1887–1986), U.S. painter. The photographer Alfred Stieglitz recognized genius in the spare lines and clear colors of the watercolors of O'Keeffe, a young art teacher living in Texas. O'Keeffe later married Stieglitz (1924) and served as his model while developing a unique style of painting that was precise, sculptured, and nonrepresentative. She was famous for large, close-up views of flowers that suggest human forms and sexual imagery; they date from the 1920s and include such paintings as *Black Iris* (1926) and *Black Flower and Blue Larkspur* (1929). After spending a summer in the New Mexico desert (1929), O'Keeffe returned to the Southwest throughout her life and drew imagery from its stark landscapes and bleached bones in such works as *Cow's Skull* (1931). Travel to Quebec's Gaspé Peninsula inspired a series of paintings that included *White Barn, No. 1* (1932). Among her later works was a series of aerial views of the earth, including a 24-foot mural executed in the 1960s. ■ See the catalogs of her exhibitions at the Art Institute of Chicago (1943) and New York's Whitney Museum (1970); Laurie Lisle, *Portrait of an Artist* (1980); Katherine Hoffman, *An Enduring Spirit* (1984); biography by Jan Garden Castro (1985); and study by Roxana Robinson (1989).

O'KELLY, SEÁN THOMAS (Seán Thomas O Ceallaigh; 1882–1966), Irish political leader. Active in nationalist political and cultural organizations, O'Kelly was a founder of the Sinn Fein party (1905) and secretary-general of the Gaelic League (1915–21). He took part in the Easter Rebellion against the British (1916) and was imprisoned for a year. O'Kelly was the first speaker (1919–21) of the Dáil Eireann (Irish parliament), served as vice president of the executive council of the Irish Free State (1932–39), and served two terms as president of Ireland (1945–59).

OKIGBO, CHRISTOPHER (1932–1967), Nigerian poet. Okigbo was the son of devout Roman Catholic parents and the grandson of a priest of a local Ibo river goddess. He studied classics at University College, Ibadan, and sought to integrate aspects of classical and modern European poetry with traditional Ibo verse in his complex and evocative poems. His later works reflected his increasing concern and involvement with contemporary African political affairs, and he died while fighting for Biafran independence during the Nigerian civil war. His best-known works appeared in *Heavensgate* (1962), *Limits,* (1964), *Labyrinths with Path of Thunder* (1971), and *Collected Poems* (1986). ▪ See study by S. A. Anozie (1972) and D. I. Nwoga, ed., *Critical Perspectives on Christopher Okigbo* (1982).

OLAH, GEORGE A. (1927–), Hungarian-born U.S. chemist. A professor of organic chemistry in Budapest and an associate director of the central research institute of the Hungarian Academy of Sciences, Olah fled to Canada after the crushing of the 1956 Hungarian revolt. He worked for the Dow Chemical Company in Ontario and later taught at Case Western Reserve University in Cleveland, Ohio (1965–77). and at the University of Southern California (1977–). Noted for his hydrocarbon research during the 1960s, Olah devised a method for stabilizing and modifying carbocations, fragments of hydrocarbon molecules that exist for a split second in the intermediate stages of chemical reactions. For his research, which led to the development of new fuels derived from petroleum, coal, and methane and to the creation of high-octane gasoline, Olah was awarded the 1994 Nobel Prize in Chemistry.

OLAND, WARNER (Werner Öhlund; 1880–1938), Swedish-born U.S. actor. A performer in stock companies and on Broadway, Oland first appeared in silent movies in 1912 and was the villain in several Pearl White serials. Frequently called upon to play oriental roles, he portrayed the evil Dr. Fu Manchu in several films before achieving international fame as the first Charlie Chan, the sagacious Chinese detective. He appeared in more than a dozen Chan movies, and few in his audience realized that he was Scandinavian and not Chinese.

OLBRACHT, IVAN (Kamil Zeman; 1882–1952), Czech novelist and essayist. A lawyer who became a journalist and editor of several socialist and communist newspapers, Olbracht achieved fame as one of Czechoslovakia's finest novelists. His masterpiece was *Nikola Šuhaj— Bandit* (1933; Eng. trans. 1954), an epic tale of a legendary Robin Hood-like robber and revolutionary of sub-Carpathian Ruthenia. Olbracht was also known for *The Strange Friendship of the Actor Jesenius* (1919), a psychological novel, and *The Bitter and the Sweet* (1937; Eng. trans. 1967), a series of stories about the poor Hasidic Jews of the Carpatho-Ukraine region. He served in the Czech parliament from 1946 until his death.

OLDENBOURG, ZOÉ (1916–), Russian-born French novelist. Oldenbourg settled in Paris with her family in 1925 and studied at the Sorbonne. Her first historical novel, *The World Is Not Enough* (1946; Eng. trans. 1948), was set in medieval France. Its sequel, *The Cornerstone* (1953; Eng. trans. 1954), won the Prix Femina and proved highly successful. She wrote about the Albigensian Crusade in a novel (*Destiny of Fire,* 1960; Eng. trans. 1961) and a history (*Massacre at Montségur,* 1959; Eng. trans. 1962). Subsequent novels included *The Crusades* (1965; Eng. trans. 1965) and *The Heirs of the Kingdom* (1970; Eng. trans. 1970), a work about a group of weavers who joined the first crusade. Unlike many historical novelists, Oldenbourg refused to pad her work with imaginary details or quaint dialogue. As a result of her careful scholarship she received serious critical attention both in France and abroad.

OLDENBURG, CLAES THURE (1929–), Swedish-born U.S. artist. Oldenburg grew up in the United States, where his father was a member of the diplomatic corps, and graduated from Yale (1950). In 1960 he achieved celebrity for his *Store* stocked with plaster copies of banal consumer goods and was regarded as a major pop artist. Later he moved into "soft sculptures" of gooey ice-cream cones and plump hamburgers. Oldenburg was a pioneer of the "happening" who found theatrical and artistic possibilities in everyday objects removed from their everyday context. ▪ See his *Raw Notes* (1973) and studies by Gena Baro (1960) and Barbara Rose (1970).

OLDFIELD, BARNEY (Berna Eli Oldfield; 1878–1946), U.S. auto-racing driver. Oldfield was the most popular of the pioneer American racing drivers, and his name was synonymous with auto racing and reckless speed during the first two decades of the century. A barnstormer with an exhibition troupe at the outset of his career, he joined Henry Ford's racing team in 1902 and drove the famous "999," He was the first man to drive a one-minute mile (59.6 seconds in 1903), and he set a world's speed record of 131.724 mph in 1910. ▪ See biography by William F. Nolan (1961).

OLESHA, YURI KARLOVICH (1899–1960), Soviet writer. Although he wrote relatively little, Olesha was acknowledged as a brilliant innovator by diverse Russian literary movements. The novel *Envy* (1927; Eng. trans. 1936, 1947; 1960 as *The Wayward Comrade and the Commissar*), his commentary on the displacement of the Intellectual in a new society, featured a conformist sausage manufacturer and reflected the influence of formalist critics. He wrote several short stories and a popular children's tale. His play *A List of Blessings* (1931; Eng. trans. 1983 in *The Complete Plays*) depicts his own ambivalent, uneasy acceptance of the Soviet regime. His humanistic works, influenced by vitalist and expressionist trends in the West, were denigrated by Soviet critics and he disappeared from the literary scene after 1938. English translations of his works are in *The Complete Short Stories* (1979). ▪ See his memoirs, *No Day Without a Line* (1965; Eng. trans. 1979), and Elizabeth Beaujour, *The Invisible Land* (1970).

OLITSKI, JULES (1922–), U.S. artist. Born in Russia, Olitski was taken to the United States as an infant. Trained in New York and Paris, he attempted, as a colorfield artist, to eliminate the use of line in his painting. He was best known for his spray-painted canvases whose areas of color dissolve into one another, creating the illusion of space. During a trip to Britain (1969), Olitski was encouraged by abstract sculptor Anthony Caro to work in three dimensions. The 20 large sculptures he constructed that year from sheets of aluminum sprayed with acrylic lacquer were exhibited at the Metropolitan Museum in New York, making Olitski the first U.S. artist exhibited there in a one-person show. He used layers of metal to create the evocative forms of the *Greenberg Variations* (1974), another series of sculptures. Olitski's later canvases, notably *Elysium* (1988) and *Bacchus Tango* (1994), had rougher surfaces and more muted colors than his earlier works, and critics noted that the layering and complexity of his sculpture carried over into his painting. ■ See study by Kenworth Moffett (1981).

OLIVETTI, ADRIANO (1901–1960), Italian industrialist. Trained as an industrial chemist, Olivetti inherited a small typewriter factory and transformed it into one of the world's largest office-machine-manufacturing firms. President of the company from 1938 until his death, Olivetti set up plants in six countries, had distributors throughout the world, and employed 25,000 workers. An anticommunist, he believed in a "Christian socialism" and provided many employee benefits and permitted workers to share in management. He was also a leader of the town-planning movement in post–World War II Italy.

OLIVIER OF BRIGHTON, LAURENCE KERR OLIVIER, BARON (1907–1989), British actor. The son of a clergyman, Olivier played his first stage role in *The Taming of the Shrew* at age 15 and went on to become a Shakespearean actor of the first order. He became a film star with *Wuthering Heights* (1939) and *Rebecca* (1940) and directed films of his own stage performances in *Hamlet* (Academy Award, 1948), *Richard III* (1955), *Othello* (1965), and *The Three Sisters* (1970). Olivier also starred in *The Entertainer* (1957; film, 1960) and played roles in several Hollywood historial epics and thrillers. He was codirector (with Ralph Richardson) of the Old Vic Theatre (1944–50) and served as director of Britain's National Theatre for ten years (1963–73). Regarded as one of the finest actors of the century, he received a knighthood (1947) and was the first actor ever made a life peer (1970). He retired from the stage in 1974 but continued to appear in films and on television. ■ See his autobiography, *Confessions of an Actor* (1982), and *On Acting* (1986), and biographies by John Cottrell (1975) and Donald Spoto (1992).

OLSEN, TILLIE (Tillie Lerner; 1913–), U.S. novelist and short-story writer. Olsen spent much of her life in San Francisco working at odd jobs and raising four daughters. Her experience and identification were strongly working class: she once remarked that the public libraries were her college. Her novel *Yonnodio: From the Thirties* (1974), written over four decades, depicted a family's attempt to survive the Depression years. The title story of *Tell Me a Riddle: A Collection* (1961) delved into the minds of an aging woman and man and prompted Dorothy Parker to say of Olsen, "She can spend no word that is not the right one." The four stories in the collection brought national attention to Olsen's work and have been repeatedly anthologized. The lectures and essays in *Silences* (1978) discussed "the relationship of circumstances—including class, color, sex; the times, climate into which one is born—to the creation of literature." She held appointments at various universities and strongly influenced other writers, particularly feminists. ■ See study by M. Pearlman and A. Werlock (1991).

OLSON, HARRY FERDINAND (1901–1982), U.S. engineer. Olson joined the RCA Research Laboratories in 1928, the same year that he wrote his Ph.D. thesis on acoustics (University of Iowa). In a long and distinguished career he made pioneering advances in loudspeakers, sound motion pictures, and high-fidelity recording equipment, and he held more than 100 patents. His velocity and directional microphone (1949) became standard equipment in radio and television broadcasting. In 1955 he developed the first electronic music synthesizer, which electronically produced sounds indistinguishable from musical instruments or the human voice. The synthesizer opened new vistas in the world of music and was used by composer Charles Wuorinen to produce *Time's Encomium* (1971), the first piece of all-electronic music to win the Pulitzer Prize.

OLYMPIO, SYLVANUS (1902–1963), president of Togo. Educated at the London School of Economics, Olympio returned to Africa (1926) to begin a commercial and political career. An active supporter of an enlarged Togoland that would reunite the Ewe tribe—separated when the former German colony was divided into French and British mandate territories after World War I—he built up a national party that sent him to the French assembly in the 1940s and won a majority of seats in the preindependence elections (1958). As premier he led the country to independence in 1960 and became its first president the next year. Olympio's authoritarian rule, close ties to France, and refusal to accept French military veterans into his army disaffected many, and he was assassinated by a group of ex-soldiers in 1963.

ONASSIS, ARISTOTLE SOCRATES (1906?–1975), Greek shipping magnate. The son of a Greek tobacco merchant from Smyrna (now Izmir, Turkey), Onassis emigrated to Argentina in 1923, at age 17; by 1930, when he was 25, he was a millionaire tobacco importer. He bought some freighters during the shipping slump of the 1930s, and by World War II he had assembled a worldwide shipping fleet. A bold operator, he amassed a fortune of $500 million. He entertained distinguished guests on his yacht *Christina* and his private Aegean island, Skorpios. After a long relationship with the soprano Maria Callas, he was married to Jacqueline Kennedy, widow of Pres. John F. Kennedy (1968–75). ▪ See biography by W. Frischauer (1968), and P. Evans, *Ari* (1986).

ONASSIS, JACQUELINE KENNEDY (Jacqueline Bouvier; 1929–1994), U.S. first lady. Born into a wealthy family, "Jackie," as she was known to the public, was educated at Vassar College, the Sorbonne, and George Washington University (B.A. 1951). She married then U.S. Senator John F. Kennedy (1953) and after his election to the presidency (1960), she restored the White House to its early 19th-century glory and brought a unique sense of elegance and cultural sophistication to presidential events. She was a fashion trendsetter and one of the most admired women in the United States. She was seated next to her husband when he was assassinated (Nov. 22, 1963) and the images of the stoic strength and dignity she displayed following the event were seared into public consciousness. She subsequently was married to Greek shipping magnate Aristotle Onassis (1968–75), one of the world's richest men, and lived in Greece. She later lived in New York City and was a book editor at Doubleday, Inc. (1978–94). ▪ See Wayne Koestenbaum, *Jackie Under My Skin* (1995); Christopher P. Andersen, *Jack and Jackie* (1996); and biographies by Stephen Birmingham (1978), David Lester (1994), and Donald Spoto (2000).

O'NEILL, EUGENE (1888–1953), U.S. playwright. Leaving Princeton after his freshman year (1906), O'Neill became a merchant seaman, tried acting (his father's profession) and reporting, then turned to writing plays. By 1916 he was providing New York's Greenwich Village Provincetown Players with one-act plays; he won consecutive Pulitzer Prizes for his first important full-length play, *Beyond the Horizon* (1920), and for *Anna Christie* (1921). Hailed as the first "serious" U.S. playwright, O'Neill rejected 19th-century farce and melodrama for symbolic expressionism in *The Emperor Jones* (1920), *Strange Interlude* (1928), and other plays of the 1920s. *Mourning Becomes Electra* (1931), a trilogy modeled after Greek tragedy; *The Iceman Cometh* (1946), set in a Bowery bar; and *Long Day's Journey into Night* (produced 1956; Pulitzer Prize), an autobiographical family tragedy, emphasized the power of deterministic forces over frail individualism. *Ah, Wilderness!* (1933) was his only comedy. O'Neill won the Nobel Prize for Literature (1936). ▪ See biographies by Louis Sheaffer (1968), Arthur and Barbara Gelb (rev. ed. 1974; rewritten ed., Vol. 1, 2000), and Normand Berlin (1982).

ONETTI, JUAN CARLOS (1909–1994), Uruguayan writer. Like various other Uruguayan novelists, Onetti spent many years(1931–34; 1941–55) in Buenos Aires. A self-styled existentialist, he wrote *The Well* (1939), reflecting the influence of contemporary French writing. His prose treated with black humor the alienation and sexual obsession of urban life. *No Man's Land* (1941; Eng. trans. 1994) depicted life in Buenos Aires. *A Brief Life* (1950; Eng. trans. 1976) and *The Shipyard* (1961; Eng. trans. 1968) both mixed elements of fantasy and realism in depicting their protagonists' efforts to escape from their meaningless and empty lives. Frequently compared to U.S. novelist William Faulkner, Onetti exerted a major influence on Latin American fiction of the 1960s and 1970s. After the military took power in Uruguay, he lived in exile in Spain (from 1975), where he won several major literary awards. His later works included *Let the Wind Speak* (1985; Eng. trans. 1996) and *Past Caring* (1993; Eng. trans. 1995). ▪ See study by Djelal Kadir (1977).

ONGANÍA, JUAN CARLOS (1914–1995), Argentine general and dictator. A middle-class graduate of Argentina's military academy, Onganía was a cavalry officer and member of the moderate constitutionalist ("blue") faction that kept clear of politics during the regime of Juan Perón. In 1962 he ousted a commander in chief who favored military dictatorship and he was named army commander by civilian president José María Guido. However, Onganía was himself chosen as president by a military junta that overthrew the civilian government in 1966. During four years as president, Onganía outlawed Argentina's political parties, dissolved congress and the supreme court, and imposed strict economic controls. His policies resulted in soaring inflation and significant labor unrest, and he was replaced by a military junta in June 1970.

ONSAGER, LARS (1903–1976), Norwegian-born U.S. chemist. A student of Dutch chemist Peter Debye in Zurich (1926–28), Onsager received a Ph.D. from Yale (1935) and taught there for the rest of his career. During the 1930s he developed a complex theory of the relationship between temperature and electricity that was described as the fourth law of thermodynamics—the thermodynamics of irreversible processes. Practical effects of his research, which earned him the 1968 Nobel Prize for Chemistry, were the synthesis of uranium-235, the basic fuel for nuclear reactors, and the desalinization of seawater.

OORT, JAN HENDRIK (1900–1992), Dutch astronomer. Oort, associated with the Leiden Observatory (1924–70; director 1945–70), studied the structure and dynamics of the galaxy. With Bertil Lindblad he developed the Lindblad-Oort theory of galactic rotation, which explained the asymmetrical movement of high-velocity stars toward one hemisphere of the sky. Oort was the first to demonstrate (1927) that the inner parts of our galaxy rotated with shorter periods than the outer parts. He later applied radio-astronomy techniques to penetrate to the core of the galaxy, and he drew a detailed galactic picture based on hydrogen emission.

OPATOSHU, JOSEPH (Joseph Meyer Opatovsky; 1886–1954), Polish-born, U.S. Yiddish-language novelist and short-story writer. Opatoshu was born into a rabbinic family and emigrated to New York City in 1907. Although trained as an engineer, he turned to literature and was one of the first to write of the immigrant Jews in America. His naturalistic novels of contemporary life included *A Story of a Horse Thief* (1912) and *The New Home* (1914). He also wrote historical novels of the Jewish past, the most notable of which were the epic *In Polish Woods* (1921; Eng. trans. 1938), an account of three generations of 19th-century Polish-Jewish life, and *The Last Revolt: The Story of Rabbi Akiba* (1948; Eng. trans. 1952), a treatment of life after the destruction of the Second Temple in Jerusalem. English translations of his short stories are in *A Day in Regensburg* (1968).

OPEL, WILHELM VON (1871–1948), German industrialist. Known as the "Henry Ford of Germany," Opel produced more than 1 million cars at the automobile works that he founded in 1897 at Rüsselsheim. He sold control of the company to General Motors for approximately $30 million (1929). Judged to be a "follower" of the Nazis by a denazification court (1947), Opel was stripped of all managerial posts in the Opel organization.

OPHULS, MARCEL (1927–), German-born French director. When he was a child, Ophuls' parents took him from Germany to France; he spent his youth in the United States and became a U.S. citizen before returning to France (1950). He worked under his father, the acclaimed director Max Ophuls, as well as with directors John Huston, Anatole Litvak, and Julien Duvivier, and then directed for television. Ophuls made two feature-length films in the mid-1960s but gained prominence for his moving and penetrating documentary *The Sorrow and the Pity* (1969), which treated the sensitive issue of the reaction of the French people to Nazi occupation during World War II. *A Sense of Loss* (1972) documented the political and religious strife in Northern Ireland and *Memory of Justice* (1976) examined Nazi German, French, and U.S. wartime atrocities in Europe, Algeria, and Vietnam. He also directed the Oscar-winning documentary, *Hotel Terminus: Klaus Barbie—His Life and Times* (1988).

OPHULS, MAX (Max Oppenheimer; 1902–1957), European film director. Born in Germany, where he was an actor and theatrical director before directing his first film (1930), Ophuls became a French citizen in 1934 and a peripatetic director. He made one film in Italy, one in Holland, and directed *Romeo and Juliet* on the Swiss stage before going to Hollywood in 1941. After several unsuccessful film projects he directed *Letter from an Unknown Woman* (1948) and *The Reckless Moment* (1949). Back in France, he made the bittersweet sexual comedies *La Ronde* (1950), *The Earrings of Madame de . . .* (1953), and his masterpiece, *Lola Montez* (1955). His films were noted for their lyrical quality and their fluid camera technique.

OPPENHEIM, LASSA FRANCIS LAWRENCE (1858–1919), German-born British jurist and legal scholar. Oppenheim received a doctorate in law from Göttingen University (1880) and taught criminal law at the universities of Freiburg and Basel before moving to Great Britain. There he was a professor of international law at the London School of Economics (1898–1908) and at Cambridge (1908–19). His most important book, *International Law: A Treatise* (2 vols., 1905–06), remained a standard reference work for more than seven decades. Oppenheim stressed that international law should be enforced by the collective action of states.

OPPENHEIMER, SIR ERNEST (1880–1957), German-born South African mining magnate. Known as the "king of diamonds," Oppenheimer was sent to Kimberley, South Africa, to represent a London diamond broker (1902) and achieved great financial success. With the backing of the U.S. financier J. P. Morgan, he set up the Anglo-American Corp. for the exploration of gold (1917). He acquired the German South West Africa diamond concession (1919) and eventually gained control of the De Beers diamond corporation and virtually monopolized the diamond industry. After establishing the Diamond Corp., Ltd. (1930), Oppenheimer also controlled worldwide diamond marketing. His investments played a key role in the economic development of South Africa and Zambia (then Northern Rhodesia), where he developed copper, lead, and zinc mines. His son, Harry F. Oppenheimer (1908–2000), who succeeded him as chairman of Anglo-American (1957–82) and De Beers (1957–84), served as a member of Parliament (1947–58) and was a consistent critic of the system of apartheid.

OPPENHEIMER, JULIUS ROBERT (1904–1967), U.S. physicist. J. Robert Oppenheimer graduated from Harvard (1925) and studied physics at Cambridge and Göttingen (Ph.D. 1927). He joined the faculties of the California Institute of Technology and the University of California at Berkeley (1929) and helped train an entire generation of American scientists in the intricacies of quantum and nuclear physics. He joined the Manhattan Project (1942) and established and administered the laboratory at Los Alamos, New Mexico, at which the first atomic bombs were made (1945). After World War II, he chaired the General Advisory Committee of the Atomic Energy Commission (1947–52). Declared a security risk (1953) for his left-wing associations, his opposition to the H-bomb, and alleged "defects in his character," he was denied access to government research. His case became an international cause célèbre, and he was finally symbolically rehabilitated when he won the Fermi Award of the Atomic Energy Commission (1963). He headed the Institute of Advanced Study at Princeton, New Jersey (1947–66). Concerned about the role of science in society, Oppenheimer wrote *Science and Common Understanding* (1954), *The Open Mind* (1955), and *Some*

Reflections on Science and Culture (1960). ■ See U.S. Atomic Energy Commission, ed., *In the Matter of J. Robert Oppenheimer: Transcript of Hearing Before Personnel Security Board* (1971); Nuel P. Davis, *Lawrence and Oppenheimer* (1968); and Alice K. Smith and Charles Weiner, eds., *Robert Oppenheimer: Letters and Recollections* (1980).

ORDÓÑEZ, ANTONIO (1931–1998), Spanish bullfighter. The son of a prominent matador who was the model for "Pedro Romero" in Ernest Hemingway's *The Sun Also Rises*, Ordóñez was trained in the deliberate and ritualistic classical style. Considered by many to be the greatest bullfighter of all time, he achieved premier status after a series of head-to-head duels in 1959 with his brother-in-law and then reigning champion Luis Dominguín. Their exploits were chronicled by Ernest Hemingway in *The Dangerous Summer* (1960). After retiring in 1962, he returned to the ring in 1965, but after his 1971 retirement he fought only once a year at the traditional Goyesca bullfight in his native town of Ronda. He appeared in more than 1,000 bullfights during his career. ■ See biography by Shay Oag, *In the Presence of Death* (1968).

ORFF, CARL (1895–1982), German composer. Orff was active as a music teacher, conductor, and editor of old music. He used historical materials in his own compositions, notably *Carmina Burana* (1937), a dramatic secular cantata adapted from a 13th-century Latin manuscript that featured primitive harmonies and rhythms and hypnotic repetitions. Orff also wrote the cantata *Catuli Carmina* (1943) and operas based on the Greek tragedies (*Antigone*, 1949; *Prometheus*, 1968). He compiled an influential five-volume series of materials for early-childhood musical education, *Music for Children* (1930–35; Eng. trans. 1950–54). ■ See study by Andreas Liess (Eng. trans. 1966).

ORLANDO, VITTORIO EMANUELE (1860–1952), Italian political leader. A constitutional lawyer and professor, Orlando was elected to the Chamber of Deputies (1897) and held several cabinet posts before becoming premier during World War I (1917). One of the Big Four (along with Woodrow Wilson, David Lloyd George, and Georges Clemenceau) at the Paris Peace Conference (1919), he argued unsuccessfully for territorial concessions in Dalmatia that had been promised to Italy in the secret Treaty of London (1915) and resigned (1919). He initially supported the fascist leader Benito Mussolini but broke with the fascists (1925) and left politics to resume his legal and teaching career. After World War II he served as first president of the constituent assembly (1946) and ran unsuccessfully for president (1948).

ORMANDY, EUGENE (1899–1985), Hungarian-born U.S. conductor. A child prodigy on the violin, Ormandy was a professor of music in Budapest at age 17. In 1921 he emigrated to the United States and for several years conducted the orchestra at the Capitol Theater, a Manhattan vaudeville movie palace. By the late 1920s and early 1930s he was regularly conducting radio broadcasts and appearing as guest conductor with many leading orchestras; in 1931 he became permanent conductor of the Minneapolis Symphony. In 1938 he succeeded Leopold Stokowski as permanent conductor of the Philadelphia Orchestra and remained at its helm until 1980. Over the years, the orchestra became known for the "Phildelphia sound," which featured a lush string tone. Ormandy was best known for his romantic interpretations of 19th-century music.

OROZCO, JOSÉ CLEMENTE (1883–1949), Mexican painter and muralist. Widely considered preeminent among modern Mexican artists, Orozco took up painting after studies in agronomy, architecture, and mathematics. His recurrent theme of oppressed individuals in misery and rebellion emerged in his series of early watercolors, *House of Tears*, and was continued when he turned to mural painting in 1922. He depicted scenes of revolution in a somber but violent style, using abrupt color contrasts. In the mid-1920s he executed a series of large murals in Mexico City's National Preparatory School, including *The Rich Banquet While the Workers Quarrel* and *The Destruction of the Old Order*. Conservative reaction to his work forced Orozco twice to flee to the United States (1917–20 and 1927–34), where he won fame for three mural series: *Prometheus* (Pomona College, California; 1930), *Struggle in the Orient/Struggle in the Occident* (New School for Social Research, New York; 1931), and the 3,000-square-foot *The Coming and Return of Quetzalcoatl* (Dartmouth College, New Hampshire; 1932–34). He was founder of the National College (1943). ■ See his *Autobiography* (Eng. trans. 1962) and studies by MacKinley Helm (1953) and Alma Reed (1956).

ORR, JOHN BOYD. *See BOYD-ORR, JOHN, 1st BARON.*

ORTEGA Y GASSET, JOSÉ (1883–1955), Spanish essayist and philosopher. Ortega, a professor of metaphysics (University of Madrid, 1910–36), editor, publisher, lecturer, and outspoken internationalist, was regarded as the foremost Spanish thinker of the century. His first crucial work, *Meditations on Quixote* (1914; Eng. trans. 1961), called for a rigorous scientific approach to philosophical questions and took issue with philosopher Miguel de Unamuno's skepticism, nationalism, and acceptance of the Catholic Church. *The Dehumanization of Art and Ideas on the Novel* (1925; Eng. trans. 1948) argued that self-expression is artistic only to the degree that it deviates from reality. He argued against popular and socially committed literature. The book that made him famous, *The Revolt of the Masses* (1929; Eng. trans. 1932), furthered his elitist sociology, describing the world as run by intellectually bankrupt "mass-men." Active politically, Ortega helped write the constitution of the Spanish republic (1931) and served in the Chamber of Deputies.

With the outbreak of the Spanish civil war, he emigrated (1936) but returned to Spain nine years later. ■ See Robert McClintock, *Man and His Circumstances: Ortega as Educator* (1971), and studies by Julian Marias (Eng. trans. 1970) and Franz Niedermayer (Eng. trans. 1973).

ORTEGA SAAVEDRA, DANIEL (1945–), Nicaraguan political leader. Ortega's middle-class parents were both activists opposed to the corrupt and dictatorial Somoza family that had assumed power with U.S. government assistance in 1933. Ortega joined the revolutionary Sandinista National Liberation Front (FSLN; 1963), a movement of armed students, peasants, and workers, and headed its urban guerrilla arm by 1967, when he was arrested for taking part in a bank robbery. Released from prison in an exchange with the government (1974), he resumed his revolutionary activities and helped build up the Sandinista forces by forging alliances with mass organizations as well as business groups and traditional political parties. The rebels overthrew the government of Anastasio Somoza Debayle (July 1979) and through the coordination of Ortega, proceeded to establish a pluralistic socialist government. It nationalized banks and Somoza family holdings, introduced trade controls, and inaugurated massive land reform, health, and literacy programs while maintaining a mixed economy and allowing limited political opposition. However, the administration of U.S. President Ronald Reagan, accusing the Sandinistas of aiding guerrillas in El Salvador and of establishing a communist dictatorship, supported anti-Sandinista rebels, the contras, with arms and money. Amid an ongoing civil war, which proved economically disastrous, Ortega was elected president of Nicaragua in 1984. During his presidential term (1984–90) the economy was weakened by U.S. trade cuts, continuing civil war, and heavy social spending. He was defeated for reelection by a 14-party conservative coalition headed by Violeta Barrios de Chamorro (1990). Ortega subsequently served as secretary-general of the FSLN (1991; reelected 1998), headed the Sandinista delegates in the National Assembly, and lost the 1996 presidential election to conservative Arnoldo Aleman, a former mayor of Managua.

ORWELL, GEORGE (Eric Arthur Blair; 1903–1950), British novelist and essayist. One of the major political writers of the century, Orwell consistently affirmed his belief in the necessity for human freedom and a truly democratic socialism. He merged this belief with a forthright skepticism of political parties and mass movements and with fears about their dehumanizing effects. Among his major works are the novel *Burmese Days* (1934), based on his experiences as a colonial policeman (1922–27), and the studies of poverty, *Down and Out in Paris and London* (1933) and *The Road to Wigan Pier* (1937). *Homage to Catalonia* (1939) recounts his experiences in the Spanish Civil War and his disillusionment with communism. He is best known for his political satires. *Animal Farm* (1946) is a short, witty fable on the evils and distortions of Stalinism. The novel *1984* (1949) is

a modern classic of a "negative Utopia," which Orwell feared might become the future of humankind. ■ See his *Collected Essays, Journalism and Letters* (4 vols., 1968) and *Lost Writings* (1985); biographies by Bernard Crick (1981), M. Shelden (1991), and J. Meyers (2000); and two-volume study by Peter Stansky and William Abrahams, *The Unknown Orwell* (1972) and *Orwell, the Transformation* (1980).

ORY, EDWARD "KID" (1886–1973), U.S. jazz trombonist, band leader, and composer. A pioneer of jazz, Ory was born into a Creole family in Louisiana. He was one of the original "tailgate" trombone men who used the instrument for rhythmic effects, primarily supporting the other musicians. From 1910 to 1919 he led one of the most famous bands in New Orleans, which included such musicians as King Oliver, Sidney Bechet, Jimmie Noone, and Louis Armstrong. Ory recorded frequently during the 1920s and was best known for "Muskrat Ramble," which was first recorded in 1926 with Louis Armstrong's *Hot Five*. Active until age 80, he profoundly influenced several generations of jazz musicians and was a major force in the post–World War II Dixieland-jazz revival.

OSBORN, FAIRFIELD (1887–1969), U.S. naturalist and conservationist. Son of paleontologist Henry Fairfield Osborn, Fairfield Osborn entered the investment business after World War I but maintained a keen interest in the natural sciences and conservation and became a trustee of the New York Zoological Society (1922). As president of the society (1940–68), he ran the Bronx Zoo and the Coney Island Aquarium with the flair of a master showman and attracted more than 3 million visitors a year. He exhibited wildlife in their natural surroundings and sponsored oceanographic research at the aquarium. His popular and influential books, *Our Plundered Planet* (1948) and *The Limits of the Earth* (1953), called for an end to mankind's destruction of the natural environment and argued for worldwide population control.

OSBORN, HENRY FAIRFIELD (1857–1935), U.S. paleontologist and museum administrator. A professor of biology (1891–96) and zoology (1896–1935) at Columbia University, Osborn was a prolific scholar and the most influential vertebrate paleontologist of his time. Associated with the American Museum of Natural History in New York City for decades (curator of vertebrate paleontology, 1891–1910; president, 1908–33), he amassed the world's largest and finest collection of vertebrate fossils and developed innovative and instructional museum displays that popularized the field of paleontology and made "dinosaur" a household word. Among his numerous books were *The Age of Mammals* (1910), *Men of the Old Stone Age* (1915), and *Origin and Evolution of Life* (1917).

OSBORNE, JOHN (1929–1994), British playwright and director. A former actor, Osborne was regarded in the 1950s as the leader of Britain's "angry young men," those nonaristocratic intellectuals who attacked the decadence and complacency of British society and government. His first play, *Look Back in Anger* (1956), caustically examined the problems faced by its working-class intellectual hero. His later plays, including *The Entertainer* (1957), *Luther* (1961), *Inadmissable Evidence* (1964), and *West of Suez* (1971), continued his dissection of society's corruption and hypocrisy. His work is characterized by brilliant rhetoric and slashing monologues. His prose was collected in *Damn You, England* (1994). He also wrote several screenplays, including that of the popular *Tom Jones* (1963). ■ See his autobiographies, *A Better Class of Person* (1981) and *Almost a Gentleman* (1991), and study by Alan Carter (1969).

OSHEROFF, DOUGLAS D. (1945–), U.S. physicist. While a graduate student at Cornell University (Ph.D. 1973), Osheroff worked on problems of low-temperature physics with professors Robert C. Richardson and David M. Lee. In 1972, the trio unexpectedly discovered superfluidity—the ability to flow without resistance—in helium-3, a rare form of liquid helium, when it was cooled to about two one-thousandths of a degree above absolute zero. The discovery enabled scientists to see, for the first time, quantum mechanical effects that previously could be observed only indirectly through the study of molecules, atoms, or subatomic particles. The discovery also provided insights into the formation of vast cosmic strings, which may have formed the first stars and galaxies microseconds after the "big bang" creation of the universe. For their research, Osheroff, Richardson, and Lee shared the 1996 Nobel Prize for Physics. Osheroff worked at Bell Labs (1972–87) and taught at Stanford University (1987–).

OSHIMA, NAGISA (1932–), Japanese motion-picture director. Oshima began his film career after leaving Kyoto University Law School in 1954. He rejected period drama and took most of his early plots from newspaper stories. He devoted himself to the political and social implications of the upheaval in Japanese life following World War II, particularly its effect on the young. *Death by Hanging* (1968) explored the traditional Japanese prejudice against Koreans in the light of the penal system. *Boy* (1969) concerned a family who threw their son in front of cars in order to collect insurance from the faked accidents. A realist, Oshima was nevertheless fascinated by the bizarre, which was particularly evident in *Ceremony* (1971), the story of three generations of a Japanese family tyrannized and manipulated by their wily grandfather. *In the Realm of the Senses* (1976), a depiction of sexual obsession, was declared obscene by the U.S. Customs Bureau and temporarily banned from being shown in the United States. He later directed *Merry Christmas, Mr. Lawrence* (1983), a Japanese-British coproduction, and *Taboo* (2000). ■ See Maureen Turim, *The Films of Oshima Nagisa* (1998).

OSMEÑA, SERGIO (1878–1961), Filipino political leader. A nationalist lawyer and editor, Osmeña cofounded the Na-

tionalist party (1907) and served as speaker of the assembly (1907–16), the house (1916–22), and president pro tempore of the senate (1923–35). He was vice president of the government-in-exile in the United States during World War II; after Pres. Quezon's death (1944), he became president of that government. After the war he attempted to reestablish American institutions in the Philippines but retired after his electoral defeat in 1946.

OSSIETZKY, CARL VON (1889–1938), German journalist and pacifist. Although an avowed pacifist, Ossietzky, the son of a former army officer, was conscripted into the German army during World War I. He helped found the No More War organization in 1922 and in 1927 he became editor of the *Weltbühne,* a respected left-wing weekly. For printing articles that exposed the secret rearmament of Germany, he was arrested and accused of treason in 1931; although released, he was sent to a concentration camp in 1933 when the Nazis came to power. Suffering from tuberculosis, he was removed to a prison hospital in 1936 and immediately awarded the 1935 Nobel Peace Prize. The Nazi government protested and forbade German citizens from accepting the Nobel Prize thereafter. ■ See his selected writings in *The Stolen Republic* (Eng. trans. 1971), and István Deák, *Weimar Germany's Left Wing Intellectuals* (1968).

OSTAIJEN, PAUL VAN (1896–1928), Belgian (Flemish) poet and essayist. Ostaijen passed from the exuberant expressionism of "metropolis lyricism" in his first volume, *Music Hall* (1916), which he published at age 20, to the more muted humanistic poetry of *The Signal* (1918). A political exile in politically tumultuous Berlin (1918–21), he experimented with drugs and began to write the painful and grotesque poetry and prose for which he is famous. The antiwar *Occupied City* (1921) and *Feasts of Fear and Agony* (Eng. trans. 1976), reflect the influence of Hugo Ball and other dadaists. *The First Book of Schmoll* (1928; Eng. trans. 1982) sought a pure poetry that Ostaijen termed "organic expressionism," attempting to separate the character of the poem from that of the poet. He also wrote short fiction and influential criticism. He died at age 32, but his intense interest in experimental forms affected the course of Flemish literature. English translations are in *Patriotism, Inc. and Other Tales* (1971).

OSTROVSKY, NIKOLAI ALEKSEYEVICH (1904–1936), Soviet novelist. Born into a working-class family in the Ukraine, Ostrovsky joined the Komsomol (communist youth organization) (1919) and fought with the bolsheviks during the civil war of 1918–20. He was a Komsomol leader until stricken with a progressive disease (1924) that eventually paralyzed and blinded him. While bedridden, he wrote the autobiographical novel, *The Making of a Hero* (1932–34: Eng. trans. 1937; appeared as *How the Steel Was Tempered,* Eng. trans. 1952), which described the heroism and revolutionary ardor of a young communist and the political awakening of the Russian workers. The novel, which remained an inspirational best-seller for decades, served as the model for an entire genre of Soviet literature, and Ostrovsky was venerated throughout the Soviet Union. He also wrote another political novel of the civil-war period, *Born of the Storm* (1934–36; Eng. trans. 1939).

OSWALD, LEE HARVEY (1939–1963), U.S. accused assassin. Emotionally disturbed as a boy, Oswald served in the U.S. Marines before defecting to the Soviet Union in 1959. He returned home to Texas with a Russian bride in 1962. He was arrested in Dallas on Nov. 22, 1963, and charged with killing Pres. John F. Kennedy. Two days later, while in custody, Oswald was shot to death by Jack Ruby, a nightclub owner. The Warren Commission concluded that Oswald had acted alone in shooting Kennedy, but speculation persisted that he may have been innocent or that he may have been part of a conspiracy. ■ See Mark Lane, *Rush to Judgment* (1966): Priscilla J. McMillan, *Marina and Lee* (1977); Edward Jay Epstein, *Legend* (1978); Anthony Summers, *Conspiracy* (1980); and Henry Hurt, *Reasonable Doubt* (1985).

OTERO, BLAS DE (1916–1979), Spanish poet. The most distinguished of the post–Spanish-civil-war poets, Otero addressed his intense poems on social and religious themes to "the immense majority." Influenced by the philosopher Miguel de Unamuno, he early agonized over the discrepancy between political anarchism and the need for a religious order, but later was increasingly committed to radical social and political change. Otero left Spain but later repatriated. Many of his poems were banned in Spain or altered by censorship. Translations of his work are in *Selected Poems: Miguel Hernández and Blas de Otero* (1972) and *All My Sonnets* (1997).

OTTO, FREI PAUL (1925–   ), German architect. The son and grandson of sculptors, Frei Otto was a pilot in World War II (1943–45). Captured by the Allies, he spent two years in France as a prisoner of war leading POW repair crews. Faced with material shortages, he experimented with the use of rubble in construction; later, with postwar prosperity, he turned to the challenge of creating lightweight coverings which are not internally supported. Otto designed suspended veils, plastic tents, and pneumatic membranes to envelop storage and exhibition areas, sports arenas, and even an entire Arctic city. Otto's doctoral thesis, *The Suspended Roof* (1953), was later published in several languages, establishing him as a prophet of what came to be called "minimal construction." His best-known projects included the West German Pavilion at Expo 67 in Montreal (1967), the Olympic Park in Munich (1967–72), and the Open Air Theater in Bad Hersfeld, Germany (1967–68). He subsequently designed schools and factories in Germany and England. ■ See studies by Conrad Roland (1970) and Philip Drew (1976).

OTTO, RUDOLF (1869–1937), German philosopher. Otto's magnum opus was *The Idea of the Holy* (1917; Eng. trans. 1923), in which he described religious experience in a comparative world context. Professor of theology at Göttingen (1904–14) and Marburg (1917–29) universities, he traveled widely to study religious origins in Africa, India, Russia, and the Far East, and he established an institute in Marburg for the comparative study of religion. A liberal Protestant, he served in the Prussian parliament (1913–18) and participated in Christian ecumenical activities. His other books included *Mysticism East and West* (1926: Eng. trans. 1932) and *The Kingdom of God and Son of Man* (1934; Eng. trans. 1938). ■ See study by Robert F. Davidson (1947).

OUD, JACOBUS JOHANNES PIETER (1890–1963), Dutch architect. One of the founders of the De Stijl movement (1917) along with Theo van Doesburg, J.J.P. Oud applied its principles of design to architecture. As city architect of Rotterdam (1918–33), he designed functional housing blocks in the austere geometric idiom of the De Stijl that contrasted dramatically with the picturesqueness and extravagant detail of the Amsterdam school. In the early 1930s he began to move away from the purity of De Stijl, by then referred to as the International Style. In several projects, notably the Shell Office Building in The Hague (1938–42), he modified modernist severity with elements of ornamentation. ■ See Gunther Stamm, *The Architecture of J.J.P. Oud* (1978).

OUSMANE, SEMBÈNE (1923–   ), Senegalese writer and filmmaker. Ousmane's experiences as a laborer in Dakar and Marseilles and his concern for ordinary people victimized by religious, class, or governmental oppression, were reflected in his realistic novels (*God's Bits of Wood,* 1960, Eng. trans. 1962; *Xala,* 1973, Eng. trans. 1976; *The Last of the Empire,* 1979, Eng. trans. 1983) and short stories (*The Money-Order with White Genesis,* 1965, Eng. trans. 1972; *Tribal Scars,* 1962, Eng. trans. 1975) set in contemporary Africa. The novel *Black Docker* (1956; Eng. trans. 1987) was autobiographical. Turning to film in order to reach a mass, non-French-reading African audience, he studied at the Gorki Film Studios in Moscow during the early 1960s and became the first internationally acclaimed African film director. Called "the father of African film," he was responsible for such highly praised works as *Black Girl* (1967), *Mandabi* (1968; based on *The Money-Order*), *Xala* (1973), *Ceddo* (1977), a controversial epic, *Camp de Thiaroye* (1988), and *Guelwaar* (1992).

OWEN, WILFRED (1893–1918), British poet. As a soldier in World War I, Owen was profoundly affected by the senseless destruction of war. Though influenced by the musicality of John Keats' poetry, he used assonance and metrical changes in anguished poems on human suffering in wartime. He was killed in action shortly before the armistice in November 1918, and his *Poems* (1920) were collected by the poet Siegfried Sassoon, who had earlier encouraged Owen in his writing. His poems were particularly influential among the left-wing poets of the 1930s, and they formed the basis of the text of Benjamin Britten's *War Requiem* (1962). ■ See biography by Jon Stallworthy (1974) and study by Gertrude M. White (1969).

OWENS, JESSE (1913–1980), U.S. track-and-field athlete. While competing for Ohio State (1935), Owens set or equaled four world records in a single hour, one of which (broad jump, 26 feet 8¼ inches) lasted for 25 years. He caused a sensation at the 1936 Olympic games in Berlin by winning gold medals in four events: 100-meter dash, 200-meter dash, broad jump and 400-meter relay. German leader Adolf Hitler, who hosted the Olympic games to showcase the feats of his Aryan "supermen," walked out of the stadium rather than congratulate a black athlete. Returning to the United States, Owens received no official recognition of his feat until 1976, 40 years after his legendary performance, when he won the Presidential Medal of Freedom. A charismatic speaker, he was famous in his later life for inspirational speaking tours. After criticizing militant black activists in *Blackthink* (1970), Owens renounced the views in that book in *I Have Changed* (1972). ■ See biography by William J. Baker (1986).

OWINGS, NATHANIEL ALEXANDER (1903–1984), U.S. architect. Owings earned a degree in architecture and engineering from Cornell (1927) and became development supervisor of the 1933 Chicago Exposition, working with Louis Skidmore to build hundreds of low-cost pavilions. In 1936 Owings and Skidmore went into a partnership that, as Skidmore, Owings and Merrill (from 1939), became one of the largest and most prolific of American architectural firms. The firm developed a team approach to architecture and was best known for its sleek International Style skyscrapers that were commissioned as headquarters by many of the country's largest corporations. An organizational genius, Owings assembled the teams responsible for such projects as the Lever House (New York, 1952), the U.S. Air Force Academy (Colorado Springs, 1954–62), the John Hancock Center (Chicago, 1970), and the Sears Tower (Chicago, 1974). He wrote *The American Aesthetic* (1969) and an autobiography, *The Spaces in Between* (1973).

OXFORD AND ASQUITH, HERBERT HENRY ASQUITH, 1st EARL OF. *See ASQUITH, HERBERT HENRY.*

OXNAM, GARFIELD BROMLEY (1891–1963), U.S. Protestant clergyman. The son of a mining engineer, Oxnam was born in the mother-lode region of California and educated at the University of Southern California (B.A. 1913). Ordained as a Methodist minister in 1916, he served as president of DePauw (Indiana) University (1928–36), and as

bishop of Omaha (1936–39), Boston (1939–44), New York (1944–52), and Washington, D.C. (1952–60), as well as president of the World Council of Churches (1948–54). He was a champion of civil liberties, social justice, the rights of labor, and Protestant ecumenism and an outspoken foe of the anticommunist crusade of Sen. Joseph McCarthy. His books included *The Ethical Ideals of Jesus in a Changing World* (1941), *Preaching in a Revolutionary Age* (1944), *I Protest* (1954), and *A Testament of Faith* (1958).

OYONO, FERDINAND LÉOPOLD (1929–   ), Cameroonian novelist, short-story writer, and diplomat. Oyono was raised in poverty by his Catholic mother, who had left his father, an important chief and official of his hometown. He worked as a choirboy and priest's servant at the local mission and received a traditional colonial education. He studied law in Paris and subsequently wrote a series of bitterly satiric novels that denounced colonial society and expressed the Africans' disillusionment with the white man's world. His best-known works were *Houseboy* (1956; Eng. trans. 1966), *The Old Man and the Medal* (1956; Eng. trans. 1967), *The Road from Europe* (1960), and *The Big Confusion* (1971). Oyono served as the Cameroon ambassador to Liberia, Belgium, and later the United Nations (1975–83) and the United Kingdom (1984–85). During the 1990s he served as foreign minister and senior minister of culture.

OZ, AMOS (1939–   ), Israeli Hebrew-language writer. Oz left his native Jerusalem at age 14 to live on a kibbutz, where he taught in the school and wrote the controversial novels and short stories that brought him international recognition. His highly symbolic works, written against the backgrounds of the Crusades, Nazi-dominated Europe, modern-day Jerusalem, and the kibbutz, dealt with the themes of persecution, suffering, guilt, and isolation. He probed the modern Israeli character while challenging many of the myths of messianic Zionism. Among his best-known works were *Elsewhere, Perhaps* (1966: Eng. trans. 1973), *My Michael* (1968; Eng. trans. 1972), *Unto Death* (1971; Eng. trans. 1978), *The Hill of Evil Counsel* (1978; Eng. trans. 1978), *Where the Jackals Howl and Other Stories* (Eng. trans. 1981), and *A Perfect Peace* (1982; Eng. trans. 1985). *In the Land of Israel* (Eng. trans. 1983), a controversial collection of articles and interviews, presented a portrait of Israeli society after the 1982 invasion of Lebanon. Oz was a leader of the Peace Now movement. His later works included the novels *Fima* (1991; Eng. trans. 1993), *Don't Call It Night* (1994; Eng. trans. 1997), and *Panther in the Basement* (1995; Eng. trans. 1997), and the essay collections, *The Slopes of Lebanon* (Eng. trans. 1989), *Israel, Palestine and Peace* (Eng. trans. 1994), and *Under This Blazing Light* (Eng. trans. 1995). He was a professor at Ben Gurion University, Beer Sheva (1986–   ).

OZAKI, YUKIO (1858–1954), Japanese politician. Japan's most prominent liberal politician, Ozaki served in every diet (parliament) from 1890 to 1953 and was mayor of Tokyo (1903–12). He led the fight for universal manhood suffrage (established 1925) and opposed Japan's expansionism abroad. The cherry trees in Washington, D.C., symbolizing Japanese–American friendship, were a gift from Ozaki.

OZAL, TURGUT (1927–1993), Turkish political leader. Trained as an electrical engineer at Istanbul Technical University (M.S. 1950), Ozal worked on government hydroelectric projects during the 1950s and served as undersecretary of the State Planning Organization (1965–71). After the 1971 military coup, Ozal worked for the World Bank in Washington, D.C. (1971–73), and in private industry in Turkey before reentering public service (1979). As undersecretary of state planning (1979–80), deputy prime minister (1980–82), and prime minister (leading the Motherland party; 1983–89), he carried out free-market economic reforms that led to an export-driven economic boom. He also increased political ties with Western Europe and the United States, although he was criticized for his harsh treatment of political prisoners and for his autocratic behavior and provocative statements. As president (1989–93) he allied Turkey to the U.S.-led coalition in the Persian Gulf War against Iraq (1991).

OZAWA, SEIJI (1935–), Japanese conductor. The son of an official in the Japanese occupation of China, Ozawa was born in Manchuria and spent his early years in Beijing (Peking). Back in Japan after World War II he received a thoroughly Western musical education, studying piano, composition, and conducting. After winning an international conducting competition in France (1959), he worked with Charles Munch, Herbert von Karajan, and Leonard Bernstein (1960–62) and directed the San Francisco Symphony (1962–65; 1970–76) and Toronto Symphony (1965–70) orchestras. A specialist in 19th- and early 20th-century music, he later headed the Boston Symphony (1973–) and codirected the Tanglewood Music Center in Massachusetts.

OZICK, CYNTHIA (1928–), U.S. writer. Born to Jewish immigrant parents who ran a drugstore in the Bronx, New York, Ozick attended New York University (B.A. 1949) and Ohio State University (M.A. 1950), writing a thesis on Henry James, whose work deeply influenced her own. She worked as an ad copywriter and gained a reputation for literary criticism, political commentary, and particularly for her short fiction. Her first collection, *The Pagan Rabbi and Other Stories* (1971), dealt with Jewish immigrants in the United States and won recognition for compelling storytelling and a sophisticated, vivid style. Later collections included *Bloodshed and Three Novellas* (1976) and *Levitation: Five Fictions* (1982), which reflected her mastery of irony and treated such subjects as moral responsibility in the post–Holocaust world, Judaism and art, and the conflicts inherent in women's lives. She also wrote the novels *Trust* (1966) *The Cannibal Galaxy* (1983), *Messiah of Stockholm* (1987), and *The Puttermesser Papers* (1997), and the essay collections, *Art and Ardor* (1983), *Metaphor and Memory* (1989), *Fame and Folly* (1996), and *Quarrel and Quandary* (2000). ■ See study by Joseph Lowin (1998).

OZU, YASUJIRO (1903–1963), Japanese film director. At age 20 Ozu went to work at Shochiku Studios and remained there for the rest of his life. In his modest, unassuming films, noted for their technical perfection and formal beauty, he explored traditional domestic relationships and provincial dramas. Most of his works dealt with middle-class Japanese families. Considered very "Japanese," Ozu's films—*Tokyo Story* (1953), *Early Spring* (1956), *An Autumn Afternoon* (1962)—began to be shown abroad only at the end of the director's life. ■ See study by Donald Richie (1974).

P

PAAR, JACK (1918–   ), U.S. television personality. Paar was a radio announcer in Cleveland and Buffalo before entertaining troops in the Pacific zone during World War II. He later was heard on his own radio program, made his film debut in *Variety Time* (1948), and was host of daytime TV shows. But he was best known for his irreverent humor and emotional outbursts while hosting (1957–62) NBC's late-night "Tonight Show," which was so popular that in its second year it was renamed "The Jack Paar Show." Audiences appreciated Paar's irritability and unpredictability; he once walked off the show to protest NBC's censorship of a joke about a water closet. Paar made several unsuccessful attempts at a comeback in the 1960s and 1970s. ■ See his autobiography, *P.S. Jack Parr* (1983).

PABST, GEORG WILHELM (1885–1967), European film director. Born in Bohemia. G. W. Pabst traveled through Europe as an actor and began his film career after World War I in Germany. He directed *Streets of Sorrow* (1925), a social comment on human misery, and *Pandora's Box* (1928), which stemmed from his interest in psychological exploration. With the Nazi assumption of power, Pabst became identified with left-wing pacifism and internationalism and moved (1933) to France, where he directed *Don Quixote,* starring the Russian singer-actor F. I. Chaliapin. He returned to Germany in 1939, however, and made two films for the Nazis during World War II. In 1948 he won a Venice Film Festival prize for *The Trial* (1948), a film about anti-Semitism. ■ See study by Lee Atwell (1977) and Eric Rentschler, ed., *The Films of G. W. Pabst* (1990).

PA CHIN. *See BA JIN.*

PACKARD, DAVID. *See HEWLETT, WILLIAM R.*

PADMORE, GEORGE (Malcolm Nurse; 1903–1959), Trinidadian-born pan-African leader. The grandson of a slave, Padmore went to the United States in 1924 and studied at Fisk University and at the law schools of Howard and New York Universities. Attracted to communism by its promise of racial equality, he joined the Communist party (1927) and was active as a Communist International (Comintern) labor organizer and journalist in the Soviet Union and Germany. Resigning from the party (1933) over the "united front" policy of accommodation with British and French colonialism, he settled in England and worked to revive the pan-African movement. He organized the International African Service Bureau (IASB) with C.L.R. James (1937) and

helped plan the 1945 pan-African Congress in Manchester. In 1957 he moved to Ghana as an adviser to Pres. Kwame Nkrumah. ■ See his *Pan-Africanism or Communism?* (1956) and James R. Hooker, *Black Revolutionary* (1967).

PADEREWSKI, IGNACE JAN (1860–1941), Polish pianist, composer, and statesman. During the 1890s, the handsome and charismatic Paderewski was the most famous and highest-paid pianist in the world. He was known for his poetic interpretations of the music of others, as well as for his own works, which included songs, an opera, a symphony, and pieces for the piano. A noted patriot, he dramatized the cause of Polish independence around the world and helped convince U.S. Pres. Woodrow Wilson to support Polish independence during World War I. He headed the government of newly reunited Poland for ten months (1919) and signed the Versailles Treaty. He resumed his concert career in 1921, often playing benefits for war victims. During World War II he headed the Polish parliament in exile (1940–41). ■ See *The Paderewski Memoirs* (1938; with Mary Lawton) and biographies by Charlotte Kellogg (1956) and Adam Zamoyski (1982).

PAGE, GERALDINE (1924–1987), U.S. actress. A leading "method" actress, Page first achieved prominence for her performance in the Off-Broadway production of *Summer and Smoke* (1952). She won numerous awards for her memorable Broadway performance in *Sweet Bird of Youth* (1959) and was nominated for Academy Awards for her acting in the films *Hondo* (1953), *Summer and Smoke* (1961), *Sweet Bird of Youth* (1962), *You're a Big Boy Now* (1967), *Pete 'n' Tillie* (1972), *Interiors* (1978), and *The Pope of Greenwich Village* (1984). She finally won an Oscar (1986) for her performance in *The Trip to Bountiful* (1985). Page also won Emmy Awards for her television performances in *A Christmas Memory* (1967) and *The Thanksgiving Visitor* (1969).

PAGE, KIRBY (1890–1957), U.S. pacifist. Ordained as a minister in the Disciples of Christ Church (1915), Page was one of America's foremost advocates of peace. He lectured throughout the country for the American Friends Service Committee and the Fellowship of Reconciliation and was editor of *The World Tomorrow* (1926–34) and contributing editor of *The Christian Century*. Warning (1932) that American capitalism was doomed, he advocated a new economic system. Among his 20 books were *The National Defense* (1931) and *War: Its Causes, Consequences and Cure* (1923).

PAGE, WALTER HINES (1855–1918), U.S. journalist and diplomat. A native of North Carolina, Page worked as a journalist and editor during the 1880s and advocated the creation of a "new south" through education, industrialization, and scientific agriculture. Opposed for his views by conservative forces, he moved to New York and Boston, where he championed reform and edited *Forum* (1890–95), the *Atlantic Monthly* (1896–99), *World's Work* (1900–13) and cofounded Doubleday books (1900). An early supporter of Pres. Woodrow Wilson, Page, an Anglophile, was appointed ambassador to Britain (1913) and did much to alleviate Anglo-American frictions. After the outbreak of World War I he fervently supported the Allied cause and incessantly wired Wilson to abandon neutrality and declare war on Germany. When Wilson finally asked Congress to declare war, he used arguments lifted from Page's memoranda. ■ See biographies by Ross Gregory (1970) and John M. Cooper, Jr. (1977) and study by Robert Rusnak (1982).

PAGNOL, MARCEL (1895–1974), French dramatist and filmmaker. Pagnol first achieved prominence with his play *Topaze* (1928; Eng. trans. 1930), a brilliant exposé of social corruption. *Marius* (1929; Eng. trans. 1957), *Fanny,* (1931), and *César* (1937), his trilogy of plays set on the Marseilles waterfront, revealed his fascination with the people of Provence. He worked on cinematic adaptations of his own plays and on films based on the writings of Jean Giono and Alphonse Daudet. In 1946 he became the first filmmaker to be elected to the Académie Française. ■ See his autobiographies, *The Days Were Too Short* (1957–59; Eng. trans. 1960), *The Time of Secrets* (1960; Eng. trans. 1962), and *The Time of Love* (1977; Eng. trans. 1979), and study by C.E.J. Caldicott (1977).

PAHLEVI, MUHAMMAD REZA SHAH (1919–1980), shah of Iran. Muhammad Reza Pahlevi succeeded to the throne (1941) after his father, Reza Pahlevi, was forced into exile by British and Russian occupation forces. Coerced into leaving the country (August 1953) by nationalist prime minister Muhammad Mussadegh. who had nationalized the oil industry, he was restored to power three days later in a countercoup engineered with the help of the U.S. Central Intelligence Agency (CIA). Subsequently the shah built up a strong central government and used the secret police (SAVAK) to suppress all opposition. Attempting to modernize the country rapidly with revenues from Iran's vast oil reserves, he developed industry, expanded the education system, carried out land reforms, and built up a huge military force. However, his increasingly despotic and corrupt government alienated intellectuals, liberals, and leftists, and his modernization programs and land reforms were attacked by Islamic fundamentalists. His economic program led to the deterioration of the agricultural sector and caused mass migrations of peasants to the cities in search of work. Opposition to his rule grew in the late 1970s and he left the country in the midst of strikes and violent demonstrations

(January 1979). An Islamic republic, led by Ayatollah Khomeini, was proclaimed later that year. The shah died in exile in Egypt. ■ See his book, *The White Revolution in Iran* (Eng. trans. 1967); Gerard deVilliers, The Imperial Shah (Eng. trans. 1976); Margaret Laing, *The Shah* (1977); and Ryszard Kapuscinski, *Shah of Shahs* (Eng. trans. 1985).

PAHLEVI, REZA SHAH (Reza Khan; 1878–1944), shah of Iran. Reza Khan was a professional soldier who overthrew the government in 1921, built up the military as the new minister of war, and served as prime minister (1923). When the Qajar dynasty was deposed (1925), he was proclaimed the new shah and adopted Pahlevi as his dynastic name. Ruling as a dictator, Reza Shah crushed regional tribal chiefs, abolished the veil for women, instituted educational reforms, and attempted to modernize and westernize the country. He also built the Trans-Iranian railroad, seized ecclesiastical income, increased taxes on foreign concessions and eliminated their special privileges, and gained control of Iran's finances from foreign influences. He abdicated in favor of his son, Muhammad Reza Pahlevi, during World War II (1941) after his pro-German stance prompted a Russian-British invasion. He was exiled to Mauritius, and then to South Africa, where he died. ■ See Cyrus Ghani, *Iran and the Rise of Reza Shah* (1998).

PAIGE, SATCHEL (Leroy Robert Paige; 1906?–1982), U.S. baseball player. One of baseball's legendary figures, Paige had pitching skills that could never be measured by official statistics since he was barred from playing in the all-white major leagues until 1948. An extraordinary athlete, known for his blistering fastball, unusual endurance, and folksy aphorisms, he was the great star of the Negro leagues for over 20 years and once pitched on 29 consecutive days. When he was finally signed by the Cleveland Indians, Paige became a rookie pitcher at age 42. Past his prime, he nevertheless had a 6–1 winning mark and helped the team win the 1948 pennant and World Series. In 1965 he made his final official appearance (the oldest man to play in a major league game), and in 1971 he was enshrined in the National Baseball Hall of Fame. He advised those seeking to emulate his staying power to "Go very lightly on the vices . . . avoid running at all times, [and] don't look back. Something might be gaining on you." ■ See his memoirs, *Maybe I'll Pitch Forever* (1962), and Mark Ribowsky, *Don't Look Back* (1994).

PAIK, NAM JUNE (1932–), Korean-born U.S. video artist and composer. The son of an industrialist, Paik left Korea with his family in 1950, settled in Tokyo, and graduated from Tokyo University (1956). He studied piano and traditional and electronic music in Germany (1956–62). In New York and several European cities during the 1960s he produced John Cage- and Dada-inspired musical "happenings" or "action concerts" that combined experimental music with absurd and unexpected theatrical activity. At the same time he invented a new art form, "video art," by manipulating the electromagnetic field of the television tube to produce unique and bizarre images on the screen. Although his first show consisting of 13 television sets (Germany, 1963) did not make an impact, he subsequently developed more sophisticated electronic techniques, gained a following in the United States, produced television shows and avant-garde video tapes, and was honored with a major retrospective at New York's Whitney Museum (1982). His best-known videos included *Global Groove* (1973), *TV Buddha* (1974), and *Family Robot* (1986). His video opera *Coyote 3* (1997) featured multiple TV screens, laser lights, and smoke, with Paik playing the piano and singing fragments of songs. ■ See study by John G. Hanhardt (1982).

PAISLEY, IAN RICHARD KYLE (1926–), Northern Ireland religious and political leader. The founder (1951) and self-proclaimed moderator of the fundamentalist Free Presbyterian Church of Ulster. Paisley was a leader of the militant Protestants in their bitter struggle with the Roman Catholics of Northern Ireland. A virulent anti-Catholic, he led numerous marches and demonstrations, many ending in violence, that opposed reforms for the Catholic minority. He served in the Northern Irish parliament (1970–72), assembly (1973–75; 1982) and constitutional convention (1975–76), and was a member of the British Parliament (from 1970). He also served in the European Parliament (1979–). His books included *Paisley, the Man and His Message* (1976), *No Pope Here* (1982), and *Understanding Events in Northern Ireland* (1995).

PALADE, GEORGE EMIL (1912–), Rumanian-born U.S. cell biologist. Palade trained at the University of Bucharest (M.D. 1940) and taught there until going to the Rockefeller Institute in New York (1946–73). In the United States he was an associate of Albert Claude, the man who adapted electron microscopy to biological studies, and he became a pioneer investigator of cell structure. He developed advanced centrifuge techniques and discovered ribosomes, the protein synthesizers of cells. Palade shared the 1974 Nobel Prize for Physiology or Medicine with Claude and Christian de Duve. He also taught at Yale (1973–90) and at the University of California at San Diego Medical School (1990–).

PALAMAS, KOSTES (1859–1943), Greek poet. The most prominent Greek literary figure for more than half a century, Palamas was a leader of the demotic movement, which successfully campaigned for the use of the vernacular Greek language in literature. A nationalist poet, he plumbed the rich folk heritage of Greece for his diverse themes. His poetry collections included *Tragedy of My Country* (1886), *Life Immovable* (1904; Eng. trans. 1919), *A Hundred Voices* (1904: Eng. trans. 1921), *The Twelve Words of the Gypsy* (1907; Eng. trans. 1964, 1969. and 1975), and *The King's Flute* (1910; Eng. trans. 1967). Palamas, who served as president of the Academy of Science and secretary of the University of Athens, was also known for his short stories,

political essays, and literary criticism. ■ See studies by Thanasis Maskaleris (1972) and Theofanis Stavrou and Constantine Trypanis (1985).

PALÉS MATOS, LUIS (1898–1959), Puerto Rican poet and essayist. Puerto Rico's most prominent poet, Palés Matos infused Spanish-language poetry with the intonations, rhythms, themes, and images of African and Afro-Caribbean folklore and dance. Not seeking sociological or anthropological accuracy, he attempted, as a white man, to evoke the exiled Afro-American through legend, folklore, and magic. He portrayed his "primitivism" as a vital creative force and as a contrast to the tensions of Western intellectualism. He also wrote notable poems concerning women. His major collections were *Tuntún de Pasa y Griferia* (1937) and *Poesias: 1915–1956* (1957). ■ See Julio Marzan, *The Numinous Site* (1995).

PALEY, GRACE (Grace Goodside; 1922–), U.S. short-story writer. Paley was born in New York City and attended Hunter College. Her fiction often used startling images, mixed with realistic New York settings and familiar dialogue, to explore the inner lives of women—women alone and in relationships. *The Little Disturbances of Man: Stories of Men and Women in Love* (1959) showed characters' changing perceptions of themselves and others in a variety of social contexts. The stories in *Enormous Changes at the Last Minute* (1974), set in city tenements, reflected an intensified political consciousness and became a film (1985); "Faith in a Tree" tells of a mother and son's involvement in a demonstration against napalm bombing in Vietnam. *Later the Same Day* (1985) revisits characters from earlier Paley stories, now older and more experienced but still grappling with issues of personal and social responsibility. *Leaning Forward* (1985) was a poetry collection. Paley was vocal in support of women's rights and against the proliferation of nuclear weapons. Her later works included the poem and story collection, *Long Walks and Intimate Talks* (1991); *New and Collected Poems* (1992); *The Collected Stories* (1994); *Just as I Thought* (1998), a collection of essays, lectures, and reminiscences; and *Begin Again: Collected Poems* (2000). ■ See literary biography by Judith Arcana (1993).

PALEY, WILLIAM SAMUEL (1901–1990), U.S. businessman. The son of a wealthy cigar manufacturer, Paley purchased (1928) a small and financially strapped radio network, United Independent Broadcasters, Inc., for $400,000, changed its name to the Columbia Broadcasting System, Inc., and built it into a multibillion-dollar communications empire. He was the broadcasting industry's foremost impresario with a genius for developing mass entertainment on both radio and television. He personally ran CBS for more than half a century (president 1928–46; chairman 1946–83) and was largely responsible for the establishment of CBS News during World War II and for the widespread popularity of television after the war. He returned to CBS as acting chairman in 1986. He also served as a trustee (from 1937) and president (1968–72) of the Museum of Modern Art (New York) and founded the Museum of Broadcasting (New York, 1976). ■ See his memoirs, *As It Happened* (1979); Lewis Paper, *Empire* (1987); and Sally Bedell Smith, *In All His Glory* (1990).

PALME, (SVEN) OLOF (JOACHIM) (1927–1986), Swedish political leader. Educated at Kenyon College (B.A. 1948), Palme returned to Sweden to study law (Stockholm University, 1951) and became active in the Social Democratic party. A protégé of Tage Erlander, he was elected to parliament (1956) and served in several cabinet posts before succeeding Erlander as party chairman (1969) and premier (1969–76). He was severely critical of U.S. involvement during the Vietnam War and called on all industrial nations to increase foreign aid to poorer countries in the Third World. His defeat in the 1976 election marked the end of the 44-year hold on power by the socialists, who created the Swedish welfare state. Palme subsequently served as a member of the Independent Commission on International Development Issues (from 1977) and as chairman of the Independent Commission on Disarmament and Security (from 1980). When the socialists won the 1982 parliamentary elections, Palme was returned to power. He was assassinated by an unknown gunman while walking on a Stockholm street (Feb. 28, 1986). In 1996 the former head of a South African apartheid-era police unit claimed that Palme was killed by one of his agents. ■ See Chris Mosey, *Cruel Awakening* (1991).

PALMER, ALEXANDER MITCHELL (1872–1936), U.S. political leader. A lifelong Quaker, A. Mitchell Palmer demonstrated a combativeness and tenacity during his years as a Democratic leader in Pennsylvania, as a representative in Congress (1909–15), and as a presidential campaign manager (1912) for Woodrow Wilson that earned him the nickname "the fighting Quaker." Named U.S. attorney general in March 1919, he freely issued injunctions against striking miners, steelworkers, and railroad workers, charging them with social revolution; he initiated (and participated in) unconstitutional dragnets and raids on private homes and organizations aimed at rounding up and deporting thousands of suspected aliens and radicals. Dubbed the "Palmer Raids." these roundups created the "red scare" of 1919–20 and were among the most flagrant violations of civil liberties up to that point in U.S. history. Adverse reaction to the raids probably cost him the 1920 Democratic presidential nomination. ■ See biography by Stanley Cohen (1963).

PALMER, ARNOLD (1929–), U.S. golfer. Palmer was one of the "big three" of modern golf (along with Gary Player and Jack Nicklaus), and the most exciting player of his time. Following a brilliant amateur career, he turned professional (1955) and in a relatively short span (1958–62) put together a remarkable string of major golf titles, including three Masters championships, the U.S. Open, and two

British Opens. In 1964 he won the Masters for the fourth time. In the mid-1960s his game began to decline as he became increasingly involved in business ventures. Nevertheless, Palmer continued to attract a tremendous following known as "Arnie's Army," and his career earnings topped the $1 million mark. ■ See biography by Mark McCormack (1967) and his autobiography, *A Golfer's Life* (1999; with James Dodson).

PALMER, (EDWARD) VANCE (1885–1959), Australian writer. A founder of Australian drama, Palmer helped organize the Pioneer Players (1922–26) in Melbourne, a group that specialized in presenting plays on Australian themes. A major literary figure, he wrote 12 novels—including *The Passage* (1930), *The Swayne Family* (1934), and *Golconda* (1948)—four volumes of short stories, two volumes of poetry, several political plays, and an influential cultural history, *The Legend of the Nineties* (1954). He was also a literary critic and a patron of young Australian writers. ■ See biography by Harry Heseltine (1970) and study by Vivian Smith (1974).

PANDIT, VIJAYA LAKSHMI (Swarup Kumari Nehru; 1900–1990), Indian nationalist and diplomat. Madame Pandit was the daughter of nationalist leader Motilal Nehru and sister of Jawaharlal Nehru. She followed in her family's footsteps and was jailed for nationalist activities. She also served as minister of public health in the government of the United Provinces (1937–39; 1946–47). After independence she led the Indian delegation to the United Nations General Assembly seven times and in 1953 became the first woman and first Asian to serve as president of that body. She also served as ambassador to the Soviet Union (1947–49), the United States (1949–51), and as Indian high commissioner to the United Kingdom (1954–61) and governor of the state of Maharashtra (1962–63) before her retirement in 1968. ■ See biography by Robert H. Andrews, *A Lamp for India* (1967), and her memoirs, *The Scope of Happiness* (1979).

PANETH, FRIEDRICH ADOLF (1887–1958), Austrian chemist. Educated in Vienna (Ph.D. 1910), Munich, and Glasgow, Paneth developed, with Georg von Hevesy, the concept of radioactive tracers (1912–13). This research technique used radioactive isotopes to "tag" atoms, permitting scientists to collect data on various chemical and physiological mechanisms, especially plant and animal metabolism. He also studied the composition of the atmosphere up to an altitude of 60 kilometers and devised a method of determining the age of earth rocks and meteorites by measuring their helium content. A refugee from the Nazis, Paneth worked in Britain (1938–53) until he returned to the Continent to head the Max Planck Institute for Chemistry at Mainz, West Germany (1953–58).

PANKEN, JACOB (1879–1968), Russian-born U.S. labor leader and judge. Born into a poor Jewish family, Panken became active in socialist politics and labor organizing while still a teenager. He was a founder of the International Ladies Garment Workers Union (ILGWU), the Amalgamated Clothing Workers of America, and the Organization for Rehabilitation through Training (ORT). Although he ran unsuccessfully for many high offices, he was elected (1917) as the first socialist judge (municipal court) in New York City and later served (1934–55) as a judge in the domestic-relations court. He wrote *Socialism in America* (1931) and *The Child Speaks* (1941).

PANKHURST, EMMELINE (Emmeline Goulden; 1858–1928), British woman-suffrage leader. A militant activist, Pankhurst founded (with her daughter Christabel and a few friends) the independent Women's Social and Political Union (WSPU) in Manchester (1903). The organization, whose membership was exclusively female and whose sole aim was the vote for women, at first adopted tactics of agitation and harassment of politicians opposed to the cause, but it soon embraced a policy of arson and destruction of property. Pankhurst was arrested on several occasions (1908–14) but released each time after participating in hunger strikes. At the outbreak of World War I she called off the suffrage campaign and supported the war effort. She joined the Conservative party late in her life and died while campaigning for a seat in Parliament, just a few weeks after the passage of the Representation of the People Act of 1928, which gave women the vote on the same basis as men. ■ See her autobiography, *My Own Story* (1914), and biography by her daughter, E. Sylvia Pankhurst (1935).

PANNEKOEK, ANTON (1873–1960), Dutch astronomer and political theorist. After receiving a Ph.D. in astronomy, Pannekoek became active in the left wing of the Social Democratic Workers' party, taught Marxist theory to workers in the Netherlands and Germany (from 1905), and contributed to socialist journals. After World War I he joined the left wing of the Dutch and German Communist parties, was a Comintern agent, and advocated council communism and the mass strike. He criticized the bolsheviks for their antidemocratic policies and for their collaboration with traditional labor unions, and was, in turn, criticized by the Comintern for his ultraleftist views. He retired from politics in the early 1920s and resumed his scientific career as a professor at the Municipal University of Amsterdam (1925–41). He studied the Milky Way, investigated ionization in stellar atmospheres, and was regarded as the founder of modern astrophysics in the Netherlands. His scientific works included *Anthropogenesis* (1945; Eng. trans. 1953) and *A History of Astronomy* (1951; Eng. trans. 1961). ■ See D. A. Smart, ed., *Pannekoek and Gorter's Marxism* (Eng. trans. 1978).

PANOFSKY, ERWIN (1892–1968), German-born art historian. A Ph.D. from the University of Freiburg (1914) who left Nazi Germany to join the Institute for Advanced Study in Princeton, New Jersey (1935–68), Panofsky examined art in the larger context of literature, philosophy, and history. His particular specialty was medieval and Renaissance symbolism, but he was also tremendously erudite on the iconography of pop culture. His extensive writings included *Studies in Iconology* (1939), a two-volume study of Albrecht Dürer (1943), and *Meaning in the Visual Arts* (1955). ■ See study by Michael Holly (1984).

PANOVA, VERA FYODOROVNA (1905-1973), Soviet novelist. Panova began a long journalistic career (1922–45) at age 17. Her first novel, *The Train* (1946; Eng. trans. 1948), was assigned to her by the Soviet writers' union: it described a hospital train during World War II. A later work, *Span of the Year* (1953; Eng. trans. 1957), was widely read and translated, but Panova was criticized in the newspaper *Pravda* for resorting to naturalism "without passing any judgment." She wrote about industrial development, but by focusing on individual characters, particularly children, she retained a measure of warmth. She also wrote *Time Walked* (1955; Eng. trans. 1957), the partly autobiographical *A Sentimental Novel* (1958), *Theses of a Novel* (1965), and numerous short stories, plays, and film scripts.

PAPADOPOULOS, GEORGE (1919–1999), Greek soldier and political leader. A career army officer who spent five years with the Greek Central Intelligence Service, Papadopoulos led the military coup that toppled Greece's democratically elected government (1967). Supposedly saving Greece from anarchy and communism, he ruled by decree, suspended civil liberties, and jailed thousands. He was premier (1967–73) and became president following the abolition of the monarchy in July 1973, but he was overthrown by another military coup in November 1973. Civilian rule was restored in 1974, and Papadopoulos was tried for revolt and high treason and sentenced to death (1975), but the sentence was later reduced to life imprisonment.

PAPAGOS, ALEXANDER (1883–1955), Greek soldier and political leader. As commander in chief of the Greek army, Papagos successfully repulsed the invading Italian armies (1940) during World War II but was defeated and taken prisoner by the Germans (1941–45). After the war he directed the successful campaign against the Greek communist rebels (1949) and was appointed field marshal. Following a dispute with King Paul, he resigned as head of the armed forces, formed a conservative political party, the Greek Rally, and served as premier (1952–55) after the party's overwhelming electoral victory (1952). Papagos improved Greek ties with the West and with Greece's Balkan neighbors.

PAPANDREOU, ANDREAS GEORGE (1919–1996), Greek political leader. The son of George Papandreou, a prominent politician, Andreas Papandreou was a left-wing student radical at the University of Athens who was granted political asylum in the United States (1939). After studying at Harvard (Ph.D. in economics, 1943), he became a U.S. citizen (1944), served in the U.S. Navy (1944–46), and taught economics at several universities including the University of California at Berkeley (1955–63). Returning to Greece after his father was elected premier (1963), he gave up his U.S. citizenship, served as minister of economic coordination, and was elected to parliament (1964). Arrested after the 1967 military coup, he was freed after eight months and spent the next seven years in exile in Stockholm and Toronto. After the restoration of democracy, he returned to Greece (1974), founded the Panhellenic Socialist Movement (1974), and served as leader of the opposition in parliament (1977–81). Elected Greece's first socialist premier (1981: reelected 1985), Papandreou established welfare state programs and pursued a pragmatic and independent foreign policy. Bribery and embezzlement scandals weakened his government in the late 1980s and he was defeated in the 1989 elections. However, he was reelected in 1993 and served as premier until forced to resign (1996) due to ill health. His books included *Man's Freedom* (1970), *Paternalistic Capitalism* (1972), and *Socialist Transformation* (1977).

PAPANDREOU, GEORGE (1888–1968), Greek political leader. First elected to parliament in 1923, Papandreou served as minister of the interior (1923) and minister of education (1929–33) before founding the Democratic Socialist party (1935). A lifelong foe of militarism and dictatorship, he was exiled (1936–40) and imprisoned during World War II by Italian occupation forces (1940–44). He escaped, became active in the resistance, and headed the Greek government-in-exile (1944–45). Back in Athens, he was premier (1945), served in several ministerial posts (1946–52), led the opposition after the rightwing election victories (1952–63), and served again as premier (1963, 1964–65) as head of the Center Union party, which he had organized in 1961. He was forced to resign after a conflict with King Constantine (1965) and was placed under house arrest following the 1967 military coup. After democracy was restored, his son Andreas Papandreou served as premier of Greece (1981–89; 1993–96).

PAPANICOLAOU, GEORGE NICHOLAS (1883–1962), Greek-born U.S. cytologist. Papanicolaou studied at the universities of Athens (M.D. 1904) and Munich (Ph.D. 1910). He served in the Greek army as a medical officer during the Balkan War (1912–13), then went to the United States (1913), where he initially worked as a salesman. He eventually worked his way up from anatomical assistant to full professor (1924–49) at Cornell Medical College. In 1927, while studying the reproductive cycles of guinea pigs and humans by using vaginal smears, he discovered the growth of cancerous cells. Subsequently, he devoted his life to persuading the medical profession that vaginal smears could be used effectively to detect curable cancer of the uterus and bladder. Ultimately the "Pap test"—a painless diagnostic procedure—was widely accepted. ■ See Daniel E. Carmichael, *The Pap Smear* (1973).

PAPEN, FRANZ VON (1879–1969), German diplomat and chancellor. A Prussian aristocrat with a military education, Papen was posted to Washington, D.C., during World War I but expelled for espionage and sabotage activities. From 1921 to 1932 he served in the Prussian diet as a right-wing member of the Catholic Center party. As chancellor (June—December 1932), he led the "barons' cabinet" that canceled German reparations and lifted the ban on Nazi paramilitary activity. An inveterate intriguer, Papen urged Pres. Paul von Hindenburg to install Nazi leader Adolf Hitler as chancellor in 1933. He subsequently served the Nazis as ambassador to Austria (1934–38), which he helped prepare for German annexation, and to Turkey (1939–44), but he was acquitted of war crimes at Nuremberg. ■ See his *Memoirs* (1952; Eng. trans. 1953) and Richard W. Rolfs, *The Sorcerer's Apprentice* (1996).

PAPINI, GIOVANNI (1881–1956), Italian critic, novelist, essayist, and political writer. Papini's long and prolific career encompassed political changes, literary shifts, and religious conversion. The 60 volumes that he wrote and the various periodicals that he founded and edited contain conflicting views on such issues as the relationship between art and society and the value of nationalism. Although he embraced and later repudiated futurism, internationalism, and agnosticism, he was one of the more influential Italian literary figures of the first quarter of the century. Some critics called his work self-serving in light of the moral ramifications of these issues in fascist Italy. His selected essays were published in *Four and Twenty Minds* (Eng. trans. 1922). Papini also wrote *The Failure* (1912; Eng. trans. 1924), which was autobiographical; *The Life of Christ* (1921: Eng. trans. 1923); and *Laborers in the Vineyard* (1929; Eng. trans. 1930).

PAPP, JOSEPH (Joseph Papirofsky; 1921–1991), U.S. theatrical producer and director. A native of New York City, Papp worked for several years as an actor and television stage manager before he founded the New York Shakespeare Festival (1954), which presented free outdoor theatrical performances, and the Public Theater (1967), which provided an Off-Broadway forum for talented young American playwrights. Many of Papp's productions achieved great success after being transplanted to Broadway. In addition to producing dozens of Shakespearean productions, Papp was best known for the musicals *Hair* (1967), *Two Gentlemen of Verona* (Tony Award, 1972), *A Chorus Line* (Tony Award, 1976), and *The Pirates of Penzance* (Pulitzer Prize and Tony Award, 1981) and the dramas *No Place to Be Somebody* (Pulitzer Prize, 1970), *Sticks and Bones* (Tony Award, 1972), *That Championship Season* (Pulitzer Prize and Tony Award, 1973) and *The Normal Heart* (1985). ■ See Stuart W. Little, *Enter Joseph Papp* (1974) and biography by Helen Epstein (1994).

PARETO, VILFREDO (1848–1923), Italian social scientist. Born in Paris, where his aristocratic father was in exile, Pareto graduated from the University of Turin (1869) to become a civil engineer and the managing director of an ironworks (1874–89). He taught political economy at Lausanne University (1893–1907), where he applied mathematics to economic and social theory. In his best-known work, *The Mind and Society* (1916; Eng. trans., 4 vols., 1935), Pareto considered history a succession of aristocracies, each ruling elite being replaced by a more powerful one. His translated works are in *Sociological Writings* (1966). ■ See Placido Bucolo, *The Other Pareto* (1980), and study by Franz Borkenau (1936).

PARK, CHUNG HEE (1917–1979), Korean military and political leader. Born into a farming family, Park was educated at a Japanese military academy and served in the Japanese army in World War II. In 1946 he switched to the South Korean army and rose to the rank of major general by 1961. In that year he led a bloodless coup d'état that deposed the democratic government of Premier John W. Chang. In 1963, as a civilian, Park was elected president and in 1971 declared a state of emergency that gave him dictatorial powers. With U.S. support, he ruthlessly suppressed opposition, denied civil rights, expanded a secret police force that operated even outside Korea, and pursued an extreme rightist, anticommunist foreign policy. His economic policies transformed South Korea from a poor rural nation into a major industrial exporting power with an annual real growth rate of more than 10 percent. He was assassinated by his colleague, the head of the Korean Central Intelligence Agency (KCIA). ■ See his books, *To Build a Nation* (1971) and *Korea Reborn* (1979).

PARK, MAUD WOOD (Maud Wood; 1871–1955), U.S. suffragist. After teaching school for eight years, she attended Radcliffe (1895–98), where in her last year she invited suffragist Alice Blackwell to speak. Distressed by the absence of young women at the 1900 convention of the National American Women Suffrage Association in Washington, D.C., Park helped form the Massachusetts College Equal Suffrage League, which was a national organization by 1908. Park also cofounded and served as executive secretary (1901–13) of the Boston Equal Suffrage Association for Good Government. In 1916, impressed by Park's grasp of legislative process, feminist leader Carrie Chapman Catt asked her to coordinate congressional work in support of a constitutional amendment giving women the vote. Park's work contributed to passage of that amendment. She was elected the first president of the League of Women Voters (1920–24) and organized the Women's Joint Congressional Committee (1924), a lobbying network representing numerous women's organizations. ■ See her *Front Door Lobby* (1960).

PARK, ROBERT EZRA (1864–1944), U.S. sociologist. Park was an itinerant reporter (1887–98) from Pennsylvania who saw the world as a laboratory of human nature. At age 35 he enrolled in a master's program at Harvard and traveled to Germany to earn a Ph.D. (1904) with a dissertation on public opinion. Working in the South with Booker T. Washington, he became a recognized expert on race relations and wrote numerous papers and essays later collected in *Race and Culture* (1950). As a member of the sociology department of the University of Chicago (1914–33). Park collaborated on *Introduction to the Science of Sociology* (1921) and wrote prolifically on urban sociology, coining the terms "marginal man" and "human ecology." ■ See his *Collected Papers* (3 vols., 1950–55); the biography by Winifred Raushenbush (1979); and Barbara B. Lal, *The Romance of Culture in an Urban Civilization* (1990).

PARK, WILLIAM HALLOCK (1863–1939), U.S. bacteriologist and public health official. The head of diphtheria research (from 1893) and director of the Bureau of Laboratories (1910–36) of the New York City Board of Health, Park was one of the foremost applied bacteriologists of his time. His development of the toxin-antitoxin treatment of diphtheria virtually eliminated the disease, and his work on bacterial contamination of milk led to compulsory pasteurization (1914) that substantially reduced the incidence of infant diarrhea as a cause of death. He also did research on poliomyelitis, influenza, pneumonia, scarlet fever, and tuberculosis. He taught bacteriology and preventive medicine at the Bellevue Hospital Medical College (later New York University College of Medicine, 1895–1937) and wrote several authoritative textbooks. ■ See Wade W. Oliver, *The Man Who Lived for Tomorrow* (1941).

PARKER, CHARLIE "BIRD" (Charles Christopher Parker, Jr.; 1920–1955), U.S. jazz musician. Parker grew up in the black ghetto of Kansas City, Missouri. He achieved fame in 1945 as one of the founders of the "bop" or "bebop" form of progressive jazz. A genius of improvisation, he was an idol of young musicians. He had an overwhelming influence on jazz performers regardless of the instrument they played and was considered by many to be the greatest alto saxophonist in jazz history. Plagued by a series of physical and emotional problems, he was addicted to drugs for many years. Parker's last public appearance, in March 1955, was at Birdland, the New York City jazz club named after him. ■ See Robert Reisner, *Bird* (1962); Ross Russell, *Bird Lives!* (1973); Gary Giddins, *Celebrating Bird* (1987); Lawrence Koch, *Yardbird Suite* (1988); and biography by Carl Woideck (1996).

PARKER, DOROTHY (Dorothy Rothschild; 1893–1967), U.S. writer and critic. She grew up in New York City and in her 20s worked on the magazine *Vanity Fair* (1917–20) with Robert Benchley and Robert Sherwood, with whom she formed a legendary luncheon group. She reigned over writers James Thurber. E. B. White, Ogden Nash, Ring Lardner, and others as queen of Manhattan's court of wits that haunted the Algonquin Hotel in the 1920s. After 1927 she was associated with the *New Yorker,* publishing incisive book reviews in her "Constant Reader" column (1927–33) that were collected in *A Month of Saturdays* (1971). But her reputation rests primarily on short stories (collected in *Here Lies,* 1939) and verse (collected in *Not So Deep as a Well,* 1936) that exposed the cruel absurdities of city living and revealed the sensitivity to thwarted idealism and frustrated love that ran beneath her cutting cynicism. Active in leftist politics during the 1930s, she was a newspaper correspondent during the Spanish Civil War. After 1933 she collaborated on numerous screenplays, including *A Star Is Born,* but her political background put her at odds with Hollywood executives during the anticommunist hysteria of the cold-war era. She is remembered for such one-liners as, "Men seldom make passes at girls who wear glasses." Parker left the bulk of her estate to Martin Luther King, Jr. ■ See John Keats, *You Might as Well Live* (1970); study by Arthur F. Kinney (1978); Leslie Frewin, *The Late Mrs. Dorothy Parker* (1986); and biography by Marion Meade (1988).

PARKS, GORDON (1912–), U.S. photographer and film director. The youngest of 15 children in a poor black Kansas family, Parks tried a dozen jobs before turning to photography. He worked briefly (1942–43) for the Farm Security Administration under Roy Stryker, whom he followed to Standard Oil as a documentary photographer (1944–48). A photo essay on Harlem gangs brought Parks to the attention of *Life* magazine, where he was a staff photographer for 20 years (1948–68). He produced notable photo essays on the civil-rights struggle and an award-winning study of a poverty-stricken family in Brazil. A talented poet and composer, Parks directed the screen version of his 1963 novel *The Learning Tree* (1969), followed by the *Shaft* films. He was the first African-American director of major Hollywood films. His books included *Arias in Silence* (1994) and *Glimpses Toward Infinity* (1996). ■ See his autobiographies, *A Choice of Weapons* (1966), *To Smile in Autumn* (1979), and *Voices in the Mirror* (1990), and Philip Brookman, *Half Past Autumn* (1997).

PARKS, ROBERT JOSEPH (1922–), U.S. aerospace scientist. A pioneer in ballistic-missile guidance, Parks directed the flights of *Mariner 2* (1962), *Mariner 4* (1965), *Rangers 6–9* (1964–65), and *Surveyor 1* (1966) while working in the National Aeronautics and Space Administration Jet Propulsion Laboratory (JPL). His most ambitious project, *Surveyor 1,* was the first American spacecraft to effect a "soft" landing (at eight miles per hour) on the moon. The successful mission enabled later space vehicles to carry out more complex tasks, paving the way for manned moon landings. Parks registered patents for the design of a guidance and control system (with William Pickering) and a guided-missile-control system (with James Burke and R. M. Stewart). He

served as the JPL's assistant, and then associate, director of flight projects (1967–83) and finally as its deputy director (1983–89).

PARKS, ROSA (1913–), U.S. civil-rights activist. Parks was a seamstress and a member of several black organizations in Montgomery, Alabama, including the National Association for the Advancement of Colored People (NAACP). When, in December 1955, she refused to give up her seat on a bus to a white passenger, she sparked a citywide boycott by blacks that lasted over a year, raised an unknown clergyman named Martin Luther King, Jr., to national prominence, and resulted in a U.S. Supreme Court decision outlawing segregation on city buses. The "mother of the civil rights movement" moved to Detroit (1957), where she became a staff assistant to Cong. John Conyers, Jr. (1965–88), and remained active in the struggle for racial equality. In 1984 she participated in protests against the South African government's policy of apartheid. ■ See her autobiography (1992; with Jim Haskins) and the biography by Douglas Brinkley (2000).

PARRA, NICANOR (1914–), Chilean poet. A professor of mathematics and theoretical physics before turning to literature, Parra was one of Latin America's most skillful, influential, and controversial poets. Influenced by existentialism and surrealism, he attempted to demythologize poetry and satirize all social institutions with his "antipoems," works that were rich with sarcasm, irony, and black humor and that utilized language and images drawn from popular culture, songs, clichés, graffiti, and slogans. Parra's antitraditional and irreverent "antipoems" were called "too dirty to be immoral" by one Chilean critic. Many of his important poems appear in *Poems and Antipoems* (1954; Eng. trans. 1967) and *Emergency Poems* (Eng. trans. 1972). ■ See also his *Sermons and Homilies of the Christ of Elqui* (1979: Eng. trans. 1984) and Edith Grassman, *The Antipoetry of Nicanor Parra* (1975).

PARRINGTON, VERNON LOUIS (1871–1929), U.S. historian. Parrington grew up in Emporia, Kansas, was educated at Harvard and at the College of Emporia, and ran for the local school board as a populist. He was well read in many fields and while teaching English at the University of Washington (1908–29) pursued his lifelong reappraisal of U.S. literature, which he analyzed from a Jeffersonian liberal perspective. In his Pulitzer Prize–winning *Main Currents in American Thought* (2 vols., 1927), a study of the liberal tradition in America, Parrington described intellectual history as a struggle between freedom and privilege that was rooted in the country's economic relations. A third unfinished volume, *The Beginnings of Critical Realism in America,* appeared posthumously (1930). The books were extremely influential during the 1930s. ■ See Richard Hofstadter, *Progressive Historians* (1979), and biography by H. Lark Hall (1994).

PARRISH, (FREDERICK) MAXFIELD (1870–1966), U.S. artist. The most popular, highest-paid illustrator of the early decades of the century, Parrish came from a Philadelphia Quaker family and studied at the Pennsylvania Academy of Fine Arts. Choosing romantic, medieval themes in the pre-Raphaelite style, he illustrated magazines and books (*The Arabian Nights, Knickerbocker's History of New York*), designed murals for hotels and other public buildings, and created some advertisements (Edison light bulbs, Jell-O). Parrish dropped into obscurity around 1940, but he enjoyed a revival of interest in his work just before his death. ▪ See studies by Coy Ludwig (1973) and Sylvia Yount (1999).

PARSONS, ELSIE WORTHINGTON (Elsie Clews; 1875–1941), U.S. anthropologist. Born into a socially prominent family, Parsons trained in sociology at Columbia University (Ph.D. 1899) and taught at Barnard College (1899–1905). She wrote a series of widely read books, including *The Family* (1905), *The Old-Fashioned Woman* (1913), and *Fear and Conventionality* (1914), that reflected her feminist beliefs and her interest in social pressures on the individual. *Religious Chastity* (1913), a daring (for the time) study of sexual practices, was published under the pseudonym of "John Main" in order to protect her husband's political career. After 1916 her focus shifted to American Indian societies. She made lengthy annual field trips and wrote such highly regarded works as *Hopi and Zuni Ceremonialism* (1933), *Mitla, Town of Souls* (1936), and *Pueblo Indian Religions* (2 vols., 1939). Parsons also published important works on West Indian and black American folklore. She headed the American Folklore Society (1919–20) and the American Ethnological Society (1923–25) and was the first woman to be elected president of the American Anthropological Association (1940). ▪ See biography by Desley Deacon (1997) and Rosemary L. Zumwalt, *Wealth and Rebellion* (1992).

PARSONS, LOUELLA O. (Louella Oettinger; 1881?–1972), U.S. newspaper columnist. The queen of the Hollywood gossip columnists, Parsons wrote of the lives and loves of the movie stars for the Hearst newspapers for over 40 years (1925–65). Extremely influential within the movie colony during its golden years, her column appeared throughout the nation and was followed by 20 million readers. She wrote *The Gay Illiterate* (1944) and *Tell It to Louella* (1961). ▪ See George Eells, *Hedda and Louella* (1972).

PARSONS, TALCOTT (1902–1979), U.S. sociologist. Trained as an economist in the United States, England, and Germany, Parsons shifted his research to sociology in the 1930s. He eventually became the most influential American sociologist and the mentor of three generations of scholars during his 46 years at Harvard University (1927–73). His first major work was *The Structure of Social Action* (1937). At a time when American sociology was largely concerned with specific, localized, empirical research. Parsons attempted to find a foundation for an abstract theory of social action, and later of social systems, that was generally applicable to all human societies. The complex Parsonian theory was elaborated in his *The Social System* (1952) and other books. Sometimes criticized as essentially conservative because it emphasized how societies resist change and peacefully resolve conflict, his work offered a major explanation of how societies function and addressed the crucial issues in modern sociology. ▪ See studies by Guy Rocher (1975), Ken Menzies (1977), and Peter Hamilton (1983), and François Borricaud, *The Sociology of Talcott Parsons* (Eng. trans. 1981).

PÄRT, ARVO (1935–), Estonian composer. While a student at the Tallinn Conservatory (1958–63), Pärt gained notoriety for *Nekrolog* (1960), an orchestral piece utilizing the 12-tone method that was considered decadent by Soviet cultural officials. His works of the 1960s featured atonality and aleatory elements, and *Credo* (1968) was banned because of its overtly religious theme. His style evolved during the 1970s and his subsequent works were composed in "tintinnabuli style," an austere method based on triadic harmonies, frequent repetition, and subtle shifts of texture. Pärt's hauntingly beautiful, hypnotic, and spiritually intense pieces, many of which were settings of biblical or medieval Christian texts, were called examples of "holy minimalism" by some critics and moved audiences throughout the world. His best known works included *Tabula Rasa* (1977), *Passio* (1981–82), *Te Deum* (1984–86), *Litany* (1994), and *Kanon Pokajanen* (1998). Pärt emigrated to the West (1980) and lived in Germany and England.

PARTCH, HARRY (1901–1974), U.S. composer. A self-taught musician and individualist, Partch was once a hobo and worked at odd jobs to support himself. His early works were based on spoken words, and he later devised a special notation for his own compositions. His microtonal music was based on an octave divided into 43 intervals instead of the traditional 12 of Western music. Among his recorded works are *And on the Seventh Day Petals Fell on Petaluma* (1964), *Daphne of the Dunes* (1958), and *Delusion of the Fury* (1969). Though recognized by critics, he received limited public acclaim, partly due to the exclusiveness of his music, which could be performed only by the bizarre instruments he created and built. Recordings that he made with colleagues (1950–74) were reissued in a four-set, *The Harry Partch Collection* (1997). ▪ See his *Genesis of a Music* (1949; rev. ed. 1974), his collected writings in *Bitter Music* (1991), and biography by Bob Gilmore (1998).

PARTRIDGE, ERIC HONEYWOOD (1894–1979), New Zealand–born lexicographer. After studying at Oxford (1921–23) and teaching briefly in Manchester and London, Partridge gave up academia to set up a small publishing house, Scholartis Press (1927–31). He turned to freelance writing during the Depression, specializing in essays on language, and began to write the books on the history and quirks of the English language that made him famous. Called "the word king" by critic Edmund Wilson, Partridge was best known for *A Dictionary of Slang and Unconventional English* (1937), *Usage and Abusage* (1942), *Origins* (1958), and *A Dictionary of Catch Phrases* (1977). ▪ See David Crystal, ed., *Eric Partridge in His Own Words* (1980).

PAŠIĆ, NIKOLA (1845–1926), Serbian and Yugoslav political leader. A founder of the Radical party (1881), which he led for the rest of his life, Pašić was the most prominent Serbian political figure in the first quarter of the century. As premier he led Serbia to wars against Turkey (1912) and Bulgaria (1913) and was Serbia's leader during World War I. Although one of the founders of the Kingdom of the Serbs, Croats, and Slovenes (1918; later Yugoslavia), he was basically a proponent of a greater Serbia. His strongly centrist policies while premier in the early 1920s were bitterly opposed by the Slovenes and Croats, and they exacerbated the regional tensions that continued to plague Yugoslavia.

PASIONARIA, LA. *See IBARRURI, DOLORES.*

PASOLINI, PIER PAOLO (1922–1975), Italian film director and writer. A Marxist poet and newspaper columnist, Pasolini wrote a novel, *Children of Life* (1954), that led to work as a scriptwriter. Drawing on his writings about Rome's working class and using nonprofessional actors, he directed his first films, *Accatone* (1961) and *Mamma Roma* (1962), controversial films about prostitutes and pimps. He turned to the Bible for his award-winning *The Gospel According to St. Matthew* (1964), casting his mother as the Virgin Mary. Pasolini drew on literary sources for a trilogy of medieval stories that celebrate sensuality: *The Decameron* (1971). *The Canterbury Tales* (1972), and *The Arabian Nights* (1974). His work often depicted homosexual themes. He had just completed *Salo; 120 Days of Sodom* (1975) when he was murdered in one of the poor Roman neighborhoods featured in his writings and films. ▪ See O. Stack, *Pasolini on Pasolini* (1969); study by Stephen Snyder (1980); biographies by Enzo Siciliano (Eng. trans. 1982) and Barth Schwartz (1992); and Sam Rohdie, *The Passion of Pier Paolo Pasolini* (1995).

PASTERNAK, BORIS LEONIDOVICH (1890–1960), Russian poet and novelist. Born into a highly cultured family in Moscow, Pasternak studied philosophy at the universities of Moscow and Marburg (Germany) and was associated with modernist poets Sergei Yesenin and Vladimir Mayakovsky prior to the 1917 Russian Revolution. His two volumes of poems, *My Sister, Life* (1922; Eng. trans. 1982) and *Theme and Variations* (1923), established his reputation as one of Russia's greatest lyric poets. The communist government criticized his difficult and highly original poetry as being subjective and apolitical, and he spent much of the 1930s translating Western classics, notably works by Shakespeare, into Russian. *Doctor Zhivago,* his narrative epic of a poet's attempt to maintain his creative integrity and faith in life amid the turmoil of war and revolution, was published in the West (Italy, 1957; Eng. trans. 1958) after being turned down by a Russian literary journal. Acclaimed as a masterpiece abroad, the book was deemed anti-Soviet by the government, and Pasternak was forced to decline the 1958 Nobel Prize for Literature. English translations of his works are in *Selected Writings* (1949), *Poetry* (1959), and *Poems* (1964). His early prose works appear in English as *The History of a Contraoctave and Childhood of Luvers* (1985). ▪ See his memoirs *Safe Conduct* (1930; Eng. trans. 1945) and *I Remember* (1956; Eng. trans. 1959); biographies by Ronald Hingley (1983) and Peter Levi (1990); and studies by J. W. Dyck (1972), Henry Gifford (1977), and Guy de Mallac (1981).

PATCHEN, KENNETH (1911–1972), U.S. poet and novelist. Patchen spent his early years at odd jobs in the United States and Canada. His first poems were political and many reflected his antiwar beliefs. Experimenting with structure, symbolism, and typography, he often produced poetry as cryptic as "The Murder of Two Men by a Young Kid Wearing Lemon-Colored Gloves," which comprised the word "wait" printed 14 times up and down the page and "now" printed once at the bottom. His collections, many of which he himself illustrated with abstract drawings, included *Before the Brave* (1936), *Selected Poems* (1946; enlarged 1958), and *Collected Poems* (1968), *The Journal of Albion Moonlight* (1941) and *Memoirs of a Shy Pornographer* (1945) were experimental novels. He was also a pioneer in the reading of poetry to the accompaniment of jazz. ▪ See Richard G. Morgan. ed., *Kenneth Patchen: A Collection of Essays* (1977), and studies by Larry R. Smith (1978) and Raymond Nelson (1984).

PATEL, VALLABHBHAI (1875–1950), Indian political leader. Patel was a successful criminal lawyer until he met nationalist leader Mahatma Gandhi in 1917 and rejected Western ways to devote himself to the nationalist cause. Although not a revolutionary, he held many posts in the Indian National Congress party, organized many of its militant nonviolent campaigns, served in local government in Ahmadabad, and was jailed often. After 1945 Patel was second only to Jawaharlal Nehru in political importance and, after independence in 1947, became deputy prime minister, minister of home affairs, and minister of states. A skilled administrator and organizer, Patel brought 562 princely states into the union and strove to maintain order between Hindus and Muslims. ▪ See biographies by N. D. Parikh (2 vols., 1953–56) and D. V. Tahmankar (1970): V. Shankar, *My Reminiscences of Sardar Patel* (2 vols., 1974–75); and R. K. Murthi, *Sardar Patel* (1976).

PATERSON, ANDREW BARTON (1864-1941), Australian poet. The author of "Waltzing Matilda" (1895), Australia's famous folk song and unofficial national anthem. "Banjo" Paterson practiced law in Sydney until 1900 and then worked as a journalist. He collected popular Australian bush songs, preserving the cheerful folk lyrics of pioneering days, and wrote his own volumes of popular verse, *The Man from Snowy River* (1895), *Rio Grande's Last Race* (1902), and *Saltbush Bill, J.P.* (1917). He also wrote two novels, *An Outback Marriage* (1906) and *The Shearer's Colt* (1936). Paterson's *Collected Verse* appeared in 1921, and his verse for children was published in *The Animals Noah Forgot* (1933), *Happy Dispatches* (1934) contains autobiographical sketches. ■ See Clement Semmler, *The Banjo of the Bush* (1966), and studies by Lorna Ollif (1971) and Colin Roderick (1993).

PATIÑO, SIMÓN ITURI (1862?—1947), Bolivian industrialist. Born into a poor Spanish-Indian family, Patiño received (1900?) the deed to a small tin mine in return for a modest loan. The mine turned out to be fabulously rich, and staking out adjacent claims, Patiño became the owner of the largest tin deposits in the world. He invested in banks, railroads, and smelting operations; his estimated worth in 1925 was $500 million. Although he spent most of his later life abroad, as minister to Spain (1920–26) and to France (1926–41), he controlled 60 percent of Bolivia's exports and decisively influenced domestic politics. His vast holdings were tax exempt, and he did nothing to alleviate the poverty of his compatriots, let alone his own exploited workers. ■ See John Hewlett, *Like Moonlight on Snow* (1947).

PATON, ALAN STEWART (1903–1988), South African writer and political leader. After ten years as a high school and college teacher, Paton served as principal of a reformatory for delinquent African boys (1935–48) and gained recognition as a leading penal reformer. His (English-language) novels, *Cry, the Beloved Country* (1948) and *Too Late the Phalarope* (1955), described the tragic effects of South Africa's racist policies and were internationally acclaimed. Called by many the conscience of white South Africa, he founded the Liberal party (1958), a multiracial political organization, to oppose apartheid, and served as its president until the government disbanded it (1968). His other writings included the short-story collection *Debbie Go Home* (1961), the novel *Ah, But Your Land is Beautiful* (1982), the collection of essays and poems *Knocking on the Door* (1976), numerous books on contemporary South African affairs, and two autobiographies, *Towards the Mountain* (1980) and *Journey Continued* (1988). ■ See study by Edward Callan (rev. ed. 1982) and biography by Peter F. Alexander (1994).

PATTERSON, ALICIA (1906-1963), U. S. American newspaper editor and publisher. Heiress of the *New York Daily News—Chicago Tribune* dynasty, Patterson was the daughter of Joseph Medill Patterson and the granddaughter of Joseph Medill; her aunt, Eleanor Medill Patterson, published the *Washington Times-Herald* (1939–48). A big-game hunter and one of the first women pilots, she worked for her father on the *News* as a reporter (1927–28) and literary critic (1923–43). With her husband, Harry F. Guggenheim, she bought a defunct Long Island (New York) newspaper (1939) and, after renaming it *Newsday,* built it into one of the country's largest suburban publications by adopting tabloid format, providing comprehensive national and international coverage as well as local news, and doing pictorial-feature and advertising spreads. With Patterson as publisher and editor, *Newsday* received an award for best U.S. tabloid (1952) and was involved in community issues, winning a Pulitzer Prize (1954) for its exposé of graft at New York racetracks.

PATTERSON, ELEANOR MEDILL (**Elinor Josephine Patterson; 1881–1948**), U.S. publisher and journalist. The granddaughter of *Chicago Tribune* publisher Joseph Medill, Eleanor Medill Patterson published two novels under her married name, Eleanor M. Gizycka. She preferred the life of a journalist to that of a socialite, and at age 48 she convinced William Randolph Hearst to put her in charge of a failing morning daily, the *Washington Herald* (1930). Within a few years she doubled the *Herald*'s circulation. She personally did investigative reporting, working incognito to expose social ills; she once spent three nights in a Salvation Army shelter for women posing as a destitute, homeless woman. In 1937, Patterson assumed management of the *Washington Times.* Two years later, when *Washington Post* publisher Eugene Meyer attempted to buy the *Herald* from Hearst, Patterson herself bought both the *Herald* and the *Times,* merging them into the successful *Washington Times-Herald.* ■ See biography by Alice Albright Hoge (1966); Paul F. Healy, *Cissy* (1966); and Ralph G. Martin, *Cissy* (1979).

PATTERSON, FLOYD (1935–), U.S. boxer. Known for speed and agility in the ring. Patterson began boxing while still a teenager and in 1952 won the Olympic middleweight championship. In 1956, at age 21, he captured the professional heavyweight title, left vacant when Rocky Marciano retired, by defeating Archie Moore. After several successful defenses he lost to Ingemar Johansson in 1959. The following year, however, he became the first heavyweight to regain his title when he upset Johansson in a rematch. He lost the crown to Sonny Liston (1962) by a first-round knockout; he spent the next decade in a vain effort to regain the title. ■ See his autobiography, *Victory over Myself* (1963).

PATTERSON, JOSEPH MEDILL (1879–1946), U.S. journalist, editor, and publisher. Born into a family of newspapermen in Chicago, Patterson graduated from Yale (B.A.

1901) and began his career working on the *Chicago Tribune* (1901–05); he was also an Illinois state legislator (1903–04) and commissioner of public works in Chicago (1905–06). He joined the Socialist party (1906) and he wrote several plays and novels based on radical themes before becoming disillusioned with socialism and returning to the *Tribune* (1910). Patterson served as a correspondent during World War I (1914–15) and later as a combat officer (1917). In 1919, he and Robert McCormick established the *New York Daily News,* whose unparalleled success stemmed from its wide use of photographs and its spicy coverage of sex and crime stories. Within six years, the *News* was the nation's largest-selling paper and its first successful tabloid. After 1925 Patterson was solely responsible for the *News.* Initially a liberal and a loyal supporter of Pres. Franklin D. Roosevelt, Patterson later became an isolationist and an archconservative, and his newspaper's editorial stance reflected the shift. He also published *Liberty* magazine (1924–31) and the *Detroit Mirror* (1931–32). His books included *The Notebook of a Neutral* (1916). ■ See John W. Tebbel, *American Dynasty* (1947; repr. 1968), and John Chapman, *Tell It to Sweeny: The Informal History of the New York Daily News* (1961).

PATTERSON, ROBERT PORTER (1891–1952), U.S. public official. A World War I hero. Patterson practiced law in New York City (1919–30) and served as a federal judge (1930–40). As under secretary of war (1940–45) he organized the army's $100 billion procurement program during World War II. He served as secretary of war (1945–47) and played a key role in the formation of the Department of Defense, which unified the U.S. armed forces. ■ See Keith E. Eiler, *Mobilizing America* (1997).

PATTERSON, WILLIAM ALLAN (1899–1980), U.S. airline executive. Patterson left his job at the Wells Fargo Bank in San Francisco (1929) to join the fledgling commercial airline industry. He helped create United Air Lines by merging four independent companies (1931) and, as its president (1934-66), was instrumental in the growth of air travel in the United States. He initiated many safety features, including two-way telephone lines, wing de-icers, lights for night flying, and instrument landing systems, in a successful effort to attract passengers. He was the first to hire young women as "stewardesses" and he helped Douglas Aircraft to develop the first all-passenger airplane, the DC-4. Under Patterson, United was the first airline committed to jet aviation. When he retired in 1966, it was the largest airline in the United States, with revenues of $900 million.

PATTON, GEORGE SMITH, JR (1885–1945), U.S. general. A West Point graduate (1909). Patton was wounded in France during World War I. During World War II he led the Allied landings in Casablanca (1942) and Sicily (1943) and commanded the 3rd Army drive through France and all the way to Czechoslovakia (1944–45). Known as "Old Blood and Guts," he was an impetuous, tough, and ruthless officer and was considered to be a military genius. His promotion to major general, however, was delayed a year after a much-publicized incident (1943) of abuse against a shell-shocked soldier. After he was dismissed as commander in occupied Germany for publicly criticizing the postwar denazification program (October 1945), he was fatally injured in an automobile accident. ■ See his *War As I Knew It* (1947) and biographies by Ladislas Farago (2 vols., 1964-81), Martin Blumenson (1985), and Carlo D'Este (1995).

PAUKER, ANA (Ana Rabinsohn; 1894?–1960), Rumanian political leader. Pauker was a Hebrew teacher and medical student (in Zurich) before becoming a full-time communist activist. She joined the party in 1921, was elected to its Central Committee in 1922, and spent the next 22 years organizing Rumanian workers and agitating against the government—when she was not in prison or in exile in the Soviet Union. In Moscow during World War II she organized a Rumanian division of the Red army and returned with it triumphantly to Bucharest in 1944. She was a cosecretary of the Communist party, played a key role In the establishment of the Cominform (1947) and the Rumanian republic (1948), and served as foreign minister (from 1947) and vice premier (1949). Although one of the most prominent figures of the international communist movement, she was branded a deviationist in 1952 and stripped of her offices.

PAUL (1901–1964), king of the Hellenes. In exile (1917–20) after his father, King Constantine, was deposed and again (1923–35) during the period of the republic, Paul was a member of the Greek government-in-exile in London during World War II. He became king of Greece (1947) upon the death of his brother, George II, and was a symbol of Greek postwar recovery. He was succeeded by his son, Constantine II.

PAUL VI (Giovanni Battista Montini; 1897–1978), Italian pope. The son of a landowning editor and member of parliament, Montini was educated by the Jesuits and ordained in 1920. After study at the papal school of foreign affairs, he served at the Vatican secretariat of state for 30 years. He was a close aide of Cardinal Pacelli, who later became Pope Pius XII. In 1954 Montini was appointed archbishop of Milan, and four years later Pope John XXIII made him a cardinal. Elected pope in 1963 and taking the name of Paul, he continued the Second Vatican Council. Church rules on fasting, mixed marriages, and use of the vernacular were relaxed, but Paul insisted on the maintenance of priestly celibacy, papal infallibility, and the prohibition of contraception. He also traveled extensively, extending relations with other churches and with communist nations. In a 1967 encyclical, he stressed the importance of the Third World in international relations. ■ See study by Alden Hatch (1966) and Wilton Wynn, *Keeper of the Keys* (1988).

PAUL, ALICE (1885–1977), U.S. social reformer and feminist. Born into a Quaker family, Paul graduated from Swarthmore College (B. A. 1905) and the University of Pennsylvania (Ph.D. 1912). She came into public view as founder of the militant Congressional Union for Woman Suffrage (1913), which emerged as the National Women's party in 1917. After woman suffrage became law (1920), Paul obtained a law degree and drafted (1923) a constitutional amendment guaranteeing equal rights for women, which she viewed as an extension of suffrage. Although it was defeated, she continued to work for women's rights and pacifism in both national and international forums. She chaired the Woman's Research Foundation (1927–37), founded the World Women's party, and was instrumental in getting an affirmation of equal rights written into the preamble of the charter of the United Nations. ■ See Christine A. Lunardini, *From Equal Suffrage to Equal Rights* (1986).

PAUL, WOLFGANG (1913–1993), German physicist. Paul studied at the University of Kiel (Ph.D. 1939) and taught at the University of Göttingen (1944–52) and at the University of Bonn (1952–81). In the 1950s he developed a device, called a Paul trap, to slow down and isolate ions (electrically charged atoms) so that they can be accurately studied. The trap became the standard method for mass separation and became an important tool in modern spectroscopy. Paul shared the 1989 Nobel Prize for Physics with Norman F. Ramsey and Hans G. Dehmelt.

PAULI, WOLFGANG (1900–1958), Swiss physicist. A child prodigy, Pauli wrote a masterful exposition of the theory of relativity at age 19. He studied in Munich (Ph.D. 1921) and Copenhagen (with Niels Bohr: 1922–23) and taught in Germany, Switzerland, and the United States. He formulated (1925) the important exclusion principle, which was essential for clarifying and describing the properties of atomic nuclei. For this work he was awarded the 1945 Nobel Prize for Physics. In 1931 he proposed the existence of the neutrino, an electrically neutral particle formed in the beta decay of nuclei. This was finally confirmed in experiments in the 1950s using nuclear-power stations.

PAULING, LINUS CARL (1901–1994), U.S. chemist. A druggist's son, Pauling studied at the California Institute of Technology (Ph.D. 1925) and taught there for 35 years. He was one of the few people in history to receive two Nobel Prizes. The first (Chemistry, 1954) recognized his work on molecular structure. Building on the work of G. N. Lewis, Ernest Rutherford, and L. V. de Broglie, he revolutionized scientists' conceptions of spatial arrangements within molecules. A decade of research on interactions among electrons produced the landmark work *The Nature of the Chemical Bond, and the Structure of Molecules and Crystals* (1939; rev. ed. 1960). Pauling's research helped scientists to determine structures of complex substances. He later wrote the text *General Chemistry* (1947) and championed vitamin C in *Vitamin C and the Common Cold* (1970). During the cold-war years, he devoted himself to warning of nuclear war and wrote *No More War!* (1958); he won the 1962 Nobel Peace Prize for his efforts. He later opposed U.S. intervention in Vietnam. ■ See biographies by Anthony Serafini (1989) and Ted and Ben Goertzel (1995).

PAULUS, FRIEDRICH (1890–1957), German general. Appointed deputy chief of staff of the German army (1940), Paulus helped plan the ill-fated invasion of the Soviet Union, which he led in 1942. He was captured at Stalingrad in early 1943 and surrendered the remnants of his army of 300,000 men—one of the turning points of World War II. Paulus remained in Soviet captivity until 1953, when he went to live in East Germany. ■ See study by Walter Gorlitz (Eng. trans. 1964).

PAUSTOVSKY, KONSTANTIN GEORGIYEVICH (1892–1968), Soviet writer. Paustovsky, who grew up in Kiev, remarked that each of his works was a journey to some corner of the Soviet Union. Writing in a variety of genres and styles, he focused on landscape, and particularly on nature being reshaped by Soviet industry. A war correspondent during World War II, he gave several fictional works a wartime setting. In his later years he coedited the anthology *Literary Moscow* (1956) and the literary miscellany *Pages from Tarusa* (1961), and acted on several occasions as spokesman for an influential group of liberal establishment writers. Revered by Soviet readers, he won the Order of Lenin in 1967. He was best known abroad for his epic six-volume autobiography, *Story of a Life* (1946–64; Eng. trans. *Story of a Life*, 1964; *Years of Hope,* 1968; *Southern Adventure,* 1969; *The Restless Years,* 1974), *The Golden Rose* (1955; Eng. trans. 1961) discusses literary technique. Further works in English are in *Selected Stories* (1970) and *Rainy Dawn and Other Stories* (1995).

PAVAROTTI, LUCIANO (1935–), Italian opera singer. The son of a talented amateur tenor, Pavarotti was introduced to the world of opera via his father's record collection. He gave up a job as an elementary schoolteacher to pursue a professional singing career and made his debut in *La Bohéme* (1961). After touring Australia with Joan Sutherland (1964), he made his debut at La Scala (1965) and later at New York's Metropolitan Opera (1968). The possessor of a brilliantly pure and sweet lyric tenor voice and an exceedingly warm and outgoing personality, Pavarotti achieved international superstar status during the 1970s. A master of the bel canto repertory, he achieved his greatest success in *The Daughter of the Regiment, L'Elisir d'Amore, I Puritani, A Masked Ball,* and *Rigoletto.* During the 1990s he toured with Plácido Domingo and José Carreras as a member of the "Three Tenors" concert series, the most lucrative production in the history of classical music. It was estimated that an audience in excess of 2 billion viewers saw the concerts on television, and video and audio tapes of the events were the best-selling classical recordings of all time. ■ See his autobiography (1981; with William Wright), *Pavarotti: My World* (1995), and study by Jurgen Kesting (Eng. trans. 1996).

PAVELIĆ, ANTE (1889–1959), Croatian political leader. A militant Croatian nationalist, Pavelić opposed the centralization of the Yugoslav state while serving in parliament (1927–29). From exile in Italy (1929) he organized a terrorist band, the Ustashe, which assassinated Yugoslavian King Alexander in Marseilles (1934). During World War II, after the Axis armies occupied Yugoslavia (1941), Pavelic was made dictator of the newly formed Croatian fascist state, which he ruled until the collapse of Nazi Germany (1945). He left Croatia and lived the rest of his life in exile in Austria, Italy, Argentina, and Spain.

PAVESE, CESARE (1908–1950), Italian novelist and poet. An editor and distinguished translator of American literature, Pavese was exiled to southern Italy by the fascists (1935–36) and joined the Communist party after World War II (1945). He decisively influenced modern Italian realism, though his own work strove not so much for realistic depiction as the recovery of experience through repetition of clusters of images. His novels treated human isolation and violence, often describing the tension between conflicting desires for solitude and active participation in life. Among his best-known works were *The Harvesters* (1941: Eng. trans. 1961), *Dialogues with Leuco* (1947; Eng. trans. 1965), *The Political Prisoner* (1949; Eng. trans. 1955), and *The Moon and the Bonfires* (1950; Eng. trans. 1953). His selected poems (1930–50) are in *A Mania for Solitude* (Eng. trans. 1969). Pavese's suicide stunned his contemporaries. His diary of the years 1935–50, *The Burning Brand* (1952; Eng. trans. 1961), and *Selected Letters* (Eng. trans. 1969) appeared posthumously. ■ See Gian-Paolo Biasin, *The Smile of the Gods* (1968), and Davide Lajolo, *An Absurd Vice* (Eng. trans. 1983).

PAVLOV, IVAN PETROVICH (1849–1936), Russian physiologist. A professor at the Imperial Medical Academy (1890–1924), Pavlov spent many years studying the physiology of the digestive glands, for which he won a Nobel Prize in 1904. Experimenting with dogs. he observed what he called the conditioned reflex, one that is learned rather than inherited and can be manipulated by various orders of conditioning. He applied his findings to human behavior, believing that mental phenomena could only be studied scientifically if reduced to quantifiable physiological data. *Conditioned Reflexes* (1926: Eng. trans. 1927) was his major work in this area. Pavlov was critical of the great human experiment of the bolshevik revolution, but the new regime continued to support his research, perhaps to confirm its own theories of social engineering. ■ See biography by Boris P. Babkin (1949) and study by Jeffrey A. Gray (1980).

PAVLOVA, ANNA (1882–1931), Russian ballerina. After seeing *The Sleeping Beauty* performed at age 8, Pavlova was determined to dance. With impeccable technique and dramatic quality, she became prima ballerina of the Imperial Ballet by age 25. Among her repertoire of 23 ballets were *Giselle* and *Chopiniana;* she was closely identified with *The Dying Swan,* the dance created for her by Michel Fokine (1905). She toured Europe (1907–08) and joined Diaghilev's Ballet Russe, dancing with Nijinsky. Worn by her rivalry with her partner, she left the troupe after one season to form her own company and toured throughout the world, giving up to 10 performances a week for more than two decades. The company presented excerpts from various ballets and featured her enchanting solo numbers. More than just a spectacular dancer, Pavlova was an international cultural phenomenon, a legend in her own time, who epitomized glamour and grace. ■ See studies by Oleg Kerensky (1973), John and Roberta Lazzarini (1980), Keith Money (1982), and Margot Fonteyn (1984).

PAYTON, WALTER (1954–1999), U.S. football player. A native of Mississippi, Payton was a star running back at Jackson State College (BA. 1975), where he set a National Collegiate Athletic Association (NCAA) record for most career points (464). With the Chicago Bears (1975–88) of the National Football League (NFL), the 5-foot, 10-inch 200-lb. Payton developed into the most powerful and elusive rusher in pro football history, breaking Jim Brown's career records for total yardage (15,459) and rushing yardage (12,312) in 1984. He also set a single-game rushing record (275 yards: Nov. 20, 1977; broken by Corey Dillon with 278 yards on Oct. 22, 2000) and surpassed Brown's career mark of 58 games in which he rushed for 100 yards or more (1984). He ultimately reached the mark in 77 games. During the 1985–86 season he set a record for rushing 100 yards or more in nine consecutive games and led the Bears to the NFL Superbowl championship. He retired as the leading ground-gainer in NFL history with 16,726 career yards (17,303 including postseason games). ■ See his autobiographies, *Sweetness* (1978) and *Never Die Easy* (2000).

PAZ, OCTAVIO (1914–1998), Mexican poet and critic. Octavio Paz abandoned his early lyrical style in favor of a more surrealist tone. A leftist who witnessed the Spanish civil war (1936–39), he wrote of his disenchantment with the Mexican revolution and the failure of socialism, and couched in stunning imagery his ideas about the relationship between the individual and society. A leading figure of modern Mexican literature, he founded and edited several influential journals, including *Taller* (1938–41). His major poetic works included *Sun Stone* (1957: Eng. trans. 1963), *Blanco* (1967: Eng. trans. 1971), and *A Draft of Shadows* (1975:

Eng. trans. 1979). Muriel Rukeyser's translations in *Early Poems, 1935–55* (1974) broadened his readership: other poems in English translation appeared in *Selected Poems* (1979, 1984). His influential prose books included *The Labyrinth of Solitude* (1952: Eng. trans. 1962), an analysis of Mexican life and culture; *Conjunctions and Disjunctions* (1969; Eng. trans. 1982), which explored the balance between feelings and ideas in society; *The Monkey Grammarian* (1974: Eng. trans. 1981), which ventured into the realm of deconstruction, putting language itself into question and treating grammar as a "critique of the universe"; and *One Earth, Four or Five Worlds* (Eng. trans. 1985), reflections on contemporary history. Paz was Mexico's ambassador to India in the 1960s, resigning in the political crisis of 1968 after Mexican police killed some 300 antigovernment demonstrators. He was awarded the 1990 Nobel Prize for Literature. ■ See studies edited by K. Chantikian (1981) and A. Roggiano (1979), and Jason Wilson, *Octavio Paz: A Study of His Poetics* (1979).

PAZ ESTENSSORO, VICTOR (1907–   ), Bolivian political leader. A middle-class economist, Paz helped found (1941) the National Revolutionary Movement (MNR). In 1943 the MNR participated in a coup d'état, and Paz was named minister of finance. He resigned from the cabinet shortly before the government was overthrown (July 1946) and went into exile in Argentina—during which period he was elected president (1951). The army attempted to block his assumption of power, but tin miners and his poor urban supporters revolted and Paz assumed the presidency in 1952. He carried out dramatic reforms, including the nationalization of tin mines and a sweeping land reform. He stepped down in 1956 but was reelected in 1960 and again in 1964. His popularity declined soon after the 1964 election, and he was overthrown by his own vice president, Gen. René Barrientos, and again exiled. He returned to Bolivia as a governmental adviser (1971) and ran unsuccessfully in the presidential elections of 1979 and 1980. Following the 1985 elections, in which he received less than the required 50 percent of the vote, he was elected president by the Bolivian congress. As president (1985–89) he carried out austerity measures and free-market policies to end hyperinflation.

PEALE, NORMAN VINCENT (1898–1993), U.S. clergyman. The son of an Ohio physician and pastor, Peale was ordained in the Methodist Episcopal Church (1922) and served as pastor of the Marble Collegiate Church in New York City (1932–84) for more than 50 years. He established a psychiatric clinic, the American Foundation of Religion and Psychiatry, next door to his church to combine religion with therapy in the treatment of mental illness. He also wrote several successful inspirational books, including *The Power of Positive Thinking* (1952), one of history's bestselling books. Determined to reach as many people as possible, Peale sermonized by radio, newsletter, television, and newspaper and magazine columns. He also broadcast his political preferences, opposing the New Deal, supporting Gen. Douglas MacArthur, questioning John F. Kennedy's fitness for the presidency as a Catholic, and befriending Pres. Richard Nixon. His wife Ruth Stafford Peale (1906–   ) was also known as a religious leader, broadcaster, and author. ■ See his autobiography, *The True Joy of Positive Living* (1984); Arthur Gordon, *One Man's Way* (rev. ed. 1972); study by Richard L. Detrich (1979); and Carol V. R. George, *God's Salesman* (1993).

PEARL, RAYMOND (1879–1940), U.S. biologist. The recipient of a Ph.D. in zoology from the University of Michigan (1902), Pearl was a pioneer in the field of biometrics, the application of statistical methods to biology. He was affiliated with Johns Hopkins University (1918–40), where he organized a department of medical statistics, and also founded two influential journals, *Quarterly Review of Biology* (1926) and *Human Biology* (1929). His many books included *The Biology of Death* (1922), *Biology of Population Growth* (1925), and the text *Introduction to Medical Biometry and Statistics* (1923).

PEARS, SIR PETER (1910–1986), British concert and opera singer. Although Pears was celebrated in his own right as a singer of oratorio, lieder, and opera, his partnership with composer Benjamin Britten contributed much to his fame. Britten wrote numerous works specifically for the tenor, including *Seven Sonnets of Michelangelo, Les Illuminations,* and the opera *Peter Grimes* (1945), and Pears sang in the premieres of Britten's *Gloriana, Billy Budd,* and *The Turn of the Screw.* Praised as often for his acting as for his singing, he made his debut at London's Covent Garden in 1948 and triumphed as David in *Die Meistersinger,* Aschenbach in Britten's *Death in Venice,* and in the title role in Mozart's *Idomeneo.* ■ See biography by Christopher Headington (1991).

PEARSE, PATRICK HENRY (1879–1916), Irish educator and revolutionist. Born in Dublin, Pearse was educated by the Irish Christian Brothers and trained in law. His love of Celtic folklore and romance drew him to the Gaelic League, and he edited its journal, *An Claidheamh Soluis.* Pearse gave up law to establish (1908) a boys' boarding and day school devoted to the heroic principles of ancient Celtic society. Few members of the school were as idealistic as Pearse, however, and all of his instructors abandoned him after the first year. Becoming involved (1913) with the activities of the Irish Volunteers, he was put in charge of military forces during the anti-British Easter Rebellion of 1916. After the surrender of the Irish insurgents, Pearse was tried by a court-martial and executed. ■ See collections of his literary (1917) and political works (1922); biography by Louis N. Le Roux (Eng. trans. 1932); and studies by Raymond J. Porter (1973), Brian P. Murphy (1991), and Sean F. Moran (1994).

PEARSON, DREW (Andrew Russell Pearson; 1897–1969), U.S. politfcal columnist. One of America's most influential and controversial journalists, Pearson wrote a daily syndicated column, "Washington Merry-Go-Round" (1932–69), which was followed by 50 million readers. Praised by many as a courageous political muckraker and damned by others as an opinionated liar and character assassin, he made a career out of exposing political corruption and wrongdoing. His disclosures led to the Senate censure of Sen. Thomas Dodd of Connecticut, contributed to the ouster of Adam Clayton Powell of New York from the House of Representatives, and were said to have resulted in the arrest of four congressmen, the defeat of many others, and the dismissal of numerous government officials. He was also involved in celebrated feuds with Presidents Franklin D. Roosevelt and Harry Truman, Sen. Joseph R. McCarthy, Gen. Douglas MacArthur, and others. ■ See his *Diaries: 1949–59* (1974); Herman Klurfeld, *Behind the Lines* (1968); and biography by Oliver Pilat (1973).

PEARSON, KARL (1857–1936), British mathematician. Pearson practiced law, wrote literary criticism, and participated in radical politics before becoming a professor at the University of London (1884–1933), where he taught applied mathematics, geometry, and eugenics. One of the founders of modern statistics and the science of biometry, he applied statistical methods to the study of such biological problems as evolution and heredity. He cofounded and edited (1901–36) the journal *Biometrika* and wrote widely in the field. ■ See biography by Egon Pearson (1938).

PEARSON, LESTER BOWLES (1897–1972), Canadian diplomat and political leader. "Mike" Pearson interrupted his studies to serve in World War I. In 1928 he began a highly successful diplomatic career. Appointed foreign minister (1948), Pearson represented Canada at many international forums, including the United Nations, which he had helped establish. In 1956 he calmed world concern over the Suez crisis by negotiating a compromise that included sending a U.N. peacekeeping force there: he subsequently won the 1957 Nobel Peace Prize. Pearson became Liberal party leader in 1958 and won the 1963 national election on the issue of stronger support for the United States in its cold war with the Soviet Union. Although personally popular, he had to contend with a growing nationalist movement among French-speaking Canadians. When French Pres. Charles de Gaulle publicly supported the nationalist movement, Pearson denounced him. Pearson retired in 1968. ■ See his memoirs, *Mike* (3 vols., 1972–74); studies by Bruce Thordarson (1974), Peter Stursberg (1978, 1980), and Robert Bothwell (1978); and biography by John English (1989).

PEARY, ROBERT EDWIN (1856–1920), U.S. explorer. A civil engineer with the U.S. Navy (1881–1911), Peary surveyed routes for an Atlantic–Pacific canal through Nicaragua (1884–85; 1886–87) before commencing his ex-

plorations of the Arctic. He led numerous expeditions to northern Greenland (from 1886), discovering vast new sections of land, bringing back large meteorites to the United States, and proving that Greenland is an island. He announced his intention to become the first to reach the North Pole (1898) and made several unsuccessful tries before reaching it, accompanied by his African-American aide Matthew A. Henson, on April 6, 1909. Among Peary's books were *Northward Over the "Great Ice"* (2 vols. 1898), *The North Pole* (1910), and *Secrets of Polar Travel* (1917). ■ The biography by John Edward Weems (1967) contains many of Peary's letters, diaries, and reports. See also William R. Hunt, *To Stand at the Pole* (1981).

PECHSTEIN, MAX (1881–1955), German artist. Pechstein, the most popular member of the German expressionist group Die Brücke, combined elements of fauvism and postimpressionism in his colorful and spontaneous works. His tendency to exotic primitivism was reinforced by a 1914 trip to the South Pacific. Dismissed from his Berlin Academy teaching position in 1933 by the Nazis as a "decadent artist." he was reinstated in 1945.

PECK, GREGORY (Eldred Gregory Peck; 1916–), U.S. actor. After graduating from the University of California (1939), Peck set out for Broadway and appeared in several short-lived plays, which led to his first film, *Days of Glory* (1944). He played a mentally ill doctor in *Spellbound* (1945) and a wrathful Ahab in *Moby Dick* (1956), but Peck, a tall, Lincolnesque actor, was often cast as a decent, responsible man vindicated by crisis, as in the social dramas *Gentleman's Agreement* (1947) and *To Kill a Mockingbird* (Academy Award, 1962). In 1972 Peck produced *The Trial of the Catonsville Nine* about radical antiwar protest. His later films included *Old Gringo* (1989) and *Other People's Money* (1991). He served as president of the Academy of Motion Picture Arts and Sciences (1967–70). ■ See study by Tony Thomas (1977) and biography by Michael Freedland (1980).

PEDERSEN, CHARLES J. (1904–1989), U.S. chemist. Pedersen, born in Korea to a Norwegian father and a Japanese mother, studied in Roman Catholic schools before coming to the United States to study chemical engineering at the University of Dayton in the 1920s. He subsequently received a master's degree from the Massachusetts Institute of Technology and worked as a researcher for Du Pont for 42 years (1927–69). During the 1960s he synthesized organic compounds that he called crown ethers, molecules with a flexible ring of carbon and oxygen atoms that bind with particular ions as the size of the ring is varied. His pioneering research laid the foundation of what is called host-guest, or supramolecular, chemistry, which allowed for the creation of synthetic molecules that could mimic the behavior of natural molecules that control all living systems. Pedersen shared the 1987 Nobel Prize in Chemistry with Donald Cram and Jean-Marie Lehn.

PEEL, WILLIAM ROBERT, 1st EARL (1867–1937), British political leader. Peel, the grandson of Sir Robert Peel, was an Oxford-educated lawyer who served in Parliament as a Unionist (1900–06; 1909–12). He served as secretary of state for India twice (1922–24 and 1928–29) and presided over the Burma Round-Table Conference (1931–32) and several top-level commissions, including the Peel Commission (1936–37), which recommended partition of Palestine.

PEERCE, JAN (Jacob Pincus Perelmuth; 1904–1984), U.S. concert and opera singer. Peerce played the violin in dance bands before being hired as a singer of operatic arias and art songs at New York City's Radio City Music Hall. He achieved stardom there and appeared onstage nearly 2,500 times (1933–39). He also had his own radio show and was named the nation's leading male radio singer in a 1936 poll. Making his operatic stage debut in 1938, he was a leading tenor at New York's Metropolitan Opera from 1941 to 1966, where he sang most of the major roles in the French and Italian repertory. ■ See his memoirs, *The Bluebird of Happiness* (1976).

PEGLER, (JAMES) WESTBROOK (1894–1969), U.S. journalist. A prominent conservative columnist for United Features Syndicate and then Hearst's King Features Syndicate (1933–62), Pegler was famous for his caustic and abusive attacks on public figures. His main targets were Pres. Franklin D. Roosevelt and members of his New Deal administration. Pegler won a 1941 Pulitzer Prize for an exposé of labor-union corruption. After losing a celebrated $175,001 libel suit to the writer Quentin Reynolds in 1954, he became increasingly right-wing, and after his break with King Features he wrote occasionally for the John Birch Society's publication, *American Opinion*. ■ See biography by Oliver Pilat (1963).

PÉGUY, CHARLES PIERRE (1873–1914), French writer. Peguy surmounted a poor childhood in Orleans to win scholarships to the elite schools of France. In 1900 he founded *Cahiers de la Quinzaine*, the leading cultural journal of the day, in which he published his work and that of others. Rejecting the trend to socialist agnosticism in favor of the pious patriotism of his youth, Péguy composed a series of long prose poems that celebrated French Catholicism. Translations of his poems are in *Basic Verities* (1943), *Men and Saints* (1944), *God Speaks* (1945), and *Portal of the Mystery of Hope* (1996). He was killed in action during World War I at the Battle of the Marne. ■ See biography by Marjorie Villiers (1966) and study by Frederic Chase St. Aubyn (1977).

PEI, IEOH MING (1917–   ), Chinese-born U.S. architect. The son of a Cantonese bank executive, I. M. Pei went to the United States in 1935 and studied architecture at the Massachusetts Institute of Technology and Harvard University. As architectural director of William Zeckendorf's New York real-estate firm (1948–55), he was intensely involved in urban renewal and city planning. Pei established his own firm in 1955, winning renown for soaring skyscrapers erected in concrete or steel and glass. After a setback in the early 1970s, when many double-paned glass windows inexplicably fell out of his 60-story John Hancock Tower in Boston, Pei quickly recovered, designing the East Wing of the National Gallery in Washington, D.C. (1978), and the John F. Kennedy Library in Dorchester, Massachusetts (1979). In the 1980s he designed the low-rise Fragrant Hill Hotel near Beijing and the Bank of China in Hong Kong, which he called "an intricate piece of geometry." His design of a 90-foot glass pyramid for the courtyard of the Louvre museum in Paris (1985) aroused controversy. He also designed the Rock-and-Roll Hall of Fame in Cleveland, Ohio (1993–95). He won the prestigious Pritzker Prize in 1983. ■ See Carter Wiseman, *The Architecture of I. M. Pei* (1990).

PELÉ (Edson Arantes do Nascimento; 1940–   ), Brazilian soccer player. Known throughout the world as the "king of soccer," Pelé was perhaps the most celebrated athlete of the 20th century. A living legend who was brilliant at ball control and playmaking, he starred for Santos for 18 years (1956–74), scored 1,220 goals, and led the Brazilian national team to World Cup championships in 1958, 1962, and 1970. He emerged from retirement by signing a multi-million dollar contract to play for the New York Cosmos (1975–77) and led the team to the 1977 North American Soccer League championship. He scored a total of 1,281 goals in 1,363 games during his career. He subsequently served as Brazil's special minister for sports (1994–98), and as a goodwill ambassador for several United Nations agencies and worked for Petrobras, the giant Brazilian oil company. ■ See his autobiography, *My Life and the Beautiful Game* (1977: with Robert L. Fish).

PELLI, CESAR ANTONIO (1926–   ), Argentinian-born U.S. architect. Pelli studied architecture at the National University of Tucumán (B.A. 1949) before moving to the United States (1952) to study at the University of Illinois (M.A. 1954). He became a naturalized U.S. citizen in 1964. His buildings, known for their lightweight appearance, creative glass surfaces, and sensitivity to their environment, were influenced by his association with Eero Saarinen (1954–64). Pelli subsequently was head of design at Gruen Associates in Los Angeles (1968–77), dean of the Yale University School of Architecture (1977–84), and founder of his own firm in New Haven, Connecticut. His best-known buildings included the Pacific Design Center, Los Angeles (1972); the U.S. Embassy in Tokyo (1972); the expansion and renovation of the Museum of Modern Art, New York City (1977–84); the World Financial Center Towers, New York City (1981–87); and the Canary Wharf Tower, London (1986). The twin, circular, 1,483-foot structures he designed for the Malaysian national oil company in Kuala Lumpur, the Petronas Towers, were the world's tallest buildings when they were completed in 1996. ■ See *Cesar Pelli: Selected and Current Works* (1993).

PENCK, ALBRECHT (1858–1945), German geologist, geographer, and cartographer. A professor at the University of Vienna (1885–1906) and Berlin (1906–26), Penck was one of the founders of geomorphology, the study of the earth's surface features. Responsible for more than 400 books and articles, he made pioneering studies of the Ice Age earth strata and promoted the production of the 1:1,000,000-scale map of the earth. His sociopolitical theories embraced the concept of *Lebensraum* ("living space") and played a major role in the revival of German nationalism after World War I. His works included *Morphological Analysis of Land Forms* (1924; Eng. trans. 1953).

PENDERECKI, KRZYSZTOF (1933–   ), Polish composer. After graduating from the Cracow Conservatory, Penderecki taught there and at Essen. He devised his own system of musical notation, concentrated on new sonorities, and received recognition as a leading avantgarde composer. His pieces incorporated the sounds of sawing and typing, and he instructed players to rattle and scrape their instruments and singers to laugh and hiss. His works included *Threnody for the Victims of Hiroshima* (1960), *St. Luke's Passion* (1965), *Slavic Mass* (1969), and *Jacob's Awakening* (1974). He adopted a traditional late-romantic style in his Symphony No. 2 (1980) and Cello Concerto No. 2 (1982). Portions of *The Polish Requiem* (1985) were written to commemorate the victims of the government suppression of worker protests in Gdansk. His later works included Sinfonietta for Strings (1990–91), Symphony No. 5 (1991–92), Symphony No. 7 (1996; written for the 3,000th anniversary of Jerusalem), and *Credo* (1998). He served as rector of the Cracow Conservatory (1972–87). ■ See biography by Wolfram Schwinger (Eng. trans. 1989).

PENDERGAST, THOMAS JOSEPH (1872–1945), U.S. political boss. Pendergast inherited the Democratic leadership post of several Kansas City, Missouri, wards from his brother (1910), and by the mid-1920s had political control of the entire city. An old-time political operator who built his machine through patronage and corruption, Pendergast launched the career of Harry S. Truman. After supporting future president Franklin D. Roosevelt at the 1932 Democratic convention, he was given control of many federal patronage jobs in the 1930s through which he further enhanced his position as one of the nation's most powerful political bosses. His power was destroyed, however, when he was convicted of income-tax evasion (1939) and sentenced to 15 months in prison. ■ See Lyle W. Dorsett, *The Pendergast Machine* (1968), and biography by Lawrence Larsen and Nancy Hulston (1997).

PENKOVSKY, OLEG VLADIMIROVICH (1919–1963), Soviet intelligence officer and double agent. Decorated for battlefield bravery in World War II, Penkovsky later joined the Soviet military intelligence (GRU). As deputy director of its foreign section, he contacted British intelligence (1960) through Greville Wynne. a British businessman visiting the Soviet Union. The CIA and British intelligence interrogated Penkovsky (1961) while he was on three official delegations to London and Paris, and engaged his services as a double agent. The Soviets uncovered his activities, tried Penkovsky (1963), and sentenced him to death. The publication of his purported memoirs, *The Penkovsky Papers* (Eng. trans. 1965), revealed a wealth of political and military data that Penkovsky had divulged about Soviet strategy: his estimates of Soviet strength affected the stance taken by the United States in the Cuba and Berlin crises of the early 1960s. Some believe the book was prepared by the CIA on the basis of data supplied by Penkovsky. ■ See Greville Wynne, *The Man from Moscow* (1967), and Jerrold Schecter and Peter Deriabin, *The Spy Who Saved the World* (1992).

PENNEY, JAMES CASH (1875–1971), U.S. businessman. Penney became a partner in a dry-goods store in Wyoming (1902) and soon bought out his partners. He started to purchase additional stores, allowing the manager of each to share in the profits. By 1913, when the J. C. Penney Co. was incorporated and the headquarters moved to New York City, there were 48 stores in the chain. Under Penney's leadership (1913–58) the firm grew rapidly, and at the time of his death the company, with 1,660 stores and annual sales of $4 billion, was the second-largest nonfood retailer in the United States. Late in life Penney achieved prominence as a philanthropist and cattle breeder. ■ See his autobiographies, *Fifty Years with the Golden Rule* (1950) and *View from the Ninth Decade* (1960), and the biography by Beatrice Plumb (1963).

PENROSE, BOIES (1860–1921), U.S. political leader. A scholarly reformer as a young man, Penrose soon cast his lot with the Pennsylvania Republican machine and served in the state legislature (1884–86), state senate (1887–96), and U.S. Senate (1897–1921). From 1904 he was the influential Pennsylvania Republican boss and in the Senate was a leader of the conservative forces who defended corporate interests and opposed progressivism. He was a consistent supporter of high tariffs and chaired the powerful Senate Finance Committee (1911–21). ■ See biography by Robert D. Bowden (1937) and Walter Davenport, *Power and Glory* (1931).

PENROSE, SIR ROGER (1931–   ), British mathematical physicist. Penrose, whose mother was a doctor and whose father was a prominent medical geneticist, studied algebraic geometry at Cambridge University (Ph.D. 1957) and taught at several universities including London (1964–73) and Oxford (1973–   ). His work with Stephen Hawking (during the 1960s and 1970s) resulted in the formulation of fundamental theorems that described black holes in space. Penrose and Hawking demonstrated that a space-time singularity, a point smaller than the nucleus of a single atom but with infinite density, exists at the center of black holes, and they theorized that the big bang that created the universe developed from such a singularity. Penrose also did innovative work in the topology of complex spaces, using tiling processes, and developed "twister theory" to provide an alternative to space-time physics. He described his controversial theories linking quantum mechanics and human consciousness in *The Emperor's New Mind* (1989) and *Shadows of the Mind* (1994). He also wrote *The Nature of Space and Time* (with Hawking; 1996) and contributed to *The Large, the Small and the Human Mind* (1997). ■ See S. Huggett and L. Mason, eds., *The Geometric Universe* (1998).

PENZIAS, ARNO (1933–), German-born U.S. physicist. Penzias, the recipient of a Ph.D. from Columbia University (1962), shared the 1978 Nobel Prize for Physics with Pyotr Kapitsa and Robert Wilson, his co-worker at the Bell Telephone Laboratories. They were honored "for the discovery of cosmic microwave background radiation." The radiation was discovered accidentally when in the mid-1960s the 20-foot horn detector set up by the two men to pick up signals from a communications satellite also produced a hissing noise. They determined that the noise was from microwave radiation coming from no identifiable direction in space but rather from the universe at large. The microwave radiation was strong evidence for the "big bang" theory of the origins of the universe, for other scientists had predicted that the original explosion would have created an "echo" of radiation that would theoretically be perpetually detectable. Penzias directed Bell's Radio Research Laboratory (1976–79) and served as Bell's vice president for research (1981–95) and chief scientist (1995–). His books included *Ideas and Information* (1989) and *Harmony* (1995).

PERELMAN, S. J. (Sidney Joseph Perelman; 1904–1979), U.S. humorist. Calling himself "a feuilletoniste . . . a writer of little leaves," Perelman was a master of hilarious parody and the light satiric essay. Winning recognition for the virtuosity of his wordplay in his *New Yorker* columns, Perelman produced a prodigious number of humorous, zanily titled collections, such as *Strictly from Hunger* (1937), *The Ill-Tempered Clavichord* (1953), and *Baby It's Cold Inside* (1970). He wrote scripts for Broadway, for Marx Brothers' movies, and for the film version of *Around the World in Eighty Days* (1956). His last collection, *The Last Laugh* (1981), contained autobiographical fragments including "The Hindsight Saga." ■ See biography by Dorothy Herrmann (1986).

PERES, SHIMON (Shimon Persky; 1923–), Polish-born Israeli political leader. Peres emigrated to Palestine with his family (1934) and was raised on a kibbutz. A leader of the Labor party youth movement, he was responsible for purchasing arms for the Jewish underground movement during the Israeli war for independence (1947–48). He became a protégé of prime minister David Ben-Gurion and served as his director general of the defense ministry (1953–59), and then deputy minister of defense (1959–63), a post he also held under prime minister Levi Eshkol (1963–65). He was elected to the Knesset (parliament) in 1959. He served as minister of defense (1974–77) and as Labor party leader after Yitzhak Rabin resigned (1977–92). An uninspiring and bland politician, he twice led the party to national election defeats at the hands of the Likud party headed by Menachem Begin (1977, 1981). However, after the inconclusive July 1984 elections, a deal was made with Likud that called for Peres to serve as prime minister of a coalition national unity government, and Likud leader Yitzhak Shamir, as foreign minister for half of the five-year term, after which time they were to switch jobs. Peres, who gained stature in office, withdrew most Israeli troops from South Lebanon and called for peace negotiations with Jordan's King Hussein. As foreign minister (1992–95) he helped negotiate the 1993 peace agreement between the Israelis and Palestinians and shared the 1994 Nobel Peace Prize with Rabin and Yasir Arafat. After Rabin's assassination Peres served as prime minister and Labor party leader (1995–96). ■ See his memoirs, *David's Sling* (Eng. trans. 1970) and *Battling for Peace* (1995); his autobiography, *Witness* (1993); and Matti Golan, *The Road to Peace* (Eng. trans. 1989).

PÉREZ, CARLOS ANDRÉS (1922–), Venezuelan political leader. Perez, who was born into a rural middle-class family, was politically active as a teenager and became a protegé of Rómalo Betancourt, one of the founders of the reformist Acción Democrática political movement. After Betancourt seized power in 1945, Pérez served as his secretary, but both were forced into exile by a right-wing military coup in 1948. After the dictatorship of Marcos Perez Jiménez was overthrown (1958), Pérez held several governmental and party posts, including interior minister (1962–63). As president of Venezuela (1974–79), he nationalized the oil industry, launched several industrial development projects, and became a champion of wealth redistribution from the industrialized nations to poor Third World countries. During his second term as president (1988–93), Pérez sponsored free-market reforms and survived two military coup attempts (1992). Accused of corruption, he was removed from office (1993), convicted of mismanaging public funds (1994), and spent more than two years under house arrest.

PÉREZ DE AYALA, RAMÓN (1880–1962), Spanish writer. Perez de Ayala first emerged as a modernist poet but found his voice in realistic fiction. His early cycle of novels was autobiographical, including *The Fox's Paw* (1912; Eng. trans. 1924). He then published a volume of three short grotesque tales called "poematic novels." *Prometheus, The Fall of the House of Limón, Sunday Sunlight* (1916; Eng. trans. 1920), in which each chapter is preceded by a "poetic" anticipation of events to come. His finest works were the experimental, linguistically masterful volumes that appeared in the 1920s: *Belarmino and Apolonio* (1921: Eng. trans. 1971), *Honeymoon, Bittermoon* (1923; Eng. trans. 1972), and *Tiger Juan* (1926; Eng. trans. 1933). Pérez de Ayala served as a diplomat in London (1932–36) under the republic. In the remaining decades of his life he published only one short-fiction collection (1962) and several essays. He also wrote literary criticism. ■ See studies by Marquerite C. Rand (1971) and John Macklin, *The Window and the Garden* (1988).

PÉREZ DE CUELLAR, JAVIER (1920–   ), Peruvian diplomat. Soon after graduating from the Catholic University in Lima with a law degree (1943). Pérez de Cuellar joined the Peruvian diplomatic service. During a 37-year career (1944–81), he served as Peru's first ambassador to the Soviet Union (1969–71) and as ambassador to the United Nations (1971–75). As U.N. Secretary-General Kurt Waldheim's special representative, he initiated negotiations between Greece and Turkey over the Cyprus problem (1975–76), and he later served as U.N. undersecretary-general for special political affairs (1979–81). Elected to replace Waldheim, he served as the fifth U.N. secretary-general (from Jan. 1, 1982). He was reelected in 1986. ■ See his memoir, *Pilgrimage for Peace* (1997).

PÉREZ ESQUIVEL, ADOLFO (1931–   ), Argentine human-rights activist. A sculptor and professor of architecture, Perez Esquivel turned to political and social activism in the 1960s. Concerned with poverty and rampant political repression in Latin America, he joined (1971) the newly founded Service for Peace and Justice in Latin America, a lay Catholic organization seeking to promote human, social, and economic rights through nonviolent means. As secretary-general of the organization (from 1974), Pérez Esquivel helped to coordinate the activities of human-rights groups throughout Latin America. He denounced and publicized the political repression of the military regime in Argentina (from 1976) and founded (1973) and edited the magazine *Peace and Justice*. His activities led to his imprisonment (1977–78) and torture as well as his being awarded the 1980 Nobel Peace Prize. He subsequently served as rector of the United Nations University for Peace, Costa Rica, and wrote *Christ in a Poncho: Testimonials of the Non-Violent Struggle in Latin America* (1983).

PERKINS, FRANCES (Fannie Perkins; 1880–1965), U.S. labor reformer and public official. Educated at Mount Holyoke College and Columbia (MS. 1910), Perkins was involved in New York groups investigating or overseeing consumer affairs, industrial safety, and hygiene. She lobbied for comprehensive factory legislation and for maximum-hour regulations for women. After chairing the New York State Industrial Board (1926–29), she served as the state's industrial commissioner under Gov. Franklin D. Roosevelt (1929–33). When Roosevelt became president, he appointed Perkins U.S. secretary of labor; she was the first woman to serve in a cabinet position. During her controversial tenure (1933–45), she implemented New Deal policies. She later served on the U.S. Civil Service Commission (1946–52). Perkins wrote on labor issues and also published *The Roosevelt I Knew* (1946). ■ See George Martin, *Madame Secretary* (1976).

PERKINS, MAXWELL EVARTS (1884–1947), U.S. editor. Perkins descended from a prominent family that included a Declaration of Independence signer. a U.S. senator, and a noted art critic. An economics major at Harvard (BA. 1907), he was briefly a *New York Times* reporter (1907–10), then went to work for Charles Scribner's Sons, a conservative old-guard publishing firm. In 1914 he transferred from the advertising to the editorial department, where he enlivened and enriched Scribner's list at a crucial point in American letters. Perkins introduced such young writers as F. Scott Fitzgerald, Ernest Hemingway, Ring Lardner, and Thomas Wolfe. (Wolfe based the character Foxhall Edwards in *You Can't Go Home Again* on Perkins.) He was the first to publish Alan Paton and James Jones, brought in the most celebrated detective fiction of the period, and suggested to Winston Churchill that he write a history of the English-speaking people. Perkins brought to his position a sound grasp of the business end of publishing and a keen instinct for what would sell. ■ See the letters collected in his *Editor to Author* (1950; rev. ed. 1979) and biography by A. Scott Berg (1978).

PERL, MARTIN L. (1927–   ), U.S. physicist. Perl worked as a chemical engineer before studying nuclear physics at Columbia University (Ph.D. 1955). He taught at the University of Michigan (1955–63) and at Stanford (1963–   ), where he did research at the Stanford Linear Accelerator Center. In a series of experiments (1974–77) he discovered the tau lepton, a fundamental subatomic particle. The discovery provided evidence, for the first time, of a third family (or generation) of fundamental particles that constitute all matter in the universe. It was critical for the completion of the "standard model" of particle physics, which holds that matter consists of 12 kinds of particles (six leptons and six quarks) that are divided into three families. For his discovery, Perl shared the 1995 Nobel Prize in Physics with Frederick Reines. ■ See his *Reflections on Experimental Science* (1996).

PERLMAN, ITZHAK (1945–   ), Israeli-born violinist. Perlman's parents emigrated from Poland to Israel. At age 4, Perlman was stricken by polio, which left his legs paralyzed. He studied violin, made his debut in Tel Aviv at age 9, and at 13 went to New York to study under Ivan Galamian at Juilliard. After he played at Carnegie Hall (1963). Perlman was quickly recognized as the preeminent violinist of his generation. He toured in the United States, Europe, and Japan, and often appeared with his friend, the violinist and violist Pinchas Zukerman.

PERLS, FRITZ (Frederick Salomon Perls; 1893–1970), German-born U.S. psychologist. Perls earned his M.D. in Berlin in 1920, was analyzed by Wilhelm Reich, and in 1933 fled the Nazis to South Africa with his wife, Dr. Laura Perls (1905–90). In the United States after World War II, they together developed the concept of Gestalt therapy (from the German word for "wholeness"). They drew on the ideas of psychoanalysts Sigmund Freud and Wilhelm Reich but rejected the Freudian emphasis on recalling early experience in individual therapy sessions and preferred to work with groups in the "here and now." This approach was elaborated by Fritz Perls in *Gestalt Therapy* (1951; with Paul Goodman and Ralph H. Hefferline) and later in *Gestalt Therapy Verbatim* (1969). Perls and his wife founded the New York Institute for Gestalt Therapy (1952). In the 1960s he was affiliated with the Esalen Institute in Big Sur, California, where he wrote a memoir, *In and Out of the Garbage Pail* (1969). Other books included *Ego, Hunger, and Aggression: The Beginning of Gestalt Therapy* (1945: rev. ed. 1969) and *The Gestalt Approach and Eye Witness to Therapy* (1973). ■ See biography by Jack Gaines (1979).

PERÓN, (MARIA) EVA (Maria Eva Duarte; 1919–1952), Argentine actress and political leader. Born into a poor family, she was a radio, stage. and screen actress in Buenos Aires before marrying military leader Juan Perón (1945). After helping him win the 1946 presidential election, she traveled around the country campaigning on behalf of his fascistic policies and gained a huge working-class following. Known as "Evita," she helped bring organized labor under Peronist control, established the Peronist Feminist party, and played a major role in securing women's suffrage. She organized her own social welfare organization that established hospitals. schools, and orphanages, and wielded an enormous amount of patronage. After her death due to cancer, she was viewed as a saint and martyr by her supporters and remained a symbol of the Peronist movement. The musical *Evita* (1978) was based on her life. ■ See biographies by John Barnes (1978), Julie M. Taylor (1979), Mary Foster Main (1980), Nicholas Fraser and Marysa Navarro (1981), and Alicia Dujovne Ortiz (Eng. trans. 1996).

PERÓN, JUAN DOMINGO (1895–1974). Argentine military and political leader. A participant in the military coup against Pres. Hipólito Irigoyen (1930), Perón witnessed the workings of fascist regimes at first hand while serving as a military attaché in Rome and Berlin during the late 1930s. He helped organize the military coup that overthrew Pres. Ramón Castillo (1943) and emerged as a popular reformist vice president and minister of labor and social security. Elected president (1946) with the help of his glamorous wife Eva (known as Evita), he organized a highly nationalistic fascist-style government. He improved conditions of the working class and nationalized banks, transport, and public utilities, while arresting political opponents, controlling the press, and suppressing civil liberties. He broke the power of the landed aristocracy and attempted to industrialize the country rapidly. Although reelected (1951), he lost support after Evita's death (1952). Economic failures and conflicts with the church and the military led to his overthrow (September 1955). After a long period of exile in Spain (1960–73), he was allowed to return home and was elected president in 1973, but he died after nine months in office. ■ See study by Robert J. Alexander (1979) and biography by Joseph A. Page (1983).

PEROT, (HENRY) ROSS (1930–   ), U.S. business executive and political leader. The son of a Texas cotton broker, Perot graduated from the U.S. Naval Academy in Annapolis, Maryland (1953), and served in the navy (1953–57) before becoming one of the International Business Machine's (IBM) most successful computer salesmen (1957–62). In 1962 he founded (with $1,000 from his wife's savings account) Electronic Data Systems, Inc. (EDS) to provide data-processing services for private companies and government agencies. Company profits soared in the mid-1960s when it gained contracts to process Medicare and Medicaid claims, and Perot made over $200 million when he took the company public in 1968. (He subsequently sold EDS to General Motors for $2.5 billion in cash and stocks in 1984 and founded another computer services firm, Perot Systems, in 1988.) During the Vietnam War he publicized the plight of U.S. POWs in North Vietnam by attempting (unsuccessfully) to deliver food, medicines, and gifts to them in December 1969. In 1979 he financed a secret mission that freed EDS employees from an Iranian maximum security prison. The spectacular rescue was described in Ken Follett's best-seller, *On Wings of Eagles* (1983). In 1992 he ran for president as an independent, pledging to lower the federal budget deficit and the national debt, and won 19 percent of the popular vote. He founded the Reform party (1995) and as its presidential candidate (1996) he ridiculed big government, preached self-reliance, and attacked the North American Free Trade Agreement (NAFTA) but managed to get only 8 percent of the vote. He wrote several books on political and economic issues. ■ See Gerald Posner, *Citizen Perot* (1996).

PERRET, AUGUSTE (1874–1954), French architect. Perret studied at the École des Beaux Arts in Paris, but he entered his family's building business before receiving a diploma. Known for introducing reinforced concrete to modern architecture, Perret built the first apartment complex designed for concrete on the Rue Franklin, Paris (1903). He used concrete reinforced with iron for the Théâtre des Champs-Élysées (1911–13), noted for its symmetry and simplicity. The graceful vaults and supports of his impressive Church of Notre Dame, Le Raincy (1922–23), were entirely formed of ferroconcrete. These buildings, and others, notably the Mobilier National, Paris (1934–35), reflected his antipathy to the severity of the dominant International Style. After World War II he was chief architect for the reconstruction of the city of Le Havre. ■ See Peter Collins, *Concrete* (1959).

PERRIN, JEAN BAPTISTE (1870–1942), French physicist. In 1895 Perrin published the results of experiments that indicated that cathode rays are composed of negatively charged particles. His experiments (1908) on the movement of tiny particles suspended in water (Brownian motion) offered support for the still-controversial atomic theory; he argued that the particles were being bombarded by microscopic molecules. From his study he was able to calculate the number of molecules in a cubic centimeter of gas at normal temperature and pressure (Avogadro's number). He received the 1926 Nobel Prize for Physics for this work. Perrin taught at the Sorbonne (University of Paris) from 1898 to 1940, when he fled to the United States after the German invasion of France. ■ See Mary Jo Nye, *Molecular Reality* (1972).

PERRY, RALPH BARTON (1876–1957), U.S. philosopher. Perry earned a Ph.D. from Harvard (1899) and taught there (1902–46). A leader of the "new realist" movement in philosophy, he revised pragmatism to stress a naturalistic theory of ethics. Perry's works included *The New Realism* (1912) and *Present Philosophical Tendencies* (1912), In *General Theory of Value* (1926), he traced morality to the conflict of instincts, desires, and feelings. He won a 1936 Pulitzer Prize for *The Thought and Character of William James* (1935).

PERSE, SAINT-JOHN (Alexis Saint-Léger Léger; 1887–1975), French poet. Born in Guadeloupe, where his family owned plantations, Saint-John Perse spent much of his life as a high-ranking French diplomat. Influenced by the verse of Paul Claudel, he focused on nature and its relationship to people and civilization in his ceremonial poetry. *Éloges* (1911: Eng. trans. 1944) and *Anabasis* (1922; Eng. trans. 1930), an epic poem based on the founding of a town by nomads, were among his earlier works. While living in the United States (1940–57) he wrote *Exile* (1942; Eng. trans. 1949), *Winds* (1946; Eng. trans. 1953), and *Seamarks* (1957; Eng. trans. 1958). In these works he discussed exile as a perpetual human condition and examined the creative and destructive results of human energy. *Chroniques* (1960: Eng. trans. 1961) and *Birds* (1962; Eng. trans. 1966) were concerned with reconciliation and serenity. Largely unknown to the general public, he was highly regarded by other poets and was awarded the 1960 Nobel Prize for Literature. Translations of his work appear in *Collected Poems* (1971, 1983). ■ See his *Letters* (Eng. trans. 1979), biography by René Galand (1972), and Erika Ostrovsky, *Under the Sign of Ambiguity* (1985).

PERSHING, JOHN JOSEPH (1860–1948), U.S. general. A cavalry officer who graduated from West Point (1886), "Black Jack" Pershing served in the campaigns against the

Sioux and Apache Indians and during the Moro insurgencies in the Philippines (1903: 1906–13). He also led the 1916 punitive expedition into Mexico. As commander in chief of the American expeditionary force in World War I, he gained a reputation as a stern disciplinarian whose object was unconditional surrender, and he returned home (1919) as a national hero. He was promoted to the unique rank of general of the armies and served as army chief of staff (1921–24). Pershing won a Pulitzer Prize for *My Experiences in the World War* (2 vols., 1931). ■ See biographies by Frederick Palmer (1948); Donald Smythe (2 vols. 1973–86); and Frank Vandiver, *Black Jack* (1977); Richard Goldhurst, *Pipe Clay and Drill* (1977); and Gene Smith, *Until the Last Trumpet Sounds* (1998).

PERTH, JAMES ERIC DRUMMOND, 16th EARL OF (1876–1951), British statesman. Drummond began his career as a private secretary and aide to the leading British statesmen of the period, including Prime Minister Herbert Asquith (1912–15) and Foreign Secretaries Edward Grey (1915–16) and Arthur Balfour (1916–18). As part of the British delegation to the Paris Peace Conference after World War I, he impressed participants with his mastery of procedure and detail. In 1919 he became the first secretary-general of the League of Nations. During his 14-year tenure, he recruited talented diplomats, forged the secretariat into a very effective technical organization, and promoted disarmament negotiations. He resigned in 1933 to become British ambassador to Italy (1933–39). Drummond acquired the title of Lord Perth in 1937 and entered the House of Lords in 1941. After World War II he became deputy leader of the Liberal party in the House of Lords. ■ See James Barros, *Office Without Power* (1979).

PERTINI, ALESSANDRO (1896–1990), Italian political leader. A lawyer who joined the Italian socialist party in 1919, Pertini was repeatedly arrested and imprisoned (1929–43) for antifascist activities during the interwar period. A member of parliament from 1946, he served as president of Italy from 1978 to 1985, a leftist symbol of resistance, courage, and integrity.

PERUTZ, MAX FERDINAND (1914–), Austrian-born British biochemist. Perutz went to Britain to study (1936) but remained there after the Nazi regime expropriated his family's business (1939) and he earned his Ph.D. at Cambridge (1940). After World War II, at the Medical Research Council's molecular biology laboratory at Cambridge (chairman, 1962–79), he presided over a brilliant team of biochemists that included Francis Crick and John Kendrew. Perutz elaborated on the work of Frederick Sanger, who had demonstrated the sequence of amino acids in a protein molecule. Using a "heavy atom" method of analyzing X-ray patterns, he determined the molecular structure of hemoglobin, a complex protein that carries oxygen in the blood. His technique was used to determine the structure of other complex substances, and he shared the 1962 Nobel Prize in Chemistry with Kendrew.

PESSOA, FERNANDO ANTONIO NOGUEIRA (1888–1935), Portuguese poet. Born in Lisbon, Pessoa received a British education in Durban, South Africa, where his stepfather was Portuguese consul. Although he wrote much of his early poetry in English, he became a major figure in the Portuguese modernist movement and contributed to the major avant-garde periodicals. A mystical, eccentric loner, preoccupied with metaphysical and existential doubts and speculations, he expressed his many-sided personality through four distinct poetic voices, his own and those of three "poets" that he invented—Alberto Caeiro, Ricardo Reis, and Alvaro de Campos. As each of these "heteronyms," as he called them, he published poems and criticism that dwelled on the same themes from widely different and often contradictory viewpoints. He published only one volume of poetry during his lifetime, but the posthumous publication of nine volumes of poems (1942–69) established his reputation as one of the great poetic geniuses of the century. English translations are in *Selected Poems* (1971: 1972; 1974; 1982; 1998), *Sixty Portuguese Poems* (1971), *Poems of Fernando Pessoa* (1986), *Message* (1992), and *Fernando Pessoa & Co.* (1998). His other works included *Always Astonished: Selected Prose* (Eng. trans. 1988) and the autobiographical *Book of Disquiet* (2 vols. 1990-91; Eng. trans 1992). ■ See Darlene Sadlier, *An Introduction to Fernando Pessoa* (1998).

PÉTAIN, (HENRI) PHILIPPE (1856–1951), French general and public official. The son of peasants. Pétain graduated from St. Cyr military academy (1878) but never saw active duty until World War I, when he declared "They shall not pass" to become the hero of Verdun (1916). Promoted to marshal of France (1918), he advocated the policy of defensive planning and border fortification that left France unprepared for World War II. Pétain served briefly as minister of war in a right-wing government (1934) and was appointed ambassador to Spain (1939). In 1940 the 84-year-old marshal was asked to negotiate an armistice with the Germans, who occupied the northern zone of France, Pétain, as "chief of state," led the collaborationist government in Vichy (1940–44), which adopted fascist-type institutions. In 1945 he was tried and convicted of treason; his death sentence was commuted to life imprisonment. ■ See biographies by Richard Griffiths (1972), Herbert R. Lottmann (1984), and Nicholas Atkin (1998).

PETER I (1844–1921), king of Serbia (1903–18) and of the Serbs, Croats, and Slovenes (Yugoslavia: 1918–21). A member of the Karadjordjević family, Peter spent 45 years in exile (1858–1903) while Serbia was ruled by the rival Obrenović family. Elected king upon the death of the last Obrenović (1903), Peter returned home and proved to be an enlightened liberal monarch who strongly supported constitutional government and instituted constitutional, military,

and educational reforms. (His son, Alexander, was named regent in 1914). During World War I Peter took part in the Serbian retreat across Albania (1915) and became a focus of national resistance. After the war he was proclaimed king of the newly formed South Slav state (1918).

PETER, PAUL, AND MARY, U.S. folksinging group. In 1962 two folksingers, **Peter Yarrow** (1938–) and **Mary Travers** (1937–), got together in New York with a stand-up comedian, **Noel Paul Stookey** (1937–), to ride the folk-music boom of the early 1960s to success. They sang in coffeehouses, at the Newport Folk Festival revivals, and won a Grammy Award for their 1963 recording of Bob Dylan's "Blowin' in the Wind." Their other popular recordings included "Puff the Magic Dragon" and "Where Have All the Flowers Gone?" After recording the hit "Leaving on a Jet Plane" (1969) the three disbanded to pursue separate careers, reuniting occasionally to benefit the causes they shared, notably nuclear disarmament.

PETERSON, OSCAR EMMANUEL (1925–), Canadian jazz pianist. The son of immigrants from the West Indies, Peterson started to play the piano at age 6 and played regularly on a Montreal radio show when he was a teenager. After receiving classical training, he played with a Canadian dance band in the 1940s and achieved fame as a performer in the United States with the "Jazz at the Philharmonic" concerts (1950–54) and later with his own trio, and finally as a solo performer. An eclectic virtuoso influenced by Art Tatum, Teddy Wilson, and Nat "King" Cole, Peterson was known for his complex harmonic and rhythmic patterns and his mastery of all jazz styles. An influential musician for more than 40 years, he recorded more than 200 albums and won several Grammy Awards. ■ See biography by Gene Lees (1988).

PETERSON, ROGER TORY (1908–1996), U.S. ornithologist and naturalist. Often compared to the 19th-century ornithologist John James Audubon, Peterson was considered the foremost ornithologist of his time in the United States. His first book, *A Field Guide to the Birds: Giving Field Marks of All Species Found in Eastern North America* (1934), which he both wrote and illustrated, was an immediate success and remained a best-seller for decades. He was associated with the National Audubon Society (from 1934) and edited the Houghton-Mifflin Field Guide Series (from 1946) and the American Naturalist Series (from 1965). His numerous books included *A Field Guide to Western Birds* (1941), *How to Know the Birds* (1949), *Wildlife in Color* (1951), *Wild America* (1955; with James Fisher), and *Penguins* (1979). ■ See John C. Devlin and Grace Naismith, *The World of Roger Tory Peterson* (1977).

PETLYURA, SIMON (1879–1926). Ukrainian nationalist leader. A founder of the Ukrainian Social Democratic Workers' party (1905), Petlyura was a nationalist who led the fight for Ukrainian independence during and after the Russian revolution. In February 1919, during the tumultuous civil war period, he headed a provisional government, but, opposed by both the Red and White armies, he fled to Poland in October 1919. From 1924 he lived as a political émigré in Paris until he was assassinated by Shalom Schwartzbard, a Jew who took revenge for the mass murders of Jews committed by Petlyura's Ukrainian army during 1919.

PETRIE, SIR (WILLIAM MATTHEW) FLINDERS (1853–1942), British archaeologist and Egyptologist. In his excavations at sites in Britain (1875–80), Egypt (1880–1924), and Palestine (1927–38), Petrie sought to "weave history out of scattered evidence." A professor at the University of London (1892–1933) he advanced the science of archaeology, developed "sequence dating," and made crucial contributions to Egyptology. Petrie established the sites of numerous ancient settlements, discovered (1899) the tombs of the first dynasty at Abydos, dated the middle Minoan period, and elaborated the relationship between ancient Egyptian and Greek cultures. Petrie continued his archaeological digs as he approached his 90th birthday. He wrote *The Revolutions of Civilization* (1911), numerous volumes on ancient Egypt, including the first three volumes of *A History of Egypt* (6 vols., 1923–27), and the autobiographical *Seventy Years in Archaeology* (1931). ■ See biography by Margaret S. Drower (1985).

PEVSNER, ANTOINE (1886–1962), Russian-Born French sculptor. Pevsner studied painting, sculpture, and architecture at Kiev Academy of Fine Arts (1902–09); he first painted abstract forms under the influence of Alexander Archipenko and Amedeo Modigliani. While a teacher in Moscow, he painted *Harmony in White* (1917), an extreme geometric abstraction, and began to view his works as "constructions," leading him to develop his wire and glass sculptures. His artistic concern was expressed in the constructivist tract, *Realistic Manifesto* (with his brother, Naum Gabo, 1920): art must derive new forms of expression through time and space. His works, although apparently solid masses, were constructed of many wires and planes that appeared to modulate under the influence of light. Pevsner emigrated (1923) to Paris, becoming a French national.

PEVSNER, SIR NIKOLAUS BERNHARD (1902–1983), German-born British art historian. The son of a wealthy German merchant, Pevsner was a lecturer at the University of Göttingen until 1933, when the Nazis came to power and he fled to Britain. He wrote a best-selling *Outline of European Architecture* (1942), became art editor of Penguin Books (1949), and taught at Cambridge (1949–55), the University of London (1945–68), and Oxford (1968–69). A prolific writer, he produced a series on *The Buildings of England* (46 vols., 1951–74), examining the relationship between design and function, style and context. He also wrote *Pioneers of the Modern Movement* (1936), *High Victorian Design* (1951), and *Studies in Art, Architecture and Design* (2 vols., 1968).

PHAM VAN DONG. *See DONG, PHAM VAN.*

PHIBUN SONGKHRAM. *See PIBUL SONGGRAM.*

PHILBY, KIM (Harold Adrian Russell Philby; 1912–1988), British intelligence officer and Soviet spy. The son of explorer and scholar St. John Philby, Kim Philby met Guy Burgess, Donald Maclean, and Anthony Blunt while he was a student at Cambridge (1929–33). They all shared anticapitalist and antifascist views, joined a secret communist cell, and agreed to spy for the Soviet Union. Philby, who was a journalist during the 1930s, joined British military intelligence in 1940 and worked on its Russian desk (1944–46). He served as first secretary of the British embassy in Washington. D.C. (1949–51) and acted as liaison between British intelligence services and the FBI and CIA. A "master spy," he transmitted a great deal of secret information to the Soviets, including plans for an allied-backed military operation in Albania (1950). Although his colleagues Burgess and Maclean, who passed secrets to the Soviets while they worked for intelligence and the foreign office, defected to the Soviet Union in 1951, Philby maintained his position until he too fled to the Soviet Union in 1963. He lived in Moscow for the rest of his life. ■ See his *My Secret War* (1968); Bruce Paige, David Leitch, and Philip Knightley, *The Philby Conspiracy* (1968); Andrew Boyle, *The Fourth Man* (1979); Douglas Sutherland, *The Great Betrayal* (1981); and Rufina Philby et al., *The Private Life of Kim Philby: The Moscow Years* (2000).

PHILIP, PRINCE. *See EDINBURGH, PHILIP MOUNTBATTEN, DUKE OF.*

PHILIPE, GÉRARD (1922–1959), French actor. Philipe was the most popular romantic actor of the post–World War II French cinema. Handsome and sensitive, he starred in the films of the greatest directors of his time (including René Clair, Max Ophuls, René Clément, and Marcel Carné) and, like James Dean and Rudolph Valentino, died at an early age. He was best known for his roles in *The Idiot* (1946), *Devil in the Flesh* (1947), *La ronde* (1950), *Beauty and the Devil* (1950), *Beauties of the Night* (1952), and *Les liaisons dangereuses* (1959).

PHILIPS, ANTON FREDERIK (1874–1951), Dutch industrialist. Anton Philips is credited with transforming the Philips Bulb and Radio Works, founded by his brother Gerard in the village of Eindhoven, into the world's largest non-American-owned electrical company. Heading the company from 1921 to 1951, Philips established a worldwide network of factories and selling outlets specializing in electrical consumer goods and other more sophisticated products. In 1924 the company began to produce one of the world's first cheap compact radio sets, and it soon rivaled the General Electric Co. in the communications field.

PHILLIPS, WILLIAM D. (1948–   ), U.S. physicist. Phillips graduated from the Massachusetts Institute of Technology (Ph.D. 1976) and did research at the U.S. National Institute of Standards and Technology in Gaithersburg, Maryland (1978–   ). His major scientific contribution was to extend the pioneering work of Steven Chu, who devised a method of using lasers to cool atoms in order to slow them down so that they could be studied in detail. Phillips and his colleagues refined the cooling technique and developed magnetic traps that cooled atoms to 40 millionths of one degree above absolute zero. The cooling techniques, further refined by Claude Cohen-Tannoudji, raised the possibility of creating ultra-accurate atomic clocks that would dramatically increase the accuracy of navigational measurements and allow for the precise measurement of gravitational forces. For their research, Phillips, Chu, and Cohen-Tannoudji shared the 1997 Nobel Prize in Physics.

PHOMVIHANE, KAYSONE. See *KAYSONE PHOMVIHANE.*

PHUMIPHOL ADULYADET. See *BHUMIBOL ADULYADEJ.*

PIAF, EDITH (Edith Giovanna Gassion; 1915–1963), French singer. Born in Paris, the daughter of an acrobat and a café singer, she was abandoned by her mother as a young girl and became a street singer at age 15. The diminutive 4-foot, 10-inch entertainer began performing in nightclubs in the early 1930s and was renamed "Piaf," Parisian slang for sparrow, by a cabaret proprietor (1935). Singing of heartbreak and disillusion in a husky and throbbing voice, she achieved popularity on radio, in films, and in theatrical appearances and became a cult figure among French intellectuals after World War II. Her anguished and defiant ballads seemed to reflect the many personal tragedies she suffered. Her best-known songs included *La vie en rose,* which she wrote, and *Mon legionnaire, Non, je ne regrette rien, Milord,* and *C'est l'amour.* She made frequent tours of Europe and the United States after 1947. ■ See her autobiography, *The Wheel of Fortune* (Eng. trans. 1965), and biographies by Simone Berteaut (Eng. trans. 1972), Monique Lange (Eng. trans. 1981), and Margaret Crosland (1985).

PIAGET, JEAN (1896–1980), Swiss psychologist. Piaget was early fascinated by zoology: he published a well-received article on mollusks at age 15 and received a doctorate in science (1918) before studying psychology in Zurich and Paris. His observations of how children get to know space, time, causality, and objectivity created a vital framework for studying human intelligence, stressing the interaction of biological and environmental factors. He theorized that from birth a child constructs and reconstructs from direct experience a model of the world, and in the process passes through a fixed, universal sequence of four mental stages. His later work linked cognitive and emotional factors in the development of intelligence. Piaget's early discoveries won international recognition in the 1920s and 1930s, but in the two decades that followed, his work was outside the mainstream of U.S. psychology. A resurgence of interest in his work occurred in the late 1950s, and his influence subsequently increased dramatically. Piaget taught at the University of Geneva (1929–54), the University of Lausanne (1938–51), and the Sorbonne (1952–63). He wrote more than 50 books and monographs, including *The Child's Conception of the World* (1926; Eng. trans. 1929), *The Origin of Intelligence in Children* (1936; Eng. trans. 1952), and *The Early Growth of Logic in the Child* (1958: Eng. trans. 1964). ■ See H. E. Gruber and J. J. Vonèche, eds., *The Essential Piaget* (1977). See also studies by Richard Evans (1973) and Margaret Boden (1980), and Jean-Claude Bringuier, *Conversations with Jean Piaget* (Eng. trans. 1980).

PIATIGORSKY, GREGOR (1903–1976), Russian-born U.S. cellist. The principal cellist of the Moscow Imperial Opera at the age of 15, Piatigorsky left the Soviet Union in 1921 and served as first cellist with the Berlin Philharmonic (1924–28) before embarking on a brilliant solo career. Internationally renowned for his exquisite tone and sensitive and poetic performances, he appeared with the world's leading orchestras and performed the world premieres of concertos by Mario Castelnuovo-Tedesco (1935), Paul Hindemith (1941), and Sir William Walton (1957). After moving to the United States at the beginning of World War II, he taught at the Curtis Institute (Philadelphia) and the University of Southern California and gave a series of celebrated recitals with violinist Jascha Heifetz and pianist Arthur Rubinstein. ■ See his autobiography, *Cellist* (1965).

PIBUL SONGGRAM or PHIBUN SONGKHRAM (1897–1964), Thai political leader. The most prominent Thai statesman of the 20th century and a founder of the modern Thai nation, Pibul came from a farming family and received a military education in Thailand (1909–14) and France (1924–27). In 1932 he was a leader of the coup that changed Thailand from an absolute to a constitutional monarchy. As premier (1938–44; 1948–57). Pibul espoused anticommunism and favored highly centralized rule by a small elite. He was an ally of Japan during World War II and an ally of the West during the cold war. After his ouster in a coup in 1957, Pibul went into exile in Japan and then became a Buddhist monk in 1960. ■ See Kobkua Suwannathat-Pian, *Thailand's Durable Premier* (1995).

PICABIA, FRANCIS (1879–1953), French artist. Picabia, whose father's family were Cuban aristocrats, began painting in an impressionist style and passed through the other major modes of 20th-century art. After experimenting with cubism (1909–11), he joined the dadaists and helped introduce the movement to the United States during World War I. Later he exhibited with the surrealists in Paris during the 1920s and 1930s. But whatever style he adopted, he was inventive and often outrageous. He was best known for his post-cubist abstractions, images of intricate but useless machines, and lyrical, transparent collages. ■ See studies by William Camfield (1978) and Maria L. Borràs (1985).

PICASSO, PABLO RUIZ (1881–1973), Spanish artist. The son of an art teacher, Picasso studied and painted in Barcelona before settling in Paris (1904). His creative life fell into periods: the introspective "blue period" (1901–04), the lyrical "rose period" (1905–07), and the period of cubist rebellion against classical representation. *Les Demoiselles d'Avignon* (1907), the first cubist painting, literally added a new dimension to the art experience. Picasso branched out into sculpture, graphics, collage, ceramics, and theater sets. His art often reflected his commitment to left-wing political causes. His *Guernica* (1937), an enormous black-and-white mural, dramatized the atrocity of the Spanish Civil War, while his lithographed doves symbolized peace. The major art figure of the century, Picasso is represented in collections worldwide; in 1980 New York's Museum of Modern Art mounted a huge retrospective of his work and published a catalog. ■ See biographies by Roland Penrose (rev. ed. 1981), Patrick O'Brian (1976), Pierre Cabanne (Eng. trans. 1977), John Richardson (1991), Arianna Stassinopoulos (1988), and Pierre Daix (Eng. trans. 1993).

PICCARD, AUGUSTE ANTOINE (1884–1962) and **JEAN FELIX PICCARD** (1884–1963), Swiss scientists. Born into a prominent academic family, the twin Piccard brothers pursued scientific careers—Auguste in physics and Jean in chemistry. Inspired by Jules Verne's writings, Auguste broke world altitude (1931) and ocean-depth (1953) records. Using a hydrogen balloon of his own design to ascend more than 50,000 feet, Auguste demonstrated the use of a pressurized cabin for manned flight. His bathyscaphe, a vehicle based on ballooning principles, took him and his son Jacques more than 10,000 feet below the surface of the Mediterranean. Jean also experimented with balloon aviation: with his wife, he ascended more than 57,000 feet (1934) and measured the effect of the magnetic field on cosmic rays. Jean also refined plastic and cellophane balloons. Auguste's son Jacques (1922–) helped his father design the bathyscaphe *Trieste* and set a submarine depth record in the vessel by descending 35,800 feet in the Pacific Ocean (1960; with Don Walsh). Jacques' son Bertrand (1958–) and Brian Jones (1947–) were the first men to circumnavigate the globe, nonstop, in a balloon (March 1–March 21, 1999). ■ See Auguste Piccard's *Earth, Sky and Sea* (Eng. trans 1956).

PICKERING, WILLIAM HAYWARD (1910–), New Zealand-born U.S. engineer and physicist. Pickering earned his Ph.D. at the California Institute of Technology (1936) and did pioneering high-altitude cosmic-ray research with Robert A. Millikan. He joined Cal Tech's Jet Propulsion Laboratory (1944) and developed the first telemetry system used in U.S. rockets. He directed the laboratory (1954–76) and carried out programs that resulted in the launching of the first U.S. artificial satellite, *Explorer 1* (1958), the *Ranger* lunar-impact flights (1964–65), and the *Mariner* flights to Venus (1962) and Mars (1964–65). The latter flights yielded the first close-up photographs of another planet and provided vast amounts of new information about the planets.

PICKETT, WILSON (1941–), U.S. singer. The composer of the 1959 hit "You're So Fine," Pickett specialized in simple repeated phrases, gospel refrains, a raucous singing style, and orange-trimmed purple jackets with ruffled lilac shirts. He signed with Atlantic Records in 1964 and gradually moved from rhythm and blues into the rock-and-roll mainstream with "In the Midnight Hour" (1964) and "Sugar Sugar" (1970).

PICKFORD, MARY (Gladys Smith; 1893–1979), U.S. film actress and business executive. Pickford was a child actress from Canada who became the world's first movie star and one of the richest women in history. Cast as a curly-haired, dewy-eyed ingenue into her thirties, she played such sentimental silent heroines as *Rebecca of Sunnybrook Farm* (1917), *Tess of the Storm Country* (1922), and *Little Annie Roonie* (1925). In 1928 she cut off her curls and made her first talkie as a small-town southern girl in *Coquette,* for which she won an Academy Award. An astute business executive, she cofounded United Artists Corp. (1919) and continued to produce films after her retirement from acting (1933). She presided over Hollywood society during the 1920s with her second husband, Douglas Fairbanks, Sr., at their estate, Pickfair. ■ See her autobiography, *Sunshine and Shadow* (1954); Robert Windeler, *Sweetheart* (1974); biographies by Scott Eyman (1990) and Eileen Whitfield (1997); and study by Kevin Brownlow (1999).

PIECK, WILHELM (1876–1960), East German political leader. Born near Berlin, where his father was a laborer, Pieck became a carpenter at age 14 and was soon active in Social Democratic politics. He was one of the founders of the revolutionary Spartacus League (1915) and the German communist party (1918) and was elected to the Reichstag in 1928 as a communist. After the Nazis came to power in 1933, Pieck went into exile, surfacing in the Soviet Union (1935) as secretary of the Comintern. He returned to Berlin in the wake of the Russian army (1945) and served as first president of the (East) German Democratic Republic (1949–60).

PIERCE, JOHN ROBINSON (1910–), U.S. engineer. At Bell Telephone Laboratories for 35 years (1936–71), Pierce did pioneering work in the development of microwave tubes, radar, and digital communication through pulse-code modulation. He was the first to write of the possibility of satellite radio communication (1955) and succeeded in persuading the U.S. government to develop the first communication satellite, *Echo 1*, launched on April 12, 1960. Its success inspired American Telephone and Telegraph to launch *Telstar* (1962) and thus revolutionize worldwide radio and television communication.

PIERCY, MARGE (1936–), U.S. writer. Born into a working-class Detroit family, Piercy graduated from the University of Michigan (BA. 1957) and Northwestern University (MA. 1958) and worked as an organizer and researcher in the anti-Vietnam War movement (1965–69) and in the women's movement (from 1969). Committed to radical social change, she chronicled the political, social, and sexual revolutions of the 1960s and 1970s in her poems and novels, many of which were semi-autobiographical. Her novels included *Going Down Fast* (1969), *Small Changes* (1973), *Woman on the Edge of Time* (1976), *The High Cost of Living* (1978), *Vida* (1980), *Braided Lives* (1982), *Fly Away Home* (1984), *Gone to Soldiers* (1987), *Available Light* (1988), *He, She and It* (1991), *The Longings of Women* (1994), and *Storm Tide* (1998). Her poetry collections included *Breaking Camp* (1968), *Hard Loving* (1969), *Living in the Open* (1976), *The Moon Is Always Female* (1980), *Circles on the Water* (1982), *Mars and Her Children* (1992), and *What Are Big Girls Made Of?* (1997).

PIGOU, ARTHUR CECIL (1877–1959), British economist. A. C. Pigou was educated at King's College, Cambridge, of which he became a fellow in 1902. From 1908 to 1943 he held the chair of political economy at Cambridge previously held by Alfred Marshall, whose views he helped disseminate. He was a neoclassical economist who believed in a national-income policy and in a moderate amount of state intervention and was best known for the development of welfare economics in such works as *Wealth and Welfare* (1912) and *The Economics of Welfare* (1920). He also made substantial contributions to the analysis of tariff policy, industrial fluctuations, unemployment, and public finance.

PIKE, JAMES ALBERT (1913–1969), U.S. theologian. Born in Oklahoma City and raised as a Catholic, Pike was a New Deal attorney in the 1930s. During wartime service in the U.S. Navy (1943–45), he decided to study theology. Ordained as an Episcopal priest (1946), he studied at Union Theological Seminary (B.D. 1951), then served as chaplain at Columbia University (1949–52) and as dean of the Cathedral of St. John the Divine in New York City (1952–58) before his appointment as bishop of California (1958). His liberal views strongly influenced Protestant religious and social thought. Often accused of heresy for questioning the Trinity and the Virgin Birth, Pike resigned his post in 1966 to become theologian-in-residence at Santa Barbara's Center

for the Study of Democratic Institutions. A prolific writer on social and religious issues, he was visiting Judea to study the origins of Christianity when he succumbed to exposure in the desert. He wrote *Beyond Anxiety* (1953), *The Church, Politics, and Society* (1955; with J. W. Pyle), and *The Next Day* (1957). ■ See William Stringfellow and Anthony Towne, *The Death and Life of Bishop Pike* (1976).

PILLAI, THAKAZHI SIVASANKARA (1914–), Indian writer. Trained as a lawyer in his native state of Kerala, Pillai wrote realistic novels and short stories and was considered the outstanding novelist in the Malayalam language. His early novels, dealing with the poverty and degradation of the outcastes of rural south India, included *The Scavenger's Son* (1947: Eng. trans. 1970) and *Two Measures of Rice* (1949; Eng. trans. 1967). His best-known novel was *Chemmeen* (1956; Eng. trans. 1962), a love story involving a Hindu and a Muslim. His other translated works included *The Iron Rod* (1974), *Rungs of the Ladder* (1976), *The Children of Ouseph* (1984), and *Kayar* (1997).

PILNYAK, BORIS (Boris Andreyevich Vogau; 1894–1941), Russian writer. Pilnyak's parents were radical intellectuals who worked among the peasants. He developed an emotional resistance to Western rationalism and in his work translated Soviet phenomena into Slavic terms, attributing the Russian Revolution (1917) to the elemental violence of old Russia. Pilnyak was the most influential Russian prose stylist of the 1920s, and he claimed to be the first "Soviet writer." He pioneered avant-garde wordplay and made extensive use of the *skaz* or storytelling technique. *The Naked Year* (1922: Eng. trans. 1928, 1975) established his reputation with its symbolic, ornamental prose and folk-epic flavor. He briefly chaired the official writers' union (1929), but when his short novel *Mahogany* (1929; Eng. trans. 1965) appeared in Berlin, he was denounced and dismissed. The official campaign against Pilnyak marked the start of Stalin's efforts to mold Soviet literature to his own ends. Pilnyak wrote *The Volga Falls to the Caspian Sea* (1930: Eng. trans. 1931) to undo the damage, but never regained official favor. During the 1930s Pilnyak daringly presided over a salon of freethinkers in his Moscow apartment. He was arrested (1937), charged with being a Trotskyist and a spy, and was presumably executed. English translations of his stories are in *The Tale of the Unextinguished Moon* (1967) and *Mother Earth* (1968). ■ See biography by Vera T. Reck (1975) and Gary Browning, *Scythian at a Typewriter* (1985).

PILSUDSKI, JOSEPH (1867–1935), Polish political leader. After five years in Siberian exile for allegedly planning to assassinate the czar, Pilsudski joined the Polish Socialist party in 1894 and edited its clandestine newspaper. More a nationalist than a socialist, he commanded the Polish Legions during World War I and in 1918 proclaimed Polish independence with himself as chief of state. Unable to work within a parliamentary system, Pilsudski retired from politics in 1922 but returned in 1926 to lead a coup. He ruled as an authoritarian dictator until his death. ∎ See his *Memoirs* (Eng. trans. 1931); biographies by William F. Reddaway (1939) and Waclaw Jedrzejewicz (1982); Joseph Rothschild, *Pilsudski's Coup d'Etat* (1966); and Richard M. Watt, *Bitter Glory* (1979).

PINCHOT, GIFFORD (1865–1946), U.S. conservationist and public official. The first professional forester in America, Pinchot headed (1898–1910) the division of forestry (department of agriculture) and was largely responsible for making conservation a public issue. He was especially influential during the presidency (1901–09) of his friend Theodore Roosevelt when millions of acres of forest land were transferred to reserves. Pinchot founded the Yale School of Forestry and was a professor there (1903–36). He invented the term "conservation" and chaired the National Conservation Association (1910–25). A founder of the Progressive party (1912), he believed that government should control the power of big business, and he served twice as a reform governor of Pennsylvania (1923–27: 1931–35). Pinchot wrote several books on forestry as well as an autobiography, *Breaking New Ground* (1947). ∎ See studies by Martin N. McGeary (1960) and Martin L. Fausold (1961).

PINCUS, GREGORY GOODWIN (1903–1967), U.S. biologist. Through his work on the physiology of reproduction, Pincus played a major role in the post–World War II breakthroughs in endocrinology and reproductive biology. His research with John Rock and M. C. Chang on the inhibition of ovulation utilizing orally active progesteronelike substances led to the development of oral contraception ("the Pill")—a discovery that had wide social and demographic implications. Pincus was a director of the Worcester (Massachusetts) Foundation for Experimental Biology (1944–67) and wrote several books including *The Eggs of Mammals* (1936) and *The Control of Fertility* (1965).

PININFARINA, BATTISTA (Giovan Battista Farina; 1895–1966), Italian automobile designer. Pininfarina, who designed his first car for Fiat (1920), founded his own automobile-body factory in Turin (1930) and almost immediately won international recognition for his elegant and functional designs. He specialized in streamlined, record-breaking racing cars for Lancia. Alfa Romeo, and Ferrari, but he also designed passenger cars for Fiat, Peugeot, and the British Motor Corp. Many of his innovations were copied by Detroit designers years after their initial appearance in Europe. His designs for the U.S. market included the 1952 Nash line, the 1959 Cadillac Eldorado Brougham. and the 1965 Chevrolet Corvette Rodine Coupe Speciale.

PINOCHET UGARTE, AUGUSTO (1915–), Chilean general and dictator. An upper-middle-class graduate of Chile's military academy (1936) and authority on geopolitics, Pinochet was promoted to brigadier general in 1968 and in 1972 to army chief of staff. Following the bloody 1973 coup d'état in which Marxist president Salvador Allende died, the military junta under Pinochet declared an "indefinite recess" of politics. It jailed, tortured, and executed political prisoners, and suspended civil rights in order to "exterminate Marxism." In 1974 Pinochet assumed sole power as chief of state. After the approval of a new constitution in a 1980 plebiscite, Pinochet was inaugurated as president for an eight-year term. A severe economic crisis in the mid-1980s led to public protests against the regime, which responded with increasingly repressive policies. After losing a 1988 plebiscite to determine whether he would stay in office, he relinquished power to a civilian government. However, he remained armed forces chief until March 1998, when he became a senator for life, a position that gave him immunity from prosecution as a government official. In October 1998 he was arrested while visiting London when Spain asked for his extradition on charges of torture and murder of hundreds of Spanish and Chilean citizens. The British government rejected his claim of immunity. However, after 16 months of house arrest, the British government ruled that he was too ill to stand trial, and he was allowed to return to Chile (2000). Subsequently the Chilean Supreme Court stripped Pinochet of his immunity (2000). ∎ See Mary H. Spooner, *Soldiers in a Narrow Land* (1994).

PINSKI, DAVID (1872–1959), Russian-born U.S. Yiddish-language dramatist and novelist. One of the few Yiddish playwrights whose works were translated into English and European languages, Pinski wrote on biblical, historical, and contemporary Jewish themes. He emigrated to New York City (1899), became a literary editor, and participated in Jewish cultural, political, working-class, and socialist-Zionist movements. He abandoned his early naturalism and produced works concerning great personalities and messianic visions. His most famous plays were *The Treasure* (Eng. trans. 1915), *The Eternal Jew* (1926), and *The Final Balance* (Eng. trans. 1926). His novels *Arnold Levenberg* (Eng. trans. 1928) and *The Generations of Noah Edon* (Eng. trans. 1931) portrayed the empty lives of assimilated American Jews who were cut off from their cultural roots. Further translations are in *Three Plays* (1918), *Ten Plays* (1920), and *Temptations: A Book of Short Stories* (1921).

PINSKY, ROBERT (1940–), U.S. poet and critic. Pinsky studied at Rutgers University (B.A. 1962) and Stanford University (Ph.D. 1966) and taught at several schools, including Wellesley College (1968–80), the University of California, Berkeley (1980–89), and Boston University (1989–). His wide-ranging, meditative poetry was collected in several volumes, including *Sadness and Happiness* (1975), *History of My Heart* (1984), *The Want Bone* (1990), *The Figured Wheel* (1996), and *Jersey Rain* (2000). He also wrote a book-length poem, *An Explanation of America* (1979), and two collections of literary essays, *The Situation of Poetry* (1977) and *Poetry and the World* (1988). Pinsky's award-winning verse translation of *The Inferno of Dante* (1995) became a best-seller. A computer aficionado, he was the computer editor of the Internet magazine *Slate* and the author of a computerized novel, *Mindwheel* (1985). While serving as U.S poet laureate (1997–2000) he wrote *The Sounds of Poetry: A Brief Guide* (1998).

PINTER, HAROLD (1930–), British playwright. The son of a poor Jewish tailor, Pinter studied briefly at the Royal Academy of Dramatic Art and was an actor before he became a dramatist. His plays, which included *The Room* (1957), *The Birthday Party* (1958), *The Caretaker* (1960), and *The Homecoming* (1965), are "comedies of menace." Written with an accurate ear for dialogue, they rely not on ingenious plot or conventional suspense, but on seemingly realistic situations, small talk, repetitions, and silences that suggest mystery and ambiguity. He dramatized human isolation, showing characters' fears and longings and their failure to communicate. *One for the Road* (1984) was a play dealing with modern political torture. Pinter also wrote highly praised screenplays. including *The Servant* (1963), *Accident* (1967), *The Go Between* (1971), *The French Lieutenant's Woman* (1981), and *Turtle Diary* (1985) and the novel *Dwarfs* (1990). ■ See his *Poems and Prose: 1949–77* (1978), *Various Voices: Prose, Poetry, Politics, 1948–1998* (1998); studies by Arlene Sykes (1970), Ronald Hayman (1973), Arnold P. Hinchliffe (rev. ed. 1981), and David Thompson (1985); and biography by Michael Billington (1996).

PINZA, EZIO (1892–1957), Italian opera and musical comedy singer. A professional bicycle racer at age 17, Pinza made a local opera debut in 1914, later graduating to Milan's La Scala and New York's Metropolitan Opera (1926–48). Tall, handsome, and a master of histrionics, he gained fame for singing the roles of Don Giovanni, Boris Godunov, Figaro, and Mephistopheles. In 1949 Pinza left opera for musical comedy, starring in *South Pacific* (1949) and *Fanny* (1954) as well as in several films. ■ See his autobiography (1958).

PIPER, WILLIAM THOMAS (1881–1970), U.S. aviation pioneer. A wealthy Pennsylvania oilman, W. T. Piper bought the bankrupt Taylor Brothers Aircraft Corp. (1931) and developed and mass-produced the "Piper Cub," the first small and inexpensive airplane. Called the "Henry Ford of aviation," Piper became the largest producer of light planes in the United States and sold more than 5,600 of them to the armed forces during World War II. During the 1950s the new twin-engine Cub was a popular executive aircraft. Piper was said to have built more airplanes than anyone else in the world. ■ See Devon Francis, *Mr. Piper and His Cubs* (1973).

PIPPIN, HORACE (1888–1946), U.S. painter. After a series of odd jobs and World War I army service, Pippin began painting during the 1920s in a bold, primitive style. His subjects were usually simple domestic scenes depicting black American life rendered in a naive, geometrically reduced scale. He was also known for his antiwar paintings and his 1942 trilogy of the John Brown saga. ■ See study by Selden Rodman (1947).

PIRANDELLO, LUIGI (1867–1936), Italian novelist and playwright. Pirandello studied in Germany before he began his literary career in Rome. After an arranged marriage, he was supported by his parents and in-laws until circumstances required him to teach to support himself. His wife, always emotionally unstable, suffered several breakdowns and was ultimately confined in a nursing home (1919). Pirandello became identified with literature of the absurd: his work probed the border region between sanity and madness. He dealt with the impossibility of understanding and with the fragility of personal identity in many of the 43 plays produced between 1910 and 1937 (of which more than half were adaptations of his short fiction). His best-known works included *The Rules of the Game* (1918; Eng. trans. 1959), *The Pleasure of Honesty* (1917; Eng. trans. 1923), *Six Characters in Search of an Author* (1921; Eng. trans. 1922), and *Tonight We Improvise* (1930: Eng. trans. 1932). His innovations in dramatic form, as well as his thematic material, greatly influenced modern theater. Pirandello won the 1934 Nobel Prize for Literature. ■ See biography by Gaspare Giudice (1963; Eng. trans. 1975) and studies by Walter Starkie (rev. ed. 1965) and Olga Ragusa (1980).

PIRE, DOMINIQUE GEORGES (1910–1969), Belgian clergyman and humanitarian, A Dominican priest who taught moral philosophy (1937–47) at the Dominican Monastery of La Sarte, Huy, Belgium, Pire was active in the anti-German resistance movement during World War II. After the war he devoted himself to the problem of refugees and displaced persons. He set up camps and established (1949) a sponsorship system for refugees. In 1956 he helped found a series of "European villages" designed to provide refugees with their own communities. For these humanitarian efforts, Pire was awarded the 1958 Nobel Peace Prize. In 1960 he established the University of Peace (Huy). He undertook other peace projects In East Pakistan (now Bangladesh), India, and elsewhere. Pire wrote *Building Peace* (Eng. trans. 1967) and *The Story of Father Dominique Pire* (as told to Hugues Vehenne; Eng. trans. 1961).

PIRENNE, HENRI (1862–1935), Belgian historian. While imprisoned by the Germans during World War I, Pirenne, an economic historian at the University of Ghent (1886–1930) learned Russian and wrote from memory a history of Europe that was later (1936) published. His major works were *Medieval Cities* (1925; Eng. trans. 1925), in which he attributed the growth of urban centers to the economic revival of the late Middle Ages, and *Mohammed and Charlemagne* (1937; Eng. trans. 1939), in which he argued that the Middle Ages began with the economic downturn occasioned by the Muslim conquest. His other important works were *His-*

tory of Belgium (7 vols.; Eng. trans. 1899–1932) and Economic and Social History of Medieval Europe (1933; Eng. trans. 1936). ■ See Alfred F. Havighurst. ed., The Pirenne Thesis (rev. ed. 1969), and biography by Bryce Lyon (1974).

PIRIE, NORMAN (1907–1997), British biochemist and physiologist. Working at Cambridge in the 1930s with Sir Frederick Bawden, Pine isolated the tobacco-mosaic virus in crystalline form. Their feat facilitated the study of macromolecules and molecular genetics, and led to discoveries about how proteins are produced. He headed the biochemistry department of Rothamsted Experimental Station (1947–72). In later years, he was an intelligent and heeded voice on the problems of population control, food productivity, and nutrition. His books included Food Resources (1969; rev. ed. 1976) and Leaf Protein and Other Aspects of Fodder Fractionation (1978; rev. ed. 1987).

PISCATOR, ERWIN (1893–1966), German theatrical director. The director of Berlin's Volksbühne and Bühne theaters during the 1920s, Piscator was a founder of modern political theater. Working with Bertolt Brecht, Piscator invented "total theater" by introducing such multimedia effects as films, newsreels, animated cartoons, flashing lights, and air-raid sirens to enhance his left-wing productions. Forced to flee the Nazis in 1933. Piscator worked in New York from 1939 to 1951, where he directed the Dramatic Workshop of the New School for Social Research. He returned to Germany (1951) and became director of West Berlin's new Freie Volksbühne Theater (1962), presenting such controversial plays as Rolf Hochhuth's The Deputy and Peter Weiss's The Investigation. ■ See John Wlllett, The Theater of Erwin Piscator (1979), and study by Gerhard F. Probst (1991).

PISTON, WALTER HAMOR, JR. (1894–1976), U.S. composer. A Harvard graduate (1924) and student of the influential French musician Nadla Boulanger, Piston composed eight symphonies (1937–65), chamber music, and concertos, in a traditional, neoclassic style. The ballet The Incredible Flutist (1938) was his first popular success. He taught at Harvard for many years (1926–60), won Pulitzer Prizes for his Third Symphony (1948) and Seventh Symphony (1961), and wrote standard texts on Harmony (1941), Counterpoint (1947), and Orchestration (1955). ■ See study by Howard Pollack (1982),

PIUS X, SAINT (Giuseppe Melchiorre Sarto; 1835–1914), Italian-born pope of the Roman Catholic Church. Ordained in 1858, Santo was a parish priest in the region of Venice before Pope Leo XIII appointed him bishop of Mantua (1884) and cardinal and patriarch of Venice (1893). He succeeded Leo XIII (1903), taking the name Pius X. A conservative, he stressed the church's spiritual mission and rejected liberal intellectual tendencies. He condemned modernist Catholic teaching that sought to recast Catholic doctrine in the light of 19th-century philosophical and historical concepts. He opposed the Christian Democratic movement and would not accept the policy of separation of church and state adopted in France in 1905. His decree (1905) urging Catholics to take communion frequently was very influential. Revered during his lifetime for his profound spirituality, after his death he was beatified (1951) and canonized (1954) by Pope Plus XII. His encyclicals and selected documents were assembled in V. A. Yzermans, ed., All Things in Christ (1954). ■ See also Katherine Burton, The Great Mantle (1950),

PIUS XI (Ambrogio Damiano Achille Ratti; 1857–1939), Italian-born pope of the Roman Catholic Church. Ratti was named cardinal and archbishop of Milan (1921) by Pope Benedict XV, whom he succeeded in 1923. As Pope Pius XI, he concluded the Lateran Treaty (1929) with fascist dictator Benito Mussolini. Mussolini assured the existence of an independent Vatican city-state and recognized the Pope's absolute sovereignty over the Vatican; in exchange, the pope recognized the kingdom of Italy and agreed to maintain permanent neutrality in diplomatic and military affairs. Eager to safeguard the rights of the church, Pius XI also entered into agreements with other European powers, including Germany (1933). Despite these agreements, he spoke out against the Nazi Third Reich, issuing two encyclicals (1937) condemning communism and fascism and denouncing Mussolini's anti-Semitic policies (1938). Pope Pius XI supported overseas missionary efforts and favored closer ties with Eastern Orthodox theologians, but remained unenthusiastic about ecumenical work with Protestants. ■ See biography by Zsolt Aradi (1958) and Peter C. Kent, The Pope and the Duce (1981).

PIUS XII (Eugenio Pacelli; 1876–1958), Italian-born pope of the Roman Catholic Church. Ordained as a priest in 1899. Pacehli studied theology and law and worked for the Vatican secretariat (1901–17). He was papal nuncio in Munich and Berlin (1917–29) before being made a cardinal (1929) and serving as the Vatican secretary of state (1930–39). He was elected pope on Mar. 2. 1939. Pius attempted to preserve cordial relations with all of the warring nations during World War II and followed a policy of neutrality. He was severely criticized after the war for not publicly condemning the Nazi genocide against the Jews. He was, however, admired for his postwar relief work and his advocacy of arms control. An outspoken anticommunist, he played a key role in weakening the Italian Communist party after the war and in bringing the Christian Democratic party to power. He was extremely conservative on doctrinal and theological questions. ■ See Katherine Burton, Witness of the Light (1958), and John Cornwell, Hitler's Pope (1999).

PLAATJE, SOLOMON TSHEKISHO (1878–1932), South African writer, scholar, and political leader. A defender of the rights of South African blacks, Plaatje founded and edited (1901–08) the first newspaper in his native Tswana language, the Tswana *Gazette,* and was the first secretary-general (1912) of the South African Native National Congress (later, the African National Congress). He tried in vain to get native South African issues discussed at the Paris Peace Conference (1919) and traveled throughout Europe, Canada, and the United States to describe the plight of the blacks of South Africa, a topic he had written about in *Native Life in South Africa* (1915). Hoping to preserve native traditional language and culture, he wrote, in English, *Sechuana Proverbs and Their European Equivalents* (1916) and *The Sechuana Phonetic Reader* (1916; with Daniel Jones). His historical novel, *Mhudi* (written 1919; published 1930; new ed. 1975), was the first published novel written in English by a black South African. His selected writings, in English, were published in 1997. ▪ See biography by Brian Willan (1984).

PLANCK, MAX KARL ERNST LUDWIG (1858–1947), German physicist. Planck studied at the universities of Berlin and Munich (Ph.D. 1879) and taught at the University of Berlin (1891–1928). Though essentially a conservative scientist, he began the modern age in physics with his development of the quantum theory (1900). Investigating black-body radiation, he proposed that energy is released not continuously, as expected in classical physics, but in energy groups called quanta, multiples of an elementary quantity, now known as Planck's constant (an expression of the ratio between quantum size and frequency). Though at first rejected, his work was later recognized as extremely important, and he was awarded the 1918 Nobel Prize for Physics. Other physicists in the 1920s used and elaborated Planck's crucial work to elucidate previously unexplained atomic phenomena. ▪ See his *Scientific Autobiography and Other Papers* (Eng. trans. 1949) and J. L. Heilbron, *The Dilemmas of an Upright Man* (1986).

PLANTE, JACQUES JOSEPH (1929–1986), Canadian ice-hockey player. Plante overcame asthma in his youth to become an outstanding goalkeeper. The best years of his long career were with the Montreal Canadiens (1952–62); he helped them to win five consecutive Stanley Cup championships (1956–60). Plante won the Vezina Trophy as the league's top goalie six times, was a member of six All-Star teams, and in 1962 was named Most Valuable Player in the National Hockey League (NHL)—an unusual honor for a goalie. He was known as "the Mask" after he became the first goaltender in the NHL to wear a protective face mask on a regular basis (1959). It subsequently became standard gear for goalies. ▪ See biography by Andy O'Brien (1973).

PLATH, SYLVIA (1932–1963), U.S. poet. A precocious child whose first poem was published when she was 8, Plath graduated from Smith College (1955) and won a Fulbright scholarship to study at Cambridge (1955–57). Her two volumes of intensely introspective and vivid poetry, *The Colos-sus* (1960) and *Ariel* (1965), helped set the confessional tone of American poetry in the 1960s. She also wrote an autobiographical novel about a nervous breakdown, *The Bell Jar* (1963), which appeared under the pseudonym Victoria Lucas shortly before Plath committed suicide at age 30. Her correspondence, edited by her mother, appeared as *Letters Home* (1975). Her *Collected Poems* (1981, Pulitzer Prize) and *Journals* (1982) were edited by her husband, the poet Ted Hughes. Her *Unabridged Journals* were published in 2000. ▪ See studies by Eileen M. Aird (1973), Edward Butsher (1976), J. Kroll (1976), and Carolyn King Barnard (1978), and Anne Stevenson, *Bitter Fame* (1989).

PLAYER, GARY (1935–   ), South African golfer. A leading competitor in the 1960s and early 1970s, Player won every one of the four major titles at least once. A small and slightly built man, he proved that golf was as much a game of fitness and finesse as of power. He won the British Open 3 times (1959, 1968, 1974), the U.S. Professional Golfers' Association title twice (1962, 1972), the U.S. Open (1965), and the Masters 3 times (1961, 1974, 1978). In addition, he won the South African Open 13 times and the Australian Open 6 times. ▪ See his autobiography (1974: with Floyd Thatcher).

PLAZA LASSO, GALO (1906–1987), Ecuadorian political leader. The son of a former president of Ecuador, Plaza studied in the United States before entering politics as a liberal democrat in 1937. He served as ambassador to Washington and delegate to the San Francisco conference on the United Nations (1945). Plaza was president of Ecuador from 1948 to 1952, an unprecedented period of domestic peace and prosperity, after which he became active in international diplomacy as a U.N. mediator in Lebanon, the Belgian Congo, and Cyprus. He served as secretary-general of the Organization of America States from 1968 to 1975. He wrote *Latin America Today and Tomorrow* (1971).

PLEKHANOV, GEORGI VALENTINOVICH (1856–1918), Russian social philosopher and historian. Plekhanov severed ties with the Russian populists (1879) because of his opposition to their terrorist tactics and left Russia (1880). In exile in Geneva he developed the social theories that are considered the foundation of Russian Marxism. He was a founder of the first Russian Marxist revolutionary organization, the League for the Emancipation of Labor (1883), and helped organize the Russian Social Democratic Labor party (1898). He collaborated (1900) with V. I. Lenin in publishing the newspaper *Iskra* ("The Spark"). Plekhanov's notion that socialism could take hold in Russia only after capitalism and industrialization were well developed formed the nucleus of menshevik thinking after the 1903 split between mensheviks and bolsheviks (though he intermittently supported bolshevik leader Lenin after that date). He returned to Russia at the time of the February (1917) revolution but was isolated and harassed when the bolsheviks seized power in October (1917) and died in a Finnish tuberculosis sanatorium. ▪ See his *Fundamental Problems of Marxism* (Eng. trans. 1929), *History of Russian Social Thought* (Eng. trans. 1938), and biography (1963) and study by Samuel Baron (1995).

PLISETSKAYA, MAYA (1925–   ), Soviet ballerina. Plisetskaya was born to a Jewish family in Moscow. She studied at the Bolshoi Ballet School, made her debut at age 11, and joined the Bolshoi troupe (1943) during World War II. She was acclaimed for her fluid, expressive style, and after the retirement (1962) of Galina Ulanova, succeeded her as the Bolshoi's prima ballerina. Plisetskaya was famous for her role in *Swan Lake;* she also danced in *Romeo and Juliet, Raymonda, The Sleeping Beauty,* and in contemporary ballets. She appeared in ballet films, such as *Master of the Russian Ballet* (1954) and *Vernal Floods* (1975); Plisetskaya choreographed *Anna Karenina* (1972), then appeared in the film adaptation (1974). She toured extensively in the West and continued dancing at galas into her seventies. She founded the Maya Plisetskaya International Ballet Competition in St. Petersburg (1994).

PLYUSHCH, LEONID (1939–   ), Soviet Ukrainian dissident. At age 19, while studying mathematics, Plyushch began an independent study of philosophy, particularly the classics of Marxism. His writings, circulated unofficially in *samizdat* (self-published) form, stressed the gap between socialist theory and the practices of the socialist state. He also protested the suppression of Ukrainian culture by Soviet authorities, and treated such varied topics as Ukrainian poetry, Tolstoyism and scientific revolution, and Dostoevsky and Marx. Plyushch was dismissed from his post at the Cybernetics Institute and was arrested on charges of anti-Soviet agitation (1972). Declared insane, he was confined to a special psychiatric hospital for three years, where his compulsory treatment involved forced medication. His case sparked considerable protest. Plyushch was discharged and permitted to emigrate to France in 1976: he became a French citizen in 1981. In the West, he criticized Soviet policies, particularly the abuse of psychiatry, while continuing to identify as a Marxist-Leninist theoretician. ■ See his autobiography, *History's Carnival* (Eng. trans. 1979).

PODHORETZ, NORMAN (1930–   ), U.S. editor. The son of a Brooklyn milkman, Podhoretz earned undergraduate degrees at Columbia and the Jewish Theological Seminary (1950) and studied at Cambridge (M.A. 1952). Returning home, he became enmeshed in New York City's literary intelligentsia and began writing for *Commentary,* an influential Jewish monthly. He attracted attention by panning a Saul Bellow novel. After military service (1953–55), Podhoretz joined the *Commentary* staff and published reviews in various publications, again winning notice for a negative review, this time of a Nelson Algren novel. At age 30, he became the editor of *Commentary* (1960–95), attracting such contributors as Irving Howe, Hannah Arendt, Lionel Trilling, and Hans Morgenthau, and reinforcing the magazine's liberal

image by serializing Paul Goodman's *Growing Up Absurd.* Distressed at student unrest, racial conflict, and anti-Semitism, Podhoretz moved to the right politically in the mid-1960s. In the decades that followed he took stands against busing, feminist causes, gay rights, and U.S. social programs. In 1982 he criticized Pres. Ronald Reagan as not sufficiently hostile to communism, *The Present Danger* (1980) and *Why We Were in Vietnam* (1982) set forth his own position against communism. He also wrote *The Bloody Crossroads: Where Literature and Politics Meet* (1986). ■ See *Making It* (1968), his controversial autobiography; *Breaking Ranks: A Political Memoir* (1979), a chronicle of Podhoretz's political evolution; *Ex-Friends* (1999), an account of his falling-out with prominent New York intellectuals; and *My Love Affair with America* (2000).

PODOLOFF, MAURICE (1890–1985), Russian-born U.S. sports administrator. A graduate of the Yale Law School (1915), Podoloff was the head of the American Hockey League and the Basketball Association of America before becoming the first president of the National Basketball Association (NBA; 1949–63). Under his leadership professional basketball became a major sport in the United States.

POHL, FREDERIK (1919–   ), U.S. science-fiction writer. A native of Brooklyn, New York, Pohl was a charter member (1938) of the Futurians. a literary group composed of politically radical science-fiction fans that included such future luminaries as Isaac Asmiov. James Blish, and Cyril Kornbluth. After service in the air force during World War II, he worked as a literary agent, edited the *Star Science Fiction Stories* series for Ballantine Books (1953–59), and edited the journals *Galaxy* and *If* (both, 1961–69). Recognized as an inventor of "sociological science fiction," he collaborated with Kornbluth on several works, including the satirical anti-utopian novel *The Space Merchants* (1952) and the award-winning short story "The Meeting" (1972). His other novels included *Man Plus* (1976), *JEM* (1979), the "Heechee trilogy" (*Gateway,* 1977; *Beyond the Blue Event Horizon,* 1980; *Heechee Rendezvous,* 1984), *Chernobyl: A Novel* (1987), *The Day the Martians Came* (1988), *The Other End of Time* (1996), *The Siege of Eternity* (1997), and *O Pioneer* (1998). He also wrote numerous other short stories, edited important anthologies, and served as an editor at Bantam Books (1973–79). ■ See his memoirs, *The Way the Future Was* (1978).

POINCARÉ, RAYMOND (1860–1934), French political leader. Poincaré was born in Lorraine (lost to Germany when he was 10) studied law at the Sorbonne in Paris, and was an attorney before his election to parliament in 1887. A conservative nationalist who favored preparedness and defensive alliances, he solidified ties with Britain and Russia during his first premiership (1912–13). He served as president of France during the World War I era (1913–20) and was premier three times after the war. When the Germans defaulted on their postwar reparations, Premier Poincaré occupied the Ruhr in 1923; following a 1926 financial crisis, he restored fiscal responsibility and confidence. He retired to Lorraine in 1929 to write his ten-volume *Memoirs* (1926–33; Eng. trans., 4 vols., 1926–31). ■ See the study by Gordon Wright (1942) and biography by J.F.V. Keiger (1997).

POIRET, PAUL (1879–1944), French fashion designer. Apprenticed to an umbrella maker, Poiret used leftover scraps of silk to make miniature ensembles. By age 17 he was working for the couturier Jacques Doucet; he soon began designing stage costumes. After designing (1900–04) for the House of Worth, he opened his own firm, becoming (1908) the first designer to do business in the Champs-Elysées section of Paris. Over the next 15 years he became Paris' fashion king, introducing exciting innovative designs and using fabrics created from designs by Raoul Dufy, Henri Matisse, and other painters. Poiret waged "war upon the corset," and he popularized exotic oriental styles. His influence diminished after 1914, when the simpler designs of Coco Chanel and others set the trend. ■ See his autobiography, *My First Fifty Years* (1931), and study by Palmer White (1973).

POITIER, SIDNEY (1927–), U.S. film actor and director. Born in Miami and raised in the Bahamas, Poitier began his acting career after World War II with the American Negro Theater in New York. He established a strong film presence as the young priest in *Cry, the Beloved Country* (1952). He won an Academy Award as the footloose handyman in *Lilies of the Field* (1963), and became the first black superstar of American film. His other popular movies included *The Defiant Ones* (1958), *A Raisin in the Sun* (1961), *Guess Who's Coming to Dinner* (1967), and *In the Heat of the Night* (1967). Poitier directed *Buck and the Preacher* (1971), *Uptown Saturday Night* (1974), and *Stir Crazy* (1980) He also starred in the TV film *Mandela and de Klerk* (1997). ■ See his autobiographies, *This Life* (1980) and *The Measure of the Man* (2000), and William Hoffman, *Sidney* (1971).

POKROVSKY, MIKHAIL NIKOLAYEVICH (1868–1932), Soviet historian. A graduate of Moscow University (1891), Pokrovsky joined the Bolshevik party in 1905 and became chairman of the Moscow Soviet after the October revolution (1917). He was the first to rewrite Russian history from a Marxist viewpoint (see his *History of Russia from the Earliest Times to the Rise of Commercial Capitalism*, Eng. trans. 1931), and he served as deputy commissar of education and rector of the Institute of Red Professors, a Marxist training school for teachers. Pokrovsky's work was later (1936) declared anti-Stalinist and anti-Leninist. Translations of his essays are in *Russia in World History* (1970).

POLANYI, JOHN C. (1929–), German-born Canadian chemist. The son of noted chemist Michael Polanyi, John C. Polanyi was raised in the United Kingdom, studied at the University of Manchester (Ph.D. 1952), and taught at the University of Toronto (1956–). He developed a technique known as infrared chemiluminescence, which enabled scientists to study chemical reactions by analyzing infrared light emitted when molecules join to form new substances. His work complemented that of Dudley R. Herschbach and Yuan T. Lee, and the three scientists shared the 1986 Nobel Prize in Chemistry for developing a new field of chemical research, reaction dynamics. Polanyi's work also influenced the development of chemical lasers. He was an advocate of nuclear arms control and was the founding chairman of the Canadian Pugwash Group (1960–78).

POLANYI, KARL PAUL (1886–1964), Austrian-U.S. economic historian. A political radical who was banished from the Austro-Hungarian Empire, Polanyi received a law degree from the University of Kolozsvar (1909). He emigrated from Austria to Britain (1933), where he taught at Oxford and the University of London during the 1930s. Thereafter, he taught at various institutions in the United States, including Columbia University (1947–53). His work shed light on the origins, principles, and theory of economic and social institutions. In his important book *The Great Transformation* (1944), Polanyi attacked economic liberalism and its theoretical bases, and characterized 19th-century laissez-faire capitalism as a passing, isolated phenomenon in history. His historical analysis of market economies also contributed to the understanding of nonmarket economies. Other books included *Essays in Economic Anthropology* (1965) and *The Livelihood of Man* (1977).

POLING, DANIEL (1884–1968), U.S. Protestant religious leader. Called an exponent of "muscular Christianity," Poling energetically espoused conservative political and social causes. He campaigned for Prohibition in his youth, served as pastor of New York City's Marble Collegiate Reform Church (1923–29), and in the 1920s gave popular radio talks of a sentimental and down-to-earth nature. Poling opposed religious pacifism during the 1930s and was a staunch anticommunist and supporter of the Vietnam War effort in the 1950s and 1960s. He edited the *Christian Herald* (1925–65), wrote numerous religious books, and served as president of the World's Christian Endeavor Union. Invited (1936) to become pastor of the Philadelphia Temple Baptist Church—a great honor, since he was not a Baptist—he accepted, eventually becoming rebaptized. During World War II, Poling headed (1942) the interventionist faction at the Baptist Convention.

POLLARD, FRITZ (Frederick Douglass Pollard; 1894–1986), U.S. football player. A speedy and agile 5-foot, 9-inch, 165-pound athlete at Brown University, Pollard was the first African-American All-American halfback (1916), the first African American to play in the Rose Bowl (1916), and the first to be inducted into the College Football Hall of Fame (1954). One of the original stars in the National Football

League, Pollard was also the first African-American coach in the league (Akron, 1920). After retiring (1926), he was a college coach (Lincoln University), businessman, and publisher. ▪ See biography by John W. Carroll (1992).

POLLOCK, JACKSON (1912–1956), U.S. artist. Pollock, a Wyoming-born student of Thomas Hart Benton at the Art Students League of New York (1929–31), gave up his easel and brush in 1947 to challenge conventional methods and values of painting. Influenced by the surrealist idea of "automatic painting," he began dripping his colors in swirls and labyrinths onto huge canvases. This was called "action painting." and despite widespread contemporary hostility to "Jack the Dripper," the technique represented the first major change in pictorial style since cubism, and Pollock came to be recognized as the most important abstract-expressionist painter. He was married to artist Lee Krasner. ▪ See studies by Alberto Bignani (Eng. trans. 1971) and Elizabeth Frank (1983); Jeffrey Potter, *To a Violent Grave* (1985); and biographies by Deborah Solomon (1987) and B. H. Friedman (1995).

POL POT (Saloth Sar; 1928–1998), Kampuchean (Cambodian) political leader. The son of a peasant, Pol Pot studied at a technical school in Phnom Penh, joined the clandestine Communist party (1946), and studied electronics in Paris (1950–53). After returning home, he was a journalist and a schoolteacher and served as secretary of the Cambodian Communist party (from 1963). He organized the Khmer Rouge guerrilla force (1963), an army that grew dramatically after Prince Sihanouk was ousted from power and the U.S. and Vietnamese forces invaded the country (1970). After capturing Phnom Penh (April 1975) the revolutionary forces attempted to create a new society by emptying cities, rooting out Western influences and European-trained intellectuals, destroying temples and pagodas, reestablishing agrarian society, and setting up huge work camps. Although most observers estimated that 3 to 4 million people died during the upheaval, government officials claimed that the figure was 20,000 to 30,000. Pol Pot served as premier from 1976 until Jan. 19, 1979, when his government was overthrown by a Vietnamese invasion force. Though charged with genocide and sentenced to death in absentia by the new government, he maintained the backing of China and attempted to overthrow the government as head of a guerrilla army. After a comprehensive peace plan for Cambodia was signed in 1991, many Khmer Rouge soldiers accepted offers of amnesty and the movement was severely weakened. In 1997 the leadership split and Pol Pot was accused of crimes against humanity by his former followers and placed under house arrest for life. He reportedly died of a heart attack in a jungle hideout. ▪ See David P. Chandler, *Brother Number One* (1992; rev. ed. 1999).

POMPIDOU, GEORGES JEAN RAYMOND (1911–1974), French political leader. Born in the Auvergne region, where his father was a professor of Spanish, Pompidou was a brilliant student. In 1944, after 10 years of teaching classics in preparatory schools, he made the acquaintance of Gen. Charles de Gaulle, whose trusted aide and confidant he remained for 25 years. In 1954 Pompidou joined the Rothschild bank, rising to become its director. After de Gaulle returned to power (1958). Pompidou helped draft the constitution of the Fifth Republic. In 1961 he was sent by Pres. de Gaulle to negotiate a truce with the Algerian rebels, and after its ratification he was appointed to lead the government. Despite his lack of parliamentary experience, Pompidou as premier (1962–68) was a pragmatic, forceful administrator, and as president (1969–74) he continued many of de Gaulle's policies. A bon vivant and man of culture, Pompidou wrote literary studies on Racine, Taine, and Baudelaire. ▪ See Philippe Alexandre, *The Duel: de Gaulle and Pompidou* (Eng. trans. 1972) and Serge Bernstein and Jean-Pierre Rioux, *The Pompidou Years, 1969–1974* (Eng. trans. 2000).

PONS, LILY (Alice Josephine Pons; 1904–1976), French-born U.S. opera singer. Renowned for her charm and glamour as well as for her brilliant coloratura voice—she had a range of two and a half octaves—Pons became an overnight sensation at her debut in *Lucia di Lammermoor* at New York's Metropolitan Opera (1931). Best known for her performances in the operas of Bellini, Donizetti, and the French school, she was a stellar attraction at the Metropolitan for 25 seasons. Singing the title role of Delibes' *Lakmé*, she was the first soprano in 50 years to reach the high F in "The Bell Song" that was originally intended. ▪ See study edited by James A. Drake and Kristin B. Ludecke (1999).

PONTOPPIDAN, HENRIK (1857–1943), Danish novelist. In his youth Pontoppidan was an idealistic Tolstoyan and tried to live the life of a country peasant. Politically radical, he expressed anticlericalism and his indignation at social injustice in a series of naturalistic novel cycles. *The Promised Land* (3 vols., 1891–95; Eng. trans. 1896), *Lykke-Per* (8 vols., 1898–1904), *and De Dødes Rige* (5 vols., 1912–16) are his major works; they described, with irony and growing pessimism, Danish life and national character. Regarded as Denmark's greatest novelist, he shared the Nobel Prize for Literature in 1917 with his compatriot K. A. Gjellerup. ▪ See study by P. M. Mitchell (1979).

PONZI, CHARLES (1877?–1949), Italian-born swindler. Ponzi emigrated to Canada as a youth, and later to the United States. During World War I he established the Securities Exchange Co. in Boston, declaring that vast profits could be made from redeeming foreign coupons. Subscribers who flocked to Ponzi's office doubled their investment in 90 days and regarded Ponzi as a financial genius and hero. Rumors of insolvency were quelled (1920) when Ponzi paid investment plus interest to all investors and served coffee and hot dogs to those who waited in line. But the next month an investigation revealed that no foreign exchanges had ever taken place and that dividends had simply been paid out of subscriptions. Ponzi was imprisoned and upon his release (1934) was arrested as an undesirable alien and deported to Italy. He emigrated to Brazil shortly before World War II broke out, and died there in poverty. ▪ See biography by Donald H. Dunn (1975).

POOLE, ERNEST COOK (1880–1950), U.S. journalist and novelist. After years of experience living and working with New York slum dwellers and Chicago stockyard workers, Poole produced a series of articles on urban life for *McClure's* and *Colliers* magazines (1903). His bestselling novel, *The Harbor* (1915), a story about the Brooklyn waterfront that critics called one of the outstanding American proletarian novels, was also based on personal experience. Poole was a correspondent in Russia, France, and Germany before and during World War I. He returned to Russia (1917) to report on village life after the revolution, and his articles were later republished in *The Dark People* (1918) and *The Village* (1918). His novel of New York life, *His Family,* won a 1917 Pulitzer Prize. ▪ See his autobiography, *The Bridge* (1940).

POPA, VASKO (1922–1991), Yugoslav poet. Considered one of the major post–World War II European poets, Popa, a literary editor, was best known for his collections *Crust* (1952), *Field of Sleeplessness* (1956), *Poems* (1956), and *Secondary Sky* (1968). His unconventional and exciting poetry, influenced by French surrealism, draws on the language and imagery of Serbian folk tradition to create universal symbols and new myths. Concise and curt, his verse is characterized by striking metaphors and is most often concerned with the universal themes of love, death, and the cosmos. English translations of his work are in *Collected Poems: 1943–1976* (1978), *Homage to the Lame Wolf* (1979), and *Collected Poems* (1997).

POPE, JOHN RUSSELL (1874–1937), U.S. architect. A graduate of Columbia University (1894) who also studied in Rome and Paris, Pope established his own architectural firm in 1900 and designed a number of major public commissions in a neoclassical style. His National Archives Building (1935) in Washington. D.C., was praised by Pres. Herbert Hoover as "an expression of the American soul." Pope also designed the Jefferson Memorial (1943) and the National Gallery (1941) in Washington, D.C., both of which were completed after the architect's death. ▪ See Royal Cortissoz, *The Architecture of John Russell Pope* (3 vols., 1924–30) and study by Steven Bedford (1998).

POPLE, JOHN A. (1925–   ), British mathematician. Pople studied at Cambridge (M.A. 1950, Ph.D. 1951) and taught at Carnegie-Mellon University, Pittsburgh, Pennsylvania (1964–91), and Northwestern University, Evanston, Illinois (1993–   ). Although he never received a degree in chemistry, Pople became a pioneer in the field of quantum chem-

istry by developing a computer program called Gaussian (1970). This enabled scientists to apply quantum calculations in order to rapidly analyze complex molecular processes. The program, which was eventually used by chemists around the world, was particularly important in the design of new drugs Pople shared the 1998 Nobel Prize in Chemistry (with Walter Kohn) for the development of his computational methods.

POPPER, SIR KARL (1902–1994), Austrian-born British philosopher. Popper studied psychology (Ph.D. 1928) and taught philosophy at Canterbury University College in New Zealand (1937–45) and at the London School of Economics (1945–69). The positivists of the Vienna Circle sponsored publication of his first book, *The Logic of Scientific Discovery* (1934: Eng. trans. 1959), but he rejected their view that scientists further knowledge strictly by deducing generalizations from empirical observation. Popper argued that scientific method begins with imaginative theorizing, and that scientists must then make strenuous efforts to falsify their theories. In his view, this crucial step—testing a theory's "falsifiability"—distinguishes scientific method from other kinds of inquiry. A scholar of broad erudition, he presented his ideas in relation to the social sciences in *The Open Society and Its Enemies* (2 vols., 1945) and *The Poverty of Historicism* (1957), in which he attacked determinism, collectivism, and Marxist theory. Popper discussed how knowledge evolves in *Objective Knowledge: An Evolutionary Approach* (1972) and linked mental and physical aspects of human life in *The Self and Its Brain* (1977; with J.C. Eccles). He also wrote *Postscript to the Logic of Scientific Discovery* (3 vols., 1982–83). ▪ See his intellectual autobiography, *Unended Quest* (1976); Paul A. Schilpp. ed., *The Philosophy of Karl Popper* (2 vols., 1974); studies by Bryan Magee (1973) and Anthony O'Hear (1980); and biography by Malachi H. Hacohen (2000).

PORSCHE, FERDINAND (1875–1951), German automotive engineer. A visionary, Porsche sought to make the automobile accessible to the masses; he designed and built the first Volkswagen or "people's car" (1936). Private companies could not afford to market the car at a salable price, but the Nazi government was set to mass-produce the auto, Europe's answer to Ford's Model T, when the onset of World War II altered production plans. After the war, the Volkswagen became one of the world's most popular cars. Porsche also designed the sports car bearing his name.

PORTER, COLE (1891–1964), U.S. composer and lyricist. Born into a wealthy Indiana family. Porter began writing songs while he was a student at Yale and Harvard. After serving in the French Foreign Legion during World War I, he studied music in Paris, lived a cosmopolitan society life on the continent, and began to contribute songs to musical plays and revues. His sophisticated Depression-era Broadway musicals (including *The Gay Divorcee,* 1932; *Anything*

Goes, 1934; *Jubilee,* 1935; *Leave It to Me,* 1938) and the Hollywood films (including *Born to Dance,* 1936 and *Rosalie,* 1937) contained such urbane and witty and graceful songs as "Night and Day," "I Get a Kick Out of You," "You're the Top," "Begin the Beguine," "Just One of Those Things," "My Heart Belongs to Daddy," and "I've Got You Under My Skin." In spite of a serious horse-riding accident (1937) in which both of his legs were crushed, leaving him in constant pain for the rest of his life, he wrote the shows *Kiss Me, Kate* (1948), *Can-Can* (1953), and *Silk Stockings* (1955) and the movie *High Society* (1956). ■ See his autobiography (1965): Robert Kimball, ed., *The Complete Lyrics* (1983); George Eells, *The Life That Late He Led* (1967); and biographies by Charles Schwartz (1977) and William McBrien (1998).

PORTER, ELIOT (1901–1990), U.S. photographer. As a youth, Porter's hobbies were bird photography and nature study, interests that remained with him as he studied at Harvard (M.D. 1929) and taught biochemistry at Harvard and Radcliffe College (1929–39). Encouraged by Alfred Stieglitz, Dorothea Lange, and Ansel Adams, he gave up his academic career and became a full-time freelance photographer in 1939. A pioneer in the use of color film, he established his reputation as a bird photographer and later was acclaimed for his contemplative, detailed color images of the wilderness. He was an ardent conservationist and he donated many of his works to the Sierra Club, which reproduced them in posters and in books to publicize the cause of preserving the natural environment. His numerous books of photography included *In Wilderness Is the Preservation of the World* (1962), *Galapagos—The Flow of Wilderness* (1968), *The Tree Where Man Was Born: The African Experience* (1972), *Birds of North America* (1972), and *Eliot Porter's Southwest* (1985).

PORTER, GEORGE, BARON PORTER OF LUDDENHAM (1920–   ), British physical chemist. Working with his professor, Ronald G. W. Norrish, while a graduate student at Cambridge (1949–55), Porter developed flash photolysis. This technique allowed investigation and measurement of extremely rapid chemical reactions by disturbing the equilibrium through short, high-intensity pulses of energy. He applied this technique to research in molecular biology, particularly the hemoglobin-oxygen reacton and the behavior of chlorophyll, and shared the 1967 Nobel Prize for Chemistry with Norrish and West German scientist Manfred Eigen. Porter was a professor at the University of Sheffield (1955–66) and director of the Royal Institution of Great Britain (1966–85). He wrote *Chemistry for the Modern World* (1962).

PORTER, HAL (1911–1984), Australian novelist, playwright, and poet. Porter, a schoolmaster, began writing in the 1930s, a time when Australian fiction stressed social realism and focused on rural life. Primarily a stylist, Porter broke

with that tradition, introducing elements of the grotesque and fantastic into poetry volumes such as *The Hexagon* (1957) and novels, including *A Handful of Pennies* (1958), *The Tilted Cross* (1961), and *The Right Thing* (1971). His short stories appeared in *Selected Stories* (1971) and *Fredo Fuss Love Life* (1974). Porter's fiction, which he called "unavoidably Australian," probed subtle class distinctions beneath the Australian veneer of egalitarianism. He also wrote three highly acclaimed autobiographical works, *The Watcher on the Cast-Iron Balcony* (1964), *The Paper Chase* (1966), and *The Extra* (1975). ■ See *The Portable Hal Porter* (1978) and biography by Mary Lord (1993).

PORTER, KATHERINE ANNE (1890–1980), U.S. short-story writer and novelist. After working as a reporter and bit-part actress, Porter published *Flowering Judas* (1930), which was praised for its spare style and psychological sensitivity. Her best-known works, *Pale Horse, Pale Rider* (1939) and *Ship of Fools* (1962)—the latter a great popular and financial success and the basis for a 1965 film—confront the problems of mania and moral failure, but Porter avoided sensationalism and coarseness, concentrating instead on the "thumbprint" of individual characters. *The Days Before* (1952) contained personal essays, articles, and book reviews. *Collected Stories* appeared in 1965 and won both the Pulitzer Prize and the National Book Award for fiction. *The Never-Ending Wrong* (1977), her last published work, dealt with the case of Nicola Sacco and Bartolomeo Vanzetti, convicted anarchists of the 1920s. ■ See Enrique Hank Lopez, *Conversations with Katherine Ann Porter* (1981), and biography by Joan Givner (1984).

PORTER, RODNEY ROBERT (1917–1985), British biochemist. Educated at Cambridge University, Porter worked at the National Institute for Medical Research (1949–60) and taught at London's St. Mary's Hospital Medical School (1960–67) and at Oxford University (from 1967). It was at the medical school that Porter conducted major research into antibodies, using an enzyme to split a molecule of gamma globulin and determining that it is composed of several chains of components. For this and related work on antibodies, he shared the 1972 Nobel Prize for Physiology or Medicine with Gerald M. Edelman.

PORTINARI, CÁNDIDO (1903–1962), Brazilian painter and muralist. With little formal education, Portinari was apprenticed to a Rio de Janeiro artist at age 15. He trained at the National Fine Arts School and supported himself by painting portraits before receiving a grant to study in Paris (1928). Early paintings, such as *The Hill* (1933) and *Coffee* (1935), used dark earth tones to depict scenes from Brazilian life; his later work was increasingly geometric and abstract. Beginning in the late 1930s, he treated historical and biblical subjects in large-scale murals, Portmnari was commissioned to fresco Rio de Janeiro's Ministry of Education (1936–45). He created four murals of Hispanic history (1941–42) for the Hispanic Foundation of the Library of Congress in Washington, D.C., and two panels, *War and Peace* (1953–54), for the United Nations General Assembly Building in New York. He also created ceramic tile murals. ■ See biography by Josias Leão (1940).

POST, EMILY (Emily Price; 1873–1960), U.S. writer and authority on etiquette. A national institution whose name was synonymous with good manners and proper social behavior, Post published her guide, *Etiquette in Society, in Business, in Politics and at Home,* in 1922. Aimed at ordinary people, the book scorned pretension, minimized formality-for-formality's-sake, and insisted that consideration for others was the basic rule of etiquette. It provided a standard of behavior for the American public, and it was a phenomenal success, going through 10 editions and 90 printings by the time of her death, Post also wrote a daily syndicated column that appeared in more than 200 newspapers and ran a national network radio program. ■ See Edwin Post, *Truly Emily Post* (1961).

POST, MARJORIE MERRIWEATHER (1887–1973), U.S. financier and philanthropist. At age 10, Post began attending board meetings of her father's company, the Postum Cereal Co. After he committed suicide (1914), she inherited the company. Although she was involved in making major decisions, she was represented by her husband on the board of directors, which would not admit women until 1936. Impressed by the possibilities of frozen food, Post acquired Clarence Birdseye's General Foods Co. and renamed Postum the General Foods Corp. (1929). She ruled high society for 40 years, with time out to accompany her third husband, Joseph E. Davies, when he served as ambassador to the Soviet Union (1936–38) and Belgium (1938–39). She lived lavishly, with a 50-room mansion in Palm Beach and a 316-foot yacht, and gave generously to such causes as the Red Cross, the Salvation Army, the Boy Scouts, Mount Vernon College, and C. W. Post College (named for her father). The actress Dina Merrill (1925–   ) was her daughter by her second husband, E. F. Hutton. ■ See William Wright, *Heiress* (1978), and Nancy Rubin, *American Empress* (1995).

POST, WILEY (1899–1935), U.S. aviator. Post worked as an oil driller, stunt parachutist, and exhibition and test pilot before becoming the private pilot of Oklahoma oilman F. C. Hall. He raced Hall's plane, the *Winnie Mae,* to victory in the Los Angeles–Chicago Bendix Trophy Race (1930) and (with navigator Harold Gatty) flew it around the world, via Britain. Russia, Siberia, and Alaska in the record time of 8 days, 15 hours, and 51 minutes (1931). The book by Post and Gatty, *Around the World in Eight Days* (1931), described the adventure. In 1933 Post repeated the journey alone, in 7 days, 18 hours, and 49 minutes, to become the first solo flyer to circle the globe. He was killed with his friend—and passenger—the humorist Will Rogers when his plane crashed near Point Barrow, Alaska.

POTOFSKY, JACOB SAMUEL (1894–1979), Russian-born U.S. labor leader. Potofsky emigrated to the United States with his family (1905) and worked as a "floor boy" in a Chicago men's clothing factory. He became involved in union activities, joined the Amalgamated Clothing Workers of America (ACWA) at its founding (1914), and served as chief aide to union president Sidney Hillman for 30 years (1916–46). As president of the ACWA (1946–72), Potofsky increased membership to 385,000 and gained a reputation as one of the nation's most socially conscious, innovative, and skillful union leaders.

POTTER, (HELEN) BEATRIX (1866–1943), British children's book author. Born into a wealthy London family, Potter had a solitary and repressed childhood. On holidays in the country she developed a love of wild animals, which years later, in the 1890s, she recorded in a series of illustrated stories she sent to a sick child. They were so well received that she privately produced two of them, *The Tale of Peter Rabbit* (1900) and *The Tailor of Gloucester* (1902). They were soon published commercially, became extremely popular, and were followed by a series of more than 25 additional books, including *The Tale of Squirrel Nutkin* (1903), *The Tale of Benjamin Bunny* (1904), *The Tale of Tom Kitten* (1907), *The Tale of the Flopsy Bunnies* (1909), and *Mrs. Tittlemouse* (1910). Simply written and illustrated with delicate watercolors, her stories unsentimentally described the lives and homes of her animal characters and were read by children—and their parents—throughout the world. ■ See *The Journals of Beatrix Potter, 1881–1897* (1966); Margaret Lane, *The Tale of Beatrix Potter* (rev. ed. 1968); and study by Judy Taylor, et al. (1987).

POULENC, FRANCIS (1899–1963), French composer. A member of the antiromantic group "The Six," Poulenc was influenced by Erik Satie. His directness, urbanity, and gallicism were apparent in works such as the ballet *Les Biches,* staged by Sergei Diaghilev in 1924, and in the satirical opera *Les Mamelles de Tirésias* ("The Breasts of Tiresias," 1947), based on a surrealistic play by Guillaume Apollinaire. His songs were among the century's finest. His later vocal works—such as the Mass (1937) for unaccompanied choir: *Figure humaine* ("The Human Face," 1942), written during the occupation of Paris (he was active in the French Resistance); and his masterpiece, the opera *Dialogues des Carmélites* (1957)—evidenced a profound humanity and strength of musical thought. ■ See his *My Friends and Myself* (Eng. trans. 1978); studies by Henri Hell (Eng. trans. 1959) and Pierre Bernac (Eng. trans. 1977); and biography by Benjamin Ivry (1996).

POULSEN, VALDEMAR (1869–1942), Danish electrical engineer. While working for the Copenhagen Telephone Co., Poulsen invented the telegraphone (1898), an electromagnetic device for recording human speech on steel wire that was the forerunner of modern magnetic tape recorders.

In 1903 he adapted an arc oscillator so that it could generate continuous radio waves. Known as the Poulsen arc, the device, when perfected, made possible long-wave radio broadcasting and wireless telephone transmissions.

POUND, EZRA (1885–1972), U.S. poet. A writer of great erudition, Pound undertook graduate studies at the University of Pennsylvania (MA. 1906) and claimed a knowledge of nine languages. Shipping out to Europe on a cattle boat (1908), he published several volumes of innovative poetry in Britain including *Personae* (1909), *Canzoni* (1911), and *Ripostes* (1912). Pound's style, which he called "imagism" (later "vorticism"), was characterized by staccato rhythms, austere imagery, and the incorporation of an occasional slang expression or Chinese ideogram. He also wrote creative translations of Greek tragedy, Anglo-Saxon epic, and Chinese poetry. As London correspondent of *Poetry* magazine, Pound befriended, encouraged, and materially aided some of the key literary figures of his day, including William Butler Yeats, T. S. Eliot, and James Joyce. The first volume of his epic lifetime work. *Cantos,* was published in Paris (1925). In 1925 he moved to Italy; during World War II he supported Italy's fascist and anti-Semitic policies in hundreds of radio broadcasts. Arrested in 1945 and charged with treason by U.S. authorities, he was found incompetent to stand trial and incarcerated for 12 years in a Washington, D.C., mental hospital. *His Pisan Cantos* (1945), written in a U.S. Army stockade, won the prestigious Bollingen Prize (1949). Released on the petition of friends in 1958, Pound spent his last years in exile in Italy. ■ See *The Letters of Ezra Pound and Wyndham Lewis* (1985); biographies by Charles Norman (1968), Noel Stock (1970; rev. ed. 1982), C. David Heymann (1976), and Alan Durant (1981); E. Fuller Torrey, *The Roots of Treason* (1984); and Humphrey Carpenter, *A Serious Character* (1988).

POUND, ROSCOE (1870–1964), U.S. jurist and botanist. The son of a judge, Pound achieved distinction both as a botanist (a rare lichen bears his name) and as a leading exponent of sociological jurisprudence. As professor at Harvard Law School (1910–47: dean, 1916–36) he held that law must be molded to society's needs. He wrote many books. including the five-volume *Jurisprudence* (1959). ■ See biography by Paul L. Sayre (1948) and studies by David Wigdor (1974) and N.E.H. Hull (1997).

POWELL, ADAM CLAYTON, JR. (1908–1972), U.S. political leader, In 1936 Powell succeeded his father as pastor of the Abyssinian Baptist Church in New York City's Harlem, the oldest and largest black congregation in the North. He also went into Democratic politics, serving in the U.S. House of Representatives for a quarter of a century (1945–67: 1969–70) and chairing the House Committee on Education and Labor (1960–67). A flamboyant and outspoken champion of civil rights, he was the most powerful African-American political leader in the United States and

had a leading role in the adoption of some 50 pieces of major social legislation. In 1966 he went to Bimini as a fugitive from a New York defamation and contempt judgment, and in 1967 he was denied his House seat for unbecoming conduct and misuse of funds. (The U.S. Supreme Court ruled in 1969 that the House had illegally barred Powell.) He was reseated for a final term in 1969 but was defeated in the 1970 primary election. ■ See his autobiography, *Adam by Adam* (1971); study by Neil Hickey and Ed Edwin (1965); biography by Charles V. Hamilton (1991); and Wil Haygood, *King of the Cats* (1993).

POWELL, ANTHONY (1905–2000), British novelist. Powell was a publisher, editor, and screenwriter. With *A Question of Upbringing* (1951), set in the 1920s at Eton and Oxford (where Powell himself was educated), he started a 12-volume series of novels, *A Dance to the Music of Time.* Wittily and with satirical skill, he wrote a complex and intricately plotted comedy of manners that chronicled the changes and social life of the British middle and upper classes. Among the titles in the series are *At Lady Molly's* (1957), *Casanova's Chinese Restaurant* (1960), and *Temporary Kings.* (1973). His four-volume autobiography, *To Keep the Ball Rolling,* was published as *Infants of the Spring* (1976), *Messengers of the Day* (1978), *Faces in My Time* (1980), and *The Strangers All Are Gone* (1982). Later works included the novel *The Fisher King* (1986), two volumes of literary criticism (*Miscellaneous Verdicts,* 1990; *Under Review,* 1994), and three volumes of his *Journals* (1995–97). ■ See studies by John D. Russell (1970) and Neil Brennan (1974).

POWELL, CECIL FRANK (1903–1969), British physicist. Educated at Cambridge (Ph.D. 1927), Powell did research involving the ionization process while he was on the faculty of the University of Bristol (1928–69). In an effort to circumvent the limitations of the Wilson Cloud Chamber, he developed and perfected (1939–45) a technique for studying charged particles that made use of photographic emulsions. The method proved effective both in high-altitude experiments involving cosmic rays and in observations of reactions generated by artificial particle accelerators. Results included Powell's discovery (1947) of the pi meson, or pion, which provided experimental confirmation for Hideki Yukawa's 1935 theory of nuclear structure. For this achievement Powell received the 1950 Nobel Prize for Physics. In the 1950s he was active in movements for peace and international scientific cooperation. *His Selected Papers* (1972) included a brief autobiography.

POWELL, COLIN LUTHER (1937–   ), U.S. military leader. The son of immigrants from Jamaica, Powell was raised in the South Bronx section of New York City and graduated from the City College of New York (CCNY; B.S. 1958). Having headed his college ROTC unit, he was commissioned in the U.S. Army upon graduation, served two tours of duty in Vietnam (1962–63, 1968–69), and became a career army officer. After earning an MBA degree from George Washington University (1971), he became a White House Fellow and subsequently served in a series of high-level command and executive department posts, including senior military assistant to the secretary of defense (1983–86). He was Pres. Ronald Reagan's national security adviser (1987–89) and was elevated to the rank of four-star general in 1989. As chairman of the Joint Chiefs of Staff (1989–93), he played a major role in the planning of the Persian Gulf War and became a highly respected and widely admired public figure. He retired from the army in 1993 as the highest-ranking African-American officer in U.S. history. Although urged by many, in 1995, to seek the Republican nomination for the U.S. presidency, he declined to run and subsequently served as U.S. secretary of state under Pres. George W. Bush (2001–   ). ▪ See his autobiography *My American Journey* (1995).

POWELL, EARL "BUD" (1924–1966), U.S. jazz pianist and composer. A pioneer of modern jazz, Powell was one of the great bebop pianists of the 1940s. His reputation was enhanced with his emotionally charged recordings and performances of the 1950s, which were noted for their incredibly fast tempos, lyric phrasings, and unpredictable tonalities. Powell's innovative career was interrupted several times due to a series of nervous breakdowns, and he left the United States for Paris (1959), where he was a major figure in the émigré jazz world. He died shortly after he returned to New York City. ▪ See Francis Paudras, *Dance of the Infidels* (Eng. trans. 1998).

POWELL, (JOHN) ENOCH (1912–1998), British political leader. Powell was a Cambridge University–trained classics scholar and a professor of Greek before his election to Parliament in 1950 as a right-wing Conservative. After serving as minister of health (1960–63) he made a bid for national leadership with demagogic speeches calling for a halt to nonwhite immigration to Britain. Resentful over the decline of empire and wealth, he also opposed British entry into the Common Market. He represented the Ulster Unionist Party in Parliament from 1974 to 1987. ▪ See studies by Andrew Roth (1970), Douglas E. Schoen (1977), and Roy Lewis (1979); biography by Robert Sheperd (1996); and Simon Heffer, *Like the Roman* (1998).

POWERS, FRANCIS GARY (1929–1977), U.S. spy pilot. While flying a U-2 high-altitude plane on a CIA reconnaissance mission over the Soviet Union, Powers was shot down by a Soviet long-range missile (May 1, 1960). The incident precipitated a major diplomatic crisis, and Soviet Premier Nikita Khrushchev canceled a scheduled summit conference with U.S. Pres. Dwight D. Eisenhower. Powers pleaded guilty to spying and was sentenced to three years in prison and seven in a labor camp. Released in exchange for convicted Soviet spy Rudolf Abel in 1962, he returned to the United States. The admission of U-2 reconnaissance flights

by Pres. Eisenhower and CIA director Allen Dulles, and the Powers-Abel exchange, in effect legitimized espionage as a tool of the intelligence trade. Powers later worked as a civilian pilot and died when the helicopter he piloted while reporting for a Los Angeles TV station crashed. ▪ See his *Operation Overflight* (1970; with Curt Gentry) and James B. Donovan, *Strangers on a Bridge* (1964).

PRADO Y UGARTECHE, MANUEL (1889–1967), Peruvian political leader. The son of a former Peruvian president, Prado earned an engineering degree, taught mathematics, and oversaw the family interests before being elected to the Chamber of Deputies (1919). An opponent of dictator Augusto Leguia, he was exiled (1921–32) but served as president of the Central Reserve Bank (1934–39) when he returned to Lima. He enjoyed popularity during his first term (1939–45) as a moderate president, but his second term (1956–62) coincided with a period of domestic crisis, and he was overthrown by the armed forces.

PRAMOEDYA ANANTA TOER (1925–   ), Indonesian writer. Pramoedya, the son of a school headmaster, graduated from the Radio Vocational School (1941) and worked for the Japanese news agency Domei during the World War II Japanese occupation (1942–45). After the war he joined the nationalist army fighting against the Dutch, edited the journal *Sadar*, and was imprisoned for his nationalist views (1947–49). After Indonesian independence (1949) he became a prominent writer and teacher and was closely associated with left-wing cultural and political movements. After the 1965 military coup led by Suharto, his house in Jakarta was burned down and he was imprisoned on the remote island of Buru (1965–79). He subsequently returned to Jakarta but remained under virtual house arrest until 1992. He wrote many works of fiction and nonfiction, notably the "Buru Quartet"—*This Earth of Mankind* (1980; Eng. trans. 1982), *A Child of All Nations* (1980; Eng. trans. 1982), *Footsteps* (1985; Eng. trans. 1995), and *House of Glass* (1988; Eng. trans. 1996)—a monumental fictional account of the birth of Indonesian nationalism. The works were composed orally while he was in prison because he was denied writing materials. They became best-sellers after they were finally published, but were quickly banned by the Suharto government. After the government fell (1998) he called for trials for all of those who committed crimes while serving under Suharto. ▪ See his memoir, *The Mute's Soliloquy* (1995; Eng. trans. 1999).

PRANDTL, LUDWIG (1875–1953), German physicist. Known as "the father of aerodynamics," Prandtl was a professor at Gottingen University (from 1904) and director of the Kaiser Wilhelm (later Max Planck) Institute for Fluid Mechanics (from 1925). His work on boundary layer theory and the nature of turbulent flow revolutionized the study of fluid mechanics. He established a world-renowned school of aerodynamics at Göttingen, developed the first German wind tunnel (1909), and did important research on airfoil theory. supersonic flow, and induced drag, which played a major role in the development of modern supersonic aircraft.

PRASAD, RAJENDRA (1884–1963), Indian nationalist. Prasad was born into an orthodox Hindu, middle-class, landowning, Bihari family. A successful lawyer, editor, and teacher, he devoted his life to the nationalist cause after he met its leader, Mahatma Gandhi, in 1917. He founded and wrote for several nationalist journals and was jailed often. Prasad held many posts, including president of the Indian National Congress party (1934, 1939, 1947) and head of the constituent assembly (1946–49), the body that completed the constitution of the republic of India. As independent India's first president (1950–62), he traveled widely in India and elsewhere in Asia. ■ See his *Autobiography* (Eng. trans. 1958) and biography by Kewal L. Panjabi (1960).

PRATOLINI, VASCO (1913–1991), Italian novelist and journalist. Pratolini was a manual laborer before pursuing a literary career, When he cofounded (1939) the magazine *Campo Marie,* he fell out of favor with the Fascist party. The magazine was shut down, and Pratolini joined underground antifascist activities. His proletarian novels, which depict class struggle, attempted to characterize the structure of Italian society and the family as a microcosm of that society. A major figure of the neorealist movement, he wrote *Naked Streets* (1944; Eng. trans. 1952), *A Tale of Poor Lovers* (1947; Eng. trans. 1949), and *Bruno Santini* (1963; Eng. trans. 1964). His trilogy, *Metello* (1955; Eng. trans. 1968), *The Waste* (1960), and *Allegory and Derision* (1966), constituted a narrative history of 20th-century Italy. ■ See his *Family Chronicle* (1960; Eng. trans. 1988) and study by Frank Rosengarten (1965).

PRATT, EDWIN JOHN (1883–1964), Canadian poet. The leading Canadian poet of his day, E. J. Pratt trained for the ministry and earned a Ph.D. (University of Toronto. 1916) in theology before turning to psychology and literature. He taught English at Toronto's Victoria College from 1919 to 1953. Writing as a Christian humanist, he created complex narrative poems that pitted humans against the forces of nature. A frequent theme was humankind's evolution from primitive beast to ethical and compassionate being. He established his reputation with *Titans* (1926), his third volume, which was followed by such poems as *The Titanic* (1935), Dunkirk (1941), and *Towards the Last Spike* (1952), a narrative about the Canadian Pacific Railroad. His best work, *Brébeuf and His Brethren* (1940), consisted of 12 books of blank verse relating the martyrdom of Jesuit missionaries among the Iroquois Indians. ■ See *Still Life, and Other Verse* (1943), his *Collected Poems* (1944 and 1958), and studies by Sandra Djwa (1974) and Robert G. Collins (1988).

PREBISCH, RAÚL (1901–1986), Argentine economist. While a professor of political economy at the University of Buenos Aires (1925–48), Prebisch served as director general of the Central Bank of Argentina (1935–43). He was executive secretary of the United Nation's Economic Commission for Latin America (1950–63) and secretary-general of the United Nations Conference on Trade and Development (UNCTAD: 1963–69). One of the most influential students of Third World economies, Prebisch contended that the contemporary terms of trade were detrimental to less developed countries and he was a major force behind the creation of the New International Economic Order. His books included *Change and Development* (Eng. trans. 1971).

PREGL, FRITZ (1869–1930), Austrian chemist, Pregl received a medical degree (1894) and taught medical chemistry at the University of Innsbruck (1910–13) and at his alma mater, the University of Graz (1913–30). When he attempted to investigate minute quantities of complex bile acids, he found standard research methods too unwieldy and he devised (1900–17) new procedures and specialized apparatus for the microanalysis of organic compounds. He received the 1923 Nobel Prize for Chemistry for this work.

PRELOG, VLADIMIR (1906–1998), Yugoslav-born Swiss organic chemist. Educated at Prague's Technical University (Ph.D. 1929), Prelog taught in Yugoslavia until the World War II German invasion (1941). He then emigrated to Switzerland and taught at the Federal Institute of Technology in Zurich (1942–76). His research in the field of stereochemistry resulted in rules for establishing whether the atoms of asymmetric molecules that contain carbon form right-handed or left-handed arrangements. Prelog used X-ray diffraction to solve the structure of several important antibiotics. Prelog shared the 1975 Nobel Prize for Chemistry with John Cornforth for his investigations of complex molecules. ■ See his *My 132 Semesters of Chemistry Studies* (1991).

PREMCHAND (Dhanpatrai Srivastava; 1880–1936), Indian writer. A pioneer of the modern Urdu and Hindi novel, Premchand (called Munshi) realistically described the social and political changes taking place in rural northern India during the first decades of the 20th century. Influenced by Mahatma Gandhi's ideology and later by socialism, he frequently described the abuses of British colonialism and the exploitation of the peasantry and untouchables. Many of his approximately 300 short stories and novels were considered seditious and were destroyed by British authorities. Among his best-known works were the novel *Gift of a Cow* (1936: Eng. trans. 1968) and the selected stories in *The World of Premchand* (Eng. trans. 1969), *Deliverance and Other Stories* (Eng. trans. 1988), *The Best of Premchand* (Eng. trans. 1997), and *Widows, Wives and Other Heroines* (Eng. trans. 1998). ■ See Robert O. Swan, *Munshi Premchand of Lamhi Village* (1969) and study by Govind N. Sharma (1978).

PREMINGER, OTTO (1905–1986), Austrian-born U.S. producer-director. Preminger studied law at the University of Vienna (LL.D. 1926), but preferred acting. He trained under Max Reinhardt, later joining his company and succeeding him as director of Vienna's Theater in der Josefstadt (1933). In 1935 he went to the United States, becoming a U.S. citizen in 1943. Following the success of his romantic mystery *Laura* (1944), Preminger landed a seven-year contract as a studio director for 20th Century-Fox. Then, as one of Hollywood's first important independent producer-directors, he helped to weaken Hollywood's studio system. He fought censorship, treated previously untouchable subjects, and defied blacklisting by openly hiring Dalton Trumbo as screenwriter for *Exodus* (1960). Preminger's films were noted for their moral complexity; many focused on such institutions as the military, the Congress, and the Catholic Church. They included *The Moon is Blue* (1953), *Anatomy of a Murder* (1959), *Advise and Consent* (1962), *The Cardinal* (1963), and *Hurry, Sundown* (1967). *Such Good Friends* (1972) and *The Human Factor* (1979) were later works. ■ See his autobiography (1977); Marion Mill Preminger, *All I Want Is Everything* (1957); and studies by Gerald Pratley (1971) and Willi Frischauer (1973).

PRENDERGAST, MAURICE BRAZIL (1859–1924), Canadian-born U.S. artist. With his brother Charles, who also became an artist, Prendergast worked his way to Europe on a cattle boat in 1886; he later made a trip to study in Paris, at the Académie Julian, and in Italy. A leading painter of his generation and one of the most advanced of the postimpressionists, he created the effect of pointillism with bright tapestries of color, such as *Central Park* (1901). *Promenade* (1914–15) was more abstract and wistful. He exhibited with The Eight at their influential 1908 show and at the controversial 1913 Armory Show in New York City. ■ See studies by H. H. Rhys (1960) and Richard Wattenmaker (1994).

PREOBRAZHENSKY, YEVGENY ALEKSEYEVICH (1886–1937), Soviet economist. Preobrazhensky joined the bolsheviks (1903), fought in the civil war, and emerged in 1920 as one of the three Communist party secretaries. The leading economic theorist (1923–27) of the "left opposition" (led by Leon Trotsky) within the party, he advocated the accelerated expansion of heavy industry. This was to be financed by forced savings in agriculture, as described in his theory of "primitive socialist accumulation." Although Joseph Stalin at first opposed his ideas and expelled Preobrazhensky from the party (1927), he adopted them after 1928. Preobrazhensky broke with Trotskyism, "confessed" his errors, and was readmitted to the party, but was arrested and shot during Stalin's 1937 purge. His most important works were *From NEP to Socialism* (Eng. trans. 1973), *The New Economics* (Eng. trans. 1965), and *The Crisis of Soviet Industrialization* (Eng. trans. 1979).

PRESLEY, ELVIS ARON (1935–1977), U.S. singer. A former truck driver from the South, a white singer who adopted the blues and the gyrations of black musicians,

Presley began a phenomenal career as the "king of rock and roll" with "Heartbreak Hotel." Released early in 1956, it eventually sold millions of copies. It was followed by "Hound Dog" and "Love Me Tender" (1956) and "All Shook Up" and "Don't Be Cruel" (1957). His manager, "Colonel" Tom Parker, turned down television and personal appearances in favor of recordings and films (such as *Love Me Tender*, 1957; *King Creole* and *Jailhouse Rock*, 1958), stage-managing every aspect of Presley's career including a ritual shearing of the ducktail hairstyle and celebrated sideburns when the singer was drafted into the army (1958). Presley's career waned in the 1960s. but he made a comeback with a Las Vegas appearance (1969) and a TV special (1970) that converted a second generation of fans. He recorded some 40 albums. In the decade following his death at age 42, fans continued to adulate the legendary Elvis. ■ See Albert Goldman, *Elvis* (1981); Jerry Hopkins, *Elvis* (1981); Priscilla Presley, *Elvis and Me* (1985); and the two-volume biography by Peter Guralnick, *Last Train to Memphis* (1994) and *Careless Love* (1999).

PRESTES, LUÍS CARLOS (1898–1990), Brazilian political leader. In 1924 Prestes, an army captain of engineers, led a mutiny against the government followed by an epic 18,000-mile, 2½-year march through the Brazilian interior, fighting a guerrilla war against government forces. The romantic revolutionary then went into exile, visited the Soviet Union (1931), joined the Communist party, and served as a Comintern agent before returning home to lead an abortive 1935 revolt. During the ensuing 30 years he was imprisoned (1935–45), amnestied, served in the Brazilian senate (1945–47), and outlawed again (1947–58: and after 1964), spending many years in underground communist politics as secretary-general of the party. Shortly after he returned to Brazil (1979), after eight years in Moscow, he was ousted from party leadership and was expelled from the party in 1984. ■ See Neill Macaulay, *The Prestes Column* (1974).

PRÉVERT, JACQUES (1900–1977), French poet and screenwriter. Briefly associated with the surrealists, Prévert wrote anarchic poetry that attacked authority and hypocrisy, but was tender and poignant in vignettes about love and human frailty. It was characterized by iconoclasm mixed with good humor. His popular poetry, written essentially to be spoken, was a racy juxtaposition of Parisian slang, free verse, repetitions, and puns. His collections like *Paroles* (1946; Eng. trans. *Selections from Paroles*, 1958) were best-sellers, and his poems, set to music, became popular songs. He wrote many screenplays, including that for Marcel Carné's celebrated *Children of Paradise* (1945). ■ See his *Words for All Seasons: Selected Poems* (Eng. trans. 1979) and *Blood and Feathers: Selected Poems* (1993); study by Claire Blakeway (1990); and biography by William E. Baker (1967).

PRICE, (MARY) LEONTYNE (1927–), U.S. opera singer. A native of Laurel, Mississippi, Price graduated from the Juilliard School of Music in New York City and achieved fame as Bess in a long-running revival of *Porgy and Bess* (1952–54). Her great love, though, was grand opera, and she was acclaimed for her television portrayal of *Tosca* (1955) and for her appearances with the San Francisco Opera Company (1957–60) and leading European companies. Her debut at La Scala (Milan) was in 1959. Price's triumphant debut at New York's Metropolitan Opera in *Il Trovatore* (1961) established her as a leading prima donna. A dramatic lyric soprano, she was best known for her portrayal of Verdi heroines, especially Aida, the role she sang at her farewell appearance at the Met (1985).

PRICHARD, KATHARINE SUSANNAH (1883–1969), Fijian-born Australian novelist. The daughter of an Australian journalist and editor, Prichard began her writing career as a freelance journalist in Australia, Britain, and the United States before establishing her reputation as a novelist with *The Pioneers* (1915). A founding member of the Australian Communist party (1920), she gained fame for her realistic and authentically Australian novels of social protest that featured exploited proletarian heroes and heroines. Among her best-known works were *Black Opal* (1921), *Working Bullocks* (1926), *Coonardoo* (1929), and *Haxby's Circus* (1930). ■ See her autobiography, *Child of the Hurricane* (1963), and studies by Jack Beasley, *The Rage for Life* (1964) and *A Gallop of Fire* (1993).

PRIDE, CHARLEY (1938–   ), U.S. country singer. As a boy Charley Pride picked cotton with his sharecropper parents. He became engrossed in the country music he heard on the radio and at age 14 bought his first guitar. Although he received little encouragement—a black singer in the Mississippi delta was expected to work in the blues tradition—he persisted. His other great ambition of playing baseball was undermined in 1964, when the New York Mets turned him down, and Pride concentrated entirely on singing. Impressed by the country sound of Pride's audition tapes, Chet Atkins signed him and cautiously promoted his records. By the time radio listeners discovered that he was black, his smooth, flexible voice was already familiar. When Pride became the first African-American singer to win the Country Music Association's Performer of the Year award (1971), he broke down the race barrier in a field of music that though markedly influenced by black music, had been open exclusively to white performers. ■ See his autobiography, *Pride* (1994; with Jim Henderson).

PRIDI PHANOMYONG (1900–1983), Thai political leader. The son of a prosperous Chinese father and a Thai mother, Pridi was educated in Thailand and France (1921–27), where he earned a doctorate and was a leader of the progressive Thai students. As the intellectual leader of the 1932 coup that overthrew the absolute monarchy, Pridi helped to write the new constitution and economic plan but

was forced into temporary exile for his utopian socialist views. He later served as minister of the interior (1935–36) and foreign minister (1936–38) and was a founder of Thammasat University. During World War II he was a member of the Regency Council and a leader of the Free Thai underground. He negotiated the postwar settlement with the Allies and served as premier for five months in 1946, but he resigned after the mysterious death of the king. After a military coup (1947) he lived in exile in China and, after 1970, in France.

PRIESTLEY, JOHN BOYNTON (1894–1984), British writer. J. B. Priestley served in World War I, graduated from Cambridge in 1921, and became a journalist in London, During a literary career that spanned seven decades. Priestley wrote 26 novels, more than 30 plays, and several volumes of literary criticism dealing with varied topics and themes. His first major success was the novel *Good Companions* (1929), which was followed by other sentimental but robust and panoramic works, notably *Bright Day* (1946) and *Lost Empires* (1965). His plays included *Dangerous Corner* (1932), *Eden End* (1935), *When We Are Married* (1938), and *An Inspector Calls* (1947). He also wrote a series of satirical books on the English character and English history. An independent leftist, he contributed essays to the *New Statesman* and was a founder of the Campaign for Nuclear Disarmament. ■ See his autobiographies, *Midnight on the Desert* (1937), *Rain upon Godshill* (1939), and *Instead of Trees* (1977); studies by A. A. DeVitis and Albert E. Kalson (1980), John J. Atkins (1981); and biographies by Vincent Brome (1988) and Judith Cook (1997).

PRIGOGINE, ILYA (1917–   ), Russian-born Belgian chemist. Prigogine was a professor of physical chemistry and theoretical physics at the Free University of Brussels and founder (1967) and director of the Center for Statistical Mechanics and Thermodynamics at the University of Texas, Austin. For his contributions to the study of how heat is created and dissipated by the activity of molecules in "open" or nonconfined systems (nonequilibrium thermodynamics), he was awarded the 1977 Nobel Prize in Chemistry. In addition to adding to knowledge of how living organisms utilize energy and to providing a theory of the origin of life—which apparently contradicted classical laws of physics—Prigogine's work made the principles of thermodynamics applicable to such diverse fields as sociology, ecology, laser technology, demography, and city planning. His books included *Introduction to the Thermodynamics of Irreversible Processes* (1954), *Order Out of Chaos* (1979), *From Being to Becoming* (1980), and *Exploring Complexity* (1989). ■ See Stuart A. Rice, ed., *For Ilya Prigogine* (1978) and *Nobel Prize Conversations* (1985).

PRIMO DE RIVERA, MIGUEL (1870–1930), Spanish general and dictator. Primo de Rivera attained the rank of lieutenant general (1919) after a military career in Cuba, the Philippines, and Morocco. As captain general in Barcelona, he gained public recognition (1922) for his efforts to bring about stability in the midst of a revolutionary climate. He participated (1923) in a military coup d'état, in which he overthrew the parliamentary government and established himself as dictator. With the cooperation of King Alfonso XIII, he suspended the constitution and imposed martial law. Although he ended the Moroccan War (1927) and instituted many social reforms, his government was opposed on all fronts. Primo finally resigned (1930) and died later that year in Paris. ■ See Dillwyn F. Ratcliff, *Prelude to Franco* (1957), and James H. Rial, *Revolution from Above* (1986).

PRIMUS, PEARL (1919–1994), Trinidadian-born dancer and choreographer. Primus studied the ritual dances of black peoples in Africa and the Caribbean and utilized them in her own choreography. She made her debut as a dancer in 1943 and was a popular cabaret performer in New York City. She then introduced (1944) her own troupe performing her own dance, *African Ceremonial*. After 1949 she researched dance, performed frequently in Africa, and served as director of performing-arts centers in Liberia and Nigeria. She also taught in New York and choreographed for Alvin Ailey's American Dance Theater and other companies. She received a Ph.D. in educational anthropology from New York University (1978).

PRINCE, HAROLD SMITH (1928–), U.S. theatrical producer and director. Active in student productions at the University of Pennsylvania (BA. 1948). Hal Prince was a protégé of Broadway director, producer, and playwright George Abbott and worked as assistant stage manager on several of his productions, including *Wonderful Town* (1953). Called the "boy wonder of Broadway" during the 1950s, Prince coproduced such award-winning musical-comedy hits as *Pajama Game* (1954), *Damn Yankees* (1955), *West Side Story* (1957), and *Fiorello* (1959). On his own he produced *A Funny Thing Happened on the Way to the Forum* (1962) and *Fiddler on the Roof* (1964). He subsequently gained a reputation as one of Broadway's most innovative directors by creating "concept" musicals, such as the Tony Award–winning *Cabaret* (1966), *Company* (1970), *Sweeney Todd* (1979), and *Evita* (1979), in which all of the elements of the show were woven together to support a specific theme. He also directed and coproduced the musical *Grind* (1985) and directed *Phantom of the Opera* (1987; Tony Award), *Kiss of the Spider Woman* (1993), and *Show Boat* (1994; Tony Award). He won a record 20 Tony Awards. ■ See biography by Carl Ilson (2000).

PRINCIP, GAVRILO (1895–1918), South Slav nationalist. A Bosnian Serb, Princip was a member of the secret Serbian terrorist organization, Black Hand. He sought to destroy the rule of Austria-Hungary in the Balkans and to unite the South Slavs into an independent nation. On June 28, 1914, Princip assassinated Archduke Francis Ferdinand, the heir to the Hapsburg throne, while he was on a visit to Sarajevo. The Austrians held Serbia responsible, declared war on July 28, and thus World War I began. Princip died of tuberculosis in an Austrian prison. ■ See Lavender Cassels, *The Archduke and the Assassin* (1984).

PRISHVIN, MIKHAIL MIKHAILOVICH (1873–1954), Soviet writer. An avid sportsman and naturalist, Prishvin emerged as an important figure at age 30. In such works as *The Springs of Berendey* (1925; expanded as *Nature's Diary*, 1937, and translated as *The Lake and the Woods*, or *Nature's Calendar*, 1976), *Crane's Birthplace* (1932), and *Honey from Beyond the Pale* (1951) he used fascinating details about nature and people symbolically to suggest larger designs of the universe. The writer Maxim Gorky once said of him, "I do not know any other writer in whom the knowledge and the love of the earth are so harmoniously united." He also wrote *Jen Sheng: The Root of Life* (1933; Eng. trans. 1936, 1980) and *The Treasure Trove of the Sun* (1945; Eng. trans. 1952). Additional works in English are in *A Selection—M. Prishvin* (1985). *The Chain of Kashchey* (1960) was autobiographical.

PRITAM, AMRITA (1919–), Indian writer. Amrita Pritam wrote prolifically in the Punjabi language; she was the moving spirit behind the *Jewelled Serpent*, a magazine of Punjabi writing. Pritam published poetry collections as well as more than a dozen novels, numerous volumes of short fiction, folk songs, essays, and travel sketches. English translations of her work appeared in *Black Rose* (1967), *Existence and Other Poems* (1968), *Selected Poems* (1970), *A Line in Water* (1975), and *Forty-nine Days* (1984), *The Haunted House and the Thirteenth Sun* (1992), *Village No. 36* (1994), and *Their Signature and Other Novelettes* (1995). *The Other Dimension* (1996) is a collection of essays. ■ See her autobiographies, *The Revenue Stamp* (Eng. trans. 1977) and *Life and Times* (1989).

PRITCHETT, SIR VICTOR SAWDON (1900–1997), British writer. V. S. Pritchett was a great traveler as a young man and wrote several highly regarded travel books. His novels and short stories—including *Elopement into Exile* (1932), *It May Never Happen* (1947), and *Mr. Beluncle* (1951)—concerned eccentric characters caught in absurd situations, described with style and affectionate irony. But Pritchett was probably best known for his literary essays (*The Living Novel*, 1947, *The Myth Makers*, 1979, and *The Tale Bearers*, 1980, are among his finest collections) and critical contributions to the *New Statesman* and the *New York Review of Books*. He also wrote biographies of Balzac (1974), Turgenev (1977), and Chekhov (1988). ■ See his *Collected Stories* (1982); *More Collected Stories* (1983); *A Man of Letters: Selected Essays* (1986); *The Pritchett Cen-*

tury (1997); his memoirs, *A Cab at the Door* (1968) and *Midnight Oil* (1971); and study by John Stinson (1997).

PROKHOROV, ALEKSANDR MIKHAILOVICH (1916–), Soviet physicist. Born in Australia to Russian émigré parents, Prokhorov was brought to Soviet Russia after the 1917 revolution and he graduated from Leningrad University (1939). After serving in World War II, he joined (1946) Moscow's Lebedev Institute of Physics. In 1954, he became head of the institute, where he developed a method of molecular amplification. This method led to the development of the maser and laser—terms that stand for Microwave/Light Amplication by Stimulated Emission of Radiation. For these advances in quantum electronics, Prokhorov shared the 1964 Nobel Prize in Physics with his coworker, Nikolai Basov, and Charles H. Townes, the American inventor of the maser. Prokhorov served as editor in chief of the *Great Soviet Encyclopedia* (1969–78).

PROKOFIEV, SERGEI SERGEEVICH (1891–1953), Russian composer. Prokofiev was a brilliant pianist and precocious musician who played his First Piano Concerto as his graduation piece from the St. Petersburg Conservatory (1914). His *Classical Symphony* and Piano Concerto No. 3 were written during the 1917 revolution, after which he visited the United States and settled in Paris, composing the opera *Love for Three Oranges* (1919) and the ballet *Prodigal Son* (1928). His works were modernistic, discordant, and witty and were brilliantly orchestrated. He returned to the Soviet Union in 1936 and turned to light music (*Peter and the Wolf*, 1936), patriotic themes (Piano Sonata No. 7, 1942; Symphony No. 5, 1944), and film scores (*Lieutenant Kije*, 1934; *Alexander Nevsky*, 1939). Although highly acclaimed during the 1930s and the World War II era, he was attacked by the government in 1948 for "decadent formalism." ■ See his memoirs (Eng. trans. 1979) and biographies by Lawrence and Elizabeth Hanson (1964) and Victor Seroff (1968).

PROUST, MARCEL (1871–1922), French novelist. The son of a well-known doctor of Catholic peasant background and a wealthy mother of Alsatian-Jewish descent, Proust was a prominent member of fashionable Parisian society of the 1890s. By 1906, after the death of his parents and debilitating bouts of asthma and various neuroses, Proust became a virtual recluse. He worked in his cork-lined bedroom insulated from street noise and dust, and he ventured out only at night, if at all. After working for years, he himself published the first volume of his masterpiece, *Remembrance of Things Past* (16 vols., 1913–27; Eng. trans. 1922–32; rev. trans. 1981). With the publication of the second volume (1919), he was immediately recognized as a literary artist and a great stylist. His semiautobiographical novel, written in the first person by a character named Marcel, is complex and allegorical; it details the rediscovery of the hidden past and self that lies concealed within everyone. A deep psychological ex-

ploration of motivation, love, and time, it is also a social comedy detailing the crumbling French aristocracy being overtaken by the rising bourgeoisie. ■ See biographies by George D. Painter (2 vols., 1959–65), Ronald Hayman (1990), Jean-Yves Tadié (1996; Eng. trans. 2000), and William C. Carter (2000) and study by Derwent May (1983).

PRUSINER, STANLEY B. (1942–), U.S. neurologist and biochemist. Prusiner studied at the University of Pennsylvania (M.D. 1968) and spent his professional career at the University of California at San Francisco (1972–). After a patient of his died (1972) of Creutzfeldt-Jacob disease, a type of rare degenerative brain disorder known as spongiform encephalopathy, Prusiner began to investigate its cause. In a series of experiments during the 1970s and 1980s he discovered that disorders that included scrapie and mad cow disease in animals, Gertsmann-Sträussler-Scheinker disease, fatal familial insomnia, and kuru in humans, are caused by a new genre of disease-causing agents that he named prions (for proteinaceous infectious particles). Because prions, which were neither viruses, fungi, bacteria, nor parasites, consisted only of proteins, and lacked genetic material, many scientists doubted that they alone could cause disease, and Prusiner's work remained controversial for many years. However, experiments in the early 1990s supported his conclusions and he was awarded the 1997 Nobel Prize in Physiology or Medicine. He edited *Prion Diseases of Humans and Animals* (1992) and *Prions Prions Prions* (1996). ■ See Richard Rhodes, *Deadly Feasts* (1997).

PRYOR, RICHARD (1940–), U.S. comedian and actor. Pryor began working as a professional comic in his hometown of Peoria, Illinois. Inspired by the success of African-American comedian Bill Cosby, he moved to New York in 1963. He gained national exposure through television appearances during the mid-1960s, but his unique brand of comedy—a biting interpretation of the black street experience—was slow to find acceptance in the mainstream of show business. In the 1970s, Pryor's audiences expanded; he won Grammy Awards for three comedy albums and appeared in such films as *The Wiz* (1978) and *Richard Pryor Live in Concert* (1979). His screenwriting credits included *Blazing Saddles* (coauthor; 1973), and he wrote material for Lily Tomlin and other comedians. Known for a tumultuous personal life that involved alcohol and cocaine abuse, Pryor narrowly escaped death when he accidentally set himself on fire while "free-basing" cocaine (1980). He made a stunning comeback, both personally and professionally, and won recognition as one of his generation's funniest comedians. However, his career was cut short again by numerous health problems, including multiple sclerosis. ■ See biographies by Fred Robbins and David Ragan (1982) and James Haskins (1984); and John and Dennis Williams, *If I Stop I'll Die* (1991).

PUCCI, EMILIO (**Marchese Emilio Pucci di Barsento;** 1914–1992), Italian fashion designer. After studying in Italy and the United States, Pucci earned a doctorate in political science at the University of Florence. He was a member of Italy's Olympic ski team (1933–34) and later served as an air force officer (1941–1952), during and after World War II. He did not launch his career as a couturier until 1950; the casual, elegant Pucci print dress was almost immediately de rigueur for the fashion-conscious woman, and the "Pucci Look" dominated fashion in the 1960s. He also designed lingerie, linens, and porcelain, and created Pucci fragrances. He served in the Italian parliament (1963–72) and was a city councillor in Florence (from 1964).

PUCCINI, GIACOMO (1858–1924), Italian opera composer. A descendant of four generations of church musicians, Puccini decided to write operas after seeing Verdi's *Aida* and he studied at the Milan conservatory (1880–83) under Amilcare Ponchielli. He established his reputation with his third opera, *La Bohéme* (1896), which was followed by *Tosca* (1900) and *Madama Butterfly* (1904). Of his later operas, *Gianni Schicchi*, from the trilogy *Il Trittico* (1918), and *Turandot,* unfinished at his death, are considered the finest. His operas reflected the influence on the Italian operatic movement of *verismo* (realism) but were tempered by tenderness and exoticism. Often innovative in his harmonies and orchestral writing, he showed an acute dramatic sense and a gift for poignant, consummately vocal melody. ■ See biographies by Mosco Carner (2d ed, 1977) and Howard Greenfeld (1980), and Stanley Jackson, *Monsieur Butterfly* (1974).

PUDOVKIN, VSEVOLOD ILLARIONOVICH (1893–1953), Russian film director. After studying chemistry at Moscow University and being wounded in World War I, Pudovkin enrolled at the State Film School, where he assisted with and acted in his teachers' films. He first directed *Chess Fever* (1925), an exercise in intercutting to produce different effects. Again utilizing his rapid cutting style, he directed the revolutionary films *Mother* (1926), *The End of St. Petersburg* (1927), and *Storm over Asia* (1928). Pudovkin's first sound films were not successful, but he continued as an actor (*Ivan the Terrible,* 1945) and directed grand historical epics in his later years. He explained his cinematic theories in *Film Technique* (Eng. trans. 1933) and *Film Acting* (Eng. trans. 1935). ■ See study by Peter Dart (1974).

PUENTE, TITO (Ernesto Antonio Puente, Jr.; 1923–2000), U.S. musician, bandleader. and composer. Born into a Puerto Rican family in New York City, Puente was often called "El Rey" or "the king of Latin music." He wrote more than 200 compositions and recorded more than 100 albums, including the all-time best-selling salsa LP, *Dance Mania* (1958). Trained on the streets of Spanish Harlem and at the Juilliard School of Music, Puente arranged his own music and played the timbales (a double tom-tom played with sticks), the trap drums, the conga drums, and the clavés as well as the piano, saxophone, and clarinet. He formed his first band in 1948,

became nationally known as an exponent of the mambo during the 1950s, and remained popular through the 1990s. Several of his albums, including *Mambo Diablo* (1985) and *Goza Mi Timbal* (1989) won Grammy Awards. ■ See biography by Steven Loza (1999).

PUIG, MANUEL (1932–1990), Argentinian novelist. Puig grew up in a provincial town and learned English as a child by watching Hollywood motion pictures. He studied film in Italy and worked briefly in the Argentinian film industry before turning to literature. His novels, which frequently explored themes of alienation and sexuality, drew upon images from film and mass media and he employed fantasy and such techniques as dialogue and interior monologue to portray the inner life of his characters. His best-known works were *Betrayed by Rita Hayworth* (1968; Eng. trans. 1971), a semiautobiographical depiction of an alienated provincial world, and *Kiss of the Spider Woman* (1976; Eng. trans. 1979; film, 1985), a story about the relationship of a Marxist political activist and an apolitical homosexual who share a cell as prisoners of the Argentinian military junta. His other works included *Heartbreak Tango* (1969; Eng. trans. 1973), *The Buenos Aires Affair* (1973; Eng. trans. 1976), *Eternal Curse on the Reader of These Pages* (1980; Eng. trans. 1982), *Blood of Requited Love* (1982; Eng. trans. 1984), and *Tropical Night Falling* (1988; Eng. trans. 1991). After his work was banned in Argentina during the 1970s, he lived in the United States, Brazil, and Mexico. ■ See biography by Suzanne Levine (2000).

PULLER, LEWIS BURWELL (1898–1971), U.S. marine. Known as "Chesty," Puller earned a reputation as the toughest marine in the corps. An outspoken, profane native of West Point, Virginia, he left the Virginia Military Institute at the outbreak of World War I and received a commission at age 20. Subsequently he fought in Haiti, Nicaragua. Guadalcanal, Cape Gloucester, Peleliu, and Korea and won four navy crosses, the bronze and silver stars, and the Legion of Merit to become the most-decorated marine in history. He was promoted to major general in 1953. ■ See Burke Davis, *Marine!* (1962).

PUNNETT, REGINALD CRUNDALL (1875–1967), British geneticist. A professor of genetics at Cambridge (1910–40), Punnett worked with William Bateson to confirm, expand, and disseminate the genetic findings of the Austrian experimenter Gregor Mendel. Together Punnett and Bateson discovered the processes of linkage and sex determination and jointly founded (1911) and edited the *Journal of Genetics*. Punnett's book, *Mendelism* (1905), helped popularize the science of genetics. He worked for more than 40 years on the breeding of poultry, and his book *Heredity in Poultry* (1923) remained a standard work for decades.

PURCELL, EDWARD MILLS (1912–1997), U.S. physicist. Purcell received a Ph.D. from Harvard (1938) and taught physics there (1938–40; 1946–80). Prior to his 1946 discovery, simultaneously with Felix Bloch, of the nuclear magnetic resonance (NMR) absorption method for measuring the magnetic fields of atomic nuclei and molecules, experiments had provided only moderately accurate measurements of gaseous substances. Purcell's method, effective for liquids and solids, enabled him to determine the unique frequency at which the nuclei of a given substance would exhibit nuclear magnetic resonance and provided a valuable tool for investigating the molecular structure of many substances. For this work he shared with Bloch the 1952 Nobel Prize for Physics. In the field of astronomy, Purcell detected the microwave radiation emission from neutral hydrogen in interstellar space at the 21-centimeter wavelength. This observation enabled astronomers to map large areas of the galaxy.

PUTIN, VLADIMIR (1952–   ), Russian political leader. While studying for a law degree at Leningrad (now Saint Petersburg) State University (1970–75) Putin was the judo champion (1974) of Leningrad. He served as a member of the KGB, the Soviet Union's secret service agency (1975–90) and worked as a spy in Germany from 1986 to 1990. He subsequently worked as an aide to Saint Petersburg's mayor Anatoly Sobchak, his former law professor, and he served as deputy mayor (1994–96). Moving to Moscow (1996), he began his meteoric rise to power as an official in President Boris Yeltsin's administration. In Aug. 1998 he became head of the Federal Security Service and in March 1999 he was chosen to lead the presidential Security Council. Appointed premier (Aug. 1999) he gained popularity by vigorously carrying out the war against rebels in Chechnya. Putin became acting president when Yeltsin resigned (Dec. 31, 1999). After he was elected president (March 2000), with 53 percent of the vote, he began to take measures to decrease the power of the obligarchy, the business elite that controls much of the Russian economy.

PYLE, ERNEST TAYLOR (1900–1945), U.S. journalist. Ernie Pyle won fame as a roving correspondent who, from 1935 to 1940, traveled throughout North America and wrote immensely popular human-interest stories concerning the lives of average citizens, During World War II he covered military operations in North Africa, Sicily, Italy. France, and the South Pacific, living with the soldiers he wrote about. He became the best-known and most beloved American correspondent by conveying, in simple language, the fears and loneliness of the American fighting man, and won a Pulitzer Prize in 1944. He was killed by Japanese gunfire while covering a battle near Okinawa. ■ See *Ernie's War* (1986), a collection of Pyle's dispatches; Lee Graham Miller, *The Story of Ernie Pyle* (1950); and study by James Tobin (1997).

PYNCHON, THOMAS (1937–   ), U.S. novelist. Pynchon was one of the most reclusive writers of his era. Very little is known about his life except that he studied physics, engineering, and English at Cornell University (B.A. 1959), served in the U.S. Navy for two years, and worked as a technical writer for Boeing Aircraft in Seattle. His wildly comic and highly detailed, complex, pessimistic novels depicted the dehumanizing effects of technology and treated such subjects as isolation, obsession, paranoia, and conspiracy in human affairs. His best-known works were *V* (1963), *The Crying of Lot 49* (1966), and *Gravity's Rainbow* (1973). *Vineland* (1990) was a humorous account of 1960s radical politics in California. The massive *Mason and Dixon* (1997) explored the tension between rationalism and chaos in a semifictional rendering of the story of the surveyors who mapped the Mason-Dixon line (1767), the boundary that divided the North from the South. ■ See studies by Joseph Slade (1990) and Judith Chambers (1992).

Q

QABBANI, NIZER (1923–1998), Syrian poet. Qabbani earned a law degree from the Syrian University, Damascus (1945); joined the foreign ministry; and served in diplomatic posts in Europe, China, and the Middle East. He resigned in 1966 and established the Nizar Qabbani publishing house in London. His sensual love poetry, which was first published in 1944, was popular throughout the Arab world, although he was frequently condemned by cultural conservatives. After the Arab defeat in the 1967 Arab-Israeli war, his poetry dealt more with political and social themes, and he criticized the authoritarianism, oppression, and backwardness of contemporary Arab society. He wrote two dozen volumes of poetry and gave public readings before large audiences. His lyrics were sung by popular Arabic vocalists. English translations of his poetry are in *Arabian Love Poems* (1993) and *On Entering the Sea* (1996).

QADDAFI, MUAMMAR AL (1942–), Libyan political leader. Born into a nomadic desert family, Qaddafi graduated from the University of Libya (1963) and the Benghazi military academy (1965), and founded the pro-Nasser Free Officers Movement (1963). In 1969 he led the successful coup against King Idris I and established a Libyan Arab republic. A revolutionary pan-Arabist and Islamic fundamentalist, he nationalized Western interests, supported revolutionary and terrorist movements in Europe, the Middle East, and Africa, and attempted to set up an austere Islamic socialist state based on principles set forth in his *Green Book* (Eng. trans. 1976). He ruled through "revolutionary committees" at all levels of society and suppressed all opposition. He was an ally of the Soviet Union, a bitter foe of Israel, and a supporter of the Palestine Liberation Organization (PLO). During the 1980s his troops intervened in the civil war in Chad. The United States imposed a trade embargo and bombed targets in Libya (1986) in retaliation for Qaddafi's support of international terrorism. United Nations sanctions were imposed on Libya (1992–99) for failing to turn over for trial Libyan citizens suspected of blowing up civilian airliners over Scotland and Africa, killing 440 people. ▪ See John K. Cooley, *Libyan Sandstorm* (1982); P. Edward Haley, *Qaddafi and the U.S. Since 1969* (1984); David Blundy and Andrew Lycett, *Qaddafi and the Libyan Revolution* (1987); and Mansour O. El-Kikhia, *Libya's Qaddafi* (1997).

QI-BAISHI (old style: CHI PAI-SHIH; 1863–1957), Chinese artist. One of the last great Chinese painters to employ the traditional style of the 17th and 18th centuries, Qi-Baishi was a skilled craftsman who educated himself in the arts of poetry, calligraphy, and painting. At the age of 40 he undertook a seven-year voyage throughout China, completing a collection of landscapes, *Little Scrolls from the Mountains*. He remained active into old age, producing meticulously detailed paintings of flowers and insects. He was honored by the People's Republic of China as a hero of culture. ▪ See study by Kai-yu Hsu and Fang-yu Wang (1979).

QIAO GUANHUA (old style: CH'IAO KUAN-HUA; 1914–1983), Chinese political leader. Qiao studied at the University of Tübingen, Germany (Ph.D., 1936) and was a prominent left-wing journalist during the 1940s. Speaking English, German, French, Russian, and Japanese, Qiao joined the foreign ministry in 1949 and traveled extensively, representing China and acting as an adviser to Premier Zhou En-lai (Chou Enlai). He played a major role in the normalization of relations between China and the United States and led the first Peoples' Republic delegation to the United Nations (1971). He was appointed foreign minister in 1974 but was ousted in 1976 for purported connections with the disgraced "gang of four" leadership. He reappeared (1982) in a minor foreign affairs post.

QUADROS, JÂNIO DA SILVA (1917–1992), Brazilian political leader. Quadros was a former teacher and lawyer, mayor, and governor (1955–59) of São Paulo, who became known for honest, efficient government. Campaigning as "the man with the broom"—millions of which were actually distributed—he was elected president of Brazil in 1960 with the largest popular vote in history. But his land and tax reforms, austerity measures, and establishment of diplomatic ties to communist governments aroused conservative opposition, and Quadros resigned after seven months in office (August 1961), beaten, he said, by "corruption, lies, and cowardliness." He was succeeded by his vice president, João Goulart. After the restoration of democracy, following 21 years of military rule, he was elected mayor of São Paulo (1985) with the support of rightist forces.

QUANT, MARY (1934–), British fashion designer. Quant opened (1955) a one-room Chelsea boutique called Bazaar and at age 21, with no formal fashion training, began designing and manufacturing the antiestablishment mini and mod fashions, notably the miniskirt, that captured the spirit of youth in the 1960s. She challenged the conventions of haute couture, using denim for evening wear and lace for day wear, and launched (1966) a line of cosmetics for the young. She won many design awards and was the first woman fashion designer to be made an officer of the Order of the British Empire (O.B.E.; 1966). She wrote *Quant by Quant* (1966) and *Mary Quant's Classic Make-Up and Beauty* (1996).

QUASIMODO, SALVATORE (1901–1968), Italian poet, translator, and critic. Quasimodo prepared for an engineering career but joined (1935) the Italian literature faculty at the Milan Conservatory. He translated classical poets, whose forms and idioms shaped his own lyric poetry. In the 1930s he was associated with the "hermetic poetry" movement, which was related to French symbolism. Between 1930 and 1938, he published five poetry collections. Quasimodo was imprisoned during World War II for antifascist activities; his postwar poetry reflected a more compassionate, humanistic consciousness. His *Discourse on Poetry* (1956; Eng. trans. 1960) advocated socially committed verse. Quasimodo won the 1959 Nobel Prize for Literature. English translations of his work are in *Selected Writings* (1960), *The Poet and the Politician* (1964), *Selected Poems* (1965), *To Give and to Have* (1969), and *Collected Poems* (1983).

QUEEN, ELLERY (Frederic Dannay, 1905–1982; and Manfred B. Lee, 1905–1971), U.S. mystery writers and editors. Ellery Queen was the name both of the pseudonymous author and of the astute detective who were created by two Brooklyn-born cousins. Dannay (born Daniel Nathan) and Lee (born Manford Lepofsky) submitted *The Roman Hat Mystery* (1928) to a mystery-novel contest, using a collective pseudonym to satisfy contest rules. Their clashing personalities resulted in a lively collaboration; the ingenious and analytical Ellery Queen quickly caught on. The authors created mysteries for their sleuth to unravel in a total of 39 novels, as well as in stories, novelettes, screenplays, and radio plays. Their best-known works included *The Four of Hearts* (1938), *Cat of Many Tails* (1949), and *The Player on the Other Side* (1963). Ellery Queen also inspired a television series. Dannay and Lee founded (1941) *Ellery Queen Mystery Magazine,* which anthologized mystery stories and encouraged both new writers and established nonmystery writers (including 12 Nobel Prize winners) to contribute. ■ See Francis M. Nevins, Jr., *Royal Bloodline* (1974).

QUENEAU, RAYMOND (1903–1976), French poet and novelist. Queneau was active as a grammarian, encyclopedia editor, and historian of mathematics. Originally a surrealist in the 1920s, under the influence of the writer L. F. Céline, he introduced colloquial speech and argot to French literary language, as in his first novel *The Bark Tree* (1933; Eng. trans. 1968). Noted for his good humor, wit, and virtuosic style, Queneau employed literary puns and droll rhymes in portraying clownish fictional characters trying to survive in an absurdist world. He was best known for *The Skin of Dreams* (1944; Eng. trans. 1948), *Exercises in Style* (1947; Eng. trans. 1958, 1981), *The Sunday of Life* (1952; Eng. trans. 1977), *Zazie* (1959; Eng. trans. 1960), and *The Flight*

of Icarus (1968; Eng. trans. 1973). English translations of his poems are in *Pounding the Pavement, Beating the Bushes, and Other Pataphysical Poems* (1986). ■ See study by Jacques Guicharnaud (Eng. trans. 1965).

QUEZON, MANUEL LUIS (1878–1944), Filipino political leader. Quezon's law studies were interrupted by the Spanish-American War (1898); he joined the insurrectionist forces and was briefly jailed by the Americans. He became a leader of the Nationalist party and member of the assembly (1907). During an extended stay as resident commissioner in the United States (1909–16), he earned a reputation as an effective lobbyist for Philippine independence. While serving in the senate (1922–35), he urged the U.S. Congress to pass the Tydings-McDuffie Act (1934), which provided for Philippine independence in 1946. Quezon became the first president of the Philippine Commonwealth (1935) and quickly consolidated his powers. He died suddenly in the United States where, during World War II, he headed the government-in-exile. ■ See his autobiography, *The Good Fight* (1946), and Elinor Goettel, *Eagle of the Philippines* (1970).

QUIDDE, LUDWIG (1858–1941), German historian and pacifist. Educated at the universities of Strasbourg and Göttingen. Quidde edited the *German Review of Historical Sciences* (1889–96). A leader in the German peace movement from the 1890s, he served as president of the German Peace Society (1914–29). As a member of the Bavarian diet (1907–14) he vociferously denounced German imperialism and lived in exile in Switzerland during World War I. After the war he served in the Weimar national assembly (1919–20), supported the League of Nations, and wrote against illegal military training. He shared the 1927 Nobel Peace Prize with Ferdinand Buisson. After the Nazis came to power (1933), he emigrated to Switzerland.

QUILL, MICHAEL JOSEPH (1905–1966), Irish-born U.S. labor leader. Active in the Irish independence movement before emigrating to the United States (1926), Quill became a New York City subway worker and helped organize the Transport Workers Union (1934). A fiery labor leader, Quill was president of the TWU from 1935 until his death and helped organize union chapters in other American cities. He also served as a member of the New York City Council (1937–39; 1943–49). ■ See L. H. Whittemore, *The Man Who Ran the Subways* (1968), and biography by Shirley Quill (1985).

QUINE, WILLARD VAN ORMAN (1908–2000), U.S. philosopher. After studying mathematics at Oberlin College, Quine studied at Harvard (Ph.D. 1932) under Alfred North Whitehead and spent his entire career there, retiring in 1978. His contact with the Vienna Circle of logical positivists in the 1930s and his friendship with Rudolf Carnap moved his thinking in the direction of symbolic logic. In an early paper (1937), Quine criticized the empiricist notion that one can distinguish between analytic statements (which deal with the relationship among concepts) and synthetic statements (which report on the course of experience). He argued that the concept on which empiricists base their distinction—that of meaning—is not sufficiently clear. For the same reason, he criticized empiricists' distinction between science and metaphysics. Best known for his effort to clarify the use of language in philosophical discourse, Quine helped to move postwar U.S. philosophy away from the linguistic philosophy of Ludwig Wittgenstein and John L. Austin. His books included *Word and Object* (1960), *Set Theory and Its Logic* (1963: rev. ed. 1969), *The Ways of Paradox* (rev. ed. 1976), and *From Stimulus to Science* (1995). ■ See his autobiography, *The Time of My Life* (1985); study by Alex Orenstein (1977); and Roger F. Gibson, Jr., *The Philosophy of W. V. Quine* (1982).

QUIRINO, ELPIDIO (1890–1956), Filipino political leader. Born in the prison of which his father was the warden, Quirino graduated from high school at age 21 and worked his way through the college of law of the University of the Philippines. He became a protégé of Manuel Quezon, served in the house of representatives (1919–25) and senate (1925–35), and held several cabinet posts during the 1930s. During World War II Quirino served in the underground and became a prisoner of war of the Japanese. He returned to government in 1945 and was president of the Philippines (1948–53). During his term in office postwar reconstruction accelerated, but rural social problems grew and his administration was weak, ineffective, corrupt, and unpopular. ■ See biography by Sol H. Gwekoh (1950).

QUISLING, VIDKUN ABRAHAM LAURITZ JONSØN (1887–1945), Norwegian political figure. Trained at Norway's War Academy, Quisling served as a military attaché in Petrograd (1918–19) and a decade later as legation secretary of the Norwegian embassy in Moscow. He served as minis-

ter of defense (1931–33), but disillusioned with both parliamentary and communistic forms of government, he founded the fascist National Unity party. Quisling actively supported the German Nazi cause in Norway in the late 1930s and collaborated on the German invasion of Norway (1940). On the night of the invasion, he made a radio broadcast announcing his appointment as premier; lacking popular support, his government lasted only six days. When no other leader of stature would collaborate, the Germans installed Quisling as minister-president with dictatorial powers (February 1942), but he remained unable to govern effectively. When Norway was liberated (1945), Quisling was tried and executed as a traitor. His name became a synonym for traitor. ■ See biographies by Ralph Hewins (1966), P. M. Hayes (1972), and Oddvar K. Hoidal (1989).

QU QIUBAI (old style: CH'Ü CH'IU-PAI; 1899–1935), Chinese political leader and literary theorist. Qu Qiubai was the pseudonym of Qu Shuang (Ch'ü Shuang). A student radical leader in Beijing (Peking; 1916–19), Qu was a member of a Marxist study group headed by Li Dazhao (Li Ta-chao), who was later a founder of the Chinese Communist party. He served as a foreign correspondent in Moscow (1920–23) and joined the Chinese Communist party in 1922. He headed the party's propaganda department (1925–27) and published Mao Zedong's (Mao Tse-tung) famous report on the peasantry (1927). As general secretary of the party (1927–28), he advocated the disastrous Guangdong (Canton) uprising and was forced out of power. Qu was the first major Marxist literary theorist in China and published numerous essays, critiques, and translations as leader of the influential Left-Wing Writers in Shanghai (1931–33). He called for a new Chinese literary language, simple to write and dedicated to serving society. After serving as commissar of education of the communist enclave in Jiangxi (Kiangsi; 1934), he was captured by the nationalist troops and publicly executed. ■ See Paul G. Pickowicz, *Marxist Literary Thought in China* (1981).

R

RAAB, JULIUS (1891–1964), Austrian political leader. Raab represented the anti-Marxist Christian Socialist party in parliament (1927–34), served as a member of the federal economic council (1934–38), and became minister of trade and transportation (1938) two months before Germany annexed Austria. Opposed to annexation, he left politics and spent the years of World War II in private industry. After the war he was a leader of the newly formed conservative Austrian People's party; as chancellor (1953–61) he championed Austrian neutrality, negotiated the withdrawal of Soviet troops, and concentrated on the economic reconstruction that brought postwar prosperity to Austria.

RABE, DAVID (1940–   ), U.S. playwright. Rabe graduated from Catholic high school and college in Dubuque, Iowa. After dropping out of the master's program in theater at Villanova University (1965), he was drafted, and spent eleven months in a hospital support unit in Vietnam. His military experiences provided the background for *The Basic Training of Pavlo Hummel* (1968), *Sticks and Bones* (1972), and *Streamers* (1975), his award-winning dramas on the brutalizing effects of the Vietnam War on its combatants. His other works included *In the Boom Boom Room* (1972), a play about a go-go dancer and the irresponsible men in her life, and *Hurlyburly* (1984), a drama depicting amorality and cynicism in contemporary society. He subsequently wrote the play *A Question of Mercy* (1998; with Richard Selzer), screenplays for *Casualties of War* (1989) and *The Firm* (1993), and the novel *Recital of the Dog* (1993).

RABI, ISIDOR ISAAC (1898–1988), U.S. physicist. Rabi was born in Poland and taken to the United States as a toddler by his father, a poor tailor. After receiving his Ph.D. (1927), he spent several years studying with prominent European physicists including Niels Bohr, Otto Stern, and Wolfgang Pauli and then taught at Columbia University (1929–67). In the 1930s Rabi devised an atomic and molecular beam resonance method for measuring the magnetic properties of atoms and molecules, which helped elucidate atomic and molecular structure. He was awarded the 1944 Nobel Prize for Physics. During World War II he helped develop microwave radar and worked on the atomic bomb project; he was later active as a government science adviser and an advocate of arms control. ■ See his *My Life and Times as a Physicist* (1960) and biography by John S. Rigden (1987).

RABIN, YITZHAK (1922–1995), Israeli military and political leader. A career military officer, Rabin served as army chief of staff (1964–68) and was a major architect of Israel's victory in the Six-Day War (1967). He subsequently was Israel's ambassador to the United States (1968–73). After the 1973 Arab-Israeli War, which caught Israel by surprise and discredited the country's leaders, he entered politics, was elected head of the Labour party (1974), and served as his country's first native-born prime minister (1974–77). He relinquished his party leadership position (1977) after it was disclosed that he had maintained an illegal bank account in Washington, D.C. Shortly thereafter, the Labour party lost the national elections to the Likud party headed by Menachem Begin. Rabin returned to power as defense minister in the National Unity government (1984–90), during which he suppressed the Palestinian uprising, the Intifada. During a second term as prime minister (1992–95), he signed a historic peace accord with the Palestinians (1993) and a peace treaty with Jordan (1994), and he shared the 1994 Nobel Peace Prize with Yasir Arafat and Shimon Peres. Shortly after signing a second peace accord with the Palestinians (1995), which called for Israeli troop withdrawals and an expansion of Palestinian home rule on the West Bank, Rabin was assassinated by a young Israeli religious extremist while attending a peace rally in Tel Aviv. ■ See *The Rabin Memoirs* (Eng. trans. 1979; rev. ed. 1996); biography by Robert Slater (1977); and study by his widow, Leah Rabin (1997).

RACHMANINOFF, SERGEI VASILYEVICH (1873–1943), Russian composer, pianist, and conductor. Born into an aristocratic and musical family, Rachmaninoff studied at the Moscow Conservatory (1885–92). Shortly after his graduation, he composed his well-known Prelude in C-sharp minor and launched a successful career as a conductor and solo virtuoso. After the Russian Revolution (1917) he emigrated to the United States and continued to concertize there and in Europe until shortly before his death. The last of the great exponents of 19th-century Russian romanticism, he wrote many works that entered the standard repertory, including the Piano Concerto No. 2 in C minor (1901), the tone poem *Isle of the Dead* (1907), Second Symphony (1907), Piano Concerto No. 3 in D minor (1909), *Rhapsody on a Theme of Paganini* (1934), and Symphony No. 3 in A minor (1936). ■ See his *Rachmaninoff's Recollections* (1934) and the biographies by Victor Seroff (1950), Sergei Bertensson and Jay Leyda (1956), Geoffrey Norris (1976), and Barrie Martyn (1990).

RADCLIFFE-BROWN, ALFRED REGINALD (1881–1955), British social anthropologist. A. R. Radcliffe-Brown played a vital role in moving the discipline of anthropology beyond the descriptive and in establishing anthropological structuralism. He advanced his basic theoretical concepts in *The Andaman Islanders* (1922; rev. 1948), in which he treated social events as natural phenomena that operate according to laws that may be identified and characterized. He taught at universities in South Africa and Australia as well as the University of Chicago (1931–37) and Oxford (1937–46). Radcliffe-Brown's works also included *The Social Organization of Australian Tribes* (1931), *Structure and Function in Primitive Society* (1952), and *Method in Social Anthropology* (1958).

RADDALL, THOMAS HEAD (1903–1994), British-born Canadian novelist. Raddall dropped out of school and worked as a wireless operator in the merchant marine in the North Atlantic and later as a bookkeeper for pulp mills in Nova Scotia, writing stories in his spare time. After 1938 he devoted himself exclusively to writing, producing historical romances that preserved the manners, customs, and speech of old Nova Scotia. His tales depended more on decisive action than on psychological subtlety: they included *His Majesty's Yankees* (1942), *The Governor's Lady* (1960), and *Hangman's Beach* (1966). He also wrote several award-winning volumes on Canadian history and six short-story collections. ■ See his memoirs, *In My Time* (1976), and study by Alan R. Young (1983).

RADEK, KARL (Karl Sobelsohn; 1885–1939?), Soviet political leader and journalist. A social democrat, Radek took part in the 1905 revolution in Warsaw and spent the next decade as a journalist in Germany and Poland. He was a bolshevik supporter and he agitated for peace in Switzerland before returning (1917) to Russia following the October revolution. After the failure of a communist uprising in Germany (1918–19), he became (1920) a leader of the Comintern in Moscow and a chief strategist of world revolution. The Comintern's ineffectiveness in Germany led to Radek's expulsion from high Comintern and party office (1924). His support of Leon Trotsky led to his exile (1928) to Siberia. He repented (1930) and returned to Moscow, where he wrote for the newspaper *Izvestia* (1931–36) and was a coauthor of the 1936 "Stalin" Constitution. Convicted in a 1937 show trial of being part of a Trotskyite conspiracy, Radek was by some accounts shot, by other accounts imprisoned in a labor camp where he died. ■ See biography by Warren Lerner (1970) and Jim Tuck, *Engine of Mischief* (1988).

RADHAKRISHNAN, SARVEPALLI (1888–1975), Indian philosopher and statesman. Born into a poor Telugu Brahman family, Radhakrishnan was educated at Madras Christian College and taught philosophy at Madras (1909–17), Mysore (1918–21), Calcutta (1921–31), and Oxford (1936–52), becoming the first Indian to hold a chair there. He was regarded as one of India's foremost philosophers and major interpreters of its intellectual and religious heritage to the West. A humanist and reformer, he sought to reinterpret Hinduism for modern times and to reconcile the religions of the world. His works included *Indian Philosophy* (2 vols., 1923–27), *The Philosophy of the Upanishads* (1924), *An Idealist View of Life* (1932), *Eastern Religions and Western Thought* (1939), and *East and West: Some Reflections* (1955). After India's independence he served as ambassador to the Soviet Union (1949–52) and vice president (1952–62) and president (1962–67) of India. ■ See Paul A. Schilpp, ed., *The Philosophy of Sarvepalli Radhakrishnan* (1952); S. J. Samartha, *Introduction to Radhakrishnan* (1964); and biographies by Sarvepalli Gopal (1989) and K. Satchidananda Murty and Ashok Vohra (1990).

RADIĆ, STJEPAN (1871–1928), Croatian political leader. A founder of the Croatian Peasant party (1905). Radić opposed the union of Croatia and Serbia and called for a separate Croat republic. After the founding of the kingdom of the Serbs, Croats, and Slovenes (1918; later Yugoslavia), Radić advocated Croatian autonomy within a federal state structure. In opposition to the central government throughout most of the 1920s, he was assassinated during a debate in parliament in June 1928.

RADIN, PAUL (1883–1959), Polish-born U.S. anthropologist and ethnographer. Educated at New York's City College and later at Columbia University (Ph.D., 1911), Radin did extensive fieldwork among several American Indian tribes, specializing in the Winnebago. To produce *Crashing Thunder* (1926), a monument of American anthropology, Radin obtained, translated, and edited the autobiography of a Winnebago Indian, the first anthropological document of its kind. His main theoretical contribution to the field was *The Method and Theory of Ethnology* (1933). His ethnographical investigation was always directed at understanding the fundamental character of human nature by focusing on the individual. His lifelong interest in primitive society is reflected in *Primitive Man as Philosopher* (1927) and *Primitive Religion* (1937).

RAEDER, ERICH (1876–1960), German admiral. Raeder joined the German navy at age 18 and served as navigator of the imperial yacht before advancing to staff and fleet service during World War I. As commander in chief (from 1928), he advocated a hit-and-run strategy by fast cruisers and submarines and was primarily responsible for rebuilding the German navy. During World War II, Raeder was instrumental in the invasions of Denmark and Norway but was removed in 1943 after differences with German dictator Adolf Hitler. He was sentenced at the Nuremberg trials to life imprisonment for war crimes but was released in 1955 because of ill health. ■ See his memoir, *My Life* (2 vols., 1956–57; Eng. trans. 1960).

RAFSANJANI, ALI AKBAR HASHEMI (1936–   ), Iranian political and religious leader. The son of a wealthy merchant, Rafsanjani began his religious education at age 14 in the city of Qom and became a disciple of Ayatollah Ruhollah Khomeini. He was arrested and tortured several times during the 1960s and 1970s for his political activities against the government of Muhammad Reza Shah Pahlevi, and he played a major role in the Islamic revolutionary movement that overthrew the Shah in 1979. He was a member of the Islamic Revolutionary Council, a founding member of the Islamic Revolutionary party, and speaker of the Majlis, the Iranian parliament (1980–89). As president of Iran (1989–97) he pursued pragmatic policies, attempting to end Iran's international isolation and to reform the economy by sponsoring liberal free-market policies. After his presidential term ended, he served as chairman of the powerful Expediency Committee, a group of experts formed to arbitrate disputes between the parliament and religious authorities.

RAHMAN, MUJIBUR ("Sheikh Mujib"; 1920–1975), Pakistani and Bangladeshi political leader. Mujib was educated in Calcutta and Dacca and was active in the Muslim League. In 1947, however, he resigned from the league to advocate East Pakistani, or Bengali, autonomy and cofounded the Awami League (1949). He spent a total of more than 10 years in prison as a result. Widespread riots forced his release in 1969. He won the 1970 national election and would have been president of Pakistan, but West Pakistani officials refused to recognize the elections, and civil war broke out. With Indian help, East Pakistan became independent Bangladesh in December 1971 and the charismatic Mujib was named prime minister in January 1972. His autocratic one-man rule, however, coincided with such social and economic deterioration that he was assassinated in a coup d'état.

RAHMAN, TUNKU ABDUL. *See ABDUL RAHMAN, TUNKU.*

RAHNER, KARL (1904–1984), German Roman Catholic theologian. Rahner was ordained a priest in 1932 and studied philosophy at the University of Freiburg (Ph.D. 1936), where he came under the influence of Martin Heidegger. Described as a "theological anthropologist," he was influenced by Thomism, Kantianism, and contemporary phenomenology and existentialism. His ability to integrate these seemingly diverse philosophical systems enabled him to exert a major influence on Roman Catholic thought. He was the official theologian at the Second Vatican Council (1962–65) and one of 30 appointed by Pope Paul VI (1969) to evaluate theological developments since the council. His liberal views influenced the development of "theology of liberation" in the Third World and of movements calling for decentralized authority within the church. His numerous books included *Spirit in the World* (1939; Eng. trans. 1968), *Hearers of the Word* (1941; Eng. trans. 1969), and *Foundations of Christian Faith* (1976; Eng. trans. 1978). ▪ See Louis Roberts, *The Achievement of Karl Rahner* (1967); Andrew Tallon, *Personal Becoming* (1981); and studies by Herbert Vorgrimler (Eng. trans. 1966) and Thomas Sheehan (1985).

RAHV, PHILIP (1908–1973), Russian-born U.S. critic and editor. Rahv emigrated to the United States as a teenager (1922), and by his mid-20s occupied an important place in American cultural life as the cofounder (with William Phillips; 1934) and editor of the *Partisan Review*—an important institution of the left-wing intelligentsia. Rahv's writings often dealt with the position of the intellectual or the artist in society. His *Image and Idea* (1949) included the landmark essay "Paleface and Redskin," in which Rahv analyzed the dichotomy between experience and consciousness in U.S. literature. Other collections included *The Myth and the Powerhouse* (1965) and *Literature and the Sixth Sense* (1969). His *Essays on Literature and Politics 1932–1972* appeared posthumously (1978). Rahv was a professor of English at Brandeis University (1957–73).

RAI, LALA LAJPAT. *See LAJPAT RAI, LALA.*

RAIMU (Jules Muraire; 1883–1946), French actor. In his teens, Raimu appeared in cafés in the south of France. He rose to fame on the Paris stage, where he starred in revues and comedies, including a 1929 production of Marcel Pagnol's *Marius*. By the 1930s Raimu was among France's best-loved actors; in that decade he made more than 30 films, beginning with Sacha Guitry's *The White and the Black* (1931). Raimu continued to appear on stage and screen during and after the World War II German occupation of France; he signed (1943) a contract with the Comédie Française.

RAINEY, MA (Gertrude Malissa Nix Pridgett; 1886–1939), U.S. singer. The first of the great black blues singers, Rainey began singing in cabarets in the early 1900s and spent many years on the vaudeville circuits. She received belated fame in 1923 when the first of her nearly 100 recordings was released. Her most famous protégée was Bessie Smith. ▪ See Sandra R. Lieb, *Mother of the Blues* (1981).

RAINIS (Jānis Pliekšāns; 1865–1929), Latvian poet and dramatist. The century's foremost Latvian literary figure, Rainis was a lawyer, newspaper editor, and political activist who was exiled by the Russians for taking part in the 1905 revolution. His poems and plays expressed his social consciousness, romantic nationalism, and concern for personal and political freedom. His most famous plays were *Fire and Night* (1905) and *The Sons of Jacob* (1919; Eng. trans. 1924). Returning to independent Latvia in 1920, he was elected to parliament, directed the National Theater, and served as minister of education. ▪ See Arvids Ziedonis, *The Religious Philosophy of Janis Rainis* (1969).

RAINWATER, (LEO) JAMES (1917–1986), U.S. physicist. Rainwater was associated with Columbia University for over four decades as student (Ph.D. 1946) and teacher (from 1946). He worked on the Manhattan atomic bomb project from 1942 to 1946. He began inquiries into the architecture of atomic nuclei as a graduate student; collaboration with Aage Bohr generated a significant theory concerning the distortion of shapes of atomic nuclei. Rainwater's theory, sparked by a 1949 seminar given by Charles H. Townes, challenged the accepted notion of a spherical nucleus. In 1975 Rainwater shared the Nobel Prize for Physics with Bohr and Ben Roy Mottelson.

RAJAGOPALACHARI, CHAKRAVARTI (1879–1972), Indian political leader. Rajagopalachari, better known as Rajaji, was a Brahman lawyer who joined nationalist leader Mahatma Gandhi's movement in 1919. A close confidant of Gandhi and a lifelong prohibitionist, he edited *Young India* during Gandhi's imprisonment and served on the Working Committee of the Indian National Congress, the executive arm of the party (1922–42). He was chief minister of his home state of Madras (now Tamil Nadu; 1937–39, 1952–54) and the first Indian governor-general of India (1948–50). In 1959 he split with the Congress party to found the conservative Swatantra party and became a critic of the government. ■ See Monica Felton, *I Meet Rajaji* (1962).

RAJK, LASZLO (1909–1949), Hungarian political leader. A veteran of the Spanish civil war, Rajk became a leader of the communist underground in Hungary during World War II. He helped to reorganize the Communist party after the war and served as minister of the interior (1946–48). Soon after his appointment in 1948 as foreign minister, he was accused of spying for Yugoslavia and the United States, tried, and executed. Rajk was rehabilitated posthumously in 1956. ■ See Béla Szász, *Volunteers for the Gallows* (Eng. trans. 1972).

RÁKOSI, MÁTYÁS (M. Rosencranz; 1892–1971), Hungarian political leader. Rákosi was an associate of Hungarian communist leader Béla Kun, and a minister in his short-lived Hungarian Soviet Republic (1919). He was an important Comintern official (1920–25) before being arrested in Hungary and sentenced to life imprisonment. Released in 1940, he resumed his work with the Comintern in Moscow, returned to Hungary during World War II with the Soviet army (1944), and helped engineer the communist takeover of power. As secretary-general of the Hungarian Communist party (1945–56), deputy prime minister (1945–52), and prime minister (1952–53), he consolidated Stalinist rule. Although removed from power in 1953, he was named premier again in 1955, serving until he fled to the Soviet Union during the 1956 Hungarian revolution.

RAKOVSKY, CHRISTIAN GEORGYEVICH (1873–1941), Bulgarian-born Soviet political leader. Rakovsky undertook revolutionary activities in Bulgaria, Rumania, Western Europe, and Russia before joining the Bolshevik party in December 1917. As premier of the Ukraine (1918–23) he

sought regional autonomy and clashed frequently with Joseph Stalin, who was creating a highly centralized, Russian-dominated state structure. After serving as Soviet ambassador to Great Britain (1923–25) and France (1925–27), he was expelled from the Communist party (1927) for supporting deposed leader Leon Trotsky. The last opposition leader to recant his views (1934), Rakovsky was permitted to rejoin the party (1935) but was imprisoned after a 1938 show trial during the great purges. ■ See his *Selected Writings on Opposition in the USSR: 1923–30* (1980) and biography by Francis Conte (Eng. trans. 1989).

RAMAN, SIR CHANDRASEKHARA VENKATA (1888–1970), Indian physicist. A professor at Calcutta University (1917–33), Raman discovered (1928) the "Raman effect," the change in the wavelength (or color) of light when it is diffused after striking different liquids, solids, or gases. The discovery is used in spectroscopy to determine a material's molecular structure, and Raman was awarded the Nobel Prize for Physics (1930) for this work. Regarded as the father of modern Indian science, he was the first Indian director at the Indian Institute of Science (1933–48), a founder of the Indian Academy of Sciences (1934), and the founder (1947) and director, until his death, of the Raman Institute in Mysore. He wrote *The New Physics* (1951).

RAMANUJAN, SRINIVASA (1887–1920), Indian mathematician. Ramanujan was an untutored mathematics prodigy who, stimulated by an old textbook, reinvented the history of mathematics, discovering in the process several new properties, functions, and algebraic series. He went to Cambridge in 1914 and was elected a fellow in 1918, but some of his later work, before his premature death from tuberculosis, was flawed by his lack of rigorous training. Ramanujan, who was also elected to the Royal Society (1918), is best remembered for his work in hypergeometric series, continued fractions, and properties of the partition function. ■ See his *Collected Papers* (1927); Godfrey H. Hardy, *Ramanujan: Twelve Lectures* (1940); biography by S. R. Ranganathan (1967); and Robert Kanigel, *The Man Who Knew Infinity* (1991).

RAMBERT, DAME MARIE (Cyvia Rambam; 1888–1982), Polish-born British dancer and ballet director. After studying and teaching eurythmics, a method of translating rhythm into bodily movements (Geneva, 1910–12), Rambert taught the technique to members of the Ballet Russe in Paris (1912–14), danced minor roles with the company, and influenced Vaslav Nijinsky's choreography for composer Igor Stravinsky's *The Rite of Spring*. In London (after 1914) she opened a ballet studio (1920) and established the Ballet Club (1930; renamed Ballet Rambert, 1934), which became one of Britain's most important ballet companies. A key figure in British dance for over 50 years, she produced more than 200 works and taught such towering ballet personalities as Alicia Markova, Agnes de Mille, Frederick Ashton, and Antony Tudor. ■ See her autobiography, *Quicksilver* (1972).

RAMO, SIMON (1913–), U.S. engineer. A research scientist with General Electric (1936–46), Ramo did pioneering microwave research and developed the GE electron microscope. At Hughes Aircraft (1946–53), he developed radar, navigation, and computer systems for guided missiles and produced the Falcon air-to-air missile. He founded (with Dean E. Wooldridge) the Ramo-Wooldridge Corp. (1953) and was chief scientist for the U.S. intercontinental-ballistic-missile (ICBM) program (1954–58). For his work in developing the Atlas, Titan, and Minuteman missiles, which were used for defense, research, and space probes during the 1950s and 1960s, Ramo was named "the leading civilian contributor" to the ICBM program by the air force. He was a director of TRW Inc. (1954–85). His books included *Introduction to Microwaves* (1945) and *America's Technology Slip* (1980).

RAMÓN Y CAJAL, SANTIAGO (1852–1934), Spanish physician and histologist. Ramón received his medical degree at the University of Saragossa and in 1877 became professor of anatomy there. Ten years later he began to study the nervous system and the brain and eventually discovered how neurons work and how nerve impulses are transmitted to cells. For this work he was awarded (with Camillo Golgi) the 1906 Nobel Prize for Physiology or Medicine. He was professor of histology at the University of Madrid (1892–1922) and then head of his own institute until his death. He wrote *Degeneration and Regeneration of the Nervous System* (1913–14; Eng. trans. 1928), *Histology* (1899–1904; Eng. trans. 1933), and the autobiography, *Recollection of My Life* (1901–07; Eng. trans. 1937, 1989). ■ See Dorothy F. Cannon, *Explorer of the Human Brain* (1949) and E. Home Craigie and William C. Gibson, *The World of Ramón y Cajal* (1968).

RAMOS, FIDEL (1928–), Filipino political leader. Born into an upper-middle-class family, Ramos graduated from the U.S. Military Academy at West Point (1950) and earned a master's degree in civil engineering at the University of Illinois (1951). He headed the Philippine Constabulary (1970–86), the arm of government responsible for domestic security, and helped Ferdinand Marcos impose martial law (1972–81). However, he subsequently supported the popular movement that drove Marcos from office and served as armed forces chief of staff (1986–88) and defense minister (1988–92) under reformist president Corazon Aquino. As president (1992–98) he made peace with leftist guerrillas, Muslim separatists, and dissident right-wing plotters within the military. He also increased the country's economic growth rate through deregulation and encouragement of foreign investment. However, high levels of poverty, underemployment, crime, and corruption continued during his years in power.

RAMOS, GRACILIANO (1892–1953), Brazilian novelist. Ramos spent many years as a civil servant in the poverty-stricken rural northeast of Brazil (1910–36). A practitioner of literary naturalism, he became a leading figure in Brazilian letters with the publication of *Anguish* (1936; Eng. trans. 1946), *São Bernardo* (1934; Eng. trans. 1979), and *Barren Lives* (1938; Eng. trans. 1965), psychological novels that explored the effects of social and economic upheaval in the northeast. He was imprisoned (1936) by dictator Getúlio Vargas for political reasons and he joined the Communist party in 1945. ■ See the autobiographical *Childhood* (1945; Eng. trans. 1979); study by Richard A. Mazzara (1974); and Celso Lemos de Oliveira, *Understanding Graciliano Ramos* (1988).

RAMOS-HORTA, JOSÉ (1949–), Timorese political leader. An advocate of East Timorese independence from Portugal, Ramos-Horta was exiled to Mozambique for anticolonial activities (1970–72). After the Portuguese withdrew and independence was declared (1975), Indonesia invaded East Timor (1975) and annexed it (1976) despite international condemnation and armed resistance by the East Timorese. Ramos-Horta fled three days before the Indonesian attack and became the leading international spokesperson for the Timorese independence movement. From his exile in Australia, where he taught law at the University of New South Wales, he toured the world publicizing the abuses of the Indonesian military and calling for a resolution to the conflict, which had taken the lives of an estimated one-third of the territory's 600,000 inhabitants. Ramos-Horta shared the 1996 Nobel Peace Prize with Bishop Carlos Ximenes Belo for working to end the crisis in East Timor. ■ See his book, *Funu: The Unfinished Saga of East Timor* (1987), and John Pilger, *Distant Voices* (1994).

RAMPAL, JEAN-PIERRE (1922–2000), French flutist. The son of a professor of flute at the Marseilles Conservatory of Music, Rampal studied both music and medicine before deciding to concentrate on his flute playing. After World War II he began the most successful solo career in the history of his instrument. Concentrating at first on the baroque repertoire, which was experiencing a resurgence of popularity, he extended his interest to such modern masters as Roussel, Prokofiev, and Hindemith. He appeared in concerts throughout the world and by the early 1970s had performed or recorded virtually every important work ever written for the flute, commissioned several new ones, and transcribed others from the violin repertoire. Rampal was known for his pure luxuriant tone and dazzling technical virtuosity. ■ See his autobiography, *Music, My Love* (1989; with Deborah Wise).

RAMSAY, SIR BERTRAM HOME (1883–1945), British military leader. The son of a brigadier general, Ramsay joined the Royal Navy as a cadet at age 15 and served as a destroyer commander in the Dover Patrol during World

War I. An expert in amphibious operations, he was called out of retirement at the start of World War II and was responsible for the massive naval evacuation of British and Allied troops from Dunkirk (1940), for which he was knighted. He later helped plan the successful Allied invasion of North Africa (1942) and the landing on Sicily (1943), and was promoted to full admiral in April 1944. As naval commander in chief of the Allied Expeditionary Force, he planned the invasion of Normandy (June 1944), the greatest combined military operation in history. He died in an air crash near Paris five months before the end of the war in Europe. ■ See his 1944 diary, *The Year of D-Day* (1994).

RAMSEY, ARTHUR MICHAEL, BARON OF CANTERBURY (1904–1988), British clergyman. A graduate of Magdalene College, Cambridge (1927), Ramsey was ordained in 1928 and served at various parishes and colleges as a teacher and vicar in the years before World War II. In 1940 he was named professor of divinity at Cambridge and in 1942 bishop of Durham. He was transferred to the archbishopric of York (1956) and served as archbishop of Canterbury from 1961 to 1974. Ramsey sought greater autonomy for the Church of England. An advocate of Christian unity, he met with Pope Paul VI (March 1966)—the first encounter between the leaders of the Roman Catholic and Anglican churches since their separation in 1534. His books included *The Gospel and the Catholic Church* (1936), *The Resurrection of Christ* (1945), *From Gore to Temple* (1960), *Canterbury Pilgrim* (1974), and *Be Still and Know* (1982). ■ See James B. Simpson, *The Hundredth Archbishop of Canterbury* (1962), and biography by Owen Chadwick (1991).

RAMSEY, FRANK PLUMPTON (1903–1930), British philosopher and mathematician. Regarded as one of the most brilliant thinkers of his generation, Ramsey was a lecturer in mathematics at Cambridge University (1924–30) before his untimely death, after an operation, at age 26. He made important contributions to the fields of mathematical logic, the philosophy of science, and the mathematical theory of probability. He also wrote two notable papers in economic theory, "A Contribution to the Theory of Taxation" (1927) and "A Mathematical Theory of Saving" (1928). His papers, edited by R. B. Braithwaite, were published posthumously as *The Foundations of Mathematics and Other Logical Essays* (1931). ■ See Nils-Eric Sahlin, *The Philosophy of F. P. Ramsey* (1990).

RAMSEY, NORMAN F. (1915–   ), U.S. physicist. Ramsey studied at Columbia University (Ph.D. 1940), helped to develop radar during World War II, and directed research groups at both the Los Almos Scientific Laboratory (1943–45) and the Brookhaven National Laboratory (1946–47). He taught at Harvard (1947–86). During the late 1940s and early 1950s he worked on the structure and properties of atoms and developed the cesium atomic clock, a device that established the international time standard, and the hydrogen maser, a laserlike device used for the precise measurement of time and frequency. He shared the 1989 Nobel Prize for Physics with Wolfgang Paul and Hans G. Dehmelt.

RAMUZ, CHARLES-FERDINAND (1878–1947), Swiss (French-language) novelist, short-story writer, and poet. Ramuz returned to his native canton of Vaud (1914) after spending 12 years in Paris and produced a body of literature that realistically re-created the life and thought of the region's peasants. Using his subjects' rough, earthy, and ungrammatical language, he wrote a penetrating series of lyrical, almost mystical novels that emphasized rural people's frequently violent and tragic struggles with nature. The novels *The End of All Men* (1922; Eng. trans. 1944), *Terror on the Mountain* (1926; Eng. trans. 1968), *Beauty on Earth* (1927; Eng. trans. 1929), and *When the Mountain Fell* (1934; Eng. trans. 1949) established his reputation as the century's most powerful and original French-Swiss writer. ■ See study by David Bevan (1979).

RAND, AYN (1905–1982), Russian-born U.S. novelist. Rand settled (1926) in the United States after graduating from Leningrad University and was a screenwriter for several years. She was best known for her long, didactic novels which celebrated selfishness, individualism, and laissez-faire capitalism. *We the Living* (1936) depicted Russian individualists confronted by dictatorship while *The Fountainhead* (1943) was a fictional account of a stubborn, individualistic architect. *Atlas Shrugged* (1957) offered a blueprint for a new society based on the vow, "I will never live for the sake of another man, nor ask any other man to live for mine." *For the New Intellectual* (1961) distilled philosophical passages from her novels to outline the theory of "rational self-interest" that she called objectivism. She also wrote *The Virtue of Selfishness* (1965) and *Capitalism: The Unknown Ideal* (1966). ■ See Nathaniel Branden, *Who Is Ayn Rand?* (1962), and Barbara Branden, *The Passion of Ayn Rand* (1986).

RAND, SALLY (Helen Gould Beck; 1904–1979), U.S. dancer. Leaving home at age 13, Sally Rand became a cigarette girl in a Kansas City club and made it to Hollywood, where in the late 1920s she won roles in several forgettable silent films. She created a sensation at the 1933 World's Fair in Chicago as a fan dancer. Illuminated by lavender lights, she danced to music by Debussy and Chopin while maneuvering two extravagant seven-foot ostrich fans around her nude body. Her fan dancing created a new genre of entertainment and helped legitimate provocative dance forms. She continued to dance in public until 1978.

RANDOLPH, ASA PHILIP (1889–1979), U.S. labor leader. A. Philip Randolph left his native Florida for New York City and studied at City College. He joined the Socialist party in 1911 and, with journalist Chandler Owen, founded the highly regarded black militant political journal, the *Messenger* (1917). Randolph, a pacifist, believed that only by integration of the labor movement could racism be conquered in the United States. He founded the all-black Brotherhood of Sleeping Car Porters (1925) and, in a job action of unprecedented length, unionized the Pullman Co. (1937). He served as president of the National Negro Congress during the 1930s and was instrumental in persuading Pres. Franklin D. Roosevelt to integrate defense plants and to set up the Fair Employment Practices Committee (1941) and in getting Pres. Harry Truman to integrate the armed forces (1948). He served as a vice president of the AFL-CIO (from 1957) and was a leader of the March on Washington (1963), the largest civil-rights demonstration in U.S. history. ■ See biographies by Jervis Anderson (1973) and Paula F. Pfeffer (1990).

RANK, JOSEPH ARTHUR RANK, 1st BARON (1888–1972), British film magnate. An employee in his father's flour business and a Methodist Sunday-school teacher, J. Arthur Rank became interested in film as a medium for spreading the Gospel and for increasing his prosperity. During the 1930s he built up the Rank Organisation, with its trademark of the bare-chested man beating a gong, into the ultimate filmmaking enterprise. Encompassing everything from production and processing to distribution and exhibition, Rank's company virtually monopolized the British film industry. A shrewd businessman, Rank later diversified into Xerox copying, hotels, and bowling alleys when film investment became less lucrative. He was raised to the peerage in 1957. ■ See Alan Wood, *Mr. Rank* (1952).

RANK, OTTO (Otto Rosenfeld; 1884–1939), Austrian-born psychoanalyst. Rank received a Ph.D. in philology (University of Vienna, 1912) and served psychoanalyst Sigmund Freud as secretary and protégé for 20 years. Applying Freud's theories to art and literature, he wrote *Art and Artist* (1907; Eng. trans. 1932) and *The Myth of the Birth of the Hero* (1909; Eng. trans. 1914). His theory of the genesis of neuroses, elaborated in *The Trauma of Birth* (1924; Eng. trans. 1929), was considered heretical by Freud, and Rank left Vienna (1924) and lived in Paris and New York, where he practiced a relatively brief, intense form of therapy devoted to reliving the birth trauma. ■ See biography by Jessie Taft (1958); E. James Lieberman, *Acts of Will* (1985); Fay B. Karpf, *Psychology and Psychotherapy of Otto Rank* (1953); and study by Esther Menaker (1982).

RANKIN, JEANNETTE (1880–1973), U.S. suffragist and pacifist. A social worker, Rankin began her suffragist activities in 1910; in 1916—two years after Montana, her native state, gave women the vote—she became the first woman elected to the U.S. Congress. A Republican, she served two terms (1917–19; 1941–43) in the House of Representatives and cast votes against U.S. entry in both world wars. She promoted women's rights, introducing the first bill to grant women citizenship independent of that of their husbands and calling for government support of education in hygiene in maternity and infancy. She was active in various women's and antiwar organizations, and at age 87 she led (1968) the Jeannette Rankin brigade of 5,000 women who expressed opposition to the Vietnam War at a Washington, D.C., demonstration. ■ See study by Hannah Josephson (1974); Sue Davidson, *A Heart in Politics* (1994); and Kevin S. Giles, *Flight of the Dove* (1980).

RANSOM, JOHN CROWE (1888–1974), U.S. poet and critic. While teaching (1914–37) at his alma mater, Vanderbilt University, Ransom founded, with students Allen Tate and Robert Penn Warren, the literary journal *Fugitive* (1922–25), which sparked the southern literary renaissance. The "Fugitives" reunited during the Depression as the "Agrarians," devoted to the triumph of nature over machine. Ransom later went to Ohio's Kenyon College, where he established and edited (1938–59) the *Kenyon Review* and published *The New Criticism* (1941), which gave the name to the critical school that rejected the Victorian stress on literature as a moral force, discounted literary biography, and advocated scrutiny of a text's literary structures. Ransom's own ironic, understated poetry was collected in *Selected Poems* (1945; enlarged and revised 1963) and in *Poems and Essays* (1955). *Beating the Bushes: Selected Essays, 1914–1970* appeared in 1972. ■ See Thomas D. Young, *Gentleman in a Dustcoat* (1976), and study by Thornton H. Parsons (1969).

RAO, RAJA (1909–   ), Indian writer. A south Indian Brahman, Raja Rao studied at the Sorbonne (Paris, 1930–33) and spent many years in France and later in the United States, where he taught philosophy at the University of Texas (from 1965). He was strongly influenced by the Gandhian movement during the 1930s, and his celebrated first novel, *Kanthapura* (1938), and short-story collection, *The Cow of the Barricades* (1947), reflect the impact of Gandhi's campaign in rural south India. His later metaphysical novels, *The Serpent and the Rope* (1960) and *The Cat and Shakespeare* (1965), deal with the concept of illusion and reality and draw on both the Indian and Western philosophical traditions. These works helped establish Rao's reputation as one of India's foremost English-language novelists. His later works included the novels *Comrade Kirillov* (1976) and *The Chessmaster and His Moves* (1978), the short-story collection *The Policeman and the Rose* (1977), and *The Meaning of India* (1996). ■ See studies by M. K. Naik (1972), C. D. Narasimhaiah (1973), and Nivedita Nanda (1992).

RAPACKI, ADAM (1909–1970), Polish political leader. The son of a leader of the pre–World War I cooperative movement in Poland, Rapacki joined the Socialist party in 1936. After spending World War II in a German prison camp, he joined Poland's new Workers' (Communist) party and was minister of education (1950–56). He survived the defeat of the Polish Stalinists in 1956 and served as foreign minister (1956–68). In 1957 Rapacki, a courtly and popular diplomat, proposed to the United Nations the establishment of an atom-free zone in Central Europe. Known as the "Rapacki Plan," the proposal was rejected by the United States, but it enhanced Poland's international prestige.

RAPAPORT, DAVID (1911–1960), Hungarian-born U.S. psychologist. In his youth Rapaport was a left-wing Zionist activist who spent two years on a kibbutz in Palestine. After receiving a Ph.D. from the Royal Hungarian University (1938), he emigrated to the United States (1938) and worked as a staff psychologist at the Menninger Clinic in Topeka, Kansas (1940–48), and at the Austen Riggs Center in Stockbridge, Massachusetts (1948–60). Rapaport was a pioneer in diagnostic testing and a leading theorist on the psychology of thought processes. He wrote *Emotions and Memory* (1942) and *The Structure of Psychoanalytic Theory* (1959), and collaborated on *Diagnostic Psychological Testing* (2 vols., 1945–46). ■ See his *Collected Papers* (1967).

RASMUSSEN, KNUD JOHAN VICTOR (1879–1933), Danish explorer and ethnologist. The son of a Danish missionary father and a part-Eskimo mother, Rasmussen was born and raised in Greenland and spent his life exploring Greenland and studying the life of the Eskimos. He participated in or led eight expeditions (1902–33), during which he founded a permanent trading post in northern Greenland called Thule (1910), mapped many of the remote areas of Greenland, and traveled by dog team across Arctic America from Greenland to Point Barrow, Alaska (1921–24), tracing Eskimo migration routes and gathering valuable ethnographic data. His books include *Eskimo Folk Tales* (Eng. trans. 1921), *Greenland by the Polar Sea* (1919; Eng. trans. 1921), and *Across Arctic America* (1925; Eng. trans. 1927). ■ See Peter Freuchen, *I Sailed With Rasmussen* (1958).

RASPUTIN, GRIGORI YEFIMOVICH (1871?–1916), Russian mystic and political figure. The charismatic peasant monk Rasputin was introduced (1905) to Czar Nicholas II and Czarina Alexandra and quickly insinuated himself into their confidence by exhibiting hypnotic powers that seemed to control the hemophilia of Alexis, heir to the throne. After 1911 Rasputin exercised an increasingly powerful influence in political affairs, despite his widely publicized dissolute behavior. Rasputin was popularly believed to be a German agent during World War I; he seemed to interfere with government administration and counseled the czar against all reform. His role in the court compromised the monarchy and the Orthodox Church in the eyes of many. Rasputin was assassinated in a plot masterminded by Prince Felix Yusupov, a relative of the czar. ■ See biographies by Alex de Jonge (1982), Joseph T. Fuhrmann (1990), and Brian Moynahan (1997); study by Michael de Enden (1982); V. M. Purishkevich, *The Murder of Rasputin* (1924; Eng. trans. 1985); and Edvard Radzinsky, *The Rasputin File* (Eng. trans. 2000).

RATHENAU, WALTER (1867–1922), German industrialist and political leader. Son of the head of Germany's largest electric-utility concern, Rathenau earned a Ph.D. in electrochemistry (1889) before joining the family firm. A reformer and idealist, he wrote books lamenting the tyranny of modern technology and advocated a decentralized economy featuring elements of capitalism and state planning. He organized raw-materials distribution during World War I and helped rationalize German industry as minister of reconstruction (1921–22). In January 1922 Rathenau, a Jew, became foreign minister of Germany; he negotiated the treaty of Rapallo recognizing the Soviet Union before his assassination by anti-Semitic rightists that June. His books included *In Days to Come* (1917; Eng. trans. 1921) and *The New Society* (1919; Eng. trans. 1921). ■ See biography by Harry Kessler (Eng. trans. 1930) and study by David Felix (1971).

RATHER, DAN (1931–), U.S. broadcast journalist. Born into a working-class Texas family during the Depression, Rather was the first member of his family to attend college. He studied at Sam Houston State Teachers College, then landed a job at a radio station. In his early career in television news, Rather covered the civil-rights movement, managed the London bureau, and reported from Vietnam. As CBS White House correspondent (1964, 1966–74), he made a name for himself with two years of aggressive reporting on the Watergate scandal, particularly his tough questioning of Pres. Richard M. Nixon at press conferences. He was coanchor of the news program *60 Minutes* (1975–81) before succeeding Walter Cronkite as anchor and managing editor of the CBS *Evening News* (1981). Making greater use of dramatic visual material and stories that show how ordinary Americans are affected by the news, Rather competed for high ratings with NBC and ABC anchors Tom Brokaw and Peter Jennings. He wrote *The Palace Guard* (1974; with Gary Gates), *The Camera Never Blinks* (1977; with Mickey Herskowitz), *The Camera Never Blinks Twice* (1994), and *Deadlines and Datelines* (1999).

RATTIGAN, SIR TERENCE MERVYN (1911–1977), British playwright. Rattigan made his reputation with two long-running farces, *French Without Tears* (1936) and *While the Sun Shines* (1943). His later commercially successful plays ranged from farce to historical dramas and included *The Winslow Boy* (1946), *The Browning Version* (1948), *Separate Tables* (1954), *Ross* (1960; based on the life of T. E. Lawrence), and *Bequest to the Nation* (1970). He also wrote numerous screenplays. Rattigan was not regarded as a deep and insightful playwright but rather as a solid craftsman of the well-made play who knew the public's taste. ■ See biographies by Michael Darlow and Gillian Hodson (1979) and Geoffrey Wansell (1997).

RAUSCHENBERG, ROBERT (1925–), U.S. artist. Rauschenberg was born in Texas of German and Indian ancestry and studied at the Kansas City Art Institute and the Académie Julian in Paris (1947). During the 1950s he began experimenting with all-white and all-black paintings that were acclaimed examples of minimalism. Then he began assembling "combines" or conglomerations of everyday objects such as buckets or hats appended to large canvases, which found their niche somewhere between abstract expressionism and pop art. He also produced large canvases utilizing a silk-screen stenciling process. His work helped break down the divisions between painting, sculpture, photography, printmaking, and technology, and he was extremely influential among young artists of the 1960s and 1970s. He designed for several dance and theater groups, notably those led by Merce Cunningham, Paul Taylor, and Trisha Brown, and founded (1984) the Rauschenberg Overseas Cultural Interchange (ROCI), a project that supports cooperation among artists around the world. ■ See study by Andrew Forge (1969); Calvin Tomkins, *Off the Wall* (1980); and biography by Mary Lynn Kotz (1990).

RAUSCHENBUSCH, WALTER (1861–1918), U.S. clergyman. Rauschenbusch was ordained in the Baptist ministry in 1886. In 1897 he joined the faculty of Rochester Theological Seminary and in 1902, the year he completed his training (D.D., University of Rochester), became professor of church history. After publishing *Christianity and the Social Crisis* (1907), he became the best-known representative of the Social Gospel movement, a liberal, idealistic movement of U.S Protestants dedicated to social reform. Rauschenbusch sought "a new order that would rest on the Christian principles of equal rights and democratic distribution of economic power." His ideas were reflected in New Deal policy in the 1930s. Later books included *Christianizing the Social Order* (1912), *The Social Principles of Jesus* (1916), and *A Theology for the Social Gospel* (1917). ■ See biography by Dores Robinson Sharpe (1942).

RAVEL, MAURICE JOSEPH (1875–1937), French composer. Ravel was a musical prodigy who studied at the Paris Conservatory for 16 years but was unsuccessful in his efforts to win the coveted Prix de Rome. A private income allowed him the luxury of conscientious musicianship, and he turned out elegant, polished impressionistic compositions at the rate of one a year. His best-known works include the piano compositions *Gaspard de La Nuit* (1908) and *Valses Nobles et sentimentales* (1911), the ballet *Daphnis et Chloë* (1912), the operatic fantasy *L'enfant et les Sortilèges* (1925), and the orchestral works *Rhapsodie Espagnol* (1907) and *Bolero* (1928). ■ See the biographies by Rollo H. Myers (1960), H. H. Stuckenschmidt (Eng. trans. 1968), and Gerald Larner (1996).

RAWLINGS, MARJORIE (Marjorie Kinnan; 1896–1953), U.S. novelist. A graduate of the University of Wisconsin (1918), Rawlings worked as a newspaper reporter for 10 years but grew increasingly frustrated because of her inability to get her short stories published. She moved (1928) to swampy backwoods Florida; the resourceful poor white farmers she encountered and the lush scenery there provided the subject matter for her novels. She is best known for *The Yearling* (1938, Pulitzer Prize), the sentimental story of a boy and his pet fawn. Rawlings contrasted garden and wilderness, bemoaning the encroachment of tourist bungalows on pioneer territory. *Cross Creek* (1942) recounted her retreat from civilization. Her *Selected Letters* appeared in 1983. ■ See *The Marjorie Rawlings Reader* (1956), Gordon E. Bigelow, *Frontier Eden* (1966), and study by Samuel Bellman (1974).

RAWLS, JOHN (1921–), U.S. philosopher. Rawls studied at Princeton University (Ph.D. 1950) and taught at Harvard University (1962–). In his major work, *A Theory of Justice* (1971), he grappled with basic social issues that had been neglected by contemporary academic philosophers. The book, which challenged utilitarianism, developed a contract theory of justice for a modern liberal society, based on the concepts of fairness and individual liberties, in which inequalities can be allowed only if they result in compensating benefits for the least advantaged members of society. The book provoked passionate debate, revitalized the discipline of political theory, and was considered one of the most significant philosophical works of the second half of the 20th century. In *Political Liberalism* (1993), Rawls responded to his critics and discussed the dilemmas posed by cultural diversity and ethical pluralism in developing a liberal theory of the good society. ■ See Robert Paul Wolff, *Understanding Rawls* (1977); Norman Daniels, ed., *Reading Rawls* (1975); Thomas W. Pogge, *Realizing Rawls* (1989); and studies by Rex Martin (1985) and H. G. Blocker and G. H. Smith, eds. (1980).

RAY, DIXY LEE (1914–1994), U.S. zoologist, educator, and public official. Ray taught science in California public schools, then finished her Ph.D. in zoology at Stanford (1945). She specialized in marine biology, and her research in the 1950s and 1960s reflected her concern with protecting the environment. Ray had taught at the University of Washington for a quarter century when Pres. Richard Nixon appointed her to the Atomic Energy Commission (1972); she later (1973–74) served as chair of that commission. After brief service in the State Department, she made a dramatic debut in elective politics, becoming Democratic governor of the state of Washington (1976). However, she lost a primary battle in a reelection bid in 1980; her blunt manner, and her support of nuclear power, unrestrained economic growth, and supertankers in Puget Sound were believed to have alienated Democrats. ■ See Louis R. Guzzo, *Is It True What They Say About Dixy?* (1981).

RAY, MAN (1890–1976), U.S. painter and photographer. Ray was an artist from Philadelphia and the only important

U.S. member of the dada and surrealist movement. He first turned to photography to reproduce his own paintings. In Paris during the 1920s and 1930s he enjoyed success as a portrait photographer and began experimenting with the photographic process. Called a poet of the darkroom, Ray created the unusual effects he called "rayographs" by casting shadows on light-sensitive paper. He also made films such as *L'Étoile de Mer* ("Star of the Sea"; 1928). ▪ See *Man Ray: Photographs* (1982) and his autobiography, *Self Portrait* (1963).

RAY, SATYAJIT (1921–1992), Indian film director. A member of a prominent Bengali artistic family, Ray studied economics, painting, and graphics. While working as an art director for a British advertising agency, he became fascinated with film, and he apprenticed (1950) with French director Jean Renoir, who was filming *The River* in India. Using nonprofessional actors in their natural environments, Ray began to make films of Indian family life, including the celebrated trilogy adapted from the novel *Pather Panchali* (*Pather Panchali,* 1955; *Aparajito,* 1956; *The World of Apu,* 1959). *The Music Room* (1958) examined the spiritual malaise of the Indian aristocracy, while *Devi* (1960) delved into Hindu superstition. Later films directed and written by Ray included *Distant Thunder* (1973), a depiction of the Bengali famine during World War II; *The Middleman* (1975), a study of the decline of traditional values in contemporary Calcutta; and *The Chess Players* (1977), an account of the Lucknow aristocracy on the eve of the British annexation in 1856. His last film, *The Stranger* (1991), was about family loyalties and trust. ▪ See Marie Seton, *Portrait of a Director* (1971), and studies by Ben Nyce (1988) and Andrew Robinson (1989).

RAYBURN, SAMUEL TALIAFERRO (1882–1961), U.S. political leader. Called "Mr. Democrat," Sam Rayburn of Texas served as a U.S. congressman (1913–61) and was Speaker of the House of Representatives (1940–47; 1949–53; 1955–61) longer than any other person. Fiercely loyal to the Democratic party and a master of legislative procedure and political persuasion, Rayburn helped mold much of the New Deal legislative program and helped push through the Marshall Plan, Pres. Harry Truman's Fair Deal program, and the Civil Rights acts of 1957 and 1960. An unideological moderate, he worked closely with every president from Franklin D. Roosevelt to John F. Kennedy and was a longtime friend and supporter of fellow Democrat and Texan Lyndon B. Johnson. ▪ See C. Dwight Dorough, *Mr. Sam* (1962); biography by Alfred Steinberg (1975); and Anthony Champagne, *Congressman Sam Rayburn* (1984).

RAYMOND, ALEXANDER GILLESPIE (1909–1956), U.S. cartoonist. In 1934 Raymond was asked by King Features Syndicate to create several Sunday features, including *Flash Gordon* (to compete with *Buck Rogers*) and *Jungle Jim* (to compete with *Tarzan*). Both strips became immensely popular, appeared in comic books, and inspired radio and movie serials and television series. A skilled draftsman who was known for his extremely realistic drawings, Raymond also collaborated on the *Secret Agent X-9* crime-fighter strip with novelist Dashiell Hammett (1934–35). After World War II service as a public information officer and artist with the U.S. Marine Corps, he initiated *Rip Kirby* (1946), a strip concerning the adventures of a sophisticated criminologist. Raymond served as president of the National Cartoonists Society (1950–52). He died in an automobile accident.

RAZAK, TUN ABDUL. *See ABDUL RAZAK, TUN.*

READ, SIR HERBERT (1893–1968), British art historian. Read was a self-described philosophic anarchist, opposed equally to the plutocracy and the proletariat. He revived interest in the discredited 19th-century romantic movement and interpreted and defended modern art movements, from cubism to surrealism and abstract art, although he had little sympathy for post-abstract expressionist art. He taught widely and wrote prolifically, including *Art Now* (1933), *The Innocent Eye* (1933), *Art and Society* (1936), and *The Philosophy of Modern Art* (1952). ▪ See his autobiography, *The Contrary Experience* (1963), and James King, *The Last Modern* (1990).

READING, RUFUS DANIEL ISAACS, 1st MARQUESS OF (1860–1935), British public official. Reading left school at age 15 to join the family business and later spent two years in the merchant navy. In 1887 he became a lawyer. Prominent in the Liberal party, he served in Parliament (1904–13) and was attorney general (1910–13), lord chief justice (1913–21), and ambassador to the United States (1918–19). From 1921 to 1926 Reading was viceroy of India during an unsettled time when nationalist leader Mahatma Gandhi's "satyagraha" (nonviolent) movement was powerful. Reading's final post was as foreign secretary in 1931. ▪ See G. R. Isaacs, 2nd Marquess of Reading, *Rufus Isaacs, First Marquis of Reading* (2 vols., 1942–45), and biography by H. Montgomery Hyde (1968).

REAGAN, RONALD WILSON (1911–), U.S. president. Reagan left his native Middle West for Hollywood (1937), where he starred in more than 50 movies (including *Knute Rockne—All American,* 1940; *King's Row,* 1942; *The Hasty Heart,* 1950; and *Bedtime for Bonzo,* 1951) and served as president of the Screen Actors Guild (1947–52; 1959–60). Although originally a New Deal Democrat, he became increasingly conservative after the late 1940s and was a spokesperson for big business during the 1950s and a prominent supporter of Republican conservative Barry Goldwater in the 1964 presidential campaign. As two-time governor of California (1967–75), Reagan became the hero of the American right wing, and after unsuccessful presidential campaigns in 1968 and 1976 he was elected (1980) president, the oldest man (age 69) ever to be elected to that office. He was reelected in 1984. He carried out a tough anti-Soviet foreign policy, sponsored programs of increased military spending, and proposed the massive space weapons system, the Strategic Defense Initiative, commonly called "Star Wars." His program of tax cuts and decreased social expenditures was known popularly as "Reaganomics." In 1987 he signed a treaty with Soviet leader Mikhail Gorbachev to eliminate intermediate-range nuclear weapons. Also in 1987, Reagan and his administration were severely criticized by Congress for initiating what became known as the Iran-Contra Affair, in which a White House agency secretly (and illegally) sold weapons to Iran and used the profits to help the contras, right-wing rebels fighting a civil war against the leftist government of Nicaragua. ■ See his autobiographies, *Where's the Rest of Me?* (1965) and *An American Life* (1990); Laurence Leamer, *Make-Believe* (1983); Laurence Barrett, *Gambling with History* (1983); and biographies by Lou Cannon (1982; 1991) and Edmund Morris, *Dutch* (1999).

REBER, GROTE (1911–), U.S. astronomer. Reber built the world's first radio telescope (1937), a bowl-shaped antenna 31 feet in diameter with which he mapped radiation from space. His early maps (1940; 1942) indicated that the visible sky was very different from the radio sky in that areas of strong radio emission were unrelated to any visible celestial object. Until after World War II, Reber operated the world's only radio telescope. However, his work inspired numerous astronomers, and eventually radio telescopes were built throughout the world. Reber did research at observatories in Hawaii (1951–54), West Virginia (1957–61), and Australia (1954–57; 1961–).

REBREANU, LIVIU (1885–1944), Rumanian novelist. One of the creators of the modern Rumanian novel, Rebreanu was educated in Budapest and Vienna and became an officer in the Austrian army. His novels depicted Rumanian village life and described the peasants' desire for land and independence. Rebeanu's most influential works were *Ion* (1920; Eng. trans. 1967), a novel of rural Transylvania at the turn of the century; *The Forest of the Hanged* (1922; Eng. trans. 1967), which dealt with Rumanian participation in World War I; and *The Uprising* (1934), a work about the 1907 peasant revolt.

RECTO, CLARO MAYO (1890–1960), Filipino political leader. Recto, a law graduate of Santo Tomás University (1914), was elected to congress in 1919. After serving in the senate (1931–35), he was president of the constitutional convention (1935) and associate justice of the supreme court (1935–41). Recto took part in the collaborationist government of José Laurel during World War II; after the war he served in the senate (from 1949) and was a critic of Philippine dependence on the United States and of U.S. military bases in his country. He ran unsuccessfully for president as head of the Nationalist Citizen's party (1957). ■ See his autobiography, *My Crusade* (1955), and study by José Maria Sison (1969).

REDFIELD, ROBERT (1897–1958), U.S. anthropologist. Redfield had already earned a law degree and a position in a legal practice when he became interested in anthropology during a 1923 visit to Mexico. Within three years he returned to Mexico to do fieldwork and in 1928 earned a Ph.D. at the University of Chicago, the institution with which he was associated throughout his lifetime. Concerned with social anthropology, he deemphasized archaeology and linguistics and focused on the cultural and social processes that illuminate the relationship between urban and folk societies and between the "great" (elite) and "little" (folk) traditions. Redfield's works included *Tepoztlán* (1930), *Chan Kom: A Maya Village* (1934), *Folk Culture of Yucatán* (1941), *A Village that Chose Progress* (1950), *The Primitive World and Its Transformations* (1953), and *Peasant Society and Culture* (1956).

REDFORD, ROBERT (1937–), U.S. actor and director. Redford grew up in southern California and studied art before turning to acting. He appeared in several films in the mid-1960s, gaining star status when he was paired with Paul Newman in *Butch Cassidy and the Sundance Kid* (1969), a combination that was repeated in *The Sting* (1973). Redford became known as much for his all-American good looks as for his starring roles. He won widespread public acclaim, but critics were generally less enthusiastic. His credits included *The Candidate* (1972), *All the President's Men* (1976), *The Natural* (1984), and *Out of Africa* (1985). He won an Academy Award for directing *Ordinary People* (1980). He directed *A River Runs Through It* (1993) and *Quiz Show* (1994) and directed and starred in *The Horse Whisperer* (1998). Also known for his support of environmental issues and the arts, Redford founded the Sundance Institute (1981) and Film Festival (1984) in Utah to aid aspiring filmmakers. ■ See biography by David Downing (1983).

REDGRAVE, VANESSA (1937–), British actress. She was born into a celebrated theatrical family; her father, Sir Michael Redgrave, and her sister and brother, Lynn and Corin Redgrave, were all actors. Vanessa Redgrave began her career with the Royal Shakespeare Company, gaining prominence on the London stage in the early 1960s. She reached an international audience on the screen; critics praised the power and delicacy of her performances in such films as *Morgan!* (1965), *Isadora* (1968), *Mary Queen of Scots* (1971), and *Julia* (1978; Academy Award). On television, she starred in such productions as *Playing for Time* (1981) and *Peter the Great* (1986). A visible political activist who repeatedly sought election to the British Parliament as a member of the Worker's Revolutionary party, Redgrave stirred controversy with her support of the Palestinian Liberation Organization (PLO). She produced and narrated the documentary film *The Palestinians* (1977). Redgrave sued the Boston Symphony Orchestra when it canceled a contract with her on political grounds (1982). The jury awarded her $100,000 for damage to her career (1984); a federal district-judge later overturned the award (1985). Her subsequent films included *Howards End* (1992) and *House of the Spirits* (1993). ■ See her autobiography (1991).

REED, SIR CAROL (1906–1976), British film director. A stage actor and dialogue director in the 1930s, Reed directed *Night Train to Munich* (1940) before making World War II military documentaries. In 1947 he received international attention for *Odd Man Out*, followed by *The Fallen Idol* (1948) and *The Third Man* (1949), a haunting story of corruption in postwar Vienna. In later years he directed *The Agony and the Ecstasy* (1965) and won an Academy Award for the musical film *Oliver!* (1968), which also won an Oscar for best picture. ■ See Nicholas Wapshott, *The Man Between* (1990) and Robert F. Moss, *The Films of Carol Reed* (1987).

REED, JOHN SILAS (1887–1920), U.S. journalist and revolutionary. Born into a wealthy but politically progressive Oregon family, Reed graduated from Harvard (1916), settled in New York's Greenwich Village, and wrote for several radical journals, including *The Masses*. He covered numerous domestic labor disorders but established his reputation as a foreign correspondent covering Pancho Villa's revolt in Mexico (1914). A war correspondent during World War I, Reed was in Russia during the bolshevik revolution, which he vividly described in *Ten Days That Shook The World* (1919). Returning to the United States in 1918 as a committed communist, Reed became a political activist, helped found the Communist Labor party of America (1919), and was a culture hero of radical intellectuals. Indicted for sedition in New York, he fled to the Soviet Union and was elected to the executive committee of the Comintern (1920) but died several weeks later of typhus. ■ See Richard O'Connor, *The Lost Revolutionary* (1967); Robert A. Rosenstone, *Romantic Revolutionary* (1975); and biography by Eric Homberger (1990).

REEVES, ROSSER (1910–1984), U.S. advertising executive. The son of a Danville, Virginia, minister, Reeves attended the University of Virginia (1928–30) and was an advertising copywriter in his home state and (after 1934) in New York City. A cofounder of Ted Bates and Co. (1940), he headed its creative department (1949–55), served as its board chairman (1955–66), and built it into the fifth largest ad agency in the world. An advocate of "hard sell" methods, he stressed the U.S.P. ("unique selling proposition") of each product he handled, including Wonder Bread, Listerine, Anacin, M&M candy, Kool cigarettes, and Carter's Little Liver Pills. Reeves also created the "Citizens for Eisenhower" radio and television campaign during the 1952 presidential election. He described his methods in *Reality in*

Advertising (1961; with Ray Martin), which became a widely used college textbook and was translated into 28 languages. Reeves was also a founder and board chairman (1958–76) of the American Chess Federation and the author of the novel *Popo* (1980).

REGAN, DONALD THOMAS (1918–), U.S. financial executive and government official. A graduate of Harvard (BA, 1940), Regan served in the marines during World War II and joined Merrill Lynch & Co., the Wall Street stock brokerage house, as an account executive in 1946. As Merrill Lynch's vice president (1959–71) and chairman and chief executive officer (1971–81), he was largely responsible for making it the nation's largest securities and brokerage firm. A financial innovator, he diversified the firm into such lucrative fields as banking, real estate, insurance, mutual funds, municipal bonds, commodity trading, and consulting. A lifelong Republican and believer in free-market practices and governmental deregulation, he served as Pres. Ronald Reagan's secretary of the treasury (1981–85) and played a major role in the passage of Reagan's 1981 tax-cut legislation. He was Reagan's White House chief of staff (1985–87) and was the principal architect of his economic policies. He wrote *A View from the Street* (1972), an account of the 1969–70 Wall Street crisis and recovery, and an autobiography, *For the Record: From Wall Street to Washington* (1988).

REHNQUIST, WILLIAM (1924–), U.S. jurist. Born in Milwaukee, Wisconsin, Rehnquist studied political science at Stanford (B.A. 1948) and Harvard (M.A. 1949) and graduated first in his class at the Stanford Law School (LL.B. 1952). After working as a Supreme Court clerk for Justice Robert H. Jackson (1952–53), he practiced law in Phoenix, Arizona, and became active in Republican conservative politics. He joined the administration of Pres. Richard M. Nixon as head of the Office of Legal Counsel in the Justice Department (1969–71) and gained a reputation for his defense of such controversial "law-and-order" tactics as "no-knock" entries, wiretapping, and pretrial detention. As an associate justice of the Supreme Court (1972–86), he was the Court's most conservative member, upholding limitations on the rights of criminal defendants and dissenting on such issues as abortion and cases upholding remedies for racial and sexual discrimination. He consistently supported the government in cases involving conflicts between the government and the individual. Named Chief Justice of the United States by Pres. Ronald Reagan (1986), he was confirmed by the Senate over strenuous objections by liberal and moderate forces. He continued to lead the Conservative faction of the court through the 1990s. He wrote *The Supreme Court: How It Was, How It Is* (1987), *Grand Inquests: The Historic Impeachments of Justice Samuel Chase and President Andrew Johnson* (1992), and *All the Laws But One: Civil Liberties in Wartime* (1998). ■ See Sue Davis, *Justice Rehnquist and the Constitution* (1989) and David Savage, *Turning Right* (1994).

REICH, STEVE (1936–), U.S. composer. Reich, a philosophy major at Cornell University (B.A. 1957), took courses at the Juilliard School of Music in New York (1958–61) and later studied with Darius Milhaud and Luciano Berio at Mills Music College in Oakland, California (M.A. 1963). He became fascinated with electronic and non-Western music and began to create and perform with his own ensemble (from 1966) experimental, minimalist compositions featuring repetitive rhythmic and melodic patterns. His music featured blends of electronic, vocal, and instrumental elements, and gained an international following in the 1970s and 1980s. His best-known works included *4 Organs* (1970), *Drumming* (1971), *Music for 18 Musicians* (1975), *Tehillim* ("Prayers"; 1981), *Movement (3) for Orchestra* (1986), *Proverb* (1995), and *City Life* (1995). ■ See his *Writings about Music* (1974).

REICH, WILHELM (1897–1957), Austrian psychiatrist. An associate of psychoanalyst Sigmund Freud in Vienna during the 1920s, Reich wrote *The Function of the Orgasm* (1927; Eng. trans. 1942), in which he stated that the discharge of sexual energy is necessary for individual health, and that sexual repression is an integral part of all authoritarian societies. He was active in the sexual-politics movement in Germany (after 1930) and attempted to synthesize Marxism and psychoanalysis, but he was expelled from both the German Communist party (1933) and the International Psychoanalytical Association (1934). He left Germany (1933) and worked in Scandinavia (1933–39), where he developed a theory of character structure and a physical therapy to treat muscular rigidities and spasms caused by underlying neuroses. In the United States (from 1939) he established an Orgone Institute ("orgone" being equated with sexual energy) and invented an orgone box, said to restore this energy and cure many illnesses, including cancer. The therapy was declared a fraud by the Food and Drug Administration, and Reich was sentenced to two years in prison, where he died. His works included *Character Analysis* (1933; Eng. trans. 1945), *Mass Psychology of Fascism* (1933; Eng. trans. 1946), the essays in *Sex-Pol* (Eng. trans. 1972), *Selected Writings* (Eng. trans. 1973), and *American Odyssey: Letters and Journals, 1940–1947* (1999). ■ See Eustace Chesser, *Salvation Through Sex* (1973); Colin Wilson, *The Quest for Wilhelm Reich* (1980); W. Edward Mann and Edward Hoffman, *The Man Who Dreamed of Tomorrow* (1980); and Myron Sharaf, *Fury on Earth* (1983).

REICHENBACH, HANS (1891–1953), German philosopher of science. A leading empiricist, Reichenbach was a founder of the Berlin Society for Empirical Philosophy and an editor (1930–40) of the journal *Erkenntnis* (later called the *Journal of Unified Science*). He left his University of Berlin professorship (1933) in protest against the Nazis and taught at the University of Istanbul (1933–38) and the University of California at Los Angeles (1938–53). He made significant contributions to the frequency theory of probability and to the study of induction, relativity, and quantum mechanics. His works included *Elements of Symbolic Logic* (1947) and *The Rise of Scientific Philosophy* (1951). ■ See William E. McMahon, *Hans Reichenbach's Philosophy of Grammar* (1976).

REICHSTEIN, TADEUS (1897–1996), Polish-born Swiss chemist and pharmacologist. Reichstein's family emigrated to Switzerland (1905) and he was educated in Zurich and earned a doctorate in organic chemistry (1922). His first important contribution was the synthesis of ascorbic acid (vitamin C) in 1933. As director of the Pharmacological Institute (1938–46) and professor of organic chemistry (1946–67) at the University of Basel, he conducted research into the hormones of the adrenal cortex, 29 of which, including cortisone, he and his associates isolated. For this work he shared the 1950 Nobel Prize for Physiology or Medicine with Edward C. Kendall and Philip S. Hench.

REID, HARRY FIELDING (1859–1944), U.S. geophysicist. Regarded as the first geophysicist in the United States, Reid graduated from Johns Hopkins University (Ph.D. 1894) and taught there from 1894 to 1930. As a result of his study of the 1906 California earthquake, he formulated the "elastic rebound theory" of the immediate source of earthquake waves—the vibrations that cause earthquakes—that was eventually accepted by scientists throughout the world.

REID, OGDEN MILLS (1882–1947), U.S. publisher. Reid was the son of an outstanding journalist, Whitelaw Reid, who gained editorial and financial control of the *New York Tribune* in 1872. After graduating from Yale Law School (1907), Reid joined the *Tribune* staff and became editor and publisher after the death of his father (1913). In 1924 Reid acquired the *New York Herald* and ran the consolidated *Herald Tribune* with the aid of his wife, Helen Rogers Reid. The *Herald Tribune* reflected Reid's moderate Republicanism and internationalism, featured such famous writers as Richard Harding Davis, Franklin P. Adams, Heywood Broun, and Walter Lippmann, and was the chief competitor of the *New York Times*.

REINER, CARL (1922–), U.S. actor, comedy writer, and director. Reiner spent the World War II years staging revues at military bases in the South Pacific. After several Broadway roles, he was hired to appear on television with Sid Caesar and Imogene Coca on "Your Show of Shows" (1950) and on Caesar's next show, "Sid Caesar Invites You" (1958), for which he won an Emmy Award as best supporting actor. Reiner went on to write for the "Dinah Shore Show" (1959), to originate and produce the "Dick Van Dyke Show" (1961–66), to direct and appear in several movies, and to record *The 2000-Year-Old Man* (1960) and *The 2000-Year-Old Man in the Year 2000* (1998; Grammy Award) with Mel Brooks. ■ See the autobiographical novel, *Enter Laughing* (1958).

REINER, FRITZ (1888–1963), Hungarian-born U.S. conductor. Reiner studied at the Music Academy in Budapest (1898–1908) and achieved an international reputation as the conductor of the Dresden Opera (1914–21). A precise, analytic master of the baton who disdained flamboyancy on the podium, Reiner insisted on rhythmic precision and clarity and was known as an uncompromising musical dictator. He helped build the Cincinnati Symphony (1922–31) and Pittsburgh Symphony (1938–48) into major American orchestras and reestablished the Chicago Symphony (1953–62) as one of the world's foremost ensembles. He was also music director of New York's Metropolitan Opera (1948–53) and led the world premieres of Béla Bartók's suite from *The Miraculous Mandarin* (1926), Roger Sessions' *The Black Maskers* (1930), and Walter Piston's *The Incredible Flutist Suite* (1940). ■ See biography by Philip Hart (1994).

REINES, FREDERICK (1918–1998), U.S. physicist. Reines studied at New York University (Ph.D. 1944) and did research in particle physics and nuclear weapons at the Los Alamos National Laboratory in New Mexico (1944–59). Working with Clyde Cowan, Jr., in the late 1950s, he was the first to detect the neutrino, a subatomic particle that has no electric charge. Its existence was theorized by scientists in the 1930s but considered impossible to detect. The discovery of the neutrino was instrumental in the early development of the "standard model" of particle physics, which states that all matter in the universe consists of 12 kinds of particles (six leptons, which include neutrinos, and six quarks) that are divided into three families. Reines later served as a professor at Case Institute of Technology (1959–66) and at the University of California at Irvine (1966–88). For his discovery he shared the 1995 Nobel Prize in Physics with Martin L. Perl.

REINHARDT, AD (Adolf Frederick Reinhardt; 1913–1967), U.S. painter. Ad Reinhardt worked for the Federal Art Project after graduating from Columbia College in 1935 and contributed satirical cartoons and articles to the New York City newspaper *P.M.* (1944–46). From geometric abstractions during the 1930s he progressed to abstract collages during the 1940s and to pure abstractions during the 1950s. "Art-as-art is nothing but art," he believed, and this philosophy culminated in a five-foot-square, symmetrically trisected painting in black (1960–62), in which the trisection is barely distinguishable. ■ See study by Lucy R. Lippard (1981).

REINHARDT, DJANGO (Jean Baptiste Reinhardt; 1910–1953), Belgian gypsy jazz guitarist. Despite the loss of the use of two fingers due to a gypsy caravan fire, Reinhardt developed a technique that enabled him to play the guitar with remarkable virtuosity. A true jazz original, he was coleader (with violinist Stéphane Grappelli) of the Quintet de Hot Club de France (Paris; 1934–39) and became known for his inimitable rhapsodic improvisations. He established an international reputation through his recordings, toured the United States with Duke Ellington (1946), and was the first European musician to influence American jazz. ■ See biography by Charles Delaunay (Eng. trans. 1961).

REINHARDT, MAX (Max Goldmann; 1873–1943), Austrian-born theatrical producer and director. One of the century's great theatrical innovators, Reinhardt directed Berlin's Deutsches Theater (1905–20) and founded and directed the Salzburg (Austria) Festival (1920–34). Utilizing new lighting techniques, stylized scenery, and the revolving stage, he directed gigantic and colorful spectacles, such as *The Miracle* (cast of 2,000; 1911) as well as intimate productions in his Kammerspiele Theater (Berlin; from 1906). His presentation of Sophocles' *Oedipus Rex* (1910) initiated a revival of classical Greek drama, and he directed world-famous productions of *The Lower Depths, A Midsummer Night's Dream,* and *Faust* as well as productions of such contemporaries as Shaw, Strindberg, Kaiser, and Pirandello. A Jew, he was forced to flee Germany when the Nazis took power (1933) and moved to the United States, where he directed a movie version of *A Midsummer Night's Dream* (1935) and ran an acting school. ■ See the memoir by his son, Gottfried Reinhardt, *The Genius* (Eng. trans. 1979), and study by J. L. Styan (1982).

REITH, JOHN CHARLES WALSHAM REITH, 1st **BARON** (1889–1971), British administrator. Known as "the father of the British Broadcasting Company," Reith was the BBC's first general manager (1922–27) and director general (1927–38). He developed the publicly owned but independent corporation into a worldwide communications network known for the high standards of its artistic and news broadcasts. Reith also served as chairman of Imperial Airways (1938–39) and its successor, British Overseas Airways Corp. (1939–40), of the Commonwealth Telecommunications Board (1946–50), and of the Colonial Development Corp. (1950–59). ■ See his autobiographies, *Into the Wind* (1949) and *Wearing Spurs* (1966).

REMARQUE, ERICH MARIA (1898–1970), German novelist. Teacher, stonecutter, racing driver, advertising man, and sports editor, Remarque turned to the novel and produced the most famous work written about World War I, *All Quiet on the Western Front* (1929; Eng. trans. 1929). Internationally acclaimed for its realism and compassion, the book reflected both Remarque's own wartime experiences and German disillusionment with the war in the late 1920s. All of his ten novels, including *The Road Back* (1931; Eng. trans. 1931), *Arch of Triumph* (1946; Eng. trans. 1946), and *The Night in Lisbon* (1962; Eng. trans. 1964), dealt with the horror of war and its aftermath, and many were made into popular movies. Remarque left Germany in 1932 and went to the United States in 1939. He was deprived of his German citizenship in 1938, and his books were burned by the Nazis. ■ See study by Christine R. Barker and R. W. Last (1979) and biography by Harley Taylor (1989).

REMI, GEORGES. *See HERGÉ.*

RENAUD, MADELEINE (1903–1994), French actress. A native of Paris, Renaud studied acting at the Conservatory of Dramatic Art and was a leading actress at the Comédie Française (1923–46). She also starred in many movies (from 1932). Known for her intelligence and beauty, Renaud was a leading interpreter of classical comedy, notably the plays of Molière and Marivaux. She married actor Jean Louis Barrault (1940) and they formed their own Compagnie Renaud-Barrault (1946) in which she expanded her repertory to include roles in plays by Lope de Vega, Chekhov, Feydeau, Anouilh, Fry, and Beckett. She continued to act until her late 80s.

RENNER, KARL (1870–1950), Austrian political leader. Born into an impoverished peasant family, Renner studied law in Vienna and was active in the moderate wing of the Austrian Social Democratic party. A member of parliament from 1907, he served as chancellor (1918–20) and headed the Austrian delegation to the Paris Peace Conference (1919). He presided over the establishment of the republic but failed to achieve Austrian union with Germany. He served as president of parliament (1930–33) but retired from public life during the Nazi occupation and World War II. After the war he formed a provisional government and skillfully negotiated Austrian unity and home rule with Allied authorities. He served as the Second Republic's first president (1945–50).

RENOIR, JEAN (1894–1979), French film director. The son of the celebrated impressionist painter Pierre Auguste Renoir, Jean Renoir created the film classics *Grand Illusion* (1937) and *The Rules of the Game* (1939), which were characterized by a "meandering" pace, soft focus, and compassionate characterizations. During World War II, he packed up a carload of his father's paintings and fled to the United States, where he directed *The Southerner* (1945) and *Woman on the Beach* (1947). He also made a film in India, *The River* (1950), as well as *French Can-Can* (1955) and *Le Petit Théâtre de Jean Renoir* (1971). He wrote *Renoir, My Father* (Eng. trans. 1962) and an autobiography, *My Life and My Films* (Eng. trans. 1974). ■ See biographies by Raymond Durgnat (1974) and Celia Bertin (Eng. trans. 1991).

RESHEVSKY, SAMUEL HERMAN (1911–1992), Polish-born U.S. chess player. A chess prodigy, Reshevsky played in exhibitions throughout Europe at the age of 6. He emigrated to the United States in 1920 and participated in many tournaments, but he withdrew from chess at age 12 to pursue his education. Returning to the game in 1935, he won the title of grand master and became one of the world's outstanding players. A frequent U.S. champion (1936; 1938; 1940; 1942; 1946; 1970–71, tie 1972) he won many international titles and wrote several chess books as well as columns on chess for numerous publications. He competed in world-class tournaments into his 70s.

RESNAIS, ALAIN (1922–   ), French film director. Resnais achieved international recognition with his short documentary film about Nazi concentration camps, *Night and Fog* (1956). Regarded as one of the most important figures of the French New Wave of the 1950s and 1960s, he experimented with concepts of time and memory and utilized complex flashback techniques in the controversial *Hiroshima mon Amour* (1959) and *Last Year at Marienbad* (1961). His other well-known films included *La Guerre est finie* (1966), *Je t'aime, Je t'aime* (1968), *Stavisky* (1974), *Providence* (1977), *Mon Oncle d'Amérique* (1978), and *La Vie est un roman* (1982). ■ See studies by John F. Kreidl (1977) and James Monaco (1979).

RESPIGHI, OTTORINO (1879–1936), Italian composer. The leading Italian composer of orchestral music of his generation, Respighi studied with Rimsky-Korsakov and Max Bruch and taught composition at the Academy of St. Cecelia in Rome from 1913 (director, 1924–26). His symphonic poems, *The Pines of Rome* (1917), *The Fountains of Rome* (1924), and *Roman Festivals* (1929), and the orchestral suite *The Birds* (1927), exemplified his rich melodic gifts and sonorous harmonies and orchestral colors. His ballet *La Boutique Fantasque* on themes of Rossini was produced by Sergei Diaghilev in 1919. ■ See the memoir by his wife, Elsa Respighi (Eng. trans. 1962).

RESTON, JAMES BARRETT (1909–1995), Scottish-born U.S. journalist. A graduate of the University of Illinois (B.S. 1932), Reston worked for the Associated Press (1934–39) as a sportswriter and London correspondent before joining the staff of the *New York Times* (1939). Assigned to Washington, D.C., after World War II, he wrote well-reasoned political columns and reportage that earned him two Pulitzer Prizes (1945 and 1957). He was the *Times'* chief Washington correspondent (1953–64) and a member of its board of directors (1973–89). ■ See his memoir, *Deadline* (1991).

RETHBERG, ELISABETH (Elisabeth Sättler; 1894–1976), German-born opera singer. A soprano, Rethberg studied piano at the Dresden Conservatory before turning to singing. In 1915 she made her debut with the Dresden State Opera, where she remained for the next seven years. She made her U.S. debut as Aïda, her most famous role, with the Metropolitan Opera in 1922. For the next 20 years she remained there, making guest appearances and giving recitals all over the world. In 1928 Rethberg returned to Dresden to create the title role in Strauss's *Die ägyptische Helena*. Her repertoire included the lighter Wagnerian roles, Madame Butterfly, the Marschallin in *Der Rosenkavalier,* and numerous Verdi heroines.

REUTHER, WALTER PHILIP (1907–1970), U.S. labor leader. A tool- and diemaker, Reuther was fired from several jobs because of his union-organizing activities. He became a United Automobile Workers (UAW) organizer in Detroit

(1935) and a leader of the sit-down strikes (1936–37) that led to the unionization of the auto industry. Reuther served as president of the UAW (1946–70) and the CIO (1952–55) and was an architect of the merger of the AFL and CIO (1955). He was vice president of the combined union until 1968, when he withdrew the UAW from the federation. He was an activist leader who worked against corruption and racism. A shrewd negotiator and labor strategist, he pioneered in securing cost-of-living pay increases, supplementary unemployment benefits, and early retirement for his union members. ■ See biographies by Frank Cormier and William J. Eaton (1970); Jean Gould and Lorena Hickok (1972); his brother Victor's memoirs, *The Brothers Reuther* (1976); study by John Barnard (1983); and Nelson Lichtenstein, *The Most Dangerous Man in Detroit* (1995).

REVELLE, ROGER (1909–1991), U.S. oceanographer and social scientist. Associated with the University of California's Scripps Institution of Oceanography, La Jolla (1931–64; director, 1950–64), Revelle led many oceanographic expeditions that contributed basic data on the sedimentary covering of the ocean floor, the depth of the Moho and the Pacific trenches, and the underwater mid-Pacific mountains. Studies of heat flow through the ocean floor and seafloor spreading tended to confirm the theory of plate tectonics that revolutionized geological thinking during the 1970s. As science adviser to the secretary of the interior (1961–63), he organized a study of soil deterioration in West Pakistan. Increasingly concerned with problems of ecology and energy resources, especially in the Third World, he directed the Center for Population Studies at Harvard (1964–76). He was also one of the first scientists to warn of global warming as a result of the use of fossil fuels.

REVSON, CHARLES (1906–1975), U.S. business executive. Son of an immigrant cigar packer, Revson (and two partners) began Revlon Inc. (1932) with an investment of $300. Marketing a new opaque, nonstreak nail polish in beauty salons throughout the country and utilizing innovative advertising techniques, Revson developed Revlon into the largest retail cosmetic and fragrance company in the United States. At the time of his death, the firm had sales totaling $605 million. ■ See Andrew Tobias, *Fire and Ice* (1976).

REXROTH, KENNETH (1905–1982), U.S. poet, translator, and critic. Rexroth was born in Indiana but made his home in San Francisco, where he was briefly associated with the "beat" poets of the 1950s. He was San Francisco correspondent for the *Nation* (1953–68). His poems, assembled in *Collected Shorter Poems* (1967), *Collected Longer Poems* (1969), and *A Kenneth Rexroth Reader* (1970), valued exuberance and direct expression over precision or control. He often read his works to jazz accompaniment. Rexroth was a brilliant translator of Chinese, Japanese, and classic Greek poetry. He also wrote literary essays, collected in *Assays*

(1962), plays, and *An Autobiographical Novel* (1966). Rexroth was also known as a painter. ■ See biography by Linda Hamalian (1991).

REYES, ALFONSO (1889–1959), Mexican writer and critic. Trained as an attorney, Reyes was best known as a scholar and essayist. His collected works filled more than 18 volumes and included essays on the Spanish golden age, travel pieces that reflect his diplomatic career (in France, Spain, Argentina, and Brazil), and intelligent essays on countless subjects. A humanist writing in the South American "Arielist tradition," he pleaded for social justice without rejection of spiritual values. He was recognized as a prose stylist; his poetry has been underrated. In his later years, Reyes directed the Colegio de Mexico and encouraged scholarship on Latin American literature. ■ See his *Position of America and Other Essays* (Eng. trans. 1950), *Mexico in a Nutshell* (Eng. trans. 1964), and study by Barbara Aponte (1972).

REYES, RAFAEL (1850–1921), Colombian dictator. Reyes was an outdoorsman who explored for rubber and quinine in the Amazon basin and distinguished himself during the long period of civil war in Colombia at the turn of the century. A leader of the Conservative party, he was elected president in 1904, establishing an authoritarian regime to further economic development. Although his term was extended to 1914, Reyes was forced to resign in 1909 after signing a treaty with the United States that recognized Panama's independence. The treaty was withdrawn and the former president went into exile.

REYMONT, WŁADYSŁAW STANISŁAW (1867–1925), Polish short-story writer and novelist. An alienated member of a large, impoverished rural family, with virtually no formal education, Reymont drew on his experiences as a tailor, traveling actor, novice in a monastery, minor railway official, and factory worker to create a body of work that earned him the 1924 Nobel Prize for Literature. His masterpiece, *The Peasants* (4 vols., 1902–09; Eng. trans. 1924–25), presents, in a grim and fatalistic manner, an epic tableau of peasant life. His other important work is *The Promised Land* (1899; Eng. trans. 1927), a novel about factory life in Łódź that attacked modern urbanization. ■ See study by Jerzy R. Krzyzanowski (1972).

REYNAUD, PAUL (1878–1966), French political leader. After graduating from the University of Paris, Reynaud became a corporation lawyer (1910). During World War I he participated in the retreat across Siberia and earned a Croix de Guerre. In 1919 he was elected to parliament as a conservative advocate of moderation in German reparations and of military preparedness. During the 1930s he spoke out against appeasement of the Axis powers. Reynaud served as minister of finance (1930, 1938–40), of justice (1932, 1938), and as premier during the last months before the fall of

France during World War II (1940). He opposed capitulation to the Germans and was imprisoned in France and Germany until 1945. He wrote numerous books and articles, served in parliament (1946–62), and helped prepare the constitution for the Fifth Republic in 1958. ▪ See his memoirs, *In the Thick of the Fight, 1930–45* (Eng. trans. 1955).

REYNOLDS, BURT (1936–   ), U.S. film actor. The son of a Florida police chief, Reynolds was a football star at Florida State University but turned to acting after an injury thwarted his plans to become a professional athlete. After appearing in several television series and low-budget adventure movies during the 1960s, he gained a large following through his appearances on television talk shows and achieved stardom in the film *Deliverance* (1972). He also gained publicity as the first male to appear nude in a magazine centerfold (*Cosmopolitan,* April 1972). Projecting a tough-tender image that appealed to both men and women, he was one of the most popular Hollywood actors of the 1970s and 1980s. His other films included *The Longest Yard* (1974), *Smokey and the Bandit* (1977), *Semi-Tough* (1977), *Starting Over* (1979), *Best Friends* (1982), and *Heat* (1987). ▪ See his *My Life* (1994) and biographies by Dianna Whitley (1979) and Sylvia Resnick (1983).

REYNOLDS, QUENTIN (1902–1965), U.S. journalist. After graduating from Brooklyn Law School (LL.B. 1931), Reynolds opted for a career in journalism. He was a reporter and sports columnist for the *New York Evening World* and the *World-Telegram,* then became a Berlin correspondent for the International News Service (1933). Impressed by a critical story on Nazi youth that he filed from Berlin, *Collier's* magazine made Reynolds an associate editor (1934). Over the next 15 years, he wrote 384 articles and stories for *Collier's.* He was best known for the human-interest stories he filed from many war zones during World War II; Reynolds also wrote seven books during the war, including the best-seller *The Wounded Don't Cry* (1941). In 1954, Reynolds, represented by attorney Louis Nizer, won a $175,001 judgment in a libel case against the Hearst newspapers and columnist Westbrook Pegler, who had blasted Reynolds' record as a war correspondent. The celebrated case became the basis for Henry Denker's Broadway play, *A Case of Libel* (1963). ▪ See his autobiography *By Quentin Reynolds* (1963).

REZA SHAH PAHLEVI. *See PAHLEVI, REZA SHAH.*

RHEE, SYNGMAN (1875–1965), Korean political leader. As a young man Rhee published the newspaper *Independence.* His nationalist views earned him a jail sentence (1897–1904), during which he was tortured, and he converted to Christianity. He studied for six years in U.S. universities, earning a Princeton Ph.D. in 1910, the same year that Japan annexed Korea. Rhee returned home but was forced to flee in 1912 and was a political exile in the United States until 1945. However, in exile he remained active politically and was a leader of the independence movement. After World War II he was returned to South Korea by U.S. forces to head the newly established Republic of Korea. As president (1948–60), Rhee was paternalistic, dictatorial, and militantly anticommunist. Accused of election fraud and corruption, he resigned amidst massive antigovernment demonstrations initiated by student groups (1960) and lived out his life in Hawaiian exile. ▪ See the laudatory biography by Robert T. Oliver (1954) and the more objective study by Richard C. Allen, *Korea's Syngman Rhee* (1960).

RHINE, JOSEPH BANKS (1895–1980), U.S. psychologist. Rhine was trained as a botanist at the University of Chicago (Ph.D. 1925) but, becoming interested in extrasensory phenomena, studied with psychologist William McDougall at Duke University, where he taught psychology (1928–65). He cofounded the Parapsychology Laboratory (1930; director 1940–65) and conducted pioneering experiments in telepathy, clairvoyance, precognition, and psychokinesis—the power of mind to control matter. Although criticized by establishment psychologists and probability theorists, he popularized the concept of extrasensory perception (ESP) and was known as the "father of parapsychology." He also founded and directed (1964–68) the Institute of Parapsychology in Durham, North Carolina. In addition to the bestselling *New Frontier of the Mind* (1937), he wrote *Extra-Sensory Perception* (1934), *The Reach of the Mind* (1947), and *New World of the Mind* (1953). ▪ See Denis Brian, *The Enchanted Voyager* (1982).

RHYS, JEAN (Ella Gwendolen Williams; 1894–1979), British novelist and short-story writer. Rhys was born and brought up in the West Indies island of Dominica. She moved to Britain at age 17, began to write in the 1920s, and was introduced into the Paris group clustered about Gertrude Stein and Ernest Hemingway. She first published a book of short fiction, *The Left Bank* (1927); the novel *Quartet* (1929) followed. Rhys' manner of scrutinizing women's experiences—combining emotional intensity with narrative distancing—was perhaps best realized in the bleak novel *After Leaving Mr. MacKenzie* (1930). She produced two more books in the 1930s, then ceased publishing until *Wide Sargasso Sea* (1966). Its appearance spurred a renewal of interest in her works, particularly by feminist readers of the 1970s, who rescued Rhys from decades of relative obscurity. ▪ See her collections *Tigers Are Better-Looking* (1968) and *Sleep It Off, Lady* (1976), *Smile Please: An Unfinished Autobiography* (1980), *Letters* (1984); studies by Thomas F. Staley (1979) and Peter Wolfe (1980); and biography by Carole Angier (1991).

RIAD, MAHMOUD (1917–1992), Egyptian soldier-diplomat. A graduate of the Egyptian military academy (1939), Riad was a career army officer before serving on the Egypt-Israeli Mixed Armistice Commission (1948–52). He participated in the 1952 overthrow of King Farouk and became a confidant of President Gamal Abdel Nasser. He served as ambassador to Syria (1955–58), representative to the United Nations (1962–64), and foreign minister (1964–72). A cool, skillful diplomat, Riad helped create the Soviet-Egyptian alliance and refused to negotiate directly with Israel. From 1972 to 1979 he was secretary-general of the Arab League.

RIBAR, IVAN (1881–1968), Yugoslav political leader. Trained as a lawyer, Ribar entered politics and was elected president of the first national assembly (1920–22) and was a leader of the opposition (1934–41). During World War II he joined the Communist party and, a close associate of Marshal Josip Broz Tito, was in charge of the civil affairs of the partisan movement. He served as president of the Executive National Committee of Liberation, which functioned as a provisional government. After the war Ribar was president of the presidium of the national assembly and carried out many of the functions of chief of state.

RIBBENTROP, JOACHIM VON (1893–1946), German Nazi foreign minister. Ribbentrop was a traveling salesman for a champagne firm until he married the owner's daughter, added "von" to his name, and entered salon society. He joined the Nazi party in 1932 and served its leader Adolf Hitler as ambassador-at-large (1935) or, as he was called derisively, "the traveling salesman of national socialism." As ambassador to Great Britain (1936–38) and as foreign minister (1938–45), he helped negotiate the alliances with Italy and Japan and signed the 1939 Nazi-Soviet nonaggression pact. In prison after World War II, he wrote *The Ribbentrop Memoirs* (1953; Eng. trans. 1954) before his execution as a war criminal. ■ See biography by Michael Bloch (1992) and John Weitz, *Hitler's Diplomat* (1992).

RIBEIRO, AQUILINO (1885–1963), Portuguese writer. Ribeiro studied at the Sorbonne in Paris (1910–14) during the first of his several periods of political exile. Republican and anticlerical in outlook, he opposed the monarchy as well as the regime of António Salazar and wrote sympathetically of the exploited peasantry and urban poor, while attacking the corrupt bureaucracy and landed classes. He was best known for the peasant novels, set in his native province of Beira, that intitiated the genre of regional literature in Portuguese fiction. He wrote biographies, historical and folkloric studies, and children's stories and was best known internationally for his masterpiece, *When the Wolves Howl* (1958; Eng. trans. 1963), a novel that described a peasant protest against a government scheme that threatened the peasants' way of life.

RIBOUD, MARC (1923–), French photographer. Riboud fought in the Resistance during World War II. He subsequently worked as an industrial engineer but gave up his job to pursue a career in photography (1952). As Henri Cartier-Bresson's protégé, he was invited to join the Magnum photo cooperative (1954) and subsequently traveled widely throughout China, elsewhere in Asia, and the Soviet Union. His detailed and complex photos appeared in magazines and in exhibitions throughout the world. ■ See his *Three Banners of China* (1966), *The Face of North Vietnam* (1970), *Visions of China: Photographs, 1957–1980* (1981), and *Marc Riboud in China: Forty Years of Photography* (1997).

RICE, ELMER LEOPOLD (Elmer Leopold Reizenstein; 1892–1967), U.S. playwright and director. Rice dropped out of high school, and later the legal profession, turning to the stage "for discussion in emotional and dramatic terms of problems that affect the lives and happiness of millions." *On Trial* (1914), a successful adaptation of the flashback technique, was followed by the experimental *The Adding Machine* (1923), in which the protagonist Mr. Zero relinquishes his job to a machine, and *Street Scene* (1929, Pulitzer Prize), a tragedy of New York tenement life. The temperamental Rice himself produced and directed many of his 50 plays, which debunked Broadway, the legislation of morality, and militarism. After resigning from the New Deal's Federal Theater Project (1936) over a censorship dispute, and later from the Playwrights TV Theater to protest blacklisting during the 1950s, he entitled his autobiography *Minority Report* (1963). ■ See studies by Frank Durham (1970) and Anthony F. Palmieri (1980).

RICE, GRANTLAND (1880–1954), U.S. journalist. One of the best-known American sportswriters of the century, Rice reported for the *New York Herald Tribune* (1914–30) before starting his nationally syndicated column "The Sportlight" (1930), which was known for its combination of colorful reporting and inspirational verse. Rice also wrote several sports books (as well as three volumes of poetry), produced many sports films, and coined numerous descriptive sports phrases, including "The Four Horsemen," a description of Notre Dame's 1924 starting backfield. He also named the All-America college football teams (for *Collier's* magazine) from 1925 through 1947. ■ See his autobiography, *The Tumult and the Shouting* (1954); Charles Fountain, *Sportswriter* (1993); and study by Mark Inabinett (1994).

RICE, JERRY (1962–), U.S. football player. An All-American at Mississippi Valley State College, Rice was drafted by the San Francisco 49ers in 1985, won the National Football League's Rookie of the Year Award, and became the greatest wide receiver in NFL history. Best known for his great speed, tremendous concentration, remarkable clutch catches, and intense training regimen, the 6-foot, 2-inch, 200-pound Rice held almost every NFL career receiving record, including (through the 2000 season) most receptions (1,281), most receiving yardage (19,247), most receiving touchdowns (176), most 100-yard receiving games (65), and most 1,000-yard receiving seasons (11). He also held the record for career touchdowns (187), breaking Jim Brown's record of 126 in 1994. Rice was also the Most Valuable Player in Super Bowl XXIII (1989) and held several Super Bowl records, including most career receptions (28), career yards (512), yards in one game (215), and career points (42).

RICH, ADRIENNE (1929–), U.S. poet and essayist. As a Radcliffe senior, Rich won the Yale Younger Poets award for *A Change of World* (1951); her second volume appeared in 1955. Her forceful, articulate poetry, especially beginning with *Snapshots of a Daughter-in-Law* (1963), reflected the long process of her emergence as a poet, political activist, lesbian feminist, and Jew. *Diving into the Wreck: Poems 1971–1972* (1973) won a National Book Award. *Twenty-One Love Poems* (1976), which celebrates the bond between women, was included in the collection *The Dream of a Common Language: Poems 1974–1977* (1978). Rich's poetry was collected in *Poems: Selected and New* (1976), *The Fact of a Doorframe: Poems Selected and New, 1950–1984* (1984), and *Your Native Land, Your Life* (1986). The prose book *Of Woman Born* (1977) treated motherhood as experience and institution, drawing on extensive research and on her own experience as the mother of three sons. Essays appeared in *On Lies, Secrets and Silence: Selected Prose 1966–1978* (1979). From the early 1970s, Rich was a leading figure in the women's movement; she spoke out against American military involvement in Southeast Asia and Central America and against the proliferation of nuclear weapons. Her later works included *Blood, Bread and Poetry: Selected Prose, 1979–1985* (1986), *An Atlas of the Difficult World: Poems, 1988–1991* (1991), *What Is Found There: Notebooks on Poetry and Politics* (1993), *Dark Fields of the Republic: Poems, 1991–1995* (1995), and *Midnight Salvage: Poems 1995–1998* (2000). ■ See Barbara Charlesworth Gelpi and Albert Gelpi, eds., *Adrienne Rich's Poetry and Prose* (1993); Wendy Martin, *An American Triptych* (1984); and studies by Judith McDaniel (1982) and Liz Yorke (1997).

RICHARD, MAURICE JOSEPH HENRI (1921–2000), Canadian ice-hockey player. A star right-winger for the Montreal Canadiens, "Rocket" Richard personified the power and physicality of professional hockey. In 18 seasons (1942–60), he led the Canadiens to eight league titles and eight Stanley Cup championships, was named to the All-Star team 13 times, and was the first player to score 50 goals in a season (1944–45). His short temper often involved him in fights, and in the 1955 play-offs he sparked a near riot in the Montreal Forum after being suspended for high-sticking a linesman. He scored 544 goals during regular season play and 82 in play-off competition.

RICHARDS, BOB (Robert Richards; 1926–), U.S. pole-vaulter. An exceptional, all-around athlete, Richards was a member of three U.S. Olympic teams (1948, 1952, 1956). He made history by capturing gold medals in the pole vault at two Olympic games (1952, 1956)—a feat that has not been duplicated. Ordained as a minister, he was called the "Vaulting Vicar," and after his retirement his appearances in breakfast-cereal commercials made him familiar to television viewers. The ultraconservative Richards ran for president of the United States in 1984 as a minor-party candidate.

RICHARDS, DICKINSON WOODRUFF (1895–1973), U.S. physician. A graduate of Yale (1917) and Columbia (M.D. 1923), Richards devoted his career to the study of the heart and lungs. He did research and taught at Columbia's College of Physicians and Surgeons from 1928 to 1961. Working with André F. Cournand (from 1931) he improved the technique of cardiac catheterization, a method of measuring blood pressure inside the heart first used by Werner Forssmann (1929). This research led to important breakthroughs in the diagnosis and treatment of heart disease, enabled doctors to assess the effects of heart drugs, and paved the way for open-heart surgery. Richards shared the 1956 Nobel Prize for Physiology or Medicine with Cournand and Forssmann.

RICHARDS, SIR GORDON (1904–), British jockey. The leading British jockey for 26 of his 34 seasons (1921–54), Richards won 4,870 races during his career. On May 4, 1950, he became the first jockey to win 4,000 races, a mark subsequently bettered by Johnny Longden and Willie Shoemaker. ■ See his autobiography, *My Story* (1955), and the biography by Michael Seth-Smith, *Knight of the Turf* (1980).

RICHARDS, IVOR ARMSTRONG (1893–1979), British literary critic. One of the founders of modern criticism, I. A. Richards approached literature through various scientific fields, including semantics and psychology. He taught at Cambridge University (1922–29) and later at Harvard (1939–63). He laid the groundwork for the Anglo-American school of literary criticism known as the New Criticism by arguing, in *Principles of Literary Criticism* (1924), that the emotive use of language in poetry differs fundamentally from the referential use of language in expository writing and therefore requires a special kind of analysis. In *Practical Criticism* (1929), he outlined a critical method that was rooted in meticulous semantic analysis but did not overlook literature's psychological functions. Together with Charles King Ogden, Richards invented Basic English, a simplified language system consisting of 850 words that he documented in *Basic English and Its Uses* (1943). His later writings included *Internal Colloquies* (1973), *Beyond* (1974), and *Complementaries: Uncollected Essays* (1976). His poetry was assembled in *New and Selected Poems* (1978). ■ See study by J. P. Schiller (1969) and biography by John Paul Russo (1989).

RICHARDS, THEODORE WILLIAM (1868–1928), U.S. chemist. On the Harvard faculty from 1894 to 1928, Richards played a major role in increasing the precision of quantitative measurement in the field of chemistry. He developed processes that enabled him to measure accurately the atomic weights of 25 elements and to confirm the existence of isotopes. He was awarded the 1914 Nobel Prize for Chemistry for his work. He also helped introduce physical chemistry to the United States and did notable research in the fields of thermochemistry and electrochemistry.

RICHARDSON, HENRY HANDEL (Ethel Richardson Robertson; 1870–1946), Australian novelist. Although she lived abroad after age 17, Richardson's remarkable fiction tapped her Australian background. She married J. G. Robertson, a student who later became a noted literary critic, and the two decisively influenced each other's work. *The Getting of Wisdom* (1910; film 1980) recalled her education at Presbyterian Ladies' College in Melbourne. Real fame came with the trilogy *The Fortunes of Richard Mahony* (1917–29; rev. ed. 1930), a realistic saga of 19th-century life based on the life of her father. It was praised in Europe and America but disparaged by certain critics at home who regretted that Australia should be represented abroad by a tragedy. Writing in lucid, spare prose, Richardson combined engrossing romance with naturalistic detail. *Myself When Young* (1948) was autobiographical. ■ See Dorothy Green, *Ulysses Bound* (1973); study by William D. Elliot (1975); and biography by Axel Clark (1990).

RICHARDSON, SIR OWEN WILLANS (1879–1959), British physicist. A professor at Princeton (1906–14) and the University of London (1914–24), Richardson discovered the fundamental physical law governing the emission of electrons from hot bodies (Richardson's law). For his work, which played a vital role in the development of vacuum tubes and the subsequent development of radio and television communication, Richardson earned the 1928 Nobel Prize for Physics. His books included *The Electron Theory of Matter* (1914) and *The Emission of Electricity from Hot Bodies* (1916). From 1924 to 1944 he was director of research at the University of London.

RICHARDSON, SIR RALPH (1902–1983), British actor. Richardson dropped out of art school (1921) to begin an acting career that lasted 63 years. He began a long association with the Old Vic in 1930, played a variety of Shakespearean and modern roles, and with his friends, colleagues, and fellow theatrical knights—he was knighted in 1947—John Gielgud and Laurence Olivier, dominated the British stage and screen for much of the century. He was codirector of the Old Vic, with Olivier, from 1944 to 1949. A beloved figure, known for his sly humor as well as for his passion and pathos, Richardson was regarded throughout much of his career as a representative of Everyman. His best-known stage roles included Falstaff in *Henry IV* (1945) and the title roles in *Peer Gynt* (1944), *Uncle Vanya* (1944), *The Alchemist* (1947), and *Cyrano de Bergerac* (1947). During the 1970s he appeared with Gielgud in memorable perform-ances in *Home* and *No Man's Land*. His notable film roles were in *The Fallen Idol* (1948), *The Heiress* (1949), *Richard III* (1955), *Long Day's Journey into Night* (1962), and *Greystoke* (1984). ■ See biographies by Garry O'Connor (1982; rev. ed. 1997) and John Miller (1995).

RICHARDSON, ROBERT C. (1937–), U.S. physicist. Richardson studied at Duke University (Ph.D. 1966) and taught at Cornell University (1967–). While performing experiments in low temperature physics (1972) with fellow researcher David M. Lee and graduate student Douglas Osheroff, Richardson and his colleagues discovered superfluidity in helium-3, a rare form of liquid helium, when it was cooled to about two one-thousandths of a degree above absolute zero. The transition to superfluidity—the ability to flow without resistance—enabled physicists to observe, for the first time, quantum mechanical effects that previously could be detected only indirectly through the study of molecules, atoms, or subatomic particles. The discovery also provided insights into the formation of vast cosmic strings that may have formed the first physical structures microseconds after the "big bang" creation of the universe. Richardson, Lee, and Osheroff shared the 1996 Nobel Prize in Physics for their research.

RICHARDSON, TONY (Cecil Antonio Richardson; 1928–1991), British theatrical and film director. An Oxford graduate (1953), Richardson was a director and producer for the BBC before directing on stage (and later filming) John Osborne's *Look Back in Anger* (1956; film 1959), the play that set the tone for the "angry young men" movement. His other productions that dealt with the problems of the working class were *The Entertainer* (1957; film 1960), *A Taste of Honey* (1960; film 1961), and *Loneliness of the Long Distance Runner* (film 1962). He also directed the films *Tom Jones* (Academy Award, 1963), *A Delicate Balance* (1973), *Joseph Andrews* (1977), and *Blue Sky* (1991). ■ See his memoir, *Long Distance Runner* (1993).

RICHET, CHARLES ROBERT (1850–1935), French physiologist and bacteriologist. Richet graduated from the University of Paris (M.D. 1877) and taught physiology there from 1887 to 1927. He did research on the properties of gastric juice, the physiology of respiration, and on the treatment of epilepsy and tuberculosis, but was best known for his work in the area of immunology. His discovery of the phenomenon of anaphylaxis laid the foundation for the study of hay fever, asthma, and other allergic disorders. For this work he was awarded the 1913 Nobel Prize in Physiology or Medicine. Richet also published poems, plays, novels, and works on pacifism and parapsychology. ■ See Stewart Wolf, *Brain, Mind, and Medicine* (1993).

RICHIER, GERMAINE (1904–1959), French sculptor. Richier studied at the Montpellier School of Fine Arts (1922–25) and produced traditional sculpture until the

1940s, when she began to develop her distinctive style. She created elongated animal and insect sculptures—especially toads, owls, bats, and spiders—whose grotesque and surreal forms reflected a preoccupation with morbidity and decay. Many of her creations were considered shocking and controversial but were later seen as pioneering examples of open-form sculpture, in which space is as important an element as the solid material of the work of art.

RICHLER, MORDECAI (1931–), Canadian novelist. Richler's fiction bears the imprint of the poverty and anti-Semitism he experienced while growing up in the Jewish district of Montreal. He fell under the influence of existentialist writers in Paris (1951–52); he began publishing upon his return. Richler pinpointed characters on the map of values drawn from the Jewish milieu and tradition. He created humor through comic distortion in such novels as *The Acrobats* (1954), which he wrote at 23; *Son of a Smaller Hero* (1955); *A Choice of Enemies* (1957); and *The Apprenticeship of Duddy Kravitz* (1959), the story of a Jewish boy turned wheeler-dealer. Later works included *Cocksure* (novel; 1968), *The Street* (short stories; 1969), *St. Urbain's Horseman* (novel; 1971), *Shovelling Trouble* (essays; 1972), *Joshua Then and Now* (novel; 1980), *Solomon Gursky Was Here* (1989), and *Barney's Version* (1997). His books on Canadian themes were *Home Sweet Home* (1984) and *Oh Canada! Oh Quebec!: Requiem for a Divided Country* (1992). *This Year in Jerusalem* (1994) is a commentary on the Palestinian-Israeli conflict and a reminiscence of his Zionist upbringing. ■ See studies by Arnold E. Davidson (1983) and Victor J. Ramraj (1983).

RICHTER, BURTON (1931–), U.S. physicist. After graduating from the Massachusetts Institute of Technology (Ph.D. 1956), Richter taught at Stanford University and was associated with the Stanford Linear Accelerator Center (director 1984–99). He designed the Stanford Positron-Electron Accelerating Ring (SPEAR), which was created to study the results of collisions of electrons and positrons at enormously high energy levels. During SPEAR experiments in 1974 Richter discovered a new subatomic particle that he called "psi." Almost simultaneously, a research team headed by Samuel C. C. Ting at the Brookhaven National Laboratory, Long Island, New York, discovered the same particle, which Ting called "J." Considered by some to be the greatest discovery in the field of elementary particles, the experimental findings earned for Richter and Ting the 1976 Nobel Prize for Physics.

RICHTER, CHARLES FRANCIS (1900–1985), U.S. geophysicist and seismologist. After receiving a Ph.D. in theoretical physics at the California Institute of Technology (1928), Richter did research at the institute's Seismological Laboratory. With seismologist Beno Gutenberg, he devised the Richter magnitude scale (1935), which measured the intensity of earthquakes (from zero to ten). It became the ac-cepted international measurement, and their book, *Seismicity of the Earth* (1941; rev. ed. 1954), became the standard reference work in the field. Richter taught at Cal Tech (1937–70) and served on the Los Angeles Earthquake Commission (from 1971).

RICHTER, CONRAD (1890–1968), U.S. novelist. Richter sold his small Ohio publishing business (1928) and moved to New Mexico to escape advancing urbanization and industrialization. His fiction championed frontier values and condemned the modern-day destruction of the natural environment. He depicted everyday living conditions of farmers, pioneers, and Indians in Ohio, his native Pennsylvania, and the Southwest. *The Trees* (1940) is an 18th-century pioneer-family portrait. *The Town* (1950, Pulitzer Prize) describes the same family's adjustment to urbanization. The Delaware Indians are the focus of *The Light in the Forest* (1953). *The Waters of Kronos* (1960) won a National Book Award. ■ See studies by Edwin W. Gaston (1965) and Marvin J. Lahood (1975).

RICHTER, HANS (1888–1976), German-born U.S. artist and filmmaker. Richter began his career as a painter in the tradition of cubism, dadaism, and expressionism, but he gave up his easel in favor of calligraphic scroll paintings in 1919. His concern with sequence and continuity led to *Rhythm 21* (1921), a pioneering abstract animated film that was an avant-garde classic. Fleeing Nazi Germany in 1940, Richter became director of the City College of New York's Institute of Film Techniques (1943–56). He continued to make films featuring his artist friends (*Dreams That Money Can Buy*, 1944–47) and wrote *Dada: Art and Anti-Art* (1964). ■ See study edited by Cleve Gray (1971).

RICHTER, SVIATOSLAV TEOFILOVICH (1915–1997), Soviet pianist. The son of a composer and musician of German extraction, Richter was a rehearsal conductor at the Odessa Opera at age 15, but he turned to the piano and studied it until he was nearly 30. His 1942 premiere of Sergei Prokofiev's Sixth Piano Sonata won him that composer's lifelong friendship and the opportunity to debut his seventh and ninth sonatas and to conduct the world premiere of his cello concerto (1952). Richter's extraordinary technique and velvet tone were amply demonstrated during his sensational U.S. debut (1960); he subsequently appeared frequently in the West and made numerous recordings. Regarded as one of the greatest pianists of the century, he developed an enormous repertory ranging from Scarlatti to Hindemith, but was best known for his interpretations of the 19th-century romantics.

RICHTHOFEN, BARON MANFRED VON (1892–1918), German pilot. The most illustrious World War I fighter pilot, Richthofen is credited with downing 80 enemy planes. Nicknamed the "Red Baron" because of his red plane, he introduced the V-formation of six or more aircraft. His daredevil career ended when he was killed during an aerial battle. In deference to his skill and daring, the British buried him with full military honors. ■ See biography by William E. Burrows (1969).

RICKENBACKER, EDWARD VERNON (1890–1973), U.S. pilot and airline executive. An outstanding race-car driver, Rickenbacker enlisted in World War I and became America's flying ace, downing 26 enemy planes in four months. "Captain Eddie" earned almost every possible military decoration, including the Congressional Medal of Honor. After the war he founded the Rickenbacker Motor Co. (1921), but after its dissolution returned to aviation and purchased Eastern Airlines (1938), which he ran as president (to 1959) and chairman of the board (1959–63). During World War II he undertook several special assignments; on one mission his plane ditched in the Pacific, and Rickenbacker spent 23 days adrift before being rescued. ■ See his autobiography (1967) and Finis Farr, *Rickenbacker's Luck* (1979).

RICKEY, BRANCH (1881–1965), U.S. baseball executive. Earning his B.A. (1906) while playing professional football and baseball, Rickey was a full-time law student at the University of Michigan (1907–11) before pursuing a career in the baseball world. As president (1917–20), field manager (1918–25), and general manager (1925–42) of the St. Louis Cardinals, Rickey devised and developed (1919) the "farm system." This system of developing new talent, in combination with his shrewd management and keen judgment of players, brought St. Louis six pennants and four world championships and made the Cardinals the most profitable team in baseball. During his tenure as president of the Brooklyn Dodgers (1942–50), Rickey broke the barrier that kept blacks from the major leagues by signing Jackie Robinson (1947) in a move that had profound sociological significance. ■ See biographies by Arthur Mann (1957), David Lipman (1966), and Murray Polner (1982) and Harvey Frommer, *Rickey and Robinson* (1982).

RICKOVER, HYMAN GEORGE (1900–1986), U.S. military leader. Born into a poor Jewish family in Russian Poland, Rickover was brought to the United States as a child and graduated from the U.S. Naval Academy at Annapolis (1922). He studied electrical engineering at Columbia University (M.S. 1929) and worked on the World War II Manhattan atomic bomb project and at the postwar Oak Ridge Atomic Research Center. As head of the navy's nuclear reactor division and the Atomic Energy Commission's naval reactor branch, the stubborn and outspoken Rickover single-mindedly pushed for the development of the nuclear submarine and was chiefly responsible for the design and production of the *Nautilus* (1954), the world's first. He also helped design the first large-scale experimental nuclear power plant in the United States (Shippingport, Pennsylvania; 1956–57). An influential figure until his forced retirement in 1982, Rickover was a vocal critic of inefficiency and waste in military contracts. He was also a noted critic of American education (*Education and Freedom,* 1959; *American Education,* 1963). ■ See study by Heather M. David (1970); biography by Norman Polmar and Thomas B. Allen (1982); and Theodore Rockwell, *The Rickover Effect* (1992).

RIDE, SALLY KRISTEN (1951–), U.S. astrophysicist and astronaut. Ride is best known for her venture into space, but her early achievements were on the tennis court. As a teenager, she attained national ranking and continued to play through college. Against the advice of one-time doubles partner Billie Jean King, Ride quit tennis and pursued graduate studies at Stanford University. After earning a Ph.D. in astrophysics (1978), Ride was one of 35 scientists selected by NASA to participate in the space program. As a mission specialist on the seventh flight of the space shuttle *Challenger* (June 1983), Sally Ride became the first American woman to fly in space. She subsequently was a professor of physics at the University of California, San Diego (1989–) and wrote *To Space and Back* (1986; with Susan Okie), *Voyager* (1992; with T. O'Shaughnessy), and *The Third Planet* (1994).

RIEFENSTAHL, LENI (1902–), German film director. Riefenstahl began her career as an actress in the pantheistic genre of German mountain films. In 1932 she directed as well as acted in *The Blue Light,* on the basis of which Nazi leader Adolf Hitler appointed her to film the 1934 Nuremberg Nazi party rally. The result, *Triumph of the Will* (1936), was a visual spectacular of torchlit parades and martial resolve and was considered a classic propaganda film. In 1936 Riefenstahl made a film of the Berlin Olympic games, *Olympiad* (1938), which premiered on Hitler's 49th birthday. After World War II she was imprisoned and blacklisted by the Allies and spent years in litigation trying to vindicate herself. She also spent many years in Africa, producing two books of still photography, *Last of the Nuba* (1974) and *People of Kau* (1976). ■ See her memoirs (Eng. trans. 1995) and the studies by Glenn Infield (1976), Renata Berg-Pan (1980), and Audrey Salkeld (1996).

RIESMAN, DAVID (1909–), U.S. social scientist. Trained in law at Harvard (LL.B. 1934), Riesman clerked for Supreme Court Justice Louis Brandeis (1935–36). After serving as assistant district attorney of New York (1942–43) and working briefly as a business executive, he taught on the social science faculty of the University of Chicago (1946–58). Riesman was surprised when the scholarly book he wrote with Reuel Denney and Nathan Glazer, *The Lonely Crowd: A Study of the Changing American Character* (1950), became a big seller. A classic of U.S. sociology, it traced the relationship between socioeconomic development and national character, coining the terms "tradition-directed," "inner-directed," and "other-directed." The book's title became a catch phrase for alienated U.S. city dwellers. Riesman later taught at Harvard (1958–80) and specialized in the sociology of higher education, documenting or predicting trends in academic life. His other works included *Individualism Reconsidered* (1954), *Abundance for What?* (1963; rev. ed. 1993), *The Perpetual Dream: Reform and Experiment in American Education* (1977), and *On Higher Education* (1980).

RIESZ, FRIGYES (1880–1956), Hungarian mathematician. Riesz was a professor at the University of Kolozsvár (Cluj) (from 1911) and Budapest (from 1945), and cofounder and editor of the journal *Acta Scientiarum Mathematicarum*. He was a pioneer of functional analysis and made significant contributions to the field. He wrote *Functional Analysis* (1952; Eng. trans. 1955).

RIETVELD, GERRIT THOMAS (1888–1964), Dutch architect and furniture designer. Rietveld was noted for his application of the principles of the De Stijl art theorists; both his famous "red-blue chair" (1918) and his Schröder House (1924) at Utrecht featured the interplay of vertical and horizontal planes and the use of primary colors. He turned exclusively to furniture design from 1936 until the end of World War II, but he later received a number of important architectural commissions, including the Dutch Pavilion at the Venice Biennale (1953–54), the Institute for Applied Art (Amsterdam; 1956), and the Van Slobbe House (Heerlen; 1964). ■ See Theodore M. Brown, *The Work of Gerrit Rietveld* (1958).

RIFBJERG, KLAUS (1931–   ), Danish writer. A film director and literary critic in the 1950s, Rifbjerg emerged as the leading figure of the lyrical modernism that dominated Danish literature in the 1960s. His focus on the encounter between consciousness and reality in *Confrontation* (1960), his third collection of poetry, and his use of modern, often unconventional syntax, typified the concerns of this lyrical renewal. His novels, more traditional in form, often probed the inner lives of people rebelling against, or escaping from, society. His critically acclaimed novel *Anna, I, Anna* (1969; Eng. trans. 1982) concerned the wife of a neurotic diplomat who crisscrosses Europe with an antisocial young hippie. Rifbjerg also wrote plays, television dramas, and films. His other works included *Selected Poems* (Eng. trans. 1975; 1984), the novel *Witness to the Future* (1981; Eng. trans. 1987), and the poem *War* (1992; Eng. trans. 1995). ■ See study by Charlotte S. Gray (1986).

RILKE, RAINER MARIA (1875–1926), Austro-German writer. One of the century's most cosmopolitan and influential lyric poets, Rilke was born in Prague, attended the universities of Prague, Munich, and Berlin, and traveled constantly throughout Europe. Influenced especially by his travels in Russia with his mistress Lou Andreas-Salomé (1899; 1900), his association with Auguste Rodin in Paris

(1902–06), and his residence at Castle Muzot in the Swiss Valais (1921–26), he dealt in his works with the themes of God, love, death, and regeneration. His best-known works were *New Poems* (1907; 1908), *Duino Elegies* and *Sonnets to Orpheus* (both 1923; many Eng. trans.), *The Tale of Love and Death of Cornet Christopher Rilke* (1906; Eng. trans. 1932), and the autobiographical novel, *The Notebook of Malte Laurids Brigge* (1910; Eng. trans. 1930, 1958, 1959). Further translations of his works in English are in *Selected Works* (2 vols., 1954–60) and *Poems, 1906–26* (1957). ■ See biographies by Elizabeth M. Butler (1946), Noro Purtscher (1950), and Wolfgang Leppmann (Eng. trans. 1984); J. F. Hendry, *Sacred Threshold* (1983); Donald Prater, *A Ringing Glass* (1986); and Ralph Freedman, *Life of a Poet* (1996).

RINEHART, MARY ROBERTS (Mary Roberts; 1876–1958), U.S. mystery writer. To recoup stock-market losses early in her marriage, Rinehart began (1903) to write, selling 45 stories during the first year. Asked to write a crime serial for *Munsey's Magazine,* she began writing best-selling mysteries including *The Circular Staircase* (1908), *The Breaking Point* (1922), *The Door* (1930), and *The Yellow Room* (1945). Her novels, about the terrorization of ordinary people, usually featured pretty heroines too thick-headed to avoid disaster and included elements of humor and romance. She also wrote plays, humorous sketches, and several travel books. For many years she was the best-selling woman writer in the United States. ■ See her autobiography, *My Story* (1931; rev. ed. 1948); Jan Cohn, *Improbable Fiction* (1980); and Charlotte MacLeod, *Had She But Known* (1994).

RINGLING, CHARLES (1863–1926), and **JOHN RINGLING** (1866–1936), U.S. circus owners. John and Charles Rüngeling, who changed their name when they entered show business, joined three of their older brothers to form a song-and-dance troupe that later developed into a circus with John as the first clown. Charles was the managerial genius behind the circus, which experienced steady growth after the acquisition of an elephant in 1888. By 1890 they were loading the circus wagons on railroad cars to make a much longer tour possible. In 1900 the circus began to absorb its competition, including Barnum and Bailey's "Greatest Show on Earth" after Bailey's death in 1907. Charles managed the circus until his death, when John took over. By 1930 the Ringling Brothers and Barnum and Bailey Circus was the biggest in the world. It used 240 rail cars for transportation, and its big top seated 10,000. After John's death, a nephew, John Ringling North (1903–85), managed the circus until 1967, when it passed from the family's hands. ■ See Richard Thomas, *John Ringling* (1960), and Henry Ringling North and Alden Hatch, *The Circus Kings* (1960).

RIPKIN, CAL, JR. (Calvin Edwin Ripkin, Jr.; 1960–   ), U.S. baseball player. The son of a minor-league baseball player and manager (who later managed the Baltimore Orioles), Ripkin was a star high school pitcher and shortstop who signed with the Baltimore Orioles organization shortly after graduation (1978). He began his remarkable major-league career as Rookie of the Year (1982) and developed into one of the greatest all-around shortstops in baseball history. He won two Most Valuable Player awards (1983, 1991), set the record for most career home runs (278) by a shortstop (1993), and held shortstop records for most consecutive errorless games (95), fewest errors in a season (3), and highest seasonal fielding percentage (.996)—all set in 1990. He also set the record for consecutive innings played (8,243), during a span of 904 games (between 1982 and 1987). Ripkin was best known, however, for beating Lou Gehrig's 56-year-old major-league record of 2,130 consecutive games played (1995), and he played in 2,632 consecutive games before ending his streak in September 1998. ■ See his *The Only Way I Know* (1997; with Mike Bryan).

RIPLEY, ROBERT LEROY (1893–1949), U.S. cartoonist. A sports cartoonist for the *New York Evening Globe* (1913–23), Ripley drew his first "Believe It or Not!" cartoon, depicting seven unusual sports records, in 1918. He soon expanded the concept and drew weekly panels illustrating oddities and bizarre facts of all kinds. A collection published in book form, *Believe It or Not* (1928), sold more than 500,000 copies, and soon the cartoon was syndicated in 326 newspapers in 38 countries around the world. In addition, Ripley developed motion-picture shorts and hosted his own radio show (from 1930) on the "Believe It or Not" theme, and he organized numerous exhibits of oddities he had collected. ■ See study by Robert Considine (1961).

RITSOS, YANNIS (1909–1990), Greek poet. During Ritsos' childhood, his prosperous family lost its fortune, his mother and brother died of tuberculosis, and his father was committed to an insane asylum. Although haunted by death and despair and victimized by frequent periods of illness, he produced a large body of poetry, rooted in the collective experience of the Greek people, proclaiming freedom, justice, and brotherhood and reflecting his Marxist beliefs. One of the most prolific and honored poets of modern Greece, he saw his books banned while he was twice incarcerated as a political prisoner (1948–52; 1967–71), but he emerged both times as a hero of the Greek left. Several of his poems, including *Epitaphios* (1936), a revolutionary lament, and *Romiosoni* (1945–47), a tribute to Greek resistance fighters of World War II, were set to music by Mikis Theodorakis. English translations of his works are in *Selected Poems* (1974; 1989), *The Fourth Dimension* (1977), *Chronicle of Exile* (1977), *Ritsos in Parenthesis* (1979), *Scripture of the Blind* (1979), *The Lady of the Vineyards* (1981), *Exile and Return* (1985), *Yannis Ritsos: Repetitions, Testimonies, Parentheses* (1991), and *Iconostasis of Anonymous Saints* (1996).

RITTER, TEX (Woodward Maurice Ritter; 1905–1974), U.S. singer and actor. Long interested in western folklore and music, Ritter dropped out of Northwestern University Law School to pursue a folksinging career. He sang cowboy and country songs on radio and on the stage during the early 1930s and (from 1936) played the role of the singing cowboy in dozens of Hollywood movies. Often called "America's most-beloved cowboy," Ritter recorded many best-selling songs including "I've Got Spurs that Jingle, Jangle, Jingle," "You Are My Sunshine," and the theme from the movie *High Noon* ("Do Not Forsake Me, Oh My Darling"). He appeared frequently with the Grand Ole Opry and was elected to both the Cowboy and Country Music Halls of Fame.

RIVERA, DIEGO (1886–1957), Mexican painter and muralist. After studying at the School of Fine Arts in Mexico City, Rivera traveled to Europe on a grant (1907) and was temporarily influenced by cubism, but he reverted to the inspiration of native folklore when he returned to Mexico (1921). A Marxist, he was primarily known for his monumental allegorical murals depicting both Mexican history and mankind's social development. He is linked with José Clemente Orozco and David Siqueiros as an innovator of popular revolutionary mural painting. He executed notable murals for the National Preparatory School (1921–23), the Ministry of Education (1923–29), the Agriculture School, Chipango (1923–27), and the National Palace (1929–35), as well as numerous pieces in the United States (1930–34). He was married to the artist Frida Kahlo. ■ See his autobiography, *My Life, My Art* (1960); Bertram D. Wolfe, *The Fabulous Life of Diego Rivera* (1963); and Patrick Marnham, *Dreaming with His Eyes Open* (1998).

RIVERA, JOSÉ DE (José A. Ruiz; 1904–1985), U.S. sculptor. Rivera grew up in Louisiana. He learned smithery and machine repair by working with his father, a sugar-mill engineer, and later by laboring in foundries. He studied drawing in Chicago (1928–31) and created his first sculptures in 1930. From the beginning of his career, he designed graceful shapes with curvilinear surfaces in highly polished metals. After the Works Progress Administration underwrote *Flight* (1938), created for Newark Airport, he was increasingly well known. Two Rivera retrospective exhibitions were mounted (1961; 1972) at the Whitney Museum of American Art in New York City. One of his stainless-steel sculptures is on permanent display in front of the Smithsonian Institution's National Museum of History and Technology in Washington, D.C.

RIVERA, JOSÉ EUSTASIO (1889–1928), Colombian novelist and poet. Schooled as a lawyer, Rivera entered public service, representing Colombia in other Latin American countries. His poetry used colorful detail and jungle rhythms to portray the violence and mystery of the wilds. Striving for an authentic Latin American novel, he wrote *The Vortex* (1924; Eng. trans. 1935), set in the jungles of Colombia. It was a powerful, poetic protest against the exploitation of rubber gatherers in the upper Amazon.

RIVERS, LARRY (Yitzroch Loiza Grossberg; 1923–), U.S. artist. A former jazz musician from the Bronx, Rivers acquired his new name while playing saxophone in hotels on the borscht circuit. After World War II he studied art and began painting abstract-expressionist canvases, into which he introduced images from memory, history, and the old masters. Rivers also experimented with stage design, poetry, acting, welded-metal sculpture, and, during the 1960s, pop art, painting mass-produced objects such as cigarette packages "with the serious grace of Tiepolo." His favorite subjects included his former mother-in-law (*Double Portrait of Berdie*, 1955) and the Russian Revolution (76 panels; 1965). A later work was *The History of Matzah; The Story of the Jews* (1984), a representation of 4,000 years of history painted on three 10-by-14 foot canvases. ■ See his *Drawings and Digressions* (1979) and his "unauthorized" autobiography, *What Did I Do?* (1992; with Arnold Weinstein).

ROA BASTOS, AUGUSTO (1917–), Paraguayan writer. Roa Bastos' sympathy for his Indian protagonists and his indignant social protest derived from his own experience; he recalled going barefoot until age 8, and he did not get beyond the fifth grade. He participated in the Chaco War (1932–35) between Bolivia and Paraguay, worked as a journalist and scriptwriter, and during political strife in Paraguay sought asylum in Argentina (1947–76). He returned but was exiled by the government in 1982 and remained in exile until 1989. He taught at the University of Toulouse, France (1976–84) and after 1985 he was active in the movement opposed to dictator Alfredo Stroessner. *Thunder in the Leaves* (1953), a short-story collection, portrays violence and despair in a mixture of Spanish and Indian languages. Roa Bastos worked in many genres. His masterpiece, the novel *Son of Man* (1960; Eng. trans. 1965), treated social corruption symbolically, applying cinematic technique to Indian legend and Christian symbolism. The historical novel dealing with a 19th-century dictator, *I the Supreme* (1974; Eng. trans. 1986), was seen by some as an allegorical attack on Paraguayan dictator Alfredo Stroessner. ■ See study by David W. Foster (1978).

ROBBE-GRILLET, ALAIN (1922–), French novelist and filmmaker. Robbe-Grillet worked for 10 years (1945–55) as an agricultural expert. As a literary theorist and writer he was the leading proponent of the "new novel," or "antinovel." Arguing that the "world is neither significant nor absurd; it simply *is*," he did not in his own novels relate a linear plot but gave only visual descriptions of objects and actions without interpretation or explanation. In his later work, realism completely disappeared. His theories are embodied in such novels as *The Erasers* (1953; Eng. trans. 1964), *Jealousy* (1957; Eng. trans. 1959), *In the Labyrinth* (1959; Eng. trans. 1960), *Project for a Revolution in New York* (1970; Eng. trans. 1972), and *Recollections of The Golden Triangle* (1978; Eng. trans. 1986), and in screenplays for Alain Resnais' *Last Year at Marienbad* (1961) and

for the films he himself directed. ■ See his *For a New Novel: Essays on Fiction* (1963; Eng. trans. 1965); his autobiography *Ghosts in the Mirror* (1985; Eng. trans. 1989); and studies by Ben F. Stoltzfus (1964) and Ilona Leki (1983).

ROBBINS, FREDERICK CHAPMAN (1916–), U.S. pediatrician and physiologist. After graduating from Harvard (M.D. 1940), Robbins served as an army medical researcher during World War II and investigated such epidemic diseases as hepatitis, typhus, and Q fever. After the war he joined the research laboratory of the Children's Hospital in Boston, where, with John Enders and Thomas Weller, he devised techniques for cultivating the poliomyelitis virus in tissue culture. This work made possible the subsequent development of the polio vaccine and improvements in the isolation and diagnosis of viruses. He shared the 1954 Nobel Prize for Physiology or Medicine with Enders and Weller. He was a professor of pediatrics at Case Western Reserve University, Cleveland (1952–80), and president of the Institute of Medicine of the National Academy of Sciences (1980–85).

ROBBINS, JEROME (Jerome Rabinowitz; 1918–1998), U.S. choreographer, director, and producer. Drawn to the dance world in his teens, Robbins studied a wide range of techniques before dancing with the American Ballet Theater (1940–48); in 1949 George Balanchine invited him to join the New York City Ballet. Robbins won acclaim for his first choreographic work, *Fancy Free* (with composer Leonard Bernstein; 1944)—a distinctly American ballet about sailors on shore leave that inspired the Broadway musical *On the Town*. Robbins created dances for other musical hits, including *West Side Story* (1957), *Gypsy* (1959), and *Fiddler on the Roof* (1964), which reflected his view that choreography must advance the plot of a dramatic work. An unusually versatile, inventive artist, he established a reputation as one of the century's great choreographers with such works as *Ballade* (1952), *Dances at a Gathering* (1969), and *Goldberg Variations* (1971). Later works included *A Suite of Dances* (1979), *Glass Pieces* (1983), *Eight Lives* (1985), and *Brandenburg* (1997). Robbins was the New York City Ballet's principal choreographer and, with Peter Martins, succeeded Balanchine as its ballet master-in-chief (1983–90). ■ See Christena L. Schlundt et al. *Dance in the Musical Theater* (1989).

ROBBINS, LIONEL CHARLES ROBBINS, BARON (1898–1984), British economist. A professor at the London School of Economics (1929–61), Robbins was a leader in the revival of liberal economic thought in Britain. In his best-known book, *An Essay on the Nature and Significance of Economic Science* (1932), he stressed the importance of scarcity in economic behavior and argued against value judgments in economics by calling for a distinction between normative and positive elements. Originally opposed to the interventionist ideas of John Maynard Keynes, he modified his views in the late 1930s and 1940s and served with Keynes at the Bretton Woods Conference (1944). Robbins chaired the influential Robbins Committee, whose 1963 report led to the expansion of higher education. He was also chairman of the *Financial Times* (1961–70), director of the *Economist* (1960–75), and chairman of the board of governors of the London School of Economics (1968–74). His other books included *The Economic Problem in Peace and War* (1947), *Classical Political Economy* (1952), *The Evolution of Modern Economic Theory* (1970), and *Autobiography of an Economist* (1971).

ROBERTS, KENNETH (1885–1957), U.S. novelist. Roberts wrote for the *Boston Post* (1909–17) and the *Saturday Evening Post* (1919–37) before turning to the carefully researched and often iconoclastic historical fiction that earned him a special Pulitzer Prize citation (1957) for "creation of greater interest in our early American history." His novels included the four-volume *Chronicles of Arundel* (1930–34), *Northwest Passage* (1937), and *Lydia Bailey* (1947). *Oliver Wiswell* (1940) was a story of the American Revolution written from the viewpoint of a Loyalist. A dowsing enthusiast, Roberts also wrote *Henry Gross and his Dowsing Rod* (1951) and *Water Unlimited* (1957). ■ See *The Kenneth Roberts Reader* (1945), the autobiographical *I Wanted to Write* (1949), and study by Jack Bales (1993).

ROBERTS, (GRANVILLE) ORAL (1918–   ), U.S. evangelist and faith healer. Roberts was born in rural Oklahoma. His mother was of Cherokee origin; his father was a Pentecostal preacher. He was ordained in the Pentacostal Holiness Church at age 17 (1936); in 1968 he was ordained in the United Methodist Church. His worldwide preaching and healing ministry spread through television broadcasts (from 1947) on which he would ask God to restore the health of ailing congregants, and through the sale of such books as *If You Need Healing, Do These Things* (1952), *God Is a Good God* (1960), and *Don't Give Up* (1980). He founded the Oral Roberts Evangelical Association (1947), a multimillion-dollar enterprise, and Oral Roberts University (1963), both in Tulsa, Oklahoma. He reported at a 1987 Bible conference that he had raised people from the dead. ■ See his autobiography, *The Call* (1972), and biography by David E. Harrell, Jr. (1985).

ROBERTS, OWEN JOSEPHUS (1875–1955), U.S. jurist. A successful Philadelphia lawyer and law professor at the University of Pennsylvania, Roberts was a special deputy U.S. attorney general during World War I and gained national attention by prosecuting those involved in the oil-reserve scandals during the 1920s. Appointed to the Supreme Court by Pres. Herbert Hoover (1930), he wrote numerous opinions but failed to develop a consistent judicial philosophy. Often a swing member of the Court, he at first opposed New Deal legislation, but later supported it. After the Japanese attack on Pearl Harbor (1941), he headed a board of inquiry into the disaster that blamed the military for "dereliction of duty" and "errors of judgment." After retiring from the

court (1945) he was dean of the University of Pennsylvania Law School (1948–51) and an active supporter of world federalism. He wrote *The Court and the Constitution* (1951).

ROBERTS, RICHARD J. (1943–   ), British molecular biologist. Roberts studied organic chemistry at the University of Sheffield, England (Ph.D. 1968), and came to the United States to do postdoctoral research at Harvard University (1969–72). He later was a researcher at the Cold Spring Harbor Laboratory in New York (1972–92) and research director of New England Biolabs in Beverly, Massachusetts (from 1992). In 1977, while studying the genes of a virus, Roberts discovered that the gene strands were discontinuous; in other words, the segments of DNA were not arranged in a continuous strand but were interrupted by stretches of DNA that contained no genetic information. Subsequent research demonstrated that these "split genes" are the most common type of genetic structure in higher organisms. It was shown that enzymes cut out the meaningless segments and that the sections containing the genetic code are spliced together to create the final messenger RNA. The discovery of split genes suggested how evolution may have been speeded up and had a great influence on basic biological research and the study of genetic diseases. Roberts shared the 1993 Nobel Prize in Physiology or Medicine with Phillip A. Sharp, who independently discovered the existence of split genes.

ROBERTSON, SIR DENNIS HOLME (1890–1963), British economist. An important theorist in the fields of monetary policy and trade cycles, D. H. Robertson taught at Trinity College, Cambridge (1914–38; 1944–57) and at the University of London (1938–44). He collaborated with his former teacher, John Maynard Keynes, during the 1920s, but broke with him during the 1930s. He came to believe that Keynes' theories were inherently inflationary and too interventionist, and he challenged his liquidity-preference theory and the multiplier effect. During World War II he handled balance of payments and overseas finance problems for the treasury, and he played a major role in the Bretton Woods monetary conference (1944). His books included *A Study of Industrial Fluctuation* (1915), *Money* (1922), *The Control of Industry* (1923), and *Banking Policy and the Price Level* (1926).

ROBERTSON, OSCAR (1938–   ), U.S. basketball player. Considered by many to be one of the greatest all-around players in basketball history, Robertson, nicknamed "the Big O," was a superb playmaker and shooter. A three-time All-American at the University of Cincinnati, the 6-foot, 5-inch-tall Robertson averaged 33.8 points and 15.2 rebounds per game during his 88-game college career (1958–60). He was a star in the National Basketball Association (NBA) with the Cincinnati Royals (1960–70) before being traded to Milwaukee, where he teamed up with Kareem Abdul-Jabbar to lead the Bucks to their first championship (1971). He retired (1974) as the all-time NBA leader in assists and free throws and the second-highest scorer in league history (26,710 points).

ROBESON, PAUL BUSTILL (1898–1976), U.S. singer and actor. The son of a runaway slave who became a Methodist minister, Robeson was an All-American football player and Phi Beta Kappa scholar at Rutgers University (B.A. 1919). He graduated from Columbia University's law school (1923), but his acting and singing interests soon took precedence over a legal career. For 30 years his rich bass-baritone renditions of spirituals and folk songs were heard from New York to Moscow. His portrayal of Brutus Jones in Eugene O'Neill's *The Emperor Jones*, of Joe in *Showboat*, and of Shakespeare's *Othello* won equal acclaim, and he appeared in several films. But cold-war America turned on him for his lifelong left-wing sympathies and civil-rights activities. Robeson was blacklisted, his passport was revoked (1950–58), and he lived in virtual exile in Europe from 1958 until 1963. He suffered from severe depression during the 1960s and 1970s and was politically inactive. ■ See his autobiography, *Here I Stand* (1958); biographies by Virginia Hamilton (1974) and Martin Duberman (1989); and study edited by Jeffrey C. Stewart (1998).

ROBINSON, BILL "BOJANGLES" (1878–1949), U.S. tap dancer and actor. One of the most famous black entertainers of the century, Robinson was considered to be the world's greatest tap dancer. A star of vaudeville and Broadway musical comedies for 25 years, he went to Hollywood (1930) and made several well-known films, including *The Littlest Rebel* (1935), *The Little Colonel* (1936), and *Rebecca of Sunnybrook Farm* (1938) with Shirley Temple. He later appeared in *The Hot Mikado* (1939) on Broadway and at the 1939 New York World's Fair. Robinson was also noted for his ability to run backward, and he set the world's record of 8.2 seconds for the 75-yard backward dash. ■ See Jim Haskins and N. R. Mitgang, *Mr. Bojangles* (1988).

ROBINSON, BOARDMAN (1876–1952), Canadian-born U.S. artist. Robinson, who studied art in Europe and did social work in New York, became a powerful political cartoonist in the "Ashcan" style of realism. He accompanied John Reed to Russia as a World War I correspondent, returning to teach at the Art Students League of New York (1919–30). His biting cartoons, which exposed social evils and the horrors of war, appeared in the radical magazines *The Masses* (1916–17) and *The Liberator* (1918–22) as well as *Harper's Weekly*, and influenced a generation of political cartoonists in the United States. Robinson also illustrated books and painted murals, such as *Man and His Toys* at New York's Radio City Music Hall (1932). ■ See study by Albert Christ-Janer (1946).

ROBINSON, EDDIE (Edward Gay Robinson; 1919–   ), U.S. football coach. The son of a Louisiana sharecropper, Robinson moved with his family to Baton Rouge when he

was a child. He was a quarterback for his high school and college (Leland; B.A. 1941) football teams and was named head football coach at Louisiana's historically black Grambling University in 1941. A charismatic perfectionist and disciplinarian who stressed the fundamentals, Robinson built a powerful football program and brought international attention to the school. His teams won 17 Southwestern Athletic Conference titles and 9 National Black College championships and frequently played before crowds of over 60,000 fans at stadiums throughout the country. He retired in 1997 after 57 years at Grambling as the winningest coach in college football history, with a record of 408 wins, 165 losses, and 15 ties. He produced over 200 professional football players, more than any other coach, including Paul (Tank) Younger, the first player from a predominantly Black college to join the NFL (1949), and Willie Davis and Willie Brown, who were elected to the National Football League (NFL) Hall of Fame.

ROBINSON, EDWARD G. (Emmanuel Goldenberg; 1893–1973), Rumanian-born U.S. actor. Robinson's classic portrayal of the brutal, cigar-chomping racketeer in the film *Little Caesar* (1930) made him a major Hollywood star and influenced the style and approach of gangster movies in the 1930s and 1940s. He played with great intensity in many gangster movies and psychological dramas, but he was also amusing in comedies and moving in historical roles, as in *Dr. Ehrlich's Magic Bullet* (1940). Despite his tough-guy movie image, Robinson was a gentle man in real life and a noted art collector. In his 60-year career he appeared in 40 Broadway plays and over 100 movies. ■ See his autobiographies, *My Father, My Son* (1958) and *All My Yesterdays* (1973), and study by Foster Hirsch (1975).

ROBINSON, EDWIN ARLINGTON (1869–1935), U.S. poet. Robinson grew up in a village in Maine, described as "Tilbury Town" in the austere, ironic poems he wrote as a young man. Forced to drop out of Harvard University (1893) for financial reasons, he struggled with poverty and obscurity for several years before Pres. Theodore Roosevelt, an admirer of his poetry, intervened to provide him with a minor government position (1905–09). Robinson first won critical recognition for *The Man Against the Sky* (1916). He won Pulitzer Prizes for his *Collected Poems* (1921; expanded 1929, 1937); for *Tristram* (1927), the third in a series of Arthurian legends; and for *The Man Who Died Twice* (1924), but he is best remembered for such short, early poems as "Miniver Cheevy" and "Richard Cory." ■ See C. P. Smith, *Where the Light Falls: A Portrait of Edwin Arlington Robinson* (1965), and studies by Hoyt C. Franchere (1968) and Emery Neff (1968).

ROBINSON, JACKIE (Jack Roosevelt Robinson; 1919–1972), U.S. baseball player. Robinson was a baseball, football, and track star at the University of California at Los Angeles (U.C.L.A.) during the late 1930s. He served in the army during World War II and afterward played professional baseball in the Negro National League and the International League. The first African American to play in the major leagues, he was a star infielder and outfielder for the Brooklyn Dodgers (1947–57) and an inspiring role model for black athletes throughout the United States. A strong hitter (.311 lifetime batting average) and daring base runner, he led the Dodgers to six National League pennants and one World Series (1955) and was largely responsible for the acceptance of black athletes in professional sports. He was the 1947 Rookie of the Year and 1949 league batting champion (.342 average) and Most Valuable Player. ■ See his autobiography, *I Never Had it Made* (1972; with Alfred Duckett); Jules Tygiel, *Baseball's Great Experiment* (1983); and biography by Arnold Rampersad (1997).

ROBINSON, JAMES HARVEY (1863–1936), U.S. historian. Robinson focused on ideas and beliefs rather than institutions and wars and was one of the founders of the "new history," which incorporated an interdisciplinary, social-science approach to traditional political history. He believed that historians and educational institutions should contribute to a more just and progressive social order. He was professor at Columbia from 1895 to 1919, when he resigned and helped to found the New School for Social Research in New York City. Robinson's best-known books were *Introduction to the History of Western Europe* (1903), *The New History* (1912), and *The Mind in the Making: The Relation of Intelligence to Social Reform* (1921). ■ See study by Luther V. Hendricks (1946).

ROBINSON, JOAN VIOLET (Joan Maurice; 1903–1983), British economist. On the faculty of Cambridge University for 40 years (1931–71), Robinson played a dominant role in the development of the Cambridge School of neoclassical economic thought, which emphasized macroeconomics and theories of growth and distribution. She was a collaborator of economist John Maynard Keynes and was also influenced by the writings of Karl Marx. A critic of laissez-faire economic theory, she was deeply concerned with the social implications of economic analysis. Beginning with her 1933 classic, *The Economics of Imperfect Competition,* and *Introduction to the Theory of Unemployment* (1937), she focused on the problems of unemployment, instability, and growth in the capitalist system. Her other books included *The Accumulation of Capital* (1956), *Freedom and Necessity* (1970), *Economic Heresies* (1971), *Introduction to Modern Economics* (1973; with John Eatwell), and *Aspects on Development and Underdevelopment* (1979). See also her collected *Economic Papers* (5 vols., 1951–79). ■ See study by James Cicarelli and Julianne Cicarelli (1996) and study edited by George Feiwel (1989).

ROBINSON, SIR ROBERT (1886–1975), British chemist. A professor at Oxford (1930–55) and president of the Royal Society (1945–50), Robinson developed an electronic theory of organic chemical reactions and played a major role in the synthesis of pencillin. He was best known, however, for his research into the chemical constituents of plants, including alkaloids and anthocyanin pigments. He determined the structure of the alkaloids morphine (1925) and strychnine (1946) and won the 1947 Nobel Prize for Chemistry. ■ See his *Memoirs of a Minor Prophet* (1976) and biography by Trevor I. Williams (1990).

ROBINSON, SUGAR RAY (Walker Smith; 1920–1989), U.S. boxer. In 1940, Robinson launched a prizefighting career that spanned more than a quarter of a century. In 1946 he captured the welterweight crown and in the following years won and lost the middleweight title five times. In 1952 he sought the light-heavyweight title, and although outboxing and outpointing his opponent, he was overcome by heat exhaustion in the 13th round. A flamboyant and popular champion, Robinson lost only 19 of his 202 professional bouts. He retired at age 45 (1965). Many boxing experts say that pound for pound, he was boxing history's outstanding all-around fighter. ■ See his autobiography, *Sugar Ray* (1970).

ROCHE, (EAMONN) KEVIN (1922–   ), Irish-born U.S. architect. Kevin Roche went to the United States to study with Mies van der Rohe in 1948, and he became Eero Saarinen's principal design associate in 1954. After Saarinen's death (1961), Roche and John Dinkeloo took over the firm and completed such structures as the Dulles International Airport Building (near Washington, D.C.), the CBS Building (New York), the TWA terminal at Kennedy Airport (New York), and the Jefferson Memorial Arch (St. Louis), many of which Roche had designed. Brilliant examples of Roche's later style were the Oakland (California) Museum, which is surmounted by a multitiered park; the Ford Foundation Headquarters in New York, which engulfs a large landscaped garden; and the new wings of the Metropolitan Museum of Art in New York City. His later designs included the E. F. Hutton Building, New York City (1980), which included many classical references, and the World Headquarters of Merck & Co., New Jersey (1993). He was awarded the 1982 Pritzker Prize.

ROCK, JOHN (1890–1984), U.S. gynecologist and obstetrician. A Roman Catholic layman, Rock was a major figure in the development of the oral contraceptive pill and an outspoken advocate of birth control. He was founding director of the Fertility and Endocrine Clinic at the Free Hospital for Women in Brookline, Massachusetts (1926–56), and a professor at the Harvard Medical School (1947–56). Working in collaboration with Miriam F. Menkin (1944), he achieved the first fertilization of a human ovum in a test tube, and several years later he began experimenting with the hormone progesterone as a means of inducing fertility in women. This research with progesterone inspired Gregory Pincus, a correspondent of Rock, to look at it as a possible birth-control agent. (Together with M. C. Chang, Pincus developed the "pill" in 1954, and it was marketed in 1960). ■ See Rock's *The Time Has Come* (1963) and Loretta McLaughlin, *The Pill, John Rock, and the Church* (1983).

ROCKEFELLER, DAVID (1915–), U.S. banker. The only one of oil magnate John D. Rockefeller's six grandchildren to pursue a business career, Rockefeller studied economics at the University of Chicago (Ph.D. 1940). Joining the Chase Manhattan Bank in 1946, he served as president (1961–69) and then chairman (1969–80) of the institution that became known as "David's bank." An influential figure in world finance, he also was a leading figure in the Trilateral Commission, a controversial international group of private individuals prominent in politics and finance, and on the Council of Foreign Relations. He served as chairman of New York's Museum of Modern Art. ■ See William S. Hoffman, *David* (1971).

ROCKEFELLER, JOHN DAVISON, JR. (1874–1960), U.S. philanthropist. The only son of oil magnate John D. Rockefeller, he became involved in the family's philanthropic activities. He and his father gave more than $3 billion to scientific, cultural, and educational institutions, including the Rockefeller Institute for Medical Research (now Rockefeller University) in New York and the Rockefeller Foundation. He served on the boards of 17 of the largest U.S. corporations and presided over the creation of Rockefeller Center in New York, which opened in 1939. His eldest child, Abby Rockefeller Mauzé (1903–1976), a philanthropist, was less well known than her five brothers, who became leaders in the world establishment of wealth and power: John D. Rockefeller III (1906–1978), Nelson A. Rockefeller (1908–1979), Laurance Spelman Rockefeller (1910–); Winthrop Rockefeller (1912–1973), and David Rockefeller (1915–). ■ See biographies by Raymond Fosdick (1956) and Cary Reich (1996) and Peter Collier and David Horowitz, *The Rockefellers* (1976).

ROCKEFELLER, JOHN DAVISON, III (1906–1978), U.S. philanthropist. The oldest and least well known of the five grandsons of oil magnate John D. Rockefeller, John D. Rockefeller III devoted his life to the family's philanthropic activities, supporting such cultural institutions as Lincoln Center for the Performing Arts and the Asia Society, both in New York City. He served as chairman of the board of the Rockefeller Foundation and of the Population Council, a research center for family planning. ■ See Peter Collier and David Horowitz, *The Rockefellers* (1976).

ROCKEFELLER, NELSON ALDRICH (1908–1979), U.S. political leader. The most politically ambitious of oil magnate John D. Rockefeller's grandsons, Nelson Rockefeller carved out a personal sphere of oil and commercial interests in Venezuela, which led to his appointment in 1940 as coordinator of the U.S. Office of Inter-American Affairs and in

1944 as assistant secretary of state for Latin America. While serving as a popular liberal Republican governor of New York (1959–73), he became leader of the eastern wing of the party, and he ran unsuccessfully for the presidential nomination in 1960, 1964, and 1968. He served as the appointed U.S. vice president under Pres. Gerald Ford (1974–76). ■ See biography by Michael S. Kramer and Sam Roberts, *I Never Wanted to Be Vice President of Anything!* (1976), and study by Robert Connery and Gerald Benjamin (1979).

ROCKNE, KNUTE KENNETH (1888–1931), Norwegian-born U.S. football coach. An outstanding scholar and football player at Notre Dame University (B.S. 1914), Rockne was head football coach at his alma mater (from 1918). In the process of compiling a record of 105 wins, 12 losses, and 5 ties, he revolutionized the game by devising the shifting backfield, perfecting the forward pass, and developing fast, deceptive offensive plays. He made Notre Dame the football capital of the United States during the 1920s and became an authentic American folk hero. His death in an airplane crash was mourned throughout the country. ■ See biographies by Arthur Daley (1960), Francis Wallace (1960), and Ray Robinson (1999).

ROCKWELL, GEORGE LINCOLN (1918–1967), U.S. Nazi leader. The son of a vaudeville comedian, Rockwell dropped out of Brown University to serve as a navy pilot (1940) and later was recalled during the Korean War with the rank of commander. During this second navy tour, he came across racist literature and was "transfixed," as he later recalled, by Adolf Hitler's book *Mein Kampf*. In 1958 Rockwell, who had failed in several careers, launched his American Nazi party in Arlington, Virginia, proclaiming himself führer and leading demonstrations that called for the separation of the races and the extermination of "Jew commies." In 1967, when party membership was estimated at no more than a few hundred, and possibly much less, Rockwell renamed his group the National Socialist White People's party to appeal to a broader group of white supremacists. Later that year he was assassinated by an expelled party member in the parking lot of a shopping center where he had been doing his laundry. ■ See Frederick J. Simonelli, *American Fuehrer* (1999).

ROCKWELL, NORMAN (1894–1978), U.S. illustrator. Rockwell became art director of *Boy's Life* at age 19 and matured into one of the most popular and best-known artists in the United States. Working methodically, he created idealized portraits of small-town life "without warts." For half a century (1926–76) the small, frail artist illustrated the world's best-selling (Boy Scout) calendar and created 317 covers for the *Saturday Evening Post* (1916–63). His "Four Freedoms" poster, inspired by Pres. Franklin D. Roosevelt's 1941 speech, were widely distributed during World War II. Rockwell published an autobiography, *My Adventures As an Illustrator* (1960), and a 1970 collection of illustrations. ■ See studies by Arthur L. Guptill (1970) and Thomas S. Buechner (1970); Donald Walton, *A Rockwell Portrait* (1978); and the definitive catalogue edited by N. L. Moffat (1986).

RODBELL, MARTIN (1925–1998), American biochemist. Rodbell graduated from the University of Washington (Ph.D. 1954) and did research in nutrition and endocrinology at the National Institutes of Health (1956–94). In the 1960s he discovered natural substances known as G-proteins (guanosine triphosphate or GTP), and described how they help cells convert signals from the environment (such as light and sound) and from chemicals within the body (such as hormones and neurotransmitters) to produce cellular chain reactions that give rise to such fundamental life processes as vision, smell, and metabolism. Subsequent research determined that G-protein activity is linked to cancer, cholera, diabetes, alcoholism, and other health disorders. For his research Rodbell shared the 1994 Nobel Prize in Physiology or Medicine with Alfred G. Gilman, who determined the chemical nature of the G-protein and purified it.

RODDENBERRY, GENE (Eugene Wesley Roddenberry; 1921–1991), U.S. writer and television producer. A decorated B-17 pilot during World War II, Roddenberry later flew for Pan American Airlines and served as a sergeant with the Los Angeles Police Department (1949–53). From 1953 to 1962 he wrote scripts for several popular television shows, including "Dragnet," "Naked City," "Highway Patrol," and "Have Gun, Will Travel." In 1964, NBC accepted his proposal for a science-fiction television series, "Star Trek," and eventually ran 79 episodes (1966–69). The show, which followed the exploits of the starship *Enterprise* and its multiracial and multinational crew—including Capt. James T. Kirk, Mr. Spock, Dr. McCoy, Lt. Sulu, Lt. Uhara, and Scotty, the ship's engineer who was frequently beaming people up—eschewed violence and promiscuity and presented an optimistic view of the future. It gained an international cult following of "Trekkies" and spawned six "Star Trek" movies (1979–91) and a sequel TV series, "Star Trek: The Next Generation," which debuted in 1987. In April 1997 his ashes, along with those of 23 others, were launched into space attached to a satellite expected to orbit the earth for up to 10 years.

RODGERS, JIMMIE (James Charles Rodgers; 1897–1933), U.S. country singer. During the same week in 1927 that the Carter Family made its first recording, Jimmie Rodgers cut his first two records in the same Tennessee studio. Guided by manager Ralph S. Peer, Rodgers' recording career flourished, and in less than six years he cut 111 songs, most of them ballads. He became famous for his rhythmic yodeling, which he combined with blues themes to become "America's Blue Yodeler." His unique sound was imitated by younger singers, including Gene Autry. Rodgers' always-weak constitution further deteriorated during the 14 years he worked

on the railroads. He succumbed to tuberculosis at age 35, at the height of his career. His recordings influenced several generations of country and western singers. ■ See biography by Nolan Porterfield (1979) and Carrie Cecil Williamson Rodgers, *My Husband Jimmie Rodgers* (1935).

RODGERS, RICHARD (1902–1979), U.S. composer. Born into a prosperous and music-loving New York City family, Rodgers composed his first song at age 14 and his first musical comedy as a 17-year-old Columbia College undergraduate. Collaborating (1918–43) with the lyricist Lorenz Hart, a former college classmate, he wrote some of Broadway's biggest musical hits, including *Garrick Gaieties* (1925), *On Your Toes* (1936), *Babes In Arms* (1937), *The Boys from Syracuse* (1938), and *Pal Joey* (1940). In partnership with Oscar Hammerstein II (1942–60), he wrote such hits as *Oklahoma!* (1943), *Carousel* (1945), *South Pacific* (1949), *The King and I* (1951), and *The Sound of Music* (1959), works that revolutionized musical comedy by integrating plot, dialogue, music, and dance in the exploration of socially significant themes. Rodgers wrote melodies for hundreds of popular songs including such standards as "Manhattan," "With a Song in My Heart," "There's a Small Hotel," "This Can't Be Love," "My Funny Valentine," "Oh, What a Beautiful Mornin'," "My Favorite Things," "Some Enchanted Evening," "Climb Every Mountain," and "It Might As Well Be Spring." He also composed the score for the TV series "Victory at Sea" (1952). ■ See his autobiography, *Musical Stages* (1975); David Ewen, *With a Song in My Heart* (1963); and biography by William G. Hyland (1998).

RODÓ, JOSÉ ENRIQUE (1871–1917), Uruguayan essayist, literary critic, and philosopher. A university professor who spent most of his life in Montevideo, Rodó was one of Latin America's most famous philosophers. He helped found (1895) and edit *The National Review of Literature and Social Sciences*, was director of the National Library (1900), and served in the Chamber of Deputies (1902–10). In his writings, which influenced two generations of Latin American idealists and intellectuals, he supported the spiritual and intellectual unity of Latin America with Spain and Europe and warned against the materialism of North America. Among his most famous works were *Ariel* (1900; Eng. trans. 1922) and *The Motives of Proteus* (1908; Eng. trans. 1929).

RODRIGUES, AMÁLIA (1920–1999), Portuguese singer. Born into an impoverished family in Lisbon, Rodrigues worked as a fruit peddler and seamstress before becoming a fado singer in taverns during the 1930s. "Fado," which means fate in Portuguese, is a haunting, passionate style whose song lyrics reflect a mixture of pessimism, longing, and nostalgia. Typically appearing in mourning clothes and accompanied by a 12-string guitar, Rodrigues extended the scope of fado and became its best-known interpreter. Beginning in 1945 she made hundreds of recordings, appeared in several movies, and gave concerts around the world. Performing into her 70s, Rodrigues became a national icon in Portugal and when she died, the prime minister ordered a three-day period of national mourning.

RODRIGUEZ, JOHNNY (Juan Raúl Rodriguez; 1952–), Mexican-U.S. country singer. As a boy, Rodriguez practiced on his father's guitar in their south Texas home. He worked in construction until heading (1972) for Nashville, where Tom T. Hall hired him as a guitarist. After "Pass Me By" (1972) and "You Always Come Back to Hurting Me" (1973) put him on the map, Rodriguez became a country-music star almost overnight—the first Mexican-American in the entertainment field to become a national celebrity. He made bilingual renditions of standard country songs. His later albums included *Run for the Border* (1994) and *You Can Say That Again* (1996).

ROEHM or RÖHM, ERNST (1887–1934), German Nazi leader. Roehm was a soldier of fortune who was wounded three times during World War I and rose to major in the German army. After meeting Adolf Hitler in 1919, he created the Nazi Sturmabteilung (SA) or brown-shirted storm troopers. Restless in peacetime, he went to Bolivia as a military instructor after the failure of the "beer-hall putsch" in Munich (1923), returning (1930) to build the SA to 2 million men. He sought to have the regular army subordinated to the SA and was Hitler's chief rival within the Nazi party. Citing the danger of a putsch, Hitler had Roehm murdered and the SA purged in 1934. ■ See Max Gallo, *The Night of the Long Knives* (Eng. trans. 1972).

ROERICH, NICHOLAS (1874–1947), Russian-born artist, archaeologist, explorer, author, internationalist, and mystic philosopher. Roerich studied painting in St. Petersburg and Paris and created monumental historical sets for Diaghilev's Ballet Russe (in Paris), including those for Igor Stravinsky's *The Rite of Spring* (1913). His mystical and symbolic paintings, many of which deal with the mysteries of nature, were purchased by museums throughout the world. He moved to New York City (1920), where he helped found Cor Ardens, an international society of art workers; Corona Mundi, an international art center; and the Roerich Museum (1928). He led expeditions to Central Asia, Inner Asia, and Tibet (1923; 1926–28; 1934–35), which he wrote about in several books, including *Himalaya* (1926), *Altai-Himalaya: A Travel Diary* (1929), and *Heart of Asia* (1930). In his attempt to foster international understanding, he sponsored international cultural conferences during the 1920s and 1930s and devised the Roerich Pact, an agreement to register all monuments and cultural and scientific institutions and to protect them from attack in wartime. The pact was signed by several governments, including the United States (1935). Roerich, who was regarded as a prophet by his followers throughout the world, also wrote *Realm of Light*

(1931) and *Gates into the Future* (1936). ■ See biography by Jacqueline Decter (1989).

ROETHKE, THEODORE (1908–1963), U.S. poet. Roethke's father was a midwestern nurseryman, and the thriving family greenhouse later figured large in Roethke's poetry as a symbol of cultivation and fruition. He earned his B.A. (1929) and M.A. (1936) from the University of Michigan and published his first book of poetry, *Open House,* in 1941. *The Lost Son and Other Poems* (1948) is considered the spiritual biography of Roethke, who suffered recurrent bouts of manic-depression. He earned a Pulitzer Prize for *The Waking* (1953). Selected prose (1966), letters (1968), and notebook excerpts (1972) appeared posthumously, as did *The Collected Poems of Theodore Roethke* (1966). ■ See Allan Seager, *The Glass House: The Life of Theodore Roethke* (1968), and Jay Parini, *Theodore Roethke: An American Romantic* (1979).

ROGERS, CARL RANSOM (1902–1987), U.S. psychologist. Rogers studied at Union Theological Seminary, then earned a Ph.D. from Columbia University Teachers College (1931). He spent a decade working with children and wrote *The Clinical Treatment of Problem Children* (1939) before joining the faculties of the University of Chicago (1945–57) and the University of Wisconsin (1957–63). He was later associated with the Center for Studies of the Person, La Jolla, California (1968–87). Convinced that psychotherapists should not try to solve problems for their patients, he began referring to the people who sought his help as "clients" to move psychology away from the medical model, and developed a nondirective, client-centered approach *Client-Centered Therapy* (1951) described his method, which departed from the more authoritarian Freudian psychology with its emphasis on the analyst's interpretations of a patient's intrapsychic conflict. He was also an innovator of the encounter group. Rogers' work strongly influenced the human potential movement in the 1970s and 1980s. *On Becoming a Person* (1961) contains an autobiographical essay. Other books included *Becoming Partners: Marriage and Its Alternatives* (1972) and *A Way of Being* (1980). ■ See Howard Kirschenbaum, *On Becoming Carl Rogers* (1979), and study by Richard Evans (1975).

ROGERS, GINGER (Virginia Katherine McMath; 1911–1995), U.S. dancer and actress. A champion Charleston dancer and vaudeville performer in her teens, Rogers introduced the songs "Embraceable You" and "But Not for Me" in George Gershwin's Broadway show *Girl Crazy* (1930), and appeared in the musical films *42nd Street* (1933) and *Gold Diggers of 1933* (1933). She was Fred Astaire's graceful and elegant partner in 10 romantic Hollywood musicals including *The Gay Divorcée* (1934), *Top Hat* (1935), *Swing Time* (1936), and *Shall We Dance* (1937). She won an Academy Award for her dramatic performance in *Kitty Foyle*

(1940) and starred in dozens of other films including *Lady in the Dark* (1944), *I'll Be Seeing You* (1945), *Monkey Business* (1952), *Forever Female* (1954), and *Harlow* (1965). Late in her career she starred on Broadway in *Hello, Dolly!* (1965–67) and in the first London production of *Mame* (1969). ■ See her autobiography, *Ginger: My Story* (1991).

ROGERS, KENNY (Kenneth Ray Rogers; 1938–   ), U.S. singer. Born in Houston, Texas, Rogers formed the Scholars, a teenage band that made the hit record "Crazy Feeling" (1957) and appeared on American Bandstand. The group's success was shortlived, and Rogers spent six years playing bass fiddle for the Bobby Doyle Trio and two singing with the New Christy Minstrels before launching Kenny Rogers and the First Edition (1967–76). The folk-rock band recorded four gold albums and nine gold singles, including the hit "Just Dropped In (To See What Condition My Condition Was In)" (1968). In 1977, Rogers made a successful transition to country music with the hit song "Lucille." His album *The Gambler* (1979) sold more than 3 million copies. He went on to record numerous hit songs, some with other country artists, including Dottie West and Dolly Parton. A congenial personality, Rogers starred in TV movies and made the film *Six Pack* (1982). His later albums included *Love Is Strange* (1990) and *Across My Heart* (1997). ■ See his *Making It with Music* (1978; with Len Epand).

ROGERS, ROY (Leonard Slye; 1911–1998), U.S. singing cowboy and actor. After a poor childhood on a farm in Duck Run, Ohio, Rogers moved to the West Coast and gradually established a reputation as a western singer on radio and in small bands. His first motion picture, *Under Western Stars* (1937), was a success, and by the mid-1940s he was among the country's 10 top-money-making actors. The formula of "a little song, a little riding, a little shooting, and a girl to be saved from hazard," combined with Rogers' pleasant good looks, seemed sufficient to produce the perfect western. With his wife and leading lady Dale Evans (1912–2001), Rogers made many movies, a television series (1955–56), and nationwide rodeo tours. His famous horse Trigger and his dog Bullet were stuffed and exhibited at Rogers' private museum. After retiring from show business, he established a large chain of Roy Rogers Family Restaurants. ■ See Rogers and Evans' autobiography, *Happy Trails* (1979), and biography by Robert W. Phillips (1995).

ROGERS, WILL (William Penn Adair Rogers; 1879–1935), U.S. humorist and actor. The son of a rancher, Rogers was a cowboy in Texas before touring with a Wild West show (1902–04) as a rope twirler. He began to add jokes and political commentary to his act and became a popular vaudeville star, appearing in several Broadway musicals as well as in Ziegfeld's *Follies* (1916–18, 1922; 1924–25). His good-natured but often sharp commentary, delivered in a southwestern drawl, made him one of the country's favorite and best-paid entertainers. His weekly (from 1922) and later daily (from 1926) columns on current affairs for the *New York Times* were eventually syndicated in 350 newspapers and solidified his reputation as America's cowboy-philosopher. He wrote several books, including *The Illiterate Digest* (1924) and *Letters of a Self-Made Diplomat to His President* (1926), and starred in such movies as *A Connecticut Yankee* (1931), *State Fair* (1933), and *David Harum* (1934). He was killed in a plane crash with his friend, pilot Wiley Post. ■ See his autobiography (1949); biographies by Richard M. Ketchum (1973) and Ben Yagoda (1993); and Ray Robinson, *American Original* (1996).

RÓHEIM, GÉZA (1891–1953), Hungarian-born U.S. psychoanalyst. Róheim was a professor of anthropology at the University of Budapest who applied a psychoanalytic approach to the study of culture. He was personally analyzed by one of psychoanalyst Sigmund Freud's closest associates, spent three years studying native peoples in Australia, Melanesia, Somaliland, and Arizona, and taught at the Budapest Institute of Psychoanalysis. He moved to the United States (1938), where he went into private practice. In his many books and papers, including *Animism, Magic and the Divine King* (1930), *The Origin and Function of Culture* (1943), *Psychoanalysis and Anthropology* (1950), and *Magic and Schizophrenia* (1955), he stressed the universal psychic experience underlying cultural diversity. ■ See Paul A. Robinson, *The Freudian Left* (1969).

ROHMER, SAX (Arthur Sarsfield Ward; 1886–1959), British novelist. After a brief career as a journalist, Rohmer wrote his first thriller, *Dr. Fu Manchu* (1913). This was followed by an exceedingly successful series of adventure thrillers featuring Fu Manchu, a mysterious oriental villain whose horrendous criminal activities and conspiracies were opposed by the stalwart British hero Nayland Smith. Such novels as *The Trail of Fu Manchu* (1934), *Shadow of Fu Manchu* (1949), and *The Return of Fu* (1959) had imaginative plots, exotic settings, and were written in simple, cliché-laden language. From "the yellow peril incarnate" in the earliest novels, Fu became an antifascist during the late 1930s and an anticommunist crusader after World War II. ■ See Cay Van Ash and Elizabeth Sax Rohmer, *Master of Villainy* (1972).

ROHRER, HEINRICH (1933–   ), Swiss physicist. A graduate of the Swiss Institute of Technology in Zurich (Ph.D. 1960), Rohrer did postgraduate work at Rutgers University (1961–63) before joining the staff of the IBM Research Laboratory in Zurich (1963). At IBM he collaborated with German physicist Gerd Binnig in developing (1981) the scanning-tunneling microscope (STM), a device that can map surfaces in such detail that individual atoms are visible. The STM was widely used in semiconductor physics and in low-temperature physics as well as in the study of ultrasmall structures and in the development of computers. He shared the 1986 Nobel Prize in Physics with Gerd Binnig and Ernst Ruska, who was credited with designing the first electron microscope.

ROH TAE WOO (1932–   ), South Korean political leader. Roh graduated from the Korean Military Academy (1955), where he was a classmate of Chun Doo Hwan, who would later become a military dictator of South Korea. He served in several top army posts and took part in the military coup that brought Chun to power (1979). He also played a major role in the brutal suppression of a protest movement in the city of Kwangju (1980), which resulted in the deaths of at least 200 students and other civilians. Roh retired from the army in 1981 and served in Chun's cabinet as minister of politial and security affairs (1981–83) and as minister of home affairs (1982–83). As minister of sports (1982) and president of the Seoul Olympic Organizing Committee, he played a key role in getting the 1988 Olympics for South Korea. He won the freely contested election in 1987 and served as president from 1988 to 1993. After democratic civilian rule was restored, Roh and Chun were both arrested (1995) and convicted (1996) of having plotted the 1979 coup and accepting hundreds of millions of dollars in bribes from businessmen. (Chun was sentenced to death for his role in the Kwangju massacre.) Roh's 22½-year prison sentence was reduced to 17 years by an appeals court. However, both Roh and Chun were pardoned and released from prison at the urging of President-elect Kim Dae-Jung (December 1997), who, as a prodemocracy activist, had been arrested by the two dictators. ▪ See Robert E. Bedeski, *The Transformation of South Korea* (1994).

ROJAS PINILLA, GUSTAVO (1900–1975), Colombian dictator. Rojas was a career army officer who studied engineering at an Indiana college (1927) and became Colombia's director of civil aeronautics in 1945. In reward for his brutal suppression of civilian riots in 1948, he was promoted to commander in chief of the armed forces (1950), which he led in a 1953 coup d'état. During four years of virtual dictatorship Rojas is said to have left 300,000 casualties. He was deposed in 1957; in 1960 he and his daughter María Eugenia, a senator, launched a populist movement, the National Popular Alliance (ANAPO), that opposed both the Liberals and the Conservatives. Rojas won 2.5 percent of the votes in the 1962 presidential election but lost by a narrow margin in the hotly disputed 1970 election.

ROKOSSOVSKY, KONSTANTIN KONSTANTINOVICH (1896–1968), Soviet marshal. Rokossovsky, who was born in Poland, served in the Russian army during World War I, and then joined the bolsheviks, fighting in the civil war and in the 1919–20 Polish campaign. During World War II he led the defense of Moscow and Stalingrad and the final thrust to Berlin through Poland, where he chose not to aid the 1944 Warsaw uprising against the Nazis. A symbol of Soviet influence in Poland, Rokossovsky served as Poland's minister of defense from 1949 to 1956, when, recalled to the Soviet Union, he served as deputy minister of defense (1956–57; 1958–62).

ROLLAND, ROMAIN (1866–1944), French playwright, novelist and biographer. A professor of art and a musicologist, Rolland was an idealistic socialist and humanist. He wrote a cycle of plays extolling revolutionary heroism. His major work was *Jean-Christophe* (10 vols., 1904–12; Eng. trans. 1910–13), a vast, moralistic novel about a brilliant German composer who lives in France. *Above the Battle* (1915; Eng. trans. 1916) was a manifesto appealing for international cooperation and pacifism during World War I. Active in left-wing movements after the war, Rolland was also interested in oriental religions and mysticism and wrote biographies of great individuals whom he considered exemplars of humanity. He was awarded the Nobel Prize for Literature in 1915. ▪ See his spiritual autobiography, *Journey Within* (1924; Eng. trans. 1947), and biography by William T. Starr (1971).

ROLLING STONES, THE (est. 1962), British singing group. Composed of **Mick Jagger** (Michael Philip Jagger; **1944–   **), **Brian Jones** (Lewis Brian Hopkin-Jones; **1942–1969**), **Keith Richards** (**1943–   **), **Charlie Watts** (Charles Robert Watts; **1941–   **), and **Bill Wyman** (William George Wyman; **1936–   **), the Rolling Stones reached the pinnacle of Britain's rock music industry within a year of their 1962 debut. Their lusty, blues-inspired music and exhibitionist performance style epitomized the 1960s and the rebellious stance of the generation that came of age in that violent era. Much of their music, composed primarily by Jagger and Richards, was noted for its aggressive sexuality. Their 1965 hit "(I Can't Get No) Satisfaction" became their trademark song. The Stones' 1969 U.S. tour, including the violent free concert at Altamont, California (where four fans died), was the subject of the documentary *Gimme Shelter* (1970). Rock music's most durable phenomenon, the Stones continued to record and tour together into the 1980s, making such albums as *Tattoo You* (1981). A 1981 U.S. tour was documented in the film *Let's Spend the Night Together* (1983). At age 42, lead vocalist Mick Jagger made his first solo album, *She's the Boss,* and entered a new age of electronic performance by making videos of five songs. Jagger and the Stones continued to tour the world, performing to sellout crowds in giant sports stadiums through the 1990s. Their later albums included *Bridges to Babylon* (1997) and *No Security* (1998). ▪ See Robert Palmer, *Rolling Stones* (1983); Stanley Booth, *Dance with the Devil* (1984); Carey Shofield, *Jagger* (1985); and Bill Wyman, *Stone Alone* (1990).

RÖLVAAG, OLE EDVART (1876–1931), Norwegian-born U.S. novelist. Rölvaag emigrated to the United States in 1896, graduated from Minnesota's St. Olaf College (1905), and became a U.S. citizen (1908). He chaired the Norwegian department of his alma mater (1906–31) and urged immigrants to retain their native language and culture. Rölvaag wrote novels that depicted Norwegian settlers in the American Midwest, showing the clash between immigrants and native cultures, and the cost of pioneer life in terms of human values. He wrote in Norwegian, then worked closely with translators on the English versions. He was best known for the epic *Giants in the Earth* (Eng. trans. 1927), the first volume of a trilogy that also included *Peder Victorious* (1929) and *Their Father's God* (1931). ■ See biography by Paul Reigstad (1972).

ROMAINS, JULES (1885–1972), French writer. After an early career as a teacher, Romains became a writer. His work is infused by his belief in unanimism, a social and utopian theory that all groups are united by a collective psychology. His play *Doctor Knock* (1923; Eng. trans. 1925) is a comic masterpiece. His major fictional work was *Men of Good Will* (27 vols., 1932–1947; Eng. trans. 1933–47), a massive epic concerning the evolution of French society from 1908 to 1933. He continued to write prolifically to the end of his life, he was elected to the Académie Française in 1946. ■ See biography by Denis Boak (1974).

ROMBERG, SIGMUND (1887–1951), Hungarian-born U.S. composer and conductor. Romberg received engineering and musical training in Vienna before emigrating to the United States (1910). He led his own café orchestra before being hired to write theater music by Jacob Shubert. Romberg composed dozens of popular Viennese-style operettas known for their rich melodies and romantic themes. *Maytime* (1917), his first big success, was followed by *Blossom Time* (1921), based on the life and music of Franz Schubert. His more-than-2,000 songs included "Deep in My Heart, Dear" and "Golden Days" from *The Student Prince* (1924); "Blue Heaven" and "One Alone" from *The Desert Song* (1926); "Lover, Come Back to Me" and "Softly, as in a Morning Sunrise" from *The New Moon* (1928); and "When I Grow Too Old to Dream" (1935). ■ See Elliot Arnold, *Deep in My Heart: A Story Based on the Life of Sigmund Romberg* (1949).

ROMER, ALFRED SHERWOOD (1894–1973), U.S. paleontologist, anatomist, and evolutionist. Romer was a professor at the University of Chicago (1923–34) and Harvard (1934–65) and director of Harvard's Museum of Comparative Zoology (1946–61). He was one of the world's leading paleontologists and spent more than 50 years studying the evolution of vertebrates. A specialist in the Permian Period (between 200 and 230 million years ago), he collected fish, amphibian, and reptile fossil specimens from around the world and utilized insights of embryology, comparative anatomy, and paleontology to study anatomical adaptation to environmental change. His books *Man and the Vertebrates* (1933), *Vertebrate Paleontology* (1933), and *The Vertebrate Body* (1949) were considered classics in the field.

ROMMEL, ERWIN JOHANNES (1891–1944), German field marshal. Rommel joined the army at age 19 and during World War I won Germany's highest military award. An infantry officer and instructor who became Nazi leader Adolf Hitler's personal bodyguard in the interwar period, during World War II he was appointed commander of the Afrika Korps (1941) in Libya. Audaciously driving his desert assault teams to several brilliant victories, he was nevertheless defeated by the British at El Alamein (1942) and subsequently forced back to Tunis. A commander in the defense against the Allies' Normandy invasion in 1944, Rommel was implicated in the July 20 attempt to assassinate Hitler. He chose suicide rather than trial. His colorful career inspired Desmond Young's *The Desert Fox* (1950), which later became a movie. ■ See also study by Charles Douglas-Home (1973); David Irving, *The Trail of the Fox* (1977); Samuel W. Mitcham, Jr., *Triumphant Fox* (1984); and David Fraser, *Knight's Cross* (1993).

ROMULO, CARLOS PENA (1899–1985), Filipino diplomat. Carlos P. Romulo studied at Columbia University (M.A. 1921), taught English at the University of the Philippines, and became a prominent journalist and newspaper publisher in Manila during the 1930s. His series of articles (1941) predicting Japanese aggression in Southeast Asia were syndicated in the United States and won a Pulitzer Prize. During World War II he was an aide to U.S. Gen. Douglas MacArthur and served in the Philippines government-in-exile in the United States. After the war he helped draft the United Nations charter (1945) and became a spokesman for newly independent Third World nations. He served as the Philippines' chief delegate to the U.N. (1945–54) and was president of the General Assembly (1949–50). A pro-American foe of communism, Romulo was ambassador to Washington (1952–53; 1955–62) and Filipino foreign minister (1950–52; 1968–84). In his later years he called for strengthening the U.N. through the acquisition of a permanent military force, the abolition of the veto in the Security Council, and the imposition of binding arbitration in cases of international conflict.

RONDON, CÂNDIDO MARIANO DA SILVA (1865–1958), Brazilian general and explorer. A graduate of Brazil's military academy (1890), Rondon was appointed in 1907 to establish telegraphic communications in the Amazon basin. In his expeditions to the "far West," including one in 1913 with former U.S. Pres. Theodore Roosevelt, he opened up 193,000 square miles of territory and charted 15 major rivers. Himself of Indian extraction, Rondon mitigated the exploitation of the natives in regions under his command and founded and headed (1910–40) the Indian Protection Service. The territory of Guaporé was renamed Rondônia in his honor (1956).

ROOSEVELT, ELEANOR (Anna Eleanor Roosevelt; 1884–1962), U.S. humanitarian and diplomat. Born into a prominent family (her uncle was Pres. Theodore Roosevelt), she was orphaned at age 10 and raised by her grandmother. She remained shy and ill at ease socially through her schooling in Britain and marriage to her distant cousin Franklin Delano Roosevelt (1905), with whom she had six children in 10 years. After her husband suffered a debilitating polio attack (1921), she became more active and visible, often serving as her husband's emissary and counselor through his 4 years in New York's governor's mansion (1928–32) and 12 years in the White House (1933–45). She made the role of first lady into a position of influence, holding press conferences, making regular radio broadcasts, and publishing newspaper columns. During World War II she was active in civilian defense work and visited troops on many fronts. A vigorous defender of human rights, she resigned from the Daughters of the American Revolution when the organization refused to let African-American singer Marian Anderson perform in Constitution Hall; she was a member of the board of the National Association for the Advancement of Colored People (NAACP). After her husband's death, Roosevelt served as a United Nations delegate (1945–52, 1961); as chair of the United Nations Commission on Human Rights (1946–52), she helped to draft the *Universal Declaration of Human Rights* and was influential in securing its adoption. Her books included *This Is My Story* (1937), *My Days* (1938), *This I Remember* (1949), *On My Own* (1958), *You Learn by Living* (1960), and her *Autobiography* (1961). ■ See also biographies by Joseph P. Lash (2 vols., 1971–72), Lorena Hickok (1980), and Blanche Wiesen Cook (2 vols., 1992–99), and Jason Berger, *New Deal for the World: Eleanor Roosevelt and American Foreign Policy* (1981).

ROOSEVELT, FRANKLIN DELANO (1882–1945), U.S. political leader. Born into a patrician family in upstate Hyde Park, New York, Roosevelt studied at the Groton School, Harvard College, and Columbia Law School. In 1905 he married his distant cousin Eleanor Roosevelt, a niece of Pres. Theodore Roosevelt. A liberal Democrat, he served as assistant secretary of the navy under Pres. Woodrow Wilson (1913–20) and ran unsuccessfully as the Democratic candidate for vice president (1920). Although partially crippled by an attack of poliomyelitis (1921), he was elected governor of New York State (1928, 1930) and established comprehensive relief programs to help alleviate effects of the Depression. Elected U.S. president an unprecedented four times (1932, 1936, 1940, 1944), he won the unswerving support of workers and farmers—and the enmity of wealthy economic conservatives—with his program of public works and reforms, known as the New Deal, which greatly expanded the role of the federal government and helped to restore the collapsed economy. Although opposed by isolationists during the late 1930s, he aided the Allies after the outbreak of World War II. Following the Japanese attack on Pearl Harbor (Dec. 7, 1941), which led to U.S. involvement in the war, he helped coordinate Allied policy at a series of conferences with British prime minister Winston Churchill and Soviet leader Joseph Stalin. He died suddenly in Warm Springs, Georgia (April 12, 1945) and was succeeded by Vice Pres. Harry S. Truman. ■ See Arthur M. Schlesinger, *The Age of Roosevelt* (3 vols., 1957–61), and biographies by Frank Freidel (4 vols., 1952–74), James MacGregor Burns (1956), Nathan Miller (1983), Ted Morgan (1985), and Kenneth S. Davis (3 vols., 1972–86).

ROOSEVELT, THEODORE (1858–1919), U.S. political leader. Born into wealth in New York City, he graduated from Harvard (1880) and served as an independent-minded Republican in the state assembly. After his first wife died (1884) "TR" ran a ranch in North Dakota for several years and wrote books on western U.S. history. He was then a reforming commissioner of police in New York (1895–97) and assistant secretary of the navy (1897–98). During the Spanish-American War he became a national hero as leader of the "Rough Riders" in Cuba (1898). He was governor of New York for two years before being nominated and elected U.S. vice president in 1900. He became president when William McKinley was assassinated (1901) and was elected to a full term in 1904, serving until 1909. His antitrust assaults on corporations shocked conservative Republicans. In protecting natural resources, he was well ahead of his time. His "Roosevelt Corollary" to the Monroe Doctrine asserted that the United States had the right to intervene militarily in the Western Hemisphere. He initiated the construction of the Panama Canal and won the Nobel Peace Prize (1906) for helping settle the Russo-Japanese War. After supporting William Howard Taft in the 1908 presidential election, he turned against him as too conservative. He ran unsuccessfully against Taft for the 1912 nomination, then split the Republican party by running as a third-party candidate. ■ See his autobiography (1913), William H. Harbaugh's biography (1961; rev. ed. 1975), and Edmund Morris, *The Rise of Theodore Roosevelt* (1979).

ROOT, ELIHU (1845–1937), U.S. cabinet officer and diplomat. A conservative corporation lawyer from New York, Root served as secretary of war (1899–1904), introducing efficient administration of the army and of the former Spanish colonies under its command. As secretary of state (1905–09), he negotiated a series of bilateral arbitration treaties as well as the 1908 Root-Takahira agreement with Japan recognizing the status quo in the Pacific. Root won a Nobel Peace Prize in 1912 and served as an appointed member of the U.S. Senate (1909–15). He also helped to found the Permanent Court of International Justice (1920–21). His books included *Military and Colonial Policy of the U.S.* (1916), *Russia and the U.S.* (1917), and *Men and Policies* (1924). ■ See biography by Philip C. Jessup (2 vols., 1938).

ROPER, ELMO BURNS, JR. (1900–1971), U.S. pollster. Roper was a former clock salesman from Nebraska who joined a New York market-research firm. In 1933 he established Roper Research Associates, Inc., which was retained by *Fortune* magazine (1935) to conduct public opinion polls over a 15-year period. Roper pioneered in the field of political polling, using scientific sampling techniques to predict election results. He gained celebrity by predicting the outcome of the 1936, 1940, and 1944 U.S. presidential elections within 1 percent of the actual vote. However, in 1948 he predicted that Thomas E. Dewey would be president, and in 1960 he picked Richard Nixon over John F. Kennedy. He wrote *You and Your Leaders* (1957) and a syndicated column, and was an editor-at-large of the *Saturday Review*.

ROREM, NED (1923–), U.S. composer. Regarded as America's leading art-song composer, Rorem studied with Virgil Thomson and Aaron Copland at the Juilliard School in New York and with Arthur Honegger in Paris. His friendships with composers Francis Poulenc, Georges Auric, and Darius Milhaud during his Paris sojourn (1951–57) also influenced his work. The publication of five volumes of elegant and explicit diaries (1966–78) brought him wide public recognition. Rorem's melodic music manifested his distaste for the avant-garde of the 1960s and 1970s. His *Air Music* (1976) won a Pulitzer Prize. He drew the texts for many of his songs from the works of 20th-century American poets. He also wrote *Setting the Tone: Essays and a Diary* (1983) and *Bright Music for Flute, Piano and String Trio* (1987). ■ See his memoir, *Knowing When to Stop* (1994), and *Lies: A Diary, 1986–1999* (2000).

ROSA, JOÃO GUIMARÃES *See GUIMARÃES ROSA, JOÃO.*

ROSE, BILLY (William Samuel Rosenberg; 1899–1966), U.S. showman. As a teenager Rose became an expert at shorthand dictation and during World War I was the chief stenographer for Bernard Baruch, head of the War Industries Board. In the 1920s he turned to show business and began to write songs, including such hits as "Me and My Shadow," "It's Only a Paper Moon," "Barney Google," "That Old Gang of Mine," and "Without a Song." Rose produced several hit Broadway shows, including *Crazy Quilt* (1931), *Jumbo* (1935), and *Carmen Jones* (1943), and founded the Backstage Club, Casino de Paree, the Diamond Horseshoe, and other highly popular New York City nightclubs. He also produced the *Aquacade* at New York's 1939–40 World's Fair. America's most successful and extravagant showman, Rose was also a shrewd real-estate and stock-market investor and a noted art collector and philanthropist. ■ See study by Earl Conrad (1968) and Polly Rose Gottlieb, *The Nine Lives of Billy Rose* (1968).

ROSE, PETE (Peter Edward Rose; 1941–), U.S. baseball player. A little leaguer at age 9, Rose played for several minor-league teams before breaking into the majors as rookie of the year with the Cincinnati Reds (1963). Known as "Charlie Hustle," he was a scrappy switch-hitting infielder and outfielder who was the spark plug of both the Reds (1963–78) and later the Philadelphia Phillies (1979–84). He re-

turned to the Reds as a player-manager (1984–89). He won three National League batting championships (1968, .335; 1969, .348; 1973, .338), and was the league's Most Valuable Player in 1973; he hit safely in 44 consecutive games in 1978, a league record. During the 1985 season he broke Ty Cobb's major-league career record of 4,191 hits, which had stood since 1928. By the time he retired he had 4,256 hits and held the major-league records for most seasons of 200 or more hits (10), most games (3,562), most at bats (14,053), and most singles (3,215). After an investigation into his gambling activities, he was banned from baseball for life by baseball commissioner A. Bartlett Giametti (1989). He was convicted of tax evasion in 1990 and served five months in prison. ■ See biography by Bill Libby (1974).

ROSEANNE (Roseanne Barr; 1952–), U.S. actress and comedian. Born into a working-class family in Salt Lake City, Utah, where she was raised both as a Mormon and as a Jew, Roseanne had a troubled adolescence and was hospitalized in a state mental institution for eight months at age 16. She later dropped out of high school, lived in a hippie commune, worked as a cocktail waitress, married, had four children, and spent several years as a housewife. Forced to return to work by economic pressures in the early 1980s, she became a stand-up comic whose routines reflected her experiences as an independent, working mother. Her success won her the starring role in "Roseanne," an ABC television comedy series (1988–97) in which she played a feisty working mother struggling with the daily hurdles of marriage, child rearing, and factory work. The show, which candidly confronted many controversial social issues, ran for 224 episodes, and became one of the most popular and influential series in television history. ■ See her autobiographies, *Roseanne* (1989) and *My Lives* (1994).

ROSENBERG, ALFRED (1893–1946), Russian-born German political leader. Forced to flee revolutionary Russia (1919) because of his outspoken anticommunism, Rosenberg went to Munich, where he joined the newly founded National Socialist party. His violently anti-Semitic and anti-Christian views and his belief in German racial purity and superiority appealed to Adolf Hitler, who appointed him editor of the party newspaper, *Völkischer Beobachter,* and chief ideologist of the Nazi movement. Rosenberg's racial and religious doctrines were set forth in *The Myth of the 20th Century* (1934). During World War II he was minister for the occupied territories in Eastern Europe (from 1941) and was subsequently convicted of war crimes at the Nuremberg trials (1946) and hanged. ■ See his *Memoirs* (Eng. trans. 1949), *Selected Writings* (Eng. trans. 1970), and Robert Cecil, *The Myth of the Master Race* (1972).

ROSENBERG, ETHEL GREENGLASS (1915–1953) **and JULIUS ROSENBERG** (1918–1953), U.S. convicted spies. The Rosenbergs were both born to Jewish immigrant parents and grew up poor on New York City's Lower East Side.

Both became involved in left-wing politics and were ardent supporters of the Soviet Union. They met at a political fund-raiser and married in 1939, the year that Julius graduated from City College. During World War II, Julius got a civilian job with the army signal corps but was fired (1945) for communist affiliations and openly pro-Soviet sympathies. The Rosenbergs were arrested for espionage (1950) on the basis of testimony given by Ethel's younger brother, David Greenglass (1922–). Greenglass had worked (1944–46) as a technician on the U.S. atomic bomb project at Los Alamos, where he had access to classified information. He claimed that the Rosenbergs directed an espionage ring and persuaded him to pass atomic-bomb secrets to the Soviets. They denied the charges but were convicted at the height of the cold war (1951) and sentenced to death by electrocution. (Greenglass was given a 15-year jail term.) The Rosenberg case aroused an international clamor; many protested the guilty verdict, others the sentence. Poland offered asylum, the French government pleaded for clemency, and Pope Pius XII protested the death sentence. The U.S. Supreme Court upheld the verdict and Pres. Dwight Eisenhower refused to exercise clemency. The Rosenbergs were the first U.S. civilians executed for treason. The Rosenberg case continued to stir controversy in the decades after their execution. ■ For differing views of the case see Walter and Miriam Schneir, *Invitation to an Inquest* (1965; rev. ed. 1983), and Ronald Radosh and Joyce Milton, *The Rosenberg File* (1983). Michael Meeropol and Robert Meeropol's *We Are Your Sons* (1975) is an account by the Rosenbergs' children. See also the study of Ethel Rosenberg by Ilene J. Philipson (1993).

ROSENFELD, MORRIS (1862–1923), Polish-born U.S. Yiddish-language poet. Rosenfeld emigrated to New York City (1886) and worked for years as a sweatshop presser. A socialist, he gained fame for his tearful songs and verses of workers' toil and trouble, collected in his *Songs of the Ghetto* (Eng. trans. 1898), *Songs of Labor and Other Poems* (Eng. trans. 1914), and *Teardrop Millionaire and Other Poems* (Eng. trans. 1955). Popular with the Jewish masses, his work was translated into several languages and soon earned him an international reputation. Unique among the worker poets, Rosenfeld also wrote on national themes—Zionism and Jewish holidays. English translations of his work are in *Morris Rosenfeld* (1964) and *Poems of Morris Rosenfeld* (1979). ■ See Leon Goldenthal, *Toil and Triumph* (1960) and Edgar J. Goldenthal, *Poet of the Ghetto* (1997).

ROSENMAN, SAMUEL IRVING (1896–1973), U.S. judge and presidential adviser. The closest adviser and favorite speech writer (1928–45) of Franklin D. Roosevelt, New York governor and then president, Rosenman wrote many of Roosevelt's campaign speeches, drafted important legislative bills and messages to Congress, and assembled the brain trust, Roosevelt's group of academic advisers. He served as a New York State Supreme Court judge (1933–43) but resigned to become presidential counsel (1943–45) and continued on as Pres. Harry Truman's counsel (1945–46) after Roosevelt's death. He edited Roosevelt's papers and addresses and wrote *Working with Roosevelt* (1952). ■ See Samuel B. Hand, *Counsel and Advise* (1979).

ROSENQUIST, JAMES ALBERT (1933–), U.S. artist. Rosenquist was a billboard painter from the Midwest who won a 1955 scholarship to the Art Students League in New York. He then returned to billboard painting, fascinated by the abstract effect of great size: a 6-foot head of Kirk Douglas, a 58-foot picture of Joanne Woodward. Rosenquist's style as a pop artist evolved in the tradition of mural painting, with images taken from commercial art of the 1940s and 1950s. His first one-man show was in 1962, and in 1965 he exhibited *F-111,* a mural with stray objects attached, which at 86 feet was even longer than the actual bomber of the title. His other works included the environmental painting *Horizon Home Sweet Home* (1970) and the huge four-canvas work, *Four New Clear Women* (1983). ■ See study by Marcia Tucker (1972).

ROSENWALD, JULIUS (1862–1932), U.S. business executive and philanthropist. As vice president (1895–1910) and president (1910–25) of Sears, Roebuck and Co., he guided the firm from a small establishment into the world's largest mail-order house and chain of retail stores. His original investment of $35,000 grew to $150 million in 30 years. Regarding gifts as social investments, he set up the Julius Rosenwald Fund (1917–48), which gave millions to build more than 5,000 public schools for rural southern blacks. Rosenwald also contributed more than $22 million of his own money to numerous charity and relief organizations, schools, and hospitals. He also made major contributions to the University of Chicago, established the Chicago Museum of Science and Industry (1929), and was president of the Federation of Jewish Charities of Chicago. ■ See biography by Alfred Q. Jarrette (1975).

ROSENZWEIG, FRANZ (1886–1929), German Jewish philosopher. Born into an assimilated family and trained in German philosophy, Rosenzweig nearly converted to Christianity. After his experience of an Orthodox Jewish Yom Kippur (Day of Atonement) service, he returned to Judaism and dedicated himself to Jewish scholarship. He wrote his most important work, *The Star of Redemption* (1921; Eng. trans. 1971), during service on the Balkan front in World War I, sending the text to his family on government postcards. Drawn from Reform, Orthodox, and Zionist thought, his philosophy attracted Jewish youth. His concern with Jewish adult education, particularly for assimilated Jews, was reflected in his essays, available in English in *On Jewish Learning* (1965). He translated the Hebrew scriptures into German in collaboration with his friend, the philosopher

Martin Buber. Rosenzweig's influence was undercut by the decimation of German Jewry during World War II, when his disciples perished or scattered. ■ See his correspondence with Eugen Rosenstock-Huessy, *Judaism Despite Christianity* (1969), and study by Nahum Glatzer (3d ed. 1998).

ROSEWALL, KEN (Kenneth Rosewall; 1934–), Australian tennis player. One of the game's great stylists, Rosewall had a long and brilliant tennis career. In 1953 he became the youngest player ever to win the Australian and French singles titles. In 1955 he again captured the Australian championship, and with Lew Hoad took the U.S., Italian, French, and British doubles crowns in 1956. Throughout the 1950s he anchored the formidable Australian Davis Cup team. A short but powerful player, Rosewall turned professional in 1957 and continued playing championship tennis. In 1970, after major tournaments were opened to professional and amateur players, Rosewall won a second U.S. singles crown—14 years after his first national championship. In 1971 and 1972 he won the professional world championship. ■ See study by Peter Rowley (1976).

ROSS, BARNEY (Barnet David Rosofsky; 1909–1967), U.S. boxer. The son of a Jewish talmudic scholar, Ross began boxing in high school and entered the Golden Gloves tournament in 1929. In 1933 he won the world lightweight and junior welterweight titles by defeating Tony Canzoneri and Jimmy McLarnin. The following year he gave up the lightweight title and lost the welterweight title, but regained it in 1935. One of the greatest welterweights of all time, he defended that title until Henry Armstrong defeated him in 1938. During World War II Ross served in the marine corps and was wounded at Guadalcanal. He received treatment for drug abuse in the service and overcame his addiction. ■ See his autobiography, *No Man Stands Alone* (1957).

ROSS, DIANA (1944–) AND THE SUPREMES, U.S. singing group. Diana Ross, **Florence Ballard (1943–1976)**, and **Mary Wilson (1943–)** met at a church gospel meeting in Detroit, formed a trio, and signed a Motown contract in 1961 with Berry Gordy, who carefully groomed them for stardom. Their first million-seller, "Where Did Our Love Go?" (1964), was followed by five successive number-one records in the course of a year: "Baby Love," "Come See About Me," "Stop in the Name of Love," "Back in My Arms Again," and "I Hear a Symphony." In 1968, after selling 12 million records, the group made a TV special and a Las Vegas farewell performance. Ross went on to a solo singing career and starred in the movies *Lady Sings the Blues* (1972), *Mahogany* (1975), and *The Wiz* (1978). She achieved superstardom in her own right with a world tour (1982) and hit albums. Her corporation, Diana Ross Enterprises, was involved with theater, film, television, and fash-

ion, ■ See her memoirs, *Secrets of a Sparrow* (1993); Geoff Brown, *Diana Ross* (1981); Mary Wilson, *Dreamgirl* (1986; with Patricia Romanowski); and J. Randy Taraborelli, *Call Her Miss Ross* (1989).

ROSS, EDWARD ALSWORTH (1866–1951), U.S. sociologist. The son of a midwestern farmer, Ross earned a Ph.D. in political economy but turned to sociology as an instrument of liberal reform. In a controversial test of academic freedom he was dismissed from the faculty of Stanford University (1900) and moved to the more progressive atmosphere of the University of Wisconsin (1906–37). Ross wrote the influential *Social Control* (1901) and *Foundations of Sociology* (1905), several popular works on the social sciences, and the widely used textbooks *Social Psychology* (1908) and *The Principles of Sociology* (1920). He also chaired the American Civil Liberties Union (1940–50). ■ See his autobiography, *Seventy Years of It* (1936), and biography by Julius Weinberg (1972).

ROSS, HAROLD WALLACE (1892–1951), U.S. editor. After editing the U.S. Army newspaper *Stars and Stripes* (1917–19), the *American Legion Weekly* (1919–23) and *Judge* magazine (1924), Ross became the founding editor of the *New Yorker* (1925). At its helm until his death, Ross molded it into one of America's most sophisticated and innovative journals and exerted a great influence on the development of humorous writing, reportage, and cartooning in the United States. He introduced the cartoon with the one-line caption, the magazine's biographical "Profiles" feature, and its humorous reporting style. He also helped establish the careers of such writers as James Thurber, E. B. White, Edmund Wilson, and Truman Capote and cartoonists Charles Addams and Peter Arno. ■ See James Thurber, *The Years with Ross* (1959); Jane Grant, *Ross, The New Yorker and Me* (1968); and Thomas Kunkel, *Genius in Disguise* (1995).

ROSS, NELLIE TAYLOE (1876–1977), U.S. public official. The wife of Wyoming governor William Bradford Ross, who died in office (1924), Nellie Tayloe Ross was elected to serve out his term (1925–27). As she was inaugurated two weeks before "Ma" Ferguson of Texas, Ross is credited with being the first elected woman governor of a state. Although she lost her bid for reelection, she served as vice chair of the Democratic National Committee (1928–34) and was the first woman director of the U.S. Mint (1933–53).

ROSS, SIR RONALD (1857–1932), British bacteriologist. Ross was born in India, educated in England (M.D. 1879), and returned (1881) to join the Indian Medical Service. In 1895 he began research on malaria, discovering (1898) the gastrointestinal parasite in the mosquito that transmits the disease, for which he won the 1902 Nobel Prize in Physiology or Medicine. He taught in Liverpool and London and directed the Ross Institute for Tropical Diseases (from 1926), which was founded in his honor. In addition to *The Prevention of Malaria* (1910), he wrote poetry, plays, and *Memoirs* (1923). ■ See John Rowland, *The Mosquito Man* (1958).

ROSSBY, CARL GUSTAV ARVID (1898–1957), Swedish-born U.S. meteorologist. A professor of meteorology at the Massachusetts Institute of Technology (1928–39), the University of Chicago (1941–50), and the University of Stockholm (1950–57), Rossby made fundamental contributions to the science of meteorology and revolutionized the field of weather forecasting. He developed new theories of large-scale air movements, developed the Rossby diagram for plotting air-mass properties and the Rossby equation for simplifying weather prediction, and described the behavior of the jet stream. He also helped the U.S. armed forces develop an extensive education program in meteorology during World War II and reorganized the Swedish government's research and science programs after 1950.

ROSSELLINI, ROBERTO (1906–1977), Italian film director. When Rossellini began directing during the 1930s, his first two films were banned by fascist censors. He won international acclaim for *Open City* (1945), shot clandestinely during World War II using local people and real locations as a setting for fiction, a style known as neorealism. His other neorealist classics were *Paisan* (1946) and *Germany Year Zero* (1947). In 1949 he made *Stromboli,* the first of several vehicles for Ingrid Bergman, who became his wife. After their divorce (1957) he returned to a war theme with *General Della Rovere* (1959). Rossellini also directed several short documentaries on historical subjects for Italian television, including *Louis XIV* (1966), which was later released in the United States as a feature film. ■ See study by José Luis Guarner (Eng. trans. 1970) and Tag Gallagher, *The Adventures of Roberto Rossellini* (1998).

ROSTOVTZEFF, MICHAEL IVANOVICH (1870–1952), Russian-born U.S. historian. Rostovtzeff taught classical philology and ancient history at the University of St. Petersburg for 20 years (1898–1918) before the bolshevik revolution caused him to emigrate to the United States. His most important work, published soon after he joined the faculty of Yale University in 1925, was *Social and Economic History of the Roman Empire* (1926), in which he supplemented the historical record with important new archaeological findings. In *A History of the Ancient World* (2 vols., 1926–28) and *Social and Economic History of the Hellenistic World* (3 vols., 1941), he incorporated social, economic, political, and cultural data.

ROSTOW, WALT WHITMAN (1916–   ), U.S. economist and government official. The son of immigrant parents, Rostow graduated from Yale (Ph.D. 1940), studied at Oxford as a Rhodes scholar (1936–38), and served in the Office of Strategic Services (OSS) during World War II. He was a professor of economic history at the Massachusetts Institute of Technology (1950–60) before becoming Pres. John F. Kennedy's deputy special assistant for national security affairs and counselor to the State Department (1961–66). He was a "hard-liner" on relations with communist governments, and as a special assistant to Pres. Lyndon B. Johnson (1966–69) he played a key role in formulating the policy of escalation during the Vietnam War. His best-known book, *The Stages of Economic Growth: A Non-Communist Manifesto* (1960), presented a generalized pattern of growth, linked to social and political developments, which he believed was as applicable to poor Third World countries as it was to the industrialized West. His other books included *Politics and the Stages of Growth* (1971), *The World Economy: History and Prospect* (1978), *Essays on a Half-Century: Ideas, Policies and Action* (1988), *History, Policy and Economic Theory: Essays in Interaction* (1990), and *The Great Population Spike and After: Reflections on the 21st Century* (1998).

ROSTROPOVICH, MSTISLAV LEOPOLDOVICH (1927–   ), Russian-born cellist. A third-generation cellist, Rostropovich studied at the Moscow Conservatory with Prokofiev and Skostakovich and won his country's highest musical honors. A musician in the grand romantic style, an affectionate and exuberant personality, he concertized all over the world and was regarded as the foremost cellist of his generation. Rostropovich spoke out against Soviet human rights violations and supported dissident author Aleksandr Solzhenitsyn. In 1970, he was placed in virtual "artistic quarantine" by Soviet authorities. Resuming his career in the West after 1974 (at age 47), he became conductor of the Washington, D.C., National Symphony Orchestra (1977–94). The Soviet Union revoked his citizenship in 1978, but it was restored in 1990. He was married to the soprano Galina Vishnevskaya.

ROTBLAT, JOSEPH (1908–   ), British physicist. Born into a wealthy Jewish family in Warsaw, Rotblat studied at the University of Warsaw (Ph.D. 1938) and went to Britain on a fellowship shortly before the German invasion of Poland (1939). He joined the Manhattan Project (February 1944) to help develop the atomic bomb, but quit for moral reasons (December 1944) when he was told that the real purpose of the bomb was to contain Russia, not to oppose Germany, and when he learned of intelligence reports indicating that Germany could not develop atomic weapons. After the war he became a British citizen and advocated a global ban on nuclear weapons, and worked for peaceful uses of nuclear energy as a professor at the University of London (1950–76) in the field of nuclear medicine. He signed a 1955 manifesto, advanced by Bertrand Russell and Albert Einstein, calling for an end to atomic weapons. In 1957 he helped organize the first annual Pugwash Conference (named for a village in Nova Scotia where the first meeting was held), which brought scientists and government officials together to ease cold war tensions and diminish the threat of nuclear war. Rotblat served as secretary-general (1957–73) and president (1988–97) of the Pugwash organization and shared the 1995 Nobel Peace Prize with it.

ROTH, PHILIP (1933–   ), U.S. novelist and short-story writer. Roth studied at the University of Chicago, a setting that he depicted in the novel *Letting Go* (1962). He published six stories in the collection *Goodbye, Columbus* (1959) for which he won a National Book Award at age 26; the title story immortalized the Jewish wedding as a motif of fiction and became a popular movie (1969). Roth gained fame with *Portnoy's Complaint* (1969), an often amusing account of a young Jew's coming of age. With this novel, Roth established himself as one of America's most reliable producers of best-sellers. His other fiction included *When She Was Good* (1967), *Our Gang* (1971), *The Breast* (1973), and *My Life as a Man* (1974). Critics saw a shift from the abrasive, self-deprecating satire of these novels to the more appreciative treatment of protagonists' Jewish identities in the trilogy comprising *The Ghost Writer* (1979), *Zuckerman Unbound* (1981), and *The Anatomy Lesson* (1983). *Zuckerman Bound* (1985) included the trilogy and an epilogue. Roth published criticism in *Reading Myself and Others* (1975). His later works included *The Counterlife* (1986), *Deception* (1990), *Sabbath's Theater* (1995), *American Pastoral* (1997; Pulitzer Prize), *I Married a Communist* (1998), and *The Human Stain* (2000). *Patrimony: A True Story* (1991) was a portrait of his father. ■ See his *The Facts: A Novelist's Autobiography* (1988); studies by Bernard F. Rodgers, Jr. (1978), Judith Jones and Guinevera Nance (1981), and Hermione Lee (1982); and Murray Baumgarten and Barbara Gottfried, *Understanding Philip Roth* (1990).

ROTHKO, MARK (Marcus Rothkovich; 1903–1970), Russian-born U.S. painter. The son of Russian Jewish immigrants, Rothko dropped out of Yale (1923) and began painting in New York City two years later. His first works were influenced by cubism and surrealism, but his work gradually became more abstract, and by the late 1940s he was internationally recognized as a leader of the abstract-expressionist movement. His canvases, which reflected his advocacy of "the simple expression of the complex thought," were created as objects of contemplation. They characteristically consisted of two or three large rectangles of pure color that float side by side within an abstract space and seem to dissolve softly into one another. Rothko committed suicide in 1970. ■ See biography by James E. B. Breslin (1993); study by Diane Waldman (1978); Lee Seldes, *The Legacy of Mark Rothko* (1978); and Dore Ashton, *About Rothko* (1983).

ROTHSCHILD, BARON EDMOND DE (1845–1934), French philanthropist. The head of the Paris branch of the famed Jewish banking family, Rothschild became involved in the program of settling European Jews in Palestine after murderous pogroms in Russia (1882). Although not politically active in the Zionist movement until after World War I, he anonymously donated millions of francs to purchase 125,000 acres, establish more than 30 settlements, and support agricultural experiments, swamp-drainage programs, and numerous industrial projects. He also contributed to the founding of Hebrew University. ■ See biographies by David Druck (1928) and Isaac Naiditch (Eng. trans. 1945) and Simon Schama, *Two Rothschilds and the Land of Israel* (1978).

ROTHSTEIN, ARTHUR (1915–1985), U.S. photographer and editor. A student of Roy Stryker's at Columbia University (B.A. 1935), Rothstein was a photographer for the Farm Security Administration (1935–40) and then for the U.S. Army during World War II. Turning to magazine photography, he became director of photography for *Look* (1946–71) and later for *Parade* magazine (from 1972). Rothstein also taught at the Columbia School of Journalism and wrote a basic text in his field, *Photojournalism* (1956). He was best known for his photos of rural poverty during the Depression, many of which are in *The Depression Years* (1978), *The American West in the Thirties* (1981), and *Arthur Rothstein's America in Photographs, 1930–1980* (1984).

ROUAULT, GEORGES (1871–1958), French artist. Rouault was born in a cellar during the Paris Commune, following the Franco-Prussian War, and apprenticed at age 14 to a craftsman who restored stained-glass windows. He studied at the École des Beaux Arts. As a painter he evolved a distinctive style, using the luminous colors, black outlines, and religious themes of stained glass in an expressionist manner. He painted powerful and somber portraits of prostitutes, clowns, outcasts, and corrupt judges. Rouault also created book illustrations, tapestries, enamels, ballet decor, and wrote poetry and memoirs (1926; 1947). ■ See studies by Lionello Venturi (Eng. trans. 1959), and Pierre Courthion (1962).

ROUCH, JEAN (1917–   ), French film director. Academically trained in literature and civil engineering, Rouch became fascinated with Africa in the early 1940s and began making anthropological documentaries there after World War II. He revolutionized the field of ethnographic filmmaking by utilizing portable cameras with synchronous sound and by interacting with and joining the activities of the subjects of the film. He made more than 80 ethnographic films, including *Les Magiciens de Wanzerbe* (*The Magicians of Wanzerbe*, 1949) and *Les Maîtres Fous* (*The Mad Masters*, 1955). He subsequently used his interactive techniques in "ethno-fiction" films that combined fiction with documentary and he became a pioneer of cinema verité and of improvised and spontaneous filmed psychodramas. These later films, which greatly influenced French cinema, included *Moi, un noir* (*I, a Black Man*, 1957), *Chronique d'un été* (*Chronicle of a Summer*, 1961) and the "Gare du Nord" episode of *Paris vu par—(Six in Paris,* 1965). He served as president of the Cinémathèque Française from 1987 to 1991. ■ See Paul Stoller, *The Cinematic Griot* (1992).

ROUS, (FRANCIS) PEYTON (1879–1970), U.S. pathologist and virologist. A graduate of Johns Hopkins (M.D. 1905), Rous conducted his first significant work in 1909, when he experimented with the cancerous tissue of chickens. After he ground up the diseased tissue, mixed it into a salt solution, filtered out the cells, and injected the solution into healthy chickens, he found that they developed malignant growths. He concluded that cancers were caused by a virus. His results were at first rejected by the medical profession but subsequent research vindicated his ideas and he was awarded (with Charles B. Huggins) the Nobel Prize for Physiology or Medicine in 1966. Rous, who conducted his research at the Rockefeller Institute for Medical Research in New York City (1909–70), also played a major role in the development of blood banks.

ROUSSEL, ALBERT CHARLES (1869–1937), French composer. Roussel began a naval career but resigned at age 25 to study composition in Paris with Vincent D'Indy. Writing in a highly individualistic, impressionist idiom, he was acclaimed for his ballets, *Le Festin d'araignée* (1912) and *Bacchus et Ariane* (1930), and the choral symphony *Évocations* (1912). His well-known works written in a neoclassical style included Suite in F major (1927), Sinfonietta for Strings (1934), and his Fourth Symphony (1934). ■ See studies by Norman Demuth (1947) and Basil Deane (1962).

ROWBOTHAM, SHEILA (1943–   ), British social historian. An Oxford-educated (B.A. 1966) socialist feminist, Rowbotham was active in the modern women's movement in England from its beginnings in the late 1960s. She was a teacher at several technical colleges and schools (1964–79) with the Workers' Education Association, wrote for socialist newspapers, and taught at several universities, including the University of Manchester (1994–   ). Her influential books, which sought to rescue women's role in history from oblivion, included *Women, Resistance and Revolution* (1972), *Hidden from History* (1973), *Women's Consciousness, Man's World* (1973), and *Beyond the Fragments: Feminism and the Making of Socialism* (1979; with H. Wainwright and L. Segal). See also her *Dreams and Dilemmas: Collected Writings* (1983), *Women in Movement* (1992), *A Century of Women* (1997), and *Threads Through Time: Writings on History and Autobiography* (1999).

ROWLAND, F. SHERWOOD (1927–   ), U.S. atmospheric chemist. Rowland studied chemistry at the University of Chicago (Ph.D. 1952) and was a professor at the University of California at Irvine (1964–   ). Following up on the research of Paul Crutzen, who showed (1970) that the earth's protective ozone layer can be destroyed by natural means, Rowland (and postdoctoral fellow Mario Molina) demon-

strated that industrially produced chlorofluorocarbons (CFCs), widely used as refrigerants, plastic foams, and aerosol-spray propellants, can also destroy the ozone layer. Their research findings were relentlessly attacked by big business and its conservative political supporters, but they eventually became widely accepted and led to international agreements (1987; 1992) by the industrial nations to end production of CFCs. For their pioneering work in environmental science, Rowland, Molina, and Crutzen shared the 1995 Nobel Prize in Chemistry.

ROXAS, MANUEL (1892–1948), Filipino political leader. After he completed his legal education at the University of the Philippines (1914), Roxas became a provincial governor (1919) and entered the Philippine congress in 1921. He helped draft the Philippine Commonwealth constitution (1934) and served in the cabinet as secretary of finance (1938–40). An aide to Gen. Douglas MacArthur during World War II, he was captured by the Japanese; he subsequently joined the collaborationist government, but he was not tried as a war criminal in 1945 due to the controversial intervention of Gen. MacArthur. After the war he founded the Liberal party and in 1946 he was elected the first president of the Philippine republic. His administration was widely criticized for its corruption, ties with the landlord class, and concessions to U.S. business and military interests. He died in office and was succeeded by Elpidio Quirino. ■ See biography by Marcial P. Lichauco (1952).

ROY, GABRIELLE (1909–1983), French-Canadian novelist. Like Roger Lemelin, Roy wrote compassionately about hand-to-mouth existence in French Canada, but she also wrote of the plight of other minorities struggling to survive in modern Canada. Her first novel, *The Tin Flute* (1945; Eng. trans. 1947, 1980), written after years of teaching and drama study, narrated the plight of a poor family during the Depression, whose misery was relieved ironically by the outbreak of World War II. *The Cashier* (1954; Eng. trans. 1955) featured a needy bank teller. *Where Nests the Waterhen* (1950; Eng. trans. 1951) was her tender and nostalgic account of isolated existence in rural Manitoba. Roy also wrote *Streets of Riches* (1955; Eng. trans. 1957), *Windflower* (1970; Eng. trans. 1970), and four semiautobiographical stories about girlhood in Manitoba, *The Road Past Altamont* (1966; Eng. trans. 1966). Her later works included the views of immigrant prairie life in *Garden in the Wind* (1975; Eng. trans. 1977) and the tales of a young schoolteacher in *Children of My Heart* (1977; Eng. trans. 1979). ■ See her *The Fragile Lights of Earth: Articles and Memories, 1942–70* (1978; Eng. trans. 1982) and her autobiography, *Enchantment and Sorrow* (Eng. trans. 1987), and studies by M. G. Hesse (1984) and Linda and William Clemente (1997).

ROY, MENABENDRA NATH (Narendranath Bhattacharya; 1887–1954), Indian revolutionary. Active in anti-

British terrorist groups prior to World War I, M. N. Roy traveled throughout Asia and the United States in search of arms. He settled in Mexico (1919), participated in the founding of the Mexican Communist party, and traveled to Moscow, where he impressed the bolshevik leader V. I. Lenin and became a leader of the Comintern. He aided in the formulation of policies on the national and colonial questions, helped found the school for Asian revolutionaries, "The Communist University for the Toilers of the East," and was the Comintern delegate in China (1927–28). Accused of "rightist deviation" in 1929, he was expelled from the Comintern and returned to India (1930), where he was jailed for six years. In 1940 he founded the Radical Democratic party and edited its journals, *Independent India* and the *Radical Humanist*. Among his books were *India in Transition* (1922), *Revolution and Counter-revolution in China* (Eng. trans. 1946), *The Russian Revolution* (1949), and *Reason, Romanticism and Revolution* (1952). ■ See *M. N. Roy's Memoirs* (1964) and biography by V. B. Karnik (1978).

ROYCE, JOSIAH (1855–1916), U.S. philosopher. Born and raised in Grass Valley, a California gold-rush town, Royce studied engineering at the University of California, then earned a Ph.D. at Johns Hopkins University (1878). Four years later, he began a lifelong career at Harvard University (1882–1916). Royce gained prominence in the early years of the century when the department he headed with William James established American philosophy as a mature discipline. His first book, *The Religious Aspect of Philosophy* (1885), made him the leading American exponent of absolute idealism, and focused philosophical debate for a generation on the existence of absolute truth and the relationship between religious and scientific thought. His ideas were somewhat tempered by the pragmatist criticisms of James, with whom Royce carried on a scholarly debate over a quarter century; after about 1900 Royce characterized his position as "absolute pragmatism." His other books included *The Spirit of Modern Philosophy* (1892), *The World and the Individual* (2 vols., 1899–1901), *The Philosphy of Loyalty* (1908), and *The Problem of Christianity* (1913). Royce's influence, enormous at the time of his death, lessened after World War I, when philosophical concerns shifted direction. He continues to be studied, however, as a representative of his generation's thought. ■ See John Clendenning, *The Life and Thought of Josiah Royce* (1985, rev. ed. 1999) and study by Robert V. Hine (1992).

RÓŻEWICZ, TADEUSZ (1921–), Polish writer. A member of the anti-Nazi underground during World War II, Różewicz began to write his influential war poems while he was studying art history at Jagiellonian University (Cracow). Viewing literature as a lie that covered up the cruelty in human society, he abandoned all traditional literary conventions (rhymes, stanzas, etc.) and produced poetry that was written in a manner similar to objective prose but was filled with emotional tension. These poems, many of which appear in *Faces of Anxiety* (Eng. trans. 1969), established a new trend in Polish literature. English translations of his poetry are also in *Selected Poems* (1976), *The Survivor and Other Poems* (1976), and *Conversation with the Prince* (1982; rev. as *They Came to See a Poet*, 1991). His grotesque and tragic plays *The Card Index* (1960; Eng. trans. 1969), *The Witnesses* (1962; Eng. trans. 1970), *The Interrupted Act* (1964; Eng. trans. 1969), and *Gone Out* (1964; Eng. trans. 1969) explored the condition of humankind while satirizing socialist society. See also *Mariage Blanc and the Hunger Artist Departs: Two Plays* (Eng. trans. 1983).

RÓZSA, MIKLÓS (1907–), Hungarian-born composer. Educated in the European romantic tradition, Rósza was a neoclassical concert composer before going to London in 1933 to score his first film. He became Hollywood's master composer for the historical epic, using authentic instrumentation and researching ethnic themes for *Quo Vadis* (1951) and *Ivanhoe* (1952). He was also skilled in the creation of suspense for psychological dramas, and his motif for a 1946 gangster movie gained familiarity on television as the "Dragnet" theme. He won Academy Awards for *Spellbound* (1945), *A Double Life* (1947), and *Ben-Hur* (1959). ■ See his autobiography, *Double Life* (1982).

RUBBIA, CARLO (1934–), Italian physicist. The son of an electrical engineer, Rubbia studied at the University of Pisa (Ph.D. 1957), did research at the European Organization for Nuclear Research (CERN, located near Geneva; from 1960), and was a professor of physics at Harvard (1970–88). At CERN he conceived of an experiment using a colliding beam accelerator that proved (1983) the existence of three subatomic particles (two W particles, one positive and one negative, and the neutral Z particle). The discovery demonstrated the unity, predicted by theoretical physicists, of two of the four fundamental forces of nature—electromagnetism and the weak force (responsible for radioactive decay)—and was considered a great step toward proving the unified field theory, linking all four natural forces: electromagnetism, the weak force, gravity, and the strong force (responsible for binding together particles of the atomic nucleus). Rubbia shared the 1984 Nobel Prize for Physics with Simon van der Meer, the CERN engineer who designed the accelerator used in the experiment. Rubbia subsequently discovered the existence of the T-top quark, one of the building blocks of matter. ■ See Gary Taubes, *Nobel Dreams* (1986).

RUBINSTEIN, ARTHUR (1887–1982), Polish-born U.S. pianist. Rubinstein gave his first recital at age 4, made his formal debut in Berlin at 11, and for 85 of his 95 years appeared in concert. In 1937 he gave a historic concert at Carnegie Hall that marked his emergence as a mature artist and one of the century's greatest pianists. During World War II Rubinstein emigrated with his family from Paris to the United States, settling in Beverly Hills, California, where in the late 1940s he performed in movies about composers. He became a U.S. citizen in 1946. In the 1950s and 1960s, he was without rival, enthralling audiences with his vast repertory (especially his renditions of Mozart and Chopin) and commanding unprecedented fees. He was known for his distinctive tone and a style that was at once passionate and intellectual. He made many recordings. ■ See his *My Young Years* (1973) and *My Many Years* (1980).

RUBINSTEIN, HELENA (1872–1965), Polish-born U.S. business executive. Rubinstein studied medicine briefly before establishing her first beauty salon in Australia, where she successfully marketed the herbal preparation Crème Valaze. She launched an international cosmetics empire, opening elaborate salons first in London (1908) and later in Paris, New York, and other cities, and entrusting their administration to her sisters. The Rubinstein range of cosmetics introduced tinted face powder and foundation and pioneered in the field of beauty aids for men. The Helena Rubinstein Foundation (established 1953) supported medical research and other health-related causes. ■ See her *My Life for Beauty* (1965) and Patrick O'Higgins, *Madame* (1971).

RUDEL, JULIUS (1921–), Austrian-born U.S. opera director and conductor. A music student in Vienna, Rudel continued his studies after emigrating with his family to New York City (1938). He joined the New York City Opera Company at its inception (1943) and performed numerous musical and administrative tasks before serving as its director and chief conductor (1957–79). A champion of modern music, he presented notable productions of 20th-century opera—including several world premieres by American composers—as well as the standard repertory. His productions of works by Mozart, Handel, and Donizetti, especially those featuring soprano Beverly Sills, were highly praised. Rudel also headed various music festivals in the United States and Europe, appeared as guest conductor with the world's major orchestras, and was musical director of the Buffalo Philharmonic (1979–85).

RÜDENBERG, REINHOLD (1883–1961), German-born electrical engineer and inventor. The son of a manufacturer, Rüdenberg received a doctorate from the Technische Hochschule in Hanover (1906) and joined the Seimens-Schuckert electrical manufacturing firm in Berlin (1908), eventually becoming its chief electrical engineer (1923–36). Although he was an expert in the areas of electric machinery, power systems, and high-voltage transmission, his greatest contribution to science was the development of the electron microscope (1931). He filed a patent for the device several days before Ernst Ruska, a fellow German engineer, reported on his own independent development of the instrument. (Ruska spent most of his career improving the micro-scope and subsequently shared the 1986 Nobel Prize in Physics for the invention.) Rüdenberg, who was Jewish, left Germany to escape from Nazi rule (1936) and eventually settled in the United States, where he served as a professor of electrical engineering at Harvard University (1938–52).

RUDOLPH, PAUL MARVIN (1918–1997), U.S. architect. A student of Walter Gropius at Harvard (M.Arch. 1947), Rudolph was best known for his wide range of innovative and unpredictable designs that reflected the influences of Le Corbusier, Frank Lloyd Wright, and Louis Kahn. He was a leading urban architect and served as chairman of Yale's department of architecture (1958–65). Among his most famous buildings were the controversial School of Art and Architecture at Yale (New Haven, 1958), the Government Service Center (Boston, 1963), and the Southeastern Massachusetts Technological Institute (North Dartmouth, 1963). During the 1970s and 1980s the popularity of modernist architecture declined in the United States and Rudolph designed large high-rise structures in Hong Kong, Singapore, and Indonesia. ■ See *Paul Rudolph: Architectural Drawings* (1982) and the study by Sybil Moholy-Nagy, *The Architecture of Paul Rudolph* (1970).

RUDOLPH, WILMA GLODEAN (1940–1994), U.S. sprinter. After childhood bouts of illness, Rudolph needed specially constructed shoes to help her walk until age 11. She was an all-state basketball star at her Tennessee high school, where she also began competing in track. A member of the 1956 and 1960 U.S. Olympic teams, she set two world records in the 100- and 200-meter sprints. In the 1960 Olympics she became the first woman on a U.S. team to win three gold medals, and the first to win both sprint events.

RUFFO, TITTA (Ruffo Cafiero Titta; 1887–1953), Italian opera singer. Called "the Caruso of baritones," Ruffo was one of the greatest performers in operatic history. The possessor of an overpowering voice, he made his debut in 1898 (U.S. debut, 1912) and was a great box-office attraction. He sang with New York's Metropolitan Opera from 1922 to 1929; his most famous roles there were in *Don Carlos, The Barber of Seville, Rigoletto, Don Giovanni*, and *Hamlet*. ■ See his autobiography, *My Parabola* (1937; Eng. trans. 1995).

RUGG, HAROLD ORDWAY (1886–1960), U.S. educator. A leading progressive, Rugg taught at Columbia Teachers College (1920–51) and specialized in restructuring the social studies curriculum by discarding dogmatic approaches and incorporating insights from the humanities and social sciences. His controversial Social Science Pamphlets (12 vols., 1921–28), published in textbook form as the *Man and His Changing Society* series (14 vols., 1929–45), presented both positive and negative aspects of U.S. society. Although widely used in the late 1930s, the books were attacked as subversive by business and patriotic groups and were banned by many communities and libraries by the mid-1940s. He wrote many other books including *Culture and Education in America* (1931), *The Teacher in School and Society* (1950), and an autobiography, *That Men May Understand* (1941). ■ See study by Peter F. Carbone, Jr. (1977).

RUKEYSER, MURIEL (1913–1980), U.S. poet. Rukeyser studied at Vassar and at Columbia University and published her first volume, *Theory of Flight* (1935), at age 22, winning the Yale Younger Poets award. *The Collected Poems of Muriel Rukeyser* (1979) assembled the work she had published in 18 volumes of poetry over nearly half a century—multipart, intricate poems that dealt with personal and political conflict. Characterized by arresting images and directness, her work reflected the sustained social vision that grew out of her political commitments and experiences: Rukeyser actively supported the Loyalist cause during the Spanish civil war; she was a vocal foe of American intervention in Vietnam; she spoke in behalf of women's rights and against the further development of nuclear power. She also wrote children's stories, essays, and biographies. ■ See Louise Kertesz, *The Poetic Vision of Muriel Rukeyser* (1980).

RULFO, JUAN (1918–1986), Mexican novelist and short-story writer. Like many Latin American fiction writers, Rulfo was decisively influenced by the U.S. novelist William Faulkner. His short-story collection *The Burning Plain* (1953; Eng. trans. 1967) contained terse, naturalistic accounts of rural Mexican life that were neither emotional nor political, but described the violence and fatalism of primitive peasant existence. His difficult, important novel *Pedro Páramo* (1955; Eng. trans. 1959, 1998), sought wisdom in Mexican history and myth; using a series of dreams, flashbacks, and interior monologues to create a timeless framework, he wrote of an archetypical rural community and its overbearing political boss. Rulfo directed the editorial department of the National Institute for Indigenous Studies and was an adviser to young writers at the Centro Mexicano de Escritores. ■ See study by Luis Leal (1983).

RUML, BEARDSLEY (1894–1960), U.S. economist, banker, and businessman. Ruml was primarily an "idea man" who had a great influence on American life. He promoted social-science research and helped create the Public Administration Clearing House (Chicago) while he was president of the Laura Spelman Rockefeller Memorial Fund (1922–29) and dean of social sciences at the University of Chicago (1931–33). He served on government committees under Presidents Herbert Hoover and Franklin D. Roosevelt and was a key New Deal adviser. Ruml also devised the "pay-as-you-go" income tax plan (1943), was chairman of Macy's department store (1945–49) and of the Federal Reserve Bank of New York (1941–47), and played a key role in the Bretton Woods Conference (1944), which set up the International Monetary Fund and the World Bank.

RUNDSTEDT, (KARL RUDOLF) GERD VON (1875–1953), German general. An aristocratic Prussian who was disdainful of the Nazis, Rundstedt nevertheless participated in Germany's secret interwar rearmament and returned from retirement in 1938 to become the greatest of Nazi dictator Adolf Hitler's generals in World War II. With brilliant precision he commanded the invasions of Poland and France, but his failure in the Russian campaign (1941) led to the first of his several dismissals. Rundstedt was commander in chief in the west (1942–45) and temporarily halted the Allied advance during the Battle of the Bulge (1944). He was captured by the Allies in 1945 and imprisoned but released (1949) due to ill health. ■ See study by John Keegan (1974) and Charles Messenger, *The Last Prussian* (1991).

RUNYON, (ALFRED) DAMON (1884–1946), U.S. journalist. Runyon, who ran away from home at 14 to serve in the Spanish-American War, became a sportswriter, war correspondent, columnist, and feature writer for the Hearst syndicate. Called "the prose laureate of the semiliterate," he focused on the human nature of New York City's "lower" social classes, gamblers, bookies, gangsters, and chorus girls, whom he described with slangy humor and affection. His collected stories included *Guys and Dolls* (1931), later a hit play and film, and *Blue Plate Special* (1934). He also wrote several film scripts, including *Lady for a Day* (1933) and *Little Miss Marker* (1934). ■ See Edwin P. Hoyt, *A Gentleman of Broadway* (1964); Tom Clark, *The World of Damon Runyon* (1978); and biography by Jimmy Breslin (1991).

RUPP, ADOLPH FREDERICK (1901–1977), U.S. basketball coach. Known as "the baron," Rupp won more college games than any other coach (879) and guided the University of Kentucky Wildcats for 43 years (1930–72). His winning percentage was .821. Outspoken and controversial, Rupp led his teams to four National Collegiate Athletic Association (NCAA) titles and one National Invitational Tournament (NIT) championship and developed 24 All-Americans. During the off-season he was a cattle breeder and tobacco farmer.

RUPPERT, JACOB (1867–1939), U.S. businessman. Active in the family brewing business in New York City, Ruppert was also a prominent sportsman and local political figure (U.S. representative, 1899–1907). His greatest interest, though, was baseball, and in 1915 he purchased (with a friend) the New York Yankees, an unprofitable, losing team. He quickly reorganized the club, hired Miller Huggins as manager (1918), brought the great player Babe Ruth to New York (1920), hired Edward G. Barrow as general manager

(1920), and built Yankee Stadium, then the nation's most modern ballpark (1923). The Yankees were soon the most successful team in baseball, winning ten pennants and seven World Series for Ruppert.

RUSHDIE, (AHMED) SALMAN (1947–   ), Indian-born British writer. Rushdie was born into a prosperous Muslim family in Bombay, just two months before India gained independence and Pakistan was created. He was sent to study at an elite private school in England at age 14 and subsequently studied history at King's College, Cambridge (M.A. 1968). Though his family migrated to Pakistan (1964), he decided to remain in England and pursue a literary career. His rich, exuberant, allegorical novels, informed by his own multicultural background and identity as an outsider, were concerned with the interconnection of the individual with the vicissitudes of national history. The novel *Midnight's Children* (1981; Booker Prize 1981) was an allegory of modern Indian history, while *Shame* (1983) utilized the techniques of magical realism to examine contemporary Pakistan. The allegorical and satirical novel *The Satanic Verses* (1989) was viewed as blasphemous by many Muslims around the world, and it was banned in India and many Islamic countries. When the Ayatollah Khomeini, Iran's supreme leader, decreed a death sentence for Rushdie and announced a $1.6 million reward for his assassin (1989), Rushdie went into hiding and was forced to live in the shadows for almost a decade. In September 1998 the Iranian government formally dissociated itself from the threat to Rushdie's life. Rushdie's other works included *The Moor's Last Sigh* (1995), a novel of modern India; *Imaginary Homelands: Essays and Criticism* (1991); and *The Ground Beneath Her Feet,* (1999), a surrealistic retelling of the Orpheus myth. ▪ See studies by J. Harrison (1992) and Catherine Cundy (1996).

RUSK, (DAVID) DEAN (1909–1994), U.S. cabinet officer. A soft-spoken Rhodes scholar from Georgia, Rusk played a major role in the execution of the Korean War as assistant secretary of state for Far Eastern affairs (1950–51). As president of the Rockefeller Foundation (1952–61), he expanded its worldwide operations. He served as U.S. secretary of state under Presidents John F. Kennedy and Lyndon B. Johnson (1961–69) and was a leading advocate of the use of force to counter communism in Vietnam. Selections from his speeches were published as *The Winds of Freedom* (1963). ▪ See his memoirs, *As I Saw It* (1990); biography by Warren I. Cohen (1980); and Thomas J. Schoenbaum, *Waging Peace and War* (1988).

RUSKA, ERNST AUGUST FRIEDRICH (1906–1988), German electrical engineer and inventor. In 1931, while a graduate student at the Technical University of Berlin (Ph.D. 1934), Ruska built the first electron microscope. Although a patent for a similar device was filed by German engineer Reinhold Rüdenberg shortly before Ruska reported on the development of his microscope, Ruska was generally cited as its inventor. He spent most of his long career as a researcher at Siemens and Halske (1937–55), the giant electronics firm, and at the Max Planck Institute, Berlin (1955–72), improving the microscope, which became one of the most significant research tools developed during the 20th century. He shared the 1986 Nobel Prize in Physics with Heinrich Rohrer and Gerd Binnig.

RUSSELL, BERTRAND ARTHUR WILLIAM RUSSELL, 3rd EARL (1872–1970), British philosopher, mathematician, and social reformer. Russell was born into a distinguished aristocratic family, studied mathematics and philosophy at Cambridge (1890–94), and taught there until being dismissed for pacifist activities (1916). His greatest scholarly work, *Principia Mathematica* (with Alfred North Whitehead; 3 vols., 1910–13), which sought to prove that mathematics was an extension of logic, was considered a landmark in the history of mathematics. In addition to numerous scholarly works, he wrote many popular books, including *ABC of Relativity* (1925), *Why I Am Not a Christian* (1927), *Marriage and Morals* (1929), *Education and the Social Order* (1932), and *History of Western Philosophy* (1945). He was awarded the 1950 Nobel Prize for Literature for his significant writings "in which he appeared as the champion of humanity and freedom of thought." An independent left-wing radical, he campaigned for women's suffrage and for pacifism in his youth and was a leader of the Campaign for Nuclear Disarmament and the anti-Vietnam War movement in his old age. ▪ See his *Basic Writings* (1903–59), *Autobiography* (3 vols., 1967–69), and biographies by Alan Wood (1957), Herbert Gottschalk (1965), Ronald W. Clark (1976), Caroline Moorehead (1993), and Ray Monk (1997).

RUSSELL, BILL (William Felton Russell; 1934–   ), U.S. basketball player. Regarded as the greatest defensive center in basketball history, the 6-foot, 10-inch-tall Russell led the University of San Francisco to 60 straight wins and two successive National Collegiate Athletic Association (NCAA) titles (1955, 1956). As a professional he led the Boston Celtics to 11 championships in 13 seasons (1956–69) and was the National Basketball Association's Most Valuable Player five times (1958; 1961–63; 1965). His shot-blocking and rebounding techniques revolutionized the game. Named player-coach of the Celtics (1967–69), he became the first African-American leader of a major U.S. pro sports team. After a four-year hiatus as a TV sports commentator, he returned to the game as head coach of the Seattle Supersonics (1973–77) and the Sacramento Kings (1987–88). ▪ See his autobiography, *Going Up for Glory* (1966), and memoirs, *Second Wind* (1979; with Taylor Branch).

RUSSELL, CHARLES EDWARD (1860–1941), U.S. journalist and politician. Russell was one of the leading muckraking journalists of the early 1900s, specializing in exposés of the railroads and the meatpacking industry. One of the few reporters to move from the newsroom into politics, he joined the Socialist party (1908) and ran (unsuccessfully) for high office in New York City and State. He was nominated for president (1916) but refused to run, and was known as a crusader for civil liberties, women's suffrage, prison reform, racial justice (he was a founder of the NAACP), and against capital punishment. His 27 books included *Lawless Wealth* (1908), *Why I Am a Socialist* (1910), and *The American Orchestra and Theodore Thomas* (Pulitzer Prize, 1927). ■ See his autobiography, *Bare Hands and Stone Walls* (1933).

RUSSELL, CHARLES MARION (1864–1926), U.S. artist. A self-taught painter of the Old West, Russell worked as a cowpuncher and trapper in Montana and lived for a time with the Indians in the Northwest Territory. He established a studio in Great Falls, Montana, in 1903, painted a mural of the explorers Lewis and Clark in the Montana State Capitol, and began selling pictures to magazines. He painted nearly 2,500 works and was the most popular interpreter of cowboy and Indian life. A museum was established in his honor in Great Falls to exhibit his paintings and sculptures. ■ See biographies by Austin Russell (1957), Harold McCracken (1957), Lola Shelton (1962), and John Taliaferro (1996).

RUSSELL, HENRY NORRIS (1877–1957), U.S. astronomer. Russell received his Ph.D. from Princeton (1900) and served on its faculty (1905–47). With Ejnar Hertzsprung, he formulated (1913) the Hertzsprung-Russell, or H-R, diagram. It depicts the relationship between the absolute magnitudes and spectral classes of stars. Although aspects of the diagram were later shown to be incorrect, it remains a cornerstone of stellar astronomy. Russell also was among the first to identify hydrogen as the dominant element in the universe. The advent of radio astronomy verified his theory of the existence of millions of solar systems like our own. His works included *On the Composition of the Sun's Atmosphere* (1929). ■ See biography by David H. DeVorkin (2000).

RUSSELL, RICHARD BREVARD, JR. (1897–1971), U.S. political leader. The son of a Georgia Supreme Court justice, Russell served as a Democratic state representative (1921–31) and governor (1931–32) before being elected to the U.S. Senate (1932), where he served until his death. He quickly became the leading voice in the southern bloc, supporting Pres. Franklin D. Roosevelt on relief and farm aid and backing lend-lease and U.S. entry into World War II. Unlike many of his southern colleagues, he did not bolt the Democratic party in 1948, and he ran unsuccessfully for the presidential nomination in 1952. During the 1950s and 1960s he turned increasingly conservative and was frequently called the Senate's most powerful member. He was a chief strategist of the anticivil-rights forces and a leader of the

states' rights movement. He also strongly supported the armed forces and presided over the expansion of the military establishment as chairman of the Senate Armed Services Committee (1951–69). ■ See biography by Gilbert C. Fite (1991) and John A. Goldsmith, *Colleagues* (1998).

RUSSELL, ROSALIND (1912–1976), U.S. actress. Russell rose to stardom as a best-dressed, career-type comedienne in such films as *His Girl Friday* (1940) and *My Sister Eileen* (1942). Her greatest role was that of the hilarious eccentric *Auntie Mame,* which she played on Broadway (1956) and in the Hollywood film (1958). She also starred in *The Women* (1939), *Sister Kenny* (1946), and *Mourning Becomes Electra* (1947). ■ See her memoirs, *Life Is a Banquet* (1977; with Chris Chase).

RUSTIN, BAYARD (1910–1987), U.S. civil-rights leader and reformer. Rustin was a leader of the pacifist Fellowship of Reconciliation (1941–53) and the first field secretary of its offshoot, the Congress of Racial Equality (1941). He was imprisoned during World War II as a conscientious objector (1943–45). A leading African-American theoretician and activist in the movement for social change through nonviolent means, Rustin was a special assistant (1955–60) to Dr. Martin Luther King, Jr. He helped organize the Southern Christian Leadership Conference and was the chief organizer of the massive March on Washington for Jobs and Freedom (1963). A believer in coalition politics and alliances with sympathetic whites, he was the major tactician of the civil-rights movement until being replaced in leadership posts by militant and separatist Black Power advocates in the mid-1960s. He headed (1964–87) the A. Philip Randolph Institute in New York, an organization working for racial equality and peace. ■ See his collected writings, *Down the Line* (1971) and *Strategies for Freedom* (1976), and biography by Jervis Anderson (1997).

RUTH, BABE (George Herman Ruth; 1895–1948), U.S. baseball player. Undoubtedly the greatest all-around player in baseball history, the legendary Ruth was the one man most identified with the sport. Starting out as a left-handed pitcher for the Boston Red Sox (1914–19), he won 94 games and lost only 46. He was the best pitcher in the American League in 1916 and set a record of 29⅔ consecutive scoreless innings in World Series competition. Sold to the New York Yankees for $125,000 (1920), he began his spectacular career as a power hitter. In 22 seasons he had a .342 batting average, hit 714 home runs, drove in 2,216 runs, scored 2,174 runs, and walked 2,056 times. Called the "Sultan of Swat," Ruth set a major-league record of 60 home runs in a 154-game season (1927). He set or tied 76 batting or pitching records, but his impact went beyond statistics. Ruth was the sports idol of the 1920s and 1930s and one of the era's leading personalities. At the twilight of his career he was traded to the Boston Braves (1935) and finished his career as a coach for the Brooklyn Dodgers (1938). In 1936 he was one of the first five players elected to the National Baseball Hall of Fame. ■ See Robert W. Creamer, *Babe* (1974), and Marshall Smelser, *The Life that Ruth Built* (1975).

RUTHERFORD, ERNEST, 1st BARON RUTHERFORD OF NELSON AND CAMBRIDGE (1871–1937), New Zealand-born British physicist. One of the century's most influential scientists, Rutherford taught at McGill University, Montreal (1898–1907), Manchester University (1907–19), and Cambridge (1919–37) and won the 1908 Nobel Prize in Chemistry. He revolutionized the world of atomic physics by developing the theory of radioactive transformation of atoms, discovering and naming alpha and beta radiation and developing the nuclear theory of atomic structure that is still accepted today. Famed as a teacher, he inspired two generations of physicists, headed the prestigious Cavendish Laboratory at Cambridge (from 1919), and served as president of the Royal Society (1925–30). ■ See biography by David Wilson (1983), study by Edward Andrade (1964), and Mario Bunge and William R. Shea, eds., *Rutherford and Physics at the Turn of the Century* (1979).

RUŽIČKA, LEOPOLD STEPHEN (1887–1976), Croatian-born Swiss organic chemist. Early in his career (from 1916), Ruzicka, a professor at the Federal Institute of Technology in Zurich (1918–26; 1929–57), investigated two active compounds important to the perfume industry, the natural odorants muskone and civetone. He found that they were composed of rings of 15 and 17 carbon atoms, disproving the theory that rings of more than 8 atoms would be too unstable to exist. In the 1930s he synthesized several male hormones, including testosterone, and shared the 1939 Nobel Prize in Chemistry with Adolf Butenandt.

RYAN, JOHN AUGUSTINE (1869–1945), U.S. Roman Catholic leader and economist. Born into a poor Irish immigrant family, Ryan was ordained in 1898. A crusader for social justice and leader of the liberal wing of the Roman Catholic Church for decades, he was a professor of moral theology and social ethics at the Catholic University of America (1915–39). Called a "radical" and "bolshevik" by many of his fellow Catholics, he responded by stating that he was applying orthodox Catholic theology and principles of social justice to the needs of modern American society. His writings (including *A Living Wage: Its Ethical and Economic Aspects,* 1906, and *Distributive Justice,* 1916) were instrumental in the creation of minimum-wage and other social-reform legislation. ■ See his autobiography, *Social Doctrine in Action* (1941), and Francis L. Broderick, *Right Reverend New Dealer* (1963).

RYAN, NOLAN (1947–), U.S. baseball player. A right-hand pitcher with a blazing fastball, Nolan Ryan played for the New York Mets (1966–71), the California Angels (1972–79), and the Houston Astros (1979–). He set a major-league single-season record of 383 strikeouts (1973) and surpassed Walter Johnson's career strikeout record of 3,508 in 1983. In 1985 he became the first pitcher in baseball history to record 4,000 strikeouts. He also was the first to pitch five no-hit games. During his 27-season career he won 324 games, struck out a record 5,714 batters, and pitched a record seven no-hitters. In the off-season he was a cattle rancher in his native Texas. He wrote *The Other Game* (1977; with Bill Libby) and *Pitching and Hitting* (1977; with Joe Torre and Joel H. Cohen).

RYDZ-ŚMIGLY, EDWARD (1886–1941), Polish military and political leader. A veteran of Joseph Pilsudski's World War I Polish Legions, Rydz-Śmigly participated in the 1926 coup and in 1935 succeeded Pilsudski as inspector general of the Polish army. In 1936 he was promoted to marshal and named "first citizen after the president," presiding over a mock-fascist "Camp of National Unity." After Poland's collapse in the face of the German invasion of 1939, Rydz-Śmigly fled to Rumania amid charges of professional incompetence.

RYKOV, ALEKSEY IVANOVICH (1881–1938), Soviet political leader. An early bolshevik, Rykov became commissar for the interior after the October revolution of 1917 and was chairman of the Supreme Council of the National Economy (1918–21). In 1922 he became a Politburo member and after Lenin's death, he served (1924–30) as premier of the Soviet Union. He was a close associate of Joseph Stalin until he opposed Stalin's rapid industrialization and collectivization plan. He recanted (1929) but was denounced as a "right deviationist" (1930) and lost his high party and government positions. After serving in the politically unimportant position of commissar for posts and telegraphs (1931–36), he was arrested (1937), convicted of treason in the show trial of 1938, and executed. ■ See Samuel A. Oppenheim, *The Practical Bolshevik* (1979).

RYLE, GILBERT (1900–1976), British philosopher. Educated at Queen's College, Oxford, Ryle was a leader in the "ordinary language" movement. As a teacher of metaphysical philosophy at Oxford (1924–68) and as editor of the periodical *Mind* (1947–71), he sought to advance philosophical thought through the precise use of language and the clear definition of concepts. His first book, *The Concept of Mind* (1949), stirred controversy by challenging the Cartesian dualism which views the body and mind as distinct substances. His other works included *Dilemmas* (1954), an analysis of seemingly irreconcilable propositions, and *Plato's Progress* (1966), a speculative historical reconstruction of the genesis of Plato's dialogues. ■ See his *Collected Papers* (2 vols., 1971); Laird Addis and Douglas Lewis, *Moore and Ryle: Two Ontologists* (1965); the articles in O. Wood, ed., *Ryle* (1970); and study by William E. Lyons (1980).

RYLE, SIR MARTIN (1918–1984), British astronomer. Ryle conducted astrophysics research at Cambridge University (1945–82) and served as the Astronomer Royal of Britain (1972–82). He developed the technique known as aperture synthesis—a method involving simultaneous operation of several small radio telescopes—allowing for data collection and mapping of galaxies, pulsars, and quasars millions of light-years from earth. Ryle was also known for his support of the "big bang" theory of the origin of the universe. He shared the 1974 Nobel Prize in Physics with Antony Hewish; they were the first astronomers to receive that distinction.

S

SAADAWI, NAWAL EL- (1930–   ), Egyptian feminist and writer. A physician who worked for the Egyptian ministry of health and edited its *Health* magazine, Nawal el-Saadawi was known throughout the Arab world for numerous volumes of fiction and nonfiction that focused on women's experience. Her study *Women and Sex* (1972) sparked controversy by calling for changes in the position of Arab women in the family. She was dismissed from her government post that year and banned from publishing in Egypt. Her book, *The Hidden Face of Eve: Women in the Arab World* (Eng. trans. 1979), appeared abroad. With a number of other women, she was arrested on orders from Pres. Anwar el-Sadat for publishing the feminist magazine *Confrontation* and imprisoned in Cairo (1981). Her other novels included *God Dies by the Nile* (Eng. trans. 1986), a political allegory; *Two Women in One* (Eng. trans. 1986), the story of a rebellious Cairo college student; *The Fall of the Imam* (1987; Eng. trans. 1988); and *Innocence of the Devil* (1992; Eng. trans. 1994). English translations of her works are in *The Nawal El Saadawi Reader* (1997). ■ See her autobiography, *A Daughter of Isis* (Eng. trans. 1999), and her *Memoirs from the Women's Prison* (1984; Eng. trans. 1986) and *My Travels Around the World* (Eng. trans. 1991), and Fedwa Malti-Douglas, *Men, Women and God(s)* (1995).

SAARINEN, (GOTTLIEB) ELIEL (1873–1950) **and EERO SAARINEN** (1910–1961), Finnish-born U.S. architects. Eliel Saarinen was Finland's leading architect before moving to the United States in 1923. He served as president (1932–48) of Michigan's Cranbrook Academy of Art, whose building he also designed. The elder Saarinen abhorred skyscrapers and designed several midwestern schools and churches in a simple, spacious style. His son Eero studied sculpture in Paris and architecture at Yale before forming a partnership with his father (1937). Together they designed an addition to the Smithsonian Institution in Washington, D.C. After his father's death, Eero Saarinen came into his own, initially rejecting his father's more romantic style and later reconciling modernism with traditional forms. Eschewing the consistency sought by the International Style of modern architecture, he took a more eclectic approach to design, and introduced new concepts, especially in domical construction. He designed the U.S. embassy in London (1960), the TWA terminal at New York's John F. Kennedy Airport (1962), Washington's Dulles International Airport (1963), and the Jefferson Memorial Arch in St. Louis (1964). Eliel Saarinen wrote *The City* (1943) and *Search for Form* (1948). ■ See study on Eliel Saarinen by Albert Christ-Janer (1979) and study on Eero Saarinen by Allan Temko (1962).

SAAVEDRA LAMAS, CARLOS (1878–1959), Argentine official. Saavedra Lamas, an aristocrat with a law degree and a record of public service, served as Argentina's minister of foreign affairs (1932–38) and asserted Argentina's influence in hemispheric affairs. He helped negotiate the 1935 truce that ended the Chaco War between Bolivia and Paraguay, for which he received the 1936 Nobel Peace Prize, and he served as president of the Assembly of the League of Nations in 1936. A nationalist who resented U.S. policies based on the Monroe Doctrine, he opposed Pres. Franklin D. Roosevelt's efforts to strengthen the inter-American system, but supported the Allies after the start of World War II. He wrote several books on international law and was president of the University of Buenos Aires (1941–43).

SÁBATO, ERNEST (1911–   ), Argentine writer. A physicist and mathematician turned novelist, Sábato wrote several highly regarded existentialist novels including *The Outsider* (1948; Eng. trans. 1950), *On Heroes and Tombs* (1961; Eng. trans. 1981), and *Angel of Darkness* (1974; Eng. trans. 1991). He drew themes from Argentina's tumultuous history and social life to represent universal psychological and political dilemmas of modern human experience. Sábato also wrote works of political and literary criticism. After the military dictatorship was replaced by a freely elected government (1983), Sábato headed the National Commission on the Disappearance of Persons, whose report (1984) implicated military and police personnel in the disappearance, torture, and murder of thousands of innocent citizens from 1976 to 1983. English translations of his essays appeared in *The Writer in the Catastrophe of Our Time* (1990). ■ See study by Harley D. Oberhelman (1970).

SABIN, ALBERT BRUCE (1906–1993), U.S. virologist. Born in Russian Poland, Sabin emigrated to the United States with his family (1921) and studied at New York University (B.S. 1928; M.D. 1931). A staff member at the Rockefeller Institute for Medical Research (1935–39) and professor at the medical school of the University of Cincinnati (1939–71), he devoted his career to the study of viruses responsible for childhood diseases. During the 1950s he developed the live-virus oral polio vaccine, which proved longer lasting and easier to administer than the vaccine developed earlier by Jonas Salk. Sabin's vaccine, which began to be widely used during the early 1960s, played a major role in the dramatic worldwide decline of polio. Sabin later served as a professor at the University of South Carolina Medical School (1974–82).

SABIN, FLORENCE RENA (1871–1953), U.S. anatomist. Sabin earned (1900) her M.D. from the Johns Hopkins Medical School, where she taught for two decades (1905–25) as the school's first full-time woman faculty member. Her major contributions included path-breaking work on the lymphatic system and on the origin of red corpuscles. She founded (1925) a department of cellular studies at the Rockefeller Institute for Medical Studies, where she conducted significant research on tuberculosis; she was the first woman elected (1925) to the U.S. National Academy of Sciences. After retirement (1938) she devoted herself to public health and preventive medicine in her native state of Colorado. ■ See study by Elinor Bluemel (1959) and Mary Kay Phelan, *Probing the Unknown* (1969).

SABU (Sabu Dastagir; 1924–1963), Indian actor. A stable boy at the court of the Maharajah of Mysore, Sabu was chosen to play the title role in *Elephant Boy* (1937), a film based on Rudyard Kipling's *Jungle Book*. He moved to Britain where he attended school and appeared in *Drums* (1938) and *The Thief of Baghdad* (1940). He migrated to Hollywood (1941), served with the U.S. Army Air Corps during World War II, and made a series of popular exotic adventure movies including *Cobra Woman* (1944), *Man-Eater of Kumoan* (1948), *Song of India* (1949), and *Savage Drums* (1951).

SACCO, NICOLA (1891–1927), and **BARTOLOMEO VANZETTI** (1888–1927), Italian-born U.S. anarchists. Sacco, a shoe-factory worker, and Vanzetti, a laborer and fish peddler, both emigrated to the United States in 1908. At the height of the post–World War I "Red scare" hysteria, both were arrested for the robbery of a shoe factory (in South Braintree, Massachusetts) and the murder of two employees (1920). They were tried and found guilty (1921), despite the shaky evidence offered by the prosecution. In seeking a rehearing, their lawyers claimed that the two were found guilty because of their radical politics and that the trial was conducted in an atmosphere of fear, repression, and prejudice. In 1925 a condemned criminal gave evidence that a gang from Rhode Island committed the crime, but the judge refused to reopen the trial. The case, a national and international cause célèbre, rallied the American intellectual, liberal, and radical communities. However, all protests for Sacco and Vanzetti were in vain, and they were electrocuted in Boston. ■ See G. L. Joughin and E. M. Morgan, *The Legacy of Sacco and Vanzetti* (1948); Roberta S. Feuerlicht, *Justice Crucified* (1977); and Paul Avrich, *Sacco and Vanzetti: The Anarchist Background* (1991). In *Postmortem* (1985), William Young and David E. Kaiser present new evidence that Sacco and Vanzetti were framed.

SACHS, NELLY (1891–1970), German poet. Born into a wealthy and cultured Jewish family in Berlin and educated by private tutors, Sachs published romantic poetry and a book of stories during the 1920s and 1930s. When the Nazis came to power, however, her carefree world was shattered and as the persecution of the Jews intensified she immersed herself in the Jewish religious and mystical literature that was to inform her later works. Through the intercession of the Swedish royal family she escaped to Sweden in 1940 and remained there for the rest of her life. Deeply shaken by the martyrdom of the Jews of Europe during World War II, she wrote a series of anguished poems that metaphorically and in universal terms described the homelessness, persecutions, suffering, and death of her people. She shared the 1966 Nobel Prize in Literature with Israeli novelist S. Y. Agnon. Translations of her work are in *O the Chimneys* (1967) and *The Seeker and Other Poems* (1970).

SADAT, (MUHAMMAD) ANWAR EL- (1918–1981), Egyptian political leader. A military-academy classmate of Gamal Abdel Nasser, the future Egyptian president, Sadat was court-martialed by the British in 1942 during World War II for favoring collaboration with the Nazis and imprisoned (1946–48) for plotting to assassinate a pro-British official. He participated in the 1952 coup that deposed King Farouk and he served as Nasser's loyal collaborator, vice president (1964–66; 1969–70), and successor to the presidency (1970–81). Sadat consolidated his power by bringing in technocrats, expelling Nasser's Soviet advisers, and, after the 1973 Arab-Israeli War, seeking a rapprochement with the United States and Israel. In a dramatic gesture of peace, he visited Israeli Prime Minister Begin in Jerusalem (1977), addressed the Israeli parliament, and signed a peace treaty with Israel (1979). For negotiating the treaty, he and Begin shared the 1978 Nobel Peace Prize. The treaty enabled Egypt to regain the Sinai peninsula, but it was denounced by most Arab governments and Sadat was virtually isolated in the Arab world. He was assassinated by Islamic fundamentalists while reviewing a military parade. ■ See his autobiography, *In Search of Identity* (1978); biographies by David Hirst and Irene Beeson (1981) and Joseph Finklestone (1995); and Mohamed Heikal, *Autumn of Fury* (1983).

SADOVEANU, MIHAIL (1880–1961), Rumanian novelist and short-story writer. One of the greatest and most prolific writers in the history of Rumanian literature, Sadoveanu depicted all aspects of Rumanian life and society in over 100 volumes of fiction. He celebrated the natural beauty of the country, as well as everyday and historical exploits. His most famous work was the epic novel *The Hatchet* (1930; Eng. trans. 1965), which dealt with a peasant murder and revenge. *Tales of War* (1906; Eng. trans. 1962) dealt with the Rumanian struggle against the Turks in 1877. See also *The Mud-Hut Dwellers* (1912; Eng. trans. 1964). Sadoveanu directed the National Theater at Iaşi (1909–19), was a member of parliament (1926), served as president of the senate (1930–31), and, after World War II, was vice president of the grand national assembly.

SAFDIE, MOSHE (1938–   ), Israeli-born architect. Safdie migrated to Canada (1955) and studied architecture at McGill University, Montreal (B.Arch. 1961). He achieved fame with his revolutionary prefabricated housing complex, Habitat, at Montreal's international exhibition Expo 67 (1967). A mass-produced, multiple-unit apartment project of stepped reinforced-concrete blocks, Habitat contained private gardens, individual access, and unobstructed views and proved that imaginative and high-quality housing could be built at low cost. He subsequently designed a 300-unit Habitat project in Puerto Rico (1968–72); the Student Union at San Francisco State College (1968); the plan for Cold Spring New Town, near Baltimore (1971); several projects in Jerusalem, including the master plan for the Western Wall Precinct (1974); and the National Gallery of Canada, Ottowa (1988). He served as a professor at Harvard University (1978–89) and wrote *Beyond Habitat* (1970), *For Everyone a Garden* (1974), *Form and Purpose* (1982), *The Language and Medium of Architecture* (1989), and *The City After the Automobile* (1997; with W. Kohn). ▪ See *Moshe Safdie: Buildings and Projects, 1967–1992* (1996).

SAGAN, CARL EDWARD (1934–1996), U.S. astronomer. A professor at Cornell University (from 1968), Sagan made important contributions to the study of planetary atmospheres, the surfaces of Venus and Mars, the origin of life on Earth, and other aspects of planetary biology. With the National Aeronautics and Space Administration he played a leading role in the Mariner, Viking, and Voyager unmanned planetary space probes. He edited *Icarus,* the journal of planetary research (1968–79), and wrote several books including *Intelligent Life in the Universe* (1966; with Soviet scientist I. S. Shklovskii), *The Cosmic Connection* (1973), *The Dragons of Eden* (Pulitzer Prize, 1977), and *Broca's Brain* (1979). He also created the television series "Cosmos" (1980) and wrote the best-selling book based on the series (1980). In 1984 he was the spokesperson for a group of prominent scientists that warned that smoke and soot resulting from a nuclear war could block out sunlight and cause a nuclear winter that would all but destroy life on Earth. His first novel, *Contact* (1985), was a best-seller. His later books, written with his wife Ann Druyan, included *Shadows of Forgotten Ancestors* (1992) and *The Demon-Haunted World* (1995). ▪ See biographies by Keay Davidson (1999) and William Poundstone (1999).

SAGAN, FRANÇOISE (Françoise Quoirez; 1935–   ), French writer. Sagan was the daughter of a wealthy industrialist. At the age of 18 she wrote her best-selling novel *Bonjour Tristesse* (1954; Eng. trans. 1955) to dispel boredom. Her other short novels included *A Certain Smile* (1956; Eng.

trans. 1956) and *Aimez-Vous Brahms?* (1959; Eng. trans. 1960). Her prose, lucid and dispassionate, focused on troubled love and the cynicism, boredom, and amorality of youth, whose spokeswoman she was considered in the 1950s. Her later works, dealing with aspects of love and loss, included the novels *The Painted Lady* (1981; Eng. trans. 1983), *Salad Days* (1980; Eng. trans. 1984), *Dear Sarah Bernhardt* (1987; Eng. trans. 1988), *Evasion* (1991; Eng. trans. 1993), and *A Fleeting Sorrow* (1994; Eng. trans. 1995), and the short-story collection *Incidental Music* (1981; Eng. trans. 1984). She also wrote plays. ▪ See the autobiographical *Nightbird: Conversations with Françoise Sagan* (1976; Eng. trans. 1980) and *With Fondest Regards* (Eng. trans. 1985).

SAGER, RUTH (1918–1997), U.S. geneticist. After studying at Columbia University (Ph.D. 1948), Sager undertook genetic studies that challenged contemporary theories by proposing the existence of a genetic transmitting system outside the chromosomes. She discovered (1953) nonchromosomal genes of the alga *chlamydomonas* and devised a method for inducing mating through nitrogen deprivation. This led to significant findings in the field of cytoplasmic heredity. She did research at the Rockefeller Institute (1953–55), Columbia (1955–65), Hunter (1966–75), and the Harvard Medical School (1975–88), and wrote *Cell Heredity* (1961; with Francis J. Ryan) and *Cytoplasmic Genes and Organelles* (1972).

SAID, EDWARD W. (1935–   ), Palestinian-born U.S. author. Said was born in Jerusalem into a well-to-do Christian family and grew up in family residences in Cairo, Beirut, and Jerusalem. He lived in Egypt during the turmoil leading up to the Arab-Israeli War of 1948, and most of his extended family became refugees during the conflict. He immigrated to the United States (1950), was educated at Princeton University (B.A. 1957) and Harvard University (Ph.D. 1964), and taught English and comparative literature at Columbia University (1963–   ). A controversial opponent of ethnocentrism in scholarship and in political life, he was best known for *Orientalism* (1978), a widely read critique of 19th-century Western scholarship on the Middle East, and *Culture and Imperialism* (1993), a study of the relationship between imperialism and Western culture. He was a powerful advocate of Palestinian national rights, a member of the Palestine National Council (1971–91), and the author of several books relating to Palestinian affairs and contemporary Western perceptions of the Middle East, including *The Question of Palestine* (1979; 1992), *Covering Islam* (1981), *After the Last Sky* (1986), *Blaming the Victims* (ed. with Christopher Hitchens, 1988), and *The End of the Peace Process* (2000). His other works included a book of essays, *The World, the Text and the Critic* (1983), and a volume on music criticism, *Musical Elaborations* (1991). ▪ See his memoir, *Out of Place* (1999).

ST. DENIS, RUTH (Ruth Dennis; 1878?–1968), U.S. dancer and choreographer. When Ruth St. Denis, a musical-comedy dancer and actress, first brought exotic oriental and Eastern dances to the American stage, she was received coolly. Like Isadora Duncan, she fared better in a European tour (1906–09). After 1909 she found more U.S. acceptance for her mystical, expressive movements, which gave a religious dimension to modern dance. She married (1914) her dancing partner Ted Shawn and established the experimental Denishawn School, which provided (1915–31) training for America's important dancers and choreographers and helped make modern dance an accepted art form. Their innovative "music visualizations," interpretive pieces based on classical music, were particularly influential. ■ See her autobiography, *An Unfinished Life* (1939); Walter Terry, *Miss Ruth* (1969); and Suzanne Shelton, *Divine Dancer* (1981).

SAINT EXUPÉRY, ANTOINE DE (1900–1944), French novelist. Saint Exupéry lived a life of adventure and danger as a military pilot (1921–23) and then a commercial pilot in Africa and South America. His novels *Southern Mail* (1928; Eng. trans. 1933), *Night Flight* (1931; Eng. trans. 1932), and the nonfiction *Wind, Sand, and Stars* (1939; Eng. trans. 1939) were based on his own experiences. In vivid and lyrical prose he recounted his joy and wonder at flying; his works contained his reflections on human existence, and on the need for brotherhood and for dedication to one's duty. His fable, *The Little Prince* (1943; Eng. trans. 1943), is popular with readers of all ages. Flying a reconnaissance mission for the Free French during World War II, he disappeared over France. ■ See his *Wartime Writings, 1939–44* (Eng. trans. 1986); biographies by Curtis Cate (1970) and Stacy Schiff (1994); and study by Joy Robinson (1984).

ST. JOHN, VINCENT (1876–1929), U.S. labor leader. A miner and union organizer (Western Federation of Miners), St. John helped established the militant Industrial Workers of the World (IWW; 1905) and was its leader from 1908 to 1915. He was a shrewd and respected leader who was dedicated to revolutionary syndicalism. He led important strikes in Lawrence, Massachusetts, and Paterson, New Jersey, and wrote *The I.W.W.: Its History, Structure and Methods* (1917).

SAINT-JOHN PERSE. *See PERSE, SAINT-JOHN.*

ST. LAURENT, LOUIS STEPHEN (1882–1973), Canadian political leader. St. Laurent, who was bilingual, practiced law and taught at Laval University Law School in Quebec (from 1914). In 1941 he agreed to become the minister of justice for the duration of World War II; he played a major role in the reconciliation of Quebec to conscription. A Liberal, St. Laurent served as minister of external affairs (1946–48) and then as prime minister (1948–57), the second French-Canadian to hold that post. His administration oc-

curred during a time of unprecedented population and economic growth. He championed greater independence from Britain and active Canadian participation in the North Atlantic Treaty Organization (NATO) and the United Nations. ■ See biography by Dale C. Thomson (1968).

ST. LAURENT, YVES (1936–   ), French fashion designer. Yves St. Laurent won a design competition and at age 17 was hired to assist the couturier who had served as judge—Christian Dior. St. Laurent worked closely with Dior, succeeding him at his death in 1957, but he alienated the firm's executives with iconoclastic creations such as leather pants suits. He was suddenly drafted into the army (1960). Discharged after an emotional breakdown, he returned to Paris, but the firm of Dior had no place for him. After litigation, he opened (1962) the House of St. Laurent; he later established (1966) the boutique St. Laurent Rive Gauche, setting a trend that punctured the bubble of exclusivity surrounding high fashion. St. Laurent decisively influenced fashion trends in the century's second half with styles reminiscent of the thirties. In the mid-1970s he introduced the *haute* peasant look. He won countless design awards, created costumes for theater and ballet, and became a celebrity in his own right. He was the subject of a retrospective exhibit at New York's Metropolitan Museum of Art (1983) and subsequently in major museums in Beijing, Paris, St. Petersburg, Sydney, and Tokyo. ■ See Axel Madsen, *Living for Design* (1979), and biography by Alice Rawsthorn (1996).

SAINTE-MARIE, BUFFY (1941–   ), Canadian-born U.S. folksinger, songwriter, and political activist. Buffy Sainte-Marie was born on an Indian reserve in Saskatchewan, Canada, to a family of Plains Cree Indian extraction, but was raised in New England by adoptive parents who were part Micmac Indian. In the early 1960s she graduated from the University of Massachusetts and began to write and perform folk music. Her song "Universal Soldier" (1963) was widely identified with the antiwar movement; Sainte-Marie was also a vocal advocate of Indian rights and wrote such songs as "Native North American Child" and "Now That the Buffalo's Gone." Her albums included *Many a Mile* (1965), *Little Wheel Spin* (1966), and *Illuminations* (1969). Although she wrote popular love songs, such as "Until It's Time for You to Go," her identification with protest movements limited her commercial possibilities, and her career waned in the United States in the 1970s. She remained popular abroad, however, and won a new audience with regular appearances on the children's TV program "Sesame Street." She won an Academy Award (1983) for writing "Up Where We Belong," the theme song for the film *An Officer and a Gentleman* (with Jack Nietzsche and Will Jennings).

SAIONJI, KIMMOCHI, PRINCE (1849–1940), Japanese political leader. Born into an imperial court family, Saionji studied in France (1871–74), where he imbibed democratic ideas, and later served as minister to Austria-Hungary, Germany, and Belgium. On his return to Japan, he helped organize the Seiyukai political party (1900), and held many posts including those of premier (1906–08; 1911–12) and chief delegate to the Paris Peace Conference (1919). Saionji was made a *genro* (elder statesman) in 1912 and was thus a close adviser to the emperor. During the 1930s he tried, in vain, to limit the power of the military in politics. ■ See Yosaburo Takekoshi, *Prince Saionji* (Eng. trans. 1933).

SAKEL, MANFRED JOSHUA (1900–1957), Austrian-born U.S. psychiatrist. Sometimes referred to as the "Pasteur of psychiatry," Sakel received his M.D. from the University of Vienna (1925) and in 1933 became research associate of the psychiatric clinic at the university. In 1937, he emigrated to the United States. Sakel's great contribution to psychiatry was his discovery, first reported in 1933, of insulin shock as a treatment for schizophrenia. It remained a standard therapy for many years. His books included *The Pharmacological Shock Treatment of Schizophrenia* (1935; Eng. trans. 1938) and *Schizophrenia* (1958).

SAKHAROV, ANDREI DMITRIYEVICH (1921–1989), Soviet physicist and social critic. Sakharov graduated from Moscow State University (1942), received his doctorate at age 26, and was the youngest scientist ever admitted to the Soviet Academy of Sciences (1953). His theoretical work, much of it done with physicist Igor Tamm, was largely responsible for the development of the Soviet hydrogen bomb. During the 1960s he emerged as an outspoken critic of the government and advocated civil liberties, scientific freedom, an end to the arms race, a rapprochement with the West, and the evolution of democratic socialism in the Soviet Union. A leader of the dissident movement, he cofounded the nongovernmental Human Rights Committee (1970) and was awarded the 1975 Nobel Peace Prize. In 1980 the Soviet government forced him out of his Moscow home and sent him into internal exile in the city of Gorky. After being allowed to return to Moscow by Soviet leader Mikhail Gorbachev (1986), he supported Gorbachev's policies of democratization and served in the Congress of People's Deputies (1989). Translations of his writings in English included *Progress, Coexistence and Intellectual Freedom* (1968), *Sakharov Speaks* (1974), *My Country and the World* (1975), *Alarm and Hope* (1978), and *Collected Scientific Works* (1982). ■ See his *Memoirs* (Eng. trans. 1990); Elena Bonner, *Alone Together* (Eng. trans. 1986); and George Bailey, *The Making of Andrei Sakharov* (1989).

SAKI. *See MUNRO, HECTOR HUGH.*

SAKMANN, BERT (1942–), German biophysicist. Sakmann studied at the University of Munich, did postdoctoral research at the University of London with Sir Bernard Katz (1971–73), received an M.D. from the University of Göttingen (1974), and did research at the Max Planck Institute

for Biophysical Chemistry in Göttingen (1973–89) and the Max Planck Institute for Medical Research in Heidelberg (1989–). Working with colleague Erwin Neher in the early 1970s, Sakmann confirmed the existence of ion channels, specialized protein molecules in the cell membrane that regulate the ability of cells to function and communicate. They developed a laboratory method, called the patch-clump technique, that utilized a tiny glass pipette fitted with a recording electrode to detect the electrical current that passes through a single ion channel. The technique revolutionized biological research as it led to new insights into the causes of diabetes, cystic fibrosis, epilepsy, and several disorders of the nervous and muscle systems. It enabled scientists to tailor drugs to act directly on the ion channel related to a specific disease. For their pioneering research Sakmann and Neher shared the 1991 Nobel Prize in Physiology or Medicine.

SALAM, ABDUS (1926–1996), Pakistani physicist. Trained at Cambridge University (Ph.D. 1952), Salam was a professor of physics at the University of London (from 1957) and director of the International Center for Theoretical Physics in Trieste, Italy (from 1964). He became the first Pakistani to win a Nobel Prize when he shared the 1979 award in physics with Sheldon L. Glashow and Steven Weinberg for work leading toward a unified-field theory of physics. Working independently, he advanced the "gauge theory" (1961), a system of equations that enabled scientists to compare seemingly diverse phenomena such as electromagnetism and the nuclear force known as "weak interaction." In this way he demonstrated a relationship between two of the four known basic forces in nature. He later attempted to unify the other two forces—the strong and gravitational interactions—into a common scheme. Salam worked toward advancing scientific training and research in developing countries.

SALAN, RAOUL ALBIN LOUIS (1899–1984), French general. A graduate of St. Cyr military academy (1919), Salan was a highly decorated soldier who served as commander in chief of French forces in Indochina and also in Algeria, where he was in charge of resisting agitation for independence during the late 1950s. Wary of Salan's popularity and anticipating his opposition to Algerian independence, Pres. Charles de Gaulle appointed Salan governor of Paris (1959–60). In 1960 Salan took refuge in Spain, and after he helped lead an abortive military rebellion in Algiers (1961), he became head of the clandestine OAS (Secret Army Organization). Apprehended in 1962, he was sentenced to life imprisonment but released after the 1968 amnesty. His rank, pension, and privileges were restored in 1982, and he was buried in Paris in the Invalides.

SALANDRA, ANTONIO (1853–1931), Italian political leader. Wealthy and conservative, Salandra was a professor of law at the University of Rome before being elected to parliament (1886). He subsequently held a series of cabinet posts and became premier in March 1914. Despite Italy's traditional alliance with Germany and Austria-Hungary, Salandra declared Italian neutrality at the outbreak of World War I. He bargained with the Allies for the acquisition of territory from Austria-Hungary and declared war on Austria (1915). He was forced to resign because of military reverses (1916) but was a delegate to the Paris Peace Conference (1919) and also served as a delegate to the League of Nations.

SALAZAR, ANTÓNIO DE OLIVEIRA (1889–1970), Portuguese political leader. A professor of economics at the University of Coimbra (from 1918), Salazar was named finance minister in 1928 and served as premier from 1932 to 1968. Influenced by Roman Catholic corporatism and Italian fascism, he wrote the constitution of 1933, which established an authoritarian corporative state. Salazar's National Union party became the only legal political organization. He supported Italy's Benito Mussolini and Spain's Francisco Franco but remained neutral during World War II and brought Portugal into the North Atlantic Treaty Organization (NATO) in 1949. During his rule, Portugal remained one of Europe's poorest and most backward countries. Salazar's last years were marked by the growth of clandestine political opposition and the beginnings of armed revolution in Portugal's African colonies. ■ See study by Hugh Kay (1970).

SALGADO, SEBASTIÃO (1944–), Brazilian photographer. Salgado received a doctorate in economics at the Sorbonne in Paris (1971) and worked for the International Coffee Organization in Africa (1971–73) before becoming a professional photographer. He was best known for his powerful black and white images that compassionately documented the exploitation and oppression of workers and peasants in the Third World. The photo collections *Other Americas* (1986) and *An Uncertain Grace* (1990) primarily depicted life in poor, remote, rural communities of Brazil. *Workers: An Archaeology of the Industrial Age* (1993) consisted of striking photos of manual labor that is slowly vanishing and included dramatic images of miners in the Serra Pelada opencast gold mine in Brazil. *Terra: Struggle of the Landless* (1997) depicted activities of the MST, the Brazilian land-occupation movement, with which Salgado was associated. His other books of photographs included *Migrations: Humanity in Transition* (2000) and *The Children: Refugees and Migrants* (2000).

SALINAS, PEDRO (1891–1951), Spanish poet and critic. A university professor for most of his life, Salinas was also a dedicated painter. His early lighthearted poems described subjects such as toy shops, fun houses, and geometric shapes. His graceful, conversational love poems elevated the commonplace, as in *My Voice Because of You* (1933; Eng. trans. 1976) and *Love's Reason* (1936). In the last volume published during his lifetime, *All Most Clear* (1949), Sali-

nas' playful tone suddenly vanishes; he views technology as a source of destruction. He continued this theme in the satirical novel *The Incredible Bomb* (1950). The posthumous collection *Confidence* (1954) seemed less fearful. Salinas, who also wrote literary criticism, lived in the United States after 1936. English translations of his poems appeared in *Lost Angel and Other Poems* (1938), *Truth of Two* (1940), *Zero* (1947), *To Live in Pronouns* (1974), and *Prelude to Pleasure* (1993). Translations of his lectures are in *Reality and the Poet in Spanish Poetry* (1966). ■ See study by John Crispin (1974).

SALINAS DE GORTARI, CARLOS (1948–), Mexican political leader. Salinas, whose father was a senator and government minister, studied politics and economics at the National University and at Harvard (Ph.D. 1978). He held high positions in the finance ministry and sponsored programs of economic liberalization as minister of budget and planning (1982–87). As president (1988–94) he privatized many state-owned businesses, cut protective tariffs, and negotiated the controversial North American Free Trade Agreement (NAFTA) with the United States and Canada. Shortly after he left office the Mexican currency collapsed, and in March 1995 his brother Raúl Salinas was arrested on charges of graft and homicide for having planned and ordered the assassination of José Francisco Ruiz Massieu, the secretary general of the ruling Institutional Revolutionary party (PRI) and a political rival of the Salinas brothers. Raúl denied the charges but Carlos was investigated for involvement in a cover-up, and he went into exile (1995), eventually settling in Ireland. He returned to Mexico (2000) to publicize his memoir, *Mexico: A Difficult Step Toward Modernity* (2000), in which he defended himself and his administration. ■ See Miguel A. Centeno, *Democracy Within Reason* (1994), and Philip L. Russell, *Mexico Under Salinas* (1994).

SALINGER, JEROME DAVID (1919–), U.S. novelist and short-story writer. Like his celebrated character Holden Caufield, J. D. Salinger was raised in New York City and had a sporadic academic record at various military schools and colleges. An infantryman in World War II, he accumulated five battle stars as well as material for early stories, many of which were first published in the *New Yorker*. After ten years' work he published *Catcher in the Rye* (1951), Holden Caufield's colloquial first-person campaign against phoniness, which set a style for youth in the 1950s. He also created the Glass family of hypersensitive geniuses, whom he housed in stories such as "A Perfect Day for Bananafish" (1948), *Franny and Zooey* (1961), and *Seymour: An Introduction* (1963). Salinger's most acclaimed stories are collected in *Nine Stories* (1953). He lived in seclusion in his later life and published little. ■ See biographies by James Lundquist (1979) and Paul Alexander (1999); Ian Hamilton, *In Search of J. D. Salinger* (1988); study by Warren French (1963; rev. ed. 1976); and the memoir by his daughter, Margaret A. Salinger, *Dream Catcher* (2000).

SALISBURY, HARRISON EVANS (1908–1993), U.S. journalist. After graduation from the University of Minnesota (1930), Salisbury went to work as a reporter for United Press, which posted him in London (1943) and Moscow (1944). He won a Pulitzer Prize (1955) after five years as the *New York Times* correspondent in Moscow (1949–54), returning to New York as a foreign-news editor. In 1966–67, Salisbury traveled to North Vietnam to report on the civilian casualties of U.S. bombing and wrote *Behind the Lines— Hanoi* (1967). His other works, which critics praised as engrossing and informative, included *The 900 Days* (1969), a history of the siege of Leningrad; *Black Night, White Snow* (1978), a dramatic presentation of the revolutions in Russia between 1905 and 1917; *Without Fear or Favor* (1980), a study of the *New York Times;* and *The Long March* (1985), an account of the 6,000-mile trek across China by Red army soldiers from 1934 to 1935. His last works were *Tiananmen Diary* (1989) and *The New Emperors* (1992). ■ See his autobiography, *Journey for Our Times* (1983), and memoir, *A Time of Change* (1988).

SALK, JONAS EDWARD (1914–   ), U.S. physician and virologist. The son of a Jewish New York City garment worker, Salk studied at City College (B.S. 1934) and New York University (M.D. 1939). He immediately immersed himself in research on dead viruses, studying their capacity to stimulate antibody production. While working at the University of Pittsburgh (1947–63), he developed the first effective polio vaccine—a series of four injections (1954). (Albert Sabin's live-virus oral vaccine later replaced this method.) Within a year, elimination of the devastating disease was within reach, and Salk's name became a household word. In 1963, he founded the Salk Institute for Biological Studies at La Jolla, California. In later years, Salk conducted research on multiple sclerosis, a degenerative disease of the nervous system, and on AIDS. He wrote about evolution and the philosophical implications of biological research in *Man Unfolding* (1972) and *The Survival of the Wisest* (1973). ■ See Richard Carter, *Breakthrough* (1967).

SALOMON, ERICH (1886–1944), German photographer. The son of a German-Jewish banker, Salomon earned a law degree (1913) but after 1927 began to practice photography. Wearing dinner clothes and using one of the new high-speed miniature cameras, he crashed diplomatic conferences and banquets, catching Europe's statesmen in "candid" moments of anger, pleasure, and fatigue. His photos, which appeared in magazines throughout Europe and the United States, created a sensation and inaugurated a new type of photojournalism. A collection of these photos was published as *Celebrated Contemporaries in Unguarded Moments* (1931). Salomon fled the Nazis (1932) to Holland but was arrested after the German occupation and sent to his death at Auschwitz concentration camp. ■ See photos in *Portrait of an Age* (1966).

SALVEMINI, GAETANO (1873–1957), Italian historian. Son of poor peasants, Salvemini began a new school of Italian historiography with his socialist-inspired studies of medieval Italian history. He also wrote *The French Revolution* (1905; Eng. trans. 1954) and a study of the Italian patriot *Mazzini* (1905; Eng. trans. 1957) before going into politics. After serving in parliament (1919–21), Salvemini was arrested for antifascist activity (1925) and fled to the United States, where he taught history at Harvard (1930–48). In exile he wrote several important works, including *The Fascist Dictatorship in Italy* (Eng. trans. 1927) and *Under the Axe of Fascism* (Eng. trans. 1936). He retired to Italy after World War II.

SAMPRAS, PETE (1971–   ), U.S. tennis player. The son of an aerospace engineer, Sampras started playing tennis at age 7 after his family moved to southern California. He dropped out of high school to turn professional (1988) and developed an aggressive serve-and-volley style of play that quickly catapulted him into the top ranks of men's tennis. With a serve clocked at 129 mph, Sampras became the youngest man ever to win the U.S. Open (1990). He subsequently won three more U.S. Opens (1993; 1995–96), seven Wimbledon championships (1993–95; 1997–2000), and two Australian Opens (1994; 1997), surpassing Roy Emerson's record of 12 Grand Slam titles. He earned a record $6.5 million in prize money during 1997, and in 1998 he became the first player to hold the number one ranking for six consecutive years.

SAMUELSON, PAUL ANTHONY (1915–   ), U.S. economist. Samuelson studied at Harvard (M.A. 1936; Ph.D. 1941) and taught at the Massachusetts Institute of Technology (1940–86). One of the best-known and influential economists of the post–World War II era, he refined the theories of British economist John Maynard Keynes and made major contributions to almost every area of economic research. He developed optimization models to analyze the economic behavior of firms, consumers, and governments as well as to study the conditions of international trade. He also made contributions to welfare economics, fiscal and monetary policy, and the study of capital, and was a major architect of the neoclassical synthesis. His textbook *Economics* (1948; 16th ed. with W. Nordhaus, 1998) influenced generations of mainstream economists and was translated into more than 20 languages. His other books included *Foundations of Economic Analysis* (1947; rev. ed. 1971) and *Collected Scientific Papers* (4 vols., 1966–78). He was awarded the 1970 Nobel Memorial Prize in Economics. ■ For a critique of his work see Marc Linder and Julius Sensat, *The Anti-Samuelson* (2 vols., 1977).

SAMUELSSON, BENGT INGEMAR (1934–   ), Swedish chemist. A student of Sune K. Bergstrom at the Karolinska Institute, Stockholm (Ph.D. in biochemistry, 1960; M.D.

1961), Samuelsson later taught there and was dean of the medical faculty (1978–83). Specializing in the study of prostaglandins—the versatile hormonelike structures that play important roles in protecting the body from disease, pain, injury, and stress—Samuelsson described the chemical processes in the body's use of prostaglandins, discovered several prostaglandin subtypes, and was the first to provide a detailed picture of arachidonic acid, the fatty acid from which prostaglandins are created. In recognition of his research he shared the 1982 Nobel Prize in Physiology or Medicine with Bergstrom and John R. Vane.

SANDBURG, CARL (1878–1967), U.S. poet. The son of Swedish immigrants, Sandburg quit school at age 13 and later served in the Spanish-American War. Although his first volume of poetry appeared in 1904, it was not until ten years later, when *Poetry* magazine published the free-verse masterpiece "Chicago," that Sandburg won critical recognition. *Chicago Poems* (1916), containing such poems as "Fog" and "Chicago," secured his reputation, but Sandburg remained a working journalist until 1945. He used blunt diction and popular jargon to express his romantic vision of a youthful, vigorous America and to urge social justice. *The People, Yes* (1936) was his epic salute to American democracy written in free verse and poetic prose. Sandburg's *Complete Poems* (1950) won a Pulitzer Prize. He also wrote the classics of biography, *Abraham Lincoln: The Prairie Years* (2 vols., 1926) and *Abraham Lincoln: The War Years* (4 vols., 1939; Pulitzer Prize). *Always the Young Strangers* (1953) is a memoir of boyhood. Sandburg's collected letters appeared in 1968. ■ See biographies by William Rogers (1970) and Penelope Niven (1991) and study by North Callahan (1970).

SANDE, EARL (1898–1968), U.S. jockey. The leading American jockey of the 1920s. Sande won 967 races (for purses of $3 million), including the Kentucky Derby three times (1923; 1925; 1930) and the Triple Crown (the Derby, Preakness, and Belmont Stakes; 1930). Man o' War, the most famous thoroughbred in racing history, was one of his mounts. Sande inspired Damon Runyon's poem, "A Handy Guy Like Sande." After his retirement he became a successful horse trainer.

SANDINO, AUGUSTO CÉSAR (1893?–1934), Nicaraguan guerrilla. The son of a coffee planter, Sandino joined a Liberal revolt (1926) and took to the hills in 1927 in opposition to the landing of U.S. Marines, conducting guerrilla skirmishes until the troops were withdrawn in 1933. His successful guerrilla tactics were later emulated by revolutionary movements throughout the world. Having gained the reputation throughout Latin America of a patriotic anti-imperialist, he was murdered by the national guard after laying down his arms. The Sandinista National Liberation Front, organized in his memory in 1961, came to power in 1979 by overthrowing the dictatorial regime of Anastasio Somoza. ■ See biography by Gregorio Selser (Eng. trans. 1982).

SANGER, FREDERICK (1918–   ), British molecular biologist. At Cambridge (Ph.D. 1943), where he spent his entire professional career, Sanger worked on the precise arrangement of amino acids in protein molecules, hoping to clarify the nature of many substances vital for biological functions, including enzymes, antibodies, and hormones. He won the 1958 Nobel Prize in Chemistry after deducing (1955) the structure of the crucial hormone insulin, which had been isolated earlier by F. G. Banting and C. H. Best. Sanger's research provided groundwork for the synthesis (1964) of insulin and for the resolution of more complex proteins by investigators such as John Kendrew and M. F. Perutz. In 1980 Sanger won a second Nobel Prize in Chemistry (shared with Walter Gilbert and Paul Berg) for determining the base sequences of nucleic acids. His research had a revolutionary effect in biology by enabling scientists to manufacture genetic material in the laboratory.

SANGER, MARGARET (Margaret Higgins; 1883–1966), U.S. social reformer. Trained as a nurse, Sanger founded and led the birth-control movement in the United States. Although harassed by the authorities, she published a radical feminist journal, *Woman Rebel* (1914), set up the first birth-control clinic (in Brooklyn, New York; 1916), and established the American Birth Control League (1921), which was later called the Planned Parenthood Association of America. A militant crusader for her cause, she lectured throughout the country, published numerous articles, and wrote several books, including *The Case for Birth Control* (1917), *Motherhood in Bondage* (1928), and *My Fight for Birth Control* (1931). She also helped establish the International Planned Parenthood Association (1953), and she espoused her cause in India and Japan. ■ See her autobiography (1938); biographies by Virginia Coigney (1969) and Madeline Gray (1979); and Ellen Chesler, *Woman of Valor* (1992).

SANTAMARIA, BARTHOLOMEW AUGUSTINE (1915–1998), Australian Roman Catholic activist. Born of Italian immigrant parents in Victoria, Santamaria became an activist for lay Catholic causes after he graduated from the University of Melbourne. He was the director of the National Secretariat of Catholic Action (1947–54), a group that encouraged lay support for pastoral work. A staunch anticommunist, Santamaria organized and directed (1943–57) the Catholic Social Movement to identify and expel suspected communists from labor unions and the Labour party. His actions in the mid-1950s, denounced by Labour party leader Herbert Vere Evatt, helped defeat Labour candidates on the federal level, split provincial labor parties, and helped prevent the Labour party from regaining power for almost two decades. Santamaria also headed the National Civic

Council (from 1957). His books included *The Price of Freedom* (1968), *Point of View* (1969), and the autobiography, *Against the Tide* (1981, rev. ed. as *Santamaria: A Memoir*, 1997). ∎ See Tom Truman, *Catholic Action and Politics* (1960).

SANTAYANA, GEORGE (1863–1952), Spanish-born philosopher and critic. A professor at Harvard (1889–1912), Santayana was a prolific and stylish writer who developed an extremely personal and idiosyncratic philosophy characterized by skepticism, materialism, and humanism. *The Sense of Beauty* (1896) was an important contribution to aesthetic theory. His masterwork, *The Life of Reason: Phases of Human Progress* (5 vols., 1905–06), was a critical study of human creativity, while his later works, *Scepticism and Animal Faith* (1923) and *The Realms of Being* (4 vols., 1927–40), dealt with the nature and types of reality. His novel *The Last Puritan* (1936) was a best-seller. ∎ See his autobiography, *Persons and Places* (3 vols., 1944–53); biography by John McCormick (1987); and studies by Mossie M. Kirkwood (1961) and Willard E. Arnett (1968).

SAPERSTEIN, ABRAHAM (1903–1966), British-born U.S. sports promoter. A social worker in Chicago's slums, Abe Saperstein organized (1927) and coached the all-black Harlem Globetrotters basketball team. Known for their tremendous basketball skill, dazzling ball handling, and hilarious antics, the Globetrotters played exhibitions in more than 80 countries and became the most famous basketball team in the world.

SAPIR, EDWARD (1884–1939), U.S. linguist and anthropologist. Born in Germany, Sapir studied American Indian linguistics and ethnology at Columbia University (Ph.D. 1909). He was a founder of linguistic anthropology and a pioneer in studies linking personality to culture. In *Time Perspective in Aboriginal Culture* (1916) he detailed how ethnographers could reconstruct cultural history in the absence of written records, thus refuting the prevailing ideas of various schools of evolutionary determinists. His important study *Language* (1921) introduced the concept of linguistic drift, the theory that grammatical change in language results from certain systematic trends in the history of a language or language family. Also a poet, essayist, and composer, Sapir headed the anthropological department at the Canadian National Museum (1910–25) and taught at the University of Chicago (1925–31) and Yale (1931–39). ∎ See biography by Regna Darnell (1990).

SAPRU, SIR TEJ BAHADUR (1875–1949), Indian political leader. An aristocratic Kashmiri Brahman, Sapru was a prominent lawyer who was a member of the imperial legislative council (1916–20) and was a law member of the viceroy's council (1920–23). He was a moderate reformer who acted as negotiator between the Indian nationalists and the British authorities and also between the Hindu and Mus-

lim factions in India. As a delegate to the Round Table Conferences in London (1930–32), he helped to bring about the Gandhi-Irwin Pact (1931). In 1944 Sapru headed a committee that investigated the Hindu-Muslim animosity and published a report opposing the partition of the two peoples.

SARAGAT, GIUSEPPE (1898–1988), Italian political leader. A socialist opponent of the fascists, Saragat spent the years from 1926 to 1943 in exile. After the war he was president of the constituent assembly (1946), which drew up Italy's republican constitution, and founded (1947) the anti-Communist Socialist Party of Italian Workers (later called the Italian Social Democratic party). After serving as deputy premier in several governments during the 1950s, he proposed an "opening to the left," which eventually (1962) enabled the government to form coalitions with left-wing socialists while isolating and excluding the Communists. Saragat served twice as minister of foreign affairs (1959–60; 1963–64) and once as president of Italy (1964–71) after a bitterly fought election. He was a strong supporter of the Atlantic Alliance and of a united Europe.

SARAMAGO, JOSÉ (1922–), Portuguese writer. Saramago was born into a poor peasant household and studied metalworking at a vocational school. Although he grew up in a home without books, he loved to read and write, and published a short novel at age 25. He wrote nothing else until the 1960s, when he published two volumes of poetry while working for a Lisbon publishing house. He joined the then illegal Communist party in 1969 and served as deputy editor of the left-wing Lisbon newspaper, *Diario de Noticias* (1974–75). After losing his job during an anti-Communist backlash, he returned to the novel and produced a string of remarkably imaginative, ironic, and compassionate works that explored basic themes of existence and human destiny. In these multifaceted allegorical works, Saramago limited orthodox punctuation, alternated between past and present tenses, and made frequent use of the supernatural and paradoxical. His best-known novels included *Baltasar and Blimunda* (1982; Eng. trans. 1987), *The Year of the Death of Ricardo Reis* (1984; Eng. trans. 1991), *The Stone Raft* (1986; Eng. trans. 1994), *The History of the Siege of Lisbon* (1989; Eng. trans. 1997), *The Gospel According to Jesus Christ* (1991; Eng. trans. 1994), *Blindness* (1995; Eng. trans. 1998), and *All the Names* (1998; Eng. trans. 2000). In 1998 he became the first Portuguese-language writer to win the Nobel Prize in Literature.

SARAZEN, GENE (Eugene Saraceni; 1902–1999), U.S. golfer. Sarazen rose from the ranks of caddies to become the first player to win all four major tournaments of professional golf: the U.S. Open (1922), British Open (1932), Masters tournament (1935), and Professional Golfers' Association (PGA) tourney (1922–23; 1933). An inventive shotmaker, he won 38 tournaments in all. Sarazen played on six U.S. Ryder Cup teams between 1927 and 1937 and lost only one individual match. His most dramatic win occurred in the 1935 Masters, when he tied Craig Wood by scoring a double eagle on the 15th hole in the last round and then won the play-off.

SARGENT, JOHN SINGER (1856–1925), U.S. painter. Sargent was born in Italy to American parents and spent most of his life abroad. He began to exhibit portraits at the Paris Salon in 1877, but after a scandal in 1884 over his portrait of the alabaster-shouldered Mme. Gautreau (*Madame X*), he moved to Britain and remained there for the rest of his life. Sargent's portraits of the British upper classes were a great success, but he considered portraiture "a pimp's profession" and dropped it in 1910 in favor of impressionistic landscape watercolors. He completed a commission to paint religious murals for the Boston Public Library in 1916; he then painted murals for Boston's Museum of Fine Art, which also has a substantial collection of Sargent's paintings. ■ See biographies by W. H. Downes (1925) and Charles M. Mount (1955); studies by Carter Ratcliff (1982) and Trevor Fairbrother (1994); and the study edited by Elaine Kilmurray and Richard Ormond (1998).

SARGESON, FRANK (1903–1982), New Zealand writer. One of his country's most distinguished and influential writers, Sargeson achieved fame for the short stories in *Conversations with My Uncle* (1936), *A Man and His Wife* (1940), and *That Summer and Other Stories* (1946). In them he satirized the puritanical and provincial attitudes of the native bourgeoisie. He frequently wrote from the viewpoint of society's dropouts and outcasts, using first-person narrative and a colloquial language that perfectly captured the spirit of the character. His highly praised novels, which further explored the ambiguities and paradoxes of life in New Zealand, included *I Saw in My Dream* (1949), *Memoirs of a Peon* (1965), *The Hangover* (1967), *Joy of the Worm* (1967), and *Man of England Now* (1972). ■ See his three volumes of memoirs, *Once Is Enough* (1973), *More Than Enough* (1975), and *Never Enough!* (1977); biography by Michael King (1995); and study by H. Winston Rhodes (1969).

SARIT THANARAT (1908–1963), Thai military and political leader. Born into a military family, Sarit was educated in military academies and became a professional soldier in 1929. He was first involved in politics in 1947, when he supported the coup d'état that overthrew the civilian government. By 1954 Sarit was the commander in chief of the Thai forces, and he served as deputy minister of defense (1951–57). In 1957 he led a coup that installed a military government and then promptly left the country for medical treatment. He returned a year later and assumed dictatorial powers. During his years as premier (1959–63), he carried out policies of rapid economic development and social reform and established close economic and military ties to the United States.

SARNOFF, DAVID (1891–1971), Russian-born U.S. business executive. Sarnoff achieved fame as a radio operator for the Marconi Wireless Telegraph Co. when he received the message from the world's largest ship, the S.S. *Titanic,* that it had hit an iceberg and was sinking (1912). An authentic rags-to-riches American success story, he rose through the ranks of the company, which was absorbed by the Radio Corp. of America (RCA) in 1919, and was elected its general manager (1921), president (1930), and board chairman (1947). He founded the National Broadcasting Co. (NBC, 1926), the first radio chain in the United States, and was a pioneer in television broadcasting during the 1940s. He was also the first to manufacture color TV sets and to transmit broadcasts (during the 1950s) in color. He retired from RCA in 1970. His son, Robert Sarnoff (1918–1997), served as NBC's president (1955–65) and RCA's president (1965–67), CEO (1967–70), and chair (1970–75). ■ See biographies by Carl Dreher (1977) and Eugene Lyons (1966) and Kenneth Bilby, *The General* (1986).

SAROYAN, WILLIAM (1908–1981), U.S. novelist and playwright. At age 26, Saroyan left his Armenian community in Fresno, California, for San Francisco and within a month he had produced and sold "The Daring Young Man on the Flying Trapeze" and 26 other pieces. Saroyan became an overnight sensation, going on to glorify the American dream in hundreds of stories, plays, and other works, including the popular song "C'mon-a My House," which was recorded by Rosemary Clooney and sold millions of copies. Characterized by the *New Yorker* as America's "greatest hit-and-run writer," Saroyan finished the play *The Time of Your Life* (1939) in six days, winning and refusing a Pulitzer Prize. His popularity waned, and he became identified principally with the novel *The Human Comedy* (1943); the movie adaptation was a hit. Saroyan's series of autobiographies began with *The Bicycle Rider in Beverly Hills* (1952); *Places Where I've Done Time* (1972) is a chronicle of aging. *My Name Is Saroyan: A Collection* (1983) appeared posthumously. ■ See studies by D. S. Calonne (1983) and Lawrence Lee and Barry Gifford (1984), and the account by his son, Aram Saroyan, *Last Rites* (1982).

SARRAUTE, NATHALIE (Nathalie Tcherniak; 1900–1999), Russian-born French novelist. A practicing lawyer until 1939, Sarraute was a proponent of the "new novel," also called the "antinovel." In her first book, *Tropisms* (1938; Eng. trans. 1964), consisting of 24 short pieces or "microdramas," she reacted against the traditional novel of plot and suspense. Instead she focused on tropism, which is a biological term for the constant small responses of an organism to a stimulus. Searching for the authenticity beneath the facade, she described the minute detailed changes in appearance and movement that reveal the unconscious. *The Use of Speech* (1980; Eng. trans. 1983) contained similar short works. Her psychological novels, in which distinctions between characters and between surface conversation and unspoken undercurrents are blurred, included *The Planetarium* (1959; Eng. trans. 1960). *The Golden Fruits* (1963; Eng. trans. 1980), *Do You Hear Them?* (1972; Eng. trans. 1973), and *"fools say"* (1976; Eng. trans. 1977). Her literary theory is presented in the essays in *The Age of Suspicion* (1956; Eng. trans. 1964). Her later works included the novels *You Don't Love Yourself* (1989; Eng. trans. 1990) and *Here* (1995; Eng. trans. 1997). ■ See her memoir *Childhood* (Eng. trans. 1984) and biography by Gretchen R. Besser (1979).

SARRIS, ANDREW (1928–), U.S. film critic. As an editor of the journal *Film Culture* (from 1955), Sarris was among the first film critics to treat experimental or underground films seriously. His articles acquainted American readers with the French critic André Bazin's auteur theory, which held that a director should be evaluated in terms of the thematic and stylistic development of his entire corpus. This generated a reappraisal of Hollywood films. Sarris edited the English-language version of *Cahiers du Cinéma,* reviewed films in the *Village Voice* (1960–89), and taught at Columbia University (1969–). He wrote *The Films of Josef Von Sternberg* (1966), *The American Cinema: Directors and Directions, 1929–1968* (1968), *Confessions of a Cultist* (1970), *Politics and Cinema* (1978), and *"You Ain't Heard Nothin' Yet," The American Talking Film: History and Memory, 1927–1949* (1998).

SARTON, GEORGE ALFRED LEON (1884–1956), Belgian-born U.S. historian of science. Sarton earned a Ph.D. in mathematics from the University of Ghent (1911) and left war-torn Europe in 1915 to pursue his lifelong study of the history of science in the United States. He lectured at Harvard (from 1916; professor 1940–51), wrote the massive *Introduction to the History of Science* (3 vols., 1927–47), founded and edited the journals *Isis* (1912) and *Osiris* (1936), and almost single-handedly established the field of the history of science as an academic discipline. His daughter was the novelist and poet May Sarton (1912–1995).

SARTRE, JEAN PAUL (1905–1980), French philosopher, novelist, dramatist, and critic. Sartre won international renown as a leading exponent of "existentialism," an oft-misunderstood philosophy of human freedom explored in his novel *Nausea* (1938; Eng. trans. 1949) and outlined in his treatise *Being and Nothingness* (1943; Eng. trans. 1956). Sartre founded (1945) *Les Temps Modernes,* a journal that exercised great influence in post–World War II intellectual circles. He attempted to reconcile Marxist political theory with his doctrine of heroic individualism in *Critique of Dialectical Reason* (1960; Eng. trans. 1976). An amazingly productive and versatile writer, Sartre published many noteworthy novels, plays, and critical works and a monumental biography of Gustave Flaubert, *The Family Idiot* (3 vols., 1971–72; Eng. trans., vol. 1, 1981). His autobiography, *Words,* appeared in 1964 (Eng. trans. 1964); in the same year he declined the Nobel Prize. He remained active in leftist politics until increasing blindness forced him to retire (1974). Sartre's *War Diaries* appeared in English in 1985. ■ See biographical introduction by Philip Thody (1972) and biography by Ronald Hayman (1987); studies by Hazel E. Barnes (1973), Peter Caws (1979), and Michael Scriven (1984); Simone de Beauvoir, *Adieux: A Farewell to Sartre* (1981; Eng. trans. 1984).

SASSOON, SIEGFRIED (1886–1967), British poet and novelist. Sassoon was born into a wealthy, artistically connected Anglo-Jewish family; he later converted to Roman Catholicism. During World War I, he was wounded and decorated for gallantry, then declared himself a pacifist and was promptly judged temporarily insane. He returned to the fighting and was wounded again. Out of his experiences and his lifelong aversion to war came the passionate and indignant, satirical war poetry of *Counterattack* (1918) and *War Poems* (1919). His fictionalized autobiography, *The Complete Memoirs of George Sherston* (3 vols., 1928–36), was a searing personal account of the war and its aftermath. He also wrote such candidly autobiographical volumes as *The Old Century and Seven More Years* (1937), *The Weald of Youth* (1942), and *Siegfried's Journal* (1945). ■ See studies by Michael Thorpe (1966) and Sanford Steinlicht (1993).

SASSOON, VIDAL (1928–), British hairstylist. Apprenticed to a hairdresser at age 14. Sassoon opened a small Bond Street (London) salon at age 26. Here he developed his technique of blow-drying hair and introduced the blunt cut. A decade later the Sassoon cut—short at the back and long at the sides—caused a sensation at a 1963 Mary Quant press show. Sassoon innovated both long and short hairstyles in the 1960s, all of which required little if any styling. He demystified the beauty parlor and credited his hairdressers when their styles appeared in the press. He also developed new hair-care products and styling tools and opened salons in six countries. Sassoon wrote *Sorry I Kept You Waiting Madam* (1968).

SATIE, ERIK ALFRED (1866–1925), French composer. Satie was a rare musical humorist, a whimsical classically trained intellectual who lived in self-imposed suburban Paris poverty after 1898. He wrote two surrealist ballets (*Parade,* 1917; *Mercure,* 1924); a collection of piano pieces (*Three Pieces in the Form of a Pear,* 1903; *Three Flabby Preludes,* 1912, to be played, according to his instructions, "sheepishly" or "with astonishment"); and a serious work for four sopranos and chamber orchestra, *Socrate* (1919). His simple, objective, and antiromantic music influenced the development of neoclassicism and the group of French composers known as "The Six." English translations of his literary works are in *The Writings of Erik Satie* (1980). ■ See the study by Rollo H. Myers (1948) and Robert Orledge, ed., *Satie Remembered* (1995).

SATO, EISAKU (1901–1975), Japanese political leader. Of samurai descent and the younger brother of former Premier Nobusuke Kishi, Sato joined the civil service immediately after college (1924). He rose slowly, became a protégé of Premier Shigeru Yoshida, and served in several cabinet posts in the 1950s and 1960s as a leader of the Liberal Democratic party. As Japan's longest-term premier (1964–72), Sato promoted his country as a major economic and political power, regained Japanese sovereignty over Okinawa and the Ryukyu Islands, and normalized relations with South Korea. In 1974 Sato shared the Nobel Peace Prize (with Sean MacBride) for curbing the spread of nuclear weapons (by signing the nonproliferation treaty) and for improving relations among nations of the Pacific.

SAUNDERS, CLARENCE (1881–1953), U.S. business executive. He started his career in the grocery business as a four-dollar-a-month clerk (1895) and by 1915 was a successful Memphis, Tennessee, wholesaler. The following year he revolutionized the industry by opening the first modern supermarket. Called King Piggly Wiggly, the store featured a continuous aisle where customers selected their own groceries, rather than the traditional counter where shoppers lined up to be served by a clerk. Barrels were replaced by individually wrapped packages. Saunders patented the store's layouts, fixtures, and fittings. Capitalizing on low prices and the novelty of the idea, he built a highly profitable chain of 1,200 Piggly Wiggly stores in 29 states before he was bankrupted by Wall Street manipulations in 1924.

SAUSSURE, FERDINAND DE (1857–1913), Swiss linguist. A specialist in Indo-European philology, Saussure taught at the School of Advanced Studies in Paris (1881–1891) and at the University of Geneva (1901–13). His pioneering book, *Course in General Linguistics* (1916; Eng. trans. 1959), composed of lecture notes edited posthumously by two of his students, was a milestone of 20th-century linguistics and a guidepost for the structuralist movement. In it he treated language as a structured, social phenomenon made up of mutually defining components. He also introduced the contrasting terms "synchronic" and "diachronic," and "langue" and "parole" to the study of linguistics, and was the first to propose the modern study of semiotics. ▪ See studies by E.F.K. Koerner (1973) and Jonathan Culler (1976).

SAVAGE, MICHAEL JOSEPH (1872–1940), New Zealand labor and political leader. Born in Australia, Savage was forced to leave school at age 14. He held several blue-collar jobs and emigrated in 1907 to New Zealand, where he became a trade-union leader and a founder of the Labour party (1916); he was elected to Parliament in 1919. In 1935 Savage was elected prime minister and headed New Zealand's first Labour government. Serving until his death, he remained popular as a "common man" and active social reformer, having introduced the 40-hour workweek, public housing, farm-price stabilization, and social security. ▪ See John A. Lee, *Simple on a Soap Box* (1964); Bruce M. Brown, *The Rise of New Zealand Labour* (1962); and Barry Gustafson, *From the Cradle to the Grave* (1986).

SAVIO, MARIO (1943?–1996), U.S. political activist. In 1964, Mario Savio emerged as a leader of the Free Speech Movement (FSM) at the University of California at Berkeley. A forerunner of the antiwar movement, FSM emerged during a dispute over students' right to display political literature on campus that grew into a conflict about educational reform and, in a larger sense, about freedom and responsibility in society. The dispute climaxed on Dec. 3, 1964, when campus and city police made the largest mass arrest in U.S. history up to that time—the first such action on a U.S. university campus. Subsequent court proceedings entered legal records as *People of California* v. *Mario Savio, and 571 Others*. Then a 22-year-old philosophy major from Queens, New York, who had been active in the civil-rights movement, Savio inspired protesters with denunciations of dehumanizing educational and social practices. He left school to become a full-time political activist. At age 40, Savio graduated Phi Beta Kappa from San Francisco State University (1984) and undertook graduate study in physics. He continued to speak out, and on the 20th anniversary of FSM urged students at Berkeley to protest U.S. actions in Central America. He subsequently taught math and philosophy at several colleges in California. ▪ See his *The Free Speech Movement and the Negro Revolution* (1965; with Raya Dunayevskaya).

SAWCHUCK, TERRY (**Terrance Gordon Sawchuck; 1929–1970**), Canadian ice-hockey player. The long career of Terry Sawchuck, the player who made the goalie's crouch famous, was disrupted by severe injuries and mental breakdowns. Nevertheless, in 20 seasons with Detroit, Chicago, and Boston he compiled a record 103 career shutouts, won the Vezina Trophy (for outstanding goaltender) four times, and was named to the All-Star team seven times. In four straight seasons at Detroit, opponents averaged under two goals per game. Sawchuck died at age 40 from a freak injury suffered in a scuffle with a teammate.

SAYERS, DOROTHY LEIGH (1893–1957), British novelist and playwright. One of Oxford's first women graduates (1915), Sayers began writing her famous mysteries to support her son, whose birth in 1924 was kept secret and who was raised by a cousin. Sayers wrote numerous brilliantly plotted, extremely literate detective novels, such as *Murder Must Advertise* (1933) and *The Nine Tailors* (1934), which were noted for their use of classical quotations and allusions. Her detective, the aristocratic, nonchalant, erudite Lord Peter Wimsey, was modeled on an Oxford professor. After 1949, she concentrated on writing religious plays and essays and scholarly translations of Dante. ■ See Janet Hitchman, *Such a Strange Lady* (1975), and biographies by Ralph E. Hone (1979), Nancy M. Tischler (1979), David Coomes (1992), and Barbara Reynolds (1993).

SAYYAB, BADR SHAKIR AL- (1926–1965), Iraqi poet. Sayyab graduated from the Teachers' Training College in Baghdad (1948) and worked as a civil servant and journalist. The most famous of the post–World War II left-wing Arabic poets, he was influential in spreading a new form of Arabic verse that differed from traditional Arabic meters. He started as a romantic poet, turned to socialist realism, but became disillusioned with communism and wrote symbolist poetry. He was influenced by the British poet T. S. Eliot and made extensive use of Arabic mythology in his verse. English translations of his works are in *Poems* (1986). ■ See Terri De Young, *Placing the Poet* (1998).

SAZONOV, SERGEI DMITREYEVICH (1861–1927), Russian political figure. Serving Czar Nicholas II as foreign minister (1910–16), Sazonov pursued a policy of close relations with France and Britain, but his Balkans policy increased tensions between Russia and Austria. After the assassination (1914) of Austrian archduke Francis Ferdinand, he advised the czar to implement a general, not partial, mobilization of Russian troops. That decision precipitated the crisis that led to Russia's disastrous participation in World War I. His advocacy of Polish autonomy as part of a postwar settlement led to his dismissal. Sazonov later emigrated to Paris (1917), where he served the antibolshevik cause during the years (1918–20) of the Russian civil war. ■ See his memoirs, *Fateful Years* (Eng. trans. 1928).

SCHACHT, HJALMAR HORACE GREELEY (1877–1970), German financier. Born in Denmark and raised in New York, where his father was a merchant, Schacht gained a reputation as a financial wizard for his efforts to stem Germany's post–World War I inflation. Appointed president of the Reichsbank (1923), he helped finance reconstruction before resigning (1930) in opposition to reparations. He supported the Nazis (from 1931), and after they came to power, he resumed his position at the Reichsbank (1933)—and was minister of economy (1934–37) as well, until dismissed in 1939 for opposing the huge military expenditures. He survived the war to found a Düsseldorf bank and act as financial consultant to developing nations. ■ See his autobiography, *Confessions of "the Old Wizard"* (Eng. trans. 1955); biography by Edward N. Peterson (1954); and study by Amos E. Simpson (1969).

SCHALLY, ANDREW VICTOR (1926–), Polish-born U.S. medical researcher. Schally left Poland after the German invasion (1939) and received his scientific training at the National Institute for Medical Research, London, and at McGill University, Montreal (Ph.D. in biochemistry, 1955). He shared the 1977 Nobel Prize in Physiology or Medicine

(with Roger Guillemin and Rosalyn Yalow) for his discovery and synthesis of hormones, produced by the hypothalamus, which regulate the pituitary gland and thus control body chemistry. His research, conducted while he was at the Baylor Medical School (1957–62) and at the New Orleans Veterans Hospital and Tulane University (from 1962), revolutionized the study of brain function. ■ See Nicholas Wade, *The Nobel Duel* (1981).

SCHAPIRO, MEYER (1904–1996), Lithuanian-born U.S. art historian. A professor at Columbia University (1928–73) and the New School for Social Research (1938–52), Schapiro wrote authoritatively on topics ranging from classical and early Christian art to modern abstraction and exerted a great influence on artists as well as scholars. Although he was the leading Marxist critic of the 1930s and early 1940s, his later work emphasized the autonomy of art as a realm of creative freedom. He was a prominent member of New York's anticommunist left-wing intelligentsia for decades. His selected papers are in *Romanesque Art* (1977), *Modern Art: Nineteenth and Twentieth Centuries* (1978), *Late Antique, Early Christian and Mediaeval Art* (1979), *Theory and Philosophy of Art: Style, Artist and Society* (1994), and *Worldview in Painting: Art and Society* (1999). Additional writings are in *Words, Script and Pictures: Semiotics and Visual Language* (1996) and *Impressionism: Reflections and Perceptions* (1997).

SCHÄRF, ADOLF (1890–1965), Austrian political leader. A lifelong socialist, Schärf was a political activist from his student days at the University of Vienna. He served briefly in parliament (1933–34) but spent most of the years prior to and during the German occupation as a leader of the socialist underground movement and was frequently jailed. After World War II, as vice-chancellor (1945–57) and president (1957–65), he helped rebuild Austria's parliamentary system, championed Austrian neutrality, and strongly supported the coalition of the conservative People's party and the Socialist party.

SCHAWLOW, ARTHUR LEONARD (1921–1999), U.S. physicist. While a researcher at the Bell Telephone Laboratories, Schawlow and his brother-in-law, the physicist and 1964 Nobel laureate Charles H. Townes, did fundamental work in quantum electronics that led to the development of the first practical laser. At Stanford University (1961–91) Schawlow continued his research and shared the 1981 Nobel Prize in Physics (with Kai Siegbahn and Nicolaas Bloembergen) for contributing to the development of laser spectroscopy. With Townes, he wrote the classic work *Microwave Spectroscopy* (1955).

SCHECHTER, SOLOMON (1847–1915), Rumanian-born Jewish scholar and theologian. Schechter studied in Vienna and Berlin before emigrating to Britain, where he taught rabbinic literature, Talmud, and Hebrew at Cambridge University (from 1890) and University College, London (from 1899). While doing research in the old synagogue in Cairo (1896), he discovered in its *geniza*—a repository for sacred manuscripts—thousands of ancient Hebrew and Arabic documents that revolutionized the study of Middle Eastern Jewish history. Schechter emigrated to New York City and served as president of the Jewish Theological Seminary (1902–15), which he helped to establish as a world center of Jewish scholarship. He was the formulator and chief spokesman of Conservative Judaism in the United States and founded the United Synagogue of America (1913). His books included *Studies in Judaism* (3 vols., 1896–1924) and *Some Aspects of Rabbinic Theology* (1909). ■ See biography by Norman Bentwich (1938) and Bernard S. Mandelbaum, ed., *The Wisdom of Solomon Schechter* (1963).

SCHEIDEMANN, PHILIPP (1865–1939), German political leader. A lifelong Social Democrat who edited his party's newspaper and was elected to the Reichstag in 1903, Scheidemann took the initiative in the disorders after World War I to proclaim a German republic (Nov. 9, 1918), later known as the Weimar Republic. He served as its first chancellor but resigned (1919) after five months in protest against the Treaty of Versailles. Scheidemann then returned to parliament (1920), became mayor of his hometown, Kassel, and survived a rightist assassination attempt (1922). He fled the country after the Nazis came to power (1933). ■ See his memoirs, *The Making of New Germany* (1928; Eng. trans. 1929).

SCHENCK, JOSEPH M. (1878–1961), Russian-born U.S. film executive. Entering the entertainment business as a co-owner (with his brother Nicholas) of several amusement parks, Schenck became interested in motion pictures and was a pioneer in the new industry. As an independent producer during World War I, Schenck helped develop the "star" system and introduced such screen luminaries as Buster Keaton, Fatty Arbuckle, and Constance and Norma Talmadge. He served as chairman (1924) and president (1927) of United Artists Corp., was a founder of Twentieth Century Pictures (1933), and was chairman of Twentieth Century-Fox (1935–52).

SCHENCK, NICHOLAS M. (1881–1969), Russian-born U.S. film executive. An associate (with his brother Joseph) of theater owner and film producer Marcus Loew, Nicholas Schenck became president of Loew's Inc. upon Loew's death (1927) and was a founder and president of Metro-Goldwyn-Mayer (1927–55), the world's largest film company. Known as "the General," Schenck controlled an entertainment empire that employed 12,000 people, and he exerted a major influence in the movie industry for more than 30 years.

SCHENDEL, ARTHUR VAN (1874–1946), Indonesian-born Dutch writer. Schendel's early romantic novels were set in medieval Italy, but after he moved to Italy (1920), he wrote realistic novels on Dutch themes. Humankind's tragic fate is the recurring motif of his celebrated works *The Johanna Maria* (1930; Eng. trans. 1935), *The Waterman* (1933; Eng. trans. 1963), *The House in Haarlem* (1935; Eng. trans. 1940), and *Grey Birds* (1937; Eng. trans. 1939). Set in the 19th century, these novels masterfully presented the Dutch character and landscape, and he was regarded as the greatest Dutch prose writer of the first half of the century. The historical novel *John Company* (1932; Eng. trans. 1983) is about the early East Indies trade.

SCHERCHEN, HERMANN (1891–1966), German conductor. Scherchen was a self-taught musician who championed contemporary composers. He made his conducting debut with the Berlin Philharmonic in 1911, toured with Arnold Schoenberg, and founded a society for new music in 1918. After fleeing the Nazis in 1933, he edited the *Musica Viva* journal in Brussels (1933–36), conducted throughout Europe and the United States, and played a major role in the development of serial and electronic music in Europe. He wrote *The Handbook of Conducting* (1929; Eng. trans. 1956) and *The Nature of Music* (1946; Eng. trans. 1950).

SCHIAPARELLI, ELSA (1890?–1973), Italian-born French fashion designer. Born into a prominent intellectual family in Rome, Schiaparelli opened (1929) a small salon in Paris and established a reputation with her novelty sweaters, sportswear, and separates. In an era of subdued elegance, Schiaparelli created daring and colorful fashions in a style that became known as "hard chic"; her 1931 collection of angular designs, featuring exaggerated shoulders and small waists, caused a sensation. Schiaparelli was the first couturiere to open a boutique (1935). Salvador Dali, Jean Cocteau, and other artists designed avant-garde fabrics for her stunning line. Schiaparelli was deliberately and consistently outrageous; "shocking pink" was her trademark. She was the first to experiment with synthetics and to introduce serendipitous touches and accessories to high fashion. She spent the World War II years in the United States, opened a New York salon in 1949, and retired in 1954. ■ See her autobiography, *Shocking Life* (1954).

SCHICK, BÉLA (1877–1967), Hungarian-born U.S. pediatrician. Schick taught (1902–23) at the University of Vienna before emigrating (1923) to the United States. He published important studies of allergies and childhood diseases, including *Scarlet Fever* (1912) and *Child Care Today* (1933), but he is best known for introducing (1913) the Schick test, a skin test that indicates susceptibility to diphtheria. ■ See biography by Antoni Gronowicz (1954).

SCHIELE, EGON (1890–1918), Austrian painter. Schiele studied at the Vienna Academy of Fine Arts (1906–09), leaving because his Gustav Klimt–influenced style was adversely criticized. A founder-member of the New Art Group (1909), Schiele concentrated on painting the human body in sharp lines with accents of intense color. The eroticism of his male and female nudes led to a brief arrest for painting immoral pictures. After World War I, during which he worked as a war artist, Schiele attracted international notice when he presented his nudes and dreamlike landscapes at the 1918 Vienna Secession exhibition. He died a few months later, at age 29, in the Spanish influenza epidemic that spread across Europe. A large retrospective exhibition of his work in 1975 enhanced critics' appreciation of his paintings and especially his drawings. ▪ See studies by Erwin Mitsch (1975), Simon Wilson (1980), and Frank Whitford (1981).

SCHIFF, DOROTHY (1903–1989), U.S. publisher. Born into a New York Jewish investment-banking family, Schiff got involved in social-welfare work during the 1930s and shed her family's Republican party affiliation to become an active Democrat and a supporter of Pres. Franklin D. Roosevelt's New Deal policies. She used her inheritance to acquire majority control of the *New York Post* in 1939. Under her personal management (1939–77), the *Post* became a tabloid but retained its liberal character and its impressive array of columnists, including Drew Pearson, Eleanor Roosevelt, Sylvia Porter, and, for a time, Schiff herself (1951–58). In 1977 she sold the newspaper to Australian publisher Rupert Murdoch. ▪ See Jeffrey Potter, *Men, Money and Magic* (1976).

SCHIFF, JACOB HENRY (1847–1920), German-born U.S. banker and philanthropist. Born into a wealthy German-Jewish family, Schiff emigrated to the United States (1865), joined the investment-banking house of Kuhn, Loeb and Co. (1873), and became head of the firm in 1885. Through the financing of railroads (notably in partnership with E. H. Harriman), Schiff became one of America's most powerful bankers and a major rival of J. P. Morgan. Internationally he floated bonds for the governments of Mexico and China and helped finance Japan's war against Russia (1904–05). Although he opposed Jewish nationalism and advocated Jewish assimilation in America, he actively supported Jewish philanthropies and cultural institutions and founded the Semitic Museum at Harvard (1903) and financed the Semitic departments at the New York Public Library and the Library of Congress. ▪ See study by Cyrus Adler (1928).

SCHLAFLY, PHYLLIS (Phyllis Stewart; 1924–   ), U.S. political activist. The president of the Illinois Federation of Republican Women (1960–64). Schlafly wrote numerous books espousing ultraconservative views, including her first, *A Choice Not an Echo* (1964), which endorsed the presidential candidacy of Sen. Barry Goldwater. *The Gravediggers* (1964; with Chester C. Ward) accused the Democratic decision makers of giving a military advantage to the Soviet Union, and *Safe—Not Sorry* (1967) identified communists as instigators of 1967 ghetto uprisings. Although she was a three-time loser for a U.S. congressional seat from Illinois, she was best known for her successful 10-year (1972–82)

campaign against the Equal Rights Amendment (ERA), during which she organized pressure groups, spoke throughout the country, and published the *Phyllis Schlafly Report* to rally public opinion against the proposed constitutional amendment. After the amendment was defeated (because it was not passed by three-fourths of the state legislatures by June 30, 1982) Schlafly led her 50,000-member Eagle Forum organization in campaigns against sex education, the nuclear freeze, and feminist influences in textbooks. Her other books included *Kissinger on the Couch* (1975), *The Power of the Positive Woman* (1977), *Ambush at Vladivostok* (1978), *Pornography's Victims* (1987), and *First Reader* (1994). ▪ See Carol Felsenthal, *The Sweetheart of the Silent Majority* (1981).

SCHLEICHER, KURT VON (1882–1934), German general. A Prussian general with political ambitions, Schleicher was defense minister in the 1932 cabinet of Franz von Papen, whom he outmaneuvered and succeeded as chancellor of the Weimar Republic (December 1932). Denied permission by Pres. Paul von Hindenburg to assume emergency powers in order to establish a military government and prevent Nazi leader Adolf Hitler from taking power, Schleicher resigned in January 1933 and was replaced by Hitler. He was murdered by the Nazis during the "night of the long knives" (June 30, 1934) when many of Hitler's opponents were killed.

SCHLESINGER, ARTHUR MEIER (1888–1965), U.S. historian. Born in Ohio to German-immigrant parents, Schlesinger earned a Ph.D. (1918) from Columbia University, where he was influenced by Charles Beard's progressive school and by the pressures of urban life. Defining history "not merely as past politics" but "as inclusive as life itself," Schlesinger established the first course in U.S. social and cultural history while teaching at the University of Iowa (1919–24). At Harvard (1924–54) he created a Ph.D. program in the history of American civilization. His books included *Colonial Merchants and the American Revolution* (1918) and *New Viewpoints in American History* (1922). He co-edited a 13-volume *History of American Life* (1927–48), of which he wrote the volume *The Rise of the City* (1933). ▪ See his autobiography, *In Retrospect* (1963).

SCHLESINGER, ARTHUR MEIER, JR. (1917–   ), U.S. historian. The son of a Harvard historian, Schlesinger graduated summa cum laude from Harvard in 1938 and published his best-selling *Age of Jackson,* for which he won a Pulitzer Prize, at age 28. During the 1950s, while teaching at Harvard, he wrote his comprehensive *Age of Roosevelt,* (3 vols., 1957–60). A politically active liberal Democrat, he served as special assistant to Presidents John F. Kennedy and Lyndon Johnson (1961–64). Schlesinger's memoir of the Kennedy administration, *A Thousand Days* (1966), won another Pulitzer Prize. He was a professor at the City University of New York (1966–94). He also wrote *The Imperial*

Presidency (1973), *Robert Kennedy and His Times* (1978), and *The Cycles of American History* (1986). *Disuniting America: Reflections on a Multicultural Society* (1992; rev. ed. 1998) attacked ethnocentric views of U.S. history and those who denied the importance of a common culture as a factor in the American past. ■ See his autobiography, *A Life in the 20th Century* (2000), and the study by Stephen P. Depoe (1994).

SCHLESINGER, JOHN (1926–   ), British film director. Born in London and educated at Oxford, Schlesinger began his film career with the British Broadcasting Corporation and made an award-winning 1961 documentary for British Transport Films. *After Billy Liar* (1963) and *Darling* (1965), both of which were well received, Schlesinger traveled to the United States to direct the highly successful *Midnight Cowboy* (1968; Academy Award). Back in London he directed *Sunday, Bloody Sunday* (1971), a sensitive study of a sexual triangle. Later films included *The Day of the Locust* (1975), *Marathon Man* (1976), *Yanks* (1979), *An Englishman Abroad* (1983), *The Falcon and the Snowman* (1984), *Madame Sousatzka* (1988), and *The Innocent* (1993). He also served as associate director of the National Theatre in London (from 1973).

SCHLIEFFEN, ALFRED VON (1833–1913), German general. A Prussian professional soldier, Schlieffen dealt with the problem of a two-front war as chief of the General Staff (1891–1905). In 1905 he proposed a plan to strike first in the West with a strong right-wing flanking movement through Belgium and northern France, and then to confront Russia. "Make the right wing strong," his last words were reputed to have been. Failure to do this in 1914 condemned the Germans to years of costly trench warfare during World War I, but a modified version of the Schlieffen plan succeeded for the Germans at the outset of World War II in 1940. ■ See Gerhard Ritter, *The Schlieffen Plan* (Eng. trans. 1958).

SCHMELING, MAXIMILIAN (1905–   ), German boxer. Better remembered as a German boxer fighting to uphold the Nazi "superman" image than for his boxing prowess. Max Schmeling won the German middleweight and light-heavyweight titles as an amateur before turning professional (1925). In 1930 he won the world heavyweight crown from Jack Sharkey on a controversial foul in an elimination tournament for the title vacated by Gene Tunney. At home, rising political leader Adolf Hitler called him a model of the Aryan superman. In 1932, Schmeling lost the crown to Sharkey in a rematch. Known for his powerful punch and endurance, Schmeling was the first man in professional boxing to defeat prizefighter Joe Louis (1936); he was knocked out by Louis in the first round of a rematch (1938). Schmeling was wounded in World War II. After the war he taught boxing and was an executive at the Coca-Cola bottling works at Essen.

SCHMIDT, BERNHARD VOLDEMAR (1879–1935), Estonian-born astronomer. Schmidt, a staff member of the Hamburg Observatory (from 1926), devised numerous mirror designs and developed (1930) the Schmidt telescope and camera. His optical system, featuring a correcting plate to eliminate spherical distortion, revolutionized astronomical photography by increasing the field of vision and sharpening the image. His instrument proved valuable in celestial observation, as well as in other technical fields such as television projection.

SCHMIDT, HELMUT HEINRICH (1918–   ), West German chancellor. Son of a Hamburg schoolteacher, Schmidt studied political economy after World War II military service and entered Social Democratic politics in 1946. A tough, efficient pragmatist who was first elected to the Bundestag in 1953, he rose through the West German cabinet from defense minister in 1969 to finance minister in 1972 and chancellor in 1974, maintaining a strict law-and-order policy against the threat of domestic disorder. As chancellor, Schmidt sought to parlay his country's growing economic strength into a stronger voice within the Western alliance. While seeking more help from the United States to counter the Soviet bloc's advantage in conventional weapons, he also supported the SALT negotiations. As the economy faltered in 1982, the Free Democratic party pulled out of the ruling coalition and Schmidt fell from power. He subsequently served as senior editor (1983–   ) and publisher (1985–89) of *Die Zeit*. His books included *The Anachronism of National Strategy* (Eng. trans. 1986). ■ See his memoirs, *Men and Powers* (1987; Eng. trans. 1989), and biography by Jonathan Carr (1985).

SCHMIDT, MAARTEN (1929–   ), Dutch-born U.S. astronomer. Schmidt's studies of the faint starlike objects called "quasi-stellar radio sources," or quasars, established that they are more distant from Earth than any other known object and are receding at more than 25,000 miles per second, a greater velocity than that of any other object. His work greatly influenced theories of the origin and age of the universe. He was associated with the California Institute of Technology (1959–96) and the Hale observatories (1959–80; director, 1978–80).

SCHMIDT-ROTTLUFF, KARL (**Karl Schmidt;** 1884–1976), German painter and woodcut artist. While an architecture student in Dresden, Schmidt-Rottluff helped found (and named) Die Brücke (1905), a community of revolutionary artists who introduced expressionism into German art. Influenced by fauvism, cubism, and African sculpture, Schmidt-Rottluff utilized vivid, dissonant colors and jagged forms in works such as *Self-Portrait with Monocle* (1910) and *Rising Moon* (1912). His powerful woodcuts, such as *Road to Emmaus* (1918), helped to revive the art in the 20th century. He remained active after Die Brücke disbanded (1913) and taught at the Prussian Academy of Art (1931–

33), but his work was banned by the Nazis and he was forbidden to paint. After World War II he taught at the Berlin Academy of Fine Arts.

SCHNABEL, ARTUR (1882–1951), Austrian pianist. An authority on Beethoven and the German classical masters, Schnabel was a legendary artist who was acclaimed as "the high priest of intellectual musicianship." He lived in Berlin (1910–33), but, as a Jew, was forced to leave when the Nazis came to power. He emigrated to the United States in 1939. During his long international concert career, in which he specialized in the music of Brahms and Schubert and which included several cycles of the complete Beethoven sonatas, he eschewed all showmanship, even refusing encores. Schnabel also composed atonal music, including three symphonies, and was a greatly sought-after teacher of piano. ■ See his memoirs, *My Life and Music* (1961); study by César Saerchinger (1957); and Konrad Wolff, *The Teaching of Artur Schnabel* (1972).

SCHNEERSON, MENACHEM MENDEL (1902–1994), U.S. religious leader. Born in the Ukraine, Schneerson was a descendant of the founder of Lubavitch (or Habad) Hasidism, a sect of Orthodox Judaism. He displayed great intellectual ability and religious erudition as a youth and joined the personal entourage of the Lubavitcher rebbe (spiritual leader) during the 1920s. After fleeing religious persecution in the Soviet Union (1929), he married the rebbe's daughter and lived in Western Europe, where he studied physics and engineering at the University Berlin and the Sorbonne, in Paris. He emigrated to the United States (1941) and succeeded his father-in-law as the Lubavitcher rebbe (1951). From his headquarters in Brooklyn, New York, he organized educational and outreach programs aimed at nonobservant Jews and created a dynamic and fast-growing worldwide movement that became a major force in modern Judaism. The charismatic Schneerson met frequently with his followers, in both public and private sessions, to offer guidance on spiritual and nonreligious matters. In the years prior to his death many of his followers believed him to be the messiah.

SCHNEIDER, EUGENE (1868–1942), French industrialist. The grandson of the founder of the vast Schneider-Creusot armaments works, Schneider headed the company from 1898 and was one of Europe's richest, most powerful men. He was a leading figure in the Comité des Forges, which controlled French iron and steel production, and founded (1920) the Union Européenne Industrielle et Financière, which controlled 182 French arms companies and 230 arms works outside of France, including a 56 percent share of the Skoda works in Czechoslovakia. He was also a member of the Chamber of Deputies (1900–25) and influenced public opinion through his control of two Paris dailies, *Le Temps* and *Journal des Débats*.

SCHNEIDER, HERMAN (1872–1939), U.S. educator. A civil engineer and professor at the University of Cincinnati (from 1903), Schneider established a work-study program in 1905 to help his students reconcile theory with practice. This was widely imitated by progressive institutions, and Schneider, subsequently dean of engineering (1906–29; 1932–39) and president (1929–32) at Cincinnati, was hailed as "the father of cooperative education." His books included *Education for Industrial Workers* (1915) and *The Problem of Vocational Guidance* (1938). ■ See Clyde W. Park, *Ambassador to Industry* (1943).

SCHNEIDERMAN, ROSE (1882–1972), U.S. labor leader. After emigrating from Poland with her family (1890), Schneiderman worked as a stitcher in a cap factory and was influential in getting women admitted to the Jewish socialist United Cloth Hat and Cap Makers Union. She played a key role in the growth of the International Ladies Garment Workers Union (ILGWU), was the eastern organizer (1917–19) of the Women's Trade Union League, and served as president (1918–49) of its New York branch. She successfully lobbied for the eight-hour day and minimum-wage laws. Probably the most widely known woman in the American trade-union movement, she became president of the National Women's Trade Union League (1926), participated in the development of New Deal programs as a member of Pres. Franklin D. Roosevelt's brain trust, and served as secretary of the New York State Department of Labor (1937–44). ■ See her autobiography, *All for One* (1967).

SCHNITTKE, ALFRED (1934–1998), Russian composer. The son of a German-born Jewish father and a Volga-German Catholic mother, Schnittke was born in a small town on the Volga River but was first exposed to classical music in Vienna (1946–48), where his father worked for a German-language Soviet newspaper. As a student (1953–61) and later teacher (1962–72) at the Moscow Conservatory, he experimented with serialism, the modernist Western 12-tone compositional technique that was denounced by Soviet cultural authorities. By the late 1960s he developed a new idiosyncratic style, "polystylistics," which synthesized themes and techniques from many different musical styles and periods of musical history. Incredibly prolific, he wrote symphonies and concertos as well as ballets, choral music, and film scores. Among his best-known works were Suite in the Old Style for Violin and Piano (or harpsichord) (1972), Quartet No. 2 for Strings (1980), Concerto for Viola and Orchestra (1985), Concerto No. 1 for Cello and Orchestra (1985–86), and the operas *Life with an Idiot* (1992) and *Historia* (1995). He came to be regarded as the most innovative Soviet composer, and his works were performed throughout the world during the 1980s and 1990s. ■ See biography by A. Ivashkin (1996).

SCHNITZLER, ARTHUR (1862–1931), Austrian writer. A practicing physician (M.D., University of Vienna, 1885),

Schnitzler wrote technical articles dealing with psychotherapy and infused his plays with insights from the growing psychological literature of his time. His sparklingly witty early plays, including *Anatol* (1893; Eng. trans. 1911), *Light-O'-Love* (1896; Eng. trans. 1929), *Reigen* (1897; Eng. trans. as *Merry Go Round*, 1953; and *Dance of Love*, 1965; filmed in French as *La Ronde*, 1950), and *Intermezzo* (1906; Eng. trans. 1915), dealt with love, sex, marriage, self-deception, and fidelity among the turn-of-the-century Viennese. In his novellas *None but the Brave* (1901; Eng. trans. 1926) and *Fraülein Else* (1924; Eng. trans. 1925) he developed the techniques of the inner monologue and stream of consciousness. His last novella, *Flight into Darkness* (1931; Eng. trans. 1931), depicted a man's descent into madness, while the play *Professor Bernhardi* (1912; Eng. trans. 1913) and the autobiographical novel *The Road to the Open* (1908; Eng. trans. 1923) dealt with anti-Semitism. ∎ See the English translations in *Viennese Novelettes* (1974) and *My Youth in Vienna* (1970) and studies by Sol Liptzin (1932), Martin Swales (1971), and Reinhard Urbach (Eng. trans. 1973).

SCHOBER, JOHANN (1874–1932), Austrian political leader. As head of the Austrian police during the turmoil of 1918 at the end of World War I, Schober prevented bloodshed by declaring allegiance to the new republican government. He served as chancellor in 1921–22, a period of constitutional reform, again in 1929–30, and as vice-chancellor and foreign minister in 1930–32, when his negotiations for an Austro-German customs union were blocked by France.

SCHOENBERG, ARNOLD (1874–1951), Austrian composer. Schoenberg's early compositions (*Verkärte Nacht*, 1899, and the monumental *Gurrelieder*, 1900–11) were written in a romantic style, but he soon moved into unfamiliar modes, adopting the 12-tone row in 1921 as a means of organizing atonality. His method had a revolutionary effect on modern music, and was further developed by his students Alban Berg and Anton Weber. A Jew, he was dismissed by the Nazis from his Berlin teaching position in 1933, and he moved to California, where he taught. He composed in every genre, from the concerto to chamber music and the symphony, culminating in his unfinished opera, *Moses und Aron* (1930–51). He wrote *Style and Idea* (Eng. trans. 1950) and *Structural Functions of Harmony* (Eng. trans. 1954). ∎ See biographies by H. H. Stuckenschmidt (Eng. trans. 1959) and Willi Reich (Eng. trans. 1971), and Dika Newlin, *Schoenberg Remembered* (1980).

SCHOLEM, GERSHOM GERHARD (1897–1982), Jewish scholar. Born in Berlin, Scholem became a Zionist and completed his doctoral thesis on an early cabalistic text (1922). Emigrating to Palestine, he taught at the Hebrew University where he developed the field of Jewish mysticism with his studies of gnosticism and cabalism. His many translated works included *Major Trends in Jewish Mysticism* (1941), *The Messianic Idea in Judaism* (1971), *Sabbatai Sevi: The Mystical Messiah* (1973), *Kabbalah* (1974), and *On Jews and Judaism in Crisis* (1976). ∎ See his memoir, *From Berlin to Jerusalem* (1980), and studies by David Biale (1979) and Joseph Dan (1988).

SCHOLES, MYRON S. (1941–), Canadian-born U.S. economist. Scholes studied finance at the University of Chicago School of Business (Ph.D. 1969) with Merton Miller and subsequently taught there (1973–83) and at Stanford University (1983–96). While teaching at the Massachusetts Institute of Technology (1968–73), he collaborated with mathematician Fischer Black (1938–95) and economist Robert C. Merton in devising a mathematical formula, known as the Black-Scholes model, for measuring the worth of stock options. The formula, published in 1973, transformed modern finance and led to the explosive growth of options trading. Subsequent modifications of the formula set in motion the enormous international market in derivatives, financial instruments whose value is linked to price fluctuations of other assets, such as stocks, bonds, and commodities. For their groundbreaking work, Scholes and Merton shared the 1997 Nobel Memorial Prize in Economics. In 1998, Long Term Capital Management, a hedge fund (specializing in speculative high-risk trades in securities around the world) that was cofounded by Scholes and Merton, nearly collapsed. The fund, and its superrich investors, were saved only after the Federal Reserve Bank of New York arranged a controversial bailout via a cash infusion of $3.6 billion put up by a consortium of banks and brokerage houses.

SCHOLLANDER, DON (1946–), U.S. swimmer. Schollander broke several U.S. and world freestyle records in the early 1960s and in 1963 was the first to swim 200 meters in less than two minutes. In Tokyo in 1964, he became the first swimmer in Olympic history to win four gold medals: he set a world mark in the 400-meter freestyle and an Olympic record in the 100-meter freestyle event; he also won medals for the 400- and 800-meter relay events. He subsequently set several world records and won a silver medal in the 1968 Olympics. Schollander later studied law at Yale University and wrote *Deep Water* (1971).

SCHRIEFFER, JOHN ROBERT (1931–), U.S. physicist. While a doctoral student of Nobel laureate John Bardeen at the University of Illinois, Schrieffer worked with Leon Cooper, a postdoctoral researcher, on the phenomenon of superconductivity of metals. Together they formulated a theoretical model (1957) that explained how at extremely low temperatures resistance to electrical currents in certain metals disappears. The BCS theory, named after the three scientists, was considered one of the major advances of

20th-century physics, and Schrieffer, Bardeen, and Cooper shared the 1972 Nobel Prize in Physics. Schrieffer taught at the University of Pennsylvania (1962–79), the University of California, Santa Barbara (1980–91), and Florida State University, Tallahassee (1992–   ), and wrote *Theory of Superconductivity* (1964).

SCHRÖDER, GERHARD (1944–   ), German political leader. Born into an impoverished family in Lower Saxony, Schröder was forced to leave school at age 14 in order to work. He completed college preparatory studies at night and did not get his law degree until 1978. A radical activist in the Social Democratic Party (SPD), he was the national chairman of the Young Socialists (1978–80) and, advocating more moderate policies, was elected to the Bundestag (1980–86). After serving as minister-president (governor) of the state of Lower Saxony (1990–98), he was elected chancellor (1998) as head of a government coalition with the Green Party. He defeated Helmut Kohl and he was the first Social Democratic chancellor in 14 years. Schröder's policies of cutting taxes for business and reducing spending for social programs dismayed many of his supporters, as did his support for NATO's bombing campaign against Serbia during the Kosovo crisis (1999). Consequently, Schröder was weakened politically and the SPD lost several local elections.

SCHRÖDINGER, ERWIN (1887–1961), Austrian physicist. Born and educated in Vienna, Schrödinger succeeded Max Planck as professor at the University of Berlin (1927). Building on L. V. de Broglie's theory of wave mechanics of the atom, he developed (1926) a crucial wave equation that described the behavior of elementary particles. This equation is a basic part of quantum mechanics. He shared the 1933 Nobel Prize in Physics with Paul Dirac for this work. Opposed to the Nazi regime, he left Germany (1933) and then Austria after the Nazis took over (1938). He settled in Ireland, where he taught at the Dublin Institute for Advanced Studies (1940–56) before returning to Vienna in 1956. ■ See study by William T. Scott (1967).

SCHULLER, GUNTHER (1925–   ), U.S. composer. The son of a New York Philharmonic violinist, Schuller played horn with the Cincinnati Symphony (1943–45) and the Metropolitan Opera (1945–59). He was self-taught as a composer, devising a "third stream" fusion of jazz and conventional techniques. He strongly supported "new" music as president of the New England Conservatory (1967–77) and as the artistic director of the Tanglewood Music Center (1974–84). His musical works included *Symphony* (1965), *American Triptych* (1965), *Poems of Time and Eternity* (1972) String Quartet No. 3 (1986), and *Of Reminiscences and Reflections* (1994; Pulitzer Prize). Schuller wrote *Horn Technique* (1962), *Early Jazz: Its Roots and Musical Development* (1968), and *The Compleat Conductor* (1997). ■ See his book, *Musings: The Musical Worlds of Gunther Schuller* (1986).

SCHULTZ, THEODORE WILLIAM (1902–1998), U.S. economist. The head of the department of economics at the University of Chicago (1946–72). Schultz was a leading agricultural economist who stressed the primacy of human resources over traditionally defined physical capital in economic production. The first to show how investments in education can affect agricultural productivity, he also studied the role of health and disease in economic development. In *Transforming Traditional Agriculture* (1964), Schultz argued against the emphasis on industrial development in Third World countries and advocated instead improving the agricultural base. He shared (with Sir Arthur Lewis) the 1979 Nobel Prize in Economics.

SCHULZ, CHARLES MONROE (1922–2000), U.S. cartoonist. In 1950 Schulz, a freelancer, sold his comic strip *Peanuts* to United Features Syndicate and went on to become one of the world's most popular cartoonists. Characterized by a simplicity of drawing style and humor, the strip grew slowly but surely in popularity and became a national vogue in the 1960s, appearing in more than 900 newspapers and prompting the manufacture of greeting cards, toys, sweat shirts, and even bed linen. Numerous *Peanuts* books were published (from 1952), and several *Peanuts* television specials appeared, including "A Charlie Brown Christmas" (1966; Emmy Award). A musical based on the strip, *You're a Good Man, Charlie Brown,* opened in New York in 1967. The strip, in which no adults ever appear, has a cast of child and animal characters: the frequently defeated, all-enduring Charlie Brown; the spiteful Lucy; the philosophical, blanket-toting Linus; and the indefatigable beagle, Snoopy.

SCHUMACHER, KURT ERNST KARL (1895-1952), German political leader. The political editor (1920) of the newspaper of the Social Democratic party (SPD), Schumacher opposed extremists of the left and right. He served in the Prussian diet (1924–31) and the Reichstag (1930–33) before being incarcerated by the Nazis (1933–43). After the war he reorganized the SPD (1945), became its chairman (1946), and built it up into West Germany's second-largest party, refusing to compromise with the Communists. He narrowly lost the 1949 elections and as the leader of the opposition, agitated for an independent, reunited, and democratic Germany and opposed the Schuman Plan as well as German membership in a European army. ■ See study by Lewis Edinger (1965).

SCHUMAN, ROBERT (1886–1963), French political leader. Born into a prosperous Lorraine family, Schuman grew up in Metz, then under German rule, and was educated in German universities. He served in the national assembly as a conservative member of the Catholic Popular Democratic party from 1919 to 1940, when he was arrested by the Gestapo. Schuman escaped from prison (1942) and subsequently fought in the French Resistance. After the war, as finance minister (1946), premier (twice: 1947–48), and foreign minister (1948–52), he was the leading spokesman for Franco-German rapprochement and European economic and political unity. He proposed (1950), with Jean Monnet, the Schuman Plan, which led to the formation of the European Coal and Steel Community (1952) and eventually to the establishment of Euratom (1958) and the Common Market (1958). Although he served as president of the Common Market's European Parliamentary Assembly (1958–60), little progress was made toward European political integration.

SCHUMAN, WILLIAM HOWARD (1910–1992), U.S. composer. A graduate of Columbia University Teachers College (B.S. 1935; M.A. 1937), Schuman was an innovator in music education who taught at Sarah Lawrence College (1935–45) before becoming president of New York's Juilliard School of Music (1945–62) and head of the Lincoln Center for the Performing Arts (1962–69). The best known of his energetic and accessible musical compositions were Symphony No. 3 (1941), Secular Cantata No. 2: *A Free Song* (1943; Pulitzer Prize), *New England Triptych* (1956), and Symphony No. 8 (1962). ■ See study by Flora R. Schreiber and Vincent Persichetti (1954).

SCHUMANN-HEINK, ERNESTINE (Ernestine Rössler; 1861–1936), Austrian opera and concert singer. Schumann-Heink, who made her operatic debut in Dresden in 1878, was a dramatic contralto who achieved great success at the Bayreuth Wagner Festival and at New York's Metropolitan Opera in the pre–World War I era. She became a U.S. citizen in 1905. In her later years she gave lieder recitals, made radio broadcasts, and at age 75 appeared in a Hollywood film, *Here's to Romance*. In her 1932 Metropolitan farewell she sang in Wagner's Ring cycle. ■ See biography by Mary Lawton (1928).

SCHUMPETER, JOSEPH ALOIS (1883–1950), Austrian-U.S. economist. One of the century's foremost political economists, Schumpeter taught at Graz (1911–14) and Bonn (1925–32) before arriving in the United States, where he taught at Harvard (1932–50). He was influenced by Marxist economics and theorized that the innovative forces in capitalism would create unstable business cycles that would ultimately result in the evolution of capitalism into socialism. However, he viewed social classes and imperialism in a broad social and political framework and not exclusively in economic terms. His best-known works were *The Theory of Economic Development* (1912; Eng. trans. 1934), *Imperialism and Social Classes* (1919–27; Eng. trans. 1951), *Business Cycles* (2 vols., 1939), *Capitalism, Socialism and Democracy* (1942), and *History of Economic Analysis* (1954). ■ See study edited by Seymour Harris (1951) and Nicolo De Vecchi, *Entrepreneurs, Institutions and Economic Change* (Eng. trans. 1995).

SCHURMAN, JACOB GOULD (1854–1942), Canadian-born U.S. educator and diplomat. Schurman studied philos-

ophy in Europe, taught at Cornell University (from 1886) and was a founder of the *Philosophical Review* (1892). As president of Cornell (1892–1920), he raised academic standards and increased the size of the campus and the university's enrollment. He took leave to chair the U.S. Philippines Commission (1899) and to serve as U.S. minister to Greece and Montenegro (1912–13). He later served as U.S. minister to China (1921–25) and ambassador to Germany (1925–30).

SCHUSCHNIGG, KURT VON (1897–1977), Austrian political leader. The minister of justice and education (1934), Schuschnigg became chancellor after the assassination of Engelbert Dollfuss (1934). An extremely controversial figure, he sought to maintain Austrian independence from Nazi Germany but was accused of paving the way for the Nazi occupation by his authoritarian policies and his steady yielding to German demands. After he announced, in defiance of German dictator Adolf Hitler, a plebiscite on the question of Austrian unification with Germany (March 1938), Hitler demanded Schuschnigg's immediate resignation, and German troops entered Austria unopposed. Schuschnigg was arrested, spent seven years in prison, and later lived and taught in the United States (1948–67) before returning to Austria. His books included *The Brutal Takeover* (1969; Eng. trans. 1971). ■ See biography by R. K. Sheridan (1942).

SCHUSTER, MAX LINCOLN (1897–1970), Austrian-born U.S. publisher. Cofounder of Simon & Schuster publishers, Schuster began a journalism career as a *New York Evening World* copyboy. He graduated (1917) from Columbia University School of Journalism, and worked as Washington correspondent for United Press. With the publication of a crossword-puzzle book (1924), Schuster and Richard Leo Simon inaugurated the publishing house later known for paperback and "how to" books, including Dale Carnegie's best-seller *How to Win Friends and Influence People* (1938). The firm developed "planned publishing," assigning book ideas to writers instead of soliciting manuscripts, and published such diverse authors as Albert Einstein, Will Durant, Arthur Murray, Robert Ripley, and Eddie Cantor. Schuster edited the bestselling *Treasury of the World's Great Letters* (1940) and remained a dominant figure in the publishing industry until his retirement in 1966.

SCHWAB, CHARLES MICHAEL (1862–1939), U.S. industrialist. Although he began his career in Andrew Carnegie's main steel plant as an unskilled laborer, Schwab quickly worked his way up and was named general superintendent (1889). A supersalesman and promoter, he acted as an intermediary between Carnegie and J. P. Morgan in the transaction that created the U.S. Steel Corp. (1901) and made Schwab the firm's first president. After a management dispute (1903), he resigned and organized the Bethlehem Steel Corp. (1904). Profiting from the increased militarism early in the century and huge World War I contracts, he built Bethlehem into one of the largest corporations in the industry. Reportedly worth $200 million at the height of his career, he speculated in unsuccessful ventures and died insolvent. ■ See Robert Hessen, *Steel Titan* (1975).

SCHWARTZ, DELMORE (1913–1966), U.S. writer and critic. Schwartz was a New York poet and frequenter of Greenwich Village taverns who attracted critical attention with the publication of the poem "Choosing Company" (1936) and the volume *In Dreams Begin Responsibilities* (1938). His poems were witty and cerebral. The youngest poet to win the Bollingen Prize for Poetry (1959), he was affiliated with various universities and also with the *Partisan Review* (1943–55) and the *New Republic* (1955–57). His works included *Vaudeville for a Princess* (1950), *Summer Knowledge: New and Selected Poems, 1938–1958* (1959), and *Successful Love and Other Stories* (1961), as well as posthumous editions of his poems (1967), essays (1970), and letters (1984). ■ See biography by James Atlas (1977) and Elizabeth Pollet, ed., *Portrait of Delmore: Journals and Notes of Delmore Schwartz, 1939–1959* (1986).

SCHWARTZ, MELVIN (1932–), U.S. physicist. Schwartz studied physics at Columbia University (Ph.D. 1958) and remained there as a professor until 1966. With colleagues Jack Steinberger (his former professor) and Leon Lederman, he performed (1960–62) a landmark experiment that generated the first artificial beam of neutrinos, subatomic particles with no electrical charge and no detectable mass. Neutrino beams subsequently became a widely used tool in particle research, particularly in the study of the "weak" nuclear force that influences radioactive nuclear decay. The experiment also revealed a hitherto unknown type of neutrino, whose existence subsequently led to the formation of the "standard model" theory describing the fundamental particles that are the components of all matter. For their research, Schwartz, Lederman, and Steinberger shared the 1988 Nobel Prize in Physics. Schwartz taught at Stanford University (1966–83); was the chief executive of Digital Pathways (1979–91), a computer company that he founded in California; and was a professor at Columbia University (1991–).

SCHWARZENBERGER, GEORG (1908–1991), German-born British legal scholar. Schwarzenberger, who earned a law degree from the University of Tubingen (1930) and a doctorate from the University of London (1936), was secretary (1934–43) and later director (from 1943) of the Institute of World Affairs in London. A member of the faculty of the University of London (1938–75), he proposed "power politics," the title of his 1941 book, as a working theory of international relations. He wrote many other books, including *A Manual of International Law* (6th ed. 1976), *International Law and Order* (1971), and *The Dynamics of International Law* (1976).

SCHWARZENEGGER, ARNOLD (1947–), Austrian-born U.S. actor. The son of a village police chief, Schwarzenegger became obsessed with bodybuilding as a teenager and in 1967, at age 20, he became the youngest man ever to win a Mr. Universe title. He went to the United States (1968) and became the most successful professional bodybuilding competitor, winning the Mr. World, Mr. Universe (five times), and Mr. Olympia (seven times) titles before retiring in 1980. His appearance in the documentary film *Pumping Iron* (1977) led to starring roles in the fantasy adventure films *Conan the Barbarian* (1982) and *Conan the Destroyer* (1984) and the science-fiction spectacular *The Terminator* (1984), which were huge international box-office hits. In spite of, or because of, his limited acting ability and his heavily accented deadpan delivery, he became a Hollywood superstar and one of the most popular personalities in the world. His macho image was enhanced with starring roles in *Total Recall* (1990), *Terminator 2: Judgment Day* (1991), and *True Lies* (1994), but he also appeared in such comedies as *Twins* (1988), *Kindergarten Cop* (1990), and *Junior* (1994). Schwarzenegger, who became a naturalized U.S. citizen in 1983, also wrote several books on bodybuilding and served as chair of the President's Council on Physical Fitness and Sports (1990).

SCHWARZKOPF, DAME ELISABETH (1915–), German-British opera and concert singer. For three decades after her professional debut in Berlin (1938). Schwarzkopf's light, lyric soprano lent itself with distinction to leading roles in operas by Mozart and Strauss staged by major companies throughout Europe. She was for years a principal with the Vienna State Opera and at La Scala, Milan, and she also won critical acclaim as a lieder singer and exponent of the songs of Hugo Wolf. She sang at London's Covent Garden during the late 1940s and was married to British record company executive Walter Legge (1953–79). Schwarzkopf's reputed Nazi sympathies delayed her American recital debut until 1953, and her opera debut until 1955, when she sang the Marschallin in a San Francisco Opera production of *Der Rosenkavalier*. In the same role, she made her Metropolitan Opera (New York) debut in 1964. ■ See biography by Alan Jefferson (1996).

SCHWARZSCHILD, KARL (1873–1916), German astronomer. Director of observatories at the University of Göttingen (1901–09) and at Potsdam (1909–16), Schwarzschild did pioneering work in many areas of astronomy. He was the first to measure a star's brightness by photography and the first to use a coarse grating in a telescope. He was also the first to describe the role of radiation in the transport of heat in the outer layers of the stars. He helped develop Niels Bohr's theory of atomic spectra and Albert Einstein's general theory of relativity, and he predicted the gravitational or Schwarzschild radius around high-density objects (or black holes).

SCHWEITZWER, ALBERT (1875–1965), Alsatian-German scholar, musician, and medical missionary. Schweitzer, the son of a Lutheran pastor, studied and taught philosophy and theology at the University of Strasbourg (Ph.D. 1899) and established his international reputation with *The Quest of the Historical Jesus* (1906; Eng. trans. 1910). He was also a world-famous organist and an expert on the life and music of Johann Sebastian Bach, whose biography he wrote in 1905 (Eng. trans. 1911). Inspired by a personal ethical philosophy he called "reverence for life," he abandoned his careers at age 30, studied medicine (M.D. 1913), and established a hospital (and later a leper colony) at Lambaréné in French Equatorial Africa (now Gabon). He remained there for most of his life, treating thousands of African patients and gaining a reputation as one of the world's leading humanitarian figures. He was awarded the 1952 Nobel Peace Prize for his work. His other books included *Civilization and Ethics* (1922; Eng. trans. 1923) and the autobiographical *On the Edge of the Primeval Forest* (1920; Eng. trans. 1922) and *Out of My Life and Thought* (1932; Eng. trans. 1933). ■ See studies by Norman Cousins (1960; 1985), Gerald McKnight (1964), and James Brabazon (1975); and biography by G. Marshall and D. Poling (2000).

SCHWIMMER, ROSIKA (1877–1948), Hungarian feminist and pacifist. Schwimmer cofounded *Feministak Egyesulete* (1904), a Hungarian feminist-pacifist organization that agitated for social reform, including women's suffrage. At the outbreak of World War I, Schwimmer appealed to U.S. Pres. Woodrow Wilson to work toward a negotiated settlement, inspired Henry Ford's peace ship expedition (1915), and organized peace conferences in neutral nations. As Hungarian ambassador to Switzerland (1918–19), she was one of modern Europe's first woman diplomats. In 1920, Schwimmer fled Hungary's anti-Semitic regime and emigrated to the United States. When she sought U.S. citizenship (1926), the Supreme Court ruled against her petition, upholding the government's conclusion that her pacifism conflicted with the naturalization bureau's requirement of willingness to "take up arms" in defense of the Constitution. Schwimmer stayed in the United States as an alien, carrying on her pacifist activities and becoming a pioneer advocate of world government.

SCHWINGER, JULIAN SEYMOUR (1918–1994), U.S. physicist. A professor at Harvard (1945–72) and the University of California at Los Angeles (from 1972), Schwinger, made theoretical assertions that were crucial in the development of the quantum theory of radiation. Combining principles of relativity and quantum theory, he worked out a mathematical formulation that clarified the interaction between charged particles and an electromagnetic field. His mathematical analysis explained a discrepancy between actual observed electron mass and the mass that had been theoretically predicted by earlier physicists (particularly by P.A.M. Dirac, who had opened the field of relativistic quantum mechanics in 1927). Schwinger demonstrated that the Dirac theory had predicted the mechanical mass, not the total mass. For this work, he shared the 1965 Nobel Prize in Physics with Richard P. Feynman and Shinichiro Tomonaga. His books included *Quantum Kinematics and Dynamics* (1970), *Particles, Sources and Fields* (2 vols., 1970–73), and *Einstein's Legacy* (1986).

SCHWITTERS, KURT (1887–1948), German artist and writer. Schwitters identified with the iconoclastic dadaists who, disillusioned by World War I, sought to undermine traditional aesthetic and social values. Scavenging the debris of middle-class life, he gradually constructed (1920–36) a giant, three-dimensional structure that he called a "Merz" building. (The magazine he edited from 1923 to 1932 also had the nonsense word "Merz" as a title.) This trash construction filled Schwitters' Hanover home when it was destroyed during World War II, but some of his collages and wordless phonetic poems survived. A second Merz building was destroyed by a fire (1951), and a third was never completed. Schwitters fled Germany (1937) when the Nazi regime condemned his work, moving to Norway and then Britain. ■ See study by Kate Steinitz (1968); Dorothea Dietrich, *The Collages of Kurt Schwitters* (1993); Jerome Rothenberg and Pierre Joris, *Poems, Performance Pieces, Proses, Plays, Poetics: Kurt Schwitters* (1993); and biography by Gwendolyn Webster (1997).

SCOPES, JOHN THOMAS (1900–1970), U.S. teacher and geologist. Scopes was in his first year as a biology teacher and athletic coach in the Dayton, Tennessee, public schools when he was tried (1925) for violating the state law forbidding the teaching of evolution, as opposed to the biblical account of creation. He sat quietly during the famous "monkey trial" while lawyers William Jennings Bryan for the prosecution and Clarence Darrow for the defense argued one of the thornier questions of the era. Scopes was convicted and fined $100. In 1927 the verdict was overturned on a technicality. Scopes later went off to the Caribbean as an oil-company geologist. The law under which he was tried was repealed in 1967. ■ See his memoir, *Center of the Storm* (1967); D. C. Ipsen, *Eye of the Whirlwind* (1973); and Edward J. Larson, *Summer for the Gods* (1997).

SCORSESE, MARTIN (1942–   ), U.S. film director. Scorsese was raised in New York City's Little Italy and aspired to become a priest. Although he switched his interest to filmmaking while studying at New York University (B.S. 1964; M.A. 1966), faith and guilt were subsequently major themes of many of his most important films. His highly personal realistic works, which explored the inner conflicts of his characters, were praised for their creative camera work and editing and for their imaginative blending of music and image. Scorsese's best-known films, *Mean Streets* (1973), *Taxi*

Driver (1976), *Raging Bull* (1980), and *Goodfellas* (1990), examined aspects of crime and violence in American society. His other movies included adaptations of Nikos Kazatzakis' *Last Temptation of Christ* (1988) and Edith Wharton's *The Age of Innocence* (1993); a biography of the Dalai Lama, *Kundun* (1997); and a story of a tormented night-shift paramedic in New York City, *Bringing Out the Dead* (1999).

SCOTT, FRANCIS REGINALD (1899–1985), Canadian poet and political leader. Frank Scott was among the Montreal group of poets who in the 1920s promoted modernism in Canadian poetry. His satires, nature lyrics, and love poems appeared in *Overture* (1945), *Events and Signals* (1954), and *The Eye of the Needle* (1957), and his metaphysical works in *Signature* (1964) and *Selected Poems* (1966). A committed socialist, he cofounded the Cooperative Commonwealth Federation party in the 1930s and was its national chairman (1942–50). He was an expert on constitutional law and civil liberties, taught (1928–64) law at McGill University, and published several works on Canadian law and social planning. His *Essays on the Constitution* (1977) and *Collected Poems* (1981) both won Governor General Awards. ■ See S. Djwa and R. Macdonald, *On F. R. Scott: Essays on His Contributions to Law, Literature and Politics* (1983), and biography by Sandra Djwa, *The Politics of the Imagination* (1987).

SCOTT, GEORGE C. (1927–1999), U.S. actor. Scott was raised in rural Appalachia and industrial Detroit. He served four years in the marines (1945–49) before studying at the University of Missouri, where he appeared in student theatrical productions. He won his first critical acclaim as *Richard III* at the New York Shakespeare Festival in 1957, then proved himself a caustic, forceful film actor in *Anatomy of a Murder* (1959) and *The Hustler* (1961). A dedicated professional with a battered face and gravelly voice, Scott excelled as both the satiric Gen. Turgidson in *Dr. Strangelove* (1963) and as the flamboyant, charismatic *Patton* (1970; Academy Award). He scored another critical and popular success in *Hospital* (1971), won a TV Emmy Award for his performances in *The Price* (1971) and *Twelve Angry Men* (1997), starred in the film *Movie Movie* (1978), and directed several Broadway shows.

SCOTT, JAMES BROWN (1866–1943), Canadian-born U.S. educator and legal scholar. Educated at Harvard (B.A. 1890), Scott was the organizer and dean of the Los Angeles Law School (1896–99) and of the University of Illinois Law School (1899–1903). He was the founder of the American Society of International Law (1906) and founded and edited its *American Journal of International Law* (1907–24). He helped establish the Carnegie Endowment for International Peace (1910; permanent secretary, 1911–40), the American Institute of International Law (1915; president, 1915–40), and the Academy of International Law (1914). He was also solicitor for the Department of State (1906–10) and was a delegate or adviser to numerous international conferences including the Paris Peace Conference (1919). He was also instrumental in the establishment of the Permanent Court of International Justice (1921). His books included *An International Court of Justice* (1916) and *Law, the State and the International Community* (1939).

SCOTT, PAUL MARK (1920–1978), British novelist. The son of a commercial artist, Scott grew up in a London suburb and served in the British army in Malaya and India during World War II. While working as an accountant and literary agent, he began to write fiction based on his wartime experiences, publishing his first novel in 1952; by 1960 he was a full-time writer. He was best known for "The Raj Quartet" (*The Jewel in the Crown*, 1966; *The Day of the Scorpion*, 1968; *The Towers of Silence*, 1971; and *A Division of the Spoils*, 1975), four interlocked novels set in India, which presented a rich tapestry of the complex relations between the British and the Indians during the last years of British rule on the subcontinent. It was filmed as *The Jewel in the Crown*, a 14-part television series, in 1984. His other novels set in India included *Johnnie Sahib* (1952), *The Birds of Paradise* (1962), and *Staying On* (1977). ■ See studies by K. Bhaskara Rao (1980) and Francine S. Weinbaum (1992) and biography by Hillary Spurling (1991).

SCOTT, ROBERT FALCON (1868–1912), British explorer. An officer in the Royal Navy, Scott led the National Antarctic Expedition (1901–04) that explored unknown areas of the continent and yielded valuable scientific information. Hoping to be the first to reach the South Pole "for the British Empire," he led a second expedition (1910–12). After an extremely difficult journey of almost three months, Scott and three companions reached the Pole on Jan. 17, 1912, only to find that the Norwegian explorer Roald Amundsen had planted the Norwegian flag there on Dec. 14, 1911. Bitterly disappointed, Scott started back to camp, but ferocious blizzards prevented his return, and he and his companions died on or about March 29. Their frozen bodies and scientific notes were discovered on Oct. 30. 1912. His diaries were published in 1905 and 1913. ■ See Reginald Pound, *Scott of the Antarctic* (1967); studies by Peter Brent (1974) and Elspeth Huxley (1978); Roland Huntford, *Scott and Amundsen* (1980); and Diana Preston, *A First Rate Tragedy* (1998).

SCRIABIN, ALEKSANDR NIKOLAEVICH (1872–1915), Russian composer. Scriabin was a solitary, unique, and eccentric musical personality, influenced successively by Friedrich Nietzsche, theosophy, and mysticism. He concentrated on piano and symphonic compositions, notably the ten piano sonatas (1892–1913), a piano concerto (1897), the *Poem of Ecstasy* (Symphony No. 4; 1908) and the *Prometheus* Symphony (No. 5; 1909). His refined and symbolic music, featuring innovative chords and a minimal use of melody, was noted for its exotic and mystical sound. He was working on a messianic epiphany of universal art, to be performed on a Tibetan peak, when he died suddenly of blood poisoning. ■ See the biographies by Faubion Bowers (2 vols., 1969; rev. ed. 1996) and Boris de Schloezer (Eng. trans. 1987).

SCRIPPS, EDWARD WYLLIS (1854–1926), U.S. newspaper publisher. Scripps published his first paper, the *Cleveland Penny Press,* in 1878. With his brothers, he acquired several other midwestern dailies and established, by 1880, the first daily-newspaper chain in the United States. In 1895, with his half brother George and Milton A. McRae, he formed the Scripps-McRae League of Newspapers. He established another chain, the Scripps Coast League, on the West Coast in 1909. His newspapers were inexpensive, liberal, prolabor, and politically independent and helped revolutionize American journalism. In 1902 he founded the Newspaper Enterprise Association to syndicate feature stories, cartoons, and illustrations, and in 1907 formed the United Press (UP), which became one of the largest worldwide news wire services. He retired in 1920. ■ See his selected writings in *Damned Old Crank* (1951) and *I Protest* (1966), and biography by Negley Cochran (1933).

SCULLIN, JAMES HENRY (1876–1953), Australian political leader. The son of a railway worker, Scullin received only a primary-school education and worked at many blue-collar jobs while he attended school at night. A labor organizer and a Labour member of Parliament (1910–13), he edited the party newspaper, *Echo,* during World War I, which supported Irish nationalists and anticonscriptionists. He returned to Parliament in 1923 and was leader of the Labour party (1928–35). As prime minister (1929–31), at the beginning of the Depression, his government was plagued by interparty and intraparty dissension and was not able to pass remedial progressive legislation. Labour was defeated in the 1931 elections, but Scullin remained in Parliament until 1949. ■ See biography by John Robertson (1975).

SEABORG, GLENN THEODORE (1912–1999), U.S. nuclear chemist. After receiving his Ph.D. from the University of California at Berkeley (1937), Seaborg joined the faculty and collaborated with Edwin M. McMillan in his research on the elements beyond uranium. Seaborg's research team was the first (1940) to isolate plutonium (element 94), and his work on the Manhattan Project led to the production of the plutonium that was used in the first atomic bombs (1945). His subsequent research (1944–58) resulted in the discovery of eight more transuranium elements (elements 95–102), and he shared the 1951 Nobel Prize in Chemistry with McMillan. Seaborg headed the U.S. Atomic Energy Commission (1961–71) and was instrumental in the growth of the nuclear-energy industry in the United States. His books included *Man and Atom* (1971; with W. R. Corliss), *Kennedy, Khrushchev and the Test Ban* (1981), and his memoir, *A Chemist in the White House* (1998).

SEALE, BOBBY (1937–), U.S. political activist. Seale grew up in Oakland, California, where, in 1966, he became a cofounder and chairman of the revolutionary Black Panther party on a platform of "power to the people." The party stressed self-defense for blacks, set up breakfast programs and free clinics in ghettos, and allied with white radicals in opposing racism and the Vietnam War. It was involved in frequent violent confrontations with the police. Carrying his politics to the 1968 Democratic national convention, Seale was indicted as one of the "Chicago Eight" for incitement to riot and was ordered bound and gagged during the 1969 trial. He was sentenced to four years in prison for contempt of court, but charges were later dropped. Returning to grass-roots politics, Seale ran unsuccessfully for mayor of Oakland (1973), after which he drifted into music and film activities, wrote cookbooks, and was a social worker with ghetto youth. ■ See his *Seize the Time* (1970) and his autobiography *A Lonely Rage* (1978).

SEARLE, RONALD (1920–), British artist. A cartoonist whose affectionate satires of British life began appearing in *Punch* in 1949 and later in the *New Yorker.* Searle invented a girls' school named St. Trinian's that was the subject of four zany films. He also worked on serious subjects, including a book of drawings from his World War II experience as a Japanese prisoner, *To the Kwai—and Back* (1986), and two books on the French artist Henri Toulouse-Lautrec (1969; 1970). Searle designed the animated sequences for such films as *Those Magnificent Men in Their Flying Machines* (1964) and *Scrooge* (1970); he also illustrated dozens of books. Some of his cat drawings appeared in *The Big Fat Cat Book* (1982). His later books included *Ronald Searle's Non-Sexist Dictionary* (1988) and *Marquis de Sade Meets Goody Two-Shoes* (1991). ■ See biography by Russell Davies (1990); *Ronald Searle in Perspective: The Best of His Work, 1938–1985* (1985); and study by Henning Bock and Pierre Dehaye (1978).

SEAVER, TOM (1944–), U.S. baseball player. A right-hand pitcher with an explosive fastball, Seaver broke into the major leagues with the New York Mets and was the 1967 Rookie of the Year. In 1969 he won 25 games, captured the National League Cy Young Award, and led the Mets to an improbable "miracle" victory over the Baltimore Orioles in the 1969 World Series. An articulate and personable athlete, Seaver was a perennial All-Star who subsequently pitched for the Cincinnati Reds (1977–82), the Mets (again, 1983), the Chicago White Sox (1984–86), and the Boston Red Sox (1986). During his career he won 311 games, recorded 3,640 strikeouts, and won three Cy Young Awards. ■ See biography by Gene Schoor (1986).

SEECKT, HANS VON (1866–1936), German general. A staff officer who planned some of Germany's World War I triumphs, Seeckt attended the Versailles Peace Conference and as head of the army (from 1920) was assigned to carry out its stipulations on the reduction of German armed forces. Thus he created a carefully selected leadership corps of 100,000 men (the nucleus of later expansion under Nazi leader Adolf Hitler) and worked with the Soviets to contravene the treaty prohibition against rearmament. He resigned in a 1926 dispute over his authorization of dueling between officers; he later served in parliament (1930–32) and was a military adviser to Chiang Kai-shek in China (1934–35). ■ See his *Thoughts of a Soldier* (Eng. trans. 1930).

SEEGER, PETE (1919–   ), U.S. folksinger. Seeger was born into an old New England family. His father was a prominent ethnomusicologist, his mother a violinist. He dropped out of Harvard (1938), joined the Young Communist League, and devoted himself to folk music. He began touring with his own group and with Woody Guthrie, performing labor and antifascist songs and organizing the Almanac Singers, a loosely knit group of performers that included Guthrie, Lee Hays, Millard Lampell, and others. After serving in World War II, Seeger founded the Weavers, who enjoyed tremendous popularity singing the old favorites "Goodnight Irene" and "On Top of Old Smoky." Called before the House Un-American Activities Committee in 1955, he had a contempt indictment dismissed on appeal but was nonetheless blacklisted for many years. Seeger's later recordings included "Where Have All the Flowers Gone?" (1961). During the 1960s and 1970s he was closely associated with the anti–Vietnam War movement. He also supported the environmental movement. ■ See his autobiography, *Where Have All the Flowers Gone* (1993; with Peter Blood); his *Incomplete Folksinger* (1972); and David L. Dunaway, *How Can I Keep from Singing* (1981).

SEFERIS, GEORGE (Georgios Seferiades; 1900–1971), Greek poet and diplomat. Regarded as the greatest Greek symbolist poet, Seferis was a member of the Greek foreign service (1925–62) and served as ambassador to the United Nations (1956–57) and Britain (1957–62). Utilizing direct and deceptively simple language, his poems evoked the Greek heritage in describing the odyssey of the soul and the survival of the past. A lifelong wanderer whose melancholy writings reflected his own quest, he was able to view stoically human transience and folly. Influenced by his friend, the English poet T. S. Eliot, Seferis was said to have brought Greek letters into the mainstream of 20th-century European literature. He won the Nobel Prize in Literature in 1963. English translations of his work are in *Poems* (1960), *Collected Poems, 1924–1955* (1967; rev. ed. 1995), and *Three Secret Poems* (1966; Eng. trans. 1969). Seferis also wrote *On the Greek Style* (1944; Eng. trans. 1966), a series of literary essays, and *A Poet's Journal: Days of 1945–51* (Eng. trans. 1974).

SEGAL, GEORGE (1924–2000), U.S. sculptor. The son of a kosher butcher in the Bronx, Segal studied art at Rutgers University and the Pratt Institute. He painted large realistic canvases before turning to sculpture in 1959. Using family and friends as models, he created unpainted, life-size plaster casts, placing them in intimate, realistic settings: *Woman Painting Her Fingernails* (1961), *Dinner Table* (1962), *Couple on a Bed* (1965). The authenticity of detail and the uncannily human quality of feeling and gesture made Segal's creations an overnight success during a period when realism was not in vogue. He also used plaster casts in *The Holocaust* (1983), a memorial in San Francisco to the Jews killed during World War II. Segal subsequently created the sculptures for the Franklin D. Roosevelt Memorial in Washington, D.C. (1997). ■ See studies by William Seitz (1972), Jan van der Marck (rev. ed. 1979), and Sam Hunter and Don Hawthorne (1985).

SEGAR, ELZIE CRISLER (1894–1938), U.S. cartoonist. Segar was a cartoonist for the *Chicago Herald* before going to New York (1919) to initiate a new strip, *Thimble Theater,* for the King Features Syndicate. Presented as a one-act play in cartoon form, the strip featured the adventures of Olive Oyl, her brother Caster Oyl, and her boyfriend Ham Gravy. Popeye, a rough and tough one-eyed sailor with bulging muscles, appeared in 1929. He became the central character and eventually the strip was renamed for him. Popeye wooed Olive Oyl and overpowered his rivals by eating spinach (the source of his strength), thus giving the vegetable a national reputation. He became one of the world's most famous comic characters and appeared in hundreds of animated cartoons produced by Max Fleischer.

SEGNI, ANTONIO (1891–1972), Italian political leader. A law professor (from 1920), Segni was a leader of the Roman Catholic Popular party (a forerunner of the Christian Democratic party) up to its dissolution by the fascists (1924). He continued teaching during the years of Benito Mussolini's government but during World War II joined the antifascist underground and helped organize the Christian Democratic party. The land-reform programs he initiated while minister of agriculture (1946–51) led right-wingers to call him the "white bolshevik." He remained a militantly anticommunist Roman Catholic, however, and served as Italy's premier (1955–57; 1959–60) and president (1962–64).

SEGOVIA, ANDRÉS (1893–1987), Spanish guitarist. Segovia began a solo concert career at age 15. He reestablished the classical guitar as a concert instrument with his popular tours and his expanded repertory. He adapted and transcribed classic compositions for the guitar and persuaded leading composers to write for him. A conservative in politics as well as music, he continued to perform into his nineties. ■ See his *Autobiography of the Years 1893–1920* (Eng. trans. 1976) and G. Clinton, ed., *Andrés Segovia* (1978).

SEGRÉ, EMILIO GINO (1905–1989), Italian-born U.S. physicist. As a student and member of Enrico Fermi's "Roman school" of physics in the late 1920s and early 1930s,

Segré conducted investigations that led to the discovery (1935) of slow neutrons. At the University of Palermo, he discovered (1936) the first artificial element, technetium. Segré was visiting researcher at the University of California at Berkeley when he was ousted (1938) from the University of Palermo faculty by Italy's fascist government. He remained at Berkeley (professor, 1946–72), becoming (1944) a U.S. citizen, and collaborated with other researchers to discover more elements, including astatine and plutonium-239. During 1943–46 he worked on the development of the atomic bomb at Los Alamos, New Mexico. With Owen Chamberlain, Segré won the 1959 Nobel Prize in Physics for the discovery (1955) of the antiproton, a particle in the atomic nucleus having the same atomic mass as a proton but an opposite charge. His books included a biography of Fermi (1970), *Nuclei and Particles* (1964; rev. ed. 1977), *From X-rays to Quarks* (Eng. trans. 1980), and *From Falling Bodies to Radio Waves* (1984). ■ See his autobiography, *A Mind Always in Motion* (1993).

SEIFERT, JAROSLAV (1901–1986), Czech poet. A proletarian poet during the early 1920s, Seifert was introduced to French surrealism on a trip to Paris (1923), and his subsequent personal works emphasized joy, love, and eroticism. His lyric poems were written in a clear and direct style and drew on natural, unaffected images and everyday experiences. Many of his works were about his native city of Prague. During World War II he wrote patriotic poems, and during the 1950s and 1960s he criticized the communist government's restrictive cultural policies. He served as chairman of the Union of Czechoslovakian Writers (1968–70) and signed Charter 77 (1977), an appeal for increased human, political, and social rights in Czechoslovakia. He was the first Czech writer to win the Nobel Prize in Literature (1984). English translations of his poems are in *The Plague Monument* (1980), *The Casting of Bells* (1983), *An Umbrella from Piccadilly* (1983), *The Early Poetry* (1997), and *The Poetry of Jaroslav Seifert* (1998).

SEINFELD, JERRY (1954–), U.S. comedian and actor. Seinfeld grew up in a suburb of New York City and studied theater and communications at Queens College (B.A. 1976). After several years as a struggling stand-up comic, he achieved fame after a series of television appearances on the "Tonight Show" in 1981. A droll, introspective commentator on the absurdities of everyday life, he became one of the most popular comedians in the United States by the mid-1980s. With his friend and fellow comic Larry David, he created (1989) a television comedy series for NBC about the daily life of an unmarried New York City stand-up comedian and his relationship with a small group of friends. The show, "Seinfeld," starring Seinfeld, became, by the mid-1990s one of the most popular and profitable shows in television history. By the time of the show's final episode (May 14, 1998), Seinfeld was reportedly earning $1 million per episode. He wrote the best-seller *Sein Language* (1993).

SELDES, GEORGE (1890–1995), U.S. journalist and author. Seldes, the brother of critic Gilbert Seldes, was born in a utopian community founded by his father in New Jersey. He was a syndicated newspaper correspondent during World War I and covered the rise of dictatorships in Europe as a reporter for the *Chicago Tribune* (1919–28). An iconoclast and self-described "progressive," he wrote several widely read books, including *You Can't Print That* (1929), an attack on press censorship; *Iron, Blood and Profits* (1934), an exposé of the armament industry; and *Sawdust Caesar* (1935), a scathing portrait of Benito Mussolini. *Lords of the Press* (1935) and *Freedom of the Press* (1938) were pioneering critiques of the U.S. newspaper industry that condemned the influence of big-business interests on the press. The muckraking newsletter, *In Fact*, which he founded and edited (1940–50), was the nation's first successful journalism review. The newsletter attacked the manipulation of government by big business, supported the labor movement, exposed the health hazards of smoking (as early as 1942), and claimed to have reached a peak of 176,000 subscribers in 1947. ■ See his autobiography, *Witness to a Century* (1987).

SELDES, GILBERT (1893–1970), U.S. author and critic. The Harvard-educated Seldes was one of the earliest writers on the popular arts in America. *The Seven Lively Arts* (1924), his controversial celebration of vaudeville, films, pop music, the circus, comic strips, and burlesque, was despised by "serious" critics, but it established his reputation. He wrote many other books, including *The Great Audience* (1950) and *The Public Arts* (1956), which analyzed the detrimental social consequences of the mass media. He was a columnist for the *New York Journal* (1931–37), a program director of the Columbia Broadcasting System (1937–45), and dean of the Annenberg School of Communications, University of Pennsylvania (1959–63). His brother was journalist George Seldes. ■ See Michael Kammen, *The Lively Arts* (1996).

SELFRIDGE, HARRY GORDON (1864–1947), U.S.-born British businessman. After making a fortune as an executive with Marshall Field and Co., the Chicago retail concern, Selfridge emigrated to London (1906), where in 1909 he opened Selfridge and Co., Ltd., a large American-style department store in Oxford Street. Selfridge used marketing and advertising techniques perfected in the United States and soon was running England's most successful store. Eventually he expanded it into a chain that employed 13,000 people and did $50 million worth of business a year. Long before he acquired British citizenship (1937), his name was a household word in his adopted country.

SELIGMAN, CHARLES GABRIEL (1873–1940), British anthropologist. Trained as a physician, C. G. Seligman was drawn to anthropology. He participated in two expeditions to New Guinea (1898; 1904) and held the first lectureship in ethnology at the University of London (1910–13) and a part-time chair in ethnology at the London School of Economics (1913–34). A pioneer field researcher, he amassed factual data on aboriginal cultures and produced several classic studies, including *The Melanesians of British New Guinea* (1910) and *The Races of Africa* (1930), and (with his wife, Brenda Salaman Seligman) *The Veddas (Ceylon)* (1911) and *Pagan Tribes of the Nilotic Sudan* (1932). He also gathered cross-cultural material to test the universality of Freudian theory. Seligman believed in the uniform mental and physical capacities of humankind in spite of racial and cultural diversity.

SELIGMAN, EDWIN ROBERT ANDERSON (1861–1939), U.S. economist and editor. Seligman graduated from Columbia University (Ph.D. 1885) and taught there in the department of political science (1885–1931). A social reformer, champion of academic freedom, and advocate of progressive taxation, he was a prolific author who helped establish the discipline of economics in the United States. He was also a founder and president (1902–04) of the American Economic Association and founder of the Encyclopedia of the Social Sciences, of which he was editor in chief (1927–35). His books included *The Economic Interpretation of History* (1902) and *The Income Tax* (1911).

SELTEN, REINHARD (1930–), German economist. Selten taught at the Free University of Berlin (1969–72) and the University of Bielefeld (1972–84) before serving on the faculty of the University of Bonn (1984–96). A pioneer in the field of game theory, he elaborated on the analysis of John F. Nash by presenting mathematical theories for discriminating between outcomes of games that are reasonable and those that are unreasonable. This enabled a player to eliminate unreasonable reactions of opponents from an analysis of such situations as business competition, trade negotiations, and international conflicts. As a visiting professor at the University of California, Berkeley (1967–68), Selten collaborated with John Harsanyi and later coauthored *A General Theory of Equilibrium Selection in Games* (1988) with him. Selten shared the 1994 Nobel Memorial Prize in Economics with Nash and Harsanyi for their work in game theory.

SELVON, SAMUEL (1923–1994), Trinidadian novelist and short-story writer. Selvon, who worked as a journalist before emigrating to London (1950), was the first Caribbean writer of East Indian origin to write of his community. His novels *A Brighter Sun* (1952) and *Turn Again, Tiger* (1958) portrayed the adjustment of a young Indian couple moving from a farm to cosmopolitan Port of Spain. Selvon's work was characterized by rich humorous dialogue and authentic regional dialects. His novel *The Lonely Londoners* (1956) was a hilarious but distressing account of West Indian immigrants in London. More serious were *The Plains of Caroni* (1969), concerning the protests of sugar-cane workers against agricultural mechanization, and *Moses Ascending*

(1975), a grim account of immigrant life. He also wrote *Moses Migrating* (1984), *Elorado West One* (1988), *Housing Lark* (1990), and *Foreday Morning: Selected Prose, 1946–1986* (1989). ■ See Austin Clarke, *A Passage Back Home* (1994).

SELYE, HANS HUGO BRUNO (1907–1982), Austrian-born Canadian physician. The son of a prominent surgeon, Selye was trained at the German University of Prague (M.D. 1929; Ph.D. in organic chemistry, 1931); he taught at McGill University, Montreal (1933–45), and directed the University of Montreal's Institute of Experimental Medicine and Surgery (1945–77). A pioneer of modern medical theory, Selye demonstrated that environmental stress causes the release of hormones that over a long period can lead to ulcers, high blood pressure, arteriosclerosis, arthritis, kidney diseases, and allergic reactions. His theory, first proposed in the 1930s, influenced medical research throughout the world and helped change popular thinking regarding the causes of human illness. In addition to dozens of technical books and hundreds of articles, he wrote the popular *Stress of Life* (1956; rev. ed. 1976), *From Dream to Discovery* (1964), *Stress Without Distress* (1974), and the autobiography *The Stress of My Life* (1977).

SELZNICK, DAVID OLIVER (1902–1965), U.S. film producer. The son of a movie producer in New York, David O. Selznick moved to Hollywood in 1926 and worked as a script editor and producer for Metro-Goldwyn-Mayer, Paramount, and RKO before heading his own company (1935–40). Specializing in lavish, high-quality productions, he was best known for *Gone With the Wind* (1939), one of the longest, most expensive, and most lucrative movies ever made. He was responsible for launching the film careers of George Cukor, Katharine Hepburn, Fred Astaire, Gregory Peck, Joseph Cotten, and Joan Fontaine, and he introduced Alfred Hitchcock (*Rebecca,* 1940) and Ingrid Bergman to American audiences. His other notable films included *Little Women* (1933), *King Kong* (1933), *Dinner at Eight* (1933), *Anna Karenina* (1935), *The Prisoner of Zenda* (1937), *Intermezzo* (1939), and *Duel in the Sun* (1946). ■ See biography by Bob Thomas (1970); the autobiography of his wife, Irene Selznick, *A Private View* (1983); and David Thomson, *Showman* (1992).

SEMENOV, NIKOLAI NIKOLAEVICH (1896–1986), Soviet physical chemist. Semenov graduated from the University of Petrograd (later Leningrad) in the year of the Bolshevik revolution (1917). He worked in Leningrad research institutes and directed the Institute of Chemical Physics of the Academy of Sciences (from 1931) until accepting a professorship at Moscow University (1944). During the 1920s he discovered branched chain reactions (occurring in explosions), formulated a general theory of such reactions, and established the chemical mechanism involved in the process. His research led to improvements in the internal combustion engine and advances in the plastics industry. He was the first Soviet scientist to win a Nobel Prize (Chemistry, 1956), which he shared with Sir Cyril Hinshelwood. He wrote *Some Problems in Chemical Kinetics and Reactivity* (Eng. trans., 2 vols., 1958–59).

SEMPLE, ELLEN CHURCHILL (1863–1932), U.S. geographer. A brilliant student of German anthropogeographer Friedrich Ratzel (in Leipzig, 1891–92), Semple was the leading American scholar of anthropogeography, the study of the geographical distribution of humankind. She lectured at the University of Chicago (1906–23) and was a professor at Clark University (1923–32). Her books, *American History and Its Geographic Conditions* (1903), *Influences of Geographic Environment* (1911), and *The Geography of the Mediterranean Region: Its Relation to Ancient History* (1932), were highly regarded when they were written, but they reflected an environmental determinism that was subsequently discounted by most scholars.

SEMYONOV, NIKOLAI. *See SEMENOV, NIKOLAI.*

SEN, AMARTYA (1933–   ), Indian economist. A native of Bengal, Sen witnessed the devastating 1943 Bengal famine as a child and studied the causes of famine, inequality, and poverty at Cambridge University (B.A. 1955; Ph.D. 1959) and during his academic career at the University of Delhi (1963–71), the London School of Economics (1971–77), Oxford (1977–88), Harvard (1987–98), and Cambridge (1998–   ). He emphasized the role of values and ethics in economic decision making and demonstrated that famines were not unavoidable natural disasters, but could be prevented by economic and political policies to help the poor. For his contributions to welfare economics, which changed the way many governments and international organizations approached problems relating to food crises, Sen received the 1998 Nobel Memorial Prize in Economics. His best-known books were *On Economic Inequality* (1973), *Poverty and Famines* (1981), *On Ethics and Economics* (1987), *Inequality Reexamined* (1994), and *Development as Freedom* (1999).

SENANAYAKE, DON STEPHEN (1884–1952), Ceylonese (Sri Lankan) political leader. Born into a devout Buddhist family, Senanayake was educated at St. Thomas College in Colombo and became a rubber planter. He entered politics as a member of the legislative council (1922), was elected to the state council (1931; chairman from 1942), and served as minister of agriculture and lands (1931–47). He formed a government in 1947 and led Ceylon to independence from Britain (1948). As premier (1948–52) he emphasized agricultural modernization, expanded the cooperative movement, brought barren lands and jungle areas under cultivation, and initiated hydroelectric installations. His son, Dudley Shelton Senanayake, later served as premier (1952–53; 1960; 1965–70).

SENDAK, MAURICE (1928–   ), U.S. illustrator, author, and opera designer. Frail and lonely as a child, Sendak sought escape in adventure books and in the creative bedtime stories his father told him. He began his career as an illustrator while he was still in high school (1945) by drawing the backgrounds for the *Mutt and Jeff* comic strip. He illustrated the first of his more than 80 books in 1951 and subsequently became one of the world's most beloved, honored, and influential children's book illustrators. His magical, finely detailed drawings that conveyed the terrors, dreams, and delights of his child heroes were featured in such books as *Where the Wild Things Are* (1963), *Higglety Pigglety Pop!* (1967), *In the Night Kitchen* (1970), *Outside Over There* (1981), *The Nutcracker* (1984), and *Swine Lake* (1999; with James Marshall). He also designed sets and costumes for many operas, including *The Magic Flute, The Love for Three Oranges,* and *The Cunning Little Vixen,* and wrote the libretto for an opera based on *Where the Wild Things Are* (1980). ■ See study by Amy Sonheim (1991).

SENGHOR, LÉOPOLD SÉDAR (1906–   ), Senegalese poet and political leader. Born into a prosperous Catholic family in a predominantly Muslim area, Senghor studied in Dakar and at the Sorbonne in Paris. A brilliant student, he was the first African awarded an *agrégation* certificate (1935), which enabled him to teach in a French high school. While in Paris during the 1930s he developed with Martinican poet Aimé Césaire and Guianan poet Léon G. Damas the concept of Negritude, which asserted the uniqueness and glory of African values and civilization. He championed modern African poetry and edited an influential anthology (1948). English translations of his poems are in *Selected Poems* (1964), *Prose and Poetry* (1965), *Nocturnes* (1971), and *Collected Poetry* (1991). A democratic socialist active in West African politics after World War II, he served in the French national assembly (1946–58) and played a major role in the Senegalese independence movement after unsuccessfully advocating a West African political and economic federation. As president of Senegal (1960–80) he maintained close ties to France and allowed little political opposition. In 1984 he became the first black member of the prestigious French Academy. ■ See his *On African Socialism* (1961; Eng. trans. 1964); the studies by Irving L. Markovitz (1969) and Jacques L. Hymans (1971); and Janet G. Vaillant, *Black French and African* (1990).

SENNETT, MACK (Michael Sinnott; 1880–1960), Canadian-born U.S. filmmaker. A former steelworker with an operatic voice, Sennett graduated from vaudeville to starring roles in D. W. Griffith's short films (1908–11). He cofounded Keystone Studios (1912), which became famous for hundreds of short slapstick comedies directed by Sennett, notably those featuring the Keystone Kops. He also discovered Charlie Chaplin, cast Gloria Swanson as a bathing beauty, produced Fatty Arbuckle's best comedies, and filmed the first flying custard pie. He remained the "King of Comedy" until the advent of sound movies in the late 1920s. ■ See his autobiography, *King of Comedy* (1954); Gene Fowlers, *Father Goose* (1974); and the study by Kalton C. Lahue (1971).

SERKIN, RUDOLF (1903–1991), Austrian-born U.S. pianist. A child prodigy, Serkin made his concert debut in Vienna at age 12 and performed throughout Europe with various ensembles led by famed pianist Adolph Busch during the 1920s and 1930s. Noted for his powerful yet sensitive and poetic performances, he was regarded as a master of the German romantic piano repertory, particularly that of Beethoven and Schubert. After emigrating to the United States (1933) he regularly appeared as a soloist with the major American orchestras, taught at the Curtis Institute of Music, Philadelphia (1938–68; director 1968–76), and helped found the Marlboro School of Music (1949) and the Marlboro Music Festival (1950) in Vermont. His son, Peter (1947–   ), was also a prominent pianist.

SERVAN-SCHREIBER, JEAN-JACQUES (1924–   ), French writer, publisher, and legislator. The son of a prominent journalist and Resistance leader, Servan-Schreiber left France during World War II and, trained by the U.S. Army Air Corps, served with the Free French forces. He wrote for *Le Monde* (1948–51) and *Paris-Presse* (1951–52) before founding, with F. Giraud, France's first newsweekly, *L'Express* (1953). Modeled after *Time* magazine, but reflecting moderately leftist views, *L'Express* was politically outspoken, and its 32-year-old publisher was drafted in 1956. When his book *Lieutenant in Africa* (1957; Eng. trans. 1958) described torture in Algeria during French repression of the nationalist rebellion there, Servan-Schreiber was tried for "undermining military morale" and acquitted. His bestselling *American Challenge* (1967; Eng. trans. 1968) warned against U.S. economic penetration of Europe. He presided over the Social Radical party (1971–75; 1977–79) and was accused of using his popular magazine to gain election to the French parliament (1970–78). He sold *L'Express* in 1979. After 1982 he headed the World Center for Information and Human Resources. His later books included *The World Challenge* (1980; Eng. trans. 1981) and *The Chosen and the Choice* (1988; Eng. trans. 1988), a study of Middle Eastern politics.

SERVICE, ROBERT WILLIAM (1874–1958), British-born Canadian poet. Service worked in a Glasgow bank before emigrating (1894) to Canada, where he spent many years in the rugged Pacific Northwest and the Yukon. Called "the Canadian Kipling," he became famous for ballads that romanticized the pioneer spirit and Klondike life in *Songs of a Sourdough* (1907), *Ballads of a Cheechako* (1909), and other collections. His most famous poems were "The Shooting of Dan McGrew" and "The Cremation of Sam McGee." He became a foreign correspondent (1912), drove an ambulance in World War I, and wrote *Rhymes of a Red Cross Man* (1916). He spent the last decades of his life mostly in France and Monte Carlo. His poetry was assembled in *Collected Verse* (1960). ■ See his autobiographies, *Ploughman of the Moon* (1945) and *Harper of Heaven* (1948); biography by Carl F. Klinck (1976); and James A. MacKay, *Vagabond of Verse* (1995).

SESSIONS, ROGER HUNTINGTON (1896–1985), U.S. composer. Sessions studied music at Harvard and Yale and taught and studied with Ernest Bloch. In 1923 he wrote the *Black Maskers* suite, his most popular composition. After work abroad, he collaborated with Aaron Copland in an influential series of concerts of contemporary music (1928–31). He later taught at Princeton (1935–45; 1953–65), the University of California at Berkeley (1945–53), and the Juilliard School of Music, New York (from 1965), and became a major force in modern American musical life. Sessions' music is characterized by strong asymmetrical rhythmic figures, polyphonic techniques, and complex thematic ideas. He wrote several symphonies, many smaller works, and two major operas, *The Trial of Lucullus* (1947) and *Montezuma* (1964). His *Concerto for Orchestra* won a 1982 Pulitzer Prize. Among his books were *The Musical Experience* (1950), *Reflections on the Musical Life in the United States* (1956), *Questions About Music* (1970), and *Roger Sessions on Music* (1979).

SEUSS, DR. (Theodor Seuss Geisel; 1904–1991), U.S. children's author, illustrator, cartoonist, and screenplay writer. Geisel was a political cartoonist for the left-wing daily newspaper *PM* in New York City during World War II (1941–43). His scripts for *Design for Death*, a 1947 documentary about Japanese warlords, and *Gerald McBoing Boing*, a 1950 animated cartoon, won Academy Awards. However, Geisel, alias Dr. Seuss, was best known as the author of such popular and whimsical children's books as *And to Think I Saw It on Mulberry Street* (1937), *The 500 Hats of Bartholomew Cubbins* (1938), and *Yertle the Turtle* (1958). *The Cat in the Hat* (1957), a successful limited-vocabulary picture-story book, launched a new trend in children's writing. His book for adults, *You're Only Old Once!* (1986), was a best-seller, as was *Oh, the Places You'll Go* (1990), which was written for both children and adults. ■ See Judith Morgan, *Dr. Seuss and Mr. Geisel* (1995; with Neil Morgan).

SEVAREID, ERIC (1912–1992), U.S. broadcast journalist. Born in North Dakota of Scandinavian ancestry, Sevareid was a member (from 1939) of the Ed Murrow team covering World War II for CBS. After the war he became a Washington radio and television correspondent, specializing in urbane commentary. He opposed Sen. Joseph McCarthy's tactics in hunting down communists, the Vietnam War, and Pres. Richard M. Nixon's administration and was an occasional critic of the superficiality of network newscasting. Before retiring (1977), he wrote two memoirs, *Not So Wild a*

Dream (1946) and *This Is Eric Sevareid* (1964). ■ See Raymond A. Schrooth, *The American Journey of Eric Sevareid* (1995).

SEVERINI, GINO (1883–1966), Italian painter. Severini studied painting and worked in Rome as a copyist (1900–06), then moved to Paris. With the poet Filippo Tommaso Marinetti, he championed Italian futurism, which glorified the machine; his own paintings, however, generally drew their imagery and dynamism from the human figure. Influenced by Pablo Picasso, Max Jacob, and Georges Braque, he evolved an idiosyncratic brand of cubism that incorporated the dynamism of futurism and the decorative qualities of pointillism. *Dynamic Hieroglyphic of the Bal Tabarin* (1910) exemplifies this blend. After 1921, he adopted the neoclassical figurative style that characterized his later works, especially the many decorative panels and mosaics that he executed for private homes during the late 1920s and 1930s. He wrote *The Artist and Society* (Eng. trans, 1946). ■ See his autobiography, *The Life of a Painter* (Eng. trans. 1995).

SEVERSKY, ALEXANDER PROCOFIEFF DE (1894–1974), Russian-born U.S. aviator and aircraft designer. A much-decorated Russian World War I pilot, De Seversky emigrated (1918) to the United States. One of his early aeronautical designs, a 100-percent-accurate bombsight (1922), was bought by the U.S. government. De Seversky joined the Army Air Corps reserve (1927) and later founded (1931) what became the Republic Aircraft Corp. He designed such innovations as wing flaps; retractable landing gear for land, water, and ice; new types of structural and instrument design; and an air-cooled engine. He also broke numerous airplane speed records. A zealous advocate of strategic air power, he detailed his beliefs in *Victory Through Air Power* (1942) and *Air Power—Key to Survival* (1950).

SEYMOUR, DAVID "CHIM" (David Szymin; 1911–1956), Polish-U.S. photographer. The son of a publisher of Yiddish books, "Chim" was born in Warsaw and studied in Leipzig and Paris. He photographed the rise of fascism during the 1930s. After covering the Spanish Civil War (1936–38), he followed a shipload of Loyalist refugees to Mexico in 1939 and himself became a refugee during World War II, which he spent in U.S. photo reconnaissance and military intelligence. A cofounder of the Magnum photo agency (1947), Seymour received an assignment from the U.N. Educational, Scientific, and Cultural Organization to photograph *Children of Europe* (1949). He was killed by Egyptian fire during the Suez crisis. A collection of his works, noted for their warmth and compassion, was published by the International Fund for Concerned Photography (1974).

SEYSS-INQUART, ARTHUR (1892–1946), Austrian public official. A leader of the Austrian Nazis, Seyss-Inquart had long advocated German-Austrian unification. As a result of German pressure on the Austrian government he was named

interior minister (Feb. 1938) and then chancellor (March 1938) on the eve of the annexation and occupation by Germany. Subsequently he was made governor of Austria and deputy governor of Poland. As Nazi high commissioner of the Netherlands (from 1940) he was responsible for the extermination of Dutch Jews and the deportation of thousands to concentration and slave labor camps. After the war he was hanged as a war criminal.

SFORZA, COUNT CARLO (1872–1952), Italian diplomat. A descendant of the powerful Renaissance family. Sforza represented Italy in China (1911–15), Serbia (1915–18), and Turkey (1918). As foreign minister (1920–21), he negotiated the Treaty of Rapallo, which settled the Italian-Yugoslav border dispute. An ardent foe of fascist leader Benito Mussolini, he resigned his post as ambassador to France (1922) and became a leader of the anti-Mussolini forces in Italy and, during his forced exile, in Europe and the United States (1927–43). After World War II he played an active role in the reorganization of Italian political life and as foreign minister again (1947–51), he worked for European unification.

SHABALALA, JOSEPH (1940–   ), South African singer. Shabalala was a member of several singing groups while he worked in a Durban factory during the mid-1950s. He returned to his family farm in Ladysmith steeped in the traditions of *iscathamiya,* a Zulu musical style that combines traditional harmonies, gospel, call and response, and step dancing. Inspired by harmonies that came to him in a dream, he formed his own 10-member a capella male choir, Ladysmith Black Mambazo, in the mid-1960s. The group won every local contest they entered, signed their first recording contract in 1970, and eventually became the most popular singing group in Africa. They gained international recognition collaborating with Paul Simon on his *Graceland* album (1986) and tour (1987). The group appeared on Broadway in *The Song of Jacob Zulu* (1993), sang at Nelson Mandela's presidential inauguration (1994), and recorded dozens of albums, including *Shaka Zulu* (1987), *Gift of the Tortoise* (1993), *Thuthukani Ngoxolo* (1996), and *Heavenly* (1997). Shabalala served as a priest in the Church of God of the Prophets and was a professor of ethnomusicology at the University of Natal.

SHACHTMAN, MAX (1904–1972), Polish-born U.S. political leader. Shachtman was a founder (1920) and leader of the American Communist party until he was expelled for "Trotskyism" (1928). He then became a leader of the American and international Trotskyist movement—which bitterly denounced the Stalinist regime in the Soviet Union—and edited several Trotskyite journals during the 1930s and 1940s. After Leon Trotsky's death (1940) Shachtman was appointed administrator of his literary estate and edited and translated many of Trotsky's works. From 1958 he was leader of the American Socialist party. His books included

The Fight for Socialism (1946) and *The Bureaucratic Revolution: The Rise of the Stalinist State* (1962). ▪ See biography by Peter Drucker (1994).

SHACKLETON, SIR ERNEST HENRY (1874–1922), British explorer. A merchant seaman, Shackleton joined Robert Falcon Scott's Antarctic Expedition (1901–04) and journeyed across the Ross Ice Shelf with Scott. He led his own expedition (1907–09) and reached within 97 miles of the South Pole. He was hailed as a hero on his return to England, was knighted, and wrote *The Heart of the Antarctic* (2 vols., 1909). His third expedition (1914), during which he hoped to cross the Antarctic, ended in disaster when his ship *Endurance* was crushed. His men drifted on ice floes and were stranded for months on ice-covered Elephant Island before being rescued on Aug. 25, 1916. His book *South* (1919) described the journey and efforts to rescue his crew. He died at sea off South Georgia Island at the onset of his fourth expedition. ▪ See biographies by Margery and James Fisher (1957) and Roland Huntford (1986) and Caroline Alexander, *The Endurance* (1998).

SHAGARI, ALHAJI SHEHU USMAN ALIYU (1925–   ), Nigerian political leader. A poet, science teacher, and educational administrator, Shehu Shagari was a founder of the Northern People's Congress (NPC; 1951) and served in the federal parliament (1954–58). He held federal cabinet positions during the 1960s but held provincial posts after the military coup of 1966. Recalled to the central government in 1970, he served as commissioner for economic development, rehabilitation, and reconstruction before assuming the key post of finance commissioner (1971–75). When the government's 12-year ban on political parties was lifted (1978), he helped found the National Party of Nigeria (NPN) and led it to victory in the 1979 elections. Thus, the pragmatic and moderate Shagari became Nigeria's first civilian president after 13 years of military control. His government, however, was perceived as being corrupt, and as the economy worsened he was overthrown by the military in Dec. 1983. He lived under house arrest from 1983 to 1986. ▪ See David Williams, *President and Power in Nigeria* (1982) and study by O. A. Ojibgo (1982).

SHAHN, BEN (1898–1969), Lithuanian-born U.S. artist. Shahn worked as a lithographer's apprentice as a teenager and graduated from the City College of New York in 1922. An individual stylist of line and color, he was the best-known social-realist artist of the 1930s. He painted a famous series on the trial of the anarchists Sacco and Vanzetti (1931–32) and assisted the Mexican artist Diego Rivera (1933) on the RCA Building murals (in New York) that were later destroyed for political reasons. Shahn was also known for his photographs of Depression subjects. After World War II he evolved a more personal, reflective mode, illustrating many books, creating posters, and teaching poetry

at Harvard (1956–57). His Harvard lectures were published as *The Shape of Content* (1957). ▪ See Selden Rodman, *Portrait of the Artist as an American* (1951); *The Complete Graphic Works* (1973); study by Frances K. Phol (1989); and biography by Howard Greenfeld (1998).

SHAMIR, YITZHAK (Yitzhak Jazernicki; 1915?–   ), Polish-born Israeli political leader. Shamir studied law in Warsaw before emigrating to Palestine (1935), where he joined the Jewish underground military organization headed by Menachem Begin. In 1940 he joined Lehi (popularly known as the Stern Gang) and helped plan the assassination of British policemen, soldiers, and government officials in its fight to drive the British out of the country. Arrested (1941, 1946) he escaped twice from British prisons. After Israeli independence (1948) he became a businessman, but later served in the Mossad, the Israeli intelligence agency (1955–65). He joined Begin's Herut party (1970), was elected to the Knesset (parliament; 1973–96), and was foreign minister in Begin's Likud government (1980–83). After Begin's resignation, Shamir served as prime minister (1983–84). Following the inconclusive elections of July 1984, he made a deal with Shimon Peres of the Labor party whereby the two leaders would share power. Under the agreement Peres would serve as prime minister and Shamir as foreign minister during the first half of the 50-month term, after which they would reverse roles for the second half of the term.

SHAMROY, LEON (1901–1974), U.S. cinematographer. Trained as a mechanical engineer, Shamroy worked in a photo lab and photographed experimental films during the 1920s. He became a cameraman for Paramount (1932) and later for 20th Century-Fox (from 1940). He was one of the first cameramen to use the zoom lens, and he shot the first movie using the cinemascope technique (*The Robe*, 1953). He won Academy Awards for *The Black Swan* (1942), *Wilson* (1944), *Leave Her to Heaven* (1945), and *Cleopatra* (1963). His other well-known films included *The King and I* (1956), *Love is a Many Splendored Thing* (1955), and *Planet of the Apes* (1968).

SHANKAR, RAVI (1920–   ), Indian sitar player. Shankar began his career as a dancer and accompanist in the dance troupe of his brother, Uday Shankar, during the 1930s. Later he founded the National Orchestra of India, was music director of All-India Radio, and became the first Indian instrumentalist to go on a world tour (1956). Playing traditional ragas on the sitar, a long-necked instrument of the lute family, he stimulated Western interest in the classical music of India. Shankar was also a teacher (notably of Beatle George Harrison) and a composer of film scores (Satyajit Ray's *Apu* trilogy, 1955–59, and Sir Richard Attenborough's *Gandhi*, 1982) and serious compositions (*Concerto for Sitar*, 1971). He also served in the Rajya Sabha, India's Upper House of Parliament (1986–92). ▪ See his *My Music, My Life* (1968).

SHANKAR, UDAY (1901?–1977), Indian dancer and choreographer. Trained in the Hindu arts by his father, Shankar studied painting in Bombay and London, where he also continued training in the dance. He performed with Anna Pavlova (1923), creating the ballets *Hindu Wedding* and *Radha-Krishna* for her. Returning to India (1929), he founded his own troupe, which in the 1930s brought new respectability to Indian dance. He synthesized ancient and modern dance forms and was regarded as one of the foremost dancers of the century. Through many well-received tours, he introduced Americans and Europeans to Indian culture. His brother was the sitarist Ravi Shankar. ■ See study by Projesh Banerji (1982).

SHANKER, ALBERT (1928–1997), U.S. labor leader. Shanker earned an M.A. from Columbia University and taught in New York City public schools (1952–59) before becoming involved full-time in the drive for teacher power. As president of the United Federation of Teachers (1964–86), the largest local in the American Federation of Teachers, he led strikes over pay and noneconomic issues, such as opposition to community control of schools, including the strike that closed New York City schools for 36 days in 1968. He won increased salaries and benefits for teachers and became a major power broker in New York politics. As president of the 600,000-member American Federation of Teachers (1974–97), he strongly defended public education and advocated school reform and rigorous academic standards. He was also a vice president of the AFL-CIO (from 1973).

SHANNON, CLAUDE ELWOOD (1916–2001), U.S. mathematician. Working at the Bell Telephone Laboratories (1941–58), Shannon contributed to the growth of information theory with his revolutionary mathematical theory of communication. He developed (1948), a procedure for expressing information in quantitative terms, using binary notation. Units of information were termed "bits." His conclusions were not only crucial to progress in circuit and computer design and other aspects of communication, but they affected biological and social sciences, linguistics, and the humanities. See his classic paper, "A Symbolic Analysis of Relay and Switching Circuits" (1938), and *The Mathematical Theory of Communication* (1949; with Warren Weaver). Shannon was a professor at the Massachusetts Institute of Technology from 1958 to 1980.

SHAPIRO, KARL (1913–2000), U.S. poet, critic, and editor. In his early poems, Shapiro wrote about his experience as an American Jewish artist; he took issue with what he viewed as anti-Semitic attitudes in works by the poets Ezra Pound and T. S. Eliot. Shapiro criticized or parodied the artifice of intellectual poetry and the New Criticism. While serving in the South Pacific during World War II, he published *Person, Place and Thing* (1942); a second wartime volume, *V-Letter,*

and Other Poems (1944), won a Pulitzer Prize. His poetry was assembled in *Poems 1940–1953* (1953) and *Collected Poems, 1940–1978* (1978). Later collections included *Love and War/Art and God* (1984), *New and Selected Poems, 1940–1986* (1987), and *The Wild Card: Selected Poems* (1998). He also wrote the satirical *Essay on Rime* (1945) in blank verse. *Beyond Criticism* (1953), *In Defense of Ignorance* (1960), and *The Poetry Wreck* (1975) are collections of essays. Shapiro also wrote criticism and edited *Poetry* magazine (1950–56) and *Prairie Schooner* (1956–66). ■ See his autobiography, *Poet* (1988), and study by Joseph Reino (1981).

SHAPLEY, HARLOW (1885–1972), U.S. astronomer. A creative researcher and theoretician who was director (1921–52) of the Harvard College Observatory, Shapley was called the "modern Copernicus"—he located the sun's position in the galaxy from a study of globular clusters. He advanced the field of galactic astronomy by determining the size and shape of the Milky Way and the location of the solar system within it. His research enabled scientists to determine which celestial objects existed outside the galaxy, and it demonstrated that many extragalactic nebulas were actually galaxies in themselves. Shapley showed that galaxies usually occur in clusters. He also researched eclipsing binary stars and introduced the use of variable stars to calculate distance. His books included *Galaxies* (1943), *Of Stars and Men* (1958), and his memoirs, *Through Rugged Ways to the Stars* (1969).

SHARANSKY, NATAN (**Anatoly Borisovich Shcharansky**; 1948–), Soviet dissident. A Jewish mathematician from Moscow, Sharansky applied for a visa to emigrate to Israel in 1973. During the next four years, he drew the particular ire of Soviet authorities by giving interviews (in fluent English) to Western correspondents and by acting informally as an effective link among various dissident movements. In 1977, 29-year-old Sharansky was accused of espionage for the U.S. Central Intelligence Agency, a charge that Pres. Jimmy Carter publicly denied. He spent nine years in prisons and labor camps before being freed as part of an East–West spy swap in February 1986 (although U.S. authorities stressed that Sharansky was not a spy). Welcomed as a hero in Israel, he joined his wife, Avital, who had long pressed for his release, took the name Natan, and vowed to continue his human rights work. He founded a political party, Yisrael B'Aliya (1996), to represent the interests of Russian immigrants, and he served in the cabinet as minister of trade and industry (1996–99) and minister of the interior (1999–2000). ■ See his autobiography, *Fear No Evil* (1988), and biography by Martin Gilbert (1986).

SHARON, ARIEL (1928–), Israeli military and political leader. Born on an agricultural cooperative near Tel Aviv, Sharon served in a paramilitary youth battalion as a teenager, joined the underground Jewish defense force, and was a company commander during Israel's war for independence (1948). During the early 1950s he gained a reputation for brutality and overstepping his authority when he headed an elite commando unit that carried out retaliatory raids on Jordanian villages. He later commanded a paratroop brigade during the Suez War (1956), commanded the Egyptian front during the Six Day War (1967), and led Israeli forces across the Suez Canal during the Yom Kippur War (1973). He advocated the annexation of all Arab lands seized during the 1967 war, and as minister of agriculture in Menachem Begin's cabinet (1977–81) he was in charge of establishing Jewish colonies on the West Bank and Gaza. Appointed defense minister (1981), he urged the invasion of Lebanon (1982) and was charged by an Israeli investigatory commission with "indirect responsibility" for the massacre of Palestinians in Beirut refugee camps carried out by Lebanese Christian militia units. Sharon resigned the defense portfolio (1983), but was appointed minister of industry and commerce (1984), minister of trade (1984–90) and housing (1990–92), minister of infrastructures (1996–98), and foreign minister (1998–99) and remained one of the most controversial figures in Israeli political life. He became leader of the Likud Party (1999–   ) and was elected prime minister (2001). ■ See his autobiography, *Warrior* (1989; with David Chanoff), and biography by Uzi Benziman (Eng. trans. 1985).

SHARP, PHILLIP A. (1944–   ), U.S. biologist. Sharp studied chemistry at the University of Illinois (Ph.D. 1969), did research at the Cold Spring Harbor Laboratory in New York (1972–74), and taught at the Massachusetts Institute of Technology (from 1974). He was a cofounder of Biogen (1978), a biotechnology company. While examining the genes of a virus, Sharp discovered (1977) that the gene strands were discontinuous: the segments of DNA encoded for proteins were not arranged in a continuous strand but were separated by stretches of DNA that contained no genetic encoding. Subsequent studies revealed that these "split genes" are the most common type of genetic structure in higher organisms. It was demonstrated that enzymes cut out the nonfunctional segments and that the functional segments of the DNA are spliced together to create the final messenger RNA molecule. The discovery convinced scientists that split genes may have speeded up the process of evolution, and the study of these genes had a great influence on biological research and the study of cancer and other diseases. Sharp shared the 1993 Nobel Prize in Physiology or Medicine with Richard J. Roberts, who independently discovered the existence of split genes.

SHARPE, WILLIAM F. (1934–   ), U.S. economist. Sharpe worked as a part-time employee at the Rand Corporation while studying for his Ph.D. in economics at the University of California at Los Angeles. At Rand he met economist Harry M. Markowitz and persuaded the economics depart-

ment at UCLA to allow Markowitz to be his mentor for his dissertation. Sharpe elaborated on Markowitz's work on portfolio theory and developed the Capital Asset Pricing Model (1964), which explained how the prices of securities are established to take into account risks and potential returns. This theory led to the development of "beta," a widely used measurement of portfolio risk that compares the risks of holding various mixes of stocks with stocks in general. Sharpe taught at the University of Washington and Stanford (1971–89; 1993–   ). His research, along with the related works of Markowitz and Merton H. Miller, created the modern discipline of financial economics and provided a theoretical underpinning for the mutual fund business. The three researchers shared the 1990 Nobel Memorial Prize in Economics.

SHASTRI, LAL BAHADUR (Lal Bahadur; 1904–1966), Indian political leader. Shastri, who came from a poor family, joined Mahatma Gandhi's noncooperation movement early in life. He rose through the ranks of the Indian National Congress party in the United Provinces (now Uttar Pradesh) and served in the state legislature (from 1937). Named Congress party general secretary (1951), he was elected to parliament (1952) and served in several cabinet posts. When Prime Minister Jawaharlal Nehru died (1964), Shastri succeeded him and generally followed Nehru's policies of moderate socialism at home and neutrality in international relations. He died suddenly while attending Indo-Pakistani peace talks in Tashkent in the Soviet Union. ■ See studies by D. R. Mankekar (1964) and R. C. Gupta (1966) and biography by C. P. Srivastava (1995).

SHAW, ANNA HOWARD (1847–1919), British-born U.S. women's suffrage leader. Shaw, whose family emigrated to the United States when she was 4, gave up careers as a Methodist minister (ordained 1880) and a physician (M.D., Boston University, 1886) in 1887 to lecture professionally on the subjects of temperance and women's suffrage. Regarded as the most effective and eloquent orator in the suffrage movement, she traveled throughout the country and served as vice president (1892–1904) and president (1904–15) of the National American Woman Suffrage Association. During World War I she headed the Woman's Committee of the United States Council of National Defense (1917–19). ■ See her autobiography, *The Story of a Pioneer* (1915), and biography by Will A. Linkugel (1991).

SHAW, ARTIE (Arthur Arshawsky; 1910–   ), U.S. jazz clarinetist and bandleader. Shaw played in bands headed by Willie "the Lion" Smith, Vincent Lopez, and Red Nichols before achieving prominence as head of his own swing band (1937). One of the most popular musicians of the late 1930s and 1940s, he recorded such hits as "Begin the Beguine," "Frenesi," "Any Old Time," and "Gloomy Sunday." A virtuoso clarinetist, Shaw also appeared as a soloist with symphony orchestras. He retired from the music world in 1955, but returned to lead the Artie Shaw Orchestra in 1983. His books included his autobiography, *The Trouble with Cinderella* (1952), three novelettes about modern divorce in *I Love You, I Hate You, Drop Dead* (1965), and *The Best of Intentions and Other Stories* (1989).

SHAW, GEORGE BERNARD (1856–1950), Irish playwright. Shaw was born into genteel poverty in Dublin. He moved (1876) to London, where he wrote unsuccessful novels and eventually became a prominent music critic. A co-founder of the socialist Fabian Society, he was a brilliant and witty speaker and pamphleteer. Influenced by the work of Henrik Ibsen, Shaw helped move contemporary British drama to a more sophisticated, more serious level. He was concerned in his work with the major intellectual and moral issues of his day, such as socialism, the English class system, and prostitution. Despite his serious intentions, his plays were witty and dazzling comedies. They included *Widower's House* (1892), his first play; *Arms and the Man* (1894); *Major Barbara* (1905); *Pygmalion* (1913), his greatest commercial success and the basis for the musical *My Fair Lady*; and *St. Joan* (1923), a deft combination of seriousness and comedy that is widely considered his finest work. Shaw intended for his plays to be read and wrote lengthy prefaces and elaborate stage directions for the published versions. His last play, *Buoyant Millions* (1949), was produced when he was past age 90. Shaw was regarded as the greatest English-language playwright since Shakespeare and was awarded the Nobel Prize in Literature (1925). ■ See the collection of autobiographical writings in *Shaw: An Autobiography* (2 vols., 1969–70, edited by Stanley Weintraub); biographies by Archibald Henderson (1932), Arnold Silver (1982), and Michael Holroyd (3 vols., 1988–91); and Maurice Valency, *The Cart and the Trumpet* (1973).

SHAW, (WARREN) WILBUR (1902–1954), U.S. auto-racing driver. A legendary figure in the racing world, Shaw was a three-time winner of the Indianapolis 500 (1937; 1939; 1940). He placed second in the race in 1933, 1935, and 1938. As president of the Indianapolis Speedway (1945–54), he helped revive the sport, which was suspended during World War II. ■ See his autobiography, *Gentlemen, Start Your Engines* (1955).

SHAWN, TED (Edwin Myers Shawn; 1891–1972), U.S. dancer, choreographer, and teacher. Intending to become a Methodist minister, Shawn studied theology in college. When, during his junior year, he suffered paralysis of the legs, ballet was prescribed as therapy. Impressed by a 1910 performance by Ruth St. Denis, who was later to become his wife (1914–31), Shawn devoted himself to modern dance. He and St. Denis founded (1915) the Denishawn School, which turned out such modern dancers as Martha Graham and Doris Humphrey. Concerned about Americans' biased view of male dancers, Shawn established and trained an all-male troupe. He also founded (1932) and directed the Ja-

cob's Pillow dance center and festival in Lee, Massachusetts. Shawn was among the first to choreograph dances based on American themes. ■ See his *One Thousand and One Night Stands* (1960) and biography by Walter Terry (1976).

SHAWQI, AHMAD (1868–1932), Egyptian poet, dramatist, and novelist. A member of a noble family, Shawqi was close to the khedival court and spent most of his life in government service. Known throughout the Arab world as the "prince of poets," he fulfilled the pre-Islamic traditional role of the poet as the spokesman of his community. Although most famous for historical verse tragedies inspired by the 17th-century French dramatist Pierre Corneille and for his political and patriotic poems, he utilized almost every conceivable type of traditional poetry to treat contemporary Arabic and Egyptian themes. His most popular play was *Majnun Layla* (Eng. trans, 1933).

SHCHARANSKY, ANATOLY. See SHARANSKY, NATAN.

SHEEAN, (JAMES) VINCENT (1899–1975), U.S. writer and journalist. Sheean was a reporter for the *New York Daily News* and the Paris edition of the *Chicago Tribune* in the early 1920s before becoming a foreign correspondent for the North American Newspaper Alliance. While covering momentous stories such as Italian fascist leader Benito Mussolini's march on Rome, the 1927 political upheaval in China, the Italian invasion of Ethiopia, the Spanish Civil War, and the assassination of Indian leader Mahatma Gandhi, he developed a reflective personal style and a socialist world view. His work influenced a generation of newspaper reporters in the 1930s and 1940s. He drew on his international experiences to write biographies, novels, and short stories and scored his greatest success with his biography of Gandhi, *Lead Kindly, Light* (1949), and his autobiographical *Personal History* (1935).

SHEELER, CHARLES (1883–1965), U.S. painter and photographer. Sheeler was influenced by the cubists and exhibited six paintings at the famous 1913 Armory Show in New York. He supported his career as a painter by commercial photography, which in turn influenced and furthered his art. In both fields he favored the abstract geometric shapes of industry and architecture, often photographing and painting in sharp focus the same subject, such as a stairway or a still life. Sheeler also completed photo essays on Chartres cathedral, Shaker architecture, and the Ford Motor Co. plant at River Rouge, Michigan. ■ See studies by Constance Rourke (1938) and Martin Friedman (1975).

SHEEN, FULTON JOHN (1895–1979), U.S. religious leader. Born into an Illinois farming family, Sheen was ordained in the Roman Catholic church (1919) and earned a Ph.D. at the University of Louvain in Belgium (1923). In 1926 he began a quarter century of teaching at Catholic University. Sheen was the first evangelist to preach regularly over the airwaves when he spoke on the radio program "The Catholic Hour" (1930). The television ministry that made him the best-known and most persuasive Catholic spokesperson in the United States dated from 1951 (the year he was consecrated auxiliary bishop of New York), when he launched "Life Is Worth Living," the television show that shocked the networks by attracting 20 million viewers. Sheen spoke out against communism, monopolistic capitalism, historical liberalism, and Freudian psychoanalysis. He converted such famous people as Clare Boothe Luce, Fritz Kreisler, and Henry Ford II to Catholicism. Archbishop Sheen was also a newspaper columnist and wrote some 50 books. ■ See his autobiography, *Treasure in Clay* (1980), and Daniel P. Noonan, *The Passion of Fulton Sheen* (1972).

SHEHU, MEHMET (1913–1981), Albanian political leader. A veteran of the Spanish Civil War and an antifascist partisan fighter during World War II, Shehu became chief of staff of the Albanian army in 1946. As premier of Albania (1954–81) and trusted aid of Communist party leader Enver Hoxha, he helped guide his country's policy of amity, followed by animosity, toward Yugoslavia in the 1940s, the Soviet Union in the 1960s, and China in the 1970s. After his reported suicide, he was denounced by Hoxha as a traitor and a secret agent of Soviet and Yugoslav intelligence services. In 1984 the Albanian government reported that Shehu was "liquidated."

SHEN CONGWEN (old style: **SHEN TS'UNG-WEN; 1902–1988**), Chinese novelist and educator. A largely self-educated liberal intellectual, Shen was a prolific author whose work celebrated the courage and dignity of the common Chinese. Most of his fiction reflected his rural and military background. He utilized a loose vernacular style and combined Western and traditional Chinese literary techniques. *The Long River* (1943) is considered Shen's best work. *The Chinese Earth* (Eng. trans. 1947, 1982) contains 15 of his short stories. For more than 20 years he was a professor of Chinese literature at several Chinese universities, including Beijing (Peking) University. Denounced by the communists, he produced no original fiction after the communist takeover in 1949. ■ See study by Hua-ling Nieh (1972); Jeffrey C. Kinkley, *The Odyssey of Shen Congwen* (1987); and Jeffrey C. Kinkley, ed., *Imperfect Paradise: Stories by Shen Congwen* (Eng. trans. 1995).

SHEN TS'UNG-WEN *See SHEN CONGWEN.*

SHEPARD, ALAN BARTLETT, JR. (1923–1998), U.S. astronaut. Shepard became America's first person in space on May 5, 1961, when he was launched into a 116-mile-high suborbital flight in the *Freedom 7* spacecraft. The near-perfect 15-minute flight, coming 23 days after Soviet astronaut Yuri Gagarin's orbit of the earth, helped restore American confidence in its space program. Shepard's flight was unique in that he manually controlled the space cap-

sule's flight. He continued to work for the National Aeronautics and Space Administration as director of astronaut training and recruitment (1965–74) and in 1971 he commanded the *Apollo 14* lunar mission and became the first person to play golf on the moon.

SHEPARD, FRANCIS PARKER (1897–1985), U.S. geologist. A faculty member of the University of Illinois (1922–42) and at the University of California's Scripps Institution of Oceanography, La Jolla (1942–85), Shepard was a pioneer marine geologist in the United States. He made notable studies of the seafloor and of the origin of submarine canyons and wrote *Submarine Geology* (1948), the first textbook on the subject. His other books included *Submarine Canyons and Other Sea Valleys* (1966; with R. F. Dill), *Our Changing Coastlines* (1971; with H. R. Wanless), *Geological Oceanography* (1977), and the popular *Earth Beneath the Sea* (1959).

SHEPARD, SAM (Samuel Shepard Rogers; 1943–), U.S. playwright, director, and actor. Born in Illinois, Shepard moved to New York City. Developing his craft in the avant-garde theater of the 1960s, he wrote one-act plays for production in cafés and churches, then graduated to Off-Off Broadway when Theater Genesis produced *Cowboys* (1964) and La Mama staged *Dog and Rocking Chair* (1965). Over the next two decades, Shepard wrote more than 40 plays, as well as poetry, short fiction, and autobiographical sketches, and was regarded as the leading playwright of his generation. He brought to the stage a distinctly American voice, with plays rooted in U.S. history and popular culture. His early work (1963–76) had elements of the fantastic; his later plays, beginning with *Curse of the Starving Class* (1976), were more personal and probing, and were often family dramas. His other plays included *The Unseen Hand* (1969), *The Tooth of Crime* (1972), *Buried Child* (1978; Pulitzer Prize), *Fool for Love* (1983), *A Lie of the Mind* (1985), and *Simpatico* (1993). He worked in film as well, and wrote the screenplay for *Paris, Texas* (1984) and *Far North* (1989), which he also directed. Shepard often acted in his own plays, and starred in the movies *Days of Heaven* (1978), *The Right Stuff* (1983), *Country* (1984), and *Fool for Love* (1985). He also wrote the short-story collection, *Cruising Paradise* (1996). ■ See biographies by Don Shewey (1985) and Ellen Oumano (1986).

SHERRINGTON, SIR CHARLES SCOTT (1857–1952), British neurophysiologist. Sherrington began investigating the anatomy of nerve paths between the brain and spinal cord while a student at Cambridge. Later, as a professor at the University of Liverpool (1895–1913) and at Oxford (1913–35), he turned his attention to the physiology of the spinal cord and demonstrated the presence of sense organs in skeletal muscles, thus explaining limb movement by reflex action. He described the function of the synapse and the fundamental mechanisms of the mammalian nervous system. In

1932, he was awarded (with Edgar D. Adrian) the Nobel Prize in Physiology or Medicine for his discoveries regarding the functions of neurons. His books included *The Integrative Action of the Nervous System* (1906) and *Man on His Nature* (1940). ■ See study by Ragnar Granit (1967).

SHERWOOD, ROBERT EMMET (1896–1955), U.S. playwright and biographer. Rejected by the U.S. Army, the 6-foot 7-inch Sherwood fought in a Scottish-Canadian regiment in World War I. Associated with *Life* magazine (1920–28), he became one of the first film columnists and a prominent member of the New York literary scene. He was a speechwriter (1940–45) for Pres. Franklin D. Roosevelt and directed the overseas branch of the Office of War Information (1942–44). His play, *Idiot's Delight* (1936), a plea for world peace, won him the first of his four Pulitzer Prizes; the others were for the plays *Abe Lincoln in Illinois* (1938) and *There Shall Be No Night* (1940) and his "intimate biography." *Roosevelt and Hopkins* (1948). He also wrote the screenplay for the movie *The Best Years of Our Lives* (1946; Academy Award). ■ See John Mason Brown, *The Worlds of Robert E. Sherwood* (1965) and *The Ordeal of a Playwright* (1970), and study by Walter J. Meserve (1970).

SHEVARDNADZE, EDUARD (1928–   ), Soviet and Georgian political leader. A native of Georgia, Shevardnadze joined the Communist party in 1948, received a university history degree by correspondence, and became a party official. As minister of the interior (1965–85) and party chief (1972–   ) of the Georgian Soviet Republic, he was known as a reformer. He supported the perestroika reform policies of Mikhail Gorbachev and as soviet foreign minister (1985–90), helped to carry out policies that improved relations with the West and led to the end of the cold war. He resigned from the Communist party (1991) and helped to form a new democratic reform movement. However, after the formal disintegration of the Soviet Union in December 1991, he returned to newly independent Georgia, helped to mediate the end of a convulsive civil war, and was named president (1992). He led Georgia into the Russian-sponsored Commonwealth of Independent States while increasing Georgian economic ties to the West, and he won landslide victories in the 1995 and 2000 presidential elections. ■ See his memoirs *The Future Belongs to Freedom* (1991; Eng. trans. 1991) and Carolyn M. Ekedahl and Melvin A. Goodman, *The Wars of Eduard Shevardnadze* (1997).

SHIDEHARA, BARON KIJURO (1872–1951), Japanese diplomat and politician. A career diplomat, Shidehara served as vice minister for foreign affairs (1915–19), ambassador to the United States (1919–22), and chief delegate to the Washington Naval Conference (1921–22). As foreign minister (1924–27; 1929–31) he advocated international cooperation, noninterference in Chinese affairs, and harmonious relations with Britain and the United States—a policy that was known as Shidehara diplomacy. He was attacked

by military and right-wing organizations and was forced to resign in 1931. After World War II he served briefly as premier (Oct. 1945–May 1946) and was speaker of the lower house of the diet (1949–51).

SHIGA, NAOYA (1883–1971), Japanese novelist and short-story writer. One of the masters of modern Japanese literature, Shiga was born into an aristocratic family and studied English literature at Tokyo Imperial University (1906–08). In 1910 he cofounded the journal *White Birch,* which inaugurated an influential literary movement emphasizing individualism and humanistic values. In the 1920s, however, he broke with the movement, and his works became more realistic, unsentimental, and descriptive. Many of his novels were semi-autobiographical. Shiga's psychological subtlety and delicate, terse style are best revealed in his works concerning difficult family and personal relationships, notably *Han's Crime* (1913; Eng. trans. 1956), *Reconciliation* (1917), and *A Dark Night's Passing* (1921–37; Eng. trans. 1976). He also wrote *The Paper Door and Other Stories* (Eng. trans. 1987). ■ See study by Francis Mathy (1974).

SHILS, EDWARD ALBERT (1911–1995), U.S. sociologist. A professor at the University of Chicago (1938–77), Shils focused on the position of the intellectual in modern society in such works as *The Intellectual Between Tradition and Modernity* (1961) and *The Intellectuals and the Powers* (1972). He concluded that intellectuals in the modern era are more likely to become attached to institutions, such as the government or the university, than they were in past eras. He also founded the journal *Minerva* (1962). Other books included *Center and Periphery: Essays in Macro-Sociology* (1975), *Culture and Its Creators* (1977), *The Calling of Sociology* (1980), *Universities, Politicians, and Bureaucrats* (1982), and *The Academic Ethic* (1984).

SHIMAZAKI, TOSON (1872–1943), Japanese poet and novelist. Shimazaki started his literary career as a romantic poet, but his novel *Broken Commandment* (1906; Eng. trans. 1974) was a pioneer work of Japanese naturalism. His writings are concerned with Japan's transition from feudal to modern times. The autobiographical novel *The Family* (1910–11; Eng. trans. 1976) was an account of the decline of two provincial families, while *Before the Dawn* (1929–35; Eng. trans. 1987), viewed the years 1853 to 1886 through his father's eyes. He also wrote *Chikuma River Sketches* (1940; Eng. trans. 1991). ■ See Edwin McClellan, *Two Japanese Novelists* (1969).

SHINN, EVERETT (1876–1953), U.S. artist. A New Jersey Quaker by birth, Shinn studied at the Pennsylvania Academy of Fine Arts and became a newspaper and magazine illustrator. A member of The Eight, he helped introduce social realism into American art in the early years of the century. Instead of scenes of New York's Bowery, however, Shinn was inclined to "uptown" subjects—music-hall, ballet, and circus themes, and theatrical portraits and sets. He also wrote and produced vaudeville melodramas in his own Greenwich Village theater. ■ See study by Edith De Shazo (1974).

SHIRAKAWA, HIDEKI (1936–), Japanese chemist. Shirakawa studied at the Tokyo Institute of Technology (Ph.D. 1966) and taught at the University of Tsukuba. During the 1970s, in collaboration with Alan G. MacDiarmid and Alan J. Heeger of the University of Pennsylvania, Shirakawa helped to develop conductive polymers, plastics that can conduct electricity like a metal. Their discovery influenced research in both chemistry and physics and played a key role in the development of molecular electronics. Conductive polymers were soon used in photographic film, computer screens, light-emitting diodes, solar cells, and mobile telephone displays. For their scientific contributions, Shirakawa, Mac-Diarmid, and Heeger shared the 2000 Nobel Prize in Chemistry.

SHIRER, WILLIAM LAWRENCE (1904–1993), U.S. journalist and author. A newspaper correspondent in Europe during the late 1920s and early 1930s, Shirer joined the staff of CBS (1937) and was highly praised for his broadcasts from Vienna, London, Prague, Berlin, and Paris (1937–40). He was one of the few foreign correspondents to cover the German army early in World War II and was the first to report on the signing of the Franco-German armistice at Compiègne (1940). His eyewitness account, *Berlin Diary: The Journal of a Foreign Correspondent, 1934–41* (1941), was an international best-seller. He remained with CBS until 1947, wrote a column for the *New York Herald Tribune* (1942–48), and broadcast the news for the Mutual Broadcasting System (1947–49). Subsequently he was a full-time freelance writer, winning the 1960 National Book Award for his monumental history *The Rise and Fall of the Third Reich* (1960). He also wrote *The Collapse of the Third Republic* (1969) and *Gandhi: A Memoir* (1979). ■ See his memoirs, *20th Century Journey* (3 vols., 1976–90).

SHKLOVSKY, VIKTOR BORISOVICH (1893–1984), Soviet critic and writer. Shklovsky published his first book in 1914, beginning a literary career that spanned seven decades. A close ally of futurist poet Vladimir Mayakovsky, he became, in the early 1920s, a theoretician of the influential formalist school of criticism, which stressed a work's form and structure and deemphasized the conditions or climate in which it was created. He was a leader of the Serapion Brothers, an informal literary group opposed to the use of literature for nonliterary ends. Opposing the Bolsheviks, who won power in the 1917 Russian Revolution, Shklovsky emigrated, but returned to the Soviet Union after two years abroad (1923). He joined the official writers' union (1934) and published essays, historical novels, screenplays, and literary criticism. Shklovsky identified the literary technique of *ostranenie* or "estrangement"—the breakdown of routine

experiences so that they are perceived as if for the first time—and applied the term in his study of the great writer Leo Tolstoy (1928). By recanting some of the more radical assertions of his youth, he survived purges of the intelligentsia. Shklovsky recalled the period 1917–22 in the autobiography *A Sentimental Journey* (1923; Eng. trans. 1971) and wrote the novels *Zoo or Letters Not About Love* (1923; Eng. trans. 1971) and *Third Factory* (1926; Eng. trans. 1977).

SHOCKLEY, WILLIAM BRADFORD (1910–1989), U.S. physicist. Shockley was born in London to American parents and was raised in California. After studying at the Massachusetts Institute of Technology (Ph.D. 1936), he worked at the Bell Telephone Laboratories. There he and his colleagues John Bardeen and W. H. Brattain discovered the transistor effect for electronic amplification. Using germanium crystals, they constructed solid-state semiconductors that were more compact and efficient than vacuum tubes. For this achievement, which had important theoretical as well as practical implications, the three shared the 1956 Nobel Prize in Physics. In the 1970s, Shockley, who taught engineering at Stanford University (1958–75), publicized his controversial view that human intelligence, as expressed in terms of IQ, hinges primarily on heredity. His lectures on the subject gave rise to charges of racism and occasioned near-riots at campuses across the country. Shockley's books included *Electrons and Holes in Semiconductors* (1950) and *Mechanics* (1966; with W. A. Gong).

SHOEMAKER, BILL (William Lee Shoemaker; 1931–), U.S. jockey. The 95-lb. 4-foot 11¼-inch Shoemaker began his phenomenal racing career in 1949. He was the leading North American rider for five years (1950; 1953–54; 1958, 1959) and leading purse winner for 10 different years. He won the Kentucky Derby four times (1955; 1959; 1965; 1986), the Belmont Stakes five times (1957; 1959; 1962; 1967; 1975), and the Preakness twice (1963; 1967). On March 3, 1985, he became the first jockey to earn $100 million with his 8,446th victory. He retired on Feb. 3, 1990, with a (then) record 8,833 victories and $123 million in purses. In 1991 he was paralyzed in an auto accident. His record was broken by Laffit Pincay, Jr., who raced to his 8,834th victory in Dec. 1999. ■ See his autobiography, *The Shoe* (1976; with Dan Smith).

SHOEMAKER, EUGENE MERLE (1928–1997), U.S. astronomer. A pioneer in the field of planetary geology, Shoemaker worked for the U.S. Geological Survey (1948–93) and taught at the California Institute of Technology (Caltech; 1962–85). He and his wife Carolyn, with whom he worked closely, were credited with identifying 32 comets and 1,125 asteroids. Their most famous discovery (made with amateur astronomer David Levy) was Comet Shoemaker-Levy (1993), whose fragments crashed into Jupiter (July 1994), creating gigantic explosions and fireballs clearly visible to astronomers on earth. He warned that comets and asteroids posed a threat to life on earth and urged scientists to search for those objects and develop technology to intercept and destroy them before they bombard the planet. As principal investigator for the National Aeronautics and Space Administration's (NASA) Apollo Moon Project in the 1960s, he mapped lunar craters, analyzed rocks brought back from the moon, and did pioneering studies of lunar geology.

SHOLEM ALEICHEM (Solomon Rabinowitz; 1859–1916), Russian-born Yiddish-language writer. Sholem Aleichem received a traditional Jewish education and served as a tutor and rabbi before turning to writing (1883) the novels, short stories, and plays that made him a beloved figure throughout the Yiddish-speaking world. Called the "Yiddish Mark Twain," he portrayed with great affection and humor the daily trials and tribulations of the poverty-stricken and oppressed Jewish masses in the Diaspora, especially in Eastern Europe. His work played a major role in elevating the quality of Yiddish literature and in popularizing it, through translations, throughout the world. He left Russia after the pogroms of 1905, lived in several European cities, and settled in New York in 1914. His best-known works were the series of tales in *Tevye the Dairyman* (1894–1916; Eng. trans. 1959; the basis of the Broadway show *Fiddler on the Roof*), *Mottel the Cantor's Son* (1907–16; Eng. trans. 1953), and *Menachem Mendel* (1892–1913; Eng. trans. 1979). Numerous other works appeared in English translation. ■ See Maurice Samuel, *The World of Sholom Aleichem* (1943), and study by Joseph and Frances Butwin (1977).

SHOLOKHOV, MIKHAIL ALEKSANDROVICH (1905–1984), Soviet novelist. Sholokhov was 23 years old when the first installments of *The Silent Don* (4 vols., 1928–40) appeared in the journal *October*. The panoramic novel set in his native Don Cossack country in southern Russia in the years surrounding the 1917 Russian Revolution was avidly read by millions of readers who identified with the exciting episodes from lives of ordinary people. *The Silent Don* was widely translated, appearing in English in two volumes: *And Quiet Flows the Don* (1934) and *The Don Flows Home to the Sea* (1940). His other major work was a less impressive two-part novel (1932–60) about the collectivization of agriculture, translated as *Virgin Soil Upturned* (1935; retitled *Seeds of Tomorrow* in the U.S. edition) and *Harvest on the Don* (1960). Sholokhov won the 1965 Nobel Prize in Literature. A member of the Supreme Soviet (from 1946) and the Central Committee of the Communist party (from 1961), he was regarded officially as the greatest Soviet prose writer and the leading practitioner of socialist realism. He often spoke out against writers who criticized the Soviet system, such as Aleksandr Solzhenitsyn, Boris Pasternak, Yuli Daniel, and Andrei Sinyavsky. Solzhenitsyn and other critics cast doubt on Sholokov's authorship of *The Silent Don;* other literary experts disagreed with these charges of plagiarism. ■ See studies by D. H. Stewart (1967) and Herman Ermolaev (1983).

SHOSTAKOVICH, DMITRI DMITRIEVICH (1906–1975), Russian composer. For his graduation from the Petrograd Conservatory, Shostakovich composed his acclaimed First Symphony (1925). His early work, including the opera *The Nose,* showed his independence and musical sophistication, and his Second and Third Symphonies (1927, 1929) won critical recognition. After the doctrine of socialist realism was proclaimed, critics assailed his opera *Lady Macbeth of Mtsensk* (1932), and Shostakovich was ostracized by the music establishment. He kept private the Fourth Symphony (1936) that marked a movement toward more expressive, emotional composition but made public his Fifth Symphony (1937), which was more ideologically acceptable. His powerful Seventh Symphony, *Leningrad* (1941), was written in his native city during World War II. After surviving another period of political disfavor (1948–53), Shostakovich composed the Tenth Symphony and again challenged the establishment with his celebrated Thirteenth Symphony, *Babi Yar* (1962); it was based on a well-known poem by Evgeny Yevtushenko that deals with Russian anti-Semitism. His son, the well-known conductor Maksim Shostakovich, emigrated to the United States (1981). ■ See the controversial memoirs *Testimony* (Eng. trans. 1979); studies by I. Martynov (1947), N. Kay (1971), and H. Ottaway (1979); and biography by Laurel E. Fay (2000).

SHOTWELL, JAMES THOMSON (1874–1965), Canadian-born U.S. historian. Having earned a Ph.D. at Columbia University (1903), Shotwell taught there until 1942. He was also president of the Carnegie Endowment for International Peace (1949–50) and editor of its 152-volume *Economic and Social History of the World War* (1921–40). Of Quaker ancestry, he was a leading advocate of world peace and was instrumental in the establishment of the International Labor Organization and the United Nations. He wrote many books, including *War as an Instrument of National Policy* (1929) and *The Long Way to Freedom* (1960). ■ See his *Autobiography* (1961) and study by Harold Josephson (1975).

SHUBERT, LEE (Levi Szemanski; 1873?–1953), and JACOB SHUBERT (Jacob Szemanski; 1880?–1963), Russian-born U.S. theatrical producers. Taken to the United States in 1882 by their poor immigrant Jewish parents, the Shuberts received no formal education before entering the theater business. Together with their brother Sam (1876?–1905), they organized stock companies, operated several theaters in upstate New York, and began to manage a theater in New York City (1900). They successfully broke the monopoly of the Klaw-Erlanger theatrical syndicate, which controlled 95 percent of American theaters, and bought up theaters in New York and major cities throughout the country. They produced a series of highly successful low-budget operettas, including *Sinbad* (1919) and *The Student Prince* (1924), and numerous vaudeville productions. By the mid-1920s they owned or controlled 35 New York theaters, produced 25 percent of all Americans plays, and controlled 75 percent of all U.S. theaters. They helped keep theater alive during the Depression of the 1930s and produced the last of their 520 productions in 1954. To avoid an antitrust suit (1950) they sold 12 theaters in six cities and gave up the booking share of the business. ■ See Jerry Stagg, *The Brothers Shubert* (1968), and Foster Hirsch, *The Boys from Syracuse* (1998).

SHUKAIRY, AHMAD (1907–1980), Palestinian political leader. Trained as a lawyer, Shukairy served as undersecretary for political affairs of the Arab League (1951–57), Saudi Arabian ambassador to the United Nations (1957–62), and Palestinian representative to the Arab League (1963). He became chairman of the Palestinian Liberation Organization (PLO) when it was established by the league (1964). A hard-liner and extremist, he called for the liquidation of the Israeli state and the physical extermination of the Jews of Israel. He was criticized for his performance during the Arab-Israeli War (1967) and was forced to resign.

SHULA, DON (1930–   ), U.S. football coach. Shula played in the National Football League before being hired by the Baltimore Colts (1963) as the youngest head coach in NFL history. After seven seasons in Baltimore, he coached the Miami Dolphins (1970–95) and became one of the most successful team leaders in professional sports. He guided the Dolphins to five Super Bowl appearances and won the championship twice (1972; 1973). His 1972 Dolphins went 17–0, the only undefeated season in NFL history. He retired in 1995 as the winningest coach ever in the NFL, having compiled an overall record of 347–173–6. He also led teams in six Super Bowls, more than any other coach. He was named to the Pro Football Hall of Fame in 1997.

SHULL, CLIFFORD G. (1915–   ), American physicist. Shull studied at New York University (Ph.D. 1941) and served as chief physicist at the Oak Ridge National Laboratory in Tennessee (1946–55), the site of one of the earliest nuclear research reactors in the United States. Working there on a team headed by Dr. Ernest O. Wollan, Shull developed neutron-scattering techniques to determine the atomic structure and properties of simple crystals. The method was subsequently used to study more complex material and aided in the development of semiconductors, superconducting materials, and catalytic converters. Shull later was a professor at the Massachusetts Institute of Technology (1955–86) and shared the 1994 Nobel Prize in Physics with Bertram M. Brockhouse.

SHULTZ, GEORGE PRATT (1920–   ), U.S. political leader. A specialist in industrial relations, Shultz taught at the Massachusetts Institute of Technology (1946–57) and the University of Chicago (1957–68; dean of the business school, 1962–68) and was an economic adviser to the Eisenhower and Kennedy administrations. He served Pres. Richard Nixon as secretary of labor (1969–70), director of

the Office of Management and Budget (1970–72), and secretary of the treasury (1972–74) before retiring to private life to join the Bechtel Corp. (president, 1975–80), a huge international engineering and construction firm with numerous projects in the Middle East. A supporter of Ronald Reagan during the 1980 presidential campaign, he was an architect of Pres. Reagan's economic policy. As his secretary of state (1982–89), Shultz pursued a tough anticommunist foreign policy, undermining radical movements and governments in the Caribbean and Central America and supporting an expansion of U.S. nuclear forces. He wrote several books including *Economic Policy Beyond the Headlines* (1978; with Kenneth W. Dam). ■ See his *Turmoil and Triumph: My Years as Secretary of State* (1993).

SHUTE, NEVIL (Nevil Shute Norway; 1899–1960), British writer and aeronautical engineer. Although Shute introduced vital aeronautical innovations, including several World War II weapons and the design of the airship R. 100, he was best known as a writer. His aeronautical expertise and numerous aerial and naval adventures provided realistic backgrounds for his more than 20 fast-paced novels, which broke British sales records. His novels included *Ordeal* (1939), *Pastoral* (1944), *No Highway* (1948), and *A Town Like Alice* (1950). He emigrated to Australia (1950), the setting for *On the Beach* (1957), a novel describing the aftermath of an atomic war. ■ See his autobiography, *Slide Rule* (1954), and study by Julian Smith (1976).

SIAD BARRE, MOHAMMED (1920?–1995), Somali political leader. The son of a nomadic desert herdsman, Siad Barre served as chief inspector of the Somali police force during the 1950s and was commander in chief of the armed forces (from 1966). He led a successful coup in 1969 and served as head of state (from 1969), president of the supreme revolutionary council (1969–76), secretary-general of the Somali Socialist Revolutionary party, and chairman of the council of ministers (from 1976). An advocate of scientific socialism, he attempted to transform his primarily nomadic society with the help of the Soviet Union, which supplied Somalia with technical aid and arms and built large naval bases in the country. After the start of the war with Ethiopia (1977), a Soviet client state, Siad Barre expelled Soviet advisers and switched to an alliance with the United States. Widespread poverty, human rights abuses, and dictatorial rule led to growing civil unrest in the late 1980s. He was overthrown in 1991, leaving Somalia without a viable central government.

SIBELIUS, JEAN JULIUS CHRISTIAN (1865–1957), Finnish composer. Born into a musical family, Sibelius was a major romantic composer whose orchestral music, notably *En Saga* (1892), *The Swan of Tuonela* (1893), and *Tapiola* (1926), evoked the natural landscape of his homeland. His most celebrated composition was *Finlandia* (1900), a symphonic poem so imbued with nationalism that it was closely associated with the movement for Finnish independence. He composed a total of seven symphonies (1899–1924), some 100 songs, and theater music, the outstanding example being the score for *The Tempest* (1926). ■ See biographies by Harold E. Johnson 1959), Robert Layton (1966), and Erik Tawaststjerna (Eng. trans. vol. I, 1976).

SICKERT, WALTER RICHARD (1860–1942), German-born British painter. The most important British impressionist painter, Sickert was a pupil of James Whistler (1882), who influenced his palette, and of Edgar Degas (1883), who influenced his subject matter and his method of positioning figures. Known for his many music-hall scenes, he was fascinated with the mundane and seamy side of English life and used low-keyed tones to heighten the dreary mood of his subjects. He founded the Camden Town (1911) and London (1913) groups of painters and was a prominent art teacher. ■ See the collection of his writings, *Free House!* (1947), and biography by Denys Sutton (1976).

SIEGBAHN, KAI (1918–), Swedish physicist. The son of Nobel Prize–winning physicist Manne Siegbahn, Kai Siegbahn received a doctorate at the University of Stockholm (1944) and taught at Uppsala University (1954–84). For his work in developing high-resolution electron spectroscopy, he shared the 1981 Nobel Prize in Physics with Arthur Schawlow and Nicolaas Bloembergen.

SIEGBAHN, (KARL) MANNE (GEORG) (1886–1978), Swedish physicist. Siegbahn's earliest experiments were conducted in the field of electromagnetism; in 1913–1914 he began the research in X-ray spectroscopy, for which he was awarded the 1924 Nobel Prize in Physics. His original contribution was the development of the techniques and equipment necessary to obtain a high resolution of X-ray spectra, permitting accurate measurement of X-ray wavelengths. By revealing that electrons are arranged in shells within the atom, he helped to confirm Niels Bohr's atomic theory. Siegbahn wrote the influential book *The Spectroscopy of X-rays* (Eng. trans. 1925), taught at the universities of Lund, Uppsala, and Stockholm, and directed (1937–64) the Nobel Institute of Physics in Stockholm. His son Kai shared the 1981 Nobel Prize in Physics.

SIEGEL, JERRY (1914–1996), and JOSEPH SHUSTER (1914–1992), U.S. cartoonists. As 17-year-old high school students, Siegel (the writer) and Shuster (the artist) collaborated to create the comic strip Superman. They sold the strip to Detective Comics (1938) for $130, and it became an instant popular success. It spawned scores of superheroes and was quickly established as a fixed American icon. Siegel and Shuster continued to work on the strip until 1948, but they had no rights to the characters and received no royalties. They initiated, but lost, many lawsuits to regain their rights to the strip and eventually left the industry. They worked at menial jobs for years and were nearly destitute when Warner Communications, the current owners of Superman, agreed (Dec. 1975) to pay each a $20,000 annuity, later increased to $30,000.

SIERPINSKI, WACLAW (1882–1969), Polish mathematician. A founder of the Warsaw school of mathematics, Sierpinski taught at the University of Warsaw (1918–60) and wrote more than 700 articles and studies in the areas of set theory, number theory, and topology. He developed new theorems and geometrical constructions and proofs and taught the first systematic course in set theory (University of Lvov, 1908). He founded (1919) and edited the journal *Fundamenta Mathematicae* and later edited *Acta Arithmetica* (from 1960). His books included *Elementary Theory of Numbers* (Eng. trans. 1946), *General Topology* (Eng. trans. 1952), and *Cardinal and Ordinal Numbers* (Eng. trans. 1958).

SIGNORET, SIMONE (Simone Kaminker; 1921–1985), French actress. Signoret, a glamorous and sensuous performer, made her film debut in 1942 and achieved stardom with *La Ronde* (1950), *Casque d'Or* (1952), *Thérèse Raquin* (1953), and *Diabolique* (1955). In 1956 she and her husband, Yves Montand, starred in Arthur Miller's *The Crucible* on the Paris stage: offstage they were prominent supporters of left-wing political causes. She gave a strong performance in the British film *Room at the Top* (1958; Academy Award). Other memorable roles were in *Ship of Fools* (1965), *Madame Rosa* (1977), and *I Sent a Letter to My Love* (1981). She also wrote the novel *Adieu, Volodya* (1985; Eng. trans. 1986). ■ See her autobiography, *Nostalgia Isn't What It Used to Be* (Eng. trans. 1978).

SIHANOUK, NORODOM (1922–), Cambodian (Kampuchean) political leader. Sihanouk ascended to the Cambodian throne in 1941 and negotiated his country's independence from France (1953). He abdicated in favor of his father (1955) to enter politics, and served as premier for 15 years. During the 1960s he struggled to maintain Cambodian independence by steering a neutral course between U.S.-backed South Vietnamese forces and communist insurgents during the war in neighboring Vietnam. He was overthrown by U.S.-backed general Lon Nol (1970) and became the nominal head of a government-in-exile (in Beijing) dominated by the communist Khmer Rouge. After they seized power in Cambodia (1975), Sihanouk, who was not a communist, returned home but was placed under house arrest. However, when Vietnamese forces invaded Cambodia and overthrew the government (1979), Sihanouk went into exile and became president of a tripartite coalition government (including the Khmer Rouge and noncommunist factions) that fought a guerrilla war (1981–89) against the Vietnamese-installed regime. After the withdrawal of Vietnamese troops (1989) he served as head of state (1989–90). He returned to Cambodia in 1991, served as president (1991–93), and became king again in September 1993. He was subsequently unable to prevent frequent violent clashes among various political factions, and he spent much of his time in his home in Beijing, China. ■ See his books, *My War with the CIA* (1973; with Wilfred Burchett) and *War and Hope* (Eng. trans. 1980), and biography by Milton Osborne (1994).

ŠIK, OTA (1919–   ), Czechoslovak economist. Šik was a member of the Central Committee of the Czech Communist party (1962–68) and director at the Economic Institute of the Academy of Sciences (1963–68). The chief architect of his country's 1968 economic reforms, he advocated the use of market factors—traditionally rejected by socialist planners as capitalistic—to reconcile the conflicting interests of producers and consumers. He also opposed the emphasis on heavy industry and contemplated massive loans from the West. He moved to Switzerland after Soviet military intervention (1968) put an end to the Czech experiment with democratic socialism. His books included *Plan and Market Under Socialism* (1965; Eng. trans. 1968), *The Third Way* (1972; Eng. trans. 1976), *The Communist Power System* (1976; Eng. trans. 1981), and *For a Humane Society* (1979; Eng. trans. 1984).

SIKORSKI, WLADYSLAW EUGENIUSZ (1881–1943), Polish soldier and public official. A veteran of the World War I Polish Legions and the 1919–20 campaign against the Soviet Union, Sikorski became Poland's chief of staff in 1921 and premier in 1922. Banned from politics after Joseph Pilsudski's 1926 coup, he returned as premier of the Polish government-in-exile in London after the German occupation in 1939. Already difficult relations with Soviet dictator Joseph Stalin were further strained in 1943 when Sikorski asked for an investigation of the Katyn massacre of Polish officers. He was killed in an air crash. ■ See his *Modern Warfare* (1943); David Irving, *Accident* (1967); and Sarah M. Terry, *Poland's Place in Europe* (1983).

SIKORSKY, IGOR IVAN (1889–1972), Russian-born U.S. aircraft designer and manufacturer. Sikorsky failed (1909–10) to design a direct-lift machine but successfully built (1913) the first multiengine plane while working as chief engineer in a Russian aviation factory. He emigrated (1919) to the United States, losing his fortune in his flight from the Bolshevik revolution. He established (1923) a company that became part of United Aircraft; his division designed land and sea craft that were widely used by both commercial and military organizations. In 1939, Sikorsky finally succeeded in building and flying the first practical helicopter. ■ See biography by Frank J. Delear (rev. ed. 1976) and Jay P. Spenser, *Whirlybirds* (1998).

SILKWOOD, KAREN GAY (1946–1974), U.S. atomic worker and union activist. While working in the Kerr-McGee Corp.'s Cimarron facility near Oklahoma City, which had a government contract to produce plutonium for nuclear reactors, Silkwood collected evidence of health and safety hazards. She arranged to turn her notes over to a *New York Times* reporter and an official of the Oil, Chemical, and Atomic Workers Union, but was killed in an automobile accident on her way to the appointment (Nov. 13, 1974). Authorities ruled her death accidental, despite the fact that no cause was established and the notes she was bringing to the meeting were not found. The Cimarron plant was shut down a month later (Dec. 1974) after several more contamination incidents. The Silkwood case moved Congress to convene hearings into health and safety problems in the nuclear industry (1976). A decade after her death, she continued to stir controversy. A civil jury awarded $10 million in damages to Silkwood's estate (1979) in connection with the plutonium contamination of her apartment (part of an alleged effort to discourage her whistle-blowing); after an appeals court reversed the decision, the U.S. Supreme Court overturned the reversal (1984) and ruled that the courts could impose punitive damages for safety violations. In August 1986, the Kerr-McGee Corp. gave the Silkwood estate $138 million in an out-of-court settlement to end the decade-long lawsuit. Her story inspired the movie *Silkwood* (1983).

SILLANPÄÄ , FRANS EEMIL (1888–1964), Finnish writer. Sillanpää was the son of a poor tenant farmer. He studied natural sciences at Helsinki University before becoming a writer. *Meek Heritage* (1919; Eng. trans. 1938) described the effects of the Finnish civil war (1918) and emphasized the workings of human nature. He achieved international fame with the novels *Fallen Asleep While Young* (1931; Eng. trans. 1933) and *People in the Summer Night* (1934; Eng. trans. 1966). Noted for his belief in the unity of nature and the universe, and for his style, which was especially lyrical and poetic in his short stories, he was awarded the Nobel Prize in Literature (1939).

SILLITOE, ALAN (1928–   ), British novelist. The son of a tannery worker, Sillitoe left school at age 14 to work in a factory. He was one of the working-class, regional novelists who brought new vigor and subject matter to British fiction in the 1950s. His first novel, *Saturday Night and Sunday Morning* (1958), examined the life of a young factory worker who finds relief from alienating work in hedonistic weekend experiences. That novel and the title story in the collection *The Loneliness of the Long Distance Runner* (1959) were made into films with screenplays by Sillitoe. His other works included the novels *The Death of William Posters* (1964), *A Start in Life* (1971), *The Widower's Son* (1976), *Her Victory* (1982), *The Lost Flying Boat* (1984), *Life Goes On* (1985), and *Last Loves* (1990) and the short-story collections *Men, Women and Children* (1973), *The Second Chance* (1981), and *Collected Stories* (1995). ■ See his autobiography, *Life Without Armour* (1995), and studies by Allen R. Penner (1972) and Stanley Atherton (1979).

SILLS, BEVERLY (Belle Silverman; 1929–), U.S. opera singer. Born in Brooklyn, New York, of Russian-Jewish descent. Sills matured from a child radio star into the most popular U.S. coloratura soprano. She made her opera debut at 17 in Philadelphia and persevered through repeated rejection to gain acceptance by the New York City Opera in 1955. By the mid-1960s she had hit her mark, making a La Scala (Milan) debut in 1969 and a belated Metropolitan Opera (New York) debut in 1975. She was best known for her interpretations of the bel canto repertory, notably *Maria Stuarda, Anna Bolena, Lucia di Lammermoor,* and the roles of Elvira in *I Puritani* and Elizabeth in *Roberto Devereux.* She also starred in Massenet's *Manon,* and sang all three female leads in Offenbach's *Tales of Hoffmann.* She later served as director of the New York City Opera (1979–88), managing director of the Metropolitan Opera (1991–94), and the chair of Lincoln Center (1994–). ■ See her autobiographies, *Bubbles* (1976) and *Beverly* (1987; with Lawrence Linderman).

SILONE, IGNAZIO (Secondo Tranquilli; 1900–1978), Italian novelist. Silone was a founder of the Italian Communist party (1921) and a leader of the antifascist underground during the 1920s. He broke with the party and lived in exile in Switzerland (1930–44), where he wrote a series of novels, including *Fontamara* (1930; rev. ed. 1958; Eng. trans. 1934, 1964), *Bread and Wine* (1937; rev. ed. 1955; Eng. trans. 1937, 1962), and *The Seed Beneath the Snow* (1941; rev. ed. 1953; Eng. trans. 1942, 1965), which expressed his antifascist sentiments and exposed the plight of the poor in southern Italy. The novels were rapidly translated, and Silone was acclaimed abroad as the leading Italian writer of his day. After World War II he briefly reentered political life and coedited the cultural review *Tempo Presente* (1956–68). His later works included *A Handful of Blackberries* (1952; Eng. trans. 1953), *The Fox and the Camellias* (1960; Eng. trans. 1961), and the autobiographical *Emergency Exit* (1965; Eng. trans. 1968), which traced his political development. During the late 1990s, documents uncovered in the national archives indicated that during the 1920s Silone apparently worked as an informant for the fascist secret police, betraying Communist cells and antifascist groups throughout Europe.

SILVER, ABBA HILLEL (1893–1963), Lithuanian-born U.S. rabbi and Zionist leader. Taken to the United States in 1902, Silver was educated at the University of Cincinnati and at Hebrew Union College and served as rabbi of the Reform Temple in Cleveland, Ohio, from 1917 until his death. Between 1938 and 1948, he headed at different times the Zionist Organization of America, American Zionist Emergency Council, United Jewish Appeal, United Palestine Appeal, and Central Conference of American Rabbis. As the head of the American section of the Jewish Agency for Palestine, Silver spoke in behalf of Zionism before the United Nations during the Palestine hearings of 1947 and played a major role in convincing the American government and people to support the Zionist plan for a Jewish state. His numerous books included *A History of Messianic Speculation in Ancient Israel* (1927), *The World Crisis and Jewish Survival* (1941), and *Where Judaism Differed* (1956). ■ See biography by Marc Lee Raphael (1989).

SILVERMAN, SIME (1873–1933), U.S. newspaper publisher. After being dismissed from his reporting job on the *New York Morning Telegraph* (1905), a sports and theatrical daily, Silverman borrowed some money and started his own show-business weekly, *Variety,* developing it into a Broadway institution. Known for its editorial fairness and independence, *Variety* was written in a lively, innovative, and slangy style that was incredibly effective. Silverman was considered one of America's most creative slang makers (he coined the term "disc jockey," among others), and his headline describing the 1929 stock-market crash, "Wall Street Lays an Egg," was regarded as a classic.

SIMAK, CLIFFORD D. (1904–1988), U.S. science-fiction writer. Simak grew up on a Wisconsin farm and later worked as a newspaperman. He began writing science fiction after reading H. G. Wells and Jules Verne, publishing his first story in 1931. His reputation was established when eight of his stories were collected in *City* (1952), a chronicle of the future that deplored the values of urban life. Journeys in time and space often figured in his fast-moving, sometimes bewildering fiction. His novels included *Way Station* (1963), *Cemetery World* (1973), *The Fellowship of the Talisman* (1978), *Project Pope* (1981), *Special Deliverance* (1982), and *Highway of Eternity* (1986). His short-story collections included *The Worlds of Clifford Simak* (1960) and *Best Science Fiction Stories of Clifford Simak* (1967).

SIMENON, GEORGES (1903–1989), Belgian-born novelist. By age 19, Simenon had moved to Paris (1922) and had begun writing popular fiction. He had no formal training, but produced more than 500 novels and novellas and countless short stories that sold millions of copies in many languages. Among his novels are psychological accounts of the frustration and isolation of inarticulate people. He created one of the world's favorite detectives in *Maigret Stonewalled* (1935; Eng. trans. 1959), and followed the adventures of the astute Inspector Maigret in some 100 novels. Unlike the writers of classic British detective novels, Simenon was concerned less with method than milieu, and in a vigorous, spare style he explored with empathy the human dimensions of crime and passion. ■ See his *Intimate Memoirs* (Eng. trans. 1984) and the autobiographical *When I Was Old* (Eng. trans. 1971); John Raymond, *Simenon in Court* (1968); Fenton S. Bresler, *Mystery of Georges Simenon* (1983); Patrick Marnham, *The Man Who Wasn't Maigret* (1993); and biography by Pierre Assouline (1997).

SIMMEL, GEORG (1858–1918), German sociologist and essayist. Simmel studied at the University of Berlin (Ph.D. 1881). As a Jew, he was denied a university chair until 1914; while he lectured at his alma mater, he was essentially an unaffiliated scholar supported by a small family inheritance. Simmel described the influence of a monetary economy on social activity and relationships in his *Philosophy of Money* (1900; Eng. trans, 1978) and was a founding member of the German Sociological Association (1910). His interests were so diffuse—from art and culture to religion and metaphysics—that he left behind many seminal ideas but failed in his effort to create a consistent system of social thought. He was regarded as a brilliant essayist. Four essays written between 1890 and 1918 appeared in English as *Georg Simmel: On Women, Sexuality, and Love* (1984). While reflecting turn-of-the-century male biases, they showed him to be a pioneer in the sociology of human emotions. ■ See Kurt Wolff, ed., *The Sociology of Georg Simmel* (1950); study edited by Peter A. Lawrence (1977); and David Frisby, *Sociological Impressionism* (1981).

SIMMONS, RUSSELL (1957–), U.S. music producer. Raised in a black middle-class family in New York City, Simmons was a gang member during his teenage years and learned about business as a seller of marijuana. While a student at City College in Harlem in the late 1970s, he began to promote rap parties and concerts and helped to launch the careers of several young rap singers, including Kurtis Blow and the group Run-DMC. As cofounder (with Rick Rubin) of Def Jam Records (1983), he discovered and promoted L. L. Cool J, the Beastie Boys, and Public Enemy and played a major role in popularizing rap and breaking down the barriers between rap and pop music. Through his magazine (*One World,* 1993–), fashion-design company (Phat Farm), and television show (*Def Comedy Jam*), Simmons spread the influence of rap and hip-hop through mainstream culture. His Rush Communications, which he founded in 1990, also produced films and television commercials.

SIMON, CLAUDE (1913–), French novelist. Simon was born in Madagascar of French parents. A painter turned "new novelist," he lived most of his life apart from a literary milieu. He first achieved prominence with *The Wind* (1957; Eng. trans. 1959). Here, as in *The Grass* (1958; Eng. trans. 1960), *The Flanders Road* (1960; Eng. trans. 1961), and *Histoire* (1967; Eng. trans. 1967), Simon abandoned a traditional story line to explore the qualities of language and perception. The U.S. author William Faulkner is the most evident literary influence on these efforts to portray human consciousness in all its complexity. In his early novels Simon often achieved richly sensuous effects, while in more experimental later works, including *Triptych* (1973; Eng. trans. 1976) and *The World About Us* (1975; Eng. trans. 1983), he sought to examine experiences of everyday life. His later works included *The Georgics* (1981; Eng. trans. 1989) and *The Acacia* (1989; Eng. trans. 1991). He was awarded the 1985 Nobel Prize in Literature. ■ See biography by Salvador Jimenez-Fajardo (1975).

SIMON, HERBERT ALEXANDER (1916–2001), U.S. economist. A versatile social scientist, Simon earned a Ph.D. in political science (1943) from the University of Chicago and joined the faculty of Carnegie-Mellon University in 1949, becoming professor of computer science and psychology (1965). He was also an authority on psychology and public administration. Simon devised a model to describe economic behavior in the real world in which the capacity for rational action is limited. Instead of "maximizing profits," business executives make decisions on the basis of limited information and seek minimally acceptable solutions to pressing problems, he believed. He was awarded the Nobel Memorial Prize in Economics in 1978 for his work on decision making. His books included *Administrative Behavior* (1947), *Models of Man* (1957), *Human Problem Solving* (1972), *Models of Thought* (1979), *Reason in Human Affairs* (1983), and *Scientific Discovery* (1987). ■ See his autobiography, *Models of My Life* (1991).

SIMON, JOHN ALLSEBROOK SIMON, 1st VISCOUNT (1873–1954), British political leader. Simon, who was educated in the classics at Oxford, became a successful lawyer, won election to Parliament (1906) as a Liberal, and served as home secretary (1915–16). He headed the 1927–30 Simon Commission on the status of India and served continuously through the 1930s as foreign secretary (1931–35), home secretary (1935–37), and chancellor of the exchequer (1937–40). He was best known as an advocate of the appeasement policy toward Nazi Germany. From 1940 to 1945 he was lord chancellor. ■ See his autobiography, *Retrospect* (1952), and biography by David Dutton (1992).

SIMON, (MARVIN) NEIL (1927–), U.S. playwright. The son of a garment salesman, Simon was a television comedy writer for a decade before *Come Blow Your Horn,* his first hit play, was produced in 1961. There followed an unprecedented string of successful Broadway plays: *Barefoot in the Park* (1963), *The Odd Couple* (1965), *Plaza Suite* (1968), *Last of the Red Hot Lovers* (1969), *The Prisoner of Second Avenue* (1971), and *The Sunshine Boys* (1972)—all situation comedies of middle-class life. *The Odd Couple* developed into a popular, long-running TV series, while several of the other plays were adapted as films. Moving from New York to Los Angeles during the mid-1970s, Simon wrote *California Suite* (1976), a play that was later filmed. Later work included three autobiographical plays, *Brighton Beach Memoirs* (1984), *Biloxi Blues* (1985; Tony Award), and *Broadway Bound* (1987), as well as *Lost in Yonkers* (1991; Pulitzer Prize), *Jake's Women* (1994), *Laughter on the 23rd Floor* (1995), *Proposals* (1997), and *The Dinner Party* (2000). Simon also wrote many screenplays. A two-volume collection of his plays appeared in 1980. ■ See his memoirs, *Rewrites* (1996) and *The Play Goes On* (1999), and studies by Edythe McGovern (1979) and Robert K. Johnson (1983).

SIMON, PAUL. *See SIMON AND GARFUNKEL.*

SIMON AND GARFUNKEL (Paul Simon, 1941– ; Art Garfunkel, 1941–), U.S. vocal and instrumental duo. Boyhood friends from New York City, Simon and Garfunkel began singing together in high school, and as Tom and Jerry recorded a hit rock song in 1957. They split up to attend college but reunited as Simon and Garfunkel (1964), singing quiet, introspective, and poetic folk-pop songs (written by Simon). Their albums, including *Sounds of Silence* (1966), *Parsley, Sage, Rosemary and Thyme* (1966), *Bookends* (1968), and *Bridge over Troubled Water* (1970), became international bestsellers. After they split up in 1970, Garfunkel starred in several movies, including *Catch-22* (1970) and *Carnal Knowledge* (1971) and recorded a few highly regarded solo albums, including *Angel Clare* (1973), *Lefty* (1988), and *Up 'Til Now* (1993). Simon, however, remained a major force in the world of pop music, with a series of albums featuring such songs as "Mother and Child Reunion," "Me and Julio Down by the Schoolyard," "Still Crazy After All These Years," and "50 Ways to Leave Your Lover." The success of the album *Graceland* (1986), based on South African township music, and *Rhythm of the Saints* (1990), based on Brazilian drumming, helped to develop an interest in the United States for world music. *Songs From the Capeman* (1997) was rooted in Salsa rhythms.

SIMONE, NINA (Eunice Kathleen Waymon; 1933–), U.S. singer, pianist, and composer. One of eight musical children, her talent at the piano was recognized and encouraged by a woman for whom her mother worked as a housekeeper. She began her career as a nightclub singer (1954) and rose to national fame with her 1959 recording of "I Love You Porgy," from Gershwin's *Porgy and Bess,* inspired by the Billie Holiday recording. Her piano style, influenced by both classical and jazz music, was difficult to classify as was her vocal style, which embodied elements of folk, jazz, gospel, and popular music. ■ See her autobiography, *I Put a Spell on You* (1993).

SIMONOV, KONSTANTIN (KIRILL) MIKHAILOVICH (1915–1979), Soviet writer. A World War II correspondent and a lesser poet, Simonov won enormous popularity with his romantic verse, "Wait for Me," a wartime poem on the power of love, reached millions of soldiers on the front and inspired numerous composers to set it to music. His widely read novels dealing with World War II included *Days and Nights* (1943–44; Eng. trans. 1945) and *The Living and the Dead* (1960; Eng. trans. 1962). Simonov was prominent in the Soviet literary establishment as editor of the journals *Literaturnaya gazeta* ("Literary Gazette"; 1950–54) and *Novy*

mir ("New World"; 1946–50; 1954–58). During his second tenure at *Novy mir,* he reflected the mood of the day by calling for "broadened socialist realism" and liberalized literary controls. English translations of his articles from *Red Star* appeared in *In One Newspaper* (1984; with Ilya Ehrenburg).

SIMONSON, LEE (1888–1967), U.S. theatrical designer. Simonson was educated at Harvard College (B.A. 1909), where he studied under George Pierce Baker. He began his professional career in New York with the Washington Square Players (1915) and was a cofounder of the Theatre Guild (1919), serving on its board of directors until 1940. He reacted against confining realistic stage designs and utilized innovative lighting and "plastic forms and spaces" to enhance the meaning of the play. His Theatre Guild productions included *Heartbreak House* (1920), *The Adding Machine* (1923), Volpone (1928), *Elizabeth the Queen* (1931), and *Idiot's Delight* (1936). Simonson was also responsible for designing the Metropolitan Opera Company's productions of Wagner's *Ring* cycle (1948). He wrote *The Stage Is Set* (1932), *The Art of Scenic Design* (1950), and the autobiographical *Part of a Lifetime* (1943).

SIMPSON, GEORGE GAYLORD (1902–1984), U.S. paleontologist. Simpson received his Ph.D. from Yale (1926) and was associated with the American Museum of Natural History in New York City for decades (1927–59). A renowned and prolific scholar, he was a professor of vertebrate paleontology at Columbia University (1945–59) and Harvard (1959–70) and was one of the world's foremost authorities on the early history of mammals and evolutionary theory. His works included *The Meaning of Evolution* (1949), *Horses* (1951), *Major Features of Evolution* (1953), *Principles of Animal Taxonomy* (1961), and *Biology and Man* (1969). ■ See his autobiography, *Concession to the Improbable* (1978).

SIMPSON, HELEN DE GUERRY (1897–1940), Australian novelist. Simpson was educated in a convent in Sydney and later in France. When World War I broke out, she went to England and worked as a message decoder and studied music at Oxford. She began writing in 1925 and established her reputation with *Boomerang* (1932), a long novel set in Europe and Australia and ending with World War I. *Woman on the Beast* (1933), *Saraband for Dead Lovers* (1935), and *Under Capricorn* (1937; film 1949) followed. Simpson also wrote several mystery novels, including *Enter Sir John* (1929), and *Re-enter Sir John* (1932), both with Clemence Dane. She was killed during a German bombing attack on London.

SIMPSON, O. J. (Orenthal James Simpson; 1947–), U.S. football player. Raised in a primarily black neighborhood in San Francisco, Simpson became a star running back for the University of Southern California, where he won the 1968

Heisman Trophy, and for the Buffalo Bills (1969–78) and San Francisco 49ers (1978–79) of the National Football League. During his pro career he set single-season records (since broken) for most yards rushing (2,003; 1973) and most touchdowns scored (23; 1975) and gained over 200 yards in a game six times. He was the NFL's Most Valuable Player (MVP) in 1973. After his retirement he was a television sports commentator (1969–86) and movie actor and started his own television production company. In 1994 he was arrested for the murder of his ex-wife, Nicole Brown Simpson, and her friend, Ronald Goldman. After a sensational, racially charged, televised trial (Jan.–Oct. 1995), which dominated the mass media and riveted the nation, Simpson was acquitted. However, in a subsequent civil trial (Oct. 1996–Feb. 1997), brought by the families of the victims, Simpson was found liable for their wrongful deaths and ordered to pay $8.5 million in compensatory damages and $25 million in punitive damages. ■ See Jeffrey Toobin, *The Run of His Life* (1996), and Daniel Petrocelli and Peter Knobler, *Triumph of Justice* (1998).

SIMS, WILLIAM SOWDEN (1858–1936), U.S. naval officer. A graduate of the U.S. Naval Academy (1880) who served as a naval attaché in Paris and St. Petersburg and as an aide to Pres. Theodore Roosevelt (1908–09), Sims was one of the most influential officers in U.S. history. He wrote a basic navigation text, enacted administrative reforms, and improved destroyer tactics and gunnery techniques. Promoted to admiral in 1917, during World War I, he commanded U.S. naval forces in European waters, where he devised "convoys" to protect merchant shipping. In 1920 he testified that navy administrative errors had prolonged that war at sea by a year. He also collaborated (with B. J. Hendrick) on the Pulitzer Prize–winning *Victory at Sea* (1920). ■ See biography by Elting E. Morison (1942).

SINATRA, FRANK (Francis Albert Sinatra; 1917?–1998), U.S. singer and actor. As a young crooner with the Harry James (1939) and Tommy Dorsey (1940–42) bands, Sinatra was besieged by hysterical bobby-soxers wherever he appeared. Singing songs such as "I'll Never Smile Again," "Let's Get Away from It All," "Try a Little Tenderness," and "Night and Day," he became one of the country's most popular entertainers and appeared in such movies as *Anchors Aweigh* (1945) and *On the Town* (1949). After a wane in popularity, he made a successful comeback in a dramatic supporting role in *From Here to Eternity* (1953), which earned him an Academy Award. Subsequently he starred in numerous movies, including *Guys and Dolls* (1955), *The Man with the Golden Arm* (1956), and *Pal Joey* (1957); appeared frequently in nightclubs, especially in Las Vegas; and became a perennially popular and dominant force in the entertainment industry. His later song hits included "All the Way," "Chicago," "Strangers in the Night," and "My Way." In 1993, his album *Frank Sinatra Duets* sold more than two million copies in the United States. ■ See biogra-

phies by Earl Wilson (1976) and Will Friedwald (1995); studies by Norm Goldstein (1982) and John Rockwell (1984); and Kitty Kelley, *His Way* (1986).

SINCLAIR, UPTON BEALL (1878–1968), U.S. novelist and reformer. Sinclair's muckraking classic *The Jungle* (1906) turned the stomachs of America with its graphic account of Chicago's meat-packing industry. With the proceeds from his best-seller, he founded a utopian community in New Jersey, which was abandoned (1907) after its building was destroyed by fire. In 1915 he compiled a pioneering volume of social protest literature, *The Cry for Justice*. He crusaded for birth control and child-labor laws, helped to found the American Civil Liberties Union, and ran repeatedly for public office on a socialist ticket. A vegetarian and teetotaler, Sinclair agitated for social justice in 79 books and hundreds of pamphlets. His account of German dictator Adolf Hitler's rise in *Dragon's Teeth* (1942), the third novel in the 11-volume "Lanny Budd" series, won a Pulitzer Prize. ■ See his *Autobiography* (1962); biography by Leon Harris (1975); and study by William Bloodworth, Jr. (1977).

SINGER, ISAAC BASHEVIS (1904–1991), Polish-born U.S. Yiddish-language writer. Influenced by the rationalism of his mother and the cabalistic mysticism of his father (a Hasidic rabbi), Singer started to write fiction while working as a translator and proofreader for a Yiddish-language newspaper in Warsaw. Emigrating to the United States (1935), where he joined his brother, the novelist I. J. Singer, he worked for the Jewish daily *Forward* in New York, which serialized most of his novels before they appeared in English translation. His works explored the theme of exile and emphasized supernatural forces and sexuality as well as aspects of asceticism and religious devotion. English translations of his writings included *Satan in Goray* (1943), *The Family Moskat* (1950), *The Magician of Lublin* (1960), *The Slave* (1962), *Enemies* (1972), *The Collected Stories* (1982), *The Penitent* (1983), *The Image and Other Stories* (1985), and *Shadows on the Hudson* (1997). *In My Father's Court* (1966), *A Little Boy in Search of God* (1976), *A Young Man in Search of Love* (1979), and *Lost in America* (1981) were autobiographical. He also wrote prize-winning children's books. In 1978 Singer was awarded the Nobel Prize in Literature. ■ See biographies by Paul Kresh (1979) and Janet Hadda (1997); study by Edward Alexander (1980); and Israel Zamir, *Journey to My Father* (Eng. trans. 1995).

SINGER, ISRAEL JOSHUA (1893–1944), Polish-born U.S. Yiddish-language novelist, playwright, and journalist. An active member of Yiddish literary groups in Kiev and Warsaw, Singer emigrated to the United States (1933), where he achieved his greatest fame. He was a master of character portrayal who produced notable epic-length novels that portrayed many generations of one family and depicted entire societies or epochs. *Yoshe Kalb* (1932; Eng. trans. as *The Sinner*, 1933; as *Yoshe Kalb*, 1965), *Blood Harvest* (1927;

Eng. trans. 1935), *The Brothers Ashkenazi* (1936; Eng. trans. 1936, 1980), and *The Family Carnovsky* (1943; Eng. trans. 1969) were Singer's most notable works. He was the older brother of the novelist Isaac Bashevis Singer. ■ See his memoir of childhood, *Of a World That Is No More* (1946; Eng. trans. 1970), and Clive Sinclair, *The Brothers Singer* (1983).

SINGH, KHUSHWANT (1915–), Indian novelist, historian, and journalist. Singh was most famous for his English-language novel *Train to Pakistan* (1955), which powerfully depicted the mass hysteria and senseless communal violence that followed the 1947 partition of the subcontinent into India and Pakistan. He also wrote the novel *I Shall Not Hear the Nightingale* (1959), the short-story collection *A Bride for the Sahib* (1967), and the nonfiction collections *Good People, Bad People* (1978), *Editor's Page* (1980), and *Sex, Scotch and Scholarship* (1992). A member of the Sikh community, he wrote and lectured extensively on the history, culture, and philosophy of his people. His books included *A History of the Sikhs: 1469–1964* (1966) and other works on Sikh history. He edited the *Illustrated Weekly of India,* a popular English-language magazine (1969–78), and the *Hindustan Times,* New Delhi (1980–83), and served in parliament (from 1980).

SINYAVSKY, ANDREI DONATOVICH (1925–1997), Russian writer. As a lecturer and senior fellow at the Gorky Institute of World Literature (1952–65), Sinyavsky wrote perceptive criticism of Soviet literature. Using the pseudonym Abram Tertz (from 1956), he wrote novels, short stories, and essays for underground circulation in the Soviet Union—and publication in the West—that reflected his abhorrence of Stalinism and socialist realism and his belief in a literature infused with the absurd and the fantastic. His best-known works were the essay *On Socialist Realism* (1959; Eng. trans. 1960), the novels *The Trial Begins* (1956; Eng. trans. 1960) and *The Makepeace Experiment* (1963; Eng. trans. 1965), and the collection *Fantastic Stories* (1961; Eng. trans. 1963). Convicted (with writer Yuli Daniel) of producing anti-Soviet propaganda (1966), he served five years in a labor camp. *A Voice from the Chorus* (1974; Eng. trans. 1976) contains notes and letters he sent to his wife from prison. He emigrated to Paris (1973) and taught Russian literature at the Sorbonne. English translations of his literary essays and book reviews are in *For Freedom of Imagination* (1971). The novel *Goodnight!* (Eng. trans. 1989) was autobiographical.

SIQUEIROS, DAVID ALFARO (1896–1974), Mexican painter and muralist. Siqueiros fought in Mexico's revolutionary war, worked as a union organizer, and was a Republican army brigade commander in the Spanish Civil War. He spent frequent periods in jail or exile due to his communist political activities. In his artwork he favored massive polemical murals—art for the people—and with Diego Rivera and

José Clemente Orozco was a leader of the muralist movement. His social realist works, which combined elements of folklore and surrealism, depicted aspects of human misery and revolutionary struggle. His best-known works include *From Porfiro's Dictatorship to the Revolution,* in the National History Museum; *Ascent of Culture,* in the National University; and *March of Humanity,* which took four years to paint and covers two acres in the garden of the Hotel de Mexico in Mexico City. ■ See his *Art and Revolution* (Eng. trans. 1975); study by Mario de Micheli (Eng. trans. 1968); and biography by Philip Stein (1994).

SIRHAN, SIRHAN BISHARA (1944–), Palestinian-born U.S. assassin. Born in Jerusalem to a Christian Palestinian Arab family, Sirhan emigrated to the United States with his family in 1957. He attended Pasadena (California) City College for two years and worked as an exercise boy at a horse ranch. On the night of the 1968 California presidential primary, he mortally wounded the Democratic victor, Sen. Robert F. Kennedy, at the Ambassador Hotel in Los Angeles. Rejecting an insanity defense in order to make a political statement about U.S. favoritism to Israel, he was convicted of first-degree murder and sentenced to death (1969). Lengthy legal maneuvers followed, and in 1972, after the California Supreme Court banned capital punishment, his sentence was reduced to life imprisonment (1972). Numerous applications for parole were denied throughout the 1990s. ■ See Robert B. Kaiser, *"R.F.K. Must Die!"* (1970).

SIRICA, JOHN JOSEPH (1904–1992), U.S. federal judge. The son of an Italian immigrant barber, Sirica was a onetime exhibition boxer who worked his way through Georgetown Law School (1926). He was active in Italian-American Republican circles, and made his reputation as a federal judge for law-and-order rulings and a high rate of reversal (1957–74). He was the senior federal judge for the District of Columbia and on the verge of retirement in 1973 when he took on the case of the burglary at the Democratic headquarters at the Watergate apartment complex. Sirica's ruling that executive privilege did not absolve Pres. Richard Nixon from a subpoena to turn over his tapes, and his subsequent sentencing of the president's top aides for conspiracy to obstruct justice, catapulted the jurist into the national limelight. His account of the Watergate affair is in *To Set the Record Straight* (1979).

SISKIND, AARON (1903–1991), U.S. photographer. Siskind was a New York City public-school English teacher who became active in the Film and Photo League during the 1930s and did significant documentary work in the city's slums. In the 1940s, however, he turned to the abstract imagery of planes and surfaces, eliminated perspective from his works, and became closely associated with abstract expressionist painters in New York. Siskind taught photography at Chicago's Institute of Design (1951–71), the Rhode Island School of Design, and elsewhere. ■ See Nathan Lyons, ed.,

Aaron Siskind, Photographer (1965), and *Places: Aaron Siskind Photographs* (1976).

SITTER, WILLEM DE (1872–1934), Dutch mathematician and astronomer. Professor of astronomy at the University of Leiden (1908–34) and director of the Leiden Observatory (1919–34), de Sitter was the first to apply Albert Einstein's general theory of relativity to the origin and expansion of the universe (1916). His work was instrumental in spreading Einstein's ideas in the English-speaking world and helped to lay the groundwork of modern cosmology. He also made notable studies of Jupiter's satellites and of the fundamental astronomical constants. His books in English included *Kosmos* (1932) and *The Astronomical Aspects of the Theory of Relativity* (1933).

SITWELL, DAME EDITH (1887–1964), British poet and critic. A member of an aristocratic family, the eccentric and controversial Edith Sitwell became famous as a coeditor (with her brothers Osbert and Sacheverell) of the annual anthology *Wheels* (1916–21), which attacked contemporary poetic styles and set a new trend in British poetry. A brilliant poetic technician and an accomplished musician, she utilized the rhythms of jazz and popular music in her early experimental and fanciful light verse. These collections—*The Mother and Other Poems* (1915), *Clowns' Houses* (1918), and *Façade* (1922)—were followed by more serious, religiously oriented works, *The Song of the Cold* (1945) and *The Canticle of the Rose* (1949). She often turned to the past for her models and allusions and frequently dressed in medieval fashions. ■ See her autobiography, *Taken Care Of* (1965), and biographies by Victoria Glendinning (1981) and Geoffrey Elborn (1981).

SITWELL, SIR OSBERT (1892–1969), British poet, essayist, and novelist. The high-spirited and iconoclastic scion of a prominent family, Sitwell began his literary career after he left the army in 1919. He first attracted notice, along with his sister Edith and brother Sacheverell, as a critic of contemporary British poetry. He was best known for his five-volume autobiography, *Left Hand! Right Hand!* (1944). *The Scarlet Tree* (1946), *Great Morning* (1947), *A Laughter in the Next Room* (1948), and *Noble Essences* (1950), which nostalgically re-created the genteel pre–World War I world in which Sitwell felt most at home. ■ See biography by Philip Ziegler (1999) and John Pearson, *The Sitwells* (1979).

SKELTON, RED (Richard Skelton; 1913–1997), U.S. comedian and actor. Skelton's father, who died two months before Red's birth, had been a circus clown. His mother was a cleaning woman at an Indianapolis circus and got him in to watch performances. Skelton decided early on an entertainment career. He worked in radio in the 1930s and after a screen test won (1940) a contract. He made dozens of movies and entertained TV viewers with "The Red Skelton Show" (1951–70), which showcased his antics and featured Skelton as Clem Kaddidlehopper, Freddie the Freeloader, and Willie Lump-Lump. Finally his ratings dropped; in 1972 he announced his retirement from show business. ■ See biography by Arthur Marx (1979).

SKIDMORE, LOUIS (1897–1962), U.S. architect. Skidmore supervised the installation of the 1933 Chicago exposition in collaboration with Nathaniel Owings. The partnership of Skidmore, Owings and Merrill, founded in 1939, developed a team approach to architectural design and expanded to include, by 1970, 1,000 architects in several branch offices. Their first large commission was the atomic research center at Oak Ridge, Tennessee (1942–46), but the firm gained national prominence with the design (by Gordon Bunshaft) of the Lever House in New York (1952), a glass-clad, setback, International Style skyscraper. The building's efficiency and sophistication set the standard for corporate architecture for the next three decades and the firm designated dozens of other influential structures including the Chase Manhattan Bank, (New York, 1961), the John Hancock Center (Chicago, 1970), and the Sears Tower (Chicago, 1974), the world's tallest building.

SKINNER, BURRHUS FREDERIC (1904–1990), U.S. psychologist. B. F. Skinner studied languages and literature at Hamilton College and was later encouraged in his literary ambitions by poet Robert Frost. He turned to graduate work in psychology at Harvard University (Ph.D. 1931), later joining its faculty (1948–71). Influenced by the work of Russian physiologist Ivan Pavlov and by his own learning experiments with rats and pigeons, Skinner became the foremost contemporary exponent of behaviorism. *The Behavior of Organisms* (1938) set forth his argument that a particular behavior may be obtained through positive reinforcement or eliminated by withholding reinforcement. He applied his conditioning techniques first to education, pioneering in the field of programmed learning and devising a teaching machine to reinforce learning by reward, and later to clinical work with psychotic patients. Skinner wrote two controversial books about the prospects of social engineering: *Walden Two* (1948), a utopian novel, and *Beyond Freedom and Dignity* (1971). *Particulars of My Life* (1977), *The Shaping of a Behaviorist* (1979), and *A Matter of Consequences* (1983) are autobiographical. With Margaret Vaughan he wrote *Enjoy Old Age* (1983). ■ See studies by Richard I. Evans (1968) and John A. Weigel (1977).

SKOU, JENS C. (1918–), Danish physicist. Skou, a professor at the University of Aarhus (1946–88), did research on local anesthetics early in his career. During the 1950s he concentrated on the study of adenosine triphosphate (ATP), a molecule that is the source of energy for all living cells, fueling such activities as nerve-impulse transmission, protein building, and muscle motion. He discovered and described an enzyme, sodium-potassium-stimulated adenosine triphosphatase (Na-K-ATPase), that acts like a pump to maintain the chemical imbalance of sodium and potassium ions inside and outside of the cell. This imbalance is necessary for the fundamental activity of transporting substances through cell membranes. Skou shared the 1997 Nobel Prize in Chemistry with Paul D. Boyer and John E. Walker for his discovery.

SKOURAS, SPYROS P. (1893–1971), Greek-born U.S. film entrepreneur. Skouras emigrated to the United States and with two brothers began (1914) a movie business with a single nickelodeon. Over the next decades, they ran a chain of movie theaters in the Midwest. Skouras assumed management of Fox Metropolitan Theaters in New York City (1932) and rose (1942) to the presidency of its parent company, 20th Century-Fox. In the two decades he held that post, Skouras promoted cinemascope and other innovative film concepts.

SLÁNSKÝ, RUDOLF SALZMANN (1901–1952), Czech political leader. A member of the Czech Communist party from 1921 and a World War II partisan fighter, Slánský served as party secretary-general (1945–51) and played a major role in the 1948 communist takeover of the government. In 1951, however, he was accused of leading a "Titoist, Zionist" plot to overthrow the regime, and he confessed under duress. After a highly publicized trial (Nov. 1952) he was executed along with seven other Jewish defendants. He was absolved, posthumously, of the charges of treason and espionage (1963). ■ See Arthur London, *The Confession* (1968; Eng. trans. 1970); Eugen Loebl, *Stalinism in Prague* (Eng. trans. 1969); and Josefa Slánský, *Report on My Husband* (Eng. trans. 1969).

SLESSOR, KENNETH (1901–1971), Australian poet. A journalist from age 19, Slessor was one of the first modernist Australian poets. His pessimistic and despairing verse was noted for its rich rhythms and pictorial description. His best-known poems included "Five Visions of Captain Cook" (1932), which evoked the literal and spiritual history of Australia; "Beach Burial" (1942), a tribute to Australian soldiers who died during World War II; and *Five Bells* (1939), an elegy to an artist friend. Slessor served as an official war correspondent during World War II. His best poems are in *One Hundred Poems* (1944) and his journalistic pieces are in *Bread and Wine* (1970). ■ See study by Herbert C. Jaffa (1971); Douglas Stewart, *A Man of Sydney* (1977); and biography by Geoffrey Dutton (1991).

SLIM, WILLIAM JOSEPH SLIM, 1st VISCOUNT (1891–1970), British military leader. During World War II, Slim led the jungle military campaign in the reconquest of Burma from the Japanese (1945). Commanding British and Indian troops in one of the most difficult campaigns in modern warfare, he gave the Japanese the greatest land defeat they ever suffered. He served as chief of the imperial general staff (1948–52), Britain's highest military post, and was governor-general of Australia (1953–60). ■ See his memoirs, *Defeat*

into Victory (1956) and *Unofficial History* (1962), and biography by Ronald Lewin (1976).

SLIPHER, VESTO MELVIN (1875–1969), U.S. astronomer. The director of the Lowell Observatory in Flagstaff, Arizona (1916–52), Slipher made numerous contributions to the field of astronomy. His discovery of the rapid rotation and enormous velocities of the spiral nebulas provided the first observational evidence for the expanding-universe theory. His numerous pioneering spectroscopic studies resulted in the chemical analyses of the atmospheres of Jupiter, Saturn, and Neptune and the discovery of sodium and calcium in interstellar space. Slipher also discovered that many diffuse nebulas shine by reflected light, and he supervised the research that led to the discovery of the planet Pluto (1930).

SLOAN, ALFRED PRITCHARD, JR. (1875–1966), U.S. industrialist. Trained at the Massachusetts Institute of Technology, Sloan headed the Hyatt Roller Bearing Co. (1901–16) before serving as president (1923–37) and board chairman (1937–56) of General Motors. During his years at GM he introduced modern managerial techniques and pioneered in automotive engineering to create one of the world's largest industrial enterprises. A prominent philanthropist, he founded the Alfred P. Sloan Foundation (1937) and the Sloan-Kettering Institute for Cancer Research in New York City (1945). ■ See his autobiography, *My Years With General Motors* (1964).

SLOAN, JOHN FRENCH (1871–1951), U.S. artist. A high school dropout with 10 years' experience as a Philadelphia newspaper artist, Sloan was a member of the pioneering group of social realists called The Eight, later called the "Ashcan school." He was the art editor of the socialist *Masses* (1911–16), ran unsuccessfully for the New York Senate in 1913, and taught at New York's Art Students League (1916–32; 1935–38). His early paintings were somber-hued scenes from New York life—*Wake of the Ferry* (1907), *Sunday, Women Drying Their Hair* (1912)—but in later years he turned to cracked-porcelain nudes and landscapes of the Southwest. A collection of Sloan's lectures was published as *Gist of Art* (1939). ■ See studies by Van Wyck Brooks (1955), Bruce St. John (1971), David Scott (1975), and John Loughery (1995).

SMALLEY, RICHARD E. (1943–   ), U.S. chemist. Smalley studied at Princeton (Ph.D. 1973) and taught at Rice University, Houston, Texas (1976–   ). While working (at Rice) with Sir Harold W. Kroto and Robert F. Curl, Jr., on carbon vaporization and long-chain carbon molecules (1985), Smalley and his colleagues discovered a previously unknown form of carbon, in which dozens of carbon atoms are linked together in a form resembling a soccer ball. The scientists whimsically named the new molecules "fullerenes" or "buckyballs" because their shape was similar to the geodesic domes designed by architect R. Buckminster Fuller. The discovery opened up a new branch of science, fullerene chemistry, which promised to yield many practical applications in fields such as ultrastrong fibers, superconductors, and lubricants. Smalley, Kroto, and Curl shared the 1996 Nobel Prize in Chemistry for their discovery.

SMALLWOOD, JOSEPH ROBERTS (1900–1991), Canadian political leader. In Canada the name Joey Smallwood is identified with the province of Newfoundland. A printer, reporter (in Canada, the United States, and Britain), editor, trade-union organizer, radio-show host, author, and hog farmer, Smallwood strongly advocated provincial status for Newfoundland. When Newfoundland became a Canadian province (1949), Smallwood, a Liberal, became its first premier and minister of economic development. Flamboyant and outspoken, he fostered an enormous growth of industry, successfully developed Newfoundland's natural resources, and sponsored social legislation. He was ousted from power after the Liberals lost the 1971 elections. ■ See his memoirs, *I Chose Canada* (1973), and *The Time Has Come to Tell* (1979).

SMEAL, ELEANOR (Eleanor Cutri; 1939–   ), U.S. feminist. Smeal studied political science at Duke University (B.A. 1961) and at the University of Florida (M.A. 1963). As a Pittsburgh homemaker, she joined the National Organization for Women (NOW) in 1970, served as the first president of its Pennsylvania chapter, and was on its national board (1973–77). She served two terms as NOW president (1977–82), then formed the political consulting firm Eleanor Smeal and Associates (1983). In 1985, she won an upset victory over incumbent Judy Goldsmith to regain the organization's presidency. While Goldsmith favored lobbying and coalition-building to achieve women's rights, Smeal urged a more confrontational approach. As president until 1987 she fought for abortion rights, campaigned to pass the Civil Rights Restoration Act of 1985, and worked to get the Equal Rights Amendment "off the back burner." She founded the Fund for the Feminist Majority (1987).

SMEDLEY, AGNES (1894?–1950), U.S. political activist, journalist, and writer. Smedley grew up in a poor Colorado coal-mining town and left home at age 16. In New York City (1916–19) she became involved in leftist politics. She lived in Berlin (1919–28), then went to China as a newspaper correspondent (1928) and spent more than a decade there. She was sympathetic to the communist cause in China and spent years with the communist forces during the civil war and the war with Japan. Smedley's books included *China Fights Back* (1938), *Battle Hymn of China* (1943), *Portraits of Chinese Women in Revolution* (1976), and *The Great Road: The Life and Times of Chu Teh* (1956), a biography of the communist military hero. Back in the United States (from 1941) she spoke out for the Chinese communist cause, but her career was ruined in 1949 after she was accused, falsely, of being a spy, and she sought refuge in Britain. Although she never joined the Communist party, she was given the honor of being buried in the National Memorial Cemetery of Revolutionary Martyrs in Beijing (Peking). ■ See her autobiographical novel *Daughter of Earth* (1929) and biography by Janice R. MacKinnon (1988).

SMITH, ALFRED EMANUEL (1873–1944), U.S. political leader. The son of poor immigrant parents, Smith grew up on New York City's Lower East Side. He became active in Tammany Hall—Manhattan's Democratic machine—as a young man and moved through the state assembly to the governorship (1919–21; 1923–28), where he gained a reputation as a reformer. Smith was the first Roman Catholic presidential candidate (1928), but he was defeated by what he called the three P's: prejudice, prohibition (he was against it), and prosperity. Disillusioned, he left politics to head the company that built and ran New York's Empire State Building. ■ See his memoirs, *Up to Now* (1929); biographies by Oscar Handlin (1958) and Matthew and Hannah Josephson (1969); and Richard O'Connor, *The First Hurrah* (1970).

SMITH, ARTHUR JAMES MARSHALL (1902–1980), Canadian poet and critic. A.J.M. Smith spearheaded the Canadian poetry revival at McGill University in Montreal during the 1920s. As a graduate student he founded and edited (1925–27; with F. R. Scott) the *McGill Fortnightly Review*, which sought to broaden the scope of Canadian literature. He advocated a scholarly approach to Canadian criticism, editing *The Book of Canadian Poetry* (1943); *The Blasted Pine* (1957; with F. R. Scott), which anthologized satire; *The Oxford Book of Canadian Verse* (1960); and *Modern Canadian Verse in English and French* (1967). His own lyric poetry was published in *News of the Phoenix* (1943), *Collected Poems* (1962), and *The Classic Shade* (1978). His essays were collected in *Towards a View of Canadian Letters* (1973) and *On Poetry and Poets* (1977). Smith taught at Michigan State University (1936–71) and became a U.S. citizen in 1941. ■ See study by John Ferns (1979).

SMITH, BESSIE (1898?–1937), U.S. blues singer. Born into a poverty-stricken southern black family, Smith became a protégée of the pioneer blues singer Ma Rainey while in her teens. She was discovered by a Columbia Records executive, and her first blues recordings (1923) brought her nationwide fame. In the period of her greatest popularity (1924–28) she recorded with Louis Armstrong, Fletcher Henderson, and other jazz greats and appeared throughout the country on the black vaudeville circuit. She was the most successful African-American entertainer in America and was known as "the empress of jazz." Smith recorded more than 150 songs; some critics regard her as the greatest artist in jazz history. Her fame dwindled after 1928 due to changing public taste and her increasing alcoholism. She died following an auto accident in Mississippi after being refused admission to an all-white hospital. ■ See Chris Albertson, *Bessie* (1973), and study by Elaine Feinstein (1985).

SMITH, DAVID (1906–1965), U.S. sculptor. While studying at the Art Students League in New York City (1926–30), Smith supported himself by working as a welder, taxi driver, and salesman. His first one-person show (1938) featured freestanding welded-metal sculptures. After working as a welder on defense projects during World War II, he created a series of monumental geometric forms called *Zigs* and *Cubi*. A versatile, prolific artist, Smith was committed to perpetual experimentation, often translating ideas from one medium to another. Working in isolation on an upstate New York farm, he created some 600 sculptures, in addition to drawings, paintings, etchings, ceramics, collages, and photographs. He died at age 59 when his pickup truck swerved off the road. ■ See his autobiographical essay (1968) and studies by Rosalind E. Krauss (1971) and Garnett McCoy (1973).

SMITH, DEAN (1931–), U.S. basketball coach. Smith played on the University of Kansas national championship basketball team (1952) and served as head coach at the University of North Carolina (1961–97). An innovative mentor, Smith was known for his integrity both on and off the court, and was a legendary figure in the sports world. His teams won at least 20 games for 27 consecutive seasons (an NCAA record), reached the Final Four in the NCAA championship 11 times, and won two national collegiate championships (1982 and 1993). Thirty of his players attained All-American status, including Michael Jordan, Billy Cunningham, and James Worthy, and the graduation rate for his players who earned letters was 97.3 percent. In addition to developing innovative court strategies, including the four-corners offense, he was known for his support of desegregation and recruitment of black athletes and assistant coaches. He retired in 1997 as the winningest coach in college basketball history, with a record of 879–254. ■ See his autobiography, *A Coach's Life* (1999; with J. Kilgo and S. Jenkins).

SMITH, GERALD LYMAN KENNETH (1898–1976), U.S. political leader. A fundamentalist and self-proclaimed rabble-rouser, Gerald L. K. Smith was a leader of the extreme right wing in America for more than 40 years. He first achieved national prominence as a colleague and supporter of Louisiana's "Kingfish," Huey P. Long, and his "soak the rich" policies. After Long's death in 1935 Smith joined the fascist movement and began his militant lifelong crusade against blacks, Jews, Catholics, communists, and labor unions. He helped organize the Union party (1936), the America First party (which ran him for U.S. president in 1944), and the Christian National Crusade (1947), and he published a monthly hate sheet, *The Cross and the Flag* (from 1942). ■ See biography by Glen Jeansonne (1988).

SMITH, HAMILTON OTHANEL (1931–), U.S. microbiologist. Smith received his M.D. degree from the Johns Hopkins Medical School (1956) and did genetic research there (from 1967). In 1969, while studying bacterial interaction with deoxyribonucleic acid (DNA), he recognized and isolated a restriction enzyme (endonuclease) that cleaved to a specific site of a DNA molecule and enabled scientists to cut and manipulate the structure of the molecule. For his research, which provided a basis for recombinant DNA research (or gene splicing), he shared the 1978 Nobel Prize in Physiology or Medicine with Daniel Nathans and Werner Arber.

SMITH, IAN (1919–), Southern Rhodesian (Zimbabwean) political leader. A World War II hero, Smith entered the Southern Rhodesian legislative assembly in 1948. He quit parliament in 1961 to protest the new constitution, which granted 15 seats to black Africans. The success of his right-wing Rhodesian Front in 1962 brought him a cabinet post, and in 1964 he became prime minister. Dedicated to the continuation of minority (white) rule, he initiated the Unilateral Declaration of Independence (UDI) from Britain (1965). His government's refusal to concede the principle of majority (black) rule provoked a civil war by African nationalists and the regime relied on military force to maintain itself. As his government was weakened by years of guerrilla warfare, Smith agreed (1979) to serve in a transitional government headed by black leader Bishop Abel Muzorewa. After Robert Mugabe's victory in the British-sponsored 1980 elections, he was excluded from the government but continued to represent white interests in the parliament of the newly independent nation, renamed Zimbabwe. He remained active in politics and his renamed Conservative Alliance of Zimbabwe party won 15 of the 20 reserved white parliamentary seats in the 1985 elections. He retained his seat in parliament until 1988, but was suspended for the 1987–88 session. ■ See his memoirs, *The Great Betrayal* (1997).

SMITH, JOE (Joe Sultzer; 1884–1981), and **CHARLES DALE** (Charles Marks; 1881–1971), U.S. comedy team. Sultzer and Marks, soon to be known as Smith and Dale, met on New York City's Lower East Side in 1898, began performing in local saloons and restaurants, and broke into vaudeville in 1901. With Dale playing the deadpan straight man and Smith supplying the punch lines, the two comedians performed as a team for more than 70 years. In addition to headlining shows at New York's Palace Theater, they appeared in films and on television. Their well-known comedy sketches included "Dr. Kronkheit" and "The New Schoolteacher." Neil Simon's 1972 play, *The Sunshine Boys* (film 1975), was partly based on the lives of Smith and Dale.

SMITH, MARGARET CHASE (Margaret Chase; 1897–1995), U.S. political leader. Born in Skowhegan, Maine,

Smith first went to Congress to serve out her late husband's term, but far surpassed him in political influence. She remained there for more than three decades, serving five terms in the U.S. House of Representatives (1940–49) before winning election to the Senate. She served in the Senate for 23 years (1949–73), longer than any other woman. She was the first Republican to challenge Sen. Joseph McCarthy on the Senate floor. The first woman to have her name put in nomination as a major-party Presidential candidate (1964), Smith won more delegate votes than any candidate other than the nominee, Sen. Barry Goldwater. ■ See her *Declaration of Conscience* (1972); biographies by Frank Graham (1964) and Marlene B. Vallin (1998); Patricia W. Wallace, *Politics of Conscience* (1995); and Janann Sherman, *No Place for a Woman* (2000).

SMITH, MICHAEL (1932–2000), British-born Canadian biochemist. Smith studied at the University of Manchester, England (Ph.D. 1956); became a Canadian citizen in 1964; and taught at the University of British Columbia, Vancouver (1966–97). During the 1970s he invented a technique called oligonucleotide site-directed mutagenesis, which enabled researchers to alter genes by splicing nucleotides, foreign genetic segments, into a single strand of DNA. The resulting mutant DNA could then be used to produce redesigned proteins. The technique was widely used in genetic engineering, and Smith shared the 1993 Nobel Prize in Chemistry with Kary B. Mullis. Smith was a founder of Zymo-Genetics, Inc., a biotechnology company (1988), and directed the Genome Sequence Center at the British Columbia Cancer Research Center (1998–2000).

SMITH, OLIVER (1918–1994), U.S. designer for theater, film, ballet, and opera. Smith began his career designing for the ballet (*Rodeo*, 1942), which later led to his appointment (1946) as codirector of the American Ballet Theatre (1946–80; 1990–92). Although he designed sets for a number of dramatic productions, including Becket (1960; Tony Award), he appeared to be most at home in the realm of musical comedy and won Tony Awards for his sets in *My Fair Lady* (1956), *West Side Story* (1957), *The Sound of Music* (1959), *Camelot* (1960), *Hello, Dolly!* (1964), and *Baker Street* (1965). His other shows included *On the Town* (1945), *Brigadoon* (1947), and *Candide* (1957). He also designed a number of film musicals, including *The Band Wagon* (1953), *Oklahoma!* (1955), and *Guys and Dolls* (1955).

SMITH, RED (Walter Wellesley Smith; 1905–1982), U.S. sportswriter. One of the most literate, erudite, and admired sportswriters of his time, Smith wrote for the *St. Louis Star* (1928–36) and *Philadelphia Record* (1936–45) before beginning a 37-year career in New York City (*New York Herald Tribune*, 1945–66; *World Journal Tribune*, 1966–67; *New York Times*, 1971–82). His syndicated column (begun in 1945) was the most widely read in the nation by the mid-1950s and appeared in more than 500 papers by the 1970s.

He won a 1976 Pulitzer Prize for distinguished commentary. His collected columns appeared in several books, including *Strawberries in the Wintertime* (1974), *The Red Smith Reader* (1982), *To Absent Friends from Red Smith* (1982), and *Red Smith on Baseball* (2000). ■ See biography by Ira Berkow, *Red* (1986).

SMITH, ROBERT HOLBROOK. *See WILSON, WILLIAM GRIFFITH.*

SMITH, TONY (1912–1980), U.S. sculptor. Smith labored in his family's waterworks foundry while training in art. He assisted (1938–40) the architect Frank Lloyd Wright, then spent two decades as an independent architect and painter. In the 1940s he was influenced by his association with abstract expressionists, including Mark Rothko and Jackson Pollock; in the 1960s he turned to sculpture. His massive creations adapted architectural forms; he used large surfaces and geometric solids in *Gracehoper* (1961), *Black Box* (1962), and *Die* (1962). His "walk-through" sculptures, such as *Bat Cave* (1971), combined his interest in architecture and sculpture and expressed his commitment to art in public settings. He was also known for the large open-form structures *Smoke* (22 feet high; 1967) and *Moondog* (17 feet high; completed posthumously, 1997), which was based on a small bronze sculpture (1967). Smith was also an influential teacher of art at several New York City universities. ■ See study by Lucy Lippard (1972).

SMITH, W. EUGENE (1918–1978), U.S. photographer. A news photographer from age 15, Smith covered numerous World War II battles and was seriously wounded on Okinawa (1945). His first picture after a long convalescence (1947) was a shot of his children, which was selected as the concluding image of the *Family of Man* exhibition and book (1955). Smith worked for seven years at *Life* magazine (1947–54), where his compassionate photo essays reflected his belief in the social responsibility of photography. Three Guggenheim fellowships (1956; 1957; 1968) enabled him to work independently and to publish *Photographs and Notes* (1969). He spent several years (1971–73) in the Japanese fishing village of Minamota, risking his livelihood and his health to tell the story of the effects of mercury pollution. His dramatic images published in *Minamota* (1975) stimulated the growth of the environmental movement. ■ See Gilles Mora and John T. Hill, eds., *W. Eugene Smith: Photographs, 1934–1975* (1999).

SMITH, WALTER BEDELL (1895–1961), U.S. general. Smith joined the national guard when he was 15, earned his commission as an army officer in 1918, and worked hard during the interwar period to make up for his lack of college or military education. As Gen. Dwight Eisenhower's Chief of Staff during World War II (1942–46) he helped plan some of the greatest military operations in history. Smith was ambassador to the Soviet Union (1946–49), head of the Central

Intelligence Agency (1950–53), and undersecretary of state (1953–54). He wrote two memoirs, *My Three Years in Moscow* (1950) and *Eisenhower's Six Great Decisions: Europe, 1944–45* (1956). ■ See D.K.R. Crosswell, *The Chief of Staff* (1991).

SMUTS, JAN CHRISTIAAN (1870–1950), South African military and political leader. Smuts, of Dutch and French Huguenot descent, studied law at Cambridge and became politically active upon his return home (1895). He was a Boer general during the Boer War (1899–1902) but later worked for reconciliation and for a united, self-governing South Africa within the British empire. Throughout his career he opposed Afrikaner nationalists who wanted an independent republic. He served as a British officer in both world wars, rising to the rank of field marshal (1941). He also participated in the Versailles Peace Conference (1919) and the founding of the League of Nations and the United Nations. But the U.N. preamble that he wrote proclaimed rights that were denied to the majority of his countrymen, for during 40 years as a Unionist member of the South African parliament, including two terms as prime minister (1919–24; 1939–48), Smuts was largely indifferent to black African welfare. ■ See biographies by W. Keith Hancock (2 vols., 1962–68) and Kenneth Ingham (1986).

SNEAD, SAM (Samuel Jackson Snead; 1912–), U.S. golfer. The colorful Snead had one of the longest and one of the most successful careers in golf history. By 1938 he was the game's top money winner. He won the British Open (1946), the U.S. Masters three times (1949; 1952; 1954), and the U.S. Professional Golfers' Association (PGA) tourney three times (1942; 1949; 1951). The only major title that eluded him was the U.S. Open, but he won well over 150 other major and minor tournaments, including 81 PGA tour wins. In his 60s he was still competing in major tournaments.

SNEEVLIET, HENDRICUS (1883–1942), Dutch revolutionary, who used the pseudonym H. Maring. A railroad worker, Sneevliet joined the Dutch Social Democratic party and became president of the Dutch railroad workers union (1909). After a labor dispute he went to the Dutch East Indies (1912) and founded (1914) the Social Democratic Association of the Indies (ISDV), a militant nationalist organization. Expelled from Java (1918), he moved to Moscow, joined the Comintern, and became its delegate in China (1921–23), where he helped establish the Chinese Communist party (July 1921). He returned to Holland (1924) and was active in the communist and union movements. He left the Dutch Communist party (1927) and founded a Trotskyist political organization, the Revolutionary Socialist party (1929), and served as its sole parliamentary deputy (1933–37). Active in the Resistance during World War II, he was captured by the Germans and executed.

SNELL, GEORGE DAVIS (1903–1996), U.S. immunogeneticist. Educated at Dartmouth and Harvard (D.Sc. 1930), Snell worked at the Jackson Laboratory, Bar Harbor, Maine (1935–73). His pioneering work (from 1944) in the genetics and immunology of tissue transplantation in mice paved the way for subsequent organ transplants in humans and made it possible to explain why individuals have different capabilities in defending themselves against certain diseases and infections. Snell named the transplant-influencing genes "histocompatibility genes" and was coauthor of *Histocompatibility* (1976; with Jean Dausset and Stanley Nathanson). He shared the 1980 Nobel Prize in Physiology or Medicine with Dausset and Baruj Benacerraf.

SNOW, CHARLES PERCY (Baron Snow of Leicester; 1905–1980), British novelist. Trained as a physicist, C. P. Snow taught at Cambridge and served as a government adviser in World War II, a civil service commissioner (1945–60), and a member of the Labour government (1964–66). He drew on this background for his novel series *Strangers and Brothers* (11 vols., 1940–70). Written in detailed, unadorned prose, Snow's novels analyzed the ethics, power plays, and politics of bureaucrats and scientists. He was also noted for his essays on the relationship between scientific and literary culture and science policy. His best-known work, *The Two Cultures and the Scientific Revolution* (1960; expanded ed., 1964), described the split between humanists and scientists. Snow was knighted (1957) and made a life peer (1964). *A Coat of Varnish* (1979), the last of his 25 books, was a serious murder mystery. ■ See the biography by Philip Snow (1983) and the study by David Shusterman (1975).

SNOW, EDGAR PARKS (1905–1972), U.S. journalist and author. Snow, who first went to China as a reporter in 1928, was the first Westerner to visit and report on the Chinese communists in their remote headquarters in Yanan (Yenan; 1936). His accounts of their programs, idealism, and discipline became the basis of his widely read book, *Red Star over China* (1937). From 1949 until the normalization of U.S.-Chinese relations in the 1970s, Snow was one of the few Americans to have regular access to China, and his books *The Other Side of the River: Red China Today* (1962) and *The Long Revolution* (1972) were based on his personal experiences there. A sympathetic observer of Chinese events, Snow was a personal friend of communist leaders Mao Zedong (Mao Tse-tung) and Zhou Enlai (Chou En-lai) and was frequently granted exclusive interviews with them. ■ See biography by John M. Hamilton (1988); Robert M. Farnsworth, *From Vagabond to Journalist* (1996); and Thomas S. Bernard, *Season of High Adventure* (1996).

SNOW, HANK (1914–1999), Canadian-born U.S. country singer. Hank Snow's country singing was well known in Canada before he emigrated (1944) to the United States. After "Brand on My Heart" (1949) and "I'm Moving On"

(1950) were promoted by Dallas disc jockeys, Snow was catapulted to fame. He joined (1950) the Grand Ole Opry, where his mellow ballads, flat-picking guitar style, and personal reserve had great appeal and influenced younger singers, including Johnny Cash. Known as the "Singing Ranger," he appeared in absurdly elaborate cowboy outfits. ■ See his autobiography (1994; with Jack Ownbey and Bob Burris).

SNOWDEN, PHILIP SNOWDEN, 1st VISCOUNT (1864–1937), British political leader. The son of a weaver, Snowden was an influential socialist and pacifist who headed the Independent Labour party (1903–06; 1917–20) and served in Parliament (1906–18; 1922–31). As chancellor of the exchequer in governments headed by Ramsay MacDonald (1924; 1929–31), he insisted on reducing taxes and expenditures, even at the expense of social-welfare programs. He clung tenaciously to the economic orthodoxies of free trade and a balanced budget, but his policies failed to curb the growing financial crisis and rising unemployment caused by the Great Depression. ■ See his *Autobiography* (2 vols., 1934) and biographies by Colin Cross (1966) and Keith Laybourn (1988).

SNOWDON, ANTHONY CHARLES ARMSTRONG-JONES, 1st EARL OF (1930–), British photographer. Armstrong-Jones received his first camera as a child recovering from polio and grew up to become a society and fashion photographer. Appointed official court photographer in 1958, he married Princess Margaret in 1960 and gave up his Pimlico studio but continued to pursue his photographic interests. They were divorced in 1978. Armstrong-Jones collaborated on *Private View* (1965), a striking color essay on the British art scene, and published several collections, including *Assignments* (1972), *Sitting* (1983), *Stills* (1987), *Public Appearances* (1991), *Wild Flowers* (1995), and *Wild Fruit* (1997). He was also known for his photo reportage and documentary films for television. He was an adviser to *Design Magazine* (1962–87) and the *London Sunday Times* (1962–90) and was provost of the Royal College of Art (1995–). ■ See *Snowdon: A Photographic Autobiography* (1979).

SOARES, MÁRIO ALBERTO NOBRE LOPES (1924–), Portuguese political leader. Brought up in a republican and liberal family, Soares was a leader of the noncommunist, antifascist youth movement during the 1940s and of the democratic socialist opposition during the 1950s and 1960s. After receiving a law degree from the Sorbonne, he opened a legal practice in Lisbon (1958), defended many enemies of the dictorial regime of António Salazar, and was forced into exile (1970–74). He headed the Portuguese Socialist party (from 1973), and after the military coup of April 1974 he served as foreign minister (1974–75), negotiating the independence of Portugal's African colonies and establishing diplomatic relations with communist and African nations.

He served as premier from July 1976 to June 1978, when his coalition government dissolved over the issue of land reform. He later headed a second coalition government (1983–85) and served as president (1986–96). ■ See the autobiographical *Portugal's Struggle for Liberty* (1972; Eng. trans. 1975), and Thomas C. Bruneau, *Politics and Nationhood* (1984).

SOCKMAN, RALPH WASHINGTON (1889–1970), U.S. Protestant clergyman. A Methodist minister in New York City for more than 40 years, Sockman was nationally known for his NBC Sunday morning radio program, "National Radio Pulpit," which ran from 1928 to 1962. His sermons brought in an average of 30,000 letters a year from listeners, and Sockman was called "broadcasting's most durable character" and regarded as one of the foremost clergymen in the United States. Among his many books were *Morals of Tomorrow* (1931), *Paradoxes of Jesus* (1936), *The Higher Happiness* (1950), *How to Believe* (1953), and *Man's First Love* (1958).

SODDY, FREDERICK (1877–1956), British chemist. Soddy worked with Ernest Rutherford at McGill University (1900–02) developing a theory of radioactive disintegration. They demonstrated how an element undergoing decay ejects subatomic particles from its nucleus, producing a series of new elements until lead is formed. The observation of nearly 50 similar but distinct intermediate elements in the process of uranium's radioactive decay seemed to contradict Mendeleev's periodic chart. Soddy resolved this contradiction when he evolved (1913) the concept of isotopes (from the Greek meaning "same place"), which are elements with identical chemical characteristics but different nuclear composition. He taught at the University of Glasgow (1904–14) and at Oxford University (1919–36) and was awarded the 1921 Nobel Prize in Chemistry. ■ See Linda Merricks, *The World Made New* (1996).

SÖDERBLOM, NATHAN (Lars Jonathan Söderblom; 1866–1931), Swedish Lutheran theologian. Ordained a minister (1893), Söderblom taught theology at the University of Uppsala (from 1901) and devoted his life to international peace and Christian unity. He was named archbishop of Uppsala and primate of Sweden in 1914. Years of ecumenical activities culminated in the creation of the Universal Christian Conference on Life and Work (Stockholm, 1925), which later merged with other organizations to form the World Council of Churches (1948). For his efforts at promoting international understanding Söderblom was awarded the 1930 Nobel Peace Prize. His translated books included *Christian Fellowship* (1923) and *The Living God* (1933). ■ See biography by Bengt Sundkler (1968).

SOKOLOW, ANNA (1910–2000), U.S. choreographer and dance teacher. The daughter of Polish-Jewish immigrants, Sokolow grew up on New York City's Lower East Side. Despite her mother's resistance, she enrolled in modern-dance classes at a settlement house. She performed in Martha Graham's troupe (1930–38), dancing in major Graham works such as *Primitive Mysteries,* and later in her own pieces. Beginning with her work of the Depression years, such as *Anti-War Cycle* and *Case History,* Sokolow infused dance with social commentary; her choreography animated the despair and alienation of working people, war victims, and refugees. *Rooms* (1955) expressed the isolation of modern city dwellers. *Dreams* (1961), which delved into the unconscious, was Sokolow's bleak statement on the Holocaust. She spent long periods teaching in Mexico and Israel and at the Juilliard School in New York (from 1957). ■ See biography by Larry Warren (1991).

SOLDATI, MARIO (1906–), Italian novelist and filmmaker. Soldati received a Jesuit education, which influenced much of his early work. He became known not only for well-crafted and "literary" fiction, including *Dinner with the Commendatore* (1952; Eng. trans. 1953), *The Capri Letters* (1954; Eng. trans. 1955), *The Confession* (1955; Eng. trans. 1958), and *The Real Silvestri* (1957; Eng. trans. 1961), but also for his cinematic achievements as a screenwriter and director during the 1940s and 1950s. His later works included the psychological novel *The Orange Envelope* (1966; Eng. trans. 1969) and the introspective fantasy *The Emerald* (1974; Eng. trans. 1977).

SOLERI, PAOLO (1919–), Italian-U.S. architect. Soleri studied architecture in Turin, Italy, then worked under the American Frank Lloyd Wright (1947–49). In 1951 he built Domed Desert House near Cave Creek, Arizona, based on his principles of "arcology," a term he coined from "architecture" and "ecology." He settled permanently in the United States in 1955. Many students were attracted to his novel techniques, and in 1961 he established the Cosanti Foundation in Scottsdale, Arizona, as a school. A visionary utopian designer, Soleri drew up plans for Mesa City, an integrated, total environment for 2 million residents in the desert, making maximum use of solar energy. His designs for Mesa City were published in *Sketchbooks* (1971). He began work on a 4,500-resident version of the city called Arcosanti in 1970. ■ See his *Arcology* (1970), *Fragments: A Selection of the Notebooks* (1981), *The Omega Seed* (1981), *Arcosanti: An Urban Laboratory?* (1984), and *Technology and Cosmogenesis* (1985).

SOLOW, ROBERT M. (1924–), U.S. economist. Solow studied at Harvard (Ph.D. 1951) with Nobel Prize–winning economist Wassily Leontief and was a professor at the Massachusetts Institute of Technology (1949–95). During the 1950s he developed a mathematical model that demonstrated that technological progress has a greater effect on long-term economic growth rates than increases in capital and labor. His work, for which he was awarded the 1987 Nobel Memorial Prize in Economics, had a tremendous impact on subsequent economic analysis and influenced many governments to spend more money on technological development, higher education, and science research. He helped to shape U.S. economic policy during the Kennedy and Johnson administrations as a staff member (1961–62) and later consultant to (1962–68) the Council of Economic Advisers. His books included *Capital Theory and the Rate of Return* (1963), *The Sources of Unemployment in the United States* (1964), *Growth Theory* (1970), *The Labor Market as Social Institution* (1990), and *A Critical Essay on Modern Macroeconomic Theory* (1995).

SOLTI, SIR GEORG (1912–1997), Hungarian-born British conductor. A student of Bartók, Kodály, and Dohnányi at the Liszt Academy of Music in Budapest (1925–30), Solti worked as an opera coach at the Budapest State Opera and assistant to Arturo Toscanini at the Salzburg Festival (1937–38). After spending World War II in Switzerland, he was principal conductor of the Bavarian State Opera, Munich (1946–52), and the Frankfurt Opera (1952–61), and appeared with major orchestras and opera companies throughout the world. He recorded the first complete issue of Richard Wagner's *Ring* cycle (1958–65) and won a record 31 Grammy awards for his notable recordings. As music director, he revitalized the Covent Garden Opera, London (1961–71), and was also director of the Orchestre de Paris (1971–75) and principal conductor of the London Philharmonic (1979–83). He achieved his greatest fame as conductor of the Chicago Symphony (1969–91), which, under his baton, was considered by many to be the world's finest orchestra. ■ See his *Memoirs* (1997) and study by Paul Robinson (1979).

SOLZHENITSYN, ALEKSANDR ISAYEVICH (1918–), Russian writer. Shortly after Solzhenitsyn graduated from the University of Rostov (1941), the Germans attacked the Soviet Union, and he was drafted into the Red army. Although twice decorated for bravery, he was arrested (1945) for criticizing Soviet dictator Joseph Stalin in letters to a friend, imprisoned in a labor camp for eight years, and exiled to Soviet Central Asia for an additional three years. His first novel, *One Day in the Life of Ivan Denisovich* (1962; Eng. trans. 1963), the first account of the horrors of the Stalinist concentration camps, was published with official praise and was a political and literary sensation. However, after Solzhenitsyn became a vocal critic of the Soviet system and a leader of the small but influential dissident movement, his works attacking Stalinism, such as *The First Circle* (1968; Eng. trans. 1968) and *Cancer Ward* (1968; Eng. trans. 1968), were banned in the Soviet Union, although they were published and widely read abroad. After he was awarded the 1970 Nobel Prize in Literature, a bitter official campaign was launched against him, and it intensified with the publication in Paris (1973) of *The Gulag Archipelago: 1918–56* (3 vols., 1973–75; Eng. trans., 3 vols., 1974–78), a massive memoir and study of the vast Soviet prison-camp system.

Stripped of his citizenship, he was deported (1974); he settled in the United States. His later works included the four-volume "Red Wheel" cycle—*August 1914* (1971; Eng. trans. 1972); *November 1916* (1984; Eng. trans. 1998); *March 1917* (1986); *April 1917* (1991)—and the autobiographical *The Oak and the Calf* (1975; Eng. trans. 1980). He returned to Russia in 1994, but there was a great loss of interest in his work and a talk show he hosted (1994–95) was canceled for lack of viewers. In *The Russian Question Toward the End of the Twentieth Century* (1995; Eng. trans. 1995), he called for a return to traditional Russian values and a repudiation of Western civilization, and in *Russia in Collapse* (1998), he attacked capitalism, NATO, the International Monetary Fund (IMF), and the Russian government. ■ See biographies by Michael Scammell (1984) and D. M. Thomas (1998) and studies by Christopher Moody (1976), Steven Allaback (1978), and Andrej Kodjak (1978).

SOMBART, WERNER (1863–1941), German economist. Sombart was a controversial historian of capitalism at the universities of Breslau and Berlin. An admirer of Marxist theories early in his career, he later rejected Marxism and became an apologist of Nazism. In his magnum opus, *Der Moderne Kapitalismus* (3 vols., 1902–27), he divided the history of capitalism into three stages, with the last and most productive stage beginning with World War I. A controversial aspect of his writings was the role that he assigned to Jews as the chief creators of capitalism. His books included *Why Is There No Socialism in the U.S.?* (1906; Eng. trans. 1976), *The Jews and Modern Capitalism* (1911; Eng. trans. 1913), *The Quintessence of Capitalism* (1913; Eng. trans. 1915), and *A New Social Philosophy* (1934; Eng. trans. 1937). ■ See study by Morton J. Plotnik (1937) and Arthur Mitzman, *Sociology and Estrangement* (1973).

SOMMERFELD, ARNOLD JOHANNES WILHELM (1868–1951), German physicist and mathematician. A professor of theoretical physics at the University of Munich (1906–40), Sommerfeld made fundamental contributions to quantum theory and developed a theory of metallic electrons. He advanced Niels Bohr's atomic theory by suggesting elliptical orbits for the electrons and proposed a quantum theory of spectral lines. His book *Atomic Structure and Spectral Lines* (1919; Eng. trans. 1923) became a standard work in the field. Called "the teacher of atomic physics in Germany," Sommerfeld counted among his students many of the outstanding scientists of the century, including Nobel Prize winners Isidor I. Rabi, Hans Bethe, Linus Pauling, Wolfgang Pauli, Peter Debye, and Werner Heisenberg.

SOMOZA DEBAYLE, ANASTASIO (1925–1980), Nicaraguan dictator. Son of Gen. Anastasio Somoza García, who established a family dictatorship in Nicaragua with the help of U.S. Marines (1933), Somoza graduated from the U.S. Military Academy at West Point (1946). He rapidly rose through the ranks of the national guard and was its de facto leader at the time of his father's assassination (1956). After the death of his brother Luis (1963), Somoza administered his family's vast land holdings and businesses, estimated to be worth $500 million, and served as president of Nicaragua (1967–72; 1974–79). Known as an anticommunist, he enjoyed support from many U.S. political and military leaders. His corrupt and authoritarian rule resulted in the growth of the Sandinista National Liberation Front, a revolutionary guerrilla movement during the 1970s, especially after Somoza was accused of profiting from aid sent to alleviate the damage caused by the devastating earthquake in Managua (1972). By 1979 Somoza had lost the support of the Carter administration in the United States, and as insurrection grew, he left the country with an estimated $100 million and fled into exile in Paraguay. He was assassinated in Asunción, the capital city. ■ See his *Nicaragua Betrayed* (1980; with Jack Cox).

SOMOZA GARCÍA, ANASTASIO (1896–1956), Nicaraguan dictator. The son of a wealthy coffee planter, Somoza studied business in the United States, married into a prominent Nicaraguan family, and entered politics at age 30. He became head of the national guard in 1933 and three years later deposed his uncle and was "elected" president. Somoza ruled as a dictator, diversifying Nicaragua's economy while amassing a huge personal fortune and maintaining close ties with the United States. He remained in power, alternating with handpicked successors, until his assassination in 1956. His son, Anastasio Somoza Debayle (1925–1980), was president (1967–72; 1974–79) and was overthrown in the revolution led by the Sandinista National Liberation Front (1979). ■ See Eduardo Crawley, *Dictators Never Die* (1979).

SONDHEIM, STEPHEN JOSHUA (1930–), U.S. composer and lyricist. Sondheim was introduced to the musical theater by family friend Oscar Hammerstein II. He studied music with Milton Babbitt and worked as a Hollywood scriptwriter before achieving prominence as the lyricist for *West Side Story* (1957) and *Gypsy* (1958). His scores were acclaimed for perfectly matching the mood and complexity of the plays for which they were written, and his songs were highly praised for their wit and sophistication. He won Tony Awards for *Company* (1970), *Follies* (1971), *A Little Night Music* (1973), *Sweeney Todd* (1979), *Into the Woods* (1987), and *Passion* (1994) and a Pulitzer Prize for *Sunday in the Park with George* (1984). ■ See Craig Zadan, *Sondheim and Co.* (1974), and biography by Meryle Secrest (1998).

SONG MEILING (old style: SOONG MEI-LING; 1897?–), Chinese political figure. The youngest daughter in a wealthy and Westernized Shanghai family, Song was the sister of banker T. V. Soong and Song Qingling, the wife of revolutionary leader Sun Yat-sen. After graduating from Wellesley College in the United States (1917), she returned to China, married nationalist leader Chiang Kai-shek (1927), persuaded him to convert to Christianity, and introduced him to Western ways. She served as Chiang's adviser, secretary, and interpreter, was the director general of his New Life Movement—an organization devoted to implementing an ideology combining Christian and Confucian values—and was a leader of the women's movement in China. During the war-torn 1940s she was a spokesperson of the nationalist government in the United States, speaking and fund-raising throughout the country. She addressed a joint session of the U.S. Congress (1943) and sought U.S. aid, unsuccessfully, during the civil war (1948). After 1945 her influence waned, and following her husband's death (1975) she lived in the United States. Her books included *This Is Our China* (1940), *China in Peace and War* (1940), and *China Shall Rise Again* (1941). ■ See Sterling Seagrave, *The Soong Dynasty* (1985).

SONG QINGLING (old style: SOONG CHING-LING; 1892–1981), Chinese political leader. Born into a wealthy and Westernized Shanghai family, Song was the sister of financier T. V. Soong and sister-in-law of nationalist leader Chiang Kai-shek. She was educated by Christian missionaries and at the Wesleyan (Georgia) College for Women in the United States. In 1914 she married revolutionary leader Sun Yat-sen and until his death (1925) was his confidante, political aide, secretary, and interpreter. After Sun's death she became sharply critical of Chiang Kai-shek, supported the left wing of the Guomindang (Kuomintang), and went into temporary exile in the Soviet Union (1927–29). However, her unique position as Sun's widow protected her, and from 1931 to 1949 she ran several welfare and refugee projects, including the China League for Civil Rights and the China Defense League, making her home a center for leftist political groups. After 1949 she served as a vice chairman of the People's Republic of China and became a revered symbol of the revolution. She joined the Communist party several weeks before her death. Her articles and speeches appeared in *The Struggle for New China* (Eng. trans. 1952). ■ See Sterling Seagrave, *The Soong Dynasty* (1985).

SONTAG, SUSAN (1933–), U.S. writer. Sontag graduated from the University of Chicago at age 18, did graduate work at Harvard and Oxford, and wrote incisive commentary on philosophy, psychology, social thought, literature, and film. Ruminations on contemporary culture, increasingly personal in tone, characterized her work. In her first collection of essays, *Against Interpretation* (1966), she defined "camp" as cultural slumming; in her second, *Styles of Radical Will* (1969), she described the North Vietnamese reeducation of prostitutes and wrote extensively on modern cinema. Catholic in her interests, she wrote two novels and wrote and directed several films in Europe. Her later works included *On Photography* (1976); *Illness as Metaphor* (1977) arose out of her own experience with cancer. Another collection, *Under the Sign of Saturn* (1980), contains essays on major European cultural figures, including Antonin Artaud, Walter Benjamin, and Elias Canetti, *A Susan Sontag Reader* appeared in 1982. She also wrote *AIDS and Its Metaphors* (1989); *The Volcano Lover: A Romance* (1992); *Alice in Bed* (1993), a play about the writer Alice James, the invalid sister of William and Henry James; and *In America* (2000), a novel about a 19th-century Polish actress in the United States. ■ See Leland Poague, *Conversations with Susan Sontag* (1995) and biography by Carl Rollyson and Lisa Paddock (2000).

SOONG, T. V. (Soong Tzu-wen; 1894–1971), Chinese financier and public official. Born into a wealthy and Westernized Shanghai family, Soong graduated from Harvard University (B.A. 1915) and became active in trade and banking circles in his home city. He was an active supporter of his brothers-in-law, political leaders Sun Yat-sen and Chiang Kai-shek. As finance minister (1925–28), governor of the central bank of China (1928–33), and chairman of the Bank of China (1935–43), he attempted to set up a modern financial system, standardize the currency, centralize the banking system, and encourage foreign investment. He also amassed one of the world's largest personal fortunes. He served as China's foreign minister (1941–45) and chaired the San Francisco Conference that organized the United Nations (1945). As premier (1945–47) he was unable to curb runaway inflation or reach a lasting agreement with communist forces. After 1949 he lived in the United States. ■ See Sterling Seagrave, *The Soong Dynasty* (1985).

SOONG CHING-LING. See *SONG QINGLING*.

SOONG MEI-LING. See *SONG MEILING*.

SOREL, GEORGES (1847–1922), French social philosopher. Sorel retired from his career as a civil engineer in 1892 to study and write about contemporary society. Influenced by Marxism and the syndicalist movement, he broke with the reform-minded socialists of the early 1900s and advocated violence and the use of revolutionary myths to bring about social change. His most famous works, *Reflections on Violence* (1908; Eng. trans. 1914) and *The Illusions of Progress* (1908; Eng. trans. 1969), influenced extremist political groups of the right and the left, including the fascist movements in Italy and Germany. Several of his essays appear in English translation in *From Georges Sorel* (1974). ■ See Jack Roth, *The Cult of Violence* (1979); study by Richard D. Humphrey (1951); James H. Meisel, *The Genesis of Georges Sorel* (1951); and John Stanley, *Sociology of Virtue* (1981).

SORGE, RICHARD (1895–1944), German-born Soviet spy. After he served in Germany in World War I, Sorge joined the German Communist party (1918), studied political science at the University of Hamburg (Ph.D. 1920), and later became a journalist, a cover he maintained in the 1930s while spying for the Soviet Union in China and Japan. Occupying a position at the German embassy in Tokyo that gave him access to sensitive information about German-Japanese relations (1938–41) and assisted by the well-placed Marxist newspaperman Hotsumi Ozaki (1921–44), Sorge was able to forecast Hitler's June 1941 invasion of the Soviet Union. However, Soviet dictator Joseph Stalin ignored the warning. When Sorge predicted, a year later, that Japan would enter the war by attacking the United States in the Pacific (rather than the Soviet Union in Siberia), Stalin believed him and moved his Siberian forces to the West. Arrested by the Japanese, Sorge and Ozaki were imprisoned (1941) by the Japanese and executed (1944) for espionage. The Kremlin posthumously conferred on Sorge their highest honor, "Hero of the Soviet Union" (1964). ■ See Charles H. Willoughby, *Shanghai Conspiracy* (1952); Hans-Otto Meissner, *The Man with Three Faces* (1955); F. W. Deakin and G. R. Storry, *The Case of Richard Sorge* (1967); and Robert Whymant, *Stalin's Spy* (1998).

SOROKIN, PITIRIM ALEXANDROVITCH (1889–1968), Russian-born U.S. sociologist. The son of peasants, Sorokin was at various times a worker, journalist, and revolutionary. He emigrated to the United States in 1924 and established the department of sociology at Harvard (1930), where he taught for 25 years. He introduced American sociology to the work being done in Europe in his encyclopedic *Contemporary Sociological Theories* (1928), and in his controversial *Social and Cultural Dynamics* (4 vols., 1937–41) he studied social and cultural values and how they have changed and been influenced over the course of recorded time. He later spent several years studying "scientific altruism." ■ See his autobiographies, *Leaves from a Russian Diary* (rev. ed. 1950) and *A Long Journey* (1963); Frank R. Cowell, *Values in Human Society* (1970); and biography by Barry V. Johnston (1995).

SOROS, GEORGE (1930–), Hungarian-born U.S. financier and philanthropist. Soros, who was born into a middle-class Jewish family in Budapest, escaped the Holocaust by using false identity papers. He moved to London (1947), where he graduated from the London School of Economics and was influenced by philosopher Karl Popper and his ideas about democratic "open societies." Soros emigrated to the United States (1956), worked as a securities analyst, established the Quantum Fund (1969), and eventually made a fortune speculating on the world currency markets. In 1992 he made more than $1 billion gambling against the British pound, and he became known as "the man who broke the Bank of England." However, he invested heavily in Russia during the late 1990s and announced a $2 billion loss in 1998. Soros was one of the world's best-known philanthropists, giving more than $1 billion to Russia and the former communist countries in Eastern Europe in order to establish democratic institutions. In the United States he gave hundreds of millions of dollars to organizations seeking to liber-alize drug laws, aid legal immigrants, improve rural and inner-city education, and enhance the dignity, comfort, and care of the dying. His pessimistic book, *The Global Crisis of Capitalism* (1998), warned against the danger of unregulated markets. His other books included *The Alchemy of Finance* (1987), *Underwriting Democracy* (1991), *Soros on Soros* (1995), and *Open Society: From Global Capitalism to Global Democracy* (2000).

SOSA, MERCEDES (1935–), Argentinian singer. Called "the voice of Latin America," Sosa was born into a poverty-stricken family in Tucumán province, in northwestern Argentina, where indigenous Andean culture thrived. She began her career at age 15 after winning an amateur competition at a local radio station, and achieved fame for her powerful renditions of songs of social concern. She was one of the leaders of the "new song movement" that revitalized Latin American music in the 1960s by blending modern sounds and traditional folk rhythms with lyrics demanding peace, freedom, and economic justice. The military dictatorship banned her music from radio and television, and she was forced to leave the country (1979–82). Returning to Argentina as civilian rule was restored, she sang of the pain of exile and the joy of witnessing the restoration of freedom and was regarded as a voice of hope for millions in Latin America. Sosa's best-known songs included "Gracias a la Vida," "Todo Cambia," and "Cucando Tengo la Tierra." Her songs of the 1980s and 1990s included jazz, rock, and pop elements.

SOUPHANOUVONG, PRINCE (1909?–1995), Laotian political leader. Souphanouvong, one of the less privileged of the royal children, studied civil engineering in Paris and designed bridges and roads in Vietnam (1938–45). He joined the anti-French nationalists after World War II and helped found the communist-nationalist Pathet Lao movement (1950), which was closely allied to the Vietminh movement in neighboring Vietnam. Souphanouvong waged war against the French until the Geneva accords (1954) ended the fighting. He participated in a short-lived coalition government (1962–63), but its collapse led to a decade of civil war. Following a cease-fire agreement (1973), Souphanouvong was named president of the coalition National Political Consultative Council (1974). After communist forces took over Vietnam and Cambodia in the spring of 1975, the Pathet Lao (now called the Lao People's Liberation army) seized the capital of Vientiane, dismissed the coalition government, abolished the monarchy, and established the Lao People's Democratic Republic with Souphanouvong as head of state and chairman of the newly created Supreme People's Council. He retired from politics in 1986.

SOUSTELLE, JACQUES (1912–1990), French anthropologist and political leader. A scholar from a working-class Protestant family, Soustelle was active as an anthropologist in Mexico during the 1930s. He was a left-wing militant and leader of several antifascist intellectual organizations and joined Gen. Charles de Gaulle and the Free French forces after the fall of France (1940) during World War II and headed intelligence operations (1943–44). After the war he served as secretary-general of the Gaullist parliamentary party (1947–52). Named governor-general of Algeria (1955), he became a leading spokesman for its economic and political integration with France. He returned to France in 1956 and played an active role in the national assembly in facilitating de Gaulle's return to power (1958) as president and served in his cabinet (1958–60). But, as he was strongly opposed to de Gaulle's policies of independence for Algeria, Soustelle broke with him and went into exile in 1961. In 1962 a warrant was issued for his arrest for subversion, and he stayed out of France until the general amnesty of 1968, after which he became the director of studies at the École Pratique des Hautes Ètudes in Paris (1969–83), served in the National Assembly (1973–78), and was named to the French Academy (1983).

SOUTINE, CHAÏM (1894–1943), Russian-born French artist. Born into a poor Jewish family near Minsk, Soutine moved to Paris in 1913 to study at the École des Beaux Arts. He adopted an expressionist style and distinctive brushwork to produce distorted portraits and visionary landscapes, in vivid colors, which displayed great emotional intensity. Repeated anxiety attacks undermined his health, and he died after surgery for a perforated ulcer. ■ See studies by Raymond Cogniat (1952) and Alfred Werner (1977) and Norman L. Kleeblat and Kenneth E. Silver, *An Expressionist in Paris* (1998).

SOUVANNA PHOUMA, PRINCE (1901–1984), Laotian political leader. Souvanna studied engineering in Paris and Grenoble before returning to French Indochina (1931) to begin a 19-year career in public-works agencies. Entering the tangled web of Laotian politics in the late 1940s as a moderate conservative, he served as premier for many years (1951–54; 1956–58; 1960; 1962–75). He represented neutralist and centrist forces who sought an alternative to both the extreme right wing and the communists, led by his half brother, Prince Souphanouvong. In 1975, communist forces seized the capital of Vientiane, ousted Souvanna's coalition government, and established the Loa People's Democratic Republic.

SOYA, CARL ERIK (1896–1983), Danish writer. Prolific in many fictional genres, Soya did not gain recognition until he was almost 50 years old. His short stories were witty and entertaining. He wrote many plays, including *Two Threads* (1943; Eng. trans. 1955). His plays were usually satirical and often shocked audiences with daring stage effects and unconventional ideas; many dealt with the concept of free will and the problems of justice and retribution. His novels included *Grandmother's House* (1943; Eng. trans. 1966), an evocation of turn-of-the-century Copenhagen through

the eyes of a young child, and *Seventeen* (3 vols., 1953–54; Eng. trans. 1961), a study of puberty. His other works included *Bedroom Mazurka: Seven Erotic Stories* (Eng. trans. 1971).

SOYER, RAPHAEL (1899–1987), Russian-born U.S. artist. The son of a teacher of Hebrew literature, Soyer was the brother of noted realist painters Moses Soyer (1899–1974) and Isaac Sayer (1907–81). He emigrated to the United States in 1912 and studied and taught art in New York City. He specialized in street scenes of New York's Lower East Side and in creating portraits of lonely "little people," for which he was acclaimed the "dean of American realism." His works were best known during the 1930s, when they captured the spirit of despair during the Depression. ■ See his *Diary of an Artist* (1977) and study by Lloyd Goodrich (1972).

SOYINKA, WOLE (Akinwande Oluwole Soyinka; 1934–), Nigerian writer. The most prominent black African playwright of the century, Soyinka mixed Nigerian myths, folklore, folk-opera techniques, dance, mime, and music with the dramatic devices of the theater of the absurd in plays that reflected the clash of African and Western values and the problems of rapidly changing contemporary African society. He was active in theater groups in Nigeria and had gained an international reputation by the mid-1960s. His best-known plays included *A Dance of the Forests* (1960), *The Trials of Brother Jero* (1960), *The Strong Breed* (1964), *Kongi's Harvest* (1964), *The Road* (1965), *Death and the King's Horsemen* (1975), and *The Beatification of Area Boy* (1994). He also wrote the novels *The Interpreters* (1965) and *Season of Anomy* (1973) and the poetry collection *Idanre* (1967). *The Man Died: Prison Notes* (1972) and the poetry collection *A Shuttle in the Crypt* (1972) were written while he was imprisoned—without charge or trial—during the Nigerian civil war (1967–69). While a professor at the *University of Ife* (from 1972) he wrote *Myth, Literature and the African World* (1976), the prose poem *Ogun Abibiman* (1976), and the autobiography *Ake: Years of Childhood* (1982). He was awarded the 1986 Nobel Prize in Literature. A vocal opponent of the military government of Gen. Sani Abacha, Soyinka lived in exile (1994–98) and taught at Emory University in Atlanta, Georgia. His later works included a family memoir, *Isara* (1989); *Ibadan: The Penkelemes Years: A Memoir, 1946–1965* (1994); *The Open Sore of a Continent: A Personal Narrative of the Nigerian Crisis* (1996); and the essay collection, *The Burden of Memory, The Muse of Forgiveness* (1999), in which he discusses negritude as well as the question of reparations. ■ See studies by Eldred Jones (1973), Gerald Moore (1978), and Derek Wright (1993).

SPAAK, PAUL HENRI (1889–1972), Belgian premier. After release from German internment during World War I, Spaak practiced law and was elected (1932) to parliament. He held cabinet posts after 1935, including that of foreign minister; he became Belgium's first socialist premier, serving in three coalition governments (1938–39; 1946; 1947–50). Spaak was foreign minister in Belgium's government-in-exile during the World War II Nazi occupation and during the postwar era (1945–49; 1954–57; 1961–65). He also served (1946) as first president of the U.N. General Assembly. An advocate of European political and economic unity, he advanced a Western European defense plan that was realized in the North Atlantic Treaty Organization pact and he was one of the organizers of European Economic Community. He served (1957–61) as secretary-general of NATO. ■ See his *The Continuing Battle: Memoirs of a European, 1936–1966* (Eng. trans. 1971) and James H. Huizinga, *Mr. Europe* (1961).

SPAATZ, CARL ANDREW (1891–1974), U.S. military leader. A graduate of West Point (1914), Spaatz was a combat pilot during World War I and served at several air bases during the interwar period. He was brigadier general at the start of World War II, commanded the U.S. air forces in Europe during the war, and was responsible for the strategic daylight bombing of Germany. After the war ended in Europe, he directed the strategic bombing of Japan, including the atomic attacks on Hiroshima and Nagasaki. He served (1947–48) as the first chief of staff of the air force when it became an independent service. ■ See David R. Mets, *Master of Airpower* (1988), and study by Richard Davis (1993).

SPALDING, ALBERT (1888–1953), U.S. violinist. The son of a partner in the sporting-goods firm of A. G. Spalding, Albert Spalding was born in Chicago and studied violin in New York, Paris, and Florence. At age 17 he made his debut in Paris, and he made his U.S. debut as a soloist with the New York Symphony in Carnegie Hall in 1908. In annual tours of the United States, Spalding established his reputation as an exquisite though restrained stylist. He played with the major U.S. and European orchestras and was the first American-born violin virtuoso to gain international acclaim. He composed several works for violin and wrote a fictionalized biography of the Italian violinist Tartini, *A Fiddle, a Sword, and a Lady* (1953). ■ See his autobiography, *Rise to Follow* (1943).

SPARK, DAME MURIEL (Muriel Sarah Camberg; 1918–), British writer. Born and raised in Edinburgh, Spark spent several years in Africa, the setting for her early stories. Her writings included literary studies of Mary Shelley (1951) and Emily Brontë (1953), as well as mildly satirical novels about charlatans and eccentrics. Spark's best-known book, *The Prime of Miss Jean Brodie* (1961), was also successful on the stage and screen. Her other novels included *The Comforters* (1957), *Memento Mori* (1959), *The Ballad of Peckham Rye* (1960), *The Mandelbaum Gate* (1965), *The Takeover* (1979), *Loitering with Intent* (1981), *The Only*

Problem (1984), *A Far Cry from Kensington* (1988), and *Reality and Dreams,* (1997). Her collected stories appeared in 1985. ■ See her autobiography, *Curriculum Vitae* (1993); study by Peter Kemp (1974); and Ruth Whittaker, *The Faith and Fiction of Muriel Spark* (1982).

SPASSKY, BORIS VASILYEVICH (1937–), Soviet chess player. An international master at 16 and grand master at 19, Spassky captured the world chess championship by defeating fellow countryman Tigran Petrosian in 1969. He lost the title to Bobby Fischer of the United States in a tournament at Reykjavik, Iceland (1972), which was the most publicized, avidly followed, and lucrative chess match up to that time. He emigrated to France during the mid-1970s. ■ See Richard Roberts, *Fischer/Spassky* (1972).

SPAULDING, CHARLES CLINTON (1874–1952), U.S. business executive. One of 14 children of a poor black North Carolina farmer, he left his home for the city of Durham at age 20 and graduated from Whitted (High) School (1898). After managing a local cooperative grocery, he joined the newly formed North Carolina Mutual and Provident Association (1899), became its general manager (1900), and by developing new markets, helped build it into the largest black life insurance company in the United States. With Spaulding as its president (1923–52), the firm, now called the North Carolina Mutual Life Insurance Co., organized a bank, bonding company, fire-insurance company, building-and-loan association, real-estate business, and two newspapers, all to offer services to the black community. The firm flourished, survived the Depression of the 1930s, and became the largest black-owned business in the country. ■ See William J. Kennedy, Jr., *The North Carolina Mutual Story* (1970), and Walter Weare, *Black Business in the New South* (1973).

SPEAKER, TRIS (Tristram Speaker; 1888–1958), U.S. baseball player. Regarded as the finest defensive outfielder of all time, Speaker—the "Gray Eagle"—was also one of baseball's greatest hitters. In 21 seasons, primarily with the Boston Red Sox (1907–15) and Cleveland Indians (1916–26), Speaker compiled a .344 batting average and amassed 3,515 hits. Baseball's highest-paid player prior to the Babe Ruth era, he was the seventh player named to the National Baseball Hall of Fame (1937).

SPEARMAN, CHARLES EDWARD (1863–1945), British psychologist. An army officer from 1883 to 1897, Spearman earned his Ph.D. at the University of Leipzig (1903), where he studied with Wilhelm Wundt, a pioneer in experimental psychology. On the faculty of University College, London (1907–31), he developed a theory of intelligence based on a general intelligence factor plus variable factors determining performance in particular tasks. His work in factor analysis opened up the way for the application of statistical methods to the study of human intelligence. His major work was *The Abilities of Man* (1927).

SPECTOR, PHIL (1940–), U.S. songwriter and record producer. Spector wrote his first hit song, "To Know Him Is to Love Him" (1958), for his high school rock-and-roll trio, The Teddy Bears. He dropped out of UCLA to pursue a career in the record business and quickly became the boy wonder of the industry, co-writing "Spanish Harlem" and producing such hits as "Corrina, Corrina," "Every Breath I Take," and "I Love How You Love Me"—all before the age of 21. Forming his own label, Philles, he perfected his "wall of sound": dense, sophisticated orchestrations featuring overdubbing and multitracking to produce a massive sound. The technique, which revolutionized rock music, was featured in such big hits as The Crystals' "Then He Kissed Me" (1963) and "Da Doo Ron Ron" (1963), The Ronettes' "Baby I Love You (1963) and "Be My Baby" (1963), and The Righteous Brothers' "You've Lost That Lovin' Feeling" (1964). Spector subsequently produced records by The Beatles, Cher, Leonard Cohen, The Ramones, and Celine Dion.

SPEER, ALBERT (1905–1981), German architect and government official. A cultured architect associated with Berlin's Technical University, Speer was an unlikely candidate for Nazi leadership. However, seduced by the prospect of redesigning Berlin as the center of a great German empire, he joined the party (1931) and became a friend and protégé of Nazi leader Adolf Hitler. As the Nazis' chief architect and head of government construction, he designed several massive projects, including the stadium in Nuremberg and the chancellery in Berlin. During World War II, Speer, a colonel in the SS, headed the ministry of armaments and munitions (1942–45) and controlled 80 percent of Germany's wartime industry. Using slave labor, he was able to increase production despite Allied bombing. At the Nuremberg trials after the war he pleaded guilty to war crimes and served a 20-year prison term. The inaccuracies in his self-serving memoirs (*Inside the Third Reich*, Eng. trans. 1970; *Spandau: The Secret Diaries*, Eng. trans. 1976; *Infiltration: The SS and German Armament*, Eng. trans. 1981) were documented in Matthias Schmidt's *Albert Speer: The End of a Myth* (Eng. trans. 1984). ■ See biography by Gitta Sereny (1995) and Dan van der Vat, *The Good Nazi* (1997).

SPELLING, AARON (1928–), U.S. television producer and writer. From the mid-1960s, Aaron Spelling was connected with some of television's most popular programs. He teamed up with Danny Thomas (1968–72) before forming Spelling-Goldberg Productions (1972–76) to produce such series as *Starsky and Hutch, Charlie's Angels, Hart to Hart,* and *Fantasy Island.* In 1977, he formed Spelling Productions, whose credits included *Vegas, Hotel, Savannah, Melrose Place,* and the phenomenally popular prime-time saga *Dynasty.* In addition, Spelling was involved, both as producer and writer, with more than 90 movies of the week for the ABC network.

SPELLMAN, FRANCIS JOSEPH (1889–1967), U.S. Roman Catholic religious leader. The archbishop of New York (from 1939) and vicar-general of the U.S. armed forces, Spellman was for years the best-known and most influential Roman Catholic leader in the United States. He was elevated to cardinal in 1946. A highly successful fund-raiser, he vastly expanded the system of Catholic schools, hospitals, and charities in New York City. He was a powerful and controversial figure in national and local politics who called for public aid to church schools, opposed birth control and pornography, and advocated censorship of movies. A militant anticommunist—the Russians dubbed him "the archangel of atomic war"—he strongly backed Sen. Joseph McCarthy's anticommunist campaign and actively supported the Vietnam War. ■ See John Cooney, *The American Pope* (1984).

SPEMANN, HANS (1869–1941), German embryologist and physiologist. The director of the Kaiser Wilhelm Institute of Biology in Berlin (1914–19) and a professor at the University of Freiburg (1919–35), Spemann won the 1935 Nobel Prize in Physiology or Medicine for his discovery of embryonic induction. Working with newt embryos, he showed that different areas of the embryo develop into functionally different organs and tissues as a result of cell differentiation that is dependent on the relative position of cells to each other and on several "organizing centers." This discovery not only helped to explain normal growth and development but also various congenital defects. It also undermined the theory that a "vital force" or an embryonic "preformation" played a role in physical development. Spemann wrote *Embryonic Development and Induction* (1936; Eng. trans. 1938).

SPENDER, SIR STEPHEN (1909–1995), British poet and critic. With his Oxford friends and contemporaries W. H. Auden and Cecil Day Lewis, Spender was noted for poetry that commented on political and social developments from a left-wing point of view. Such works included *Poems* (1933) and *The Still Centre* (1939). Briefly a Communist, he openly broke with the party and moved toward political liberalism. His later poetry was meditative and lyrical. His idealistic humanism and honesty characterized all of his work. Active as a teacher, critic, and translator, he was an editor of *Horizon* (1939–41), a founding editor of the liberal anticommunist journal *Encounter* (1953–67), and a professor at the University of London (1970–77). ■ See his *Collected Poems 1928–1985* (1986); the autobiography, *World Within World* (1951); *The Thirties and After: Poetry, Politics, People: 1933–1970* (1978); *Journals 1939–1983* (1986); study by Andrew Weatherhead (1975); and biography by Hugh David (1992).

SPENGLER, OSWALD (1880–1936), German philosopher of history. Amid the destruction and doom of World War I Spengler wrote his *Decline of the West* (2 vols., 1918–22; Eng. trans. 1926–28), comparing the life cycles and world views of classical, Indian, Arabic, and Western civilizations. He believed that Western civilization, characterized by the triumph of the "Faustian will to power," was condemned like the others to inevitable decline. ▪ See study by H. Stuart Hughes (1952) and John F. Fennelly, *Twilight of the Evening Lands* (1972).

SPERRY, ELMER AMBROSE (1860–1930), U.S. engineer and inventor. Sperry registered more than 400 patents for his inventions, but he is best known for his design of gyroscopic compasses and stabilizers. His Sperry Gyroscope Co. (estab. 1910) later became the giant Sperry Rand Corp. First used on the battleship *Delaware* (1911), the gyrocompass proved superior to the magnetic compass and was adopted by the navy. His design of the stabilizer for ships and aircraft (1913–14) greatly increased travel comfort; navies around the world used it. Sperry also invented (1918) the high-intensity arc searchlight. ▪ See biography by Thomas P. Hughes (1971).

SPERRY, ROGER WOLCOTT (1913–1994), U.S. psychobiologist. After receiving a doctorate in zoology (University of Chicago, 1941), Sperry pursued a career combining psychology and biology at Harvard, the Yerkes Laboratories in Primate Biology (Atlanta), and the University of Chicago. As professor of psychobiology at the California Institute of Technology at Pasadena (1954–84), he did pioneering brain research with animals and later with human subjects that proved that the right and left hemispheres of the brain have different functions, and that both, independently, have the ability to learn. In addition, he demonstrated that the right hemisphere was primarily responsible for intuitive thinking and comprehending spatial relationships. Sperry shared the 1981 Nobel Prize in Physiology or Medicine with David H. Hubel and Torsten N. Wiesel. ▪ See *Nobel Prize Conversations* (1985).

SPIEGEL, SAM (1904–1985), Austrian-born U.S. film producer. After studying at the University of Vienna, Spiegel produced films in Europe before emigrating to the United States in 1939. An independent producer in Hollywood from the early 1940s, he worked closely with directors and screenwriters to produce a series of popular, high-quality films, including the Academy Award winners *On the Waterfront* (1954), *The Bridge on the River Kwai* (1957), and *Lawrence of Arabia* (1962). His other movies included *The Stranger* (1945), *The African Queen* (1953), *Suddenly Last Summer* (1960), and *The Last Tycoon* (1976).

SPIELBERG, STEVEN (1947–   ), U.S. film director, writer, and producer. The son of an electronics-firm executive, Spielberg grew up in several middle-class suburban communities. Fascinated with movies from his early childhood, he made dozens of 8mm and 16mm films at home and studied film at college. After directing the TV movie *Duel* (1971) and then *Sugarland Express* (1974), he directed the adventure film *Jaws* (1975), wrote and directed the science-fiction movie *Close Encounters of the Third Kind* (1977), and directed the action adventure film *Raiders of the Lost Ark* (1981), three of the biggest box-office hits in movie history. His brilliantly filmed fantasy of a lovable and intelligent child-sized space creature stranded in a suburban community in California, *E.T.* (1982), created a nationwide sensation and spawned a fad for E.T. dolls, toys, T-shirts, and posters. Spielberg also directed *Indiana Jones and the Temple of Doom* (1984), *The Color Purple* (1985), *Schindler's List* (1993; Academy Award), *Jurassic Park* (1993), *The Lost World* (1997), *Amistad* (1997), and *Saving Private Ryan* (1998; Academy Award for Direction). In 1994 he founded a new studio, DreamWorks SKG, with fellow Hollywood producers David Geffen and Jeffrey Katzenberg. His credits as a producer included *Poltergeist* (1982; screenwriter and producer), *Twilight Zone—the Movie* (1983), and *Gremlins* (1984). ▪ See biographies by Andrew Yule (1996) and Joseph McBride (1997).

SPILLANE, MICKEY (Frank Morrison Spillane; 1918–   ), U.S. novelist. Spillane grew up in Brooklyn, New York, and began his career writing comic-book story lines. He wrote hard-boiled crime fiction featuring the tough-guy detective Mike Hammer. Spillane's emphasis on violence, sex, and sadism brought notoriety and commercial success in the 1950s, but his popularity waned in the less restrictive 1960s and 1970s. His early books, *I, the Jury* (1947), *My Gun Is Quick* (1950), *The Big Kill* (1951), and *One Lonely Night* (1951), each sold more than 5 million copies and were the all-time most popular American crime novels, topped only by Mario Puzo's *The Godfather* (1969). Later titles included *The Death Dealers* (1967), *The Erection Set* (1972), *The Killing Man* (1989), and *Black Alley* (1996). He also wrote an award-winning children's book, *The Day the Sea Rolled Back* (1979).

SPINGARN, ARTHUR BARNETT (1878–1971), U.S. lawyer and civil-rights leader. Born into a wealthy Jewish family in New York City, Spingarn joined the National Association for the Advancement of Colored People (NAACP) at its founding (1909) and served as its vice president and chaired its legal committee (1911–40). He and his defense team won numerous Supreme Court victories that eroded the structure of segregation in the United States and fostered equality between blacks and whites in education and voting rights. During his tenure as president of the NAACP (1940–66) the organization won the landmark 1954 Supreme Court decision outlawing segregation in public schools, and its membership grew from 85,000 to more than 400,000 members.

SPINGARN, JOEL ELIAS (1875–1939), U.S. scholar and social reformer. Spingarn taught comparative literature at Columbia University (1899–1911) and was a founder and member of the publishing firm of Harcourt, Brace (1919–32). One of the most influential exponents of the aesthetic school of literary criticism, he wrote *A History of Literary Criticism in the Renaissance* (1899), *The New Criticism* (1911), and *Creative Criticism* (1917). Spingarn is best remembered, however, for his role in the founding of the National Association for the Advancement of Colored People (1909), which he served as chairman (1913–19) and president (1930–39).

SPÍNOLA, ANTÓNIO SEBASTIÃO RIBEIRO DE (1910–1996). Portuguese military and political leader. An aristocratic career army officer, Spínola served as governor and military commander in Portuguese Guinea (1968–72). Returning home as a popular hero, he was named deputy chief of staff of the armed forces (1973–74). Realizing that the unwinnable colonial wars in Guinea, Angola, and Mozambique were bankrupting the country, Spínola called for a negotiated solution and for increased political freedom at home in his book *Portugal and the Future* (Feb. 1974), which became a sensational best-seller. Although he did not take part in the military coup (April 1974) that overthrew the government of Marcello Caetano, Spínola was appointed president by the new military leaders (May 15, 1974). He restored democratic rights and began negotiations that eventually led to the independence of the African colonies. However, as pressures from the left increased, Spínola resigned (Sept. 30, 1974) and temporarily retired from politics. He led an abortive coup in March 1975.

SPITTELER, CARL (1845–1924), Swiss (German-language) poet, novelist, and critic. Called by the French writer Romain Rolland "the greatest German poet since Goethe, the only master of the epic since Milton." Spitteler was best known for his mythical epic poems *Prometheus and Epimetheus* (1880–81; revised as *Suffering Prometheus*, 1924: Eng. trans. 1931) and *Olympian Spring* (1900–05). His autobiographical novel, *Imago* (1906), which dealt with the unconscious and its stimulation to creativity, inspired the psychiatrist Sigmund Freud and his colleagues to name their psychoanalytic periodical after it. His other works included the novel *The Little Misogynists* (1907; Eng. trans. 1923). Spitteler won the 1919 Nobel Prize in Literature.

SPITZ, MARK ANDREW (1950–), U.S. Olympic swimmer. One of the greatest freestyle swimmers in history, Spitz was the only athlete to win seven gold medals in a single Olympic games (Munich, 1972). He won two gold medals in the 1968 Olympics in Mexico City (both in team relay races), but was disappointed at not winning an individual event. In 1972 (the year he graduated from Indiana University), however, he won four individual events, including world-record performances in the 100- and 200-meter freestyle races.

SPOCK, BENJAMIN MCLANE (1903–1998), U.S. pediatrician and writer. Spock was on the Yale crew team that won a gold medal at the 1924 Olympic games. He graduated the next year, then studied medicine at Columbia University (M.D. 1929). His *Common Sense Book of Baby and Child Care* (1946), one of the most influential mass-market books ever published, sold more than 30 million copies to several generations of parents. His reassuring advice departed from more rigid child-rearing guides by urging parents to use their own good judgment. Rev. Norman Vincent Peale and others blamed the rebellious stance of youth in the 1960s on Dr. Spock's book. A political activist, Spock was the 1968 presidential candidate of the left-wing People's party. He criticized U.S. involvement in Vietnam, advocated nuclear disarmament, and was arrested a dozen times for civil disobedience. In the seventh edition of *Baby and Child Care* (1998), Spock advocated a strict vegetarian diet for children after age 2. He wrote numerous other books including his memoirs, *Spock on Spock* (1989). ■ See biography by Thomas Maier (1998).

SPRINGER, AXEL CAESAR (1912–1985), German publisher. After working on his father's newspaper, Springer established his own publishing empire after World War II. He rose to prominence with four West German newspapers, which together accounted for nearly half the country's circulation of dailies. His publications included the tabloid *Bild Zeitung,* Europe's best-selling daily newspaper; *Die Welt,* an influential Bonn daily; two Berlin dailies; two Sunday papers; and two weeklies specializing in TV and radio news. His company, the Axel Springer Publishing Group, also encompassed the Ullstein and Propylaen book publishing firms. His publications, including the prestigious *Die Welt,* followed Springer's political stance: he supported the free-market economy, reunification of Germany, and the reconciliation of Germans and Jews, and he opposed communism. He was closely associated with the Christian Democratic party, and left-wing activists often protested his conservative positions.

SPRINGSTEEN, BRUCE (1949–), U.S. singer and songwriter. Best known for highly personal rock ballads celebrating blue-collar life, Springsteen's brand of rock and roll transformed him from a rock singer to a rock hero. Born in New Jersey, he developed a passion for rock and roll as a teenager. Springsteen built a solid reputation in the clubs on the New Jersey shore until he landed a record contract (1972). He was heavily promoted as the new Bob Dylan and, after the release of his LP *Born to Run* (1975), appeared on the covers of *Time* and *Newsweek* the same week. Although the publicity was a case of too much too soon, Springsteen continued to attract a strong and loyal following. After a three-year hiatus, the release of his LP *Born in the U.S.A.* (1984), and the tremendously successful video and tour that followed, reconfirmed his status as a contemporary rock hero, and "the Boss." Subsequent albums included *Tunnel of Love* (1987) and *The Ghost of Tom Joad* (1995), and songs included "Streets of Philadelphia" (1994; Grammy Award and Academy Award) and "Dead Man Walking." ■ See studies by Robert Hilburn (1985) and Christopher Sandford (1999) and Jim Cullen, *Born in the U.S.A.* (1997).

SPROUL, ROBERT GORDON (1891–1975), U.S. educator. The president of the University of California for 28 years (1930–1958), Sproul built the multicampus system into one of the world's largest and most highly regarded. Although a controversial figure, frequently attacked by the right-wing press for allowing "communist penetration" of the university, he weathered many political storms, including one involving a faculty loyalty oath (1949). Sproul raised vast sums of money, both public and private, for the university, quadrupled the size of the library, and attracted numerous Nobel laureates and other distinguished scholars to the faculty. ■ See George A. Pettitt, *Twenty-Eight Years in the Life of a University President* (1966).

SRAFFA, PIERO (1898–1983), Italian-born theoretical economist. A friend of Italian communist leader Antonio Gramsci and critic of the fascist government of Benito Mussolini, Sraffa accepted an offer by British economist John Maynard Keynes to teach at Cambridge University (1927) and he remained there for the rest of his life. His seminal article in the *Economic Journal* (1926), which exposed shortcomings in the orthodox model of perfect competition and stressed the importance of monopolistic conditions, helped lay the groundwork for new theories of prices, value, and distribution. His book, *Production of Commodities by Means of Commodities: Prelude to a Critique of Economic Theory* (1960), criticized the foundations of neoclassical economics, influenced Marxist economic theories, and consolidated his position as a leader of the Cambridge post-Keynesian school of economic theory. An admirer of 19th-century economist David Ricardo, Sraffa spent many years editing and annotating Ricardo's *Works and Correspondence* (11 vols., 1951–73; with Maurice Dobb). ■ See Ian Steedman, *Marx After Sraffa* (1977).

STAËL, NICOLAS DE (1914–1955), Russian-born French painter. An important abstract painter of the School of Paris, de Staël began as a nonfigurative painter whose works embodied rhythmically structured blocks and cubes of luminescent color that suggested architectural motifs and subjects from nature. Shifting to a more representational style in the 1950s, he executed paintings of soccer players, landscapes (such as *Agrigente*, 1954), and still lifes. He used brilliant flat colors and a minimum of detail to distill the essence of a familiar scene. Extremely poor throughout his adult life, de

Staël had achieved wealth and fame by the time he committed suicide. ■ See biography by Douglas Cooper (1961).

STAFFORD, JEAN (1915–1979), U.S. novelist and short-story writer. Stafford grew up in Colorado; her father wrote westerns under the pen name Jack Wonder. Her first novel, *Boston Adventure* (1944), won praise for precise description and sure craft. A portrayal of various strata of Boston society, it created the sense of claustrophobia that characterized Stafford's later fiction. She wrote two more novels and children's books but was best known for her short fiction, cast in traditional forms. *The Collected Stories* (1969) won a Pulitzer Prize. ■ See study by Mary E. W. Walsh (1985) and Ann Hulbert, *The Interior Castle* (1992).

STAGG, AMOS ALONZO (1862–1965), U.S. sportsman. An innovator in baseball (he developed the headlong slide) and basketball (he coached the University of Chicago, the winner of the first college game with five men on a side, 1896). Stagg was most famous as a football coach. In a career spanning 71 years, he introduced the huddle, the direct pass from center, the man in motion, the end around run, the line shift, and cross-blocking and was regarded as football's greatest pioneer. He won seven conference championships during his 41-year tenure as coach of the University of Chicago (1892–1932) and won coach-of-the-year honors at the age of 81 while at the College of the Pacific (1943). His total of 315 career victories was surpassed only by Bear Bryant (323) and Eddie Robinson, the Grambling coach, who won his 324th game in 1985. ■ See his autobiography, *Touchdown!* (1927), and Ellis Lucia, *Mr. Football* (1970).

STÅHLBERG, KAARLO JUHO (1865–1952), Finnish political leader. An opponent of Russian domination of Finland, Ståhlberg was a leader of the Constitutionalist party (1904–18) and professor of law at the University of Helsinki (1908–18). He headed the committee (1914–19) that drafted the republican Finnish constitution (1919) and served as the first president of independent Finland (1919–25). He ran unsuccessfully for president in 1931 and 1937.

STALIN, JOSEPH (Iosif Vissarionovich Dzhugashvili; 1879–1953), Soviet political leader. Born into a poor family in the Georgian town of Gori, Stalin studied at a theological seminary (1894–99) but was expelled before his graduation. He was attracted to the underground revolutionary Marxist movement (1901), joined the Bolsheviks (1903), and became a disciple of V. I. Lenin. Although a member of the inner circle of the Bolshevik party by 1913, he played only a minor role in the 1917 revolution. He was elevated to the Politburo of the party (1919) and was named general secretary of the party's Central Committee in 1922. He used that position, which gave him control of the party's personnel, to consolidate his power after Lenin's death (1924), and by 1928 Stalin had outmaneuvered his Bolshevik rivals, including Leon Trotsky, and assumed full control of the party and state apparatus. He launched (1928) the policy of rapid industrialization and agricultural collectivization that cost the lives of millions of innocent people but established the Soviet Union as a great industrial power. He solidified his control during the 1930s by the means of pervasive police terror, executions, mass internal deportations, show trials of alleged enemies of the state, and systematic self-glorification. His armies helped defeat the Germans in World War II (1941–45), and he exerted control over the nations of Eastern Europe and built up the Soviet nuclear arsenal after the war. Many of his totalitarian policies and the "cult of personality" were later denounced by party leader Nikita Khrushchev (1956), and the most brutal aspects of Stalinism were modified. ■ See Roy A. Medvedev, *Let History Judge* (Eng. trans. 1972), and biographies by Isaac Deutscher (1949; 2d ed. 1967), Robert C. Tucker (1973; 1990), Adam Ulam (1973), and Dmitri Volkogonov (1983; Eng. trans. 1991).

STAMBULISKI, ALEXANDER (1879–1923), Bulgarian political leader. The leader of the Bulgarian Agrarian Union (Peasant's party), Stambuliski opposed Bulgaria's entry into World War I on the side of the Central Powers and was imprisoned (1915–18). After the war he led an insurrection that forced King Ferdinand to abdicate, and he served as premier from 1919 to 1923. Strongly antiurban and antiindustry, he redistributed lands to the peasantry, instituted judicial and governmental reforms, and founded the Green International, an international peasant alliance set up to counter the "Red" and "White" internationals. He was overthrown by a military coup in June 1923. ■ See John D. Bell, *Peasants in Power* (1977).

STANFIELD, ROBERT LORNE (1914–), Canadian politician. Born into a wealthy family, Stanfield was educated at Dalhousie University and Harvard (LL.B. 1939). He practiced law in Nova Scotia (from 1940) and was elected to the provincial legislature as a Progressive Conservative (1949). From 1956 to 1967 he was premier of Nova Scotia. In 1967 Stanfield was elected to Parliament and chosen head of the Progressive Conservative party. As leader of the opposition, however, he lost three successive elections to Pierre Trudeau and resigned the leadership in 1976. He left Parliament in 1979 and subsequently headed the Institute for Research on Public Policy (1981–87) and the Commonwealth Foundation (1987–91). ■ See E. D. Haliburton, *My Years with Stanfield* (1972), and study by Geoffrey Stevens (1973).

STANISLAVSKY, CONSTANTIN (Konstantin Sergeyevich Alekseyev; 1863–1938), Russian actor, director, teacher, and producer. A cofounder (1898) and director of the world-famous Moscow Art Theater. Stanislavsky reacted to the artificial and highly romantic acting style of 19th-century Russian theater by developing a method of acting that emphasized the psychological truth of the characterization and the actor's inner identification with his role. He directed and

starred in many celebrated plays, notably those of Chekhov, Gorky, and Gogol. His tour of Europe and the United States (1922–24) aroused great interest in the "Stanislavsky method," and it subsequently had a profound influence on modern theater, particularly in the United States, where it was adapted by the Actors Studio in New York. He described his concepts in *An Actor Prepares* (Eng. trans. 1936), *Building a Character* (Eng. trans. 1949), and *Creating a Role* (Eng. trans. 1961). ■ See his autobiography, *My Life in Art* (Eng. trans. 1924), and biographies by David Magarshack (1950) and E. Poliakova (Eng. trans. 1982).

STANLEY, KIM (Patricia Reid; 1925–), U.S. actress. Kim Stanley studied psychology as an undergraduate in New Mexico and Texas, then worked as a model and waitress in New York City before studying with Elia Kazan and Lee Strasberg at the Actors Studio. There she developed the "method acting" that made her one of the most intense dramatic actresses on the American stage. Stanley was best known for her award-winning performances in *Picnic* (1953) and *Bus Stop* (1955), as well as for her roles in *Cat on a Hot Tin Roof* (1958), *A Touch of the Poet* (1958), and *The Three Sisters* (1964). She preferred stage acting to film work but made several memorable films (including *The Goddess,* 1958; *Seance on a Wet Afternoon,* 1964; and *Frances,* 1982) and appeared as well on television; she won an Emmy Award for her 1963 TV role in *A Cardinal Act of Mercy.* She left the stage to teach acting.

STANLEY, WENDELL MEREDITH (1904–1971), U.S. biochemist. W. M. Stanley played collegiate football and was diverted from a coaching career by a chance conversation with a chemistry professor. He received a Ph.D. from the University of Illinois (1929) and taught at the Rockefeller Institute for Medical Research (1931–48) and the University of California at Berkeley (1948–71). He was the first to purify and crystallize a virus (tobacco mosaic virus, 1935) and prove that viruses are nucleoproteins and can be studied by physical and chemical methods. During World War II Stanley developed a vaccine against the influenza virus. In 1946 he shared the Nobel Prize in Chemistry with James Sumner and John Northrop, who had also crystallized proteins.

STANTON, FRANK NICHOLAS (1908–), U.S. radio and television executive. Trained as a psychologist at Ohio State (Ph.D. 1935), Station left academia to work for the Columbia Broadcasting System. He served as president of CBS (1946–71) and helped develop the company into the largest advertising and communications medium in the world. Primarily concerned with questions of organization, policy, and news presentation, he was an outspoken advocate of freedom of the press and the leading statesman of the broadcast industry. However, he was also chiefly responsible for the network's policy of blacklisting alleged left-wing actors and writers during the 1950s and 1960s. He frequently testified before Congress and was mainly responsible for convincing it to suspend the equal-time rule and allow the broadcast of the presidential-election debate between John F. Kennedy and Richard Nixon (1960). Stanton also served as chairman of the American Red Cross (1973–79).

STARHEMBERG, ERNST RÜDIGER VON (1899-1956), Austrian political leader. Although he participated in Adolf Hitler's "beer hall putsch" in Munich (1923), Starhemberg broke with Hitler but maintained his ideology and attempted to establish an indigenous Austrian fascist system. He was leader (1930) of the Heimwehr, a fascist paramilitary organization, and a founder (1932) of the government-sponsored Fatherland Front, a right-wing party coalition; he was appointed vice-chancellor in 1934. In 1936 he was expelled from the government, the Heimwehr was dissolved, and Starhemberg left the country after the unification of Austria and Germany (1938). During World War II he served briefly in the British and Free French air forces. He emigrated to Argentina (1942) but returned to Austria in 1955. ■ See his memoirs, *Between Hitler and Mussolini* (1942).

STARK, JOHANNES (1874–1957), German physicist. Stark was educated at the University of Munich (Ph.D. 1897) and held various academic posts from 1900 to 1922. He demonstrated (1913) the splitting of spectral lines in an electric field, a phenomenon that became known as the "Stark effect." For this discovery and for his observation of the Doppler effect in the high-velocity atoms of canal rays (1905), he received the 1919 Nobel Prize in Physics. His work helped to establish quantum theory, although Stark later irrationally denounced the theory as un-Aryan. He became an enthusiastic Nazi party member, an anti-Semitic race theorist, and wrote a book on Nazi leader Adolf Hitler. After World War II he was sentenced (1947) to four years in a labor camp.

STARLING, ERNEST HENRY (1866–1927), British physiologist. Starling studied medicine before undertaking research at University College at Oxford (1899). He gained a reputation for devising brilliant experimental techniques. Starling's collaboration with Sir William Bayliss led to the discovery of the substance that he named the hormone, after the Greek word meaning "to set in motion." The hormone was a substance secreted by one organ, and carried in the bloodstream, that stimulates a specific effect on another organ. After 1902 he did pioneering work on the heart's pumping action and formulated Starling's law of the heart: the energy of the contraction is a function of the length of the muscle fibers. During World War I he worked on antidotes to poison gases. His *Principles of Human Physiology* (1912) was an important reference book. ■ See Charles Evans, *Reminiscences of Bayliss and Starling* (1964).

STARR, CHAUNCEY (1912–　), U.S. physicist and electrical engineer. Starr worked on the Manhattan atomic bomb project (1942–46) and was technical director of the pilot uranium plant at Oak Ridge, Tennessee. At North American Aviation (1946–66), he headed research groups that pioneered in the development of the sodium-cooled nuclear reactor, which was the forerunner of the fast-breeder power reactor, and the organic-cooled reactor, which was the basis of the heavy-water reactor used for electric power production and water desalinization. He was best known for the creation of the compact and lightweight zirconium-hydride reactor that was designed to power satellites and spacecraft. The launching (1965) and successful operation of his 970-pound *SNAP-10A* power plant marked the beginning of the nuclear space age. Starr was dean of the engineering school at the University of California, Los Angeles (1966–73), and founder and president of the Electric Power Research Institute (1973–78).

STAUDINGER, HERMANN (1881–1965), German chemist. A professor at Zurich (1912–26) and Freiburg (1926–51), Staudinger developed his theories of molecular organization during the 1920s. He demonstrated that polymers were long chainlike structures consisting of smaller molecules and that they could be built up synthetically by various chemical means without losing their individuality. Staudinger's work made possible the development of synthetic rubber, fibers, and plastics, and he won the 1953 Nobel Prize in Chemistry.

STAUFFENBERG, CLAUS VON (1907–1944), German anti-Nazi conspirator. A career officer from a distinguished German family, Stauffenberg was disturbed by the anti-Semitism and brutality he witnessed on the Russian front during World War II. Severely wounded in 1943, he spent his long convalescence plotting to assassinate Nazi dictator Adolf Hitler and replace Nazism with social democracy. But Stauffenberg's bomb failed to kill Hitler on July 20, 1944; his coconspirators failed to seize the reins of power, and he was himself summarily executed that day. ■ See biography by Joachim Kramarz (1967).

STAUNING, THORVALD (1873–1942), Danish political leader. Stauning was president of the cigar-makers union and secretary of the Social Democratic party before his election to parliament (1906). During his years as premier (1924–26; 1929–42) he introduced pioneering social-welfare reforms and reduced military expenditures. After the German invasion (1940) during World War II, Stauning remained in power as head of a coalition government.

STAVISKY, SERGE ALEXANDRE (1886–1934), French swindler. The son of Russian Jews who emigrated to France before the turn of the century, Stavisky drifted into the Parisian underworld as a young man. In 1926 he was arrested for defrauding stockbrokers of 7 million francs and served 18 months while awaiting a trial that was postponed indefinitely because of his influential connections. Stavisky grew rich by floating fraudulent municipal bonds, using his wealth to buy newspapers, racehorses, and officials. In 1934, after several prominent politicians were implicated in his bond swindles, he allegedly committed suicide. Many believed that he was killed by the police to protect the politicians, and subsequent violent right-wing street demonstrations against official corruption brought down the government and threatened, for several months, the future of parliamentary democracy in France.

STEAD, CHRISTINA ELLEN (1902–1983), Australian novelist. Stead graduated from Sydney University Teachers' College (1922). She left Australia in 1928 and spent most of her life in Europe. Although she often set her novels in Australia, she was more concerned with individual than with national experience. *The Man Who Loved Children* (1940), set in the United States, revealed the disastrous effect of male chauvinism on a family. She published several novels in the 1940s that commented sardonically on sexual mores and materialism in America. In *Dark Places of the Heart* (1966), a novel set in industrial northern England in the early 1950s, she explored the character of a radical lesbian. Her short fiction was published in *The Salzburg Tales* (1934), *The Puzzleheaded Girl* (1967), and *Ocean of Story: The Uncollected Stories of Christina Stead* (1986), and excerpts from 11 of her novels appeared in *A Christina Stead Reader* (1979). ■ See studies by R. G. Geering (1969) and Joan Lidoff (1982) and biography by Hazel Rowley (1994).

STEBBINS, GEORGE LEDYARD (1906–2000), U.S. botanist. The recipient of a Harvard Ph.D. (1931), G. Ledyard Stebbins was a professor at the University of California at Davis (1947–73) and founder of its department of genetics. He was the first to artificially synthesize a new species of plant able to grow in a natural environment (1944) and the first to apply the modern synthetic theory of evolution to plant evolution (in *Variation and Evolution in Plants*, 1950). In addition to several textbooks he wrote *Processes of Organic Evolution* (1966) and *Flowering Plants: Evolution Above the Species Level* (1974).

STEFANSSON, VILHJALMUR (1879–1962), Canadian-born U.S. explorer and ethnologist. The son of Icelandic immigrant parents, Stefansson studied anthropology and archaeology in the United States and Iceland. He made three major expeditions to remote regions of Arctic Canada (1906–07; 1908–12; 1913–18), during which he explored many uncharted regions and gained valuable information about Eskimo life and culture. After his retirement (1919) he lectured widely on the Arctic regions, discussing the value of the Arctic's resources and predicting transpolar crossings by airplane and submarine. He advised the U.S. government on Alaskan defense during World War II and advised Pan American Airways on polar air routes from 1932 to 1945. He wrote many popular books including *My Life with the Eskimo* (1913), *The Friendly Arctic* (1921), and his auto-

biography, *Discovery* (1964). ■ See study by Richard Diubaldo (1978) and Erick Berry, *Mr. Arctic* (1966).

STEFFENS, (JOSEPH) LINCOLN (1866–1936), U.S. journalist. As editor of *McClure's* magazine (1901–06) and later as a freelance writer, Steffens spearheaded the "muckraking" movement that exposed corruption in U.S. business and government. (See his *Shame of the Cities,* 1904.) Increasingly pessimistic about prospects for reform, he became interested in revolutionary socialism. "I have seen the future, and it works," he announced after a 1919 trip to the Soviet Union. In 1927 he retired to his native California, where he wrote a bestselling *Autobiography* (2 vols., 1931) and edited a weekly newspaper. ■ See biography by Justin Kaplan (1974) and studies by Patrick F. Palermo (1978) and Robert Stinson (1979).

STEICHEN, EDWARD JEAN (1879–1973), U.S. photographer, painter, and curator. Steichen was born in Luxembourg, grew up in Michigan, and became one of the most celebrated U.S. photographers. A leader of the pre–World War I Photo Secession movement, he turned to advertising and fashion photography (1923–38) and contributed stylish portraits to *Vogue* and *Vanity Fair*. During World War II he organized a department in the U.S. Navy to photograph the war at sea. From 1947 to 1962 Steichen was director of photography at the Museum of Modern Art in New York, where he mounted the enormously successful "Family of Man" exhibition (1955), which was seen by 9 million people. ■ See his autobiography, *A Life in Photography* (1963); his photos in *Edward Steichen* (1978) and *Steichen: The Master Prints, 1895–1914* (1978); and studies by Penelope Niven (1997), J. Smith (1999) and J. Steichen (2000).

STEIN, SIR AUREL (1862–1943), Hungarian-born British archaeologist. A great explorer of Asia, Stein went to India in 1888 as a college principal and published a Sanskrit edition and an English translation of the ancient Indian *Chronicle of the Kings of Kashmir* (1900). He then embarked on four major expeditions into central Asia and China (1900–30), tracing ancient caravan routes and the campaigns of Alexander the Great, all of which he described in 12 volumes. During the 1930s he investigated the prehistoric relationships between the Mesopotamian. Indus Valley, and ancient Iranian civilizations. Stein remained active as an explorer into his eighties. ■ See the biographies by Jeannette Mirsky (1977) and Annabel Walker (1995).

STEIN, EDITH (1891–1942), German philosopher and nun. Born into a wealthy Jewish family, Stein became an atheist and studied philosophy with Edmund Husserl, the father of phenomenology, at Göttingen and Freiburg universities (Ph.D. 1916). She converted to Roman Catholicism (1922) and became a well-known university lecturer and writer on Catholic philosophy, phenomenology, women, and education before becoming a Carmelite nun (1934). Her books included *Finite and Eternal Being* (1950), an attempt to synthesize Thomism and phenomenology, and *The Science of the Cross* (1950; Eng. trans. 1960), a phenomenological study of St. John of the Cross. Forced by the Nazis to flee Germany (1938), she escaped to a convent in Holland but was seized by the Gestapo (1942) and taken to Auschwitz, the concentration camp where she died in the gas chamber. She was considered a modern martyr by the church and was beatified in 1987 and proclaimed a saint by Pope John Paul II in 1998. ■ See her *Life in a Jewish Family: Her Unfinished Autobiographical Account* (Eng. trans. 1986); the biography by Waltraud Herbstrith (Eng. trans. 1985); and Hilda C. Graef, *The Scholar and the Cross* (1955).

STEIN, GERTRUDE (1874–1946), U.S. writer. The daughter of a wealthy businessman, Stein grew up in California and studied at Radcliffe (B.A. 1898) and Johns Hopkins Medical School. She left for Paris (1903) and began her important modern-art collection when she met the artists Braque and Matisse as well as Picasso, who painted a celebrated portrait of her (1906). Stein presided for 43 years over the Paris salon frequented by European artists and writers, as well as the "lost generation" of American expatriates of the 1920s. Her famous phrase, "a rose is a rose is a rose is a rose," suggested that writing must entail a repetitive and nonassociative sequence of images that, like movie frames, flow together to create a fictional present. She insisted that punctuation interfered with this animation process. Stein decisively influenced Sherwood Anderson, Ernest Hemingway, and other writers. Her own writing at its best was incomparably witty and penetrating, and at its worst, unreadable. It included *Three Lives* (1909); *The Making of Americans* (1925); *The Autobiography of Alice B. Toklas* (1933), Stein's own life viewed from the perspective of her lifelong lover; *Everybody's Autobiography* (1937); *Picasso* (1938); and *Wars I Have Seen* (1945). Her literary theory included *Composition as Exploration* (1926). Selections of her work are contained in *Selected Writings 1909–44* (1946), *Operas and Plays 1913–30* (1932), and *Look at Me Now and Here I Am: Writings and Lectures 1911–45* (1967). ■ See study by Richard Bridgman (1970) and James R. Mellow, *Charmed Circle* (1974).

STEIN, WILLIAM HOWARD (1911–1980), U.S. biochemist. Stein earned a Columbia University Ph.D. (1938), joined the faculty of the Rockefeller University, and began a collaboration with Stanford Moore into the problems of cellular protein synthesis (1939). They performed pioneering studies into the structure and activity of the enzyme ribonuclease (RNA) and shared (with Christian Anfinsen) the 1972 Nobel Prize in Chemistry. Stein and Moore subsequently analyzed the action of deoxyribonuclease (DNA). Because RNA and DNA control the chemistry of life, Stein and Moore's research raised hopes for modifying defective enzymes in order to prevent inherited diseases and mental re-

tardation. Stein edited (1968–69) the *Journal of Biological Chemistry*.

STEINBECK, JOHN (1902–1968), U.S. novelist. Steinbeck's early novels, such as *Tortilla Flat* (1935) and *Of Mice and Men* (1937), were well received, but real fame came with *The Grapes of Wrath* (1939), based on his Depression-era experiences among the "Okies." The allegory's vivid narrative and moving portrayals depicted the migration from Oklahoma's dust bowl to the "promised land" of California. Although some libraries banned the book as subversive, Steinbeck's plea for social solidarity appealed to readers who despaired of the individual's ability to deal with economic crisis, and it sparked widespread indignation over the plight of America's disinherited. The novel sold 3 million copies in the United States, making Steinbeck an unwilling celebrity. He failed to sustain the brilliance of that novel in such later works as *Cannery Row* (1944), *East of Eden* (1952), and *The Winter of Our Discontent* (1961), and his 1962 Nobel Prize aroused some critical indignation. Steinbeck took to travels in midlife, recording his experiences in *A Russian Journal* (1948) and *Travels with Charley in Search of America* (1962). ■ See biographies by Jay Parini (1995) and Jackson J. Benson (1983); Thomas Kiernan, *The Intricate Music* (1979); and studies by Joseph Fontenrose (1964) and Warren French (rev. ed. 1984).

STEINBERG, SAUL (1914–1999), Rumanian-born U.S. painter and cartoonist. Educated as an architect in Milan, Italy (1933–40), Steinberg gradually turned from architecture to art and cartooning; his drawings soon found their way into *Life* and *Harper's Bazaar*. He emigrated to the United States (1942), and his work was honored by inclusion in the "14 Americans" show at New York's Museum of Modern Art (1946). His cartoons and covers for the *New Yorker* were admired for their complicated designs of thin, elegant ink lines, their witty combinations of diverse items, and their elaborate detail. Steinberg also painted murals; a lifetime project was *Parades,* a panorama of nations and eras, much of which was acquired by the Metropolitan Museum of Art in New York. His work appeared in *The Passport* (1954), *The Inspector* (1973), and *Saul Steinberg* (1978), and *The Discovery of America* (1993). His best-known work was a depiction of a Manhattanite's view of the world, which first appeared on a *New Yorker* cover (March 29, 1976).

STEINBERGER, JACK (1921–), German-born U.S. physicist. The son of a Jewish community leader, Steinberger was able to leave Germany after the Nazis came to power and settle in the United States (1934). During World War II he worked in the Radiation Laboratory of the Massachusetts Institute of Technology and subsequently studied physics at the University of Chicago (Ph.D. 1948) and taught at Columbia University (1950–71). Working with Melvin Schwartz (his former student) and Leon Lederman, he performed (1960–62) a landmark experiment that produced the first artificial beam of neutrinos, subatomic particles with no electrical charge and no detectable mass. The experiment provided physicists with a powerful tool with which to study the "weak" nuclear force that influences radioactive decay of atoms. The experiment also revealed a new type of neutrino, the muon neutrino, whose existence led to the formulation of the "standard model" theory, which describes the fundamental particles that are the basic components of all matter. For their research Steinberger, Lederman, and Schwartz shared the 1988 Nobel Prize in Physics. Steinberger worked at the European Center for Nuclear Research (CERN) in Geneva (1968–86).

STEINEM, GLORIA (1934–   ), U.S. journalist and feminist. The granddaughter of a prominent feminist leader, Steinem grew up in a poor neighborhood in Toledo, Ohio, graduated from Smith College (B.A. 1956), and studied in India for two years (1956–58). She achieved prominence as a freelance journalist during the 1960s and established a column in *New York* magazine (1968), "The City Politic," which reflected her left-liberal social and political views. Attracted to the nascent feminist movement in 1968, she became one of its major spokeswomen and fund-raisers and helped found the National Women's Political Caucus (1971), the Women's Action Alliance (1971), and the Coalition of Labor Union Women (1974). She was the founding editor (1972–87) of *Ms.* magazine, the most widely read feminist periodical in the United States. Her books included *Outrageous Acts and Everyday Rebellions* (1983); *Marilyn* (1986); *Revolution from Within: A Book of Self-Esteem* (1992); and *Moving Beyond Words* (1993), a volume of essays on the powerlessness of women. ▪ See biography by Sidney L. Stern (1997).

STEINER, MAXIMILIAN RAOUL (1888–1971), Austrian-born U.S. film composer. Steiner, who came from a prominent Viennese musical family, emigrated to the United States in 1914 and became a Broadway conductor and orchestrator. He moved to Hollywood in 1929 to pioneer in the composition and orchestration of lush symphonic-style music for films. Utilizing special effects and psychological drama, he coordinated his music with the visual track of such classics as *King Kong* (1933), *Gone With the Wind* (1939), and *The Treasure of Sierra Madre* (1948). He scored more than 200 films and won Academy Awards for *The Informer* (1935), *Now Voyager* (1942), and *Since You Went Away* (1944).

STEINER, RUDOLF (1861–1925), Austrian social philosopher. Steiner edited the poetic and scientific works of German writer Johann Wolfgang von Goethe (1889–96) and wrote *Philosophy of Spiritual Activity* (1894; Eng. trans. 1922), which was influenced by Goethe's thought. He became increasingly involved with spiritualism and the occult and devised a new philosophy called "anthroposophy," a synthesis of 19th-century philosophical ideas and theosophical material. Described as a "spiritual science," anthroposophy explained life in terms of humankind's spiritual nature and taught that people have faculties for spiritual comprehension that can be developed through pure thought. Steiner founded the Anthroposophical Society (1912) and inspired the Waldorf School movement, which spread throughout Europe and the United States. ▪ See his autobiography, *The Course of My Life* (1925; Eng. trans. 1951), and study by Stewart C. Easton (1980).

STEINMAN, DAVID BARNARD (1886–1960), U.S. engineer. An independent bridge designer and consultant, Steinman made pioneering theoretical and experimental aerodynamic studies of suspension bridges that allowed for the construction of extremely long yet fundamentally stable structures. He designed more than 400 bridges, including the Florianópolis (Brazil, 1926), Sydney Harbor (Australia, 1932), Triborough (New York City, 1936), and the Mackinac Straits (Michigan, 1957). He wrote *Bridges and Their Builders* (1941), *Suspension Bridges* (1954), and *Mackinac Bridge at Mackinac* (1957). ▪ See William Ratigan, *Highways Over Broad Waters* (1959).

STEINMETZ, CHARLES PROTEUS (**Karl August Rudolf Steinmetz;** 1865–1923), German-born U.S. electrical engineer. Steinmetz, a hunchback who was four feet tall, was forced to leave Germany (1888) because of his socialist activities. He emigrated (1889) to the United States, where he distinguished himself by explaining the power loss resulting from magnetic resistance. Finding that alternating current could partially remedy this loss, he conducted an elaborate theoretical study that not only simplified the complex field but also accelerated the commercial use of alternating current. His investigation of lightning led to the development of lightning arresters to protect electrical-power lines. From 1893 until his death, Steinmetz was associated with the General Electric Co. He taught at Union College (after 1902). Although primarily a theoretician, Steinmetz received approximately 200 patents for his electrical-engineering inventions. ▪ See Ernest Caldecott and Philip Alger, comps., *Steinmetz the Philosopher* (1965); John A. Miller, *Modern Jupiter* (1958); and biographies by Sigmund A. Lavine (1955) and Ronald R. Kline (1992).

STELLA, FRANK PHILIP (1936–   ), U.S. artist. The son of a Massachusetts gynecologist, Stella graduated from Phillips Academy (1954) and Princeton (1958), where he began painting in an abstract-expressionist style. He abandoned the style, though, and won recognition for his "black" paintings and had a one-man show at New York's Museum of Modern Art in 1960. He was regarded as a leader in the development of minimal art, and his experiments with abstract shapes culminated in a 1965 series on irregular polygons and a 1967 *Protractor* series of huge, shaped canvases with architectural contours. His complex *Cone* *and Pillar* series was exhibited in New York City in 1985. ▪ See Richard H. Axsom, *The Prints of Frank Stella* (1983), and the illustrated biography by Sidney Guberman (1995).

STELLA, JOSEPH (1877–1946), Italian-born U.S. painter. The major futurist painter on the American scene, Stella was fascinated by the lines of force created in the New World by steel and electricity. His subject was the surging romance of engineering—the skyscrapers, subways, bridges, and other visual archetypes of New York. Stella's best-known paintings were *Brooklyn Bridge* (1917–18), *Battle of Lights, Coney Island* (1913), and *New York Interpreted* (1920–22). In the 1930s he painted a series of lush tropical landscapes with surrealistic elements. ▪ See study by Irma B. Jaffe (1970).

STENGEL, CASEY (Charles Dillon Stengel; 1891–1975), U.S. baseball player and manager. An outfielder with the Brooklyn Dodgers, Pittsburgh Pirates, Philadelphia Phillies, New York Giants, and Boston Braves (1912–25), Stengel appeared in two World Series (1922; 1923) and had a lifetime batting average of .284. He was a coach and manager in the major and minor leagues (1932–48) before managing the New York Yankees (1949–60), the team he led to 10 American League pennants and seven World Series championships, including a record five straight (1949–53). He subsequently managed the newly organized New York Mets (1962–65). His humor and quotable malapropisms, dubbed "Stengelese" by the press, made him one of baseball's most popular and colorful personalities. ▪ See Maury Allen, *You Could Look It Up* (1979), and biography by Robert W. Creamer (1984).

STENMARK, INGEMAR (1956–), Swedish skier. Born and raised near the Arctic Circle in Swedish Lapland, Stenmark began to ski at age 5, was coached by his father, and won his first national competition at age 8. A specialist in the slalom and giant slalom noted for his precise, graceful style and his tremendous balance and agility, he won his first World Cup event in December 1974 and was the World Cup champion in 1976, 1977, and 1978. Only a change in the scoring rules in 1978, reinstating equal weight in point scoring to the downhill race—not Stenmark's forte—deprived him of subsequent championships. He won two gold medals at the Lake Placid Olympic Games (1980) and was the first man to win three consecutive world slalom titles (1980–82). By winning his 63rd individual race in January 1982, he broke Annemarie Moser-Proell's record and became the most successful skier in World Cup history. He retired at the end of the 1989 season.

STEPHENS, JAMES (1882?–1950), Irish writer. Stephens grew up in the slums of Dublin and had little formal education. He began his writing career contributing to *Sinn Fein*, the newspaper of the Irish Republican party. *The Crock of Gold* (1912), which combined fantasy with reality, estab-lished his reputation as a novelist and allowed him to write full-time. He vowed to give Ireland a "new mythology," and the novels *Deirdre* (1923) and *In the Land of Youth* (1924) were part of this effort. His writing was both lyrical and ironic, reflecting his mastery of Irish folklore. He wrote little in his later years and eventually moved to Britain, where he did frequent broadcasts for the BBC. ▪ See his *Collected Poems* (1954), *A James Stephens Reader* (1962), and studies by Hilary Pyle (1965) and Augustine Martin (1977).

STERN, ISAAC (1920–), Russian-born U.S. violinist. Taken to San Francisco when he was one year old, Stern was the first great violinist to have been completely trained in the United States. He made his debut with the San Francisco Philharmonic at age 11 and gave his first New York recital in 1937. After his triumphant Carnegie Hall debut (1943), he was regarded as one of the most brilliant virtuosos of the century. Over the next four decades he performed throughout the world and made recordings of all of the great concertos, from Bach to 20th-century masters. He appeared frequently as part of a trio with pianist Eugene Istomin and cellist Leonard Rose (1962–83). He was instrumental in the creation of the National Endowment for the Arts, and after helping to save Carnegie Hall from demolition in 1959, he served as its president (1960–). ▪ See his autobiography, *My First 79 Years* (1999; with Chaim Potok).

STERN, LINA SOLOMONOVNA (1878–1968), Soviet physiologist. Born in Latvia and brought up and educated in Switzerland, Stern left her professorship in Geneva (1925) and emigrated to the Soviet Union. She was director of the Moscow Institute of Physiology (1925–49) and was the first woman to be elected to the Soviet Academy of Sciences (1939). The most prominent woman scientist in the Soviet Union, she wrote more than 400 works on physiology and pioneered in the study of the chemical foundation of physiological processes. After winning the Stalin Prize (1943), she was removed from her post (1948) but was restored to her position after dictator Joseph Stalin's death in 1953.

STERN, OTTO (1888–1969), German-born physicist. Stern worked under Albert Einstein and taught physics at several universities. Forced to leave Germany after the Nazis took power, he emigrated to the United States, where he taught at the Carnegie Institute of Technology in Pittsburgh (1933–45). In the 1920s and 1930s he subjected molecular beams, molecules of gases injected into a vacuum, to magnetic fields. In a series of experiments he proved the existence of atomic magnetic movement and gave direct evidence for the confirmation of the basic ideas of quantum theory. He received the 1943 Nobel Prize in Physics. Using the same molecular-beam method, Stern confirmed L. V. de Broglie's earlier prediction of the wave properties of electrons.

STERNBERG, JOSEF VON. *See VON STERNBERG, JOSEF.*

STETTINIUS, EDWARD REILLY, JR. (1900–1949), U.S. industrialist and public official. Stettinius arrived in Washington, D.C., as a General Motors' lobbyist with the New Deal administration, but he remained to take on a variety of government appointments. In 1938 he became chairman of the board of U.S. Steel, a $100,000-a-year job that he gave up in 1939 to serve successively as a $1-a-year administrator in war resources, lend-lease, production management, and the state department. Stettinius was appointed secretary of state in 1944, resigning in 1945 to serve as the first U.S. representative to the United Nations (1945–46), an organization he helped to establish. ▪ See his *Diaries: 1943–46* (1975), *Roosevelt and the Russians: The Yalta Conference* (1949) and study by R. L. Walker (1965).

STEVENS, GEORGE (1905–1975), U.S. film director. Stevens went to Hollywood as a cameraman (1921) and filmed many of the early Laurel and Hardy shorts. He achieved fame as a director with such classics as *Alice Adams* (1935), *Swing Time* (1936), *Gunga Din* (1939), *Woman of the Year* (1942), and *Talk of the Town* (1942). During World War II he headed an army film unit that covered the liberation of Dachau concentration camp and the capture of German dictator Adolf Hitler's Berchtesgaden hideaway. After the war he directed *I Remember Mama* (1948), *Shane* (1952), and *The Diary of Anne Frank* (1959) and won Academy Awards for *A Place in the Sun* (1951) and *Giant* (1956).

STEVENS, WALLACE (1879–1955), U.S. poet. Stevens studied literature at Harvard, became a lawyer (1904), and from 1917 until his death was a Hartford, Connecticut, insurance company executive. The poet Marianne Moore, who visited his office, recalled a polished mahogany desk with nothing on it. Stevens' drive to impose order on his life is reflected in his poetry. He characterized imagination as "the power that enables us to perceive the normal in the abnormal, the opposite of chaos in chaos." He treated this theme in his first collection, *Harmonium* (1923), which included the acclaimed "Sunday Morning," and in his second collection, *Ideas of Order* (1935). His poetry is noted for its musicality and effective use of alliteration. His *Collected Poems* (1954) won the Pulitzer Prize. He also wrote a book of essays on poetry, *The Necessary Angel* (1951). *Collected Poetry and Prose* appeared in 1997. ▪ See biographies by Samuel F. Morse (1970), Milton J. Bates (1985), and Joan Richardson (2 vols., 1986–88); Peter Brazeau, *Paris of a World: Wallace Stevens Remembered* (1983); and studies by Frank Kermode (1979) and Harold Bloom (1977).

STEVENSON, ADLAI EWING (1900–1965), U.S. political leader. The son of a publishing executive and grandson of a U.S. vice president, Stevenson graduated from Princeton (1922) and went to work on a family newspaper in Illinois while completing his law degree. After World War II service in Washington and participation in the creation of the

United Nations, Stevenson returned to Illinois to run as a reform candidate for governor in 1948, his first and only electoral victory. Twice chosen as the Democratic presidential nominee (1952; 1956), he raised the level of political debate with his wit, eloquence, and idealism, but lost both races to Dwight D. Eisenhower. Stevenson served as U.S. ambassador to the United Nations (1961–65), where he had to defend policies he had only a subsidiary role in making. His son, Adlai E. Stevenson III, served as U.S. senator from Illinois (1970–81). ▪ See biographies by Herbert J. Muller (1967), John B. Martin (1976), and Porter McKeever (1989).

STEWARD, JULIAN HAYNES (1902–1972), U.S. cultural anthropologist. Steward founded cultural ecology, which explained social systems according to their environment and technology, and was a leading exponent of cultural evolution. While associated with the U.S. Bureau of American Ethnology at the Smithsonian Institution (1935–46), he edited the monumental *Handbook of South American Indians* (7 vols., 1946–59), and while a professor at Columbia University (1946–52) directed a massive study of the people of Puerto Rico (published 1956). He wrote *Area Research: Theory and Practice* (1950), a work that influenced the development of multidisciplinary area studies. At the University of Illinois, Urbana (1952–72), he directed many cross-cultural peasant studies and edited *Contemporary Change in Traditional Societies* (3 vols., 1967). His influential scholarly articles are in *Theory and Culture Change* (1955) and *Evolution and Ecology* (1977).

STEWART, ALICE (Alice Naish; 1906–   ), British epidemiologist. Stewart, both of whose parents were prominent medical doctors and professors, trained as a clinical physician, served on the faculty of Oxford University (1941–74), and was elected a fellow of the Royal College of Physicians (1946). She was a pioneer in studying the hazardous effects of low-level radiation on human beings, and her scientific reports generated much controversy. Her findings during the 1950s that X rays were dangerous to unborn children, gained worldwide acceptance by the 1970s and led to the ending of X rays for pregnant women. Her study during the 1970s of the effects of low-level radiation on workers at the Hanford nuclear weapons plant in Washington State showed that exposure to less than half of the federal safety limit resulted in higher levels of cancer than expected. She claimed that safety standards for radiation exposure were based on flawed analyses of the official 1951 studies of the survivors of the Hiroshima and Nagasaki bombings, and as a result the risks from low-level radiation were seriously underestimated. She spoke of the dangers of low-level radiation at public gatherings, scientific conference, and congressional hearings. ▪ See Gayle Greene, *The Woman Who Knew Too Much* (1999).

STEWART, DOUGLAS (1913–1985), New Zealand-born Australian writer. One of the most versatile modern Australian literary figures, Stewart was known for his verse plays (*Ned Kelly*, 1943; *The Fire on the Snow*, 1944; *The Golden Lover*, 1944; *Shipwreck*, 1947), poetry (*Sun Orchids*, 1952; *Collected Poems*, 1967), and his influential literary criticism (*The Flesh and the Spirit*, 1948; *The Broad Stream*, 1975). He was the literary editor of the *Sydney Bulletin* (1939–61) and edited several volumes of bush songs, ballads, and poems. *The Seven Rivers* (1966) contained his reminiscences. ■ See his *Springtime in Taranaki: An Autobiography of Youth* (1983) and study by Clement Semmler (1974).

STEWART, ELLEN (1931–), U.S. theatrical producer. Stewart was born in New Orleans, studied fashion design in New York in the 1950s, and worked as a seamstress at Saks Fifth Avenue, becoming a custom designer. She founded (1961) the Café La Mama—an experimental theater club— when she rented a claustrophobic basement in New York City's East Village. Many important playwrights had their first stagings at La Mama, which was later housed in its own building and supported by foundation grants. Stewart was responsible for the first American staging (1962) of a work by British writer Harold Pinter; she produced plays by then unknowns including Sam Shepard, Rochelle Owens, and Megan Terry. Stewart's La Mama was soon recognized as a center of theatrical pioneering. Numerous other La Mama companies assembled and performed throughout the world. In 1985 she won a prestigious MacArthur Foundation fellowship.

STEWART, JACKIE (John Young Stewart; 1939–), Scottish auto-racing driver. A three-time world driving champion (1969; 1971; 1973), Stewart won a record 27 Grand Prix races and more than $1 million during his racing career. An outspoken advocate of increased safety standards in auto racing, Stewart retired in 1973 after several of his colleagues were killed in racing accidents. ■ See his *Faster! A Racer's Diary* (1972; with Peter Manso) and *On the Road* (1983).

STEWART, JAMES (1908–1997), U.S. actor. Stewart studied architecture at Princeton before making his acting debut on Broadway in 1932. A tall country boy with an engaging drawl, he won great acclaim as the idealistic young politician in the film *Mr. Smith Goes to Washington* (1939) and as Elwood P. Dowd, the amiable eccentric whose best friend is an invisible giant rabbit—*Harvey* (stage, 1940; film, 1950). Stewart won an Academy Award for *The Philadelphia Story* (1940) and also starred in *It's A Wonderful Life* (1946), *The Spirit of St. Louis* (1957), and in director Alfred Hitchcock's thrillers *Rear Window* (1954) and *Vertigo* (1958). He was a spokesman for conservative causes and a brigadier general in the air force reserve. ■ See Jhan Robbins, *Everybody's Man* (1984).

STEWART, POTTER (1915–1985), U.S. jurist. Stewart graduated from Yale Law School (1941) and practiced law in New York and Cincinnati before being appointed to the U.S. Court of Appeals for the 6th District (1954). Elevated to the Supreme Court by Pres. Dwight D. Eisenhower (1959), Stewart, a moderate, frequently voted with the court's conservative bloc, but at times was a swing member. He wrote several notable dissenting opinions during the 1960s and often argued on narrow constitutional grounds. He retired in 1981.

STIBITZ, GEORGE ROBERT (1904–1995), U.S. mathematician. After receiving a Ph.D. in physics from Cornell University (1930), Stibitz did research for the Bell Telephone Laboratories in New York City (1930–41), where he worked on telephone relay-switching equipment. To help quickly work out the complex mathematical calculations involved in his projects, he built (1937) a primitive, desktop binary adder out of dry-cell batteries, strips of metal, and flashlight bulbs attached to old telephone relays. With the help of colleague Samuel Williams, he expanded his contraption into the closet-size Model I Complex Calculator (1940), which is considered to be the world's first operational digital computer. (A smaller, cruder version of a digital computer was built, independently, in 1938 by Konrad Zuse in Germany.) He also demonstrated what was considered to be the first remote computer operation by sending problems by teletype from Dartmouth College in Hanover, New Hampshire, to Bell Labs in New York and receiving answers within seconds. During World War II he worked on the military uses of binary computers. He later taught at the Dartmouth Medical School (1964–73), where he did pioneering work in the application of computers to biomedical problems.

STIEGLITZ, ALFRED (1864–1946), U.S. photographer. Stieglitz was drawn to photography while studying mechanical engineering in Germany (1883). More than any other photographer, he was responsible for the recognition of photography as an art form. Initially influenced by the values of painting, he gradually developed a peculiarly photographic aesthetic, which he fostered through competitions, exhibitions, and publications. Stieglitz's multimedia Photo-Secession movement and gallery at 291 Fifth Avenue, New York, together with his magazine *Camera Work*, dominated modern American art and photography from 1902 to 1917. He introduced the works of artists such as Rodin, Matisse, Cézanne, and Picasso to America. His best-known photos were those of New York City taken at the turn of the century, a series of cloud images, and a series of portraits of his wife, the artist Georgia O'Keeffe. ■ See *Stieglitz, Photographs and Writings* (1983); study by William Homer (1983); and biographies by Dorothy Norman (1973) and Sue Davidson Lowc (1983).

STIGLER, GEORGE JOSEPH (1911–1991), U.S. economist. Stigler was long associated with the University of

Chicago (Ph.D. 1938; professor from 1958) and its "Chicago school" of conservative economics, which emphasized monetarism, free markets, reduced government spending, and minimal governmental regulation. For his seminal work on regulation, on industrial structures, and on the functioning of markets, he was awarded the 1982 Nobel Prize in Economics. He also advanced a "theory of the economics of information," made pioneering studies in the economic analysis of law, and wrote extensively on the history of economics. His books included *Production and Distribution Theories* (1941), *The Theory of Price* (1946), *The Behavior of Industrial Prices* (1970; with J. K. Kindahl), *The Citizen and the State* (1975), and *The Economist as Preacher* (1983).

STILL, CLYFFORD (1904–1980), U.S. artist. As a teacher on the West Coast (California School of Fine Arts, San Francisco: 1946–50) and in New York City, Still influenced the development of abstract expressionism, although he viewed himself as part of no movement or school in his attempt to develop a uniquely American aesthetic vision. An antitraditionalist and one of the most original artists of his time, he was best known for his very large and totally abstract works of the 1940s and 1950s, which consisted of jagged forms and open color fields painted in a manner that conveyed an immediacy and a limitless sense of scale. Shortly before his death he was the subject of the largest one-man exhibition (78 paintings) ever held for a living artist at New York's Metropolitan Museum of Art. ▪ See study and catalog edited by John P. O'Neill (1979).

STILL, WILLIAM GRANT (1895–1978), U.S. composer. Still studied music with Edgar Varèse and was an arranger of jazz compositions for W. C. Handy and Paul Whiteman. Most of his music was devoted to black themes: *Afro-American Symphony* (1931), *Lenox Avenue* (for orchestra and chorus, 1937), and the opera, *Troubled Island* (1938). He was the first African-American conductor of a major U.S. symphony orchestra (Los Angeles Philharmonic, 1936). He also directed and arranged music for radio, television, film, and theater. ▪ See studies by Verna Arvey (1939), Robert B. Haas (1972), and Catherine P. Smith (2000).

STIMSON, HENRY LEWIS (1867–1950), U.S. lawyer and public official. A Harvard-educated Wall Street lawyer, Stimson served as a cabinet appointee of three U.S. presidents. He was William H. Taft's secretary of war (1911–13) and Herbert Hoover's secretary of state (1929–33). A persistent opponent of U.S. isolationism and European appeasement, he wrote the Stimson Doctrine (1932), which refused to recognize Japanese rule in Manchuria. As Pres. Franklin D. Roosevelt's secretary of war (1940–45), Stimson supervised mobilization for World War II. ▪ See the autobiographical, *On Active Service in Peace and War* (1948; with McGeorge Bundy); Richard N. Current, *Secretary Stimson*

(1954); Elting E. Morison, *Turmoil and Tradition* (1960); and Godfrey Hodgson, *The Colonel* (1990).

STIVENS, DALLAS GEORGE (1911–   ), Australian novelist and short-story writer. Dal Stivens injected warm humor and coarse wit into his finest novel, the satirical *Jimmy Brockett: Portrait of a Notable Australian* (1951). His works reflected his preoccupation with the tension between illusion and reality. *The Wide Arch* (1958), a mystery with striking similarities to *Hamlet*, and *A Horse of Air* (1970), whose explorer hero sets out on a quest to find the rare "night parrot," were experimental parodies. His short stories appeared in several volumes including *The Tramp* (1936), *The Courtship of Uncle Henry* (1946), *Selected Stories* (1969), and *The Unicorn* (1976).

STOCKHAUSEN, KARLHEINZ (1928–   ), German composer. Stockhausen worked as a dance-hall pianist in order to study musicology at the University of Cologne. He began experimenting with electronic music and composed *Electronic Studies* (1953). Moving to the field of aleatory or chance music, Stockhausen composed *Klavierstüke XI* (1956), which consists of 19 musical fragments to be played in any order, speed, and loudness. He also experimented with spatial effects, arranging his instruments in three groups to achieve a live stereo effect in *Gruppen* (1959) and using four orchestras and choruses in *Carré* (1960). But Stockhausen's most radical innovation was to incorporate sounds such as grunts and handclapping in *Momente* (1962). Despite the avant-garde nature of his music, he enjoyed both critical and popular esteem. His works of the 1970s were increasingly mystical. He completed the first segment of a planned seven-part opera, *Licht* (Light), in 1978. ▪ See his discussion of music and life in *Towards a Cosmic Music* (1989) and study by Karl H. Worner (Eng. trans. 1973).

STOCKMAN, DAVID ALAN (1946–   ), U.S. public official. Son of a Michigan farmer, Stockman acquired rural, middle-class, midwestern conservative values. He graduated (1968) from Michigan State University, where he had led an anti-Vietnam War movement, and then briefly studied for a divinity degree at Harvard. For a while, he helped develop policy for Republican members of Congress. Returning to Michigan, Stockman was elected to the U.S. House in 1976. Revealing impressive knowledge and skill, he pursued his supply-side economic goals: lowering taxes to spur investment and productivity, and reducing government involvement in the private sector. As Pres. Ronald Reagan's director of the Office of Management and Budget (1981–85), he orchestrated a major cut in taxes and massive shifts in spending from social welfare programs to defense. The economy improved, but federal budget deficits ballooned. He resigned to enter investment banking in New York City. ▪ See his memoirs, *The Triumph of Politics: Why the Reagan Revolu-*

tion Failed (1986); biography by Owen Ullmann (1986); and John Greenya and Anne Urban, *The Real David Stockman* (1986).

STOCKTON, EARL OF. *See MACMILLAN, HAROLD, EARL OF STOCKTON.*

STODDARD, THEODORE LOTHROP (1883–1950), U.S. publicist of nativism. Stoddard earned a Ph.D. from Harvard (1914) in preparation for his work as a propagandist for white racism. In his writings—*The Rising Tide of Color Against White-World Supremacy* (1920) and *The Revolt Against Civilization: The Menace of the Underman* (1922)—he warned against the yellow and brown races—and bolshevism—as threats to white Anglo-Saxon civilization. He also advocated eugenics as the final solution, short of which he urged immigration restrictions to prevent the "inferior races" of Southern and Eastern Europe from entering the country. His views were widely accepted in the United States during the 1920s.

STOKOWSKI, LEOPOLD (1882–1977), U.S. conductor. Stokowski was born in London of Polish-Irish parentage and educated at Oxford and the Royal College of Music. In 1905 he moved to the United States, where he reigned for 26 years (1912–38) as conductor of the Philadelphia Orchestra, broadening its repertoire to include modern classics and his own transcriptions of J. S. Bach, and elevating it to world status. A tall, distinctive figure with a ruff of fair hair and a flair for the dramatic, Stokowski performed in the films *The Big Broadcast of 1937* (1936) and *Fantasia* (1940) and helped popularize classical music. Some criticized him for taking liberties with scores, while others praised his efforts to improve the quality of sound recording. After leaving Philadelphia, he worked with a number of different orchestras, founding the American Symphony of New York in 1962 and remaining active into his nineties. ■ See his *Music for All of Us* (1943); studies by Abram Chasms (1979) and Oliver Daniel (1983); and William A. Smith, *The Mystery of Leopold Stokowski* (1990).

STOLYPIN, PIOTR ARKADEVICH (1862–1911), Russian political leader. Under Czar Nicholas II, Stolypin served as premier and minister of the interior (1906–11). A member of the nobility, he attempted to quash revolutionary fervor, using both repressive measures and social reform. He ordered court-martial proceedings that resulted in the execution of hundreds of rebels (1906–07). Stolypin also instituted land reforms (1906) aimed at creating a conservative core of peasant landowners. He dissolved the first and second Dumas and ensured a sympathetic third Duma by revising the election law (1907). He took no initiatives against reactionary elements responsible for anti-Jewish pogroms. He was assassinated by a double agent, a revolutionary serving as a police operative. ■ See Maria Petrovna von Bock, *Reminiscences of My Father* (Eng. trans. 1970), and

studies by Mary S. Conroy (1976) and George Tokmakoff (1981).

STOMMEL, HENRY MELSON (1920–1992), U.S. oceanographer. A research associate at the Woods Hole Oceanographic Institution (1944–60), Stommel made pioneering contributions to the understanding of the behavior of oceans. He worked out the first theory of the Gulf Stream (1947), devised a method for determining the absolute velocity of mean ocean currents (1977), and initiated observational and statistical gathering programs in Bermuda, the Mediterranean, and the Indian Ocean. He taught at Harvard (1960–63), the Massachusetts Institute of Technology (1963–78), and at Woods Hole (from 1978). His books included *The Gulf Stream* (1958; 2nd ed. 1965).

STONE, EDWARD DURRELL (1902–1978), U.S. architect. An Arkansas-born architecture student at Harvard and the Massachusetts Institute of Technology (1925–26), Stone began his career designing the Art Deco interior of New York's Radio City Music Hall. He collaborated (with Philip Goodwin) on New York's Museum of Modern Art (1937) in the modern International Style idiom, but he gradually evolved toward a more extravagant use of ornamentation, as with the U.S. embassy in New Delhi, India (1954), and the John F. Kennedy Center for the Performing Arts in Washington, D.C. (1971). He also designed skyscrapers for General Motors in New York (1968) and Standard Oil in Chicago (1974). ■ See his autobiography, *The Evolution of an Architect* (1962), and his *Recent and Future Architecture* (1967).

STONE, HARLAN FISKE (1872–1946), U.S. jurist. The son of a New Hampshire farmer, Stone worked his way through Columbia Law School (LL.B. 1898) as a history teacher and remained at Columbia as a popular professor of law and dean (1910–24). He also worked intermittently as a Wall Street lawyer before his appointment (1924) as U.S. attorney general and shortly afterward (1925) as associate justice of the Supreme Court. An advocate of "reasonable accommodation of law to changing economic and social needs," Stone was a member of the court's liberal wing and upheld much of the New Deal legislation. In 1941 he was appointed chief justice. ■ See biography by Alpheus T. Mason (1956).

STONE, I. F. (Isidor Feinstein; 1907–1989), U.S. journalist. I. F. Stone, who published his own newspaper, *The Progressive,* at age 14, was an editorial writer for several Philadelphia newspapers before joining the editorial staffs of the *New York Post* (1933–39) and the *Nation* magazine (1938–46). An independent muckraking socialist, Stone gained a reputation for his honest, insightful, and biting critiques of federal governmental bureaucracy, military spending, and cold-war policies. He independently wrote and published *I. F. Stone's Weekly* (1953–72), a four-page newsletter that was one of the few U.S. journals of dissent during the 1950s and one of the leading anti–Vietnam War periodicals of the 1960s. Widely read in government and academic circles, it reached a circulation of 74,000 subscribers by the time Stone ceased its publication (Jan. 1, 1972). Stone's books included *Underground to Palestine* (1946), *The Hidden History of the Korean War* (1952), *The Haunted Fifties* (1964), and *In a Time of Torment* (1967). ■ See biography by Robert C. Cottrell (1992).

STONE, IRVING (Irving Tennenbaum; 1903–1989), U.S. writer. Stone studied political science and worked his way through the University of California at Berkeley (B.A. 1923) as a saxophonist in a dance band. He did research in Europe for his biographical novel about the painter Vincent van Gogh, *Lust for Life* (1934; film 1956), which pioneered fictional "bio-history." His *Clarence Darrow for the Defense* (1941) was a more traditional biography, written with the aid of the late attorney's literary estate, but Stone returned to the novel form with *Love Is Eternal* (1954), about first lady Mary Lincoln; *The Agony and the Ecstasy* (1961; film 1965), about the artist Michelangelo; *Passions of the Mind* (1971), about psychoanalyst Sigmund Freud; *The Origin* (1980), about Charles Darwin; and *Depths of Glory* (1985), about Camille Pissarro (1985).

STONE, MELVILLE ELIJAH (1848–1929), U.S. journalist. Born in Illinois, Stone was instrumental in establishing (1875) Chicago's original penny paper, the *Daily News,* and later (1881) the *Morning News.* But he was best known for his management (1893–1921) of the Associated Press (AP), which he built into a major institution of American journalism. He fought a prolonged legal battle that resulted in the Supreme Court ruling (1918) that news reports were subject to copyright laws. ■ See his memoirs, *Fifty Years a Journalist* (1921).

STONE, OLIVER (1946–   ), U.S. film director, screenwriter, and producer. Born in New York City, the son of a stockbroker, Stone dropped out of Yale at age 19 and enlisted in the U.S. Army (1967). He served as a combat soldier in the Vietnam War and was awarded a Purple Heart and Bronze Star. He subsequently studied film under Martin Scorsese at New York University (B.F.A. 1971) and began his professional career as a screenwriter, winning an Academy Award for his screenplay *Midnight Express* (1978). As a director he specialized in iconoclastic political films and became one of Hollywood's most controversial figures. He won Academy Awards for directing two films about the war in Vietnam, *Platoon* (1986) and *Born on the Fourth of July* (1989). He was best known for *JFK* (1991), a film about a conspiracy to assassinate Pres. John F. Kennedy that challenged the official version of Kennedy's death. His other films included *Wall Street* (1987), a depiction of greed among stockbrokers; *Natural Born Killers* (1994), a movie about a murderous couple that Stone called satire; and *Nixon* (1995), a complex film biography of Pres. Richard

Nixon. His novel, *A Child's Night Dream,* written when he was 19, was published in 1997.

STONE, SIR (JOHN) RICHARD (NICHOLAS) (1913–1991), British economist. The son of a judge, Stone studied economics under John Maynard Keynes at Cambridge (B.A. 1935) and later worked with Keynes as a government statistician in analyzing the British economy at the outset of World War II. As director of the department of applied economics (1945–55) and professor of finance and accounting (1955–80) at Cambridge, he developed detailed uniform accounting systems, similar to those used by corporations, to measure national income and spending. The systems of accounts, which included data regarding households, businesses, and government, enabled officials to measure economic trends and compare economic performance with other nations. They were adapted by many international organizations, including the United Nations, World Bank, and International Monetary Fund. Stone was awarded the 1984 Nobel Prize in Economics. His books included *National Income and Expenditure* (1944; with J. E. Meade), *Mathematical Models for the Economy* (1970), and *Aspects of Economic and Social Modelling* (1980).

STOPES, MARIE CHARLOTTE CARMICHAEL (1880–1958), British advocate of birth control and sex education. Trained as a paleobotanist at London University and the University of Munich (Ph.D. 1904), Stopes was the first woman on the science staff of Manchester University (1904). In 1916 she began a crusade to disseminate information on contraception and founded (London, 1921) the first birth control clinic in Britain. She wrote *Married Love* (1918), a best-seller banned in the United States until 1931, and *Contraception: Its Theory, History and Practice* (1923). ■ See Keith Briant, *Passionate Paradox* (1962); Ruth Hall, *Passionate Crusader* (1977); and biography by June Rose (1992).

STOPH, WILLI (1919–   ), East German political leader. Stoph joined the communist youth movement at age 14 while apprenticed to a mason, and after World War II he helped to build the East German party. He served as minister of the interior (1952–55) during the workers' uprisings of 1953, and as his country's first minister of defense (1956–60) announced that all East Germans should learn to shoot. As premier (1964–73; 1976–89), Stoph began to negotiate the normalization of relations with West Germany. After the disintegration of the East German government and the unification of Germany, he was arrested (1991) and tried on charges relating to the shooting of fugitives attempting to cross the border to West Germany after the construction of the Berlin Wall in the 1960s. However, before a verdict was reached his prosecution was halted due to his ill health.

STOPPARD, SIR TOM (Tom Straussler; 1937–   ), British playwright. Born in Czechoslovakia, Stoppard went to

Britain via Singapore and India while still a child. He began a career in journalism but turned to writing plays in 1960. Stoppard attracted international attention with *Rosencrantz and Guildenstern Are Dead* (1967; Tony Award), an ironic perspective on Shakespeare's *Hamlet,* which Stoppard wrote while in Berlin on a Ford Foundation grant. Subsequent plays, all well received, included *The Real Inspector Hound* (1968); *Jumpers* (1972), a witty dissection of some philosophical problems of modern existence; *Travesties: Every Good Boy Deserves Favor* (1974) and *The Professional Foul* (1978), two plays on the abuse of human rights in Eastern Europe; and *The Real Thing* (1982), a sophisticated look at love. Stoppard's plays exhibit verbal flair and detached ingenuity. He also wrote for radio, screen, and television. His later works included the plays *Hapgood* (1988), *Arcadia* (1994), and *The Invention of Love* (1997) and the screenplays for *Empire of the Sun* (1987), *Billy Bathgate* (1991), and *Shakespeare in Love* (1998; with Marc Norman; Academy Award). ■ See studies by Ronald Hayman (1977) and Felicia H. Londré (1981) and Mel Gussow, *Conversations with Stoppard* (1995).

STOREY, DAVID (1933–), British writer. The son of a coal miner, Storey financed his studies by playing rugby. His successful first novel, *This Sporting Life* (1960), concerned an inarticulate rugby star and his landlady. In this, and other novels such as *Pasmore* (1974), *A Temporary Life* (1974), and *A Prodigal Child* (1983), he focused on the effects of his characters' revolt against their working-class origins. He also wrote plays, drawing on his experience in sports (*The Changing Room,* 1972) and as a schoolteacher in London's East End. The award-winning *Home* (1971) concerned the empty lives of two men in a mental institution. He also wrote the novel *A Serious Man* (1998).

STÖRMER, HORST (1949–), German physicist. Störmer studied at Stuttgart University (Ph.D. 1977), did research at Bell Laboratories, New Jersey (1977–97), and taught at Columbia University (1998–). Working with Bell colleague Daniel C. Tsui, he discovered (1982) the phenomenon known as the fractional quantum Hall effect. Störmer demonstrated that at temperatures near absolute zero, electrons that are exposed to an extremely powerful magnetic field condense to form a quantum fluid and seem to split into thirds and have a fraction of the electric charge of an electron. The discovery, which offered insights into the inner structure and dynamics of matter, was explained by Bell researcher Robert B. Laughlin, and Störmer, Tsui, and Laughlin shared the 1998 Nobel Prize in Physics.

STOUT, REX (1886–1975), U.S. novelist. After a colorful career that included running a successful business and writing popular adventure stories, Stout launched (1934) his entertaining series of detective novels featuring Nero Wolfe, a massive, cerebral, literate detective. Wolfe's eccentricities in-

cluded the growing of prize orchids, a love of good food and beer, and an aversion to leaving his New York town house to solve a case. Among the 46 Nero Wolfe mysteries were *Too Many Cooks* (1938) and *The Doorbell Rang* (1966), which featured the FBI as Wolfe's opponent. During World War II Stout headed the War Writers Board and after the war he was active in the movement for world government. ■ See biography by John McAleer (1977).

STOW, (JULIAN) RANDOLPH (1935–), Australian novelist and poet. Stow pursued his interest in anthropology in travels to central Australia and New Guinea; the same interest informed his fiction, which emphasizes setting and explores archetypal symbols and myth. His novels included *A Haunted Land* (1956). *The Bystander* (1957), *Tourmaline* (1963), *The Merry-Go-Round in the Sea* (1965), *Visitants* (1979), *The Green Girl as Elderflower* (1980), and *The Suburbs of Hell* (1984). He also wrote poetry, collected in *Act One* (1957), *Outrider* (1962), and *A Counterfeit Silence* (1969). A selection of stories, poems, and essays were published in *Randolph Stow* (1990). ■ See study by Ray Willbanks (1978).

STRACHEY, (EVELYN) JOHN (1901–1963), British writer and political leader. Strachey, whose father was editor of the conservative *Spectator,* became involved in socialist causes while a student at Oxford. Elected as a Labour deputy to Parliament (1929), he resigned (1931) to rethink more radical social alternatives, which he elaborated upon in his Marxist books *The Coming Struggle for Power* (1932) and *The Nature of the Capitalist Crisis* (1935). Strachey returned to Parliament (1945–63) as "the most mature ideological thinker of the Labour movement," the *London Times* said. As minister of food (1946–50) he imposed peacetime rationing, and as war minister (1950–51) he came reluctantly to accept nuclear deterrence. His later books included *Contemporary Capitalism* (1959) and *On the Prevention of War* (1962). ■ See biographies by Hugh Thomas (1973) and Noel Thompson (1993).

STRACHEY, (GILES) LYTTON (1880–1932), British biographer and critic. Strachey was a prominent member of the Bloomsbury group, a loose collection of intellectuals and artists including Virginia Woolf, John Maynard Keynes, and Clive Bell. He wrote on French literature but achieved prominence with his elegantly written biographies of Victorian and other British historical figures. Though his work had weaknesses as biography, it greatly influenced other writers with its subtle and artistic style and debunking tone. In *Eminent Victorians* (1918) Strachey described such cherished figures as Florence Nightingale as boring, pompous, and ambitious, and also ridiculed the church, public schools, and imperialism. Other studies included *Queen Victoria* (1921) and *Elizabeth and Essex* (1928). ■ Michael Holroyd wrote the standard biography (rev. ed. 1971).

STRAND, MARK (1934–), Canadian-born U.S. poet. Strand studied painting under Josef Albers at Yale (B.F.A. 1959), but turned his attention to poetry after graduation. His sparse, conversational poems ranged from brooding works filled with menace and foreboding to joyous and witty verse celebrating life. Among his best-known books of verse were *Sleeping with One Eye Open* (1964), *The Story of Our Lives* (1973), *Selected Poems* (1980), *The Continuous Life* (1990), and *Blizzard of One* (1998; Pulitzer Prize). He taught at several major universities, including Yale, Princeton, Harvard, the University of Utah, and Johns Hopkins, and served as poet laureate of the United States (1990–91). He also wrote children's books, art criticism, and a collection of short stories, *Mr. and Mrs. Baby* (1985). ■ See study by David Kirby (1990).

STRAND, PAUL (1890–1976), U.S. photographer. Born in New York City, Strand studied with Lewis W. Hine (1907) and developed a lifelong interest in realistic photography. At age 26 he had his first photo exhibition at Photo-Secession's "291" gallery. His early works featured the abstract architectural forms of New York City, but he later turned to still lifes of the wilderness in microcosm. From the 1930s he was concerned with economic and social issues and made several notable documentaries, including *Redes* (*The Wave;* 1935), about a Mexican fisherman's strike, and *Native Land* (1942), about civil rights violations in the United States. In 1950 Strand moved to France and subsequently produced striking photo essays on Italian peasants (1954), Hebrides fishermen (1962), and Egyptian fellahin (1969). ■ See his *Time in New England* (1950) and *Strand, Sixty Years of Photographs* (1976).

STRASBERG, LEE (1901–1982), Austrian-born U.S. actor, director, and teacher. Strasberg trained at the American Laboratory Theater in New York City with Richard Boleslavski and Maria Ouspenskaya, former students of Russian director Constantin Stanislavsky, who developed the naturalistic style of acting that became known as "the method." He began his career as a stage manager and actor with the Theater Guild (1924). With Harold Clurman and Cheryl Crawford he formed the Group Theater (1931), a highly experimental and noncommercial ensemble for which he directed *Men in White* (1933) and *Johnny Johnson* (1936). He joined the Actors Studio (1947), the "temple" of method acting, and as artistic director (from 1948) he helped train such well-known actors as Marlon Brando, Paul Newman, Julie Harris, Kim Stanley, Geraldine Page, Al Pacino, and Robert DeNiro. He established the Lee Strasberg Institute of Theater (1969) and made his screen debut in the *The Godfather Part II* (1974). ■ See biography by Cindy Heller Adams (1980).

STRATEMEYER, EDWARD (1862–1930), U.S. writer and publisher. Inspired by Horatio Alger and popular dime novelists, Stratemeyer began to write juvenile adventure stories

while working as a clerk in a family-owned tobacco store. He sold his first story in 1888, and edited several popular journals published by Street and Smith during the 1890s. He gained nationwide popularity with an 1898 novel, *Under Dewey at Manila,* which told the story of three young men serving on a battleship during the Spanish-American War. Their further adventures were recounted in the *Old Glory* and *Soldiers of Fortune* series. The subsequent success of the first three volumes of the *Rover Boys* series (1899), inspired Stratemeyer to create formulas and characters for other series and hire a team of writers, all using the same pseudonym, to produce the novels for an ever-expanding readership. Ultimately, 30 volumes of *Rover Boys* books were published between 1899 and 1926, selling more than 5 million copies. Stratemeyer, called the "king of juvenile literature" personally wrote over 150 books and was responsible for outlining and editing more than 650 others. His Stratemeyer Literary Syndicate, established in 1906, produced many of the most enduringly popular juvenile books in literary history, including the *Tom Swift, Hardy Boys, Bobbsey Twins,* and *Nancy Drew* series. ■ See Carol Billman, *The Secret of the Stratemeyer Syndicate* (1986), and study by Deidre Johnson (1993).

STRATTON, SAMUEL WESLEY (1861–1931), U.S. physicist and educator. A professor of mathematics and physics at the new University of Chicago (1892–1901), Stratton drafted the bill establishing the Federal Bureau of Standards and served as its first director (1901–23). The bureau became an important national research center under Stratton's leadership. He was later president of the Massachusetts Institute of Technology (1923–30).

STRAUS, NATHAN (1848–1931), German-born U.S. merchant and philanthropist. After working in the family crockery business, Straus became co-owner (with his brother Isidor) of R. H. Macy and Co. in New York City and developed it into the world's largest department store. Straus was also a leader in the field of child health and promoted the pasteurization of milk. He was responsible for the establishment (by 1920) of almost 300 milk-distribution centers in the United States and throughout the world. Straus was proclaimed (1923) the person who did the most for New York City's welfare in the first quarter of the century.

STRAUS, OSCAR SOLOMON (1850–1926), U.S. diplomat and public official. A brother of merchants Isidor and Nathan Straus, Oscar Straus served as minister to Ottoman Turkey (1887–89; 1898–1900; 1909–10) and was the first Jew to serve in the cabinet (secretary of commerce and labor, 1906–09). He served four terms on The Hague Permanent Court of Arbitration (1902; 1908; 1912; 1920) and was a special adviser to Pres. Woodrow Wilson during the Versailles Peace Conference (1919). Like his brothers, Straus supported many Jewish cultural and charitable organizations and used his influence to promote the rights of Jewish minorities in Palestine, Russia, and various European countries. ■ See the autobiographical *Under Four Administrations* (1922).

STRAUSS, FRANZ JOSEF (1915–1988), West German political leader. Strauss, a cofounder of the Bavarian Christian Social Union (CSU), was elected to the Bundestag in 1949. An advocate of West German rearmament and of the acquisition of nuclear weapons, he became defense minister in 1956 but was forced to resign in the aftermath of the 1962 "*Spiegel* affair," when he was implicated in harsh police measures against the news magazine. He served as finance minister (1966–69) and premier of Bavaria (1978–88). He was the unsuccessful candidate of the CSU and Christian Democratic Union for chancellor in 1980. Though widely admired for his political acumen and his intellect, he had been judged to be too right-wing for the chancellorship. He was later (1983) denied a seat in the cabinet of Chancellor Heimut Kohl's conservative coalition government.

STRAUSS, LEO (1899–1973), German-born U.S. political philosopher. Strauss was born into an orthodox Jewish family, served in the German army during World War I, and studied philosophy at the University of Hamburg (Ph.D. 1921). He was a research assistant at the Academy of Jewish Research in Berlin until he fled Nazi persecution and settled in the United States (1937), where he taught at the New School for Social Research (1938–49) and the University of Chicago (1949–67). In his controversial writings and lectures he presented a powerful critique of modern liberalism, relativistic social science, and egalitarian democracy, which, in his view, produced mediocrity, conformism, and amoral leadership. He advocated, instead, the revival of classical rationalism, as epitomized in the Socratic way of life, the quest for classical natural law that consisted of unchanging moral truths, and the restoration of the humanities to a predominant position in education. His teachings played an important role in the revival of conservative thought in the United States, and his rigorous approach to textual analysis influenced a generation of political philosophers who were called "Straussians." Among his most important books were *Spinoza's Critique of Religion* (1930; Eng. trans. 1965), which contains an autobiographical essay; *Persecution and the Art of Writing* (1952); *Natural Right and History* (1953); *What Is Political Philosophy?* (1959); *The City and Man* (1964); and *Xenophon's Socratic Discourse* (1970). ■ See study by Shadia B. Drury (1997).

STRAUSS, RICHARD (1864–1949), German composer. The son of a well-known horn player, Strauss wrote a polka at age 6, a march at 12, and at 17 a symphony performed in Munich and New York. He became known as "Richard the Second," successor to Wagner, for his lush symphonic poems replete with psychological motifs, including *Don Juan* (1888), *Till Eulenspiegel's Merry Pranks* (1895), *Thus Spake*

Zarathustra (1896), and *Don Quixote* (1898). He was also a widely traveled conductor, but is best remembered for his 15 operas, including *Salomé* (1905), *Elektra* (1909), *Der Rosenkavalier* (1911), and *Arabella* (1933). ■ See Strauss's *Recollections and Reflections* (Eng. trans. 1953); studies by Norman Del Mar (3 vols., 1969–73), Ernst Krause (Eng. trans. 1969), and Michael Kennedy (1976); and biographies by Matthew Boyden (1999), Tim Ashley (1999), and Michael Kennedy (1999).

STRAVINSKY, IGOR FYODOROVICH (1882–1971), Russian-born U.S. composer. A onetime law student, Stravinsky studied music with Rimsky-Korsakov. He achieved fame in Paris with the ballets *The Firebird* (1910) and *Petrushka* (1911) composed for impresario Sergei Diaghilev. The premiere performance of *The Rite of Spring* (1913) touched off a near riot with its explosive new tonal language; it used complicated polyrhythms, polytonalities, and percussive dissonances. Stravinsky next devoted himself to neoclassicism, exemplified in such works as *Symphony of Psalms* (1930), Symphony in C (1940), and Mass in G (1948). In his seventies he turned to the serialism he had rejected in earlier years, marking another restless shift in styles. *Canticum Sacrum* (1956) and the ballet *Agon* (1957) were products of this period. Stravinsky's undaunted experimentation profoundly influenced the development of 20th-century music. He wrote *Chronicle of My Life* (2 vols., 1936; rev. ed. 1972) and *Poetics of Music* (1947), and published a series of personally revealing books of "conversation" with Robert Craft (1959; 1960; 1962; 1972). ■ See his *Selected Correspondence* (1982–85); studies by Eric Walter White (1979) and Mikhail Druskin (1983); and Robert Craft's biography (1992) and *Chronicle of a Friendship* (rev. ed. 1994).

STREEP, MERYL (Mary Louise Streep; 1949–   ), U.S. actress. Born in suburban New Jersey, Streep attended Vassar College (B.A. 1971), where her dramatic talent was first noticed. She worked in summer stock, then entered Yale Drama School, where she performed some 40 roles. She won acclaim on the New York stage in such plays as *The Taming of the Shrew* and *The Cherry Orchard,* won an Emmy Award (1978) for her role in the TV miniseries *Holocaust,* and went on to a series of movie roles that solidified her reputation as the most talented and intelligent actress of her generation. Her credits included *The Deer Hunter* (1979), *The Seduction of Joe Tynan* (1979), *Kramer vs. Kramer* (1979; Academy Award), *The French Lieutenant's Woman* (1981), *Sophie's Choice* (1982; Academy Award), *Silkwood* (1983), and *Out of Africa* (1985), *The Bridges of Madison County* (1995), *Dancing at Lughnasa* (1998), and *One True Thing* (1998). ■ See biography by Eugene E. Pfaff (1987; with Mark Emerson).

STREETON, SIR ARTHUR ERNEST (1867–1943), Australian artist. A member of his country's Heidelberg School of impressionists (from 1886), Streeton concentrated almost exclusively on landscapes. He painted Australia as the promised land, with awe and reverence, working outdoors to capture the fleeting effects of light on the countryside. The heroic impressionism typified by his work dominated Australian painting for more than 50 years. Streeton was knighted in 1937, and his work is considered a national institution. ▪ See study by Ann Galbally (1969).

STREISAND, BARBRA (1942–　), U.S. singer and film actress. A singer with an intensely dramatic style, Streisand won her first nightclub engagement in a talent contest in New York in 1961. The following year she appeared on Broadway in *I Can Get It for You Wholesale*. When she arrived in Hollywood to star in two latter-day film musicals, *Funny Girl* (1968; Academy Award), and *Hello Dolly* (1969), Streisand already had a large and loyal following as a singer and had appeared frequently on television and in nightclubs. Turning to comedy, she developed an exaggerated, screwball style in *The Owl and the Pussycat* (1970) and *What's Up Doc?* (1972). She also produced and acted in a contemporary remake of *A Star is Born* (1976) and directed and acted in a film version of I. B. Singer's short story *Yentl* (1983), *Prince of Tides* (1991), and *The Mirror Has Two Faces* (1996). ▪ See Rene Jordan, *The Greatest Star* (1975), and biographies by James Spada and Christopher Nickens (1981), Donald Zec and Anthony Fowles (1981), Shaun Considine (1985), and Anne Edwards (1997).

STRESEMANN, GUSTAV (1878–1929), German political leader. Stresemann was born into the Berlin bourgeoisie and wrote a Ph.D. dissertation on the bottled-beer industry. A Reichstag deputy from 1907, he remained a monarchist and annexationist through World War I. After the war he supported the new republic and sought to restore Germany's status in Europe. In 1923 he served briefly as chancellor, then becoming foreign minister and surviving from one government to another (1923–29) by the force of his personality, although he was bitterly attacked by right-wing nationalists. Stresemann shared with Aristide Briand the 1926 Nobel Peace Prize for his role in negotiating the Treaty of Locarno (1925), which settled Germany's western frontiers and ended its isolation. He also signed a treaty with the Soviet Union and brought Germany into the League of Nations (1926). ▪ See study by Henry Ashby Turner, Jr. (1963).

STRIJDOM, JOHANNES GERHARDUS (1893–1958), South African political leader. A lawyer and civil servant from Cape province, Strijdom was an uncompromising white supremacist known as the "Lion of Waterberg," the Transvaal parliamentary district he represented as a Nationalist party member (1929–58). As prime minister (1954–58) he embodied the principle of *baasskap*, or white domination, and expanded the apartheid laws introduced by his predecessor, Daniel Malan.

STROESSNER, ALFREDO (1912–　), Paraguayan dictator. The son of a German immigrant, Stroessner was a professional soldier who became chief of staff in 1951 and came to power via a 1954 coup d'état. With the support of the army and the compliance of the Colorado party, he suppressed opposition, suspended civil rights, and ruled for over 30 years as a dictator despite the appearance of elections held every five years. A virulent anticommunist at home and abroad, Stroessner maintained close ties with the United States and did little to change the semifeudal nature of Paraguayan society. He was overthrown in a military coup (1989) and subsequently lived in exile in Brazil. ▪ See Paul H. Lewis. *Paraguay Under Stroessner* (1980).

STROHEIM, ERICH VON. *See VON STROHEIM, ERICH.*

STRÖMGREN, BENGT GEORG DANIEL (1908–1987), Swedish astrophysicist. Strömgren, who succeeded his father as director of the Copenhagen Observatory (1940–57), determined that luminous gas clouds in space were ionized hydrogen surrounded by unionized hydrogen. By calculating the radius of the ionized spheres in our galaxy, later known as "Strömgren spheres," scientists were able to estimate the size of such regions in other galaxies and to determine galactic distances. Strömgren also did research on the composition of stars and pioneered in the classification of stellar spectra by utilizing photoelectric techniques. He was a professor at the University of Chicago (1952–57) and joint director of the Yerkes (Wisconsin) and McDonald (Texas) observatories (1951–57). He was also a member of the Institute for Advanced Studies at Princeton, New Jersey (1957–67), and professor at the University of Copenhagen (1967–78).

STRONG, ANNA LOUISE (1885–1970), U.S. journalist. The daughter of a midwestern Congregationalist minister, Strong graduated from Oberlin (B.A. 1905) and became the youngest woman ever to receive a Ph.D. from the University of Chicago (1908). She subsequently worked in the labor movement in Seattle, became bitterly disillusioned with American life, and went to Moscow (1920) for the American Friends Service Committee. Committed to communism, she spent the rest of her life writing popular and colorful books and articles that sympathetically described developments in the communist world, especially in the Soviet Union and China. From 1958 until her death she lived in Beijing, where she published the monthly *Letter from China*, a valuable source of information on Chinese domestic and international politics that was distributed throughout the world. ▪ See biography by Tracy B. Strong and Helene Keyssar, *Right in her Soul* (1983).

STRONG, BENJAMIN (1877–1928), U.S. banker. An officer of the Bankers' Trust Co. (from 1903), Strong was appointed governor of the newly formed Federal Reserve Bank of New York (1914), and he dominated the entire Federal Reserve System until his death. He modified existing policies during the mid-1920s to allow for easy money in order to influence the level of business activity. He believed that the Federal Reserve's open-market policies could prevent any serious economic crisis, but he died on the eve of the century's greatest depression. ▪ See biography by Lester V. Chandler (1958).

STRONG, KEN (Kenneth Strong; 1906–1978), U.S. football player. One of the finest running backs in gridiron history, Strong had a phenomenal college career for New York University, leading the nation in scoring in 1928 with 162 points and 2,100 yards rushing. After playing for the Staten Island Stapletons (1929–32), he joined the New York Giants (1933) and led the team to a league championship in 1934 and to three division titles. A complete football player in the days when the same personnel handled offense and defense, Strong excelled in running, passing, blocking, punting, and placekicking. He retired in 1939 but was lured back by the Giants to serve as a kicking specialist for nine more years.

STROUD, ROBERT (1890–1963), U.S. convict and ornithologist. A school dropout and runaway from Seattle, Stroud was convicted of murdering two men, one in 1909 and the other, a prison guard, in 1916. He spent a total of 54 years in prison, 42 of them in solitary confinement. While in the Leavenworth (Kansas) federal prison he took an interest in birds, studied chemistry, medicine, and pharmacology by correspondence, and constructed cages out of cigar boxes for pet canaries. He wrote *Stroud's Digest on the Diseases of Birds* (1942), a classic in its field. Transferred to Alcatraz prison in 1942 and forbidden to keep his pets, he turned to the study of languages, including Greek. Considered dangerously antisocial, he was denied parole and died in prison. ▪ Thomas E. Gaddis wrote *Birdman of Alcatraz* (1955), which was made into a film in 1962.

STRUVE, OTTO (1897–1963), Russian-born U.S. astronomer. Born into a family of distinguished astronomers, Struve emigrated to the United States in 1921 and made advances in almost every area of modern astronomy. He directed the Yerkes and McDonald observatories (1932–47) and later directed the Leuschner Observatory (Berkeley, California) and the National Radio Astronomy Observatory (West Virginia). Perhaps his most crucial contribution was the discovery of large gaseous clouds between stars. The finding of interstellar hydrogen shed light on galactic structure and stellar evolution and gave impetus to the new field of radio astronomy. Struve pioneered the study of stellar radiation, stellar spectroscopy, and binary stars. He advocated the theory that intelligent life exists on other planets. ▪ See Allan H. Batten, *Resolute and Undertaking Characters* (1988).

STRYKER, ROY EMERSON (1893–1975), U.S. photo editor. A one-time cowboy from Kansas, Stryker completed two years at the Colorado School of Mines before transferring to Columbia University (B.A. 1924; M.A. 1926), where he studied under Rexford Tugwell and taught economics. He followed Tugwell into Pres. Franklin D. Roosevelt's New Deal administration. As head of the historical section of the Farm Security Administration (1935–43), Stryker hired top photographers, including Walker Evans, Ben Shahn, Dorothea Lange, Carl Mydans, and Gordon Parks, to document all aspects of rural and smalltown life during the Depression. Some of these 270,000 photos were later published as *In This Proud Land* (1973). After World War II, Stryker directed documentary projects for the Standard Oil Co. of New Jersey and the Jones and Laughlin Steel Corp. ▪ See F. Jack Hurley, *Portrait of a Decade* (1972), and study by Steven W. Plattner (1983).

STURGEON, THEODORE (Edward Hamilton Waldo; 1918–1985), U.S. science-fiction writer. During three years at sea as an engine-room wiper, Sturgeon sold 40 short stories. Once he began producing science fiction (1939), he wrote full-time. His early stories were fairly typical, light pieces, but he soon began writing the horror fantasies for which he became famous; many appeared in the magazine *Weird Tales. More Than Human* (1953) was among his best-known novels. His works, such as the story "The World Well Lost" (1953), were among the first to treat sexuality—heterosexual and homosexual—in science fiction. After 1961 Sturgeon regularly reviewed science fiction. He also wrote TV scripts for "Star Trek" and other serials. In 1972 he published *Sturgeon Is Alive and Well*. Other books included *The Worlds of Theodore Sturgeon* (1972), *The Golden Helix* (1979), and *Alien Cargo* (1984).

STURZO, LUIGI (1871–1959), Italian priest and political leader. Ordained in 1894, Sturzo taught both philosophy and sociology but gave up his academic career as he became active in the political organization of miners, craftsmen, and peasants. In 1919 he founded the Italian Popular party, a Roman Catholic political organization, which won 101 of 508 seats in the Chamber of Deputies. As the party's political secretary he was powerful in Italian political life and a leader of the antifascist opposition until forced out of politics (1923) as a result of fascist pressure on the Vatican. In exile in France, Britain, and the United States (1924–46), he wrote numerous philosophical and political works. He returned to Italy as his movement was being revived as the Christian Democratic party, which became the dominant political force in post–World War II Italy.

STYNE, JULE (Julius Stein; 1905–1994), British-born U.S. composer. A former child prodigy on the piano, Styne abandoned a classical concert career for one in pop music. He went to Hollywood as a vocal coach in the 1930s and later teamed with lyricist Sammy Cahn to write bright, happy scores for films that included the Academy Award–winning song, "Three Coins in the Fountain" (1954). Between 1947 and 1972 he wrote the music for 16 Broadway musicals, including *Gentlemen Prefer Blondes* (1949), *Bells Are Ringing* (1956), *Gypsy* (1959), and *Funny Girl* (1964). His hit songs included "Let It Snow, Let It Snow," "Diamonds Are a Girl's Best Friend," "The Party's Over," "Everything's Coming Up Roses," "Make Someone Happy," and "People." ▪ See Theodore Taylor, *Jule* (1979).

STYRON, WILLIAM (1925–), U.S. novelist. Styron began writing during his undergraduate years at Duke University. After graduation (1947) he left the South but returned repeatedly in his fiction to his hometown of Newport News, Virginia, which he fictionalized as Port Warwick. Melodrama and overworked prose marred his first novel, *Lie Down in Darkness* (1951), which chronicled the disintegration of a Virginia family in a tone reminiscent of the novels of William Faulkner. In *The Long March* (1957) he adapted the stream-of-consciousness technique. After forming a friendship with novelist James Baldwin in the 1960s, Styron wrote *The Confessions of Nat Turner* (1967; Pulitzer Prize), a first-person narrative of a slave revolt. *Sophie's Choice* (1979; film, 1982), told from the viewpoint of a novice author, depicts the continuing victimization of a Polish woman who is liberated from a Nazi concentration camp but ultimately does not survive the effects of the Holocaust. *This Quiet Dust* (1982) assembled Styron's reflections on literature and politics. His later works included *Darkness Visible: A Memoir of Madness* (1990), about his fall into depression during the mid-1980s, and the autobiographical *A Tidewater Morning: Three Tales from Youth* (1993). Styron, also a book critic for *Harper's,* claimed to dislike the slow and painful work of writing. ▪ See James L. West, 3d, *Conversations with William Styron* (1985); studies by Marc L. Ratner (1972) and Melvin J. Friedman (1974); and A. D. Casciato and J. L. West, eds., *Critical Essays on William Styron* (1982).

SUHARTO (1921–), Indonesian political leader. Suharto worked as a bank clerk before joining the Dutch colonial army. During the World War II Japanese occupation, he served with the Japanese defense forces and fought in the anti-Dutch guerrilla movement after the war. He rose through the military ranks after independence (1949) and as a general in charge of forces in Djakarta (1965) he led the army in suppressing an allegedly communist-inspired coup attempt. More than 300,000 supposed communists and leftists were slaughtered throughout the country and Pres. Sukarno soon lost the public's confidence. Suharto took control of the government in 1966 and was subsequently named acting president (1967). First elected in 1968, he was re-elected in 1971, 1977, and 1983. Reversing Sukarno's policies, Suharto developed close economic ties with the West and Japan. The economy was helped by the exploitation of vast oil reserves, but Indonesia remained one of the world's poorest countries. Suharto's government was accused of rampant corruption and was frequently cited for human rights violations. A severe economic downturn in the late 1990s led to high inflation, bankruptcies, food shortages, and, in the spring of 1998, widespread antigovernment demonstrations and rioting. In May 1998, Suharto resigned from office, replaced by his vice president, B. J. Habibie. His family's worth at the time was estimated to be $30–40 billion. ▪ See Hamish McDonald, *Suharto's Indonesia* (1980); Bilveer Singh, *Succession Politics in Indonesia* (1999); and Adam Schwarz, *A Nation in Waiting* (2000).

SÜHBAATAR (or SUKHE-BATOR), DAMDINY (1893–1923), Mongolian military and political leader. Born in Urga (now Ulan Bator), the son of a serf, Sühbaatar was inducted into the army (1912). He was trained as a machine gunner in the Russian army and became a hero during the anti-Japanese battles in 1916. In 1919 he formed one of the two Mongolian revolutionary communist groups, served as a member of the Central Committee of the Mongolian People's Revolutionary party, and was a founder of the Mongolian People's army (1921). Aided by Russian Red army forces, the Mongolians defeated the Chinese (May 1921) and an army of White Russians (May–Aug. 1921) and established a revolutionary government. Sühbaatar served as minister of war in the new government. ▪ See Owen Lattimore, *Nationalism and Revolution in Mongolia* (1955).

SUKARNO (1901–1970), Indonesian political leader. Sukarno was a civil engineer before he began his career as a leader of the anti-Dutch nationalist movement (1927). Jailed and exiled during the 1930s, he worked with the Japanese puppet government during World War II and declared Indonesia's independence at the end of the war (Aug. 17, 1945). After four years of conflict and negotiation with the Dutch, Indonesia became formally independent in 1949 with Sukarno as its president. A charismatic leader, he helped forge a unique national identity for the heterogeneous Indonesian people. In 1956 he declared a policy of "guided democracy," by which he dispensed with parliamentary democracy and the free enterprise system and ruled as a dictator. Ideologically committed to a vague combination of nationalism, communism, and Islam, he was unable to solve Indonesia's economic problems or control rampant inflation, and his government became known for its widespread corruption. His foreign policy was nominally nonaligned, but he maintained close ties with China and the Soviet Union and railed against Western imperialism. Following the suppression of an allegedly communist-led coup attempt (1965) by the army forces of Gen. Suharto, some 300,000 reputed communists and leftists were slaughtered throughout the country and Sukarno's government lost public support. He was forced to relinquish much of his power to Suharto (1966), who became acting president in 1967 and elected president in 1968. ▪ See his autobiography (1965), and biographies by J. D. Legge (1972) and C.L.M. Penders (1974).

SUKHE-BATOR, DAMDINY. *See SUHBAATAR, DAMDINY.*

SULLIVAN, EDWARD VINCENT (1902–1974), U.S. newspaper columnist and television personality. Ed Sullivan was a sports reporter in the 1920s and in the 1930s hosted a radio variety show that introduced Jack Benny over the airwaves. He wrote "Little Old New York," a daily column reporting on the Broadway scene, which appeared in the *New York Daily News* (1933–74). Sullivan presided over television's hugely successful and durable variety program "The Ed Sullivan Show" (1948–71). Each Sunday evening millions of Americans would watch the rather nervous, uneffusive Sullivan introduce into his "really big show," a mix of circus acts, chorus-line routines, old standbys, and new faces. He had a genius for spotting genuine talent, and he introduced to network viewers Dean Martin and Jerry Lewis, Elvis Presley, and the Beatles. ■ See Michael Harris, *Always on Sunday* (1968), and Jerry Bowles, *A Thousand Sundays* (1980).

SULLIVAN, HARRY STACK (1892–1949), U.S. psychiatrist. Sullivan, who earned his M.D. at the Chicago College of Medicine and Surgery (1917), demonstrated a striking ability to communicate with and treat schizophrenics in small groups while working at a Maryland hospital during the 1920s. As a founder and president of the William Alanson White Foundation in New York (1934–43) and of the Washington (D.C.) School of Psychiatry (1936–47), he trained graduate therapists in his interpersonal theory of psychiatry, rejecting Freudian sexual determinism in favor of a social and environmental approach to personality development. Several of his papers were collected in *Conceptions of Modern Psychiatry* (1940), *Schizophrenia as a Human Process* (1962), and *The Fusion of Psychiatry and Social Science* (1964). ■ See biography by Arthur H. Chapman (1976), and Helen Swick Perry, *Psychiatrist of America* (1982).

SULZBERGER, ARTHUR HAYS (1891–1968), U.S. newspaper publisher. Born into a prominent Jewish family, Sulzberger graduated from Columbia University (1913) and married the daughter of Adolph Ochs, the publisher of the *New York Times*. He joined the staff in 1919 and succeeded Ochs as publisher (1935–61). Sulzberger expanded the news and features coverage of the paper, enlarged the staff, pioneered in transmitting photos by wire, and steered a liberal but independent political course. During his years at the helm (he served as chairman of the board until his death), the worldwide influence of the *Times* expanded greatly, and its daily circulation increased by 40 percent and Sunday circulation doubled. His son, Arthur Ochs "Punch" Sulzberger (1926–   ), served as president and publisher of the *Times* (from 1963). ■ See the memoirs of Sulzberger's widow, Iphigene Ochs Sulzberger, *Iphigene* (1981).

SUMNER, JAMES BATCHELLER (1887–1955), U.S. biochemist. The German chemist Richard Willstätter sparked a controversy in the 1920s by insisting that enzymes were not proteins. Challenging this Nobel Prize laureate was the unknown biochemist James B. Sumner, who had pursued a career in research despite the boyhood loss of his left arm (and he was left-handed). Retraining his right hand, he earned a B.A. (1910) and Ph.D. (1914) at Harvard and later taught at the Cornell University Medical School (1929–55). In 1926 Sumner prepared urease, the first enzyme in crystalline form, and showed that it was indeed a protein. His work was later confirmed by other researchers including John Northrop, with whom Sumner and W. M. Stanley shared the 1946 Nobel Prize in Chemistry.

SUNDAY, BILLY (William Ashley Sunday; 1863–1935), U.S. evangelist. After earning a living as a professional baseball player (1883–90), Sunday began leading religious revivals (1896). A fundamentalist who was ordained a Presbyterian minister (1903), Sunday was a charismatic showman who delivered dramatic, fiery sermons. He was a leader in the movement to prohibit the sale of liquor in the United States. His revivals were attended by millions of Americans, and he amassed a fortune during his career. After 1920 his popularity decreased. ■ See studies by William G. McLoughlin (1955) and Lee Thomas (1961) and Roger Bruns, *Preacher* (1992).

SUN YAT-SEN (1866–1925), Chinese political leader. Born into a peasant family in Guangdong (Kwangtung) province. Sun was raised in Hawaii, studied medicine in Hong Kong (M.D. 1892), and converted to Christianity. Opposed to the Manchu dynasty, he became involved in revolutionary politics in 1894 and led an abortive revolt in Guangzhou (Canton; 1895). He spent the next 16 years traveling the world, organizing and fundraising among overseas Chinese. In Tokyo (1905) he founded the Tongmenghui (T'ung Meng Hui), the Chinese United League, a political movement based on his Three Principles of the People: nationalism, democracy, and socialism. He returned to China during the revolution that overthrew the Manchus (1911) and served briefly as president of the provisional government (1912), but resigned in favor of his rival, Yüan Shih-kai, in order to preserve unity. He helped establish the Guomindang (Kuomintang), or Nationalist party (1912), but soon broke with Yüan and returned to Japan. After Yüan's death (1916), Sun returned to his power base in Southern China, reorganized the party, and took power briefly in Guangzhou (1917). After turning to the Soviet Union for aid and advice, he regained power (1923), formed an alliance with the Communist party (1924), and reorganized the Guomindang along Soviet lines, with the army under strict political control. He died of cancer before the movement was able to unite China, but remained a national hero to both the Communist and Nationalist movements. ■ See study by Harold Z. Schiffrin (1968) and biography by Marie-Claire Bergère (Eng. trans. 1998).

SUN YAT-SEN, MADAME. *See SONG QINGLING.*

SUSLOV, MIKHAIL ANDREYEVICH (1902–1982), Soviet political leader. Born into a poor peasant family, Suslov participated in the Bolshevik revolution and joined the Communist party at age 19. Trained as an economist, he taught at Moscow University and worked his way up through the party hierarchy. A loyal Stalinist, he organized party purges in the Urals and the Ukraine during the 1930s, participated in the deportation of ethnic minorities from the Caucasus in 1944, and supervised the political integration of Lithuania into the Soviet Union at the end of World War II. He was a national party secretary (from 1947), a member of the ruling Politburo (from 1955), and the chief party ideologist for more than three decades. An ideological conservative opposed to liberalizing trends at home and abroad, he played a leading role in the anti-Titoist policies of the 1940s, the suppression of the 1956 Hungarian revolt and the 1968 Czech liberalization movement, and the ouster of Premier Nikita Khrushchev (1964). He later urged that the Solidarity movement in Poland be suppressed (1980–81).

SUSSKIND, DAVID (1920–1987), U.S. television, film, and theatrical producer. A Harvard graduate (1942), Susskind became a talent agent after World War II and started producing dramatic shows for television (1952). One of the most prolific producers in the industry, Susskind was responsible for scores of notable productions for the "Philco TV Playhouse," the "Kaiser Aluminum Hour," "Armstrong Circle Theater," "Du Pont Show of the Month," "Kraft Television Theater," and "The Play of the Week" during the 1950s and early 1960s, the golden age of U.S. television. He presented award-winning productions through the 1970s, including *The Price* (1971), *The Glass Menagerie* (1973), and *Eleanor and Franklin* (1976–77). His movies included *Edge of the City* (1957), *A Raisin in the Sun* (1961), *Requiem for a Heavyweight* (1962), *All the Way Home* (1963), and *Alice Doesn't Live Here Anymore* (1974). He also hosted his own syndicated television talk shows, "Open End" (1958–67) and "The David Susskind Show" (1967–86).

SUTHERLAND, EARL WILBUR, JR. (1915–1974), U.S. pharmacologist and physiologist. Sutherland studied at Washington University, St. Louis (M.D. 1942). His early research, which began there in 1947 in cooperation with Nobel laureate Carl Cori, focused on the process by which adrenaline regulates the degradation of glycogen to glucose in the liver. Later, while teaching at the Case Western Reserve University in Cleveland, he found that the process hinged on a previously unknown chemical substance that he isolated and named cyclic AMP. He showed that cyclic AMP played a critical role in the mechanism by which many hormones control various metabolic activities. For helping to explain how hormones work, he was awarded the 1971 No-

bel Prize in Physiology or Medicine. He taught at Vanderbilt University from 1963 to 1973.

SUTHERLAND, GRAHAM VIVIAN (1903–1980), British painter. Sutherland began his career as an etcher, but became known in the 1930s for oil and watercolor landscapes that combined elements of romanticism and surrealism. He was an official war artist during World War II and produced haunting images of destruction. His expressionistic *Crucifixion* (1944) is considered to be one of the major religious works of the century. He painted penetrating portraits of Somerset Maugham (1949) and Lord Beaverbrook (1957) and his portrait of Sir Winston Churchill (1955) became a cause célèbre when Churchill expressed his dissatisfaction and refused to have it shown publicly. ■ See biography by Roger Berthoud (1982) and Douglas Cooper, *The Work of Graham Sutherland* (1961).

SUTHERLAND, DAME JOAN (1926–), Australian opera singer. Regarded as one of the greatest sopranos of the century. Sutherland received overnight fame for her Covent Garden (London) performance in the title role of *Lucia di Lammermoor* (1959). She was also acclaimed for her performances in *Rigoletto, Norma,* and *The Tales of Hoffmann.* The foremost bel canto singer of her era, she was a leading soprano at New York's Metropolitan Opera (from 1961), sang at the world's major opera houses, and was named commander of the British Empire by Queen Elizabeth II (1961). She appeared frequently with her husband, conductor Richard Bonynge. ■ See her autobiography, *A Prima Donna's Progress* (1997); biography by Norma Major (1987); and Brian Adams, *La Stupenda* (1983).

SUTTON, WALTER STANBOROUGH (1877–1916), U.S. geneticist. While a graduate student at Columbia University, Sutton wrote two papers, "Morphology of the Chromosome Group in *Brachystola magna*" (1902) and "The Chromosomes in Heredity" (1903), that revolutionized the field of genetics. His research, based on the Austrian experimenter Gregor Mendel's theories, determined that chromosomes carry the units of inheritance and that they occur in pairs, one of maternal and the other of paternal derivation. He thus established the theory of the chromosomal basis of heredity. Sutton received an M.D. degree from Columbia University (1907) and practiced surgery in New York City; Kansas City, Kansas; and Kansas City, Missouri.

SUTTON, WILLIE (**William Francis Sutton**; 1901–1980), U.S. bank robber. Willie Sutton was a master criminal and tireless jailbreaker. In 1930, after a five-year jail term for safecracking, he launched a new career as "Willie the Actor"—talking his way into bank strong rooms disguised as a mail carrier, fire fighter, or even as a police officer. He claimed to have stolen more than $2 million from banks alone, but he had little chance to enjoy this money since he spent 33 years in jail. Sutton was last arrested in 1952, after six years on the run, and sentenced to a 30-year jail term. Released (1969) due to failing health, he applied for public assistance. He wrote *I, Willie Sutton* (1953; with Quentin Reynolds) and *Where the Money Was* (1976; with Edward Linn).

SUTZKEVER, ABRAHAM (1913–   ), Polish-born Israeli Yiddish-language poet. A member of the literary and artistic group "Young Vilna," Sutzkever survived the Vilna ghetto (1941), fought the Nazis as a partisan during World War II, and subsequently settled in Israel (1947), where he founded (1949) and edited the outstanding Yiddish literary quarterly, *Di Goldene Keyt*. His sensual, lyric poems often used surrealist imagery. Among Sutzkever's many published volumes were *Poems* (1937), *The Fortress* (1945), *Vilna Ghetto* (1946), *Siberia* (1952; Eng. trans. 1961), *Collected Works* (1963), *Green Aquarium* (1975; Eng. trans. 1982), *Burnt Pearls: Ghetto Poems* (Eng. trans. 1981), *The Fiddle Rose* (Eng. trans. 1990), and *Laughter Beneath the Forest* (Eng. trans. 1996). Selected prose and poetry appeared in *A. Sutzkever* (Eng. trans. 1991). ■ See biography by Joseph Leftwich (1971).

SUVERO, MARK DI (1933–   ), U.S. sculptor. Di Suvero's Italian parents emigrated (1941) from China to California. Shortly after his first one-person exhibition in New York City, he suffered (1957) a near-fatal fall in an elevator. While recovering, di Suvero helped establish the Park Place Gallery, the first cooperative gallery in New York's SoHo district. In the mid-1960s he began constructing large-scale, moving, outdoor sculptures that invite contact—pulling, pushing, even riding. His *Peace Tower* in Los Angeles protested U.S. intervention in Vietnam. Di Suvero's political disenchantment led him to leave the United States (1971) for Europe, where he continued to create and show sculpture in various countries. A 1975 exhibition at the Whitney Museum and outdoor sites throughout New York City were greeted with unrestrained enthusiasm by critics and the public. His large steel constructions won various prizes and awards.

SUZMAN, HELEN (Helen Gavronsky; 1917–   ), South African political leader. The daughter of an immigrant Jewish businessman, Suzman graduated from the University of Witwatersrand and later taught economics there (1944–52). A member of the United party, she represented a predominantly English-speaking suburban district of Johannesburg in parliament (1953–89) and cofounded the liberal Progressive party in 1959. As the party's only member of parliament (1961–74), she waged a one-woman crusade in favor of universal suffrage and a bill of rights and against the evils of apartheid, detention without charge, forced labor, and prison brutality. The party grew, changed its name—to the Progressive Reform party (1975) and the Progressive Fed-

eral party (1977)—and became the official opposition, with 27 seats, after the 1981 elections. She later served as president of the South African Institute of Race Relations (1991–93). ■ See her memoirs, *In No Uncertain Terms* (1993), and Joanna Strangwayes-Booth, *A Cricket in the Thorn Tree* (1976).

SUZUKI, DAISETSU TEITARO (1870–1966), Japanese Buddhist scholar. D. T. Suzuki studied at Tokyo University and later (1897–1909) in the United States. A renowned scholar of Zen Buddhism, he taught at major academic institutions in Japan, Europe, and the United States and brought the teachings of Zen Buddhism to the West. Suzuki wrote prolifically, including *Essays in Zen Buddhism* (3 vols., 1927–33), *The Training of the Buddhist Monk* (1934), *An Introduction to Zen Buddhism* (1949), and *Mysticism: Christian and Buddhist* (1957).

SUZUKI, SHINICHI (1898–1998), Japanese music teacher. Suzuki, whose father ran Japan's largest violin factory, studied violin in Berlin (1921–28), founded the Tokyo String Orchestra, and was president of the Teikoku Music School. He devised a revolutionary method of musical instruction based on the principle of language. Children learn to speak before they can read, he reasoned, so by means of exposure, imitation, and reinforcement they could learn to play the violin. First put into practice with a group of three-to-five-year-old children in his school (1950), Suzuki's theories and "talent education movement" spread all over the world with dramatic results. ■ See study by Masaaki Honda (1976).

SVEDBERG, THEODOR (1884–1971), Swedish chemist. A professor at the University of Uppsala (1912–49), Svedberg investigated colloids, substances whose particles are larger than molecules; they therefore do not form a true solution and do not settle out without artificial inducement. Such an inducement was introduced when Svedberg used (1923) the ultracentrifuge to isolate colloidal particles. From the rate of settling, Svedberg could deduce the size and shape of the particles. Although soluble, some large molecules (including proteins and polymers) resemble colloids, and Svedberg's methods permitted chemists to gather data on these molecules by observing their settling rates. Svedberg won the 1926 Nobel Prize in Chemistry. He later collaborated with his student Arne Tiselius to devise electrophoresis, a more modern tool for studying proteins.

SVERDRUP, HARALD ULRIK (1888–1957), Norwegian oceanographer. Sverdrup served as scientific director of the Norwegian north-polar expedition aboard the *Maud* (1918–25) and directed the University of California's Scripps Institution of Oceanography at La Jolla (1936–48) and the Norwegian Polar Institute in Oslo (from 1948). His monumental and comprehensive book *The Oceans: Their Physics, Chemistry and General Biology* (1942; with Martin W.

Johnson and Richard H. Fleming) had an international impact and provided a foundation for research during and after World War II. His research into tides and wave heights contributed to the success of amphibious landings during the war. Sverdrup also developed a theory explaining that the source of the salinity of the Pacific Ocean was the Antarctic circumpolar current from the Indian Ocean. He also contributed to the theory that explains equatorial countercurrents.

SVEVO, ITALO (Ettore Schmitz; 1861–1928), Italian novelist. Born into a prosperous Jewish family in Trieste, Svevo prepared for a business career but yearned to be a writer. He wrote the novels *A Life* (1892; Eng. trans. 1963) and *As a Man Grows Older* (1898; Eng. trans. 1932), but discouraged by negative reviews, he returned to the business world. Since that life required travel, he studied English; he showed his novels to his tutor, the Irish writer James Joyce, who encouraged him. Svevo published *Confessions of Zeno* (1923; Eng. trans. 1930), which was warmly received abroad, especially in France, where he was dubbed "the Italian Proust." Influenced by Sigmund Freud, he was one of the first to apply psychoanalytic insights to the novel. His ironic, sparse, and introspective works were largely autobiographical and preoccupied with the themes of guilt, death, and the passage of time. *The Nice Old Man and the Pretty Girls* (1929; Eng. trans. 1930), *Short Sentimental Journey* (1949; Eng. trans. 1967), and *Further Confessions of Zeno* (Eng. trans. 1969) appeared posthumously. ■ See biography by John Gatt-Rutter (1988) and studies by P. N. Furbank (1966), Naomi Lebowitz (1978), and Beno Weiss (1987).

SVOBODA, LUDVIK (1895–1979), Czech military and political leader. A career army officer, Svoboda fled to the Soviet Union after the German occupation of Prague (1939) and headed the Czech army corps serving under Soviet command (1941–45). A national hero after World War II, he served as defense minister and deputy premier and joined the Communist party in 1948. Victimized by the Stalinist purges of the early 1950s, he was rehabilitated in 1956, headed the Czech Military Academy, and served as president of Czechoslovakia (1968–75). He supported the liberal regime (1968) of Alexander Dubček.

SWANSON, GLORIA (Gloria Svensson; 1899–1983), American actress. One of the most successful and highly paid silent-film stars, the Chicago-born Swanson got her first movie part at age 17 in *The Fable of Elvira*. Thin and chic, Swanson established her image as the glamour queen of the 1920s with several sophisticated comedies of manners (*Don't Change Your Husband*, 1918; *Male and Female*, 1919; *Why Change Your Wife?*, 1920). In 1928 she produced and starred in *Sadie Thompson*. She made only one successful sound film, *The Trespasser* (1929) and grudgingly retired in 1934. "Who needed sound? We had faces, then," complained the silent diva in the decayed splendor of *Sunset Boulevard* (1950), Swanson's comeback classic. She also established several successful businesses, including a clothing and a "natural" cosmetics firm. ■ See her autobiography, *Swanson on Swanson* (1980), and the study by Richard M. Hudson and Raymond Lee (1970).

SWEENEY, JOHN JOSEPH (1934–), U.S. labor leader. Sweeney grew up in an immigrant Irish, working-class family in New York City and attended Transport Workers Union meetings with his father. He received a bachelor's degree in economics from Iona College (1956) and began his 20-year career as an officer of the New York City local of the Service Employees International Union (SEIU) in 1960. As local president (1976–80), he led two successful city-wide strikes and increased local union membership from 45,000 to 70,000. During his tenure as national SEIU president (1980–95), Sweeney vigorously recruited public-sector employees, health care workers, women, and minorities, and increased union membership by more than 75 percent, making the SEIU the third largest union in the United States. He sponsored research on job-related medical disorders and supported federal legislation requiring universal health care and family and medical leave benefits. After being elected (1995) president of the American Federation of Labor and Congress of Industrial Organizations (AFL-CIO), Sweeney concentrated on increasing union membership, which had fallen to less than 15 percent of the labor force, and on enhancing the power of labor in local, state, and national electoral politics.

SWEEZY, PAUL M. (1910–), U.S. economist. Sweezy was a founder (1949) and editor (with Leo Huberman) of the influential journal *Monthly Review: An Independent Socialist Magazine* and taught at several major universities including Harvard, Yale, Cornell, and Stanford. He was one of the major figures in the revival of Marxist economic thought in the 1960s and 1970s. His books included *The Theory of Capitalist Development* (1942), *The Present as History* (1953), *Monopoly Capital* (1966; with Paul Baran), *Four Lectures on Marxism* (1981), and *The Irreversible Crisis* (1980; with Harry Magdoff).

SWING, RAYMOND GRAM (1887–1968), U.S. radio commentator. One of America's most popular newsmen, Swing was called "the best-known voice in the world." He was a radio news commentator and analyst for the Columbia and Mutual broadcast systems during the 1930s and 1940s, a reporter on American affairs for the British Broadcasting Corp. (1935–45), and a political commentator for the Voice of America (1951–53; 1959–64). At the height of his career he was said to be reaching approximately 37 million listeners throughout the world. He was known for his sober, intelligent reports delivered in a calm and reasoned manner. His popularity declined after the House Un-

American Activities Committee harassed him for his liberal views (1945). ■ See his autobiography, *Good Evening* (1964).

SWOPE, GERARD (1872–1957), U.S. industrialist. An engineering graduate of the Massachusetts Institute of Technology (1895), Swope was an executive with the Western Electric Co. before serving as president of General Electric (1922–40; 1942–44). He diversified GE's production to make the firm one of the largest producers of electrical appliances; he instituted unemployment insurance, profit sharing, and cost-of-living wage adjustments for the firm's workers, which resulted in smooth labor relations throughout his long tenure. He served on many governmental advisory and regulatory boards. Also a leader in public housing, Swope served as chairman of the New York City Housing Authority from 1940–42. ■ See biography by David Loth (1958).

SWOPE, HERBERT BAYARD (1882–1958), U.S. journalist and public official. One of the century's foremost American journalists, Swope was a reporter and editor for the *New York World* (1909–29). He achieved fame as a crime reporter (1912), won a Pulitzer Prize (1917) for his war reporting from Germany, and "scooped" the world by becoming the first reporter to get the text of the League of Nations Covenant (1919). As a crusading liberal editor (1920–29), he launched numerous investigations, including a Pulitzer Prize–winning exposé of the Ku Klux Klan (1921). He was the innovator of the widely imitated "Op Ed" (opposite editorial) page, which featured columns and reviews by prominent writers. After 1929 he was an adviser to many political and business figures. During World War II he was a consultant to the secretary of war and after the war served as an assistant to Bernard Baruch, the U.S. delegate to the United Nations Atomic Energy Commission. ■ See Ely J. Kahn, Jr., *The World of Swope* (1965), and Alfred Allan Lewis, *Top of the World* (1977).

SYNGE, (EDMUND) JOHN MILLINGTON (1871–1909), Irish dramatist. Synge was a leader of the Irish literary renaissance and codirector (from 1904), with W. B. Yeats and Lady Gregory, of the Abbey Theatre (Dublin). Inspired by Yeats, he studied traditional life and culture in the remote Aran Islands (from 1898) and infused his (English-language) plays with the folklore and Anglo-Irish dialect of the Irish peasantry. Although basically sympathetic portrayals, several of his intense and poetic works were attacked because of their frankness and their apparent slight to the country people. His best-known plays were *The Shadow of the Glen* (1903), *Riders to the Sea* (1904), and his comic masterpiece, *The Playboy of the Western World* (1907). *The Aran Islands* (1907) recorded Synge's impressions of the islands. ■ See studies by David H. Greene and Edward M. Stephens (1959; rev. ed. 1989), Donna Gerstenberger (1964), Robin Skelton (1971), and David M. Kiely (1994).

SYNGE, RICHARD LAURENCE MILLINGTON (1914–1994), British biochemist. The son of a stockbroker, Synge was known for the development (1941) of paper-partition chromatography, a quick and inexpensive method of separating the components of complex mixtures. He shared with his collaborator Archer Martin the 1952 Nobel Prize in Chemistry. Synge applied this technique to unravel the molecular structure of the simple protein gramicidin S. His research anticipated the work of investigators such as Frederick Sanger, who determined the exact sequence of amino acids in protein molecules. He worked at the Wool Industries Research Association (1941–43), the Lister Institute (1943–48), the Rowett Research Institute (1948–67), and the Food Research Institute (1967–76) and taught at the University of East Anglia (1968–84).

SZASZ, THOMAS STEPHEN (1920–   ), Hungarian-born U.S. psychiatrist. Born into a wealthy Jewish family, Szasz emigrated to the United States in 1938, studied medicine at the University of Cincinnati (M.D. 1944), and trained in psychiatry at the University of Chicago (1946–50). A well-known critic of his profession, Szasz wrote that "mental illness" is a mythological concept used by the state to control deviants and thereby limit individual freedom in American society. In his view, conditions comprising "mental illness" are social and moral problems, but not medical ones. Szasz repeatedly warned against replacing a theological world view with a therapeutic one. He was an uncompromising libertarian and humanist who argued persuasively against involuntary psychiatric examination and hospitalization and believed that the psychoanalytic relationship should be free of coercion and control. Szasz was professor of psychiatry at the Upstate Medical Center, State University of New York, Syracuse (1956–90). His books included *The Myth of Mental Illness* (1961), *Law, Liberty and Psychiatry* (1963), *The Manufacture of Madness* (1971), *The Myth of Psychotherapy* (1978), *Our Right to Drugs: The Case for a Free Market* (1992), *Cruel Compassion: Psychiatric Control of Society's Unwanted* (1994), and *The Meaning of Mind* (1996). ■ See Richard E. Vatz and Lee S. Weinberg, eds., *Thomas Szasz: Primary Values and Major Contentions* (1983).

SZELL, GEORGE (1897–1970), U.S. conductor. Born in Hungary, Szell was a child prodigy who composed music and made his piano debut at age 11 with the Vienna Symphony. At 17 he replaced a scheduled conductor with the Vienna Symphony, and he conducted for several years with the Berlin State Opera (1924–29) before he made his first American appearance (1930). In 1939, while returning to Europe from an Australian tour, he was stranded in New York by World War II, which he spent as a conductor with the Metropolitan Opera. In 1946 Szell, who had a reputation as a martinet, was appointed music director of the Cleveland Symphony. Over the next 24 years he built that orchestra into one of the world's finest, with frequent European tours and Carnegie Hall concerts devoted primarily to the Austro-German School of Haydn, Mozart, Beethoven, Schumann, Brahms, Mahler, and Richard Strauss.

SZENT-GYORGYI, ALBERT (1893–1986), Hungarian-born U.S. biochemist. Born and educated in Budapest, Szent-Gyorgyi fled from the Bolshevik revolution in 1919 and settled in the Netherlands. He earned a Ph.D. at Cambridge University (1927). Szent-Gyorgyi won a 1937 Nobel Prize in Physiology or Medicine for contributions to two areas of biochemistry. He identified the catalytic role of fumaric and succinic acids in cellular respiration. Extending this important work on cell metabolism to plant tissues, he isolated hexuronic acid (renaming it ascorbic acid) from plants and showed that it was identical with vitamin C. Later he returned to Hungary and investigated the chemistry of muscular contraction. Szent-Gyorgyi emigrated to the United States in 1947, directed cancer research at the Marine Biology Laboratories at Woods Hole, Massachusetts, and became a citizen in 1955. He wrote books on many subjects, including *On Oxidation, Fermentation, Vitamins, Health and Disease* (1940), *The Chemistry of Muscular Contraction* (1951), *Bioenergetics* (1957), *Introduction to Submolecular Biology* (1960), *Bioelectronics* (1968), *Crazy Ape* (1970), *The Living State with Remarks on Cancer* (1972), and *Electronic Biology and Cancer* (1976).

SZIGETI, JOSEPH (1892–1973), Hungarian-born U.S. violinist. A child prodigy, Szigeti made his formal debut at age 13 in Berlin. He was a brilliant technician who matured into a sensitive and intelligent musician. By eschewing the exhibitionism prevalent among concert violinists when he began his career, he helped influence modern violin playing. He was among the first to perform the music of Béla Bartók, Darius Milhaud, Ernest Bloch, Serge Prokofiev, and other contemporary composers. Noteworthy among his numerous recordings is a series of Beethoven works he performed with Bartók at the piano. He made his American debut in 1925, settled in the United States in 1940, and performed throughout the world until his retirement in 1960. ■ See his reminiscences, *With Strings Attached* (1967).

SZILARD, LEO (1898–1964), U.S. physicist. Born in Hungary, Szilard was educated at the University of Berlin (Ph.D. 1922) and taught physics in Germany. A Jew, he was forced to flee Germany when the Nazis came to power. He eventually settled in the United States (1937). He was the first scientist to conceptualize (1934) the idea of a nuclear chain reaction and to confirm (1939) the practicality of a nuclear reaction using uranium. Realizing the enormous military potential of uranium fission and the fact that the Germans were working on it, Szilard and Eugene Wigner persuaded Albert Einstein to write his famous letter (1939) to President Franklin D. Roosevelt explaining the importance of government research on nuclear fission. The result was the establishment of the Manhattan Project to develop the atomic bomb. With Enrico Fermi, Szilard built the world's first self-sustaining nuclear reactor (1942). Regretting his work on the atomic bomb, Szilard protested against its use and fought for nuclear disarmament. After World War II he did research in biophysics. His recollections and correspondence were edited by Spencer Weart and Gertrud W. Szilard (1978). ■ See William Lanouette, *Genius in the Shadows* (1992).

SZOLD, HENRIETTA (1860–1945), U.S. Zionist leader. Szold came from a family active in aiding Jewish immigrants from Europe. She taught school in Baltimore, cofounded (1889) an evening school for recent Jewish immigrants, and served as editor for the Jewish Publication Society of America (1892–1916). Szold first visited Palestine in 1909 and became convinced that Zionism was the hope for Jewish cultural and spiritual development; to this end she founded Hadassah (1912), a women's Zionist organization dedicated to improving health conditions in Palestine. After Szold migrated to Palestine (1920) she was elected to the World Zionist Organization executive committee (1927) and was active in coordinating the emigration of Jewish children from Germany after the Nazi rise to power in 1933 and in organizing a modern system of social service. ■ See biography by Irving Fineman (1961) and Joan Dash, *Summoned to Jerusalem* (1979).

SZYMANOWSKI, KAROL (1882–1937), Polish composer. Szymanowski grew up in the Ukraine, studied at the Warsaw Conservatory, and cofounded the "Young Poland in Music" group (1905) in Berlin. His music, including the frequently performed *Mythes* (1915) for violin and piano, showed the influence of German romanticism, Russian mysticism, and French impressionism until 1920, when he became prominent in the musical life of newly independent Poland and composed his *Stabat Mater* (1929) and *Sinfonia Concertante* (1932) in a more nationalistic idiom. ■ See biography by Teresa Chylinska (Eng. trans. 1993).

SZYMBORSKA, WISLAWA (1923–), Polish poet. Szymborska studied literature and sociology at Jagiellonian University in Cracow (1945–48). Her verse was first published in a Cracow newspaper (1945), and she was a columnist for the weekly *Literary Life* (1953–81). Her early works, which she later disclaimed, were written in the style of socialist realism. However, after 1957 she published several volumes of delicate, witty, and unpretentious poems that described the quirks and ironies of everyday life and personal relationships. Her simple language, nonchalance, and sense of humor belied her concern with complex philosophical issues. Although little known outside of Poland, she became one of her country's most popular poets and was awarded the 1996 Nobel Prize in Literature. English-language translations of her collections include *Sounds, Feelings and Thoughts* (1981), *People on a Bridge* (1990), and *View with a Grain of Sand* (1995).

T

TAFT, LORADO (1860–1936), U.S. sculptor. Taft studied at the University of Illinois, where his father taught science, and at the École des Beaux Arts (1850–85) in Paris. Composing idealized figures into graceful allegories, he designed fountains for the Union Station Plaza in Washington, D.C. (1908), and the *Fountain of the Great Lakes* (1913) and *Fountain of Time* (1922) in Chicago. Taft also taught at the Chicago Art Institute (from 1886), played a major role in art education in the United States, and wrote *The History of American Sculpture* (1903) and *Modern Tendencies in Sculpture (1921)*.

TAFT, ROBERT ALPHONSO (1889–1953), U.S. senator. The son of U.S. Pres. William H. Taft, Robert Taft became known as "Mr. Republican" during a long career in the Ohio legislature (1921–38) and the U.S. Senate (1939–53). A leading conservative member of his party and an unsuccessful candidate for its 1940, 1948, and 1952 presidential nominations, he was an isolationist who opposed U.S. entry into World War II and cosponsored the 1947 Taft-Hartley Act, which restricted many activities in labor unions. Taft also wrote *A Foreign Policy for Americans* (1951). ▪ See James St. Patterson, *Mr. Republican* (1972).

TAFT, WILLIAM HOWARD (1857–1930), U.S. president and jurist. A second-generation lawyer from Ohio, Taft was a state and federal judge who proved himself an able and sympathetic governor of the Philippines (1901–4) after the Spanish-American War. Appointed secretary of war (1904–8) by his friend Theodore Roosevelt, Taft, a Republican, succeeded Roosevelt as president, earning a reputation for honesty and efficiency during his single term in the White House (1909–13). Although he pursued the antitrust activities of his predecessor, his alliance with the conservative wing of the party alienated Roosevelt and the progressives. Taft was nominated by the Republicans for reelection (1912), but the intraparty dispute prompted Roosevelt to run for president on his own Bull Moose (Progressive) party, thus splitting the Republican vote and guaranteeing the election of Democrat Woodrow Wilson. Taft subsequently chaired the War Labor Board during World War I and served as chief justice of the U.S. Supreme Court (1921–30). His son Robert A. Taft (1889–1953) was an influential U.S. senator. ▪ See biographies by Henry F. Pringle (2 vols., 1939) and Judith I. Anderson (1981), and Paolo E. Coletta, *The Presidency of William H. Taft* (1973).

TAGORE, SIR RABINDRANATH (1861–1941), Indian poet, philosopher, dramatist, and social reformer. Born into a wealthy and talented Bengali family, Tagore was one of the century's most prolific and multifaceted literary masters. His poetry, exemplified by the collection *Gitanjali* (1910; Eng. trans. 1912), expressed a universal love of humankind, of God, and of the beauties of nature and earned him the 1913 Nobel Prize in Literature. His dozens of publications included the novels *Gora* (1910; Eng. trans. 1924) and *The Home and the World* (1916; Eng. trans. 1919), the play *Chitra* (1892; Eng. trans. 1914), the short-story collections *The Housewarming* (Eng. trans. 1965) and *Hungry Stones* (Eng. trans. 1970), the philosophical essay collections *The Religion of Man* (Eng. trans. 1931) and *Sadhana* (Eng. trans. 1913), and several books of songs. He introduced new poetic forms into the Bengali language and created a new style of vocal music that combined classical ragas, semiclassical love songs, and folk music. He traveled widely and played a major role in introducing Indian culture to the West and Western culture to India. Tagore founded an international nontraditional school at Shantiniketan (1901), which grew into the Visva-Bharati University (1924), and set up a model experimental village, Shriniketan. ▪ See his *My Reminiscences* (Eng. trans. 1917); Amiya Chakravarty, ed., *A Tagore Reader* (1961); studies by Krishna Kripalani (1962) and Mary M. Lago (1976); and biography by Krishna Dutta and Andrew Robinson (1995).

TAHA HUSAYN. *See HUSAYN, TAHA.*

TAIROV, ALEKSANDR YAKOVLEVICH (**A. Y. Kornblit;** 1885–1950), Soviet stage director. After graduating (1913) from St. Petersburg University's law faculty, Tairov acted in St. Petersburg under Vsevolod Meyerhold's direction and began directing his own productions. He moved to Moscow, where with his wife, the actress Alisa Roonen, he cofounded (1914) the Kamerny (Chamber) Theater, which he directed for 35 years (1914–49). He characterized himself as a "neorealist;" Tairov's innovative stagecraft eschewed the techniques of Meyerhold's "conditioned" productions. Tairov incorporated commedia dell'arte elements into his productions and introduced to Moscow audiences contemporary foreign plays by G. B. Shaw, Eugene O'Neill, and others. Collaboration with stage designer Aleksandra Ekster resulted in colorful, platformed stage sets in the cubist mode. His productions stunned audiences when he toured Europe (1925–30). Though severely restricted by Stalinist overseers in the 1930s and 1940s, Tairov continued his work nearly until his death. He wrote *Notes of a Director* (Eng. trans. 1969).

TAKAHASHI, KOREKIYO (1854–1936), Japanese political and financial leader. Takahashi studied English and went to the United States in 1867. He returned in 1868 to teach and became a Christian convert. He launched a second career in 1881 as a civil servant; a third career as a banker (after 1892) proved extremely successful, and he was named president of the Bank of Japan (1911). He joined the Seiyukai political party (1913) and was finance minister in six cabinets between 1913 and 1936. He served briefly as premier from November 1921 to June 1922. Trying to balance demands of the financial community and the military, he resisted all-out armaments spending, and he was assassinated during an uprising of young radical officers on Feb. 26, 1936.

TAKAMINE, JOKICHI (1854–1922), Japanese-U.S. chemist. Born in Japan, Takamine graduated from the Imperial University in Tokyo (1879). He organized a fertilizer manufacturing company and isolated a starch-digesting enzyme, takadiastase, which was used in the distilling industry and in medicines. He moved to the United States (1890), joined Parker, Davis and Co., and succeeded (1901) in isolating a substance from the adrenal glands that is now known as adrenaline or epinephrine. Although the concept of the hormone had not yet been formulated, it was eventually acknowledged that Takamine had been the first to isolate a pure hormone. He also aided scientific and industrial development in Japan and helped establish the Imperial Research Institute (1913).

TAKEMITSU, TORU (1930–1996), Japanese composer. An avant-garde composer in the Western tradition of chromatic, quasi-serial composition, Takemitsu dispensed with traditional harmony and rhythm. In his spare, atmospheric music he concentrated on texture and frequently utilized silence. He also experimented with tape and aleatory music. His works included *Requiem* (1957), *November Steps* (1967), *Asterism* (1968), *In an Autumn Garden* (1973–79), *Toward the Sea* (1986–88), *Waves* (1976), and *How Slow the Wind* (1994) and innovative film scores for *Woman in the Dunes* and *Kwaidan* (both 1964) and *Ran* (1985). He composed many pieces for traditional Japanese instruments in a European manner.

TALBERT, MAY BURNETT (1866–1923), U.S. civil-rights leader. Talbert was born in Oberlin, Ohio, and graduated from Oberlin College at age 19. She was active in the black community in Buffalo, New York, for many years and was president (1916–21) of the National Association of Colored Women. She was also a director of the National Association for the Advancement of Colored People and active on behalf of both women's rights and civil rights.

TALLCHIEF, MARIA (1925–), U.S. ballerina. Tallchief was born to a Scots-Irish mother; her father was a chief in Oklahoma's Osage tribe. Tallchief debuted (1942) with Serge Denham's Ballet Russe de Monte Carlo in Canada and during the next three years danced roles in *Schéhérazade, Etude,*

Danse Indienne, and other ballets. At New York's Ballet Society and the New York City Ballet (1947–60; 1963–65), Tallchief was prima ballerina and danced in ballets choreographed by George Balanchine, to whom she was married (1946–52). She gained an international reputation for her elegant and technically brilliant interpretations and helped popularize ballet in America through her many television appearances. She was best known for her performance in Balanchine's *Firebird*. She was the founding director of the Chicago City Ballet (1979–87) and the ballet director of the Lyric Opera of Chicago. ■ See her autobiography (1997; with Larry Kaplan); Olga Maynard, *Bird of Fire* (1961); and biography by Elisabeth P. Myers (1967).

TALMA, LOUISE (1906–), French-born U.S. composer. Talma studied composition with Nadia Boulanger in Paris and earned an M.A. from Columbia University (1933). She spent her career on the faculty of New York City's Hunter College (1928–79). The first woman composer elected to the National Institute of Arts and Letters (1974), Talma gained an international reputation with such works as *Three Madrigals* (1929), *String Quartet* (1954), *A Time to Remember* (1966–67), *Voices of Peace* (1973), *Celebration for Women's Chorus and Orchestra* (1977), and *Thirteen Ways of Looking at a Blackbird for Tenor, Oboe, and Piano* (1979). Thornton Wilder wrote the libretto for Talma's opera. *The Alcestiad* (1955–58).

TALMADGE, EUGENE (1884–1946), U.S. political leader. Talmadge earned a law degree from the University of Georgia (1907) but preferred to conduct his political campaigns in shirtsleeves and red suspenders, as a dirt farmer. As Georgia's commissioner of agriculture (1927–33) he attacked the fertilizer trusts and city slickers; as governor (1933–37; 1941–43) he used the national guard to crush strikes and dismissed state university professors who professed a belief in racial equality. He also opposed the disbursement of federal relief funds. Reelected governor in 1946, Talmadge died before taking office; he was succeeded (1947) by his son Herman. ■ See William Anderson, *The Wild Man from Sugar Creek* (1975).

TAMAYO, RUFINO (1899–1991), Mexican painter. After study at the Academy of San Carlos (1917–21), Tamayo supervised the department of ethnographic drawing at the National Museum of Anthropology and was greatly impressed by Indian tribal sculpture. He combined pre-Columbian folk themes with European avant-garde styles and was particularly influenced by Pablo Picasso and Georges Braque. Opposed to the cult of Mexican revolutionary mural painters, Tamayo sought to emphasize the aesthetic qualities of a painting, not its social message. His murals *Birth of Nationality* and *Mexico Today* (Palace of Fine Arts, 1952–53) preceded his receiving the São Paulo Biennial Grand Prize. He also completed murals for the Conference Hall of the United Nations Educational, Scientific and Cultural Organization

(Paris, 1958) and the Montreal Expo (1967). ■ See study by Jacques Lassaigne (1982).

TAMBO, OLIVER (1917–1993), South African political leader. After finishing St. Peter's Secondary School in Johannesburg, Tambo attended the University of Fort Hare in Cape Province (1938–41) and earned a law degree by correspondence course. In the 1940s, with Nelson Mandela and others, he formed the African National Congress (ANC) Youth League which ultimately transformed the ANC into a militant liberation movement. In the 1950s, while practicing law in Johannesburg (1951–60), Tambo took an active role in the nationalist movement, and he was banned from attending meetings (1954–56) and detained (1956–57). While serving as deputy president of the African National Congress (1958–67), he was again banned (1959–64). In 1960, the year the ANC was outlawed, Tambo escaped to London, and later moved to Zambia. In exile, Tambo became ANC president (1967) and remained a leading nationalist. In the 1980s he stepped up the ANC's guerrilla campaign against South Africa's white minority government, vowing, in 1986, "rapid, extensive escalation" of the armed struggle against apartheid. After the ANC was legalized, Tambo returned to South Africa (1990) and was replaced as ANC president by Nelson Mandela (1991).

TAMIRIS, HELEN (Helen Becker; 1902?–1966), U.S. dancer and choreographer. Tamiris studied ballet with Michel Fokine and modern dance at the Isadora Duncan School in New York. She abandoned a career in nightclubs and musical revues for the concert stage (1927) and was one of the first modern dancers to utilize jazz, Negro spirituals, and themes of social protest in her performances. She directed her own School of American Dance (1930–45), was principal choreographer of the Federal Theater Project (1936–39), and choreographed such prominent Broadway shows as *Showboat* (revival 1946), *Annie Get Your Gun* (1948), *Touch and Go* (1949), *Fanny* (1954), and *Plain and Fancy* (1955). ■ See study by Christena L. Schlundt (1972).

TAMM, IGOR YEVGENIEVICH (1895–1971), Soviet physicist. A professor at the University of Moscow (1924–57), Tamm was one of the Soviet Union's foremost nuclear physicists. Much of his work utilized both the theory of relativity and quantum mechanics at a time when both were officially out of favor in the Soviet Union. He did pioneering work in semiconductor physics (1933), formulated the beta theory of nuclear forces (1934), conducted experiments in controlled nuclear reactions (1950), and played a major role in the training of Soviet physicists. He was best known for his research determining the properties of the Cherenkov effect, the light waves emitted by electrons moving in a transparent medium at a speed greater than the speed of light in the medium. For his research, which played an important role in the detection and measurement of elementary particles through the development of the Cherenkov counter,

Tamm shared the 1958 Nobel Prize in Physics with compatriots Pavel A. Cherenkov and Ilya M. Frank. He advocated increased freedom for scientists in the Soviet Union.

TANAKA, KAKUEI (1918–1993), Japanese political leader. Born into a poor family, Tanaka worked his way through technical school and founded a construction business that prospered during World War II. He was first elected to the diet (parliament) in 1947, and rose through the ranks of the Liberal Democratic party. He was finance minister (1962–64) and minister of international trade and industry (1964–72) before serving as premier (1972–74). He was forced to resign because of alleged political financial irregularities; in 1976 he was indicted for accepting bribes from Lockheed, the American company, while he was premier. After a trial lasting nearly seven years, he was convicted in 1983 but did not serve a prison term because of appeals. Even after his indictment, however, Tanaka remained a powerful figure in party and national politics. He wrote *Building a New Japan* (Eng. trans. 1983).

TANDY, JESSICA (1909–1994), British-born U.S. actress. Tandy played Shakespearean roles in Britain, sharing the stage with such stars as John Gielgud and Alec Guinness, but not until the 1960s did she play Shakespeare in America because, as she put it, "Nobody asked me until now." Critics praised her performance as Lady Macbeth in the 1961 Stratford Festival. Tandy was a particularly versatile character actress, perhaps best known for her Tony Award-winning interpretation of Blanche du Bois in *A Streetcar Named Desire* (1947). She costarred with husband Hume Cronyn in productions such as *The Fourposter* (1951), *The Honeys* (1955), and *The Gin Game* (1977), for which she won a second Tony Award. She won a third Tony Award for her portrayal of an Appalachian widow in *Foxfire* (1982). Tandy also appeared in motion-picture and television roles and with Cronyn on the radio and TV series "The Marriage." Her movies included *The Seventh Cross* (1944), *Fried Green Tomatoes* (1991), and *Driving Miss Daisy* (1988), for which she won an Academy Award for best actress.

TANGE, KENZO (1913–), Japanese architect. A professor at Tokyo University (1946–74), Tange began his most creative architectural work after World War II. His first prominent design was the Hiroshima Peace Hall (1949–55), which showed the influence of Le Corbusier. Tange's special contribution to architecture was the synthesis of modern techniques and materials and traditional Japanese forms. In the 1960s, his buildings became more dramatic in scope, as evidenced by the swirling shapes of the National Gymnasium (1961–64) designed for the 1964 Olympic games. Also a city planner, Tange developed an innovative reorganization scheme to extend Tokyo city over the bay (1960), designed the master plan and theme pavilion for the 1970 Osaka Exposition, and developed urban plans for Skopje, Yugoslavia (1965–66), Bologna, Italy (1971–74), and San

Francisco (1971). He was also noted for the Tokyo Prince Hotel (1983–87). He was awarded the 1987 Pritzker Prize. ■ See studies by Robin Boyd (1962), Paolo Riani (1969), and Udo Kultermann, ed. (1970).

TANGUAY, EVA (1878–1947), Canadian-born U.S. entertainer. The queen of musical comedy at the turn of the century, Tanguay switched to vaudeville (1906) and became the field's highest-paid performer. An enthusiastic and flamboyant entertainer whose onstage and offstage activities were highly publicized, she wowed her audiences with such risqué songs as "I Don't Care," "I Want Someone to Go Wild with Me," and "It's All Been Done Before but Not the Way I Do It." Her songs, scanty costumes, and gleeful abandon onstage reflected the social and sexual ferment of her era. Her career ended shortly after she lost her fortune in the 1929 stock-market crash.

TANGUY, YVES (1900–1955), French artist. Tanguy traveled the world as a soldier and sailor before joining the surrealist movement (1925) as a self-taught artist. He painted bizarre, unreal subjects with great precision; landscapes and dreamscapes full of spectral forms or great amorphous conglomerations. He emigrated to the United States (1939) and influenced the early development of abstract expressionism. ■ See study by André Breton (1946).

TANIZAKI, JUNICHIRO (1886–1965), Japanese novelist and short-story writer. A leader of the neoromantic school of Japanese literature, Tanizaki combined adherence to Japanese tradition with a fascination for the West. Influenced by Western writers Edgar Allan Poe, Charles Baudelaire, and Oscar Wilde, he was obsessed with cruelty, sexual aberration, and mysterious demonic forces, and he infused sensual themes and vivid imagery into his writing. Among his greatest works were *A Blind Man's Tale* (1931; Eng. trans. 1963), *The Story of Shunkin* (1933; Eng. trans. 1936), *The Makioka Sisters* (1948; Eng. trans. 1957), *The Key* (1956; Eng. trans. 1961), and *Diary of a Mad Old Man* (1961–62; Eng. trans. 1965). *Naomi,* a partly autobiographical work that was originally serialized in the 1920s, appeared in English translation in 1985. He also adapted into modern Japanese the 11th-century classic *The Tale of Genji.* ■ See Gwenn Petersen, *The Moon in the Water* (1979).

TANNER, HENRY OSSAWA (1859–1937), U.S. artist. Born in Pittsburgh into a long line of black clergymen, Tanner studied with Thomas Eakins at the Philadelphia Academy of Fine Arts and in Paris at the Académie Julian. A naturalistic painter of dramatic biblical scenes—*The Resurrection of Lazarus,* which was purchased by the French government, *Daniel in the Lion's Den,* and *The Return of the Holy Women*—Tanner remained in France for most of his life and was elected to the Legion of Honor (1923). His best-known works, depicting blacks, were *The Banjo Lesson* and *The Thankful Poor.* His landscape *Sand Dunes at Sunset, At-* *lantic City* was the first painting by an African American to be part of the White House art collection (1996). His success inspired many artists of the Harlem renaissance and he was the first African American elected to full membership in the National Academy of Art and Design. ■ See biography by Marcia M. Mathews (1969).

TÀPIES, ANTONI (1923–), Spanish painter. Tàpies grew up in Barcelona, where as an adolescent he was affected by the barbarities of the civil war. He later abandoned law training to paint. Largely self-taught, he was influenced by artists Paul Klee and Jean Dubuffet. His early works were collages made of string, newspaper, and cardboard, but beginning in 1950 he produced earthtone paintings using relief-surface techniques. He experimented with texture, mixing paint with sand, pulverized marble, and other materials; applied to canvas, the paint was often wrinkled, scratched, or cut, exposing a base of a different color. Distorted letters, geometrical forms, and found objects were sometimes superimposed on a roughly textured background. A founder (1957) of the controversial El Paso group, which championed expressive abstraction, or informalism, Tàpies is credited with bringing contemporary abstract art to Spain. ■ See studies by Blai Bonet (Eng. trans. 1969), Alejandro Cirici Pellicer (Eng. trans. 1972), P. Gimferrer (1975), and R. Penrose (1974).

TARBELL, IDA MINERVA (1857–1944), U.S. editor and writer. After studying at the Sorbonne in Paris (1891–94), Tarbell served as an editor of *McClure's Magazine* (1894–1906), a leading muckraking journal, and championed honest government and trust-busting. In 1904 she wrote the *History of the Standard Oil Company,* which exposed the ruthless practices of big business and the wasteful exploitation of natural resources. From 1906 to 1915 she worked with Lincoln Steffens and other muckrakers on the *American Magazine.* A liberal rather than a radical, she was not an uncompromising critic of big business, and in later years wrote sympathetic accounts of business and businessmen. She also wrote several books on Abraham Lincoln and on women's issues. ■ See her autobiography, *All in the Day's Work* (1939); biography by Kathleen Brady (1984); and Robert C. Kochersberger, Jr., ed., *More Than a Muckraker* (1994).

TARKENTON, FRAN (Francis Asbury Tarkenton; 1940–), U.S. football player. The son of a Methodist minister, Tarkenton was an All-American quarterback at the University of Georgia (1959–61) who was drafted to play pro ball by the newly formed Minnesota Vikings of the National Football League (NFL). An unorthodox scrambler, he was a threat both as a runner and a passer. As a star with the Vikings (1961–66; 1972–78) and the New York Giants (1967–71) he established lifetime NFL records for passes attempted (6,467), passes completed (3,686), yards gained passing (47,003), and touchdown passes (342). Quiet and reserved off field, he was a member of the Fellowship of Christian Athletes. He wrote the mystery novel *Murder at the Superbowl* (1986; with Herb Resnicow).

TARKINGTON, (NEWTON) BOOTH (1869–1946), U.S. novelist. A lifelong resident of Indianapolis, Indiana, Tarkington recorded the manners and morals of midwestern middle-class family life. His novels were mildly satirical; the characters seem more misdirected than evil. *Alice Adams* (1921) and *The Magnificent Ambersons* (1918) won Pulitzer Prizes, though they are perhaps less well known than Tarkington's sentimental accounts of boyhood and adolescence: *Penrod* (1914) and *Seventeen* (1916). He also wrote many plays, notably *Clarence* (produced 1921), as well as essays and short stories. ▪ See his reminiscences, *The World Does Move* (1928); Susannah Mayberry, *My Amiable Uncle* (1984); biography by James L. Woodress (1955); and study by Keith J. Fennimore (1974).

TARSKI, ALFRED (1902–1983), Polish-born U.S. mathematician and logician. Tarski taught at the University of California at Berkeley (1942–68), where he molded the careers of many mathematicians. A major figure in modern mathematics and philosophy, he made important contributions to general algebra, measurement theory, mathematical logic, and set theory. He was a key figure in the development of metamathematics, which mathematicians use to examine theorems and postulates for internal consistency. His work influenced the development of symbolic logic, and he is credited with advancing the semantic method, a procedure for examining the relationship between an expression and the object to which it refers. His books included *The Concept of Truth in the Languages of Deductive Sciences* (1933), *Introduction to Logic and the Methodology of Deductive Sciences* (1936), *Undecidable Theories* (1953), and *Logic, Semantics, Metamathematics* (1956).

TASCHEREAU, LOUIS ALEXANDRE (1876–1952), Canadian political leader. A practicing lawyer from an old and distinguished family, Taschereau served as a Liberal member of the Quebec legislature (1900–36) and as Quebec's minister of public works and labor (1907–19) and as attorney general (1919–36). As premier of Quebec (1920–36), he promoted industrial development and opened up large areas of the northwest for settlement. His son Robert (1896–1970) served as chief justice of Canada from 1963 to 1967. ▪ See Bernard L. Vigod, *Quebec Before Duplessis* (1986).

TATA, J.R.D. (Jehangir Ratanji Dadabhoy Tata; 1904–1993), Indian industrialist. Tata, a Parsi, was born into one of India's richest and most powerful industrial families. He joined the family business, Tata Sons Ltd., a giant iron and steel holding company, in 1922. He founded Tata Airlines (1932), which developed into Air India, and served as chairman of Tata Sons (1938–91). Over the years he diversified the company into engineering, soap, trucks, luxury hotels, and numerous other industries, and by the time of his retirement he controlled more than 80 companies with annual revenues of more that $4 billion. Tata also created the Family Planning Foundation, the Tata Institute of Fundamental Research, and several charitable trusts.

TATE, ALLEN (1899–1979), U.S. critic, poet, and educator. A 1922 graduate of Vanderbilt University, Tate was a founder and editor of the influential journal *The Fugitive* (1922–25), which published the conservative views of an influential southern literary cluster. He later edited (1944–46) the *Sewanee Review*. Tate's writings included biographies of Stonewall Jackson (1928) and Jefferson Davis (1929) and the novel *The Fathers* (1938), but he was best known for the cerebral poetry assembled in *Collected Poems, 1919–1976* (1977) and for critical writings such as *Reactionary Essays on Poetry and Ideas* (1936), *On the Limits of Poetry* (1948), *The Man of Letters in the Modern World* (1955), and *Collected Essays* (1959). ▪ See his *Memoirs and Opinions* (1975); biography by James Squires (1971); study by Robert S. Dupree (1983); and J. Larry Allums, ed., *Tate and the Poetic Way* (1984).

TATI, JACQUES (Jacques Tatischeff; 1908–1982), French movie director and actor. A popular pantomimist and music-hall entertainer of the 1930s, Tati wrote, directed, and starred in *Jour de Fête* (1949), a brilliant satire on the post–World War II American-inspired obsession with speed and efficiency. In other comic masterpieces that emphasized visual humor—*Mr. Hulot's Holiday* (1953), *Mon Oncle* (1958), *Playtime* (1968), and *Traffic* (1971)—Tati played the character of the awkward yet innocent Mr. Hulot, whose misadventures and foibles exposed the growing conformity, mechanization, and dehumanization of modern Parisian and Western European society. ▪ See study by Penelope Gilliatt (1976); and biography by David Bellos (1999).

TATLIN, VLADIMIR EVGRAFOVICH (1885–1953), Russian painter and sculptor. Tatlin studied at the Moscow School of Fine Arts (c. 1909–11). He painted works noted for their flatness in color and curved forms before visiting Paris (1913), where he was influenced by Pablo Picasso's collages of cardboard, wood, and metal. Returning to Moscow, Tatlin contributed to the development of Russian constructivism with his "painting-reliefs" that used industrial materials. Although his *Monument for the Third International* was never constructed, a scale model using glass and a spiral iron framework was exhibited at the 8th Congress of the Soviets (1920). In the 1920s he was active in cultural organizations and worked in applied art, designing furniture and clothing and evolving a mode of design he called the "New Way of Life." He experimented with an insectlike glider, worked in theater design, and painted nudes and still lifes in his later years. ▪ See study by John Milner (1983).

TATUM, ART (1909–1956), U.S. jazz pianist. Virtually blind from birth, Tatum was a self-taught musician who rose to prominence in the jazz world in the mid-1930s. Considered by many to be the most technically brilliant jazz pianist in history, Tatum mastered all jazz styles and was the most influential pianist of his era. He was originally a solo performer but formed a trio in 1943. He recorded frequently during the last few years of his life. ■ See James Lester, *Too Marvelous for Words* (1994).

TATUM, EDWARD LAWRIE (1909–1975), U.S. geneticist and biochemist. Tatum studied at the University of Wisconsin (Ph.D. 1934) and taught at Stanford (1937–45; 1948–57), Yale (1945–48), and Rockefeller University (1957–75). With George W. Beadle, he undertook research (1937–41) demonstrating that genes regulate specific biochemical processes in organisms, and with Joshua Lederberg he showed (1946) that genetic recombination in bacteria amounted to a form of sexual reproduction. His work with molds, bacteria, and yeast helped to establish the field of molecular genetics, and he shared the 1958 Nobel Prize in Physiology or Medicine with Beadle and Lederberg.

TATUM, GOOSE (Reese Tatum; 1921–1967), U.S. basketball player. Known as the "Clown Prince of Basketball," Tatum was the star of the Harlem Globetrotters (1942–54) and the founder of the Harlem Magicians. A brilliant, razzle-dazzle ball handler, accurate shooter, and unsurpassed court comedian, the 6-foot, 3-inch-tall Tatum had an arm span of 84 inches, and large hands that made it easy for him to palm the ball and fool his opponents. In addition to his clowning he averaged 25 points per game.

TAUBE, HENRY (1915–   ), Canadian-born U.S. chemist. A pioneer of modern inorganic chemistry, Taube studied at the University of Saskatchewan (M.S. 1937) and the University of California, Berkeley (Ph.D. 1940). He became a U.S. citizen in 1942 and taught at the University of Chicago (1946–62) and at Stanford University (1962–90). His major work was in the area of inorganic reactions in solution, and he was best known for his studies of the mechanism of electron transfer in oxidation-reduction reactions. Taube's research contributed to the study of biological catalysts (enzymes) and was applied by the chemical industry to the selection of compounds for use as catalysts, superconductors, and pigments. He was awarded the 1983 Nobel Prize in Chemistry.

TAUBER, RICHARD (Ernst Seiffert; 1892–1948), Austrian-born opera and concert singer. Tauber made his debut at age 21 as Tamino in Mozart's *The Magic Flute,* which was directed by his father at the New State Theater in Chemnitz. This performance led to a five-year contract with the Dresden Opera, by the end of which Tauber was well known all over the German-speaking world for his performances of

Mozart. Abroad, however, the tenor became better known for his performances in the operettas of Franz Lehar and Johann Strauss. His theme song was "Yours Is My Heart Alone" from Lehar's *The Land of Smiles.* In 1938 Tauber moved to England, where he appeared often at London's Covent Garden; he became a British subject in 1940. ■ See Charles Castle, *This Was Richard Tauber* (1971).

TAUSSIG, HELEN BROOKE (1898–1986), U.S. pediatrician and cardiologist. A graduate of the Johns Hopkins Medical School (M.D. 1927) and the first woman appointed a full professor at the school (1959), Taussig made important contributions in the field of heart research. She conceived the idea that many infants and children suffering from a condition of inadequate airing of the blood due to a constriction of the pulmonary artery could be helped by increasing blood circulation to the lungs by means of an artificial bypass. Together with surgeon Alfred Blalock (1944), she devised the "blue baby operation" which greatly stimulated surgical correction of congenital heart defects. She wrote *Congenital Malformations of the Heart* (1947; 2nd ed. 1960).

TAWNEY, RICHARD HENRY (1880–1962), British economic historian. Tawney was a Fabian socialist, an Oxford graduate (1903) who taught working-class student tutorials and successfully lobbied for progressive labor legislation. He was president of the Workers' Educational Association (1928–44) and taught at the London School of Economics (1919–49). His writings on *The Agrarian Problem in the Sixteenth Century* (1912), *The Acquisitive Society* (1921), and *Religion and the Rise of Capitalism* (1926) deeply influenced contemporary concepts of economic history, morality, and social justice. ■ See study by Ross Terrill (1973).

TAYAMA, KATAI (1871–1930), Japanese novelist. One of the most influential Japanese literary figures during the first 20 years of the century, Tayama was the leading figure of Japanese naturalism. Influenced by the French writers Guy de Maupassant, Émile Zola, and the Goncourt brothers, he concentrated on sordid details of his life and helped establish the autobiographical or "I-novel" as a major literary form in Japan. Among his most famous novels were *One Soldier* (1907; Eng. trans. 1956), *The Quilt* (1907; Eng. trans. 1981), *Life* (1908), *Wife* (1908–09), *Country Teacher* (1909; Eng. trans. 1984), and *Bondage* (1910). ■ See his memoirs, *Literary Life in Tokyo, 1885–1915* (1917; Eng. trans. 1987).

TAYLOR, ALAN JOHN PERCIVALE (1906–1990), British historian. After graduating with honors from Oxford (B.A. 1927; M.A. 1932), A.J.P. Taylor continued his study of central European history in Vienna. Author of *The Habsburg Monarchy* (1941), *The Struggle for Mastery in Europe, 1848–1918* (1954), *The Origins of the Second World War*

(1961), and *English History: 1914–1945* (1965), as well as numerous contributions to scholarly and popular journals, Taylor was considered a maverick historian for his irony and iconoclasm. He lectured at Manchester University (1930–38) and served as an Oxford fellow (1938–76), tutor in modern history (1938–63), and university lecturer in international history (1953–63). ∎ See his autobiography, *Personal History* (1983).

TAYLOR, (JOSEPH) DEEMS (1885–1966), U.S. composer and writer. During a long career in music, Taylor worked as a critic (1917–32), radio commentator (1936–43), CBS network consultant, and president of the American Society of Composers, Authors and Publishers (ASCAP; 1942–48) as well as a writer and composer. His musical works included two operas, *The King's Henchman* (1926) and *Peter Ibbetson* (1931). He wrote *Of Music and Men* (1937), *The Well Tempered Listener* (1940), *Music to My Ears* (1949), and *Some Enchanted Evenings* (1953).

TAYLOR, ELIZABETH (1932–   ), U.S. film actress. Born in London, Taylor was evacuated during World War II to Hollywood, where she became a child actress with *Lassie Come Home* (1943) and *National Velvet* (1944). Growing up into a buxom, black-haired beauty with violet eyes, she starred in *Giant* (1956), *Cat on a Hot Tin Roof* (1958), and *Butterfield 8* (Academy Award, 1960). While earning $1 million as *Cleopatra* (1963), Taylor conducted a highly public romance with Richard Burton, who became her fourth husband (1964) and costar in *Who's Afraid of Virginia Woolf?* (Academy Award, 1966) and *The Taming of the Shrew* (1967). They were separated several times and were divorced—for the second time—in 1976. Taylor subsequently appeared on Broadway in *The Little Foxes* (1981). She remained a celebrity as her career waned in the 1980s and 1990s and raised millions of dollars to fight AIDS. ∎ See Dick Sheppard, *Elizabeth* (1974); Brenda Maddox, *Who's Afraid of Elizabeth Taylor?* (1977); and biographies by Kitty Kelley (1981), Bill Adler (1982), and Alexander Walker (1990).

TAYLOR, JOSEPH H., JR. (1941–   ), U.S. physicist. Taylor studied astronomy at Harvard University (Ph.D. 1968) and taught at the University of Massachusetts, Amherst (1969–81), where one of his graduate students was Russell A. Hulse. During a search for pulsars with the radio telescope at Arecibo, Puerto Rico (1974), the two researchers discovered the first binary pulsar, two dense, rapidly spinning neutron stars rotating around a common center of mass with one emitting pulsing radio waves. They found that the rotational speed of the pulsars was increasing as was their proximity to each other, and they theorized that the orbital decay was due to energy loss in the form of gravitational waves. Their work constituted the first indirect experimental evidence to support the existence of gravitational waves and supported Albert Einstein's theory of gravity. Taylor and

Hulse shared the 1993 Nobel Prize in Physics for their discovery. Taylor continued his research on pulsars after becoming a professor at Princeton University (1980–   ).

TAYLOR, LAURETTE (Helen Laurette Cooney; 1884–1946), U.S. actress. Taylor began her career as a vaudeville performer at age 13 and achieved stardom on Broadway (after 1909) in a series of sentimental comedies written by John Hartley Manners, whom she married in 1912. She was best known for the title role in *Peg o' My Heart* (1912), which she played in 604 consecutive performances. Taylor remained popular throughout the 1920s but drifted into alcoholism and appeared in few roles after her husband's death (1928). Although she had relatively few commercial successes in her career, she was considered by some critics to be the greatest actress of her time. She made a spectacular comeback in *The Glass Menagerie* (1945), giving one of the more memorable performances in Broadway history. ∎ See *Laurette* (1955), a biography written by her daughter Marguerite Taylor Courtney.

TAYLOR, MAXWELL DAVENPORT (1901–1987), U.S. general. The only child of a Missouri railroad attorney, a graduate of West Point (1922), and a scholar of languages, Taylor was a World War II paratroop commander who became U.S. Army chief of staff in 1955. He resigned (1959) in opposition to Pres. Dwight D. Eisenhower's administration's reliance on massive nuclear retaliation. Pres. John Kennedy adopted Taylor as his personal military representative in 1961, appointed him chairman of the Joint Chiefs of Staff (1962), and pursued the general's policy of limited conventional warfare in Vietnam, where Taylor served as U.S. ambassador (1964–65). He wrote *The Uncertain Trumpet* (1959), *Responsibility and Response* (1967), and his memoirs, *Swords and Plowshares* (1972). ∎ See biography by John M. Taylor (1989).

TAYLOR, PAUL (1930–   ), U.S. modern dancer and choreographer. Taylor began to study dance while a college student majoring in painting, and during summer breaks he worked under Martha Graham, José Limón, and Doris Humphrey. He performed in Graham's troupe (from 1955), winning acclaim in the late 1950s as a soloist in many new roles. He formed (1954) his own dance troupe and left (1962) Graham's company to devote himself to choreographic efforts. He staged experimental, suggestive dances, whose titles were often as puzzling as the dances themselves, and made numerous international tours with his company. Among his best-known works were *Seven New Dances* (1957), *Aureole* (1962), *Esplanade* (1975), *American Genesis* (1975), *Airs* (1978), and *Company B* (1991). ∎ See his autobiography, *Private Domain* (1987).

TAYLOR, RICHARD E. (1929–   ), Canadian-U.S. physicist. Taylor was born in Medicine Hat, then a small prairie town in Alberta, and studied at the University of Alberta

(B.S. 1950; M.S. 1952). He moved to California to study physics at Stanford University (Ph.D. 1962) and taught there (1962–). In collaboration with Henry W. Kendall and Jerome Friedman at the two-mile-long, high-energy particle accelerator at the Stanford Linear Accelerator Center (1967–73), Taylor performed electron-scattering experiments that confirmed the existence of the subatomic particles known as quarks, the fundamental building blocks of protons and neutrons. The three researchers also identified gluons, electrically neutral particles that bind quarks together. Taylor, Kendall, and Friedman shared the 1990 Nobel Prize in Physics for their experiments.

TAYLOR, ROBERT (Spangler Arlington Brugh; 1911–1969), U.S. film actor. A cellist and drama student from Nebraska, Taylor achieved great popularity during the 1930s as one of Hollywood's most glamorous actors. Under contract to MGM for 25 years, he specialized in romantic leads (*Camille*, 1936) and knightly roles (*Ivanhoe*, 1952). *Billy the Kid* (1941) is considered one of his best films. A handsome man of limited acting ability, Taylor left MGM in 1959, worked on TV in "The Detectives" (1959–62), and ended his career with several quickie westerns.

TAYLOR, TELFORD (1908–1998), U.S. attorney. A graduate of Williams College and Harvard Law School (1932), Taylor went to Washington, D.C., in 1933 to work for the New Deal administration. After World War II army service, he was promoted to brigadier general and chief U.S. prosecutor at the Nuremberg war-crimes trials (1946–49). The tribunal served no useful purpose except as a cautionary example, he argued in a 1970 book, *Nuremberg and Vietnam,* pointing out the potential criminality of U.S. conduct in Vietnam. He was also a critic of Sen. Joseph McCarthy during the 1950s and an opponent of the war in Vietnam during the 1960s and 1970s. A professor at Columbia (1958–76) and Cardozo (from 1976) law schools, Taylor also wrote books about Soviet Jewish dissidents, *Courts of Terror* (1976), and pre–World War II appeasement, *Munich: The Price of Peace* (1979). He also wrote *The Anatomy of the Nuremberg Trials* (1992).

TAYMUR, MAHMUD (1894–1973), Egyptian short-story writer. His name is also spelled Tymur. Born into a wealthy and intellectual family, Taymur was one of the century's most influential Arabic writers. A pioneer of the Arabic short story, he exposed human foibles and failings in numerous stories of life in Cairo. Many of his characters—from poor and disreputable elements of society—became famous throughout Egypt. Taymur also wrote plays, travel books, literary criticism, and edited a magazine devoted to the short story. His translated works included *Tales from Egyptian Life* (1949) and *The Call of the Unknown* (1964).

TCHELITCHEW, PAVEL (1898–1957), Russian-born U.S. artist. Tchelitchew was a member of the Russian upper classes who fled the 1917 revolution to Berlin, where he received his first commissions to design stage sets. In Paris he worked for the ballet impresario Sergei Diaghilev and was a leader of the neoromantic opposition to abstract art. Tchelitchew, who emigrated to the United States in 1934, experimented with changing perspectives and surrealistic elements in his multifaceted "metamorphoses." He also painted portraits, including several of the British poet Edith Sitwell. ■ See Parker Tyler, *The Divine Comedy of Pavel Tchelitchew* (1967).

TCHERNICHOWSKY, SAUL. *See TSCHERNICHOWSKY, SAUL.*

TEAGARDEN, JACK (Weldon John Teagarden; 1905–1964). U.S. jazz musician and singer. One of the few white jazz masters, Teagarden was a self-taught trombonist whose style was widely imitated. From his arrival on the jazz scene in the late 1920s—his recording debut was in 1927—he demonstrated a brilliant technique, tremendous range, and a continuous flow of melodic innovations and improvisations. He toured with his own band (1939–47; 1951–59) and played with Louis Armstrong (1947–51). ■ See biography by Jay D. Smith and Len Guttridge (1960).

TEAGLE, WALTER CLARK (1878–1962), U.S. industrialist. Born into an oil family, Teagle worked for New Jersey Standard Oil and Imperial Oil of Canada before becoming head of the Standard Oil Co. (New Jersey). As president (1917–37) and board chairman (1937–42), he was credited with expanding the oil-export field, acquiring foreign sources of oil, and building up Standard's tanker fleet. Teagle was also known for his enlightened labor practices—he established an 8-hour day (1925) and 40-hour week (1932)—and served the New Deal as a member of the Industrial Advisory Board and National Labor Board. ■ See biography by Bennett H. Wall and George S. Gibbs (1974).

TEAGUE, WALTER DORWIN (1883–1960), U.S. industrial designer. Trained at the Art Students League in New York (1903–07), Teague founded his own company (1926) and was a pioneering figure in U.S. industrial design. With clients such as Eastman Kodak, National Cash Register, General Foods, Du Pont, Ford, and U.S. Steel, Teague achieved fame with designs of cameras, automobiles, office machines, service stations, and airline and train interiors. He designed numerous exhibitions for the New York World's Fair (1939) and did the interior of the Air Force Academy, Colorado Springs, Colorado. He wrote *Design This Day* (1940) and *Land of Plenty* (1947).

TEASDALE, SARA (1884–1933), U.S. poet. Born in Missouri, Teasdale toured Europe and the Near East during her twenties, writing *Sonnets to Duse and Other Poems* (1907). *Helen of Troy and Other Poems* (1911) brought her critical recognition, and *Love Songs* (1917) a special Poetry Society

Prize. Teasdale stood apart from the literary experimentation of her time, writing in the romantic tradition. Her finest poems are short personal lyrics, bare of imagery, that articulate mood, not eternal truths. After her divorce (1929), she lived as a semi-invalid and committed suicide shortly before the appearance of her collection, *Strange Victory* (1933). *Collected Poems* (1937) was published posthumously. ▪ See biographies by Margaret H. Carpenter (1960) and William Drake (1979).

TEBALDI, RENATA (1922–   ), Italian opera singer. Chosen by conductor Arturo Toscanini to sing at the post–World War II reopening of La Scala in Milan (1946), Tebaldi soon became the leading soprano there (1949–54) and developed into one of the foremost singers of the postwar era. Famous for her serene and elegant style of singing, she was widely acclaimed for her portrayals of Verdi and Puccini heroines, notably in such operas as *Tosca, Aida, Madama Butterfly,* and *Otello.* She made her U.S. debut with the San Francisco Opera (1950) and sang with New York's Metropolitan Opera from 1955 to 1973. ▪ See her autobiography (1999); studies by Victor Seroff (1961) and Kenn Harris (1974); and biography by Carlamaria Casanova (1987; Eng. trans. 1995).

TEDDER, ARTHUR WILLIAM TEDDER, 1st BARON (1890–1967), British air marshal. A Cambridge history graduate (1912), Tedder served in the Royal Flying Corps during World War I. During World War II, as chief of the Royal Air Force Middle East command (1940–43), he helped drive the Germans from North Africa, and his bombing strategy while Mediterranean commander (1943) helped assure the success of the Allied offensive in Sicily and mainland Italy. From December 1943 until the end of the war he was deputy supreme commander (to Gen. Dwight Eisenhower) of all Allied forces. His concentrated bombing of German communications lines contributed greatly to the successful D-Day Normandy landings (June 6, 1944) and to the German defeat in Western Europe. After the war he served as air chief of staff (1946–50). ▪ See his memoirs, *With Prejudice* (1966).

TEILHARD DE CHARDIN, PIERRE (1881–1955), French paleontologist and philosopher. Teilhard received extensive training in the natural sciences, geology, and paleontology during and after his preparation for ordination (1911) as a Jesuit priest; in 1922 he completed doctoral studies in paleontology at the Sorbonne. Teilhard returned from his first expedition (1923–24) to China to a teaching post at the Institut Catholique in Paris, but his Jesuit superiors mistrusted his attempts to reconcile religious faith with his notion of evolution. Forbidden to teach in France or to publish any but purely scientific writings, he returned (1926) to China, where he collaborated in work that led to the discovery of Peking Man, and he remained there for 20 years. In his im-

mensely influential and controversial writings, all published posthumously, he integrated a scientific understanding of evolution with sophisticated and optimistic theological views on the human being's place in the universe. His best-known work was *The Phenomenon of Man* (1938–40; pub. 1955; Eng. trans. 1959). ▪ See biographies by Claude Cuénot (Eng. trans. 1965), Robert Speaight (1967), and Mary and Ellen Lukas (1977); and Ursula King, *Spirit of Fire* (1996).

TE KANAWA, DAME KIRI (1944–   ), New Zealand opera singer. A New Zealand lyric soprano of Maori parentage, Te Kanawa attended St. Mary's College in Auckland, then studied at the London Opera Centre and made her London debut in 1969. In 1970, she gave her first performance at the Royal Opera House, Covent Garden. Her first major role was the Countess in Mozart's *Marriage of Figaro* in San Francisco (1972). She made her Met debut as *Desdemona* in 1974. Te Kanawa was most familiar to opera enthusiasts in London, where she appeared regularly at Covent Garden in such roles as Elvira in *Don Giovanni,* Mimi in *La Bohème,* and Tatiana in *Eugene Onegin.* She won acclaim for her warm, vibrant voice, her simple style, and her stunning stage presence. ▪ See biography by David Fingleton (1983) and Garry Jenkins, *Kiri* (1998).

TELLER, EDWARD (1908–   ), Hungarian-born U.S. physicist. Teller studied at Leipzig (Ph.D. 1930) and taught at Göttingen (1931–33) before fleeing from Nazi Germany. He studied with Niels Bohr in Copenhagen (1934) and emigrated to the United States, where he worked with Enrico Fermi in producing the first nuclear chain reaction (University of Chicago, 1942). He worked (1943–45) on the Manhattan Project, which the U.S. government established to produce an atomic bomb, and subsequently formulated the theoretical foundations for the hydrogen bomb, which was first exploded in 1952. One of the most controversial scientists of his time, Teller, the "father of the H-bomb," advocated U.S. nuclear supremacy over the Soviet Union, supported the buildup of nuclear weapons (including weapons in space), and opposed the nuclear test ban treaty. He was one of the architects of Pres. Ronald Reagan's Strategic Defense Initiative (SDI) or "Star Wars." He subsequently advocated the use of missile interceptors and nuclear explosions to prevent asteroids from colliding with the Earth. He headed the weapons laboratory at Livermore, California (1958–60), and was a professor of physics at the University of California, Berkeley (1953–75), and associate director of its Lawrence Livermore Radiation Laboratory (1974–75). His writings include *The Legacy of Hiroshima* (1962; with Allen Brown), *Our Nuclear Future* (1958; with Albert L. Latter), *Energy from Heaven and Earth* (1979), *Better a Shield than a Sword* (1981), and *Conversations on the Dark Secrets of Physics* (1991). ▪ See Stanley A. Blumberg and Gwinn Owens, *Energy and Conflict* (1976), and biography by Stanley A. Blumberg (1990).

TEMIN, HOWARD MARTIN (1934–1994), U.S. virologist. Temin did graduate work at the California Institute of Technology with biologist Renato Dulbecco (1955–59) before joining the faculty of the University of Wisconsin (1960). In 1970 he confirmed his own theory of a reverse pattern of genetic information channeling, from RNA to DNA, which helped scientists understand how viruses could cause a normal cell to become malignant. He shared the 1975 Nobel Prize in Physiology or Medicine with Dulbecco and David Baltimore.

TEMPLE, SHIRLEY (1928–   ), U.S. film actress. From her debut at age 3, Temple sang, tap-danced, and charmed her way through the Depression to become the greatest child star in Hollywood history. Urged on by her mother, the dimpled, curly-haired tot starred in *The Little Colonel* (1935), *Wee Willie Winkie* (1937), and *Rebecca of Sunnybrook Farm* (1938). She was less successful as an adolescent in *Miss Annie Rooney* (1942) and she made her last film in 1949. Temple later hosted a TV show and, as Shirley Temple Black, became active in conservative Republican politics; she was appointed a U.S. representative to the United Nations (1969) and served as ambassador to Ghana (1974–76), White House chief of protocol (1976–77), and ambassador to Czechoslovakia (1989–92). ■ See her autobiography, *Child Star* (1988), and studies by Jeanine Basinger (1975) and Lester and Irene David (1983).

TEMPLE, WILLIAM (1881–1944). British theologian. Temple's father, Frederick Temple, served as archbishop of Canterbury (1896–1902). Before ordination, William Temple studied philosophy at Oxford and was involved in education and social work, areas that held his lifetime interest. His social and international concerns brought him international respect as bishop of Manchester (1921–29) and archbishop of York (1929–42). While archbishop of Canterbury (1942–44), he sought Christian principles to help guide the world at war. He worked toward greater autonomy for the Church of England and supported the ecumenical movement; he was a moving spirit behind the formation of the World Council of Churches (1948). A Christian socialist, he believed that Christian revelation occurred through personal encounters and preached in idealistic terms that helped to make Labour party tenets more palatable to the public. In this way, he contributed to their 1945 victory. His publications included *Nature, Man and God* (1934), *Christianity and the Social Order* (1942), and *The Church Looks Forward* (1944). ■ See studies by Frederic A. Iremonger (1948), Joseph F. Fletcher (1963), and John Kent (1992).

TEMPLEMAN, WILLIAM GLADSTONE (1911–1970), British agricultural scientist. Associated with the Jealott's Hill Research Station (1933–69), Templeman pioneered in the discovery of hormone-selective weed killers. His work with synthetic chemicals during the early 1940s (with W. A. Sexton and R. E. Slade) led to the worldwide use of herbicides and to increased yields of cereal crops throughout the world.

TEMPLEWOOD, SAMUEL JOHN HOARE, 1st VISCOUNT. *See HOARE, SAMUEL JOHN.*

TENG HSIAO-PING. *See DENG XIAOPING.*

TENNANT, KYLIE (1912–1988), Australian novelist. Tennant searched the crannies of her society, gathering material for her realistic tragicomic novels. More interested in social conglomerates than in the individual psyche, she sometimes overpopulated her books. Tennant contrasted city and country: *Foveaux* (1939), *Ride on Stranger* (1943), and *Time Enough Later* (1943) described urban maladies; *The Battlers* (1941), *Lost Haven* (1947), and *The Honey Flow* (1956) evoked the beauty of rural Australia. She also wrote plays, history, poetry, and travel books. Among Tennant's later works were the biography *Evatt: Politics and Justice* (1970) and the autobiographical memoir *The Man on the Headland* (1971). She was a critic for the *Sydney Morning Herald* (1953–76). ■ See her autobiography, *The Missing Heir* (1986), and Margaret Dick, *The Novels of Kylie Tennant* (1966).

TENZING NORGAY (1914–1986), Nepalese Sherpa mountaineer. A participant as a porter and later *sirdar* (head porter) in numerous Himalayan mountain-climbing expeditions from 1935 onward, Tenzing became the first person (with Sir Edmund Hillary) to reach the summit of the 29,028-foot Mt. Everest, the world's highest mountain (May 29, 1953). In his later years he was a director of the Himalayan Mountaineering Institute in Darjeeling, India. ■ See his autobiographies, *Tiger of the Snows* (1955) and *After Everest* (1977), and Yves Malartic, *Tenzing of Everest* (Eng. trans. 1954).

TERESA, MOTHER. *See MOTHER TERESA.*

TERESHKOVA, VALENTINA VLADIMIROVNA (1937–   ), Soviet cosmonaut. Tereshkova was an amateur parachutist before joining the cosmonaut-training program. On June 16, 1963, she became the first woman in space when she was launched into orbit in the *Vostok VI* spacecraft. During the 71-hour, 48-orbit flight, her vehicle orbited with the previously launched *Vostok V;* at one point; the two crafts were only 3.1 miles apart. Tereshkova's performance confirmed Soviet test results that women can withstand the physical and emotional stress of space flight as well as, if not better than, men. Tereshkova headed the Soviet Women's Committee (1968–87) and was a member of the Supreme Soviet Presidium (1974–90), and the Central Committee of the Communist party (1971–90), served as a people's deputy (1989–91), and headed the Center for International Scientific and Cultural Cooperation (1994–   ).

TERKEL, STUDS (Louis Terkel; 1912–   ), U.S. oral historian, writer, and broadcaster. Terkel was born in New York City; from age 11 he lived in Chicago. When his father became ill, his mother managed a hotel, where Terkel spent hours talking to local people who socialized there. He graduated from the University of Chicago (1932) and completed its law school (1934), but turned away from the legal profession. In his mid-twenties he broke into broadcasting with "Wax Museum" (1945), a radio interview show that developed his knack for getting people to talk. He later hosted the Chicago TV show "Studs' Place" (1950–53). He wrote newspaper columns on jazz and published *Giants of Jazz* (1957) but became best known for books that recorded candid accounts of the experiences of Americans from all walks of life. *Division Street: America* (1967) reflected despair among city dwellers; *Hard Times* (1970) chronicled the Great Depression; *Working* (1974) contained accounts of how people earn a livelihood; and *American Dreams: Lost and Found* (1980) recorded 100 accounts of people's dreams and what happened to them. *The Good War: An Oral History of World War II* (1984) won a Pulitzer Prize. His later books included *The Great Divide: Second Thoughts on the American Dream* (1988), *Race: How Blacks and Whites Think and Feel About the American Obsession* (1992), *Coming of Age: The Story of Our Century by Those Who've Lived It* (1996), and *Spectator: Talk About Movies and Plays with the People Who Make Them* (1999). ■ See his autobiography, *Talking to Myself* (1977), and biography by Tony Parker (1996).

TERMAN, LEWIS MADISON (1877–1956), U.S. psychologist. A member of the faculty of Stanford University (1910–43), Terman pioneered in the measurement of intelligence and achievement. He constructed the Stanford-Binet intelligence test (1916), the English-language version of the French Binet-Simon test that served as the standardized IQ test for more than 30 years. *The Measurement of Intelligence* (1916) was a guide for the use of the test and the IQ scale. He believed in the heritability of intelligence and inaugurated (1921) a long-term study of gifted children (*Genetic Studies of Genius*, 5 vols., 1926–59) that showed that they maintained high achievement over time and tended to become healthy and stable adults. Terman also helped develop the U.S. Army intelligence tests during World War I, and was coauthor of the Stanford Achievement Tests during the 1920s. His other books included *Sex and Personality* (1936) and *Psychological Factors in Marital Happiness* (1938). ■ See May V. Seagoe, *Terman and the Gifted* (1975), and biography by Henry Minton (1988).

TERRA, GABRIEL (1873–1942), Uruguayan political leader. Terra was basically a technocrat, a professor of political economy, and cabinet minister who was a Colorado party deputy to the Uruguayan congress (1905–25). Elected president in 1930, he dissolved the legislative and the national council (1933), promulgated a new constitution (1934) that enhanced presidential powers, and ruled until 1938, when he yielded to his elected successor, his brother-in-law, Gen. Alfredo Baldomir.

TERRY, PAUL HOUGHTON (1887–1971), U.S. cartoonist. A pioneer in animated cartoons, Terry produced more than 1,000 films in a career lasting 40 years (1915–55) and introduced numerous animation techniques that simplified the production of cartoon films. He produced the famous silent series *Aesop's Film Fables* during the 1920s and during the 1930s created the Terrytoon series, which "starred" such characters as Mighty Mouse and Heckle and Jeckle.

TERTZ, ABRAM. *See SINYAVSKY, ANDREI.*

TERZAGHI, KARL (1883–1963), Austrian-born U.S. engineer. A graduate of the Technische Hochschule in Graz (D. Sc. 1912), Terzaghi founded the field of soil mechanics—the study of the properties and utilization of soil under stress. His book, *Erdbaumechanik* ("soil mechanics," 1925), established the field as a branch of mechanical and civil engineering. He taught at the Massachusetts Institute of Technology (1925–29), the Technische Hochschule in Vienna (1929–38), and Harvard (1946–56) in addition to working as a consulting engineer on projects throughout the world. Selections of his writings and a brief biography appeared in *From Theory to Practice in Soil Mechanics* (1960).

TETRAZZINI, LUISA (1871–1940), Italian opera singer. Tetrazzini was born and educated in Florence, where she made her debut in 1895 as Meyerbeer's *L'Africaine*. She sang in operas all over Italy, South America, Poland, and Russia before first attracting international attention in a performance of *La Traviata* at London's Covent Garden in 1907. A great coloratura known for her vocal technique and her brilliant singing of staccato passages, Tetrazzini made her debut in New York's Metropolitan Opera in 1908, followed by a successful U.S. tour and a season with the Chicago Opera Company (1913–14). ■ See her reminiscences, *My Life of Song* (1921), and biography by Charles N. Gattey (1995).

TEY, JOSEPHINE (Elizabeth MacKintosh; 1896–1952), Scottish mystery writer. A physical education teacher, Tey spent her last 28 years caring for her ailing parents in rural Scotland and writing. She wrote novels, historical plays, biographies, and short fictions (some under the pseudonym Gordon Daviot), but was best known for her eight sophisticated mystery novels, including *The Man in the Queue* (1929) and *The Singing Sands* (1952). Most featured Scotland Yard inspector Alan Grant. In *The Daughter of Time* (1951), Grant tries to clear the name of King Richard III. *Miss Pym Disposes* (1946) is based on Tey's experiences in a physical-training college. ■ See study by Sandra Roy (1980).

THAELMANN (or THÄLMANN), ERNST (1886–1944), German political leader. A leader of the left wing of the German Communist party, Thaelmann served as party chairman from 1925 and held high Comintern posts during the 1920s and 1930s. He served in the Reichstag (1924–33) and was the Communist candidate for president in 1925 and 1932, when he received more than 5 million votes. He went underground after Adolf Hitler came to power but was soon arrested and sent to Buchenwald concentration camp where he was executed in August 1944.

THALBERG, IRVING GRANT (1899–1936), U.S. film producer. The "boy genius" of Hollywood, Thalberg became studio manager of Universal Pictures at age 21 and Metro-Goldwyn-Mayer's vice president in charge of production at age 24. In 12 years at MGM (1924–36), he displayed great skill in picking talent, editing scripts, and supervising production; he was known for the consistently high artistic standards of his films. Among his best-known productions were *The Big Parade* (1925), *Grand Hotel* (1932), *The Barretts of Wimpole Street* (1934), *Mutiny on the Bounty* (1935), The Marx Brothers' *A Night at the Opera* (1935), *Camille* (1936), and *The Good Earth* (1937). ■ See biography by Bob Thomas (1969).

THANT, U (1909–1974), Burmese diplomat. The son of a prosperous farmer, Thant was a classmate of U Nu at Rangoon University. He worked as an educational administrator during the 1930s and 1940s and after independence (1948) he held several Burmese government posts, including that of permanent representative to the United Nations (1957–61). As secretary-general of the United Nations (1961–71), Thant was an activist who was often critical of the superpowers. He was concerned with such major events as the Cuban missile crisis, the Congo civil war, and the conflict in Southeast Asia. He was criticized in the West for withdrawing U.N. forces from Egypt (1967) shortly before the outbreak of the Arab Israeli War. ■ See his memoirs, *View from the UN* (1978), and biography by June Bingham (1966).

THARP, TWYLA (1941–), U.S. dancer and choreographer. Tharp studied music and dance as a child and took both ballet and modern-dance lessons while a student at Barnard College in New York. After performing with the Paul Taylor Dance Company (1963–65), she formed her own small troupe (1965) and began to choreograph and dance offbeat, witty, and technically precise works that combined modern and traditional dance movements. She gained critical and popular acclaim during the 1970s with her innovative jazz ballets, *Eight Jelly Rolls, The Bix Pieces, Raggedy Dances, Deuce Coupe,* and *Sue's Leg,* and she also choreographed the movie *Hair* (1979). Her works were performed by the City Center Joffrey Ballet and the American Ballet Theatre as well as by her own company. Tharp's works from the 1980s and 1990s included *In the Upper Room, On the Wing, How Near Heaven,* and *Known by Heart.* ■ See her autobiography, *Push Comes to Shove* (1992).

THATCHER, MARGARET (Margaret Roberts; 1925–), British political leader. The daughter of a prosperous small-town grocer who also served as mayor, Thatcher studied chemistry at Oxford (B.Sc. 1947) and was president of the University Conservative Association. After several years as a research chemist she studied law, worked as a tax attorney, and was elected to Parliament as a Conservative from a suburban London district (1959). A leader of her party's right wing, she served as secretary of state for health and science in the government of Edward Heath (1970–74) and was elected party leader in 1975. Britain's first woman prime minister (1979–90), she sought to shift the economy toward private enterprise by selling off state-owned enterprises, and pursued monetarist financial policies. She also cut welfare-state programs, reduced funding for education and the arts, and introduced legislation to curb union power. Although inflation dropped to 5 percent per annum by 1985, the unemployment rate rose to nearly 14 percent. An outspoken anticommunist, she generally supported the foreign policies of the conservative U.S. Reagan administration. Her government received wide support for recapturing the Falkland Islands (Malvinas) from Argentina (1982). By the late 1980s her autocratic style, controversial economic policies, and advocacy of an unpopular "poll tax" alienated her from many Conservative party members and leaders. She resigned in 1990, replaced by John Major. Thatcher was the longest-serving British prime minister of the century and was made a life peer in 1992. ■ See her memoirs, *The Downing Street Years* (1993) and *The Path to Power* (1995); studies by Nicholas Wapshott and George Brock (1983), Bruce Arnold (1984), and Russell Lewis (1984); and Hugo Young, *The Iron Lady* (1989).

THEILER, MAX (1899–1972), South African–born, U.S. microbiologist. Born in Pretoria and educated in Cape Town and London, Theiler worked in the department of tropical medicine at the Harvard Medical School (1922–30). There he carried out important research on amebic dysentery and rat-bite fever. He did research at the Rockefeller Institute for Medical Research in New York City from 1930 to 1964. His great contribution to medicine was the development of a vaccine for yellow fever (1937), for which he won the 1951 Nobel Prize in Physiology or Medicine.

THEODORAKIS, MIKIS (Michalis Theodorakis; 1925–), Greek composer. After embracing Marxism as a resistance fighter against the Germans during World War II, Theodorakis spent most of his life attempting to revolutionize Greek culture and politics. Greece's most popular composer, he infused his orchestral, theatrical, and popular music with militant and revolutionary themes. He was a leader of the left-wing Lambrikis youth movement (1963) and was elected to parliament (1964). However, he was jailed by the military junta from 1967 to 1970. In exile from 1970 to 1974, he was an outspoken critic of the regime. He was best known abroad for his film scores for *Zorba the Greek* (1964), *Z*

(1969), and *State of Siege* (1973) and for his infectious "bouzouki" melodies, derived from Greek folk music. After returning to Greece he again served in parliament (1981–86). In the late 1980s he supported the conservative New Democratic party and served in parliament (1989–93) and as a minister of state (1990–92). His later musical works included the cantata *Sadoukeon Passion* (1982), Symphony No. 7 (1983), and the operas *Medea* (1990) and *Elektra* (1993). ■ See his *Journal of Resistance* (Eng. trans. 1973) and studies by George Giannaris (1972) and Gail Holst (1980).

THEORELL, (AXEL) HUGO TEODOR (1903–1982), Swedish biochemist. Theorell received his M.D. from the Karolinska Institute in Stockholm (1930), but after an attack of polio left him crippled, he turned his energies to research. He was the first to isolate the oxygen-carrying protein, myoglobin, in crystalline form (1932). Later, he isolated (1934) the sugar-converting yellow enzyme and discovered that it is composed of two parts: the nonprotein coenzyme, which acts as a catalyst, and the apoenzyme, which is pure protein. His research yielded the first detailed study of enzyme action and the first detailed analysis of a coenzyme. For his pioneering research on oxidation enzymes, he was awarded the Nobel Prize in Physiology or Medicine (1955). His other accomplishments included the devising of a blood test for drunkenness. From 1937 to 1970 he directed the biochemistry department at the Karolinska Institute.

THIBAUD, JACQUES (1880–1953), French violinist. After studying at the Paris Conservatory, Thibaud made his first foreign tour as a soloist in 1899, soon gaining a reputation as the leading master of the French school of classic violin playing. He produced an exceptionally pure tone and was best known for his performances of music by Mozart, Beethoven, Franck, Fauré, and Debussy. In addition to solo recitals, he appeared frequently as part of a trio with pianist Alfred Cortot and cellist Pablo Casals.

THICH NHAT HANH (1926–), Vietnamese-born religious leader and peace activist. A Buddhist monk from the age of 16, Thich Nhat Hanh founded the first Buddhist high school in Vietnam (1952) and was a cofounder of Van Hanh Buddhist University in Saigon (1959). In the early 1960s he studied comparative religion at Princeton and Columbia universities. Upon returning to war-torn Vietnam (1963), he popularized a movement—he called it "engaged Buddhism"— that combined traditional meditation and nonviolent civil disobedience in the quest for peace and social justice. He founded the School of Youth for Social Service (1964), which had attracted 10,000 members by 1975. Touring Europe and the United States (1966), he advocated a peaceful solution to the conflict in Vietnam and was prohibited from returning to his homeland. He was given asylum in France, where he established a retreat center that became a haven for peace and social activists from around the world. He fre-

quently visited the United States, where his advocacy of a socially engaged spiritual philosophy attracted thousands of followers. He wrote more than 75 books of prose, poetry, and prayers, including *Vietnam: Lotus in a Sea of Fire* (Eng. trans. 1967), *Vietnam Poems* (Eng. trans. 1972), *The Miracle of Mindfulness* (Eng. trans. 1987), *The Heart of Understanding* (Eng. trans. 1988), and *Hermitage Among the Clouds* (Eng. trans. 1993). His guided meditations are in *The Blooming of a Lotus* (Eng. trans. 1993).

THIEU, NGUYEN VAN (1923–), Vietnamese political leader. Thieu, who was born into a family of small landowners and fishermen, joined the nationalist Vietminh organization in 1945. He left it (1946) to enlist in a military academy, and he served in the French colonial army (1949–54). As an officer in the South Vietnamese army (from 1954), Thieu supported Pres. Ngo Dinh Diem and only reluctantly took part in the coup that overthrew him (1963). In 1965 he became titular head of state in a military government headed by Nguyen Cao Ky. As president of South Vietnam during the critical years of the Vietnam War (1967–75), he led an authoritarian government that suppressed opposition and was charged with nepotism and corruption. Despite massive U.S. military and economic aid, his forces were unable to defeat communist-led insurgents. As his army and government were collapsing (1975), Thieu fled to Taiwan and then to Britain. He eventually settled in the U.S.

THOMAS, ALBERT (1878–1932), French statesman and historian. Thomas was assistant editor of the socialist newspaper *L'Humanité* (founded 1904) and a leader of the moderate faction within the French Socialist party. A member of the Chamber of Deputies (1910–21), he served as minister of munitions (1916–17) during World War I. He was active in the labor movement and was the first director of the International Labor Organization (ILO; 1919–32). ■ See Edward J. Phelan, *Yes and Albert Thomas* (1950).

THOMAS, (MARTHA) CAREY (1857–1935), U.S. feminist and educator. Despite her parents' objections, Thomas studied at Cornell, then earned a Ph.D. at Zurich (1882). She helped organize Bryn Mawr College for women (1884), serving as dean and English professor, and later as president (1894–1922). After observing worker education in British settlement houses, Thomas established Bryn Mawr's summer school for women in industry (1921). A leading suffragist, she presided over the National College Equal Suffrage League (1906–13). ■ See her writings in Marjorie H. Dobkin, ed., *The Making of a Feminist* (1979), and the biography by Edith Finch (1947).

THOMAS, DYLAN MARLAIS (1914–1953), Welsh-born British poet. Although he published fewer than 100 poems, Thomas was the most popular and one of the most critically acclaimed English-language writers of his time. A poet of the rural world who frequently evoked his Welsh heritage, he most often wrote of birth, childhood innocence, sex, and death. Influenced by surrealism, his highly personal, exuberant, and difficult poetry was marked by puns and wordplays. He achieved great fame in the United States and Britain through his readings, recordings, and radio broadcasts (1945–53). Shy, insecure, self-destructive, and frequently in debt, Thomas lived a bohemian life and was an alcoholic in his last years. Among his best-known works were the poetry collections *Deaths and Entrances* (1946) and *In Country Sleep* (1951), the humorous autobiographical sketch *Portrait of the Artist as a Young Dog* (1940), and the radio play *Under Milk Wood* (1954). ■ See his *Collected Poems* (1953); biographies by John Ackerman (1964), Constantine Fitzgibbon (1965), Paul Ferris (1977), and Jonathan Fryer (1993); and Andrew Sinclair, *Dylan the Bard* (1999).

THOMAS, E. DONNALL (1920–   ), U.S. oncologist. Thomas graduated from Harvard Medical School (M.D. 1946) and served as a clinical professor at Columbia University (1956–63) and as chief oncologist at the University of Washington, Seattle (1963–90). Specializing during the 1950s in the treatment of leukemia, the most incurable form of cancer at the time, Thomas performed successful bone marrow transplants in dogs and then (1956) with identical twins. However, the problem of deadly immune-system rejection of transplanted tissue remained for patients who were not identical twins. Utilizing immunosuppressant drugs and matching tissue types, Thomas overcame the problem and performed (1970) the first successful marrow transplant on a leukemia patient who was not a twin. Subsequent research allowed for transplants from unrelated donors and by 1987 more than 20,000 transplants were performed with survival rates of over 80 percent for certain types of children's leukemia. Thomas shared the 1990 Nobel Prize in Physiology or Medicine with Joseph E. Murray.

THOMAS, LOWELL JACKSON (1892–1981), U.S. news broadcaster, world traveler, and author. Thomas first achieved recognition while in his early twenties by leading two expeditions to remote regions of Alaska and by reporting on his trip through a highly successful lecture tour. A foreign correspondent during World War I, he was commissioned by Pres. Woodrow Wilson to record the history of the war on film and was attached at one time or another to all of the Allied armies. During his mission he met British Col. T. E. Lawrence, joined him in the Arabian desert, and was an eyewitness to his famous desert campaigns. Thomas' book, *With Lawrence in Arabia* (1924), recounted his experiences. In 1930 he inaugurated his daily network news program; he was on the air for 46 years, longer than anyone in the history of network radio. He continued his travels to remote corners of the world, including Tibet (1949), and produced numerous travelogues. ■ See his autobiographies, *Good Evening Everybody* (1976) and *So Long Until Tomorrow* (1977).

THOMAS, NORMAN MATTOON (1884–1968), U.S. political leader. A graduate of Princeton (1905) and the Union Theological Seminary (1911), Thomas was motivated by "grotesque inequalities, conspicuous waste, gross exploitation, and unnecessary poverty" to leave the Presbyterian Church in 1918 and become a socialist. He assumed leadership of the American Socialist party (1926) and became a perennial candidate for public office (including, six times [1928–48], the U.S. presidency). A brilliant orator, Thomas was also a prolific writer whose works included *The Conscientious Objector in America* (1923), *Human Exploitation in the U.S.* (1934), *A Socialist's Faith* (1951), *Great Dissenters* (1961), and *Socialism Reexamined* (1963). ■ See biographies by Harry Fleischmann (rev. ed. 1969) and W. A. Swanberg (1976).

THOMAS, WILLIAM ISAAC (1863–1947), U.S. sociologist. Thomas received a Ph.D. from the University of Chicago (1896) and studied anthropology and sociology in Germany. While teaching at the University of Chicago (1894–1918), he wrote *Sex and Society* (1907) and *Source Book for Social Origins* (1909). A pioneer of social psychology, he was particularly interested in cultural change and personality development, and he helped establish the empirical base of sociology with works such as *The Polish Peasant in Europe and America* (5 vols., 1918–21; with Florian Znaniecki) and *The Unadjusted Girl* (1923).

THOMASHEVSKY, BORIS (1868–1939), Russian-born U.S. actor and theatrical director. A pioneer in the Yiddish theater in the United States, Thomashevsky was active for more than half a century. He appeared in all types of productions, from musical comedies to Shakespearean dramas, and always commanded a large popular following. He built (1912) the National Theater in New York City's Lower East Side, which was a center of Yiddish-language show business for decades, and he introduced many well-known performers, including Bertha Kalish, Joseph Schildkraut, and Sophie Tucker.

THOMPSON, DALEY (1958–   ), British athlete. The son of a Nigerian father and a Scottish mother, Daley graduated from a state-supported boarding school at age 16 and was forced to leave home when he announced his plans to become a decathlete, a competitor in the grueling 10-event track and field specialty. With help from a government stipend, he trained full-time, became the youngest man ever to get 8,000 points in the event (1977), and won the decathlon event at the Commonwealth Games (1978). A world-class sprinter, he won the decathlon championship at the 1980 Olympics (in Moscow), the 1982 Commonwealth Games and European Championship, and the 1983 World Championship. He became the second man in history—Bob Mathias was the first—to win two Olympic decathlon gold medals when he won the event in the 1984 Olympics (in Los Angeles). He repeated as Commonwealth and European champion in 1986. ■ See biography by Skip Rozin (1983).

THOMPSON, DOROTHY (1894–1961), U.S. journalist. A 1935 newsweekly poll ranked Thompson the most important woman in the United States, after the first lady. She started as a foreign correspondent during the 1920s, began a thrice-weekly syndicated column in 1936, and for 20 years contributed a monthly column to the *Ladies' Home Journal.* She was best known for her aggressive antifascist reporting and commentary during the 1930s. Thompson's books included *The New Russia* (1928) and *Listen, Hans* (1942). She was married to novelist Sinclair Lewis (1927–42). ■ See biography by Marion K. Sanders (1973) and Peter Kurth, *American Cassandra* (1990).

THOMPSON, EDWARD HERBERT (1865–1935), U.S. archeologist. An amateur archaeologist with a lifelong interest in Mayan civilization, Thompson served as U.S. consul in the Yucatán (1885–1909) and spent much of his time exploring the Mayan archaeological sites at Chichén Itzá, including the temple, terraced pyramid, and astronomical observatory. His most famous achievement was the dredging and underwater exploration of the Sacred Well, a small oval-shaped lake into which human sacrifices and artifacts were thrown to propitiate the rain god who was believed to live at the bottom of the well. He described his discoveries in *People of the Serpent* (1932).

THOMPSON, EDWARD PALMER (1924–1993), British historian and peace activist. After military service in World War II, E. P. Thompson graduated from Cambridge University. Active in the Communist party until 1956, he subsequently became a leader of the independent New Left movement and chaired the editorial board of the *New Left Review.* An advocate of studying "history from below," he wrote the landmark book, *The Making of the English Working Class* (1963) and founded the Center for the Study of Social History at Warwick University. His biography of William Morris (1955; rev. ed. 1977) and writings on crime and society in *Whigs and Hunters* (1975) and *Albion's Fatal Tree* (1975) enhanced his reputation as a major Marxist historian. During the 1970s and 1980s he was the leader of the European Nuclear Disarmament (END) movement. See his political essays in *Poverty of Theory* (1978) and *Writing by Candlelight* (1980), and his writings on disarmament in *Protest and Survive* (1980) and *Beyond the Cold War* (1982). His later works included *Customs in Common* (1991), *Making History* (1994), *The Romantics: England in a Revolutionary Age* (1997), and *Witness Against the Beast* (1993), a study of William Blake.

THOMPSON, LLEWELLYN E., JR. (1904–1972), U.S. diplomat. The son of a Colorado rancher, Thompson graduated from the University of Colorado (1928) and joined the foreign service (1929). He served as U.S. consul in Moscow and London during World War II and helped negotiate the complex Trieste Settlement (1954) and the Austrian State Treaty (1955) after years of quiet diplomacy. A model diplomat whose skills and expertise were universally admired, Thompson served as ambassador to Moscow twice during the cold war era (1957–62; 1967–69) and helped ease U.S.-Soviet tensions. A confidant of Soviet Premier Nikita Khrushchev, he helped arrange the Camp David meeting between Khrushchev and Pres. Dwight D. Eisenhower (1959) and the Vienna summit between Khrushchev and Pres. John F. Kennedy (1961), and helped negotiate the cultural exchange, nuclear test ban, and strategic arms limitation (SALT) treaties. He also played a major role in resolving the Cuban missile crisis of 1962.

THOMSON, SIR GEORGE PAGET (1892–1975), British physicist. Thomson was the son of the Nobel Prize–winning physicist Sir Joseph J. Thomson. After World War I he worked under his father at the Cavendish Laboratory at Cambridge. While a professor at the University of Aberdeen (1922–30), he conducted experiments (1926) that proved that electrons were diffracted in crystal in a pattern that followed L. V. de Broglie's wave theory of subatomic particles. He shared (with Clinton Davisson) the Nobel Prize in Physics (1937) for his pioneering work. He also taught at the Imperial College of Science in London (1930–52) and was involved in atomic-power research. His books included *The Atom* (1930), *The Wave Mechanics of Free Electrons* (1930), and *Theory and Practice of Electron Diffraction* (1939; with W. Cochrane).

THOMSON, SIR JOSEPH JOHN (1856–1940), British physicist. The Cavendish Professor of Experimental Physics (1884–1919) at Cambridge University and head of the Cavendish Laboratory, J. J. Thomson played a revolutionary role in modern physics by his discovery of the electron (1897). His later studies established the principles of mass spectroscopy (1912) and demonstrated the existence of isotopes among nonradioactive elements (1912). He built the Cavendish Laboratory into a world center of atomic research; seven of his students received Nobel Prizes. He himself received the 1906 Nobel Prize in Physics for his research into the conduction of electricity by gases. ■ See his autobiographical *Recollections and Reflections* (1936) and biographies by Robert J. S. Rayleigh (1942) and G. P. Thomson (1965).

THOMSON, TOM (1877–1917), Canadian artist. Largely self-taught as an artist, Thomson sold his first large canvas, *A Northern Lake* (1913), to the government of Ontario. He spent his last summers sketching in Algonquin Provincial Park and his winters in Toronto painting brilliantly textured scenes of the Canadian northland, notably *The West Wind* (1917) and *The Jack Pine* (1917). ■ See studies by Blodwen Davies (rev. ed. 1967), Joan Murray (1971), and Ottelyn Addison (1975).

THOMSON, VIRGIL (1896–1989), U.S. composer. Although his talents matured among the Paris impressionists, Thomson wrote profoundly American music, often evoking the 19th-century Midwest. Using dissonance sparingly, building tension by abrupt key changes, he transformed simple, modal melodies—folk hymns and ballads—into works of wit and sophistication: *Symphony on a Hymn Tune* (1928); *Four Saints in Three Acts* (1928) and *The Mother of Us All* (1947), operas with texts by Gertrude Stein; *The Filling Station* (1938), for ballet; the score for the film *Louisiana Story* (Pulitzer Prize, 1949); and *Missa Pro Defunctis* (1960). He continued working into his eighties, with such works as *Fanfare for Peace* (1979). From 1940 to 1954 Thomson was music critic for the *New York Herald Tribune*. Selections of his writings are in *American Music Since 1910* (1971) and *The Virgil Thomson Reader* (1981). ■ See his autobiography (1966) and biographies by Kathleen Hoover and John Cage (1959) and Anthony Tommasini (1997).

THOMSON OF FLEET, ROY HERBERT THOMSON, 1st BARON (1894–1976), British newspaper publisher. The son of a barber, Thomson failed in several business ventures before setting up a small radio station in northern Canada (1931). He purchased a small weekly newspaper (1933) and then spent 20 years developing a chain of Canadian newspapers and radio stations. Emigrating to Britain (1953), he purchased the *Scotsman* of Edinburgh and became involved in Scottish television. Thomson continued to enlarge his holdings, eventually acquiring the *Sunday Times* (1962) and the *London Times* (1967). His publishing empire eventually encompassed some 285 stations in Britain, Canada, Africa, Asia, and the West Indies. Thomson contributed to the development of independent newspaper publishing since his management was business oriented and not concerned with exploiting the media for personal or political motives. ■ See his autobiography, *After I Was Sixty* (1975), and biography by Russell Braddon (1966).

'T HOOFT, GERARDUS (1946–), Dutch physicist. 'T Hooft was a student of Martinus J. G. Veltman at the University of Utrecht (Ph.D. 1972) and later taught physics there (1977–). In the early 1970s, 't Hooft and Veltman devised refined mathematical calculations that enabled physicists to understand the quantum structure of electroweak subatomic interactions. (Electroweak interactions are believed to be the basis of electromagnetism and the "weak" nuclear force, which, along with gravity and the "strong" force, are recognized as the four fundamental forces of nature.) The work of 't Hooft and Veltman led to the detection of previously unknown particles, including the top quark, and they shared the 1999 Nobel Prize in Physics.

THOREZ, MAURICE (1900–1964), French political leader. Thorez followed his father and grandfather into the coal mines at age 12, became a socialist at age 19 and a communist the following year. He became secretary-general of the

French Communist party in 1930, a position he held until his death. He was elected to the Chamber of Deputies in 1932 and helped form the popular-front alliance of left-wing parties in 1934. In 1940, during World War II, Thorez went underground, surfacing in 1943 in the Soviet Union. He resumed his parliamentary career in 1945 as minister of state and leader of the largest bloc in the national assembly, but was dismissed from the government in 1947. The stocky, self-taught Thorez was forced to recant his nationalism in 1948, but he remained a Stalinist even after the Soviet leader's repudiation. ■ See his autobiography, *Son of the People* (Eng. trans. 1938).

THORNDIKE, DAME SYBIL (1882–1976), British actress. Thorndike's work developed in the century's early decades at the Gaiety Theatre in Manchester, known for fostering naturalistic acting; in the 1920s she helped enhance the reputation of the Old Vic company. She was seen most often in *Saint Joan,* a role that George Bernard Shaw wrote for her (1923), and which she played some 2,000 times. But far from typecast, she won critical acclaim in a variety of parts, particularly in classic comedy and Shakespeare; she even played Prince Hal in *Henry V* and the Fool in *King Lear.* Britain's foremost actress in a career that spanned seven decades, Dame Sybil Thorndike was a vocal advocate of women's rights, trade unionism, and the peace movement. ■ See her *My Dear One* (1984).

THORPE, JIM (James Francis Thorpe; 1888–1953), U.S. athlete. Thorpe, who was of mixed European and Native American (Sauk and Fox) descent, achieved fame as an All-American football player (1911; 1912) at the Carlisle (Pennsylvania) Indian School. He won the decathlon and the pentathlon at the 1912 Olympic games in Stockholm, but was stripped of his medals the following year after the disclosure that he had earned money playing baseball in 1909 and 1910. (His medals were restored posthumously by the International Olympic Committee in 1982.) The scandal did not affect his popularity as a sports superhero, and he played both professional baseball (1913–19) and professional football (1917–29). He also served as first president (1920–21) of the American Professional Football Association, which later became the National Football League. In 1950 he was selected by nearly 400 sportswriters, in an Associated Press poll, as the greatest athlete of the first half of the century. ■ See Jack Newcombe, *Best of the Athletic Boys* (1975), and study by Robert W. Wheeler (1981).

THUKU, HARRY (1895–1970), Kenyan political leader. Trained as a clerk, Thuku became secretary (1920) of the Kikuyu Central Association, the earliest East African nationalist organization. In 1921 he cofounded the East African Association to protect African labor interests and served as its president. After advocating civil disobedience, he was arrested and deported (1922) and came to symbolize anticolonialism. Released in 1930, he became president of the Kikuyu

Central Association (1932–35), but his moderate political views caused dissension and the association split into factions. Thuku founded the Kikuyu Provincial Association (1935), a group dedicated to legal, nonviolent opposition to British rule. Subsequently, he played a minor role in the Kenyan struggle for independence. ■ See his autobiography (1970).

THURBER, JAMES (1894–1961), U.S. humorist and comic artist. Thurber met *New Yorker* editor E. B. White at a party and talked his way onto the staff—as managing editor (1927). He gave up that position (1933), but continued to exert decisive influence on the magazine's tone with his satirical sketches, anecdotes, and stories, as well as his drawings of predatory women, timid men, and improbable animals, mostly canine. The daydreaming hero of his celebrated story "The Secret Life of Walter Mitty" (1947) was immortalized by a scholarly British medical journal, which referred to "the Walter Mitty syndrome." Thurber himself ridiculed psychoanalysis in *Is Sex Necessary?* (1925; with E. B. White) and *Let Your Mind Alone* (1937). His plays included *The Male Animal* (1940; with Elliott Nugent), which mocked collegiate rah-rah, and the revue, *The Thurber Carnival* (1960). Thurber, who went completely blind in midlife, recalled his *New Yorker* career in *The Years with Ross* (1959). ■ See his *Selected Letters* (1981); biographies by Burton Bernstein (1975), Neil A. Grauer (1994), and Harrison Kinney (1995); and study by Robert D. Arner (1979).

THURMOND, (JAMES) STROM (1902–   ), U.S. senator. A schoolteacher from South Carolina, Thurmond studied law by correspondence and was elected to the state legislature in 1933. He also served as a circuit-court judge and was a much-decorated soldier during World War II, after which he served as governor of South Carolina (1947–51) and was nominated as an unsuccessful Dixiecrat candidate for the presidency (1948). Elected to the U.S. Senate (1954), Thurmond conducted a record 24-hour filibuster against civil-rights legislation (1957). After shifting affiliation from Democratic to Republican in 1964, he was a key factor in Richard Nixon's "southern strategy" for election to the presidency in 1968. He exercised a strong voice on the Senate Judiciary (chairman 1981–87; 1995–   ) and Armed Services committees and served as president pro tempore of the Senate (from 1981). The oldest man to ever serve in Congress, Thurmond was elected to an eighth term in 1996 and became the longest-serving senator in U.S. history (41 years, 10 months, 12 days) on May 25, 1997. ■ See Alberta Lachicotte, *Rebel Senator* (1966), and biography by Jack Bass and Marlyn W. Thompson, *Ol' Strom* (1999).

THURSTON, HOWARD (1869–1936) U.S. magician and illusionist. A performer for 45 years, Thurston ran the last of the big-time traveling magic shows, employing 40 assistants and transporting numerous animals and 250 trunks filled with equipment. He was the leading illusionist of his era and was best known for sawing a woman in half, making a piano and piano player disappear, and "the Levitation of Princess Karnac." Thurston toured the world several times and frequently entertained royalty. ■ See his autobiography, *My Life of Magic* (1929).

THURSTONE, LOUIS LEON (1887–1955), U.S. psychologist. Originally trained as an engineer, Thurstone switched to psychology and was a professor at the University of Chicago (1924–52). A pioneer in applying statistical methods to psychological research, he was one of America's most influential social scientists. Thurstone developed widely used attitude and intelligence tests and demonstrated that test performance was influenced by several factors including spatial visualization, perceptual ability, memory, reasoning, and verbal comprehension and fluency. His most important works were *The Vectors of Mind* (1935) and *Multiple-Factor Analysis* (1947).

THYSSEN, FRITZ (1873–1951), German industrialist. Upon the death of his father August (1842–1927), Fritz Thyssen inherited an iron and steel empire that controlled most of Germany's ore reserves and employed 200,000 workers. An early financial supporter of Adolf Hitler and the Nazi party, he organized the Harzburg front, an alliance of Nazis and industrialists that enabled Hitler to take power in 1933. Eventually he became disenchanted with the Nazis and fled to France, but he was captured and spent the war years in a concentration camp. After the war he was convicted of being a "minor Nazi," and he later emigrated to Argentina, where he died. ■ See his apologia, *I Paid Hitler* (Eng. trans. 1941).

TIAN HAN (old style: T'IEN HAN; 1898–1968), Chinese playwright. The pioneer of modern Chinese theater, Tian first became seriously involved with dramatic literature while a student in Tokyo. The publication of two plays in the journal of the Creation Society (1922) brought him widespread recognition. In 1928 he founded the South China Society, a dramatic organization that staged performances throughout China and became the center of the new theater movement. An early proponent of romanticism, he later advocated class struggle and joined the Communist party (1931). He is best known for modernizing Chinese stage techniques, revamping the archaic Chinese stage dialogue, and encouraging new teaching and training methods for the theater. The major force in the Beijing (Peking) theater world during the 1950s, his works included *The White Snake: A Peking Opera* (Eng. trans. 1957). His "historical" play *Kuan Han-ch'ing* (1958; Eng. trans. 1961) was a masked attack on the government and he was subsequently persecuted during the Cultural Revolution of the 1960s. He died in prison.

TIBBETT, LAWRENCE MERVIL (1896–1960), U.S. opera singer. A star at New York's Metropolitan Opera for 25 years (1925–50), Tibbett sang nearly all of the major baritone roles in the French and Italian repertory. The title role of Louis Gruenberg's *The Emperor Jones* (1933) was created for him, and he appeared in the premieres of operas by Deems Taylor and Howard Hanson. Tibbett was also heard frequently on radio shows and seen in several motion pictures and Broadway musicals. ■ See his autobiography, *The Glory Road* (1933), and Hertzel Weinstat, *Dear Rogue* (1996).

T'IEN HAN. *See TIAN HAN.*

TIFFANY, LOUIS COMFORT (1848–1933), U.S. artist, designer, and philanthropist. The son of a prominent merchant who innovated sterling-silver designs and patronized the arts, Tiffany studied in Paris and painted in oils and watercolors. After experimenting with stained glass, he established his own factory (1878) and became known for iridescent and freely formed *favrile* glass, produced in the Art Nouveau style. His impressionistic glass lamps, jewelry, and pottery were extremely popular in the United States and Europe in the pre–World War I era. Tiffany established (1919) a foundation, bearing his name, for art students. ■ See study by Robert Koch (1964).

TIKHONOV, NIKOLAI SEMYONOVICH (1896–1979), Soviet poet and short-story writer. Tikhonov had his literary upbringing in the experimental atmosphere of the 1920s. His popular ballads, lauding manhood and heroic feats, influenced Soviet youth in the 1920s and 1930s. Despite the romantic tone of his writing, he increasingly accepted official literary dicta, and by the 1930s he was already considered by some to be a "government writer." Appointed general secretary of the official writers' union in 1944, he was dismissed by dictator Joseph Stalin's literary overseer, A. A. Zhdanov, two years later. In the late 1950s, Tikhonov played a vocal role in the campaign against his former mentor, the internationally acclaimed writer Boris Pasternak.

TIKHONRAVOV, MIKHAIL KLAVDIEVICH (1900–1974), Soviet rocket engineer. A pioneer in the field of rocketry and spacecraft, Tikhonravov graduated from the Zhukovsky Air Force Engineering Academy (1925). He began research into aerodynamics during the 1920s and designed his first successful rocket in 1933. Collaborating for more than 30 years with Sergei Korolev, the head of the Soviet space program, he helped develop long-range ballistic missiles, pilot-operated spaceships, and automatic space stations.

TILDEN, BILL (William Tatem Tilden II; 1893–1953), U.S. tennis player. Named by sportswriters (1950) as the greatest tennis player of the first half of the century, he won his first U.S. national titles in doubles matches when he teamed up with Mary K. Browne (1913) and Vincent Richards (1918). Thereafter he won the doubles title four times (1921–23; 1927) and the singles six times (1921–25; 1929). With a big serve and consistent baseline play, Tilden anchored the U.S.

Davis Cup team for 11 years (1920–30). He also won three British singles titles at Wimbledon (1920; 1921; 1930). In 1931 Tilden turned professional and for the next 20 years competed on the pro tour, capturing several championships. ■ See his autobiography, *My Story: A Champion's Memoirs* (1948), and biography by Frank Deford (1976).

TILDY, ZOLTÁN (1889–1961), Hungarian political leader. A Protestant minister who became active in Hungarian politics after World War I as a member of the Smallholders party, Tildy was elected to parliament in 1936, and was chosen as prime minister (1945) and later president (1946) of Hungary. He resigned in 1948 in protest against the process of Sovietization. Tildy reappeared briefly in the 1956 revolutionary government, then was imprisoned for three years after the Soviet intervention.

TILLICH, PAUL JOHANNES (1886–1965), German-born U.S. theologian. Tillich earned a Ph.D. in the philosophy of religion at the University of Breslau (1911) and was ordained in the Evangelical Lutheran church the following year. After serving as a chaplain in the German army in World War I, he was prominent in the Religious Socialist movement. Opposing Nazism, he left Germany for the United States (1933), where he taught at Union Theological Seminary, Harvard, and the Chicago Divinity School, and decisively influenced theology, social thought, and the academic study of religion. Seeking to make religion more responsive to everyday human experience, Tillich incorporated psychological principles into his religious framework. He rejected Protestant orthodoxy, asserting that each generation must interpret the Christian message in its own terms. His major work was the three-volume *Systematic Theology* (1951–63). ■ See Carl J. Armbruster, *The Vision of Paul Tillich* (1967), and biography by Wilhelm and Marion Pauck (1976).

TIMERMAN, JACOBO (1923–1999), Argentine newspaper publisher, writer, and political activist. To escape pogroms, Timerman's Jewish family emigrated from the Ukraine to Argentina when he was 5. A lifelong Zionist, he was active during World War II in the Youth League for Freedom, which promoted the Allied cause during a period when Argentina supported the Nazis; he was arrested for his political activities in 1944. He studied engineering, but from 1947 was a writer, editor, and publisher, working in the print and broadcast media. Rising to prominence in Argentina's publishing world, he published two news magazines in the 1960s, then founded *La Opinión* (1971), a liberal newspaper that denounced the government's campaign of terror and documented officially sanctioned anti-Semitism. In 1977, the Argentine junta seized the newspaper and imprisoned Timerman for 29 months. He recounted the torture and anti-Semitism he experienced during captivity in *Prisoner Without a Name, Cell Without a Number* (Eng. trans. 1981). When he was released in 1979, his citizenship was revoked and he was deported to Israel, where he again stirred controversy by condemning government policy in the book *The Longest War—Israel in Lebanon* (Eng. trans. 1982). After Raúl Alfonsin won election in Argentina, Timerman returned to Buenos Aires (1984) and was named chief editor of the daily newspaper *La Razón*. His later works included *Chile: Death in the South* (Eng. trans. 1987) and *Cuba: A Journey* (Eng. trans. 1990).

TIMMERMANS, FELIX (1886–1947), Belgian (Flemish) writer and painter. After surviving a serious illness, Timmermans rejected his previous pessimistic view of life and wrote a series of novels and short stories, including *Pallieter* (1916; Eng. trans. 1924), which celebrated life and nature. His colorfully written works presented a lyrical and idyllic view of small-town life in Flanders and were filled with folkloric elements. Among his other works were romanticized biographies of the artist Pieter Brueghel (1928; Eng. trans. as *Droll Peter,* 1930) and St. Francis (1932; Eng. trans. as *The Perfect Joy of St. Francis,* 1952); the children's Christmas classic, *The Christ Child in Flanders* (1917; Eng. trans. 1961); and *The Triptych of the Three Kings* (1923; Eng. trans. 1936).

TIMOSHENKO, SEMYON KONSTANTINOVICH (1895–1970), Soviet marshal. Timoshenko, who joined the Bolsheviks in 1917, won prominence during the Russian civil war (1918–20) and was one of the few commanders to survive the army purges of the 1930s. As commissar of defense (1940–41) he instituted training and organizational reforms that helped the Red army to prevail in World War II. He contributed significantly to the Soviet victory over Finnish forces (1940). His forces delayed the German advance on Moscow (1941) and liberated Rostov from German occupation (1941). Timoshenko also led Soviet troops on the northwest front, in the Caucasus, and in Bressarabia, and after the war he headed the Belorussian military (1949–60).

TINBERGEN, JAN (1903–1994), Dutch economist. The older brother of zoologist and Nobel laureate Nikolaas Tinbergen, Jan Tinbergen was educated at the University of Leiden and taught at the Eramus University, Rotterdam (previously called the Netherlands School of Economics; 1933–73). He made crucial contributions to economic theory in the 1930s. Tinbergen's analysis of U.S. economic development in *Business Cycles in the USA, 1919–32* (1939) influenced business-cycle theory and suggested methods for economic stabilization. After World War II he directed the Netherlands Central Planning Bureau (1945–55). Using formal statistical techniques for policy analysis and planning, Tinbergen pioneered in the field of econometrics, defending his methods in a famous debate with John Maynard Keynes. His other works included *Econometrics* (1941; Eng. trans. 1951), *Economic Policy: Principles and Design* (1956), *Shaping the World Economy* (1962), *Central Planning* (1964), *Development Planning* (1967; Eng. trans. 1968), *Income Distribution* (1975), *Production, Income and Welfare* (1985),

and *World Security and Equity* (1990). He shared the first Nobel Memorial Prize in Economics (1969) with Ragnar Frisch.

TINBERGEN, NIKOLAAS (1907–1988), Dutch-British zoologist. A cofounder with Konrad Lorenz of the science of ethology (the study of animal behavior), Tinbergen taught at Oxford University (1949–74) and became a British citizen in 1954. He was best known for his studies of the stimuli that trigger specific behavioral responses in animals, and he demonstrated that these responses are adapted to an animal's needs. He analyzed the psychological and environmental basis of behavior in such animals and insects as gulls, wasps, butterflies, and foxes and wrote of the importance of such animal studies to the understanding of human behavior, especially human aggression. His publications included *The Study of Instinct* (1951), *Social Behavior in Animals* (1953), and *The Animal in Its World* (2 vols., 1972–73, with E. A. Tinbergen). A brother of Nobel laureate in economics Jan Tinbergen, he shared with Lorenz and Karl von Frisch the 1973 Nobel Prize in Physiology or Medicine.

TING, SAMUEL CHAO CHUNG (1936–   ), U.S. physicist. Born in Ann Arbor, Michigan, where his father was a student at the University of Michigan, Ting spent his early years in China and on Taiwan before returning to the United States (1956). After receiving his Ph.D. (University of Michigan, 1962), he taught at Columbia University, worked at the European Nuclear Research Center (CERN) in Geneva, and became a professor of physics at the Massachusetts Institute of Technology (1967). In experiments performed (1974) at New York's Brookhaven National Laboratory, Ting's research groups discovered a new subatomic particle, which he called "J," by firing a stream of protons at a stationary target of beryllium. Almost simultaneously, a team headed by Burton Richter at Stanford University discovered the same particle, which Richter called "Psi." Called the greatest discovery in the field of elementary particles, the Psi/J experiments earned for Ting and Richter the 1976 Nobel Prize in Physics.

TING LING. *See DING LING.*

TINGUELY, JEAN (1925–1991), Swiss sculptor. After attending the Basel School of Fine Arts intermittently (1941–45), Jean Tinguely worked on abstract paintings, constructions in metal and wood with paper, and grass structures. Beginning in 1952, he developed mechanical sculptures called *Métamécaniques* ("beyond the machine"), wire and sheet-metal devices that moved and often produced sounds or odors. His experiments went beyond "kinetic art" to "performance art." One of his *Painting Machines* (1955) produced 40,000 paintings while emitting sounds and fumes. The culmination of this genre was *Homage to New York* (1960), which was supposed to destroy itself during a "happening" in the garden of New York City's Museum of Modern Art but malfunctioned and caused a fire. His show in Moscow (1990) included the gigantic *Altar of Western Affluence and Totalitarian Commercialism,* a warning against the evils of a consumer society. ■ See study by K. G. Pontus Hultén (Eng. trans. 1975).

TIOMKIN, DMITRI (1899–1979), Russian-born U.S. film composer. Tiomkin, who composed some of the best film music for westerns, was a pianist from the St. Petersburg Conservatory who emigrated to the United States in 1925. He composed some 160 Hollywood film scores, borrowing heavily from both the European and American classical and folk repertory. The best-known Hollywood film composer, he wrote the scores for *Lost Horizon* (1937), *Duel in the Sun* (1947), and *Giant* (1956), and he won Academy Awards for *High Noon* (1952), *The High and the Mighty* (1954), and *The Old Man and the Sea* (1958). ■ See his autobiography, *Please Don't Hate Me* (1960).

TIPPETT, SIR MICHAEL KEMP (1905–1998), British composer. Trained at the Royal College of Music, London (1923–28; 1930–32), Tippett served as music director of Morley College, London (1940–51), and achieved fame for his *Concerto for Double String Orchestra* (1939) and oratorio *A Child of Our Time* (1943), a politically explicit work reflecting his antifascist and pacifist views. He was a conscientious objector during World War II. His music, which ignored traditional forms, incorporated complex tonal harmonies, rhythms, and counterpoint with elements of jazz and English Renaissance music. It was influenced by the work of composer Igor Stravinsky. His other well-known works included the operas *The Midsummer Marriage* (1952), *King Priam* (1961), *The Knot Garden* (1970), and *The Ice Break* (1976); the choral works *The Vision of St. Augustine* (1965) and *The Mask of Time* (1984); and Symphony No. 2 (1957) and Symphony No. 3 (1972). His later works included *The Blue Guitar* (1983) and *The Mask of Time for Orchestra and Chorus* (1981–84). ■ See his autobiography, *Those Twentieth Century Blues* (1991), his collection of essays, *Moving into Aquarius* (1959; 2nd ed. 1974) and *Music of the Angels* (1980), and studies by David Matthews (1979) and Meirion Bowen (1981).

TIRPITZ, ALFRED VON (1849–1930), German admiral. Tirpitz served as a cruiser squadron commander in east Asia before becoming secretary of state for the navy (1897–1916). He sponsored Germany's plan to achieve naval parity with Britain by 1917, which resulted in an international arms race and increased tensions. At the start of World War I, Tirpitz was refused command of the fleet he had created, and in 1916 he resigned over the government's failure to implement all-out submarine warfare—which was adopted the following year. He served in the Reichstag (1924–28) as a deputy of the German National People's party. ■ See his *My Memoirs* (2 vols.; Eng. trans. 1919) and Jonathon Steinberg, *Yesterday's Deterrent* (1965).

TISELIUS, ARNE (1902–1971), Swedish biochemist. Tiselius received his Ph.D. (1930) from the University of Uppsala and taught there until 1968. While working under Theodor Svedberg, he became interested in techniques for differentiating colloids and heavy molecules. He contrived "the Tiselius apparatus," a U-shaped tube for use in electrophoresis, a procedure for separating heavy molecules (such as proteins) under the influence of an electric field. Tiselius' methods proved particularly applicable to the study of complex blood-serum proteins. He also developed adsorption analysis, utilizing chromatographic methods, which permits separation and analysis of proteins, sugars, salts, acids, and other types of compounds. Tiselius won the 1948 Nobel Prize in Chemistry.

TISO, JOZEF (1887–1947), Slovak priest and political leader. After World War I Tiso joined the Slovak People's party, a clerical movement that sought autonomy from Czechoslovakia. He succeeded Andrej Hlinka as the party's chairman (1938). When Slovakia was granted autonomy after the Munich Pact (1938), Tiso was named premier and subsequently president of the newly founded German puppet state, the Slovak republic (1939–45). Tiso ran a fascist state on the German Nazi model before his government was deposed by the Soviet and Czech armies. Tried and convicted of treason and war crimes, he was executed in Bratislava.

TISZA, COUNT ISTVÁN (1861–1918), Hungarian political leader. The son of a Hungarian premier, Count Tisza was a chauvinistic premier who ran Hungary (1903–05; 1913–17) in behalf of its landed interests. He continued to repress the subject nationalities of the Austro-Hungarian monarchy until the bitter end, resigning in 1917 in opposition to suffrage reform. A supporter of the World War I alliance with Germany, Tisza was blamed by many for Hungary's suffering during the war and was assassinated on the eve of the declaration of Hungarian independence. ■ See study by Gabor Vermes (1985).

TITCHENER, EDWARD BRADFORD (1867–1927), British-born U.S. psychologist. A student of Wilhelm Wundt, the founder of experimental psychology, at Leipzig (Ph.D. 1892), Titchener taught at Cornell University (1892–1927) and helped establish the field of experimental psychology in the United States. The leader of the structural school of psychology, he emphasized the scientific nature of psychology as opposed to its applications and concerned himself with the examination and description of conscious experience from the point of view of the experiencing individual. He was an editor of the *American Journal of Psychology* (1895–1925) and founder of the Society of Experimental Psychology (1904). He wrote more than 200 articles and eight books, including the monumental *Experimental Psychology* (4 vols.; 1901–05) and *A Textbook of Psychology* (1910).

TITCHMARSH, EDWARD CHARLES (1899–1963), British mathematician. A professor of geometry at Oxford (from 1931), Titchmarsh made important contributions to several branches of mathematical analysis, including Fourier series and integrals and the Riemann zeta-function. His research on eigenfunctions of differential equations played an important role in the development of quantum theory. Titchmarsh was also known for his systemization of existing knowledge. His books included the widely used text *The Theory of Functions* (1932) and *Mathematics for the General Reader* (1948).

TITMUSS, RICHARD MORRIS (1907–1973), British social administrator. The self-taught son of a farmer, Titmuss wrote three books on social problems (1938–42) while employed by an insurance company. He participated in a civilian history of World War II, and with *Problems of Social Policy* (1949) he advanced to a professorship of social administration at the London School of Economics. He was an adviser to the Labour party on social-security reform, and his *Essays on "The Welfare State"* (1958) influenced party policies in the 1960s. Titmuss also influenced U.S. legislation with his study of the commercial blood market, *The Gift Relationship* (1970).

TITO, JOSIP BROZ (1892–1980), Yugoslav military and political leader. Born in Croatia, the son of a peasant, Josip Broz was a metalworker and mechanic before serving in the Austrian army during World War I. Captured by the Russians (1915), he fought with the Red army during the civil war and became an organizer for the clandestine Yugoslav Communist party when he returned to Zagreb (1920). He survived Yugoslav imprisonment (1928–34) and the Soviet purges of the 1930s to become head of the Yugoslav Communist party in 1937. (He adopted the party name "Tito" in 1934). His 300,000-member partisan movement gained wide support in its struggle against German and Italian occupying armies during World War II, and Tito took control of the government after the war, establishing a federalized, socialist Yugoslav state. Resisting Stalinist pressures, he became the first communist leader to break with the Soviet Union (1948) and created a "Titoist" brand of communism featuring workers' self-management and the allowance of free market forces and consumerism. In his 35 years of power—as premier and later president for life—he played a major role in the development of the nonaligned movement. ■ See biographies by Phyllis Auty (rev. ed. 1974) and Richard West (1995).

TITTLE, Y. A. (Yelberton Abraham Tittle; 1926–), U.S. football player. One of the most brilliant quarterbacks in football history, Tittle played for the Baltimore Colts (1948–50), San Francisco 49ers (1951–60), and New York Giants (1961–64). An accurate and tricky passer, he had his best years with the Giants, leading them to two division titles and winning Most Valuable Player honors (1961; 1963). He was All-Pro three times (1957; 1962; 1963). He completed 2,427 passes, gained 33,070 yards, and threw 212 touchdown passes during his career.

TITULESCU, NICHOLAS (1882–1941), Rumanian political leader. Titulescu studied law in Paris, returning home to teach at the universities of Iaşi and Bucharest and to write on politico-legal issues such as land and electoral reform. Elected to parliament in 1912, he served as minister of finance (1917–18; 1920–21) and as Rumania's delegate to the Paris Peace Conference. He was his country's delegate to the League of Nations (1920–36), where he was a leader in the movement for peaceful coexistence and collective security. As Rumania's foreign minister (1927–28; 1932–36), he helped to negotiate French-sponsored Balkan Entente of 1934.

TOBEY, MARK (1890–1976), U.S. painter. Tobey began his career as an illustrator and portraitist in Chicago and New York (1911–22). In Seattle (1922–31) and Britain (1931–38) he experimented with many different styles, but after several trips to China and Japan (1934–36), during which he studied Buddhist philosophy and calligraphy, he developed a technique called "white writing" or "white line." A synthesis of oriental brushwork and Western form and content, it enabled him to portray, in abstract terms, his vision of a reality beyond everyday perceptions while still preserving allusions to the natural world. Acclaimed internationally after World War II as one of the most original American artists of the century, Tobey had many one-man exhibits in the United States and Europe. ■ See study by Wieland Schmied (1966).

TOBIN, DANIEL JOSEPH (1875–1955), Irish-born U.S. labor leader. Shortly after emigrating to the United States at age 14, Tobin drove a horse team for a Boston trucking firm. He joined the local chapter of the International Brotherhood of Teamsters, Chauffeurs, Warehousemen and Helpers of America (commonly called the Teamsters Union), befriended American Federation of Labor (AFL) president Samuel Gompers, and became a union activist. He served as union president from 1907 to 1952. Although accused of racketeering and using abusive tactics, the union grew during Tobin's reign to 1.25 million members, and it was one of the most powerful unions in the country. Tobin was also a vice president of the AFL (1933–52) and a close adviser to Pres. Franklin D. Roosevelt.

TOBIN, JAMES (1918–), U.S. economist. A leading neo-Keynesian theorist, Tobin taught at Yale (1950–88) and served as a member of Pres. John F. Kennedy's Council of Economic Advisers (1961–62). For his analysis of the relationship of financial markets to production, consumption, prices, and investment, he was awarded the 1981 Nobel

Prize in Economics. His books included *National Economic Policy* (1966), *The New Economics—One Decade Older* (1974), *Full Employment and Growth* (1996), and *Money, Credit and Capital* (1997).

TODD, ALEXANDER ROBERTUS, BARON TODD OF TRUMPINGTON (1907–1997), British biochemist. A professor of organic chemistry at Manchester (1938–44) and Cambridge (1944–71), Todd worked on the structure and synthesis of vitamins B_1, E, B_{12}, and other chemical substances of importance to pharmacological research. He was best known, however, for his research on the chemical structure and synthesis of nucleotides, nucleosides, and nucleotide coenzymes, the building blocks of nucleic acids, which are the components of genes. His work was of fundamental importance to the study of the workings of the genes, and he won the 1957 Nobel Prize in Chemistry. Todd chaired the British government's Advisory Council on Scientific Policy (1952–64) and was president of the Royal Society (1975–80). ■ See his autobiography, *Time to Remember* (1983).

TODD, MICHAEL (Avrom Hirsch Goldbogen; 1909–1958). U.S. producer. A flamboyant impresario, Mike Todd presented a flame dancer at the 1933 Chicago World's Fair and in 1936 began producing Broadway burlesque revues starring Gypsy Rose Lee and Mae West. Moving into film in the 1950s, Todd established a theater chain and a production company that he later sold to associates. He gave his name to Todd-AO, a new 65mm film process, and helped develop cinerama. Having made and lost several fortunes, Todd spent lavishly on the Academy Award winning *Around the World in 80 Days* (1956), his sole film as a producer. The investment paid off with big box office receipts, but he didn't live much longer to enjoy his good fortune. Shortly after marrying actress Elizabeth Taylor, Todd was killed in a plane crash. ■ See Art Cohn, *The Nine Lives of Michael Todd* (1958), and biography by Michael Todd, Jr., and Susan M. Todd (1983).

TODMAN, WILLIAM SELDEN. *See GOODSON, MARK.*

TOER, PRAMOEDYA ANANTA. *See PRAMOEDYA ANANTA TOER.*

TOGLIATTI, PALMIRO (1893–1964), Italian political leader. A Turin University law graduate, Togliatti was a founder of the Italian Communist party (1921). In exile (1926–44) he was loyal to Soviet dictator Joseph Stalin and a member of the Comintern secretariat. After World War II, however, he advocated polycentrism, sought an "Italian road to socialism," accepted democratic methods and constitutional means of achieving power, and served in the government as vice premier (1944–45) and minister of justice (1945). Although ousted from the government by anticommunist forces, Togliatti remained, until his death, the most powerful communist leader in Western Europe. His posthu-

mously published political memorandum called for greater freedom in the Soviet Union and supported increased autonomy for national Communist parties.

TOJO, HIDEKI (1884–1948), Japanese military and political leader. Of samurai descent, Tojo attended military school, followed by three years of study in Europe (1919–22). He rose rapidly in the military establishment and by 1937 was chief of staff of the Kwantung army in Manchuria. Tojo became war minister in 1940 and premier in 1941. He always represented the ultramilitarist army position during World War II, but by 1944 Japanese losses forced his resignation. After Japan's surrender in 1945 he unsuccessfully attempted suicide; he was hanged in 1948 after a two-year trial on charges of war crimes. ■ See studies by Robert J. Butow (1961) and Courtney Browne (1967).

TOKYO ROSE (Iva Toguri D'Aquino; 1916–), Japanese-U.S. propagandist. Born in Los Angeles, D'Aquino went to Japan in 1941 to visit a sick relative and was unable to return after the Japanese attacked Pearl Harbor. She barely spoke Japanese and refused to renounce her American citizenship, but she was one of 13 women announcers forced to work for Radio Tokyo and broadcast anti-American propaganda in order to demoralize Allied servicemen in the Pacific. They were all dubbed "Tokyo Rose" by U.S. soldiers. When she returned home in 1949, she was convicted of treason and stripped of her citizenship, though some of her colleagues were not prosecuted. After six years in prison she retired to privacy in Chicago. In 1976 several prosecution witnesses revealed that they were coerced to testify against her at her trial, and she was pardoned by Pres. Gerald Ford in Jan. 1977. ■ See Masayo Duus, *Tokyo Rose* (1979), and Russell W. Howe, *The Hunt for "Tokyo Rose"* (1990).

TOLAND, GREGG (1904–1948), U.S. cinematographer. As a teenager Toland became an assistant cameraman on two-reel comedies at Fox. Working with cinematographer George Barnes after 1926, he devised the first soundproof blimp, established a method to maintain focus on moving shots, and developed the deep-focus photographic technique. After his first solo film in 1931, Toland shot a succession of classics: *Les Misérables* (1935), *Dead End* (1937), *Wuthering Heights* (1939; Academy Award), *The Grapes of Wrath* (1940), and *Citizen Kane* (1941). Working with director John Ford's U.S. Navy Camera Unit during World War II, he shot (1943) a prize-winning campaign film, *December 7th*. Toland returned to Hollywood to shoot *The Best Years of Our Lives* (1946) before his death from heart disease.

TOLKIEN, JOHN RONALD REVEL (1892–1973), South African-born British scholar and novelist. A professor of English at Oxford (1925–59), Tolkien created the mythological world of Middle Earth in the phenomenally successful fantasies *The Hobbit* (1938) and *The Lord of the Rings* trilogy (1954–56). Filled with people, elves, trolls, wizards, and hobbits—small, fat, good-natured creatures who laughed deeply, dressed in bright colors, and loved peace and quiet—Middle Earth attracted millions of young readers during the 1960s. Both praised and belittled by critics, Tolkien's novels, which he claimed were not allegories, were replete with parallels to *The Ring of the Nibelungen,* the Scandinavian epics, and other early European romances. *The Silmarillon* (1977), published posthumously, is the history of Tolkien's imaginary world prior to the events recorded in the Hobbit chronicles. ■ See his *The Monsters and the Critics and Other Essays* (1984); biographies by Humphrey Carpenter (1977) and Daniel Grotta-Kurska (1977); and study by Deborah and Ivor Rogers (1980).

TOLLER, ERNST (1893–1939), German playwright and poet. A pacifist and revolutionary socialist, Toller served as the first president of the Central Committee of the Bavarian Socialist Republic (April 1919). Imprisoned (1919–24) for his role in the short-lived revolution, Toller wrote a series of hard-hitting expressionistic plays of social protest that brought him fame while he was still incarcerated. Most notable were *Transfiguration* (1919; Eng. trans. 1936), *Masses and Man* (1922; Eng. trans. 1923), *The Machine Wreckers* (1922; Eng. trans. 1923), and *Brokenbrow* (1924; Eng. trans. 1926). His best-known poems appeared in *The Swallow Book* (1924; Eng. trans. 1924). A Jew, he fled Germany in 1932 and lectured widely in Europe and the United States against the Nazis. He committed suicide in New York City. ■ See his autobiography, *I Was a German* (1933; Eng. trans. 1934); study by Malcolm Pittock (1979); and Richard Dove, *He Was a German* (1990).

TOLMAN, EDWARD CHACE (1886–1959), U.S. psychologist. E. C. Tolman, who earned a Ph.D. in psychology from Harvard University (1915), taught at the University of California at Berkeley (1918–54). Rejecting the mechanistic behaviorist scheme of stimulus and response as too simplistic an explanation of human activity, he developed the study of "purposive behaviorism," a holistic approach, influenced by Gestalt psychology, which stressed the goal-directed nature of behavior. His major work was *Purposive Behavior in Animals and Men* (1932). He also led the struggle for academic freedom during the loyalty-oath controversy at Berkeley in the early 1950s. ■ See his *Collected Papers in Psychology* (1951).

TOLSON, MELVIN BEAUNORUS (1898–1966), U.S. poet. Tolson was an African American recognized by the critic and poet Karl Shapiro as "a great poet [who] has been living in our midst for decades, and is almost totally unknown, even by literati [and] poets." He was born in Mississippi, educated at Fisk, Lincoln, and Columbia (M.A. 1940) universities, and spent most of his teaching career at Wiley College in Texas (1924–47) and at Langston University in Oklahoma (1947–65). He also served four terms as mayor of the town of Langston. His poetry collection *Rendezvous with*

America (1944) was highly praised. Commissioned to commemorate Liberia's centennial, he composed the acclaimed *Libretto for the Republic of Liberia* (1953). *Harlem Gallery, Book I: The Curator* (1965) used traditional forms and tight structure to create a Harlem panorama. His collected columns from the *Washington Tribune* (1937–44) are in *Caviar and Cabbage* (1982). ■ See biography by Robert M. Farnsworth (1984) and study by Joy Flasch (1972).

TOLSTOY, ALEXEI NIKOLAEVICH (1883–1945), Soviet novelist. A distant relative of the great writer Leo Tolstoy, he wrote stories of Russian provincial life that demonstrated considerable narrative skill. An opponent of the Bolsheviks, Tolstoy emigrated to Paris (1919), where he wrote his best novels, the autobiographical *Nikita's Childhood* (1920; Eng. trans. 1945) and the first part of the trilogy *The Road to Calvary* (1921–40; Eng. trans. 1945). Tolstoy was welcomed back to the Soviet Union (1923), where he became an establishment writer. *Bread* (1937; Eng. trans. 1938), which fictitiously portrayed the dictator Joseph Stalin as the heroic defender of Tsaritsyn (later Stalingrad) during the Russian civil war (1918–20), was apparently designed to protect his comfortable existence during the worst years of the purges. His unfinished work, *Peter the First* (1929–45; Eng. trans. 1956), was considered by many to be the finest historical novel ever written in the Soviet Union. Tolstoy also wrote a classic of Soviet science fiction, *Aelita,* or *The Decline of Mars* (1922; Eng. trans. 1985).

TOMBAUGH, CLYDE WILLIAM (1906–1997), U.S. astronomer. Tombaugh, who could not afford to attend college, fashioned a nine-inch telescope using machine parts he found on his father's farm. In his early twenties, he landed a job as an assistant at Lowell Observatory in Arizona (1929). There, he sighted the planet Pluto (1930), whose existence Percival Lowell had earlier posited. The historic discovery resulted from his painstaking comparison of photographs of the sky taken on consecutive days. His feat resulted in a scholarship to the University of Kansas (B.A. 1936; M.A. 1939). Tombaugh also discovered galactic and globular star clusters, variable stars, asteroids, and clusters of nebulas. He made geological surveys of the surfaces of Mars and the moon and helped design telescopic mirrors. He taught at New Mexico State University (1955–73) and wrote *Out of the Darkness: The Planet Pluto* (1980; with Patrick Moore). ■ See biography by David H. Levy (1991).

TOMLIN, LILY (**Mary Jean Tomlin;** 1939–), U.S. actress. Tomlin grew up in Detroit and studied at Wayne State University. Moving to New York (1966), she landed a job as secretary to a casting director, performed at various clubs, and appeared Off-Broadway. She performed on the last "Garry Moore Show" and then on the TV comedy hit *Laugh-In* (1969–72), where she delighted viewers with a one-woman cast of characters that included the telephone operator

Ernestine, 5-year-old Edith Ann, and Suzy Sorority. With Jane Wagner writing much of her material, Tomlin won Emmy Awards (1973; 1975; 1981) for her TV specials, made records, and appeared on Broadway in *Appearing Nightly* (1977; Tony Award) and *The Search for Intelligent Life in the Universe* (1985; Tony Award, 1986). Her movie credits included *Nashville* (1975), *Nine to Five* (1980), *All of Me* (1984), *And the Band Played On* (1993), and *Tea with Mussolini* (1999). She also appeared on the TV show "Murphy Brown" (1996–98). Tomlin was a visible supporter of women's and gay rights.

TOMONAGA, SHINICHIRO or SIN-ITIRO (1906–1979), Japanese physicist. Educated in his native Japan, Tomonaga worked under Werner Heisenberg in Germany (1937–39). A theoretical physicist, he developed a coupling theory to explain aspects of the proton and neutron. During World War II he proposed a solution to problems in electrodynamic quantum theory that was in accord with the special theory of relativity. For this work, which permitted a greater understanding of elementary particles in high-energy physics, he shared the 1965 Nobel Prize in Physics with Richard Feynman and Julian Schwinger. Tomonaga was a professor (from 1941) and president (1956–62) of the Tokyo University of Education. He wrote *Quantum Mechanics* (2 vols.; Eng. trans. 1962–66).

TOMSKY, MIKHAIL PAVLOVICH (1880–1936), Soviet political leader. Born into a worker's family, Tomsky joined the Russian Social Democratic Labor party (1904), supported its Bolshevik faction, and organized the Reval (now Tallin, Estonia) Soviet (workers' council) during the 1905 revolution. After the October 1917 revolution he headed the trade union movement in Moscow and later chaired the central council of Soviet trade unions (1922–29). He was also active in the Comintern and a member of the ruling Soviet Politburo (1922–29). Opposed to dictator Joseph Stalin's policy of forced collectivization and of rapid industrialization, he was removed from his union and party posts along with other members of the "right opposition" and forced to recant. Threatened during the first of the great purge trials (1936), Tomsky committed suicide.

TONEGAWA, SUSUMU (1939–   ), Japanese molecular biologist. Tonegawa studied at Kyoto University (B.A. 1963) and at the University of California, San Diego (Ph.D. 1969), did research at the Basel (Switzerland) Institute for Immunology (1971–81), and taught at the Massachusetts Institute of Technology (1981–   ). During the 1970s he discovered the genetic mechanism by which limited numbers of cells in the immune system, through constant rearrangement and mutation, produce apparently unlimited numbers of specialized antibodies in order to fight diverse diseases. For his pioneering work he won the 1987 Nobel Prize in Physiology or Medicine.

TÖNNIES, FERDINAND JULIUS (1855–1936), German sociologist. An authority on the British political philosopher Thomas Hobbes, Tönnies taught at the University of Kiel for 50 years, until dismissed by the Nazis in 1933. In his classic, *Community and Society* (1887; Eng. trans. 1957), he introduced concepts that powerfully affected modern sociological thought. He used the term *Gemeinschaft* (community) to characterize the type of community typical of small, isolated villages, where life is highly integrated and relationships tend to be close and enduring; he used the term *Gesellschaft* (society) to describe the less coherent, more fragmented type of community typical of large urban centers, where relationships tend to be impersonal and transitory. His model of the transition from one type of community to the other had profound implications for his time, when industrialization and urbanization were at the root of tremendous social upheaval. In his *Introduction to Sociology* (1931), Tönnies drew a distinction between abstract, applied, and practical sociology. ■ See his selected writings, *On Sociology* (Eng. trans. 1971), and Arthur Mitzman, *Sociology and Estrangement* (1973).

TOOMER, JEAN (1894–1967), U.S. novelist. Toomer prepared for a law career at the City College of New York and the University of Wisconsin. He undertook his experimental fiction in the 1920s, emerging as a major figure of the Harlem renaissance with the publication of *Cane* (1923), a sequence of encounters linked by lyric poems. Despite critics' praise, *Cane* sold only 500 copies on publication and remained largely unread. Toomer's work was influenced by his study with the Russian mystic Gurdjieff. Toomer established a Gurdjieff Institute in Wisconsin, devoted to consciousness expansion and meditation. A selection of his writings appears in *The Wayward and the Seeking* (1980). ■ See biography by Nellie Y. McKay (1984); studies by Brian J. Benson and Mabel M. Dillard (1980) and Charles Scruggs and Lee Van Demarr (1998); and Cynthia E. Kerman and Richard Eldridge, *The Lives of Jean Toomer* (1987).

TORRES RESTREPO, CAMILO (1929–1966), Colombian priest, sociologist, and revolutionary. Chaplain of the National University, founder of its sociology department, and dean of its Advanced School of Public Administration, Torres concluded by the early 1960s that only a mass "united popular movement" could bring social justice to Colombia. Hoping to overthrow the ruling elite peacefully, he left the priesthood and organized a united front of popular movements. He soon moved further to the left, joined the National Liberation army, and issued a call for Colombians to prepare for a war of revolution. He died during a battle with government troops (1966) and was subsequently considered a martyr of the Latin American left. ■ See his *Revolutionary Writings* (Eng. trans. 1969); John Alvarez Garcia and Christian Restrepo Calle, eds., *Camilo Torres: His Life and His Message* (1968); and John Gerassi, ed., *Revolutionary Priest* (1971).

TORRIJOS HERRERA, OMAR (1929–1981), Panamanian political leader. A lieutenant colonel in the Panamanian national guard, Torrijos led the coup that overthrew Pres. Arnulfo Arias (1968), and he dominated Panamanian politics from February 1969 until his death in a plane crash 12 years later. He assumed the rank of brigadier general in 1969 and served as chief of government from 1972 to 1978. Supported by the peasantry and left-wing students, Torrijos carried out significant economic and political reforms. A fiery, nationalistic orator who frequently denounced United States domination of the Panama Canal, he was best known for negotiating the 1977 treaties that provided for transfer of the canal to Panamanian sovereignty by the year 2000.

TOSCANINI, ARTURO (1867–1957), Italian conductor. While touring Brazil as a 19-year-old cellist with an Italian opera company, Toscanini made his conducting debut as a last-minute replacement for an ailing colleague (1886). He quickly earned a reputation for exacting musicianship, insisting on fidelity to the composer's score rather than the romantic self-expression then in fashion. In 1898 Toscanini was appointed artistic director of Milan's La Scala opera, and 10 years later he became a conductor with the Metropolitan Opera in New York. He returned to La Scala after World War I, but with the rise of Italian fascism returned to the United States to conduct the New York Philharmonic, which became one of the world's leading orchestras under his baton (1928–36). Through his intense emotional and subtle intellectual grasp of music, Toscanini was able to exert a magnetic control over his musicians, leading them to landmark performances of both traditional and modern compositions. At age 70, he began conducting the National Broadcasting Company (NBC) Symphony, which was created for him. Over the next 17 years (1937–54), he became one of the first conductors to reach vast audiences through broadcasts and recordings. ■ See Howard Taubman, *The Maestro* (1951), and biography by George R. Marek (1975).

TOURÉ, (AHMED) SÉKOU (1922–1984), Guinean political leader. A zealous union organizer in the postal and treasury departments, Touré participated in the formation of the intercolonial nationalist movement, Rassemblement Democratique Africain (RDA) in 1946 and by 1952 he headed its local branch, the Parti Démocratique de Guinée (PDG). He was elected mayor of Conakry (1955), representative to the French national assembly (1957), and vice president of the government council (1957). He led the campaign for complete independence rather than continued association with France in the elections of 1958, the year he became president of Guinea. Claiming to be a socialist, he became a hero of African radicals as he limited Western economic influence and pursued policies based on self-reliance and mass political organization. However, his government was an oppressive one-party dictatorship and he liquidated thousands of his opponents during purges of the 1970s. As the economy deteriorated he eased internal repression, advocated a more gradualist and pro-Western foreign policy, and invited private U.S. investment (1982). ■ See 'Lapido Adamolekun, *Sékou Touré's Guinea* (1976).

TOURNIER, MICHEL (1924–), French writer. A student of law and philosophy at the universities of Paris and Tübingen (Germany), Tournier was a journalist, television producer, literary editor, and essayist. He was best known for *Friday* (1967; Eng. trans. 1969) and *The Ogre* (1970; Eng. trans. 1972; Prix Goncourt), two highly imaginative philosophical novels that were filled with complex symbols and allusions. His other works included the novels *Gemini* (1975; Eng. trans. 1981), *The Four Wise Men* (1980; Eng. trans. 1982), *The Golden Droplet* (1985; Eng. trans. 1987), and *The Mirror of Ideas* (1994; Eng. trans. 1998) and the short-story collections *The Fetishist* (1978; Eng. trans. 1984) and *The Midnight Love Feast* (1989; Eng. trans. 1991). He was named to the Legion of Honor in 1984. ■ See his autobiography, *The Wind Spirit* (1977; Eng. trans 1988), and the study by William Cloonan (1985).

TOWNES, CHARLES HARD (1915–), U.S. physicist. An industrial researcher and professor, Townes worked on microwave spectroscopy during World War II. He and A. L. Schawlow made the first maser (an acronym for Microwave Amplification by Stimulated Emission of Radiation) in 1953. The maser was the forerunner of the laser, which produces remarkably intense, short-wavelength light, and was used in such highly diversified fields as surgery, welding, holography, communications, and surveying. Townes shared the 1964 Nobel Prize in Physics with Nikolai Basov and Aleksandr Prochorov for this work in quantum electronics. He wrote *Microwave Spectroscopy* (1955; with Schawlow) and taught at Columbia University (1948–61), the Massachusetts Institute of Technology (1961–67), and the University of California at Berkeley (1967–86).

TOWNSEND, FRANCIS EVERETT (1867–1960), U.S. physician. A native of the Midwest, Townsend was practicing medicine in southern California during the Depression when he became convinced of the need for a national old-age pension. The "Townsend Plan," published by the *Long Beach Press-Telegram* (1933), called for pensions of $200 monthly to be raised through a sales tax. Citizens over 60 would be eligible, provided only that they spend the money within a month. The Townsend movement claimed millions of zealous adherents throughout the country at its height, but it was preempted by passage of the Social Security Act (1935) and the gradual improvement of economic conditions. ■ See his autobiography, *New Horizons* (1943), and Abraham Holtzman, *The Townsend Movement* (1963).

TOYNBEE, ARNOLD JOSEPH (1889–1975), British historian. Toynbee studied classics at Oxford (1907–11), worked for British intelligence during World War I, and attended the Paris Peace Conference (1919). While teaching Byzantine and Greek history at London University (1919–24), he conceived the idea of a comparative study of world civilization. In *A Study of History*, eventually published in 12 volumes (1934–61), he described a life cycle of genesis, growth, and decay in civilizations, with religion acting as a regenerating force. From 1925 to 1955 he was research professor of international history at the University of London and director of studies for the Royal Institute of International Affairs. His *Experiences* (1969) contains autobiographical information. ▪ See Edward T. Gargan, ed., *The Intent of Toynbee's History* (1961), and studies by Ronald N. Stromberg (1972), Kenneth Winetrout (1975), and William H. McNeill (1989).

TRACY, SPENCER (1900–1967), U.S. actor. In 1930 Tracy arrived in Hollywood via the U.S. Navy, the American Academy of Dramatic Arts, and Broadway. His best early film was *The Power and the Glory* (1933), followed by Academy Award–winning performances in *Captains Courageous* (1937) and *Boys Town* (1938). An unassuming midwesterner who could be gruff and shrewd or engaging and sympathetic, Tracy inclined to the latter in his relationship with Katharine Hepburn, with whom he made nine films including *Pat and Mike* (1952) and *Guess Who's Coming to Dinner?* (1967). In two of his best late films, Tracy played a conniving politician in *The Last Hurrah* (1958) and the lawyer Clarence Darrow in *Inherit the Wind* (1960). ▪ See Garson Kanin, *Tracy and Hepburn* (1971), and the biographies by Larry Swindell (1972) and Bill Davidson (1987).

TRAVEN, B. (Otto Feige?; 1890?–1969), German-born (?) novelist. Due to Traven's own strenuous efforts at obfuscation, few facts of his life have been clearly established. He lived in Germany from 1907 to 1922 and probably used the name Ret Marut. He was most likely an actor (1907–15), magazine writer (1912–19), and publisher of an anarchist journal (1917–22). After involvement in the anarchist movement following World War I, he moved to Mexico, (1924), where he remained for more than 40 years. His realistic short stories and novels, written in German, depicted cruelty and greed and reflected his anticapitalist and anti-imperialist views. Among his best known works, which were extremely popular in Europe, were *The Death Ship* (1926; Eng. trans. 1934) and *The Treasure of the Sierra Madre* (1927; Eng. trans. 1934; film, 1948). English translations of his short fiction are in *By the Man Nobody Knows* (1961), *The Night Visitor* (1966), *Kidnapped Saint* (1975), and *To the Honorable Miss S.* (1981). ▪ See study by Michael Baumann (1976); Judy Stone, *The Mystery of B. Traven* (1977); Will Wyatt, *The Secret of the Sierra Madre* (1980); and the biography by K. S. Guthke (Eng. trans. 1991).

TRAVERS, P. L. (Helen Lyndon Goff; 1906–1996), Australian-born British writer. An actress, dancer, and jour-

nalist who adopted the professional name Pamela Lyndon Travers before settling in England (1924), she published poems and theater criticism in journals during the 1920s. As a result of friendships with poets George William Russell (known as A. E.) and William Butler Yeats, Travers became fascinated with Celtic folklore, mysticism, magic, and Eastern religions, all of which influenced her subsequent work. Her children's story, *Mary Poppins* (1934), about a stern, prim English nanny with magical powers, was an immediate success. It sold millions of copies, was translated into more than 20 languages, inspired numerous sequels, and was the basis of a popular Walt Disney movie (1964). Her other books included *Friend Monkey* (1973); *About Sleeping Beauty* (1975); a collection of essays exploring myths and tradition, *What the Bee Knows* (1989); and a biography of the Russian mystic G. I. Gurdjieff (1973).

TRENET, CHARLES (1913–2001), French singer and songwriter. A legendary entertainer in France, Trenet displayed talent in music, art, and drama as a young boy. He published poetry and theatrical reviews at the age of 15 and completed an unpublished novel at 17. After moving to Paris (1930), he collaborated on a musical film score, published poetry, and befriended such cultural luminaries as Max Jacob, Maurice Utrillo, Antonin Artaud, and Jean Cocteau. He made his debut as part of a singing duo in 1933, and performed on radio and in cabarets. He appeared as a music hall soloist for the first time in 1938, wearing a dark shirt, white tie, red carnation, and soft felt hat that became his trademark. His popular high-spirited optimistic songs of the 1930s, influenced by jazz and swing, included "Je chante," "Boum," "J'ai ta main," and "Y'a d'la joie" ("There's Happiness Everywhere"). His nostalgic "Douce France" (1943) took on patriotic significance during World War II. After the war he toured the world and his songs "La Mer" ("Beyond the Sea") and "Que reste-t'il de nos amours?" ("I Wish You Love") became huge international hits. Active through the 1990s, Trenet wrote hundreds of songs and several novels during his long career and was awarded the Legion of Honor.

TRESCA, CARLO (1879–1943), Italian-born U.S. labor and political leader. Tresca, who was born into a wealthy family, emigrated to the United States in 1904 to devote his life to the labor movement. A journalist as well as activist, he lived and wrote with gusto and courage, frequently landing in jail for strike activities and for advocating other radical causes such as birth control. He was a spokesman for the Italian working class and was active in the Industrial Workers of the World (IWW) before World War I. He continued his labor agitation as an independent radical after the war and became a hero of the noncommunist left. He was assassinated in New York City by persons unknown, but he had bitter enemies on both the right, as a leading antifascist, and the left, as an opponent of Stalinism. ▪ See Dorothy Gallagher, *All the Right Enemies* (1988).

TREVELYAN, GEORGE MACAULEY (1876–1962), British historian. Great-nephew of the historian Thomas Macauley, Trevelyan studied at Cambridge but rejected the university (1903) in favor of a full-time writing career. Following a literary, humanistic approach in preference to the current "scientific" trend in history, he produced a colorful trilogy on the Italian patriot Giuseppe Garibaldi (1907–11) and a best-selling single-volume history of England (1926), and completed the last three volumes of his great-uncle's *History of England* (1930–34). These works, as well as the highly acclaimed *English Social History* (1944), reflected his liberal outlook. He returned to teach at Cambridge from 1927 to 1951. ■ See his autobiography (1949), biographies by John H. Plumb (1951) and David Cannadine (1992), and the memoir by Mary Trevelyan Moorman (1980).

TREVOR-ROPER, HUGH REDWALD (1914–), British historian. H. R. Trevor-Roper was an expert on Elizabethan history whose interests also ranged to the contemporary. As an intelligence officer during World War II he gathered the material for his best-known book, *The Last Days of Hitler* (1947), described by one reviewer as "more readable than a novel." He wrote *The Philby Affair* (1968) about his acquaintance, the cold war spy Kim Philby. In a more scholarly vein, Trevor-Roper wrote *The Rise of Christian Europe* (1965) and *The European Witch Craze of the Sixteenth and Seventeenth Centuries* (1969). His later works included *Hermit of Peking: The Hidden Life of Sir Edmund Backhouse* (1977) and *Princes and Artists* (1976), a study of Habsburg patronage. He also edited *The Goebbels Diaries: The Last Days* (1978). After 23 years on the faculty at Oxford, he moved to Cambridge (1980–87). He was elevated to the peerage (1979) as Baron Dacre of Glanton.

TRIFONOV, YURI VALENTINOVICH (1925–1981), Soviet writer. When Trifonov was 12, his father, a Bolshevik revolutionary, was killed at the height of the Stalinist purges (1937), and his mother was sent to a prison camp. He lived with his grandmother. Soon after graduating from Gorky Literary Institute in Moscow (1949), Trifonov won a Stalin Prize at age 28 for his novel *Students* (1950; Eng. trans. 1953). By the mid-1960s, he had gained a reputation as a writer of the "urban school" and was publishing ideologically provocative fiction characterized by keen psychological insight and intriguing narrative structure. He is best known for novels of the 1970s that were of two basic types. The first depicted the moral conflicts of contemporary Moscow intellectuals and included *Taking Stock* (1970; Eng. trans. 1977), *The Long Goodbye* (1971; Eng. trans. 1977), and *Another Life* (1975; Eng. trans. 1983). The second portrayed older, disillusioned protagonists who trace the links between past and present, and included *The House on the Embankment* (1976; Eng. trans. 1983), *The Old Man* (1978; Eng. trans. 1984), and *Place and Time* (1981). Trifonov died of complications following routine kidney surgery.

TRILLING, LIONEL (1905–1975), U.S. critic, teacher, and fiction writer. Trilling studied at Columbia University (B.A. 1925; Ph.D. 1938) and taught there for more than four decades (1931–75). He wrote important studies of Matthew Arnold (1939) and E. M. Forster (1943), writers who embodied the liberal, humanist tradition to which he adhered. Trilling established himself as one of the century's leading critics by treating the relationship between literary ideas and social thought in elegant essays collected in *The Liberal Imagination* (1950), *The Opposing Self* (1955), and *A Gathering of Fugitives* (1956). A fascination with the ideas of psychoanalyst Sigmund Freud informed Trilling's later work, which linked the workings of the mind with the workings of art. *Beyond Culture* (1965), *Sincerity and Authenticity* (1972), and *The Last Decade: Essays and Reviews, 1965–1975* (1979) contained his later writings. He wrote the novel *The Middle of the Journey* (1947) and the short stories collected in *Of This Time, Of That Place* (1979). His wife was the critic Diana R. Trilling (1905–1996). ■ See studies by William Chace (1981), J. Edward Shoben, Jr. (1982), and Mark Krupnick (1986); and Diana Trilling, *The Beginning of the Journey* (1993).

TRIMBLE, (WILLIAM) DAVID (1944–), Northern Ireland political leader. Trimble taught law at Queens University, Belfast, his alma mater, and served as a member of the Northern Ireland Constitutional Convention (1975–76). A militant Protestant who opposed any compromise with the Roman Catholic community in Northern Ireland, he served in the British Parliament (1990–) and as leader of the Ulster Unionist Party (1995–), the largest Protestant political party in the province. In the mid-1990s he modified his hard-line positions, met with political leaders of the Irish Republican Army, his arch enemy, and participated in peace talks (1996–98) that culminated in the signing of the Good Friday Agreement (April 1998). The pact provided for a respite in sectarian violence and the creation of a new Northern Ireland Assembly. Trimble served as the first minister of the new legislature and shared the 1998 Nobel Peace Prize with Northern Ireland Catholic political leader John Hume.

TRIPPE, JUAN (1899–1981), U.S. business executive. After his graduation from Yale (1921), Trippe, the son of an investment banker, became involved in the fledgling commercial aviation industry. In 1927 he founded Pan American World Airlines and within 10 years had put together an international network capable of competing against subsidized foreign airlines. Under Trippe's leadership (1927–68), Pan Am inaugurated the first international airmail flights (1927), the first commercial flights across the Pacific (1935) and Atlantic (1939) oceans, and initiated low-cost trips to Europe (1952). ■ See Robert Daley, *An American Saga* (1980), and Marilyn Bender and Selig Altschul, *The Chosen Instrument* (1982).

TROELTSCH, ERNST (1865–1923), German theologian, historian, and sociologist. Trained in theology at the universities of Erlangen and Berlin, Troeltsch taught philosophy at the universities of Heidelberg (1894–1914) and Berlin (1915–23). An important theoretician of liberal Protestant theology, he was best known for his comprehensive historical presentation of Christian social teaching. Troeltsch introduced sociological methods into the study of theology and history and studied the ways that social and cultural factors shape the development of religion and its institutions, but he rejected the Marxist view of religion. He also served as a member of the Berlin Landtag (diet). His major works included *The Social Teachings of the Christian Churches* (1908–11; Eng. trans. 1931), *History and Its Problems* (1922), and the posthumous volume, *Christian Thought* (1923; Eng. trans. 1923). Translations of his writings were edited by Robert Morgan and Michael Pye (1977). His essays appeared in *Religion in History* (Eng. trans. 1991). ■ See also the volume edited by J. P. Clayton (1976) and Robert J. Rubanowice, *Crisis in Consciousness* (1982).

TROTSKY, LEON (Lev Davidovich Bronstein; 1879–1940), Russian political leader. Born into a Jewish family in the Ukraine, Trotsky was imprisoned for revolutionary activities at age 19 and sent to Siberia. He escaped and joined socialist leader V. I. Lenin in London. He emerged during the 1905 revolution as a leader of the first St. Petersburg Soviet, but was again arrested and sent to Siberia. He escaped and spent several years organizing abroad. Trotsky combined a penetrating intellect with strong organizing and oratorical ability. He was also an independent thinker who challenged Lenin's principle of a centralized party organization. In 1917, however, he allied with the Bolsheviks and as chairman of the Petrograd Soviet helped to organize the October revolution and the seizure of power from the provisional government. He became commissar of foreign affairs and then of war, creating the Red army and guiding it to victory in the Russian civil war (1918–20). He began to lose influence during Lenin's illness, and upon Lenin's death (1924) he was defeated in a power struggle by a coalition of opponents, of whom Joseph Stalin emerged as leader. In the mid-1920s, Trotsky sparked strenuous debate over Stalin's goal of "socialism in one country," which conflicted with his own commitment to "permanent revolution" on an international scale. Trotsky was expelled from the party (1927) and later from the country (1929). In exile he wrote the *History of the Russian Revolution* (3 vols.; Eng. trans. 1932) and worked toward forging the Fourth International, a revolutionary socialist movement that he offered as an alternative to Stalinist communism. Trotsky was assassinated by a Stalinist agent in Mexico. Selections of his writings are in *The Basic Writings of Trotsky* (1963) and *The Age of Permanent Revolution* (1964). ■ See his autobiography, *My Life* (Eng. trans. 1930); Isaac Deutscher's trilogy, *The Prophet Armed* (1954), *The Prophet Unarmed* (1959), and *The Prophet Outcast*

(1963); and biographies by Joel Carmichael (1975), Victor Serge and Natalia Trotsky (1975), Robert D. Warth (1977), Ronald Segal (1979), and Dimitri Volkogonov (Eng. trans. 1996).

TROTTER, WILLIAM MONROE (1872–1934), U.S. journalist. A Harvard graduate (B.A. 1895; M.A. 1896), Trotter gave up a business career to devote his life to the fight against racial discrimination. The most militant African-American spokesman of his time, Trotter founded (1901) and edited (1901–34) the weekly *Boston Guardian* and spoke out strongly against the moderate policies of Booker T. Washington. Although he collaborated with W.E.B. DuBois in founding the Niagara movement for civil rights (1905), he refused to join him in the NAACP as he feared it was too moderate an organization. He founded, instead, the National Equal Rights League to agitate for equality, but it never received the support or recognition of the larger and more moderate black organizations. Many of Trotter's nonviolent protest tactics, however, were adopted by later generations of black activists. ■ See Stephen R. Fox, *The Guardian of Boston* (1970).

TROYAT, HENRI (Lev Tarassov; 1911–), Russian-born French novelist and biographer. Troyat's family fled the Bolshevik regime and settled in Paris, where he studied law. His novel *Faux Jour* ("False Light"; 1935), a study of a son's rebellion against his father, won him early acclaim. *The Web* (1938; Eng. trans. 1984) received the Prix Goncourt. In 1941 Troyat resigned from the French civil service to devote himself to writing. The influence of the great Russian novelist Leo Tolstoy is evident in his epic trilogy, *My Father's House* (1947; Eng. trans. 1952), *The Red and the White* (1948; Eng. trans. 1956), and *Strangers on Earth* (1950; Eng. trans. 1958), which deals with the fate of a middle-class Russian family in the half century before the revolution of 1917. In 1959 Troyat was elected to the Académie Française. He also wrote notable biographies of Pushkin (1946; Eng. trans. 1950), Tolstoy (1965; Eng. trans. 1967), Gogol (1971; Eng. trans. 1973), Catherine the Great (1977; Eng. trans. 1980), Chekhov (1984; Eng. trans. 1986), Turgenev (1985; Eng. trans. 1988), and Gorky (1986; Eng. trans. 1989). *Sylvie* (1980; Eng. trans. 1982) and *Sylvie, Her Teenage Years* (1986; Eng. trans. 1988) represented a view of postwar France through the eyes of a child. ■ See study by Nicholas Hewitt (1984).

TRUDEAU, GARRY (Garretson Beckman Trudeau; 1948–), U.S. cartoonist. While a student at Yale, Trudeau edited the campus humor magazine and, for the Yale *Daily News*, started a comic strip, *Bull Tales* (1968), satirizing local Yale celebrities. After graduating, he signed up with the newly formed Universal Press Syndicate, which was looking for a political cartoon that would appeal to youth. The name of the strip was changed to *Doonesbury*—after one of its leading characters—and it made its debut (in 28 newspapers) in 1970. Featuring both fictional and real-life characters, the strip brilliantly satirized contemporary political and social life in the United States and was soon appearing in more than 400 newspapers. Trudeau won the Pulitzer Prize (1975) for cartooning and published numerous *Doonesbury* collections in book form.

TRUDEAU, PIERRE ELLIOTT (1919–2000), Canadian political leader. Born into a wealthy French-Canadian family in Montreal, Trudeau studied law at the University of Montreal and political economy at Harvard, the École des Sciences Politiques in Paris, and the London School of Economics. A labor and civil-rights lawyer during the 1950s, he cofounded the influential left-liberal magazine *Cité Libre* ("free city"; 1950), and taught law at Montreal University (1961–65). He joined the Liberal party, was elected to Parliament (1965), and was appointed minister of justice and attorney-general (1967–68) before serving his long tenure as prime minister (1968–79; 1980–84). A charismatic and flamboyant leader, he was committed to reconciling the differences between English and French Canadians and to maintaining a unified federal political structure. He made both French and English the official languages throughout the Canadian administration and led the successful struggle against the Quebec separatist movement (1980). He also presided over the severance of British control over the Canadian constitution and gained approval of a new constitution that included a charter of rights (1981). Internationally he campaigned for disarmament and for an enhanced and more equitable role for Third World countries in the international economic structure. His books included *Federalism and the French Canadians* (1968), *Conversations with Canadians* (1972), *Against the Current* (1996), and *The Essential Trudeau* (1998). ▪ See his *Memoirs* (1993); the study by George Radwanski (1978), and Richard Gwyn, *The Northern Magus* (1980).

TRUFFAUT, FRANÇOIS (1932–1984), French film director. Truffaut grew up poor in Paris and landed in a reformatory at age 15. His lifelong fascination with film led to a position as film critic for *Cahiers du Cinema* during the 1950s. In 1959, with two short films to his credit as a director, he made the autobiographical *The 400 Blows,* which won a Cannes Film Festival prize, enjoyed great popularity for its unconventional charm, and established his reputation as a leader of the New Wave cinema. Truffaut's second feature, *Shoot the Piano Player* (1960), was a takeoff on the American genre of "B" thrillers, while *Jules and Jim* (1961) was a charming tragicomic love triangle, all in love with all. Truffaut subsequently made several more semiautobiographical films and in his *Day for Night* (1973) played the lead as a film director. His other films included *Small Change* (1976), *The Story of Adele H.* (1976), and *The Last Metro* (1980). ▪ See studies by Don Allen (1974) and Annette Insdorf (1978) and biography by Antoine de Baecque and Serge Toubiana (1996; Eng. trans. 1999).

TRUJILLO MOLINA, RAFAEL LEONIDAS (1891–1961), dictator of the Dominican Republic. During the occupation of the Dominican Republic by U.S. marines (1916–24), Trujillo was trained as an officer in the national guard and became its chief of staff (1927). He led a military revolt and became president in 1930 by intimidating and murdering his opponents; he remained in power for 31 years by the same means. Sectors of the economy were modernized, but civil rights and opposition political parties were suppressed. Trujillo renamed cities, provinces, and streets after himself and his family and amassed a fortune estimated at $500 million. He was assassinated by dissident military officers aided by the U.S. Central Intelligence Agency (CIA). ▪ See biographies by Germán E. Ornes (1958) and Robert Crassweller (1966); Jesus Galindez Suarez, *The Era of Trujillo* (1956; Eng. trans. 1973); Howard J. Wiarda, *Dictatorship and Development* (1968); and study by Bernard Diederich (1978).

TRUMAN, HARRY S. (1884–1972), U.S. political leader. A World War I veteran and an unsuccessful clothing store owner, Truman entered Missouri politics as a protégé of Democratic boss Thomas Pendergast and served as a county judge (1926–34). Elected to the U.S. Senate (1934; 1940) he supported New Deal legislation and attracted national attention (1942) with his investigation of World War II profiteering. He was selected as Pres. Franklin D. Roosevelt's vice-presidential running mate in 1944 and succeeded to the presidency when Roosevelt died on April 12, 1945. Truman ordered the atomic bomb dropped on Japan (1945) and pursued an aggressive postwar policy of "containing" communism via the Truman Doctrine and the Marshall Plan (1947). After his unexpected defeat of Thomas Dewey in the 1948 presidential election, Truman helped establish the North Atlantic Treaty Organization (NATO; 1949), but he was unable to end the civil war in China, and he intervened militarily in Korea (1950). Domestically, Congress blocked his liberal "Fair Deal" social legislation, and Sen. Joseph R. McCarthy's anticommunist witch hunt gained strength and targeted Secretary of State Dean Acheson and Secretary of Defense George Marshall. Truman declined to run for reelection in 1952 and retired to Independence, Missouri. ▪ See his *Memoirs* (2 vols.; 1955–56); Merle Miller, *Plain Speaking* (1974); Robert J. Donovan, *Conflict and Crisis* (1977) and *Tumultuous Years* (1982); and biography by David McCullough (1992).

TRUMBO, (JAMES) DALTON (1905–1976), U.S. screenwriter. Trumbo came into public view with publication of his antiwar novel, *Johnny Got His Gun* (1939), and during World War II became one of Hollywood's most sought-after scriptwriters; his credits included *Kitty Foyle* (1940), *A Guy Named Joe* (1943), and *Thirty Seconds Over Tokyo* (1944). After he was convicted of contempt of Congress (1947) for refusing to cooperate with the House Un-American Activities Committee (HUAC) regarding alleged Communist party membership, Trumbo—one of the "Hollywood Ten"—was jailed and blacklisted. He later wrote several scripts under assumed names, winning an Oscar for *The Brave One* (1956) under the name Robert Rich. Not until 1960 did his own name appear; in that year he received credit for *Exodus* and *Spartacus*. Trumbo later wrote such scripts as *The Sandpiper* (1965) and *The Fixer* (1968). *Additional Dialogue* (1970) contained his selected letters. ■ See biography by Bruce Cook (1977).

TRUNGPA, CHOGYAM (1939–1987), Tibetan-born Buddhist religious leader. Considered to be the tenth incarnation of a great Tibetan teacher, Trungpa was raised in Buddhist monasteries, where he received scholastic and meditative training. He fled to India when Chinese troops occupied Tibet (1959) and devoted his life to the preservation and dissemination of Buddhist spiritual teachings. After attending Oxford University (1963–67) he moved to the United States (1970) and established (in Boulder, Colorado) Vajradhatu, a nationwide association of meditation communities and centers, and the Nalanda Foundation, which includes the Naropa Institute. His teachings influenced important Western cultural figures such as Allen Ginsberg, John Cage, Gregory Bateson, and R. D. Laing. His books in English included *Born in Tibet* (1966; with E. C. Roberts), *Cutting Through Spiritual Materialism* (1973), *Journey Without Goal* (1981), *The Teachings of the Theravadin Tradition* (1984), *Exchanging Self for Others* (1984), and *Crazy Wisdom* (1991).

TS'AI YUAN-P'EI. *See CAI YUANPEI.*

TS'AO YU. *See CAO YU.*

TSCHERNICHOWSKY, SAUL (1875–1943), Russian-born Hebrew-language poet. A student of language, literature, and science, Tschernichowsky studied medicine in Heidelberg and Lausanne and worked as a physician in Russia (1907–22). He emigrated to Berlin (1922) and lived in Palestine after 1931. Regarded as the first modern Hebrew poet, he used a variety of poetic forms and was known for his thematic and linguistic innovations. His love and nature poetry, reflecting his pantheist philosophy, represented a fusion of Hellenism and Judaism. He looked to the vigorous ancient Hebrews as his ideal and called for modern Jews to embrace beauty and nature and to free themselves from the stagnant environment of the ghetto. In addition to being a prolific poet, he translated many works into Hebrew, including the *Iliad*, the *Odyssey, Oedipus Rex,* and the Finnish saga *Kalevala*. ■ The study by Eisig Silberschlag (1968) contains English translations of his poems.

TSEDENBAL, YUMJAGIYN (1916–1991), Mongolian political leader. Tsedenbal studied in the Soviet Union, taught economics in Ulan Bator, and became finance minister and chairman of the trade-industrial bank at age 23. As general secretary of the Central Committee of the Mongolian People's Revolutionary party (1940–54), he was the country's second most powerful leader after premier Choibalsan. After Choibalsan's death (1952), Tsedenbal dominated both party and government as chairman of the council of ministers (1952–74), chairman of the presidium of the Great People's Khural (from 1974), and party general secretary (from 1958). Under Tsedenbal's leadership, Mongolia became industrialized and maintained close economic and military ties with the Soviet Union while relations with China deteriorated. He was overthrown in 1984 and lived the remainder of his life in exile in Moscow. In 1990 he was expelled from the Communist party and stripped of his state titles.

TSHOMBE, MOÏSE KAPENDA (1919–1969), Congolese political leader. A member of a wealthy commercial family of the Lunda tribe, Tshombe favored an independent Congo (now Zaïre) composed of a loose confederation of states in which he and his Belgian industrial supporters could exploit the mineral resources of Katanga (now Shaba) province. As provisional president of Katanga, he seceded from the Congo during the intervention crisis of 1960. When U.N. troops finally regained Katanga, he fled the country (1963). Recalled by Pres. Joseph Kasavubu in 1964 to serve as premier, he employed Belgian mercenaries to quell tribal civil war. Amid growing tensions, Tshombe was overthrown by Joseph Mobutu in 1965; he fled into exile, where he remained until his death. ■ See his *My Fifteen Months in Government* (Eng. trans. 1967); Anthony Bouscaren, *Tshombe* (1967); and Ian Colvin, *The Rise and Fall of Moïse Tshombe* (1968).

TSIOLKOVSKY, KONSTANTIN EDUARDOVICH (1857–1935), Russian aerospace scientist. Although Tsiolkovsky conducted few practical experiments, he was a renowned aeronautical theorist. While teaching school, he developed (1903) his theory that a liquid-fuel reaction engine was necessary for a rocket, due to the oxygen lack in the upper atmosphere. He also posited the theory of mass ratio, the ratio of the mass of the rocket before and after fuel consumption, and demonstrated the necessity of multistaged rockets for space travel. He was elected (1919) to the Soviet Academy of Sciences, and his home was made a state museum after his death. ■ See his novel *Beyond the Planet Earth* (Eng. trans. 1960); the biography by A. Kosmodemyansky (Eng. trans. 1956); and V. N. Sokolsky. *K. E. Tsiolkovsky: Selected Works* (Eng. trans. 1968).

TSUI, DANIEL C. (1939–), Chinese-born U.S. physicist. Tsui studied at the University of Chicago (Ph.D. 1967), did research at Bell Laboratories (1968–82), and taught at Princeton University (1982–). Working with Bell colleague Horst Störmer, he devised (1982) an experiment with electrons that led to discovery of the phenomenon known as the fractional quantum Hall effect. This means that at temperatures near absolute zero, electrons exposed to an ultrapowerful magnetic field were a fluid and appear to be split into thirds. The effect, which offered insights into the inner structure and dynamics of matter, was explained by Bell Laboratories theorist Robert B. Laughlin, and Tsui, Störmer, and Laughlin shared the 1998 Nobel Prize in Physics.

TSVET (or TSWETT), MIKHAIL SEMENOVICH (1872–1919), Russian botanist. A graduate of the University of Geneva (Ph.D. 1896) and professor in Warsaw (1908–16), Tsvet did important research on plant pigments and discovered that there are several forms of chlorophyll (1900). Later, he discovered the technique of chromatography while separating plant pigments by passing solutions of ground leaves, ether, and alcohol through a column of powdered chalk. He observed the formation of sharply defined colored bands and realized that small amounts of pigments were being selectively absorbed and that this simple and quick technique could be used to identify and analyze chemical compounds. Chromatography was virtually ignored when first conceived but was widely used during the 1930s and after.

TSVETAEVA, MARINA IVANOVNA (1892–1941), Russian poet. Tsvetaeva wrote rhythmic, spontaneous lyrics that reflected her background; her mother was a musician. She began writing and publishing before the Russian Revolution (1917); she settled (1922) in Paris, publishing such volumes as *Mileposts* (1922) and *Poems to Blok* (1922). *A Fine Fellow* (1924) is her verse rendition of a folktale about a vampire. Tsvetaeva was considered among the most remarkable poets writing in Russian, but from 1925 to 1961 she remained unpublished in her homeland. She returned (1939) to the Soviet Union for personal rather than political reasons. Her husband, a former White army officer and therefore considered politically untrustworthy, was shot (1941). Later that year, Tsvetaeva committed suicide. Translations of her work are in *Selected Poems* (1971; 1986); *A Captive Spirit: Selected Prose* (1980); *The Demesne of the Swans* (1980); *In the Inmost Hour of the Soul* (1989); and *Art in the Light of Conscience: Eight Essays on Poetry* (1992). ■ See Elaine Feinstein, *A Captive Lion* (1987); Simon Karlinsky, *Marina Tsvetaeva* (1985); and Ellendea Proffer, ed., *Tsvetaeva: A Pictorial Biography* (1980).

TUBB, ERNEST (1914–1984), U.S. country musician. When Jimmie Rodgers died in 1933, 19-year-old Tubb phoned his widow to ask for a snapshot of his idol. She invited Tubb to visit her, admired his renditions of Rodgers' songs, and helped promote his career. By the early 1940s, Tubb was a star in his own right, broadcasting his own songs like the million-seller "I'm Walking the Floor Over You" (1941). He played in four movies, and after a dazzling Nashville debut (1942) became a Grand Ole Opry regular. Known as the Texas Troubador, Tubb was instrumental in the continuing success of the Opry, helping to establish the use of the term "country" rather than "hillbilly" to characterize the music it popularized. He teamed up with such vocalists as the Andrews Sisters, Red Roley, Minnie Pearl, and, later, Loretta Lynn. He played himself in the film *Coal Miner's Daughter* (1980). ■ See biography by Ronnie Pugh (1996).

TUBMAN, WILLIAM VACANARAT SHADRACH (1895–1971), president of Liberia. A member of a prominent family, Tubman was trained as a lawyer and elected to the national assembly (1923). He was appointed to the Liberian supreme court (1937), remaining active in the ruling True Whig party. Tubman was elected president in 1943 and held that office from 1944 until his death. While maintaining the dominance of the American-Liberian elite, he focused his efforts on integrating the outlying counties into the national economy and on encouraging foreign investment. He continued Liberia's close ties with the West while reducing its economic dependency on the United States. ■ See biography by Robert A. Smith (1967).

TUCHOLSKY, KURT (1890–1935), German journalist and satirist. A socialist and pacifist who was associated with the *Weltbühne*, Germany's leading left-wing periodical during the 1920s, Tucholsky was one of the most brilliant satirists and cultural and political critics of the Weimar period in Germany. In his essays, poetry, lyrics, and theatrical and literary criticism, he attacked fascism, militarism, nationalism, privilege, and injustice. After becoming disillusioned with the Weimar Republic, he settled in Sweden (1929), where he committed suicide in 1935. English translations of his writings are in *The World Is a Comedy* (1957) and *What If . . . ?* (1968). ■ See study by Harold L. Poor (1968).

TUCKER, RICHARD (Reuben Ticker; 1914–1975), U.S. opera singer. Born in Brooklyn, Tucker made his debut at age 6, singing alto at the Allen Street Synagogue on New York's Lower East Side. Before his marriage to Sara Perelmuth, sister of Metropolitan Opera tenor Jan Peerce, Tucker was a fur salesman who had never heard a Met performance. Establishing a friendly rivalry with Peerce, he studied voice and sang at the Met for 30 seasons (1945–74). As lead tenor in more than 30 roles, he styled himself after Enrico Caruso, distinguishing himself with his sweet yet powerful voice. He was best known for his performances in *Aïda, La Bohème,* and *Pagliacci*. ■ See biography by James A. Drake (1984).

TUDJMAN, FRANJO (1922–1999), Croatian political leader. Tudjman served with Tito's partisans during World War II, became a Communist, and rose through the ranks of the Yugoslav army, retiring as a general in 1961. He then served as director of the Institute of the History of the Worker's Movement in Zagreb and as a professor of political science at the University of Zagreb. However, his support of Croatian nationalism led to his dismissal from the posts (1967), expulsion from the Communist party, and imprisonment (1972; 1982–83). As Communist rule weakened in Yugoslavia, he founded the MDZ (Croation Democratic Union; 1989), a movement favoring self-determination, and was elected president of the Croatian Republic (1990). After Croatia declared its independence (1991), Tudjman led his government in a bitter civil war against the Serb minority and ultimately captured areas of Croatia inhabited by Serbs (1995). He headed a repressive ultranationalist government and was reelected president in 1995 and 1997. With the presidents of Serbia and Bosnia he signed the U.S.-sponsored Dayton Accords (1995) that ended the war in Bosnia.

TUDOR, ANTONY (1909–1987), British dancer and choreographer. Tudor began studying ballet (with Marie Rambert) at the advanced age of 19. He was a dancer with her company, Ballet Club (1930–38), and created such important works as *Jardin aux Lilas, Dark Elegies,* and *Judgment of Paris.* He was a choreographer at New York's Ballet (now American Ballet) Theater (1939–50) and became known for developing the psychological ballet, a dance form that expressed immediate and intense emotions through the use of subtle movements and gestures. His best-known works were *Pillar of Fire, Romeo and Juliet, Undertow,* and *Dim Lustre.* He taught dance at New York's Juilliard School (from 1951), was ballet director at the Metropolitan Opera (1957–63), artistic director of the Royal Swedish Ballet (1963–64), and associate director of the American Ballet Theatre (1974–80). ■ See biography by Donna Perlmutter, *Shadowplay* (1991).

TUGWELL, REXFORD GUY (1891–1979), U.S. public official. Tugwell was an economist at Columbia University (1920–37) when he was drafted into Pres. Franklin D. Roosevelt's brains trust, serving as assistant secretary (1933) and undersecretary of agriculture (1934–36). He also directed the Federal Resettlement Administration (1936–38), helping displaced farm families and other victims of the Depression to achieve "a more abundant life," a New Deal expression he coined. He later served as governor of Puerto Rico (1941–46) and helped formulate the plans for "Operation Bootstrap." As a senior fellow at the Center for the Study of Democratic Institutions in Santa Barbara, California (1966–78), he drafted a model for a new constitution for the United States. He wrote many books including *The Brains Trust* (1968), *The Emerging Constitution* (1975), and the autobiographical *The Light of Other Days* (1962). ■ See his memoir, *To the Lesser Heights of Morningside* (1982), and biography by Michael V. Namorato (1988).

TUKHACHEVSKY, MIKHAIL NIKOLAYEVICH (1893–1937), Soviet marshal. An officer in the czarist army (from 1914), Tukhachevsky joined the Bolsheviks (1918) and became a Red army commander in the Russian civil war (1918–20) and in the Russo-Polish conflict of 1921. He was involved in quashing the Kronstadt rebellion (1921). As chief of staff (1925–28) and deputy military commissar (from 1931) he was instrumental in strengthening and modernizing the Red army. In June 1937, however, he was charged with treason and executed. The subsequent purge of top military leaders, based on trumped-up charges, virtually wiped out the top officer corps of the Soviet military. Tukhachevsky's name was posthumously cleared by party leader Nikita Khrushchev (1958). ■ See Victor Alexandrov,

The Tukhachevsky Affair (Eng. trans. 1964), and Thomas G. Butson, *The Tsar's Lieutenant* (1984).

TUNKIN, GRIGORY IVANOVICH (1906–1993), Soviet diplomat. Tunkin graduated from the Moscow Law Institute (1935). Entering the Soviet diplomatic service in 1939, he was posted in Canada (1942–44) and the People's Republic of Korea (1948–51). Tunkin also taught international law at Moscow University, headed the treaties and legal department of the Soviet foreign affairs ministry (1952–65), and was a member of the U.N. commission on international law (1957–66). He chaired the Soviet Association of International Law (from 1957). He made important contributions to the Marxist theory of international law in the post-Stalin era, and his views of interstate relations provided the juridical basis for the Soviet policies of East-West cooperation and peaceful coexistence during the cold war. His books included *Theory of International Law* (1970, Eng. trans 1974).

TUNNEY, GENE (James Joseph Tunney; 1897–1978), U.S. boxer. A high school dropout from New York City who joined the marines at age 19, Tunney won the light-heavyweight championship of the U.S. expeditionary forces in Europe just at the close of World War I. Returning home, he captured the light-heavyweight world crown by defeating Georges Charpentier, lost the title, then regained it. A methodical, intelligent boxer, Tunney stunned the boxing world by defeating Jack Dempsey in 10 rounds for the world heavyweight title (1926). In 1928 he rebuffed Dempsey's challenge in the famous "long count" match. Knocked to the floor by Dempsey in the seventh round, Tunney had four extra seconds in which to recover when the referee waited for Dempsey to move to a neutral corner. The following year, Tunney retired. During World War II, he was director of athletics and physical fitness for the U.S. Navy. His son, John Tunney (1934–), represented California in the U.S. Senate (1971–77). ■ See his autobiography, *A Man Must Fight* (1932), and Bruce J. Evensen, *When Dempsey Fought Tunney* (1996).

TURATI, FILIPPO (1857–1932), Italian political leader. A wealthy lawyer from Milan, Turati was a cofounder (1892) of the Italian Socialist party and leading advocate of nonviolent, reformist socialism. The party won nearly one million votes just prior to World War I and over a million and a half votes in the 1921 election. After the fascists took power (1922) the socialists were supressed. In 1926 Turati made a dramatic escape from his fascist foes by small boat to Corsica and then Paris, where he served as leader of an antifascist coalition until his death.

TURINA, JOAQUÍN (1882–1949), Spanish composer. After nearly 10 years of study in Paris, Turina returned home in 1914 to emphasize the most characteristically Spanish folk elements in his compositions. He won acclaim for his *Sinfonia Sevillana* (1920), a picturesque evocation of his native city, and his *Danzas fantásticas* (1920, for orchestra) was also very popular. His other compositions include the opera *Jardín de Oriente* (1923), the string quartet *La Oración del torero* (1925), and *La Leyenda de la Giralda* (1927) for piano. Turina was also a conductor, a newspaper critic, and author of a music encyclopedia.

TURING, ALAN MATHISON (1912–1954), British mathematician. Turing studied mathematics at Oxford (1931–35) and made important contributions to mathematical logic while a doctoral student at Princeton (Ph.D. 1938). A pioneer in computer theory, he helped design and construct the Automatic Computing Engine (ACE) at the National Physical Laboratory at Teddington (1945–48) and the Manchester Automatic Digital Machine (MADAM) at the University of Manchester (after 1949). He developed early programming techniques and theorized that machines could be made to think. He also applied mathematical and mechanical theory to the form and growth of living organisms. ▪ See biographies by Sara Turing (1959) and Andrew Hodges (1983).

TURNBULL, COLIN (1924–1994), British-born U.S. social anthropologist. Turnbull studied in Britain, then conducted research in India (1949–51) and subsequently, in the Congo and East Africa. He was associated with the American Museum of Natural History in New York City (1959–69) and taught at George Washington University (1976–85). His best-known books, dealing sensitively with social change and human relationships in contemporary Africa, included *The Forest People* (1961), *The Lonely African* (1962), *Tradition and Change in African Tribal Life* (1966), *The Mountain People* (1972), and *The Human Cycle* (1983).

TURNER, FREDERICK JACKSON (1861–1932), U.S. historian. Born in Wisconsin, Jackson earned his Ph.D. at Johns Hopkins (1890) and taught at the University of Wisconsin (1889–1910) and at Harvard (1910–24). His "frontier" theory of American history, originally presented as a paper at the 1893 World's Fair meeting of the American Historical Society and later published as *The Frontier in American History* (1920), influenced a generation of U.S. historians. Turner considered the frontier a democratizing influence on American life and character, fostering such virtues as curiosity, practicality, and restless expansion. He won a Pulitzer Prize for a collection of essays, *The Significance of Sections in American History* (1932). ▪ See biographies by Ray Allen Billington (1973) and Allan G. Bogue (1998) and study by James D. Bennett (1975).

TURNER, TED (Robert Edward Turner 3d; 1938–), U.S. business executive and sportsman. Using as a base the outdoor advertising business in Georgia that he had inherited from his father (1963), Turner expanded into television in 1970. By 1975 he had transformed a small Atlanta UHF station into the first "super station" (WTBS) by transmitting programs by satellite to cable networks throughout the nation. In June 1980 he established the Cable News Network (CNN), television's first 24-hour newscast. After failing in his attempt to purchase CBS, he bought the MGM/UA Entertainment Company for $1.5 billion (1985). An avid sportsman, he purchased the Atlanta Braves baseball team and the Atlanta Hawks basketball team (1976), and won the America's Cup yachting race against the Australians (1977). He subsequently created separate sports, cartoon, classic-movie, and headline-news channels and merged with Time-Warner (1996) to form one of the largest media conglomerates in the world. In 1997 Turner pledged $1 billion to the United Nations over a 10-year period. He was also one of the top landowners in the United States, having purchased more than 1.2 million acres of ranchland during the 1980s, and he owned the nation's largest herd of buffalo. He was married to actress Jane Fonda (from 1991). ▪ See study by Roger Vaughan (1978) and Robert Goldberg, *Citizen Turner* (1995).

TURNER, TINA (Anna Mae Bullock; 1940–), U.S. singer. In her youth, Turner did field work on the Tennessee cotton plantation managed by her father, then lived with her mother in St. Louis. There she made her singing debut (1956) with Ike Turner and the Kings of Rhythm. She became Ike Turner's lead singer, and after their marriage, they formed the Ike and Tina Turner Revue. The revue gained popularity throughout the 1960s and early 1970s, winning a Grammy Award in 1971. Although Tina Turner was considered the group's dynamo on stage, with her powerful voice and provocative dancing, it was Ike Turner who controlled every aspect of the group's act. Tina Turner left the revue and her marriage during a 1976 tour, walking away virtually penniless. She gradually rebuilt her career and with the release of her album *Private Dancer* (1984), she earned both a Grammy Award and superstardom in her own right. ▪ See her autobiography, *I, Tina* (1986), and Ron Wynn, *Tina* (1985).

TURNER, VICTOR WITTER (1920–1983), British anthropologist. Born in Glasgow, Scotland, Turner took up English literature at University College in London (1938–41), served in the British army (1941–46), then resumed his studies, switching to the anthropology department (B.A. 1949). He earned a Ph.D. from the University of Manchester (1955). Turner combined meticulous ethnography with provocative theory in a career that focused on the study of ritual and the interpretation of symbolism. His fruitful fieldwork among the Ndembu tribe of Zambia (1950–54) produced several books, including *Schism and Continuity in an African Society* (1957), *The Forest of Symbols* (1967), *The Drums of Affliction* (1968), and *Revelation and Divination in Ndembu Ritual* (1975). Other books included *The Ritual Process: Structure and Anti-Structure* (1969), *Dramas, Fields, and Metaphors* (1974), *Process, Performance, and Pilgrimage* (1980), and *From Ritual to Theater: The Human*

Seriousness of Play (1982). Turner taught in the United States at Cornell (1964–68), the University of Chicago (1968–77), and the University of Virginia (1977–83).

TUTU, DESMOND MPILO (1931–   ), South African religious leader. Tutu gave up a teaching career for the ministry and was ordained an Anglican priest in 1960. He was named the first black Anglican dean of Johannesburg (1975) and served as bishop of Lesotho before being appointed the first black general secretary of the South African Council of Churches (1978), an organization representing 12 million people. In this post he became an internationally known leader in the struggle against apartheid, advocating nonviolence and interracial reconciliation. He campaigned in the West for economic pressures against the South African government to force it to change its policies toward the majority black population. In 1984 Tutu won the Nobel Peace Prize and was named the first black bishop of Johannesburg. As archbishop of Cape Town (1986–96) he was titular head of the Anglican Church in South Africa. After the fall of the apartheid system, Tutu was the chair of the Truth and Reconciliation Commission (1995–98), whose controversial 1998 report concluded that from the late 1970s through early 1990 the former white supremacist government carried out numerous abductions and killings of its political enemies and systematically covered up its unlawful activities. The report also stated that the African National Congress (ANC) and the Zulu-based Inkatha Freedom Party were also guilty of killing civilians and committing other violations of human rights. His books include *Crying in the Wilderness* (1982) and *Hope and Suffering* (1984).

TUTUOLA, AMOS (1920–1997), Nigerian writer. Born into a poor Christian family, Tutuola received little formal education but was steeped in the folklore and oral tradition of his native Yoruba people. His first prose epic, *The Palm-Wine Drinkard and His Dead Palm-Wine Tapster in the Dead's Town* (1952), was one of the first works of African fiction widely read in the West. A fantastic tale filled with humor, horror, and exotic supernatural events, and written in a unique idiosyncratic form of Nigerian English, the story was replete with African myths as well as Christian and European elements. His subsequent works, similar to the first, recorded the adventures of a hero or heroine in a jungle forest filled with monsters, gods, ghosts, pygmies, satyrs, and magicians; they included *My Life in the Bush of Ghosts* (1954), *The Feather Woman of the Jungle* (1962), *Abaiyi and His Inherited Poverty* (1967), *The Witch-Herbalist of the Remote Town* (1982), *Pauper, Brawler and Slanderer* (1987), and *Simbi and the Satyr of the Dark Jungle* (1988). ▪ See studies by Harold R. Collins (1969) and Oyekan Owomoyela (1999).

TUWIM, JULIAN (1894–1953), Polish poet. Raised in a middle-class Jewish family from Lodz, Tuwim graduated from Warsaw University and led the post–World War I Skamander group of poets. He wrote short, light, lyric and humorous poems that were traditional in their rhymes but innovative in their rhythms, juxtapositions, and especially in their use of unusual Polish words. His works during the 1930s attacked Poland's militarists and capitalists. Regarded as the major Polish poet between the wars, he is most famous for his antifascist poem *Ball at the Opera* (1936) and the collections *Gypsy Bible and Other Poems* (1933) and *The Burning Essence* (1936). Tuwim left Poland in 1939 and wrote his book-length lyric epic *Polish Flowers* (1940–44; published 1949) while in exile. He returned to Warsaw in 1946. English translations of his work are in *The Dancing Socrates and Other Poems* (1968).

TVARDOVSKY, ALEKSANDR TRIFONOVICH (1910–1971), Soviet poet and editor. Tvardovsky was an accomplished and popular poet, but he made a greater mark as the controversial editor of the journal *Novy Mir* ("new world"; 1950–54; 1958–70). Removed from that position in 1954 when he published articles advocating greater liberalization, he was reinstated in 1958 when party leader Nikita Khrushchev loosened control over the literary establishment. Under his direction, *Novy Mir* became a forum for the intelligentsia, publishing such authors as Vladimir Dudintsev, Ilya Ehrenburg, and Konstantin Paustovsky. Aleksandr Solzhenitsyn's *One Day in the Life of Ivan Denisovich* (1963) first appeared in Tvardovsky's journal. Tvardovsky won a Lenin Prize in 1961, but as political winds shifted he lost favor and was dismissed from his post for a second time (1970). Translations of his work are in *Tyorkin and the Stovemakers* (1974).

TYMUR, MAHMUD. *See TAYMUR, MAHMUD.*

TYNYANOV, YURI (1896–1943), Soviet critic and writer. Tynyanov studied at Petrograd (now Leningrad) University, and by age 29 was a university professor and noted scholar. He wrote on the theory of parody, and he analyzed the work of Aleksandr Pushkin and other writers in *Archaists and Innovators* (1929), which earned him a solid place among the formalist critics. His *Gogol and Dostoevsky* (1921) and *On Literary Evolution* (1927; Eng. trans. 1971) are important critical works. He won popularity with his biographies, including one of Pushkin (1936–37), and his fiction, including the tales *Second Lieutenant Asfor* (1927; Eng. trans. 1965) and *The Wax Figure* (1930). Other works available in English translation included *Death and Diplomacy in Persia* (Eng. trans. 1974), about the writer Aleksandr Griboedov, and *The Problem of Verse Language* (Eng. trans. 1981).

"TYPHOID MARY." *See MALLON, MARY.*

TZARA, TRISTAN (1896–1963), Rumanian-born French poet and critic. Various sources give his original name as

Samuel Rosenstock, Rosenfeld, or Rosenstein. At age 19, Tzara emigrated to France; he wrote in French. Although he produced numerous books of poetry, five plays, and many critical essays, he was known less for these than for his role as a founder of the dada movement, whose principles he enunciated in his *Seven Dada Manifestos* (1916–20; Eng. trans. 1979) and in the review *Dada* (1917–21). It was Tzara who fished the word "dada" (meaning "hobbyhorse") out of the Larousse dictionary. He used it to designate a literary and artistic movement that rejected common usage in matters of language, form, and meaning, and staged provocative literary events in order to challenge the bourgeois values that he blamed for the devastating violence of World War I. Tzara later figured in the surrealist movement, but after breaking with the movement's theoretician, André Breton (1934), he became more involved in political activism than literary theory. Tzara joined the Communist party in 1936 and was active in the Resistance in World War II. His best-known poem was *Approximate Man* (1931; Eng. trans. 1973). English translations of his work are assembled in *Selected Poems* (1975), *Primele Poeme—First Poems* (1976), and *Chanson Dada* (1987). ▪ See biography by Elmer Peterson (1971) and M. A. Caws, *The Poetry of Dada and Surrealism* (1970).

U

UDERZO, ALBERTO. *See GOSCINNY RENÉ.*

ULAM, STANISLAW MARCIN (1909–1984), Polish-born U.S. mathematician. Trained at the Polytechnic Institute at Lvov (D.Sc. 1933), Ulam went to the United States at the invitation of the Institute for Advanced Study at Princeton (1936). After teaching at Harvard and the University of Wisconsin, he joined the Manhattan atom bomb project at Los Alamos, New Mexico (1943), and devised the "Monte Carlo" method of finding approximate answers to complex mathematical problems. The method was widely applied in nuclear physics, weapons design, mathematical economy, and operations research. He also played a major role in developing the hydrogen bomb, planning for nuclear propulsion of space vehicles, and developing electronic computers. He served as research adviser to the Los Alamos Laboratory of the University of California and was professor of mathematics at the University of Colorado (1966–77). He wrote *A Collection of Mathematical Problems* (1960), *Sets, Numbers and Universes* (1974), and an autobiography, *Adventures of a Mathematician* (1976).

ULANOVA, GALINA (1910–1998), Soviet ballerina. Ulanova was born into a family of dancers. She made her debut (1928) with the Maryinsky Ballet (known as the Kirov Ballet, 1935–91) and became prima ballerina of the Bolshoi Theater (1944). Her extraordinary dancing and acting in such works as *Swan Lake, Giselle,* and Lavrovsky's *Romeo and Juliet* helped to give the Bolshoi company its imposing stature in the ballet world. After Ulanova retired (1962), she continued to teach at the Bolshoi. ■ See Albert E. Kahn, *Days with Ulanova* (1962).

ULBRICHT, WALTER (1893–1973), East German political leader. A socialist carpenter who became a Communist functionary, Ulbricht was assigned to liquidate anti-Stalinist Loyalists during the Spanish Civil War. He went to the Soviet Union in 1938 and remained there during World War II, returning home with the Soviet army of occupation. As secretary-general of East Germany's Socialist Unity (communist) party from 1950 to 1971 and head of state, in effect, after 1960. Ulbricht was responsible for the forced collectivization of agriculture, the building of the Berlin Wall (1961), and the suppression of internal dissent ■ See biography by Carola Stern (Eng. trans. 1965).

ULLSTEIN, HANS (1859–1935), LOUIS ULLSTEIN (1863–1933), FRANZ ULLSTEIN (1868–1945), RUDOLF ULLSTEIN (1874–1964), and HERMANN ULLSTEIN (1875–1943), German publishers. The five Ullstein brothers built the House of Ullstein—founded by their father Leopold (1826–99)—into the world's largest private publishing house. They published newspapers and illustrated magazines that sold in the millions and ran one of the largest book-publishing concerns in Germany. However, being Jews, they were forced to sell their company (1934) for one-fifth of its value after the Nazis came to power. Their company became a Nazi party publisher, and the brothers went into exile. After World II the greatly diminished empire was restored to the family, but they sold it to publishing magnate Axel Springer in 1960. ■ See Hermann Ullstein, *The Rise and Fall of the House of Ullstein* (1943).

UM KALTHOUM (Fatma-el-Zahraa Ibrahim; 1900?–1975), Egyptian singer and actress. Um Kalthoum was probably the most famous Arabic woman of the century. She was a singing idol for more than 50 years and appeared in numerous stage and movie productions. Utilizing both classical and popular Arabic, she sang profoundly emotional songs that, in the Islamic tradition, would frequently last from one to two hours. She sang of love, patriotism, and religion in a style marked by its elliptical repetitiveness. Her monthly concerts, broadcast from Cairo and heard throughout the Arab world, were eagerly awaited by all ages and classes of the population.

UNAMUNO Y JUGO, MIGUEL DE (1864–1936), Spanish philosophical writer. Of Basque descent, Unamuno was a professor of Greek and Latin. A leading figure in the "Generation of 1898," he stressed the subjective vision of life in all his work. After publishing the realistic novel *Peace in War* (1897; Eng. trans. 1983), he adopted the modernist style, referring to his later novels such as *Mist* (1914; Eng. trans. 1923), *Abel Sánchez* (1917; Eng. trans. 1947), and *St. Emmanuel the Good, Martyr* (1933; Eng. trans. 1956) as "narratives of intimate realities." Unamuno's poetry cannot be categorized; he wrote short lyrics, such as "In a Castilian Village Cemetery," and long blank-verse poems, including *The Christ of Velázquez* (1920; Eng. trans. 1924). He also wrote plays, but Unamuno may be best known for his philosophical writings. *The Tragic Sense of Life in Men and Nations* (1913; Eng. trans. 1968) concerns his personal struggle with the inevitability of death. *Our Lord Don Quixote* (1905; Eng. trans. 1967) argues that Don Quixote represents an ironic reversal of his creator Cervantes' own tragic sense of life. ■ See biography by Julián Marías (1966); Margaret T. Rudd, *The Lone Heretic* (1963); and Victor Ouimette, *Reason Aflame* (1974).

UNDERWOOD, OSCAR WILDER (1862–1929), U.S. political leader. One of the most respected legislators of his time, Underwood served as U.S. representative (1895–1915) and U.S. senator (1915–27) from Alabama. Although a conservative, he supported Pres. Woodrow Wilson's New Freedom legislation, and as Democratic floor leader and chairman of the House Ways and Means Committee he was instrumental in the passage of the Underwood-Simmons Act (1913), which lowered tariffs; the Federal Reserve Act (1913); and the Clayton Antitrust Act (1914). A strong candidate for the Democratic presidential nomination in 1912 (the first southerner in decades to be seriously considered), Underwood was denied the 1924 nomination mainly due to his denunciation of the Ku Klux Klan and Prohibition. ■ See his autobiography, *Drifting Sands of Party Politics* (1928), and biography by Evans C. Johnson (1980).

UNDSET, SIGRID (1882–1949), Norwegian novelist. Undset's archaeologist father inspired her love for the past. After his death she worked in an office, and she wrote her first novel in 1907. Her initial success was *Jenny* (1911; Eng. trans. 1921), a novelist study of a gifted girl's problems in finding happiness. The autobiographical novel *The Longest Years* (1934; Eng. trans. 1935) described her childhood. Her most famous work was *Kristin Lavransdatter* (3 vols., 1920–22; Eng. trans. 1923–27), a historical novel set in 14th-century Norway. Her numerous other novels and historical cycles also portrayed the problems of idealistic women in past and present society and were greatly influenced by her conversion to Roman Catholicism (1924). Although she won the Nobel Prize in Literature (1928), her later work was regarded as tendentious. ■ See study by Carl Bayerschmidt (1970).

UNGARETTI, GIUSEPPE (1888–1970), Italian poet. Born and raised in Egypt, Ungaretti studied in Paris (1912), where he was greatly influenced by the French symbolists. He wrote his first book of poetry while a soldier in World War I. With Eugenio Montale and Salvatore Quasimodo he founded the "hermetic poetry" movement and revolutionized Italian poetry, which had been ornamented, rhythmical, and rhetorical. Eschewing traditional forms, he used simple syntax and no punctuation or rhyme in his poetry. Using a controlled, condensed style, Ungaretti's poetry employed the emotional force of words in a pure form. His work was often elliptical, symbolic, occasionally obscure, and intensely personal. He taught Italian literature in Brazil (1936–42) and Rome (1942–63) and was a noted translator. English translations of his work are in *Life of a Man* (1958) and *Selected Poems* (1971; 1975). ■ See study by Frederic J. Jones (1977).

UNRUH, FRITZ VON (1885–1970), German writer. The son of a Prussian general, Unruh was persuaded by theatrical director Max Reinhardt (1912) to give up his military career to become a full-time writer. He criticized the military in the drama *Officers* (1912), in the dramatic poem *Before the Decision* (1919), and in the narrative *Way of Sacrifice* (1918; Eng. trans. 1928), but he served in the military for the duration of World War I. He espoused pacifism after the war. One of the most poetically gifted of the German expressionists, he reflected in his works his internationalist, antiauthoritarian, and humanitarian beliefs. He was politically active during the 1920s, and his *Bonaparte* (1927; Eng. trans. 1928) predicted a German dictatorship. He left Germany before it came (1932) and did not return permanently until 1962.

UNTERMEYER, LOUIS (1885–1977), U.S. writer and anthologist. Untermeyer came from an upper-middle-class German-Jewish family in New York City and worked for 20 years in the family jewelry business before retiring in 1923 to devote himself full-time to poetry. He had already edited *Modern American Poetry* (1919), an anthology that would go through multiple editions. He also wrote biographies, a treatise on candy making, memoirs (*From Another World*, 1939; *Bygones*, 1965), and poetry, the best of which was published as *Long Feud* (1962). But it was primarily through his many anthologies of British and American poetry that he influenced the literary tastes of several generations. He produced, in all, some 90 books.

UNTERMYER, SAMUEL (1858–1940), U.S. lawyer. Untermyer was one of the most respected, busiest, and highest-paid trial lawyers of his time. In a career lasting more than 50 years, he participated in many of the country's most important trials and public investigations and profoundly affected the passage of reform legislation. His investigations as counsel for the U.S. House of Representatives' Pujo Committee (1912–13) investigating the "money trust" led to the passage of the Clayton Antitrust Act, the Federal Reserve Act, and the creation of the Federal Trade Commission. During World War I he chaired a federal board that formulated income-tax and excess-profits legislation. In 1927 he served as counsel in a successful libel suit brought against Henry Ford for printing anti-Semitic materials in his *Dearborn Independent*. An avid supporter of the New Deal, Untermyer was also one of the first Americans to denounce Nazi Germany.

U NU. *See NU, U.*

UNWIN, SIR STANLEY (1884–1968), British publisher and author. When his father's print works burned down, Unwin left school at age 14 to work as an office boy. In 1904 he joined the publishing firm of his stepuncle, T. Fisher Unwin, concentrating on foreign rights. At age 28 he established his own firm, George Allen & Unwin, Ltd. (1914). An architect of Britain's book trade, Unwin built an impressive list of serious nonfiction by such authors as Bertrand Russell, Julian Huxley, and Sigmund Freud. He had ties to the socialist Fabian Society, sparked controversy by publishing books by conscientious objectors during World War I, and in the years between the world wars issued works by such left-wing authors as Harold J. Laski and Leon Trotsky. At the urging of his 10-year-old son, Unwin published J.R.R. Tolkien's *The Hobbit* (1937), and later, *The Lord of the Rings* (1954–55). Unwin's book *The Truth About Publishing* (1926) was required reading for generations of publishing professionals. ■ See his autobiography, *The Truth About a Publisher* (1960).

UPDIKE, JOHN (1932–), U.S. writer. Hoping to draw cartoons for the *New Yorker,* Updike followed his Harvard B.A. (1954) degree with art training in Britain. He eventually landed a job on the magazine, but as a writer for the "Talk of the Town" (1955–57); he remained a frequent contributor. Updike's novels included *The Poorhouse Fair* (1959), *Rabbit Run* (1960), *The Centaur* (1963), *Couples* (1968), *Bech: A Book* (1970), and *Rabbit Redux* (1971). One of America's foremost novelists, he treated traditional themes and everyday situations using complex verbal textures: his prose was often metaphorical and lyrical. *Rabbit Is Rich* (1981), the third in the series depicting the American "everyman" Harry "Rabbit" Angstrom, won both a Pulitzer Prize and an American Book Award. It was followed by *Bech Is Back* (1982), *The Witches of Eastwick* (1984), *Roger's Version* (1986), *Rabbit at Rest* (1990; Pulitzer Prize), *In the Beauty of the Lilies* (1996), *Bech at Bay* (1998), and *Gertrude and Claudius* (2000). His short-story collections included *Trust Me* (1987) and *The Afterlife and Other Stories* (1994). *Hugging the Shore* (1983), *Odd Jobs* (1991), and *More Matter* (1999), contained essays and criticism. ■ See his memoirs, *Self-Consciousness* (1989); the biography by S. H. Uphaus (1980); studies by Donald Greiner (1984) and Robert Detweiler (rev. ed. 1984); and James Plath, ed., *Conversations with John Updike* (1994).

URBAN, JOSEPH MARIA (1872–1933), Austrian-born U.S. theatrical designer and architect. Urban emigrated (1911) to the United States from Vienna, where he had worked as a designer, bringing with him many techniques still foreign to the American theater. He designed a number of sets for the Boston Opera Company before moving to New York, where he designed for both the Metropolitan Opera Company and Ziegfeld's *Follies*. In addition, he designed furniture, interiors, homes, and public buildings as well as the Ziegfeld Theater and the New School for Social Research, both in New York City.

UREY, HAROLD CLAYTON (1893–1981), U.S. physical chemist and geochemist. Urey, a professor at Columbia University (1929–45), won the 1934 Nobel Prize in Chemistry after he spearheaded the discovery (1931) of deuterium, a heavy form of hydrogen. Deuterium is valued by chemists as a tracer and by atomic physicists as the main energy source for the hydrogen bomb as well as the means of securing power from uranium fission. During World War II, Urey directed work on the separation of isotopes for the Manhattan atom bomb project, but after the war he advocated nuclear disarmament and world government. As a faculty member

at the University of Chicago (1945–58) and the University of California, San Diego (1958–70), he worked out detailed theories about the origin of the solar system and the origin of life on earth. ■ See his book, *The Planets: Their Origin and Development* (1952).

URIS, LEON MARCUS (1924–), U.S. writer. A high-school dropout from Baltimore, Uris drew on his own experience in the marine corps in writing his first popular novel, *Battle Cry* (1953). His subsequent novels were all based on extensive research into events of contemporary history: *Exodus* (1958), about the birth of Israel; *Mila 18* (1961), about the 1943 Warsaw ghetto uprising; *QB VII* (1970), about a Nazi war criminal; and *Trinity* (1976), about the Irish conflict. *The Haj* (1984) was set in the Middle East. Uris also collaborated with his wife Jill on photo essays on Ireland (1975; 1982) and Jerusalem (1984). His later novels included *Redemption* (1995) and *A God in Ruins* (1999). ■ See study by Kathleen S. Cain (1998).

USSACHEVSKY, VLADIMIR (1911–1990), U.S. composer. Born into a Russian family in Manchuria, Ussachevsky emigrated to the United States (1930) and studied with Howard Hanson at the Eastman Conservatory (Ph.D. 1939) and Otto Luening at Columbia University, where he taught in the music department (1947–80). In 1951 he began to experiment with tape transformation of sounds and timbre; from this he went on to more sophisticated electronic sound processes, becoming one of the pioneers of electronic music. He later experimented with computer music. He was codirector (from 1959) of the Columbia-Princeton Electronic Music Center; he also composed notable choral works that were influenced by his early exposure to Russian Orthodox church music. His compositions included *Sonic Contours* (1952), *Rhapsodic Variations* (1953–54; with Luening), *A Piece for Tape Recorder* (1956), *Conflict* (1971), *Creation* (1973–75), and *Divertimento* (1980–81).

U THANT. *See* THANT, U.

UTRILLO, MAURICE (1883–1955), French painter. Utrillo was the illegitimate son of the acrobat, artists' model, and sometime artist Suzanne Valadon. He had a poverty-stricken childhood that led him to adolescent alcoholism, which his mother sought to control by encouraging him to paint. Although he had no formal training, he produced hundreds of canvases. The dark colors of his first paintings gave way to a brighter palette leading to his "white period" (1908–14), so called because of his use of zinc white to portray ordinary scenes with heightened sensitivity and melancholy. Utrillo sought to render his surroundings as he saw them and depicted the solitude and emptiness of the streets, houses, and cafés of Montmartre. By the 1920s he was one of the most famous and successful Parisian painters. ■ See Robert Coughlin, *The Wine of Genius* (1951), and Peter De Polnay, *Enfant Terrible* (rev. ed. 1969).

V

VAIHINGER, HANS (1852–1933), German philosopher. A professor at the University of Halle (1884–1906), Vaihinger was a renowned authority on the German philosopher Immanuel Kant; he founded the journal *Kantstudien* (1896) and the Kant Society (1904). In his major work, *The Philosophy of "As If"* (1911; Eng. trans. 1924), he argued that human beings construct fictions to satisfy their needs and then proceed to treat reality "as if" it agreed with their inventions. Interested in evolution, he stirred controversy by defining humankind as "a species of monkey suffering from megalomania." ■ See Heinrich F. Wolf, *Philosophy for the Common Man* (1951)

VAKHTANGOV, YEVGENI (1883–1922), Soviet actor and director. A pupil of noted director Constantin Stanislavsky, Vakhtangov was a member of the Moscow Art Theater and was responsible for some of the most innovative productions of the postrevolutionary theater. He was best known for infusing his productions with fantastic, satirical, and grotesque but realistic effects. Among his best known presentations were *Macbeth* (1914), *The Dybbuk* (1922), and *Turandot* (1922). From 1920 he produced plays in his own studio, the Third Workshop, which was renamed the Vakhtangov Theater. He was also the first director of the Hebrew-language Habima Theater (from 1917), which moved to Palestine (1931) and became (1953) Israel's national theater. ■ See Ruben Simonov, *Stanislavsky's Protégé* (Eng. trans., 1969).

VALENTINO, RUDOLPH (Rodolfo d'Antonguolla; 1895–1926), U.S. movie idol. An immigrant (1913) from southern Italy, Valentino worked as a gardener and professional dancing partner in New York before appearing in a dance-hall scene in a 1918 Hollywood movie. His first major role was in *The Four Horsemen of the Apocalypse* (1921), after which Valentino, with his brilliantined hair and smoldering eyes, became the archetype of the arrogant lover in *The Shiek* (1921). His other films included *Blood and Sand* (1922), *Monsieur Beaucaire* (1924), and *The Eagle* (1925). The first male star with sex appeal, Valentino had an extraordinary popular following that did not forget him after his premature death from peritonitis ■ See biographies by Alexander Walker (1976) and Noel Botham and Peter Donnelly (1977).

VALÉRY, PAUL (1871–1945), French poet and essayist. Valéry's early poetry was influenced by the symbolists. After an emotional crisis in the 1890s he ceased publishing and abandoned poetry. He then worked in the ministry of war

and for a news agency (1900–22). After the publication of *The Young Fate* (1917; Eng. trans. 1971) and *Charms* (1922; Eng. trans. 1971), and his critical and philosophical essays, he was regarded as the greatest French poet of the century and elected to the Académie Française (1925). His poetry was sensuous and melodious, noted for its striking abstract and concrete images. Most of his work was concerned with the problems of artistic creation and the relationship between meditative thought and involvement in life. Translations of his works are in *Paul Valéry: An Anthology* (1977) and *Collected Works* (15 vols., 1956–75). ■ See studies by Henry A. Grubbs (1968), Christine M. Crow (1982), and Walter C. Putnam (1995).

VALLEE, RUDY (Hubert Prior Vallee; 1901–1986), U.S. singer and actor. Vallee was a self-taught saxophonist, bandleader, and crooner who interrupted his education at Yale (B.A. 1927) to perform on the tea-dance circuit with a repertoire including his school's "Whiffenpoof Song." His radio program, "The Fleischmann Hour" (1929–39), with his theme song "My Time Is Your Time," was radio's first variety show. Vallee wrote the words and music for "The Vagabond Lover," and starred in the 1929 film of that name. He also appeared as a stuffy millionaire in *The Palm Beach Story*, a 1942 film, and played a serious role in the 1947 film of *I Remember Mama*. He made a comeback in the 1961 Broadway musical, *How to Succeed in Business Without Really Trying*. ■ See his memoirs, *Vagabond Dreams Come True* (1930), *My Time Is Your Time* (1962), and *Let the Chips Fall* (1975).

VALLE-INCLÁN, RAMÓN MARÍA DEL (1866–1936), Spanish writer. A legendary member of the "Generation of 1898," Valle-Inclán was one of the leading figures of the Spanish modernist movement. An extravagant and colorful personality, he wrote notable poems, novels, and plays that at first reflected a turn-of-the-century decadence, but later demonstrated his concern with contemporary society and his antibourgeois iconoclasm. His best-known works included a semiautobiographical novel about a modern-day Don Juan, *The Pleasant Memoirs of the Marquis de Bradomin* (4 parts, 1902–05; Eng. trans. 1924); a novel concerning an archetypal Latin American dictator, *The Tyrant* (1926; Eng. trans. 1929); and the mocking avant-garde dramas *The Dragon's Head* (1910; Eng. trans. 1918), *Divine Words* (1920; Eng. trans. 1968), and *Bohemian Lights* (1920; Eng. trans. 1976). ■ See studies by Verity Smith (1973) and Xavier Vila (1994).

VALLEJO, CÉSAR (1892–1938), Peruvian poet. Vallejo came from a pious Catholic family and never escaped the poverty of his childhood. His mother and paternal grandmother were Indians; Vallejo wrote about Indian culture and experience, drawing on the intensity of Indian language and the intuitive wisdom of Indian legends. His first volume, *Black Heralds* (1918; Eng. trans. 1990), suggested the inadequacy of traditional poetic forms. Imprisoned (1920) on trumped-up arson charges, he wrote *Trilce* (1922; Eng. trans. 1973), an iconoclastic series of poems, in jail. Dismissed from a teaching post on political grounds, he emigrated (1923) to Paris, where he led a bohemian existence and joined (1931) the Communist party. He wrote socialist-realist fiction in the 1930s, including the novel *Tungsten* (1931; Eng. trans. 1988). The poetry published posthumously in *Human Poems* (1939; Eng. trans. 1968) told of the anguish of the Spanish Civil War; *Spain, Let This Cup Pass from Me* (1940; Eng. trans. 1972) expressed his guilt at his own inability to help. English translations of his works are in *The Complete Posthumous Poetry* (1978) and *Selected Poems* (1981). ■ See study by Jean Franco (1976) and Adam Sharman, ed., *The Poetry and Poetics of César Vallejo* (1997).

VALLETTA, VITTORIO (1883–1967), Italian industrialist. A brilliant young Turin economics professor and corporate consultant, Valletta was hired by Giovanni Agnelli, the founder of FIAT, to help rebuild the industrial firm after World War I. He rose rapidly through the ranks and conceived of the idea of mass-producing minicars in Italy. After World War II Valletta served as president of FIAT (1946–66) and built it into one of Europe's biggest auto producers and one of the world's largest industrial complexes, producing steel, aircraft, trucks, ships, and more than 100,000 separate components. He was known for his profit-sharing plan and private welfare programs for his workers. His 1966 agreement with the Soviet government to build a car assembly plant that would produce 600,000 cars annually was the largest single automotive contract in history.

VAN ALLEN, JAMES ALFRED (1914–), U.S. physicist. Van Allen studied at the University of Iowa (Ph.D. 1939) and taught there from 1951. He was one of the organizers of the International Geophysical Year (IGY) of 1957–58. His research on terrestrial magnetism and his use of rockets for studying the upper atmosphere advanced the field of space exploration. His most notable achievement, however, was the discovery of two doughnut-shaped zones of charged particles encircling the earth, now called the Van Allen radiation belts. The particles, arising from solar flares and from cosmic rays, were first detected by a Geiger counter that Van Allen installed in *Explorer I,* the first U.S. satellite (1958). His books include *Origins of Magnetospheric Physics* (1983).

VAN ANDA, CARR VATTEL (1864–1945), U.S. journalist and editor. The legendary managing editor of the *New York Times* (1904–25), Van Anda developed the newspaper into the preeminent news operation in the United States. He played an important role in expanding the paper's staff of foreign and domestic correspondents, in developing the idea of the *Times* as "the newspaper of record," and in founding the *New York Times Index.* He was acclaimed for organizing the paper's complete coverage of World War I and the Paris Peace Conference and for his reports on science (Albert Einstein's theory of relativity) and exploration (the discovery of the North and South poles). ■ See Barnett Fine, *A Giant of the Press* (1933).

VAN BUREN, ABIGAIL (Pauline Esther Friedman Phillips; 1918–), U. S. columnist. A journalism major at Morningside College, Sioux City, Iowa, Van Buren was the twin sister and rival of Ann Landers (Esther Pauline Friedman), whom she followed into the advice-column business in 1956. Beginning in the *San Francisco Chronicle,* the "Dear Abby" column with its flip, astringent advice to the lovelorn and just plain troubled was syndicated to 800 newspapers by 1968. Van Buren advised her readers against smoking, drinking, or premarital sex, recommending instead marriage and humor, religion, psychiatry, and cold showers. She was active in many charitable and philanthropic organizations. ■ See *The Best of Dear Abby* (1982) and Janice Pottker, *Dear Ann, Dear Abby* (1987).

VANCE, CYRUS ROBERTS (1917–), U.S. public official. Vance was a Yale law graduate (1942) who moved from Wall Street litigation to international negotiation. During the 1960s he served as secretary of the army, deputy secretary of defense, and diplomatic troubleshooter, becoming known as a supporter but not a vocal advocate of the Vietnam War. For his loyalty, skills as a negotiator, and streak of "moral idealism," he was named secretary of state in 1977 by Pres. Jimmy Carter. He played a major role in negotiations leading to the SALT II nuclear arms treaty with the Soviet Union (1979) and the Camp David treaty between Israel and Egypt (1979). Vance resigned in 1980, following the failed attempt to rescue U.S. diplomatic hostages in Iran, an attempt he did not support. He subsequently served as cochair of a United Nations–European Community Peace Conference on Yugoslavia (1992–93) and as a special U.N. representative in South Africa (1992) and Nagorno-Karabakh (1992). ■ See his memoirs, *Hard Choices* (1983), and biography by David S. McLellan (1985).

VANČURA, VLADISLAV (1891–1942), Czech novelist. A practicing physician, Vančura was known as one of the most original and influential Czech prose writers of the years between the two world wars. His work is marked by strong plots, rich language, and an innovative experimental style. Known for his communist beliefs, Vančura expressed a hatred for war and social oppression in his novels, which frequently depicted social outcasts as heroes. His best-known works were *The Baker Jan Marhoul* (1924), *Markéta Lazarová* (1931), *The End of the Old Times* (1934; Eng. trans., 1965), and *Three Rivers* (1936). He was murdered by the Germans as one of the reprisals for the assassination of the Nazi official Reinhard Heydrich by Czech Resistance fighters.

VAN DE GRAAFF, ROBERT JEMISON (1901–1967), U.S. physicist. Educated at the University of Alabama, the Sorbonne, and Oxford (Ph.D. 1928), Van de Graaff invented the electrostatic high-voltage generator while a researcher at Princeton (1929). Called the Van de Graaff generator, it enabled scientists to obtain precisely controlled accelerations of charged nuclear particles and electrons at high velocities. It was used in nuclear-physics research and in industry and was adapted for radiation therapy for the treatment of tumors (1937). Van de Graaff was on the faculty of the Massachusetts Institute of Technology (1931–60) and cofounded the High Voltage Engineering Corp. (1946) to manufacture the accelerator.

VANDENBERG, ARTHUR HENDRICK (1884–1951), U.S. senator. Vandenberg worked his way up from copyboy to become editor at age 22 of the *Grand Rapids* (Michigan) *Herald*. By age 32 he had become a power in state Republican politics. Elected to the U.S. Senate in 1928, he was known for his effusive oratory on behalf of reapportionment at home and neutrality abroad. But Vandenberg's most famous speech was his renunciation (1945) of isolationism, which signaled bipartisan support for the emerging global anticommunist policies of the cold war. He wrote three books on Alexander Hamilton (during the 1920s), and his *Private Papers* were published in 1952. ■ See biography by C. David Tompkins (1970).

VANDERBILT, AMY (1908–1974), U.S. journalist and author. A leading authority on etiquette, Vanderbilt was a syndicated columnist for the United Features Syndicate (1954–68) and the *Los Angeles Times* (1968–74). Her column appeared in over 100 newspapers and reached more than 40 million readers. She wrote the monumental *Amy Vanderbilt's Complete Book of Etiquette* (1952), which established her as a major arbiter of manners. She also hosted her own television (1954–60) and radio (1960–62) shows and was official consultant to various organizations, including the U.S. Department of State.

VAN DER MEER, SIMON (1925–), Dutch physicist. Van der Meer received a doctorate in physical engineering from the Technical University in Delft (1956) and worked at the European Organization for Nuclear Research (CERN, located near Geneva; 1956–90). As a senior engineer at CERN he developed a mechanism crucial in controlling the antiproton beam in the colliding-beam experiment devised by Carlo Rubbia (1983). The experiment proved the existence of three subatomic particles (two W particles, one positive

and one negative, and the neutral Z particle). The discovery demonstrated the unity, predicted by theoretical physicists, of two of the four fundamental forces of nature—electromagnetism and the weak force (responsible for radioactive decay)—and was considered a great step toward proving the unified field theory, linking all four natural forces: electromagnetism, the weak force, gravity, and the strong force (responsible for binding together particles of the atomic nucleus). For his contribution to the experiment, Van der Meer shared the 1984 Nobel Prize in Physics with Rubbia.

VANDERVELDE, ÉMILE (1866–1938), Belgian political leader. A leader of the international socialist movement, Vandervelde entered the Belgian parliament in 1894 and held many posts in coalition governments from 1914 to 1937, including minister of justice (1918–21) and foreign minister (1925–27). He advocated universal suffrage, the eight-hour workday, penal reform, and an internationalist, antimilitarist foreign policy. He played a major role in negotiating the Treaty of Locarno (1925). Vandervelde taught political economy at the University of Brussels (1924–37) and wrote several works on socialism and labor history, including *Collectivism and Industrial Evolution* (Eng. trans. 1901), *Three Aspects of the Russian Revolution* (Eng. trans. 1918), and *Socialism versus the State* (Eng. trans. 1919).

VAN DEVANTER, WILLI (1859–1941), U.S. jurist. A prominent lawyer and judge in Wyoming (1884–97). Van Devanter served as an assistant U.S. attorney general (1897–1903) and federal appeals judge (1903–10) before being appointed to the Supreme Court by Pres. William Howard Taft (1910). An ultraconservative supporter of individual property rights and big business and an opponent of big government, Van Devanter was a powerful foe of Pres. Franklin D. Roosevelt's policies and was part of the judicial coalition that declared many key New Deal measures unconstitutional. His resignation on May 18, 1937, the day that the Senate Judiciary Committee was voting on a bill to enable the government to increase the number of judges on the Supreme Court, helped defeat the measure.

VAN DINE, S. S. (**Williard Huntington Wright;** 1888–1939), U.S. mystery writer. Van Dine was a literary and art critic who collaborated on *Europe after 8:15* (1914), studies of nightlife in Europe, with H. L. Mencken and George Jean Nathan. He worked vigorously until confined to bed by a heart ailment. He then read and collected detective novels and resolved to write his own for an elite readership. His upper-crust sleuth, the erudite Philo Vance, became the most popular detective of the late 1920s and early 1930s. He appeared in 12 intricately plotted novels, including *The Canary Murder Case* (1927) and *The Bishop Murder Case* (1929). Van Dine edited *The Great Detective Stories* (1927) and published "Twenty Rules for Writing Detective Stories" (1928). ■ See John Loughery, *Alias S. S. Van Dine* (1992).

VAN DOREN, CARL CLINTON (1885–1950), U.S. writer and literary critic. Born on a farm in Illinois, Van Doren studied classics at the University of Illinois (B.A. 1907) and earned a Ph.D. from Columbia University (1911). As a member of the Columbia faculty (1911–30) he sparked a renewal of interest in American literature. He served as literary editor of the *Nation* (1919–22) and of *Century Magazine* (1922–25) and wrote *The American Novel* (1921; rev. ed. 1940), a standard in its field, and *American and British Literature Since 1890* (with his brother Mark, 1925; rev. ed. 1939). Moving into the field of history, Van Doren wrote a Pulitzer Prize–winning biography of Benjamin Franklin (1939) as well as *The Great Rehearsal* (1948), a study of the 1787 constitutional convention. ■ See his autobiography, *Three Worlds* (1936).

VAN DOREN, MARK (1894–1972), U.S. writer and teacher. Following in the footsteps of his older brother Carl, Mark Van Doren earned a Ph.D. from Columbia University (1920) and remained there as a favorite member of the faculty for nearly 40 years. He succeeded his brother as literary editor at the *Nation* (1924–28), later serving as the magazine's film critic (1935–38). Van Doren wrote more than 50 books, including critical studies of Shakespeare, Dryden, and Thoreau, essays, one play, and many volumes of poetry characterized by a deep love of nature. He won a Pulitzer Prize for his *Collected Poems* (1939), and his *Liberal Education* (1943) remained influential in its field. ■ See his autobiography (1958).

VAN DUSEN, HENRY PITNEY (1897–1975), U.S. Protestant theologian. An advocate of the "social gospel" during his undergraduate days at Princeton, Van Dusen became a prominent liberal Protestant churchman and a leader of the ecumenical movement. He was on the faculty (from 1926) and president (1945–63) of the Union Theological Seminary in New York City and a founder of the World Council of Churches (1948). His books included *World Christianity* (1947) and *One Great Ground of Hope: Christian Missions and Christian Unity* (1961).

VAN DUYN, MONA (1921–   ), U.S. poet. Born and educated in Iowa, Van Duyn taught English at several midwestern universities, including the University of Louisville, Kentucky (1946–50), and Washington University, St. Louis (1950–67). In her poetry she used humorous colloquial language and diverse subjects from everyday life to examine an array of personal, emotional, and philosophical issues. Her works were both popular and highly regarded by critics, and her collections won both the National Book Award (*To See, To Take,* 1970) and the Pulitzer Prize (*Near Changes,* 1990). Her other volumes included *Valentines to the Wide World* (1959), *Merciful Disguises* (1973), *If It Be Not I: Collected Poems, 1959–82* (1993), and *Firefall* (1993). She was also cofounder and coeditor of *Perspective: A Quarterly of Lit-*erature (1947–67) and served as U.S. poet laureat (1992–93). ■ See Michael Burns, ed., *Discovery and Reminiscence: Essays on the Poetry of Mona Van Duyn* (1998).

VANE, JOHN ROBERT (1927–   ), British chemist and pharmacologist. Vane studied at Oxford (Ph.D. 1953) and taught at Yale and the University of London's Institute of Basic Medical Sciences before moving to the Wellcome Research Laboratories, Beckenham, England (1973–1985). Concentrating his research on the chemistry of prostaglandins—the hormonelike structures that play important roles in protecting the body from disease, pain, injury, and stress—Vane discovered the subtype prostacyclin (1976), which inhibits the blood clots that may lead to heart attacks and strokes. Vane also discovered (1971) that aspirin blocks the formation of prostaglandins, thus solving the long-standing mystery of how the drug works in treating pain, fever, and inflammation. Vane shared the 1982 Nobel Prize in Physiology or Medicine with Sune K. Bergstrom and Bengt I. Samuelsson.

VAN HEUSEN, JAMES (Edward Chester Babcock; 1913–   ), U.S. composer. Van Heusen was a radio announcer before achieving prominence in the pop-music field in the late 1930s. During World War II he was a test pilot. He wrote extensively for Frank Sinatra and Bing Crosby, composing the music for the "Road" movies that Crosby made with Bob Hope. Among the upbeat songs from his many Broadway, film, and television scores were the Academy Award–winners "Swinging on a Star" (1944), "All the Way" (1957), "High Hopes" (1959), and "Call Me Irresponsible" (1963); the Emmy Award winner "Love and Marriage" (1955); and "Personality" (1946), "The Tender Trap" (1955), "The Second Time Around" (1960), and "My Kind of Town" (1964).

VANIER, GEORGE PHILIAS (1888–1967), Canadian soldier and statesman. Vanier was born in Montreal, where he practiced law before serving as a lieutenant in World War I. He returned a hero, with one leg amputated and several medals, and remained in the military after the war. Until he retired to private life in 1954, he served in more military and diplomatic posts than any Canadian of his time, including an ambassadorship to France (1944–54). Vanier later served as governor-general of Canada (1959–67), the first French-Canadian to hold that post. He traveled widely, urging Canadian unity. ■ See study by Robert Speaight (1970).

VAN MEEGEREN, HANS (1889–1947), Dutch artist and art forger. Panned by the critics as second-rate, Van Meegeren decided to prove that he was a great painter by passing off his works as those of "old masters." He succeeded. At the time of his death, he was conceded to be one of the greatest art forgers of all time by having fooled the art world with seven "newly discovered" works of Vermeer and

Pieter de Hooch, which he painted between 1936 and 1942. The paintings fetched nearly $3 million from collectors (including Nazi leader Hermann Goering); when he admitted his forgeries, he stunned the art world and became a popular hero in Holland. He was sentenced to one year's imprisonment, but he died before he could serve his time.

VANSITTART, ROBERT GILBERT VANSITTART, 1st BARON (1881–1957), British diplomat. An erudite, upper-class career foreign-service officer, Vansittart was permanent undersecretary of state for foreign affairs (1930–38) and adviser to the foreign secretary (1938–41). He was a noted Germanophobe, advocated a tough anti-German policy, and strongly urged that Britain rearm. His views, referred to as "Vansittartism," were not heeded by the government during the 1930s, but he continued to urge that Germany be permanently demilitarized and its people be reeducated after World War II. ■ See his *Lessons of My Life* (1943) and his autobiography, *The Mist Procession* (1958).

VAN SWERINGEN, ORIN PAXTON (1879–1936), and MANTIS JAMES VAN SWERINGEN (1881–1935), U.S. railroad executives. The Van Sweringen brothers accidentally entered the railroad business when they were forced to build a streetcar line in Shaker Heights, Ohio, a run-down tract of land on the outskirts of Cleveland that they developed into a fashionable suburb. In 1916 they purchased the New York, Chicago, and St. Louis Railroad (called the Nickel Plate) and over the next 15 years bought the Toledo, St. Louis and Western; the Lake Erie and Western; the Chesapeake and Ohio; the Erie; the Pere Marquette; and the Missouri Pacific. By 1932 they controlled 21,000 miles of rail, but as the Depression deepened, their empire weakened, and was broken up following their deaths.

VAN VECHTEN, CARL (1880–1964), U.S. writer. A music and drama critic for the *New York Times* and *New York Press* prior to World War I, Van Vechten became a leading figure of the New York literary world of the 1920s. He wrote works of musical criticism, several witty and popular novels of life in the 1920s, including *Peter Whiffle* (1922), *The Tattooed Countess* (1924), *Nigger Heaven* (1926), and *Spider Boy* (1928), and edited the works of Gertrude Stein (1946; 1949). A supporter and collector of the literature and music of American blacks, he founded (1941) the James Weldon Johnson Memorial Collection of Negro Arts and Letters at Yale University. At age 52 he gave up writing to pursue a successful career as a portrait photographer of some of the leading celebrities of his time, including prominent black artists and intellectuals. ■ See his *Sacred and Profane Memories* (1932) and *Fragments from an Unwritten Autobiography* (2 vols., 1955), and biographies by Edward G. Lueders (1965) and Bruce Kellner (1968).

VAN VLECK, JOHN HASBROUCK (1899–1980), U.S. mathematical physicist. The son of a professor of mathe-

matics, Van Vleck was affiliated with Harvard University for more than three decades. He conducted path-breaking research in the field of modern quantum mechanics, developing a theory of magnetism that built on contributions by Niels Bohr. Van Vleck investigated the magnetic properties of chemical bonds and advanced knowledge of free molecules and of ions in the solid state. His book *The Theory of Electric and Magnetic Susceptibilities* (1932) was the first comprehensive work on quantum magnetics, and he was known as "the father of modern magnetism." His achievements were recognized by a 1977 Nobel Prize in Physics, which he shared with Philip W. Anderson and Nevill F. Mott. The trio's discoveries provided the basis for such electronic devices as high-speed computers, copying machines, lasers, and tape recorders.

VANZETTI, BARTOLOMEO. *See SACCO, NICOLA.*

VARDA, AGNÈS (1928–), French filmmaker. Born in Brussels to a French-Greek family, Agnès Varda was raised in France. She studied photography, served as the stills photographer for the Théâtre National Populaire, and was involved as well in painting, sculpture, and journalism. Turning to filmmaking, she made shorts for the French Tourist Office, and made her feature film debut with the innovative *La pointe courte* (1954). Varda served as screenwriter, director, and producer of her films, which often treated social and political issues and were noted for their elaborate visual detail and their juxtaposition of provocative themes. Her work figured prominently in France's New Wave of filmmaking, which translated into cinematic terms the techniques of the "new novel." Her films included *Cleo from Five to Seven* (1961), *Salut les Cubains* (1964), *Le Bonheur* (1965), *One Stings, the Other Doesn't* (1977), *Vagabond* (1985), *Jacquot de Nantes* (1991), and *101 Nights* (1995). She also made documentaries on the Vietnam War and the Black Panthers. ■ See study by Alison Smith (1998).

VARE, GLENNA (Glenna Collett; 1903–1989), U.S. golfer. The leading figure in women's golf in the 1920s, she captured the U.S. Women's amateur championship in 1922, then regained the title five times (1925; 1928–30; 1935). In the mid-1920s, she won 59 out of 60 straight matches in tournament play. Vare won the French title in 1925; she made four unsuccessful attempts at the British title. Virginia van Wie ended Vare's dominance of the sport in the early 1930s by winning three consecutive titles (1931–34); Vare reclaimed the championship in 1935. The Vare trophy, awarded annually to the woman professional with the best scoring average, was named in her honor. Vare was the women's senior champion in 1960.

VARÈSE, EDGARD (Edgar Varèse; 1883–1965), French-U.S. composer. Varèse, who was trained as an engineer, was at the forefront of avant-garde music for half a century. He composed most of his mature compositions after moving to the United States in 1916 (*Hyperprism*, 1923; *Intégrales*, 1925; *Ionisation*, 1931; *Déserts*, 1954; *Poéme Electronique*, 1958). One of the first composers to experiment with electronic music, Varèse wrote controversial dissonant works utilizing asymmetrical rhythms and unconventional harmonics. He founded several organizations to promote contemporary music. ■ See Louise Varèse, *Varèse: A Looking-glass Diary* (1972), and biography by Fernand Ouelette (Eng. trans. 1968).

VARGAS, GETÚLIO DORNELLES (1883–1954), Brazilian political leader. Born into a prominent political family, Vargas served in the national congress (1922–26) and was the federal finance minister (1926–28) and the governor of the state of Rio Grande do Sul (1928–30) before running unsuccessfully for the presidency as a reform candidate (1930). His backers, however, charged fraud and plotted a successful revolt (October 1930) that brought Vargas to supreme power, which he maintained for 15 years. Although a constitutional government was established in 1934, Vargas overthrew it in a 1937 coup and subsequently presided over a semifacist regime that transformed Brazil into a modern state. He expanded the role of the central government, spurred industrial development, and sponsored social reforms and benefits for workers while suppressing personal liberties. He was overthrown by the military (Oct. 1945) but was reelected president (1950) and served until economic difficulties and numerous scandals made his position untenable. Rather than accept an ultimatum by military to resign, he committed suicide (Aug. 24, 1954). ■ See biography by John. W. F. Dulles (1967).

VARGAS LLOSA, MARIO (1936–   ), Peruvian novelist. Vargas Llosa's first novel, *The Time of the Hero* (1962; Eng. trans. 1966), was based on his own school days in a military academy and criticized *machismo*, the cult of virility. Critics praised the book and viewed it, in retrospect, as a starting point in a "boom" in Latin American fiction. Vargas Llosa established a reputation as Peru's leading contemporary writer with such novels as *Conversation in the Cathedral* (1969; Eng. trans. 1975), which described the dictatorship of Manuel Odría (1948–56); *Captain Pantoja and the Special Service* (1973; Eng. trans. 1978), a popular satirical novel about an officer assigned to organize prostitutes in remote military outposts; *Aunt Julia and the Scriptwriter* (1977; Eng. trans. 1982), a semiautobiographical comic novel that inspired a top-rated TV series in Colombia; and the award-winning *War of the End of the World* (1981; Eng. trans. 1983), a historical epic set in turn-of-the-century Brazil. *The Real Life of Alejandro Mayta* (1984; Eng. trans. 1986) told the story of a fictional Peruvian revolutionary from various perspectives. A political leftist committed to social justice, Vargas Llosa lived in exile in Europe for 18 years; after returning to Peru in 1974, he spoke out when the leftist military government suppressed dissent and he moved

to the right. A best-selling author in Europe and South America, he was also a scholar, critic, and playwright, and hosted a TV talk show in Peru in the 1980s. After running, unsuccessfully, as a conservative candidate for president of Peru in the 1990 elections, he wrote the novels *Death in the Andes* (1993; Eng. trans. 1996) and *The Notebooks of Don Rigoberto* (1997; Eng. trans. 1998) and the essay collection *Making Waves* (Eng. trans. 1997). ■ See his memoir, *A Fish in the Water* (1993; Eng. trans. 1994), the study by L. A. Díez (1970), and study edited by C. Rossman and A. W. Friedman (1978).

VARMUS, HAROLD (1939–   ), U.S. virologist. The son of a physician, Varmus switched from studying 17th-century English literature at Harvard (M.A. 1962) to pursuing medical studies at Columbia University (M.D. 1966). After a stint as a researcher in molecular biology at the National Institutes of Health (1968–70), he abandoned clinical medicine to teach and do research in microbiology at the University of California Medical School in San Francisco (1970–93). In collaboration with colleague J. Michael Bishop and postdoctoral fellows Dominique Stehelin and Deborah Spector, Varmus ushered in a new era of cancer research in the early 1970s by demonstrating that normal genes, responsible for cellular growth and division, can malfunction when disrupted by mutations or chemicals (carcinogens) and cause cancer. For their research, which overturned the theory that cancer was caused by viral genes, Varmus and Bishop shared the 1989 Nobel Prize for Physiology or Medicine. Subsequently, Varmus served as director of the National Institutes of Health (1993–99) and president and chief executive of Memorial Sloan-Kettering Cancer Center in New York City (2000–   ). His books included *Genes and Biology of Cancer* (1993; with R. A. Weinberg).

VASARELY, VICTOR (1908–1997), French painter. The Hungarian-born Vasarely settled in Paris in 1930 and worked in advertising and decoration while he developed a painting technique influenced by constructivism, a relief style using modern industrial materials. During the 1940s he began to create geometric abstractions in which movement was suggested by visual ambiguity and the use of optical illusions. These kinetic works, later featuring dazzling interactive colors, were perfected during the 1950s and 1960s, and Vasarely was hailed as the pioneer of the op art movement. ■ See his *Vasarely* (Eng. trans. 1964) and *Vasarely II* (Eng. trans. 1970).

VASCONCELOS, JOSÉ (1882–1959), Mexican educator, political leader, author, and philosopher. Vasconcelos called for a synthesis of Mexican life based on the indigenous Indian culture, which would transcend what he saw as the narrow limits of Western culture. After serving as rector of the National University (1920–21), he became minister of education (1921–24) and expanded public education and improved the rate of literacy. Entering electoral politics, he lost the 1929 presidential election and was forced into exile. In his later years he was a zealous Roman Catholic and an apologist for the Spanish tradition. He returned to Mexico (1940) and was named director of the National Library, a post he held until his death. His best-known works were *La Raza Cósmica* (1925) and a multivolume autobiography that appeared in an abridged English translation as *A Mexican Ulysses* (1963). ▪ See studies by Gabriella De Beer (1966) and John H. Haddox (1967).

VÁSQUEZ, HORACIO (1860–1936), president of the Dominican Republic. Vásquez was the dominant political figure in his country during the first three decades of the century, an era marked by political instability and an increasing U.S. influence. A three-time president (1899; 1902–03; 1924–30), he launched an era of modest economic progress and reasonable public honesty during the 1920s. As political feuding worsened at the beginning of the Depression, however, he was accused of corruption and of being a puppet of the United States. He was ousted from the presidency in a revolt led by Rafael Trujillo (1930) and exiled.

VAUGHAN WILLIAMS, RALPH (1872–1958), British composer. National music is the "expression of the soul of a nation," wrote Vaughan Williams, who helped to free the British soul from German dominance by incorporating folk songs, hymns, street tunes, even the chimes of Big Ben into his compositions. These included the orchestral work *Fantasia on a Theme by Thomas Tallis* (1910), Mass in G Minor (1923), the opera *Sir John in Love* (1930), featuring the Elizabethan song "Greensleeves," and nine symphonies (1910–58). He taught at the Royal College of Music and wrote *National Music* (1934). ▪ See studies by Alan Dickinson (1963) and Ursula Vaughan Williams (1964).

VAVILOV, NIKOLAI IVANOVICH (1887–1943?), Soviet botanist and geneticist. A student of the geneticist William Bateson of Cambridge, Vavilov was a professor of botany at the University of Saratov (1917–21). He was then appointed head of the Bureau of All-Union Applied Botany and Breeding (later known as the Institute of Horticulture) and began his monumental and comprehensive study of the origin of cultivated plants. He set up research stations throughout the Soviet Union, gathered thousands of plant specimens from around the world, and postulated that there were 12 world centers of origin at which the greatest concentration of diversity in cultivated plant species occurred. During the 1930s he was denounced by the "official" geneticist, T. D. Lysenko, as a purveyor of "Mendelist-Morganist genetics" and he was ousted from his directorship of the institute (1940). Imprisonment in a labor camp and death followed. His books included *The Origin, Variation, Immunity and Breeding of Cultivated Plants* (Eng. trans. 1951).

VEBLEN, OSWALD (1880–1960). U.S. mathematician. A nephew of the sociologist Thorstein Veblen. Veblen earned his Ph.D. at the University of Chicago (1903) and taught at Princeton University (1905–32). He developed the school of mathematics at Princeton's Institute for Advanced Study (1932–50), educating countless young mathematicians in addition to working himself on the foundations of geometry, Veblen was a pioneer in the theory of topology (*Analysis Situs*, 1922), and coauthor of *Foundations of Differential Geometry* (1932; with J.H.C. Whitehead), *Geometry of Complex Domains* (1936; with Wallace Givens), and a standard text of *Projective Geometry* (2 vols., 1910–18; with J. W. Young).

VEBLEN, THORSTEIN (1857–1929), U.S. economist and social critic. One of 12 children of Norwegian immigrants, Veblen received a Ph.D. from Yale in 1884. While teaching at the University of Chicago (1892–1906), he wrote a critique of capitalism that was little known in its own day but had a major impact on later social thought. In *The Theory of the Leisure Class* (1899) he coined the phrase "conspicuous consumption," attacked the values and status-seeking of "captains of industry," and laid groundwork for the institutional economics of John Kenneth Galbraith, Robert Heilbroner, and others. Veblen broadened his critique in numerous writings, including *The Theory of Business Enterprise* (1904) and *Absentee Ownership* (1923). After leaving Chicago, he taught at Stanford (1906–09), the University of Missouri (1911–18), and the New School for Social Research (1918–26). ▪ See studies by Joseph Dorfman (1934) and David Riesman (1975); John P. Diggins, *The Bard of Savagery* (1978); and biography by Elizabeth Jorgensen (1999).

VEIL, SIMONE (Simone Jacob; 1927–   ), French government official. Born into a cultivated Jewish family, Veil and her sister and mother were deported to Nazi concentration camps (1944). She survived to study law in Paris and to advance through France's ministry of justice as an authority on the legal status of women, children, and prisoners. As minister of health and social services (1974–79) she successfully led the controversial campaign to legalize abortion (1974), upgraded health services for the poor, sponsored medical-school reforms, and launched a nationwide antismoking campaign. Veil later served as president of the European parliament (1979–81) and chaired its legal affairs committee. She subsequently served as France's minister of social affairs, health, and urban development (1993–95).

VELASCO IBARRA, JOSÉ MARÍA (1893–1979), Ecuadorian political leader. Five-time president of Ecuador (1934–35; 1944–47; 1952–56; 1960–61; 1968–72). Velasco Ibarra was his country's most important political figure of the century. He was a brilliant orator who appealed mostly to the urban lower classes, but he had neither a well-defined political program to implement once in office nor an ongoing political organization to support him. Thus, he was overthrown four times and served out only his 1952–56 term.

Among his achievements were the destruction of the stranglehold the corrupt Liberal party had on Ecuadorian politics and the construction of new roads and schools throughout the country.

VELÁQUEZ SÁNCHEZ, FIDEL (1900–1997), Mexican labor leader. Born in a small town near Mexico City, Veláquez left school before finishing the sixth grade, worked in a dairy, and founded the Union of Milk Workers (1921). He was a member of the executive committee of the newly formed Confederation of Mexican Workers (CTM; 1936–40) and served as its secretary general for more than half a century (1940–46; 1947–97). Considered the second most powerful political figure in Mexico after the president, he played a major role in gaining legal recognition for the right to strike and gained substantial wage increases for workers in the 1950s and 1960s. However, for most of his later career, the conservative and anti-Communist union leader supported the austerity measures of the governing Institutional Revolutionary party (PRI) and helped to legitimize its rule. His policies, which led to stability and social peace, alienated many workers, particularly in the 1980s and 1990s, as salaries and living standards declined. In the 1990s Veláquez supported the North American Free Trade Agreement (NAFTA), encouraged the privatization of state-owned enterprises, and condemned the Zapatista uprising in Chiapas. ■ See George W. Grayson, *The Mexican Labor Machine* (1989).

VELDE, HENRY VAN DE (1863–1957), Belgian artist and writer. One of the originators of the art nouveau style, Velde turned from painting to the applied arts after a nervous collapse (1889). He made his most important contributions to modern design as a teacher in Germany, where his interior design exhibition (1897) secured his reputation. Influenced by the British arts and crafts movement, he designed a wide variety of useful objects, from bookbindings to jewelry, dresses, ceramics, and tableware, all in the curvilinear forms of art nouveau. His last executed designs were for the Belgian pavilions at the Paris (1937) and New York (1939) international exhibitions.

VELIKOVSKY, IMMANUEL (1895–1979), Russian-born astronomical theorist. Trained as a medical doctor and psychologist, Velikovsky worked in Berlin, Jerusalem, Zurich, and Vienna before emigrating to the United States (1939). He stirred up the scientific world with the publication of his theory of cosmic collisions in *Worlds in Collision* (1950), which asserted that a comet collided twice with the earth in approximately 1500 B.C. causing cataclysmic upheavals. Using an unorthodox "astrohistorical" approach, Velikovsky supplied evidence for his theory from mythology and the history of ancient civilizations. Although his work proved a huge commercial success, most scientists discounted its scientific accuracy. Some of Velikovsky's astronomical hypotheses, such as the emission of radio waves from Jupiter,

have been experimentally verified. He also wrote *Ages in Chaos* (1952), a reexamination of ancient Egyptian history, and *Earth in Upheaval* (1955), a presentation of evidence supporting his catastrophe theory. ■ See the articles in *Velikovsky Reconsidered* (1976) collected by the editors of *Pensée*; Donald Goldsmith, ed., *Scientists Confront Velikovsky* (1977); Alfred de Grazia, ed., *The Velikovsky Affair* (rev. ed. 1978); and Henry H. Bauer, *Beyond Velikovsky* (1984).

VELOSO, CAETANO (1942–   ), Brazilian singer and songwriter. A native of Bahia in northeastern Brazil, Veloso was a pioneer, in the late 1960s, of tropicalismo, an eclectic style that transformed Brazilian popular music. In such songs as "Tropicalia" and "Alegria, Alegria" he fused Afro-Brazilian rhythms, bossa nova harmonies, and elements of North American and British rock music and became a superstar. Although his poetic lyrics were oblique and often surreal, he was seen as a threat by the military government and arrested (1968) and forced (1969) into a 2½-year exile in England. Upon his return to Brazil, he continued to mix both native and foreign influences in his innovative songs, and his lyrics frequently commented on Brazil's social problems. His best-known albums included *Circuladô, Estrangeiro,* and *Livro.* He also wrote several widely read books of poetry.

VELTMAN, MARTINUS, J. G. (1931–   ), Dutch physicist. Veltman studied at the University of Utrecht (Ph.D. 1963) and taught there (1966–81) and at the University of Michigan (1981–97). In the late 1960s he developed a computer program, Schoonship, for performing calculations in quantum field theories. In the 1970s, with his graduate student Geradus 't Hooft, he devised mathematical calculations that allowed scientists to elucidate the quantum structure of electroweak interactions and to predict new electroweak effects. (Electroweak interactions are believed to be the basis of electromagenetism and the "weak" force, which along with gravity and the "strong" force—that binds atomic nuclei together—are recognized as the fundamental forces of nature.) The work of Veltman and 't Hooft enabled physicists to detect previously unknown subatomic particles, including the top quark, and they shared the 1999 Nobel Prize in Physics.

VENING MEINESZ, FELIX ANDRIES (1887–1966), Dutch geodesist and geophysicist. After obtaining a degree in civil engineering (1910), Vening Meinesz was employed by the Geodetic Commission of the Netherlands to make a gravity survey of the country. He invented a pendulum apparatus (1923–28) that not only accurately measured the gravity on the unstable water-soaked Dutch soil but also, when carried in a submarine, precisely measured gravity in the oceans. He made 11 submarine expeditions from 1923 to 1937, cruising all of the oceans and gathering data that made possible the complete mapping of the earth. He was professor at Utrecht (1927–38) and at the Dutch Technical

University in Delft (1938–57). His books included *The Earth and its Gravity Field* (1958; with W. A. Heiskanen) and *The Earth's Crust and Mantle* (1964).

VENIZELOS, ELEUTHERIOS (1864–1936), Greek political leader. The most prominent Greek political figure of the century, Venizelos began his career in his native Crete by leading a successful revolt against the Turks (1897). During his eight terms as premier (1910–33) he was regarded as an international diplomat of the highest rank. He led Greece during the Balkan Wars (1912–13), which resulted in the doubling of Greece's territory and population. His maneuvering to bring Greece into World War I on the side of the Allies (1917) resulted in further territorial expansion. A democrat and a reformer, he led the Liberal party during the Second Republic (1924–35), until he fled Greece, following an abortive antimonarchist revolt organized by his supporters. He died in Paris. ■ See study by Herbert A. Gibbons (1923).

VENTURI, ROBERT (1925–), U.S. architect and writer. A graduate of Princeton (M.A. 1950), Venturi sought to release architecture from the confines of the early modern movement's functionalism. Developing an architecture practice with his wife, city planner Denise Scott Brown, and partner John Rauch, he introduced pop art features into his designs. Drawing inspiration from the commercial landscapes of Las Vegas and Levittown, Venturi developed a plain, yet sophisticated style. He claimed that residents of his buildings could "put their plastic flowers on the windowsills" without violating his designs. His structures included the Humanities Building at the State University of New York, Purchase (1973), the Seattle Art Museum (1991), and the new wing of the National Gallery in London (1991). He was awarded the 1991 Pritzker Prize. His books included the influential volume *Complexity and Contradiction in Architecture* (1966; 2nd ed. 1977); *Learning from Las Vegas* (1972; with Denise Scott Brown and Steven Izenour), a treatment of U.S. suburbs; *A View from the Campidoglio: Selected Essays, 1953–84* (1985); and *Iconography and Electronics upon a Generic Architecture* (1996). ■ See D. Dunster, ed., *Venturi and Rauch: the Public Buildings* (1978).

VERCORS (Jean Bruller; 1902–1991), French novelist, illustrator, and essayist. *The Silence of the Sea* (1942; Eng. trans. 1944) made Vercors famous during World War II. Published by Les Éditions de Minuit, the clandestine press he helped found, it recounts a young German officer's disillusionment with Nazism. *The Guiding Star* (1943; Eng. trans. in *Three Short Novels*, 1947) chronicles the difficulties of an East European immigrant to France. Despite his intense concern with social justice, Vercors never committed himself to any political group. The essays contained in *Plus ou moins homme* ("More or Less human"; 1950) explore modern ethical problems. His later novels included *Sylva*

(1961; Eng. trans. 1962) and *The Raft of the Medusa* (1969; Eng. trans. 1971). He published his memoirs in *For the Time Being* (1960; Eng. trans. 1960) and *The Battle of Silence* (1967; Eng. trans. 1968).

VERÍSSIMO, ÉRICO LOPES (1905–1975), Brazilian writer. Veríssimo's popular and highly acclaimed novels notably *Crossroads* (1935; Eng. trans. 1943). *Consider the Lilies of the Field* (1938; Eng. trans. 1947), and *The Rest Is Silence* (1942; Eng. trans. 1946), reflect the inner conflicts caused by the rapid social and cultural changes taking place in his native state of Rio Grande do Sul in southern Brazil. He was best known for the historical novel *Time and the Wind* (3 vols., 1949–62; vols. I and II. Eng. trans. 1951), which traced the turbulent history of his native state through the fortunes of one family from the 1740s through the late 19th century. He also wrote in English, *Brazilian Literature: An Outline* (1945) and directed the department of cultural affairs of the Pan American Union (1953–56).

VERNADSKY, VLADIMIR IVANOVICH (1863–1945), Russian mineralogist and geochemist. A pioneer in the field of geochemistry, Vernadsky was a professor at the University of Moscow (1890–1911) who early in his career made important studies of the structure and genesis of silicates and aluminosilicates. Subsequently he formulated geochemical classifications of the elements, made pioneering studies of radioactive minerals, and developed the theory of the biosphere—one of the basic components of ecology—through his studies of living organisms and their effect on the earth's crust and atmosphere. He also founded and directed the State Radium Institute (1922–39) and the Department of Living Matter (later the Biogeochemical Laboratory) of the Academy of Sciences (1927–45). ■ See study by Rudolph K. Balandin (Eng. trans. 1982).

VERTOV, DZIGA (Denis Arkadevich Kaufman; 1896–1954), Soviet director. The Kaufman family—whose three sons Denis, Mikhail, and Boris, all made names in cinema history—left (1915) Bialystok in Russian Poland and settled in Moscow during World War I. Denis, who took the pseudonym Dziga Vertov, wrote poetry in the futurist mode, experimented with sound recordings, and at age 20 began innovative work in film. In the early 1920s, working with the small group Kino-glaz ("film eye"), he used combinations of cinematic techniques to shape filmed "actuality" material, and worked on *Kino-Pravda* ("film truth"; 1922–25), a series of 23 newsreels. Vertov became head (1924) of the new Kultkino studio; his experimental films documented the achievements of Soviet power. Vertov's full-length films, the avant-garde *Man with a Movie Camera* (1929), as well as *Enthusiasm* (1930) and *Three Songs of Lenin* (1934), influenced documentary filmmakers in the Soviet Union and the West. In the late 1930s, Stalinist arbiters of culture denounced Vertov as a "formalist." He made only one subsequent full-length movie, *Lullaby* (1937). ■ See Annette

Michelson, ed., *KinoEye: The Writings of Dziga Vertov* (1984).

VERWOERD, HENDRIK FRENSCH (1901–1996), Dutch-born South African political leader, Verwoerd, who was an infant when his family migrated to South Africa, taught social psychology and sociology at Stellenbosch University (1927–37) and edited an Afrikaner Nationalist party newspaper (1937–48) that attacked "British-Jewish imperialism." He gained prominence in the Nationalist party and was appointed a senator after the party gained power in 1948. As minister of native affairs (1950–58) and prime minister (1958–66), Verwoerd enforced and expanded apartheid legislation, forced the repatriation of urban blacks to tribal reserves, and withdrew (1961) from the Commonwealth of Nations after South Africa became a republic. He was stabbed to death on the floor of parliament by a government messenger. ■ See study by Alexander Hepple (1967).

VESAAS, TARJEI (1897–1970), Norwegian writer. Born into a farming family, Vesaas traveled widely and later ran his own farm. Regarded as a leading writer of his generation, he explored in his early novels the value of a life lived close to the soil. In the 1930s and 1940s his works, such as the novel *The Seed* (1940; Eng. trans. 1964) and *House in the Dark* (1945; Eng. trans. 1976), examined major political and social problems, including the Nazi occupation of Norway. His style became more simple and flinty, and his increasingly symbolic and enigmatic narrative evoked the fiction of Franz Kafka. Among his later works were the novels *The Birds* (1957; Eng. trans., 1968) and *The Boat in the Evening* (1968; Eng. trans. 1971), and the poetry collection *Land of Hidden Fires* (1953; Eng. trans. 1973). ■ See study by Kenneth G. Chapman (1970).

VESTDIJK, SIMON (1898–1971), Dutch writer. Vestdijk abandoned his medical practice (1933) to pursue a literary career and published nearly 100 books, including 38 novels and more than 20 volumes of poetry. A self-described psychological realist, he exposed, in rich detail, the barrenness of provincial life in his novels and frequently wrote of youthful and tragic love. Among his best-known works were the eight-volume "autobiography" of Anton Wachter and *The Garden Where the Brass Band Played* (1950; Eng. trans. 1965). He also wrote meticulously researched historical novels, including *Rum Island* (1940; Eng. trans. 1963), a pirate adventure set in 18th-century Jamaica, and several volumes on music, religion, and astrology.

VEZINA, GEORGES (1887–1926), Canadian ice-hockey player. Hockey's first great goaltender, Vezina began playing with the Montreal Canadiens in 1910 and for 15 years was a key team member. With Vezina defending the nets, the Canadiens captured the National Hockey Association championship twice, the National Hockey League title three times, and the Stanley Cup twice. He played in 328 consecutive league games and 39 playoffs. Vezina succumbed to tuberculosis at age 39. His memory was perpetuated in the Vezina Trophy awarded annually to the league's outstanding goaltender.

VIAN, BORIS (1920–1959), French novelist and dramatist. At age 12, Vian suffered an attack of rheumatic fever; the resultant heart condition eventually killed him. Notwithstanding, he worked as an engineer during World War II and was prominent in postwar existentialist circles. For a time he was a jazz trumpeter. His violent, erotic *I Spit on Your Graves* (1946; Eng. trans. 1998), which he claimed he had merely translated, scandalized the public; later, he announced that he wrote it in 10 days to win a bet and that it had no literary value. Among his serious novels were *Froth on the Daydream* (1947; Eng. trans. 1967), a tragic love story, and *Heartsnatcher* (1953; Eng. trans. 1968), an unsentimental observation of children in rebellion against adult tyranny. *The Empire Builders* (1959; Eng. trans. 1967), a satire of social and political institutions, was his most successful play. He also wrote the novel *Mood Indigo* (1968; Eng. trans. 1968), *Blues for a Black Cat and Other Stories* (Eng. trans. 1992), and more than 400 popular songs. ■ See study by Alfred Cismaru (1974).

VICKERY, WILLIAM S. (1914–1996), Canadian-born U.S. economist. The son of an executive of an international relief organization, Vickery was a conscientious objector during World War II and spent his life trying to solve social problems using insights from economic analysis. He studied at Columbia University in New York (M.A. 1937; Ph.D. 1947) and spent his entire teaching career (1947–82) there. His pioneering work in the theory of incentives under asymmetric information, instances in which agents involved in economic transactions have different information from their counterparts, was applied in many diverse, real-world situations to try to produce the most socially desirable behavior, or price. The theory, extended by James A. Mirrlees, was applied to income and commodity taxation, the regulation of public utilities, the pricing of public transport, and the theory of auctions and environmental policy. Vickery and Mirrlees shared the 1996 Nobel Memorial Prize in Economics for their pioneering work.

VICTOR EMMANUEL III (1869–1947), King of Italy (1900–1946). Victor Emmanuel III ascended to the throne on the assassination of his father, Humbert I. Unable to cope with domestic political turmoil after World War I, he turned power over to the fascist leader Benito Mussolini (1922), whose conquests made the Italian king emperor of Ethiopia (1936–43) and king of Albania (1939–43), but whose power reduced him to a figurehead. The king, after Italian reverses in World War II, dismissed the fascist leader in 1943 but remained so unpopular that in 1946 he abdicated in favor of his son, Hubert II, going into exile in Egypt.

VIDAL, GORE (Eugene Luther Vidal, Jr.; 1925–), U.S. writer. Descended from a prominent political family, Vidal was considered a literary boy wonder with the publication of his first novel *Williwaw* (1946), written while he was serving in the army. His other early successes included the plays *Visit to a Small Planet* (1955) and *The Best Man* (1960). A cynic and literary gadfly, he attacked the crassness, conformity, and parochialism of American life and concentrated on themes of power, corruption, and the flouting of convention in his numerous novels. His best-known works of fiction were the iconoclastic series on American politics, *Washington, D.C.* (1967), *Burr* (1973), *1876* (1976), *Lincoln* (1984), *Empire* (1987), *Hollywood: A Novel of America in the 1920s* (1990), *Smithsonian Institution* (1998), and *The Golden Age* (2000); "the mad hymn to bisexuality" *Myra Breckinridge* (1968); and the historical novels *Julian* (1964) and *Creation* (1981). *Live from Golgotha: The Gospel According to Gore Vidal* (1992) was an irreverent account of the origins of Christianity, and *United States: Essays, 1952–1992* (1993) won the National Book Award. He was also a noted essayist, critic, and TV commentator; he ran (unsuccessfully) for public office several times. ■ See his memoir, *Palimpsest* (1995); *Views from a Window: Conversations with Gore Vidal* (1980; with Robert J. Stanton); Bernard Dick; *The Apostle Angel* (1979); the biography by Fred Kaplan (1999); and the study edited by Jay Parini (1992).

VIGO, JEAN (1905–1934), French film director. Son of an anarchist who died mysteriously, Vigo made his first film, *A Propros de Nice* (1930), after undergoing treatment for tuberculosis in Nice. The film contrasted the idle rich of the Riviera to the town's poor and anticipated cinema verité in its technique. Cameraman Boris Kaufman, brother of Soviet film director Dziga Vertov, shot all of Vigos films. *Zéro de Conduite* (1933), a surrealist attack on boarding-school education in which the children revolt, combined dream and fantasy in a highly sensitive and forceful statement. The film was banned by the French government until 1945. *L'Atalante* (1934), a love story taking place on a barge in the Seine, showed its working-class milieu unflinchingly and at the same time created a dreamlike atmosphere in one of the great achievements in cinema. Despite a career shortened by an early death, Vigo influenced generations of filmmakers. ■ See studies by P. E. Salles Gomes (Eng. trans. 1972) and John M. Smith (1972).

VILLA, PANCHO (Doroteo Arango; 1878?–1923), Mexican revolutionary leader, Villa began his legendary military career as a peasant bandit chieftain. In 1910 he participated in the successful revolt against dictator Porfirio Diaz. He supported the short-lived democratic presidency of Francisco Madero and revolted against Victoriano Huerta, who overthrew Madero. Allied with another rebel, Venustiano Carranza, he helped overthrow Huerta. Villa soon broke with Carranza and remained in rebellion during the entire Carranza presidency (1914–20). In 1916, in an attempt to discredit Carranza and take revenge on the United States for supporting Carranza, he executed several U.S. citizens in Mexico and attacked the town of Columbus, New Mexico. Pres. Woodrow Wilson sent a U.S. Army force under Gen. John J. Pershing on a punitive expedition into Villa's home state of Chihuahua, but Villa was never captured and he emerged from the campaign as a popular hero. Although he retired from politics in 1920, he was assassinated in 1923. ■ See his *Memoirs* (Eng. trans. 1965) and biographies by William D. Lansford (1965) and Friedrich Katz (1998).

VILLA-LOBOS, HEITOR (1878–1959), Brazilian composer. As a youth, Villa-Lobos wandered in the Brazilian interior, absorbing native rhythms and melodies. Pedagogue as well as folklorist, he took charge of national music education in 1932 and later established the Brazilian Academy of Music (1945). He is believed to have composed more than 1,500 compositions in every genre from opera to film score and guitar solo, combining Afro-Brazilian, Indian, and Portuguese folk melodies and rhythms with Western European classical music. His best-known works are the 14 *Chôros* (1920–29) and the nine *Bachianas Brasileiras* (1930–44). ■ See biography by Eero Tarasti (Eng. trans. 1995).

VILLARD, OSWALD GARRISON (1872–1949), U.S. journalist. The son of railroad magnate Henry Villard and grandson of abolitionist William Lloyd Garrison, Villard inherited both wealth and powerful moral convictions. As president and editor of the *New York Evening Post* (1897–1918) and the liberal magazine the *Nation* (1918–32), he condemned America's role in both the Spanish-American War and World War I, and crusaded for racial equality, minority rights, women's suffrage, and union rights, and against political corruption, tariffs, and trusts. Though one of the century's foremost American liberals, he isolated himself from liberal opinion in the late 1930's by maintaining his pacifist views and by refusing to support U.S. rearmament or aid to the *Allies* during World War II. ■ See his autobiography, *Fighting Years* (1939), and studies by D. Joy Humes (1960) and Michael Wreszin (1965).

VILLELLA, EDWARD (1936–), U.S. ballet dancer. When Villella began attending his sister's dance classes at George Balanchine's School of American Ballet, the instructors noted his talent; he won a scholarship and studied there for five years. He attended New York Maritime College, where he was campus welterweight champion, but left to join the New York City Ballet (1957). He won acclaim for his athletic, yet sensitive, performances in many roles, particularly in Balanchine's *The Prodigal Son* (1960). He served as artistic director of the Eglevsky Ballet Company (1979–84) and the Miami City Ballet (1985–). ■ See his memoirs, *Prodigal Son* (1992; with Larry Kaplan).

VILLON, JACQUES (Gaston Duchamp; 1875–1963), French painter. The older brother of artists Raymond Duchamp-Villon and Marcel Duchamp, Villon assumed the name of his favorite poet, François Villon, while he was a student. Influenced by Toulouse-Lautrec, he contributed to humorous magazines and created posters for Montmartre cabarets before developing his unusual cubist style, exemplified by *Marching Soldiers* (1913). He later turned to symbolic abstracts (1919–29) in shades of gray and brown. To earn a living, he made notable engraved reproductions of modern paintings; his geometric style later became more colorful. During World War II, Villon painted the landscapes, including *Garden with Pumpkins* (1942), that first brought him public attention. In his last paintings, he fused the strains of impressionism, cubism, realism, and abstraction with which he had earlier experimented.

VINER, JACOB (1892–1970), Canadian-born U.S. economist. Viner was a graduate of McGill University (1914) and Harvard (Ph.D. 1922). He spent most of his academic career at the University of Chicago (1919–46) and at Princeton (1946–60). Viner served as a consultant to the Treasury Department (1934–47), where he took part in the initial planning of the Social Security program, and to the State Department (1943–52). A trade specialist, he wrote *Studies in the Theory of International Trade* (1937) and *International Trade and Economic Development* (1952). He also made major contributions to the theory of cost and production and wrote extensively on the influence of Christian theology on the growth of European economic doctrines. ■ See his *Religious Thought and Economic Society* (1978) and his collected essays in *The Long View and the Short* (1958)

VINOGRADOFF, SIR PAUL GAVRILOVICH (1854–1925), Anglo-Russian scholar. Russian by birth and education, Vinogradoff was a liberal, cosmopolitan scholar who completed his master's thesis on Italian feudalism and his doctoral dissertation on English agrarian history, *Villainage in England* (Eng. trans. 1892). To protest czarist repression he resigned his professorship at the University of Moscow (1901) and emigrated to Britain, where he was professor of jurisprudence at Oxford (1903–25). Other works by Vinogradoff included *The Growth of the Manor* (1905), *Roman Law in Medieval Europe* (1909), and *Outlines of Historical Jurisprudence* (2 vols., 1920–22).

VINSON, CARL (1883–1981), U.S. political leader. A Democratic congressman from Georgia, Vinson served in the U.S. House of Representatives longer than anyone else (1914–65). Known as the "Swamp Fox" and "Mr. Defense," he chaired the Naval Affairs Committee (1931–47) and became the navy's foremost congressional advocate. He backed appropriations for preparedness and opposed excess profits on navy contracts. After World War II he continued to influence defense spending as chairman of the Armed Services Committee (1950–64). In 1980 a nuclear aircraft carrier was named in his honor.

VINSON, FREDERICK MOORE (1890–1953), U.S. jurist. Vinson served as a Democratic congressman from Kentucky (1923–29; 1931–38) before being appointed as a judge on the U.S. Court of Appeals for the District of Columbia (1938–43). A tax and fiscal expert, he directed the Office of Economic Stabilization (1943–45) and was Pres. Harry S. Truman's secretary of the treasury (19454–46). He played a major role in the founding of the International Monetary Fund and the International Bank for Reconstruction and Development. Truman appointed him chief justice of the U.S. Supreme Court (1946), where he was an exponent of a liberal interpretation of the Constitution. He was an advocate of civil rights, but he almost always upheld the government's claims against individuals in civil-liberties cases. He upheld sweeping governmental powers for dealing with social and economic problems and issued a vigorous dissent when the court ruled that Pres. Truman's seizure of the steel industry was unconstitutional (1952).

VIONNET, MADELEINE (1876–1975), French couturiere. Apprenticed to a dressmaker for five years, starting at age 11, Vionnet worked with several well-known designers before opening her own house in Paris in 1912. She revolutionized dress design with her invention of the bias cut, which enabled dresses to be shaped to the body, and dominated the world of high fashion during the 1920s and 1930s. Her many technical innovations influenced later designers.

VIRTANEN, ARTTURI ILMARI (1895–1973), Finnish biochemist. A professor at the University of Helsinki (1924–48) and director of Helsinki's Biochemical Research Institute (from 1931), Virtanen specialized in chemistry relating to nutrition and agriculture and made his most important contributions through research in plant fermentation. His AIV method for preserving green fodder in an acid medium provided northern countries with an economical means of feeding cattle in the winter. Virtanen won the 1945 Nobel Prize for Chemistry; he later served (1948–63) as president of Finland's State Academy of Science and Arts. ■ See his book, *Cattle Fodder and Human Nutrition* (1938).

VISCONTI, LUCHINO (1906–1976), Italian film director. An aristocrat by birth and Marxist by persuasion, Visconti began his career in film as an assistant to French director Jean Renoir (1935). Called the father of the Italian neorealist school, he made a first film., *Ossessione* (1942), that was banned by the fascist government. Later during World War II Visconti was himself arrested and nearly executed, saved by the arrival of American troops in Italy. *La Terra Trema* (1948), *Rocco and His Brothers* (1960), which won Visconti his first international fame, and *The Leopard* (1963) formed his trilogy on Sicily. While his early films stressed naturalism, the later films (*The Damned,* 1969) were operatic in character though extraordinarily attentive to detail. He was also acclaimed for his interpretation of Thomas Mann's *Death in Venice* (1971). Active in theater and opera as well as cinema, Visconti introduced the works of writers Tennessee Williams, Arthur Miller, Jean Paul Satre, and Jean Cocteau to Italy. ■ See study by Geoffery Nowell-Smith (1974); Monica Stirling, *A Screen of Time* (1979); and biography by Gala Servadio (1983).

VISHINSKY, ANDREI YANUARIEVICH. *See VYSHINSKY, ANDREI YANUARIEVICH.*

VISHNIAC, ROMAN (1897–1990), Russian-born U.S. photographer and biologist. Vishniac left the Soviet Union in 1920 after earning an M.D. and a doctorate in zoology and settled in Berlin, where he worked as a biologist. He also studied optics and made several photo expeditions to document the Jewish ghettos of Eastern Europe just prior to World War II. After emigrating to the United States in 1940, he began experimenting in photomicrography, successfully taking pictures of living microscopic animals and eventually photographing the world through the eye of a firefly. Vishniac became a research associate (1957) and later professor at the Albert Einstein College of Medicine in New York and, in 1960, project director of a National Science Foundation film series on "Living Biology." ■ See his *Polish Jews* (1947), *Building Blocks of Life* (1971), and *A Vanished World* (1983).

VITTORINI, ELIO (1908–1966), Italian writer. Vittorini introduced Italian readers to the works of Edgar Allan Poe, D. H. Lawrence, William Faulkner, William Saroyan, and John Steinbeck through translations undertaken during the 1930s. He wrote a major antifascist novel, *In Sicily* (1941; Eng. trans. 1949), and emerged after World War II as one of Italy's most influential critics and novelists. He founded and edited two major cultural periodicals. *Il Politecnico* (1945–47) and *Il Menabò* (1959–67), and wrote several important novels reflecting his independent Marxist outlook, including *The Dark and the Light* (Eng. trans. 1960), *The Twilight of the Elephant* (1947; Eng. trans. 1951; as *Tune for an Elephant,* 1955), and *The Women of Messina* (1949; rev. ed. 1964; Eng. trans. 1973). ■ See study by Joy H. Potter (1979).

VLAMINCK, MAURICE DE (1876–1958), French painter. A bohemian musician and bicycle racer with no formal art training, Vlaminck was inspired to paint by his friendship with André Derain and his enthusiastic response to the works of Vincent van Gogh. Vlaminck's energetic canvases of the early years of the century featured the dramatic use of pure color, and he was one of the originators of fauvism. Subsequently (1908–14) he fell under the influence of Paul Cézanne and increasingly demonstrated concern with for-

mal composition. His late paintings, primarily expressionistic landscapes, were more realistic than his early works and more somber in color.

VLASOV, ANDREI ANDREYEVICH (1900–1946), Soviet general. Vlasov's seminary studies were cut short by the 1917 revolution. Conscripted into the Red army (1919), he rose meteorically through the ranks. He joined the Communist party (1930) and ultimately achieved the rank of lieutenant general. During World War II, his armies helped defend Kiev and Moscow, but while attempting to disrupt the Leningrad blockade, they were encircled. The army was annihilated and Vlasov surrendered to the Germans (1942). An anti-Stalinist, he was allowed to form the Russian Liberation Army made up of Russian prisoners of war and civilian prisoners in Germany, in order to fight against the Soviet Union. Actually, Vlasov had no control over the army and it served a propaganda function only, until it saw limited action in late 1944 and early 1945. He surrendered to the Americans near Prague (May 1945) but was returned to Soviet authorities and executed. In the Soviet Union his name became synonymous with treason. ■ See study by Sven Steenberg (Eng. trans. 1970), and Jurgen Thorwald, *The Illusion* (Eng. trans. 1975).

VOEGELIN, ERIC (1901–1985), German-born U.S. philosopher. Voegelin received a doctorate in law from the University of Vienna and taught there (from 1929). Having written several books attacking racial and authoritarian political ideologies, he was forced to leave his post when the Nazis annexed Austria (1938), and he emigrated to the United States. A scholar with broad knowledge of ancient and modern cultures and steeped in several academic disciplines, he attempted to create a comprehensive philosophy of human existence through an analysis of symbols underlying political institutions and ideologies. He claimed that the source of modern totalitarianism was ancient gnosticism and its drive toward human perfection. Voegelin taught at Louisiana State University (1943–58), the University of Munich (1958–69), and at the Hoover Institution, Stanford University (from 1969), and was best known for *The New Science of Politics* (1952) and *Order and History* (4 vols. 1956–74), ■ See Ellis Sandoz, *The Voegelinian Revolution* (1981) and the studies by Eugene Webb (1981) and Barry Cooper (1999).

VOLCKER, PAUL A. (1927–), U.S., economist and public official. Educated at Princeton (B.A. 1949). Harvard (M.A. 1951), and the London School of Economics. Volcker worked for the Chase Manhattan Bank (1957–61; vice president 1965–68) and was deputy undersecretary (1961–65) and undersecretary (1969–74) of the treasury. A monetarist, he served as president of the Federal Reserve Bank of New York (1975–79) and chairman of the Federal Reserve Board (1979–87). Called the second-most-powerful man in Washington during the first term of Pres. Ronald Reagan, he carried out a controversial policy of high interest rates and shrinking money supplies that was praised by some for reducing inflation but criticized by others for causing a stagnant economy and a high unemployment rate. During Reagan's second term Volcker advocated increased monetary growth. ■ See biography by William R. Neikirk (1987).

VOLLARD, AMBROISE (1867–1939), French art dealer and publisher. One of the early champions of modernism, Vollard held many historic avant-garde art exhibitions at his Paris gallery, including the first one-man shows of Cézanne (1895), Picasso (1901), and Matisse (1904). He supported many of the then-unknown "modern" artists by buying their unwanted works and later made a fortune by selling them after their reputations had been established. Vollard published many high-quality books with original prints by Bonnard, Chagall, Rouault, Duffy, Redon, and others and wrote anecdotal biographies of *Cézonne* (1914; Eng. trans 1923), *Renoir* (1919; Eng. trans. 1925), and *Degas* (1924; Eng. trans. 1927). ■ See his autobiography, *Recollections of a Picture Dealer* (Eng. trans. 1936).

VOLTERRA, VITO (1860–1940), Italian mathematician. A child prodigy, Volterra studied advanced mathematics at age 11 and received a Ph.D. in physics from the University of Pisa at age 22. As a professor of mathematical physics at the University of Rome (1900–31), he became internationally renowned for his contributions to the fields of higher analysis (especially the theory of functionals and the solution of integral equations), electromagnetism, elasticity, celestial mechanics, and biometrics. During World War I he helped to develop military dirigibles and was the first to propose the use of helium in airships. He served in the Italian senate (1905–30), spoke out forcefully against fascism, and was dismissed from the University of Rome (1931) for refusing to sign a loyalty oath to the fascist government. His books included *Theory of Functionals and of Integral and Integro-Differential Equations* (Eng. trans. 1930; reprinted 1959 with a biography).

VON BRAUN, WERNHER (1912–1977), German-born U.S. aerospace scientist. One of Germany's early rocket scientists, Von Braun pioneered the development of the V-2 rocket used against Britain in World War II. As the war was ending he arranged the surrender of himself and many of the engineers on his team to the Americans, calculating that the United States would permit him to continue space research. Von Braun headed the U.S. Army ballistic-weapons program and was assigned responsibility for developing the Redstone and Jupiter rockets. His teams also orbited America's first satellite, *Explorer* (1958). As director of the National Aeronautics and Space Administration (NASA) Space Flight Center (1960–70) he oversaw the development of *Saturn V,* the launch vehicle for *Apollo 8*—the first spacecraft to travel to the moon (1969). Von Braun, who was granted U.S. citizen-

ship in 1955, also served as NASA's deputy administrator for planning (1970–72). His books included *Space Frontier* (rev. ed. 1971) and *History of Rocketry and Space Travel* (rev. ed. 1969). ■ See Erik Bergaust, *Reaching for the Stars* (1960); biography by Helen B. Walters (1964); Frederick I. Ordway III and Mitchell R. Sharpe, *The Rocket Team* (1979); and Dennis Piszkíewicz, *The Nazi Rocketeers* (1995).

VO NGUYEN GIAP. *See GIAP, VO NGUYEN.*

VON HAYEK, FRIEDRICH AUGUST. *See HAYEK, FRIEDRICH AUGUST VON.*

VON KLITZING, KLAUS (1943–), West German physicist. Klaus von Klitzing studied physics at the Technical University in Brunswick, received his doctorate at the University of Würzburg (1972), and did research at the Max Planck Institute for Solid State Physics in Stuttgart (1980–). His experiment on the quantized Hall effect, performed in a high-field magnetic laboratory in Grenoble, France (1980), demonstrated that electrical resistance occurs in extremely precise units at regular intervals, irrespective of the size, thickness, or material through which the electric current if flowing. The discovery, which allowed for the extremely precise (accurate to one part in a million) measurement of the conductivity of electronic components, opened up a new area of research and had immediate practical application in the electronics and computer industries. Von Klitzing won the 1985 Nobel Prize in Physics for his research.

VON MISES, LUDWIG EDLER. *See MISES, LUDWIG EDLER VON.*

VONNEGUT, KURT, JR. (1922–), U.S. writer. After serving in World War II, Vonnegut studied at the University of Chicago and worked in public relations. Turning to writing full-time in 1950, he tackled the great social and moral themes of the day in a gently satirical manner and mildly fantastical style. *Player Piano* (1952), his first novel, dealt with automation and dehumanization, and *Cat's Cradle* (1963), with the end of the world; *Slaughterhouse-Five* (1969) was a futuristic treatment of Vonnegut's experiences as a World War II prisoner of war in Dresden, Germany. *Breakfast of Champions* (1973) depicted life in middle America and, as Vonnegut proclaimed at its end, purged the ghosts of his first 50 years of life. However, subsequent novels, including *Jailbird* (1979), reintroduce familiar faces from Vonnegut's cast. Several meet their end when a neutron bomb is accidentally detonated in *Deadeye Dick* (1982). *Galapagos* (1985) takes place after civilization is destroyed in the late 20th century. His later works included *Hocus Pocus* (1990) and *Timequake* (1997). ■ See his *Fates Worse than Death: An Autobiographical Collage of the 1980s* (1991); biography by Jerome Klinkowitz (1982); and study by Stanley Schatt (1976).

VON STERNBERG, JOSEPH (Jo Sternberg; 1894–1969), Austrian-U.S. film director. Born in Vienna, Von Sternberg divided his youth between Europe and the United States. He established his reputation as a director with a Hollywood gangster film (*Underworld*, 1927) before directing the German classic, *The Blue Angel* (1930), which starred Marlene Dietrich. Back in Hollywood, Von Sternberg created a series of successful vehicles for his sultry blond star: *Morocco* (1930), *Blonde Venus* (1932), *The Scarlet Empress* (1934)—all involving bizarre plots and revolving around the beautifully contrived Dietrich. Von Sternberg directed a few movies during the last 20 years of his life (*Jet Pilot*, 1951), but he never again equaled the success of the Dietrich films. ■ See his autobiography, *Fun in a Chinese Laundry* (1965).

VON STROHEIM, ERICH (1885–1957), Austrian-born U.S. film actor and director. An actor from Vienna Von Stroheim emigrated to the United States in 1906 and played small parts in the classics *Birth of a Nation* (1915) and *Intolerance* (1916). He began directing with *Blind Husbands* (1918) and *Foolish Wives* (1921), casting himself in both as an old-world aristocrat seducing American women. Egotistical and extravagant, Von Stroheim created continuous difficulties with his producers while directing *Greed* (1923), *The Merry Widow* (1925), and *Queen Kelly* (1928). In 1936 he moved to France, where he played the saber-scarred Prussian in *Grand Illusion* (1937). In the Hollywood production of *Sunset Boulevard* (1950) he played a former director reduced to the status of a butler. ■ See Peter Noble, *Hollywood Scapegoat* (1951); studies by Joel Finler (1968) and Thomas Q. Curtiss (1971); and biography by Arthur Lenig (1999).

VON SYDOW, MAX (Carl Adolf von Sydow; 1929–), Swedish actor. Von Sydow trained at the Royal Dramatic Theater School in Stockholm (1948–51) while making his film debut in 1949. Tall and gaunt, with a long gloomy face, he became a member of director Ingmar Bergman's group, starring in the films *The Seventh Seal* (1957), *The Virgin Spring* (1960), and *Hour of the Wolf* (1968), with smaller roles in other Bergman's films. Von Sydow also made several American films, including *The Greatest Story Ever Told* (1965), *The Exorcist* (1973), *Day of the Condor* (1975), *Hannah and Her Sisters* (1986), and *Awakenings* (1990), and starred in the Swedish epics *The Emigrants* (1971), *The Flight of the Eagle* (1982), and *Pelle the Conqueror* (1987). ■ See biography by Peter Cowie (1982).

VOORHIS, (HORACE) JEREMIAH (1901–1984), U.S. political leader. A wealthy Yale graduate, Jerry Voorhis was an idealistic socialist who worked as a laborer and used his inheritance to found a school in California for underprivileged boys. Inspired by the New Deal of Pres. Franklin D. Roosevelt, he joined the Democratic party and was elected to Congress from the Los Angeles area (1936). A dedicated legislator, he amassed one of the most liberal voting records in the House of Representatives and was reelected four times. He was defeated in the 1946 election campaign by neophyte Republican challenger Richard M. Nixon, who attacked Voorhis' character and waged an effective telephone smear campaign. Voorhis subsequently was executive director of the Cooperative League of the U.S.A. in Chicago. His books included *Confessions of a Congressman* (1974) and *The Strange Case of Richard Milhous Nixon* (1972). ■ See study by Paul Bullock (1978).

VOROSHILOV, KLEMENT YEFREMOVICH (1881–1969), Soviet marshall and political leader. A bolshevik from 1903, Voroshilov distinguished himself as a Red army commander in the Russian civil war (1918–20). A loyal ally of Communist party leader Joseph Stalin, he served as defense commissar (1925–40), and (with S. K. Timoshenko) reorganized the Red army. He was appointed to the Politburo in 1926 and was named a marshal in 1935. During World War II he was held responsible for losses to the Finns and for failing to prevent the German blockade of Leningrad. After Stalin's death, Voroshilov served as president of the Soviet Union (1953–60), a largely ceremonial post. When party chief Nikita Khrushchev publicly accused him of complicity in the 1957 "antiparty faction" that attempted to oust Khruschchev from power, Voroshilov acknowledged his mistake, swore loyalty to the party leadership, and was allowed to keep his high posts.

VORSTER, BALTHAZAR JOHANNES (1915–1983), South African political leader. An Afrikaner, Vorster earned a law degree from Stellenbosch University (1938). He was an anti-British activist and was jailed during World War II (1942–44) for neo-Nazi activity. He later joined the white supremacist Nationalist party and was elected to parliament in 1953. "The rights of free speech, assembly, and protest are getting out of hand," he announced in 1961, and proceeded, as minister of justice (1961–66), to curb them. Succeeding the assassinated Hendrik Verwoerd as prime minister (1966–78), Vorster maintained the apartheid system and internal repression but attempted to achieve better relations with South Africa's neighbors. He was elected to the ceremonial post of president in September 1978 but resigned in June 1979 after being implicated in a government financial scandal. ■ See study by John D'Oliveira (1977).

VOZNESENSKY, ANDREI ANDREYEVICH (1933–), Soviet poet. Born into a highly cultured Moscow family, Voznesensky studied architecture but turned to poetry after his student project was destroyed by a fire at the Architectural Institute (1957). The most accomplished of a group of young poets who emerged during the early 1960s, he displayed a remarkable virtuosity in his use of unconventional associations, neologisms, slang, and scientific terminology in works ranging from love poetry to surrealistic satires to musings on American technology. He gave mass poetry readings in sports stadiums, became a cultural hero to many young Russians, and frequently traveled abroad but was often rebuked by official critics and ideologues for his criticism of government censorship and his digs at the Soviet establishment. English translations of his work are in *Selected Poems* (1964; 1966), *Antiworlds and the Fifth Ace* (1967), *Story Under Full Sail* (1974), *Nostalgia for the Present* (1978), and *An Arrow in the Walls: Selected Poetry and Prose* (1987).

VREELAND, DIANA (Diana Dalziel; 1903– 1989), French-born U.S. fashion editor. Vreeland was the daughter of a wealthy Scottish father and an American mother whose Paris home was a gathering place of the leading artists of the pre–World War I era. After the family moved to New York (1914), she lived the life of a debutante, married a banker (1924), and wrote a snobbish, highly popular, and frequently satirized fashion and advice column ("Why Don't You . . . ?") for *Harper's Bazaar* magazine (1936–39). As that magazine's fashion editor (1939–62) she was recognized as one of the country's leading fashion reporters and trend setters, and as editor in chief of *Vogue* (1963–71) she popularized eccentric and youthful styles (for example, boots, pants for women, and the peasant look), coined the term "beautiful people," and exerted an extraordinary influence on popular American fashion and culture. She was special consultant to the New York Metropolitan Museum of Art's Costume Institute (from 1971) and mounted a series of extremely popular fashion exhibitions. ■ See her informal memoir, *D.V.* (1984).

VUILLARD, (JEAN) ÉDOUARD (1868–1940), French painter. Vuillard studied in Paris at the École des Beaux Arts (1886–88) and the Académie Julian (1889), where he was influenced by the Nabi ("prophet") artists Maurice Denis, Pierre Bonnard, and Paul Sérusier, with whom he exhibited (to 1899). Known as an "intimist" painter, Vuillard created scenes of the subdued and cultured upper-middle class in domestic settings. His work embodied aspects of the work of Claude Monet, Paul Gauguin, and Georges Seurat, as well as of the linear techniques and flat colors of Japanese prints. Noted for his decorative panels, Vuillard designed ornamentation for the Théâtre des Champs-Élysées foyer (Paris, 1912–13) and the League of Nations Palace (Geneva, 1938). In his later years he painted impressionistic portraits. ■ See

studies by Claude Roger-Marx (1946) and John Russell (1971).

VYGOTSKY, LEV SEMENOVICH (1896–1934), Soviet psychologist. While enrolled at the University of Moscow, Vygotsky delved into various disciplines of the social sciences as well as into linguistics, philosophy, and the arts. He did not focus exclusively on psychological research until age 28; at age 38, he succumbed to tuberculosis. However, his single decade of research resulted in a cultural-historical theory of personality development that became the most important strand in the new Marxist-restructured Soviet psychology. Working at Moscow's Institute of Psychology (1924–34), he used innovative methods to study the role of cultural and social factors in the development of cognition. His ideas about how language and thinking are linked influenced such Soviet psychologists as his student, Aleksandr Lurta, and such Western psychologists as Jean Piaget. His best-known work, *Thought and Language* (1934; Eng. trans. 1962), introduced a theory of intellectual development. Other works available in English translation include *The Psychology of Art* (1971) and *Mind in Society* (1978), a collection of four theoretical essays.

VYSHINSKY (or VISHINSKY), ANDREI YANUARIEVICH (1883–1954), Soviet jurist and diplomat. Vyshinsky joined the Social Democrat party (1902), studied law in Kiev, and served in the Red army during the Russian civil war (1918–20). A menshevik until he became a bolshevik in 1920, he taught law (1923–25) and was rector (1925–28) at Moscow University, and gained a reputation as a leading theorist of Soviet law. As chief public prosecutor (1935–39), he was dictator Joseph Stalin's principal legal aide in the Communist party purges and the vengeful courtroom accuser of the "old bolsheviks" (whom he termed "mad dogs") at the Moscow show trials (1936–38). He later served as deputy foreign minister (1940–49); when he succeeded V. M. Molotov as minister of foreign affairs (1949–53), he was known for his virulent attacks on the West. He died in New York City, where he was the Soviet representative to the United Nations (1953–54). ■ See his *Law of the Soviet State* (Eng. trans. 1948) and his selected speeches in *The USSR and World Peace* (Eng. trans. 1949).

W

WAGNER, OTTO (1841–1918), Austrian architect. Wagner designed buildings in a neo-Renaissance style and Viennese municipal railway stations in the Art Nouveau idiom before becoming a champion of a rational, simple, and efficient modern architecture in the 1890s. He came to believe in the primacy of function over decoration and was primarily concerned with adapting architecture to the needs of modern city life. His glass and aluminum Postal Savings Bank in Vienna (1904–06) was a landmark in the development of modern architecture. Wagner was an influential professor at the Vienna Academy (from 1894) and wrote the noted textbook *Modern Architecture* (1896; Eng. trans. 1902). ■ See study by Heinz Geretsegger and Max Peinter (Eng. trans. 1970).

WAGNER, ROBERT FERDINAND (1877–1953), German-born U.S. political leader. A child of the New York City slums, Wagner earned a law degree, then entered Democratic politics. Elected to the state assembly (1904) and the state senate (1908), he campaigned for workers' compensation and against unsafe factories and substandard housing. He continued his commitment to social welfare as a state supreme-court justice (1919–26). In 1926 he was elected to the U.S. Senate, where he remained until he retired in 1949. Perhaps the most successful legislator in Senate history, he was the prime mover behind such New Deal legislation as the 1933 National Industrial Recovery Act, the National Labor Relations Act that bears his name (1935), the Social Security Act (1935), and the bill setting up the National Housing Authority (1937). A liberal and compassionate man, he was one of the leading architects of the modern American welfare state. His son, Robert Wagner, Jr., served as mayor of New York City (1954–65). ■ See J. Joseph Huthmacher, *Senator Robert F. Wagner and the Rise of Urban Liberalism* (1968).

WAGNER, ROBERT FERDINAND, JR. (1910–1991), U.S. political leader. Son of U.S. Sen. Robert Wagner, Sr., he served as a Democrat in the New York State Assembly (1938–41) and was Manhattan borough president (1949–53) before serving three terms as mayor of New York City (1954–65), a feat matched only by Fiorello La Guardia. (Edward I. Koch was elected to a third term in 1985.) An uncharismatic but thoroughly professional politician, Wagner bolted his party's regular Tammany organization in 1961 and with the help of the emerging reform wing of the party beat the regulars' candidate for the nomination. He served as U.S. ambassador to Spain (1968–69) before returning to New York City to seek, unsuccessfully, the 1969 Democratic mayoralty nomination.

WAGNER VON JAUREGG (or **WAGNER-JAUREGG**), **JULIUS** (1857–1940), Austrian neurologist and psychiatrist. Wagner von Jauregg, a professor at the University of Vienna (1881–80; 1893–1928), contributed to psychiatry when he proposed (1887) that nervous or mental disorders be treated by deliberately inducing a fever in the patient. In 1917 he inoculated patients suffering from incurable syphilitic paralysis with malaria and noted dramatic improvement in the condition of paralysis. Although the malaria treatment was superseded by the use of antibiotic drugs, Wagner von Jauregg's method was the forerunner of shock therapy, and he was awarded the 1927 Nobel Prize in Physiology or Medicine.

WAIN, JOHN (1925–1994), British poet and novelist. Wain was educated at Oxford (B.A. 1946), taught English literature (1947–55), and wrote much criticism and a biography of Samuel Johnson (1974). He was once grouped with Britain's "angry young men," and his first picaresque novels, such as *Hurry on Down* (1953), were humorous and satirical descriptions of young people caught in a smothering, middle-class society. His later works included *Strike the Father Dead* (1962), *A Winter in the Hills* (1970), *The Pardoner's Tale* (1978), *Dear Shadows: Portraits from Memory* (1986), *Where the Rivers Meet* (1988), *Comedies* (1990), and *Hungry Generations* (1994). His poetry (*Poems: 1949–1979*, 1980) was characterized by its wit and clever verbal dexterity. He was a professor of poetry at Oxford (1973–78) and wrote *Professing Poetry* (1978). ■ See the autobiographical *Sprightly Running* (1962), biography by Elizabeth Hatziolou (1997), and study by Dale Salwak (1981).

WAINWRIGHT, JONATHAN MAYHEW (1883–1953), U.S. Army officer. At the outset of World War II Wainwright was second in command (to Gen. Douglas MacArthur) of the U.S. forces in the Philippines. After MacArthur's departure to Australia (March 1942), Wainwright's forces, though hopelessly outnumbered, heroically fought on Bataan for three months before withdrawing to Corregidor Island, where his isolated army finally surrendered on May 6, 1942. He was imprisoned for three years by the Japanese, but he was rescued in time to attend the surrender ceremonies in Tokyo (Sept. 1945). Given a hero's welcome home after the war, Wainwright received the Congressional Medal of Honor and was promoted to full general. ■ See his memoirs, *General Wainwright's Story* (1946).

WAJDA, ANDRZEJ (1927–   ), Polish filmmaker. Wajda studied at the Lodz film school, and won recognition for an early trilogy (1955–58). It included *Ashes and Diamonds* (1958), which was filmed in the wake of de-Stalinization, and depicted positively the attempt of underground dissidents to assassinate Communist officials. *Everything for Sale* (1968) portrayed Wajda's friend, actor Zbigniew Cybulski, who had died in 1967. *Man of Marble* (1976), which was made after censors rejected the script for 13 consecutive years, recounts the efforts of a woman filmmaker to document the sudden fall from grace of a naive hero of labor who had been exploited for propaganda purposes. *Man of Iron* (1981) celebrates new possibilities in a Poland affected by the Solidarity movement. (He later served as a Solidarity representative in the Polish Senate, 1989–91.) *Danton* (1982), a controversial film about the French Revolution, shows the devastating effects of using violence to quash political resistance and preserve state power. *Dr. Korczak* (1990) and *The Ring with a Crowned Eagle* (1993) were based on World War II themes. He subsequently directed *Pan Tadeusz* (1999). The leading Polish filmmaker of his generation, Wajda was known for brilliant composition, thematic complexity, and stylistic versatility, and was a major figure of Eastern European film. He also worked extensively in the theater. ■ See his memoir, *Double Vision: My Life in Film* (Eng. trans. 1989), and Boleslaw Michalek, *The Cinema of Andrzej Wajda* (Eng. trans. 1973).

WAKSMAN, SELMAN ABRAHAM (1888–1973), U.S. microbiologist. Born in the Ukraine, Waksman emigrated to the United States in 1910. He studied at the University of California at Berkeley (Ph.D. 1918) and taught at Rutgers University (1918–58). Waksman devoted his early research to the study of humus, the microorganisms found in soil, and the effects of these microbes on one another. This work led him (1939) to a systematic search for antibiotics (a term he coined) produced by these microbes and to the discovery of streptomycin (1943). This was the first antibiotic able to control tuberculosis and many other infectious diseases. For this discovery Waksman received the 1952 Nobel Prize in Physiology or Medicine. His books included *Principles of Soil Microbiology* (1927), *Streptomycin* (1949), and *The Actinomycetes* (3 vols., 1959–62). ■ See his autobiography, *My Life with the Microbes* (1954).

WALCOTT, DEREK (1930–), West Indian poet and playwright. Walcott was born to an English-speaking family in St. Lucia, where he was exposed to a mix of languages, including standard and patois French. He was of British and African parentage. Walcott studied at St. Mary's College in St. Lucia (B.A. 1953) and the University of the West Indies in Jamaica, where he taught comparative literature until 1958. In the 1950s, he began writing folk drama and in the 1960s directed the Trinidad Theater Workshop. His plays were collected in *Dreams on Monkey Mountain and Other Plays* (1970); later plays included *O Babylon!* (1976) and *Remembrance* (1979). Walcott was best known, however, for the dense poetry that combines his inventive vivid imagery and Caribbean dialect with the formal structures of English literature. His poems were assembled in *Collected Poems, 1948–1984* (1985). *Another Life* (1973), a long, lyrical poem, was autobiographical. From the mid-1970s, Walcott taught at various universities in the United States. He won a prestigious MacArthur fellowship in 1981. His later works included *Omeros* (1990), an epic-length poem of the Caribbean inspired by the *Odyssey* of Homer; *The Odyssey: A Stage Version* (1993); *What the Twilight Says: Essays* (1998); and *Tiepolo's Hound* (2000), a long narrative poem celebrating art and nature. He was awarded the 1992 Nobel Prize for Literature. ■ See William Baer, ed., *Conversations with Derek Walcott* (1996), and studies by Robert D. Hammer and John Thieme (1999).

WALD, GEORGE (1906–1997), U.S. biochemist. Born on New York City's Lower East Side to immigrant parents, Wald studied at New York University (B.S. 1927) and received a Ph.D. in zoology from Columbia University (1932). He spent two years as a fellow in the Berlin laboratory of chemist Otto Warburg, where he identified vitamin A in the retina and contributed to scientists' understanding of the link between vision and nutrition. Wald spent the rest of his career at Harvard (1932–77). In the 1940s he delved further into the process of vision, discovering the chemical reactions involved in the function of the rods. In the late 1950s, collaborating with Paul K. Brown, he identified the pigments of the eye that respond to yellow-green light and illuminated the cause of color blindness. For this work, Wald shared the 1967 Nobel Prize in Physiology or Medicine with Haldan K. Hartline and Ragnar Granit. An early, vocal opponent of the Vietnam War, Wald spent his postretirement years lecturing on the dangers of nuclear weapons and the arms race. His books included *General Education in a Free Society* (1945) and *Twenty-Six Afternoons of Biology: An Introductory Laboratory Manual* (1962).

WALD, LILLIAN D. (1867–1940), U.S. nurse and social worker. After graduating from nursing school in New York City, Wald moved to the Lower East Side, the home of thousands of recently arrived, poverty-stricken Jewish immigrants. Dedicating her life to serving these people, she set up the Henry Street Settlement (1893), which provided a visiting-nurse service as well as artistic and recreational activities. The settlement gained an international reputation, and Wald remained there until 1933. She also initiated the world's first public-school nursing system (1902), suggested a home-nursing service adopted by the Red Cross and the Metropolitan Life Insurance Co., originated the idea of the U.S. Children's Bureau (established in 1912), and helped found and became the first president of the National Organization for Public Health Nursing (1912). Wald was active in many humanitarian and reform organizations. ■ *The House on Henry Street* (1915) and *Windows on Henry Street* (1934) are autobiographical. See Doris Daniels, *Always a Sister* (1989).

WALDHEIM, KURT (1918–), Austrian diplomat. Waldheim's legal studies at the University of Vienna were interrupted when he was drafted into the German army during World War II (1939). Wounded while serving on the Eastern front (1941), he claimed to have been released from the army (1942) and permitted to resume his studies. He received his doctorate of law in 1944 and entered the diplomatic service (1945). He was Austria's permanent observer at the United Nations (1955–56), envoy and ambassador to Canada (1956–60), director general for political affairs in the foreign ministry (1960–64), U.N. ambassador (1964–68; 1970–71) and foreign minister (1968–70). After running unsuccessfully for president of Austria as a candidate of the conservative People's party (1971), Waldheim served as U.N. secretary-general (1972–82). He supervised U.N. peacekeeping operations in Africa, Cyprus, and the Middle East, and helped organize relief projects in Bangladesh, Cambodia, and Nicaragua. While he was again running for the presidency of Austria (1986) it was reported that he had been an intelligence officer with a German army in the Balkans (1942–45) that killed thousands of partisans and civilians in Yugoslavia and deported Jews from Greece. Waldheim claimed that he was merely an interpreter and that he had no knowledge of war crimes. Despite the controversy brought about by these revelations, he won the election with 53.9 percent of the votes cast. His memoirs, *In the Eye of the Storm* (Eng. trans. 1986), does not mention his service in the Balkans. An international panel of historians issued a 200-page report in 1988 claiming that Waldheim knew of war crimes committed by his units but that he had not committed any crimes. ▪ See studies by Robert Herzstein (1988) and Richard Bassett (1989); Shirley Hazzard, *Countenance of Truth* (1990); and Eli Rosenbaum, *Betrayal* (1993).

WALESA, LECH (1943–), Polish labor and political leader. The son of a carpenter, Walesa received vocational training and worked as an electrician at the Lenin Shipyard in Gdansk (1967–76), the scene of violent antigovernment demonstrations in 1970. He was dismissed from his job for unauthorized labor agitation, but he remained active in the underground union movement. A founder of the free labor union known as Solidarity (1979), Walesa led the strike movement of July–August 1980 that involved over 300,000 workers. He signed the historic agreement with the government (Aug. 31, 1980) that granted workers the right to form independent unions, the right to strike, and significant wage increases. Solidarity eventually attracted an estimated 10 million members, but martial law was declared on Dec. 13, 1981; the union was suppressed, and Walesa and thousands of its leading members were imprisoned. After being released (Nov. 1982), Walesa went back to work as an electrician in Gdansk. He continued to lead Solidarity (through 1990) and he was awarded the 1983 Nobel Peace Prize. He subsequently chaired the talks with the Communist government that led to free elections (1989) that were won by Sol-

idarity candidates and brought an end to Communist rule. Walesa was elected president of Poland in December 1990, but was defeated for a second term in 1995 primarily because of dissatisfaction with the economic results of rapid market reforms that restored capitalism to Poland. ▪ See his autobiography, *The Struggle and the Triumph* (Eng. trans. 1992); R. Eringer, *Strike for Freedom* (1982); *The Book of Lech Walesa* (1982); and Roger Boyes, *The Naked President* (1994).

WALEY, ARTHUR (Arthur David Schloss; 1889–1966), British translator and critic. Educated at Cambridge, Waley was the assistant keeper of prints and drawings at the British Museum (1912–30) and a lecturer on oriental studies. His translations of Japanese and Chinese classics, among the first and the finest of their time, strongly influenced such poets as Ezra Pound and T. S. Eliot and made oriental literature accessible to the general reader. Among his many translations are *170 Chinese Poems* (1917), *Japanese Poems* (1919), and *The Tale of Genji* (6 vols., 1925–32). He also wrote several historical and literary studies but never traveled to China or Japan. ▪ See Ivan Morris, ed., *Madly Singing in the Mountains* (1970), and Alison Waley, *A Half of Two Lives* (1983).

WALGREEN, CHARLES RUDOLPH (1873–1939), U.S. business executive. Trained as a pharmacist in Chicago, he bought his first drugstore in 1902, organized the Walgreen Co. after purchasing his seventh store (1916), and eventually built up the largest chain of drugstores in America. Known as "the father of the modern drugstore," he pioneered open display merchandising, introduced modern store equipment, and popularized the drugstore lunch counter and soda fountain. The "malted" was reportedly introduced in one of his stores. At the time of his death there were nearly 500 Walgreen stores in 215 cities coast-to-coast.

WALKER, ALICE (1944–), U.S. writer. Born into a poor black family in rural Georgia, Walker studied at Sarah Lawrence College (B.A. 1965), participated in the civil-rights movement, and taught literature and writing at several colleges. Her works, concerned with the problems of black families and particularly of black women, included the poetry collections *Once* (1968), *Revolutionary Petunias* (1973), *Good Night, Willie Lee, I'll See You in the Morning* (1979), and *Horses Make a Landscape Look More Beautiful* (1984); the novels *The Third Life of Grange Copeland* (1970) and *Meridian* (1976); and the short-story collections *In Love and Trouble* (1974) and *You Can't Keep a Good Woman Down* (1981). Her novel *The Color Purple* (1982), written as a series of letters between two sisters, one in the rural South and the other in Africa, won the 1983 Pulitzer Prize in Fiction. It was filmed in 1985. Her later works included the novels *The Temple of My Familiar* (1989), *Possessing the Secret of Joy* (1992), *By the Light of My Father's Smile* (1998), and *The Way Forward Is with a Broken Heart*

(2000); *Her Blue Body Everything We Know: Earthling Poems, 1965–1990* (1991), *Warrior Marks: Female Genital Mutilation and the Sexual Blinding of Women* (1993; with Pratibha Parmar), and *Anything We Love Can Be Saved: A Writer's Activism: Essays, Speeches, Statements and Letters* (1997). ■ See study by Donna Winchell (1992).

WALKER, JAMES JOHN (1881–1946), U.S. political leader. A dapper lawyer and one-time songwriter, Jimmy Walker won an upset victory (with the support of Tammany Hall—Manhattan's Democratic political machine) to become mayor of New York in 1925. Witty and popular, he had extensive contacts in the Broadway and entertainment world and became a world-famous celebrity. His administration made improvements in transit, sanitation, and health care, but it was also marked by fraud, corruption, and incompetence, according to a state investigation. Unable to explain some large financial transactions, Walker resigned in 1932 and took refuge in Europe for several years. ■ See Gene Fowler, *Beau James* (1949), and George Walsh, *Gentleman Jimmy Walker* (1974).

WALKER, JOHN E. (1941–), British molecular biologist. Walker studied at Oxford University (D.Phil. 1969) and did research at the Medical Research Council Laboratory of Molecular Biology, Cambridge (1974–). During the 1980s he began studying adenosine triphosphate (ATP), a molecule that is the source of energy for all living cells, ultimately responsible for such diverse processes as transmitting nerve impulses, activating muscle contractions, and building proteins. Expanding the pioneering work of Paul D. Boyer, Walker mapped the structure of ATP synthase, the enzyme that plays a key role in the formation of ATP, and confirmed Boyer's hypothesis regarding the unusual molecular mechanism of the enzyme. Walker shared the 1997 Nobel Prize in Chemistry with Boyer and Jens C. Skou for his discoveries.

WALKER, KATH. *See NOONUCCAL, OODGEROO.*

WALKER, MICKEY (Edward Patrick Walker; 1901–1981), U.S. boxer. Walker, whose mother was a boxing fan, was nicknamed the "toy bulldog" for his tenacity in the ring. A versatile fighter whose weight ranged from 147 to 170 pounds during his career, he boxed in four different weight classes. He won the welterweight crown at age 21 (1922) and the middleweight title four years later. After losing to light heavyweights Tommy Loughran and Maxie Rosenbloom, he fought heavyweight Jack Sharkey to a 15-round draw in 1931. He was knocked out the next year by Max Schmeling. During his 17-year career (1919–35), Walker fought 160 professional bouts, winning 60 by knockouts and 33 by decision. He was married six times to four women, and squandered $4 million. After his retirement, he studied art and attained considerable success as a primitive painter. ■ See his autobiography, *The Will to Conquer* (1953).

WALKER, RALPH THOMAS (1889–1973), U.S. architect. A graduate of the Massachusetts Institute of Technology (1911), Walker was senior partner of the firm Vorhees, Walker, Smith and Smith, which designed the New York Telephone Co. (1923–26) and the Irving Trust (1929–32) buildings in Manhattan, the AFL-CIO building in Washington, D.C. (1956), and the Eastman Memorial in Rochester, New York. He was also known for his pioneering designs of research facilities (Bell Telephone Laboratories, 1939; Argonne National Laboratories, 1952) and for the buildings he designed for the New York World's Fair (1939). He was hailed by his peers as "the architect of the century" in 1957 for his catalytic role on civic, professional, and national planning committees. ■ See his *The Fly in the Amber: Comments on the Making of Architecture* (1957) and *Ralph Walker, Architect* (1957).

WALLACE, DEWITT (William Roy DeWitt Wallace; 1889–1981), U.S. publisher. Wallace studied at Macalester College in Minnesota (1907–9), where his father was president, and later transferred to the University of California at Berkeley, but did not earn a degree. In the period between Macalester and Berkeley (1910–11), he jotted on cards the highlights of articles from current magazines that caught his interest. Based on this card file, he later conceived the idea of a pocket-sized magazine that would consist entirely of condensed "articles of lasting interest" from other publications. In 1920, he and his wife, Lila Bell Acheson Wallace, assembled the first issue and called it the *Reader's Digest*. It was an instant success, and by the time of Wallace's death, its circulation had reached 30.5 million copies each month, attracting more than 100 million readers in 163 countries (in 16 languages). It typically featured humor, watered-down science, self-improvement, and advice on health, child rearing, and sex. The magazine reflected Wallace's political views, which were strongly conservative and anticommunist. The Wallaces made contributions to many causes through the Reader's Digest Foundation. ■ See James Playsted Wood, *Of Lasting Interest: The Story of the Reader's Digest* (1967); John Heidenry, *Theirs Was the Kingdom* (1993); and Peter Canning, *American Dreamers* (1996).

WALLACE, GEORGE CORLEY (1919–1998), U.S. political leader. A law graduate of the University of Alabama (1942), he served as a circuit-court judge (1953–59), and became known as a segregationist. Elected Democratic governor of Alabama in 1962, he achieved a national reputation for confronting federal marshals during the integration of the University of Alabama (1963). His social conservatism, antipathy to Washington, and appeal to white working-class voters prefigured much of the politics of the 1970s, 1980s, and 1990s and predated many of the conservative policies of Richard Nixon and Ronald Reagan. He was succeeded as governor by his wife Lurleen in 1967. He won 9.9 million votes as a conservative third-party presidential candidate in 1968 but was shot and partially paralyzed while campaigning (as a Democrat) in 1972. He was reelected governor of Alabama in 1970 and 1974 and, moderating his views and apologizing for his earlier opposition to civil rights, was elected to an unprecedented fourth term in 1982 with strong black support. ■ See his *Stand Up for America* (1976), the biography by Marshall Frady (1968), and study by Michael Dorman (1976).

WALLACE, HENRY AGARD (1888–1965), U.S. political leader. Wallace, whose father was the U.S. secretary of agriculture under presidents Harding and Coolidge, edited the family's agricultural journal and developed a high-yield strain of hybrid corn before becoming involved in politics. He switched his allegiance from the Republican to the Democratic party in 1928. As Franklin D. Roosevelt's activist secretary of agriculture (1933–40) and vice president (1941–45), he epitomized the philosophy of a "New Deal" for the common person. While secretary of commerce (1945–46), he broke with Pres. Harry Truman over cold-war policies and was forced to resign. Advocating cooperation with the Soviet Union and criticizing the growth of fascism at home, Wallace ran unsuccessfully for president on the Progressive party ticket (1948). ■ See biographies by Dwight MacDonald (1948) and Edward L. and Frederick H. Schapsmeier (2 vols., 1968–71); the study by Graham J. White (1995); and John C. Culver and John Hyde, *American Dreamer* (2000).

WALLACE, IRVING (1916–1990), U.S. writer. A former magazine journalist and occasional Hollywood screenwriter, Wallace wrote a succession of best-selling novels embroidering on real people or events, including *The Chapman Report* (1960), about a Kinsey-type sex survey; *The Prize* (1962), about Nobel Prize intrigue; and *The Seventh Secret* (1986), about Hitler's last days. With his son David Wallechinsky and others, he broke new publishing ground with such reference books as *The People's Almanac* (1975, 1978, 1981) and a spin-off, *The Book of Lists* (1977, 1980), and *Significa* (1983). He also wrote *The Intimate Sex Lives of Famous People* (1982). ■ See John Leverence, *Wallace: A Writer's Profile* (1974).

WALLACE, MIKE (1918–   ), U.S. television journalist. Mike Wallace began broadcasting as a student announcer for the University of Michigan's radio station. In the 1940s he acted on radio shows such as "The Lone Ranger," "The Green Hornet," "Ma Perkins," and "The Guiding Light" and worked in radio entertainment as a navy officer in World War II. Later Wallace hosted or narrated numerous television programs and appeared in a forgotten Broadway comedy, *Reclining Figure* (1954). But it was in producing and broadcasting news—particularly in conducting tough interviews—that he made his mark. On *Nightbeat*, and later on *Mike Wallace Interviews*, he grilled political figures, stars, celebrities, and other people in the news, producing lively and revealing glimpses of their lives. After 1968 Wallace was a host of CBS's "60 Minutes," television's most popular news program, which often took a hard look at controversial subjects. ■ See his autobiography, *Close Encounters* (1984; with Gary P. Gates).

WALLACE, RICHARD HORATIO EDGAR (1875–1932), British novelist. Born out of wedlock to an actress, Wallace left school at age 12. After military service, he became a journalist. He sold his first successful novel, *The Four Just Men* (1905), for only £75, but he later made a fortune with a constant stream of potboiler thrillers and mystery stories that sold millions of copies. To maintain his lavish lifestyle he churned out in 28 years over 170 novels, 15 plays (one of which he wrote over a weekend), and innumerable magazine and newspaper articles. Yet he was in debt when he died in Hollywood, where he was working on the script of *King Kong*. His best-known works included *Sanders of the River* (1911), *The Mind of Mr. J. G. Reeder* (1925), and *The Terror* (1930). ■ See his autobiography, *People* (1926), and biography by Margaret Lane (rev. ed. 1964).

WALLAS, GRAHAM (1858–1932), British political scientist. Wallas was an Oxford graduate (1881) and early Fabian socialist (1886–1904) who was active in local politics as well as academia. He taught at the London School of Economics (1895–1923) and was university professor of political science at the University of London (1914–23). Wallas favored a "psychodynamic approach" to the study of politics, bypassing laws and institutions to focus on the nonrational, subconscious components of political behavior. His writings included *Human Nature in Politics* (1908) and *The Great Society* (1914). ■ See Martin J. Wiener, *Between Two Worlds* (1972), and studies by Sugwon Kang (1972) and Terence H. Qualter (1979).

WALLENBERG, RAOUL (1912–1947?), Swedish diplomat. Born into one of Sweden's wealthiest industrial and banking families, Wallenberg traveled widely in his youth and graduated from the University of Michigan, with a degree in architecture and city planning (1935). He subsequently worked in firms in South Africa, Palestine, and Sweden. During World War II, when the Germans occupied Hungary (1944) and began deporting the Jewish population to death camps in Poland, Wallenberg was sent to Budapest as a special diplomatic envoy of neutral Sweden to try to rescue as many Jews as possible. By issuing special passports, fabricating identification papers, bribing guards and government officials, establishing safe houses, and making false or exaggerated claims to Nazi officials, he was personally able to save an estimated 100,000 Jews between July and December 1944. After the Soviet Army liberated Budapest (Jan. 1945), Wallenberg was arrested by Soviet authorities and never seen again. Although rumors persisted that he remained alive for decades, the Russian government announced in 1991 that Wallenberg had died in prison in 1947. ■ See John Bierman, *Righteous Gentile* (1981), and biography by Kati Marton (1995).

WALLENDA, KARL (1905–1978), German-born circus performer. The son of a trapeze artist, Wallenda joined a high-wire act as a teenager, formed his own troupe in 1922, and in 1925 created the first high-wire pyramid with his brother and two other men. An immediate sensation, the "Great Wallendas" joined the U.S. Ringling Brothers Circus (1928) to become the most famous daredevil act in circus history. The troupe first performed its unique seven-person, three-tiered pyramid in 1947 as the climax of its act but discontinued it after an accident during a performance in Detroit killed two members of the troupe. Wallenda fell to his death while trying to walk along a wire strung between two 10-story hotels in San Juan, Puerto Rico. His career was the longest in recorded circus history. ■ See biography by Ron Morris (1976).

WALLER, FATS (Thomas Wright Waller; 1904–1943), U.S. jazz musician, singer, and composer. The son of a prominent African-American New York City Protestant minister who thought jazz was "music from the devil's workshop," Waller nevertheless became a protégé of James P. Johnson, the founder of the "stride" school of jazz piano. He achieved fame in the late 1920s as a pianist (Oscar Levant called him the "black Horowitz"), band leader, comedy singer, and composer ("Ain't Misbehavin'," "Honeysuckle Rose"). Waller's numerous recordings, made after 1934, were known for their parodic treatment of current popular songs, and he was one of the few jazz innovators to have a lucrative commercial career. ■ See Ed Kirkeby, Ain't Misbehavin' (1966); biographies by Joel Vance (1977) and Maurice Waller (1977); and Paul Machlin, Stride (1985).

WALLERSTEIN, IMMANUEL (1930–   ), U.S. sociologist. A professor at Columbia University (1958–71), Wallerstein gained a reputation as a leading student of African affairs with his books Africa: The Politics of Independence (1961), The Road to Independence (1964), and Africa: The Politics of Unity (1967). As distinguished professor of sociology at the State University of New York at Binghamton (from 1976) and founding director of its Fernand Braudel Center, he utilized a sophisticated neo-Marxian analysis in The Modern World System, a highly influential historical study in three volumes: Capitalist Agriculture and the Origins of the European World Economy in the 16th Century (1974), Mercantilism and the Consolidation of the European World Economy 1600–1750 (1980), and The Second Era of the Great Expansion of the Capitalist World Economy, 1730–1840s (1989). He also wrote The Capitalist World Economy (1980), Unthinking Social Science: The Limits of Nineteenth-Century Paradigms (1991), and After Liberation (1995) and edited Review, a journal of world system analysis.

WALLING, WILLIAM ENGLISH (1877–1936), U.S. labor reformer and political leader. Born into a wealthy and prominent family, Walling was educated at Harvard and the University of Chicago. One of the leading progressives of his generation, he helped found the National Women's Trade Union League (1903) and the National Association for the Advancement of Colored People (NAACP; 1909) and was an active member of the Socialist party (1910–17) until he resigned because of its antiwar policy during World War I. Disillusioned with the antidemocratic aspects of the Russian Revolution, he modified his earlier revolutionary positions and, after the war, worked full-time for the reformist American Federation of Labor (AFL). In 1935 he headed the Labor Chest, an organization set up to help workers in fascist countries. His books included The Larger Aspects of Socialism (1913), Progressivism—and After (1914), and American Labor and American Democracy (1926). ■ See James R. Boylan, Revolutionary Lives (1998).

WALLIS, HAL B. (1899–1986), U.S. film producer. Wallis worked in movie exhibition and publicity, became head of production (1928–31; 1933–44) at Warner Brothers, then established (1944) his own independent production company. His great success was due in part to his eye for film talent; Wallis "discovered" such stars as Errol Flynn, Burt Lancaster, Kirk Douglas, and Elvis Presley. He produced many film classics, including Little Caesar (1930), The Maltese Falcon (1941), Casablanca (1943), and Gunfight at the OK Corral (1956); he later produced several acclaimed costume dramas, including Becket (1964) and Anne of the Thousand Days (1969). ■ See his autobiography Starmaker (1980).

WALPOLE, SIR HUGH SEYMOUR (1884–1941), New Zealand–born British novelist and critic. Following a Cambridge education (1903–06) and a brief stint of teaching at a boys' preparatory school, Walpole began his literary career. He gained recognition and financial success with Fortitude (1913) and The Duchess of Wrexe (1914). A prolific but uneven writer, he wrote popular historical novels, such as the "Herries Chronicle": Rogue Herries (1930), Judith Paris (1931), The Fortress (1932), and Vanessa (1933); horror stories; and a trilogy based on his childhood: Jeremy (1919), Jeremy and Hamlet (1923), and Jeremy at Crale (1927). He also wrote plays, short stories, criticism, and biographies. Roman Fountain (1940) was autobiographical. ■ See biography by Rupert Hart-Davis (1952) and study by Elizabeth Steele (1972).

WALSH, STELLA (Stanislawa Walasiewicz; 1911–1980), Polish-U.S. track athlete. Walsh was brought to the United States from Poland as an infant. After 1930, when she became the first woman to run 100 yards in under 11 seconds, track enthusiasts expected a strong showing from her in the 1932 Olympics. However, she faced economic hurdles during these Depression years. When she was laid off from her job, the only offer forthcoming was a sports-related position that would have disqualified her from amateur competition, including the Olympics. She got no help from U.S. sources, and one day before she was due to become a U.S. citizen, agreed to take a job at the Polish consulate in New York and compete for Poland. She captured a gold medal by running 100 meters in 11.9 seconds at the Los Angeles Olympics; in 1936 she won a silver medal for Poland in the same event. The world record she set in 1935 by running 200 meters in 23.6 seconds stood for 17 years. Some blamed her decision to compete for Poland on the lack of U.S. support for women athletes; others criticized Walsh herself. She was not granted U.S. citizenship until 1947. Walsh was fatally shot outside a store where she was buying streamers to welcome Polish Olympic athletes to the United States.

WALTER, BRUNO (Bruno Walter Schlesinger; 1876–1962), German-born U.S. conductor. Born into a middle-class Jewish family in Berlin, Walter studied music there at the Stern Conservatory. He became (1894) an assistant to Gustav Mahler, then director of the Hamburg Opera, and later followed Mahler to the Vienna Opera (1901). He subsequently directed the Munich Opera (1913–22) and headed the Berlin State Opera (1925–29). Prohibited by the Nazis from working in Germany after 1933, Walter returned to the Vienna Opera until 1938. In 1939 he emigrated to the United States, where he was a frequent guest conductor with the New York Philharmonic (1941–60) and the Metropolitan Opera (1941–59). He was best known for his performances and recordings of the German-Viennese school of composers, including the music of Mozart, Haydn, Bruckner, Richard Strauss, and Mahler, of whom he also wrote a 1936 biography. Walter's autobiography, *Theme and Variations* (1946), revealed the conductor's literary knowledge and personal charm.

WALTERS, BARBARA (1931–), U.S. television journalist. Walters began working in television fresh out of Sarah Lawrence College. She became (1961) a writer for the NBC morning program "Today" and two years later won a regular on-camera spot due to her articulate reporting and assertive interviewing. Walters was promoted (1964) to "Today" cohost while continuing special reports and later hosting "Not for Women Only." She impressed audiences with her forceful style and sometimes unexpected remarks. Her distinctive diction (her *r*'s sounded like *w*'s) became increasingly familiar in American households; when in 1976 she was offered a million-dollar contract by ABC to become the first woman to anchor a network news telecast, as well as television's highest-paid newscaster, the deal made headlines across the nation. She subsequently cohosted ABC's news show "20/20" (1979–). She wrote *How to Talk with Practically Anybody About Practically Anything* (1971).

WALTON, ERNEST THOMAS SINTON (1903–1995), Irish physicist. While working at the Cavendish Laboratory at Cambridge, Walton undertook (1928) experiments intended to generate, artificially, streams of fast subatomic nuclei. With J. D. Cockcroft he developed the first nuclear-particle accelerator (the Cockcroft-Walton generator) and in 1931 bombarded the nuclei of lithium with protons to produce the first artificial nuclear reaction without the use of radioactive substances. For this achievement they shared the 1951 Nobel Prize in Physics. Walton received his Ph.D. at Cambridge (1934) and taught at Trinity College in Dublin (1947–74).

WALTON, SAMUEL MOORE (1918–1992), U.S. retailer. Sam Walton, the most successful merchant of his era, was the son of a rural banker. He studied economics at the University of Missouri (B.A. 1940) and opened his first store, a franchise, in Newport, Arkansas (1945). Convinced that large discount stores could thrive in small towns and rural areas, locations that had been bypassed by large chains, Walton opened his first Wal-Mart store in Rogers, Arkansas, in 1962. Business increased rapidly; by 1972 he owned 64 stores and by 1983, 642. Walton's formula was to offer low prices, enormous variety, and personal service to customers; incentive bonuses and profit-sharing plans to employees; and increased jobs, tax revenues, and charity assistance to communities where he planned to open stores. Although accused of driving many small-town retailers out of business, Walton's chain continued its remarkable growth, and by 1991 Wal-Mart surpassed Sears Roebuck to become the largest retailer in the United States with sales over $43 billion. Walton was identified by *Forbes* magazine as the "richest man in America" (1985–91) and at the time of his death he had established 1,735 stores in 43 states and employed 80,000 people. ■ See biographies by Vance H. Trimble (1990) and Austin Teutsch (1991) and Bob Ortega, *In Sam We Trust* (1998).

WALTON, SIR WILLIAM TURNER (1902–1983), British composer. While a student at Oxford, Walton composed *Façade* (1923), a piece of sophisticated irreverence accompanied by Edith Sitwell poetry. His later works included an oratorio (*Belshazzar's Feast*, 1931), two symphonies (1935; 1960), a violin concerto (1939), and several film scores, all featuring propulsive rhythms and romantic sonorities. He also wrote coronation music for King George VI (1937) and Queen Elizabeth II (1953). ■ See study by Frank Howes (1965) and biographies by Neil Tierney (1984) and Susana Walton (1988).

WANG, AN (1920–1990), Chinese-born U.S. physicist and business executive. The son of a high school teacher, Wang graduated from Jiao Tong University in Shanghai (1940), came to the United States in 1945, and studied applied physics at Harvard (M.S. 1946; Ph.D. 1948). A specialist in the new field of computers, he invented the magnetic core memory and sold the patent to IBM. He established Wang Laboratories in Cambridge, Massachusetts (1951), and built it into one of the world's largest office automation systems firms. Sales for fiscal 1985 were $2.3 billion. Wang, whose 40 percent share of the company was worth more than $700 million, was one of the richest men in the United States and a leading philanthropist in Boston. ■ See his autobiography, *Lessons* (1986; with Eugene Linden).

WANG CHING-WEI. *See WANG JINGWEI.*

WANGENSTEEN, OWEN HARDING (1898–1981), U.S. surgeon. The chief of surgery at the University of Minnesota (1930–67), Wangensteen did pioneering work in the surgical treatment of cancer, appendicitis, ulcers, and various disorders of the alimentary canal. Stressing research and laboratory experimentation, he played a leading role in the development of open-heart surgery during the 1950s and trained generations of innovative surgeons, including the pioneers of heart-transplant surgery, Christian N. Barnard and Norman E. Shumway. In addition to numerous technical papers, he wrote (with his wife Sarah) a history, *The Rise of Surgery: From Empiric Craft to Scientific Discipline* (1979).

WANG JINGWEI (old style: **WANG CHING-WEI; 1883–1944**), Chinese revolutionary leader. Born into the gentry, Wang met the revolutionary Sun Yat-sen and himself became a revolutionary while in Tokyo studying law. Jailed briefly for an unsuccessful assassination attempt on the prince regent in 1910, he was released after the 1911 revolution and emerged as a national hero. He was Sun's close confidant (1917–25) and a bitter rival of Chiang Kai-shek, the chief of the nationalist Guomindang (Kuomintang) army. After Sun's death (1925) he headed a short-lived leftist government in Wuhan (1927). Following the Japanese takeover of Manchuria, Wang was reconciled with Chiang and served as Chiang's relatively powerless premier (1932–35). After the outbreak of the Sino-Japanese War (1937), Wang was convinced of China's inability to defeat Japan. He broke with the nationalists, urged a peace settlement, and headed the puppet government of Japanese-occupied China in Nanjing (Nanking) from 1940 to 1944.

WARBURG, ABY (1886–1929), German art historian. Warburg's conception of art history extended beyond connoisseurship and the study of form. He concentrated on the evolution of particular symbols or images to illuminate cultural phenomena. His examination of the art world in Florence during the Renaissance was a starting point for his consideration of the evolution of Western civilization from classical antiquity. In the 1920s, Fritz Saxl transformed Warburg's library in Hamburg into a center for humanistic studies. When the Nazis came to power in Germany, the Warburg Institute became part of the University of London. ■ See the intellectual biography by E. H. Gombrich (1970).

WARBURG, FELIX MORITZ (1871–1937), German-born U.S. financier and philanthropist. Warburg emigrated to the United States (1894), married the daughter of investment banker Jacob Schiff, and became a partner in Schiff's firm, Kuhn, Loeb and Co. (1897). His primary interests, however, were education, social welfare, and philanthropy. He was a major contributor to the Henry Street Settlement, the Educational Alliance, and other institutions catering to New York City's poor. He helped found the Federation for the Support of Jewish Philanthropic Societies (1917) and the American Jewish Joint Distribution Committee (1915), a war-relief organization. Although never a Zionist, he aided Jewish settlements in Palestine, headed the Jewish Agency (1929–30), opposed the partition of Palestine (1937), and supported the Hebrew University in Jerusalem. ■ See David Farrer, *The Warburgs* (1975).

WARBURG, OTTO HEINRICH (1883–1970), German biochemist. Warburg was associated with the Kaiser Wilhelm (later Max Planck) Institute for Cell Physiology from 1913 until his death (director from 1953). His research, reported in five books and some 500 papers, made fundamental contributions to biochemistry. Warburg devised innovative experimental methods to investigate photosynthesis, cellular respiration, and cancer; his techniques were applied to industry and medicine. In 1931, he received the Nobel Prize in Physiology or Medicine for illuminating the nature of cell metabolism by isolating and identifying a crucial respiratory enzyme. Investigating the metabolism of cancer cells, Warburg posited that they are able to grow in the absence of oxygen. A Jew, Warburg was prevented from accepting a second Nobel Prize in 1934 by decree of Nazi leader Adolf Hitler. His books included *Heavy Metal Prosthetic Groups and Enzyme Action* (Eng. trans. 1949) and *New Methods of Cell Physiology* (Eng. trans. 1962). ■ See Hans Krebs, *Otto Warburg: Cell Physiologist, Biochemist, and Eccentric* (1981).

WARBURG, PAUL MORITZ (1868–1932), German-born U.S. banker and philanthropist. Born into a well-known banking family, Warburg joined the banking house of Kuhn, Loeb and Co. in New York City in 1902, the year he emigrated to America. An expert on European central banking systems, Warburg advocated banking reforms in the United States after the panic of 1907; he served as one of the five appointed members of the first Federal Reserve Board (1914–18) and as a member of its advisory council (1921–26). Warburg was one of the few bankers to warn the public of the impending stock market crash in 1929. He was also a leading figure in Jewish philanthropic organizations. ■ See David Farrer, *The Warburgs* (1975).

WARD, BARBARA. *See JACKSON OF LODSWORTH, BARBARA MARY JACKSON, BARONESS.*

WARD, DOUGLAS TURNER (1930–   ), U.S. actor, playwright, and director. Born into a poor black family on a Louisiana plantation, Ward studied acting in New York City, appeared in several Broadway, Off-Broadway, and television dramas in the late 1950s and early 1960s, and wrote the acclaimed one-act satires *Happy Ending* and *Days of*

Absence (1965). He cofounded (1967; with Robert Hooks and Gerald S. Krone) the Negro Ensemble Company, which presented dramatic works of promising young black playwrights and provided an outlet for black actors, directors, and technicians. As its artistic director (1967–92), Ward starred in *Ceremonies in Dark Old Men* (1969), directed and starred in *The River Niger* (1972–73), and directed *A Soldier's Play* (1981).

WARD, HARRY FREDERICK (1873–1966), British-born U.S. minister. An ordained Methodist minister and a professor of Christian ethics at the Union Theological Seminary in New York City (1916–41), Ward was a lifelong social crusader who worked for radical change in the United States. He served as national chairman of the American Civil Liberties Union (1920–40), general secretary of the Methodist Federation of Social Service (1911–44), and chairman of the American League for Peace and Democracy (1934–40). Although long a peace advocate, he denounced the isolationist position in the face of Nazi aggression and urged U.S. entry into World War II. His books included *The New Social Order* (1919), *Our Economic Morality and the Ethic of Jesus* (1929), and *Democracy and Social Change* (1940). ■ See Eugene P. Link, *Labor-Religion Prophet* (1984).

WARD, ROBERT (1917–   ), U.S. composer. Ward studied at the Eastman and Juilliard schools of music. His lyrical, melodic compositions were marked by rhythmic variety and colorful sonorities. He was influenced by jazz and American folk-song melodies. His best-known work, the opera *The Crucible* (1961), won a Pulitzer Prize. His other works included Fifth Symphony—*Canticles for America* (1976), *Sonic Structure for Orchestra* (1980), *The Scarlett Letter Suite* (1990), *Serenade for Mallarmé* (1991), the operas *Minutes till Midnight* (1982) and *Roman Fever* (1993), and the song cycle *Sacred Canticles* (1994). He served as president of the North Carolina School of the Arts (1967–74) and taught at Duke University (1978–87).

WARHOL, ANDY (Andrew Warhola; 1930?–1987), U.S. artist and filmmaker. A commercial artist from Pittsburgh, Warhol began painting comic-book art during the late 1950s. He progressed to the mechanical reproduction of such everyday objects as flowers, soup cans, and cola bottles, which were celebrated as icons of advanced industrial society, and was the best-known pop artist of the 1960s and 1970s. He also cast his friends in crude underground films that were memorable chiefly for their extreme length, lack of action, and voyeuristic conception (*Chelsea Girls*, 1966; *Trash*, 1970). In 1968 he was shot and wounded by one of his starlets, but he recovered to remain a cult figure of jet-set society. His views on art are in *The Philosophy of Andy Warhol* (1975). ■ See his *POPism* (1980; with Pat Hackett); studies by John Coplans (1970) and Rainer Crone (Eng. trans. 1970); Pat Hackett, ed., *The Andy Warhol Diaries* (1989); and Victor Bockris, *The Life and Death of Andy Warhol* (1989).

WARING, FRED (1900–1984), U.S. choral conductor. Waring founded the Pennsylvanians, a band and choral ensemble specializing in soft melodies and lush orchestrations, while he was a student at the University of Pennsylvania and dropped out of school to tour with the group. It gained a national following by the early 1920s and made the first electronic recording (1925) and the first all-musical film (*Syncopation*, 1929). It was the first vocal-orchestra to have its own coast-to-coast radio (1933) and television (1949) show, and popularized such songs as "Sleep," "Dream, Dream, Dream," and "I Love Music." Waring composed approximately 200 songs and led the Pennsylvanians, and its successor group, the Young Pennsylvanians, until 1980. He also invented one of the first food processors, the "Waring Blendor" (1937). ■ See study by Virginia Waring (1997).

WARNER, JACK L. (Jack Eichelbaum; 1892–1978), U.S. film producer. Youngest son of an immigrant Polish peddler, Jack Warner went into the film business with his brothers Sam, Harry, and Albert in 1903. Moving to Hollywood in 1918, the brothers successfully gambled on the introduction of sound, producing the first talkie, *The Jazz Singer*, in 1927, and overnight Warner Brothers became a major film studio. With Jack dictating discipline and economy as head of production, the studio produced stark social dramas starring Bette Davis, Humphrey Bogart, and James Cagney. In the late 1940s, Warner Brothers also moved into the vanguard of TV production, which helped finance such throwbacks as *My Fair Lady* (1964) and *Camelot* (1967), both personally produced by Jack. ■ See his memoirs, *My First Hundred Years in Hollywood* (1965).

WARNER, POP (Glenn Scobey Warner; 1871–1954), U.S. football coach. Warner earned a law degree from Cornell (1894), but preferred a coaching career. From 1895 to 1938 he coached teams at Georgia, Cornell, Carlisle, Pittsburgh, Stanford, and Temple, compiling a record of 312 wins, 104 losses, and 32 ties. Warner dominated football with innovations that permanently altered the game, including the single- and double-wing formations, the spiral punt, and the rolling body block. He introduced headgear, blocking dummies, and many other refinements. Pop Warner coached 47 All-American players, including backfield phenomena Jim Thorpe and Ernie Nevers.

WARNER, SYLVIA TOWNSEND (1893–1978), British writer. Warner coedited a 10-volume work on Tudor church music, along with writing poetry, novels, short stories, and biography. Her witty and compassionate fiction frequently concerned characters whose aspirations were thwarted. Her novel *Lolly Willowes* (1926) was the first Book-of-the-Month Club selection in the United States; her subtle, polished short stories often dealt with the occult and the fantastic, on which she was a great authority, and ran regularly in the *New Yorker* after 1935. *The Corner That Held Them* (1948), a novel set in 14th-century Britain, is considered her best book, while her biography of the novelist T. H. White (1967) is also highly regarded. ▪ See her *Scenes of Childhood* (1982), *Collected Poems* (1982), *Letters* (1983), and *Diaries* (1994), and biography by Claire Harman (1989).

WARNER, WILLIAM LLOYD (1898–1970), U.S. social anthropologist. W. Lloyd Warner taught at Harvard (1929–35) and the University of Chicago (1935–60). His study of Australian aborigines (*A Black Civilization*, 1937) prompted him to apply the research methods of cultural anthropology to contemporary social problems. He was particularly interested in class structure and status, which he explored in his "Yankee City" series (5 vols., 1941–59) and in *Social Class in America* (1949). Warner divided U.S. classes into lower, middle, and upper, each having a lower and upper subclass. He also analyzed the caste-class structure of race relations in the South. In a study of *Big Business Leaders in America* (1955), he concluded there was increasing mobility between the classes.

WARREN, EARL (1891–1974), U.S. jurist. Warren was a crime-busting district attorney of Alameda County, California (1925–39), a progressive Republican governor (1943–53) of California, and a libertarian chief justice during his 16 years on the U.S. Supreme Court (1953–69). He conceived of the court as a "people's court," translating the law into comprehensible language within a framework of four-square morality. "In the field of public education the doctrine of 'separate but equal' has no place," he wrote in his landmark *Brown* v. *Board of Education* opinion (1954), and subsequently extended integration to transportation, parks, and restaurants. Warren's court also expanded the substance of civil and individual liberties and transformed representative government with its "one-man one-vote" opinion. He also headed the commission that investigated the assassination of Pres. John F. Kennedy. ▪ See his *Memoirs* (1977); biographies by Jack Pollack (1979) and G. Edward White (1982); study by Bernard Schwartz (1983); and Ed Cray, *Chief Justice* (1997).

WARREN, HARRY (1893–1981), U.S. songwriter. Born into an impoverished immigrant Italian family, Warren left high school to join a carnival band. His first song was published in 1922, and he wrote his first big hit, "I Love My Baby," in 1923. In collaboration with lyricist Al Dubin he wrote dozens of songs for the popular musical films of the 1930s and 1940s, including "Lullaby of Broadway" (Academy Award, 1935), "Shuffle Off to Buffalo," "Don't Give Up the Ship," and "You Must Have Been a Beautiful Baby." He also wrote "Hello, Frisco, Hello," "Chattanooga Choo Choo," and "You'll Never Know" (Academy Award, 1943) with Mack Gordon, and "On the Atchison, Topeka and Santa Fe" (Academy Award, 1945) with Johnny Mercer. He continued to write hit songs through the 1960s. ▪ See study by Tony Thomas (1975).

WARREN, LEONARD (1911–1960), U.S. opera singer. A singer in the chorus of New York's Radio City Music Hall,

Warren won the Metropolitan Opera's auditions (1938) and remained with the company for the next 22 years. Regarded by many as the finest baritone of his era, Warren was best known for his roles in Verdi operas (especially *Rigoletto*) and was a great public favorite. He died of a cerebral hemorrhage at the height of his career during a performance of Verdi's *La Forza del Destino* at the Metropolitan Opera House; he collapsed amidst great applause before a capacity audience after having finished the aria "Urna fatale del mio destino" ("fatal urn of my destiny").

WARREN, ROBERT PENN (1905–1989), U.S. novelist and poet. Robert Penn Warren enrolled at Vanderbilt (1921), intending to study electrical engineering. Influenced by Prof. John Crowe Ransom, he turned instead to literature, becoming a member of Ransom's Fugitive group and later of the anti-industrial Agrarians. A proponent of the New Criticism, Warren collaborated with Cleanth Brooks in editing (1935–42) the influential *Southern Review* and writing the textbooks *Understanding Poetry* (1938) and *Understanding Fiction* (1943). He taught at several universities, including Yale (1951–73). An extremely versatile writer, he won three Pulitzer Prizes—two for poetry collections, *Promises* (1957) and *Now and Then: Poems, 1976–1978* (1979), and one for the novel based on the Louisiana politician Huey Long, *All the King's Men* (1946). His writing was characterized by its southern regionalism, its technical dexterity, and its symbolic energy. His other writings were collected in *New and Selected Poems, 1923–1985* (1985) and *New and Selected Essays* (1989). In 1986 he was designated as the country's first official poet laureate. ▪ See F. C. Watkins and J. T. Hiers, eds., *Robert Penn Warren Talking: Interviews, 1950–1978* (1980); Barnett Guttenberg, *Web of Being* (1975); study by Katherine Snipes (1984); and biography by Joseph Blotner (1997).

WASHINGTON, HENRY STEPHENS (1867–1934), U.S. geologist. A pioneer in the chemical study of igneous rock, Washington conducted petrological investigations throughout the world. His books *Chemical Analyses of Igneous Rocks* (1903; enlarged 1917) and *Manual of the Chemical Analysis of Rocks* (1904) established standards of analysis that were used for decades. An independent researcher for much of his early career, he was associated with the Geophysical Laboratory of the Carnegie Institution, Washington, D.C., after 1912. He also wrote *Composition of the Earth's Crust* (1924).

WASSERBURG, GERALD JOSEPH (1927–), U.S. geophysicist. A faculty member of the California Institute of Technology (from 1955), Wasserburg utilized methods of chemical physics to study the age and development of the earth, moon, and meteorites. With his colleagues he developed (1965) a computer-controlled mass spectrometer (Lunatic I) that greatly improved the precision of radioactive-isotope measurement. He joined the National Aeronautics and Space Administration (NASA) lunar advisory group (1967) and was able to date almost all of the lunar material returned by the (U.S.) Apollo and (Soviet) Luna missions.

WASSERMAN, AUGUST PAUL VON (1866–1925), German bacteriologist. After studying at the universities of Erlangen, Vienna, Munich, and Strasbourg (M.D. 1889), Wasserman joined the staff of the Robert Koch Institute for Infectious Diseases (Berlin) in 1890. He became famous for developing (1906; with Albert Neisser and Carl Bruck) a diagnostic test for syphilis, known as the Wasserman test. He also developed an antitoxin treatment for diphtheria and inoculations against typhoid, cholera, and tetanus. While serving as director of the department of experimental therapy at the Kaiser Wilhelm Institute (Berlin; 1913–25) he devised a diagnostic test for tuberculosis.

WATERS, ETHEL (1896–1977), U.S. singer and actress. Raised in the black slums of Philadelphia, Waters worked as a chambermaid and scrubwoman before starting her nightclub and vaudeville singing career at age 17. She soon gained a reputation for singing "St. Louis Blues" and sang in New York City's Harlem (1925) and appeared on Broadway in *Africana*, an all-black musical revue (1927). She later starred in Irving Berlin's *As Thousands Cheer* (1933) and in *Cabin in the Sky* (1940). Although she made famous such songs as "Dinah," "Heat Wave," and "Am I Blue," Waters was equally well known for her highly praised dramatic performances in the movie *Pinky* (1949) and *The Member of the Wedding* (Broadway show, 1950; film, 1952). ■ See her autobiography, *His Eye Is on the Sparrow* (1951).

WATERS, MUDDY (McKinley Morganfield; 1915–1983), U.S. blues singer and guitarist. Raised in a sharecropper's cabin on a plantation in the Mississippi delta, Waters learned to sing the delta blues, the traditional migratory music of rural southern blacks, during his childhood. He was discovered and first recorded (1941) by Library of Congress musicologist Alan Lomax; he moved to Chicago (1943), where he established a reputation for his authentic and aggressive down-home sound and for introducing amplification and irregular beats to the music. His Chicago form of rhythm and blues influenced the development of rock-and-roll and soul music of the 1950s and 1960s, and he recorded several Grammy Award–winning albums. His best-known songs included "Rollin' Stone," "Got My Mojo Working," "Honey Bee," and "Hoochie Choochie Man." ■ See James Rooney, *Bossmen* (1971).

WATSON, ARTHEL "DOC" (1923–   ), U.S. country and bluegrass musician. North Carolina's blind musician "Doc" Watson became known by performing in folk festivals during the 1960s. He was famous for his extraordinary, tricky guitar picking and for his extreme versatility. Watson's repertoire ranged from traditional folk songs and hymns to country music and sophisticated bluegrass. He frequently recorded with his family, particularly his son Merle (1949–   ).

WATSON, JAMES DEWEY (1928–   ), U.S. biologist. A student of Nobel laureate Hermann J. Muller, Watson received his doctorate in biology from the University of Indiana (1950). In 1951 he conducted research at the Cavendish Laboratory, Cambridge University, where he met Francis Crick, thus beginning a partnership that resulted in their joint formulation of the double-helical model of the DNA (deoxyribonucleic acid) molecule. This discovery, which revealed the chemical basis of heredity and inaugurated a revolution in genetic research, won for them, and Maurice Wilkins, the 1962 Nobel Prize in Physiology or Medicine. Watson, who taught at Harvard from 1955 to 1976, served as director (1968–93) and president (1994–   ) of the Cold Spring (New York) Biological Laboratories, where he concentrated on cancer research. His books included *The Double Helix* (1968), a personal account of the discovery of the DNA structure; *The Molecular Biology of the Gene* (1965; 4th ed. 1986), a widely used textbook; and *A Passion for DNA* (2000).

WATSON, JOHN BROADUS (1878–1958), U.S. psychologist. A professor at Johns Hopkins University (1908–20), Watson changed the course of the history of psychology with his 1913 paper, "Psychology as a Behaviorist Views It," which formally stated, for the first time, the principles of behaviorism that subsequently dominated psychology in the United States for decades. Watson thought that studies of consciousness, mental states, and the soul were irrelevant to psychology, whose purpose, he believed, was to predict and control behavior, which could be modified through conditioning. He denied the influence of instinct and heredity and stressed learning and the environment as essential to human and animal behavior. Watson performed numerous experiments on white rats, monkeys, and birds and in 1918 initiated a series of classic experiments with human infants. His books included *Behavior: An Introduction to Comparative Psychology* (1914), *Psychology from the Standpoint of a Behaviorist* (1919), and the popularly written *Behaviorism* (1925) and *Psychological Care of Infant and Child* (1928). After resigning from Johns Hopkins following a scandal involving his divorce (1920), Watson became an advertising executive. ■ See biography by David Cohen (1979) and Kerry W. Buckley, *Mechanical Man* (1989).

WATSON, THOMAS JOHN (1874–1956), U.S. business executive. Having successfully sold pianos, sewing machines, and cash registers, Watson in 1914 undertook to manufacture and sell business machines as president of the 400-employee Computer-Tabulating-Recording Co. A rigid, hardworking, and paternalistic leader, he built his industrial "family"—International Business Machines—into the world's largest computer-making enterprise with offices in some 80 nations. At his death, IBM had assets of $629 million, and its abbreviated name symbolized the age of information technology. ■ See Thomas and Marva Belden, *The Lengthening Shadow* (1962), and William Rodgers, *Think* (1969).

WATSON, THOMAS JOHN, JR. (1914–1993), U.S. businessman. The son of the head of International Business Machines (IBM), Watson succeeded his father as president (1952–61), chairman (1961–71), and chairman of the executive board (1972–79) of the company. Called by *Fortune* magazine "the most successful capitalist who ever lived," he guided the firm during the period of its greatest growth, in the early years of the electronic computer revolution, and molded it into the giant of the industry. From 1979 to 1981 he served as U.S. ambassador to the Soviet Union. ■ See his memoirs, *Father, Son & Co.* (1990; with Peter Petre), and William Rodgers, *Think* (1969).

WATSON-WATT, SIR ROBERT (1892–1973), Scottish physicist. Born in Scotland and educated there as an electrical engineer and physicist, Watson-Watt held a variety of governmental scientific posts (1915–45). Working as a meteorologist, he had used radarlike devices to locate thunderstorms as early as 1919. Starting in 1935, he began the secret development of the first practical radar system, which detected airplanes by means of reflected radio waves. His system gave the British early warning of enemy airplane attacks during World War II and helped the Royal Air Force win the Battle of Britain against the Germans (1940). He was knighted (1942) and given a special £50,000 award for his invention. ■ See his autobiography, *The Pulse of Radar* (1959), and John Rowland, *The Radar Man* (1963).

WATTS, ANDRE (1946–   ), U.S. pianist. Born in Germany, the son of a Hungarian mother and a black American soldier, Watts studied at the Philadelphia Academy of Music and at 16 made his debut over national television with the New York Philharmonic. Concentrating on the romantic repertory, especially the difficult works of Franz Liszt, he soon made an international career as an outstanding pianist.

WAUGH, EVELYN ARTHUR ST. JOHN (1903–1966), British novelist. Educated at Oxford, where he claimed he led an "idle, dissolute, and extravagant life," Waugh briefly studied art and failed as a schoolmaster. Such novels as *Decline and Fall* (1928), *Vile Bodies* (1930), and *Scoop* (1938), brilliant, witty satires on upper-class society and follies, established his reputation. They were noted for their memorable comic characters and black comedy, exemplified by poor Tony Last in *A Handful of Dust* (1934) who was forced for the remainder of his life to read Dickens to an illiterate savage. Waugh's post–World War II work, notably *Brideshead Revisited* (1945), reflected his deep religious feelings as a Roman Catholic convert (1930). Basically a moralist and traditionalist, his work was filled with nostal-gia for an earlier age and he expressed distaste for modern culture and society. His *Complete Stories* were published in 1999. ■ See his autobiography, *A Little Learning* (1964), and *Letters* (1980); the biographies by Christopher Sykes (1975), Selina Hastings (1995), Douglas L. Patey (1998), and David Wykes (1999); and study by David Pryce-Jones (1973).

WAVELL, ARCHIBALD PERCIVAL WAVELL, 1st EARL (1883–1950), British military leader. During World War II, as commander in chief of British forces in the Middle East (1939–41), Wavell led his troops to victories against the Italians in North Africa and East Africa (Dec. 1940–May 1941). However, he was unable to stop the German advance in Greece and Crete, and after being forced to retreat by German Gen. Erwin Rommel's forces in North Africa, he was transferred to India and Southeast Asia, where his forces lost Malaya, Singapore, and Burma to the Japanese (Dec. 1941–May 1942). He was succeeded as Allied Pacific commander by Gen. Douglas MacArthur (April 1942) and subsequently served as viceroy of India (1943–47). ■ See *Wavell: The Viceroy's Journal* (1973); study by John Connell (1965); and Ronald Lewin, *The Chief* (1980).

WAYNE, JOHN (Marion Morrison; 1907–1979), U.S. film actor. After winning a football scholarship to the University of Southern California, Wayne got a summer job as a Hollywood propman, which led to his being cast in a string of quickie westerns during the 1930s. *Stagecoach* (1939) was his first popular success. Over the years Wayne played soldiers, sailors, pilots, and big-game hunters, but he remained the archetypal western hero—big, tough, resourceful, and true. His best westerns were *Fort Apache* (1948), *She Wore a Yellow Ribbon* (1949), *Rio Bravo* (1959), and *True Grit* (1969), for which he won an Academy Award. Long active in conservative politics (during the 1950s he headed the Motion Picture Alliance for the Preservation of American Ideals), Wayne directed as well as starred in *The Green Berets* (1968), a film supportive of the war in Vietnam. ■ See Maurice Zolotow, *Shooting Star* (1974); biography by George Carpozi, Jr. (1979); and Garry Wills, *John Wayne's America* (1997).

WEAVER, ROBERT CLIFTON (1907–1997), U.S. economist and government official. After studying at Harvard (M.A. 1931; Ph.D. 1934), Weaver was an adviser on housing, manpower, and minority problems to various New Deal agencies and, as the head of a black "brain trust," the most prominent African American in Washington. After World War II he was New York State rent commissioner (1955–59) and administrator of the Federal Housing and Home Finance Agency (1961–66). He served as Pres. Lyndon Johnson's secretary of housing and urban development (1966–68), the first African American to achieve cabinet rank. He subsequently taught at several universities in New York City.

■ See his *Negro Labor* (1946), *The Negro Ghetto* (1948), *The Urban Complex* (1964), and *Dilemmas of Urban America* (1965).

WEAVER, WARREN (1894–1978), U.S. communications theorist. Weaver taught at his alma mater, the University of Wisconsin (1920–32), before joining the Rockefeller Foundation (director of national sciences, 1932–55; vice president, 1955–59) and the Alfred P. Sloan Foundation (vice president, 1959–64), where he dispensed millions of dollars in medical and scientific grants. A pioneer in the field of cybernetics and the mathematical theory of probability, he wrote *The Mathematical Theory of Communication* (1949; with C. E. Shannon), a seminal work. He was also an authority on the work of another mathematician, Lewis Carroll's *Alice in Wonderland*, and wrote *Alice in Many Tongues* (1964). ■ See his selected writings, *Science and Imagination* (1967), and his autobiography, *Scene of Change* (1970).

WEAVERS, THE, U.S. singing group. Composed of **Pete Seeger** (1919–), **Lee Hays** (1914–1981), **Ronnie Gilbert** (1933–), and **Fred Hellerman** (1927–), the Weavers started a folk-music boom with their 1949 debut at the Village Vanguard in New York. Many of their songs, performed in concert, on radio, and on TV, became hits; their first record (1950), with "Tzena, Tzena," on one side and "Goodnight Irene" on the other, was a hit. They became known for reditions of such songs as "If I Had a Hammer," "Lonesome Traveler," and "Wasn't That a Time?" Blacklisted during the early 1950s for leftist sympathies, the Weavers were unable to get jobs and disbanded in 1952. They reunited at Carnegie Hall in 1955 and were so well received that they stayed together until 1963. A 25th anniversary of that concert was held in 1980. The film documentary *Wasn't That a Time!* (1982) recorded the events surrounding the anniversary concert. Pete Seeger continued to perform and record folk music. Ronnie Gilbert, who was also an actress, revived her singing career in 1984 when she toured and recorded the album *Lifeline* with Holly Near; she recorded *The Spirit Is Free* in 1985. Fred Hellerman continued to record and produce records. ■ See Doris Willens, *Lonesome Traveler: The Life of Lee Hays* (1988).

WEBB, (MARTHA) BEATRICE POTTER (1858–1943) **and SIDNEY JAMES WEBB** (1st Baron Passfield; 1859–1947), British economists and social reformers. Beatrice Potter, the daughter of a rich industrialist, was a social worker and wrote several books on Britian's economic and social life before her marriage to Sidney Webb in 1892. Sidney Webb, the son of an accountant and shopkeeper, worked as a civil servant in the colonial office before being admitted to the bar (1885). Together they became pillars of the Fabian Society and set out to reform Britain's sociopolitical system. Their intellectual socialism deeply affected British radical thought and institutions in the early decades of the century.

They collaborated on *The History of Trade Unionism* (1894), *Industrial Democracy* (1897), and an exhaustive *History of English Local Government* (7 vols., 1903–30). They founded the *New Statesman* (1913) and played a major role in establishing the London School of Economics. After joining the Labour party (1914), they rose to its leadership. Sidney drafted the policy statement that guided the party's 1918, 1922, and 1924 election campaigns, was a member of the party's national executive (1915–25), and held various posts in the Labour governments of Prime Minister Ramsay MacDonald. In 1932, the Webbs traveled to the Soviet Union, reporting their enthusiastic reactions in *Soviet Communism: A New Civilization?* (1935). ■ See Beatrice Webb's penetrating diaries (4 vols.; 1982–86); the Webbs' combined collected letters (3 vols., 1978); and *Our Partnership* (1948, repr. 1975). See also biographies by M. A. Hamilton (1933) and Lisanne Radice (1984); Jeanne MacKenzie, *Victorian Courtship* (1979); and Carole Seymour-Jones, *Beatrice Webb: Woman of Conflict* (1992).

WEBER, MAX (1864–1920), German sociologist. The son of a prosperous liberal politician, Weber passed his bar exam at age 22 and was a full professor of economics at the University of Freiburg at age 30. He was a polymath, a universal intellect with a command of history, economics, philosophy, culture, and law. Perhaps the most influential social scientist of the century, he insisted on eliminating value judgments in social analysis and proposed the use of abstract models, or "ideal types," to study society. His best-known work, *The Protestant Ethic and the Spirit of Capitalism* (1904; Eng. trans. 1930), linked the growth of modern capitalism to Protestant religious beliefs. He did studies of Chinese, Indian, and the ancient Jewish religion and society, and analyzed the relationship between world views, economic organization, and social structure in *Economy and Society* (1922; Eng. trans. 1968). He also published comparative studies of authority and domination and emphasized the importance of bureaucracy in modern Western societies. A left-liberal, Weber was a critic of Emperor William II, a vociferous opponent of World War I, and one of the creators of the constitution of the postwar Weimar Republic (1918). *From Max Weber* (1946), edited by H. H. Gerth and C. Wright Mills, contains a selection of his writings and a biographical essay. ■ See study by Reinhard Bendix (1960); biography by Marianne Weber (Eng. trans. 1975); Wolfgang J. Mommsen, *Max Weber and German Politics, 1890–1920* (Eng. trans. 1985); and studies by Dirk Käsler (Eng. trans. 1988) and John P. Diggins (1996).

WEBER, MAX (1881–1961), Russian-born U.S. painter. Weber was brought to the United States at age 10. He studied art in New York (1898–1900) and later in Paris (1905–09), where he was influenced by Henri Matisse and the fauves. Returning to New York, Weber helped introduce such avant-garde European art movements as cubism and fauvism to American artists. The painting *Chinese Restau-*

rant (1915) exemplified his cubist period. In later decades Weber adopted a more representational style; some of his paintings, such as *Adoration of the Moon* (1944), drew on Hasidic Jewish culture. Weber taught at the Art Students League and published *Essays on Art* (1916) and *Primitives* (1926).

WEBERN, ANTON VON (1883–1945), Austrian composer. Webern earned a Ph.D. in music from the University of Vienna (1906) and studied privately with composer Arnold Schoenberg. His early compositions were atonal, concise, and short—"every glance is a poem," he explained—but by 1924 he had adopted Schoenberg's 12-tone system, which he used more radically and more consistently than his teacher. His *String Trio* (1927) and *Symphony* (1928) were composed in this style. Webern was accidentally shot by a U.S. soldier at the end of World War II. ■ See biographies by Friedrich Wildgans (1966) and Hans and Rosaleen Moldenhauer (1979) and study by Kathryn Bailey (1998).

WEBSTER, MARGARET (1905–1972), British-U.S. actress and director. The daughter of actress Dame May Whitty, Webster made her debut (1917) at age 12 in the war-charity production *Women's Tribute*, playing Youth. Her first professional role came seven years later in *The Trojan Women* (1924). Webster's acting—particularly her diction—won acclaim on the British and American stage, but she achieved even greater distinction as a Shakespearean director. She directed New York productions of *Richard II* (1937), *Hamlet* (1938), and *Henry IV* (1939); her 1943 staging of *Othello* (starring Paul Robeson) broke records for a Shakespearean production with a run of 296 successive performances. Webster also directed opera productions in the 1950s. She lectured extensively and wrote *Shakespeare Without Tears* (1942). ■ See her autobiographies, *The Same Only Different* (1970) and *Don't Put Your Daughter on the Stage* (1972).

WEEGEE (Arthur Fellig; 1899–1968), Austrian-born U.S. photographer. Weegee left school at age 14 and began his career as an itinerant street photographer. He later lived near Manhattan (New York City) police headquarters and, using a police radio, arrived on the scene to snap action-packed news pictures of crime and violence and of more four-alarm fires than any other photographer in history. His stark photos, published by New York newspapers and photosyndicates during the 1930s and 1940s, earned him an international reputation. "My murder victims," he once said, "always fall faceup and they almost always wear pearl-gray hats." ■ See *Naked City* (1945), *Weegee's People* (1946), his autobiography (1961), and Miles Barth, *Weegee's World* (1997).

WEGENER, ALFRED LOTHAR (1880–1930), German geologist, meteorologist, and Arctic explorer. Noted for research into Arctic climatology, Wegener made four polar expeditions (1906–08; 1912–13; 1929; 1930) and wrote an important study of the thermodynamics of the atmosphere. He was best known, however, for developing the theory of continental drift (1912). Described in his widely read book, *The Origins of Continents and Oceans* (1915; Eng. trans. 1924), the theory stated that the earth's continents were originally one large landmass that gradually separated and drifted apart. He argued that the continents were still changing, and that the geographic poles have wandered. Although at first discredited, the theory was subsequently accepted by geographers. ■ See biography by Martin Schwarzbach (1986).

WEIDENREICH, FRANZ (1873–1948), German physical anthropologist and anatomist. Trained in medicine (M.D., 1899) and biology, Weidenreich concentrated on studies in hematology and anatomy. The relationship of the skeleton to evolution led him to anthropological investigation. A Jew, Weidenreich left Germany (1934) shortly after the Nazis came to power and he spent seven years in China (1935–41) collaborating with Chinese scholars and Pierre Teilhard de Chardin, the French paleontologist, in the excavation and analysis of Peking Man fossils. He was best known for his important series of monographs, particularly his descriptions of Peking Man (1943) and Java (or Solo) Man (1948). In the 1940s he was associated with the American Museum of Natural History in New York. His works included *Apes, Giants and Man* (1947), *Giant Early Man from Java and South China* (1945), and *Shorter Anthropological Papers* (1949).

WEIDMAN, CHARLES (1901–1975), U.S. dancer, choreographer, and teacher. Weidman began his half century of involvement in modern dance by performing in the troupe directed by Ruth St. Denis and Ted Shawn (1920–27). With Doris Humphrey he left that troupe to direct their own school (1927–45), which promoted greater male interest in dance. Weidman founded the Theater Dance Company (1948) and established the Expression of the Two Arts Theater with artist Mikhail Santaro (1960). Weidman's style combined cerebral abstract movements with comedy and mime, as evidenced in his *Atavism* (1936), *Flickers* (1962), and *Fables of Our Time* (1948). ■ See Eleanor King, *Transformations* (1978).

WEIL, ANDRÉ (1906–1998), French mathematician. Weil studied at the University of Paris (Ph.D. 1928) and was a founding member of the influential Bourbaki group of French mathematicians. He taught at universities in India, France, and Brazil before settling in the United States as a professor at the University of Chicago (1947–58) and at the Institute for Advanced Studies in Princeton, New Jersey (1958–76). His fundamental contributions to the fields of algebraic geometry had applications in the transmission of computer data and the study of elementary particle physics. He also made major advances in the areas of number theory and topological group theory and was considered by many of his colleagues to be the greatest mathematician of the century. He was the brother of philosopher Simone Weil (1909–1943). His books included *Foundations of Algebraic Geometry* (1946) and *Number Theory* (1984).

WEIL, SIMONE (1909–1943), French essayist and mystic. Daughter of well-to-do Jewish parents, Weil studied philosophy and after 1931 taught in secondary schools, also working as a factory hand and later as a farm servant. Her strong identification with the downtrodden at first directed her toward left-wing social and political activism. After 1936 she turned to Christianity, though she never joined the church. In 1942, during World War II, her family fled France for Britain; there she ruined her health with self-imposed privations that led to her death. Her "spiritual autobiography," *Waiting for God* (1949; Eng. trans. 1951), and other volumes containing her philosophical, often mystical, reflections including *Gravity and Grace* (1947; Eng. trans. 1952), *The Need for Roots* (1949; Eng. trans. 1952), and *Oppression and Liberty* (1955; Eng. trans. 1958), were published posthumously. Her brother was the mathematician André Weil (1906–1998). ■ See the *Simone Weil Reader* (1977) and biographies by Simone Pétrement (1973; Eng. trans. 1976), David McLellan (1989), Gabriella Fiori (Eng. trans. 1989), and Thomas R. Nevin (1991).

WEILL, KURT (1900–1950), German-born composer. Concerned with reaching the masses, Weill devised a new art form, the "song play," which combined musical comedy and opera. The themes dealt with contemporary political and social issues and the music was infused with jazz and popular dance rhythms. He collaborated with Bertolt Brecht on *The Threepenny Opera* (1927), a provocative and hugely successful updating of John Gay's *Beggar's Opera*, and *The Rise and Fall of the City of Mahagonny* (1929), a rowdy satire of capitalism in decay. Weill fled Nazi Germany (1933) and moved to the United States (1935), where he wrote the scores for the musical comedies *Knickerbocker Holiday* (1938; it included "September Song") and *Lady in the Dark* (1947) and for the musical plays *Street Scene* (1947) and *Lost in the Stars* (1949). He also wrote the music for *The Eternal Road* (1937), a dramatic pageant that incorporated biblical elements with the story of the persecution of the Jews in modern times. ■ See Ronald Sanders, *The Days Grow Short* (1980), and biography by Jürgen Schebera (1997).

WEINBERG, SIDNEY JAMES (1891–1969), U.S. financier. Although he was raised in a Brooklyn, New York, slum, and his formal schooling ended with the eighth grade, Weinberg worked his way up from assistant janitor (1907) to senior partner (1930) of the investment banking house of Goldman, Sachs and Co. A financial wizard, he was a much sought-after adviser and was known for decades as "Mr. Wall Street." His two biggest deals were the sale of $650 million worth of Ford Motor Co. stock for the Ford Foundation (1956) and the underwriting of $350 million worth of Sears, Roebuck debentures (1958)—the largest such transaction up to that time.

WEINBERG, STEVEN (1933–), U.S. physicist. Weinberg was a classmate of Sheldon L. Glashow at New York's Bronx High School of Science and Cornell University. The two physicists shared the 1979 Nobel Prize for Physics with Pakistani Abdus Salam for work leading toward a unified-force theory. Working independently, Weinberg developed what became known as the Weinberg-Salam Theory of Weak Interactions, which, in part, asserts that two basic natural forces—electromagnetism and the "weak interaction" (the force that causes radioactive decay in some atomic nuclei)—are aspects of a single natural phenomenon. The predictions made by Weinberg and Salam in the 1960s were confirmed by experiments in the 1970s that established the existence of a weak neutral current in the atomic nucleus. Weinberg taught at the University of California, Berkeley (1960–69), the Massachusetts Institute of Technology (1969–73), Harvard (1977–83), and the University of Texas (1982–). He wrote *Gravitation and Cosmology: Principles and Applications of the General Theory of Relativity* (1972); *The First Three Minutes* (1977), a popular work on the origins of the universe; *The Discovery of Subatomic Particles* (1983); and *Dreams of a Final Theory* (1992).

WEINGARTNER, FELIX (1863–1942), Austrian conductor and composer. One of the most prominent musical interpreters of his generation, Weingartner was best known for his performance of the works of Beethoven and Wagner. He conducted the Royal Opera in Berlin (1891–98), the Vienna State Opera (1908–10; 1935–36), the Vienna Philharmonic (1919–27), and directed the Basel Conservatory (1927–34). He traveled widely and conducted in the United States and South America as well as in Europe. He wrote six symphonies and eight operas, edited the works of Berlioz and Haydn, and wrote several books on conducting and musical interpretation. ■ See his autobiography, *Buffets and Rewards* (Eng. trans. 1937), and study edited by Christopher Dyment (1976).

WEINREICH, MAX (1894–1969), Latvian-born U.S. Yiddish linguist. A founder (1925) and longtime scientific director of the YIVO Institute for Jewish Research in Vilna (Vilnius) and later (1940–50) in New York, Weinreich was the leading exponent of a school of broad Jewish humanistic research. He was the first professor of Yiddish language in the United States (1947; at the City College of New York). Besides his activities as a teacher, journalist, editor, and translator, Weinreich published works on diverse themes in *Pictures from Yiddish Literary History* (1928), *The Way to Our Youth* (1935), *Psychoanalysis* (1937), and *Hitler's Professors* (1946; Eng. trans., 1947). His major work, *His-*

tory of the Yiddish Language (1973; Eng. trans. 2 vols., 1980), was a milestone analysis of language and society.

WEINREICH, URIEL (1926–1967), Polish-born U.S. linguist. Son of Yiddish linguist Max Weinreich, Uriel Weinreich emigrated to the United States (1940) and contributed widely to general linguistics. His *Languages in Contact* (1953) was a seminal work in bilingualism. His originality in semantics, dialectology, lexicography, and the history of linguistic theory was impressive, reflected only in part in the posthumous publications *Explorations in Semantic Theory* (1972) and *On Semantics* (1980). As a professor of Yiddish language, literature, and culture at Columbia University (from 1959), Weinreich initiated and directed the monumental dialectical research project, the Language and Culture Atlas of Ashkenazic Jewry. His contributions to Yiddish studies included *College Yiddish* (1949), *Modern English-Yiddish, Yiddish-English Dictionary* (1968), and *The Field of Yiddish* (editor; 3 vols., 1954; 1965; 1969).

WEIR, PETER (1944–), Australian film director. The son of a prosperous real-estate broker, Weir gave up his university studies to work for his father's firm. After living in Europe for more than a year, he returned home determined to pursue a career in show business. He worked (1969–73) for the Commonwealth Film Unit (later known as Film Australia), which produced government documentaries, before directing the haunting enigmatic films that established his reputation, *Picnic at Hanging Rock* (1975) and *The Last Wave* (1977). These and subsequent films, including *Gallipoli* (1980), *The Year of Living Dangerously* (1982), and Hollywood films *Witness* (1985), *The Mosquito Coast* (1986), and *Green Card* (1990), examined themes of culture clash and social isolation. *Dead Poets Society* (1989) was about an unconventional prep school teacher, and *The Truman Show* (1998) was the story of a man whose life, unbeknownst to him, was broadcast around the world 24 hours a day as a live television drama. ■ See Don Shiach, *The Films of Peter Weir: Visions of Alternative Realities* (1993), and the study by Marek Haltof (1996).

WEISS, PETER (1916–1982), German-born Swedish writer. The son of a wealthy Jewish textile manufacturer, Weiss fled Nazi persecution in Germany (1934) and settled in Sweden (1939), where he became a noted painter and experimental and documentary filmmaker during the 1940s and 1950s. His autobiographical novels *Leave Taking* (1961; Eng. trans. 1962) and *Vanishing Point* (1962; Eng. trans. 1966; published together as *Exile*, 1968) were highly acclaimed, but he was best known for his play *Marat/Sade* (1964; Eng. trans. 1965; Tony Award, 1966). The play utilized elements of the theater of Bertolt Brecht and Antonin Artaud and was regarded as one of the masterpieces of post–World War II European theater. An independent Marxist thinker and activist, Weiss condemned Nazi war crimes (*The Investigation*, 1965; Eng. trans. 1966),

Portuguese colonialism (*The Song of the Lusitanian Bogey*, 1967; Eng. trans. 1970), and U.S. imperialism (*Discourse on Vietnam*, 1967; Eng. trans. 1970) in his other notable semi-documentary plays. ■ See study by Otto F. Best (1976).

WEISSKOPF, VICTOR FREDERICK (1908–), Austrian-born U.S. physicist. After receiving his Ph.D. from Göttingen University (1931), Weisskopf worked (1931–37) in Berlin, Cambridge, Zurich, and Copenhagen with the outstanding physicists of Europe. He emigrated to the United States to escape Nazi anti-Semitic policies and worked as a group leader on the Manhattan Project (1943–46), which produced the first atomic bombs. After World War II he advocated nuclear disarmament, helped found the *Bulletin of Atomic Scientists*, worked for the free exchange of scientific data of all countries, and taught physics at the Massachusetts Institute of Technology (1946–74). From 1961 to 1965 he headed the 14-nation European Center for Nuclear Research (CERN) in Geneva. He wrote *Theoretical Nuclear Physics* (1952; with John M. Blatt), *Knowledge and Wonder* (1962), *Physics in the Twentieth Century* (1972), and *The Privilege of Being a Physicist* (1988). ■ See his autobiography, *The Joy of Insight: Passions of a Physicist* (1991).

WEISSMULLER, JOHNNY (1904–1984), U.S. swimmer and actor. The son of Austrian immigrants, Weissmuller gained fame as a powerful swimmer in the 1920s. He set 67 world records before reaching age 25. Weissmuller was the U.S. outdoor champion in the 100-, 200-, 400-, and 800-meter freestyle events (1922–27). At the 1924 and 1928 Olympic games he won five gold medals for the 100- and 200-meter freestyle and the 800-meter relay. Turning professional, he endorsed swimsuits and won roles in motion pictures, starring in nearly 20 Tarzan movies (1932–48) opposite Maureen O'Sullivan, who played Jane. Television reruns of the films made his chest-thumping figure familiar to generations of Americans. In the 1950s he starred in the TV series *Jungle Jim*. ■ See Narda Onyx, *Water, World and Weissmuller* (1964).

WEIZMANN, CHAIM (1874–1952), Zionist leader and president of Israel. Born and educated in Russia, Weizmann was active in the Zionist movement from his youth. He was trained as a chemist and lectured in Swiss and British universities, becoming a British subject in 1910. His important practical discoveries in organic chemistry helped the British munitions industry and gave him connections with the British government that led to his assuming a leadership position in the Zionist movement during World War I. His efforts resulted in the British government's issuance of the Balfour Declaration (1917), which supported the establishment of a Jewish homeland in Palestine. Subsequently, Weizmann was president of the World Zionist Organization (1921–31; 1935–46). When the state of Israel was established (1948) he was elected its first president. Weizmann was also the founder of what became the Weizmann Institute of Science in Rehovot, Israel. ■ See his autobiography, *Trail and Error* (1949), and biographies by Harold Blumberg (1975), Barnet Litvinoff (1976), and Jehuda Reinharz (1985).

WEIZSÄCKER, BARON CARL FRIEDRICH VON (1912–), German astrophysicist and philosopher of science. Weizsäcker developed (1942–45) a theory of the origin of the planets that relied on dust aggregation rather than on the previously accepted sun-star collision hypothesis. Taking into account new knowledge of the chemical elements, Weizsäcker based his theory on the German metaphysician Immanuel Kant's conception of a rotating nebula. He posited that the dust particles that did not dissipate in the nebula would gradually accumulate to form planets. He also wrote extensively on the relationship of science to philosophical and political issues. Weizsäcker taught at the Max Planck Institute, Göttingen (1946–57), and the universities of Hamburg (1957–69) and Munich (1970–80).

WELCH, JOSEPH NYE (1890–1960), U.S. lawyer. A native of Iowa, Welch worked his way through Grinnell College and won a scholarship to Harvard Law School (graduated 1917). A successful trial lawyer in Boston, he won national attention for his role as special counsel for the army in the televised 1954 Army-McCarthy hearings. Charging Senator Joseph R. McCarthy from Wisconsin with improper influence in the promotion of protégé G. David Schine, Welch emerged as a crusty character with a sharp sense of irony. The hearings helped to discredit McCarthy and he was censured by the Senate in December 1954. Welch later did some work as a TV narrator and played the role of a judge in the film *Anatomy of a Murder* (1956).

WELCH, ROBERT H. W., JR. (1899–1985), U.S. businessman and political activist. Welch was born on a North Carolina farm and attended the U.S. Naval Academy and Harvard Law School without graduating. After many years as a candy manufacturer (1922–56), he became active in extremist right-wing politics and founded the monthly *American Opinion* (1956). Having written *The Life of John Birch* (1954), he founded (1958) and presided over (1958–83) the John Birch Society, named in honor of the U.S. intelligence officer killed by Chinese communists. Dismissed by some as a crank—he considered Pres. Dwight Eisenhower a member of the communist conspiracy and the United Nations a front for the Comintern—Welch nonetheless attracted a considerable following. ■ See his book *The Politician* (1963) and biography by G. Edward Griffin (1975).

WELENSKY, SIR ROY (1907–1991), Rhodesian political leader. Born into a poor white immigrant family, Welensky was a heavyweight boxing champion before becoming a railway engineer and successful union organizer. A member of the legislature of Northern Rhodesia (1938–53), he promoted the establishment of the Federation of Rhodesia and Nyasaland, also known as the Central African Federation (now the independent nations of Zambia, Zimbabwe, and Malawi) and served it as a cabinet member (1953–56) and prime minister (1956–63). His gradual approach to majority rule was unacceptable to the British government, intransigent white settlers, and black African nationalists, and the federation dissolved in 1963. Opposed to the independence, under white rule, of Southern Rhodesia, he was badly defeated in an attempt to win a seat in the legislative assembly (1964). He retired from politics and subsequently moved to Britain. ■ See his *Welensky's 4000 Days* (1964); J.R.T. Wood, *The Welensky Papers* (1983); and Garry Allighan, *The Welensky Story* (1962).

WELK, LAWRENCE (1903–1992), U.S. bandleader and television personality. Born in North Dakota of German immigrant parents, Welk preserved his accent and his homespun approach to music during his rise through radio and the dance hall to television celebrity. He entertained (1955–70) middle-aged America on Saturday nights with his "champagne music" and guest performers. After 1970, the show continued to be offered in syndication and (from 1987) on public television. With his famous "ah-one, ah-two," he led his 27-piece band in rather staid pop tunes; his theme song was "I'm Forever Blowing Bubbles." Welk's New Year's Eve show was a perennial feature of holiday entertainment. ■ See his *Wunnerful, Wunnerful* (1971) and *Ah-one, Ah-two!* (1974).

WELLER, THOMAS HUCKLE (1915–), U.S. physiologist and parasitologist. A Harvard graduate, (M.D. 1940), Weller first became interested in tissue-culture technique as a medical student. While serving in the army during World War II, he studied various tropical diseases. After the war (1947) he joined with John Enders in establishing a research laboratory at Harvard, where he headed the Department of Tropical Public Health (1954–81). There, he and Enders along with Frederick C. Robbins cultivated poliomyelitis viruses in human nonnerve tissue culture (1949), a feat that led to the development of a polio vaccine. For this work Weller shared the 1954 Nobel Prize in Physiology or Medicine with Enders and Robbins. He also isolated and propagated the causative agents of chicken pox, rubella (German measles), and shingles.

WELLES, (GEORGE) ORSON (1915–1985), U.S. producer, actor, and director. A child prodigy from Wisconsin, Welles made his theater debut at age 16 in Dublin before touring the United States with Katharine Cornell's company. A tall man with a deep, resonant voice, Welles directed the Mercury Theater group's highly successful radio dramatizations, including a 1938 adaptation of H. G. Wells' *War of the Worlds* that caused a panic. By age 26 the precocious genius had written, directed, and starred in *Citizen Kane* (1941), an American film classic about the rise to power of a newspaper magnate closely resembling William Randolph Hearst. In this and other films (*The Magnificent Ambersons*,

1942; *Touch of Evil*, 1958), Welles' pioneered new techniques in photography, cutting, and dialogue, although some of his film productions ran into financial and artistic difficulties. Welles gave a small but memorable performance in *The Third Man* (1949) and also acted in *The Long Hot Summer* (1958). ■ See study by Joseph McBride (1977); biography by Barbara Leaming (1985); and David Thomson, *Rosebud* (1996).

WELLES, SUMNER (1892–1961), U.S. diplomat. A graduate of Groton and Harvard (1914), Welles was regarded as the nation's foremost governmental expert on Latin America. He was assistant secretary (1933; 1934–37) and later undersecretary of state (1937–43) for Latin American affairs and was the chief architect of Pres. Franklin D. Roosevelt's "Good Neighbor Policy." Differences with Secretary of State Cordell Hull caused him to resign in 1943. His writings included *Naboth's Vineyard: The Dominican Republic, 1844–1924* (2 vols., 1928), a mildly critical account of U.S. expansionism; *The World of Four Freedoms* (1942); *We Need Not Fail* (1948); and *Seven Decisions That Shaped History* (1950). ■ See biography by Benjamin Welles (1997).

WELLMAN, WILLIAM AUGUSTUS (1896–1975), U.S. film director. Wellman was a World War I flying ace who got into film, legend has it, by landing a small plane on the polo field of actor Douglas Fairbanks, Sr. Wellman acted in a 1919 Fairbanks film before making his debut as a director in 1923. In 1929 he directed *Wings*, which won the first Academy Award for best film. He was coauthor as well as director of the original show-business drama, *A Star Is Born* (1937), but the tough-talking, hard-drinking director was better known for dramatic action films like *Public Enemy* (1931), *Beau Geste* (1939), *The Oxbow Incident* (1943), and *The High and the Mighty* (1954). ■ See his memoir, *A Short Time for Insanity* (1974).

WELLS, HERBERT GEORGE (1866–1946), British writer. H. G. Wells was a schoolteacher and journalist before making his name as a science-fiction writer in 1895 with the publication of *The Time Machine*. Refining his talent for making the impossible seem plausible, he wrote *The Island of Dr. Moreau* (1896), *The Invisible Man* (1897), and *The War of the Worlds* (1898). In his fiction he foresaw many of the technological and social changes that were to take place during the 20th century. Wells was an active socialist, a member of the Fabian Society (1903–08), and the author of many pamphlets on world peace and world federation. *The Outline of History* (1920; rev. ed. 1939), which he wrote at great speed, remained a best-seller for years. ■ See his *Experiment in Autobiography* (2 vols., 1934); biographies by Anthony West (1894), David C. Smith (1986), and Norman and Jeanne MacKenzie (1973); and study by Richard Costa (rev. ed. 1985).

WELTY, EUDORA (1909–), U.S. novelist and short-story writer. Welty attended Mississippi College for Women and later studied advertising. She spent all her life in Jackson, Mississippi. Although her fiction drew from the southern gothic tradition, populating Mississippi towns with grotesque and alienated but disarming characters, she was not a strictly regional writer. Welty came into the public eye with stories collected in *A Curtain of Green* (1941) and *The Wide Net* (1943). *The Golden Apples* (1949) and *The Bride Of Innisfallen* (1955) were story cycles. Her novels included *Delta Wedding* (1946) and the comic *The Ponder Heart* (1954), which was adapted for the stage (1957). Her reputation grew after 1970, when she published *Losing Battles*, a novel about poor Mississippi hill people. *The Optimist's Daughter* (1972) won a Pulitzer Prize. *The Collected Stories* appeared in 1980. Welty's essays were assembled in *The Eye of the Story* (1978), and her autobiography, *One Writer's Beginnings* (1984), was a best-seller. ■ See her *Stories, Essays and Memoir* (1998); biographies by A. J. Devlin (1983) and Ann Waldron (1998); and studies by Elizabeth Evans (1981) and Michael Kreyling (1980).

WEN I-TO. *See WEN YI-DUO.*

WENNER-GREN, AXEL LEONARD (1881–1961), Swedish financier and industrialist. As representative of the Swedish Lux Co., a producer of light bulbs, Wenner-Gren landed the contract for lighting the newly built Panama Canal (1914). He founded the Electrolux Co. and made a huge fortune selling vacuum cleaners and refrigerators. One of the world's richest men—he was said to be worth $1 billion—he had extensive holdings in Mexico, Canada, and Europe. However, he was blacklisted by the U.S. government for alleged dealings with the Nazis during World War II. A noted philanthropist, he established the Wenner-Gren Fund and reportedly dispersed between $25 and $50 million to various scientific and health foundations.

WENNERSTRÖM, STIG (1906–), Swedish spy. Beginning his career in the Swedish navy (1929), Wennerström learned Russian and was posted to the Moscow embassy as an air attaché (1940). He then served in the Swedish military intelligence (1941–48) as an expert on the Soviet Union and rose to the rank of lieutenant colonel; he had access to vital military secrets that he began to sell to the Soviets during tours of duty in Moscow (1949–52), Washington (1952–57), and Stockholm (1957–63). He revealed the newest aircraft of the North Atlantic Treaty Organization (NATO) as well as the entire radar defenses of Sweden. He fell under suspicion, but his superiors could not believe in his guilt until a suspicious housekeeper produced incontrovertible evidence. Arrested in 1963, he was sentenced (1964) to life imprisonment but his sentence was reduced to 20 years (1972) and he was released in 1974. ■ See H. K. Ronblom, *The Spy Without a Country* (1965), and Thomas Whiteside, *An Agent in Place* (1967).

WEN YI-DUO (old style: WEN I-TO; 1899–1946), Chinese poet. The leading poet of the 1920s, Wen contributed to the development of the new vernacular style by combining Chinese and Western techniques and images. Although politically active, he became increasingly pessimistic regarding the contemporary political situation and withdrew from public life to pursue a purely academic and research career (1928). During the Sino-Japanese War (1937–45) he resumed his political activity, became increasingly critical of the ruling Guomindang (Kuomintang) party, and was named a director of the China Democratic League (1944), a liberal, noncommunist confederation advocating Western-style democracy and national reconstruction. He was assassinated in 1946. ■ See his *Red Candle: Selected Poems* (Eng. trans. 1972) and study by Kai-yu Hsü (1980).

WERFEL, FRANZ (1890–1945), Austrian writer. In the century's second decade, Werfel was the most popular poet of the expressionist movement; his lyric verse spoke of universal human values and the evils of war. Werfel also wrote modernist plays, traditional historical drama, religious plays, and widely read fiction. His novels reflected a Jewish intellectual's troubled response to the political turmoil and oppression of his day as well as his fascination with music and Christianity. They included *Verdi* (1924; Eng. trans. 1947), *The Pascarella Family* (1931; Eng. trans. 1932), *The Forty Days of Musa Dagh* (1933; Eng. trans. 1934), *The Song of Bernadette* (1941; Eng. trans. 1942), and *Jakobowsky and the Colonel* (1944; Eng. trans. 1944). A selection of his poetry in translation appeared in 1945. Werfel fled Nazi-dominated Austria for France; he then traveled (1940) by foot to Spain, eventually settling in the United States. ■ See study edited by L. B. Fotlin (1961) and biographies by Lionel B. Steiman (1985) and Peter S. Jungk (1991).

WERNER, BUDDY (Wallace Werner; 1936–1974), U.S. skier. U.S. downhill champion (1957) and combined Alpine champion (1959; 1963), Buddy Werner was the first male American skier to seriously challenge Europeans in international competition. In the 1964 Olympics he placed 8th in the slalom and 17th in the downhill. Shortly afterward he was killed in an avalanche in Switzerland. ■ See John R. Burroughs, *I Never Look Back* (1967).

WERTHEIMER, MAX (1880–1943), German psychologist. Trained in Prague, Berlin, and Würzburg (Ph.D. 1904). Wertheimer conducted experiments in perception with Kurt Koffka and Wolfgang Köhler (1912) that led to the founding of the Gestalt school of psychology. Rejecting the atomistic assumptions of contemporary psychology, the Gestalt view was that learning, thinking, and perception involved the appreciation of patterned and structured wholes and not merely isolated and individual elements. The Gestalt approach emphasized the integrative aspects of experience and had a profound effect on 20th-century social science and psychotherapy. Wertheimer taught at Frankfurt (1912–16; 1929–33) and Berlin (1916–29) but left Germany on the eve of the Nazi electoral victory (1933) and emigrated to the United States, where he taught at the New School for Social Research in New York. He wrote numerous articles on the application of Gestalt concepts to perception as well as to problems of truth, social ethics, and freedom. He also wrote *Productive Thinking* (1945), a Gestalt view of creative thinking. ■ See Abraham and Edith Luchins, *Wertheimer's Seminars Revisited* (3 vols., 1970), and *Revisting Wertheimer's Seminars* (2 vols., 1978).

WERTMÜLLER, LINA (1928?–), Italian film director. After graduating (1951) from theater school, Wertmüller became a puppeteer. She met (1962) director Federico Fellini and assisted him in directing his film 8½. She quickly set out on her own, winning (1963) a Locarno Film Festival award for her first work, *The Lizards*. Financial difficulties caused a hiatus of several years; in the 1970s Wertmüller made the controversial films *The Seduction of Mimi* (1972), *Love and Anarchy* (1973), *Swept Away* (1974), and *Seven Beauties* (1976), which were seriocomic studies of sex and politics. Her films reflected antifascist sentiments rooted in her early years in fascist Italy. Some critics hailed her work; others asserted that she made a burlesque of human suffering. She was a director of the Experimental Cinema Center in Rome (1988–94). ■ See Ernest Ferlita and John R. May, *The Parables of Lina Wertmüller* (1977).

WESKER, ARNOLD (1932–), British playwright. Born into a Yiddish-speaking immigrant family in London's East End, Wesker attended state schools and held a series of manual jobs before achieving recognition as the author of socially conscious plays. He was best known for his trilogy: *Chicken Soup with Barley* (1958), *Roots* (1959), and *I'm Talking About Jerusalem* (1960), which concerned members of an Anglo-Jewish family during the 1930s and 1940s. *The Kitchen* (1960), an allergory of the struggle and competition of the social world, and *Chips with Everything* (1962), which had the Royal Air Force as its setting, were also highly acclaimed. Wesker helped found and direct (1961–71) *Centre 42*, a union-backed organization formed to bring cultural programs to industrial workers. His later works included the plays *The Journalists* (1980), *Caritas* (1981), *Annie Wobbler* (1982), *Wild Spring* (1992), and *Tokyo* (1994); the short-story collections *Love Letters on Blue Paper* (1974), *Said the Old Man to the Young Man* (1978), and *The King's Daughter* (1996); and the essay collections *Fears of Fragmentation* (1970) and *Words as Definitions of Experience* (1976). He served as president of the International Committee of Playwrights (1979–83). ■ See his autobiography, *As Much as I Dare, 1932–59* (1994), and studies by Harold U. Ribalow (1966), Ronald Hayman (1973), Glenda Leeming (1983), and Reade W. Dornan (1994).

WEST, JERRY (1938–), U.S. basketball player. A 6-foot, 3-inch guard, West was an All-American at the University of West Virginia (1956–60) and perennial All-Star in the National Basketball Association with the Los Angeles Lakers

(1960–74). A hard driver and a graceful and deadly shooter, he scored 25,192 points and averaged 27.0 points per game during regular-season play and 29.1 points per game during play-off competition. He also was credited with 6,238 assists and led the league in scoring in 1970, averaging 31.2 points per game. After he retired as a player, he served as the Lakers' coach (1976–79), general manager (1982–94), and executive vice president (1994–2000).

WEST, MAE (1893–1980), U.S. actress. From an amateur talent-show debut in Brooklyn, West rose to success in vaudeville as mistress of provocative sexual innuendo. She wrote much of her own material, including the play *Diamond Lil* (1928), which she later filmed as *She Done Him Wrong* (1933) with Cary Grant. At age 40 West arrived in Hollywood, a rococo figure in curls, feather boa, and Cheshire-cat face, to film *Night After Night* (1932). Like her plays, West's films led to legal battles over censorship. With *Klondike Annie* (1936), Hollywood retreated into wholesomeness. In 1943, West returned to the Broadway stage in her *Catherine Was Great.* Her autobiography, *Goodness Had Nothing to Do with It* (1959), takes its title from West's comeback to the line, "My goodness, what beautiful diamonds!" ■ See David Hanna, *Come Up and See Me Sometime* (1976); biographies by George Eells and Stanley Musgrove (1982) and Maurice Leonard (1991); and Emily W. Leider, *Becoming Mae West* (1997).

WEST, MORRIS (1916–1999), Australian novelist. After West left the Christian Brothers Order (1939), he became an intelligence officer, a political aide, and a radio serializer, but he never abandoned his quest for religious and moral identity. This search dominated his novels, including *The Big Story* (1957) and *The Devil's Advocate* (1959). The bestseller *The Shoes of the Fisherman* (1963), whose characters were based on the French philosopher Pierre Teilhard de Chardin and Pope John XXIII, became a popular movie. West treated contemporary political issues in *The Ambassador* (1965), which explored the complexity of American involvement in Vietnam, and in *The Tower of Babel* (1968), about the events leading up to the Six Day War (1967) in the Mideast. His other novels included *Summer of the Red Wolf* (1971), *Harlequin* (1974), *The Clowns of God* (1981), *The World Is Made of Glass* (1983), *Cassidy* (1986), *Lazarus* (1990), *The Lovers* (1993), and *Vanishing Point* (1996). ■ See his memoir, *A View from the Ridge* (1996).

WEST, NATHANAEL (Nathan Weinstein; 1903–1940), U.S. writer. West supported himself after graduation from Brown University (1924) by working as a hotel manager in New York City. After publishing *Miss Lonelyhearts* (1933), which depicted the seamy underside of big-city life, he went to Hollywood as a screenwriter. Fascinated by the grotesque and latent violence of life on the fringes of the movie colony, he wrote the second of his Depression-era classics of American literature, *The Day of the Locust* (1939). West was killed in an auto accident. His *Complete Works* were published in 1957. ■ See biography by Jay Martin (1970) and studies by Stanley Edgar Hyman (1962), Victor Comerchero (1964), and Kingsley Widmer (1982).

WEST, DAME REBECCA (Cicily Isabel Fairfield; 1892–1983), British journalist, critic, and novelist. A socialist activist, advocate of female suffrage, and contributor to radical periodicals in her youth, West became a well-known political journalist noted for her wit, perception, analytical powers, and wide-ranging interests. Her most celebrated work was *Black Lamb and Grey Falcon* (1941), a massive journal of a 1937 trip through Yugoslavia. She also achieved fame for her articles on the war-crimes trials after World War II, which were collected in *The Meaning of Treason* (1947). *The Court and the Castle* (1957) was a highly acclaimed work of literary criticism. Her novels, written from a feminist perspective, included *The Return of a Soldier* (1918), *The Thinking Reed* (1936), the autobiographical *The Fountain Overflows* (1957), and its sequel, *This Real Night* (1985). ■ See studies by Peter Wolfe (1971) and Motley F. Deakin (1980) and biography by Carl Rollyson (1996).

WESTMORELAND, WILLIAM CHILDS (1914–   ), U.S. general. A graduate of West Point (1936), Westmoreland saw action with the army in World War II and in the Korean War. He commanded the 101st Airborne Division (1958–60), served as superintendent of West Point (1960–63), commanded the 18th Airborne Division (1963–64), and received four-star rank in 1964. As commander of all U.S. military forces in Vietnam (1964–68), he was influential in increasing the number of U.S. ground forces in the war and in developing the tactic of "search and destroy" missions. Although he sent Washington optimistic reports on the course of the war, the Tet offensive (February 1968) set back American military progress. As U.S. casualties mounted, the war—and Westmoreland—became increasingly unpopular at home, and he was replaced by Gen. Creighton W. Abrams. He subsequently served as chief of staff of the army (1968–72). ■ See his memoir, *A Soldier Reports* (1976), and biographies by Ernest B. Furgurson (1968) and Samuel Zaffiri (1994).

WESTON, EDWARD (1886–1958), U.S. photographer. Weston was an apolitical, asocial photographer who sought purity of texture and shape in such forms as clouds, cacti, gourds, and nudes. In the 1930s he was the center of a West Coast photography group called "f/64" after the smallest lens opening, hence the most sharply defined image. He received the first Guggenheim fellowship in photography in 1937 and spent two years photographing in California and the Southwest. ■ See his diaries, *The Daybooks of Edward Weston* (2 vols. 1961–66), *Edward Weston: Fifty Years* (1973; rev. ed. 1979), and *Edward Weston on Photography* (1983); and Chris Wilson and Wendy Madar, *Through Another Lens* (1998).

WEYGAND, MAXIME (1867–1965), French general. Born in Brussels, Weygand graduated from the French military academy at St. Cyr and became a French citizen. He served as chief of staff to Marshal Ferdinand Foch during World War I, then acted as an adviser to the Polish army during the Russo-Polish War (1920). A devout Catholic and an outspoken royalist, Weygand was recalled from the Near East during World War II to command French forces in the final weeks before the fall of France in 1940. He then acted as the collaborationist Vichy government's defense minister and representative in French Africa (1940–41). Imprisoned by the Gestapo (1942–45), he was exonerated after the war (1948) of the charge of collaborating with the Germans. ▪ See his memoirs, *Recalled to Service* (Eng. trans. 1952), and study by P.C.F. Bankwitz (1967).

WEYL, HERMANN (1885–1955), German mathematician. The most brilliant student of David Hilbert at Göttingen (Ph.D. 1908), Weyl taught there (1910–13; 1930–33) and at the University of Zurich (1913–30) before leaving Nazi Germany for the United States (1933), where he joined the original faculty of the Institute for Advanced Study, Princeton, New Jersey (1933–51). One of the century's most universal mathematicians, Weyl made fundamental contributions to many areas, including mathematical physics, differential equations, topology, group theory, relativity theory, and logic. He was also noted as a historian of the philosophy of science. His books included *Space, Time, Matter* (1918; Eng. trans. 1921), *The Theory of Groups and Quantum Mechanics* (1928; Eng. trans. 1931), and *Philosophy of Mathematics and Natural Sciences* (1949).

WHARTON, EDITH (Edith Newbold Jones; 1862–1937), U.S. novelist. Wharton's wealthy family educated her in the United States and abroad. Her psychological novels, influenced by her friend and fellow novelist Henry James, treated ironically the effect of money and class on character. Her most widely read works were *The House of Mirth* (1905), *Ethan Frome* (1911), *The Custom of the Country* (1913), and *The Age of Innocence* (1920; Pulitzer Prize). She also wrote *The Writing of Fiction* (1925). Her later work suffered from the constraints of writing for women's magazines. Wharton lived in France after 1907 and was buried at Versailles. ▪ See her autobiography, *A Backward Glance* (1934); biographies by R.W.B. Lewis (1975) and Eleanor Dwight (1994); and study by Margaret B. McDowell (1976).

WHEELER, BURTON K. (1882–1975), U.S. political leader. A liberal Democratic senator from Montana (1923–47), Wheeler left his party briefly to run for vice president on the Progressive party ticket headed by Robert La Follette (1924). He was an early supporter of the New Deal but broke with Pres. Franklin Roosevelt over his "court-packing" scheme (1937). Wheeler was best known for his opposition to lend-lease and his outspoken isolationist views prior to

U.S. entry into World War II. ▪ See his autobiography, *Yankee from the West* (1962).

WHEELER, SIR (ROBERT ERIC) MORTIMER (1890–1976), British archaeologist. One of the pioneers of modern archaeology, Wheeler was best known for his excavations of Roman and pre-Roman settlements in England and Wales and his excavations of the Indus Valley civilization at Harappa and Mohenjo-Daro in India and Pakistan. He was keeper and secretary of the London Museum (1926–44), director-general of archaeology, India (1944–48), secretary of the British Academy (1949–68), and fellow (1922–76) and professor of archaeology (1948–55) at the University of London. His books included *The Indus Civilization* (1953), *Archaeology from the Earth* (1954), *Roman Art and Architecture* (1964), and his autobiography, *Still Digging* (1955). ▪ See biography by Jacquetta Hawkes, *Adventurer in Archaeology* (1982).

WHEELER, WAYNE BIDWELL (1869–1927), U.S. prohibitionist. An Ohio lawyer, Wheeler was an activist in the Anti-Saloon League of America (from 1893), which used its substantial influence to support political candidates favoring prohibition. As the league's general counsel in Washington, D.C. (1915–27), he was one of the capital's most powerful lobbyists and played a leading role in congressional passage of the 18th (Prohibition) Amendment (1919) and its ratification by the states. ▪ See biography by Justin Steuart (1928).

WHELAN, GROVER MICHAEL ALOYSIUS AUGUSTINE (1886–1962), U.S. businessman and public official. Holder of numerous municipal offices in New York City during the 1920s (including that of police commissioner), Whelan was best known as the city's official—but unpaid—greeter of celebrities (1925–29) and was credited with originating the ticker-tape parades up lower Broadway. Called "the doorman of the Western hemisphere," Whelan always appeared elegantly dressed—sporting a carefully groomed mustache and white carnation—and he became a symbol of New York City. Indeed, the dramatist Elmer Rice wrote that "London has the British Royal Family and New York has Grover Whelan." He also served as general manager of Wanamaker's Department Store (1924–34), president of the New York World's Fair (1939–40), and New York's civilian-defense director (1943). ▪ See his autobiography, *Mr. New York* (1955).

WHIPPLE, GEORGE HOYT (1878–1976), U.S. physician and educator. A graduate of Johns Hopkins (M.D. 1905), where he trained in pathology under William H. Welch, Whipple became associate professor of pathology at that institution (1911). From 1914 to 1921 he was professor of medicine at the University of California, Berkeley, and director of the Hooper Foundation for Medical Research. During this period he discovered that the liver plays an essential role in blood formation and that a liver diet can cure cases of pernicious anemia. For this discovery he shared the 1934 Nobel Prize for Physiology or Medicine with George Minot and William P. Murphy. Whipple helped to organize and served as the first dean (1921–53) of the University of Rochester (New York) Medical School. ▪ See biography by George W. Corner (1963).

WHITE, ALMA (Mollie Alma Bridwell; 1862–1946), U.S. theologian. White came under the influence of Methodist holiness or "second blessing" preachers during her childhood in Kentucky. She first preached from the pulpit of her husband, a Methodist preacher in Colorado. Her emotional preaching at camp meetings and her establishment of missions brought her into conflict with church authorities. She founded (1901) her own fundamentalist sect, the Pentecostal Union, and presided over it as bishop. The church's name was changed to the Pillar of Fire in 1917. White supported the Ku Klux Klan and issued books praising it as an agency of God. Her autobiography, *Looking Back from Beulah* (1902), contains a history of her church. ▪ See also her *Story of My Life* (6 vols., 1919–34) and Susie C. Stanley, *Feminist Pillar of Fire* (1993).

WHITE, BYRON RAYMOND (1917–   ), U.S. jurist. An All-American football player at the University of Colorado, White then played professional football (1938), studied at Oxford University under a Rhodes Scholarship, served as a naval intelligence officer during World War II, and received a law degree from Yale (1946). He was a clerk for Chief Justice Fred Vinson, then practiced law in Colorado. He campaigned in 1960 for a wartime friend, John F. Kennedy, who was running for president. After his election, Kennedy named White deputy attorney general. Appointed by Kennedy to the U.S. Supreme Court (1962) amid controversy over his lack of judicial experience, White became one of its more conservative members, notably in the field of criminal law. He wrote a strong dissent in *Miranda v. Arizona* (1966), which required that police give suspects explicit warning before interrogation, and supported the right of prosecutors to use evidence obtained by an invalid search warrant (*U.S. v. Leon*, 1984). He dissented in the 1973 *Roe v. Wade* decision, which granted women the right of abortion, and wrote the majority opinion in *Bowers v. Hardwick* (1986), which gave states the right to outlaw adult consensual homosexual sex. However, he often sided with the liberals in supporting school busing, affirmative action, and expanded voting rights. He retired from the court in 1993. ▪ See Dennis J. Hutchinson, *The Man Who Once Was Whizzer White* (1998).

WHITE, (CHARLES) DAVID (1862–1935), U.S. paleobotanist and geologist. After graduating from Cornell University (1886), White began a 49-year research and administrative career with the U.S. Geological Survey. He served as the survey's chief geologist (1912–22) and was also the curator of

paleobotany of the U.S. National Museum (1903–35). He made many important studies of coal and oil formation and was best known for his carbon-ratio theory (1915), which enabled researchers to determine the rank of coal on the evolutionary scale and also to predict the amount of liquid and gaseous hydrocarbons present in certain types of coal. This insight tremendously aided the growth of the petroleum industry. He also did pioneering research into oil shale and headed surveys that estimated U.S. coal and oil reserves.

WHITE, EDWARD DOUGLASS (1845–1921), U.S. jurist. A Democratic senator from Louisiana (from 1891), White was appointed to the U.S. Supreme Court by Pres. Grover Cleveland (1894) and elevated to the position of chief justice by Pres. William Howard Taft (1910). The first associate justice to head the court, White held the post until his death. A conservative and nationalist, he supported congressional powers over interstate commerce (1917) and federal emergency powers during wartime (1917), and denied constitutional protection to residents of Hawaii and other "unincorporated" territories of the United States (1901–05), but he developed no consistent judicial philosophy. He was best known for invoking (1911) the vague "rule of reason" to the interpretation of the Sherman Antitrust Act, which made only "unreasonable" restraint of trade illegal and thus undercut efforts to curb monopolies. ▪ See study by Robert B. Highsaw (1981).

WHITE, ELWIN BROOKS (1899–1985), U.S. humorist. E. B. White worked as a journalist and in an advertising agency before Harold Ross, editor of a struggling new magazine, spotted poems and pieces submitted by White and persuaded him to join (1925) the *New Yorker* staff, beginning his lifelong association with the magazine. White contributed satires, verse and essays, and much of the "Talk of the Town" column. He also wrote (1938–43) a column "One Man's Meat" for *Harper's*. His many books included two juvenile classics *Stuart Little* (1945) and *Charlotte's Web* (1952). He wrote *Is Sex Necessary?* (1929; with James Thurber) and collected his writings in such popular volumes as *Every Day Is Saturday* (1934), *Quo Vadimus?* (1939), *One Man's Meat* (1942), *The Second Tree from the Corner* (1954), and *Poems and Sketches of E. B. White* (1981). He also revised William Strunk, Jr.'s, *The Elements of Style* (1959). ▪ See biography by Scott Elledge (1984).

WHITE, GEORGE (George Weitz; 1890–1968), U.S. theatrical producer. A Broadway song-and-dance man, White produced his first show, an eight-girl musical revue, in 1918. From 1921 to 1939 he produced 13 editions of his spectacular chorus-girl-filled *Scandals*, which were among the most popular and successful musical revues of the time. He introduced such performers as Helen Morgan, Ethel Merman, Eleanor Powell, Ann Miller, and Kate Smith and such popular dances as the black bottom and the Charleston. He also produced *Manhattan Mary* (1927) and *Flying High* (1930).

WHITE, HARRY DEXTER (1892–1948), U.S. economist and public official. A Harvard-trained economist, White left an academic career to join the Treasury Department (1934) as director of monetary research. During his 13-year career, he managed the department's $2-billion currency stabilization fund, served as a trustee of the Export-Import Bank of Washington, and devised the Morgenthau Plan for the deindustrialization of Germany after World War II. He also formulated the postwar international finance plans adopted at the 44-nation Bretton Woods Conference (1944), and he subsequently served as assistant secretary of the treasury and U.S. executive director of the International Monetary Fund (IMF; 1946–47). Accused, during the height of the cold war, of being part of a communist conspiracy, he left his government posts and, in testimony before the House Committee on Un-American Activities, denied that he was a communist and that he had given information to a Soviet spy ring during World War II. He died of a heart attack shortly thereafter. ▪ See biography by D. Rees (1973).

WHITE, JOSH (1908–1969), U.S. folksinger. The son of a black South Carolina minister, White believed he had a religious calling to work for the blind minstrels of the South. He traveled with them, learning folk ballads, the blues, and prison songs. In 1932 he played the role of one of his mentors, Blind Lemon Jefferson, in the Broadway play *John Henry*, and soon became a renowned popularizer of the blues, performing and recording such songs as "Sometimes I Feel Like a Motherless Child," "Frankie and Johnny," and "Free and Equal Blues." On the eve of World War II, his album of *Chain Gang Songs* made him famous. In later years he often performed for college audiences. ▪ See biography by Elijah Wald (2000).

WHITE, LESLIE ALVIN (1900–1975), U.S. cultural anthropologist. One of the leading theoreticians in American anthropology, White taught at the University of Michigan (1930–70) and helped develop its very strong anthropology department. Influenced by the theories of Karl Marx and Lewis H. Morgan, White believed that technology was the most important determinant of human culture, and he was a leading exponent of cultural evolution. His controversial books included *The Science of Culture* (1949) and *The Evolution of Culture* (1959).

WHITE, MINOR (1908–1976), U.S. photographer. White began to experiment with photography seriously in 1937 and worked as a photographer with the Works Progress Administration (1938–41). A student and associate of Alfred Stieglitz, Edward Weston, and Ansel Adams, he sought to bring to photography a spiritual, mystical quality and was one of the most influential creative and abstract photographers of the post–World War II era. White organized exhibitions, cofounded (1952) and edited the journal *Aperture*, wrote extensively, and taught at several schools including the California School of Fine Arts (1946–52) and the Mas-

sachusetts Institute of Technology (1965–74). ▪ See study by James Baker Hall (1978).

WHITE, PATRICK VICTOR MARTINDALE (1912–1990), Australian author. A graduate of Cambridge University (B.A. 1935), White spent many years abroad before returning to Australia (a great "emptiness") after World War II. He published his first novel, *Happy Valley* (1939), in London, but he did not receive international recognition until the appearance of *The Tree of Man* (1955) and *Voss* (1957). His later novels included *Riders of the Chariot* (1961), *The Solid Mandala* (1966), *The Eye of the Storm* (1973), *A Fringe of Leaves* (1976), and *The Twyborn Affair* (1980). His books, which are infused with allegory and symbolism, described the loneliness and frustrations of ordinary Australians and attacked the social conformity of bourgeois Australian society. As a deeply religious and mystical writer, however, he offered a vision of transcendence based on humility and integrity. He was awarded the 1973 Nobel Prize for Literature. ▪ See his autobiography, *Flaws in the Glass* (1981), and *Letters* (1996); studies by Alan Lawson (1974), Brian Kiernan (1980), and John A. Weigel (1983); and biography by David Marr (1992).

WHITE, PAUL DUDLEY (1886–1973), U.S. physician and cardiologist. A founder of the American Heart Association (1922), White taught at the Harvard Medical School (1914–56) and was a pioneer in the reseach and treatment of heart disease. He was one of the first to use the electrocardiograph, an intrument for measuring and recording electric activity of the various parts of the heart, and the first to suggest a direct relationship between diet, exercise, mental stress, and heart disease. White's book *Heart Disease* (1931) became a standard reference work for the medical profession. ▪ See his autobiography (1971), study by E. Grey Dimond (1965) and Paul Oglesby, *Take Heart* (1986).

WHITE, PEARL (1889–1938), U.S. film actress. One of the most popular of the silent-movie stars, White achieved fame as the heroine of *The Perils of Pauline* (1914), an early serial thriller. Each of the 20 installments left Pauline in apparently inescapable danger (for example, on the verge of being run over by a speeding train), and it was only during the next episode, presented the following week, that her last-minute, hair-raising escape was shown. She appeared on several other action serials (including *The Exploits of Elaine, The Black Secret,* and *The Iron Claw*) and 10 feature films before retiring to France (1924) to lead a life of luxury and enjoy the $2 million she was said to have earned during her relatively short career. ▪ See biography by Manuel Weltman and Raymond Lee (1969).

WHITE, WALTER FRANCIS (1893–1955), U.S. civil-rights leader. Although an African American, the blue-eyed and fair-skinned Walter White could have passed easily in white society; instead he actively aligned himself with the civil-rights movement. After graduation from Atlanta University (1916), he helped organize Atlanta's chapter of the National Association for the Advancement of Colored People and was NAACP national secretary from 1931 to 1955. His appearance allowed him to pose as a white reporter and investigate lynchings and race riots in the South. Lobbying in Congress for antilynching and antipoll-tax legislation and writing for several newspapers and journals, he helped create a more liberal stance toward civil rights by the federal government during the 1930s and 1940s. His books included *Rope and Faggot: A Biography of Judge Lynch* (1929). ■ See his autobiography, *A Man Called White* (1948), and Poppy Cannon, *A Gentle Knight* (1956).

WHITE, WILLIAM ALLEN (1868–1944), U.S. journalist. White attended Emporia College and the University of Kansas before becoming a journalist. As editor and publisher of the *Emporia Gazette* (from 1895) he attracted national notice when he opposed Democratic leader William Jennings Bryan and the Populists in an editorial "What's the Matter with Kansas?" (1896). Although long a supporter of liberal Republicanism, he broke with the party in 1912 when he backed Theodore Roosevelt's Bull Moose presidential campaign. A spokesman for tolerant middle-class rural America, he was known as "the sage of Emporia" and was associated with the muckraking journalists; he supported the League of Nations and the New Deal, and opposed the Ku Klux Klan. He won Pulitzer Prizes for the editorial "To an Anxious Friend" (1923) and his (posthumously published) *Autobiography* (1946). ■ See biography by John McKee (1975); Sally F. Griffith, *Home Town News* (1989); and Edward A. Agran, *Too Good a Town* (1998).

WHITEHEAD, ALFRED NORTH (1861–1947), British mathematician and philosopher. Whitehead studied (1880–84) mathematics and subsequently taught (1884–1910) at Trinity College, Cambridge. A decade of collaboration with his protégé Bertrand Russell resulted in the three-volume monument *Principia Mathematica* (1910–13), which undertook to demonstrate that mathematics could be deduced from the principles of formal logic. In the 1920s he wrote on the philosophy of science and at age 62 accepted a post at Harvard University, where he pursued work in metaphysics (1924–37). *Process and Reality: An Essay in Cosmology* (1929) used complex and specific terminology to formulate a comprehensive "philosophy of organism"; Whitehead believed that conventional categories of philosophy did not express the interconnections among matter, time, and space, or allow the statement of general metaphysical principles. Whitehead's other writings included *Science and the Modern World* (1925), *The Aims of Education and Other Essays* (1929), *Essays in Science and Philosophy* (1947), and *Dialogues* (1954). *Wit and Wisdom of Alfred North Whitehead* (1947) assembled excerpts from his writings. ■ See the "Autobiographical Notes" published in *The Philosophy of Alfred North Whitehead* (1941); biography by Victor Low

(vol. 1, 1985); I. Leclerc, ed., *The Relevance of Whitehead* (1961); and study by Paul G. Kuntz (1984).

WHITEHEAD, JOHN HENRY CONSTANTINE (1904–1960), Indian-born British mathematician. The son of the bishop of Madras and nephew of famed mathematician Alfred North Whitehead, J.H.C. Whitehead studied at Oxford and Princeton (Ph.D. 1932) and served as professor of pure mathematics at Oxford (1947–60). He was internationally known for his pioneering work in differential geometry and topology. *The Mathematical Works of J.H.C. Whitehead* (4 vols., 1962) contains biographical information.

WHITEMAN, PAUL (1890–1967), U.S. bandleader. The most popular dance bandleader of the 1920s, Whiteman performed in America's leading nightclubs and ballrooms. He developed a personal style of orchestration and performance called "symphonic jazz," a fusion of classical music with contemporary jazz. Although he was dubbed the "King of Jazz," his music was a watered-down "respectable" version of the jazz being developed by black musicians of the time. He commissioned and conducted the first performance of George Gershwin's *Rhapsody in Blue* (1924), appeared in Ziegfeld's *Follies* and George White's *Scandals,* and was featured in the movie *King of Jazz* (1930). He was regularly heard on radio broadcasts of the 1930s and 1940s. ■ See his *How to Be a Bandleader* (1948; with Leslie Lieber), and Thomas A. DeLong, *Pops* (1984).

WHITLAM, (EDWARD) GOUGH (1960–   ), Australian political leader. Born into an upper-class family, Whitlam served in the air force in World War II and practiced law from 1947. Elected as a Labour member of Parliament in 1952, he rose to party leadership in 1967 despite his nonworking-class background and served as prime minister from 1972 to 1975. As Labour's first head of government since 1949, Whitlam ended conscription, recalled Australian troops from Vietnam, advanced women's rights, recognized the People's Republic of China, and tried to "buy back" Australia from U.S. interests. As economic conditions deteriorated, however, a scandal that involved money borrowed from Arab interests and a stalemate in the legislature holding up money bills led to the governor-general's unprecedented action of dissolving Whitlam's government. He lost the subsequent election (December 1975) and resigned from Parliament in 1978, but served on many national and international commissions. His books included *The Whitlam Government* (1985), *National and International Maturity* (1991), and *Abiding Interests* (1997). ■ See Laurie Oakes and David Solomon, *The Making of an Australian Prime Minister* (1973); Paul Kelly, *The Unmaking of Gough* (1976); and Alan Reid, *The Whitlam Venture* (1976).

WHITNEY, (CHARLOTTE) ANITA (1867–1955), U.S. political leader. A socially prominent Californian whose ancestors sailed on the *Mayflower,* Whitney did social work in

New York after graduation from Wellesley College (B.S. 1889). She was active in the woman suffrage movement and in 1914 joined the Socialist party. Whitney was one of the left-wing socialists who split off in 1919 to form the Communist party, of which she became California state chairman in 1936. She was a member of the party's national committee and ran frequently for public office, without success. ▪ See Al Richmond, *Native Daughter* (1942).

WHITNEY, GERTRUDE VANDERBILT (Gertrude Vanderbilt; 1875–1942), U.S. sculptor. Born to wealth, Whitney studied under private tutors and at the Art Students League of New York and then in Paris. She established a hospital in France during World War I and developed sketches of soldiers, nurses, and civilians into sculptural reliefs commemorating victims of war; the best known were two panels for the Victory Arch (New York City: 1918–19), *The Washington Heights War Memorial* (New York City: 1921), and the St. Nazaire (France) Monument (1926). She was also known for architectural and fountain sculpture, including the *El Dorado Fountain* (San Francisco: 1915). Her Whitney Studio Club, founded in New York City in 1918, became a center for avant-garde art in America and led to the establishment (1930) of the Whitney Museum of American Art. Whitney wrote the novel *Walking the Dusk* (1932) under the name L. J. Webb. ▪ See biography by B. H. Friedman (1978).

WHITNEY, JOHN HAY (1904–1982), U.S. public official and publisher. Heir to one of America's greatest fortunes and to a family tradition of public service, "Jock" Whitney had distinguished careers in several fields. In the 1930s he was an international polo star and a Broadway and Hollywood financier. After serving as an intelligence officer during World War II, he became active in postwar Republican politics and served as ambassador to Great Britain (1957–61). He also established the John Hay Whitney Foundation (1946) and was a prominent thoroughbred horse breeder and art collector. In 1958 Whitney acquired control of the *New York Herald Tribune* and served as its publisher and editor (1961–67). Through the Whitney Communications Corp. he controlled such publications as *Parade Magazine, Art in America,* and the *International Herald Tribune.* ▪ See E. J. Kahn, Jr., *Jock* (1981).

WHITTLE, SIR FRANK (1907–1996), British aeronautical engineer. A test pilot in the Royal Air Force during the early 1930s, Whittle studied mechanical sciences at Cambridge (M.A. 1937) and invented the turbojet technique of aircraft propulsion. Although he built and patented a turbojet engine in 1930, it was not until 1941 that his jet turbine engine was used to propel an airplane. Whittle retired from the RAF in 1948 and was knighted. He moved to the United States in 1976 and served as a research professor at the U.S. Naval Academy at Annapolis, Maryland. ▪ See his *Jet: The Story of a Pioneer* (1953) and biography by John Golley (1987).

WHORF, BENJAMIN LEE (1897–1941), U.S. linguist. A chemical engineer employed as a fire-prevention expert by the Hartford Fire Insurance Co., Whorf was an amateur scholar who carried out extensive research in American Indian languages (Hopi, Maya, Aztec) and comparative linguistics as a hobby. He was a part-time graduate student of Edward Sapir (Yale University, 1931–32), who influenced his controversial theory of linguistic relativity that stated that the structure and grammar of one's language influences one's patterns of thought, perception, and action. His major writings are in J. B. Carroll, ed., *Language, Thought and Reality* (1956).

WIELAND, HEINRICH OTTO (1877–1957), German organic chemist. The son of a chemist, Wieland was a professor at the University of Munich (1925–52). He was awarded the 1927 Nobel Prize for Chemistry for significant breakthroughs in steroid chemistry made when he elucidated the structure of bile acids. He later was entangled in an illuminating scientific conflict: while the physiologist Otto Heinrich Warburg believed that oxidation was the crucial reaction in metabolic functions, Wieland asserted that dehydrogenation was the basic process. Both were right, and their controversy advanced the understanding of metabolism. Wieland opposed the Nazi regime in Germany, and although several of his students were tried for treason (1944), he survived World War II.

WIENER, NORBERT (1894–1964), U.S. mathematician. Wiener began reading at age 3, enrolled at Tufts University at 11, earned a Harvard Ph.D. at 18, and taught at the Massachusetts Institute of Technology (1919–60). During World War II, he was concerned with the rapid computation of factors crucial to antiaircraft measures. This work required more sophisticated computers than those available, and Wiener therefore delved into the mathematical foundation of communications systems. He recorded his vital findings in *Cybernetics* (1948; rev. ed. 1961); his title used this term for the first time. (It was derived from the Greek for "steersman.") His work led to the creation of a new discipline concerned with control, communication, and organization. In 1947 Wiener ceased military research and devoted himself to publicizing the issues raised by an automated society in such books as *The Human Use of Human Beings* (1950) and *God and Golem, Inc.* (1964). ▪ See his autobiographies, *Ex-Prodigy* (1953) and *I Am a Mathematician* (1956), and Steve Heims, *John von Neumann and Norbert Wiener* (1981).

WIESCHAUS, ERIC F. (1947–), U.S. biologist. Wieschaus studied biology at Yale (Ph.D. 1974), did research at the University of Zurich's Zoological Institute (1975–78) and Heidelberg's European Molecular Biology Laboratory (1978–81), and taught at Princeton University (1981–). Working in the late 1970s with his colleague at Heidelberg, Christine Nüsslein-Volhard, he followed up on the pioneering studies of genetic mutations of the fruit fly Drosophila done by Edward B. Lewis in the 1940s. By breeding 40,000 fly families to study the fly's 20,000 genes, they were able to discover the small number of master genes that determine the early structural development of the embryo. Their research opened up a new approach to the study of developmental biology, and they shared the 1995 Nobel Prize in Physiology or Medicine with Lewis.

WIESEL, ELIE (1928–   ), Rumanian-born U.S. writer. Born into a religious Jewish family in the Transylvanian town of Sighet, Wiesel was deported by the Germans during World War II to Auschwitz and Buchenwald concentration camps, where most members of his family were killed. Liberated from the camps at the end of the war (1945), he studied at the Sorbonne in Paris (1948–51) and worked for several years as a French- and Hebrew-language journalist. He realized, however, that his primary role as a Holocaust survivor was "to bear witness" and relate the experience of the victims of the Nazis to the world at large, and he began to write (1954) a series of powerful books that greatly increased public awareness of the destruction of European Jewry during the war. The best known of these works were the memoir *Night* (1958; Eng. trans. 1960), followed by the novels *Dawn* (1960; Eng. trans. 1961) and *The Gates of the Forest* (1966; Eng. trans. 1966). *The Fifth Son* (1985) is about the child of Holocaust survivors. He also wrote notable works on the plight of Soviet Jews (*The Jews of Silence,* 1966), modern Israel (*A Beggar in Jerusalem,* 1970), and Hasidism (*Souls on Fire,* 1972; *Somewhere a Master,* 1982), as well as several volumes of essays and biblical portraits. *Against Silence* (3 vols., 1985) is a collection of essays, lectures, interviews, and commentaries. He became a U.S. citizen (1963) and taught at New York's City College (1972–76) and Boston University (from 1976). He chaired the U.S. Holocaust Memorial Council (1980–86) and was awarded a Congressional Medal for his work (1985). In 1986 he was the recipient of the Nobel Peace Prize. ■ See his *From the Kingdom of Memory: Reminiscences* (1990); two volumes of memoirs, *All Rivers Run to the Sea* (1995) and *And the Sea Is Never Full* (1999); and studies by Ellen N. Stern (1982) and Robert McAfee Brown (1983).

WIESEL, TORSTEN NILS (1924–   ), Swedish neurobiologist. Wiesel received a medical degree from Stockholm's Karolinska Institute (1954) and did neurological research at the Johns Hopkins Medical School (1955–59), where he began a long and fruitful collaboration with David Hubel. Together they moved to the faculty of the Harvard Medical School (1959–83), where they continued their study of the complex matter in which the brain processes visual information. For their pioneering work with cats and monkeys, in which they determined specific functions of individual nerve cells in the brain's visual cortex, they shared the 1981 Nobel Prize in Physiology or Medicine with Roger W. Sperry and David H. Hubel. He subsequently taught at Rockefeller University in New York City (1983–   ) and served as its presi-

dent (1992–98). During the 1996–97 academic year, he was the highest-paid university president in the United States, earning $546,966 in salary and benefits.

WIESENTHAL, SIMON (1908–   ), Austrian war crimes investigator. An architect in Poland before World War II, Wiesenthal, a Jew, was imprisoned in a Nazi forced labor camp during the war (1941–43); he escaped but was soon recaptured (1944) and sent to the Mauthausen (Austria) concentration camp. Freed by U.S. troops on May 5, 1945, Wiesenthal was reunited with his wife, whom he had presumed dead; they had lost 89 relatives in the Holocaust. After the war he worked for the U.S. Army gathering evidence against Nazi war criminals. Afterward, as a private citizen, he founded the Jewish Documentation Center in Linz, Austria (1947–54), reestablishing the center in Vienna in 1961. Committed to documenting the Nazi effort to exterminate all Jews, Wiesenthal located more than 1,000 Nazi war criminals. In 1960, after an arduous search in cooperation with Israeli agents, Wiesenthal used a tip from a fellow stamp collector to locate Adolf Eichmann, chief of the Gestapo's anti-Jewish operations, in Argentina. Later that year he apprehended Karl Silberbauer, the Gestapo officer who had arrested Anne Frank, and effectively stopped the effort to discredit Frank's diary. His books, in English translation, included *The Sunflower: On the Possibility and Limits of Forgiveness* (1970; rev. ed. 1997), *Sails of Hope: The Secret Mission of Christopher Columbus* (1973), *Every Day a Rememberance Day: A Chronicle of Jewish Martyrdom* (1987), and *Justice Not Vengeance* (1987). ■ See his *I Hunted Eichmann* (Eng. trans. 1961) and *The Murderers Among Us* (Eng. trans. 1967); Iris Nobel, *Nazi Hunter* (1979); and biography by Hella Pick (1996).

WIGGIN, ALBERT HENRY (1868–1951), U.S. banker. The youngest vice president in the history of the Chase National Bank (1904), Wiggin was elevated to the presidency (1911) at age 43; by the time he stepped down in 1930 he had built up the relatively small institution into the world's largest bank. He established a security affiliate, maintained close ties with the country's largest corporations, and arranged several mergers with New York banks, including one with the Equitable Trust Co. (1930), which was dominated by the Rockefeller family and had resources of more than $1 billion. Wiggins' reputation was severely tarnished after a 1933 Senate investigation charged him with using Chase investments for his private profit. Although he denied any wrongdoing, he was repudiated by the bank and personally paid $2 million in an out-of-court settlement of a $100-million lawsuit brought against the bank by Chase shareholders.

WIGHTMAN, HAZEL HOTCHKISS (Hazel Hotchkiss; 1886–1974), U.S. tennis player. Wightman's tennis career spanned five decades. She won her first national titles (singles, doubles, and mixed doubles) in 1909 and attracted national attention when she repeated this feat the next two years. In 1919 she captured her fourth national singles title and donated a trophy for international women's team competition that became known as the Wightman Cup tournament (1923). She made best use of her smash and volley in doubles play, winning the British title (with Wills Moody in 1924) and six U.S. championships. In 1954, at age 68, Wightman won the seniors' doubles crown, the last of some 45 national titles.

WIGMAN, MARY (Marie Weigmann; 1886–1973), German dancer, choreographer, and teacher. When Wigman first enrolled in Delcroze's School of Dance (1911), she was thought awkward. She later studied with Rudolf von Laban, (1913–19), who believed in freeing movement from music. Rejecting the constraints of classical ballet, Wigman evolved an expressionistic style of dance, stressing spontaneity and communication, and was regarded as the founder of modern dance in Europe. She directed the influential Mary Wigman Zentralschule in Dresden (1920–41), but the Nazis regarded her style of dance as "un-German" and she was forced to leave her school. After emigrating (1949) to West Berlin, she founded another school (1950), which was a major center of European modern dance. She performed until 1953 but continued working into her eighties as choreographer and trainer; more than 500 Wigman dances were listed in her illustrated *Language of Dance* (Eng. trans. 1966). She influenced American modern dance through such students as Hanya Holm. ■ See Walter Sorell, ed., *The Mary Wigman Book: Her Writings* (1975).

WIGMORE, JOHN HENRY (1863–1943), U.S. legal scholar. A professor at Northwestern University Law School (1893–1929; dean, 1901–29), Wigmore played a major role in the modernization of legal education in the United States. Called "the first law writer in the country," he was a prolific author and editor, responsible for more than 100 volumes dealing with evidence, comparative law, criminal law, torts, and legal history. He was best known for *Treatise on the Anglo-American System of Evidence in Trials at Common Law* (4 vols., 1904–05; expanded to 10 vols., 1940), *The Principles of Judicial Proof* (1913), and *Panorama of the World's Legal Systems* (3 vols., 1928). ■ See biography by William R. Roalfe (1977).

WIGNER, EUGENE PAUL (1902–1995), Hungarian-born U.S. mathematical physicist. Because Wigner made fundamental advances in various fields of physics, the Nobel Prize for Physics awarded to him in 1963 carried a general citation: "for systematically improving and extending the methods of quantum mechanics and applying them widely." He shared the award with Maria Goeppert-Mayer and J. Hans D. Jensen. His early work on symmetry principles resulted in a seminal book on *Group Theory* (Eng. trans. 1959). In the 1930s he studied nuclear binding energies; he applied mathematical group theory to the energy levels of certain nuclei, and in this way explained observed regularities. In 1938 he focused on the problem of obtaining energy from nuclear fission; some of his theoretical advances were basic to Enrico Fermi's first controlled chain reaction. While a professor at Princeton University (1938–71), he played a major role in persuading the U.S. government to establish the Manhattan Project to produce an atomic reactor (1942). ■ See his book of essays, *Symmetries and Reflections* (1967), and *The Recollections of Eugene P. Wigner as Told to Andrew Szanton* (1992).

WILBUR, RAY LYMAN (1875–1949), U.S. educator. A Stanford University graduate (B.A. 1896) and professor of medicine (1909–16), Wilbur served as president of the university from 1916 to 1943. He took leave from academia to work for former classmate Herbert Hoover's World War I food administration (1917), and again to serve as Pres. Hoover's secretary of the interior (1929–33). He was also a leader in the field of public health and a founder and chairman (1925–29; 1948–49) of the Institute of Pacific Relations. ■ See his *Memoirs* (1960).

WILBUR, RICHARD (1921–), U.S. poet and translator. A polished, versatile poet trained at Amherst and Harvard, Wilbur published traditional verse on a broad spectrum of themes in *The Beautiful Changes* (1947) and *Things of This World* (1957, Pulitzer Prize). He drew from French literature and translated Molière. Wilbur, who began writing as a response to World War II, declared that he was conducting "a public quarrel with the aesthetics of Edgar Allan Poe." Other works included *The Poems of Richard Wilbur* (1963), *Opposites* (1973), *Responses: Prose Pieces, 1948–1976* (1976), *New and Collected Poems* (1988; Pulitzer Prize), *Beyond the Outsider* (1991), *The Catbird's Seat: Prose Pieces, 1963–1995* (1997), and *Mayflies: New Poems and Translations* (2000). He served as U.S. poet laureate (1987–88). ■ See study by Donald L. Hill (1967) and William Butts, ed., *Conversations with Richard Wilbur* (1990).

WILDER, BILLY (1906–), Austrian-born U.S. screenwriter and director. A newspaper reporter in Vienna and Berlin, Wilder had written 20 screenplays before the Nazi rise to power prompted his move to Hollywood in 1934. He specialized in "smart romances," producing some of director Ernst Lubitsch's best scripts (*Bluebeard's Eighth Wife,* 1938; *Ninotchka,* 1939) before he turned to directing in 1942. Wilder's most memorable directing efforts were all dramas: *The Lost Weekend* (1945), a study in alcoholism; *Sunset Boulevard* (1950), the classic about a superannuated silent-film star; and *Stalag 17* (1953), a prison-camp film. Wilder also directed *The Apartment* (1960), *The Fortune Cookie* (1966), and two of Marilyn Monroe's best efforts, *The Seven Year Itch* (1955) and *Some Like It Hot* (1959). ■ See studies by Axel Madsen (1969), Maurice Zolotow

(1977), and Bernard F. Dick (1980); biography by Ed Sikov, *On Sunset Boulevard* (1998); and Cameron Crowe, *Conversations with Wilder* (1999).

WILDER, LAURA INGALLS (Laura Ingalls; 1867–1957), U.S. author. A child of the American frontier, Wilder wrote a series of children's books, based on her youth, known as the "Little House Series" (*Little House in the Big Woods* [1932], *Little House on the Prairie* [1935], etc.). She gave a straightforward, detailed, unromanticized account of day-to-day life in her pioneer family, always from a child's perspective. A hardworking farm woman most of her life, Wilder published her first book when she was 65. A Laura Ingalls Wilder Award (for children's literature) was established in 1954. In 1974 a television series loosely based on the enduringly popular books was launched; it met with immediate and long-lasting success. ▪ See Donald Zochert, *Laura* (1976), and John E. Miller, *Becoming Laura Ingalls Wilder* (1998).

WILDER, THORNTON (1897–1975), U.S. novelist and playwright. Born in Wisconsin and raised in China, Wilder studied archaeology and taught literature at the University of Chicago (1930–37). His Pulitzer Prize–winning novel, *The Bridge of San Luis Rey* (1927)—in which the disparate lives of five people converge in the same fatal accident—won international recognition. The absence of props and the presence of an informative stage manager universalized the immensely popular play *Our Town* (1938; Pulitzer Prize); purposeful anachronisms achieved a similar effect in *The Skin of Our Teeth* (1942; Pulitzer Prize). *The Matchmaker* (1954) became the Broadway musical hit *Hello Dolly* (1963). Wilder received the first National Medal for Literature (1965) and the National book Award for *The Eighth Day* (1968). *American Characteristics, and Other Essays* (1979) appeared posthumously. ▪ See biographies by Richard H. Goldstone (1975) and Linda Simon (1979), and Gilbert A. Harrison, *The Enthusiast* (1983).

WILEY, HARVEY WASHINGTON (1844–1930), U.S. chemist and public official. A graduate of Indiana Medical College (1871) and Harvard (B.S. 1873), Wiley served as state chemist of Indiana and professor of chemistry at Purdue University (1874–83). From 1883 to 1912 he was chief chemist in the U.S. Department of Agriculture, where he built up the Bureau of Chemistry from six to more than 500 employees, campaigned vigorously against food adulteration, and was the principal force behind the passage of the Pure Food and Drug Act of 1906. After retiring from government service (1912), Wiley devoted the rest of his life to the cause of pure food and health. He wrote a monthly column for *Good Housekeeping* magazine (1912–30), lectured widely, and wrote several books, including *Not by Bread Alone* (1915) and *Health Reader* (1916). ▪ See his autobiography (1930).

WILGRESS, (LEOLYN) DANA (1892–1969), Canadian diplomat. Educated at McGill University (B.A. 1914), Wilgress began a distinguished diplomatic career in 1914 when he joined the Commercial Intelligence Service of the Department of Trade and Commerce. He served in Omsk, Vladivostok, and in China, as well as in Europe and South America. When he transferred to the Department of External Affairs, he served as Canadian minister to the Soviet Union (1941–47), Switzerland (1947–49), and Britain (1949–52), and then as undersecretary of state (1952–53). He later was representative to the North Atlantic Treaty Organization council (1953–58) and chairman of the Canada–U.S. Permanent Joint Defense Board (1959–66). ▪ See his *Memoirs* (1967).

WILHELM II, KAISER. *See WILLIAM II.*

WILHELMINA (1880–1962), queen of the Netherlands. Wilhelmina succeeded to the throne in 1890 on the death of her father, William III, and served under her mother's regency until she was inaugurated queen in 1898. She was an extremely popular ruler and helped maintain Dutch neutrality in World War I. During World War II she left her country after the German invasion (May 1940), and from her headquarters in London she symbolized Dutch resistance to the Nazis. She returned to the Netherlands (1945) and abdicated in favor of her daughter, Juliana (1948). ▪ See her autobiography, *Lonely but Not Alone* (1959; Eng. trans. 1960).

WILKINS, SIR (GEORGE) HUBERT (1888–1958), Australian-born explorer, scientist, and adventurer. Trained as an engineer and photographer, Wilkins left Australia at age 20 and became a corespondent and photographer for a London newspaper. Fascinated with polar exploration, he participated in Vilhjalmur Stefansson's Arctic Expedition (1913–17), the British Imperial Antarctic Expedition (1920–21), and Sir Ernest Shackleton's last Antarctic Expedition (1921–22). He made several pioneering Arctic flights (1926–28) and was knighted for being the first to fly (with pilot Carl Ben Eielson) from Point Barrow, Alaska, to Spitsbergen, Norway (1928). He and Eielson were also the first to fly in Antarctica (1928). Wilkins later made pioneering though unsuccessful attempts to reach the North Pole by submarine (1931). All of his journeys yielded valuable geographical and meteorological information. His books included *Flying the Arctic* (1928) and *Under the North Pole* (1931). ▪ See biographies by John Grierson (1960) and Lowell Thomas (1961).

WILKINS, MAURICE HUGH FREDERICK (1916–), New Zealand-born British biophysicist. A graduate in physics from Birmingham University (Ph.D. 1940), Wilkins joined King's College, University of London (1946), where he began to study the structure of DNA (deoxyribonucleic acid) using X-ray diffraction analysis. His studies indicated that the molecular arrangement of DNA was regular and had the shape of a double helix. Based on the work of Wilkins and his colleague Rosalind Franklin, James Watson and Sir Francis Crick were able to prove that the DNA molecule was indeed a double helix and to construct a model of the molecule. For his part in this discovery, Wilkins shared the 1962 Nobel Prize for Physiology or Medicine with Watson and Crick. He later served as professor of molecular biology (1963–80) and biophysics (1970–81) at King's College.

WILKINS, ROY (1901–1981), U.S. civil-rights leader. The grandson of a slave, Wilkins began his lifelong career with the National Association for the Advancement of Colored People while still an undergraduate at the University of Minnesota (B.A. 1923). After graduating, he became a journalist with a black weekly in Kansas City, Missouri, and later edited the NAACP organ, *Crisis,* for 15 years (1934–49). Investigating, picketing, writing, and urging civil rights for blacks, he advanced (1955) to head the NAACP, where, until 1977, he skilfully maintained a middle ground between the white establishment and black militants. ■ See his autobiography, *Standing Fast* (1982).

WILKINSON, SIR GEOFFREY (1921–1996), British chemist. While an assistant professor at Harvard (1951–55), Wilkinson investigated "sandwich compounds" and explained how metals and organic substances can merge and form organometallic molecules. Similar theoretical studies were done by German chemist Ernst Otto Fischer, and they shared the 1973 Nobel Prize for Chemistry. Their work held out promise for the development of gasoline additives that would reduce automobile-exhaust pollution. Wilkinson returned to Britain and was professor of chemistry at Imperial College, London (1956–88).

WILLARD, FRANK HENRY (1893–1958), U.S. cartoonist. A cartoonist for the *Chicago Herald* (1914–17) and King Features Syndicate (1920–23), Willard was persuaded by *New York Daily News* publisher Joseph M. Patterson to create a new strip. The result was *Moon Mullins* (1923), which featured the mooching, impolite, and uninhibited Moon, who was most at home in a pool parlor, and such characters as Lady Plushbottom, Mushmouth, and Little Egypt. Moon was one of the few comic-strip characters who, true to form, did not sign up during World War II. *Moon Mullins* eventually ran in more than 400 newspapers.

WILLEBRANDT, MABEL (Mabel Walker; 1889–1963), U.S. lawyer and public official. One of America's most prominent lawyers, Willebrandt was the first woman to serve as an assistant attorney general of the United States (1921–29) and was in charge of all cases involving federal tax laws and the enforcement of the 18th (Prohibition) Amendment. As the chief prosecutor in prohibition cases,

she gained nationwide fame and was called "Prohibition Portia." She also headed the Bureau of Federal Prisons, was the first woman public defender in police courts (Los Angeles), and the first woman to head a committee of the American Bar Association. ■ See her memoir, *The Inside of Prohibition* (1929), and study by Dorothy M. Brown (1984).

WILLIAM II (Kaiser Wilhelm II; 1859–1941), emperor of Germany. The last of the Hohenzollerns, William II was an impulsive young military officer when he succeeded his father, Frederick III, in 1888. His first battle was a contest of wills with Chancellor Otto von Bismarck, whom he successfully forced out in 1890. But his intervention in Germany's domestic and foreign affairs was erratic. Seeking international influence, he alternately courted and spurned Britain and Russia, with the effect that Germany was left alone with its Habsburg ally, Austria-Hungary, on the eve of World War I. Forced to abdicate after Germany's defeat in 1918, he retired to Holland. He wrote *The Kaiser's Memoirs* (Eng. trans. 1922) and *My Early Life* (Eng. trans. 1926). ■ See Michael Balfour, *The Kaiser and His Times* (1964); Virginia Cowles, *The Kaiser* (1964); Alan W. Palmer, *The Kaiser* (1978); and the biography by Lamar Cecil (2 vols., 1989–96).

WILLIAMS, BERT (Egbert Austin Williams; 1876–1922), Bahamian-born U.S. entertainer. One of the most famous black entertainers of the century, Williams sang, danced, and clowned his way to stardom as a member of the vaudeville team of Walker and Williams (1895–1909). Although a cultivated and studious man, he portrayed the stereotyped, dim-witted "shuffling" black, which was the only black character acceptable to white audiences at the time. Considered one of the greatest comedians of his day, he appeared in several Broadway shows and was the comedy star of Ziegfeld's *Follies* for 10 years (1910–19). ■ See biography by Eric L. Smith (1992).

WILLIAMS, BETTY. *See CORRIGAN, MAIREAD.*

WILLIAMS, EDWARD BENNETT (1920–1988), U.S. attorney. A graduate of Georgetown University Law School (1945), Williams opened his own office in Washington, D.C., in 1949 and soon made a name as defense attorney for leading public officials in legal trouble. His clients included Sen. Joseph McCarthy, Rep. Adam Clayton Powell, and presidential aide Bobby Baker. Williams won an acquittal for Teamster official Jimmy Hoffa on bribery charges even though Hoffa was arrested with incriminating documents. An avid sportsman, Williams became president of the Washington Redskins football team (1965–85) and owner of the Baltimore Orioles baseball club (1979–88). ■ See his *One Man's Freedom* (1962); study by Robert Pack (1983); and Evan Thomas, *The Man to See* (1992).

WILLIAMS, ERIC EUSTACE (1911–1981), Trinidad and Tobago political leader and scholar. Williams studied at Oxford (Ph.D. 1938) and taught social and political science at Howard University (1939–53). His dissertation, published as *Capitalism and Slavery* (1944), was a classic account of the contribution of slavery to the growth of capitalism in Britain. His other scholarly books included *The Negro in the Caribbean* (1942), *History of the People of Trinidad and Tobago* (1964), *British Historians and the West Indies* (1966), and *From Columbus to Castro: The History of the Caribbean, 1492–1969* (1970). He was active in the Caribbean Commission during the 1940s and 1950s and returned to Trinidad to establish the People's National Movement (PNM; 1955). Elected chief minister in 1956, he helped guide Trinidad and Tobago to independence in 1962 and served as prime minister until his death. A controversial democratic socialist, he sponsored programs of economic development but strove unsuccessfully for Caribbean political and economic integration. ■ See his autobiography, *Inward Hunger* (1969), and *Eric E. Williams Speaks: Essays on Colonialism and Independence* (1993).

WILLIAMS, HANK (Hiram Hank Williams; 1923–1953), U.S. country singer. Williams was raised in Alabama by his mother, a church organist. He took up the guitar early and worked his way through local bands to the Grand Ole Opry. Nashville publishers Fred Rose and Roy Acuff began refining and publishing Williams' songs. Under Rose's management, Williams turned out hit after hit, combining pop and country in such songs as "Cold Cold Heart," "I'm So Lonesome I Could Cry," and "Your Cheatin' Heart." Singing a repertoire made up almost entirely of his own songs, Williams was a magnetic stage presence. But his alcoholism, drug addiction, and stormy personal life undermined his career, which lagged in the early 1950s. When he died of alcohol-related heart disease in 1953, 25,000 people attended his funeral. The MGM film *Your Cheatin' Heart* (1964) mythologized his life. A 10-CD set, *The Complete Hank Williams* (1998), contained all of his recorded music. His son Hank Williams, Jr. (1949–) was a well-known performer and songwriter. ■ See biographies by Jay Caress (1979) and Colin Escott (1994).

WILLIAMS, HENRY SYLVESTER (1869–1911), Trinidadian pan-African activist. A lawyer from Trinidad, Williams organized the first pan-African conference in London (1900) and traveled to the United States and the West Indies to promote the cause. He settled in South Africa (1903) to practice law and appeal for native rights, but he returned to London and became involved in left-wing British politics (1905–08). He returned to Trinidad in 1908. His nephew was the radical activist George Padmore. ■ See study by Owen C. Mathurin (1976).

WILLIAMS, JODY (1950–), U.S. peace activist. Williams, the daughter of a county judge in Vermont, became politically active protesting the war in Vietnam and U.S. policies in Central America. After earning a degree from the Johns Hopkins School of Advanced International Studies (1984), she was coordinator of the Nicaragua-Honduras Education Project and associate director of Medical Aid to El Salvador. In 1991 she joined Robert Muller, the president of Vietnam Veterans of America, who had lost the use of his legs during the Vietnam War, and the head of Medico International, a German medical relief organization, to form the International Campaign to Ban Landmines. As coordinator, Williams organized a grassroots international effort to outlaw and destroy antipersonnel landmines, which killed or maimed an estimated 26,000 people a year. The movement gained prominence when Canadian foreign minister Lloyd Axworthy began drafting a treaty to ban landmines (1996), and the effort was endorsed by the pope, former president Jimmy Carter, and Diana, princess of Wales. A treaty banning landmines was signed by 121 countries in December 1997, but the United States and China refused to sign the treaty. For her efforts Williams shared the 1997 Nobel Peace Prize with the International Campaign to Ban Landmines. She wrote (with Shawn Roberts) *After the Guns Fall Silent: The Enduring Legacy of Landmines* (1995).

WILLIAMS, MARY LOU (Mary Elfrieda Scruggs: 1910–1981), U.S. jazz pianist, composer, and arranger. Called "the first lady of jazz," Williams was a prominent fixture in the jazz world from the late 1920s until 1980. Renowned for her swinging piano renditions, she was a soloist and arranger with Andy Kirk's band (1929–42) and a leading interpreter of the bebop music of the 1940s. She wrote and arranged for Benny Goodman, Dizzy Gillespie, Cab Calloway, and the Dorsey Brothers, and was best known for her compositions, "Roll 'Em," "Camel Hop," "Walkin' but Swingin'," "Trumpets No End," and "In the Land of Oo-Bla Dee." She played her long composition, *The Zodiac Suite*, with the New York Philharmonic (1946). After her conversion to Roman Catholicism (1957), she wrote several religiously oriented pieces, including the joyful and swinging, *Mary Lou's Mass* (originally called *Music for Peace*; 1969). ■ See Linda Dahl, *Morning Glory* (2000).

WILLIAMS, RAYMOND HENRY (1921–1988), Welsh cultural historian and social critic. Brought up in a working-class family in a Welsh border village, Williams attended Trinity College, Cambridge (M.A. 1946) on a state scholarship. He taught adult education at Oxford University (1946–61) before joining the faculty at Cambridge, where he taught (from 1961) courses in literature and drama. An independent radical thinker, Williams was considered the foremost Marxist literary historian of his generation. He wrote path-breaking scholarly works such as *Culture and Society: 1780–1950* (1958), *The Long Revolution* (1961), *The Country and the City* (1972), *Keywords: A Vocabulary of Culture and Society* (1976), *Marxism and Literature* (1977), and *Problems in Materialism and Culture* (1980). His essays appeared in the posthumously published *The Politics of Modernism* (1989). He also wrote several novels, including *Border Country* (1960). ▪ See his *Politics and Letters* (1979) for background on his life and thought and the biography by Fred Inglis (1995).

WILLIAMS, TED (Theodore Samuel Williams; 1918–), U.S. baseball player. Ted Williams, known as "the Kid" and the "Splendid Splinter," was one of the greatest hitters in baseball history. In a career lasting 19 seasons with the Boston Red Sox (starting in 1939 but interrupted twice for military service), he compiled a batting average of .344, hit 521 home runs, won six American League batting championships, and was twice named the league's Most Valuable Player (1946; 1949). Although a perfectionist when it came to hitting—he batted .406 in 1941 and won his last batting crown at the age of 40 (1958)—Williams had little interest in the art of fielding. He was notorious for his quick temper and his frequent run-ins with fans and sportswriters. All was forgiven after he retired, however, and he was elected to the National Baseball Hall of Fame (1966) by a record number of the votes cast, more than 93 percent. ▪ See his autobiography, *My Turn at Bat* (1969).

WILLIAMS, TENNESSEE (Thomas Lanier Williams; 1911–1983), U.S. playwright. Williams began writing during his sickly childhood in Mississippi. He infused the intense frustration of lower-class life in the deep South into emotionally charged plays which affected post-World War II theater in the United States. The roles in his more than two dozen full-length plays, including *The Glass Menagerie* (1945), *A Streetcar Named Desire* (1947, Pulitzer Prize), *Cat on a Hot Tin Roof* (1955, Pulitzer Prize), and *Night of the Iguana* (1961), challenged the country's leading actors. Williams was a master of stage effects and scene construction. His women are generally volatile, tragic characters; he contended that only southern women can deliver lyrical dialogue naturally. Some critics considered his work overly preoccupied with sex (both heterosexual and homosexual); others appreciated his exploration of sex and violence as keys to human vulnerability and isolation. His health and career waned in the 1960s; *Small Craft Warnings* (1972) was the only one of his later plays to win critical acclaim. He also wrote two novels, short stories (*Collected Stories*, 1985), verse, and *Memoirs* (1975). ▪ See studies by Signi L. Falk (1978) and Felicia Londré (1979); biographies by Dakin Williams and Shepherd Mead (1983), Dotson Rader (1985), and Lyle Leverich (1995); and Donald Spoto, *Kindness of Strangers* (1985).

WILLIAMS, WILLIAM APPLEMAN (1921–1990), U.S. historian. The first and most influential of the revisionist historians of America's role in the 20th century, Williams was educated at the U.S. Naval Academy (B.S. 1944) and at the University of Wisconsin (Ph.D. 1950). A neo-Marxist, he attributed the open-door policy to capitalism in search of world markets and described the cold war as a continuing effort to make the world safe for capitalism. In *The Tragedy* of *American Diplomacy* (1959) and *The Roots of the Modern American Empire* (1969), Williams cast the United States as a counterrevolutionary world leader. He also wrote *The Contours of American History* (1961), *The Great Evasion* (1964), and *Empire as a Way of Life* (1980). He taught at the University of Wisconsin (1960–68) and Oregon State University (1968–86). ▪ See biography by Paul Buhle (1995).

WILLIAMS, WILLIAM CARLOS (1883–1963), U.S. poet. Williams was born, practiced medicine, and died in suburban Rutherford, New Jersey. The poets Ezra Pound and Hilda Doolittle inspired Williams to practice the art of experimental poetry as well as obstetrics and pediatrics. Extending imagism to what he termed "objectivism," he stripped his lines of extraneous detail, retaining detached, sensory observations, in his *Collected Earlier Poems* (1951), *Collected Later Poems* (1950; rev. 1963), and *Pictures from Brueghel and Other Poems* (1962, Pulitzer Prize). He is best known for *Paterson* (5 vols., 1946–58), a gargantuan poem that universalized the cultural milieu of a New Jersey city. His collected nonverse works appear in *The Great American Novel* (1923), essays; *Many Loves* (1961), plays; *The Farmers' Daughters* (1961), stories; *Autobiography* (1951); and *Selected Letters* (1957). *The Doctor Stories* (1984), compiled and published posthumously, recounted episodes from Williams' practice. ▪ See biographies by Reed Whittemore (1975) and Paul Mariani (1981) and John Lowney, *The American Avant-garde Tradition* (1997).

WILLIAMSON, ROBIN (1943–), British singer, musician, and songwriter. A native of Edinburgh, Williamson cofounded the Incredible String Band (1965), a folk group that created a unique style incorporating elements of traditional, rock, honky-tonk, spirituals, and African and Indian music. The exhilarating and often mystical songs were played on a wide variety of instruments, including the sitar. Their albums, which became closely associated with the hippie and alternate music culture, included *5,000 Spirits, or the Layers of the Onion* (1967), *The Hangman's Beautiful Daughter* (1968), and *U* (1970). After the band broke up (1974), Williamson performed with a new group, the Merry Band (1976–79), and subsequently recorded and toured as a soloist. He immersed himself in traditional Celtic music and literature and gained a reputation as a "20th-century bard" for his numerous recordings of traditional songs and stories. His solo albums, including *Songs of Love and Parting* (1981), *Legacy of the Scottish Harpers* (1986), *Songs for Children of All Ages* (1987), and *Celtic Harp Airs and Dance Tunes* (1997), displayed his prodigious talents as a singer, storyteller, and harpist. He also wrote several books on Celtic traditions and composed scores for television and mixed-media theatrical productions.

WILLKIE, WENDELL LEWIS (1892–1944), U.S. industrialist and political leader. A Wall Street lawyer (1929–33),

Willkie served as president of Commonwealth and Southern (1933–39), a giant utility holding company that battled against the federal government's Tennessee Valley Authority (TVA) for control of regional electric power. Although a Democrat, he became a symbol of the business community's opposition to New Deal economic policies and was nominated as the Republican presidential candidate to run against incumbent Franklin D. Roosevelt in 1940. Although he lost the election, he helped move the Republicans away from isolationism, actively supported aid for the Allied powers in World War II, and toured Britain, China, the Soviet Union, and the Middle East as Roosevelt's personal representative (1941–42). His best-selling account of the trip, *One World* (1943), advocated international cooperation and the establishment of a postwar peacekeeping organization. ■ See biographies by Mary E. Dillon (1952) and E. Barnard (1966) and S. Neal, *Dark Horse* (1984).

WILLS, HELEN NEWINGTON (1905–1998), U.S. tennis player. Called the "queen of courts," Wills overpowered opponents with dazzling ground strokes and fierce concentration. Between 1923 and 1938 she captured seven U.S. single titles, eight British titles, and four French titles. She also won the Wightman Cup singles title 18 times. At the peak of her career she totally dominated women's tennis, winning every set that she played in tournament competition between 1927 and 1933. During the years of her marriage to Frederick S. Moody, Jr. (1929–37), she competed as Helen Wills Moody. She wrote *Tennis* (1928) and *Fifteen–Thirty* (1937). ■ See Larry Engelmann, *The Goddess and the American Girl* (1988).

WILLSTÄTTER, RICHARD (1872–1942), German biochemist. The Russian botanist Mikhail S. Tsvett received little attention when his findings on the chemical structure of plant pigments (including chlorophyll)—facilitated by his development of chromatography—were published (1906) in Russian. When Willstätter, a professor in Zurich (1905–12) and Munich (from 1916), introduced the same technique and achieved similar results several years later, he won the 1915 Nobel Prize for Chemistry. In the 1920s, Willstätter asserted that enzymes are not proteins, a theory that influenced a decade of research before it was proved wrong. Although he had contributed to the German effort in World War I, designing an effective gas mask, the Jewish Willstätter resigned (1924) his post at the University of Munich to protest against the anti-Semitic academic establishment. He remained in Germany until Nazi harassment forced him to flee (1939) to Switzerland. ■ See his memoirs, *From My Life* (1949; Eng. trans. 1965).

WILMUT, IAN (1944–), British embryologist. Wilmut studied with prominent reproductive scientist G. Eric Lamming at the University of Nottingham (B.Sc. 1967) and pursued research in the field of animal genetic engineering at Cambridge University (Ph.D. 1971). As a researcher with the Animal Breeding Research Station, affiliated with the University of Edinburgh (Scotland) and later known as the Roslin Institute (1974–), he did pioneering work in genetic research and particularly in cloning, a procedure that many scientists believed would never be possible. In early 1996, using a mammary cell from an adult sheep and an unfertilized egg (whose nucleus was removed) from a second sheep, Wilmut and his team were able to fuse the two cells and implant the resultant embryo in a surrogate mother sheep. A fetus developed and on July 5, 1996, Dolly (named after singer Dolly Parton), the world's first mammal cloned from fully developed adult cells, was born. The successful experiment was kept secret until February 1997, when Dolly's survival was assured, and Wilmut and his team were able to patent their technique. ■ See his *The Second Creation* (2000; with K. Campbell and C. Tudge) and Gina Kolata, *Clone* (1998).

WILSON, SIR ANGUS (1913–1991), British novelist. Educated at Oxford (B.A. 1936), Wilson worked as a staff member (1936–55) of the British Museum and taught English literature (1963–78) at the University of East Anglia. His short stories, in *Such Darling Dodos* (1950), and novels, including *Hemlock and After* (1952) and *Anglo-Saxon Attitudes* (1956), were characterized by their psychological insight and their description and satire of the British middle class. *No Laughing Matter* (1967), an experimental and ambitious novel, traced the lives of six children of a London family from 1912 to 1962 against the background of contemporary political and social developments. A liberal humanist, Wilson explored the theme of social responsibility in *As If by Magic* (1973) and the conflict of culture and anarchy in *Setting the World on Fire* (1980). *The Wild Garden; or Speaking of Writing* (1963) contains an autobiographical essay. He also wrote *Reflections in a Writer's Eye: Travel Pieces* (1986). ■ See his selected critical writings in *Diversity and Depth in Fiction* (1983); studies by Jay L. Halio (1964) and Peter Faulkner (1980); and biography by Margaret Drabble (1995).

WILSON, AUGUST (1945–), U.S. playwright. Born to an interracial couple and raised in the poor, black Hill District of Pittsburgh, Pennsylvania, Wilson cofounded an activist theater company during the 1960s in order to raise the political consciousness of his community. As a playwright he was influenced by the Black Power movement and the ideas of Malcolm X, as well as the blues, and he drew on his own experiences in writing a cycle of dramas depicting the black experience in America during the 20th century. Each of the plays was set in a different decade, and examined the issues of self-discovery and the search for identity in environments of racism and poverty. The dramas included the Pulitzer Prize–winning *Fences* (1987) and *The Piano Lesson* (1990) as well as *Ma Rainey's Black Bottom* (1984), *Joe Turner's Come and Gone* (1986), *Two Trains Running* (1990), and *Seven Guitars* (1995). Most of Wilson's works premiered at the Yale School of Drama and were directed by Lloyd Richards, the longtime dean of the school. ▪ See Mary L. Bogumil, *Understanding August Wilson* (1999), and the study by Peter Wolfe (1999).

WILSON, CHARLES ERWIN (1890–1961), U.S. industrialist and public official. An automotive engineer, Wilson served as president of General Motors (1941–53), molding it into America's biggest producer of war material. He served as secretary of defense (1953–57) and advocated a policy of massive retaliation, increased nuclear-weapons production, and an expansion of the air force. Outspoken and controversial, he achieved notoriety for his remark that "what was good for our country was good for General Motors, and vice versa," which the press reported as, "What's good for General Motors is good for the country." ▪ See study by E. Bruce Geelhoed (1979).

WILSON, CHARLES THOMSON REES (1869–1959), British physicist. C.T.R. Wilson graduated from Cambridge University (1892) and worked there with J. J. Thomson. At the Cavendish Laboratory, he conducted experiments (1896–97) showing that charged atoms (ions), not dust particles, are the necessary nuclei of condensation in artificial cloud formation. In 1911 he produced a sophisticated version of the famous Wilson Cloud Chamber, in which tiny condensed-water droplets revealed the paths of charged particles; this invention became a highly significant tool for the study of nuclear physics. For it he shared with Arthur Compton the 1927 Nobel Prize for Physics. He served as professor of natural philosophy at Cambridge from 1925 to 1934.

WILSON, COLIN HENRY (1931–   ), British critic and novelist. Wilson left school at age 16, worked at odd jobs, and served in the Royal Air Force (1949–50). In his early 20s he began writing *The Outsider* (1956), the book that deplored the spiritual hollowness of modern society and won him celebrity as an "angry young man." It was followed by numerous philosophical and critical works, as well as novels and plays. Wilson's books treated an unusual variety of subjects, as these titles indicate: *Origins of the Sexual Impulse* (1963), *Rasputin and the Fall of the Romanovs* (1964), *Bernard Shaw: A Reassessment* (1969), *The Occult* (1971), *New Pathways in Psychology* (1972), *Poetry and Mysticism* (1970; rev. ed. 1986), *Hesse, Reich, Borges* (1974), and *Starseekers* (1980). His novels included *Ritual in the Dark* (1960) and *Lingard* (1970). ▪ See *The Essential Colin Wilson* (1984) and study by Nicolas Tredell (1982).

WILSON, DAGMAR (1916–   ), U.S. political activist. A journalist's daughter, Wilson spent her early years in Europe, returning to the United States at the outset of World War II. From 1946 she worked as a freelance artist, illustrating numerous children's books and volumes of fairy tales. Alarmed by nuclear armament in the 1950s, Wilson

joined SANE (1959). Two years later, she proposed a strike by women to dramatize their opposition to nuclear weapons. Within six weeks, 50,000 women in 60 cities—many of them housewives and mothers—were prepared to join her, and Women Strike for Peace was established (1961). Envisioned as a one-day event, it became a national women's antiwar effort. In 1962, Wilson was summoned to testify before the House Un-American Activities Committee (HUAC) on charges of alleged communist infiltration, which she denied. In 1965 she was convicted on charges of contempt of Congress after refusing to testify before a closed HUAC session; the conviction was overturned on a technicality. In 1967 she was arrested during an antiwar demonstration. She subsequently withdrew from the leadership of Women Strike for Peace. The group she had founded remained an active force in national politics, however. Its first national and political director was Bella Abzug.

WILSON, EDMUND (1895–1972), U.S. critic and writer. One of the most eclectic and important writers of the century, Edmund Wilson produced literary and social criticism that spanned many cultures and fields. After graduating (1916) from Princeton, he edited *Vanity Fair* (1920–21) and worked on the *New Republic* (1926–31) and the *New Yorker* (1944–48). Wilson wrote plays and poems, the novel *I Thought of Daisy* (1929), and a volume of short stories, *Memoirs of Hecate County* (1949). His sociological interests were reflected in a number of cultural studies, including *The American Jitters* (1932), *Red, Black, Blond and Olive* (1956), and *O Canada* (1965). Among his most notable works are *Axel's Castle* (1931), a study of symbolist literature, and *To the Finland Station* (1940), a study of the European revolutionary tradition. His diaries appeared posthumously as *The Twenties* (1975), *The Thirties* (1980), *The Forties* (1983), and *The Fifties* (1986). *A Piece of My Mind* (1956) and *A Prelude* (1967) were autobiographical. ▪ See studies by Paul Sherman (1965), Leonard Kriegl (1971), Richard H. Costa (1980), and David Castronovo (1985), and biography by Jeffrey Meyers (1995).

WILSON, EDWARD OSBORNE (1929–   ), U.S. biologist. As a student of entomology at the University of Alabama and at Harvard (Ph.D. 1955), Wilson did pioneering research on ants. Subsequent studies while a member of Harvard's faculty (from 1956) established his reputation as one of the world's foremost authorities on social insects. His work was summarized in *Insect Societies* (1971). In his books *Sociobiology: The New Synthesis* (1975) and *On Human Nature* (Pulitzer Prize, 1978), he extended his scope to include social structures or all organisms and contended that certain patterns of social behavior in humans are genetically based. These works helped to shape a new discipline (sociobiology) but also aroused tremendous controversy within the academic community as Wilson was attacked by those arguing for the cultural and environmental basis of human behavior. His subsequent works included *The Ants* (with

Bert Holldobler; Pulitzer Prize, 1990), *In Search of Nature* (1996), and *Consilience* (1998), an attempt to unify all of the major branches of knowledge by finding common foundations. ■ See Arthur L. Caplan, ed., *The Sociobiology Debate* (1978) and Ashley Montagu, ed., *Sociobiology Examined* (1980).

WILSON, (JAMES) HAROLD, BARON OF RIEVAULX (1916–1995), British political leader. A graduate of Oxford, Wilson entered the civil service, then turned to politics and was elected to Parliament as a member of the Labour party (1945). He held several positions in the Labour government, including president of the board of trade (1947–51). He left the government in 1951 to protest cuts in social-welfare sending, and thereafter emerged as a leader of the party's left wing. He failed in one attempt at the party leadership (1960), but succeeded on a second try in 1963. In 1964, Labour won a narrow victory in the parliamentary election, and Wilson became prime minister. He won a bigger majority in the 1966 election. In a shift of geographical emphasis, Wilson announced a withdrawal of all military bases east of the Suez Canal and applied for membership in the European Market. He was unable to prevent Rhodesia's unilateral declaration of independence. Austerity measures at home appeared to give the economy a lift, but Wilson nonetheless went down to a surprise defeat in the 1970 parliamentary election. He regained power in 1974 as head of a minority government but then unexpectedly resigned in 1976. Widespread allegations that extreme right-wing leaders of the British counterintelligence service acted to bring down his government were discussed in David Leigh's *The Wilson Plot* (1988). He was created a life peer in 1983. ■ See his *A Personal Record* (1971), *Final Term* (1979), and *Memoirs* (1986) and the biographies by Austen Morgan (1992) and Philip Ziegler (1993).

WILSON, JOHN TUZO (1908–1993), Canadian geologist and geophysicist. A professor at the University of Toronto (1946–74), J. Tuzo Wilson made important studies of continental structure, faulting, and ocean-floor shifting and was a leading exponent of the theory of plate tectonics or continental drift. As president of the International Union of Geodesy and Geophysics (1957–60), he played a major role in the International Geophysical Year (IGY; 1957–58), the most extensive international scientific undertaking carried out up to that time. He later served as director general of the Ontario Science Center (1974–85) and Chancellor of York University, Toronto (1983–86). Wilson edited *Continents Adrift* (1972) and *Continents Adrift and Continents Aground* (1976) and wrote *IGY: Year of the New Moons* (1959) and two books based on trips to China, *One Chinese Moon* (1959) and *Unglazed China* (1973).

WILSON, KENNETH GEDDES (1936–), U.S. physicist. The son of a Harvard chemistry professor, Wilson studied with Murray Gell-Mann at the California Institute of Tech-

nology (Ph.D. 1961) and taught at Cornell University (1963–88) and Ohio State University (1988–). A theoretical physicist, he utilized "renormalization group theory" to develop equations to explain the so-called critical points at which matter changes under the influence of pressure and temperature, such as when water boils into steam, metals melt into liquid, and iron bars lose their magnetism. His analysis, which involved accounting for an almost infinite number of interacting atoms and molecules, led to advances in diverse areas of metallurgy, physics, meteorology, and biology, and he won the 1982 Nobel Prize in Physics.

WILSON, ROBERT WOODROW (1936–), U.S. physicist. Wilson, the recipient of a Ph.D. from the California Institute of Technology (1962), was a researcher for the Bell Telephone Laboratories (1964) when he and colleague Arno Penzias noted an initially unexplainable hissing noise from an antenna designed to receive signals from the *Echo* communications satellite. They identified the hissing as microwave noise that had no direction in space; it was coming from outside the galaxy—in fact, from the universe at large. This discovery of cosmic microwave background radiation earned Wilson and Penzias the 1978 Nobel Prize in Physics. Its significance lay in part in the fact that it provided evidence for a phenomenon predicted independently by physicists who in the late 1940s hypothesized that radiation emitted by the "big bang"—which they associated with the origins of the universe—would perpetually fill the universe with the microwave radiation. Wilson headed Bell's Radio Physics Research Department (1976–94) and the Harvard Smithsonian Center for Astrophysics (1994–).

WILSON, TEDDY (1912–1986), U.S. jazz pianist and composer. Wilson studied piano and violin, then in 1935 played jazz piano for the Benny Goodman Trio (with Goodman and Gene Krupa), the first interracial group of the swing era. He established a band (1939–40) to play his own compositions and arrangements and later taught at the Juilliard School of Music in New York. Even after swing-era jazz went out of style, he continued to broadcast, record, and tour with small ensembles, helping to create a second vogue for his music. He was a respected orchestrator. ■ See his *Teddy Wilson Talks Jazz* (1996).

WILSON, WILLIAM BAUCHOP (1862–1934), Scottish-born U.S. labor leader and public official. A mine worker from childhood. Wilson was a labor agitator and a founder (1890) of the United Mine Workers of America (UMW). He was UMW secretary-treasurer (1900–08) and served three terms as a Democratic congressman from Pennsylvania (1907–13), during which he was instrumental in establishing the eight-hour day, the Children's Bureau, the Bureau of Mines, and the Department of Labor. As the nation's first secretary of labor (1913–1921), he organized the new department, sponsored programs in the field of labor welfare, reorganized the Bureau of Immigration and Naturalization, established the U.S. Employment Service, and developed agencies for meditation and collective bargaining.

WILSON, WILLIAM GRIFFITH (1895–1971), and ROBERT HOLBROOK SMITH (1879–1950), founders of Alcoholics Anonymous. Wilson, a onetime New York stockbroker, and Smith, a surgeon, met at Akron, Ohio, meetings of the Oxford Group, a fellowship that stressed honest self-appraisal and making amends for past wrongs. They formed a partnership to encourage each other in their struggle for sobriety and formed Alcoholics Anonymous (AA) to extend that support to others. They dated the formation of AA from the June day in 1935 when Smith stopped drinking. Over the next 50 years, AA grew into a worldwide movement with more than 30,000 local groups in some 90 countries. In the 1980s, it claimed more than a million members. *Alcoholics Anonymous* (1939), a book compiled by the two founders (who were known to AA members as Bill W. and Dr. Bob) contained Wilson's "Twelve Steps" for recovery. Known as the "Big Book," it sold 3 million copies by the 1980s. Lois Wilson, wife of AA's cofounder, helped to establish Al-Anon (1951), an organization that helps friends and relatives of alcoholics. ■ See Robert Thomsen, *Bill W.* (1975); Ernest Kurtz, *Not-God: A History of Alcoholics Anonymous* (1979); and Lois Wilson, *Lois Remembers* (1979).

WILSON, (THOMAS) WOODROW (1856–1924), U.S. political leader. The son of Presbyterian minister, Wilson was raised in the South, graduated from Princeton University (1879), taught jurisprudence and political economy there (1890–1902), and served as its reformist president (1902–10). An idealist and moralist Democrat, he was governor of New Jersey (1911–12) before being elected U.S. president (1912). Domestically he carried out his "New Freedom" program of progressive reforms by establishing the Federal Trade Commission and Federal Reserve Board and reducing tariffs, introducing the first income tax, and sponsoring antitrust legislation and laws protecting labor unions. Although he observed strict neutrality at the outset of World War I and was reelected (1916) pledging to keep the United States out of the war, the revelation of anti-U.S. intrigues by Germany in Mexico and the resumption of German unrestricted submarine warfare persuaded Wilson to enter the war on the side of Allies (April 1917). He sought a peace based on democracy, self-determination, arms limitations, adjustment of territorial claims, and the establishment of a League of Nations, all outlined in his Fourteen Points speech (January 1918). However, during the Paris Peace Conference (1919) at the war's end, Wilson's idealistic vision was thwarted by the nationalistic and punitive policies of the European Allies. Returning home, he suffered a physical collapse (September 1919) while campaigning for Senate passage of the peace treaty. The Senate, dominated by isolationist forces, voted down the treaty and thereby blocked U.S. membership in the League of Nations. Wilson was incapacitated during the last 18 months of his presidency and thereafter retired from public life. ■ See biography by Arthur Link (5 vols., 1947–65).

WINCHELL, WALTER (1897–1972), U.S. newspaper columnist. A school dropout at age 13, Winchell was a vaudeville performer before joining the *New York Evening Graphic* as a gossip columnist (1924). He later wrote a nationally syndicated column for the *New York Daily Mirror* (1929–63), and in 1932 he started a highly opinionated radio news broadcast that remained on the air until the early 1950s. He was noted for his punning and phrase making and for the Broadway idiom he used to express himself. An influential figure in show business, political, and society circles, he was always controversial, especially during the cold war when his politics turned to the right and he supported Sen. Joseph McCarthy and became a "red-baiter." ■ See his autobiography, *Winchell Exclusive* (1975), and biographies by Bob Thomas (1971), Herman Klurfeld (1976), and Neal Gabler (1994).

WINDAUS, ADOLF (1876–1959), German chemist. The head of the chemical institute of Göttingen University (1915–44), Windaus spent more than three decades studying complex alcohols known as sterols. He discovered the structure of cholesterol, which helped establish the chemical study of sex hormones, and did important research on digitalis, which was used in various drugs to treat heart ailments. For his research in the chemistry of foods and his synthesis of the component of vitamin D (ergosterol), which helps to prevent and cure rickets, Windaus was awarded the 1928 Nobel Prize in Chemistry.

WINDSOR, DUKE OF. *See EDWARD VIII.*

WINFREY, OPRAH (1954–), U.S. television talk-show host. Born to unwed teenage parents, Winfrey was raised on a pig farm by her poverty-stricken grandmother in rural Mississippi. After a troubled adolescence she went to live in Nashville with her father, who taught her the values of education and discipline. She gained a scholarship to study speech and drama at Tennessee State University (B.A. 1987) and started her television career as the first African-American coanchor of a news program in Nashville (1973–76). After hosting a successful morning talk show in Baltimore (1977–83), she became the host of "A.M. Chicago" (1984), which became nationally syndicated as "The Oprah Winfrey Show" (1986–). With her guests sharing their most personal problems with the audience, Winfrey helped establish the talk show as public (often bizarre) therapy, and it reached more than 15 million daily viewers. She founded her own production company (1986) and was regarded, by the 1990s, as the world's highest paid entertainer. As an actress she appeared in *The Color Purple* (1985), *Native Son* (1986), and the television miniseries "The Women of Brewster Place" (1989), which her company produced. She also produced and starred in the film *Beloved* (1998). She founded the successful women's magazine, *O: The Oprah Magazine* (2000).

WINGATE, ORDE CHARLES (1903–1944), British soldier. Wingate was an "irregular," an eccentric officer who specialized in commando and guerrilla operations. Assigned to Palestine paramilitary intelligence (1936–39), he helped form Jewish defense squads that became the core of the subsequent Israeli army. During World War II he led successful Ethiopian guerrilla operations against the Italians, formed "Wingate's raiders" to harass the superior Japanese force in Burma, and helped train "Merrill's marauders," a U.S. guerrilla regiment in Burma. He died in a plane crash. ■ See biography by Christopher Sykes (1959) and John Bierman and Colin Smith, *Fire in the Night* (1999).

WINNICOTT, DONALD WOODS (1896–1971), British pediatrician, child psychiatrist, and psychoanalyst. Trained in pediatrics, D. W. Winnicott joined the staff of London's Paddington Green Children's Hospital in 1923 and remained there for four decades. During the 1920s he became interested in the application of psychoanalysis to work with children, which had been pioneered by psychoanalysts Anna Freud and Melanie Klein. His *Clinical Notes on Disorders of Childhood* (1931) was one of the first duties in the field of pediatrics to connect medical and psychiatric concerns. Winnicott began practicing psychoanalysis in the mid-1930s, exerting strong influence on the theory of object relations and stressing, from the early 1950s, the universal role of transitional phenomena and transitional objects in human development. He also introduced new techniques for clinical work with young children. Other books included *The Child and the Family* (1957), *The Child and the Outside World* (1957), *Collected Papers: Through Paediatrics to Psycho-Analysis* (1958), and *The Family and Individual Development* (1965). *Playing and Reality* (1971) and *Therapeutic Consultations in Child Psychiatry* (1971) appeared shortly after his death. *Home Is Where We Start From* (1986) assembled his essays. ■ See Madeleine Davis and David Wallbridge, *Boundary and Space* (1981).

WINTERS, (ARTHUR) YVOR (1900–1968), U.S. critic and poet. Winters studied at Stanford University (Ph.D. 1934), where he spent his 40-year career as a professor of English. A leading critic of his generation, Winters advanced the moralist position, arguing that literature's function rests upon an "act of moral judgment." He argued that poetry should embody rational, clear statements about life that are morally uplifting and are subject to objective evaluation. Other critics questioned his taste—he complained about the obscurantism of Edgar Allan Poe, Nathaniel Hawthorne, and Herman Melville, and rated the British poet Robert Bridges superior to T. S. Eliot—but regarded his essays as classics of literary theory. He wrote such critical works as *In Defense of Reason* (1947), which contained his major writings on U.S. literature, *The Function of Criticism* (1957),

Yvor Winters on Modern Poets (1959), and *Forms of Discovery* (1967). He won the coveted Bolligen Prize (1960) for his own poetry, which was assembled in *Collected Poems* (1952; rev. ed. 1960) and *The Early Poems of Yvor Winters* (1966).

WIRTH, LOUIS (1897–1952), German-born U.S. sociologist. Taken to the United States at age 14, Wirth earned an A.B., M.A. and Ph.D. at the University of Chicago, where he later taught (from 1926). He was influenced by Marxism and pacifism, conceiving of sociology as an instrument of social betterment and taking an activist role in social work, housing development, and race relations. Wirth's major work described the ecology of the community: *The Ghetto* (1928), *Our Cities: Their Role in the National Economy* (1937), and *Community Life and Social Policy* (1956), a posthumous collection of essays.

WISE, STEPHEN SAMUEL (1874–1949), U.S. Jewish religious leader and Zionist. Born in Hungary, Wise was raised in the United States and educated at Columbia University (Ph.D. 1901). A leader of Reform Judaism, he founded (in New York City) the Free Synagogue (1907), which he served as rabbi for 43 years, and the Jewish Institute of Religion (1922), which trained students for the rabbinate. Wise was prominent in social and political reform movements and a cofounder of the National Association for the Advancement of Colored People (1909) and the American Civil Liberties Union (1920), though his greatest contributions were in Jewish communal activities. He was a leader of the American Zionist movement and a founder and president of both the American Jewish Congress (1916) and the World Jewish Congress (1936). ■ See his autobiography, *Challenging Years* (1949); Melvin Urofsky, *A Voice That Spoke for Justice* (1982); and Robert D. Shapiro, *A Reform Rabbi in the Progressive Era* (1988).

WISEMAN, FREDERICK (1930–), U.S. film director. Wiseman graduated from Yale Law School (1954) and practiced and taught law for several years before becoming involved in filmmaking as the producer of a documentary version of a novel about delinquents in Harlem, *The Cool World* (1964). He subsequently made more than two dozen sophisticated documentary films that revealed, in a detached yet compelling manner, the workings of numerous American institutions. Wiseman's films, which he called "reality fictions," were all unstaged and contained no narration, on-camera interviews, background music, nor additional lighting. However, the social reality he filmed was given structure and perspective through an extensive editing process, and his works were regarded as presenting unique insights into contemporary American culture. His subjects included a prison for the criminally insane (*Titicut Follies,* 1967), a public school (*High School,* 1962), a police department (*Law and Order,* 1969), an urban hospital (*Hospital,* 1970), a welfare office (*Welfare,* 1975), a primate research center

(*Primate,* 1974), a meatpacking plant (*Meat,* 1975), a resort for the wealthy (*Aspen,* 1991), a department store (*The Store,* 1983), a ballet company (*Ballet,* 1995), a housing project (*Public Housing,* 1997), and a New England community (*Belfast, Maine,* 1999). ▪ See Thomas W. Benson and Carolyn Anderson, *Reality Fictions* (1989), and B. K. Grant, *Voyages of Discovery* (1992).

WISSLER, CLARK (1870–1947), U.S. anthropologist. Trained at Columbia University (Ph.D., 1901), Wissler switched to anthropology under the influence of Franz Boas, the professor who dominated American anthropology early in the century. In 1902 he began his four-decade association with the American Museum of Natural History in New York (curator of department of anthropology, 1905–42). In *The American Indian* (1917), Wissler guided the interpretation of ethnographic data by suggesting that the geographical distribution of certain cultural characteristics is related to physical environment. He formulated the concept of "culture area," which he further elaborated in *Man and Culture* (1923) and *The Relation of Nature to Man in Aboriginal America* (1926). Wissler also taught (1924–40) at Yale University.

WISTER, OWEN (1860–1938), U.S. writer. Born into a prominent Philadelphia family, Wister graduated from Harvard College (1882) and became a lawyer (1889). He spent summers on ranches in Wyoming and, like his Harvard classmate and lifelong friend Theodore Roosevelt, he fell in love with the American west. He began to write about the region and after *Harper's* published two of his sketches (1891) he decided to pursue a literary career. He wrote several collections of stories featuring ranchers and cowboys, but was best known for the humorous novel *The Virginian* (1902). It featured a brave but shy "tenderfoot" hero who became the model of the cowboy in modern fiction and popular culture. The novel helped to create the mythology of the West and inspired a play, several films, and a television series. Wister's journals and letters were published as *Owen Wister Out West* (1958). He also wrote novels set in the East and several biographies and works of nonfiction. ▪ See biography by Darwin Payne (1985).

WITKIEWICZ, STANISLAW IGNACY (1885–1939), Polish writer, artist, and philosopher. Attacked by contemporary critics and considered by many to be insane, Witkiewicz was rediscovered during the 1950s and 1960s and subsequently regarded as one of the century's major literary figures. His pessimistic, surrealistic, and grotesque plays, filled with black humor, predated the theater of the absurd by more than 25 years. His best-known plays, including *The Water Hen* (produced 1922; published 1962; Eng. trans. 1968), *The Crazy Locomotive* (1923/1962/1968), and *The Shoemakers* (1934/1948/1968) dealt with the destruction of the individual and the triumph of technology. His anti-utopian novels *Farewell to Autumn* (1927) and *Insatiability*

(1930; Eng. trans. 1977; 1996) predicted the collapse of European civilization and the triumph of totalitarianism. He committed suicide after Germany and Russia invaded Poland during World War II. English translations of his works are in *The Madman and the Nun and Other Plays* (1968), *Tropical Madness* (1972), and *The Beelzebub Sonata: Plays, Essays and Documents* (1980). ▪ See Daniel Gerould, *Witkacy* (1981).

WITTE, COUNT SERGEI YULYEVICH (1849–1915), Russian political leader. Witte was born into a Baltic German family in Tiflis (now Tblisi) and studied in Odessa. He was an administrator of provincial railways; in later ministerial posts, he was responsible for commerce, industry, finance, and communication (1892?–1903). An advocate of modernization, he was instrumental in construction of the Trans-Siberian and Chinese Eastern railways; he introduced the gold standard and reorganized the state bank, and fostered industrial growth with the use of foreign capital. His policies favored the new class of industrialists but resulted in depressed living standards for the peasantry and were resisted by the landed nobility. Although dismissed by Czar Nicholas II in 1903, he was recalled to negotiate an end to the Russo-Japanese War at Portsmouth, New Hampshire (1905), and subsequently persuaded the czar to establish a constitutional government. As Russia's first premier (1905–06), he suppressed the revolutionary movement and secured loans from the British and French. However, the czar distrusted him and replaced his government with a more conservative one. ▪ See his *Memoirs* (Eng. trans. 1921) and studies by Vladimir Brenner (Eng. trans. 1979), Theodore H. von Laue (1963), and Howard D. Mehlinger (1972).

WITTEN, EDWARD (1951–   ), U.S. mathematical physicist. Witten, the son of a physics professor, studied history at Brandeis University (B.A. 1971), worked in George McGovern's 1972 presidential campaign, and became a political journalist. However, he soon returned to academia and earned a doctorate in physics from Princeton University (1976). He subsequently did postdoctoral work at Harvard (1976–80), and served as professor of physics at Princeton (1980–87) and at the Institute for Advanced Study (1987–   ). One of the most innovative theoreticians of his generation, Witten was best known for his work on superstring theory (1984), which provided a possible means of unifying quantum physics with gravity. He utilized a topological analysis to support the existence of a 10-dimensional universe, which would explain, if true, the nature of all matter and energy and allow for a "grand unified theory." His subsequent work in knot theory, quark behavior, and supersymmetry bolstered the theoretical bases of string theory. Witten, who was awarded the Fields Medal (1990), wrote *Superstring Theory* (with M. B. Green and J. M. Schwarz; 2 vols., 1987).

WITTGENSTEIN, LUDWIG JOSEF JOHANN (1889–1951), Austrian-born British philosopher. The son of an industrialist, Wittgenstein was raised in an intellectual and cultured environment. His early interest in mechanics led to mechanical engineering and aeronautical training in Germany and Britain. After reading Bertrand Russell's *Principles of Mathematics,* he studied under Russell at Cambridge (1912–13) and developed the ideas articulated in his *Tractatus Logico-Philosophicus* (1922; Eng. trans. 1922), written during service in the Austrian army in World War I. This 80-page work on the nature of thought and language demonstrated a series of seven propositions, including Wittgenstein's idea that "A proposition is a picture of reality. A proposition is a model of reality as we think it to be." The work influenced the Vienna Circle of logical positivists. After a 15-year period when he abandoned the formal study of philosophy, he returned to Cambridge (1929–47), where he lectured and gathered a small cult following. He became a naturalized British citizen in 1938. A major figure in philosophy between the wars, Wittgenstein produced two systems of philosophic thought: theories of logic and theories of language. Most of his works were published posthumously, including *Philosophical Investigations* (Eng. trans. 1953), which related philosophical problems to illusions rooted in linguistic ambiguity, and his notes for students, recorded during the 1930s, published as *Preliminary Studies for the "Philosophical Investigations," Generally Known as the Blue and Brown Books* (1958). ▪ See biographies by Anthony Kenney (1973) and Ray Monk (1991); and Allan Janik and Stephen Toulmin, *Wittgenstein's Vienna* (1973).

WITTIG, GEORG (1897–1987), German organic chemist. At age 82, Wittig shared the 1979 Nobel Prize in Chemistry (with Herbert C. Brown) for work accomplished some 30 years earlier. The prize acknowledged the Wittig synthesis, or Wittig reaction, which made feasible large-scale manufacture of hundreds of pharmaceutical and industrial chemicals at reasonable cost. He invented a technique facilitating the joining of large molecules; he developed chains consisting of carbon, hydrogen, and phosphorus atoms that function as temporary links joining large molecules until permanent chemical links can be established. Wittig directed the Chemical Institute of the University of Tubingen (1944–56) and was a professor at the University of Heidelberg (1956–67).

WODEHOUSE, SIR PELHAM GRENVILLE (1881–1975), British-born U.S. novelist. P. G. Wodehouse worked in a bank before becoming a newspaper columnist and magazine writer. After 1909 he spent most of his time in the United States and France. He published several boys' tales and began (1914) generating the amusing fiction for which he became known, at the rate of two books per year. Most were set in the parlors of Edwardian England (and later in the 1920s); his stylized characters, including Psmith, Bertie Wooster, and his man Jeeves, played out farcical variations on a few plots in such novels as *Leave It to Psmith* (1923), *Carry on Jeeves* (1925), *The Code of the Woosters* (1938),

and *Frozen Assets* (1964). He also wrote plays and movie scripts and collaborated with Guy Bolton and Jerome Kern on several musical comedies. While living in France during World War II, Wodehouse fell into Nazi custody; his subsequent radio broadcasts from Berlin spurred controversy. He never returned to Britain and became a U.S. citizen in 1956. *Performing Flea: A Self-Portrait in Letters* (1953) and *Over Seventy* (1957) were autobiographical. ▪ See biographies by Joseph Connolly (1980), Frances Donaldson (1982), David A. Jasen (rev. ed. 1982), and Barry Phelps (1992).

WOLF, CHRISTA (1929–), East German writer. Wolf attended the universities of Jena and Leipzig, then worked as an editor for various publishers and literary journals, including *New German Literature.* After publishing *Divided Heaven: A Novel of Germany Today* (1963; Eng. trans. 1965), Wolf won her country's National Prize for Art and Literature (1964). Two years later, she drew criticism at home with *The Quest for Christa T.* (1966; Eng. trans. 1970), a novel that violated the strictures of socialist realism and expressed disillusionment with East German ideology. Published in West Germany, it was praised in the West for its complexity and craft, became a best-seller, and brought Wolf international attention. *A Model Childhood* (1976; Eng. trans. 1982), experimental fiction, reflected Wolf's experiences growing up in Nazi Germany. *No Place on Earth* (1979; Eng. trans. 1982), a novel set in Germany in 1804, also mixed fact and fiction. *The Reader and the Writer* (1972; Eng. trans. 1978) collected her essays. Wolf traveled in the West but continued to live in East Germany. She was a vocal opponent of nuclear armaments. She also wrote *Cassandra: A Novel and Four Essays* (1983; Eng. trans. 1984), the novel *Accident: A Day's News* (1987; Eng. trans. 1989), and *The Author's Dimension: Selected Essays* (1987; Eng. trans. 1993). After the collapse of communism in the East and the unification of Germany (1990), she was attacked by several West German critics for the privilege and rank she was granted by the East German government and for her brief, informal collaboration with its secret police. Her later works included *What Remains and Other Stories* (1993; Eng. trans. 1995), *Parting from Phantoms: Selected Writings, 1990–1994* (1994; Eng. trans. 1997), and *Medea: A Modern Retelling* (1996; Eng. trans. 1998). ▪ See studies by Gail Finney (1999), Anna K. Kuhn (1988), and Margit Resch (1997).

WOLFE, THOMAS (1900–1938), U.S. novelist. After a short-lived career as student playwright at Harvard, Wolfe joined the faculty of New York University (1924) and soon began the first of his autobiographical novels, *Look Homeward, Angel* (1929). His candid, detailed accounts of interactions in his native Asheville, North Carolina, were enthusiastically received everywhere except Asheville. Two more novels were published during Wolfe's lifetime. His most famous works, *The Web and the Rock* (1939) and *You Can't Go Home Again* (1940)—stories of a man's search for meaning in a spiritually destructive world—were extracted posthumously from manuscripts. Although Wolfe's powerful, lyric flowing interior monologues are frequently uncontrolled, his fiction is, in his own words, rich "in space and color and time." His *Letters to His Mother* (1943), *Selected Letters* (1956), and *Notebooks* (1970) were published posthumously. Wolfe's *The Autobiography of an American Novelist* (1983) contains two lectures written shortly before his death. ▪ See biographies by Richard G. Walser (1977) and Elizabeth Nowell (1960); study by Richard L. Steele (1976); and David Herbert Donald, *Look Homeward* (1987).

WOLFE, TOM (Thomas Kennerly Wolfe; 1931–), U.S. writer. The foremost exponent of a "new journalism," Tom Wolfe was born in Virginia and earned a Ph.D. in American studies from Yale (1956). As a feature writer of *New York* magazine and *Esquire*, he combined the techniques of fiction with factual reporting and a generous borrowing from sociology and the comic strips. A collection of Wolfe's articles on pop culture was published as *The Kandy-Kolored Tangerine-Flake Streamline Baby* (1965), followed by a "nonfiction novel" on the evolution of the drug culture, *The Electric Kool-Aid Acid Test* (1968). He also wrote essays attacking radical chic (*Radical Chic and Mau-Mauing the Flak Catchers*, 1970), modern art (*The Painted Word*, 1976), and modern architecture (*From Bauhaus to Our House*, 1981). *The Right Stuff* (1979; film 1983) was a study of the early years of the U.S. space program focusing on the seven original astronauts. The bitterly sarcastic novel *Bonfire of the Vanities* (1987; film 1990) depicted greed, political ambition, and racial hostility in contemporary New York City, while *A Man in Full* (1998) dealt with racial politics, criminality, and greed in Atlanta in the 1990s. Selections from his works are in *The Purple Decades* (1982).

WOLFSON, HARRY AUSTRYN (1887–1974), Lithuanian-born U.S. historian. Wolfson arrived at Harvard on a scholarship in 1908 (Ph.D. 1915) and taught there for the rest of his life as an authority on Jewish medieval scholarship, comparative religion, and Greek, Christian, Hebrew, and Islamic philosophy. His work helped establish Jewish studies in the United States, and he was instrumental in establishing the Harvard College Library's Judaica Collection. Wolfson wrote many books, including *The Philosophy of Spinoza* (1934), *Philo* (1947), *The Philosophy of the Church Fathers* (1956), and *Studies in the History of Philosophy and Religion* (1973). ▪ See Leo Schwartz, *Wolfson of Harvard* (1978).

WOLFSON, SIR ISAAC (1897–1991), British businessman and philanthropist. A school dropout who became a traveling salesman, Wolfson joined Great Universal Stores in 1932. By 1946, he was chairman of the board (a position he shared with his son, Sir Leonard Wolfson, from 1984 to 1987, when he became honorary life president). Under his leadership, "GUS" grew into the largest mail-order concern

outside the United States. He founded the Wolfson Foundation (1955), which supported health, educational, and youth activities, and Wolfson College, Oxford (1966). He endowed academic chairs at Oxford and Cambridge and supported a nursing and medical school. He was also a strong supporter of Israel and Jewish causes. He was made a baronet in 1962.

WOLKER, JIŘÍ (1900–1924), Czech poet. Wolker arrived in Prague in 1919 to study law but soon became involved in the literary life of the capital. His first volume of poetry, *A Guest in the House* (1921), proclaimed the essential goodness and unity of humankind, while his second and last volume, the influential *Grievous Hour* (1922), reflected his commitment to the exploited proletariat and his belief in communism. Wolker expressed strong youthful emotions through powerful images and was known as a poet of the young as well as the most prominent proletarian poet. Although he died of tuberculosis at an early age, his work influenced many poets in subsequent years.

WOLPE, STEFAN (1902–1972), German-born U.S. composer. A native of Berlin. Wolpe was associated during the 1920s with the Bauhaus School and the left-wing theater of Bertolt Brecht and wrote proletarian revolutionary songs, piano pieces, and choral works. He left Nazi Germany in 1933 and emigrated via Palestine to the United States (1938), where he taught at several universities. Wolpe composed complex atonal chamber music, operas, and cantatas, with traces of jazz and folk themes. His best-known works included *Enactments* for three pianos (1950–53) and *Symphony* (1955–56).

WONDER, STEVIE (Steveland Judkins Morris; 1950–), U.S. singer, musician, and composer. Born blind, Wonder grew up in Detroit's black ghetto and signed a record contract with Motown Records, the creators of the slick soul sound, at age 12. He recorded his first gold record at age 13 and developed into one of the most popular and respected musicians in the United States, creating a new music that successfully bridged the gap between rock and soul music. He played the piano, drums, organ, harmonica, and synthesizer on numerous Grammy Award-winning records including the singles "Superstition" (1972), "You Are the Sunshine of My Life" (1972), "Living for the City" (1973), "I Wish" (1977), "For Your Love" (1995) and the albums *Innervisions* (1973), *Fulfillingness' First Finale* (1974), and *Songs in the Key of Life* (1976). He was active in the movement protesting apartheid in South Africa, and he won a special award for this work (1985). ▪ See biography by Ray Cumming Fox (1977) and Jim Haskins, *The Stevie Wonder Scrapbook* (1978).

WOOD, GRANT (1892–1942), U.S. artist. Wood was a skilled craftsman who studied (at night) at the Chicago Art Institute, and then in Europe, where he was fascinated by the early German masters. He returned home to paint meticulously detailed landscapes and portraits of his native Iowa. The owl-eyed, purse-lipped portraits of *American Gothic* (1930) and *Daughters of Revolution* (1932) brought him overnight fame as a regional painter. Wood also supervised a New Deal arts project and taught at the University of Iowa (from 1934). ■ See Darrell Garwood, *Artist in Iowa* (1944), and study by Wanda M. Corn (1983).

WOOD, LEONARD (1860–1927), U.S. colonial administrator. Wood was an army doctor (Harvard Medical School, M.D. 1884) with strong political connections. After helping his friend Theodore Roosevelt raise and organize the Rough Riders to fight in the Spanish-American War (1898), he served as military governor of Cuba (1899–1902), where he laid the basis for civilian government and improved health conditions. As army chief of staff (1910–14), Wood favored universal military training and preparedness and was a well-known and popular figure. After an unsuccessful bid for the Republican presidential nomination (1920), he served as governor-general of the Philippines (1921–27). ■ See biography by Hermann Hagedorn (1931).

WOOD, ROBERT EKLINGTON (1879–1969), U.S. business executive. An army officer (1900–15), Wood served in Panama during construction of the canal. He returned to the military in 1917 and emerged from fighting in Europe during World War I with the rank of brigadier general (1918). He worked for the mail-order firm of Montgomery Ward (1919–24) before joining its competitor, Sears, Roebuck and Co. (1924). As president (1928–39) and chairman of the board (from 1939) he was instrumental in the expansion and diversification of Sears, so that by his retirement (1954) it was the world's largest merchandising company, with more than 800 retail stores and 11 mail-order plants. During the late 1930s he tried to keep the United States out of World War II and chaired the America First Committee (1940–41). ■ See James C. Worthy, *Shaping an American Institution* (1984).

WOODEN, JOHN (1910–), U.S. basketball coach. Wooden was an All-American college basketball player before beginning his sensational coaching career. For over a quarter of a century he coached the University of California at Los Angeles (UCLA) Bruins (1948–75), winning an unprecedented 10 national championships. However, success did not come overnight; it took 16 seasons (1948–64) before he put together his first national championship team. In 1973–74, Wooden's team won 88 straight games. He coached such players as Kareem Abdul-Jabbar (then Lew Alcindor) and Bill Walton. ■ See biography by Dwight Chapin and Jeff Prugh, *The Wizard of Westwood* (1973).

WOODRUFF, HALE A. (1900–1980), U.S. painter and educator. Born in the Midwest, Woodruff studied art in Indiana and Massachusetts and later in France and Mexico.

During the Harlem renaissance of the 1920s, he won recognition for his use of color and design. His canvases of the 1930s and 1940s were quiet landscapes suggesting the ambience of southern towns; he turned in the 1950s to dramatic abstract works. He was best known for panels of black neighborhoods painted in the 1930s under Work Projects Administration subsidy and for murals depicting an 1839 slave mutiny executed at Alabama's Talladega College (1938). Critics noted Woodruff's early use of African imagery and stressed his role in organizing the first national exhibition of black art, the Atlanta University Annual (1942). A retrospective of his work was mounted at Harlem's Studio Museum (1979).

WOODRUFF, ROBERT WINSHIP (1889–1985), U.S. business executive. Woodruff was the son of a Georgia banker and industrialist who led a group of businessmen in purchasing the Atlanta-based Coca-Cola Co. (1919). He served as vice president and general manager of the White Motor Co. in Cleveland (1919–23) before being called home to rescue the foundering soft-drink company. As the firm's dominant force for decades (president, 1923–39; chairman, 1939–55; finance committee chairman, 1955–81), he greatly expanded the company—and its profits—and developed its international markets. Over the years Coke became a widely recognized symbol of the United States. Woodruff was the most powerful civic leader in Atlanta and one of the richest men in the South. He made huge philanthropic donations to Atlanta cultural and health institutions, including $210 million to Emory University.

WOODS, TIGER (Eldrick Woods; 1975–), U.S. golfer. Woods, whose father was African American and whose mother was Thai, was taught to play golf as a young child. Rigorously trained by his father, an ex-Green Beret, Woods won an international junior title at the age of 8, won a record three consecutive U.S. Junior Amateur Championships (1991–93), and a record three consecutive U.S. Amateur titles (1994–96). He left Stanford University (1996) to become a professional and won the 1997 Masters tournament by a record 12 strokes with a score of 270. He was the youngest Masters champion in history and the first man of color ever to win a major golfing title. An extremely graceful player known for his long drives and intense concentration, he quickly became one of the world's most popular athletes. He won eight tournaments in 1999, including the PGA Championship, and won a record $6,616,885 in prize money that year. In 2000 he won the U.S. Open by a record 15 strokes and the British Open with a record score of 19 under par (269), becoming the youngest player, at age 24, to win all four major championships. Later that summer Woods captured his second consecutive PGA Championship, in a playoff, after shooting a record 18-under par 270.

WOODSON, CARTER GODWIN (1875–1950), U.S. educator and historian. The son of poverty-stricken former slaves, Woodson worked in the Kentucky coal mines as a youth and received little formal education until he was nearly 20. After graduating from high school (1896), however, he attended Berea College (1896–98), received a B.A. (1907) and an M.A. (1908) from the University of Chicago, and a Ph.D. from Harvard (1912), and dedicated his life to the cause of black history in the United States. To overcome the neglect and bias of white scholars in the field, Woodson founded the Association for the Study of Negro Life and History (1915), the *Journal of Negro History* (1916), the *Negro History Bulletin* (1937), and inaugurated Negro History Week (1926). He also founded Associated Publishers, Inc. (1921), which was devoted to publishing books on black history and culture. Woodson's scholarly works included *A Century of Negro Migration* (1918), *The Negro in Our History* (1922), *The Rural Negro (1930)*, and *African Heroes and Heroines* (1939). ▪ See biography by Jacqueline A. Goggin (1993).

WOODSWORTH, JAMES SHAVER (1874–1942), Canadian reformer and political leader. Ordained a Methodist minister in 1896, J. S. Woodsworth became interested in social reform after a year in Britain visiting slum areas. He resigned his ministry in 1918 for labor organizing. In 1921 he was elected an independent Labour member of Parliament (from Winnipeg) and spent the next 21 years fighting for social reform and labor and radical agrarian causes. From 1932 he headed the socialist Cooperative Commonwealth Federation (CCF) party. A pacifist, he was the only member of Parliament to vote against participation in World War II (1939). ▪ See biography by Grace MacInnis (1953) and Kenneth McNaught, *A Prophet in Politics* (1959).

WOODWARD, COMER VANN (1908–1999), U.S. historian. A historian of the American south, C. Vann Woodward was born in Arkansas, earned his Ph.D. from the University of North Carolina (1937), and taught at Johns Hopkins (1946–61) and Yale (1961–77). His many outstanding works on the South and the racial question included *Origins of the New South* (1951), *The Strange Career of Jim Crow* (1955), *The Burden of Southern History* (1960), and *American Counterpoint* (1971). *Mary Chestnut's Civil War* (1982), which he edited, won a Pulitzer Prize. His later works included *Thinking Back: The Perils of Writing History* (1986), *The Future of the Past* (1989), and *The Old World's New World* (1991).

WOODWARD, ROBERT BURNS (1917–1979), U.S. organic chemist. The winner of the 1965 Nobel Prize in Chemistry, Woodward was called the greatest synthetic organic chemist of modern times. A professor at Harvard (1937–79), he determined the structures of many complex natural molecules and successfully synthesized substances such as quinine (1944), cholesterol and cortisone (1951), lysergic acid (LSD; 1954), reserpine (1956), chlorophyll (1960), tetracycline (1962), and vitamin B_{12} (1971). He also played a major role in determining the complex molecular structure of penicillin (1945). His research in stereochemistry yielded new concepts, such as the conservation of orbital symmetry as well as new synthetic procedures.

WOODWARD, ROBERT UPSHUR (1943–), U.S. journalist. The son of an Illinois circuit-court judge, Woodward attended Yale on an ROTC scholarship and served five years as a naval officer. As a police reporter for the *Washington Post*, he was assigned to cover the June 1972 burglary of Democratic headquarters at the Watergate apartment complex. Together with reporter Carl Bernstein, he traced the burglary all the way into the White House, with the help of Woodward's mystery source, "Deep Throat." "Woodstein" described their Pulitzer Prize–winning (1973) story, which resulted in the resignation of Pres. Richard Nixon, in two books, *All The President's Men* (1974) and *The Final Days* (1976). Woodward also wrote the exposé *The Brethren: Inside the Supreme Court* (1979; with Scott Armstrong); *Veil: The Secret Wars of the CIA, 1981–1987* (1987); *The Agenda: Inside the Clinton White House* (1994); *The Choice* (1996), a study of the 1996 presidential election; and *Shadow: Five Presidents and the Legacy of Watergate* (1999).

WOOLF, LEONARD SIDNEY (1880–1969), British writer and publisher. Born into a wealthy Jewish family, Woolf was educated at Cambridge (B.A. 1902) and served as a civil servant in Ceylon (1904–11). Upon his return to London he became a leader of the influential band of intellectuals known as the Bloomsbury group and wrote numerous books on politics and social conditions—including *After the Deluge* (3 vols., 1931–53)—which reflected his anticolonialist, internationalist, and Fabian socialist viewpoint. He also was an editor of several journals, including *Nation* (1923–30) and *Political Quarterly* (1931–59), and a high-level adviser to the Labour party. Together with his wife Virginia Woolf, whom he married in 1912, he founded the Hogarth Press (1917), which published her novels as well as early works of T. S. Eliot, E. M. Forster, Robert Graves, Christopher Isherwood, W. H. Auden, and Harold Laski. ▪ See his celebrated five-volume autobiography (1960–69) and study by Peter Alexander (1992).

WOOLF, VIRGINIA (Adeline Virginia Stephen; 1882–1941), British writer. The daughter of the noted man of letters Sir Leslie Stephen, Virginia Woolf was a leader of the influential band of artists, writers, and intellectuals in London called the Bloomsbury group. It included such figures as Clive Bell, Lytton Strachey, E. M. Forster, John Maynard Keynes, Victoria Sackville-West, Roger Fry, and Leonard Woolf, whom she married (1912) and with whom she established the Hogarth Press (1917). A pioneer of the modern novel, Woolf broke with the realist tradition and wrote a series of subjective, impressionistic, and plotless novels, including *Mrs. Dalloway* (1925), *To the Lighthouse* (1927),

The Waves (1931), and *Between the Acts* (1942), which were concerned with her characters' consciousness, creative imagination, and perception of time. Her *Complete Shorter Fiction* appeared in 1985. Her feminist perspectives, reflected in the novels, were clearly stated in the critical essays in *A Room of One's Own* (1929) and *Three Guineas* (1938). Frequently plagued by incapacitating spells of depression, Woolf committed suicide in 1941. ▪ See her diaries (5 vols., 1977–84); biographies by Quentin Bell (1972), Lyndall Gordon (1985), Hermione Lee (1997), and Nigel Nicolson (2000); and study by Peter Alexander (1992).

WOOLLCOTT, ALEXANDER (1887–1943), U.S. writer and actor. Woollcott was a wit-about-town and raconteur who for a generation played an influential role in New York literary and dramatic circles. He was the *New York Times* drama critic (1914–22), later moving to the *Herald* (1922–24), *Sun* (1924–25), and *World* (1925–28), and was the "Town Crier" of radio (1929–40). He played a character based on himself in *The Man Who Came to Dinner*, a 1939 play by George S. Kaufman and Moss Hart. He wrote several books, including *While Rome Burns* (1934). ▪ See biography by Edwin P. Hoyt (1973) and Howard Teichmann, *Smart Aleck* (1976).

WOOLLEY, SIR (CHARLES) LEONARD (1880–1960), British archaeologist. After receiving a degree in theology from Oxford, Woolley turned to archaeology and did fieldwork in Nubia (1907–11); Carchemish, the ancient Hittite city on the Euphrates (with T. E. Lawrence; 1912–14, 1919); and at Tell el Amarna in Egypt (1921–22). His greatest success came at Ur of the Chaldees in southern Iraq, where as director of the British Museum and University of Pennsylvania expedition (1922–34) he unearthed the art, architecture, written documents, and royal treasures of the Sumerian civilization, which were nearly 5,000 years old. His work attracted international attention and the Ur region became known as "the cradle of civilization." His later fieldwork was done in Syria (1936–37) and southeastern Turkey (1937–39; 1946–49). He wrote numerous scholarly works in addition to the more popular *Dead Towns and Living Men* (1920), *Ur of the Chaldees* (1929), *Digging Up the Past* (1931), and *Excavations at Ur* (1954).

WOOLTON, FREDERICK JAMES MARQUIS, 1st EARL OF (1883–1964), British business executive and political leader. Marquis did social work in Liverpool from 1906 to 1914, and was appointed World War I controller of civilian boots; after the war he went into the retail business, rising to chairman of Lewis' stores (1936). During World War II he served as a nonparty minister of food (1940–43) and minister of reconstruction (1943–45). As chairman of the Conservative party (1946–55), he broadened its social base and created the machinery for its return to power in 1951, when he again served in the cabinet (1951–55). He was created an earl in 1956. ▪ See his *Memoirs* (1959).

WOUK, HERMAN (1915–   ), U.S. novelist. The son of Jewish immigrants, Wouk wrote gags for radio comics, including Fred Allen, and also wrote radio plays to promote World War II bonds. Decorated for naval service in the Pacific, he wrote *The Caine Mutiny* (1951, Pulitzer Prize), a novel about an incident aboard a destroyer during World War II, and *The Winds of War* (1971) and *War and Remembrance* (1975), which traced the lives of a navy commander and his family during the war. His other works included the best-sellers *Marjorie Morningstar* (1955), *Youngblood Hawke* (1962), and *Inside, Outside* (1985), and the nonfiction book *This Is My God* (1959), a study of orthodox Judaism. He also wrote *The Hope* (1993) and *The Glory* (1994), novels about the growth of Israel from the 1940s through the early 1980s, and *The Will to Live On* (2000), personal reflections on Judaism. ▪ See studies by Arnold Beichman (1984) and Laurence W. Mazzeno (1994).

WRANGEL, BARON PYOTR NIKOLAYEVICH (1878–1928), Russian general. A mining engineer, Wrangel fought in the Russo-Japanese War (1904–05) and in World War I before joining (late 1917) the White forces that were engaged in combat against the Bolsheviks in the south of Russia. Wrangel succeeded Anton Denikin as commander in chief of the White army (April 1920), restoring discipline to the demoralized troops and winning some ground on the Crimean front. He also agitated for a land-reform program. Ultimately Wrangel was forced to retreat, and he evacuated his forces to Constantinople (Nov. 1920). He died in exile in Brussels. ▪ See his *Memoirs* (Eng. trans. 1929), later published as *Always with Honour* (Eng. trans. 1957).

WRIGHT, FRANK LLOYD (1867–1959), U.S. architect. Largely a self-taught architect, Wright began his seven-decade career in the 1890s with his so-called Prairie Houses—long, low bungalows that blended into the landscape, of which Chicago's Robie House (1909) is the finest example. He pioneered in the application of cubist spatial concepts and modern technology to architecture. Wright believed that buildings should embrace their sites and reflect the values of the people who inhabit them. His ideas and values helped to shape 20th-century architecture and design. Working at Taliesin, his estate in Wisconsin, and at Taliesin West, his home and school near Phoenix, Wright influenced a generation of architects. His well-known buildings included the Imperial Hotel, Tokyo (1916–20), the "Fallingwater" weekend retreat near Pittsburgh (1936), the Johnson Wax office block in Racine, Wisconsin (1936), the Guggenheim Museum in New York (1956), and the Marin County (California) Civic Center (1957–60). He wrote some 20 books, including *An Organic Architecture* (1939). ▪ See his *Autobiography* (1932; rev. eds. 1943, 1962) and *Letters to Apprentices* (1983). See also biography by Robert C. Twombley (1979); H. Allen Brooks, ed., *Writings on Wright* (1981); E. Kaufmann and B. Raeburn, eds., *Frank Lloyd Wright: Writings and Buildings* (1960); and Bruce B. Pfeiffer, ed., *Collected Writings* (2 vols., 1993).

WRIGHT, JUDITH (1915–), Australian writer. The outstanding Australian poet of her generation, Wright was educated at the University of Sydney. In the best of her early philosophical poems, she focused on the procreative forces of nature and the powers of love. Her later work was more pessimistic in its depiction of human alienation from the natural environment. In her poems of social protest she condemned the war in Vietnam, the exploitation of the Aborigines, and the destruction and pollution of the Australian countryside. She was the cofounder (1962) and president (1962–74) of the Wildlife Preservation Society of Queensland. Her volumes included *The Moving Image* (1946), *Woman to Man* (194), *The Two Fires* (1955), and *Alive* (1973). She also wrote an influential work of literary criticism, *Preoccupations in Australian Poetry* (1965), a volume of essays. *Because I Was Invited* (1976), and a historical account of the effects of European migration on the aboriginal inhabitants of New South Wales and Queensland, *The Cry for the Dead* (1981). Her later works included *Born of the Conquerors: Selected Essay* (1991) and the poetry collections *Collected Poems: 1942–1985* (1994), *A Human Pattern* (1990), and *Going on Talking* (1992). ■ See *The Double Tree: Selected Poems, 1942–1976* (1978); studies by A. D. Hope (1975) and Shirley Walker (1981); and Veronica Brady, *South of My Days* (1998).

WRIGHT, QUINCY (1890–1970), U.S. political scientist. An expert on international law trained at the University of Illinois (Ph.D. 1915), Wright taught at the University of Chicago (1923–56). Originally a supporter of the League of Nations, he developed the historical, cultural, and legal arguments for a renewed world organization in his *Study of War* (2 vols., 1942; rev. ed. 1965). A technical adviser to the International Military Tribunal at Nuremberg in 1945, Wright also served as a consultant to the U.S. government on various issues. He wrote *The Study of International Relations* (1955) and continued to speak out even after his retirement in 1956, opposing the 1962 quarantine of Cuba as illegal, and favoring self-determination in Southeast Asia.

WRIGHT, RICHARD (1908–1960), U.S. novelist. Wright drew on his plantation experiences to record and protest the abuse of black Americans. *Uncle Tom's Children* (1938), a collection of stories based on his Mississippi childhood, won several awards and established his reputation. He was a member of the Communist party (1932–44) and worked on several radical journals and newspapers. His best-known work was *Native Son* (1940), a complex novel about life in Chicago's black ghetto; a film adaptation starred Wright. After publishing a second best-seller, the autobiographical *Black Boy* (1945), he expatriated (1947) to Paris, where he supported the struggles against colonialism and neocolonialism, wrote on Third World issues, and influenced a generation of black American writers, including James Baldwin, Ralph Ellison, and Chester Himes. Wright's other publications included novels, short stories, lectures, and the folk

history *Twelve Million Black Voices* (1941), *American Hunger* (1977) was a sequel to *Black Boy*. *The Richard Wright Reader* (1978) included excerpts from his fiction and nonfiction. ■ See the biography by Constance Webb (1968); Michel Fabre, *The Unfinished Quest of Richard Wright* (Eng. trans. 1973); and study by Robert Felgar (1980).

WRIGHT, RUSSEL (1904?–1976), U.S. industrial designer. Wright never finished college or earned formal design credentials, but he introduced modernist concepts in furnishings and housewares that molded American tastes in the late 1930s. Many of his dinnerware, flatware, and furniture designs were acquired by the Metropolitan Museum of Art and other museums, but Wright's influence stemmed from the fact that the products he conceived were mass-produced at affordable prices. Americans spent more than $50 million between 1937 and 1954 on his American Modern Dinnerware, a rimless pattern. His innovative use of line and materials was applied to products from draperies to automobile seat covers. In the 1960s Wright designed parks and nature sanctuaries. He was the coauthor, with his wife, of *Mary and Russel Wright's Guide to Easier Living* (1951). ■ See study by William J. Hennessey (1983).

WRIGHT, WILBUR (1867–1912), and ORVILLE WRIGHT (1871–1948), U.S. aviation pioneers. Owners of a bicycle shop in Dayton, Ohio, the Wright brothers began to study the theory and art of flying during, the 1890s. Self-taught, they experimented with gliders, built the first wind tunnel in the United States (1901), and constructed their own engine, which resulted, on Dec. 17, 1903 (on sand dunes near Kitty Hawk, North Carolina), in the world's first manned, powered flights in a heavier-than-air craft. Traveling in a 12-horsepower, 750-pound machine, Orville flew 120 feet in 12 seconds, and Wilbur, 852 feet in 59 seconds. The brothers received a patent for their flying machine (1906), signed a contract with the War Department to produce a 40-mph airplane (1909), and set up the American Wright Corp. (1909) to manufacture planes and train pilots. After Wilbur's death, Orville retired from business activities (1914) to do private research; he served as a member of the National Advisory Committee for Aeronautics (1915–48). ■ See Fred C. Kelly, *The Wright Brothers* (1943); Harry Combs and Martin Caiden, *Kill Devil Hill* (1979); Fred Howard, *Wilbur and Orville* (1987); and Tom D. Crouch, *The Bishop's Boys* (1989).

WRIGHT, WILLARD HUNTINGTON. *See VAN DINE, S. S.*

WRIGLEY, WILLIAM, JR. (1861–1932), U.S. businessman. The man who taught the world how to chew gum, Wrigley started his chewing-gum business in 1891 and by 1908 was the world's largest gum producer. A born salesman and promoter, he spent huge sums advertising his product—especially his new (1899) "spearmint" flavor—in 30 languages.

By the time of his death he had built factories in England, Germany, Canada, and Australia and had annual sales of $75 million. Wrigley also held a controlling interest in the Chicago Cubs baseball team, which played in Wrigley Field, and purchased (1919) Santa Catalina Island, off the California coast, which he developed into a major resort.

WU, CHIEN-SHIUNG (1912–1997), Chinese-born U.S. physicist. Wu studied at the National Central University in China; after emigrating (1936) to the United States, she received a Ph.D. (1940) from the University of California at Berkeley. On the faculty of Columbia University (1944–81) she gained a reputation as one of the world's leading experimental physicists. After physicists Tsung-dao Lee and Chen Ning Yang theorized (1956) that the conservation of the parity principle does not hold for weak interactions of subatomic particles, Wu designed and executed research on beta decay of oriented nuclei that confirmed their thinking. Lee and Yang won the 1957 Nobel Prize in Physics; Wu did not. In 1963 she and her colleagues experimentally confirmed a new fundamental theory of nuclear physics, the theory of conservation of vector current in nuclear beta decay, proposed by Richard Feynman and Murray Gell-Mann (1958). She wrote *Beta Decay* (1965; with S. Moszkowski) and *Muon Physics* (3 vols., 1976–77).

WUORINEN, CHARLES (1938–), U.S. composer. Wuorinen received degrees from Columbia University (B.A. 1961; M.A. 1963), taught there (1964–71), and helped found (1962) the avant-garde Group for Contemporary Music. His wide range of works included symphonies and other pieces for orchestra, vocal music, opera, solo, instrumental, and chamber works, and electronic music. He used 12-tone technique in the Third Symphony (1959) and Piano Concerto (1966) and serialism in his later works, including String Quartet (1971). He won the first Pulitzer Prize (1970) for an all-electronic composition, *Time's Encomium*, which he also scored for traditional orchestra. His later works included *New York Notes for Chamber Orchestra* (1982) and *Quartet No. 3 for Strings* (1987).

WU PEIFU (1874–1939), Chinese warlord. Born into a merchant family, Wu received a classical and military education and by 1902 was associated with Yuan Shih-kai, the military leader of north China. After the 1911 revolution, Wu became a brigade commander and following Yuan's death (1916) he consolidated his power and by 1922 he was the most powerful warlord in north China. A relatively progressive leader, Wu lost popularity after brutally suppressing a railroad workers' strike (1923) and for preparing to unite China by military means. After his armies were defeated by Zhang Zuolin (Chang Tso-lin; 1924) and by the Guomindang's (Kuomintang) Northern Expedition (1926), he went into internal exile (1926–1931) where he studied Buddhism and Confucianism. Returning to Peking (1932) he refused to join any side but after the outbreak of the Sino-Japanese

War (1937), he agreed to lead a Japanese equipped army against the communists. However, the Japanese were unwilling to agree to his demands: a 500,000 man army and an agreement to withdraw from China.

WURSTER, WILLIAM WILSON (1895–1973), U.S. architect. A native of California who graduated from the University of California at Berkeley (1919) and studied regional planning at Harvard, Wurster established his own firm in San Francisco (1926) to design houses and country clubs in a straightforward and economical regional idiom. Wurster was dean of architecture at the Massachusetts Institute of Technology (1944–50) and at Berkeley (1950–59) and dean of Berkeley's new College of Environmental Design (1959–63). His 50-member firm designed San Francisco's Ghirardelli Square complex (1962–67) and Bank of America headquarters (1970–71).

WYETH, ANDREW NEWELL (1917–), U.S. artist. The son of a top magazine illustrator, Wyeth was a solitary, sickly child growing up in the Pennsylvania backcountry with his father as teacher. He spent his summers in Maine. He had his first show at age 20 with a collection of watercolors of old houses, hills, and fields. He continued to concentrate on the seasons of rural New England and also painted notable portraits. Many of his works convey a mood of melancholy and desolation. Wyeth's realistic style was almost photographic, yet his best work—such as *Christina's World* (1948), one of the most famous American paintings—evokes a quality of unreality. He received nationwide publicity (1985) for the Helga series, 246 paintings and drawings of his neighbor, which were exhibited at the National Gallery of Art in Washington, D.C. (1987). ■ See his autobiography (1995); Thomas Hoving, *Two Worlds of Andrew Wyeth* (1978); and the biography by Richard Meryman (1997).

WYLER, WILLIAM (1902–1981), German-born U.S. film director. Wyler came to the United States (1922) at the invitation if his distant cousin Carl Laemmle, the head of Universal Pictures. He worked his way up from publicity agent and script clerk to director of feature-length films in the 1930s and earned a reputation as a taskmaster and perfectionist. He developed into one of the most successful directors in Hollywood history, winning Academy Awards for *Mrs. Miniver* (1942), *The Best Years of Our Lives* (1946), and *Ben-Hur* (1959) and directing such other memorable films as *Jezebel* (1938), *Wuthering Heights* (1939), *The Little Foxes* (1941), *Roman Holiday* (1953), *The Children's Hour* (1962), and *Funny Girl* (1968). ■ See biography by Axel Madsen (1973); study by Michael Anderegg (1979); and Jan Herman, *A Talent for Trouble* (1996).

WYNDHAM, JOHN (John Wyndham Parkes Lucas Benyon Harris; 1903–1969), British science-fiction writer. After his literary debut (1931) in U.S. science-fiction magazines, he published numerous books under the pseudonyms John Benyon Harris, John Benyon, Lucas Parkes, and John Wyndham. his writing was distinguished by a sense of style and a narrative skill uncommon to science fiction. Wyndham's early works, while not devoid of social consciousness, were action oriented. His popular novel *The Day of the Triffids* (1951), which described a society struggling to survive after a blinding attack by hybrid creatures, marked a shift in emphasis to the psychological. Many of Wyndham's later novels were social allegories. *The Midwich Cuckoos* (1957) became the film *Village of the Damned* (1960). ▪ See his stories in *The Best of John Wyndham* (1973).

WYNETTE, TAMMY (1942–1998), U.S. country singer. A onetime beautician, Wynette was rejected by four record companies before Billy Sherrill signed her for the Epic label (1966). Her successful first release, "Apartment No. 9," was followed by the big hits "I Don't Wanna Play House" (1967) and "D-I-V-O-R-C-E" (1968). "Stand By Your Man" (1967) sold millions of copies, becoming a country-music classic. Sherrill, coauthor of many of Wynette's hits, promoted her image as a loyal, long-suffering woman whose values were unaffected by the women's movement. Wynette recorded romantic duets with David Houston as well as with George Jones, to whom she was married during the 1970s. She was the Country Music Association's female vocal artist of the year in 1968, 1969, and 1970. Wynette continued recording into the 1990s, with such albums as *Sometimes When We Touch* (1985), *Higher Ground* (1987), and *One* (1995; with George Jones). During her career she recorded more than 50 albums and sold more than 30 million recordings. ▪ See her *Stand By Your Man* (1979; with Joan Dew) and biography by her daughter Jackie Daly (2000; with Tom Carter).

WYNN, ED (Isaiah Edwin Leopold; 1886–1966), U.S. entertainer. A popular favorite for more than 60 years, Wynn began his career as a vaudeville comedian. He was a star performer by 1904 and was featured in Ziegfeld's *Follies* of 1914 and 1915. A lisping, giggling master of zany comedy and outrageous joking and clowning, Wynn wrote, produced, and starred in several shows during the 1920s and became known as "the Perfect Fool," the title of his most successful show (1921). From 1932 through 1939 he starred as "Texaco's Fire Chief," one of the nation's most popular radio programs. He turned to dramatic acting in the 1950s, appeared in several major television dramas (including *Requiem for a Heavyweight*, 1956) and movies, and was nominated for an Oscar for his role in *The Diary of Anne Frank* (1959).

WYSZYŃSKI, STEFAN (1901–1981), Polish religious leader. A Catholic priest with a Ph.D. in sociology and a wartime record in the anti-Nazi resistance, Wyszyński was appointed archbishop of Gniezno and Warsaw and Primate of Poland in 1949 and cardinal in 1953. He was imprisoned (1953–56) for protesting against communist repression of the church; after his release he continued to chastise Poland's leaders as "godless cultural barbarians" but maintained an uneasy coexistence with the government. Fearful of Soviet intervention and internal chaos, he was a moderating force on the Solidarity labor union and acted as an arbitrator between the union and the Communist party (1980–81). ▪ See his *Freedom Within* (Eng. trans. 1984) and biography by Andrzej Micewski (Eng. trans. 1984).

X

XENAKIS, IANNIS (1922-), Rumanian-born Greek-French composer. A veteran of the World War II anti-Nazi Resistance, Xenakis financed his music study in Paris by working as an engineer for the architect Le Corbusier (1948–59). He utilized probability theory, game theory, and computers to determine pitch, duration, and dynamics in a musical style he called "stochastic." *Metastasis* (1954) was his pioneering effort in this vein. He described his compositions *Pithoprakta* (1955–56) and *Syrmos* (1959) as aural transcriptions of curves and planes. His later works included the choral pieces *Nuit* (1967–68) and *Cendrées* (1973–74); the orchestral work *Eridanos* (1973); and *Psappha,* for percussion instruments (1975); and *Mists,* for piano (1980). He founded the Center for Mathematical and Automated Music (Paris, 1966) and wrote *Formalized Music* (1971; rev. ed. 1992). His later musical compositions included *Jalons* (1986), *Okho for 3 Percussionists* (1989), and *Kai for Chamber Ensemble* (1995). ■ See biography by Nouritza Matossian (1986).

XOXE, KOCI (1911–1949), Albanian political leader. A blacksmith by trade, Xoxe rose to lieutenant general in Albania's World War II liberation army and then to secretary-general (1946) of its Communist party, vice president of the national constituent assembly, deputy prime minister, and minister of the interior. His plans for the merger of Albania into a Yugoslav federation were blocked by the Yugoslav-Soviet conflict, and in 1949 he was sentenced to death and executed for anti-Soviet activities.

XU ZHIMO (old style: HSÜ CHIH-MO; 1896–1931), Chinese poet. Xu was also known as Nan-hu and Shizhe (Shih-che). After receiving a classical education at Beijing (Peking) University (1916–18), Xu left China and attended Clark, Columbia, and finally Cambridge University, where he abandoned his interest in politics and decided to pursue a literary career. After his return home (1922), he became a leader of the modern poetry movement that aimed at creating a new style of poetry by wedding vernacular Chinese to Western poetic forms. Xu was influential for his own successful linguistic experimentation as well as for his essays, criticism, and translations, which helped spread the knowledge of Western literature to his Chinese colleagues. He is recognized as the first successful modern poet in the Chinese language. A flying enthusiast, Xu died in an airplane crash.

Y

YALOW, ROSALYN (Rosalyn Sussman; 1921–), U.S. medical researcher. Yalow was a product of the Bronx public school system and New York's Hunter College, where she was the college's first physics major (1941). During a 22-year collaboration with Solomon Berson (1950–72) at the Bronx Veterans Administration Hospital, she helped develop an extremely sensitive technique for measuring minute concentrations of hormones, vitamins, enzymes, and other biologically active substances that could not be detected by other means. Called radioimmunoassay (RIA), the test had a revolutionary impact on medical research and was called one of the most important research developments of the century. Yalow shared the 1977 Nobel Prize for Physiology or Medicine with Roger Guillemin and Andrew V. Schally. She also taught at the Mt. Sinai School of Medicine and the Albert Einstein College of Medicine in New York City. ■ See biography by Eugene Straus (1998).

YAMAMOTO, ISOROKU (1884–1943), Japanese admiral. Yamamoto graduated from a military academy in 1904 and was severely wounded in the Russo-Japanese War of 1904–05. He held important posts in the navy and naval air corps, including that of naval attaché at the Japanese embassy in Washington, D.C. (1926–28). Although opposed to the Japanese-German alliance and Japanese entry into World War II, Yamamoto was commander in chief of the combined fleet and planned the successful attack on Pearl Harbor. His forces were defeated at the Battle of Midway (June 1942), a turning point of the war in the Pacific. He was killed when his plane was shot down over the Solomon Islands after the United States broke the Japanese code and learned of his whereabouts. ■ See John D. Potter, *Yamamoto* (1965), and Agawa Hiroyuki, *The Reluctant Admiral* (Eng. trans. 1980).

YAMANI, SHEIKH AHMED ZAKI (1930–), Saudi Arabian government official. The son and grandson of legal scholars, Yamani studied law in Egypt and the United States, where he earned a degree at Harvard. Returning to Saudi Arabia, he served as legal adviser to the council of ministers (1958–60) and as minister of state (1960–62). As minister of petroleum and mineral resources (1962–86), he was determined to use oil revenues to bring industrialization and modernization to Saudi Arabia and to alter the relationship between the Arab and Western worlds. Remaining pro-American and procapitalist in outlook, he negotiated a favorable new royalty arrangement with the Arabian American Oil Co. and supported the creation of a cartel, the Organization of Petroleum Exporting Countries (OPEC). In the wake of the 1973 Arab-Israeli War, Yamani instigated

cuts in production and a temporary embargo on the United States and other allies of Israel that created a temporary worldwide oil shortage and a sharp rise in prices. For years afterward Saudi Arabia restricted its output and urged other OPEC members to do the same in order to keep up oil prices. However, as worldwide demand decreased due to conservation measures and competition from non-OPEC oil, it reversed its policy in 1985 and doubled its output. When oil prices declined precipitously in late 1985 and early 1986, Yamani again urged producers to cut their output. He was unexpectedly removed from his post in October 1986. ■ See study by Jeffrey Robinson (1988).

YAMASAKI, MINORU (1912–1986), U.S. architect. Yamasaki worked summers in Alaskan fish canneries to put himself through the University of Washington (B.Arch. 1934). His breakthrough as an architect came in 1956 with the vaulted, futuristic St. Louis Air Terminal, and his Federal Science Pavilion for the Century 21 World's Fair in Seattle (1962) was hailed for its synthesis of Japanese and Western models. Later he returned to "pseudostructuralism" with the 110-story World Trade Center towers in New York City (1973–74). ■ See his autobiography, *A Life in Architecture* (1979).

YAMASHITA, TOMOYUKI (1885–1946), Japanese general. Yamashita served in the army all of his adult life, rising to the rank of lieutenant general by 1937. During World War II he swept through Malaya and captured Singapore (1942), which earned him the rank of general and the nickname "Tiger of Malaya." As commander of Japanese forces in the Philippines (1944–45), Yamashita surrendered to Allied forces. His trial and execution by hanging for war crimes has been criticized because it is not clear how much he knew about atrocities committed by members of his army. ■ See Adolf F. Reel, *The Case of General Yamashita* (1949).

YÁÑEZ, AGUSTÍN (1904–1980), Mexican novelist. A pioneer of modern Mexican fiction, Yáñez was also a lawyer, an educational administrator, and a U.N. delegate. His exploration of Mexican history and character was informed by his familiarity with classical Spanish literature, as well as with modern European writers. His major work, *The Edge of the Storm* (1947; Eng. trans. 1971), grew out of the outline for a short novel and is said to have influenced the flowering of Mexican fiction. He used stream of consciousness and symbolism to build on the traditional social novel. He scrutinized the psychological impact of social and religious upheaval by writing about the effect of the Mexican revolution on life in a village in the state of Jalisco, which he served as governor. His other works included *The Lean Lands* (1962; Eng. trans. 1969), a novel about the downfall of the local political leader and the growth of industry sponsored by the central government.

YANG, CHEN NING (1922–   ), Chinese-born physicist. The son of a mathematics professor, Yang arrived in the United States on a fellowship (1945) and studied physics with Edward Teller and Enrico Fermi at the University of Chicago (Ph.D. 1948). From 1949 to 1965 he was associated with the Institute for Advanced Study, Princeton, where he met Tsung-dao Lee, with whom he shared the 1957 Nobel Prize for Physics. Together they proved theoretically that the apparently universal law of parity conservation, which held that atomic particles behaved the same way as their mirror images, was invalid when elementary particles decay. Their theory, proved experimentally by Chien-shiung Wu (1957), was a revolutionary advance in the study of particle physics. After 1965, Yang held the Albert Einstein chair of physics at the State University of New York at Stony Brook.

YAN XISHAN (old style: **YEN HSI-SHAN;** 1883–1960), Chinese warlord. Yan's military training began in 1901, when his father's small bank failed, and continued in Japan, where he joined the revolutionary leader Sun Yatsen. Returning to China as a colonel in the New Shanxi (Shansi) army, he declared Shanxi independent of the Manchu government during the 1911 revolution and totally ruled Shanxi province by 1917. During the next 32 years he maintained his power, defeated enemies, and conducted a campaign of social reform that earned Shanxi the reputation of the "model province." His program included fostering women's rights, public education, and curbing the power of the local gentry. During World War II, Yan cooperated with the Japanese, and after their defeat (1945), he used Japanese troops to fight the Communists. In 1949 he fled with the Nationalists to Taiwan, where he served briefly as premier (1949–50) and presidential adviser. ■ See Donald G. Gillan, *Warlord* (1967).

YEAGER, CHARLES ELWOOD (1923–   ), U.S. pilot. On Oct. 14, 1947, Yeager, a veteran World War II fighter pilot, became the first person to break the sound barrier. Selected to fly the Bell X-1 research plane on the basis of his skill and small size, Yeager piloted the rocket plane to a level-flight speed of 670 miles per hour, exceeding the speed of sound (662 miles per hour at 40,000 feet). Colonel Yeager also set (1953) a world speed record when he flew the air force's X-1A rocket plane at 1,650 miles per hour. He received numerous honors, including the Collier and MacKay trophies. In 1997, on the fiftieth anniversary of his flight that broke the sound barrier, Yeager, then a retired 74-year-old brigadier general, repeated the performance by piloting an F-15D jet fighter over the Mojave Desert. ■ See William R.

Lundgren, *Across the High Frontier* (1955), and his autobiography, *Yeager* (1985; with Leo Janos).

YEATS, WILLIAM BUTLER (1865–1939), Irish poet and dramatist. Regarded by many critics as the greatest English-language poet of the century, Yeats was the major figure of the Irish literary renaissance and a cofounder of the Irish National Theater Company, which developed into the Abbey Theatre in Dublin. His early symbolic and lyrical works celebrated Irish myths and legends and played an important role in awakening Irish nationalism, while his later works, including *The Tower* (1928), *The Winding Stair* (1933), and *The Last Poems* (1940), were concerned with youth, love, old age, and his cyclical view of history, which he had outlined in his prose work *A Vision* (1925; rev. ed., 1937). His works reflected his lifelong interest in the occult, mysticism, theosophy, astrology, and Eastern religions. Among his best-known poems were "Easter 1916," "The Second Coming," and "Sailing to Byzantium." He served in the Irish senate (1922–28) and won the 1923 Nobel Prize in Literature. ■ See *The Autobiographies* (1956), *Memoirs* (1972), *Collected Poems* (1956), and *Collected Plays* (1963); studies by Denis Donoghue (1971), Frank Tuohy (1976), and Douglas Archibald (1983); biographies by Roy Foster (1997) and Terence Brown (1999); and Brenda Maddox, *Yeats's Ghosts* (1999).

YELTSIN, BORIS (1931–   ), Russian political leader. Born into a poor family in the Sverdlovsk region (Ekaterinburg) of Russia, Yeltsin worked as a construction engineer and joined the Communist party in 1961, becoming a full-time official in 1968. He was named the top party leader in the Sverdlovsk region (1976) and was named Moscow party chief by Mikhail Gorbachev (1985). An outspoken advocate of rapid economic and political reform, he criticized Gorbachev's policies as too slow, and he was ousted from his leadership position (1987). However, he was elected to the Congress of People's Deputies of the USSR (1989) and to the Congress of People's Deputies of the Russian Republic (1990). As chair of the Russian Congress, he emerged as a major rival of Gorbachev, resigned from the Communist party (1990), proposed a rapid transformation to a free-market economy, and was elected president of the Russian Republic (June 1991). In August 1991 he resisted a coup against the central government in Moscow by Communist hard-liners, and he subsequently banned the Communist party and played a major role in dismantling the Soviet Union. After Gorbachev resigned (December 1991), Yeltsin replaced him in the Kremlin. As president (1991–99), he restored elements of capitalism, Western-style democracy, and basic individual freedoms to Russia, but his years in power were marked by growing poverty, income disparity, criminality and corruption, and the emergence of a group of fabulously wealthy businessmen who controlled the economy. ■ See his autobiography, *Against the Grain* (Eng. trans. 1990); his memoir, *Midnight Diaries* (2000; Eng. trans. 2000); and biography by Leon Aron (2000).

YEN HSI-SHAN. *See YAN XISHAN.*

YERKES, ROBERT MEARNS (1876–1956), U.S. psychologist. A pioneer in the experimental study of animal behavior, Yerkes taught at Harvard (1902–17) and Yale (1924–44) and founded (1929) and directed the Yale Laboratories of Primate Biology (Oak Park, Florida), which was renamed the Yerkes Laboratory when he retired in 1942. He made numerous studies of the perception and intelligence of various animals, including humans, but was internationally known for his studies of the great apes. His books included *The Mental Life of Monkeys and Apes* (1916), *The Great Apes* (1929), and *Chimpanzees: A Laboratory Colony* (1943).

YESENIN, SERGEI ALEKSANDROVICH (1895–1925), Soviet poet. Born into a prosperous peasant family, he called himself "the last village poet." Yesenin welcomed the 1917 Russian Revolution, after which he soon gained a cult following. He belonged to a short-lived group, the Imagists (1919–24), which juxtaposed coarse and elegant elements in their artistic works. His best-known works of this period were *Confessions of a Hooligan* (1921; Eng. trans. 1973) and *Moscow of the Taverns* (1922). After the dissolution of his marriage to the free-spirited American dancer Isadora Duncan, he wed a granddaughter of the writer Leo Tolstoy (1925). Yesenin became increasingly dependent on alcohol and drugs; morbid self-contempt pervaded such poems as "Letters to My Mother" (1924), "The Man in Black" (1925), and "Anna Snegina" (1925), as well as the brief *Autobiography* (1925) he wrote shortly before hanging himself in a Leningrad hotel. His son Aleksandr Esenin-Volpin, mathematician, poet, and human-rights activist, emigrated (1972) to the United States. ■ See his biography in letters and memoirs edited by J. Davies (1982), biography by Gordon McVay (1976), and study by Constantine Ponamareff (1978). The study by Yuri Prokushev (Eng. trans. 1979) contains translations of his verse.

YEVTUSHENKO, YEVGENY ALEKSANDROVICH (1933–   ), Soviet poet. Yevtushenko studied at the Gorky Literary Institute (Moscow, 1951–54) and emerged during the late 1950s as the most prominent literary spokesman of his generation. The nonconformity, candor, and sense of human sympathy in his poetry, combined with his attacks on Stalinism, won him a wide following and numerous denunciations by Communist party officials. However, he frequently read his works before mass audiences at home and abroad and considered himself a loyal communist. Although he wrote many poems on personal themes, he is best known for his "civic poetry," notably such works as "Zima Junction" (1956), concerned with the immediate post-Stalin era; "Babi Yar" (1961), an exposé of German and Russian anti-Semitism; "The Heirs of Stalin" (1962), an attack on the persistence of Stalinism; and "Bratsk Station" (1965), a panoramic view of Russia's past and present. English translations of his work are in *Bratsk Station and Other New*

Poems (1966), *The Poetry of Yevgeny Yevtushenko* (1967, 1981), *Stolen Apples* (1971), *Yevtushenko Reader* (1972), *From Desire to Desire* (1976), and *The Face Behind the Face* (1979). His first novel, *Wild Berries* (1981; Eng. trans. 1984), sold millions of copies in the Soviet Union. He also wrote and directed the "semiautobiographical" film, *The Kindergarten* (1983). His later works included *Collected Poems, 1952–1990* (Eng. trans. 1993), *Fatal Half Measures: The Culture of Democracy in the Soviet Union* (Eng. trans. 1991), and *Don't Die Before You're Dead* (1993; Eng. trans. 1995). ■ See *A Precocious Autobiography* (1962; Eng. trans. 1963).

YEZHOV, NIKOLAI IVANOVICH (1894–1939?), Soviet political leader. Yezhov joined the Communist party in 1917 and served as a political commissar in the Red army. He was a member of the Central Committee of the Soviet Communist party from 1934 and headed the people's commissariat of internal affairs (NKVD) during the 1936–38 period. Under his direction, the NKVD carried out dictator Joseph Stalin's purges; Yezhov's name became synonymous with the Great Terror (*Yezhovshchina*). Yezhov was succeeded (1938) by Lavrenti Beria and was probably assassinated the following year; the exact circumstances of his death have never been established.

YOKOMITSU, RIICHI (1898–1947), Japanese novelist and short-story writer. He was also known as Toshikazu Yokomitsu. Revolting against both the naturalist and proletarian schools of Japanese literature, Yokomitsu was the leading theoretician and one of the foremost contributors to the school of neoimpressionism. Influenced by the European avant-garde futurists, dadaists, and expressionists of the 1920s, Yokomitsu presented sensual impressions in sharp and startlingly new ways. Among his best-known works were *The Fly* (1923; Eng. trans. 1965), *Head and Stomach* (1924), *The Sun* (1924), and *Machine* (1930; Eng. trans. 1961). After 1930 his works, notably *Family Crest* (1934) and *Lonely Journey* (1937–46), became more psychologically oriented and reflected his concern for the plight of the excessively self-conscious intellectual in the modern world. English translations are in *Time, and Others* (1965) and *Love, and Other Stories* (1974). ■ See study by Donald Keene (1980).

YORK, SERGEANT (Alvin Cullum York; 1887–1964), U.S. soldier. An elementary-school dropout from the mountains of Tennessee, York was refused conscientious-objector status during World War I and was inducted into the army (1917). During the Battle of the Argonne Forest in France (Oct. 8, 1918), York, a remarkable sharpshooter, single-handedly killed 25 Germans and captured 132 prisoners and 35 machine guns. When asked to explain how he did it, he answered, "I surrounded 'em." The most popular American hero of World War I, he amassed more than 50 decorations, including the Congressional Medal of Honor and the Croix de Guerre. He became a farmer after the war, and his auto-biography (1928) was made into the popular film *Sergeant York* (1940), starring Gary Cooper. ∎ See biography by David D. Lee (1985).

YOSHIDA, SHIGERU (1878–1967), Japanese diplomat and political leader. In 1880, Yoshida was adopted by a wealthy family, and he inherited a fortune. After completing his education in 1906, he joined the foreign ministry. A liberal and an opponent of military rule, Yoshida retired in 1938 after serving in many posts, including ambassador to Britain. Just before the end of World War II he was put in prison for his efforts to hasten the Japanese surrender. Yoshida was foreign minister in the first postwar government, and he then served as prime minister (1946–54, except for 16 months). He pushed through a new constitution and pursued a tough, pragmatic policy to lift Japan from the ravages of war and establish the basis for Japan's modern economic boom. He allied his country with the Western powers. ∎ See *The Yoshida Memoirs* (Eng. trans. 1962), and John Dower, *Empire and Aftermath* (1979).

YOSHINO, SAKUZO (1878–1933), Japanese political leader and educator. A leader of the Christian Socialist movement, Yoshino was a professor in the law faculty at Tokyo University. His magazine and newspaper articles, calling for popular participation in governmental affairs, universal suffrage, and civilian control over the army, were widely read and influenced the democratic movement in Japan. He founded the Reimeikai (a society for the advancement of democratic thought; 1918), a consumers' cooperative union (1919), and helped fund the Social Popular party (1926). He also set up an association for the study of Meiji culture and coedited a 24-volume series of Meiji source material (1927–30), which demonstrated the historical roots of liberal democracy in Japan.

YOUMANS, VINCENT (1898–1946), U.S. composer. An enlistee during World War I, Youmans was assigned to produce musicals and write songs for the entertainment of naval trainees. After the war he became a staff pianist in New York's Tin Pan Alley and was soon one of its leading lights. He was best known for his shows *Wildflower* (1923), *No, No, Nanette* (1925), and *Hit the Deck* (1927), and his songs, "Tea for Two," "I Want to Be Happy," "More Than You Know," "Without a Song," "Rise 'n' Shine," and "Time on My Hands." ∎ See Gerald Bordman, *Days to Be Happy, Years to Be Sad* (1982).

YOUNG, ANDREW JACKSON, JR. (1932–), U.S. political leader. Young was born into New Orleans' black bourgeoisie and was ordained in the predominantly white United Church of Christ (1955). He worked for the National Council of Churches in New York (1957–61) before joining the Southern Christian Leadership Conference. He collaborated with Dr. Martin Luther King, Jr., served as the SCLC's exec-utive director (1964–70), and was a major strategist of the civil-rights movement during the 1960s. In 1972 Young won election to Congress as a Democrat from a largely white district in Georgia. A policy adviser to Pres. Jimmy Carter, Young served as his ambassador to the United Nations (1977–79). His outspoken statements on domestic and international affairs, however, frequently created difficulties for the Carter administration, and he resigned under pressure. He was elected mayor of Atlanta, Georgia, in 1981 and reelected in 1985. He wrote *An Easy Burden: The Civil Rights Movement and the Transformation of America* (1996). ∎ See biography by Carl Gardner (1978).

YOUNG, ART (Arthur Henry Young; 1866–1943), U.S. cartoonist. Young's socialist convictions were reflected in his humorous and compassionate political cartoons, which aimed at exposing the evils and hypocrisy of American capitalism. A coeditor of *The Masses* (1911–18), he later published *Good Morning* (1919–21) and contributed to the *Liberator,* the *New Masses,* and *The New Yorker.* He was arrested as a pacifist during World War I and was active in the campaigns for women's suffrage, racial equality, the abolition of child labor, and labor organizing. He twice ran (unsuccessfully) for state office in New York (1913; 1918). A collection of his cartoons is in *The Best of Art Young* (1936). His books include *On My Way* (1928), *Art Young's Inferno* (1934), and his autobiography (1939).

YOUNG, CHIC (Murat Young; 1901–1973), U.S. cartoonist. Encouraged by his mother, a painter, Young studied art, began to draw cartoons in 1920, and joined the King Features Syndicate in 1923. His strips featuring "dumb blond" types, *The Affairs of Jane* (1920), *Beautiful Bab* (1922), and *Dumb Dora* (1924), were predecessors of the famous *Blondie* (1930), which became an American institution. Blondie Bumstead, *née* Boopadoop, was a dizzy flapper who grew increasingly practical after her marriage to the trouble-prone Dagwood. The strip focused on the foibles of middle-class family life and was the world's most widely circulated comic strip, appearing in more than 1,600 newspapers, in 60 countries. It generated 28 movies from 1938 to 1951 and later a television series and a novel.

YOUNG, COLEMAN ALEXANDER (1918–1997), U.S. political leader. Young grew up in Detroit and did union organizing while working for the Ford Motor Co. and the U.S. Post Office. After serving in an elite black flying unit during World War II, he worked as a county organizer for the CIO and founded the National Negro Labor Council to gain equal job opportunities for blacks. As a Democratic Michigan state senator (1964–73), he championed both labor and black causes. Elected mayor of Detroit an unprecedented five times (1973; 1977; 1981; 1985; 1989). Young improved relations between the police and the black community, kept the city solvent during the auto industry downturn, and sponsored the revitalization of the city's riverfront area, but was unable to reverse the high levels of unemployment and poverty. ■ See his autobiography, *Hard Stuff* (1994), and the biography by Wilbur Rich (1989).

YOUNG, CY (Denton True Young; 1867–1955), U.S. baseball player. Major-league baseball's most illustrious pitcher, Young starred on five different teams in both the National and American leagues for 22 seasons (1890–1911) and won a record 511 games. A hurler of legendary stamina, he won 20 or more games for 16 seasons (including 30 or more five times), completed more games than any other major-league pitcher (751), and held the record for most innings pitched in a lifetime (7,356). He was elected to the National Baseball Hall of Fame in 1937. The award presented every season to the outstanding pitcher in each major league was named for him (1956). ■ See biography by Ralph H. Romig (1964).

YOUNG, ELLA FLAGG (1845–1918), U.S. educator. Active in Chicago education for over 50 years, Young was an associate of John Dewey at the University of Chicago and a leading figure in American progressive education. As district superintendent (1887–99) and superintendent of schools (1909–15; the first woman to head a major U.S. school system), she advocated independent thinking and personal responsibility on the party of students and instituted curriculum revisions, vocational courses, physical training, and sex education. She was also a colleague of social reformer Jane Addams and the first woman president of the National Education Association (1910–11). ■ See biography by Joan K. Smith (1979).

YOUNG, LESTER WILLIS (1909–1959), U.S. jazz musician. Originally a drummer in his father's ministrel-show band, Young switched to the tenor saxophone at age 13 and developed into one of the most influential jazz saxophonists of all time. He was most responsible for the switch from hot to cool (or progressive) jazz, symbolized on the saxophone by a transition from a rich, full, vibrato tone to a spare, laconic, and metallic one. Young played with Count Basie's band (1936–40), with which he made his first recordings, and later recorded extensively with Billie Holiday. ■ See study by Lewis Porter (1985), and Luc Delannoy, *Pres* (1993).

YOUNG, LORETTA (Gretchen Young; 1913–2000), U.S. actress. One of the four Young daughters who played in movies before they were teenagers, Young stayed with her film career, starring in nearly 100 features and winning (1947) an Oscar for *The Farmer's Daughter.* Young's dramatic television series "The Loretta Young Show" won two Emmy Awards and became standard TV fare in the 1950s, as each week the graceful actress swirled into view in up-to-date gowns; the gowns were not up-to-date 20 years later when NBC was rerunning the series. Young, displeased to be considered "high camp," sued the network for over a million dollars for broadcasting the shows without her consent,

and she won. ■ See her autobiography, *The Things I Had to Learn* (1961; with Helen Ferguson).

YOUNG, OWEN D. (1874–1962), U.S. lawyer, diplomat, and industrialist. Young began his career as an attorney specializing in public-utility securities in Boston. He was invited to become general counsel of General Electric in 1913 and served as its board chairman (1922–39; 1942–44). In 1919 he helped strengthen the U.S. position in international communications by participating in the creation of the Radio Corporation of America (RCA), also serving as chairman of the board (1919–29). While serving as a director of the Federal Reserve Bank of New York (1923–40), he coauthored the Dawes plan (1924; with Charles G. Dawes), which reformed the German economy and provided a new timetable for the payment of World War I reparations to the Allies. He later set forth the Young plan (1930), which reduced German reparations to levels that were pegged to Germany's ability to pay. After World War II he chaired the committee that recommended the establishment of the State University of New York (1949). ■ See study by Ida Tarbell (1932) and biography by Josephine and Everett Case (1982).

YOUNG, WHITNEY MOORE, JR. (1921–1971), U.S. civil-rights leader. Young served in an all-black unit in the army during World War II and received a degree in social work after the war (University of Minnesota, 1947). He worked for the National Urban League in St. Paul and Omaha and then served as dean of the Atlanta University School of Social Work (1954–61). As executive director of the Urban League (1961–71) he participated in civil-rights marches, helped create the Urban Coalition (1967) to ease inner-city economic problems, and gained a national reputation as an articulate leader of the civil-rights movement. He developed a "domestic Marshall Plan" (1963), later incorporated in antipoverty legislation. ■ See his books, *To Be Equal* (1964) and *Beyond Racism* (1969), and Dennis C. Dickerson, *Militant Mediator* (1998).

YOUNGHUSBAND, SIR FRANCIS EDWARD (1863–1942), British explorer. The first Englishman to reach India overland from China, Younghusband also explored Manchuria and attempted unsuccessfully to scale Mt. Everest. He led the 1903–04 diplomatic and military mission to Tibet that opened that remote outpost to British trade. Later he was president of the Royal Geographic Society (1919–22). A mystic and idealist, he worked to further worldwide religious harmony. His books included *India and Tibet* (1910) and *Modern Mystics* (1935). ■ See biographies by George Seaver (1953), Anthony Verrier (1991), and Patrick French (1994), and Peter Fleming, *Bayonets to Lhasa* (1961).

YOURCENAR, MARGUERITE (Marguerite de Crayencour; 1903–1987), Belgian-born French writer. Raised in an aristocratic household and educated entirely by governesses and tutors, Yourcenar began to write at age 14 and published a book of verse at 18. During the next half century she traveled widely and wrote many erudite and polished novels, plays, essays, and poems drawing on such varied sources as fascist Italy, ancient Greek and Roman history, Hindu mysticism, black American poetry and spirituals, 16th-century Europe, and her personal experiences in the eastern Mediterranean. Her works, known for their keen psychological analysis, complex characters, and fascinating historical reconstruction, included the historical novels *Coup de Grace* (1939; Eng. trans. 1957), *Memoirs of Hadrian* (1951; Eng. trans. 1954), and *The Abyss* (1968; Eng. trans. 1976), the prose poems *Fires* (1936; Eng. trans. 1981), and the short-story collection *Oriental Tales* (1938; rev. ed. 1982; Eng. trans. 1985). Although she emigrated to the United States (1939), her work remained highly regarded in France, and she was the first woman elected to the Académie Française (1980). Her later works included the three stories in *Two Lives and a Dream* (Eng. trans. 1987), *A Blue Tale and Other Stories* (Eng. trans. 1995), and *The Mighty Sculptor, Time* (1988; Eng. trans. 1992). *The Dark Brain of Piranesi* (Eng. trans. 1984) was a book of essays. ■ See her autobiographies, *Dear Departed* (1974; Eng. trans. 1991) and *How Many Years* (1977; Eng. trans. 1995); study by Pierre Horn (1985); and biography by Josyane Savigneau (1993).

YUAN SHI-KAI (old style: YÜAN SHIH-K'AI; 1859–1916), Chinese military and political leader. Born into a landowning family in Honan province, Yuan began his military career in 1880. After serving as the government's chief representative in Korea (1883–94), he built up the largest and best equipped army in China. He helped suppress the reform movement of 1898 as well as the Boxer rebellion (1900), and was appointed governor of Zhili (Chihli) province (1901–07) and high commissioner for north China. During the revolutionary upheavals of 1911, he manipulated the abdication of the Manchu emperor and assumed the presidency of the newly proclaimed republic (1912) with the support of military leaders and foreign bankers. He quickly began to undermine the democratic forces within the government, dissolved the parliament (1914), and established a dictatorship. His decision to establish a new dynasty with himself as emperor (1915) alienated many of his supporters and led to armed revolts throughout the country. He rescinded his plan in March 1916, and died of natural causes three months later. ■ See biography by Jerome Ch'en (2d ed. 1972); Ernest P. Young, *The Presidency of Yüan Shih-k'ai* (1977); and Stephen R. MacKinnon, *Power and Politics in Late Imperial China* (1981).

YUKAWA, HIDEKI (1907–1981), Japanese physicist. In the mid-1930s, Yukawa, the son of a Kyoto University geology professor, began his investigations into the forces that bind atomic nuclei. It had been pointed out that the positive elec-

tromagnetic force within the nucleus ought to result in the mutual repulsion of the particles involved. In order to account for the more powerful binding force, Yukawa postulated the existence of a new fundamental particle intermediate in mass between the proton and the electron and evolved a theory of the transfer of such particles within the atomic nucleus. The discovery (1947) of a particle now known as the pi meson afforded experimental confirmation of Yukawa's hypothesis; he received the 1949 Nobel Prize in Physics, becoming the first Japanese granted a Nobel award. He taught at Kyoto University (1939–48; 1954–70) and Columbia University (1949–54), and wrote *Creativity and Intuition* (Eng. trans. 1973) and *Tabibito—the Traveler* (Eng. trans. 1982).

YUNUS, MUHAMMAD (1941–   ), Bangladeshi banker. Yunus, who was born into a wealthy business family, studied economics at Vanderbilt University, Tennessee (Ph.D. 1972), and taught economics at the University of Chittagong (1972–   ) in southern Bangladesh. Moved by the poverty afflicting the rural areas of his country, he was angered that banks would not lend even small amounts of money to those who needed it most—poor, illiterate, landless peasant women who had no collateral. To solve the problem, Yunus formed his own Grameen ("rural" in Bengali) Bank (1983), charging 2 percent annual interest on loans averaging $75–$100 and requiring borrowers to save money. To encourage peer pressure as well as community support, Yunus required that loans be made only to groups of five borrowers, with each one being responsible for repaying her share of the loan. The bank became an immediate success. By the late 1990s more than 1,000 branches were opened in Bangladesh and other countries in Asia and Africa. The bank, which lent more than $1.5 billion to more than 2.1 million borrowers, enabled millions of peasants to raise themselves out of abject poverty and had a 98 percent repayment record.

YUPANQUI, ATAHUALPA (Hector Roberto Chavero; 1908–1992), Argentinian singer, musician, and poet. Born to a Basque mother and a Native-American father, he adopted the name of the last chief of the Incas (Atahualpa) and the founder of the Inca Empire in the 15th century (Yupanqui). He sang and composed songs that denounced social injustice, celebrated the culture of the South American peasant, and depicted the beauty of his native country. His performances around the world, for more than 40 years, helped revive interest in traditional Argentine folk songs and heralded the "nueva cancion" (new song) movement of protest songs that spread throughout Latin America and the Caribbean during the 1960s. He moved to Paris in 1948 and was associated with many leading artists and intellectuals, including Edith Piaf, Pablo Picasso, and Paul Éluard.

Z

ZADKINE, OSSIP (1890–1967), Russian-born French sculptor and teacher. A distinctive and inventive cubist sculptor, Zadkine studied in London and Paris, fought in the French army during World War I, and became a French citizen in 1921. He took a great interest in primitive art and combined its bold, starkly simple elements with dynamic contours to suggest lyrical movement and convey expressive power. A Jew, he fled from France (1940) and lived in New York City during World War II. He is best known for a monumental bronze sculpture that epitomizes his unique blend of neoclassical and cubist styles—the Rotterdam monument *The Destroyed City* (1951–53), which depicts an agonized, mutilated giant. ■ See study by Ionel Jianu (1964).

ZAGHLUL PASHA, SAAD (1857?–1927), Egyptian political leader. Zaghlul was influenced by reformers when he was a student at the Muslim University of al-Azhar in Cairo. He practiced law, became active in moderate nationalist politics, and served as minister of education (1906–8) and justice (1910–12). Opposed to Egypt being a British protectorate, he formed a delegation (wafd) to protest British rule directly to the high commissioner (1918). This group was eventually transformed into the Wafd party, a popular nationalist movement that pressed for independence as well as for social, educational, and judicial reforms. Having been sent into exile (1919–21; 1921–23), Zaghlul returned as a national hero, and in January 1924 became premier of the independent kingdom of Egypt. Although he was forced out by British pressure in November of that year, he remained the dominant force in Egyptian politics until his death.

ZAHARIAS, BABE DIDRIKSON (Mildred Didrikson; 1914–1956), U.S. athlete. One of the century's great athletes, Babe Zaharias was an All-American high-school basketball player (1930), then turned to track and field. In the 1932 Olympic games she set world records in all three events open to women: the javelin throw, the 80-meter hurdles, and the high jump. (Her high-jump record was disallowed on a technicality, and she won two gold medals). Zaharias was also an expert swimmer, rifle shot, tennis player, and she starred on touring basketball, softball, and baseball teams. She once pitched in a St. Louis Cardinals exhibition game. In 1934 she turned to golf, but after winning the Texas Open the following year she was banned (1935–43) from amateur golf because of an unauthorized endorsement. In 1946 she won the U.S. Women's Amateur tournament and the next year won 17 consecutive golf titles, including the British Women's Amateur championship. After turning professional (1948), she won the U.S. Women's Open three times (1948,

1950, 1954) and was the leading money winner for four straight years (1948–51). She died of cancer at age 42. ■ See her autobiography, *This Life I've Led* (1955); William O. Johnson and Nancy P. Williamson, *Whatta-gal!* (1977); and Susas E. Cayleff, *Babe* (1995).

ZAHAROFF, SIR BASIL (Basileios Zacharias; 1850–1936), Turkish-born armaments dealer and financier. Called a "merchant of death" and popularly known as the "mystery man of Europe," Zaharoff became one of the world's richest and most hated men through the sale of armaments for the Nordenfelt (Swedish) and later Vickers-Armstrong (British) munitions firms. An intimate of many leading European statesmen, he was accused of fomenting wars and political intrigues; he supplied arms for the Boer War, the Russo-Japanese War, the Balkan Wars, and World War I. He was knighted by the British and decorated by the French for his intelligence work during World War I. ■ See Donald McCormick, *Peddler of Death* (1965).

ZAHIR SHAH, MOHAMMAD (1914–), Afghan monarch. Educated in Kabul and in France, Zahir Shah served as minister of education and in 1933 ascended the throne after the assassination of his father, King Nadir Shah. Under the control of the royal family, he was only a figurehead. However, in 1964 he introduced a constitutional government and asserted his power. He maintained neutrality in international relations and sponsored several development projects, but Afghanistan's poverty was aggravated by a three-year famine (1970–73). The general discontent led to Zahir Shah's ouster (by a coup led by Daud Khan in July 1973) while he was in Italy for medical reasons. He formally abdicated and remained in exile.

ZAMYATIN, YEVGENY IVANOVICH (1884–1937), Russian writer. In his early years, Zamyatin studied naval engineering, engaged in Bolshevik activities, and was twice arrested and exiled. After the 1917 Russian Revolution he was a founder of the Serapion Brothers, a loosely formed literary group that opposed the use of literature for nonliterary ends. Zamyatin left his naval-engineering post to instruct such Soviet writers as Ilf and Petrov and Mikhail Zoshchenko. His scientific bent affected his fiction; Zamyatin was preoccupied with the construction and distortion of physical reality. Opposing the insistence of writer Maxim Gorky that Soviet writers imitate the classics, Zamyatin called himself a neorealist and used startling language and imagery in such remarkable tales as *The Cave* (1922; Eng. trans. 1923) and in such plays as *The Flea* (1926). When *We* (1920–21; Eng.

trans. 1924), his anti-utopian novel condemning social collectivization, was published abroad (apparently without his permission), he was expelled from the official writers' union and he reportedly wrote to dictator Joseph Stalin requesting permission to emigrate. Denounced as an anti-Soviet "internal émigré," Zamyatin left Russia (1931) and settled in France. English translations of his works are in *The Dragon and Other Stories* (1967), *A Soviet Heretic: Essays* (1970), and *Islanders, and the Fisher of Men* (1984). ■ See biography by Alex M. Shane (1968) and Gary Kern, ed., *Zamyatin's We* (1985).

ZANGWILL, ISRAEL (1864–1926), British writer. The most prominent Anglo-Jewish writer of his time, Zangwill achieved fame for his novels of Jewish ghetto life in London: *Children of the Ghetto* (1892), *Ghetto Tragedies* (1893), and *King of the Schnorrers* (1894). His play *The Melting Pot* (1908), about the Americanization of Jewish immigrants in New York, was a hit on Broadway. An early member of the Zionist movement (from 1896), Zangwill broke with it (1905) to found the Jewish Territorial Organization (president, 1905–25), which sought a land for homeless and persecuted Jews but not necessarily in Palestine. His essays on the Jewish question were collected in *Voice of Jerusalem* (1920). ■ See biographies by Joseph Leftwich (1957) and Elsie Adams (1971).

ZANUCK, DARRYL F. (1902–1979), U.S. film producer. A screenwriter from Wahoo, Nebraska, Zanuck progressed from writing scripts featuring the dog Rin-Tin-Tin in 1924 to overseeing production at Warner Brothers (1929) and at Twentieth Century-Fox (1935). Early films produced by Zanuck include the socially significant *The Grapes of Wrath* (1940), *The Ox-Bow Incident* (1943), and *Gentleman's Agreement* (1947). After 21 years at Fox, Zanuck became an independent producer, personally directing *The Longest Day* (1962), but he returned (1962) to take control of the studio after a power struggle. In 1971 he was replaced by his son Richard (1934–). ■ See Mel Gussow's biography, *Don't Say Yes Until I Finish Talking* (1971); study by Leo Guild (1970); biography by Leonard Mosley (1984); and George F. Custen, *Twentieth Century's Fox* (1997).

ZAPATA, EMILIANO (1879–1919), Mexican revolutionary leader. A peasant of almost pure Indian stock, Zapata received no formal education and only minimal military training. In 1910, when Francisco Madero called for a revolt against the 35-year dictatorship of Porfirio Díaz, Zapata responded and organized a rebellion in his home state. His forces contributed to the victory over Díaz (1911), but when Madero failed to distribute land to the peasants, Zapata formulated his own agrarian reform plan—the Plan of Ayala—and gained widespread support. His peasant army was in continuous revolt against Madero and Madero's successor, Victoriano Huerta (1911–14). Zapata then joined forces with Pancho Villa to fight against Huerta's successor, Venus-

tiano Carranza. In areas under Zapata's control, he distributed land, set up cooperatives, and established Mexico's first agricultural credit organization and is thus credited with bringing the agrarian issue to the forefront of the Mexican revolution. He was assassinated by Carranza agents (1919). ■ See John Womack, *Zapata and the Mexican Revolution* (1968); biography by Roger Parkinson (1975); and study by Peter Newell (1997).

ZAPOTOCKY, ANTONÍN (1884–1957), Czech political leader. The son of a founder of the Czech Socialist party, Zapotocky was a founder (1921) and secretary-general (1923) of the Czech Communist party. He was elected to parliament (1925) and led the communist trade unions (1929–39) before being incarcerated by the Germans (1939–45) during World War II. After the war he was chairman of the Constituent National Assembly and also chairman of the Revolutionary Trade Union movement, which represented all of the nation's organized labor. A leader of the 1948 communist coup, Zapotocky became premier and subsequently president (1953–57) of Czechoslovakia.

ZATOPEK, EMIL (1922–2000), Czech long-distance runner. One of the greatest long-distance runners in the history of track, Zatopek won four gold medals in Olympic competition for the 10,000 meters (1948, 1952) and 5,000 meters and the marathon (1952). In the 11 years up to 1952 he set six new world records in distances from 5,000 to 30,000 meters. He was married to Dana Zatopkova (1922–), who won the gold medal in javelin throwing at the 1952 Olympic games.

ZECKENDORF, WILLIAM (1905–1976), U.S. business executive. The son of a retailer, William Zeckendorf dropped out of college (New York University) in 1925 to begin a long career of real-estate wheeling and dealing in New York City. He conducted negotiations for the Rockefellers and put together the site for the United Nations headquarters. In 1949 he bought out the old New York firm of Webb and Knapp, which he had joined in 1933, and worked with architect I. M. Pei in urban-renewal projects in Denver, Dallas, Washington, D.C., Philadelphia, and Montreal. The flamboyant Zeckendorf reportedly controlled a half-billion dollars in property by the early 1960s, but his tenuous loan structure collapsed and he went bankrupt in 1965. ■ See his autobiography (1970).

ZEDILLO PONCE DE LEON, ERNESTO (1951–), Mexican political leader. Born into a lower-middle class family in Mexico City, Zedillo studied economics at the National Polytechnic Institute in Mexico City and at Yale University (M.A. 1977; Ph.D. 1981). He worked at the Banco de Mexico, the country's central bank, and subsequently served as minister of budget and planning (1988–92) and minister of education (1992–93). He supported economic liberalization and Mexico's entry into the North American

Free Trade Agreement (NAFTA). As president (1994–2000) he initiated significant judicial and political reforms. His devaluation of the peso and tight money policies during his first months in office eventually led to economic growth. However, by 1998, the economy faltered, inflation and unemployment rose, per capita income fell, and the crime rate surged.

ZEFFIRELLI, FRANCO (Gianfranco Corsi; 1923–), Italian director and stage designer. After studying architecture at the University of Florence and the Accademia di Belle Arti, Zeffirelli took up stage design and acting. He established himself as a scenic designer for Luchino Visconti's opera productions in the late 1940s and was assistant director on several Visconti films. In the 1950s, he won acclaim for his own lavish productions of opera (often featuring soprano Maria Callas) and of theater (particularly Shakespeare), gaining a reputation for his vivid eroticism and opulent sets and costumes. From the late 1960s he was known primarily as a film director, whose credits included *The Taming of the Shrew* (1967), *Romeo and Juliet* (1968), *Brother Sun and Sister Moon* (1972), *The Champ* (1979), *Endless Love* (1981), *La Traviata* (1983), *Otello* (1986), and *Tea with Mussolini* (1999). He also made the TV movie *Jesus of Nazareth* (1977) and directed major productions at New York's Metropolitan Opera. ■ See his autobiography (1986).

ZEITLIN, SOLOMON (1892?–1976), Russian-born Jewish historian. In the century's first decade, Zeitlin studied at Baron David Günzburg's Academy of Jewish Learning in St. Petersburg. He later emigrated to the United States and taught at the University of Pennsylvania. A leading authority on rabbinics and Jewish history, Zeitlin's ideas often flouted conventional wisdom. He dated the Dead Sea Scrolls to the Middle Ages and debated historian Arnold Toynbee on the legitimacy of Jewish claims to Palestine. The moving force behind *The Jewish Quarterly Review*, Zeitlin was known for his extraordinary erudition and prolific publications: a 1970 annotated bibliography listed 406 articles or books. His works include the three-volume *Studies in the Early History of Judaism* (1973–76).

ZELAYA, JOSÉ SANTOS (1853–1919), Nicaraguan political leader. A French-educated Liberal politician, Zelaya seized power in 1893 and ended 30 years of Conservative party rule. Playing one faction off against the other, he remained in power for 16 years, during which he secularized and expanded the educational system, developed railroad and steamer transportation, and modernized agriculture and industry while enriching himself through graft. His modernization program resulted in violent conservative opposition, and his regime became increasingly dictatorial. He frequently interfered in the affairs of neighboring governments and hoped to set up a Central American Federation under his leadership. He opposed U.S. penetration in Central

America, and the U.S. government supported the revolutionaries who succeeded in overthrowing him in 1909. Zelaya lived the last decade of his life in Mexico, Spain, and the United States.

ZEPPELIN, COUNT FERDINAND VON (1838–1917), German aircraft designer. After attaining the rank of general in the Germany army, von Zeppelin retired (1891) and devoted himself to designing a rigid, motor-powered dirigible balloon. The first of his airships, called zeppelins, was flown on July 2, 1900. Before World War I, many traversed distances of over 1,000 miles. Their use during the war for dropping bombs was limited by their vulnerability to storms and gunfire. The zeppelin eventually became the first regular means of passenger air transport. ■ See W. Robert Nitske, *The Zeppelin Story* (1977).

ZERNIKE, FRITS (1888–1966), Dutch physicist. On the faculty of the University of Groningen for his entire career (1915–58), Zernike developed a phase-contrast method for the improvement of astronomical telescopes (1934) and immediately realized its application to the microscope. The phase-contrast microscope made it possible to observe and study living cells without staining and thus killing them. His microscope, which came into general use after World War II, became an extremely valuable tool in medicine and biological research and earned Zernike the 1953 Nobel Prize in Physics.

ŻEROMSKI, STEFAN (1864–1925), Polish novelist, short-story writer, and playwright. The most important Polish fiction writer during the first quarter of the century, Żeromski was called "the conscience of Polish literature." The son of an impoverished nobleman, he was a socialist sympathizer who was obsessed with social injustice and armed struggles of the past. Known for their compassion, lyricism, and melodrama, Żeromski's novels realistically depicted, for the first time, the evils of the Polish social system and featured idealistic and socially motivated heroes. *Homeless People* (1900), an account of a sensitive intellectual's reaction to the poverty of the masses; *Ashes* (3 vols., 1904; Eng. trans. 1928), a historical epic of life during the Napoleonic wars; *The Faithful River* (1912; Eng. trans. 1943), a novel of the 1863 national uprising; and *Before the Spring* (1925), a novel depicting the social problems that followed World War I, were among his best works.

ZETKIN, CLARA (Clara Eissner; 1857–1933), German political leader. A prominent feminist and socialist theoretician and orator, Clara Zetkin was a member of the left wing of the Social Democratic party (SPD; 1881–1917), a founder of the Second International (1889), and founding editor of the SPD's women's journal, *Die Gleichheit* (1892–1917). She was a founder (with Rosa Luxemburg, Karl Liebknecht, and others) of the radical Spartacus League (1916), a founder of the German Communist party (KPD; 1919), and a Communist member of the Reichstag (1920–33). A close friend of the Russian revolutionary V. I. Lenin, she supported the 1917 Bolshevik revolution in Russia and spent much of her time (after 1921) in Moscow. She was elected to the presidium of the Third International (1921) but lost much of her influence after Lenin's death (1924). ■ See her *Selected Writings* (Eng. trans. 1984).

ZEWAIL, AHMED HASSAN (1946–   ), Egyptian-born chemist. Zewail studied at the University of Alexandria and at the University of Pennsylvania (Ph.D. 1974) and taught at the California Institute of Technology (Caltech; 1976–   ). During the 1980s he developed an ultrafast laser technique that enabled scientists to see how atoms in molecules rearrange themselves during a chemical reaction. Called "femtosecond spectroscopy," the technique measured the reactions of atoms in units of time called femtoseconds. (A femtosecond is one quadrillionth of a second.) Zewail's innovation, which revolutionized chemistry, led to advances in the study of catalysts, the design of miniature electronic components, and the understanding of such processes as photosynthesis and animal vision. For devising what has been called the world's fastest camera, Zewail was awarded the 1999 Nobel Prize in Chemistry.

ZHANG GUOTAO (old style: CHANG KUO-T'AO; 1897–1979), Chinese political leader. Raised in a wealthy family, Zhang attended Beijing (Peking) National University, where he was a student leader during the May 4, 1919, demonstrations. He became a Marxist and was a founder of the Chinese Communist party (1921). He organized labor movements and visited the Soviet Union several times as a Comintern delegate. During the early 1930s he controlled a communist army and enclave that was independent of the forces of Mao Zedong (Mao Tse-tung). However, due to his differences with Mao and a major loss of troops in 1935 attributed to his military and political errors, he left the communist movement (1938) and was a powerless Guomindang (Kuomintang) official from 1938 to 1945. After the communist victory in the civil war (1949) he lived in Hong Kong (to 1968) and Canada.

ZHANG XUELIANG (old style: CHANG HSUEH-LIANG; 1898–   ), Chinese warlord. The son of Zhang Zuolin (Chang Tso-lin), the Manchurian warlord, Zhang Xueliang, the "young marshal," joined his father's army and succeeded him in 1928. He defied his father's allies, the Japanese, and pledged the allegiance of Manchuria to the new nationalist government headed by Chiang Kai-shek. Forced out of Manchuria by the Japanese (1931), Zhang was angered at Chiang for waging war only against the communists and for refusing to fight the occupiers. He made a secret agreement with the Chinese communists and kidnapped Chiang (the Xi'an [Sian] Incident, 1936, releasing him when he promised to join the communists in an anti-Japanese war. After returning to the capital (Nanjing [Nanking]) Chiang took revenge by having Zhang arrested, convicted, and placed under house arrest. After Chiang's national government fled to Taiwan (1949), Zhang was brought there and remained in confinement until 1991.

ZHANG YIMOU (1951–   ), Chinese film director. Born into a family with a history of ties to the anti-Communist Guomindang movement, Zhang was not allowed to join the Communist party and was forced to give up school to spend several years (1966–76) as a farmhand and factory worker during the Cultural Revolution. He taught himself photography (1974) and studied cinematography at the newly reopened Beijing Film Academy (1978–82). A leading member of "Fifth Generation" filmmakers, as 1982 Academy graduates were called, he first gained public attention for his camera work on *Yellow Earth* (1983) and *The Big Parade* (1985). He subsequently directed *Red Sorghum* (1988), *Ju Dou* (1990), and *Raise the Red Lantern* (1991), which depicted the oppression of women in traditional Confucian society. The epic *To Live* (1994) traced the hardships of a family during the years of Communist rule in China, while *Shanghai Triad* (1995) was a film set in the pre–World War II era. *Keep Cool* (1997) was a comedy set in contemporary times. Most of Zhang's films were banned in China. In 1998 he directed a spectacular production of Puccini's opera *Turandot,* which was staged in Beijing's Forbidden City and broadcast throughout the world. He also directed *Not One Less* (2000).

ZHANG ZUOLIN (old style: CHANG TSO-LIN; 1873–1928), Chinese warlord. Zhang, the "old marshal," was an uneducated peasant who began his military career before the age of 20. He organized his own army in Manchuria and with the help of the Japanese, he ruled Manchuria and other parts of northern China as his private domain (1919–28). He opposed the revolutionary nationalism of Sun Yat-sen. In 1924 he spread his rule to Beijing (Peking), but he was forced to retreat (1928) by the Guomindang (Kuomintang) nationalist armies headed by Chiang Kai-shek. He was killed on his way home when Japanese extremists, hoping that Japan would occupy Manchuria, blew up the train he was on. ■ See study by Gavan McCormack (1977).

ZHAO ZIYANG (old style: CHAO TZU-YANG; 1919–   ), Chinese political leader. Born in Henan (Honan) province, the son of a landlord and grain merchant, Zhao joined the Communist party in 1938 and worked as a party official during World War II. After the establishment of the People's Republic of China (1949), he worked in rural development and became provincial first party secretary in Guangdong (Kwangtung) province (1965). Denounced during the Cultural Revolution (1967) as a "revisionist" and "counterrevolutionary" for his moderate economic policies, he was purged from his position and remained in obscurity for several years. However, he was rehabilitated, returned to Guangdong (1972), and resumed his post as provincial secretary (1974). As governor and party first secretary of Sichuan (Szechwan) province (1975–80), he initiated pragmatic and flexible reforms (including material incentives for workers based on productivity, greater autonomy for factory managers, expansion of the amount of land for private farm plots, and the revival of free peasant markets) that resulted in dramatic increases in industrial production and agricultural output. He was named to the politburo (1979) and was brought to Beijing (Peking) by Deng Xiaoping (Teng Hsiao-ping; 1980). Zhao's policies served as the basis of reforms adopted throughout the country, and he served as premier (1980–87) and general secretary of the Communist party (1987–89). He pursued conciliatory relations with the Western powers and expanded trade and cultural and scientific exchanges with them. During the enormous Tiananmen Square demonstrations in Beijing in the spring of 1989 he favored granting concessions to the protesters. As a result, he was ousted from the Political Bureau in late May, just prior to the government's violent crackdown, and was officially stripped of power in late June. ■ See biography by Wei Chao (Eng. trans. 1989).

ZHDANOV, ANDREI ALEKSANDROVICH (1896–1948), Soviet political and military leader. A close associate of dictator Joseph Stalin, Zhdanov was secretary of the Leningrad Communist party committee (1934–44) and was named to full membership in the Politburo (1939). A military leader during World War II, he was active (1939–40) on the Finnish front and in the defense of Leningrad. He wielded great influence in cultural affairs; Zhdanov's speech at the 1934 First Congress of Soviet Writers enunciated the principles of socialist realism. Zhdanovism reigned in the postwar period (1946–53); he denounced (1946) Anna Akhmatova, Boris Pasternak, and other nonconformist writers for their "cosmopolitanism" and "vulgarity" and closed or censured the journals that had published their work. He also restricted music, drama, cinema, and other cultural expressions. Zhdanov was also the leading spokesman of the Cominform (established 1947), which enunciated a militantly anti-Western position in the years after World War II. ■ See his *Essays on Literature, Philosophy and Music* (Eng. trans. 1950); Werner G. Hahn, *Postwar Soviet Politics* (1982); and Gavriel D. Ra'anan, *International Policy Formation in the USSR* (1983).

ZHITLOWSKY, CHAIM (1865–1943), Russian-born U.S. leader of secular Jewish culture. An essayist, philosopher, and orator in Yiddish, German, and Russian, Zhitlowsky played a major role in the Yiddish cultural movement. In Europe he contributed to socialist periodicals and helped found the Russian Social Revolutionary party (1893). After settling in New York (1908), he edited the journal *Dos Naye Lebn* (1908–13), in which he expounded an anti-Zionist secularist philosophy for agnostic Jews. He deplored assimilationists but propounded a vibrant culture based on the Yiddish language. He was a founding editor of the Yiddish-language newspaper *Day* (1914). Excerpts from his mem-

oirs are in Lucy S. Dawidowicz, ed., *The Golden Tradition* (1967). ■ See David H. Weinberg, *Between Tradition and Modernity* (1996).

ZHIVKOV, TODOR (1911–1998), Bulgarian political leader. A printer by trade, Zhivkov was active in Bulgarian communist circles during the 1930s and as a World War II partisan leader under the name of "Marko." Official communist sources claim that he led the coup that overthrew the pro-German regime in September 1944. Rising to the posts of secretary of the Bulgarian Communist party in 1954, premier in 1962, and president in 1971, he ran Bulgaria as a faithful ally of the Soviet Union. Under his leadership, Bulgaria was the first socialist country to complete collectivization of agriculture, and it participated in the 1968 invasion of Czechoslovakia. Zhivkov was removed from office (1989) in the bloodless coup by reformers within the Bulgarian Communist party. In 1992 he was convicted of embezzlement and sentenced to seven years of house arrest, but he was acquitted of the charges by Bulgaria's highest court in 1996. ■ *Todor Zhivkov: Stateman and Builder of New Bulgaria* (Eng. trans. 1982) contains biographical information.

ZHOU ENLAI (old style: CHOU EN-LAI; 1898–1976), Chinese political leader. The son of wealthy landowners, Zhou was a student radical who participated in the May Fourth Movement (1919). While studying in France and Germany (1920–24), he founded a branch of the Chinese Communist party in Paris (1922) and joined the nationalist Guomindang (Kuomintang, 1924). Back in China, he served as political head of the Whampoa Military Academy (1924–26) and helped to organize worker and peasant uprisings in Shanghai and Nanchang (1927). He barely escaped Guomindang repression (1927), went underground, and joined Mao Zedong (Mao Tse-tung) and his guerrilla movement in Jiangxi (Kiangsi) province (1931). He built up the Red army and helped organize and lead the Long March (1934–35). After Mao became party chief (1934–35) Zhou supported his policies. He negotiated a united front with the Guomindang to fight the Japanese (1937–45), became the chief diplomat for the communists in their external dealings, and played an important role in the civil war (1945–49) that resulted in the establishment of the People's Republic of China (1949). As prime minister (1949–76), he created a solid administrative base for the new government, and as foreign minister (1949–58) he represented China at numerous international conferences. He was a moderating influence during the Great Leap Forward (1958) and the Cultural Revolution (1966–69), and was largely responsible for the reestablishment of diplomatic ties with Japan and the United States during the 1970s. ■ See biographies by John McCook Roots (1977), Dick Wilson (1984), and Percy Jucheng Fang and Lucy Guinong J. Fang (1986).

ZHOU ZUOREN (old style: CHOU TSO-JEN; 1885–1966), Chinese essayist and translator. Zhou, the brother of the famed fiction writer Lu Xun (Lu Hsun), received a thorough classical as well as a Western education. He was an activist in several radical literary organizations that were founded during the revolutionary ferment of the 1919 May Fourth Movement and advocated a new literature based upon social realism and vernacular Chinese. Chou translated works of Greek, Roman, English, Japanese, Russian, and East European authors and published 30 collections of influential essays concerning literature and society. He was sentenced to life imprisonment after World War II for serving as head of the Bureau of Education (1941–43) in the Japanese puppet government, but was pardoned in 1949 and continued his literary work in Beijing (Peking). ■ See study by Ernst Wolff (1971) and David E. Pollard, *A Chinese Look at Literature* (1973).

ZHU DE (old style: CHU THE; 1886–1976), Chinese military and political leader. Zhu De, called the "father" of the Red army, began his military training early, and participated in the 1911 revolution. From 1912 to 1920 he led a warlord existence. In 1922 he went to Germany, where he joined the Chinese Communist party with the support of party leader Zhou Enlai (Chou En-lai). An associate of Mao Zedong (Mao Tse-tung; from 1928) he became the head of the communist armies in China (1930) and led them through the Long March (1934–35), the resistance to the Japanese occupation (1937–45), and the victorious civil war against the nationalists (1946–49). He gave up his military posts in 1954 and subsequently held high official positions, including that of chairman of the standing committee of the National People's Congress. ■ See Agnes Smedley, *The Great Road* (1956).

ZHU RONGZI (1928–   ), Chinese political leader. A native of Hunan province, Zhu was orphaned as a young child and raised by relatives. He joined the Communist party (1949) while studying electrical engineering at Beijing's prestigious Qinghua University and graduated in 1951. Zhu worked for the State Planning Commission but was branded a "rightist" (1957) after the "Hundred Flowers" campaign and again (1970) during the Cultural Revolution and was banished to the countryside to do rural labor in both cases. Rehabilitated in 1979 and sponsored by Deng Xiaoping, he served as vice minister of the State Economic Commission (1983–88) and mayor of Shanghai (1988–91), and gained a reputation as an efficient, pragmatic, and reform-minded administrator who successfully courted foreign investors. He was promoted to deputy prime minister (1991) and Politburo member (1992) and was given control over the economy in 1993. His austerity measures successfully lowered inflation while spurring exports and maintaining high growth rates and high levels of foreign investment. He subsequently served as premier (1998–   ).

ZHUKOV, GEORGI KONSTANTINOVICH (1896–1974), Soviet military leader. Zhukov, the son of a peasant, was drafted into the czarist army (1915). He allied with the Bolsheviks and joined the Red army (1918), rapidly winning command of a cavalry regiment during the Russian civil war (1918–20). In the 1930s he studied tank warfare and applied the principles he developed to defeat Japanese invaders in Mongolia (1939). Zhukov was a key figure during World War II, winning almost legendary fame as the "undefeatable general." He participated in the defense of Leningrad (1941), commanded the Moscow front (1941), launched the offensives that relieved Stalingrad (1942), and commanded the Russian thrust to Berlin (1945). He was minister of defense (1955–57) under Nikita Khrushchev but was dismissed and denounced for obstructing party work in the military and for encouraging a Zhukov cult. He was rehabilitated (1965) after Khrushchev's fall. ■ See his *Memoirs* (Eng. trans. 1971); *Marshal Zhukov's Greatest Battles* (Eng. trans. 1969); biography by Otto P. Chaney (1971; 1996); and David M. Glautz, *Zhukov's Greatest Defeat* (1999).

ZIA UL-HAQ, MOHAMMAD (1924–1988), Pakistani political leader. A career army officer (commissioned in May 1945), Zia was apparently a loyal follower of Prime Minister Zulfikar Ali Bhutto, who promoted him to general and appointed him chief of staff of the army in March 1976. However, after rioting, charges of fraud, and months of political turmoil followed the March 1977 elections, Zia overthrew Bhutto in a bloodless coup (July 1977), banned all political parties and trade unions, and became president in September 1978. Bhutto was found guilty of murder-conspiracy charges and, despite clemency appeals from world leaders, was hanged on April 4, 1979. Zia, a devout Muslim, introduced strict Islamic social, fiscal, and penal laws and punishments, increased Pakistan's ties to Third World countries, and reestablished closer ties to the United States after the Soviet invasion of neighboring Afghanistan in 1979. He and most of Pakistan's army leadership were killed in a midair explosion of a military aircraft. ■ See Craig Baxter, ed., *Zia's Pakistan* (1985), and Shahid J. Burki, *Pakistan Under the Military* (1991).

ZIEGFELD, FLORENZ (1869–1932), U.S. theatrical producer. Ziegfeld entered show business as a manager during the World's Columbia Exposition in Chicago (1893) and achieved fame as a producer of a series of lavish Broadway musical comedies starring French actress Anna Held (from 1896), whom he later married. His greatest success came with the production of *The Follies of 1907*, a glamorous, romantic, and colorful musical revue that was modeled on the Folies-Bergère in Paris. The show, which aimed to "glorify the American girl," featured beautiful chorus girls, opulent costumes, highly stylized dance routines, and sophisticated humor and political satire. Presented annually until 1931 (except for 1926, 1928, and 1929), the *Follies* transformed the musical theater in the United States. They featured music by Irving Berlin, Jerome Kern, Victor Herbert, and Rudolf Friml and helped develop such talents as Will Rogers, Fanny

Brice, W. C. Fields, Eddie Cantor, and Ed Wynn. Ziegfeld also produced such Broadway hits as *Sally* (1920), *Showboat* (1927), and *Rio Rita* (1927). Gambling debts and the stock-market crash in 1929 ruined Ziegfeld financially. ■ See biography by Charles Higham (1972) and Randolph Carter, *The World of Flo Ziegfeld* (1974).

ZIEGLER, KARL (1898–1973), German organic chemist. Ziegler received his Ph.D. at the University of Marburg (1923) and taught at several universities before directing the Max Planck Institute for coal research (1943–69). During the 1950s he devised a process that utilized chemical catalysts to produce strengthened polyethylene plastics. His polymerization technique allowed for the mass production of high-quality plastics, rubber, fibers, and film for industrial and domestic use. For his research he shared the 1963 Nobel Prize in Chemistry with Giulio Natta.

ZIMBALIST, EFREM (1890–1985), Russian-born U.S. violinist and composer. Zimbalist studied with his father, a conductor, and later with Leopold Auer (1901–07) at the St. Petersburg Conservatory. He won critical acclaim when he appeared in Berlin (1907), and after his successful American debut in Boston (1911), in which he performed Glazunov's A minor violin concerto, he settled in the United States. A leading violinist of his generation, he was acclaimed for his unhurried, penetrating, and dignified interpretations. Zimbalist also directed (1941–68) Philadelphia's Curtis Institute of Music and composed several works for violin, cello, and orchestra. His son Efrem Zimbalist, Jr. (1923–) was a well-known actor; his granddaughter Stephanie Zimbalist (1956–) was an actress.

ZIMMERN, SIR ALFRED ECKHARD (1879–1957), British historian. The son of a merchant in the China trade, Zimmern was a scholar of ancient history and contemporary politics. He was active on behalf of the League of Nations and the United Nations and directed the School of International Studies at Geneva (1925–39). He taught international relations at Oxford (1930–44) and wrote *The Greek Commonwealth* (1911), *The League of Nations and the Rule of Law* (1936), and *The American Road to World Peace* (1953).

ZINKERNAGEL, ROLF M. (1944–), Swiss immunologist. Zinkernagel studied at the University of Basel (M.D. 1970) and at the Australian National University, Canberra (Ph.D. 1975), and taught pathology and immunology at the University of Zurich, Switzerland (1979–). While a postdoctoral research fellow at the John Curtin School of Medical Research in Canberra, he collaborated with Peter C. Doherty on immune system studies (1973–75). Using laboratory mice, they discovered how white blood cells (cytotoxic T cells or killer T cells), responsible for hunting and killing virus-infected cells in the body, recognize infected cells and leave normal body cells alone. They discovered

that the white cells simultaneously recognize two separate protein signals from the target cell, one indicating that the cell is part of the "self" and not a foreign invader, and the other indicating that the cell is infected. Their findings revealed the fundamental nature of the immune response and led to new approaches to the treatment of such diseases as cancer, AIDS, diabetes, and multiple sclerosis. For their research, Zinkernagel and Doherty shared the 1996 Nobel Prize in Physiology or Medicine.

ZINN, HOWARD (1922–), U.S. historian. Zinn served in the U.S. Army Air Corps during World War II, studied at Columbia University (Ph.D. 1958), and taught history and political science at Spelman College, Atlanta, Georgia (1956–63), and Boston University (1964–88). He was active in the civil-rights and anti–Vietnam War movements and concentrated on the role of the working class, the poor, and minority groups in his writings on American history. His best-known work, *A People's History of the United States* (1980; rev. ed. 1995), sold more than 500,000 copies. His other books included *SNCC: The New Abolitionists* (1964), *The Southern Mystique* (1964), *The Politics of History* (1970), *Declarations of Independence* (1990), and *The Zinn Reader: Writings on Disobedience and Democracy* (1997). ■ See his autobiography, *You Can't Be Neutral on a Moving Train* (1994).

ZINNEMANN, FRED (1907–1997), Austrian-born U.S. film director. Born in Vienna, the son of a doctor, Zinnemann abandoned plans for a legal career to study filmmaking in Paris. He moved to Hollywood (1929) and assisted several leading directors during the 1930s. Beginning in the 1940s he directed a series of humanistic films that dealt with social issues and crises of moral courage, and he was recognized as a pioneering Hollywood neorealist. His best-known works included the Academy Award–winning *From Here to Eternity* (1953) and *A Man for All Seasons* (1966) as well as such Hollywood classics as *The Search* (1948), *The Men* (1950), *High Noon* (1952), *The Member of the Wedding* (1953), *The Nun's Story* (1959), and *Julia* (1977). He also directed the musical *Oklahoma!* (1955) and two Academy Award–winning short documentaries, *That Mothers Might Live* (1938) and *Benjy* (1951). ■ See his autobiography, *A Life in the Movies* (1992).

ZINOVIEV, GRIGORI EVSEYEVICH (O.G.A. Radomyslsky; 1883–1936), Soviet political leader. Zinoviev joined the Bolsheviks (1903) and lived abroad (1908–17) working closely with V. I. Lenin. After the 1917 Russian Revolution he served as Petrograd party chief (1921–26) and helped win support for the new government. While he was president of the Communist International (Comintern; 1919–26) the famous "Zinoviev letter" was circulated; the 1924 communication, allegedly written by Zinoviev, outlined plans for an uprising in Britain and played a major role in the defeat of the first British Labour government. Zinoviev was named to the Politburo (1921) and had enormous power in the early 1920s. After Lenin's death (1924) he assumed collective rule with Joseph Stalin and Lev Kamenev, but his influence diminished. He was instrumental in the political demise of Leon Trotsky (1925), but when opposed by Stalin, he joined with Trotsky (1926) and both of them were expelled from the party (1927). After repudiating his stance, he was readmitted (1928), but he never regained his earlier stature. Expelled again in 1932 and 1934, he was accused by Stalin of complicity in the assassination of Sergei Kirov (1934). Forced to confess during the most famous of the purge trials (1936), he was found guilty and executed. ■ See his *History of the Bolshevik Party* (1923; Eng. trans. 1973).

ZINSSER, HANS (1878–1940), U.S. bacteriologist. Born in New York and educated at Columbia Medical School (M.D. 1903), Zinsser became the world's leading authority on typhus. After isolating the typhus germ, he worked with his colleagues at the Harvard Medical School (from 1923) to develop a typhus vaccine (1940). A poet and epic conversationalist, Zinsser wrote *Rats, Lice and History* (1935), a popular work in the history of typhus, as well as textbooks on infectious disease and an autobiography, *As I Remember Him,* in the form of a memoir of a friend, "R.S.," or "romantic self" (1940).

ZNANIECKI, FLORIAN WITOLD (1882–1958), Polish sociologist. After earning a Ph.D. in philosophy from the University of Cracow (1910), Znaniecki was invited (1914) to come to the United States to collaborate on *The Polish Peasant in Europe and America* (5 vols., 1918–20), a classic of comparative sociology. Back in Poland he established the first department of sociology (University of Poznan) and founded the Polish Institute of Sociology (1922). On a later trip to teach in the United States he was stranded by World War II and taught at the University of Illinois (1940–50). Znaniecki's writings in English, including *Cultural Sciences* (1952), attempted to bridge the gap between sociology and social psychology, with particular attention to the role of creativity.

ZOG I (**Ahmed Bey Zogu;** 1895–1961), king of Albania. The son of a Muslim clan chieftain, Zog served as commander of the Albanian armed forces (1920), premier (1922–24), and president (1925) and was proclaimed king in 1928. His autocratic rule was aimed at forging an Albanian national consciousness to take precedence over clan and regional loyalties. Zog's reign was marked by relative tranquility, modest reforms, and economic progress, but Italian influence grew in all spheres and Albania became virtually a puppet state of Italian dictator Benito Mussolini. In 1939 the Italians invaded and declared Albania a protectorate; Zog fled. After World War II Zog's hopes of returning to Albania were shattered by the establishment of a communist government, and he remained in exile in Egypt, the United States, and France. ■ See study by Bernd-Jürgen Fischer (1934).

ZORACH, WILLIAM (1887–1966), Lithuanian-born U.S. sculptor. Zorach studied art in Cleveland, New York City, and Paris. Influenced by the cubists and fauves, Zorach figured among the avant-garde in American painting and exhibited at the landmark 1913 Armory Show in New York City. In the next several years he turned to carving, a medium in which he was self-taught. A sculptor of traditional forms, he won commissions for *Spirit of the Dance* (1932) at New York's Radio City Music Hall, *Benjamin Franklin* (1936–37) at the Post Office Building in Washington, D.C., and the relief *Man and Work* (1954) for the Mayo Clinic in Rochester, Minnesota. A teacher at the Art Students League in New York City (1929–60), Zorach wrote *Zorach Explains Sculpture* (1947) and the autobiography *Art Is My Life* (1967). ■ See study by John J. Baur (1959).

ZOSHCHENKO, MIKHAIL MIKHAILOVICH (1895–1958), Russian humorist. Zoshchenko was wounded in World War I and during the Russian civil war (1918–20) joined the Red army. He gleaned situational and linguistic absurdities from Soviet life and worked them into hugely popular short stories collected in *Respected Citizens* (1926), *Nervous People* (1927; Eng. trans. 1963), *Short Stories* (1932), and *Private Life* (1933). In *Youth Restored* (1932; Eng. trans. 1985), a novella about an unhappy middle-aged man who discovers the secret of rejuvenation and lives to regret it, Zoshchenko parodied scientific discourse. In the unfinished novel *Before Sunrise* (1943; Eng. trans. 1974), he searched for the roots of his own chronic melancholia, achieving irony by carefully arranging autobiographical episodes and finally turning to Pavlov and Freud for answers. He made some concessions to ideology with made-to-order works like *Stories About Lenin* (1940), but was nevertheless expelled (1946) from the official writers' union when Andrei Zhdanov, literary overseer for dictator Joseph Stalin, objected to the tale *The Adventures of a Monkey* (1945). Zoshchenko's career never recovered from this blow. Translations of his stories are collected in *Scenes from the Bathhouse* (1961), *The Woman Who Could Not Read and Other Tales* (1973), *The Wonderful Dog and Other Tales* (1973), *Nervous People and Other Stories* (1975), and *Man Is Not a Flea* (1989). ■ See study by Linda H. Scatton (1993).

ZSIGMONDY, RICHARD (1865–1929), Austrian-born German chemist. With the help of Henry F. W. Siedentopf of the Zeiss Co., Zsigmondy designed and constructed (1903) the first ultramicroscope, which enabled him to do the pioneering research in colloidal chemistry. For this work he won the 1925 Nobel Prize in Chemistry. From 1907 to 1929 he directed the Institute for Inorganic Chemistry at the University of Göttingen.

ZUCKMAYER, CARL (1896–1977), German playwright, poet, and novelist. A prolific author who worked with the dramatists Bertolt Brecht and Gerhart Hauptmann and the producer Max Reinhardt in his early days, Zuckmayer was known for his wit, vitality, and contempt for established values and for his memorable characters. His most famous play was *The Captain from Köpenick* (1930; Eng. trans. 1932), a satire on German militarism and obedience that was regarded as one of the greatest comedies in German literature. He was also known for *The Merry Vineyard* (1925), *The Devil's General* (1946), *The Cold Light* (1955), and *Schinderhannes* (1927), a Robin Hood tale set in Napoleonic times that depicted the church and the state as the real robbers. He also wrote several screenplays, including *The Blue Angel* (1930). He emigrated to the United States (1939) and settled in Switzerland after World War II. ■ See his autobiographies, *Second Wind* (1940; in English) and *A Part of Myself* (1969; Eng. trans. 1970), and studies by Arnold Bauer (Eng. trans. 1976) and Siegfried Mews (1981).

ZUKERMAN, PINCHAS (1948–   ), Israeli-born violinist, violist, and conductor. His parents were concentration camp survivors from Poland who resettled in Tel Aviv. Zukerman's father had been a violinist in the Warsaw Philharmonic; Zukerman took up the instrument at age 7 and was soon recognized as a prodigy. He studied in Tel Aviv, then at age 14 went to New York (1962) as a protégé of Isaac Stern, who wanted him to study at Juilliard under Ivan Galamian. He made his New York debut with the New York Philharmonic (1969) and toured extensively thereafter. He appeared frequently with his friend, violinist Itzhak Perlman. He was known particularly for his violin and viola performances of the German late romantics. Zukerman, who studied conducting while at Juilliard, made his debut as a conductor in 1974 and led the St. Paul Chamber Orchestra (1980–87). He subsequently served as music director of the National Arts Centre Orchestra of Ottawa, Canada (1998–   ).

ZUKOR, ADOLPH (1873–1976), Hungarian-born U.S. film executive. One of the first Hollywood tycoons, Zukor went into the penny-arcade business in 1903. The Famous Players Film Co., which he established in 1913 to make movies of successful plays, soon evolved into Paramount Pictures with contract stars such as Mary Pickford and Rudolph Valentino. Under Zukor's leadership Paramount produced the early classics *The Sheik* (1921) and *The Ten Commandments* (1923). As president of Paramount (1917–35) and later chairman of the board, Zukor concerned himself mainly with film distribution. He acquired some cinema chains and controlled others by means of "block booking," which required an exhibitor to accept a series of films in order to get the one he wanted. A tiny man of great longevity, Zukor celebrated his 100th birthday at a Hollywood gala. ■ See his autobiography, *The Public Is Never Wrong* (1953).

ZUSE, KONRAD (1910–1995), German computer scientist. Zuse studied civil engineering at the Technical University in Berlin (1927–35) and worked as a design engineer at the Henschel Aircraft Company. In order to help solve complicated calculations related to his work, he developed (1936–38), in his spare time (with the help of Helmut Schreyer), the world's first binary digital computer (the Z1). The device, built in his parents' living room, was small and crude. (Independently, in the United States, George Stibitz produced a similar device.) However, Zuse subsequently completed (1941) an operational program-controlled electromechanical digital computer (the Z3). (Both devices were destroyed in air raids during World War II.) A more advanced model, the Z4, survived the war and was eventually taken to Zurich, Switzerland (1950), where it was installed in the Federal Polytechnical Institute. Zuse founded his own computer company (1950), which became part of the Siemens conglomerate in 1967. ■ See his autobiography, *The Computer—My Life* (1970; Eng. trans. 1993).

ZWEIG, ARNOLD (1887–1968), German novelist. Originally concerned with intellectualism and sensibility, Zweig turned after World War I to realistic novels of social criticism. His eight-volume epic dealing with the war and its effects on German society included his best-known novel, *The Case of Sergeant Grischa* (1927; Eng. trans. 1927), a powerful indictment of militarism. Other novels in the series included *Young Woman of 1914* (1931; Eng. trans. 1932) and *Education Before Verdun* (1935; Eng. trans. 1936). A socialist, pacifist, and Zionist, Zweig emigrated to Palestine in 1934 but returned to (East) Germany in 1948. He served as president of the East German Academy of Arts (1950–53) and was also a member of parliament. ■ See study by George Salamon (1975).

ZWEIG, STEFAN (1881–1942), Austrian writer. Born into a wealthy Viennese Jewish family, Zweig was a pacifist, a believer in a pan-European community, and was among the first authors to utilize Freudian insights in his work. One of the world's most translated writers during the 1920s and 1930s, he was best known for his character studies of famous personalities (*Master Builders,* 1934, Eng. trans. 1939; *Three Masters,* 1920, Eng. trans. 1930; *Mental Healers,* 1931, Eng. trans. 1932), and his intuitive full-length biographies (*Marie Antoinette,* 1932, Eng. trans. 1933; *Erasmus,* 1934, Eng. trans. 1934; *Mary Stuart,* 1935, Eng. trans. 1935). His fiction included the novellas *Amok* (1922; Eng. trans. 1931), *Conflicts* (1927; Eng. trans. 1927), and *The Royal Game* (1942; Eng. trans. 1945) and the novel *Beware of Pity* (1938; Eng. trans. 1939). He left Austria (1934) and lived for several years in England and the United States before moving to Brazil (1941). In despair at the destruction of European civilization during World War II, he committed suicide in Petropolis, Brazil. ■ See his autobiography, *The World of Yesterday* (Eng. trans. 1943); the biography by Elizabeth Allday (1972); and D. A. Prater, *European of Yesterday* (1972).

ZWICKY, FRITZ (1898–1974), Bulgarian-born Swiss astronomer, physicist, and jet-propulsion pioneer. Associated with the California Institute of Technology from 1925 to 1972, Zwicky made pioneering studies (with Walter Baade) during the 1930s showing that supernovas are completely different in nature from ordinary novas and that they occur only two or three times every 1,000 years. He studied many galaxies in detail and discovered 18 supernovas. As research director of Aerojet Engineering Corp. (1943–49), he did innovative work on jet engines and jet-assisted takeoff units for heavy-laden aircraft. His books included *Discovery, Invention, Research* (Eng. trans. 1969).

ZWORYKIN, VLADIMIR KOSMA (1889–1982), Russian-born U.S. engineer and inventor. Zworykin came to the United States after World War I and earned a Ph.D. at the University of Pittsburgh (1926) while working for Westinghouse (1920–29). The "father of television," Zworykin helped to design (1929) the kinescope picture tube that reconstructed the television image, and he laid the groundwork for the all-electronic television system by inventing (1931) the iconoscope, the first practical TV camera. As head of the electronics research laboratory of the Radio Corp. of America (RCA; 1929–54), Zworykin made contributions to other electronic equipment, most significantly the electron microscope, which made visible such structures as viruses and protein chains. He held some 120 U.S. patents.

INDEX

EDUCATION

ENGINEERING AND INVENTION

PHILOSOPHY

PHOTOGRAPHY

PHYSICS

POLITICAL SCIENCE

POLITICS AND LAW

Africa

THEOLOGY

See Religion and Theology

MISCELLANEOUS